# O
# 19

# FOOTBALL

NATIONAL COLLEGIATE ATHLETIC ASSOCIATION

[ISSN 0735-5475]

## THE NATIONAL COLLEGIATE ATHLETIC ASSOCIATION
6201 College Boulevard
Overland Park, Kansas 66211-2422
913/339-1906
July 1993

**Compiled By:** Richard M. Campbell, *Assistant Statistics Coordinator;* John D. Painter, *Assistant Statistics Coordinator;* Sean W. Straziscar, *Assistant Statistics Coordinator.*

**Edited By:** J. Gregory Summers, *Assistant Director of Publishing.*

**Designed By:** Victor M. Royal, *Director of Graphics.*

**Cover Photography By:** *Young Company, Kansas City, Missouri.*

# Contents

# DIVISION I-A RECORDS

In 1992, Houston quarterback Jimmy Klingler tied the Division I-A record for most touchdown passes by a sophomore (32) and generated 342.5 yards per game in total offense, the 10th-best season average in history.

Under a three-division reorganization plan adopted by the special NCAA Convention of August 1973, teams classified major-college in football on August 1, 1973, were placed in Division I. College-division teams were divided into Division II and Division III. At the NCAA Convention of January 1978, Division I was divided into Division I-A and Division I-AA for football only.

From 1937, when official national statistics rankings began, through 1969, individual rankings were by totals. Beginning in 1970, most season individual rankings were by per-game averages. In total offense, rushing and scoring, it is yards or points per game; in receiving, catches per game and yards per game; in interceptions, catches per game; and in punt and kickoff returns, yards per return. Punting always has been by average, and all team rankings have been per game. Beginning in 1979, passers were rated in all divisions on **Efficiency Rating Points**, which are derived from a formula that compares passers to the national averages for 14 seasons of two-platoon Division I football starting with the 1965 season. One hundred points equals the 14-year averages for all players in Division I. Those averages break down to 6.29 yards per attempt, 47.14 percent completions, 3.97 percent touchdown passes and 6.54 percent interceptions. The formula assumes that touchdowns are as good as interceptions are bad; therefore, these two figures offset each other for the average player. To determine Efficiency Rating Points, multiply a passer's yards per attempt by 8.4, add his completion percentage, add his touchdown percentage times 3.3, then subtract his interception percentage times two.

Passers must have a minimum of 15 attempts per game to determine rating points because fewer attempts could allow a player to win the championship with fewer than 100 attempts in a season. A passer must play in at least 75 percent of his team's games to qualify for the rankings (e.g., a player on a team with a nine-game season could qualify by playing in seven games; thus, a passer with 105 attempts could qualify for the national rankings).

All individual and team records and rankings include regular-season games only. Career records of other players who played in both Division I and Divisions II or III—such as Grambling's Doug Williams—will be found where they played the majority of their career. Williams played three of his four seasons in Division II; thus, his career records are in the Division II section.

Statistics in some team categories were not tabulated until the advent of the computerized statistics program in 1966. The records listed in those categories begin with the 1966 season and are so indicated.

In 1954, the regular-season schedule was limited to a maximum of 10 games, and in 1970, to a limit of 11 games, excluding postseason competition.

A player whose career includes statistics for parts of five seasons (or an active player who will have five seasons) because he was granted an additional season of competition for reasons of hardship (Bylaw 14.2.5) or a freshman redshirt (Bylaw 14.2.1) are denoted by [$].

### Collegiate Records
Individual collegiate records are determined by comparing the best records in all four divisions (I-A, I-AA, II and III) in comparable categories. Included are career records of players who played half of their careers in two divisions (such as Dennis Shaw of San Diego State, Howard Stevens of Randolph-Macon and Louisville, and Tom Ehrhardt of LIU-C. W. Post and Rhode Island). For individual collegiate career leaders, see page 281.

# COLLEGE FOOTBALL'S FIRST GAME

## November 6, 1869

It all started on a cold day. There was, in fact, a threat of snow in the air that November day when a team of 25 and some faithful followers boarded a train in Princeton for New Brunswick, New Jersey. There, starting at 3 o'clock after a leisurely dinner, some billiards and some girl-watching, Rutgers and Princeton played the first game of intercollegiate football. At that point, the history of football began.

The football that was played that day, on a field where the Rutgers gymnasium now stands, bore no resemblance to the football of today. It was, essentially, soccer. There were 25 men on a side. There was no running with the ball, or throwing it. It had to be kicked or headed. Scoring was done by kicking the ball through the opponent's goal and, according to the rules, "goals must be eight paces," presumably eight yards between two posts stuck in the ground. After each goal (or game, as it was called), the teams changed sides. Time was not important, except in the case of darkness. A game was decided by the number of goals kicked. In this case, the one kicking six first was the winner. The field was 120 yards long and 75 yards wide, a vacant lot with a wooden fence on one side across from the old Rutgers campus.

Accounts of this game are rather hazy, as might be expected. The best is from the Rutgers *Targum,* the student paper, and it speaks, somewhat dramatically, of "grim men, silently stripping" before the kickoff. What they stripped to it doesn't say, but it wasn't much. The players simply took off their hats, coats and vests, and they were ready. No uniforms. The only color was provided by scarlet turbans the Rutgers boys wore on their heads.

As was frequently the case in those days, teams had their own rules. William S. Gummere, the Princeton captain later to become chief justice of the New Jersey Supreme Court, acceded to Rutgers captain William Leggett, and the game was played under Rutgers rules. This was one of the few juridical mistakes Mr. Gummere ever made. Rutgers won the game, 6 goals to 4, after Princeton had overcome an early deficit to draw even at 4-all.

However, another game was played later that month at Princeton, this one under Princeton rules, which permitted free kicks if anyone caught the ball on the fly or the first bounce. Unaccustomed to this sort of business, Rutgers was shut out, 8-0.

---

*Account by Len Elliott, sports editor, The Newark News, 1939-1968, as printed in One Hundred Years of Princeton Football 1869-1969, William C. Stryker ('50), editor. Reprinted from the 1991 Princeton University football media guide.*

# INDIVIDUAL RECORDS

## TOTAL OFFENSE
### (Rushing Plus Passing)

### Most Plays

**Quarter**
35—Mike Romo, Southern Methodist vs. Rice, Nov. 10, 1990 (4th; 31 passes, 4 rushes); Chris Rowland, Washington vs. California, Oct. 6, 1973 (4th; 31 passes, 4 rushes)

**Half**
53—Matt Vogler, Texas Christian vs. Houston, Nov. 3, 1990 (2nd; 47 passes, 6 rushes)

**Game**
94—Matt Vogler, Texas Christian vs. Houston, Nov. 3, 1990 (696 yards)

**Season**
704—David Klingler, Houston, 1990 (5,221 yards)

**2 Yrs**
1,294—David Klingler, Houston, 1990-91 (8,447 yards)

**3 Yrs**
1,548—Ty Detmer, Brigham Young, 1988-91 (13,456 yards)

**Career**
(4 yrs.) 1,795—Ty Detmer, Brigham Young, 1988-91 (14,665 yards)

### Most Plays Per Game

**Season**
64.0—David Klingler, Houston, 1990 (704 in 11)

**2 Yrs**
61.6—David Klingler, Houston, 1990-91 (1,294 in 21)

**Career**
48.5—Doug Gaynor, Long Beach St., 1984-85 (1,067 in 22)

### Most Plays by a Freshman

**Game**
76—Sandy Schwab, Northwestern vs. Michigan, Oct. 23, 1982 (431 yards)

**Season**
504—Sandy Schwab, Northwestern, 1982 (2,555 yards)
Also holds per-game record at 45.8 (504 in 11)

### Most Yards Gained

**Quarter**
340—Andre Ware, Houston vs. Southern Methodist, Oct. 21, 1989 (2nd)

**Half**
510—Andre Ware, Houston vs. Southern Methodist, Oct. 21, 1989 (1st)

**Game**
732—David Klingler, Houston vs. Arizona St., Dec. 2, 1990 (716 passing, 16 rushing)

**Season**
5,221—David Klingler, Houston, 1990 (81 rushing, 5,140 passing)

**2 Yrs**
9,455—Ty Detmer, Brigham Young, 1989-90 (-293 rushing, 9,748 passing)

**3 Yrs**
10,664—Ty Detmer, Brigham Young, 1988-90 (-336 rushing, 11,000 passing)

**Career**
(4 yrs.) 14,665—Ty Detmer, Brigham Young, 1988-91 (-366 rushing, 15,031 passing)

### Most Yards Gained Per Game

**Season**
474.6—David Klingler, Houston, 1990 (5,221 in 11)

**2 Yrs**
402.2—David Klingler, Houston, 1990-91 (8,447 in 21)

**Career**
318.8—Ty Detmer, Brigham Young, 1988-91 (14,665 in 46)

### Most Yards Gained, First Two Seasons
6,710—Doug Gaynor, Long Beach St., 1984-85
Also holds per-game record at 305.0

### Most Seasons Gaining 4,000 Yards or More
3—Ty Detmer, Brigham Young, 1989-91

### Most Seasons Gaining 3,000 Yards or More
3—Ty Detmer, Brigham Young, 1989-91

### Most Seasons Gaining 2,500 Yards or More
3—Shane Matthews, Florida, 1990-92; Ty Detmer, Brigham Young, 1989-91; Shawn Moore, Virginia, 1988-90; Erik Wilhelm, Oregon St., 1986-88; Brian McClure, Bowling Green, 1983-85; Randall Cunningham, Nevada-Las Vegas, 1982-84; Doug Flutie, Boston College, 1982-84; John Elway, Stanford, 1980-82

### Most Yards Gained by a Freshman

**Game**
458—Bob Hoernschemeyer, Indiana vs. Nebraska, Oct. 9, 1943 (37 plays)

**Season**
2,975—Todd Ellis, South Caro., 1986 (436 plays)
Also holds per-game record at 270.5

### Most Yards Gained by a Sophomore

**Game**
625—Scott Mitchell, Utah vs. Air Force, Oct. 15, 1988 (631 passing, -6 rushing)

**Season**
4,433—Ty Detmer, Brigham Young, 1989 (12 games, 497 plays)
Per-game record—390.8, Scott Mitchell, Utah, 1988

### Most Yards Gained in First Game of Career
483—Billy Stevens, UTEP vs. North Texas, Sept. 18, 1965

### Most Yards Gained, Two, Three and Four Consecutive Games

**2 Games**
1,310—David Klingler, Houston, 1990 (578 vs. Eastern Wash., Nov. 17; 732 vs. Arizona St., Dec. 2)

**3 Games**
1,651—David Klingler, Houston, 1990 (341 vs. Texas, Nov. 10; 578 vs. Eastern Wash., Nov. 17; 732 vs. Arizona St., Dec. 2)

**4 Games**
2,276—David Klingler, Houston, 1990 (625 vs. Texas Christian, Nov. 3; 341 vs. Texas, Nov. 10; 578 vs. Eastern Wash., Nov. 17; 732 vs. Arizona St., Dec. 2)

**Most Games Gaining 300 Yards or More**
**Season**
12—Ty Detmer, Brigham Young, 1990
**Career**
33—Ty Detmer, Brigham Young, 1988-91

**Most Consecutive Games Gaining
300 Yards or More**
**Season**
12—Ty Detmer, Brigham Young, 1990
**Career**
19—Ty Detmer, Brigham Young, 1989-90

**Most Games Gaining 400 Yards or More**
**Season**
9—David Klingler, Houston, 1990
**Career**
13—Ty Detmer, Brigham Young, 1988-91

**Most Consecutive Games Gaining
400 Yards or More**
**Season**
5—Ty Detmer, Brigham Young, 1990
Also holds career record at 5

**Most Yards Gained Against One Opponent**
**Career**
1,483—Ty Detmer, Brigham Young vs. San
Diego St., 1988-91

**Most Yards Gained Per Game Against
One Opponent**
**Career**
*(Min. 3 games)* 383.7—Gary Schofield, Wake
Forest vs. Maryland, 1981-83 (1,151 yards)
*(Min. 4 games)* 370.8—Ty Detmer, Brigham
Young vs. San Diego St., 1988-91 (1,483
yards)

**Most Yards Gained by Two Opposing Players**
**Game**
1,321—Matt Vogler, Texas Christian (696) &
David Klingler, Houston (625), Nov. 3, 1990

**Gaining 1,000 Yards Rushing and
1,000 Yards Passing**
**Season**
Michael Carter (QB), Hawaii, 1991 (1,092 rushing, 1,172 passing); Brian Mitchell (QB),
Southwestern La., 1989 (1,311 rushing, 1,966
passing); Dee Dowis (QB), Air Force, 1989
(1,286 rushing, 1,285 passing); Darian Hagan
(QB), Colorado, 1989 (1,004 rushing, 1,002
passing); Bart Weiss (QB), Air Force, 1985
(1,032 rushing, 1,449 passing); Reggie Collier
(QB), Southern Miss., 1981 (1,005 rushing,
1,004 passing); Johnny Bright (HB), Drake,
1950 (1,232 rushing, 1,168 passing)

**A Quarterback Gaining 2,000 Yards Rushing
and 4,000 Yards Passing**
**Career**
Major Harris, West Va., 1987-89 (2,030 rushing,
4,834 passing); Brian Mitchell, Southwestern
La., 1986-89 (3,335 rushing, 5,447 passing);
Rickey Foggie, Minnesota, 1984-87 (2,038
rushing, 4,903 passing); John Bond, Mississippi St., 1980-83 (2,280 rushing, 4,621 passing); Prince McJunkins, Wichita St., 1979-82
(2,047 rushing, 4,544 passing)

**A Quarterback Gaining 300 Yards Passing
and 100 Yards Rushing**
**Game**
Donald Douglas, Houston vs. Southern Methodist, Oct. 19, 1991 (319 passing, 103 rushing); Randy Welniak, Wyoming vs. Air Force,
Sept. 24, 1988 (359 passing, 108 rushing)

**A Quarterback Gaining 200 Yards Rushing
and 200 Yards Passing**
**Game**
Brian Mitchell, Southwestern La. vs. Colorado
St., Nov. 21, 1987 (271 rushing, 205 passing);
Steve Gage, Tulsa vs. New Mexico, Nov. 8,
1986 (212 rushing, 209 passing); Reds Bag-
nell, Pennsylvania vs. Dartmouth, Oct. 14,
1950 (214 rushing, 276 passing)

**Teams Having a 3,000-Yard Passer,
1,000-Yard Rusher and 1,000-Yard
Receiver in the Same Year**
Pacific (Cal.), 1991 (Troy Kopp [3,767 passer],
Aaron Turner [1,604 receiver] and Ryan
Benjamin [1,581 rusher]); Houston, 1989
(Andre Ware [4,699 passer], Manny Hazard
[1,689 receiver] and Chuck Weatherspoon
[1,146 rusher]); Colorado St., 1983 (Terry
Nugent [3,319 passer], Jeff Champine [1,002
receiver] and Steve Bartalo [1,113 rusher]);
Southern Methodist, 1968 (Chuck Hixson
[3,103 passer], Jerry LeVias [1,131 receiver]
and Mike Richardson [1,034 rusher])

**Highest Average Gain Per Play**
**Game**
*(Min. 37-62 plays)* 12.76—Mike Perez, San Jose
St. vs. Pacific (Cal.), Oct. 25, 1986 (42 for 536)
*(Min. 63 plays)* 9.92—David Klingler, Houston
vs. Texas Christian, Nov. 3, 1990 (63 for 625)
**Season**
*(Min. 3,000 yards)* 8.92—Ty Detmer, Brigham
Young, 1989 (497 for 4,433)
**Career**
*(Min. 7,500 yards)* 8.17—Ty Detmer, Brigham
Young, 1988-91 (1,795 for 14,665)

**Most Touchdowns Responsible For
(TDs Scored and Passed For)**
**Game**
11—David Klingler, Houston vs. Eastern Wash.,
Nov. 17, 1990 (passed for 11)
**Season**
55—David Klingler, Houston, 1990 (scored 1,
passed for 54)
**2 Yrs**
85—David Klingler, Houston, 1990-91 (scored
2, passed for 83)
**3 Yrs**
122—Ty Detmer, Brigham Young, 1989-91
(scored 14, passed for 108)
**Career**
135—Ty Detmer, Brigham Young, 1988-91
(scored 14, passed for 121)

**Most Touchdowns Responsible For Per Game**
**Season**
5.0—David Klingler, Houston, 1990 (55 in 11)
**2 Yrs**
4.05—David Klingler, Houston, 1990-91 (85 in
21)
**3 Yrs**
3.39—Ty Detmer, Brigham Young, 1989-91
(122 in 36)
**Career**
2.93—Ty Detmer, Brigham Young, 1988-91
(135 in 46)
Collegiate record—3.60, Dennis Shaw, San
Diego St., 1968-69 (72 in 20)

**Most Points Responsible For
(Points Scored and Passed For)**
**Game**
66—David Klingler, Houston vs. Eastern Wash.,
Nov. 17, 1990 (passed for 11 TDs)

**Season**
334—David Klingler, Houston, 1990 (scored 1 TD, passed for 54 TDs, accounted for 2 two-point conversions)

**2 Yrs**
514—David Klingler, Houston, 1990-91 (scored 2 TDs, passed for 83 TDs, accounted for 2 two-point conversions)

**3 Yrs**
582—Ty Detmer, Brigham Young, 1988-90 (scored 10 TDs, passed for 86 TDs, accounted for 3 two-point conversions)

**Career**
820—Ty Detmer, Brigham Young, 1988-91 (scored 14 TDs, passed for 121 TDs, accounted for 5 two-point conversions)

**Most Points Responsible For Per Game**
**Season**
30.4—David Klingler, Houston, 1990 (334 in 11)
**2 Yrs**
22.8—Jim McMahon, Brigham Young, 1980-81 (502 in 22)
**3 Yrs**
17.1—Ty Detmer, Brigham Young, 1988-90 (582 in 34)
**Career**
17.8—Ty Detmer, Brigham Young, 1988-91 (820 in 46)
Collegiate record—21.6, Dennis Shaw, San Diego St., 1968-69 (432 in 20)

**Scoring 200 Points and Passing for 200 Points**
**Career**
Rick Leach, Michigan, 1975-78 (scored 204, passed for 270)

# RUSHING

**Most Rushes**

**Quarter**
20—Kent Kitzmann, Minnesota vs. Illinois, Nov. 12, 1977 (3rd); Steve Owens, Oklahoma vs. Oklahoma St., Nov. 29, 1969 (3rd); O. J. Simpson, Southern Cal vs. Oregon St., Nov. 16, 1968 (4th)
**Half**
34—Tony Sands, Kansas vs. Missouri, Nov. 23, 1991 (2nd, 240 yards)
**Game**
58—Tony Sands, Kansas vs. Missouri, Nov. 23, 1991 (396 yards)
**Season**
403—Marcus Allen, Southern Cal, 1981 (2,342 yards)
**2 Yrs**
757—Marcus Allen, Southern Cal, 1980-81 (3,905 yards)
**Career**
(3 yrs.) 994—Herschel Walker, Georgia, 1980-82 (5,259 yards)
(4 yrs.) 1,215—Steve Bartalo, Colorado St., 1983-86 (4,813 yards)

**Most Rushes Per Game**
**Season**
39.6—Ed Marinaro, Cornell, 1971 (356 in 9)
**2 Yrs**
36.0—Marcus Allen, Southern Cal, 1980-81 (757 in 21)
**Career**
34.0—Ed Marinaro, Cornell, 1969-71 (918 in 27)

**Most Rushes by a Freshman**
**Game**
45—James McDougal, Wake Forest vs. Clemson, Oct. 9, 1976 (249 yards)
**Season**
292—Steve Bartalo, Colorado St., 1983 (1,113 yards)

**Most Rushes Per Game by a Freshman**
**Season**
29.2—Steve Bartalo, Colorado St., 1983 (292 in 10)

**Most Consecutive Rushes by Same Player**
**Game**
16—William Howard, Tennessee vs. Mississippi, Nov. 15, 1986 (during two possessions)

**Most Rushes in Two Consecutive Games**
**Season**
102—Lorenzo White, Michigan St., 1985 (53 vs. Purdue, Oct. 26; 49 vs. Minnesota, Nov. 2)

**Most Yards Gained**

**Quarter**
214—Andre Herrera, Southern Ill. vs. Northern Ill., Oct. 23, 1976 (1st, 17 rushes)
**Half**
287—Stacey Robinson, Northern Ill. vs. Fresno St., Oct. 6, 1990 (1st; 114 in first quarter, 173 in second quarter; 20 rushes)
**Game**
396—Tony Sands, Kansas vs. Missouri, Nov. 23, 1991 (58 rushes) (240 yards on 34 carries, second half)
**Season**
2,628—Barry Sanders, Oklahoma St., 1988 (344 rushes, 11 games)
**2 Yrs**
3,905—Marcus Allen, Southern Cal, 1980-81 (757 rushes)
**Career**
(3 yrs.) 5,259—Herschel Walker, Georgia, 1980-82 (994 rushes)
(4 yrs.) 6,082—Tony Dorsett, Pittsburgh, 1973-76 (1,074 rushes)

**Most Yards Gained Per Game**
**Season**
238.9—Barry Sanders, Oklahoma St., 1988 (2,628 in 11)
**2 Yrs**
186.0—Marcus Allen, Southern Cal, 1980-81 (3,905 in 21)
**Career**
174.6—Ed Marinaro, Cornell, 1969-71 (4,715 in 27)

**Most Yards Gained by a Freshman**
**Game**
386—Marshall Faulk, San Diego St. vs. Pacific (Cal.), Sept. 14, 1991 (37 rushes)
**Season**
1,616—Herschel Walker, Georgia, 1980 (274 rushes)
Per-game record—158.8, Marshall Faulk, San Diego St., 1991 (1,429 in 9)

## Most Yards Gained by a Sophomore

**Game**
342—Charlie Davis, Colorado vs. Oklahoma St., Nov. 13, 1971 (34 rushes)

**Season**
1,908—Lorenzo White, Michigan St., 1985 (386 rushes)
Also holds per-game record at 173.5 (1,908 in 11)

## Freshmen Gaining 1,000 Yards or More

**Season**
By 31 players (see chart after Annual Rushing Champions). Most recent: Winslow Oliver, New Mexico, 1992 (1,063); Deland McCullough, Miami (Ohio), 1992 (1,026); Marshall Faulk, San Diego St., 1991 (1,429); Greg Hill, Texas A&M, 1991 (1,216); David Small, Cincinnati, 1991 (1,004)

## Two Freshmen, Same Team, Gaining 1,000 Yards or More

**Season**
Mike Smith (1,062) & Gwain Durden (1,049), Tenn.-Chatt., 1977

## Earliest Game a Freshman Reached 1,000 Yards

**Season**
7—Marshall Faulk, San Diego St., 1991 (1,157 vs. Colorado St., Nov. 9); Emmitt Smith, Florida, 1987 (1,011 vs. Temple, Oct. 17)

## First Player to Gain 1,000 Yards or More

**Season**
Byron "Whizzer" White, Colorado, 1937 (1,121)

## Earliest Game Gaining 1,000 Yards or More

**Season**
5—Marcus Allen, Southern Cal, 1981 (1,136); Ernest Anderson, Oklahoma St., 1982 (1,042); Ed Marinaro, Cornell, 1971 (1,026); Ricky Bell, Southern Cal, 1976 (1,008); Barry Sanders, Oklahoma St., 1988 (1,002)

## Most Yards Gained by a Quarterback

**Game**
308—Stacey Robinson, Northern Ill. vs. Fresno St., Oct. 6, 1990 (22 rushes)

**Season**
1,443—Stacey Robinson, Northern Ill., 1989 (223 rushes)
Also holds per-game record at 131.2 (1,443 in 11)

**Career**
3,612—Dee Dowis, Air Force, 1986-89 (543 rushes)
Per-game record—109.1, Stacey Robinson, Northern Ill., 1988-90 (2,727 in 25)

## Longest Gain by a Quarterback

**Game**
98—Mark Malone, Arizona St. vs. Utah St., Oct. 27, 1979 (TD)

## Most Games Gaining 100 Yards or More

**Season**
11—By 9 players. Most recent: Barry Sanders, Oklahoma St., 1988

**Career**
33—Tony Dorsett, Pittsburgh, 1973-76 (43 games); Archie Griffin, Ohio St., 1972-75 (42 games)

## Most Games Gaining 100 Yards or More by a Freshman

**Season**
9—Tony Dorsett, Pittsburgh, 1973; Ron "Po" James, New Mexico St., 1968
Consecutive record 8 by James

## Most Consecutive Games Gaining 100 Yards or More

**Career**
31—Archie Griffin, Ohio St. Began Sept. 15, 1973 (vs. Minnesota), ended Nov. 22, 1975 (vs. Michigan)

## Most Games Gaining 200 Yards or More

**Season**
8—Marcus Allen, Southern Cal, 1981

**Career**
11—Marcus Allen, Southern Cal, 1978-81 (in 21 games during 1980-81)

## Most Games Gaining 200 Yards or More by a Freshman

**Season**
4—Herschel Walker, Georgia, 1980

## Most Consecutive Games Gaining 200 Yards or More

**Season**
5—Barry Sanders, Oklahoma St., 1988 (320 vs. Kansas St., Oct. 29; 215 vs. Oklahoma, Nov. 5; 312 vs. Kansas, Nov. 12; 293 vs. Iowa St., Nov. 19; 332 vs. Texas Tech, Dec. 3); Marcus Allen, Southern Cal, 1981 (210 vs. Tennessee, Sept. 12; 274 vs. Indiana, Sept. 19; 208 vs. Oklahoma, Sept. 26; 233 vs. Oregon St., Oct. 3; 211 vs. Arizona, Oct. 10)

## Most Games Gaining 300 Yards or More

**Season**
4—Barry Sanders, Oklahoma St., 1988

**Career**
4—Barry Sanders, Oklahoma St., 1986-88

## Most Yards Gained, Two, Three, Four and Five Consecutive Games

**2 Games**
626—Mike Pringle, Cal St. Fullerton, 1989 (357 vs. New Mexico St., Nov. 4; 269 vs. Long Beach St., Nov. 11)

**3 Games**
937—Barry Sanders, Oklahoma St., 1988 (312 vs. Kansas, Nov. 12; 293 vs. Iowa St., Nov. 19; 332 vs. Texas Tech, Dec. 3)

**4 Games**
1,152—Barry Sanders, Oklahoma St., 1988 (215 vs. Oklahoma, Nov. 5; 312 vs. Kansas, Nov. 12; 293 vs. Iowa St., Nov. 19; 332 vs. Texas Tech, Dec. 3)

**5 Games**
1,472—Barry Sanders, Oklahoma St., 1988 (320 vs. Kansas St., Oct. 29; 215 vs. Oklahoma, Nov. 5; 312 vs. Kansas, Nov. 12; 293 vs. Iowa St., Nov. 19; 332 vs. Texas Tech, Dec. 3)

## Most Seasons Gaining 1,500 Yards or More

**Career**
3—Herschel Walker, Georgia, 1980-82; Tony Dorsett, Pittsburgh, 1973, 75-76

## Most Seasons Gaining 1,000 Yards or More

**Career**
4—Amos Lawrence, North Caro., 1977-80; Tony Dorsett, Pittsburgh, 1973-76
Collegiate record tied by Howard Stevens, Randolph-Macon, 1968-69, Louisville, 1971-72

## Two Players, Same Team, Each Gaining 1,000 Yards or More

**Season**
21 times. Most recent: Nebraska, 1992—Calvin Jones (1,210) & Derek Brown (1,011)

*Division I-A Individual Records*                                    13

## Two Players, Same Team, Each Gaining 200 Yards or More
**Game**
Gordon Brown, 214 (23 rushes) & Steve Gage (QB), 206 (26 rushes), Tulsa vs. Wichita St., Nov. 2, 1985

## Two Opposing I-A Players Each Gaining 200 Yards or More
**Game**
Barry Sanders, Oklahoma St. (215) & Mike Gaddis, Oklahoma (213), Nov. 5, 1988; George Swarn, Miami (Ohio) (239) & Otis Cheathem, Western Mich. (219), Sept. 8, 1984

## Most Yards Gained by Two Opposing Players
**Game**
553—Marshall Faulk, San Diego St. (386) & Ryan Benjamin, Pacific (Cal.) (167), Sept. 14, 1991

## Most Yards Gained by Two Players, Same Team
**Game**
476—Tony Sands (396) & Chip Hilleary (80), Kansas vs. Missouri, Nov. 23, 1991
**Season**
2,997—Barry Sanders (2,628) & Gerald Hudson (Sanders' backup, 369), Oklahoma St., 1988 Also hold per-game record at 272.5
**Career**
8,193—Eric Dickerson (4,450) & Craig James (3,743), Southern Methodist, 1979-82 (alternated at the same position during the last 36 games)

## Most Yards Gained in First Game of a Career
220—Alan Thompson, Wisconsin vs. Oklahoma, Sept. 20, 1969

## Most Yards Gained by a Freshman in the First Game of Career
212—Greg Hill, Texas A&M vs. Louisiana St., Sept. 14, 1991 (30 carries)

## Most Yards Gained in an Opening Game of a Season
343—Tony Jeffery, Texas Christian vs. Tulane, Sept. 13, 1986 (16 rushes)

## Most Yards Gained Against One Opponent
**Career**
754—Tony Dorsett, Pittsburgh vs. Notre Dame, 1973-76 (96 rushes)

## Most Yards Gained Per Game Against One Opponent
**Career**
*(Min. 2 games)* 245.5—Ed Marinaro, Cornell vs. Rutgers, 1969, 1971 (491 yards, 79 rushes)
*(Min. 3 games)* 216.3—Herschel Walker, Georgia vs. Florida, 1980-82 (649 yards, 119 rushes)

## Highest Average Gain Per Rush
**Game**
*(Min. 8-14 rushes)* 30.2—Kevin Lowe, Wyoming vs. South Dak. St., Nov. 10, 1984 (10 for 302)
*(Min. 15-25 rushes)* 21.4—Tony Jeffery, Texas Christian vs. Tulane, Sept. 13, 1986 (16 for 343)
*(Min. 26 rushes)* 13.7—Eddie Lee Ivery, Georgia Tech vs. Air Force, Nov. 11, 1978 (26 for 356)

**Season**
*(Min. 101-213 rushes)* 9.63—Chuck Weatherspoon, Houston, 1989 (119 for 1,146)
*(Min. 214-281 rushes)* 7.81—Mike Rozier, Nebraska, 1983 (275 for 2,148)
*(Min. 282 rushes)* 7.64—Barry Sanders, Oklahoma St., 1988 (344 for 2,628)
Glenn Davis, Army, 1945, holds the record for a minimum of 75 rushes—11.51 (82 for 944)
**Career**
*(Min. 300-413 rushes)* 8.26—Glenn Davis, Army, 1943-46 (358 for 2,957)
*(Min. 414-780 rushes)* 7.16—Mike Rozier, Nebraska, 1981-83 (668 for 4,780)
*(Min. 781 rushes)* 6.13—Archie Griffin, Ohio St., 1972-75 (845 for 5,177)

## Most Touchdowns Scored by Rushing
**Game**
8—Howard Griffith, Illinois vs. Southern Ill., Sept. 22, 1990 (5, 51, 7, 41, 5, 18, 5, 3 yards; Griffith scored three touchdowns [51, 7, 41] on consecutive carries and scored four touchdowns in the third quarter)
**Season**
37—Barry Sanders, Oklahoma St., 1988 (11 games)
Also holds per-game record at 3.36 (37 in 11)
**Career**
64—Anthony Thompson, Indiana, 1986-89

## Most Games Scoring Two or More Touchdowns by Rushing
**Season**
11—Barry Sanders, Oklahoma St., 1988

## Most Consecutive Games Scoring Two or More Touchdowns by Rushing
**Career**
12—Barry Sanders, Oklahoma St. (last game of 1987, all 11 in 1988)

## Most Touchdowns Scored by Rushing by a Freshman
**Game**
7—Marshall Faulk, San Diego St. vs. Pacific (Cal.), Sept. 14, 1991
**Season**
21—Marshall Faulk, San Diego St., 1991
Also holds per-game record at 2.33 (21 in 9)

## Most Rushing Touchdowns Scored by a Quarterback
**Game**
6—Dee Dowis, Air Force vs. San Diego St., Sept. 1, 1989 (55, 28, 12, 16, 60, 17 yards; 249 yards rushing on 13 carries)
**Season**
19—Stacey Robinson, Northern Ill., 1990, 1989; Brian Mitchell, Southwestern La., 1989; Fred Solomon, Tampa, 1974
**Career**
47—Brian Mitchell, Southwestern La., 1986-89 (in 43 games)

## Most QB Touchdowns Over Two Consecutive Seasons
38—Stacey Robinson, Northern Ill., 1989-90 (19 and 19)

## Most Yards Gained by Two Brothers
**Season**
3,690—Barry Sanders, Oklahoma St. (2,628) & Byron Sanders, Northwestern (1,062), 1988

# PASSING

## Highest Passing Efficiency Rating Points
### Game
*(Min. 12-24 atts.)* 403.4—Tim Clifford, Indiana vs. Colorado, Sept. 26, 1980 (14 attempts, 11 completions, 0 interceptions, 345 yards, 5 TD passes)

*(Min. 25-49 atts.)* 273.8—Tom Tunnicliffe, Arizona vs. Pacific (Cal.), Oct. 23, 1982 (28 attempts, 21 completions, 0 interceptions, 427 yards, 6 TD passes)

*(Min. 50 atts.)* 197.8—David Klingler, Houston vs. Eastern Wash., Nov. 17, 1990 (58 attempts, 41 completions, 2 interceptions, 572 yards, 11 TD passes)

### Season
*(Min. 15 atts. per game)* 176.9—Jim McMahon, Brigham Young, 1980 (445 attempts, 284 completions, 18 interceptions, 4,571 yards, 47 TD passes)

### Career
*(Min. 200 comps.)* 162.73—Ty Detmer, Brigham Young, 1988-91 (1,530 attempts, 958 completions, 65 interceptions, 15,031 yards, 121 TD passes)

## Highest Passing Efficiency Rating Points by a Freshman
### Season
*(Min. 15 atts. per game)* 148.0—Kerwin Bell, Florida, 1984 (184 attempts, 98 completions, 7 interceptions, 1,614 yards, 16 TD passes)

## Most Passes Attempted
### Quarter
32—Jack Trudeau, Illinois vs. Purdue, Oct. 12, 1985 (4th, completed 14)

### Half
48—David Klingler, Houston vs. Southern Methodist, Oct. 20, 1990 (1st, completed 32)

### Game
79—Matt Vogler, Texas Christian vs. Houston, Nov. 3, 1990 (completed 44)

### Season
643—David Klingler, Houston, 1990 (11 games, completed 374)

### 2 Yrs
1,140—David Klingler, Houston, 1990-91 (completed 652)

### 3 Yrs
1,377—Ty Detmer, Brigham Young, 1989-91 (completed 875)

### Career
*(4 yrs.)* 1,530—Ty Detmer, Brigham Young, 1988-91 (completed 958)

## Most Passes Attempted Per Game
### Season
58.5—David Klingler, Houston, 1990 (643 in 11)

### Career
39.6—Mike Perez, San Jose St., 1986-87 (792 in 20)

## Most Passes Attempted by a Freshman
### Game
71—Sandy Schwab, Northwestern vs. Michigan, Oct. 23, 1982 (completed 45)

### Season
503—Mike Romo, Southern Methodist, 1989 (completed 282)

## Most Passes Completed
### Quarter
21—Mike Romo, Southern Methodist vs. Rice, Nov. 10, 1990 (4th, attempted 31)

### Half
32—David Klingler, Houston vs. Southern Methodist, Oct. 20, 1990 (1st, attempted 48)

### Game
48—David Klingler, Houston vs. Southern Methodist, Oct. 20, 1990 (attempted 76)

### Season
374—David Klingler, Houston, 1990 (11 games, attempted 643)

### 2 Yrs
652—David Klingler, Houston, 1990-91 (attempted 1,140)
Also holds per-game record at 31.0 (652 in 21)

### 3 Yrs
875—Ty Detmer, Brigham Young, 1989-91 (attempted 1,377)
Per-game record—24.8, David Klingler, Houston, 1989-91 (720 in 29)

### Career
*(4 yrs.)* 958—Ty Detmer, Brigham Young, 1988-91 (attempted 1,530)

## Most Passes Completed Per Game
### Season
34.0—David Klingler, Houston, 1990 (374 in 11)

### Career
25.9—Doug Gaynor, Long Beach St., 1984-85 (569 in 22)

## Most Passes Completed by a Freshman
### Game
45—Sandy Schwab, Northwestern vs. Michigan, Oct. 23, 1982 (attempted 71)

### Season
282—Mike Romo, Southern Methodist, 1989 (attempted 503)
Also holds per-game record at 25.6 (282 in 11)

## Most Consecutive Passes Completed
### Game
22—Chuck Long, Iowa vs. Indiana, Oct. 27, 1984

### Season
22—Chuck Long, Iowa vs. Indiana, Oct. 27, 1984; Steve Young, Brigham Young, 1982 (completed last 8 attempts vs. Utah St., Oct. 30, and first 14 vs. Wyoming, Nov. 6)

## Most Passes Completed, Two, Three and Four Consecutive Games
### 2 Games
82—David Klingler, Houston, 1990 (48 vs. Southern Methodist, Oct. 20; 34 vs. Arkansas, Oct. 27) and (41 vs. Eastern Wash., Nov. 17; 41 vs. Arizona St., Dec. 2)

### 3 Games
118—David Klingler, Houston, 1990-91 (41 vs. Eastern Wash., Nov. 17, 1990; 41 vs. Arizona St., Dec. 2, 1990; 36 vs. Louisiana Tech, Aug. 31, 1991) and 1990 (48 vs. Southern Methodist, Oct. 20; 34 vs. Arkansas, Oct. 27; 36 vs. Texas Christian, Nov. 3)

### 4 Games
144—Andre Ware, Houston, 1989 (42 vs. Texas Christian, Nov. 4; 29 vs. Texas, Nov. 11; 37 vs. Texas Tech, Nov. 25; 36 vs. Rice, Dec. 2)

## Highest Percentage of Passes Completed
### Game
*(Min. 20-29 comps.)* 92.6%—Rick Neuheisel, UCLA vs. Washington, Oct. 29, 1983 (25 of 27)

*(Min. 30-39 comps.)* 83.3%—Todd Santos, San Diego St. vs. Utah, Sept. 12, 1987 (35 of 42)

*(Min. 40 comps.)* 81.1%—Rich Campbell, Cali-

fornia vs. Florida, Sept. 13, 1980 (43 of 53)

**Season**
*(Min. 150 atts.)* 71.3%—Steve Young, Brigham Young, 1983 (306 of 429)
**Career**
*(Min. 875-999 atts.)* 65.2%—Steve Young, Brigham Young, 1981-83 (592 of 908)
*(Min. 1,000-1,099 atts.)* 64.6%—$Chuck Long, Iowa, 1981-85 (692 of 1,072)
*(Min. 1,100 atts.)* 63.9%—Jack Trudeau, Illinois, 1981, 1983-85 (736 of 1,151)
$ *See page 8 for explanation.*

### Highest Percentage of Passes Completed by a Freshman
**Season**
*(Min. 200 atts.)* 66.2%—Grady Benton, Arizona St., 1992 (149 of 225)

### Most Passes Had Intercepted
**Game**
9—John Reaves, Florida vs. Auburn, Nov. 1, 1969 (attempted 66)
**Season**
34—John Eckman, Wichita St., 1966 (attempted 458)
Also holds per-game record at 3.4 (34 in 10)
**Career**
*(3 yrs.)* 68—Zeke Bratkowski, Georgia, 1951-53 (attempted 734)
*(4 yrs.)* 73—Mark Herrmann, Purdue, 1977-80 (attempted 1,218)
Per-game record—2.31, Steve Ramsey, North Texas, 1967-69 (67 in 29)

### Lowest Percentage of Passes Had Intercepted
**Season**
*(Min. 150-349 atts.)* 0.00%—Matt Blundin, Virginia, 1991 (0 of 224)
*(Min. 350 atts.)* 1.56%—Dan McGwire, San Diego St., 1990 (7 of 449)
**Career**
*(Min. 600-799 atts.)* 1.75%—Damon Allen, Cal St. Fullerton, 1981-84 (11 of 629)
*(Min. 800-1,049 atts.)* 2.42%—Gino Torretta, Miami (Fla.), 1989-92 (24 of 991)
*(Min. 1,050 atts.)* 2.91%—Brett Favre, Southern Miss., 1987-90 (34 of 1,169)

### Most Passes Attempted Without an Interception
**Game**
68—David Klingler, Houston vs. Baylor, Oct. 6, 1990 (completed 35)
**Entire Season**
224—Matt Blundin, Virginia, 1991 (completed 135)

### Most Consecutive Passes Attempted Without an Interception
**Season**
224—Matt Blundin, Virginia, 1991 (went entire 11-game season without an interception)
**Career**
231—Matt Blundin, Virginia, 1990-91 (started with 7 straight in last game of 1990 and continued with 224 through 1991 season)

### Most Consecutive Passes Attempted With Just One Interception
**Career**
329—Damon Allen, Cal St. Fullerton, 1983-84 (during 16 games; began Oct. 8, 1983, vs. Nevada, ended Nov. 3, 1984, vs. Fresno St. Interception occurred vs. Idaho, Sept. 15, 1984)

### Most Consecutive Passes Attempted Without an Interception at the Start of a Career
138—Mike Gundy, Oklahoma St., 1986 (during 8 games)

### Most Yards Gained
**Quarter**
340—Andre Ware, Houston vs. Southern Methodist, Oct. 21, 1989 (2nd)
**Half**
517—Andre Ware, Houston vs. Southern Methodist, Oct. 21, 1989 (1st, completed 25 of 41)
**Game**
716—David Klingler, Houston vs. Arizona St., Dec. 2, 1990 (41 of 70)
**Season**
*(12 games)* 5,188—Ty Detmer, Brigham Young, 1990 (completed 361 of 562)
*(11 games)* 5,140—David Klingler, Houston, 1990 (completed 374 of 643)
**2 Yrs**
9,748—Ty Detmer, Brigham Young, 1989-90 (completed 626 of 974)
**3 Yrs**
13,779—Ty Detmer, Brigham Young, 1989-91 (completed 875 of 1,377)
**Career**
*(4 yrs.)* 15,031—Ty Detmer, Brigham Young, 1988-91 (completed 958 of 1,530)

### Most Yards Gained Per Game
**Season**
467.3—David Klingler, Houston, 1990 (5,140 in 11)
**2 Yrs**
406.2—Ty Detmer, Brigham Young, 1989-90 (9,748 in 24)
**3 Yrs**
382.8—Ty Detmer, Brigham Young, 1989-91 (13,779 in 36)
**Career**
326.8—Ty Detmer, Brigham Young, 1988-91 (15,031 in 46)

### Most Yards Gained by a Freshman
**Game**
469—Ben Bennett, Duke vs. Wake Forest, Nov. 8, 1980
**Season**
3,020—Todd Ellis, South Caro., 1986
Also holds per-game record at 274.5 (3,020 in 11)

### Most Yards Gained by a Sophomore
**Game**
631—Scott Mitchell, Utah vs. Air Force, Oct. 15, 1988
**Season**
4,560—Ty Detmer, Brigham Young, 1989
Per-game record—392.9, Scott Mitchell, Utah, 1988 (4,322 in 11)

### Most Seasons Gaining 2,000 Yards or More
**Career**
4—Alex Van Pelt, Pittsburgh, 1989-92 (2,527-2,427-2,796-3,163); T. J. Rubley, Tulsa, 1987-89, 1991 (2,058-2,497-2,292-2,054); Tom Hodson, Louisiana St., 1986-89 (2,261-2,125-2,074-2,655); Todd Santos, San Diego St., 1984-87 (2,063-2,877-2,553-3,932); Kevin Sweeney, Fresno St., 1983-86 (2,359-3,259-2,604-2,363)

### Most Yards Gained, Two, Three and Four Consecutive Games
**2 Games**
1,288—David Klingler, Houston, 1990 (572 vs. Eastern Wash., Nov. 17; 716 vs. Arizona St.,

Dec. 2)

**3 Games**
1,798—David Klingler, Houston, 1990-91 (572 vs. Eastern Wash., Nov. 17, 1990; 716 vs. Arizona St., Dec. 2, 1990; 510 vs. Louisiana Tech, Aug. 31, 1991)

**4 Games**
2,150—David Klingler, Houston, 1990 (563 vs. Texas Christian, Nov. 3; 299 vs. Texas, Nov. 10; 572 vs. Eastern Wash., Nov. 17; 716 vs. Arizona St., Dec. 2)

**Most Games Gaining 200 Yards or More**
**Season**
12—Ty Detmer, Brigham Young, 1990, 1989; Robbie Bosco, Brigham Young, 1985, 1984
**Career**
38—Ty Detmer, Brigham Young, 1988-91

**Most Consecutive Games Gaining 200 Yards or More**
**Season**
12—Ty Detmer, Brigham Young, 1990, 1989; Robbie Bosco, Brigham Young, 1984
**Career**
27—Ty Detmer, Brigham Young (from Sept. 2, 1989, to Sept. 21, 1991)

**Most Games Gaining 300 Yards or More**
**Season**
12—Ty Detmer, Brigham Young, 1989, 1990
**Career**
33—Ty Detmer, Brigham Young, 1988-91

**Most Consecutive Games Gaining 300 Yards or More**
**Season**
12—Ty Detmer, Brigham Young, 1990, 1989
**Career**
24—Ty Detmer, Brigham Young (from Sept. 2, 1989, to Dec. 1, 1990)

**Most Games Gaining 400 Yards or More**
**Season**
9—David Klingler, Houston, 1990
**Career**
12—Ty Detmer, Brigham Young, 1988-90

**Most Yards Gained by Two Opposing Players**
**Game**
1,253—Matt Vogler, Texas Christian (690) & David Klingler, Houston (563), Nov. 3, 1990

**Two Players, Same Team, Each Passing for 250 Yards or More**
**Game**
Andre Ware (517) & David Klingler (254), Houston vs. Southern Methodist, Oct. 21, 1989; Steve Cottrell (311) & John Elway (270), Stanford vs. Arizona St., Oct. 24, 1981

**Most Yards Gained in an Opening Game of a Season**
511—Scott Mitchell, Utah vs. Idaho St., Sept. 10, 1988

**Most Yards Gained Against One Opponent**
**Career**
1,495—Ty Detmer, Brigham Young vs. New Mexico, 1988-91

**Most Yards Gained Per Game Against One Opponent**
**Career**
(Min. 3 games) 410.7—Gary Schofield, Wake Forest vs. Maryland, 1981-83 (1,232 yards)
(Min. 4 games) 373.8—Ty Detmer, Brigham Young vs. New Mexico, 1988-91 (1,495 yards)

**Most Yards Gained Per Attempt**
**Game**
(Min. 40-59 atts.) 13.93—Marc Wilson, Brigham Young vs. Utah, Nov. 5, 1977 (41 for 571)
(Min. 60 atts.) 10.52—Scott Mitchell, Utah vs. Air Force, Oct. 15, 1988 (60 for 631)
**Season**
(Min. 412 atts.) 11.07—Ty Detmer, Brigham Young, 1989 (412 for 4,560)
**Career**
(Min. 1,000 atts.) 9.82—Ty Detmer, Brigham Young, 1988-91 (1,530 for 15,031)

**Most Yards Gained Per Completion**
**Game**
(Min. 22-41 comps.) 22.8—Marc Wilson, Brigham Young vs. Utah, Nov. 5, 1977 (26 for 571)
(Min. 42 comps.) 15.7—Matt Vogler, Texas Christian vs. Houston, Nov. 3, 1990 (44 for 690)
**Season**
(Min. 109-204 comps.) 18.2—Doug Williams, Grambling, 1977 (181 for 3,286)
(Min. 205 comps.) 17.2—Ty Detmer, Brigham Young, 1989 (265 for 4,560)
**Career**
(Min. 275-399 comps.) 17.2—Danny White, Arizona St., 1971-73 (345 for 5,932)
(Min. 400 comps.) 15.7—Shawn Moore, Virginia, 1987-90 (421 for 6,629)

**Most Touchdown Passes**
**Quarter**
6—David Klingler, Houston vs. Louisiana Tech, Aug. 31, 1991 (2nd)
**Half**
7—Dennis Shaw, San Diego St. vs. New Mexico St., Nov. 15, 1969 (1st)
**Game**
11—David Klingler, Houston vs. Eastern Wash., Nov. 17, 1990
**Season**
54—David Klingler, Houston, 1990 (11 games)
**2 Yrs**
83—David Klingler, Houston, 1990-91
Also holds per-game record at 3.95 (83 in 21)
**3 Yrs**
108—Ty Detmer, Brigham Young, 1989-91
**Career**
121—Ty Detmer, Brigham Young, 1988-91

**Most Touchdown Passes Per Game**
**Season**
4.91—David Klingler, Houston, 1990 (54 in 11)
**Career**
2.84—David Klingler, Houston, 1988-91 (91 in 32)
Collegiate record—2.90, Dennis Shaw, San Diego St., 1968-69 (58 in 20)

**Highest Percentage of Passes for Touchdowns**
**Season**
(Min. 175-374 atts.) 11.6%—Dennis Shaw, San Diego St., 1969 (39 of 335)
(Min. 375 atts.) 10.6%—Jim McMahon, Brigham Young, 1980 (47 of 445)
**Career**
(Min. 400-499 atts.) 9.74%—Rick Leach, Michigan, 1975-78 (45 of 462)
(Min. 500 atts.) 9.09%—Danny White, Arizona St., 1971-73 (59 of 649)

**Most Consecutive Games Throwing a Touchdown Pass**
**Career**
35—Ty Detmer, Brigham Young (from Sept. 7, 1989, to Nov. 23, 1991)

*Division I-A Individual Records*                                      17

## Most Consecutive Passes Completed for Touchdowns

**Game**
6—Brooks Dawson, UTEP vs. New Mexico, Oct. 28, 1967 (first six completions of the game)

## Most Touchdown Passes in First Game of a Career
5—John Reaves, Florida vs. Houston, Sept. 20, 1969

## Most Touchdown Passes by a Freshman

**Game**
6—Bob Hoernschemeyer, Indiana vs. Nebraska, Oct. 9, 1943
**Season**
20—Todd Ellis, South Caro., 1986

## Most Touchdown Passes in Freshman and Sophomore Seasons
45—Ty Detmer, Brigham Young, 1988 (13) & 1989 (32)

## Most Touchdown Passes by a Sophomore
32—Jimmy Klingler, Houston, 1992; Ty Detmer, Brigham Young, 1989

## Most Touchdown Passes at Conclusion of Junior Year
86—Ty Detmer, Brigham Young, 1988 (13), 1989 (32) & 1990 (41)

## Most Touchdown Passes, Same Passer and Receiver

**Season**
19—Elvis Grbac to Desmond Howard, Michigan, 1991; Andre Ware to Manny Hazard, Houston, 1989
**Career**
33—Troy Kopp to Aaron Turner, Pacific (Cal.), 1989-92

## Most Passes Attempted Without a Touchdown Pass

**Season**
266—Stu Rayburn, Kent, 1984 (completed 125)

## Fewest Times Sacked Attempting to Pass
**Season**
*(Min. 300 atts.)* 4—Steve Walsh, Miami (Fla.), 1988, in 390 attempts. Last 4 games of the season: Tulsa, 1 for -8 yards; Louisiana St., 1 for -2; Arkansas, 1 for -12; Brigham Young, 1 for -9.

# RECEIVING

## Most Passes Caught
**Game**
22—Jay Miller, Brigham Young vs. New Mexico, Nov. 3, 1973 (263 yards)
**Season**
142—Manny Hazard, Houston, 1989 (1,689 yards)
**Career**
*(2 yrs.)* 220—Manny Hazard, Houston, 1989-90 (2,635 yards)
*(3 yrs.)* 261—Howard Twilley, Tulsa, 1963-65 (3,343 yards)
*(4 yrs.)* 266—Aaron Turner, Pacific (Cal.), 1989-92 (4,345 yards)

## Most Passes Caught Per Game
**Season**
13.4—Howard Twilley, Tulsa, 1965 (134 in 10)
**Career**
10.5—Manny Hazard, Houston, 1989-90 (220 in 21)

## Most Passes Caught by Two Players, Same Team
**Season**
212—Howard Twilley (134) & Neal Sweeney (78), Tulsa, 1965 (2,662 yards, 24 TDs)
**Career**
453—Mark Templeton (262) & Charles Lockett (191), Long Beach St., 1983-86 (4,871 yards, 30 TDs)

## Most Passes Caught in Consecutive Games
38—Manny Hazard, Houston, 1989 (19 vs. Texas Christian, Nov. 4; 19 vs. Texas, Nov. 11)

## Most Consecutive Games Catching a Pass
**Career**
44—Gary Williams, Ohio St., 1979-82 (every game)

## Most Passes Caught by a Tight End
**Game**
17—Jon Harvey, Northwestern vs. Michigan, Oct. 23, 1982 (208 yards); Emilio Vallez, New Mexico vs. UTEP, Oct. 27, 1967 (257 yards)

## Most Passes Caught Per Game by a Tight End
**Season**
6.36—Chuck Scott, Vanderbilt, 1983 (70 in 11); Mark Dowdell, Bowling Green, 1983 (70 in 11)
**Career**
5.39—Gordon Hudson, Brigham Young, 1980-83 (178 in 33)

## Most Passes Caught by a Running Back
**Game**
18—Mark Templeton, Long Beach St. vs. Utah St., Nov. 1, 1986 (173 yards)
**Season**
99—Mark Templeton, Long Beach St., 1986 (688 yards)
**Career**
262—Mark Templeton, Long Beach St., 1983-86 (1,969 yards)

## Most Passes Caught by a Freshman
**Game**
18—Richard Woodley (WR), Texas Christian vs. Texas Tech, Nov. 10, 1990 (180 yards)
**Season**
61—Jason Wolf, Southern Methodist, 1989 (676 yards)
Also holds per-game record at 5.55

## Catching at Least 50 Passes and Gaining at Least 1,000 Yards Rushing
**Season**
By 10 players. Most recent: Ryan Benjamin, Pacific (Cal.), 1991 (51 catches and 1,581 yards rushing)
Darrin Nelson, Stanford, holds record for most seasons at 3 (1977-78, 1981)

## Catching at Least 60 Passes and Gaining at Least 1,000 Yards Rushing
Johnny Johnson, San Jose St., 1988 (61 catches

and 1,219 yards rushing); Brad Muster, Stanford, 1986 (61 catches and 1,053 yards rushing); Darrin Nelson, Stanford, 1981 (67 catches and 1,014 yards rushing)

### Most Yards Gained
**Game**
349—Chuck Hughes, UTEP vs. North Texas, Sept. 18, 1965 (caught 10)
**Season**
1,779—Howard Twilley, Tulsa, 1965 (caught 134)
**Career**
4,345—Aaron Turner, Pacific (Cal.), 1989-92 (caught 266)

### Most Yards Gained Per Game
**Season**
177.9—Howard Twilley, Tulsa, 1965 (1,779 in 10)
**Career**
128.6—Howard Twilley, Tulsa, 1963-65 (3,343 in 26)

### Most Yards Gained by a Tight End
**Game**
259—Gordon Hudson, Brigham Young vs. Utah, Nov. 21, 1981 (caught 13)
**Season**
1,156—Chris Smith, Brigham Young, 1990 (caught 68)
**Career**
2,484—Gordon Hudson, Brigham Young, 1980-83 (caught 178)

### Most Yards Gained Per Game by a Tight End
**Season**
102.0—Mike Moore, Grambling, 1977 (1,122 in 11)
**Career**
75.3—Gordon Hudson, Brigham Young, 1980-83 (2,484 in 33)

### Most Yards Gained by a Freshman
**Game**
243—Darnay Scott, San Diego St. vs. Brigham Young, Nov. 16, 1991 (caught 8)
**Season**
870—Cormac Carney, Air Force, 1978 (caught 57)
Also holds per-game record at 79.1

### Most Games Gaining 100 Yards or More
**Season**
11—Aaron Turner, Pacific (Cal.), 1991
Also holds consecutive record at 11
**Career**
23—Aaron Turner, Pacific (Cal.), 1989-92 (in 44 games played)

### Most Games Gaining 200 Yards or More
**Season**
5—Howard Twilley, Tulsa, 1965
Also holds consecutive record at 3

### Most Yards Gained by Two Players, Same Team
**Game**
640—Rick Eber (322) & Harry Wood (318), Tulsa vs. Idaho St., Oct. 7, 1967 (caught 33, 6 TDs)
**Season**
2,662—Howard Twilley (1,779) & Neal Sweeney (883), Tulsa, 1965

### Two Players, Same Team, Each Gaining 1,000 yards
Charles Johnson (1,149; 57 catches) & Michael Westbrook (1,060; 76 catches), Colorado, 1992; Andy Boyce (1,241; 79 catches) &

Chris Smith (1,156; 68 catches), Brigham Young, 1990; Patrick Rowe (1,392; 71 catches) & Dennis Arey (1,118; 68 catches), San Diego St., 1990; Jason Phillips (1,443; 108 catches) & James Dixon (1,103; 102 catches), Houston, 1988

### Two Players, Same Team, Ranked No. 1 & No. 2 in Final Receiving Rankings
**Season**
Jason Phillips (No. 1, 9.8 catches per game) & James Dixon (No. 2, 9.3 catches per game), Houston, 1988

### Three Players, Same Team, Each Catching 60 Passes or More
Patrick Rowe (71), Dennis Arey (68) & Jimmy Raye (62), San Diego St., 1990

### Most 1,000-Yard Receiving Seasons
3—Aaron Turner, Pacific (Cal.), 1990-92 (1,264 in 1990; 1,604 in 1991; 1,171 in 1992); Clarkston Hines, Duke, 1987-89 (1,084 in 1987; 1,067 in 1988; 1,149 in 1989); Marc Zeno, Tulane, 1985-87 (1,137 in 1985; 1,033 in 1986; 1,206 in 1987)

### Highest Average Gain Per Reception
**Game**
*(Min. 3-4 receps.)* 72.7—Terry Gallaher, East Caro. vs. Appalachian St., Sept. 13, 1975 (3 for 218; 82, 77, 59 yards)
*(Min. 5-9 receps.)* 52.6—Alex Wright, Auburn vs. Pacific (Cal.), Sept. 9, 1989 (5 for 263; 78, 60, 41, 73, 11 yards)
*(Min. 10 receps.)* 34.9—Chuck Hughes, UTEP vs. North Texas, Sept. 18, 1965 (10 for 349)
*(Min. 30-49 receps.)* 27.9—Elmo Wright, Houston, 1968 (43 for 1,198)
*(Min. 50 receps.)* 24.4—Henry Ellard, Fresno St., 1982 (62 for 1,510)
**Career**
*(Min. 75-104 receps.)* 25.7—Wesley Walker, California, 1973-76 (86 for 2,206)
*(Min. 105 receps.)* 22.0—Herman Moore, Virginia, 1988-90 (114 for 2,504)

### Highest Average Gain Per Reception by a Tight End
**Season**
*(Min. 30 receps.)* 22.6—Jay Novacek, Wyoming, 1984 (33 for 745)
**Career**
*(Min. 75 receps.)* 19.2—Clay Brown, Brigham Young, 1978-80 (88 for 1,691)

### Most Touchdown Passes Caught
**Game**
6—Tim Delaney, San Diego St. vs. New Mexico St., Nov. 15, 1969 (16 receptions)
**Season**
22—Manny Hazard, Houston, 1989 (142 receptions)
Per-game record—2.25, Tom Reynolds, San Diego St., 1969 (18 in 8)
**Career**
43—Aaron Turner, Pacific (Cal.), 1989-92 (266 receptions)

### Most Games Catching a Touchdown Pass
**Season**
10—Desmond Howard, Michigan, 1991; Aaron Turner, Pacific (Cal.), 1991; Herman Moore, Virginia, 1990; Manny Hazard, Houston, 1989
**Career**
26—Aaron Turner, Pacific (Cal.), 1989-92 (caught a total of 43 in 44 games); Terance

*Division I-A Individual Records*                                       19

Mathis, New Mexico, 1985-87, 1989 (caught a total of 36 in 44 games)

### Most Consecutive Games Catching a Touchdown Pass
**Season**
10—Desmond Howard, Michigan, 1991
**Career**
12—Desmond Howard, Michigan (last two games of 1990 and first 10 games of 1991); Aaron Turner, Pacific (Cal.) (last three games of 1990 and first nine games of 1991)

### Most Touchdown Passes Caught by a Tight End
**Season**
18—Dennis Smith, Utah, 1989 (73 receptions)
**Career**
24—Dennis Smith, Utah, 1987-89 (156 receptions); Dave Young, Purdue, 1977-80 (172 receptions)

### Highest Percentage of Passes Caught for Touchdowns
**Season**
(Min. 10 TDs) 58.8%—Kevin Williams, Southern Cal, 1978 (10 of 17)
**Career**
(Min. 20 TDs) 35.3%—Kevin Williams, Southern Cal, 1977-80 (24 of 68)

Also holds record for touchdown frequency: 1 TD every 2.83 catches

### Highest Average Yards Per Touchdown Pass
**Season**
(Min. 10) 56.1—Elmo Wright, Houston, 1968 (11 for 617 yards; 87, 50, 75, 2, 80, 79, 13, 67, 61, 43, 60 yards)

### Most Touchdown Passes Caught, 50 Yards or More
**Season**
8—Henry Ellard, Fresno St., 1982 (68, 51, 80, 61, 67, 72, 80, 72 yards); Elmo Wright, Houston, 1968 (87, 50, 75, 80, 79, 67, 61, 60 yards)

### Most Consecutive Passes Caught for Touchdowns
6—Gerald Armstrong, Nebraska, 1992 (1 vs. Utah, Sept. 5; 1 vs. Arizona St., Sept. 26; 1 vs. Oklahoma St., Oct. 10; 1 vs. Colorado, Oct. 31; 2 vs. Kansas, Nov. 7); Carlos Carson, Louisiana St., 1977 (5 vs. Rice, Sept. 24; 1 vs. Florida, Oct. 1; first receptions of his career)

### Most Touchdown Passes Caught by a Freshman
**Season**
10—Dwight Collins, Pittsburgh, 1980

# PUNTING

### Most Punts
**Game**
36—Charlie Calhoun, Texas Tech vs. Centenary, Nov. 11, 1939 (1,318 yards; 20 were returned, 8 went out of bounds, 6 were downed, 1 was blocked [blocked kicks counted against the punter until 1955] and 1 went into the end zone for a touchback. Thirty-three of the punts occurred on first down during a heavy downpour in the game played at Shreveport, Louisiana)
**Season**
101—Jim Bailey, Va. Military, 1969 (3,507 yards)
**Career**
(3 yrs.) 276—Jim Bailey, Va. Military, 1969-71 (10,127 yards)
(4 yrs.) 320—Cameron Young, Texas Christian, 1976-79 (12,947 yards)

### Highest Average Per Punt
**Game**
(Min. 5-9 punts) 60.4—Lee Johnson, Brigham Young vs. Wyoming, Oct. 8, 1983 (5 for 302; 53, 44, 63, 62, 80 yards)
(Min. 10 punts) 53.6—Jim Benien, Oklahoma St. vs. Colorado, Nov. 13, 1971 (10 for 536)
**Season**
(Min. 40-49 punts) 49.8—Reggie Roby, Iowa, 1981 (44 for 2,193)
(Min. 50-74 punts) 48.2—Ricky Anderson, Vanderbilt, 1984 (58 for 2,793)
(Min. 75 punts) 45.8—Bucky Scribner, Kansas, 1982 (76 for 3,478)
**Career**
(Min. 150-199 punts) 45.6—Reggie Roby, Iowa, 1979-82 (172 for 7,849)
(Min. 200-249 punts) 44.7—Ray Guy, Southern Miss., 1970-72 (200 for 8,934)
(Min. 250 punts) 44.3—Bill Smith, Mississippi, 1983-86 (254 for 11,260)

### Highest Average Per Punt by a Freshman
**Season**
(Min. 40 punts) 47.0—Tom Tupa, Ohio St., 1984 (41 for 1,927)

### Most Yards on Punts
**Game**
1,318—Charlie Calhoun, Texas Tech vs. Centenary, Nov. 11, 1939 (36 punts)
**Season**
4,138—Johnny Pingel, Michigan St., 1938 (99 punts)
**Career**
12,947—Cameron Young, Texas Christian, 1976-79 (320 punts)

### Most Games With a 40-Yard Average or More
**Career**
(Min. 4 punts) 36—Bill Smith, Mississippi, 1983-86 (punted in 44 games)

### Most Punts, 50 Yards or More
**Season**
31—Chuck Ramsey, Wake Forest, 1973 (87 punts); Marv Bateman, Utah, 1971 (68 punts)
**Career**
(2 yrs.) 51—Marv Bateman, Utah, 1970-71 (133 punts)
(3 yrs.) 61—Russ Henderson, Virginia, 1976-78 (226 punts)
(4 yrs.) 88—Bill Smith, Mississippi, 1983-86 (254 punts)

### Most Consecutive Games With at Least One Punt of 50 Yards or More
**Career**
32—Bill Smith, Mississippi, 1983-86

### Most Punts in a Career Without Having One Blocked
300—Tony DeLeone, Kent, 1981-84
Also holds consecutive record at 300

### Longest Punt
99—Pat Brady, Nevada vs. Loyola (Cal.), Oct. 28, 1950

### Ranking in Top 12 in Both Punting and Field Goals
Daron Alcorn, Akron, 1992 (No. 11 in punting, 43.6-yard average and tied for No. 9 in field goals, 1.64 per game); Dan Eichloff, Kansas,

1991 (No. 12 in punting, 42.3-yard average and No. 3 in field goals, 1.64 per game); Chris Gardocki, Clemson, 1990 (No. 4 in punting, 44.3-yard average and No. 4 in field goals, 1.73 per game), 1989 (No. 10 in punting, 42.7-yard average and No. 6 in field goals, 1.82 per game); Rob Keen, California, 1988 (No. 11 in punting, 42.6-yard average and No. 3 in field goals, 1.91 per game); Steve Little, Arkansas, 1977 (No. 4 in punting, 44.3-yard average and No. 2 in field goals, 1.73 per game)

# INTERCEPTIONS

### Most Passes Intercepted
**Game**
5—Dan Rebsch, Miami (Ohio) vs. Western Mich., Nov. 4, 1972 (88 yards); Byron Beaver, Houston vs. Baylor, Sept. 22, 1962 (18 yards); Walt Pastuszak, Brown vs. Rhode Island, Oct. 8, 1949 (47 yards); Lee Cook, Oklahoma St. vs. Detroit, Nov. 28, 1942 (15 yards)
**Season**
14—Al Worley, Washington, 1968 (130 yards)
**Career**
29—Al Brosky, Illinois, 1950-52 (356 yards)

### Most Passes Intercepted Per Game
**Season**
1.40—Al Worley, Washington, 1968 (14 in 10)
**Career**
1.07—Al Brosky, Illinois, 1950-52 (29 in 27)

### Most Passes Intercepted by a Linebacker
**Season**
9—Bill Sibley, Texas A&M, 1941 (57 yards)

### Most Passes Intercepted by a Freshman
**Game**
3—Torey Hunter, Washington St. vs. Arizona St., Oct. 19, 1991 (22 yards); Shawn Simms, Bowling Green vs. Toledo, Oct. 24, 1981 (46 yards)
**Season**
13—George Shaw, Oregon, 1951 (136 yards)
Also holds per-game record at 1.30 (13 in 10)

### Most Yards on Interception Returns
**Game**
182—Ashley Lee, Virginia Tech vs. Vanderbilt, Nov. 12, 1983 (2 interceptions)

**Season**
302—Charles Phillips, Southern Cal, 1974 (7 interceptions)
**Career**
501—Terrell Buckley, Florida St., 1989-91 (21 interceptions)

### Most Touchdowns Scored on Interception Returns
**Game**
3—Johnny Jackson, Houston vs. Texas, Nov. 7, 1987 (31, 53, 97 yards)
**Season**
3—By many players. Most recent: Johnny Jackson, Houston, 1987 (8 interceptions); Erik McMillan, Missouri, 1987 (5 interceptions)
**Career**
5—Ken Thomas, San Jose St., 1979-82 (14 interceptions); Jackie Walker, Tennessee, 1969-71 (11 interceptions)

### Highest Average Gain Per Interception
**Game**
(Min. 2 ints.) 91.0—Ashley Lee, Virginia Tech vs. Vanderbilt, Nov. 12, 1983 (2 for 182)
**Season**
(Min. 5 ints.) 50.6—Norm Thompson, Utah, 1969 (5 for 253)
**Career**
(Min. 15 ints.) 26.5—Tom Pridemore, West Va., 1975-77 (15 for 398)

### Most Consecutive Games Intercepting a Pass
15—Al Brosky, Illinois, began Nov. 11, 1950 (vs. Iowa), ended Oct. 18, 1952 (vs. Minnesota)

# PUNT RETURNS

### Most Punt Returns
**Game**
20—Milton Hill, Texas Tech vs. Centenary, Nov. 11, 1939 (110 yards)
**Season**
55—Dick Adams, Miami (Ohio), 1970 (578 yards)
Also holds per-game record at 5.50
**Career**
153—Vai Sikahema, Brigham Young, 1980-81, 1984-85 (1,312 yards)

### Most Yards on Punt Returns
**Game**
219—Golden Richards, Brigham Young vs. North Texas, Sept. 10, 1971 (5 returns)
**Season**
791—Lee Nalley, Vanderbilt, 1948 (43 returns)
Also holds per-game record at 79.1
**Career**
1,695—Lee Nalley, Vanderbilt, 1947-49 (109 returns)

### Highest Average Gain Per Return
**Game**
(Min. 3-4 rets.) 59.7—Chip Hough, Air Force vs. Southern Methodist, Oct. 9, 1971 (3 for 179)
(Min. 5 rets.) 43.8—Golden Richards, Brigham Young vs. North Texas, Sept. 10, 1971 (5 for 219)
**Season**
(Min. 1.2 rets. per game) 25.9—Bill Blackstock, Tennessee, 1951 (12 for 311)
(Min. 1.5 rets. per game) 25.0—George Sims, Baylor, 1948 (15 for 375)
**Career**
(Min. 1.2 rets. per game) 23.6—Jack Mitchell, Oklahoma, 1946-48 (39 for 922)
(Min. 1.5 rets. per game) 20.5—Gene Gibson, Cincinnati, 1949-50 (37 for 760)

### Most Touchdowns Scored on Punt Returns
**Game**
2—By many players. Most recent: Jeff Sweitzer, Akron vs. Northern Ariz., Nov. 4, 1989 (53 and 70 yards in first and second quarters)
**Season**
4—James Henry, Southern Miss., 1987; Golden Richards, Brigham Young, 1971; Cliff Branch, Colorado, 1971
**Career**
7—Johnny Rodgers, Nebraska, 1970-72 (2 in 1970, 3 in 1971, 2 in 1972); Jack Mitchell, Oklahoma, 1946-48 (3 in 1946, 1 in 1947, 3 in 1948)

*Division I-A Individual Records*                    21

# KICKOFF RETURNS

**Most Kickoff Returns**

**Game**
11—Trevor Cobb, Rice vs. Houston, Dec. 2, 1989 (166 yards)

**Season**
44—Frank Collins, Utah, 1974 (907 yards)

**Career**
114—Joe Redding, Southwestern La., 1985-88 (2,642 yards)

**Most Returns Per Game**

**Season**
4.6—Dwayne Owens, Oregon St., 1990 (41 in 9)

**Career**
3.0—Steve Odom, Utah, 1971-73 (99 in 33)

**Most Yards on Kickoff Returns**

**Game**
241—Jerry Blitz, Harvard vs. Princeton, Nov. 8, 1952 (7 returns)

**Season**
1,014—Dwayne Owens, Oregon St., 1990 (41 returns)

**Career**
2,642—Joe Redding, Southwestern La., 1985-88 (114 returns)

**Most Yards Returned Per Game**

**Season**
112.7—Dwayne Owens, Oregon St., 1990 (1,014 in 9)

**Career**
78.2—Steve Odom, Utah, 1971-73 (2,582 in 33)

**Highest Average Gain Per Return**

**Game**
*(Min. 3 rets.)* 72.7—Anthony Davis, Southern Cal vs. Notre Dame, Dec. 2, 1972 (3 for 218)

**Season**
*(Min. 1.2 rets. per game)* 40.1—Paul Allen,
Brigham Young, 1961 (12 for 481)
*(Min. 1.5 rets. per game)* 38.2—Forrest Hall, San Francisco, 1946 (15 for 573)

**Career**
*(Min. 1.2 rets. per game)* 36.2—Forrest Hall, San Francisco, 1946-47 (22 for 796)
*(Min. 1.5 rets. per game)* 31.0—Overton Curtis, Utah St., 1957-58 (32 for 991)

**Most Touchdowns Scored on Kickoff Returns**

**Game**
2—Stacey Corley, Brigham Young vs. Air Force, Nov. 11, 1989 (99 & 85 yards); *Raghib Ismail, Notre Dame vs. Michigan, Sept. 16, 1989 (88 & 92 yards); Raghib Ismail, Notre Dame vs. Rice, Nov. 5, 1988 (87 & 83 yards); Anthony Davis, Southern Cal vs. Notre Dame, Dec. 2, 1972 (97 & 96 yards); Ollie Matson, San Francisco vs. Fordham, Oct. 20, 1951 (94 & 90 yards); Ron Horwath, Detroit vs. Hillsdale, Sept. 22, 1950 (96 & 96 yards); Paul Copoulos, Marquette vs. Iowa Pre-Flight, Nov. 6, 1943 (85 & 82 yards)

**Season**
3—Terance Mathis, New Mexico, 1989; Willie Gault, Tennessee, 1980; Anthony Davis, Southern Cal, 1974; Stan Brown, Purdue, 1970; Forrest Hall, San Francisco, 1946

**Career**
6—Anthony Davis, Southern Cal, 1972-74
* Ismail is the only player in history to score twice in two games.

**Scoring a Touchdown on Team's Opening Kickoff of Two Seasons**

**Season**
Barry Sanders, Oklahoma St., 1988 (100 yards vs. Miami, Ohio, Sept. 10) & 1987 (100 yards vs. Tulsa, Sept. 5)

# TOTAL KICK RETURNS
### (Combined Punt and Kickoff Returns)

**Most Kick Returns**

**Game**
20—Milton Hill, Texas Tech vs. Centenary, Nov. 11, 1939 (20 punts, 110 yards)

**Season**
70—Keith Stephens, Louisville, 1986 (28 punts, 42 kickoffs, 1,162 yards); Dick Adams, Miami (Ohio), 1970 (55 punts, 15 kickoffs, 944 yards)

**Career**
199—Tony James, Mississippi St., 1989-92 (121 punts, 78 kickoffs, 3,194 yards)

**Most Yards on Kick Returns**

**Game**
247—Tyrone Hughes, Nebraska vs. Kansas St., Oct. 6, 1991 (8 returns); Golden Richards, Brigham Young vs. North Texas, Sept. 10, 1971 (7 returns)

**Season**
1,228—Steve Odom, Utah, 1972
Per-game record—116.2, Dion Johnson, East Caro., 1990 (1,046 yards, with 167 on punt returns and 879 on kickoff returns in 9 games)

**Career**
3,194—Tony James, Mississippi St., 1989-92 (1,332 on punts, 1,862 on kickoffs)

**Gaining 1,000 Yards on Punt Returns and 1,000 Yards on Kickoff Returns**

**Career**
Tony James, Mississippi St., 1989-92 (1,332 & 1,862); Willie Drewrey, West Va., 1981-84 (1,072 & 1,302); Anthony Carter, Michigan 1979-82 (1,095 & 1,504); Devon Ford, Appalachian St., 1973-76 (1,197 & 1,761); Troy Slade, Duke, 1973-75 (1,021 & 1,757)

**Highest Average Per Kick Return (Min. 1.2 Punt Returns and 1.2 Kickoff Returns Per Game)**

**Season**
27.2—Erroll Tucker, Utah, 1985 (40 for 1,087; 16 for 389 on punt returns, 24 for 698 on kickoff returns)

**Highest Average Per Kick Return (Min. 1.3 Punt Returns and 1.3 Kickoff Returns Per Game)**

**Career**
22.0—Erroll Tucker, Utah, 1984-85 (79 for 1,741; 38 for 650 on punt returns, 41 for 1,091 on kickoff returns)

**Averaging 20 Yards Each on Punt Returns and Kickoff Returns (Min. 1.2 Returns Per Game Each)**

Season
By 7 players. Most recent: Lee Gissendaner, Northwestern, 1992 (21.8 on punt returns, 15 for 327; 22.4 on kickoff returns, 17 for 381)

**Most Touchdowns Scored on Kick Returns (Must Have at Least One Punt Return and One Kickoff Return)**

Game
2—By 5 players. Most recent: Eric Blount, North Caro. vs. William & Mary, Oct. 5, 1991 (1 punt, 1 kickoff)

Season
5—Robert Woods, Grambling, 1977 (3 punts, 2 kickoffs); Pinky Rohm, Louisiana St., 1937 (3 punts, 2 kickoffs)

Career
8—Johnny Rodgers, Nebraska, 1970-72 (7 punts, 1 kickoff); Cliff Branch, Colorado, 1970-71 (6 punts, 2 kickoffs)

**Winning Both Punt Return and Kickoff Return Championships**

Season
Erroll Tucker, Utah, 1985

Career
Erroll Tucker, Utah, 1985; Ira Matthews, Wisconsin, kickoff returns (1976) and punt returns (1978)

# ALL RUNBACKS

(Combined Interceptions, Punt Returns and Kickoff Returns)

**Scoring More Than One Touchdown in Each Category**

Season
Erroll Tucker, Utah, 1985 (3 interceptions, 2 punt returns, 2 kickoff returns)

**Scoring One Touchdown in Each Category**

Season
Scott Thomas, Air Force, 1985; Mark Haynes, Arizona St., 1974; Dick Harris, South Caro., 1970

**Highest Average Per Runback**

Season
(Min. 40 returns) 28.3—Erroll Tucker, Utah, 1985 (6 for 216 on interceptions, 16 for 389 on punt returns, 24 for 698 on kickoff returns; total 46 for 1,303)

**Highest Average Per Runback (At Least 7 Interceptions and Min. 1.3 Punt Returns and 1.3 Kickoff Returns Per Game)**

Career
22.6—Erroll Tucker, Utah, 1984-85 (8 for 224 on interceptions, 38 for 650 on punt returns, 41 for 1,091 on kickoff returns; total 87 for 1,965)

**Most Touchdowns on Interceptions, Punt Returns and Kickoff Returns (Must Have at Least One Touchdown in Each Category)**

Season
7—Erroll Tucker, Utah, 1985 (3 interceptions, 2 punt returns, 2 kickoff returns)

Career
8—Erroll Tucker, Utah, 1984-85 (3 interceptions, 3 punt returns, 2 kickoff returns)

# OPPONENT'S KICKS BLOCKED

**Most Opponent's Punts Blocked By**

Game
4—Ken Irvin, Memphis St. vs. Arkansas, Sept. 26, 1992 (4 punts)

Season
8—James Francis (LB), Baylor, 1989 (11 games); Jimmy Lisko, Arkansas St., 1975 (11 games)

**Most Opponent's Total Kicks Blocked By (Includes Punts, PAT Attempts, FG Attempts)**

Game
4—Ken Irvin, Memphis St. vs. Arkansas, Sept. 26, 1992 (4 punts)

Career
19—James Ferebee, New Mexico St., 1978-81 (8 FG attempts, 6 PAT attempts, 5 punts)

**Most Touchdowns Scored on Blocked Punts**

Season
3—Joe Wessel, Florida St., 1984

# ALL-PURPOSE RUNNING

### (Yardage Gained From Rushing, Receiving and All Runbacks)

**Most Plays**

**Game**

58—Tony Sands, Kansas vs. Missouri, Nov. 23, 1991 (58 rushes)

**Season**

432—Marcus Allen, Southern Cal, 1981 (403 rushes, 29 receptions)

**Career**

*(3 yrs.)* 1,034—Herschel Walker, Georgia, 1980-82 (994 rushes, 26 receptions, 14 kickoff returns)

*(4 yrs.)* 1,347—Steve Bartalo, Colorado St., 1983-86 (1,215 rushes, 132 receptions)

**Most Yards Gained**

**Game**

422—Marshall Faulk, San Diego St. vs. Pacific (Cal.), Sept. 14, 1991 (386 rushing, 11 receiving, 25 kickoff returns)

**Season**

3,250—Barry Sanders, Oklahoma St., 1988 (2,628 rushing, 106 receiving, 95 punt returns, 421 kickoff returns; 11 games)

**Career**

*(3 yrs.)* 5,749—Herschel Walker, Georgia, 1980-82 (5,259 rushing, 243 receiving, 247 kickoff returns; 1,034 plays)

*(4 yrs.)* 7,172—$Napoleon McCallum, Navy, 1981-85 (4,179 rushing, 796 receiving, 858 punt returns, 1,339 kickoff returns; 1,138 plays)

$ See page 8 for explanation.

**Most Yards Gained Per Game**

**Season**

295.5—Barry Sanders, Oklahoma St., 1988 (3,250 in 11 games)

**Career**

237.8—Ryan Benjamin, Pacific (Cal.), 1990-92 (5,706 in 24 games; 3,119 rushing, 1,063 receiving, 100 punt returns, 1,424 kickoff returns)

Collegiate record—7,564, Howard Stevens, Randolph-Macon, 1968-69, and Louisville,

1971-72 (5,297 rushing, 738 receiving, 781 punt returns, 748 kickoff returns)

**Most Yards Gained by a Freshman**

**Game**

422—Marshall Faulk, San Diego St. vs. Pacific (Cal.), Sept. 14, 1991 (386 rushing, 11 receiving, 25 kickoff returns)

**Season**

1,805—Herschel Walker, Georgia, 1980 (1,616 rushing, 70 receiving, 119 kickoff returns; 287 plays)

Per-game record—184.8, Marshall Faulk, San Diego St., 1991 (1,663 in 9)

**Most Seasons With 2,000 or More Yards**

2—Ryan Benjamin, Pacific (Cal.), 1991 (2,995) & 1992 (2,597); Sheldon Canley, San Jose St., 1989 (2,513) & 1990 (2,213); Chuck Weatherspoon, Houston, 1989 (2,391) & 1990 (2,038); Napoleon McCallum, Navy, 1983 (2,385) & 1985 (2,330); Howard Stevens, Randolph-Macon, 1968 (2,115) & Louisville, 1972 (2,132)

**Highest Average Gain Per Play**

**Season**

*(Min. 1,500 yards, 100-124 plays)* 18.5—Henry Bailey, Nevada-Las Vegas, 1992 (1,883 on 102)

*(Min. 1,500 yards, 125 plays)* 15.72—Terance Mathis, New Mexico, 1989 (2,138 on 136)

**Career**

*(Min. 5,000 yards, 275-374 plays)* 17.4—Anthony Carter, Michigan, 1979-82 (5,197 on 298)

*(Min. 5,000 yards, 375 plays)* 14.64—Terance Mathis, New Mexico, 1985-87, 1989 (6,691 on 457)

**Most Yards Gained by Two Players, Same Team**

**Career**

9,751—Ryan Benjamin (5,706) & Aaron Turner (4,045), Pacific (Cal.), 1990-92 (does not include Turner's freshman year in 1989 but does include Benjamin's in 1990)

# SCORING

### Most Points Scored
### (By Non-Kickers)

**Game**

48—Howard Griffith, Illinois vs. Southern Ill., Sept. 22, 1990 (8 TDs on runs of 5, 51, 7, 41, 5, 18, 5, 3 yards)

**Season**

234—Barry Sanders, Oklahoma St., 1988 (39 TDs in 11 games)

**2 Yrs**

312—Barry Sanders, Oklahoma St., 1987-88 (52 TDs in 22 games)

**Career**

*(3 yrs.)* 336—Steve Owens, Oklahoma, 1967-69 (56 TDs)

*(4 yrs.)* 394—Anthony Thompson, Indiana, 1986-89 (65 TDs, 4 PATs)

**Most Points Scored Per Game**

**Season**

21.27—Barry Sanders, Oklahoma St., 1988 (234 in 11)

**2 Yrs**

14.2—Barry Sanders, Oklahoma St., 1987-88 (312 in 22)

**Career**

11.9—Bob Gaiters, New Mexico St., 1959-60 (203 in 17)

**Most Points Scored by a Freshman**

**Game**

44—Marshall Faulk, San Diego St. vs. Pacific (Cal.), Sept. 14, 1991 (7 TDs, 1 two-point conversion)

**Season**

140—Marshall Faulk, San Diego St., 1991 (23 TDs, 1 two-point conversion)

Also holds per-game record at 15.6 (140 in 9)

**Most Touchdowns Scored**

**Game**

8—Howard Griffith, Illinois vs. Southern Ill., Sept. 22, 1990 (all 8 by rushing on runs of 5, 51, 7, 41, 5, 18, 5, 3 yards)

**Season**

39—Barry Sanders, Oklahoma St., 1988 (11 games)

Also holds per-game record at 3.55 (39 in 11)

**2 Yrs**

52—Barry Sanders, Oklahoma St., 1987-88 (22

games)
Also holds per-game record at 2.36 (52 in 22)
**Career**
*(3 yrs.)* 56—Steve Owens, Oklahoma, 1967-69 (all by rushing)
Per-game record—1.93, Ed Marinaro, Cornell, 1969-71 (52 in 27)
*(4 yrs.)* 65—Anthony Thompson, Indiana, 1986-89 (64 rushing, 1 pass reception)

**Most Touchdowns Scored, Two and Three Consecutive Games**
**2 Games**
11—Kelvin Bryant, North Caro., 1981 (6 vs. East Caro., Sept. 12; 5 vs. Miami, Ohio, Sept. 19)
**3 Games**
15—Kelvin Bryant, North Caro., 1981 (6 vs. East Caro., Sept. 12; 5 vs. Miami, Ohio, Sept. 19; 4 vs. Boston College, Sept. 26)

**Most Touchdowns Scored by a Freshman**
**Game**
7—Marshall Faulk, San Diego St. vs. Pacific (Cal.), Sept. 14, 1991 (all by rushing)
**Season**
23—Marshall Faulk, San Diego St., 1991 (21 rushing, 2 pass receptions)
Also holds per-game record at 2.56 (23 in 9)

**Most Consecutive Games Scoring a Touchdown**
**Career**
23—Bill Burnett, Arkansas (from Oct. 5, 1968, through Oct. 31, 1970; 47 touchdowns)

**Most Games Scoring a Touchdown**
**Season**
11—By many players. Most recent: Barry Sanders, Oklahoma St., 1988
**Career**
31—Ted Brown, North Caro. St., 1975-78; Tony Dorsett, Pittsburgh, 1973-76; Glenn Davis, Army, 1943-46

**Most Games Scoring Two or More Touchdowns**
**Season**
11—Barry Sanders, Oklahoma St., 1988
**Career**
17—Tony Dorsett, Pittsburgh, 1973-76; Steve Owens, Oklahoma, 1967-69; Glenn Davis, Army, 1943-46

**Most Consecutive Games Scoring Two or More Touchdowns**
**Season**
11—Barry Sanders, Oklahoma St., 1988
**Career**
13—Barry Sanders, Oklahoma St. (from Nov. 14, 1987, through 1988)

**Most Games Scoring Three or More Touchdowns**
**Season**
9—Barry Sanders, Oklahoma St., 1988

**Most Consecutive Games Scoring Three or More Touchdowns**
**Season**
5—Barry Sanders, Oklahoma St., 1988 (from Sept. 10 through Oct. 15); Paul Hewitt, San Diego St., 1987 (from Oct. 10 through Nov. 7)

**Most Touchdowns and Points Scored by Two Players, Same Team**
**Season**
54 and 324—Barry Sanders (39-234) & Hart Lee Dykes (15-90), Oklahoma St., 1988
**Career**
97 and 585—Glenn Davis (59-354) & Doc

Blanchard (38-231), Army, 1943-46
**Passing for a Touchdown and Scoring Touchdowns by Rushing and Receiving**
**Game**
By many players. Most recent: Keith Byars, Ohio St. vs. Iowa, Sept. 22, 1984

**Passing for a Touchdown and Scoring on a Pass Reception and Punt Return**
**Game**
By many players. Most recent: Scott Schwedes, Syracuse vs. Temple, Oct. 26, 1985

**Most Extra Points Attempted by Kicking**
**Game**
14—Terry Leiweke, Houston vs. Tulsa, Nov. 23, 1968 (13 made)
**Season**
71—Kurt Gunther, Brigham Young, 1980 (64 made)
**Career**
217—Roman Anderson, Houston, 1988-91 (213 made)

**Most Extra Points Made by Kicking**
**Game**
13—Derek Mahoney, Fresno St. vs. New Mexico, Oct. 5, 1991 (13 attempts); Terry Leiweke, Houston vs. Tulsa, Nov. 23, 1968 (14 attempts)
**Season**
67—Cary Blanchard, Oklahoma St., 1988 (67 attempts)
Also holds per-game record at 6.09 (67 in 11)
**Career**
213—Roman Anderson, Houston, 1988-91 (217 attempts)
Per-game record—5.15, Al Limahelu, San Diego St., 1969-70 (103 in 20)

**Best Perfect Record of Extra Points Made**
**Season**
67 of 67—Cary Blanchard, Oklahoma St., 1988

**Highest Percentage of Extra Points Made**
**Career**
*(Min. 100 atts.)* 100%—David Browndyke, Louisiana St., 1986-89 (109 of 109); Pete Stoyanovich, Indiana 1985-88 (101 of 101); Van Tiffin, Alabama, 1983-86 (135 of 135)

**Most Consecutive Extra Points Made**
**Game**
13—Derek Mahoney, Fresno St. vs. New Mexico, Oct. 5, 1991 (13 attempts)
**Season**
67—Cary Blanchard, Oklahoma St., 1988 (67 attempts)
**Career**
157—Carlos Huerta, Miami (Fla.), 1988-91

**Most Points Scored by Kicking**
**Game**
24—Mike Prindle, Western Mich. vs. Marshall, Sept. 29, 1984 (7 FGs, 3 PATs)
**Season**
131—Roman Anderson, Houston, 1989 (22 FGs, 65 PATs)
Also holds per-game record at 11.91 (131 in 11)
**Career**
423—Roman Anderson, Houston, 1988-91 (70 FGs, 213 PATs)
Also holds per-game record at 9.61 (423 in 44)

**Highest Percentage of Extra Points and Field Goals Made**
**Season**
*(Min. 30 PATs and 15 FGs made)* 98.3%—Chuck Nelson, Washington, 1982 (34 of 34

PATs, 25 of 26 FGs)
*(Min. 40 PATs and 20 FGs made)* 97.3%—Chris
Jacke, UTEP, 1988 (48 of 48 PATs, 25 of 27
FGs)
**Career**
*(Min. 100 PATs and 50 FGs made)* 93.3%—John
Lee, UCLA, 1982-85 (116 of 117 PATs, 79 of
92 FGs)

### Most Two-Point Attempts Made
**Game**
6—Jim Pilot, New Mexico St. vs. Hardin-Simmons, Nov. 25, 1961 (all by running, attempted 7)

**Season**
6—Howard Twilley, Tulsa, 1964 (all on pass
receptions); Jim Pilot, New Mexico St., 1961
(all by running); Pat McCarthy, Holy Cross,
1960 (all by running)
**Career**
13—Pat McCarthy, Holy Cross, 1960-62 (all by
running)

### Most Successful Two-Point Passes
**Season**
12—John Hangartner, Arizona St., 1958 (attempted 21)
**Career**
19—Pat McCarthy, Holy Cross, 1960-62 (attempted 33)

# DEFENSIVE EXTRA POINTS

### Most Defensive Extra Points Scored
**Game**
1—By 23 players. Most recent: Lee Rubin,
Penn St. vs. Pittsburgh, Nov. 21, 1992 (kick
return)
**Season**
1—By 23 players. Most recent: Lee Rubin,
Penn St. vs. Pittsburgh, Nov. 21, 1992 (kick
return)

### Longest Return of a Defensive
### Extra-Point Attempt
**Game**
100—William Price (CB), Kansas St. vs. Indiana
St., Sept. 7, 1991 (intercepted pass three
yards deep in Indiana St. end zone); Curt
Newton (LB), Washington St. vs. Oregon St.,
Oct. 20, 1990 (returned conversion pass

attempt from Washington St. goal line); Quin-
tin Parker (DB), Illinois vs. Wisconsin, Oct.
28, 1989 (returned kick from Illinois goal
line); Lee Ozmint (LB), Alabama vs. Louisiana
St., Nov. 11, 1989 (intercepted pass at Alabama goal line)

### First Defensive Extra-Point Attempt
**Season**
Thomas King (S), Southwestern La. vs. Cal St.
Fullerton, Sept. 3, 1988 (returned blocked
kick 6 yards)

### Most Defensive Extra-Point Kicks Blocked
**Game**
2—Nigel Codrington (DB), Rice vs. Notre
Dame, Nov. 5, 1988 (1 resulted in a score)
Also holds season record at 2

# FUMBLE RETURNS (Since 1992)
### Most Fumble Returns
**Game**
1—By many players

# FIELD GOALS

### Most Field Goals Attempted
**Game**
9—Mike Prindle, Western Mich. vs. Marshall,
Sept. 29, 1984 (7 made)
**Season**
38—Jerry DePoyster, Wyoming, 1966 (13 made)
Also holds per-game record at 3.80
**Career**
*(3 yrs.)* 93—Jerry DePoyster, Wyoming, 1965-
67 (36 made)
Also holds per-game record at 3.10
*(4 yrs.)* 105—Philip Doyle, Alabama, 1987-90
(78 made); Luis Zendejas, Arizona St., 1981-
84 (78 made)
Doyle holds per-game record at 2.44 (105 in 43)

### Most Field Goals Made
**Quarter**
4—By 4 players. Most recent: David Hardy,
Texas A&M vs. Texas-Arlington, Sept. 18,
1982 (2nd)
**Half**
5—Dat Ly, New Mexico St. vs. Kansas, Oct. 1,
1988 (1st); Dale Klein, Nebraska vs. Missouri,
Oct. 19, 1985 (1st)
**Game**
7—Dale Klein, Nebraska vs. Missouri, Oct. 19,
1985 (32, 22, 43, 44, 29, 43, 43 yards), 7
attempts; Mike Prindle, Western Mich. vs.
Marshall, Sept. 29, 1984 (32, 44, 42, 23, 48, 41,

27 yards), 9 attempts
**Season**
29—John Lee, UCLA, 1984 (33 attempts)
**2 Yrs**
50—John Lee, UCLA, 1984-85 (57 attempts)
**Career**
80—Jeff Jaeger, Washington, 1983-86 (99 attempts)

### Most Field Goals Made Per Game
**Season**
2.64—John Lee, UCLA, 1984 (29 in 11)
**Career**
1.84—John Lee, UCLA, 1982-85 (79 in 43)

### Best Perfect Record of Field Goals Made
**Game**
7 of 7—Dale Klein, Nebraska vs. Missouri, Oct.
19, 1985

### Most Field Goals Made by a Freshman
**Game**
6—*Mickey Thomas, Virginia Tech vs. Vanderbilt, Nov. 4, 1989 (6 attempts)
**Season**
23—Collin Mackie, South Caro., 1987 (30 attempts)
* *Conventional-style kicker.*

## Highest Percentage of Field Goals Made
**Season**
*(Min. 15 atts.)* 96.2%—Chuck Nelson, Washington, 1982 (25 of 26)
**Career**
*(Min. 45-54 atts.)* 87.8%—Bobby Raymond, Florida, 1983-84 (43 of 49)
*(Min. 55 atts.)* 85.9%—John Lee, UCLA, 1982-85 (79 of 92)

## Most Consecutive Field Goals Made
**Season**
25—Chuck Nelson, Washington, 1982 (first 25, missed last attempt of season vs. Washington St., Nov. 20)
**Career**
30—Chuck Nelson, Washington, 1981-82 (last 5 in 1981, from Southern Cal, Nov. 14, and first 25 in 1982, ending with last attempt vs. Washington St., Nov. 20)

## Most Games Kicking a Field Goal
**Career**
40—Gary Gussman, Miami (Ohio), 1984-87 (in 44 games played)

## Most Consecutive Games Kicking a Field Goal
19—Gary Gussman, Miami (Ohio), 1986-87; Larry Roach, Oklahoma St., 1983-84

## Most Field Goals Made, 60 Yards or More
**Game**
2—Tony Franklin, Texas A&M vs. Baylor, Oct. 16, 1976 (65 & 64 yards)
**Season**
3—Russell Erxleben, Texas, 1977 (67 vs. Rice, Oct. 1; 64 vs. Baylor, Oct. 16; 60 vs. Texas Tech, Oct. 29) (4 attempts)
**Career**
3—Russell Erxleben, Texas, 1975-78 (see Season Record above)

## Most Field Goals Attempted, 60 Yards or More
**Season**
5—Tony Franklin, Texas A&M, 1976 (2 made)
**Career**
11—Tony Franklin, Texas A&M, 1975-78 (2 made)

## Most Field Goals Made, 50 Yards or More
**Game**
3—Sergio Lopez-Chavero, Wichita St. vs. Drake, Oct. 27, 1984 (54, 54, 51 yards); Jerry DePoyster, Wyoming vs. Utah, Oct. 8, 1966 (54, 54, 52 yards)
**Season**
8—Fuad Reveiz, Tennessee, 1982 (10 attempts)
20—Jason Hanson, Washington St., 1988-91 (35 attempts)

## Most Field Goals Attempted, 50 Yards or More
**Season**
17—Jerry DePoyster, Wyoming, 1966 (5 made)
**Career**
38—Tony Franklin, Texas A&M, 1975-78 (16 made)

## Highest Percentage of Field Goals Made, 50 Yards or More
**Season**
*(Min. 10 atts.)* 80.0%—Fuad Reveiz, Tennessee, 1982 (8 of 10)
**Career**
*(Min. 15 atts.)* 60.9%—Max Zendejas, Arizona, 1982-85 (14 of 23)

## Most Field Goals Made, 40 Yards or More
**Game**
5—Alan Smith, Texas A&M vs. Arkansas St., Sept. 17, 1983 (44, 45, 42, 59, 57 yards)
**Season**
14—Chris Jacke, UTEP, 1988 (16 attempts)
**Career**
39—Jason Hanson, Washington St., 1988-91 (66 attempts) (19 of 31, 40-49 yards; 20 of 35, 50 or more yards)

## Most Field Goals Attempted, 40 Yards or More
**Season**
25—Jerry DePoyster, Wyoming, 1966 (6 made)
**Career**
66—Jason Hanson, Washington St., 1988-91 (39 made)

## Highest Percentage of Field Goals Made, 40 Yards or More
**Season**
*(Min. 10 made)* 90.9%—John Carney, Notre Dame, 1984 (10 of 11)
**Career**
*(Min. 20 made)* 69.4%—John Lee, UCLA, 1982-85 (25 of 36)

## Highest Percentage of Field Goals Made, 40-49 Yards
**Season**
*(Min. 10 made)* 100%—John Carney, Notre Dame, 1984 (10 of 10)
**Career**
*(Min. 15 made)* 82.6%—Jeff Jaeger, Washington, 1983-86 (19 of 23)

## Most Consecutive Field Goals Made, 40-49 Yards
**Career**
12—John Carney, Notre Dame, 1984-85

## Highest Percentage of Field Goals Made, Under 40 Yards
**Season**
*(Min. 16 made)* 100%—Philip Doyle, Alabama, 1989 (19 of 19); Scott Slater, Texas A&M, 1986 (16 of 16); Bobby Raymond, Florida, 1984 (18 of 18); John Lee, UCLA, 1984 (16 of 16); Randy Pratt, California, 1983 (16 of 16); Paul Woodside, West Va., 1982 (23 of 23)
**Career**
*(Min. 30-39 made)* 97.0%—Bobby Raymond, Florida, 1983-84 (32 of 33)
*(Min. 40 made)* 96.4%—John Lee, UCLA, 1982-85 (54 of 56)

## Longest Average Distance Field Goals Made
**Game**
*(Min. 4 made)* 49.5—Jeff Heath, East Caro. vs. Texas-Arlington, Nov. 6, 1982 (58, 53, 42, 45 yards)
**Season**
*(Min. 10 made)* 50.9—Jason Hanson, Washington St., 1991 (10 made)
**Career**
*(Min. 25 made)* 42.4—Russell Erxleben, Texas, 1975-78 (49 made)

## Longest Average Distance Field Goals Attempted
**Season**
*(Min. 20 atts.)* 51.2—Jason Hanson, Washington St., 1991 (22 attempts)
**Career**
*(Min. 40 atts.)* 44.7—Russell Erxleben, Texas, 1975-78 (78 attempts)

**Most Times Kicking Two or More Field Goals in a Game**
**Season**
10—Paul Woodside, West Va., 1982
**Career**
27—Kevin Butler, Georgia, 1981-84

**Most Times Kicking Three or More Field Goals in a Game**
**Season**
6—Joe Allison, Memphis St., 1992; Luis Zendejas, Arizona St., 1983
**Career**
13—Luis Zendejas, Arizona St., 1981-84

**Most Times Kicking Four or More Field Goals in a Game**
**Season**
4—Matt Bahr, Penn St., 1978
**Career**
6—John Lee, UCLA, 1982-85
Also holds career record for most times kicking four or more field goals in a game at 8

**Longest Field Goal Made**
67—Joe Williams, Wichita St. vs. Southern Ill., Oct. 21, 1978; Steve Little, Arkansas vs. Texas, Oct. 15, 1977; Russell Erxleben, Texas vs. Rice, Oct. 1, 1977

**Longest Indoor Field Goal Made**
57—Juan Carrillo, Cal St. Fullerton vs. Northern Ariz., Oct. 15, 1977

**Longest Field Goal Made Without Use of a Kicking Tee**
62—Jason Hanson, Washington St. vs. Nevada-Las Vegas, Sept. 28, 1991

**Longest Field Goal Made by a Freshman**
59—Barry Childers, Marshall vs. Western Caro., Oct. 25, 1980; Tony Franklin, Texas A&M vs. Rice, Nov. 15, 1975

**Longest Field Goal Made on First Attempt of a Career**
61—Ralf Mojsiejenko, Michigan St. vs. Illinois, Sept. 11, 1982

**Most Field Goals Made in First Game of a Career**
5—Jose Oceguera, Long Beach St. vs. Kansas St., Sept. 3, 1983 (5 attempts); Nathan Ritter, North Caro. St. vs. East Caro., Sept. 9, 1978 (6 attempts); Joe Liljenquist, Brigham Young vs. Colorado St., Sept. 20, 1969 (6 attempts)

**Most Games in Which Field Goal(s) Provided the Winning Margin**
**Season**
6—Henrik Mike-Mayer, Drake, 1981
**Career**
10—Jeff Ward, Texas, 1983-86; John Lee, UCLA, 1982-85; Dan Miller, Miami (Fla.), 1978-81

---

# TEAM RECORDS

## SINGLE GAME—OFFENSE
### TOTAL OFFENSE

**Most Plays**
112—Montana vs. Montana St., Nov. 1, 1952 (475 yards)

**Most Plays, Both Teams**
196—San Diego St. (99) & North Texas (97), Dec. 4, 1971 (851 yards)

**Fewest Plays**
12—Texas Tech vs. Centenary, Nov. 11, 1939 (10 rushes, 2 passes, -1 yard)

**Fewest Plays, Both Teams**
33—Texas Tech (12) & Centenary (21), Nov. 11, 1939 (28 rushes, 5 passes, 30 yards)

**Most Yards Gained**
1,021—Houston vs. Southern Methodist, Oct. 21, 1989 (250 rushing, 771 passing, 86 plays)

**Most Yards Gained, Both Teams**
1,563—Houston (827) & Texas Christian (736), Nov. 3, 1990 (187 plays)

**Fewest Yards Gained**
Minus 47—Syracuse vs. Penn St., Oct. 18, 1947 (-107 rushing, gained 60 passing, 49 plays)

**Fewest Yards Gained, Both Teams**
30—Texas Tech (-1) & Centenary (31), Nov. 11, 1939 (33 plays)

**Most Yards Gained by a Losing Team**
736—Texas Christian vs. Houston, Nov. 3, 1990 (lost 35-56)

**Both Teams Gaining 600 Yards or More**
In 12 games. Most recent: Houston (684) & Texas Tech (636), Nov. 30, 1991 (182 plays); Brigham Young (767) & San Diego St. (695), Nov. 16, 1991 (168 plays); San Jose St. (616) & Pacific (Cal.) (603), Oct. 19, 1991 (157 plays)

**Fewest Yards Gained by a Winning Team**
22—Citadel vs. Davidson, Nov. 23, 1946 (won 21-13)

**Highest Average Gain Per Play (Min. 75 Plays)**
11.9—Houston vs. Southern Methodist, Oct. 21, 1989 (86 for 1,021)

**Most Touchdowns Scored by Rushing and Passing**
15—Wyoming vs. Northern Colo., Nov. 5, 1949 (9 rushing, 6 passing)

### RUSHING

**Most Rushes**
99—Missouri vs. Colorado, Oct. 12, 1968 (421 yards)

**Most Rushes, Both Teams**
141—Colgate (82) & Bucknell (59), Nov. 6, 1971 (440 yards)

**Fewest Rushes**
5—Houston vs. Texas Tech, Nov. 25, 1989 (36 yards)

**Fewest Rushes, Both Teams**
28—Texas Tech (10) & Centenary (18), Nov. 11, 1939 (23 yards)

**Most Yards Gained**
768—Oklahoma vs. Kansas St., Oct. 15, 1988 (72 rushes)

**Most Yards Gained, Both Teams**
1,039—Lenoir-Rhyne (837) & Davidson (202), Oct. 11, 1975 (111 rushes)

**Fewest Yards Gained, Both Teams**
Minus 24—San Jose St. (-102) & UTEP (78), Oct. 22, 1966 (75 rushes)

**Most Yards Gained, Both Teams, Major-College Opponents**
956—Oklahoma (711) & Kansas St. (245), Oct. 23, 1971 (111 rushes)

**Most Yards Gained Without Loss**
677—Nebraska vs. New Mexico St., Sept. 18, 1982 (78 rushes)

**Most Yards Gained by a Losing Team**
525—Air Force vs. New Mexico, Nov. 2, 1991 (70 rushes, lost 32-34)

**Highest Average Gain Per Rush (Min. 50 Rushes)**
11.9—Alabama vs. Virginia Tech, Oct. 27, 1973 (63 for 748)

**Most Players on One Team Each Gaining 100 Yards or More**
4—Army vs. Montana, Nov. 17, 1984 (Doug Black 183, Nate Sassaman 155, Clarence Jones 130, Jarvis Hollingsworth 124); Alabama vs. Virginia Tech, Oct. 27, 1973 (Jimmy Taylor 142, Wilbur Jackson 138, Calvin Culliver 127, Richard Todd 102); Texas vs. Southern Methodist, Nov. 1, 1969 (Jim Bertelsen 137, Steve Worster 137, James Street 121, Ted Koy 111); Arizona vs. Arizona, Nov. 10, 1951 (Bob Tarwater 140, Harley Cooper 123, Duane Morrison 118, Buzz Walker 113)

**Most Touchdowns Scored by Rushing**
12—UTEP vs. New Mexico St., Nov. 25, 1948

## PASSING

**Most Passes Attempted**
81—Houston vs. Southern Methodist, Oct. 20, 1990 (completed 53)

**Most Passes Attempted, Both Teams**
135—Texas Christian (79) & Houston (56), Nov. 3, 1990 (completed 81)

**Fewest Passes Attempted**
0—By many teams. Most recent: Oklahoma vs. Colorado, Nov. 15, 1986

**Fewest Passes Attempted, Both Teams**
1—Michigan St. (0) & Maryland (1), Oct. 20, 1944 (not completed)

**Most Passes Attempted Without a Completion**
18—West Va. vs. Temple, Oct. 18, 1946

**Most Passes Attempted Without Interception**
72—Houston vs. Texas Christian, Nov. 4, 1989 (completed 47)

**Most Passes Attempted Without Interception, Both Teams**
114—Illinois (67) & Purdue (47), Oct. 12, 1985 (completed 67)

**Most Consecutive Passes Attempted Without a Rushing Play**
32—North Caro. St. vs. Duke, Nov. 11, 1989 (3rd & 4th quarters, completed 16)

**Most Passes Completed**
53—Houston vs. Southern Methodist, Oct. 20, 1990 (attempted 81)

**Most Passes Completed, Both Teams**
81—Texas Christian (44) & Houston (37), Nov. 3, 1990 (attempted 135)

**Best Perfect Game (1.000 Pct.)**
11 of 11—North Caro. vs. William & Mary, Oct. 5, 1991; Air Force vs. Northwestern, Sept. 17, 1988; Oregon St. vs. UCLA, Oct. 2, 1971; Southern Cal vs. Washington, Oct. 9, 1965

**Highest Percentage of Passes Completed**
*(Min. 15-24 comps.)* 95.0%—Mississippi vs. Tulane, Nov. 6, 1982 (19 of 20)
*(Min. 25-34 comps.)* 92.6%—UCLA vs. Wash-

ington, Oct. 29, 1983 (25 of 27)
*(Min. 35 comps.)* 81.1%—California vs. Florida, Sept. 13, 1980 (43 of 53)

**Highest Percentage of Passes Completed, Both Teams (Min. 40 Completions)**
84.6%—UCLA & Washington, Oct. 29, 1983 (44 of 52)

**Most Passes Had Intercepted**
10—California vs. UCLA, Oct. 21, 1978 (52 attempts); Detroit Mercy vs. Oklahoma St., Nov. 28, 1942

**Most Yards Gained**
771—Houston vs. Southern Methodist, Oct. 21, 1989 (completed 40 of 61)

**Most Yards Gained, Both Teams**
1,253—Texas Christian (690) & Houston (563), Nov. 3, 1990 (135 attempts)

**Fewest Yards Gained, Both Teams**
Minus 13—North Caro. (-7 on 1 of 3 attempts) & Pennsylvania (-6 on 2 of 12 attempts), Nov. 13, 1943

**Most Yards Gained Per Attempt**
*(Min. 30-39 atts.)* 14.6—Arizona St. vs. Stanford, Oct. 24, 1981 (35 for 511)
*(Min. 40 atts.)* 15.9—UTEP vs. North Texas, Sept. 18, 1965 (40 for 634)

**Most Yards Gained Per Completion**
*(Min. 15-24 comps.)* 31.9—UTEP vs. New Mexico, Oct. 28, 1967 (16 for 510)
*(Min. 25 comps.)* 25.4—UTEP vs. North Texas, Sept. 18, 1965 (25 for 634)

**Most Touchdown Passes**
11—Houston vs. Eastern Wash., Nov. 17, 1990

**Most Touchdown Passes, Major-College Opponents**
10—Houston vs. Southern Methodist, Oct. 21, 1989; San Diego St. vs. New Mexico St., Nov. 15, 1969

*Division I-A Team Records*

**Most Touchdown Passes, Both Teams**
14—Houston (11) & Eastern Wash. (3), Nov. 17, 1990

**Most Touchdown Passes, Both Teams, Major-College Opponents**
13—San Diego St. (10) & New Mexico St. (3), Nov. 15, 1969

# PUNTING

**Most Punts**
39—Texas Tech vs. Centenary, Nov. 11, 1939 (1,377 yards)
38—Centenary vs. Texas Tech, Nov. 11, 1939 (1,248 yards)

**Most Punts, Both Teams**
77—Texas Tech (39) & Centenary (38), Nov. 11, 1939 (2,625 yards) (The game was played in a heavy downpour in Shreveport, Louisiana. Forty-two punts were returned, 19 went out of bounds, 10 were downed, 1 went into the end zone for a touchback, 4 were blocked and 1 was fair caught. Sixty-seven punts [34 by Texas Tech and 33 by Centenary] occurred on first-down plays, including 22 consecutively in the third and fourth quarters. The game was a scoreless tie.)

**Fewest Punts**
0—By many teams. Most recent: Nebraska vs. Colorado St., Sept. 14, 1991 (won 71-14); New Mexico St. vs. UTEP, Sept. 14, 1991 (lost 21-22)

**Fewest Punts by a Losing Team**
0—By many teams. Most recent: New Mexico St. vs. UTEP, Sept. 14, 1991 (lost 21-22)

**Highest Average Per Punt**
*(Min. 5-9 punts)* 60.4—Brigham Young vs. Wyoming, Oct. 8, 1983 (5 for 302)
*(Min. 10 punts)* 53.6—Oklahoma St. vs. Colorado, Nov. 13, 1971 (10 for 536)

**Highest Average Per Punt, Both Teams (Min. 10 Punts)**
55.3—Brigham Young & Wyoming, Oct. 8, 1983 (11 for 608)

# PUNT RETURNS

**Most Punt Returns**
22—Texas Tech vs. Centenary, Nov. 11, 1939 (112 yards)

**Most Punt Returns, Both Teams**
42—Texas Tech (22) & Centenary (20), Nov. 11, 1939 (233 yards)

**Most Yards on Punt Returns**
319—Texas A&M vs. North Texas, Sept. 21, 1946 (10 returns)

**Highest Average Gain Per Return (Min. 5 Returns)**
44.2—Denver vs. Colorado Col., Sept. 17, 1954 (6 for 265)

**Most Touchdowns Scored on Punt Returns**
3—Holy Cross vs. Brown, Sept. 21, 1974; Louisiana St. vs. Mississippi, Dec. 5, 1970; Wichita St. vs. Northern St. (S.D.), Oct. 22, 1949; Wisconsin vs. Iowa, Nov. 8, 1947

# KICKOFF RETURNS

**Most Kickoff Returns**
14—Arizona St. vs. Nevada, Oct. 12, 1946 (290 yards)

**Most Yards on Kickoff Returns**
295—Cincinnati vs. Memphis St., Oct. 30, 1971 (8 returns)

**Highest Average Gain Per Return (Min. 6 Returns)**
46.2—Southern Cal vs. Washington St., Nov. 7, 1970 (6 for 277)

**Most Touchdowns Scored on Kickoff Returns**
2—By many teams. Most recent: Brigham Young vs. Air Force, Nov. 11, 1989; Notre Dame vs. Michigan, Sept. 16, 1989; New Mexico St. vs. Drake, Oct. 15, 1983 (consecutive returns)

**Touchdowns Scored on Back-to-Back Kickoff Returns, Both Teams**
2—By many teams. Most recent: Wisconsin & Northern Ill., Sept. 14, 1985

# TOTAL KICK RETURNS

### (Combined Punt and Kickoff Returns)

**Most Yards on Kick Returns**
376—Florida St. vs. Virginia Tech, Nov. 16, 1974 (9 returns)

**Highest Average Gain Per Return (Min. 7 Returns)**
41.8—Florida St. vs. Virginia Tech, Nov. 16, 1974 (9 for 376)

# SCORING

**Most Points Scored**
103—Wyoming vs. Northern Colo. (0), Nov. 5, 1949 (15 TDs, 13 PATs)

**Most Points Scored Against a Major-College Opponent**
100—Houston vs. Tulsa (6), Nov. 23, 1968 (14 TDs, 13 PATs, 1 FG)

**Most Points Scored, Both Teams**
124—Oklahoma (82) & Colorado (42), Oct. 4, 1980

**Most Points Scored by a Losing Team**
51—San Diego St. vs. Wyoming (52), Oct. 6, 1990

**Most Points, Both Teams in a Tie Game**
104—Brigham Young (52) & San Diego St. (52), Nov. 16, 1991

**Most Points Scored in One Quarter**
49—Fresno St. vs. New Mexico, Oct. 5, 1991 (2nd quarter); Davidson vs. Furman, Sept. 27, 1969 (2nd quarter); Houston vs. Tulsa, Nov. 23, 1968 (4th quarter)

**Most Points Scored in One Half**
76—Houston vs. Tulsa, Nov. 23, 1968 (2nd half)

**Most Touchdowns Scored**
15—Wyoming vs. Northern Colo., Nov. 5, 1949 (9 rushing, 6 passing)

**Most Touchdowns Scored, Both Teams**
18—Oklahoma (12) & Colorado (6), Oct. 4, 1980

**Most Extra Points Made by Kicking**
13—Fresno St. vs. New Mexico, Oct. 5, 1991 (attempted 13); Houston vs. Tulsa, Nov. 23, 1968 (attempted 14); Wyoming vs. Northern Colo., Nov. 5, 1949 (attempted 15)

**Most Two-Point Attempts Scored**
7—Pacific (Cal.) vs. San Diego St., Nov. 22, 1958 (attempted 9)

**Most Defensive Extra-Point Attempts**
2—Northern Ill. vs. Akron, Nov. 3, 1990 (2 interception returns); Rice vs. Notre Dame, Nov. 5, 1988 (2 kick returns; 1 scored)

**Most Defensive Extra-Point Attempts Scored**
1—By 23 teams. Most recent: Penn St. vs. Pittsburgh, Nov. 21, 1992 (kick return)

**Most Field Goals Made**
7—Nebraska vs. Missouri, Oct. 19, 1985 (attempted 7); Western Mich. vs. Marshall, Sept. 29, 1984 (attempted 9)

**Most Field Goals Made, Both Teams**
9—Southwestern La. (5) & Central Mich. (4), Sept. 9, 1989 (attempted 11)

**Most Field Goals Attempted**
9—Western Mich. vs. Marshall, Sept. 29, 1984 (made 7)

**Most Field Goals Attempted, Both Teams**
12—Clemson (6) & Georgia (6), Sept. 17, 1983 (made 6)

**Most Field Goals Missed**
7—Louisiana St. vs. Florida, Nov. 25, 1972 (attempted 8)

# FIRST DOWNS

**Most First Downs**
44—Nebraska vs. Utah St., Sept. 7, 1991 (33 rush, 10 pass, 1 penalty)

**Most First Downs, Both Teams**
72—New Mexico (37) & San Diego St. (35), Sept. 27, 1986

**Fewest First Downs by a Winning Team**
0—Michigan vs. Ohio St., Nov. 25, 1950 (won

9-3); North Caro. St. vs. Virginia, Sept. 30, 1944 (won 13-0)

**Most First Downs by Rushing**
36—Nebraska vs. New Mexico St., Sept. 18, 1982

**Most First Downs by Passing**
30—Brigham Young vs. Colorado St., Nov. 7, 1981; Tulsa vs. Idaho St., Oct. 7, 1967

# FUMBLES

**Most Fumbles**
17—Wichita St. vs. Florida St., Sept. 20, 1969 (lost 10)

**Most Fumbles, Both Teams**
27—Wichita St. (17) & Florida St. (10), Sept. 20, 1969 (lost 17)

**Most Fumbles Lost**
10—Wichita St. vs. Florida St., Sept. 20, 1969 (17 fumbles)

**Most Fumbles Lost, Both Teams**
17—Wichita St. (10) & Florida St. (7), Sept. 20, 1969 (27 fumbles)

**Most Fumbles Lost in a Quarter**
5—San Diego St. vs. California, Sept. 18, 1982 (1st quarter); East Caro. vs. Southwestern La., Sept. 13, 1980 (3rd quarter on 5 consecutive possessions)

# PENALTIES

**Most Penalties Against**
24—San Jose St. vs. Fresno St., Oct. 4, 1986 (199 yards)

**Most Penalties, Both Teams**
36—San Jose St. (24) & Fresno St. (12), Oct. 4, 1986 (317 yards)

**Fewest Penalties, Both Teams**
0—By many teams. Most recent: Army & Navy,

Dec. 6, 1986

**Most Yards Penalized**
238—Arizona St. vs. UTEP, Nov. 11, 1961 (13 penalties)

**Most Yards Penalized, Both Teams**
421—Grambling (16 for 216 yards) & Texas Southern (17 for 205 yards), Oct. 29, 1977

# TURNOVERS

**(Number of Times Losing the Ball on Interceptions and Fumbles)**

**Most Turnovers Lost**
13—Georgia vs. Georgia Tech, Dec. 1, 1951 (8 interceptions, 5 fumbles)

**Most Turnovers, Both Teams**
20—Wichita St. (12) & Florida St. (8), Sept. 20, 1969 (17 fumbles, 3 interceptions)

*Division I-A Team Records*

**Most Total Plays Without a Turnover (Rushes, Passes, All Runbacks)**
110—Baylor vs. Rice, Nov. 13, 1976; California vs. San Jose St., Oct. 5, 1968 (also did not fumble)

**Most Total Plays Without a Turnover, Both Teams**
184—Arkansas (93) & Texas A&M (91), Nov. 2, 1968

**Most Total Plays Without a Turnover or a Fumble, Both Teams**
158—Stanford (88) & Oregon (70), Nov. 2, 1957

**Most Turnovers by a Winning Team**
11—Purdue vs. Illinois, Oct. 2, 1943 (9 fumbles, 2 interceptions; won 40-21)

**Most Passes Had Intercepted by a Winning Team**
7—Pittsburgh vs. Army, Nov. 15, 1980 (54 attempts; won 45-7)

**Most Fumbles Lost by a Winning Team**
9—Arizona St. vs. Utah, Oct. 14, 1972 (10 fumbles; won 59-48); Purdue vs. Illinois, Oct. 2, 1943 (10 fumbles; won 40-21)

# SINGLE GAME—DEFENSE
## TOTAL DEFENSE

**Fewest Plays Allowed**
12—Centenary vs. Texas Tech, Nov. 11, 1939 (10 rushes, 2 passes; -1 yard)

**Fewest Yards Allowed**
Minus 47—Penn St. vs. Syracuse, Oct. 18, 1947

(-107 rushing, 60 passing; 49 plays)

**Most Yards Allowed**
1,021—Southern Methodist vs. Houston, Oct. 21, 1989 (250 rushing, 771 passing)

## RUSHING DEFENSE

**Fewest Rushes Allowed**
5—Texas Tech vs. Houston, Nov. 25, 1989 (36 yards)

**Fewest Rushing Yards Allowed**
Minus 109—Toledo vs. Northern Ill., Nov. 11, 1967 (33 rushes)

## PASS DEFENSE

**Fewest Attempts Allowed**
0—By many teams. Most recent: Colorado vs. Oklahoma, Nov. 15, 1986

**Fewest Completions Allowed**
0—By many teams. Most recent: San Jose St. vs. Cal St. Fullerton, Oct. 10, 1992 (11 attempts)

**Lowest Completion Percentage Allowed (Min. 10 Attempts)**
.000—San Jose St. vs. Cal St. Fullerton, Oct. 10, 1992 (0 of 11 attempts); Temple vs. West Va., Oct. 18, 1946 (0 of 18 attempts)

**Fewest Yards Allowed**
Minus 16—Va. Military vs. Richmond, Oct. 5, 1957 (2 completions)

**Most Passes Intercepted By**
11—Brown vs. Rhode Island, Oct. 8, 1949 (136 yards)

**Most Passes Intercepted By Against a Major-College Opponent**
10—UCLA vs. California, Oct. 21, 1978; Oklahoma St. vs. Detroit Mercy, Nov. 28, 1942

**Most Yards on Interception Returns**
240—Kentucky vs. Mississippi, Oct. 1, 1949 (6 returns)

**Most Touchdowns on Interception Returns**
4—Houston vs. Texas, Nov. 7, 1987 (198 yards; 3 TDs in the fourth quarter)

## FIRST DOWNS

**Fewest First Downs Allowed**
0—By many teams. Most recent: North Caro. St. vs. Western Caro., Sept. 1, 1990

## OPPONENT'S KICKS BLOCKED

**Most Opponent's Punts Blocked**
4—Memphis St. vs. Arkansas, Sept. 26, 1992 (10 attempts); Michigan vs. Ohio St., Nov. 25, 1950; Southern Methodist vs. Texas-Arlington, Sept. 30, 1944

**Most Opponent's Punts Blocked, One Quarter**
3—Purdue vs. Northwestern, Nov. 11, 1989 (4 attempts)

## TURNOVERS GAINED
### (Number of Times Gaining the Ball on Interceptions and Fumbles)

**Most Turnovers Gained**
13—Georgia Tech vs. Georgia, Dec. 1, 1951 (8 interceptions, 5 fumbles)

**Most Consecutive Opponents' Series Resulting in Turnovers**
7—Florida vs. Florida St., Oct. 7, 1972 (3 interceptions, 4 fumbles lost; first seven series of the game)

## FUMBLE RETURNS (SINCE 1992)

**Most Touchdowns on Fumble Returns**
2—Toledo vs. Arkansas St., Sept. 5, 1992

**Longest Return of a Fumble**
97 yards—East Caro. vs. West Va., Nov. 7, 1992

## DEFENSIVE EXTRA POINTS

**Most Defensive Extra Points Scored Against**
1—By many teams. Most recent: Pittsburgh vs. Penn St., Nov. 21, 1992 (kick return)

**Most Defensive Extra-Point Attempts Against**
2—Akron vs. Northern Ill., Nov. 3, 1990 (2 interception returns); Notre Dame vs. Rice, Nov. 5, 1988 (2 blocked kick returns, 1 scored)

# SEASON—OFFENSE
## TOTAL OFFENSE

**Most Yards Gained Per Game**
624.9—Houston, 1989 (6,874 in 11)

**Most Yards Gained**
6,874—Houston, 1989 (11 games)

**Highest Average Gain Per Play**
7.61—Brigham Young, 1989 (852 for 6,485)

**Gaining 300 Yards or More Per Game Rushing and 200 Yards or More Per Game Passing**
Arizona St., 1973 (310.2 rushing, 255.3 passing);

Houston, 1968 (361.7 rushing, 200.3 passing)

**Most Plays Per Game**
92.4—Notre Dame, 1970 (924 in 10)

**Most Touchdowns Rushing and Passing**
84—Nebraska, 1983
Also holds per-game record at 7.0

## RUSHING

**Most Yards Gained Per Game**
472.4—Oklahoma, 1971 (5,196 in 11)

**Highest Average Gain Per Rush**
7.64—Army, 1945 (424 for 3,238)

**Highest Average Gain Per Rush (Min. 500 Rushes)**
6.83—Oklahoma, 1971 (761 for 5,196)

**Most Rushes Per Game**
73.9—Oklahoma, 1974 (813 in 11)

**Most Touchdowns Rushing Per Game**
5.1—Texas, 1970, 1969; Oklahoma, 1956 (each 51 in 10)

## PASSING

**Most Yards Gained Per Game**
511.3—Houston, 1989 (5,624 in 11)

**Most Yards Gained**
5,624—Houston, 1989 (11 games)

**Highest Average Gain Per Attempt**
*(Min. 225-349 atts.)* 10.07—Syracuse, 1987 (250 for 2,518)
*(Min. 350 atts.)* 10.93—Brigham Young, 1989 (433 for 4,732)

**Highest Average Gain Per Completion**
*(Min. 100-174 comps.)* 19.1—Houston, 1968 (105 for 2,003)
*(Min. 175-224 comps.)* 18.0—Grambling, 1977 (187 for 3,360)
*(Min. 225 comps.)* 16.96—Brigham Young, 1989 (279 for 4,732)

**Most Passes Attempted Per Game**
63.1—Houston, 1989 (694 in 11)

**Most Passes Completed Per Game**
39.4—Houston, 1989 (434 in 11)

**Highest Percentage Completed (Min. 150 Attempts)**
70.8%—Long Beach St., 1985 (323 of 456)

**Lowest Percentage Had Intercepted**
*(Min. 300-399 atts.)* 1.13%—Georgia, 1991 (4 of 355)
*(Min. 400 atts.)* 1.53%—Miami (Fla.), 1992 (7 of 457)

**Most Touchdown Passes Per Game**
5.0—Houston, 1989 (55 in 11)

**Most Touchdown Passes**
55—Houston, 1989 (11 games)

**Fewest Touchdown Passes**
0—By 5 teams since 1975. Most recent: Air Force, 1990 (11 games, 90 attempts)

**Highest Passing Efficiency Rating Points (Min. 150 Attempts)**
174.45—Brigham Young, 1989 (433 attempts, 279 completions, 15 interceptions, 4,732 yards, 33 TD passes)

**A Team With a 3,000-Yard Passer, 1,000-Yard Receiver and 1,000-Yard Rusher**
Houston, 1989 (Andre Ware 4,699 passing, Manny Hazard 1,689 receiving, Chuck Weatherspoon 1,146 rushing); Colorado St., 1983 (Terry Nugent 3,319 passing, Jeff Champine 1,002 receiving, Steve Bartalo 1,113 rushing); Southern Methodist, 1968 (Chuck Hixson 3,103 passing, Jerry LeVias 1,131 receiving, Mike Richardson 1,034 rushing)

**A Team With Two 1,000-Yard Receivers**
Colorado, 1992 (Charles Johnson, 1,149 & Michael Westbrook, 1,060); San Diego St., 1990 (Patrick Rowe, 1,392 & Dennis Arey, 1,118); Brigham Young, 1990 (Andy Boyce, 1,241 & Chris Smith, 1,156); Houston, 1988 (Jason Phillips, 1,444 & James Dixon, 1,103)

**A Team With the No. 1 & No. 2 Receivers**
Houston, 1988 (Jason Phillips, No. 1, 9.82 catches per game & James Dixon, No. 2, 9.27 catches per game)

**Most 100-Yard Receiving Games in a Season, One Team**
19—San Diego St., 1990 (Patrick Rowe 9, Dennis Arey 8 & Jimmy Raye 2)

# PUNTING

**Most Punts Per Game**
13.9—Tennessee, 1937 (139 in 10)

**Fewest Punts Per Game**
2.0—Nevada, 1948 (18 in 9)

**Highest Punting Average**
50.6—Brigham Young, 1983 (24 for 1,215 yards)

**Highest Punting Average (Min. 40 Punts)**
47.6—Vanderbilt, 1984 (59 for 2,810)

**Highest Net Punting Average**
45.0—Brigham Young, 1983 (24 for 1,215 yards, 134 yards in punts returned)

**Highest Net Punting Average (Min. 40 Punts)**
44.4—Colorado St., 1976 (72 for 3,323, 123 yards in punts returned)

# PUNT RETURNS

**Most Punt Returns Per Game**
6.9—Texas A&M, 1943 (69 in 10)

**Fewest Punt Returns Per Game**
0.55—Iowa, 1971 (6 in 11)

**Most Punt-Return Yards Per Game**
114.5—Colgate, 1941 (916 in 8)

**Highest Average Gain Per Return**
(Min. 15-29 rets.) 25.2—Arizona St., 1952 (18 for 454 yards)
(Min. 30 rets.) 22.4—Oklahoma, 1948 (43 for 963)

**Most Touchdowns Scored on Punt Returns (From 1966)**
7—Southern Miss., 1987 (on 46 returns)

# KICKOFF RETURNS

**Most Kickoff Returns Per Game**
7.3—Cal St. Fullerton, 1990 (80 in 11)

**Fewest Kickoff Returns Per Game**
0.7—Boston College, 1939 (7 in 10)

**Most Kickoff-Return Yards Per Game**
134.7—Virginia Tech, 1973 (1,482 in 11)

**Highest Average Gain Per Return**
(Min. 25-34 rets.) 30.3—Florida St., 1992 (27 for 819)
(Min. 35 rets.) 27.5—Rice, 1973 (39 for 1,074)

**Most Touchdowns Scored on Kickoff Returns (From 1966)**
4—Dayton, 1974 (on 44 returns)

# SCORING

**Most Points Per Game**
56.0—Army, 1944 (504 in 9)

**Most Points Scored**
624—Nebraska, 1983 (12 games)

**Highest Scoring Margin**
52.1—Army, 1944 (scored 504 points for 56.0 average and allowed 35 points for 3.9 average in 9 games)

**Most Points Scored, Two Consecutive Games**
177—Houston, 1968 (77-3 vs. Idaho, Nov. 16, and 100-6 vs. Tulsa, Nov. 23)

**Most Touchdowns Per Game**
8.22—Army, 1944 (74 in 9)

**Most Touchdowns**
89—Nebraska, 1983 (12 games)

**Most Extra Points Made by Kicking**
77—Nebraska, 1983 (77 in 12, attempted 85) Also holds per-game record at 6.4

**Most Consecutive Extra Points Made by Kicking**
67—Oklahoma St., 1988 (attempted 67)

**Most Two-Point Attempts Made Per Game**
2.22—Rutgers, 1958 (20 in 9, attempted 31)

**Most Defensive Extra-Point Attempts**
3—Rice, 1988 (1 vs. Southwestern La., Sept. 24, blocked kick return; 2 vs. Notre Dame, Nov. 5, 2 blocked kick returns, 1 scored)

**Most Defensive Extra-Point Attempts Scored**
1—By 23 teams. Most recent: Penn St., 1992 (kick return vs. Pittsburgh, Nov. 21)

**Most Field Goals Per Game**
2.64—UCLA, 1984 (29 in 11)

# FIRST DOWNS

**Most First Downs Per Game**
30.9—Brigham Young, 1983 (340 in 11)

**Most Rushing First Downs Per Game**
21.4—Oklahoma, 1974 (235 in 11)

**Most Passing First Downs Per Game**
19.8—Brigham Young, 1990 (237 in 12)

# FUMBLES

**Most Fumbles**
73—Cal St. Fullerton, 1992 (lost 41)

**Most Fumbles Lost**
41—Cal St. Fullerton, 1992 (fumbled 73 times)

*1993 NCAA FOOTBALL*

**Fewest Own Fumbles Lost**
2—Dayton, 1968; UCLA, 1952; Tulsa, 1942; Washington, 1941

**Most Consecutive Fumbles Lost**
14—Oklahoma, 1983 (during 5 games, Oct. 8-Nov. 5)

## PENALTIES

**Most Penalties Per Game**
12.9—Grambling, 1977 (142 in 11, 1,476 yards)

**Most Yards Penalized Per Game**
134.2—Grambling, 1977 (1,476 in 11, 142 penalties)

## TURNOVERS (GIVEAWAYS)
### (Passes Had Intercepted and Fumbles Lost)

**Fewest Turnovers**
8—Miami (Ohio), 1966 (4 interceptions, 4 fumbles lost)

**Most Turnovers**
61—Tulsa, 1976 (24 interceptions, 37 fumbles lost); North Texas, 1971 (33 interceptions, 28 fumbles lost)

**Fewest Turnovers Per Game**
0.80—Miami (Ohio), 1966 (8 in 10 games)

**Most Turnovers Per Game**
6.1—Mississippi St., 1949 (55 in 9 games; 25 interceptions, 30 fumbles lost)

# SEASON—DEFENSE
## TOTAL DEFENSE

**Fewest Yards Allowed Per Game**
69.9—Santa Clara, 1937 (559 in 8)

**Fewest Rushing and Passing Touchdowns Allowed Per Game**
0.0—Tennessee, 1939; Duke, 1938

**Lowest Average Yards Allowed Per Play**
1.71—Texas A&M, 1939 (447 for 763)

**Lowest Average Yards Allowed Per Play**
*(Min. 600-699 plays)* 2.51—Nebraska, 1967 (627 for 1,576)
*(Min. 700 plays)* 2.69—Toledo, 1971 (734 for 1,795)

**Most Yards Allowed Per Game**
536.0—Kansas, 1988 (5,896 in 11)

## RUSHING DEFENSE

**Fewest Yards Allowed Per Game**
17.0—Penn St., 1947 (153 in 9)

**Most Yards Lost by Opponents Per Game**
70.1—Wyoming, 1968 (701 in 10, 458 rushes)

**Lowest Average Yards Allowed Per Rush**
0.64—Penn St., 1947 (240 for 153)

**Lowest Average Yards Allowed Per Rush**
*(Min. 400-499 rushes)* 1.26—North Texas, 1966 (408 for 513)
*(Min. 500 rushes)* 2.06—Nebraska, 1971 (500 for 1,031)

## PASS DEFENSE

**Fewest Yards Allowed Per Game**
13.1—Penn St., 1938 (105 in 8)

**Fewest Yards Allowed Per Attempt**
*(Min. 200-299 atts.)* 3.41—Toledo, 1970 (251 for 856)
*(Min. 300 atts.)* 3.78—Notre Dame, 1967 (306 for 1,158)

**Fewest Yards Allowed Per Completion**
*(Min. 100-149 comps.)* 9.36—Oklahoma, 1986 (128 for 1,198)
*(Min. 150 comps.)* 9.56—Miami (Fla ), 1983 (176 for 1,683)

**Lowest Completion Percentage Allowed**
*(Min. 150-199 atts.)* 31.1%—Virginia, 1952 (50 of 161)
*(Min. 200 atts.)* 33.3%—Notre Dame, 1967 (102 of 306)

**Fewest Touchdowns Allowed by Passing**
0—By many teams. Most recent: Louisiana St., 1959; North Texas, 1959

**Lowest Pass Efficiency Defensive Rating**
**(From 1990)**
77.37—Texas, 1991 (304 attempts, 115 completions, 15 interceptions, 1,513 yards, 7 TDs)

**Most Passes Intercepted By Per Game**
4.13—Pennsylvania, 1940 (33 in 8)

**Highest Percentage Intercepted By**
**(Min. 200 Attempts)**
17.9%—Army, 1944 (36 of 201)

**Most Yards Gained on Interception Returns**
782—Tennessee, 1971 (25 interceptions)

**Most Interception Yards Per Game**
72.5—Texas, 1943 (580 in 8)

**Highest Average Per Interception Return**
*(Min. 10-14 ints.)* 36.3—Oregon St., 1959 (12 for 436)
*(Min. 15 ints.)* 31.3—Tennessee, 1971 (25 for 782)

**Most Touchdowns on Interception Returns**
7—Tennessee, 1971 (25 interceptions; 287 pass attempts against)

# PUNTING

**Most Opponent's Punts Blocked By**
11—Arkansas St., 1975 (11 games, 95 punts against)

# PUNT RETURNS

**Fewest Returns Allowed**
5—Notre Dame, 1968 (52 yards)

**Fewest Yards Allowed**
2—Miami (Fla.), 1989 (12 returns)

**Lowest Average Yards Allowed Per Punt Return**
0.17—Miami (Fla.), 1989 (12 for 2 yards)

# KICKOFF RETURNS

**Lowest Average Yards Allowed Per Kickoff Return**
8.35—Richmond, 1951 (23 for 192 yards)

# SCORING

**Fewest Points Allowed Per Game**
0.0—Tennessee, 1939 (10 games); Duke, 1938 (9 games)

**Most Points Allowed and Points Allowed Per Game**
544 and 49.5—UTEP, 1973 (11 games)

# FUMBLES

**Most Opponent's Fumbles Recovered**
36—Brigham Young, 1977; North Texas, 1972

# TURNOVERS (TAKEAWAYS)

(Opponent's Passes Intercepted and Fumbles Recovered)

**Most Opponent's Turnovers**
57—Tennessee, 1970 (36 interceptions, 21 fumbles lost)

**Highest Margin of Turnovers Per Game Over Opponents**
4.0—UCLA, 1952 (36 in 9; 13 giveaways vs. 49 takeaways)
Also holds total-margin record at 36

**Most Opponent's Turnovers Per Game**
5.44—UCLA, 1954 (49 in 9); UCLA, 1952 (49 in 9); Pennsylvania, 1950 (49 in 9); Wyoming, 1950 (49 in 9)

**Highest Margin of Turnovers Per Game by Opponents**
3.1—Southern Miss., 1969 (31 in 10; 45 giveaways vs. 14 takeaways)

# DEFENSIVE EXTRA POINTS

**Most Defensive Extra-Point Attempts Against**
2—Notre Dame, 1988 (2 kick returns, 1 scored); Southwestern La., 1988 (2 kick returns, none scored)

**Most Defensive Extra Points Scored Against**
2—Oklahoma, 1992 (vs. Texas Tech, Sept. 3, and vs. Oklahoma St., Nov. 14)

# CONSECUTIVE RECORDS

**Most Consecutive Victories**
47—Oklahoma, 1953-57

**Most Consecutive Games Without Defeat**
48—Oklahoma, 1953-57 (1 tie)

**Most Consecutive Losses**
34—Northwestern, from Sept. 22, 1979, vs. Syracuse through Sept. 18, 1982, vs. Miami (Ohio)
Ended with 31-6 victory over Northern Ill., Sept. 25, 1982

**Most Consecutive Games Without a Victory on the Road**
46—Northwestern (including one tie), from Nov. 23, 1974, through Oct. 30, 1982

**Most Consecutive Games Without a Tie**
299—Miami (Fla.) (current), from Nov. 11, 1966

**Most Consecutive Games Without Being Shut Out**
246—UCLA, from Oct. 2, 1971, to Oct. 24, 1992 (ended by Arizona St. with 20-0 victory)

**Most Consecutive Shutouts (Regular Season)**
17—Tennessee, from Nov. 5, 1938, through Oct. 12, 1940

**Most Consecutive Quarters Opponents Held Scoreless (Regular Season)**
71—Tennessee, from 2nd quarter vs. Louisiana St., Oct. 29, 1938, to 2nd quarter vs. Alabama, Oct. 19, 1940

**Most Consecutive Victories at Home**
57—Alabama (at Tuscaloosa), from Oct. 26, 1963, through Oct. 23, 1982

**Most Consecutive Winning Seasons**
31—Nebraska (current), from 1962

**Most Consecutive Non-Losing Seasons**
49—Penn St., 1939-1987

**Most Consecutive Non-Winning Seasons**
28—Rice, 1964-91

*1993 NCAA FOOTBALL*

**Most Consecutive Seasons Winning Nine or More Games**
24—Nebraska (current), from 1969

**Most Consecutive Seasons Playing in a Bowl Game**
25—Alabama, from 1959 through 1983

**Most Consecutive Games Scoring on a Pass**
37—Brigham Young, from Nov. 31, 1981, through Sept. 7, 1985

**Most Consecutive Games Passing for 200 Yards or More**
64—Brigham Young, from Sept. 13, 1980, through Oct. 19, 1985

**Most Consecutive Games Without a Shutout**
214—Tulane (current), from Dec. 29, 1973

**Most Consecutive Extra Points Made**
262—Syracuse, from Nov. 18, 1978, to Sept. 9, 1989. (By the following kickers: Dave Jacobs, last PAT of 1978; Gary Anderson, 72 from 1979 through 1981; Russ Carpentieri, 17 in 1982; Don McAulay, 62 from 1983 through 1985; Tim Vesling, 71 in 1986 and 1987; Kevin Greene, 37 in 1988; John Biskup, 2 in 1989.)

## ADDITIONAL RECORDS

**Highest-Scoring Tie Game**
52-52—Brigham Young & San Diego St., Nov. 16, 1991

**Most Tie Games in a Season**
4—Central Mich., 1991 (11 games); UCLA, 1939 (10 games); Temple, 1937 (9 games)

**Most Scoreless Tie Games in a Season**
4—Temple, 1937 (9 games)

**Most Consecutive Scoreless Tie Games**
2—Alabama, 1954 vs. Georgia, Oct. 30 & vs. Tulane, Nov. 6; Georgia Tech, 1938 vs. Florida, Nov. 19 & vs. Georgia, Nov. 26

**Last Scoreless Tie Game**
Nov. 19, 1983—Oregon & Oregon St.

**Most Points Overcome to Win a Game (Between Division I-A Teams)**
31—Ohio St. (41), Minnesota (37), Oct. 28, 1989 (trailed 0-31 with 4:29 remaining in 2nd quarter); Maryland (42), Miami (Fla.) (40), Nov. 10, 1984 (trailed 0-31 with 12:35 remaining in 3rd quarter)

**Most Points Scored in Fourth Quarter to Win a Game**
28—Washington St. (49) vs. Stanford (42), Oct. 20, 1984 (trailed 14-42 with 5:38 remaining in third quarter and scored 35 consecutive points)

**Most Points Scored in a Brief Period of Time**
41 in 2:55 of possession time during six drives— Nebraska vs. Colorado, Oct. 15, 1983 (6 TDs, 5 PATs in 3rd quarter. Drives occurred during 9:10 of total playing time in the period); 21 in 1:24 of total playing time—San Jose St. (42) vs. Fresno St. (7), Nov. 17, 1990 (3 TDs, 3 PATs in second quarter; 1:17 of possession time on two drives and one intercepted pass returned for a TD)

**Most Improved Won-Lost Record**
8 games—Purdue, 1943 (9-0) from 1942 (1-8); Stanford, 1940 (10-0, including a bowl win) from 1939 (1-7-1)

**Most Improved Won-Lost Record Following Winless Season**
7 games—Florida, 1980 (8-4-0, including a bowl win) from 1979 (0-10-1)

# ANNUAL CHAMPIONS, ALL-TIME LEADERS

## TOTAL OFFENSE

### Career Yards Per Game

| Player, Team | Years | Games | Plays | Yards | TDR‡ | Yd. PG |
|---|---|---|---|---|---|---|
| Ty Detmer, Brigham Young ............. | 1988-91 | 46 | *1,795 | *14,665 | *135 | *318.8 |
| Mike Perez, San Jose St. ............... | 1986-87 | 20 | 875 | 6,182 | 37 | 309.1 |
| Doug Gaynor, Long Beach St. .......... | 1984-85 | 22 | 1,067 | 6,710 | 45 | 305.0 |
| Tony Eason, Illinois .................... | 1981-82 | 22 | 1,016 | 6,589 | 43 | 299.5 |
| David Klingler, Houston ................ | 1988-91 | 32 | 1,431 | 9,327 | 93 | 291.5 |
| Steve Young, Brigham Young .......... | 1981-83 | 31 | 1,177 | 8,817 | 74 | 284.4 |
| Doug Flutie, Boston College ........... | 1981-84 | 42 | 1,558 | 11,317 | 74 | 269.5 |
| Brent Snyder, Utah St. ................. | 1987-88 | 22 | 1,040 | 5,916 | 43 | 268.9 |
| Shane Matthews, Florida ............... | 1989-92 | 35 | 1,397 | 9,241 | 82 | 264.0 |
| Larry Egger, Utah ...................... | 1985-86 | 22 | 903 | 5,651 | 42 | 256.9 |
| Jim Plunkett, Stanford ................. | 1968-70 | 31 | 1,174 | 7,887 | 62 | 254.4 |
| Troy Kopp, Pacific (Cal.) .............. | 1989-92 | 40 | 1,595 | 10,037 | 90 | 250.9 |
| Randall Cunningham, Nev.-Las Vegas .. | 1982-84 | 33 | 1,330 | 8,224 | 67 | 249.2 |
| Erik Wilhelm, Oregon St. .............. | 1985-88 | 37 | 1,689 | 9,062 | 55 | 244.9 |
| Todd Dillon, Long Beach St. ........... | 1982-83 | 23 | 1,031 | 5,588 | 38 | 243.0 |
| Bernie Kosar, Miami (Fla.)............. | 1983-84 | 23 | 847 | 5,585 | 48 | 242.8 |
| Alex Van Pelt, Pittsburgh .............. | 1989-92 | 41 | 1,570 | 10,814 | 58 | 240.3 |
| Jack Trudeau, Illinois .................. | 1981, 83-85 | 34 | 1,318 | 8,096 | 56 | 238.1 |
| Chuck Hixson, Southern Methodist ..... | 1968-70 | 29 | 1,358 | 6,884 | 50 | 237.4 |
| Robbie Bosco, Brigham Young ......... | 1983-85 | 35 | 1,159 | 8,299 | 72 | 237.1 |

| Player, Team | Years | Games | Plays | Yards | TDR‡ | Yd. PG |
|---|---|---|---|---|---|---|
| Dan McGwire, Iowa/San Diego St....... | 1986-87, 89-90 | 32 | 1,067 | 7,557 | 50 | 236.2 |
| Johnny Bright, Drake ................... | 1949-51 | 25 | 825 | 5,903 | 64 | 236.1 |
| Brian McClure, Bowling Green ......... | 1982-85 | 42 | 1,630 | 9,774 | 67 | 232.7 |
| Marc Wilson, Brigham Young .......... | 1977-79 | 33 | 1,183 | 7,602 | 68 | 230.4 |
| Todd Santos, San Diego St. ............. | 1984-87 | 46 | 1,722 | 10,513 | 71 | 228.5 |
| Pat Sullivan, Auburn ................... | 1969-71 | 30 | 970 | 6,844 | 71 | 228.1 |
| John Reaves, Florida................... | 1969-71 | 32 | 1,258 | 7,283 | 58 | 227.6 |
| Steve Ramsey, North Texas ............. | 1967-69 | 29 | 1,132 | 6,568 | 71 | 226.5 |
| Steve Clarkson, San Jose St. ............ | 1979-82 | 31 | 1,124 | 6,995 | 68 | 225.6 |
| Gifford Nielsen, Brigham Young ........ | 1975-77 | 24 | 871 | 5,391 | 58 | 224.6 |

* *Record.*   ‡ *Touchdowns-responsible-for are player's TDs scored and passed for.*

Several high-powered quarterbacks have come and gone since 1983, but Brigham Young signal-caller Steve Young's average of 395.1 yards per game in total offense that season is still the fourth best in Division I-A history.

| Season Yards Per Game |||||||
|---|---|---|---|---|---|---|
| Player, Team | Year | Games | Plays | Yards | TDR‡ | Yd. PG |
| David Klingler, Houston ...................... | †1990 | 11 | *704 | *5,221 | *55 | *474.6 |
| Andre Ware, Houston ....................... | †1989 | 11 | 628 | 4,661 | 49 | 423.7 |
| Ty Detmer, Brigham Young ............... | 1990 | 12 | 635 | 5,022 | 45 | 418.5 |
| Steve Young, Brigham Young ............... | †1983 | 11 | 531 | 4,346 | 41 | 395.1 |
| Scott Mitchell, Utah ......................... | †1988 | 11 | 589 | 4,299 | 29 | 390.8 |
| Jim McMahon, Brigham Young ............... | †1980 | 12 | 540 | 4,627 | 53 | 385.6 |
| Ty Detmer, Brigham Young ................. | 1989 | 12 | 497 | 4,433 | 38 | 369.4 |
| Troy Kopp, Pacific (Cal.) ................... | 1990 | 9 | 485 | 3,276 | 32 | 364.0 |
| Jim McMahon, Brigham Young .............. | †1981 | 10 | 487 | 3,458 | 30 | 345.8 |
| Jimmy Klingler, Houston ..................... | †1992 | 11 | 544 | 3,768 | 34 | 342.5 |

*1993 NCAA FOOTBALL*

| Player, Team | Year | Games | Plays | Yards | TDR‡ | Yd. PG |
|---|---|---|---|---|---|---|
| Anthony Dilweg, Duke | 1988 | 11 | 539 | 3,713 | 26 | 337.6 |
| Bill Anderson, Tulsa | †1965 | 10 | 580 | 3,343 | 35 | 334.3 |
| Ty Detmer, Brigham Young | †1991 | 12 | 478 | 4,001 | 39 | 333.4 |
| Dan McGwire, San Diego St. | 1990 | 11 | 484 | 3,664 | 28 | 333.1 |
| Mike Perez, San Jose St. | †1986 | 9 | 425 | 2,969 | 14 | 329.9 |
| Robbie Bosco, Brigham Young | †1984 | 12 | 543 | 3,932 | 35 | 327.7 |
| Doug Flutie, Boston College | 1984 | 11 | 448 | 3,603 | 30 | 327.5 |
| Jim Everett, Purdue | †1985 | 11 | 518 | 3,589 | 24 | 326.3 |
| Todd Dillon, Long Beach St. | †1982 | 11 | 585 | 3,587 | 23 | 326.1 |
| Marc Wilson, Brigham Young | †1979 | 11 | 488 | 3,580 | 32 | 325.5 |

*Record.   † National champion.   ‡ Touchdowns-responsible-for are player's TDs scored and passed for.*

## Career Yards

| Player, Team | Years | Plays | Yards Rush | Yards Pass | Total | Avg. |
|---|---|---|---|---|---|---|
| Ty Detmer, Brigham Young | 1988-91 | *1,795 | -366 | *15,031 | *14,665 | #8.17 |
| Doug Flutie, Boston College | 1981-84 | 1,558 | 738 | 10,579 | 11,317 | 7.26 |
| Alex Van Pelt, Pittsburgh | 1989-92 | 1,570 | -99 | 10,913 | 10,814 | 6.89 |
| Todd Santos, San Diego St. | 1984-87 | 1,722 | -912 | 11,425 | 10,513 | 6.11 |
| Kevin Sweeney, Fresno St. | $1982-86 | 1,700 | -371 | 10,623 | 10,252 | 6.03 |
| Troy Kopp, Pacific (Cal.) | 1989-92 | 1,595 | -221 | 10,258 | 10,037 | 6.29 |
| Brian McClure, Bowling Green | 1982-85 | 1,630 | -506 | 10,280 | 9,774 | 6.00 |
| Jim McMahon, Brigham Young | 1977-78, 80-81 | 1,325 | 187 | 9,536 | 9,723 | 7.34 |
| Terrence Jones, Tulane | 1985-88 | 1,620 | 1,761 | 7,684 | 9,445 | 5.83 |
| David Klingler, Houston | 1988-91 | 1,431 | -103 | 9,430 | 9,327 | 6.52 |
| Shawn Jones, Georgia Tech | 1989-92 | 1,609 | 855 | 8,441 | 9,296 | 5.78 |
| Shane Matthews, Florida | 1989-92 | 1,397 | -46 | 9,287 | 9,241 | 6.61 |
| T. J. Rubley, Tulsa | 1987-89, 91 | 1,541 | -244 | 9,324 | 9,080 | 5.89 |
| Brad Tayles, Western Mich. | 1989-92 | 1,675 | 354 | 8,717 | 9,071 | 5.42 |
| John Elway, Stanford | 1979-82 | 1,505 | -279 | 9,349 | 9,070 | 6.03 |
| Erik Wilhelm, Oregon St. | 1985-88 | 1,689 | -331 | 9,393 | 9,062 | 5.37 |
| Ben Bennett, Duke | 1980-83 | 1,582 | -553 | 9,614 | 9,061 | 5.73 |
| Chuck Long, Iowa | $1981-85 | 1,410 | -176 | 9,210 | 9,034 | 6.41 |
| Todd Ellis, South Caro. | 1986-89 | 1,517 | -497 | 9,519 | 9,022 | 5.95 |
| Tom Hodson, Louisiana St. | 1986-89 | 1,307 | -177 | 9,115 | 8,938 | 6.84 |
| Scott Mitchell, Utah | 1987-89 | 1,306 | -145 | 8,981 | 8,836 | 6.77 |
| Steve Young, Brigham Young | 1981-83 | 1,177 | 1,084 | 7,733 | 8,817 | 7.49 |
| Brian Mitchell, Southwestern La. | 1986-89 | 1,521 | 3,335 | 5,447 | 8,782 | 5.77 |
| Jeremy Leach, New Mexico | 1988-91 | 1,695 | -762 | 9,382 | 8,620 | 5.09 |
| Mark Herrmann, Purdue | 1977-80 | 1,354 | -744 | 9,188 | 8,444 | 6.24 |
| Robbie Bosco, Brigham Young | 1983-85 | 1,158 | -101 | 8,400 | 8,299 | 7.17 |
| Troy Taylor, California | 1986-89 | 1,490 | 110 | 8,126 | 8,236 | 5.53 |
| Randall Cunningham, Nev.-Las Vegas | 1982-84 | 1,330 | 204 | 8,020 | 8,224 | 6.18 |
| Steve Slayden, Duke | 1984-87 | 1,546 | 125 | 8,004 | 8,129 | 5.26 |
| Jack Trudeau, Illinois | 1981, 83-85 | 1,318 | -50 | 8,146 | 8,096 | 6.14 |
| Mark Barsotti, Fresno St. | 1988-91 | 1,192 | 768 | 7,321 | 8,089 | 6.79 |
| Gene Swick, Toledo | 1972-75 | 1,579 | 807 | 7,267 | 8,074 | 5.11 |
| Andre Ware, Houston | 1987-89 | 1,194 | -144 | 8,202 | 8,058 | 6.75 |
| Joe Adams, Tennessee St. | 1977-80 | 1,256 | -677 | 8,649 | 7,972 | 6.35 |
| Rodney Peete, Southern Cal | 1985-88 | 1,226 | 309 | 7,640 | 7,949 | 6.48 |
| Shawn Moore, Virginia | 1987-90 | 1,177 | 1,268 | 6,629 | 7,897 | 6.71 |
| Jim Plunkett, Stanford | 1968-70 | 1,174 | 343 | 7,544 | 7,887 | 6.72 |
| Art Schlichter, Ohio St. | 1978-81 | 1,316 | 1,285 | 6,584 | 7,869 | 5.98 |
| Mike Gundy, Oklahoma St. | 1986-89 | 1,275 | -248 | 8,072 | 7,824 | 6.14 |
| John Holman, Northeast La. | 1979-82 | 1,376 | -25 | 7,827 | 7,802 | 5.67 |
| Gino Torretta, Miami (Fla.) | 1989-92 | 1,101 | 32 | 7,690 | 7,722 | 7.01 |
| Jack Thompson, Washington St. | 1975-78 | 1,345 | -120 | 7,818 | 7,698 | 5.72 |
| Dan Marino, Pittsburgh | 1979-82 | 1,376 | -270 | 7,905 | 7,635 | 6.44 |
| Brett Favre, Southern Miss. | 1987-90 | 1,362 | -89 | 7,695 | 7,606 | 5.58 |
| Marc Wilson, Brigham Young | 1977-79 | 1,183 | -35 | 7,637 | 7,602 | 6.43 |
| Dan McGwire, Iowa/San Diego St. | 1986-87, 89-90 | 1,067 | -607 | 8,164 | 7,557 | 7.08 |
| John Paye, Stanford | 1983-86 | 1,174 | -131 | 7,669 | 7,538 | 5.23 |
| Scott Campbell, Purdue | 1980-83 | 1,305 | -110 | 7,636 | 7,526 | 5.77 |

*Record.   $ See page 8 for explanation.   # Record for minimum of 6,500 yards.*

**Career Yards Record Progression**
**(Record Yards—Player, Team, Seasons Played)**

**3,481**—Davey O'Brien, Texas Christian, 1936-38; **3,882**—Paul Christman, Missouri, 1938-40; **4,602**—Frank Sinkwich, Georgia, 1940-42; **4,627**—Bob Fenimore, Oklahoma St., 1943-46; **4,871**—Charlie

Justice, North Caro., 1946-49; **5,903**—Johnny Bright, Drake, 1949-51; **6,354**—Virgil Carter, Brigham Young, 1964-66; **6,568**—Steve Ramsey, North Texas, 1967-69; **7,887**—Jim Plunkett, Stanford, 1968-70; **8,074**—Gene Swick, Toledo, 1972-75; **8,444**—Mark Herrmann, Purdue, 1977-80; **9,723**—Jim McMahon, Brigham Young, 1977-78, 1980-81; **11,317**—Doug Flutie, Boston College, 1981-84; **14,665**—Ty Detmer, Brigham Young, 1988-91.

## Season Yards

| Player, Team | Year | Games | Plays | Yards Rush | Yards Pass | Total | Avg. |
|---|---|---|---|---|---|---|---|
| David Klingler, Houston | †1990 | 11 | *704 | 81 | 5,140 | *5,221 | 7.42 |
| Ty Detmer, Brigham Young | 1990 | 12 | 635 | -106 | *5,188 | 5,022 | 7.91 |
| Andre Ware, Houston | †1989 | 11 | 628 | -38 | 4,699 | 4,661 | 7.42 |
| Jim McMahon, Brigham Young | †1980 | 12 | 540 | 56 | 4,571 | 4,627 | 8.57 |
| Ty Detmer, Brigham Young | 1989 | 12 | 497 | -127 | 4,560 | 4,433 | @8.92 |
| Steve Young, Brigham Young | †1983 | 11 | 531 | 444 | 3,902 | 4,346 | 8.18 |
| Scott Mitchell, Utah | †1988 | 11 | 589 | -23 | 4,322 | 4,299 | 7.30 |
| Robbie Bosco, Brigham Young | 1985 | 13 | 578 | -132 | 4,273 | 4,141 | 7.16 |
| Ty Detmer, Brigham Young | †1991 | 12 | 478 | -30 | 4,031 | 4,001 | 8.37 |
| Robbie Bosco, Brigham Young | †1984 | 12 | 543 | 57 | 3,875 | 3,932 | 7.24 |
| Jimmy Klingler, Houston | †1992 | 11 | 544 | -50 | 3,818 | 3,768 | 6.93 |
| Anthony Dilweg, Duke | 1988 | 11 | 539 | -111 | 3,824 | 3,713 | 6.89 |
| Todd Santos, San Diego St. | †1987 | 12 | 562 | -244 | 3,932 | 3,688 | 6.56 |
| Troy Kopp, Pacific (Cal.) | 1991 | 12 | 496 | -81 | 3,767 | 3,686 | 7.43 |
| Dan McGwire, San Diego St. | 1990 | 11 | 484 | -169 | 3,833 | 3,664 | 7.57 |
| Doug Flutie, Boston College | 1984 | 11 | 448 | 149 | 3,454 | 3,603 | 8.04 |
| Jim Everett, Purdue | †1985 | 11 | 518 | -62 | 3,651 | 3,589 | 6.93 |
| Todd Dillon, Long Beach St. | †1982 | 11 | 585 | 70 | 3,517 | 3,587 | 6.13 |
| Marc Wilson, Brigham Young | †1979 | 11 | 488 | -140 | 3,720 | 3,580 | 7.34 |
| Sam King, Nevada-Las Vegas | 1981 | 12 | 507 | -216 | 3,778 | 3,562 | 7.03 |
| Matt Kofler, San Diego St. | 1981 | 11 | 594 | 191 | 3,337 | 3,528 | 5.94 |
| Steve Young, Brigham Young | 1982 | 11 | 481 | 407 | 3,100 | 3,507 | 7.29 |
| John Kaleo, Maryland | 1992 | 11 | 588 | 80 | 3,392 | 3,472 | 5.90 |
| Doug Gaynor, Long Beach St. | 1985 | 12 | 589 | -96 | 3,563 | 3,467 | 5.89 |
| Jim McMahon, Brigham Young | 1981 | 10 | 487 | -97 | 3,555 | 3,458 | 7.10 |

*Record. † National champion. @ Record for minimum of 3,000 yards.*

## Single-Game Yards

| Yds. | Rush | Pass | Player, Team (Opponent) | Date |
|---|---|---|---|---|
| 732 | 16 | 716 | David Klingler, Houston (Arizona St.) | Dec. 2, 1990 |
| 696 | 6 | 690 | Matt Vogler, Texas Christian (Houston) | Nov. 3, 1990 |
| 625 | 62 | 563 | David Klingler, Houston (Texas Christian) | Nov. 3, 1990 |
| 625 | -6 | 631 | Scott Mitchell, Utah (Air Force) | Oct. 15, 1988 |
| 612 | -1 | 613 | Jimmy Klingler, Houston (Rice) | Nov. 28, 1992 |
| 603 | 4 | 599 | Ty Detmer, Brigham Young (San Diego St.) | Nov. 16, 1991 |
| 601 | 37 | 564 | Troy Kopp, Pacific, Cal. (New Mexico St.) | Oct. 20, 1990 |
| 599 | 86 | 513 | Virgil Carter, Brigham Young (UTEP) | Nov. 5, 1966 |
| 594 | -28 | 622 | Jeremy Leach, New Mexico (Utah) | Nov. 11, 1989 |
| 585 | -36 | 621 | Dave Wilson, Illinois (Ohio St.) | Nov. 8, 1980 |
| 582 | 11 | 571 | Marc Wilson, Brigham Young (Utah) | Nov. 5, 1977 |
| 578 | 6 | 572 | David Klingler, Houston (Eastern Wash.) | Nov. 17, 1990 |
| 562 | 25 | 537 | Ty Detmer, Brigham Young (Washington St.) | Sept. 7, 1989 |
| 552 | -13 | 565 | Jim McMahon, Brigham Young (Utah) | Nov. 21, 1981 |
| 548 | 12 | 536 | Dave Telford, Fresno St. (Pacific, Cal.) | Oct. 24, 1987 |
| 540 | -45 | 585 | Robbie Bosco, Brigham Young (New Mexico) | Oct. 19, 1985 |
| 540 | 104 | 436 | Archie Manning, Mississippi (Alabama) | Oct. 4, 1969 |
| 539 | 1 | 538 | Jim McMahon, Brigham Young (Colorado St.) | Nov. 7, 1981 |
| 537 | 2 | 535 | Shane Montgomery, North Caro. St. (Duke) | Nov. 11, 1989 |
| 537 | -24 | 561 | Tony Adams, Utah St. (Utah) | Nov. 11, 1972 |
| 536 | 28 | 508 | Mike Perez, San Jose St. (Pacific, Cal.) | Oct. 25, 1986 |
| 532 | 0 | 532 | Jeff Van Raaphorst, Arizona St. (Florida St.) | Nov. 3, 1984 |
| 531 | 13 | 518 | Jeff Graham, Long Beach St. (Hawaii) | Oct. 29, 1988 |
| 528 | -40 | 568 | David Lowery, San Diego St. (Brigham Young) | Nov. 16, 1991 |
| 528 | -2 | 530 | Dan McGwire, San Diego St. (New Mexico) | Nov. 17, 1990 |
| 527 | 17 | 510 | David Klingler, Houston (Louisiana Tech) | Aug. 31, 1991 |
| 525 | -29 | 554 | Greg Cook, Cincinnati (Ohio) | Nov. 16, 1968 |
| 524 | 118 | 406 | Ned James, New Mexico (Wyoming) | Nov. 1, 1986 |
| 521 | -39 | 560 | Ty Detmer, Brigham Young (Utah St.) | Nov. 24, 1990 |
| 521 | 57 | 464 | Whit Taylor, Vanderbilt (Tennessee) | Nov. 28, 1981 |

*1993 NCAA FOOTBALL*

| Yds. | Rush | Pass | Player, Team (Opponent) | Date |
|---|---|---|---|---|
| 519 | -14 | 533 | David Klingler, Houston (Texas Tech) | Nov. 30, 1991 |
| 517 | 45 | 472 | Doug Flutie, Boston College (Miami, Fla.) | Nov. 23, 1984 |
| 517 | 73 | 444 | Matt Kofler, San Diego St. (Iowa St.) | Oct. 10, 1981 |
| 516 | -42 | 558 | Chuck Hartlieb, Iowa (Indiana) | Oct. 29, 1988 |
| 516 | 31 | 485 | Jim McMahon, Brigham Young (Utah St.) | Oct. 18, 1980 |
| 516 | -11 | 527 | Don Strock, Virginia Tech (Houston) | Oct. 7, 1972 |
| 513 | 2 | 511 | Scott Mitchell, Utah (Idaho St.) | Sept. 10, 1988 |
| 512 | -22 | 534 | Paul Justin, Arizona St. (Washington St.) | Oct. 28, 1989 |
| 512 | -14 | 526 | Joe Theismann, Notre Dame (Southern Cal) | Nov. 28, 1970 |

## Annual Champions

| Year | Player, Team | Class | Plays | Rush | Yards Pass | Total |
|---|---|---|---|---|---|---|
| 1937 | Byron "Whizzer" White, Colorado | Sr. | 224 | 1,121 | 475 | 1,596 |
| 1938 | Davey O'Brien, Texas Christian | Sr. | 291 | 390 | 1,457 | 1,847 |
| 1939 | Kenny Washington, UCLA | Sr. | 259 | 811 | 559 | 1,370 |
| 1940 | Johnny Knolla, Creighton | Sr. | 298 | 813 | 607 | 1,420 |
| 1941 | Bud Schwenk, Washington (Mo.) | Sr. | 354 | 471 | 1,457 | 1,928 |
| 1942 | Frank Sinkwich, Georgia | Sr. | 341 | 795 | 1,392 | 2,187 |
| 1943 | Bob Hoernschemeyer, Indiana | Fr. | 355 | 515 | 1,133 | 1,648 |
| 1944 | Bob Fenimore, Oklahoma St. | So. | 241 | 897 | 861 | 1,758 |
| 1945 | Bob Fenimore, Oklahoma St. | Jr. | 203 | 1,048 | 593 | 1,641 |
| 1946 | Travis Tidwell, Auburn | Fr. | 339 | 772 | 943 | 1,715 |
| 1947 | Fred Enke, Arizona | So. | 329 | 535 | 1,406 | 1,941 |
| 1948 | Stan Heath, Nevada | Sr. | 233 | -13 | 2,005 | 1,992 |
| 1949 | Johnny Bright, Drake | So. | 275 | 975 | 975 | 1,950 |
| 1950 | Johnny Bright, Drake | Jr. | 320 | 1,232 | 1,168 | 2,400 |
| 1951 | Dick Kazmaier, Princeton | Sr. | 272 | 861 | 966 | 1,827 |
| 1952 | Ted Marchibroda, Detroit Mercy | Sr. | 305 | 176 | 1,637 | 1,813 |
| 1953 | Paul Larson, California | Jr. | 262 | 141 | 1,431 | 1,572 |
| 1954 | George Shaw, Oregon | Sr. | 276 | 178 | 1,358 | 1,536 |
| 1955 | George Welsh, Navy | Sr. | 203 | 29 | 1,319 | 1,348 |
| 1956 | John Brodie, Stanford | Sr. | 295 | 9 | 1,633 | 1,642 |
| 1957 | Bob Newman, Washington St. | Jr. | 263 | 53 | 1,391 | 1,444 |
| 1958 | Dick Bass, Pacific (Cal.) | Jr. | 218 | 1,361 | 79 | 1,440 |
| 1959 | Dick Norman, Stanford | Jr. | 319 | 55 | 1,963 | 2,018 |
| 1960 | Bill Kilmer, UCLA | Sr. | 292 | 803 | 1,086 | 1,889 |
| 1961 | Dave Hoppmann, Iowa St. | Jr. | 320 | 920 | 718 | 1,638 |
| 1962 | Terry Baker, Oregon St. | Sr. | 318 | 538 | 1,738 | 2,276 |
| 1963 | George Mira, Miami (Fla.) | Sr. | 394 | 163 | 2,155 | 2,318 |
| 1964 | Jerry Rhome, Tulsa | Sr. | 470 | 258 | 2,870 | 3,128 |
| 1965 | Bill Anderson, Tulsa | Sr. | 580 | -121 | 3,464 | 3,343 |
| 1966 | Virgil Carter, Brigham Young | Sr. | 388 | 363 | 2,182 | 2,545 |
| 1967 | Sal Olivas, New Mexico St. | Sr. | 368 | -41 | 2,225 | 2,184 |
| 1968 | Greg Cook, Cincinnati | Sr. | 507 | -62 | 3,272 | 3,210 |
| 1969 | Dennis Shaw, San Diego St. | Sr. | 388 | 12 | 3,185 | 3,197 |

Beginning in 1970, ranked on per-game (instead of total) yards

| Year | Player, Team | Class | Games | Plays | Rush | Yards Pass | Total | Avg. |
|---|---|---|---|---|---|---|---|---|
| 1970 | Pat Sullivan, Auburn | Jr. | 10 | 333 | 270 | 2,586 | 2,856 | 285.6 |
| 1971 | Gary Huff, Florida St. | Jr. | 11 | 386 | -83 | 2,736 | 2,653 | 241.2 |
| 1972 | Don Strock, Virginia Tech | Sr. | 11 | 480 | -73 | 3,243 | 3,170 | 288.2 |
| 1973 | Jesse Freitas, San Diego St. | Sr. | 11 | 410 | -92 | 2,993 | 2,901 | 263.7 |
| 1974 | Steve Joachim, Temple | Sr. | 10 | 331 | 277 | 1,950 | 2,227 | 222.7 |
| 1975 | Gene Swick, Toledo | Sr. | 11 | 490 | 219 | 2,487 | 2,706 | 246.0 |
| 1976 | Tommy Kramer, Rice | Sr. | 11 | 562 | -45 | 3,317 | 3,272 | 297.5 |
| 1977 | Doug Williams, Grambling | Sr. | 11 | 377 | -57 | 3,286 | 3,229 | 293.5 |
| 1978 | Mike Ford, Southern Methodist | So. | 11 | 459 | -50 | 3,007 | 2,957 | 268.8 |
| 1979 | Marc Wilson, Brigham Young | Sr. | 11 | 488 | -140 | 3,720 | 3,580 | 325.5 |
| 1980 | Jim McMahon, Brigham Young | Jr. | 12 | 540 | 56 | 4,571 | 4,627 | 385.6 |
| 1981 | Jim McMahon, Brigham Young | Sr. | 10 | 487 | -97 | 3,555 | 3,458 | 345.8 |
| 1982 | Todd Dillon, Long Beach St. | Jr. | 11 | 585 | 70 | 3,517 | 3,587 | 326.1 |
| 1983 | Steve Young, Brigham Young | Sr. | 11 | 531 | 444 | 3,902 | 4,346 | 395.1 |
| 1984 | Robbie Bosco, Brigham Young | Jr. | 12 | 543 | 57 | 3,875 | 3,932 | 327.7 |
| 1985 | Jim Everett, Purdue | Sr. | 11 | 518 | -62 | 3,651 | 3,589 | 326.3 |
| 1986 | Mike Perez, San Jose St. | Jr. | 9 | 425 | 35 | 2,934 | 2,969 | 329.9 |
| 1987 | Todd Santos, San Diego St. | Sr. | 12 | 562 | -244 | 3,932 | 3,688 | 307.3 |
| 1988 | Scott Mitchell, Utah | So. | 11 | 589 | -23 | 4,322 | 4,299 | 390.8 |
| 1989 | Andre Ware, Houston | Jr. | 11 | 628 | -38 | 4,699 | 4,661 | 423.7 |

*Division I-A Annual Champions, All-Time Leaders*      41

| Year | Player, Team | Class | Games | Plays | Yards Rush | Pass | Total | Avg. |
|---|---|---|---|---|---|---|---|---|
| 1990 | David Klingler, Houston | Jr. | 11 | *704 | 81 | 5,140 | *5,221 | *174.6 |
| 1991 | Ty Detmer, Brigham Young | Sr. | 12 | 478 | -30 | 4,031 | 4,001 | 333.4 |
| 1992 | Jimmy Klingler, Houston | So. | 11 | 544 | -50 | 3,818 | 3,768 | 342.5 |

* Record.

# RUSHING
## Career Yards Per Game

| Player, Team | Years | Games | Plays | Yards | TD | Yd. PG |
|---|---|---|---|---|---|---|
| Ed Marinaro, Cornell | 1969-71 | 27 | 918 | 4,715 | 50 | *174.6 |
| O. J. Simpson, Southern Cal | 1967-68 | 19 | 621 | 3,124 | 33 | 164.4 |
| Herschel Walker, Georgia | 1980-82 | 33 | 994 | 5,259 | 49 | 159.4 |
| Tony Dorsett, Pittsburgh | 1973-76 | 43 | 1,074 | *6,082 | 55 | 141.4 |
| Mike Rozier, Nebraska | 1981-83 | 35 | 668 | 4,780 | 49 | 136.6 |
| Howard Stevens, Louisville | §1971-72 | 20 | 509 | 2,723 | 25 | 136.2 |
| Jerome Persell, Western Mich. | 1976-78 | 31 | 842 | 4,190 | 39 | 135.2 |
| Rudy Mobley, Hardin-Simmons | 1942,46 | 19 | 414 | 2,543 | 32 | 133.8 |
| Vaughn Dunbar, Indiana | 1990-91 | 22 | 565 | 2,842 | 24 | 129.2 |
| Steve Owens, Oklahoma | 1967-69 | 30 | 905 | 3,867 | 56 | 128.9 |
| Charles White, Southern Cal | 1976-79 | 44 | 1,023 | 5,598 | 46 | 127.2 |
| Johnny Bright, Drake | 1949-51 | 25 | 513 | 3,134 | 39 | 125.4 |
| Woody Green, Arizona St. | 1971-73 | 30 | 601 | 3,754 | 33 | 125.1 |
| Archie Griffin, Ohio St. | 1972-75 | 42 | 845 | 5,177 | 25 | 123.3 |
| Anthony Thompson, Indiana | 1986-89 | 41 | 1,089 | 4,965 | *64 | 121.1 |
| Mark Kellar, Northern Ill. | 1971-73 | 31 | 743 | 3,745 | 32 | 120.8 |
| Paul Gipson, Houston | 1966-68 | 23 | 447 | 2,769 | 25 | 120.4 |
| John Cappelletti, Penn St. | ‡1972-73 | 22 | 519 | 2,639 | 29 | 120.0 |
| Steve Bartalo, Colorado St. | 1983-86 | 41 | *1,215 | 4,813 | 46 | 117.4 |
| Louie Giammona, Utah St. | 1973-75 | 30 | 756 | 3,499 | 21 | 116.6 |
| Paul Palmer, Temple | 1983-86 | 42 | 948 | 4,895 | 39 | 116.5 |
| Bill Marek, Wisconsin | 1972-75 | 32 | 719 | 3,709 | 44 | 115.9 |
| Darren Lewis, Texas A&M | 1987-90 | 44 | 909 | 5,012 | 44 | 113.9 |
| Dick Jauron, Yale | 1970-72 | 26 | 515 | 2,947 | 27 | 113.3 |
| Bo Jackson, Auburn | 1982-85 | 38 | 650 | 4,303 | 43 | 113.2 |
| Joe Morris, Syracuse | 1978-81 | 38 | 813 | 4,299 | 25 | 113.1 |
| Eugene "Mercury" Morris, West Tex. St. | 1966-68 | 30 | 541 | 3,388 | 34 | 112.9 |

* Record. § Competed two years in Division I-A and two years in Division II (Randolph-Macon, 1968-69). Four-year totals: 5,297 yards, 139.4 average. ‡ Defensive back in 1971.

## Season Yards Per Game

| Player, Team | Year | Games | Plays | Yards | TD | Yd. PG |
|---|---|---|---|---|---|---|
| Barry Sanders, Oklahoma St. | †1988 | 11 | 344 | *2,628 | *37 | *238.9 |
| Marcus Allen, Southern Cal | †1981 | 11 | *403 | 2,342 | 22 | 212.9 |
| Ed Marinaro, Cornell | †1971 | 9 | 356 | 1,881 | 24 | 209.0 |
| Charles White, Southern Cal | †1979 | 10 | 293 | 1,803 | 18 | 180.3 |
| Mike Rozier, Nebraska | †1983 | 12 | 275 | 2,148 | 29 | 179.0 |
| Tony Dorsett, Pittsburgh | †1976 | 11 | 338 | 1,948 | 21 | 177.1 |
| Ollie Matson, San Francisco | †1951 | 9 | 245 | 1,566 | 20 | 174.0 |
| Lorenzo White, Michigan St. | †1985 | 11 | 386 | 1,908 | 17 | 173.5 |
| Herschel Walker, Georgia | 1981 | 11 | 385 | 1,891 | 18 | 171.9 |
| O. J. Simpson, Southern Cal | †1968 | 10 | 355 | 1,709 | 22 | 170.9 |
| Ernest Anderson, Oklahoma St. | †1982 | 11 | 353 | 1,877 | 8 | 170.6 |
| Ricky Bell, Southern Cal | †1975 | 11 | 357 | 1,875 | 13 | 170.5 |

* Record. † National champion.

## Career Yards

| Player, Team | Years | Plays | Yards | Avg. | Long |
|---|---|---|---|---|---|
| Tony Dorsett, Pittsburgh | 1973-76 | 1,074 | *6,082 | 5.66 | 73 |
| Charles White, Southern Cal | 1976-79 | 1,023 | 5,598 | 5.47 | 79 |
| Herschel Walker, Georgia | 1980-82 | 994 | 5,259 | 5.29 | 76 |
| Archie Griffin, Ohio St. | 1972-75 | 845 | 5,177 | ††6.13 | 75 |
| Darren Lewis, Texas A&M | 1987-90 | 909 | 5,012 | 5.51 | 84 |
| Anthony Thompson, Indiana | 1986-89 | 1,089 | 4,965 | 4.56 | 52 |
| George Rogers, South Caro. | 1977-80 | 902 | 4,958 | 5.50 | 80 |
| Trevor Cobb, Rice | 1989-92 | 1,091 | 4,948 | 4.54 | 79 |
| Paul Palmer, Temple | 1983-86 | 948 | 4,895 | 5.16 | 78 |
| Steve Bartalo, Colorado St. | 1983-86 | *1,215 | 4,813 | 3.96 | 39 |

*1993 NCAA FOOTBALL*

| Player, Team | Years | Plays | Yards | Avg. | Long |
|---|---|---|---|---|---|
| Mike Rozier, Nebraska | 1981-83 | 668 | 4,780 | #7.16 | 93 |
| Ed Marinaro, Cornell | 1969-71 | 918 | 4,715 | 5.14 | 79 |
| Marcus Allen, Southern Cal | 1978-81 | 893 | 4,682 | 5.24 | 45 |
| Ted Brown, North Caro. St. | 1975-78 | 860 | 4,602 | 5.35 | 95 |
| Thurman Thomas, Oklahoma St. | 1984-87 | 898 | 4,595 | 5.12 | 66 |
| Terry Miller, Oklahoma St. | 1974-77 | 847 | 4,582 | 5.41 | 81 |
| Darrell Thompson, Minnesota | 1986-89 | 911 | 4,518 | 4.96 | 98 |
| Lorenzo White, Michigan St. | 1984-87 | 991 | 4,513 | 4.55 | 73 |
| Eric Dickerson, Southern Methodist | 1979-82 | 790 | 4,450 | 5.63 | 80 |
| Earl Campbell, Texas | 1974-77 | 765 | 4,443 | 5.81 | ‡‡83 |
| Amos Lawrence, North Caro. | 1977-80 | 881 | 4,391 | 4.98 | 62 |
| Bo Jackson, Auburn | 1982-85 | 650 | 4,303 | 6.62 | 80 |
| Joe Morris, Syracuse | 1978-81 | 813 | 4,299 | 5.29 | 75 |
| Reggie Taylor, Cincinnati | 1983-86 | 876 | 4,242 | 4.48 | ‡‡68 |
| Mike Mayweather, Army | 1987-90 | 832 | 4,212 | 5.06 | 52 |
| Jerome Persell, Western Mich. | 1976-78 | 842 | 4,190 | 4.98 | 86 |
| Napoleon McCallum, Navy | $1981-85 | 908 | 4,179 | 4.60 | 60 |
| Tico Duckett, Michigan St. | 1989-92 | 824 | 4,176 | 5.07 | 88 |
| George Swarn, Miami (Ohio) | 1983-86 | 881 | 4,172 | 4.74 | 98 |
| Curtis Adams, Central Mich. | 1981-84 | 761 | 4,162 | 5.47 | 87 |
| Allen Pinkett, Notre Dame | 1982-85 | 889 | 4,131 | 4.65 | 76 |
| James Gray, Texas Tech | 1986-89 | 742 | 4,066 | 5.48 | 72 |
| Robert Lavette, Georgia Tech | 1981-84 | 914 | 4,066 | 4.45 | 83 |
| Stump Mitchell, Citadel | 1977-80 | 756 | 4,062 | 5.37 | 77 |
| Dalton Hilliard, Louisiana St. | 1982-85 | 882 | 4,050 | 4.59 | 66 |
| Charles Alexander, Louisiana St. | 1975-78 | 855 | 4,035 | 4.72 | 64 |
| Darrin Nelson, Stanford | 1977-78, 80-81 | 703 | 4,033 | 5.74 | 80 |
| Joe Washington, Oklahoma | 1972-75 | 656 | 3,995 | 6.09 | 71 |
| Mike Voight, North Caro. | 1973-76 | 826 | 3,971 | 4.81 | 84 |
| Jamie Morris, Michigan | 1984-87 | 742 | 3,944 | 5.32 | 74 |
| Eric Bieniemy, Colorado | 1987-90 | 699 | 3,940 | 5.64 | 69 |
| Emmitt Smith, Florida | 1987-89 | 700 | 3,928 | 5.61 | 96 |
| Ron "Po" James, New Mexico St. | 1968-71 | 818 | 3,884 | 4.75 | 69 |
| Steve Owens, Oklahoma | 1967-69 | 905 | 3,867 | 4.27 | ‡‡49 |
| Mike Williams, New Mexico | 1975-78 | 857 | 3,862 | 4.51 | 36 |
| Sonny Collins, Kentucky | 1972-75 | 777 | 3,835 | 4.94 | 66 |
| Eric Wilkerson, Kent | 1985-88 | 735 | 3,830 | 5.21 | 74 |
| Billy Sims, Oklahoma | $1975-79 | 538 | 3,813 | 7.09 | ‡‡71 |
| James McDougald, Wake Forest | 1976-79 | 880 | 3,811 | 4.33 | 62 |
| Tony Sands, Kansas | 1988-91 | 778 | 3,788 | 4.87 | 66 |

* Record.  $ See page 8 for explanation.  ‡‡ Did not score.  †† Record for minimum of 781 carries.  # Record for minimum of 414 carries.

## Career Yards Record Progression
### (Record Yards—Player, Team, Seasons Played)

**1,961**—Marshall Goldberg, Pittsburgh, 1936-38; **2,105**—Tom Harmon, Michigan, 1938-40; **2,271**—Frank Sinkwich, Georgia, 1940-42; **2,301**—Bill Daley, Minnesota, 1940-42, Michigan, 1943; **2,957**—Glenn Davis, Army, 1943-46; **3,095**—Eddie Price, Tulane, 1946-49; **3,238**—John Papit, Virginia, 1947-50; **3,381**—Art Luppino, Arizona, 1953-56; **3,388**—Eugene "Mercury" Morris, West Tex. St., 1966-68; **3,867**—Steve Owens, Oklahoma, 1967-69; **4,715**—Ed Marinaro, Cornell, 1969-71; **5,177**—Archie Griffin, Ohio St., 1972-75; **6,082**—Tony Dorsett, Pittsburgh, 1973-76.

## Season Yards

| Player, Team | Year | Games | Plays | Yards | Avg. |
|---|---|---|---|---|---|
| Barry Sanders, Oklahoma St. | †1988 | 11 | 344 | *2,628 | ‡7.64 |
| Marcus Allen, Southern Cal | †1981 | 11 | *403 | 2,342 | 5.81 |
| Mike Rozier, Nebraska | †1983 | 12 | 275 | 2,148 | #7.81 |
| Tony Dorsett, Pittsburgh | †1976 | 11 | 338 | 1,948 | 5.76 |
| Lorenzo White, Michigan St. | †1985 | 11 | 386 | 1,908 | 4.94 |
| Herschel Walker, Georgia | 1981 | 11 | 385 | 1,891 | 4.91 |
| Ed Marinaro, Cornell | †1971 | 9 | 356 | 1,881 | 5.28 |
| Ernest Anderson, Oklahoma St. | †1982 | 11 | 353 | 1,877 | 5.32 |
| Ricky Bell, Southern Cal | †1975 | 11 | 357 | 1,875 | 5.25 |
| Paul Palmer, Temple | †1986 | 11 | 346 | 1,866 | 5.39 |
| Charles White, Southern Cal | †1979 | 10 | 293 | 1,803 | 6.15 |
| Anthony Thompson, Indiana | †1989 | 11 | 358 | 1,793 | 5.01 |
| Obie Graves, Cal St. Fullerton | 1978 | 12 | 275 | 1,789 | 6.51 |
| Bo Jackson, Auburn | 1985 | 11 | 278 | 1,786 | 6.42 |
| George Rogers, South Caro. | †1980 | 11 | 297 | 1,781 | 6.00 |

*Division I-A Annual Champions, All-Time Leaders*　　　　43

| Player, Team | Year | Games | Plays | Yards | Avg. |
|---|---|---|---|---|---|
| Billy Sims, Oklahoma | †1978 | 11 | 231 | 1,762 | 7.63 |
| Charles White, Southern Cal | 1978 | 12 | 342 | 1,760 | 5.15 |
| Robert Newhouse, Houston | 1971 | 11 | 277 | 1,757 | 6.34 |
| Herschel Walker, Georgia | 1982 | 11 | 335 | 1,752 | 5.23 |
| Earl Campbell, Texas | †1977 | 11 | 267 | 1,744 | 6.53 |
| Mike Pringle, Cal St. Fullerton | 1989 | 11 | 296 | 1,727 | 5.83 |
| Don McCauley, North Caro. | 1970 | 11 | 324 | 1,720 | 5.31 |

* *Record.* † *National champion.* ‡ *Record for minimum of 282 carries.* # *Record for minimum of 214 carries.*

## Single-Game Yards

| Yds. | Player, Team (Opponent) | Date |
|---|---|---|
| 396 | Tony Sands, Kansas (Missouri) | Nov. 23, 1991 |
| 386 | Marshall Faulk, San Diego St. (Pacific, Cal.) | Sept. 14, 1991 |
| 377 | Anthony Thompson, Indiana (Wisconsin) | Nov. 11, 1989 |
| 357 | Mike Pringle, Cal St. Fullerton (New Mexico St.) | Nov. 4, 1989 |
| 357 | Rueben Mayes, Washington St. (Oregon) | Oct. 27, 1984 |
| 356 | Eddie Lee Ivery, Georgia Tech (Air Force) | Nov. 11, 1978 |
| 350 | Eric Allen, Michigan St. (Purdue) | Oct. 30, 1971 |
| 349 | Paul Palmer, Temple (East Caro.) | Oct. 11, 1986 |
| 347 | Ricky Bell, Southern Cal (Washington St.) | Oct. 9, 1976 |
| 347 | Ron Johnson, Michigan (Wisconsin) | Nov. 16, 1968 |
| 343 | Tony Jeffery, Texas Christian (Tulane) | Sept. 13, 1986 |
| 342 | Roosevelt Leaks, Texas (Southern Methodist) | Nov. 3, 1973 |
| 342 | Charlie Davis, Colorado (Oklahoma St.) | Nov. 13, 1971 |
| 340 | Eugene "Mercury" Morris, West Tex. St. (Montana St.) | Oct. 5, 1968 |
| 332 | Barry Sanders, Oklahoma St. (Texas Tech) | Dec. 3, 1988 |
| 328 | Derrick Fenner, North Caro. (Virginia) | Nov. 15, 1986 |
| 326 | George Swarn, Miami, Ohio (Eastern Mich.) | Nov. 16, 1985 |
| 326 | Fred Wendt, UTEP (New Mexico St.) | Nov. 25, 1948 |
| 322 | Greg Allen, Florida St. (Western Caro.) | Oct. 31, 1981 |
| 321 | Frank Mordica, Vanderbilt (Air Force) | Nov. 18, 1978 |
| 320 | Barry Sanders, Oklahoma St. (Kansas St.) | Oct. 29, 1988 |
| 319 | Andre Herrera, Southern Ill. (Northern Ill.) | Oct. 23, 1976 |
| 319 | Jim Pilot, New Mexico St. (Hardin-Simmons) | Nov. 25, 1961 |
| 316 | Emmitt Smith, Florida (New Mexico) | Oct. 21, 1989 |
| 316 | Mike Adamle, Northwestern (Wisconsin) | Oct. 18, 1969 |
| 312 | Mark Brus, Tulsa (New Mexico St.) | Oct. 27, 1990 |
| 312 | Barry Sanders, Oklahoma St. (Kansas) | Nov. 12, 1988 |
| 310 | Tony Alford, Colorado St. (Utah) | Oct. 28, 1989 |
| 310 | Mitchell True, Pacific, Cal. (UC Davis) | Nov. 18, 1972 |
| 308 | Stacey Robinson (QB), Northern Ill. (Fresno St.) | Oct. 6, 1990 |
| 307 | Curtis Kuykendall, Auburn (Miami, Fla.) | Nov. 24, 1944 |
| 304 | Barry Sanders, Oklahoma St. (Tulsa) | Oct. 1, 1988 |
| 304 | Sam Dejarnette, Southern Miss. (Florida St.) | Sept. 25, 1982 |
| 304 | Bill Marek, Wisconsin (Minnesota) | Nov. 23, 1974 |
| 303 | Tony Dorsett, Pittsburgh (Notre Dame) | Nov. 15, 1975 |
| 302 | Jason Davis, Louisiana Tech (Southwestern La.) | Sept. 29, 1990 |
| 302 | Kevin Lowe, Wyoming (South Dak. St.) | Nov. 10, 1984 |
| 300 | Marshall Faulk, San Diego St. (Hawaii) | Nov. 14, 1992 |

## Annual Champions

| Year | Player, Team | Class | Plays | Yards |
|---|---|---|---|---|
| 1937 | Byron "Whizzer" White, Colorado | Sr. | 181 | 1,121 |
| 1938 | Len Eshmont, Fordham | So. | 132 | 831 |
| 1939 | John Polanski, Wake Forest | So. | 137 | 882 |
| 1940 | Al Ghesquiere, Detroit Mercy | Sr. | 146 | 957 |
| 1941 | Frank Sinkwich, Georgia | Jr. | 209 | 1,103 |
| 1942 | Rudy Mobley, Hardin-Simmons | So. | 187 | 1,281 |
| 1943 | Creighton Miller, Notre Dame | Sr. | 151 | 911 |
| 1944 | Wayne "Red" Williams, Minnesota | Jr. | 136 | 911 |
| 1945 | Bob Fenimore, Oklahoma St. | Jr. | 142 | 1,048 |
| 1946 | Rudy Mobley, Hardin-Simmons | Sr. | 227 | 1,262 |
| 1947 | Wilton Davis, Hardin-Simmons | So. | 193 | 1,173 |
| 1948 | Fred Wendt, UTEP | Sr. | 184 | 1,570 |
| 1949 | John Dottley, Mississippi | Jr. | 208 | 1,312 |
| 1950 | Wilford White, Arizona St. | Sr. | 199 | 1,502 |
| 1951 | Ollie Matson, San Francisco | Sr. | 245 | 1,566 |

*1993 NCAA FOOTBALL*

| Year | Player, Team | Class | Plays | Yards |
|---|---|---|---|---|
| 1952 | Howie Waugh, Tulsa | Sr. | 164 | 1,372 |
| 1953 | J. C. Caroline, Illinois | So. | 194 | 1,256 |
| 1954 | Art Luppino, Arizona | So. | 179 | 1,359 |
| 1955 | Art Luppino, Arizona | Jr. | 209 | 1,313 |
| 1956 | Jim Crawford, Wyoming | Sr. | 200 | 1,104 |
| 1957 | Leon Burton, Arizona St. | Sr. | 117 | 1,126 |
| 1958 | Dick Bass, Pacific (Cal.) | Jr. | 205 | 1,361 |
| 1959 | Pervis Atkins, New Mexico St. | Jr. | 130 | 971 |
| 1960 | Bob Gaiters, New Mexico St. | Sr. | 197 | 1,338 |
| 1961 | Jim Pilot, New Mexico St. | So. | 191 | 1,278 |
| 1962 | Jim Pilot, New Mexico St. | Jr. | 208 | 1,247 |
| 1963 | Dave Casinelli, Memphis St. | Sr. | 219 | 1,016 |
| 1964 | Brian Piccolo, Wake Forest | Sr. | 252 | 1,044 |
| 1965 | Mike Garrett, Southern Cal | Sr. | 267 | 1,440 |
| 1966 | Ray McDonald, Idaho | Sr. | 259 | 1,329 |
| 1967 | O. J. Simpson, Southern Cal | Jr. | 266 | 1,415 |
| 1968 | O. J. Simpson, Southern Cal | Sr. | 355 | 1,709 |
| 1969 | Steve Owens, Oklahoma | Sr. | 358 | 1,523 |

*Beginning in 1970, ranked on per-game (instead of total) yards*

| Year | Player, Team | Class | Games | Plays | Yards | Avg. |
|---|---|---|---|---|---|---|
| 1970 | Ed Marinaro, Cornell | Jr. | 9 | 285 | 1,425 | 158.3 |
| 1971 | Ed Marinaro, Cornell | Sr. | 9 | 356 | 1,881 | 209.0 |
| 1972 | Pete VanValkenburg, Brigham Young | Sr. | 10 | 232 | 1,386 | 138.6 |
| 1973 | Mark Kellar, Northern Ill. | Sr. | 11 | 291 | 1,719 | 156.3 |
| 1974 | Louie Giammona, Utah St. | Jr. | 10 | 329 | 1,534 | 153.4 |
| 1975 | Ricky Bell, Southern Cal | Jr. | 11 | 357 | 1,875 | 170.5 |
| 1976 | Tony Dorsett, Pittsburgh | Sr. | 11 | 338 | 1,948 | 177.1 |
| 1977 | Earl Campbell, Texas | Sr. | 11 | 267 | 1,744 | 158.5 |
| 1978 | Billy Sims, Oklahoma | Jr. | 11 | 231 | 1,762 | 160.2 |
| 1979 | Charles White, Southern Cal | Sr. | 10 | 293 | 1,803 | 180.3 |
| 1980 | George Rogers, South Caro. | Sr. | 11 | 297 | 1,781 | 161.9 |
| 1981 | Marcus Allen, Southern Cal | Sr. | 11 | *403 | 2,342 | 212.9 |
| 1982 | Ernest Anderson, Oklahoma St. | Jr. | 11 | 353 | 1,877 | 170.6 |
| 1983 | Mike Rozier, Nebraska | Sr. | 12 | 275 | 2,148 | 179.0 |
| 1984 | Keith Byars, Ohio St. | Jr. | 11 | 313 | 1,655 | 150.5 |
| 1985 | Lorenzo White, Michigan St. | So. | 11 | 386 | 1,908 | 173.5 |
| 1986 | Paul Palmer, Temple | Sr. | 11 | 346 | 1,866 | 169.6 |
| 1987 | Elbert "Ickey" Woods, Nevada-Las Vegas | Sr. | 11 | 259 | 1,658 | 150.7 |
| 1988 | Barry Sanders, Oklahoma St. | Jr. | 11 | 344 | *2,628 | *238.9 |
| 1989 | Anthony Thompson, Indiana | Sr. | 11 | 358 | 1,793 | 163.0 |
| 1990 | Gerald Hudson, Oklahoma St. | Sr. | 11 | 279 | 1,642 | 149.3 |
| 1991 | Marshall Faulk, San Diego St. | Fr. | 9 | 201 | 1,429 | 158.8 |
| 1992 | Marshall Faulk, San Diego St. | So. | 10 | 265 | 1,630 | 163.0 |

* *Record.*

### Freshman 1,000-Yard Rushers

| Player, Team | Year | Yards |
|---|---|---|
| Ron "Po" James, New Mexico St. | 1968 | 1,291 |
| Tony Dorsett, Pittsburgh | 1973 | 1,586 |
| James McDougald, Wake Forest | 1976 | 1,018 |
| Mike Harkrader, Indiana | 1976 | 1,003 |
| Amos Lawrence, North Caro. | 1977 | 1,211 |
| Darrin Nelson, Stanford | 1977 | 1,069 |
| Mike Smith, Tenn.-Chatt. | 1977 | 1,062 |
| Gwain Durden, Tenn.-Chatt. | 1977 | 1,049 |
| Allen Ross, Northern Ill. | 1977 | 1,036 |
| Allen Harvin, Cincinnati | 1978 | 1,238 |
| Joe Morris, Syracuse | 1978 | 1,001 |
| Ron Lear, Marshall | 1979 | 1,162 |
| Herschel Walker, Georgia | 1980 | *1,616 |
| Kerwin Bell, Kansas | 1980 | 1,114 |
| Joe McIntosh, North Caro. St. | 1981 | 1,190 |
| Steve Bartalo, Colorado St. | 1983 | 1,113 |
| Spencer Tillman, Oklahoma | 1983 | 1,047 |
| D. J. Dozier, Penn St. | 1983 | 1,002 |
| Eddie Johnson, Utah | 1984 | 1,021 |
| Darrell Thompson, Minnesota | 1986 | 1,240 |

*Division I-A Annual Champions, All-Time Leaders*　　　45

| Player, Team | Year | Yards |
|---|---|---|
| Emmitt Smith, Florida | 1987 | 1,341 |
| Reggie Cobb, Tennessee | 1987 | 1,197 |
| Bernie Parmalee, Ball St. | 1987 | 1,064 |
| Curvin Richards, Pittsburgh | 1988 | 1,228 |
| Chuck Webb, Tennessee | 1989 | 1,236 |
| Robert Smith, Ohio St. | 1990 | 1,064 |
| Marshall Faulk, San Diego St. | 1991 | 1,429 |
| Greg Hill, Texas A&M | 1991 | 1,216 |
| David Small, Cincinnati | 1991 | 1,004 |
| Deland McCullough, Miami (Ohio) | 1992 | 1,026 |
| Winslow Oliver, New Mexico | 1992 | 1,063 |

* Record for freshman.

# QUARTERBACK RUSHING
## Season Yards

| Player, Team | Year | Games | Plays | Yards | TD | Avg. |
|---|---|---|---|---|---|---|
| Stacey Robinson, Northern Ill. | 1989 | 11 | 223 | *1,443 | *19 | 6.47 |
| Dee Dowis, Air Force | 1987 | 12 | 194 | 1,315 | 10 | 6.78 |
| Brian Mitchell, Southwestern La. | 1989 | 11 | 237 | 1,311 | *19 | 5.53 |
| Fred Solomon, Tampa | 1974 | 11 | 193 | 1,300 | *19 | 6.74 |
| Dee Dowis, Air Force | 1989 | 12 | 172 | 1,286 | 18 | *7.48 |
| Stacey Robinson, Northern Ill. | 1990 | 11 | 193 | 1,238 | *19 | 6.41 |
| Rob Perez, Air Force | 1991 | 12 | 233 | 1,157 | 10 | 4.97 |
| Jack Mildren, Oklahoma | 1971 | 11 | 193 | 1,140 | 17 | 5.91 |
| Nolan Cromwell, Kansas | 1975 | 11 | 218 | 1,124 | 9 | 5.16 |
| Michael Carter, Hawaii | 1991 | 12 | 221 | 1,092 | 16 | 4.94 |
| Tory Crawford, Army | 1986 | 11 | *244 | 1,075 | 15 | 4.41 |
| Bart Weiss, Air Force | 1985 | 12 | 180 | 1,032 | 12 | 5.73 |
| Jimmy Sidle, Auburn | 1963 | 10 | 185 | 1,006 | 10 | 5.44 |
| Reggie Collier, Southern Miss. | 1981 | 11 | 153 | 1,005 | 12 | 6.57 |
| Darian Hagan, Colorado | 1989 | 11 | 186 | 1,004 | 17 | 5.40 |

* Record.

## Career Yards

| Player, Team | Years | Games | Plays | Yards | TD | Yd. PG |
|---|---|---|---|---|---|---|
| Dee Dowis, Air Force | 1986-89 | 47 | 543 | *3,612 | 41 | 76.9 |
| Brian Mitchell, Southwestern La. | 1986-89 | 43 | 678 | 3,335 | *47 | 77.6 |
| Fred Solomon, Tampa | 1971-74 | 43 | 557 | 3,299 | 39 | 76.7 |
| Stacey Robinson, Northern Ill. | 1988-90 | 25 | 429 | 2,727 | 38 | *109.1 |
| Jamelle Holieway, Oklahoma | 1985-88 | 38 | 505 | 2,699 | 30 | 71.0 |
| Bill Hurley, Syracuse | 1975-79 | 46 | *685 | 2,551 | 19 | 55.5 |
| Bill Deery, William & Mary | 1972-74 | 33 | 443 | 2,401 | 19 | 72.8 |
| Reggie Collier, Southern Miss. | 1979-82 | 39 | 446 | 2,304 | 26 | 59.1 |
| John Bond, Mississippi St. | 1980-83 | 44 | 572 | 2,280 | 24 | 51.8 |
| Tory Crawford, Army | 1984-87 | 31 | 495 | 2,255 | 34 | 72.7 |
| Alton Grizzard, Navy | 1987-90 | 38 | 599 | 2,174 | 15 | 57.2 |
| Roy DeWalt, Texas-Arlington | 1975, 77-79 | 38 | 468 | 2,136 | 27 | 56.2 |
| Bucky Richardson, Texas A&M | 1987-88, 90-91 | 41 | 370 | 2,095 | 30 | 51.1 |
| Rocky Long, New Mexico | 1969-71 | 31 | 469 | 2,071 | 21 | 66.8 |
| Steve Davis, Oklahoma | 1973-75 | 33 | 515 | 2,069 | 33 | 62.7 |
| Steve Taylor, Nebraska | 1985-88 | 37 | 429 | 2,065 | 30 | 55.8 |
| Rick Leach, Michigan | 1975-78 | 43 | 440 | 2,053 | 34 | 47.7 |
| Prince McJunkins, Wichita St. | 1979-82 | 44 | 613 | 2,047 | 27 | 46.5 |
| Rickey Foggie, Minnesota | 1984-87 | 41 | 510 | 2,038 | 24 | 49.7 |
| Major Harris, West Va. | 1987-89 | 33 | 386 | 2,030 | 18 | 51.5 |
| Steve Gage, Tulsa | 1983-84, 86 | 33 | 522 | 2,029 | 30 | 61.5 |
| Darian Hagan, Colorado | 1988-91 | 41 | 489 | 2,007 | 27 | 49.0 |

* Record.

*1993 NCAA FOOTBALL*

# PASSING

### Career Passing Efficiency
### (Minimum 500 Completions)

| Player, Team | Years | Att. | Cmp. | Int. | Pct. | Yds. | TD | Pts. |
|---|---|---|---|---|---|---|---|---|
| Ty Detmer, Brigham Young ....... | 1988-91 | *1,530 | *958 | 65 | .626 | *15,031 | *121 | *162.7 |
| Jim McMahon, Brigham Young ... | 1977-78, 80-81 | 1,060 | 653 | 34 | .616 | 9,536 | 84 | 156.9 |
| Steve Young, Brigham Young ..... | 1981-83 | 908 | 592 | 33 | **.652 | 7,733 | 56 | 149.8 |
| Robbie Bosco, Brigham Young ... | 1983-85 | 997 | 638 | 36 | .640 | 8,400 | 66 | 149.4 |
| Chuck Long, Iowa ............... | $1981-85 | 1,072 | 692 | 46 | ‡.646 | 9,210 | 64 | 147.8 |
| Andre Ware, Houston ............ | 1987-89 | 1,074 | 660 | 28 | .615 | 8,202 | 75 | 143.3 |
| Doug Gaynor, Long Beach St. .... | 1984-85 | 837 | 569 | 35 | .680 | 6,793 | 35 | 141.6 |
| Dan McGwire, Iowa/San Diego St. | 1986-87, 89-90 | 973 | 575 | 30 | .591 | 8,164 | 49 | 140.0 |
| John Elway, Stanford ............ | 1979-82 | 1,246 | 774 | 39 | .621 | 9,349 | 77 | 139.3 |
| David Klingler, Houston .......... | 1988-91 | 1,261 | 726 | 38 | .576 | 9,430 | 91 | 138.2 |
| Scott Mitchell, Utah .............. | 1987-89 | 1,165 | 669 | 38 | .574 | 8,981 | 68 | 137.7 |
| Shane Matthews, Florida ......... | 1989-92 | 1,202 | 722 | 46 | .601 | 9,287 | 74 | 137.6 |
| Marc Wilson, Brigham Young ..... | 1977-79 | 937 | 535 | 46 | .571 | 7,637 | 61 | 137.2 |
| R. Cunningham, Nev.-Las Vegas .. | 1982-84 | 1,029 | 597 | 29 | .580 | 8,020 | 59 | 136.8 |
| Kerwin Bell, Florida .............. | 1984-87 | 953 | 549 | 35 | .576 | 7,585 | 56 | 136.5 |
| Tom Hodson, Louisiana St. ....... | 1986-89 | 1,163 | 674 | 41 | .580 | 9,115 | 69 | 136.3 |
| Rodney Peete, Southern Cal ..... | 1985-88 | 972 | 571 | 32 | .587 | 7,640 | 52 | 135.8 |
| Troy Kopp, Pacific (Cal.) ......... | 1989-92 | 1,374 | 798 | 47 | .581 | 10,258 | 87 | 134.9 |
| Joe Adams, Tennessee St. ........ | 1977-80 | 1,100 | 604 | 60 | .549 | 8,649 | 81 | 134.4 |
| Mike Gundy, Oklahoma St. ....... | 1986-89 | 1,037 | 606 | 37 | .584 | 8,072 | 54 | 133.9 |
| Todd Santos, San Diego St. ....... | 1984-87 | 1,484 | 910 | 57 | .613 | 11,425 | 70 | 133.9 |
| Tony Eason, Illinois ............... | 1981-82 | 856 | 526 | 29 | .615 | 6,608 | 37 | 133.8 |
| Danny McCoin, Cincinnati ........ | 1984-87 | 899 | 544 | 26 | .605 | 6,801 | 39 | 132.6 |
| Rich Campbell, California ........ | 1977-80 | 891 | 574 | 42 | .644 | 6,933 | 33 | 132.6 |
| Jim Everett, Purdue .............. | $1981-85 | 923 | 550 | 30 | .596 | 7,158 | 40 | 132.5 |
| Matt Rodgers, Iowa .............. | 1988-91 | 844 | 516 | 30 | .611 | 6,308 | 40 | 132.5 |
| Doug Flutie, Boston College ..... | 1981-84 | 1,270 | 677 | 54 | .533 | 10,579 | 67 | 132.2 |
| Gino Torretta, Miami (Fla.) ........ | 1989-92 | 991 | 555 | 24 | .560 | 7,690 | 47 | 132.0 |
| Jack Trudeau, Illinois ............ | 1981, 83-85 | 1,151 | 736 | 38 | †.639 | 8,146 | 51 | 131.4 |
| Kevin Sweeney, Fresno St. ........ | $1982-86 | 1,336 | 731 | 48 | .547 | 10,623 | 66 | 130.6 |
| Bill Musgrave, Oregon ........... | 1987-90 | 1,018 | 582 | 38 | .572 | 7,631 | 55 | 130.6 |
| Gene Swick, Toledo .............. | 1972-75 | 938 | 556 | 45 | .593 | 7,267 | 44 | 130.3 |
| Jason Verduzco, Illinois .......... | 1989-92 | 986 | 622 | 29 | .631 | 6,974 | 40 | 130.0 |
| Brian McClure, Bowling Green ... | 1982-85 | 1,427 | 900 | 58 | .631 | 10,280 | 63 | 130.0 |

### (400-499 Completions)

| Player, Team | Years | Att. | Cmp. | Int. | Pct. | Yds. | TD | Pts. |
|---|---|---|---|---|---|---|---|---|
| Vinny Testaverde, Miami (Fla.) ........ | 1982, 84-86 | 674 | 413 | 25 | .613 | 6,058 | 48 | 152.9 |
| Troy Aikman, Oklahoma/UCLA ....... | 84-85, 87-88 | 637 | 401 | 18 | .630 | 5,436 | 40 | 149.7 |
| Chuck Hartlieb, Iowa................. | 1985-88 | 716 | 461 | 17 | .643 | 6,269 | 34 | 148.9 |
| Elvis Grbac, Michigan ................ | 1989-92 | 754 | 477 | 29 | .633 | 5,859 | 64 | 148.9 |
| Gifford Nielsen, Brigham Young ...... | 1975-77 | 708 | 415 | 29 | .586 | 5,833 | 55 | 145.3 |

| Player, Team | Years | Att. | Cmp. | Int. | Pct. | Yds. | TD | Pts. |
|---|---|---|---|---|---|---|---|---|
| Tom Ramsey, UCLA ................. | 1979-82 | 691 | 411 | 33 | .595 | 5,844 | 48 | 143.9 |
| Shawn Moore, Virginia ............... | 1987-90 | 762 | 421 | 32 | .552 | 6,629 | 55 | 143.8 |
| Jerry Rhome, Southern Meth./Tulsa .. | 1961, 63-64 | 713 | 448 | 23 | .628 | 5,472 | 47 | 142.6 |
| Bernie Kosar, Miami (Fla.) ............. | 1983-84 | 743 | 463 | 29 | .623 | 5,971 | 40 | 139.8 |
| Craig Erickson, Miami (Fla.) .......... | 1987-90 | 752 | 420 | 22 | .559 | 6,056 | 46 | 137.8 |
| Dave Yarema, Michigan St. ........... | $1982-86 | 727 | 447 | 29 | .615 | 5,569 | 41 | 136.5 |
| Gary Huff, Florida St. ................. | 1970-72 | 796 | 436 | 42 | .548 | 6,378 | 52 | 133.1 |
| Jeff Francis, Tennessee .............. | 1985-88 | 768 | 476 | 26 | .620 | 5,867 | 31 | 132.7 |
| Mike Perez, San Jose St. .............. | 1986-87 | 792 | 471 | 30 | .595 | 6,194 | 36 | 132.6 |
| Jeff Van Raaphorst, Arizona St. ....... | 1984-86 | 811 | 473 | 36 | .583 | 6,250 | 42 | 131.3 |

**(325-399 Completions)**

| Player, Team | Years | Att. | Cmp. | Int. | Pct. | Yds. | TD | Pts. |
|---|---|---|---|---|---|---|---|---|
| Jim Harbaugh, Michigan .............. | 1983-86 | 582 | 368 | 19 | .632 | 5,215 | 31 | 149.6 |
| Danny White, Arizona St. ............. | 1971-73 | 649 | 345 | 36 | .532 | 5,932 | 59 | 148.9 |
| Jim Karsatos, Ohio St. ................ | 1983-86 | 573 | 330 | 19 | .576 | 4,698 | 36 | 140.6 |
| Jerry Tagge, Nebraska ............... | 1969-71 | 581 | 348 | 19 | .599 | 4,704 | 33 | 140.1 |
| Garrett Gabriel, Hawaii............... | 1987-90 | 661 | 356 | 31 | .539 | 5,631 | 47 | 139.5 |
| Rick Mirer, Notre Dame .............. | 1989-92 | 698 | 377 | 23 | .540 | 5,996 | 41 | 139.0 |
| Gary Sheide, Brigham Young ........ | 1973-74 | 594 | 358 | 31 | .603 | 4,524 | 45 | 138.8 |
| Dan Speltz, Cal St. Fullerton .......... | 1988-89 | 583 | 350 | 19 | .600 | 4,595 | 33 | 138.4 |
| Don McPherson, Syracuse............ | $1983-87 | 687 | 367 | 29 | .534 | 5,812 | 46 | 138.1 |
| Sam King, Nevada-Las Vegas ........ | 1979-81 | 625 | 360 | 29 | .576 | 5,393 | 30 | 136.6 |
| Jesse Freitas, Stanford/San Diego St.. | 1970, 72-73 | 547 | 338 | 33 | .618 | 4,408 | 28 | 134.3 |
| Jeff Blake, East Caro. ................ | 1988-91 | 667 | 360 | 20 | .540 | 5,133 | 43 | 133.9 |
| Alan Risher, Louisiana St. ............ | 1980-82 | 615 | 381 | 24 | .620 | 4,585 | 31 | 133.4 |

*\* Record. \*\* Record for minimum of 875 attempts. ‡ Record for minimum of 1,000 attempts. † Record for minimum of 1,100 attempts. $ See page 8 for explanation.*

**Season Passing Efficiency**
**(Minimum 15 Attempts Per Game)**

| Player, Team | Year | G. | Att. | Cmp. | Int. | Pct. | Yds. | TD | Pts. |
|---|---|---|---|---|---|---|---|---|---|
| Jim McMahon, Brigham Young ..... | #†1980 | 12 | 445 | 284 | 18 | .638 | 4,571 | 47 | *176.9 |
| Ty Detmer, Brigham Young ......... | †1989 | 12 | 412 | 265 | 15 | .643 | 4,560 | 32 | 175.6 |
| Jerry Rhome, Tulsa ................. | #†1964 | 10 | 326 | 224 | 4 | .687 | 2,870 | 32 | 172.6 |
| Elvis Grbac, Michigan............... | †1991 | 11 | 228 | 152 | 5 | .667 | 1,955 | 24 | 169.0 |
| Ty Detmer, Brigham Young ......... | #1991 | 12 | 403 | 249 | 12 | .618 | 4,031 | 35 | 168.5 |
| Steve Young, Brigham Young ....... | #†1983 | 11 | 429 | 306 | 10 | *.713 | 3,902 | 33 | 168.5 |
| Vinny Testaverde, Miami (Fla.) ...... | †1986 | 10 | 276 | 175 | 9 | .634 | 2,557 | 26 | 165.8 |
| Brian Dowling, Yale ................. | 1968 | 9 | 160 | 92 | 10 | .575 | 1,554 | 19 | 165.8 |
| Don McPherson, Syracuse.......... | †1987 | 11 | 229 | 129 | 11 | .563 | 2,341 | 22 | 164.3 |
| Dave Wilson, Ball St. ................ | 1977 | 11 | 177 | 115 | 7 | .650 | 1,589 | 17 | 164.2 |
| Bob Berry, Oregon .................. | 1963 | 10 | 171 | 101 | 7 | .591 | 1,675 | 16 | 164.0 |
| Jim Harbaugh, Michigan ........... | †1985 | 11 | 212 | 139 | 6 | .656 | 1,913 | 18 | 163.7 |
| Troy Aikman, UCLA................. | 1987 | 11 | 243 | 159 | 6 | .654 | 2,354 | 16 | 163.6 |
| Turk Schonert, Stanford............. | †1979 | 11 | 221 | 148 | 6 | .670 | 1,922 | 19 | 163.0 |
| Brian Broomell, Temple ............. | 1979 | 11 | 214 | 120 | 11 | .561 | 2,103 | 22 | 162.3 |
| Dennis Shaw, San Diego St. ........ | †1969 | 10 | 335 | 199 | 26 | .594 | 3,185 | 39 | 162.2 |
| Timm Rosenbach, Washington St. ... | †1988 | 11 | 302 | 199 | 10 | .659 | 2,791 | 23 | 162.0 |
| Davey O'Brien, Texas Christian ..... | ¢#†1938 | 10 | 167 | 93 | 4 | .557 | 1,457 | 19 | 161.7 |
| Chuck Hartlieb, Iowa................ | 1987 | 12 | 299 | 196 | 8 | .656 | 2,855 | 19 | 161.4 |
| David Brown, Duke ................. | 1989 | 9 | 163 | 104 | 6 | .638 | 1,479 | 14 | 161.0 |
| Shawn Moore, Virginia .............. | †1990 | 10 | 241 | 144 | 8 | .598 | 2,262 | 21 | 160.7 |
| Chuck Long, Iowa .................. | 1983 | 10 | 236 | 144 | 8 | .610 | 2,434 | 14 | 160.4 |
| Jeff Garcia, San Jose St. ............ | 1991 | 9 | 160 | 99 | 5 | .619 | 1,519 | 12 | 160.1 |
| Matt Blundin, Virginia ............... | 1991 | 9 | 224 | 135 | 0 | .603 | 1,902 | 19 | 159.6 |
| Kerwin Bell, Florida ................. | 1985 | 11 | 288 | 180 | 8 | .625 | 2,687 | 21 | 159.4 |
| Mike Gundy, Oklahoma St. ......... | 1988 | 11 | 236 | 153 | 12 | .648 | 2,163 | 19 | 158.2 |
| Danny White, Arizona St. ........... | 1973 | 11 | 265 | 146 | 12 | .551 | 2,609 | 23 | 157.4 |
| Stan Heath, Nevada................. | #†1948 | 9 | 222 | 126 | 9 | .568 | 2,005 | 22 | 157.2 |
| Jim Harbaugh, Michigan ............ | 1986 | 11 | 254 | 167 | 8 | .658 | 2,557 | 10 | 157.0 |
| Shawn Moore, Virginia .............. | 1989 | 11 | 221 | 125 | 7 | .566 | 2,078 | 18 | 156.1 |
| Dan Speltz, Cal St. Fullerton ........ | 1989 | 11 | 309 | 214 | 11 | .693 | 2,671 | 20 | 156.1 |
| Ty Detmer, Brigham Young ......... | 1990 | 12 | 562 | 361 | 28 | .642 | *5,188 | 41 | 155.9 |
| Doug Williams, Grambling .......... | #1977 | 11 | 352 | 181 | 18 | .514 | 3,286 | 38 | 155.2 |
| John Huarte, Notre Dame.......... | 1964 | 10 | 205 | 114 | 11 | .556 | 2,062 | 16 | 155.1 |
| Jim McMahon, Brigham Young ..... | #†1981 | 10 | 423 | 272 | 7 | .643 | 3,555 | 30 | 155.0 |

*1993 NCAA FOOTBALL*

| Player, Team | Year | G. | Att. | Cmp. | Int. | Pct. | Yds. | TD | Pts. |
|---|---|---|---|---|---|---|---|---|---|
| Elvis Grbac, Michigan .............. | †1992 | 9 | 169 | 112 | 12 | .663 | 1,465 | 15 | 154.2 |
| Steve Sloan, Alabama .............. | 1965 | 10 | 160 | 97 | 3 | .606 | 1,453 | 10 | 153.8 |
| Tom Ramsey, UCLA ................ | †1982 | 11 | 311 | 191 | 10 | .614 | 2,824 | 21 | 153.5 |
| Martin Vaughn, Pennsylvania ....... | 1973 | 9 | 206 | 114 | 8 | .553 | 1,926 | 17 | 153.3 |
| Dick Doheny, Fordham ............ | 1949 | 8 | 140 | 87 | 5 | .621 | 1,127 | 13 | 153.3 |

*Record.   † National pass-efficiency champion.   # National total-offense champion.   ¢ Available records before 1946 do not include TD passes except for O'Brien and relatively few other passers; thus, passing efficiency points cannot be compiled for those players without TD passes.*

### Annual Passing Efficiency Leaders
### (%Minimum 11 Attempts Per Game)

**1946**—Bill Mackrides, Nevada, 176.9; **1947**—Bobby Layne, Texas, 138.9; **1948**—Stan Heath, Nevada, 157.2 (#†); **1949**—Bob Williams, Notre Dame, 159.1; **1950**—Claude Arnold, Oklahoma, 157.3; **1951**—Dick Kazmaier, Princeton, 155.3 (#); **1952**—Ron Morris, Tulsa, 177.4; **1953**—Bob Garrett, Stanford, 142.2 (†); **1954**—Pete Vann, Army, 166.5; **1955**—George Welsh, Navy, 146.1 (#†); **1956**—Tom Flores, Pacific (Cal.), 147.5; **1957**—Lee Grosscup, Utah, 175.5; **1958**—John Hangartner, Arizona St., 150.1; **1959**—Charley Johnson, New Mexico St., 135.7; **1960**—Eddie Wilson, Arizona, 140.8; **1961**—Ron DiGravio, Purdue, 140.1; **1962**—John Jacobs, Arizona St., 153.9; **1963**—Bob Berry, Oregon, 164.0; **1964**—Jerry Rhome, Tulsa, 172.6 (#†).

### (Minimum 15 Attempts Per Game)

**1946**—Ben Raimondi, Indiana, 117.0; **1947**—Charley Conerly, Mississippi, 125.8 (†); **1948**—Stan Heath, Nevada, 157.2 (#†); **1949**—Dick Doheny, Fordham, 153.3; **1950**—Dick Doheny, Fordham, 149.5; **1951**—Babe Parilli, Kentucky, 130.8; **1952**—Gene Rossi, Cincinnati, 149.7; **1953**—Bob Garrett, Stanford, 142.2 (†); **1954**—Len Dawson, Purdue, 145.8; **1955**—George Welsh, Navy, 146.1 (#†); **1956**—Bob Reinhart, San Jose St., 121.3; **1957**—Bob Newman, Washington St., 126.5 (#); **1958**—Randy Duncan, Iowa, 135.1; **1959**—Charley Johnson, New Mexico St., 135.7; **1960**—Charley Johnson, New Mexico St., 134.1; **1961**—Eddie Wilson, Arizona, 134.2; **1962**—Terry Baker, Oregon St., 146.5 (#); **1963**—Bob Berry, Oregon, 164.0; **1964**—Jerry Rhome, Tulsa, 172.6 (#†).

### (Minimum 15 Attempts Per Game)

| Year | Player, Team | G. | Att. | Cmp. | Int. | Pct. | Yds. | TD | Pts. |
|---|---|---|---|---|---|---|---|---|---|
| 1965 | Steve Sloan, Alabama ................. | 10 | 160 | 97 | 3 | .606 | 1,453 | 10 | 153.8 |
| 1966 | Dewey Warren, Tennessee ........... | 10 | 229 | 136 | 7 | .594 | 1,716 | 18 | 142.2 |
| 1967 | Bill Andrejko, Villanova .............. | 10 | 187 | 114 | 6 | .610 | 1,405 | 13 | 140.6 |
| 1968 | Brian Dowling, Yale .................. | 9 | 160 | 92 | 10 | .575 | 1,554 | 19 | 165.8 |
| 1969 | #Dennis Shaw, San Diego St. ......... | 10 | 335 | 199 | 26 | .594 | 3,185 | 39 | 162.2 |
| 1970 | Jerry Tagge, Nebraska ............... | 11 | 165 | 104 | 7 | .630 | 1,383 | 12 | 149.0 |
| 1971 | Jerry Tagge, Nebraska ............... | 12 | 239 | 143 | 4 | .598 | 2,019 | 17 | 150.9 |
| 1972 | John Hufnagel, Penn St. ............. | 11 | 216 | 115 | 8 | .532 | 2,039 | 15 | 148.0 |
| 1973 | Danny White, Arizona St. ............ | 11 | 265 | 146 | 12 | .551 | 2,609 | 23 | 157.4 |
| 1974 | #Steve Joachim, Temple .............. | 10 | 221 | 128 | 13 | .579 | 1,950 | 20 | 150.1 |
| 1975 | James Kubacki, Harvard ............. | 8 | 137 | 77 | 9 | .562 | 1,273 | 11 | 147.6 |
| 1976 | Steve Haynes, Louisiana Tech ....... | 10 | 216 | 120 | 11 | .556 | 1,981 | 16 | 146.9 |
| 1977 | Dave Wilson, Ball St. ................ | 11 | 177 | 115 | 7 | .650 | 1,589 | 17 | 164.2 |
| 1978 | Paul McDonald, Southern Cal ....... | 11 | 194 | 111 | 7 | .572 | 1,667 | 18 | 152.8 |

*(See page 54 for annual leaders beginning in 1979)*

*† National pass-efficiency champion.   # National total-offense champion.   % In many seasons during 1946-64, only a few passers threw as many as 15 passes per game; thus, a lower minimum was used.*

### Career Yards

| Player, Team | Years | Att. | Cmp. | Int. | Pct. | Yards | TD | Long |
|---|---|---|---|---|---|---|---|---|
| Ty Detmer, Brigham Young ....... | 1988-91 | *1,530 | *958 | 65 | .626 | *15,031 | *121 | 76 |
| Todd Santos, San Diego St. ....... | 1984-87 | 1,484 | 910 | 57 | .613 | 11,425 | 70 | 84 |
| Alex Van Pelt, Pittsburgh ......... | 1989-92 | 1,463 | 845 | 59 | .578 | 10,913 | 64 | 91 |
| Kevin Sweeney, Fresno St. ........ | $1982-86 | 1,336 | 731 | 48 | .547 | 10,623 | 66 | 95 |
| Doug Flutie, Boston College ...... | 1981-84 | 1,270 | 677 | 54 | .533 | 10,579 | 67 | 80 |
| Brian McClure, Bowling Green ... | 1982-85 | 1,427 | 900 | 58 | .631 | 10,280 | 63 | 90 |
| Troy Kopp, Pacific (Cal.) ......... | 1989-92 | 1,374 | 798 | 47 | .581 | 10,258 | 87 | 80 |
| Ben Bennett, Duke ............... | 1980-83 | 1,375 | 820 | 57 | .596 | 9,614 | 55 | 88 |
| Jim McMahon, Brigham Young ... | 1977-78, 80-81 | 1,060 | 653 | 34 | .616 | 9,536 | 84 | 80 |
| Todd Ellis, South Caro. .......... | 1986-89 | 1,266 | 704 | 66 | .556 | 9,519 | 49 | 97 |
| David Klingler, Houston .......... | 1988-91 | 1,261 | 726 | 38 | .576 | 9,430 | 91 | 95 |
| Erik Wilhelm, Oregon St. ......... | 1985-88 | 1,480 | 870 | 61 | .588 | 9,393 | 52 | ‡74 |
| Jeremy Leach, New Mexico ....... | 1988-91 | 1,432 | 735 | 62 | .513 | 9,382 | 50 | 82 |
| John Elway, Stanford ............. | 1979-82 | 1,246 | 774 | 39 | .621 | 9,349 | 77 | 70 |
| T. J. Rubley, Tulsa ............... | 1987-89, 91 | 1,336 | 682 | 54 | .510 | 9,324 | 73 | 75 |
| Shane Matthews, Florida ......... | 1989-92 | 1,202 | 722 | 46 | .601 | 9,287 | 74 | 70 |
| Chuck Long, Iowa ............... | $1981-85 | 1,072 | 692 | 46 ‡‡ | .646 | 9,210 | 64 | 89 |
| Mark Herrmann, Purdue .......... | 1977-80 | 1,218 | 717 | *73 | .589 | 9,188 | 62 | 75 |
| Tom Hodson, Louisiana St. ....... | 1986-89 | 1,163 | 674 | 41 | .580 | 9,115 | 69 | 80 |
| Scott Mitchell, Utah .............. | 1987-89 | 1,165 | 669 | 38 | .574 | 8,981 | 68 | 72 |

| Player, Team | Years | Att. | Cmp. | Int. | Pct. | Yards | TD | Long |
|---|---|---|---|---|---|---|---|---|
| Brad Tayles, Western Mich. ....... | 1989-92 | 1,370 | 663 | 67 | .484 | 8,717 | 49 | 84 |
| Joe Adams, Tennessee St. ........ | 1977-80 | 1,100 | 604 | 60 | .549 | 8,649 | 81 | 71 |
| Shawn Jones, Georgia Tech ...... | 1989-92 | 1,217 | 652 | 50 | .536 | 8,441 | 51 | 82 |
| Robbie Bosco, Brigham Young ... | 1983-85 | 997 | 638 | 36 | .640 | 8,400 | 66 | ‡89 |
| Andre Ware, Houston ............. | 1987-89 | 1,074 | 660 | 28 | .615 | 8,202 | 75 | 87 |
| Dan McGwire, Iowa/San Diego St. | 1986-87, 89-90 | 973 | 575 | 30 | .591 | 8,164 | 49 | 71 |
| Jack Trudeau, Illinois ............. | 1981, 83-85 | 1,151 | 736 | 38 | †.639 | 8,146 | 51 | 83 |
| Troy Taylor, California ............. | 1986-89 | 1,162 | 683 | 46 | .588 | 8,126 | 51 | 79 |
| Mike Gundy, Oklahoma St. ....... | 1986-89 | 1,037 | 606 | 37 | .584 | 8,072 | 54 | ‡84 |
| Jeff Graham, Long Beach St. ..... | 1985-88 | 1,175 | 664 | 42 | .565 | 8,063 | 42 | 85 |
| R. Cunningham, Nev.-Las Vegas .. | 1982-84 | 1,029 | 597 | 29 | .580 | 8,020 | 59 | 69 |
| Steve Slayden, Duke .............. | 1984-87 | 1,204 | 699 | 53 | .581 | 8,004 | 48 | 73 |
| Dan Marino, Pittsburgh ........... | 1979-82 | 1,084 | 626 | 64 | .577 | 7,905 | 74 | 65 |
| John Holman, Northeast La. ...... | 1979-82 | 1,201 | 593 | 54 | .494 | 7,827 | 51 | 85 |
| Jack Thompson, Washington St... | 1975-78 | 1,086 | 601 | 49 | .553 | 7,818 | 53 | 80 |
| Bobby Fuller, Appalachian St./ South Caro...................... | 1987-88, 90-91 | 1,061 | 596 | 32 | .562 | 7,746 | 52 | 79 |
| Steve Young, Brigham Young ..... | 1981-83 | 908 | 592 | 33 | **.652 | 7,733 | 56 | 63 |
| Brett Favre, Southern Miss. ....... | 1987-90 | 1,169 | 613 | 34 | .524 | 7,695 | 52 | 80 |
| Gino Torretta, Miami (Fla.) ....... | 1989-92 | 991 | 555 | 24 | .560 | 7,690 | 47 | 99 |
| Terrence Jones, Tulane .......... | 1985-88 | 1,042 | 570 | 41 | .547 | 7,684 | 46 | 76 |
| John Paye, Stanford ............. | 1983-86 | 1,198 | 715 | 44 | .597 | 7,669 | 38 | 80 |
| Rodney Peete, Southern Cal ..... | 1985-88 | 972 | 571 | 32 | .587 | 7,640 | 52 | ‡68 |
| Marc Wilson, Brigham Young ..... | 1977-79 | 937 | 535 | 46 | .571 | 7,637 | 61 | 72 |
| Scott Campbell, Purdue.......... | 1980-83 | 1,060 | 609 | 41 | .575 | 7,636 | 45 | 77 |
| Bill Musgrave, Oregon ........... | 1987-90 | 1,018 | 582 | 38 | .572 | 7,631 | 55 | 83 |

*Record. $ See page 8 for explanation. ‡ Did not score. † Record for minimum of 1,100 attempts. ‡‡ Record for minimum of 1,000 attempts. ** Record for minimum of 875 attempts.

## Career Yards Record Progression
### (Record Yards — Player, Team, Seasons Played)

3,075—Billy Patterson, Baylor, 1936-38; 3,777—Bud Schwenk, Washington (Mo.), 1939-41; 4,004—Johnny Rauch, Georgia, 1945-48; 4,736—John Ford, Hardin-Simmons, 1947-50; 4,863—Zeke Bratkowski, Georgia, 1951-53; 5,472—Jerry Rhome, Southern Methodist, 1961, Tulsa, 1963-64; 6,495—Billy Stevens, UTEP, 1965-67; 7,076—Steve Ramsey, North Texas, 1967-69; 7,544—Jim Plunkett, Stanford, 1968-70; 7,549—John Reaves, Florida, 1969-71; 7,818—Jack Thompson, Washington St., 1975-78; 9,188—Mark Herrmann, Purdue, 1977-80; 9,536—Jim McMahon, BrighamYoung, 1977-78, 80-81; 9,614—Ben Bennett, Duke, 1980-83; 10,579—Doug Flutie, Boston College, 1981-84; 10,623—Kevin Sweeney, Fresno St., $1982-86; 11,425—Todd Santos, San Diego St., 1984-87; 15,031—Ty Detmer, Brigham Young, 1988-91.

$ See page 8 for explanation.

## Career Yards Per Game

| Player, Team | Years | G. | Att. | Cmp. | Int. | Pct. | Yds. | TD | Yd. PG |
|---|---|---|---|---|---|---|---|---|---|
| Ty Detmer, Brigham Young ...... | 1988-91 | 46 | *1,530 | *958 | 65 | .626 | *15,031 | *121 | *326.8 |
| Mike Perez, San Jose St. ......... | 1986-87 | 20 | 792 | 471 | 30 | .595 | 6,194 | 36 | 309.7 |
| Doug Gaynor, Long Beach St. ... | 1984-85 | 22 | 837 | 569 | 35 | .680 | 6,793 | 35 | 308.8 |
| Tony Eason, Illinois .............. | 1981-82 | 22 | 856 | 526 | 29 | .614 | 6,608 | 37 | 300.4 |
| David Klingler, Houston ......... | 1988-91 | 32 | 1,261 | 726 | 38 | .576 | 9,430 | 91 | 294.7 |
| Brent Snyder, Utah St. .......... | 1987-88 | 22 | 875 | 472 | 36 | .539 | 6,105 | 39 | 277.5 |
| Shane Matthews, Florida ......... | 1989-92 | 35 | 1,202 | 722 | 46 | .601 | 9,287 | 74 | 265.3 |
| Larry Egger, Utah ............... | 1985-86 | 22 | 799 | 470 | 31 | .588 | 5,749 | 39 | 261.3 |
| Bernie Kosar, Miami (Fla.)........ | 1983-84 | 23 | 743 | 463 | 29 | .623 | 5,971 | 40 | 259.6 |

*Record.

## Career Touchdown Passes

| Player, Team | Years | Games | TD Passes |
|---|---|---|---|
| Ty Detmer, Brigham Young ........................... | 1988-91 | 46 | *121 |
| David Klingler, Houston ............................. | 1988-91 | 32 | 91 |
| Troy Kopp, Pacific (Cal.) ............................ | 1989-92 | 40 | 87 |
| Jim McMahon, Brigham Young ....................... | 1977-78, 80-81 | 44 | 84 |
| Joe Adams, Tennessee St. .......................... | 1977-80 | 41 | 81 |
| John Elway, Stanford ............................... | 1979-82 | 43 | 77 |
| Andre Ware, Houston ............................... | 1987-89 | 29 | 75 |
| Shane Matthews, Florida............................. | 1989-92 | 35 | 74 |
| Dan Marino, Pittsburgh ............................. | 1979-82 | 40 | 74 |
| T. J. Rubley, Tulsa .................................. | 1987-89, 91 | 47 | 73 |
| Todd Santos, San Diego St. ......................... | 1984-87 | 46 | 70 |
| Tom Hodson, Louisiana St. .......................... | 1986-89 | 44 | 69 |
| Steve Ramsey, North Texas ......................... | 1967-69 | 29 | 69 |
| Scott Mitchell, Utah ................................ | 1987-89 | 33 | 68 |
| Doug Flutie, Boston College ......................... | 1981-84 | 42 | 67 |

*1993 NCAA FOOTBALL*

| Player, Team | Years | Games | TD Passes |
|---|---|---|---|
| Kevin Sweeney, Fresno St. . . . . . . . . . . . . . . . . . . . . . . . . . . | 1983-86 | 47 | 66 |
| Robbie Bosco, Brigham Young . . . . . . . . . . . . . . . . . . . . . | 1983-85 | 35 | 66 |
| Elvis Grbac, Michigan . . . . . . . . . . . . . . . . . . . . . . . . . . . . . | 1989-92 | 41 | 64 |
| Alex Van Pelt, Pittsburgh . . . . . . . . . . . . . . . . . . . . . . . . . . | 1989-92 | 45 | 64 |
| Chuck Long, Iowa . . . . . . . . . . . . . . . . . . . . . . . . . . . . . . . . | $1981-85 | 45 | 64 |

*Record.   $ See page 8 for explanation.*

## Season Yards

| Player, Team | Year | Games | Att. | Cmp. | Int. | Pct. | Yards | TD | Long |
|---|---|---|---|---|---|---|---|---|---|
| Ty Detmer, Brigham Young . . . . . . . . . . . | 1990 | 12 | 562 | 361 | 28 | .642 | *5,188 | 41 | 69 |
| David Klingler, Houston . . . . . . . . . . . . . . | 1990 | 11 | *643 | *374 | 20 | .582 | 5,140 | *54 | 95 |
| Andre Ware, Houston . . . . . . . . . . . . . . . . . | 1989 | 11 | 578 | 365 | 15 | .631 | 4,699 | 46 | 87 |
| Jim McMahon, Brigham Young . . . . . . . . | †1980 | 12 | 445 | 284 | 18 | .638 | 4,571 | 47 | 80 |
| Ty Detmer, Brigham Young . . . . . . . . . . . | †1989 | 12 | 412 | 265 | 15 | .643 | 4,560 | 32 | 67 |
| Scott Mitchell, Utah . . . . . . . . . . . . . . . . . . . | 1988 | 11 | 533 | 323 | 15 | .606 | 4,322 | 29 | 72 |
| Robbie Bosco, Brigham Young . . . . . . . . | 1985 | 13 | 511 | 338 | 24 | .661 | 4,273 | 30 | ‡89 |
| Ty Detmer, Brigham Young . . . . . . . . . . . | 1991 | 12 | 403 | 249 | 12 | .618 | 4,031 | 35 | 97 |
| Todd Santos, San Diego St. . . . . . . . . . . . | 1987 | 12 | 492 | 306 | 15 | .622 | 3,932 | 26 | 74 |
| Steve Young, Brigham Young . . . . . . . . . | †1983 | 11 | 429 | 306 | 10 | *.713 | 3,902 | 33 | 63 |
| Robbie Bosco, Brigham Young . . . . . . . . | 1984 | 12 | 458 | 283 | 11 | .618 | 3,875 | 33 | 54 |
| Dan McGwire, San Diego St. . . . . . . . . . . | 1990 | 11 | 449 | 270 | 7 | .601 | 3,833 | 27 | 71 |
| Anthony Dilweg, Duke . . . . . . . . . . . . . . . . | 1988 | 11 | 484 | 287 | 18 | .593 | 3,824 | 24 | 65 |
| Jimmy Klingler, Houston . . . . . . . . . . . . . . | 1992 | 11 | 504 | 303 | 18 | .601 | 3,818 | 32 | 82 |
| Sam King, Nevada-Las Vegas . . . . . . . . . | 1981 | 12 | 433 | 255 | 19 | .589 | 3,778 | 18 | 71 |
| Troy Kopp, Pacific (Cal.) . . . . . . . . . . . . . . | 1991 | 12 | 449 | 275 | 16 | .612 | 3,767 | 37 | 68 |
| Marc Wilson, Brigham Young . . . . . . . . . | 1979 | 12 | 427 | 250 | 15 | .585 | 3,720 | 29 | ‡76 |
| Dan McGwire, San Diego St. . . . . . . . . . . | 1989 | 12 | 440 | 258 | 19 | .586 | 3,651 | 16 | 57 |
| Jim Everett, Purdue . . . . . . . . . . . . . . . . . . . | 1985 | 11 | 450 | 285 | 11 | .633 | 3,651 | 23 | 70 |
| Bernie Kosar, Miami (Fla.) . . . . . . . . . . . . . | 1984 | 12 | 416 | 262 | 16 | .630 | 3,642 | 25 | 85 |
| Jeremy Leach, New Mexico . . . . . . . . . . . | 1989 | 12 | 511 | 282 | 20 | .552 | 3,573 | 22 | 82 |
| Doug Gaynor, Long Beach St. . . . . . . . . | 1985 | 12 | 452 | 321 | 18 | .710 | 3,563 | 19 | 57 |
| Jim McMahon, Brigham Young . . . . . . . . | †1981 | 10 | 423 | 272 | 7 | .643 | 3,555 | 30 | ‡67 |
| Todd Dillon, Long Beach St. . . . . . . . . . . | 1982 | 11 | 504 | 289 | 21 | .573 | 3,517 | 19 | ‡73 |

*Record.   † National pass-efficiency champion.   ‡ Did not score.*

## Season Yards Per Game

| Player, Team | Year | Games | Att. | Cmp. | Int. | Pct. | Yards | TD | Yd. PG |
|---|---|---|---|---|---|---|---|---|---|
| David Klingler, Houston . . . . . . . . . . . | 1990 | 11 | *643 | *374 | 20 | .582 | 5,140 | *54 | *467.3 |
| Ty Detmer, Brigham Young . . . . . . . | 1990 | 12 | 562 | 361 | 28 | .642 | *5,188 | 41 | 432.3 |
| Andre Ware, Houston . . . . . . . . . . . . | 1989 | 11 | 578 | 365 | 15 | .631 | 4,699 | 46 | 427.2 |
| Scott Mitchell, Utah . . . . . . . . . . . . . . | 1988 | 11 | 533 | 323 | 15 | .606 | 4,322 | 29 | 392.9 |
| Jim McMahon, Brigham Young . . . | †1980 | 12 | 445 | 284 | 18 | .638 | 4,571 | 47 | 380.9 |
| Ty Detmer, Brigham Young . . . . . . . | †1989 | 12 | 412 | 265 | 15 | .643 | 4,560 | 32 | 380.0 |
| Troy Kopp, Pacific (Cal.) . . . . . . . . . | 1990 | 9 | 428 | 243 | 14 | .568 | 3,311 | 31 | 367.9 |
| Jim McMahon, Brigham Young . . . | †1981 | 10 | 423 | 272 | 7 | .643 | 3,555 | 30 | 355.5 |
| Steve Young, Brigham Young . . . . . | †1983 | 11 | 429 | 306 | 10 | *.713 | 3,902 | 33 | 354.7 |
| Dan McGwire, San Diego St. . . . . . . | 1990 | 11 | 449 | 270 | 7 | .601 | 3,833 | 27 | 348.5 |
| Anthony Dilweg, Duke . . . . . . . . . . . | 1988 | 11 | 484 | 287 | 18 | .593 | 3,824 | 24 | 347.6 |
| Jimmy Klingler, Houston . . . . . . . . . | 1992 | 11 | 504 | 303 | 18 | .601 | 3,818 | 32 | 347.1 |
| Bill Anderson, Tulsa . . . . . . . . . . . . . . | †1965 | 10 | 509 | 296 | 14 | .582 | 3,464 | 30 | 346.4 |
| David Klingler, Houston . . . . . . . . . . | 1991 | 10 | 497 | 278 | 17 | .559 | 3,388 | 29 | 338.8 |
| Marc Wilson, Brigham Young . . . . . | 1979 | 12 | 427 | 250 | 15 | .585 | 3,720 | 29 | 338.2 |

*Record.   † National pass-efficiency champion.*

## Season Touchdown Passes

| Player, Team | Year | Games | TD Passes |
|---|---|---|---|
| David Klingler, Houston . . . . . . . . . . . . . . . . . . . . . . . . . . . . . . . | 1990 | 11 | *54 |
| Jim McMahon, Brigham Young . . . . . . . . . . . . . . . . . . . . . . . . . . | 1980 | 12 | 47 |
| Andre Ware, Houston . . . . . . . . . . . . . . . . . . . . . . . . . . . . . . . . . | 1989 | 11 | 46 |
| Ty Detmer, Brigham Young . . . . . . . . . . . . . . . . . . . . . . . . . . . . | 1990 | 12 | 41 |
| Dennis Shaw, San Diego St. . . . . . . . . . . . . . . . . . . . . . . . . . . . | 1969 | 10 | 39 |
| Doug Williams, Grambling . . . . . . . . . . . . . . . . . . . . . . . . . . . . | 1977 | 11 | 38 |
| Troy Kopp, Pacific (Cal.) . . . . . . . . . . . . . . . . . . . . . . . . . . . . . | 1991 | 12 | 37 |
| Ty Detmer, Brigham Young . . . . . . . . . . . . . . . . . . . . . . . . . . . . | 1991 | 12 | 35 |
| Dan Marino, Pittsburgh . . . . . . . . . . . . . . . . . . . . . . . . . . . . . . . | 1981 | 11 | 34 |
| Steve Young, Brigham Young . . . . . . . . . . . . . . . . . . . . . . . . . . | 1983 | 11 | 33 |
| Robbie Bosco, Brigham Young . . . . . . . . . . . . . . . . . . . . . . . . . | 1984 | 12 | 33 |
| Jerry Rhome, Tulsa . . . . . . . . . . . . . . . . . . . . . . . . . . . . . . . . . . | 1964 | 10 | 32 |
| Ty Detmer, Brigham Young . . . . . . . . . . . . . . . . . . . . . . . . . . . . | 1989 | 12 | 32 |
| Jimmy Klingler, Houston . . . . . . . . . . . . . . . . . . . . . . . . . . . . . | 1992 | 11 | 32 |
| Troy Kopp, Pacific (Cal.) . . . . . . . . . . . . . . . . . . . . . . . . . . . . . | 1990 | 9 | 31 |

*Record.*

## Single-Game Yards

| Yds. | Player, Team (Opponent) | Date |
|---|---|---|
| 716 | David Klingler, Houston (Arizona St.) | Dec. 2, 1990 |
| 690 | Matt Vogler, Texas Christian (Houston) | Nov. 3, 1990 |
| 631 | Scott Mitchell, Utah (Air Force) | Oct. 15, 1988 |
| 622 | Jeremy Leach, New Mexico (Utah) | Nov. 11, 1989 |
| 621 | Dave Wilson, Illinois (Ohio St.) | Nov. 8, 1980 |
| 613 | Jimmy Klingler, Houston (Rice) | Nov. 28, 1992 |
| 599 | Ty Detmer, Brigham Young (San Diego St.) | Nov. 16, 1991 |
| 585 | Robbie Bosco, Brigham Young (New Mexico) | Oct. 19, 1985 |
| 572 | David Klingler, Houston (Eastern Wash.) | Nov. 17, 1990 |
| 571 | Marc Wilson, Brigham Young (Utah) | Nov. 5, 1977 |
| 568 | David Lowery, San Diego St. (Brigham Young) | Nov. 16, 1991 |
| 565 | Jim McMahon, Brigham Young (Utah) | Nov. 21, 1981 |
| 564 | Troy Kopp, Pacific, Cal. (New Mexico St.) | Oct. 20, 1990 |
| 563 | David Klingler, Houston (Texas Christian) | Nov. 3, 1990 |
| 561 | Tony Adams, Utah St. (Utah) | Nov. 11, 1972 |
| 560 | Ty Detmer, Brigham Young (Utah St.) | Nov. 24, 1990 |
| 558 | Chuck Hartlieb, Iowa (Indiana) | Oct. 29, 1988 |
| 554 | Greg Cook, Cincinnati (Ohio) | Nov. 16, 1968 |
| 538 | Jim McMahon, Brigham Young (Colorado St.) | Nov. 7, 1981 |
| 537 | Ty Detmer, Brigham Young (Washington St.) | Sept. 7, 1989 |
| 536 | Dave Telford, Fresno St. (Pacific, Cal.) | Oct. 24, 1987 |
| 536 | Todd Santos, San Diego St. (Stanford) | Oct. 17, 1987 |
| 536 | David Spriggs, New Mexico St. (Southern Ill.) | Sept. 30, 1978 |
| 535 | Shane Montgomery, North Caro. St. (Duke) | Nov. 11, 1989 |
| 534 | Paul Justin, Arizona St. (Washington St.) | Oct. 28, 1989 |
| 533 | David Klingler, Houston (Texas Tech) | Nov. 30, 1991 |
| 532 | Jeff Van Raaphorst, Arizona St. (Florida St.) | Nov. 3, 1984 |
| 530 | Dan McGwire, San Diego St. (New Mexico) | Nov. 17, 1990 |
| 527 | Don Strock, Virginia Tech (Houston) | Oct. 7, 1972 |
| 526 | Joe Theismann, Notre Dame (Southern Cal) | Nov. 28, 1970 |

## Career Yards Per Attempt
### (Minimum 900 Attempts)

| Player, Team | Years | Att. | Cmp. | Pct. | Yards | Yards Per Cmp. | Per Att. |
|---|---|---|---|---|---|---|---|
| Ty Detmer, Brigham Young | 1988-91 | *1,530 | *958 | .626 | *15,031 | *15.69 | *9.82 |
| Jim McMahon, Brigham Young | 1977-78, 80-81 | 1,060 | 653 | .616 | 9,536 | 14.60 | 9.00 |
| Chuck Long, Iowa | $1981-85 | 1,072 | 692 | #.646 | 9,210 | 13.31 | 8.59 |
| Steve Young, Brigham Young | 1981-85 | 908 | 592 | ††.652 | 7,733 | 13.06 | 8.52 |
| Robbie Bosco, Brigham Young | 1983-85 | 997 | 638 | .640 | 8,400 | 13.17 | 8.43 |
| Dan McGwire, Iowa/San Diego St. | 1986-87, 89-90 | 973 | 575 | .591 | 8,164 | 14.20 | 8.39 |
| Doug Flutie, Boston College | 1981-84 | 1,270 | 677 | .533 | 10,579 | 15.63 | 8.33 |
| Marc Wilson, Brigham Young | 1977-79 | 937 | 535 | .571 | 7,637 | 14.27 | 8.15 |
| Kerwin Bell, Florida | 1984-87 | 953 | 549 | .576 | 7,585 | 13.82 | 7.96 |
| Kevin Sweeney, Fresno St. | $1982-86 | 1,336 | 731 | .547 | 10,623 | 14.53 | 7.95 |
| Joe Adams, Tennessee St. | 1977-80 | 1,100 | 604 | .549 | 8,649 | 14.32 | 7.86 |
| Rodney Peete, Southern Cal | 1985-88 | 972 | 571 | .587 | 7,640 | 13.38 | 7.86 |
| Tom Hodson, Louisiana St. | 1986-89 | 1,163 | 674 | .580 | 9,115 | 13.52 | 7.84 |
| Jim Plunkett, Stanford | 1968-70 | 962 | 530 | .551 | 7,544 | 14.23 | 7.84 |
| Randall Cunningham, Nev.-Las Vegas | 1982-84 | 1,029 | 597 | .580 | 8,020 | 13.43 | 7.79 |

*Record. $ See page 8 for explanation. # Record for minimum of 1,000 attempts. †† Record for minimum of 875 attempts.

## Single-Game Attempts

| No. | Player, Team (Opponent) | Date |
|---|---|---|
| 79 | Matt Vogler, Texas Christian (Houston) | Nov. 3, 1990 |
| 76 | David Klingler, Houston (Southern Methodist) | Oct. 20, 1990 |
| 75 | Chris Vargas, Nevada (McNeese St.) | Sept. 19, 1992 |
| 73 | Jeff Handy, Missouri (Oklahoma St.) | Oct. 17, 1992 |
| 73 | Troy Kopp, Pacific, Cal. (Hawaii) | Oct. 27, 1990 |
| 73 | Shane Montgomery, North Caro. St. (Duke) | Nov. 11, 1989 |
| 72 | Matt Vogler, Texas Christian (Texas Tech) | Nov. 10, 1990 |
| 71 | Jimmy Klingler, Houston (Rice) | Nov. 28, 1992 |
| 71 | Sandy Schwab, Northwestern (Michigan) | Oct. 23, 1982 |
| 70 | David Klingler, Houston (Texas Tech) | Nov. 30, 1991 |
| 70 | David Klingler, Houston (Arizona St.) | Dec. 2, 1990 |
| 70 | Dave Telford, Fresno St. (Utah St.) | Nov. 14, 1987 |
| 69 | Dave Wilson, Illinois (Ohio St.) | Nov. 8, 1980 |
| 69 | Chuck Hixson, Southern Methodist (Ohio St.) | Sept. 28, 1968 |
| 68 | David Klingler, Houston (Baylor) | Oct. 6, 1990 |

*1993 NCAA FOOTBALL*

| No. | Player, Team (Opponent) | Date |
|---|---|---|
| 68 | Jeremy Leach, New Mexico (Utah) | Nov. 11, 1989 |
| 68 | Steve Smith, Stanford (Notre Dame) | Oct. 7, 1989 |
| 68 | Andre Ware, Houston (Arizona St.) | Sept. 23, 1989 |
| 67 | Mike Hohensee, Minnesota (Ohio St.) | Nov. 7, 1981 |
| 66 | Drew Bledsoe, Washington St. (Montana) | Sept. 5, 1992 |
| 66 | Jack Trudeau, Illinois (Purdue) | Oct. 12, 1985 |
| 66 | John Reaves, Florida (Auburn) | Nov. 1, 1969 |
| 65 | Jimmy Klingler, Houston (Texas Christian) | Oct. 31, 1992 |
| 65 | Scott Mitchell, Utah (UTEP) | Oct. 1, 1988 |
| 65 | Mike Bates, Miami, Ohio (Toledo) | Oct. 24, 1987 |
| 65 | Craig Burnett, Wyoming (San Diego St.) | Nov. 15, 1986 |
| 65 | Gary Schofield, Wake Forest (Maryland) | Oct. 16, 1982 |
| 65 | Jim McMahon, Brigham Young (Colorado St.) | Nov. 7, 1981 |
| 65 | Brooks Dawson, UTEP (UC Santa Barb.) | Sept. 14, 1968 |
| 65 | Bill Anderson, Tulsa (Southern Ill.) | Oct. 30, 1965 |
| 65 | Bill Anderson, Tulsa (Memphis St.) | Oct. 9, 1965 |

## Single-Game Completions

| No. | Player, Team (Opponent) | Date |
|---|---|---|
| 48 | David Klingler, Houston (Southern Methodist) | Oct. 20, 1990 |
| 46 | Jimmy Klingler, Houston (Rice) | Nov. 28, 1992 |
| 45 | Sandy Schwab, Northwestern (Michigan) | Oct. 23, 1982 |
| 44 | Matt Vogler, Texas Christian (Houston) | Nov. 3, 1990 |
| 44 | Chuck Hartlieb, Iowa (Indiana) | Oct. 29, 1988 |
| 44 | Jim McMahon, Brigham Young (Colorado St.) | Nov. 7, 1981 |
| 43 | Jeff Handy, Missouri (Oklahoma St.) | Oct. 17, 1992 |
| 43 | Chris Vargas, Nevada (McNeese St.) | Sept. 19, 1992 |
| 43 | Gary Schofield, Wake Forest (Maryland) | Oct. 17, 1981 |
| 43 | Dave Wilson, Illinois (Ohio St.) | Nov. 8, 1980 |
| 43 | Rich Campbell, California (Florida) | Sept. 13, 1980 |
| 42 | Jimmy Klingler, Houston (Texas Christian) | Oct. 31, 1992 |
| 42 | Troy Kopp, Pacific, Cal. (Hawaii) | Oct. 27, 1990 |
| 42 | Andre Ware, Houston (Texas Christian) | Nov. 4, 1989 |
| 42 | Dan Speltz, Cal St. Fullerton (Utah St.) | Oct. 7, 1989 |
| 42 | Robbie Bosco, Brigham Young (New Mexico) | Oct. 19, 1985 |
| 42 | Bill Anderson, Tulsa (Southern Ill.) | Oct. 30, 1965 |
| 41 | David Klingler, Houston (Texas Tech) | Nov. 30, 1991 |
| 41 | David Klingler, Houston (Arizona St.) | Dec. 2, 1990 |
| 41 | David Klingler, Houston (Eastern Wash.) | Nov. 17, 1990 |
| 41 | Jeremy Leach, New Mexico (Utah) | Nov. 11, 1989 |
| 41 | Scott Mitchell, Utah (UTEP) | Oct. 1, 1988 |
| 41 | Doug Gaynor, Long Beach St. (Utah St.) | Sept. 7, 1985 |
| 40 | Mike Romo, Southern Methodist (Rice) | Nov. 10, 1990 |
| 40 | Andre Ware, Houston (Arizona St.) | Sept. 23, 1989 |
| 40 | Dave Telford, Fresno St. (Utah St.) | Nov. 14, 1987 |
| 40 | Todd Santos, San Diego St. (Stanford) | Oct. 17, 1987 |
| 40 | Larry Egger, Utah (UTEP) | Nov. 29, 1986 |
| 40 | John Paye, Stanford (San Diego St.) | Oct. 5, 1985 |
| 40 | Gary Schofield, Wake Forest (Maryland) | Oct. 16, 1982 |
| 40 | Jim McMahon, Brigham Young (North Texas) | Nov. 8, 1980 |

## Annual Champions

| Year | Player, Team | Class | Att. | Cmp. | Int. | Pct. | Yds. | TD |
|---|---|---|---|---|---|---|---|---|
| 1937 | Davey O'Brien, Texas Christian | Jr. | 234 | 94 | 18 | .402 | 969 | — |
| 1938 | Davey O'Brien, Texas Christian | Sr. | 167 | 93 | 4 | .557 | 1,457 | — |
| 1939 | Kay Eakin, Arkansas | Sr. | 193 | 78 | 18 | .404 | 962 | — |
| 1940 | Billy Sewell, Washington St. | Sr. | 174 | 86 | 17 | .494 | 1,023 | — |
| 1941 | Bud Schwenk, Washington (Mo.) | Sr. | 234 | 114 | 19 | .487 | 1,457 | — |
| 1942 | Ray Evans, Kansas | Jr. | 200 | 101 | 9 | .505 | 1,117 | — |
| 1943 | Johnny Cook, Georgia | Fr. | 157 | 73 | 20 | .465 | 1,007 | — |
| 1944 | Paul Rickards, Pittsburgh | So. | 178 | 84 | 20 | .472 | 997 | — |
| 1945 | Al Dekdebrun, Cornell | Sr. | 194 | 90 | 15 | .464 | 1,227 | — |
| 1946 | Travis Tidwell, Auburn | Fr. | 158 | 79 | 10 | .500 | 943 | 5 |
| 1947 | Charlie Conerly, Mississippi | Sr. | 233 | 133 | 7 | .571 | 1,367 | 18 |
| 1948 | Stan Heath, Nevada | Sr. | 222 | 126 | 9 | .568 | 2,005 | 22 |
| 1949 | Adrian Burk, Baylor | Sr. | 191 | 110 | 6 | .576 | 1,428 | 14 |
| 1950 | Don Heinrich, Washington | Jr. | 221 | 134 | 9 | .606 | 1,846 | 14 |
| 1951 | Don Klosterman, Loyola (Cal.) | Sr. | 315 | 159 | 21 | .505 | 1,843 | 9 |

| Year | Player, Team | Class | Att. | Cmp. | Int. | Pct. | Yds. | TD |
|------|--------------|-------|------|------|------|------|------|-----|
| 1952 | Don Heinrich, Washington | Sr. | 270 | 137 | 17 | .507 | 1,647 | 13 |
| 1953 | Bob Garrett, Stanford | Sr. | 205 | 118 | 10 | .576 | 1,637 | 17 |
| 1954 | Paul Larson, California | Sr. | 195 | 125 | 8 | .641 | 1,537 | 10 |
| 1955 | George Welsh, Navy | Sr. | 150 | 94 | 6 | .627 | 1,319 | 8 |
| 1956 | John Brodie, Stanford | Sr. | 240 | 139 | 14 | .579 | 1,633 | 12 |
| 1957 | Ken Ford, Hardin-Simmons | Sr. | 205 | 115 | 11 | .561 | 1,254 | 14 |
| 1958 | Buddy Humphrey, Baylor | Sr. | 195 | 112 | 8 | .574 | 1,316 | 7 |
| 1959 | Dick Norman, Stanford | Jr. | 263 | 152 | 12 | .578 | 1,963 | 11 |
| 1960 | Harold Stephens, Hardin-Simmons | Sr. | 256 | 145 | 14 | .566 | 1,254 | 3 |
| 1961 | Chon Gallegos, San Jose St. | Sr. | 197 | 117 | 13 | .594 | 1,480 | 14 |
| 1962 | Don Trull, Baylor | Jr. | 229 | 125 | 12 | .546 | 1,627 | 11 |
| 1963 | Don Trull, Baylor | Sr. | 308 | 174 | 12 | .565 | 2,157 | 12 |
| 1964 | Jerry Rhome, Tulsa | Sr. | 326 | 224 | 4 | .687 | 2,870 | 32 |
| 1965 | Bill Anderson, Tulsa | Sr. | 509 | 296 | 14 | .582 | 3,464 | 30 |
| 1966 | John Eckman, Wichita St. | Jr. | 458 | 195 | *34 | .426 | 2,339 | 7 |
| 1967 | Terry Stone, New Mexico | Jr. | 336 | 160 | 19 | .476 | 1,946 | 9 |
| 1968 | Chuck Hixson, Southern Methodist | So. | 468 | 265 | 23 | .566 | 3,103 | 21 |
| 1969 | John Reaves, Florida | So. | 396 | 222 | 19 | .561 | 2,896 | 24 |

*Beginning in 1970, ranked on per-game (instead of total) completions*

| Year | Player, Team | Cl. | G. | Att. | Cmp. | Avg. | Int. | Pct. | Yds. | TD |
|------|--------------|-----|-----|------|------|------|------|------|------|-----|
| 1970 | Sonny Sixkiller, Washington | So. | 10 | 362 | 186 | 18.6 | 22 | .514 | 2,303 | 15 |
| 1971 | Brian Sipe, San Diego St. | Sr. | 11 | 369 | 196 | 17.8 | 21 | .531 | 2,532 | 17 |
| 1972 | Don Strock, Virginia Tech | Sr. | 11 | 427 | 228 | 20.7 | 27 | .534 | 3,243 | 16 |
| 1973 | Jesse Freitas, San Diego St. | Sr. | 11 | 347 | 227 | 20.6 | 17 | .654 | 2,993 | 21 |
| 1974 | Steve Bartkowski, California | Sr. | 11 | 325 | 182 | 16.5 | 7 | .560 | 2,580 | 12 |
| 1975 | Craig Penrose, San Diego St. | Sr. | 11 | 349 | 198 | 18.0 | 24 | .567 | 2,660 | 15 |
| 1976 | Tommy Kramer, Rice | Sr. | 11 | 501 | 269 | 24.5 | 19 | .537 | 3,317 | 21 |
| 1977 | Guy Benjamin, Stanford | Sr. | 10 | 330 | 208 | 20.8 | 15 | .630 | 2,521 | 19 |
| 1978 | Steve Dils, Stanford | Sr. | 11 | 391 | 247 | 22.5 | 15 | .632 | 2,943 | 22 |

*Beginning in 1979, ranked on Passing Efficiency Rating Points (instead of per-game completions)*

| Year | Player, Team | Cl. | G. | Att. | Cmp. | Int. | Pct. | Yds. | TD | Pts. |
|------|--------------|-----|-----|------|------|------|------|------|-----|------|
| 1979 | Turk Schonert, Stanford | Sr. | 11 | 221 | 148 | 6 | .670 | 1,922 | 19 | 163.0 |
| 1980 | Jim McMahon, Brigham Young | Jr. | 12 | 445 | 284 | 18 | .638 | 4,571 | 47 | *176.9 |
| 1981 | Jim McMahon, Brigham Young | Sr. | 10 | 423 | 272 | 7 | .643 | 3,555 | 30 | 155.0 |
| 1982 | Tom Ramsey, UCLA | Sr. | 11 | 311 | 191 | 10 | .614 | 2,824 | 21 | 153.5 |
| 1983 | Steve Young, Brigham Young | Sr. | 11 | 429 | 306 | 10 | *.713 | 3,902 | 33 | 168.5 |
| 1984 | Doug Flutie, Boston College | Sr. | 11 | 386 | 233 | 11 | .604 | 3,454 | 27 | 152.9 |
| 1985 | Jim Harbaugh, Michigan | Jr. | 11 | 212 | 139 | 6 | .656 | 1,913 | 18 | 163.7 |
| 1986 | Vinny Testaverde, Miami (Fla.) | Sr. | 10 | 276 | 175 | 9 | .634 | 2,557 | 26 | 165.8 |
| 1987 | Don McPherson, Syracuse | Sr. | 11 | 229 | 129 | 11 | .563 | 2,341 | 22 | 164.3 |
| 1988 | Timm Rosenbach, Washington St. | Jr. | 11 | 302 | 199 | 10 | .659 | 2,791 | 23 | 162.0 |
| 1989 | Ty Detmer, Brigham Young | So. | 12 | 412 | 265 | 15 | .643 | 4,560 | 32 | 175.6 |
| 1990 | Shawn Moore, Virginia | Sr. | 10 | 241 | 144 | 8 | .598 | 2,262 | 21 | 160.7 |
| 1991 | Elvis Grbac, Michigan | Jr. | 11 | 228 | 152 | 5 | .667 | 1,955 | 24 | 169.0 |
| 1992 | Elvis Grbac, Michigan | Sr. | 9 | 169 | 112 | 12 | .663 | 1,465 | 15 | 154.2 |

*\* Record.*

# RECEIVING

## Career Catches Per Game

| Player, Team | Years | Games | Catches | Yards | TD | Ct. PG |
|--------------|-------|-------|---------|-------|-----|--------|
| Manny Hazard, Houston | 1989-90 | 21 | 220 | 2,635 | 31 | *10.5 |
| Howard Twilley, Tulsa | 1963-65 | 26 | 261 | 3,343 | 32 | 10.0 |
| Jason Phillips, Houston | 1987-88 | 22 | 207 | 2,319 | 18 | 9.4 |
| Neal Sweeney, Tulsa | 1965-66 | 18 | 134 | 1,623 | 11 | 7.4 |
| David Williams, Illinois | 1983-85 | 33 | 245 | 3,195 | 22 | 7.4 |
| James Dixon, Houston | 1987-88 | 22 | 161 | 1,762 | 14 | 7.3 |
| John Love, North Texas | 1965-66 | 20 | 144 | 2,124 | 17 | 7.2 |
| Fred Gilbert, UCLA/Houston | 1989, 91-92 | 22 | 158 | 1,672 | 14 | 7.2 |
| Ron Sellers, Florida St. | 1966-68 | 30 | 212 | 3,598 | 23 | 7.1 |
| Barry Moore, North Texas | 1968-69 | 20 | 140 | 2,183 | 12 | 7.0 |
| Mike Kelly, Davidson | 1967-69 | 23 | 156 | 2,114 | 17 | 6.8 |
| Guy Liggins, San Jose St. | 1986-87 | 22 | 149 | 2,191 | 16 | 6.8 |
| Dave Petzke, Northern Ill. | 1977-78 | 22 | 148 | 1,960 | 16 | 6.7 |
| Loren Richey, Utah | 1985-86 | 21 | 140 | 1,746 | 13 | 6.7 |
| Tom Reynolds, San Diego St. | 1969,71 | 18 | 117 | 1,955 | 25 | 6.5 |

| Player, Team | Years | Games | Catches | Yards | TD | Ct. PG |
|---|---|---|---|---|---|---|
| Tim Delaney, San Diego St. ......... | 1968-70 | 29 | 180 | 2,535 | 22 | 6.2 |
| Larry Willis, Fresno St. ............. | 1983-84 | 23 | 142 | 2,260 | 14 | 6.2 |
| Phil Odle, Brigham Young ......... | 1965-67 | 30 | 183 | 2,548 | 25 | 6.1 |
| Aaron Turner, Pacific (Cal.) ........ | 1989-92 | 44 | *266 | *4,345 | *43 | 6.0 |
| Mike Mikolayunas, Davidson........ | 1968-70 | 29 | 175 | 1,768 | 14 | 6.0 |
| Terance Mathis, New Mexico ....... | 1985-87,89 | 44 | 263 | 4,254 | 36 | 6.0 |
| Rick Eber, Tulsa .................... | 1966-67 | 20 | 119 | 1,902 | 15 | 6.0 |
| Hugh Campbell, Washington St. .... | 1960-62 | 30 | 176 | 2,453 | 22 | 5.9 |
| Vern Burke, Oregon St. ............. | 1962-63 | 20 | 117 | 1,801 | 19 | 5.9 |

* Record.

| | Season Catches Per Game | | | | | |
|---|---|---|---|---|---|---|
| Player, Team | Year | Games | Catches | Yards | TD | Ct. PG |
| Howard Twilley, Tulsa ....................... | †1965 | 10 | 134 | *1,779 | 16 | *13.4 |
| Manny Hazard, Houston .................... | †1989 | 11 | *142 | 1,689 | *22 | 12.9 |
| Jason Phillips, Houston ..................... | †1988 | 11 | 108 | 1,444 | 15 | 9.8 |
| Fred Gilbert, Houston ...................... | †1991 | 11 | 106 | 957 | 7 | 9.6 |
| Jerry Hendren, Idaho ...................... | †1969 | 10 | 95 | 1,452 | 12 | 9.5 |
| Howard Twilley, Tulsa ....................... | †1964 | 10 | 95 | 1,178 | 13 | 9.5 |
| Sherman Smith, Houston ................... | †1992 | 11 | 103 | 923 | 6 | 9.4 |
| James Dixon, Houston ..................... | 1988 | 11 | 102 | 1,103 | 11 | 9.3 |
| David Williams, Illinois ..................... | †1984 | 11 | 101 | 1,278 | 8 | 9.2 |
| Glenn Meltzer, Wichita St. ................. | †1966 | 10 | 91 | 1,115 | 4 | 9.1 |
| Jay Miller, Brigham Young ................. | †1973 | 11 | 100 | 1,181 | 8 | 9.1 |

* Record.  † National champion.

Tulsa's Howard Twilley averaged 13.4 catches per game in 1965 and 9.5 per game in 1964, seasons that rank first and fifth, respectively, on the Division I-A all-time list for catches per game.

## Career Catches

| Player, Team | Years | Catches | Yards | Avg. | TD |
|---|---|---|---|---|---|
| Aaron Turner, Pacific (Cal.) | 1989-92 | *266 | *4,345 | 16.3 | *43 |
| Terance Mathis, New Mexico | 1985-87, 89 | 263 | 4,254 | 16.2 | 36 |
| Mark Templeton, Long Beach St. (RB) | 1983-86 | 262 | 1,969 | 7.5 | 11 |
| Howard Twilley, Tulsa | 1963-65 | 261 | 3,343 | 12.8 | 32 |
| David Williams, Illinois | 1983-85 | 245 | 3,195 | 13.0 | 22 |
| Marc Zeno, Tulane | 1984-87 | 236 | 3,725 | 15.8 | 25 |
| Jason Wolf, Southern Methodist | 1989-92 | 235 | 2,232 | 9.5 | 17 |
| Manny Hazard, Houston | 1989-90 | 220 | 2,635 | 12.0 | 31 |
| Darrin Nelson, Stanford (RB) | 1977-78, 80-81 | 214 | 2,368 | 11.1 | 16 |
| Ron Sellers, Florida St. | 1966-68 | 212 | 3,598 | ‡17.0 | 23 |
| Jason Phillips, Houston | 1987-88 | 207 | 2,319 | 11.2 | 18 |
| Hart Lee Dykes, Oklahoma St. | 1985-88 | 203 | 3,171 | 15.6 | 29 |
| Keith Edwards, Vanderbilt | 1980, 82-84 | 200 | 1,757 | 8.8 | 3 |
| Bobby Slaughter, Louisiana Tech | 1987-90 | 198 | 2,544 | 12.9 | 14 |
| Richard Buchanan, Northwestern | 1987-90 | 197 | 2,474 | 12.6 | 22 |
| Gerald Harp, Western Caro. | 1977-80 | 197 | 3,305 | 16.8 | 26 |
| Matt Bellini, Brigham Young (RB) | 1987-90 | 196 | 2,544 | 13.0 | 13 |
| Brad Muster, Stanford (FB) | 1984-87 | 196 | 1,669 | 8.5 | 6 |
| Greg Primus, Colorado St. | 1989-92 | 192 | 3,200 | 16.7 | 16 |
| Charles Lockett, Long Beach St. | 1983-86 | 191 | 2,902 | 15.1 | 19 |
| Clarkston Hines, Duke | 1986-89 | 189 | 3,318 | 17.6 | 38 |
| Ricky Proehl, Wake Forest | 1986-89 | 188 | 2,949 | 15.7 | 25 |
| Boo Mitchell, Vanderbilt | 1985-88 | 188 | 2,964 | 15.8 | 9 |
| Monty Gilbreath, San Diego St. | 1986-89 | 187 | 2,241 | 12.0 | 8 |
| Eric Henley, Rice | 1988-91 | 186 | 2,200 | 11.8 | 16 |
| Jeff Champine, Colorado St. | 1980-83 | 184 | 2,811 | 15.3 | 21 |
| Wendell Davis, Louisiana St. | 1984-85 | 183 | 2,708 | 14.8 | 19 |
| Phil Odle, Brigham Young | 1965-67 | 183 | 2,548 | 13.9 | 25 |
| Mark Szlachcic, Bowling Green | 1989-92 | 182 | 2,507 | 13.8 | 18 |
| Kelly Blackwell, Texas Christian (TE) | 1988-91 | 181 | 2,155 | 11.9 | 13 |
| Tim Delaney, San Diego St. | 1968-70 | 180 | 2,535 | 14.1 | 22 |
| Michael Smith, Kansas St. | 1988-91 | 179 | 2,457 | 13.7 | 11 |
| Walter Murray, Hawaii | 1982-85 | 178 | 2,865 | 16.1 | 20 |
| Gordon Hudson, Brigham Young (TE) | 1980-83 | 178 | 2,484 | 14.0 | 22 |
| Rick Beasley, Appalachian St. | 1978-80 | 178 | 3,124 | 17.6 | 23 |
| Stan Hunter, Bowling Green | 1982-85 | 176 | 2,679 | 15.2 | 21 |
| Rodney Carter, Purdue | 1982-85 | 176 | 1,786 | 10.1 | 5 |
| Hugh Campbell, Washington St. | 1960-62 | 176 | 2,453 | 13.9 | 22 |
| John Jefferson, Arizona St. | 1974-77 | 175 | 2,824 | 16.1 | 19 |
| Mike Mikolayunas, Davidson | 1968-70 | 175 | 1,768 | 10.1 | 14 |

* Record.   ‡ Record for minimum of 200 catches.

## Season Catches

| Player, Team | Year | Games | Catches | Yards | TD |
|---|---|---|---|---|---|
| Manny Hazard, Houston | †1989 | 11 | *142 | 1,689 | *22 |
| Howard Twilley, Tulsa | †1965 | 10 | 134 | *1,779 | 16 |
| Jason Phillips, Houston | †1988 | 11 | 108 | 1,444 | 15 |
| Fred Gilbert, Houston | †1991 | 11 | 106 | 957 | 7 |
| Sherman Smith, Houston | †1992 | 11 | 103 | 923 | 6 |
| James Dixon, Houston | 1988 | 11 | 102 | 1,103 | 11 |
| David Williams, Illinois | †1984 | 11 | 101 | 1,278 | 8 |
| Jay Miller, Brigham Young | †1973 | 11 | 100 | 1,181 | 8 |
| Jason Phillips, Houston | †1987 | 11 | 99 | 875 | 3 |
| Mark Templeton, Long Beach St. (RB) | †1986 | 11 | 99 | 688 | 2 |
| Rodney Carter, Purdue | †1985 | 11 | 98 | 1,099 | 4 |
| Keith Edwards, Vanderbilt | †1983 | 11 | 97 | 909 | 0 |
| Jerry Hendren, Idaho | †1969 | 10 | 95 | 1,452 | 12 |
| Howard Twilley, Tulsa | †1964 | 10 | 95 | 1,178 | 13 |
| Richard Buchanan, Northwestern | 1989 | 11 | 94 | 1,115 | 9 |
| Aaron Turner, Pacific (Cal.) | 1991 | 11 | 92 | 1,604 | 18 |
| Dave Petzke, Northern Ill. | †1978 | 11 | 91 | 1,217 | 11 |
| Glenn Meltzer, Wichita St. | †1966 | 10 | 91 | 1,115 | 4 |

* Record.   † National champion.

*1993 NCAA FOOTBALL*

## Season Touchdown Receptions

| Player, Team | Year | Games | TD |
|---|---|---|---|
| Manny Hazard, Houston | 1989 | 11 | *22 |
| Desmond Howard, Michigan | 1991 | 11 | 19 |
| Aaron Turner, Pacific (Cal.) | 1991 | 11 | 18 |
| Dennis Smith, Utah | 1989 | 12 | 18 |
| Tom Reynolds, San Diego St. | 1971 | 10 | 18 |
| Mario Bailey, Washington | 1991 | 11 | 17 |
| Clarkston Hines, Duke | 1989 | 11 | 17 |
| Dan Bitson, Tulsa | 1989 | 11 | 16 |
| Howard Twilley, Tulsa | 1965 | 10 | 16 |
| Jason Phillips, Houston | 1988 | 11 | 15 |
| Henry Ellard, Fresno St. | 1982 | 11 | 15 |

* Record.

## Single-Game Catches

| No. | Player, Team (Opponent) | Date |
|---|---|---|
| 22 | Jay Miller, Brigham Young (New Mexico) | Nov. 3, 1973 |
| 20 | Rick Eber, Tulsa (Idaho St.) | Oct. 7, 1967 |
| 19 | Manny Hazard, Houston (Texas) | Nov. 11, 1989 |
| 19 | Manny Hazard, Houston (Texas Christian) | Nov. 4, 1989 |
| 19 | Ron Fair, Arizona St. (Washington St.) | Oct. 28, 1989 |
| 19 | Howard Twilley, Tulsa (Colorado St.) | Nov. 27, 1965 |
| 18 | Richard Woodley, Texas Christian (Texas Tech) | Nov. 10, 1990 |
| 18 | Mark Templeton, Long Beach St. (RB) (Utah St.) | Nov. 1, 1986 |
| 18 | Howard Twilley, Tulsa (Southern Ill.) | Oct. 30, 1965 |
| 17 | Loren Richey, Utah (UTEP) | Nov. 29, 1986 |
| 17 | Keith Edwards, Vanderbilt (Georgia) | Oct. 15, 1983 |
| 17 | Jon Harvey, Northwestern (Michigan) | Oct. 23, 1982 |
| 17 | Don Roberts, San Diego St. (California) | Sept. 18, 1982 |
| 17 | Tom Reynolds, San Diego St. (Utah St.) | Oct. 22, 1971 |
| 17 | Mike Mikolayunas, Davidson (Richmond) | Oct. 11, 1969 |
| 17 | Jerry Hendren, Idaho (Southern Miss.) | Oct. 4, 1969 |
| 17 | Emilio Vallez, New Mexico (New Mexico St.) | Oct. 27, 1967 |
| 17 | Chuck Hughes, UTEP (Arizona St.) | Oct. 30, 1965 |

## Career Yards

| Player, Team | Years | Catches | Yards | Avg. | TD |
|---|---|---|---|---|---|
| Aaron Turner, Pacific (Cal.) | 1989-92 | *266 | *4,345 | 16.3 | *43 |
| Terance Mathis, New Mexico | 1985-87, 89 | 263 | 4,254 | 16.2 | 36 |
| Marc Zeno, Tulane | 1984-87 | 236 | 3,725 | 15.8 | 25 |
| Ron Sellers, Florida St. | 1966-68 | 212 | 3,598 | 17.0 | 23 |
| Elmo Wright, Houston | 1968-70 | 153 | 3,347 | ‡21.9 | 34 |
| Howard Twilley, Tulsa | 1963-65 | 261 | 3,343 | 12.8 | 32 |
| Clarkston Hines, Duke | 1986-89 | 189 | 3,318 | 17.6 | 38 |
| Gerald Harp, Western Caro. | 1977-80 | 197 | 3,305 | 16.8 | 26 |
| Dan Bitson, Tulsa | 1987-89, 91 | 163 | 3,300 | 20.2 | 29 |
| Greg Primus, Colorado St. | 1989-92 | 192 | 3,200 | 16.7 | 16 |
| David Williams, Illinois | 1983-85 | 245 | 3,195 | 13.0 | 22 |
| Hart Lee Dykes, Oklahoma St. | 1985-88 | 203 | 3,171 | 15.6 | 29 |
| Rick Beasley, Appalachian St. | 1978-80 | 178 | 3,124 | 17.6 | 23 |
| Ricky Proehl, Wake Forest | 1986-89 | 188 | 2,949 | 15.7 | 25 |
| Henry Ellard, Fresno St. | 1979-82 | 138 | 2,947 | 21.4 | 25 |
| Kendal Smith, Utah St. | 1985-88 | 169 | 2,943 | 17.4 | 25 |
| Charles Lockett, Long Beach St. | 1983-86 | 191 | 2,902 | 15.1 | 19 |
| Chuck Hughes, UTEP | 1964-66 | 162 | 2,882 | 17.8 | 19 |
| Walter Murray, Hawaii | 1982-85 | 178 | 2,865 | 16.1 | 20 |
| Boo Mitchell, Vanderbilt | 1985-88 | 188 | 2,864 | 15.8 | 9 |
| ¢Ryan Yarborough, Wyoming | 1990-92 | 162 | 2,845 | 17.6 | 26 |
| John Jefferson, Arizona St. | 1974-77 | 175 | 2,824 | 16.1 | 19 |

* Record.  ¢ Active player.  ‡ Record for minimum of 105 catches.

## Career Touchdown Receptions

| Player, Team | Years | Games | TD |
|---|---|---|---|
| Aaron Turner, Pacific (Cal.) | 1989-92 | 44 | *43 |
| Clarkston Hines, Duke | 1986-89 | 44 | 38 |
| Terance Mathis, New Mexico | 1985-87, 89 | 44 | 36 |
| Elmo Wright, Houston | 1968-70 | 30 | 34 |
| Steve Largent, Tulsa | 1973-75 | 30 | 32 |

| Player, Team | Years | Games | TD |
|---|---|---|---|
| Howard Twilley, Tulsa | 1963-65 | 30 | 32 |
| Manny Hazard, Houston | 1989-90 | 21 | 31 |
| Sean Dawkins, California | 1990-92 | 33 | 30 |
| Desmond Howard, Michigan | 1989-91 | 33 | 30 |
| Jade Butcher, Indiana | 1967-69 | 30 | 30 |
| Dan Bitson, Tulsa | 1987-89, 91 | 44 | 29 |

\* Record.

## Season Yards

| Player, Team | Year | Catches | Yards | Avg. | TD |
|---|---|---|---|---|---|
| Howard Twilley, Tulsa | †1965 | 134 | *1,779 | 13.3 | 16 |
| Manny Hazard, Houston | †1989 | *142 | 1,689 | 11.9 | *22 |
| Aaron Turner, Pacific (Cal.) | †1991 | 92 | 1,604 | 17.4 | 18 |
| Chuck Hughes, UTEP | 1965 | 80 | 1,519 | 19.0 | 12 |
| Henry Ellard, Fresno St. | 1982 | 62 | 1,510 | ††24.4 | 15 |
| Ron Sellers, Florida St. | †1968 | 86 | 1,496 | 17.4 | 12 |
| Jerry Hendren, Idaho | †1969 | 95 | 1,452 | 15.3 | 12 |
| Jason Phillips, Houston | †1988 | 108 | 1,444 | 13.4 | 15 |

\* Record.   † National champion.   †† Record for minimum of 50 catches.

## Single-Game Yards

| Yds. | Player, Team (Opponent) | Date |
|---|---|---|
| 349 | Chuck Hughes, UTEP (North Texas) | Sept. 18, 1965 |
| 322 | Rick Eber, Tulsa (Idaho St.) | Oct. 7, 1967 |
| 318 | Harry Wood, Tulsa (Idaho St.) | Oct. 7, 1967 |
| 316 | Jeff Evans, New Mexico St. (Southern Ill.) | Sept. 30, 1978 |
| 290 | Tom Reynolds, San Diego St. (Utah St.) | Oct. 22, 1971 |
| 289 | Wesley Walker, California (San Jose St.) | Oct. 2, 1976 |
| 288 | Mike Siani, Villanova (Xavier) | Oct. 30, 1971 |
| 284 | Don Clune, Pennsylvania (Harvard) | Oct. 30, 1971 |
| 283 | Chris Castor, Duke (Wake Forest) | Nov. 6, 1982 |
| 282 | Larry Willis, Fresno St. (Montana St.) | Nov. 17, 1984 |
| 278 | Derek Graham, Princeton (Yale) | Nov. 14, 1981 |

## Annual Champions

| Year | Player, Team | Class | Ct. | Yards | TD |
|---|---|---|---|---|---|
| 1937 | Jim Benton, Arkansas | Sr. | 47 | 754 | — |
| 1938 | Sam Boyd, Baylor | Sr. | 32 | 537 | — |
| 1939 | Ken Kavanaugh, Louisiana St. | Sr. | 30 | 467 | — |
| 1940 | Eddie Bryant, Virginia | So. | 30 | 222 | 2 |
| 1941 | Hank Stanton, Arizona | Sr. | 50 | 820 | — |
| 1942 | Bill Rogers, Texas A&M | Sr. | 39 | 432 | — |
| 1943 | Neil Armstrong, Oklahoma St. | Fr. | 39 | 317 | — |
| 1944 | Reid Moseley, Georgia | So. | 32 | 506 | — |
| 1945 | Reid Moseley, Georgia | Jr. | 31 | 662 | — |
| 1946 | Neil Armstrong, Oklahoma St. | Sr. | 32 | 479 | 1 |
| 1947 | Barney Poole, Mississippi | Jr. | 52 | 513 | 8 |
| 1948 | Johnny "Red" O'Quinn, Wake Forest | Jr. | 39 | 605 | 7 |
| 1949 | Art Weiner, North Caro. | Sr. | 52 | 762 | 7 |
| 1950 | Gordon Cooper, Denver | Jr. | 46 | 569 | 8 |
| 1951 | Dewey McConnell, Wyoming | Sr. | 47 | 725 | 9 |
| 1952 | Ed Brown, Fordham | Sr. | 57 | 774 | 6 |
| 1953 | John Carson, Georgia | Sr. | 45 | 663 | 4 |
| 1954 | Jim Hanifan, California | Sr. | 44 | 569 | 7 |
| 1955 | Hank Burnine, Missouri | Sr. | 44 | 594 | 2 |
| 1956 | Art Powell, San Jose St. | So. | 40 | 583 | 5 |
| 1957 | Stuart Vaughan, Utah | Sr. | 53 | 756 | 5 |
| 1958 | Dave Hibbert, Arizona | Jr. | 61 | 606 | 4 |
| 1959 | Chris Burford, Stanford | Sr. | 61 | 756 | 6 |
| 1960 | Hugh Campbell, Washington St. | So. | 66 | 881 | 10 |
| 1961 | Hugh Campbell, Washington St. | Jr. | 53 | 723 | 5 |
| 1962 | Vern Burke, Oregon St. | Jr. | 69 | 1,007 | 10 |
| 1963 | Lawrence Elkins, Baylor | Jr. | 70 | 873 | 8 |
| 1964 | Howard Twilley, Tulsa | Jr. | 95 | 1,178 | 13 |
| 1965 | Howard Twilley, Tulsa | Sr. | 134 | *1,779 | 16 |
| 1966 | Glenn Meltzer, Wichita St. | So. | 91 | 1,115 | 4 |
| 1967 | Bob Goodridge, Vanderbilt | Sr. | 79 | 1,114 | 6 |
| 1968 | Ron Sellers, Florida St. | Sr. | 86 | 1,496 | 12 |
| 1969 | Jerry Hendren, Idaho | Sr. | 95 | 1,452 | 12 |

*1993 NCAA FOOTBALL*

*Beginning in 1970, ranked on per-game (instead of total) catches*

| Year | Player, Team | Class | G. | Ct. | Avg. | Yards | TD |
|---|---|---|---|---|---|---|---|
| 1970 | Mike Mikolayunas, Davidson .............. | Sr. | 10 | 87 | 8.7 | 1,128 | 8 |
| 1971 | Tom Reynolds, San Diego St. ............. | Sr. | 10 | 67 | 6.7 | 1,070 | 7 |
| 1972 | Tom Forzani, Utah St. ...................... | Sr. | 11 | 85 | 7.7 | 1,169 | 8 |
| 1973 | Jay Miller, Brigham Young ................ | So. | 11 | 100 | 9.1 | 1,181 | 8 |
| 1974 | Dwight McDonald, San Diego St. ......... | Sr. | 11 | 86 | 7.8 | 1,157 | 7 |
| 1975 | Bob Farnham, Brown ..................... | Jr. | 9 | 56 | 6.2 | 701 | 2 |
| 1976 | Billy Ryckman, Louisiana Tech........... | Sr. | 11 | 77 | 7.0 | 1,382 | 10 |
| 1977 | Wayne Tolleson, Western Caro. .......... | Sr. | 11 | 73 | 6.6 | 1,101 | 7 |
| 1978 | Dave Petzke, Northern Ill. ................. | Sr. | 11 | 91 | 8.3 | 1,217 | 11 |
| 1979 | Rick Beasley, Appalachian St............. | Jr. | 11 | 74 | 6.7 | 1,205 | 12 |
| 1980 | Dave Young, Purdue ...................... | Sr. | 11 | 67 | 6.1 | 917 | 8 |
| 1981 | Pete Harvey, North Texas ................ | Sr. | 9 | 57 | 6.3 | 743 | 3 |
| 1982 | Vincent White, Stanford .................. | Sr. | 10 | 68 | 6.8 | 677 | 8 |
| 1983 | Keith Edwards, Vanderbilt................ | Jr. | 11 | 97 | 8.8 | 909 | 8 |
| 1984 | David Williams, Illinois .................. | Jr. | 11 | 101 | 9.2 | 1,278 | 8 |
| 1985 | Rodney Carter, Purdue................... | Sr. | 11 | 98 | 8.9 | 1,099 | 4 |
| 1986 | Mark Templeton, Long Beach St. (RB) .... | Sr. | 11 | 99 | 9.0 | 688 | 2 |
| 1987 | Jason Phillips, Houston .................. | Jr. | 11 | 99 | 9.0 | 875 | 3 |
| 1988 | Jason Phillips, Houston .................. | Sr. | 11 | 108 | 9.8 | 1,444 | 15 |
| 1989 | Manny Hazard, Houston ................. | Jr. | 11 | *142 | 12.9 | 1,689 | *22 |

*Beginning in 1990, ranked on both per-game catches and yards per game*

### Per-Game Catches

| Year | Player, Team | Class | G. | Ct. | Avg. | Yards | TD |
|---|---|---|---|---|---|---|---|
| 1990 | Manny Hazard, Houston .................. | Sr. | 10 | 78 | 7.8 | 946 | 9 |
| 1991 | Fred Gilbert, Houston .................... | Jr. | 11 | 106 | 9.6 | 957 | 7 |
| 1992 | Sherman Smith, Houston ................ | Jr. | 11 | 103 | 9.4 | 923 | 6 |

### Yards Per Game

| Year | Player, Team | Class | G. | Ct. | Yards | Avg. | TD |
|---|---|---|---|---|---|---|---|
| 1990 | Patrick Rowe, San Diego St. ............. | Jr. | 11 | 71 | 1,392 | 126.6 | 8 |
| 1991 | Aaron Turner, Pacific (Cal.) .............. | Jr. | 11 | 92 | 1,604 | 145.8 | 18 |
| 1992 | Lloyd Hill, Texas Tech.................... | Jr. | 11 | 76 | 1,261 | 114.6 | 12 |

* *Record.*

# SCORING

## Career Points Per Game

| Player, Team | Years | Games | TD | XPt. | FG | Pts. | Pt. PG |
|---|---|---|---|---|---|---|---|
| Bob Gaiters, New Mexico St. ................ | 1959-60 | 17 | 32 | 11 | 0 | 203 | *11.9 |
| Ed Marinaro, Cornell ....................... | 1969-71 | 27 | 52 | 6 | 0 | 318 | 11.8 |
| Bill Burnett, Arkansas ...................... | 1968-70 | 26 | 49 | 0 | 0 | 294 | 11.3 |
| Steve Owens, Oklahoma ................... | 1967-69 | 30 | ‡56 | 0 | 0 | ‡336 | 11.2 |
| Eddie Talboom, Wyoming .................. | 1948-50 | 28 | 34 | 99 | 0 | 303 | 10.8 |
| O. J. Simpson, Southern Cal ............... | 1967-68 | 19 | 33 | 0 | 0 | 198 | 10.4 |
| Rudy Mobley, Hardin-Simmons ............. | 1942, 46 | 19 | 32 | 0 | 0 | 192 | 10.1 |
| Howard Twilley, Tulsa ...................... | 1963-65 | 26 | 32 | 67 | 0 | 259 | 10.0 |
| Blaise Bryant, Iowa St. ..................... | 1989-90 | 20 | 32 | 6 | 0 | 198 | 9.9 |
| Tom Harmon, Michigan ..................... | 1938-40 | 24 | 33 | 33 | 2 | 237 | 9.9 |
| Jackie Parker, Mississippi St. .............. | 1952-53 | 19 | 24 | 41 | 0 | 185 | 9.7 |
| Roman Anderson, Houston ................. | 1988-91 | 44 | 0 | *213 | 70 | *423 | 9.6 |
| Anthony Thompson, Indiana................ | 1986-89 | 41 | *65 | 4 | 0 | 394 | 9.6 |
| Johnny Bright, Drake ...................... | 1949-51 | 25 | 40 | 0 | 0 | 240 | 9.6 |
| Glenn Davis, Army ........................ | 1943-46 | 37 | 59 | 0 | 0 | 354 | 9.6 |
| Stan Koslowski, Holy Cross................. | 1943, 45 | 17 | 23 | 24 | 0 | 162 | 9.5 |
| Mack Herron, Kansas St..................... | 1968-69 | 20 | 31 | 2 | 0 | 188 | 9.4 |
| Stacey Robinson, Northern Ill. (QB) ........ | 1988-90 | 25 | 38 | 6 | 0 | 234 | 9.4 |
| Pervis Atkins, New Mexico St................ | 1959-60 | 20 | 29 | 13 | 0 | 187 | 9.4 |
| Bernard White, Bowling Green.............. | 1984-85 | 22 | 34 | 0 | 0 | 204 | 9.3 |
| Floyd Little, Syracuse ..................... | 1964-66 | 30 | 46 | 2 | 0 | 278 | 9.3 |
| Felix "Doc" Blanchard, Army................ | 1944-46 | 25 | 38 | 3 | 0 | 231 | 9.2 |
| Bobby Reynolds, Nebraska ................ | 1950-52 | 23 | 28 | 40 | 1 | 211 | 9.2 |
| Anthony Davis, Southern Cal .............. | 1972-74 | 33 | 50 | 2 | 0 | 302 | 9.2 |

* *Record.* ‡ *Three-year totals record.*

## Season Points Per Game

| Player, Team | Year | Games | TD | XPt. | FG | Pts. | Pt. PG |
|---|---|---|---|---|---|---|---|
| Barry Sanders, Oklahoma St. ................ | †1988 | 11 | *39 | 0 | 0 | *234 | *21.3 |
| Bobby Reynolds, Nebraska ................. | †1950 | 9 | 22 | 25 | 0 | 157 | 17.4 |
| Art Luppino, Arizona ....................... | †1954 | 10 | 24 | 22 | 0 | 166 | 16.6 |
| Ed Marinaro, Cornell ....................... | †1971 | 9 | 24 | 4 | 0 | 148 | 16.4 |
| Lydell Mitchell, Penn St. ................... | 1971 | 11 | 29 | 0 | 0 | 174 | 15.8 |

| Player, Team | Year | Games | TD | XPt. | FG | Pts. | Pt. PG |
|---|---|---|---|---|---|---|---|
| Marshall Faulk, San Diego St. | †1991 | 9 | 23 | 2 | 0 | 140 | 15.6 |
| Byron "Whizzer" White, Colorado | †1937 | 8 | 16 | 23 | 1 | 122 | 15.3 |

* Record. † National champion.

## Career Points (Non-Kickers)

| Player, Team | Years | TD | XPt. | FG | Pts. |
|---|---|---|---|---|---|
| Anthony Thompson, Indiana | 1986-89 | *65 | 4 | 0 | *394 |
| Tony Dorsett, Pittsburgh | 1973-76 | 59 | 2 | 0 | 356 |
| Glenn Davis, Army | 1943-46 | 59 | 0 | 0 | 354 |
| Art Luppino, Arizona | 1953-56 | 48 | 49 | 0 | 337 |
| Steve Owens, Oklahoma | 1967-69 | ‡56 | 0 | 0 | ‡336 |
| Wilford White, Arizona St. | 1947-50 | 48 | 27 | 4 | 327 |
| Barry Sanders, Oklahoma St. | 1986-88 | 54 | 0 | 0 | 324 |
| Allen Pinkett, Notre Dame | 1982-85 | 53 | 2 | 0 | 320 |
| Pete Johnson, Ohio St. | 1973-76 | 53 | 0 | 0 | 318 |
| Ed Marinaro, Cornell | 1969-71 | 52 | 6 | 0 | 318 |
| Herschel Walker, Georgia | 1980-82 | 52 | 2 | 0 | 314 |
| James Gray, Texas Tech | 1986-89 | 52 | 0 | 0 | 312 |
| Mike Rozier, Nebraska | 1981-83 | 52 | 0 | 0 | 312 |
| Ted Brown, North Caro. St. | 1975-78 | 51 | 6 | 0 | 312 |
| John Harvey, UTEP | 1985-88 | 51 | 0 | 0 | 306 |
| Eddie Talboom, Wyoming | 1948-50 | 34 | 99 | 0 | 303 |
| Anthony Davis, Southern Cal | 1972-74 | 50 | 2 | 0 | 302 |
| Dalton Hilliard, Louisiana St. | 1982-85 | 50 | 0 | 0 | 300 |
| Billy Sims, Oklahoma | $1975-79 | 50 | 0 | 0 | 300 |
| Charles White, Southern Cal | 1976-79 | 49 | 2 | 0 | 296 |
| Nolan Jones, Arizona St. | 1958-61 | 30 | 77 | 13 | 296 |
| Steve Bartalo, Colorado St. | 1983-86 | 49 | 0 | 0 | 294 |
| Bill Burnett, Arkansas | 1968-70 | 49 | 0 | 0 | 294 |
| Brian Mitchell, Southwestern La. | 1986-89 | 47 | 4 | 0 | 286 |
| Keith Byars, Ohio St. | 1982-85 | 48 | 0 | 0 | 286 |
| Rick Badanjek, Maryland | 1982-85 | 46 | 10 | 0 | 286 |

* Record. ‡ Three-year totals record. $ See page 8 for explanation.

## Career Points (Kickers)

| Player, Team | Years | PAT | PAT Att. | FG | FG Att. | Pts. |
|---|---|---|---|---|---|---|
| Roman Anderson, Houston | 1988-91 | *213 | *217 | 70 | 101 | *423 |
| Carlos Huerta, Miami (Fla.) | 1988-91 | 178 | 181 | 73 | 91 | 397 |
| Jason Elam, Hawaii | $1988-92 | 158 | 161 | 79 | 100 | 395 |
| Derek Schmidt, Florida St. | 1984-87 | 174 | 178 | 73 | 102 | 393 |
| Luis Zendejas, Arizona St. | 1981-84 | 134 | 135 | 78 | *105 | 368 |
| Jeff Jaeger, Washington | 1983-86 | 118 | 123 | *80 | 99 | 358 |
| John Lee, UCLA | 1982-85 | 116 | 117 | 79 | 92 | 353 |
| Max Zendejas, Arizona | 1982-85 | 122 | 124 | 77 | 104 | 353 |
| Kevin Butler, Georgia | 1981-84 | 122 | 125 | 77 | 98 | 353 |
| Philip Doyle, Alabama | 1987-90 | 105 | 108 | 78 | *105 | %345 |
| Andy Trakas, San Diego St. | 1989-92 | 170 | 178 | 56 | 82 | 338 |
| Barry Belli, Fresno St. | 1984-87 | 116 | 123 | 70 | 99 | 326 |
| Jason Hanson, Washington St. | 1988-91 | 136 | 141 | 62 | 95 | 322 |
| R. D. Lashar, Oklahoma | 1987-90 | 194 | 200 | 42 | 60 | 320 |
| Collin Mackie, South Caro. | 1987-90 | 112 | 113 | 69 | 95 | 319 |
| Cary Blanchard, Oklahoma St. | 1987-90 | 150 | 151 | 54 | 73 | #314 |
| Fuad Reveiz, Tennessee | 1981-84 | 101 | 103 | 71 | 95 | 314 |
| Sean Fleming, Wyoming | 1988-91 | 150 | 155 | 54 | 92 | 312 |
| Van Tiffin, Alabama | 1983-86 | 135 | 135 | 59 | 87 | 312 |
| Jess Atkinson, Maryland | 1981-84 | 128 | 131 | 60 | 82 | 308 |
| Gary Gussman, Miami (Ohio) | 1984-87 | 102 | 104 | 68 | 94 | 306 |
| Greg Cox, Miami (Fla.) | 1984-87 | 162 | 169 | 47 | 64 | 303 |
| Scott Sisson, Georgia Tech | 1989-92 | 119 | 121 | 60 | 88 | 299 |
| Rusty Hanna, Toledo | 1989-92 | 94 | 99 | 68 | 99 | 298 |
| Tim Lashar, Oklahoma | 1983-86 | 168 | 170 | 43 | 65 | 297 |
| John Biskup, Syracuse | 1989-92 | 125 | 132 | 57 | 78 | 296 |
| Quin Rodriguez, Southern Cal | 1987-90 | 139 | 146 | 52 | 68 | 295 |

* Record.  % Includes one TD reception.  # Includes one two-point conversion.  $ See page 8 for explanation.

*1993 NCAA FOOTBALL*

## Season Points

| Player, Team | Year | TD | XPt. | FG | Pts. |
|---|---|---|---|---|---|
| Barry Sanders, Oklahoma St. | †1988 | *39 | 0 | 0 | *234 |
| Mike Rozier, Nebraska | †1983 | 29 | 0 | 0 | 174 |
| Lydell Mitchell, Penn St. | 1971 | 29 | 0 | 0 | 174 |
| Art Luppino, Arizona | †1954 | 24 | 22 | 0 | 166 |
| Bobby Reynolds, Nebraska | †1950 | 22 | 25 | 0 | 157 |
| Anthony Thompson, Indiana | †1989 | 25 | 4 | 0 | 154 |
| Fred Wendt, UTEP | †1948 | 20 | 32 | 0 | 152 |
| Pete Johnson, Ohio St. | †1975 | 25 | 0 | 0 | 150 |

* Record. † National champion.

## Single-Game Points

| No. | Player, Team (Opponent) | Date |
|---|---|---|
| 48 | Howard Griffith, Illinois (Southern Ill.) | Sept. 22, 1990 |
| 44 | Marshall Faulk, San Diego St. (Pacific, Cal.) | Sept. 14, 1991 |
| 43 | Jim Brown, Syracuse (Colgate) | Nov. 17, 1956 |
| 42 | Arnold "Showboat" Boykin, Mississippi (Mississippi St.) | Dec. 1, 1951 |
| 42 | Fred Wendt, UTEP (New Mexico St.) | Nov. 25, 1948 |
| 38 | Dick Bass, Pacific, Cal. (San Diego St.) | Nov. 22, 1958 |
| 37 | Jimmy Nutter, Wichita St. (Northern St., S.D.) | Oct. 22, 1949 |
| 36 | Calvin Jones, Nebraska (Kansas) | Nov. 9, 1991 |
| 36 | Blake Ezor, Michigan St. (Northwestern) | Nov. 18, 1989 |
| 36 | Dee Dowis, Air Force (San Diego St.) | Sept. 2, 1989 |
| 36 | Kelvin Bryant, North Caro. (East Caro.) | Sept. 12, 1981 |
| 36 | Andre Herrera, Southern Ill. (Northern Ill.) | Oct. 23, 1976 |
| 36 | Anthony Davis, Southern Cal (Notre Dame) | Dec. 2, 1972 |
| 36 | Tim Delaney, San Diego St. (New Mexico St.) | Nov. 15, 1969 |
| 36 | Tom Francisco, Virginia Tech (Va. Military) | Nov. 24, 1966 |
| 36 | Howard Twilley, Tulsa (Louisville) | Nov. 6, 1965 |
| 36 | Pete Pedro, West Tex. St. (UTEP) | Sept. 30, 1961 |
| 36 | Tom Powers, Duke (Richmond) | Oct. 21, 1950 |

## Annual Champions

| Year | Player, Team | Class | TD | XPt. | FG | Pts. |
|---|---|---|---|---|---|---|
| 1937 | Byron "Whizzer" White, Colorado | Sr. | 16 | 23 | 1 | 122 |
| 1938 | Parker Hall, Mississippi | Sr. | 11 | 7 | 0 | 73 |
| 1939 | Tom Harmon, Michigan | Jr. | 14 | 15 | 1 | 102 |
| 1940 | Tom Harmon, Michigan | Sr. | 16 | 18 | 1 | 117 |
| 1941 | Bill Dudley, Virginia | Sr. | 18 | 23 | 1 | 134 |
| 1942 | Bob Steuber, Missouri | Sr. | 18 | 13 | 0 | 121 |
| 1943 | Steve Van Buren, Louisiana St. | Sr. | 14 | 14 | 0 | 98 |
| 1944 | Glenn Davis, Army | So. | 20 | 0 | 0 | 120 |
| 1945 | Felix "Doc" Blanchard, Army | Jr. | 19 | 1 | 0 | 115 |
| 1946 | Gene Roberts, Tenn.-Chatt. | Sr. | 18 | 9 | 0 | 117 |
| 1947 | Lou Gambino, Maryland | Jr. | 16 | 0 | 0 | 96 |
| 1948 | Fred Wendt, UTEP | Sr. | 20 | 32 | 0 | 152 |
| 1949 | George Thomas, Oklahoma | Sr. | 19 | 3 | 0 | 117 |
| 1950 | Bobby Reynolds, Nebraska | So. | 22 | 25 | 0 | 157 |
| 1951 | Ollie Matson, San Francisco | Sr. | 21 | 0 | 0 | 126 |
| 1952 | Jackie Parker, Mississippi St. | Jr. | 16 | 24 | 0 | 120 |
| 1953 | Earl Lindley, Utah St. | Sr. | 13 | 3 | 0 | 81 |
| 1954 | Art Luppino, Arizona | So. | 24 | 22 | 0 | 166 |
| 1955 | Jim Swink, Texas Christian | Jr. | 20 | 5 | 0 | 125 |
| 1956 | Clendon Thomas, Oklahoma | Jr. | 18 | 0 | 0 | 108 |
| 1957 | Leon Burton, Arizona St. | Jr. | 16 | 0 | 0 | 96 |
| 1958 | Dick Bass, Pacific (Cal.) | Jr. | 18 | 8 | 0 | 116 |
| 1959 | Pervis Atkins, New Mexico St. | Jr. | 17 | 5 | 0 | 107 |
| 1960 | Bob Gaiters, New Mexico St. | Sr. | 23 | 7 | 0 | 145 |
| 1961 | Jim Pilot, New Mexico St. | So. | 21 | 12 | 0 | 138 |
| 1962 | Jerry Logan, West Tex. St. | Sr. | 13 | 32 | 0 | 110 |
| 1963 | Cosmo Iacavazzi, Princeton | Jr. | 14 | 0 | 0 | 84 |
| | Dave Casinelli, Memphis St. | Sr. | 14 | 0 | 0 | 84 |
| 1964 | Brian Piccolo, Wake Forest | Sr. | 17 | 9 | 0 | 111 |
| 1965 | Howard Twilley, Tulsa | Sr. | 16 | 31 | 0 | 127 |
| 1966 | Ken Hebert, Houston | Jr. | 11 | 41 | 2 | 113 |
| 1967 | Leroy Keyes, Purdue | Jr. | 19 | 0 | 0 | 114 |
| 1968 | Jim O'Brien, Cincinnati | Jr. | 12 | 31 | 13 | 142 |
| 1969 | Steve Owens, Oklahoma | Sr. | 23 | 0 | 0 | 138 |

*Division I-A Annual Champions, All-Time Leaders*

Beginning in 1970, ranked on per-game (instead of total) points

| Year | Player, Team | Class | Games | TD | XPt. | FG | Pts. | Avg. |
|------|-------------|-------|-------|-----|------|-----|------|------|
| 1970 | Brian Bream, Air Force | Jr. | 10 | 20 | 0 | 0 | 120 | 12.0 |
| | Gary Kosins, Dayton | Jr. | 9 | 18 | 0 | 0 | 108 | 12.0 |
| 1971 | Ed Marinaro, Cornell | Sr. | 9 | 24 | 4 | 0 | 148 | 16.4 |
| 1972 | Harold Henson, Ohio St. | So. | 10 | 20 | 0 | 0 | 120 | 12.0 |
| 1973 | Jim Jennings, Rutgers | Sr. | 11 | 21 | 2 | 0 | 128 | 11.6 |
| 1974 | Bill Marek, Wisconsin | Jr. | 9 | 19 | 0 | 0 | 114 | 12.7 |
| 1975 | Pete Johnson, Ohio St. | Jr. | 11 | 25 | 0 | 0 | 150 | 13.6 |
| 1976 | Tony Dorsett, Pittsburgh | Sr. | 11 | 22 | 2 | 0 | 134 | 12.2 |
| 1977 | Earl Campbell, Texas | Sr. | 11 | 19 | 0 | 0 | 114 | 10.4 |
| 1978 | Billy Sims, Oklahoma | Jr. | 11 | 20 | 0 | 0 | 120 | 10.9 |
| 1979 | Billy Sims, Oklahoma | Sr. | 11 | 22 | 0 | 0 | 132 | 12.0 |
| 1980 | Sammy Winder, Southern Miss. | Jr. | 11 | 20 | 0 | 0 | 120 | 10.9 |
| 1981 | Marcus Allen, Southern Cal | Sr. | 11 | 23 | 0 | 0 | 138 | 12.5 |
| 1982 | Greg Allen, Florida St. | So. | 11 | 21 | 0 | 0 | 126 | 11.5 |
| 1983 | Mike Rozier, Nebraska | Sr. | 12 | 29 | 0 | 0 | 174 | 14.5 |
| 1984 | Keith Byars, Ohio St. | Jr. | 11 | 24 | 0 | 0 | 144 | 13.1 |
| 1985 | Bernard White, Bowling Green | Sr. | 11 | 19 | 0 | 0 | 114 | 10.4 |
| 1986 | Steve Bartalo, Colorado St. | Sr. | 11 | 19 | 0 | 0 | 114 | 10.4 |
| 1987 | Paul Hewitt, San Diego St. | Jr. | 12 | 24 | 0 | 0 | 144 | 12.0 |
| 1988 | Barry Sanders, Oklahoma St. | Jr. | 11 | *39 | 0 | 0 | *234 | *21.3 |
| 1989 | Anthony Thompson, Indiana | Sr. | 11 | 25 | 4 | 0 | 154 | 14.0 |
| 1990 | Stacey Robinson, Northern Ill. (QB) | Sr. | 11 | 19 | 6 | 0 | 120 | 10.9 |
| 1991 | Marshall Faulk, San Diego St. | Fr. | 9 | 23 | 2 | 0 | 140 | 15.6 |
| 1992 | Garrison Hearst, Georgia | Jr. | 11 | 21 | 0 | 0 | 126 | 11.5 |

* Record.

# INTERCEPTIONS
## Career Interceptions

| Player, Team | Years | No. | Yards | Avg. |
|-------------|-------|-----|-------|------|
| Al Brosky, Illinois | 1950-52 | *29 | 356 | 12.3 |
| Martin Bayless, Bowling Green | 1980-83 | 27 | 266 | 9.9 |
| John Provost, Holy Cross | 1972-74 | 27 | 470 | 17.4 |
| Tracy Saul, Texas Tech | 1989-92 | 25 | 425 | 17.0 |
| Tony Thurman, Boston College | 1981-84 | 25 | 221 | 8.8 |
| Tom Curtis, Michigan | 1967-69 | 25 | 440 | 17.6 |
| Jeff Nixon, Richmond | 1975-78 | 23 | 377 | 16.4 |
| Bennie Blades, Miami (Fla.) | 1984-87 | 22 | 355 | 16.1 |
| Jim Bolding, East Caro. | 1973-76 | 22 | 143 | 6.5 |
| Terrell Buckley, Florida St. | 1989-91 | 21 | *501 | 23.9 |
| Chuck Cecil, Arizona | 1984-87 | 21 | 241 | 11.5 |
| Barry Hill, Iowa St. | 1972-74 | 21 | 202 | 9.6 |
| Mike Sensibaugh, Ohio St. | 1968-70 | 21 | 226 | 10.8 |
| Kevin Smith, Texas A&M | 1988-91 | 20 | 289 | 14.5 |
| Mark Collins, Cal St. Fullerton | 1982-85 | 20 | 193 | 9.7 |
| Anthony Young, Temple | 1981-84 | 20 | 230 | 11.5 |
| Chris Williams, Louisiana St. | 1977-80 | 20 | 91 | 4.6 |
| Charles Jefferson, McNeese St. | 1975-78 | 20 | 95 | 4.8 |
| Artimus Parker, Southern Cal | 1971-73 | 20 | 268 | 13.4 |
| Dave Atkinson, Brigham Young | 1971-73 | 20 | 222 | 11.1 |
| Jackie Wallace, Arizona | 1970-72 | 20 | 250 | 12.5 |
| Tom Wilson, Colgate | 1964-66 | 20 | 215 | 10.8 |
| Lynn Chandnois, Michigan St. | 1946-49 | 20 | 410 | 20.5 |
| Bobby Wilson, Mississippi | 1946-49 | 20 | 369 | 18.5 |

* Record.

## Season Interceptions

| Player, Team | Year | No. | Yards |
|-------------|------|-----|-------|
| Al Worley, Washington | †1968 | *14 | 130 |
| George Shaw, Oregon | †1951 | 13 | 136 |
| Terrell Buckley, Florida St. | †1991 | 12 | 238 |
| Cornelius Price, Houston | †1989 | 12 | 187 |
| Bob Navarro, Eastern Mich. | †1989 | 12 | 73 |
| Tony Thurman, Boston College | †1984 | 12 | 99 |
| Terry Hoage, Georgia | †1982 | 12 | 51 |
| Frank Polito, Villanova | †1971 | 12 | 261 |
| Bill Albrecht, Washington | 1951 | 12 | 140 |
| Hank Rich, Arizona St. | †1950 | 12 | 135 |

* Record.  † National champion.

*1993 NCAA FOOTBALL*

## Annual Champions

| Year | Player, Team | Class | No. | Yards |
|------|--------------|-------|-----|-------|
| 1938 | Elmer Tarbox, Texas Tech | Sr. | 11 | 89 |
| 1939 | Harold Van Every, Minnesota | Sr. | 8 | 59 |
| 1940 | Dick Morgan, Tulsa | Jr. | 7 | 210 |
| 1941 | Bobby Robertson, Southern Cal | Sr. | 9 | 126 |
| 1942 | Ray Evans, Kansas | Jr. | 10 | 76 |
| 1943 | Jay Stoves, Washington | Sr. | 7 | 139 |
| 1944 | Joe Stuart, California | Jr. | 7 | 76 |
| 1945 | Jake Leicht, Oregon | So. | 9 | 195 |
| 1946 | Larry Hatch, Washington | So. | 8 | 114 |
| 1947 | John Bruce, William & Mary | Jr. | 9 | 78 |
| 1948 | Jay Van Noy, Utah St. | Jr. | 8 | 228 |
| 1949 | Bobby Wilson, Mississippi | Sr. | 10 | 70 |
| 1950 | Hank Rich, Arizona St. | Sr. | 12 | 135 |
| 1951 | George Shaw, Oregon | Fr. | 13 | 136 |
| 1952 | Cecil Ingram, Alabama | Jr. | 10 | 163 |
| 1953 | Bob Garrett, Stanford | Sr. | 9 | 80 |
| 1954 | Gary Glick, Colorado St. | Jr. | 8 | 168 |
| 1955 | Sam Wesley, Oregon St. | Jr. | 7 | 61 |
| 1956 | Jack Hill, Utah St. | Sr. | 7 | 132 |
| 1957 | Ray Toole, North Texas | Sr. | 7 | 133 |
| 1958 | Jim Norton, Idaho | Jr. | 9 | 222 |
| 1959 | Bud Whitehead, Florida St. | Jr. | 6 | 111 |
| 1960 | Bob O'Billovich, Montana | Jr. | 7 | 71 |
| 1961 | Joe Zuger, Arizona St. | Sr. | 10 | 121 |
| 1962 | Byron Beaver, Houston | Sr. | 10 | 56 |
| 1963 | Dick Kern, William & Mary | Sr. | 8 | 116 |
| 1964 | Tony Carey, Notre Dame | Jr. | 8 | 121 |
| 1965 | Bob Sullivan, Maryland | Sr. | 10 | 61 |
| 1966 | Henry King, Utah St. | Sr. | 11 | 180 |
| 1967 | Steve Haterius, West Tex. St. | Sr. | 11 | 90 |
| 1968 | Al Worley, Washington | Sr. | *14 | 130 |
| 1969 | Seth Miller, Arizona St. | Sr. | 11 | 63 |

*Beginning in 1970, ranked on per-game (instead of total) number*

| Year | Player, Team | Class | Games | No. | Avg. | Yards |
|------|--------------|-------|-------|-----|------|-------|
| 1970 | Mike Sensibaugh, Ohio St. | Sr. | 8 | 8 | 1.00 | 40 |
| 1971 | Frank Polito, Villanova | So. | 10 | 12 | 1.20 | 261 |
| 1972 | Mike Townsend, Notre Dame | Jr. | 10 | 10 | 1.00 | 39 |
| 1973 | Mike Gow, Illinois | Jr. | 11 | 10 | 0.91 | 142 |
| 1974 | Mike Haynes, Arizona St. | Jr. | 11 | 10 | 0.91 | 115 |
| 1975 | Jim Bolding, East Caro. | Jr. | 10 | 10 | 1.00 | 51 |
| 1976 | Anthony Francis, Houston | Jr. | 11 | 10 | 0.91 | 118 |
| 1977 | Paul Lawler, Colgate | Sr. | 9 | 7 | 0.78 | 53 |
| 1978 | Pete Harris, Penn St. | Jr. | 11 | 10 | 0.91 | 155 |
| 1979 | Joe Callan, Ohio | Sr. | 9 | 9 | 1.00 | 110 |
| 1980 | Ronnie Lott, Southern Cal | Sr. | 11 | 8 | 0.73 | 166 |
|  | Steve McNamee, William & Mary | Sr. | 11 | 8 | 0.73 | 125 |
|  | Greg Benton, Drake | Sr. | 11 | 8 | 0.73 | 119 |
|  | Jeff Hipp, Georgia | Sr. | 11 | 8 | 0.73 | 104 |
|  | Mike Richardson, Arizona St. | So. | 11 | 8 | 0.73 | 89 |
|  | Vann McElroy, Baylor | Jr. | 11 | 8 | 0.73 | 73 |
| 1981 | Sam Shaffer, Temple | Sr. | 10 | 9 | 0.90 | 76 |
| 1982 | Terry Hoage, Georgia | Jr. | 10 | 12 | 1.20 | 51 |
| 1983 | Martin Bayless, Bowling Green | Sr. | 11 | 10 | 0.91 | 64 |
| 1984 | Tony Thurman, Boston College | Sr. | 11 | 12 | 1.09 | 99 |
| 1985 | Chris White, Tennessee | Sr. | 11 | 9 | 0.82 | 168 |
|  | Kevin Walker, East Caro. | Sr. | 11 | 9 | 0.82 | 155 |
| 1986 | Bennie Blades, Miami (Fla.) | Jr. | 11 | 10 | 0.91 | 128 |
| 1987 | Keith McMeans, Virginia | Fr. | 10 | 9 | 0.90 | 35 |
| 1988 | Kurt Larson, Michigan St. (LB) | Sr. | 11 | 8 | 0.73 | 78 |
|  | Andy Logan, Kent | Sr. | 11 | 8 | 0.73 | 54 |
| 1989 | Cornelius Price, Houston | Jr. | 11 | 12 | 1.09 | 187 |
|  | Bob Navarro, Eastern Mich. | Jr. | 11 | 12 | 1.09 | 73 |
| 1990 | Jerry Parks, Houston | Jr. | 11 | 8 | 0.73 | 124 |
| 1991 | Terrell Buckley, Florida St. | Jr. | 12 | 12 | 1.00 | 238 |
| 1992 | Carlton McDonald, Air Force | Sr. | 11 | 8 | 0.73 | 109 |

* Record.

# PUNTING

## Career Average (Minimum 150 Punts)

| Player, Team | Years | No. | Yards | Avg. | Long |
|---|---|---|---|---|---|
| Reggie Roby, Iowa | 1979-82 | 172 | 7,849 | *45.6 | 69 |
| Greg Montgomery, Michigan St. | 1985-87 | 170 | 7,721 | 45.4 | 86 |
| Tom Tupa, Ohio St. | 1984-87 | 196 | 8,854 | 45.2 | 75 |
| Barry Helton, Colorado | 1984-87 | 153 | 6,873 | 44.9 | 68 |
| Ray Guy, Southern Miss. | 1970-72 | 200 | 8,934 | 44.7 | 93 |
| Bucky Scribner, Kansas | 1980-82 | 217 | 9,670 | 44.6 | 70 |
| Greg Horne, Arkansas | 1983-86 | 180 | 8,002 | 44.5 | 72 |
| Ray Criswell, Florida | 1982-85 | 161 | 7,153 | 44.4 | 73 |
| Russell Erxleben, Texas | 1975-78 | 214 | 9,467 | 44.2 | 80 |
| Mark Simon, Air Force | 1984-86 | 156 | 6,898 | 44.2 | 64 |
| Johnny Evans, North Caro. St. | 1974-77 | 185 | 8,143 | 44.0 | 81 |
| Chuck Ramsey, Wake Forest | 1971-73 | 205 | 9,010 | 44.0 | 70 |
| Jimmy Colquitt, Tennessee | 1981-84 | 201 | 8,816 | 43.9 | 70 |
| John Teltschik, Texas | 1982-85 | 217 | 9,496 | 43.8 | 81 |

* Record.

## Career Average (Minimum 250 Punts)

| Player, Team | Years | No. | Yards | Avg. | Long |
|---|---|---|---|---|---|
| Bill Smith, Mississippi | 1983-86 | 254 | 11,260 | *44.3 | 92 |
| Jim Arnold, Vanderbilt | 1979-82 | 277 | 12,171 | 43.9 | 79 |
| Ralf Mojsiejenko, Michigan St. | 1981-84 | 275 | 11,997 | 43.6 | 72 |
| Jim Miller, Mississippi | 1976-79 | 266 | 11,549 | 43.4 | 82 |
| Russ Henderson, Virginia | 1975-78 | 276 | 11,957 | 43.3 | 74 |
| Maury Buford, Texas Tech | 1978-81 | 293 | 12,670 | 43.2 | 75 |
| Chris Becker, Texas Christian | 1985-88 | 265 | 11,407 | 43.0 | 77 |
| Mark Bounds, West Tex. St./Texas Tech | ✓1988-91 | 252 | 10,842 | 43.0 | 89 |
| Ron Keller, New Mexico | 1983-86 | 252 | 10,737 | 42.6 | 77 |
| James Gargus, Texas Christian | 1981-84 | 255 | 10,862 | 42.6 | 74 |

* Record. ✓ Transferred to Texas Tech after West Tex. St. dropped football program in 1990.

## Season Average
### (Qualifiers for Championship)

| Player, Team | Year | No. | Yards | Avg. |
|---|---|---|---|---|
| Reggie Roby, Iowa | †1981 | 44 | 2,193 | *49.8 |
| Kirk Wilson, UCLA | †1956 | 30 | 1,479 | 49.3 |
| Zack Jordan, Colorado | †1950 | 38 | 1,830 | 48.2 |
| Ricky Anderson, Vanderbilt | †1984 | 58 | 2,793 | ‡48.2 |
| Reggie Roby, Iowa | †1982 | 52 | 2,501 | 48.1 |
| Marv Bateman, Utah | †1971 | 68 | 3,269 | 48.1 |
| Owen Price, UTEP | †1940 | 30 | 1,440 | 48.0 |
| Jack Jacobs, Oklahoma | 1940 | 31 | 1,483 | 47.8 |
| Bill Smith, Mississippi | 1984 | 44 | 2,099 | 47.7 |
| Ed Bunn, UTEP | †1992 | 41 | 1,955 | 47.7 |

* Record. † National champion. ‡ Record for minimum of 50 punts.

## Annual Champions

| Year | Player, Team | Class | No. | Yards | Avg. |
|---|---|---|---|---|---|
| 1937 | Johnny Pingel, Michigan St. | Jr. | 49 | 2,101 | 42.9 |
| 1938 | Jerry Dowd, St. Mary's (Cal.) | Sr. | 62 | 2,711 | 43.7 |
| 1939 | Harry Dunkle, North Caro. | So. | 37 | 1,725 | 46.6 |
| 1940 | Owen Price, UTEP | Jr. | 30 | 1,440 | 48.0 |
| 1941 | Owen Price, UTEP | Sr. | 40 | 1,813 | 45.3 |
| 1942 | Bobby Cifers, Tennessee | Jr. | 37 | 1,586 | 42.9 |
| 1943 | Harold Cox, Arkansas | Fr. | 37 | 1,518 | 41.0 |
| 1944 | Bob Waterfield, UCLA | Sr. | 60 | 2,575 | 42.9 |
| 1945 | Howard Maley, Southern Methodist | Sr. | 59 | 2,458 | 41.7 |
| 1946 | Johnny Galvin, Purdue | Sr. | 30 | 1,286 | 42.9 |
| 1947 | Leslie Palmer, North Caro. St. | Sr. | 65 | 2,816 | 43.3 |
| 1948 | Charlie Justice, North Caro. | Jr. | 62 | 2,728 | 44.0 |
| 1949 | Paul Stombaugh, Furman | Sr. | 57 | 2,550 | 44.7 |
| 1950 | Zack Jordan, Colorado | So. | 38 | 1,830 | 48.2 |
| 1951 | Chuck Spaulding, Wyoming | Jr. | 37 | 1,610 | 43.5 |
| 1952 | Des Koch, Southern Cal | Jr. | 47 | 2,043 | 43.5 |
| 1953 | Zeke Bratkowski, Georgia (QB) | Sr. | 50 | 2,132 | 42.6 |
| 1954 | A. L. Terpening, New Mexico | Sr. | 41 | 1,869 | 45.6 |
| 1955 | Don Chandler, Florida | Sr. | 22 | 975 | 44.3 |
| 1956 | Kirk Wilson, UCLA | So. | 30 | 1,479 | 49.3 |

| Year | Player, Team | Class | No. | Yards | Avg. |
|---|---|---|---|---|---|
| 1957 | Dave Sherer, Southern Methodist | Jr. | 36 | 1,620 | 45.0 |
| 1958 | Bobby Walden, Georgia | So. | 44 | 1,991 | 45.3 |
| 1959 | John Hadl, Kansas | So. | 43 | 1,960 | 45.6 |
| 1960 | Dick Fitzsimmons, Denver | So. | 25 | 1,106 | 44.2 |
| 1961 | Joe Zuger, Arizona St. | Sr. | 31 | 1,305 | 42.1 |
| 1962 | Joe Don Looney, Oklahoma | Jr. | 34 | 1,474 | 43.4 |
| 1963 | Danny Thomas, Southern Methodist | Jr. | 48 | 2,110 | 44.0 |
| 1964 | Frank Lambert, Mississippi | Sr. | 50 | 2,205 | 44.1 |
| 1965 | Dave Lewis, Stanford | Jr. | 29 | 1,302 | 44.9 |
| 1966 | Ron Widby, Tennessee | Sr. | 48 | 2,104 | 43.8 |
| 1967 | Zenon Andrusyshyn, UCLA | So. | 34 | 1,502 | 44.2 |
| 1968 | Dany Pitcock, Wichita St. | Sr. | 71 | 3,068 | 43.2 |
| 1969 | Ed Marsh, Baylor | Jr. | 68 | 2,965 | 43.6 |
| 1970 | Marv Bateman, Utah | Jr. | 65 | 2,968 | 45.7 |
| 1971 | Marv Bateman, Utah | Sr. | 68 | 3,269 | 48.1 |
| 1972 | Ray Guy, Southern Miss. | Sr. | 58 | 2,680 | 46.2 |
| 1973 | Chuck Ramsey, Wake Forest | Sr. | 87 | 3,896 | 44.8 |
| 1974 | Joe Parker, Appalachian St. | So. | 63 | 2,788 | 44.3 |
| 1975 | Tom Skladany, Ohio St. | Jr. | 36 | 1,682 | 46.7 |
| 1976 | Russell Erxleben, Texas | So. | 61 | 2,842 | 46.6 |
| 1977 | Jim Miller, Mississippi | So. | 66 | 3,029 | 45.9 |
| 1978 | Maury Buford, Texas Tech | Fr. | 71 | 3,131 | 44.1 |
| 1979 | Clay Brown, Brigham Young | Jr. | 43 | 1,950 | 45.3 |

*Beginning in 1980, ranked on minimum 3.6 punts per game*

| Year | Player, Team | Class | No. | Yards | Long | Avg. |
|---|---|---|---|---|---|---|
| 1980 | Steve Cox, Arkansas | Sr. | 47 | 2,186 | 86 | 46.5 |
| 1981 | Reggie Roby, Iowa | Jr. | 44 | 2,193 | 68 | *49.8 |
| 1982 | Reggie Roby, Iowa | Sr. | 52 | 2,501 | 66 | 48.1 |
| 1983 | Jack Weil, Wyoming | Sr. | 52 | 2,369 | 86 | 45.6 |
| 1984 | Ricky Anderson, Vanderbilt | Sr. | 58 | 2,793 | 82 | @48.2 |
| 1985 | Mark Simon, Air Force | Jr. | 53 | 2,506 | 71 | 47.3 |
| 1986 | Greg Horne, Arkansas | Sr. | 49 | 2,313 | 65 | 47.2 |
| 1987 | Tom Tupa, Ohio St. (QB) | Sr. | 63 | 2,963 | 72 | 47.0 |
| 1988 | Keith English, Colorado | Sr. | 51 | 2,297 | 77 | 45.0 |
| 1989 | Tom Rouen, Colorado | So. | 36 | 1,651 | 63 | 45.8 |
| 1990 | Cris Shale, Bowling Green | Sr. | 66 | 3,087 | 81 | 46.8 |
| 1991 | Mark Bounds, Texas Tech | Sr. | 53 | 2,481 | 78 | 46.8 |
| 1992 | Ed Bunn, UTEP | Sr. | 41 | 1,955 | 73 | 47.7 |

*\* Record. @ Record for minimum of 50 punts.*

# PUNT RETURNS

### Career Average
### (Minimum 1.2 Returns Per Game)

| Player, Team | Years | No. | Yards | TD | Long | Avg. |
|---|---|---|---|---|---|---|
| Jack Mitchell, Oklahoma | 1946-48 | 39 | 922 | **7 | 70 | *23.6 |
| Gene Gibson, Cincinnati | 1949-50 | 37 | 760 | 4 | 75 | 20.5 |
| Eddie Macon, Pacific (Cal.) | 1949-51 | 48 | 907 | 4 | **100 | 18.9 |
| Jackie Robinson, UCLA | 1939-40 | 37 | 694 | 2 | 89 | 18.8 |
| Mike Fuller, Auburn | 1972-74 | 50 | 883 | 3 | 63 | 17.7 |
| Bobby Dillon, Texas | 1949-51 | 47 | 830 | 1 | 84 | 17.7 |
| Erroll Tucker, Utah | 1984-85 | 38 | 650 | 3 | 89 | 17.1 |
| George Hoey, Michigan | 1966-68 | 31 | 529 | 1 | 60 | 17.1 |
| Jack Christiansen, Colorado St. | 1948-50 | 37 | 626 | 2 | 89 | 16.9 |
| Henry Pryor, Rutgers | 1948-49 | 37 | 625 | 1 | 85 | 16.9 |
| Adolph Bellizeare, Pennsylvania | 1972-74 | 33 | 557 | 3 | 73 | 16.9 |
| Ken Hatfield, Arkansas | 1962-64 | 70 | 1,135 | 5 | 95 | 16.2 |
| Gene Rossides, Columbia | 1945-48 | 53 | 851 | 3 | 70 | 16.1 |
| Bill Hillenbrand, Indiana | 1941-42 | 65 | 1,042 | 2 | 88 | 16.0 |

*\* Record. \*\* Record tied.*

### Season Average
### (Minimum 1.2 Returns Per Game)

| Player, Team | Year | No. | Yards | Avg. |
|---|---|---|---|---|
| Bill Blackstock, Tennessee | 1951 | 12 | 311 | *25.9 |
| George Sims, Baylor | 1948 | 15 | 375 | 25.0 |
| Gene Derricotte, Michigan | 1947 | 14 | 347 | 24.8 |
| Erroll Tucker, Utah | †1985 | 16 | 389 | 24.3 |
| George Hoey, Michigan | 1967 | 12 | 291 | 24.3 |
| Floyd Little, Syracuse | 1965 | 18 | 423 | 23.5 |

*\* Record. † National champion.*

## Annual Champions
### (Ranked on Total Yards Until 1970)

| Year | Player, Team | Class | No. | Yards | Avg. |
|------|--------------|-------|-----|-------|------|
| 1939 | Bosh Pritchard, Va. Military | So. | 42 | 583 | 13.9 |
| 1940 | Junie Hovious, Mississippi | Sr. | 33 | 498 | 15.1 |
| 1941 | Bill Geyer, Colgate | Sr. | 33 | 616 | 18.7 |
| 1942 | Bill Hillenbrand, Indiana | Jr. | 23 | 481 | 20.9 |
| 1943 | Marion Flanagan, Texas A&M | Jr. | 49 | 475 | 9.7 |
| 1944 | Joe Stuart, California | Jr. | 39 | 372 | 9.5 |
| 1945 | Jake Leicht, Oregon | So. | 28 | 395 | 14.1 |
| 1946 | Harry Gilmer, Alabama | Jr. | 37 | 436 | 11.8 |
| 1947 | Lindy Berry, Texas Christian | So. | 42 | 493 | 11.7 |
| 1948 | Lee Nalley, Vanderbilt | Jr. | 43 | *791 | 18.4 |
| 1949 | Lee Nalley, Vanderbilt | Sr. | 35 | 498 | 14.2 |
| 1950 | Dave Waters, Wash. & Lee | Jr. | 30 | 445 | 14.8 |
| 1951 | Tom Murphy, Holy Cross | So. | 25 | 533 | 21.3 |
| 1952 | Horton Nesrsta, Rice | Jr. | 44 | 536 | 12.2 |
| 1953 | Paul Giel, Minnesota | Sr. | 17 | 288 | 16.9 |
| 1954 | Dicky Maegle, Rice | Sr. | 15 | 293 | 19.5 |
| 1955 | Mike Sommer, Geo. Washington | So. | 24 | 330 | 13.8 |
| 1956 | Bill Stacy, Mississippi St. | Jr. | 24 | 290 | 12.1 |
| 1957 | Bobby Mulgado, Arizona St. | Sr. | 14 | 267 | 19.1 |
| 1958 | Howard Cook, Colorado | Sr. | 24 | 242 | 10.1 |
| 1959 | Pervis Atkins, New Mexico St. | Jr. | 16 | 241 | 15.1 |
| 1960 | Lance Alworth, Arkansas | Jr. | 18 | 307 | 17.1 |
| 1961 | Lance Alworth, Arkansas | Sr. | 28 | 336 | 12.0 |
| 1962 | Darrell Roberts, Utah St. | Sr. | 16 | 333 | 20.8 |
| 1963 | Ken Hatfield, Arkansas | Jr. | 21 | 350 | 16.7 |
| 1964 | Ken Hatfield, Arkansas | Sr. | 31 | 518 | 16.7 |
| 1965 | Nick Rassas, Notre Dame | Sr. | 24 | 459 | 19.1 |
| 1966 | Vic Washington, Wyoming | Jr. | 34 | 443 | 13.0 |
| 1967 | Mike Battle, Southern Cal | Jr. | 47 | 570 | 12.1 |
| 1968 | Roger Wehrli, Missouri | Sr. | 41 | 478 | 11.7 |
| 1969 | Chris Farasopoulous, Brigham Young | Jr. | 35 | 527 | 15.1 |

*Beginning in 1970, ranked on average per return (instead of total yards)‡*

| Year | Player, Team | Class | No. | Yards | TD | Long | Avg. |
|------|--------------|-------|-----|-------|-----|------|------|
| 1970 | Steve Holden, Arizona St. | So. | 17 | 327 | 2 | 94 | 19.2 |
| 1971 | Golden Richards, Brigham Young | Jr. | 33 | 624 | **4 | 87 | 18.9 |
| 1972 | Randy Rhino, Georgia Tech | So. | 25 | 441 | 1 | 96 | 17.6 |
| 1973 | Gary Hayman, Penn St. | Sr. | 23 | 442 | 1 | 83 | 19.2 |
| 1974 | John Provost, Holy Cross | Sr. | 13 | 238 | 2 | 85 | 18.3 |
| 1975 | Donnie Ross, New Mexico St. | Sr. | 21 | 338 | 1 | #81 | 16.1 |
| 1976 | Henry Jenkins, Rutgers | Sr. | 30 | 449 | 0 | #40 | 15.0 |
| 1977 | Robert Woods, Grambling | Sr. | ††11 | 279 | 3 | 72 | 25.4 |
| 1978 | Ira Matthews, Wisconsin | Sr. | 16 | 270 | 3 | 78 | 16.9 |
| 1979 | Jeffrey Shockley, Tennessee St. | Sr. | 27 | 456 | 1 | 79 | 16.9 |
| 1980 | Scott Woerner, Georgia | Sr. | 31 | 488 | 2 | 67 | 15.7 |
| 1981 | Glen Young, Mississippi St. | Jr. | 19 | 307 | 2 | 87 | 16.2 |
| 1982 | Lionel James, Auburn | Jr. | 25 | 394 | 0 | #63 | 15.8 |
| 1983 | Jim Sandusky, San Diego St. | Sr. | 20 | 381 | 1 | 90 | 19.0 |
| 1984 | Ricky Nattiel, Florida | So. | 22 | 346 | 1 | 67 | 15.7 |
| 1985 | Erroll Tucker, Utah | Sr. | 16 | 389 | 2 | 89 | 24.3 |
| 1986 | Rod Smith, Nebraska | Jr. | ‡‡12 | 227 | 1 | 63 | 18.9 |
| 1987 | Alan Grant, Stanford | Jr. | 27 | 446 | 2 | 77 | 16.5 |
| 1988 | Deion Sanders, Florida St. | Sr. | 33 | 503 | 1 | 76 | 15.2 |
| 1989 | Larry Hargrove, Ohio | Sr. | 17 | 309 | 1 | 83 | 18.2 |
| 1990 | Dave McCloughan, Colorado | Sr. | 32 | 524 | 2 | 90 | 16.4 |
| 1991 | Bo Campbell, Virginia Tech | Jr. | 15 | 273 | 0 | 45 | 18.2 |
| 1992 | Lee Gissendaner, Northwestern | Jr. | 15 | 327 | 1 | 72 | 21.8 |

*\* Record. \*\*Record tied. # Did not score. †† Declared champion; with three more returns (making 1.3 per game) for zero yards still would have highest average. ‡ Ranked on minimum 1.5 returns per game, 1970-73; 1.2 from 1974. ‡‡ Declared champion; with two more returns (making 1.2 per game) for zero yards still would have highest average.*

### Annual Punt Return Leaders (1939-69) Based on Average Per Return
#### (Minimum 1.2 Returns Per Game)

**1939**—Jackie Robinson, UCLA, 20.0; **1940**—Jackie Robinson, UCLA, 21.0; **1941**—Walt Slater, Tennessee, 20.4; **1942**—Billy Hillenbrand, Indiana, 20.9; **1943**—Otto Graham, Northwestern, 19.7; **1944**—Glenn Davis, Army, 18.4; **1945**—Jake Leicht, Oregon, 14.8; **1946**—Harold Griffin, Florida, 20.1; **1947**—Gene Derricotte, Michigan, 24.8; **1948**—George Sims, Baylor, 25.0; **1949**—Gene Evans,

66

Wisconsin, 21.8; **1950**—Lindy Hanson, Boston U., 22.5; **1951**—Bill Blackstock, Tennessee, 25.9; **1952**—Gil Reich, Kansas, 17.2; **1953**—Bobby Lee, New Mexico, 19.4; **1954**—Dicky Maegle, Rice, 19.5; **1955**—Ron Lind, Drake, 21.1; **1956**—Ron Lind, Drake, 19.1; **1957**—Bobby Mulgado, Arizona St., 19.1; **1958**—Herb Hallas, Yale, 23.4; **1959**—Jacque MacKinnon, Colgate, 17.5; **1960**—Pat Fischer, Nebraska, 21.2; **1961**—Tom Larscheid, Utah St., 23.4; **1962**—Darrell Roberts, Utah St., 20.8; **1963**—Rickie Harris, Arizona, 17.4; **1964**—Ken Hatfield, Arkansas, 16.7; **1965**—Floyd Little, Syracuse, 23.5; **1966**—Don Bean, Houston, 20.2; **1967**—George Hoey, Michigan, 24.3; **1968**—Rob Bordley, Princeton, 20.5; **1969**—George Hannen, Davidson, 22.4.

# KICKOFF RETURNS
### Career Average
### (Minimum 1.2 Returns Per Game)

| Player, Team | Years | No. | Yards | Avg. |
|---|---|---|---|---|
| Forrest Hall, San Francisco | 1946-47 | 22 | 796 | *36.2 |
| Anthony Davis, Southern Cal | 1972-74 | 37 | 1,299 | 35.1 |
| Overton Curtis, Utah St. | 1957-58 | 32 | 991 | 31.0 |
| Fred Montgomery, New Mexico St. | 1991-92 | 39 | 1,191 | 30.5 |
| Altie Taylor, Utah St. | 1966-68 | 40 | 1,170 | 29.3 |
| Stan Brown, Purdue | 1968-70 | 49 | 1,412 | 28.8 |
| Henry White, Colgate | 1974-77 | 41 | 1,180 | 28.8 |
| Donald Dennis, West Tex. St. | 1964-65 | 27 | 777 | 28.8 |
| Bobby Ward, Memphis St. | 1973-74 | 27 | 770 | 28.5 |
| Paul Loughran, Temple | 1970-72 | 40 | 1,123 | 28.1 |
| Jim Krieg, Washington | 1970-71 | 31 | 860 | 27.7 |

* *Record.*

### Season Average
### (Minimum 1.2 Returns Per Game)

| Player, Team | Year | No. | Yards | Avg. |
|---|---|---|---|---|
| Paul Allen, Brigham Young | 1961 | 12 | 481 | *40.1 |
| Forrest Hall, San Francisco | †1946 | 15 | 573 | **38.2 |
| Tony Ball, Tenn.-Chatt. | †1977 | 13 | 473 | 36.4 |
| George Marinkov, North Caro. St. | 1954 | 13 | 465 | 35.8 |
| Bob Baker, Cornell | 1964 | 11 | 386 | 35.1 |

* *Record.* ** *Record for minimum of 1.5 returns per game.* † *National champion.*

### Annual Champions
### (Ranked on Total Yards Until 1970)

| Year | Player, Team | Class | No. | Yards | Avg. |
|---|---|---|---|---|---|
| 1939 | Nile Kinnick, Iowa | Sr. | 15 | 377 | 25.1 |
| 1940 | Jack Emigh, Montana | Sr. | 18 | 395 | 21.9 |
| 1941 | Earl Ray, Wyoming | So. | 23 | 496 | 21.6 |
| 1942 | Frank Porto, California | Sr. | 17 | 483 | 28.4 |
| 1943 | Paul Copoulos, Marquette | So. | 11 | 384 | 34.9 |
| 1944 | Paul Copoulos, Marquette | Jr. | 14 | 337 | 24.1 |
| 1945 | Al Dekdebrun, Cornell | Sr. | 14 | 321 | 22.9 |
| 1946 | Forrest Hall, San Francisco | Jr. | 15 | 573 | *38.2 |
| 1947 | Doak Walker, Southern Methodist | So. | 10 | 387 | 38.7 |
| 1948 | Bill Gregus, Wake Forest | Jr. | 19 | 503 | 26.5 |
| 1949 | Johnny Subda, Nevada | Sr. | 18 | 444 | 24.7 |
| 1950 | Chuck Hill, New Mexico | Jr. | 27 | 729 | 27.0 |
| 1951 | Chuck Hill, New Mexico | Sr. | 17 | 504 | 29.6 |
| 1952 | Curly Powell, Va. Military | Sr. | 27 | 517 | 19.1 |
| 1953 | Max McGee, Tulane | Sr. | 17 | 371 | 21.8 |
| 1954 | Art Luppino, Arizona | So. | 20 | 632 | 31.6 |
| 1955 | Sam Woolwine, Va. Military | Jr. | 22 | 471 | 21.4 |
| 1956 | Sam Woolwine, Va. Military | Sr. | 18 | 503 | 27.9 |
| 1957 | Overton Curtis, Utah St. | Jr. | 23 | 695 | 30.2 |
| 1958 | Sonny Randle, Virginia | Sr. | 21 | 506 | 24.1 |
| 1959 | Don Perkins, New Mexico | Sr. | 15 | 520 | 34.7 |
| 1960 | Bruce Samples, Brigham Young | Sr. | 23 | 577 | 25.1 |
| 1961 | Dick Mooney, Idaho | Sr. | 23 | 494 | 21.5 |
| 1962 | Donnie Frederick, Wake Forest | Sr. | 29 | 660 | 22.8 |
| 1963 | Gary Wood, Cornell | Sr. | 19 | 618 | 32.5 |
| 1964 | Dan Bland, Mississippi St. | Jr. | 20 | 558 | 27.9 |
| 1965 | Eric Crabtree, Pittsburgh | Sr. | 25 | 636 | 25.4 |
| 1966 | Marcus Rhoden, Mississippi St. | Sr. | 26 | 572 | 22.0 |
| 1967 | Joe Casas, New Mexico | Sr. | 23 | 602 | 26.2 |
| 1968 | Mike Adamle, Northwestern | So. | 34 | 732 | 21.5 |
| 1969 | Stan Brown, Purdue | Jr. | 26 | 698 | 26.8 |

*Division I-A Annual Champions, All-Time Leaders*         67

*Beginning in 1970, ranked on average per return (instead of total yards)‡*

| Year | Player, Team | Class | No. | Yards | Avg. |
|------|--------------|-------|-----|-------|------|
| 1970 | Stan Brown, Purdue | Sr. | 19 | 638 | 33.6 |
| 1971 | Paul Loughran, Temple | Jr. | 15 | 502 | 33.5 |
| 1972 | Larry Williams, Texas Tech | So. | 16 | 493 | 30.8 |
| 1973 | Steve Odom, Utah | Sr. | 21 | 618 | 29.4 |
| 1974 | Anthony Davis, Southern Cal | Sr. | ††11 | 467 | 42.5 |
| 1975 | John Schultz, Maryland | Sr. | 13 | 403 | 31.0 |
| 1976 | Ira Matthews, Wisconsin | So. | 14 | 415 | 29.6 |
| 1977 | Tony Ball, Tenn.-Chatt. | Fr. | 13 | 473 | 36.4 |
| 1978 | Drew Hill, Georgia Tech | Sr. | 19 | 570 | 30.0 |
| 1979 | Stevie Nelson, Ball St. | Fr. | 18 | 565 | 31.4 |
| 1980 | Mike Fox, San Diego St. | So. | †11 | 361 | 32.8 |
| 1981 | Frank Minnifield, Louisville | Jr. | 11 | 334 | 30.4 |
| 1982 | Carl Monroe, Utah | Sr. | 14 | 421 | 30.1 |
| 1983 | Henry Williams, East Caro. | Jr. | 19 | 591 | 31.1 |
| 1984 | Keith Henderson, Texas Tech | Fr. | 13 | 376 | 28.9 |
| 1985 | Erroll Tucker, Utah | Sr. | 24 | 698 | 29.1 |
| 1986 | Terrance Roulhac, Clemson | Sr. | 17 | 561 | 33.0 |
| 1987 | Barry Sanders, Oklahoma St. | So. | 14 | 442 | 31.6 |
| 1988 | Raghib Ismail, Notre Dame | Fr. | #12 | 433 | 36.1 |
| 1989 | Tony Smith, Southern Miss. | So. | 14 | 455 | 32.5 |
| 1990 | Dale Carter, Tennessee | Jr. | 17 | 507 | 29.8 |
| 1991 | Fred Montgomery, New Mexico St. | Jr. | 25 | 734 | 29.4 |
| 1992 | Fred Montgomery, New Mexico St. | Sr. | 14 | 457 | 32.6 |

* *Record.* # *Declared champion; with two more returns (making 1.3 per game) for zero yards still would have highest average.* † *Declared champion; with one more return (making 1.2 per game) for zero yards still would have highest average.* †† *Declared champion; with three more returns (making 1.3 per game) for zero yards still would have highest average.* ‡ *Ranked on minimum 1.5 returns per game, 1970-73; 1.2 from 1974.*

### Annual Kickoff Return Leaders (1939-69) Based on Average Per Return
### (Minimum 1.2 Returns Per Game)

**1939**—Nile Kinnick, Iowa, 25.1; **1940**—Bill Geyer, Colgate, 27.0; **1941**—Vern Lockard, Colorado, 24.4; **1942-45**—Not compiled; **1946**—Forrest Hall, San Francisco, 38.2; **1947**—Skippy Minisi, Pennsylvania, 28.8; **1948**—Jerry Williams, Washington St., 29.9; **1949**—Billy Conn, Georgetown, 31.1; **1950**—Johnny Turco, Holy Cross, 27.4; **1951**—Bob Mischak, Army, 31.3; **1952**—Carroll Hardy, Colorado, 32.2; **1953**—Carl Bolt, Wash. & Lee, 27.1; **1954**—George Marinkov, North Caro. St., 35.8; **1955**—Jim Brown, Syracuse, 32.0; **1956**—Paul Hornung, Notre Dame, 31.0; **1957**—Overton Curtis, Utah St., 30.2; **1958**—Marshall Starks, Illinois, 26.3; **1959**—Don Perkins, New Mexico, 34.7; **1960**—Tom Hennessey, Holy Cross, 33.4; **1961**—Paul Allen, Brigham Young, 40.1; **1962**—Larry Coyer, Marshall, 30.2; **1963**—Gary Wood, Cornell, 32.5; **1964**—Bob Baker, Cornell, 35.1; **1965**—Tom Barrington, Ohio St., 34.3; **1966**—Frank Moore, Louisville, 27.9; **1967**—Altie Taylor, Utah St., 31.9; **1968**—Kerry Reardon, Iowa, 32.1; **1969**—Chris Farasopoulous, Brigham Young, 32.2.

# ALL-PURPOSE RUNNING
### Career Yards Per Game

| Player, Team | Years | Rush | Rcv | Int | PR | KOR | Yds. | Yd. PG |
|--------------|-------|------|-----|-----|-----|-----|------|--------|
| Ryan Benjamin, Pacific (Cal.) | 1990-92 | 3,119 | 1,063 | 0 | 100 | 1,424 | 5,706 | *237.8 |
| Sheldon Canley, San Jose St. | 1988-90 | 2,513 | 828 | 0 | 5 | 1,800 | 5,146 | 205.8 |
| Howard Stevens, Louisville | §1971-72 | 2,723 | 389 | 0 | 401 | 360 | 3,873 | 193.7 |
| O. J. Simpson, Southern Cal | 1967-68 | 3,124 | 235 | 0 | 0 | 307 | 3,666 | 192.9 |
| Ed Marinaro, Cornell | 1969-71 | 4,715 | 225 | 0 | 0 | 0 | 4,940 | 183.0 |
| Herschel Walker, Georgia | 1980-82 | 5,259 | 243 | 0 | 0 | 247 | 5,749 | 174.2 |
| Louie Giammona, Utah St. | 1973-75 | 3,499 | 171 | 0 | 188 | 1,345 | 5,203 | 173.4 |
| Pervis Atkins, New Mexico St. | 1959-60 | 1,582 | 769 | 66 | 459 | 557 | 3,433 | 171.7 |

* *Record.* § *Competed two years in Division I-A and two years in Division II (Randolph-Macon, 1968-69). Four-year average: 199.1.*

### Season Yards Per Game

| Player, Team | Year | Rush | Rcv | Int | PR | KOR | Yds. | Yd. PG |
|--------------|------|------|-----|-----|-----|-----|------|--------|
| Barry Sanders, Oklahoma St. | †1988 | *2,628 | 106 | 0 | 95 | 421 | *3,250 | *295.5 |
| Ryan Benjamin, Pacific (Cal.) | †1991 | 1,581 | 612 | 0 | 4 | 798 | 2,995 | 249.6 |
| Byron "Whizzer" White, Colorado | †1937 | 1,121 | 0 | 103 | 587 | 159 | 1,970 | 246.3 |
| Mike Pringle, Cal St. Fullerton | †1989 | 1,727 | 249 | 0 | 0 | 714 | 2,690 | 244.6 |
| Paul Palmer, Temple | †1986 | 1,866 | 110 | 0 | 0 | 657 | 2,633 | 239.4 |
| Ryan Benjamin, Pacific (Cal.) | †1992 | 1,441 | 434 | 0 | 96 | 626 | 2,597 | 236.1 |
| Marcus Allen, Southern Cal | †1981 | 2,342 | 217 | 0 | 0 | 0 | 2,559 | 232.6 |
| Sheldon Canley, San Jose St. | 1989 | 1,201 | 353 | 0 | 0 | 959 | 2,513 | 228.5 |
| Ollie Matson, San Francisco | †1951 | 1,566 | 58 | 18 | 115 | 280 | 2,037 | 226.3 |
| Art Luppino, Arizona | †1954 | 1,359 | 50 | 84 | 68 | 632 | 2,193 | 219.3 |

*1993 NCAA FOOTBALL*

| Player, Team | Year | Rush | Rcv | Int | PR | KOR | Yds. | Yd. PG |
|---|---|---|---|---|---|---|---|---|
| Chuck Weatherspoon, Houston ....... | 1989 | 1,146 | 735 | 0 | 715 | 95 | 2,391 | 217.4 |
| Anthony Thompson, Indiana .......... | 1989 | 1,793 | 201 | 0 | 0 | 394 | 2,388 | 217.1 |
| Napoleon McCallum, Navy ........... | †1983 | 1,587 | 166 | 0 | 272 | 360 | 2,385 | 216.8 |
| Ed Marinaro, Cornell ................. | †1971 | 1,881 | 51 | 0 | 0 | 0 | 1,932 | 214.7 |
| Howard Stevens, Louisville ........... | †1972 | 1,294 | 221 | 0 | 337 | 240 | 2,132 | 213.2 |
| Napoleon McCallum, Navy ........... | †1985 | 1,327 | 358 | 0 | 157 | 488 | 2,330 | 211.8 |
| Keith Byars, Ohio St................. | †1984 | 1,655 | 453 | 0 | 0 | 176 | 2,284 | 207.6 |
| Mike Rozier, Nebraska ............... | 1983 | 2,148 | 106 | 0 | 0 | 232 | 2,486 | 207.2 |

* Record.   † National champion.

| Player, Team | Career Yards Years | Rush | Rcv | Int | PR | KOR | Yds. | Yd. PP |
|---|---|---|---|---|---|---|---|---|
| Napoleon McCallum, Navy ....... | $1981-85 | 4,179 | 796 | 0 | 858 | 1,339 | *7,172 | 6.3 |
| Darrin Nelson, Stanford .......... | 1977-78, 80-81 | 4,033 | 2,368 | 0 | 471 | 13 | 6,885 | 7.1 |
| Terance Mathis, New Mexico .... | 1985-87, 89 | 329 | *4,254 | 0 | 115 | 1,993 | 6,691 | 14.6 |
| Tony Dorsett, Pittsburgh ......... | 1973-76 | *6,082 | 406 | 0 | 0 | 127 | 6,615 | 5.9 |
| Paul Palmer, Temple ............. | 1983-86 | 4,895 | 705 | 0 | 12 | 997 | 6,609 | 6.1 |
| Charles White, Southern Cal ..... | 1976-79 | 5,598 | 507 | 0 | 0 | 440 | 6,545 | 6.0 |
| Trevor Cobb, Rice................ | 1989-92 | 4,948 | 892 | 0 | 21 | 651 | 6,512 | 5.3 |
| Glyn Milburn, Oklahoma/Stanford | 1988, 90-92 | 2,302 | 1,495 | 0 | 1,145 | 1,246 | 6,188 | 8.1 |
| Anthony Thompson, Indiana..... | 1986-89 | 4,965 | 713 | 0 | 0 | 412 | 6,090 | 5.1 |
| Archie Griffin, Ohio St........... | 1972-75 | 5,177 | 286 | 0 | 0 | 540 | 6,003 | 6.7 |
| Ron "Po" James, New Mexico St. | 1968-71 | 3,884 | 217 | 0 | 8 | 1,870 | 5,979 | 6.5 |
| Eric Wilkerson, Kent ............ | 1985-88 | 3,830 | 506 | 0 | 0 | 1,638 | 5,974 | 7.0 |
| Steve Bartalo, Colorado St. ...... | 1983-86 | 4,813 | 1,079 | 0 | 0 | 0 | 5,892 | 4.4 |
| Wilford White, Arizona St........ | 1947-50 | 3,173 | 892 | 212 | 798 | 791 | 5,866 | 9.2 |
| Joe Washington, Oklahoma...... | 1972-75 | 3,995 | 253 | 0 | 807 | 726 | 5,781 | 7.3 |
| Herschel Walker, Georgia ........ | 1980-82 | 5,259 | 243 | 0 | 0 | 247 | ‡5,749 | 5.6 |
| George Swarn, Miami (Ohio) .... | 1983-86 | 4,172 | 1,057 | 0 | 0 | 498 | 5,727 | 5.6 |
| Chuck Weatherspoon, Houston .. | 1987-90 | 3,247 | 1,375 | 0 | 611 | 482 | 5,715 | 9.7 |
| Ryan Benjamin, Pacific (Cal.) .... | 1990-92 | 3,119 | 1,063 | 0 | 100 | 1,424 | ‡5,706 | 8.8 |
| Eric Metcalf, Texas ............. | 1985-88 | 2,661 | 1,394 | 0 | 1,076 | 574 | 5,705 | 6.7 |
| George Rogers, South Caro...... | 1977-80 | 4,958 | 371 | 0 | 0 | 339 | 5,668 | 5.9 |
| Jamie Morris, Michigan ......... | 1984-87 | 3,944 | 703 | 0 | 0 | 984 | 5,631 | 6.4 |
| Joe Morris, Syracuse............ | 1978-81 | 4,299 | 278 | 0 | 0 | 1,023 | 5,600 | 6.3 |
| James Brooks, Auburn .......... | 1977-80 | 3,523 | 219 | 0 | 128 | 1,726 | 5,596 | 7.6 |
| Johnny Rodgers, Nebraska ..... | 1970-72 | 745 | 2,479 | 0 | 1,515 | 847 | ‡5,586 | 13.8 |
| Thurman Thomas, Oklahoma St. | 1984-87 | 4,595 | 551 | 0 | 143 | 237 | 5,526 | 5.5 |
| Mike Rozier, Nebraska .......... | 1981-83 | 4,780 | 216 | 0 | 0 | 449 | ‡5,445 | 7.7 |

* Record.   ‡ Three-year totals.   $ See page 8 for explanation.

| Player, Team | Season Yards Year | Rush | Rcv | Int | PR | KOR | Yds. | Yd. PP |
|---|---|---|---|---|---|---|---|---|
| Barry Sanders, Oklahoma St. ........... | †1988 | *2,628 | 106 | 0 | 95 | 421 | *3,250 | 8.3 |
| Ryan Benjamin, Pacific (Cal.) ........... | †1991 | 1,581 | 612 | 0 | 4 | 798 | 2,995 | 9.6 |
| Mike Pringle, Cal St. Fullerton .......... | †1989 | 1,727 | 249 | 0 | 0 | 714 | 2,690 | 7.6 |
| Paul Palmer, Temple ................... | †1986 | 1,866 | 110 | 0 | 0 | 657 | 2,633 | 6.8 |
| Ryan Benjamin, Pacific (Cal.) ........... | †1992 | 1,441 | 434 | 0 | 96 | 626 | 2,597 | 8.1 |
| Marcus Allen, Southern Cal ............. | †1981 | 2,342 | 217 | 0 | 0 | 0 | 2,559 | 5.9 |
| Sheldon Canley, San Jose St. ........... | 1989 | 1,201 | 353 | 0 | 0 | 959 | 2,513 | 7.4 |
| Mike Rozier, Nebraska ................. | 1983 | 2,148 | 106 | 0 | 0 | 232 | 2,486 | 8.4 |
| Chuck Weatherspoon, Houston ......... | 1989 | 1,146 | 735 | 0 | 415 | 95 | 2,391 | 10.7 |
| Anthony Thompson, Indiana............. | 1989 | 1,793 | 201 | 0 | 0 | 394 | 2,388 | 5.8 |
| Napoleon McCallum, Navy ............. | †1983 | 1,587 | 166 | 0 | 272 | 360 | 2,385 | 6.1 |
| Napoleon McCallum, Navy.............. | †1985 | 1,327 | 358 | 0 | 157 | 488 | 2,330 | 6.3 |
| Keith Byars, Ohio St................... | †1984 | 1,655 | 453 | 0 | 0 | 176 | 2,284 | 6.4 |
| Glyn Milburn, Stanford ................ | †1990 | 729 | 632 | 0 | 267 | 594 | 2,222 | 8.4 |
| Vaughn Dunbar, Indiana ............... | 1991 | 1,699 | 252 | 0 | 0 | 262 | 2,213 | 5.9 |
| Sheldon Canley, San Jose St. ........... | 1990 | 1,248 | 386 | 0 | 5 | 574 | 2,213 | 6.3 |
| Johnny Johnson, San Jose St. ........... | 1988 | 1,219 | 668 | 0 | 0 | 315 | 2,202 | 7.1 |
| Art Luppino, Arizona ................... | †1954 | 1,359 | 50 | 84 | 68 | 632 | 2,193 | 10.4 |
| Rick Calhoun, Cal St. Fullerton .......... | 1986 | 1,398 | 125 | 0 | 138 | 522 | 2,183 | 7.0 |
| Terance Mathis, New Mexico ........... | 1989 | 38 | 1,315 | 0 | 0 | 785 | 2,138 | 15.7 |
| Howard Stevens, Louisville.............. | †1972 | 1,294 | 221 | 0 | 377 | 240 | 2,132 | 6.4 |

* Record.   † National champion.

*Division I-A Annual Champions, All-Time Leaders*          69

## All-Purpose Single-Game Highs

| Yards | Player, Team (Opponent) | Date |
|---|---|---|
| 422 | Marshall Faulk, San Diego St. (Pacific, Cal.) | Sept. 14, 1991 |
| 417 | Paul Palmer, Temple (East Caro.) | Nov. 10, 1986 |
| 417 | Greg Allen, Florida St. (Western Caro.) | Oct. 31, 1981 |
| 416 | Anthony Thompson, Indiana (Wisconsin) | Nov. 11, 1989 |
| 402 | Ryan Benjamin, Pacific, Cal. (Utah St.) | Nov. 21, 1992 |
| 401 | Chuck Hughes, UTEP (North Texas) (349 on receptions) | Sept. 18, 1965 |
| 397 | Eric Allen, Michigan St. (Purdue) | Oct. 30, 1971 |
| 388 | Ryan Benjamin, Pacific, Cal. (Cal St. Fullerton) | Oct. 5, 1991 |
| 387 | Kendal Smith, Utah St. (San Jose St.) | Oct. 22, 1988 |
| 387 | Ron Johnson, Michigan (Wisconsin) | Nov. 16, 1968 |
| 386 | Barry Sanders, Oklahoma St. (Kansas) | Nov. 12, 1988 |
| 379 | Glyn Milburn, Stanford (California) | Nov. 17, 1990 |
| 375 | Rueben Mayes, Washington St. (Oregon St.) | Nov. 3, 1984 |
| 374 | Tony Dorsett, Pittsburgh (Penn St.) | Nov. 22, 1975 |
| 373 | Barry Sanders, Oklahoma St. (Oklahoma) | Nov. 5, 1988 |
| 372 | Chuck Weatherspoon, Houston (Eastern Wash.) | Nov. 17, 1990 |

## Annual Champions

| Year | Player, Team | Cl. | Rush | Rcv | Int | PR | KOR | Yds. | Yd. PG |
|---|---|---|---|---|---|---|---|---|---|
| 1937 | Byron "Whizzer" White, Colorado | Sr. | 1,121 | 0 | 103 | 587 | 159 | 1,970 | 246.3 |
| 1938 | Parker Hall, Mississippi | Sr. | 698 | 0 | 128 | 0 | 594 | 1,420 | 129.1 |
| 1939 | Tom Harmon, Michigan | Jr. | 868 | 110 | 98 | 0 | 132 | 1,208 | 151.0 |
| 1940 | Tom Harmon, Michigan | Sr. | 844 | 0 | 20 | 244 | 204 | 1,312 | 164.0 |
| 1941 | Bill Dudley, Virginia | Sr. | 968 | 60 | 76 | 481 | 89 | 1,674 | 186.0 |
| 1942 | records not available | — | — | — | — | — | — | — | — |
| 1943 | Stan Koslowski, Holy Cross | Fr. | 784 | 63 | 50 | 438 | 76 | 1,411 | 176.4 |
| 1944 | Red Williams, Minnesota | Jr. | 911 | 0 | 0 | 242 | 314 | 1,467 | 163.0 |
| 1945 | Bob Fenimore, Oklahoma St. | Jr. | 1,048 | 12 | 129 | 157 | 231 | 1,577 | 197.1 |
| 1946 | Rudy Mobley, Hardin-Simmons | Sr. | 1,262 | 13 | 79 | 273 | 138 | 1,765 | 176.5 |
| 1947 | Wilton Davis, Hardin-Simmons | So. | 1,173 | 79 | 0 | 295 | 251 | 1,798 | 179.8 |
| 1948 | Lou Kusserow, Columbia | Sr. | 766 | 463 | 19 | 130 | 359 | 1,737 | 193.0 |
| 1949 | Johnny Papit, Virginia | Jr. | 1,214 | 0 | 0 | 0 | 397 | 1,611 | 179.0 |
| 1950 | Wilford White, Arizona St. | Sr. | 1,502 | 225 | 0 | 64 | 274 | 2,065 | 206.5 |
| 1951 | Ollie Matson, San Francisco | Sr. | 1,566 | 58 | 18 | 115 | 280 | 2,037 | 226.3 |
| 1952 | Billy Vessels, Oklahoma | Sr. | 1,072 | 165 | 10 | 120 | 145 | 1,512 | 151.2 |
| 1953 | J. C. Caroline, Illinois | So. | 1,256 | 52 | 0 | 129 | 33 | 1,470 | 163.3 |
| 1954 | Art Luppino, Arizona | So. | 1,359 | 50 | 84 | 68 | 632 | 2,193 | 219.3 |
| 1955 | Jim Swink, Texas Christian | Jr. | 1,283 | 111 | 46 | 64 | 198 | 1,702 | 170.2 |
|  | Art Luppino, Arizona | Jr. | 1,313 | 74 | 0 | 62 | 253 | 1,702 | 170.2 |
| 1956 | Jack Hill, Utah St. | Sr. | 920 | 215 | 132 | 21 | 403 | 1,691 | 169.1 |
| 1957 | Overton Curtis, Utah St. | Jr. | 616 | 193 | 60 | 44 | 695 | 1,608 | 160.8 |
| 1958 | Dick Bass, Pacific (Cal.) | Jr. | 1,361 | 121 | 5 | 164 | 227 | 1,878 | 187.8 |
| 1959 | Pervis Atkins, New Mexico St. | Jr. | 971 | 301 | 23 | 241 | 264 | 1,800 | 180.0 |
| 1960 | Pervis Atkins, New Mexico St. | Sr. | 611 | 468 | 23 | 218 | 293 | 1,613 | 161.3 |
| 1961 | Jim Pilot, New Mexico St. | So. | 1,278 | 20 | 0 | 161 | 147 | 1,606 | 160.6 |
| 1962 | Gary Wood, Cornell | Jr. | 889 | 7 | 0 | 69 | 430 | 1,395 | 155.0 |
| 1963 | Gary Wood, Cornell | Sr. | 818 | 15 | 0 | 57 | 618 | 1,508 | 167.6 |
| 1964 | Donny Anderson, Texas Tech | Jr. | 966 | 396 | 0 | 28 | 320 | 1,710 | 171.0 |
| 1965 | Floyd Little, Syracuse | Jr. | 1,065 | 248 | 0 | 423 | 254 | 1,990 | 199.0 |
| 1966 | Frank Quayle, Virginia | So. | 727 | 420 | 0 | 30 | 439 | 1,616 | 161.6 |
| 1967 | O. J. Simpson, Southern Cal | Jr. | 1,415 | 109 | 0 | 0 | 176 | 1,700 | 188.9 |
| 1968 | O. J. Simpson, Southern Cal | Sr. | 1,709 | 126 | 0 | 0 | 131 | 1,966 | 196.6 |
| 1969 | Lynn Moore, Army | Sr. | 983 | 44 | 0 | 223 | 545 | 1,795 | 179.5 |
| 1970 | Don McCauley, North Caro. | Sr. | 1,720 | 235 | 0 | 0 | 66 | 2,021 | 183.7 |
| 1971 | Ed Marinaro, Cornell | Sr. | 1,881 | 51 | 0 | 0 | 0 | 1,932 | 214.7 |
| 1972 | Howard Stevens, Louisville | Sr. | 1,294 | 221 | 0 | 377 | 240 | 2,132 | 213.2 |
| 1973 | Willard Harrell, Pacific (Cal.) | Jr. | 1,319 | 18 | 0 | 88 | 352 | 1,777 | 177.7 |
| 1974 | Louie Giammona, Utah St. | Jr. | 1,534 | 79 | 0 | 16 | 355 | 1,984 | 198.4 |
| 1975 | Louie Giammona, Utah St. | Sr. | 1,454 | 33 | 0 | 124 | 434 | 2,045 | 185.9 |
| 1976 | Tony Dorsett, Pittsburgh | Sr. | 1,948 | 73 | 0 | 0 | 0 | 2,021 | 183.7 |
| 1977 | Earl Campbell, Texas | Sr. | 1,744 | 111 | 0 | 0 | 0 | 1,855 | 168.6 |
| 1978 | Charles White, Southern Cal | Jr. | 1,760 | 191 | 0 | 0 | 145 | 2,096 | 174.7 |
| 1979 | Charles White, Southern Cal | Sr. | 1,803 | 138 | 0 | 0 | 0 | 1,941 | 194.1 |
| 1980 | Marcus Allen, Southern Cal | Jr. | 1,563 | 231 | 0 | 0 | 0 | 1,794 | 179.4 |
| 1981 | Marcus Allen, Southern Cal | Sr. | 2,342 | 217 | 0 | 0 | 0 | 2,559 | 232.6 |
| 1982 | Carl Monroe, Utah | Sr. | 1,507 | 108 | 0 | 0 | 421 | 2,036 | 185.1 |
| 1983 | Napoleon McCallum, Navy | Jr. | 1,587 | 166 | 0 | 272 | 360 | 2,385 | 216.8 |
| 1984 | Keith Byars, Ohio St. | Jr. | 1,655 | 453 | 0 | 0 | 176 | 2,284 | 207.6 |
| 1985 | Napoleon McCallum, Navy | Sr. | 1,327 | 358 | 0 | 157 | 488 | 2,330 | 211.8 |
| 1986 | Paul Palmer, Temple | Sr. | 1,866 | 110 | 0 | 0 | 657 | 2,633 | 239.4 |

| Year | Player, Team | Cl. | Rush | Rcv | Int | PR | KOR | Yds. | Yd. PG |
|------|--------------|-----|------|-----|-----|-----|-----|------|--------|
| 1987 | Eric Wilkerson, Kent .................. | Jr. | 1,221 | 269 | 0 | 0 | 584 | 2,074 | 188.6 |
| 1988 | Barry Sanders, Oklahoma St. .......... | Jr. | *2,628 | 106 | 0 | 95 | 421 | *3,250 | *295.5 |
| 1989 | Mike Pringle, Cal St. Fullerton ......... | Sr. | 1,727 | 249 | 0 | 0 | 714 | 2,690 | 244.6 |
| 1990 | Glyn Milburn, Stanford................ | So. | 729 | 632 | 0 | 267 | 594 | 2,222 | 202.0 |
| 1991 | Ryan Benjamin, Pacific (Cal.) .......... | Jr. | 1,581 | 612 | 0 | 4 | 798 | 2,995 | 249.6 |
| 1992 | Ryan Benjamin, Pacific (Cal.) .......... | Sr. | 1,441 | 434 | 0 | 96 | 626 | 2,597 | 236.1 |

* Record.

Georgia's Kevin Butler is tied for sixth in Division I-A in career field goals with 77. He was 50 of 56 under 40 yards, and his kicks provided the winning margin in seven games.

# FIELD GOALS

### Career Field Goals

(One-inch tees were permitted in 1949, two-inch tees were permitted in 1965, and use of tees was eliminated in 1989. The goal posts were widened from 18 feet, 6 inches to 23 feet, 4 inches in 1959 and were narrowed back to 18 feet, 6 inches in 1991.)

| Player, Team | Years | Total | Pct. | Under 40 Yds. | 40 Plus | Long | ‡Won |
|--------------|-------|-------|------|---------------|---------|------|------|
| Jeff Jaeger, Washington (S) .......... | 1983-86 | *80-99 | .808 | 59-68 | 21-31 | 52 | 5 |
| John Lee, UCLA (S) ................. | 1982-85 | 79-92 | *.859 | 54-56 | 25-36 | 52 | **10 |
| Jason Elam, Hawaii (S) .............. | $1988-92 | 79-100 | .790 | 50-55 | 29-45 | 56 | 3 |
| Philip Doyle, Alabama (S) ............ | 1987-90 | 78-*105 | .743 | 57-61 | 21-44 | 53 | 6 |
| Luis Zendejas, Arizona St. (S) ........ | 1981-84 | 78-*105 | .743 | 53-59 | 25-46 | 55 | 1 |
| Kevin Butler, Georgia (S) ............ | 1981-84 | 77-98 | .786 | 50-56 | 27-42 | 60 | 7 |
| Max Zendejas, Arizona (S) ........... | 1982-85 | 77-104 | .740 | 47-53 | 30-51 | 57 | 7 |
| Carlos Huerta, Miami (Fla.) (S) ....... | 1988-91 | 73-91 | .802 | 56-60 | 17-31 | 52 | 3 |
| Derek Schmidt, Florida St. (S) ....... | 1984-87 | 73-104 | .702 | 44-55 | 29-49 | 54 | 1 |
| Fuad Reveiz, Tennessee (S) .......... | 1981-84 | 71-95 | .747 | 45-53 | 26-42 | 60 | 7 |

| Player, Team | Years | Total | Pct. | Under 40 Yds. | 40 Plus | Long | ‡Won |
|---|---|---|---|---|---|---|---|
| Roman Anderson, Houston (S) ....... | 1988-91 | 70-101 | .802 | *61-*72 | 9-29 | 53 | 3 |
| Barry Belli, Fresno St. (S) ............ | 1984-87 | 70-99 | .707 | 47-53 | 23-46 | 55 | 5 |
| Collin Mackie, South Caro. (S)....... | 1987-90 | 69-95 | .726 | 48-57 | 21-38 | 52 | 5 |
| Gary Gussman, Miami (Ohio) (S) .... | 1984-87 | 68-94 | .723 | 50-57 | 18-37 | 53 | 2 |
| Rusty Hanna, Toledo (S) ............. | 1989-92 | 68-99 | .687 | 51-58 | 17-41 | 51 | 3 |
| Larry Roach, Oklahoma St. (S) ....... | 1981-84 | 68-101 | .673 | 46-54 | 22-47 | 56 | 5 |
| Paul Woodside, West Va. (S) .......... | 1981-84 | 65-81 | .802 | 45-49 | 20-32 | 55 | 5 |
| John Diettrich, Ball St. (S) ............ | 1983-86 | 63-90 | .700 | 42-50 | 21-40 | 62 | 5 |
| Jason Hanson, Washington St. (S).... | 1988-91 | 63-96 | .656 | 24-30 | *39-*66 | 62 | 4 |
| Kenny Stucker, Ball St. (S) ............ | 1988-91 | 62-87 | .713 | 45-51 | 17-36 | 52 | 4 |
| David Browndyke, Louisiana St. (S)... | 1986-89 | 61-75 | .813 | 49-53 | 12-22 | 52 | 3 |
| Todd Gregoire, Wisconsin (S)......... | 1984-87 | 61-81 | .753 | 48-56 | 13-25 | 54 | 6 |
| Todd Wright, Arkansas (S) ............ | 1989-92 | 60-79 | .759 | 41-47 | 19-32 | 50 | 2 |
| Jess Atkinson, Maryland (S) .......... | 1981-84 | 60-82 | .732 | 40-48 | 20-34 | 50 | 5 |
| Scott Sisson, Georgia Tech (S) ....... | 1989-92 | 60-88 | .682 | 45-53 | 15-35 | 51 | 6 |
| Obed Ariri, Clemson (S) .............. | 1977-80 | 60-92 | .652 | 47-55 | 13-37 | 57 | 5 |
| Chuck Nelson, Washington (S) ....... | 1980-82 | 59-72 | .819 | 47-53 | 12-19 | 51 | 5 |
| Van Tiffin, Alabama (S)............... | 1983-86 | 59-87 | .678 | 32-38 | 27-49 | 57 | 5 |
| John Hopkins, Stanford (S) .......... | 1987-90 | 59-88 | .670 | 43-50 | 16-38 | 54 | 4 |
| Jeff Ward, Texas (S)................. | 1983-86 | 58-78 | .744 | 36-41 | 22-37 | 57 | **10 |
| Jeff Shudak, Iowa St. (S)............. | 1987-90 | 58-79 | .734 | 38-45 | 20-34 | 55 | 5 |

* Record.   ** Record tied.   ‡ Number of games in which his field goal(s) provided the winning margin.   $ See page 8 for explanation.

## Season Field Goals

| Player, Team | Year | Total | Pct. | Under 40 Yds. | 40 Plus | Long | ‡Won |
|---|---|---|---|---|---|---|---|
| John Lee, UCLA (S) .................. | †1984 | *29-33 | .879 | 16-16 | 13-17 | 51 | 5 |
| Paul Woodside, West Va. (S) .......... | †1982 | 28-31 | .903 | 23-23 | 5-8 | 45 | 2 |
| Luis Zendejas, Arizona St. (S)........ | †1983 | 28-37 | .757 | 19-22 | 9-15 | 52 | 1 |
| Fuad Reveiz, Tennessee (S) .......... | 1982 | 27-31 | .871 | 14-14 | 13-17 | 60 | 2 |
| Chuck Nelson, Washington (S) ....... | 1982 | 25-26 | *.962 | 22-23 | 3-3 | 49 | 1 |
| Chris Jacke, UTEP (S) ............... | 1988 | 25-27 | .926 | 11-11 | *14-16 | 52 | 2 |
| John Diettrich, Ball St. (S) ........... | †1985 | 25-29 | .862 | 16-17 | 9-12 | 54 | 2 |
| Kendall Trainor, Arkansas (S) ........ | †1988 | 24-27 | .889 | 14-15 | 10-12 | 58 | 4 |
| Carlos Reveiz, Tennessee (S) ........ | 1985 | 24-28 | .857 | 12-14 | 12-14 | 52 | 2 |
| Chris White, Illinois (S)............... | 1984 | 24-28 | .857 | 16-17 | 8-11 | 52 | 1 |
| Philip Doyle, Alabama (S)............. | †1990 | 24-29 | .828 | 16-17 | 8-12 | 47 | 2 |
| Bruce Kallmeyer, Kansas (S) ......... | 1983 | 24-29 | .828 | 13-14 | 11-15 | 57 | 1 |
| Mike Prindle, Western Mich. (S)....... | 1984 | 24-30 | .800 | 17-20 | 7-10 | 56 | 1 |
| Joe Allison, Memphis St. (S) ......... | †1992 | 23-25 | .920 | 13-14 | 10-11 | 51 | 1 |
| Bobby Raymond, Florida (S) ......... | 1984 | 23-26 | .885 | 18-18 | 5-8 | 51 | 1 |
| Mike Bass, Illinois (S) .............. | 1982 | 23-26 | .885 | 12-13 | 11-13 | 53 | 1 |
| Kevin Butler, Georgia (S).............. | 1984 | 23-28 | .821 | 12-14 | 11-14 | 60 | 2 |
| Collin Mackie, South Caro. (S)........ | †1987 | 23-30 | .767 | 17-21 | 6-9 | 49 | 0 |
| Obed Ariri, Clemson (S) .............. | †1980 | 23-30 | .767 | 18-19 | 5-11 | 52 | 3 |
| Derek Schmidt, Florida St. (S) ........ | †1987 | 23-31 | .742 | 16-21 | 7-10 | 53 | 0 |

* Record.   † National champion.   ‡ Number of games in which his field goal(s) provided the winning margin.   (S) Soccer-style kicker.

## Single-Game Field Goals

| No. | Player, Team (Opponent) | Date |
|---|---|---|
| 7 | Dale Klein, Nebraska (Missouri) .................................................Oct. 19, 1985 |
| 7 | Mike Prindle, Western Mich. (Marshall) ..........................................Sept. 29, 1984 |
| 6 | Rusty Hanna, Toledo (Northern Ill.) ..............................................Nov. 21, 1992 |
| 6 | Philip Doyle, Alabama (Southwestern La.) .........................................Oct. 6, 1990 |
| 6 | Sean Fleming, Wyoming (Arkansas St.) ..........................................Sept. 15, 1990 |
| 6 | Bobby Raymond, Florida (Kentucky) .............................................Nov. 17, 1984 |
| 6 | John Lee, UCLA (San Diego St.) ................................................Sept. 8, 1984 |
| 6 | Bobby Raymond, Florida (Florida St.) .............................................Dec. 3, 1983 |
| 6 | Alan Smith, Texas A&M (Arkansas St.) ..........................................Sept. 17, 1983 |
| 6 | Al Del Greco, Auburn (Kentucky) ................................................Oct. 9, 1982 |
| 6 | Vince Fusco, Duke (Clemson) ..................................................Oct. 16, 1976 |
| 6 | Frank Nester, West Va. (Villanova) ...............................................Sept. 9, 1972 |
| 6 | Charley Gogolak, Princeton (Rutgers).............................................Sept. 25, 1965 |

*1993 NCAA FOOTBALL*

## Annual Champions
(From 1959-90, goal posts were 23 feet, 4 inches; and from 1991, narrowed to 18 feet, 6 inches.)

| Year | Player, Team | Total | PG | Pct. | Under 40 Yds. | 40 Plus | Long | ‡Won |
|------|--------------|-------|----|----|------|------|------|------|
| 1959 | Karl Holzwarth, Wisconsin (C) | 7-8 | 0.8 | .875 | 7-8 | 0-0 | 29 | 4 |
| 1960 | Ed Dyas, Auburn (C) | 13-18 | 1.3 | .722 | 13-17 | 0-1 | 37 | 2 |
| 1961 | Greg Mather, Navy (C) | 11-15 | 1.1 | .733 | 9-12 | 2-3 | 45 | 1 |
| 1962 | Bob Jencks, Miami (Ohio) (C) | 8-11 | 0.8 | .727 | 7-9 | 1-2 | 52 | 3 |
|      | Al Woodall, Auburn (C) | 8-20 | 0.8 | .400 | 8-13 | 0-7 | 35 | 0 |
| 1963 | Billy Lothridge, Georgia Tech (C) | 12-16 | 1.2 | .750 | 10-14 | 2-2 | 41 | 3 |
| 1964 | Doug Moreau, Louisiana St. (C) | 13-20 | 1.3 | .650 | 13-20 | 0-0 | 36 | 0 |
| 1965 | Charley Gogolak, Princeton (S) | 16-23 | 1.8 | .696 | 7-10 | 9-13 | 54 | 0 |
| 1966 | Jerry DePoyster, Wyoming (C) | 13-*38 | 1.3 | .342 | 7-13 | 6-*25 | 54 | 1 |
| 1967 | Gerald Warren, North Caro. St. (C) | 17-22 | 1.7 | .773 | 13-14 | 4-8 | 47 | 1 |
| 1968 | Bob Jacobs, Wyoming (C) | 14-29 | 1.4 | .483 | 10-15 | 4-14 | 51 | 2 |
| 1969 | Bob Jacobs, Wyoming (C) | 18-27 | 1.8 | .667 | 13-16 | 5-11 | 43 | 2 |

*Beginning in 1970, ranked on per-game (instead of total) made*

| Year | Player, Team | Total | PG | Pct. | Under 40 Yds. | 40 Plus | Long | ‡Won |
|------|--------------|-------|----|----|------|------|------|------|
| 1970 | Kim Braswell, Georgia (C) | 13-17 | 1.3 | .765 | 11-14 | 2-3 | 43 | 0 |
| 1971 | Nick Mike-Mayer, Temple (S) | 12-17 | 1.3 | .706 | 8-10 | 4-7 | 48 | 1 |
| 1972 | Nick Mike-Mayer, Temple (S) | 13-20 | 1.4 | .650 | 10-11 | 3-9 | 44 | 3 |
| 1973 | Rod Garcia, Stanford (S) | 18-29 | 1.6 | .621 | 10-14 | 8-15 | 59 | 2 |
| 1974 | Dave Lawson, Air Force (C) | 19-31 | 1.7 | .613 | 13-14 | 6-17 | 60 | 1 |
| 1975 | Don Bitterlich, Temple (S) | 21-31 | 1.9 | .677 | 13-14 | 8-17 | 56 | 0 |
| 1976 | Tony Franklin, Texas A&M (S) | 17-26 | 1.6 | .654 | 9-12 | 8-14 | 65 | 0 |
| 1977 | Paul Marchese, Kent (S) | 18-27 | 1.8 | .667 | 13-15 | 5-12 | 51 | 2 |
| 1978 | Matt Bahr, Penn St. (S) | 22-27 | 2.0 | .815 | 19-20 | 3-7 | 50 | 3 |
| 1979 | Ish Ordonez, Arkansas (S) | 18-22 | 1.6 | .818 | 12-14 | 6-8 | 50 | 2 |
| 1980 | Obed Ariri, Clemson (S) | 23-30 | 2.1 | .767 | 18-19 | 5-11 | 52 | 3 |
| 1981 | Bruce Lahay, Arkansas (S) | 19-24 | 1.7 | .792 | 12-15 | 7-9 | 49 | 4 |
|      | Kevin Butler, Georgia (S) | 19-26 | 1.7 | .731 | 11-14 | 8-12 | 52 | 0 |
|      | Larry Roach, Oklahoma St. (S) | 19-28 | 1.7 | .679 | 12-14 | 7-14 | 56 | 3 |
| 1982 | Paul Woodside, West Va. (S) | 28-31 | 2.6 | .903 | 23-23 | 5-8 | 45 | 2 |
| 1983 | Luis Zendejas, Arizona St. (S) | 28-37 | 2.6 | .757 | 19-22 | 9-15 | 52 | 1 |
| 1984 | John Lee, UCLA (S) | *29-33 | *2.6 | .879 | 16-16 | 13-17 | 51 | 5 |
| 1985 | John Diettrich, Ball St. (S) | 25-29 | 2.3 | .862 | 16-17 | 9-12 | 54 | 2 |
| 1986 | Chris Kinzer, Virginia Tech (C) | 22-27 | 2.0 | .815 | 14-17 | 8-10 | 50 | 5 |
| 1987 | Collin Mackie, South Caro. (S) | 23-30 | 2.1 | .767 | 17-21 | 6-9 | 49 | 0 |
|      | Derek Schmidt, Florida St. (S) | 23-31 | 2.1 | .742 | 16-21 | 7-10 | 53 | 0 |
| 1988 | Kendall Trainor, Arkansas (S) | 24-27 | 2.2 | .889 | 14-15 | 10-12 | 58 | 4 |
| 1989 | Philip Doyle, Alabama (S) | 22-25 | 2.0 | .880 | 19-19 | 3-6 | 44 | 2 |
|      | Gregg McCallum, Oregon (S) | 22-29 | 2.0 | .759 | 15-15 | 7-14 | 47 | 2 |
|      | Roman Anderson, Houston (S) | 22-34 | 2.0 | .647 | 17-20 | 5-14 | 51 | 0 |
| 1990 | Philip Doyle, Alabama (S) | 24-29 | 2.2 | .828 | 16-17 | 8-12 | 47 | 2 |
| 1991 | Doug Brien, California (S) | 19-28 | 1.7 | .679 | 15-20 | 4-8 | 50 | 2 |
| 1992 | Joe Allison, Memphis St. (S) | 23-25 | 2.1 | .920 | 13-14 | 10-11 | 51 | 1 |

* *Record.* ‡ *Number of games in which his field goal(s) provided the winning margin.* (C) *Conventional kicker.* (S) *Soccer-style kicker.*

# ALL-TIME LONGEST PLAYS

*Since 1941, official maximum length of all plays fixed at 100 yards.*

## Rushing

| Yds. | Player, Team (Opponent) | Year |
|------|-------------------------|------|
| 99 | Kelsey Finch, Tennessee (Florida) | 1977 |
| 99 | Ralph Thompson, West Tex. St. (Wichita St.) | 1970 |
| 99 | Max Anderson, Arizona St. (Wyoming) | 1967 |
| 99 | Gale Sayers, Kansas (Nebraska) | 1963 |
| 98 | Darrell Thompson, Minnesota (Michigan) | 1987 |
| 98 | George Swarn, Miami, Ohio (Western Mich.) | 1984 |
| 98 | Mark Malone, Arizona St. (Utah St.) | 1979 |
| 98 | Stanley Howell, Mississippi St. (Southern Miss.) | 1979 |
| 98 | Steve Atkins, Maryland (Clemson) | 1978 |
| 98 | Granville Amos, Va. Military (William & Mary) | 1964 |
| 98 | Jim Thacker, Davidson (Geo. Washington) | 1952 |
| 98 | Bill Powell, California (Oregon St.) | 1951 |
| 98 | Al Yannelli, Bucknell (Delaware) | 1946 |
| 98 | Meredith Warner, Iowa St. (Iowa Pre-Flight) | 1943 |

*Division I-A Annual Champions, All-Time Leaders*          73

## Passing

| Yds. | Passer-Receiver, Team (Opponent) | Year |
|---|---|---|
| 99 | Gino Torretta-Horace Copeland, Miami, Fla. (Arkansas) | 1991 |
| 99 | Scott Ankrom-James Maness, Texas Christian (Rice) | 1984 |
| 99 | Cris Collinsworth-Derrick Gaffney, Florida (Rice) | 1977 |
| 99 | Terry Peel-Robert Ford, Houston (San Diego St.) | 1972 |
| 99 | Terry Peel-Robert Ford, Houston (Syracuse) | 1970 |
| 99 | Colin Clapton-Eddie Jenkins, Holy Cross (Boston U.) | 1970 |
| 99 | Bo Burris-Warren McVea, Houston (Washington St.) | 1966 |
| 99 | Fred Owens-Jack Ford, Portland (St. Mary's, Cal.) | 1947 |
| 98 | Tom Dubs-Richard Hill, Ohio (Kent) | 1991 |
| 98 | Paul Oates-Sean Foster, Long Beach St. (San Diego St.) | 1989 |
| 98 | Barry Garrison-Al Owens, New Mexico (Brigham Young) | 1987 |
| 98 | Kelly Donohoe-Willie Vaughn, Kansas (Colorado) | 1987 |
| 98 | Jeff Martin-Mark Flaker, Drake (New Mexico St.) | 1976 |
| 98 | Pete Woods-Joe Stewart, Missouri (Nebraska) | 1976 |
| 98 | Dan Hagemann-Jack Steptoe, Utah (New Mexico) | 1976 |
| 98 | Bruce Shaw-Pat Kenney, North Caro. St. (Penn St.) | 1972 |
| 98 | Jerry Rhome-Jeff Jordan, Tulsa (Wichita St.) | 1963 |
| 98 | Bob Dean-Norman Dawson, Cornell (Navy) | 1947 |

## Interception Returns

*Since 1941, 59 players have returned interceptions 100 yards. The most recent:*

| Yds. | Player, Team (Opponent) | Year |
|---|---|---|
| 100 | John Hardy, California (Wisconsin) | 1990 |
| 100 | Ed Givens, Army (Lafayette) | 1990 |
| 100 | Greg Jackson, Louisiana St. (Mississippi St.) | 1988 |
| 100 | Dennis Price, UCLA (California) | 1987 |

## Punt Returns

| Yds. | Player, Team (Opponent) | Year |
|---|---|---|
| 100‡ | Richie Luzzi, Clemson (Georgia) | 1968 |
| 100‡ | Don Guest, California (Washington St.) | 1966 |
| 100 | Jimmy Campagna, Georgia (Vanderbilt) | 1952 |
| 100 | Hugh McElhenny, Washington (Southern Cal) | 1951 |
| 100 | Frank Brady, Navy (Maryland) | 1951 |
| 100 | Bert Rechichar, Tennessee (Wash. & Lee) | 1950 |
| 100 | Eddie Macon, Pacific, Cal. (Boston U.) | 1950 |

‡ *Return of field-goal attempt.*

## Kickoff Returns

*Since 1941, 166 players have returned kickoffs 100 yards. The most recent:*

| Yds. | Player, Team (Opponent) | Year |
|---|---|---|
| 100 | Fred Montgomery, New Mexico St. (Long Beach St.) | 1991 |
| 100 | Anthony Prior, Washington St. (Southern Cal) | 1991 |
| 100 | Ricky Turner, Pittsburgh (West Va.) | 1990 |
| 100 | Kurt Johnson, Kentucky (Georgia) | 1989 |
| 100 | Carlos Snow, Ohio St. (Pittsburgh) | 1988 |
| 100 | Pierre Goode, Alabama (Mississippi) | 1988 |
| 100 | Eric Mortensen, Brigham Young (Utah St.) | 1988 |
| 100† | Barry Sanders, Oklahoma St. (Miami, Ohio) | 1988 |
| 100 | Barry Sanders, Oklahoma St. (Kansas) | 1987 |
| 100† | Barry Sanders, Oklahoma St. (Tulsa) | 1987 |

† *Team's first kickoff return of the season.*

## Punts

| Yds. | Player, Team (Opponent) | Year |
|---|---|---|
| 99 | Pat Brady, Nevada (Loyola, Cal.) | 1950 |
| 96 | George O'Brien, Wisconsin (Iowa) | 1952 |
| 94 | John Hadl, Kansas (Oklahoma) | 1959 |
| 94 | Carl Knox, Texas Christian (Oklahoma St.) | 1947 |
| 94 | Preston Johnson, Southern Methodist (Pittsburgh) | 1940 |

## Fumble Returns (Since 1992)

| Yds. | Player, Team (Opponent) | Year |
|---|---|---|
| 97 | Ernie Lewis, East Caro. (West Va.) | 1992 |
| 96 | Jeff Arneson, Illinois (Ohio St.) | 1992 |
| 91 | Michael Barber, Clemson (Tenn.-Chatt.) | 1992 |
| 91 | Cassius Ware, Mississippi (Auburn) | 1992 |

*1993 NCAA FOOTBALL*

## Field Goals

| Yds. | Player, Team (Opponent) | Year |
|---|---|---|
| 67 | Joe Williams, Wichita St. (Southern Ill.) | 1978 |
| 67 | Steve Little, Arkansas (Texas) | 1977 |
| 67 | Russell Erxleben, Texas (Rice) | 1977 |
| 65 | Tony Franklin, Texas A&M (Baylor) | 1976 |
| 64 | Russell Erxleben, Texas (Oklahoma) | 1977 |
| 64 | Tony Franklin, Texas A&M (Baylor) | 1976 |
| 63 | Morten Andersen, Michigan St. (Ohio St.) | 1981 |
| 63 | Clark Kemble, Colorado St. (Arizona) | 1975 |
| 62† | Jason Hanson, Washington St. (Nevada-Las Vegas) | 1991 |
| 62 | John Diettrich, Ball St. (Ohio) | 1986 |
| 62 | Chip Lohmiller, Minnesota (Iowa) | 1986 |
| 62 | Tom Whelihan, Missouri (Colorado) | 1986 |
| 62 | Dan Christopulos, Wyoming (Colorado St.) | 1977 |
| 62 | Iseed Khoury, North Texas (Richmond) | 1977 |
| 62 | Dave Lawson, Air Force (Iowa St.) | 1975 |
| 61 | Dan Eichloff, Kansas (Ball St.) | 1992 |
| 61 | Mark Porter, Kansas St. (Nebraska) | 1988 |
| 61 | Ralf Mojsiejenko, Michigan St. (Illinois) | 1982 |
| 61 | Steve Little, Arkansas (Tulsa) | 1976 |
| 61 | Wayne Latimer, Virginia Tech (Florida St.) | 1975 |
| 61 | Ray Guy, Southern Miss. (Utah St.) | 1972 |
| 60 | Joe Nedney, San Jose St. (Wyoming) | 1992 |
| 60 | Don Shafer, Southern Cal (Notre Dame) | 1986 |
| 60 | Steve DeLine, Colorado St. (Air Force) | 1985 |
| 60 | Kevin Butler, Georgia (Clemson) | 1984 |
| 60 | Chris Perkins, Florida (Tulane) | 1984 |
| 60 | Fuad Reveiz, Tennessee (Georgia Tech) | 1982 |
| 60 | Russell Erxleben, Texas (Texas Tech) | 1977 |
| 60 | Bubba Hicks, Baylor (Rice) | 1975 |
| 60 | Dave Lawson, Air Force (Colorado) | 1974 |
| 60 | Tony Di Rienzo, Oklahoma (Kansas) | 1973 |
| 60 | Bill McClard, Arkansas (Southern Methodist) | 1970 |

† *Longest collegiate field goal without use of a kicking tee. Also longest field goal with narrower (18'6")
goal posts.*

### LIST OF UNDERCLASSMEN WHO WERE CERTIFIED FOR
### THE 1992 NATIONAL FOOTBALL LEAGUE DRAFT

Patrick Akos, Vanderbilt, TE; Richie Anderson, Penn St., RB; Patrick Bates, Texas A&M, DB; Keith Battle, North Caro. St., LB; Jerome Bettis, Notre Dame, FB; Drew Bledsoe, Washington St., QB; Phillip Bobo, Washington St., WR; Derek Brown, Nebraska, RB; Tom Carter, Notre Dame, DB; Don Cheney, South Caro., WR; Curtis Conway, Southern Cal, WR/KR; Russell Copeland, Memphis St., WR; Sean Dawkins, California, WR; Thomas England, Winston-Salem, WR; Reginald Gillard, Grambling, WR; Roger Harper, Ohio St., DB; Andre Hastings, Georgia, WR; Garrison Hearst, Georgia, RB; Othello Henderson, UCLA, DB; Billy Joe Hobert, Washington, QB; Marvin Jones, Florida St., LB; Michael McClendon, North Ala., LB; Natrone Means, North Caro., RB; Dean Noel, Delaware, RB; Sterling Palmer, Florida St., LB; Marvin Patton, Texas A&I, RB; Mike Reid, North Caro. St., DB; Leonard Renfro, Colorado, DT; Lester Ridley, Iowa St., DB; Kelly Rush, Florida St., DE; Robert Smith, Ohio St., RB; Walter Tate, Auburn, DL; Charles Thompson, Central St. (Ohio), QB; Olanda Truitt, Mississippi St., WR; Kevin Williams, Miami (Fla.), WR/KR; Ronald Williams, Clemson, RB; James Willis, Auburn, LB; Frank Wycheck, Maryland, TE.

# TEAM CHAMPIONS

## ANNUAL OFFENSE CHAMPIONS

| Year | Total Offense | Avg. | Rushing | Avg. | Passing | Avg. |
|---|---|---|---|---|---|---|
| 1937 | Colorado | 375.4 | Colorado | 310.0 | Arkansas | 185.0 |
| 1938 | Fordham | 341.6 | Fordham | 297.1 | Texas Christian | 164.1 |
| 1939 | Ohio St. | 309.3 | Wake Forest | 290.3 | Texas Christian | 148.5 |
| 1940 | Lafayette | 368.2 | Lafayette | 306.4 | Cornell | 186.3 |
| 1941 | Duke | 372.2 | Missouri | 307.7 | Arizona | 177.7 |
| 1942 | Georgia | 429.5 | Hardin-Simmons | 307.4 | Tulsa | 233.9 |
| 1943 | Notre Dame | 418.0 | Notre Dame | 313.7 | Brown | 133.1 |
| 1944 | Tulsa | 434.7 | Army | 298.6 | Tulsa | 206.3 |
| 1945 | Army | 462.7 | Army | 359.8 | St. Mary's (Cal.) | 161.3 |
| 1946 | Notre Dame | 441.3 | Notre Dame | 340.1 | Nevada | 198.1 |

| Year | Total Offense | Avg. | Rushing | Avg. | Passing | Avg. |
|------|---------------|------|---------|------|---------|------|
| 1947 | Michigan | 412.7 | Detroit Mercy | 319.7 | Michigan | 173.9 |
| 1948 | Nevada | 487.0 | UTEP | 378.3 | Nevada | 255.0 |
| 1949 | Notre Dame | 434.8 | UTEP | 333.2 | Fordham | 183.4 |
| 1950 | Arizona St. | 470.4 | Arizona St. | 347.0 | Southern Methodist | 214.6 |
| 1951 | Tulsa | 480.1 | Arizona St. | 334.8 | Loyola (Cal.) | 210.6 |
| 1952 | Tulsa | 466.6 | Tulsa | 321.5 | Fordham | 225.8 |
| 1953 | Cincinnati | 409.5 | Oklahoma | 306.9 | Stanford | 179.5 |
| 1954 | Army | 448.7 | Army | 322.0 | Purdue | 177.3 |
| 1955 | Oklahoma | 410.7 | Oklahoma | 328.9 | Navy | 185.1 |
| 1956 | Oklahoma | 481.7 | Oklahoma | 391.0 | Washington St. | 206.8 |
| 1957 | Arizona St. | 444.9 | Colorado | 322.4 | Utah | 195.2 |
| 1958 | Iowa | 405.9 | Pacific (Cal.) | 259.6 | Army | 172.2 |
| 1959 | Syracuse | 451.5 | Syracuse | 313.6 | Stanford | 227.8 |
| 1960 | New Mexico St. | 419.6 | Utah St. | 312.0 | Washington St. | 185.5 |
| 1961 | Mississippi | 418.7 | New Mexico St. | 299.1 | Wisconsin | 188.4 |
| 1962 | Arizona St. | 384.4 | Ohio St. | 278.9 | Tulsa | 199.3 |
| 1963 | Utah St. | 395.3 | Nebraska | 262.6 | Tulsa | 244.8 |
| 1964 | Tulsa | 461.8 | Syracuse | 251.0 | Tulsa | 317.9 |
| 1965 | Tulsa | 427.8 | Nebraska | 290.0 | Tulsa | 346.4 |
| 1966 | Houston | 437.2 | Harvard | 269.0 | Tulsa | 272.0 |
| 1967 | Houston | 427.9 | Houston | 270.9 | UTEP | 301.1 |
| 1968 | Houston | 562.0 | Houston | 361.7 | Cincinnati | 335.8 |
| 1969 | San Diego St. | 532.2 | Texas | 363.0 | San Diego St. | 374.2 |
| 1970 | Arizona St. | 514.5 | Texas | 374.5 | Auburn | 288.5 |
| 1971 | Oklahoma | 566.5 | Oklahoma | *472.4 | San Diego St. | 251.4 |
| 1972 | Arizona St. | 516.5 | Oklahoma | 368.8 | Virginia Tech | 304.4 |
| 1973 | Arizona St. | 565.5 | UCLA | 400.3 | San Diego St. | 305.0 |
| 1974 | Oklahoma | 507.7 | Oklahoma | 438.8 | Colorado St. | 261.8 |
| 1975 | California | 458.5 | Arkansas St. | 340.5 | San Diego St. | 291.3 |
| 1976 | Michigan | 448.1 | Michigan | 362.6 | Brigham Young | 307.8 |
| 1977 | Colgate | 486.1 | Oklahoma | 328.9 | Brigham Young | 341.6 |
| 1978 | Nebraska | 501.4 | Oklahoma | 427.5 | Southern Methodist | 276.2 |
| 1979 | Brigham Young | 521.4 | East Caro. | 368.5 | Brigham Young | 368.3 |
| 1980 | Brigham Young | 535.0 | Nebraska | 378.3 | Brigham Young | 409.8 |
| 1981 | Arizona St. | 498.7 | Oklahoma | 334.3 | Brigham Young | 356.9 |
| 1982 | Nebraska | 518.6 | Nebraska | 394.3 | Long Beach St. | 326.8 |
| 1983 | Brigham Young | 584.2 | Nebraska | 401.7 | Brigham Young | 381.2 |
| 1984 | Brigham Young | 486.5 | Army | 345.3 | Brigham Young | 346.2 |
| 1985 | Brigham Young | 500.2 | Nebraska | 374.3 | Brigham Young | 354.5 |
| 1986 | San Jose St. | 481.4 | Oklahoma | 404.7 | San Jose St. | 312.5 |
| 1987 | Oklahoma | 499.7 | Oklahoma | 428.8 | San Jose St. | 338.1 |
| 1988 | Utah | 526.8 | Nebraska | 382.3 | Utah | 395.9 |
| 1989 | Houston | *624.9 | Nebraska | 375.3 | Houston | *511.3 |
| 1990 | Houston | 586.8 | Northern Ill. | 344.6 | Houston | 473.9 |
| 1991 | Fresno St. | 541.9 | Nebraska | 353.2 | Houston | 372.8 |
| 1992 | Houston | 519.5 | Nebraska | 328.2 | Houston | 407.1 |

* Record.

## SCORING OFFENSE

| Year | Team | Avg. | Year | Team | Avg. | Year | Team | Avg. |
|------|------|------|------|------|------|------|------|------|
| 1937 | Colorado | 31.0 | 1957 | Arizona St. | 39.7 | 1977 | Grambling | 42.0 |
| 1938 | Dartmouth | 28.2 | 1958 | Rutgers | 33.4 | 1978 | Oklahoma | 40.0 |
| 1939 | Utah | 28.4 | 1959 | Syracuse | 39.0 | 1979 | Brigham Young | 40.6 |
| 1940 | Boston College | 32.0 | 1960 | New Mexico St. | 37.4 | 1980 | Brigham Young | 46.7 |
| 1941 | Texas | 33.8 | 1961 | Utah St. | 38.7 | 1981 | Brigham Young | 38.7 |
| 1942 | Tulsa | 42.7 | 1962 | Wisconsin | 31.7 | 1982 | Nebraska | 41.1 |
| 1943 | Duke | 37.2 | 1963 | Utah St. | 31.7 | 1983 | Nebraska | 52.0 |
| 1944 | Army | *56.0 | 1964 | Tulsa | 38.4 | 1984 | Boston College | 36.7 |
| 1945 | Army | 45.8 | 1965 | Arkansas | 32.4 | 1985 | Fresno St. | 39.1 |
| 1946 | Georgia | 37.2 | 1966 | Notre Dame | 36.2 | 1986 | Oklahoma | 42.4 |
| 1947 | Michigan | 38.3 | 1967 | UTEP | 35.9 | 1987 | Oklahoma | 43.5 |
| 1948 | Nevada | 44.4 | 1968 | Houston | 42.5 | 1988 | Oklahoma St. | 47.5 |
| 1949 | Army | 39.3 | 1969 | San Diego St. | 46.4 | 1989 | Houston | 53.5 |
| 1950 | Princeton | 38.8 | 1970 | Texas | 41.2 | 1990 | Houston | 46.5 |
| 1951 | Maryland | 39.2 | 1971 | Oklahoma | 44.9 | 1991 | Fresno St. | 44.2 |
| 1952 | Oklahoma | 40.7 | 1972 | Arizona St. | 46.6 | 1992 | Fresno St. | 40.5 |
| 1953 | Texas Tech. | 38.9 | 1973 | Arizona St. | 44.6 | * Record. | | |
| 1954 | UCLA | 40.8 | 1974 | Oklahoma | 43.0 | | | |
| 1955 | Oklahoma | 36.5 | 1975 | Ohio St. | 34.0 | | | |
| 1956 | Oklahoma | 46.6 | 1976 | Michigan | 38.7 | | | |

*1993 NCAA FOOTBALL*

# ANNUAL TEAM DEFENSE CHAMPIONS

| Year | Total Defense | Avg. | Rushing | Avg. | Passing | $Avg. |
|------|---------------|------|---------|------|---------|-------|
| 1937 | Santa Clara | *69.9 | Santa Clara | 25.3 | Harvard | 31.0 |
| 1938 | Alabama | 77.9 | Oklahoma | 43.3 | Penn St. | *13.1 |
| 1939 | Texas A&M | 76.3 | Texas A&M | 41.5 | Kansas | 34.1 |
| 1940 | Navy | 96.0 | Texas A&M | 44.3 | Harvard | 33.3 |
| 1941 | Duquesne | 110.6 | Duquesne | 56.0 | Purdue | 27.1 |
| 1942 | Texas | 117.3 | Boston College | 48.9 | Harvard | 45.4 |
| 1943 | Duke | 121.7 | Duke | 39.4 | North Caro. | 36.5 |
| 1944 | Virginia | 96.8 | Navy | 53.8 | Michigan St. | 26.7 |
| 1945 | Alabama | 109.9 | Alabama | 33.9 | Holy Cross | 37.7 |
| 1946 | Notre Dame | 141.7 | Oklahoma | 58.0 | Holy Cross | 53.7 |
| 1947 | Penn St. | 76.8 | Penn St. | *17.0 | North Caro. St. | 39.3 |
| 1948 | Georgia Tech | 151.3 | Georgia Tech | 74.9 | Northwestern | 54.1 |
| 1949 | Kentucky | 153.8 | Oklahoma | 55.6 | Miami (Fla.) | 54.7 |
| 1950 | Wake Forest | 163.2 | Ohio St. | 64.0 | Tennessee | 67.5 |
| 1951 | Wisconsin | 154.8 | San Francisco | 51.6 | Wash. & Lee | 67.9 |
| 1952 | Tennessee | 166.7 | Michigan St. | 83.9 | Virginia | 50.3 |
| 1953 | Cincinnati | 184.3 | Maryland | 83.9 | Richmond | 40.3 |
| 1954 | Mississippi | 172.3 | UCLA | 73.2 | Alabama | 45.8 |
| 1955 | Army | 160.7 | Maryland | 75.9 | Florida | 42.0 |
| 1956 | Miami (Fla.) | 189.4 | Miami (Fla.) | 106.9 | Villanova | 43.8 |
| 1957 | Auburn | 133.0 | Auburn | 67.4 | Georgia Tech | 33.4 |
| 1958 | Auburn | 157.5 | Auburn | 79.6 | Iowa St. | 39.0 |
| 1959 | Syracuse | 96.2 | Syracuse | 19.3 | Alabama | 45.7 |
| 1960 | Wyoming | 149.6 | Wyoming | 82.4 | Iowa St. | 30.2 |
| 1961 | Alabama | 132.6 | Utah St. | 50.8 | Pennsylvania | 56.9 |
| 1962 | Mississippi | 142.2 | Minnesota | 52.2 | New Mexico | 56.8 |
| 1963 | Southern Miss. | 131.2 | Mississippi | 77.3 | UTEP | 43.8 |
| 1964 | Auburn | 164.7 | Washington | 61.3 | Kent | 53.6 |
| 1965 | Southern Miss. | 161.1 | Michigan St. | 45.6 | Toledo | 69.8 |
| 1966 | Southern Miss. | 163.7 | Wyoming | 38.5 | Toledo | 70.4 |
| 1967 | Nebraska | 157.6 | Wyoming | 42.3 | Nebraska | 90.1 |
| 1968 | Wyoming | 206.8 | Arizona St. | 57.0 | Kent | 107.6 |
| 1969 | Toledo | 209.1 | Louisiana St. | 38.9 | Dayton | 90.0 |
| 1970 | Toledo | 185.8 | Louisiana St. | 52.2 | Toledo | 77.8 |
| 1971 | Toledo | 179.5 | Michigan | 63.3 | Texas Tech | 60.1 |
| 1972 | Louisville | 202.5 | Louisville | 82.1 | Vanderbilt | 80.3 |
| 1973 | Miami (Ohio) | 177.4 | Miami (Ohio) | 77.0 | Nebraska | 39.9 |
| 1974 | Notre Dame | 195.2 | Notre Dame | 102.8 | Iowa | 65.7 |
| 1975 | Texas A&M | 183.8 | Texas A&M | 80.3 | Va. Military | 51.1 |
| 1976 | Rutgers | 179.2 | Rutgers | 83.9 | Western Mich. | 78.5 |
| 1977 | Jackson St. | 207.0 | Jackson St. | 67.8 | Tennessee St. | 67.9 |
| 1978 | Penn St. | 203.9 | Penn St. | 54.5 | Boston College | 65.1 |
| 1979 | Yale | 175.4 | Yale | 75.0 | Western Caro. | 77.5 |
| 1980 | Pittsburgh | 205.5 | Pittsburgh | 65.3 | Kansas St. | 91.4 |
| 1981 | Pittsburgh | 224.8 | Pittsburgh | 62.4 | Nebraska | 100.1 |
| 1982 | Arizona St. | 228.9 | Virginia Tech | 49.5 | Missouri | 123.5 |
| 1983 | Texas | 212.0 | Virginia Tech | 69.4 | Ohio | 115.3 |
| 1984 | Nebraska | 203.3 | Oklahoma | 68.8 | Texas Tech | 114.8 |
| 1985 | Oklahoma | 193.5 | UCLA | 70.3 | Oklahoma | 103.6 |
| 1986 | Oklahoma | 169.6 | Oklahoma | 60.7 | Oklahoma | 108.9 |
| 1987 | Oklahoma | 208.1 | Michigan St. | 61.5 | Oklahoma | 102.4 |
| 1988 | Auburn | 218.1 | Auburn | 63.2 | Baylor | 117.8 |
| 1989 | Miami (Fla.) | 216.5 | Southern Cal | 61.5 | Kansas St. | 129.3 |
| 1990 | Clemson | 216.9 | Washington | 66.8 | Alabama | 82.47 |
| 1991 | Texas A&M | 222.4 | Clemson | 53.4 | Texas | 77.37 |
| 1992 | Alabama | 194.2 | Alabama | 55.0 | Western Mich. | 83.16 |

*Record.  $ Beginning in 1990, ranked on passing-efficiency defense rating points instead of per-game yardage allowed.*

## SCORING DEFENSE

| Year | Team | Avg. | Year | Team | Avg. | Year | Team | Avg. |
|------|------|------|------|------|------|------|------|------|
| 1937 | Santa Clara | 1.1 | 1942 | Tulsa | 3.2 | 1947 | Penn St. | 3.0 |
| 1938 | Duke | **0.0 | 1943 | Duke | 3.8 | 1948 | Michigan | 4.9 |
| 1939 | Tennessee | **0.0 | 1944 | Army | 3.9 | 1949 | Kentucky | 4.8 |
| 1940 | Tennessee | 2.6 | 1945 | St. Mary's (Cal.) | 4.0 | 1950 | Army | 4.4 |
| 1941 | Duquesne | 2.9 | 1946 | Notre Dame | 2.7 | 1951 | Wisconsin | 5.9 |

*Division I-A Team Champions*

| Year | Team | Avg. | Year | Team | Avg. | Year | Team | Avg. |
|------|------|------|------|------|------|------|------|------|
| 1952 | Southern Cal | 4.7 | 1967 | Oklahoma | 6.8 | 1982 | Arkansas | 10.5 |
| 1953 | Maryland | 3.1 | 1968 | Georgia | 9.8 | 1983 | Virginia Tech | 8.3 |
| 1954 | UCLA | 4.4 | 1969 | Arkansas | 7.6 | 1984 | Nebraska | 9.5 |
| 1955 | Georgia Tech | 4.6 | 1970 | Dartmouth | 4.7 | 1985 | Michigan | 6.8 |
| 1956 | Georgia Tech | 3.3 | 1971 | Michigan | 6.4 | 1986 | Oklahoma | 6.6 |
| 1957 | Auburn | 2.8 | 1972 | Michigan | 5.2 | 1987 | Oklahoma | 7.5 |
| 1958 | Oklahoma | 4.9 | 1973 | Ohio St. | 4.3 | 1988 | Auburn | 7.2 |
| 1959 | Mississippi | 2.1 | 1974 | Michigan | 6.8 | 1989 | Miami (Fla.) | 9.3 |
| 1960 | Louisiana St. | 5.0 | 1975 | Alabama | 6.0 | 1990 | Central Mich. | 8.9 |
| 1961 | Alabama | 2.2 | 1976 | Michigan | 7.4 | 1991 | Miami (Fla.) | 9.1 |
| 1962 | Louisiana St. | 3.4 | | Rutgers | 7.4 | 1992 | Arizona | 8.9 |
| 1963 | Mississippi | 3.7 | 1977 | North Caro. | 7.4 | | | |
| 1964 | Arkansas | 5.7 | 1978 | Ball St. | 7.5 | | | |
| 1965 | Michigan St. | 6.2 | 1979 | Alabama | 5.3 | | | |
| 1966 | Alabama | 3.7 | 1980 | Florida St. | 7.7 | | | |
| | | | 1981 | Southern Miss. | 8.1 | | | |

*\* Record tied.*

## OTHER ANNUAL TEAM CHAMPIONS

| Year | Punting | #Avg. | Punt Returns | Avg. | Kickoff Returns | Avg. |
|------|---------|-------|--------------|------|-----------------|------|
| 1937 | Iowa | 43.0 | — | | — | |
| 1938 | Arkansas | 41.6 | — | | — | |
| 1939 | Auburn | 43.3 | UCLA | 16.3 | Wake Forest | 32.9 |
| 1940 | Auburn | 42.3 | UCLA | 16.2 | Minnesota | 36.4 |
| 1941 | Clemson | 42.3 | Colgate | 18.7 | Tulane | 32.1 |
| 1942 | Tulsa | 41.3 | — | | — | |
| 1943 | Michigan | 39.2 | Columbia | 20.9 | Navy | 28.8 |
| 1944 | UCLA | 43.0 | New York U. | 22.0 | — | |
| 1945 | Miami (Fla.) | 39.9 | — | | — | |
| 1946 | UTEP | 41.2 | Columbia | 16.8 | William & Mary | 31.7 |
| 1947 | Duke | 41.9 | Florida | 19.7 | Southern Methodist | 31.4 |
| 1948 | North Caro. | 44.0 | Oklahoma | †22.4 | Wyoming | 27.4 |
| 1949 | Furman | 44.7 | Wichita St. | 18.3 | Army | 34.1 |
| 1950 | Colorado | 45.1 | Texas A&M | 17.6 | Wyoming | 29.3 |
| 1951 | Alabama | 41.8 | Holy Cross | 17.7 | Marquette | 25.0 |
| 1952 | Colorado | 43.3 | Arizona St. | ‡25.2 | Wake Forest | 25.1 |
| 1953 | Georgia | 41.2 | Kansas St. | 23.8 | Texas Tech | 23.8 |
| 1954 | New Mexico | 42.6 | Miami (Fla.) | 19.7 | Arizona | 26.1 |
| 1955 | Michigan St. | 41.2 | North Caro. | 22.5 | Southern Cal | 25.8 |
| 1956 | Colorado St. | 42.2 | Cincinnati | 17.7 | Georgia Tech | 24.6 |
| 1957 | Utah St. | 40.1 | North Texas | 17.5 | Notre Dame | 27.6 |
| 1958 | Georgia | 41.9 | Notre Dame | 17.6 | Tulsa | 25.8 |
| 1959 | Brigham Young | 43.2 | Wyoming | 16.6 | Auburn | 25.8 |
| 1960 | Georgia | 43.7 | Arizona | 17.7 | Yale | 26.7 |
| 1961 | Arizona St. | 42.1 | Memphis St. | 17.4 | Harvard | 25.9 |
| 1962 | Wyoming | 42.6 | West Tex. St. | 18.4 | Alabama | 28.9 |
| 1963 | Southern Methodist | 41.4 | Army | 18.1 | Memphis St. | 27.7 |
| 1964 | Mississippi | 44.1 | UTEP | 16.9 | Cornell | 27.1 |
| 1965 | Arizona St. | 44.0 | Georgia Tech | 23.0 | Dartmouth | 28.7 |
| 1966 | Tennessee | 43.4 | Brown | 21.0 | Notre Dame | 29.6 |
| 1967 | Houston | 44.4 | Memphis St. | 16.3 | Air Force | 25.3 |
| 1968 | Wichita St. | 43.2 | Army | 17.4 | Louisville | 25.7 |
| 1969 | Georgia | 43.5 | Davidson | 21.3 | Brigham Young | 28.7 |
| 1970 | Utah | 45.0 | Wichita St. | 28.5 | South Caro. | 26.5 |
| 1971 | Utah | 46.7 | Mississippi St. | 20.8 | Miami (Fla.) | 24.1 |
| 1972 | Southern Miss. | 45.1 | Georgia Tech | 17.3 | Michigan | 26.9 |
| 1973 | Wake Forest | 44.1 | Utah | 23.4 | Rice | +27.5 |
| 1974 | Ohio St. | 44.9 | Auburn | 16.6 | Southern Cal | 25.7 |
| 1975 | Ohio St. | 44.1 | New Mexico St. | 15.3 | Maryland | $29.5 |
| 1976 | Colorado St. | **44.4 | Wichita St. | 15.0 | South Caro. | 27.0 |
| 1977 | Mississippi | 43.4 | Grambling | 16.9 | Miami (Ohio) | 24.6 |
| 1978 | Texas | 41.7 | McNeese St. | 15.7 | Utah St. | 26.7 |
| 1979 | Mississippi | 42.4 | Tennessee St. | 16.9 | Brigham Young | 26.3 |
| 1980 | Florida St. | 42.6 | Georgia | 16.5 | Oklahoma | 33.2 |
| 1981 | Michigan | 43.1 | North Caro. St. | 13.4 | Iowa | 29.1 |

| Year | Punting | #Avg. | Punt Returns | Avg. | Kickoff Returns | Avg. |
|------|---------|-------|--------------|------|-----------------|------|
| 1982 | Vanderbilt | 42.1 | Auburn | 15.8 | Utah | 25.5 |
| 1983 | Brigham Young | *45.0 | San Diego St. | 17.0 | Tennessee | 28.8 |
| 1984 | Ohio St. | 44.0 | Florida | 13.8 | Texas Tech | 25.2 |
| 1985 | Colorado | 43.6 | Utah | 20.7 | Air Force | 27.0 |
| 1986 | Michigan | 43.1 | Arizona St. | 17.9 | Clemson | 26.1 |
| 1987 | Ohio St. | 40.7 | Stanford | 15.4 | Oklahoma St. | 23.7 |
| 1988 | Brigham Young | 42.9 | Florida St. | 15.5 | Notre Dame | 24.2 |
| 1989 | Colorado | 43.8 | Ohio | 18.2 | Colorado | 26.1 |
| 1990 | Pittsburgh | 41.2 | Michigan | 15.6 | Nebraska | 27.8 |
| 1991 | Texas Tech | 40.6 | Alabama | 16.9 | New Mexico St. | 25.2 |
| 1992 | Nebraska | 41.7 | Northwestern | 21.8 | Florida St. | 30.3 |

*# Beginning in 1975, ranked on net punting average.  \* Record for net punting average, minimum of 40 punts.  + Record for minimum of 35 kickoff returns.  $ Record for minimum of 25 kickoff returns.  † Record for minimum of 30 punt returns.  ‡ Record for minimum of 15 punt returns.*

# ANNUAL TOUGHEST-SCHEDULE LEADERS

The NCAA's toughest-schedule program (which began in 1977) is based on what all Division I-A opponents did against other Division I-A teams when not playing the team in question. Games against non-I-A teams are deleted, and nine intradivision games are required to qualify. (Bowl games are not included.) The leaders:

| Year | Team (+Record) | ¢Opponents' Record W | L | T | Pct. |
|------|----------------|------|------|------|------|
| 1977 | Miami (Fla.) (3-8-0) | 66 | 42 | 2 | .609 |
|      | Penn St. (10-1-0) | 61 | 39 | 2 | .608 |
| 1978 | Notre Dame (8-3-0) | 77 | 31 | 2 | .709 |
|      | Southern Cal (11-1-0) | 79 | 40 | 1 | .663 |
| 1979 | UCLA (5-6-0) | 71 | 37 | 2 | .655 |
|      | South Caro. (8-3-0) | 69 | 38 | 2 | .642 |
| 1980 | Florida St. (10-1-0) | 70 | 34 | 0 | .673 |
|      | Miami (Fla.) (8-3-0) | 64 | 33 | 1 | .658 |
| 1981 | Penn St. (9-2-0) | 71 | 33 | 2 | .679 |
|      | Temple (5-5-0) | 71 | 33 | 2 | .669 |
| 1982 | Penn St. (10-1-0) | 63 | 34 | 2 | .646 |
|      | Kentucky (0-10-1) | 63 | 34 | 5 | .642 |
| 1983 | Auburn (10-1-0) | 70 | 31 | 3 | .688 |
|      | UCLA (6-4-1) | 68 | 37 | 5 | .641 |
| 1984 | Penn St. (6-5-0) | 58 | 36 | 3 | .613 |
|      | Georgia (7-4-0) | 60 | 39 | 4 | .602 |
| 1985 | Notre Dame (5-6-0) | 72 | 29 | 3 | .707 |
|      | Alabama (8-2-1) | 65 | 32 | 5 | .662 |
| 1986 | Florida (6-5-0) | 64 | 29 | 3 | .682 |
|      | Louisiana St. (9-2-0) | 67 | 36 | 2 | .648 |
| 1987 | Notre Dame (8-3-0) | 71 | 34 | 2 | .673 |
|      | Florida St. (10-1-0) | 60 | 29 | 4 | .667 |

## TOP 10 TOUGHEST-SCHEDULE LEADERS FOR 1988-92

**1988**

| Team | ¢Opp. Record | Pct. |
|------|--------------|------|
| 1. Virginia Tech | 74-36-0 | .673 |
| 2. Arizona | 70-37-3 | .650 |
| 3. North Caro. | 69-38-3 | .641 |
| 4. Florida St. | 68-38-1 | .640 |
| 5. Southern Cal | 68-39-4 | .631 |
| 6. Oregon St. | 69-41-2 | .625 |
| 7. Maryland | 67-40-3 | .623 |
| 8. Miami (Fla.) | 68-41-2 | .622 |
| 9. Navy | 66-41-1 | .616 |
| 10. East Caro. | 66-43-0 | .606 |

**1989**

| Team | ¢Opp. Record | Pct. |
|------|--------------|------|
| 1. Notre Dame | 74-38-4 | .655 |
| 2. Louisiana St. | 67-41-1 | .619 |
| 3. Colorado St. | 67-42-3 | .612 |
| 4. Florida St. | 65-41-2 | .611 |
| 4. Texas | 65-41-2 | .611 |
| 6. South Caro. | 57-36-2 | .611 |
| 7. Auburn | 64-42-1 | .603 |
| 8. Oregon St. | 64-42-3 | .601 |
| 9. Tennessee | 62-41-2 | .600 |
| 9. Maryland | 62-41-2 | .600 |

*Division I-A Team Champions*

| 1990 | | | | 1991 | | |
|------|------|-----|---|------|------|-----|
| **Team** | **¢Opp.**<br>**Record** | **Pct.** | | **Team** | **¢Opp.**<br>**Record** | **Pct.** |
| 1. Colorado | 72-42-3 | .628 | | 1. South Caro. | 57-31-2 | .644 |
| 2. Stanford | 67-39-4 | .627 | | 2. Florida | 66-37-1 | .639 |
| 3. Purdue | 60-36-3 | .621 | | 3. Louisiana St. | 60-38-0 | .612 |
| 4. Notre Dame | 63-38-5 | .618 | | 4. Florida St. | 64-40-3 | .612 |
| 5. Texas | 65-40-3 | .616 | | 5. Maryland | 62-39-3 | .611 |
| 6. Miami (Fla.) | 65-41-5 | .608 | | 6. Southern Cal | 67-43-0 | .609 |
| 7. Virginia Tech | 59-38-3 | .605 | | 7. Oklahoma St. | 62-40-3 | .605 |
| 8. Georgia | 62-41-2 | .600 | | 8. Northern Ill. | 44-30-4 | .590 |
| 9. Maryland | 60-40-2 | .598 | | 9. Tennessee | 63-44-0 | .589 |
| 10. Penn St. | 63-43-4 | .591 | | 10. Houston | 61-43-2 | .585 |

**1992**

| **Team** | **¢Opp.**<br>**Record** | **Pct.** |
|------|------|-----|
| 1. Southern Cal | 68-38-4 | .636 |
| 2. Stanford | 73-43-4 | .625 |
| 3. Florida | 72-46-1 | .609 |
| 4. Northwestern | 64-41-7 | .603 |
| 5. Arizona | 64-43-1 | .597 |
| 6. Missouri | 55-37-5 | .593 |
| 7. Arkansas | 58-40-0 | .592 |
| 8. Oregon St. | 65-46-0 | .586 |
| Louisiana St. | 64-45-2 | .586 |
| 10. Iowa | 65-46-7 | .581 |

+ Not including bowl games.   ¢ When not playing the team listed.

# ANNUAL MOST-IMPROVED TEAMS

| Year | Team | $Games<br>Improved | From | | To | | Coach |
|------|------|------|------|------|------|------|------|
| 1937 | California | 4½ | 1936 | 6-5-0 | 1937 | *10-0-1 | Stub Allison |
|      | Syracuse | 4½ | 1936 | 1-7-0 | 1937 | 5-2-1 | #Ossie Solem |
| 1938 | Texas Christian | 5½ | 1937 | 4-4-2 | 1938 | *11-0-0 | Dutch Meyer |
| 1939 | Texas A&M | 5½ | 1938 | 4-4-1 | 1939 | *11-0-0 | Homer Norton |
| 1940 | Stanford | 8 | 1939 | 1-7-1 | 1940 | *10-0-0 | #Clark Shaughnessy |
| 1941 | Vanderbilt | 4½ | 1940 | 3-6-1 | 1941 | 8-2-0 | Red Sanders |
| 1942 | Utah St. | 5½ | 1941 | 0-8-0 | 1942 | 6-3-1 | Dick Romney |
| 1943 | Purdue | 8 | 1942 | 1-8-0 | 1943 | 9-0-0 | Elmer Burnham |
| 1944 | Ohio St. | 6 | 1943 | 3-6-0 | 1944 | 9-0-0 | #Carroll Widdoes |
| 1945 | Miami (Fla.) | 7 | 1944 | 1-7-1 | 1945 | *9-1-1 | Jack Harding |
| 1946 | Illinois | 5 | 1945 | 2-6-1 | 1946 | *8-2-0 | Ray Eliot |
|      | Kentucky | 5 | 1945 | 2-8-0 | 1946 | 7-3-0 | #Paul "Bear" Bryant |
| 1947 | California | 6½ | 1946 | 2-7-0 | 1947 | 9-1-0 | #Lynn "Pappy" Waldorf |
| 1948 | Clemson | 6 | 1947 | 4-5-0 | 1948 | *11-0-0 | Frank Howard |
| 1949 | Tulsa | 5 | 1948 | 0-9-1 | 1949 | 5-4-1 | J. O. Brothers |
| 1950 | Brigham Young | 5 | 1949 | 0-11-0 | 1950 | 4-5-1 | Chick Atkinson |
|      | Texas A&M | 5 | 1949 | 1-8-1 | 1950 | *7-4-0 | Harry Stiteler |
| 1951 | Georgia Tech | 6 | 1950 | 5-6-0 | 1951 | *11-0-1 | Bobby Dodd |
| 1952 | Alabama | 4½ | 1951 | 5-6-0 | 1952 | *10-2-0 | Harold "Red" Drew |
| 1953 | Texas Tech | 7 | 1952 | 3-7-1 | 1953 | *11-1-0 | DeWitt Weaver |
| 1954 | Denver | 5 | 1953 | 3-5-2 | 1954 | 9-1-0 | Bob Blackman |
| 1955 | Texas A&M | 6½ | 1954 | 1-9-0 | 1955 | 7-2-1 | Paul "Bear" Bryant |
| 1956 | Iowa | 5 | 1955 | 3-5-1 | 1956 | *9-1-0 | Forest Evashevski |
| 1957 | Notre Dame | 5 | 1956 | 2-8-0 | 1957 | 7-3-0 | Terry Brennan |
|      | Texas | 5 | 1956 | 1-9-0 | 1957 | +6-4-1 | #Darrell Royal |
| 1958 | Air Force | 6 | 1957 | 3-6-1 | 1958 | ‡9-0-1 | #Ben Martin |
| 1959 | Washington | 6½ | 1958 | 3-7-0 | 1959 | *10-1-0 | Jim Owens |
| 1960 | Minnesota | 5½ | 1959 | 2-7-0 | 1960 | +8-2-0 | Murray Warmath |
|      | North Caro. St. | 5½ | 1959 | 1-9-0 | 1960 | 6-3-1 | Earle Edwards |
| 1961 | Villanova | 6 | 1960 | 2-8-0 | 1961 | *8-2-0 | Alex Bell |
| 1962 | Southern Cal | 6 | 1961 | 4-5-1 | 1962 | *11-0-0 | John McKay |
| 1963 | Illinois | 6 | 1962 | 2-7-0 | 1963 | *8-1-1 | Pete Elliott |
| 1964 | Notre Dame | 6½ | 1963 | 2-7-0 | 1964 | 9-1-0 | #Ara Parseghian |
| 1965 | UTEP | 6½ | 1964 | 0-8-2 | 1965 | *8-3-0 | #Bobby Dobbs |
| 1966 | Dayton | 6½ | 1965 | 1-8-1 | 1966 | 8-2-0 | John McVay |

| Year | Team | $Games Improved | From | | To | | Coach |
|------|------|-----------------|------|------|------|------|--------|
| 1967 | Indiana | 7 | 1966 | 1-8-1 | 1967 | +9-2-0 | John Pont |
| 1968 | Arkansas | 5 | 1967 | 4-5-1 | 1968 | *10-1-0 | Frank Broyles |
| 1969 | UCLA | 5½ | 1968 | 3-7-0 | 1969 | 8-1-1 | Tommy Prothro |
| 1970 | Tulsa | 5 | 1969 | 1-9-0 | 1970 | 6-4-0 | #Claude Gibson |
| 1971 | Army | 5 | 1970 | 1-9-1 | 1971 | 6-4-0 | Tom Cahill |
| | Georgia | 5 | 1970 | 5-5-0 | 1971 | *11-1-0 | Vince Dooley |
| 1972 | Pacific (Cal.) | 5 | 1971 | 3-8-0 | 1972 | 8-3-0 | Chester Caddas |
| | Southern Cal | 5 | 1971 | 6-4-1 | 1972 | *12-0-0 | John McKay |
| | UCLA | 5 | 1971 | 2-7-1 | 1972 | 8-3-0 | Pepper Rodgers |
| 1973 | Pittsburgh | 5 | 1972 | 1-10-0 | 1973 | +6-5-1 | #Johnny Majors |
| 1974 | Baylor | 5½ | 1973 | 2-9-0 | 1974 | +8-4-0 | Grant Teaff |
| 1975 | Arizona St. | 5 | 1974 | 7-5-0 | 1975 | *12-0-0 | Frank Kush |
| 1976 | Houston | 7 | 1975 | 2-8-0 | 1976 | *10-2-0 | Bill Yeoman |
| 1977 | Miami (Ohio) | 7 | 1976 | 3-8-0 | 1977 | 10-1-0 | Dick Crum |
| 1978 | Tulsa | 6 | 1977 | 3-8-0 | 1978 | 9-2-0 | John Cooper |
| 1979 | Wake Forest | 6½ | 1978 | 1-10-0 | 1979 | +8-4-0 | John Mackovic |
| 1980 | Florida | 7 | 1979 | 0-10-1 | 1980 | *8-4-0 | Charley Pell |
| 1981 | Clemson | 5½ | 1980 | 6-5-0 | 1981 | *12-0-0 | Danny Ford |
| 1982 | New Mexico | 6 | 1981 | 4-7-1 | 1982 | 10-1-0 | Joe Morrison |
| | Southwestern La. | 6 | 1981 | 1-9-1 | 1982 | 7-3-1 | Sam Robertson |
| 1983 | Kentucky | 5½ | 1982 | 0-10-1 | 1983 | +6-5-1 | Jerry Claiborne |
| | Memphis St. | 5½ | 1982 | 1-10-0 | 1983 | 6-4-1 | Rex Dockery |
| 1984 | Army | 6 | 1983 | 2-9-0 | 1984 | *8-3-1 | Jim Young |
| 1985 | Colorado | 5½ | 1984 | 1-10-0 | 1985 | +7-5-0 | Bill McCartney |
| | Fresno St. | 5½ | 1984 | 6-6-0 | 1985 | *11-0-1 | Jim Sweeney |
| 1986 | San Jose St. | 7 | 1985 | 2-8-1 | 1986 | *10-2-0 | Claude Gilbert |
| 1987 | Syracuse | 6 | 1986 | 5-6-0 | 1987 | ‡11-0-1 | Dick MacPherson |
| 1988 | West Va. | 5 | 1987 | 6-6-0 | 1988 | +11-1-0 | Don Nehlen |
| | Washington St. | 5 | 1987 | 3-7-1 | 1988 | *9-3-0 | Dennis Erickson |
| 1989 | Tennessee | 5½ | 1988 | 5-6-0 | 1989 | *11-1-0 | Johnny Majors |
| 1990 | Temple | 6 | 1989 | 1-10-0 | 1990 | 7-4-0 | Jerry Berndt |
| 1991 | Tulsa | 6½ | 1990 | 3-8-0 | 1991 | *10-2-0 | Dave Rader |
| 1992 | Hawaii | 6 | 1991 | 4-7-1 | 1992 | *11-2-0 | Bob Wagner |

$ To determine games improved, add the difference in victories between the two seasons to the difference in losses, then divide by two; ties not counted. Bowl victory (*), loss (+), tie (‡) included in record.   # First year as head coach at that college.

## ALL-TIME MOST-IMPROVED TEAMS

| Games | Team (Year) | Games | Team (Year) |
|-------|-------------|-------|-------------|
| 8 | Purdue (1943) | 6½ | Wake Forest (1979) |
| 8 | Stanford (1940) | 6½ | Toledo (1967) |
| 7 | San Jose St. (1986) | 6½ | Dayton (1966) |
| 7 | Florida (1980) | 6½ | UTEP (1965) |
| 7 | Miami (Ohio) (1977) | 6½ | Notre Dame (1964) |
| 7 | Houston (1976) | 6½ | Washington (1959) |
| 7 | Indiana (1967) | 6½ | Texas A&M (1955) |
| 7 | Texas Tech (1953) | 6½ | California (1947) |
| 7 | Miami (Fla.) (1945) | | |
| 6½ | Tulsa (1991) | | |

## 1992 MOST-IMPROVED TEAMS

| College (Coach) | 1992 | 1991 | $Games Improved |
|-----------------|------|------|-----------------|
| Hawaii (Bob Wagner) | 11-2-0 | 4-7-1 | 6 |
| Wake Forest (Bill Dooley) | 8-4-0 | 3-8-0 | 4½ |
| Washington St. (Mike Price) | 9-3-0 | 4-7-0 | 4½ |
| Boston College (Tom Coughlin) | 8-3-1 | 4-7-0 | 4 |
| New Mexico St. (Jim Hess) | 6-5-0 | 2-9-0 | 4 |
| Oklahoma St. (Pat Jones) | 4-6-1 | 0-10-1 | 4 |
| Southern Methodist (Tom Rossley) | 5-6-0 | 1-10-0 | 4 |
| Mississippi (Billy Brewer) | 9-3-0 | 5-6-0 | 3½ |
| Louisville (Howard Schnellenberger) | 5-6-0 | 2-9-0 | 3 |
| Northern Ill. (Charlie Sadler) | 5-6-0 | 2-9-0 | 3 |
| Southern Cal (Larry Smith) | 6-5-1 | 3-8-0 | 3 |
| Southern Miss. (Jeff Bower) | 7-4-0 | 4-7-0 | 3 |
| Oregon (Rich Brooks) | 6-6-0 | 3-8-0 | 2½ |
| Toledo (Gary Pinkel) | 8-3-0 | 5-5-1 | 2½ |
| Arizona (Dick Tomey) | 6-5-1 | 4-7-0 | 2 |

| College (Coach) | 1992 | 1991 | $Games Improved |
|---|---|---|---|
| Michigan St. (George Perles) | 5-6-0 | 3-8-0 | 2 |
| Nevada-Las Vegas (Jim Strong) | 6-5-0 | 4-7-0 | 2 |
| Rice (Fred Goldsmith) | 6-5-0 | 4-7-0 | 2 |

$ To determine games improved, add the difference in victories between the two seasons to the difference in losses, then divide by two; ties not counted.

# ALL-TIME TEAM WON-LOST RECORDS

Classified as Division I-A for the last 10 years. Won-lost-tied record includes bowl games.

## PERCENTAGE (TOP 25)

| Team | Yrs. | Won | Lost | Tied | Pct.† | *Bowls W | L | T | Total Games |
|---|---|---|---|---|---|---|---|---|---|
| Notre Dame# | 104 | 712 | 210 | 41 | .761 | 11 | 6 | 0 | 963 |
| Michigan | 113 | 731 | 238 | 36 | .745 | 11 | 13 | 0 | 1,005 |
| Alabama | 98 | 682 | 234 | 43 | .734 | 25 | 17 | 3 | 959 |
| Oklahoma | 98 | 650 | 237 | 52 | .720 | 19 | 10 | 1 | 939 |
| Texas | 100 | 682 | 268 | 31 | .711 | 16 | 16 | 2 | 981 |
| Southern Cal | 100 | 622 | 249 | 52 | .702 | 22 | 13 | 0 | 923 |
| Ohio St. | 103 | 649 | 264 | 52 | .699 | 12 | 13 | 0 | 965 |
| Penn St. | 106 | 664 | 289 | 41 | .689 | 17 | 10 | 2 | 994 |
| Nebraska$ | 103 | 662 | 289 | 40 | .688 | 14 | 17 | 0 | 991 |
| Tennessee | 96 | 627 | 274 | 52 | .685 | 18 | 15 | 0 | 953 |
| Central Mich. | 92 | 475 | 249 | 36 | .649 | 3 | 1 | 1 | 760 |
| Washington✓ | 103 | 555 | 306 | 49 | .637 | 12 | 8 | 1 | 910 |
| Army | 103 | 582 | 322 | 50 | .636 | 2 | 1 | 1 | 954 |
| Miami (Ohio) | 104 | 542 | 301 | 42 | .636 | 5 | 2 | 1 | 885 |
| Louisiana St.✓ | 99 | 568 | 319 | 46 | .633 | 11 | 16 | 1 | 933 |
| Georgia | 99 | 584 | 327 | 53 | .633 | 15 | 13 | 3 | 964 |
| Arizona St. | 80 | 438 | 250 | 24 | .632 | 9 | 5 | 1 | 712 |
| Florida St.✓ | 46 | 304 | 175 | 16 | .630 | 13 | 7 | 2 | 495 |
| Auburn✓ | 100 | 547 | 335 | 46 | .614 | 12 | 9 | 2 | 928 |
| Colorado | 103 | 549 | 345 | 35 | .610 | 5 | 12 | 0 | 929 |
| Michigan St. | 96 | 515 | 322 | 43 | .610 | 5 | 5 | 0 | 880 |
| Miami (Fla.) | 66 | 402 | 257 | 19 | .607 | 10 | 9 | 0 | 678 |
| Bowling Green | 74 | 383 | 240 | 50 | .606 | 2 | 3 | 0 | 673 |
| Minnesota | 109 | 551 | 352 | 43 | .605 | 2 | 3 | 0 | 946 |
| UCLA | 74 | 429 | 276 | 37 | .603 | 10 | 7 | 1 | 742 |

## ALPHABETICAL LISTING

| Team | Yrs. | Won | Lost | Tied | Pct.† | *Bowls W | L | T | Total Games |
|---|---|---|---|---|---|---|---|---|---|
| Air Force | 37 | 206 | 189 | 13 | .521 | 6 | 5 | 1 | 408 |
| Alabama | 98 | 682 | 234 | 43 | .734 | 25 | 17 | 3 | 959 |
| Arizona | 88 | 449 | 311 | 33 | .587 | 2 | 6 | 1 | 793 |
| Arizona St. | 80 | 438 | 250 | 24 | .632 | 9 | 5 | 1 | 712 |
| Arkansas | 99 | 545 | 356 | 39 | .601 | 9 | 15 | 3 | 940 |
| Army | 103 | 582 | 322 | 50 | .636 | 2 | 1 | 1 | 954 |
| Auburn✓ | 100 | 547 | 335 | 46 | .614 | 12 | 9 | 2 | 928 |
| Ball St. | 68 | 316 | 255 | 30 | .551 | 0 | 1 | 0 | 601 |
| Baylor | 90 | 463 | 396 | 43 | .537 | 8 | 7 | 0 | 902 |
| Boston College | 94 | 488 | 348 | 35 | .580 | 3 | 5 | 0 | 871 |
| Bowling Green | 74 | 383 | 240 | 50 | .606 | 2 | 3 | 0 | 673 |
| Brigham Young | 68 | 364 | 302 | 26 | .545 | 5 | 11 | 1 | 692 |
| California | 97 | 521 | 375 | 51 | .577 | 4 | 6 | 1 | 947 |
| Central Mich. | 92 | 475 | 249 | 36 | .649 | 3 | 1 | 0 | 760 |
| Cincinnati | 105 | 437 | 453 | 51 | .492 | 1 | 1 | 0 | 941 |
| Clemson | 97 | 517 | 353 | 45 | .584 | 11 | 7 | 0 | 915 |
| Colorado | 103 | 549 | 345 | 35 | .610 | 5 | 12 | 0 | 929 |
| Colorado St. | 94 | 352 | 428 | 33 | .453 | 1 | 1 | 0 | 813 |
| Duke | 80 | 411 | 313 | 31 | .565 | 3 | 4 | 0 | 755 |
| East Caro. | 57 | 280 | 260 | 12 | .518 | 2 | 0 | 0 | 552 |
| Eastern Mich. | 100 | 364 | 372 | 46 | .495 | 1 | 0 | 0 | 782 |
| Florida | 86 | 480 | 330 | 39 | .588 | 9 | 11 | 0 | 849 |
| Florida St.✓ | 46 | 304 | 175 | 16 | .630 | 13 | 7 | 2 | 495 |
| Fresno St. | 71 | 423 | 276 | 28 | .601 | 7 | 1 | 0 | 727 |
| Georgia | 99 | 584 | 327 | 53 | .633 | 15 | 13 | 3 | 964 |

*1993 NCAA FOOTBALL*

| Team | Yrs. | Won | Lost | Tied | Pct.† | *Bowls W | L | T | Total Games |
|---|---|---|---|---|---|---|---|---|---|
| Georgia Tech | 100 | 550 | 363 | 43 | .598 | 17 | 8 | 0 | 956 |
| Hawaii | 77 | 408 | 281 | 25 | .589 | 1 | 1 | 0 | 714 |
| Houston | 47 | 281 | 209 | 14 | .571 | 7 | 5 | 1 | 504 |
| Illinois | 103 | 491 | 401 | 49 | .548 | 4 | 6 | 0 | 941 |
| Indiana | 105 | 374 | 484 | 44 | .439 | 3 | 4 | 0 | 902 |
| Iowa | 104 | 459 | 426 | 38 | .518 | 6 | 5 | 1 | 923 |
| Iowa St. | 101 | 418 | 452 | 45 | .481 | 0 | 4 | 0 | 915 |
| Kansas | 103 | 472 | 446 | 58 | .513 | 2 | 5 | 0 | 976 |
| Kansas St.✓ | 97 | 317 | 535 | 41 | .378 | 0 | 1 | 0 | 893 |
| Kent | 70 | 257 | 348 | 27 | .428 | 0 | 1 | 0 | 632 |
| Kentucky✓ | 102 | 484 | 441 | 44 | .522 | 5 | 2 | 0 | 969 |
| Louisiana St.✓ | 99 | 568 | 319 | 46 | .633 | 11 | 16 | 1 | 933 |
| Louisville✓ | 74 | 316 | 346 | 17 | .478 | 2 | 1 | 1 | 679 |
| Maryland | 100 | 503 | 429 | 42 | .538 | 6 | 9 | 2 | 974 |
| Memphis St.✓ | 77 | 349 | 342 | 32 | .505 | 1 | 0 | 0 | 723 |
| Miami (Fla.) | 66 | 402 | 257 | 19 | .607 | 10 | 9 | 0 | 678 |
| Miami (Ohio) | 104 | 542 | 301 | 42 | .636 | 5 | 2 | 0 | 885 |
| Michigan | 113 | 731 | 238 | 36 | .745 | 11 | 13 | 0 | 1,005 |
| Michigan St. | 96 | 515 | 322 | 43 | .610 | 5 | 5 | 0 | 880 |
| Minnesota | 109 | 551 | 352 | 43 | .605 | 2 | 3 | 0 | 946 |
| Mississippi✓ | 98 | 508 | 374 | 35 | .573 | 14 | 11 | 0 | 917 |
| Mississippi St.✓ | 93 | 403 | 423 | 37 | .488 | 4 | 4 | 0 | 863 |
| Missouri | 102 | 504 | 418 | 50 | .544 | 8 | 11 | 0 | 972 |
| Navy | 112 | 542 | 418 | 57 | .561 | 3 | 4 | 1 | 1,017 |
| Nebraska$ | 103 | 662 | 289 | 40 | .688 | 14 | 17 | 0 | 991 |
| Nevada-Las Vegas | 25 | 159 | 114 | 4 | .581 | 1 | 0 | 0 | 277 |
| New Mexico | 94 | 355 | 414 | 31 | .463 | 2 | 2 | 1 | 800 |
| New Mexico St. | 97 | 358 | 422 | 32 | .461 | 2 | 0 | 1 | 812 |
| North Caro. | 102 | 538 | 392 | 54 | .574 | 7 | 10 | 0 | 984 |
| North Caro. St. | 101 | 427 | 428 | 55 | .499 | 7 | 7 | 1 | 910 |
| Northern Ill. | 91 | 414 | 346 | 51 | .542 | 1 | 0 | 0 | 811 |
| Northwestern | 105 | 369 | 514 | 42 | .422 | 1 | 0 | 0 | 925 |
| Notre Dame# | 104 | 712 | 210 | 41 | .761 | 12 | 6 | 0 | 963 |
| Ohio | 97 | 417 | 400 | 47 | .510 | 0 | 2 | 0 | 864 |
| Ohio St. | 103 | 649 | 264 | 52 | .699 | 12 | 13 | 0 | 965 |
| Oklahoma | 98 | 650 | 237 | 52 | .720 | 19 | 10 | 1 | 939 |
| Oklahoma St. | 91 | 407 | 419 | 47 | .493 | 9 | 3 | 0 | 873 |
| Oregon | 97 | 428 | 399 | 46 | .517 | 3 | 6 | 0 | 873 |
| Oregon St. | 96 | 388 | 434 | 50 | .474 | 2 | 2 | 0 | 872 |
| Pacific (Cal.) | 74 | 334 | 376 | 23 | .471 | 3 | 1 | 1 | 733 |
| Penn St. | 106 | 664 | 289 | 41 | .689 | 17 | 10 | 1 | 994 |
| Pittsburgh | 103 | 563 | 375 | 42 | .596 | 8 | 10 | 0 | 980 |
| Purdue | 105 | 470 | 397 | 45 | .540 | 4 | 1 | 0 | 912 |
| Rice✓ | 81 | 345 | 437 | 31 | .443 | 4 | 3 | 0 | 813 |
| Rutgers | 123 | 526 | 475 | 41 | .525 | 0 | 1 | 0 | 1,042 |
| San Diego St. | 70 | 394 | 267 | 32 | .592 | 2 | 3 | 0 | 693 |
| San Jose St. | 74 | 377 | 306 | 38 | .549 | 4 | 3 | 0 | 721 |
| South Caro. | 99 | 440 | 429 | 43 | .506 | 0 | 8 | 0 | 912 |
| Southern Cal | 100 | 622 | 249 | 52 | .702 | 22 | 13 | 0 | 923 |
| Southern Methodist@ | 76 | 389 | 347 | 51 | .527 | 4 | 6 | 1 | 787 |
| Southern Miss.✓ | 76 | 414 | 280 | 25 | .593 | 2 | 6 | 0 | 719 |
| Southwestern La. | 85 | 398 | 383 | 32 | .509 | 0 | 1 | 0 | 813 |
| Stanford | 86 | 476 | 322 | 47 | .591 | 8 | 7 | 1 | 845 |
| Syracuse | 103 | 577 | 379 | 48 | .599 | 8 | 6 | 1 | 1,004 |
| Temple | 94 | 366 | 381 | 52 | .491 | 1 | 1 | 0 | 799 |
| Tennessee | 96 | 627 | 274 | 52 | .685 | 18 | 15 | 0 | 953 |
| Texas | 100 | 682 | 268 | 31 | .711 | 16 | 16 | 2 | 981 |
| Texas A&M | 98 | 539 | 359 | 47 | .595 | 10 | 9 | 0 | 945 |
| Texas Christian | 96 | 436 | 439 | 56 | .498 | 4 | 9 | 1 | 931 |
| Texas Tech | 68 | 379 | 315 | 32 | .544 | 4 | 13 | 1 | 726 |
| Toledo | 72 | 341 | 315 | 22 | .519 | 4 | 1 | 0 | 678 |
| Tulane✓ | 99 | 415 | 449 | 38 | .481 | 2 | 6 | 0 | 902 |
| Tulsa | 88 | 470 | 313 | 26 | .597 | 4 | 7 | 0 | 809 |
| UCLA | 74 | 429 | 276 | 37 | .603 | 10 | 7 | 1 | 742 |
| Utah | 99 | 466 | 358 | 31 | .563 | 2 | 1 | 0 | 855 |
| Utah St. | 95 | 410 | 360 | 31 | .531 | 0 | 4 | 0 | 801 |
| UTEP | 75 | 290 | 388 | 29 | .431 | 5 | 3 | 0 | 707 |
| Vanderbilt | 103 | 498 | 421 | 50 | .540 | 1 | 1 | 1 | 969 |
| Virginia | 103 | 494 | 454 | 48 | .520 | 2 | 3 | 0 | 996 |
| Virginia Tech | 99 | 504 | 377 | 46 | .569 | 1 | 5 | 0 | 927 |

*Division I-A All-Time Team Won-Lost Records*

83

| Team | Yrs. | Won | Lost | Tied | Pct.† | *Bowls W | *Bowls L | *Bowls T | Total Games |
|---|---|---|---|---|---|---|---|---|---|
| Wake Forest........................ | 91 | 324 | 479 | 33 | .407 | 2 | 2 | 0 | 836 |
| Washington✓ | 103 | 555 | 306 | 49 | .637 | 12 | 8 | 1 | 910 |
| Washington St. .................... | 96 | 396 | 392 | 45 | .502 | 3 | 2 | 0 | 833 |
| West Va............................ | 100 | 546 | 378 | 45 | .587 | 8 | 7 | 0 | 969 |
| Western Mich...................... | 87 | 406 | 306 | 23 | .568 | 0 | 1 | 0 | 735 |
| Wisconsin ......................... | 103 | 468 | 400 | 49 | .537 | 1 | 5 | 0 | 917 |
| Wyoming........................... | 96 | 390 | 404 | 28 | .491 | 4 | 5 | 0 | 822 |

**The following are not listed above because of reclassification to Division I-A:**

| Team | Yrs. | Won | Lost | Tied | Pct.† | *Bowls W | *Bowls L | *Bowls T | Total Games |
|---|---|---|---|---|---|---|---|---|---|
| Akron ............................. | 92 | 409 | 354 | 36 | .534 | 0 | 0 | 0 | 799 |
| Arkansas St. ...................... | 76 | 342 | 296 | 36 | .534 | 0 | 0 | 0 | 674 |
| Louisiana Tech .................... | 89 | 451 | 306 | 37 | .591 | 0 | 0 | 1 | 794 |
| Nevada............................ | 82 | 381 | 329 | 32 | .535 | 0 | 1 | 0 | 742 |

† Ties computed as half won and half lost.  * Record in a major bowl game only (i.e., a team's opponent was classified as a major-college team that season or it was classified as a major-college team at the time.)  # Leader since 1948. Notre Dame displaced all-time leader Yale .8082 to .8081 after the 1947 season.  $ Record adjusted in 1989 (8 less victories, 1 less defeat).  @ Football program suspended 1987-88.  ✓ Includes games forfeited or changed by action of the NCAA Council.

## VICTORIES

| Team | Wins | Team | Wins | Team | Wins |
|---|---|---|---|---|---|
| Michigan ................. | 731 | Virginia ................... | 494 | Mississippi St.✓ .......... | 403 |
| Notre Dame .............. | 712 | Illinois ................... | 491 | Miami (Fla.) .............. | 402 |
| Alabama................. | 682 | Boston College ........... | 488 | Southwestern La.......... | 398 |
| Texas .................... | 682 | Kentucky✓ ............... | 484 | Washington St. ........... | 396 |
| Penn St. ................. | 664 | Florida.................... | 480 | San Diego St. ............ | 394 |
| Nebraska$................ | 662 | Stanford ................. | 476 | Wyoming ................. | 390 |
| Oklahoma ............... | 650 | Central Mich. ............. | 475 | Southern Methodist ...... | 389 |
| Ohio St. ................. | 649 | Kansas .................. | 472 | Oregon St. ............... | 388 |
| Tennessee ............... | 627 | Purdue .................. | 470 | Bowling Green ........... | 383 |
| Southern Cal ............ | 622 | Tulsa ................... | 470 | Texas Tech .............. | 379 |
| Georgia ................. | 584 | Wisconsin ............... | 468 | San Jose St. ............. | 377 |
| Army .................... | 582 | Utah .................... | 466 | Indiana .................. | 374 |
| Syracuse ................ | 577 | Baylor ................... | 463 | Northwestern ............ | 369 |
| Louisiana St.✓ .......... | 568 | Iowa .................... | 459 | Temple .................. | 366 |
| Pittsburgh ............... | 563 | Louisiana Tech .......... | 451 | Brigham Young .......... | 364 |
| Washington✓ ............ | 555 | Arizona .................. | 449 | Eastern Mich............. | 364 |
| Minnesota ............... | 551 | South Caro. .............. | 440 | New Mexico St. .......... | 358 |
| Georgia Tech ............ | 550 | Arizona St. .............. | 438 | New Mexico ............. | 355 |
| Colorado ................ | 549 | Cincinnati ............... | 437 | Colorado St.............. | 352 |
| Auburn✓ ................ | 547 | Texas Christian .......... | 436 | Memphis St.✓ ........... | 349 |
| West Va. ................ | 546 | UCLA ................... | 429 | Rice✓ ................... | 345 |
| Arkansas ................ | 545 | Oregon .................. | 428 | Toledo ................... | 341 |
| Miami (Ohio) ............ | 542 | North Caro. St. .......... | 427 | Pacific (Cal.) ............ | 334 |
| Navy..................... | 542 | Fresno St. ............... | 423 | Wake Forest ............. | 324 |
| Texas A&M .............. | 539 | Iowa St. ................. | 418 | Kansas St.✓ ............. | 317 |
| North Caro. ............. | 538 | Ohio..................... | 417 | Ball St. .................. | 316 |
| Rutgers.................. | 526 | Tulane✓ ................. | 415 | Louisville✓ .............. | 316 |
| California................ | 521 | Northern Ill. ............. | 414 | Florida St.✓ ............. | 304 |
| Clemson ................ | 517 | Southern Miss.✓ ......... | 414 | UTEP..................... | 290 |
| Michigan St. ............ | 515 | Duke .................... | 411 | Houston ................. | 281 |
| Mississippi✓ ............ | 508 | Utah St. ................. | 410 | East Caro. ............... | 280 |
| Missouri ................ | 504 | Akron ................... | 409 | Kent ..................... | 257 |
| Virginia Tech ............ | 504 | Hawaii ................. | 408 | Air Force ................ | 206 |
| Maryland ................ | 503 | Oklahoma St.............. | 407 | Nevada-Las Vegas........ | 159 |
| Vanderbilt ............... | 498 | Western Mich. ........... | 406 | | |

**The following are not listed above because of reclassification to Division I-A:**

Louisiana Tech ............451
Akron ....................409
Nevada ...................381
Arkansas St..............342

$ Record adjusted by Nebraska in 1989 (8 less victories).   ✓ Includes games forfeited or changed by action of the NCAA Council.

# RECORDS IN THE 1990s

## (1990-91-92, including bowls and playoffs)

### BY PERCENTAGE

| Team | W-L-T | Pct.† | Team | W-L-T | Pct.† |
|---|---|---|---|---|---|
| Miami (Fla.) | 33-3-0 | .917 | Tulsa | 17-17-0 | .500 |
| Florida St. | 32-5-0 | .865 | Oregon | 17-18-0 | .486 |
| Washington | 31-5-0 | .861 | Utah | 17-18-0 | .486 |
| Alabama | 31-6-0 | .838 | Boston College | 16-17-1 | .485 |
| Texas A&M | 31-6-1 | .829 | Michigan St. | 16-17-1 | .485 |
| Michigan | 28-5-3 | .819 | Akron | 15-16-2 | .485 |
| Nevada% | 32-8-0 | .800 | Arizona St. | 16-17-0 | .485 |
| Colorado | 28-6-3 | .797 | Rutgers | 16-17-0 | .485 |
| Notre Dame | 29-7-1 | .797 | West Va. | 15-16-2 | .485 |
| Florida | 28-8-0 | .778 | Colorado St. | 17-19-0 | .472 |
| Fresno St. | 27-8-1 | .764 | Washington St. | 16-18-0 | .471 |
| Nebraska | 27-8-1 | .764 | Memphis St. | 15-17-1 | .470 |
| Syracuse | 27-8-2 | .757 | Utah St. | 15-17-1 | .470 |
| Tennessee | 27-8-2 | .757 | Army | 15-18-0 | .455 |
| Bowling Green | 24-8-2 | .735 | Rice | 15-18-0 | .455 |
| Penn St. | 27-10-0 | .730 | South Caro. | 14-17-2 | .455 |
| Clemson | 24-10-1 | .700 | Texas Tech | 15-18-0 | .455 |
| Brigham Young | 26-11-2 | .692 | Texas Christian | 14-18-1 | .439 |
| North Caro. St. | 25-11-1 | .689 | Nevada-Las Vegas | 14-19-0 | .424 |
| Toledo | 22-10-1 | .682 | Wake Forest | 14-20-0 | .412 |
| Georgia Tech | 24-11-1 | .681 | Virginia Tech | 13-19-1 | .409 |
| Oklahoma | 22-10-2 | .676 | Northern Ill. | 13-20-0 | .394 |
| San Jose St. | 22-10-2 | .676 | Arkansas | 12-21-1 | .368 |
| Virginia | 23-11-1 | .671 | Pittsburgh | 12-21-1 | .368 |
| Ohio St. | 23-11-2 | .667 | Iowa St. | 11-20-2 | .364 |
| Louisiana Tech | 21-10-3 | .662 | Louisiana St. | 12-21-0 | .364 |
| North Caro. | 22-11-1 | .662 | Pacific (Cal.) | 12-22-0 | .353 |
| Georgia | 23-12-0 | .657 | Maryland | 11-22-1 | .338 |
| Mississippi | 23-12-0 | .657 | Kentucky | 11-22-0 | .333 |
| Iowa | 23-12-1 | .653 | Wisconsin | 11-22-0 | .333 |
| Air Force | 24-13-0 | .649 | Duke | 10-22-1 | .318 |
| Stanford | 23-13-0 | .639 | Missouri | 10-22-1 | .318 |
| Central Mich. | 19-10-5 | .632 | Minnesota | 10-23-0 | .303 |
| Western Mich. | 20-12-1 | .621 | Purdue | 10-23-0 | .303 |
| East Caro. | 21-13-0 | .618 | Temple | 10-23-0 | .303 |
| Texas | 21-13-0 | .618 | Vanderbilt | 10-23-0 | .303 |
| Baylor | 21-13-1 | .614 | Southwestern La. | 9-23-1 | .288 |
| California | 21-13-1 | .614 | New Mexico St. | 9-24-0 | .273 |
| Hawaii | 22-14-1 | .608 | Oklahoma St. | 8-23-2 | .273 |
| UCLA | 20-14-0 | .588 | UTEP | 8-25-1 | .250 |
| San Diego St. | 19-14-2 | .571 | Cincinnati | 8-25-0 | .242 |
| Illinois | 20-15-1 | .569 | Northwestern | 8-25-0 | .242 |
| Miami (Ohio) | 17-13-3 | .561 | New Mexico | 8-27-0 | .229 |
| Southern Miss. | 19-15-0 | .559 | Navy | 7-26-0 | .212 |
| Ball St. | 18-15-0 | .545 | Southern Methodist | 7-26-0 | .212 |
| Houston | 18-15-0 | .545 | Tulane | 7-26-0 | .212 |
| Auburn | 18-14-2 | .544 | Eastern Mich. | 6-26-1 | .197 |
| Indiana | 18-15-2 | .543 | Arkansas St.* | 5-26-1 | .172 |
| Mississippi St. | 19-16-0 | .543 | Kent | 5-28-0 | .152 |
| Kansas St. | 17-16-0 | .515 | Ohio | 4-27-2 | .152 |
| Kansas | 17-16-1 | .515 | Cal St. Fullerton# | 5-29-0 | .147 |
| Louisville | 17-16-1 | .515 | Oregon St. | 3-29-1 | .106 |
| Wyoming | 18-17-1 | .514 | | | |
| Arizona | 17-17-1 | .500 | | | |
| Southern Cal | 17-17-2 | .500 | | | |

† Ties counted as half won and half lost.   % Nevada joined I-A in 1992.   * Arkansas St. joined I-A in 1992.   # Cal St. Fullerton dropped football after the 1992 season.

## VICTORIES
### (Minimum 20 Victories)

| Team | Wins | Team | Wins | Team | Wins |
|---|---|---|---|---|---|
| Miami (Fla.) | 33 | Brigham Young | 26 | San Jose St. | 22 |
| Florida St. | 32 | North Caro. St. | 25 | Toledo | 22 |
| Nevada% | 32 | Air Force | 24 | Baylor | 21 |
| Alabama | 31 | Bowling Green | 24 | California | 21 |
| Texas A&M | 31 | Clemson | 24 | East Caro. | 21 |
| Washington | 31 | Georgia Tech | 24 | Louisiana Tech | 21 |
| Notre Dame | 29 | Georgia | 23 | Texas | 21 |
| Colorado | 28 | Iowa | 23 | Illinois | 20 |
| Florida | 28 | Mississippi | 23 | UCLA | 20 |
| Michigan | 28 | Ohio St. | 23 | Western Mich. | 20 |
| Fresno St. | 27 | Stanford | 23 | | |
| Nebraska | 27 | Virginia | 23 | | |
| Penn St. | 27 | Hawaii | 22 | | |
| Syracuse | 27 | North Caro. | 22 | | |
| Tennessee | 27 | Oklahoma | 22 | | |

% Nevada joined I-A in 1992.

# WINNINGEST TEAMS BY DECADE
## BY PERCENTAGE
### (Bowls and playoffs included)
#### 1980-89

| Rank | Team | W-L-T | Pct.† | Rank | Team | W-L-T | Pct.† |
|---|---|---|---|---|---|---|---|
| 1. | Nebraska | 93-17-0 | .846 | 11. | Florida St. | 77-26-3 | .741 |
| 2. | Miami (Fla.) | 87-19-0 | .821 | 12. | Auburn | 76-29-1 | .722 |
| 3. | Brigham Young | 92-23-0 | .800 | 13. | Washington | 75-29-1 | .717 |
| 4. | Oklahoma | 84-21-2 | .794 | 14. | Alabama | 75-30-2 | .710 |
| 5. | Georgia | 82-21-4 | .785 | | Arkansas | 75-30-2 | .710 |
| 6. | Penn St. | 81-24-1 | .769 | 16. | Ohio St. | 74-31-2 | .701 |
| 7. | UCLA | 78-23-5 | .759 | 17. | Florida | 69-32-3 | .678 |
| 8. | Southern Methodist | 61-19-1 | .759 | 18. | Fresno St. | 69-33-1 | .675 |
| 9. | Clemson | 76-23-4 | .757 | 19. | Southern Cal | 69-33-2 | .673 |
| 10. | Michigan | 79-27-2 | .741 | 20. | Arizona St. | 67-32-3 | .672 |

#### 1970-79

| Rank | Team | W-L-T | Pct.† | Rank | Team | W-L-T | Pct.† |
|---|---|---|---|---|---|---|---|
| 1. | Oklahoma | 102-13-3 | .877 | 11. | Arizona St. | 90-28-0 | .763 |
| 2. | Alabama | 103-16-1 | .863 | 12. | Yale@ | 67-21-2 | .756 |
| 3. | Michigan | 96-16-3 | .848 | 13. | San Diego St. | 82-26-2 | .755 |
| 4. | Tennessee St.* | 85-17-2 | .827 | 14. | Miami (Ohio) | 80-26-2 | .750 |
| 5. | Nebraska | 98-20-4 | .820 | 15. | Central Mich.# | 80-27-3 | .741 |
| 6. | Penn St. | 96-22-0 | .814 | 16. | Arkansas | 79-31-5 | .709 |
| 7. | Ohio St. | 91-20-3 | .811 | 17. | Houston | 80-33-2 | .704 |
| 8. | Notre Dame | 91-22-0 | .805 | 18. | Louisiana Tech# | 77-34-2 | .690 |
| 9. | Southern Cal | 93-21-5 | .803 | 19. | McNeese St.# | 75-33-4 | .688 |
| 10. | Texas | 88-26-1 | .770 | 20. | Dartmouth@ | 60-27-3 | .683 |

#### 1960-69

| Rank | Team | W-L-T | Pct.† | Rank | Team | W-L-T | Pct.† |
|---|---|---|---|---|---|---|---|
| 1. | Alabama | 85-12-3 | .865 | 11. | Memphis St. | 70-25-1 | .734 |
| 2. | Texas | 80-18-2 | .810 | 12. | Arizona St. | 72-26-1 | .732 |
| 3. | Arkansas | 80-19-1 | .805 | 13. | Louisiana St. | 70-25-5 | .725 |
| 4. | Mississippi | 72-20-6 | .765 | | Nebraska | 72-27-1 | .725 |
| 5. | Bowling Green | 71-22-2 | .758 | 15. | Wyoming | 69-26-4 | .717 |
| 6. | Dartmouth@ | 68-22-0 | .756 | 16. | Princeton@ | 64-26-0 | .711 |
| | Ohio St. | 67-21-2 | .756 | 17. | Utah St. | 68-29-3 | .695 |
| 8. | Missouri | 72-22-6 | .750 | 18. | Purdue | 64-28-3 | .689 |
| | Southern Cal | 73-23-4 | .750 | 19. | Syracuse | 68-31-0 | .687 |
| 10. | Penn St. | 73-26-0 | .737 | 20. | Florida | 66-30-4 | .680 |
| | | | | | Miami (Ohio) | 66-30-4 | .680 |
| | | | | | Tennessee | 65-29-6 | .680 |

† Ties computed as half won and half lost.   * In I-A less than 8 years, now a member of I-AA.   @ Now a member of I-AA.   # A member of I-A less than 8 years.

# NATIONAL CHAMPIONS FROM 1936 TO 1949

Based on Associated Press poll of sportswriters and broadcasters, United Press International poll of coaches, Football Writers Association of America's Grantland Rice Award, and National Football Foundation and Hall of Fame's MacArthur Bowl award. The national champion was selected before bowl games as follows: AP (1936-64 and 1966-67); UP-UPI (1950-73); FWAA (1954); NFF-HF (1959-70).

| Year | Team | *Record | Coach | †Years |
|------|------|---------|-------|--------|
| 1936 | Minnesota | 7-1-0 | Bernie Bierman | 5-15 |
| 1937 | Pittsburgh | 9-0-1 | Jock Sutherland | 13-18 |
| 1938 | Texas Christian | 10-0-0 W | Leo "Dutch" Meyer | 5-5 |
| 1939 | Texas A&M | 10-0-0 W | Homer Norton | 6-16 |
| 1940 | Minnesota | 8-0-0 | Bernie Bierman | 9-19 |
| 1941 | Minnesota | 8-0-0 | Bernie Bierman | 10-20 |
| 1942 | Ohio St. | 9-1-0 | Paul Brown | 2-2 |
| 1943 | Notre Dame | 9-1-0 | Frank Leahy | 3-5 |
| 1944 | Army | 9-0-0 | Earl "Red" Blaik | 4-11 |
| 1945 | Army | 9-0-0 | Earl "Red" Blaik | 5-12 |
| 1946 | Notre Dame | 8-0-1 | Frank Leahy | 4-6 |
| 1947 | Notre Dame | 9-0-0 | Frank Leahy | 5-7 |
| 1948 | Michigan | 9-0-0 | Bennie Oosterbaan | 1-1 |
| 1949 | Notre Dame | 10-0-0 | Frank Leahy | 7-9 |

* Regular-season record (bowl game win or loss is indicated by W or L).   † Years head coach at that college and total years at four-year colleges.

# NATIONAL CHAMPIONS FROM 1950

Associated Press (AP) from 1950; United Press International (UPI‡) from 1950-1990; Football Writers Association of America (FW) from 1954; National Football Foundation and Hall of Fame (NFF) from 1959-1990; USA Today/Cable News Network (USA/CNN) from 1991, and United Press International/ National Football Foundation and Hall of Fame (UPI/NFF) from 1991.

Note: The following T-formation quarterbacks led their teams to two consecutive national championships: John Lujack, Notre Dame (1946-47); Jimmy Harris, Oklahoma (1955-56); Jerry Tagge, Nebraska (1970-71), and Steve Davis, Oklahoma (1974-75). Bruce Smith, a single-wing tailback, led Minnesota to titles in 1940 and 1941. Lujack started the last four games for Notre Dame's 1943 national champions after Angelo Bertelli started the first six games then joined the Marines.

| Year | Team | ‡Selected By | *Record | Coach | †Year(s) |
|------|------|--------------|---------|-------|----------|
| 1950 | Oklahoma | AP-UPI | 10-0-0 L | Bud Wilkinson | 4-4 |
| 1951 | Tennessee | AP-UPI | 10-0-0 L | Bob Neyland | 20-20 |
| 1952 | Michigan St. | AP-UPI | 9-0-0 | Biggie Munn | 6-9 |
| 1953 | Maryland | AP-UPI | 10-0-0 L | Jim Tatum | 7-9 |
| 1954 | UCLA | UPI-FW | 9-0-0 | Red Sanders | 6-12 |
|  | Ohio St. | AP | 9-0-0 W | Woody Hayes | 4-9 |
| 1955 | Oklahoma | (All 3) | 10-0-0 W | Bud Wilkinson | 9-9 |
| 1956 | Oklahoma | (All 3) | 10-0-0 | Bud Wilkinson | 10-10 |
| 1957 | Ohio St. | UPI-FW | 8-1-0 W | Woody Hayes | 7-12 |
|  | Auburn | AP | 10-0-0 | Ralph Jordan | 7-7 |
| 1958 | Louisiana St. | AP-UPI | 10-0-0 W | Paul Dietzel | 4-4 |
|  | Iowa | FW | 7-1-1 W | Forest Evashevski | 5-8 |
| 1959 | Syracuse | (All 4) | 10-0-0 W | Ben Schwartzwalder | 11-14 |
| 1960 | Minnesota | AP-UPI-NFF | 8-1-0 L | Murray Warmath | 7-9 |
|  | Mississippi | FW | 9-0-1 W | John Vaught | 14-14 |
| 1961 | Alabama | AP-UPI-NFF | 10-0-0 W | Paul "Bear" Bryant | 4-17 |
|  | Ohio St. | FW | 8-0-1 | Woody Hayes | 11-16 |
| 1962 | Southern Cal | (All 4) | 10-0-0 W | John McKay | 3-3 |
| 1963 | Texas | (All 4) | 10-0-0 W | Darrell Royal | 7-10 |
| 1964 | Alabama | AP-UPI | 10-0-0 L | Paul "Bear" Bryant | 7-20 |
|  | Arkansas | FW | 10-0-0 W | Frank Broyles | 3-4 |
|  | Notre Dame | NFF | 9-1-0 | Ara Parseghian | 1-14 |
| 1965 | Alabama | AP-FW (tie) | 8-1-1 W | Paul "Bear" Bryant | 8-21 |
|  | Michigan St. | UPI-FW (tie)-NFF | 10-0-0 L | Duffy Daugherty | 12-12 |
| 1966 | Notre Dame | AP-UPI-NFF (tie) | 9-0-1 | Ara Parseghian | 3-17 |
|  | Michigan St. | NFF (tie) | 9-0-1 | Duffy Daugherty | 13-13 |
| 1967 | Southern Cal | (All 4) | 9-1-0 W | John McKay | 8-8 |
| 1968 | Ohio St. | (All 4) | 9-0-0 W | Woody Hayes | 18-23 |
| 1969 | Texas | (All 4) | 10-0-0 W | Darrell Royal | 13-16 |
| 1970 | Nebraska | AP-FW | 10-0-1 W | Bob Devaney | 9-14 |
|  | Texas | UPI-NFF (tie) | 10-0-0 L | Darrell Royal | 14-17 |
|  | Ohio St. | NFF (tie) | 9-0-0 L | Woody Hayes | 20-25 |
| 1971 | Nebraska | (All 4) | 12-0-0 W | Bob Devaney | 10-15 |
| 1972 | Southern Cal | (All 4) | 11-0-0 W | John McKay | 13-13 |

Halfback Joe Washington, Oklahoma's all-time leading rusher, capped his great collegiate career in 1975 by rushing for 871 yards and scoring 11 touchdowns to lead the Sooners to the national championship.

| Year | Team | ‡Selected By | *Record | Coach | †Year(s) |
|------|------|--------------|---------|-------|----------|
| 1973 | Notre Dame | AP-FW-NFF | 10-0-0 | Ara Parseghian | 10-23 |
|      | Alabama | UPI | 11-0-0 L | Paul "Bear" Bryant | 16-29 |
| 1974 | Southern Cal | UPI-FW-NFF | 9-1-1 W | John McKay | 15-15 |
|      | Oklahoma | AP | 11-0-0 | Barry Switzer | 2-2 |
| 1975 | Oklahoma | (All 4) | 10-1-0 W | Barry Switzer | 3-3 |
| 1976 | Pittsburgh | (All 4) | 11-1-0 W | Johnny Majors | 4-9 |
| 1977 | Notre Dame | (All 4) | 10-1-0 W | Dan Devine | 3-19 |
| 1978 | Alabama | AP-FW-NFF | 10-1-0 W | Paul "Bear" Bryant | 21-34 |
|      | Southern Cal | UPI | 11-1-0 W | John Robinson | 3-3 |
| 1979 | Alabama | (All 4) | 11-0-0 W | Paul "Bear" Bryant | 22-35 |
| 1980 | Georgia | (All 4) | 11-0-0 W | Vince Dooley | 17-17 |
| 1981 | Clemson | (All 4) | 11-0-0 W | Danny Ford | #4-4 |
| 1982 | Penn St. | (All 4) | 10-1-0 W | Joe Paterno | 17-17 |
| 1983 | Miami (Fla.) | (All 4) | 10-1-0 W | Howard Schnellenberger | 5-5 |
| 1984 | Brigham Young | (All 4) | 12-0-0 W | LaVell Edwards | 13-13 |
| 1985 | Oklahoma | (All 4) | 10-1-0 W | Barry Switzer | 13-13 |
| 1986 | Penn St. | (All 4) | 11-0-0 W | Joe Paterno | 21-21 |
| 1987 | Miami (Fla.) | (All 4) | 11-0-0 W | Jimmy Johnson | 3-9 |
| 1988 | Notre Dame | (All 4) | 11-0-0 W | Lou Holtz | 3-19 |
| 1989 | Miami (Fla.) | (All 4) | 10-1-0 W | Dennis Erickson | 1-8 |
| 1990 | Colorado | AP-FW-NFF | 11-1-1 W | Bill McCartney | 9-9 |
|      | Georgia Tech | UPI | 11-0-1 W | Bobby Ross | 4-14 |
| 1991 | Washington | USA/CNN-UPI/NFF-FW | 12-0-0 W | Don James | 17-21 |
|      | Miami (Fla.) | AP | 12-0-0 W | Dennis Erickson | 3-10 |
| 1992 | Alabama | (All 4) | 13-0-0 W | Gene Stallings | 3-10 |

*Regular-season record (bowl game win or loss is indicated by W or L). † Years head coach at that college and total years as a head coach at four-year colleges. ‡ United Press (UP), 1950-57; UPI from 1958-90 after merger with International News Service. USA/CNN took over coaches poll in 1991. # Includes last game of 1978 season.

# NATIONAL POLL RANKINGS

## DICKINSON SYSTEM
### (1924-40)

The Dickinson System was a mathematical point system devised by Frank G. Dickinson, a professor of economics at Illinois. The annual Dickinson ratings were emblematic of the national championship and the basis for awarding the Rissman National Trophy and the Knute K. Rockne Intercollegiate Memorial Trophy. Notre Dame gained permanent possession of the Rissman Trophy (named for Jack F. Rissman, a Chicago clothing manufacturer) after its third victory in 1930. Minnesota retired the Rockne Trophy (named in honor of the famous Notre Dame coach) after winning it for a third time in 1940. Subsequently, the Associated Press annual national champions were awarded the Williams Trophy and the Reverend J. Hugh O'Donnell Trophy. In 1947, Notre Dame retired the Williams Trophy (named after Dr. Henry L. Williams, Minnesota coach, and sponsored by the M Club of Minnesota). In 1956, Oklahoma retired the O'Donnell Trophy (named for Notre Dame's president and sponsored by Notre Dame alumni). Beginning with the 1957 season, the award was known as the AP Trophy, and since 1983 the award has been known as the Paul "Bear" Bryant Trophy.

| Yr. | | Yr. | | Yr. | | Yr. | |
|---|---|---|---|---|---|---|---|
| 1924 | Notre Dame | 1929 | Notre Dame | 1934 | Minnesota | 1939 | Southern Cal |
| 1925 | Dartmouth | 1930 | Notre Dame | 1935 | Southern Meth. | 1940 | Minnesota |
| 1926 | Stanford | 1931 | Southern Cal | 1936 | Minnesota | | |
| 1927 | Illinois | 1932 | Michigan | 1937 | Pittsburgh | | |
| 1928 | Southern Cal | 1933 | Michigan | 1938 | Notre Dame | | |

## DUNKEL SYSTEM
### (From 1929 to present)

A power index system devised by Dick Dunkel Sr. (1929-71); from 1972 by Dick Dunkel Jr.

| Yr. | | Yr. | | Yr. | | Yr. | |
|---|---|---|---|---|---|---|---|
| 1929 | Notre Dame | 1949 | Notre Dame | 1964 | Michigan | 1979 | Alabama |
| 1930 | Notre Dame | 1950 | Tennessee | 1965 | Michigan St. | 1980 | Oklahoma |
| 1931 | Southern Cal | 1951 | Maryland | 1966 | Notre Dame | 1981 | Penn St. |
| 1932 | Southern Cal | 1952 | Michigan St. | 1967 | Notre Dame | 1982 | Penn St. |
| 1933 | Ohio St. | 1953 | Notre Dame | 1968 | Ohio St. | 1983 | Miami (Fla.) |
| 1934 | Alabama | 1954 | UCLA | 1969 | Texas | 1984 | Florida |
| 1935 | Princeton | 1955 | Oklahoma | 1970 | Nebraska | 1985 | Oklahoma |
| 1936 | Minnesota | 1956 | Oklahoma | 1971 | Nebraska | 1986 | Oklahoma |
| 1937 | California | 1957 | Michigan St. | 1972 | Southern Cal | 1987 | Miami (Fla.) |
| 1938 | Tennessee | 1958 | Louisiana St. | 1973 | Oklahoma | 1988 | Notre Dame |
| 1939 | Texas A&M | 1959 | Mississippi | 1974 | Oklahoma | 1989 | Miami (Fla.) |
| 1940 | Tennessee | 1960 | Mississippi | 1975 | Oklahoma | 1990 | Florida St. |
| 1941 | Minnesota | 1961 | Alabama | 1976 | Southern Cal | 1991 | Washington |
| 1942 | Ohio St. | 1962 | Southern Cal | 1977 | Notre Dame | 1992 | Alabama |
| 1943 | Notre Dame | 1963 | Texas | 1978 | Oklahoma | | |
| 1944 | Army | | | | | | |
| 1945 | Army | | | | | | |
| 1946 | Notre Dame | | | | | | |
| 1947 | Michigan | | | | | | |
| 1948 | Michigan | | | | | | |

## WILLIAMSON SYSTEM
### (1932-63)

A power rating system chosen by Paul Williamson, a geologist and member of the Sugar Bowl committee.

| Yr. | | Yr. | | Yr. | | Yr. | |
|---|---|---|---|---|---|---|---|
| 1932 | Southern Cal | 1942 | Georgia | 1952 | Michigan St. | 1962 | Southern Cal |
| 1933 | Southern Cal | 1943 | Notre Dame | 1953 | Notre Dame | 1963 | Texas |
| 1934 | Alabama | 1944 | Army | 1954 | Ohio St. | | |
| 1935 | Louisiana St. | 1945 | Army | 1955 | Oklahoma | | |
| 1936 | Louisiana St. | 1946 | Georgia | 1956 | Oklahoma | | |
| 1937 | Pittsburgh | 1947 | Notre Dame | 1957 | Auburn | | |
| 1938 | Texas Christian | 1948 | Michigan | 1958 | Louisiana St. | | |
| 1939 | Texas A&M | 1949 | Notre Dame | 1959 | Syracuse | | |
| 1940 | Tennessee | 1950 | Oklahoma | 1960 | Mississippi | | |
| 1941 | Texas | 1951 | Tennessee | 1961 | Alabama | | |

# LITKENHOUS SYSTEM
### (1934-76)

A difference-by-score formula developed by Edward E. Litkenhous, a professor of chemical engineering at Vanderbilt, and his brother, Frank.

| Yr. | | Yr. | | Yr. | | Yr. | |
|---|---|---|---|---|---|---|---|
| 1934 | Minnesota | 1949 | Notre Dame | 1959 | Syracuse | 1969 | Texas |
| 1935 | Minnesota | 1950 | Oklahoma | 1960 | Iowa | 1970 | Texas |
| 1936 | Minnesota | 1951 | Tennessee | 1961 | Alabama | 1971 | Nebraska |
| 1937 | Pittsburgh | 1952 | Michigan St. | 1962 | Mississippi | 1972 | Southern Cal |
| 1938 | Tennessee | 1953 | Notre Dame | 1963 | Texas | 1973 | Alabama |
| 1939 | Cornell | 1954 | UCLA | 1964 | Alabama | 1974 | Oklahoma |
| 1940 | Minnesota | 1955 | Oklahoma | 1965 | Michigan St. | 1975 | Ohio St. |
| 1941 | Minnesota | 1956 | Oklahoma | 1966 | Notre Dame | 1976 | Michigan |
| 1942 | Georgia | 1957 | Ohio St. | 1967 | Tennessee | | |
| 1943 | Notre Dame | 1958 | Louisiana St. | 1968 | Georgia | | |
| 1944 | Army | | | | | | |
| 1945 | Army | | | | | | |
| 1946 | Notre Dame | | | | | | |
| 1947 | Michigan | | | | | | |
| 1948 | Michigan | | | | | | |

# ATHLETIC FOUNDATION
### (1883-1982)

Originally in the name of the Helms Athletic Foundation (1936-69), the foundation was established by the founding sponsor, Paul H. Helms, Los Angeles sportsman and philanthropist. After Helms' death in 1957, United Savings & Loan Association became its benefactor during 1970-72. A merger of United Savings and Citizens Savings was completed in 1973, and the Athletic Foundation became known as Citizens Savings Athletic Foundation. In 1982, The First Interstate Bank assumed sponsorship for its final rankings. In 1941, Bill Schroeder, managing director of the Helms Athletic Foundation, retroactively selected the national football champions for the period beginning in 1883 (the first year of a scoring system) through 1941. Thereafter, Schroeder, who passed away in 1988, then chose, with the assistance of a Hall Board, the annual national champion after the bowl games.

| Yr. | | Yr. | | Yr. | | Yr. | |
|---|---|---|---|---|---|---|---|
| 1883 | Yale | 1908 | Pennsylvania | 1933 | Michigan | 1958 | Louisiana St. |
| 1884 | Yale | 1909 | Yale | 1934 | Minnesota | 1959 | Syracuse |
| 1885 | Princeton | 1910 | Harvard | 1935 | Minnesota | 1960 | Washington |
| 1886 | Yale | 1911 | Princeton | 1936 | Minnesota | 1961 | Alabama |
| 1887 | Yale | 1912 | Harvard | 1937 | California | 1962 | Southern Cal |
| 1888 | Yale | 1913 | Harvard | 1938 | Texas | 1963 | Texas |
| 1889 | Princeton | 1914 | Army | | Christian | 1964 | Arkansas |
| 1890 | Harvard | 1915 | Cornell | 1939 | Texas A&M | 1965 | Michigan St. |
| 1891 | Yale | 1916 | Pittsburgh | 1940 | Stanford | 1966 | Notre Dame & |
| 1892 | Yale | 1917 | Georgia Tech | 1941 | Minnesota | | Michigan St. |
| 1893 | Princeton | 1918 | Pittsburgh | 1942 | Wisconsin | 1967 | Southern Cal |
| 1894 | Yale | 1919 | Harvard | 1943 | Notre Dame | 1968 | Ohio St. |
| 1895 | Pennsylvania | 1920 | California | 1944 | Army | 1969 | Texas |
| 1896 | Princeton | 1921 | Cornell | 1945 | Army | 1970 | Nebraska |
| 1897 | Pennsylvania | 1922 | Cornell | 1946 | Army & | 1971 | Nebraska |
| 1898 | Harvard | 1923 | Illinois | | Notre Dame | 1972 | Southern Cal |
| 1899 | Harvard | 1924 | Notre Dame | 1947 | Michigan & | 1973 | Notre Dame |
| 1900 | Yale | 1925 | Alabama | | Notre Dame | 1974 | Oklahoma & |
| 1901 | Michigan | 1926 | Alabama & | 1948 | Michigan | | Southern Cal |
| 1902 | Michigan | | Stanford | 1949 | Notre Dame | 1975 | Ohio St. & |
| 1903 | Princeton | 1927 | Illinois | 1950 | Oklahoma | | Oklahoma |
| 1904 | Pennsylvania | 1928 | Georgia Tech | 1951 | Michigan St. | 1976 | Pittsburgh |
| 1905 | Chicago | 1929 | Notre Dame | 1952 | Michigan St. | 1977 | Notre Dame |
| 1906 | Princeton | 1930 | Notre Dame | 1953 | Notre Dame | 1978 | Alabama, |
| 1907 | Yale | 1931 | Southern Cal | 1954 | UCLA & | | Oklahoma & |
| | | 1932 | Southern Cal | | Ohio St. | | Southern Cal |
| | | | | 1955 | Oklahoma | 1979 | Alabama |
| | | | | 1956 | Oklahoma | 1980 | Georgia |
| | | | | 1957 | Auburn | 1981 | Clemson |
| | | | | | | 1982 | Penn St. & |
| | | | | | | | Southern |
| | | | | | | | Methodist |

# NATIONAL FOOTBALL FOUNDATION AND HALL OF FAME MacARTHUR BOWL NATIONAL CHAMPIONS

### (1959-1990)

National Football Foundation and Hall of Fame national champions before 1991 were awarded the MacArthur Bowl. Beginning in 1991, the No. 1 team in the United Press International/National Football Foundation final poll received the MacArthur Bowl. The first year that the National Football Foundation and Hall of Fame selected the national champion after the bowl games was 1971.

| Yr. | | Yr. | | Yr. | | Yr. | |
|---|---|---|---|---|---|---|---|
| 1959 | Syracuse | 1969 | Texas | 1979 | Alabama | 1989 | Miami (Fla.) |
| 1960 | Minnesota | 1970 | Texas & | 1980 | Georgia | 1990 | Colorado |
| 1961 | Alabama | | Ohio St. | 1981 | Clemson | | |
| 1962 | Southern Cal | 1971 | Nebraska | 1982 | Penn St. | | |
| 1963 | Texas | 1972 | Southern Cal | 1983 | Miami (Fla.) | | |
| 1964 | Notre Dame | 1973 | Notre Dame | 1984 | Brigham | | |
| 1965 | Michigan St. | 1974 | Southern Cal | | Young | | |
| 1966 | Notre Dame & | 1975 | Oklahoma | 1985 | Oklahoma | | |
| | Michigan St. | 1976 | Pittsburgh | 1986 | Penn St. | | |
| 1967 | Southern Cal | 1977 | Notre Dame | 1987 | Miami (Fla.) | | |
| 1968 | Ohio St. | 1978 | Alabama | 1988 | Notre Dame | | |

## No. 1 vs. No. 2

The No. 1 and No. 2 teams in the Associated Press poll (begun in 1936) have faced each other 27 times (18 in regular-season games and nine in bowl games). The No. 1 team has won 16, with two games ending in ties.

| Date | Score | Stadium (Site) |
|---|---|---|
| 10-9-43 | No. 1 Notre Dame 35, No. 2 Michigan 12 | Michigan Stadium (Ann Arbor) |
| 11-20-43 | No. 1 Notre Dame 14, No. 2 Iowa Pre-Flight 13 | Notre Dame (South Bend) |
| 12-2-44 | No. 1 Army 23, No. 2 Navy 7 | Municipal (Baltimore) |
| 11-10-45 | No. 1 Army 48, No. 2 Notre Dame 0 | Yankee (New York) |
| 12-1-45 | No. 1 Army 32, No. 2 Navy 13 | Municipal (Philadelphia) |
| 11-9-46 | No. 1 Army 0, No. 2 Notre Dame 0 (tie) | Yankee (New York) |
| 1-1-63 | No. 1 Southern Cal 42, No. 2 Wisconsin 37 (Rose Bowl) | Rose Bowl (Pasadena) |
| 10-12-63 | No. 2 Texas 28, No. 1 Oklahoma 7 | Cotton Bowl (Dallas) |
| 1-1-64 | No. 1 Texas 28, No. 2 Navy 6 (Cotton Bowl) | Cotton Bowl (Dallas) |
| 11-19-66 | No. 1 Notre Dame 10, No. 2 Michigan St. 10 (tie) | Spartan (East Lansing) |
| 9-28-68 | No. 1 Purdue 37, No. 2 Notre Dame 22 | Notre Dame (South Bend) |
| 1-1-69 | No. 1 Ohio St. 27, No. 2 Southern Cal 16 (Rose Bowl) | Rose Bowl (Pasadena) |
| 12-6-69 | No. 1 Texas 15, No. 2 Arkansas 14 | Razorback (Fayetteville) |
| 11-25-71 | No. 1 Nebraska 35, No. 2 Oklahoma 31 | Owen Field (Norman) |
| 1-1-72 | No. 1 Nebraska 38, No. 2 Alabama 6 (Orange Bowl) | Orange Bowl (Miami) |
| 1-1-79 | No. 2 Alabama 14, No. 1 Penn St. 7 (Sugar Bowl) | Sugar Bowl (New Orleans) |
| 9-26-81 | No. 1 Southern Cal 28, No. 2 Oklahoma 24 | Coliseum (Los Angeles) |
| 1-1-83 | No. 2 Penn St. 27, No. 1 Georgia 23 (Sugar Bowl) | Sugar Bowl (New Orleans) |
| 10-19-85 | No. 1 Iowa 12, No. 2 Michigan 10 | Kinnick (Iowa City) |
| 9-27-86 | No. 2 Miami (Fla.) 28, No. 1 Oklahoma 16 | Orange Bowl (Miami) |
| 1-2-87 | No. 2 Penn St. 14, No. 1 Miami (Fla.) 10 (Fiesta Bowl) | Sun Devil (Tempe) |
| 11-21-87 | No. 2 Oklahoma 17, No. 1 Nebraska 7 | Memorial (Lincoln) |
| 1-1-88 | No. 2 Miami (Fla.) 20, No. 1 Oklahoma 14 (Orange Bowl) | Orange Bowl (Miami) |
| 11-26-88 | No. 1 Notre Dame 27, No. 2 Southern Cal 10 | Coliseum (Los Angeles) |
| 9-16-89 | No. 1 Notre Dame 24, No. 2 Michigan 19 | Michigan (Ann Arbor) |
| 11-16-91 | No. 2 Miami (Fla.) 17, No. 1 Florida St. 16 | Doak Campbell (Tallahassee) |
| 1-1-93 | No. 2 Alabama 34, No. 1 Miami (Fla.) 13 (Sugar Bowl) | Superdome (New Orleans) |

*Division I-A National Poll Rankings*

# ASSOCIATED PRESS (WRITERS AND BROADCASTERS)
## FINAL POLLS

### 1936
Team
1. Minnesota
2. Louisiana St.
3. Pittsburgh
4. Alabama
5. Washington
6. Santa Clara
7. Northwestern
8. Notre Dame
9. Nebraska
10. Pennsylvania
11. Duke
12. Yale
13. Dartmouth
14. Duquesne
15. Fordham
16. Texas Christian
17. Tennessee
18. Arkansas
    Navy
20. Marquette

### 1937
Team
1. Pittsburgh
2. California
3. Fordham
4. Alabama
5. Minnesota
6. Villanova
7. Dartmouth
8. Louisiana St.
9. Notre Dame
   Santa Clara
11. Nebraska
12. Yale
13. Ohio St.
14. Holy Cross
    Arkansas
16. Texas Christian
17. Colorado
18. Rice
19. North Caro.
20. Duke

### 1938
Team
1. Texas Christian
2. Tennessee
3. Duke
4. Oklahoma
5. Notre Dame
6. Carnegie Mellon
7. Southern Cal
8. Pittsburgh
9. Holy Cross
10. Minnesota
11. Texas Tech
12. Cornell
13. Alabama
14. California
15. Fordham
16. Michigan
17. Northwestern
18. Villanova
19. Tulane
20. Dartmouth

### 1939
Team
1. Texas A&M
2. Tennessee
3. Southern Cal
4. Cornell
5. Tulane
6. Missouri
7. UCLA
8. Duke
9. Iowa
10. Duquesne
11. Boston College
12. Clemson
13. Notre Dame
14. Santa Clara
15. Ohio St.
16. Georgia Tech
17. Fordham
18. Nebraska
19. Oklahoma
20. Michigan

### 1940
Team
1. Minnesota
2. Stanford
3. Michigan
4. Tennessee
5. Boston College
6. Texas A&M
7. Nebraska
8. Northwestern
9. Mississippi St.
10. Washington
11. Santa Clara
12. Fordham
13. Georgetown
14. Pennsylvania
15. Cornell
16. Southern Methodist
17. Hardin-Simmons
18. Duke
19. Lafayette

### 1941
Team
1. Minnesota
2. Duke
3. Notre Dame
4. Texas
5. Michigan
6. Fordham
7. Missouri
8. Duquesne
9. Texas A&M
10. Navy
11. Northwestern
12. Oregon St.
13. Ohio St.
14. Georgia
15. Pennsylvania
16. Mississippi St.
17. Mississippi
18. Tennessee
19. Washington St.
20. Alabama

### 1942
Team
1. Ohio St.
2. Georgia
3. Wisconsin
4. Tulsa
5. Georgia Tech
6. Notre Dame
7. Tennessee
8. Boston College
9. Michigan
10. Alabama
11. Texas
12. Stanford
13. UCLA
14. William & Mary
15. Santa Clara
16. Auburn
17. Washington St.
18. Mississippi St.
19. Minnesota
    Holy Cross
    Penn St.

### 1943
Team
1. Notre Dame
2. Iowa Pre-Flight
3. Michigan
4. Navy
5. Purdue
6. Great Lakes
7. Duke
8. Del Monte P-F
9. Northwestern
10. March Field
11. Army
12. Washington
13. Georgia Tech
14. Texas
15. Tulsa
16. Dartmouth
17. Bainbridge NTS
18. Colorado Col.
19. Pacific (Cal.)
20. Pennsylvania

### 1944
Team
1. Army
2. Ohio St.
3. Randolph Field
4. Navy
5. Bainbridge NTS
6. Iowa Pre-Flight
7. Southern Cal
8. Michigan
9. Notre Dame
10. March Field
11. Duke
12. Tennessee
13. Georgia Tech
    Norman P-F
15. Illinois
16. El Toro Marines
17. Great Lakes
18. Fort Pierce
19. St. Mary's P-F
20. Second Air Force

### 1945
Team
1. Army
2. Alabama
3. Navy
4. Indiana
5. Oklahoma St.
6. Michigan
7. St. Mary's (Cal.)
8. Pennsylvania
9. Notre Dame
10. Texas
11. Southern Cal
12. Ohio St.
13. Duke
14. Tennessee
15. Louisiana St.
16. Holy Cross
17. Tulsa
18. Georgia
19. Wake Forest
20. Columbia

### 1946
Team
1. Notre Dame
2. Army
3. Georgia
4. UCLA
5. Illinois
6. Michigan
7. Tennessee
8. Louisiana St.
9. North Caro.
10. Rice
11. Georgia Tech
12. Yale
13. Pennsylvania
14. Oklahoma
15. Texas
16. Arkansas
17. Tulsa
18. North Caro. St.
19. Delaware
20. Indiana

### *1947
Team
1. Notre Dame
2. Michigan
3. Southern Methodist
4. Penn St.
5. Texas
6. Alabama
7. Pennsylvania
8. Southern Cal
9. North Caro.
10. Georgia Tech
11. Army
12. Kansas
13. Mississippi
14. William & Mary
15. California
16. Oklahoma
17. North Caro. St.
18. Rice
19. Duke
20. Columbia

## 1948
**Team**
1. Michigan
2. Notre Dame
3. North Caro.
4. California
5. Oklahoma
6. Army
7. Northwestern
8. Georgia
9. Oregon
10. Southern Methodist
11. Clemson
12. Vanderbilt
13. Tulane
14. Michigan St.
15. Mississippi
16. Minnesota
17. William & Mary
18. Penn St.
19. Cornell
20. Wake Forest

## 1949
**Team**
1. Notre Dame
2. Oklahoma
3. California
4. Army
5. Rice
6. Ohio St.
7. Michigan
8. Minnesota
9. Louisiana St.
10. Pacific (Cal.)
11. Kentucky
12. Cornell
13. Villanova
14. Maryland
15. Santa Clara
16. North Caro.
17. Tennessee
18. Princeton
19. Michigan St.
20. Missouri
    Baylor

## 1950
**Team**
1. Oklahoma
2. Army
3. Texas
4. Tennessee
5. California
6. Princeton
7. Kentucky
8. Michigan St.
9. Michigan
10. Clemson
11. Washington
12. Wyoming
13. Illinois
14. Ohio St.
15. Miami (Fla.)
16. Alabama
17. Nebraska
18. Wash. & Lee
19. Tulsa
20. Tulane

## 1951
**Team**
1. Tennessee
2. Michigan St.
3. Maryland
4. Illinois
5. Georgia Tech
6. Princeton
7. Stanford
8. Wisconsin
9. Baylor
10. Oklahoma
11. Texas Christian
12. California
13. Virginia
14. San Francisco
15. Kentucky
16. Boston U.
17. UCLA
18. Washington St.
19. Holy Cross
20. Clemson

## 1952
**Team**
1. Michigan St.
2. Georgia Tech
3. Notre Dame
4. Oklahoma
5. Southern Cal
6. UCLA
7. Mississippi
8. Tennessee
9. Alabama
10. Texas
11. Wisconsin
12. Tulsa
13. Maryland
14. Syracuse
15. Florida
16. Duke
17. Ohio St.
18. Purdue
19. Princeton
20. Kentucky

## 1953
**Team**
1. Maryland
2. Notre Dame
3. Michigan St.
4. Oklahoma
5. UCLA
6. Rice
7. Illinois
8. Georgia Tech
9. Iowa
10. West Va.
11. Texas
12. Texas Tech
13. Alabama
14. Army
15. Wisconsin
16. Kentucky
17. Auburn
18. Duke
19. Stanford
20. Michigan

## 1954
**Team**
1. Ohio St.
2. UCLA
3. Oklahoma
4. Notre Dame
5. Navy
6. Mississippi
7. Army
8. Maryland
9. Wisconsin
10. Arkansas
11. Miami (Fla.)
12. West Va.
13. Auburn
14. Duke
15. Michigan
16. Virginia Tech
17. Southern Cal
18. Baylor
19. Rice
20. Penn St.

## 1955
**Team**
1. Oklahoma
2. Michigan St.
3. Maryland
4. UCLA
5. Ohio St.
6. Texas Christian
7. Georgia Tech
8. Auburn
9. Notre Dame
10. Mississippi
11. Pittsburgh
12. Michigan
13. Southern Cal
14. Miami (Fla.)
15. Miami (Ohio)
16. Stanford
17. Texas A&M
18. Navy
19. West Va.
20. Army

## 1956
**Team**
1. Oklahoma
2. Tennessee
3. Iowa
4. Georgia Tech
5. Texas A&M
6. Miami (Fla.)
7. Michigan
8. Syracuse
9. Michigan St.
10. Oregon St.
11. Baylor
12. Minnesota
13. Pittsburgh
14. Texas Christian
15. Ohio St.
16. Navy
17. Geo. Washington
18. Southern Cal
19. Clemson
20. Colorado

## 1957
**Team**
1. Auburn
2. Ohio St.
3. Michigan St.
4. Oklahoma
5. Navy
6. Iowa
7. Mississippi
8. Rice
9. Texas A&M
10. Notre Dame
11. Texas
12. Arizona St.
13. Tennessee
14. Mississippi St.
15. North Caro. St.
16. Duke
17. Florida
18. Army
19. Wisconsin
20. Va. Military

## 1958
**Team**
1. Louisiana St.
2. Iowa
3. Army
4. Auburn
5. Oklahoma
6. Air Force
7. Wisconsin
8. Ohio St.
9. Syracuse
10. Texas Christian
11. Mississippi
12. Clemson
13. Purdue
14. Florida
15. South Caro.
16. California
17. Notre Dame
18. Southern Methodist
19. Oklahoma St.
20. Rutgers

## 1959
**Team**
1. Syracuse
2. Mississippi
3. Louisiana St.
4. Texas
5. Georgia
6. Wisconsin
7. Texas Christian
8. Washington
9. Arkansas
10. Alabama
11. Clemson
12. Penn St.
13. Illinois
14. Southern Cal
15. Oklahoma
16. Wyoming
17. Notre Dame
18. Missouri
19. Florida
20. Pittsburgh

*Division I-A National Poll Rankings*

## 1960
**Team**
1. Minnesota
2. Mississippi
3. Iowa
4. Navy
5. Missouri
6. Washington
7. Arkansas
8. Ohio St.
9. Alabama
10. Duke
11. Kansas
12. Baylor
13. Auburn
14. Yale
15. Michigan St.
16. Penn St.
17. New Mexico St.
18. Florida
19. Syracuse
    Purdue

## 1961
**Team**
1. Alabama
2. Ohio St.
3. Texas
4. Louisiana St.
5. Mississippi
6. Minnesota
7. Colorado
8. Michigan St.
9. Arkansas
10. Utah St.
11. Missouri
12. Purdue
13. Georgia Tech
14. Syracuse
15. Rutgers
16. UCLA
17. Rice
    Penn St.
    Arizona
20. Duke

## 1962
**Team**
1. Southern Cal
2. Wisconsin
3. Mississippi
4. Texas
5. Alabama
6. Arkansas
7. Louisiana St.
8. Oklahoma
9. Penn St.
10. Minnesota
Only 10 ranked

## 1963
**Team**
1. Texas
2. Navy
3. Illinois
4. Pittsburgh
5. Auburn
6. Nebraska
7. Mississippi
8. Alabama
9. Oklahoma
10. Michigan St.
Only 10 ranked

## 1964
**Team**
1. Alabama
2. Arkansas
3. Notre Dame
4. Michigan
5. Texas
6. Nebraska
7. Louisiana St.
8. Oregon St.
9. Ohio St.
10. Southern Cal
Only 10 ranked

## 1965
**Team**
1. Alabama
2. Michigan St.
3. Arkansas
4. UCLA
5. Nebraska
6. Missouri
7. Tennessee
8. Louisiana St.
9. Notre Dame
10. Southern Cal
Only 10 ranked

## 1966
**Team**
1. Notre Dame
2. Michigan St.
3. Alabama
4. Georgia
5. UCLA
6. Nebraska
7. Purdue
8. Georgia Tech
9. Miami (Fla.)
10. Southern Methodist
Only 10 ranked

## 1967
**Team**
1. Southern Cal
2. Tennessee
3. Oklahoma
4. Indiana
5. Notre Dame
6. Wyoming
7. Oregon St.
8. Alabama
9. Purdue
10. Penn St.
Only 10 ranked

## 1968
**Team**
1. Ohio St.
2. Penn St.
3. Texas
4. Southern Cal
5. Notre Dame
6. Arkansas
7. Kansas
8. Georgia
9. Missouri
10. Purdue
11. Oklahoma
12. Michigan
13. Tennessee
14. Southern Methodist
15. Oregon St.
16. Auburn
17. Alabama
18. Houston
19. Louisiana St.
20. Ohio

## 1969
**Team**
1. Texas
2. Penn St.
3. Southern Cal
4. Ohio St.
5. Notre Dame
6. Missouri
7. Arkansas
8. Mississippi
9. Michigan
10. Louisiana St.
11. Nebraska
12. Houston
13. UCLA
14. Florida
15. Tennessee
16. Colorado
17. West Va.
18. Purdue
19. Stanford
20. Auburn

## 1970
**Team**
1. Nebraska
2. Notre Dame
3. Texas
4. Tennessee
5. Ohio St.
6. Arizona St.
7. Louisiana St.
8. Stanford
9. Michigan
10. Auburn
11. Arkansas
12. Toledo
13. Georgia Tech
14. Dartmouth
15. Southern Cal
16. Air Force
17. Tulane
18. Penn St.
19. Houston
20. Oklahoma
    Mississippi

## 1971
**Team**
1. Nebraska
2. Oklahoma
3. Colorado
4. Alabama
5. Penn St.
6. Michigan
7. Georgia
8. Arizona St.
9. Tennessee
10. Stanford
11. Louisiana St.
12. Auburn
13. Notre Dame
14. Toledo
15. Mississippi
16. Arkansas
17. Houston
18. Texas
19. Washington
20. Southern Cal

## 1972
**Team**
1. Southern Cal
2. Oklahoma
3. Texas
4. Nebraska
5. Auburn
6. Michigan
7. Alabama
8. Tennessee
9. Ohio St.
10. Penn St.
11. Louisiana St.
12. North Caro.
13. Arizona St.
14. Notre Dame
15. UCLA
16. Colorado
17. North Caro. St.
18. Louisville
19. Washington St.
20. Georgia Tech

## 1973
**Team**
1. Notre Dame
2. Ohio St.
3. Oklahoma
4. Alabama
5. Penn St.
6. Michigan
7. Nebraska
8. Southern Cal
9. Arizona St.
    Houston
11. Texas Tech
12. UCLA
13. Louisiana St.
14. Texas
15. Miami (Ohio)
16. North Caro. St.
17. Missouri
18. Kansas
19. Tennessee
20. Maryland
    Tulane

## 1974
**Team**
1. Oklahoma
2. Southern Cal
3. Michigan
4. Ohio St.
5. Alabama
6. Notre Dame
7. Penn St.
8. Auburn
9. Nebraska
10. Miami (Ohio)
11. North Caro. St.
12. Michigan St.
13. Maryland
14. Baylor
15. Florida
16. Texas A&M
17. Mississippi St.
    Texas
19. Houston
20. Tennessee

## 1975
**Team**
1. Oklahoma
2. Arizona St.
3. Alabama
4. Ohio St.
5. UCLA
6. Texas
7. Arkansas
8. Michigan
9. Nebraska
10. Penn St.
11. Texas A&M
12. Miami (Ohio)
13. Maryland
14. California
15. Pittsburgh
16. Colorado
17. Southern Cal
18. Arizona
19. Georgia
20. West Va.

## 1976
**Team**
1. Pittsburgh
2. Southern Cal
3. Michigan
4. Houston
5. Oklahoma
6. Ohio St.
7. Texas A&M
8. Maryland
9. Nebraska
10. Georgia
11. Alabama
12. Notre Dame
13. Texas Tech
14. Oklahoma St.
15. UCLA
16. Colorado
17. Rutgers
18. Kentucky
19. Iowa St.
20. Mississippi St.

## 1977
**Team**
1. Notre Dame
2. Alabama
3. Arkansas
4. Texas
5. Penn St.
6. Kentucky
7. Oklahoma
8. Pittsburgh
9. Michigan
10. Washington
11. Ohio St.
12. Nebraska
13. Southern Cal
14. Florida St.
15. Stanford
16. San Diego St.
17. North Caro.
18. Arizona St.
19. Clemson
20. Brigham Young

## 1978
**Team**
1. Alabama
2. Southern Cal
3. Oklahoma
4. Penn St.
5. Michigan
6. Clemson
7. Notre Dame
8. Nebraska
9. Texas
10. Houston
11. Arkansas
12. Michigan St.
13. Purdue
14. UCLA
15. Missouri
16. Georgia
17. Stanford
18. North Caro. St.
19. Texas A&M
20. Maryland

## 1979
**Team**
1. Alabama
2. Southern Cal
3. Oklahoma
4. Ohio St.
5. Houston
6. Florida St.
7. Pittsburgh
8. Arkansas
9. Nebraska
10. Purdue
11. Washington
12. Texas
13. Brigham Young
14. Baylor
15. North Caro.
16. Auburn
17. Temple
18. Michigan
19. Indiana
20. Penn St.

## 1980
**Team**
1. Georgia
2. Pittsburgh
3. Oklahoma
4. Michigan
5. Florida St.
6. Alabama
7. Nebraska
8. Penn St.
9. Notre Dame
10. North Caro.
11. Southern Cal
12. Brigham Young
13. UCLA
14. Baylor
15. Ohio St.
16. Washington
17. Purdue
18. Miami (Fla.)
19. Mississippi St.
20. Southern Methodist

## 1981
**Team**
1. Clemson
2. Texas
3. Penn St.
4. Pittsburgh
5. Southern Methodist
6. Georgia
7. Alabama
8. Miami (Fla.)
9. North Caro.
10. Washington
11. Nebraska
12. Michigan
13. Brigham Young
14. Southern Cal
15. Ohio St.
16. Arizona St.
17. West Va.
18. Iowa
19. Missouri
20. Oklahoma

## 1982
**Team**
1. Penn St.
2. Southern Methodist
3. Nebraska
4. Georgia
5. UCLA
6. Arizona St.
7. Washington
8. Clemson
9. Arkansas
10. Pittsburgh
11. Louisiana St.
12. Ohio St.
13. Florida St.
14. Auburn
15. Southern Cal
16. Oklahoma
17. Texas
18. North Caro.
19. West Va.
20. Maryland

## 1983
**Team**
1. Miami (Fla.)
2. Nebraska
3. Auburn
4. Georgia
5. Texas
6. Florida
7. Brigham Young
8. Michigan
9. Ohio St.
10. Illinois
11. Clemson
12. Southern Methodist
13. Air Force
14. Iowa
15. Alabama
16. West Va.
17. UCLA
18. Pittsburgh
19. Boston College
20. East Caro.

*Division I-A National Poll Rankings*                    95

**1984**

Team
1. Brigham Young
2. Washington
3. Florida
4. Nebraska
5. Boston College
6. Oklahoma
7. Oklahoma St.
8. Southern Methodist
9. UCLA
10. Southern Cal
11. South Caro.
12. Maryland
13. Ohio St.
14. Auburn
15. Louisiana St.
16. Iowa
17. Florida St.
18. Miami (Fla.)
19. Kentucky
20. Virginia

**1985**

Team
1. Oklahoma
2. Michigan
3. Penn St.
4. Tennessee
5. Florida
6. Texas A&M
7. UCLA
8. Air Force
9. Miami (Fla.)
10. Iowa
11. Nebraska
12. Arkansas
13. Alabama
14. Ohio St.
15. Florida St.
16. Brigham Young
17. Baylor
18. Maryland
19. Georgia Tech
20. Louisiana St.

**1986**

Team
1. Penn St.
2. Miami (Fla.)
3. Oklahoma
4. Arizona St.
5. Nebraska
6. Auburn
7. Ohio St.
8. Michigan
9. Alabama
10. Louisiana St.
11. Arizona
12. Baylor
13. Texas A&M
14. UCLA
15. Arkansas
16. Iowa
17. Clemson
18. Washington
19. Boston College
20. Virginia Tech

**1987**

Team
1. Miami (Fla.)
2. Florida St.
3. Oklahoma
4. Syracuse
5. Louisiana St.
6. Nebraska
7. Auburn
8. Michigan St.
9. UCLA
10. Texas A&M
11. Oklahoma St.
12. Clemson
13. Georgia
14. Tennessee
15. South Caro.
16. Iowa
17. Notre Dame
18. Southern Cal
19. Michigan
20. Arizona St.

**1988**

Team
1. Notre Dame
2. Miami (Fla.)
3. Florida St.
4. Michigan
5. West Va.
6. UCLA
7. Southern Cal
8. Auburn
9. Clemson
10. Nebraska
11. Oklahoma St.
12. Arkansas
13. Syracuse
14. Oklahoma
15. Georgia
16. Washington St.
17. Alabama
18. Houston
19. Louisiana St.
20. Indiana

**†1989**

Team
1. Miami (Fla.)
2. Notre Dame
3. Florida St.
4. Colorado
5. Tennessee
6. Auburn
7. Michigan
8. Southern Cal
9. Alabama
10. Illinois
11. Nebraska
12. Clemson
13. Arkansas
14. Houston
15. Penn St.
16. Michigan St.
17. Pittsburgh
18. Virginia
19. Texas Tech
20. Texas A&M
21. West Va.
22. Brigham Young
23. Washington
24. Ohio St.
25. Arizona

**1990**

Team
1. Colorado
2. Georgia Tech
3. Miami (Fla.)
4. Florida St.
5. Washington
6. Notre Dame
7. Michigan
8. Tennessee
9. Clemson
10. Houston
11. Penn St.
12. Texas
13. Florida
14. Louisville
15. Texas A&M
16. Michigan St.
17. Oklahoma
18. Iowa
19. Auburn
20. Southern Cal
21. Mississippi
22. Brigham Young
23. Virginia
24. Nebraska
25. Illinois

**1991**

Team
1. Miami (Fla.)
2. Washington
3. Penn St.
4. Florida St.
5. Alabama
6. Michigan
7. Florida
8. California
9. East Caro.
10. Iowa
11. Syracuse
12. Texas A&M
13. Notre Dame
14. Tennessee
15. Nebraska
16. Oklahoma
17. Georgia
18. Clemson
19. UCLA
20. Colorado
21. Tulsa
22. Stanford
23. Brigham Young
24. North Caro. St.
25. Air Force

**1992**

Team
1. Alabama
2. Florida St.
3. Miami (Fla.)
4. Notre Dame
5. Michigan
6. Syracuse
7. Texas A&M
8. Georgia
9. Stanford
10. Florida
11. Washington
12. Tennessee
13. Colorado
14. Nebraska
15. Washington St.
16. Mississippi
17. North Caro. St.
18. Ohio St.
19. North Caro.
20. Hawaii
21. Boston College
22. Kansas
23. Mississippi St.
24. Fresno St.
25. Wake Forest

* On January 6, 1948, in a special postseason poll after the Rose Bowl, the Associated Press voted Michigan No. 1 and Notre Dame No. 2. However, the postseason poll did not supersede the final regular-season poll of December 6, 1947.   † Beginning in 1989 season, AP selected top 25 teams instead of 20.

# ASSOCIATED PRESS
## WEEKLY LEADERS

The weekly dates are for Tuesday, the most frequent release date of the poll, except when the final poll was taken after January 1-2 bowl games. A team's record includes its last game before the weekly poll. A new weekly leader's rank the previous week is indicated in parentheses after its record. Final poll leaders (annual champions) are in bold face. (Note: Only 10 teams were ranked in the weekly polls during 1962, 1963, 1964, 1965, 1966 and 1967; 20 were ranked in all other seasons until 1989, when 25 were ranked.)

| Date | 1936 | | |
|---|---|---|---|
| 10-20 | Minnesota ....................(3-0) | | |
| 10-27 | Minnesota ....................(4-0) | | |
| 11-3 | Northwestern .............(5-0) (3) | | |
| 11-10 | Northwestern ................(6-0) | | |
| 11-17 | Northwestern ...............(7-0) | | |
| 11-24 | Minnesota ................(7-1) (2) | | |
| **12-1** | **Minnesota ...................(7-1)** | | |
| | **1937** | | |
| 10-20 | California ....................(5-0) | | |
| 10-27 | California ....................(6-0) | | |
| 11-2 | California ....................(7-0) | | |
| 11-9 | Pittsburgh .............(6-0-1) (3) | | |
| 11-16 | Pittsburgh.................(7-0-1) | | |
| 11-23 | Pittsburgh.................(8-0-1) | | |
| **11-30** | **Pittsburgh ................(9-0-1)** | | |
| | **1938** | | |
| 10-18 | Pittsburgh ...................(4-0) | | |
| 10-25 | Pittsburgh ...................(5-0) | | |
| 11-1 | Pittsburgh ...................(6-0) | | |
| 11-8 | Texas Christian ...........(7-0) (2) | | |
| 11-15 | Notre Dame .............(7-0) (2) | | |
| 11-22 | Notre Dame .................(8-0) | | |
| 11-29 | Notre Dame .................(8-0) | | |
| **12-6** | **Texas Christian .........(10-0) (2)** | | |
| | **1939** | | |
| 10-17 | Pittsburgh ...................(3-0) | | |
| 10-24 | Tennessee ..............(4-0) (5) | | |
| 10-31 | Tennessee...................(5-0) | | |
| 11-7 | Tennessee...................(6-0) | | |
| 11-14 | Tennessee...................(7-0) | | |
| 11-21 | Texas A&M ...............(9-0) (2) | | |
| 11-28 (tie) | Texas A&M ..................(9-0) | | |
| (tie) | Southern Cal ..........(6-0-1) (4) | | |
| 12-5 | Texas A&M ................(10-0) | | |
| **12-12** | **Texas A&M ...............(10-0)** | | |
| | **1940** | | |
| 10-15 | Cornell ......................(2-0) | | |
| 10-22 | Cornell ......................(3-0) | | |
| 10-29 | Cornell ......................(4-0) | | |
| 11-5 | Cornell ......................(5-0) | | |
| 11-12 | Minnesota ...............(6-0) (2) | | |
| 11-19 | Minnesota...................(7-0) | | |
| 11-26 | Minnesota...................(8-0) | | |
| **12-3** | **Minnesota ..................(8-0)** | | |
| | **1941** | | |
| 10-14 | Minnesota....................(2-0) | | |
| 10-21 | Minnesota....................(3-0) | | |
| 10-28 (tie) | Minnesota...................(4-0) | | |
| (tie) | Texas .....................(5-0) (2) | | |
| 11-4 | Texas .......................(6-0) | | |
| 11-11 | Minnesota ...............(6-0) (2) | | |
| 11-18 | Minnesota...................(7-0) | | |
| 11-25 | Minnesota...................(8-0) | | |
| **12-2** | **Minnesota ..................(8-0)** | | |
| | **1942** | | |
| 10-13 | Ohio St. ......................(3-0) | | |
| 10-20 | Ohio St. ......................(4-0) | | |
| 10-27 | Ohio St. ......................(5-0) | | |
| 11-3 | Georgia...................(7-0) (2) | | |
| 11-10 | Georgia .....................(8-0) | | |
| 11-17 | Georgia .....................(9-0) | | |
| 11-24 | Boston College ...........(8-0) (3) | | |
| **12-1** | **Ohio St. ...............(9-1-0) (3)** | | |

| | 1943 | |
|---|---|---|
| 10-5 | Notre Dame .................(2-0) | |
| 10-12 | Notre Dame .................(3-0) | |
| 10-19 | Notre Dame .................(4-0) | |
| 10-26 | Notre Dame .................(5-0) | |
| 11-2 | Notre Dame .................(6-0) | |
| 11-9 | Notre Dame .................(7-0) | |
| 11-16 | Notre Dame .................(8-0) | |
| 11-23 | Notre Dame .................(9-0) | |
| **11-30** | **Notre Dame .............(9-1-0)** | |
| | **1944** | |
| 10-10 | Notre Dame .................(2-0) | |
| 10-17 | Notre Dame .................(3-0) | |
| 10-24 | Notre Dame .................(4-0) | |
| 10-31 | Army .....................(5-0) (2) | |
| 11-7 | Army ........................(6-0) | |
| 11-14 | Army ........................(7-0) | |
| 11-21 | Army ........................(8-0) | |
| 11-28 | Army ........................(8-0) | |
| **12-5** | **Army.........................(9-0)** | |
| | **1945** | |
| 10-9 | Army .......................(2-0-0) | |
| 10-16 | Army .......................(3-0-0) | |
| 10-23 | Army .......................(4-0-0) | |
| 10-30 | Army .......................(5-0-0) | |
| 11-6 | Army .......................(6-0-0) | |
| 11-13 | Army .......................(7-0-0) | |
| 11-20 | Army .......................(8-0-0) | |
| 11-27 | Army .......................(8-0-0) | |
| **12-4** | **Army........................(9-0-0)** | |
| | **1946** | |
| 10-8 | Texas......................(3-0-0) | |
| 10-15 | Army ...................(4-0-0) (2) | |
| 10-22 | Army .......................(5-0-0) | |
| 10-29 | Army .......................(6-0-0) | |
| 11-5 | Army .......................(7-0-0) | |
| 11-12 | Army .......................(7-0-1) | |
| 11-19 | Army .......................(8-0-1) | |
| 11-26 | Army .......................(8-0-1) | |
| **12-3** | **Notre Dame ...........(8-0-1) (2)** | |
| | **1947*** | |
| 10-7 | Notre Dame ...............(1-0-0) | |
| 10-14 | Michigan ...............(3-0-0) (2) | |
| 10-21 | Michigan ..................(4-0-0) | |
| 10-28 | Notre Dame ...........(4-0-0) (2) | |
| 11-4 | Notre Dame ...............(5-0-0) | |
| 11-11 | Notre Dame ...............(6-0-0) | |
| 11-18 | Michigan ...............(8-0-0) (2) | |
| 11-25 | Notre Dame ...........(8-0-0) (2) | |
| 12-2 | Notre Dame ...............(8-0-0) | |
| **12-9** | **Notre Dame ..............(9-0-0)** | |
| | **1948** | |
| 10-5 | Notre Dame ...............(2-0-0) | |
| 10-12 | North Caro................(3-0-0) (2) | |
| 10-19 | Michigan ..............(4-0-0) (4) | |
| 10-26 | Michigan ..................(5-0-0) | |
| 11-2 | Notre Dame ...........(6-0-0) (2) | |
| 11-9 | Michigan ...............(7-0-0) (2) | |
| 11-16 | Michigan ..................(8-0-0) | |
| 11-23 | Michigan ..................(9-0-0) | |
| **11-30** | **Michigan..................(9-0-0)** | |
| | **1949** | |
| 10-4 | Michigan .................(2-0-0) | |
| 10-11 | Notre Dame ...........(3-0-0) (2) | |

| 10-18 | Notre Dame | (4-0-0) |
| 10-25 | Notre Dame | (4-0-0) |
| 11-1 | Notre Dame | (5-0-0) |
| 11-8 | Notre Dame | (6-0-0) |
| 11-15 | Notre Dame | (7-0-0) |
| 11-22 | Notre Dame | (8-0-0) |
| **11-29** | **Notre Dame** | **(9-0-0)** |

**1950**

| 10-3 | Notre Dame | (1-0-0) |
| 10-10 | Army | (2-0-0) (4) |
| 10-17 | Army | (3-0-0) |
| 10-24 | Southern Methodist | (5-0-0) (3) |
| 10-31 | Southern Methodist | (5-0-0) |
| 11-7 | Army | (6-0-0) (2) |
| 11-14 | Ohio St. | (6-1-0) (2) |
| 11-21 | Oklahoma | (8-0-0) (2) |
| **11-28** | **Oklahoma** | **(9-0-0)** |

**1951**

| 10-2 | Michigan St. | (2-0-0) |
| 10-9 | Michigan St. | (3-0-0) |
| 10-16 | California | (4-0-0) (2) |
| 10-23 | Tennessee | (4-0-0) (2) |
| 10-30 | Tennessee | (5-0-0) |
| 11-6 | Tennessee | (6-0-0) |
| 11-13 | Michigan St. | (7-0-0)(5) |
| 11-20 | Tennessee | (8-0-0) (2) |
| 11-27 | Tennessee | (9-0-0) |
| **12-4** | **Tennessee** | **(10-0-0)** |

**1952**

| 9-30 | Michigan St. | (1-0-0) |
| 10-7 | Wisconsin | (2-0-0) (8) |
| 10-14 | Michigan St. | (3-0-0)(2) |
| 10-21 | Michigan St. | (4-0-0) |
| 10-28 | Michigan St. | (5-0-0) |
| 11-4 | Michigan St. | (6-0-0) |
| 11-11 | Michigan St. | (7-0-0) |
| 11-18 | Michigan St. | (8-0-0) |
| 11-25 | Michigan St. | (9-0-0) |
| **12-1** | **Michigan St.** | **(9-0-0)** |

**1953**

| 9-29 | Notre Dame | (1-0-0) |
| 10-6 | Notre Dame | (2-0-0) |
| 10-13 | Notre Dame | (2-0-0) |
| 10-20 | Notre Dame | (3-0-0) |
| 10-27 | Notre Dame | (4-0-0) |
| 11-3 | Notre Dame | (5-0-0) |
| 11-10 | Notre Dame | (6-0-0) |
| 11-17 | Notre Dame | (7-0-0) |
| 11-24 | Maryland | (10-0-0) (2) |
| **12-1** | **Maryland** | **(10-0-0)** |

**1954**

| 9-21 | Oklahoma | (1-0-0) |
| 9-28 | Notre Dame | (1-0-0) (2) |
| 10-5 | Oklahoma | (2-0-0) (2) |
| 10-12 | Oklahoma | (3-0-0) |
| 10-19 | Oklahoma | (4-0-0) |
| 10-26 | Ohio St. | (5-0-0) (4) |
| 11-2 | UCLA | (7-0-0) (3) |
| 11-9 | UCLA | (8-0-0) |
| 11-16 | Ohio St. | (8-0-0) (2) |
| 11-23 | Ohio St. | (9-0-0) |
| **11-30** | **Ohio St.** | **(9-0-0)** |

**1955**

| 9-20 | UCLA | (1-0-0) |
| 9-27 | Maryland | (2-0-0) (5) |
| 10-4 | Maryland | (3-0-0) |
| 10-11 | Michigan | (3-0-0) (2) |
| 10-18 | Michigan | (4-0-0) |
| 10-25 | Maryland | (6-0-0) (2) |
| 11-1 | Maryland | (7-0-0) |
| 11-8 | Oklahoma | (7-0-0) (2) |
| 11-15 | Oklahoma | (8-0-0) |
| 11-22 | Oklahoma | (9-0-0) |
| **11-29** | **Oklahoma** | **(10-0-0)** |

**1956**

| 9-25 | Oklahoma | (0-0-0) |
| 10-2 | Oklahoma | (1-0-0) |
| 10-9 | Oklahoma | (2-0-0) |
| 10-16 | Oklahoma | (3-0-0) |
| 10-23 | Michigan St. | (4-0-0) (2) |
| 10-30 | Oklahoma | (5-0-0) |
| 11-6 | Oklahoma | (6-0-0) |
| 11-13 | Tennessee | (7-0-0) (3) |
| 11-20 | Oklahoma | (8-0-0) (2) |
| 11-27 | Oklahoma | (9-0-0) |
| **12-4** | **Oklahoma** | **(10-0-0)** |

**1957**

| 9-24 | Oklahoma | (1-0-0) |
| 10-1 | Oklahoma | (1-0-0) |
| 10-8 | Oklahoma | (2-0-0) |
| 10-15 | Michigan St. | (3-0-0) (2) |
| 10-22 | Oklahoma | (4-0-0) (2) |
| 10-29 | Texas A&M | (6-0-0) (2) |
| 11-5 | Texas A&M | (7-0-0) |
| 11-12 | Texas A&M | (8-0-0) |
| 11-19 | Michigan St. | (7-1-0)(4) |
| 11-26 | Auburn | (9-0-0) (2) |
| **12-3** | **Auburn** | **(10-0-0)** |

**1958**

| 9-23 | Ohio St. | (0-0-0) |
| 9-30 | Oklahoma | (1-0-0) (2) |
| 10-7 | Auburn | (2-0-0) (2) |
| 10-14 | Army | (3-0-0) (3) |
| 10-21 | Army | (4-0-0) |
| 10-28 | Louisiana St. | (6-0-0) (3) |
| 11-4 | Louisiana St. | (7-0-0) |
| 11-11 | Louisiana St. | (8-0-0) |
| 11-18 | Louisiana St. | (9-0-0) |
| 11-25 | Louisiana St. | (10-0-0) |
| **12-2** | **Louisiana St.** | **(10-0-0)** |

**1959**

| 9-22 | Louisiana St. | (1-0-0) |
| 9-29 | Louisiana St. | (2-0-0) |
| 10-6 | Louisiana St. | (3-0-0) |
| 10-13 | Louisiana St. | (4-0-0) |
| 10-20 | Louisiana St. | (5-0-0) |
| 10-27 | Louisiana St. | (6-0-0) |
| 11-3 | Louisiana St. | (7-0-0) |
| 11-10 | Syracuse | (7-0-0) (4) |
| 11-17 | Syracuse | (8-0-0) |
| 11-24 | Syracuse | (9-0-0) |
| 12-1 | Syracuse | (9-0-0) |
| **12-8** | **Syracuse** | **(10-0-0)** |

**1960**

| 9-20 | Mississippi | (1-0-0) |
| 9-27 | Mississippi | (2-0-0) |
| 10-4 | Syracuse | (2-0-0) (2) |
| 10-11 | Mississippi | (4-0-0) (2) |
| 10-18 | Iowa | (4-0-0) (2) |
| 10-25 | Iowa | (5-0-0) |
| 11-1 | Iowa | (6-0-0) |
| 11-8 | Minnesota | (7-0-0) (3) |
| 11-15 | Missouri | (9-0-0) (2) |
| 11-22 | Minnesota | (8-1-0) (4) |
| **11-29** | **Minnesota** | **(8-1-0)** |

**1961**

| 9-26 | Iowa | (0-0-0) |
| 10-3 | Iowa | (1-0-0) |
| 10-10 | Mississippi | (3-0-0) (2) |
| 10-17 | Michigan St. | (3-0-0) (5) |
| 10-24 | Michigan St. | (4-0-0) |
| 10-31 | Michigan St. | (5-0-0) |
| 11-7 | Texas | (7-0-0) (3) |
| 11-14 | Texas | (8-0-0) |
| 11-21 | Alabama | (9-0-0) (2) |
| 11-28 | Alabama | (9-0-0) |
| **12-5** | **Alabama** | **(10-0-0)** |

**1962**

| 9-25 | Alabama | (1-0-0) |

| | | |
|---|---|---|
| 10-2 | Ohio St. | (1-0-0) (2) |
| 10-9 | Alabama | (3-0-0) (2) |
| 10-16 | Texas | (4-0-0) (2) |
| 10-23 | Texas | (5-0-0) |
| 10-30 | Northwestern | (5-0-0) (3) |
| 11-6 | Northwestern | (6-0-0) |
| 11-13 | Alabama | (8-0-0) (3) |
| 11-20 | Southern Cal | (8-0-0) (2) |
| 11-27 | Southern Cal | (9-0-0) |
| **12-4** | **Southern Cal** | **(10-0-0)** |

**1963**

| | | |
|---|---|---|
| 9-24 | Southern Cal | (1-0-0) |
| 10-1 | Oklahoma | (1-0-0) (3) |
| 10-8 | Oklahoma | (2-0-0) |
| 10-15 | Texas | (4-0-0) (3) |
| 10-22 | Texas | (5-0-0) |
| 10-29 | Texas | (6-0-0) |
| 11-5 | Texas | (7-0-0) |
| 11-12 | Texas | (8-0-0) |
| 11-19 | Texas | (9-0-0) |
| 11-26 | Texas | (9-0-0) |
| 12-3 | Texas | (10-0-0) |
| **12-10** | **Texas** | **(10-0-0)** |

**1964**

| | | |
|---|---|---|
| 9-29 | Texas | (2-0-0) |
| 10-6 | Texas | (3-0-0) |
| 10-13 | Texas | (3-0-0) |
| 10-20 | Ohio St. | (4-0-0)(2) |
| 10-27 | Ohio St. | (5-0-0) |
| 11-3 | Notre Dame | (6-0-0)(2) |
| 11-10 | Notre Dame | (7-0-0) |
| 11-17 | Notre Dame | (8-0-0) |
| 11-24 | Notre Dame | (9-0-0) |
| **12-1** | **Alabama** | **(10-0-0) (2)** |

**1965**

| | | |
|---|---|---|
| 9-21 | Notre Dame | (1-0-0) |
| 9-28 | Texas | (2-0-0) (3) |
| 10-5 | Texas | (3-0-0) |
| 10-12 | Texas | (4-0-0) |
| 10-19 | Arkansas | (5-0-0) (3) |
| 10-26 | Michigan St. | (6-0-0) (2) |
| 11-2 | Michigan St. | (7-0-0) |
| 11-9 | Michigan St. | (8-0-0) |
| 11-16 | Michigan St. | (9-0-0) |
| 11-23 | Michigan St. | (10-0-0) |
| 11-30 | Michigan St. | (10-0-0) |
| **1-4** | **Alabama** | **(9-1-1) (4)** |

**1966**

| | | |
|---|---|---|
| 9-20 | Michigan St. | (1-0-0) |
| 9-27 | Michigan St. | (2-0-0) |
| 10-4 | Michigan St. | (3-0-0) |
| 10-11 | Michigan St. | (4-0-0) |
| 10-18 | Notre Dame | (4-0-0) (2) |
| 10-25 | Notre Dame | (5-0-0) |
| 11-1 | Notre Dame | (6-0-0) |
| 11-8 | Notre Dame | (7-0-0) |
| 11-15 | Notre Dame | (8-0-0) |
| 11-22 | Notre Dame | (8-0-1) |
| 11-29 | Notre Dame | (9-0-1) |
| **12-5** | **Notre Dame** | **(9-0-1)** |

**1967**

| | | |
|---|---|---|
| 9-19 | Notre Dame | (0-0-0) |
| 9-26 | Notre Dame | (1-0-0) |
| 10-3 | Southern Cal | (3-0-0) (2) |
| 10-10 | Southern Cal | (4-0-0) |
| 10-17 | Southern Cal | (5-0-0) |
| 10-24 | Southern Cal | (6-0-0) |
| 10-31 | Southern Cal | (7-0-0) |
| 11-7 | Southern Cal | (8-0-0) |
| 11-14 | UCLA | (7-0-1) (2) |
| 11-21 | Southern Cal | (9-1-0) (4) |
| **11-28** | **Southern Cal** | **(9-1-0)** |

**1968**

| | | |
|---|---|---|
| 9-17 | Purdue | (0-0-0) |
| 9-24 | Purdue | (1-0-0) |
| 10-1 | Purdue | (2-0-0) |
| 10-8 | Purdue | (3-0-0) |
| 10-15 | Southern Cal | (4-0-0) (2) |
| 10-22 | Southern Cal | (5-0-0) |
| 10-29 | Southern Cal | (5-0-0) |
| 11-5 | Southern Cal | (6-0-0) |
| 11-12 | Southern Cal | (7-0-0) |
| 11-19 | Southern Cal | (8-0-0) |
| 11-26 | Ohio St. | (9-0-0) (2) |
| 12-2 | Ohio St. | (9-0-0) |
| **12-9** | **Ohio St.** | **(10-0-0)** |

**1969**

| | | |
|---|---|---|
| 9-23 | Ohio St. | (0-0-0) |
| 9-30 | Ohio St. | (1-0-0) |
| 10-7 | Ohio St. | (2-0-0) |
| 10-14 | Ohio St. | (3-0-0) |
| 10-21 | Ohio St. | (4-0-0) |
| 10-28 | Ohio St. | (5-0-0) |
| 11-4 | Ohio St. | (6-0-0) |
| 11-11 | Ohio St. | (7-0-0) |
| 11-18 | Ohio St. | (8-0-0) |
| 11-25 | Texas | (8-0-0) (2) |
| 12-2 | Texas | (9-0-0) |
| 12-9 | Texas | (10-0-0) |
| **1-4** | **Texas** | **(11-0-0)** |

**1970**

| | | |
|---|---|---|
| 9-15 | Ohio St. | (0-0-0) |
| 9-22 | Ohio St. | (0-0-0) |
| 9-29 | Ohio St. | (1-0-0) |
| 10-6 | Ohio St. | (2-0-0) |
| 10-13 | Ohio St. | (3-0-0) |
| 10-20 | Ohio St. | (4-0-0) |
| 10-27 | Texas | (5-0-0) (2) |
| 11-3 | Texas | (6-0-0) |
| 11-10 | Texas | (7-0-0) |
| 11-17 | Texas | (8-0-0) |
| 11-24 | Texas | (8-0-0) |
| 12-1 | Texas | (9-0-0) |
| 12-8 | Texas | (10-0-0) |
| **1-6** | **Nebraska** | **(11-0-1) (3)** |

**1971**

| | | |
|---|---|---|
| 9-14 | Nebraska | (1-0-0) |
| 9-21 | Nebraska | (2-0-0) |
| 9-28 | Nebraska | (3-0-0) |
| 10-5 | Nebraska | (4-0-0) |
| 10-12 | Nebraska | (5-0-0) |
| 10-19 | Nebraska | (6-0-0) |
| 10-26 | Nebraska | (7-0-0) |
| 11-2 | Nebraska | (8-0-0) |
| 11-9 | Nebraska | (9-0-0) |
| 11-16 | Nebraska | (10-0-0) |
| 11-23 | Nebraska | (10-0-0) |
| 11-30 | Nebraska | (11-0-0) |
| 12-7 | Nebraska | (12-0-0) |
| **1-4** | **Nebraska** | **(13-0-0)** |

**1972**

| | | |
|---|---|---|
| 9-12 | Southern Cal | (1-0-0) |
| 9-19 | Southern Cal | (2-0-0) |
| 9-26 | Southern Cal | (3-0-0) |
| 10-3 | Southern Cal | (4-0-0) |
| 10-10 | Southern Cal | (5-0-0) |
| 10-17 | Southern Cal | (6-0-0) |
| 10-24 | Southern Cal | (7-0-0) |
| 10-31 | Southern Cal | (8-0-0) |
| 11-7 | Southern Cal | (9-0-0) |
| 11-14 | Southern Cal | (9-0-0) |
| 11-21 | Southern Cal | (10-0-0) |
| 11-28 | Southern Cal | (10-0-0) |
| 12-5 | Southern Cal | (11-0-0) |
| **1-3** | **Southern Cal** | **(12-0-0)** |

**1973**

| | | |
|---|---|---|
| 9-11 | Southern Cal | (0-0-0) |
| 9-18 | Southern Cal | (1-0-0) |

| 9-25 | Southern Cal ............. (2-0-0) |
| 10-2 | Ohio St. ............... (2-0-0) (3) |
| 10-9 | Ohio St. ..................... (3-0-0) |
| 10-16 | Ohio St. ..................... (4-0-0) |
| 10-23 | Ohio St. ..................... (5-0-0) |
| 10-30 | Ohio St. ..................... (6-0-0) |
| 11-6 | Ohio St. ..................... (7-0-0) |
| 11-13 | Ohio St. ..................... (8-0-0) |
| 11-20 | Ohio St. ..................... (9-0-0) |
| 11-27 | Alabama ................ (10-0-0) (2) |
| 12-4 | Alabama ................... (11-0-0) |
| **1-3** | **Notre Dame ........... (11-0-0)(3)** |

**1974**

| 9-10 | Oklahoma .................. (0-0-0) |
| 9-17 | Notre Dame ........... (1-0-0) (2) |
| 9-24 | Ohio St. ............... (2-0-0) (2) |
| 10-1 | Ohio St. ..................... (3-0-0) |
| 10-8 | Ohio St. ..................... (4-0-0) |
| 10-15 | Ohio St. ..................... (5-0-0) |
| 10-22 | Ohio St. ..................... (6-0-0) |
| 10-29 | Ohio St. ..................... (7-0-0) |
| 11-5 | Ohio St. ..................... (8-0-0) |
| 11-12 | Oklahoma ............. (8-0-0) (2) |
| 11-19 | Oklahoma ................. (9-0-0) |
| 11-26 | Oklahoma ............... (10-0-0) |
| 12-3 | Oklahoma ............... (11-0-0) |
| **1-3** | **Oklahoma ............... (11-0-0)** |

**1975**

| 9-9 | Oklahoma .................. (0-0-0) |
| 9-16 | Oklahoma .................. (1-0-0) |
| 9-23 | Oklahoma .................. (2-0-0) |
| 9-30 | Oklahoma .................. (3-0-0) |
| 10-7 | Ohio St. ............... (4-0-0) (2) |
| 10-14 | Ohio St. ..................... (5-0-0) |
| 10-21 | Ohio St. ..................... (6-0-0) |
| 10-28 | Ohio St. ..................... (7-0-0) |
| 11-4 | Ohio St. ..................... (8-0-0) |
| 11-11 | Ohio St. ..................... (9-0-0) |
| 11-18 | Ohio St. ................... (10-0-0) |
| 11-25 | Ohio St. ................... (11-0-0) |
| 12-2 | Ohio St. ................... (11-0-0) |
| **1-3** | **Oklahoma............. (11-1-0) (3)** |

**1976**

| 9-14 | Michigan ................... (1-0-0) |
| 9-21 | Michigan ................... (2-0-0) |
| 9-28 | Michigan ................... (3-0-0) |
| 10-5 | Michigan ................... (4-0-0) |
| 10-12 | Michigan ................... (5-0-0) |
| 10-19 | Michigan ................... (6-0-0) |
| 10-26 | Michigan ................... (7-0-0) |
| 11-2 | Michigan ................... (8-0-0) |
| 11-9 | Pittsburgh ............. (9-0-0) (2) |
| 11-16 | Pittsburgh............... (10-0-0) |
| 11-23 | Pittsburgh............... (10-0-0) |
| 11-30 | Pittsburgh............... (11-0-0) |
| **1-5** | **Pittsburgh ................ (12-0-0)** |

**1977**

| 9-13 | Michigan ................... (1-0-0) |
| 9-20 | Michigan ................... (2-0-0) |
| 9-27 | Oklahoma ............... (3-0-0) (3) |
| 10-4 | Southern Cal ........... (4-0-0) (2) |
| 10-11 | Michigan ............... (5-0-0) (3) |
| 10-18 | Michigan ................... (6-0-0) |
| 10-25 | Texas .................... (6-0-0) (2) |
| 11-1 | Texas......................... (7-0-0) |
| 11-8 | Texas......................... (8-0-0) |
| 11-15 | Texas......................... (9-0-0) |
| 11-22 | Texas....................... (10-0-0) |
| 11-29 | Texas ..................... (11-0-0) |
| **1-4** | **Notre Dame........... (11-1-0) (5)** |

**1978**

| 9-12 | Alabama ................... (1-0-0) |
| 9-19 | Alabama ................... (2-0-0) |
| 9-26 | Oklahoma ........... (3-0-0) (tie 3) |

| 10-3 | Oklahoma .................. (4-0-0) |
| 10-10 | Oklahoma .................. (5-0-0) |
| 10-17 | Oklahoma .................. (6-0-0) |
| 10-24 | Oklahoma .................. (7-0-0) |
| 10-31 | Oklahoma .................. (8-0-0) |
| 11-7 | Oklahoma .................. (9-0-0) |
| 11-14 | Penn St. ............... (10-0-0) (2) |
| 11-21 | Penn St.................... (10-0-0) |
| 11-28 | Penn St.................... (11-0-0) |
| 12-5 | Penn St.................... (11-0-0) |
| **1-4** | **Alabama ............... (11-1-0) (2)** |

**1979**

| 9-11 | Southern Cal .............. (1-0-0) |
| 9-18 | Southern Cal .............. (2-0-0) |
| 9-25 | Southern Cal .............. (3-0-0) |
| 10-2 | Southern Cal .............. (4-0-0) |
| 10-9 | Southern Cal .............. (5-0-0) |
| 10-16 | Alabama ................ (5-0-0) (2) |
| 10-23 | Alabama ................... (6-0-0) |
| 10-30 | Alabama ................... (7-0-0) |
| 11-6 | Alabama ................... (8-0-0) |
| 11-13 | Alabama ................... (9-0-0) |
| 11-20 | Alabama ................. (10-0-0) |
| 11-27 | Alabama ................. (11-0-0) |
| 12-4 | Ohio St. ............... (11-0-0) (3) |
| **1-3** | **Alabama ............... (12-0-0) (2)** |

**1980**

| 9-9 | Ohio St. ..................... (0-0-0) |
| 9-16 | Alabama ................ (1-0-0) (2) |
| 9-23 | Alabama ................... (2-0-0) |
| 9-30 | Alabama ................... (3-0-0) |
| 10-7 | Alabama ................... (4-0-0) |
| 10-14 | Alabama ................... (5-0-0) |
| 10-21 | Alabama ................... (6-0-0) |
| 10-28 | Alabama ................... (7-0-0) |
| 11-4 | Notre Dame ........... (7-0-0) (3) |
| 11-11 | Georgia .................. (9-0-0) (2) |
| 11-18 | Georgia ................. (10-0-0) |
| 11-25 | Georgia ................. (10-0-0) |
| 12-2 | Georgia ................. (11-0-0) |
| 12-9 | Georgia ................. (11-0-0) |
| **1-4** | **Georgia................. (12-0-0)** |

**1981**

| 9-8 | Michigan ................... (0-0-0) |
| 9-15 | Notre Dame ........... (1-0-0) (4) |
| 9-22 | Southern Cal ......... (2-0-0) (2) |
| 9-29 | Southern Cal ............. (3-0-0) |
| 10-6 | Southern Cal ............. (4-0-0) |
| 10-13 | Texas .................. (4-0-0) (3) |
| 10-20 | Penn St. ............... (5-0-0) (2) |
| 10-27 | Penn St. ................... (6-0-0) |
| 11-3 | Pittsburgh ............. (7-0-0) (2) |
| 11-10 | Pittsburgh ............... (8-0-0) |
| 11-17 | Pittsburgh ............... (9-0-0) |
| 11-24 | Pittsburgh............... (10-0-0) |
| 12-1 | Clemson .............. (11-0-0) (2) |
| **1-3** | **Clemson.................. (12-0-0)** |

**1982**

| 9-7 | Pittsburgh ................. (0-0-0) |
| 9-14 | Washington............. (1-0-0) (2) |
| 9-21 | Washington ............... (2-0-0) |
| 9-28 | Washington ............... (3-0-0) |
| 10-5 | Washington ............... (4-0-0) |
| 10-12 | Washington ............... (5-0-0) |
| 10-19 | Washington ............... (6-0-0) |
| 10-26 | Pittsburgh ............. (6-0-0) (2) |
| 11-2 | Pittsburgh ............... (7-0-0) |
| 11-9 | Georgia.................. (9-0-0) (3) |
| 11-16 | Georgia ................. (10-0-0) |
| 11-23 | Georgia ................. (10-0-0) |
| 11-30 | Georgia ................. (11-0-0) |
| 12-7 | Georgia ................. (11-0-0) |
| **1-3** | **Penn St................ (11-1-0) (2)** |

**1983**

| | | |
|---|---|---|
| 9-6 | Nebraska | (1-0-0) |
| 9-13 | Nebraska | (2-0-0) |
| 9-20 | Nebraska | (3-0-0) |
| 9-27 | Nebraska | (4-0-0) |
| 10-4 | Nebraska | (5-0-0) |
| 10-11 | Nebraska | (6-0-0) |
| 10-18 | Nebraska | (7-0-0) |
| 10-25 | Nebraska | (8-0-0) |
| 11-1 | Nebraska | (9-0-0) |
| 11-8 | Nebraska | (10-0-0) |
| 11-15 | Nebraska | (11-0-0) |
| 11-22 | Nebraska | (11-0-0) |
| 11-29 | Nebraska | (12-0-0) |
| 12-6 | Nebraska | (12-0-0) |
| **1-3** | **Miami (Fla.)** | **(11-1-0) (5)** |

**1984**

| | | |
|---|---|---|
| 9-4 | Miami (Fla.) | (2-0-0) |
| 9-11 | Nebraska | (1-0-0) (2) |
| 9-18 | Nebraska | (2-0-0) |
| 9-25 | Nebraska | (3-0-0) |
| 10-2 | Texas | (2-0-0) (2) |
| 10-9 | Texas | (3-0-0) |
| 10-16 | Washington | (6-0-0) (2) |
| 10-23 | Washington | (7-0-0) |
| 10-30 | Washington | (8-0-0) |
| 11-6 | Washington | (9-0-0) |
| 11-13 | Nebraska | (9-1-0) (2) |
| 11-20 | Brigham Young | (11-0-0) (3) |
| 11-27 | Brigham Young | (12-0-0) |
| 12-4 | Brigham Young | (12-0-0) |
| **1-3** | **Brigham Young** | **(13-0-0)** |

**1985**

| | | |
|---|---|---|
| 9-3 | Oklahoma | (0-0-0) |
| 9-10 | Auburn | (1-0-0) (2) |
| 9-17 | Auburn | (2-0-0) |
| 9-24 | Auburn | (2-0-0) |
| 10-1 | Iowa | (3-0-0) (3) |
| 10-8 | Iowa | (4-0-0) |
| 10-15 | Iowa | (5-0-0) |
| 10-22 | Iowa | (6-0-0) |
| 10-29 | Iowa | (7-0-0) |
| 11-5 | Florida | (7-0-1) (2) |
| 11-12 | Penn St. | (9-0-0) (2) |
| 11-19 | Penn St. | (10-0-0) |
| 11-26 | Penn St. | (11-0-0) |
| 12-3 | Penn St. | (11-0-0) |
| **1-3** | **Oklahoma** | **(11-1-0) (4)** |

**1986**

| | | |
|---|---|---|
| 9-9 | Oklahoma | (1-0-0) |
| 9-16 | Oklahoma | (1-0-0) |
| 9-23 | Oklahoma | (2-0-0) |
| 9-30 | Miami (Fla.) | (4-0-0) (2) |
| 10-7 | Miami (Fla.) | (5-0-0) |
| 10-14 | Miami (Fla.) | (6-0-0) |
| 10-21 | Miami (Fla.) | (7-0-0) |
| 10-28 | Miami (Fla.) | (7-0-0) |
| 11-4 | Miami (Fla.) | (8-0-0) |
| 11-11 | Miami (Fla.) | (9-0-0) |
| 11-18 | Miami (Fla.) | (10-0-0) |
| 11-25 | Miami (Fla.) | (10-0-0) |
| 12-2 | Miami (Fla.) | (11-0-0) |
| **1-4** | **Penn St.** | **(12-0-0) (2)** |

**1987**

| | | |
|---|---|---|
| 9-8 | Oklahoma | (1-0-0) |
| 9-15 | Oklahoma | (2-0-0) |
| 9-22 | Oklahoma | (2-0-0) |
| 9-29 | Oklahoma | (3-0-0) |
| 10-6 | Oklahoma | (4-0-0) |
| 10-13 | Oklahoma | (5-0-0) |
| 10-20 | Oklahoma | (6-0-0) |
| 10-27 | Oklahoma | (7-0-0) |
| 11-3 | Oklahoma | (8-0-0) |
| 11-10 | Oklahoma | (9-0-0) |
| 11-17 | Nebraska | (9-0-0) (2) |
| 11-24 | Oklahoma | (11-0-0) (2) |
| 12-1 | Oklahoma | (11-0-0) |
| 12-8 | Oklahoma | (11-0-0) |
| **1-3** | **Miami (Fla.)** | **(12-0-0) (2)** |

**1988**

| | | |
|---|---|---|
| 9-6 | Miami (Fla.) | (1-0-0) |
| 9-13 | Miami (Fla.) | (1-0-0) |
| 9-20 | Miami (Fla.) | (2-0-0) |
| 9-27 | Miami (Fla.) | (3-0-0) |
| 10-4 | Miami (Fla.) | (4-0-0) |
| 10-11 | Miami (Fla.) | (4-0-0) |
| 10-18 | UCLA | (6-0-0) (2) |
| 10-25 | UCLA | (7-0-0) |
| 11-1 | Notre Dame | (8-0-0) (2) |
| 11-8 | Notre Dame | (9-0-0) |
| 11-15 | Notre Dame | (9-0-0) |
| 11-22 | Notre Dame | (10-0-0) |
| 11-29 | Notre Dame | (11-0-0) |
| 12-6 | Notre Dame | (11-0-0) |
| **1-3** | **Notre Dame** | **(12-0-0)** |

**1989**

| | | |
|---|---|---|
| 9-5 | Notre Dame | (1-0-0) |
| 9-12 | Notre Dame | (1-0-0) |
| 9-19 | Notre Dame | (2-0-0) |
| 9-26 | Notre Dame | (3-0-0) |
| 10-3 | Notre Dame | (4-0-0) |
| 10-10 | Notre Dame | (5-0-0) |
| 10-17 | Notre Dame | (6-0-0) |
| 10-24 | Notre Dame | (7-0-0) |
| 10-31 | Notre Dame | (8-0-0) |
| 11-7 | Notre Dame | (9-0-0) |
| 11-14 | Notre Dame | (10-0-0) |
| 11-21 | Notre Dame | (11-0-0) |
| 11-28 | Colorado | (11-0-0) (2) |
| 12-5 | Colorado | (11-0-0) |
| **1-2** | **Miami (Fla.)** | **(11-1-0) (2)** |

Consensus all-American linebacker Michael Stonebreaker led a Notre Dame defense that allowed just 12.3 points per game during the 1988 regular season, sparking the Irish to the top ranking in all four major polls.

| | 1990 | | | |
|---|---|---|---|---|
| 9-4 | Miami (Fla.) ...............(0-0-0) | 10-28 | Florida St. .................(8-0-0) |
| 9-11 | Notre Dame ...........(0-0-0) (2) | 11-4 | Florida St. .................(9-0-0) |
| 9-18 | Notre Dame ...............(1-0-0) | 11-11 | Florida St. ................(10-0-0) |
| 9-25 | Notre Dame ...............(2-0-0) | 11-18 | Miami (Fla.) .............(9-0-0) (2) |
| 10-2 | Notre Dame ...............(3-0-0) | 11-25 | Miami (Fla.) ...............(10-0-0) |
| 10-9 | Michigan ...............(3-1-0) (3) | 12-2 | Miami (Fla.) ...............(11-0-0) |
| 10-16 | Virginia .................(6-0-0) (2) | **1-2** | **Miami (Fla.)** ..............**(12-0-0)** |
| 10-23 | Virginia....................(7-0-0) | | |
| 10-30 | Virginia....................(7-0-0) | | **1992** |
| 11-6 | Notre Dame ...........(7-1-0) (2) | 9-8 | Miami (Fla.) ...............(1-0-0) |
| 11-13 | Notre Dame ...............(8-1-0) | 9-15 | Miami (Fla.) ...............(1-0-0) |
| 11-20 | Colorado .............(10-1-1) (2) | 9-22 | Miami (Fla.) ...............(2-0-0) |
| 11-27 | Colorado.................(10-1-1) | 9-29 | Washington.............(3-0-0) (2) |
| 12-4 | Colorado.................(10-1-1) | 10-6 | Washington ...............(4-0-0) |
| **1-2** | **Colorado** ................**(11-1-1)** | 10-13 | Washington ...............(5-0-0) |
| | **1991** | 10-20 | Miami (Fla.)† ..........(6-0-0) (2) |
| 9-3 | Florida St. .................(1-0-0) | 10-27 | Miami (Fla.) ...............(7-0-0) |
| 9-10 | Florida St. .................(2-0-0) | 11-3 | Washington.............(8-0-0) (2) |
| 9-17 | Florida St. .................(3-0-0) | 11-10 | Miami (Fla.) ...............(8-0-0) |
| 9-23 | Florida St. .................(3-0-0) | 11-17 | Miami (Fla.) ...............(9-0-0) |
| 9-30 | Florida St. .................(4-0-0) | 11-24 | Miami (Fla.) ..............(10-0-0) |
| 10-7 | Florida St. .................(5-0-0) | 12-1 | Miami (Fla.) ..............(11-0-0) |
| 10-14 | Florida St. .................(6-0-0) | 12-8 | Miami (Fla.) ..............(11-0-0) |
| 10-21 | Florida St. .................(7-0-0) | **1-2** | **Alabama** .............(13-0-0) (2) |

* On January 6, 1948, in a special postseason poll after the Rose Bowl, The Associated Press voted Michigan No. 1 and Notre Dame No. 2. However, the postseason poll did not supersede the final regular-season poll of December 9, 1947.   † Miami (Fla.) and Washington actually tied for first place in The Associated Press poll for the first time in 51 years, but Miami (Fla.) had one more first-place vote, 31-30, than Washington.

# UNITED PRESS INTERNATIONAL/
# NATIONAL FOOTBALL FOUNDATION

United Press (UP), 1950-57; United Press International (UPI) from 1958 after merger with International News Service (INS). Served as the coaches' poll until 1991, when it was taken over by USA Today/Cable News Network (CNN) poll.

| 1950 | 1951 | 1952 | 1953 |
|---|---|---|---|
| **Team** | **Team** | **Team** | **Team** |
| 1. Oklahoma | 1. Tennessee | 1. Michigan St. | 1. Maryland |
| 2. Texas | 2. Michigan St. | 2. Georgia Tech | 2. Notre Dame |
| 3. Tennessee | 3. Illinois | 3. Notre Dame | 3. Michigan St. |
| 4. California | 4. Maryland | 4. Oklahoma | 4. UCLA |
| 5. Army | 5. Georgia Tech | Southern Cal | 5. Oklahoma |
| 6. Michigan | 6. Princeton | 6. UCLA | 6. Rice |
| 7. Kentucky | 7. Stanford | 7. Mississippi | 7. Illinois |
| 8. Princeton | 8. Wisconsin | 8. Tennessee | 8. Texas |
| 9. Michigan St. | 9. Baylor | 9. Alabama | 9. Georgia Tech |
| 10. Ohio St. | 10. Texas Christian | 10. Wisconsin | 10. Iowa |
| 11. Illinois | 11. Oklahoma | 11. Texas | 11. Alabama |
| 12. Clemson | 12. California | 12. Purdue | 12. Texas Tech |
| 13. Miami (Fla.) | 13. Notre Dame | 13. Maryland | 13. West Va. |
| 14. Wyoming | 14. San Francisco | 14. Princeton | 14. Wisconsin |
| 15. Washington | Purdue | 15. Ohio St. | 15. Kentucky |
| Baylor | Washington St. | Pittsburgh | 16. Army |
| 17. Alabama | 17. Holy Cross | 17. Navy | 17. Stanford |
| 18. Wash. & Lee | UCLA | 18. Duke | 18. Duke |
| 19. Navy | Kentucky | 19. Houston | 19. Michigan |
| 20. Nebraska | 20. Kansas | Kentucky | 20. Ohio St. |
| Wisconsin | | | |
| Cornell | | | |

**1954**
Team
1. UCLA
2. Ohio St.
3. Oklahoma
4. Notre Dame
5. Navy
6. Mississippi
7. Army
8. Arkansas
9. Miami (Fla.)
10. Wisconsin
11. Southern Cal
    Maryland
    Georgia Tech
14. Duke
15. Michigan
16. Penn St.
17. Southern Methodist
18. Denver
19. Rice
20. Minnesota

**1955**
Team
1. Oklahoma
2. Michigan St.
3. Maryland
4. UCLA
5. Ohio St.
6. Texas Christian
7. Georgia Tech
8. Auburn
9. Mississippi
10. Notre Dame
11. Pittsburgh
12. Southern Cal
13. Michigan
14. Texas A&M
15. Army
16. Duke
17. West Va.
18. Miami (Fla.)
19. Iowa
20. Navy
    Stanford
    Miami (Ohio)

**1956**
Team
1. Oklahoma
2. Tennessee
3. Iowa
4. Georgia Tech
5. Texas A&M
6. Miami (Fla.)
7. Michigan
8. Syracuse
9. Minnesota
10. Michigan St.
11. Baylor
12. Pittsburgh
13. Oregon St.
14. Texas Christian
15. Southern Cal
16. Wyoming
17. Yale
18. Colorado
19. Navy
20. Duke

**1957**
Team
1. Ohio St.
2. Auburn
3. Michigan St.
4. Oklahoma
5. Iowa
6. Navy
7. Rice
8. Mississippi
9. Notre Dame
10. Texas A&M
11. Texas
12. Arizona St.
13. Army
14. Duke
    Wisconsin
16. Tennessee
17. Oregon
18. Clemson
    UCLA
20. North Caro. St.

**1958**
Team
1. Louisiana St.
2. Iowa
3. Army
4. Auburn
5. Oklahoma
6. Wisconsin
7. Ohio St.
8. Air Force
9. Texas Christian
10. Syracuse
11. Purdue
12. Mississippi
13. Clemson
14. Notre Dame
15. Florida
16. California
17. Northwestern
18. Southern Methodist

**1959**
Team
1. Syracuse
2. Mississippi
3. Louisiana St.
4. Texas
5. Georgia
6. Wisconsin
7. Washington
8. Texas Christian
9. Arkansas
10. Penn St.
11. Illinois
12. Southern Cal
13. Alabama
14. Penn St.
15. Oklahoma
16. Northwestern
    Michigan St.
18. Wyoming
19. Auburn
    Missouri

**1960**
Team
1. Minnesota
2. Iowa
3. Mississippi
4. Missouri
5. Wisconsin
6. Navy
7. Arkansas
8. Ohio St.
9. Kansas
10. Alabama
11. Duke
    Baylor
    Michigan St.
14. Auburn
15. Purdue
16. Florida
17. Texas
18. Yale
19. New Mexico St.
    Tennessee

**1961**
Team
1. Alabama
2. Ohio St.
3. Louisiana St.
4. Texas
5. Mississippi
6. Minnesota
7. Colorado
8. Arkansas
9. Michigan St.
10. Utah St.
11. Purdue
    Missouri
13. Georgia Tech
14. Duke
15. Kansas
16. Syracuse
17. Wyoming
18. Wisconsin
19. Miami (Fla.)
    Penn St.

**1962**
Team
1. Southern Cal
2. Wisconsin
3. Mississippi
4. Texas
5. Alabama
6. Arkansas
7. Oklahoma
8. Louisiana St.
9. Penn St.
10. Minnesota
11. Georgia Tech
12. Missouri
13. Ohio St.
14. Duke
    Washington
16. Northwestern
    Oregon St.
18. Arizona St.
    Illinois
    Miami (Fla.)

**1963**
Team
1. Texas
2. Navy
3. Pittsburgh
4. Illinois
5. Nebraska
6. Auburn
7. Mississippi
8. Oklahoma
9. Alabama
10. Michigan St.
11. Mississippi St.
12. Syracuse
13. Arizona St.
14. Memphis St.
15. Washington
16. Penn St.
    Southern Cal
    Missouri
19. North Caro.
20. Baylor

**1964**
Team
1. Alabama
2. Arkansas
3. Notre Dame
4. Michigan
5. Texas
6. Nebraska
7. Louisiana St.
8. Oregon St.
9. Ohio St.
10. Southern Cal
11. Florida St.
12. Syracuse
13. Princeton
14. Penn St.
    Utah
16. Illinois
    New Mexico
18. Tulsa
    Missouri
20. Mississippi
    Michigan St.

**1965**
Team
1. Michigan St.
2. Arkansas
3. Nebraska
4. Alabama
5. UCLA
6. Missouri
7. Tennessee
8. Notre Dame
9. Southern Cal
10. Texas Tech
11. Ohio St.
12. Florida
13. Purdue
14. Louisiana St.
15. Georgia
16. Tulsa
17. Mississippi
18. Kentucky
19. Syracuse
20. Colorado

*Division I-A National Poll Rankings*

## 1966
**Team**
1. Notre Dame
2. Michigan St.
3. Alabama
4. Georgia
5. UCLA
6. Purdue
7. Nebraska
8. Georgia Tech
9. Southern Methodist
10. Miami (Fla.)
11. Florida
12. Mississippi
13. Arkansas
14. Tennessee
15. Wyoming
16. Syracuse
17. Houston
18. Southern Cal
19. Oregon St.
20. Virginia Tech

## 1967
**Team**
1. Southern Cal
2. Tennessee
3. Oklahoma
4. Notre Dame
5. Wyoming
6. Indiana
7. Alabama
8. Oregon St.
9. Purdue
10. UCLA
11. Penn St.
12. Syracuse
13. Colorado
14. Minnesota
15. Florida St.
16. Miami (Fla.)
17. North Caro. St.
18. Georgia
19. Houston
20. Arizona St.

## 1968
**Team**
1. Ohio St.
2. Southern Cal
3. Penn St.
4. Georgia
5. Texas
6. Kansas
7. Tennessee
8. Notre Dame
9. Arkansas
10. Oklahoma
11. Purdue
12. Alabama
13. Oregon St.
14. Florida St.
15. Michigan
16. Southern Methodist
17. Missouri
18. Ohio
    Minnesota
20. Houston
    Stanford

## 1969
**Team**
1. Texas
2. Penn St.
3. Arkansas
4. Southern Cal
5. Ohio St.
6. Missouri
7. Louisiana St.
8. Michigan
9. Notre Dame
10. UCLA
11. Tennessee
12. Nebraska
13. Mississippi
14. Stanford
15. Auburn
16. Houston
17. Florida
18. Purdue
    San Diego St.
    West Va.

## 1970
**Team**
1. Texas
2. Ohio St.
3. Nebraska
4. Tennessee
5. Notre Dame
6. Louisiana St.
7. Michigan
8. Arizona St.
9. Auburn
10. Stanford
11. Air Force
12. Arkansas
13. Houston
    Dartmouth
15. Oklahoma
16. Colorado
17. Georgia Tech
    Toledo
19. Penn St.
    Southern Cal

## 1971
**Team**
1. Nebraska
2. Alabama
3. Oklahoma
4. Michigan
5. Auburn
6. Arizona St.
7. Colorado
8. Georgia
9. Tennessee
10. Louisiana St.
11. Penn St.
12. Texas
13. Toledo
14. Houston
15. Notre Dame
16. Stanford
17. Iowa St.
18. North Caro.
19. Florida St.
20. Arkansas
    Mississippi

## 1972
**Team**
1. Southern Cal
2. Oklahoma
3. Ohio St.
4. Alabama
5. Texas
6. Michigan
7. Auburn
8. Penn St.
9. Nebraska
10. Louisiana St.
11. Tennessee
12. Notre Dame
13. Arizona St.
14. Colorado
    North Caro.
16. Louisville
17. UCLA
    Washington St.
19. Utah St.
20. San Diego St.

## 1973
**Team**
1. Alabama
2. Oklahoma
3. Ohio St.
4. Notre Dame
5. Penn St.
6. Michigan
7. Southern Cal
8. Texas
9. UCLA
10. Arizona St.
11. Nebraska
    Texas Tech
13. Houston
14. Louisiana St.
15. Kansas
    Tulane
17. Miami (Ohio)
18. Maryland
19. San Diego St.
    Florida

## *1974
**Team**
1. Southern Cal
2. Alabama
3. Ohio St.
4. Notre Dame
5. Michigan
6. Auburn
7. Penn St.
8. Nebraska
9. North Caro. St.
10. Miami (Ohio)
11. Houston
12. Florida
13. Maryland
14. Baylor
15. Texas A&M
    Tennessee
17. Mississippi St.
18. Michigan St.
19. Tulsa

## 1975
**Team**
1. Oklahoma
2. Arizona St.
3. Alabama
4. Ohio St.
5. UCLA
6. Arkansas
7. Texas
8. Michigan
9. Nebraska
10. Penn St.
11. Maryland
12. Texas A&M
13. Arizona
    Pittsburgh
15. California
16. Miami (Ohio)
17. Notre Dame
    West Va.
19. Georgia
    Southern Cal

## 1976
**Team**
1. Pittsburgh
2. Southern Cal
3. Michigan
4. Houston
5. Ohio St.
6. Oklahoma
7. Nebraska
8. Texas A&M
9. Alabama
10. Georgia
11. Maryland
12. Notre Dame
13. Texas Tech
14. Oklahoma St.
15. UCLA
16. Colorado
17. Rutgers
18. Iowa St.
19. Baylor
    Kentucky

## 1977
**Team**
1. Notre Dame
2. Alabama
3. Arkansas
4. Penn St.
5. Texas
6. Oklahoma
7. Pittsburgh
8. Michigan
9. Washington
10. Nebraska
11. Florida St.
12. Ohio St.
    Southern Cal
14. North Caro.
15. Stanford
16. North Texas
    Brigham Young
18. Arizona St.
19. San Diego St.
    North Caro. St.

## 1978
**Team**
1. Southern Cal
2. Alabama
3. Oklahoma
4. Penn St.
5. Michigan
6. Notre Dame
7. Clemson
8. Nebraska
9. Texas
10. Arkansas
11. Houston
12. UCLA
13. Purdue
14. Missouri
15. Georgia
16. Stanford
17. Navy
18. Texas A&M
19. Arizona St.
    North Caro. St.

## 1979
**Team**
1. Alabama
2. Southern Cal
3. Oklahoma
4. Ohio St.
5. Houston
6. Pittsburgh
7. Nebraska
8. Florida St.
9. Arkansas
10. Purdue
11. Washington
12. Brigham Young
13. Texas
14. North Caro.
15. Baylor
16. Indiana
17. Temple
18. Penn St.
19. Michigan
20. Missouri

## 1980
**Team**
1. Georgia
2. Pittsburgh
3. Oklahoma
4. Michigan
5. Florida St.
6. Alabama
7. Nebraska
8. Penn St.
9. North Caro.
10. Notre Dame
11. Brigham Young
12. Southern Cal
13. Baylor
14. UCLA
15. Ohio St.
16. Purdue
17. Washington
18. Miami (Fla.)
19. Florida
20. Southern Methodist

## 1981
**Team**
1. Clemson
2. Pittsburgh
3. Penn St.
4. Texas
5. Georgia
6. Alabama
7. Washington
8. North Caro.
9. Nebraska
10. Michigan
11. Brigham Young
12. Ohio St.
13. Southern Cal
14. Oklahoma
15. Iowa
16. Arkansas
17. Mississippi St.
18. West Va.
19. Southern Miss.
20. Missouri

## 1982
**Team**
1. Penn St.
2. Southern Methodist
3. Nebraska
4. Georgia
5. UCLA
6. Arizona St.
7. Washington
8. Arkansas
9. Pittsburgh
10. Florida St.
11. Louisiana St.
12. Ohio St.
13. North Caro.
14. Auburn
15. Michigan
16. Oklahoma
17. Alabama
18. Texas
19. West Va.
20. Maryland

## 1983
**Team**
1. Miami (Fla.)
2. Nebraska
3. Auburn
4. Georgia
5. Texas
6. Florida
7. Brigham Young
8. Ohio St.
9. Michigan
10. Illinois
11. Southern Methodist
12. Alabama
13. UCLA
14. Iowa
15. Air Force
16. West Va.
17. Penn St.
18. Oklahoma St.
19. Pittsburgh
20. Boston College

## 1984
**Team**
1. Brigham Young
2. Washington
3. Nebraska
4. Boston College
5. Oklahoma St.
6. Oklahoma
7. Florida
8. Southern Methodist
9. Southern Cal
10. UCLA
11. Maryland
12. Ohio St.
13. South Caro.
14. Auburn
15. Iowa
16. Louisiana St.
17. Virginia
18. West Va.
19. Kentucky
    Florida St.

## 1985
**Team**
1. Oklahoma
2. Michigan
3. Penn St.
4. Tennessee
5. Air Force
6. UCLA
7. Texas A&M
8. Miami (Fla.)
9. Iowa
10. Nebraska
11. Ohio St.
12. Arkansas
13. Florida St.
14. Alabama
15. Baylor
16. Fresno St.
17. Brigham Young
18. Georgia Tech
19. Maryland
20. Louisiana St.

## 1986
**Team**
1. Penn St.
2. Miami (Fla.)
3. Oklahoma
4. Nebraska
5. Arizona St.
6. Ohio St.
7. Michigan
8. Auburn
9. Alabama
10. Arizona
11. Louisiana St.
12. Texas A&M
13. Baylor
14. UCLA
15. Iowa
16. Arkansas
17. Washington
18. Boston College
19. Clemson
20. Florida St.

## 1987
**Team**
1. Miami (Fla.)
2. Florida St.
3. Oklahoma
4. Syracuse
5. Louisiana St.
6. Nebraska
7. Auburn
8. Michigan St.
9. Texas A&M
10. Clemson
11. UCLA
12. Oklahoma St.
13. Tennessee
14. Georgia
15. South Caro.
16. Iowa
17. Southern Cal
18. Michigan
19. Texas
20. Indiana

## 1988
**Team**
1. Notre Dame
2. Miami (Fla.)
3. Florida St.
4. Michigan
5. West Va.
6. UCLA
7. Auburn
8. Clemson
9. Southern Cal
10. Nebraska
11. Oklahoma St.
12. Syracuse
13. Arkansas
14. Oklahoma
15. Georgia
16. Washington St.
17. North Caro. St.
    Alabama
19. Indiana
20. Wyoming

## 1989
**Team**
1. Miami (Fla.)
2. Florida St.
3. Notre Dame
4. Colorado
5. Tennessee
6. Auburn
7. Alabama
8. Michigan
9. Southern Cal
10. Illinois
11. Clemson
12. Nebraska
13. Arkansas
14. Penn St.
15. Virginia
16. Texas Tech
    Michigan St.
18. Brigham Young
19. Pittsburgh
20. Washington

*Division I-A National Poll Rankings*

### #1990
**Team**
1. Georgia Tech
2. Colorado
3. Miami (Fla.)
4. Florida St.
5. Washington
6. Notre Dame
7. Tennessee
8. Michigan
9. Clemson
10. Penn St.
11. Texas
12. Louisville
13. Texas A&M
14. Michigan St.
15. Virginia
16. Iowa
17. Brigham Young
    Nebraska
19. Auburn
20. San Jose St.
21. Syracuse
22. Southern Cal
23. Mississippi
24. Illinois
25. Virginia Tech

### ¢1991
**Team**
1. Washington
2. Miami (Fla.)
3. Penn St.
4. Florida St.
5. Alabama
6. Michigan
7. Florida
8. California
9. East Caro.
10. Iowa
11. Syracuse
12. Notre Dame
13. Texas A&M
14. Tennessee
15. Nebraska
16. Oklahoma
17. Clemson
18. Colorado
19. UCLA
20. Georgia
21. Tulsa
22. Stanford
23. North Caro. St.
24. Brigham Young
25. Ohio St.

### 1992
**Team**
1. Alabama
2. Florida St.
3. Miami (Fla.)
4. Notre Dame
5. Michigan
6. Syracuse
7. Texas A&M
8. Georgia
9. Stanford
10. Florida
11. Washington
12. Tennessee
13. Colorado
14. Nebraska
15. Washington St.
16. Mississippi
17. North Caro. St.
18. North Caro.
19. Ohio St.
20. Hawaii
21. Boston College
22. Kansas
23. Fresno St.
24. Penn St.
25. Mississippi St.

*\* Beginning in 1974, by agreement with the American Football Coaches Association, teams on probation by the NCAA were ineligible for ranking and national championship consideration by the UPI Board of Coaches. # Beginning in 1990 season, UPI selected top 25 teams instead of 20. ¢ Beginning in 1991, the No. 1 team in the final UPI/NFF ratings will receive the MacArthur Bowl, awarded by the NFF since 1959 to recognize its national champion. The National Football Foundation and Hall of Fame MacArthur Bowl national champions before 1991 are listed in the national championship section.*

# UNITED PRESS INTERNATIONAL/NATIONAL FOOTBALL FOUNDATION POLL
## WEEKLY LEADERS

| Date | 1992 | | | |
|------|------|---|---|---|
| 9-8 | Miami (Fla.) ................(1-0-0) | | 11-3 | Washington ................(8-0-0) |
| 9-15 | Miami (Fla.) ................(1-0-0) | | 11-10 | Miami (Fla.).............(8-0-0) (2) |
| 9-22 | Miami (Fla.) ................(2-0-0) | | 11-17 | Miami (Fla.) ..............(9-0-0) |
| 9-29 | Miami (Fla.) ................(3-0-0) | | 11-24 | Miami (Fla.) ..............(10-0-0) |
| 10-6 | Washington.............(4-0-0) (2) | | 12-1 | Miami (Fla.) ..............(11-0-0) |
| 10-13 | Washington ................(5-0-0) | | 12-8 | Miami (Fla.) ..............(11-0-0) |
| 10-20 | Washington ................(6-0-0) | | **1-2** | **Alabama** ..............(13-0-0) (2) |
| 10-27 | Washington ................(7-0-0) | | | |

# USA TODAY/CABLE NEWS NETWORK (COACHES)
## (Since 1982)

Took over as coaches' poll in 1991.

### 1982
**Team**
1. Penn St.
2. Southern Methodist
3. Nebraska
4. Georgia
5. UCLA
6. Arizona St.
7. Pittsburgh
8. Arkansas
9. Clemson
10. Washington
11. Louisiana St.
12. Florida St.
13. Ohio St.
14. Southern Cal
15. Oklahoma
16. Auburn
17. West Va.
18. Maryland
19. North Caro.
20. Texas
21. Michigan
22. Alabama
23. Tulsa
24. Iowa
25. Florida

### 1983
**Team**
1. Miami (Fla.)
2. Auburn
3. Nebraska
4. Georgia
5. Texas
6. Brigham Young
7. Michigan
8. Ohio St.
9. Florida
10. Clemson
11. Illinois
12. Southern Methodist
13. Alabama
14. Air Force
15. West Va.
16. Iowa
17. Tennessee
18. UCLA
19. Pittsburgh
20. Penn St.
21. Oklahoma
22. Boston College
23. Oklahoma St.
24. Maryland
25. East Caro.

## 1984
**Team**
1. Brigham Young
2. Washington
3. Florida
4. Nebraska
5. Oklahoma
6. Boston College
7. Oklahoma St.
8. Southern Methodist
9. Maryland
10. South Caro.
11. Southern Cal
12. UCLA
13. Louisiana St.
14. Ohio St.
15. Auburn
16. Miami (Fla.)
17. Florida St.
18. Virginia
19. Kentucky
20. Iowa
21. West Va.
22. Army
23. Georgia
24. Air Force
25. Notre Dame

## 1985
**Team**
1. Oklahoma
2. Penn St.
3. Michigan
4. Tennessee
5. Florida
6. Miami (Fla.)
7. Air Force
8. Texas A&M
9. UCLA
10. Iowa
11. Nebraska
12. Alabama
13. Ohio St.
14. Florida St.
15. Arkansas
16. Brigham Young
17. Maryland
18. Georgia Tech
19. Baylor
20. Auburn
21. Louisiana St.
22. Army
23. Fresno St.
24. Georgia
25. Oklahoma St.

## 1986
**Team**
1. Penn St.
2. Miami (Fla.)
3. Oklahoma
4. Nebraska
5. Arizona St.
6. Ohio St.
7. Auburn
8. Michigan
9. Alabama
10. Louisiana St.
11. Arizona
12. Texas A&M
13. UCLA
14. Baylor
15. Boston College
16. Iowa
17. Arkansas
18. Clemson
19. Washington
20. Virginia Tech
21. Florida St.
22. Stanford
23. Georgia
24. North Caro. St.
25. San Diego St.

## 1987
**Team**
1. Miami (Fla.)
2. Florida St.
3. Oklahoma
4. Syracuse
5. Nebraska
6. Louisiana St.
7. Auburn
8. Michigan St.
9. Texas A&M
10. UCLA
11. Clemson
12. Oklahoma St.
13. Georgia
14. Tennessee
15. Iowa
16. Notre Dame
17. Southern Cal
18. South Caro.
19. Michigan
20. Texas
21. Pittsburgh
22. Indiana
23. Penn St.
24. Ohio St.
25. Alabama

## 1988
**Team**
1. Notre Dame
2. Miami (Fla.)
3. Florida St.
4. UCLA
5. Michigan
6. West Va.
7. Southern Cal
8. Nebraska
9. Auburn
10. Clemson
11. Oklahoma St.
12. Syracuse
13. Oklahoma
14. Arkansas
15. Washington St.
16. Georgia
17. Alabama
18. North Caro. St.
19. Houston
20. Indiana
21. Wyoming
22. Louisiana St.
23. Colorado
24. Southern Miss.
25. Brigham Young

## 1989
**Team**
1. Miami (Fla.)
2. Notre Dame
3. Florida St.
4. Colorado
5. Tennessee
6. Auburn
7. Southern Cal
8. Michigan
9. Alabama
10. Illinois
11. Nebraska
12. Clemson
13. Arkansas
14. Houston
15. Penn St.
16. Virginia
17. Michigan St.
18. Texas Tech
19. Pittsburgh
20. Texas A&M
21. West Va.
22. Brigham Young
23. Syracuse
24. Ohio St.
25. Washington

## 1990
**Team**
1. Colorado
2. Georgia Tech
3. Miami (Fla.)
4. Florida St.
5. Washington
6. Notre Dame
7. Tennessee
8. Michigan
9. Clemson
10. Texas
11. Penn St.
12. Houston
13. Florida
14. Louisville
15. Michigan St.
16. Texas A&M
17. Oklahoma
18. Iowa
19. Auburn
20. Brigham Young
21. Mississippi
22. Southern Cal
23. Nebraska
24. Illinois
25. Virginia

## 1991
**Team**
1. Washington
2. Miami (Fla.)
3. Penn St.
4. Florida St.
5. Alabama
6. Michigan
7. California
8. Florida
9. East Caro.
10. Iowa
11. Syracuse
12. Notre Dame
13. Texas A&M
14. Oklahoma
15. Tennessee
16. Nebraska
17. Clemson
18. UCLA
19. Georgia
20. Colorado
21. Tulsa
22. Stanford
23. Brigham Young
24. Air Force
25. North Caro. St.

## 1992
**Team**
1. Alabama
2. Florida St.
3. Miami (Fla.)
4. Notre Dame
5. Michigan
6. Texas A&M
7. Syracuse
8. Georgia
9. Stanford
10. Washington
11. Florida
12. Tennessee
13. Colorado
14. Nebraska
15. North Caro. St.
16. Mississippi
17. Washington St.
18. North Caro.
19. Ohio St.
20. Hawaii
21. Boston College
22. Fresno St.
23. Kansas
24. Penn St.
25. Wake Forest

*Division I-A National Poll Rankings*

# USA TODAY/CNN (COACHES) POLL
## WEEKLY LEADERS

| Date | 1992 | | | |
|------|------|---|---|---|
| 9-8 | Miami (Fla.) ...............(1-0-0) | | 11-3 | Miami (Fla.) ...............(8-0-0) |
| 9-15 | Miami (Fla.) ...............(1-0-0) | | 11-10 | Miami (Fla.) ...............(8-0-0) |
| 9-22 | Miami (Fla.) ...............(2-0-0) | | 11-17 | Miami (Fla.) ...............(9-0-0) |
| 9-29 | Washington............(3-0-0) (2) | | 11-24 | Miami (Fla.) ..............(10-0-0) |
| 10-6 | Washington ...............(4-0-0) | | 12-1 | Miami (Fla.) ..............(11-0-0) |
| 10-13 | Miami (Fla.) ............(5-0-0) (2) | | 12-8 | Miami (Fla.) ..............(11-0-0) |
| 10-20 | Miami (Fla.) ...............(6-0-0) | | **1-2** | **Alabama** .............**(13-0-0) (2)** |
| 10-27 | Miami (Fla.) ...............(7-0-0) | | | |

# GAMES IN WHICH A NO. 1-RANKED
# TEAM WAS DEFEATED OR TIED

Listed here are 104 games in which the No. 1-ranked team in the Associated Press poll was defeated or tied. An asterisk (*) indicates the home team, an (N) a neutral site. In parentheses after the winning or tying team is its rank in the previous week's poll (NR indicates it was not ranked), its won-lost record entering the game and its score. The defeated or tied No. 1-ranked team follows with its score, and in parentheses is its rank in the poll the following week. Before 1965, the polls were final before bowl games. (Note: Only 10 teams were ranked in the weekly polls during 1962, 1963, 1964, 1965, 1966 and 1967; 20 teams all other seasons except 1989, when 25 teams were ranked.)

| | |
|---|---|
| 10-31-36 | *Northwestern (3, 4-0) 6, Minnesota 0 (2) |
| 11-21-36 | *Notre Dame (11, 5-2) 26, Northwestern 6 (7) |
| 10-30-37 | (Tie) Washington (NR, 3-2-1) 0, *California 0 (2) |
| 10-29-38 | Carnegie Mellon (t19, 4-1) 20, *Pittsburgh 10 (3) |
| 12-2-38 | *Southern Cal (8, 7-2) 13, Notre Dame 0 (5) |
| 10-14-39 | Duquesne (NR, 3-0) 21, *Pittsburgh 13 (18) |
| 11-8-41 | (Tie) Baylor (NR, 3-4) 7, *Texas 7 (2) |
| 10-31-42 | *Wisconsin (6, 5-0-1) 17, Ohio St. 7 (6) |
| 11-21-42 | (N) Auburn (NR, 4-4-1) 27, Georgia 13 (5) |
| 11-28-42 | Holy Cross (NR, 4-4-1) 55, *Boston College 12 (8) |
| 11-27-43 | *Great Lakes NTS (NR, 9-2-0) 19, Notre Dame 14 (1) |
| 11-9-46 | (Tie) (N) Notre Dame (2, 5-0-0) 0, Army 0 (1) |
| 10-8-49 | Army (7, 2-0) 21, *Michigan 7 (7) |
| 10-7-50 | Purdue (NR, 0-1) 28, *Notre Dame 14 (10) |
| 11-4-50 | *Texas (7, 4-1) 23, Southern Methodist 20 (7) |
| 11-18-50 | *Illinois (10, 6-1) 14, Ohio St. 7 (8) |
| 1-1-51 | (Sugar Bowl) Kentucky (7, 10-1-0) 13, Oklahoma 7 (1) |
| 10-20-51 | Southern Cal (11, 4-1) 21, *California 14 (9) |
| 1-1-52 | (Sugar Bowl) Maryland (3, 9-0) 28, Tennessee 13 (1) |
| 10-11-52 | *Ohio St. (NR, 1-1-0) 23, Wisconsin 14 (12) |
| 11-21-53 | (Tie) Iowa (20, 5-3-0) 14, *Notre Dame 14 (2) |
| 1-1-54 | (Orange Bowl) Oklahoma (4, 8-1-1) 7, Maryland 0 (1) |
| 10-2-54 | Purdue (19, 1-0-0) 27, *Notre Dame 14 (8) |
| 9-24-55 | *Maryland (5, 1-0-0) 7, UCLA 0 (7) |
| 10-27-56 | *Illinois (NR, 1-3-0) 20, Michigan St. 13 (4) |
| 10-19-57 | Purdue (NR, 0-3-0) 20, *Michigan St. 13 (8) |
| 11-16-57 | *Rice (20, 4-3-0) 7, Texas A&M 6 (4) |
| 10-25-58 | (Tie) *Pittsburgh (NR, 4-1-0) 14, Army 14 (3) |
| 11-7-59 | *Tennessee (13, 4-1-1) 14, Louisiana St. 13 (3) |
| 11-5-60 | *Minnesota (3, 6-0-0) 27, Iowa 10 (5) |
| 11-12-60 | Purdue (NR, 2-4-1) 23, *Minnesota 14 (4) |
| 11-19-60 | Kansas (NR, 6-2-1) 23, *Missouri 7 (5) |
| 1-1-61 | (Rose Bowl) Washington (6, 9-1) 17, Minnesota 7 (1) |
| 11-4-61 | *Minnesota (NR, 4-1-0) 13, Michigan St. 0 (6) |
| 11-18-61 | Texas Christian (NR, 2-4-1) 6, *Texas 0 (5) |
| 10-6-62 | *UCLA (NR, 0-0-0) 9, Ohio St. 7 (10) |
| 10-27-62 | (Tie) *Rice (NR, 0-3-1) 14, Texas 14 (5) |
| 11-10-62 | *Wisconsin (8, 5-1-0) 37, Northwestern 6 (9) |
| 11-17-62 | *Georgia Tech (NR, 5-2-1) 7, Alabama 6 (6) |
| 9-28-63 | Oklahoma (3, 1-0-0) 17, *Southern Cal 12 (8) |

108                                                  *1993 NCAA FOOTBALL*

| | |
|---|---|
| 10-12-63 | (N)Texas (2, 3-0-0) 28, Oklahoma 7 (6) |
| 10-17-64 | Arkansas (8, 4-0-0) 14, *Texas 13 (6) |
| 11-28-64 | *Southern Cal (NR, 6-3-0) 20, Notre Dame 17 (3) |
| 1-1-65 | (Orange Bowl) Texas (5, 9-1) 21, Alabama 17 (1) |
| 9-25-65 | *Purdue (6, 1-0-0) 25, Notre Dame 21 (8) |
| 10-16-65 | *Arkansas (3, 4-0-0) 27, Texas 24 (5) |
| 1-1-66 | (Rose Bowl) UCLA (5, 7-2-1) 14, Michigan St. 12 (2) |
| 11-19-66 | (Tie) *Michigan St. (2, 9-0-0) 10, Notre Dame 10 (1) |
| 9-30-67 | *Purdue (10, 1-0-0) 28, Notre Dame 21 (6) |
| 11-11-67 | *Oregon St. (NR, 5-2-1) 3, Southern Cal 0 (4) |
| 11-18-67 | *Southern Cal (4, 8-1-0) 21, UCLA 20 (4) |
| 10-12-68 | *Ohio St. (4, 2-0-0) 13, Purdue 0 (5) |
| 11-22-69 | *Michigan (12, 7-2-0) 24, Ohio St. 12 (4) |
| 1-1-71 | (Cotton Bowl) Notre Dame (6, 8-1-1) 24, Texas 11 (3) |
| 9-29-73 | (Tie) Oklahoma (8, 1-0-0) 7, *Southern Cal 7 (4) |
| 11-24-73 | (Tie) *Michigan (4, 10-0-0) 10, Ohio St. 10 (3) |
| 12-31-73 | (Sugar Bowl) Notre Dame (3, 10-0-0) 24, Alabama 23 (4) |
| 11-9-74 | *Michigan St. (NR, 4-3-1) 16, Ohio St. 13 (4) |
| 1-1-76 | (Rose Bowl) UCLA (11, 8-2-1) 23, Ohio St. 10 (4) |
| 11-6-76 | *Purdue (NR, 3-5-0) 16, Michigan 14 (4) |
| 10-8-77 | Alabama (t7, 3-1-0) 21, *Southern Cal 20 (6) |
| 10-22-77 | *Minnesota (NR, 4-2-0) 16, Michigan 0 (6) |
| 1-2-78 | (Cotton Bowl) Notre Dame (5, 10-1-0) 38, Texas 10 (4) |
| 9-23-78 | (N) Southern Cal (7, 2-0-0) 24, Alabama 14 (3) |
| 11-11-78 | *Nebraska (4, 8-1-0) 17, Oklahoma 14 (4) |
| 1-1-79 | (Sugar Bowl) Alabama 14 (2, 10-1-0) 14, Penn St. 7 (4) |
| 10-13-79 | (Tie) Stanford (NR, 3-2-0) 21, *Southern Cal 21 (4) |
| 1-1-80 | (Rose Bowl) Southern Cal (3, 10-0-1) 17, Ohio St. 16 (4) |
| 11-1-80 | (N) Mississippi St. (NR, 6-2-0) 6, Alabama 3 (6) |
| 11-8-80 | (Tie) *Georgia Tech (NR, 1-7-0) 3, Notre Dame 3 (6) |
| 9-12-81 | *Wisconsin (NR, 0-0-0) 21, Michigan 14 (11) |
| 9-19-81 | *Michigan (11, 0-1-0) 25, Notre Dame 7 (13) |
| 10-10-81 | Arizona (NR, 2-2-0) 13, *Southern Cal 10 (7) |
| 10-17-81 | *Arkansas (NR, 4-1-0) 42, Texas 11 (10) |
| 10-31-81 | *Miami (Fla.) (NR, 4-2-0) 17, Penn St. 14 (5) |
| 11-28-81 | Penn St. (11, 8-2-0) 48, *Pittsburgh 14 (10) |
| 11-6-82 | Notre Dame (NR, 5-1-1) 31, *Pittsburgh 16 (8) |
| 1-1-83 | (Sugar Bowl) Penn St. (2, 10-1-0) 27, Georgia 23 (4) |
| 1-2-84 | (Orange Bowl) Miami (Fla.) (5, 10-1-0) 31, Nebraska 30 (4) |
| 9-8-84 | *Michigan (14, 0-0-0) 22, Miami (Fla.) 14 (5) |
| 9-29-84 | *Syracuse (NR, 2-1-0) 17, Nebraska 9 (8) |
| 10-13-84 | (N) (Tie) Oklahoma (3, 4-0-0) 15, Texas 15 (3) |
| 11-10-84 | *Southern Cal (12, 7-1-0) 16, Washington 7 (5) |
| 11-17-84 | Oklahoma (6, 7-1-1) 17, *Nebraska 7 (7) |
| 9-28-85 | *Tennessee (NR, 0-0-1) 38, Auburn 20 (14) |
| 11-2-85 | *Ohio St. (7, 6-1-0) 22, Iowa 13 (6) |
| 11-9-85 | (N) Georgia (17, 6-1-1) 24, Florida 3 (11) |
| 1-1-86 | (Orange Bowl) Oklahoma (4, 9-1-0) 25, Penn St. 10 (3) |
| 9-27-86 | *Miami (Fla.) (2, 3-0-0) 28, Oklahoma 16 (6) |
| 1-2-87 | (Fiesta Bowl) Penn St. (2, 11-0-0) 14, Miami (Fla.) 10 (2) |
| 11-21-87 | Oklahoma (2, 11-0-0) 17, *Nebraska 7 (2) |
| 1-1-88 | (Orange Bowl) Miami (Fla.) (2, 11-1-0) 20, Oklahoma 14 (3) |
| 10-15-88 | *Notre Dame (4, 5-0-0) 31, Miami (Fla.) 30 (4) |
| 10-29-88 | Washington St. (NR, 4-3-0) 34, *UCLA 30 (6) |
| 11-25-89 | *Miami (Fla.) (7, 9-1-0) 27, Notre Dame 10 (5) |
| 1-1-90 | (Orange Bowl) Notre Dame (4, 11-1-0) 21, Colorado 6 (4) |
| 9-8-90 | *Brigham Young (16, 1-0-0) 28, Miami (Fla.) 21 (10) |
| 10-6-90 | Stanford (NR, 1-3-0) 36, *Notre Dame 31 (8) |
| 10-13-90 | Michigan St. (NR, 1-2-1) 28, *Michigan 27 (10) |
| 11-3-90 | Georgia Tech (16, 6-0-1) 41, *Virginia 38 (11) |
| 11-17-90 | Penn St. (18, 7-2-0) 24, *Notre Dame 21 (7) |
| 11-16-91 | Miami (Fla.) (2, 8-0-0) 17, *Florida St. 16 (3) |
| 11-7-92 | *Arizona (12, 5-2-1) 16, Washington 3 (6) |
| 1-1-93 | (Sugar Bowl) Alabama (2, 12-0) 34, Miami (Fla.) 13 (3) |

*Division I-A National Poll Rankings*

# UNDEFEATED, UNTIED TEAMS

Regular-season games only, minimum of five games played against opponents above the high-school level. Subsequent bowl win is indicated by (†), loss (‡) and tie ($). Unscored-on teams are indicated by (●).

| Year | College | Wins | Year | College | Wins | Year | College | Wins |
|---|---|---|---|---|---|---|---|---|
| 78 | Princeton | 6 | 12 | Harvard | 9 | 26 | Alabama | $9 |
| 82 | Yale | 8 | | Notre Dame | 7 | | Stanford | $10 |
| 83 | Yale | 8 | | Penn St. | 8 | | Utah | 7 |
| 85 | Princeton | 9 | | Washington | 6 | 27 | (None) | |
| 87 | Yale | 9 | | Wisconsin | 7 | 28 | Boston College | 9 |
| 88 | Yale | ●13 | 13 | Auburn | 8 | | Detroit | 9 |
| 89 | Princeton | 10 | | Chicago | 7 | | Georgia Tech | †9 |
| 90 | Harvard | 11 | | Harvard | 9 | 29 | Notre Dame | 9 |
| 91 | Yale | ●13 | | Michigan St. | 7 | | Pittsburgh | ‡9 |
| 92 | Minnesota | 5 | | Nebraska | 8 | | Purdue | 8 |
| | Purdue | 8 | | Notre Dame | 7 | | Tulane | 9 |
| | Yale | ●13 | | Washington | 7 | | Utah | 7 |
| 93 | Minnesota | 6 | 14 | Army | 9 | 30 | Alabama | †9 |
| | Princeton | 11 | | Illinois | 7 | | Notre Dame | 10 |
| 94 | Pennsylvania | 12 | | Tennessee | 9 | | Utah | 8 |
| | Va. Military | 5 | | Texas | 8 | | Washington St. | ‡9 |
| | Yale | 16 | | Wash. & Lee | 9 | 31 | Tulane | ‡11 |
| 95 | Pennsylvania | 14 | 15 | Colorado St. | 7 | 32 | Colgate | ●9 |
| 96 | Louisiana St. | 6 | | Columbia | 5 | | Michigan | 8 |
| 97 | Pennsylvania | 15 | | Cornell | 9 | | Southern Cal | †9 |
| 98 | Harvard | 11 | | Nebraska | 8 | 33 | Princeton | 9 |
| | Kentucky | ●7 | | Oklahoma | 10 | 34 | Alabama | †9 |
| | Michigan | 10 | | Pittsburgh | 8 | | Minnesota | 8 |
| | North Caro. | 9 | | Washington | 7 | 35 | Minnesota | 8 |
| 99 | Kansas | 10 | | Washington St. | †6 | | Princeton | 9 |
| | Sewanee | 12 | 16 | Army | 9 | | Southern Meth. | ‡12 |
| 00 | Clemson | 6 | | Ohio St. | 7 | 36 | (None) | |
| | Texas | 6 | | Pittsburgh | 8 | 37 | Alabama | ‡9 |
| | Tulane | ●5 | | Tulsa | 10 | | Colorado | ‡8 |
| | Yale | 12 | 17 | Denver | 9 | | Santa Clara | ‡8 |
| 01 | Harvard | 12 | | Georgia Tech | 9 | 38 | Duke | ‡●9 |
| | Michigan | †●10 | | Pittsburgh | 9 | | Georgetown | 8 |
| | Wisconsin | 9 | | Texas A&M | ●8 | | Oklahoma | ‡10 |
| 02 | Arizona | ●5 | | Washington St. | 6 | | Tennessee | †10 |
| | California | 8 | 18 | Michigan | 5 | | Texas Christian | †10 |
| | Michigan | 11 | | Oklahoma | 6 | | Texas Tech | ‡10 |
| | Nebraska | ●10 | | Texas | 9 | 39 | Cornell | 8 |
| 03 | Nebraska | 11 | | Virginia Tech | 7 | | Tennessee | †●10 |
| | Princeton | 11 | | Washington (Mo.) | 6 | | Texas A&M | †10 |
| 04 | Auburn | 5 | 19 | Notre Dame | 9 | 40 | Boston College | †10 |
| | Michigan | 10 | | Texas A&M | ●10 | | Lafayette | 9 |
| | Minnesota | 13 | 20 | Boston College | 8 | | Minnesota | 8 |
| | Pennsylvania | 12 | | California | †8 | | Stanford | †9 |
| | Pittsburgh | 10 | | Notre Dame | 9 | | Tennessee | ‡10 |
| | Vanderbilt | 9 | | Ohio St. | ‡7 | 41 | Duke | ‡9 |
| 05 | Chicago | 10 | | Southern Cal | 6 | | Duquesne | 8 |
| | Stanford | 8 | | Texas | 9 | | Minnesota | 8 |
| | Yale | 10 | | Va. Military | 9 | 42 | Tulsa | ‡10 |
| 06 | New Mexico St. | 5 | 21 | California | $9 | 43 | Purdue | 9 |
| | Washington St. | ●6 | | Cornell | 8 | 44 | Army | 9 |
| | Wisconsin | 5 | | Iowa | 7 | | Ohio St. | 9 |
| 07 | Oregon St. | ●6 | 22 | California | 9 | 45 | Alabama | †9 |
| 08 | Kansas | 9 | | Cornell | 8 | | Army | 9 |
| | Louisiana St. | 10 | | Drake | 7 | | Oklahoma St. | †8 |
| 09 | Arkansas | 7 | | Iowa | 7 | 46 | Georgia | †10 |
| | Colorado | ●6 | | Princeton | 8 | | Hardin-Simmons | †10 |
| | Washington | 7 | | Tulsa | 7 | | UCLA | ‡10 |
| | Yale | ●10 | 23 | Colorado | 9 | 47 | Michigan | †9 |
| 10 | Colorado | 6 | | Cornell | 8 | | Notre Dame | 9 |
| | Illinois | ●7 | | Illinois | 8 | | Penn St. | $9 |
| | Pittsburgh | ●9 | | Michigan | 8 | 48 | California | ‡10 |
| | Washington | 6 | | Southern Methodist | 9 | | Clemson | †10 |
| 11 | Colorado | 6 | | Yale | 8 | | Michigan | 9 |
| | Oklahoma | 8 | 24 | Notre Dame | †9 | 49 | Army | 9 |
| | Utah St. | ●5 | 25 | Alabama | †9 | | California | ‡10 |
| | Washington | 7 | | Dartmouth | 8 | | Notre Dame | 10 |

| Year | College | Wins | Year | College | Wins | Year | College | Wins |
|---|---|---|---|---|---|---|---|---|
|  | Oklahoma | †10 |  | Arkansas | †10 |  | Arkansas St. | 11 |
| 50 | Oklahoma | ‡10 |  | Princeton | 9 |  | Ohio St. | ‡11 |
|  | Princeton | 9 | 65 | Arkansas | ‡10 | 76 | Maryland | ‡11 |
|  | Wyoming | †9 |  | Dartmouth | 9 |  | Pittsburgh | †11 |
| 51 | Maryland | †9 |  | Michigan St. | ‡10 |  | Rutgers | 11 |
|  | Michigan St. | 9 |  | Nebraska | ‡10 | 77 | Texas | ‡11 |
|  | Princeton | 9 | 66 | Alabama | †11 | 78 | Penn St. | ‡11 |
|  | San Francisco | 9 | 67 | Wyoming | ‡10 | 79 | Alabama | †11 |
|  | Tennessee | ‡10 | 68 | Ohio | ‡10 |  | Brigham Young | ‡11 |
| 52 | Georgia Tech | †11 |  | Ohio St. | †9 |  | Florida St. | ‡11 |
|  | Michigan St. | 9 |  | Penn St. | †10 |  | McNeese St. | ‡11 |
| 53 | Maryland | ‡10 | 69 | Penn St. | †10 |  | Ohio St. | ‡11 |
| 54 | Ohio St. | †9 |  | San Diego St. | †10 | 80 | Georgia | †11 |
|  | Oklahoma | 10 |  | Texas | †10 | 81 | Clemson | †11 |
|  | UCLA | 9 |  | Toledo | †10 | 82 | Georgia | ‡11 |
| 55 | Maryland | ‡10 | 70 | Arizona St. | †10 | 83 | Nebraska | ‡12 |
|  | Oklahoma | †10 |  | Dartmouth | 9 |  | Texas | ‡11 |
| 56 | Oklahoma | 10 |  | Ohio St. | ‡9 | 84 | Brigham Young | ‡12 |
|  | Tennessee | ‡10 |  | Texas | ‡10 | 85 | Bowling Green | ‡11 |
|  | Wyoming | 10 |  | Toledo | †11 |  | Penn St. | ‡11 |
| 57 | Arizona St. | 10 | 71 | Alabama | ‡11 | 86 | Miami (Fla.) | ‡11 |
|  | Auburn | 10 |  | Michigan | †11 |  | Penn St. | †11 |
| 58 | Louisiana St. | †10 |  | Nebraska | †12 | 87 | Miami (Fla.) | †11 |
| 59 | Syracuse | †10 |  | Toledo | †11 |  | Oklahoma | ‡11 |
| 60 | New Mexico St. | †10 | 72 | Southern Cal | †11 |  | Syracuse | $11 |
|  | Yale | 9 | 73 | Alabama | ‡11 | 88 | Notre Dame | †11 |
| 61 | Alabama | †10 |  | Miami (Ohio) | †10 |  | West Va. | ‡11 |
|  | Rutgers | 9 |  | Notre Dame | †10 | 89 | Colorado | ‡11 |
| 62 | Dartmouth | 9 |  | Penn St. | †11 | 90 | (None) |  |
|  | Mississippi | †9 | 74 | Alabama | †11 | 91 | Miami (Fla.) | †11 |
|  | Southern Cal | †10 |  | Oklahoma | 11 |  | Washington | †11 |
| 63 | Texas | †10 | 75 | Arizona St. | †11 | 92 | Alabama | †12 |
| 64 | Alabama | ‡10 |  |  |  |  |  |  |

# THE SPOILERS
### (From 1937 Season)

Following is a list of the spoilers of major-college teams that lost their perfect (undefeated, untied) record in their **final** game of the season, including a bowl game (in parentheses). Confrontations of two undefeated, untied teams at the time are in bold face. An asterisk (*) indicates the home team in a regular-season game, a dagger (†) indicates a neutral site.

| Date | Spoiler | Victim | Score |
|---|---|---|---|
| 1-1-38 | California | Alabama (Rose) | 13-0 |
| 1-1-38 | Rice | Colorado (Cotton) | 28-14 |
| 12-3-38 | *Southern Cal | Notre Dame | 13-0 |
| 1-2-39 | Southern Cal | Duke (Rose) | 7-3 |
| 1-2-39 | **Tennessee** | **Oklahoma (Orange)** | 17-0 |
| 1-2-39 | St. Mary's (Cal.) | Texas Tech (Cotton) | 20-13 |
| 12-2-39 | *Duquesne | Detroit Mercy | tie 10-10 |
| 1-1-40 | Southern Cal | Tennessee (Rose) | 14-0 |
| 1-1-41 | **Boston College** | **Tennessee (Sugar)** | 19-13 |
| 1-1-42 | Oregon St. | Duke (Rose) | 20-16 |
| 11-27-43 | *Great Lakes | Notre Dame | 19-14 |
| 1-1-44 | Southern Cal | Washington (Rose) | 29-0 |
| 11-25-44 | *Virginia | Yale | tie 6-6 |
| 1-1-47 | Illinois | UCLA (Rose) | 45-14 |
| 1-1-48 | Southern Methodist | Penn St. (Cotton) | tie 13-13 |
| 11-27-48 | †Navy | Army | tie 21-21 |
| 12-2-48 | *Southern Cal | Notre Dame | tie 14-14 |
| 1-1-49 | Northwestern | California (Rose) | 20-14 |
| 1-2-50 | Ohio St. | California (Rose) | 17-14 |
| 12-2-50 | †Navy | Army | 14-2 |
| 1-1-51 | Kentucky | Oklahoma (Sugar) | 13-7 |
| 1-1-52 | **Maryland** | **Tennessee (Sugar)** | 28-13 |
| 11-22-52 | Southern Cal | *UCLA | 14-12 |
| 1-1-54 | Oklahoma | Maryland (Orange) | 7-0 |
| 1-2-56 | **Oklahoma** | **Maryland (Orange)** | 20-6 |
| 1-1-57 | Baylor | Tennessee (Sugar) | 13-7 |
| 11-28-64 | *Southern Cal | Notre Dame | 20-17 |
| 1-1-65 | Texas | Alabama (Orange) | 21-17 |
| 11-20-65 | **Dartmouth** | ***Princeton** | 28-14 |
| 1-1-66 | UCLA | Michigan St. (Rose) | 14-12 |

*Division I-A Undefeated, Untied Teams*

| Date | Spoiler | Victim | Score |
|------|---------|--------|-------|
| 1-1-66 | Alabama | Nebraska (Orange) | 39-28 |
| 1-1-66 | Louisiana St. | Arkansas (Cotton) | 14-7 |
| 11-19-66 | **Notre Dame** | ***Michigan St.** | tie 10-10 |
| 1-1-68 | Louisiana St. | Wyoming (Sugar) | 20-13 |
| 11-23-68 | *Harvard | Yale | tie 29-29 |
| 12-27-68 | Richmond | Ohio (Tangerine) | 49-42 |
| 11-22-69 | *Michigan | Ohio St. | 24-12 |
| 11-22-69 | *Princeton | Dartmouth | 35-7 |
| 11-21-70 | *Ohio St. | **Michigan** | 20-9 |
| 1-1-71 | Stanford | Ohio St. (Rose) | 27-17 |
| 1-1-71 | Notre Dame | Texas (Cotton) | 24-11 |
| 1-1-72 | Stanford | Michigan (Rose) | 13-12 |
| 1-1-72 | **Nebraska** | **Alabama (Orange)** | 38-6 |
| 11-25-72 | *Ohio St. | Michigan | 14-11 |
| 11-24-73 | **Ohio St.** | *Michigan | tie 10-10 |
| 12-31-73 | **Notre Dame** | **Alabama (Sugar)** | 24-23 |
| 11-23-74 | *Ohio St. | Michigan | 12-10 |
| 11-23-74 | *Harvard | Yale | 21-16 |
| 1-1-75 | Notre Dame | Alabama (Orange) | 13-11 |
| 1-1-76 | UCLA | Ohio St. (Rose) | 23-10 |
| 1-1-77 | Houston | Maryland (Cotton) | 30-21 |
| 11-19-77 | *Delaware | Colgate | 21-3 |
| 1-2-78 | Notre Dame | Texas (Cotton) | 38-10 |
| 1-1-79 | Alabama | Penn St. (Sugar) | 14-7 |
| 11-17-79 | Harvard | *Yale | 22-7 |
| 12-15-79 | Syracuse | McNeese St. (Independence) | 31-7 |
| 12-21-79 | Indiana | Brigham Young (Holiday) | 38-37 |
| 1-1-80 | Southern Cal | Ohio St. (Rose) | 17-16 |
| 1-1-80 | Oklahoma | Florida St. (Orange) | 24-7 |
| 1-1-83 | Penn St. | Georgia (Sugar) | 27-23 |
| 1-2-84 | Georgia | Texas (Cotton) | 10-9 |
| 1-2-84 | Miami (Fla.) | Nebraska (Orange) | 31-30 |
| 12-14-85 | Fresno St. | Bowling Green (California) | 51-7 |
| 1-1-86 | Oklahoma | Penn St. (Orange) | 25-10 |
| 1-2-87 | **Penn St.** | **Miami (Fla.) (Fiesta)** | 14-10 |
| 1-1-88 | Auburn | Syracuse (Sugar) | tie 16-16 |
| 1-1-88 | **Miami (Fla.)** | **Oklahoma (Orange)** | 20-14 |
| 1-2-89 | **Notre Dame** | **West Va. (Fiesta)** | 34-21 |
| 1-1-90 | Notre Dame | Colorado (Orange) | 21-6 |
| 1-1-93 | Notre Dame | Texas A&M (Cotton) | 28-3 |
| 1-1-93 | **Alabama** | **Miami (Fla.) (Sugar)** | 34-13 |

# STREAKS AND RIVALRIES

## LONGEST WINNING STREAKS
### (Includes Bowl Games)

| Wins | Team | Years | Ended by | Score |
|------|------|-------|----------|-------|
| 47 | Oklahoma | 1953-57 | Notre Dame | 7-0 |
| 39 | Washington | 1908-14 | Oregon St. | 0-0 |
| 37 | Yale | 1890-93 | Princeton | 6-0 |
| 37 | Yale | 1887-89 | Princeton | 10-0 |
| 35 | Toledo | 1969-71 | Tampa | 21-0 |
| 34 | Pennsylvania | 1894-96 | Lafayette | 6-4 |
| 31 | Oklahoma | 1948-50 | Kentucky | *13-7 |
| 31 | Pittsburgh | 1914-18 | Cleveland Naval Reserve | 10-9 |
| 31 | Pennsylvania | 1896-98 | Harvard | 10-0 |
| 30 | Texas | 1968-70 | Notre Dame | *24-11 |
| 29 | Miami (Fla.) | 1990-93 | Alabama | *34-13 |
| 29 | Michigan | 1901-03 | Minnesota | 6-6 |
| 28 | Alabama | 1978-80 | Mississippi St. | 6-3 |
| 28 | Oklahoma | 1973-75 | Kansas | 23-3 |
| 28 | Michigan St. | 1950-53 | Purdue | 6-0 |

| Wins | Team | Years | Ended by | Score |
|------|------|-------|----------|-------|
| 27 | Nebraska | 1901-04 | Colorado | 6-0 |
| 26 | Cornell | 1921-24 | Williams | 14-7 |
| 26 | Michigan | 1903-05 | Chicago | 2-0 |
| 25 | Brigham Young | 1983-85 | UCLA | 27-24 |
| 25 | Michigan | 1946-49 | Army | 21-7 |
| 25 | Army | 1944-46 | Notre Dame | 0-0 |
| 25 | Southern Cal | 1931-33 | Oregon St. | 0-0 |
| 24 | Princeton | 1949-52 | Pennsylvania | 13-7 |
| 24 | Minnesota | 1903-05 | Wisconsin | 16-12 |
| 24 | Yale | 1894-95 | Boston AC | 0-0 |
| 24 | Harvard | 1890-91 | Yale | 10-0 |
| 24 | Yale | 1882-84 | Princeton | 0-0 |
| 23 | Alabama# | 1991-93 | Current | |
| 23 | Notre Dame | 1988-89 | Miami (Fla.) | 27-10 |
| 23 | Nebraska | 1970-71 | UCLA | 20-17 |
| 23 | Penn St. | 1968-70 | Colorado | 41-13 |
| 23 | Tennessee | 1937-39 | Southern Cal | *14-0 |
| 23 | Harvard | 1901-02 | Yale | 23-0 |
| 22 | Washington | 1990-92 | Arizona | 16-3 |
| 22 | Nebraska | 1982-83 | Miami (Fla.) | *31-30 |
| 22 | Ohio St. | 1967-69 | Michigan | 24-12 |
| 22 | Arkansas | 1963-65 | Louisiana St. | *14-7 |
| 22 | Harvard | 1912-14 | Penn St. | 13-13 |
| 22 | Yale | 1904-06 | Princeton | 0-0 |
| 21 | Arizona St. | 1969-71 | Oregon St. | 24-18 |
| 21 | San Diego St. | 1968-70 | Long Beach St. | 27-11 |
| 21 | Notre Dame | 1946-48 | Southern Cal | 14-14 |
| 21 | Minnesota | 1933-36 | Northwestern | 6-0 |
| 21 | Colorado | 1908-12 | Colorado St. | 21-0 |
| 21 | Pennsylvania | 1903-05 | Lafayette | 6-6 |
| 21 | Yale | 1900-01 | Army | 5-5 |
| 21 | Harvard | 1898-99 | Yale | 0-0 |
| 20 | Oklahoma | 1986-87 | Miami (Fla.) | *20-14 |
| 20 | Tennessee | 1950-51 | Maryland | *28-13 |
| 20 | Notre Dame | 1929-31 | Northwestern | 0-0 |
| 20 | Alabama | 1924-26 | Stanford | *7-7 |
| 20 | Iowa | 1920-23 | Illinois | 9-6 |
| 20 | Notre Dame | 1919-21 | Iowa | 10-7 |

* Streak ended in bowl game.   # Current streak.

# LONGEST UNBEATEN STREAKS
## (Includes Bowl Games; May Include Ties)

| No. | Wins | Ties | Team | Years | Ended by | Score |
|-----|------|------|------|-------|----------|-------|
| 63 | 59 | 4 | Washington | 1907-17 | California | 27-0 |
| 56 | 55 | 1 | Michigan | 1901-05 | Chicago | 2-0 |
| 50 | 46 | 4 | California | 1920-25 | Olympic Club | 15-0 |
| 48 | 47 | 1 | Oklahoma | 1953-57 | Notre Dame | 7-0 |
| 48 | 47 | 1 | Yale | 1885-89 | Princeton | 10-0 |
| 47 | 42 | 5 | Yale | 1879-85 | Princeton | 6-5 |
| 44 | 42 | 2 | Yale | 1894-96 | Princeton | 24-6 |
| 42 | 39 | 3 | Yale | 1904-08 | Harvard | 4-0 |
| 39 | 37 | 2 | Notre Dame | 1946-50 | Purdue | 28-14 |
| 37 | 36 | 1 | Oklahoma | 1972-75 | Kansas | 23-3 |
| 37 | 37 | 0 | Yale | 1890-93 | Princeton | 6-0 |
| 35 | 35 | 0 | Toledo | 1969-71 | Tampa | 21-0 |
| 35 | 34 | 1 | Minnesota | 1903-05 | Wisconsin | 16-12 |
| 34 | 33 | 1 | Nebraska | 1912-16 | Kansas | 7-3 |
| 34 | 34 | 0 | Pennsylvania | 1894-96 | Lafayette | 6-4 |
| 34 | 32 | 2 | Princeton | 1884-87 | Harvard | 12-0 |
| 34 | 29 | 5 | Princeton | 1877-82 | Harvard | 1-0 |
| 33 | 30 | 3 | Tennessee | 1926-30 | Alabama | 18-6 |
| 33 | 31 | 2 | Georgia Tech | 1914-18 | Pittsburgh | 32-0 |
| 33 | 30 | 3 | Harvard | 1911-15 | Cornell | 10-0 |
| 32 | 31 | 1 | Nebraska | 1969-71 | UCLA | 20-17 |
| 32 | 30 | 2 | Army | 1944-47 | Columbia | 21-20 |
| 32 | 31 | 1 | Harvard | 1898-00 | Yale | 28-0 |
| 31 | 30 | 1 | Penn St. | 1967-70 | Colorado | 41-13 |
| 31 | 30 | 1 | San Diego St. | 1967-70 | Long Beach St. | 27-11 |

| No. | Wins | Ties | Team | Years | Ended by | Score |
|-----|------|------|------|-------|----------|-------|
| 31 | 29 | 2 | Georgia Tech | 1950-53 | Notre Dame | 27-14 |
| 31 | 31 | 0 | Oklahoma | 1948-50 | Kentucky | 13-7 |
| 31 | 31 | 0 | Pittsburgh | 1914-18 | Cleveland Naval | 10-9 |
| 31 | 31 | 0 | Pennsylvania | 1896-98 | Harvard | 10-0 |
| 30 | 30 | 0 | Texas | 1968-70 | Notre Dame | 24-11 |
| 30 | 25 | 5 | Penn St. | 1919-22 | Navy | 14-0 |
| 30 | 28 | 2 | Pennsylvania | 1903-06 | Swarthmore | 4-0 |
| 29 | 29 | 0 | Miami (Fla.) | 1990-93 | Alabama | 34-13 |
| 28 | 28 | 0 | Alabama | 1978-80 | Mississippi St. | 6-3 |
| 28 | 26 | 2 | Southern Cal | 1978-80 | Washington | 20-10 |
| 28 | 28 | 0 | Michigan St. | 1950-53 | Purdue | 6-0 |
| 28 | 26 | 2 | Army | 1947-50 | Navy | 14-2 |
| 28 | 24 | 4 | Minnesota | 1933-36 | Northwestern | 6-0 |
| 28 | 26 | 2 | Tennessee | 1930-33 | Duke | 10-2 |
| 27 | 26 | 1 | Southern Cal | 1931-33 | Stanford | 13-7 |
| 27 | 24 | 3 | Notre Dame | 1910-14 | Yale | 28-0 |
| 27 | 27 | 0 | Nebraska | 1901-04 | Colorado | 6-0 |

## LONGEST HOME WINNING STREAKS
### (Includes Bowl Games)

| Wins | Team | Years | Ended by | Score |
|------|------|-------|----------|-------|
| 57 | Alabama | 1963-82 | Southern Miss. | 38-29 |
| 51 | Miami (Fla.) | 1985-93 | Current | |
| 50 | Michigan | 1901-07 | Pennsylvania | 6-0 |
| 40 | Notre Dame | 1907-18 | Great Lakes | 7-7 |
| 33 | Nebraska | 1901-06 | Iowa St. | 14-2 |
| 30 | Auburn | 1952-61 | Kentucky | 14-12 |
| 28 | Michigan | 1969-73 | Ohio St. | 0-0 |
| 27 | Vanderbilt | 1903-07 | Michigan | 8-0 |
| 25 | Ohio St. | 1972-76 | Missouri | 22-21 |
| 24 | Georgia | 1980-83 | Auburn | 13-7 |
| 24 | Georgia Tech | 1916-19 | Wash. & Lee | 3-0 |
| 24 | Virginia | 1899-04 | Navy | 5-0 |
| 23 | Tulane | 1929-32 | Vanderbilt | 6-6 |
| 23 | Michigan St. | 1904-08 | Michigan | 0-0 |
| 23 | Michigan | 1897-00 | Ohio St. | 0-0 |
| 22 | Wyoming | 1965-70 | Air Force | 41-17 |
| 22 | Minnesota | 1933-37 | Notre Dame | 7-6 |
| 21 | Mississippi | 1952-59 | Louisiana St. | 10-10 |
| 21 | North Caro. | 1893-00 | Virginia Tech | 0-0 |
| 20 | Fresno St. | 1987-90 | Utah St. | 24-24 |
| 20 | Rutgers | 1974-78 | Colgate | 14-9 |
| 20 | Mississippi St. | 1939-45 | Mississippi | 7-6 |
| 20 | Southern Cal | 1927-29 | California | 15-7 |
| 20 | Southern Cal | 1919-23 | California | 13-7 |

## LONGEST LOSING STREAKS

| Losses | Team | Years | Ended by | Score |
|--------|------|-------|----------|-------|
| 34 | Northwestern | 1979-82 | Northern Ill. | 31-6 |
| 28 | Virginia | 1958-61 | William & Mary | 21-6 |
| 28 | Kansas St. | 1944-48 | Arkansas St. | 37-6 |
| 27 | New Mexico St. | 1988-90 | Cal St. Fullerton | 43-9 |
| 27 | Eastern Mich. | 1980-82 | Kent | 9-7 |
| 26 | Colorado St. | 1960-62 | Pacific (Cal.) | 20-0 |
| 20 | Florida St. | 1972-74 | Miami (Fla.) | 21-14 |
| 18 | Wake Forest | 1962-63 | South Caro. | 20-19 |
| 17 | Memphis St. | 1981-82 | Arkansas St. | 12-0 |
| 17 | Tulane | 1961-63 | South Caro. | 20-7 |
| 17 | Kansas | 1953-55 | Washington St. | 13-0 |
| 16 | Indiana | 1983-85 | Louisville | 41-28 |
| 16 | Vanderbilt | 1961-62 | Tulane | 20-0 |

114      *1993 NCAA FOOTBALL*

# MOST-PLAYED RIVALRIES
## (Still Ongoing Unless Indicated)

| Games | Opponents (Series leader listed first) | Rivalry Record | First Game |
|---|---|---|---|
| 102 | Minnesota-Wisconsin | 55-39-8 | 1890 |
| 101 | Missouri-Kansas | 48-44-9 | 1891 |
| 99 | Nebraska-Kansas | 75-21-3 | 1892 |
| 99 | Baylor-Texas Christian | 46-46-7 | 1899 |
| 99 | Texas-Texas A&M | 64-30-5 | 1894 |
| 97 | North Caro.-Virginia | 53-40-4 | 1892 |
| 97 | Miami (Ohio)-Cincinnati | 53-38-6 | 1888 |
| 96 | Auburn-Georgia | 45-44-7 | 1892 |
| 96 | Oregon-Oregon St. | 47-39-10 | 1894 |
| 95 | Purdue-Indiana | 58-31-6 | 1891 |
| 95 | Stanford-California | 47-37-11 | 1892 |
| 93 | Army-Navy | 43-43-7 | 1890 |
| 92 | Penn St.-Pittsburgh | 47-41-4 | 1893 |
| 90 | Louisiana St.-Tulane | *61-22-7 | 1893 |
| 90 | #Auburn-Georgia Tech | 47-39-4 | 1892 |
| 90 | Clemson-South Caro. | 53-33-4 | 1896 |
| 90 | Kansas-Kansas St. | 61-24-5 | 1902 |
| 90 | Oklahoma-Kansas | 60-24-6 | 1903 |
| 90 | Utah-Utah St. | 59-27-4 | 1892 |
| 89 | Michigan-Ohio St. | 50-33-6 | 1897 |
| 89 | Mississippi-Mississippi St. | 52-31-6 | 1901 |
| 88 | Tennessee-Kentucky | 56-23-9 | 1893 |
| 87 | Texas-Oklahoma | 51-32-4 | 1900 |
| 87 | Oklahoma-Oklahoma St. | 69-11-7 | 1904 |
| 87 | Georgia-Georgia Tech | 47-35-5 | 1893 |
| 86 | Tennessee-Vanderbilt | 55-26-5 | 1892 |
| 86 | Illinois-Northwestern | 45-36-5 | 1892 |
| 85 | Michigan-Michigan St. | 56-24-5 | 1898 |
| 85 | Pittsburgh-West Va. | 55-27-3 | 1895 |
| 85 | Washington-Washington St. | 54-25-6 | 1900 |

*Disputed series record: Tulane claims 23-60-7 record.   # Have not met since 1989.*

## ADDITIONAL RECORDS

**Longest Uninterrupted Series**
90 games—Kansas-Oklahoma (from 1903)
87 games—Kansas-Nebraska (from 1906)
86 games—Minnesota-Wisconsin (from 1907)
83 games—Wake Forest-North Caro. (from 1910)

**Most Consecutive Wins Over a Major Opponent in an Uninterrupted Series**
32—Oklahoma over Kansas St., 1937-68
27—Texas over Rice, 1966-92

**Most Consecutive Current Wins Over a Major Opponent**
29—Notre Dame over Navy, 1964-92 (56-9-1 in the rivalry)
27—Texas over Rice, 1966-92 (58-20-1 in the rivalry)
24—Nebraska over Kansas, 1969-92 (75-21-3 in the rivalry)
24—Nebraska over Kansas St., 1969-92 (65-10-2 in the rivalry)
22—Oklahoma over Kansas St., 1971-92 (63-11-4 in the rivalry)

**Most Consecutive Games Without a Loss Against a Major Opponent**
34—Oklahoma over Kansas St., 1935-68 (1 tie)

# CLIFFHANGERS

Regular-season Division I-A games won on the final play (since 1971, when first recorded). The extra point is listed when it provided the margin of victory after the winning touchdown on the game's final play.

| Date | Opponents, Score | Game-winning play |
|---|---|---|
| 9-25-71 | Marshall 15, Xavier (Ohio) 13 | Terry Gardner 13 pass from Reggie Oliver |
| 10-9-71 | California 30, Oregon St. 27 | Steve Sweeney 7 pass from Jay Cruze |
| 10-23-71 | Washington St. 24, Stanford 23 | Don Sweet 27 FG |
| 11-6-71 | Kentucky 14, Vanderbilt 7 | Darryl Bishop 43 interception return |
| 11-4-72 | Louisiana St. 17, Mississippi 16 | Brad Davis 10 pass from Bert Jones (Rusty Jackson kick) |

| Date | Opponents, Score | Game-winning play |
|------|------------------|-------------------|
| 11-18-72 | California 24, Stanford 21 | Steve Sweeney 7 pass from Vince Ferragamo |
| 9-15-73 | Lamar 21, Howard Payne 17 | Larry Spears 14 pass from Jabo Leonard |
| 9-22-73 | Hawaii 13, Fresno St. 10 | Reinhold Stuprich 29 FG |
| 11-17-73 | New Mexico 23, Wyoming 21 | Bob Berg 43 FG |
| 11-23-74 | Stanford 22, California 20 | Mike Langford 50 FG |
| 9-20-75 | Indiana St. 23, Southern III. 21 | Dave Vandercook 50 FG |
| 10-18-75 | Cal St. Fullerton 32, UC Riverside 31 | John Choukair 52 FG |
| 11-8-75 | West Va. 17, Pittsburgh 14 | Bill McKenzie 38 FG |
| 11-8-75 | Stanford 13, Southern Cal 10 | Mike Langford 37 FG |
| 11-15-75 | North Caro. 17, Tulane 15 | Tom Biddle 40 FG |
| 11-6-76 | Eastern Mich. 30, Central Mich. 27 | Ken Dudal 38 FG |
| 9-30-78 | Virginia Tech 22, William & Mary 19 | Ron Zollicoffer 50 pass from David Lamie |
| 10-21-78 | Arkansas St. 6, McNeese St. 3 | Doug Dobbs 42 FG |
| 11-9-78 | San Jose St. 33, Pacific (Cal.) 31 | Rick Parma 5 pass from Ed Luther |
| 10-6-79 | Stanford 27, UCLA 24 | Ken Naber 56 FG |
| 10-20-79 | Nevada-Las Vegas 43, Utah 41 | Todd Peterson 49 FG |
| 10-27-79 | Michigan 27, Indiana 21 | Anthony Carter 45 pass from John Wangler |
| 11-10-79 | Penn St. 9, North Caro. St. 7 | Herb Menhardt 54 FG |
| 11-17-79 | Air Force 30, Vanderbilt 29 | Andy Bark 14 pass from Dave Ziebart |
| 11-24-79 | Arizona 27, Arizona St. 24 | Brett Weber 27 FG |
| 9-13-80 | Southern Cal 20, Tennessee 17 | Eric Hipp 47 FG |
| 9-13-80 | Illinois 20, Michigan St. 17 | Mike Bass 38 FG |
| 9-20-80 | Notre Dame 29, Michigan 27 | Harry Oliver 51 FG |
| 9-27-80 | Tulane 26, Mississippi 24 | Vince Manalla 29 FG |
| 10-18-80 | Connecticut 18, Holy Cross 17 | Ken Miller 4 pass from Ken Sweitzer (Keith Hugger pass from Sweitzer) |

Penn State's Herb Menhardt kicked 14 field goals in 20 attempts in 1979, including a 54-yarder on the final play of the game to beat North Carolina State, 9-7.

| Date | Opponents, Score | Game-winning play |
|------|------------------|-------------------|
| 10-18-80 | Washington 27, Stanford 24 | Chuck Nelson 25 FG |
| 11-1-80 | Tulane 24, Kentucky 22 | Vince Manalla 22 FG |
| 11-15-80 | Florida 17, Kentucky 15 | Brian Clark 34 FG |
| 10-16-82 | Arizona 16, Notre Dame 13 | Max Zendejas 48 FG |
| 10-23-82 | Illinois 29, Wisconsin 28 | Mike Bass 46 FG |
| 11-20-82 | California 25, Stanford 20 | 57 (5 laterals) kickoff return involving, in order: Kevin Moen, Richard Rodgers, Dwight Garner, Rodgers, Mariet Ford and Moen |
| 10-8-83 | Iowa St. 38, Kansas 35 | Marc Bachrodt 47 FG |
| 10-29-83 | Bowling Green 15, Central Mich. 14 | Stan Hunter 8 pass from Brian McClure |
| 11-5-83 | Baylor 24, Arkansas 21 | Marty Jimmerson 24 FG |
| 11-12-83 | Pacific (Cal.) 30, San Jose St. 26 | Ron Woods 85 pass from Mike Pitz |
| 11-12-83 | Miami (Fla.) 17, Florida St. 16 | Jeff Davis 19 FG |
| 11-26-83 | Arizona 17, Florida St. 15 | Max Zendejas 45 FG |
| 9-8-84 | Southwestern La. 17, Louisiana Tech 14 | Patrick Broussard 21 FG |
| 9-15-84 | Syracuse 13, Northwestern 12 | Jim Tait 2 pass from Todd Norley (Don McAulay kick) |
| 10-13-84 | UCLA 27, Washington St. 24 | John Lee 47 FG |
| 11-17-84 | Southwestern La. 18, Tulsa 17 | Patrick Broussard 45 FG |
| 11-17-84 | Temple 19, West Va. 17 | Jim Cooper 36 FG |
| 11-23-84 | Boston College 47, Miami (Fla.) 45 | Gerard Phelan 48 pass from Doug Flutie |
| 9-14-85 | Clemson 20, Virginia Tech 17 | David Treadwell 36 FG |
| 9-14-85 | Oregon St. 23, California 20 | Jim Nielsen 20 FG |
| 9-14-85 | Utah 29, Hawaii 27 | Andre Guardi 19 FG |
| 9-21-85 | New Mexico St. 22, UTEP 20 | Andy Weiler 32 FG |
| 10-5-85 | Mississippi St. 31, Memphis St. 28 | Artie Cosby 54 FG |
| 10-5-85 | Illinois 31, Ohio St. 28 | Chris White 38 FG |
| 10-12-85 | Tulsa 37, Long Beach St. 35 | Jason Staurovsky 46 FG |
| 10-19-85 | Northwestern 17, Wisconsin 14 | John Duvic 42 FG |
| 10-19-85 | Iowa 12, Michigan 10 | Rob Houghtlin 29 FG |
| 10-19-85 | Utah 39, San Diego St. 37 | Andre Guardi 42 FG |
| 11-30-85 | Alabama 25, Auburn 23 | Van Tiffin 52 FG |
| 9-13-86 | Oregon 32, Colorado 30 | Matt MacLeod 35 FG |
| 9-13-86 | Wyoming 23, Pacific (Cal.) 20 | Greg Worker 38 FG |
| 9-20-86 | Clemson 31, Georgia 28 | David Treadwell 46 FG |
| 9-20-86 | Southern Cal 17, Baylor 14 | Don Shafer 32 FG |
| 10-18-86 | Michigan 20, Iowa 17 | Mike Gillette 34 FG |
| 10-25-86 | Syracuse 27, Temple 24 | Tim Vesling 32 FG |
| 11-1-86 | North Caro. St. 23, South Caro. 22 | Danny Peebles 33 pass from Erik Kramer |
| 11-1-86 | North Caro. 32, Maryland 30 | Lee Gliarmis 28 FG |
| 11-8-86 | Southern Miss. 23, East Caro. 21 | Rex Banks 31 FG |
| 11-15-86 | Minnesota 20, Michigan 17 | Chip Lohmiller 30 FG |
| 11-29-86 | Notre Dame 38, Southern Cal 37 | John Carney 19 FG |
| 9-12-87 | Youngstown St. 20, Bowling Green 17 | John Dowling 36 FG |
| 9-19-87 | Utah 31, Wisconsin 28 | Scott Lieber 39 FG |
| 10-10-87 | Marshall 34, Louisville 31 | Keith Baxter 31 pass from Tony Petersen |
| 10-17-87 | Texas 16, Arkansas 14 | Tony Jones 18 pass from Bret Stafford |
| 11-12-88 | New Mexico 24, Colorado St. 23 | Tony Jones 28 pass from Jeremy Leach |
| 9-16-89 | Southern Methodist 31, Connecticut 30 | Mike Bowen 4 pass from Mike Romo |
| 9-30-89 | Kansas St. 20, North Texas 17 | Frank Hernandez 12 pass from Carl Straw |
| 10-7-89 | Florida 16, Louisiana St. 13 | Arden Czyzewski 41 FG |
| 10-14-89 | Southern Miss. 16, Louisville 10 | Darryl Tillman 79 pass from Brett Favre |
| 10-28-89 | Virginia 16, Louisville 15 | Jake McInerney 37 FG |
| 11-4-89 | Toledo 19, Western Mich. 18 | Romauldo Brown 9 pass from Kevin Meger |
| 11-4-89 | Northern Ill. 23, Southwestern La. 20 | Stacey Robinson 7 run |
| 9-8-90 | Utah 35, Minnesota 29 | Lavon Edwards 91 run of blocked FG |
| 9-29-90 | North Caro. St. 12, North Caro. 9 | Damon Hartman 56 FG |
| 10-20-90 | Alabama 9, Tennessee 6 | Philip Doyle 47 FG |
| 10-6-90 | Colorado 33, Missouri 31 | Charles S. Johnson 1 run |
| 11-3-90 | Southern Miss. 14, Southwestern La. 13 | Michael Welch 11 pass from Brett Favre (Jim Taylor kick) |
| 11-17-90 | Stanford 27, California 25 | John Hopkins 39 FG |
| 11-24-90 | Michigan 16, Ohio St. 13 | J. D. Carlson 37 FG |
| 9-7-91 | Central Mich. 27, Southwestern La. 24 | L. J. Muddy 2 pass from Jeff Bender |
| 9-21-91 | California 23, Arizona 21 | Doug Brien 33 FG |
| 9-21-91 | Georgia Tech 24, Virginia 21 | Scott Sisson 33 FG |
| 9-21-91 | Louisiana Tech 17, Eastern Mich. 14 | Chris Bonoil 54 FG |
| 10-12-91 | Ball St. 10, Eastern Mich. 8 | Kenny Stucker 41 FG |
| 11-2-91 | Kentucky 20, Cincinnati 17 | Doug Pelphrey 53 FG |

*Division I-A Cliffhangers*

| Date | Opponents, Score | Game-winning play |
|------|------------------|-------------------|
| 11-2-91 | Tulsa 13, Southern Miss. 10 | Eric Lange 24 FG |
| 9-5-92 | Louisiana Tech 10, Baylor 9 | Chris Bonoil 30 FG |
| 9-19-92 | Southern Miss. 16, Louisiana Tech 13 | Johnny Lomoro 46 FG |
| 10-3-92 | Texas A&M 19, Texas Tech 17 | Terry Venetoulias 21 FG |
| 10-3-92 | Georgia Tech 16, North Caro. St. 13 | Scott Sisson 29 FG |
| 10-3-92 | San Jose St. 26, Wyoming 24 | Joe Nedney 60 FG |
| 10-24-92 | Maryland 27, Duke 25 | Marcus Badgett 38 pass from John Kaleo |
| 10-31-92 | Rutgers 50, Virginia Tech 49 | Chris Brantley 15 pass from Bryan Fortay |
| 11-14-92 | UCLA 9, Oregon 6 | Louis Perez 40 FG |

## "CARDIAC SEASONS"
### (From 1937; won-lost record in parentheses)
### Games Decided by Two Points or Less

6—Kansas, 1973 (3-2-1): Tennessee 27-28, Nebraska 9-10, Iowa St. 22-20, Oklahoma St. 10-10, Colorado 17-15, Missouri 14-13 (season record: 7-3-1)

5—Illinois, 1992 (2-2-1): Minnesota 17-18, Ohio St. 18-16, Northwestern 26-27, Wisconsin 13-12, Michigan 22-22 (season record: 6-4-1)

5—Columbia, 1971 (4-1-0): Princeton 22-20, Harvard 19-21, Yale 15-14, Rutgers 17-16, Dartmouth 31-29 (season record: 6-3-0)

5—Missouri, 1957 (2-2-1): Vanderbilt 7-7, Southern Methodist 7-6, Nebraska 14-13, Kansas St. 21-23, Kansas 7-9 (season record: 5-4-1)

### Games Decided by Three Points or Less

7—Bowling Green, 1980 (2-5-0): Ohio 20-21, Ball St. 24-21, Western Mich. 17-14, Kentucky 20-21, Long Beach St. 21-23, Eastern Mich. 16-18, Richmond 17-20 (season record: 4-7-0)

7—Columbia, 1971 (4-3-0): Lafayette 10-3, Princeton 22-20, Harvard 19-21, Yale 15-14, Rutgers 17-16, Cornell 21-24, Dartmouth 31-29 (season record: 6-3-0)

6—Illinois, 1992 (3-2-1): Minnesota 17-18, Ohio St. 18-16, Northwestern 26-27, Wisconsin 13-12, Purdue 20-17, Michigan 22-22 (season record: 6-4-1)

6—Central Mich., 1991 (2-0-4): Ohio 17-17, Southwestern La. 27-24, Akron 31-29, Toledo 16-16, Miami (Ohio) 10-10, Eastern Mich. 14-14 (season record: 6-1-4)

6—Air Force, 1967 (2-2-2): Oklahoma St. 0-0, California 12-14, North Caro. 10-8, Tulane 13-10, Colorado St. 17-17, Army 7-10 (season record: 2-6-2)

6—Missouri, 1957 (3-2-1): Vanderbilt 7-7, Southern Methodist 7-6, Nebraska 14-13, Colorado 9-6, Kansas St. 21-23, Kansas 7-9 (season record: 5-4-1)

# DIVISION I-A STADIUMS

## STADIUMS LISTED ALPHABETICALLY BY SCHOOL

| School | Stadium | Conference | Year Built | Capacity | Surface |
|--------|---------|------------|------------|----------|---------|
| Air Force | Falcon | Western Athletic | 1962 | 53,533 | Grass |
| Akron | ✓Rubber Bowl | Mid-American | 1940 | 35,482 | Turf |
| Alabama | ✓Legion Field | Southeastern | 1927 | 83,091 | Turf |
| | Bryant-Denny | Southeastern | 1929 | 70,123 | PAT |
| Arizona | Arizona | Pacific-10 | 1928 | 58,000 | Grass |
| Arizona St. | Sun Devil | Pacific-10 | 1958 | 74,783 | Grass |
| Arkansas | ✓War Memorial | Southeastern | 1948 | 53,250 | Turf |
| | Razorback | Southeastern | 1938 | 51,000 | Turf |
| Arkansas St. | Indian | Big West | 1974 | 33,410 | Grass |
| Army | Michie | Independent | 1924 | 39,929 | Turf |
| Auburn | Jordan-Hare | Southeastern | 1939 | 85,214 | Grass |
| Ball St. | Ball St. | Mid-American | 1967 | 16,319 | Grass |
| Baylor | Floyd Casey | Southwest | 1950 | 48,500 | Turf |
| Boston College | Alumni | Big East | 1957 | 32,000 | Turf |
| Bowling Green | Doyt Perry | Mid-American | 1966 | 30,599 | Grass |
| Brigham Young | Cougar | Western Athletic | 1964 | 65,000 | Grass |
| California | Memorial | Pacific-10 | 1923 | 75,662 | Turf |
| Central Mich. | Kelly/Shorts | Mid-American | 1972 | 20,086 | Turf |
| Cincinnati | Nippert | Independent | 1916 | 35,000 | Turf |
| Clemson | Memorial | Atlantic Coast | 1942 | 81,473 | Grass |
| Colorado | Folsom Field | Big Eight | 1924 | 51,748 | Turf |
| Colorado St. | Hughes | Western Athletic | 1968 | 30,000 | Grass |

| School | Stadium | Conference | Year Built | Capacity | Surface |
|---|---|---|---|---|---|
| Duke | Wallace Wade | Atlantic Coast | 1929 | 33,941 | Grass |
| East Caro. | Ficklen Memorial | Independent | 1963 | 35,000 | Grass |
| Eastern Mich. | Rynearson | Mid-American | 1969 | 30,200 | Turf |
| Florida | Florida Field | Southeastern | 1929 | 83,000 | Grass |
| Florida St. | Doak Campbell | Atlantic Coast | 1950 | 72,000 | PAT |
| Fresno St. | Bulldog | Western Athletic | 1980 | 41,031 | Grass |
| Georgia | Sanford | Southeastern | 1929 | 85,434 | Grass |
| Georgia Tech | Dodd/Grant Field | Atlantic Coast | 1914 | 46,000 | Turf |
| Hawaii | ✓Aloha | Western Athletic | 1975 | 50,000 | Turf |
| Houston | ✓Astrodome@ | Southwest | 1965 | 60,000 | Turf |
| Illinois | Memorial | Big Ten | 1923 | 69,200 | Turf |
| Indiana | Memorial | Big Ten | 1960 | 52,354 | Turf |
| Iowa | Kinnick | Big Ten | 1929 | 70,311 | PAT |
| Iowa St. | Jack Trice Field | Big Eight | 1975 | 50,000 | Turf |
| Kansas | Memorial | Big Eight | 1921 | 50,250 | Turf |
| Kansas St. | KSU | Big Eight | 1968 | 42,000 | Turf |
| Kent | Dix | Mid-American | 1969 | 30,520 | Grass |
| Kentucky | Common- wealth | Southeastern | 1973 | 58,000 | Grass |
| Louisiana St. | Tiger | Southeastern | 1924 | 80,150 | Grass |
| Louisiana Tech | Joe Aillet | Big West | 1968 | 30,600 | Grass |
| Louisville | ✓Cardinal | Independent | 1956 | 35,500 | Turf |
| Maryland | Byrd | Atlantic Coast | 1950 | 45,000 | Grass |
| Memphis St. | ✓Liberty Bowl | Independent | 1965 | 62,425 | PAT |
| Miami (Fla.) | ✓Orange Bowl | Big East | 1935 | 74,712 | PAT |
| Miami (Ohio) | Fred Yager | Mid-American | 1983 | 25,183 | Grass |
| Michigan | Michigan | Big Ten | 1927 | 102,501 | PAT |
| Michigan St. | Spartan | Big Ten | 1957 | 76,000 | Turf |
| Minnesota | ✓Metrodome@ | Big Ten | 1982 | 62,345 | Turf |
| Mississippi | ✓Miss. Memorial | Southeastern | 1953 | 62,500 | Grass |
| | Vaught- Hemingway | Southeastern | 1941 | 42,577 | Grass |
| Mississippi St. | ✓Miss. Memorial | Southeastern | 1953 | 62,500 | Grass |
| | Scott Field | Southeastern | 1935 | 40,656 | PAT |
| Missouri | Faurot Field | Big Eight | 1926 | 62,000 | Turf |
| Navy | Navy-MC | Independent | 1959 | 30,000 | Grass |
| Nebraska | Memorial | Big Eight | 1923 | 73,650 | Turf |
| Nevada | Mackay | Big West | 1965 | 31,545 | Grass |
| Nevada-Las Vegas | ✓Silver Bowl | Big West | 1971 | 31,000 | Turf |
| New Mexico | University | Western Athletic | 1960 | 30,646 | Grass |
| New Mexico St. | Aggie Memorial | Big West | 1978 | 30,300 | Grass |
| North Caro. | Kenan | Atlantic Coast | 1927 | 52,000 | Grass |
| North Caro. St. | Carter-Finley | Atlantic Coast | 1966 | 47,000 | Grass |
| Northern Ill. | Huskie | Big West | 1965 | 30,998 | Turf |
| Northwestern | Dyche | Big Ten | 1926 | 49,256 | Turf |
| Notre Dame | Notre Dame | Independent | 1930 | 59,075 | Grass |
| Ohio | Peden | Mid-American | 1929 | 20,000 | Grass |
| Ohio St. | Ohio | Big Ten | 1922 | 91,470 | PAT |
| Oklahoma | Owen Field | Big Eight | 1924 | 75,004 | Turf |
| Oklahoma St. | Lewis | Big Eight | 1920 | 50,614 | Turf |
| Oregon | Autzen | Pacific-10 | 1967 | 41,678 | Turf |
| Oregon St. | Parker | Pacific-10 | 1953 | 35,547 | Turf |
| Pacific (Cal.) | Stagg Memorial | Big West | 1950 | 30,000 | Grass |
| Penn St. | Beaver | Big Ten | 1960 | 93,967 | Grass |
| Pittsburgh | Pitt | Big East | 1925 | 56,500 | Turf |
| Purdue | Ross-Ade | Big Ten | 1924 | 67,861 | PAT |
| Rice | Rice | Southwest | 1950 | 70,000 | Turf |
| Rutgers | ✓Giants | Big East | 1976 | 76,000 | Turf |
| | Rutgers | Big East | 1938 | 25,000 | Grass |
| San Diego St. | ✓Jack Murphy | Western Athletic | 1967 | 62,809 | Grass |

| School | Stadium | Conference | Year Built | Capacity | Surface |
|---|---|---|---|---|---|
| San Jose St. | Spartan | Big West | 1932 | 31,218 | Grass |
| South Caro. | Williams-Brice | Southeastern | 1934 | 72,400 | Grass |
| Southern Cal | ✓Los Angeles Coliseum | Pacific-10 | 1923 | 92,516 | Grass |
| Southern Methodist | Ownby | Southwest | 1926 | 23,783 | Turf |
| | Cotton Bowl | Southwest | 1938 | 71,615 | Turf |
| Southern Miss. | Roberts | Independent | 1976 | 33,000 | Grass |
| Southwestern La. | Cajun Field | Big West | 1971 | 31,000 | Grass |
| Stanford | Stanford | Pacific-10 | 1921 | 85,500 | Grass |
| Syracuse | Carrier Dome@ | Big East | 1980 | 50,000 | Turf |
| Temple | ✓Veterans | Big East | 1971 | 66,592 | Turf |
| Tennessee | Neyland | Southeastern | 1921 | 91,902 | Turf |
| Texas | Memorial | Southwest | 1924 | 77,809 | Turf |
| Texas A&M | Kyle Field | Southwest | 1925 | 70,210 | Turf |
| Texas Christian | Amon Carter | Southwest | 1929 | 46,000 | Grass |
| Texas Tech | Jones | Southwest | 1947 | 50,500 | Turf |
| Toledo | Glass Bowl | Mid-American | 1937 | 26,248 | Turf |
| Tulane | ✓Superdome@ | Independent | 1975 | 72,704 | Turf |
| Tulsa | Skelly | Independent | 1930 | 40,385 | Turf |
| UCLA | ✓Rose Bowl | Pacific-10 | 1922 | 99,563 | Grass |
| UTEP | ✓Sun Bowl | Western Athletic | 1963 | 51,270 | Turf |
| Utah | Robert Rice | Western Athletic | 1927 | 35,000 | Turf |
| Utah St. | E. L. Romney | Big West | 1968 | 30,257 | Grass |
| Vanderbilt | Vanderbilt | Southeastern | 1922** | 41,000 | Turf |
| Virginia | Scott | Atlantic Coast | 1931 | 42,000 | Turf |
| Virginia Tech | Lane | Big East | 1965 | 51,000 | Grass |
| Wake Forest | Groves | Atlantic Coast | 1968 | 31,500 | Grass |
| Washington | Husky | Pacific-10 | 1920 | 72,500 | Turf |
| Washington St. | Martin | Pacific-10 | 1972 | 40,000 | Turf |
| West Va. | Mountaineer Field | Big East | 1980 | 63,500 | Turf |
| Western Mich. | Waldo | Mid-American | 1939 | 30,000 | PAT |
| Wisconsin | Camp Randall | Big Ten | 1917 | 77,745 | Turf |
| Wyoming | War Memorial | Western Athletic | 1950 | 33,500 | Grass |

## STADIUMS LISTED BY CAPACITY
### (TOP 25)

| School | Stadium | Surface | Capacity |
|---|---|---|---|
| Michigan | Michigan | PAT | 102,501 |
| UCLA | ✓Rose Bowl | Grass | 99,563 |
| Penn St. | Beaver | Grass | 93,967 |
| Southern Cal | ✓Los Angeles Coliseum | Grass | 92,516 |
| Tennessee | Neyland | Turf | 91,902 |
| Ohio St. | Ohio | PAT | 91,470 |
| Stanford | Stanford | Grass | 85,500 |
| Georgia | Sanford | Grass | 85,434 |
| Auburn | Jordan-Hare | Grass | 85,214 |
| Alabama | ✓Legion Field | Turf | 83,091 |
| Florida | Florida Field | Grass | 83,000 |
| Clemson | Memorial | Grass | 81,473 |
| Louisiana St. | Tiger | Grass | 80,150 |
| Texas | Memorial | Turf | 77,809 |
| Wisconsin | Camp Randall | Turf | 77,745 |
| Michigan St. | Spartan | Turf | 76,000 |
| Rutgers† | ✓Giants | Turf | 76,000 |
| California | Memorial | Turf | 75,662 |
| Oklahoma | Owen Field | Turf | 75,004 |
| Arizona St. | Sun Devil | Grass | 74,783 |
| Miami (Fla.) | ✓Orange Bowl | PAT | 74,712 |
| Nebraska | Memorial | Turf | 73,650 |
| Tulane | ✓Superdome@ | Turf | 72,704 |
| Washington | Husky | Turf | 72,500 |
| South Caro. | Williams-Brice | Grass | 72,400 |

✓ *Not located on campus.*  @ *Indoor facility.*

** *Vanderbilt Stadium was renovated almost completely in 1981.*  † *Rutgers also plays games in an on-campus facility, Rutgers Stadium (25,000 capacity).*

*1993 NCAA FOOTBALL*

**NOTES ON OFF-CAMPUS FACILITIES:**
*Legion Field is located in Birmingham and is home to approximately half of Alabama's home games.*
*War Memorial Stadium is located in Little Rock.*
*Aloha Stadium is located in Honolulu.*
*The Astrodome is located approximately 10 miles from the Houston campus.*
*Mississippi plays some home games a year at Mississippi Memorial Stadium in Jackson. Mississippi St.*
*also plays home games at Mississippi Memorial Stadium.*
*Giants Stadium is located in East Rutherford, New Jersey.*
**Surface Legend:** *Turf—Any of several types of artificial turfs (name brands include AstroTurf, All-Pro, Omniturf, SuperTurf, etc.); Grass—Natural grass surface; PAT—Prescription Athletic Turf (a "natural-artificial" surface featuring a network of pipes connected to pumps capable of sucking water from the natural turf or watering it. The pipes are located 18 inches from the surface and covered with a mixture of sand and filler. The turf also is lined with heating coils to keep it from freezing in temperatures below 32 degrees).*

# FAMOUS MAJOR-COLLEGE DYNASTIES

The following are singled out because of their historical significance, and all represent an outstanding record as well as more than one national championship.

**Notre Dame (1919-30)**
Under Knute Rockne, the Fighting Irish posted an overall record of 101-11-3 (.891 winning percentage) and captured three national titles during this 12-year period. Rockne, who died in an airplane crash in 1931, did not accomplish this by himself, with athletes like George Gipp and the legendary Four Horsemen (Harry Stuhldreher, Elmer Layden, Jim Crowley and Don Miller ) around. The longest winning streak was 22 games, which began in 1918 under Gipp, but the South Benders had three other streaks of at least 15 games in the period.

**Minnesota (1933-41)**
Bernie Bierman, known as "The Silver Fox" for his prematurely gray hair, led the Golden Gophers through their best era. In the nine-year span, Minnesota posted a 58-9-5 (.840) record and won five national titles (1934, 1936, 1940 and 1941 outright and 1935 shared). Bierman oversaw five undefeated teams in the span, and the longest winning streak was 28 games. Defense was a trademark of the Gophers, who notched 23 shutouts in the 72 games. The top offensive player was 1941 Heisman Trophy winner Bruce Smith.

**Notre Dame (1946-53)**
Under head coach Frank Leahy, Notre Dame began another streak almost as successful as the Rockne era. Leahy led the Irish to a national title in 1943, and beginning in 1946, Notre Dame set off on a 63-8-6 (.857) journey that yielded three more national championships (1946, 1947 and 1949) in four years. The longest unbeaten streak stretched to 39 games. The top players were Heisman Trophy winners Johnny Lujack (1947), Leon Hart (1949) and John Lattner (1953).

**Oklahoma (1948-58)**
Many felt this particular span featured the greatest accomplishment in modern-day collegiate football—Oklahoma's Bud Wilkinson-led 47-game winning streak from 1953-57. The Sooners posted a 107-8-2 (.923) mark during the 11-year stretch that included three consensus national titles (1950, 1955 and 1956). Halfback Billy Vessels, the 1952 Heisman winner, was the outstanding individual player in the streak, but Wilkinson's teams were typified by overall speed and quickness.

**Alabama (1959-67)**
Paul "Bear" Bryant's return to his alma mater started a chain of events that eventually yielded one of the greatest dynasties in history. During the nine-year span, Bryant's teams fashioned an 83-10-6 (.869) record and captured three national prizes (1961, 1964 and 1965). His players included Joe Namath, Ken Stabler, Pat Trammell, Ray Perkins, Steve Sloan and Lee Roy Jordan, an eclectic group that featured no Heisman winners. All his players knew how to do was win football games, and the 1963-67 teams never lost a home game.

**Southern Cal (1967-79)**
Two coaches—John McKay and John Robinson—shared this dynasty, which posted a 122-23-7 (.826) record and four national titles (1967, 1972 and 1974 under McKay and 1978 under Robinson). The longest unbeaten streak was 28 games. Southern Cal had two Heisman winners—O. J. Simpson (1968) and Charles White (1979)—and 18 consensus all-Americans in the 13-year period.

**Alabama (1971-80)**
This was the second great run for the Crimson Tide under Bryant. Alabama reeled off a 28-game unbeaten streak and posted a 107-13-0 (.892) record during the 10-year span, including national championships in 1973, 1978 and 1979. Again, there were no Heisman winners for Bryant, but he had a list of players like John Hannah, Steadman Shealy, Jeff Rutledge, Tony Nathan and Major Ogilvie. Bryant died in 1983 as the winningest college coach.

**Oklahoma (1971-80)**
Barry Switzer led the Sooner dynasty to a 102-14-2 (.873) record that included a 37-game unbeaten string and 10 Big Eight championships. Back-to-back national titles in 1974 and 1975 were the result of enormous talent and Switzer's coaching. Some of the Sooner all-Americans during the 10-year period included Jack Mildren, Greg Pruitt, Lucious Selmon, Rod Shoate, Tinker Owens, Dewey Selmon, Lee

Roy Selmon, Joe Washington, Billy Brooks and George Cumby. Heisman Trophy winner Billy Sims (1978) was the biggest name in a Sooner rushing attack that was virtually unstoppable.

**Miami (Fla.) (1983-92)**
The loss to Alabama in the Sugar Bowl ended a real streak for the Hurricanes, going for a fifth national title since 1983. Few would argue that during the 1980s under three different coaches—Howard Schnellenberger, Jimmy Johnson and Dennis Erickson—the Hurricanes were the most successful team in America. With a 107-13-0 (.892) record that included national titles in 1983, 1987, 1989 and 1991, the Hurricanes served notice that an undefeated season was a possibility every year.

# MAJOR-COLLEGE STATISTICS TRENDS†

**(Average Per Game, Both Teams)**

| Year | Rushing Plays | Yds. | Avg. | Att. | Passing Cmp. | Pct. | Yds. | Av. Att. | Total Offense Plays | Yds. | Avg. | Scoring TD | FG | Pts. |
|---|---|---|---|---|---|---|---|---|---|---|---|---|---|---|
| 1937 | — | 267.6 | — | 26.0 | 9.9 | .381 | 129.0 | 4.96 | — | 396.8 | — | — | — | 20.2 |
| 1938 | 81.6 | 280.2 | 3.43 | 28.0 | 10.4 | .371 | 140.2 | 5.01 | 109.6 | 420.4 | 3.85 | 3.50 | 0.12 | 23.5 |
| 1939 | 81.6 | 271.8 | 3.33 | 27.6 | 10.3 | .374 | 132.8 | 4.81 | 109.2 | 404.6 | 3.70 | 3.32 | 0.18 | 22.7 |
| 1940 | 83.8 | 281.0 | 3.35 | 29.6 | 11.5 | .386 | 156.0 | 5.26 | 113.4 | 437.0 | 3.85 | 3.94 | 0.16 | 26.6 |
| 1941 | 84.4 | 282.4 | 3.35 | 30.0 | 11.7 | .392 | 161.2 | 5.38 | 114.4 | 443.6 | 3.88 | 4.06 | 0.12 | 27.5 |
| 1946 | 84.6 | 304.8 | 3.60 | 31.0 | 12.1 | .389 | 176.6 | 5.69 | 115.6 | 481.4 | 4.16 | 4.78 | 0.08 | 32.1 |
| 1947 | 84.6 | 317.4 | 3.75 | 30.5 | 12.6 | .414 | 180.2 | 5.91 | 115.1 | 497.6 | 4.32 | 4.73 | 0.07 | 31.8 |
| 1948 | 87.4 | 324.4 | 3.71 | 31.7 | 13.4 | .423 | 188.4 | 5.95 | 119.0 | 513.0 | 4.31 | 5.04 | 0.09 | 34.2 |
| 1949 | 94.4 | 361.2 | 3.83 | 35.3 | 15.1 | .431 | 220.1 | 6.24 | 129.7 | 581.3 | 4.48 | 5.71 | 0.08 | 38.8 |
| 1950 | 94.0 | 360.3 | 3.83 | 35.0 | 15.3 | .438 | 216.9 | 6.19 | 129.0 | 577.2 | 4.47 | 5.58 | 0.07 | 37.8 |
| 1951 | 97.1 | 365.0 | 3.76 | 37.7 | 16.8 | .446 | 227.1 | 6.02 | 134.9 | 592.1 | 4.39 | 5.72 | 0.09 | 38.8 |
| 1952 | 96.6 | 352.7 | 3.65 | 36.7 | 16.2 | .441 | 223.6 | 6.09 | 133.4 | 576.3 | 4.32 | 5.36 | 0.14 | 36.7 |
| 1953 | 90.1 | 353.1 | 3.92 | 30.4 | 13.0 | .428 | 183.4 | 6.03 | 120.5 | 536.4 | 4.45 | 5.07 | 0.09 | 34.2 |
| 1954 | 90.9 | 368.1 | *4.05 | 29.7 | 13.0 | .437 | 182.2 | 6.14 | 120.6 | 550.2 | 4.56 | 5.17 | 0.09 | 34.7 |
| 1955 | 92.1 | 353.3 | 3.83 | 27.1 | 11.8 | .435 | 169.3 | 6.24 | 119.2 | 522.6 | 4.38 | 4.74 | 0.10 | 32.1 |
| 1956 | 98.3 | 386.2 | 3.93 | 28.2 | 12.3 | .437 | 171.8 | 6.09 | 126.5 | 558.0 | 4.41 | 4.90 | 0.09 | 33.0 |
| 1957 | 98.5 | 355.0 | 3.60 | 28.8 | 12.8 | .444 | 171.0 | 5.94 | 127.2 | 526.0 | 4.14 | 4.61 | 0.11 | 31.1 |
| 1958 | 94.2 | 341.4 | 3.62 | 32.2 | 14.7 | .458 | 195.3 | 6.06 | 126.4 | 536.7 | 4.24 | 4.61 | 0.18 | 32.0 |
| 1959 | 92.4 | 332.0 | 3.59 | 33.0 | 14.9 | .451 | 197.0 | 5.96 | 125.4 | 529.0 | 4.21 | 4.50 | 0.34 | 31.7 |
| 1960 | 90.6 | 339.7 | 3.75 | 31.5 | 14.3 | .454 | 187.1 | 5.94 | 122.1 | 526.8 | 4.31 | 4.37 | 0.38 | 31.1 |
| 1961 | 91.1 | 333.3 | 3.66 | 31.8 | 14.3 | .448 | 189.4 | 5.95 | 122.9 | 522.7 | 4.25 | 4.46 | 0.47 | 32.0 |
| 1962 | 90.5 | 328.0 | 3.63 | 34.4 | 15.9 | .463 | 209.9 | 6.10 | 124.9 | 537.9 | 4.31 | 4.59 | 0.42 | 32.7 |
| 1963 | 88.2 | 320.0 | 3.63 | 35.2 | 16.2 | .461 | 210.5 | 5.98 | 123.4 | 530.6 | 4.30 | 4.38 | 0.53 | 31.6 |
| 1964 | 87.4 | 299.3 | 3.43 | 35.8 | 16.9 | .472 | 219.9 | 6.14 | 123.2 | 519.2 | 4.21 | 4.13 | 0.59 | 30.1 |
| 1965 | 90.2 | 298.7 | 3.31 | 41.5 | 19.3 | .464 | 246.4 | 5.93 | 131.7 | 545.0 | 4.14 | 4.51 | 0.83 | 33.3 |
| 1966 | 88.5 | 297.3 | 3.36 | 43.9 | 20.6 | .470 | 266.3 | 6.07 | 132.3 | 563.6 | 4.26 | 4.70 | 0.84 | 34.9 |
| 1967 | 94.6 | 309.3 | 3.27 | 45.8 | 21.4 | .467 | 279.6 | 6.10 | 140.4 | 588.9 | 4.19 | 4.95 | 0.91 | 36.8 |
| 1968 | 99.4 | 341.5 | 3.44 | 50.7 | 24.1 | .474 | 315.4 | 6.22 | *150.1 | 657.0 | 4.38 | 5.77 | 0.92 | 42.4 |
| 1969 | 98.9 | 343.6 | 3.47 | 50.9 | 24.0 | .471 | 314.1 | 6.17 | 149.8 | 657.7 | 4.39 | 5.80 | 1.08 | 43.2 |
| 1970 | 98.5 | 351.3 | 3.57 | 49.9 | 23.3 | .467 | 305.3 | 6.12 | 148.4 | 656.6 | 4.42 | 5.66 | 1.13 | 42.6 |
| 1971 | 99.3 | 364.3 | 3.67 | 43.4 | 20.1 | .463 | 264.6 | 6.10 | 142.6 | 628.9 | 4.41 | 5.38 | 1.08 | 40.4 |
| 1972 | 99.6 | 369.0 | 3.70 | 43.9 | 20.3 | .462 | 273.7 | 6.24 | 143.5 | 642.7 | 4.48 | 5.42 | 1.22 | 41.1 |
| 1973 | 100.2 | 385.5 | 3.85 | 40.8 | 19.2 | .472 | 261.7 | 6.41 | 141.0 | 647.2 | 4.59 | 5.50 | 1.29 | 41.9 |
| 1974 | 103.7 | 403.6 | 3.89 | 37.6 | 17.8 | .474 | 244.6 | 6.50 | 141.3 | 648.2 | 4.59 | 5.27 | 1.26 | 40.3 |
| 1975 | *103.8 | *408.9 | 3.94 | 36.7 | 17.3 | .473 | 239.2 | 6.52 | 140.5 | 648.1 | 4.61 | 5.14 | 1.48 | 40.1 |
| 1976 | 102.7 | 397.5 | 3.87 | 38.1 | 18.1 | .474 | 246.9 | 6.49 | 140.8 | 644.4 | 4.58 | 5.13 | 1.49 | 40.0 |
| 1977 | 102.5 | 389.2 | 3.80 | 40.3 | 19.5 | .483 | 269.0 | 6.67 | 142.9 | 658.2 | 4.61 | 5.34 | 1.46 | 41.5 |
| 1978 | 101.7 | 385.2 | 3.79 | 42.4 | 20.6 | .486 | 277.7 | 6.55 | 144.1 | 662.9 | 4.60 | 5.28 | 1.51 | 41.1 |
| 1979 | 98.1 | 375.8 | 3.83 | 43.1 | 21.2 | .491 | 278.6 | 6.47 | 141.2 | 654.4 | 4.63 | 5.09 | 1.53 | 39.9 |
| 1980 | 95.3 | 366.6 | 3.74 | 46.6 | 23.3 | .500 | 303.7 | 6.52 | 141.9 | 660.3 | 4.65 | 5.22 | 1.61 | 41.0 |
| 1981 | 92.6 | 338.8 | 3.66 | 50.6 | 25.4 | .502 | 329.4 | 6.51 | 143.2 | 668.2 | 4.67 | 5.14 | 1.73 | 41.0 |
| 1982 | 90.2 | 338.5 | 3.75 | 55.2 | 28.9 | .522 | 364.8 | 6.61 | 145.4 | 703.3 | 4.84 | 5.42 | 2.04 | 43.8 |
| 1983 | 89.2 | 338.9 | 3.80 | 53.9 | 28.8 | .536 | 365.5 | 6.79 | 143.1 | 704.5 | 4.92 | 5.45 | 2.11 | 44.2 |
| 1984 | 89.4 | 336.2 | 3.76 | 53.5 | 28.2 | .527 | 362.2 | 6.77 | 142.9 | 698.4 | 4.89 | 5.32 | 2.30 | 44.1 |
| 1985 | 89.1 | 338.3 | 3.80 | 54.5 | 29.3 | .537 | 372.2 | 6.82 | 143.6 | 710.5 | 4.95 | 5.48 | 2.18 | 44.7 |
| 1986 | 88.4 | 335.8 | 3.80 | 54.4 | 29.2 | .537 | 370.2 | 6.81 | 142.8 | 706.0 | 4.95 | 5.59 | 2.14 | 45.4 |
| 1987 | 88.8 | 348.4 | 3.92 | 54.1 | 28.5 | .526 | 367.1 | 6.78 | 142.9 | 715.5 | 5.01 | 5.65 | 2.25 | 46.1 |
| 1988 | 88.0 | 349.1 | 3.97 | 54.1 | 28.6 | .529 | 371.5 | 6.87 | 142.1 | 720.6 | 5.07 | 5.82 | *2.31 | 47.5 |
| 1989 | 85.4 | 332.8 | 3.90 | *57.0 | *30.8 | *.540 | *401.8 | *7.05 | 142.4 | *734.6 | *5.16 | 5.94 | 2.26 | 48.2 |
| 1990 | 86.1 | 335.3 | 3.90 | 56.6 | 30.2 | .534 | 394.3 | 6.96 | 142.7 | 729.6 | 5.11 | *6.07 | 2.16 | *48.8 |
| 1991 | 86.6 | 339.4 | 3.91 | 54.4 | 29.1 | .535 | 379.2 | 6.98 | 141.0 | 718.7 | 5.10 | 5.90 | 1.77 | 46.2 |
| 1992 | 85.3 | 331.2 | 3.89 | 56.2 | 29.8 | .530 | 380.9 | 6.77 | 141.5 | 712.1 | 5.03 | 5.67 | 2.08 | 45.8 |

*Record.  † Records not compiled in 1942-45 except for Scoring Points Per Game: 1942 (31.3); 1943 (31.3); 1944 (32.6); 1945 (32.2).

*1993 NCAA FOOTBALL*

# ADDITIONAL MAJOR-COLLEGE STATISTICS TRENDS†

Rules changes and statistics changes affecting trends: PUNTING—Beginning in 1965, 20 yards not deducted from a punt into the end zone for a touchback. INTERCEPTIONS—Interception yards not compiled, 1958-65. KICKOFF RETURNS—During 1937-45, if a kickoff went out of bounds, the receiving team put the ball in play on its 35-yard line instead of a second kickoff; in 1984 (rescinded in 1985), a 30-yard-line touchback for kickoffs crossing the goal line in flight and first touching the ground out of the end zone; in 1986, kickoffs from the 35-yard line. PUNT RETURNS—In 1967, interior linemen restricted from leaving until the ball is kicked.

| | Punting | | | Interceptions | | | Punt Returns | | | Kickoff Returns | | | |
| | | | | (Average Per Game, Both Teams) | | | | | | | | | |
| Year | No. | Avg. | Net Avg. | No. | Avg. Ret. | Yds. | No. | Avg. Ret. | Yds. | No. | Avg. Ret. | Yds. | Pct. Ret'd |
|---|---|---|---|---|---|---|---|---|---|---|---|---|---|
| 1937 | 18.4 | 36.3 | — | 3.36 | — | — | — | — | — | — | — | — | — |
| 1938 | 18.6 | 37.2 | — | 3.40 | 9.19 | 31.6 | — | — | — | — | — | — | — |
| 1939 | *18.7 | 36.7 | — | 3.34 | 9.84 | 33.0 | *8.84 | 9.40 | 83.2 | 4.28 | 19.3 | 82.6 | .764 |
| 1940 | 18.1 | 36.6 | — | 3.58 | 10.05 | 36.0 | 8.41 | 10.58 | 89.0 | 4.64 | *20.4 | 95.0 | .753 |
| 1941 | 17.7 | 36.1 | — | *3.62 | 11.28 | 40.8 | 8.54 | 11.10 | *94.8 | 4.82 | 20.2 | 97.2 | .768 |
| 1946 | 14.6 | 35.7 | — | 3.50 | 11.79 | 41.2 | 7.40 | 11.32 | 83.8 | 6.02 | 18.9 | 113.8 | .870 |
| 1947 | 13.4 | 36.4 | 30.3 | 3.21 | 11.93 | 38.3 | 6.94 | 11.73 | 81.4 | 6.07 | 18.9 | 114.5 | .884 |
| 1948 | 12.6 | 36.3 | 30.2 | 3.20 | 12.59 | 40.3 | 6.18 | *12.16 | 75.1 | 6.34 | 18.5 | 117.2 | .873 |
| 1949 | 12.5 | 36.6 | 30.3 | 3.37 | *13.23 | *44.6 | 6.41 | 12.13 | 77.7 | 7.02 | 17.9 | 125.5 | .885 |
| 1950 | 12.0 | 36.3 | 30.8 | 3.21 | 11.99 | 38.5 | 6.07 | 10.72 | 65.1 | 6.92 | 16.6 | 114.8 | .889 |
| 1951 | 12.8 | 35.9 | 30.7 | 3.34 | 12.00 | 40.1 | 6.20 | 10.58 | 65.6 | 7.06 | 17.0 | 119.7 | .884 |
| 1952 | 12.5 | 36.4 | 31.6 | 3.19 | 11.60 | 37.0 | 6.13 | 9.95 | 61.0 | 6.89 | 17.6 | 121.4 | .908 |
| 1953 | 10.4 | 34.9 | 29.7 | 2.74 | 12.12 | 33.2 | 5.13 | 10.66 | 54.7 | 6.54 | 17.8 | 116.4 | .903 |
| 1954 | 9.7 | 34.9 | 29.4 | 2.71 | 12.48 | 33.8 | 4.84 | 11.16 | 54.0 | 6.64 | 18.4 | 122.0 | *.910 |
| 1955 | 9.8 | 34.9 | 29.8 | 2.52 | 12.96 | 33.5 | 4.78 | 10.54 | 50.4 | 6.17 | 18.5 | 114.4 | .892 |
| 1956 | 10.1 | 35.1 | 30.1 | 2.57 | 12.86 | 33.1 | 4.97 | 10.07 | 50.1 | 6.37 | 18.0 | 114.8 | .906 |
| 1957 | 10.6 | 34.8 | 30.2 | 2.52 | 11.95 | 30.1 | 5.06 | 9.57 | 48.4 | 6.09 | 18.7 | 114.1 | .897 |
| 1958 | 11.1 | 35.4 | 30.9 | 2.65 | — | — | 5.13 | 9.70 | 49.8 | 6.03 | 18.9 | 113.9 | .880 |
| 1959 | 11.0 | 35.9 | 31.5 | 2.66 | — | — | 5.34 | 9.06 | 48.4 | 6.18 | 18.7 | 115.6 | .892 |
| 1960 | 10.2 | 36.0 | 31.4 | 2.48 | — | — | 4.78 | 9.73 | 46.5 | 6.09 | 18.8 | 114.6 | .890 |
| 1961 | 10.3 | 35.5 | 31.1 | 2.44 | — | — | 4.85 | 9.44 | 45.8 | 6.12 | 18.3 | 112.2 | .873 |
| 1962 | 10.4 | 35.7 | 31.3 | 2.50 | — | — | 4.72 | 9.66 | 45.6 | 6.20 | 19.6 | 121.4 | .876 |
| 1963 | 10.3 | 36.3 | 32.5 | 2.38 | — | — | 4.68 | 9.71 | 45.4 | 6.15 | 20.1 | 123.7 | .880 |
| 1964 | 10.6 | 36.4 | 32.5 | 2.39 | — | — | 4.65 | 8.99 | 41.8 | 5.86 | 19.6 | 114.6 | .862 |
| 1965 | 11.7 | 38.5 | 33.9 | 2.84 | — | — | 5.46 | 9.99 | 54.5 | 6.30 | 18.8 | 118.6 | .849 |
| 1966 | 11.8 | 37.5 | 33.5 | 3.00 | 12.07 | 36.2 | 5.26 | 8.82 | 46.4 | 6.48 | 18.7 | 121.6 | .849 |
| 1967 | 12.9 | 36.8 | 31.6 | 3.04 | 11.39 | 34.6 | 6.83 | 9.92 | 67.7 | 6.61 | 18.7 | 123.3 | .831 |
| 1968 | 13.3 | 37.4 | 33.3 | 3.22 | 11.51 | 37.1 | 6.01 | 8.95 | 53.8 | 7.27 | 19.1 | 139.1 | .829 |
| 1969 | 13.1 | 37.5 | 33.4 | 3.39 | 11.07 | 37.5 | 6.00 | 9.00 | 54.0 | 7.34 | 18.9 | 138.7 | .818 |
| 1970 | 12.6 | 37.4 | 33.2 | 3.32 | 11.65 | 38.7 | 5.78 | 9.28 | 53.7 | 7.37 | 19.0 | 140.2 | .828 |
| 1971 | 12.3 | 37.6 | 33.4 | 2.97 | 11.75 | 34.9 | 5.78 | 9.04 | 52.3 | 7.14 | 19.2 | 137.2 | .834 |
| 1972 | 12.1 | 37.2 | 33.4 | 3.07 | 11.54 | 35.4 | 5.44 | 8.61 | 46.8 | 6.99 | 19.0 | 132.8 | .803 |
| 1973 | 11.6 | 37.8 | 34.1 | 2.72 | 11.30 | 30.8 | 5.03 | 8.65 | 43.5 | 7.08 | 19.6 | 138.4 | .797 |
| 1974 | 11.2 | 37.6 | 34.2 | 2.46 | 11.30 | 27.8 | 4.80 | 7.92 | 38.0 | 6.75 | 19.1 | 128.5 | .784 |
| 1975 | 10.8 | 38.1 | 35.0 | 2.42 | 11.26 | 27.2 | 4.77 | 7.19 | 34.3 | 6.39 | 19.3 | 123.3 | .733 |
| 1976 | 11.3 | 38.0 | 35.1 | 2.45 | 11.44 | 28.0 | 4.83 | 6.83 | 33.0 | 6.28 | 18.3 | 114.7 | .722 |
| 1977 | 11.5 | 38.0 | 35.0 | 2.51 | 11.05 | 27.8 | 4.89 | 7.10 | 34.6 | 6.32 | 18.4 | 116.1 | .711 |
| 1978 | 12.0 | 38.0 | 34.9 | 2.68 | 10.83 | 29.0 | 5.02 | 7.39 | 37.1 | 6.36 | 18.7 | 119.1 | .665 |
| 1979 | 11.6 | 37.7 | 34.8 | 2.62 | 10.66 | 27.9 | 4.76 | 7.09 | 33.8 | 6.03 | 18.8 | 113.7 | .637 |
| 1980 | 11.6 | 38.3 | 35.4 | 2.74 | 10.85 | 29.7 | 4.88 | 7.01 | 34.2 | 5.81 | 19.0 | 110.2 | .651 |
| 1981 | 11.9 | 38.9 | 35.9 | 2.76 | 10.22 | 28.2 | 4.90 | 7.22 | 35.4 | 5.72 | 18.8 | 107.8 | .636 |
| 1982 | 11.7 | *39.8 | *36.5 | 2.78 | 10.70 | 29.7 | 4.79 | 8.00 | 38.3 | 5.37 | 19.3 | 103.7 | .561 |
| 1983 | 11.0 | 39.5 | 35.9 | 2.74 | 10.43 | 28.6 | 4.94 | 7.95 | 39.3 | 5.29 | 19.2 | 101.6 | .549 |
| 1984 | 11.1 | 39.7 | 36.3 | 2.61 | 10.07 | 26.3 | 4.94 | 7.61 | 37.6 | 6.05 | 18.6 | 112.3 | .621 |
| 1985 | 11.0 | 39.6 | 36.1 | 2.59 | 10.47 | 27.1 | 4.89 | 7.92 | 38.8 | 5.88 | 19.4 | 114.0 | .603 |
| 1986 | 10.7 | 39.2 | 35.4 | 2.59 | 10.99 | 28.5 | 5.01 | 8.23 | 41.3 | 7.55 | 19.8 | 149.2 | .770 |
| 1987 | 10.7 | 38.6 | 34.7 | 2.64 | 10.82 | 28.6 | 4.95 | 8.31 | 41.1 | 7.78 | 19.1 | 149.0 | .780 |
| 1988 | 10.4 | 38.4 | 34.7 | 2.47 | 11.17 | 28.0 | 4.78 | 7.96 | 38.1 | *7.94 | 19.4 | 154.2 | .778 |
| 1989 | 10.4 | 38.5 | 34.3 | 2.56 | 10.75 | 27.6 | 4.72 | 8.46 | 39.9 | 7.83 | 19.7 | *154.3 | .776 |
| 1990 | 10.6 | 38.6 | 34.3 | 2.46 | 11.40 | 28.0 | 4.89 | 9.33 | 45.7 | 7.58 | 19.6 | 148.9 | .738 |
| 1991 | 10.5 | 38.4 | 34.3 | 2.35 | 11.30 | 26.6 | 5.00 | 8.74 | 43.7 | 6.86 | 19.4 | 133.1 | .741 |
| 1992 | 11.2 | 39.0 | 34.9 | 2.39 | 11.00 | 26.3 | 5.25 | 9.04 | 47.5 | 6.60 | 20.1 | 132.7 | .732 |

† Records not compiled in 1942-45.   * Record.

*Division I-A Statistical Trends*                                                                123

# MAJOR-COLLEGE TIE GAMES

The record for most tie games in a single week is six—on October 27, 1962; September 28, 1963, and October 9, 1982.

| Year | No. | Games | Pct. | Scoreless | Year | No. | Games | Pct. | Scoreless |
|------|-----|-------|------|-----------|------|-----|-------|------|-----------|
| 1954 | 15 | 551 | 2.72 | 2 | 1974 | 18 | 749 | 2.40 | 0 |
| 1955 | 22 | 536 | 4.10 | 1 | 1975 | 16 | 785 | 2.04 | 0 |
| 1956 | 28 | 558 | 5.02 | 2 | 1976 | 13 | 796 | 1.63 | 1 |
| 1957 | 24 | 570 | 4.21 | 4 | 1977 | 16 | 849 | 1.88 | 1 |
| *1958 | 19 | 578 | 3.29 | 2 | 1978 | 16 | 816 | 1.96 | 1 |
| 1959 | 13 | 578 | 2.25 | 4 | 1979 | 17 | 811 | 2.10 | 1 |
| 1960 | 23 | 596 | 3.86 | 4 | 1980 | 12 | 810 | 1.48 | 0 |
| 1961 | 11 | 574 | 1.92 | 1 | 1981 | 17 | 788 | 2.16 | 0 |
| 1962 | 20 | 602 | 3.32 | 2 | 1982 | 14 | 599 | 2.34 | 0 |
| 1963 | 25 | 605 | 4.13 | 4 | 1983 | 13 | 631 | 2.06 | †1 |
| 1964 | 19 | 613 | 3.10 | 2 | 1984 | 15 | 626 | 2.40 | 0 |
| 1965 | 19 | 619 | 3.07 | 4 | 1985 | 13 | 623 | 2.09 | 0 |
| 1966 | 13 | 626 | 2.08 | 0 | 1986 | 10 | 619 | 1.62 | 0 |
| 1967 | 14 | 611 | 2.29 | 1 | 1987 | 13 | 615 | 2.11 | 0 |
| 1968 | 17 | 615 | 2.76 | 1 | 1988 | 12 | 616 | 1.94 | 0 |
| 1969 | 9 | 621 | 1.45 | 0 | 1989 | 15 | 614 | 2.44 | 0 |
| 1970 | 7 | 667 | 1.05 | 0 | 1990 | 15 | 623 | 2.41 | 0 |
| 1971 | 12 | 726 | 1.65 | 1 | 1991 | 14 | 617 | 2.27 | 0 |
| 1972 | 14 | 720 | 1.94 | 1 | 1992 | 13 | 619 | 2.10 | 0 |
| 1973 | 18 | 741 | 2.43 | 2 | | | | | |

* First year of two-point conversion rule.   † Last scoreless tie game: Nov. 19, 1983, Oregon vs. Oregon St.

# HIGHEST-SCORING TIE GAMES

**(Home team is listed first)**

| Score | Date | Opponents | Score | Date | Opponents |
|-------|------|-----------|-------|------|-----------|
| 52-52 | 11-16-91 | San Diego St.-Brigham Young | 35-35 | 9-21-68 | Washington-Rice |
| 48-48 | 9-8-79 | San Jose St.-Utah St. | 35-35 | 11-18-67 | Navy-Vanderbilt |
| 43-43 | 11-12-88 | Duke-North Caro. St. | 35-35 | 12-11-48 | †Pacific (Cal.)—Hardin-Simmons |
| 41-41 | 9-23-89 | San Diego St.-Cal St. Fullerton | 34-34 | 10-6-90 | Iowa St.-Kansas |
| 40-40 | 11-8-75 | Idaho-Weber St. | 33-33 | 10-1-83 | California-Arizona |
| 39-39 | 11-7-82 | Texas Tech-Texas Christian | 33-33 | 9-24-49 | Texas Christian-Oklahoma St. |
| 37-37 | 9-23-67 | *Alabama-Florida St. | 33-33 | 10-31-31 | Yale-Dartmouth |
| 36-36 | 9-30-72 | Georgia Tech-Rice | | | |
| 35-35 | 11-16-91 | San Jose St.-Hawaii | | | |
| 35-35 | 12-9-89 | Hawaii-Air Force | | | |
| 35-35 | 9-23-89 | Colorado St.-Eastern Mich. | | | |
| 35-35 | 10-7-78 | Ohio St.-Southern Methodist | | | |
| 35-35 | 10-19-74 | Idaho-Montana | | | |
| 35-35 | 10-9-71 | New Mexico-New Mexico St. | | | |
| 35-35 | 9-27-69 | Minnesota-Ohio | | | |

* At Birmingham.   † Grape Bowl, Lodi, Calif.

# HOME-FIELD RECORDS

**(Includes host teams at neutral-site games)**

| Year | Games | Home Team Won | Lost | Tied | Pct. | Year | Games | Home Team Won | Lost | Tied | Pct. |
|------|-------|------|------|------|------|------|-------|------|------|------|------|
| 1966 | 626 | 365 | 248 | 13 | .594 | 1981 | 788 | 457 | 314 | 17 | .591 |
| 1967 | 611 | 333 | 264 | 14 | .557 | 1982 | 599 | 368 | 217 | 14 | .626 |
| 1968 | 615 | 348 | 250 | 17 | .580 | 1983 | 631 | 364 | 254 | 13 | .587 |
| 1969 | 621 | 366 | 246 | 9 | .596 | 1984 | 626 | 371 | 240 | 15 | .605 |
| 1970 | 667 | 399 | 261 | 7 | .603 | 1985 | 623 | 371 | 239 | 13 | .606 |
| 1971 | 726 | 416 | 298 | 12 | .581 | 1986 | 619 | 363 | 246 | 10 | .595 |
| 1972 | 720 | 441 | 265 | 14 | .622 | 1987 | 615 | 387 | 215 | 13 | *.640 |
| 1973 | 741 | 439 | 284 | 18 | .605 | 1988 | 616 | 370 | 234 | 12 | .610 |
| 1974 | 749 | 457 | 274 | 18 | .622 | 1989 | 614 | 365 | 234 | 15 | .607 |
| 1975 | 785 | 434 | 335 | 16 | .563 | 1990 | 623 | 373 | 235 | 15 | .611 |
| 1976 | 796 | 463 | 320 | 13 | .590 | 1991 | 617 | 362 | 241 | 14 | .598 |
| 1977 | 849 | 501 | 332 | 16 | .600 | 1992 | 619 | 388 | 218 | 13 | .637 |
| 1978 | 816 | 482 | 318 | 16 | .601 | | | | | | |
| 1979 | 811 | 460 | 334 | 17 | .578 | | | | | | |
| 1980 | 809 | 471 | 327 | 12 | .589 | | | | | | |

* Record.

# FIELD-GOAL TRENDS
## (1938-1968)

**(Goal posts widened from 18 feet, 6 inches to 23 feet, 4 inches in 1959)**

| Year | Made | Year | Made | Year | Made | Atts. | Pct. |
|------|------|------|------|------|------|-------|------|
| 1938 | 47 | 1951 | 53 | 1960 | 224 | | |
| 1939 | 80 | 1952 | 83 | 1961 | 277 | | |
| 1940 | 84 | 1953 | 50 | 1962 | 261 | | |
| 1941 | 59 | 1954 | 48 | 1963 | 314 | | |
| 1942-45 | * | 1955 | 57 | 1964 | 368 | | |
| 1946 | 44 | 1956 | 53 | 1965 | 484 | 1,035 | .468 |
| 1947 | 38 | 1957 | 64 | 1966 | 522 | 1,125 | .464 |
| 1948 | 53 | 1958 | 103 | 1967 | 555 | 1,266 | .438 |
| 1949 | 46 | 1959 | 199 | 1968 | 566 | 1,287 | .440 |
| 1950 | 46 | | | | | | |

\* Records not compiled.

# FIELD-GOAL TRENDS (FROM 1969)

**(Includes Field Goal Attempts by Divisions I-AA, II and III Opponents)**

| Year | Made | Atts. | Pct. | 16-39 | Pct. | 16-49 | Pct. | 40-49 | Pct. | 50 Plus | Pct. | 60 Plus |
|------|------|-------|------|-------|------|-------|------|-------|------|---------|------|---------|
| | | | | | | Totals | | | | Breakdown by Distances | | |
| 1969 | 669 | 1,402 | .477 | 538-872 | .617 | 654-1,267 | .516 | 116-395 | .294 | 15-135 | .111 | 0-8 |
| 1970 | 754 | 1,548 | .487 | 614-990 | .620 | 740-1,380 | .536 | 126-390 | .323 | 14-168 | .083 | 1-9 |
| 1971 | 780 | 1,625 | .480 | 607-1,022 | .594 | 760-1,466 | .518 | 153-444 | .345 | 20-159 | .126 | 0-11 |
| 1972 | 876 | 1,828 | .479 | 705-1,150 | .613 | 855-1,641 | .521 | 150-491 | .305 | 21-187 | .112 | 1-12 |
| 1973 | 958 | 1,920 | .499 | 728-1,139 | .639 | 914-1,670 | .547 | 186-531 | .350 | 44-250 | .176 | 1-21 |
| 1974 | 947 | 1,905 | .497 | 706-1,096 | .644 | 906-1,655 | .547 | 200-559 | .358 | 41-250 | .164 | 1-17 |
| 1975 | 1,164 | 2,237 | .520 | 849-1,255 | .676 | 1,088-1,896 | .574 | 239-641 | .373 | 76-341 | .223 | 4-32 |
| 1976 | 1,187 | 2,330 | .509 | 854-1,301 | .656 | 1,131-1,997 | .566 | 277-696 | .398 | 56-333 | .168 | 3-24 |
| 1977 | 1,238 | 2,514 | .492 | 882-1,315 | .671 | 1,160-2,088 | .556 | 278-773 | .360 | 78-426 | .183 | 6-40 |
| 1978 | 1,229 | 2,113 | .582 | 938-1,361 | .689 | 1,193-1,982 | .602 | 255-621 | .411 | 36-131 | .275 | 1-4 |

| Year | Made | Atts. | Pct. | Under 20 | 20-29 | 30-39 | 40-49 | 50-59 | 60 Plus |
|------|------|-------|------|----------|-------|-------|-------|-------|---------|
| 1979 | 1,241 | 2,129 | .583 | 34-43 | 455-601 | 425-706 | 286-600 | 41-173 | 0-6 |
| 1980 | 1,302 | 2,241 | .581 | 31-39 | 408-529 | 452-696 | 317-682 | 37-175 | 0-7 |
| 1981 | 1,360 | 2,254 | .603 | 42-48 | 471-598 | 461-731 | 335-698 | 58-169 | 1-10 |
| 1982 | 1,224 | 1,915 | .639 | 31-34 | 384-475 | 415-597 | 319-604 | 73-190 | 2-15 |
| 1983 | 1,329 | 2,025 | .656 | 34-37 | 417-508 | 477-636 | 329-628 | 72-201 | 0-15 |
| 1984 | 1,442 | 2,112 | .683 | 44-49 | 450-532 | 503-681 | 363-630 | 80-206 | 2-14 |
| 1985 | 1,360 | 2,106 | .646 | 40-47 | 416-511 | 478-657 | 341-647 | 84-227 | 1-17 |
| 1986 | 1,326 | 2,034 | .652 | 45-48 | 445-525 | 448-641 | 340-629 | 44-182 | 4-9 |
| 1987 | 1,381 | 2,058 | .671 | 45-48 | 484-559 | 469-638 | 311-604 | 72-200 | 0-9 |
| 1988 | 1,421 | 2,110 | .673 | 33-35 | 487-573 | 495-664 | 337-610 | 68-217 | 1-11 |
| 1989# | 1,389 | 2,006 | *.692 | 50-53 | 497-565 | 471-655 | 319-573 | 52-154 | 0-6 |
| 1990 | 1,348 | 2,011 | .670 | 39-42 | 477-546 | 454-626 | 319-625 | 59-167 | 0-5 |
| 1991$ | 1,092 | 1,831 | .596 | 31-32 | 395-519 | 366-612 | 254-531 | 45-132 | 1-5 |
| 1992 | 1,288 | 1,986 | .649 | 32-38 | 464-569 | 447-673 | 294-577 | 49-126 | 2-3 |

\* Record.   # First year after kicking tee became illegal.   $ First year after goal-post width narrowed back to 18'6" from 23'4".

# FIELD-GOAL TRENDS BY SOCCER-STYLE AND CONVENTIONAL KICKERS (DIVISION I-A KICKERS ONLY)

(Pete Gogolak of Cornell was documented as the first soccer-style kicker in college football history. The Hungarian-born kicker played at Cornell from 1961 through 1963. He set a national major-college record of 44 consecutive extra-point conversions and finished 54 of 55 for his career. His younger brother, Charley, also a soccer-styler, kicked at Princeton from 1963 through 1965.)

### SOCCER-STYLE

| Year | †No. | Made | Atts. | Pct. | 16-39 | Pct. | 16-49 | Pct. | 40-49 | Pct. | 50 Plus | Pct. | 60 Plus |
|------|------|------|-------|------|-------|------|-------|------|-------|------|---------|------|---------|
| | Totals | | | | | | Breakdown by Distances | | | | | | |
| 1975 | 70 | 528 | 1,012 | .522 | 370-540 | .685 | 479-816 | .587 | 109-276 | .395 | 49-196 | .250 | 1-17 |
| 1976 | 84 | 517 | 1,019 | .507 | 350-517 | .677 | 477-831 | .574 | 127-314 | .404 | 40-188 | .213 | 3-16 |
| 1977 | 96 | 665 | 1,317 | .505 | 450-649 | .693 | 615-1,047 | .587 | 165-398 | .415 | 50-270 | .185 | 2-27 |
| 1978 | 98 | 731 | 1,244 | .588 | 540-768 | .703 | 703-1,148 | .612 | 163-380 | .429 | 28-96 | .292 | 1-3 |

| Year | †No. | Made | Atts. | Pct. | Under 20 | 20-29 | 30-39 | 40-49 | 50-59 | 60 Plus |
|---|---|---|---|---|---|---|---|---|---|---|
| | | **Totals** | | | | **Breakdown by Distances** | | | | |
| 1979 | 116 | 839 | 1,413 | .594 | 23-28 | 288-380 | 282-455 | 214-419 | 32-126 | 0-5 |
| 1980 | 121 | 988 | 1,657 | .596 | 26-32 | 327-416 | 342-522 | 261-540 | 32-147 | 0-5 |
| 1981 | 138 | 1,108 | 1,787 | .620 | 32-36 | 377-476 | 376-576 | 279-551 | 43-142 | 1-6 |
| 1982 | 105 | 1,026 | 1,548 | .663 | 26-27 | 317-375 | 346-482 | 273-495 | 62-156 | 2-13 |
| 1983 | 110 | 1,139 | 1,724 | .661 | 29-31 | 345-416 | 403-541 | 294-543 | 68-179 | 0-14 |
| 1984 | 127 | 1,316 | 1,898 | *.694 | 43-47 | 414-480 | 438-589 | 341-572 | 78-197 | 2-13 |
| 1985 | 133 | 1,198 | 1,838 | .652 | 35-41 | 369-452 | 415-578 | 306-560 | 72-191 | 1-16 |
| 1986 | 128 | 1,201 | 1,829 | .657 | 37-40 | 398-467 | 410-575 | 313-576 | 39-162 | 4-9 |
| 1987 | 122 | 1,275 | 1,892 | .674 | 40-43 | 458-523 | 424-574 | 290-566 | 63-177 | 0-9 |
| 1988 | 140 | 1,317 | 1,947 | .676 | 31-33 | 445-521 | 468-630 | 311-562 | 61-201 | 1-11 |
| 1989 | 138 | 1,313 | 1,897 | .692 | 49-52 | 462-526 | 441-612 | 310-551 | 51-150 | 0-6 |
| 1990 | 135 | 1,282 | 1,890 | .678 | 36-38 | 450-515 | 432-589 | 308-590 | 56-154 | 0-4 |
| 1991 | 132 | 1,048 | 1,763 | .594 | 30-31 | 381-500 | 349-589 | 243-512 | 44-130 | 1-1 |
| 1992 | 135 | 1,244 | 1,926 | .646 | 31-37 | 447-554 | 429-647 | 288-561 | 47-124 | 2-3 |

## CONVENTIONAL

| Year | †No. | Made | Atts. | Pct. | 16-39 | Pct. | 16-49 | Pct. | 40-49 | Pct. | 50 Plus | Pct. | 60 Plus |
|---|---|---|---|---|---|---|---|---|---|---|---|---|---|
| | | **Totals** | | | **Breakdown by Distances** | | | | | | | | |
| 1975 | 116 | 564 | 1,085 | .520 | 427-640 | .667 | 541-959 | .564 | 114-319 | .357 | 23-126 | .183 | 3-13 |
| 1976 | 101 | 608 | 1,192 | .510 | 460-720 | .639 | 594-1,065 | .558 | 134-345 | .388 | 14-127 | .110 | 0-7 |
| 1977 | 98 | 513 | 1,054 | .487 | 384-586 | .655 | 487-916 | .532 | 103-330 | .312 | 26-138 | .188 | 4-14 |
| 1978 | 86 | 440 | 761 | .578 | 352-516 | .682 | 434-729 | .595 | 82-213 | .385 | 6-32 | .188 | 0-0 |

| Year | †No. | Made | Atts. | Pct. | Under 20 | 20-29 | 30-39 | 40-49 | 50-59 | 60 Plus |
|---|---|---|---|---|---|---|---|---|---|---|
| 1979 | 70 | 333 | 585 | .569 | 10-14 | 140-185 | 111-198 | 63-150 | 9-37 | 0-1 |
| 1980 | 62 | 258 | 471 | .548 | 5-7 | 81-113 | 110-174 | 56-142 | 6-33 | 0-2 |
| 1981 | 50 | 195 | 367 | .531 | 8-9 | 70-97 | 69-126 | 41-112 | 7-22 | 0-1 |
| 1982 | 25 | 103 | 195 | .528 | 3-4 | 36-50 | 34-62 | 25-59 | 5-18 | 0-2 |
| 1983 | 23 | 112 | 181 | .619 | 4-5 | 40-55 | 46-58 | 22-50 | 0-12 | 0-1 |
| 1984 | 10 | 44 | 76 | .579 | 0-1 | 17-26 | 20-33 | 7-15 | 0-1 | 0-0 |
| 1985 | 12 | 81 | 138 | .587 | 3-4 | 22-29 | 29-40 | 19-44 | 8-20 | 0-1 |
| 1986 | 8 | 58 | 89 | .652 | 4-4 | 21-28 | 17-27 | 14-24 | 2-6 | 0-0 |
| 1987 | 4 | 35 | 50 | .700 | 4-4 | 10-14 | 14-16 | 6-9 | 1-7 | 0-0 |
| 1988 | 5 | 26 | 40 | .650 | 0-0 | 17-21 | 5-7 | 4-10 | 0-2 | 0-0 |
| 1989 | 2 | 37 | 47 | *.787 | 1-1 | 19-20 | 12-16 | 5-9 | 0-1 | 0-0 |
| 1990 | 2 | 23 | 38 | .605 | 1-1 | 8-10 | 8-9 | 4-13 | 2-5 | 0-0 |
| 1991 | 2 | 16 | 24 | .667 | 0-0 | 5-9 | 6-7 | 5-7 | 0-1 | 0-0 |
| 1992 | 1 | 12 | 18 | .667 | 0-0 | 5-6 | 6-8 | 1-4 | 0-0 | 0-0 |

*Record.  † Number of kickers attempting at least one field goal.*

## AVERAGE YARDAGE OF FIELD GOALS
## (DIVISION I-A KICKERS ONLY)

| Year | Soccer-Style | | | Conventional | | | Nation | | |
|---|---|---|---|---|---|---|---|---|---|
| | Made | Missed | Total | Made | Missed | Total | Made | Missed | Total |
| 1975 | 35.1 | 43.2 | 39.0 | 33.1 | 41.3 | 37.0 | 34.1 | 42.2 | 37.9 |
| 1976 | 35.0 | 43.1 | 39.0 | 33.2 | 40.7 | 36.9 | 34.0 | 41.8 | 37.9 |
| 1977 | 34.7 | 44.3 | 39.5 | 33.3 | 41.9 | 37.7 | 34.1 | 43.2 | 38.7 |
| 1978 | 34.0 | 39.9 | 36.4 | 31.9 | 38.3 | 34.6 | 33.2 | 39.3 | 35.7 |
| 1979 | 33.7 | 39.9 | 36.2 | 31.9 | 38.0 | 34.5 | 33.2 | 39.3 | 35.7 |
| 1980 | 34.0 | 40.7 | 36.7 | 33.4 | 39.6 | 36.2 | 33.8 | 40.4 | 36.6 |
| 1981 | 33.9 | 40.1 | 36.2 | 33.2 | 38.6 | 35.7 | 33.8 | 39.8 | 36.1 |
| 1982 | 34.8 | 41.8 | 37.2 | 34.0 | 39.8 | 36.7 | 34.7 | 41.5 | 37.1 |
| 1983 | 34.7 | 42.1 | 37.2 | 32.3 | 40.5 | 35.5 | 34.5 | 41.9 | 37.0 |
| 1984 | 34.4 | 41.8 | 36.7 | 32.3 | 34.9 | 33.4 | 34.3 | 41.5 | 36.5 |
| 1985 | 34.5 | 41.3 | 36.8 | 35.4 | 41.7 | 38.0 | 34.5 | 41.3 | 36.9 |
| 1986 | 33.9 | 41.6 | 36.6 | 32.5 | 38.6 | 34.7 | 33.9 | 41.4 | 36.5 |
| 1987 | 33.5 | 41.8 | 36.2 | 32.3 | 41.4 | 35.1 | 33.5 | 41.8 | 36.2 |
| 1988 | 33.9 | 41.7 | 36.4 | 30.0 | 37.6 | 32.7 | 32.0 | 39.3 | 34.4 |
| 1989 | 33.5 | 41.2 | 35.9 | 30.5 | 39.6 | 32.4 | 33.4 | 41.2 | 35.8 |
| 1990 | 33.4 | 41.3 | 36.0 | 33.4 | 42.0 | 36.7 | 33.4 | 41.3 | 36.0 |
| 1991 | 33.2 | 40.7 | 35.8 | 28.6 | 31.9 | 40.7 | 35.9 | 40.4 | 36.1 |
| 1992 | 34.1 | 41.2 | 36.7 | 30.1 | 37.8 | 32.7 | 37.2 | 41.3 | 37.8 |

## DIVISION I-A EXTRA-POINT TRENDS
### (From start of two-point attempts)

| Year | Games | Percent of Total Tries | | Kick Attempts | | | Two-Point Attempts | | |
|---|---|---|---|---|---|---|---|---|---|
| | | Kick | 2-Pt. | Atts. | Made | Pct. | Atts. | Made | Pct. |
| 1958 | 578 | .486 | *.514 | 1,295 | 889 | .686 | *1,371 | *613 | .447 |
| 1959 | 578 | .598 | .402 | 1,552 | 1,170 | .754 | 1,045 | 421 | .403 |
| 1960 | 596 | .701 | .299 | 1,849 | 1,448 | .783 | 790 | 345 | .437 |
| 1961 | 574 | .723 | .277 | 1,842 | 1,473 | .800 | 706 | 312 | .442 |
| 1962 | 602 | .724 | .276 | 1,987 | 1,549 | .780 | 757 | 341 | .450 |
| 1963 | 605 | .776 | .224 | 2,057 | 1,659 | .807 | 595 | 256 | .430 |
| 1964 | 613 | .814 | .186 | 2,053 | 1,704 | .830 | 469 | 189 | .403 |
| 1965 | 619 | .881 | .119 | 2,460 | 2,083 | .847 | 331 | 134 | .405 |
| 1966 | 626 | .861 | .139 | 2,530 | 2,167 | .857 | 410 | 165 | .402 |
| 1967 | 611 | .869 | .131 | 2,629 | 2,252 | .857 | 397 | 160 | .403 |
| 1968 | 615 | .871 | .129 | 3,090 | 2,629 | .851 | 456 | 181 | .397 |
| 1969 | 621 | .880 | .120 | 3,168 | 2,781 | .878 | 432 | 170 | .394 |
| 1970 | 667 | .862 | .138 | 3,255 | 2,875 | .883 | 522 | 246 | *.471 |
| 1971 | 726 | .889 | .111 | 3,466 | 3,081 | .889 | 433 | 173 | .400 |
| 1972 | 720 | .872 | .128 | 3,390 | 3,018 | .890 | 497 | 219 | .441 |
| 1973 | 741 | .893 | .107 | 3,637 | 3,258 | .896 | 435 | 180 | .414 |
| 1974 | 749 | .885 | .115 | 3,490 | 3,146 | .901 | 455 | 211 | .464 |
| 1975 | 785 | .891 | .109 | 3,598 | 3,266 | .908 | 440 | 171 | .389 |
| 1976 | 796 | .877 | .123 | 3,579 | 3,241 | .906 | 502 | 203 | .404 |
| 1977 | 849 | .891 | .109 | *4,041 | *3,668 | .908 | 495 | 209 | .422 |
| 1978 | 816 | .884 | .116 | 3,808 | 3,490 | .916 | 498 | 208 | .418 |
| 1979 | 811 | .897 | .103 | 3,702 | 3,418 | .923 | 424 | 176 | .415 |
| 1980 | 810 | .895 | .105 | 3,785 | 3,480 | .919 | 442 | 170 | .384 |
| 1981 | 788 | .901 | .099 | 3,655 | 3,387 | .927 | 403 | 172 | .427 |
| 1982 | 599 | .901 | .099 | 2,920 | 2,761 | .946 | 320 | 120 | .375 |
| 1983 | 631 | .896 | .104 | 3,080 | 2,886 | .937 | 356 | 151 | .424 |
| 1984 | 626 | .889 | .111 | 2,962 | 2,789 | .942 | 370 | 173 | .468 |
| 1985 | 623 | .899 | .101 | 3,068 | 2,911 | .949 | 345 | 121 | .351 |
| 1986 | 619 | .905 | .095 | 3,132 | 2,999 | .958 | 330 | 131 | .397 |
| 1987 | 615 | .892 | .108 | 3,094 | 2,935 | .949 | 375 | 163 | .435 |
| 1988 | 616 | .899 | .101 | 3,215 | 3,074 | .956 | 363 | 156 | .430 |
| 1989 | 614 | .888 | .112 | 3,233 | 3,090 | .956 | 409 | 179 | .438 |
| 1990 | 623 | *.911 | .089 | 3,429 | 3,291 | *.960 | 335 | 138 | .412 |
| 1991 | 617 | .906 | .094 | 3,279 | 3,016 | .920 | 342 | 128 | .374 |
| 1992 | 619 | .899 | .101 | 3,156 | 2,967 | .940 | 353 | 159 | .450 |

* Record.

## DIVISION I-A EXTRA-POINT KICK ATTEMPTS
### (1938-1957)

| Year | Pct. Made | Year | Pct. Made | Year | Pct. Made | Year | Pct. Made |
|---|---|---|---|---|---|---|---|
| 1938 | .608 | 1946 | .657 | 1951 | .711 | 1956 | .666 |
| 1939 | .625 | 1947 | .657 | 1952 | .744 | 1957 | .653 |
| 1940 | .607 | 1948 | .708 | 1953 | .650 | | |
| 1941 | .638 | 1949 | .738 | 1954 | .656 | | |
| 1942-45 | * | 1950 | .713 | 1955 | .669 | | |

* Not compiled.

## ALL-DIVISIONS DEFENSIVE EXTRA-POINT TRENDS

In 1988, the NCAA Football Rules Committee adopted a rule that gave defensive teams an opportunity to score two points on point-after-touchdown tries. The two points were awarded for returning an interception or advancing a blocked kick for a touchdown on point-after tries.

| DIVISION I-A Year | Games | Kick Ret./TDs | Int. Ret./TDs | Total Ret./TDs |
|---|---|---|---|---|
| 1988 | 616 | 8/2 | 6/0 | 14/2 |
| 1989 | 614 | 12/3 | 9/2 | 21/5 |
| 1990 | 623 | 9/3 | 5/2 | 14/5 |
| 1991 | 617 | 9/3 | 10/3 | 19/6 |
| 1992 | 619 | 8/5 | 1/0 | 9/5 |

*Division I-A Statistical Trends*

| DIVISION I-AA Year | Games | Kick Ret./TDs | Int. Ret./TDs | Total Ret./TDs |
|---|---|---|---|---|
| 1988 | 553 | 4/1 | 7/1 | 11/2 |
| 1989 | 554 | 11/4 | 4/2 | 15/6 |
| 1990 | 548 | 7/3 | 4/2 | 11/5 |
| 1991 | 560 | 12/3 | 9/2 | 21/5 |
| 1992 | 553 | 9/5 | 8/5 | 17/10 |

| DIVISION II Year | Games | Kick Ret./TDs | Int. Ret./TDs | Total Ret./TDs |
|---|---|---|---|---|
| 1988 | 580 | 19/4 | 9/0 | 28/4 |
| 1989 | 590 | 18/8 | 11/3 | 29/11 |
| 1990 | 596 | 9/3 | 2/2 | 11/5 |
| 1991 | 575 | 10/3 | 8/2 | 18/5 |
| 1992 | 580 | 9/4 | 7/3 | 16/7 |

| DIVISION III Year | Games | Kick Ret./TDs | Int. Ret./TDs | Total Ret./TDs |
|---|---|---|---|---|
| 1988 | 994 | 29/8 | 25/3 | 54/11 |
| 1989 | 1,012 | 16/5 | 13/4 | 29/9 |
| 1990 | 1,020 | 25/10 | 16/6 | 41/16 |
| 1991 | 1,006 | 18/7 | 14/5 | 32/12 |
| 1992 | 1,028 | 14/6 | 17/7 | 31/13 |

| ALL DIVISIONS—NATIONWIDE Year | Games | Kick Ret./TDs | Int. Ret./TDs | Total Ret./TDs |
|---|---|---|---|---|
| 1988 | 2,743 | 60/15 | 47/4 | 107/19 |
| 1989 | 2,770 | 57/20 | 37/11 | 94/31 |
| 1990 | 2,787 | 50/19 | 27/12 | 77/31 |
| 1991 | 2,758 | 49/16 | 41/12 | 90/28 |
| 1992 | 2,780 | 40/20 | 33/15 | 73/35 |

# ALL-DIVISIONS FUMBLE-RECOVERY RETURNS

In 1990, the NCAA Football Rules Committee adopted a rule that gave the defense an opportunity to advance fumbles that occur beyond the neutral zone (or line of scrimmage). In 1992, the rule was changed to allow defenses to advance any fumble regardless of position behind or beyond the line of scrimmage. Here are the number of fumble recoveries by division that were advanced, and whether a score resulted.

| DIVISION I-A Year | Games | Fumble Rec./TDs |
|---|---|---|
| 1990 | 623 | 51/17 |
| 1991 | 617 | 60/16 |
| 1992 | 619 | 126/34 |

| DIVISION I-AA Year | Games | Fumble Rec./TDs |
|---|---|---|
| 1990 | 548 | 34/16 |
| 1991 | 560 | 42/13 |
| 1992 | 553 | 96/42 |

| DIVISION II Year | Games | Fumble Rec./TDs |
|---|---|---|
| 1990 | 596 | 46/25 |
| 1991 | 575 | 43/19 |
| 1992 | 580 | 77/39 |

| DIVISION III Year | Games | Fumble Rec./TDs |
|---|---|---|
| 1990 | 1,020 | 55/19 |
| 1991 | 1,006 | 62/22 |
| 1992 | 1,028 | 94/47 |

| ALL DIVISIONS—NATIONWIDE Year | Games | Fumble Rec./TDs |
|---|---|---|
| 1990 | 2,787 | 186/77 |
| 1991 | 2,758 | 207/70 |
| 1992 | 2,780 | 393/162 |

# COLLEGE FOOTBALL RULES CHANGES

## THE BALL

| | |
|---|---|
| 1869 | Round, rubber Association ball. |
| 1875 | Egg-shaped, leather-covered Rugby ball. |
| 1896 | Prolate spheroid, without specific measurements. |
| 1912 | 28-28½ inches around ends, 22½-23 inches around middle, weight 14-15 ounces. |
| 1929 | 28-28½ inches around ends, 22-22½ inches around middle, weight 14-15 ounces. |
| 1934 | 28-28½ inches around ends, 21¼-21½ inches around middle, weight 14-15 ounces. |
| 1952 | Ball may be inclined no more than 45 degrees by snapper. |
| 1956 | Rubber-covered ball permitted. |
| 1973 | Teams allowed to use ball of their choice while in possession. |
| 1978 | Ball may not be altered, and new or nearly new balls added. |
| 1982 | 10⅞ to 11⁷⁄₁₆ inches long, 20¾ to 21¼ inches around middle, and 27¾ to 28½ inches long-axis circumference. |
| 1993 | Rubber or composition ball ruled illegal. |

## THE FIELD

| | |
|---|---|
| 1869 | 120 yards by 75 yards; uprights 24 feet apart. |
| 1871 | 166⅔ yards by 100 yards. |
| 1872 | 133⅓ yards by 83⅓ yards. |
| 1873 | Uprights 25 feet apart. |
| 1876 | 110 yards by 53⅓ yards. Uprights 18½ feet apart; crossbar 10 feet high. |
| 1882 | Field marked with transverse lines every five yards. This distance to be gained in three downs to retain possession. |
| 1912 | Field 120 yards by 53⅓ yards, including two 10-yard end zones. |
| 1927 | Goal posts moved back 10 yards, to end line. |
| 1957 | Team area at 35-yard lines. |
| 1959 | Uprights widened to 23 feet, 4 inches. |
| 1966 | Pylons placed in corners of end zone and at goal lines. |
| 1991 | Uprights moved back to 18 feet, 6 inches. |
| 1993 | Hash marks moved six feet, eight inches closer to center of field to 60 feet from each sideline. |

## POINTS

| | |
|---|---|
| 1869 | All goals count 1 each. |
| 1883 | Safety 1, touchdown 2, goal after TD 4, goal from field 5. |
| 1884 | Safety 2, touchdown 4, goal after TD 2. |
| 1898 | Touchdown 5, goal after TD 1. |
| 1904 | Goal from field 4. |
| 1909 | Goal from field 3. |
| 1912 | Touchdown 6. |
| 1922 | Try-for-point by scrimmage play from 5-yard line. |
| 1929 | Try-for-point by scrimmage play from 2-yard line. |
| 1958 | One-point & two-point conversion (from 3-yard line). |
| 1958 | One-point safety added. |
| 1974 | Ball must go between the uprights for a successful field goal, over the uprights previously scored. |
| 1976 | Forfeit score changed from 1-0 to score at time of forfeit if the offended team is ahead at time of forfeit. |
| 1984 | Try may be eliminated at end of game if both captains agree. |

## PLAYERS

| | |
|---|---|
| 1869 | Each team consisted of 25 players. |
| 1873 | Each team consisted of 20 players. |
| 1876 | Each team consisted of 15 players. |
| 1880 | Each team consisted of 11 players. |
| 1895 | Only one man in motion forward before the snap. No more than three players behind the line. One player permitted in motion toward own goal line. |
| 1910 | Seven players required on line. |
| 1911 | Illegal to conceal ball beneath a player's clothing. |
| 1915 | Numbering of players recommended. |
| 1937 | Number front and back mandatory with 6-inch Arabic in front and 10-inch in the rear. |
| 1939 | All players must wear head protectors. |
| 1951 | Face masks legal. |
| 1966 | Mandatory numbering of five players on the line 50-79. |
| 1982 | Tearaway jersey eliminated by charging a timeout. |
| 1983 | Mandatory white jersey for visiting teams. |

*College Football Rules Changes*

# SUBSTITUTIONS

| 1876 | Fifteen players to a team and few if any substitutions. |
| 1882 | Replacements for disqualified or injured players. |
| 1897 | Substitutions may enter the game any time at discretion of captains. |
| 1922 | Players withdrawn during the first half may be returned during the second half. A player withdrawn in the second half may not return. |
| 1941 | A player may substitute any time but may not be withdrawn or the outgoing player returned to the game until one play had intervened. Platoon football made possible. |
| 1948 | Unlimited substitution on change of team possession. |
| 1953 | Two-platoon abolished and players allowed to enter the game only once in each quarter. |
| 1954-64 | Changes each year toward more liberalized substitution rule and platoon football. |
| 1965 | Platoon football returns. Unlimited substitutions between periods, after a score or try. |
| 1974 | Substitutes must be in for one play and replaced players out for one play. |
| 1993 | Players who are bleeding or whose uniforms are saturated with blood must come out of the game until their return has been approved by medical personnel. |

# PASSING GAME

| 1906 | One forward pass legalized behind the line if made five yards right or left of center. Ball went to opponents if it failed to touch a player of either side before touching the ground. Either team could recover a pass touched by an opponent. One pass each scrimmage down. |
| 1910 | Pass interference does not apply 20 yards beyond the line of scrimmage. Passer must be five yards behind the line of scrimmage. One forward pass permitted during each down. |
| 1914 | Roughing the passer added. |
| 1923 | Handing the ball forward is an illegal forward pass and receivers going out of bounds and returning prohibited. |
| 1934 | Three changes encourage use of pass. (1) First forward pass in series of downs can be incomplete in the end zone without loss of ball except on fourth down. (2) Circumference of ball reduced, making it easier to throw. (3) Five-yard penalty for more than one incomplete pass in same series of downs eliminated. |
| 1941 | Fourth-down forward pass incomplete in end zone no longer a touchback. Ball goes to opponent at spot where put in play. |
| 1945 | Forward pass may be thrown from anywhere behind the line, encouraging use of modern T formation. |
| 1968 | Compulsory numbering system makes only players numbered other than 50-79 eligible forward-pass receivers. |
| 1976 | Offensive blocking changed to provide half extension of arms to assist pass blocking. |
| 1980 | Retreat blocking added with full arm extension to assist pass blocking, and illegal use of hands reduced to five yards. |
| 1982 | Pass interference only on a catchable forward pass. Forward pass intentionally grounded to conserve time permitted. |
| 1983 | First down added to roughing the passer. |
| 1985 | Retreat block deleted and open hands and extended arms permitted anywhere on the field. |

# GENERAL CHANGES

| 1876 | Holding and carrying the ball permitted. |
| 1880 | Eleven players on a side and a scrimmage line established. |
| 1882 | Downs and yards to gain enter the rules. |
| 1883 | Scoring system established. |
| 1906 | Forward passes permitted. Ten yards for first down. |
| 1920 | Clipping defined. |
| 1922 | Try-for-point introduced. Ball brought out five yards from goal line for scrimmage, allowing try for extra point by place kick, drop kick, run or forward pass. |
| 1925 | Kickoff returned to 40-yard line. Clipping made a violation, with penalty of 25 yards. |
| 1927 | One-second pause imposed on shift. Thirty seconds allowed for putting ball in play. Huddle limited to 15 seconds. To encourage use of lateral pass, missed backward pass other than from center declared dead ball when it hits the ground and cannot be recovered by opponents. |
| 1929 | All fumbles ruled dead at point of recovery. |
| 1932 | Most far-reaching changes in nearly a quarter of a century set up safeguards against hazards of game. (1) Ball declared dead when any portion of player in possession, except his hands or feet, touches ground. (2) Use of flying block and flying tackle barred under penalty of five yards. (3) Players on defense forbidden to strike opponents on head, neck or face. (4) Hard and dangerous equipment must be covered with padding. |
| 1937 | Numerals on front and back of jerseys required. |
| 1941 | Legal to hand ball forward behind the neutral zone. |
| 1948 | One-inch kicking tees permitted. |
| 1949 | Blockers required to keep hands against their chest. |
| 1951 | Fair catch restored. |
| 1952 | Penalty for striking with forearm, elbow or locked hands, or for flagrantly rough play or unsportsmanlike conduct, changed from 15 yards to mandatory suspension. |

| 1957 | Penalty for grabbing face mask. |
| 1959 | Distance penalties limited to one-half distance to offending team's goal line. |
| 1965 | Two-inch kicking tees permitted. |
| 1967 | Coaching from sideline permitted. |
| 1971 | Crack-back block (blocking below waist) illegal. |
| 1972 | Freshman eligibility restored. |
| 1977 | Clock started on snap after a penalty. |
| 1978 | Unsuccessful field goal returned to the previous spot. |
| 1983 | Offensive encroachment changed . . . no offensive player permitted in or beyond the neutral zone after snapper touches ball. |
| 1985 | One or both feet on ground required for blocking below waist foul. |
| 1986 | Kickoff from the 35-yard line. |
| 1988 | Defensive team allowed to score two points on return of blocked extra-point kick attempt or interception of extra-point pass attempt. |
| 1989 | Kicking tees eliminated for field goals and extra-point attempts. |
| 1990 | Defense allowed to advance fumbles that occur beyond the neutral zone. |
| 1991 | Width between goal-post uprights reduced from 23 feet, 4 inches to 18 feet, 6 inches. Kickoffs out of bounds allow receiving team to elect to take ball 30 yards beyond yard line where kickoff occurred. |
| 1992 | Defense allowed to advance fumbles regardless of where they occur. Changes ruling of 1990 fumble advancement. |
| 1993 | Guard-around or "fumblerooski" play ruled illegal. |

# DIVISION I-AA RECORDS

Princeton running back Keith Elias set the Division I-AA record for most rushing yards in two consecutive games (572) and tied the record for most yards gained in three straight games (711) on his way to leading the division in rushing in 1992 with a per-game average of 157.5, fifth best on the all-time I-AA list.

# INDIVIDUAL RECORDS

## TOTAL OFFENSE

### (Rushing Plus Passing)

**Most Plays**

**Quarter**
31—Mike Hanlin, Morehead St. vs. Austin Peay, Oct. 10, 1981 (4th)

**Half**
48—John Witkowski, Columbia vs. Dartmouth, Nov. 6, 1982 (2nd)

**Game**
89—Thomas Leonard, Mississippi Val. vs. Texas Southern, Oct. 25, 1986 (440 yards)

**Season**
611—Neil Lomax, Portland St., 1979 (3,966 yards)

**Career**
1,901—Neil Lomax, Portland St., 1977-80 (13,345 yards)

**Most Plays Per Game**

**Season**
56.4—Willie Totten, Mississippi Val., 1984 (564 in 10)

**Career**
45.3—Willie Totten, Mississippi Val., 1982-85 (1,812 in 40)

**Most Plays by a Freshman**

**Game**
79—Adrian Breen, Morehead St. vs. Austin Peay, Oct. 8, 1983 (206 yards)

**Season**
462—Greg Wyatt, Northern Ariz., 1986 (2,695 yards)
Per-game record—44.7, Jason Whitmer, Idaho St., 1987 (402 in 9)

**Most Yards Gained**

**Quarter**
278—Willie Totten, Mississippi Val. vs. Kentucky St., Sept. 1, 1984 (2nd)

**Half**
404—Todd Hammel, Stephen F. Austin vs. Northeast La., Nov. 11, 1989 (1st)

**Game**
643—Jamie Martin, Weber St. vs. Idaho St., Nov. 23, 1991 (624 passing, 19 rushing)

**Season**
4,572—Willie Totten, Mississippi Val., 1984 (4,557 passing, 15 rushing)

**2 Yrs**
8,314—Willie Totten, Mississippi Val., 1984-85 (8,255 passing, 59 rushing)

**3 Yrs**
11,647—Neil Lomax, Portland St., 1978-80 (11,550 passing, 97 rushing)

**Career**
*(4 yrs.)* 13,345—Neil Lomax, Portland St., 1977-80 (13,220 passing, 125 rushing)

**Most Yards Gained Per Game**

**Season**
457.2—Willie Totten, Mississippi Val., 1984 (4,572 in 10)

**Career**
325.2—Willie Totten, Mississippi Val., 1982-85 (13,007 in 40)

**Most Seasons Gaining 3,000 Yards or More**
3—Jamie Martin, Weber St., 1990-92; Sean Payton, Eastern Ill., 1984-86; Neil Lomax, Portland St., 1978-80

**Most Yards Gained by a Freshman**

**Game**
478—Steve McNair, Alcorn St. vs. Howard, Oct. 5, 1991 (42 plays)

**Season**
3,137—Steve McNair, Alcorn St., 1991
Also holds per-game record at 313.7

**Most Yards Gained, Two, Three and Four Consecutive Games**

**2 Games**
1,088—Willie Totten, Mississippi Val., 1984 (561 vs. Southern-B.R., Sept. 29; 527 vs. Grambling, Oct. 13)

**3 Games**
1,576—Willie Totten, Mississippi Val., 1984 (488 vs. Jackson St., Sept. 22; 561 vs. Southern-B.R., Sept. 29; 527 vs. Grambling, Oct. 13)

**4 Games**
2,068—Willie Totten, Mississippi Val., 1984 (561 vs. Southern-B.R., Sept. 29; 527 vs. Grambling, Oct. 13; 359 vs. Texas Southern, Oct. 20; 621 vs. Prairie View, Oct. 27)

**Most Games Gaining 300 Yards or More**

**Season**
10—Willie Totten, Mississippi Val., 1984; Neil Lomax, Portland St., 1980

**Career**
28—Neil Lomax, Portland St., 1977-80

**Most Consecutive Games Gaining 300 Yards or More**

**Season**
10—Willie Totten, Mississippi Val., 1984

**Career**
13—Neil Lomax, Portland St., 1979-80

**Most Games Gaining 400 Yards or More**

**Season**
7—Willie Totten, Mississippi Val., 1984

**Career**
13—Willie Totten, Mississippi Val., 1982-85

**Most Consecutive Games Gaining 400 Yards or More**

**Season**
5—Willie Totten, Mississippi Val., 1984

**Most Games Gaining 500 Yards or More**

**Season**
4—Willie Totten, Mississippi Val., 1984
Also holds career record at 4 (1982-85)

**Most Yards Gained Against One Opponent**

**Career**
1,713—Willie Totten, Mississippi Val. vs. Prairie View, 1982-85
Also holds per-game record at 428.3 (1,713 in 4)

**Gaining 1,000 Yards Rushing and 1,000 Yards Passing**

**Season**
Tracy Ham (QB), Ga. Southern, 1986 (1,048 rushing, 1,772 passing)

**Gaining 2,000 Yards Rushing and 4,000 Yards Passing**

**Career**
Bill Vergantino (QB), Delaware, 1989-92 (2,287 rushing, 6,177 passing); Tracy Ham (QB),

Ga. Southern, 1984-86 (2,506 rushing, 4,871 passing)

**Highest Average Gain Per Play**
**Game**
  *(Min. 39-49 plays)* 12.2—Todd Hammel, Stephen F. Austin vs. Northeast La., Nov. 11, 1989 (46 for 562)
  *(Min. 50-59 plays)* 9.82—Scott Semptimphelter, Lehigh vs. Lafayette, Nov. 21, 1992 (51 for 501)
  *(Min. 60 plays)* 9.70—Willie Totten, Mississippi Val. vs. Prairie View, Oct. 27, 1984 (64 for 621)
**Season**
  *(Min. 2,500-3,299 yards)* 9.57—Frank Baur, Lafayette, 1988 (285 for 2,727)
  *(Min. 3,300 yards)* 8.36—Jeff Wiley, Holy Cross, 1987 (445 for 3,722)
**Career**
  *(Min. 4,000-4,999 yards)* 7.55—Reggie Lewis, Sam Houston St., 1986-87 (653 for 4,929)
  *(Min. 5,000 yards)* 7.34—Jay Johnson, Northern Iowa, 1989-92 (928 for 6,813)

**Most Touchdowns Responsible For**
**(TDs Scored and Passed For)**
**Game**
  9—Willie Totten, Mississippi Val. vs. Prairie View, Oct. 27, 1984 (passed for 8, scored 1) &

vs. Kentucky St., Sept. 1, 1984 (passed for 9); Neil Lomax, Portland St. vs. Delaware St., Nov. 8, 1980 (passed for 8, scored 1)
**Season**
  61—Willie Totten, Mississippi Val., 1984 (passed for 56, scored 5)
  Also holds per-game record at 6.1 (61 in 10)
**Career**
  157—Willie Totten, Mississippi Val., 1982-85 (passed for 139, scored 18)
  Also holds per-game record at 3.93 (157 in 40)

**Most Points Responsible For**
**(Points Scored and Passed For)**
**Game**
  56—Willie Totten, Mississippi Val. vs. Kentucky St., Sept. 1, 1984 (passed for 9 TDs and 1 two-point conversion)
**Season**
  368—Willie Totten, Mississippi Val., 1984 (passed for 56 TDs, scored 5 TDs and passed for 1 two-point conversion)
  Also holds per-game record at 36.8 (368 in 10)
**Career**
  946—Willie Totten, Mississippi Val., 1982-85 (passed for 139 TDs, scored 18 TDs and passed for 1 two-point conversion)
  Also holds per-game record at 23.7 (946 in 40)

# RUSHING

**Most Rushes**
**Quarter**
  19—Mal Najarian, Boston U. vs. Northeastern, Sept. 30, 1978 (4th)
**Half**
  32—David Clark, Dartmouth vs. Pennsylvania, Nov. 18, 1989 (2nd)
**Game**
  52—James Black, Akron vs. Austin Peay, Nov. 19, 1983 (295 yards)
**Season**
  351—James Black, Akron, 1983 (1,568 yards)
**Career**
  963—Kenny Gamble, Colgate, 1984-87 (5,220 yards)

**Most Rushes Per Game**
**Season**
  34.0—James Black, Akron, 1982 (306 in 9)
**Career**
  23.7—Paul Lewis, Boston U., 1981-84 (878 in 37)

**Most Consecutive Carries by Same Player**
**Game**
  14—Dave Mixon, Tennessee Tech vs. Morehead St., Oct. 22, 1983 (during 4 series)

**Most Yards Gained**
**Quarter**
  194—Otto Kelly, Nevada vs. Idaho, Nov. 12, 1983 (3rd, 8 rushes)
**Half**
  263—Joe Delaney, Northwestern (La.) vs. Nicholls St., Oct. 28, 1978 (2nd, 19 rushes)
**Game**
  345—Russell Davis, Idaho vs. Portland St., Oct. 3, 1981 (20 rushes)
**Season**
  1,883—Rich Erenberg, Colgate, 1983 (302 rushes)
**Career**
  5,333—Frank Hawkins, Nevada, 1977-80 (945 rushes)

**Most Yards Gained Per Game**
**Season**
  172.2—Gene Lake, Delaware St., 1984 (1,722 in 10)
**Career**
  *(2 yrs.)* 124.7—Rich Erenberg, Colgate, 1982-83 (2,618 in 21 games)
  *(3 yrs.)* 133.0—Mike Clark, Akron, 1984-86 (4,257 in 32)
  *(4 yrs.)* 124.3—Kenny Gamble, Colgate, 1984-87 (5,220 in 42)

**Most Yards Gained by a Freshman**
**Game**
  304—Tony Citizen, McNeese St. vs. Prairie View, Sept. 6, 1986 (30 rushes)
**Season**
  1,620—Markus Thomas, Eastern Ky., 1989 (232 rushes)

**Most Yards Gained Per Game by a Freshman**
**Season**
  147.3—Markus Thomas, Eastern Ky., 1989 (1,620 in 11)

**Most Yards Gained by a Quarterback**
**Game**
  309—Eddie Thompson, Western Ky. vs. Southern Ill., Oct. 31, 1992 (28 rushes)
**Season**
  1,152—Jack Douglas, Citadel, 1991 (266 rushes)
  Also holds per-game record at 104.7
**Career**
  3,674—Jack Douglas, Citadel, 1989-92 (832 rushes)

**Most Games Gaining 100 Yards or More**
**Season**
  11—Frank Hawkins, Nevada, 1980
**Career**
  29—Kenny Gamble, Colgate, 1984-87 (42 games); Frank Hawkins, Nevada, 1977-80 (43 games)

*Division I-AA Individual Records*

### Most Consecutive Games Gaining
### 100 Yards or More
**Season**
11—Frank Hawkins, Nevada, 1980
**Career**
20—Frank Hawkins, Nevada, 1979-80

### Most Games Gaining 100 Yards or More
### by a Freshman
8—David Wright, Indiana St., 1992; Markus Thomas, Eastern Ky., 1989

### Most Games Gaining 200 Yards or More
**Season**
4—Kenny Gamble, Colgate, 1986; Rich Erenberg, Colgate, 1983
**Career**
6—Kenny Gamble, Colgate, 1984-87

### Most Consecutive Games Gaining
### 200 Yards or More
**Season**
4—Rich Erenberg, Colgate, 1983

### Most Yards Gained, Two, Three and
### Four Consecutive Games
**2 Games**
572—Keith Elias, Princeton, 1992 (299 vs. Lafayette, Sept. 26; 273 vs. Lehigh, Oct. 3)
**3 Games**
711—Keith Elias, Princeton, 1992 (299 vs. Lafayette, Sept. 26; 273 vs. Lehigh, Oct. 3; 139 vs. Brown, Oct. 10); Gene Lake, Delaware St., 1984 (143 vs. Central St., Ohio, Oct. 27; 232 vs. Howard, Nov. 3; 336 vs. Liberty, Nov. 10)
**4 Games**
874—Gene Lake, Delaware St., 1984 (163 vs. Towson St., Oct. 20; 143 vs. Central St., Ohio, Oct. 27; 232 vs. Howard, Nov. 3; 336 vs. Liberty, Nov. 10)

### Most Seasons Gaining 1,000 Yards or More
**Career**
3—By 15 players. Most recent: Markus Thomas, Eastern Ky., 1989, 1991-92; Joe Segreti, Holy Cross, 1988-90; Elroy Harris, Eastern Ky., 1985, 1987-88; Kenny Gamble, Colgate, 1985-87; James Crawford, Eastern Ky., 1985-87

### Two Players, Same Team, Each Gaining
### 1,000 Yards or More
Northeast La., 1992—Greg Robinson (1,011) & Roosevelt Potts (1,004); Yale, 1991—Chris Kouri (1,101) & Nick Crawford (1,024); William & Mary, 1990—Robert Green (1,185) & Tyrone Shelton (1,020); Citadel, 1988—Adrian Johnson (1,091) & Gene Brown (1,006); Eastern Ky., 1986—Elroy Harris (1,152) & James Crawford (1,070); Eastern Ky., 1985—James Crawford (1,282) & Elroy Harris (1,134); Nevada, 1983—Otto Kelly (1,090) & Tony Corley (1,006); Jackson St., 1978—Perry Harrington (1,105) & Jeffrey Moore (1,094)

### Most Yards Gained by Two Players, Same Team
**Game**
445—Joe Delaney (299) & Brett Knecht (146), Northwestern (La.) vs. Nicholls St., Oct. 28, 1978
**Season**
2,429—Frank Hawkins (1,683) & John Vicari (746), Nevada, 1979

### Most Yards Gained in an Opening Game
### of a Season
304—Tony Citizen, McNeese St. vs. Prairie View, Sept. 6, 1986 (30 rushes)

### Most Yards Gained in
### First Game of a Career
304—Tony Citizen, McNeese St. vs. Prairie View, Sept. 6, 1986 (30 rushes)

### Highest Average Gain Per Rush
**Game**
*(Min. 15-19 rushes)* 19.1—Gene Brown, Citadel vs. Va. Military, Nov. 12, 1988 (15 for 286)
*(Min. 20 rushes)* 17.3—Russell Davis, Idaho vs. Portland St., Oct. 3, 1981 (20 for 345)
**Season**
*(Min. 150-199 rushes)* 7.74—Harvey Reed, Howard, 1986 (179 for 1,386)
*(Min. 200 rushes)* 7.29—Mike Clark, Akron, 1986 (245 for 1,786)
**Career**
*(Min. 350-599 rushes)* 7.30—Keith Williams, Southwest Mo. St., 1982-85 (369 for 2,694)
*(Min. 600 rushes)* 6.57—Markus Thomas, Eastern Ky., 1989-92 (784 for 5,149)

### Most Touchdowns Scored by Rushing
**Game**
6—Gene Lake, Delaware St. vs. Howard, Nov. 3, 1984; Gill Fenerty, Holy Cross vs. Columbia, Oct. 29, 1983; Henry Odom, South Caro. St. vs. Morgan St., Oct. 18, 1980
**Season**
24—Geoff Mitchell, Weber St., 1991
**Career**
55—Kenny Gamble, Colgate, 1984-87

### Most Touchdowns Scored Per Game
### by Rushing
**Season**
2.2—Geoff Mitchell, Weber St., 1991 (24 in 11)
**Career**
1.52—Elroy Harris, Eastern Ky., 1985, 1987-88 (47 in 31)

### Most Touchdowns Scored by Rushing
### by a Quarterback
**Season**
18—Tracy Ham, Ga. Southern, 1986
**Career**
48—Jack Douglas, Citadel, 1989-92
Also holds per-game record at 1.09 (48 in 44)

### Longest Play
99—Phillip Collins, Southwest Mo. St. vs. Western Ill., Sept. 16, 1989; Pedro Bacon, Western Ky. vs. Livingston, Sept. 13, 1986 (only rush of the game); Hubert Owens, Mississippi Val. vs. Ark.-Pine Bluff, Sept. 20, 1980

# PASSING

### Highest Passing Efficiency Rating Points
**Game**
*(Min. 15-24 atts.)* 322.9—Mike Smith, Northern Iowa vs. Indiana St., Nov. 13, 1986 (16 attempts, 14 completions, 0 interceptions, 252 yards, 5 TD passes)

*(Min. 25-44 atts.)* 283.3—Mike Smith, Northern Iowa vs. McNeese St., Nov. 8, 1986 (27 attempts, 22 completions, 0 interceptions, 413 yards, 6 TD passes)
*(Min. 45 atts.)* 220.8—Todd Hammel, Stephen F. Austin vs. Northeast La., Nov. 11, 1989 (45

attempts, 31 completions, 3 interceptions, 571 yards, 8 TD passes)

**Season**
*(Min. 15 atts. per game)* 181.3—Michael Payton, Marshall, 1991 (216 attempts, 143 completions, 5 interceptions, 2,333 yards, 19 TD passes)

**Career**
*(Min. 300-399 comps.)* 148.9—Jay Johnson, Northern Iowa, 1989-92 (744 attempts, 397 completions, 25 interceptions, 7,049 yards, 51 TD passes)
*(Min. 400 comps.)* 146.8—Willie Totten, Mississippi Val., 1982-85 (1,555 attempts, 907 completions, 75 interceptions, 12,711 yards, 139 TD passes)

### Most Passes Attempted
**Quarter**
28—Paul Peterson, Idaho St. vs. Cal Poly SLO, Oct. 22, 1983 (4th)

**Half**
42—Doug Pederson, Northeast La. vs. Stephen F. Austin, Nov. 11, 1989 (1st, completed 27); Mike Machurek, Idaho St. vs. Weber St., Sept. 20, 1980 (2nd, completed 18)

**Game**
77—Neil Lomax, Portland St. vs. Northern Colo., Oct. 20, 1979 (completed 44)

**Season**
518—Willie Totten, Mississippi Val., 1984 (completed 324)
Also holds per-game record at 51.8

**Career**
1,606—Neil Lomax, Portland St., 1977-80 (completed 938)
Per-game record—42.9, Stan Greene, Boston U., 1989-90 (944 in 22)

### Most Passes Attempted by a Freshman
**Game**
66—Chris Swartz, Morehead St. vs. Tennessee Tech, Oct. 17, 1987 (completed 35)

**Season**
392—Greg Wyatt, Northern Ariz., 1986 (completed 250)
Per-game record—37.8, Jason Whitmer, Idaho St., 1987 (340 in 9)

### Most Passes Completed
**Quarter**
18—Kirk Schulz, Villanova vs. Central Conn. St., Oct. 10, 1987 (3rd); Willie Totten, Mississippi Val. vs. Grambling, Oct. 31, 1984 (2nd) & vs. Kentucky St., Sept. 1, 1984 (2nd)

**Half**
27—Doug Pederson, Northeast La. vs. Stephen F. Austin, Nov. 11, 1989 (1st, attempted 42)

**Game**
47—Jamie Martin, Weber St. vs. Idaho St., Nov. 23, 1991 (attempted 62)

**Season**
324—Willie Totten, Mississippi Val., 1984 (attempted 518)
Also holds per-game record at 32.4

**Career**
938—Neil Lomax, Portland St., 1977-80 (attempted 1,606)
Per-game record—23.8, Stan Greene, Boston U., 1989-90 (524 in 22)

### Most Passes Completed by a Freshman
**Game**
35—Chris Swartz, Morehead St. vs. Tennessee Tech, Oct. 17, 1987 (attempted 66)

**Season**
250—Greg Wyatt, Northern Ariz., 1986 (attempted 392)
Also holds per-game record at 22.7 (250 in 11)

### Most Passes Completed, Freshman and Sophomore Seasons
518—Greg Wyatt, Northern Ariz., 1986-87 (attempted 804)

### Most Consecutive Passes Completed
**Game**
19—Kirk Schulz, Villanova vs. Central Conn. St., Oct. 10, 1987

### Most Consecutive Pass Completions to Start Game
18—Scott Auchenbach, Bucknell vs. Colgate, Nov. 11, 1989

### Highest Percentage of Passes Completed
**Game**
*(Min. 20-29 comps.)* 87.9%—Donny Simmons, Western Ill. vs. Indiana St., Oct. 24, 1992 (29 of 33)
*(Min. 30 comps.)* 81.6%—Eric Beavers, Nevada vs. Idaho St., Nov. 17, 1984 (31 of 38)

**Season**
*(Min. 200 atts.)* 68.2%—Jason Garrett, Princeton, 1988 (204 of 299)

**Career**
*(Min. 500-749 atts.)* 66.9%—Jason Garrett, Princeton, 1987-88 (366 of 550)
*(Min. 750 atts.)* 61.9%—Michael Payton, Marshall, 1989-92 (542 of 876)

### Most Passes Had Intercepted
**Game**
7—Dan Crowley, Towson St. vs. Maine, Nov. 16, 1991 (53 attempts); Carlton Jenkins, Mississippi Val. vs. Prairie View, Oct. 31, 1987 (34 attempts); Charles Hebert, Southeastern La. vs. Northwestern (La.), Nov. 12, 1983 (23 attempts); Mick Spoon, Idaho St. vs. Montana, Oct. 21, 1978 (attempted 35)

**Season**
29—Willie Totten, Mississippi Val., 1985 (492 attempts)
Also holds per-game record at 2.64 (29 in 11)

**Career**
75—Willie Totten, Mississippi Val., 1982-85
Per-game record—2.0, John Witkowski, Columbia, 1981-83 (60 in 30)

### Lowest Percentage of Passes Had Intercepted
**Season**
*(Min. 175-324 atts.)* 0.84%—Jeff Mladenich, Boise St., 1991 (2 of 239)
*(Min. 325 atts.)* 1.22%—Bill Lazor, Cornell, 1992 (4 of 328)

**Career**
*(Min. 500-749 atts.)* 1.82%—Jason Garrett, Princeton, 1987-88 (10 of 550)
*(Min. 750 atts.)* 2.67%—Brad Lebo, Montana, 1989-92 (25 of 938)

### Most Passes Attempted Without Interception
**Game**
68—Tony Petersen, Marshall vs. Western Caro., Nov. 14, 1987 (completed 34)

### Most Consecutive Passes Attempted Without Interception
**Season**
176—Jason Garrett, Princeton, 1988 (in 7 games, from Sept. 17 through Oct. 29)

**Career**
199—Thomas Debow, Tennessee Tech, began Sept. 17, 1988, ended Oct. 14, 1989

## Most Yards Gained

**Quarter**
278—Willie Totten, Mississippi Val. vs. Kentucky
St., Sept. 1, 1984 (2nd)

**Half**
383—Michael Payton, Marshall vs. Va. Military,
Nov. 16, 1991 (1st)

**Game**
624—Jamie Martin, Weber St. vs. Idaho St.,
Nov. 23, 1991

**Season**
4,557—Willie Totten, Mississippi Val., 1984

**Career**
13,220—Neil Lomax, Portland St., 1977-80

### Most Yards Gained Per Game

**Season**
455.7—Willie Totten, Mississippi Val., 1984
(4,557 in 10)

**Career**
320.1—Tom Ehrhardt, Rhode Island, 1984-85
(6,722 in 21)

### Most Yards Gained by a Freshman

**Game**
469—Jason Whitmer, Idaho St. vs. Weber St.,
Nov. 21, 1987

**Season**
2,895—Steve McNair, Alcorn St., 1991
Also holds per-game record at 289.5 (2,895 in
10)

### Most Yards Gained, Freshman and Sophomore Seasons

6,436—Steve McNair, Alcorn St., 1991-92

### Most Yards Gained, Two, Three and Four Consecutive Games

**2 Games**
1,105—Todd Hammel, Stephen F. Austin, 1989
(534 vs. Sam Houston St., Nov. 4; 571 vs.
Northeast La., Nov. 11)

**3 Games**
1,624—Willie Totten, Mississippi Val., 1984 (526
vs. Jackson St., Sept. 22; 553 vs. Southern-
B.R., Sept. 29; 545 vs. Grambling, Oct. 13)

**4 Games**
2,065—Willie Totten, Mississippi Val., 1984 (553
vs. Southern-B.R., Sept. 29; 545 vs. Grambling, Oct. 13; 368 vs. Texas Southern, Oct. 20;
599 vs. Prairie View, Oct. 27)

### Most Games Gaining 200 Yards or More

**Season**
11—By 12 players. Most recent: Chris Hakel,
William & Mary, 1991; Jamie Martin, Weber
St., 1991; John Friesz, Idaho, 1989; Todd
Hammel, Stephen F. Austin, 1989

**Career**
36—Neil Lomax, Portland St., 1977-80 (42
games)

### Most Consecutive Games Gaining 200 Yards or More

**Season**
11—By 10 players. Most recent: Chris Hakel,
William & Mary, 1991; Jamie Martin, Weber
St., 1991; Jeff Wiley, Holy Cross, 1987; Tony
Petersen, Marshall, 1987

**Career**
28—Neil Lomax, Portland St., 1978-80

### Most Games Gaining 300 Yards or More

**Season**
10—John Friesz, Idaho, 1989; Willie Totten,
Mississippi Val., 1984

**Career**
28—Neil Lomax, Portland St., 1977-80

## Most Consecutive Games Gaining 300 Yards or More

**Season**
10—John Friesz, Idaho, 1989; Willie Totten,
Mississippi Val., 1984

**Career**
13—Neil Lomax, Portland St., 1979-80

### Most Yards Gained Against One Opponent

**Career**
1,675—Willie Totten, Mississippi Val. vs. Prairie
View, 1982-85
Also holds per-game record at 418.8 (1,675 in
4)

### Most Yards Per Attempt

**Game**
(Min. 30-44 atts.) 16.1—Gilbert Renfroe, Tennessee St. vs. Dist. Columbia, Nov. 5, 1983
(30 for 484)
(Min. 45 atts.) 12.69—Todd Hammel, Stephen
F. Austin vs. Northeast La., Nov. 11, 1989 (45
for 571)

**Season**
(Min. 250-324 atts.) 10.31—Mike Smith, Northern Iowa, 1986 (303 for 3,125)
(Min. 325 atts.) 9.51—John Friesz, Idaho, 1989
(425 for 4,041)

**Career**
(Min. 500-999 atts.) 9.47—Jay Johnson, North-
ern Iowa, 1989-92 (744 for 7,049)
(Min. 1,000 atts.) 8.23—Neil Lomax, Portland
St., 1977-80 (1,606 for 13,220)

### Most Yards Gained Per Completion

**Game**
(Min. 15-19 comps.) 22.79—Matt Griffin, New
Hampshire vs. Hofstra, Sept. 21, 1991 (19 for
433)
(Min. 20 comps.) 22.55—Michael Payton, Marshall vs. Va. Military, Nov. 16, 1991 (22 for
496)

**Season**
(Min. 200 comps.) 16.4—Todd Hammel, Stephen F. Austin, 1989 (238 for 3,914)

**Career**
(Min. 350-399 comps.) 17.76—Jay Johnson,
Northern Iowa, 1989-92 (397 for 7,049)
(Min. 400 comps.) 15.31—Todd Hammel, Ste-
phen F. Austin, 1986-89 (443 for 6,784)

### Most Touchdown Passes

**Quarter**
7—Neil Lomax, Portland St. vs. Delaware St.,
Nov. 8, 1980 (1st)

**Half**
7—Neil Lomax, Portland St. vs. Delaware St.,
Nov. 8, 1980 (1st)

**Game**
9—Willie Totten, Mississippi Val. vs. Kentucky
St., Sept. 1, 1984

**Season**
56—Willie Totten, Mississippi Val., 1984
Also holds per-game record at 5.6 (56 in 10)

**Career**
139—Willie Totten, Mississippi Val., 1982-85
Also holds per-game record at 3.48 (139 in 40)

### Most Consecutive Games Throwing a Touchdown Pass

**Career**
27—Willie Totten, Mississippi Val., 1983-85

### Most Touchdown Passes, Same Passer and Receiver

**Season**
27—Willie Totten to Jerry Rice, Mississippi Val.,
1984

**Career**
47—Willie Totten to Jerry Rice, Mississippi Val., 1982-84

**Highest Percentage of Passes for Touchdowns**
**Season**
(Min. 200-299 atts.) 11.7%—Mike Williams, Grambling, 1980 (28 of 239)

(Min. 300 atts.) 10.8%—Willie Totten, Mississippi Val., 1984 (56 of 518)
**Career**
(Min. 500-749 atts.) 8.46%—Mike Williams, Grambling, 1977-80 (44 of 520)
(Min. 750 atts.) 7.06%—Eric Beavers, Nevada, 1983-86 (77 of 1,094)

# RECEIVING

**Most Passes Caught**
**Game**
24—Jerry Rice, Mississippi Val. vs. Southern-B.R., Oct. 1, 1983 (219 yards)
**Season**
115—Brian Forster, Rhode Island, 1985 (1,617 yards)
**Career**
301—Jerry Rice, Mississippi Val., 1981-84 (4,693 yards)

**Most Passes Caught Per Game**
**Season**
11.5—Brian Forster, Rhode Island, 1985 (115 in 10)
**Career**
7.3—Jerry Rice, Mississippi Val., 1981-84 (301 in 41)

**Most Passes Caught by a Tight End**
**Game**
18—Brian Forster, Rhode Island vs. Brown, Sept. 28, 1985 (327 yards)
**Season**
115—Brian Forster, Rhode Island, 1985 (1,617 yards)
Also holds per-game record at 11.5 (115 in 10)
**Career**
245—Brian Forster, Rhode Island, 1983-85, 1987 (3,410 yards)

**Most Passes Caught by a Running Back**
**Game**
21—David Pandt, Montana St. vs. Eastern Wash., Sept. 21, 1985 (169 yards)
**Season**
78—Gordie Lockbaum, Holy Cross, 1987 (1,152 yards)
**2 Yrs**
135—Gordie Lockbaum, Holy Cross, 1986-87 (2,012 yards)
Also holds per-game record at 6.1 (135 in 22)
**Career**
182—Merril Hoge, Idaho St., 1983-86 (1,734 yards)

**Most Passes Caught by Two Players, Same Team**
**Season**
183—Jerry Rice (103 for 1,682 yards and 27 TDs) & Joe Thomas (80 for 1,119 yards and 11 TDs), Mississippi Val., 1984
**Career**
420—Darrell Colbert (217 for 3,177 yards and 33 TDs) & Donald Narcisse (203 for 2,429 yards and 26 TDs), Texas Southern, 1983-86

**Most Yards Gained**
**Game**
370—Michael Lerch, Princeton vs. Brown, Oct. 12, 1991 (caught 9)
**Season**
1,682—Jerry Rice, Mississippi Val., 1984 (caught 103)
**Career**
4,693—Jerry Rice, Mississippi Val., 1981-84 (caught 301)

**Most Yards Gained Per Game**
**Season**
168.2—Jerry Rice, Mississippi Val., 1984 (1,682 in 10)
**Career**
114.5—Jerry Rice, Mississippi Val., 1981-84 (4,693 in 41)

**Most Yards Gained by a Tight End**
**Game**
327—Brian Forster, Rhode Island vs. Brown, Sept. 28, 1985 (caught 18)
**Season**
1,617—Brian Forster, Rhode Island, 1985 (caught 115)
Also holds per-game record at 161.7 (1,617 in 10)
**Career**
3,410—Brian Forster, Rhode Island, 1983-85, 87 (caught 245)

**Most Yards Gained by a Running Back**
**Game**
220—Alvin Atkinson, Davidson vs. Furman, Nov. 3, 1979 (caught 9)
**Season**
1,152—Gordie Lockbaum, Holy Cross, 1987 (caught 78)
Also holds per-game record at 104.7 (1,152 in 11)

**Most Yards Gained by Two Players, Same Team**
**Season**
2,801—Jerry Rice (1,682, 103 caught and 27 TDs) & Joe Thomas (1,119, 80 caught and 11 TDs), Mississippi Val., 1984
**Career**
5,806—Roy Banks (3,177, 184 caught and 38 TDs) & Cal Pierce (2,629, 163 caught and 13 TDs), Eastern Ill., 1983-86

**Highest Average Gain Per Reception**
**Game**
(Min. 5-9 receps.) 44.6—John Taylor, Delaware St. vs. St. Paul's, Sept. 21, 1985 (5 for 223)
(Min. 10 receps.) 29.0—Jason Cristino, Lehigh vs. Lafayette, Nov. 21, 1992 (11 for 319)
**Season**
(Min. 30-39 receps.) 26.3—Brian Allen, Idaho, 1983 (31 for 814)
(Min. 40-59 receps.) 25.0—Mark Stock, Va. Military, 1986 (45 for 1,123)
(Min. 60 receps.) 20.7—Golden Tate, Tennessee St., 1983 (63 for 1,307)
**Career**
(Min. 90-124 receps.) 24.3—John Taylor, Delaware St., 1982-85 (100 for 2,426)
(Min. 125 receps.) 20.0—Tracy Singleton, Howard, 1979-82 (159 for 3,187)

**Most Games Gaining 100 Yards or More**
**Career**
23—Jerry Rice, Mississippi Val., 1981-84 (in 41 games played)

## Most Touchdown Passes Caught
**Game**
 5—Rennie Benn, Lehigh vs. Indiana (Pa.), Sept. 14, 1985 (266 yards); Jerry Rice, Mississippi Val. vs. Prairie View, Oct. 27, 1984 & vs. Kentucky St., Sept. 1, 1984
**Season**
 27—Jerry Rice, Mississippi Val., 1984
**Career**
 50—Jerry Rice, Mississippi Val., 1981-84

### Most Touchdown Passes Caught Per Game
**Season**
 2.7—Jerry Rice, Mississippi Val., 1984 (27 in 10)

**Career**
 1.22—Jerry Rice, Mississippi Val., 1981-84 (50 in 41)

### Most Games Catching a Touchdown Pass
**Season**
 10—Jerry Rice, Mississippi Val., 1984
 Also holds consecutive record at 10 (1984)

**Career**
 26—Jerry Rice, Mississippi Val., 1981-84
 Also holds consecutive record at 17 (1983-84)

# PUNTING
### Most Punts
**Game**
 16—Matt Stover, Louisiana Tech vs. Northeast La., Nov. 18, 1988 (567 yards)
**Season**
 98—Barry Hickingbotham, Louisiana Tech, 1987 (3,821 yards)
**Career**
 301—Barry Bowman, Louisiana Tech, 1983-86 (11,441 yards)

### Highest Average Per Punt
**Game**
 (Min. 5-9 punts) 55.7—Harold Alexander, Appalachian St. vs. Citadel, Oct. 3, 1992 (6 for 334); Jody Farmer, Montana vs. Nevada, Oct. 1, 1988 (9 for 501)
 (Min. 10 punts) 52.2—Stuart Dodds, Montana St. vs. Northern Ariz., Oct. 20, 1979 (10 for 522)
**Season**
 (Min. 60 punts) 47.0—Harold Alexander, Appalachian St., 1991 (64 for 3,009)
**Career**
 (Min. 150 punts) 44.4—Pumpy Tudors, Tenn.-Chatt., 1989-91 (181 for 8,041)

### Longest Punt
 91—Bart Helsley, North Texas vs. Northeast La., Nov. 17, 1990

# INTERCEPTIONS
### Most Passes Intercepted
**Game**
 5—Mark Cordes, Eastern Wash. vs. Boise St., Sept. 6, 1986 (48 yards); Michael Richardson, Northwestern (La.) vs. Southeastern La., Nov. 12, 1983 (128 yards); Karl Johnson, Jackson St. vs. Grambling, Oct. 23, 1982 (29 yards)
**Season**
 12—Dean Cain, Princeton, 1987 (98 yards)
 Also holds per-game record at 1.2 (12 in 10)
**Career**
 28—Dave Murphy, Holy Cross, 1986-89 (309 yards)
 Per-game record—0.73, Dean Cain, Princeton, 1985-87 (22 in 30)

### Most Yards on Interception Returns
**Game**
 216—Keiron Bigby, Brown vs. Yale, Sept. 29, 1984 (3 interceptions) (first career game)
**Season**
 216—Keiron Bigby, Brown, 1984 (3 interceptions)
**Career**
 452—Rick Harris, East Tenn. St., 1986-88 (20 interceptions)

### Most Touchdowns Scored on Interception Returns
**Game**
 2—By five players. Most recent: Lance Guidry, McNeese St. vs. Stephen F. Austin, Nov. 7, 1992; Bill Curry, Maine vs. Liberty, Oct. 10, 1992
**Season**
 4—Robert Turner, Jackson St., 1990 (9 interceptions, 212 yards)
**Career**
 4—Robert Turner (DB), Jackson St., 1990 (9 interceptions); Ken Braden (LB), Southwest Mo. St., 1984-87 (8 interceptions); Roger Robinson (DB), Tennessee St., 1981-84 (12 interceptions)

### Highest Average Gain Per Interception
**Game**
 (Min. 3 ints.) 72.0—Keiron Bigby, Brown vs. Yale, Sept. 29, 1984 (3 for 216)
**Season**
 (Min. 3 ints.) 72.0—Keiron Bigby, Brown, 1984 (3 for 216)
**Career**
 (Min. 12 ints.) 24.9—Roger Robinson, Tennessee St., 1981-84 (12 for 299)

# PUNT RETURNS
### Most Punt Returns
**Game**
 9—By 12 players. Most recent: Brad Jordan, Fordham vs. Pennsylvania, Oct. 3, 1992 (64 yards)
**Season**
 55—Tommy Houk, Murray St., 1980 (442 yards)
 Also holds per-game record at 5.0 (55 in 11)
**Career**
 117—David McCrary, Tenn.-Chatt., 1982-85 (1,230 yards)
 Per-game record—3.8, Tommy Houk, Murray St., 1979-80 (84 in 22)

### Most Yards on Punt Returns
**Game**
 216—Gary Harrell, Howard vs. Morgan St.,

Nov. 3, 1990 (7 returns); Willie Ware, Mississippi Val. vs. Washburn, Sept. 15, 1984 (7 returns)

**Season**

561—Willie Ware, Mississippi Val., 1985 (31 returns)

Also holds per-game record at 51.0 (561 in 11)

**Career**

1,230—David McCrary, Tenn.-Chatt., 1982-85 (117 returns)

### Highest Average Gain Per Return

**Game**

*(Min. 5 rets.)* 30.9—Gary Harrell, Howard vs. Morgan St., Nov. 3, 1990 (7 for 216); Willie Ware, Mississippi Val. vs. Washburn, Sept. 15, 1984 (7 for 216)

**Season**

*(Min. 1.2 rets. per game)* 23.0—Tim Egerton, Delaware St., 1988 (16 for 368)

**Career**

*(Min. 1.2 rets. per game)* 16.4—Willie Ware, Mississippi Val., 1982-85 (61 for 1,003)

### Most Touchdowns Scored on Punt Returns

**Game**

2—By four players. Most recent: Sebron Spivey, Southern Ill. vs. Southeast Mo. St., Oct. 19, 1985

**Season**

4—Kenny Shedd, Northern Iowa, 1992 (27 returns); Howard Huckaby, Florida A&M, 1988 (26 returns)

**Career**

7—Kenny Shedd, Northern Iowa, 1989-92

### Longest Punt Return

98—Barney Bussey, South Caro. St. vs. Johnson Smith, Oct. 10, 1981

### Most Consecutive Games Returning Punt for Touchdown

3—Troy Jones, McNeese St., 1989 (vs. Mississippi Col., Sept. 2; vs. Samford, Sept. 9; vs. Northeast La., Sept. 16)

# KICKOFF RETURNS

### Most Kickoff Returns

**Game**

10—Merril Hoge, Idaho St. vs. Weber St., Oct. 25, 1986 (179 yards)

**Season**

50—David Primus, Samford, 1989 (1,411 yards)

**Career**

118—Clarence Alexander, Mississippi Val., 1986-89 (2,439 yards)

### Most Kickoff Returns Per Game

**Season**

4.55—David Primus, Samford, 1989 (50 in 11)

**Career**

2.95—Clarence Alexander, Mississippi Val., 1986-89 (118 in 40); Lorenza Rivers, Tennessee Tech, 1985, 1987 (62 in 21)

### Most Yards on Kickoff Returns

**Game**

262—Herman Hunter, Tennessee St. vs. Mississippi Val., Nov. 13, 1982 (6 returns)

**Season**

1,411—David Primus, Samford, 1989 (50 returns)

**Career**

2,439—Clarence Alexander, Mississippi Val., 1986-89 (118 returns)

### Most Yards Per Game on Kickoff Returns

**Season**

128.3—David Primus, Samford, 1989 (1,411 in 11)

**Career**

60.98—Clarence Alexander, Mississippi Val., 1986-89 (2,439 in 40)

### Highest Average Gain Per Return

**Game**

*(Min. 5 rets.)* 45.6—Jerome Stelly, Western Ill. vs. Youngstown St., Nov. 7, 1981 (5 for 228)

**Season**

*(Min. 1.2 rets. per game)* 34.7—Craig Richardson, Eastern Wash., 1984 (21 for 729)

**Career (Min. 1.2 Returns Per Game)**

*(Min. 30-44 rets.)* 29.7—Troy Brown, Marshall, 1991-92 (32 for 950)

*(Min. 45 rets.)* 29.3—Charles Swann, Indiana St., 1989-91 (45 for 1,319)

### Most Touchdowns Scored on Kickoff Returns

**Game**

2—Kerry Hayes, Western Caro. vs. Va. Military, Oct. 10, 1992 (90 & 94 yards); Paul Ashby, Alabama St. vs. Grambling, Nov. 9, 1991 (97 & 94 yards); David Lucas, Florida A&M vs. North Caro. A&T, Oct. 12, 1991 (99 & 93 yards); Jerome Stelly, Western Ill. vs. Youngstown St., Nov. 7, 1981 (99 & 97 yards)

**Season**

3—Troy Brown, Marshall, 1991; David Lucas, Florida A&M, 1991

**Career**

3—By nine players. Most recent: Troy Brown, Marshall, 1992; Chris Pierce, Rhode Island, 1992

# TOTAL KICK RETURNS

### (Combined Punt and Kickoff Returns)

### Most Kick Returns

**Game**

12—Craig Hodge, Tennessee St. vs. Morgan St., Oct. 24, 1987 (8 punts, 4 kickoffs, 318 yards)

**Season**

64—Joe Markus, Connecticut, 1981 (34 punts, 30 kickoffs, 939 yards)

**Career**

199—Herman Hunter, Tennessee St., 1981-84 (103 punts, 96 kickoffs, 3,232 yards)

### Most Yards on Kick Returns

**Game**

319—Craig Hodge, Tennessee St. vs. Morgan St., Oct. 24, 1987 (12 returns, 206 on punts, 113 on kickoffs)

**Season**

1,469—David Primus, Samford, 1989 (1,411 on kickoffs, 58 on punts)

Also holds per-game record at 133.5 (1,469 in 11)

Northern Iowa's Kenny Shedd last season became only the second Division I-AA player to gain more than 1,000 yards on both kickoff returns and punt returns in a career. Shedd finished with 1,081 in punt returns and 1,359 in kickoff returns, including a record-tying seven touchdowns. The versatile flanker also was among the 1992 Division I-AA leaders in all-purpose yardage (158.6 yards per game) and receiving yards per game (84.2).

**Career**
3,232—Herman Hunter, Tennessee St., 1981-84 (974 on punts, 2,258 on kickoffs)
Also holds per-game record at 75.2 (3,232 in 43)

**Gaining 1,000 Yards on Punt Returns and 1,000 Yards on Kickoff Returns**
**Career**
Kenny Shedd, Northern Iowa, 1989-92 (1,081 on punts and 1,359 on kickoffs); Joe Markus, Connecticut, 1979-82 (1,012 on punts and 1,185 on kickoffs)

**Highest Average Per Kick Return**
**Game**
*(Min. 6 rets.)* 42.3—Herman Hunter, Tennessee St. vs. Mississippi Val., Nov. 13, 1982 (7 for 296)

**Season**
*(Min. 40 rets.)* 26.7—David Primus, Samford, 1989 (55 for 1,469)
**Career**
*(Min. 60 rets.)* 20.9—Bill LaFreniere, Northeastern, 1978-81 (112 for 2,336)

**Most Touchdowns Scored on Kick Returns**
**Season**
4—Troy Brown, Marshall, 1991 (3 kickoffs and 1 punt); Howard Huckaby, Florida A&M, 1988 (4 punts); Willie Ware, Mississippi Val., 1985 (2 punts and 2 kickoffs)
**Career**
7—Kenny Shedd, Northern Iowa, 1989-92 (7 punts); Willie Ware, Mississippi Val., 1982-85 (5 punts and 2 kickoffs)

## ALL-PURPOSE RUNNING
### (Yardage Gained From Rushing, Receiving and All Runbacks)
### Most Plays
**Game**
54—Ron Darby, Marshall vs. Western Caro., Nov. 12, 1988 (47 rushes, 4 receptions, 3 kickoff returns; 329 yards)
**Season**
364—Toby Davis, Illinois St., 1992 (341 rushes, 17 receptions, 6 kickoff returns; 1,762 yards)

**Career**
1,096—Kenny Gamble, Colgate, 1984-87 (963 rushes, 43 receptions, 10 punt returns, 80 kickoff returns; 7,623 yards)

### Most Yards Gained
**Game**
463—Michael Lerch, Princeton vs. Brown, Oct.

12, 1991 (15 rushing, 370 receiving, 78 kickoff returns; 16 plays)

**Season**

2,425—Kenny Gamble, Colgate, 1986 (1,816 rushing, 178 receiving, 40 punt returns, 391 kickoff returns; 343 plays)

**Career**

7,623—Kenny Gamble, Colgate, 1984-87 (5,220 rushing, 536 receiving, 104 punt returns, 1,763 kickoff returns; 1,096 plays)

### Most Yards Gained Per Game

**Season**

220.5—Kenny Gamble, Colgate, 1986 (2,425 in 11)

**Career**

189.1—David Meggett, Towson St., 1987-88 (3,403 in 18)

### Most Yards Gained by a Freshman

**Season**

2,014—David Wright, Indiana St., 1992 (1,313 rushing, 108 receiving, 593 kickoff returns; 254 plays)

### Highest Average Gain Per Play

**Game**

*(Min. 20 plays)* 20.6—Herman Hunter, Tennessee St. vs. Mississippi Val., Nov. 13, 1982 (453 on 22)

**Season**

*(Min. 1,000 yards, 100 plays)* 19.68—Otis Washington, Western Caro., 1988 (2,086 on 106)

**Career**

*(Min. 4,000 yards, 350 plays)* 14.8—Pete Mandley, Northern Ariz., 1979-80, 1982-83 (5,925 on 401)

# SCORING

### Most Points Scored

**Game**

36—By five players. Most recent: Erwin Matthews, Richmond vs. Massachusetts, Sept. 19, 1987 (6 TDs, including 1 TD and 6 points in OT)

**Season**

170—Geoff Mitchell, Weber St., 1991 (28 TDs, 2 PATs)

**Career**

385—Marty Zendejas, Nevada, 1984-87 (72 FGs, 169 PATs)

### Most Points Scored Per Game

**Season**

16.2—Jerry Rice, Mississippi Val., 1984 (162 in 10)

**Career**

10.0—David Meggett, Towson St., 1987-88 (180 in 18)

### Most Touchdowns Scored

**Game**

6—By five players. Most recent: Erwin Matthews, Richmond vs. Massachusetts, Sept. 19, 1987 (1 TD in OT)

**Season**

28—Geoff Mitchell, Weber St., 1991

**Career**

60—Charvez Foger, Nevada, 1985-88

### Most Touchdowns Scored Per Game

**Season**

2.7—Jerry Rice, Mississippi Val., 1984 (27 in 10)

**Career**

1.67—David Meggett, Towson St., 1987-88 (30 in 18)

### Most Touchdowns Scored by a Freshman

**Season**

18—Charvez Foger, Nevada, 1985

Also holds per-game record at 1.8 (18 in 10)

### Most Extra Points Attempted by Kicking

**Game**

15—John Kincheloe, Portland St. vs. Delaware St., Nov. 8, 1980 (15 made)

**Season**

74—John Kincheloe, Portland St., 1980 (70 made)

Per-game record—7.2, Jonathan Stokes, Mississippi Val., 1984 (72 in 10)

**Career**

175—Thayne Doyle, Idaho, 1988-91 (160 made); Marty Zendejas, Nevada, 1984-87 (169 made)

### Most Extra Points Made by Kicking

**Game**

15—John Kincheloe, Portland St. vs. Delaware St., Nov. 8, 1980 (15 attempts)

**Season**

70—John Kincheloe, Portland St., 1980 (74 attempts)

Per-game record—6.8, Jonathan Stokes, Mississippi Val., 1984 (68 in 10)

**Career**

169—Marty Zendejas, Nevada, 1984-87 (175 attempts)

Also holds per-game record at 3.84 (169 in 44)

### Best Perfect Record of Extra Points Made

**Season**

51 of 51—Jim Hodson, Lafayette, 1988

### Highest Percentage of Extra Points Made

**Career**

*(Min. 100-119 atts.)* 100%—Anders Larsson, Montana St., 1985-88 (101 of 101)

*(Min. 120 atts.)* 99.2%—Brian Mitchell, Marshall/Northern Iowa, 1987, 1989-91 (130 of 131)

### Most Consecutive Extra Points Made

**Game**

15—John Kincheloe, Portland St. vs. Delaware St., Nov. 8, 1980

**Season**

51—Jim Hodson, Lafayette, 1988

**Career**

121—Brian Mitchell, Marshall/Northern Iowa, 1987, 1989-91

### Most Points Scored by Kicking

**Game**

24—Goran Lingmerth, Northern Ariz. vs. Idaho, Oct. 25, 1986 (8 FGs)

**Season**

109—Brian Mitchell, Northern Iowa, 1990 (26 FGs, 31 PATs)

**Career**

385—Marty Zendejas, Nevada, 1984-87 (72 FGs, 169 PATs)

### Most Points Scored by Kicking Per Game

**Season**

9.9—Brian Mitchell, Northern Iowa, 1990 (109 in 11)

**Career**

9.09—Tony Zendejas, Nevada, 1981-83 (300 in 33)

### Most Defensive Extra-Point Returns, One Game, Single Player

2—Joe Lee Johnson, Western Ky. vs. Indiana

St., Nov. 10, 1990 (both kick returns, scored on neither)

### Most Defensive Extra Points Scored
**Game**
1—By many players
**Season**
2—Jackie Kellogg, Eastern Wash. vs. Weber St., Oct. 6, 1990 (90-yard interception return) & vs. Portland St., Oct. 27, 1990 (94-yard interception return)

### Longest Return of a Defensive Extra Point
100—Rich Kinsman (DB), William & Mary vs. Lehigh, Nov. 14, 1992; Morgan Ryan (DB), Montana St. vs. Sam Houston St., Sept. 7, 1991 (interception return)

### First Defensive Extra-Point Attempts
Mike Rogers (DB), Davidson vs. Lehigh, Sept.

10, 1988 (30-yard interception return); Dave Benna (LB), Towson St. vs. Northeastern, Sept. 10, 1988 (35-yard interception return)

### Most Two-Point Attempts
**Season**
11—Jamie Martin, Weber St., 1990; Brent Woods, Princeton, 1982

### Most Successful Two-Point Passes
**Game**
3—Brent Woods, Princeton vs. Lafayette, Nov. 6, 1982 (attempted 3)
**Season**
7—Jamie Martin, Weber St., 1992 (attempted 7)
**Career**
15—Jamie Martin, Weber St., 1989-92 (attempted 28)

# KICK BLOCKS

### Most Kicks Blocked
**Game**
3—Adrian Hardy, Northwestern (La.) vs. Arkansas St., Oct. 3, 1992 (2 PATs, 1 FG)

**Career**
9—Adrian Hardy, Northwestern (La.), 1989-92 (3 PATs, 6 FGs)

# FIELD GOALS

### Most Field Goals Attempted
**Game**
8—Goran Lingmerth, Northern Ariz. vs. Idaho, Oct. 25, 1986 (made 8)
**Season**
33—Tony Zendejas, Nevada, 1982 (made 26)
**Career**
102—Kirk Roach, Western Caro., 1984-87 (made 71)

### Most Field Goals Made
**Quarter**
4—Ryan Weeks, Tennessee Tech vs. Tenn.-Chatt., Sept. 9, 1989 (3rd); Tony Zendejas, Nevada vs. Northern Ariz., Oct. 16, 1982 (4th)
**Half**
5—Ryan Weeks, Tennessee Tech vs. Tenn.-Chatt., Sept. 9, 1989 (2nd); Tony Zendejas, Nevada vs. Northern Ariz., Oct. 16, 1982 (2nd); Dean Biasucci, Western Caro. vs. Mars Hill, Sept. 18, 1982 (1st)
**Game**
8—Goran Lingmerth, Northern Ariz. vs. Idaho, Oct. 25, 1986 (39, 18, 20, 33, 46, 27, 22, 35 yards; by quarters—1, 3, 2, 2), 8 attempts
**Season**
26—Brian Mitchell, Northern Iowa, 1990 (27 attempts); Tony Zendejas, Nevada, 1982 (33 attempts)
**Career**
72—Marty Zendejas, Nevada, 1984-87 (90 attempts)

### Most Field Goals Made Per Game
**Season**
2.36—Brian Mitchell, Northern Iowa, 1990 (26 in 11); Tony Zendejas, Nevada, 1982 (26 in 11)
**Career**
2.12—Tony Zendejas, Nevada, 1981-83 (70 in 33)

### Highest Percentage of Field Goals Made
**Season**
*(Min. 20 atts.)* 96.3%—Brian Mitchell, Northern Iowa, 1990 (26 of 27)

**Career**
*(Min. 50 atts.)* 81.4%—Tony Zendejas, Nevada, 1981-83 (70 of 86)

### Most Consecutive Field Goals Made
**Game**
8—Goran Lingmerth, Northern Ariz. vs. Idaho, Oct. 25, 1986
**Season**
21—Brian Mitchell, Northern Iowa, 1990
**Career**
26—Brian Mitchell, Northern Iowa, 1990-91

### Most Consecutive Games Kicking a Field Goal
**Career**
33—Tony Zendejas, Nevada, 1981-83 (at least one in every game played)

### Most Field Goals Made, 50 Yards or More
**Game**
3—Jesse Garcia, Northeast La. vs. McNeese St., Oct. 29, 1983 (52, 56, 53 yards)
**Season**
7—Kirk Roach, Western Caro., 1987 (12 attempts); Jesse Garcia, Northeast La., 1983 (12 attempts)
**Career**
11—Kirk Roach, Western Caro., 1984-87 (26 attempts)

### Highest Percentage of Field Goals Made, 50 Yards or More
**Season**
*(Min. 6 atts.)* 83.3%—Tim Foley, Ga. Southern, 1987 (5 of 6)
**Career**
*(Min. 10 atts.)* 90.9%—Tim Foley, Ga. Southern, 1984-87 (10 of 11)

### Most Field Goals Made, 40 Yards or More
**Season**
12—Marty Zendejas, Nevada, 1985 (15 attempts)
**Career**
30—Marty Zendejas, Nevada, 1984-87 (45 attempts)

### Highest Percentage of Field Goals Made, 40 Yards or More
**Season**
*(Min. 8 made)* 100.0%—Tim Foley, Ga. Southern, 1985 (8 of 8)
**Career**
*(Min. 15 made)* 72.0%—Tim Foley, Ga. Southern, 1984-87 (18 of 25)

### Highest Percentage of Field Goals Made, 40-49 Yards
**Season**
*(Min. 8 made)* 90.0%—Marty Zendejas, Nevada, 1985 (9 of 10)
**Career**
*(Min. 12 made)* 72.0%—Tony Zendejas, Nevada, 1981-83 (18 of 25)

### Highest Percentage of Field Goals Made, Under 40 Yards
**Season**
*(Min. 15 made)* 100.0%—Brian Mitchell, Northern Iowa, 1990 (23 of 23); Kirk Roach, Western Caro., 1986 (17 of 17); Matt Stover, Louisiana Tech, 1986 (15 of 15)
**Career**
*(Min. 25 made)* 93.3%—Marty Zendejas, Nevada, 1984-87 (42 of 45)

### Most Times Kicking Two or More Field Goals in a Game
**Season**
10—Brian Mitchell, Northern Iowa, 1991
**Career**
25—Kirk Roach, Western Caro., 1984-87

### Most Times Kicking Three or More Field Goals in a Game
**Season**
7—Brian Mitchell, Northern Iowa, 1991
**Career**
11—Brian Mitchell, Marshall/Northern Iowa, 1987, 1989-91

### Most Consecutive Quarters Kicking a Field Goal
**Season**
7—Scott Roper, Arkansas St., 1986 (last 3 vs. McNeese St., Oct. 25; all 4 vs. North Texas, Nov. 1)

### Longest Average Distance Field Goals Made
**Game**
*(Min. 3 made)* 53.7—Jesse Garcia, Northeast La. vs. McNeese St., Oct. 29, 1983 (52, 56, 53 yards)
**Season**
*(Min. 14 made)* 45.0—Jesse Garcia, Northeast La., 1983 (15 made)
**Career**
*(Min. 35 made)* 37.5—Roger Ruzek, Weber St., 1979-82 (46 made)

### Longest Average Distance Field Goals Attempted
**Season**
*(Min. 20 atts.)* 45.9—Jesse Garcia, Northeast La., 1983 (26 attempts)
**Career**
*(Min. 60 atts.)* 40.5—Kirk Roach, Western Caro., 1984-87 (102 attempts)

### Longest Field Goal Made
63—Scott Roper, Arkansas St. vs. North Texas, Nov. 7, 1987; Tim Foley, Ga. Southern vs. James Madison, Nov. 7, 1987

### Longest Field Goal Made by a Freshman
60—David Cool, Ga. Southern vs. James Madison, Nov. 5, 1988

### Most Field Goals Made by a Freshman
**Game**
5—Chuck Rawlinson, Stephen F. Austin vs. Prairie View, Sept. 10, 1988 (5 attempts); Marty Zendejas, Nevada vs. Idaho St., Nov. 17, 1984 (5 attempts); Mike Powers, Colgate vs. Army, Sept. 10, 1983 (6 attempts)
**Season**
22—Marty Zendejas, Nevada, 1984 (27 attempts)

### Most Field Goals Made in First Game of a Career
5—Mike Powers, Colgate vs. Army, Sept. 10, 1983 (6 attempts)

### Most Games in Which Field Goal(s) Provided the Winning Margin
**Career**
11—John Dowling, Youngstown St., 1984-87

### Longest Return of a Missed Field Goal
89—Pat Bayers, Western Ill. vs. Youngstown St., Nov. 6, 1982 (TD)

# TEAM RECORDS

## SINGLE GAME—OFFENSE
### TOTAL OFFENSE

**Most Plays**
113—Villanova vs. Connecticut, Oct. 7, 1989 (553 yards)

**Most Plays, Both Teams**
196—Villanova (113) & Connecticut (83), Oct. 7, 1989 (904 yards)

**Most Yards Gained**
876—Weber St. vs. Idaho St., Nov. 23, 1991 (252 rushing, 624 passing)

**Most Yards Gained, Both Teams**
1,418—Howard (740) & Bethune-Cookman (678), Sept. 19, 1987 (161 plays)

**Most Yards Gained by a Losing Team**
678—Bethune-Cookman vs. Howard, Sept. 19, 1987 (lost 51-58)

**Fewest Yards Gained by a Winning Team**
31—Middle Tenn. St. vs. Murray St., Oct. 17, 1981 (won 14-9)

**Highest Average Gain Per Play (Min. 55 Plays)**
12.7—Marshall vs. Va. Military, Nov. 16, 1991 (62 for 789)

**Most Touchdowns Scored by Rushing and Passing**
14—Portland St. vs. Delaware St., Nov. 8, 1980 (10 passing, 4 rushing)

# RUSHING

**Most Rushes**
90—Va. Military vs. East Tenn. St., Nov. 17, 1990 (311 yards)

**Most Rushes, Both Teams**
125—Austin Peay (81) & Murray St. (44), Nov. 17, 1990 (443 yards); Southwest Mo. St. (71) & Northern Ill. (54), Oct. 17, 1987 (375 yards)

**Fewest Rushes**
11—Western Ill. vs. Northern Iowa, Oct. 24, 1987 (-11 yards); Mississippi Val. vs. Kentucky St., Sept. 1, 1984 (17 yards)

**Most Yards Gained**
681—Southwest Mo. St. vs. Mo. Southern St., Sept. 10, 1988 (83 rushes)

**Most Yards Gained, Both Teams**
762—Arkansas St. (604) & East Tex. St. (158), Sept. 26, 1987 (102 rushes)

**Most Yards Gained by a Losing Team**
429—Nevada vs. Weber St., Nov. 6, 1982 (lost 43-46, 3 OT)

**Highest Average Gain Per Rush (Min. 45 Rushes)**
11.2—Southwest Mo. St. vs. Northeast Mo. St., Oct. 5, 1985 (45 for 505)

**Most Touchdowns Scored by Rushing**
10—Arkansas St. vs. East Tex. St., Sept. 26, 1987

# PASSING

**Most Passes Attempted**
77—Portland St. vs. Northern Colo., Oct. 20, 1979 (completed 44 for 499 yards)

**Most Passes Attempted, Both Teams**
122—Idaho (62) & Idaho St. (60), Sept. 24, 1983 (completed 48 for 639 yards)

**Fewest Passes Attempted**
1—By many teams. Most recent: Northeastern vs. Towson St., Sept. 9, 1989 (completed 1)

**Fewest Passes Attempted, Both Teams**
11—Western Ky. (6) & North Caro. A&T (5), Nov. 19, 1988 (completed 2); Arkansas St. (8) & Memphis St. (3), Nov. 27, 1982 (completed 6)

**Most Passes Attempted Without Interception**
72—Marshall vs. Western Caro., Nov. 14, 1987 (completed 35)

**Most Passes Completed**
50—Mississippi Val. vs. Prairie View, Oct. 27, 1984 (attempted 66 for 642 yards); Mississippi Val. vs. Southern-B.R., Sept. 29, 1984 (attempted 70 for 633 yards)

**Most Passes Completed, Both Teams I-AA**
77—Northeast La. (46) & Stephen F. Austin (31), Nov. 11, 1989 (attempted 116 for 1,190 yards)

**Most Passes Completed, Both Teams**
80—Hofstra (50) & Fordham (30), Oct. 19, 1991 (attempted 120 for 987 yards)

**Fewest Passes Completed**
0—By many teams. Most recent: Citadel vs. East Tenn. St., Sept. 19, 1992; Delaware St. vs. North Caro. A&T, Nov. 9, 1991

**Fewest Passes Completed, Both Teams**
2—North Caro. A&T (0) & Western Ky. (2), Nov. 19, 1988 (attempted 11)

**Highest Percentage Completed**
*(Min. 30-44 atts.)* 81.6%—Nevada vs. Idaho St., Nov. 17, 1984 (31 of 38)
*(Min. 45 atts.)* 75.7%—Mississippi Val. vs. Prairie View, Oct. 27, 1984 (50 of 66)

**Lowest Percentage Completed (Min. 20 Attempts)**
9.5%—Florida A&M vs. Central St. (Ohio), Oct. 11, 1986 (2 of 21)

**Most Passes Had Intercepted**
10—Boise St. vs. Montana, Oct. 28, 1989 (55 attempts); Mississippi Val. vs. Grambling, Oct. 17, 1987 (47 attempts)

**Most Yards Gained**
699—Mississippi Val. vs. Kentucky St., Sept. 1, 1984

**Most Yards Gained, Both Teams**
1,190—Northeast La. (619) & Stephen F. Austin (571), Nov. 11, 1989

**Most Yards Gained Per Attempt (Min. 25 Attempts)**
17.4—Marshall vs. Va. Military, Nov. 16, 1991 (37 for 642)

**Most Yards Gained Per Completion**
*(Min. 10-24 comps.)* 33.0—Jackson St. vs. Southern-B. R., Oct. 13, 1990 (14 for 462)
*(Min. 25 comps.)* 22.9—Marshall vs. Va. Military, Nov. 16, 1991 (28 for 642)

**Most Touchdown Passes**
11—Mississippi Val. vs. Kentucky St., Sept. 1, 1984

**Most Touchdown Passes, Both Teams**
14—Mississippi Val. (8) & Texas Southern (6), Oct. 26, 1985

# PUNTING

**Most Punts**
16—Louisiana Tech vs. Northeast La., Nov. 19, 1988 (567 yards)

**Highest Average Per Punt (Min. 5 Punts)**
55.7—Appalachian St. vs. Citadel, Oct. 3, 1992 (6 for 334); Montana vs. Nevada, Oct. 1, 1988 (9 for 501)

**Highest Average Per Punt (Min. 10 Punts)**
52.2—Montana St. vs. Northern Ariz., Oct. 20, 1979 (10 for 522)

**Fewest Punts**
0—By many teams. Most recent: Southwest Mo. St. vs. Southern Ill., Nov. 7, 1992; Dartmouth vs. Brown, Nov. 16, 1991

**Fewest Punts, Both Teams**
0—Ga. Southern & James Madison, Nov. 15, 1986

**Most Opponent's Punts Blocked By**
4—Middle Tenn. St. vs. Mississippi Val., Oct. 8, 1988 (7 punts); Montana vs. Montana St., Oct. 31, 1987 (13 punts)

# PUNT RETURNS

**Most Punt Returns**
12—Northern Iowa vs. Youngstown St., Oct. 20, 1984 (83 yards)

**Most Yards on Punt Returns**
221—Howard vs. Morgan St., Nov. 3, 1990 (8 returns)

**Highest Average Gain Per Return (Min. 6 Returns)**
30.9—Mississippi Val. vs. Washburn, Sept. 15, 1984 (7 for 216, 2 TDs)

**Most Touchdowns Scored on Punt Returns**
2—By nine teams. Most recent: Lehigh vs. Davidson, Sept. 10, 1988 (includes a blocked punt return)

# KICKOFF RETURNS

**Most Kickoff Returns**
15—Delaware St. vs. Portland St., Nov. 8, 1980 (209 yards)

**Most Yards on Kickoff Returns**
277—Idaho St. vs. Texas A&I, Sept. 12, 1987 (10 returns)

**Highest Average Gain Per Return**
*(Min. 3-5 rets.)* 50.5—Eastern Ky. vs. Murray St., Oct. 28, 1978 (4 for 202)
*(Min. 6 rets.)* 46.3—Western Caro. vs. Va. Military, Oct. 10, 1992 (6 for 278)

**Most Touchdowns Scored on Kickoff Returns**
2—Western Caro. vs. Va. Military, Oct. 10, 1992; Western Ill. vs. Youngstown St., Nov. 7, 1981

# TOTAL KICK RETURNS
## (Combined Punt and Kickoff Returns)

**Most Yards on Kick Returns**
318—Tennessee St. vs. Morgan St., Oct. 24, 1987 (12 returns)

**Highest Average Gain Per Return (Min. 6 Returns)**
46.8—Connecticut vs. Yale, Sept. 24, 1983 (6 for 281)

# SCORING

**Most Points Scored**
105—Portland St. vs. Delaware St., Nov. 8, 1980 (15 TDs, 15 PATs)

**Most Points Scored, Both Teams**
122—Weber St. (63) & Eastern Wash. (59), Sept. 28, 1991 (17 TDs, 14 PATs, 2 FGs)

**Most Points Scored by a Losing Team**
59—Eastern Wash. vs. Weber St. (63), Sept. 28, 1991

**Most Points Scored Each Quarter**
*1st:* 49—Portland St. vs. Delaware St., Nov. 8, 1980
*2nd:* 50—Alabama St. vs. Prairie View, Oct. 26, 1991
*3rd:* 35—Portland St. vs. Delaware St., Nov. 8, 1980
*4th:* 35—Southeastern La. vs. Delta St., Nov. 8, 1980

**Most Points Scored Each Half**
*1st:* 73—Montana St. vs. Eastern Ore., Sept. 14, 1985
*2nd:* 49—Northern Iowa vs. Wis.-Whitewater, Oct. 13, 1984; Southeastern La. vs. Delta St., Nov. 8, 1980

**Most Touchdowns Scored**
15—Portland St. vs. Delaware St., Nov. 8, 1980

**Most Touchdowns Scored, Both Teams**
17—Weber St. (9) & Eastern Wash. (8), Sept. 28, 1991; Furman (9) & Davidson (8), Nov. 3, 1979

**Most Extra Points Made by Kicking**
15—Portland St. vs. Delaware St., Nov. 8, 1980 (15 attempts)

**Most Two-Point Attempts Made**
5—Weber St. vs. Eastern Wash., Oct. 6, 1990 (5 passes attempted)

**Most Field Goals Made**
8—Northern Ariz. vs. Idaho, Oct. 25, 1986 (8 attempts)

**Most Field Goals Attempted**
8—Northern Ariz. vs. Idaho, Oct. 25, 1986 (made 8)

**Most Field Goals Made, Both Teams**
9—Nevada (5) & Weber St. (4), Nov. 6, 1982 (11 attempts, 3 OT); Nevada (5) & Northern Ariz. (4), Oct. 9, 1982 (12 attempts)

**Most Safeties Scored**
3—Alabama St. vs. Albany St. (Ga.), Oct. 15, 1988

**Most Defensive Extra Points Scored**
2—Va. Military vs. Davidson, Nov. 4, 1989 (Jeff Barnes, 95-yard interception return, and Wayne Purcell, 90-yard interception return)

**Most Defensive Extra-Point Attempts**
2—Western Ky. vs. Indiana St., Nov. 10, 1990 (2 interception returns); Va. Military vs. Davidson, Nov. 4, 1989 (2 interception returns)

# FIRST DOWNS

**Most First Downs**
46—Weber St. vs. Idaho St., Nov. 23, 1991 (12 rushing, 31 passing, 3 penalty)

**Most First Downs, Both Teams**
72—Bethune-Cookman (40) & Howard (32), Sept. 19, 1987

**Most First Downs by Rushing**
29—By six teams. Most recent: Arkansas St. vs. Southern Ill., Nov. 5, 1988; Southwest Mo. St. vs. Mo. Southern St., Sept. 10, 1988

**Most First Downs by Passing**
31—Weber St. vs. Idaho St., Nov. 23, 1991

**Most First Downs by Penalty**
11—Towson St. vs. Liberty, Oct. 21, 1990

## FUMBLES

**Most Fumbles**
16—Delaware St. vs. Portland St., Nov. 8, 1980 (lost 6)

**Most Fumbles, Both Teams**
20—Prairie View (11) & Southern-B.R. (9), Sept. 24, 1983 (lost 7); Morgan St. (11) & South Caro. St. (9), Oct. 14, 1978 (lost 9)

**Most Fumbles Lost**
8—By four teams. Most recent: Morgan St. vs. North Caro. A&T, Sept. 22, 1990 (12 fumbles)

**Most Fumbles Lost, Both Teams**
12—Austin Peay (8) & Mars Hill (4), Nov. 17, 1979 (18 fumbles); Virginia St. (7) & Howard (5), Oct. 13, 1979 (16 fumbles)

## PENALTIES

**Most Penalties Against**
23—Idaho vs. Idaho St., Oct. 10, 1992 (204 yards)

**Most Penalties, Both Teams**
39—In four games. Most recent: Jackson St. (22) & Grambling (17), Oct. 24, 1987 (370 yards)

**Most Yards Penalized**
260—Southern-B.R. vs. Howard, Nov. 4, 1978 (22 penalties)

**Most Yards Penalized, Both Teams**
423—Southern-B.R. (260) & Howard (163), Nov. 4, 1978 (37 penalties)

## TURNOVERS
### (Passes Had Intercepted and Fumbles Lost)

**Most Turnovers**
12—Texas Southern vs. Lamar, Sept. 6, 1980 (4 interceptions, 8 fumbles lost)

**Most Turnovers, Both Teams**
15—Stephen F. Austin (8) & Nicholls St. (7), Sept. 22, 1990 (8 interceptions, 7 fumbles lost); Bucknell (8) & Hofstra (7), Sept. 8, 1990 (10 interceptions, 5 fumbles lost)

# SINGLE GAME—DEFENSE
## TOTAL DEFENSE

**Fewest Plays Allowed**
31—Howard vs. Dist. Columbia, Sept. 2, 1989 (32 yards)

**Fewest Yards Allowed**
Minus 12—Eastern Ill. vs. Kentucky St., Nov. 13, 1982 (-67 rushing, 55 passing)

## RUSHING DEFENSE

**Fewest Rushes Allowed**
10—Ga. Southern vs. Valdosta St., Sept. 12, 1992 (21 yards)

**Fewest Rushing Yards Allowed**
Minus 88—Austin Peay vs. Morehead St., Oct. 8, 1983 (31 rushes)

## PASS DEFENSE

**Fewest Attempts Allowed**
1—By five teams. Most recent: Towson St. vs. Northeastern, Sept. 9, 1989 (1 completed)

**Fewest Completions Allowed**
0—By many teams. Most recent: Colgate vs. Army, Nov. 18, 1989 (2 attempts); Illinois St. vs. Arkansas St., Nov. 11, 1989 (3 attempts); Marshall vs. Va. Military, Oct. 28, 1989 (4 attempts)

**Lowest Completion Percentage Allowed (Min. 30 Attempts)**
11.8%—Southern-B.R. vs. Nicholls St., Oct. 11, 1980 (4 of 34)

**Fewest Yards Allowed**
Minus 2—Florida A&M vs. Albany St. (Ga.),

Oct. 16, 1982

**Most Passes Intercepted By**
10—Montana vs. Boise St., Oct. 28, 1989 (55 attempts); Grambling vs. Mississippi Val., Oct. 17, 1987 (47 attempts)

**Most Times Opponent Tackled for Loss Attempting to Pass**
13—Austin Peay vs. Morehead St., Oct. 8, 1983 (110 yards)

**Most Interceptions Returned for Touchdowns**
3—Delaware St. vs. Akron, Oct. 17, 1987 (5 for 124 yards); Montana vs. Eastern Wash., Nov. 12, 1983 (4 for 134 yards); Tenn.-Chatt. vs. Southwestern La., Sept. 17, 1983 (4 for 122 yards)

## KICK BLOCKS

**Most Kicks Blocked**
3—Northwestern (La.) vs. Arkansas St., Oct. 3, 1992 (2 PATs, 1 FG)

**Most Punts Blocked**
4—Middle Tenn. St. vs. Mississippi Val., Oct. 8, 1988 (7 punts); Montana vs. Montana St., Oct. 31, 1987 (13 punts)

# SEASON—OFFENSE

## TOTAL OFFENSE

**Most Yards Gained Per Game**
640.1—Mississippi Val., 1984 (6,401 in 10)

**Highest Average Gain Per Play**
7.39—Mississippi Val., 1984 (866 for 6,401)

**Most Plays Per Game**
89.6—Weber St., 1991 (986 in 11)

**Most Touchdowns by Rushing and Passing Per Game**
8.4—Mississippi Val., 1984 (84 in 10)

## RUSHING

**Most Yards Gained Per Game**
381.6—Howard, 1987 (3,816 in 10)

**Highest Average Gain Per Rush**
6.60—Howard, 1987 (578 for 3,816)

**Most Rushes Per Game**
69.8—Northeastern, 1986 (698 in 10)

**Most Touchdowns by Rushing Per Game**
4.5—Howard, 1987 (45 in 10)

## PASSING

**Most Yards Gained Per Game**
496.8—Mississippi Val., 1984 (4,968 in 10)

**Highest Average Gain Per Attempt**
*(Min. 250-399 atts.)* 10.17—Marshall, 1991 (298 for 3,032)
*(Min. 400 atts.)* 9.25—Idaho, 1989 (445 for 4,117)

**Highest Average Gain Per Completion**
*(Min. 125-199 comps.)* 19.27—Jackson St., 1990 (156 for 3,006)
*(Min. 200 comps.)* 16.6—Stephen F. Austin, 1989 (240 for 3,985)

**Most Passes Attempted Per Game**
55.8—Mississippi Val., 1984 (558 in 10)

**Most Passes Completed Per Game**
35.1—Mississippi Val., 1984 (351 in 10)

**Highest Percentage Completed**
*(Min. 200-449 atts.)* 68.4%—Princeton, 1988 (206 of 301)
*(Min. 450 atts.)* 62.9%—Mississippi Val., 1984 (351 of 558)

**Lowest Percentage Had Intercepted**
*(Min. 200-399 atts.)* 1.00%—Princeton, 1988 (3 of 301)
*(Min. 400 atts.)* 1.22%—Lamar, 1988 (5 of 411)

**Most Consecutive Passes Attempted Without an Interception**
275—Lamar, 1988 (during 8 games, Sept. 3 to Oct. 29)

**Most Touchdown Passes Per Game**
6.4—Mississippi Val., 1984 (64 in 10)

**Highest Passing Efficiency Rating Points**
173.5—Marshall, 1991 (298 attempts, 186 completions, 8 interceptions, 3,032 yards, 28 TDs)

## PUNTING

**Most Punts Per Game**
9.64—Louisiana Tech, 1987 (106 in 11)

**Fewest Punts Per Game**
2.4—Howard, 1987 (24 in 10)

**Highest Punting Average**
47.0—Appalachian St., 1991 (64 for 3,009)

**Highest Net Punting Average**
42.8—Western Caro., 1984 (49 for 2,127 yards; 32 yards returned)

**Most Punts Had Blocked**
8—Western Ky., 1982

## PUNT RETURNS

**Most Punt Returns Per Game**
5.4—Murray St., 1980 (59 in 11)

**Fewest Punt Returns Per Game**
0.64—Southern Ill., 1991 (7 in 11); Prairie View, 1991 (7 in 11); Youngstown St., 1990 (7 in 11)

**Most Punt-Return Yards Per Game**
56.1—South Caro. St., 1981 (617 in 11)

**Highest Average Gain Per Punt Return**
*(Min. 20-29 rets.)* 18.6—Richmond, 1985 (23 for 427)
*(Min. 30 rets.)* 18.1—Mississippi Val., 1985 (31 for 561)

**Most Touchdowns Scored on Punt Returns**
5—Southern Ill., 1985

## KICKOFF RETURNS

**Most Kickoff Returns Per Game**
7.0—Prairie View, 1991 (77 in 11; 1,128 yards); Idaho St., 1987 (77 in 11; 1,577 yards); Davidson, 1986 (63 in 9; 1,104 yards)

**Fewest Kickoff Returns Per Game**
1.4—North Texas, 1983 (15 in 11)

**Most Kickoff-Return Yards Per Game**
143.4—Idaho St., 1987 (1,577 in 11; 77 returns)

**Highest Average Gain Per Kickoff Return (Min. 20 Returns)**
29.5—Eastern Ky., 1986 (34 for 1,022)

# COMBINED RETURNS
### (Interceptions, Punt Returns and Kickoff Returns)

**Most Touchdowns Scored**
9—Delaware St., 1987 (5 interceptions, 3 punt returns, 1 kickoff return)

## SCORING

**Most Points Per Game**
60.9—Mississippi Val., 1984 (609 in 10)

**Most Touchdowns Per Game**
8.7—Mississippi Val., 1984 (87 in 10)

**Most Extra Points Made by Kicking Per Game**
7.7—Mississippi Val., 1984 (77 in 10)

**Most Consecutive Extra Points Made by Kicking**
51—Lafayette, 1988

**Most Two-Point Attempts Made**
9—Weber St., 1992 (11 attempts)

**Most Defensive Extra-Point Attempts**
2—Western Ky., 1990; Eastern Wash., 1990; Va. Military, 1989

**Most Defensive Extra Points Scored**
2—Eastern Wash., 1990 (2 interception returns); Va. Military, 1989 (2 interception returns)

**Most Field Goals Made Per Game**
2.4—Northern Iowa, 1990 (26 in 11); Nevada, 1982 (26 in 11)

**Most Safeties Scored**
5—Jackson St., 1986

## FIRST DOWNS

**Most First Downs Per Game**
31.7—Mississippi Val., 1984 (317 in 10)

**Most Rushing First Downs Per Game**
17.9—Howard, 1987 (179 in 10)

**Most Passing First Downs Per Game**
21.4—Mississippi Val., 1984 (214 in 10)

**Most First Downs by Penalty Per Game**
3.7—Texas Southern, 1987 (41 in 11; 134 penalties by opponents); Alabama St., 1984 (41 in 11; 109 penalties by opponents)

## FUMBLES

**Most Fumbles Per Game**
5.3—Prairie View, 1984 (58 in 11)

**Most Fumbles Lost Per Game**
3.1—Delaware St., 1980 (31 in 10); Idaho, 1978 (31 in 10)

**Fewest Own Fumbles Lost**
3—By four teams. Most recent: Tennessee St., 1987 (10 fumbles)

## PENALTIES

**Most Penalties Per Game**
13.7—Grambling, 1984 (151 in 11; 1,206 yards)

**Most Yards Penalized Per Game**
125.5—Tennessee St., 1982 (1,255 in 10; 132 penalties)

## TURNOVERS

**Fewest Turnovers**
10—Appalachian St., 1985 (3 fumbles, 7 interceptions)

**Most Turnovers**
59—Texas Southern, 1980 (27 fumbles, 32 interceptions)

**Highest Turnover Margin Per Game Over Opponents**
2.5—Appalachian St., 1985; Florida A&M, 1981

# SEASON—DEFENSE
## TOTAL DEFENSE

**Fewest Yards Allowed Per Game**
149.9—Florida A&M, 1978 (1,649 in 11)

**Fewest Rushing and Passing Touchdowns Allowed Per Game**
0.7—Western Mich., 1982 (8 in 11)

**Lowest Average Yards Allowed Per Play**
2.4—South Caro. St., 1978 (719 for 1,736)

## RUSHING DEFENSE

**Fewest Yards Allowed Per Game**
44.5—Grambling, 1984 (489 in 11)

**Lowest Average Yards Allowed Per Rush**
1.3—Florida A&M, 1978 (419 for 535)

**Fewest Rushing Touchdowns Allowed Per Game**
0.3—Florida A&M, 1978 (3 in 11)

# PASS DEFENSE

**Fewest Yards Allowed Per Game**
59.9—Bethune-Cookman, 1981 (659 in 11)

**Fewest Yards Allowed Per Attempt**
**(Min. 200 Attempts)**
3.98—Middle Tenn. St., 1988 (251 for 999)

**Fewest Yards Allowed Per Completion**
**(Min. 100 Completions)**
9.08—Middle Tenn. St., 1988 (110 for 999)

**Lowest Completion Percentage Allowed**
*(Min. 200-299 atts.)* 32.3%—Alcorn St., 1979 (76 of 235)
*(Min. 300 atts.)* 34.2%—Tennessee St., 1986 (107 of 313)

**Fewest Touchdowns Allowed by Passing**
1—Middle Tenn. St., 1990; Nevada, 1978

**Lowest Passing Efficiency Defense Rating**
**(Since 1990)**
70.01—South Caro. St., 1991 (278 attempts, 97 completions, 21 interceptions, 1,360 yards, 8 TDs)

**Most Passes Intercepted By, Per Game**
3.2—Florida A&M, 1981 (35 in 11)

**Highest Percentage Intercepted By**
13.4—Florida A&M, 1981 (35 of 262)

**Most Yards Gained on Interceptions**
498—Jackson St., 1985 (28 interceptions)

**Most Yards Gained Per Game on Interceptions**
49.8—Jackson St., 1985 (498 in 10)

**Highest Average Per Interception Return**
**(Min. 15 Returns)**
21.6—Jackson St., 1986 (23 for 497)

**Most Touchdowns on Interception Returns**
7—Jackson St., 1985

# PUNTING

**Most Opponent's Punts Blocked By**
9—Middle Tenn. St., 1988 (73 punts)

# PUNT RETURNS

**Lowest Average Yards Allowed Per**
**Punt Return**
0.96—Yale, 1988 (24 for 23)

**Fewest Returns Allowed**
7—Furman, 1984 (11 games, 8 yards)

# KICKOFF RETURNS

**Lowest Average Yards Allowed Per**
**Kickoff Return**
11.0—Lafayette, 1980 (20 for 220)

# SCORING

**Fewest Points Allowed**
6.5—South Caro. St., 1978 (72 in 11)

# FUMBLES

**Most Opponent's Fumbles Recovered**
29—Western Ky., 1982 (43 fumbles)

# FUMBLE RETURNS (SINCE 1992)

**Most Fumbles Returned for Touchdowns**
2—Citadel, 1992 (vs. Arkansas, Sept. 5 & vs. Western Caro., Oct. 24)

# TURNOVERS

**Most Opponent's Turnovers Per Game**
4.8—Grambling, 1985 (53 in 11)

# ADDITIONAL RECORDS

**Most Consecutive Victories**
20—Holy Cross, 1990-91

**Most Consecutive Home Victories**
38—Ga. Southern, from Oct. 5, 1985, through Sept. 22, 1990 (includes 10 I-AA playoff games)

**Most Consecutive Losses**
44—Columbia, from Nov. 12, 1983, through Oct. 1, 1988 (ended Oct. 8, 1988, with 16-13 win over Princeton)

**Most Consecutive Games Without a Win**
47—Columbia, from Oct. 22, 1983, through Oct. 1, 1988, including two ties (ended Oct. 8, 1988, with 16-13 win over Princeton)

**Most Consecutive Games Without**
**Being Shut Out**
193—Boise St., from Sept. 21, 1968, through Nov. 10, 1984

**Most Shutouts in a Season**
5—South Caro. St., 1978

**Most Consecutive Quarters Holding Opponents Scoreless**
14—McNeese St., 1985; Bucknell, 1979

**Most Consecutive Games Without a Tie**
315—Richmond (current)

**Last Scoreless-Tie Game**
Oct. 26, 1985—McNeese St. & North Texas

**Most Consecutive Passes Attempted Without an Interception**
297—Lamar (in 9 games from Nov. 21, 1987, to Oct. 29, 1988)

**Most Points Overcome to Win a Game**
35—Nevada (55) vs. Weber St. (49), Nov. 2, 1991 (trailed 14-49 with 12:16 remaining in 3rd quarter)
32—Morehead St. (36) vs. Wichita St. (35), Sept. 20, 1986 (trailed 3-35 with 9:03 remaining in 3rd quarter)

**Most Points Overcome in Fourth Quarter to Win a Game**
28—Delaware St. (38) vs. Liberty (37), Oct. 6, 1990 (trailed 9-37 with 13:00 remaining in 4th quarter)

**Most Overtime Periods in a Game**
6—Villanova vs. Connecticut, Oct. 7, 1989 (score after regulation time was 21-21; Villanova won, 41-35)

### Score By Periods

| | | | *Regulation* | |
|---|---|---|---|---|
| Connecticut | 0 | 14 | 0 | 7—21 |
| Villanova | 0 | 0 | 14 | 7—21 |
| | | | *Overtime* | |
| Connecticut | 0 | 0 | 7 | 0 | 7 | 0—35 |
| Villanova | 0 | 0 | 7 | 0 | 7 | 6—41 |

There were 11 TDs, 10 PATs. Game time was 3:40. Villanova's Jeff Johnson scored the winning TD on a 3-yard run (his third TD of the game).

6—Rhode Island vs. Maine, Sept. 18, 1982 (score after regulation time was 21-21; Rhode Island won, 58-55)

### Score By Periods

| | | | *Regulation* | |
|---|---|---|---|---|
| Rhode Island | 7 | 7 | 0 | 7—21 |
| Maine | 0 | 7 | 0 | 14—21 |
| | | | *Overtime* | |
| Rhode Island | 7 | 7 | 3 | 7 | 7 | 6—58 |
| Maine | 7 | 7 | 3 | 7 | 7 | 3—55 |

There were 15 TDs, 14 PATs, 3 FGs. Game time was 3:46, including 51 minutes of overtime. Rhode Island's T. J. Del Santo scored the winning TD on a 2-yard run (his fourth TD of the game) after Maine kicked a field goal in the sixth overtime.

**Most Consecutive Overtime Games Played**
2—Connecticut, 1989 (Connecticut 35, Villanova 41, 6 OT, Oct. 7; and Connecticut 39, Massachusetts 33, 1 OT, Oct. 14); Maine, 1982 (Maine 55, Rhode Island 58, 6 OT, Sept. 18; and Maine 45, Boston U. 48, 4 OT, Sept. 25)

**Most Consecutive Extra-Point Kicks Made**
134—Boise St. (began Oct. 27, 1984; ended Nov. 12, 1988)

**Most Consecutive Winning Seasons**
27—Grambling (1960-86)

**Most Improved Won-Lost Record**
9½ games—Montana St., 1984 (12-2-0, including 3 Division I-AA playoff games) from 1983 (1-10-0)

---

# ANNUAL CHAMPIONS, ALL-TIME LEADERS

## TOTAL OFFENSE
### Career Yards Per Game

| Player, Team | Years | Games | Plays | Yards | TDR‡ | Yd. PG |
|---|---|---|---|---|---|---|
| Willie Totten, Mississippi Val. | 1982-85 | 40 | 1,812 | 13,007 | *157 | *325.2 |
| Neil Lomax, Portland St. | 1977-80 | 42 | *1,901 | *13,345 | 120 | 317.7 |
| Tom Ehrhardt, Rhode Island | #1984-85 | 21 | 1,010 | 6,492 | 66 | 309.1 |
| Tod Mayfield, West Tex. St. | ¢1984-86 | 24 | 1,165 | 7,316 | 58 | 304.8 |
| Jamie Martin, Weber St. | 1989-92 | 41 | 1,838 | 12,287 | 93 | 299.7 |
| Stan Greene, Boston U. | 1989-90 | 22 | 1,167 | 6,408 | 49 | 291.3 |
| John Friesz, Idaho | 1986-89 | 35 | 1,459 | 10,187 | 79 | 291.1 |
| Vern Harris, Idaho St. | 1984-85 | 19 | 813 | 5,302 | 36 | 279.1 |
| Grady Bennett, Montana | 1988-90 | 31 | 1,389 | 8,304 | 69 | 267.9 |
| Sean Payton, Eastern Ill. | 1983-86 | 39 | 1,690 | 10,298 | 91 | 264.1 |
| John Witkowski, Columbia | 1981-83 | 30 | 1,330 | 7,748 | 58 | 258.3 |
| Dave Stireman, Weber St. | 1984-85 | 21 | 762 | 5,396 | 43 | 257.0 |
| Ken Hobart, Idaho | 1980-83 | 44 | 1,847 | 11,127 | 105 | 252.9 |
| Mike Machurek, Idaho St. | 1980-81 | 20 | 805 | 4,974 | 43 | 248.7 |
| Tony Petersen, Marshall | 1986-87 | 20 | 756 | 4,940 | 31 | 247.0 |
| Jeff Wiley, Holy Cross | 1985-88 | 40 | 1,428 | 9,877 | 76 | 246.9 |
| Doug Butler, Princeton | 1983-85 | 29 | 1,137 | 7,157 | 52 | 246.8 |
| Tom Ciaccio, Holy Cross | 1988-91 | 37 | 1,283 | 9,066 | 87 | 245.0 |
| Greg Wyatt, Northern Ariz. | 1986-89 | 42 | 1,753 | 10,277 | 75 | 244.7 |
| Chris Hakel, William & Mary | 1988-91 | 28 | 915 | 6,458 | 56 | 239.2 |

| Player, Team | Years | Games | Plays | Yards | TDR‡ | Yd. PG |
|---|---|---|---|---|---|---|
| Bob Jean, New Hampshire ............... | 1985-88 | 32 | 1,287 | 7,621 | 59 | 238.2 |
| Michael Proctor, Murray St. .............. | 1986-89 | 43 | 1,577 | 9,886 | 66 | 230.0 |
| Jason Garrett, Princeton ................. | 1987-88 | 20 | 731 | 4,555 | 24 | 227.8 |
| Paul Peterson, Idaho St. ................. | 1982-83 | 22 | 1,057 | 4,967 | 36 | 225.8 |
| Frank Baur, Lafayette ................... | 1985, 87-89 | 38 | 1,312 | 8,579 | 72 | 225.8 |
| Eric Beavers, Nevada ................... | 1983-86 | 40 | 1,307 | 9,025 | 85 | 225.6 |

*Record.* ‡ *Touchdowns-responsible-for are player's TDs scored and passed for.* # *Two years in Division I-AA and two years in Division II (LIU-C. W. Post). Four-year totals: 9,793 yards and 232.2 average.* ¢ *Two years in Division I-AA (1984-85) and one year in Division II (1986).*

## Season Yards Per Game

| Player, Team | Year | Games | Plays | Yards | TDR‡ | Yd. PG |
|---|---|---|---|---|---|---|
| Willie Totten, Mississippi Val. .................. | †1984 | 10 | 564 | *4,572 | *61 | *457.2 |
| Steve McNair, Alcorn St. ...................... | †1992 | 10 | 519 | 4,057 | 39 | 405.7 |
| Jamie Martin, Weber St......................... | †1991 | 11 | 591 | 4,337 | 37 | 394.3 |
| Neil Lomax, Portland St. ....................... | †1980 | 11 | 550 | 4,157 | 42 | 377.9 |
| Neil Lomax, Portland St. ....................... | †1979 | 11 | *611 | 3,966 | 31 | 360.5 |
| John Friesz, Idaho ............................ | †1989 | 11 | 464 | 3,853 | 31 | 350.3 |
| Todd Hammel, Stephen F. Austin ............. | 1989 | 11 | 487 | 3,822 | 38 | 347.5 |
| Tom Ehrhardt, Rhode Island ................. | †1985 | 10 | 529 | 3,460 | 35 | 346.0 |
| Ken Hobart, Idaho ........................... | †1983 | 11 | 578 | 3,800 | 37 | 345.5 |
| Dave Stireman, Weber St. .................... | 1985 | 11 | 502 | 3,759 | 33 | 341.7 |
| Willie Totten, Mississippi Val. .................. | 1985 | 11 | 561 | 3,742 | 43 | 340.2 |
| Jeff Wiley, Holy Cross......................... | †1987 | 11 | 445 | 3,722 | 34 | 338.4 |
| Jamie Martin, Weber St. ...................... | †1990 | 11 | 508 | 3,713 | 25 | 337.6 |
| Sean Payton, Eastern Ill. ..................... | 1984 | 11 | 584 | 3,661 | 31 | 332.8 |
| Tod Mayfield, West Tex. St.................... | 1985 | 10 | 526 | 3,328 | 21 | 332.8 |
| Neil Lomax, Portland St. ...................... | †1978 | 11 | 519 | 3,524 | 27 | 320.4 |

*Record.* † *National champion.* ‡ *Touchdowns-responsible-for are player's TDs scored and passed for.*

## Career Yards

| Player, Team | Years | Plays | Yards | Avg. |
|---|---|---|---|---|
| Neil Lomax, Portland St. ............................ | 1977-80 | *1,901 | *13,345 | 7.02 |
| Willie Totten, Mississippi Val. ....................... | 1982-85 | 1,812 | 13,007 | *7.18 |
| Jamie Martin, Weber St............................. | 1989-92 | 1,838 | 12,287 | 6.68 |
| Ken Hobart, Idaho ................................. | 1980-83 | 1,847 | 11,127 | 6.02 |
| Sean Payton, Eastern Ill. ........................... | 1983-86 | 1,690 | 10,298 | 6.09 |
| Greg Wyatt, Northern Ariz.......................... | 1986-89 | 1,753 | 10,277 | 5.86 |
| John Friesz, Idaho ................................. | 1986-89 | 1,459 | 10,187 | 6.98 |
| Michael Proctor, Murray St. ........................ | 1986-89 | 1,577 | 9,886 | 6.27 |
| Jeff Wiley, Holy Cross.............................. | 1985-88 | 1,428 | 9,877 | 6.92 |
| Matt DeGennaro, Connecticut ...................... | 1987-90 | 1,619 | 9,269 | 5.73 |
| Tom Ciaccio, Holy Cross........................... | 1988-91 | 1,283 | 9,066 | 7.07 |
| Eric Beavers, Nevada ............................. | 1983-86 | 1,307 | 9,025 | 6.91 |
| Marty Horn, Lehigh ................................ | 1982-85 | 1,612 | 8,956 | 5.56 |
| Kirk Schulz, Villanova ............................. | 1986-89 | 1,534 | 8,900 | 5.80 |
| Robbie Justino, Liberty ............................ | 1989-92 | 1,469 | 8,803 | 5.99 |
| Chris Swartz, Morehead St. ........................ | 1987-90 | 1,559 | 8,648 | 5.55 |
| Frank Baur, Lafayette ........................... | 1985, 87-89 | 1,312 | 8,579 | 6.54 |
| Fred Gatlin, Nevada ............................... | %1989-92 | 1,330 | 8,568 | 6.44 |
| ¢Doug Nussmeier, Idaho .......................... | 1990-92 | 1,156 | 8,540 | 7.39 |
| Steve Calabria, Colgate ........................... | 1981-84 | 1,342 | 8,532 | 6.36 |
| Mike Buck, Maine ................................. | 1986-89 | 1,288 | 8,457 | 6.57 |
| Jason Whitmer, Idaho St. .......................... | 1987-90 | 1,618 | 8,449 | 5.22 |
| Scott Davis, North Texas ........................... | 1987-90 | 1,548 | 8,436 | 5.45 |
| Grady Bennett, Montana ........................... | 1988-90 | 1,389 | 8,304 | 5.98 |
| Bill Vergantino, Delaware .......................... | 1989-92 | 1,459 | 8,225 | 5.64 |
| Stan Yagiello, William & Mary ..................... | $1981-85 | 1,492 | 8,168 | 5.47 |
| Mike Smith, Northern Iowa ........................ | 1984-87 | 1,163 | 8,145 | 7.00 |
| Bob Bleier, Richmond ............................. | 1983-86 | 1,313 | 7,991 | 6.09 |
| Alan Hooker, North Caro. A&T ..................... | 1984-87 | 1,476 | 7,787 | 5.28 |
| John Witkowski, Columbia ......................... | 1981-83 | 1,330 | 7,748 | 5.83 |
| Michael Payton, Marshall .......................... | 1989-92 | 1,106 | 7,744 | 7.00 |
| Kelly Bradley, Montana St. ......................... | 1983-86 | 1,547 | 7,740 | 5.00 |
| Jeff Cesarone, Western Ky. ........................ | 1984-87 | 1,502 | 7,694 | 5.12 |

*Record.* $ *See page 8 for explanation.* ¢ *Active player.* % *Played 1992 season in Division I-A.*

*Division I-AA Annual Champions, All-Time Leaders*      153

## Season Yards

| Player, Team | Year | Games | Plays | Yards | Avg. |
|---|---|---|---|---|---|
| Willie Totten, Mississippi Val. | †1984 | 10 | 564 | *4,572 | 8.11 |
| Jamie Martin, Weber St. | †1991 | 11 | 591 | 4,337 | 7.34 |
| Neil Lomax, Portland St. | †1980 | 11 | 550 | 4,157 | 7.56 |
| Steve McNair, Alcorn St. | †1992 | 10 | 519 | 4,057 | 7.82 |
| Neil Lomax, Portland St. | †1979 | 11 | *611 | 3,966 | 6.49 |
| John Friesz, Idaho | †1989 | 11 | 464 | 3,853 | 8.30 |
| Todd Hammel, Stephen F. Austin | 1989 | 11 | 487 | 3,822 | 7.85 |
| Ken Hobart, Idaho | †1983 | 11 | 578 | 3,800 | 6.57 |
| Dave Stireman, Weber St. | 1985 | 11 | 502 | 3,759 | 7.49 |
| Willie Totten, Mississippi Val. | 1985 | 11 | 561 | 3,742 | 6.67 |
| Jeff Wiley, Holy Cross | †1987 | 11 | 445 | 3,722 | *8.36 |
| Jamie Martin, Weber St. | †1990 | 11 | 508 | 3,713 | 7.31 |
| Sean Payton, Eastern Ill. | 1984 | 11 | 584 | 3,661 | 6.27 |
| Todd Brunner, Lehigh | 1989 | 11 | 504 | 3,639 | 7.22 |
| Neil Lomax, Portland St. | †1978 | 11 | 519 | 3,524 | 6.79 |
| Glenn Kempa, Lehigh | 1991 | 11 | 513 | 3,511 | 6.84 |
| John Friesz, Idaho | 1987 | 11 | 543 | 3,489 | 6.43 |
| Doug Nussmeier, Idaho | 1991 | 11 | 472 | 3,460 | 7.33 |
| Tom Ehrhardt, Rhode Island | †1985 | 10 | 529 | 3,460 | 6.54 |
| Kelly Bradley, Montana St. | 1984 | 11 | 598 | 3,455 | 5.78 |

*Record.  † National champion.*

## Single-Game Yards

| Yds. | Player, Team (Opponent) | Date |
|---|---|---|
| 643 | Jamie Martin, Weber St. (Idaho St.) | Nov. 23, 1991 |
| 621 | Willie Totten, Mississippi Val. (Prairie View) | Oct. 27, 1984 |
| 604 | Steve McNair, Alcorn St. (Jackson St.) | Nov. 21, 1992 |
| 595 | Doug Pederson, Northeast La. (Stephen F. Austin) | Nov. 11, 1989 |
| 587 | Vern Harris, Idaho St. (Montana) | Oct. 12, 1985 |
| 566 | Tom Ehrhardt, Rhode Island (Connecticut) | Nov. 16, 1985 |
| 562 | Todd Hammel, Stephen F. Austin (Northeast La.) | Nov. 11, 1989 |
| 561 | Willie Totten, Mississippi Val. (Southern-B.R.) | Sept. 29, 1984 |
| 549 | Steve McNair, Alcorn St. (Jacksonville St.) | Oct. 31, 1992 |
| 547 | Tod Mayfield, West Tex. St. (New Mexico St.) | Nov. 16, 1985 |
| 546 | Dave Stireman, Weber St. (Montana) | Nov. 2, 1985 |
| 543 | Ken Hobart, Idaho (Southern Colo.) | Sept. 10, 1983 |
| 539 | Jamie Martin, Weber St. (Montana St.) | Sept. 26, 1990 |
| 536 | Willie Totten, Mississippi Val. (Kentucky St.) | Sept. 1, 1984 |
| 527 | Willie Totten, Mississippi Val. (Grambling) | Oct. 13, 1984 |
| 519 | Bernard Hawk, Bethune-Cookman (Ga. Southern) | Oct. 6, 1984 |

## Annual Champions

| Year | Player, Team | Class | Games | Plays | Yards | Avg. |
|---|---|---|---|---|---|---|
| 1978 | Neil Lomax, Portland St. | So. | 11 | 519 | 3,524 | 320.4 |
| 1979 | Neil Lomax, Portland St. | Jr. | 11 | *611 | 3,966 | 360.5 |
| 1980 | Neil Lomax, Portland St. | Sr. | 11 | 550 | 4,157 | 377.9 |
| 1981 | Mike Machurek, Idaho St. | Sr. | 9 | 363 | 2,645 | 293.9 |
| 1982 | Brent Woods, Princeton | Sr. | 10 | 577 | 3,079 | 307.9 |
| 1983 | Ken Hobart, Idaho | Sr. | 11 | 578 | 3,800 | 345.5 |
| 1984 | Willie Totten, Mississippi Val. | Jr. | 10 | 564 | *4,572 | *457.2 |
| 1985 | Tom Ehrhardt, Rhode Island | Sr. | 10 | 529 | 3,460 | 346.0 |
| 1986 | Brent Pease, Montana | Sr. | 10 | 499 | 3,094 | 309.4 |
| 1987 | Jeff Wiley, Holy Cross | Jr. | 11 | 445 | 3,722 | 338.4 |
| 1988 | John Friesz, Idaho | Jr. | 10 | 424 | 2,751 | 275.1 |
| 1989 | John Friesz, Idaho | Sr. | 11 | 464 | 3,853 | 350.3 |
| 1990 | Jamie Martin, Weber St. | So. | 11 | 508 | 3,713 | 337.6 |
| 1991 | Jamie Martin, Weber St. | Jr. | 11 | 591 | 4,337 | 394.3 |
| 1992 | Steve McNair, Alcorn St. | So. | 10 | 519 | 4,057 | 405.7 |

*Record.*

# RUSHING

## Career Yards Per Game§

| Player, Team | Years | Games | Plays | Yards | TD | Yd. PG |
|---|---|---|---|---|---|---|
| Mike Clark, Akron | 1984-86 | 32 | 804 | 4,257 | 24 | *133.0 |
| Rich Erenberg, Colgate | 1982-83 | 21 | 464 | 2,618 | 22 | 124.7 |
| Kenny Gamble, Colgate | 1984-87 | 42 | *963 | 5,220 | *55 | 124.3 |
| Frank Hawkins, Nevada | 1977-80 | 43 | 945 | *5,333 | 39 | 124.0 |
| Elroy Harris, Eastern Ky. | 1985, 87-88 | 31 | 648 | 3,829 | 47 | 123.5 |

*1993 NCAA FOOTBALL*

| Player, Team | Years | Games | Plays | Yards | TD | Yd. PG |
|---|---|---|---|---|---|---|
| Gill Fenerty, Holy Cross .................. | 1983-85 | 30 | 622 | 3,618 | 26 | 120.6 |
| Markus Thomas, Eastern Ky. ............. | 1989-92 | 43 | 784 | 5,149 | 51 | 119.7 |
| Buford Jordan, McNeese St. ............. | 1982-83 | 19 | 436 | 2,123 | 17 | 111.7 |
| Derrick Harmon, Cornell ................. | 1981-83 | 28 | 545 | 3,074 | 26 | 109.8 |
| Paul Lewis, Boston U. .................... | 1982-84 | 37 | 878 | 3,995 | 50 | 108.0 |
| Derrick Franklin, Indiana St. ............. | 1989-91 | 30 | 710 | 3,231 | 23 | 107.7 |
| Charvez Foger, Nevada .................. | 1985-88 | 42 | 864 | 4,484 | 52 | 106.8 |
| James Crawford, Eastern Ky. ............ | 1985-87 | 32 | 661 | 3,404 | 22 | 106.4 |
| Bryan Keys, Pennsylvania ................ | 1987-89 | 30 | 609 | 3,137 | 34 | 104.6 |
| Fine Unga, Weber St. .................... | 1987-88 | 22 | 406 | 2,298 | 19 | 104.5 |
| Judd Garrett, Princeton .................. | 1987-89 | 30 | 687 | 3,109 | 32 | 103.6 |
| Stanford Jennings, Furman .............. | 1982-83 | 22 | 390 | 2,267 | 25 | 103.0 |

* Record.  § The following players competed two years in Division I-AA and two years in Division I-A: Rich Erenberg, Colgate (four years: 3,689 yards and 94.6 average); Buford Jordan, McNeese St. (four years: 4,106 yards and 100.1 average), and Stanford Jennings, Furman (four years: 3,868 yards and 90.0 average).

## Season Yards Per Game

| Player, Team | Year | Games | Plays | Yards | TD | Yd. PG |
|---|---|---|---|---|---|---|
| Gene Lake, Delaware St. ..................... | †1984 | 10 | 238 | 1,722 | 20 | *172.2 |
| Rich Erenberg, Colgate .................... | †1983 | 11 | 302 | *1,883 | 20 | 171.2 |
| Kenny Gamble, Colgate ................... | †1986 | 11 | 307 | 1,816 | **21 | 165.1 |
| Mike Clark, Akron.......................... | 1986 | 11 | 245 | 1,786 | 8 | 162.4 |
| Keith Elias, Princeton ...................... | †1992 | 10 | 245 | 1,575 | 18 | 157.5 |
| Frank Hawkins, Nevada .................... | †1980 | 11 | 307 | 1,719 | 9 | 156.3 |
| Brad Baxter, Alabama St. .................. | 1986 | 11 | 302 | 1,705 | 13 | 155.0 |
| Elroy Harris, Eastern Ky. .................. | 1988 | 10 | 277 | 1,543 | **21 | 154.3 |
| Frank Hawkins, Nevada .................... | †1979 | 11 | 293 | 1,683 | 13 | 153.0 |
| Carl Smith, Maine .......................... | †1989 | 11 | 305 | 1,680 | 20 | 152.7 |
| Harvey Reed, Howard ...................... | †1987 | 10 | 211 | 1,512 | 20 | 151.2 |
| John Settle, Appalachian St. .............. | 1986 | 11 | 317 | 1,661 | 20 | 151.0 |
| Garry Pearson, Massachusetts ............... | †1982 | 11 | 312 | 1,631 | 13 | 148.3 |
| Lorenzo Bouier, Maine ...................... | 1980 | 11 | 349 | 1,622 | 9 | 147.5 |

* Record.  ** Record tied.  † National champion.

## Career Yards@

| Player, Team | Years | Plays | Yards | Avg. | Long |
|---|---|---|---|---|---|
| Frank Hawkins, Nevada ...................... | 1977-80 | 945 | *5,333 | 5.64 | 50 |
| Kenny Gamble, Colgate ...................... | 1984-87 | *963 | 5,220 | 5.42 | 91 |
| Markus Thomas, Eastern Ky. .................. | 1989-92 | 784 | 5,149 | 6.57 | 90 |
| Cedric Minter, Boise St. ..................... | 1977-80 | 752 | 4,475 | 5.95 | 77 |
| John Settle, Appalachian St. ................. | 1983-86 | 891 | 4,409 | 4.95 | 88 |
| Mike Clark, Akron........................... | 1984-86 | 804 | 4,257 | 5.29 | †65 |
| Warren Marshall, James Madison ............. | $1982-86 | 737 | 4,168 | 5.66 | 59 |
| Carl Tremble, Furman ....................... | 1989-92 | 696 | 4,149 | 5.96 | 65 |
| Harvey Reed, Howard ....................... | 1984-87 | 635 | 4,142 | *6.52 | 85 |
| Paul Lewis, Boston U........................ | 1981-84 | 878 | 3,995 | 4.55 | 80 |
| Joe Ross, Ga. Southern ..................... | 1987-90 | 687 | 3,876 | 5.64 | 75 |
| Garry Pearson, Massachusetts ................ | 1979-82 | 808 | 3,859 | 4.78 | 71 |
| Elroy Harris, Eastern Ky. ...........1985, 87-88 | | 648 | 3,829 | 5.91 | 64 |
| Lorenzo Bouier, Maine ...................... | 1979-82 | 879 | 3,827 | 4.35 | 77 |
| Lewis Tillman, Jackson St. ................... | $1984-88 | 779 | 3,824 | 4.91 | 39 |
| Joe Campbell, Middle Tenn. St. ............... | 1988-91 | 638 | 3,823 | 5.99 | 81 |
| Carl Smith, Maine ........................... | 1988-91 | 759 | 3,815 | 5.03 | 89 |
| Brad Baxter, Alabama St. .................... | 1985-88 | 773 | 3,732 | 4.83 | 71 |
| Toby Davis, Illinois St........................ | 1989-92 | 825 | 3,702 | 4.49 | 34 |
| Gill Fenerty, Holy Cross ..................... | 1983-85 | 622 | 3,618 | 5.82 | 76 |
| Burton Murchison, Lamar.................... | 1984-87 | 665 | 3,598 | 5.41 | 76 |

* Record.  † Did not score.  $ See page 8 for explanation.  @ The following players competed two years in Division I-AA and two years in Division I-A: Rich Erenberg, Colgate (four years: 3,689 yards); Buford Jordan, McNeese St. (four years: 4,106 yards), and Stanford Jennings, Furman (four years: 3,868 yards).

## Season Yards

| Player, Team | Year | Games | Plays | Yards | Avg. |
|---|---|---|---|---|---|
| Rich Erenberg, Colgate ....................... | †1983 | 11 | 302 | *1,883 | 6.24 |
| Kenny Gamble, Colgate ...................... | †1986 | 11 | 307 | 1,816 | 5.92 |
| Mike Clark, Akron............................ | 1986 | 11 | 245 | 1,786 | ‡7.29 |
| Gene Lake, Delaware St...................... | †1984 | 10 | 238 | 1,722 | 7.24 |
| Frank Hawkins, Nevada ...................... | †1980 | 11 | 307 | 1,719 | 5.60 |

| Player, Team | Year | Games | Plays | Yards | Avg. |
|---|---|---|---|---|---|
| Brad Baxter, Alabama St. ..................... | 1986 | 11 | 302 | 1,705 | 5.65 |
| Frank Hawkins, Nevada ...................... | †1979 | 11 | 293 | 1,683 | 5.74 |
| Carl Smith, Maine ........................... | †1989 | 11 | 305 | 1,680 | 5.51 |
| John Settle, Appalachian St. ................. | 1986 | 11 | 317 | 1,661 | 5.24 |
| Garry Pearson, Massachusetts ............... | †1982 | 11 | 312 | 1,631 | 5.23 |
| Lorenzo Bouier, Maine ....................... | 1980 | 11 | 349 | 1,622 | 4.65 |
| Markus Thomas, Eastern Ky.................. | 1989 | 11 | 232 | 1,620 | 6.98 |
| Keith Elias, Princeton ....................... | †1992 | 10 | 245 | 1,575 | 6.43 |
| James Black, Akron.......................... | 1983 | 11 | *351 | 1,568 | 4.47 |
| Toby Davis, Illinois St......................... | 1992 | 11 | 341 | 1,561 | 4.58 |
| Carl Tremble, Furman......................... | 1992 | 11 | 228 | 1,555 | 6.82 |
| Burton Murchison, Lamar..................... | †1985 | 11 | 265 | 1,547 | 5.84 |
| Jerome Bledsoe, Massachusetts .............. | †1991 | 11 | 264 | 1,545 | 5.85 |
| Elroy Harris, Eastern Ky. ..................... | 1988 | 10 | 277 | 1,543 | 5.57 |
| Cedric Minter, Boise St........................ | 1978 | 11 | 258 | 1,526 | 5.91 |

*Record. † National champion. ‡ Record for minimum of 200 carries.*

### Single-Game Yards

| Yds. | Player, Team (Opponent) | Date |
|---|---|---|
| 345 | Russell Davis, Idaho (Portland St.)............................................ | Oct. 3, 1981 |
| 337 | Gill Fenerty, Holy Cross (Columbia) .......................................... | Oct. 29, 1983 |
| 336 | Gene Lake, Delaware St. (Liberty) ........................................... | Nov. 10, 1984 |
| 323 | Matt Johnson, Harvard (Brown) .............................................. | Nov. 9, 1991 |
| 312 | Surkano Edwards, Samford (Tenn.-Martin) .................................... | Nov. 14, 1992 |
| 309 | Eddie Thompson, Western Ky. (Southern Ill.)................................. | Oct. 29, 1992 |
| 305 | Lucius Floyd, Nevada (Montana St.)........................................... | Sept. 27, 1986 |
| 304 | Tony Citizen, McNeese St. (Prairie View) .................................... | Sept. 6, 1986 |
| 302 | Lorenzo Bouier, Maine (Northeastern)........................................ | Nov. 1, 1980 |
| 300 | Markus Thomas, Eastern Ky. (Marshall) ...................................... | Oct. 21, 1989 |
| 299 | Keith Elias, Princeton (Lafayette) ........................................... | Sept. 26, 1992 |
| 299 | Joe Delaney, Northwestern, La. (Nicholls St.) ................................ | Oct. 28, 1978 |
| 293 | Terence Thompson, Eastern Ky. (Akron) ..................................... | Sept. 26, 1981 |
| 293 | Frank Hawkins, Nevada (San Fran. St.) ...................................... | Sept. 30, 1978 |

### Annual Champions

| Year | Player, Team | Class | Games | Plays | Yards | Avg. |
|---|---|---|---|---|---|---|
| 1978 | Frank Hawkins, Nevada ............... | So. | 10 | 259 | 1,445 | 144.5 |
| 1979 | Frank Hawkins, Nevada ............... | Jr. | 11 | 293 | 1,683 | 153.0 |
| 1980 | Frank Hawkins, Nevada ............... | Sr. | 11 | 307 | 1,719 | 156.3 |
| 1981 | Gregg Drew, Boston U. ............... | Jr. | 10 | 309 | 1,257 | 125.7 |
| 1982 | Garry Pearson, Massachusetts ........ | Sr. | 11 | 312 | 1,631 | 148.3 |
| 1983 | Rich Erenberg, Colgate ............... | Sr. | 11 | 302 | *1,883 | 171.2 |
| 1984 | Gene Lake, Delaware St............... | Jr. | 10 | 238 | 1,722 | *172.2 |
| 1985 | Burton Murchison, Lamar............. | So. | 11 | 265 | 1,547 | 140.6 |
| 1986 | Kenny Gamble, Colgate ............... | Jr. | 11 | 307 | 1,816 | 165.1 |
| 1987 | Harvey Reed, Howard ................. | Sr. | 10 | 211 | 1,512 | 151.2 |
| 1988 | Elroy Harris, Eastern Ky. ............. | Jr. | 10 | 277 | 1,543 | 154.3 |
| 1989 | Carl Smith, Maine .................... | So. | 11 | 305 | 1,680 | 152.7 |
| 1990 | Walter Dean, Grambling .............. | Sr. | 11 | 221 | 1,401 | 127.4 |
| 1991 | Al Rosier, Dartmouth ................. | Sr. | 10 | 258 | 1,432 | 143.2 |
| 1992 | Keith Elias, Princeton ................. | Jr. | 10 | 245 | 1,575 | 157.5 |

*Record.*

## QUARTERBACK RUSHING
### Career Yards (Since 1978)

| Player, Team | Years | Games | Plays | Yards | TD | Yd. PG |
|---|---|---|---|---|---|---|
| Jack Douglas, Citadel.............. | 1989-92 | 44 | *832 | *3,674 | *48 | *83.5 |
| Tracy Ham, Ga. Southern .......... | 1984-86 | 33 | 511 | 2,506 | 32 | 75.9 |
| Tony Scales, Va. Military ........... | 1989-92 | 44 | 561 | 2,475 | 19 | 56.3 |
| Raymond Gross, Ga. Southern ..... | 1987-90 | 42 | 695 | 2,290 | 20 | 54.5 |
| Bill Vergantino, Delaware .......... | 1989-92 | 44 | 656 | 2,287 | 34 | 52.0 |
| Dwane Brown, Arkansas St. ........ | 1984-87 | 42 | 595 | 2,192 | 33 | 52.2 |
| Roy Johnson, Arkansas St. ........ | 1988-91 | 43 | 558 | 2,182 | 22 | 50.7 |
| DeAndre Smith, Southwest Mo. St. .. | 1987-90 | 42 | 558 | 2,140 | 36 | 50.9 |
| Ken Hobart, Idaho .................. | 1980-83 | 44 | 628 | 1,827 | 26 | 41.5 |
| Darin Kehler, Yale .................. | 1987-90 | 28 | 402 | 1,643 | 13 | 58.7 |

*Record.*

| Player, Team | Year | Games | Plays | Yards | TD | Avg. |
|---|---|---|---|---|---|---|
| Jack Douglas, Citadel ............... | 1991 | 11 | *266 | *1,152 | 13 | 4.33 |
| Tony Scales, Va. Military ............ | 1991 | 11 | 185 | 1,105 | 8 | 5.97 |
| Tracy Ham, Ga. Southern ........... | 1986 | 11 | 207 | 1,048 | *18 | 5.06 |
| Nick Crawford, Yale ................. | 1991 | 10 | 210 | 1,024 | 8 | 4.98 |
| Gene Brown, Citadel ................ | 1988 | 9 | 152 | 1,006 | 13 | 6.62 |
| Jack Douglas, Citadel ............... | 1992 | 11 | 178 | 926 | 13 | 5.20 |
| Roy Johnson, Arkansas St. ......... | 1989 | 11 | 193 | 925 | 6 | 4.79 |
| Darin Kehler, Yale .................. | 1989 | 10 | 210 | 903 | 6 | 4.30 |
| Jim O'Leary, Northeastern .......... | 1986 | 10 | 195 | 884 | 10 | 4.53 |
| Earl Easley, Arkansas St. ........... | 1988 | 11 | 196 | 861 | 11 | 4.39 |
| Brad Brown, Northwestern (La.) .... | 1990 | 11 | 192 | 843 | 8 | 4.39 |
| DeAndre Smith, Southwest Mo. St. . | 1989 | 11 | 176 | 841 | 12 | 4.78 |
| Eddie Thompson, Western Ky. ...... | 1992 | 9 | 113 | 837 | 9 | *7.41 |
| Gilbert Price, Southwest Tex. St. .... | 1991 | 11 | 244 | 837 | 8 | 3.43 |
| Jack Douglas, Citadel ............... | 1990 | 11 | 211 | 836 | 13 | 3.96 |
| Ken Hobart, Idaho .................. | 1980 | 11 | 209 | 829 | 7 | 3.97 |

* Record.

# PASSING

## Career Passing Efficiency
### (Minimum 300 Completions)

| Player, Team | Years | Att. | Cmp. | Int. | Pct. | Yards | TD | Pts. |
|---|---|---|---|---|---|---|---|---|
| Jay Johnson, Northern Iowa ........ | 1989-92 | 744 | 397 | 25 | .534 | 7,049 | 51 | *148.9 |
| Willie Totten, Mississippi Val........ | 1982-85 | 1,555 | 907 | *75 | .583 | 12,711 | *139 | 146.8 |
| Kenneth Biggles, Tennessee St...... | 1981-84 | 701 | 397 | 28 | .566 | 5,933 | 57 | 146.6 |
| Mike Smith, Northern Iowa ......... | 1984-87 | 943 | 557 | 43 | .591 | 8,219 | 58 | 143.5 |
| Neil Lomax, Portland St. ........... | 1977-80 | *1,606 | *938 | 55 | .584 | *13,220 | 106 | 142.5 |
| Tom Ciaccio, Holy Cross............ | 1988-91 | 1,073 | 658 | 46 | .613 | 8,603 | 72 | 142.2 |
| Jim Zaccheo, Nevada .............. | 1987-88 | 554 | 326 | 27 | .588 | 4,750 | 35 | 142.0 |
| Eric Beavers, Nevada .............. | 1983-86 | 1,094 | 646 | 37 | .591 | 8,626 | 77 | 141.8 |
| Jason Garrett, Princeton ........... | 1987-88 | 550 | 368 | 10 | *.669 | 4,274 | 20 | 140.6 |
| Connell Maynor, Winston-Salem/<br>  North Caro. A&T ................. | 1987, 89-91 | 661 | 365 | 31 | .552 | 5,390 | 50 | 139.3 |
| Jamie Martin, Weber St............. | 1989-92 | 1,544 | 934 | 56 | .605 | 12,207 | 87 | 138.2 |
| Ricky Jones, Alabama St. .......... | 1988-91 | 644 | 324 | 30 | .503 | 5,472 | 49 | 137.5 |
| Jeff Carlson, Weber St.............. | 1984, 86-88 | 723 | 384 | 33 | .531 | 6,147 | 47 | 136.9 |
| Chris Hakel, William & Mary ....... | 1988-91 | 812 | 489 | 26 | .602 | 6,447 | 40 | 136.7 |
| Jeff Wiley, Holy Cross.............. | 1985-88 | 1,208 | 723 | 63 | .599 | 9,698 | 71 | 136.3 |
| Tom Ehrhardt, Rhode Island ....... | ††1984-85 | 919 | 526 | 35 | .572 | 6,722 | 66 | 134.8 |
| Mike Buck, Maine .................. | 1986-89 | 1,134 | 637 | 41 | .562 | 8,721 | 68 | 133.4 |
| Frankie DeBusk, Furman........... | 1987-90 | 634 | 333 | 29 | .525 | 5,414 | 35 | 133.3 |
| Frank Novak, Lafayette ............ | 1981-83 | 834 | 478 | 36 | .573 | 6,378 | 51 | 133.1 |
| Robbie Justino, Liberty ............ | 1989-92 | 1,267 | 769 | 51 | .607 | 9,548 | 54 | 132.6 |
| Rick Worman, Eastern Wash. ...... | **1982, 84-85 | 673 | 382 | 23 | .568 | 5,013 | 41 | 132.6 |
| Glenn Kempa, Lehigh .............. | 1989-91 | 901 | 520 | 27 | .577 | 6,722 | 49 | 132.3 |
| Gilbert Renfroe, Tennessee St. ..... | 1982-85 | 721 | 370 | 23 | .513 | 5,556 | 48 | 131.6 |
| Tod Mayfield, West Tex. St......... | ##1984-86 | 1,035 | 630 | 38 | .609 | 7,424 | 55 | 131.3 |
| Tracy Ham, Ga. Southern .......... | 1984-86 | 568 | 301 | 31 | .530 | 4,881 | 29 | 131.1 |
| Matt DeGennaro, Connecticut ...... | 1987-90 | 1,319 | 803 | 49 | .609 | 9,288 | 73 | 130.9 |
| Ken Hobart, Idaho ................. | 1980-83 | 1,219 | 629 | 42 | .516 | 9,300 | 79 | 130.2 |

* Record. $ See page 8 for explanation. ** At Fresno St. in 1982. ## Two years in Division I-AA (1984-85) and one year in Division II (1986). †† Two years in Division I-AA and two years in Division II (LIU-C. W. Post).

## Season Passing Efficiency
### (Minimum 15 Attempts Per Game)

| Player, Team | Year | G | Att. | Cmp. | Int. | Pct. | Yards | TD | Pts. |
|---|---|---|---|---|---|---|---|---|---|
| Michael Payton, Marshall .......... | †1991 | 9 | 216 | 143 | 5 | .622 | 2,333 | 19 | *181.3 |
| Frank Baur, Lafayette .............. | †1988 | 10 | 256 | 164 | 11 | .641 | 2,621 | 23 | 171.1 |
| Bobby Lamb, Furman .............. | †1985 | 11 | 181 | 106 | 6 | .586 | 1,856 | 18 | 170.9 |
| Jay Fiedler, Dartmouth ............. | †1992 | 10 | 273 | 175 | 13 | .641 | 2,748 | 25 | 169.4 |
| Mike Smith, Northern Iowa ......... | †1986 | 11 | 303 | 190 | 16 | .627 | 3,125 | 27 | 168.2 |
| Willie Totten, Mississippi Val........ | †1983 | 9 | 279 | 174 | 9 | .624 | 2,566 | 29 | 167.5 |
| Lonnie Galloway, Western Caro. .... | 1992 | 11 | 211 | 128 | 12 | .607 | 2,181 | 20 | 167.4 |
| Eriq Williams, James Madison ...... | 1991 | 11 | 192 | 107 | 7 | .557 | 1,914 | 19 | 164.8 |
| Willie Totten, Mississippi Val........ | †1984 | 10 | *518 | *324 | 22 | .626 | *4,557 | *56 | 163.6 |
| Jeff Wiley, Holy Cross.............. | †1987 | 11 | 400 | 265 | 17 | .663 | 3,677 | 34 | 163.0 |

Dartmouth quarterback Jay Fiedler led Division I-AA in passing efficiency in 1992 with a rating of 169.4, the fourth-best rating in division history. The junior completed 64 percent of his passes and threw 25 touchdown strikes.

| Player, Team | Year | G | Att. | Cmp. | Int. | Pct. | Yards | TD | Pts. |
|---|---|---|---|---|---|---|---|---|---|
| Todd Hammel, Stephen F. Austin ... | †1989 | 11 | 401 | 238 | 13 | .594 | 3,914 | 34 | 162.8 |
| Mike Williams, Grambling ........... | †1980 | 11 | 239 | 127 | 5 | .531 | 2,116 | 28 | 162.0 |
| John Friesz, Idaho ................... | 1989 | 11 | 425 | 260 | 8 | .612 | 4,041 | 31 | 161.4 |
| Wendal Lowrey, Northeast La. ...... | 1992 | 11 | 227 | 147 | 9 | .648 | 2,190 | 16 | 161.1 |
| Donny Simmons, Western Ill. ....... | 1992 | 11 | 281 | 182 | 11 | .648 | 2,496 | 25 | 160.9 |
| David Charpia, Furman ............. | 1983 | 9 | 155 | 99 | 4 | .635 | 1,419 | 12 | 160.1 |
| Joe Aliotti, Boise St................. | †1979 | 11 | 219 | 144 | 7 | .658 | 1,870 | 19 | 159.7 |
| Gilbert Renfroe, Tennessee St. ...... | 1984 | 11 | 165 | 95 | 5 | .576 | 1,458 | 17 | 159.7 |
| Mike Buck, Maine ................... | 1989 | 11 | 264 | 170 | 3 | .644 | 2,315 | 19 | 159.5 |
| Bobby Lamb, Furman ............... | 1984 | 11 | 191 | 106 | 7 | .555 | 1,781 | 19 | 159.3 |
| Kenneth Biggles, Tennessee St...... | 1984 | 11 | 258 | 157 | 7 | .609 | 2,242 | 24 | 159.1 |
| Michael Payton, Marshall ........... | 1992 | 11 | 313 | 200 | 11 | .639 | 2,788 | 26 | 159.1 |
| Shawn Knight, William & Mary ...... | 1992 | 11 | 195 | 124 | 5 | .636 | 1,892 | 11 | 158.6 |
| Ricky Jordan, Jackson St. ......... | 1992 | 11 | 215 | 119 | 9 | .553 | 2,124 | 18 | 157.6 |
| Hugh Swilling, Furman.............. | 1991 | 9 | 153 | 85 | 5 | .556 | 1,422 | 14 | 157.3 |

* Record.  † National champion.

| Player, Team | Years | Att. | Cmp. | Int. | Pct. | Yards | TD |
|---|---|---|---|---|---|---|---|
| **Career Yards** | | | | | | | |
| Neil Lomax, Portland St. ............. | 1977-80 | *1,606 | *938 | 55 | .584 | *13,220 | 106 |
| Willie Totten, Mississippi Val. ......... | 1982-85 | 1,555 | 907 | *75 | .583 | 12,711 | *139 |
| Jamie Martin, Weber St............... | 1989-92 | 1,544 | 934 | 56 | .605 | 12,207 | 87 |
| John Friesz, Idaho ................... | 1986-89 | 1,350 | 801 | 40 | .593 | 10,697 | 77 |
| Greg Wyatt, Northern Ariz............ | 1986-89 | 1,510 | 926 | 49 | .613 | 10,697 | 70 |
| Sean Payton, Eastern Ill. ............ | 1983-86 | 1,408 | 756 | 55 | .537 | 10,655 | 75 |
| Jeff Wiley, Holy Cross................ | 1985-88 | 1,208 | 723 | 63 | .599 | 9,698 | 71 |
| Robbie Justino, Liberty .............. | 1989-92 | 1,267 | 769 | 51 | .607 | 9,548 | 64 |
| Kirk Schulz, Villanova ................ | 1986-89 | 1,297 | 774 | 70 | .597 | 9,305 | 70 |
| Ken Hobart, Idaho ................... | 1980-83 | 1,219 | 629 | 42 | .516 | 9,300 | 79 |

| Player, Team | Years | Att. | Cmp. | Int. | Pct. | Yards | TD |
|---|---|---|---|---|---|---|---|
| Matt DeGennaro, Connecticut ........ | 1987-90 | 1,319 | 803 | 49 | .609 | 9,288 | 73 |
| Marty Horn, Lehigh .................. | 1982-85 | 1,390 | 744 | 64 | .535 | 9,120 | 62 |
| Jason Whitmer, Idaho St. ............. | 1987-90 | 1,349 | 721 | 53 | .534 | 9,081 | 55 |
| Chris Swartz, Morehead St. .......... | 1987-90 | 1,408 | 774 | 47 | .550 | 9,027 | 56 |
| Michael Proctor, Murray St. .......... | 1986-89 | 1,148 | 578 | 45 | .503 | 8,682 | 52 |
| Eric Beavers, Nevada ................ | 1983-86 | 1,094 | 646 | 37 | .590 | 8,626 | 77 |
| Tom Ciaccio, Holy Cross.............. | 1988-91 | 1,073 | 658 | 46 | .613 | 8,603 | 72 |
| Steve Calabria, Colgate .............. | 1981-84 | 1,143 | 626 | 68 | .548 | 8,555 | 54 |
| Mike Buck, Maine.................... | 1986-89 | 1,102 | 619 | 39 | .562 | 8,491 | 67 |
| Jeff Cesarone, Western Ky. .......... | 1984-87 | 1,339 | 714 | 39 | .533 | 8,404 | 45 |
| Frank Baur, Lafayette ................ | 1985, 87-89 | 1,103 | 636 | 46 | .577 | 8,399 | 62 |
| Fred Gatlin, Nevada................... | %1989-92 | 1,116 | 613 | 46 | .549 | 8,312 | 63 |
| Stan Yagiello, William & Mary ........ | $1981-85 | 1,247 | 737 | 36 | .591 | 8,249 | 51 |
| Mike Smith, Northern Iowa ........... | 1984-87 | 943 | 557 | 43 | .591 | 8,219 | 58 |
| Kelly Bradley, Montana St. ........... | 1983-86 | 1,238 | 714 | 45 | .577 | 8,152 | 60 |
| Bob Bleier, Richmond................. | 1983-86 | 1,169 | 672 | 56 | .575 | 8,057 | 54 |
| John Gregory, Marshall .............$#1985, 86-89 | | 1,074 | 552 | 45 | .513 | 7,896 | 59 |
| Chris Goetz, Towson St. .............. | 1987-90 | 1,172 | 648 | 51 | .553 | 7,882 | 42 |
| ¢Doug Nussmeier, Idaho ............. | 1990-92 | 921 | 561 | 27 | .609 | 7,864 | 58 |
| Paul Singer, Western Ill. .............. | 1985-88 | 1,171 | 646 | 43 | .552 | 7,850 | 61 |
| John Witkowski, Columbia ............ | 1981-83 | 1,176 | 613 | 60 | .521 | 7,849 | 56 |
| Grady Bennett, Montana ............. | 1987-90 | 1,097 | 641 | 42 | .584 | 7,778 | 55 |
| Bernard Hawk, Bethune-Cookman ... | 1982-85 | 1,120 | 554 | 51 | .495 | 7,737 | 56 |
| Bob Jean, New Hampshire............ | 1985-88 | 1,126 | 567 | 49 | .504 | 7,704 | 51 |

* Record.   $ See page 8 for explanation.   # At Southeastern La. in 1985.   ¢ Active player.   % Played 1992 season in Division I-A.

## Career Yards Per Game

| Player, Team | Years | G | Att. | Cmp. | Yards | TD | Yd. PG |
|---|---|---|---|---|---|---|---|
| Willie Totten, Mississippi Val. ............. | 1982-85 | 40 | 1,555 | 907 | 12,711 | *139 | *317.8 |
| Neil Lomax, Portland St. ................. | 1977-80 | 42 | *1,606 | *938 | *13,220 | 106 | 314.8 |
| John Friesz, Idaho ..................... | 1986-89 | 35 | 1,350 | 801 | 10,697 | 77 | 305.6 |
| Jamie Martin, Weber St. ................ | 1989-92 | 41 | 1,544 | 934 | 12,207 | 87 | 297.7 |
| Sean Payton, Eastern Ill. ............... | 1983-86 | 37 | 1,408 | 756 | 10,655 | 75 | 288.0 |
| Greg Wyatt, Northern Ariz. .............. | 1986-89 | 42 | 1,510 | 926 | 10,697 | 70 | 254.7 |

* Record.

## Career Touchdown Passes

| Player, Team | Years | Games | TD Passes |
|---|---|---|---|
| Willie Totten, Mississippi Val............................................ | 1982-85 | 40 | *139 |
| Neil Lomax, Portland St. ............................................... | 1977-80 | 42 | 106 |
| Jamie Martin, Weber St. ............................................... | 1989-92 | 41 | 87 |
| Ken Hobart, Idaho .................................................... | 1980-83 | 44 | 79 |
| John Friesz, Idaho .................................................... | 1986-89 | 35 | 77 |
| Eric Beavers, Nevada ................................................. | 1983-86 | 40 | 77 |
| Sean Payton, Eastern Ill. .............................................. | 1983-86 | 39 | 75 |
| Matt DeGennaro, Connecticut .......................................... | 1987-90 | 43 | 73 |
| Tom Ciaccio, Holy Cross............................................... | 1988-91 | 37 | 72 |
| Jeff Wiley, Holy Cross................................................. | 1985-88 | 41 | 71 |
| Kirk Schulz, Villanova ................................................. | 1986-89 | 42 | 70 |
| Greg Wyatt, Northern Ariz.............................................. | 1986-89 | 42 | 70 |

* Record.

**Special Note:** Tom Ehrhardt played two years at LIU-C. W. Post (Division II) and two years at Rhode Island (Division I-AA) and totaled 92 career touchdown passes. For I-AA, he totaled 66.

## Season Touchdown Passes

| Player, Team | Year | Games | TD Passes |
|---|---|---|---|
| Willie Totten, Mississippi Val.......................................... | 1984 | 10 | *56 |
| Willie Totten, Mississippi Val.......................................... | 1985 | 11 | 39 |
| Neil Lomax, Portland St. .............................................. | 1980 | 11 | 37 |
| Jamie Martin, Weber St. .............................................. | 1991 | 11 | 35 |
| Tom Ehrhardt, Rhode Island .......................................... | 1985 | 10 | 35 |
| Todd Hammel, Stephen F. Austin ...................................... | 1989 | 11 | 34 |
| Jeff Wiley, Holy Cross................................................ | 1987 | 11 | 34 |
| Doug Hudson, Nicholls St............................................. | 1986 | 11 | 32 |
| Ken Hobart, Idaho ................................................... | 1983 | 11 | 32 |
| Glenn Kempa, Lehigh................................................. | 1991 | 11 | 31 |
| John Friesz, Idaho ................................................... | 1989 | 11 | 31 |
| Brent Pease, Montana................................................ | 1986 | 11 | 30 |
| Kelly Bradley, Montana St. ........................................... | 1984 | 11 | 30 |

* Record.

_Division I-AA Annual Champions, All-Time Leaders_

## Season Yards

| Player, Team | Year | G | Att. | Cmp. | Int. | Pct. | Yards | TD |
|---|---|---|---|---|---|---|---|---|
| Willie Totten, Mississippi Val. | †1984 | 10 | *518 | *324 | 22 | .626 | *4,557 | *56 |
| Jamie Martin, Weber St. | 1991 | 11 | 500 | 310 | 17 | .620 | 4,125 | 35 |
| Neil Lomax, Portland St. | 1980 | 11 | 473 | 296 | 12 | .626 | 4,094 | 37 |
| John Friesz, Idaho | 1989 | 11 | 425 | 260 | 8 | .612 | 4,041 | 31 |
| Neil Lomax, Portland St. | 1979 | 11 | 516 | 299 | 16 | .579 | 3,950 | 26 |
| Todd Hammel, Stephen F. Austin | †1989 | 11 | 401 | 238 | 13 | .594 | 3,914 | 34 |
| Sean Payton, Eastern Ill. | 1984 | 11 | 473 | 270 | 15 | .571 | 3,843 | 28 |
| Jamie Martin, Weber St. | 1990 | 11 | 428 | 256 | 15 | .598 | 3,700 | 23 |
| Willie Totten, Mississippi Val. | 1985 | 11 | 492 | 295 | 29 | .600 | 3,698 | 39 |
| Jeff Wiley, Holy Cross | †1987 | 11 | 400 | 265 | 17 | .663 | 3,677 | 34 |
| John Friesz, Idaho | 1987 | 11 | 502 | 311 | 14 | .620 | 3,677 | 28 |
| Ken Hobart, Idaho | 1983 | 11 | 477 | 268 | 19 | .562 | 3,618 | 32 |
| Glenn Kempa, Lehigh | 1991 | 11 | 474 | 286 | 15 | .603 | 3,565 | 31 |
| Tom Ehrhardt, Rhode Island | 1985 | 10 | 497 | 283 | 19 | .569 | 3,542 | 35 |
| Steve McNair, Alcorn St. | 1992 | 10 | 427 | 231 | 11 | .541 | 3,541 | 29 |
| Tony Petersen, Marshall | 1987 | 11 | 466 | 251 | 25 | .539 | 3,529 | 22 |
| Todd Brunner, Lehigh | 1989 | 11 | 450 | 273 | 19 | .607 | 3,516 | 26 |
| Kelly Bradley, Montana St. | 1984 | 11 | 499 | 289 | 20 | .579 | 3,508 | 30 |
| Neil Lomax, Portland St. | †1978 | 11 | 436 | 241 | 22 | .553 | 3,506 | 25 |

* Record.   † National pass-efficiency champion.

## Season Yards Per Game

| Player, Team | Year | G | Att. | Cmp. | Int. | Pct. | Yards | TD | Yd.PG |
|---|---|---|---|---|---|---|---|---|---|
| Willie Totten, Mississippi Val. | †1984 | 10 | *518 | *324 | 22 | .626 | *4,557 | *56 | *455.7 |
| Jamie Martin, Weber St. | 1991 | 11 | 500 | 310 | 17 | .620 | 4,125 | 35 | 375.0 |
| Neil Lomax, Portland St. | 1980 | 11 | 473 | 296 | 12 | .626 | 4,094 | 37 | 372.2 |
| John Friesz, Idaho | 1989 | 11 | 425 | 260 | 8 | .612 | 4,041 | 31 | 367.4 |
| Neil Lomax, Portland St. | 1979 | 11 | 516 | 299 | 16 | .579 | 3,950 | 26 | 359.1 |
| Todd Hammel, Stephen F. Austin | †1989 | 11 | 401 | 238 | 13 | .594 | 3,914 | 34 | 355.8 |
| Tom Ehrhardt, Rhode Island | 1985 | 10 | 497 | 283 | 19 | .569 | 3,542 | 35 | 354.2 |
| Steve McNair, Alcorn St. | 1992 | 10 | 427 | 231 | 11 | .541 | 3,541 | 29 | 354.1 |
| Sean Payton, Eastern Ill. | 1984 | 11 | 473 | 270 | 15 | .571 | 3,843 | 28 | 349.4 |
| Jamie Martin, Weber St. | 1990 | 11 | 428 | 256 | 15 | .598 | 3,700 | 23 | 336.4 |
| Willie Totten, Mississippi Val. | 1985 | 11 | 492 | 295 | 29 | .600 | 3,698 | 39 | 336.2 |

* Record.   † National pass-efficiency champion.

## Single-Game Yards

| Yds. | Player, Team (Opponent) | Date |
|---|---|---|
| 624 | Jamie Martin, Weber St. (Idaho St.) | Nov. 23, 1991 |
| 619 | Doug Pederson, Northeast La. (Stephen F. Austin) | Nov. 11, 1989 |
| 599 | Willie Totten, Mississippi Val. (Prairie View) | Oct. 27, 1984 |
| 589 | Vern Harris, Idaho St. (Montana) | Oct. 12, 1985 |
| 571 | Todd Hammel, Stephen F. Austin (Northeast La.) | Nov. 11, 1989 |
| 566 | Tom Ehrhardt, Rhode Island (Connecticut) | Nov. 16, 1985 |
| 553 | Willie Totten, Mississippi Val. (Southern-B.R.) | Sept. 29, 1984 |
| 547 | Jamie Martin, Weber St. (Montana St.) | Sept. 26, 1992 |
| 545 | Willie Totten, Mississippi Val. (Grambling) | Oct. 13, 1984 |
| 537 | Tod Mayfield, West Tex. (New Mexico St.) | Nov. 16, 1985 |
| 536 | Willie Totten, Mississippi Val. (Kentucky St.) | Sept. 1, 1984 |
| 534 | Todd Hammel, Stephen F. Austin (Sam Houston St.) | Nov. 4, 1989 |
| 527 | Bernard Hawk, Bethune-Cookman (Ga. Southern) | Oct. 6, 1984 |
| 527 | Ken Hobart, Idaho (Southern Colo.) | Sept. 10, 1983 |
| 526 | Willie Totten, Mississippi Val. (Jackson St.) | Sept. 22, 1984 |

## Single-Game Attempts

| No. | Player, Team (Opponent) | Date |
|---|---|---|
| 77 | Neil Lomax, Portland St. (Northern Colo.) | Oct. 20, 1979 |
| 74 | Paul Peterson, Idaho St. (Nevada) | Oct. 1, 1983 |
| 71 | Doug Pederson, Northeast La. (Stephen F. Austin) | Nov. 11, 1989 |
| 70 | Greg Farland, Rhode Island (Boston U.) | Oct. 18, 1986 |
| 69 | Steve McNair, Alcorn St. (Jacksonville St.) | Oct. 31, 1992 |
| 68 | Tony Petersen, Marshall (Western Caro.) | Nov. 14, 1987 |
| 67 | Michael Payton, Marshall (Western Caro.) | Oct. 31, 1992 |
| 67 | Vern Harris, Idaho St. (Montana) | Oct. 12, 1985 |
| 67 | Rick Worman, Eastern Wash. (Nevada) | Oct. 12, 1985 |
| 67 | Tod Mayfield, West Tex. St. (Indiana St.) | Oct. 5, 1985 |

| No. | Player, Team (Opponent) | Date |
|---|---|---|
| 67 | Tom Ehrhardt, Rhode Island (Brown) | Sept. 28, 1985 |
| 66 | Chris Swartz, Morehead St. (Tennessee Tech) | Oct. 17, 1987 |
| 66 | Sean Cook, Texas Southern (Texas A&I) | Sept. 6, 1986 |
| 66 | Kelly Bradley, Montana St. (Eastern Wash.) | Sept. 21, 1985 |
| 66 | Bernard Hawk, Bethune-Cookman (Ga. Southern) | Oct. 6, 1984 |
| 66 | Willie Totten, Mississippi Val. (Southern-B.R.) | Sept. 29, 1984 |
| 66 | Paul Peterson, Idaho St. (Cal Poly SLO) | Oct. 22, 1983 |

### Single-Game Completions

| No. | Player, Team (Opponent) | Date |
|---|---|---|
| 47 | Jamie Martin, Weber St. (Idaho St.) | Nov. 23, 1991 |
| 46 | Doug Pederson, Northeast La. (Stephen F. Austin) | Nov. 11, 1989 |
| 46 | Willie Totten, Mississippi Val. (Southern-B.R.) | Sept. 29, 1984 |
| 45 | Willie Totten, Mississippi Val. (Prairie View) | Oct. 27, 1984 |
| 44 | Neil Lomax, Portland St. (Northern Colo.) | Oct. 20, 1979 |
| 42 | Tod Mayfield, West Tex. St. (Indiana St.) | Oct. 5, 1985 |
| 42 | Kelly Bradley, Montana St. (Eastern Wash.) | Sept. 21, 1985 |
| 42 | Rusty Hill, North Texas (Tulsa) | Nov. 20, 1982 |

### Annual Champions

| Year | Player, Team | Cl. | G. | Att. | Cmp. | Avg. | Int. | Pct. | Yds. | TD |
|---|---|---|---|---|---|---|---|---|---|---|
| 1978 | Neil Lomax, Portland St. | So. | 11 | 436 | 241 | 21.9 | 22 | .553 | 3,506 | 25 |

*Beginning in 1979, ranked on Passing Efficiency Rating Points (instead of per-game completions)*

| Year | Player, Team | Cl. | G. | Att. | Cmp. | Int. | Pct. | Yds. | TD | Pts. |
|---|---|---|---|---|---|---|---|---|---|---|
| 1979 | Joe Aliotti, Boise St. | Jr. | 11 | 219 | 144 | 7 | .658 | 1,870 | 19 | 159.7 |
| 1980 | Mike Williams, Grambling | Sr. | 11 | 239 | 127 | 5 | .531 | 2,116 | 28 | 162.0 |
| 1981 | Mike Machurek, Idaho St. | Sr. | 9 | 313 | 188 | 11 | .601 | 2,752 | 22 | 150.1 |
| 1982 | Frank Novak, Lafayette | Jr. | 10 | 257 | 154 | 12 | .599 | 2,257 | 20 | 150.0 |
| 1983 | Willie Totten, Mississippi Val. | So. | 9 | 279 | 174 | 9 | .624 | 2,566 | 29 | 167.5 |
| 1984 | Willie Totten, Mississippi Val. | Jr. | 10 | *518 | *324 | 22 | .626 | *4,557 | *56 | 163.6 |
| 1985 | Bobby Lamb, Furman | Sr. | 11 | 181 | 106 | 6 | .586 | 1,856 | 18 | 170.9 |
| 1986 | Mike Smith, Northern Iowa | Jr. | 11 | 303 | 190 | 16 | .627 | 3,125 | 27 | 168.2 |
| 1987 | Jeff Wiley, Holy Cross | Jr. | 11 | 400 | 265 | 17 | .663 | 3,677 | 34 | 163.0 |
| 1988 | Frank Baur, Lafayette | Jr. | 10 | 256 | 164 | 11 | .641 | 2,621 | 23 | 171.1 |
| 1989 | Todd Hammel, Stephen F. Austin | Sr. | 11 | 401 | 238 | 13 | .594 | 3,914 | 34 | 162.8 |
| 1990 | Connell Maynor, North Caro. A&T | Jr. | 11 | 191 | 123 | 10 | .644 | 1,699 | 16 | 156.3 |
| 1991 | Michael Payton, Marshall | Jr. | 9 | 216 | 143 | 5 | .662 | 2,333 | 19 | *181.3 |
| 1992 | Jay Fiedler, Dartmouth | Jr. | 10 | 273 | 175 | 13 | .641 | 2,748 | 25 | 169.4 |

*\* Record.*

# RECEIVING

### Career Catches Per Game

| Player, Team | Years | Games | Catches | Yards | TD | Ct. PG |
|---|---|---|---|---|---|---|
| Jerry Rice, Mississippi Val. | 1981-84 | 41 | *301 | *4,693 | *50 | *7.3 |
| Kevin Guthrie, Princeton | 1981-83 | 28 | 193 | 2,645 | 16 | 6.9 |
| Eric Yarber, Idaho | 1984-85 | 19 | 129 | 1,920 | 17 | 6.8 |
| Brian Forster, Rhode Island (TE) | 1983-85, 87 | 38 | 245 | 3,410 | 31 | 6.5 |
| Kasey Dunn, Idaho | 1988-91 | 42 | 268 | 3,847 | 25 | 6.4 |
| Gordie Lockbaum, Holy Cross (RB) | ‡1986-87 | 22 | 135 | 2,012 | 17 | 6.1 |
| Derek Graham, Princeton | 1981, 83-84 | 29 | 176 | 2,819 | 19 | 6.1 |
| Stuart Gaussoin, Portland St. | 1978-80 | 23 | 135 | 1,909 | 14 | 5.9 |
| Don Lewis, Columbia | 1981-83 | 30 | 176 | 2,207 | 11 | 5.9 |
| Mike Barber, Marshall | 1985-88 | 36 | 209 | 3,250 | 20 | 5.8 |
| Sebastian Brown, Bethune-Cookman | 1984-85 | 20 | 116 | 1,830 | 17 | 5.8 |
| Rennie Benn, Lehigh | 1982-85 | 41 | 237 | 3,662 | 44 | 5.8 |
| Daren Altieri, Boston U. | 1987-90 | 39 | 225 | 2,518 | 15 | 5.8 |
| Bill Reggio, Columbia | 1981-83 | 30 | 170 | 2,384 | 26 | 5.7 |

*\* Record.   ‡ Defensive back in 1984-85.*

### Season Catches Per Game

| Player, Team | Year | Games | Catches | Yards | TD | Ct. PG |
|---|---|---|---|---|---|---|
| Brian Forster, Rhode Island (TE) | †1985 | 10 | *115 | 1,617 | 12 | *11.5 |
| Jerry Rice, Mississippi Val. | 1984 | 10 | 103 | *1,682 | *27 | 10.3 |
| Jerry Rice, Mississippi Val. | †1983 | 10 | 102 | 1,450 | 14 | 10.2 |
| Stuart Gaussoin, Portland St. | †1979 | 9 | 90 | 1,132 | 8 | 10.0 |
| Kevin Guthrie, Princeton | 1983 | 10 | 88 | 1,259 | 9 | 8.8 |

| Player, Team | Year | Games | Catches | Yards | TD | Ct. PG |
|---|---|---|---|---|---|---|
| Alfred Pupunu, Weber St. (TE) ......... | †1991 | 11 | 93 | 1,204 | 12 | 8.5 |
| Derek Graham, Princeton .............. | 1983 | 10 | 84 | 1,363 | 11 | 8.4 |
| Don Lewis, Columbia ................. | †1982 | 10 | 84 | 1,000 | 6 | 8.4 |
| Peter Macon, Weber St. ............... | †1989 | 11 | 92 | 1,047 | 6 | 8.4 |
| Marvin Walker, North Texas ............ | 1982 | 11 | 91 | 934 | 11 | 8.3 |

*Record.   † National champion.*

## Career Catches

| Player, Team | Years | Catches | Yards | Avg. | TD |
|---|---|---|---|---|---|
| Jerry Rice, Mississippi Val. ................. | 1981-84 | *301 | *4,693 | 15.6 | *50 |
| Kasey Dunn, Idaho ........................ | 1988-91 | 268 | 3,847 | 14.4 | 25 |
| Brian Forster, Rhode Island ................ | 1983-85, 87 | 245 | 3,410 | 13.9 | 31 |
| Mark Didio, Connecticut ................... | 1988-91 | 239 | 3,535 | 14.8 | 21 |
| Rennie Benn, Lehigh....................... | 1982-85 | 237 | 3,662 | 15.5 | 44 |
| Daren Altieri, Boston U. .................... | 1987-90 | 225 | 2,518 | 11.2 | 15 |
| Darrell Colbert, Texas Southern ............ | 1983-86 | 217 | 3,177 | 14.6 | 33 |
| Mike Barber, Marshall ..................... | 1985-88 | 209 | 3,520 | 16.8 | 20 |
| William Brooks, Boston U. ................. | 1982-85 | 204 | 3,154 | 15.5 | 26 |
| Donald Narcisse, Texas Southern .......... | 1983-86 | 203 | 2,429 | 12.0 | 26 |
| Alex Davis, Connecticut.................... | 1989-92 | 202 | 2,567 | 12.7 | 24 |
| Shawn Collins, Northern Ariz............... | 1985-88 | 201 | 2,764 | 13.8 | 24 |
| Leland Melvin, Richmond .................. | 1982-85 | 198 | 2,669 | 13.5 | 16 |
| Curtis Olds, New Hampshire............... | 1985-88 | 193 | 3,028 | 15.7 | 23 |
| Kevin Guthrie, Princeton ................... | 1981-83 | 193 | 2,645 | 13.7 | 16 |
| Sergio Hebra, Maine ...................... | 1984-87 | 189 | 2,612 | 13.8 | 17 |
| John Perry, New Hampshire ............... | 1989-92 | 186 | 2,798 | 15.0 | 19 |
| Glenn Antrum, Connecticut................ | 1985-88 | 186 | 2,552 | 13.7 | 14 |
| Joe Thomas, Mississippi Val............... | 1982-85 | 186 | 2,816 | 15.1 | 36 |
| Roy Banks, Eastern Ill. ................... | 1983-86 | 184 | 3,177 | 17.3 | 38 |
| Merril Hoge, Idaho St. (RB) ............... | 1983-86 | 182 | 1,734 | 9.5 | 13 |
| George Delaney, Colgate .................. | 1988-91 | 181 | 2,938 | 16.2 | 25 |
| Robert Brady, Villanova ................... | 1986-89 | 180 | 2,725 | 15.1 | 28 |
| Cisco Richard, Northeast La............... | 1987-90 | 179 | 1,874 | 10.5 | 12 |
| Peter Macon, Weber St. ................... | 1986-89 | 177 | 2,151 | 12.1 | 16 |

*Record.*

## Season Catches

| Player, Team | Year | Games | Catches | Yards | TD |
|---|---|---|---|---|---|
| Brian Forster, Rhode Island (TE) .............. | †1985 | 10 | *115 | 1,617 | 12 |
| Jerry Rice, Mississippi Val. .................... | †1984 | 10 | 103 | *1,682 | *27 |
| Jerry Rice, Mississippi Val. .................... | †1983 | 10 | 102 | 1,450 | 14 |
| Alfred Pupunu, Weber St. (TE) ................ | †1991 | 11 | 93 | 1,204 | 12 |
| Peter Macon, Weber St. ...................... | †1989 | 11 | 92 | 1,047 | 6 |
| Marvin Walker, North Texas .................. | 1982 | 11 | 91 | 934 | 11 |
| Stuart Gaussoin, Portland St. ................ | †1979 | 9 | 90 | 1,132 | 8 |
| Mark Didio, Connecticut ..................... | 1991 | 11 | 88 | 1,354 | 8 |
| Kasey Dunn, Idaho ......................... | †1990 | 11 | 88 | 1,164 | 7 |
| Donald Narcisse, Texas Southern ............ | †1986 | 11 | 88 | 1,074 | 15 |
| Kevin Guthrie, Princeton ..................... | 1983 | 10 | 88 | 1,259 | 9 |
| Kasey Dunn, Idaho ......................... | 1991 | 11 | 85 | 1,263 | 6 |
| Derek Graham, Princeton .................... | 1983 | 10 | 84 | 1,363 | 11 |
| Don Lewis, Columbia ....................... | †1982 | 10 | 84 | 1,000 | 6 |

*Record.   † National champion.*

## Single-Game Catches

| No. | Player, Team (Opponent) | Date |
|---|---|---|
| 24 | Jerry Rice, Mississippi Val. (Southern-B.R.)...................................... | Oct. 1, 1983 |
| 22 | Marvin Walker, North Texas (Tulsa) ........................................... | Nov. 20, 1982 |
| 21 | David Pandt, Montana St. (Eastern Wash.) ..................................... | Sept. 21, 1985 |
| 18 | Jerome Williams, Morehead St. (Eastern Ky.) .................................. | Nov. 18, 1989 |
| 18 | Brian Forster, Rhode Island (Brown)........................................... | Sept. 28, 1985 |
| 17 | Lifford Jackson, Louisiana Tech (Kansas St.) ................................... | Oct. 1, 1988 |
| 17 | Brian Forster, Rhode Island (Lehigh) .......................................... | Oct. 12, 1985 |
| 17 | Jerry Rice, Mississippi Val. (Southern-B.R.) .................................... | Sept. 29, 1984 |
| 17 | Jerry Rice, Mississippi Val. (Kentucky St.) ..................................... | Sept. 1, 1984 |

*1993 NCAA FOOTBALL*

## Career Yards

| Player, Team | Years | Catches | Yards | Avg. | TD |
|---|---|---|---|---|---|
| Jerry Rice, Mississippi Val. | 1981-84 | *301 | *4,693 | 15.6 | *50 |
| Kasey Dunn, Idaho | 1988-91 | 268 | 3,847 | 14.4 | 25 |
| Rennie Benn, Lehigh | 1982-85 | 237 | 3,662 | 15.5 | 44 |
| Mark Didio, Connecticut | 1988-91 | 239 | 3,535 | 14.8 | 21 |
| Mike Barber, Marshall | 1985-88 | 209 | 3,520 | 16.8 | 20 |
| Brian Forster, Rhode Island (TE) | 1983-85, 87 | 245 | 3,410 | 13.9 | 31 |
| Tracy Singleton, Howard | 1979-82 | 159 | 3,187 | ‡20.0 | 16 |
| Roy Banks, Eastern Ill. | 1983-86 | 184 | 3,177 | 17.3 | 38 |
| Darrell Colbert, Texas Southern | 1983-86 | 217 | 3,177 | 14.6 | 33 |
| William Brooks, Boston U. | 1982-85 | 204 | 3,154 | 15.5 | 26 |

*Record.  ‡ Record for minimum of 125 catches.*

## Season Yards

| Player, Team | Year | Catches | Yards | Avg. | TD |
|---|---|---|---|---|---|
| Jerry Rice, Mississippi Val. | †1984 | 103 | *1,682 | 16.3 | *27 |
| Brian Forster, Rhode Island | †1985 | *115 | 1,617 | 14.1 | 12 |
| Jerry Rice, Mississippi Val. | †1983 | 102 | 1,450 | 14.2 | 14 |
| Derek Graham, Princeton | 1983 | 84 | 1,363 | 16.2 | 11 |
| Mark Didio, Connecticut | †1991 | 88 | 1,354 | 15.4 | 8 |
| Golden Tate, Tennessee St. | 1983 | 63 | 1,307 | 20.7 | 13 |

*Record.  † National champion.*

## Single-Game Yards

| Yds. | Player, Team (Opponent) | Date |
|---|---|---|
| 370 | Michael Lerch, Princeton (Brown) | Oct. 12, 1991 |
| 330 | Nate Singleton, Grambling (Virginia Union) | Sept. 14, 1991 |
| 327 | Brian Forster, Rhode Island (Brown) | Sept. 28, 1985 |
| 319 | Jason Cristino, Lehigh (Lafayette) | Nov. 21, 1992 |
| 299 | Treamelle Taylor, Nevada (Montana) | Oct. 14, 1989 |
| 299 | Brian Forster, Rhode Island (Lehigh) | Oct. 12, 1985 |
| 294 | Jerry Rice, Mississippi Val. (Kentucky St.) | Sept. 1, 1984 |
| 285 | Jerry Rice, Mississippi Val. (Jackson St.) | Sept. 22, 1984 |
| 279 | Jerry Rice, Mississippi Val. (Southern-B.R.) | Oct. 1, 1983 |
| 266 | Rennie Benn, Lehigh (Indiana, Pa.) | Sept. 14, 1985 |
| 263 | Mark Stock, Va. Military (East Tenn. St.) | Nov. 22, 1986 |
| 262 | Andre Motley, Marshall (Tenn.-Chatt.) | Oct. 20, 1990 |
| 262 | Kenneth Gilstrap, Tennessee Tech (Morehead St.) | Oct. 17, 1987 |
| 253 | Chris Johnson, Indiana St. (Illinois St.) | Oct. 18, 1986 |
| 252 | Jeff Sanders, William & Mary (Miami, Ohio) | Sept. 11, 1982 |
| 251 | Lifford Jackson, Louisiana Tech (Kansas St.) | Oct. 1, 1988 |

## Annual Champions

| Year | Player, Team | Class | G. | Ct. | Avg. | Yards | TD |
|---|---|---|---|---|---|---|---|
| 1978 | Dan Ross, Northeastern | Sr. | 11 | 68 | 6.2 | 988 | 7 |
| 1979 | Stuart Gaussoin, Portland St. | Jr. | 9 | 90 | 10.0 | 1,132 | 8 |
| 1980 | Kenny Johnson, Portland St. | So. | 11 | 72 | 6.5 | 1,011 | 11 |
| 1981 | Ken Harvey, Northern Iowa | Sr. | 11 | 78 | 7.1 | 1,161 | 15 |
| 1982 | Don Lewis, Columbia | Jr. | 10 | 84 | 8.4 | 1,000 | 6 |
| 1983 | Jerry Rice, Mississippi Val. | Jr. | 10 | 102 | 10.2 | 1,450 | 14 |
| 1984 | Jerry Rice, Mississippi Val. | Sr. | 10 | 103 | 10.3 | *1,682 | *27 |
| 1985 | Brian Forster, Rhode Island (TE) | Jr. | 10 | *115 | *11.5 | 1,617 | 12 |
| 1986 | Donald Narcisse, Texas Southern | Sr. | 11 | 88 | 8.0 | 1,074 | 15 |
| 1987 | Mike Barber, Marshall | Jr. | 11 | 78 | 7.1 | 1,237 | 7 |
|  | Gordie Lockbaum, Holy Cross (RB) | Sr. | 11 | 78 | 7.1 | 1,152 | 9 |
| 1988 | Glenn Antrum, Connecticut | Sr. | 11 | 77 | 7.0 | 1,130 | 7 |
| 1989 | Peter Macon, Weber St. | Sr. | 11 | 92 | 8.4 | 1,047 | 6 |

*Beginning in 1990, ranked on both per-game catches and yards per game*

## Per-Game Catches

| Year | Player, Team | Class | G. | Ct. | Avg. | Yards | TD |
|---|---|---|---|---|---|---|---|
| 1990 | Kasey Dunn, Idaho | Jr. | 11 | 88 | 8.0 | 1,164 | 7 |
| 1991 | Alfred Pupunu, Weber St. (TE) | Sr. | 11 | 93 | 8.5 | 1,204 | 12 |
| 1992 | Glenn Krupa, Southeast Mo. St. | Sr. | 11 | 77 | 7.0 | 773 | 4 |

*Division I-AA Annual Champions, All-Time Leaders*      163

## Yards Per Game

| Year | Player, Team | Class | G. | Ct. | Yards | Avg. | TD |
|------|-------------|-------|-----|-----|-------|------|-----|
| 1990 | Kasey Dunn, Idaho | Jr. | 11 | 88 | 1,164 | 105.8 | 7 |
| 1991 | Mark Didio, Connecticut | Sr. | 11 | 88 | 1,354 | 123.1 | 8 |
| 1992 | Jason Cristino, Lehigh | Sr. | 11 | 65 | 1,282 | 116.5 | 9 |

* Record.

# SCORING

## Career Points Per Game §

| Player, Team | Years | Games | TD | XPt. | FG | Pts. | Pt. PG |
|-------------|-------|-------|-----|------|-----|------|--------|
| David Meggett, Towson St. | 1987-88 | 18 | 30 | 0 | 0 | 180 | *10.0 |
| Elroy Harris, Eastern Ky. | 1985, 87-88 | 31 | 47 | 6 | 0 | 288 | 9.3 |
| Tony Zendejas, Nevada | 1981-83 | 33 | 0 | 90 | 70 | 300 | 9.1 |
| Gerald Harris, Ga. Southern | 1984-86 | 31 | 45 | 2 | 0 | 272 | 8.8 |
| Marty Zendejas, Nevada | 1984-87 | 44 | 0 | *169 | *72 | *385 | 8.8 |
| Charvez Foger, Nevada | 1985-88 | 42 | *60 | 2 | 0 | 362 | 8.6 |
| Paul Lewis, Boston U. | 1981-84 | 37 | 51 | 2 | 0 | 308 | 8.3 |
| Judd Garrett, Princeton | 1987-89 | 30 | 41 | 1 | 0 | 248 | 8.3 |
| Andre Garron, New Hampshire | 1982-85 | 30 | 41 | 0 | 0 | 246 | 8.2 |
| Micky Penaflor, Northern Ariz. | 1986-88 | 22 | 0 | 66 | 38 | 180 | 8.2 |
| Kenny Gamble, Colgate | 1984-87 | 42 | 57 | 0 | 0 | 342 | 8.1 |
| Barry Bourassa, New Hampshire | 1989-92 | 39 | 51 | 0 | 0 | 306 | 7.8 |
| Markus Thomas, Eastern Ky. | 1989-92 | 43 | 53 | 4 | 0 | 322 | 7.5 |
| Jerry Rice, Mississippi Val. | 1981-84 | 41 | 50 | 2 | 0 | 302 | 7.4 |
| Joel Sigel, Portland St. | 1977-80 | 41 | 50 | 2 | 0 | 302 | 7.4 |
| Brian Mitchell, Marshall/Northern Iowa | 1987, 89-91 | 44 | 0 | 130 | 64 | 322 | 7.3 |
| George Benyola, Louisiana Tech | 1984-85 | 22 | 0 | 40 | 40 | 160 | 7.3 |
| Roberto Moran, Boise St. | 1985-86 | 22 | 0 | 57 | 34 | 159 | 7.2 |
| Harvey Reed, Howard | 1984-87 | 41 | 48 | 6 | 0 | 294 | 7.2 |
| Thayne Doyle, Idaho | 1988-91 | 43 | 0 | 160 | 49 | 307 | 7.1 |
| Dwight Stone, Middle Tenn. St. | 1985-86 | 22 | 26 | 0 | 0 | 156 | 7.1 |
| Stanford Jennings, Furman | 1982-83 | 22 | 26 | 0 | 0 | 156 | 7.1 |
| Rich Erenberg, Colgate | 1982-83 | 21 | 23 | 10 | 0 | 148 | 7.0 |

* Record.  § The following players competed two years in Division I-AA and two years in Division I-A: Stanford Jennings, Furman (four years: 262 points and 6.1 average); Rich Erenberg, Colgate (four years: 202 points and 5.2 average), and Buford Jordan, McNeese St. (four years: 266 points and 6.5 average).

## Season Points Per Game

| Player, Team | Year | Games | TD | XPt. | FG | Pts. | Pt. PG |
|-------------|------|-------|-----|------|-----|------|--------|
| Jerry Rice, Mississippi Val. | †1984 | 10 | 27 | 0 | 0 | 162 | *16.2 |
| Geoff Mitchell, Weber St. | †1991 | 11 | *28 | 1 | 0 | *170 | 15.5 |
| Sherriden May, Idaho | †1992 | 11 | 25 | 0 | 0 | 150 | 13.6 |
| Elroy Harris, Eastern Ky. | †1988 | 10 | 21 | 2 | 0 | 128 | 12.8 |
| Sean Sanders, Weber St. | †1987 | 10 | 21 | 0 | 0 | 126 | 12.6 |
| Rich Erenberg, Colgate | †1983 | 11 | 21 | 10 | 0 | 136 | 12.4 |
| Harvey Reed, Howard | 1987 | 10 | 20 | 2 | 0 | 122 | 12.2 |
| Paul Lewis, Boston U. | 1983 | 10 | 20 | 2 | 0 | 122 | 12.2 |
| Gordie Lockbaum, Holy Cross | 1987 | 11 | 22 | 0 | 0 | 132 | 12.0 |
| Gordie Lockbaum, Holy Cross | †1986 | 11 | 22 | 0 | 0 | 132 | 12.0 |
| Gene Lake, Delaware St. | 1984 | 10 | 20 | 0 | 0 | 120 | 12.0 |
| Ernest Thompson, Ga. Southern | 1988 | 10 | 19 | 2 | 0 | 116 | 11.6 |
| Barry Bourassa, New Hampshire | 1991 | 11 | 21 | 0 | 0 | 126 | 11.5 |
| Kenny Gamble, Colgate | 1986 | 11 | 21 | 0 | 0 | 126 | 11.5 |
| Gerald Harris, Ga. Southern | 1984 | 9 | 17 | 0 | 0 | 102 | 11.3 |
| Keith Elias, Princeton | 1992 | 10 | 18 | 2 | 0 | 110 | 11.0 |
| Harvey Reed, Howard | 1986 | 10 | 18 | 2 | 0 | 110 | 11.0 |
| Toby Davis, Illinois St. | 1992 | 11 | 20 | 0 | 0 | 120 | 10.9 |
| Carl Smith, Maine | †1989 | 11 | 20 | 0 | 0 | 120 | 10.9 |
| Joe Segreti, Holy Cross | 1988 | 11 | 20 | 0 | 0 | 120 | 10.9 |
| Luther Turner, Sam Houston St. | 1987 | 11 | 20 | 0 | 0 | 120 | 10.9 |
| John Settle, Appalachian St. | 1986 | 11 | 20 | 0 | 0 | 120 | 10.9 |

* Record.  † National champion.

## Career Points (Non-Kickers)

| Player, Team | Years | TD | XPt. | Pts. |
|-------------|-------|-----|------|------|
| Charvez Foger, Nevada | 1985-88 | *60 | 2 | 362 |
| Kenny Gamble, Colgate | 1984-87 | 57 | 0 | 342 |
| Markus Thomas, Eastern Ky. | 1989-92 | 53 | 4 | 322 |
| Paul Lewis, Boston U. | 1981-84 | 51 | 2 | 308 |
| Barry Bourassa, New Hampshire | 1989-92 | 51 | 0 | 306 |

| Player, Team | Years | TD | XPt. | Pts. |
|---|---|---|---|---|
| Erick Torain, Lehigh | 1987-90 | 50 | 6 | 306 |
| Jerry Rice, Mississippi Val. | 1981-84 | 50 | 2 | 302 |
| Joel Sigel, Portland St. | 1977-80 | 50 | 2 | 302 |
| Harvey Reed, Howard | 1984-87 | 48 | 6 | 294 |
| Jack Douglas, Citadel (QB) | 1989-92 | 48 | 0 | 288 |
| Elroy Harris, Eastern Ky. | 1985, 87-88 | 47 | 6 | 288 |
| Joe Campbell, Middle Tenn. St. | 1988-91 | 45 | 2 | 272 |
| Gerald Harris, Ga. Southern | 1984-86 | 45 | 2 | 272 |
| Carl Tremble, Furman | 1989-92 | 45 | 0 | 270 |
| Norm Ford, New Hampshire | 1986-89 | 45 | 0 | 270 |
| John Settle, Appalachian St. | 1983-86 | 44 | 4 | 268 |
| Ernest Thompson, Ga. Southern | 1985, 87-89 | 44 | 2 | 266 |
| Rennie Benn, Lehigh | 1982-85 | 44 | 2 | 266 |
| Joe Segreti, Holy Cross | 1987-90 | 44 | 0 | 264 |
| Gordie Lockbaum, Holy Cross | 1984-87 | 44 | 0 | 264 |
| Frank Hawkins, Nevada | 1977-80 | 44 | 0 | 264 |

* Record.

## Career Points
## (Kickers)

| Player, Team | Years | PAT | PAT Att. | FG | FG Att. | Pts. |
|---|---|---|---|---|---|---|
| Marty Zendejas, Nevada | 1984-87 | *169 | *175 | *72 | 90 | *385 |
| Brian Mitchell, Marshall/Northern Iowa | 1987, 89-91 | 130 | 131 | 64 | 81 | 322 |
| Thayne Doyle, Idaho | 1988-91 | 160 | 174 | 49 | 75 | 307 |
| Kirk Roach, Western Caro. | 1984-87 | 89 | 91 | 71 | *102 | 302 |
| Tim Foley, Ga. Southern | 1984-87 | 151 | 156 | 50 | 62 | 301 |
| Dewey Klein, Marshall | 1988-91 | 156 | 165 | 48 | 66 | 300 |
| Tony Zendejas, Nevada | 1981-83 | 90 | 96 | 70 | 86 | 300 |
| Steve Christie, William & Mary | 1986-89 | 108 | 116 | 57 | 83 | 279 |
| Franco Grilla, Central Fla. | 1989-92 | 141 | 147 | 45 | 69 | 278 |
| Mike Black, Boise St. | 1988-91 | 122 | 127 | 51 | 75 | 275 |
| Kirk Duce, Montana | 1988-91 | 131 | 141 | 47 | 78 | 272 |
| Paul Hickert, Murray St. | 1984-87 | 116 | 121 | 49 | 79 | 263 |
| Dean Biasucci, Western Caro. | 1980-83 | 101 | 106 | 54 | 80 | 263 |
| Matt Stover, Louisiana Tech | #1986-89 | 70 | 72 | 64 | 88 | 262 |
| Kelly Potter, Middle Tenn. St. | 1981-84 | 105 | 109 | 52 | 78 | 261 |
| Billy Hayes, Sam Houston St. | 1985-88 | 117 | 120 | 47 | 71 | 258 |
| Michael O'Neal, Samford | 1989-92 | 142 | 152 | 38 | 60 | 256 |
| Jim Hodson, Lafayette | 1987-90 | 134 | 140 | 40 | 66 | 254 |
| Dave Parkinson, Delaware St. | 1985-88 | 134 | 143 | 40 | 77 | 254 |
| Chuck Rawlinson, Stephen F. Austin | 1988-91 | 106 | 110 | 49 | 69 | 253 |
| Paul Politi, Illinois St. | 1983-86 | 101 | 103 | 50 | 78 | 251 |
| Teddy Garcia, Northeast La. | 1984-87 | 78 | 81 | 56 | 88 | 246 |
| Paul McFadden, Youngstown St. | 1980-83 | 87 | 90 | 52 | 90 | 243 |

* Record.   # Member of Division I-A 1989 only.

## Season Points

| Player, Team | Year | TD | XPt. | FG | Pts. |
|---|---|---|---|---|---|
| Geoff Mitchell, Weber St. | †1991 | *28 | 2 | 0 | *170 |
| Jerry Rice, Mississippi Val. | †1984 | 27 | 0 | 0 | 162 |
| Sherriden May, Idaho | †1992 | 25 | 0 | 0 | 150 |
| Rich Erenberg, Colgate | †1983 | 21 | 10 | 0 | 136 |
| Gordie Lockbaum, Holy Cross | 1987 | 22 | 0 | 0 | 132 |
| Gordie Lockbaum, Holy Cross | †1986 | 22 | 0 | 0 | 132 |
| Elroy Harris, Eastern Ky. | †1988 | 21 | 1 | 0 | 128 |
| Barry Bourassa, New Hampshire | 1991 | 21 | 0 | 0 | 126 |
| Sean Sanders, Weber St. | †1987 | 21 | 0 | 0 | 126 |
| Kenny Gamble, Colgate | 1986 | 21 | 0 | 0 | 126 |
| Harvey Reed, Howard | 1987 | 20 | 2 | 0 | 122 |
| Paul Lewis, Boston U. | 1983 | 20 | 2 | 0 | 122 |
| Toby Davis, Illinois St. | 1992 | 20 | 0 | 0 | 120 |
| Carl Smith, Maine | †1991 | 20 | 0 | 0 | 120 |
| Joe Segreti, Holy Cross | 1988 | 20 | 0 | 0 | 120 |
| Luther Turner, Sam Houston St. | 1987 | 20 | 0 | 0 | 120 |
| John Settle, Appalachian St. | 1986 | 20 | 0 | 0 | 120 |
| Gene Lake, Delaware St. | 1984 | 20 | 0 | 0 | 120 |

* Record.   † National champion.

*Division I-AA Annual Champions, All-Time Leaders*

## Annual Champions

| Year | Player, Team | Class | Games | TD | XPt. | FG | Pts. | Avg. |
|------|--------------|-------|-------|-----|------|-----|------|------|
| 1978 | Frank Hawkins, Nevada | So. | 10 | 17 | 0 | 0 | 102 | 10.2 |
| 1979 | Joel Sigel, Portland St. | Jr. | 10 | 16 | 0 | 0 | 96 | 9.6 |
| 1980 | Ken Jenkins, Bucknell | Jr. | 10 | 16 | 0 | 0 | 96 | 9.6 |
| 1981 | Paris Wicks, Youngstown St. | Jr. | 11 | 17 | 2 | 0 | 104 | 9.5 |
| 1982 | Paul Lewis, Boston U. | So. | 10 | 18 | 0 | 0 | 108 | 10.8 |
| 1983 | Rich Erenberg, Colgate | Sr. | 11 | 21 | 10 | 0 | 136 | 12.4 |
| 1984 | Jerry Rice, Mississippi Val. | Sr. | 10 | 27 | 0 | 0 | 162 | *16.2 |
| 1985 | Charvez Foger, Nevada | Fr. | 10 | 18 | 0 | 0 | 108 | 10.8 |
| 1986 | Gordie Lockbaum, Holy Cross | Jr. | 11 | 22 | 0 | 0 | 132 | 12.0 |
| 1987 | Sean Sanders, Weber St. | Sr. | 10 | 21 | 0 | 0 | 126 | 12.6 |
| 1988 | Elroy Harris, Eastern Ky. | Jr. | 10 | 21 | 1 | 0 | 128 | 12.8 |
| 1989 | Carl Smith, Maine | So. | 11 | 20 | 0 | 0 | 120 | 10.9 |
| 1990 | Barry Bourassa, New Hampshire | So. | 9 | 16 | 0 | 0 | 96 | 10.7 |
| 1991 | Geoff Mitchell, Weber St. | Sr. | 11 | *28 | 1 | 0 | *170 | 15.5 |
| 1992 | Sherriden May, Idaho | So. | 11 | 25 | 0 | 0 | 150 | 13.6 |

* Record.

# PUNTING
### Career Average
### (Minimum 150 Punts)

| Player, Team | Years | No. | Yards | Long | Avg. |
|--------------|-------|-----|-------|------|------|
| Pumpy Tudors, Tenn.-Chatt. | 1989-91 | 181 | 8,041 | 79 | *44.4 |
| Case de Bruijn, Idaho St. | 1978-81 | 256 | 11,184 | 76 | 43.7 |
| George Cimadevilla, East Tenn. St. | 1983-86 | 225 | 9,676 | 72 | 43.0 |
| Harold Alexander, Appalachian St. | 1989-92 | 259 | 11,100 | 78 | 42.9 |
| John Christopher, Morehead St. | 1979-82 | 298 | 12,633 | 62 | 42.4 |
| Colin Godfrey, Tennessee St. | 1989-92 | 213 | 9,012 | 69 | 42.3 |
| Russell Griffith, Utah St./Weber St. | 1983, 85-86 | 187 | 7,908 | 67 | 42.3 |
| Bret Wright, Southeastern La. | 1981-83 | 165 | 6,963 | 66 | 42.2 |
| Jeff Kaiser, Idaho St. | 1982-84 | 156 | 6,571 | 88 | 42.1 |
| Greg Davis, Citadel | 1983-86 | 263 | 11,076 | 81 | 42.1 |
| Mark Royals, Appalachian St. | 1983-85 | 223 | 9,372 | 67 | 42.0 |

* Record.

### Season Average
### (Qualifiers for Championship)

| Player, Team | Year | No. | Yards | Avg. |
|--------------|------|-----|-------|------|
| Harold Alexander, Appalachian St. | †1991 | 64 | 3,009 | *47.0 |
| Case de Bruijn, Idaho St. | †1981 | 42 | 1,928 | 45.9 |
| Colin Godfrey, Tennessee St. | †1990 | 57 | 2,614 | 45.9 |
| Stuart Dodds, Montana St. | †1979 | 59 | 2,689 | 45.6 |
| Pumpy Tudors, Tenn.-Chatt. | 1991 | 53 | 2,414 | 45.5 |
| Paul Asbury, Southwest Tex. St. | 1990 | 39 | 1,749 | 44.9 |
| Tom Sugg, Idaho | 1991 | 53 | 2,371 | 44.7 |
| Mike Rice, Montana | †1985 | 62 | 2,771 | 44.7 |
| Case de Bruijn, Idaho St. | 1979 | 73 | 3,261 | 44.7 |
| George Cimadevilla, East Tenn. St. | 1985 | 66 | 2,948 | 44.7 |
| Greg Davis, Citadel | †1986 | 61 | 2,723 | 44.6 |
| Pumpy Tudors, Tenn.-Chatt. | 1990 | 63 | 2,810 | 44.6 |
| Pat Velarde, Marshall | †1983 | 64 | 2,852 | 44.6 |
| Bart Bradley, Sam Houston St. | 1986 | 44 | 1,957 | 44.5 |
| Harold Alexander, Appalachian St. | †1992 | 55 | 2,445 | 44.5 |
| Curtis Moody, Texas Southern | 1985 | 64 | 2,844 | 44.4 |
| Terry Belden, Northern Ariz. | 1991 | 43 | 1,908 | 44.4 |
| Terry Belden, Northern Ariz. | 1992 | 59 | 2,614 | 44.3 |
| Bret Wright, Southeastern La. | 1983 | 66 | 2,923 | 44.3 |
| George Cimadevilla, East Tenn. St. | 1986 | 65 | 2,876 | 44.2 |
| Case de Bruijn, Idaho St. | †1980 | 67 | 2,945 | 44.0 |

* Record.   † National champion.

### Annual Champions

| Year | Player, Team | Class | No. | Yards | Avg. |
|------|--------------|-------|-----|-------|------|
| 1978 | Nick Pavich, Nevada | So. | 47 | 1,939 | 41.3 |
| 1979 | Stuart Dodds, Montana St. | Sr. | 59 | 2,689 | 45.6 |
| 1980 | Case de Bruijn, Idaho St. | Jr. | 67 | 2,945 | 44.0 |
| 1981 | Case de Bruijn, Idaho St. | Sr. | 42 | 1,928 | 45.9 |
| 1982 | John Christopher, Morehead St. | Sr. | 93 | 4,084 | 43.9 |

| Year | Player, Team | Class | No. | Yards | Avg. |
|------|--------------|-------|-----|-------|------|
| 1983 | Pat Velarde, Marshall | Sr. | 64 | 2,852 | 44.6 |
| 1984 | Steve Kornegay, Western Caro. | Jr. | 49 | 2,127 | 43.4 |
| 1985 | Mike Rice, Montana | Jr. | 62 | 2,771 | 44.7 |
| 1986 | Greg Davis, Citadel | Sr. | 61 | 2,723 | 44.6 |
| 1987 | Eric Stein, Eastern Wash. | Sr. | 74 | 3,193 | 43.2 |
| 1988 | Mike McCabe, Illinois St. | Sr. | 69 | 3,042 | 44.1 |
| 1989 | Pumpy Tudors, Tenn.-Chatt. | So. | 65 | 2,817 | 43.3 |
| 1990 | Colin Godfrey, Tennessee St. | So. | 57 | 2,614 | 45.9 |
| 1991 | Harold Alexander, Appalachian St. | Jr. | 64 | 3,009 | *47.0 |
| 1992 | Harold Alexander, Appalachian St. | Sr. | 55 | 2,445 | 44.5 |

* Record.

# INTERCEPTIONS
## Career Interceptions

| Player, Team | Years | No. | Yards | Avg. |
|--------------|-------|-----|-------|------|
| Dave Murphy, Holy Cross | 1986-89 | *28 | 309 | 11.0 |
| Issiac Holt, Alcorn St. | 1981-84 | 24 | 319 | 13.3 |
| Bill McGovern, Holy Cross | 1981-84 | 24 | 168 | 7.0 |
| William Carroll, Florida A&M | 1989-92 | 23 | 328 | 14.3 |
| Kevin Smith, Rhode Island | 1987-90 | 23 | 287 | 12.5 |
| Mike Prior, Illinois St. | 1981-84 | 23 | 211 | 9.2 |
| Frank Robinson, Boise St. | 1988-91 | 22 | 203 | 9.2 |
| Dean Cain, Princeton | 1985-87 | 22 | 203 | 9.2 |
| Dave Roberts, Youngstown St. | 1989-92 | 22 | 131 | 6.0 |
| George Floyd, Eastern Ky. | 1978-81 | 21 | 318 | 15.1 |
| Kevin Dent, Jackson St. | 1985-88 | 21 | 280 | 13.3 |
| Chris Demarest, Northeastern | 1984-87 | 21 | 255 | 12.1 |
| Greg Greely, Nicholls St. | 1981-84 | 21 | 218 | 10.4 |
| Mark Seals, Boston U. | 1985-88 | 21 | 169 | 8.0 |
| Jeff Smith, Illinois St. | 1985-88 | 21 | 152 | 7.2 |
| Rick Harris, East Tenn. St. | 1986-88 | 20 | *452 | 22.6 |
| Leslie Frazier, Alcorn St. | 1977-80 | 20 | 269 | 13.5 |
| Mark Kelso, William & Mary | 1981-84 | 20 | 171 | 8.6 |
| Ricky Thomas, South Caro. St. | 1988-91 | 19 | 374 | 19.7 |
| Michael Richardson, Northwestern (La.) | 1981-84 | 19 | 344 | 18.1 |
| Mike Genetti, Northeastern | 1980-83 | 19 | 296 | 15.6 |
| George Schmitt, Delaware | 1980-82 | 19 | 280 | 14.7 |
| Joe Burton, Delaware St. | 1983-86 | 19 | 248 | 13.1 |
| Dwayne Harper, South Caro. St. | 1984-87 | 19 | 163 | 8.6 |

* Record.

## Season Interceptions

| Player, Team | Year | No. | Yards |
|--------------|------|-----|-------|
| Dean Cain, Princeton | †1987 | *12 | 98 |
| Aeneas Williams, Southern-B. R. | ‡1990 | 11 | 173 |
| Claude Pettaway, Maine | ‡1990 | 11 | 161 |
| Everson Walls, Grambling | †1980 | 11 | 145 |
| Anthony Young, Jackson St. | †1978 | 11 | 108 |
| Bill McGovern, Holy Cross | †1984 | 11 | 102 |
| Kevin Dent, Jackson St. | ‡1986 | 10 | 192 |
| George Schmitt, Delaware | †1982 | 10 | 186 |
| Neale Henderson, Southern-B.R. | †1979 | 10 | 151 |
| Mike Genetti, Northeastern | †1981 | 10 | 144 |
| Chris Demarest, Northeastern | 1987 | 10 | 129 |
| Eric Thompson, New Hampshire | ‡1986 | 10 | 94 |
| Bob Mahr, Lafayette | 1981 | 10 | 48 |
| Mike Armentrout, Southwest Mo. St. | †1983 | 10 | 42 |
| Anthony Anderson, Grambling | †1986 | 10 | 37 |
| Cedric Walker, Stephen F. Austin | 1990 | 10 | 11 |

* Record.   † National champion.   ‡ National championship shared.

## Annual Champions
### (Ranked on Per-Game Average)

| Year | Player, Team | Class | Games | No. | Avg. | Yards |
|------|--------------|-------|-------|-----|------|-------|
| 1978 | Anthony Young, Jackson St. | Sr. | 11 | 11 | 1.00 | 108 |
| 1979 | Neale Henderson, Southern-B.R. | Sr. | 11 | 10 | 0.91 | 151 |
| 1980 | Everson Walls, Grambling | Sr. | 11 | 11 | 1.00 | 145 |
| 1981 | Mike Genetti, Northeastern | So. | 10 | 10 | 1.00 | 144 |
| 1982 | George Schmitt, Delaware | Sr. | 11 | 10 | 0.91 | 186 |

| Year | Player, Team | Class | Games | No. | Avg. | Yards |
|------|--------------|-------|-------|-----|------|-------|
| 1983 | Mike Armentrout, Southwest Mo. St. ...... | Jr. | 11 | 10 | 0.91 | 42 |
| 1984 | Bill McGovern, Holy Cross ................ | Sr. | 11 | 11 | 1.00 | 102 |
| 1985 | Mike Cassidy, Rhode Island .............. | Sr. | 10 | 9 | 0.90 | 169 |
|      | George Duarte, Northern Ariz. ........... | Jr. | 10 | 9 | 0.90 | 150 |
| 1986 | Kevin Dent, Jackson St. .................. | So. | 11 | 10 | 0.91 | 192 |
|      | Eric Thompson, New Hampshire......... | Sr. | 11 | 10 | 0.91 | 94 |
|      | Anthony Anderson, Grambling ........... | Sr. | 11 | 10 | 0.91 | 37 |
| 1987 | Dean Cain, Princeton .................... | Sr. | 10 | *12 | *1.20 | 98 |
| 1988 | Kevin Smith, Rhode Island ............... | So. | 10 | 9 | 0.90 | 94 |
| 1989 | Mike Babb, Weber St. .................... | Sr. | 11 | 9 | 0.82 | 90 |
| 1990 | Aeneas Williams, Southern-B. R. ......... | Sr. | 11 | 11 | 1.00 | 173 |
|      | Claude Pettaway, Maine.................. | Sr. | 11 | 11 | 1.00 | 161 |
| 1991 | Warren McIntire, Delaware ............... | Jr. | 11 | 9 | 0.82 | 208 |
| 1992 | Dave Roberts, Youngstown St. ........... | Sr. | 11 | 9 | 0.82 | 39 |

* Record.

# PUNT RETURNS
## Career Average
### (Minimum 1.2 Returns Per Game)

| Player, Team | Years | No. | Yards | Avg. |
|--------------|-------|-----|-------|------|
| Willie Ware, Mississippi Val. .......................... | 1982-85 | 61 | 1,003 | *16.4 |
| Tim Egerton, Delaware St. ........................... | 1986-89 | 59 | 951 | 16.1 |
| Chris Darrington, Weber St........................... | 1984-86 | 26 | 415 | 16.0 |
| John Armstrong, Richmond ......................... | 1984-85 | 31 | 449 | 14.5 |
| Kenny Shedd, Northern Iowa ........................ | 1989-92 | 79 | 1,081 | 13.7 |
| Joe Fuller, Northern Iowa ........................... | 1982-85 | 69 | 888 | 12.9 |
| Eric Yarber, Idaho .................................. | 1984-85 | 32 | 406 | 12.7 |
| Troy Brown, Marshall ............................... | 1991-92 | 36 | 455 | 12.6 |
| Trumaine Johnson, Grambling ....................... | 1979-82 | 53 | 662 | 12.5 |
| Tony Merriwether, North Texas ...................... | 1982-83 | 41 | 507 | 12.4 |
| Thaylen Armstead, Grambling ....................... | 1989-91 | 44 | 540 | 12.3 |
| Barney Bussey, South Caro. St. ..................... | 1980-83 | 47 | 573 | 12.2 |
| Cornell Johnson, Southern-B.R. ..................... | 1990-92 | 40 | 482 | 12.1 |
| John Taylor, Delaware St. ........................... | 1982-85 | 48 | 576 | 12.0 |

* Record.

## Season Average
### (Minimum 1.2 Returns Per Game and Qualifiers for Championship)

| Player, Team | Year | No. | Yards | Avg. |
|--------------|------|-----|-------|------|
| Tim Egerton, Delaware St. ............................. | †1988 | 16 | 368 | *23.0 |
| Ryan Priest, Lafayette.................................. | †1982 | 12 | 271 | 22.6 |
| Craig Hodge, Tennessee St............................. | †1987 | 19 | 398 | 21.0 |
| John Armstrong, Richmond ............................ | †1985 | 19 | 391 | 20.6 |
| Willie Ware, Mississippi Val. ............................ | †1984 | 19 | 374 | 19.7 |
| Mark Hurt, Alabama St. ................................ | 1988 | 10 | 185 | 18.5 |
| Howard Huckaby, Florida A&M ......................... | 1988 | 26 | 478 | 18.4 |
| Ashley Ambrose, Mississippi Val. ...................... | †1991 | 28 | 514 | 18.4 |
| Quincy Miller, South Caro. St........................... | †1992 | 17 | 311 | 18.3 |
| Barney Bussey, South Caro. St.......................... | †1981 | 14 | 255 | 18.2 |
| Chris Darrington, Weber St............................. | †1986 | 16 | 290 | 18.1 |
| Willie Ware, Mississippi Val. ............................ | 1985 | 31 | *561 | 18.1 |
| Kerry Lawyer, Boise St. ................................ | 1992 | 18 | 325 | 18.1 |
| Kenny Shedd, Northern Iowa ........................... | 1992 | 27 | 477 | 17.7 |
| Clarence Alexander, Mississippi Val. .................... | 1986 | 22 | 380 | 17.3 |
| Henry Richard, Northeast La. .......................... | †1989 | 15 | 258 | 17.2 |
| Carl Williams, Texas Southern ......................... | 1981 | 16 | 269 | 16.8 |
| Jerome Bledsoe, Massachusetts ........................ | 1988 | 17 | 285 | 16.8 |

* Record.  † National champion.

## Annual Champions

| Year | Player, Team | Class | No. | Yards | Avg. |
|------|--------------|-------|-----|-------|------|
| 1978 | Ray Smith, Northern Ariz............................. | Sr. | 13 | 181 | 13.9 |
| 1979 | Joseph Markus, Connecticut.......................... | Fr. | 17 | 219 | 12.9 |
| 1980 | Trumaine Johnson, Grambling........................ | So. | ††13 | 226 | 17.4 |
| 1981 | Barney Bussey, South Caro. St. ...................... | So. | 14 | 255 | 18.2 |
| 1982 | Ryan Priest, Lafayette ............................... | Fr. | 12 | 271 | 22.6 |

| Year | Player, Team | Class | No. | Yards | Avg. |
|------|-------------|-------|-----|-------|------|
| 1983 | Joe Fuller, Northern Iowa .......................... | So. | 22 | 344 | 15.6 |
| 1984 | Willie Ware, Mississippi Val. ........................ | Jr. | 19 | 374 | 19.7 |
| 1985 | John Armstrong, Richmond ........................ | Sr. | 19 | 391 | 20.6 |
| 1986 | Chris Darrington, Weber St. ........................ | Sr. | 16 | 290 | 18.1 |
| 1987 | Craig Hodge, Tennessee St. ........................ | Sr. | 19 | 398 | 21.0 |
| 1988 | Tim Egerton, Delaware St. .......................... | Jr. | 16 | 368 | *23.0 |
| 1989 | Henry Richard, Northeast La. ....................... | Jr. | 15 | 258 | 17.2 |
| 1990 | Gary Harrell, Howard ............................... | Fr. | 26 | 417 | 16.0 |
| 1991 | Ashley Ambrose, Mississippi Val. ................... | Sr. | 28 | 514 | 18.4 |
| 1992 | Quincy Miller, South Caro. St. ...................... | Jr. | 17 | 311 | 18.3 |

* Record.   †† Declared champion; with one more return (making 1.3 per game) for zero yards, still would have highest average.

# KICKOFF RETURNS
## Career Average
### (Minimum 1.2 Returns Per Game)

| Player, Team | Years | No. | Yards | Avg. |
|-------------|-------|-----|-------|------|
| Troy Brown, Marshall ............................. | 1991-92 | 32 | 950 | *29.7 |
| Charles Swann, Indiana St. ........................ | 1989-91 | 45 | 1,319 | 29.3 |
| Craig Richardson, Eastern Wash. ................... | 1983-86 | 71 | 2,021 | 28.5 |
| Daryl Holcombe, Eastern Ill. ....................... | 1986-89 | 49 | 1,379 | 28.1 |
| Curtis Chappell, Howard ........................... | 1984-87 | 42 | 1,177 | 28.0 |
| Jerry Parrish, Eastern Ky. ......................... | 1978-81 | 61 | 1,668 | 27.3 |
| Tony James, Eastern Ky. ........................... | 1982-84 | 57 | 1,552 | 27.2 |
| Frank Selto, Idaho St. ............................. | 1986-87 | 30 | 803 | 26.8 |
| Chris Hickman, Northeast La. ...................... | 1991-92 | 30 | 798 | 26.6 |
| Chris Pollard, Dartmouth .......................... | 1986-88 | 52 | 1,376 | 26.5 |
| John Jarvis, Howard ............................... | 1986-88 | 39 | 1,031 | 26.4 |
| Ronald Scott, Southern-B.R. ....................... | 1982-85 | 38 | 1,003 | 26.4 |
| Rob Tesch, Montana St. ............................ | 1989-92 | 50 | 1,317 | 26.3 |
| Vernon Williams, Eastern Wash. .................... | 1986-88 | 40 | 1,052 | 26.3 |
| Steve Ortman, Pennsylvania ....................... | 1982-84 | 31 | 808 | 26.1 |
| John Armstrong, Richmond ........................ | 1984-85 | 32 | 826 | 25.8 |
| Renard Coleman, Montana ......................... | 1985-88 | 57 | 1,465 | 25.7 |
| Michael Haynes, Northern Ariz. .................... | 1986-87 | 36 | 925 | 25.7 |
| Kevin Gainer, Bethune-Cookman ................... | 1988-90 | 42 | 1,070 | 25.5 |
| Archie Herring, Youngstown St. .................... | 1987-90 | 79 | 2,005 | 25.4 |
| Kenny Shedd, Northern Iowa ...................... | 1989-92 | 54 | 1,359 | 25.2 |
| Jerome Stelly, Western Ill. ......................... | 1981-82 | 42 | 1,024 | 24.4 |
| Chris Pierce, Rhode Island ......................... | 1989-92 | 63 | 1,521 | 24.1 |
| Albert Brown, Western Ill. .......................... | 1985-86 | 30 | 723 | 24.1 |
| Sylvester Stamps, Jackson St. ..................... | 1980, 82-83 | 42 | 1,012 | 24.1 |
| Ray Brown, Southeastern La. ...................... | 1983-84 | 30 | 719 | 24.0 |

* Record.

**Special Note:** Leader in number and yardage: Herman Hunter, Tennessee St., 1981-84, with 96 returns for 2,258 yards.

## Season Average
### (Minimum 1.2 Returns Per Game)

| Player, Team | Year | No. | Yards | Avg. |
|-------------|------|-----|-------|------|
| Craig Richardson, Eastern Wash. ................... | †1984 | 21 | 729 | *34.7 |
| Marcus Durgin, Samford ........................... | †1992 | 15 | 499 | 33.3 |
| Dave Meggett, Towson St. ......................... | †1988 | 13 | 418 | 32.2 |
| Charles Swann, Indiana St. ........................ | †1990 | 20 | 642 | 32.1 |
| Archie Herring, Youngstown St. .................... | 1990 | 18 | 575 | 31.9 |
| Davlin Mullen, Western Ky. ........................ | †1982 | 18 | 574 | 31.9 |
| Danny Copeland, Eastern Ky. ...................... | †1986 | 26 | 812 | 31.2 |
| Chris Chappell, Howard ........................... | 1986 | 17 | 528 | 31.1 |
| Dave Loehle, New Hampshire ...................... | †1978 | 15 | 460 | 30.7 |
| Paul Ashby, Alabama St. ........................... | †1991 | 17 | 520 | 30.6 |
| Juan Jackson, North Caro. A&T ..................... | 1986 | 16 | 487 | 30.4 |
| Kevin Gainer, Bethune-Cookman ................... | 1990 | 21 | 635 | 30.2 |
| Howard Huckaby, Florida A&M ..................... | †1987 | 20 | 602 | 30.1 |
| Tony James, Eastern Ky. ........................... | †1983 | 17 | 511 | 30.1 |
| Robert Johnson, Idaho St. ......................... | 1992 | 14 | 416 | 29.7 |
| Jerry Parrish, Eastern Ky. ......................... | †1981 | 18 | 534 | 29.7 |
| John Armstrong, Richmond ........................ | 1984 | 18 | 531 | 29.5 |
| Renard Coleman, Montana ......................... | 1987 | 20 | 588 | 29.4 |

* Record.   † National champion.

## Annual Champions

| Year | Player, Team | Class | No. | Yards | Avg. |
|------|-------------|-------|-----|-------|------|
| 1978 | Dave Loehle, New Hampshire | Jr. | 15 | 460 | 30.7 |
| 1979 | Garry Pearson, Massachusetts | Fr. | 12 | 348 | 29.0 |
| 1980 | Danny Thomas, North Caro. A&T | Fr. | 15 | 381 | 25.4 |
| 1981 | Jerry Parrish, Eastern Ky. | Sr. | 18 | 534 | 29.7 |
| 1982 | Davlin Mullen, Western Ky. | Sr. | 18 | 574 | 31.9 |
| 1983 | Tony James, Eastern Ky. | Jr. | 17 | 511 | 30.1 |
| 1984 | Craig Richardson, Eastern Wash. | So. | 21 | 729 | *34.7 |
| 1985 | Rodney Payne, Murray St. | Fr. | 16 | 464 | 29.0 |
| 1986 | Danny Copeland, Eastern Ky. | Jr. | 26 | 812 | 31.2 |
| 1987 | Howard Huckaby, Florida A&M | So. | 20 | 602 | 30.1 |
| 1988 | Dave Meggett, Towson St. | Sr. | 13 | 418 | 32.2 |
| 1989 | Scott Thomas, Liberty | Fr. | 13 | 373 | 28.7 |
| 1990 | Charles Swann, Indiana St. | Jr. | 20 | 642 | 32.1 |
| 1991 | Paul Ashby, Alabama St. | Jr. | 17 | 520 | 30.6 |
| 1992 | Marcus Durgin, Samford | Jr. | 15 | 499 | 33.3 |

* Record.

# ALL-PURPOSE RUNNING

### Career Yards Per Game

| Player, Team | Years | Rush | Rcv | Int. | PR | KOR | Yds. | Yd. PG |
|---|---|---|---|---|---|---|---|---|
| Dave Meggett, Towson St. | 1987-88 | 1,658 | 788 | 0 | 212 | 745 | 3,403 | *189.1 |
| Kenny Gamble, Colgate | 1984-87 | 5,220 | 536 | 0 | 104 | 1,763 | *7,623 | 181.5 |
| Rich Erenberg, Colgate | #1982-83 | 2,618 | 423 | 0 | 268 | 315 | 3,624 | 172.6 |
| Fine Unga, Weber St. | 1987-88 | 2,298 | 391 | 0 | 7 | 967 | 3,663 | 166.5 |
| Gill Fenerty, Holy Cross | 1983-85 | 3,618 | 477 | 0 | 1 | 731 | 4,827 | 160.9 |
| Barry Bourassa, New Hampshire | 1989-92 | 2,960 | 1,307 | 0 | 306 | 1,370 | 5,943 | 152.4 |
| Judd Garrett, Princeton | 1987-89 | 3,109 | 1,385 | 0 | 0 | 10 | 4,510 | 150.3 |
| Treamelle Taylor, Nevada | 1987-90 | 0 | 1,926 | 0 | 662 | 687 | 3,275 | 148.9 |
| Troy Brown, Marshall | 1991-92 | 138 | 1,716 | 0 | 455 | 950 | 3,259 | 148.1 |
| Andre Garron, New Hampshire | 1982-85 | 2,901 | 809 | 0 | 8 | 651 | 4,369 | 145.6 |
| Carl Boyd, Northern Iowa | 1983, 85-87 | 2,735 | 1,987 | 0 | 0 | 183 | 4,905 | 144.3 |
| Merril Hoge, Idaho St. | 1983-86 | 2,713 | 1,734 | 0 | 1 | 1,005 | 5,453 | 139.8 |
| Pete Mandley, Northern Ariz. | 79-80, 82-83 | 436 | 2,598 | 11 | 901 | 1,979 | 5,925 | 137.8 |
| Frank Hawkins, Nevada | 1977-80 | *5,333 | 519 | 0 | 0 | 0 | 5,852 | 136.1 |
| Derrick Harmon, Cornell | 1981-83 | 3,074 | 679 | 0 | 5 | 42 | 3,800 | 135.7 |
| Dorron Hunter, Morehead St. | 1977-80 | 1,336 | 1,320 | 0 | 510 | 1,970 | 5,136 | 135.2 |

* Record.  # Two years in Division I-AA and two years in Division I-A. Four-year totals: 5,695 yards and 146.0 average.

### Season Yards Per Game

| Player, Team | Year | Rush | Rcv | Int. | PR | KOR | Yds. | Yd. PG |
|---|---|---|---|---|---|---|---|---|
| Kenny Gamble, Colgate | †1986 | 1,816 | 178 | 0 | 40 | 391 | *2,425 | *220.5 |
| Michael Clemons, William & Mary | 1986 | 1,065 | 516 | 0 | 330 | 423 | 2,334 | 212.2 |
| Rich Erenberg, Colgate | †1983 | *1,883 | 214 | 0 | 126 | 18 | 2,241 | 203.7 |
| Dave Meggett, Towson St. | †1987 | 814 | 572 | 0 | 78 | 327 | 1,791 | 199.0 |
| Gordie Lockbaum, Holy Cross | 1986 | 827 | 860 | 34 | 0 | 452 | 2,173 | 197.6 |
| Gill Fenerty, Holy Cross | †1985 | 1,368 | 187 | 0 | 1 | 414 | 1,970 | 197.0 |
| Barry Bourassa, New Hampshire | †1991 | 1,130 | 426 | 0 | 0 | 596 | 2,152 | 195.6 |
| Barry Bourassa, New Hampshire | †1990 | 957 | 276 | 0 | 133 | 368 | 1,734 | 192.7 |
| Merril Hoge, Idaho St. | 1985 | 1,041 | 708 | 0 | 0 | 364 | 2,113 | 192.1 |
| Andre Garron, New Hampshire | 1983 | 1,009 | 539 | 0 | 0 | 359 | 1,907 | 190.7 |
| Kenny Gamble, Colgate | 1987 | 1,411 | 151 | 0 | 64 | 471 | 2,097 | 190.6 |
| Otis Washington, Western Caro. | †1988 | 64 | 907 | 0 | 0 | 1,113 | 2,086 | 189.6 |
| Ken Jenkins, Bucknell | †1980 | 1,270 | 293 | 0 | 65 | 256 | 1,884 | 188.4 |
| Kenny Gamble, Colgate | 1985 | 1,361 | 162 | 0 | 0 | 520 | 2,043 | 185.7 |
| Gordie Lockbaum, Holy Cross | 1987 | 403 | 1,152 | 0 | 209 | 277 | 2,041 | 185.6 |
| Dominic Corr, Eastern Wash. | †1989 | 796 | 52 | 0 | 0 | 807 | 1,655 | 183.9 |
| Al Rosier, Dartmouth | 1991 | 1,432 | 113 | 0 | 0 | 290 | 1,835 | 183.5 |
| Jerome Bledsoe, Massachusetts | 1991 | 1,545 | 178 | 0 | 0 | 293 | 2,016 | 183.3 |
| David Wright, Indiana St. | †1992 | 1,313 | 108 | 0 | 0 | 593 | 2,014 | 183.1 |
| Mark Stock, Va. Military | 1988 | 90 | 1,161 | 0 | 260 | 500 | 2,011 | 182.8 |
| Jamie Jones, Eastern Ill. | 1991 | 1,403 | 299 | 0 | 0 | 305 | 2,007 | 182.5 |
| Pete Mandley, Northern Ariz. | †1982 | 36 | 1,067 | 0 | 344 | 532 | 1,979 | 179.9 |
| Kelvin Anderson, Southeast Mo. St. | 1992 | 1,371 | 171 | 0 | 0 | 253 | 1,795 | 179.5 |
| Dave Meggett, Towson St. | 1988 | 844 | 216 | 0 | 134 | 418 | 1,612 | 179.1 |
| Carl Smith, Maine | 1989 | 1,680 | 169 | 0 | 0 | 120 | 1,969 | 179.0 |

* Record.  † National champion.

*1993 NCAA FOOTBALL*

## Career Yards §

| Player, Team | Years | Rush | Rcv | Int. | PR | KOR | Yds. | Yd. PP |
|---|---|---|---|---|---|---|---|---|
| Kenny Gamble, Colgate ......... | 1984-87 | 5,220 | 536 | 0 | 104 | 1,763 | *7,623 | 7.0 |
| Barry Bourassa, New Hampshire .. | 1989-92 | 2,960 | 1,307 | 0 | 306 | 1,370 | 5,943 | 7.5 |
| Pete Mandley, Northern Ariz...... | 1979-80, 82-83 | 436 | 2,598 | 11 | 901 | 1,979 | 5,925 | *14.8 |
| Frank Hawkins, Nevada ......... | 1977-80 | *5,333 | 519 | 0 | 0 | 0 | 5,852 | 5.8 |
| Jamie Jones, Eastern III. ......... | 1988-91 | 3,466 | 816 | 0 | 66 | 1,235 | 5,583 | 6.2 |
| Merril Hoge, Idaho St............. | 1983-86 | 2,713 | 1,734 | 0 | 1 | 1,005 | 5,453 | 6.6 |
| Herman Hunter, Tennessee St. ... | 1981-84 | 1,049 | 1,129 | 0 | 974 | *2,258 | 5,410 | 10.5 |
| Cedric Minter, Boise St. .......... | 1977-80 | 4,475 | 525 | 0 | 49 | 267 | 5,316 | 6.5 |
| Charvez Foger, Nevada .......... | 1985-88 | 4,484 | 821 | 0 | 0 | 0 | 5,305 | 5.7 |
| Garry Pearson, Massachusetts ... | 1979-82 | 3,859 | 466 | 0 | 0 | 952 | 5,277 | 5.9 |
| John Settle, Appalachian St. ..... | 1983-86 | 4,409 | 526 | 0 | 0 | 319 | 5,254 | 5.3 |
| Dorron Hunter, Morehead St. .... | 1977-80 | 1,336 | 1,320 | 0 | 510 | 1,970 | 5,136 | 9.6 |

* Record.  § Rich Erenberg, Colgate, competed two years in Division I-AA and two years in Division I-A (four-year total: 5,695 yards), and Dwight Walker, Nicholls St., competed two years in Division I-AA and two years in Division II (four-year total: 5,200 yards).

## Season Yards

| Player, Team | Year | Rush | Rcv | Int. | PR | KOR | Yds. | Yd. PP |
|---|---|---|---|---|---|---|---|---|
| Kenny Gamble, Colgate ................. | †1986 | 1,816 | 178 | 0 | 40 | 391 | *2,425 | 7.1 |
| Michael Clemons, William & Mary ....... | 1986 | 1,065 | 516 | 0 | 330 | 423 | 2,334 | 6.7 |
| Rich Erenberg, Colgate ................. | †1983 | *1,883 | 214 | 0 | 126 | 18 | 2,241 | 6.7 |
| Gordie Lockbaum, Holy Cross .......... | 1986 | 827 | 860 | 34 | 0 | 452 | 2,173 | 9.7 |
| Barry Bourassa, New Hampshire ........ | †1991 | 1,130 | 426 | 0 | 0 | 596 | 2,152 | 7.5 |
| Merril Hoge, Idaho St..................... | 1985 | 1,041 | 708 | 0 | 0 | 364 | 2,113 | 7.4 |
| Kenny Gamble, Colgate ................. | 1987 | 1,411 | 151 | 0 | 64 | 471 | 2,097 | 6.5 |
| Otis Washington, Western Caro. ......... | †1988 | 66 | 907 | 0 | 0 | 1,113 | 2,086 | *19.7 |
| Kenny Gamble, Colgate ................. | 1985 | 1,361 | 162 | 0 | 0 | 520 | 2,043 | 7.3 |
| Gordie Lockbaum, Holy Cross .......... | 1987 | 403 | 1,152 | 0 | 209 | 277 | 2,041 | 10.4 |
| Jerome Bledsoe, Massachusetts ......... | 1991 | 1,545 | 178 | 0 | 0 | 293 | 2,016 | 6.7 |
| David Wright, Indiana St.................. | †1992 | 1,313 | 108 | 0 | 0 | 593 | 2,014 | 7.9 |
| Mark Stock, Va. Military .................. | 1988 | 90 | 1,161 | 0 | 260 | 500 | 2,011 | 14.0 |
| Jamie Jones, Eastern III. ................. | 1991 | 1,403 | 299 | 0 | 0 | 305 | 2,007 | 7.2 |
| Pete Mandley, Northern Ariz.............. | †1982 | 36 | 1,067 | 0 | 344 | 532 | 1,979 | 18.7 |
| Gill Fenerty, Holy Cross .................. | †1985 | 1,368 | 187 | 0 | 1 | 414 | 1,970 | 6.8 |

* Record.  † National champion.

## All-Purpose Single-Game Highs

| Yds. | Player, Team (Opponent) | Date |
|---|---|---|
| 463 | Michael Lerch, Princeton (Brown) ................................................. | Oct. 12, 1991 |
| 453 | Herman Hunter, Tennessee St. (Mississippi Val.) ............................... | Nov. 13, 1982 |
| 395 | Scott Oliaro, Cornell (Yale) ........................................................ | Nov. 3, 1990 |
| 386 | Gill Fenerty, Holy Cross (Columbia) ............................................. | Oct. 29, 1983 |
| 378 | Joe Delaney, Northwestern, La. (Nicholls St.) .................................. | Oct. 28, 1978 |
| 372 | Gary Harrell, Howard (Morgan St.) ............................................... | Nov. 3, 1990 |
| 372 | Treamelle Taylor, Nevada (Montana) ............................................. | Oct. 14, 1989 |
| 369 | Flip Johnson, McNeese St. (Southwestern La.) .................................. | Nov. 15, 1986 |
| 367 | Chris Darrington, Weber St. (Idaho St.) .......................................... | Oct. 25, 1986 |
| 365 | Erwin Matthews, Richmond (Delaware) .......................................... | Sept. 26, 1987 |
| 361 | Patrick Robinson, Tennessee St. (Jackson St.) .................................. | Sept. 12, 1992 |
| 352 | Andre Garron, New Hampshire (Lehigh) .......................................... | Oct. 15, 1983 |
| 345 | Russell Davis, Idaho (Weber St.) .................................................. | Oct. 2, 1982 |
| 341 | Barry Bourassa, New Hampshire (Delaware) .................................... | Oct. 5, 1991 |
| 340 | Gene Lake, Delaware St. (Liberty) ................................................ | Nov. 10, 1984 |
| 335 | Judd Garrett, Princeton (Harvard) ................................................ | Oct. 22, 1988 |
| 329 | Barry Bourassa, New Hampshire (Maine) ........................................ | Sept. 22, 1990 |
| 329 | Ron Darby, Marshall (Youngstown St.) ........................................... | Nov. 19, 1988 |
| 329 | Keith Williams, Southwest Mo. St. (Illinois St.) ................................. | Sept. 14, 1985 |

## Annual Champions

| Year | Player, Team | Cl. | Rush | Rcv | Int. | PR | KOR | Yds. | Yd. PG |
|---|---|---|---|---|---|---|---|---|---|
| 1978 | Frank Hawkins, Nevada .............. | So. | 1,445 | 211 | 0 | 0 | 0 | 1,656 | 165.6 |
| 1979 | Frank Hawkins, Nevada .............. | Jr. | 1,683 | 123 | 0 | 0 | 0 | 1,806 | 164.2 |
| 1980 | Ken Jenkins, Bucknell ............... | Jr. | 1,270 | 293 | 0 | 65 | 256 | 1,884 | 188.4 |
| 1981 | Garry Pearson, Massachusetts ....... | Jr. | 1,026 | 105 | 0 | 0 | 450 | 1,581 | 175.7 |
| 1982 | Pete Mandley, Northern Ariz.......... | Jr. | 36 | 1,067 | 0 | 344 | 532 | 1,979 | 179.9 |

*Division I-AA Annual Champions, All-Time Leaders*

| Year | Player, Team | Cl. | Rush | Rcv | Int. | PR | KOR | Yds. | Yd. PG |
|------|--------------|-----|------|-----|------|----|----|------|--------|
| 1983 | Rich Erenberg, Colgate .............. | Sr. | *1,883 | 214 | 0 | 126 | 18 | 2,241 | 203.7 |
| 1984 | Gene Lake, Delaware St. ............. | Jr. | 1,722 | 37 | 0 | 0 | 0 | 1,759 | 175.9 |
| 1985 | Gill Fenerty, Holy Cross .............. | Sr. | 1,368 | 187 | 0 | 1 | 414 | 1,970 | 197.0 |
| 1986 | Kenny Gamble, Colgate ............. | Jr. | 1,816 | 178 | 0 | 40 | 391 | *2,425 | *220.5 |
| 1987 | Dave Meggett, Towson St. ........... | Jr. | 814 | 572 | 0 | 78 | 327 | 1,791 | 199.0 |
| 1988 | Otis Washington, Western Caro. ..... | Sr. | 66 | 907 | 0 | 0 | 1,113 | 2,086 | 189.6 |
| 1989 | Dominic Corr, Eastern Wash.......... | Sr. | 796 | 52 | 0 | 0 | 807 | 1,655 | 183.9 |
| 1990 | Barry Bourassa, New Hampshire .... | So. | 957 | 276 | 0 | 133 | 368 | 1,734 | 192.7 |
| 1991 | Barry Bourassa, New Hampshire .... | Jr. | 1,130 | 426 | 0 | 0 | 596 | 2,152 | 195.6 |
| 1992 | David Wright, Indiana St............. | Fr. | 1,313 | 108 | 0 | 0 | 593 | 2,014 | 183.1 |

*Record.

**Indiana State tailback David Wright led Division I-AA in all-purpose yardage (2,014 yards, 183.1 per game) as a freshman in 1992. Wright was among the top 10 in kickoff returns (27.0 average, eighth) and finished 13th in rushing (119.4 yards per game).**

## FIELD GOALS
### Career Field Goals

| Player, Team | Years | Total | Pct. | Under 40 Yds. | 40 Plus | Long |
|--------------|-------|-------|------|---------------|---------|------|
| Marty Zendejas, Nevada (S)............... | 1984-87 | *72-90 | .800 | 42-45 | 30-45 | 54 |
| Kirk Roach, Western Caro. (S) ............. | 1984-87 | 71-*102 | .696 | 45-49 | 26-53 | 57 |
| Tony Zendejas, Nevada (S) ................ | 1981-83 | 70-86 | *.814 | 45-49 | 25-37 | 58 |
| Brian Mitchell, Marshall/Northern Iowa (S) | 1987, 89-91 | 64-81 | .790 | 48-55 | 16-26 | 57 |
| Matt Stover, Louisiana Tech (S) ........... | 1986-89 | 64-88 | .727 | 36-42 | 28-46 | 57 |
| Steve Christie, William & Mary (S) ........ | 1986-89 | 57-83 | .686 | 39-49 | 18-34 | 53 |
| Teddy Garcia, Northeast La. (S)............ | 1984-87 | 56-88 | .636 | 35-43 | 21-45 | 55 |
| Bjorn Nittmo, Appalachian St. (S).......... | 1985-88 | 55-74 | .743 | 35-40 | 20-34 | 54 |
| Kelly Potter, Middle Tenn. St. (S) ........... | 1981-84 | 52-78 | .667 | 37-49 | 15-29 | 57 |
| Paul McFadden, Youngstown St. (S) ....... | 1980-83 | 52-90 | .578 | 28-42 | 24-48 | 54 |

| Player, Team | Years | Total | Pct. | Under 40 Yds. | 40 Plus | Long |
|---|---|---|---|---|---|---|
| Mike Black, Boise St. (S) .................. | 1988-91 | 51-75 | .680 | 35-43 | 16-32 | 48 |
| Tim Foley, Ga. Southern (S) .............. | 1984-87 | 50-62 | .806 | 32-37 | 18-25 | **63 |
| Paul Politi, Illinois St. (S) ................. | 1983-86 | 50-78 | .641 | 34-48 | 16-30 | 50 |
| Thayne Doyle, Idaho St. (S) .................. | 1988-91 | 49-75 | .653 | 35-51 | 14-24 | 52 |
| Chuck Rawlinson, Stephen F. Austin (S) ... | 1988-91 | 49-69 | .710 | 34-43 | 15-26 | 58 |
| Scott Roper, Texas-Arlington/Ark. St. (S) ..1985, 86-87 | | 49-75 | .653 | 35-43 | 14-32 | **63 |
| Paul Hickert, Murray St. (S) ................ | 1984-87 | 49-79 | .620 | 34-48 | 15-31 | 62 |
| Dewey Klein, Marshall (S)................. | 1988-91 | 48-66 | .727 | 37-47 | 11-19 | 54 |
| John Dowling, Youngstown St. (S)........ | 1984-87 | 48-76 | .632 | 36-44 | 12-32 | 49 |
| Kirk Duce, Montana (S) .................... | 1988-91 | 47-78 | .603 | 37-51 | 10-27 | 51 |
| Billy Hayes, Sam Houston St. (S) .......... | 1985-88 | 47-71 | .662 | 37-55 | 10-16 | 54 |
| Roger Ruzek, Weber St. (S) ............... | 1979-82 | 46-78 | .590 | 28-37 | 18-41 | 51 |

*Record.  ** Record tied.  (S) Soccer-style kicker.*

## Season Field Goals

| Player, Team | Year | Total | Pct. | Under 40 Yds. | 40 Plus | Long |
|---|---|---|---|---|---|---|
| Brian Mitchell, Northern Iowa (S) ......... | †1990 | **26-27 | *.963 | 23-23 | 3-4 | 45 |
| Tony Zendejas, Nevada (S) ............... | †1982 | **26-*33 | .788 | 18-20 | 8-13 | 52 |
| Kirk Roach, Western Caro. (S) ........... | †1986 | 24-28 | .857 | 17-17 | 7-11 | 52 |
| George Benyola, Louisiana Tech (S) ...... | †1985 | 24-31 | .774 | 15-18 | 9-13 | 53 |
| Goran Lingmerth, Northern Ariz. (S) ...... | 1986 | 23-29 | .793 | 16-19 | 7-10 | 55 |
| Tony Zendejas, Nevada (S) ............... | †1983 | 23-29 | .793 | 14-15 | 9-14 | 58 |
| Mike Dodd, Boise St. (S) .................. | †1992 | 22-31 | .710 | 16-21 | 6-10 | 50 |
| Marty Zendejas, Nevada (S)............... | †1984 | 22-27 | .815 | 12-13 | 10-14 | 52 |
| Kevin McKelvie, Nevada (S)............... | 1990 | 21-24 | .875 | 16-17 | 5-7 | 52 |
| Matt Stover, Louisiana Tech (S) ........... | 1986 | 21-25 | .840 | 15-15 | 6-10 | 53 |
| Scott Roper, Arkansas St. (S) ............. | 1986 | 21-28 | .750 | 15-17 | 6-11 | 50 |
| Tony Zendejas, Nevada (S) ............... | †1981 | 21-24 | .875 | 13-14 | 8-10 | 55 |
| Darren Goodman, Idaho St. (S) ........... | 1990 | 20-28 | .714 | 12-14 | 8-14 | 53 |
| Steve Christie, William & Mary (S) ........ | †1989 | 20-29 | .690 | 16-17 | 4-12 | 53 |
| Teddy Garcia, Northeast La. (S) ........... | 1987 | 20-28 | .714 | 10-11 | 10-17 | 55 |

*Record.  ** Record tied.  † National champion.  (S) Soccer-style kicker.*

## Annual Champions
### (Ranked on Per-Game Average)

| Year | Player, Team | Total | PG | Pct. | Under 40 Yds. | 40 Plus | Long |
|---|---|---|---|---|---|---|---|
| 1978 | Tom Sarette, Boise St. (S) ............. | 12-20 | 1.2 | .600 | 8-10 | 4-10 | 47 |
| 1979 | Wilfredo Rosales, Alcorn St. (S) ....... | 13-20 | 1.3 | .650 | 10-11 | 3-9 | 45 |
|  | Sandro Vitiello, Massachusetts (S) .... | 13-22 | 1.3 | .591 | 10-12 | 3-10 | 47 |
| 1980 | Scott Norwood, James Madison (S) .. | 15-21 | 1.5 | .714 | 10-11 | 5-10 | 48 |
| 1981 | Tony Zendejas, Nevada (S) .......... | 21-24 | 1.9 | .875 | 13-14 | 8-10 | 55 |
| 1982 | Tony Zendejas, Nevada (S) .......... | **26-*33 | **2.4 | .788 | 18-20 | 8-13 | 52 |
| 1983 | Tony Zendejas, Nevada (S) .......... | 23-29 | 2.1 | .793 | 14-15 | 9-14 | 58 |
| 1984 | Marty Zendejas, Nevada (S).......... | 22-27 | 2.0 | .815 | 12-13 | 10-14 | 52 |
| 1985 | George Benyola, Louisiana Tech (S) .. | 24-31 | 2.2 | .774 | 15-18 | 9-13 | 53 |
| 1986 | Kirk Roach, Western Caro. (S) ........ | 24-28 | 2.2 | .857 | 17-17 | 7-11 | 52 |
| 1987 | Micky Penaflor, Northern Ariz. (S)..... | 19-27 | 1.9 | .704 | 12-16 | 7-11 | 51 |
| 1988 | Chris Lutz, Princeton (S) .............. | 19-24 | 1.9 | .792 | 19-21 | 0-3 | 39 |
| 1989 | Steve Christie, William & Mary (S) .... | 20-29 | 1.8 | .690 | 16-17 | 4-12 | 53 |
| 1990 | Brian Mitchell, Northern Iowa (S) ..... | **26-27 | **2.4 | *.963 | 23-23 | 3-4 | 45 |
| 1991 | Brian Mitchell, Northern Iowa (S) .... | 19-24 | 1.7 | .792 | 15-16 | 4-8 | 57 |
| 1992 | Mike Dodd, Boise St. (S) .............. | 22-31 | 2.0 | .710 | 16-21 | 6-10 | 50 |

*Record.  ** Record tied.  (S) Soccer-style kicker.*

# LONGEST PLAYS

*Since 1941, official maximum length of all plays fixed at 100 yards.*

## Rushing

| Yds. | Player, Team (Opponent) | Year |
|---|---|---|
| 99 | Phillip Collins, Southwest Mo. St. (Western Ill.) ............................................. | 1989 |
| 99 | Pedro Bacon, Western Ky. (Livingston) ................................................... | 1986 |
| 99 | Hubert Owens, Mississippi Val. (Ark.-Pine Bluff) ......................................... | 1980 |
| 98 | Johnny Gordon, Nevada (Montana St.) .................................................... | 1984 |
| 97 | Norman Bradford, Grambling (Prairie View) ............................................... | 1992 |

| Yds. | Player, Team (Opponent) | Year |
|---|---|---|
| 97 | David Clark, Dartmouth (Harvard) | 1989 |
| 97 | David Clark, Dartmouth (Princeton) | 1988 |
| 96 | Kelvin Anderson, Southeast Mo. St. (Murray St.) | 1992 |
| 96 | Andre Lockhart, Tenn.-Chatt. (East Tenn. St.) | 1986 |
| 95 | Jerry Ellison, Tenn.-Chatt. (Boise St.) | 1992 |
| 95 | Joe Sparksman, James Madison (William & Mary) | 1990 |
| 94 | Mark Vigil, Idaho (Simon Fraser) | 1980 |
| 93 | Jimmy Henderson, Columbia (Yale) | 1984 |
| 93 | Terence Thompson, Eastern Ky. (Akron) | 1981 |

## Passing

| Yds. | Passer-Receiver, Team (Opponent) | Year |
|---|---|---|
| 99 | Todd Donnan-Troy Brown, Marshall (East Tenn. St.) | 1991 |
| 99 | Antoine Ezell-Tyrone Davis, Florida A&M (Bethune-Cookman) | 1991 |
| 99 | Jay Johnson-Kenny Shedd, Northern Iowa (Oklahoma St.) | 1990 |
| 99 | John Bonds-Hendricks Johnson, Northern Ariz. (Boise St.) | 1990 |
| 99 | Scott Stoker-Victor Robinson, Northwestern, La. (Northeast La.) | 1989 |
| 98 | Antoine Ezell-Tim Daniel, Florida A&M (Delaware St.) | 1991 |
| 98 | John Friesz-Lee Allen, Idaho (Northern Ariz.) | 1989 |
| 98 | Fred Gatlin-Treamelle Taylor, Nevada (Montana) | 1989 |
| 98 | Steve Monaco-Emerson Foster, Rhode Island (Holy Cross) | 1988 |
| 98 | Frank Baur-Maurice Caldwell, Lafayette (Columbia) | 1988 |
| 98 | David Gabianelli-Craig Morton, Dartmouth (Columbia) | 1986 |
| 98 | Joe Pizzo-Bryan Calder, Nevada (Eastern Wash.) | 1984 |
| 98 | Bobby Hebert-Randy Liles, Northwestern, La. (Southeastern La.) | 1980 |
| 97 | Nate Harrison-Brian Thomas, Southern-B.R. (Dist. Columbia) | 1989 |
| 97 | Jerome Baker-John Taylor, Delaware St. (St. Paul's) | 1985 |
| 97 | John McKenzie-Chris Burkett, Jackson St. (Mississippi Val.) | 1983 |
| 96 | Greg Wyatt-Shawn Collins, Northern Ariz. (Montana St.) | 1988 |
| 96 | Rick Fahnestock-Albert Brown, Western Ill. (Northern Iowa) | 1986 |
| 96 | Jeff Cesarone-Keith Paskett, Western Ky. (Akron) | 1985 |
| 96 | Mike Williams-Trumaine Johnson, Grambling (Jackson St.) | 1980 |

## Interception Returns

| Yds. | Player, Team (Opponent) | Year |
|---|---|---|
| 100 | Derek Grier, Marshall (East Tenn. St.) | 1991 |
| 100 | Ricky Fields, Samford (Concord, W. Va.) | 1990 |
| 100 | Warren Smith, Stephen F. Austin (Nicholls St.) | 1990 |
| 100 | Rob Pouliot, Montana St. (Boise St.) | 1988 |
| 100 | Rick Harris, East Tenn. St. (Davidson) | 1986 |
| 100 | Bruce Alexander, Stephen F. Austin (Lamar) | 1986 |
| 100 | Guy Carbone, Rhode Island (Lafayette) | 1985 |
| 100 | Moses Aimable, Northern Iowa (Western Ill.) | 1985 |
| 100 | Kervin Fontennette, Southeastern La. (Nicholls St.) | 1985 |
| 100 | Jim Anderson, Princeton (Cornell) | 1984 |
| 100 | Keiron Bigby, Brown (Yale) | 1984 |
| 100 | Vencie Glenn, Indiana St. (Wayne St., Mich.) | 1984 |
| 100 | George Floyd, Eastern Ky. (Youngstown St.) | 1980 |

## Punt Returns

| Yds. | Player, Team (Opponent) | Year |
|---|---|---|
| 98 | Willie Ware, Mississippi Val. (Bishop) | 1985 |
| 98 | Barney Bussey, South Caro. St. (Johnson Smith) | 1981 |
| 96 | Carl Williams, Texas Southern (Grambling) | 1981 |
| 95 | Clarence Weathers, Delaware St. (Salisbury St.) | 1980 |
| 93 | Joe Fuller, Northern Iowa (Wis.-Whitewater) | 1984 |

## Kickoff Returns

*Twenty-nine players have returned kickoffs 100 yards. The most recent:*

| Yds. | Player, Team (Opponent) | Year |
|---|---|---|
| 100 | Leon Brown, Eastern Ky. (Western Ky.) | 1992 |
| 100 | Eddie Godfrey, Western Ky. (Louisville) | 1990 |
| 100 | Roman Carter, Idaho (Cal St. Chico) | 1990 |
| 100 | Dominic Corr, Eastern Wash. (Weber St.) | 1989 |
| 100 | Leon Brown, Eastern Ky. (Austin Peay) | 1989 |
| 100 | Dave Meggett, Towson St. (Northeastern) | 1988 |
| 100 | Dominic Corr, Eastern Wash. (Illinois St.) | 1987 |
| 100 | Barry Chubb, Colgate (Lafayette) | 1986 |
| 100 | Marco Kornegay, Morgan St. (Norfolk St.) | 1986 |

*1993 NCAA FOOTBALL*

## Punts

| Yds. | Player, Team (Opponent) | Year |
|------|-------------------------|------|
| 91 | Bart Helsley, North Texas (Northeast La.) | 1990 |
| 89 | Jim Carriere, Connecticut (Maine) | 1987 |
| 88 | Jeff Kaiser, Idaho St. (UTEP) | 1983 |
| 87 | John Starnes, North Texas (Texas-Arlington) | 1983 |
| 85 | Don Alonzo, Nicholls St. (Northwestern, La.) | 1980 |
| 84 | Billy Smith, Tenn.-Chatt. (Appalachian St.) | 1988 |
| 83 | Jason Harkins, Appalachian St. (Citadel) | 1986 |
| 82 | Tim Healy, Delaware (Boston U.) | 1987 |
| 82 | John Howell, Tenn.-Chatt. (Vanderbilt) | 1982 |

## Field Goals

| Yds. | Player, Team (Opponent) | Year |
|------|-------------------------|------|
| 63 | Scott Roper, Arkansas St. (North Texas) | 1987 |
| 63 | Tim Foley, Ga. Southern (James Madison) | 1987 |
| 62 | Paul Hickert, Murray St. (Eastern Ky.) | 1986 |
| 58 | Rich Emke, Eastern Ill. (Northern Iowa) | 1986 |
| 58 | Tony Zendejas, Nevada (Boise St.) | 1983 |

# TEAM CHAMPIONS

## OFFENSE

| Year | Total Offense | Avg. | Rushing | Avg. |
|------|---------------|------|---------|------|
| 1978 | Portland St. | 477.4 | Jackson St. | 314.5 |
| 1979 | Portland St. | 460.7 | Jackson St. | 288.4 |
| 1980 | Portland St. | 504.3 | North Caro. A&T | 322.1 |
| 1981 | Idaho | 438.8 | Idaho | 266.3 |
| 1982 | Drake | 444.8 | Delaware | 258.4 |
| 1983 | Idaho | 479.5 | Furman | 287.1 |
| 1984 | Mississippi Val. | *640.1 | Delaware St. | 377.3 |
| 1985 | Weber St. | 516.1 | Southwest Mo. St. | 298.7 |
| 1986 | Nevada | 492.0 | Northeastern | 336.0 |
| 1987 | Holy Cross | 552.2 | Howard | *381.6 |
| 1988 | Lehigh | 485.6 | Eastern Ky. | 303.0 |
| 1989 | Idaho | 495.9 | Ga. Southern | 329.2 |
| 1990 | William & Mary | 498.7 | Delaware St. | 298.7 |
| 1991 | Weber St. | 581.4 | Va. Military | 316.9 |
| 1992 | Alcorn St. | 502.9 | Citadel | 345.5 |

| Year | Scoring | Avg. | Passing | Avg. |
|------|---------|------|---------|------|
| 1978 | Nevada | 35.6 | Portland St. | 367.1 |
| 1979 | Portland St. | 34.3 | Portland St. | 368.9 |
| 1980 | Portland St. | 49.2 | Portland St. | 434.9 |
| 1981 | Delaware | 34.1 | Idaho St. | 325.7 |
| 1982 | Delaware | 34.1 | West Tex. St. | 313.7 |
| 1983 | Mississippi Val. | 39.2 | Idaho | 336.1 |
| 1984 | Mississippi Val. | *60.9 | Mississippi Val. | *496.8 |
| 1985 | Mississippi Val. | 41.5 | Rhode Island | 384.3 |
| 1986 | Nevada | 39.4 | Eastern Ill. | 326.1 |
| 1987 | Holy Cross | 46.5 | Holy Cross | 358.4 |
| 1988 | Lafayette | 38.2 | Lehigh | 330.1 |
| 1989 | Grambling | 37.1 | Idaho | 374.3 |
| 1990 | Jackson St. | 38.0 | Weber St. | 342.2 |
| 1991 | Nevada | 45.1 | Weber St. | 389.1 |
| 1992 | Marshall | 42.4 | Alcorn St. | 360.5 |

## DEFENSE

| Year | Total Defense | Avg. | Rushing | Avg. |
|------|---------------|------|---------|------|
| 1978 | Florida A&M | *149.9 | Florida A&M | 48.6 |
| 1979 | Alcorn St. | 166.3 | Alcorn St. | 56.7 |
| 1980 | Massachusetts | 193.5 | South Caro. St. | 61.8 |
| 1981 | South Caro. St. | 204.0 | South Caro. St. | 60.8 |
| 1982 | South Caro. St. | 191.4 | South Caro. St. | 59.4 |

| Year | Total Defense | Avg. | Rushing | Avg. |
|---|---|---|---|---|
| 1983 | Grambling | 206.0 | Jackson St. | 79.2 |
| 1984 | Tennessee St. | 187.0 | Grambling | *44.5 |
| 1985 | Arkansas St. | 258.8 | Jackson St. | 63.0 |
| 1986 | Tennessee St. | 178.5 | Eastern Ky. | 62.8 |
| 1987 | Southern-B.R. | 202.8 | Southern-B.R. | 64.5 |
| 1988 | Alcorn St. | 215.4 | Stephen F. Austin | 83.5 |
| 1989 | Howard | 220.0 | Montana | 70.2 |
| 1990 | Middle Tenn. St. | 244.8 | Delaware St. | 77.2 |
| 1991 | South Caro. St. | 208.9 | Boise St. | 84.4 |
| 1992 | South Caro. St. | 250.9 | Villanova | 77.8 |

| Year | Scoring | Avg. | Passing | $Avg. |
|---|---|---|---|---|
| 1978 | South Caro. St. | *6.5 | Southern-B.R. | 85.6 |
| 1979 | Lehigh | 7.2 | Mississippi Val. | 64.2 |
| 1980 | Murray St. | 9.1 | Howard | 93.8 |
| 1981 | Jackson St. | 9.4 | Bethune-Cookman | *59.9 |
| 1982 | Western Mich. | 7.1 | Northeastern | 98.8 |
| 1983 | Grambling | 8.6 | Louisiana Tech | 111.4 |
| 1984 | Northwestern (La.) | 9.0 | Louisiana Tech | 105.5 |
| 1985 | Appalachian St. | 9.9 | Dartmouth | 110.3 |
| 1986 | Tennessee St. | 8.3 | Bethune-Cookman | 99.8 |
| 1987 | Holy Cross | 10.0 | Alcorn St. | 101.3 |
| 1988 | Furman | 9.7 | Middle Tenn. St. | 90.8 |
| 1989 | Howard | 10.5 | Tenn.-Chatt. | 104.4 |
| 1990 | Middle Tenn. St. | 9.2 | Middle Tenn. St. | 78.83 |
| 1991 | Villanova | 12.0 | South Caro. St. | *70.01 |
| 1992 | Citadel | 13.0 | Middle Tenn. St. | 76.93 |

** Record. $ Beginning in 1990, ranked on passing-efficiency defense rating points instead of per-game yardage allowed.*

# ANNUAL TOUGHEST-SCHEDULE LEADERS

The Division I-AA toughest-schedule program, which began in 1982, is based on what all Division I-AA opponents did against other Division I-AA and Division I-A teams when *not* playing the team in question. Games against non-I-AA and I-A teams are deleted. (Playoff or postseason games are not included.) The top two leaders by year:

| | | ¢Opponents' Record | | | |
|---|---|---|---|---|---|
| Year | Team (†Record) | W | L | T | Pct. |
| 1982 | Massachusetts (5-6-0) | 50 | 30 | 1 | .623 |
| | Lehigh (4-6-0) | 44 | 31 | 0 | .587 |
| 1983 | Florida A&M (7-4-0) | 42 | 23 | 3 | .640 |
| | Grambling (8-1-2) | 49 | 31 | 0 | .613 |
| 1984 | North Texas (2-9-0) | 55 | 35 | 2 | .609 |
| | Va. Military (1-9-0) | 53 | 37 | 2 | .587 |
| 1985 | South Caro. St. (5-6-0) | 43 | 20 | 1 | .680 |
| | Lehigh (5-6-0) | 47 | 33 | 1 | .586 |
| 1986 | James Madison (5-5-1) | 46 | 28 | 1 | .620 |
| | Bucknell (3-7-0) | 43 | 27 | 0 | .614 |
| 1987 | Ga. Southern (8-3-0) | 47 | 31 | 0 | .603 |
| | Northeastern (6-5-0) | 50 | 37 | 0 | .575 |
| 1988 | Northwestern (La.) (9-2-0) | 54 | 36 | 2 | .598 |
| | Ga. Southern (9-2-0) | 43 | 31 | 1 | .580 |
| 1989 | Liberty (7-3-0) | 39 | 22 | 2 | .635 |
| | Western Caro. (3-7-1) | 46 | 34 | 2 | .573 |
| 1990 | Ga. Southern (8-3-0) | 53 | 25 | 1 | .677 |
| | Western Ky. (2-8-0) | 55 | 36 | 1 | .603 |
| 1991 | Bucknell (1-9-0) | 53 | 29 | 1 | .645 |
| | William & Mary (5-6-0) | 62 | 43 | 0 | .590 |
| 1992 | Va. Military (3-8-0) | 46 | 36 | 0 | .561 |
| | Harvard (3-7-0) | 51 | 40 | 0 | .560 |

*† Not including playoff or postseason games. ¢ When not playing the team listed.*

# TOP 10 TOUGHEST-SCHEDULE LEADERS
## FOR 1988-92†

| 1988 Team | ¢Opp. Record | Pct. |
|---|---|---|
| 1. Northwestern (La.) | 54-36-2 | .598 |
| 2. Ga. Southern | 43-31-1 | .580 |
| 3. McNeese St. | 53-41-0 | .564 |
| 4. Colgate | 53-42-3 | .556 |
| 5. Eastern Wash. | 50-40-0 | .556 |
| Lafayette | 45-36-0 | .556 |
| 7. Louisiana Tech | 61-49-0 | .555 |
| 8. Northeastern | 52-44-0 | .542 |
| 9. Weber St. | 48-41-0 | .539 |
| 10. Western Caro. | 52-45-2 | .535 |

| 1989 Team | ¢Opp. Record | Pct. |
|---|---|---|
| 1. Liberty | 39-22-2 | .635 |
| 2. Western Caro. | 46-34-2 | .573 |
| 3. Northwestern (La.) | 54-41-0 | .568 |
| 4. Western Ky. | 57-44-2 | .563 |
| 5. Boston U. | 52-41-2 | .558 |
| 6. Villanova | 57-45-2 | .558 |
| 7. Southern Ill. | 49-39-1 | .556 |
| 8. Tennessee St. | 50-40-1 | .555 |
| 9. Northeastern | 50-41-1 | .549 |
| 10. Western Ill. | 40-33-0 | .548 |

| 1990 Team | ¢Opp. Record | Pct. |
|---|---|---|
| 1. Ga. Southern | 53-25-1 | .677 |
| 2. Western Ky. | 55-36-1 | .603 |
| 3. Liberty | 47-35-1 | .572 |
| 4. Eastern Wash. | 47-36-0 | .566 |
| 5. Arkansas St. | 60-48-0 | .556 |
| 6. Holy Cross | 55-44-1 | .555 |
| 7. William & Mary | 57-46-0 | .553 |
| 8. Tenn.-Chatt. | 54-44-1 | .551 |
| 9. Tennessee St. | 47-40-0 | .540 |
| 10. Austin Peay | 48-41-1 | .539 |

| 1991 Team | ¢Opp. Record | Pct. |
|---|---|---|
| 1. Bucknell | 53-29-1 | .645 |
| 2. William & Mary | 62-43-0 | .590 |
| 3. North Texas | 51-36-5 | .582 |
| 4. Liberty | 45-33-0 | .577 |
| 5. Morgan St. | 41-30-1 | .576 |
| 6. Massachusetts | 60-47-0 | .561 |
| 7. Fordham | 46-36-1 | .560 |
| 8. Connecticut | 59-47-0 | .557 |
| 9. Idaho | 48-39-0 | .552 |
| 10. Ga. Southern | 43-35-1 | .551 |

| 1992 Team | ¢Opp. Record | Pct. |
|---|---|---|
| 1. Va. Military | 46-36-0 | .561 |
| 2. Harvard | 51-40-0 | .560 |
| 3. Florida A&M | 47-37-0 | .560 |
| 4. Appalachian St. | 53-43-1 | .552 |
| 5. McNeese St. | 52-42-4 | .551 |
| 6. Maine | 50-41-2 | .548 |
| 7. Massachusetts | 51-42-2 | .547 |
| 8. James Madison | 45-37-3 | .547 |
| 9. New Hampshire | 56-47-0 | .544 |
| 10. Delaware St. | 40-34-1 | .540 |

† Not including playoff or postseason games.   ¢ When not playing the team listed.

# ALL-TIME TEAM WON-LOST RECORDS

Includes records as a senior college only, minimum of 20 seasons of competition. Bowl and playoff games are included, and each tie game is computed as half won and half lost.

## BY PERCENTAGE (TOP 25)

| Team | Yrs. | Won | Lost | Tied | Pct.† | *Playoffs W-L-T | Total Games |
|---|---|---|---|---|---|---|---|
| Yale | 120 | 770 | 257 | 55 | .737 | 0-0-0 | 1,082 |
| Tennessee St.# | 65 | 419 | 144 | 30 | .732 | 8-2-1 | 593 |
| Grambling | 50 | 381 | 136 | 15 | .730 | 9-6-0 | 532 |
| Florida A&M | 60 | 415 | 162 | 18 | .713 | 2-1-1 | 595 |
| Princeton | 123 | 698 | 287 | 49 | .699 | 0-0-0 | 1,034 |
| Boise St. | 25 | 196 | 88 | 2 | .689 | 7-6-0 | 286 |
| Harvard | 118 | 698 | 315 | 50 | .680 | 1-0-0 | 1,063 |
| Fordham | 94 | 670 | 328 | 52 | .663 | 2-3-0 | 1,050 |
| Jackson St. | 47 | 299 | 163 | 12 | .643 | 1-8-0 | 474 |
| Dartmouth | 111 | 584 | 321 | 45 | .638 | 0-0-0 | 950 |
| Eastern Ky. | 69 | 410 | 237 | 27 | .628 | 16-13-0 | 674 |
| Pennsylvania | 116 | 684 | 409 | 42 | .621 | 0-1-0 | 1,135 |
| South Caro. St. | 66 | 352 | 210 | 27 | .621 | 5-4-0 | 589 |
| Southern-B.R. | 71 | 403 | 247 | 25 | .616 | 4-0-0 | 675 |
| Ga. Southern | 24 | 153 | 97 | 7 | .609 | 20-2-0 | 257 |

| Team | Yrs. | Won | Lost | Tied | Pct.† | *Playoffs W-L-T | Total Games |
|------|------|-----|------|------|-------|-----------------|-------------|
| Appalachian St. | 63 | 380 | 241 | 29 | .607 | 3-9-0 | 650 |
| Bethune-Cookman | 54 | 292 | 186 | 22 | .606 | 6-2-0 | 500 |
| Hofstra | 52 | 290 | 188 | 9 | .605 | 2-7-0 | 487 |
| Middle Tenn. St. | 76 | 423 | 272 | 27 | .605 | 8-8-0 | 722 |
| Dayton | 85 | 467 | 305 | 26 | .602 | 16-11-0 | 798 |
| Alcorn St. | 69 | 336 | 217 | 37 | .601 | 1-3-0 | 590 |
| Butler | 103 | 469 | 309 | 35 | .598 | 0-3-0 | 813 |
| Western Ky. | 74 | 395 | 264 | 31 | .595 | 7-4-0 | 690 |
| McNeese St. | 42 | 254 | 172 | 14 | .593 | 4-5-0 | 440 |
| Cornell | 105 | 544 | 371 | 34 | .591 | 0-0-0 | 949 |

## ALPHABETICAL LISTING

| Team | Yrs. | Won | Lost | Tied | Pct.† | *Playoffs W-L-T | Total Games |
|------|------|-----|------|------|-------|-----------------|-------------|
| Alabama St. | 87 | 349 | 332 | 41 | .512 | 1-0-0 | 722 |
| Alcorn St. | 69 | 336 | 217 | 37 | .601 | 1-3-0 | 590 |
| Appalachian St. | 63 | 380 | 241 | 29 | .607 | 3-9-0 | 650 |
| Austin Peay | 56 | 215 | 326 | 16 | .400 | 0-0-0 | 557 |
| Bethune-Cookman | 54 | 292 | 186 | 22 | .606 | 6-2-0 | 500 |
| Boise St. | 25 | 196 | 88 | 2 | .689 | 7-6-0 | 286 |
| Boston U. | 73 | 289 | 339 | 28 | .462 | 1-4-0 | 656 |
| Brown | 107 | 471 | 469 | 40 | .501 | 0-1-0 | 980 |
| Bucknell | 107 | 472 | 436 | 51 | .519 | 1-0-0 | 959 |
| Buffalo | 79 | 283 | 320 | 29 | .471 | 0-0-0 | 632 |
| Butler | 103 | 469 | 309 | 35 | .598 | 0-3-0 | 813 |
| Cal St. Northridge | 31 | 141 | 175 | 4 | .447 | 0-2-0 | 320 |
| Cal St. Sacramento | 39 | 177 | 207 | 7 | .462 | 2-3-0 | 391 |
| Canisius | 47 | 202 | 159 | 24 | .556 | 0-1-0 | 385 |
| Central Conn. St. | 54 | 200 | 228 | 22 | .469 | 0-0-0 | 450 |
| Citadel | 85 | 384 | 393 | 32 | .494 | 2-3-0 | 809 |
| Colgate | 102 | 477 | 366 | 49 | .562 | 1-2-0 | 892 |
| Columbia | 102 | 311 | 497 | 41 | .390 | 1-0-0 | 849 |
| Connecticut | 94 | 367 | 404 | 38 | .477 | 0-0-0 | 809 |
| Cornell | 105 | 544 | 371 | 34 | .591 | 0-0-0 | 949 |
| Dartmouth | 111 | 584 | 321 | 45 | .638 | 0-0-0 | 950 |
| Davidson | 95 | 322 | 462 | 44 | .415 | 0-1-0 | 828 |
| Dayton | 85 | 467 | 305 | 26 | .602 | 16-11-0 | 798 |
| Delaware | 101 | 498 | 343 | 42 | .588 | 18-10-0 | 883 |
| Delaware St. | 47 | 206 | 228 | 8 | .475 | 1-0-0 | 642 |
| Drake | 99 | 436 | 419 | 28 | .510 | 2-3-0 | 883 |
| Duquesne | 45 | 185 | 192 | 18 | .491 | 1-0-0 | 395 |
| East Tenn. St. | 69 | 279 | 336 | 27 | .456 | 1-0-0 | 642 |
| Eastern Ill. | 92 | 353 | 392 | 43 | .475 | 8-6-0 | 788 |
| Eastern Ky. | 69 | 410 | 237 | 27 | .628 | 16-13-0 | 674 |
| Eastern Wash. | 82 | 348 | 293 | 23 | .541 | 2-3-0 | 664 |
| Evansville | 67 | 243 | 341 | 22 | .419 | 1-1-0 | 606 |
| Florida A&M | 60 | 415 | 162 | 18 | .713 | 2-1-1 | 595 |
| Fordham | 94 | 670 | 328 | 52 | .663 | 2-3-0 | 1,050 |
| Furman | 79 | 429 | 332 | 36 | .561 | 10-6-0 | 797 |
| Ga. Southern | 24 | 153 | 97 | 7 | .609 | 20-2-0 | 257 |
| Georgetown | 81 | 385 | 262 | 31 | .591 | 0-2-0 | 678 |
| Grambling | 50 | 381 | 136 | 15 | .730 | 9-6-0 | 532 |
| Harvard | 118 | 698 | 315 | 50 | .680 | 1-0-0 | 1,063 |
| Hofstra | 52 | 290 | 188 | 9 | .605 | 2-7-0 | 487 |
| Holy Cross | 97 | 519 | 352 | 55 | .590 | 0-2-0 | 926 |
| Howard | 96 | 378 | 307 | 42 | .549 | 0-0-0 | 727 |
| Idaho | 95 | 349 | 424 | 25 | .453 | 4-8-0 | 798 |
| Idaho St. | 88 | 375 | 327 | 20 | .533 | 3-1-0 | 722 |
| Illinois St. | 93 | 345 | 405 | 63 | .463 | 0-0-0 | 813 |
| Indiana St. | 76 | 290 | 324 | 20 | .473 | 1-2-0 | 634 |
| Jackson St. | 47 | 299 | 163 | 12 | .643 | 1-8-0 | 474 |
| James Madison | 20 | 114 | 97 | 3 | .540 | 1-2-0 | 214 |
| Lafayette | 111 | 559 | 446 | 36 | .554 | 0-0-0 | 1,041 |
| Lehigh | 109 | 502 | 496 | 44 | .503 | 4-4-0 | 1,042 |
| Liberty | 20 | 95 | 101 | 4 | .485 | 0-0-0 | 200 |
| Maine | 101 | 391 | 358 | 38 | .521 | 0-3-0 | 787 |
| Marshall | 89 | 364 | 430 | 44 | .461 | 12-3-0 | 838 |
| Massachusetts | 110 | 420 | 438 | 51 | .490 | 2-5-0 | 909 |
| McNeese St. | 42 | 254 | 172 | 14 | .593 | 4-5-0 | 440 |

*1993 NCAA FOOTBALL*

| Team | Yrs. | Won | Lost | Tied | Pct.† | *Playoffs W-L-T | Total Games |
|------|------|-----|------|------|-------|-----------------|-------------|
| Middle Tenn. St. | 76 | 423 | 272 | 27 | .605 | 8-8-0 | 722 |
| Mississippi Val. | 40 | 166 | 199 | 9 | .456 | 0-1-0 | 374 |
| Montana | 93 | 338 | 420 | 26 | .447 | 2-5-0 | 784 |
| Montana St. | 89 | 339 | 352 | 34 | .491 | 7-1-2 | 725 |
| Morehead St. | 63 | 218 | 327 | 22 | .404 | 0-0-0 | 567 |
| Morgan St. | 72 | 350 | 241 | 30 | .588 | 1-2-0 | 621 |
| Murray St. | 68 | 347 | 280 | 34 | .551 | 0-2-1 | 661 |
| New Hampshire | 96 | 391 | 345 | 54 | .529 | 1-3-0 | 790 |
| Nicholls St. | 21 | 106 | 122 | 4 | .466 | 1-1-0 | 232 |
| North Caro. A&T | 69 | 333 | 275 | 39 | .545 | 1-6-0 | 647 |
| North Texas | 77 | 398 | 314 | 32 | .556 | 1-4-0 | 744 |
| Northeast La. | 42 | 196 | 230 | 8 | .461 | 5-2-0 | 434 |
| Northeastern | 57 | 213 | 250 | 17 | .461 | 0-1-0 | 480 |
| Northern Ariz. | 68 | 285 | 306 | 22 | .483 | 1-2-0 | 613 |
| Northern Iowa | 94 | 455 | 314 | 47 | .586 | 5-6-0 | 816 |
| Northwestern (La.) | 84 | 390 | 313 | 33 | .552 | 2-1-0 | 736 |
| Pennsylvania | 116 | 684 | 409 | 42 | .621 | 0-1-0 | 1,135 |
| Prairie View | 66 | 327 | 296 | 31 | .524 | 1-3-0 | 654 |
| Princeton | 123 | 698 | 287 | 49 | .699 | 0-0-0 | 1,034 |
| Rhode Island | 92 | 314 | 402 | 41 | .442 | 2-4-0 | 757 |
| Richmond | 109 | 381 | 509 | 52 | .432 | 2-3-0 | 942 |
| Sam Houston St. | 77 | 344 | 340 | 34 | .503 | 4-3-1 | 718 |
| Samford | 76 | 305 | 304 | 46 | .501 | 2-2-0 | 655 |
| San Diego | 25 | 112 | 114 | 8 | .495 | 0-0-0 | 234 |
| South Caro. St. | 66 | 352 | 210 | 27 | .621 | 5-4-0 | 589 |
| Southeast Mo. St. | 80 | 340 | 329 | 37 | .508 | 0-0-0 | 706 |
| Southern-B.R. | 71 | 403 | 247 | 25 | .616 | 4-0-0 | 675 |
| Southern Ill. | 77 | 306 | 368 | 33 | .456 | 3-0-0 | 707 |
| Southern Utah | 30 | 150 | 133 | 5 | .530 | 0-0-0 | 288 |
| Southwest Mo. St. | 81 | 354 | 337 | 40 | .512 | 1-5-0 | 731 |
| Southwest Tex. St. | 78 | 391 | 281 | 27 | .579 | 6-1-0 | 699 |
| St. Francis (Pa.) | 44 | 141 | 192 | 12 | .426 | 0-0-0 | 345 |
| St. John's (N.Y.) | 24 | 119 | 94 | 7 | .557 | 0-0-0 | 220 |
| St. Mary's (Cal.) | 64 | 312 | 224 | 19 | .579 | 1-2-0 | 555 |
| St. Peter's | 21 | 44 | 117 | 1 | .275 | 0-0-0 | 162 |
| Stephen F. Austin$ | 66 | 252 | 372 | 28 | .408 | 5-2-0 | 652 |
| Tenn.-Chatt. | 85 | 412 | 363 | 33 | .530 | 0-1-0 | 808 |
| Tenn.-Martin | 36 | 162 | 201 | 5 | .447 | 1-0-0 | 368 |
| Tennessee St.# | 65 | 419 | 144 | 30 | .732 | 8-2-1 | 593 |
| Tennessee Tech | 71 | 298 | 350 | 31 | .462 | 0-3-0 | 679 |
| Texas Southern | 47 | 277 | 232 | 27 | .495 | 1-0-0 | 486 |
| Towson St. | 24 | 133 | 110 | 4 | .547 | 3-4-0 | 247 |
| Troy St. | 62 | 305 | 262 | 14 | .537 | 9-1-0 | 581 |
| Va. Military | 102 | 417 | 470 | 43 | .472 | 0-0-0 | 930 |
| Valparaiso | 72 | 283 | 324 | 24 | .468 | 0-1-0 | 631 |
| Villanova | 95 | 439 | 361 | 41 | .546 | 2-5-1 | 841 |
| Wagner | 62 | 269 | 233 | 17 | .535 | 5-3-0 | 519 |
| Weber St. | 31 | 156 | 167 | 3 | .483 | 1-2-0 | 326 |
| Western Caro. | 59 | 242 | 316 | 23 | .436 | 3-2-0 | 581 |
| Western Ill. | 89 | 366 | 326 | 37 | .527 | 1-4-0 | 729 |
| Western Ky. | 74 | 395 | 264 | 31 | .595 | 7-4-0 | 690 |
| William & Mary | 97 | 415 | 436 | 37 | .488 | 2-5-0 | 888 |
| Yale | 120 | 770 | 257 | 55 | .737 | 0-0-0 | 1,082 |
| Youngstown St. | 52 | 283 | 209 | 16 | .573 | 11-7-0 | 508 |
| **I-AA teams lacking 20 seasons:** | | | | | | | |
| Ala.-Birmingham | 2 | 11 | 6 | 2 | .631 | 0-0-0 | 19 |
| Central Fla. | 14 | 73 | 74 | 1 | .497 | 2-1-0 | 148 |
| Charleston So. | 2 | 5 | 13 | 0 | .278 | 0-0-0 | 18 |
| Iona | 15 | 65 | 80 | 3 | .449 | 0-0-0 | 148 |
| Marist | 15 | 48 | 83 | 3 | .369 | 0-0-0 | 134 |
| Siena | 5 | 11 | 34 | 0 | .244 | 0-0-0 | 45 |

## VICTORIES

| Team | Wins | Team | Wins | Team | Wins |
|------|------|------|------|------|------|
| Yale | 770 | Dartmouth | 584 | Delaware | 498 |
| Harvard | 698 | Lafayette | 559 | Colgate | 477 |
| Princeton | 698 | Cornell | 544 | Bucknell | 472 |
| Pennsylvania | 684 | Holy Cross | 519 | Brown | 471 |
| Fordham | 670 | Lehigh | 502 | Butler | 469 |

*Division I-AA All-Time Team Won-Lost Records*  179

| Team | Wins | Team | Wins | Team | Wins |
|---|---|---|---|---|---|
| Dayton | 467 | Idaho | 349 | Morehead St. | 218 |
| Northern Iowa | 455 | Eastern Wash. | 348 | Austin Peay | 215 |
| Villanova | 439 | Murray St. | 347 | Northeastern | 213 |
| Drake | 436 | Illinois St. | 345 | Delaware St. | 206 |
| Furman | 429 | Sam Houston St. | 344 | Canisius | 202 |
| Middle Tenn. St. | 423 | Southeast Mo. St. | 340 | Central Conn. St. | 200 |
| Massachusetts | 420 | Montana St. | 339 | Boise St. | 196 |
| Tennessee St.# | 419 | Montana | 338 | Northeast La. | 196 |
| Va. Military | 417 | Alcorn St. | 336 | Duquesne | 185 |
| Florida A&M | 415 | North Caro. A&T | 333 | Cal St. Sacramento | 177 |
| William & Mary | 415 | Prairie View | 327 | Mississippi Val. | 166 |
| Tenn.-Chatt. | 412 | Davidson | 322 | Tenn.-Martin | 162 |
| Eastern Ky. | 410 | Rhode Island | 314 | Weber St. | 156 |
| Southern-B.R. | 403 | St. Mary's (Cal.) | 312 | Ga. Southern | 153 |
| North Texas | 398 | Columbia | 311 | Southern Utah | 150 |
| Western Ky. | 395 | Southern Ill. | 306 | Cal St. Northridge | 141 |
| Maine | 391 | Samford | 305 | St. Francis (Pa.) | 141 |
| New Hampshire | 391 | Troy St. | 305 | Towson St. | 133 |
| Southwest Tex. St. | 391 | Jackson St. | 299 | St. John's (N.Y.) | 119 |
| Northwestern (La.) | 390 | Tennessee Tech | 298 | James Madison | 114 |
| Georgetown | 385 | Bethune-Cookman | 292 | San Diego | 112 |
| Citadel | 384 | Hofstra | 290 | Nicholls St. | 106 |
| Grambling | 381 | Indiana St. | 290 | Liberty | 95 |
| Richmond | 381 | Boston U. | 289 | Central Fla. | 73 |
| Appalachian St. | 380 | Northern Ariz. | 285 | Iona | 65 |
| Howard | 378 | Buffalo | 283 | Marist | 48 |
| Idaho St. | 375 | Valparaiso | 283 | St. Peter's | 44 |
| Connecticut | 367 | Youngstown St. | 283 | Ala.-Birmingham | 11 |
| Western Ill. | 366 | East Tenn. St. | 279 | Siena | 11 |
| Marshall | 364 | Texas Southern | 277 | Charleston So. | 5 |
| Southwest Mo. St. | 354 | Wagner | 269 | | |
| Eastern Ill. | 353 | McNeese St. | 254 | | |
| South Caro. St. | 352 | Stephen F. Austin$ | 252 | | |
| Morgan St. | 350 | Evansville | 243 | | |
| Alabama St. | 349 | Western Caro. | 242 | | |

*Also includes any participation in major bowl games.* † *Ties computed as half won and half lost.* # *Tennessee State's participation in 1981 and 1982 Division I-AA championships (1-2 record) voided.* $ *Stephen F. Austin's participation in 1989 Division I-AA championship (3-1 record) voided.*

# RECORDS IN THE 1990s

## (1990-91-92; Includes Playoffs)

### BY PERCENTAGE

| Team | W-L-T | Pct.† | Team | W-L-T | Pct.† |
|---|---|---|---|---|---|
| Youngstown St. | 34-7-1 | .821 | Cornell | 19-11-0 | .633 |
| Eastern Ky. | 31-7-0 | .816 | Princeton | 19-11-0 | .633 |
| Holy Cross | 26-6-1 | .803 | Southwest Mo. St. | 21-12-1 | .632 |
| Northern Iowa | 31-8-0 | .795 | Central Fla. | 22-13-0 | .629 |
| North Caro. A&T | 27-8-0 | .771 | Furman | 22-13-0 | .629 |
| Middle Tenn. St. | 30-9-0 | .769 | Boise St. | 22-14-0 | .611 |
| Dartmouth | 22-6-2 | .767 | Massachusetts | 19-12-1 | .609 |
| Samford | 27-9-1 | .743 | Jackson St. | 20-13-0 | .606 |
| Alabama St. | 24-8-2 | .735 | Montana | 20-13-0 | .606 |
| Delaware | 27-10-0 | .730 | Appalachian St. | 21-14-0 | .600 |
| Villanova | 25-10-0 | .714 | Florida A&M | 20-14-0 | .588 |
| Marshall | 29-12-0 | .707 | McNeese St. | 20-14-2 | .583 |
| Ga. Southern | 26-11-0 | .703 | Lehigh | 19-14-0 | .576 |
| Citadel | 25-11-0 | .694 | Sam Houston St. | 18-13-3 | .574 |
| William & Mary | 24-11-0 | .686 | South Caro. St. | 18-14-0 | .563 |
| Northeast La. | 24-11-1 | .681 | Southwest Tex. St. | 18-14-1 | .561 |
| Grambling | 23-11-0 | .676 | Weber St. | 19-15-0 | .559 |
| Idaho | 24-12-0 | .667 | Alcorn St. | 16-13-1 | .550 |
| Delaware St. | 21-11-0 | .656 | Lafayette | 18-15-0 | .545 |
| New Hampshire | 21-11-2 | .647 | Liberty | 18-15-0 | .545 |

| Team | W-L-T | Pct.† | Team | W-L-T | Pct.† |
|---|---|---|---|---|---|
| Northwestern (La.) | 18-15-0 | .545 | Maine | 12-21-0 | .364 |
| Yale | 16-14-0 | .533 | Morehead St. | 12-21-0 | .364 |
| Mississippi Val. | 16-14-1 | .532 | Northern Ariz. | 12-21-0 | .364 |
| Eastern Wash. | 17-16-0 | .515 | Rhode Island | 12-21-0 | .364 |
| Western Ill. | 17-16-1 | .515 | Tenn.-Martin# | 12-21-0 | .364 |
| James Madison | 18-17-0 | .514 | Western Caro. | 12-21-0 | .364 |
| Colgate | 15-18-0 | .455 | Va. Military | 11-22-0 | .333 |
| Howard | 15-18-0 | .455 | Northeastern | 10-22-1 | .318 |
| Illinois St. | 15-18-0 | .455 | Montana St. | 10-23-0 | .303 |
| Tenn.-Chatt. | 15-18-0 | .455 | Richmond | 10-23-0 | .303 |
| Tennessee St. | 15-18-0 | .455 | Western Ky. | 9-22-0 | .290 |
| Tennessee Tech | 15-18-0 | .455 | Idaho St. | 9-23-1 | .288 |
| Texas Southern | 14-18-1 | .439 | Nicholls St. | 9-23-1 | .288 |
| Connecticut | 14-19-0 | .424 | Towson St. | 8-24-0 | .250 |
| Eastern Ill. | 14-19-0 | .424 | Austin Peay | 8-25-0 | .242 |
| Harvard | 12-17-1 | .417 | East Tenn. St. | 8-25-0 | .242 |
| North Texas | 13-19-1 | .409 | Stephen F. Austin | 7-25-1 | .227 |
| Pennsylvania | 12-18-0 | .400 | Murray St. | 7-26-0 | .212 |
| Indiana St. | 13-20-0 | .394 | Columbia | 5-25-0 | .167 |
| Southern-B.R. | 13-20-0 | .394 | Fordham | 4-26-0 | .133 |
| Southern Ill. | 13-20-0 | .394 | Morgan St. | 4-28-0 | .125 |
| Bethune-Cookman | 12-19-0 | .387 | Brown | 3-27-0 | .100 |
| Bucknell | 12-20-0 | .375 | Prairie View* | 0-22-0 | .000 |
| Southeast Mo. St. | 12-20-0 | .375 | | | |
| Boston U. | 12-21-0 | .364 | | | |

† Ties counted as half won and half lost.　　* Did not play in 1990.　　# Joined I-AA in 1991.

## VICTORIES
### (Minimum 20 Wins)

| Team | Wins | Team | Wins |
|---|---|---|---|
| Youngstown St. | 34 | William & Mary | 24 |
| Eastern Ky. | 31 | Grambling | 23 |
| Northern Iowa | 31 | Boise St. | 22 |
| Middle Tenn. St. | 30 | Central Fla. | 22 |
| Marshall | 29 | Dartmouth | 22 |
| Delaware | 27 | Furman | 22 |
| North Caro. A&T | 27 | Appalachian St. | 21 |
| Samford | 27 | Delaware St. | 21 |
| Ga. Southern | 26 | New Hampshire | 21 |
| Holy Cross | 26 | Southwest Mo. St. | 21 |
| Citadel | 25 | Florida A&M | 20 |
| Villanova | 25 | Jackson St. | 20 |
| Alabama St. | 24 | McNeese St. | 20 |
| Idaho | 24 | Montana | 20 |
| Northeast La. | 24 | | |

# RECORDS IN THE 1980s
### (Playoffs Included)

## BY PERCENTAGE

| Rank | Team | W-L-T | Pct.† | Rank | Team | W-L-T | Pct.† |
|---|---|---|---|---|---|---|---|
| 1 | Eastern Ky. | 88-24-2 | .781 | 11 | Delaware | 68-36-0 | .654 |
| 2 | Furman | 83-23-4 | .773 | 12 | Middle Tenn. St. | 65-36-0 | .644 |
| 3 | Ga. Southern | 68-22-1 | *.753 | 13 | Boise St. | 66-38-0 | .635 |
| 4 | Jackson St. | 71-25-5 | .728 | 14 | Southwest Tex. St. | 66-39-0 | .629 |
| 5 | Grambling | 68-30-3 | .688 | 15 | Murray St. | 61-36-2 | .626 |
| 6 | Nevada-Reno‡ | 71-35-1 | .668 | 16 | Northern Iowa | 64-38-2 | .625 |
| 7 | Holy Cross | 67-33-2 | .667 | 17 | Towson St. | 60-36-2 | .622 |
| 8 | Tennessee St. | 64-32-4 | .660 | 18 | Alcorn St. | 56-34-0 | .622 |
| 9 | Eastern Ill. | 70-36-1 | .659 | 19 | Northeast La. | 64-39-0 | .621 |
| 10 | Idaho | 69-36-0 | .657 | 20 | South Caro. St. | 55-34-1 | .617 |

† Ties counted as half won and half lost.　　* Includes two nonvarsity seasons and five varsity seasons; varsity record, 55-14-0 for .797.　　‡ Later changed name to Nevada.

# UNDEFEATED, UNTIED TEAMS

Regular-season games only, from 1978. Subsequent loss in Division I-AA championship is indicated by (††).

| Yr. | College | Wins | Yr. | College | Wins |
|-----|---------|------|-----|---------|------|
| 1978 | Nevada | ††11 | 1987 | Holy Cross | 11 |
| 1982 | *Eastern Ky. | 10 | 1989 | *Ga. Southern | 11 |
| 1984 | Tennessee St. | 11 | 1990 | Youngstown St. | ††11 |
| | Alcorn St. | ††9 | 1991 | Holy Cross | 11 |
| 1985 | Middle Tenn. St. | ††11 | | Nevada | ††11 |
| 1986 | Nevada | ††11 | | | |
| | Pennsylvania | 10 | | | |

* *Won Division I-AA championship.*

# DIVISION I-AA FINAL POLL LEADERS

**(Released before division championship playoffs)**

| Year | Team, Record* | Coach | †Record in Championship |
|------|---------------|-------|-------------------------|
| 1978 | Nevada (10-0-0) | Chris Ault | 0-1 Lost in semifinals |
| 1979 | Grambling (8-2-0) | Eddie Robinson | Did not compete |
| 1980 | South Caro. St. (10-0-0) | Bill Davis | Did not compete |
| 1981 | Eastern Ky. (9-1-0) | Roy Kidd | 2-1 Runner-up |
| 1982 | Eastern Ky. (10-0-0) | Roy Kidd | 3-0 Champion |
| 1983 | Southern Ill. (10-1-0) | Rey Dempsey | 3-0 Champion |
| 1984 | Alcorn St. (9-0-0) | Marino Casem | 0-1 Lost in quarterfinals |
| 1985 | Middle Tenn. St. (11-0-0) | James Donnelly | 0-1 Lost in quarterfinals |
| 1986 | Nevada (11-0-0) | Chris Ault | 2-1 Lost in semifinals |
| 1987 | Holy Cross (11-0-0) | Mark Duffner | Did not compete |
| 1988 | Idaho (9-1-0) | Keith Gilbertson | 2-1 Lost in semifinals |
| 1989 | Ga. Southern (11-0-0) | Erk Russell | 4-0 Champion |
| 1990 | Middle Tenn. St. (10-1-0) | James Donnelly | 1-1 Lost in quarterfinals |
| 1991 | Nevada (11-0-0) | Chris Ault | 1-1 Lost in quarterfinals |
| 1992 | tie Citadel (10-1-0) | Charlie Taaffe | 1-1 Lost in quarterfinals |
| | Northeast La. (9-2-0) | Dave Roberts | 1-1 Lost in quarterfinals |

* *Final poll record; in some cases, a team had one or two games remaining before the championship playoffs.* † *Number of teams in the championship: 4 (1978-80); 8 (1981); 12 (1982-85); 16 (1986-).*

# THE SPOILERS

**(From 1978 Season)**

Following is a list of the spoilers of Division I-AA teams that lost their perfect (undefeated, untied) record in their **season-ending** game, including the Division I-AA championship playoffs. An asterisk (*) indicates a championship playoff game and a dagger (†) indicates the home team in a regular-season game.

| Date | Spoiler | Victim | Score |
|------|---------|--------|-------|
| 12-9-78 | *Massachusetts | Nevada | 44-21 |
| 11-15-80 | †Grambling | South Caro. St. | 26-3 |
| 11-22-80 | †Murray St. | Western Ky. | 49-0 |
| 12-1-84 | *Louisiana Tech | Alcorn St. | 44-21 |
| 12-7-85 | *Ga. Southern | Middle Tenn. St. | 28-21 |
| 11-22-86 | Boston College | †Holy Cross | 56-26 |
| 12-19-86 | *Ga. Southern | Nevada | 48-38 |
| 11-19-88 | *Cornell | Pennsylvania | 19-6 |
| 11-24-90 | *Central Fla. | Youngstown St. | 20-17 |
| 12-7-91 | *Youngstown St. | Nevada | 30-28 |

*1993 NCAA FOOTBALL*

# MOST-PLAYED RIVALRIES

## (Current Rivalry)

| Games | Opponents (Rivalry leader listed first) | Rivalry Record | First Game |
|---|---|---|---|
| 128 | Lafayette-Lehigh | 70-53-5 | 1884 |
| 115 | Yale-Princeton | 63-42-10 | 1873 |
| 109 | Yale-Harvard | 59-42-8 | 1875 |
| 102 | William & Mary-Richmond | 50-47-5 | 1898 |
| 99 | Pennsylvania-Cornell | 55-39-5 | 1893 |
| 97 | Yale-Brown | 69-23-5 | 1880 |
| 96 | Harvard-Dartmouth | 50-41-5 | 1882 |
| 92 | Montana-Montana St. | 55-32-5 | 1897 |
| 92 | Harvard-Brown | 68-22-2 | 1893 |
| 85 | Princeton-Harvard | 46-32-7 | 1877 |
| 84 | Princeton-Pennsylvania | 59-24-1 | 1876 |
| 83 | Connecticut-Rhode Island | 43-32-8 | 1897 |
| 81 | Illinois St.-Eastern Ill. | 40-33-8 | 1901 |
| 80 | Maine-New Hampshire | 37-35-8 | 1903 |
| 80 | Cornell-Columbia | 52-25-3 | 1889 |
| 78 | Cornell-Colgate | 46-29-3 | 1896 |

# CLIFFHANGERS

Regular-season Division I-AA games won on the final play in regulation time. The extra point is listed when it provided the margin of victory after the winning touchdown on the game's final play.

| Date | Opponents, Score | Game-winning play |
|---|---|---|
| 10-21-78 | Western Ky. 17, Eastern Ky. 16 | Kevin McGrath 25 FG |
| 9-8-79 | Northern Ariz. 22, Portland St. 21 | Ken Fraser 15 pass from Brian Potter (Mike Jenkins pass from Potter) |
| 10-18-80 | Connecticut 18, Holy Cross 17 | Ken Miller 4 pass from Ken Sweitzer (Keith Hugger pass from Sweitzer) |
| 11-15-80 | Morris Brown 19, Bethune-Cookman 18 | Ray Mills 1 run (Carlton Johnson kick) |
| 9-26-81 | Abilene Christian 41, Northwestern (La.) 38 | David Russell 17 pass from Loyal Proffitt |
| 10-10-81 | LIU-C. W. Post 37, James Madison 36 | Tom DeBona 10 pass from Tom Ehrhardt |
| 11-13-82 | Pennsylvania 23, Harvard 21 | Dave Shulman 27 FG |
| 10-1-83 | Connecticut 9, New Hampshire 7 | Larry Corn 7 run |
| 9-8-84 | Southwestern La. 17, Louisiana Tech 16 | Patrick Broussard 21 FG |
| 9-15-84 | Lehigh 10, Connecticut 7 | Dave Melick 45 FG |
| 9-15-84 | William & Mary 23, Delaware 21 | Jeff Sanders 18 pass from Stan Yagiello |
| 10-13-84 | Lafayette 20, Connecticut 13 | Ryan Priest 2 run |
| 10-20-84 | Central Fla. 28, Illinois St. 24 | Jeff Farmer 30 punt return |
| 10-27-84 | Western Ky. 33, Morehead St. 31 | Arnold Grier 50 pass from Jeff Cesarone |
| 9-7-85 | Central Fla. 39, Bethune-Cookman 37 | Ed O'Brien 55 FG |
| 10-26-85 | Va. Military 39, William & Mary 38 | Al Comer 3 run (James Wright run) |
| 8-30-86 | Texas Southern 38, Prairie View 35 | Don Espinoza 23 FG |
| 9-20-86 | Delaware 33, West Chester 31 | Fred Singleton 3 run |
| 10-4-86 | Northwestern (La.) 17, Northeast La. 14 | Keith Hodnett 27 FG |
| 10-11-86 | Eastern Ill. 31, Northern Iowa 30 | Rich Ehmke 58 FG |
| 9-12-87 | Youngstown St. 20, Bowling Green 17 | John Dowling 36 FG |
| 10-3-87 | Northeast La. 33, Northwestern (La.) 31 | Jackie Harris 48 pass from Stan Humphries |
| 10-10-87 | Marshall 34, Louisville 31 | Keith Baxter 31 pass from Tony Petersen |
| 10-17-87 | Princeton 16, Lehigh 15 | Rob Goodwin 38 FG |
| 11-12-87 | South Caro. St. 15, Grambling 13 | William Wrighten 23 FG |
| 9-24-88 | Holy Cross 30, Princeton 26 | 70 kickoff return; Tim Donovan 55 on lateral from Darin Cromwell (15) |
| 10-15-88 | Weber St. 37, Nevada 31 | Todd Beightol 57 pass from Jeff Carlson |
| 10-29-88 | Nicholls St. 13, Southwest Tex. St. 10 | Jim Windham 33 FG |
| 9-2-89 | Alabama St. 16, Troy St. 13 | Reggie Brown 28 pass from Antonius Smith |
| 9-16-89 | Western Caro. 26, Tenn.-Chatt. 20 | Terrell Wagner 68 interception return |
| 9-23-89 | Northwestern (La.) 18, McNeese St. 17 | Chris Hamler 25 FG |
| 10-14-89 | East Tenn. St. 24, Tenn.-Chatt. 23 | George Searcy 1 run |
| 9-29-90 | Southwest Tex. St. 33, Nicholls St. 30 | Robbie Roberson 32 FG |
| 10-6-90 | Grambling 27, Alabama A&M 20 | Dexter Butcher 28 pass from Shawn Burras |
| 11-2-91 | Grambling 30, Texas Southern 27 | Gilad Landau 37 FG |

*Division I-AA Most-Played Rivalries*

| Date | Opponents, Score | Game-winning play |
|------|------------------|-------------------|
| 9-19-92 | Eastern Ky. 26, Northeast La. 21 | Sean Little recovered fumble in end zone |
| 10-10-92 | Appalachian St. 27, James Madison 21 | Craig Styron 44 pass from D. J. Campbell |
| 11-14-92 | Towson St. 33, Northeastern 32 | Mark Orlando 10 pass from Dan Crowley |

## LONGEST WINNING STREAKS

**(From 1978; must have been I-AA members during that period. Includes playoff games.)**

| Wins | Team | Years | Ended by | Score |
|------|------|-------|----------|-------|
| 20 | Holy Cross | 1990-92 | Army | 7-17 |
| 18 | Eastern Ky. | 1982-83 | Western Ky. | 10-10 |
| 16 | Ga. Southern | 1989-90 | Middle Tenn. St. | 13-16 |
| 14 | Delaware | 1979-80 | Lehigh | 20-27 |
| 13 | Holy Cross | 1988-89 | Army | 9-45 |
| 13 | Nevada | 1986 | Ga. Southern | 38-48 |
| 13 | Tennessee St. | 1983-85 | Western Ky. | 17-22 |
| 12 | Nevada | 1989-90 | Boise St. | 14-30 |
| 12 | Furman | 1989 | Stephen F. Austin | 19-21 |
| 12 | Holy Cross | 1987-88 | Army | 3-23 |
| 12 | Southern Ill. | 1982-83 | Wichita St. | 6-28 |
| 12 | Florida A&M | 1978-79 | Tennessee St. | 3-20 |

## LONGEST UNBEATEN STREAKS

**(From 1978. Includes playoff games and may include ties.)**

| No. | Wins | Ties | Team | Years | Ended by |
|-----|------|------|------|-------|----------|
| 20 | 20 | 0 | Holy Cross | 1990-92 | Army |
| 19 | 18 | 1 | Eastern Ky. | 1982-83 | Murray St. |
| 17 | 16 | 1 | Alabama St. | 1990-92 | Alcorn St. |
| 17 | 16 | 1 | Grambling | 1977-78 | Florida A&M |
| 16 | 16 | 0 | Ga. Southern | 1989-90 | Middle Tenn. St. |
| 14 | 14 | 0 | Delaware | 1979-80 | Lehigh |
| 13 | 13 | 0 | Holy Cross | 1988-89 | Army |
| 13 | 13 | 0 | Nevada | 1986 | Ga. Southern |
| 13 | 13 | 0 | Tennessee St. | 1983-85 | Western Ky. |
| 13 | 12 | 1 | Mississippi Val. | 1983-84 | Alcorn St. |
| 13 | 12 | 1 | Eastern Ill. | 1981-82 | Tennessee St. |
| 12 | 12 | 0 | Nevada | 1989-90 | Boise St. |
| 12 | 12 | 0 | Furman | 1989 | Stephen F. Austin |
| 12 | 12 | 0 | Holy Cross | 1987-88 | Army |
| 12 | 11 | 1 | Tennessee St. | 1985-86 | Alabama St. |
| 12 | 12 | 0 | Southern Ill. | 1982-83 | Wichita St. |
| 12 | 11 | 1 | Tennessee St. | 1981-83 | Jackson St. |
| 12 | 12 | 0 | Florida A&M | 1978-79 | Tennessee St. |
| 10 | 9 | 1 | Stephen F. Austin | 1989 | Ga. Southern |
| 10 | 9 | 1 | Holy Cross | 1983 | Boston College |
| 10 | 9 | 1 | Jackson St. | 1980 | Grambling |

## HOME WINNING STREAKS

**(From 1978. Must have been I-AA members during that period.)**

| Wins | Team | Years | Ended by |
|------|------|-------|----------|
| 38 | Ga. Southern | 1985-90 | Eastern Ky. |
| 30 | Eastern Ky. | 1978-83 | Western Ky. |
| 25 | Northern Iowa | 1989-92 | Youngstown St. |
| 23 | Northern Iowa | 1983-87 | Montana |
| 22 | Nevada | 1989-91 | Youngstown St. |
| 20 | Arkansas St. | 1984-87 | Northwestern (La.) |
| 16 | Southwest Tex. St. | 1981-83 | Central St. (Ohio) |
| 16 | Citadel | 1980-82 | East Tenn. St. |
| 15 | Holy Cross | 1987-89 | Massachusetts |
| 13 | William & Mary | 1988-91 | Delaware |

| Wins | Team | Years | Ended by |
|---|---|---|---|
| 12 | Idaho .......................... | 1988-89 ......... | Eastern Ill. |
| 12 | Delaware St. ................... | 1983-86 ......... | Northeastern |
| 12 | Eastern Ill....................... | 1981-83 ......... | Indiana St. |

# REGULAR-SEASON OVERTIME GAMES

In 1981, the NCAA Football Rules Committee approved an overtime tie-breaker system to decide a tie game for the purpose of determining a conference champion. The following conferences have used the tie-breaker system to decide conference-only tie games. In an overtime period, one end of the field is used and each team gets an offensive series beginning at the 25-yard line. Each team shall have possession until it has scored, failed to gain a first down or has lost possession. The team scoring the greater number of points after completion of both possessions is declared the winner. The periods continue until a winner is determined.

## BIG SKY CONFERENCE

| Date | Opponents, Score | No. OTs | Score, Reg. |
|---|---|---|---|
| 10-31-81 | ‡Weber St. 24, Northern Ariz. 23 ............................. | 1 | 17-17 |
| 11-21-81 | ‡Idaho St. 33, Weber St. 30 ................................. | 3 | 23-23 |
| 10-2-82 | ‡Montana St. 30, Idaho St. 27 ............................... | 3 | 17-17 |
| 11-6-82 | Nevada 46, ‡Weber St. 43 ................................... | 3 | 30-30 |
| 10-13-84 | ‡Montana St. 44, Nevada 41 ................................. | 4 | 21-21 |
| 9-17-88 | Boise St. 24, ‡Northern Ariz. 21 ............................. | 2 | 14-14 |
| 10-15-88 | ‡Montana 33, Northern Ariz. 26 .............................. | 2 | 26-26 |
| 9-15-90 | ‡Weber St. 45, Idaho St. 38 ................................. | 2 | 31-31 |
| 9-29-90 | ‡Nevada 31, Idaho 28 ...................................... | 1 | 28-28 |
| 11-3-90 | Eastern Wash. 33, ‡Idaho St. 26............................. | 1 | 26-26 |
| 11-10-90 | Montana St. 28, ‡Eastern Wash. 25 .......................... | 1 | 25-25 |
| 10-26-91 | Eastern Wash. 34, ‡Idaho 31 ................................ | 2 | 24-24 |
| 11-16-91 | Montana 35, ‡Idaho 34....................................... | 1 | 28-28 |

## MID-EASTERN ATHLETIC CONFERENCE

| Date | Opponents, Score | No. OTs | Score, Reg. |
|---|---|---|---|
| 11-1-86 | ‡North Caro. A&T 30, Bethune-Cookman 24 ................. | 1 | 24-24 |

## OHIO VALLEY CONFERENCE

| Date | Opponents, Score | No. OTs | Score, Reg. |
|---|---|---|---|
| 10-13-84 | Youngstown St. 17, ‡Austin Peay 13 .......................... | 1 | 10-10 |
| 11-3-84 | ‡Murray St. 20, Austin Peay 13............................... | 2 | 10-10 |
| 10-19-85 | ‡Middle Tenn. St. 31, Murray St. 24 .......................... | 2 | 17-17 |
| 11-2-85 | ‡Middle Tenn. St. 28, Youngstown St. 21 ..................... | 2 | 14-14 |
| 10-4-86 | ‡Austin Peay 7, Middle Tenn. St. 0 ........................... | 1 | 0-0 |
| 10-10-87 | ‡Austin Peay 20, Morehead St. 13............................ | 1 | 13-13 |
| 11-7-87 | ‡Youngstown St. 20, Murray St. 13 ........................... | 1 | 13-13 |
| 10-1-88 | Tennessee Tech 16, ‡Murray St. 13 .......................... | 1 | 10-10 |
| 10-29-88 | Eastern Ky. 31, ‡Murray St. 24 .............................. | 1 | 24-24 |
| 11-18-89 | Eastern Ky. 38, ‡Morehead St. 31 ........................... | 3 | 24-24 |
| 11-10-90 | ‡Tennessee Tech 20, Austin Peay 14 ......................... | 1 | 14-14 |
| 11-17-90 | Murray St. 31, ‡Austin Peay 24............................... | 3 | 24-24 |
| 11-7-92 | ‡Eastern Ky. 21, Murray St. 18 .............................. | 1 | 18-18 |

## YANKEE CONFERENCE

| Date | Opponents, Score | No. OTs | Score, Reg. |
|---|---|---|---|
| 9-18-82 | Rhode Island 58, ‡Maine 55................................... | 6 | 21-21 |
| 9-25-82 | ‡Boston U. 48, Maine 45 ..................................... | 4 | 24-24 |
| 10-27-84 | Maine 13, ‡Connecticut 10 ................................... | 1 | 10-10 |
| 9-13-86 | New Hampshire 28, ‡Delaware 21 ............................ | 1 | 21-21 |
| 11-15-86 | ‡Connecticut 21, Rhode Island 14 ............................ | 1 | 14-14 |
| 9-19-87 | ‡Richmond 52, Massachusetts 51 ............................. | 4 | 28-28 |
| 9-19-87 | New Hampshire 27, ‡Boston U. 20 ............................ | 3 | 17-17 |
| 10-31-87 | Maine 59, ‡Delaware 56...................................... | 2 | 49-49 |
| 11-21-87 | ‡Delaware 17, Boston U. 10 .................................. | 1 | 10-10 |
| 9-24-88 | Villanova 31, ‡Boston U. 24 .................................. | 1 | 24-24 |

*Division I-AA Home Winning Streaks*

| Date | Opponents, Score | No. OTs | Score, Reg. |
|---|---|---|---|
| 10-8-88 | ‡Richmond 23, New Hampshire 17 ........................... | 1 | 17-17 |
| 10-7-89 | ‡Villanova 41, Connecticut 35 ............................... | 6 | 21-21 |
| 11-16-91 | Boston U. 29, ‡Connecticut 26 ............................. | 2 | 23-23 |

‡ *Home team.*

# DIVISION I-AA STADIUMS

**(115 Teams, 115 Stadiums)**
**LISTED ALPHABETICALLY BY SCHOOL**

| School | Stadium | Conference | Year Built | Capacity | Surface |
|---|---|---|---|---|---|
| Ala.-Birmingham .............. | ✓Legion Field | Independent | 1927 | 83,091 | Turf |
| Alabama St. ................... | ✓Cramton Bowl | SWAC | NA | 24,600 | Grass |
| Alcorn St. .................... | Jack Spinks | SWAC | 1930 | 25,000 | Grass |
| Appalachian St. ............... | Kidd Brewer | Southern | 1962 | 18,000 | Turf |
| Austin Peay ................... | Municipal | Ohio Valley | 1946 | 10,000 | Turf |
| Bethune-Cookman ........... | Municipal | MEAC | NA | 10,000 | Grass |
| Boise St. ..................... | Bronco | Big Sky | 1970 | 22,600 | Blue Turf |
| Boston U. ..................... | Nickerson Field | Yankee | 1930 | 17,369 | Turf |
| Brown........................ | Brown | Ivy | 1925 | 20,000 | Grass |
| Bucknell ..................... | Mathewson | Patriot | 1924 | 13,100 | Grass |
| Buffalo ....................... | UB Stadium | Independent | 1992 | 16,500 | Grass |
| Butler ....................... | Butler Bowl | Independent | 1927 | 19,000 | Grass |
| Cal St. Northridge............ | North Campus | Independent | 1971 | 6,000 | Grass |
| Cal St. Sacramento ........... | Hornet | Independent | NA | 26,000 | Grass |
| Canisius ..................... | Demske | MAAC | 1989 | 1,000 | Turf |
| Central Conn. St. ............. | Arute Field | Independent | 1969 | 5,000 | Grass |
| Central Fla. .................. | *✓Florida Citrus | Independent | 1989 | 70,000 | Grass |
| Charleston So. ................ | CSU Field | Independent | NA | 1,500 | Grass |
| Citadel ...................... | Johnson Hagood | Southern | 1948 | 22,500 | Grass |
| Colgate ...................... | Andy Kerr | Patriot | 1937 | 12,500 | Grass |
| Columbia .................... | Lawrence Wien | Ivy | 1984 | 17,000 | Grass |
| Connecticut.................. | Memorial | Yankee | 1953 | 16,200 | Grass |
| Cornell ...................... | Schoellkopf | Ivy | 1915 | 27,000 | Turf |
| Dartmouth ................... | Memorial Field | Ivy | 1923 | 20,416 | Grass |
| Davidson..................... | Richardson | Independent | 1924 | 5,200 | Grass |
| Dayton ....................... | Welcome | Pioneer | 1949 | 11,000 | Turf |
| Delaware..................... | Delaware | Yankee | 1952 | 23,000 | Grass |
| Delaware St. ................. | Alumni Field | MEAC | 1957 | 5,000 | Grass |
| Drake ....................... | Drake | Pioneer | 1925 | 18,000 | Grass |
| Duquesne .................... | South High | Independent | NA | 7,000 | Turf |
| East Tenn. St. ................ | @Memorial | Southern | 1977 | 12,000 | Turf |
| Eastern Ill.................... | O'Brien | Gateway | 1970 | 10,000 | Grass |
| Eastern Ky.................... | Roy Kidd | Ohio Valley | 1969 | 20,000 | Grass |
| Eastern Wash................. | Woodward | Big Sky | 1967 | 6,000 | Grass |
| Evansville.................... | McCutchan | Independent | 1985 | 3,000 | Grass |
| Florida A&M ................. | Bragg Memorial | MEAC | 1957 | 25,500 | Grass |
| Fordham ..................... | Jack Coffey Field | Patriot | 1930 | 9,000 | Grass |
| Furman ...................... | Paladin | Southern | 1981 | 16,000 | Grass |
| Ga. Southern................. | Paulson | Southern | 1984 | 18,000 | Grass |
| Georgetown ................. | Kehoe Field | MAAC | NA | 2,000 | Turf |
| Grambling ................... | Robinson | SWAC | 1983 | 22,000 | Grass |
| Harvard ...................... | Harvard | Ivy | 1903 | 37,289 | Grass |
| Hofstra ...................... | Hofstra | Independent | 1963 | 7,500 | Turf |
| Holy Cross ................... | Fitton Field | Patriot | 1924 | 23,500 | Grass |
| Howard ...................... | Greene | MEAC | 1986 | 7,500 | Turf |
| Idaho ....................... | @Kibbie Dome | Big Sky | 1975 | 16,000 | Turf |
| Idaho St. ..................... | @Holt Arena | Big Sky | 1970 | 12,000 | Turf |
| Illinois St. ................... | Hancock | Gateway | 1963 | 15,000 | Turf |
| Indiana St. ................... | Memorial | Gateway | 1970 | 20,500 | Turf |
| Iona......................... | Mazzella Field | MAAC | 1989 | 1,200 | Turf |
| Jackson St. ................... | ✓Miss. Memorial | SWAC | 1949 | 62,500 | Grass |
| James Madison ............... | Bridgeforth | Yankee | 1975 | 12,800 | Turf |
| Lafayette .................... | Fisher Field | Patriot | 1926 | 13,750 | Grass |
| Lehigh ...................... | Goodman | Patriot | 1988 | 16,000 | Grass |
| Liberty ...................... | Liberty University | Independent | 1989 | 12,000 | Turf |

*1993 NCAA FOOTBALL*

| School | Stadium | Conference | Year Built | Capacity | Surface |
|---|---|---|---|---|---|
| Maine | Alumni | Yankee | 1942 | 10,000 | Grass |
| Marist | Leonidoff | Independent | 1972 | 2,500 | Grass |
| Marshall | Marshall University | Southern | 1991 | 28,000 | Turf |
| Massachusetts | McGuirk | Yankee | 1965 | 16,000 | Grass |
| McNeese St. | Cowboy | Southland | 1965 | 20,000 | Grass |
| Middle Tenn. St. | Johnny Floyd | Ohio Valley | 1969 | 15,000 | Turf |
| Mississippi Val. | Magnolia | SWAC | 1958 | 10,500 | Grass |
| Montana | Wash.-Grizzly | Big Sky | 1986 | 14,000 | Grass |
| Montana St. | Reno Sales | Big Sky | 1973 | 15,197 | Grass |
| Morehead St. | Jayne | Ohio Valley | 1964 | 10,000 | Turf |
| Morgan St. | Hughes | MEAC | NA | 10,000 | Grass |
| Murray St. | Stewart | Ohio Valley | 1973 | 16,800 | Turf |
| New Hampshire | Cowell | Yankee | 1936 | 9,571 | Grass |
| Nicholls St. | John Guidry | Southland | 1972 | 12,800 | Grass |
| North Caro. A&T | Aggie | MEAC | 1981 | 17,500 | Grass |
| North Texas | Fouts Field | Southland | 1952 | 20,000 | Turf |
| Northeast La. | Malone | Southland | 1978 | 23,277 | Grass |
| Northeastern | E. S. Parsons | Yankee | 1933 | 7,000 | Turf |
| Northern Ariz. | @Walkup Skydome | Big Sky | 1977 | 15,300 | Turf |
| Northern Iowa | @UNI-Dome | Gateway | 1976 | 16,400 | Turf |
| Northwestern (La.) | Turpin | Southland | 1976 | 16,522 | Turf |
| Pennsylvania | Franklin Field | Ivy | 1895 | 60,546 | Turf |
| Prairie View | Blackshear | SWAC | NA | 6,600 | Grass |
| Princeton | Palmer | Ivy | 1914 | 45,725 | Grass |
| Rhode Island | Meade | Yankee | 1928 | 10,000 | Grass |
| Richmond | Richmond | Yankee | 1929 | 22,611 | Turf |
| Sam Houston St. | Bowers | Southland | 1986 | 14,000 | Turf |
| Samford | Siebert | Independent | NA | 6,700 | Grass |
| San Diego | USD Torero | Pioneer | NA | 4,000 | Grass |
| Siena | Siena Field | MAAC | NA | 500 | Grass |
| South Caro. St. | Dawson Bulldog | MEAC | 1955 | 14,000 | Grass |
| Southeast Mo. St. | Houck | Ohio Valley | 1930 | 10,000 | Grass |
| Southern-B. R. | Mumford | SWAC | 1928 | 24,000 | Grass |
| Southern Ill. | McAndrew | Gateway | 1975 | 17,324 | Turf |
| Southern Utah | Coliseum | Independent | 1967 | 4,500 | Grass |
| Southwest Mo. St. | Plaster Field | Gateway | 1941 | 16,600 | Turf |
| Southwest Tex. St. | Bobcat | Southland | 1981 | 14,104 | Grass |
| St. Francis (Pa.) | Pine Bowl | Independent | NA | 1,500 | Grass |
| St. John's (N. Y.) | Redmen Field | MAAC | 1961 | 3,000 | Turf |
| St. Mary's (Cal.) | St. Mary's Field | Independent | 1976 | 3,500 | Grass |
| St. Peter's | Jaroschak | MAAC | NA | 500 | Grass |
| Stephen F. Austin | Homer Bryce | Southland | 1973 | 14,575 | Turf |
| Tenn.-Chatt. | Chamberlain | Southern | 1947 | 10,501 | Grass |
| Tenn.-Martin | Pacer | Ohio Valley | 1964 | 8,000 | Grass |
| Tennessee St. | W. J. Hale | Ohio Valley | 1953 | 16,000 | Grass |
| Tennessee Tech | Tucker | Ohio Valley | 1966 | 16,500 | Turf |
| Texas Southern | ✓Robertson | SWAC | 1965 | 25,000 | Grass |
| Towson St. | Minnegan | Independent | 1978 | 5,000 | Grass |
| Troy St. | Memorial | Independent | 1950 | 12,000 | Grass |
| Va. Military | Alumni Field | Southern | 1962 | 10,000 | Grass |
| Valparaiso | Brown Field | Pioneer | 1947 | 5,000 | Grass |
| Villanova | Villanova | Yankee | 1929 | 13,400 | Turf |
| Wagner | Fischer Memorial | Independent | NA | 5,000 | Grass |
| Weber St. | Wildcat | Big Sky | 1966 | 17,500 | Grass |
| Western Caro. | E. J. Whitmire | Southern | 1974 | 12,000 | Turf |
| Western Ill. | Hanson Field | Gateway | 1948 | 15,000 | Grass |
| Western Ky. | L. T. Smith | Gateway | 1968 | 17,500 | Grass |
| William & Mary | Walter Zable | Yankee | 1935 | 15,000 | Grass |
| Yale | Yale Bowl | Ivy | 1914 | 70,896 | Grass |
| Youngstown St. | Stambaugh | Independent | 1982 | 16,000 | Turf |

## LISTED BY CAPACITY (TOP 28)

| School | Stadium | Surface | Capacity |
|---|---|---|---|
| Ala.-Birmingham | ✓Legion Field | Turf | 83,091 |
| Yale | Yale Bowl | Grass | 70,896 |
| Central Fla. | *✓Florida Citrus | Grass | 70,000 |
| Jackson St. | ✓Miss. Memorial | Grass | 62,500 |
| Pennsylvania | Franklin Field | Turf | 60,546 |

*Division I-AA Stadiums*

| School | Stadium | Surface | Capacity |
|---|---|---|---|
| Princeton ..................................... | Palmer | Grass | 45,725 |
| Harvard ....................................... | Harvard | Grass | 37,289 |
| Marshall....................................... | Marshall University | Turf | 28,000 |
| Cornell ........................................ | Schoellkopf | Turf | 27,000 |
| Cal St. Sacramento .......................... | Hornet | Grass | 26,000 |
| Florida A&M .................................. | Bragg Memorial | Grass | 25,500 |
| Alcorn St. ..................................... | Jack Spinks | Grass | 25,000 |
| Texas Southern .............................. | ✓Robertson | Grass | 25,000 |
| Alabama St..................................... | ✓Cramton Bowl | Grass | 24,600 |
| Southern-B. R. ............................... | Mumford | Grass | 24,000 |
| Holy Cross .................................... | Fitton Field | Grass | 23,500 |
| Northeast La. ................................. | Malone | Grass | 23,277 |
| Delaware....................................... | Delaware | Grass | 23,000 |
| Richmond...................................... | Richmond | Turf | 22,611 |
| Boise St. ...................................... | Bronco | Blue Turf | 22,600 |
| Citadel ........................................ | Johnson Hagood | Grass | 22,500 |
| Grambling ..................................... | Robinson | Grass | 22,000 |
| Indiana St. .................................... | Memorial | Turf | 20,500 |
| Dartmouth ..................................... | Memorial Field | Grass | 20,416 |
| Brown.......................................... | Brown | Grass | 20,000 |
| Eastern Ky..................................... | Roy Kidd | Grass | 20,000 |
| McNeese St. .................................. | Cowboy | Grass | 20,000 |
| North Texas ................................... | Fouts Field | Turf | 20,000 |

✓ *Not located on campus.*  @ *Indoor facility.*

* *Florida Citrus: Renovated by adding 19,000 seats in 1989. An earlier renovation in 1975 brought attendance from 9,000 to 51,000.*

**Surface Legend:** Turf—Any of several types of artificial turfs (name brands include AstroTurf, All-Pro, Omniturf, SuperTurf, etc.); Grass—Natural grass surface.

# STATISTICS TRENDS

**(Average Per Game, Both Teams)**

| | Rushing | | | Passing | | | | | Total Offense | | | Scoring | | |
|---|---|---|---|---|---|---|---|---|---|---|---|---|---|---|
| Year | Plays | Yds. | Avg. | Att. | Cmp. | Pct. | Yds. | Avg. P/Att. | Plays | Yds. | Avg. | TD | FG | Pts. |
| 1978 | *96.7 | *343.5 | 3.55 | 41.4 | 19.1 | 46.2 | 258.6 | 6.24 | 138.1 | 602.1 | 4.36 | 5.20 | 1.03 | 39.0 |
| 1979 | 94.1 | 329.3 | 3.50 | 40.9 | 18.4 | 45.0 | 250.4 | 6.13 | 135.0 | 579.7 | 4.30 | 4.79 | 1.23 | 36.9 |
| 1980 | 90.3 | 329.6 | 3.65 | 44.8 | 20.8 | 46.5 | 288.8 | 6.45 | 135.1 | 618.4 | 4.58 | 5.15 | 1.18 | 39.2 |
| 1981 | 88.5 | 309.9 | 3.50 | 49.7 | 23.7 | 47.7 | 322.9 | 6.49 | 138.2 | 632.8 | 4.58 | 5.42 | 1.38 | 41.7 |
| 1982 | 88.8 | 313.1 | 3.53 | 52.2 | 25.6 | 48.9 | 332.0 | 6.35 | 141.0 | 645.1 | 4.57 | 5.24 | 1.59 | 41.0 |
| 1983 | 87.8 | 310.3 | 3.54 | 52.4 | 25.9 | 49.4 | 334.5 | 6.38 | 140.2 | 644.8 | 4.60 | 5.38 | 1.58 | 42.1 |
| 1984 | 85.7 | 305.1 | 3.56 | 55.7 | 27.9 | 50.0 | 361.9 | 6.49 | 141.4 | 666.9 | 4.72 | 5.59 | 1.60 | 43.6 |
| 1985 | 84.7 | 315.2 | 3.72 | *57.7 | *29.1 | 50.4 | *374.6 | 6.49 | *142.4 | 689.8 | 4.84 | 5.67 | 1.61 | 44.2 |
| 1986 | 84.8 | 315.8 | 3.72 | 56.5 | 28.1 | 49.7 | 372.8 | 6.60 | 141.3 | 688.6 | 4.87 | 5.80 | 1.72 | 45.4 |
| 1987 | 86.2 | 317.2 | 3.68 | 54.2 | 27.1 | 50.1 | 351.1 | 6.48 | 140.4 | 668.3 | 4.76 | 5.55 | 1.81 | 44.0 |
| 1988 | 86.3 | 322.5 | 3.74 | 52.9 | 26.5 | 50.2 | 345.4 | 6.53 | 139.2 | 667.9 | 4.80 | 5.59 | *1.81 | 44.2 |
| 1989 | 84.9 | 320.4 | 3.77 | 55.4 | 28.4 | 51.3 | 372.0 | 6.71 | 140.3 | 692.4 | 4.93 | 5.43 | 1.49 | 45.5 |
| 1990 | 85.3 | 323.0 | 3.79 | 55.6 | 28.1 | 50.6 | 374.0 | 6.73 | 140.9 | 697.0 | 4.95 | 5.96 | 1.67 | 46.4 |
| 1991 | 86.4 | 341.2 | 3.95 | 53.7 | 27.9 | *51.9 | 369.3 | 6.87 | 140.1 | *710.5 | 5.07 | *6.38 | 1.33 | *48.1 |
| 1992 | 86.0 | 342.8 | *3.99 | 52.0 | 26.9 | 51.7 | 358.8 | *6.89 | 138.0 | 701.6 | *5.08 | 6.32 | 1.36 | 47.7 |

* *Record.*

## ADDITIONAL STATISTICS TRENDS

**(Average Per Game, Both Teams)**

| | Punting | | | Interceptions | | | Punt Returns | | | Kickoff Returns | | |
|---|---|---|---|---|---|---|---|---|---|---|---|---|
| Year | No. | Avg. | Net Avg. | No. | Avg. Ret. | Yds. | No. | Avg. Ret. | Yds. | No. | Avg. Ret. | Yds. |
| 1978 | *12.2 | 36.5 | 33.6 | 2.84 | 11.92 | 33.9 | 4.78 | 7.49 | 35.8 | 6.45 | 18.4 | 118.4 |
| 1979 | 11.9 | 36.5 | 33.4 | 2.88 | 11.39 | 32.8 | 4.82 | 7.46 | 35.9 | 6.11 | 18.4 | 112.3 |
| 1980 | 11.6 | 37.0 | 33.7 | 2.74 | 10.06 | 27.6 | 4.87 | 7.94 | 38.7 | 6.17 | 17.4 | 107.4 |
| 1981 | 11.8 | 37.2 | 33.9 | *3.19 | 10.63 | *33.9 | 4.99 | 7.77 | 38.8 | 6.54 | 18.4 | 120.1 |
| 1982 | 12.0 | 37.1 | 34.0 | 2.99 | 10.15 | 30.3 | 4.88 | 7.63 | 37.2 | 6.15 | 19.0 | 116.8 |

| Year | Punting No. | Punting Avg. | Punting Net Avg. | Interceptions No. | Interceptions Avg. Ret. | Interceptions Yds. | Punt Returns No. | Punt Returns Avg. Ret. | Punt Returns Yds. | Kickoff Returns No. | Kickoff Returns Avg. Ret. | Kickoff Returns Yds. |
|---|---|---|---|---|---|---|---|---|---|---|---|---|
| 1983 | 11.9 | 37.3 | 34.1 | 3.03 | 9.99 | 30.2 | *5.17 | 7.58 | 39.2 | 6.11 | 18.6 | 113.8 |
| 1984 | 11.6 | 37.3 | 33.9 | 3.05 | 10.40 | 31.7 | 5.10 | 7.84 | 40.0 | 6.46 | 18.6 | 120.0 |
| 1985 | 11.4 | 37.6 | *34.2 | 3.02 | 10.56 | 31.9 | 5.09 | 7.52 | 38.3 | 6.39 | 18.1 | 115.7 |
| 1986 | 11.2 | *37.6 | 34.0 | 3.01 | 10.90 | 32.8 | 5.09 | 7.92 | 40.3 | *8.04 | 19.4 | *155.7 |
| 1987 | 11.2 | 36.8 | 33.4 | 2.80 | 10.57 | 29.7 | 4.96 | 7.51 | 37.3 | 7.91 | 19.0 | 149.1 |
| 1988 | 10.9 | 36.3 | 32.8 | 2.68 | 10.61 | 28.4 | 4.80 | 7.96 | 38.3 | 7.90 | 18.8 | 148.6 |
| 1989 | 11.0 | 36.1 | 32.8 | 2.62 | 10.40 | 27.3 | 4.63 | 7.93 | 36.7 | 7.92 | 18.9 | 149.4 |
| 1990 | 10.8 | 36.7 | 32.7 | 2.76 | *11.94 | 32.9 | 4.97 | 8.46 | 42.0 | 8.03 | 18.9 | 151.7 |
| 1991 | 10.6 | 36.6 | 32.6 | 2.70 | 10.81 | 29.1 | 4.92 | 8.57 | 42.2 | 7.68 | 19.1 | 146.7 |
| 1992 | 10.6 | 36.6 | 32.2 | 2.41 | 10.24 | 24.6 | 5.05 | *9.35 | *47.2 | 7.63 | *19.5 | 148.7 |

* Record.

# I-AA FINAL REGULAR-SEASON TOP 20 POLLS

## 1982
Team
1. Eastern Ky.
2. Louisiana Tech
3. Delaware
4. Tennessee St.
5. Eastern Ill.
6. Furman
7. South Caro. St.
8. Jackson St.
9. Colgate
10. Grambling
11. Idaho
12. Northern Ill.
13. Holy Cross
14. Bowling Green
15. Boise St.
16. Western Mich.
17. Tenn.-Chatt.
18. Northwestern (La.)
19. Montana
20. Lafayette

## 1983
Team
1. Southern Ill.
2. Furman
3. Holy Cross
4. North Texas
5. Indiana St.
6. Eastern Ill.
7. Colgate
8. Eastern Ky.
9. Western Caro.
10. Grambling
11. Nevada
12. Idaho St.
13. Boston U.
    Northeast La.
15. Jackson St.
16. Middle Tenn. St.
17. Tennessee St.
18. South Caro. St.
19. Mississippi Val.
20. New Hampshire

## 1984
Team
1. Alcorn St.
2. Montana St.
    Rhode Island
4. Boston U.
5. Indiana St.
6. Middle Tenn. St.
    Mississippi Val.
8. Eastern Ky.
9. Louisiana Tech
10. Arkansas St.
11. New Hampshire
12. Richmond
13. Murray St.
14. Western Caro.
15. Holy Cross
16. Furman
17. Tenn.-Chatt.
18. Northern Iowa
19. Delaware
20. McNeese St.

## 1985
Team
1. Middle Tenn. St.
2. Furman
    Nevada
4. Northern Iowa
5. Idaho
6. Arkansas St.
7. Rhode Island
8. Grambling
9. Ga. Southern
10. Akron
11. Eastern Wash.
12. Appalachian St.
    Delaware St.
14. Louisiana Tech
15. Jackson St.
16. William & Mary
17. Murray St.
18. Richmond
19. Eastern Ky.
20. Alcorn St.

## 1986
Team
1. Nevada
2. Arkansas St.
3. Eastern Ill.
4. Ga. Southern
5. Holy Cross
6. Appalachian St.
7. Pennsylvania
8. William & Mary
9. Jackson St.
10. Eastern Ky.
11. Sam Houston St.
12. Nicholls St.
13. Delaware
14. Tennessee St.
15. Furman
16. Idaho
17. Southern Ill.
18. Murray St.
19. Connecticut
20. North Caro. A&T

## 1987
Team
1. Holy Cross
2. Appalachian St.
3. Northeast La.
4. Northern Iowa
5. Idaho
6. Ga. Southern
7. Eastern Ky.
8. James Madison
9. Jackson St.
10. Weber St.
11. Western Ky.
12. Arkansas St.
13. Maine
14. Marshall
15. Youngstown St.
16. North Texas
17. Richmond
18. Howard
19. Sam Houston St.
20. Delaware St.

## 1988
Team
1. Stephen F. Austin
2. Idaho
3. Ga. Southern
4. Western Ill.
5. Furman
6. Jackson St.
7. Marshall
8. Eastern Ky.
9. Citadel
10. Northwestern (La.)
11. Massachusetts
12. North Texas
13. Boise St.
14. Florida A&M
    Pennsylvania
16. Western Ky.
17. Connecticut
18. Grambling
19. Montana
20. New Hampshire

## 1989
Team
1. Ga. Southern
2. Furman
3. Stephen F. Austin
4. Holy Cross
    Idaho
6. Montana
7. Appalachian St.
8. Maine
9. Southwest Mo. St.
10. Middle Tenn. St.
    William & Mary
12. Eastern Ky.
13. Grambling
14. Youngstown St.
15. Eastern Ill.
16. Villanova
17. Jackson St.
18. Connecticut
19. Nevada
20. Northern Iowa

*Division I-AA Statistics Trends*

## 1990
**Team**
1. Middle Tenn. St.
2. Youngstown St.
3. Ga. Southern
4. Nevada
5. Eastern Ky.
6. Southwest Mo. St.
7. William & Mary
8. Holy Cross
9. Massachusetts
10. Boise St.
11. Northern Iowa
12. Furman
13. Idaho
14. Northeast La.
15. Citadel
16. Jackson St.
17. Dartmouth
18. Central Fla.
19. New Hampshire
    North Caro. A&T

## 1991
**Team**
1. Nevada
2. Eastern Ky.
3. Holy Cross
4. Northern Iowa
5. Alabama St.
6. Delaware
7. Villanova
8. Marshall
9. Middle Tenn. St.
10. Samford
11. New Hampshire
12. Sam Houston St.
13. Youngstown St.
14. Western Ill.
15. Weber St.
16. James Madison
17. Appalachian St.
18. Northeast La.
19. McNeese St.
20. Citadel
    Furman

## 1992

| Team (Record) | How Season Ended |
|---|---|
| 1. Citadel (10-1) | Eliminated by Youngstown St., 17-42, in championship quarterfinals. |
| Northeast La. (9-2) | Eliminated by Delaware, 18-41, in championship quarterfinals. |
| 3. Northern Iowa (10-1) | Eliminated by Youngstown St., 7-19, in championship semifinals. |
| 4. Middle Tenn. St. (9-2) | Eliminated by Marshall, 21-35, in championship quarterfinals. |
| 5. Idaho (9-2) | Eliminated by McNeese St., 20-23, in championship first round. |
| 6. Marshall (8-3) | Defeated Youngstown St., 31-28, in Division I-AA championship game. |
| 7. Youngstown St. (8-2-1) | Lost to Marshall, 28-31, in Division I-AA championship game. |
| 8. Delaware (9-2) | Eliminated by Marshall, 7-28, in championship semifinals. |
| 9. Samford (9-2) | Eliminated by Delaware, 21-56, in championship first round. |
| 10. Villanova (9-2) | Eliminated by Youngstown St., 20-23, in championship first round. |
| 11. McNeese St. (8-3) | Eliminated by Northern Iowa, 14-17, in championship quarterfinals. |
| 12. Eastern Ky. (9-2) | Eliminated by Marshall, 0-44, in championship first round. |
| 13. William & Mary (9-2) | Ended regular season with a 34-19 victory over Richmond. |
| 14. Eastern Wash. (7-3) | Eliminated by Northern Iowa, 14-17, in championship first round. |
| 15. Florida A&M (7-3) | Ended regular season with a 21-35 loss to Bethune-Cookman. |
| 16. Appalachian St. (7-4) | Eliminated by Middle Tenn. St., 10-35, in championship first round. |
| 17. North Caro. A&T (9-2) | Eliminated by Citadel, 0-44, in championship first round. |
| 18. Alcorn St. (7-3) | Eliminated by Northeast La., 27-78, in championship first round. |
| 19. Liberty (7-4) | Ended regular season with a 49-27 victory over Delaware St. |
| 20. Western Ill. (7-4) | Ended regular season with a 6-37 loss to Northern Iowa. |

## 1992 WEEK-BY-WEEK POLLS

| Final Poll—Nov. 22 | 11/16 | 11/9 | 11/2 | 10/26 | 10/19 | 10/12 | 10/5 | 9/28 | 9/21 | 9/14 | *8/17 |
|---|---|---|---|---|---|---|---|---|---|---|---|
| 1. Citadel | 1t | 2 | 3t | 6 | 6 | 4 | 5 | 6 | 8 | 9 | — |
| Northeast La. | 1t | 1 | 3t | 5 | 5 | 8 | 9 | 9 | 11t | 10 | 4t |
| 3. Northern Iowa | 3 | 4 | 1 | 1 | 1 | 1 | 1 | 2t | 4 | 4 | 4t |
| 4. Middle Tenn. St. | 4 | 5 | 7 | 4 | 4 | 7 | 9 | 8 | 10 | 12 | 10 |
| 5. Idaho | 5 | 6 | 2 | 3 | 2 | 3 | 4 | 5 | 6 | 6 | 9 |
| 6. Marshall | 6 | 10 | 5 | 2 | 3 | 5 | 6 | 1 | 2 | 2 | 2 |
| 7. Youngstown St. | 7t | 7 | 9 | 10t | 13 | 6 | 7 | 7 | 1 | 1 | 1 |
| 8. Delaware | 10 | 3 | 6 | 7 | 7 | 12 | 12 | 12 | 7 | 8 | 7t |
| 9. Samford | 9 | 12 | 8 | 8 | 8t | 13 | 17 | 18 | ** | ** | 13 |
| 10. Villanova | 7t | 9 | 11 | 14 | 8t | 2 | 2 | 2t | 3 | 3 | 3 |
| 11. McNeese St. | 11 | 13 | 14 | 15 | ** | ** | 13 | 13 | 19 | 14t | 15 |
| 12. Eastern Ky. | 12 | 15 | 15 | 16 | 17 | 11 | 3 | 4 | 5 | 5 | 6 |
| 13. William & Mary | 13 | 17t | 16t | 10t | 10 | 10 | 10 | 10 | 14 | 17 | ** |
| 14. Eastern Wash. | 14t | 20t | 18 | 19 | 20t | 16 | 20 | 20t | — | — | — |
| 15. Florida A&M | 14t | 8 | 10 | 12 | 15 | 9 | 11 | 11 | 20 | 13 | — |
| 16. Appalachian St. | 18 | ** | — | — | — | — | — | — | — | — | — |
| 17. North Caro. A&T | ** | 17t | 19 | 18 | 18 | 18 | 15 | 15 | ** | ** | — |
| 18. Alcorn St. | — | ** | — | ** | — | ** | — | ** | — | — | — |
| 19. Liberty | — | — | — | — | — | — | — | — | — | — | — |
| 20. Western Ill. | — | 19 | ** | ** | — | — | — | — | ** | — | ** |

t Tie.   * Preseason.   ** Received votes.   — Not ranked.

# BLACK COLLEGE NATIONAL CHAMPIONS

Selected by the Pittsburgh Courier, 1920-1980, and compiled by Collie Nicholson, former Grambling sports information director; William Nunn Jr., Pittsburgh Courier sports editor, and Eric "Ric" Roberts, Pittsburgh Courier sports writer and noted black college sports historian. Selected from 1981 by the Sheridan Broadcasting Network, 411 Seventh Ave., Suite 1500, Pittsburgh, Pa. 15219-1905. Records include postseason games.

| Year | Team | Won | Lost | Tied | Coach |
|------|------|-----|------|------|-------|
| 1920 | Howard | 7 | 0 | 0 | Edward Morrison |
|  | Talladega | 5 | 0 | 1 | Jubie Bragg |
| 1921 | Talladega | 6 | 0 | 1 | Jubie Bragg |
|  | Wiley | 7 | 0 | 1 | Jason Grant |
| 1922 | Hampton | 6 | 1 | 0 | Gideon Smith |
| 1923 | Virginia Union | 6 | 0 | 1 | Harold Martin |
| 1924 | Tuskegee | 9 | 0 | 1 | Cleve Abbott |
|  | Wiley | 8 | 0 | 1 | Fred Long |
| 1925 | Tuskegee | 8 | 0 | 1 | Cleve Abbott |
|  | Howard | 6 | 0 | 2 | Louis Watson |
| 1926 | Tuskegee | 10 | 0 | 0 | Cleve Abbott |
|  | Howard | 7 | 0 | 0 | Louis Watson |
| 1927 | Tuskegee | 9 | 0 | 1 | Cleve Abbott |
|  | Bluefield St. (Va.) | 8 | 0 | 1 | Harry Jefferson |
| 1928 | Bluefield St. (Va.) | 8 | 0 | 1 | Harry Jefferson |
|  | Wiley | 8 | 0 | 1 | Fred Long |
| 1929 | Tuskegee | 10 | 0 | 0 | Cleve Abbott |
| 1930 | Tuskegee | 11 | 0 | 1 | Cleve Abbott |
| 1931 | Wilberforce | 9 | 0 | 0 | Harry Graves |
| 1932 | Wiley | 9 | 0 | 0 | Fred Long |
| 1933 | Morgan St. | 9 | 0 | 0 | Edward Hurt |
| 1934 | Kentucky St. | 9 | 0 | 0 | Henry Kean |
| 1935 | Texas College | 9 | 0 | 0 | Arnett Mumford |
| 1936 | West Va. St. | 8 | 0 | 0 | Adolph Hamblin |
|  | Virginia St. | 7 | 0 | 2 | Harry Jefferson |
| 1937 | Morgan St. | 7 | 0 | 0 | Edward Hurt |
| 1938 | Florida A&M | 8 | 0 | 0 | Bill Bell |
| 1939 | Langston | 9 | 0 | 0 | Felton "Zip" Gayles |
| 1940 | Morris Brown | 9 | 1 | 0 | Artis Graves |
| 1941 | Morris Brown | 8 | 1 | 0 | William Nicks |
| 1942 | Florida A&M | 9 | 0 | 0 | Bill Bell |
| 1943 | Morgan St. | 5 | 0 | 0 | Edward Hurt |
| 1944 | Morgan St. | 6 | 1 | 0 | Edward Hurt |
| 1945 | Wiley | 10 | 0 | 0 | Fred Long |
| 1946 | Tennessee St. | 10 | 1 | 0 | Henry Kean |
|  | Morgan St. | 8 | 0 | 0 | Edward Hurt |
| 1947 | Tennessee St. | 10 | 0 | 0 | Henry Kean |
|  | Shaw | 10 | 0 | 0 | Brutus Wilson |
| 1948 | Southern-B.R. | 12 | 0 | 0 | Arnett Mumford |
| 1949 | Southern-B.R. | 10 | 0 | 1 | Arnett Mumford |
|  | Morgan St. | 8 | 0 | 0 | Edward Hurt |
| 1950 | Southern-B.R. | 10 | 0 | 1 | Arnett Mumford |
|  | Florida A&M | 8 | 1 | 1 | Alonzo "Jake" Gaither |
| 1951 | Morris Brown | 10 | 1 | 0 | Edward "Ox" Clemons |
| 1952 | Florida A&M | 8 | 2 | 0 | Alonzo "Jake" Gaither |
|  | Texas Southern | 10 | 0 | 1 | Alexander Durley |
|  | Lincoln (Mo.) | 8 | 0 | 1 | Dwight Reed |
|  | Virginia St. | 8 | 1 | 0 | Sylvester "Sal" Hall |
| 1953 | Prairie View | 12 | 0 | 0 | William Nicks |
| 1954 | Tennessee St. | 10 | 1 | 0 | Henry Kean |
|  | Southern-B.R. | 10 | 1 | 0 | Arnett Mumford |
|  | Florida A&M | 8 | 1 | 0 | Alonzo "Jake" Gaither |
|  | Prairie View | 10 | 1 | 0 | William Nicks |
| 1955 | Grambling | 10 | 0 | 0 | Eddie Robinson |
| 1956 | Tennessee St. | 10 | 0 | 0 | Howard Gentry |
| 1957 | Florida A&M | 9 | 0 | 0 | Alonzo "Jake" Gaither |
| 1958 | Prairie View | 10 | 0 | 1 | William Nicks |
| 1959 | Florida A&M | 10 | 0 | 0 | Alonzo "Jake" Gaither |
| 1960 | Southern-B.R. | 9 | 1 | 0 | Arnett Mumford |
| 1961 | Florida A&M | 10 | 0 | 0 | Alonzo "Jake" Gaither |
| 1962 | Jackson St. | 10 | 1 | 0 | John Merritt |
| 1963 | Prairie View | 10 | 1 | 0 | William Nicks |
| 1964 | Prairie View | 9 | 0 | 0 | William Nicks |

| Year | Team | Won | Lost | Tied | Coach |
|------|------|-----|------|------|-------|
| 1965 | Tennessee St. | 9 | 0 | 1 | John Merritt |
| 1966 | Tennessee St. | 10 | 0 | 0 | John Merritt |
| 1967 | Morgan St. | 8 | 0 | 0 | Earl Banks |
| | Grambling | 9 | 1 | 0 | Eddie Robinson |
| 1968 | Alcorn St. | 9 | 1 | 0 | Marino Casem |
| | North Caro. A&T | 8 | 1 | 0 | Hornsby Howell |
| 1969 | Alcorn St. | 8 | 0 | 1 | Marino Casem |
| 1970 | Tennessee St. | 11 | 0 | 0 | John Merritt |
| 1971 | Tennessee St. | 9 | 1 | 0 | John Merritt |
| 1972 | Grambling | 11 | 2 | 0 | Eddie Robinson |
| 1973 | Tennessee St. | 10 | 0 | 0 | John Merritt |
| 1974 | Grambling | 11 | 1 | 0 | Eddie Robinson |
| | Alcorn St. | 9 | 2 | 0 | Marino Casem |
| 1975 | Grambling | 10 | 2 | 0 | Eddie Robinson |
| 1976 | South Caro. St. | 10 | 1 | 0 | Willie Jeffries |
| 1977 | South Caro. St. | 9 | 1 | 1 | Willie Jeffries |
| | Grambling | 10 | 1 | 0 | Eddie Robinson |
| | Florida A&M | 11 | 0 | 0 | Rudy Hubbard |
| 1978 | Florida A&M | 12 | 1 | 0 | Rudy Hubbard |
| 1979 | Tennessee St. | 8 | 3 | 0 | John Merritt |
| 1980 | Grambling | 10 | 2 | 0 | Eddie Robinson |
| 1981 | South Caro. St. | 10 | 3 | 0 | Bill Davis |
| 1982 | Tennessee St. | *9 | 0 | 1 | John Merritt |
| 1983 | Grambling | 8 | 1 | 2 | Eddie Robinson |
| 1984 | Alcorn St. | 9 | 1 | 0 | Marino Casem |
| 1985 | Jackson St. | 8 | 3 | 0 | W. C. Gorden |
| 1986 | Central St. (Ohio) | 10 | 1 | 1 | Billy Joe |
| 1987 | Central St. (Ohio) | 10 | 1 | 1 | Billy Joe |
| 1988 | Central St. (Ohio) | 11 | 2 | 0 | Billy Joe |
| 1989 | Central St. (Ohio) | 10 | 2 | 0 | Billy Joe |
| 1990 | #Central St. (Ohio) | 11 | 1 | 0 | Billy Joe |
| 1991 | ¢Alabama St. | 11 | 0 | 1 | Houston Markham |
| 1992 | $Grambling | 10 | 2 | 0 | Eddie Robinson |

* Tennessee State's participation in the 1982 Division I-AA championship (1-1 record) voided.    # NAIA Division I national champion.    ¢ Alabama St. defeated North Caro. A&T, 36-13, in the inaugural Alamo Heritage Bowl, the first bowl game for the historically black schools.    $ Grambling defeated Florida A&M, 45-15, in the second Heritage Bowl.

*1993 NCAA FOOTBALL*

New Haven running back Roger Graham can hold his finger aloft for good reason: He was No. 1 among Division II rushers in 1992. The sophomore ran for 1,717 yards, the sixth-highest total in Division II history, and averaged more than 8.5 yards per carry.

Official national statistics for all nonmajor four-year colleges began in 1946 with a limited postseason survey. In 1948, the service was expanded to include weekly individual and team statistics rankings in all categories except interceptions, punt returns and kickoff returns; these categories were added to official individual rankings and records in 1970.

From 1946, individual rankings were by totals. Beginning in 1970, most season individual rankings were by per-game averages. In total offense, rushing and scoring, yards or points per game determine rankings; in receiving and interceptions, catches per game; in punt and kickoff returns, yards per return; and in field goals, number made per game. Punting always has been by average, and all team rankings have been per game.

Beginning in 1979, passers were ranked in all divisions on Efficiency Rating Points (see page 8 for explanation).

Before 1967, rankings and records included all four-year colleges that reported their statistics to the NCAA. Beginning with the 1967 season, rankings and records included only members of the NCAA.

In 1973, College Division teams were divided into Division II and Division III under a three-division reorganization plan adopted by the special NCAA Convention on August 1, 1973. Career records of players who played in both Divisions II and III will be found where they played the majority of their careers (i.e., two of the last three or three of the last four years). In the event an individual's four-year or two-year career is divided evenly between classifications (or between member and nonmember status), the player's career statistics are entered in the collegiate record category.

Collegiate records for all NCAA divisions can be determined by comparing records for all four divisions. Collegiate records are listed only if they involve players with divided careers.

All individual and team statistics rankings include regular-season games only.

# INDIVIDUAL RECORDS

## TOTAL OFFENSE
### (Rushing Plus Passing)

### Most Plays

**Game**
85—Dave Walter, Michigan Tech vs. Ferris St., Oct. 18, 1986 (457 yards)
**Season**
594—Chris Hegg, Northeast Mo. St., 1985 (3,782 yards)
Per-game record—58.3, Dave Walter, Michigan Tech, 1986 (525 in 9)
**2 Yrs**
1,107—Pat Brennan, Franklin, 1983-84 (6,487 yards)
Also holds per-game record at 55.4 (1,107 in 20)
**3 Yrs**
1,542—Earl Harvey, N.C. Central, 1985-87 (8,266 yards)
**Career**
(4 yrs.) 2,045—Earl Harvey, N.C. Central, 1985-88 (10,667 yards)
Also holds per-game record at 52.4 (2,045 in 39)

### Most Plays by a Freshman

**Season**
538—Earl Harvey, N.C. Central, 1985 (3,008 yards)
Also holds per-game record at 53.8 (538 in 10)

### Most Yards Gained

**Game**
584—Tracy Kendall, Alabama A&M vs. Clark Atlanta, Nov. 4, 1989 (70 rushing, 514 passing)
**Season**
3,782—Chris Hegg, Northeast Mo. St., 1985 (41 rushing, 3,741 passing)
**2 Yrs**
6,487—Pat Brennan, Franklin, 1983-84 (-344 rushing, 6,831 passing)
**3 Yrs**
8,266—Earl Harvey, N.C. Central, 1985-87 (14 rushing, 8,252 passing)
**Career**
(4 yrs.) 10,667—Earl Harvey, N.C. Central, 1985-88 (46 rushing, 10,621 passing)

## Most Yards Gained Per Game
**Season**
350.4—Rob Tomlinson, Cal St. Chico, 1989 (3,504 in 10)
**Career**
281.0—Jayson Merrill, Western St., 1990-91 (5,619 in 20)

## Most Seasons Gaining 3,000 Yards or More
2—Pat Brennan, Franklin, 1983 (3,239) & 1984 (3,248)

## Most Seasons Gaining 2,500 Yards or More
3—Jim Lindsey, Abilene Christian, 1968 (2,740), 1969 (2,646) & 1970 (2,654)

### Gaining 2,500 Yards Rushing and 3,000 Yards Passing
**Career**
Jeff Bentrim, North Dak. St., 1983-86 (2,946 rushing, 3,453 passing)

### Most Yards Gained by a Freshman
**Game**
482—Matthew Montgomery, Hampton vs. Tuskegee, Oct. 26, 1991
**Season**
3,008—Earl Harvey, N.C. Central, 1985 (538 plays)
Also holds per-game record at 300.8 (3,008 in 10)

## Most Games Gaining 300 Yards or More
**Season**
8—Chris Hegg, Northeast Mo. St., 1985

**Career**
15—June Jones, Portland St., 1975-76; Jim Lindsey, Abilene Christian, 1967-70

### Highest Average Gain Per Play
**Season**
*(Min. 350 plays)* 8.33—Bob Toledo, San Fran. St., 1967 (409 for 3,407)
**Career**
*(Min. 950 plays)* 7.64—Doug Williams, Grambling, 1974-77 (1,072 for 8,195)

### Most Touchdowns Responsible For
### (TDs Scored and Passed For)
**Game**
10—Bruce Swanson, North Park vs. North Central, Oct. 12, 1968 (passed for 10)
Also holds record for Most Points Responsible For at 60
**Season**
46—Bob Toledo, San Fran. St., 1967 (scored 1, passed for 45)
Also holds per-game record at 4.6 (46 in 10) and record for Most Points Responsible For at 276
**Career**
106—Earl Harvey, N.C. Central, 1985-88 (scored 20, passed for 86)

### Most Points Responsible For
### (Points Scored and Passed For)
**Career**
636—Earl Harvey, N.C. Central, 1985-88 (scored 120, passed for 516)

# RUSHING

### Most Rushes
**Game**
62—Nelson Edmonds, Northern Mich. vs. Wayne St. (Mich.), Oct. 26, 1991 (291 yards)
**Season**
350—Leon Burns, Long Beach St., 1969 (1,659 yards)
Per-game record—38.6, Mark Perkins, Hobart, 1968
**2 Yrs**
648—Steve Roberts, Butler, 1987-88 (2,917 yards)
**Career**
1,072—Bernie Peeters, Luther, 1968-71 (4,435 yards)
Also holds per-game record at 29.8 (1,072 in 36)

### Most Consecutive Rushes by the Same Player
**Game**
13—Michael Mann, Indiana (Pa.) vs. Edinboro, Nov. 7, 1992; Randy Walker, Wheaton (Ill.) vs. North Park, Nov. 4, 1972 (during one ball possession)

### Most Yards Gained
**Half**
213—Chad Guthrie, Northeast Mo. St. vs. Southwest Baptist, Oct. 3, 1992 (16 rushes)
**Game**
382—Kelly Ellis, Northern Iowa vs. Western Ill., Oct. 13, 1979 (40 rushes)
**Season**
2,011—Johnny Bailey, Texas A&I, 1986 (271 rushes)
**2 Yrs**
3,609—Johnny Bailey, Texas A&I, 1986-87 (488 rushes)
**3 Yrs**
5,051—Johnny Bailey, Texas A&I, 1986-88

(717 rushes)
**Career**
6,320—Johnny Bailey, Texas A&I, 1986-89 (885 rushes)

### Most Yards Gained Per Game
**Season**
182.8—Johnny Bailey, Texas A&I, 1986 (2,011 in 11)
**2 Yrs**
171.9—Johnny Bailey, Texas A&I, 1986-87 (3,609 in 21)
**Career**
*(Min. 3,000 yards)* 162.1—Johnny Bailey, Texas A&I, 1986-89 (6,320 in 39)

### Most Yards Gained by a Freshman
**Game**
370—Jim Hissam, Marietta vs. Bethany (W. Va.), Nov. 15, 1958 (22 rushes)
**Season**
2,011—Johnny Bailey, Texas A&I, 1986 (271 rushes)
Also holds per-game record at 182.8 (2,011 in 11)

### Most Yards Gained in First Game of a Career
238—Johnny Bailey, Texas A&I vs. Texas Southern, Sept. 6, 1986

### Most Yards Gained by
### Two Players, Same Team
**Game**
514—Thelbert Withers (333) & Derrick Ray (181), N.M. Highlands vs. Fort Lewis, Oct. 17, 1992
**Season**
3,526—Johnny Bailey (2,011) & Heath Sherman (1,515), Texas A&I, 1986
Also hold per-game record at 320.5 (3,526 in 11)

### Career
*(3 yrs.)* 8,594—Johnny Bailey (5,051) & Heath Sherman (3,543), Texas A&I, 1986-88 (1,317 rushes)

### Two Players, Same Team, Each Gaining 200 Yards or More
#### Game
Ed Tillison, 272 (29 rushes, 2 TDs) & Jeremy Wilson, 204 (18 rushes, 1 TD), Northwest Mo. St. vs. Neb.-Kearney, Nov. 11, 1990; Jeremy Monroe, 220 (23 rushes, 5 TDs) & Mark Kieliszewski, 212 (18 rushes, 1 TD), Michigan Tech vs. Trinity (Ill.), Nov. 3, 1990; Johnny Bailey, 207 (23 rushes, 0 TDs) & Heath Sherman, 206 (17 rushes, 3 TDs), Texas A&I vs. East Central Okla., Sept. 20, 1986; Johnny Bailey, 244 (21 rushes, 3 TDs) & Heath Sherman, 216 (22 rushes, 4 TDs), Texas A&I vs. North Dak., Sept. 13, 1986 (consecutive games)

### Two Players, Same Team, Each Gaining 1,000 Yards or More
#### Season
11 times. Most recent: Pittsburg St., 1991—Darren Dawson (1,176) & Ronald Moore (1,040); Pittsburg St., 1990—Darren Dawson (1,170) & Ronald Moore (1,013)

### Most Games Gaining 100 Yards or More
#### Season
11—Ronald Moore, Pittsburg St., 1992; Johnny Bailey, Texas A&I, 1986
Bailey also holds freshman record at 11
#### Career
33—Johnny Bailey, Texas A&I, 1986-89 (39 games)

### Most Consecutive Games Gaining 100 Yards or More
#### Season
11—Johnny Bailey, Texas A&I, 1986
Also holds freshman record at 11
#### Career
24—Peter Gorniewicz, Colby, 1971-73

### Most Games Gaining 200 Yards or More
#### Season
5—Johnny Bailey, Texas A&I, 1986
Also holds freshman record at 5
#### Career
11—Johnny Bailey, Texas A&I, 1986-89 (39 games)

### Most Consecutive Games Gaining 200 Yards or More
#### Season
4—Johnny Bailey, Texas A&I, 1986 (first games of his career)

### Most Yards Gained, Four and Five Consecutive Games
#### 4 Games
975—Zed Robinson, Southern Utah, Oct. 5-Oct. 26, 1991
#### 5 Games
1,075—Zed Robinson, Southern Utah, Oct. 5-Nov. 2, 1991

### Most Yards Gained by a Quarterback
#### Game
323—Shawn Graves, Wofford vs. Lenoir-Rhyne, Sept. 15, 1990 (23 rushes)
#### Season
1,483—Shawn Graves, Wofford, 1989 (241 rushes)

### Career
5,128—Shawn Graves, Wofford, 1989-92 (730 rushes)

### Most Rushes by a Quarterback
#### Career
730—Shawn Graves, Wofford, 1989-92

### Most Yards Gained by a Freshman in First Game of Career
238—Johnny Bailey, Texas A&I vs. Texas Southern, Sept. 6, 1986

### Most Seasons Gaining 1,000 Yards or More
#### Career
4—Johnny Bailey, Texas A&I, 1986-89; Vincent Allen, Indiana St., 1973-75, 77

### Highest Average Gain Per Rush
#### Game
*(Min. 20 rushes)* 17.5—Don Polkinghorne, Washington (Mo.) vs. Wash. & Lee, Nov. 23, 1957 (21 for 367)
#### Season
*(Min. 140 rushes)* 10.5—Billy Johnson, Widener, 1972 (148 for 1,556)
*(Min. 200 rushes)* 8.59—Roger Graham, New Haven, 1992 (200 for 1,717)
*(Min. 250 rushes)* 7.42—Johnny Bailey, Texas A&I, 1986 (271 for 2,011)
#### Career
*(Min. 300 rushes)* 9.09—Billy Johnson, Widener, 1971-73 (411 for 3,735)
*(Min. 500 rushes)* 8.49—Bill Rhodes, Western St., 1953-56 (506 for 4,294)

### Most Touchdowns Scored by Rushing
#### Game
8—Junior Wolf, Panhandle St. vs. St. Mary (Kan.), Nov. 8, 1958
#### Season
28—Terry Metcalf, Long Beach St., 1971
#### Career
72—Shawn Graves, Wofford, 1989-92
Per-game record—1.83, Jeff Bentrim, North Dak. St., 1983-86 (64 in 35)

### Most Touchdowns Scored by Rushing by a Freshman
#### Season
24—Shawn Graves, Wofford, 1989
Also holds per-game record at 2.18 (24 in 11)

### Most Touchdowns Scored by Rushing by a Quarterback
#### Season
24—Shawn Graves, Wofford, 1989
Per-game record—2.3, Jeff Bentrim, North Dak. St. (23 in 10)
#### Career
72—Shawn Graves, Wofford, 1989-92
Per-game record—1.83, Jeff Bentrim, North Dak. St., 1983-86 (64 in 35)

### Most Touchdowns Scored by Rushing by Two Players, Same Team
#### Season
41—Roger Graham (22) & A. J. Livingston (19), New Haven, 1992; Heath Sherman (23) & Johnny Bailey (18), Texas A&I, 1986
Per-game record—4.10, Roger Graham & A. J. Livingston, New Haven, 1992 (41 in 10)
#### Career
106—Heath Sherman (55) & Johnny Bailey (51), Texas A&I, 1985-88

# PASSING

## Highest Passing Efficiency Rating Points

**Season**

*(Min. 15 atts. per game)* 210.1—Boyd Crawford, Col. of Idaho, 1953 (120 attempts, 72 completions, 6 interceptions, 1,462 yards, 21 TD passes)

*(Min. 100 comps.)* 189.0—Chuck Green, Wittenberg, 1963 (182 attempts, 114 completions, 8 interceptions, 2,181 yards, 19 TD passes)

*(Min. 200 comps.)* 159.7—Chris Petersen, UC Davis, 1986 (311 attempts, 218 completions, 7 interceptions, 2,622 yards, 22 TD passes)

**Career**

*(Min. 375 comps.)* 164.0—Chris Petersen, UC Davis, 1985-86 (553 attempts, 385 completions, 13 interceptions, 4,988 yards, 39 TD passes)

## Most Passes Attempted

**Game**

72—Kurt Otto, North Dak. vs. Texas A&I, Sept. 13, 1986 (completed 41); Kaipo Spencer, Santa Clara vs. Portland St., Oct. 11, 1975 (completed 37); Joe Stetser, Cal St. Chico vs. Oregon Tech, Sept. 23, 1967 (completed 38)

**Season**

515—Tod Mayfield, West Tex. St., 1986 (completed 317)

**Career**

1,442—Earl Harvey, N.C. Central, 1985-88 (completed 690)

## Most Passes Attempted Per Game

**Season**

50.2—Pat Brennan, Franklin, 1984 (502 in 10)

**Career**

46.2—Tim Von Dulm, Portland St., 1969-70 (924 in 20)

## Most Passes Completed

**Game**

44—Tom Bonds, Cal Lutheran vs. St. Mary's (Cal.), Nov. 22, 1986 (attempted 59)

**Season**

317—Tod Mayfield, West Tex. St., 1986 (attempted 515)

**Career**

733—Andy Breault, Kutztown, 1989-92 (attempted 1,259)

## Most Passes Completed Per Game

**Season**

28.8—Tod Mayfield, West Tex. St., 1986 (317 in 11)

**Career**

25.0—Tim Von Dulm, Portland St., 1969-70 (500 in 20)

## Most Passes Completed by a Freshman

**Game**

41—Neil Lomax, Portland St. vs. Montana St., Nov. 19, 1977 (59 attempts, 469 yards, 6 TDs)

## Most Consecutive Passes Completed

**Game**

20—Rod Bockwoldt, Weber St. vs. South Dak. St., Nov. 6, 1976

**Season**

23—Mike Ganey, Allegheny, 1967 (completed last 16 attempts vs. Carnegie Mellon, Oct. 9, and first 7 vs. Oberlin, Oct. 16)

## Highest Percentage of Passes Completed

**Game**

*(Min. 20 comps.)* 90.9%—Rod Bockwoldt, Weber St. vs. South Dak. St., Nov. 6, 1976 (20 of 22)

*(Min. 35 comps.)* 70.1%—Kurt Beathard, Towson St. vs. Lafayette, Nov. 2, 1985 (40 of 51)

**Season**

*(Min. 225 atts.)* 70.1%—Chris Petersen, UC Davis, 1986 (218 of 311)

*(Min. 350 atts.)* 66.0%—Chris Hatcher, Valdosta St., 1992 (264 of 400)

**Career**

*(Min. 500 atts.)* 69.6%—Chris Petersen, UC Davis, 1985-86 (385 of 553)

## Most Passes Had Intercepted

**Game**

9—Pat Brennan, Franklin vs. Saginaw Valley, Sept. 24, 1983; Henry Schafer, Johns Hopkins vs. Haverford, Oct. 16, 1965

**Season**

32—Joe Stetser, Cal St. Chico, 1967 (attempted 464)

**Career**

83—Mike Houston, St. Joseph's (Ind.), 1978-81 (attempted 1,031)

## Lowest Percentage of Passes Had Intercepted

**Season**

*(Min. 200 atts.)* 0.75%—Larry Caswell, Rhode Island, 1967 (2 of 266)

*(Min. 300 atts.)* 1.93%—Scott Jones, South Dak., 1985 (6 of 311)

**Career**

*(Min. 500 atts.)* 2.35%—Chris Petersen, UC Davis, 1985-86 (13 of 553)

*(Min. 700 atts.)* 2.63%—Jack Hull, Grand Valley St., 1988-91 (22 of 835)

## Most Passes Attempted Without Interception

**Game**

70—Tim Von Dulm, Portland St. vs. Eastern Wash., Nov. 21, 1970

**Season**

113—Jeff Allen, New Hampshire, 1975

## Most Consecutive Passes Attempted Without Interception

211—Ken Suhl, New Haven, during 10 games from Sept. 5 to Nov. 14, 1992

## Most Yards Gained

**Game**

592—John Charles, Portland St. vs. Cal Poly SLO, Nov. 16, 1991

**Season**

3,741—Chris Hegg, Northeast Mo. St., 1985

**2 Yrs**

6,831—Pat Brennan, Franklin, 1983-84

**3 Yrs**

8,252—Earl Harvey, N.C. Central, 1985-87

**Career**

10,621—Earl Harvey, N.C. Central, 1985-88

## Most Yards Gained Per Game

**Season**

351.3—Bob Toledo, San Fran. St., 1967 (3,513 in 10)

**Career**

298.4—Tim Von Dulm, Portland St., 1969-70 (5,967 in 20)

## Most Yards Gained by a Freshman

**Game**

469—Neil Lomax, Portland St. vs. Montana St., Nov. 19, 1977

**Season**
3,190—Earl Harvey, N.C. Central, 1985

**Most Games Gaining 200 Yards or More**
**Season**
11—Tod Mayfield, West Tex. St., 1986; Chris Hegg, Northeast Mo. St., 1985
**Career**
29—Dave DenBraber, Ferris St., 1984-87

**Most Consecutive Games Gaining
200 Yards or More**
**Career**
15—John Charles, Portland St., 1991-92; Tim Von Dulm, Portland St., 1969-70

**Most Games Gaining 300 Yards or More**
**Season**
8—Earl Harvey, N.C. Central, 1985; Chris Hegg, Northeast Mo. St., 1985
**Career**
15—Earl Harvey, N.C. Central, 1987-88

**Most Consecutive Games Gaining
300 Yards or More**
**Season**
5—Earl Harvey, N.C. Central, 1985; Tim Von Dulm, Portland St., 1970; Jim Lindsey, Abilene Christian, 1968
**Career**
8—Earl Harvey, N.C. Central, 1985-86

**Most Yards Gained Per Attempt**
**Season**
*(Min. 300 atts.)* 11.28—Jayson Merrill, Western St., 1991 (309 for 3,484)
**Career**
*(Min. 500 atts.)* 10.57—John Charles, Portland St., 1991-92 (510 for 5,389)
*(Min. 700 atts.)* 9.02—Bruce Upstill, Col. of Emporia, 1960-63 (769 for 6,935)

**Most Yards Gained Per Completion**
**Season**
*(Min. 125 comps.)* 18.70—Matt Cook, Mo. Southern St., 1991 (141 for 2,637)
*(Min. 175 comps.)* 17.87—Jayson Merrill, Western St., 1991 (195 for 3,484)
**Career**
*(Min. 300 comps.)* 17.77—Jayson Merrill, West-

ern St., 1990-91 (328 for 5,830)
*(Min. 450 comps.)* 17.38—Doug Williams, Grambling, 1974-77 (484 for 8,411)

**Most Touchdown Passes**
**Quarter**
5—Kevin Russell, Calif. (Pa.) vs. Frostburg St., Nov. 5, 1983 (2nd quarter)
**Game**
10—Bruce Swanson, North Park vs. North Central, Oct. 12, 1968
**Season**
45—Bob Toledo, San Fran. St., 1967
Also holds per-game record at 4.5 (45 in 10)
**Career**
93—Doug Williams, Grambling, 1974-77
Per-game record—2.7, Bob Toledo, San Fran. St., 1966-67 (53 in 20)

**Most Touchdown Passes by a Freshman**
**Game**
6—Earl Harvey, N.C. Central vs. Johnson Smith, Nov. 9, 1985
**Season**
22—Earl Harvey, N.C. Central, 1985

**Highest Percentage of Passes for Touchdowns**
**Season**
*(Min. 150 atts.)* 16.0%—John Ford, Hardin-Simmons, 1949 (26 of 163)
*(Min. 300 atts.)* 11.4%—Bob Toledo, San Fran. St., 1967 (45 of 396)
**Career**
*(Min. 500 atts.)* 12.2%—Al Niemela, West Chester, 1985-88 (73 of 600)

**Most Consecutive Games
Throwing a Touchdown Pass**
**Career**
21—Andy Breault, Kutztown, 1990-91 (all 11 in 1990, all 10 in 1991); Earl Harvey, N.C. Central, 1985-87 (last 5 in 1985, all 10 in 1986, first 6 in 1987)

**Most Games Throwing a Touchdown Pass**
**Career**
38—Doug Williams, Grambling, 1974-77 (played in 40 games)

# RECEIVING

**Most Passes Caught**
**Game**
23—Barry Wagner, Alabama A&M vs. Clark Atlanta, Nov. 4, 1989 (370 yards)
**Season**
106—Barry Wagner, Alabama A&M, 1989 (1,812 yards)
**Career**
253—Chris Myers, Kenyon, 1967-70 (3,897 yards)

**Most Passes Caught Per Game**
**Season**
10.1—Bruce Cerone, Emporia St., 1968 (91 in 9)
**Career**
8.6—Ed Bell, Idaho St., 1968-69 (163 in 19)

**Most Consecutive Games Catching a Pass**
**Career**
42—Gary Compton, East Tex. St., 1987-90 (42 of 42 games played)

**Most Passes Caught by a Tight End**
**Game**
15—By six players. Most recent: Mark Martin,

Cal St. Chico vs. San Fran. St., Oct. 21, 1989 (223 yards)
**Season**
77—Bob Tucker, Bloomsburg, 1967 (1,325 yards)
**Career**
199—Barry Naone, Portland St., 1985-88 (2,237 yards)

**Most Passes Caught by a Running Back**
**Season**
94—Billy Joe Masters, Evansville, 1987 (960 yards)
Also holds per-game record at 9.4 (94 in 10)
**Career**
200—Mark Steinmeyer, Kutztown, 1988-91 (2,118 yards)
Per-game record—5.4, Mark Marana, Northern Mich., 1979-80 (107 in 20)

**Most Passes Caught by a Freshman**
**Season**
66—Don Hutt, Boise St., 1971 (928 yards)

### Most Passes Caught by
### Two Players, Same Team
**Career**
363—Robert Clark (210) & Robert Green (153), N.C. Central, 1983-86 (6,528 yards, 49 TDs)

### Most Yards Gained
**Game**
370—Barry Wagner, Alabama A&M vs. Clark Atlanta, Nov. 4, 1989 (caught 23)
**Season**
1,812—Barry Wagner, Alabama A&M, 1989 (caught 106)
**Career**
4,354—Bruce Cerone, Yankton/Emporia St., 1966-69 (caught 241)

### Most Yards Gained Per Game
**Season**
164.7—Barry Wagner, Alabama A&M, 1989 (1,812 in 11)
**Career**
137.3—Ed Bell, Idaho St., 1968-69 (2,608 in 19)

### Most Yards Gained by a Tight End
**Game**
290—Bob Tucker, Bloomsburg vs. Susquehanna, Oct. 7, 1967 (caught 15)
**Season**
1,325—Bob Tucker, Bloomsburg, 1967 (caught 77)
**Career**
2,494—Dan Anderson, Northwest Mo. St., 1982-85 (caught 186)

### Most Yards Gained by a Running Back
**Game**
209—Don Lenhard, Bucknell vs. Delaware, Nov. 19, 1966 (caught 11)
**Season**
960—Billy Joe Masters, Evansville, 1987 (caught 94)
Also holds per-game record at 96.0 (960 in 10)
**Career**
2,118—Mark Steinmeyer, Kutztown, 1988-91 (caught 200)

### Most Yards Gained by
### Two Players, Same Team
**Career**
6,528—Robert Clark (4,231) & Robert Green (2,297), N.C. Central, 1983-86 (caught 363, 49 TDs)

### Highest Average Gain Per Reception
**Season**
*(Min. 30 receps.)* 32.5—Tyrone Johnson, Western St., 1991 (32 for 1,039)
*(Min. 40 receps.)* 27.6—Chris Harkness, Ashland, 1987 (41 for 1,131)
*(Min. 55 receps.)* 24.0—Rod Smith, Mo. Southern St., 1991 (60 for 1,439)
**Career**
*(Min. 135 receps.)* 21.8—Willie Richardson, Jackson St., 1959-62 (166 for 3,616)
*(Min. 180 receps.)* 20.1—Robert Clark, N.C. Central, 1983-86 (210 for 4,231)

### Highest Average Gain Per Reception
### by a Running Back
**Season**
*(Min. 40)* 19.4—John Smith, Boise St., 1975 (45 for 854)
**Career**
*(Min. 80)* 18.1—John Smith, Boise St., 1972-75 (89 for 1,608)

### Most Touchdown Passes Caught
**Game**
8—Paul Zaeske, North Park vs. North Central, Oct. 12, 1968 (11 receptions)
**Season**
20—Ed Bell, Idaho St., 1969 (96 receptions)
Per-game record—2.0, Shannon Sharpe, Savannah St., 1989 (18 in 9); Ed Bell, Idaho St., 1969 (20 in 10)
**Career**
49—Bruce Cerone, Yankton/Emporia St., 1966-69 (241 receptions)
Per-game record—1.6, Ed Bell, Idaho St., 1968-69 (30 in 19)

### Most Touchdown Passes Caught
### by a Tight End
**Game**
5—Mike Palomino, Portland St. vs. Cal Poly SLO, Nov. 16, 1991; Alex Preuss, Grand Valley St. vs. Winona St., Sept. 17, 1988
**Season**
13—Bob Tucker, Bloomsburg, 1967

### Most Touchdown Passes Caught
### by a Running Back
**Season**
11—John Smith, Boise St., 1975
**Career**
24—John Smith, Boise St., 1972-75

### Most Touchdown Passes Caught
### by a Freshman
**Season**
11—Douglas Grant, Savannah St., 1990; Harold Roberts, Austin Peay, 1967

### Highest Percentage of Passes
### Caught for Touchdowns
**Season**
*(Min. 10 TDs)* 68.8%—Jim Callahan, Temple, 1966 (11 of 16)
**Career**
*(Min. 20 TDs)* 30.0%—Bob Cherry, Wittenberg, 1960-63 (27 of 90)

### Most Consecutive Passes
### Caught for Touchdowns
**Season**
10—Jim Callahan, Temple, 1966 (first 5 games, first games of career)

### Most Consecutive Games
### Catching a Touchdown Pass
**Career**
14—Jeff Tiefenthaler, South Dak. St., from Oct. 27, 1984, through Nov. 9, 1985

### Most Games Catching a Touchdown Pass
**Career**
25—Jeff Tiefenthaler, South Dak. St., 1983-86 (in 36 games)

# PUNTING

### Most Punts
**Game**
32—Jan Jones, Sam Houston St. vs. East Tex. St., Nov. 2, 1946 (1,203 yards)

**Season**
98—John Tassi, Lincoln (Mo.), 1981 (3,163 yards)

**Career**
328—Dan Brown, Nicholls St., 1976-79 (12,883 yards)

**Highest Average Per Punt**

**Game**
(Min. 5 punts) 57.5—Tim Baer, Colorado Mines vs. Fort Lewis, Oct. 25, 1986 (8 for 460)

**Season**
(Min. 20 punts) 49.1—Steve Ecker, Shippensburg, 1965 (32 for 1,570)
(Min. 40 punts) 46.3—Mark Bounds, West Tex. St., 1990 (69 for 3,198)

**Career**
(Min. 100 punts) 44.3—Steve Lewis, Jacksonville St., 1989-92 (100 for 4,434)

# INTERCEPTIONS (From 1970)

## Most Passes Intercepted

**Quarter**
3—Anthony Devine, Millersville vs. Cheyney, Oct. 13, 1990 (3rd; 90 yards); Mike McDonald, Southwestern La. vs. Lamar, Oct. 24, 1970 (4th; 25 yards)

**Game**
5—By five players. Most recent: Gary Evans, Northeast Mo. St. vs. Missouri-Rolla, Oct. 18, 1975

**Season**
14—By five players. Most recent: Luther Howard, Delaware St., 1972 (99 yards); Eugene Hunter, Fort Valley St., 1972 (211 yards)

**Career**
37—Tom Collins, Indianapolis, 1982-85 (390 yards)

## Most Passes Intercepted by Per Game

**Season**
1.56—Luther Howard, Delaware St., 1972 (14 in 9); Eugene Hunter, Fort Valley St., 1972 (14 in 9); Tom Rezzuti, Northeastern, 1971 (14 in 9)

## Most Yards on Interception Returns

**Game**
152—Desmond Brown, Tuskegee vs. Morris Brown, Sept. 15, 1990 (2 interceptions)

**Season**
300—Mike Brim, Virginia Union, 1986 (8 interceptions)

**Career**
504—Anthony Leonard, Virginia Union, 1973-76 (17 interceptions)

## Highest Average Gain Per Interception

**Season**
(Min. 6 ints.) 40.0—Steve Smith, Bowie St., 1992 (6 for 240)

**Career**
(Min. 10 ints.) 37.4—Greg Anderson, Montana, 1974-76 (11 for 411)
(Min. 15 ints.) 29.6—Anthony Leonard, Virginia Union, 1973-76 (17 for 504)

## Most Touchdowns Scored on Interceptions

**Season**
4—Clay Blalack, Tenn.-Martin, 1976 (8 interceptions)

# PUNT RETURNS (From 1970)

## Most Punt Returns

**Game**
10—Armin Anderson, UC Davis vs. Cal St. Chico, Oct. 22, 1983 (42 yards)

**Season**
61—Armin Anderson, UC Davis, 1984 (516 yards)

**Career**
153—Armin Anderson, UC Davis, 1983-85 (1,207 yards)

## Most Yards on Punt Returns

**Game**
265—Billy Johnson, Widener vs. St. John's (N.Y.), Sept. 23, 1972 (4 returns)

**Season**
603—Rob Richmond, Hampden-Sydney, 1971 (46 returns)

**Career**
1,207—Armin Anderson, UC Davis, 1983-85 (153 returns)

## Highest Average Gain Per Return

**Game**
(Min. 4 rets.) 66.3—Billy Johnson, Widener vs. St. John's (N.Y.), Sept. 23, 1972 (4 for 265)

**Season**
(Min. 1.2 rets. per game) 34.1—Billy Johnson, Widener, 1972 (15 for 511)

**Career**
(Min. 1.2 rets. per game) 24.7—Billy Johnson, Widener, 1971-73 (40 for 989)

## Most Touchdowns Scored on Punt Returns

**Game**
3—By four players. Most recent: Virgil Seay, Troy St. vs. Livingston, Sept. 29, 1979

**Season**
4—Michael Fields, Mississippi Col., 1984; Billy Johnson, Widener, 1972

**Career**
7—Billy Johnson, Widener, 1971-73

# KICKOFF RETURNS (From 1970)

## Most Kickoff Returns

**Game**
9—Darron Turner, Tenn.-Martin vs. Jacksonville St., Oct. 21, 1989; Thad Kuehnl, Michigan Tech vs. Northern Mich., Sept. 5, 1987; Matthew Williams, Northeast La. vs. Jacksonville St., Nov. 3, 1973

**Season**
47—Sean Tarrant, Lincoln (Mo.), 1986 (729 yards)
Also holds per-game record at 4.3 (47 in 11)

**Career**
115—Sean Tarrant, Lincoln (Mo.), 1985-88 (1,901 yards)

## Most Yards on Kickoff Returns

**Game**
276—Matt Pericolosi, Central Conn. St. vs. Hofstra, Sept. 14, 1991 (6 returns); Tom Dufresne, Hamline vs. Minn.-Duluth, Sept. 30, 1972 (7 returns)

**Season**
983—Doug Parrish, San Fran. St., 1990 (34 returns)

**Career**
2,291—Joe Wingate, Northwest Mo. St., 1970-73 (99 returns)

### Highest Average Gain Per Return

**Game**
(Min. 3 rets.) 71.7—Clarence Martin, Cal Poly SLO vs. Cal Poly Pomona, Nov. 20, 1982 (3 for 215)

**Season**
(Min. 1.2 rets. per game) 39.4—Danny Lee, Jacksonville St., 1992 (12 for 473)

**Career**
(Min. 1.2 rets. per game) 34.0—Glen Printers, Southern Colo., 1973-74 (25 for 851)

### Most Touchdowns Scored on Kickoff Returns

**Game**
2—Clarence Martin, Cal Poly SLO vs. Cal Poly Pomona, Nov. 20, 1982 (successive); Tom Dufresne, Hamline vs. Minn.-Duluth, Sept. 30, 1972·

**Season**
3—Danny Lee, Jacksonville St., 1992; Dave Ludy, Winona St., 1992; Otha Hill, Central St. (Ohio), 1979

**Career**
5—Dave Ludy, Winona St., 1991-92

## TOTAL KICK RETURNS
### (Combined Punt and Kickoff Returns)

**Most Kick Returns**

**Season**
63—Bobby Yates, Central Mo. St., 1990 (31 kickoffs, 32 punts, 840 yards)

**Most Consecutive Touchdowns on Kick Returns**

**Game**
2—Victor Barnes, Nebraska-Omaha vs. Neb.-Kearney, Sept. 8, 1990 (94-yard kickoff return & 79-yard punt return)

## ALL RUNBACKS
### (Combined Interceptions, Punt Returns and Kickoff Returns)

**Most Touchdowns Scored on Interceptions, Punt Returns and Kickoff Returns**

**Season**
6—Anthony Leonard, Virginia Union, 1974 (2 interceptions, 2 punt returns, 2 kickoff returns)

**Career**
13—Anthony Leonard, Virginia Union, 1973-76 (3 interceptions, 6 punt returns, 4 kickoff returns)

**Most Touchdowns Scored on Punt Returns and Kickoff Returns**

**Career**
10—Anthony Leonard, Virginia Union, 1973-76 (6 punt returns, 4 kickoff returns)

**Longest Return of a Missed Field Goal**
100—Kalvin Simmons, Clark Atlanta vs. Morris Brown, Sept. 5, 1987 (actually from 6 yards in end zone)

## OPPONENT'S PUNTS BLOCKED

**Career**
13—Bernard Ford, Central Fla., 1985-87

## ALL-PURPOSE RUNNING
### (Yardage Gained From Rushing, Receiving and All Runbacks)

**Most Plays**

**Season**
415—Steve Roberts, Butler, 1989 (325 rushes, 49 receptions, 21 punt returns, 20 kickoff returns)

**Career**
1,195—Steve Roberts, Butler, 1986-89 (1,026 rushes, 120 receptions, 21 punt returns, 28 kickoff returns)

**Most Yards Gained**

**Game**
525—Andre Johnson, Ferris St. vs. Clarion, Sept. 16, 1989 (19 rushing, 235 receiving, 10 punt returns, 261 kickoff returns; 17 plays)

**Season**
2,669—Steve Roberts, Butler, 1989 (1,450 rushing, 532 receiving, 272 punt returns, 415 kickoff returns; 415 plays)
Freshman record (2,425) and freshman per-game record (220.5) held by Johnny Bailey, Texas A&I (11 games), 1986

**Career**
7,803—Johnny Bailey, Texas A&I, 1986-89 (6,302 rushing, 452 receiving, 20 punt returns, 1,011 kickoff returns)

**Most Yards Gained by Two Players, Same Team**

**Season**
4,076—Johnny Bailey (2,425) and Heath Sherman (1,651), Texas A&I, 1986
Also hold per-game record at 370.5 (4,076 in 11)

**Most Yards Gained Per Game**

**Season**
266.9—Steve Roberts, Butler, 1989 (2,669 in 10)

**Career**
205.1—Howard Stevens, Randolph-Macon, 1968-69 (3,691 in 18)
Also holds collegiate per-game record at 199.1 (7,564 in 38) at Randolph-Macon, 1968-69, and Louisville, 1971-72

**Highest Average Gain Per Play**

**Game**
(Min. 15 plays) 30.9—Andre Johnson, Ferris St. vs. Clarion, Sept. 16, 1989 (525 on 17)

**Season**
(Min. 1,500 yards, 150 plays) 12.94—Billy Johnson, Widener, 1972 (2,265 on 175)

**Career**
*(Min. 4,000 yards, 300 plays)* 11.28—Billy Johnson, Widener, 1971-73 (5,404 on 479)

# SCORING

### Most Points Scored
**Game**
48—Paul Zaeske, North Park vs. North Central,
Oct. 12, 1968 (8 TDs); Junior Wolf, Panhandle
St. vs. St. Mary (Kan.), Nov. 8, 1958 (8 TDs)
**Season**
178—Terry Metcalf, Long Beach St., 1971 (29
TDs, 4 PATs)
**3 Yrs**
400—Walter Payton, Jackson St., 1972-74 (59
TDs, 40 PATs, 2 FGs)
**Career**
464—Walter Payton, Jackson St., 1971-74 (66
TDs, 53 PATs, 5 FGs)

### Most Points Scored Per Game
**Season**
21.0—Carl Herakovich, Rose-Hulman, 1958
(168 in 8)
**Career**
13.4—Ole Gunderson, St. Olaf, 1969-71 (362 in
27)

### Most Touchdowns Scored
**Game**
8—Paul Zaeske, North Park vs. North Central,
Oct. 12, 1968 (all on pass receptions); Junior
Wolf, Panhandle St. vs. St. Mary (Kan.), Nov.
8, 1958 (all by rushing)
**Season**
29—Terry Metcalf, Long Beach St., 1971
**Career**
*(3 yrs.)* 62—Billy Johnson, Widener, 1971-73
*(4 yrs.)* 72—Shawn Graves, Wofford, 1989-92

### Most Touchdowns Scored Per Game
**Season**
3.1—Carl Herakovich, Rose-Hulman, 1958 (25
in 8)
**Career**
2.2—Billy Johnson, Widener, 1971-73 (62 in 28)

### Most Touchdowns and Points Scored by a Freshman
**Season**
24 & 144—Shawn Graves, Wofford, 1989
Also holds per-game records at 2.2 & 13.1 (24 &
144 in 11)

### Most Touchdowns and Points Scored by a Quarterback
**Season**
24 & 144—Shawn Graves, Wofford, 1989
Per-game records—2.3 &13.8, Jeff Bentrim,
North Dak. St., 1986 (23 & 138 in 10)
**Career**
72 & 438—Shawn Graves, Wofford, 1989-92
Per-game records—1.8 & 11.0, Jeff Bentrim,
North Dak. St., 1983-86 (64 & 386 in 35)

### Most Touchdowns and Points Scored by Two Players, Same Team
**Season**
42 & 254—Heath Sherman (23 & 138) & Johnny
Bailey (19 & 116), Texas A&I, 1986
Also hold per-game records at 3.8 & 23.1 (42 &
254 in 11)
**3 Yrs**
110 & 666—Heath Sherman (56 & 336) &
Johnny Bailey (54 & 330), Texas A&I, 1986-
88

**Wofford quarterback Shawn Graves finished his stellar collegiate career in 1992 as the Division II all-time leader in touchdowns (72) and rushing yards by a quarterback (5,128). His 438 points ranks third on the all-time collegiate list.**

### Most Consecutive Games Scoring a Touchdown
**Career**
25—Billy Johnson, Widener, 1971-73

### Most Field Goals Made
**Game**
6—Steve Huff, Central Mo. St. vs. Southeast
Mo. St., Nov. 2, 1985 (37, 45, 37, 24, 32, 27
yards), 6 attempts
**Season**
20—Pat Beaty, North Dak., 1988 (26 attempts);
Tom Jurich, Northern Ariz., 1977 (29 attempts)
**Career**
64—Mike Wood, Southeast Mo. St., 1974-77
(109 attempts)

### Most Field Goals Made Per Game
**Season**
1.9—Dennis Hochman, Sonoma St., 1986 (19
in 10); Jaime Nunez, Weber St., 1971 (19 in
10)
**Career**
1.5—Mike Wood, Southeast Mo. St., 1974-77
(64 in 44)

### Most Consecutive Field Goals Made
**Career**
14—Keith Kasnic, Tenn.-Martin, 1982-83; Kurt Seibel, South Dak., 1982-83

### Longest Field Goal
67—Tom Odle, Fort Hays St. vs. Washburn, Nov. 5, 1988
*Special reference:* Ove Johannson, Abilene Christian (not an NCAA-member college at the time), kicked a 69-yard field goal against East Tex. St., Oct. 16, 1976

### Most Field Goals Attempted
**Game**
7—Jim Turcotte, Mississippi Col. vs. Troy St., Oct. 3, 1981 (made 2)
**Season**
35—Mike Wood, Southeast Mo. St., 1977 (made 16)
Per-game record—3.3, Skipper Butler, Texas-Arlington, 1968 (33 in 10)
**Career**
109—Mike Wood, Southeast Mo. St., 1974-77 (made 64)
Per-game record—2.7, Jaime Nunez, Weber St., 1969-71 (83 in 31)

### Highest Percentage of Field Goals Made
**Season**
*(Min. 15 atts.)* 88.2%—Howie Guarini, Shippensburg, 1990 (15 of 17); Kurt Seibel, South Dak., 1983 (15 of 17)
*(Min. 20 atts.)* 86.4%—Dennis Hochman, Sonoma St., 1986 (19 of 22)
**Career**
*(Min. 35 made)* 80.0%—Billy May, Clarion, 1977-80 (48 of 60)

### Most Extra Points Made by Kicking
**Game**
14—Art Anderson, North Park vs. North Central, Oct. 12, 1968 (attempted 15); Matt Johnson, Connecticut vs. Newport Naval Training, Oct. 22, 1949 (attempted 17)
**Season**
65—Peter Capvano, New Haven, 1992 (attempted 70); Miguel Sagaro, Grand Valley St., 1989 (attempted 66)
**Career**
163—Miguel Sagaro, Grand Valley St., 1989-92 (attempted 179)

### Most Extra Points Attempted by Kicking
**Game**
17—Matt Johnson, Connecticut vs. Newport Naval Training, Oct. 22, 1949 (made 14)
**Season**
74—Bill McFarland, Pacific (Cal.), 1949 (made 54)
**Career**
179—Miguel Sagaro, Grand Valley St., 1989-92 (made 163); James Jenkins, Pittsburg St., 1988-91 (made 156)

### Highest Percentage of Extra Points Made by Kicking
**Season**
*(Min. 50 atts.)* 100.0%—Bryan Thompson, Angelo St., 1982 (51 of 51); Ken Blazei, North Dak. St., 1968 (50 of 50)
**Career**
*(Min. 90 atts.)* 98.9%—Mark DeMoss, Liberty, 1980-83 (92 of 93)
*(Min. 100 atts.)* 97.1%—Dan Worrell, Montana, 1968-71 (101 of 104)

### Most Consecutive Extra Points Made by Kicking
**Season**
51—Bryan Thompson, Angelo St., 1989 (51 attempts)
**Career**
82—Mark DeMoss, Liberty, 1980-83

### Most Points Scored by Kicking
**Game**
20—Clarence Joseph, Central St. (Ohio) vs. Kentucky St., Oct. 16, 1982 (5 FGs, 5 PATs)
**Season**
92—Tom Jurich, Northern Ariz., 1977 (20 FGs, 32 PATs)
Per-game record—8.8, Jay Masek, Chadron St., 1990 (88 in 10)
**Career**
266—Eddie Loretto, UC Davis, 1985-88 (46 FGs, 128 PATs)
Per-game record *(Min. 145 pts.)*—8.3, Dave Austinson, Northeast Mo. St., 1981-82 (149 in 18)
Per-game record *(Min. 175 pts.)*—6.65, Eddie Loretto, UC Davis, 1985-88 (266 in 40)

## DEFENSIVE EXTRA POINTS

### Most Defensive Extra Points Scored
**Game and Season**
1—Several times. Most recent: Jermal Pulliam (DE), Jacksonville St. vs. Kentucky St., Nov. 14, 1992 (90-yard interception return)

### Longest Defensive Extra Point Blocked-Kick Return
97—Dominic Kurtyan (DB), West Chester vs. Kutztown, Oct. 7, 1988 (TD)

### Longest Defensive Extra Point Fumble Return
87—Rod Beauchamp (DB), Colorado Mines vs. Hastings, Sept. 3, 1988

### Longest Defensive Extra Point Interception Return
90—Jermal Pulliam (DE), Jacksonville St. vs. Kentucky St., Nov. 14, 1992

# TEAM RECORDS

## SINGLE GAME—OFFENSE
### TOTAL OFFENSE

**Most Yards Gained**
910—Hanover vs. Franklin, Oct. 30, 1948 (426 rushing, 484 passing; 75 plays)

**Most Plays**
117—Texas A&I vs. Angelo St., Oct. 30, 1982 (96 rushes, 21 passes; 546 yards)

**Highest Average Gain Per Play**
12.1—Hanover vs. Franklin, Oct. 30, 1948 (75 for 910)

**Most Touchdowns Scored by Rushing and Passing**
15—North Park vs. North Central, Oct. 12, 1968 (4 by rushing, 11 by passing)

**Most Touchdowns Scored by Rushing and Passing, Both Teams**
20—North Park (15) & North Central (5), Oct. 12, 1968

**Most Yards Gained by a Losing Team**
645—Texas A&I vs. West Tex. St., Nov. 1, 1986 (lost 49-54)

## RUSHING

**Most Yards Gained**
719—Coe vs. Beloit, Oct. 16, 1971 (73 rushes)

**Most Rushes**
97—Hobart vs. Union (N.Y.), Oct. 23, 1971 (444 yards)

**Highest Average Gain Per Rush (Min. 50 Rushes)**
10.5—St. Olaf vs. Beloit, Nov. 8, 1969 (51 for 537)

**Most Touchdowns Scored by Rushing**
12—Coe vs. Beloit, Oct. 16, 1971

**Most Players, One Team, Each Gaining 100 Yards or More**
5—South Dak. vs. St. Cloud St., Nov. 1, 1986 (James Hambrick 125, Darryl Colvin 123, Tony Higgins 118, Dave Elle 109, Joe Longueville [QB] 106; team gained 581)

## PASSING

**Most Passes Attempted**
84—Livingston vs. Jacksonville St., Nov. 7, 1992 (completed 49)

**Most Passes Attempted, Both Teams**
121—Franklin (68) & Saginaw Valley (53), Sept. 22, 1984 (completed 63)

**Most Passes Completed**
49—Livingston vs. Jacksonville St., Nov. 7, 1992 (attempted 84)

**Most Passes Completed, Both Teams**
67—Indiana (Pa.) (34) & Lehigh (33), Sept. 14, 1985 (attempted 92)

**Most Passes Had Intercepted**
11—Hamline vs. Concordia-M'head, Nov. 5, 1955; Rhode Island vs. Brown, Oct. 8, 1949

**Most Passes Attempted Without Interception**
63—Hamline vs. St. John's (Minn.), Oct. 8, 1955 (completed 34)

**Highest Percentage of Passes Completed (Min. 20 Attempts)**
90.0%—Northwestern (La.) vs. Southwestern La., Nov. 12, 1966 (20 of 22)

**Most Yards Gained**
678—Portland St. vs. Eastern Mont., Nov. 20, 1976

**Most Yards Gained, Both Teams**
904—New Haven (455) & West Chester (449), Oct. 5, 1990

**Most Touchdown Passes**
11—North Park vs. North Central, Oct. 12, 1968

**Most Touchdown Passes, Both Teams**
14—North Park (11) & North Central (3), Oct. 12, 1968

## PUNTING

**Most Punts**
32—Sam Houston St. vs. East Tex. St., Nov. 2, 1946 (1,203 yards)

**Most Punts, Both Teams**
63—Sam Houston St. (32) & East Tex. St. (31), Nov. 2, 1946

**Highest Average Per Punt (Min. 5 Punts)**
57.5—Colorado Mines vs. Fort Lewis, Oct. 21, 1989 (8 for 460)

## PUNT RETURNS

**Most Yards on Punt Returns**
265—Widener vs. St. John's (N.Y.), Sept. 23, 1972 (4 returns)

**Most Touchdowns Scored on Punt Returns**
3—Troy St. vs. Livingston, Sept. 29, 1979; Widener vs. St. John's (N.Y.), Sept. 23, 1972

## SCORING

**Most Points Scored**
125—Connecticut vs. Newport Naval Training, Oct. 22, 1949

**Most Points Scored Against a College Opponent**
106—Fort Valley St. vs. Knoxville, Oct. 11, 1969 (14 TDs, 2 PATs, 9 two-point conversions, 1 safety)

**Most Points Scored by a Losing Team**
60—New Haven vs. Southern Conn. St. (64), Oct. 25, 1991

**Most Points Scored, Both Teams**
136—North Park (104) & North Central (32), Oct. 12, 1968

**Most Points Scored in Two Consecutive Games**
172—Tuskegee, 1966 (93-0 vs. Morehouse, Oct. 14; 79-0 vs. Lane, Oct. 22)

**Most Touchdowns Scored**
17—Connecticut vs. Newport Naval Training, Oct. 22, 1949

**Most Touchdowns Scored Against a College Opponent**
15—North Park vs. North Central, Oct. 12, 1968; Alcorn St. vs. Paul Quinn, Sept. 9, 1967; Iowa Wesleyan vs. William Penn, Oct. 31, 1953

**Most Points After Touchdown Made by Kicking**
14—North Park vs. North Central, Oct. 12, 1968 (attempted 15); Connecticut vs. Newport Naval Training, Oct. 22, 1949 (attempted 17)

**Most Two-Point Attempts**
11—Fort Valley St. vs. Knoxville, Oct. 11, 1969 (made 9)

**Most Two-Point Attempts Made**
9—Fort Valley St. vs. Knoxville, Oct. 11, 1969 (attempted 11)

**Most Field Goals Made**
6—Central Mo. St. vs. Southeast Mo. St., Nov. 2, 1985 (6 attempts)

**Most Defensive Extra Points Scored**
1—By many teams. Most recent: Jacksonville St. vs. Kentucky St., Nov. 14, 1992 (90-yard interception return)

**Most Defensive Extra-Point Opportunities**
2—North Dak. St. vs. Augustana (S.D.), Sept. 24, 1988 (2 interceptions; none scored)

## FIRST DOWNS

**Most Total First Downs**
42—Delaware vs. Baldwin-Wallace, Oct. 6, 1973

**Most First Downs by Penalty**
14—La Verne vs. Northern Ariz., Oct. 11, 1958

**Most Total First Downs, Both Teams**
66—North Dak. (36) & Texas A&I (30), Sept. 13, 1986; Ferris St. (33) & Northwood (33), Oct. 26, 1985

## PENALTIES

**Most Penalties**
28—Northern Ariz. vs. La Verne, Oct. 11, 1958 (155 yards)

**Most Penalties, Both Teams**
42—N.C. Central (23) & St. Paul's (19), Sept. 13, 1986 (453 yards)

**Most Yards Penalized**
293—Cal Poly SLO vs. Portland St., Oct. 31, 1981 (26 penalties)

**Most Yards Penalized, Both Teams**
453—N.C. Central (256) & St. Paul's (197), Sept. 13, 1986 (42 penalties)

## FUMBLES

**Most Fumbles**
16—Carthage vs. North Park, Nov. 14, 1970 (lost 7)

# SINGLE GAME—DEFENSE
## TOTAL DEFENSE

**Fewest Total Offense Plays Allowed**
29—North Park vs. Concordia (Ill.), Sept. 26, 1964

**Fewest Total Offense Yards Allowed**
Minus 55—San Diego St. vs. U.S. Int'l, Nov. 27, 1965 (59 plays)

**Fewest Rushes Allowed**
7—Indianapolis vs. Valparaiso, Oct. 30, 1982 (-57 yards)

**Fewest Rushing Yards Allowed**
Minus 95—San Diego St. vs. U.S. Int'l, Nov. 27, 1965 (35 plays)

**Fewest Pass Completions Allowed**
0—By many teams. Most recent: New Haven vs. Springfield, Oct. 31, 1992 (4 attempts)

**Fewest Passing Yards Allowed**
Minus 19—Ashland vs. Heidelberg, Sept. 25, 1948 (4 completions)

**Most Times an Opponent Tackled for Loss Attempting to Pass**
19—Southern Conn. St. vs. Albany (N.Y.), Oct. 6, 1984

## PUNTING

**Most Opponent's Punts Blocked By**
5—Winston-Salem vs. N.C. Central, Oct. 4, 1986; Southeastern La. vs. Troy St., Oct. 7, 1978 (holds record for most consecutive punts blocked with 4)

## INTERCEPTIONS

**Most Passes Intercepted By**
11—St. Cloud St. vs. Bemidji St., Oct. 31, 1970 (45 attempts); Concordia-M'head vs. Hamline, Nov. 5, 1955 (37 attempts)

**Most Touchdowns on Interception Returns**
3—By many teams. Most recent: Fort Valley St. vs. North Ala., Oct. 12, 1991

# SEASON—OFFENSE
## TOTAL OFFENSE

**Most Yards Gained Per Game**
624.1—Hanover, 1948 (4,993 in 8)

**Most Yards Gained**
5,969—Texas A&I, 1986 (899 plays, 11 games)

**Highest Average Gain Per Play**
9.20—Hanover, 1948 (543 for 4,993)

**Highest Average Gain Per Play**
**(Min. 800 Plays)**
6.64—Texas A&I, 1986 (899 for 5,969)

**Most Plays Per Game**
88.7—Cal St. Chico, 1967 (887 in 10)

## RUSHING

**Most Yards Gained Per Game**
404.7—Col. of Emporia, 1954 (3,643 in 9)

**Most Yards Gained**
4,347—Texas A&I, 1986 (689 rushes, 11 games)

**Highest Average Gain Per Rush**
8.38—Hanover, 1948 (382 for 3,203)

**Highest Average Gain Per Rush**
**(Min. 500 Rushes)**
7.07—William Jewell, 1952 (537 for 3,795)

**Highest Average Gain Per Rush**
**(Min. 600 Rushes)**
6.31—Texas A&I, 1986 (689 for 4,347)

**Most Rushes Per Game**
78.9—Panhandle St., 1963 (789 in 10)

## PASSING

**Most Yards Gained Per Game**
404.1—Portland St., 1976 (4,445 in 11)

**Highest Average Gain Per Attempt**
**(Min. 175 Attempts)**
10.8—Western St., 1991 (330 for 3,574)

**Highest Average Gain Per Completion**
*(Min. 100 comps.)* 19.4—Calif. (Pa.), 1966 (116 for 2,255)
*(Min. 200 comps.)* 17.6—Western St., 1991 (203 for 3,574)

**Most Passes Attempted Per Game**
51.8—Portland St., 1970 (518 in 10)

**Most Passes Completed Per Game**
29.9—West Tex. St., 1986 (329 in 11)

**Fewest Passes Completed Per Game**
0.4—Hobart, 1971 (4 in 9)

**Highest Percentage Completed**
*(Min. 200 atts.)* 70.2%—UC Davis, 1986 (226 of 322)
*(Min. 350 atts.)* 65.6%—Valdosta St., 1992 (273 of 416)

**Lowest Percentage of Passes**
**Had Intercepted**
**(Min. 275 Attempts)**
1.34%—UC Davis, 1988 (4 of 298)

**Most Touchdown Passes Per Game**
4.9—San Fran. St., 1967 (49 in 10)

**Highest Passing Efficiency Rating Points**
*(Min. 200 atts.)* 183.8—Wittenberg, 1963 (216 attempts, 138 completions, 10 interceptions, 2,457 yards, 22 TDs)
*(Min. 300 atts.)* 180.2—Western St., 1991 (330 attempts, 203 completions, 12 interceptions, 3,574 yards, 35 TDs)

## PUNTING

**Most Punts Per Game**
10.0—Wash. & Lee, 1968 (90 in 9)

**Fewest Punts Per Game**
1.9—Kent, 1954 (17 in 9)

**Highest Punting Average**
48.0—Adams St., 1966 (36 for 1,728)

## PUNT RETURNS

**Most Punt Returns**
64—UC Davis, 1984 (557 yards)

**Most Touchdowns Scored on Punt Returns**
4—Central Ark., 1992; Norfolk St., 1992; Texas A&I, 1992; Eastern N. Mex., 1991; Mississippi Col., 1984; Widener, 1972

## KICKOFF RETURNS

**Most Kickoff Returns**
70—Wayne St. (Neb.), 1988 (926 yards)

## SCORING

**Most Points Per Game**
54.7—Florida A&M, 1961 (492 in 9)

**Most Touchdowns Per Game**
7.7—Pacific (Cal.), 1949 (85 in 11)

**Most Consecutive Extra Points**
**Made by Kicking**
51—Angelo St., 1989

**Most Consecutive Field Goals Made**
13—UC Davis, 1976

**Most Two-Point Attempts Per Game**
6.8—Florida A&M, 1961 (61 in 9, scored 69 TDs)

**Most Two-Point Attempts Made Per Game**
3.6—Florida A&M, 1961 (32 in 9, attempted 61)

**Most Field Goals Made**
20—North Dak., 1988 (attempted 26); Northern
Ariz., 1977 (attempted 29)

**Most Defensive Extra Points Scored**
1—By many teams

**Most Defensive Extra-Point Opportunities**
3—Central Okla., 1989 (2 blocked kick returns,
1 interception; one scored); Northern Colo.,
1988 (2 blocked kick returns, 1 interception;
none scored)

# PENALTIES

**Most Penalties Against**
146—Gardner-Webb, 1992 (1,344 yards)
Per-game record—14.3, N.C. Central, 1986
(143 in 10)

**Most Yards Penalized**
1,356—Hampton, 1977 (124 penalties, 11
games)

## TURNOVERS (GIVEAWAYS) (From 1985)
### (Passes Had Intercepted and Fumbles Lost)

**Fewest Turnovers**
9—North Dak. St., 1991 (1 interception, 8
fumbles lost)

**Most Turnovers**
61—Cheyney, 1990 (36 interceptions, 25 fumbles lost)

**Fewest Turnovers Per Game**
1.0—North Dak. St., 1991 (9 in 9)

**Most Turnovers Per Game**
5.8—Livingstone, 1986 (58 in 10)

# SEASON—DEFENSE
## TOTAL DEFENSE

**Fewest Yards Allowed Per Game**
44.4—John Carroll, 1962 (311 in 7)

**Lowest Average Yards Allowed Per Play**
1.0—John Carroll, 1962 (310 for 311 yards)

**Lowest Average Yards Allowed Per Play
(Min. 500 Plays)**
1.51—Tennessee St., 1966 (511 for 771)

**Lowest Average Yards Allowed Per Play
(Min. 600 Plays)**
1.81—Alcorn St., 1976 (603 for 1,089)

**Fewest Rushing and Passing Touchdowns
Allowed Per Game**
0.0—Albany St. (Ga.), 1960 (0 in 9)

## RUSHING DEFENSE

**Fewest Yards Allowed Per Game**
Minus 16.7—Tennessee St., 1967 (-150 in 9)

**Lowest Average Yards Allowed Per Rush**
Minus 0.5—Tennessee St., 1967 (296 for -150
yards)

**Lowest Average Yards Allowed Per Rush
(Min. 325 Rushes)**
0.41—Merchant Marine, 1969 (359 for 146)

**Lowest Average Yards Allowed Per Rush
(Min. 400 Rushes)**
1.25—Luther, 1971 (414 for 518)

## PASS DEFENSE

**Fewest Yards Allowed Per Game**
10.1—Ashland, 1948 (91 in 9)

**Fewest Yards Allowed Per Attempt**
(Min. 200 atts.) 3.07—Virginia St., 1971 (205 for
630)
(Min. 300 atts.) 3.16—Southwest Mo. St., 1966
(315 for 996)

**Fewest Yards Allowed Per Completion
(Min. 100 Completions)**
8.78—Long Beach St., 1965 (144 for 1,264)

**Lowest Completion Percentage Allowed
(Min. 250 Attempts)**
24.1%—Southwest Mo. St., 1966 (76 of 315)

**Most Passes Intercepted By Per Game**
3.9—Whitworth, 1959 (35 in 9); Delaware, 1946
(35 in 9)

**Fewest Passes Intercepted By
(Min. 150 Attempts)**
1—Gettysburg, 1972 (175 attempts; 0 yards
returned)

**Highest Percentage Intercepted By**
(Min. 150 atts.) 21.7%—Stephen F. Austin, 1949
(35 of 161)
(Min. 275 atts.) 11.8%—Missouri-Rolla, 1978
(35 of 297)

**Most Touchdowns on Interception Returns**
7—Gardner-Webb, 1992 (35 interceptions);
Fort Valley St., 1991 (15 interceptions); Virginia Union, 1986 (31 interceptions)

**Lowest Passing Efficiency Rating Points
by Opponents
(Min. 250 Attempts)**
41.7—Fort Valley St., 1985 (allowed 283 attempts, 90 completions, 1,039 yards, 2 TDs
and intercepted 33)

# BLOCKED KICKS

**Most Blocked Kicks**
27—Winston-Salem, 1986 (16 punts, 7 field
goal attempts, 4 point-after-touchdown kicks)

## SCORING

**Fewest Points Allowed Per Game**
0.0—Albany St. (Ga.), 1960 (0 in 9 games)

**Most Points Allowed Per Game**
64.5—Rose-Hulman, 1961 (516 in 8)

**Most Defensive Extra-Point Opportunities**
3—Central Okla., 1989 (2 blocked kick returns, 1 interception; one scored); Northern Colo., 1988 (2 blocked kick returns, 1 interception; none scored)

## TURNOVERS (TAKEAWAYS) (From 1985)
### (Opponent's Passes Intercepted and Fumbles Recovered)

**Highest Margin of Turnovers Per Game Over Opponents**
2.5—North Ala., 1990 (plus 25 in 10; 14 giveaways vs. 39 takeaways); St. Joseph's (Ind.), 1986 (plus 25 in 10; 18 giveaways vs. 43 takeaways)

**Most Opponent's Turnovers Per Game**
5.09—Gardner-Webb, 1992 (56 in 11)

**Most Opponent's Turnovers**
56—Gardner-Webb, 1992 (35 interceptions, 21 fumble recoveries)

## ADDITIONAL RECORDS

**Most Consecutive Victories**
41—Missouri Valley, 1941-48 (did not field teams during 1943-45)
*Special reference:* Texas A&I, from Nov. 17, 1973, through Oct. 1, 1977 (a period during which it was not an NCAA-member college), won 42 consecutive games. The streak ended Oct. 8, 1977, with a 25-25 tie vs. Abilene Christian

**Most Consecutive Games Unbeaten (From 1946)**
38—Doane, 1965-70 (2 ties)
*Special reference:* Texas A&I, from Nov. 17, 1973, through Oct. 29, 1977 (a period during which it was not an NCAA-member college), was unbeaten during 46 games (including one tie). The streak ended Nov. 5, 1977, with a 7-6 loss to East Tex. St.

**Most Consecutive Games Without Being Shut Out**
178—North Dak. (from Oct. 7, 1967, through Nov. 10, 1984; ended with 41-0 loss to Northern Ariz., Aug. 31, 1985)

**Most Points Overcome to Win a Game**
27—New Haven (58) vs. West Chester (57), Oct. 5, 1990 (trailed 24-51 with 5:51 remaining in 3rd quarter)

**Most Consecutive Losses**
39—St. Paul's, 1948-53

**Most Consecutive Games Without a Victory**
49—Paine, 1954-61 (1 tie)

**Most Consecutive Games Without a Tie**
329—West Chester (from Oct. 26, 1945, to Oct. 31, 1980; ended with 24-24 tie vs. Cheyney, Nov. 8, 1980)

**Most Tie Games in a Season**
5—Wofford, 1948 (consecutive)

**Highest-Scoring Tie Game**
43-43—Trinity (Conn.) & Rensselaer, Oct. 11, 1969

**Most Consecutive Quarters Without Yielding a Rushing Touchdown**
51—Butler (from Sept. 25, 1982, to Oct. 15, 1983)

**Most Consecutive Point-After-Touchdown Kicks Made**
123—Liberty (1978-83)

**Most Improved Won-Lost Record**
11 games—Northern Mich., 1975 (13-1-0), including 3 Division II playoff victories, from 1974 (0-10-0)

# ANNUAL CHAMPIONS, ALL-TIME LEADERS

## TOTAL OFFENSE

### Career Yards

| Player, Team | Years | Plays | Yards |
|---|---|---|---|
| Earl Harvey, N.C. Central | 1985-88 | *2,045 | *10,667 |
| Sam Mannery, Calif. (Pa.) | 1987-90 | 1,669 | 9,125 |
| Andy Breault, Kutztown | 1989-92 | 1,459 | 8,975 |
| Steward Perez, Chadron St. | 1988-91 | 1,072 | 8,443 |
| Jim Lindsey, Abilene Christian | 1967-70 | 1,510 | 8,385 |
| Dave Walter, Michigan Tech | 1983-86 | 1,660 | 8,345 |
| Maurice Heard, Tuskegee | 1988-91 | 1,289 | 8,321 |
| Jack Hull, Grand Valley St. | 1988-91 | 1,196 | 8,221 |
| Doug Williams, Grambling | 1974-77 | 1,072 | 8,195 |
| Dave DenBraber, Ferris St. | 1984-87 | 1,522 | 8,115 |
| Tracy Kendall, Alabama A&M | 1988-91 | 1,480 | 8,112 |
| Bill Bair, Mansfield | 1989-92 | 1,352 | 8,101 |
| Ned Cox, Angelo St. | 1983-86 | 1,831 | 8,097 |
| Steve Wray, Franklin | 1978-82 | 1,370 | 7,606 |
| Carl Wright, Virginia Union | 1989-91 | 1,104 | 7,517 |

| Player, Team | Years | Plays | Yards |
|---|---|---|---|
| John St. Jacques, Santa Clara ........................ | 1988-89, 91-92 | 1,219 | 7,505 |
| John Schultz, Augustana (S.D.) ..................... | 1982-85 | 1,328 | 7,474 |
| Tom Nelson, St. Cloud St............................. | 1980-83 | 1,421 | 7,430 |
| Donald Smith, Langston ............................. | 1958-61 | 998 | 7,376 |
| Tom Bonds, Cal Lutheran ............................ | 1984-87 | 1,439 | 7,374 |
| Al Niemela, West Chester ........................... | 1985-88 | 1,259 | 7,359 |
| Loyal Proffitt, Abilene Christian ..................... | 1981-84 | 1,418 | 7,337 |
| Pat Brennan, Franklin .............................. | 1981-84 | 1,286 | 7,316 |
| Chris Crawford, Portland St. ........................ | 1985-88 | 1,178 | 7,310 |
| Ted Wahl, South Dak. St............................. | 1985-88 | 1,172 | 7,253 |
| Scott Butler, Delta St. .............................. | 1981-84 | 1,358 | 7,229 |
| Bruce Upstill, Col. of Emporia ...................... | 1960-63 | 922 | 7,122 |
| Mike Houston, St. Joseph's (Ind.) ................... | 1978-81 | 1,298 | 7,104 |

*Record.*

## Season Yards

| Player, Team | Year | Games | Plays | Yards |
|---|---|---|---|---|
| Chris Hegg, Northeast Mo. St. ...................... | †1985 | 11 | *594 | *3,782 |
| Tod Mayfield, West Tex. St........................... | †1986 | 11 | 555 | 3,533 |
| Rob Tomlinson, Cal St. Chico ....................... | †1989 | 10 | 533 | 3,504 |
| June Jones, Portland St. ............................ | †1976 | 11 | 465 | 3,463 |
| Bob Toledo, San Fran. St. ........................... | †1967 | 10 | 409 | 3,407 |
| Jayson Merrill, Western St........................... | †1991 | 10 | 337 | 3,400 |
| Richard Strasser, San Fran. St. ..................... | 1985 | 10 | 536 | 3,259 |
| Pat Brennan, Franklin .............................. | †1984 | 10 | 583 | 3,248 |
| Pat Brennan, Franklin .............................. | †1983 | 10 | 524 | 3,239 |
| Phil Basso, Liberty ................................. | 1984 | 11 | 456 | 3,227 |
| John Craven, Gardner-Webb ........................ | 1992 | 11 | 453 | 3,216 |
| Andy Breault, Kutztown ............................. | †1990 | 11 | 562 | 3,173 |
| Jim McMillan, Boise St. ............................. | †1974 | 10 | 403 | 3,101 |
| Tracy Kendall, Alabama A&M ........................ | 1989 | 11 | 451 | 3,079 |
| Thad Trujillo, Fort Lewis ............................ | 1992 | 10 | 477 | 3,047 |
| Darin Slack, Central Fla. ............................ | 1987 | 11 | 491 | 3,037 |
| Dan Koster, Southwest St............................ | 1983 | 11 | 567 | 3,032 |
| Jermaine Whitaker, N.M. Highlands .................. | 1992 | 11 | 422 | 3,009 |
| Earl Harvey, N.C. Central............................ | 1985 | 10 | 538 | 3,008 |
| Jim Zorn, Cal Poly Pomona ......................... | †1973 | 11 | 499 | 3,000 |

*Record.   † National champion.*

## Single-Game Yards

| Yds. | Player, Team (Opponent) | Date |
|---|---|---|
| 584 | Tracy Kendall, Alabama A&M (Clark Atlanta) .................................. | Nov. 4, 1989 |
| 571 | John Charles, Portland St. (Cal Poly SLO) ................................... | Nov. 16, 1991 |
| 562 | Bob Toledo, San Fran. St. (Cal St. Hayward) ................................ | Oct. 21, 1967 |
| 555 | A. J. Vaughn, Wayne St., Mich. (Wis.-Milwaukee).......................... | Sept. 30, 1967 |
| 536 | Earl Harvey, N.C. Central (Jackson St.) .................................... | Aug. 30, 1986 |
| 528 | Rob Tomlinson, Cal St. Chico (Southern Conn. St.) ......................... | Oct. 7, 1989 |
| 526 | Dwayne Butler, Dist. Columbia (Central St., Ohio) .......................... | Nov. 20, 1982 |
| 526 | Dennis Shaw, San Diego St. (Southern Miss.)............................... | Nov. 9, 1968 |
| 519 | Maurice Heard, Tuskegee (Alabama A&M) .................................. | Nov. 10, 1990 |
| 517 | Jeff Petrucci, Calif., Pa. (Edinboro) ....................................... | Nov. 9, 1968 |
| 506 | Kurt Otto, North Dak. (Texas A&I) ......................................... | Sept. 13, 1986 |
| 505 | Jim Zorn, Cal Poly Pomona (Southern Utah) ................................ | Sept. 14, 1974 |

## Career Yards Per Game

| Player, Team | Years | Games | Plays | Yards | Yd. PG |
|---|---|---|---|---|---|
| Jayson Merrill, Western St................. | 1990-91 | 20 | 641 | 5,619 | *281.0 |
| Chris Petersen, UC Davis ................. | 1985-86 | 20 | 735 | 5,532 | 276.6 |
| Tim Von Dulm, Portland St. ............... | 1969-70 | 20 | 989 | 5,501 | 275.1 |
| Troy Mott, Wayne St. (Neb.)............... | 1991-92 | 20 | 943 | 5,212 | 260.6 |
| Earl Harvey, N.C. Central................. | 1985-88 | 41 | *2,045 | *10,667 | 260.2 |
| Chris Hegg, Northeast Mo. St. ............ | ‡1982, 84-85 | 21 | 932 | 5,412 | 257.7 |
| Jim Zorn, Cal Poly Pomona ............... | 1973-74 | 21 | 946 | 5,364 | 255.4 |
| Pat Brennan, Franklin .................... | 1981-84 | 30 | 1,286 | 7,316 | 243.9 |
| June Jones, Hawaii/Portland St. .......... | 1974, 75-76 | 23 | 760 | 5,601 | 243.5 |
| Carl Wright, Virginia Union............... | 1989-91 | 31 | 1,104 | 7,517 | 242.5 |
| Steve Wray, Franklin ..................... | 1978-82 | 32 | 1,370 | 7,606 | 237.7 |
| Jim Lindsey, Abilene Christian ........... | 1967-70 | 36 | 1,510 | 8,385 | 232.9 |

*Record.   ‡ Played in one game at Northern Iowa in 1982.*

## Season Yards Per Game

| Player, Team | Year | Games | Plays | Yards | Yd. PG |
|---|---|---|---|---|---|
| Rob Tomlinson, Cal St. Chico | †1989 | 10 | 533 | 3,504 | *350.4 |
| Chris Hegg, Northeast Mo. St. | †1985 | 11 | *594 | *3,782 | 343.8 |
| Bob Toledo, San Fran. St. | †1967 | 10 | 409 | 3,407 | 340.7 |
| Jayson Merrill, Western St. | †1991 | 10 | 337 | 3,400 | 340.0 |
| John Charles, Portland St. | †1992 | 8 | 303 | 2,708 | 338.5 |
| George Bork, Northern Ill. | †1963 | 9 | 413 | 2,945 | 327.2 |
| Richard Strasser, San Fran. St. | 1985 | 10 | 536 | 3,259 | 325.9 |
| Pat Brennan, Franklin | †1984 | 10 | 583 | 3,248 | 324.8 |
| Pat Brennan, Franklin | †1983 | 10 | 524 | 3,239 | 323.9 |
| Tod Mayfield, West Tex. St. | †1986 | 11 | 555 | 3,533 | 321.2 |
| June Jones, Portland St. | †1976 | 11 | 465 | 3,463 | 314.8 |
| Jim McMillan, Boise St. | †1974 | 10 | 403 | 3,101 | 310.1 |

* Record.   † National champion.

## Annual Champions

| Year | Player, Team | Class | Plays | Yards |
|---|---|---|---|---|
| 1946 | Buster Dixon, Abilene Christian | Sr. | 170 | 960 |
| 1947 | Jim Peterson, Hanover | So. | 108 | 1,449 |
| 1948 | Jim Peterson, Hanover | Jr. | 130 | 1,589 |
| 1949 | Connie Callahan, Morningside | Sr. | 311 | 2,006 |
| 1950 | Bob Heimerdinger, Northern Ill. | Jr. | 286 | 1,782 |
| 1951 | Bob Heimerdinger, Northern Ill. | Sr. | 292 | 1,775 |
| 1952 | Don Gottlob, Sam Houston St. | Sr. | 303 | 2,470 |
| 1953 | Ralph Capitani, Northern Iowa | Jr. | 317 | 1,755 |
| 1954 | Bill Engelhardt, Nebraska-Omaha | So. | 243 | 1,645 |
| 1955 | Jim Stehlin, Brandeis | Sr. | 222 | 1,455 |
| 1956 | Dick Jamieson, Bradley | So. | 240 | 1,925 |
| 1957 | Stan Jackson, Cal Poly Pomona | Jr. | 301 | 2,145 |
| 1958 | Stan Jackson, Cal Poly Pomona | Sr. | 334 | 2,478 |
| 1959 | Gary Campbell, Whittier | Sr. | 309 | 2,383 |
| 1960 | Charles Miller, Austin | Sr. | 287 | 1,966 |
| 1961 | Denny Spurlock, Whitworth | Sr. | 224 | 1,684 |
| 1962 | George Bork, Northern Ill. | Jr. | 397 | 2,398 |
| 1963 | George Bork, Northern Ill. | Sr. | 413 | 2,945 |
| 1964 | Jerry Bishop, Austin | Jr. | 332 | 2,152 |
| 1965 | Ron Christian, Northern Ill. | Sr. | 377 | 2,307 |
| 1966 | Joe Stetser, Cal St. Chico | Jr. | 406 | 2,382 |
| 1967 | Bob Toledo, San Fran. St. | Sr. | 409 | 3,407 |
| 1968 | Terry Bradshaw, Louisiana Tech | Jr. | 426 | 2,987 |
| 1969 | Tim Von Dulm, Portland St. | Jr. | 462 | 2,736 |

*Beginning in 1970, ranked on per-game (instead of total) yards*

| Year | Player, Team | Cl. | G | Plays | Yards | Avg. |
|---|---|---|---|---|---|---|
| 1970 | Jim Lindsey, Abilene Christian | Sr. | 9 | 440 | 2,654 | 294.9 |
| 1971 | Randy Mattingly, Evansville | Jr. | 9 | 402 | 2,234 | 248.2 |
| 1972 | Bob Biggs, UC Davis | Sr. | 9 | 381 | 2,356 | 261.8 |
| 1973 | Jim Zorn, Cal Poly Pomona | Jr. | 11 | 499 | 3,000 | 272.7 |
| 1974 | Jim McMillan, Boise St. | Sr. | 10 | 403 | 3,101 | 310.1 |
| 1975 | Lynn Hieber, Indiana (Pa.) | Sr. | 10 | 402 | 2,503 | 250.3 |
| 1976 | June Jones, Portland St. | Sr. | 11 | 465 | 3,463 | 314.8 |
| 1977 | Steve Mariucci, Northern Mich. | Sr. | 8 | 270 | 1,780 | 222.5 |
| 1978 | Charlie Thompson, Western St. | Jr. | 9 | 304 | 2,138 | 237.6 |
| 1979 | Phil Kessel, Northern Mich. | Jr. | 9 | 368 | 2,164 | 240.4 |
| 1980 | Curt Strasheim, Southwest St. | Jr. | 10 | 501 | 2,565 | 256.5 |
| 1981 | Steve Wray, Franklin | Jr. | 10 | 488 | 2,726 | 272.6 |
| 1982 | Steve Wray, Franklin | Sr. | 8 | 382 | 2,114 | 264.3 |
| 1983 | Pat Brennan, Franklin | Jr. | 10 | 524 | 3,239 | 323.9 |
| 1984 | Pat Brennan, Franklin | Sr. | 10 | 583 | 3,248 | 324.8 |
| 1985 | Chris Hegg, Northeast Mo. St. | Sr. | 11 | *594 | *3,782 | 343.8 |
| 1986 | Tod Mayfield, West Tex. St. | Sr. | 11 | 555 | 3,533 | 312.2 |
| 1987 | Randy Hobson, Evansville | Sr. | 10 | 457 | 2,964 | 296.4 |
| 1988 | Mark Sedinger, Northern Colo. | Sr. | 10 | 413 | 2,828 | 282.8 |
| 1989 | Rob Tomlinson, Cal St. Chico | So. | 10 | 533 | 3,504 | *350.4 |
| 1990 | Andy Breault, Kutztown | Jr. | 11 | 562 | 3,173 | 288.5 |
| 1991 | Jayson Merrill, Western St. | Sr. | 10 | 337 | 3,400 | 340.0 |
| 1992 | John Charles, Portland St. | Sr. | 8 | 303 | 2,708 | 338.5 |

* Record.

210

# RUSHING

## Career Yards

| Player, Team | Years | Plays | Yards | Avg. |
|---|---|---|---|---|
| Johnny Bailey, Texas A&I | 1986–89 | 885 | *6,320 | 7.14 |
| Shawn Graves, Wofford | 1989–92 | 730 | 5,128 | 7.02 |
| Chris Cobb, Eastern Ill. | 1976–79 | 930 | 5,042 | 5.42 |
| Harry Jackson, St. Cloud St. | 1986–89 | 915 | 4,890 | 5.34 |
| Jerry Linton, Panhandle St. | 1959–62 | 648 | 4,839 | 7.47 |
| Jim VanWagner, Michigan Tech | 1973–76 | 958 | 4,788 | 5.00 |
| Heath Sherman, Texas A&I | 1985–88 | 804 | 4,654 | 5.79 |
| Steve Roberts, Butler | 1986–89 | 1,026 | 4,623 | 4.51 |
| Don Aleksiewicz, Hobart | 1969–72 | 819 | 4,525 | 5.53 |
| Dale Mills, Northeast Mo. St. | 1957–60 | 751 | 4,502 | 5.99 |
| Leo Lewis, Lincoln (Mo.) | 1951–54 | 623 | 4,458 | 7.16 |
| Bernie Peeters, Luther | 1968–71 | *1,072 | 4,435 | 4.14 |
| Larry Schreiber, Tennessee Tech | 1966–69 | 878 | 4,421 | 5.04 |
| Brad Rowland, McMurry | 1947–50 | 683 | 4,347 | 6.36 |
| Vincent Allen, Indiana St. | 1973–75, 77 | 832 | 4,335 | 5.21 |
| Ronald Moore, Pittsburg St. | 1989–92 | 619 | 4,299 | 6.95 |
| Bill Rhodes, Western St. | 1953–56 | 506 | 4,294 | *8.49 |
| Lem Harkey, Col. of Emporia | 1951–54 | 502 | 4,232 | 8.43 |
| Curtis Delgardo, Portland St. | 1987–90 | 703 | 4,178 | 5.94 |
| Ricke Stonewall, Millersville | 1981–84 | 648 | 4,169 | 6.43 |

* Record.

## Season Yards

| Player, Team | Year | Games | Plays | Yards | Avg. |
|---|---|---|---|---|---|
| Johnny Bailey, Texas A&I | †1986 | 11 | 271 | *2,011 | 7.42 |
| Ronald Moore, Pittsburg St. | 1992 | 11 | 239 | 1,864 | 7.80 |
| Zed Robinson, Southern Utah | 1991 | 11 | 254 | 1,828 | 7.20 |
| Jim Holder, Panhandle St. | †1963 | 10 | 275 | 1,775 | 6.45 |
| Mike Thomas, Nevada-Las Vegas | †1973 | 11 | 274 | 1,741 | 6.35 |
| Roger Graham, New Haven | †1992 | 10 | 200 | 1,717 | 8.59 |
| Terry Metcalf, Long Beach St. | 1971 | 12 | 273 | 1,673 | 6.13 |
| Troy Mills, Cal St. Sacramento | 1991 | 10 | 223 | 1,668 | 7.48 |
| Leon Burns, Long Beach St. | †1969 | 11 | *350 | 1,659 | 4.74 |
| Chad Guthrie, Northeast Mo. St. | 1991 | 11 | 302 | 1,649 | 5.46 |
| Bob White, Western N. Mex. | †1951 | 9 | 202 | 1,643 | 8.13 |
| Thelbert Withers, N.M. Highlands | 1992 | 11 | 240 | 1,621 | 6.75 |
| Don Aleksiewicz, Hobart | †1971 | 9 | 276 | 1,616 | 5.86 |

* Record. † National champion.

## Single-Game Yards

| Yds. | Player, Team (Opponent) | Date |
|---|---|---|
| 382 | Kelly Ellis, Northern Iowa (Western Ill.) | Oct. 13, 1979 |
| 373 | Dallas Garber, Marietta (Wash. & Jeff.) | Nov. 7, 1959 |
| 370 | Jim Baier, Wis.-River Falls (Wis.-Stevens Point) | Nov. 5, 1966 |
| 370 | Jim Hissam, Marietta (Bethany, W. Va.) | Nov. 15, 1958 |
| 367 | Don Polkinghorne, Washington, Mo. (Wash. & Lee) | Nov. 23, 1957 |
| 363 | Richie Weaver, Widener (Moravian) | Oct. 17, 1970 |
| 356 | Ole Gunderson, St. Olaf (Monmouth, Ill.) | Oct. 11, 1969 |
| 350 | Ricke Stonewall, Millersville (New Haven) | Nov. 13, 1982 |
| 343 | Zed Robinson, Southern Utah (Santa Clara) | Oct. 12, 1991 |
| 343 | Jesse Lakes, Central Mich. (Wis.-Milwaukee) | Sept. 27, 1969 |
| 337 | Harry Jackson, St. Cloud St. (South Dak.) | Nov. 4, 1989 |
| 333 | Thelbert Withers, N.M. Highlands (Fort Lewis) | Oct. 17, 1992 |
| 327 | Bill Rhodes, Western St. (Adams St.) | Oct. 20, 1956 |
| 323 | Shawn Graves, Wofford (Lenoir-Rhyne) | Sept. 15, 1990 |
| 323 | Gary Nelson, Wartburg (Buena Vista) | Oct. 26, 1968 |

## Career Yards Per Game

| Player, Team | Years | Games | Plays | Yards | Yd. PG |
|---|---|---|---|---|---|
| Johnny Bailey, Texas A&I | 1986–89 | 39 | 885 | *6,320 | *162.1 |
| Ole Gunderson, St. Olaf | 1969–71 | 27 | 639 | 4,060 | 150.4 |
| Brad Hustad, Luther | 1957–59 | 27 | 655 | 3,943 | 146.0 |
| Joe Iacone, West Chester | 1960–62 | 27 | 565 | 3,767 | 139.5 |
| Billy Johnson, Widener | 1971–73 | 28 | 411 | 3,737 | 133.5 |
| Don Aleksiewicz, Hobart | 1969–72 | 34 | 819 | 4,525 | 133.1 |
| Jim VanWagner, Michigan Tech | 1973–76 | 36 | 958 | 4,788 | 133.0 |
| Steve Roberts, Butler | 1986–89 | 35 | 1,026 | 4,623 | 132.1 |

* Record.

## Season Yards Per Game

| Player, Team | Year | Games | Plays | Yards | TD | Yd. PG |
|---|---|---|---|---|---|---|
| Johnny Bailey, Texas A&I | †1986 | 11 | 271 | *2,011 | 18 | *182.8 |
| Bob White, Western N. Mex. | †1951 | 9 | 202 | 1,643 | 20 | 182.6 |
| Kevin Mitchell, Saginaw Valley | †1989 | 8 | 236 | 1,460 | 6 | 182.5 |
| Don Aleksiewicz, Hobart | †1971 | 9 | 276 | 1,616 | 19 | 179.6 |
| Jim Holder, Panhandle St. | †1963 | 10 | 275 | 1,775 | 9 | 177.5 |
| Jim Baier, Wis.-River Falls | †1966 | 9 | 240 | 1,587 | 17 | 176.3 |
| Billy Johnson, Widener | †1972 | 9 | 148 | 1,556 | 23 | 172.9 |
| Hank Treesh, Hanover | †1948 | 8 | 100 | 1,383 | 17 | 172.9 |
| Dave Kiarsis, Trinity (Conn.) | †1970 | 8 | 201 | 1,374 | 10 | 171.8 |
| Roger Graham, New Haven | †1992 | 10 | 200 | 1,717 | 22 | 171.7 |

*Record.  † National champion.*

## Annual Champions

| Year | Player, Team | Class | Plays | Yards |
|---|---|---|---|---|
| 1946 | V. T. Smith, Abilene Christian | So. | 99 | 733 |
| 1947 | John Williams, Jacksonville St. | Jr. | 150 | 931 |
| 1948 | Hank Treesh, Hanover | Jr. | 100 | 1,383 |
| 1949 | Odie Posey, Southern-B.R. | Jr. | 121 | 1,399 |
| 1950 | Meriel Michelson, Eastern Wash. | Sr. | 180 | 1,234 |
| 1951 | Bob White, Western N. Mex. | Jr. | 202 | 1,643 |
| 1952 | Al Conway, William Jewell | Sr. | 134 | 1,325 |
| 1953 | Elroy Payne, McMurry | So. | 183 | 1,274 |
| 1954 | Lem Harkey, Col. of Emporia | Sr. | 121 | 1,146 |
| 1955 | Gene Scott, Centre | Sr. | 107 | 1,138 |
| 1956 | Bill Rhodes, Western St. | Sr. | 130 | 1,200 |
| 1957 | Brad Hustad, Luther | So. | 219 | 1,401 |
| 1958 | Dale Mills, Northeast Mo. St. | So. | 186 | 1,358 |
| 1959 | Dale Mills, Northeast Mo. St. | Jr. | 248 | 1,385 |
| 1960 | Joe Iacone, West Chester | So. | 199 | 1,438 |
| 1961 | Bobby Lisa, St. Mary (Kan.) | Jr. | 156 | 1,082 |
| 1962 | Jerry Linton, Panhandle St. | Sr. | 272 | 1,483 |
| 1963 | Jim Holder, Panhandle St. | Sr. | 275 | 1,775 |
| 1964 | Jim Allison, San Diego St. | Sr. | 174 | 1,186 |
| 1965 | Allen Smith, Findlay | Jr. | 207 | 1,240 |
| 1966 | Jim Baier, Wis.-River Falls | Sr. | 240 | 1,587 |
| 1967 | Dickie Moore, Western Ky. | Jr. | 208 | 1,444 |
| 1968 | Howard Stevens, Randolph-Macon | Fr. | 191 | 1,468 |
| 1969 | Leon Burns, Long Beach St. | Jr. | *350 | 1,659 |

*Beginning in 1970, ranked on per-game (instead of total) yards*

| Year | Player, Team | Cl. | G | Plays | Yards | Avg. |
|---|---|---|---|---|---|---|
| 1970 | Dave Kiarsis, Trinity (Conn.) | Sr. | 8 | 201 | 1,374 | 171.8 |
| 1971 | Don Aleksiewicz, Hobart | Jr. | 9 | 276 | 1,616 | 179.6 |
| 1972 | Billy Johnson, Widener | So. | 9 | 148 | 1,556 | 172.9 |
| 1973 | Mike Thomas, Nevada-Las Vegas | Jr. | 11 | 274 | 1,741 | 158.3 |
| 1974 | Jim VanWagner, Michigan Tech | So. | 9 | 246 | 1,453 | 161.4 |
| 1975 | Jim VanWagner, Michigan Tech | Jr. | 9 | 289 | 1,331 | 147.9 |
| 1976 | Ted McKnight, Minn.-Duluth | Sr. | 10 | 220 | 1,482 | 148.2 |
| 1977 | Bill Burnham, New Hampshire | Sr. | 10 | 281 | 1,422 | 142.2 |
| 1978 | Mike Harris, Northeast Mo. St. | Sr. | 11 | 329 | 1,598 | 145.3 |
| 1979 | Chris Cobb, Eastern Ill. | Sr. | 11 | 293 | 1,609 | 146.3 |
| 1980 | Louis Jackson, Cal Poly SLO | Sr. | 10 | 287 | 1,424 | 142.4 |
| 1981 | Rick Porter, Slippery Rock | Sr. | 9 | 208 | 1,179 | 131.0 |
| 1982 | Ricke Stonewall, Millersville | So. | 10 | 191 | 1,387 | 138.7 |
| 1983 | Mark Corbin, Central St. (Ohio) | So. | 10 | 208 | 1,502 | 150.2 |
| 1984 | Charles Sanders, Slippery Rock | Jr. | 10 | 269 | 1,280 | 128.0 |
| 1985 | Dan Sonnek, South Dak. St. | So. | 11 | 303 | 1,518 | 138.0 |
| 1986 | Johnny Bailey, Texas A&I | Fr. | 11 | 271 | *2,011 | *182.8 |
| 1987 | Johnny Bailey, Texas A&I | So. | 10 | 217 | 1,598 | 159.8 |
| 1988 | Johnny Bailey, Texas A&I | Jr. | 10 | 229 | 1,442 | 144.2 |
| 1989 | Kevin Mitchell, Saginaw Valley | Jr. | 8 | 236 | 1,460 | 182.5 |
| 1990 | David Jones, Chadron St. | Sr. | 10 | 225 | 1,570 | 157.0 |
| 1991 | Quincy Tillmon, Emporia St. | So. | 9 | 259 | 1,544 | 171.6 |
| 1992 | Roger Graham, New Haven | So. | 10 | 200 | 1,717 | 171.7 |

*Record.*

# PASSING

## Career Passing Efficiency
### (Minimum 375 Completions)

| Player, Team | Years | Att. | Cmp. | Int. | Pct. | Yds. | TD | Pts. |
|---|---|---|---|---|---|---|---|---|
| Chris Petersen, UC Davis ........... | 1985-86 | 553 | 385 | 13 | *.696 | 4,988 | 39 | *164.0 |
| Jim McMillan, Boise St. ............. | 1971-74 | 640 | 382 | 29 | .597 | 5,508 | 58 | 152.8 |
| Jack Hull, Grand Valley St.......... | 1988-91 | 835 | 485 | 22 | .581 | 7,120 | 64 | 149.7 |
| Bruce Upstill, Col. of Emporia ...... | 1960-63 | 769 | 438 | 36 | .570 | 6,935 | 48 | 144.0 |
| George Bork, Northern Ill. ......... | 1960-63 | 902 | 577 | 33 | .640 | 6,782 | 60 | 141.8 |
| Steve Mariucci, Northern Mich. ..... | 1974-77 | 678 | 380 | 33 | .561 | 6,022 | 41 | 140.9 |
| Scott Barry, UC Davis .............. | 1982-84 | 588 | 377 | 16 | .641 | 4,421 | 33 | 140.4 |
| June Jones, Hawaii/Portland St. .... | 1974, 75-76 | 666 | 376 | 35 | .565 | 5,809 | 41 | 139.5 |
| Doug Williams, Grambling ......... | 1974-77 | 1,009 | 484 | 52 | .480 | 8,411 | *93 | 138.1 |
| Chris Crawford, Portland St. ........ | 1985-88 | 954 | 588 | 35 | .616 | 7,543 | 48 | 137.3 |
| Trevor Spradley, Southwest Baptist . | 1990-92 | 712 | 441 | 27 | .619 | 5,881 | 29 | 137.2 |
| Dan Miles, Southern Ore. .......... | 1964-67 | 871 | 577 | 56 | .662 | 6,531 | 52 | 136.1 |
| Al Niemela, West Chester .......... | 1985-88 | 1,063 | 600 | 36 | .564 | 7,853 | 73 | 134.4 |
| Steward Perez, Chadron St......... | 1988-91 | 1,015 | 565 | 60 | .557 | 8,186 | 69 | 134.0 |
| Denny Spurlock, Whitworth ........ | 1958-61 | 723 | 388 | 48 | .537 | 5,526 | 63 | 133.4 |
| Jeff Tisdel, Nevada ................. | 1974-77 | 776 | 394 | 34 | .508 | 6,098 | 59 | 133.1 |

\* Record.

## Season Passing Efficiency
### (Minimum 15 Attempts Per Game)

| Player, Team | Year | G | Att. | Cmp. | Int. | Pct. | Yds. | TD | Pts. |
|---|---|---|---|---|---|---|---|---|---|
| Boyd Crawford, Col. of Idaho ....... | †1953 | 8 | 120 | 72 | 6 | .600 | 1,462 | 21 | *210.1 |
| Chuck Green, Wittenberg ........... | †1963 | 9 | 182 | 114 | 8 | .626 | 2,181 | 19 | 189.0 |
| Jayson Merrill, Western St........... | †1991 | 10 | 309 | 195 | 11 | .631 | 3,484 | 35 | 187.9 |
| Jim Feely, Johns Hopkins .......... | †1967 | 7 | 110 | 69 | 5 | .627 | 1,264 | 12 | 186.2 |
| John Charles, Portland St. .......... | 1991 | 11 | 247 | 147 | 7 | .595 | 2,619 | 32 | 185.5 |
| Steve Smith, Western St. ............ | †1992 | 10 | 271 | 180 | 5 | .664 | 2,719 | 30 | 183.5 |
| Jim Peterson, Hanover ............. | †1948 | 8 | 125 | 81 | 12 | .648 | 1,571 | 12 | 182.9 |
| John Wristen, Southern Colo........ | †1982 | 8 | 121 | 68 | 2 | .562 | 1,358 | 13 | 182.5 |
| John Charles, Portland St. .......... | 1992 | 8 | 263 | 179 | 7 | .681 | 2,770 | 24 | 181.3 |
| Richard Basil, Savannah St......... | †1989 | 9 | 211 | 120 | 7 | .569 | 2,148 | 29 | 180.9 |
| Jim Cahoon, Ripon ................. | †1964 | 8 | 127 | 74 | 7 | .583 | 1,206 | 19 | 176.4 |
| Ken Suhl, New Haven .............. | 1992 | 10 | 239 | 148 | 5 | .619 | 2,336 | 26 | 175.7 |
| Tony Aliucci, Indiana (Pa.) ......... | †1990 | 10 | 181 | 111 | 10 | .613 | 1,801 | 21 | 172.0 |
| John Costello, Widener ............. | †1956 | 9 | 149 | 74 | 10 | .497 | 1,702 | 17 | 169.8 |
| Kurt Coduti, Michigan Tech ........ | 1992 | 9 | 155 | 92 | 3 | .594 | 1,518 | 15 | 169.7 |
| Chris Petersen, UC Davis .......... | †1985 | 10 | 242 | 167 | 6 | .690 | 2,366 | 17 | 169.4 |
| Mike Rieker, Lehigh ................ | †1977 | 11 | 230 | 137 | 14 | .596 | 2,431 | 23 | 169.2 |
| Steve Michuta, Grand Valley St..... | †1981 | 8 | 173 | 114 | 11 | .659 | 1,702 | 17 | 168.3 |
| James Armendariz, Southern Utah.. | 1991 | 11 | 184 | 109 | 5 | .592 | 1,839 | 17 | 168.0 |
| Mitch Nicholson, Winston-Salem ... | 1990 | 11 | 171 | 85 | 5 | .497 | 1,651 | 22 | 167.2 |

\* Record. † National champion.

## Annual Passing Efficiency Leaders
### (Minimum 11 Attempts Per Game)

**1948**—Jim Peterson, Hanover, 182.9; **1949**—John Ford, Hardin-Simmons, 179.6; **1950**—Edward Ludorf, Trinity (Conn.), 167.8; **1951**—Vic Lesch, Western Ill., 182.4; **1952**—Jim Gray, East Tex. St., 205.5; **1953**—Boyd Crawford, Col. of Idaho, *210.1; **1954**—Bill Englehardt, Nebraska-Omaha, 170.7; **1955**—Robert Alexander, Trinity (Conn.), 208.7; **1956**—John Costello, Widener, 169.8; **1957**—Doug Maison, Hillsdale, 200.0; **1958**—Kurt Duecker, Ripon, 161.7; **1959**—Fred Whitmire, Humboldt St., 188.7; **1960**—Larry Cline, Otterbein, 195.2.

\* Record.

### (Minimum 15 Attempts Per Game)

| Year | Player, Team | G | Att. | Cmp. | Int. | Pct. | Yds. | TD | Pts. |
|---|---|---|---|---|---|---|---|---|---|
| 1961 | Denny Spurlock, Whitworth ........... | 10 | 189 | 115 | 16 | .609 | 1,708 | 26 | 165.2 |
| 1962 | Roy Curry, Jackson St................. | 10 | 194 | 104 | 8 | .536 | 1,862 | 15 | 151.5 |
| 1963 | Chuck Green, Wittenberg ............. | 9 | 182 | 114 | 8 | .626 | 2,181 | 19 | 189.0 |
| 1964 | Jim Cahoon, Ripon ................... | 8 | 127 | 74 | 7 | .583 | 1,206 | 19 | 176.4 |
| 1965 | Ed Buzzell, Ottawa ................... | 9 | 238 | 118 | 5 | .496 | 2,170 | 31 | 165.0 |
| 1966 | Jim Alcorn, Clarion .................. | 9 | 199 | 107 | 4 | .538 | 1,714 | 24 | 161.9 |
| 1967 | Jim Feely, Johns Hopkins ............. | 7 | 110 | 69 | 5 | .627 | 1,264 | 12 | 186.2 |
| 1968 | Larry Green, Doane .................. | 9 | 182 | 97 | 7 | .533 | 1,592 | 22 | 159.0 |
| 1969 | George Kaplan, Northern Colo. ....... | 9 | 155 | 92 | 5 | .594 | 1,396 | 16 | 162.6 |
| 1970 | Gary Wichard, LIU-C. W. Post ......... | 9 | 186 | 100 | 5 | .538 | 1,527 | 12 | 138.6 |

| Year | Player, Team | G | Att. | Cmp. | Int. | Pct. | Yds. | TD | Pts. |
|------|--------------|---|------|------|------|------|------|-----|------|
| 1971 | Peter Mackey, Middlebury............. | 8 | 180 | 101 | 4 | .561 | 1,597 | 19 | 161.0 |
| 1972 | David Hamilton, Fort Valley St......... | 9 | 180 | 99 | 9 | .550 | 1,571 | 24 | 162.3 |
| 1973 | Jim McMillan, Boise St. ............... | 11 | 179 | 110 | 5 | .615 | 1,525 | 17 | 158.8 |
| 1974 | Jim McMillan, Boise St. ............... | 10 | 313 | 192 | 15 | .613 | 2,900 | 33 | 164.4 |
| 1975 | Joe Sterrett, Lehigh .................. | 11 | 228 | 135 | 13 | .592 | 2,114 | 22 | 157.5 |
| 1976 | Mike Makings, Western St. ............ | 10 | 179 | 90 | 6 | .503 | 1,617 | 14 | 145.3 |
| 1977 | Mike Rieker, Lehigh .................. | 11 | 230 | 137 | 14 | .596 | 2,431 | 23 | 169.2 |
| 1978 | Mike Moroski, UC Davis .............. | 10 | 205 | 119 | 9 | .581 | 1,689 | 17 | 145.9 |

*(See page 216 for annual leaders beginning in 1979.)*

## Career Yards

| Player, Team | Years | Att. | Cmp. | Int. | Pct. | Yards | TD |
|--------------|-------|------|------|------|------|-------|-----|
| Earl Harvey, N.C. Central.......... | 1985-88 | *1,442 | *690 | 81 | .479 | *10,621 | 86 |
| Andy Breault, Kutztown........... | 1989-92 | 1,259 | 733 | 63 | .582 | 9,086 | 86 |
| Sam Mannery, Calif. (Pa.) ......... | 1987-90 | 1,283 | 649 | 68 | .506 | 8,680 | 64 |
| Dave DenBraber, Ferris St. ........ | 1984-87 | 1,254 | 661 | 45 | .527 | 8,536 | 52 |
| Jim Lindsey, Abilene Christian .... | 1967-70 | 1,237 | 642 | 69 | .519 | 8,521 | 61 |
| Maurice Heard, Tuskegee ........ | 1988-91 | 1,134 | 556 | 54 | .490 | 8,434 | 87 |
| Doug Williams, Grambling ........ | 1974-77 | 1,009 | 484 | 52 | .480 | 8,411 | *93 |
| Steward Perez, Chadron St....... | 1988-91 | 1,015 | 565 | 60 | .557 | 8,186 | 69 |
| Steve Wray, Franklin .............. | 1978-82 | 1,230 | 592 | 48 | .481 | 8,123 | 62 |
| John St. Jacques, Santa Clara .... | 1988-89, 91-92 | 1,060 | 543 | 36 | .512 | 7,968 | 68 |
| Al Niemela, West Chester ........ | 1985-88 | 1,063 | 600 | 36 | .564 | 7,853 | 73 |
| Ned Cox, Angelo St. .............. | 1983-86 | 1,205 | 589 | 58 | .489 | 7,843 | 56 |
| Loyal Proffitt, Abilene Christian ... | 1981-84 | 1,157 | 550 | 80 | .475 | 7,824 | 54 |
| Tom Bonds, Cal Lutheran ........ | 1984-87 | 1,137 | 625 | 52 | .550 | 7,773 | 57 |
| Pat Brennan, Franklin ............ | 1981-84 | 1,123 | 535 | 62 | .476 | 7,717 | 53 |
| Chris Crawford, Portland St. ...... | 1985-88 | 954 | 588 | 35 | .616 | 7,543 | 48 |
| Bill Bair, Mansfield ............... | 1989-92 | 1,041 | 617 | 44 | .593 | 7,531 | 56 |
| Chris Fagan, Millersville ......... | 1989-92 | 1,098 | 556 | 52 | .506 | 7,362 | 48 |
| Tom Bertoldi, Northern Mich. ..... | 1980-83 | 987 | 524 | 50 | .531 | 7,330 | 45 |
| Tracy Kendall, Alabama A&M ..... | 1988-91 | 1,117 | 564 | 54 | .505 | 7,205 | 49 |
| Jack Hull, Grand Valley St........ | 1988-91 | 835 | 485 | 22 | .581 | 7,120 | 64 |
| Bob Caress, Bradley .............. | 1962-65 | 1,156 | 610 | 62 | .528 | 7,115 | 64 |
| Greg Calcagno, Santa Clara ..... | 1984-87 | 1,004 | 566 | 39 | .564 | 7,011 | 43 |
| Kim McQuilken, Lehigh .......... | 1971-73 | 925 | 516 | 42 | .558 | 6,996 | 37 |
| Bruce Upstill, Emporia St......... | 1960-63 | 769 | 438 | 36 | .570 | 6,935 | 48 |

\* *Record.*

## Season Yards

| Player, Team | Year | Games | Att. | Cmp. | Int. | Pct. | Yards | TD |
|--------------|------|-------|------|------|------|------|-------|-----|
| Chris Hegg, Northeast Mo. St. ........ | 1985 | 11 | 503 | 284 | 20 | .565 | *3,741 | 32 |
| Tod Mayfield, West Tex. St............ | 1986 | 11 | *515 | *317 | 20 | .615 | 3,664 | 31 |
| June Jones, Portland St. ............. | †1976 | 11 | 423 | 238 | 24 | .563 | 3,518 | 25 |
| Bob Toledo, San Fran. St. ............ | 1967 | 10 | 396 | 211 | 24 | .533 | 3,513 | *45 |
| Pat Brennan, Franklin ................ | 1983 | 10 | 458 | 226 | 30 | .493 | 3,491 | 25 |
| Jayson Merrill, Western St............ | †1991 | 10 | 309 | 195 | 11 | .631 | 3,484 | 35 |
| Pat Brennan, Franklin ................ | 1984 | 10 | 502 | 238 | 20 | .474 | 3,340 | 18 |
| Phil Basso, Liberty .................. | 1984 | 11 | 426 | 250 | 15 | .587 | 3,326 | 24 |
| John Craven, Gardner-Webb ........ | 1992 | 11 | 423 | 240 | 16 | .567 | 3,320 | 32 |
| Richard Strasser, San Fran. St. ....... | 1985 | 10 | 452 | 250 | 19 | .553 | 3,317 | 20 |
| Rob Tomlinson, Cal St. Chico ......... | 1989 | 10 | 437 | 254 | 16 | .581 | 3,237 | 19 |
| Earl Harvey, N.C. Central............ | 1985 | 10 | 392 | 188 | 19 | .480 | 3,190 | 22 |
| Andy Breault, Kutztown.............. | 1990 | 11 | 474 | 269 | 19 | .568 | 3,143 | 23 |
| Jay McLucas, New Haven ............ | 1990 | 10 | 402 | 209 | 18 | .520 | 3,114 | 23 |
| George Bork, Northern Ill. ........... | †1963 | 9 | 374 | 244 | 12 | .652 | 3,077 | 32 |
| Darin Slack, Central Fla. ............. | 1987 | 11 | 420 | 219 | 18 | .521 | 3,054 | 26 |
| Randy Hobson, Evansville ........... | 1987 | 10 | 386 | 242 | 16 | .626 | 3,042 | 23 |
| Tim Von Dulm, Portland St. .......... | †1970 | 10 | 490 | 259 | 23 | .529 | 3,041 | 25 |

\* *Record.* † *National champion.*

## Single-Game Yards

| Yds. | Player, Team (Opponent) | Date |
|------|--------------------------|------|
| 592 | John Charles, Portland St. (Cal Poly SLO) ..................................... | Nov. 16, 1991 |
| 568 | Bob Toledo, San Fran. St. (Cal St. Hayward) ..................................... | Oct. 21, 1967 |
| 550 | Earl Harvey, N.C. Central (Jackson St.) ..................................... | Aug. 30, 1986 |
| 539 | Maurice Heard, Tuskegee (Alabama A&M) ..................................... | Nov. 10, 1990 |
| 525 | Rob Tomlinson, Cal St. Chico (Southern Conn. St.) ............................. | Oct. 7, 1989 |

*1993 NCAA FOOTBALL*

| Yds. | Player, Team (Opponent) | Date |
|---|---|---|
| 524 | Dennis Shaw, San Diego St. (Southern Miss.) | Nov. 9, 1968 |
| 514 | Tracy Kendall, Alabama A&M (Clark Atlanta) | Nov. 4, 1989 |
| 506 | Jeff King, Bloomsburg (Lock Haven) | Sept. 19, 1992 |
| 506 | Tod Mayfield, West Tex. St. (Texas A&I) | Nov. 1, 1986 |
| 502 | John Linhart, Slippery Rock (Clarion) | Nov. 7, 1992 |
| 502 | Mike Packer, Lock Haven (Delaware Valley) | Oct. 24, 1970 |
| 501 | Bob Toledo, San Fran. St. (Humboldt St.) | Nov. 4, 1967 |
| 500 | Jerry Bishop, Austin (East Cent. Okla.) | Nov. 2, 1963 |

### Single-Game Attempts

| No. | Player, Team (Opponent) | Date |
|---|---|---|
| 72 | Kurt Otto, North Dak. (Texas A&I) | Sept. 13, 1986 |
| 72 | Kaipo Spencer, Santa Clara (Portland St.) | Oct. 11, 1975 |
| 72 | Joe Stetser, Cal St. Chico (Oregon Tech) | Sept. 23, 1967 |
| 71 | Pat Brennan, Franklin (Ashland) | Nov. 3, 1984 |

### Single-Game Completions

| No. | Player, Team (Opponent) | Date |
|---|---|---|
| 44 | Tom Bonds, Cal Lutheran (St. Mary's, Cal.) | Nov. 22, 1986 |
| 43 | George Bork, Northern Ill. (Central Mich.) | Nov. 9, 1963 |
| 42 | Marty Washington, Livingston (Mississippi Col.) | Oct. 17, 1992 |
| 42 | Chris Teal, West Ga. (Valdosta St.) | Oct. 19, 1991 |
| 42 | Tim Von Dulm, Portland St. (Eastern Wash.) | Nov. 21, 1970 |
| 41 | Kurt Otto, North Dak. (Texas A&I) | Sept. 13, 1986 |
| 41 | Neil Lomax, Portland St. (Montana St.) | Nov. 19, 1977 |
| 40 | Kurt Beathard, Towson St. (Lafayette) | Nov. 2, 1985 |
| 39 | Jeff King, Bloomsburg (Lock Haven) | Sept. 19, 1992 |
| 39 | Pat Brennan, Franklin (Saginaw Valley) | Sept. 22, 1984 |
| 39 | Mark Beans, Shippensburg (Edinboro) | Sept. 24, 1983 |
| 39 | Curt Strasheim, Southwest St. (Moorhead St.) | Nov. 14, 1981 |
| 39 | Craig Blackford, Evansville (Ball St.) | Oct. 17, 1970 |

### Career Yards Per Game

| Player, Team | Years | G. | Att. | Cmp. | Int. | Pct. | Yards | TD | Avg. |
|---|---|---|---|---|---|---|---|---|---|
| Tim Von Dulm, Portland St. ....... | 1969-70 | 20 | 924 | 500 | 41 | .541 | 5,967 | 51 | *298.4 |
| Jayson Merrill, Western St......... | 1990-91 | 20 | 580 | 328 | 25 | .566 | 5,830 | 56 | 291.5 |
| John Charles, Portland St. ....... | 1991-92 | 19 | 510 | 326 | 14 | .639 | 5,389 | 56 | 283.6 |
| Earl Harvey, N.C. Central......... | 1985-88 | 40 | *1,442 | *690 | 81 | .479 | *10,621 | 86 | 265.5 |
| Pat Brennan, Franklin ............. | 1981-84 | 30 | 1,123 | 535 | 62 | .476 | 7,717 | 53 | 257.2 |
| Jay McLucas, New Haven......... | 1989-90 | 20 | 699 | 370 | 30 | .529 | 5,139 | 37 | 257.0 |
| Steve Wray, Franklin ............. | 1978-82 | 32 | 1,230 | 592 | 48 | .481 | 8,123 | 62 | 253.8 |
| Chris Hegg, Northeast Mo. St. .... | ‡1982, 84-85 | 21 | 772 | 410 | 33 | .531 | 5,306 | 44 | 252.7 |
| Troy Mott, Wayne St. (Neb.)....... | 1991-92 | 20 | 757 | 437 | 37 | .577 | 5,003 | 25 | 250.2 |
| Chris Petersen, UC Davis ........ | 1985-86 | 20 | 553 | 385 | 13 | *.696 | 4,988 | 39 | 249.4 |
| Jeff Phillips, Central Mo. St........ | 1986-88 | 26 | 892 | 496 | 54 | .556 | 6,294 | 46 | 242.1 |
| June Jones, Hawaii/Portland St... | 1974, 75-76 | 24 | 666 | 376 | 35 | .565 | 5,809 | 41 | 242.0 |
| Rex Lamberti, Abilene Christian .. | 1984-86 | 24 | 829 | 439 | 29 | .530 | 5,807 | 56 | 242.0 |
| Rich Ingold, Indiana (Pa.) ........ | #1981, 83-85 | 27 | 862 | 503 | 36 | .584 | 6,494 | 50 | 240.5 |
| Joe Stetser, Cal St. Chico ........ | 1966-67 | 20 | 813 | 394 | 48 | .485 | 4,803 | 40 | 240.2 |
| Leonard Williams, Tenn.-Martin ... | 1990-91 | 19 | 594 | 305 | 21 | .513 | 4,518 | 40 | 237.8 |
| Jim Lindsey, Abilene Christian .... | 1967-70 | 36 | 1,237 | 642 | 69 | .519 | 8,521 | 61 | 236.7 |

*Record.   ‡ Played in one game at Northern Iowa in 1982.   # Played in one game at South Carolina in 1981.

### Season Yards Per Game

| Player, Team | Year | Games | Att. | Cmp. | Int. | Pct. | Yards | TD | Avg. |
|---|---|---|---|---|---|---|---|---|---|
| Bob Toledo, San Fran. St. ........ | 1967 | 10 | 396 | 211 | 24 | .533 | 3,513 | *45 | *351.3 |
| Pat Brennan, Franklin ............. | 1983 | 10 | 458 | 226 | 30 | .493 | 3,491 | 25 | 349.1 |
| Jayson Merrill, Western St........ | †1991 | 10 | 309 | 195 | 11 | .631 | 3,484 | 35 | 348.4 |
| John Charles, Portland St. ........ | 1992 | 8 | 263 | 179 | 7 | .681 | 2,770 | 24 | 346.3 |
| George Bork, Northern Ill. ........ | †1963 | 9 | 374 | 244 | 12 | .652 | 3,077 | 32 | 341.9 |
| Chris Hegg, Northeast Mo. St. ... | †1985 | 11 | 503 | 284 | 20 | .565 | *3,741 | 32 | 340.1 |
| Pat Brennan, Franklin ............. | 1984 | 10 | 502 | 238 | 20 | .474 | 3,340 | 18 | 334.0 |
| Tod Mayfield, West Tex. St........ | 1986 | 11 | *515 | *317 | 20 | .615 | 3,664 | 31 | 333.1 |
| Richard Strasser, San Fran. St. ... | 1985 | 10 | 452 | 250 | 19 | .553 | 3,317 | 20 | 331.7 |
| Rob Tomlinson, Cal St. Chico.... | 1989 | 10 | 437 | 254 | 16 | .581 | 3,237 | 19 | 323.7 |

| Player, Team | Year | Games | Att. | Cmp. | Int. | Pct. | Yards | TD | Avg. |
|---|---|---|---|---|---|---|---|---|---|
| June Jones, Portland St. ......... | †1976 | 11 | 423 | 238 | 24 | .563 | 3,518 | 25 | 319.8 |
| Earl Harvey, N.C. Central........ | 1985 | 10 | 392 | 188 | 19 | .480 | 3,190 | 22 | 319.0 |
| Jay McLucas, New Haven........ | 1990 | 10 | 402 | 209 | 18 | .520 | 3,114 | 23 | 311.4 |
| Randy Hobson, Evansville ....... | 1987 | 10 | 386 | 242 | 16 | .626 | 3,042 | 23 | 304.2 |
| Tim Von Dulm, Portland St. ...... | †1970 | 10 | 490 | 259 | 23 | .529 | 3,041 | 25 | 304.1 |
| Phil Basso, Liberty/Northern Ill. ... | 1984 | 11 | 426 | 250 | 15 | .587 | 3,326 | 24 | 302.4 |

* Record.  † National champion.

## Annual Champions

| Year | Player, Team | Cl. | Att. | Cmp. | Int. | Pct. | Yds. | TD |
|---|---|---|---|---|---|---|---|---|
| 1946 | Hank Caver, Presbyterian ................. | Sr. | 128 | 59 | 13 | .461 | 790 | 7 |
| 1947 | James Batchelor, East Tex. St. ............ | Sr. | 184 | 94 | 10 | .511 | 1,114 | 9 |
| 1948 | Sam Gary, Swarthmore .................. | Jr. | 153 | 93 | 11 | .608 | 1,218 | 16 |
| 1949 | Sam McGowan, New Mexico St. .......... | Sr. | 219 | 112 | 22 | .511 | 1,712 | 12 |
| 1950 | Andy MacDonald, Central Mich. .......... | Jr. | 200 | 109 | 12 | .545 | 1,577 | 15 |
| 1951 | Andy MacDonald, Central Mich. .......... | Sr. | 183 | 114 | 7 | .623 | 1,560 | 12 |
| 1952 | Wes Bair, Illinois St. ...................... | So. | 242 | 135 | 18 | .558 | 1,375 | 14 |
| 1953 | Pence Dacus, Southwest Tex. St. ......... | Sr. | 207 | 113 | 10 | .546 | 1,654 | 11 |
| 1954 | Tommy Egan, Brandeis ................... | Sr. | 144 | 87 | 8 | .604 | 1,050 | 11 |
| 1955 | Jerry Foley, Hamline .................... | Fr. | 167 | 87 | 8 | .521 | 1,034 | 6 |
| 1956 | James Stehlin, Brandeis ................. | Sr. | 206 | 116 | 11 | .563 | 1,155 | 6 |
| 1957 | Jay Roelen, Pepperdine.................. | Sr. | 214 | 106 | 16 | .495 | 1,428 | 13 |
| 1958 | Stan Jackson, Cal Poly Pomona .......... | Sr. | 256 | 123 | 14 | .480 | 1,994 | 16 |
| 1959 | Gary Campbell, Whittier ................. | Sr. | 183 | 111 | 4 | .607 | 1,717 | 12 |
| 1960 | Denny Spurlock, Whitworth .............. | Jr. | 257 | 135 | 16 | .525 | 1,892 | 14 |
| 1961 | Tom Gryzwinski, Defiance ............... | Jr. | 258 | 127 | 17 | .492 | 1,684 | 14 |
| 1962 | George Bork, Northern Ill. ............... | Jr. | 356 | 232 | 11 | .652 | 2,506 | 22 |
| 1963 | George Bork, Northern Ill. ............... | Sr. | 374 | 244 | 12 | .652 | 3,077 | 32 |
| 1964 | Jerry Bishop, Austin .................... | Jr. | 300 | 182 | 16 | .607 | 2,246 | 17 |
| 1965 | Bob Caress, Bradley ..................... | Sr. | 393 | 210 | 21 | .534 | 2,167 | 24 |
| 1966 | Paul Krause, Dubuque ................... | Sr. | 318 | 179 | 22 | .563 | 2,210 | 16 |
| 1967 | Joe Stetser, Cal St. Chico ................ | Sr. | 464 | 220 | *32 | .474 | 2,446 | 14 |
| 1968 | Jim Lindsey, Abilene Christian ............ | So. | 396 | 204 | 19 | .515 | 2,717 | 18 |
| 1969 | Tim Von Dulm, Portland St. ............... | Jr. | 434 | 241 | 18 | .555 | 2,926 | 26 |

*Beginning in 1970, ranked on per-game (instead of total) completions*

| Year | Player, Team | Cl. | G. | Att. | Cmp. | Avg. | Int. | Pct. | Yds. | TD |
|---|---|---|---|---|---|---|---|---|---|---|
| 1970 | Tim Von Dulm, Portland St. ....... | Sr. | 10 | 490 | 259 | *25.9 | 23 | .529 | 3,041 | 25 |
| 1971 | Bob Baron, Rensselaer............ | Sr. | 9 | 302 | 168 | 18.7 | 13 | .556 | 2,105 | 15 |
| 1972 | Bob Biggs, UC Davis ............. | Sr. | 9 | 327 | 186 | 20.7 | 16 | .569 | 2,291 | 15 |
| 1973 | Kim McQuilken, Lehigh .......... | Sr. | 11 | 326 | 196 | 17.8 | 13 | .601 | 2,603 | 19 |
| 1974 | Jim McMillan, Boise St. .......... | Sr. | 10 | 313 | 192 | 19.2 | 15 | .613 | 2,900 | 13 |
| 1975 | Dan Hayes, UC Riverside ......... | Sr. | 10 | 316 | 171 | 17.1 | 20 | .541 | 2,215 | 21 |
| 1976 | June Jones, Portland St. .......... | Sr. | 11 | 423 | 238 | 21.6 | 24 | .563 | 3,518 | 25 |
| 1977 | Ed Schultz, Moorhead St. ......... | Sr. | 10 | 304 | 187 | 18.7 | 16 | .615 | 1,943 | 21 |
| 1978 | Jeff Knapple, Northern Colo....... | Sr. | 10 | 349 | 178 | 17.8 | 21 | .510 | 2,191 | 16 |

*Beginning in 1979, ranked on Passing Efficiency Rating Points (instead of per-game completions)*

| Year | Player, Team | Cl. | G. | Att. | Cmp. | Int. | Pct. | Yds. | TD | Pts. |
|---|---|---|---|---|---|---|---|---|---|---|
| 1979 | Dave Alfaro, Santa Clara .............. | Jr. | 9 | 168 | 110 | 9 | .655 | 1,721 | 13 | 166.3 |
| 1980 | Willie Tullis, Troy St.................... | Sr. | 10 | 203 | 108 | 8 | .532 | 1,880 | 15 | 147.5 |
| 1981 | Steve Michuta, Grand Valley St........ | Sr. | 8 | 173 | 114 | 11 | .659 | 1,702 | 17 | 168.3 |
| 1982 | John Wristen, Southern Colo......... | Jr. | 8 | 121 | 68 | 2 | .562 | 1,358 | 13 | 182.5 |
| 1983 | Kevin Parker, Fort Valley St. .......... | Jr. | 9 | 168 | 87 | 8 | .518 | 1,539 | 18 | 154.6 |
| 1984 | Brian Quinn, Northwest Mo. St. ....... | Sr. | 10 | 178 | 96 | 2 | .539 | 1,561 | 14 | 151.3 |
| 1985 | Chris Petersen, UC Davis ............ | Jr. | 10 | 242 | 167 | 6 | .690 | 2,366 | 17 | 169.4 |
| 1986 | Chris Petersen, UC Davis ............ | Sr. | 10 | 311 | 218 | 7 | ‡.701 | 2,622 | 22 | 159.7 |
| 1987 | Dave Biondo, Ashland ................ | Jr. | 10 | 177 | 95 | 11 | .536 | 1,828 | 14 | 154.0 |
| 1988 | Al Niemela, West Chester ............ | Sr. | 10 | 217 | 138 | 9 | .635 | 1,932 | 21 | 161.9 |
| 1989 | Richard Basil, Savannah St. .......... | Sr. | 9 | 211 | 120 | 7 | .568 | 2,148 | 29 | 180.9 |
| 1990 | Tony Aliucci, Indiana (Pa.) ........... | Jr. | 10 | 181 | 111 | 10 | .613 | 1,801 | 21 | 172.0 |
| 1991 | Jayson Merrill, Western St............. | Sr. | 10 | 309 | 195 | 11 | .631 | 3,484 | 35 | 187.9 |
| 1992 | Steve Smith, Western St. .............. | Sr. | 10 | 271 | 180 | 5 | .664 | 2,719 | 30 | 183.5 |

* Record.  ‡ Record for minimum of 225 attempts.

# RECEIVING

## Career Catches

| Player, Team | Years | No. | Yards | TD |
|---|---|---|---|---|
| Chris Myers, Kenyon | 1967-70 | *253 | 3,897 | 33 |
| Bruce Cerone, Yankton/Emporia St. | 1966-67, 68-69 | 241 | *4,354 | *49 |
| Harold "Red" Roberts, Austin Peay | 1967-70 | 232 | 3,005 | 31 |
| Jerry Hendren, Idaho | 1967-69 | 230 | 3,435 | 27 |
| Mike Healey, Valparaiso | 1982-85 | 228 | 3,212 | 26 |
| William Mackall, Tenn.-Martin | 1985-88 | 224 | 2,488 | 16 |
| Robert Clark, N.C. Central | 1983-86 | 210 | 4,231 | 38 |
| Terry Fredenberg, Wis.-Milwaukee | 1965-68 | 206 | 2,789 | 24 |
| Dan Bogar, Valparaiso | 1981-84 | 204 | 2,816 | 26 |
| Rich Otte, Northeast Mo. St. | 1980-83 | 202 | 2,821 | 16 |
| Mark Steinmeyer, Kutztown (RB) | 1988-91 | 200 | 2,118 | 23 |
| Barry Naone, Portland St. (TE) | 1985-88 | 199 | 2,237 | 8 |
| Jon Braff, St. Mary's (Cal.) (TE) | 1985-88 | 193 | 2,461 | 20 |
| Shannon Sharpe, Savannah St. | 1986-89 | 192 | 3,744 | 40 |
| Bill Wick, Carroll (Wis.) | 1966-69 | 190 | 2,967 | 20 |
| Don Hutt, Boise St. | 1971-73 | 187 | 2,716 | 30 |
| Steve Hansley, Northwest Mo. St. | 1983-85 | 186 | 2,898 | 24 |
| Dan Anderson, Northwest Mo. St. (TE) | 1982-85 | 186 | 2,494 | 16 |

* Record.

## Season Catches

| Player, Team | Year | Games | No. | Yards | TD |
|---|---|---|---|---|---|
| Barry Wagner, Alabama A&M | †1989 | 11 | *106 | 1,812 | 17 |
| Mike Healey, Valparaiso | †1985 | 10 | 101 | 1,279 | 11 |
| Ed Bell, Idaho St. | †1969 | 10 | 96 | 1,522 | *20 |
| Dick Hewins, Drake | †1968 | 10 | 95 | 1,316 | 13 |
| Billy Joe Masters, Evansville | †1987 | 10 | ¢94 | ¢960 | 4 |
| Stan Carraway, West Tex. St. | †1986 | 11 | 94 | 1,175 | 9 |
| Manley Sarnowsky, Drake | †1966 | 10 | 92 | 1,114 | 7 |
| Bruce Cerone, Emporia St. | 1968 | 9 | 91 | 1,479 | 15 |
| Rodney Robinson, Gardner-Webb | 1992 | 11 | 89 | 1,496 | 16 |
| Harvey Tanner, Murray St. | †1967 | 10 | 88 | 1,019 | 3 |

* Record.  † National champion.  ¢ Record for a running back.

## Single-Game Catches

| No. | Player, Team (Opponent) | Date |
|---|---|---|
| 23 | Barry Wagner, Alabama A&M (Clark Atlanta) | Nov. 4, 1989 |
| 20 | Harold Roberts, Austin Peay (Murray St.) | Nov. 8, 1969 |
| 19 | Matt Carman, Livingston (Jacksonville St.) | Nov. 7, 1992 |
| 19 | Aaron Marsh, Eastern Ky. (Northwood) | Oct. 14, 1967 |
| 19 | George LaPorte, Union, N.Y. (Rensselaer) | Oct. 16, 1965 |
| 18 | Carl Bruere, N.M. Highlands (Western St.) | Oct. 12, 1991 |
| 18 | Billy Joe Masters, Evansville (Ashland) | Oct. 31, 1987 |
| 18 | Bruce Cerone, Emporia St. (Washburn) | Nov. 9, 1968 |
| 18 | Dick Donlin, Hamline (St. John's, Minn.) | Oct. 8, 1955 |

## Career Catches Per Game

| Player, Team | Years | Games | No. | Yards | TD | Ct. PG |
|---|---|---|---|---|---|---|
| Ed Bell, Idaho St. | 1968-69 | 19 | 163 | 2,608 | 30 | *8.6 |
| Jerry Hendren, Idaho | 1967-69 | 30 | 230 | 3,435 | 27 | 7.7 |
| Gary Garrison, San Diego St. | 1964-65 | 20 | 148 | 2,188 | 26 | 7.4 |
| Chris Myers, Kenyon | 1967-70 | 35 | *253 | 3,897 | 33 | 7.2 |

* Record.

## Season Catches Per Game

| Player, Team | Year | Games | No. | Yards | TD | Ct. PG |
|---|---|---|---|---|---|---|
| Bruce Cerone, Emporia St. | 1968 | 9 | 91 | 1,479 | 15 | *10.1 |
| Mike Healey, Valparaiso | †1985 | 10 | 101 | 1,279 | 11 | 10.1 |
| Barry Wagner, Alabama A&M | †1989 | 11 | *106 | *1,812 | 17 | 9.6 |
| Ed Bell, Idaho St. | †1969 | 10 | 96 | 1,522 | *20 | 9.6 |
| Jerry Hendren, Idaho | 1968 | 9 | 86 | 1,457 | 14 | 9.6 |
| Dick Hewins, Drake | †1968 | 10 | 95 | 1,316 | 13 | 9.5 |
| Billy Joe Masters, Evansville | †1987 | 10 | ¢94 | ¢960 | 4 | ¢9.4 |
| Joe Dittrich, Southwest St. | †1980 | 9 | 83 | 974 | 7 | 9.2 |
| Manley Sarnowsky, Drake | †1966 | 10 | 92 | 1,114 | 7 | 9.2 |

* Record.  † National champion.  ¢ Record for a running back.

## Career Yards

| Player, Team | Years | Catches | Yards | Avg. | TD |
|---|---|---|---|---|---|
| Bruce Cerone, Yankton/Emporia St. ... | 1966-67, 68-69 | 241 | *4,345 | 18.1 | *49 |
| Robert Clark, N.C. Central ............ | 1983-86 | 210 | 4,231 | ‡‡20.1 | 38 |
| Chris Myers, Kenyon.................. | 1967-70 | *253 | 3,897 | 15.4 | 33 |
| Shannon Sharpe, Savannah St. ....... | 1986-89 | 192 | 3,744 | 19.5 | 40 |
| Jeff Tiefenthaler, South Dak. St........ | 1983-86 | 173 | 3,621 | 20.9 | 31 |
| Willie Richardson, Jackson St. ........ | 1959-62 | 166 | 3,616 | ††21.8 | 36 |

* Record.  ‡‡ Record for a minimum of 180 catches.  †† Record for a minimum of 135 catches.

## Season Yards

| Player, Team | Year | Catches | Yards | Avg. | TD |
|---|---|---|---|---|---|
| Barry Wagner, Alabama A&M ............. | †1989 | *106 | *1,812 | 17.1 | 17 |
| Dan Fulton, Nebraska-Omaha ............ | 1976 | 67 | 1,581 | 23.6 | 16 |
| Jeff Tiefenthaler, South Dak. St........... | 1986 | 73 | 1,534 | 21.0 | 11 |
| Ed Bell, Idaho St. ........................ | †1969 | 96 | 1,522 | 15.9 | *20 |
| Rodney Robinson, Gardner-Webb ........ | †1992 | 89 | 1,496 | 16.8 | 16 |
| Bruce Cerone, Emporia St. .............. | 1968 | 91 | 1,479 | 16.3 | 15 |
| Jerry Hendren, Idaho ................... | 1968 | 86 | 1,457 | 16.9 | 14 |

* Record.  † National champion.

## Annual Champions

| Year | Player, Team | Class | No. | Yards | TD |
|---|---|---|---|---|---|
| 1946 | Hugh Taylor, Oklahoma City ......................... | Jr. | 23 | 457 | 8 |
| 1947 | Bill Klein, Hanover ................................... | So. | 52 | 648 | 12 |
| 1948 | Bill Klein, Hanover ................................... | Jr. | 43 | 812 | 6 |
| 1949 | Cliff Coggin, Southern Miss. .......................... | Sr. | 53 | 1,087 | 9 |
| 1950 | Jack Bighead, Pepperdine ........................... | Jr. | 38 | 551 | 6 |
| 1951 | Jim Stefoff, Kalamazoo ............................. | Jr. | 45 | 680 | 5 |
| 1952 | Jim McKinzie, Northern Ill............................ | Sr. | 44 | 703 | 6 |
| 1953 | Dick Beetsch, Northern Iowa ........................ | So. | 54 | 837 | 9 |
| 1954 | R. C. Owens, Col. of Idaho.......................... | Sr. | 48 | 905 | 7 |
| 1955 | Dick Donlin, Hamline ................................ | Sr. | 41 | 480 | 2 |
| 1956 | Tom Rychlec, American Int'l .......................... | Sr. | 40 | 353 | 3 |
| 1957 | Tom Whitaker, Nevada ............................... | Jr. | 40 | 527 | 4 |
| 1958 | Bruce Shenk, West Chester .......................... | Sr. | 39 | 580 | 9 |
| 1959 | Fred Tunnicliffe, UC Santa Barb....................... | So. | 48 | 1,087 | 11 |
| 1960 | Ken Gregory, Whittier ................................ | Sr. | 74 | 1,018 | 4 |
| 1961 | Marty Baumhower, Defiance .......................... | Jr. | 57 | 708 | 4 |
| 1962 | Hugh Rohrschneider, Northern Ill. .................... | Jr. | 76 | 795 | 5 |
| 1963 | Hugh Rohrschneider, Northern Ill. .................... | Sr. | 75 | 1,036 | 14 |
| 1964 | Steve Gilliatt, Parsons ............................... | So. | 81 | 984 | 12 |
| 1965 | George LaPorte, Union (N.Y.) ......................... | Sr. | 74 | 724 | 5 |
| 1966 | Manley Sarnowsky, Drake............................ | Sr. | 92 | 1,114 | 7 |
| 1967 | Harvey Tanner, Murray St............................ | Jr. | 88 | 1,019 | 3 |
| 1968 | Dick Hewins, Drake ................................. | Sr. | 95 | 1,316 | 13 |
| 1969 | Ed Bell, Idaho St. ................................... | Sr. | 96 | 1,522 | *20 |

*Beginning in 1970, ranked on per-game (instead of total) catches*

| Year | Player, Team | Cl. | G | Ct. | Avg. | Yards | TD |
|---|---|---|---|---|---|---|---|
| 1970 | Steve Mahaffey, Wash. & Lee ............. | Sr. | 9 | 74 | 8.2 | 897 | 2 |
| 1971 | Kalle Kontson, Rensselaer ................ | Sr. | 9 | 69 | 7.7 | 1,031 | 7 |
| 1972 | Freddie Scott, Amherst .................. | Jr. | 8 | 66 | 8.3 | 936 | 12 |
| 1973 | Ron Gustafson, North Dak. ............... | Jr. | 10 | 67 | 6.7 | 1,210 | 10 |
| 1974 | Andy Sanchez, Cal Poly Pomona ......... | Sr. | 10 | 62 | 6.2 | 903 | 0 |
| 1975 | Butch Johnson, UC Riverside............. | Sr. | 8 | 67 | 8.4 | 1,027 | 8 |
| 1976 | Bo Darden, Shaw ...................... | So. | 9 | 57 | 6.3 | 863 | 4 |
| 1977 | Jeff Tesch, Moorhead St................. | Sr. | 10 | 67 | 6.7 | 760 | 9 |
| 1978 | Mike Chrobot, Butler..................... | Sr. | 10 | 55 | 5.5 | 628 | 5 |
|  | Tom Ferguson, Cal St. Hayward .......... | Jr. | 10 | 55 | 5.5 | 698 | 6 |
|  | Mark McDaniel, Northern Colo. .......... | Sr. | 10 | 55 | 5.5 | 761 | 6 |
| 1979 | Robbie Ray, Franklin ..................... | Sr. | 10 | 63 | 6.3 | 987 | 3 |
| 1980 | Joe Dittrich, Southwest St................ | Sr. | 9 | 83 | 9.2 | 974 | 7 |
| 1981 | Paul Choudek, Southwest St.............. | Sr. | 10 | 70 | 7.0 | 747 | 5 |
| 1982 | Jay Barnett, Evansville ................... | Sr. | 10 | 81 | 8.1 | 1,181 | 12 |
| 1983 | Perry Kemp, Calif. (Pa.) .................. | Sr. | 10 | 74 | 7.4 | 1,101 | 9 |
| 1984 | Dan Bogar, Valparaiso .................. | Sr. | 10 | 73 | 7.3 | 861 | 11 |
| 1985 | Mike Healey, Valparaiso .................. | Sr. | 10 | 101 | 10.1 | 1,279 | 11 |
| 1986 | Stan Carraway, West Tex. St.............. | Sr. | 11 | 94 | 8.5 | 1,175 | 9 |
| 1987 | Billy Joe Masters, Evansville ............. | Sr. | 10 | ¢94 | ¢9.4 | ¢960 | 4 |
| 1988 | Todd Smith, Morningside ................ | Sr. | 11 | 86 | 7.8 | 1,006 | 8 |
| 1989 | Barry Wagner, Alabama A&M ............. | Sr. | 11 | *106 | 9.6 | *1,812 | 17 |

| Year | Player, Team | Cl. | G | Ct. | Avg. | Yards | TD |
|------|--------------|-----|---|-----|------|-------|-----|
| 1990 | Mark Steinmeyer, Kutztown ............... | Jr. | 11 | 86 | 7.8 | 940 | 5 |
| 1991 | Jesse Lopez, Cal St. Hayward............. | Sr. | 10 | 86 | 8.6 | 861 | 4 |
| 1992 | Randy Bartosh, Southwest Baptist ........ | Sr. | 8 | 65 | 8.1 | 860 | 2 |

\* *Record.*   ¢ *Record for a running back.*

### Receiving Yards Per Game

| Year | Player, Team | Cl. | G | Ct. | Yards | Avg. | TD |
|------|--------------|-----|---|-----|-------|------|-----|
| 1990 | Ernest Priester, Edinboro .................. | Sr. | 8 | 45 | 1,060 | 132.5 | 14 |
| 1991 | Rod Smith, Mo. Southern St............... | Jr. | 11 | 60 | 1,439 | 130.8 | 15 |
| 1992 | Rodney Robinson, Gardner-Webb ........ | Sr. | 11 | 89 | 1,496 | 136.0 | 16 |

# SCORING

### Career Points

| Player, Team | Years | TD | XPt. | FG | Pts. |
|--------------|-------|-----|------|-----|------|
| Walter Payton, Jackson St............................. | 1971-74 | 66 | 53 | 5 | *464 |
| Shawn Graves, Wofford .............................. | 1989-92 | *72 | 3 | 0 | 438 |
| Johnny Bailey, Texas A&I ............................ | 1986-89 | 70 | 3 | 0 | 426 |
| Dale Mills, Northeast Mo. St. ......................... | 1957-60 | 64 | 23 | 0 | 407 |
| Garney Henley, Huron ............................... | 1956-59 | 63 | 16 | 0 | 394 |
| Steve Roberts, Butler ............................... | 1986-89 | 63 | 4 | 0 | 386 |
| Jeff Bentrim, North Dak. St........................... | 1983-86 | 64 | 2 | 0 | 386 |
| Leo Lewis, Lincoln (Mo.) ............................ | 1951-54 | 64 | 0 | 0 | 384 |
| Heath Sherman, Texas A&I .......................... | 1985-88 | 63 | 0 | 0 | 378 |
| Billy Johnson, Widener .............................. | 1971-73 | 62 | 0 | 0 | 372 |
| Tank Younger, Grambling ............................ | 1945-48 | 60 | 9 | 0 | 369 |
| Bill Cooper, Muskingum .............................. | 1957-60 | 54 | 37 | 1 | 364 |

\* *Record.*

### Season Points

| Player, Team | Year | TD | XPt. | FG | Pts. |
|--------------|------|-----|------|-----|------|
| Terry Metcalf, Long Beach St............................ | 1971 | *29 | 4 | 0 | *178 |
| Jim Switzer, Col. of Emporia ............................ | †1963 | 28 | 0 | 0 | 168 |
| Carl Herakovich, Rose-Hulman ......................... | †1958 | 25 | 18 | 0 | 168 |
| Ted Scown, Sul Ross St. ................................ | †1948 | 28 | 0 | 0 | 168 |
| Ronald Moore, Pittsburg St.............................. | 1992 | 27 | 4 | 0 | 166 |
| Leon Burns, Long Beach St. ............................ | †1969 | 27 | 2 | 0 | 164 |
| Mike Deutsch, North Dak................................ | 1972 | 27 | 0 | 0 | 162 |
| Billy Johnson, Widener ................................. | †1972 | 27 | 0 | 0 | 162 |

\* *Record.*  † *National champion.*

### Career Points Per Game

| Player, Team | Years | Games | TD | XPt. | FG | Pts. | Pt. PG |
|--------------|-------|-------|-----|------|-----|------|--------|
| Ole Gunderson, St. Olaf ................ | 1969-71 | 27 | 60 | 2 | 0 | 362 | *13.4 |
| Billy Johnson, Widener ................. | 1971-73 | 28 | 62 | 0 | 0 | 372 | 13.3 |
| Leon Burns, Long Beach St. ............ | 1969-70 | 22 | 47 | 2 | 0 | 284 | 12.9 |
| Dale Mills, Northeast Mo. St. ........... | 1957-60 | 36 | 64 | 23 | 0 | 407 | 11.3 |
| Walter Payton, Jackson St.............. | 1971-74 | 42 | 66 | 53 | 5 | *464 | 11.0 |
| Steve Roberts, Butler ................. | 1986-89 | 35 | 63 | 4 | 0 | 386 | 11.0 |
| Jeff Bentrim, North Dak. St. ........... | 1983-86 | 35 | 64 | 2 | 0 | 386 | 11.0 |
| Shawn Graves, Wofford ................ | 1989-92 | 40 | *72 | 3 | 0 | 438 | 11.0 |
| Johnny Bailey, Texas A&I .............. | 1986-89 | 39 | 70 | 3 | 0 | 426 | 10.9 |
| Garney Henley, Huron ................. | 1956-59 | 37 | 63 | 16 | 0 | 394 | 10.6 |

\* *Record.*

### Season Points Per Game

| Player, Team | Year | Games | TD | XPt. | FG | Pts. | Pt. PG |
|--------------|------|-------|-----|------|-----|------|--------|
| Carl Herakovich, Rose-Hulman ......... | †1958 | 8 | 25 | 18 | 0 | 168 | *21.0 |
| Jim Switzer, Col. of Emporia ........... | †1963 | 9 | 28 | 0 | 0 | 168 | 18.7 |
| Billy Johnson, Widener ................ | †1972 | 9 | 27 | 0 | 0 | 162 | 18.0 |
| Carl Garrett, N. M. Highlands .......... | †1966 | 9 | 26 | 2 | 0 | 158 | 17.6 |
| Ted Scown, Sul Ross St. ............... | †1948 | 10 | 28 | 0 | 0 | 168 | 16.8 |

\* *Record.*  † *National champion.*

## Annual Champions

| Year | Player, Team | Class | TD | XPt. | FG | Pts. |
|------|-------------|-------|-----|------|-----|------|
| 1946 | Joe Carter, Florida N&I | So. | 21 | 26 | 0 | 152 |
| 1947 | Darwin Horn, Pepperdine | Jr. | 19 | 1 | 0 | 115 |
| | Chuck Schoenherr, Wheaton (Ill.) | So. | 19 | 1 | 0 | 115 |
| 1948 | Ted Scown, Sul Ross St. | So. | 28 | 0 | 0 | 168 |
| 1949 | Sylvester Polk, Md.-East. Shore | Jr. | 19 | 15 | 0 | 129 |
| 1950 | Carl Taseff, John Carroll | Sr. | 23 | 0 | 0 | 138 |
| 1951 | Paul Yackey, Heidelberg | Jr. | 22 | 0 | 0 | 132 |
| 1952 | Al Conway, William Jewell | Sr. | 22 | 1 | 0 | 133 |
| 1953 | Leo Lewis, Lincoln (Mo.) | Jr. | 22 | 0 | 0 | 132 |
| 1954 | Jim Podoley, Central Mich. | Jr. | 18 | 1 | 0 | 109 |
| | Dick Nyers, Indianapolis | Sr. | 16 | 13 | 0 | 109 |
| 1955 | Nate Clark, Hillsdale | Jr. | 24 | 0 | 0 | 144 |
| 1956 | Larry Houdek, Kan. Wesleyan | Sr. | 19 | 0 | 0 | 114 |
| 1957 | Lenny Lyles, Louisville | Sr. | 21 | 6 | 0 | 132 |
| 1958 | Carl Herakovich, Rose-Hulman | Sr. | 25 | 18 | 0 | 168 |
| 1959 | Garney Henley, Huron | Sr. | 22 | 9 | 0 | 141 |
| 1960 | Bill Cooper, Muskingum | Sr. | 23 | 14 | 0 | 152 |
| 1961 | John Murio, Whitworth | Jr. | 15 | 33 | 2 | 129 |
| 1962 | Mike Goings, Bluffton | So. | 22 | 0 | 0 | 132 |
| 1963 | Jim Switzer, Col. of Emporia | Sr. | 28 | 0 | 0 | 168 |
| 1964 | Henry Dyer, Grambling | Jr. | 17 | 2 | 0 | 104 |
| | Dunn Marteen, Cal St. Los Angeles | Sr. | 11 | 38 | 0 | 104 |
| 1965 | Allen Smith, Findlay | Jr. | 24 | 2 | 0 | 146 |
| 1966 | Carl Garrett, N. M. Highlands | So. | 26 | 2 | 0 | 158 |
| 1967 | Bert Nye, West Chester | Jr. | 19 | 13 | 0 | 127 |
| 1968 | Howard Stevens, Randolph-Macon | Fr. | 23 | 4 | 0 | 142 |
| 1969 | Leon Burns, Long Beach St. | Jr. | 27 | 2 | 0 | 164 |

*Beginning in 1970, ranked on per-game (instead of total) points*

| Year | Player, Team | Class | G | TD | XPt. | FG | Pts. | Avg. |
|------|-------------|-------|----|-----|------|-----|------|------|
| 1970 | Mike DiBlasi, Mount Union | Sr. | 9 | 22 | 0 | 0 | 132 | 14.7 |
| 1971 | Larry Ras, Michigan Tech | Sr. | 9 | 24 | 0 | 0 | 144 | 16.0 |
| 1972 | Billy Johnson, Widener | Jr. | 9 | 27 | 0 | 0 | 162 | 18.0 |
| 1973 | Walter Payton, Jackson St. | Jr. | 11 | 24 | 13 | 1 | 160 | 14.5 |
| 1974 | Walter Payton, Jackson St. | Sr. | 10 | 19 | 6 | 1 | 123 | 12.3 |
| 1975 | Dale Kasowski, North Dak. | Sr. | 7 | 16 | 4 | 0 | 100 | 14.3 |
| 1976 | Ted McKnight, Minn.-Duluth | Sr. | 10 | 24 | 0 | 0 | 144 | 14.4 |
| 1977 | Bill Burnham, New Hampshire | Sr. | 10 | 22 | 0 | 0 | 132 | 13.2 |
| 1978 | Marschell Brunfield, Youngstown St. | Sr. | 9 | 14 | 0 | 0 | 84 | 9.3 |
| | Charlie Thompson, Western St. | Sr. | 9 | 14 | 0 | 0 | 84 | 9.3 |
| 1979 | Robby Robson, Youngstown St. | Jr. | 10 | 20 | 0 | 0 | 120 | 12.0 |
| 1980 | Amory Bodin, Minn.-Duluth | Sr. | 10 | 19 | 2 | 0 | 116 | 11.6 |
| 1981 | George Works, Northern Mich. | Jr. | 10 | 21 | 0 | 0 | 126 | 12.6 |
| 1982 | George Works, Northern Mich. | Sr. | 10 | 23 | 0 | 0 | 138 | 13.8 |
| 1983 | Clarence Johnson, North Ala. | Jr. | 10 | 16 | 0 | 0 | 96 | 9.6 |
| 1984 | Jeff Bentrim, North Dak. St. | So. | 9 | 14 | 0 | 0 | 84 | 9.3 |
| 1985 | Jeff Bentrim, North Dak. St. | Jr. | 8 | 18 | 2 | 0 | 110 | ††13.8 |
| 1986 | Jeff Bentrim, North Dak. St. | Sr. | 10 | 23 | 0 | 0 | 138 | 13.8 |
| 1987 | Johnny Bailey, Texas A&I | So. | 10 | 20 | 0 | 0 | 120 | 12.0 |
| 1988 | Steve Roberts, Butler | Jr. | 10 | 23 | 4 | 0 | 142 | 14.2 |
| 1989 | Jimmy Allen, St. Joseph's (Ind.) | Jr. | 10 | 23 | 0 | 0 | 138 | 13.8 |
| 1990 | Ernest Priester, Edinboro | Sr. | 8 | 16 | 0 | 0 | 96 | 12.0 |
| 1991 | Quincy Tillmon, Emporia St. | So. | 9 | 19 | 0 | 0 | 114 | 12.7 |
| 1992 | David McCartney, Chadron St. | Jr. | 10 | 25 | 4 | 0 | 154 | 15.4 |

†† *Declared champion; with one more game (to meet 75 percent of games played minimum) for zero points, still would have highest per-game average.*

# PUNTING

### Career Average
### (Minimum 100 Punts)

| Player, Team | Years | No. | Yards | Avg. |
|-------------|-------|-----|-------|------|
| Steve Lewis, Jacksonville St. | 1989-92 | 100 | 4,434 | *44.34 |
| Tim Baer, Colorado Mines | 1986-89 | 235 | 10,406 | 44.28 |
| Jeff Guy, Western St. | 1983-85 | 113 | 4,967 | 44.0 |
| Russ Pilcher, Carroll (Mont.) | 1964-66 | 124 | 5,424 | 43.7 |
| Russell Gonzales, Morris Brown | 1976-77 | 111 | 4,833 | 43.5 |

*1993 NCAA FOOTBALL*

| Player, Team | Years | No. | Yards | Avg. |
|---|---|---|---|---|
| Gerald Circo, Cal St. Chico ......................... | 1964-65 | 103 | 4,470 | 43.4 |
| Trent Morgan, Cal St. Northridge ................... | 1987-88 | 128 | 5,531 | 43.2 |
| Bryan Wagner, Cal St. Northridge .................. | 1981-84 | 203 | 8,762 | 43.2 |
| Tom Kolesar, Nevada................................. | 1973-74 | 140 | 6,032 | 43.1 |
| Jimmy Morris, Angelo St. ........................... | 1991-92 | 101 | 4,326 | 42.8 |
| Don Geist, Northern Colo. .......................... | 1981-84 | 263 | 11,244 | 42.8 |
| Jan Chapman, San Diego.......................... | 1958-60 | 106 | 4,533 | 42.8 |
| Eric Fadness, Fort Lewis ........................... | 1989-92 | 209 | 8,905 | 42.6 |
| Warner Robertson, Md.-East. Shore................. | 1968-70 | 131 | 5,578 | 42.6 |

\* *Record.*

## Season Average
### (Qualifiers for Championship)

| Player, Team | Year | No. | Yards | Avg. |
|---|---|---|---|---|
| Steve Ecker, Shippensburg............................ | †1965 | 32 | 1,570 | *49.1 |
| Don Cockroft, Adams St. ............................. | †1966 | 36 | 1,728 | 48.0 |
| Jack Patterson, William Jewell ......................... | 1965 | 29 | 1,377 | 47.5 |
| Art Calandrelli, Canisius ............................ | †1949 | 25 | 1,177 | 47.1 |
| Grover Perkins, Southern-B.R. ........................ | †1961 | 22 | 1,034 | 47.0 |
| Erskine Valrie, Alabama A&M .......................... | 1966 | 36 | 1,673 | 46.5 |
| Mark Bounds, West Tex. St. ............................ | †1990 | 69 | 3,198 | 46.3 |
| Bruce Swanson, North Park............................ | †1967 | 53 | 2,455 | 46.3 |
| Lyle Johnston, Weber St. ............................. | 1965 | 29 | 1,340 | 46.2 |

\* *Record.*   † *National champion.*

## Annual Champions

| Year | Player, Team | Class | No. | Yards | Avg. |
|---|---|---|---|---|---|
| 1948 | Arthur Teixeira, Central Mich......................... | Sr. | 42 | 1,867 | 44.5 |
| 1949 | Art Calandrelli, Canisius ........................... | Jr. | 25 | 1,177 | 47.1 |
| 1950 | Flavian Weidekamp, Butler........................... | Sr. | 41 | 1,762 | 43.0 |
| 1951 | Curtiss Harris, Savannah St. ........................ | Sr. | 42 | 1,854 | 44.1 |
| 1952 | Virgil Stan, Western St............................... | Sr. | 37 | 1,622 | 43.8 |
| 1953 | Bill Bradshaw, Bowling Green ....................... | Jr. | 50 | 2,199 | 44.0 |
| 1954 | Bill Bradshaw, Bowling Green ....................... | Sr. | 28 | 1,228 | 43.9 |
| 1955 | Don Baker, North Texas ............................. | Sr. | 30 | 1,349 | 45.0 |
| 1956 | Marion Zody, Ashland................................ | Jr. | 34 | 1,475 | 43.4 |
| 1957 | Lawson Persley, Mississippi Val. .................... | Sr. | 36 | 1,659 | 46.1 |
| 1958 | Tom Lewis, Lake Forest ............................. | Jr. | 24 | 1,089 | 45.4 |
| 1959 | Buck Grover, Salem ................................. | Fr. | 27 | 1,203 | 44.6 |
| 1960 | Joe Roy, N. M. Highlands ........................... | So. | 40 | 1,744 | 43.6 |
| 1961 | Grover Perkins, Southern-B.R. ....................... | Fr. | 22 | 1,034 | 47.0 |
| 1962 | Ron Crouse, Catawba................................ | Jr. | 37 | 1,653 | 44.7 |
| 1963 | Steve Bailey, Kentucky St. .......................... | Sr. | 39 | 1,747 | 44.8 |
| 1964 | Russ Pilcher, Carroll (Mont.) ....................... | So. | 34 | 1,545 | 45.4 |
| 1965 | Steve Ecker, Shippensburg.......................... | Sr. | 32 | 1,570 | *49.1 |
| 1966 | Don Cockroft, Adams St. ........................... | Sr. | 36 | 1,728 | 48.0 |
| 1967 | Bruce Swanson, North Park ......................... | Jr. | 53 | 2,455 | 46.3 |
| 1968 | Warner Robertson, Md.-East. Shore.................. | Fr. | 61 | 2,699 | 44.2 |
| 1969 | Warner Robertson, Md.-East. Shore.................. | So. | 37 | 1,629 | 44.0 |
| 1970 | John Bonner, Tenn.-Chatt. .......................... | Sr. | 73 | 3,243 | 44.4 |
| 1971 | Ken Gamble, Fayetteville St. ........................ | Sr. | 47 | 2,092 | 44.5 |
| 1972 | Raymond Key, Jackson St............................ | Jr. | 44 | 1,883 | 42.8 |
| 1973 | Jerry Pope, Louisiana Tech ......................... | Fr. | 48 | 2,064 | 43.0 |
| 1974 | Mike Shawen, Middle Tenn. St. ...................... | Sr. | 62 | 2,720 | 43.9 |
| 1975 | Mike Wood, Southeast Mo. St. ...................... | Jr. | 40 | 1,729 | 43.2 |
| 1976 | Russell Gonzales, Morris Brown .................... | So. | 54 | 2,474 | 45.8 |
| 1977 | Jeff Gossett, Eastern Ill............................. | Jr. | 62 | 2,668 | 43.0 |
| 1978 | Bill Moats, South Dak. ............................. | Sr. | 77 | 3,377 | 43.9 |
| 1979 | Bob Fletcher, Northeast Mo. St. ..................... | Sr. | 79 | 3,409 | 43.2 |
| 1980 | Sean Landeta, Towson St. ........................... | So. | 47 | 2,038 | 43.4 |
| 1981 | Gregg Lowery, Jacksonville St. ...................... | Jr. | 64 | 2,787 | 43.5 |
| 1982 | Don Geist, Northern Colo. .......................... | So. | 66 | 2,966 | 44.4 |
| 1983 | Jeff Guy, Western St................................. | So. | 39 | 1,734 | 44.5 |
| 1984 | Jeff Guy, Western St................................. | Jr. | 46 | 2,012 | 43.7 |
| 1985 | Jeff Williams, Slippery Rock ........................ | Sr. | 46 | 1,977 | 43.0 |
| 1986 | Tim Baer, Colorado Mines .......................... | Fr. | 62 | 2,797 | 45.1 |
| 1987 | Jeff McComb, Southern Utah ....................... | Sr. | 42 | 1,863 | 44.4 |

*Division II Annual Champions, All-Time Leaders*

| Year | Player, Team | Class | No. | Yards | Avg. |
|------|--------------|-------|-----|-------|------|
| 1988 | Tim Baer, Colorado Mines | Jr. | 65 | 2,880 | 43.9 |
| 1989 | Tim Baer, Colorado Mines | Sr. | 55 | 2,382 | 43.3 |
| 1990 | Mark Bounds, West Tex. St. | Jr. | 69 | 3,198 | 46.3 |
| 1991 | Doug O'Neill, Cal Poly SLO | Sr. | 42 | 1,895 | 45.1 |
| 1992 | Jimmy Morris, Angelo St. | So. | 45 | 2,001 | 44.5 |

* Record.

East Texas State defensive back Pat Williams led Division II in interceptions (13) and interceptions per game (1.18) as a junior in 1992.

# INTERCEPTIONS

### Career Interceptions

| Player, Team | Years | No. | Yards | Avg. |
|--------------|-------|-----|-------|------|
| Tom Collins, Indianapolis | 1982-85 | *37 | 390 | 10.5 |
| Dean Diaz, Humboldt St. | 1980-83 | 31 | 328 | 10.6 |
| Scott Wiedeman, Adams St. | 1988-91 | 31 | 289 | 9.3 |
| Bill Grantham, Missouri-Rolla | 1977-80 | 29 | 263 | 9.1 |
| Buster West, Gust. Adolphus | 1967-70 | 26 | 192 | 7.4 |
| Tony Woods, Bloomsburg | 1982-85 | 26 | 105 | 4.0 |
| Greg Mercier, Ripon | 1968-70 | 25 | 243 | 9.7 |
| Gary Rubeling, Towson St. | 1980-83 | 25 | 122 | 4.9 |

* Record.

### Season Interceptions

| Player, Team | Year | No. | Yards |
|--------------|------|-----|-------|
| Eugene Hunter, Fort Valley St. | †1972 | **14 | 211 |
| Luther Howard, Delaware St. | †1972 | **14 | 99 |
| Tom Rezzuti, Northeastern | †1971 | **14 | 153 |
| Jim Blackwell, Southern-B.R. | †1970 | **14 | 196 |
| Carl Ray Harris, Fresno St. | 1970 | **14 | 98 |

** Record tied.   † National champion.

| Year | Player, Team | Class | Games | No. | Avg. | Yards |
|------|--------------|-------|-------|-----|------|-------|
| 1970 | Jim Blackwell, Southern-B.R. | Sr. | 11 | **14 | 1.27 | 196 |
| 1971 | Tom Rezzuti, Northeastern | Jr. | 9 | **14 | **1.56 | 153 |
| 1972 | Eugene Hunter, Fort Valley St. | So. | 9 | **14 | **1.56 | 211 |
|      | Luther Howard, Delaware St. | Sr. | 9 | **14 | **1.56 | 99 |
| 1973 | Mike Pierce, Northern Colo. | Sr. | 7 | 7 | 1.00 | 158 |
|      | James Smith, Shaw | So. | 8 | 8 | 1.00 | 94 |
| 1974 | Terry Rusin, Wayne St. (Mich.) | Fr. | 10 | 10 | 1.00 | 62 |
| 1975 | Jim Poettgen, Cal Poly Pomona | Jr. | 11 | 12 | 1.09 | 156 |
| 1976 | Johnny Tucker, Tennessee Tech | Sr. | 11 | 10 | 0.91 | 74 |
| 1977 | Mike Ellis, Norfolk St. | So. | 11 | 12 | 1.09 | 257 |
|      | Cornelius Washington, Winston-Salem | Sr. | 11 | 12 | 1.09 | 128 |
| 1978 | Bill Grantham, Missouri-Rolla | So. | 11 | 11 | 1.00 | 109 |
| 1979 | Jeff Huffman, Michigan Tech | Sr. | 10 | 11 | 1.10 | 97 |
| 1980 | Mike Lush, East Stroudsburg | Sr. | 10 | 12 | 1.20 | 208 |
| 1981 | Bobby Futrell, Elizabeth City St. | So. | 9 | 11 | 1.22 | 159 |
| 1982 | Greg Maack, Central Mo. St. | Sr. | 10 | 11 | 1.10 | 192 |
| 1983 | Matt Didio, Wayne St. (Mich.) | Sr. | 10 | 13 | 1.30 | 131 |
| 1984 | Bob Jahelka, LIU-C. W. Post | Sr. | 8 | 9 | 1.13 | 83 |
| 1985 | Duvaal Callaway, Fort Valley St. | Sr. | 11 | 10 | 0.91 | 175 |
|      | Tony Woods, Bloomsburg | Sr. | 11 | 10 | 0.91 | 10 |
| 1986 | Doug Smart, Winona St. | Jr. | 8 | 10 | 1.25 | 56 |
| 1987 | Mike Petrich, Minn.-Duluth | Jr. | 11 | 9 | 0.82 | 151 |
| 1988 | Pete Jaros, Augustana (S.D.) | Jr. | 11 | 13 | 1.18 | 120 |
| 1989 | Jacque DeMatteo, Clarion | Jr. | 8 | 6 | 0.75 | 21 |
| 1990 | Eric Turner, East Tex. St. | Jr. | 11 | 10 | 0.91 | 105 |
| 1991 | Jeff Fickes, Shippensburg | Sr. | 11 | 12 | 1.09 | 154 |
| 1992 | Pat Williams, East Tex. St. | Jr. | 11 | 13 | 1.18 | 145 |

** Record tied.

# PUNT RETURNS

## Career Average
### (Minimum 1.2 Returns Per Game)

| Player, Team | Years | No. | Yards | Avg. |
|--------------|-------|-----|-------|------|
| Billy Johnson, Widener | 1971-73 | 40 | 989 | *24.7 |
| Robbie Martin, Cal Poly SLO | 1978-80 | 69 | 1,168 | 16.9 |
| Roscoe Word, Jackson St. | 1970-73 | 35 | 554 | 15.8 |
| Darryl Skinner, Hampton | 1983-86 | 53 | 835 | 15.8 |
| Michael Fields, Mississippi Col. | 1984-85 | 50 | 695 | 13.9 |

* Record.

## Season Average
### (Minimum 1.2 Returns Per Game)

| Player, Team | Year | No. | Yards | Avg. |
|--------------|------|-----|-------|------|
| Billy Johnson, Widener | †1972 | 15 | 511 | *34.1 |
| William Williams, Livingstone | †1976 | 16 | 453 | 28.3 |
| Terry Egerdahl, Minn.-Duluth | †1975 | 13 | 360 | 27.7 |
| Ennis Thomas, Bishop | †1971 | 18 | 450 | 25.0 |
| Chuck Goehl, Monmouth (Ill.) | 1972 | 17 | 416 | 24.5 |

* Record. † National champion.

## Annual Champions

| Year | Player, Team | Class | No. | Yards | Avg. |
|------|--------------|-------|-----|-------|------|
| 1970 | Kevin Downs, Ill. Benedictine | Jr. | 11 | 255 | 23.2 |
| 1971 | Ennis Thomas, Bishop | So. | 18 | 450 | 25.0 |
| 1972 | Billy Johnson, Widener | Jr. | 15 | 511 | *34.1 |
| 1973 | Roscoe Word, Jackson St. | Sr. | 19 | 316 | 16.6 |
| 1974 | Greg Anderson, Montana | So. | 13 | 263 | 20.2 |
| 1975 | Terry Egerdahl, Minn.-Duluth | Sr. | 13 | 360 | 27.7 |
| 1976 | William Williams, Livingstone | So. | 16 | 453 | 28.3 |
| 1977 | Armando Olivieri, New York Tech | So. | 14 | 270 | 19.3 |
| 1978 | Dwight Walker, Nicholls St. | Fr. | 16 | 284 | 17.8 |
| 1979 | Ricky Eberhart, Morris Brown | Fr. | 18 | 401 | 22.3 |
| 1980 | Ron Bagby, Puget Sound | So. | 16 | 242 | 15.1 |
| 1981 | Ron Trammell, East Tex. St. | Jr. | 29 | 467 | 16.1 |
| 1982 | Darrel Green, Texas A&I | Sr. | 19 | 392 | 20.6 |
| 1983 | Steve Carter, Albany St. (Ga.) | Sr. | 27 | 511 | 18.9 |
| 1984 | Michael Fields, Mississippi Col. | Jr. | 23 | 487 | 21.2 |

| Year | Player, Team | Class | No. | Yards | Avg. |
|------|------|-------|-----|-------|------|
| 1985 | Darryl Skinner, Hampton | Jr. | 19 | 426 | 22.4 |
| 1986 | Ben Frazier, Cheyney | So. | 14 | 246 | 17.6 |
| 1987 | Ronald Day, Savannah St. | Sr. | 12 | 229 | 19.1 |
| 1988 | Donnie Morris, Norfolk St. | Jr. | 12 | 283 | 23.6 |
| 1989 | Dennis Mailhot, East Stroudsburg | Jr. | 16 | 284 | 17.8 |
| 1990 | Ron West, Pittsburg St. | Jr. | 23 | 388 | 16.9 |
| 1991 | Doug Grant, Savannah St. | So. | 19 | 331 | 17.4 |
| 1992 | Doug Grant, Savannah St. | Jr. | 15 | 366 | 24.4 |

* Record.

# KICKOFF RETURNS

## Career Average
### (Minimum 1.2 Returns Per Game)

| Player, Team | Years | No. | Yards | Avg. |
|------|-------|-----|-------|------|
| Glen Printers, Southern Colo. | 1973-74 | 25 | 851 | *34.0 |
| Karl Evans, Mo. Southern St. | 1991-92 | 32 | 959 | 30.0 |
| Clarence Chapman, Eastern Mich. | 1973-75 | 45 | 1,278 | 28.4 |
| Greg Wilson, East Tenn. St. | 1975-78 | 37 | 1,032 | 27.9 |
| Bernie Rose, Samford/North Ala. | 1973, 74-76 | 64 | 1,715 | 26.8 |
| Roscoe Word, Jackson St. | 1970-73 | 74 | 1,980 | 26.8 |

* Record.

## Season Average
### (Minimum 1.2 Returns Per Game)

| Player, Team | Year | No. | Yards | Avg. |
|------|------|-----|-------|------|
| Danny Lee, Jacksonville St. | †1992 | 12 | 473 | *39.4 |
| Roscoe Word, Jackson St. | †1973 | 18 | 650 | 36.1 |
| Steve Levenseller, Puget Sound | †1978 | 17 | 610 | 35.9 |
| Winston Horshaw, Shippensburg | †1991 | 15 | 536 | 35.7 |
| Anthony Rivera, Western St. | 1991 | 18 | 635 | 35.3 |
| Dave Ludy, Winona St. | 1992 | 25 | 881 | 35.2 |
| Mike Scullin, Baldwin-Wallace | †1970 | 14 | 492 | 35.1 |
| Rufus Smith, Eastern N. Mex. | †1985 | 11 | 386 | 35.1 |
| Greg Anderson, Montana | †1974 | 10 | 335 | 33.5 |
| Kevin McDevitt, Butler | †1975 | 12 | 395 | 32.9 |

* Record.  † National champion.

## Annual Champions

| Year | Player, Team | Class | No. | Yards | Avg. |
|------|------|-------|-----|-------|------|
| 1970 | Mike Scullin, Baldwin-Wallace | So. | 14 | 492 | 35.1 |
| 1971 | Joe Brockmeyer, Western Md. | Jr. | 16 | 500 | 31.3 |
| 1972 | Rick Murphy, Indiana St. | Jr. | 22 | 707 | 32.1 |
| 1973 | Roscoe Word, Jackson St. | Sr. | 18 | 650 | 36.1 |
| 1974 | Greg Anderson, Montana | So. | 10 | 335 | 33.5 |
| 1975 | Kevin McDevitt, Butler | Jr. | 12 | 395 | 32.9 |
| 1976 | Henry Vereen, Nevada-Las Vegas | So. | 20 | 628 | 31.4 |
| 1977 | Dickie Johnson, Southern Colo. | Jr. | 13 | 385 | 29.6 |
| 1978 | Steve Levenseller, Puget Sound | Sr. | 17 | 610 | 35.9 |
| 1979 | Otha Hill, Central St. (Ohio) | Sr. | 18 | 526 | 29.2 |
| 1980 | Charlie Taylor, Southeast Mo. St. | Sr. | 13 | 396 | 30.5 |
| 1981 | Willie Canady, Fort Valley St. | Jr. | 13 | 415 | 31.9 |
| 1982 | Clarence Martin, Cal Poly SLO | So. | 11 | 360 | 32.7 |
| 1983 | David Anthony, Southern Ore. | Jr. | 14 | 436 | 31.1 |
| 1984 | Larry Winters, St. Paul's | Sr. | 20 | 644 | 32.2 |
| 1985 | Rufus Smith, Eastern N. Mex. | Fr. | 11 | 386 | 35.1 |
| 1986 | John Barron, Butler | So. | 21 | 653 | 31.1 |
| 1987 | Albert Fann, Cal St. Northridge | Fr. | 16 | 468 | 29.3 |
| 1988 | Pierre Fils, New Haven | So. | 12 | 378 | 31.5 |
| 1989 | Dennis Mailhot, East Stroudsburg | Jr. | 11 | 359 | 32.6 |
| 1990 | Alfred Banks, Livingston | Sr. | 17 | 529 | 31.1 |
| 1991 | Winston Horshaw, Shippensburg | Jr. | 15 | 536 | 35.7 |
| 1992 | Danny Lee, Jacksonville St. | Sr. | 12 | 473 | *39.4 |

* Record.

# ALL-PURPOSE RUNNING

## Annual Champions

| Year | Player, Team | Cl. | Rush | Rcv. | Int. | PR | KOR | Yds. | Yd. PG |
|------|--------------|-----|------|------|------|----|----|------|--------|
| 1992 | Johnny Cox, Fort Lewis ........... | Jr. | 95 | 1,331 | 0 | 80 | 679 | 2,185 | 218.5 |

# FIELD GOALS

## Career Field Goals

| Player, Team | Years | Made | Atts. | Pct. |
|--------------|-------|------|-------|------|
| Mike Wood, Southeast Mo. St. (S) ................. | 1974-77 | *64 | *109 | .587 |
| Pat Beaty, North Dak. (S) ........................... | 1985-88 | 52 | 82 | .634 |
| Bob Gilbreath, Eastern N. Mex. (S) ................ | 1986-89 | 50 | 77 | .649 |
| Ed O'Brien, Central Fla. (S) ......................... | 1984-87 | 50 | 77 | .649 |
| Bill May, Clarion (C) ................................. | 1977-80 | 48 | 60 | *.800 |
| Ed Detwiler, East Stroudsburg ..................... | 1989-92 | 48 | 87 | .552 |
| Mike Thomas, Angelo St. (S) ....................... | 1980-83 | 47 | 68 | .691 |
| Steve Huff, Central Mo. St. (C) ..................... | 1982-85 | 47 | 80 | .588 |
| Phil Brandt, Central Mo. St. (S) .................... | 1987-90 | 46 | 66 | .697 |
| Howie Guarini, Shippensburg (S) ................... | 1988-91 | 45 | 62 | .726 |
| James Knowles, North Ala. (C) ..................... | 1982-85 | 45 | 77 | .584 |
| Ed Hotz, Southeast Mo. St. (S) ..................... | 1978-81 | 45 | 77 | .584 |
| Kurt Seibel, South Dak. (C) ......................... | 1980-83 | 44 | 62 | .710 |
| Jason Monday, Lenoir-Rhyne ........................ | 1989-92 | 44 | 64 | .688 |
| Pat Bolton, Montana St. (C) ......................... | 1972-75 | 44 | 76 | .579 |
| Skipper Butler, Texas-Arlington (C) ................ | 1966-69 | 44 | 101 | .436 |

*Record.  (C) Conventional kicker.  (S) Soccer-style kicker.

## Season Field Goals

| Player, Team | Year | Made | Atts. | Pct. |
|--------------|------|------|-------|------|
| Pat Beaty, North Dak. (S) ........................... | †1988 | **20 | 26 | .769 |
| Tom Jurich, Northern Ariz. (C) ...................... | †1977 | **20 | 29 | .690 |
| Dennis Hochman, Sonoma St. (S) ................... | †1986 | 19 | 22 | .864 |
| Cory Solberg, North Dak. (S) ....................... | †1989 | 19 | 27 | .704 |
| Jaime Nunez, Weber St. (S) ......................... | †1971 | 19 | 32 | .594 |
| Bernard Henderson, Albany St. (Ga.) (S) ........... | †1985 | 18 | 26 | .692 |
| Ki Tok Chu, Tenn.-Martin (S) ........................ | 1988 | 17 | 22 | .773 |
| Jack McTyre, Valdosta St. (S) ....................... | 1990 | 17 | 23 | .739 |
| Dino Beligrinis, Winston-Salem (S) ................. | 1988 | 17 | 23 | .739 |
| Ed O'Brien, Central Fla. (S) ......................... | †1987 | 17 | 26 | .654 |
| Mike Wood, Southeast Mo. St. (S) .................. | 1976 | 17 | 33 | .515 |

** Record tied.  (C) Conventional kicker.  (S) Soccer-style kicker.

## Annual Champions

| Year | Player, Team | Class | Made | Atts. | Pct. | PG |
|------|--------------|-------|------|-------|------|-----|
| 1970 | Chris Guerrieri, Alfred (S) .................... | Sr. | 11 | 21 | .524 | 1.38 |
| 1971 | Jaime Nunez, Weber St. (S) ................ | Sr. | 19 | 32 | .594 | **1.90 |
| 1972 | Randy Walker, Northwestern (La.) (C) ........ | Jr. | 13 | 19 | .684 | 1.30 |
| 1973 | Reinhold Struprich, Hawaii (S) ................ | Jr. | 15 | 23 | .652 | 1.36 |
| 1974 | Mike Wood, Southeast Mo. St. (S) ............ | Fr. | 16 | 23 | .696 | 1.45 |
| 1975 | Wolfgang Taylor, Western St. (S) .............. | Sr. | 14 | 21 | .667 | 1.56 |
| 1976 | Rolf Benirschke, UC Davis (S) ................ | Sr. | 14 | 19 | .737 | 1.56 |
| 1977 | Tom Jurich, Northern Ariz. (C) ................ | Sr. | **20 | 29 | .690 | 1.81 |
| 1978 | Frank Friedman, Cal St. Northridge (S) ....... | Jr. | 15 | 22 | .682 | 1.50 |
| 1979 | Bill May, Clarion (C) ........................ | Jr. | 16 | 21 | .762 | 1.60 |
| 1980 | Nelson McMurain, North Ala. (S) ............. | Jr. | 14 | 22 | .636 | 1.40 |
|      | Sean Landeta, Towson St. (S) ................ | So. | 14 | 28 | .500 | 1.40 |
| 1981 | Russ Meier, South Dak. St. (S) ............... | Fr. | 16 | 21 | .762 | 1.60 |
| 1982 | Joey Malone, Alabama A&M (C) .............. | Fr. | 15 | 21 | .714 | 1.36 |
|      | Rick Ruszkiewicz, Edinboro (S) .............. | Sr. | 15 | 24 | .625 | 1.36 |
| 1983 | Mike Thomas, Angelo St. (S) ................ | Sr. | 16 | 22 | .727 | 1.45 |
| 1984 | Terry Godfrey, South Dak. (S) ................ | Jr. | 16 | 26 | .615 | 1.60 |
| 1985 | Bernard Henderson, Albany St. (Ga.) (S) ..... | Sr. | 18 | 26 | .692 | 1.64 |
| 1986 | Dennis Hochman, Sonoma St. (S) ............ | Sr. | 19 | 22 | .864 | **1.90 |
| 1987 | Ed O'Brien, Central Fla. (S) .................. | Sr. | 17 | 26 | .654 | 1.70 |
| 1988 | Pat Beaty, North Dak. (S) .................... | Sr. | **20 | 26 | .769 | 1.82 |
| 1989 | Cory Solberg, North Dak. (S) ................ | Jr. | 19 | 27 | .704 | 1.73 |
| 1990 | Jack McTyre, Valdosta St. (S) ................ | Sr. | 17 | 23 | .739 | 1.70 |
| 1991 | Billy Watkins, East Tex. St. (S) ............... | So. | 15 | 24 | .625 | 1.36 |
| 1992 | Mike Estrella, St. Mary's (Cal.) (S) ............ | Jr. | 15 | 27 | .556 | 1.67 |

** Record tied.  (C) Conventional kicker.  (S) Soccer-style kicker.

*Division II Annual Champions, All-Time Leaders*

# LONGEST PLAYS

*Since 1941, official maximum length of all plays fixed at 100 yards.*

## Rushing

| Yds. | Player, Team (Opponent) | Year |
|------|-------------------------|------|
| 99 | Thelbert Withers, N.M. Highlands (Fort Lewis) | 1992 |
| 99 | Lester Frye, Edinboro (Calif., Pa.) | 1991 |
| 99 | Kelvin Minefee, Southern Utah (Mesa St.) | 1988 |
| 99 | Fred Deutsch, Springfield (Wagner) | 1977 |
| 99 | Sammy Croom, San Diego (Azusa Pacific) | 1972 |
| 99 | John Stenger, Swarthmore (Widener) | 1970 |
| 99 | Jed Knuttila, Hamline (St. Thomas, Minn.) | 1968 |
| 99 | Dave Lanoha, Colorado Col. (Texas Lutheran) | 1967 |
| 99 | Tom Pabst, UC Riverside (Cal Tech) | 1965 |
| 99 | George Phillips, Concord (Davis & Elkins) | 1961 |
| 99 | Gerry White, Connecticut (Rhode Island) | 1960 |
| 99 | Leo Williams, St. Augustine's (Morris) | 1960 |
| 99 | George Phelps, Cornell College (Monmouth, Ill.) | 1959 |
| 99 | Mark Lydon, Tufts (Bowdoin) | 1958 |
| 99 | David Wells, Tufts (Williams) | 1956 |
| 99 | Jack Moskal, Case Reserve (Case Tech) | 1956 |
| 99 | Lou Mariano, Kent (Case Reserve) | 1954 |
| 99 | Ron Temple, Cal St. Chico (Southern Ore.) | 1953 |
| 99 | Ellis Horton, Eureka (Rose-Hulman) | 1952 |
| 99 | Pat Abbruzzi, Rhode Island (New Hampshire) | 1951 |

## Passing

*Pass plays have resulted in 99-yard completions 13 times. The most recent:*

| Yds. | Passer-Receiver, Team (Opponent) | Year |
|------|----------------------------------|------|
| 99 | Rob Rayl-John Unger, Valparaiso (Hillsdale) | 1992 |
| 99 | Bret Comp-Ken Kopetchny, East Stroudsburg (Mansfield) | 1990 |
| 99 | Mike Turk-Titus Dixon, Troy St. (Nicholls St.) | 1986 |
| 99 | Keith Young-John Ragin, Dist. Columbia (Fayetteville St.) | 1985 |
| 99 | Nick Pannunzo-Herman Heard, Southern Colo. (Adams St.) | 1982 |
| 99 | Tim Ebersole-Ed Noon, Shippensburg (Indiana, Pa.) | 1982 |
| 99 | John Guercio-Tom Bennett, LIU-C. W. Post (Juniata) | 1980 |
| 99 | Mike Moroski-Calvin Ellison, UC Davis (Puget Sound) | 1978 |
| 99 | Gary Duesenberg-Harvey King, North Park (Ill. Wesleyan) | 1970 |

## Field Goals

| Yds. | Player, Team (Opponent) | Year |
|------|-------------------------|------|
| 67 | Tom Odle, Fort Hays St. (Washburn) | 1988 |
| 63 | Joe Duren, Arkansas St. (McNeese St.) | 1974 |
| 62 | Mike Flater, Colorado Mines (Western St.) | 1973 |
| 61 | Duane Christian, Cameron (Southwestern Okla.) | 1976 |
| 61 | Mike Wood, Southeast Mo. St. (Lincoln, Mo.) | 1975 |
| 61 | Bill Shear, Cortland St. (Hobart) | 1966 |
| 60 | Mike Panasuk, Ferris St. (St. Joseph's, Ind.) | 1990 |
| 60 | Ed Beaulac, Sonoma St. (St. Mary's, Cal.) | 1989 |
| 60 | Roger McCoy, Grand Valley St. (Grand Rapids) | 1976 |
| 60 | Skipper Butler, Texas-Arlington (East Tex. St.) | 1968 |

## Punts

| Yds. | Player, Team (Opponent) | Year |
|------|-------------------------|------|
| 97 | Earl Hurst, Emporia St. (Central Mo. St.) | 1964 |
| 96 | Gary Frens, Hope (Olivet) | 1966 |
| 96 | Jim Jarrett, North Dak. (South Dak.) | 1957 |
| 93 | Elliot Mills, Carleton (Monmouth, Ill.) | 1970 |
| 93 | Kaspar Fitins, Taylor (Georgetown, Ky.) | 1966 |
| 93 | Leeroy Sweeney, Pomona-Pitzer (UC Riverside) | 1960 |

*Since 1941, many players have returned interceptions, punts and kickoffs 100 yards. For the 1992 season leaders, see page 640.*

# TEAM CHAMPIONS

## ANNUAL TEAM OFFENSE CHAMPIONS

| Year | Total Offense Team | Avg. | Rushing Team | Avg. | Passing Team | Avg. |
|------|------|------|------|------|------|------|
| 1948 | Hanover | *624.1 | Hanover | 400.4 | Hanover | 223.8 |
| 1949 | Pacific (Cal.) | 505.3 | Southern-B.R. | 382.9 | Baldwin-Wallace | 196.9 |
| 1950 | West Tex. St. | 465.3 | St. Lawrence | 356.1 | Northern Ill. | 187.0 |
| 1951 | Western Ill. | 473.6 | Western N. Mex. | 379.2 | Central Mich. | 213.8 |
| 1952 | Sam Houston St. | 448.2 | William Jewell | 345.0 | Sam Houston St. | 263.0 |
| 1953 | Col. of Idaho | 476.3 | McPherson | 375.9 | Southern Conn. St. | 193.5 |
| 1954 | Col. of Emporia | 469.7 | Col. of Emporia | *404.8 | Northern Iowa | 206.1 |
| 1955 | Centre | 431.0 | Centre | 373.4 | Hamline | 210.7 |
| 1956 | Florida A&M | 475.0 | Tufts | 359.9 | Widener | 207.7 |
| 1957 | Denison | 430.8 | Denison | 372.1 | Cal Poly Pomona | 236.0 |
| 1958 | Mo. Valley | 449.6 | Huron | 353.3 | Cal Poly Pomona | 217.6 |
| 1959 | Whittier | 461.3 | Bemidji St. | 326.6 | Whittier | 199.3 |
| 1960 | Muskingum | 456.4 | Muskingum | 355.2 | Whitworth | 213.6 |
| 1961 | Florida A&M | 413.6 | Huron | 313.1 | Cal Poly Pomona | 244.1 |
| 1962 | Baker | 438.4 | Northern St. | 355.3 | Northern Ill. | 285.6 |
| 1963 | Col. of Emporia | 517.1 | Luther | 356.0 | Northern Ill. | 349.3 |
| 1964 | San Diego St. | 422.6 | Cal St. Los Angeles | 325.9 | Parsons | 301.3 |
| 1965 | Long Beach St. | 439.5 | Huron | 303.3 | Southern Ore. | 268.9 |
| 1966 | Weber St. | 460.1 | Neb.-Kearney | 370.1 | San Diego St. | 268.1 |
| 1967 | San Fran. St. | 490.0 | North Dak. St. | 299.6 | San Fran. St. | 387.0 |
| 1968 | Louisiana Tech | 459.1 | Delaware | 315.8 | Louisiana Tech | 316.4 |
| 1969 | Delaware | 488.9 | St. Olaf | 369.1 | Portland St. | 308.6 |
| 1970 | Grambling | 457.7 | Delaware | 385.9 | Portland St. | 313.8 |
| 1971 | Delaware | 515.6 | Delaware | 371.2 | LIU-C. W. Post | 262.5 |
| 1972 | Hobart | 457.3 | Hobart | 380.7 | Maryville (Tenn.) | 277.8 |
| 1973 | Boise St. | 466.5 | Bethune-Cookman | 308.8 | Lehigh | 275.0 |
| 1974 | Boise St. | 516.9 | Central Mich. | 324.6 | Boise St. | 334.5 |
| 1975 | Portland St. | 472.4 | North Dak. | 344.4 | Portland St. | 361.7 |
| 1976 | Portland St. | 497.5 | Montana St. | 287.5 | Portland St. | *404.1 |
| 1977 | Portland St. | 506.7 | South Caro. St. | 321.5 | Portland St. | 378.5 |
| 1978 | Western St. | 487.0 | Western St. | 320.2 | Northern Mich. | 242.3 |
| 1979 | Delaware | 450.5 | Mississippi Col. | 314.5 | Northern Mich. | 284.2 |
| 1980 | Southwest Tex. St. | 423.0 | Minn.-Duluth | 307.3 | Northern Mich. | 269.6 |
| 1981 | Southwest Tex. St. | 482.3 | Millersville | 322.9 | Franklin | 306.5 |
| 1982 | Northern Mich. | 450.4 | Mississippi Col. | 297.0 | Evansville | 313.0 |
| 1983 | Central St. (Ohio) | 491.1 | Jamestown | 297.7 | Franklin | 358.0 |
| 1984 | North Dak. St. | 455.3 | North Dak. St. | 334.7 | Franklin | 334.0 |
| 1985 | Northeast Mo. St. | 471.4 | Saginaw Valley | 300.4 | Northeast Mo. St. | 345.1 |
| 1986 | Texas A&I | 542.6 | Texas A&I | 395.2 | West Tex. St. | 345.5 |
| 1987 | Texas A&I | 486.4 | Texas A&I | 330.5 | Evansville | 306.6 |
| 1988 | Cal St. Sacramento | 486.0 | North Dak. St. | 373.1 | Central Fla. | 292.2 |
| 1989 | Grand Valley St. | 446.3 | Wofford | 373.7 | Cal St. Chico | 328.8 |
| 1990 | Chadron St. | 479.6 | North Dak. St. | 364.2 | New Haven | 335.4 |
| 1991 | Western St. | 549.8 | Wofford | 347.9 | Western St. | 357.4 |
| 1992 | New Haven | 587.7 | Pittsburg St. | 353.8 | Gardner-Webb | 367.8 |

### Scoring Offense

| Year | Team | Avg. | Year | Team | Avg. |
|------|------|------|------|------|------|
| 1948 | Sul Ross St. | 43.1 | 1963 | Col. of Emporia | 42.4 |
| 1949 | Pacific (Cal.) | 50.0 | 1964 | San Diego St. | 42.3 |
| 1950 | West Tex. St. | 37.2 | 1965 | Ottawa | 43.2 |
| 1951 | Western Ill. | 42.1 | 1966 | N. M. Highlands | 48.1 |
| 1952 | East Tex. St. | 49.6 | 1967 | Waynesburg | 53.7 |
| 1953 | Col. of Idaho | 42.4 | 1968 | Doane | 52.9 |
| 1954 | Col. of Emporia | 43.2 | 1969 | St. Olaf | 45.2 |
| 1955 | Central Mich. | 36.3 | 1970 | Wittenberg | 40.0 |
| 1956 | Florida A&M | 45.9 | 1971 | Michigan Tech | 42.4 |
| 1957 | Denison | 38.6 | 1972 | Fort Valley St. | 45.0 |
| 1958 | Wheaton (Ill.) | 44.6 | 1973 | Western Ky. | 37.7 |
| 1959 | Florida A&M | 42.6 | 1974 | Boise St. | 44.6 |
| 1960 | Florida A&M | 52.8 | 1975 | Bethune-Cookman | 37.9 |
| 1961 | Florida A&M | *54.7 | 1976 | Northern Mich. | 43.0 |
| 1962 | Florida A&M | 42.0 | 1977 | South Caro. St. | 38.4 |

| Year | Team | Avg. |
|---|---|---|
| 1978 | Western St. | 45.2 |
| 1979 | Delaware | 35.5 |
| 1980 | Minn.-Duluth | 35.4 |
| 1981 | Southwest Tex. St. | 37.5 |
| 1982 | Northeast Mo. St. | 40.0 |
| 1983 | Central St. (Ohio) | 43.6 |
| 1984 | North Dak. St. | 39.0 |
| 1985 | UC Davis | 37.6 |
| 1986 | Texas A&I | 43.1 |
| 1987 | West Chester | 34.5 |
|  | Central Fla. | 34.5 |
| 1988 | North Dak. St. | 39.6 |
|  | Texas A&I | 39.6 |
| 1989 | Grand Valley St. | 44.5 |
| 1990 | Indiana (Pa.) | 44.2 |
| 1991 | Western St. | 46.1 |
| 1992 | New Haven | 50.5 |

* Record.

# ANNUAL TEAM DEFENSE CHAMPIONS

| Year | Total Defense Team | Avg. | Rushing Defense Team | Avg. | Pass Defense Team | $Avg. |
|---|---|---|---|---|---|---|
| 1948 | Morgan St. | 104.4 | Morgan St. | 44.8 | Ashland | *10.1 |
| 1949 | Southern Conn. St. | 95.6 | Hanover | 43.5 | Wilmington (Ohio) | 39.8 |
| 1950 | Southern Conn. St. | 93.6 | Lewis & Clark | 50.3 | Vermont | 34.4 |
| 1951 | Southern Conn. St. | 84.3 | Southern Conn. St. | 17.1 | Alfred | 52.0 |
| 1952 | West Chester | 128.4 | East Tex. St. | 48.5 | Cortland St. | 45.9 |
| 1953 | Shippensburg | 81.9 | Shippensburg | 53.6 | Shippensburg | 28.3 |
| 1954 | Geneva | 106.3 | Tennessee St. | 29.2 | St. Augustine's | 26.5 |
| 1955 | Col. of Emporia | 102.0 | Muskingum | 52.5 | Ithaca | 15.5 |
| 1956 | Tennessee St. | 118.9 | Hillsdale | 51.1 | West Va. Tech | 29.1 |
| 1957 | West Chester | 90.2 | West Chester | 27.9 | Lake Forest | 25.0 |
| 1958 | Rose-Hulman | 95.8 | Ithaca | 48.4 | Coast Guard | 25.4 |
| 1959 | Maryland St. | 75.3 | Maryland St. | 36.3 | Huron | 21.9 |
| 1960 | Maryland St. | 104.8 | West Chester | 41.4 | Susquehanna | 27.3 |
| 1961 | Florida A&M | 85.3 | Florida A&M | 20.1 | Westminster (Utah) | 24.8 |
| 1962 | John Carroll | *44.4 | John Carroll | -1.0 | Principia | 27.8 |
| 1963 | West Chester | 100.8 | St. John's (Minn.) | 12.9 | Western Caro. | 39.3 |
| 1964 | Morgan St. | 126.4 | Fort Valley St. | 39.7 | Eastern Mont. | 44.1 |
| 1965 | Morgan St. | 91.5 | Morgan St. | 15.0 | Minot St. | 44.5 |
| 1966 | Tennessee St. | 85.7 | Tennessee St. | 13.9 | Manchester | 54.7 |
| 1967 | Tennessee St. | 61.6 | Tennessee St. | *-16.7 | Mount Union | 61.4 |
| 1968 | Alcorn St. | 103.4 | Alcorn St. | 8.8 | Bridgeport | 47.6 |
| 1969 | Livingstone | 148.5 | Kings Point | 16.2 | Wabash | 72.0 |
| 1970 | Delaware St. | 103.5 | Delaware St. | -4.9 | Hampden-Sydney | 62.9 |
| 1971 | Hampden-Sydney | 115.6 | Northern Colo. | 27.5 | Western Ky. | 57.7 |
| 1972 | Wis.-Whitewater | 143.8 | Alcorn St. | 49.8 | Howard | 48.8 |
| 1973 | Livingstone | 114.9 | Alcorn St. | 45.9 | East Stroudsburg | 37.6 |
| 1974 | Livingstone | 120.5 | Livingstone | 53.0 | Tennessee St. | 52.6 |
| 1975 | South Caro. St. | 100.6 | Alcorn St. | 15.9 | N.C. Central | 60.2 |
| 1976 | Alcorn St. | 108.9 | Alcorn St. | 32.5 | Morris Brown | 60.8 |
| 1977 | Virginia Union | 160.3 | Virginia Union | 63.6 | Delaware St. | 64.3 |
| 1978 | East Stroudsburg | 153.8 | East Stroudsburg | 52.2 | Concordia-M'head | 55.8 |
| 1979 | Virginia Union | 138.2 | Virginia Union | 41.0 | Kentucky St. | 62.3 |
| 1980 | Concordia-M'head | 191.7 | Missouri-Rolla | 34.6 | Norfolk St. | 71.5 |
| 1981 | Fort Valley St. | 148.3 | Fort Valley St. | 46.9 | Bowie St. | 75.7 |
| 1982 | Jamestown | 187.9 | Butler | 71.1 | Elizabeth City St. | 49.0 |
| 1983 | Virginia Union | 143.7 | Butler | 38.2 | Elizabeth City St. | 65.0 |
| 1984 | Virginia St. | 180.6 | Norfolk St. | 53.8 | Virginia St. | 80.4 |
| 1985 | Fort Valley St. | 162.2 | Norfolk St. | 50.9 | Fort Valley St. | 94.5 |
| 1986 | Virginia Union | 163.5 | Central St. (Ohio) | 44.5 | Virginia Union | 84.7 |
| 1987 | Alabama A&M | 167.1 | West Chester | 67.2 | Alabama A&M | 72.5 |
| 1988 | Alabama A&M | 175.8 | Cal Poly SLO | 56.4 | Alabama A&M | 84.3 |
| 1989 | Winston-Salem | 185.7 | Texas A&I | 60.7 | Mo. Southern St. | 93.0 |
| 1990 | Sonoma St. | 218.5 | Sonoma St. | 58.3 | Angelo St. | 65.4 |
| 1991 | Ashland | 195.5 | Sonoma St. | 63.6 | Carson-Newman | 64.9 |
| 1992 | Ashland | 211.5 | Ashland | 64.4 | East Tex. St. | 61.8 |

## Scoring Defense

| Year | Team | Avg. | Year | Team | Avg. |
|---|---|---|---|---|---|
| 1959 | Huron | 2.1 | 1964 | Central (Iowa) | 4.8 |
| 1960 | Albany St. (Ga.) | *0.0 | 1965 | St. John's (Minn.) | 2.2 |
| 1961 | Florida A&M | 2.8 | 1966 | Morgan St. | 3.6 |
| 1962 | John Carroll | 2.9 | 1967 | Waynesburg | 4.3 |
| 1963 | Massachusetts | 1.3 | 1968 | Central Conn. St. | 4.4 |

| Year | Team | Avg. |
|------|------|------|
| 1969 | Carthage .............6.0 | |
| 1970 | Hampden-Sydney ......2.8 | |
| 1971 | Hampden-Sydney ......3.4 | |
| 1972 | Ashland.................5.6 | |
| 1973 | Virginia Union .........3.8 | |
| 1974 | Minn.-Duluth ..........5.5 | |
| 1975 | South Caro. St. .........2.9 | |
| 1976 | South Caro. St. .........3.4 | |
| 1977 | Minn.-Duluth ...........7.8 | |
| 1978 | Southwestern La. .......7.1 | |
| 1979 | Virginia Union .........6.1 | |
| 1980 | Minn.-Duluth ..........7.6 | |
| 1981 | Moorhead St. ...........5.0 | |
| 1982 | Jamestown .............5.9 | |
| 1983 | Towson St...............5.8 | |

| Year | Team | Avg. |
|------|------|------|
| 1984 | Cal Poly SLO ..........9.0 | |
| 1985 | Fort Valley St...........6.3 | |
| 1986 | North Dak. St. .........6.8 | |
| 1987 | Tuskegee ..............9.1 | |
| 1988 | Alabama A&M .........7.5 | |
| 1989 | Jacksonville St. .........7.0 | |
| 1990 | Cal Poly SLO ..........11.3 | |
| 1991 | Butler ..................7.1 | |
| 1992 | Ferris St................10.5 | |

* *Record.* $ *Beginning in 1990, based on passing efficiency ranking instead of yards per game.*

## OTHER ANNUAL TEAM CHAMPIONS

| Year | Net Punting | Avg. | Punt Returns | Avg. | Kickoff Returns | Avg. |
|------|-------------|------|--------------|------|-----------------|------|
| 1992 | Fort Lewis .............37.9 | | Savannah St. ..........21.2 | | Jacksonville St. ........34.0 | |

| Year | Turnover Margin | Mar. |
|------|-----------------|------|
| 1992 | Hillsdale ...............2.2 | |

# STREAKS AND RIVALRIES

## ** LONGEST STREAKS
### (From 1931; includes postseason games)

### Winning Streaks

| Wins | Team | Years |
|------|------|-------|
| 34 | Hillsdale .................1954-57 | |
| 32 | Wilkes.....................1965-69 | |
| 31 | Morgan St.................1965-68 | |
| 31 | Mo. Valley................1946-48 | |
| 29 | East Tex. St...............1951-53 | |
| 25 | San Diego St. ............1965-67 | |
| 25 | Peru St. ..................1951-54 | |
| 25 | Maryland St. .............1948-51 | |
| 24 | North Dak. St.............1964-66 | |
| 24 | Wesleyan .................1945-48 | |

### Unbeaten Streaks

| No. | Wins | Ties | Team | Years |
|-----|------|------|------|-------|
| 54 | 47 | 7 | Morgan St................1931-38 | |
| 38 | 36 | 2 | Doane .....................1965-70 | |
| 37 | 35 | 2 | Southern-B.R..............1947-51 | |
| 35 | 34 | 1 | North Dak. St.............1968-71 | |
| 31 | 29 | 2 | St. Ambrose .............1935-38 | |
| 30 | 29 | 1 | Wittenberg .............1961-65 | |
| 30 | 29 | 1 | East Tex. St...............1951-53 | |
| 28 | 27 | 1 | Wesleyan ................†1942-48 | |
| 28 | 27 | 1 | Case Reserve ............1934-37 | |
| 27 | 26 | 1 | Juniata...................1956-59 | |

** *During 1973-77 (a period when it was not an NCAA-member college), Texas A&I won 42 consecutive games and was unbeaten during 46 consecutive games (including one tie).* † *Did not field teams 1943-44.*

## MOST-PLAYED RIVALRIES

| Games | Opponents (Series leader listed first) | Series Record | First Game |
|-------|----------------------------------------|---------------|------------|
| 97 | North Dak.-North Dak. St......................................... | 52-42-3 | 1894 |
| 93 | South Dak.-South Dak. St......................................... | 47-39-7 | 1889 |
| 88 | Colorado Mines-Colorado Col. ................................. | 46-37-5 | 1889 |
| 83 | South Dak.-Morningside ........................................ | 50-28-5 | 1898 |
| 82 | Tuskegee-Morehouse ........................................... | 51-25-6 | 1902 |
| 81 | Virginia Union-Hampton ........................................ | 41-37-3 | 1906 |
| 79 | North Dak. St.-South Dak. St. ................................... | 41-33-5 | 1903 |

# ALL-TIME WON-LOST RECORDS

Includes records as a senior college only, minimum of 20 seasons of competition since 1937. Postseason games are included, and each tie game is computed as half won and half lost.

### TOP 25—BY PERCENTAGE

| Team | Yrs. | Won | Lost | Tied | Pct. |
|------|------|-----|------|------|------|
| West Chester.................. | 64 | 413 | 166 | 16 | .708 |
| Texas A&I .................... | 64 | 432 | 193 | 16 | .686 |
| Neb.-Kearney ................ | 69 | 387 | 213 | 26 | .639 |
| Indiana (Pa.) ................. | 63 | 347 | 195 | 23 | .635 |
| Central Okla.................. | 87 | 476 | 266 | 46 | .633 |

### TOP 25—BY VICTORIES

| Team | Wins |
|------|------|
| Hillsdale ....................484 | |
| Tuskegee ...................477 | |
| Central Okla. ...............476 | |
| North Dak. St. ..............474 | |
| Pittsburg St. ................470 | |

## TOP 25—BY PERCENTAGE

| Team | Yrs. | Won | Lost | Tied | Pct. |
|---|---|---|---|---|---|
| Grand Valley St. | 22 | 139 | 82 | 1 | .628 |
| Pittsburg St. | 85 | 470 | 277 | 46 | .622 |
| Minn.-Duluth | 60 | 307 | 183 | 23 | .621 |
| Virginia Union | 92 | 426 | 253 | 44 | .620 |
| Mesa St. | 17 | 109 | 66 | 5 | .619 |
| Tuskegee | 95 | 477 | 286 | 50 | .617 |
| Northeast Mo. St. | 85 | 435 | 265 | 35 | .616 |
| Hillsdale | 100 | 484 | 298 | 45 | .612 |
| Carson-Newman | 69 | 387 | 241 | 29 | .611 |
| East Stroudsburg | 65 | 333 | 210 | 18 | .610 |
| North Dak. St. | 96 | 474 | 298 | 34 | .609 |
| Angelo St. | 29 | 186 | 119 | 6 | .608 |
| Fort Valley St. | 47 | 259 | 165 | 20 | .606 |
| Jacksonville St. | 60 | 325 | 211 | 27 | .601 |
| North Dak. | 96 | 447 | 308 | 29 | .589 |
| Virginia St. | 81 | 398 | 259 | 48 | .584 |
| Central Ark. | 81 | 396 | 282 | 41 | .579 |
| Southern Conn. St. | 45 | 235 | 170 | 10 | .578 |
| East Tex. St. | 75 | 393 | 287 | 31 | .575 |
| Northern Mich. | 79 | 322 | 243 | 25 | .567 |

## TOP 25—BY VICTORIES

| Team | Wins |
|---|---|
| North Dak. | 447 |
| Northeast Mo. St. | 435 |
| Texas A&I | 432 |
| Northern St. | 428 |
| Virginia Union | 426 |
| South Dak. St. | 416 |
| Washburn | 416 |
| West Chester | 413 |
| South Dak. | 407 |
| Springfield | 407 |
| Virginia St. | 398 |
| Central Ark. | 396 |
| East Tex. St. | 393 |
| Carson-Newman | 387 |
| Neb.-Kearney | 387 |
| Hampton | 385 |
| Mississippi Col. | 381 |
| Elon | 379 |
| Presbyterian | 376 |
| Lenoir-Rhyne | 374 |

## ALPHABETICAL
(No minimum seasons of competition.)

| Team | Yrs. | Won | Lost | Tied | Pct. |
|---|---|---|---|---|---|
| Abilene Christian | 71 | 355 | 291 | 32 | .547 |
| Adams St. | 58 | 255 | 221 | 16 | .535 |
| Alabama A&M | 55 | 249 | 223 | 25 | .526 |
| Albany St. (Ga.) | 47 | 210 | 203 | 21 | .508 |
| American Int'l | 56 | 226 | 232 | 20 | .494 |
| Angelo St. | 29 | 186 | 119 | 6 | .608 |
| Ashland | 70 | 320 | 264 | 29 | .546 |
| Assumption | 5 | 13 | 29 | 1 | .314 |
| Augustana (S.D.) | 72 | 280 | 326 | 13 | .463 |
| Bemidji St. | 67 | 218 | 308 | 23 | .418 |
| Bentley | 5 | 30 | 13 | 1 | .693 |
| Bloomsburg | 65 | 247 | 272 | 20 | .477 |
| Bowie St. | 21 | 69 | 127 | 5 | .356 |
| Cal Poly SLO | 52 | 276 | 211 | 9 | .566 |
| Cal St. Chico | 69 | 281 | 318 | 21 | .470 |
| Cal St. Hayward | 29 | 125 | 158 | 7 | .443 |
| Calif. (Pa.) | 63 | 235 | 265 | 19 | .471 |
| Cameron | 25 | 136 | 115 | 8 | .541 |
| Carson-Newman | 69 | 387 | 241 | 29 | .611 |
| Catawba | 73 | 346 | 333 | 26 | .509 |
| Central Ark. | 81 | 396 | 282 | 41 | .579 |
| Central Mo. St. | 96 | 367 | 417 | 50 | .470 |
| Central Okla. | 87 | 476 | 266 | 46 | .633 |
| Chadron St. | 78 | 333 | 284 | 15 | .539 |
| Cheyney | 39 | 79 | 258 | 4 | .238 |
| Clarion | 64 | 294 | 224 | 17 | .565 |
| Clark Atlanta | 54 | 172 | 252 | 23 | .411 |
| Colorado Mines | 103 | 308 | 426 | 30 | .423 |
| Concord | 68 | 305 | 273 | 27 | .526 |
| Delta St. | 63 | 289 | 286 | 21 | .503 |
| East Stroudsburg | 65 | 333 | 210 | 18 | .610 |
| East Tex. St. | 75 | 393 | 287 | 31 | .575 |
| Eastern N. Mex. | 49 | 246 | 229 | 12 | .517 |
| Edinboro | 64 | 227 | 273 | 24 | .456 |
| Elizabeth City St. | 51 | 222 | 216 | 18 | .507 |
| Elon | 71 | 379 | 290 | 18 | .565 |
| Emporia St. | 95 | 371 | 402 | 44 | .481 |
| Fairmont St. | 79 | 339 | 273 | 44 | .550 |
| Fayetteville St. | 47 | 156 | 252 | 23 | .389 |
| Ferris St. | 64 | 217 | 285 | 32 | .436 |
| Fort Hays St. | 71 | 313 | 332 | 46 | .486 |
| Fort Lewis | 29 | 101 | 163 | 3 | .384 |
| Fort Valley St. | 47 | 259 | 165 | 20 | .606 |
| Gannon | 5 | 29 | 15 | 1 | .656 |
| Gardner-Webb | 23 | 115 | 127 | 2 | .475 |

| Team | Yrs. | Won | Lost | Tied | Pct. |
|------|------|-----|------|------|------|
| Glenville St. | 80 | 230 | 312 | 37 | .429 |
| Grand Valley St. | 22 | 139 | 82 | 1 | .628 |
| Hampton | 91 | 385 | 316 | 34 | .547 |
| Henderson St. | 85 | 367 | 309 | 43 | .540 |
| Hillsdale | 100 | 484 | 298 | 45 | .612 |
| Humboldt St. | 65 | 290 | 252 | 18 | .534 |
| Indiana (Pa.) | 63 | 347 | 195 | 23 | .635 |
| Indianapolis | 55 | 232 | 244 | 22 | .488 |
| Jacksonville St. | 60 | 325 | 211 | 27 | .601 |
| Johnson Smith | 65 | 263 | 282 | 34 | .484 |
| Kentucky St. | 64 | 272 | 315 | 25 | .465 |
| Kutztown | 62 | 204 | 286 | 21 | .420 |
| Ky. Wesleyan | 32 | 89 | 131 | 16 | .411 |
| Lenoir-Rhyne | 73 | 374 | 298 | 34 | .554 |
| LIU-C. W. Post | 36 | 197 | 142 | 5 | .580 |
| Livingston | 51 | 194 | 257 | 14 | .432 |
| Livingstone | 44 | 170 | 220 | 14 | .438 |
| Lock Haven | 64 | 242 | 306 | 25 | .444 |
| Mankato St. | 67 | 284 | 264 | 27 | .517 |
| Mansfield | 63 | 200 | 295 | 30 | .410 |
| Mars Hill | 29 | 127 | 153 | 10 | .455 |
| Mass.-Lowell | 13 | 65 | 54 | 2 | .545 |
| Mercyhurst | 12 | 60 | 44 | 3 | .575 |
| Mesa St. | 17 | 109 | 66 | 5 | .619 |
| Michigan Tech | 70 | 243 | 234 | 17 | .509 |
| Miles | 23 | 43 | 155 | 6 | .225 |
| Millersville | 61 | 262 | 232 | 20 | .529 |
| Minn.-Duluth | 60 | 307 | 183 | 23 | .621 |
| Minn.-Morris | 31 | 161 | 128 | 10 | .555 |
| Mississippi Col. | 80 | 381 | 290 | 34 | .565 |
| Missouri-Rolla | 87 | 330 | 381 | 35 | .466 |
| Mo. Southern St. | 25 | 133 | 114 | 6 | .538 |
| Mo. Western St. | 23 | 98 | 134 | 7 | .425 |
| Moorhead St. | 75 | 321 | 273 | 29 | .539 |
| Morehouse | 93 | 320 | 330 | 49 | .493 |
| Morningside | 91 | 326 | 401 | 35 | .451 |
| Morris Brown | 67 | 302 | 270 | 37 | .526 |
| N.C. Central | 62 | 311 | 236 | 24 | .566 |
| Neb.-Kearney | 69 | 387 | 213 | 26 | .639 |
| Nebraska-Omaha | 76 | 315 | 310 | 30 | .504 |
| New Haven | 20 | 99 | 92 | 4 | .518 |
| Newberry | 79 | 291 | 422 | 33 | .412 |
| N.M. Highlands | 66 | 225 | 289 | 26 | .441 |
| Norfolk St. | 32 | 158 | 142 | 6 | .526 |
| North Ala. | 44 | 245 | 186 | 16 | .566 |
| North Dak. | 96 | 447 | 308 | 29 | .589 |
| North Dak. St. | 96 | 474 | 298 | 34 | .609 |
| Northeast Mo. St. | 85 | 435 | 265 | 35 | .616 |
| Northern Colo. | 80 | 300 | 320 | 24 | .484 |
| Northern Mich. | 79 | 322 | 243 | 25 | .567 |
| Northern St. | 87 | 428 | 251 | 33 | .624 |
| Northwest Mo. St. | 75 | 304 | 336 | 32 | .476 |
| Northwood | 31 | 123 | 148 | 6 | .455 |
| Pace | 15 | 56 | 83 | 2 | .404 |
| Pittsburg St. | 85 | 470 | 277 | 46 | .622 |
| Portland St. | 38 | 193 | 193 | 7 | .500 |
| Presbyterian | 80 | 376 | 356 | 35 | .513 |
| Quincy | 7 | 31 | 33 | 1 | .485 |
| Sacred Heart | 2 | 5 | 13 | 0 | .278 |
| Saginaw Valley | 18 | 92 | 92 | 3 | .500 |
| San Fran. St. | 60 | 236 | 290 | 21 | .451 |
| Savannah St. | 40 | 150 | 204 | 13 | .426 |
| Shepherd | 69 | 288 | 257 | 26 | .527 |
| Shippensburg | 63 | 298 | 246 | 21 | .546 |
| Slippery Rock | 65 | 310 | 234 | 28 | .566 |
| Sonoma St. | 14 | 57 | 84 | 1 | .405 |
| South Dak. | 97 | 407 | 382 | 34 | .515 |
| South Dak. St. | 95 | 416 | 348 | 38 | .542 |
| Southern Conn. St. | 45 | 235 | 170 | 10 | .578 |
| Southwest Baptist | 10 | 39 | 58 | 2 | .404 |

| Team | Yrs. | Won | Lost | Tied | Pct. |
|------|------|-----|------|------|------|
| Southwest St. | 25 | 97 | 144 | 5 | .404 |
| Springfield | 99 | 407 | 363 | 55 | .527 |
| St. Cloud St. | 65 | 299 | 242 | 21 | .551 |
| St. Francis (Ill.) | 7 | 43 | 27 | 0 | .614 |
| St. Joseph's (Ind.) | 73 | 228 | 281 | 23 | .452 |
| Stonehill | 5 | 23 | 17 | 3 | .570 |
| Texas A&I | 64 | 432 | 193 | 16 | .686 |
| Tuskegee | 95 | 477 | 286 | 50 | .617 |
| UC Davis | 74 | 347 | 288 | 32 | .544 |
| Valdosta St. | 11 | 62 | 48 | 3 | .562 |
| Virginia St. | 81 | 398 | 259 | 48 | .584 |
| Virginia Union | 92 | 426 | 253 | 44 | .620 |
| Washburn | 101 | 416 | 438 | 40 | .488 |
| Wayne St. (Mich.) | 75 | 261 | 327 | 29 | .447 |
| Wayne St. (Neb.) | 67 | 280 | 326 | 38 | .464 |
| West Chester | 64 | 413 | 166 | 16 | .708 |
| West Ga. | 14 | 59 | 84 | 0 | .413 |
| West Liberty St. | 66 | 318 | 255 | 35 | .552 |
| West Tex. St. | 81 | 354 | 379 | 22 | .483 |
| West Va. Tech | 73 | 262 | 298 | 35 | .470 |
| Western St. | 70 | 281 | 298 | 13 | .486 |
| Wingate | 7 | 28 | 40 | 0 | .412 |
| Winona St. | 92 | 247 | 400 | 31 | .387 |
| Winston-Salem | 49 | 253 | 199 | 19 | .557 |
| Wofford | 84 | 354 | 385 | 35 | .480 |

## WIRE SERVICE NATIONAL CHAMPIONS

### (1958-74)

(For what was then known as College Division teams. Selections by United Press International from 1958 and Associated Press from 1960.)

| Year | Team | Coach | *Record |
|------|------|-------|---------|
| 1958 | Southern Miss. | Thad "Pie" Vann | 9-0-0 |
| 1959 | Bowling Green | Doyt Perry | 9-0-0 |
| 1960 | Ohio | Bill Hess | 10-0-0 |
| 1961 | Pittsburg St. | Carnie Smith | 9-0-0 |
| 1962 | Southern Miss. (UPI) | Thad "Pie" Vann | 9-1-0 |
| | Florida A&M (AP) | Jake Gaither | 9-0-0 |
| 1963 | Delaware (UPI) | Dave Nelson | 8-0-0 |
| | Northern Ill. (AP) | Howard Fletcher | 9-0-0 |
| 1964 | Cal St. Los Angeles (UPI) | Homer Beatty | 9-0-0 |
| | Wittenberg (AP) | Bill Edwards | 8-0-0 |
| 1965 | North Dak. St. | Darrell Mudra | 10-0-0 |
| 1966 | San Diego St. | Don Coryell | 10-0-0 |
| 1967 | San Diego St. | Don Coryell | 9-1-0 |
| 1968 | San Diego St. (UPI) | Don Coryell | 9-0-1 |
| | North Dak. St. (AP) | Ron Erhardt | 9-0-0 |
| 1969 | North Dak. St. | Ron Erhardt | 9-0-0 |
| 1970 | Arkansas St. | Bennie Ellender | 10-0-0 |
| 1971 | Delaware | Harold "Tubby" Raymond | 9-1-0 |
| 1972 | Delaware | Harold "Tubby" Raymond | 10-0-0 |
| 1973 | Tennessee St. | John Merritt | 10-0-0 |
| 1974 | Louisiana Tech (UPI) | Maxie Lambright | 10-0-0 |
| | Central Mich. (AP) | Roy Kramer | 9-1-0 |

* *Regular season.*

## NCAA DIVISION II FINAL POLL LEADERS

### (Released before the division championship playoffs)

| Year | Team, Record* | Coach | †Record in Championship Playoffs |
|------|---------------|-------|----------------------------------|
| 1975 | North Dak. (9-0-0) | Jerry Olson | 0-1 Lost in first round |
| 1976 | Northern Mich. (10-0-0) | Gil Krueger | 1-1 Lost in semifinals |
| 1977 | North Dak. St. (8-1-1) | Jim Wacker | 1-1 Lost in semifinals |
| 1978 | Winston-Salem (10-0-0) | Bill Hayes | Did not compete |
| 1979 | Delaware (9-1-0) | Harold "Tubby" Raymond | 3-0 Champion |

| Year | Team, Record* | Coach | †Record in Championship Playoffs |
|------|---------------|-------|----------------------------------|
| 1980 | Eastern Ill. (8-2-0) | Darrell Mudra | 2-1 Runner-up |
| 1981 | Southwest Tex. St. (9-0-0) | Jim Wacker | 3-0 Champion |
| 1982 | Southwest Tex. St. (11-0-0) | Jim Wacker | 3-0 Champion |
| 1983 | UC Davis (9-0-0) | Jim Sochor | 1-1 Lost in semifinals |
| 1984 | North Dak. St. (9-1-0) | Don Morton | 2-1 Runner-up |
| 1985 | UC Davis (9-1-0) | Jim Sochor | 0-1 Lost in first round |
| 1986 | North Dak. St. (10-0-0) | Earle Solomonson | 3-0 Champion |
| 1987 | Texas A&I (9-1-0) | Ron Harms | Did not compete |
| 1988 | North Dak. St. (10-0-0) | Rocky Hager | 4-0 Champion |
| 1989 | Texas A&I (10-0-0) | Ron Harms | 0-1 Lost in first round |
| 1990 | North Dak. St. (10-0-0) | Rocky Hager | 4-0 Champion |
| 1991 | Indiana (Pa.) (10-0-0) | Frank Cignetti | 2-1 Lost in semifinals |
| 1992 | Pittsburg St. (11-0-0) | Chuck Broyles | 3-1 Runner-up |

* Final poll record; in some cases, a team had one game remaining before the championship play-offs.   † Number of teams in the championship: 8 (1975-87); 16 (1988-).

# UNDEFEATED, UNTIED TEAMS

### (Regular-season games only)

In 1948, official national statistics rankings began to include all nonmajor four-year colleges. Until the 1967 season, rankings and records included all four-year colleges that reported their statistics to the NCAA. Beginning with the 1967 season, statistics (and won-lost records) included only members of the NCAA.

Since 1981, conference playoff games have been included in a team's regular-season statistics and won-lost record (previously, such games were considered postseason contests).

The regular-season list includes games in which a home team served as a predetermined, preseason host of a "bowl game" regardless of its record and/or games scheduled before the season, thus eliminating as postseason designation the Orange Blossom Classic, annually hosted by Florida A&M, and the Prairie View Bowl, annually hosted by Prairie View, for example.

Figures are regular-season wins only. A subsequent postseason win(s) is indicated by (*), a loss by (†) and a tie by (‡).

| Year | College | Wins | Year | College | Wins | Year | College | Wins |
|------|---------|------|------|---------|------|------|---------|------|
| 1948 | Alma | 8 | | West Liberty St. | *8 | | Juniata | 7 |
| | Bloomsburg | 9 | | Wis.-La Crosse | *9 | | Northern St. | 8 |
| | Denison | 8 | | Wis.-Whitewater | 6 | | N'western (Wis.) | 6 |
| | Heidelberg | 9 | 1951 | Bloomsburg | 8 | | Peru St. | 8 |
| | Michigan Tech | 7 | | Bucknell | 9 | | Prairie View | 10 |
| | Missouri Valley | †‡9 | | Col. of Emporia | 8 | | Shippensburg | 8 |
| | Occidental | *8 | | Ill. Wesleyan | 8 | | St. Olaf | 8 |
| | Southern-B.R. | *11 | | Lawrence | 7 | | Westminster (Pa.) | 8 |
| | Sul Ross St. | ‡10 | | Northern Ill. | 9 | | Wis.-La Crosse | ‡9 |
| | Wesleyan | 8 | | Principia | 6 | | Wis.-Platteville | 6 |
| 1949 | Ball St. | 8 | | South Dak. Tech | 8 | 1954 | Ashland | 7 |
| | Emory & Henry | *†10 | | St. Michael's | 6 | | Carleton | 8 |
| | Gannon | 8 | | Susquehanna | 6 | | Central Conn. St. | 6 |
| | Hanover | †8 | | Trenton St. | 6 | | Col. of Emporia | †9 |
| | Lewis | 8 | | Valparaiso | 9 | | Delta St. | 8 |
| | Md.-East. Shore | 8 | | Western Md. | 8 | | Hastings | *8 |
| | Morgan St. | 8 | 1952 | Beloit | 8 | | Hobart | 8 |
| | Pacific (Cal.) | 11 | | Clarion | *8 | | Juniata | 8 |
| | St. Ambrose | 8 | | East Tex. St. | *10 | | Luther | 9 |
| | St. Vincent | *9 | | Fairmont St. | 6 | | Miles | 8 |
| | Trinity (Conn.) | 8 | | Idaho St. | 8 | | Nebraska-Omaha | *9 |
| | Wayne St. (Neb.) | 9 | | Lenoir-Rhyne | †8 | | N'western (Wis.) | 6 |
| | Wofford | 11 | | Northeastern Okla. | †9 | | Pomona-Pitzer | 8 |
| 1950 | Abilene Christian | *10 | | Peru St. | 10 | | Principia | 7 |
| | Canterbury | 8 | | Rochester | 8 | | Southeastern La. | 9 |
| | Florida St. | 8 | | Shippensburg | 7 | | Tennessee St. | †10 |
| | Frank. & Marsh. | 9 | | St. Norbert | 6 | | Trinity (Conn.) | 7 |
| | Lehigh | 9 | | West Chester | 7 | | Trinity (Tex.) | 9 |
| | Lewis & Clark | *8 | 1953 | Cal Poly SLO | 8 | | Whitworth | 8 |
| | Md.-East. Shore | 8 | | Col. of Emporia | 8 | | Widener | 7 |
| | Mission House | 6 | | Col. of Idaho | †8 | | Worcester Tech | 6 |
| | New Hampshire | 8 | | Defiance | †8 | 1955 | Alfred | 8 |
| | St. Lawrence | 8 | | East Tex. St. | ‡10 | | Centre | 8 |
| | St. Norbert | 7 | | Florida A&M | 10 | | Coe | 8 |
| | Thiel | 7 | | Indianapolis | 8 | | Col. of Emporia | 9 |
| | Valparaiso | †9 | | Iowa Wesleyan | †9 | | Drexel | 8 |

| Year | College | Wins |
|---|---|---|
| | Grambling | 10 |
| | Heidelberg | 9 |
| | Hillsdale | 9 |
| | Juniata | ‡8 |
| | Md.-East. Shore | 9 |
| | Miami (Ohio) | 9 |
| | Muskingum | 8 |
| | Northern St. | †9 |
| | Parsons | 8 |
| | Shepherd | 8 |
| | Southeast Mo. St. | 9 |
| | Trinity (Conn.) | 7 |
| | Whitworth | 9 |
| | Wis.-Stevens Point | 8 |
| 1956 | Alfred | 7 |
| | Central Mich. | 9 |
| | Hillsdale | 9 |
| | Lenoir-Rhyne | 10 |
| | Milton | 6 |
| | Montana St. | ‡9 |
| | Neb.-Kearney | 9 |
| | Redlands | 9 |
| | Sam Houston St. | *9 |
| | Southern Conn. St. | 9 |
| | St. Thomas (Minn.) | 8 |
| | Tennessee St. | 10 |
| | Westminster (Pa.) | 8 |
| 1957 | Elon | 6 |
| | Fairmont St. | 7 |
| | Florida A&M | 9 |
| | Hillsdale | †9 |
| | Hobart | 6 |
| | Idaho St. | 9 |
| | Jamestown | 7 |
| | Juniata | 7 |
| | Lock Haven | 8 |
| | Middle Tenn. St. | 10 |
| | Pittsburg St. | *10 |
| | Ripon | 8 |
| | St. Norbert | 8 |
| | West Chester | 9 |
| 1958 | Calif. (Pa.) | 8 |
| | Chadron St. | 8 |
| | Gust. Adolphus | †8 |
| | Missouri Valley | †8 |
| | N'eastern Okla. | **9 |
| | Neb.-Kearney | 9 |
| | Northern Ariz. | *†10 |
| | Rochester | 8 |
| | Rose-Hulman | 8 |
| | Sewanee | 8 |
| | Southern Miss. | 9 |
| | St. Benedict's | †10 |
| | Wheaton (Ill.) | 8 |
| 1959 | Bowling Green | 9 |
| | Butler | 9 |
| | Coe | 8 |
| | Fairmont St. | 9 |
| | Florida A&M | 10 |
| | Hofstra | 9 |
| | John Carroll | 7 |
| | Lenoir-Rhyne | *†9 |
| | San Fran. St. | 10 |
| | Western Ill. | 9 |
| 1960 | Albright | 9 |
| | Arkansas Tech | †10 |
| | Humboldt St. | *†10 |
| | Langston | 9 |
| | Lenoir-Rhyne | *‡10 |
| | Montclair St. | 8 |
| | Muskingum | 9 |
| | Northern Iowa | †9 |
| | Ohio | 10 |

| Year | College | Wins |
|---|---|---|
| | Ottawa | 9 |
| | Wagner | 9 |
| | West Chester | 9 |
| | Whitworth | 9 |
| | Willamette | 8 |
| 1961 | Albion | 8 |
| | Baldwin-Wallace | 9 |
| | Butler | 9 |
| | Central Okla. | 9 |
| | Florida A&M | 10 |
| | Fresno St. | *9 |
| | Linfield | *†10 |
| | Mayville St. | 8 |
| | Millikin | 8 |
| | Northern St. | 9 |
| | Ottawa | 9 |
| | Pittsburg St. | **9 |
| | Wash. & Lee | 9 |
| | Wheaton (Ill.) | 6 |
| | Whittier | †9 |
| 1962 | Carthage | 8 |
| | Central Okla. | **9 |
| | Col. of Emporia | †10 |
| | Earlham | 8 |
| | East Stroudsburg | †8 |
| | John Carroll | 7 |
| | Kalamazoo | 8 |
| | Lenoir-Rhyne | *†10 |
| | Northern St. | †9 |
| | Parsons | 9 |
| | St. John's (Minn.) | 9 |
| | Susquehanna | 9 |
| | Wittenberg | 9 |
| 1963 | Alabama A&M | 8 |
| | Central Wash. | 9 |
| | Coast Guard | †8 |
| | Col. of Emporia | 10 |
| | Delaware | 8 |
| | John Carroll | 7 |
| | Lewis & Clark | 8 |
| | Luther | 9 |
| | McNeese St. | 8 |
| | N'eastern Okla. | *10 |
| | Neb.-Kearney | †9 |
| | Northeastern | †8 |
| | Northern Ill. | *9 |
| | Prairie View | *†9 |
| | Ripon | 8 |
| | Sewanee | 6 |
| | Southwest Mo. St. | †9 |
| | Southwest Tex. St. | 10 |
| | St. John's (Minn.) | **8 |
| | Wis.-Eau Claire | 7 |
| 1964 | Albion | 8 |
| | Amherst | 8 |
| | Cal St. Los Angeles | 9 |
| | Concordia-M'head | *†9 |
| | Frank. & Marsh. | 8 |
| | Montclair St. | 7 |
| | Prairie View | 9 |
| | Wagner | 10 |
| | Western St. | †9 |
| | Westminster (Pa.) | 8 |
| | Wittenberg | 8 |
| 1965 | Ball St. | ‡9 |
| | East Stroudsburg | *9 |
| | Fairmont St. | †8 |
| | Georgetown (Ky.) | 9 |
| | Ill. Wesleyan | 8 |
| | Ithaca | 8 |
| | Middle Tenn. St. | 10 |
| | Morgan St. | 9 |
| | North Dak. St. | *10 |

| Year | College | Wins |
|---|---|---|
| | Northern Ill. | †9 |
| | Ottawa | 9 |
| | Springfield | 9 |
| | St. John's (Minn.) | **9 |
| | Sul Ross St. | †10 |
| | Tennessee St. | ‡9 |
| 1966 | Central (Iowa) | †9 |
| | Clarion | *9 |
| | Defiance | 9 |
| | Morgan St. | *8 |
| | Muskingum | †9 |
| | Northwestern (La.) | 9 |
| | San Diego St. | *10 |
| | Tennessee St. | *9 |
| | Waynesburg | **9 |
| | Wilkes | 9 |
| | Wis.-Whitewater | *†9 |

*Beginning in 1967,
NCAA members only.*

| Year | College | Wins |
|---|---|---|
| 1967 | Alma | 8 |
| | Central (Iowa) | 9 |
| | Doane | ‡8 |
| | Lawrence | 8 |
| | Morgan St. | 8 |
| | North Dak. St. | †9 |
| | Northern Mich. | †9 |
| | Wagner | 9 |
| | West Chester | *†9 |
| | Wilkes | 8 |
| 1968 | Alma | 8 |
| | Doane | *9 |
| | East Stroudsburg | ‡8 |
| | Indiana (Pa.) | †9 |
| | North Dak. St. | *9 |
| | Randolph-Macon | 9 |
| 1969 | Albion | 8 |
| | Carthage | 9 |
| | Defiance | 9 |
| | Doane | 8 |
| | Montana | †10 |
| | North Dak. St. | *9 |
| | Northern Colo. | 10 |
| | Wesleyan | 8 |
| | Wittenberg | *9 |
| 1970 | Arkansas St. | *10 |
| | Jacksonville St. | 10 |
| | Montana | †10 |
| | St. Olaf | 9 |
| | Tennessee St. | *10 |
| | Westminster (Pa.) | **8 |
| | #Wittenberg | 9 |
| 1971 | Alfred | 8 |
| | Hampden-Sydney | †10 |
| | Westminster (Pa.) | †‡8 |
| 1972 | Ashland | 11 |
| | Bridgeport | *10 |
| | Delaware | 10 |
| | Doane | †10 |
| | Frank. & Marsh. | 9 |
| | Heidelberg | **9 |
| | Louisiana Tech | *11 |
| | Middlebury | 8 |
| | Monmouth (Ill.) | 9 |
| 1973 | Tennessee St. | 10 |
| | Western Ky. | **†10 |
| 1974 | Louisiana Tech | *†10 |
| | Michigan Tech | 9 |
| | Nevada-Las Vegas | *†11 |
| 1975 | East Stroudsburg | *9 |
| | North Dak. | †9 |
| 1976 | East Stroudsburg | ‡9 |
| 1977 | Florida A&M | 11 |

| Year | College | Wins | Year | College | Wins | Year | College | Wins |
|------|---------|------|------|---------|------|------|---------|------|
| | UC Davis ..........*†10 | | | UC Davis .........**†10 | | 1989 | Grand Valley St. ....†11 | |
| | Winston-Salem .....†11 | | 1983 | Central St. (Ohio) **†10 | | | Jacksonville St. ..***†10 | |
| 1978 | Western St. .........*†9 | | | UC Davis ..........*†10 | | | Pittsburg St. .......*†11 | |
| | Winston-Salem ....*†10 | | 1984 | (None) | | | Texas A&I ..........†10 | |
| 1979 | (None) | | 1985 | Bloomsburg .......*†11 | | 1990 | North Dak. St. ...****10 | |
| 1980 | Minn.-Duluth ........10 | | 1986 | North Dak. St. ....***10 | | | Pittsburg St. .......**†10 | |
| | Missouri-Rolla .......10 | | | UC Davis ..........†10 | | 1991 | Carson-Newman ...†10 | |
| 1981 | Northern Mich. ....*†10 | | | Virginia Union ......†11 | | | Indiana (Pa.)......**†10 | |
| | Shippensburg .....*†11 | | 1987 | (None) | | | Jacksonville St. ...***†9 | |
| | Virginia Union ......†11 | | 1988 | North Dak. St. ...****10 | | 1992 | New Haven .......**†10 | |
| 1982 | North Dak. St. .....*†11 | | | St. Mary's (Cal.).....10 | | | Pittsburg St. .....***†11 | |
| | Southwest Tex. St. ***11 | | | | | | | |

# Later forfeited all games.

# THE SPOILERS

(Compiled since 1973, when the three-division reorganization plan was adopted by the special NCAA Convention.) Following is a list of the spoilers of Division II teams that lost their perfect (undefeated, untied) record in their **season-ending** game, including the Division II championship playoffs. An asterisk (*) indicates an NCAA championship playoff game, a pound sign (#) indicates an NAIA championship playoff game, and a dagger (†) indicates the home team in a regular-season game. A game involving two undefeated, untied teams is in bold face.

| Date | Spoiler | Victim | Score |
|------|---------|--------|-------|
| 12-15-73 | *Louisiana Tech | Western Ky. | 34-0 |
| 11-30-74 | *Louisiana Tech | Western Caro. | 10-7 |
| 11-15-75 | †LIU-C. W. Post | American Int'l | 21-0 |
| 11-15-75 | Eastern N. Mex. | †Northern Colo. | 16-14 |
| 11-29-75 | *Livingston | North Dak. | 34-14 |
| 11-20-76 | †Shippensburg | East Stroudsburg | tie14-14 |
| 12-3-77 | ‡South Caro. St. | Winston-Salem | 10-7 |
| 12-3-77 | *Lehigh | UC Davis | 39-30 |
| 12-2-78 | *Delaware | Winston-Salem | 41-0 |
| 11-28-81 | *Shippensburg | Virginia Union | 40-27 |
| 12-5-81 | *North Dak. St. | Shippensburg | 18-6 |
| 12-5-81 | *Southwest Tex. St. | Northern Mich. | 62-0 |
| 12-4-82 | *UC Davis | North Dak. St. | 19-14 |
| 12-11-82 | **Southwest Tex. St.** | **UC Davis** | 34-9 |
| 12-3-83 | *North Dak. St. | UC Davis | 26-17 |
| 12-10-83 | *North Dak. St. | Central St. (Ohio) | 41-21 |
| 12-7-85 | *North Ala. | Bloomsburg | 34-0 |
| 11-15-86 | West Chester | †Millersville | 7-3 |
| 11-29-86 | *Troy St. | Virginia Union | 31-7 |
| 11-29-86 | *South Dak. | UC Davis | 26-23 |
| 12-10-88 | *Adams St. | Pittsburg St. | 13-10 |
| 11-18-89 | *Mississippi Col. | Texas A&I | 34-19 |
| 11-18-89 | *Indiana (Pa.) | Grand Valley St. | 34-24 |
| 11-25-89 | *Angelo St. | Pittsburg St. | 24-21 |
| 12-9-89 | *Mississippi Col. | Jacksonville St. | 3-0 |
| 12-1-90 | **North Dak. St.** | **Pittsburg St.** | 39-29 |
| 11-23-91 | #Western St. | Carson-Newman | 38-21 |
| 12-7-91 | **Jacksonville St.** | **Indiana (Pa.)** | 27-20 |
| 12-14-91 | *Pittsburg St. | Jacksonville St. | 23-6 |
| 12-5-92 | *Jacksonville St. | New Haven | 46-35 |
| 12-12-92 | *Jacksonville St. | Pittsburg St. | 17-13 |

‡ Gold Bowl.

# CLIFFHANGERS

Regular-season Division II games *won on the final play of the game* (from 1973). The extra point is listed when it provided the margin of victory after the winning touchdown.

| Date | Opponents, Score | Game-winning play |
|------|------------------|-------------------|
| 10-12-74 | Westminster (Pa.) 23, Indiana (Pa.) 20 | Rick Voltz 20 FG |
| 11-23-74 | Arkansas St. 22, McNeese St. 20 | Joe Duren 56 FG |
| 10-11-75 | Indiana (Pa.) 16, Westminster (Pa.) 14 | Tom Alper 37 FG |
| 10-18-75 | Cal St. Fullerton 32, UC Riverside 31 | John Choukair 52 FG |
| 9-25-76 | Portland St. 50, Montana 49 | Dave Stief 2 pass from June Jones |

*Division II Undefeated, Untied Teams*

| Date | Opponents, Score | Game-winning play |
|------|------------------|-------------------|
| 10-30-76 | South Dak. St. 16, Northern Iowa 13 | Monte Mosiman 53 pass from Dick Weikert |
| 10-27-77 | Albany (N.Y.) 42, Maine 39 | Larry Leibowitz 19 FG |
| 10-6-79 | Indiana (Pa.) 31, Shippensburg 24 | Jeff Heath 4 run |
| 9-6-80 | Ferris St. 20, St. Joseph's (Ind.) 15 | Greg Washington 17 pass from (holder) John Gibson (after bad snap on 34 FG attempt) |
| 11-15-80 | Morris Brown 19, Bethune-Cookman 18 | Ray Mills 1 run (Carlton Jackson kick) |
| 11-15-80 | Tuskegee 23, Alabama A&M 21 | Korda Joseph 45 FG |
| 9-26-81 | Abilene Christian 41, Northwestern (La.) 38 | David Russell 17 pass from Loyal Proffitt |
| 9-26-81 | Cal St. Chico 10, Santa Clara 7 | Mike Sullivan 46 FG |
| 10-10-81 | LIU-C. W. Post 37, James Madison 36 | Tom DeBona 10 pass from Tom Ehrhardt (Ehrhardt run) |
| 10-9-82 | Westminster (Pa.) 3, Indiana (Pa.) 0 | Ron Bauer 35 FG |
| 9-17-83 | Central Mo. St. 13, Sam Houston St. 10 | Steve Huff 27 FG |
| 9-22-84 | Clarion 16, Shippensburg 13 | Eric Fairbanks 26 FG |
| 9-29-84 | Angelo St. 18, Eastern N. Mex. 17 | Ned Cox 3 run |
| 10-13-84 | Northwest Mo. St. 35, Central Mo. St. 34 | Pat Johnson 20 FG |
| 10-13-84 | UC Davis 16, Cal St. Chico 13 | Ray Sullivan 48 FG |
| 11-3-84 | Bloomsburg 34, West Chester 31 | Curtis Still 50 pass from Jay Dedea |
| 11-20-84 | Central Fla. 28, Illinois St. 24 | Jeff Farmer 30 punt return |
| 9-7-85 | Central Fla. 39, Bethune-Cookman 37 | Ed O'Brien 55 FG |
| 9-13-86 | Michigan Tech 34, St. Norbert 30 | Jim Wallace 41 pass from Dave Walter |
| 9-20-86 | Delaware 33, West Chester 31 | Fred Singleton 3 run |
| 10-18-86 | Indianapolis 25, Evansville 24 | Ken Bruce 18 FG |
| 10-24-87 | Indianapolis 27, Evansville 24 | Doug Sabotin 2 pass from Tom Crowell |
| 11-7-87 | Central Mo. St. 35, Northeast Mo. St. 33 | Phil Brandt 25 FG |
| 9-3-88 | Alabama A&M 17, North Ala. 16 | Edmond Allen 30 FG |
| 9-17-89 | Morehouse 22, Fort Valley St. 21 | David Boone 18 pass from Jimmie Davis |
| 11-11-89 | East Stroudsburg 22, Central Conn. St. 19 | Frank Magolon 4 pass from Tom Taylor |
| 10-13-90 | East Stroudsburg 23, Bloomsburg 21 | Ken Kopetchny 3 pass from Bret Comp |
| 11-10-90 | Southern Conn. St. 12, Central Conn. St. 10 | Paul Boulanger 48 FG |
| 9-21-91 | Livingston 22, Albany St. (Ga.) 21 | Matt Carman 24 pass from Deon Timmons (Anthony Armstrong kick) |
| 10-26-91 | Central Mo. St. 38, Northeast Mo. St. 37 | Chris Pyatt 45 FG |

# DIVISION II STATISTICS TRENDS

**(For valid comparisons from 1973, when College Division teams were divided into Division II and Division III)**

**(Average Per Game, Both Teams)**

| | Rushing | | | Passing | | | | | Total Offense | | | Scoring | | |
|------|-------|-------|------|------|------|------|-------|---------|-------|-------|------|------|------|------|
| Year | Plays | Yds. | Avg. | Att. | Cmp. | Pct. | Yds. | Av. Att. | Plays | Yds. | Avg. | TD | FG | Pts. |
| 1973 | 95.1 | 339.1 | 3.57 | 40.0 | 17.6 | .442 | 243.0 | 6.08 | 135.1 | 582.1 | 4.31 | 5.06 | 0.83 | 36.4 |
| 1974 | 95.1 | 312.6 | 3.29 | 38.9 | 17.3 | .445 | 244.8 | 6.28 | 134.0 | 557.3 | 4.16 | 5.10 | 0.86 | 37.9 |
| 1975 | 94.6 | 337.1 | 3.56 | 38.9 | 17.4 | .448 | 241.2 | 6.21 | 133.5 | 578.3 | 4.33 | 4.98 | 0.89 | 37.1 |
| 1976 | 94.7 | 331.4 | 3.50 | 39.8 | 18.2 | .457 | 251.8 | 6.32 | 134.5 | 583.2 | 4.34 | 5.03 | 0.93 | 37.4 |
| 1977 | *96.7 | *347.6 | 3.59 | 40.6 | 18.4 | .453 | 252.4 | 6.21 | 137.3 | 599.9 | 4.37 | 5.16 | 0.91 | 38.2 |
| 1978 | 95.9 | 338.5 | 3.52 | 41.1 | 18.4 | .448 | 248.5 | 6.05 | 137.0 | 587.0 | 4.29 | 5.11 | 0.98 | 38.6 |
| 1979 | 91.6 | 309.4 | 3.38 | 41.9 | 18.9 | .450 | 251.6 | 6.00 | 133.4 | 560.9 | 4.20 | 4.73 | 1.03 | 35.8 |
| 1980 | 90.5 | 307.5 | 3.40 | 44.7 | 20.7 | .463 | 275.2 | 6.16 | 135.2 | 582.6 | 4.31 | 5.02 | 1.04 | 37.8 |
| 1981 | 89.1 | 293.2 | 3.29 | 47.9 | 21.9 | .457 | 291.7 | 6.09 | 137.0 | 584.9 | 4.27 | 4.95 | 1.08 | 37.4 |
| 1982 | 86.5 | 288.2 | 3.32 | 52.2 | 24.5 | .469 | 322.0 | 6.17 | 138.6 | 610.2 | 4.40 | 5.25 | 1.24 | 39.6 |
| 1983 | 86.3 | 290.7 | 3.37 | 52.1 | 25.0 | .479 | 329.0 | 6.31 | 138.4 | 619.7 | 4.48 | 5.27 | 1.23 | 39.2 |
| 1984 | 83.8 | 284.3 | 3.39 | 52.0 | 25.0 | .481 | 329.5 | 6.33 | 135.8 | 613.8 | 4.52 | 5.25 | 1.23 | 38.7 |
| 1985 | 83.3 | 288.0 | 3.46 | *54.8 | *26.4 | .483 | 341.2 | 6.23 | 138.1 | 629.2 | 4.56 | 5.46 | 1.30 | 41.8 |
| 1986 | 83.6 | 297.7 | 3.56 | 53.7 | 26.0 | .484 | 336.8 | 6.27 | 137.3 | 634.5 | 4.62 | 5.78 | 1.27 | 43.9 |
| 1987 | 85.6 | 303.7 | 3.55 | 49.2 | 23.8 | .483 | 311.0 | 6.31 | 134.9 | 614.7 | 4.56 | 5.29 | 1.28 | 40.4 |
| 1988 | 87.7 | 318.8 | 3.64 | 49.2 | 23.8 | .484 | 319.5 | 6.49 | 136.9 | 638.3 | 4.66 | 5.83 | 1.29 | 44.2 |
| 1989 | 87.3 | 332.0 | 3.80 | 50.1 | 24.3 | *.485 | 323.0 | 6.45 | 137.4 | 655.0 | 4.77 | 5.94 | 1.24 | 45.1 |
| 1990 | 87.3 | 336.6 | *3.86 | 52.8 | 25.6 | .485 | *346.6 | 6.57 | *140.0 | *683.2 | *4.88 | *6.19 | 1.29 | *46.7 |
| 1991 | 87.4 | 335.5 | 3.84 | 52.7 | 25.5 | .484 | 344.8 | 6.54 | 140.0 | 680.3 | 4.86 | 6.09 | *1.31 | 46.4 |
| 1992 | 88.1 | 335.1 | 3.80 | 51.2 | 24.8 | .484 | 342.8 | *6.70 | 139.3 | 677.9 | 4.87 | 6.01 | 1.30 | 46.2 |

* Record.

# ADDITIONAL DIVISION II STATISTICS TRENDS

### (Average Per Game, Both Teams)

| Year | †Teams | Games | Punting | | PAT Kick Attempts | | Two-Point Attempts | | Field Goals |
| | | | No. | Avg. | Pct. Made | Pct. of Total Tries | Pct. Made | Pct. of Total Tries | Pct. Made |
|---|---|---|---|---|---|---|---|---|---|
| 1973 | 131 | 1,326 | 11.5 | 36.0 | .833 | .876 | .419 | .124 | .439 |
| 1974 | 136 | 1,388 | 11.4 | *36.8 | .830 | .859 | .432 | .141 | .472 |
| 1975 | 126 | 1,282 | 11.0 | 36.3 | .837 | .874 | .464 | .126 | .476 |
| 1976 | 122 | 1,244 | 11.6 | 36.2 | .841 | .878 | .419 | .122 | .461 |
| 1977 | 124 | 1,267 | 11.7 | 36.1 | .832 | .874 | .436 | .126 | .442 |
| 1978 | 91 | 921 | 11.9 | 35.9 | .830 | .880 | .452 | .120 | .519 |
| 1979 | 99 | 1,016 | 12.1 | 35.2 | .854 | .861 | .459 | .139 | .543 |
| 1980 | 103 | 1,040 | 11.7 | 35.6 | .852 | .864 | .438 | .136 | .512 |
| 1981 | 113 | 1,138 | *12.2 | 35.6 | .856 | .861 | .440 | .139 | .531 |
| 1982 | 118 | 1,196 | 12.2 | 36.4 | .862 | .877 | .431 | .123 | .560 |
| 1983 | 115 | 1,175 | 11.9 | 36.1 | .866 | .847 | .428 | .153 | .564 |
| 1984 | 112 | 1,150 | 11.8 | 36.4 | .876 | .875 | .448 | .125 | .567 |
| 1985 | 107 | 1,098 | 11.5 | 35.9 | *.905 | .864 | .414 | .136 | .549 |
| 1986 | 109 | 1,124 | 11.1 | 36.5 | .870 | .865 | .466 | .135 | *.576 |
| 1987 | 105 | 1,100 | 11.4 | 35.7 | .857 | .865 | .435 | .135 | .547 |
| 1988 | 111 | 1,114 | 11.2 | 35.6 | .886 | .868 | .399 | .132 | .555 |
| 1989 | 106 | 1,084 | 10.9 | 36.7 | .873 | .845 | .376 | *.155 | .567 |
| 1990 | 105 | 1,065 | 11.3 | 35.7 | .876 | *.885 | *.474 | .115 | .568 |
| 1991 | 114 | 1,150 | 10.9 | 36.1 | .882 | .880 | .426 | .120 | .572 |
| 1992 | 115 | 1,145 | 11.0 | 35.9 | .888 | .870 | .442 | .130 | .575 |

* Record.   † Teams reporting statistics, not the total number of teams in the division.

# DIVISION III RECORDS

Worcester State defensive back Chris Butts returns one of his 12 interceptions in 1992, when he led Division III in both total interceptions and interceptions per game (1.33). Only four players in division history have picked off more passes in a season.

Division III football records are based on the performances of Division III teams since the three-division reorganization plan was adopted by the special NCAA Convention in August 1973.

# INDIVIDUAL RECORDS

## TOTAL OFFENSE
### (Rushing Plus Passing)

### Most Plays
**Quarter**
33—Aaron Keen, Washington (Mo.) vs. Trinity (Tex.), Oct. 3, 1992 (4th)
**Half**
59—Mike Wallace, Ohio Wesleyan vs. Denison, Oct. 3, 1981 (2nd)
**Game**
91—Jordan Poznick, Principia vs. Blackburn, Oct. 10, 1992 (81 passes, 10 rushes; 538 yards)
**Season**
614—Tim Peterson, Wis.-Stout, 1989 (3,244 yards)
Per-game record—64.9, Jordan Poznick, Principia, 1992 (519 in 8)
**2 Yrs**
1,165—Kirk Baumgartner, Wis.-Stevens Point, 1987-88 (7,502 yards)
Per-game record—55.6, Keith Bishop, Wheaton (Ill.), 1984-85 (1,000 in 18)
**3 Yrs**
1,695—Kirk Baumgartner, Wis.-Stevens Point, 1987-89 (11,042 yards)
Also holds per-game record at 53.0 (1,695 in 32)
**Career**
(4 yrs.) 2,007—Kirk Baumgartner, Wis.-Stevens Point, 1986-89 (12,767 yards)
Also holds per-game record at 49.0 (2,007 in 41)

### Most Plays by a Freshman
**Season**
479—Jason Cooperider, Denison, 1989 (2,301 yards)
Also holds per-game record at 47.9 (479 in 10)

### Most Yards Gained
**Game**
596—John Love, North Park vs. Elmhurst, Oct. 13, 1990 (533 passing, 63 rushing)
**Season**
3,790—Kirk Baumgartner, Wis.-Stevens Point, 1988 (-38 rushing, 3,828 passing)
Per-game record—354.8, Keith Bishop, Wheaton (Ill.), 1983 (3,193 in 9)
**2 Yrs**
7,502—Kirk Baumgartner, Wis.-Stevens Point, 1987-88 (-81 rushing, 7,583 passing)
Also holds per-game record at 349.0 (7,330 in 21, 1988-89)

**3 Yrs**
11,042—Kirk Baumgartner, Wis.-Stevens Point, 1987-89 (-233 rushing, 11,275 passing)
Also holds per-game record at 345.1 (11,042 in 32)
**Career**
(4 yrs.) 12,767—Kirk Baumgartner, Wis.-Stevens Point, 1986-89 (-261 rushing, 13,028 passing)
Also holds per-game record at 311.4 (12,767 in 41)

### Most Yards Gained by a Freshman
**Season**
2,554—Brad Hensley, Kenyon, 1991 (441 plays)
Per-game record—271.8, Chris Ings, Wabash, 1992 (2,446 in 9)

### Most Games Gaining 300 Yards or More
**Season**
8—Kirk Baumgartner, Wis.-Stevens Point, 1989
**Career**
26—Kirk Baumgartner, Wis.-Stevens Point, 1986-89

### Most Consecutive Games Gaining 300 Yards or More
**Season**
6—Kirk Baumgartner, Wis.-Stevens Point, 1987

### Gaining 4,000 Yards Rushing and 2,000 Yards Passing
**Career**
Chris Spriggs, Denison, 1983-86 (4,248 rushing & 2,799 passing)
Also holds record for yards gained by a running back at 7,047

### Gaining 3,000 Yards Rushing and 3,000 Yards Passing
**Career**
Clay Sampson (TB), Denison, 1977-80 (3,726 rushing & 3,194 passing)

### Highest Average Gain Per Play
**Season**
(Min. 2,500 yards) 8.66—Walter Briggs, Montclair St., 1986 (297 for 2,571)

**Career**
(Min. 6,000 yards) 6.96—Walter Briggs, Montclair St., 1983-86 (972 for 6,769)

### Most Touchdowns Responsible For (TDs Scored and Passed For)
**Career**
123—Kirk Baumgartner, Wis.-Stevens Point, 1986-89 (110 passing, 13 rushing)
Also holds per-game record at 3.00 (123 in 41)

## RUSHING

### Most Rushes
**Game**
58—Bill Kaiser, Wabash vs. DePauw, Nov. 9, 1985 (211 yards)

**Season**
380—Mike Birosak, Dickinson, 1989 (1,798 yards)
Also holds per-game record at 38.0 (380 in 10)

## Career

1,112—Mike Birosak, Dickinson, 1986-89 (4,662 yards)

Per-game record—32.7, Chris Sizemore, Bridge-water (Va.), 1972-74 (851 in 26)

### Most Rushes by a Quarterback
#### Season
231—Jeff Saveressig, Wis.-River Falls, 1988 (1,095 yards)

Also holds per-game record at 25.7 (231 in 9)

### Most Consecutive Rushes by the Same Player
#### Game
46—Dan Walsh, Montclair St. vs. Ramapo, Sept. 30, 1989 (during 13 ball possessions)
#### Season
51—Dan Walsh, Montclair St., 1989 (Sept. 23 to Sept. 30)

### Most Yards Gained
#### Half
310—Leroy Horn, Montclair St. vs. Jersey City St., Nov. 9, 1985 (21 rushes)
#### Game
382—Pete Baranek, Carthage vs. North Central, Oct. 5, 1985 (24 rushes)
#### Season
2,035—Ricky Gales, Simpson, 1989 (297 rushes)

Also holds per-game record at 203.5 (2,035 in 10)
#### 2 Yrs
3,326—Ricky Gales, Simpson, 1988-89 (530 rushes)

Also holds per-game record at 175.1 (3,326 in 19)
#### 3 Yrs
4,476—Joe Dudek, Plymouth St., 1983-85 (662 rushes)

Per-game record—165.3, Terry Underwood, Wagner, 1986-88 (3,803 in 23)
#### Career
(4 yrs.) 5,570—Joe Dudek, Plymouth St., 1982-85 (785 rushes)

Per-game record—151.8, Terry Underwood, Wagner, 1985-88 (5,010 in 33)

### Most Yards Gained by a Freshman
#### Season
1,283—Jason Wooley, Worcester Tech, 1990 (209 rushes)

Per-game record—148.4, Chris Harper, Carthage, 1990 (1,187 in 8)

### Most Rushing Yards Gained by a Quarterback
#### Game
235—Mark Cota, Wis.-River Falls vs. Minn.-Morris, Sept. 13, 1986 (27 rushes)
#### Season
1,279—Mark Cota, Wis.-River Falls, 1986 (227 rushes)

Also holds per-game record at 127.9 (1,279 in 10)
#### Career
2,171—Sam Juarascio, DePauw, 1972-75 (407 rushes)

### Longest Gain by a Quarterback
#### Game
98—Jon Hinds, Principia vs. Illinois Col., Sept.

20, 1986 (TD)

### Most Games Gaining 100 Yards or More
#### Career
30—Joe Dudek, Plymouth St., 1982-85 (41 games)

### Most Consecutive Games Gaining 100 Yards or More
#### Career
18—Hank Wineman, Albion, 1990-91

### Most Games Gaining 200 Yards or More
#### Season
8—Ricky Gales, Simpson, 1989 (consecutive)
#### Career
11—Ricky Gales, Simpson, 1988-89

### Most Seasons Gaining 1,000 Yards or More
#### Career
4—Joe Dudek, Plymouth St., 1982-85; Rich Kowalski, Hobart, 1972-75

### Two Players, Same Team, Each Gaining 1,000 Yards or More
#### Season
By seven teams. Most recent: Thomas More, 1992—Ryan Reynolds (1,042) (TB) & Derrick Jett (1,021) (FB)

### Most Yards Gained Rushing by Two Players, Same Team
#### Game
472—Jon Warga (TB) 264 & Jeff Stockdale (FB) 208, Wittenberg vs. Emory & Henry, Oct. 27, 1990
#### Season
2,590—Jon Warga (TB) 1,836 & Jeff Stockdale (FB) 727, Wittenberg, 1990 (10 games)

### Highest Average Gain Per Rush
#### Game
(Min. 15 rushes) 19.1—Billy Johnson, Widener vs. Swarthmore, Nov. 10, 1973 (15 for 286)

(Min. 24 rushes) 15.9—Pete Baranek, Carthage vs. North Central, Oct. 5, 1985 (24 for 382)
#### Season
(Min. 140 rushes) 8.89—Billy Johnson, Widener, 1973 (168 for 1,494)

(Min. 195 rushes) 7.49—Sandy Rogers, Emory & Henry, 1986 (231 for 1,730)
#### Career
(Min. 500 rushes) 7.10—Joe Dudek, Plymouth St., 1982-85 (785 for 5,570)

### Most Touchdowns Scored by Rushing
#### Game
6—Eric Leiser, Eureka vs. Concordia (Wis.), Nov. 2, 1991; Rob Sinclair, Simpson vs. Upper Iowa, Nov. 10, 1990
#### Season
27—Stanley Drayton, Allegheny, 1991

Also holds per-game record at 3.0 (27 in 9)
#### Career
76—Joe Dudek, Plymouth St., 1982-85

Also holds per-game record at 1.85 (76 in 41)

### Most Rushing Touchdowns Scored by a Quarterback
#### Season
16—Mark Cota, Wis.-River Falls, 1986

Also holds per-game record at 1.60 (16 in 10)

# PASSING

### Highest Passing Efficiency Rating Points
#### Season
(Min. 15 atts. per game) *203.3—Joe Blake, Simpson, 1989 (144 attempts, 93 completions, 3 interceptions, 1,705 yards, 19 TDs)

(Min. 25 atts. per game) 181.0—Pat Mayew, St. John's (Minn.), 1991 (247 attempts, 154 completions, 4 interceptions, 2,408 yards, 30 TDs)

**Career**
(Min. 325 comps.) 153.3—Joe Blake, Simpson, 1987-90 (672 attempts, 399 completions, 15 interceptions, 6,183 yards, 43 TDs)

* Declared champion; with six more pass attempts (making 15 per game), all interceptions, still would have highest efficiency (187.3).

## Most Passes Attempted
**Quarter**
31—Mike Wallace, Ohio Wesleyan vs. Denison, Oct. 3, 1981 (4th)
**Half**
57—Mike Wallace, Ohio Wesleyan vs. Denison, Oct. 3, 1981 (2nd)
**Game**
81—Jordan Poznick, Principia vs. Blackburn, Oct. 10, 1992 (completed 48)
**Season**
527—Kirk Baumgartner, Wis.-Stevens Point, 1988 (completed 276)
Per-game record—56.4, Jordan Poznick, Principia, 1992 (451 in 8)
**2 Yrs**
993—Kirk Baumgartner, Wis.-Stevens Point, 1987-88 (completed 519)
**3 Yrs**
1,448—Kirk Baumgartner, Wis.-Stevens Point, 1987-89 (completed 766)
**Career**
(4 yrs.) 1,696—Kirk Baumgartner, Wis.-Stevens Point, 1986-89 (completed 883)
Per-game record—42.3, Keith Bishop, Ill. Wesleyan, 1981; Wheaton (Ill.), 1983-85 (1,311 in 31)

### Most Passes Attempted by a Freshman
**Season**
384—Brad Hensley, Kenyon, 1991 (completed 198)
Per-game record—46.3, Jordan Poznick, Principia, 1990 (278 in 6)

## Most Passes Completed
**Quarter**
21—Rob Bristow, Pomona-Pitzer vs. Whittier, Oct. 19, 1985 (4th)
**Half**
36—Mike Wallace, Ohio Wesleyan vs. Denison, Oct. 3, 1981 (2nd)
**Game**
50—Tim Lynch, Hofstra vs. Fordham, Oct. 19, 1991 (attempted 69)
**Season**
276—Kirk Baumgartner, Wis.-Stevens Point, 1988 (attempted 527)
Per-game record—30.1, Jordan Poznick, Principia, 1992 (241 in 8)
**2 Yrs**
523—Kirk Baumgartner, Wis.-Stevens Point, 1988-89 (attempted 982)
**3 Yrs**
766—Kirk Baumgartner, Wis.-Stevens Point, 1987-89 (attempted 1,448)
**Career**
(4 yrs.) 883—Kirk Baumgartner, Wis.-Stevens Point, 1986-89 (attempted 1,696)
Per-game record—24.9, Keith Bishop, Ill. Wesleyan, 1981; Wheaton (Ill.), 1983-85 (772 in 31)

### Most Passes Completed by a Freshman
**Season**
199—Luke Hanks, Otterbein, 1990 (attempted 370)
Per-game record—21.8, Jordan Poznick, Principia, 1990 (131 in 6)

## Highest Percentage of Passes Completed
**Game**
(Min. 20 comps.) 84.6%—Bob Krepfle, Wis.-La Crosse vs. Anderson, Oct. 6, 1984 (22 of 26)
(Min. 25 comps.) 83.3%—Scott Driggers, Colorado Col. vs. Neb. Wesleyan, Sept. 10, 1983 (35 of 42)
**Season**
(Min. 250 atts.) 64.0%—Willie Reyna, La Verne, 1992 (176 of 275)
**Career**
(Min. 550 atts.) 62.2%—Brian Moore, Baldwin-Wallace, 1981-84 (437 of 703)
(Min. 750 atts.) 60.0%—Scott Driggers, Colorado Col., 1981-84 (613 of 1,022)

## Most Consecutive Passes Completed
**Game**
17—Jim Ballard, Mount Union vs. Ill. Wesleyan, Nov. 28, 1992; William Snyder, Carnegie Mellon vs. Wooster, Oct. 20, 1990
**Season**
20—Dick Puccio, Cortland St. vs. Brockport St., Oct. 12, and Albany (N.Y.), Oct. 19, 1991

## Most Passes Had Intercepted
**Game**
8—Jason Clark, Ohio Northern vs. John Carroll, Nov. 9, 1991; Jim Higgins, Brockport St. vs. Buffalo St., Sept. 29, 1990; Dennis Bogacz, Wis.-Oshkosh vs. Wis.-Stevens Point, Oct. 29, 1988; Kevin Karwath, Canisius vs. Liberty, Nov. 19, 1979
**Season**
43—Steve Hendry, Wis.-Superior, 1982 (attempted 480)
Also holds per-game record at 3.9 (43 in 11)
**Career**
117—Steve Hendry, Wis.-Superior, 1980-83 (attempted 1,343)
Per-game record—3.2, Willie Martinez, Oberlin, 1973-74 (58 in 18)

## Lowest Percentage of Passes Had Intercepted
**Season**
(Min. 150 atts.) 0.89%—Brett Russ, Union (N.Y.), 1991 (2 of 224)
**Career**
(Min. 600 atts.) 1.93%—Mark Casale, Montclair St., 1980-83 (16 of 828)

## Most Passes Attempted Without Interception
**Game**
61—Mark Krajnik, Occidental vs. La Verne, Oct. 18, 1986 (32 completions); Brion Demski, Wis.-Stevens Point vs. Wis.-Superior, Oct. 16, 1981 (31 completions)
**Season**
124—Tim Tenhet, Sewanee, 1982

## Most Consecutive Passes Attempted Without an Interception
**Season**
205—Kirk Baumgartner, Wis.-Stevens Point, 1989 (during 6 games; began Sept. 16 vs. Wis.-Platteville, ended Oct. 21 vs. Wis.-Whitewater)

## Most Yards Gained
**Game**
585—Tim Lynch, Hofstra vs. Fordham, Oct. 19, 1991
**Season**
3,828—Kirk Baumgartner, Wis.-Stevens Point, 1988
Also holds per-game record at 369.2 (3,692 in 10, 1989)
**2 Yrs**
7,583—Kirk Baumgartner, Wis.-Stevens Point,

1987-88

**3 Yrs**

11,275 — Kirk Baumgartner, Wis.-Stevens Point, 1987-89

**Career**

(4 yrs.) 13,028 — Kirk Baumgartner, Wis.-Stevens Point, 1986-89

Also holds per-game record at 317.8 (13, 028 in 41)

### Most Yards Gained by a Freshman

**Season**

2,520 — Brad Hensley, Kenyon, 1991

Per-game record — 268.8, Dennis Bogacz, Wis.-Oshkosh, 1988 (2,150 in 8)

### Most Games Passing for 200 Yards or More

**Season**

10 — Kirk Baumgartner, Wis.-Stevens Point, 1989, 1988, 1987

**Career**

32 — Kirk Baumgartner, Wis.-Stevens Point, 1986-89

### Most Consecutive Games Passing for 200 Yards or More

**Season**

10 — Kirk Baumgartner, Wis.-Stevens Point, 1989 (entire season)

**Career**

27 — Keith Bishop, Ill. Wesleyan, 1981; Wheaton (Ill.), 1983-85

### Most Games Passing for 300 Yards or More

**Season**

9 — Kirk Baumgartner, Wis.-Stevens Point, 1989

**Career**

24 — Kirk Baumgartner, Wis.-Stevens Point, 1986-89

### Most Consecutive Games Passing for 300 Yards or More

**Season**

9 — Kirk Baumgartner, Wis.-Stevens Point, 1989 (began Sept. 9 vs. St. Norbert, through Nov. 4 vs. Wis.-Superior)

**Career**

13 — Kirk Baumgartner, Wis.-Stevens Point, 1988-89 (began Oct. 22, 1988, vs. Wis.-Stout, through Nov. 4, 1989, vs. Wis.-Superior)

### Most Yards Gained by Two Opposing Players

**Game**

928 — Brion Demski, Wis.-Stevens Point (477) & Steve Hendry, Wis.-Superior (451), Oct. 17, 1981 (completed 70 of 123)

### Most Yards Gained Per Attempt

**Season**

(Min. 175 atts.) 10.49 — George Muller, Hofstra, 1980 (189 for 1,983)

(Min. 275 atts.) 9.10 — Jim Ballard, Mount Union,

1992 (292 for 2,656)

**Career**

(Min. 600 atts.) 9.20 — Joe Blake, Simpson, 1987-90 (672 for 6,183)

(Min. 950 atts.) 8.22 — John Clark, Wis.-Eau Claire, 1987-90 (1,119 for 9,196)

### Most Yards Gained Per Completion

**Season**

(Min. 100 comps.) 19.7 — David Parker, Bishop, 1981 (114 for 2,242)

(Min. 200 comps.) 15.5 — Kirk Baumgartner, Wis.-Stevens Point, 1987 (243 for 3,755)

**Career**

(Min. 300 comps.) 18.3 — David Parker, Bishop, 1981-84 (378 for 6,934)

(Min. 425 comps.) 15.1 — Rob Light, Moravian, 1986-89 (438 for 6,624)

### Most Touchdown Passes

**Quarter**

4 — By seven players. Most recent: Steve Austin, Mass.-Boston vs. Framingham St., Nov. 14, 1992 (3rd)

**Game**

8 — Steve Austin, Mass.-Boston vs. Framingham St., Nov. 14, 1992; Kirk Baumgartner, Wis.-Stevens Point vs. Wis.-Superior, Nov. 4, 1989

**Season**

39 — Kirk Baumgartner, Wis.-Stevens Point, 1989

Also holds per-game record at 3.90 (39 in 10)

**Career**

110 — Kirk Baumgartner, Wis.-Stevens Point, 1986-89

Also holds per-game record at 2.68 (110 in 41)

### Highest Percentage of Passes for Touchdowns

**Season**

(Min. 200 atts.) 13.49% — Jimbo Fisher, Samford, 1987 (34 of 252)

(Min. 300 atts.) 8.87% — Craig Solomon, Rhodes, 1978 (29 of 327)

**Career**

(Min. 625 atts.) 10.84% — Gary Collier, Emory & Henry, 1984-87 (80 of 738)

(Min. 800 atts.) 7.59% — Scott Scesney, St. John's (N.Y.), 1986-89 (71 of 935)

### Most Touchdown Passes by a Freshman

**Season**

25 — David Parker, Bishop, 1981

Per-game record — 2.44, Jim Ballard, Wilmington (Ohio), 1990 (22 in 9)

### Most Consecutive Games Throwing a Touchdown Pass

**Career**

27 — Dan Stewart, Union (N.Y.) (from Nov. 14, 1981, through Nov. 10, 1984)

# RECEIVING

### Most Passes Caught

**Game**

23 — Sean Munroe, Mass.-Boston vs. Mass. Maritime, Oct. 10, 1992 (332 yards)

**Season**

106 — Theo Blanco (RB), Wis.-Stevens Point, 1987 (1,616 yards)

Per-game record — 12.3, Matt Newton, Principia, 1992 (98 in 8)

**Career**

258 — Bill Stromberg, Johns Hopkins, 1978-81 (3,776 yards)

Also holds per-game record at 7.2 (258 in 36)

### Most Passes Caught by a Tight End

**Game**

16 — Shawn Graham, St. Thomas (Minn.) vs. Hamline, Nov. 13, 1982

**Season**

72 — Don Moehling, Wis.-Stevens Point, 1988 (1,290 yards)

**Career**

171 — Jim Maransky, Albright, 1986-89 (2,128 yards)

### Most Passes Caught by a Running Back

**Game**

17 — Theo Blanco, Wis.-Stevens Point vs. Wis.-

Oshkosh, Oct. 31, 1987 (271 yards); Tim
Mowery, Wis.-Superior vs. Wis.-Stevens Point,
Oct. 17, 1981 (154 yards)

**Season**
106—Theo Blanco, Wis.-Stevens Point, 1987
(1,616 yards)

**Career**
169—Mike Christman, Wis.-Stevens Point,
1983-86 (2,190 yards)

### Most Passes Caught by a Freshman
**Season**
67—Bill Stromberg, Johns Hopkins, 1978
(1,027 yards)

### Most Passes Caught by Two Players, Same Team
**Season**
158—Theo Blanco (RB) 106 & Aatron Kenney
(WR) 52, Wis.-Stevens Point, 1987 (2,713
yards, 24 TDs)

### Most Passes Caught by Three Players, Same Team
**Season**
217—Theo Blanco (WR) 80, Don Moehling
(TE) 72 & Jim Mares (RB) 65, Wis.-Stevens
Point, 1988. Totaled 2,959 yards and 19 TDs
(team totals: 285-3,924-26)

### Most Consecutive Games Catching a Pass
**Career**
36—Chris Bisaillon, Ill. Wesleyan, 1989-92
(entire career); David Lauber, Wheaton (Ill.),
1985, 87-89; Bill Stromberg, Johns Hopkins,
1978-81 (entire career)

### Most Yards Gained
**Game**
332—Sean Munroe, Mass.-Boston vs. Mass.
Maritime, Oct. 10, 1992 (caught 23)

**Season**
1,693—Sean Munroe, Mass.-Boston, 1992
(caught 95)
Also holds per-game record at 188.1 (1,693 in
9)

**Career**
3,846—Dale Amos, Frank. & Marsh., 1986-89
(caught 233)
Per-game record—110.1, Tim McNamara, Trinity (Conn.), 1981-84 (2,313 in 21)

### Most Yards Gained by a Tight End
**Game**
267—Tom Mullady, Rhodes vs. Rose-Hulman,
Nov. 11, 1978 (caught 13)

**Season**
1,290—Don Moehling, Wis.-Stevens Point, 1988
(caught 72)

**Career**
2,663—Don Moehling, Wis.-Stevens Point,
1986-89 (caught 152)

### Most Yards Gained by a Running Back
**Game**
271—Theo Blanco, Wis.-Stevens Point vs. Wis.-
Oshkosh, Oct. 31, 1987 (caught 17)

**Season**
1,616—Theo Blanco, Wis.-Stevens Point, 1987
(caught 106)

**Career**
2,190—Mike Christman, Wis.-Stevens Point,
1983-86 (caught 169)

### Most Yards Gained by Two Players, Same Team
**Season**
2,713—Theo Blanco (RB) 1,616 & Aatron Kenney (WR) 1,097, Wis.-Stevens Point, 1987
(158 receptions, 24 TDs)

### Highest Average Gain Per Reception
**Game**
(Min. 3 receps.) 68.3—Paul Jaeckel, Elmhurst
vs. Ill. Wesleyan, Oct. 8, 1983 (3 for 205)
(Min. 5 receps.) 56.8—Tom Casperson, Trenton
St. vs. Ramapo, Nov. 15, 1980 (5 for 284)

**Season**
(Min. 35 receps.) 26.9—Marty Redlawsk, Concordia (Ill.), 1985 (38 for 1,022)
(Min. 50 receps.) 23.5—Evan Elkington, Worcester Tech, 1989 (52 for 1,220)

**Career**
(Min. 125 receps.) 20.0—Marty Redlawsk, Concordia (Ill.), 1984-87 (131 for 2,620)
(Min. 150 receps.) 19.4—John Aromando, Trenton St., 1981-84 (165 for 3,197)

### Highest Average Gain Per Reception by a Running Back
**Season**
(Min. 50 receps.) 17.5—Barry Rose, Wis.-Stev-
ens Point, 1989 (67 for 1,171)

### Most Touchdown Passes Caught
**Game**
5—By 10 players. Most recent: Sean Munroe,
Mass.-Boston vs. Framingham St., Nov. 14,
1992

**Season**
20—John Aromando, Trenton St., 1983
Also holds per-game record at 2.0 (20 in 10)

**Career**
55—Chris Bisaillon, Ill. Wesleyan, 1989-92 (223
receptions)
Also holds per-game record at 1.53 (55 in 36)

### Most Touchdown Passes Caught by a Freshman
**Season**
12—Chris Bisaillon, Ill. Wesleyan, 1989

### Highest Percentage of Passes Caught for Touchdowns
**Season**
(Min. 12 TDs) 54.3%—Keith Gilliam, Randolph-
Macon, 1984 (19 of 35)

**Career**
(Min. 20 TDs) 28.0%—Pat Schwanke, Lawrence, 1979-82 (28 of 100)

### Most Consecutive Passes Caught for Touchdowns
9—Keith Gilliam, Randolph-Macon, 1984 (during four games)

# PUNTING

### Most Punts
**Game**
17—Jerry Williams, Frostburg St. vs. Salisbury
St., Sept. 30, 1978

**Season**
106—Bob Blake, Wis.-Superior, 1977 (3,404
yards)
Per-game record—11.0, Mark Roedelbronn,
FDU-Madison, 1990 (99 in 9)

**Career**
263—Chris Gardner, Loras, 1987-90 (9,394
yards)

### Highest Average Per Punt
**Season**
(Min. 40 punts) 44.9—Bob Burwell, Rose-Hul-
man, 1978 (61 for 2,740)

**Career**
(Min. 110 punts) 42.1—Mike Manson, Ill. Benedictine, 1975-78 (120 for 5,056)

# INTERCEPTIONS

### Most Passes Intercepted
**Game**
5—By eight players. Most recent: Chris Butts, Worcester St. vs. Fitchburg St., Oct. 10, 1992
**Season**
15—Mark Dorner, Juniata, 1987 (202 yards) Also holds per-game record at 1.5 (15 in 10)
**Career**
34—Ralph Gebhardt, Rochester, 1972-75 (406 yards)

### Most Consecutive Games Intercepting a Pass
**Season**
9—Brent Sands, Cornell College, 1992 Also holds career record at 9

### Most Yards on Interception Returns
**Game**
164—Rick Conner, Western Md. vs. Dickinson, Oct. 15, 1983 (89-yard interception and 75-yard lateral after an interception)

**Season**
358—Rod Pesek, Whittier, 1987 (10 interceptions)
**Career**
479—Eugene Hunter, Fort Valley St., 1972-74 (29 interceptions)

### Highest Average Gain Per Interception
**Season**
(Min. 7 ints.) 35.8—Rod Pesek, Whittier, 1987 (10 for 358)
**Career**
(Min. 20 ints.) 20.4—Todd Schoelzel, Wis.-Oshkosh, 1985-88 (22 for 448)

### Most Touchdowns Scored on Interceptions
**Game**
2—By many players. Most recent: Aaron Brown, Capital vs. Bethany (W. Va.), Sept. 14, 1991
**Season**
3—By eight players. Most recent: Will Hall, Millsaps, 1992 (6 interceptions); Michael Sikma, Carroll (Wis.), 1992 (4 interceptions)

# PUNT RETURNS

### Most Punt Returns
**Game**
10—Ellis Wangelin, Wis.-River Falls vs. Wis.-Platteville, Oct. 12, 1985 (87 yards)
**Season**
48—Rick Bealer, Lycoming, 1989 (492 yards)
**Career**
126—Mike Caterbone, Frank. & Marsh., 1980-83 (1,141 yards)

### Most Yards on Punt Returns
**Game**
212—Melvin Dillard, Ferrum vs. Newport News App., Oct. 13, 1990 (6 returns)
**Season**
688—Melvin Dillard, Ferrum, 1990 (25 returns)
**Career**
1,198—Chuck Downey, Stony Brook, 1984-87 (59 returns)

### Highest Average Gain Per Return
**Season**
(Min. 1.2 rets. per game) 31.2—Chuck Downey, Stony Brook, 1986 (17 for 530)
**Career**
(Min. 1.2 rets. per game) 22.9—Keith Winston, Knoxville, 1986-87 (30 for 686)
(Min. 50 rets.) 20.3—Chuck Downey, Stony Brook, 1984-87 (59 for 1,198)

### Most Touchdowns Scored on Punt Returns
**Game**
2—By six players. Most recent: James Spriggs, Sewanee vs. Ky. Wesleyan, Nov. 14, 1992 (87 & 76 yards)
**Season**
4—Chris Warren, Ferrum, 1989 (18 returns); Keith Winston, Knoxville, 1986 (14 returns); Chuck Downey, Stony Brook, 1986 (17 returns); Matt Pekarske, Wis.-La Crosse, 1986 (37 returns)
**Career**
7—Chuck Downey, Stony Brook, 1984-87 (59 returns)

**Coe's Jason Martin led Division III in kickoff returns in 1992 with an average return of 39.8 yards, a Division III record and the second-best season average in collegiate history (minimum 1.2 returns per game).**

# KICKOFF RETURNS

### Most Kickoff Returns

**Game**
9—Larry Schurder, North Park vs. Elmhurst, Sept. 17, 1983 (229 yards)
**Season**
42—Phil Puryear, Wooster, 1990 (834 yards); Dirk Blood, Ohio Northern, 1987 (973 yards)
**Career**
85—Tom Southall, Colorado Col., 1981-84 (1,876 yards)

### Most Yards on Kickoff Returns

**Game**
279—Chuck Downey, Stony Brook vs. Trenton St., Oct. 5, 1984 (7 returns)
**Season**
973—Dirk Blood, Ohio Northern, 1987 (42 returns)
**Career**
1,876—Tom Southall, Colorado Col., 1981-84

(85 returns)

### Highest Average Gain Per Return

**Game**
*(Min. 3 rets.)* 68.0—Victor Johnson, Elmhurst vs. Wheaton (Ill.), Sept. 15, 1979 (3 for 204)
**Season**
*(Min. 1.2 rets. per game)* 39.8—Jason Martin, Coe, 1992 (11 for 438)
**Career**
*(Min. 1.2 rets. per game)* 29.2—Daryl Brown, Tufts, 1974-76 (38 for 1,111)

### Most Touchdowns Scored on Kickoff Returns

**Game**
2—By many players. Most recent: Bill Nashwinter, Buffalo St. vs. Alfred, Oct. 27, 1990
**Season**
4—Byron Womack, Iona, 1989
**Career**
6—Byron Womack, Iona, 1988-91

# TOTAL KICK RETURNS
### (Combined Punt and Kickoff Returns)

### Most Yards on Kick Returns

**Game**
354—Chuck Downey, Stony Brook vs. Trenton St., Oct. 5, 1984 (7 kickoff returns for 279 yards, 1 punt return for 75 yards)

### Gaining 1,000 Yards on Punt Returns and 1,000 Yards on Kickoff Returns

**Career**
Chuck Downey, Stony Brook, 1984-87 (1,281 on kickoff returns, 1,198 on punt returns)

### Most Touchdowns on Kick Returns

**Game**
3—Chuck Downey, Stony Brook vs. Trenton St., Oct. 5, 1984 (2 kickoff returns 98 & 95 yards, 1 punt return 75 yards)
**Season**
5—Chris Warren, Ferrum, 1989 (4 punt returns, 1 kickoff return); Chuck Downey, Stony

Brook, 1986 (4 punt returns, 1 kickoff return)
**Career**
10—Chuck Downey, Stony Brook, 1984-87 (7 punt returns, 3 kickoff returns)

### Highest Average Per Kick Return (Min. 1.2 Returns Per Game Each)

**Career**
23.6—Chuck Downey, Stony Brook, 1984-87 (59 for 1,198 on punt returns, 46 for 1,281 on kickoff returns)

### Averaging 20 Yards Each on Punt Returns and Kickoff Returns (Min. 1.2 Returns Per Game Each)

**Career**
Chuck Downey, Stony Brook, 1984-87 (20.3 on punt returns, 59 for 1,198; 27.8 on kickoff returns, 46 for 1,281)

# ALL RUNBACKS
### (Combined Interceptions, Punt Returns and Kickoff Returns)

### Most Touchdowns on Interceptions, Punt Returns and Kickoff Returns

**Season**
6—Chuck Downey, Stony Brook, 1986 (4 punt returns, 1 kickoff return, 1 interception return)

**Career**
11—Chuck Downey, Stony Brook, 1984-87 (7 punt returns, 3 kickoff returns, 1 interception return)

# PUNTS BLOCKED BY

### Most Punts Blocked By

**Game**
3—Jim Perryman, Millikin vs. Carroll (Wis.), Nov. 1, 1980
**Season**
9—Jim Perryman, Millikin, 1980

**Career**
13—Frank Lyle, Millsaps, 1979-82
(Daryl Hobson, Ill. Benedictine DB, blocked 9 punts during 17 games in 1987-88)

# ALL-PURPOSE RUNNING
### (Yardage Gained From Rushing, Receiving and All Runbacks)
### Most Plays

**Season**
383—Mike Birosak, Dickinson, 1989 (380 rushes, 3 receptions)
**Career**
1,158—Eric Frees, Western Md., 1988-91 (1,059 rushes, 34 receptions, 58 kickoff returns, 7 punt returns)

### Most Yards Gained

**Game**
402—Dan Nienhuis, Carleton vs. Hamline, Sept. 28, 1985 (88 rushing, 94 receiving, 66 punt returns, 154 kickoff returns; 33 plays)
**Season**
2,418—Theo Blanco, Wis.-Stevens Point, 1987 (454 rushing, 1,616 receiving, 245 punt re-

turns, 103 kickoff returns; 271 plays)
Per-game record—243.1, Kirk Matthieu, Maine Maritime, 1992 (2,188 in 9)

**Career**
6,878—Eric Frees, Western Md., 1988-91 (5,281 rushing, 392 receiving, 47 punt returns, 1,158 kickoff returns; 1,158 plays)
Per-game record—197.4, Gary Trettel, St. Thomas (Minn.), 1988-90 (5,724 in 29)

### Highest Average Gain Per Play

**Season**
*(Min. 1,500 yards, 125 plays)* 10.21—Billy Johnson, Widener, 1973 (1,868 in 183)

**Career**
*(Min. 4,000 yards, 300 plays)* 10.82—Theo Blanco, Wis.-Stevens Point, 1985-88 (4,698 yards on 434). Successively played RB, TE, RB and WR during his career

# SCORING

### Most Points Scored

**Season**
168—Stanley Drayton, Allegheny, 1991 (28 TDs)
Also holds per-game record at 16.8 (168 in 10)

**Career**
474—Joe Dudek, Plymouth St., 1982-85 (79 TDs)
Also holds per-game record at 11.6 (474 in 41)

### Two Players, Same Team, Each Scoring 100 Points or More

**Season**
Denis McDermott (126) & Manny Tsantes (102), St. John's (N.Y.), 1989; Theo Blanco (102) & Aatron Kenney (102), Wis.-Stevens Point, 1987

### Most Touchdowns Scored

**Season**
28—Stanley Drayton, Allegheny, 1991
Also holds per-game record at 2.8 (28 in 10)

**Career**
79—Joe Dudek, Plymouth St., 1982-85
Also holds per-game record at 1.9 (79 in 41)

### Most Games Scoring a Touchdown

**Career**
33—Joe Dudek, Plymouth St., 1982-85 (41 games)

### Most Games Scoring Two or More Touchdowns

**Career**
24—Joe Dudek, Plymouth St., 1982-85 (41 games)

### Most Extra Points Attempted by Kicking

**Game**
14—Kurt Christenson, Concordia-M'head vs. Macalester, Sept. 24, 1977 (made 13)

**Season**
63—Tim Mercer, Ferrum, 1989 (made 62)

**Career**
194—Tim Mercer, Ferrum, 1987-90 (made 183)

### Most Extra Points Made by Kicking

**Game**
13—Kurt Christenson, Concordia-M'head vs. Macalester, Sept. 24, 1977 (attempted 14)

**Season**
62—Tim Mercer, Ferrum, 1989 (attempted 63)

**Career**
183—Tim Mercer, Ferrum, 1987-90 (attempted 194)

### Highest Percentage of Extra Points Made (Best Perfect Season)

100.0%—Mike Duvic, Dayton, 1989 (46 of 46)

### Highest Percentage of Extra Points Made

**Career**
*(Min. 80 atts.)* 100.0%—Mike Farrell, Adrian, 1983-85 (84 of 84)
*(Min. 100 atts.)* 98.5%—Rims Roof, Coe, 1982-85 (135 of 137)

### Most Consecutive Extra Points Made by Kicking

**Game**
13—Kurt Christenson, Concordia-M'head vs. Macalester, Sept. 24, 1977

**Career**
102—Rims Roof, Coe (from Sept. 24, 1983, through Nov. 9, 1985)

### Most Points Scored by Kicking

**Game**
20—Jim Hever, Rhodes vs. Millsaps, Sept. 22, 1984 (6 FGs, 2 PATs)

**Season**
102—Ken Edelman, Mount Union, 1990 (20 FGs, 42 PATs)
Also holds per-game record at 10.2 (102 in 10)

**Career**
274—Ken Edelman, Mount Union, 1987-90 (52 FGs, 118 PATs)
Also holds per-game record at 6.9 (274 in 40)

### Most Successful Two-Point Pass Attempts

**Game**
4—Rob Bristow, Pomona-Pitzer vs. Whittier, Oct. 19, 1985 (all in 4th quarter); Dave Geissler, Wis.-Stevens Point vs. Wis.-La Crosse, Sept. 21, 1985 (all in 4th quarter)

**Season**
7—Kirk Baumgartner, Wis.-Stevens Point, 1988 (8 attempts); Gary Collier, Emory & Henry, 1987 (11 attempts); Dave Geissler, Wis.-Stevens Point, 1985 (8 attempts)

**Career**
11—Dave Geissler, Wis.-Stevens Point, 1982-85 (14 attempts)
Rob Bristow, Pomona-Pitzer, 1983-86, holds record for highest percentage of successful two-point pass attempts (best perfect record) at 9 of 9

### Most Two-Point Passes Caught

**Season**
4—Rob Brooks, Albright, 1992; Don Moehling, Wis.-Stevens Point, 1988; Mike Christman, Wis.-Stevens Point, 1985

# DEFENSIVE EXTRA POINTS

### Most Defensive Extra Points Scored

**Game**
1—By many players

**Season**
2—Dan Fichter, Brockport St., 1990 (2 blocked kick returns)

### Longest Defensive Extra Point Blocked Kick Return

97—Keith Mottram (CB), Colorado Col. vs. Austin, Oct. 10, 1992 (scored)

### Longest Defensive Extra Point Interception

100—By four players. Most recent: Chris

Schleeper (FS), Quincy vs. Ill. Wesleyan, Sept. 29, 1990 (scored)

**First Defensive Extra Point Scored**
Steve Nieves (DB), St. John's (N.Y.) vs. Iona, Sept. 10, 1988 (83-yard blocked kick return)

## FIELD GOALS

### Most Field Goals Made
**Game**
6—Jim Hever, Rhodes vs. Millsaps, Sept. 22, 1984 (30, 24, 42, 44, 46, 30 yards; attempted 8)
**Season**
20—Ken Edelman, Mount Union, 1990 (attempted 27)
Also holds per-game record at 2.00 (20 in 10)
**Career**
52—Ken Edelman, Mount Union, 1987-90, (attempted 71)
Also holds per-game record at 1.30 (52 in 40) (Min. 30)

### Most Field Goals Attempted
**Game**
8—Jim Hever, Rhodes vs. Millsaps, Sept. 22, 1984 (made 6)
**Season**
29—Scott Ryerson, Central Fla., 1981 (made 18)

**Career**
71—Ken Edelman, Mount Union, 1987-90 (made 52); Doug Hart, Grove City, 1985-88 (made 40)

### Highest Percentage of Field Goals Made
**Season**
(Min. 15 atts.) 93.8%—Steve Graeca, John Carroll, 1988 (15 of 16)
**Career**
(Min. 50 atts.) *77.6%—Mike Duvic, Dayton, 1986-89 (38 of 49)
* Declared champion; with one more attempt (making 50), failed, still would have highest percentage (76.0).

### Longest Field Goal Made
62—Dom Antonini, Rowan vs. Salisbury St., Sept. 18, 1976

### Most Field Goals Attempted Without Success
**Season**
11—Scott Perry, Moravian, 1986

# TEAM RECORDS

## SINGLE GAME—OFFENSE
### TOTAL OFFENSE

**Most Plays**
112—Gust. Adolphus vs. Bethel (Minn.), Nov. 2, 1985 (65 passes, 47 rushes; 493 yards)

**Most Plays, Both Teams**
214—Gust. Adolphus (112) & Bethel (Minn.) (102), Nov. 2, 1985 (143 passes, 71 rushes; 930 yards)

**Most Yards Gained**
761—LIU-C. W. Post vs. Alfred, Nov. 14, 1992

(528 passing, 233 rushing)

**Most Yards Gained, Both Teams**
1,360—Millikin (694) & Wheaton (Ill.) (666), Nov. 12, 1983 (166 plays)

**Most Touchdowns Scored by Rushing and Passing**
14—Concordia-M'head vs. Macalester, Sept. 24, 1977 (12 rushing, 2 passing)

### RUSHING

**Most Rushes**
92—Wis.-River Falls vs. Wis.-Platteville, Oct. 21, 1989 (464 yards)

**Most Yards Gained Rushing**
642—Wis.-River Falls vs. Wis.-Superior, Oct.

14, 1989 (88 rushes)

**Most Touchdowns Scored by Rushing**
12—Concordia-M'head vs. Macalester, Sept. 24, 1977

### PASSING

**Most Passes Attempted**
81—Principia vs. Blackburn, Oct. 10, 1992 (completed 48)

**Most Passes Attempted, Both Teams**
143—Bethel (Minn.) (78) & Gust. Adolphus (65), Nov. 2, 1985 (completed 65)

**Most Passes Attempted Without an Interception**
61—Occidental vs. La Verne, Oct. 18, 1986 (completed 32); Wis.-Stevens Point vs. Wis.-Superior, Oct. 16, 1981 (completed 31)

**Most Passes Completed**
50—Hofstra vs. Fordham, Oct. 19, 1991 (attempted 69)

**Most Passes Completed, Both Teams**
72—Wis.-Superior (41) & Wis.-Stevens Point (31), Oct. 17, 1981 (attempted 131)

**Highest Percentage of Passes Completed (Min. 35 Attempts)**
78.9%—Wheaton (Ill.) vs. North Park, Oct. 8, 1983 (30 of 38)

**Most Yards Gained**
585—Hofstra vs. Fordham, Oct. 19, 1991

**Most Yards Gained, Both Teams**
1,036—Knox (576) & Cornell College (460), Oct. 11, 1986 (attempted 92, completed 59)

**Most Touchdown Passes**
8—Mass.-Boston vs. Framingham St., Nov. 14, 1992; Wis.-Stevens Point vs. Wis.-Superior, Nov. 4, 1989

**Most Touchdown Passes, Both Teams**
11—Emory & Henry (6) & Samford (5), Oct. 24, 1987; Cornell College (6) & Knox (5), Oct. 11, 1986

# PUNT RETURNS

**Most Touchdowns Scored on Punt Returns**
2—By many teams. Most recent: Widener vs. Susquehanna, Oct. 20, 1990; Widener vs.

Albright, Oct. 13, 1990 (consecutive games, 3 returns on blocked punts)

# KICKOFF RETURNS

**Most Yards on Kickoff Returns**
279—Stony Brook vs. Trenton St., Oct. 5, 1984

# SCORING

**Most Points Scored**
97—Concordia-M'head vs. Macalester, Sept. 24, 1977

**Most Points Scored, Both Teams**
111—Carroll (Wis.) (58) & Ill. Wesleyan (53), Nov. 11, 1989

**Most Points Scored by a Losing Team**
53—Ill. Wesleyan vs. Carroll (Wis.) (58), Nov. 11, 1989

**Most Points Overcome to Win a Game**
33—Salisbury St. vs. Randolph-Macon, Sept. 15, 1984 (trailed 33-0 with 14:18 left in 2nd quarter; won 34-33); Wis.-Platteville vs. Wis.-Eau Claire, Nov. 8, 1980 (trailed 33-0 with 7:00 left in 2nd quarter; won 52-43)

**Most Points Scored in a Brief Period of Time**
21 in 2:11—Merchant Marine vs. Bentley, Sept. 30, 1989 (turned 0-0 game into 21-0 in 1st quarter; won 30-14)
32 in 4:04—Wis.-Stevens Point vs. Wis.-La Crosse, Sept. 21, 1985 (trailed 3-27 and 11-35 in 4th quarter; ended in 35-35 tie)

**Most Points Scored in First Varsity Game**
63—Bentley vs. Brooklyn (26), Sept. 24, 1988

**Most Touchdowns Scored**
14—Concordia-M'head vs. Macalester, Sept. 24, 1977

**Most Extra Points Made by Kicking**
13—Concordia-M'head vs. Macalester, Sept. 24, 1977 (attempted 14)

**Most Field Goals Made**
6—Rhodes vs. Millsaps, Sept. 22, 1984 (attempted 8)

**Most Field Goals Attempted**
8—Rhodes vs. Millsaps, Sept. 22, 1984 (made 6)

**Most Defensive Extra-Point Returns Scored**
1—By many teams

**Most Defensive Extra-Point Opportunities**
2—Frank. & Marsh. vs. Johns Hopkins, Nov. 7, 1992 (1 interception & 1 kick return; none scored); Wis.-River Falls vs. Wis.-La Crosse, Nov. 11, 1989 (2 kick returns; 1 scored); Wis.-Platteville vs. Wis.-Oshkosh, Oct. 15, 1988 (2 interceptions; none scored); Buffalo St. vs. Brockport St., Oct. 1, 1988 (1 interception & 1 kick return; none scored)

# TURNOVERS
### (Most Times Losing the Ball on Interceptions and Fumbles)

**Most Turnovers**
13—St. Olaf vs. St. Thomas (Minn.), Oct. 12, 1985 (10 interceptions, 3 fumbles); Mercyhurst vs. Buffalo St., Oct. 23, 1982 (12 fumbles, 1 interception); Albany (N.Y.) vs. Rochester

Inst., Oct. 1, 1977

**Most Turnovers, Both Teams**
24—Albany (N.Y.) (13) & Rochester Inst. (11), Oct. 1, 1977

# FIRST DOWNS

**Most Total First Downs**
40—Upper Iowa vs. Loras, Nov. 7, 1992 (19 rushing, 17 passing, 4 by penalty)

# PENALTIES

**Most Penalties Against**
25—Norwich vs. Coast Guard, Sept. 29, 1985 (192 yards)

# SINGLE GAME—DEFENSE
## TOTAL DEFENSE

**Fewest Yards Allowed**
Minus 50—Ithaca vs. Springfield, Oct. 11, 1975 (-94 rushing, 44 passing)

## RUSHING DEFENSE

**Fewest Rushes Allowed**
10—Augustana (Ill.) vs. Ill. Wesleyan, Oct. 11, 1983 (28 yards); Wis.-Superior vs. Wis.-Stevens Point, Oct. 17, 1981 (-3 yards)

**Fewest Yards Allowed**
Minus 112—Coast Guard vs. Wesleyan, Oct. 7, 1989 (23 plays)

## PASS DEFENSE

**Fewest Attempts Allowed**
0—By many teams. Most recent: Concordia-M'head vs. Macalester, Oct. 12, 1991

**Fewest Completions Allowed**
0—By many teams. Most recent: Frank. & Marsh. vs. Gettysburg, Nov. 14, 1992 (2 attempts)

**Fewest Yards Allowed**
Minus 6—Central (Iowa) vs. Simpson, Oct. 19, 1985 (1 completion)

**Most Passes Intercepted By**
10—St. Thomas (Minn.) vs. St. Olaf, Oct. 12, 1985 (91 yards; 50 attempts)

**Most Players Intercepting a Pass**
8—Samford vs. Anderson, Oct. 11, 1986 (8 interceptions in the game)

## PUNTS BLOCKED BY

**Most Opponent's Punts Blocked By**
4—Ill. Benedictine vs. Olivet Nazarene, Oct. 22, & vs. Aurora, Oct. 29, 1988 (consecutive games, resulting in 4 TDs and 1 safety).

Blocked 9 punts in three consecutive games, vs. MacMurray, Oct. 15, Olivet Nazarene and Aurora, resulting in 4 TDs and 2 safeties

## FIRST DOWNS

**Fewest First Downs Allowed**
0—Case Reserve vs. Wooster, Sept. 21, 1985

# SEASON—OFFENSE
## TOTAL OFFENSE

**Most Yards Gained Per Game**
523.1—Samford, 1987 (5,231 in 10)

**Highest Average Gain Per Play**
8.14—Ferrum, 1990 (534 for 4,350)

**Most Plays Per Game**
85.6—Hampden-Sydney, 1978 (856 in 10)

**Most Touchdowns Scored Per Game by Rushing and Passing**
7.0—Samford, 1987 (70 in 10; 40 passing, 30 rushing)

## RUSHING

**Most Yards Gained Per Game**
434.7—Ferrum, 1990 (3,912 in 9)

**Highest Average Gain Per Rush**
8.32—Ferrum, 1990 (470 for 3,912)

**Most Rushes Per Game**
71.4—Wis.-River Falls, 1988 (714 in 10)

**Most Touchdowns Scored Per Game by Rushing**
5.4—Ferrum, 1990 (49 in 9)

## PASSING

**Most Yards Gained Per Game**
403.5—Hofstra, 1991 (4,035 in 10)

**Fewest Yards Gained Per Game**
18.4—Wis.-River Falls, 1983 (184 in 10)

**Highest Average Gain Per Attempt**
*(Min. 250 atts.)* 9.86—Ill. Benedictine, 1974 (259 for 2,554)
*(Min. 350 atts.)* 8.71—Wheaton (Ill.), 1983 (393 for 3,424)

**Highest Average Gain Per Completion (Min. 200 Completions)**
15.4—Wis.-Stevens Point, 1987 (249 for 3,836)

**Most Passes Attempted Per Game**
58.5—Hofstra, 1991 (585 in 10)

**Fewest Passes Attempted Per Game**
4.0—Wis.-River Falls, 1988 (40 in 10)

**Most Passes Completed Per Game**
34.4—Hofstra, 1991 (344 in 10)

**Fewest Passes Completed Per Game**
1.3—Wis.-River Falls, 1983 (13 in 10)

**Highest Percentage Completed**
*(Min. 200 atts.)* 65.2%—Kenyon, 1978 (148 of 227)
*(Min. 300 atts.)* 63.5%—Mount Union, 1992 (205 of 323)

**Lowest Percentage of Passes Had Intercepted (Min. 150 Attempts)**
0.7%—San Diego, 1990 (1 of 153)

**Most Touchdown Passes Per Game**
4.0—Samford, 1987 (40 in 10)

**Highest Passing Efficiency Rating Points**
*(Min. 15 atts. per game)* 191.7—Simpson, 1989 (163 attempts, 101 completions, 3 interceptions, 1,804 yards, 20 TDs)
*(Min. 300 atts.)* 171.7—Samford, 1987 (303 attempts, 165 completions, 7 interceptions, 2,825 yards, 40 TDs)

## PUNTING

**Most Punts Per Game**
11.0—FDU-Madison, 1990 (99 in 9)

**Fewest Punts Per Game**
2.4—Frostburg St., 1990 (24 in 10)

**Highest Punting Average**
44.6—Occidental, 1982 (55 for 2,454)

## SCORING

**Most Points Per Game**
51.7—Samford, 1987 (517 in 10)

**Most Touchdowns Per Game**
7.4—Samford, 1987 (74 in 10)

**Best Perfect Record on Extra Points Made by Kicking**
49 of 49—Dayton, 1989

**Most Two-Point Attempts Per Game**
2.8—N'western (Wis.), 1990 (17 in 6)

**Most Field Goals Made Per Game**
2.0—Mount Union, 1990 (20 in 10)

**Highest Scoring Margin**
38.2—Hofstra, 1990 (averaged 47.2 and allowed 9.0 in 10 games)

**Most Touchdowns on Blocked Punt Returns**
5—Widener, 1990

**Most Safeties**
4—Alfred, 1992; Central (Iowa), 1992; Westfield St., 1992; Wis.-Stevens Point, 1990

**Most Defensive Extra-Point Returns Scored**
2—Eureka, 1991; Brockport St., 1990

**Most Defensive Extra Point Blocked Kick Returns**
3—Assumption, 1992 (1 scored); Ohio Wesleyan, 1991 (0 scored); Brockport St., 1990 (2 scored)

**Most Defensive Extra Point Interceptions**
2—Swarthmore, 1989 (1 scored); Wis.-Platteville, 1988 (none scored)

## PENALTIES

**Most Penalties Per Game**
13.3—Kean, 1990 (133 in 10, 1,155 yards)

**Most Yards Penalized Per Game**
121.9—Hofstra, 1991 (1,219 in 10, 124 penalties)

### TURNOVERS (GIVEAWAYS) (FROM 1985)
#### (Passes Had Intercepted and Fumbles Lost)

**Fewest Turnovers**
8—North Central, 1989 (7 interceptions, 1 fumble lost); Occidental, 1988 (2 interceptions, 6 fumbles lost)
Per-game record—0.89, North Central, 1989 (8 in 9); Occidental, 1988 (8 in 9)

**Most Turnovers**
52—William Penn, 1985 (19 interceptions, 33 fumbles lost)
Per-game record—5.2, William Penn, 1985 (52 in 10)

# SEASON—DEFENSE
## TOTAL DEFENSE

**Fewest Yards Allowed Per Game**
94.0—Knoxville, 1977 (940 in 10)

**Lowest Average Yards Allowed Per Play**
(Min. 500 plays) 1.76—Bowie St., 1978 (576 for 1,011)

(Min. 650 plays) 2.03—Plymouth St., 1987 (733 for 1,488)

**Fewest Rushing and Passing Touchdowns Allowed Per Game**
0.3—Montclair St., 1984 (3 in 10)

## RUSHING DEFENSE

**Fewest Yards Allowed Per Game**
Minus 2.3—Knoxville, 1977 (-23 in 10 games)

**Lowest Average Yards Allowed Per Rush**
(Min. 275 rushes) Minus 0.07—Knoxville, 1977 (333 for -23)

(Min. 400 rushes) 1.00—Lycoming, 1976 (400 for 399)

**Fewest Touchdowns by Rushing Allowed**
0—Union (N.Y.), 1983 (9 games); New Haven, 1978 (9 games)

## PASS DEFENSE

**Fewest Yards Allowed Per Game**
48.5—Mass. Maritime, 1978 (388 in 8)

**Fewest Yards Allowed Per Attempt**
(Min. 150 atts.) 2.87—Plymouth St., 1982 (170 for 488)
(Min. 225 atts.) 3.27—Plymouth St., 1987 (281 for 919)

**Fewest Yards Allowed Per Completion**
**(Min. 100 Completions)**
8.64—Baldwin-Wallace, 1990 (151 for 1,305)

**Lowest Completion Percentage Allowed**
(Min. 150 atts.) 24.3%—Doane, 1973 (41 of 169)
(Min. 250 atts.) 33.5%—Plymouth St., 1987 (94 of 281)

**Highest Percentage Intercepted By**
**(Min. 200 Attempts)**
15.2%—Rose-Hulman, 1977 (32 of 210)

**Most Passes Intercepted By**
35—Plymouth St., 1987 (12 games, 281 attempts against, 348 yards returned)
Per-game record—3.4, Montclair St., 1981 (34 in 10)

**Fewest Passes Intercepted By**
**(Min. 125 Attempts)**
1—Bates, 1987 (134 attempts against in 8 games, 0 yards returned)

**Most Yards on Interception Returns**
576—Emory & Henry, 1987 (31 interceptions)

**Most Touchdowns Scored on Interceptions**
6—Coe, 1992 (22 interceptions, 272 passes against); Augustana (Ill.), 1987 (23 interceptions, 229 passes against)

**Fewest Touchdown Passes Allowed**
0—By many teams. Most recent: Dayton, 1980 (11 games)

**Lowest Passing Efficiency Rating Points Allowed Opponents**
(Min. 150 atts.) 27.8—Plymouth St., 1982 (allowed 170 attempts, 53 completions, 488 yards, 1 TD & intercepted 25 passes)
(Min. 275 atts.) 43.1—Plymouth St., 1987 (allowed 281 attempts, 94 completions, 919 yards, 6 TDs & intercepted 35 passes)

## PUNTING

**Most Opponent's Punts Blocked By**
11—Ill. Benedictine, 1987 (78 punts against in 10 games). Blocked 17 punts in 18 games during 1987-88, resulting in 5 TDs and 3 safeties

## SCORING

**Fewest Points Allowed Per Game**
3.4—Millsaps, 1980 (31 in 9)

**Fewest Touchdowns Allowed**
4—Baldwin-Wallace, 1981 (10 games); Millsaps, 1980 (9 games); Bentley, 1990 (8 games)

**Most Shutouts**
6—Cortland St., 1989; Plymouth St., 1982 (consecutive)

**Most Consecutive Shutouts**
6—Plymouth St., 1982

**Most Points Allowed Per Game**
59.1—Macalester, 1977 (532 in 9; 76 TDs, 64 PATs, 4 FGs)

**Most Defensive Extra-Point Attempts by Opponents**
5—Norwich, 1992 (4 blocked kick returns, 1 interception; none scored)

## TURNOVERS (TAKEAWAYS) (FROM 1985)

### (Opponent's Passes Intercepted and Fumbles Recovered)

**Highest Margin of Turnovers Per Game Over Opponents**
2.90—Macalester, 1986 (29 in 10; 29 giveaways vs. 58 takeaways)

**Most Takeaways**
58—Macalester, 1986 (28 interceptions, 30 fumbles gained)
Per-game record—5.8, Macalester, 1986 (58 in 10)

## ADDITIONAL RECORDS

**Most Consecutive Victories**
37—Augustana (Ill.) (from Sept. 17, 1983, through 1985 Division III playoffs; ended with 0-0 tie vs. Elmhurst, Sept. 13, 1986)

**Most Consecutive Regular-Season Victories**
49—Augustana (Ill.) (from Oct. 25, 1980, through 1985; ended with 0-0 tie vs. Elmhurst, Sept. 13, 1986)

**Most Consecutive Games Without Defeat**
60—Augustana (Ill.), (from Sept. 17, 1983, through Nov. 22, 1987; ended with 38-36 loss to Dayton, Nov. 29, 1987, in Division III playoffs and included one tie)

**Most Consecutive Regular-Season Games Without Defeat**
70—Augustana (Ill.) (from Oct. 25, 1980, through Oct. 1, 1988; ended with 24-21 loss to Carroll, Wis., Oct. 8, 1988)

**Most Consecutive Winning Seasons**
34—Wittenberg (from 1955 through 1988; ended with 4-5 record in 1989)

**Most Consecutive Games Without Being Shut Out**
195—Carnegie Mellon (current from Sept. 30, 1972)

**Most Consecutive Losses**
50—Macalester (from Oct. 5, 1974, to Nov. 10, 1979; ended with 17-14 win over Mount Senario, Sept. 6, 1980)

**Most Consecutive Games Without a Tie**
371—Widener (from Oct. 29, 1949, to Nov. 11, 1989; ended with 14-14 tie against Gettysburg, Sept. 8, 1990)

**Highest-Scoring Tie Game**
40-40—Wagner & Montclair St., Sept. 11, 1982

**Last Scoreless Tie Game**
Oct. 4, 1986—Delaware Valley & Moravian

**Most Consecutive Quarters Without Yielding a Touchdown by Rushing**
61—Augustana (Ill.) (in 16 games from Sept. 27, 1986, to Nov. 7, 1987; 77 including four 1986 Division III playoff games); Union (N.Y.) (in 16 games from Oct. 23, 1982, to Sept. 29, 1984)

**Most Consecutive Quarters Without Yielding a Touchdown by Passing**
44—Swarthmore (from Oct. 31, 1981, to Nov. 13, 1982)

**Most Improved Won-Lost Record (Including Postseason Games)**
7 games—Susquehanna, 1986 (11-1-0) from 1985 (3-7-0); Maryville (Tenn.), 1976 (7-2-0) from 1975 (0-9-0)

# ANNUAL CHAMPIONS, ALL-TIME LEADERS

## TOTAL OFFENSE

### Career Yards

| Player, Team | Years | Plays | Yards |
|---|---|---|---|
| Kirk Baumgartner, Wis.-Stevens Point | 1986-89 | *2,007 | *12,767 |
| Tim Peterson, Wis.-Stout | 1986-89 | 1,558 | 9,701 |
| Keith Bishop, Ill. Wesleyan/Wheaton (Ill.) | 1981, 83-85 | 1,467 | 9,052 |
| Dave Geissler, Wis.-Stevens Point | 1982-85 | 1,695 | 8,990 |
| Dennis Bogacz, Wis.-Oshkosh/Wis.-Whitewater | 1988-89, 90-91 | 1,394 | 8,850 |

| Player, Team | Years | Plays | Yards |
|---|---|---|---|
| John Clark, Wis.-Eau Claire ......................... | 1987-90 | 1,354 | 8,838 |
| Matt Jozokos, Plymouth St. ......................... | 1987-90 | 1,234 | 8,188 |
| Darryl Kosut, William Penn ........................ | 1983-86 | 1,583 | 7,817 |
| Steve Osterberger, Drake ......................... | 1987-90 | 1,263 | 7,520 |
| David Parker, Bishop ............................. | 1981-84 | 1,257 | 7,516 |
| John Rooney, Ill. Wesleyan ........................ | 1982-84 | 1,260 | 7,393 |
| Larry Barretta, Lycoming ......................... | 1983-86 | 1,205 | 7,320 |
| John Wortham, Earlham ........................... | 1989-92 | 1,574 | 7,296 |
| Shane Fulton, Heidelberg .......................... | 1983-86 | 1,344 | 7,203 |
| Scott Scesney, St. John's (N.Y.) .................... | 1986-89 | 1,048 | 7,196 |
| Ron Devorsky, Hiram ............................. | 1984-87 | 1,178 | 7,059 |
| Ed Dougherty, Lycoming .......................... | 1988-91 | 1,320 | 7,055 |
| Craig Solomon, Rhodes ........................... | 1975-78 | 1,261 | 7,055 |
| Chris Spriggs, Denison ........................... | 1983-86 | 1,219 | 7,047 |
| ¢Jim Ballard, Wilmington (Ohio)/Mount Union ..... | 1990, 91-92 | 1,020 | 7,043 |
| Bill Hyland, Iona ................................. | 1989-92 | 1,240 | 7,041 |
| Gary Collier, Emory & Henry ....................... | 1984-87 | 1,089 | 7,036 |
| Clay Sampson, Denison ........................... | 1977-80 | 1,225 | 6,920 |
| Rob Light, Moravian .............................. | 1986-89 | 1,226 | 6,886 |
| Mike Culver, Juniata ............................. | 1983-86 | 1,098 | 6,834 |

*\* Record.   ¢ Active player.*

## Season Yards

| Player, Team | Year | Games | Plays | Yards |
|---|---|---|---|---|
| Kirk Baumgartner, Wis.-Stevens Point ................ | †1988 | 11 | 604 | *3,790 |
| Kirk Baumgartner, Wis.-Stevens Point ................ | 1987 | 11 | 561 | 3,712 |
| Kirk Baumgartner, Wis.-Stevens Point ................ | †1989 | 10 | 530 | 3,540 |
| Tim Peterson, Wis.-Stout .......................... | 1989 | 10 | *614 | 3,244 |
| Keith Bishop, Wheaton (Ill.) ........................ | †1983 | 9 | 421 | 3,193 |
| Scott Isphording, Hanover ......................... | 1992 | 10 | 484 | 3,150 |
| Tim Peterson, Wis.-Stout .......................... | 1987 | 11 | 393 | 3,052 |
| Steve Austin, Mass.-Boston ........................ | 1992 | 9 | 466 | 3,003 |
| Keith Bishop, Wheaton (Ill.) ........................ | †1985 | 9 | 521 | 2,951 |
| Dennis Bogacz, Wis.-Oshkosh ...................... | 1989 | 10 | 417 | 2,939 |
| Brion Demski, Wis.-Stevens Point ................... | †1981 | 10 | 503 | 2,895 |
| Larry Barretta, Lycoming ......................... | †1986 | 10 | 453 | 2,875 |
| Shane Fulton, Heidelberg .......................... | 1985 | 10 | 485 | 2,858 |
| Mark Peterson, Neb. Wesleyan ..................... | 1983 | 10 | 425 | 2,846 |
| Leroy Williams, Upsala ........................... | 1992 | 10 | 476 | 2,822 |
| Keith Bishop, Wheaton (Ill.) ........................ | †1984 | 9 | 479 | 2,777 |
| Rhory Moss, Hofstra .............................. | †1990 | 9 | 372 | 2,775 |
| Dave Geissler, Wis.-Stevens Point .................. | 1985 | 11 | 456 | 2,756 |
| Jordan Poznick, Principia .......................... | †1992 | 8 | 519 | 2,747 |
| Bill Lech, Coe ................................... | 1989 | 9 | 404 | 2,743 |

*\* Record.   † National champion.*

## Single-Game Yards

| Yds. | Player, Team (Opponent) | Date |
|---|---|---|
| 596 | John Love, North Park (Elmhurst) .............................................. | Oct. 13, 1990 |
| 564 | Tim Lynch, Hofstra (Fordham) ................................................ | Oct. 19, 1991 |
| 538 | Jordan Poznick, Principia (Blackburn) .......................................... | Oct. 10, 1992 |
| 534 | Cliff Scott, Buffalo (New Haven) .............................................. | Sept. 12, 1992 |
| 528 | Steve Austin, Mass.-Boston (Mass. Maritime) .................................. | Oct. 10, 1992 |
| 527 | Rob Shippy, Concordia, Ill. (Concordia, Wis.) ................................... | Oct. 5, 1985 |
| 515 | Seamus Crotty, Hamilton (Middlebury) ........................................ | Oct. 27, 1984 |
| 512 | Bob Monroe, Knox (Cornell College) .......................................... | Oct. 11, 1986 |
| 511 | Kirk Baumgartner, Wis.-Stevens Point (Wis.-Superior) .......................... | Nov. 4, 1989 |
| 511 | Kirk Baumgartner, Wis.-Stevens Point (Wis.-Stout) ............................. | Oct. 24, 1987 |
| 509 | Michael Ferraro, LIU-C. W. Post (Alfred) ...................................... | Nov. 14, 1992 |
| 509 | Craig Solomon, Rhodes (Rose-Hulman) ........................................ | Nov. 11, 1978 |
| 507 | George Beisel, Hofstra (LIU-C. W. Post) ....................................... | Sept. 18, 1991 |
| 506 | Todd Coolidge, Susquehanna (Muhlenberg) .................................... | Sept. 12, 1987 |
| 504 | Jeff Hagan, Coast Guard (Trinity, Conn.) ...................................... | Oct. 26, 1985 |

## Career Yards Per Game

| Player, Team | Years | Games | Plays | Yards | Yd. PG |
|---|---|---|---|---|---|
| Kirk Baumgartner, Wis.-Stevens Point ....... | 1986-89 | 41 | *2,007 | *12,767 | *311.4 |
| Willie Reyna, La Verne ...................... | 1991-92 | 17 | 551 | 4,996 | 293.9 |
| Keith Bishop, Ill. Wesleyan/Wheaton (Ill.) ... | 1981, 83-85 | 31 | 1,467 | 9,052 | 292.0 |
| John Rooney, Ill. Wesleyan .................. | 1982-84 | 27 | 1,260 | 7,393 | 273.8 |
| Tim Peterson, Wis.-Stout ................... | 1986-89 | 36 | 1,558 | 9,701 | 269.5 |

*Division III Annual Champions, All-Time Leaders*                                253

| Player, Team | Years | Games | Plays | Yards | Yd. PG |
|---|---|---|---|---|---|
| Robert Farra, Claremont-M-S ............... | 1978-79 | 16 | 690 | 4,179 | 261.2 |
| Dennis Bogacz, Wis.-Oshkosh/ | | | | | |
| Wis.-Whitewater ......................... | 1988-89, 90-91 | 38 | 1,394 | 8,850 | 232.9 |
| John Clark, Wis.-Eau Claire ................ | 1987-90 | 38 | 1,354 | 8,838 | 232.6 |
| Mark Peterson, Neb. Wesleyan ............. | 1982-84 | 28 | 1,151 | 6,367 | 227.4 |
| Scott Scesney, St. John's (N.Y.) ............ | 1986-89 | 32 | 1,048 | 7,196 | 224.9 |
| Rob Bristow, Pomona-Pitzer ............... | 1983-86 | 29 | 1,290 | 6,465 | 222.9 |
| Dave Geissler, Wis.-Stevens Point .......... | 1982-85 | 42 | 1,695 | 8,990 | 214.0 |
| Jeff Beer, Bethany (W. Va.) ................. | 1978-80 | 25 | 878 | 5,228 | 209.1 |
| John Love, North Park .................... | 1988-90 | 27 | 1,182 | 5,613 | 207.9 |
| Seamus Crotty, Hamilton .................. | 1982-85 | 31 | 1,225 | 6,402 | 206.5 |
| Jeff Voris, DePauw ....................... | 1986-89 | 28 | 993 | 5,754 | 205.5 |
| Matt Jozokos, Plymouth St. ................ | 1987-90 | 40 | 1,234 | 8,188 | 204.7 |
| Steve Osterberger, Drake .................. | 1987-90 | 37 | 1,263 | 7,520 | 203.2 |
| Tim Tully, Wheaton (Ill.) ................... | 1989-92 | 33 | 1,064 | 6,669 | 202.1 |
| Marty Barrett, Buffalo ..................... | 1980-82 | 32 | 1,280 | 6,466 | 202.1 |

* Record.

## Season Yards Per Game

| Player, Team | Year | Games | Plays | Yards | Yd. PG |
|---|---|---|---|---|---|
| Keith Bishop, Wheaton (Ill.) .................. | †1983 | 9 | 421 | 3,193 | *354.8 |
| Kirk Baumgartner, Wis.-Stevens Point ........ | †1989 | 10 | 530 | 3,540 | 354.0 |
| Kirk Baumgartner, Wis.-Stevens Point ........ | †1988 | 11 | 604 | *3,790 | 344.5 |
| Jordan Poznick, Principia ................... | †1992 | 8 | 519 | 2,747 | 343.4 |
| Kirk Baumgartner, Wis.-Stevens Point ........ | 1987 | 11 | 561 | 3,712 | 337.5 |
| Steve Austin, Mass.-Boston .................. | 1992 | 9 | 466 | 3,003 | 333.7 |
| Willie Reyna, La Verne ...................... | †1991 | 8 | 220 | 2,633 | 329.1 |
| Keith Bishop, Wheaton (Ill.) .................. | †1985 | 9 | 521 | 2,951 | 327.9 |
| Tim Peterson, Wis.-Stout .................... | 1989 | 10 | *614 | 3,244 | 324.4 |
| Scott Isphording, Hanover ................... | 1992 | 10 | 484 | 3,150 | 315.0 |
| Keith Bishop, Wheaton (Ill.) .................. | †1984 | 9 | 479 | 2,777 | 308.6 |
| Rhory Moss, Hofstra ........................ | †1990 | 9 | 372 | 2,775 | 308.3 |
| Bill Lech, Coe ............................. | 1989 | 9 | 404 | 2,743 | 304.8 |
| Robert Farra, Claremont-M-S ................ | †1978 | 9 | 427 | 2,685 | 298.3 |
| Rob Shippy, Concordia (Ill.) ................. | 1985 | 9 | 370 | 2,682 | 298.0 |
| Brett Butler, Wabash ....................... | 1989 | 9 | 449 | 2,666 | 296.2 |
| Dennis Bogacz, Wis.-Oshkosh ............... | 1989 | 10 | 417 | 2,939 | 293.9 |
| Brion Demski, Wis.-Stevens Point ............ | †1981 | 10 | 503 | 2,895 | 289.5 |

* Record.   † National champion.

## Annual Champions

| Year | Player, Team | Cl. | G | Plays | Yards | Avg. |
|---|---|---|---|---|---|---|
| 1973 | Bob Dulich, San Diego ...................... | Jr. | 11 | 340 | 2,543 | 231.2 |
| 1974 | Larry Cenotto, Pomona-Pitzer ............... | Sr. | 9 | 436 | 2,127 | 236.3 |
| 1975 | Ricky Haygood, Millsaps ..................... | Jr. | 9 | 332 | 2,176 | 241.8 |
| 1976 | Rollie Wiebers, Buena Vista .................. | So. | 9 | 353 | 2,198 | 244.2 |
| 1977 | Tom Hamilton, Occidental ................... | Sr. | 9 | 358 | 2,050 | 227.8 |
| 1978 | Robert Farra, Claremont-M-S ................ | Jr. | 9 | 427 | 2,685 | 298.3 |
| 1979 | Clay Sampson, Denison ..................... | Jr. | 9 | 412 | 2,255 | 250.6 |
| 1980 | Jeff Beer, Bethany (W. Va.) .................. | Sr. | 9 | 372 | 2,331 | 259.0 |
| 1981 | Brion Demski, Wis.-Stevens Point ............ | Sr. | 10 | 503 | 2,895 | 289.5 |
| 1982 | Dave McCarrell, Wheaton (Ill.) ............... | Sr. | 9 | 387 | 2,503 | 278.1 |
| 1983 | Keith Bishop, Wheaton (Ill.) .................. | So. | 9 | 421 | 3,193 | *354.8 |
| 1984 | Keith Bishop, Wheaton (Ill.) .................. | Jr. | 9 | 479 | 2,777 | 308.6 |
| 1985 | Keith Bishop, Wheaton (Ill.) .................. | Sr. | 9 | 521 | 2,951 | 327.9 |
| 1986 | Larry Barretta, Lycoming ................... | Sr. | 10 | 453 | 2,875 | 287.5 |
| 1987 | Todde Greenough, Willamette ................ | Jr. | 9 | 436 | 2,567 | 285.2 |
| 1988 | Kirk Baumgartner, Wis.-Stevens Point ........ | Jr. | 11 | 604 | *3,790 | 344.5 |
| 1989 | Kirk Baumgartner, Wis.-Stevens Point ........ | Sr. | 10 | 530 | 3,540 | 354.0 |
| 1990 | Rhory Moss, Hofstra ........................ | Jr. | 9 | 372 | 2,775 | 308.3 |
| 1991 | Willie Reyna, La Verne ...................... | Jr. | 8 | 220 | 2,633 | 329.1 |
| 1992 | Jordan Poznick, Principia ................... | Jr. | 8 | 519 | 2,747 | 343.4 |

* Record.

*1993 NCAA FOOTBALL*

# RUSHING

## Career Yards

| Player, Team | Years | Plays | Yards | Avg. |
|---|---|---|---|---|
| Joe Dudek, Plymouth St. | 1982-85 | 785 | *5,570 | ‡7.10 |
| Eric Frees, Western Md. | 1988-91 | 1,059 | 5,281 | 4.99 |
| Terry Underwood, Wagner | 1985-88 | 742 | 5,010 | 6.75 |
| Mike Birosak, Dickinson | 1986-89 | *1,112 | 4,662 | 4.19 |
| Rich Kowalski, Hobart | 1972-75 | 907 | 4,631 | 5.11 |
| ¢Kirk Matthieu, Maine Maritime | $1989-92 | 836 | 4,513 | 5.40 |
| Jim Romagna, Loras | 1989-92 | 983 | 4,493 | 4.57 |
| Chris Babirad, Wash. & Jeff. | 1989-92 | 683 | 4,419 | 6.47 |
| Willie Beers, John Carroll | 1989-92 | 848 | 4,332 | 5.11 |
| Remon Smith, Randolph-Macon | 1984-87 | 737 | 4,249 | 5.77 |
| Chris Spriggs, Denison | 1983-86 | 787 | 4,248 | 5.40 |
| Scott Reppert, Lawrence | 1979-82 | 757 | 4,211 | 5.56 |
| Alonzo Patterson, Wagner | 1979-82 | 816 | 4,177 | 5.12 |
| Von Cummings, Defiance | 1989-92 | 810 | 4,131 | 5.10 |
| Peter Gorniewicz, Colby | 1971-74 | 1,024 | 4,113 | 4.02 |
| Bryce Tuohy, Heidelberg | 1986-89 | 905 | 4,067 | 4.49 |
| Ricky Gales, Nebraska-Omaha/Simpson | 1986-87, 88-89 | 701 | 4,061 | 5.79 |
| Brian Grandison, Wooster | 1988-91 | 899 | 4,042 | 4.50 |
| Jay Wessler, Illinois Col. | 1977-80 | 807 | 4,016 | 4.98 |
| Sandy Rogers, Emory & Henry | 1983-86 | 641 | 4,005 | 6.25 |
| Tim McDaniel, Centre | 1988-91 | 920 | 3,897 | 4.24 |
| Ted Pretasky, Wis.-La Crosse | 1985-88 | 698 | 3,877 | 5.55 |
| Wes Stearns, Merchant Marine | 1989-92 | 736 | 3,875 | 5.26 |
| Roscoe Mitchell, Fort Valley St. | 1976-79 | 848 | 3,869 | 4.56 |
| Evan Lipp, Marietta | 1984-87 | 900 | 3,844 | 4.27 |

* Record.  ‡ Record for minimum of 500 carries.  ¢ Active player.  $ See page 8 for explanation.

## Season Yards

| Player, Team | Year | Games | Plays | Yards | Avg. |
|---|---|---|---|---|---|
| Ricky Gales, Simpson | †1989 | 10 | 297 | *2,035 | 6.85 |
| Jon Warga, Wittenberg | †1990 | 10 | 254 | 1,836 | 7.23 |
| Terry Underwood, Wagner | †1988 | 9 | 245 | 1,809 | 6.75 |
| Mike Birosak, Dickinson | 1989 | 10 | *380 | 1,798 | 4.73 |
| Kirk Matthieu, Maine Maritime | †1992 | 9 | 327 | 1,733 | 5.30 |
| Sandy Rogers, Emory & Henry | †1986 | 11 | 231 | 1,730 | +7.49 |
| Anthony Russo, St. John's (N.Y.) | †1991 | 10 | 287 | 1,685 | 5.87 |
| John Bernatavitz, Dickinson | 1990 | 10 | 266 | 1,666 | 6.26 |
| Hank Wineman, Albion | 1991 | 9 | 307 | 1,629 | 5.31 |
| Gary Trettel, St. Thomas (Minn.) | 1990 | 10 | 293 | 1,620 | 5.53 |
| Joe Dudek, Plymouth St. | †1985 | 11 | 216 | 1,615 | 7.48 |
| Eric Frees, Western Md. | 1990 | 10 | 295 | 1,594 | 5.40 |
| Chris Babirad, Wash. & Jeff. | 1992 | 9 | 243 | 1,589 | 6.54 |
| George Rainey, Wis.-Whitewater | 1987 | 11 | 279 | 1,567 | 5.62 |
| Rob Johnson, Western Md. | 1992 | 10 | 330 | 1,560 | 4.73 |
| Eric Frees, Western Md. | 1991 | 10 | 304 | 1,545 | 5.08 |
| Clay Sampson, Denison | †1979 | 9 | 323 | 1,517 | 4.70 |
| Chuck Evans, Ferris St. | 1976 | 10 | 224 | 1,509 | 6.74 |
| Chris Babirad, Wash. & Jeff. | 1991 | 9 | 224 | 1,508 | 6.73 |
| Gary Trettel, St. Thomas (Minn.) | 1989 | 10 | 256 | 1,502 | 5.87 |

* Record.  † National champion.  + Record for minimum of 195 carries.

## Single-Game Yards

| Yds. | Player, Team (Opponent) | Date |
|---|---|---|
| 382 | Pete Baranek, Carthage (North Central) | Oct. 5, 1985 |
| 363 | Terry Underwood, Wagner (Hofstra) | Oct. 15, 1988 |
| 354 | Terry Underwood, Wagner (Western Conn. St.) | Oct. 3, 1986 |
| 342 | Dave Bednarek, Wis.-River Falls (Wis.-Stevens Point) | Oct. 29, 1983 |
| 337 | Kirk Matthieu, Maine Maritime (Curry) | Oct. 27, 1990 |
| 337 | Ted Helsel, St. Francis, Pa. (Gallaudet) | Nov. 3, 1979 |
| 334 | Oliver Bridges, Stony Brook (Pace) | Nov. 16, 1991 |
| 329 | Don Williams, Lowell (Colby) | Oct. 4, 1985 |
| 326 | Mike Krueger, Tufts (Amherst) | Oct. 25, 1980 |
| 321 | Jack Davis, Hobart (Brockport St.) | Nov. 5, 1977 |
| 317 | Greg Novarro, Bentley (St. John's, N.Y.) | Nov. 14, 1992 |
| 314 | Anthony Russo, St. John's, N.Y. (Georgetown) | Nov. 7, 1992 |
| 312 | Don Taylor, Central, Iowa (Dubuque) | Oct. 9, 1976 |

| Yds. | Player, Team (Opponent) | Date |
|---|---|---|
| 311 | Jason Wooley, Worcester Tech (MIT) | Nov. 10, 1990 |
| 311 | Mike Birosak, Dickinson (Gettysburg) | Nov. 4, 1989 |
| 311 | Roy Heffernan, Middlebury (Worcester Tech) | Oct. 4, 1975 |

## Career Yards Per Game

| Player, Team | Years | Games | Plays | Yards | Yd. PG |
|---|---|---|---|---|---|
| Terry Underwood, Wagner | 1985-88 | 33 | 742 | 5,010 | *151.8 |
| Joe Dudek, Plymouth St. | 1982-85 | 41 | 785 | *5,570 | 135.9 |
| Eric Frees, Western Md. | 1988-91 | 40 | 1,059 | 5,281 | 132.0 |
| Rich Kowalski, Hobart | 1972-75 | 36 | 907 | 4,631 | 128.6 |
| Peter Gorniewicz, Colby | 1971-74 | 32 | 1,024 | 4,113 | 128.5 |
| Scott Reppert, Lawrence | 1979-82 | 33 | 757 | 4,211 | 127.6 |
| Chris Babirad, Wash. & Jeff. | 1989-92 | 35 | 683 | 4,419 | 126.3 |
| Tim Barrett, John Carroll | 1972-74 | 29 | 662 | 3,621 | 124.9 |

* Record.

## Season Yards Per Game

| Player, Team | Year | Games | Plays | Yards | TD | Yd. PG |
|---|---|---|---|---|---|---|
| Ricky Gales, Simpson | †1989 | 10 | 297 | *2,035 | 26 | *203.5 |
| Terry Underwood, Wagner | †1988 | 9 | 245 | 1,809 | 21 | 201.0 |
| Kirk Matthieu, Maine Maritime | †1992 | 9 | 327 | 1,733 | 16 | 192.6 |
| Jon Warga, Wittenberg | †1990 | 10 | 254 | 1,836 | 15 | 183.6 |
| Hank Wineman, Albion | †1991 | 9 | 307 | 1,629 | 14 | 181.0 |
| Eric Grey, Hamilton | 1991 | 8 | 217 | 1,439 | 13 | 179.9 |
| Mike Birosak, Dickinson | 1989 | 10 | *380 | 1,798 | 18 | 179.8 |
| Chris Babirad, Wash. & Jeff. | 1992 | 9 | 243 | 1,589 | 22 | 176.6 |
| Clay Sampson, Denison | †1979 | 9 | 323 | 1,517 | 13 | 168.6 |
| Anthony Russo, St. John's (N.Y.) | 1991 | 10 | 287 | 1,685 | 18 | 168.5 |
| Chris Babirad, Wash. & Jeff. | 1991 | 9 | 224 | 1,508 | 18 | 167.6 |
| John Bernatavitz, Dickinson | 1990 | 10 | 266 | 1,666 | 15 | 166.6 |
| Billy Johnson, Widener | †1973 | 9 | 168 | 1,494 | 21 | 166.0 |
| Scott Reppert, Lawrence | †1982 | 8 | 254 | 1,323 | 14 | 165.4 |
| Chris Dabrow, Claremont-M-S | †1987 | 9 | 265 | 1,486 | 13 | 165.1 |
| Wes Stearns, Merchant Marine | 1992 | 9 | 247 | 1,477 | 12 | 164.1 |
| Trent Nauholz, Simpson | 1992 | 8 | 254 | 1,302 | 21 | 162.8 |
| Gary Trettel, St. Thomas (Minn.) | 1990 | 10 | 293 | 1,620 | 19 | 162.0 |
| Tom Shaffner, Defiance | 1973 | 9 | 251 | 1,450 | 19 | 161.1 |

* Record. † National champion.

## Annual Champions

| Year | Player, Team | Cl. | G | Plays | Yards | Avg. |
|---|---|---|---|---|---|---|
| 1973 | Billy Johnson, Widener | Sr. | 9 | 168 | 1,494 | 166.0 |
| 1974 | Tim Barrett, John Carroll | Sr. | 9 | 256 | 1,409 | 156.6 |
| 1975 | Ron Baker, Monmouth (Ill.) | Sr. | 8 | 200 | 1,116 | 139.5 |
| 1976 | Chuck Evans, Ferris St. | Jr. | 10 | 224 | 1,509 | 150.9 |
| 1977 | Don Taylor, Central (Iowa) | Sr. | 9 | 267 | 1,329 | 147.7 |
| 1978 | Dino Hall, Rowan | Sr. | 10 | 239 | 1,330 | 133.0 |
| 1979 | Clay Sampson, Denison | Jr. | 9 | 323 | 1,517 | 168.6 |
| 1980 | Scott Reppert, Lawrence | So. | 8 | 223 | 1,223 | 152.9 |
| 1981 | Scott Reppert, Lawrence | Jr. | 9 | 250 | 1,410 | 156.7 |
| 1982 | Scott Reppert, Lawrence | Sr. | 8 | 254 | 1,323 | 165.4 |
| 1983 | John Franco, Wagner | Sr. | 8 | 175 | 1,166 | 145.8 |
| 1984 | Gary Errico, Mass.-Lowell | Sr. | 9 | 165 | 1,404 | 156.0 |
| 1985 | Bruce Montella, Chicago | Sr. | 9 | 265 | 1,372 | 152.4 |
| 1986 | Sandy Rogers, Emory & Henry | Sr. | 11 | 231 | 1,730 | 157.3 |
| 1987 | Chris Dabrow, Claremont-M-S | Sr. | 9 | 265 | 1,486 | 165.1 |
| 1988 | Terry Underwood, Wagner | Sr. | 9 | 245 | 1,809 | 201.0 |
| 1989 | Ricky Gales, Simpson | Sr. | 10 | 297 | *2,035 | *203.5 |
| 1990 | Jon Warga, Wittenberg | Sr. | 10 | 254 | 1,836 | 183.6 |
| 1991 | Hank Wineman, Albion | Sr. | 9 | 307 | 1,629 | 181.0 |
| 1992 | Kirk Matthieu, Maine Maritime | Jr. | 9 | 327 | 1,733 | 192.6 |

* Record.

*1993 NCAA FOOTBALL*

# PASSING

## Career Passing Efficiency
### (Minimum 325 Completions)

| Player, Team | Years | Att. | Cmp. | Int. | Pct. | Yds. | TD | Pts. |
|---|---|---|---|---|---|---|---|---|
| Joe Blake, Simpson | 1987-90 | 672 | 399 | 15 | .594 | 6,183 | 43 | *153.3 |
| Willie Reyna, La Verne | 1991-92 | 542 | 346 | 19 | .638 | 4,712 | 37 | 152.4 |
| Gary Collier, Emory & Henry | 1984-87 | 738 | 386 | 33 | .523 | 6,103 | 80 | 148.6 |
| Greg Heeres, Hope | 1981-84 | 630 | 347 | 21 | .537 | 5,120 | 53 | 144.4 |
| Bruce Crosthwaite, Adrian | 1984-87 | 618 | 368 | 31 | .596 | 4,959 | 45 | 141.0 |
| Matt Jozokos, Plymouth St. | 1987-90 | 1,003 | 527 | 39 | .525 | 7,658 | 95 | 140.2 |
| Joe Coviello, Frank. & Marsh. | 1973-76 | 591 | 334 | 36 | .565 | 4,651 | 52 | 139.5 |
| John Clark, Wis.-Eau Claire | 1987-90 | 1,119 | 645 | 42 | .576 | 9,196 | 63 | 137.7 |
| Joe Shield, Trinity (Conn.) | 1981-84 | 845 | 476 | 39 | .563 | 6,646 | 52 | 133.5 |
| David Broecker, Wabash | 1979-82 | 633 | 369 | 45 | .583 | 4,895 | 45 | 132.5 |
| Dick Puccio, Cortland St. | 1988-91 | 727 | 451 | 34 | .620 | 5,301 | 40 | 131.9 |
| Mike Culver, Juniata | 1983-86 | 756 | 406 | 41 | .537 | 5,799 | 56 | 131.7 |
| Robb Disbennett, Salisbury St. | 1982-85 | 633 | 359 | 40 | .567 | 5,023 | 40 | 131.6 |
| Kirk Baumgartner, Wis.-Stevens Point | 1986-89 | *1,696 | *883 | 57 | .521 | *13,028 | *110 | 131.3 |
| Walter Briggs, Montclair St. | 1983-86 | 832 | 417 | 36 | .501 | 6,489 | 59 | 130.4 |
| Brian Cox, Beloit | 1988-91 | 620 | 337 | 43 | .544 | 4,641 | 50 | 130.0 |
| Randy Muetzel, St. Thomas (Minn.) | 1979-82 | 613 | 339 | 20 | .553 | 4,462 | 36 | 129.3 |
| Larry Barretta, Lycoming | 1983-86 | 732 | 361 | 26 | .493 | 5,345 | 57 | 129.3 |
| Ed Dougherty, Lycoming | 1988-91 | 1,025 | 589 | 47 | .575 | 7,108 | 69 | 128.7 |
| Keith Bishop, Ill. Wesleyan/Wheaton (Ill.) | 1981, 83-5 | 1,311 | 772 | 65 | .589 | 9,579 | 71 | 128.2 |
| Kevin King, Ripon | 1978-81 | 635 | 348 | 43 | .548 | 5,029 | 39 | 128.1 |

* Record.

## Season Passing Efficiency
### (Minimum 15 Attempts Per Game)

| Player, Team | Year | G | Att. | Cmp. | Int. | Pct. | Yds. | TD | Pts. |
|---|---|---|---|---|---|---|---|---|---|
| Joe Blake, Simpson | ††1989 | 10 | 144 | 93 | 3 | .645 | 1,705 | 19 | *203.3 |
| Mitch Sanders, Bridgeport | 1973 | 10 | 151 | 84 | 7 | .556 | 1,551 | 23 | 182.9 |
| Pat Mayew, St. John's (Minn.) | †1991 | 9 | 247 | 154 | 4 | .623 | 2,408 | 30 | ‡181.0 |
| Jimbo Fisher, Samford | †1987 | 10 | 252 | 139 | 5 | .551 | 2,394 | 34 | 175.4 |
| Gary Collier, Emory & Henry | 1987 | 11 | 249 | 152 | 10 | .610 | 2,317 | 33 | 174.8 |
| James Grant, Ramapo | 1989 | 9 | 147 | 91 | 7 | .619 | 1,441 | 17 | 172.7 |
| Gary Urwiler, Eureka | 1991 | 10 | 171 | 103 | 5 | .602 | 1,656 | 18 | 170.3 |
| Steve Keller, Dayton | †1992 | 10 | 153 | 99 | 5 | .647 | 1,350 | 17 | 168.9 |
| Robb Disbennett, Salisbury St. | †1985 | 10 | 153 | 94 | 6 | .614 | 1,462 | 16 | 168.4 |
| Scott Scesney, St. John's (N.Y.) | 1989 | 10 | 244 | 131 | 9 | .536 | 2,314 | 31 | 167.8 |
| Jim Ballard, Mount Union | 1992 | 10 | 292 | 186 | 8 | .637 | 2,656 | 29 | 167.4 |
| Chuck Hooker, Cornell College | 1985 | 9 | 186 | 108 | 10 | .581 | 1,818 | 21 | 166.7 |
| Steve Varley, St. John's (Minn.) | 1989 | 9 | 162 | 106 | 8 | .654 | 1,476 | 16 | 164.6 |
| Brad Forsyth, Ill. Wesleyan | 1989 | 9 | 159 | 100 | 4 | .628 | 1,380 | 16 | 163.9 |
| Cody Dearing, Randolph-Macon | †1984 | 10 | 226 | 125 | 12 | .553 | 2,139 | 27 | 163.4 |
| Paul Foye, Amherst | 1985 | 8 | 133 | 87 | 7 | .654 | 1,161 | 14 | 163.0 |
| Matt Dillon, Cornell College | 1978 | 9 | 166 | 98 | 7 | .590 | 1,567 | 16 | 161.7 |
| Aaron Van Dyke, Cornell College | 1976 | 9 | 154 | 91 | 12 | .591 | 1,611 | 14 | 161.4 |
| John Koz, Baldwin-Wallace | 1991 | 10 | 239 | 153 | 4 | .640 | 1,014 | 21 | 160.5 |
| George Muller, Hofstra | †1980 | 10 | 189 | 115 | 14 | .608 | 1,983 | 15 | 160.4 |

* Record.  † National champion.  †† Declared champion; with six more pass attempts (making 15 per game), all interceptions, still would have highest efficiency (187.3).  ‡ Record for minimum of 25 attempts per game.

## Career Yards

| Player, Team | Years | Att. | Cmp. | Int. | Pct. | Yards | TD |
|---|---|---|---|---|---|---|---|
| Kirk Baumgartner, Wis.-Stevens Point | 1986-89 | *1,696 | *883 | 57 | .521 | *13,028 | *110 |
| Keith Bishop, Ill. Wesleyan/Wheaton (Ill.) | 1981, 83-85 | 1,311 | 772 | 65 | .589 | 9,579 | 71 |
| Dennis Bogacz, Wis.-Oshkosh/ Wis.-Whitewater | 1988-89, 90-91 | 1,275 | 654 | 59 | .513 | 9,536 | 66 |
| Dave Geissler, Wis.-Stevens Point | 1982-85 | 1,346 | 789 | 57 | .586 | 9,518 | 65 |
| John Clark, Wis.-Eau Claire | 1987-90 | 1,119 | 645 | 42 | .576 | 9,196 | 63 |
| Tim Peterson, Wis.-Stout | 1986-89 | 1,185 | 653 | 62 | .551 | 8,881 | 59 |
| Matt Jozokos, Plymouth St. | 1987-90 | 1,003 | 527 | 39 | .525 | 7,658 | 95 |
| Bill Hyland, Iona | 1989-92 | 1,017 | 511 | 55 | .502 | 7,382 | 57 |
| Shane Fulton, Heidelberg | 1983-86 | 1,024 | 587 | 55 | .573 | 7,372 | 50 |
| Paul Brandenburg, Ripon | 1984-87 | 1,181 | 607 | 66 | .514 | 7,320 | 39 |

| Player, Team | Years | Att. | Cmp. | Int. | Pct. | Yards | TD |
|---|---|---|---|---|---|---|---|
| Craig Solomon, Rhodes ................... | 1975-78 | 1,022 | 542 | 70 | .530 | 7,314 | 71 |
| Rob Bristow, Pomona-Pitzer .............. | 1983-86 | 1,155 | 628 | 60 | .544 | 7,120 | 27 |
| Ed Dougherty, Lycoming ................. | 1988-91 | 1,025 | 589 | 47 | .575 | 7,108 | 69 |
| ¢Jim Ballard, Wilmington (Ohio)/Mount Union................................... | 1990, 91-92 | 885 | 514 | 30 | .581 | 7,075 | 78 |
| Steve Osterberger, Drake ................. | 1987-90 | 981 | 536 | 33 | .546 | 7,021 | 53 |
| Ron Devorsky, Hiram ..................... | 1984-87 | 1,028 | 542 | 59 | .527 | 7,012 | 50 |
| Gary Walljasper, Wartburg ................ | 1981-84 | 974 | 521 | 50 | .535 | 6,992 | 49 |
| Marty Barrett, Buffalo .................... | 1980-83 | 956 | 513 | 53 | .537 | 6,945 | 44 |
| David Parker, Bishop ..................... | 1981-84 | 938 | 378 | 63 | .403 | 6,934 | 69 |
| Scott Scesney, St. John's (N.Y.) ........... | 1986-89 | 945 | 463 | 44 | .490 | 6,914 | 72 |
| John Wortham, Earlham .................. | 1989-92 | 1,189 | 615 | 74 | .517 | 6,812 | 38 |
| Scott Driggers, Colorado Col............... | 1981-84 | 1,022 | 612 | 54 | .599 | 6,709 | 40 |

* Record.  ¢ Active player.

## Season Yards

| Player, Team | Year | Games | Att. | Cmp. | Int. | Pct. | Yards | TD |
|---|---|---|---|---|---|---|---|---|
| Kirk Baumgartner, Wis.-Stevens Point.... | 1988 | 11 | *527 | *276 | 16 | .524 | *3,828 | 25 |
| Kirk Baumgartner, Wis.-Stevens Point.... | 1987 | 11 | 466 | 243 | 22 | .521 | 3,755 | 31 |
| Kirk Baumgartner, Wis.-Stevens Point.... | 1989 | 10 | 455 | 247 | 9 | .542 | 3,692 | *39 |
| Keith Bishop, Wheaton (Ill.) .............. | 1983 | 9 | 375 | 236 | 19 | *.629 | 3,274 | 24 |
| Keith Bishop, Wheaton (Ill.) .............. | 1985 | 9 | 457 | 262 | 22 | .573 | 3,171 | 25 |
| Scott Isphording, Hanover .............. | 1992 | 10 | 359 | 207 | 19 | .576 | 3,098 | 24 |
| Dennis Bogacz, Wis.-Oshkosh ........... | 1989 | 10 | 378 | 219 | 18 | .579 | 3,051 | 18 |
| Steve Austin, Mass.-Boston .............. | 1992 | 9 | 396 | 181 | 25 | .457 | 2,991 | 29 |
| Keith Bishop, Wheaton (Ill.) .............. | 1984 | 9 | 440 | 259 | 21 | .589 | 2,968 | 21 |
| Tim Peterson, Wis.-Stout ................ | 1989 | 10 | 445 | 256 | 15 | .575 | 2,956 | 20 |
| Brion Demski, Wis.-Stevens Point ....... | 1981 | 10 | 452 | 222 | 20 | .491 | 2,889 | 16 |
| Shane Fulton, Heidelberg ................ | 1985 | 10 | 393 | 222 | 24 | .565 | 2,876 | 19 |
| Tim Peterson, Wis.-Stout ................ | 1987 | 11 | 302 | 180 | 19 | .596 | 2,871 | 18 |
| Chris Creighton, Kenyon ................ | 1990 | 10 | 398 | 231 | 18 | .580 | 2,843 | 29 |
| Kevin Enterlein, Pace ................... | 1986 | 10 | 427 | 205 | 28 | .480 | 2,829 | 20 |
| John Clark, Wis.-Eau Claire .............. | 1989 | 10 | 344 | 199 | 14 | .578 | 2,785 | 22 |
| Ed Smith, Ill. Benedictine ................ | 1992 | 10 | 320 | 184 | 16 | .575 | 2,770 | 25 |
| Robert Farra, Claremont-M-S ............ | †1978 | 9 | 359 | 196 | 15 | .546 | 2,770 | 20 |

* Record.  † National champion.

## Single-Game Yards

| Yds. | Player, Team (Opponent) | Date |
|---|---|---|
| 585 | Tim Lynch, Hofstra (Fordham) ............................................... | Oct. 19, 1991 |
| 533 | John Love, North Park (Elmhurst) ............................................ | Oct. 13, 1990 |
| 532 | Bob Monroe, Knox (Cornell College)......................................... | Oct. 11, 1986 |
| 523 | Kirk Baumgartner, Wis.-Stevens Point (Wis.-Stout) ........................... | Oct. 24, 1987 |
| 513 | Craig Solomon, Rhodes (Rose-Hulman) ...................................... | Nov.11, 1978 |
| 509 | Bob Krepfle, Wis.-La Crosse (Wis.-River Falls) ............................... | Nov. 12, 1983 |
| 507 | George Beisel, Hofstra (LIU-C. W. Post)...................................... | Sept. 28, 1991 |
| 506 | Keith Bishop, Wheaton, Ill. (Ill. Wesleyan) ................................... | Oct. 29, 1983 |
| 505 | Kirk Baumgartner, Wis.-Stevens Point (Wis.-Superior) ........................ | Nov. 4, 1989 |
| 504 | Jordan Poznick, Principia (Blackburn) ....................................... | Oct. 10, 1992 |
| 504 | Rob Shippy, Concordia, Ill. (Concordia, Wis.)................................. | Oct. 5, 1985 |
| 503 | Dave Detrick, Wis.-Superior (Wis.-Oshkosh).................................. | Sept. 16, 1989 |
| 501 | Keith Bishop, Wheaton, Ill. (North Park) ..................................... | Oct. 12, 1985 |

## Single-Game Completions

| Cmp. | Player, Team (Opponent) | Date |
|---|---|---|
| 50 | Tim Lynch, Hofstra (Fordham) ............................................... | Oct. 19, 1991 |
| 48 | Jordan Poznick, Principia (Blackburn) ....................................... | Oct. 10, 1992 |
| 47 | Mike Wallace, Ohio Wesleyan (Denison)...................................... | Oct. 3, 1981 |
| 42 | Tim Lynch, Hofstra (Towson St.) ............................................ | Nov. 2, 1991 |
| 42 | Keith Bishop, Wheaton, Ill. (Millikin) ........................................ | Sept. 14, 1985 |
| 41 | Michael Doto, Hofstra (Central Conn. St.) .................................... | Sept. 14, 1991 |
| 41 | Todd Monken, Knox (Cornell College) ....................................... | Oct. 8, 1988 |
| 40 | Dave Geissler, Wis.-Stevens Point (Wis.-Eau Claire) .......................... | Nov. 12, 1983 |
| 39 | Rob Bristow, Pomona-Pitzer (La Verne) ..................................... | Oct. 12, 1985 |
| 39 | Steve Hendry, Wis.-Superior (Wis.-Stevens Point) ............................ | Oct. 17, 1981 |
| 38 | George Beisel, Hofstra vs. Southern Conn. St................................. | Oct. 9, 1992 |
| 38 | Jeff Voris, DePauw (Findlay)................................................. | Oct. 31, 1987 |
| 38 | Todde Greenough, Willamette (Southern Ore.) ............................... | Sept. 26, 1987 |
| 38 | Pat Moyer, Maryville, Tenn. (Cumberland) ................................... | Oct. 5, 1985 |

## Career Yards Per Game

| Player, Team | Years | G | Att. | Cmp. | Int. | Pct. | Yards | TD | Avg. |
|---|---|---|---|---|---|---|---|---|---|
| Kirk Baumgartner, Wis.-Stevens Pt. | 1986-89 | 41 | *1,696 | *883 | 57 | .521 | *13,028 | *110 | *317.8 |
| Keith Bishop, Ill. Wes./Wheaton ... | 1981, 83-85 | 31 | 1,311 | 772 | 65 | .589 | 9,579 | 71 | 309.0 |
| Willie Reyna, La Verne ........... | 1991-92 | 17 | 542 | 346 | 19 | .638 | 4,712 | 37 | 277.2 |
| Robert Farra, Claremont-M-S ..... | 1978-79 | 16 | 579 | 313 | 24 | .541 | 4,360 | 31 | 272.5 |
| Dennis Bogacz, Wis.-Oshkosh/ Wis.-Whitewater ............... | 1988-89, 90-1 | 38 | 1,275 | 654 | 59 | .513 | 9,536 | 66 | 250.9 |
| Tim Peterson, Wis.-Stout .......... | 1986-89 | 36 | 1,185 | 653 | 62 | .551 | 8,881 | 59 | 246.7 |
| Rob Bristow, Pomona-Pitzer ...... | 1983-86 | 29 | 1,155 | 628 | 60 | .544 | 7,120 | 27 | 245.5 |
| John Rooney, Ill. Wesleyan ....... | 1982-84 | 27 | 986 | 489 | 47 | .496 | 6,576 | 55 | 243.6 |
| John Clark, Wis.-Eau Claire ....... | 1987-90 | 38 | 1,119 | 645 | 42 | .576 | 9,196 | 63 | 242.0 |
| Dave Geissler, Wis.-Stevens Pt. ... | 1982-85 | 42 | 1,346 | 789 | 57 | .586 | 9,518 | 65 | 226.6 |
| Scott Scesney, St. John's (N.Y.) ... | 1986-89 | 32 | 945 | 463 | 44 | .490 | 6,914 | 72 | 216.1 |
| Jeff Voris, DePauw ................ | 1986-89 | 28 | 910 | 504 | 25 | .554 | 6,035 | 56 | 215.5 |
| Paul Brandenburg, Ripon ......... | 1984-87 | 34 | 1,181 | 607 | 66 | .514 | 7,320 | 39 | 215.3 |

* Record.

## Season Yards Per Game

| Player, Team | Year | G | Att. | Cmp. | Int. | Pct. | Yards | TD | Avg. |
|---|---|---|---|---|---|---|---|---|---|
| Kirk Baumgartner, Wis.-Stevens Point.. | 1989 | 10 | 455 | 247 | 9 | .543 | 3,692 | *39 | *369.2 |
| Keith Bishop, Wheaton (Ill.) ............ | 1983 | 9 | 375 | 236 | 19 | *.629 | 3,274 | 24 | 363.8 |
| Keith Bishop, Wheaton (Ill.) ............ | 1985 | 9 | 457 | 262 | 22 | .573 | 3,171 | 25 | 352.3 |
| Kirk Baumgartner, Wis.-Stevens Point.. | 1988 | 11 | *527 | *276 | 16 | .524 | *3,828 | 25 | 348.0 |
| Kirk Baumgartner, Wis.-Stevens Point.. | 1987 | 11 | 466 | 243 | 22 | .521 | 3,755 | 31 | 341.4 |
| Steve Austin, Mass.-Boston ............ | 1992 | 9 | 396 | 181 | 25 | .457 | 2,991 | 29 | 332.3 |
| Keith Bishop, Wheaton (Ill.) ............ | 1984 | 9 | 440 | 259 | 21 | .589 | 2,968 | 21 | 329.8 |
| Jordan Poznick, Principia ............. | 1992 | 8 | 451 | 241 | 13 | .534 | 2,618 | 21 | 327.3 |
| Willie Reyna, La Verne ................ | 1991 | 8 | 267 | 170 | 6 | .636 | 2,543 | 16 | 317.9 |
| Scott Isphording, Hanover ............ | 1992 | 10 | 359 | 207 | 19 | .576 | 3,098 | 24 | 309.8 |
| Robert Farra, Claremont-M-S .......... | †1978 | 9 | 359 | 196 | 15 | .546 | 2,770 | 20 | 307.8 |
| Dennis Bogacz, Wis.-Oshkosh ......... | 1989 | 10 | 378 | 219 | 18 | .580 | 3,051 | 18 | 305.1 |

* Record.   † National champion.

Principia quarterback Jordan Poznick's 327.3 yards passing per game in 1992 was the eighth best in Division III history. The junior also led the division in total offense with 343.4 yards per game.

### Annual Champions

| Year | Player, Team | Cl. | G | Att. | Cmp. | Avg. | Int. | Pct. | Yds. | TD |
|------|-------------|-----|---|------|------|------|------|------|------|-----|
| 1973 | Pat Clements, Kenyon | Jr. | 9 | 239 | 133 | 14.8 | 17 | .556 | 1,738 | 12 |
| 1974 | Larry Cenotto, Pomona-Pitzer | Sr. | 9 | 294 | 147 | 16.3 | 23 | .500 | 2,024 | 15 |
| 1975 | Ron Miller, Elmhurst | Sr. | 8 | 205 | 118 | 14.8 | 15 | .576 | 1,398 | 7 |
| 1976 | Tom Hamilton, Occidental | Jr. | 8 | 235 | 131 | 16.4 | 10 | .557 | 1,988 | 10 |
| 1977 | Tom Hamilton, Occidental | Sr. | 9 | 323 | 171 | 19.0 | 17 | .529 | 2,132 | 13 |
| 1978 | Robert Farra, Claremont-M-S | Jr. | 9 | 359 | 196 | 21.8 | 15 | .546 | 2,770 | 20 |

*Beginning in 1979, ranked on Passing Efficiency Rating Points, minimum of 15 attempts per game (instead of per-game completions).*

| Year | Player, Team | Cl. | G | Att. | Cmp. | Int. | Pct. | Yds. | TD | Pts. |
|------|-------------|-----|---|------|------|------|------|------|-----|------|
| 1979 | David Broecker, Wabash | Fr. | 9 | 145 | 81 | 9 | .559 | 1,311 | 13 | 149.0 |
| 1980 | George Muller, Hofstra | Sr. | 10 | 189 | 115 | 14 | .608 | 1,983 | 15 | 160.4 |
| 1981 | Larry Atwater, Coe | Sr. | 9 | 172 | 92 | 10 | .535 | 1,615 | 15 | 147.2 |
| 1982 | Mike Bennett, Cornell College | Sr. | 9 | 154 | 83 | 8 | .539 | 1,436 | 17 | 158.3 |
| 1983 | Joe Shield, Trinity (Conn.) | Jr. | 8 | 238 | 135 | 13 | .567 | 2,185 | 19 | 149.1 |
| 1984 | Cody Dearing, Randolph-Macon | Sr. | 10 | 226 | 125 | 12 | .553 | 2,139 | 27 | 163.4 |
| 1985 | Robb Disbennett, Salisbury St. | Sr. | 10 | 153 | 94 | 6 | .614 | 1,462 | 16 | 168.4 |
| 1986 | Gary Collier, Emory & Henry | Jr. | 11 | 171 | 88 | 6 | .514 | 1,509 | 21 | 158.9 |
| 1987 | Jimbo Fisher, Samford | Sr. | 10 | 252 | 139 | 5 | .551 | 2,394 | 34 | 175.4 |
| 1988 | Steve Flynn, Central (Iowa) | Jr. | 8 | 133 | 82 | 6 | .616 | 1,190 | 10 | 152.5 |
| 1989 | Joe Blake, Simpson | ††Jr. | 10 | 144 | 93 | 3 | .645 | 1,705 | 19 | *203.3 |
| 1990 | Dan Sharley, Dayton | †††Sr. | 10 | 149 | 95 | 2 | .637 | 1,377 | 12 | 165.1 |
| 1991 | Pat Mayew, St. John's (Minn.) | Sr. | 9 | 247 | 154 | 4 | .623 | 2,408 | 30 | 181.0 |
| 1992 | Steve Keller, Dayton | Sr. | 10 | 153 | 99 | 5 | .647 | 1,350 | 17 | 168.9 |

* *Record.*  †† *Declared champion; with six more pass attempts (making 15 per game), all interceptions, still would have highest efficiency (187.3).*  ††† *Declared champion; with one more attempt (making 15 per game), an interception, still would have highest efficiency (162.8).*

### Annual Passing Efficiency Leaders
### (Before 1979)
### (Minimum 15 Attempts Per Game)

| Year | Player, Team | G | Att. | Cmp. | Int. | Pct. | Yds. | TD | Pts. |
|------|-------------|---|------|------|------|------|------|-----|------|
| 1973 | Mitch Sanders, Bridgeport | 10 | 151 | 84 | 7 | .556 | 1,551 | 23 | 182.9 |
| 1974 | Tom McGuire, Ill. Benedictine | 10 | 221 | 142 | 16 | .643 | 2,206 | 16 | 157.5 |
| 1975 | Jim Morrow, Wash. & Jeff. | 9 | 137 | 82 | 7 | .599 | 1,283 | 11 | 154.8 |
| 1976 | Aaron Van Dyke, Cornell College | 9 | 154 | 91 | 12 | .591 | 1,611 | 14 | 161.4 |
| 1977 | Matt Winslow, Middlebury | 8 | 130 | 79 | 5 | .608 | 919 | 17 | 155.6 |
| 1978 | Matt Dillon, Cornell College | 9 | 166 | 98 | 7 | .590 | 1,567 | 16 | 161.7 |

# RECEIVING

### Career Catches

| Player, Team | Years | No. | Yards | TD |
|-------------|-------|-----|-------|-----|
| Bill Stromberg, Johns Hopkins | 1978-81 | *258 | 3,776 | 39 |
| Dale Amos, Frank. & Marsh. | 1986-89 | 233 | *3,846 | 35 |
| Scott Fredrickson, Wis.-Stout | 1986-89 | 233 | 3,390 | 23 |
| Mike Whitehouse, St. Norbert | 1986-89 | 230 | 3,480 | 37 |
| Mike Funk, Wabash | 1985, 87-89 | 228 | 2,858 | 33 |
| Dan Daley, Pomona-Pitzer | 1985-88 | 227 | 2,598 | 10 |
| Jim Jorden, Wheaton (Ill.) | 1982-85 | 225 | 3,022 | 22 |
| Chris Bisaillon, Ill. Wesleyan | 1989-92 | 223 | 3,670 | *55 |
| Theo Blanco, Wis.-Stevens Point | 1985-88 | 223 | 3,139 | 18 |
| Ed Brady, Ill. Wesleyan | 1981-84 | 220 | 2,907 | 22 |
| Walter Kalinowski, Catholic | 1983-86 | 219 | 2,430 | 16 |
| Jim Bradford, Carleton | 1988-91 | 212 | 3,719 | 32 |
| Mike Cottle, Juniata | 1985-88 | 212 | 2,607 | 36 |
| John Ward, Cornell College | 1979-82 | 211 | 3,085 | 30 |
| Ron Severance, Otterbein | 1989-91 | 207 | 2,378 | 17 |
| Vince Dortch, Jersey City St. | 1983-86 | 206 | 3,037 | 28 |
| Chris Murphy, Georgetown | 1989-92 | 205 | 2,817 | 26 |
| Scott Faessler, Framingham St. | 1989-92 | 201 | 2,121 | 8 |
| Rick Fry, Occidental | 1974-77 | 200 | 3,073 | 18 |
| Todd Stoner, Kenyon | 1981-84 | 197 | 3,191 | 31 |
| Steve Feyrer, Ripon | 1983-86 | 196 | 2,852 | 19 |

* *Record.*

*1993 NCAA FOOTBALL*

## Season Catches

| Player, Team | Year | Games | No. | Yards | TD |
|---|---|---|---|---|---|
| Theo Blanco, Wis.-Stevens Point | 1987 | 11 | *106 | 1,616 | 8 |
| Matt Newton, Principia | †1992 | 8 | 98 | 1,487 | 14 |
| Sean Munroe, Mass.-Boston | 1992 | 9 | 95 | *1,693 | 17 |
| Ron Severance, Otterbein | 1990 | 10 | 92 | 1,049 | 8 |
| Scott Faessler, Framingham St. | †1990 | 9 | 92 | 916 | 5 |
| Mike Funk, Wabash | †1989 | 9 | 87 | 1,169 | 12 |
| Ted Taggart, Kenyon | 1989 | 10 | 87 | 1,004 | 7 |
| Jim Jorden, Wheaton (Ill.) | †1985 | 9 | 87 | 1,011 | 8 |
| Ron Severance, Otterbein | †1991 | 10 | 85 | 929 | 4 |
| Scott Fredrickson, Wis.-Stout | 1989 | 10 | 83 | 1,102 | 7 |
| Rick Fry, Occidental | †1977 | 9 | 82 | 1,222 | 5 |
| Jim Myers, Kenyon | †1974 | 9 | 82 | 1,483 | 12 |
| Wayne Morris, Hofstra | 1991 | 10 | 80 | 890 | 7 |
| Theo Blanco, Wis.-Stevens Point | †1988 | 10 | 80 | 1,009 | 7 |
| Bob Glanville, Lewis & Clark | 1985 | 9 | 80 | 1,054 | 9 |
| Ed Brady, Ill. Wesleyan | †1983 | 9 | 80 | 873 | 7 |
| Roger Little, Dubuque | 1988 | 10 | 79 | 1,025 | 7 |
| Walt Kalinowski, Catholic | 1985 | 11 | 79 | 875 | 4 |

*Record. † National champion.*

## Single-Game Catches

| No. | Player, Team (Opponent) | Date |
|---|---|---|
| 23 | Sean Munroe, Mass.-Boston (Mass. Maritime) | Oct. 10, 1992 |
| 20 | Rich Johnson, Pace (Fordham) | Nov. 7, 1987 |
| 20 | Pete Thompson, Carroll, Wis. (Augustana, Ill.) | Nov. 4, 1978 |
| 18 | Ed Sullivan, Catholic (Carnegie Mellon) | Nov. 7, 1992 |
| 17 | Matt Newton, Principia (Concordia, Ill.) | Nov. 7, 1992 |
| 17 | Danny Cole, Lake Forest (Monmouth, Ill.) | Sept. 29, 1990 |
| 17 | Dan Daley, Pomona-Pitzer (Occidental) | Oct. 15, 1988 |
| 17 | Theo Blanco, Wis.-Stevens Point (Wis.-Oshkosh) | Oct. 31, 1987 |
| 17 | Tim Mowery, Wis.-Superior (Wis.-Stevens Point) | Oct. 17, 1971 |
| 16 | Ken Morton, Dubuque (Wis.-Whitewater) | Sept. 6, 1986 |
| 16 | Shawn Graham, St. Thomas, Minn. (Hamline) | Nov. 13, 1982 |
| 16 | Steve Forsythe, Frostburg St. (Allegheny) | Sept. 18, 1982 |
| 16 | John Dettmann, Wis.-Oshkosh (Wis.-River Falls) | Oct. 10, 1981 |
| 16 | Jay True, DePauw (Butler) | Nov. 4, 1978 |
| 16 | Rick Fry, Occidental (Azusa Pacific) | Sept. 24, 1977 |
| 16 | Pete Bylsma, Wheaton, Ill. (Millikin) | Oct. 19, 1974 |

## Career Catches Per Game

| Player, Team | Years | Games | No. | Yards | TD | Ct. PG |
|---|---|---|---|---|---|---|
| Bill Stromberg, Johns Hopkins | 1978-81 | 36 | *258 | 3,776 | 39 | *7.2 |
| Tim McNamara, Trinity (Conn.) | 1981-84 | 21 | 146 | 2,313 | 19 | 7.0 |
| Ron Severance, Otterbein | 1989-91 | 30 | 207 | 2,378 | 17 | 6.9 |
| Chuck Braun, Wis.-Stevens Point | 1980-81 | 18 | 124 | 1,914 | 19 | 6.9 |
| Jim Jorden, Wheaton (Ill.) | 1982-85 | 33 | 225 | 3,022 | 22 | 6.8 |
| Mike Whitehouse, St. Norbert | 1986-89 | 35 | 230 | 3,480 | 37 | 6.6 |
| Dan Daley, Pomona-Pitzer | 1985-88 | 35 | 227 | 2,598 | 10 | 6.5 |
| Rich Johnson, Pace | 1985-87 | 29 | 188 | 2,614 | 8 | 6.5 |
| Chris Bisaillon, Ill. Wesleyan | 1989-92 | 36 | 223 | 3,670 | *55 | 6.2 |
| Rick Fry, Occidental | 1974-77 | 33 | 200 | 3,073 | 18 | 6.1 |
| Mike Funk, Wabash | 1985, 87-89 | 38 | 228 | 2,858 | 33 | 6.0 |
| Scott Faessler, Framingham St. | 1989-92 | 34 | 201 | 2,121 | 8 | 5.9 |
| Ted Taggart, Kenyon | 1988-90 | 28 | 165 | 2,034 | 20 | 5.9 |
| Pat McNamara, Trinity (Conn.) | 1977-79 | 24 | 141 | 2,280 | 20 | 5.9 |
| Theo Blanco, Wis.-Stevens Point | 1985-88 | 38 | 223 | 3,139 | 18 | 5.9 |
| Dale Amos, Frank. & Marsh. | 1986-89 | 40 | 233 | *3,846 | 35 | 5.8 |
| Scott Fredrickson, Wis.-Stout | 1986-89 | 40 | 233 | 3,390 | 23 | 5.8 |

*Record.*

## Season Catches Per Game

| Player, Team | Year | Games | No. | Yards | TD | Ct. PG |
|---|---|---|---|---|---|---|
| Matt Newton, Principia | †1992 | 8 | 98 | 1,487 | 14 | *12.3 |
| Sean Munroe, Mass.-Boston | 1992 | 9 | 95 | *1,693 | 17 | 10.6 |
| Scott Faessler, Framingham St. | †1990 | 9 | 92 | 916 | 5 | 10.2 |
| Mike Funk, Wabash | †1989 | 9 | 87 | 1,169 | 12 | 9.7 |
| Jim Jorden, Wheaton (Ill.) | †1985 | 9 | 87 | 1,011 | 8 | 9.7 |

| Player, Team | Year | Games | No. | Yards | TD | Ct. PG |
|---|---|---|---|---|---|---|
| Theo Blanco, Wis.-Stevens Point .......... | 1987 | 11 | *106 | 1,616 | 8 | 9.6 |
| Rick Fry, Occidental ...................... | †1976 | 8 | 74 | 1,214 | 8 | 9.3 |
| Ron Severance, Otterbein................. | 1990 | 10 | 92 | 1,049 | 8 | 9.2 |
| Rick Fry, Occidental ...................... | †1977 | 9 | 82 | 1,222 | 5 | 9.1 |
| Jim Myers, Kenyon ...................... | †1974 | 9 | 82 | 1,483 | 12 | 9.1 |
| Bob Glanville, Lewis & Clark .............. | 1985 | 9 | 80 | 1,054 | 9 | 8.9 |
| Ed Brady, Ill. Wesleyan ................... | †1983 | 9 | 80 | 873 | 7 | 8.9 |
| John Tucci, Amherst ...................... | †1986 | 8 | 70 | 1,025 | 8 | 8.8 |
| Ted Taggart, Kenyon ..................... | 1989 | 10 | 87 | 1,004 | 7 | 8.7 |

* Record.  † National champion.

### Annual Champions (Catches Per Game)

| Year | Player, Team | Cl. | G | No. | Avg. | Yards | TD |
|---|---|---|---|---|---|---|---|
| 1973 | Ron Duckett, Trinity (Conn.) .............. | Sr. | 8 | 57 | 7.1 | 834 | 7 |
| 1974 | Jim Myers, Kenyon ...................... | Sr. | 9 | 82 | 9.1 | 1,483 | 12 |
| 1975 | C. J. DeWitt, Bridgewater (Va.) ........... | Sr. | 9 | 64 | 7.1 | 836 | 2 |
| 1976 | Rick Fry, Occidental ..................... | Jr. | 8 | 74 | 9.3 | 1,214 | 8 |
| 1977 | Rick Fry, Occidental ..................... | Sr. | 9 | 82 | 9.1 | 1,222 | 5 |
| 1978 | Pat McNamara, Trinity (Conn.) ........... | Jr. | 8 | 67 | 8.4 | 1,024 | 11 |
| 1979 | Theodore Anderson, Fisk ................. | Jr. | 7 | 49 | 7.0 | 699 | 2 |
| 1980 | Bill Stromberg, Johns Hopkins............ | Jr. | 9 | 66 | 7.3 | 907 | 11 |
| 1981 | Bill Stromberg, Johns Hopkins............ | Sr. | 9 | 78 | 8.7 | 924 | 10 |
| 1982 | Jim Gustafson, St. Thomas (Minn.) ....... | Sr. | 10 | 72 | 7.2 | 990 | 5 |
| 1983 | Ed Brady, Ill. Wesleyan .................. | Jr. | 9 | 80 | 8.9 | 873 | 7 |
| 1984 | Tim McNamara, Trinity (Conn.) .......... | Sr. | 8 | 67 | 8.4 | 1,004 | 10 |
| 1985 | Jim Jorden, Wheaton (Ill.) ............... | Sr. | 9 | 87 | 9.7 | 1,011 | 8 |
| 1986 | John Tucci, Amherst ..................... | Sr. | 8 | 70 | 8.8 | 1,025 | 8 |
| 1987 | Chris Vogel, Knox........................ | So. | 9 | 78 | 8.7 | 1,326 | 15 |
| 1988 | Theo Blanco, Wis.-Stevens Point.......... | Sr. | 10 | 80 | 8.0 | 1,009 | 7 |
| 1989 | Mike Funk, Wabash ...................... | Sr. | 9 | 87 | 9.7 | 1,169 | 12 |
| 1990 | Scott Faessler, Framingham St. ........... | So. | 9 | 92 | 10.2 | 916 | 5 |
| 1991 | Ron Severance, Otterbein................. | Sr. | 10 | 85 | 8.5 | 929 | 4 |
| 1992 | Matt Newton, Principia ................... | Jr. | 8 | 98 | *12.3 | 1,487 | 14 |

* Record.

### Annual Champions (Yards Per Game)

| Year | Player, Team | Cl. | G | No. | Yards | TD | Avg. |
|---|---|---|---|---|---|---|---|
| 1990 | Ray Shelley, Juniata ..................... | Sr. | 10 | 54 | 1,147 | 12 | 114.7 |
| 1991 | Rodd Patten, Framingham St.............. | So. | 8 | 49 | 956 | 13 | 119.5 |
| 1992 | Sean Munroe, Mass.-Boston .............. | Sr. | 9 | 95 | *1,693 | 17 | *188.1 |

### Career Yards

| Player, Team | Years | Catches | Yards | Avg. | TD |
|---|---|---|---|---|---|
| Dale Amos, Frank. & Marsh. .............. | 1986-89 | 233 | *3,846 | 16.5 | 35 |
| Bill Stromberg, Johns Hopkins............ | 1978-81 | *258 | 3,776 | 14.6 | 39 |
| Jim Bradford, Carleton................... | 1988-91 | 212 | 3,719 | 17.5 | 32 |
| Chris Bisaillon, Ill. Wesleyan ............. | 1989-92 | 223 | 3,670 | 16.5 | *55 |
| Mike Whitehouse, St. Norbert ............ | 1986-89 | 230 | 3,480 | 15.1 | 37 |
| Scott Fredrickson, Wis.-Stout ............ | 1986-89 | 233 | 3,390 | 14.5 | 23 |
| John Aromando, Trenton St. .............. | 1981-84 | 165 | 3,197 | 19.4 | 39 |
| Todd Stoner, Kenyon.................... | 1981-84 | 197 | 3,191 | 16.2 | 31 |
| Theo Blanco, Wis.-Stevens Point .......... | 1985-88 | 223 | 3,139 | 14.1 | 18 |
| John Ward, Cornell College............... | 1979-82 | 211 | 3,085 | 14.6 | 30 |
| Rick Fry, Occidental ..................... | 1974-77 | 200 | 3,073 | 15.4 | 18 |

* Record.

### Season Yards

| Player, Team | Year | Catches | Yards | Avg. | TD |
|---|---|---|---|---|---|
| Sean Munroe, Mass.-Boston .............. | †1992 | 95 | *1,693 | 17.8 | 17 |
| Theo Blanco, Wis.-Stevens Point .......... | 1987 | *106 | 1,616 | 15.2 | 8 |
| Matt Newton, Principia ................... | 1992 | 98 | 1,487 | 15.2 | 14 |
| Jim Myers, Kenyon ...................... | †1974 | 82 | 1,483 | 18.1 | 12 |
| Beau Almodobar, Norwich ................ | 1984 | 71 | 1,375 | 19.4 | 10 |
| Chris Vogel, Knox........................ | †1987 | 78 | 1,326 | 17.0 | 15 |
| Dale Amos, Frank. & Marsh. .............. | 1989 | 72 | 1,302 | 18.1 | 15 |
| Don Moehling, Wis.-Stevens Point ........ | 1988 | 72 | 1,290 | 17.9 | 7 |
| Jim Bradford, Carleton................... | 1989 | 69 | 1,238 | 17.9 | 6 |
| Rick Fry, Occidental ..................... | †1977 | 82 | 1,222 | 14.9 | 5 |

| Player, Team | Year | Catches | Yards | Avg. | TD |
|---|---|---|---|---|---|
| Evan Elkington, Worcester Tech .......... | 1989 | 52 | 1,220 | +23.5 | 16 |
| Rick Fry, Occidental .................... | †1976 | 74 | 1,214 | 16.4 | 8 |
| Mike Howey, Moravian ................... | 1989 | 61 | 1,203 | 19.7 | 7 |
| Scott Fredrickson, Wis.-Stout ............ | 1987 | 70 | 1,185 | 16.9 | 7 |
| Bill Bagley, Frostburg St................. | 1984 | 70 | 1,182 | 16.9 | 10 |

*Record. † National champion. + Record for minimum of 50 receptions.*

### Single-Game Yards

| No. | Player, Team (Opponent) | Date |
|---|---|---|
| 332 | Sean Munroe, Mass.-Boston (Mass. Maritime)................................ | Oct. 10, 1992 |
| 309 | Dale Amos, Frank. & Marsh. (Western Md.)................................. | Oct. 24, 1987 |
| 303 | Chuck Braun, Wis.-Stevens Point (Wis.-Superior) ......................... | Oct. 17, 1981 |
| 303 | Rick Fry, Occidental (Claremont-M-S) .................................... | Oct. 30, 1976 |
| 301 | Greg Holmes, Carroll, Wis. (North Central)............................... | Nov. 7, 1981 |
| 296 | Joe Richards, Johns Hopkins (Georgetown) .............................. | Oct. 26, 1991 |
| 296 | Vince Hull, Minn.-Morris (Bemidji St.) .................................. | Oct. 10, 1981 |
| 295 | Aatron Kenney, Wis.-Stevens Point (Wis.-Stout) ......................... | Oct. 24, 1987 |
| 293 | Mike Stotz, Catholic (Bridgewater, Va.)................................. | Nov. 15, 1980 |
| 292 | Andy Steckel, Western Md. (Gettysburg) ................................ | Sept. 15, 1990 |
| 287 | Matt Newton, Principia (Concordia, Wis.) ............................... | Nov. 7, 1992 |
| 287 | Chris Bisaillon, Ill. Wesleyan (Carroll, Wis.)............................. | Sept. 15, 1990 |
| 285 | Jim Bradford, Carleton (Gust. Adolphus)................................ | Oct. 20, 1990 |
| 284 | Tom Casperson, Trenton St. (Ramapo) ................................. | Nov. 15, 1980 |
| 280 | Chris Vogel, Knox (Ripon) ............................................ | Oct. 3, 1987 |

# SCORING

### Career Points

| Player, Team | Years | TD | XPt. | FG | Pts. |
|---|---|---|---|---|---|
| Joe Dudek, Plymouth St.......................... | 1982-85 | *79 | 0 | 0 | *474 |
| Chris Bisaillon, Ill. Wesleyan ..................... | 1989-92 | 61 | 12 | 0 | 378 |
| Chris Babirad, Wash. & Jeff. ..................... | 1989-92 | 62 | 2 | 0 | 374 |
| Terry Underwood, Wagner ....................... | 1985-88 | 58 | 0 | 0 | 348 |
| Jim Romagna, Loras ............................ | 1989-92 | 57 | 2 | 0 | 344 |
| Stanley Drayton, Allegheny ...................... | 1989-92 | 56 | 0 | 0 | 336 |
| Cary Osborn, Wis.-Eau Claire .................... | 1987-90 | 55 | 0 | 0 | 330 |
| Tim McDaniel, Centre........................... | 1988-91 | 54 | 0 | 0 | 324 |
| A. J. Pagano, Wash. & Jeff. ...................... | 1984-87 | 53 | 5 | 0 | 323 |
| Ricky Gales, Nebraska-Omaha/Simpson .......... | 1986-87, 88-89 | 51 | 10 | 0 | 316 |
| Greg Corning, Wis.-River Falls ................... | 1984-87 | 52 | 2 | 0 | 314 |
| Vance Mueller, Occidental ....................... | 1982-85 | 51 | 8 | 0 | 314 |
| Scott Barnyak, Carnegie Mellon ................. | 1987-90 | 49 | 14 | 0 | 308 |
| Prentes Wilson, Ill. Benedictine ................. | 1987-90 | 50 | 0 | 0 | 300 |
| Eric Frees, Western Md.......................... | 1988-91 | 49 | 4 | 0 | 298 |
| Michael Waithe, Curry .......................... | 1984-87 | 49 | 0 | 0 | 294 |
| Jeff Norman, St. John's (Minn.) .................. | 1974-77 | 25 | 119 | 8 | 293 |
| Joe Thompson, Augustana (Ill.).................. | 1973-76 | 48 | 4 | 0 | 292 |
| Mark Kelly, Wartburg........................... | 1989-92 | 48 | 0 | 0 | 288 |
| Ryan Kolpin, Coe .............................. | 1987-90 | 48 | 0 | 0 | 288 |

*Record.*

### Season Points

| Player, Team | Year | TD | XPt. | FG | Pts. |
|---|---|---|---|---|---|
| Stanley Drayton, Allegheny ...................... | †1991 | *28 | 0 | 0 | *168 |
| Ricky Gales, Simpson........................... | †1989 | 26 | 10 | 0 | 166 |
| Greg Novarro, Bentley .......................... | 1992 | 25 | 0 | 0 | 150 |
| Joe Dudek, Plymouth St.......................... | 1985 | 25 | 0 | 0 | 150 |
| Bruce Naszimento, Jersey City St. ............... | 1973 | 25 | 0 | 0 | 150 |
| Chris Babirad, Wash. & Jeff. ..................... | †1992 | 24 | 0 | 0 | 144 |
| Scott Barnyak, Carnegie Mellon ................. | †1990 | 22 | 6 | 0 | 138 |
| Ryan Kolpin, Coe .............................. | †1990 | 23 | 0 | 0 | 138 |
| Ron Corbett, Cornell College .................... | 1982 | 23 | 0 | 0 | 138 |
| Billy Johnson, Widener ......................... | †1973 | 23 | 0 | 0 | 138 |
| Chris Babirad, Wash. & Jeff. ..................... | 1991 | 22 | 2 | 0 | 134 |
| Thomas Lee, Anderson .......................... | 1992 | 22 | 0 | 0 | 132 |
| Tim McDaniel, Centre........................... | 1990 | 22 | 0 | 0 | 132 |
| Chris Hipsley, Cornell College ................... | †1976 | 14 | 42 | 2 | 132 |
| Carey Bender, Coe ............................. | 1992 | 21 | 4 | 0 | 130 |

*Division III Annual Champions, All-Time Leaders*

| Player, Team | Year | TD | XPt. | FG | Pts. |
|---|---|---|---|---|---|
| Trent Nauholz, Simpson | †1992 | 21 | 2 | 0 | 128 |
| Karl Kohl, Catholic | 1989 | 21 | 2 | 0 | 128 |
| Denis McDermott, St. John's (N.Y.) | 1989 | 21 | 0 | 0 | 126 |
| Terry Underwood, Wagner | †1988 | 21 | 0 | 0 | 126 |
| Prentes Wilson, Ill. Benedictine | 1988 | 21 | 0 | 0 | 126 |
| Joe Dudek, Plymouth St. | †1984 | 21 | 0 | 0 | 126 |

\* Record.  † National champion.

## Career Points Per Game

| Player, Team | Years | Games | TD | XPt. | FG | Pts. | Pt. PG |
|---|---|---|---|---|---|---|---|
| Joe Dudek, Plymouth St. | 1982-85 | 41 | *79 | 0 | 0 | *474 | *11.6 |
| Chris Babirad, Wash. & Jeff. | 1989-92 | 35 | 62 | 2 | 0 | 374 | 10.7 |
| Terry Underwood, Wagner | 1985-88 | 33 | 58 | 0 | 0 | 348 | 10.5 |
| Chris Bisaillon, Ill. Wesleyan | 1989-92 | 36 | 61 | 12 | 0 | 378 | 10.5 |
| Stanley Drayton, Allegheny | 1989-92 | 32 | 56 | 0 | 0 | 336 | 10.5 |
| Greg Novarro, Bentley | 1990-92 | 24 | 42 | 0 | 0 | 252 | 10.5 |
| Ryan Kolpin, Coe | 1987-90 | 28 | 48 | 0 | 0 | 288 | 10.3 |
| A. J. Pagano, Wash. & Jeff. | 1984-87 | 36 | 53 | 5 | 0 | 323 | 9.0 |
| Gary Trettel, St. Thomas (Minn.) | 1988-90 | 29 | 43 | 0 | 0 | 258 | 8.9 |
| Vance Mueller, Occidental | 1982-85 | 36 | 51 | 8 | 0 | 314 | 8.7 |
| Jeff Norman, St. John's (Minn.) | 1974-77 | 34 | 25 | 119 | 8 | 293 | 8.6 |
| Denis McDermott, St. John's (N.Y.) | 1987-89 | 30 | 43 | 0 | 0 | 258 | 8.6 |
| Joe Thompson, Augustana (Ill.) | 1973-76 | 34 | 48 | 4 | 0 | 292 | 8.6 |
| Tim McDaniel, Centre | 1988-91 | 38 | 54 | 0 | 0 | 324 | 8.5 |
| Jeff Wittman, Ithaca | 1989-92 | 32 | 45 | 0 | 0 | 270 | 8.4 |
| Jay Wessler, Illinois Col. | 1977-80 | 34 | 46 | 6 | 0 | 282 | 8.3 |
| Scott Reppert, Lawrence | 1979-82 | 33 | 45 | 0 | 0 | 270 | 8.2 |
| Pedro Bowman, Duquesne | 1981-84 | 34 | 46 | 2 | 0 | 278 | 8.2 |

\* Record.

## Season Points Per Game

| Player, Team | Year | Games | TD | XPt. | FG | Pts. | Pt. PG |
|---|---|---|---|---|---|---|---|
| Stanley Drayton, Allegheny | †1991 | 10 | *28 | 0 | 0 | *168 | *16.8 |
| Ricky Gales, Simpson | †1989 | 10 | 26 | 10 | 0 | 166 | 16.6 |
| Chris Babirad, Wash. & Jeff. | †1992 | 9 | 24 | 0 | 0 | 144 | 16.0 |
| Trent Nauholz, Simpson | †1992 | 8 | 21 | 2 | 0 | 128 | 16.0 |
| Billy Johnson, Widener | †1973 | 9 | 23 | 0 | 0 | 138 | 15.3 |
| Greg Novarro, Bentley | 1992 | 10 | 25 | 0 | 0 | 150 | 15.0 |
| Bruce Naszimento, Jersey City St. | 1973 | 10 | 25 | 0 | 0 | 150 | 15.0 |
| Chris Babirad, Wash. & Jeff. | 1991 | 9 | 22 | 2 | 0 | 134 | 14.9 |
| Chris Hipsley, Cornell College | †1976 | 9 | 14 | 42 | 2 | 132 | 14.7 |
| Carey Bender, Coe | 1992 | 9 | 21 | 4 | 0 | 130 | 14.4 |
| Michael Waithe, Curry | †1987 | 8 | 19 | 0 | 0 | 114 | 14.3 |
| Rick Bell, St. John's (Minn.) | †1982 | 9 | 21 | 2 | 0 | 128 | 14.2 |
| Terry Underwood, Wagner | †1988 | 9 | 21 | 0 | 0 | 126 | 14.0 |
| Scott Barnyak, Carnegie Mellon | †1990 | 10 | 22 | 6 | 0 | 138 | 13.8 |
| Ryan Kolpin, Coe | †1990 | 10 | 23 | 0 | 0 | 138 | 13.8 |
| Kevin Weaver, Wash. & Lee | †1985 | 8 | 17 | 8 | 0 | 110 | 13.8 |
| Joe Dudek, Plymouth St. | 1985 | 11 | 25 | 0 | 0 | 150 | 13.6 |

\* Record.  † National champion.

## Annual Champions

| Year | Player, Team | Class | G | TD | XPt. | FG | Pts. | Avg. |
|---|---|---|---|---|---|---|---|---|
| 1973 | Billy Johnson, Widener | Sr. | 9 | 23 | 0 | 0 | 138 | 15.3 |
| 1974 | Joe Thompson, Augustana (Ill.) | So. | 9 | 17 | 0 | 0 | 102 | 11.3 |
| 1975 | Ron Baker, Monmouth (Ill.) | Sr. | 8 | 15 | 2 | 0 | 92 | 11.5 |
| 1976 | Chris Hipsley, Cornell College | So. | 9 | 14 | 42 | 2 | 132 | 14.7 |
| 1977 | Chip Zawoiski, Widener | Sr. | 9 | 18 | 0 | 0 | 108 | 12.0 |
| 1978 | Roger Andrachik, Baldwin-Wallace | Sr. | 8 | 16 | 0 | 0 | 96 | 12.0 |
| 1979 | Jay Wessler, Illinois Col. | Jr. | 8 | 16 | 4 | 0 | 100 | 12.5 |
| 1980 | Daryl Johnson, Wabash | Jr. | 9 | 20 | 0 | 0 | 120 | 13.3 |
| 1981 | Scott Reppert, Lawrence | Jr. | 9 | 15 | 0 | 0 | 90 | 10.0 |
| | Daryl Johnson, Wabash | Sr. | 9 | 15 | 0 | 0 | 90 | 10.0 |
| 1982 | Rick Bell, St. John's (Minn.) | Sr. | 9 | 21 | 2 | 0 | 128 | 14.2 |
| 1983 | John Aromando, Trenton St. | Jr. | 10 | 20 | 0 | 0 | 120 | 12.0 |
| 1984 | Joe Dudek, Plymouth St. | Jr. | 10 | 21 | 0 | 0 | 126 | 12.6 |
| 1985 | Kevin Weaver, Wash. & Lee | Jr. | 8 | 17 | 8 | 0 | 110 | 13.8 |
| 1986 | Jim Korfonta, Hamilton | Sr. | 8 | 16 | 0 | 0 | 96 | 12.0 |
| | Russ Kring, Mount Union | Jr. | 10 | 20 | 0 | 0 | 120 | 12.0 |
| 1987 | Michael Waithe, Curry | Sr. | 8 | 19 | 0 | 0 | 114 | 14.3 |

*1993 NCAA FOOTBALL*

| Year | Player, Team | Class | G | TD | XPt. | FG | Pts. | Avg. |
|------|-------------|-------|---|----|----|----|------|------|
| 1988 | Terry Underwood, Wagner ............... | Sr. | 9 | 21 | 0 | 0 | 126 | 14.0 |
| 1989 | Ricky Gales, Simpson.................... | Sr. | 10 | 26 | 10 | 0 | 166 | 16.6 |
| 1990 | Scott Barnyak, Carnegie Mellon ........ | Sr. | 10 | 22 | 6 | 0 | 138 | 13.8 |
|  | Ryan Kolpin, Coe ....................... | Sr. | 10 | 23 | 0 | 0 | 138 | 13.8 |
| 1991 | Stanley Drayton, Allegheny ............. | Jr. | 10 | *28 | 0 | 0 | *168 | *16.8 |
| 1992 | Chris Babirad, Wash. & Jeff. ........... | Sr. | 9 | 24 | 0 | 0 | 144 | 16.0 |
|  | Trent Nauholz, Simpson ................ | Jr. | 8 | 21 | 2 | 0 | 128 | 16.0 |

* Record.

# PUNTING

## Career Average
### (Minimum 100 Punts)

| Player, Team | Years | No. | Yards | Avg. |
|-------------|-------|-----|-------|------|
| Mike Manson, Ill. Benedictine ...................... | 1975-78 | 120 | 5,056 | *42.13 |
| Kirk Seufert, Memphis St./Rhodes ................. | 1981, 83-84 | 109 | 4,587 | 42.08 |
| Dan Osborn, Occidental ............................ | 1981-83 | 157 | 6,528 | 41.6 |
| Thomas Murray, Catholic .......................... | 1983-84 | 122 | 5,028 | 41.2 |
| Scott Lanz, Bethany (W. Va.) ...................... | 1975-78 | 235 | 9,592 | 40.8 |
| Jim Allshouse, Adrian ............................. | 1972-75 | 210 | 8,525 | 40.6 |

* Record.

## Season Average
### (Qualifiers for Championship)

| Player, Team | Year | No. | Yards | Avg. |
|-------------|------|-----|-------|------|
| Bob Burwell, Rose-Hulman ......................... | †1978 | 61 | 2,740 | *44.9 |
| Charles McPherson, Clark Atlanta .................... | 1978 | 50 | 2,237 | 44.7 |
| Dan Osborn, Occidental ............................ | †1982 | 55 | 2,454 | 44.6 |
| Mike Manson, Ill. Benedictine ...................... | †1976 | 36 | 1,587 | 44.1 |
| Linc Welles, Bloomsburg............................ | †1973 | 39 | 1,708 | 43.8 |
| Kirk Seufert, Rhodes ............................... | †1983 | 44 | 1,921 | 43.7 |
| Kelvin Albert, Knoxville ............................ | †1987 | 30 | 1,308 | 43.6 |

* Record.   † National champion.

## Annual Champions

| Year | Player, Team | Class | No. | Yards | Avg. |
|------|-------------|-------|-----|-------|------|
| 1973 | Linc Welles, Bloomsburg.............................. | Sr. | 39 | 1,708 | 43.8 |
| 1974 | Sylvester Cunningham, Fort Valley St. ................ | So. | 40 | 1,703 | 42.6 |
| 1975 | Larry Hersh, Shepherd ............................... | Jr. | 58 | 2,519 | 43.4 |
| 1976 | Mike Manson, Ill. Benedictine ........................ | So. | 36 | 1,587 | 44.1 |
| 1977 | Scott Lanz, Bethany (W. Va.) ........................ | Jr. | 78 | 3,349 | 42.9 |
| 1978 | Bob Burwell, Rose-Hulman ........................... | Sr. | 61 | 2,740 | *44.9 |
| 1979 | Jay Lenstrom, Neb. Wesleyan ........................ | Sr. | 64 | 2,641 | 41.3 |
| 1980 | Duane Harrison, Bridgewater (Va.) ................... | Sr. | 43 | 1,792 | 41.7 |
| 1981 | Dan Paro, Denison ................................... | Jr. | 54 | 2,223 | 41.2 |
| 1982 | Dan Osborn, Occidental ............................. | Jr. | 55 | 2,454 | 44.6 |
| 1983 | Kirk Seufert, Rhodes ................................ | Jr. | 44 | 1,921 | 43.7 |
| 1984 | Thomas Murray, Catholic ............................ | Sr. | 59 | 2,550 | 43.2 |
| 1985 | Dave Lewis, Muhlenberg ............................. | So. | 55 | 2,290 | 41.6 |
|  | Mike Matzen, Coe.................................... | Sr. | 55 | 2,290 | 41.6 |
| 1986 | Darren Estes, Millsaps .............................. | Jr. | 45 | 1,940 | 43.1 |
| 1987 | Kelvin Albert, Knoxville ............................. | So. | 30 | 1,308 | 43.6 |
| 1988 | Bobby Graves, Sewanee ............................. | So. | 57 | 2,445 | 42.9 |
| 1989 | Paul Becker, Kenyon ................................ | Sr. | 57 | 2,307 | 40.5 |
| 1990 | Bill Nolan, Carroll (Wis.) ............................ | Sr. | 33 | 1,322 | 40.1 |
| 1991 | Jeff Stolte, Chicago ................................. | So. | 54 | 2,295 | 42.5 |
| 1992 | Robert Ray, San Diego .............................. | So. | 44 | 1,860 | 42.3 |

* Record.

# INTERCEPTIONS

## Career Interceptions

| Player, Team | Years | No. | Yards | Avg. |
|-------------|-------|-----|-------|------|
| Ralph Gebhardt, Rochester .......................... | 1972-75 | *34 | 406 | 11.9 |
| Eugene Hunter, Fort Valley St. ...................... | 1972-74 | 29 | *479 | 16.5 |
| Brian Fetterolf, Aurora ............................. | 1986-89 | 28 | 390 | 13.9 |
| Rick Bealer, Lycoming .............................. | 1987-90 | 28 | 279 | 10.0 |
| Tim Lennon, Curry.................................. | 1986-89 | 27 | 190 | 7.0 |

| Player, Team | Years | No. | Yards | Avg. |
|---|---|---|---|---|
| Mike Hintz, Wis.-Platteville | 1983-86 | 27 | 183 | 6.8 |
| Mark Dorner, Juniata | 1984-87 | 26 | 443 | 17.0 |
| Cory Mabry, Susquehanna | 1988-91 | 26 | 400 | 15.4 |
| Jeff Hughes, Ripon | 1975-78 | 26 | 333 | 12.8 |
| Neal Guggemos, St. Thomas (Minn.) | 1982-85 | 25 | 377 | 15.1 |
| Dave Adams, Carleton | 1984-87 | 25 | 327 | 13.1 |
| Will Hill, Bishop | 1983-86 | 25 | 261 | 10.4 |
| Tom Devine, Juniata | 1979-82 | 25 | 248 | 9.9 |
| Gary Ellis, Rose-Hulman | 1974-77 | 25 | 226 | 9.1 |

* Record.

## Season Interceptions

| Player, Team | Year | No. | Yards |
|---|---|---|---|
| Mark Dorner, Juniata | †1987 | *15 | 202 |
| Steve Nappo, Buffalo | †1986 | 13 | 155 |
| Chris McMahon, Catholic | †1984 | 13 | 105 |
| Ralph Gebhardt, Rochester | †1973 | 13 | 105 |
| Brian Barr, Gettysburg | 1985 | 12 | 144 |
| John Bernard, Buffalo | †1983 | 12 | 143 |
| Mick McConkey, Neb. Wesleyan | †1982 | 12 | 111 |
| Chris Butts, Worcester St. | †1992 | 12 | 109 |
| Tom Devine, Juniata | †1981 | 12 | 91 |

* Record.   † National champion.

## Annual Champions
### (Ranked on Average Per Game)

| Year | Player, Team | Class | Games | No. | Avg. | Yards |
|---|---|---|---|---|---|---|
| 1973 | Ralph Gebhardt, Rochester | So. | 9 | 13 | 1.44 | 105 |
| 1974 | Kevin Birkholz, Carleton | Jr. | 9 | 11 | 1.22 | 137 |
| 1975 | Mark Persichetti, Wash. & Jeff. | So. | 9 | 10 | 1.11 | 97 |
| 1976 | Gary Jantzer, Southern Ore. | Sr. | 9 | 10 | 1.11 | 63 |
| 1977 | Greg Jones, FDU-Madison | So. | 9 | 10 | 1.11 | 106 |
|  | Mike Jones, Norwich | So. | 9 | 10 | 1.11 | 98 |
| 1978 | Don Sutton, San Fran. St. | Fr. | 8 | 10 | 1.25 | 43 |
| 1979 | Greg Holland, Simpson | Fr. | 9 | 11 | 1.22 | 150 |
| 1980 | Tim White, Lawrence | Sr. | 8 | 10 | 1.25 | 131 |
| 1981 | Tom Devine, Juniata | Sr. | 9 | 12 | 1.33 | 91 |
| 1982 | Mick McConkey, Neb. Wesleyan | Sr. | 9 | 12 | 1.33 | 111 |
| 1983 | John Bernard, Buffalo | Sr. | 10 | 12 | 1.20 | 143 |
| 1984 | Chris McMahon, Catholic | Sr. | 9 | 13 | 1.44 | 140 |
| 1985 | Kim McManis, Lane | Sr. | 9 | 11 | 1.22 | 165 |
| 1986 | Steve Nappo, Buffalo | Sr. | 11 | 13 | 1.18 | 155 |
| 1987 | Mark Dorner, Juniata | Sr. | 10 | *15 | *1.50 | 202 |
| 1988 | Tim Lennon, Curry | Jr. | 9 | 11 | 1.22 | 86 |
| 1989 | Ron Davies, Coast Guard | So. | 9 | 11 | 1.22 | 90 |
| 1990 | Craig Garritano, FDU-Madison | Jr. | 9 | 10 | 1.11 | 158 |
|  | Brad Bohn, Neb. Wesleyan | So. | 9 | 10 | 1.11 | 90 |
|  | Frank Greer, Sewanee | So. | 9 | 10 | 1.11 | 67 |
|  | Harold Krebs, Merchant Marine | Sr. | 9 | 10 | 1.11 | 19 |
| 1991 | Murray Meadows, Millsaps | Sr. | 9 | 11 | 1.22 | 46 |
| 1992 | Chris Butts, Worcester St. | Jr. | 9 | 12 | 1.33 | 109 |

* Record.

# PUNT RETURNS

## Career Average
### (Minimum 1.2 Returns Per Game)

| Player, Team | Years | No. | Yards | Avg. |
|---|---|---|---|---|
| Keith Winston, Knoxville | 1986-87 | 30 | 686 | *22.9 |
| Robert Middlebrook, Knoxville | 1984-85 | 21 | 473 | 22.5 |
| Kevin Doherty, Mass. Maritime | 1976-78, 80 | 45 | 939 | 20.9 |
| Chuck Downey, Stony Brook | 1984-87 | 59 | *1,198 | +20.3 |
| Mike Askew, Kean | 1980-81 | 28 | 555 | 19.8 |
| Willie Canady, Fort Valley St. | 1979-82 | 41 | 772 | 18.8 |

* Record.   + Record for minimum of 50 returns.

## Season Average
### (Minimum 1.2 Returns Per Game)

| Player, Team | Year | No. | Yards | Avg. |
|---|---|---|---|---|
| Chuck Downey, Stony Brook | †1986 | 17 | 530 | *31.2 |
| Kevin Doherty, Mass. Maritime | †1976 | 11 | 332 | 30.2 |
| Robert Middlebrook, Knoxville | †1984 | 9 | 260 | 28.9 |
| Joe Troise, Kean | †1974 | 12 | 342 | 28.5 |
| Melvin Dillard, Ferrum | †1990 | 25 | *688 | 27.5 |
| Chris Warren, Ferrum | †1989 | 18 | 421 | 23.4 |
| Kevin Doherty, Mass. Maritime | 1978 | 11 | 246 | 22.4 |

* Record.   † National champion.

## Annual Champions

| Year | Player, Team | Class | No. | Yards | ‡Avg. |
|---|---|---|---|---|---|
| 1973 | Al Shepherd, Monmouth (Ill.) | Sr. | 18 | 347 | 19.3 |
| 1974 | Joe Troise, Kean | Fr. | 12 | 342 | 28.5 |
| 1975 | Mitch Brown, St. Lawrence | So. | 25 | 430 | 17.2 |
| 1976 | Kevin Doherty, Mass. Maritime | Fr. | 11 | 332 | 30.2 |
| 1977 | Charles Watkins, Knoxville | Sr. | 15 | 278 | 18.5 |
| 1978 | Dennis Robinson, Wesleyan | Sr. | ††9 | 263 | 29.2 |
| 1979 | Steve Moffett, Maryville (Tenn.) | Jr. | 19 | 357 | 18.8 |
| 1980 | Mike Askew, Kean | Jr. | 16 | 304 | 19.0 |
| 1981 | Mike Askew, Kean | Sr. | 12 | 251 | 20.9 |
| 1982 | Tom Southall, Colorado Col. | So. | 13 | 281 | 21.6 |
| 1983 | Edmond Donald, Millsaps | Jr. | 15 | 320 | 21.3 |
| 1984 | Robert Middlebrook, Knoxville | So. | 9 | 260 | 28.9 |
| 1985 | Dan Schone, Illinois Col. | Fr. | 11 | 231 | 21.0 |
| 1986 | Chuck Downey, Stony Brook | Jr. | 17 | 530 | *31.2 |
| 1987 | Keith Winston, Knoxville | Sr. | 16 | 343 | 21.4 |
| 1988 | Dennis Tarr, Framingham St. | Jr. | 9 | 178 | 19.8 |
| 1989 | Chris Warren, Ferrum | Sr. | 18 | 421 | 23.4 |
| 1990 | Melvin Dillard, Ferrum | Sr. | 25 | *688 | 27.5 |
| 1991 | Jordan Nixon, Augustana (Ill.) | Sr. | 27 | 473 | 17.5 |
| 1992 | Vic Moncato, FDU-Madison | So. | †††10 | 243 | 24.3 |

* Record.   ‡ Ranked on minimum of 1.5 returns per game in 1973; 1.2 from 1974.   †† Declared champion; with one more return (making 1.25 per game) for zero yards, still would have highest average (26.3).   ††† Declared champion; with one more return (making 1.22 per game) for zero yards, still would have highest average (22.1).

# KICKOFF RETURNS

## Career Average
### (Minimum 1.2 Returns Per Game)

| Player, Team | Years | No. | Yards | Avg. |
|---|---|---|---|---|
| Daryl Brown, Tufts | 1974-76 | 38 | 1,111 | *29.2 |
| Mike Askew, Kean | 1980-81 | 33 | 938 | 28.4 |
| Chuck Downey, Stony Brook | 1984-87 | 46 | 1,281 | 27.8 |
| Scott Reppert, Lawrence | 1979-82 | 44 | 1,134 | 25.8 |
| Rick Rosenfeld, Western Md. | 1973-76 | 69 | 1,732 | 25.1 |

* Record.

## Season Average
### (Minimum 1.2 Returns Per Game)

| Player, Team | Year | No. | Yards | Avg. |
|---|---|---|---|---|
| Jason Martin, Coe | †1992 | 11 | 438 | *39.8 |
| Nate Kirtman, Pomona-Pitzer | †1990 | 14 | 515 | 36.8 |
| Tom Myers, Coe | †1983 | 11 | 401 | 36.5 |
| Ron Scott, Occidental | 1983 | 10 | 363 | 36.3 |
| Alan Hill, DePauw | 1980 | 12 | 434 | 36.2 |
| Al White, Wm. Paterson | 1990 | 12 | 427 | 35.6 |
| Byron Womack, Iona | †1989 | 15 | 531 | 35.4 |
| Darnell Marshall, Carroll (Wis.) | 1989 | 17 | 586 | 34.5 |
| Daryl Brown, Tufts | †1976 | 11 | 377 | 34.3 |
| Rich Jinnette, Methodist | 1992 | 15 | 514 | 34.3 |
| Sean Healy, Coe | 1989 | 11 | 372 | 33.8 |
| Anthony Drakeford, Ferrum | †1987 | 15 | 507 | 33.8 |
| Ryan Reynolds, Thomas More | 1992 | 14 | 473 | 33.8 |
| Glenn Koch, Tufts | †1986 | 14 | 472 | 33.7 |

* Record.   † National champion.

## Annual Champions

| Year | Player, Team | Class | No. | Yards | ‡Avg. |
|------|-------------|-------|-----|-------|-------|
| 1973 | Greg Montgomery, Wis.-Whitewater | So. | 17 | 518 | 30.5 |
| 1974 | Tom Oleksa, Muhlenberg | Sr. | 15 | 467 | 31.1 |
| 1975 | Jeff Levant, Beloit | Jr. | 15 | 434 | 28.9 |
| 1976 | Daryl Brown, Tufts | Sr. | 11 | 377 | 34.3 |
| 1977 | Charlie Black, Marietta | Jr. | 14 | 465 | 33.2 |
| 1978 | Russ Atchison, Centre | So. | 11 | 284 | 25.8 |
| 1979 | Jim Iannone, Rochester | Jr. | 13 | 411 | 31.6 |
| 1980 | Mike Askew, Kean | So. | ††10 | 415 | 41.5 |
| 1981 | Gene Cote, Wesleyan | Sr. | 16 | 521 | 32.6 |
| 1982 | Jim Hachey, Bri'water (Mass.) | Jr. | 16 | 477 | 29.8 |
| 1983 | Tom Myers, Coe | So. | 11 | 401 | 36.5 |
| 1984 | Mike Doetsch, Trinity (Conn.) | Jr. | 13 | 434 | 33.4 |
| 1985 | Gary Newsom, Lane | So. | 10 | 319 | 31.9 |
| 1986 | Glenn Koch, Tufts | Sr. | 14 | 472 | 33.7 |
| 1987 | Anthony Drakeford, Ferrum | Sr. | 15 | 507 | 33.8 |
| 1988 | Harold Owens, Wis.-La Crosse | Jr. | 10 | 508 | 29.9 |
| 1989 | Byron Womack, Iona | Sr. | 15 | 531 | 35.4 |
| 1990 | Nate Kirtman, Pomona-Pitzer | Jr. | 14 | 515 | 36.8 |
| 1991 | Tom Reason, Albion | So. | 13 | 423 | 32.5 |
| 1992 | Jason Martin, Coe | So. | 11 | 438 | *39.8 |

*Record. ‡ Ranked on minimum of 1.5 returns per game in 1973; 1.2 from 1974. †† Declared champion; with one more return (making 1.2 per game) for zero yards, still would have highest average (37.7).

# FIELD GOALS

### Career Field Goals

| Player, Team | Years | Made | Atts. | Pct. |
|-------------|-------|------|-------|------|
| Ken Edelman, Mount Union (S) | 1987-90 | *52 | **71 | .732 |
| Ted Swan, Colorado Col. (S) | 1973-76 | 43 | 57 | .754 |
| Jim Hever, Rhodes (S) | 1982-85 | 42 | 66 | .636 |
| Manny Matsakis, Capital (C) | 1980-83 | 40 | 66 | .606 |
| Doug Hart, Grove City (S) | 1985-88 | 40 | **71 | .563 |
| Mike Duvic, Dayton (S) | 1986-89 | 38 | 49 | $.776 |
| Jeff Reitz, Lawrence (C) | 1974-77 | 37 | 60 | .617 |
| Dan Deneher, Montclair St. (S) | 1978-79, 81-82 | 37 | 65 | .569 |
| Jim Flynn, Gettysburg (S) | 1982-85 | 37 | 68 | .544 |

*Record. ** Record tied. $ Declared record; with one more attempt (making 50), failed, still would have highest percentage (.760). (C) Conventional kicker. (S) Soccer-style kicker.

### Season Field Goals

| Player, Team | Year | Made | Atts. | Pct. |
|-------------|------|------|-------|------|
| Ken Edelman, Mount Union (S) | †1990 | *20 | 27 | .741 |
| Scott Ryerson, Central Fla. (S) | †1981 | 18 | *29 | .621 |
| Steve Graeca, John Carroll (S) | †1988 | 15 | 16 | *.938 |
| Ken Edelman, Mount Union (S) | 1988 | 15 | 17 | .882 |
| Gary Potter, Hamline (C) | †1984 | 15 | 21 | .714 |
| Jeff Reitz, Lawrence (C) | †1975 | 15 | 26 | .577 |

*Record. † National champion. (C) Conventional kicker. (S) Soccer-style kicker.

### Annual Champions

| Year | Player, Team | Class | Made | Atts. | Pct. | PG |
|------|-------------|-------|------|-------|------|-----|
| 1973 | Chuck Smeltz, Susquehanna (C) | Jr. | 10 | 14 | .714 | 1.11 |
| 1974 | Ted Swan, Colorado Col. (S) | So. | 13 | 15 | .867 | 1.44 |
| 1975 | Jeff Reitz, Lawrence (C) | So. | 15 | 26 | .577 | 1.67 |
| 1976 | Mark Sniegocki, Bethany (W. Va.) (C) | So. | 11 | 14 | .786 | 1.22 |
| 1977 | Bob Unruh, Wheaton (Ill.) (S) | Jr. | 11 | 14 | .786 | 1.22 |
| 1978 | Craig Walker, Western Md. (C) | So. | 13 | 24 | .542 | 1.44 |
| 1979 | Jeff Holter, Concordia-M'head (S) | Jr. | 12 | 15 | .800 | 1.33 |
| 1980 | Jeff Holter, Concordia-M'head (S) | Sr. | 13 | 19 | .684 | 1.30 |
| 1981 | Scott Ryerson, Central Fla. (S) | So. | 18 | *29 | .621 | 1.80 |
| 1982 | Manny Matsakis, Capital (C) | Jr. | 13 | 20 | .650 | 1.44 |
| 1983 | Mike Farrell, Adrian (S) | So. | 12 | 21 | .571 | 1.33 |
| 1984 | Gary Potter, Hamline (C) | Jr. | 15 | 21 | .714 | 1.50 |
| 1985 | Joe Bevelhimer, Wabash (C) | Sr. | 14 | 22 | .636 | 1.40 |
|  | Jim Hever, Rhodes (S) | Sr. | 14 | 23 | .609 | 1.40 |
| 1986 | Tim Dewberry, Occidental (C) | Sr. | 13 | 21 | .619 | 1.44 |
| 1987 | Doug Dickason, John Carroll (S) | Sr. | 13 | 21 | .619 | 1.44 |

| Year | Player, Team | Class | Made | Atts. | Pct. | PG |
|------|--------------|-------|------|-------|------|-----|
| 1988 | Steve Graeca, John Carroll (S) | Fr. | 15 | 16 | *.938 | 1.67 |
| 1989 | Dave Bergmann, San Diego (S) | So. | 14 | 18 | .778 | 1.56 |
|      | Rich Egal, Merchant Marine (S) | Fr. | 14 | 22 | .636 | 1.56 |
| 1990 | Ken Edelman, Mount Union (S) | Sr. | *20 | 27 | .741 | *2.00 |
| 1991 | Greg Harrison, Union (N.Y.) (S) | So. | 12 | 16 | .750 | 1.33 |
| 1992 | Todd Holthaus, Rose-Hulman (S) | Jr. | 13 | 19 | .684 | 1.30 |

* Record. (C) Conventional kicker. (S) Soccer-style kicker.

# LONGEST PLAYS

*Since 1941, official maximum length of all plays fixed at 100 yards.*

### Rushing

| Yds. | Player, Team (Opponent) | Year |
|------|-------------------------|------|
| 99 | Arnie Boigner, Ohio Northern (Muskingum) | 1992 |
| 99 | Reese Wilson, MacMurray (Eureka) | 1986 |
| 99 | Don Patria, Rensselaer (Mass.-Lowell) | 1981 |
| 99 | Kevin Doherty, Mass. Maritime (New Haven) | 1980 |
| 99 | Sam Halliston, Albany, N.Y. (Norwich) | 1977 |
| 98 | Rich Vargas, Wis.-Stout (Wis.-Oshkosh) | 1992 |
| 98 | Ted Pretasky, Wis.-La Crosse (Wis.-River Falls) | 1987 |
| 98 | Jon Hinds, Principia (Illinois Col.) | 1986 |
| 98 | Alex Schmidt, Muhlenberg (Lebanon Valley) | 1984 |
| 98 | Eric Batt, Ohio Northern (Ohio Wesleyan) | 1982 |
| 98 | Mike Shannon, Centre (Sewanee) | 1978 |

### Passing

| Yds. | Passer-Receiver, Team (Opponent) | Year |
|------|----------------------------------|------|
| 99 | Marc Klausner-Eric Frink, Pace (Hobart) | 1992 |
| 99 | Carlos Nazario-Ray Marshall, St. Peter's (Georgetown) | 1991 |
| 99 | Mike Jones-Warren Tweedy, Frostburg St. (Waynesburg) | 1990 |
| 99 | Chris Etzler-Andy Nowlin, Bluffton (Urbana) | 1990 |
| 99 | John Clark-Pete Balistrieri, Wis.-Eau Claire (Minn.-Duluth) | 1989 |
| 99 | Kelly Sandidge-Mark Green, Centre (Sewanee) | 1988 |
| 99 | Mike Francis-John Winter, Carleton (Trinity, Tex.) | 1983 |
| 99 | Rich Boling-Lewis Borsellino, DePauw (Valparaiso) | 1976 |
| 99 | John Wicinski-Donnell Lipford, John Carroll (Allegheny) | 1975 |
| 99 | Jack Berry-Mercer West, Wash. & Lee (Hampden-Sydney) | 1974 |
| 99 | Gary Shope-Rick Rudolph, Juniata (Moravian) | 1973 |

### Interception Returns

*Seventeen players have returned interceptions 100 yards. The most recent:*

| Yds. | Player, Team (Opponent) | Year |
|------|-------------------------|------|
| 100 | Scott Schuster, Stony Brook (Pace) | 1992 |
| 100 | Randy Ashe, Loras (Quincy) | 1991 |
| 100 | Bill Zagger, Stony Brook (Merchant Marine) | 1990 |
| 100 | Dana Cruickshank, Dubuque (Upper Iowa) | 1987 |
| 100 | Todd Schoelzel, Wis.-Oshkosh (Wis.-Platteville) | 1987 |

### Punt Returns

| Yds. | Player, Team (Opponent) | Year |
|------|-------------------------|------|
| 99 | Robert Middlebrook, Knoxville (Miles) | 1985 |
| 98 | Mark Griggs, Wooster (Oberlin) | 1980 |
| 98 | Ron Mabry, Emory & Henry (Maryville, Tenn.) | 1973 |
| 97 | Rob Allard, Nichols (Curry) | 1991 |
| 96 | Marvin Robbins, Salisbury St. (Wesley) | 1987 |
| 96 | Gary Martin, Muskingum (Wooster) | 1976 |
| 95 | Brian Sarver, William Penn (Dubuque) | 1992 |
| 95 | Stan Thompson, Knoxville (Livingstone) | 1982 |

### Kickoff Returns

*Forty players have returned kickoffs 100 yards. The most recent:*

| Yds. | Player, Team (Opponent) | Year |
|------|-------------------------|------|
| 100 | Eric Green, Ill. Benedictine (Carthage) | 1992 |
| 100 | Nate Kirtman, Pomona-Pitzer (Redlands) | 1990 |

| Yds. | Player, Team (Opponent) | Year |
|---|---|---|
| 100 | Phil Bryant, Wilmington, Ohio (Tiffin) | 1990 |
| 100 | Steve Burns, Mass.-Boston (Curry) | 1989 |
| 100 | Wayne Morris, Hofstra (Pace) | 1989 |

### Punts

| Yds. | Player, Team (Opponent) | Year |
|---|---|---|
| 90 | Dan Heeren, Coe (Lawrence) | 1974 |
| 86 | David Anastasi, Buffalo (John Carroll) | 1989 |
| 86 | Dana Loucks, Buffalo (Frostburg St.) | 1987 |
| 86 | John Pavlik, Wabash (Centre) | 1978 |
| 83 | Geoff Hansen, Gust. Adolphus (Augustana, S.D.) | 1992 |
| 82 | John Massab, Albion (Adrian) | 1982 |
| 82 | Mike Manson, Ill. Benedictine (Monmouth, Ill.) | 1976 |
| 81 | Jason Berg, Mass. Maritime (Mass.-Lowell) | 1990 |
| 81 | Tom Illig, Ohio Wesleyan (Wittenberg) | 1975 |

### Field Goals

| Yds. | Player, Team (Opponent) | Year |
|---|---|---|
| 62 | Dom Antonini, Rowan (Salisbury St.) | 1976 |
| 59 | Chris Gustafson, Carroll, Wis. (North Park) | 1985 |
| 59 | Hartmut Strecker, Dayton (Iowa St.) | 1977 |
| 57 | Scott Fritz, Wartburg (Simpson) | 1982 |
| 57 | Kevin Shea, St. Mary's, Cal. (Oregon Tech) | 1976 |

# TEAM CHAMPIONS AND WINNING STREAKS

## ANNUAL TEAM OFFENSE CHAMPIONS

| Year | Total Offense Team | Avg. | Rushing Team | Avg. | Passing Team | Avg. |
|---|---|---|---|---|---|---|
| 1973 | San Diego | 441.0 | Widener | 361.7 | San Diego | 231.7 |
| 1974 | Ithaca | 487.9 | Albany (N.Y.) | 361.6 | Ill. Benedictine | 255.4 |
| 1975 | Frank. & Marsh. | 439.4 | Widener | 345.8 | St. Norbert | 227.7 |
| 1976 | St. John's (Minn.) | 451.8 | St. John's (Minn.) | 348.9 | Occidental | 255.4 |
| 1977 | St. John's (Minn.) | 437.5 | St. John's (Minn.) | 315.3 | Southwestern | 257.8 |
| 1978 | Lawrence | 432.6 | Ithaca | 320.1 | Claremont-M-S | 331.7 |
| 1979 | Norwich | 465.2 | Norwich | 383.1 | Claremont-M-S | 250.1 |
| 1980 | Widener | 459.0 | Widener | 317.5 | Occidental | 255.9 |
| 1981 | Middlebury | 446.5 | Augustana (Ill.) | 313.6 | Wis.-Stevens Point | 288.9 |
| 1982 | West Ga. | 470.6 | West Ga. | 319.6 | Wheaton (Ill.) | 308.7 |
| 1983 | Elmhurst | 483.3 | Augustana (Ill.) | 345.7 | Wheaton (Ill.) | *380.4 |
| 1984 | Alma | 465.1 | Augustana (Ill.) | 338.4 | Wheaton (Ill.) | 351.6 |
| 1985 | St. Thomas (Minn.) | 446.9 | Denison | 351.0 | Wheaton (Ill.) | 371.6 |
| 1986 | Mount Union | 452.8 | Wis.-River Falls | 361.4 | Pace | 286.9 |
| 1987 | Samford | *523.1 | Augustana (Ill.) | 369.1 | Wis.-Stout | 314.6 |
| 1988 | Wagner | 465.9 | Tufts | 369.0 | Wis.-Stevens Point | 356.7 |
| 1989 | Simpson | 514.0 | Wis.-River Falls | 388.5 | Wis.-Stevens Point | 380.4 |
| 1990 | Hofstra | 505.7 | Ferrum | *434.7 | Hofstra | 342.2 |
| 1991 | St. John's (Minn.) | 503.8 | Ferrum | 361.4 | St. John's (Minn.) | 302.8 |
| 1992 | Mount Union | 463.7 | Wis.-River Falls | 315.6 | Mass.-Boston | 337.0 |

* Record.

### Scoring Offense

| Year | Team | Avg. | Year | Team | Avg. |
|---|---|---|---|---|---|
| 1973 | San Diego | 40.1 | 1983 | Elmhurst | 38.1 |
| 1974 | Frank. & Marsh. | 45.1 | 1984 | Hope | 40.3 |
| 1975 | Frank. & Marsh. | 38.2 | 1985 | Salisbury St. | 39.5 |
| 1976 | St. John's (Minn.) | 42.5 | 1986 | Dayton | 40.8 |
| 1977 | Lawrence | 38.2 | 1987 | Samford | *51.7 |
| 1978 | Georgetown | 36.5 | 1988 | Central (Iowa) | 37.6 |
| 1979 | Wittenberg | 39.7 | 1989 | Ferrum | 46.7 |
| 1980 | Widener | 43.3 | 1990 | Ferrum | 47.3 |
| 1981 | Lawrence | 35.3 | 1991 | Union (N.Y.) | 46.1 |
| 1982 | West Ga. | 42.1 | 1992 | Coe | 46.4 |

* Record.

270

# ANNUAL TEAM DEFENSE CHAMPIONS

| | Total Defense | | | Rushing Defense | | | Pass Defense | |
|---|---|---|---|---|---|---|---|---|
| **Year** | **Team** | **Avg.** | **Team** | **Avg.** | | **Team** | **$Avg.** | |
| 1973 | Doane | 144.3 | Oregon Col. | 61.2 | | Nichols | 53.0 | |
| 1974 | Alfred | 153.6 | Millersville | 57.2 | | Findlay | 49.2 | |
| 1975 | Lycoming | 133.1 | Cal Lutheran | 62.4 | | Wash. & Jeff. | 56.0 | |
| 1976 | Albion | 129.9 | Lycoming | 44.3 | | Mass. Maritime | *48.5 | |
| 1977 | Knoxville | *94.0 | Knoxville | *-2.3 | | Hofstra | 49.4 | |
| 1978 | Bowie St. | 112.3 | Western Md. | 43.4 | | Bowie St. | 64.7 | |
| 1979 | Catholic | 116.9 | Catholic | 46.4 | | Wagner | 59.5 | |
| 1980 | Maine Maritime | 127.2 | Maine Maritime | 3.2 | | Williams | 63.8 | |
| 1981 | Millsaps | 147.6 | Augustana (Ill.) | 30.7 | | Plymouth St. | 66.9 | |
| 1982 | Plymouth St. | 122.2 | Lycoming | 34.2 | | Plymouth St. | 48.8 | |
| 1983 | Lycoming | 154.5 | DePauw | 41.6 | | Muhlenberg | 76.4 | |
| 1984 | Swarthmore | 159.2 | Swarthmore | 40.0 | | Bri'water (Mass.) | 68.7 | |
| 1985 | Augustana (Ill.) | 149.1 | Augustana (Ill.) | 35.1 | | Bri'water (Mass.) | 77.3 | |
| 1986 | Augustana (Ill.) | 136.2 | Dayton | 13.5 | | Knoxville | 83.2 | |
| 1987 | Plymouth St. | 135.3 | Lycoming | 35.4 | | Jersey City St. | 67.0 | |
| 1988 | Plymouth St. | 143.6 | Worcester St. | 43.9 | | Colorado Col. | 78.9 | |
| 1989 | Frostburg St. | 119.7 | Frostburg St. | 49.7 | | Frostburg St. | 70.0 | |
| 1990 | Bentley | 139.8 | Ohio Wesleyan | 18.9 | | Bentley | 47.4 | |
| 1991 | Wash. & Jeff. | 143.0 | Wash. & Jeff. | 64.6 | | Wash. & Jeff. | 50.3 | |
| 1992 | Bentley | 184.5 | Bri'water (Mass.) | 43.2 | | St. Peter's | 51.7 | |

*Record.   $ Beginning in 1990, ranked on passing efficiency defense rating points instead of per-game yardage allowed.*

## Scoring Defense

| Year | Team | Avg. | Year | Team | Avg. |
|---|---|---|---|---|---|
| 1973 | Fisk | 6.4 | 1983 | Carnegie Mellon | 5.3 |
| | Slippery Rock | 6.4 | 1984 | Union (N.Y.) | 4.6 |
| 1974 | Central (Iowa) | 6.9 | 1985 | Augustana (Ill.) | 4.7 |
| | Rhodes | 6.9 | 1986 | Augustana (Ill.) | 5.1 |
| 1975 | Millsaps | 5.0 | 1987 | Plymouth St. | 6.2 |
| 1976 | Albion | 5.4 | 1988 | Plymouth St. | 6.5 |
| 1977 | Central (Iowa) | 5.0 | 1989 | Millikin | 4.8 |
| 1978 | Minn.-Morris | 5.9 | 1990 | Bentley | 4.5 |
| 1979 | Carnegie Mellon | 4.9 | 1991 | Mass.-Lowell | 5.4 |
| 1980 | Millsaps | *3.4 | 1992 | Dayton | 6.7 |
| 1981 | Baldwin-Wallace | 3.9 | | | |
| 1982 | West Ga. | 4.6 | | | |

*Record.*

# OTHER ANNUAL TEAM CHAMPIONS

| Year | Net Punting | Avg. | Punt Returns | Avg. | Kickoff Returns | Avg. |
|---|---|---|---|---|---|---|
| 1992 | San Diego | 39.2 | Occidental | 18.7 | Thomas More | 27.7 |

| Year | Turnover Margin | Avg. |
|---|---|---|
| 1992 | Illinois Col. | 2.44 |

# LONGEST STREAKS
**(Minimum two seasons in Division III; includes postseason games.)**

| | Winning Streaks | | | | Unbeaten Streaks | | |
|---|---|---|---|---|---|---|---|
| **Wins** | **Team** | **Years** | **No.** | **Wins** | **Ties** | **Team** | **Years** |
| 37 | Augustana (Ill.) | 1983-85 | 60 | 59 | 1 | Augustana (Ill.) | 1983-87 |
| 24 | Allegheny | 1990-91 | 25 | 24 | 1 | Dayton | 1989-90 |
| 23 | Williams | 1988-91 | 24 | 24 | 0 | Allegheny | 1990-91 |
| 22 | Dayton | 1989-90 | 24 | 23 | 1 | Wabash | 1979-81 |
| 22 | Augustana (Ill.) | 1986-87 | 23 | 23 | 0 | Williams | 1988-91 |
| 21 | Dayton | 1979-81 | 22 | 21 | 1 | Dayton | 1979-81 |
| 20 | Plymouth St. | 1987-88 | 21 | 20 | 1 | Baldwin-Wallace | 1977-79 |
| 19 | Plymouth St. | 1981-82 | 20 | 20 | 0 | Plymouth St. | 1987-88 |
| 18 | Lawrence | 1980-81 | 20 | 18 | 2 | St. John's (Minn.) | 1975-76 |
| 18 | Ithaca | 1979-80 | | | | | |

# LONGEST DIVISION III SERIES

| Games | Opponents<br>(Series leader listed first) | Series<br>Record | First<br>Game |
|---|---|---|---|
| 107 | Williams-Amherst | 58-45-4 | 1884 |
| 106 | Albion-Kalamazoo | 68-34-4 | 1896 |
| 104 | Bowdoin-Colby | 59-37-8 | 1892 |
| 103 | Monmouth (Ill.)-Knox | 48-45-10 | 1891 |
| 102 | Coe-Cornell College | 54-44-4 | 1891 |
| 99 | DePauw-Wabash | 45-45-9 | 1890 |
| 98 | Amherst-Wesleyan | 50-39-9 | 1882 |
| 98 | Williams-Wesleyan | 58-35-5 | 1881 |
| 97 | Hampden-Sydney—Randolph-Macon | 50-36-11 | 1893 |
| 96 | Union (N.Y.)-Hamilton | 46-38-12 | 1890 |
| 95 | Colby-Bates | 50-37-8 | 1893 |

# ALL-TIME WON-LOST RECORDS

Includes records as a senior college only, minimum 20 seasons of competition since 1937. Postseason games are included, and each tie game is computed as half won and half lost.

## TOP 25—BY PERCENTAGE

| Team | Yrs. | Won | Lost | Tied | Pct. |
|---|---|---|---|---|---|
| Plymouth St. | 23 | 149 | 61 | 7 | .703 |
| Wis.-La Crosse | 68 | 401 | 176 | 40 | .682 |
| St. John's (Minn.) | 82 | 390 | 194 | 23 | .661 |
| Ithaca | 60 | 308 | 167 | 11 | .645 |
| Cal Lutheran | 31 | 195 | 106 | 6 | .645 |
| Montclair St. | 62 | 310 | 178 | 20 | .630 |
| Wis.-Whitewater | 68 | 345 | 199 | 21 | .629 |
| Wittenberg | 99 | 536 | 311 | 32 | .628 |
| Augustana (Ill.) | 80 | 399 | 232 | 28 | .627 |
| Concordia-M'head | 73 | 365 | 210 | 37 | .627 |
| Gust. Adolphus | 77 | 378 | 224 | 21 | .624 |
| Baldwin-Wallace | 88 | 425 | 257 | 30 | .618 |
| Millikin | 87 | 425 | 268 | 28 | .609 |
| Lawrence | 99 | 441 | 286 | 29 | .603 |
| Williams | 107 | 501 | 324 | 46 | .602 |
| Central (Iowa) | 84 | 408 | 267 | 26 | .601 |
| Albany (N.Y.) | 20 | 117 | 78 | 0 | .600 |
| Widener | 112 | 512 | 336 | 38 | .599 |
| St. Thomas (Minn.) | 87 | 409 | 269 | 32 | .599 |
| Wash. & Jeff. | 101 | 507 | 337 | 40 | .596 |
| Wis.-River Falls | 67 | 316 | 211 | 32 | .594 |
| Wabash | 106 | 474 | 326 | 59 | .586 |
| Albion | 106 | 451 | 317 | 43 | .583 |
| Whittier | 83 | 401 | 284 | 36 | .581 |
| Salisbury St. | 21 | 117 | 84 | 4 | .580 |

## TOP 25—BY VICTORIES

| Team | Wins |
|---|---|
| Wittenberg | 536 |
| Widener | 512 |
| Wash. & Jeff. | 507 |
| Frank. & Marsh. | 501 |
| Williams | 501 |
| Amherst | 490 |
| Wabash | 474 |
| Ohio Wesleyan | 459 |
| Gettysburg | 458 |
| Denison | 455 |
| Albion | 451 |
| Centre | 445 |
| Lawrence | 441 |
| Mount Union | 437 |
| Muskingum | 437 |
| Coe | 432 |
| Tufts | 429 |
| DePauw | 428 |
| Swarthmore | 426 |
| Baldwin-Wallace | 425 |
| Millikin | 425 |
| Rochester | 424 |
| Wesleyan | 424 |
| Trinity (Conn.) | 423 |
| Ill. Wesleyan | 416 |

## ALPHABETICAL
(No minimum seasons of competition.)

| Team | Yrs. | Won | Lost | Tied | Pct. |
|---|---|---|---|---|---|
| Adrian | 90 | 285 | 363 | 17 | .441 |
| Albany (N.Y.) | 20 | 117 | 78 | 0 | .600 |
| Albion | 106 | 451 | 317 | 43 | .583 |
| Albright | 80 | 319 | 372 | 21 | .463 |
| Alfred | 94 | 365 | 279 | 44 | .563 |
| Allegheny | 98 | 366 | 333 | 44 | .522 |
| Alma | 96 | 380 | 324 | 27 | .538 |
| Amherst | 113 | 490 | 364 | 53 | .569 |
| Anderson | 46 | 197 | 201 | 12 | .495 |
| Augsburg | 61 | 132 | 342 | 18 | .287 |
| Augustana (Ill.) | 80 | 399 | 232 | 28 | .627 |
| Aurora | 7 | 39 | 20 | 1 | .658 |
| Baldwin-Wallace | 88 | 425 | 257 | 30 | .618 |
| Bates | 97 | 277 | 395 | 46 | .418 |
| Beloit | 102 | 341 | 408 | 47 | .458 |

*1993 NCAA FOOTBALL*

| Team | Yrs. | Won | Lost | Tied | Pct. |
|---|---|---|---|---|---|
| Bethany (W. Va.) | 92 | 278 | 431 | 33 | .397 |
| Bethel (Minn.) | 40 | 116 | 229 | 8 | .340 |
| Blackburn | 4 | 6 | 27 | 0 | .182 |
| Bluffton | 70 | 222 | 309 | 23 | .421 |
| Bowdoin | 99 | 339 | 380 | 43 | .473 |
| Bri'water (Mass.) | 33 | 134 | 140 | 6 | .489 |
| Bridgewater (Va.) | 48 | 117 | 259 | 10 | .316 |
| Brockport St. | 46 | 114 | 244 | 2 | .319 |
| Buena Vista | 88 | 340 | 310 | 28 | .522 |
| Buffalo St. | 12 | 46 | 63 | 0 | .422 |
| Cal Lutheran | 31 | 195 | 106 | 6 | .645 |
| Capital | 69 | 271 | 261 | 27 | .509 |
| Carleton | 98 | 407 | 295 | 25 | .577 |
| Carnegie Mellon | 83 | 377 | 295 | 29 | .558 |
| Carroll (Wis.) | 89 | 345 | 265 | 38 | .562 |
| Carthage | 96 | 349 | 326 | 41 | .516 |
| Case Reserve | 23 | 87 | 118 | 4 | .426 |
| Catholic | 47 | 183 | 193 | 12 | .487 |
| Central (Iowa) | 84 | 408 | 267 | 26 | .601 |
| Centre | 100 | 445 | 331 | 37 | .570 |
| Chicago | 73 | 312 | 298 | 33 | .511 |
| Claremont-M-S | 35 | 118 | 187 | 4 | .388 |
| Coast Guard | 69 | 233 | 307 | 49 | .437 |
| Coe | 100 | 432 | 315 | 38 | .575 |
| Colby | 99 | 281 | 396 | 32 | .419 |
| Colorado Col. | 107 | 415 | 373 | 34 | .526 |
| Concordia (Ill.) | 54 | 165 | 238 | 18 | .413 |
| Concordia-M'head | 73 | 365 | 210 | 37 | .627 |
| Cornell College | 102 | 415 | 343 | 33 | .546 |
| Cortland St. | 66 | 271 | 226 | 27 | .543 |
| Curry | 28 | 94 | 136 | 5 | .411 |
| Defiance | 70 | 274 | 291 | 20 | .485 |
| Delaware Valley | 45 | 171 | 200 | 10 | .462 |
| Denison | 103 | 455 | 350 | 56 | .561 |
| DePauw | 105 | 428 | 394 | 41 | .520 |
| Dickinson | 104 | 367 | 454 | 54 | .450 |
| Dubuque | 70 | 258 | 293 | 25 | .470 |
| Earlham | 102 | 299 | 439 | 23 | .408 |
| Elmhurst | 73 | 229 | 346 | 23 | .402 |
| Emory & Henry | 77 | 393 | 318 | 19 | .551 |
| Eureka | 59 | 125 | 309 | 26 | .300 |
| FDU-Madison | 19 | 45 | 117 | 1 | .279 |
| Ferrum | 8 | 58 | 27 | 1 | .680 |
| Fitchburg St. | 9 | 7 | 72 | 0 | .089 |
| Framingham St. | 19 | 71 | 96 | 1 | .426 |
| Frank. & Marsh. | 105 | 501 | 358 | 47 | .579 |
| Franklin | 92 | 326 | 390 | 31 | .457 |
| Frostburg St. | 32 | 135 | 156 | 7 | .465 |
| Gallaudet | 93 | 201 | 407 | 19 | .336 |
| Gettysburg | 100 | 458 | 385 | 41 | .541 |
| Grinnell | 102 | 328 | 445 | 33 | .427 |
| Grove City | 98 | 381 | 376 | 60 | .503 |
| Guilford | 87 | 225 | 458 | 25 | .335 |
| Gust. Adolphus | 77 | 378 | 224 | 21 | .624 |
| Hamilton | 99 | 318 | 375 | 47 | .461 |
| Hamline | 101 | 343 | 341 | 30 | .501 |
| Hampden-Sydney | 98 | 406 | 352 | 28 | .534 |
| Hanover | 100 | 336 | 339 | 29 | .498 |
| Hartwick | 21 | 42 | 105 | 10 | .299 |
| Heidelberg | 97 | 384 | 378 | 41 | .504 |
| Hiram | 94 | 231 | 451 | 32 | .346 |
| Hobart | 99 | 343 | 400 | 40 | .464 |
| Hope | 83 | 320 | 252 | 37 | .556 |
| Ill. Benedictine | 71 | 233 | 266 | 23 | .468 |
| Ill. Wesleyan | 101 | 416 | 323 | 41 | .560 |
| Illinois Col. | 96 | 334 | 369 | 36 | .476 |
| Ithaca | 60 | 308 | 167 | 11 | .645 |
| Jersey City St. | 25 | 85 | 146 | 2 | .369 |
| John Carroll | 70 | 314 | 251 | 35 | .553 |
| Johns Hopkins | 108 | 345 | 407 | 56 | .462 |

| Team | Yrs. | Won | Lost | Tied | Pct. |
|------|------|-----|------|------|------|
| Juniata | 70 | 300 | 253 | 21 | .541 |
| Kalamazoo | 98 | 321 | 379 | 41 | .461 |
| Kean | 21 | 85 | 114 | 6 | .429 |
| Kenyon | 103 | 292 | 465 | 46 | .392 |
| Knox | 99 | 336 | 425 | 43 | .445 |
| La Verne | 67 | 248 | 290 | 18 | .462 |
| Lake Forest | 100 | 338 | 360 | 55 | .485 |
| Lawrence | 99 | 441 | 286 | 29 | .603 |
| Lebanon Valley | 92 | 331 | 408 | 36 | .450 |
| Loras | 64 | 269 | 219 | 30 | .548 |
| Luther | 79 | 344 | 268 | 21 | .560 |
| Lycoming | 43 | 206 | 158 | 11 | .564 |
| Macalester | 90 | 224 | 401 | 29 | .365 |
| MacMurray | 8 | 30 | 44 | 1 | .407 |
| Maine Maritime | 47 | 190 | 171 | 9 | .526 |
| Manchester | 67 | 205 | 319 | 20 | .395 |
| Marietta | 98 | 332 | 427 | 35 | .440 |
| Maryville (Tenn.) | 95 | 363 | 386 | 35 | .485 |
| Mass.-Boston | 5 | 17 | 27 | 1 | .389 |
| Mass.-Dartmouth | 5 | 19 | 26 | 0 | .422 |
| Mass. Maritime | 20 | 101 | 75 | 1 | .573 |
| Menlo | 7 | 31 | 31 | 1 | .500 |
| Merchant Marine | 48 | 204 | 222 | 13 | .479 |
| Methodist | 4 | 2 | 38 | 0 | .050 |
| Middlebury | 96 | 322 | 333 | 42 | .492 |
| Millikin | 87 | 425 | 268 | 28 | .609 |
| Millsaps | 70 | 294 | 268 | 36 | .522 |
| MIT | 5 | 11 | 25 | 1 | .311 |
| Monmouth (Ill.) | 100 | 410 | 374 | 39 | .522 |
| Montclair St. | 62 | 310 | 178 | 20 | .630 |
| Moravian | 59 | 245 | 236 | 20 | .509 |
| Mount Union | 96 | 437 | 378 | 34 | .535 |
| Muhlenberg | 93 | 380 | 400 | 41 | .488 |
| Muskingum | 98 | 437 | 318 | 37 | .575 |
| Neb. Wesleyan | 84 | 368 | 320 | 42 | .533 |
| Nichols | 34 | 144 | 121 | 6 | .542 |
| North Central | 88 | 305 | 344 | 35 | .471 |
| North Park | 35 | 71 | 230 | 6 | .241 |
| Norwich | 94 | 279 | 391 | 31 | .420 |
| N'western (Wis.) | 94 | 286 | 301 | 30 | .488 |
| Oberlin | 102 | 351 | 431 | 39 | .451 |
| Occidental | 91 | 374 | 315 | 26 | .541 |
| Ohio Northern | 94 | 347 | 382 | 34 | .477 |
| Ohio Wesleyan | 102 | 459 | 389 | 44 | .539 |
| Olivet | 92 | 259 | 409 | 33 | .393 |
| Otterbein | 103 | 330 | 468 | 43 | .418 |
| Plymouth St. | 23 | 149 | 61 | 7 | .703 |
| Pomona-Pitzer | 95 | 322 | 352 | 31 | .479 |
| Principia | 59 | 173 | 271 | 16 | .393 |
| Randolph-Macon | 105 | 379 | 375 | 55 | .502 |
| Redlands | 83 | 360 | 339 | 27 | .514 |
| Rensselaer | 103 | 271 | 471 | 46 | .373 |
| Rhodes | 81 | 292 | 297 | 37 | .496 |
| Ripon | 99 | 394 | 287 | 46 | .574 |
| Rochester | 104 | 424 | 369 | 38 | .533 |
| Rose-Hulman | 97 | 323 | 407 | 29 | .445 |
| Rowan | 33 | 151 | 141 | 7 | .517 |
| Salisbury St. | 21 | 117 | 84 | 4 | .580 |
| Sewanee | 98 | 409 | 358 | 39 | .532 |
| Simpson | 87 | 343 | 403 | 37 | .462 |
| St. John Fisher | 5 | 17 | 30 | 0 | .362 |
| St. John's (Minn.) | 82 | 390 | 194 | 23 | .661 |
| St. Lawrence | 98 | 336 | 335 | 29 | .501 |
| St. Norbert | 59 | 262 | 220 | 20 | .542 |
| St. Olaf | 75 | 340 | 248 | 20 | .576 |
| St. Thomas (Minn.) | 87 | 409 | 269 | 32 | .599 |
| Stony Brook | 10 | 40 | 48 | 1 | .455 |
| Susquehanna | 94 | 328 | 377 | 38 | .467 |
| Swarthmore | 112 | 426 | 402 | 36 | .514 |
| Thiel | 88 | 291 | 342 | 36 | .462 |

| Team | Yrs. | Won | Lost | Tied | Pct. |
|---|---|---|---|---|---|
| Thomas More | 3 | 22 | 8 | 0 | .733 |
| Trenton St. | 68 | 240 | 251 | 30 | .489 |
| Trinity (Conn.) | 108 | 423 | 311 | 42 | .572 |
| Trinity (Tex.) | 88 | 304 | 398 | 49 | .437 |
| Tufts | 111 | 429 | 417 | 46 | .507 |
| Union (N.Y.) | 105 | 376 | 381 | 62 | .497 |
| Upper Iowa | 90 | 272 | 350 | 25 | .440 |
| Upsala | 67 | 233 | 305 | 18 | .435 |
| Ursinus | 100 | 293 | 472 | 54 | .391 |
| Wabash | 106 | 474 | 326 | 59 | .586 |
| Wartburg | 57 | 219 | 252 | 12 | .466 |
| Wash. & Jeff. | 101 | 507 | 337 | 40 | .596 |
| Wash. & Lee | 99 | 381 | 415 | 38 | .480 |
| Washington (Mo.) | 95 | 367 | 388 | 28 | .487 |
| Waynesburg | 89 | 334 | 307 | 37 | .520 |
| Wesley | 7 | 25 | 40 | 0 | .385 |
| Wesleyan | 111 | 424 | 413 | 42 | .506 |
| Western Conn. St. | 21 | 65 | 130 | 2 | .335 |
| Western Md. | 98 | 406 | 373 | 46 | .520 |
| Western New Eng. | 12 | 44 | 63 | 0 | .411 |
| Westfield St. | 11 | 45 | 58 | 0 | .437 |
| Wheaton (Ill.) | 80 | 322 | 293 | 29 | .523 |
| Whittier | 83 | 401 | 284 | 36 | .581 |
| Widener | 112 | 512 | 336 | 38 | .599 |
| Wilkes | 47 | 171 | 218 | 8 | .441 |
| William Penn | 92 | 256 | 428 | 35 | .380 |
| Williams | 107 | 501 | 324 | 46 | .602 |
| Wilmington (Ohio) | 60 | 233 | 256 | 13 | .477 |
| Wis.-Eau Claire | 74 | 276 | 282 | 34 | .495 |
| Wis.-La Crosse | 68 | 401 | 176 | 40 | .682 |
| Wis.-Oshkosh | 66 | 210 | 289 | 30 | .425 |
| Wis.-Platteville | 84 | 285 | 275 | 31 | .508 |
| Wis.-River Falls | 67 | 316 | 211 | 32 | .594 |
| Wis.-Stevens Point | 93 | 349 | 302 | 43 | .534 |
| Wis.-Stout | 73 | 196 | 365 | 33 | .358 |
| Wis.-Whitewater | 68 | 345 | 199 | 21 | .629 |
| Wittenberg | 99 | 536 | 311 | 32 | .628 |
| Wm. Paterson | 21 | 89 | 112 | 4 | .444 |
| Wooster | 94 | 393 | 347 | 41 | .529 |
| Worcester St. | 8 | 31 | 38 | 0 | .449 |
| Worcester Tech | 103 | 240 | 390 | 30 | .386 |

# NCAA DIVISION III FINAL POLL LEADERS

(Released before the division championship playoffs.)

| Year | Team, Record* | Coach | †Record in Championship Playoffs |
|---|---|---|---|
| 1975 | Ithaca (8-0-0) | Jim Butterfield | 2-1 Runner-up |
| 1976 | St. John's (Minn.) (7-0-1) | John Gagliardi | 3-0 Champion |
| 1977 | Wittenberg (8-0-0) | Dave Maurer | Did not compete |
| 1978 | Minn.-Morris (9-0-0) | Al Molde | 1-1 Lost in semifinals |
| 1979 | Wittenberg (8-0-0) | Dave Maurer | 2-1 Runner-up |
| 1980 | Ithaca (10-0-0) | Jim Butterfield | 2-1 Runner-up |
| 1981 | Widener (9-0-0) | Bill Manlove | 3-0 Champion |
| 1982 | Baldwin-Wallace (10-0-0) | Bob Packard | 0-1 Lost in first round |
| 1983 | Augustana (Ill.) (9-0-0) | Bob Reade | 3-0 Champion |
| 1984 | Augustana (Ill.) (9-0-0) | Bob Reade | 3-0 Champion |
| 1985 | Augustana (Ill.) (9-0-0) | Bob Reade | 4-0 Champion |
| 1986 | Dayton (10-0-0) | Mike Kelly | 0-1 Lost in first round |
| 1987 | Augustana (Ill.) (9-0-0) | Bob Reade | 1-1 Lost in quarterfinals |
| 1988 | **East Region** | | |
| | Cortland St. (9-0-0) | Dennis Kayser | 1-1 Lost in quarterfinals |
| | **North Region** | | |
| | Dayton (9-1-0) | Mike Kelly | 0-1 Lost in first round |
| | **South Region** | | |
| | Ferrum (9-0-0) | Hank Norton | 2-1 Lost in semifinals |
| | **West Region** | | |
| | Central (Iowa) (8-0-0) | Ron Schipper | 3-1 Runner-up |

| Year | Team, Record* | Coach | †Record in Championship Playoffs |
|---|---|---|---|
| 1989 | **East Region**<br>Union (N.Y.) (9-0-0) | Al Bagnoli | 3-1 Runner-up |
| | **North Region**<br>Dayton (8-0-1) | Mike Kelly | 4-0 Champion |
| | **South Region**<br>Rhodes (7-0-0) | Mike Clary | Did not compete |
| | **West Region**<br>Central (Iowa) (8-0-0) | Ron Schipper | 1-1 Lost in quarterfinals |
| 1990 | **East Region**<br>Hofstra (9-0-0) | Joe Gardi | 2-1 Lost in semifinals |
| | **North Region**<br>Dayton (9-0-0) | Mike Kelly | 1-1 Lost in quarterfinals |
| | **South Region**<br>Ferrum (8-0-0) | Hank Norton | 0-1 Lost in first round |
| | **West Region**<br>Wis.-Whitewater (9-0-0) | Bob Berezowitz | 0-1 Lost in first round |
| 1991 | **East Region**<br>Ithaca (7-1-0) | Jim Butterfield | 4-0 Champion |
| | **North Region**<br>Allegheny (10-0-0) | Ken O'Keefe | 1-1 Lost in quarterfinals |
| | **South Region**<br>Lycoming (8-0-0) | Frank Girardi | 1-1 Lost in quarterfinals |
| | **West Region**<br>St. John's (Minn.) (9-0-0) | John Gagliardi | 2-1 Lost in semifinals |
| 1992 | **East Region**<br>Rowan (9-0-0) | John Bunting | 2-1 Lost in semifinals |
| | **North Region**<br>Dayton (9-0-0) | Mike Kelly | 0-1 Lost in first round |
| | **South Region**<br>Wash. & Jeff. (8-0-0) | John Luckhardt | 3-1 Runner-up |
| | **West Region**<br>Central (Iowa) (9-0-0) | Ron Schipper | 1-1 Lost in quarterfinals |

\* *Final poll record.*
† *Number of teams in the championship: 8 (1975-84); 16 (1985-).*

# UNDEFEATED, UNTIED TEAMS

### (Regular-season games only.)

Following is a list of undefeated and untied teams since 1973, when College Division teams were divided into Division II and Division III under a three-division reorganization plan adopted by the special NCAA Convention on August 1, 1973. Since 1981, conference playoff games have been included in a team's won-lost record (previously, such games were considered postseason contests). Figures indicate the regular-season wins (minimum seven games against four-year varsity opponents). A subsequent postseason win(s) in the Division III championship or a conference playoff game (before 1981) is indicated by (*), a loss by (†) and a tie by (‡).

| Year | College | Wins | Year | College | Wins | Year | College | Wins |
|---|---|---|---|---|---|---|---|---|
| 1973 | Fisk | 9 | 1980 | Adrian | 9 | | Case Reserve | 9 |
| | Wittenberg | ***9 | | Baldwin-Wallace | †9 | | Central (Iowa) | **†9 |
| 1974 | Albany (N.Y.) | 9 | | Bethany (W. Va.) | †9 | | Dayton | †9 |
| | Central (Iowa) | **9 | | Dayton | ***11 | | Hope | 9 |
| | Frank. & Marsh. | 9 | | Ithaca | **†10 | | Occidental | †10 |
| | Ithaca | *†9 | | Millsaps | 9 | | Plymouth St. | †10 |
| | Towson St. | 10 | | Widener | *†10 | 1985 | Augustana (Ill.) | ****9 |
| 1975 | Cal Lutheran | *†9 | 1981 | Alfred | †10 | | Carnegie Mellon | †8 |
| | Ithaca | **†9 | | Augustana (Ill.) | †9 | | Central (Iowa) | ***†9 |
| | Widener | *†9 | | Lawrence | *†9 | | Denison | †10 |
| | Wittenberg | ***†9 | | West Ga. | †9 | | Lycoming | †10 |
| 1976 | Albion | 9 | | Widener | ***†10 | | Mount Union | *†10 |
| 1977 | Central (Iowa) | †9 | 1982 | Augustana (Ill.) | ***†9 | | Union (N.Y.) | †9 |
| | Cornell College | †8 | | Baldwin-Wallace | †10 | 1986 | Central (Iowa) | **†10 |
| | Wittenberg | †9 | | Plymouth St. | 10 | | Dayton | †10 |
| 1978 | Baldwin-Wallace | ‡***8 | | St. John's (Minn.) | †9 | | Ithaca | **†10 |
| | Illinois Col. | 9 | | St. Lawrence | *†9 | | Mount Union | *†10 |
| | Minn.-Morris | *†10 | | Wabash | 10 | | Salisbury St. | ***†10 |
| | Wittenberg | ‡**†8 | | West Ga. | ***9 | | Susquehanna | *†10 |
| 1979 | Carnegie Mellon | *†9 | 1983 | Augustana (Ill.) | ****9 | | Union (N.Y.) | 9 |
| | Dubuque | †9 | | Carnegie Mellon | †9 | 1987 | Augustana (Ill.) | *†9 |
| | Jamestown | 7 | | Hofstra | †10 | | Gust. Adolphus | †10 |
| | Tufts | 9 | | Worcester Tech | 8 | | Wash. & Jeff. | *†9 |
| | Widener | *†9 | 1984 | Amherst | 8 | 1988 | Cortland St. | *†10 |
| | Wittenberg | ***†8 | | Augustana (Ill.) | ***9 | | Ferrum | **†9 |

| Year | College | Wins | Year | College | Wins | Year | College | Wins |
|---|---|---|---|---|---|---|---|---|
| 1989 | Central (Iowa) | *†9 | | Wis.-Whitewater | †10 | | Thomas More | 10 |
| | Millikin | *†9 | 1991 | Allegheny | *†10 | | Union (N.Y.) | *†9 |
| | Union (N.Y.) | ***†10 | | Baldwin-Wallace | †10 | 1992 | Aurora | †9 |
| | Williams | 8 | | Dayton | ***†10 | | Central (Iowa) | *†9 |
| 1990 | Carnegie Mellon | †10 | | Dickinson | †10 | | Cornell College | 10 |
| | Dayton | *†10 | | Eureka | 10 | | Dayton | †10 |
| | Hofstra | **†10 | | Lycoming | *†9 | | Emory & Henry | *†10 |
| | Lycoming | ***†9 | | Mass.-Lowell | †10 | | Ill. Wesleyan | *†9 |
| | Mount Union | †10 | | Simpson | †10 | | Mount Union | ***†10 |
| | Wash. & Jeff. | *†9 | | St. John's (Minn.) | **†9 | | Rowan | **†10 |
| | Williams | 8 | | | | | | |

# THE SPOILERS

**(Since 1973, when the three-division reorganization plan was adopted by the special NCAA Convention, creating Divisions II and III.)**

Following is a list of the spoilers of Division III teams that lost their perfect (undefeated, untied) record in their **season-ending** game, including the Division III championship playoffs. An asterisk (*) indicates a Division III championship playoff game and a dagger (†) indicates the home team in a regular-season game. A game involving two undefeated, untied teams is in bold face.

| Date | Spoiler | Victim | Score |
|---|---|---|---|
| 11-17-73 | †Williams | Amherst | 30-14 |
| 12-7-74 | *Central (Iowa) | Ithaca | 10-8 |
| 11-8-75 | Cornell College | †Lawrence | 17-16 |
| 11-22-75 | *Ithaca | Widener | 23-14 |
| 12-6-75 | *Wittenberg | Ithaca | 28-0 |
| 11-12-77 | Norwich | †Middlebury | 34-20 |
| 11-12-77 | Ripon | †Cornell College | 10-7 |
| 11-19-77 | †Baldwin-Wallace | Wittenberg | 14-7 |
| 11-19-77 | *Widener | Central (Iowa) | 19-0 |
| 11-25-78 | *Wittenberg | Minn.-Morris | 35-14 |
| 11-17-79 | *Ithaca | Dubuque | 27-7 |
| 11-17-79 | ‡Findlay | Jamestown | 41-15 |
| 11-24-79 | *Wittenberg | Widener | 17-14 |
| 11-24-79 | *Ithaca | Carnegie Mellon | 15-6 |
| 12-1-79 | *Ithaca | Wittenberg | 14-10 |
| 11-8-80 | DePauw | †Wabash | tie 22-22 |
| 11-22-80 | *Widener | Bethany (W. Va.) | 43-12 |
| 11-22-80 | *Dayton | Baldwin-Wallace | 34-0 |
| 11-29-80 | *Dayton | Widener | 28-24 |
| 12-6-80 | #*Dayton | Ithaca | 63-0 |
| 11-14-81 | †DePauw | Wabash | 21-14 |
| 11-14-81 | †St. Mary's (Cal.) | San Diego | 31-14 |
| 11-21-81 | *Widener | West Ga. | 10-3 |
| 11-21-81 | *Dayton | Augustana (Ill.) | 19-7 |
| 11-21-81 | *Montclair St. | Alfred | 13-12 |
| 11-28-81 | *Dayton | Lawrence | 38-0 |
| 11-13-82 | †Widener | Swarthmore | 24-7 |
| 11-20-82 | ‡N'western (Iowa) | St. John's (Minn.) | 33-28 |
| 11-20-82 | *Augustana (Ill.) | Baldwin-Wallace | 28-22 |
| 11-27-82 | *Augustana (Ill.) | St. Lawrence | 14-0 |
| 12-4-82 | **West Ga.** | **Augustana (Ill.)** | 14-0 |
| 11-19-83 | *Salisbury St. | Carnegie Mellon | 16-14 |
| 11-19-83 | *Union (N.Y.) | Hofstra | 51-19 |
| 11-10-84 | St. John's (N.Y.) | †Hofstra | 19-16 |
| 11-10-84 | †St. Olaf | Hamline | tie 7-7 |
| 11-17-84 | *Union (N.Y.) | Plymouth St. | 26-14 |
| 11-17-84 | *Central (Iowa) | Occidental | 23-22 |
| 11-17-84 | *Augustana (Ill.) | Dayton | 14-13 |
| 12-8-84 | **Augustana (Ill.)** | **Central (Iowa)** | 21-12 |
| 11-23-85 | *Gettysburg | Lycoming | 14-10 |
| 11-23-85 | **Mount Union** | **Denison** | 35-3 |
| 11-23-85 | *Salisbury St. | Carnegie Mellon | 35-22 |
| 11-23-85 | *Ithaca | Union (N.Y.) | 13-12 |
| 12-7-85 | **Augustana (Ill.)** | **Central (Iowa)** | 14-7 |
| 11-15-86 | †Lawrence | Coe | 14-10 |

| Date | Spoiler | Victim | Score |
|------|---------|--------|-------|
| 11-22-86 | *Mount Union | Dayton | 42-36 |
| 11-22-86 | *Ithaca | Union (N.Y.) | OT 24-17 |
| 11-29-86 | *Concordia-M'head | Central (Iowa) | 17-14 |
| 11-29-86 | *Salisbury St. | Susquehanna | 31-17 |
| 11-29-86 | *Augustana (Ill.) | Mount Union | 16-7 |
| 12-6-86 | *Salisbury St. | Ithaca | 44-40 |
| 12-13-86 | *Augustana (Ill.) | Salisbury St. | 31-3 |
| 11-11-87 | St. Norbert | †Monmouth (Ill.) | 20-15 |
| 11-21-87 | *St. John's (Minn.) | Gust. Adolphus | 7-3 |
| 11-28-87 | *Emory & Henry | Wash. & Jeff. | 23-16 |
| 11-28-87 | $*Dayton | Augustana (Ill.) | 38-36 |
| 11-12-88 | †St. Norbert | Monmouth (Ill.) | 12-0 |
| 11-19-88 | Coast Guard | †Plymouth St. | 28-19 |
| 11-26-88 | *Ithaca | Cortland St. | 24-17 |
| 12-3-88 | *Ithaca | Ferrum | 62-28 |
| 11-11-89 | †Baldwin-Wallace | John Carroll | 25-19 |
| 11-11-89 | †Bri'water (Mass.) | Mass.-Lowell | 14-10 |
| 11-11-89 | †Centre | Rhodes | 13-10 |
| 11-18-89 | †Alfred | Bri'water (Mass.) | 30-27 |
| 11-25-89 | *St. John's (Minn.) | Central (Iowa) | 27-24 |
| 11-25-89 | *Dayton | Millikin | 28-16 |
| 12-9-89 | *Dayton | Union (N.Y.) | 17-7 |
| 11-10-90 | Trenton St. | †Ramapo | 9-0 |
| 11-10-90 | †Waynesburg | Frostburg St. | 28-18 |
| 11-17-90 | *Allegheny | Mount Union | 26-15 |
| 11-17-90 | *Lycoming | Carnegie Mellon | 17-7 |
| 11-17-90 | *St. Thomas (Minn.) | Wis.-Whitewater | 24-23 |
| 11-24-90 | *Allegheny | Dayton | 31-23 |
| 11-24-90 | *Lycoming | Wash. & Jeff. | 24-0 |
| 12-1-90 | *Lycoming | Hofstra | 20-10 |
| 12-8-90 | *Allegheny | Lycoming | OT 21-14 |
| 11-9-91 | †Coe | Beloit | 26-10 |
| 11-23-91 | *Union (N.Y.) | Mass.-Lowell | 55-16 |
| 11-23-91 | *Dayton | Baldwin-Wallace | 27-10 |
| 11-30-91 | *Dayton | Allegheny | OT 28-25 |
| 11-30-91 | *Ithaca | Union (N.Y.) | 35-23 |
| 11-30-91 | *Susquehanna | Lycoming | 31-24 |
| 12-7-91 | *Dayton | St. John's (Minn.) | 19-7 |
| 12-14-91 | *Ithaca | Dayton | 34-20 |
| 11-7-92 | Cornell College | †Coe | 37-20 |
| 11-7-92 | Union (N.Y.) | †Rochester | 14-10 |
| 11-21-92 | *Ill. Wesleyan | Aurora | 21-12 |
| 11-21-92 | *Mount Union | Dayton | 27-10 |
| 11-28-92 | *Mount Union | Ill. Wesleyan | 49-27 |
| 11-28-92 | *Wash. & Jeff. | Emory & Henry | 51-15 |
| 11-28-92 | *Wis.-La Crosse | Central (Iowa) | 34-9 |
| 12-5-92 | *Wash. & Jeff. | Rowan | 18-13 |
| 12-5-92 | *Wis.-La Crosse | Mount Union | 29-24 |

‡ *NAIA championship playoff game.   # Defeated three consecutive perfect-record teams in the Division III championship play-offs.   $ Ended Augustana's (Ill.) 60-game undefeated streak.*

# CLIFFHANGERS

Regular-season Division III games won on the final play of the game in regulation time (from 1973). The extra point is listed when it provided the margin of victory after the winning touchdown.

| Date | Opponents, Score | Game-winning play |
|------|------------------|-------------------|
| 9-22-73 | Hofstra 21, Seton Hall 20 | Tom Calder 15 pass from Steve Zimmer (Jim Hogan kick) |
| 9-18-76 | Ohio Wesleyan 23, DePauw 20 | Tom Scurfield 48 pass from Bob Mauck |
| 10-27-77 | Albany (N.Y.) 42, Maine 39 | Larry Leibowitz 19 FG |
| 9-22-79 | Augustana (Ill.) 19, Carthage 18 | John Stockton 14 pass from Mark Schick |
| 10-6-79 | Carleton 17, Lake Forest 14 | Tim Schoonmaker 46 FG |
| 11-10-79 | Dayton 24, St. Norbert 22 | Jim Fullenkamp 21 FG |
| 9-13-80 | Cornell College 14, Lawrence 13 | John Bryant 8 pass from Matt Dillon (Keith Koehler kick) |

| Date | Opponents, Score | Game-winning play |
|---|---|---|
| 9-27-80 | Muhlenberg 41, Johns Hopkins 38 | Mickey Mottola 1 run |
| 10-25-80 | Mass.-Lowell 15, Marist 13 | Ed Kulis 3 run |
| 10-17-81 | Carleton 22, Ripon 21 | John Winter 23 pass from Billy Ford (Dave Grein kick) |
| 10-2-82 | Frostburg St. 10, Mercyhurst 7 | Mike Lippold 34 FG |
| 11-6-82 | Williams 27, Wesleyan 24 | Marc Hummon 33 pass from Robert Connolly |
| 10-7-83 | Johns Hopkins 19, Ursinus 17 | John Tucker 10 pass from Mark Campbell |
| 10-8-83 | Susquehanna 17, Widener 14 | Todd McCarthy 20 FG |
| 10-29-83 | Frank. & Marsh. 16, Swarthmore 15 | Billy McLean 51 pass from Niall Rosenzweig |
| 9-24-84 | Muhlenberg 3, Frank. & Marsh. 0 | Tom Mulroy 26 FG |
| 10-26-85 | Buffalo 13, Brockport St. 11 | Dan Friedman 37 FG |
| 11-9-85 | Frank. & Marsh. 29, Johns Hopkins 28 | Brad Ramsey 1 run (Ken Scalet pass from John Travagline) |
| 9-18-86 | Beloit 16, Lakeland 13 | Sean Saturnio 38 pass from Ed Limon |
| 9-20-86 | Susquehanna 43, Lycoming 42 | Rob Sochovka 40 pass from Todd Coolidge (Randy Pozsar kick) |
| 10-18-86 | Ill. Wesleyan 25, Elmhurst 23 | Dave Anderson 11 pass from Doug Moews |
| 9-5-87 | Wash. & Jeff. 17, Ohio Wesleyan 16 | John Ivory 28 FG |
| 9-26-87 | Gust. Adolphus 19, Macalester 17 | Dave Fuecker 8 pass from Dean Kraus |
| 10-3-87 | Wis.-Whitewater 10, Wis.-Platteville 7 | Dave Emond 25 FG |
| 10-24-87 | Geneva 9, St. Francis (Pa.) 7 | John Moores 19 FG |
| 10-1-88 | Canisius 17, Rochester 14 | Jim Ehrig 34 FG |
| 10-1-88 | Cortland St. 24, Western Conn. St. 21 | Ted Nagengast 35 FG |
| 10-8-88 | UC Santa Barb. 20, Sonoma St. 18 | Harry Konstantinopoulos 52 FG |
| 10-8-88 | Hamilton 13, Bowdoin 10 | Nate O'Steen 19 FG |
| 11-5-88 | Colby 20, Middlebury 18 | Eric Aulenback 1 run |
| 11-12-88 | Wis.-River Falls 24, Wis.-Stout 23 | Andy Feil 45 FG |
| 10-7-89 | Moravian 13, Juniata 10 | Mike Howey 75 pass from Rob Light |
| 10-21-89 | Western New Eng. 17, Bentley 14 | Leo Coughlin 17 FG |
| 10-21-89 | Thiel 19, Carnegie Mellon 14 | Bill Barber 4 pass from Jeff Sorenson |
| 9-8-90 | Emory & Henry 22, Wash. & Lee 21 | Todd Woodall 26 pass from Pat Walker |
| 9-15-90 | Otterbein 20, Capital 17 | Korey Brown 39 FG |
| 10-27-90 | Hamline 26, Gust. Adolphus 24 | Mike Sunnarborg 2 pass from Bob Hackney |
| 11-10-90 | Colby 23, Bowdoin 20 | Paul Baisley 10 pass from Bob Ward |
| 9-7-91 | Central (Iowa) 26, Gust. Adolphus 25 | Brian Krob 1 pass from Shad Flynn |
| 9-13-91 | St. John's (N.Y.) 30, Iona 27 | John Ledwith 42 FG |
| 10-5-91 | Trinity (Conn.) 30, Williams 27 | John Mullaney 5 pass from James Lane |
| 10-26-91 | DePauw 12, Anderson 7 | Steve Broderick 65 pass from Brian Goodman |
| 10-17-92 | Elmhurst 30, North Central 28 | Eric Ekstrom 2 pass from Jack Lamb |

## REGULAR-SEASON OVERTIME GAMES

In 1981, the NCAA Football Rules Committee approved an overtime tie-breaker system to decide a tie game for the purpose of determining a conference champion. The following conferences are currently using the tie-breaker system to decide conference-only tie games. The number of overtimes is indicated in parentheses.

### IOWA INTERCOLLEGIATE ATHLETIC CONFERENCE

| Date | Opponents, Score | Date | Opponents, Score |
|---|---|---|---|
| 9-26-81 | William Penn 24, Wartburg 21 (1 OT) | 9-26-87 | William Penn 19, Upper Iowa 13 (2 OT) |
| 9-25-82 | Dubuque 16, Buena Vista 13 (1 OT) | 11-7-87 | William Penn 17, Loras 10 (1 OT) |
| 10-2-82 | Luther 25, Dubuque 22 (1 OT) | 10-10-92 | Simpson 20, Loras 14 (1 OT) |
| 10-30-82 | Wartburg 27, Dubuque 24 (3 OT) | 11-14-92 | Luther 17, Buena Vista 10 (1 OT) |
| 10-4-86 | Luther 28, Wartburg 21 (1 OT) | | |

### MIDWEST COLLEGIATE ATHLETIC CONFERENCE

| Date | Opponents, Score | Date | Opponents, Score |
|---|---|---|---|
| 10-25-86 | Lake Forest 30, Chicago 23 (1 OT) | 9-30-89 | Illinois Col. 26, Ripon 20 (3 OT) |
| 10-26-86 | Lawrence 7, Beloit 0 (1 OT) | 10-27-90 | Beloit 16, St. Norbert 10 (1 OT) |

### NEW ENGLAND FOOTBALL CONFERENCE
#### (From 1987)

| Date | Opponents, Score | Date | Opponents, Score |
|---|---|---|---|
| 10-31-87 | Nichols 21, Mass.-Lowell 20 (1 OT) | 10-28-89 | Worcester St. 27, Nichols 20 (1 OT) |
| 9-17-88 | Mass.-Lowell 22, Worcester St. 19 (2 OT) | 11-7-92 | Mass.-Dartmouth 21, Westfield St. 14 (3 OT) |
| 9-30-89 | Worcester St. 23, Mass.-Dartmouth 20 (1 OT) | | |

### SOUTHERN CALIFORNIA INTERCOLLEGIATE ATHLETIC CONFERENCE

| Date | Opponents, Score | Date | Opponents, Score |
|---|---|---|---|
| 10-18-86 | La Verne 53, Occidental 52 (1 OT) | 10-27-90 | Occidental 47, Claremont-M-S 41 (1 OT) |
| 9-26-87 | Claremont-M-S 33, Occidental 30 (1 OT) | 10-17-92 | Cal Lutheran 17, Occidental 14 (1 OT) |

# ALL-TIME WINNINGEST NON-NCAA MEMBER TEAMS

Minimum of 20 seasons of varsity competition. Postseason games are included, and each tie game is computed as half won and half lost.

## BY PERCENTAGE

| Team | Yrs. | Won | Lost | Tied | Pct. | Post-season |
|------|------|-----|------|------|------|-------------|
| Missouri Valley | 69 | 443 | 168 | 33 | .714 | 7-6-2 |
| N'western (Iowa) | 33 | 215 | 105 | 7 | .668 | 13-8-0 |
| Linfield | 78 | 388 | 209 | 30 | .643 | 17-12-0 |
| Central St. (Ohio) | 71 | 391 | 214 | 31 | .639 | 15-9-0 |
| Arkansas Tech | 72 | 394 | 233 | 36 | .639 | 0-1-0 |
| William Jewell | 104 | 494 | 283 | 52 | .627 | 1-1-0 |
| Minot St. | 68 | 289 | 167 | 29 | .626 | 2-3-0 |
| Pacific Lutheran | 58 | 314 | 189 | 27 | .618 | 16-9-1 |
| St. Ambrose | 59 | 293 | 188 | 27 | .603 | 0-1-0 |
| Westminster (Pa.) | 97 | 466 | 306 | 50 | .597 | 22-8-1 |
| Baker | 85 | 425 | 288 | 39 | .591 | 5-4-0 |
| Dickinson St. | 67 | 276 | 190 | 25 | .588 | 4-6-0 |
| Central Wash. | 74 | 329 | 235 | 22 | .580 | 5-7-0 |
| Carroll (Mont.) | 71 | 282 | 203 | 16 | .579 | 1-4-0 |
| Peru St. | 92 | 421 | 308 | 49 | .573 | 6-2-0 |
| Puget Sound | 84 | 362 | 270 | 35 | .569 | 0-1-0 |
| Hastings | 94 | 391 | 291 | 51 | .568 | 2-3-0 |
| Doane | 97 | 418 | 317 | 50 | .564 | 1-1-1 |
| N'eastern Okla. St. | 70 | 334 | 262 | 30 | .558 | 6-8-0 |
| Bethany (Kan.) | 80 | 377 | 297 | 30 | .557 | 2-6-0 |
| Valley City St. | 79 | 302 | 239 | 28 | .555 | 1-2-0 |
| Jamestown | 72 | 303 | 243 | 26 | .552 | 0-1-0 |
| Western Ore. | 77 | 306 | 247 | 17 | .552 | 0-3-0 |
| Ouachita Baptist | 86 | 389 | 314 | 42 | .550 | 1-3-0 |
| Benedictine | 60 | 291 | 238 | 17 | .549 | 3-2-0 |
| Southern Ark. | 61 | 306 | 255 | 21 | .544 | 1-0-1 |
| Ottawa | 85 | 381 | 318 | 39 | .543 | 0-0-0 |
| S'western (Kan.) | 87 | 401 | 337 | 47 | .541 | 2-3-0 |
| Willamette | 92 | 371 | 313 | 39 | .540 | 0-2-0 |
| S'western Okla. St. | 83 | 363 | 329 | 37 | .523 | 2-2-0 |
| Lewis & Clark | 47 | 213 | 195 | 12 | .521 | 1-2-0 |
| East Central | 80 | 368 | 338 | 38 | .520 | 1-5-0 |
| South Dak. Tech | 90 | 314 | 302 | 43 | .509 | 0-0-0 |
| Howard Payne | 87 | 371 | 357 | 41 | .509 | 1-2-0 |
| Geneva | 98 | 400 | 388 | 50 | .507 | 2-1-0 |
| Austin | 92 | 366 | 369 | 39 | .498 | 2-4-0 |
| Black Hills St. | 90 | 310 | 321 | 35 | .492 | 0-0-0 |
| Concordia (Neb.) | 53 | 219 | 227 | 20 | .491 | 0-0-0 |
| Southern Ore. | 59 | 234 | 245 | 16 | .489 | 0-0-0 |
| Langston | 69 | 287 | 301 | 29 | .489 | 1-4-0 |
| S'eastern Okla. St. | 82 | 331 | 355 | 43 | .484 | 1-1-0 |
| Huron | 90 | 303 | 328 | 39 | .481 | 0-1-0 |
| Kan. Wesleyan | 83 | 314 | 340 | 38 | .461 | 0-0-0 |
| Western Wash. | 76 | 273 | 296 | 34 | .481 | 0-0-0 |
| Teikyo Westmar | 78 | 278 | 304 | 34 | .479 | 0-1-0 |
| Midland Lutheran | 98 | 331 | 373 | 40 | .472 | 0-0-0 |
| McMurry | 67 | 277 | 332 | 33 | .457 | 1-2-0 |

# INDIVIDUAL COLLEGIATE RECORDS

*Barry Sanders' 1988 season remains perhaps the best ever by a collegiate rusher. The Oklahoma State running back set single-season records for rushing yards (2,628), rushing yards per game (238.9) and scoring (234 points). Each of these records is well ahead of the second-place entry on the respective all-time list.*

# INDIVIDUAL COLLEGIATE RECORDS

Individual collegiate records are determined by comparing the best records in all four divisions (I-A, I-AA, II and III) in comparable categories. Included are career records of players who played half their careers in two divisions (e.g., Dennis Shaw of San Diego St., Howard Stevens of Randolph-Macon and Louisville, and Tom Ehrhardt of LIU-C. W. Post and Rhode Island).

## TOTAL OFFENSE

### Career Yards Per Game
### (Minimum 20 Games)

| Player, Team (Division[s]) | Years | Games | Plays | Yards | TDR‡ | Yd. PG |
|---|---|---|---|---|---|---|
| Willie Totten, Mississippi Val. (I-AA) ...... | 1982-85 | 40 | 1,812 | 13,007 | *157 | *325.2 |
| Ty Detmer, Brigham Young (I-A) .......... | 1988-91 | 46 | 1,795 | *14,665 | 135 | 318.8 |
| Neil Lomax, Portland St. (II; I-AA)........ | 1977; 78-80 | 42 | 1,901 | 13,345 | 120 | 317.7 |
| Kirk Baumgartner, Wis.-Stevens Point (III) | 1986-89 | 41 | 2,007 | 12,767 | 110 | 311.4 |
| Mike Perez, San Jose St. (I-A) ........... | 1986-87 | 20 | 875 | 6,182 | 37 | 309.1 |
| Doug Gaynor, Long Beach St. (I-A) ...... | 1984-85 | 22 | 1,067 | 6,710 | 45 | 305.0 |
| Tod Mayfield, West Tex. St. (I-AA; II) ...... | 1984-85; 86 | 24 | 1,165 | 7,316 | 58 | 304.8 |
| Jamie Martin, Weber St. (I-AA)........... | 1989-92 | 41 | 1,838 | 12,287 | 93 | 299.7 |
| Tony Eason, Illinois (I-A) ................ | 1981-82 | 22 | 1,016 | 6,589 | 43 | 299.5 |
| Keith Bishop, Ill. Wes./Wheaton (Ill.) (III).. | 1981, 83-85 | 31 | 1,467 | 9,052 | 77 | 292.0 |
| David Klingler, Houston (I-A) ............ | 1988-91 | 32 | 1,431 | 9,327 | 93 | 291.5 |
| Stan Greene, Boston U. (I-AA) ........... | 1989-90 | 22 | 1,167 | 6,408 | 49 | 291.3 |
| John Friesz, Idaho (I-AA) ................ | 1986-89 | 35 | 1,459 | 10,187 | 79 | 291.1 |
| Steve Young, Brigham Young (I-A)....... | 1981-83 | 31 | 1,177 | 8,817 | 74 | 284.4 |
| Jayson Merrill, Western St. (II) ........... | 1990-91 | 20 | 641 | 5,619 | 57 | 281.0 |
| Andre Ware, Houston (I-A) .............. | 1987-89 | 29 | 1,194 | 8,058 | 81 | 277.9 |
| Chris Petersen, UC Davis (II) ............ | 1985-86 | 20 | 735 | 5,532 | 52 | 276.6 |
| Tim Von Dulm, Portland St. (II) .......... | 1969-70 | 20 | 989 | 5,501 | 51 | 275.1 |
| John Rooney, Ill. Wesleyan (III) ......... | 1982-84 | 27 | 1,260 | 7,363 | 71 | 273.8 |
| Tim Peterson, Wis.-Stout (III) ............ | 1986-89 | 36 | 1,558 | 9,701 | 59 | 269.5 |
| Doug Flutie, Boston College (I-A)........ | 1981-84 | 42 | 1,558 | 11,317 | 74 | 269.5 |
| Bret Snyder, Utah St. (I-A) .............. | 1987-88 | 22 | 1,040 | 5,916 | 43 | 268.9 |
| Dennis Shaw, San Diego St. (II; I-A) ...... | 1968; 69 | 20 | 682 | 5,371 | 72 | 268.6 |

\* Record.   ‡ Touchdowns-responsible-for are player's TDs scored and passed for.

### Season Yards Per Game

| Player, Team (Division) | Year | Games | Plays | Yards | TDR‡ | Yd. PG |
|---|---|---|---|---|---|---|
| David Klingler, Houston (I-A) .............. | †1990 | 11 | *704 | *5,221 | 55 | *474.6 |
| Willie Totten, Mississippi Val. (I-AA) ......... | †1984 | 10 | 564 | 4,572 | *61 | 457.2 |
| Andre Ware, Houston (I-A).................. | †1989 | 11 | 628 | 4,661 | 49 | 423.7 |
| Ty Detmer, Brigham Young (I-A) ............ | 1990 | 12 | 635 | 5,022 | 45 | 418.5 |
| Steve McNair, Alcorn St. (I-AA) ............. | †1992 | 10 | 519 | 4,057 | 39 | 405.7 |
| Steve Young, Brigham Young (I-A).......... | †1983 | 11 | 531 | 4,346 | 41 | 395.1 |
| Jamie Martin, Weber St. (I-AA)............. | †1991 | 11 | 591 | 4,337 | 37 | 394.3 |
| Scott Mitchell, Utah (I-A).................. | †1988 | 11 | 589 | 4,299 | 29 | 390.8 |
| Jim McMahon, Brigham Young (I-A)........ | †1980 | 12 | 540 | 4,627 | 53 | 385.6 |
| Neil Lomax, Portland St. (I-AA) ............ | †1980 | 11 | 550 | 4,157 | 42 | 377.9 |
| Ty Detmer, Brigham Young (I-A) ............ | 1989 | 12 | 497 | 4,433 | 38 | 369.4 |
| Troy Kopp, Pacific (Cal.) (I-A) .............. | 1990 | 9 | 485 | 3,276 | 32 | 364.0 |
| Neil Lomax, Portland St. (I-AA) ............ | †1979 | 11 | 611 | 3,966 | 31 | 360.5 |
| Keith Bishop, Wheaton (Ill.) (III) ........... | †1983 | 9 | 421 | 3,193 | 24 | 354.8 |
| Kirk Baumgartner, Wis.-Stevens Point (III) ... | †1989 | 10 | 530 | 3,540 | 39 | 354.0 |
| Rob Tomlinson, Cal St. Chico (II) ........... | †1989 | 10 | 533 | 3,504 | 26 | 350.4 |
| John Friesz, Idaho (I-AA) ................. | †1989 | 11 | 464 | 3,853 | 31 | 350.3 |
| Todd Hammel, Stephen F. Austin (I-AA) ..... | 1989 | 11 | 487 | 3,822 | 38 | 347.5 |
| Tom Ehrhardt, Rhode Island (I-AA) ......... | †1985 | 10 | 529 | 3,460 | 35 | 346.0 |
| Jim McMahon, Brigham Young (I-A)........ | †1981 | 10 | 487 | 3,458 | 30 | 345.8 |
| Ken Hobart, Idaho (I-AA) .................. | †1983 | 11 | 578 | 3,800 | 37 | 345.5 |
| Kirk Baumgartner, Wis.-Stevens Point (III) ... | †1988 | 11 | 604 | 3,790 | 27 | 344.5 |
| Chris Hegg, Northeast Mo. St. (II)........... | †1985 | 11 | 594 | 3,782 | 35 | 343.8 |
| Jordan Poznick, Principia (III)............. | †1992 | 8 | 519 | 2,747 | 25 | 343.4 |
| Jimmy Klingler, Houston (I-A) .............. | †1992 | 11 | 544 | 3,768 | 34 | 342.5 |
| Dave Stireman, Weber St. (I-AA) ........... | 1985 | 11 | 502 | 3,759 | 33 | 341.7 |
| Bob Toledo, San Fran. St. (II) ............. | †1967 | 10 | 409 | 3,407 | 46 | 340.7 |
| Willie Totten, Mississippi Val. (I-AA) ......... | 1985 | 11 | 561 | 3,742 | 43 | 340.2 |

\* Record.   † National total-offense champion.   ‡ Touchdowns-responsible-for are player's TDs scored and passed for.

*1993 NCAA FOOTBALL*

## Career Yards

| Player, Team (Division[s]) | Years | Plays | Yards | Avg. |
|---|---|---|---|---|
| Ty Detmer, Brigham Young (I-A) | 1988-91 | 1,795 | *14,665 | *8.17 |
| Neil Lomax, Portland St. (II; I-AA) | 1977; 78-80 | 1,901 | 13,345 | 7.02 |
| Willie Totten, Mississippi Val. (I-AA) | 1982-85 | 1,812 | 13,007 | 7.18 |
| Kirk Baumgartner, Wis.-Stevens Point (III) | 1986-89 | 2,007 | 12,767 | 6.36 |
| Jamie Martin, Weber St. (I-AA) | 1989-92 | 1,838 | 12,287 | 6.68 |
| Doug Flutie, Boston College (I-A) | 1981-84 | 1,558 | 11,317 | 7.26 |
| Ken Hobart, Idaho (I-AA) | 1980-83 | 1,847 | 11,127 | 6.02 |
| Alex Van Pelt, Pittsburgh (I-A) | 1989-92 | 1,570 | 10,814 | 6.89 |
| Earl Harvey, N.C. Central (II) | 1985-88 | *2,045 | 10,667 | 5.22 |
| Todd Santos, San Diego St. (I-A) | 1984-87 | 1,722 | 10,513 | 6.11 |
| Sean Payton, Eastern Ill. (I-AA) | 1983-86 | 1,690 | 10,298 | 6.09 |
| Greg Wyatt, Northern Ariz. (I-AA) | 1986-89 | 1,753 | 10,277 | 5.86 |
| Kevin Sweeney, Fresno St. (I-A) | $1982-86 | 1,700 | 10,252 | 6.03 |
| John Friesz, Idaho (I-AA) | 1986-89 | 1,459 | 10,187 | 6.98 |
| Troy Kopp, Pacific (Cal.) (I-A) | 1989-92 | 1,595 | 10,037 | 6.29 |
| Michael Proctor, Murray St. (I-AA) | 1986-89 | 1,577 | 9,886 | 6.27 |
| Jeff Wiley, Holy Cross (I-AA) | 1985-88 | 1,428 | 9,877 | 6.92 |
| Tom Ehrhardt, LIU-C. W. Post (II); R. I. (I-AA) | 1981-82; 84-85 | 1,674 | 9,793 | 5.85 |
| Brian McClure, Bowling Green (I-A) | 1982-85 | 1,630 | 9,774 | 6.00 |
| Jim McMahon, Brigham Young (I-A) | 1977-78, 80-81 | 1,325 | 9,723 | 7.34 |
| Tim Peterson, Wis.-Stout (III) | 1986-89 | 1,558 | 9,701 | 6.23 |
| Terrence Jones, Tulane (I-A) | 1985-88 | 1,620 | 9,445 | 5.83 |
| David Klingler, Houston (I-A) | 1988-91 | 1,431 | 9,327 | 6.52 |
| Shawn Jones, Georgia Tech (I-A) | 1989-92 | 1,609 | 9,296 | 5.78 |
| Matt DeGennaro, Connecticut (I-AA) | 1987-90 | 1,619 | 9,269 | 5.73 |
| Shane Matthews, Florida (I-A) | 1989-92 | 1,397 | 9,241 | 6.61 |
| Sam Mannery, Calif. (Pa.) (II) | 1987-90 | 1,669 | 9,125 | 5.47 |
| T. J. Rubley, Tulsa (I-A) | 1987-89, 91 | 1,541 | 9,080 | 5.89 |
| Brad Tayles, Western Mich. (I-AA) | 1989-92 | 1,675 | 9,071 | 5.42 |
| John Elway, Stanford (I-A) | 1979-82 | 1,505 | 9,070 | 6.03 |
| Tom Ciaccio, Holy Cross (I-AA) | 1988-91 | 1,283 | 9,066 | 7.07 |
| Erik Wilhelm, Oregon St. (I-A) | 1985-88 | 1,689 | 9,062 | 5.37 |
| Ben Bennett, Duke (I-A) | 1980-83 | 1,582 | 9,061 | 5.73 |
| Keith Bishop, Ill. Wesleyan/Wheaton (Ill.) (III) | 1981, 83-85 | 1,467 | 9,052 | 6.17 |
| Chuck Long, Iowa (I-A) | $1981-85 | 1,411 | 9,034 | 6.40 |

* Record.   $ See page 8 for explanation.

## Season Yards

| Player, Team (Division) | Year | Games | Plays | Yards | Avg. |
|---|---|---|---|---|---|
| David Klingler, Houston (I-A) | †1990 | 11 | *704 | *5,221 | 7.42 |
| Ty Detmer, Brigham Young (I-A) | 1990 | 12 | 635 | 5,022 | 7.91 |
| Andre Ware, Houston (I-A) | †1989 | 11 | 628 | 4,661 | 7.42 |
| Jim McMahon, Brigham Young (I-A) | †1980 | 12 | 540 | 4,627 | 8.57 |
| Willie Totten, Mississippi Val. (I-AA) | †1984 | 10 | 564 | 4,572 | 8.11 |
| Ty Detmer, Brigham Young (I-A) | 1989 | 12 | 497 | 4,433 | @8.92 |
| Steve Young, Brigham Young (I-A) | †1983 | 11 | 531 | 4,346 | 8.18 |
| Jamie Martin, Weber St. (I-AA) | †1991 | 11 | 591 | 4,337 | 7.34 |
| Scott Mitchell, Utah (I-A) | †1988 | 11 | 589 | 4,299 | 7.30 |
| Neil Lomax, Portland St. (I-AA) | †1980 | 11 | 550 | 4,157 | 7.56 |
| Robbie Bosco, Brigham Young (I-A) | 1985 | 13 | 578 | 4,141 | 7.16 |
| Steve McNair, Alcorn St. (I-AA) | †1992 | 10 | 519 | 4,057 | 7.82 |
| Ty Detmer, Brigham Young (I-A) | †1991 | 12 | 478 | 4,001 | 8.37 |
| Neil Lomax, Portland St. (I-AA) | †1979 | 11 | 611 | 3,966 | 6.49 |
| Robbie Bosco, Brigham Young (I-A) | †1984 | 12 | 543 | 3,932 | 7.24 |
| John Friesz, Idaho (I-AA) | †1989 | 11 | 464 | 3,853 | 8.30 |
| Todd Hammel, Stephen F. Austin (I-AA) | 1989 | 11 | 487 | 3,822 | 7.85 |
| Ken Hobart, Idaho (I-AA) | 1983 | 11 | 578 | 3,800 | 6.57 |
| Kirk Baumgartner, Wis.-Stevens Point (III) | †1988 | 11 | 604 | 3,790 | 6.27 |
| Chris Hegg, Northeast Mo. St. (II) | †1985 | 11 | 594 | 3,782 | 6.37 |
| Jimmy Klingler, Houston (I-A) | †1992 | 11 | 544 | 3,768 | 6.93 |
| Dave Stireman, Weber St. (I-AA) | 1985 | 11 | 502 | 3,759 | 7.49 |
| Willie Totten, Mississippi Val. (I-AA) | 1985 | 11 | 561 | 3,742 | 6.67 |
| Jeff Wiley, Holy Cross (I-AA) | †1987 | 11 | 445 | 3,722 | 8.36 |
| Jamie Martin, Weber St. (I-AA) | 1990 | 11 | 508 | 3,713 | 7.31 |
| Anthony Dilweg, Duke (I-A) | 1988 | 11 | 539 | 3,713 | 6.89 |
| Kirk Baumgartner, Wis.-Stevens Point (III) | 1987 | 11 | 561 | 3,712 | 6.62 |

* Record.   † National total-offense champion.   @ Record for minimum of 3,000 yards.

## Single-Game Yards

| Yds. | Div. | Player, Team (Opponent) | Date |
|---|---|---|---|
| 732 | I-A | David Klingler, Houston (Arizona St.) | Dec. 2, 1990 |
| 696 | I-A | Matt Vogler, Texas Christian (Houston) | Nov. 3, 1990 |
| 643 | I-AA | Jamie Martin, Weber St. (Idaho St.) | Nov. 23, 1991 |
| 625 | I-A | David Klingler, Houston (Texas Christian) | Nov. 3, 1990 |
| 625 | I-A | Scott Mitchell, Utah (Air Force) | Oct. 15, 1988 |
| 621 | I-AA | Willie Totten, Mississippi Val. (Prairie View) | Oct. 27, 1984 |
| 612 | I-A | Jimmy Klingler, Houston (Rice) | Nov. 28,1992 |
| 604 | I-AA | Steve McNair, Alcorn St. (Jackson St.) | Nov. 21, 1992 |
| 603 | I-A | Ty Detmer, Brigham Young (San Diego St.) | Nov. 16, 1991 |
| 601 | I-A | Troy Kopp, Pacific, Cal. (New Mexico St.) | Oct. 20, 1990 |
| 599 | I-A | Virgil Carter, Brigham Young (UTEP) | Nov. 5, 1966 |
| 596 | III | John Love, North Park (Elmhurst) | Oct. 13, 1990 |
| 595 | I-AA | Doug Pederson, Northeast La. (Stephen F. Austin) | Nov. 11, 1989 |
| 594 | I-A | Jeremy Leach, New Mexico (Utah) | Nov. 11, 1989 |
| 587 | I-AA | Vern Harris, Idaho St. (Montana) | Oct. 12, 1985 |
| 585 | I-A | Dave Wilson, Illinois (Ohio St.) | Nov. 8, 1980 |
| 584 | II | Tracy Kendall, Alabama A&M (Clark Atlanta) | Nov. 4, 1989 |
| 582 | I-A | Marc Wilson, Brigham Young (Utah) | Nov. 5, 1977 |
| 578 | I-A | David Klingler, Houston (Eastern Wash.) | Nov. 17, 1990 |
| 571 | II | John Charles, Portland St. (Cal Poly SLO) | Nov. 16, 1991 |
| 566 | I-AA | Tom Ehrhardt, Rhode Island (Connecticut) | Nov. 16, 1985 |
| 564 | III | Tim Lynch, Hofstra (Fordham) | Oct. 19, 1991 |
| 562 | I-AA | Todd Hammel, Stephen F. Austin (Northeast La.) | Nov. 11, 1989 |
| 562 | I-A | Ty Detmer, Brigham Young (Washington St.) | Sept. 7, 1989 |
| 562 | II | Bob Toledo, San Fran. St. (Cal St. Hayward) | Oct. 21, 1967 |
| 561 | I-AA | Willie Totten, Mississippi Val. (Southern-B.R.) | Sept. 29, 1984 |
| 555 | II | A. J. Vaughn, Wayne St., Mich. (Wis.-Milwaukee) | Sept. 30, 1967 |

# RUSHING

## Career Yards Per Game
### (Minimum 18 Games)

| Player, Team (Division[s]) | Years | G | Plays | Yards | TD | Yd. PG |
|---|---|---|---|---|---|---|
| Ed Marinaro, Cornell (I-A) | 1969-71 | 27 | 918 | 4,715 | 50 | *174.6 |
| O.J. Simpson, Southern Cal (I-A) | 1967-68 | 19 | 621 | 3,214 | 33 | 164.4 |
| Johnny Bailey, Texas A&I (II) | 1986-89 | 39 | 885 | *6,320 | 66 | 162.1 |
| Herschel Walker, Georgia (I-A) | 1980-82 | 33 | 994 | 5,259 | 49 | 159.4 |
| Terry Underwood, Wagner (III) | 1985-88 | 33 | 742 | 5,010 | 52 | 151.8 |
| Ole Gunderson, St. Olaf (II) | 1969-71 | 27 | 639 | 4,060 | 56 | 150.4 |
| Brad Hustad, Luther (II) | 1957-59 | 27 | 655 | 3,943 | 25 | 146.0 |
| Tony Dorsett, Pittsburgh (I-A) | 1973-76 | 43 | 1,074 | 6,082 | 55 | 141.4 |
| Joe Iacone, West Chester (II) | 1960-62 | 27 | 565 | 3,767 | 40 | 139.5 |
| Howard Stevens, Rand.-Macon (II); Louisville (I-A) | 1968-69; 71-72 | 38 | 891 | 5,297 | 58 | 139.4 |
| Mike Rozier, Nebraska (I-A) | 1981-83 | 35 | 668 | 4,780 | 50 | 136.6 |
| Joe Dudek, Plymouth St. (III) | 1982-85 | 41 | 785 | 5,570 | *76 | 135.9 |
| Jerome Persell, Western Mich. (I-A) | 1976-78 | 31 | 842 | 4,190 | 39 | 135.2 |

* Record.

## Season Yards Per Game

| Player, Team (Division) | Year | Games | Plays | Yards | TD | Yd. PG |
|---|---|---|---|---|---|---|
| Barry Sanders, Oklahoma St. (I-A) | †1988 | 11 | 344 | *2,628 | *37 | *238.9 |
| Marcus Allen, Southern Cal (I-A) | †1981 | 11 | *403 | 2,342 | 22 | 212.9 |
| Ed Marinaro, Cornell (I-A) | †1971 | 9 | 356 | 1,881 | 24 | 209.0 |
| Ricky Gales, Simpson (III) | †1989 | 10 | 297 | 2,035 | 26 | 203.5 |
| Terry Underwood, Wagner (III) | †1988 | 9 | 245 | 1,809 | 21 | 201.0 |
| Kirk Matthieu, Maine Maritime (III) | †1992 | 9 | 327 | 1,733 | 16 | 192.6 |
| Jon Warga, Wittenberg (III) | †1990 | 10 | 254 | 1,836 | 15 | 183.6 |
| Johnny Bailey, Texas A&I (II) | †1986 | 11 | 271 | 2,011 | 18 | 182.8 |
| Bob White, Western N. Mex. (II) | †1951 | 9 | 202 | 1,643 | 20 | 182.6 |
| Kevin Mitchell, Saginaw Valley (II) | 1989 | 8 | 236 | 1,460 | 6 | 182.5 |
| Hank Wineman, Albion (III) | †1991 | 9 | 307 | 1,629 | 14 | 181.0 |
| Charles White, Southern Cal (I-A) | †1979 | 10 | 293 | 1,803 | 18 | 180.3 |
| Eric Grey, Hamilton (III) | 1991 | 8 | 217 | 1,439 | 13 | 179.9 |
| Mike Birosak, Dickinson (III) | 1989 | 10 | 380 | 1,798 | 18 | 179.8 |
| Don Aleksiewicz, Hobart (II) | †1971 | 9 | 276 | 1,616 | 19 | 179.6 |

| Player, Team (Division) | Year | Games | Plays | Yards | TD | Yd. PG |
|---|---|---|---|---|---|---|
| Mike Rozier, Nebraska (I-A) | †1983 | 12 | 275 | 2,148 | 29 | 179.0 |
| Jim Holder, Panhandle St. (II) | †1963 | 10 | 275 | 1,775 | 9 | 177.5 |
| Tony Dorsett, Pittsburgh (I-A) | †1976 | 11 | 338 | 1,948 | 21 | 177.1 |
| Chris Babirad, Wash. & Jeff. (III) | 1992 | 9 | 243 | 1,589 | 22 | 176.6 |
| Jim Baier, Wis.-River Falls (II) | †1966 | 9 | 240 | 1,587 | 17 | 176.3 |
| Ollie Matson, San Francisco (I-A) | †1951 | 9 | 245 | 1,566 | 20 | 174.0 |

* Record.   † National champion.

## Career Yards

| Player, Team (Division[s]) | Years | Plays | Yards | Avg. |
|---|---|---|---|---|
| Johnny Bailey, Texas A&I (II) | 1986-89 | 885 | *6,320 | 7.14 |
| Tony Dorsett, Pittsburgh (I-A) | 1973-76 | 1,074 | 6,082 | 5.66 |
| Charles White, Southern Cal (I-A) | 1976-79 | 1,023 | 5,598 | 5.47 |
| Joe Dudek, Plymouth St. (III) | 1982-85 | 785 | 5,570 | 7.10 |
| Frank Hawkins, Nevada (I-AA) | 1977-80 | 945 | 5,333 | 5.64 |
| Howard Stevens, Rand.-Macon (II); Louisville (I-A) | 1968-69; 71-72 | 891 | 5,297 | 5.95 |
| Eric Frees, Western Md. (III) | 1988-91 | 1,059 | 5,281 | 4.99 |
| Herschel Walker, Georgia (I-A) | 1980-82 | 994 | 5,259 | 5.29 |
| Kenny Gamble, Colgate (I-AA) | 1984-87 | 963 | 5,220 | 5.42 |
| Archie Griffin, Ohio St. (I-A) | 1972-75 | 845 | 5,177 | 6.13 |
| Markus Thomas, Eastern Ky. (I-AA) | 1989-92 | 784 | 5,149 | 6.57 |
| Shawn Graves, Wofford (QB) (II) | 1989-92 | 730 | 5,128 | 7.02 |
| Chris Cobb, Eastern Ill. (II) | 1976-79 | 930 | 5,042 | 5.42 |
| Darren Lewis, Texas A&M (I-A) | 1987-90 | 909 | 5,012 | 5.51 |
| Terry Underwood, Wagner (III) | 1985-88 | 742 | 5,010 | 6.75 |
| Anthony Thompson, Indiana (I-A) | 1986-89 | 1,089 | 4,965 | 4.56 |
| George Rogers, South Caro. (I-A) | 1977-80 | 902 | 4,958 | 5.50 |
| Trevor Cobb, Rice (I-A) | 1989-92 | 1,091 | 4,948 | 4.54 |
| Paul Palmer, Temple (I-A) | 1983-86 | 948 | 4,895 | 5.16 |
| Harry Jackson, St. Cloud St. (II) | 1986-89 | 915 | 4,890 | 5.34 |
| Jerry Linton, Panhandle St. (II) | 1959-62 | 648 | 4,839 | ‡7.47 |
| Steve Bartalo, Colorado St. (I-A) | 1983-86 | *1,215 | 4,813 | 3.96 |

* Record.   ‡ Record for minimum of 600 carries.

## Season Yards

| Player, Team (Division) | Year | Games | Plays | Yards | Avg. |
|---|---|---|---|---|---|
| Barry Sanders, Oklahoma St. (I-A) | †1988 | 11 | 344 | *2,628 | @7.64 |
| Marcus Allen, Southern Cal (I-A) | †1981 | 11 | *403 | 2,342 | 5.81 |
| Mike Rozier, Nebraska (I-A) | †1983 | 12 | 275 | 2,148 | ††7.81 |
| Ricky Gales, Simpson (III) | †1989 | 10 | 297 | 2,035 | 6.85 |
| Johnny Bailey, Texas A&I (II) | †1986 | 11 | 271 | 2,011 | 7.42 |
| Tony Dorsett, Pittsburgh (I-A) | †1976 | 11 | 338 | 1,948 | 5.76 |
| Lorenzo White, Michigan St. (I-A) | †1985 | 11 | 386 | 1,908 | 4.94 |
| Herschel Walker, Georgia (I-A) | †1981 | 11 | 385 | 1,891 | 4.91 |
| Rich Erenberg, Colgate (I-AA) | †1983 | 11 | 302 | 1,883 | 6.24 |
| Ed Marinaro, Cornell (I-A) | †1971 | 9 | 356 | 1,881 | 5.28 |
| Ernest Anderson, Oklahoma St. (I-A) | †1982 | 11 | 353 | 1,877 | 5.32 |
| Ricky Bell, Southern Cal (I-A) | †1975 | 11 | 357 | 1,875 | 5.25 |
| Paul Palmer, Temple (I-A) | †1986 | 11 | 346 | 1,866 | 5.39 |
| Ronald Moore, Pittsburg St. (II) | 1992 | 11 | 239 | 1,864 | 7.80 |
| Jon Warga, Wittenberg (III) | †1990 | 10 | 254 | 1,836 | 7.23 |
| Zed Robinson, Southern Utah (II) | 1991 | 11 | 254 | 1,828 | 7.20 |
| Kenny Gamble, Colgate (I-AA) | †1986 | 11 | 307 | 1,816 | 5.92 |
| Terry Underwood, Wagner (III) | †1988 | 9 | 245 | 1,809 | 6.75 |
| Charles White, Southern Cal (I-A) | †1979 | 10 | 293 | 1,803 | 6.15 |

* Record.   † National champion.   †† Record for minimum of 214 carries.   @ Record for minimum of 282 carries.

## Single-Game Yards

| Yds. | Div. | Player, Team (Opponent) | Date |
|---|---|---|---|
| 396 | I-A | Tony Sands, Kansas (Missouri) | Nov. 23, 1991 |
| 386 | I-A | Marshall Faulk, San Diego St. (Pacific, Cal.) | Sept. 14, 1991 |
| 382 | III | Pete Baranek, Carthage (North Central) | Oct. 5, 1985 |
| 382 | II | Kelly Ellis, Northern Iowa (Western Ill.) | Oct. 13, 1979 |
| 377 | I-A | Anthony Thompson, Indiana (Wisconsin) | Nov. 11, 1989 |
| 373 | II | Dallas Garber, Marietta (Wash. & Jeff.) | Nov. 7, 1959 |
| 370 | II | Jim Baier, Wis.-River Falls (Wis.-Stevens Point) | Nov. 5, 1966 |
| 370 | II | Jim Hissam, Marietta (Bethany, W. Va.) | Nov. 15, 1958 |
| 367 | II | Don Polkinghorne, Washington, Mo. (Wash. & Lee) | Nov. 23, 1957 |
| 363 | III | Terry Underwood, Wagner (Hofstra) | Oct. 15, 1988 |

*Individual Collegiate Records*

| Yds. | Div. | Player, Team (Opponent) | Date |
|---|---|---|---|
| 363 | II | Richie Weaver, Widener (Moravian) | Oct. 17, 1970 |
| 357 | I-A | Mike Pringle, Cal St. Fullerton (New Mexico St.) | Nov. 4, 1989 |
| 357 | I-A | Rueben Mayes, Washington St. (Oregon) | Oct. 27, 1984 |
| 356 | I-A | Eddie Lee Ivery, Georgia Tech (Air Force) | Nov. 11, 1978 |
| 356 | II | Ole Gunderson, St. Olaf (Monmouth, Ill.) | Oct. 11, 1969 |
| 354 | III | Terry Underwood, Wagner (Western Conn. St.) | Oct. 3, 1986 |
| 350 | II | Ricke Stonewall, Millersville (New Haven) | Nov. 13, 1982 |
| 350 | I-A | Eric Allen, Michigan St. (Purdue) | Oct. 30, 1971 |

# PASSING

## Career Passing Efficiency
### (Minimum 475 Completions)

| Player, Team (Division[s]) | Years | Att. | Cmp. | Int. | Pct. | Yds. | TD | Pts. |
|---|---|---|---|---|---|---|---|---|
| Ty Detmer, Brigham Young (I-A) | 1988-91 | 1,530 | *958 | 65 | .626 | *15,031 | 121 | *162.7 |
| Jim McMahon, Brigham Young (I-A) | 1977-78, 80-81 | 1,060 | 653 | 34 | .616 | 9,536 | 84 | 156.9 |
| Steve Young, Brigham Young (I-A) | 1981-83 | 908 | 592 | 33 | .652 | 7,733 | 56 | 149.8 |
| Jack Hull, Grand Valley St. (II) | 1988-91 | 835 | 485 | 22 | .581 | 7,120 | 64 | 149.7 |
| Robbie Bosco, Brigham Young (I-A) | 1983-85 | 997 | 638 | 36 | .640 | 8,400 | 66 | 149.4 |
| Elvis Grbac, Michigan (I-A) | 1989-92 | 754 | 477 | 29 | .633 | 5,859 | 64 | 148.9 |
| Chuck Long, Iowa (I-A) | $1981-85 | 1,072 | 692 | 46 | .646 | 9,210 | 64 | 147.8 |
| Willie Totten, Mississippi Val. (I-AA) | 1982-85 | 1,555 | 907 | *75 | .583 | 12,711 | *139 | 146.8 |
| Mike Smith, Northern Iowa (I-AA) | 1984-87 | 943 | 557 | 43 | .591 | 8,219 | 58 | 143.5 |
| Neil Lomax, Portland St. (II; I-AA) | 1977; 78-80 | 1,606 | 938 | 55 | .584 | 13,220 | 106 | 142.5 |
| Tom Ciaccio, Holy Cross (I-AA) | 1988-91 | 1,073 | 658 | 46 | .613 | 8,603 | 72 | 142.2 |
| George Bork, Northern Ill. (II) | 1960-63 | 902 | 577 | 33 | .640 | 6,782 | 60 | 141.8 |
| Eric Beavers, Nevada (I-AA) | 1983-86 | 1,094 | 646 | 37 | .591 | 8,626 | 77 | 141.8 |
| Doug Gaynor, Long Beach St. (I-A) | 1984-85 | 837 | 569 | 35 | .680 | 6,793 | 35 | 141.6 |
| Matt Jozokos, Plymouth St. (III) | 1987-90 | 1,003 | 527 | 39 | .525 | 7,658 | 95 | 140.2 |
| Dan McGwire, Iowa/San Diego St. (I-A) | 1986-87, 89-90 | 973 | 575 | 30 | .591 | 8,164 | 49 | 140.0 |
| John Elway, Stanford (I-A) | 1979-82 | 1,246 | 774 | 39 | .621 | 9,349 | 77 | 139.3 |
| Jamie Martin, Weber St. (I-AA) | 1989-92 | 1,544 | 934 | 56 | .605 | 12,207 | 87 | 138.2 |
| David Klingler, Houston (I-A) | 1988-91 | 1,261 | 726 | 38 | .576 | 9,430 | 91 | 138.2 |
| Doug Williams, Grambling (II; I-A) | 1974-76; 77 | 1,009 | 484 | 52 | .480 | 8,411 | 93 | 138.1 |

*Record.  $ See page 8 for explanation.*

## Career Passing Efficiency
### (Minimum 325-474 Completions)

| Player, Team (Division[s]) | Years | Att. | Cmp. | Int. | Pct. | Yds. | TD | Pts. |
|---|---|---|---|---|---|---|---|---|
| John Charles, Portland St. (II) | 1991-92 | 510 | 326 | 14 | .639 | 5,389 | 56 | *183.4 |
| Tony Aliucci, Indiana (Pa.) (II) | 1988-91 | 579 | 350 | 24 | .604 | 5,655 | 53 | 164.4 |
| Jayson Merrill, Western St. (II) | 1990-91 | 580 | 328 | 25 | .566 | 5,830 | 56 | 164.2 |
| Chris Petersen, UC Davis (II) | 1985-86 | 553 | 385 | 13 | *.696 | 4,988 | 39 | 164.0 |
| Dennis Shaw, San Diego St. (II; I-A) | 1968; 69 | 575 | 333 | 41 | .579 | 5,324 | 58 | 154.7 |
| Joe Blake, Simpson (III) | 1987-90 | 672 | 399 | 15 | .594 | 6,183 | 43 | 153.3 |
| Vinny Testaverde, Miami (Fla.) (I-A) | 1982, 84-86 | 674 | 413 | 25 | .613 | 6,058 | 48 | 152.9 |
| Jim McMillan, Boise St. (II) | 1971-74 | 640 | 382 | 29 | .597 | 5,508 | 58 | 152.8 |
| Willie Reyna, La Verne (III) | 1991-92 | 542 | 346 | 19 | .638 | 4,712 | 37 | 152.4 |
| Troy Aikman, Oklahoma/UCLA (I-A) | 84-85, 87-88 | 637 | 401 | 18 | .630 | 5,436 | 40 | 149.7 |
| Jim Harbaugh, Michigan (I-A) | 1983-86 | 582 | 368 | 19 | .632 | 5,215 | 31 | 149.6 |
| Chuck Hartlieb, Iowa (I-A) | 1985-88 | 716 | 461 | 17 | .643 | 6,269 | 34 | 148.9 |
| Jay Johnson, Northern Iowa (I-AA) | 1989-92 | 744 | 397 | 25 | .534 | 7,049 | 51 | 148.9 |
| Danny White, Arizona St. (I-A) | 1971-73 | 649 | 345 | 36 | .532 | 5,932 | 59 | 148.9 |
| Gary Collier, Emory & Henry (III) | 1984-87 | 738 | 386 | 33 | .523 | 6,103 | 80 | 148.6 |
| Kenneth Biggles, Tennessee St. (I-AA) | 1981-84 | 701 | 397 | 28 | .566 | 5,933 | 57 | 146.6 |
| Gifford Nielsen, Brigham Young (I-A) | 1975-77 | 708 | 415 | 29 | .586 | 5,833 | 55 | 145.3 |
| Greg Heeres, Hope (III) | 1981-84 | 630 | 347 | 21 | .537 | 5,120 | 53 | 144.4 |
| Bruce Upstill, Col. of Emporia (II) | 1960-63 | 769 | 438 | 36 | .570 | 6,935 | 48 | 144.0 |
| Tom Ramsey, UCLA (I-A) | 1979-82 | 691 | 411 | 33 | .595 | 5,844 | 48 | 143.9 |
| Shawn Moore, Virginia (I-A) | 1987-90 | 762 | 421 | 32 | .552 | 6,629 | 55 | 143.8 |
| Jerry Rhome, SMU/Tulsa (I-A) | 1961, 63-64 | 713 | 448 | 23 | .628 | 5,472 | 47 | 142.6 |
| Jim Zaccheo, Nevada (I-AA) | 1987-88 | 554 | 326 | 27 | .588 | 4,750 | 35 | 142.0 |
| Bruce Crosthwaite, Adrian (III) | 1984-87 | 618 | 368 | 31 | .596 | 4,959 | 45 | 141.0 |
| Steve Mariucci, Northern Mich. (II) | 1974-77 | 678 | 380 | 33 | .561 | 6,022 | 41 | 140.9 |
| Jim Karsatos, Ohio St. (I-A) | 1983-86 | 573 | 330 | 19 | .576 | 4,698 | 36 | 140.6 |
| Jason Garrett, Princeton (I-AA) | 1987-88 | 550 | 368 | 10 | .669 | 4,274 | 20 | 140.6 |
| Scott Barry, UC Davis (II) | 1982-84 | 588 | 377 | 16 | .641 | 4,421 | 33 | 140.4 |
| Jerry Tagge, Nebraska (I-A) | 1969-71 | 581 | 348 | 19 | .599 | 4,704 | 33 | 140.1 |

*Record.*

## Season Passing Efficiency
### (Minimum 30 Attempts Per Game)

| Player, Team (Division) | Year | G | Att. | Cmp. | Int. | Pct. | Yds. | TD | Pts. |
|---|---|---|---|---|---|---|---|---|---|
| Jayson Merrill, Western St. (II) ........ | †1991 | 10 | 309 | 195 | 11 | .631 | 3,484 | 35 | *187.9 |
| John Charles, Portland St. (II) ........ | 1992 | 8 | 263 | 179 | 7 | .681 | 2,770 | 24 | 181.3 |
| Jim McMahon, Brigham Young (I-A) .. | †1980 | 12 | 445 | 284 | 18 | .638 | 4,571 | 47 | 176.9 |
| Ty Detmer, Brigham Young (I-A) ...... | †1989 | 12 | 412 | 265 | 15 | .643 | 4,560 | 32 | 175.6 |
| Jerry Rhome, Tulsa (I-A) .............. | †1964 | 10 | 326 | 224 | 4 | .687 | 2,870 | 32 | 172.6 |
| Ty Detmer, Brigham Young (I-A) ...... | 1991 | 12 | 403 | 249 | 12 | .618 | 4,031 | 35 | 168.5 |
| Steve Young, Brigham Young (I-A) ... | †1983 | 11 | 429 | 306 | 10 | *.713 | 3,902 | 33 | 168.5 |
| Willie Totten, Mississippi Val. (I-AA) ... | †1983 | 9 | 279 | 174 | 9 | .624 | 2,566 | 29 | 167.5 |
| Jim McMillan, Boise St. (II) ........... | †1974 | 10 | 313 | 192 | 15 | .613 | 2,900 | 33 | 164.4 |
| Willie Totten, Mississippi Val. (I-AA) ... | †1984 | 10 | 518 | 324 | 22 | .626 | 4,557 | *56 | 163.6 |
| Jeff Wiley, Holy Cross (I-AA) .......... | †1987 | 11 | 400 | 265 | 17 | .663 | 3,677 | 34 | 163.0 |
| Todd Hammel, Stephen F. Austin (I-AA) | †1989 | 11 | 401 | 238 | 13 | .594 | 3,914 | 34 | 162.8 |
| Dennis Shaw, San Diego St. (I-A) ..... | †1969 | 10 | 335 | 199 | 26 | .594 | 3,185 | 39 | 162.2 |
| John Friesz, Idaho (I-AA) ............. | 1989 | 11 | 425 | 260 | 8 | .612 | 4,041 | 31 | 161.4 |
| Willie Reyna, La Verne (III) ........... | 1991 | 8 | 267 | 170 | 6 | .636 | 2,543 | 16 | 158.8 |
| George Bork, Northern Ill. (II) ........ | 1963 | 9 | 374 | 244 | 12 | .652 | 2,824 | 32 | 156.2 |
| Neil Lomax, Portland St. (I-AA) ...... | 1980 | 11 | 473 | 296 | 12 | .626 | 4,094 | 37 | 156.0 |
| Ty Detmer, Brigham Young (I-A) ...... | 1990 | 12 | 562 | 361 | 28 | .642 | *5,188 | 41 | 155.9 |
| Doug Williams, Grambling (I-A) ...... | 1977 | 11 | 352 | 181 | 18 | .514 | 3,286 | 38 | 155.2 |
| Jim McMahon, Brigham Young (I-A) .. | †1981 | 10 | 423 | 272 | 7 | .643 | 3,555 | 30 | 155.0 |
| Andy Breault, Kutztown (II) ........... | 1991 | 10 | 360 | 225 | 20 | .625 | 2,927 | 37 | 153.4 |
| Chuck Long, Iowa (I-A) .............. | 1985 | 11 | 351 | 231 | 15 | .658 | 2,978 | 26 | 153.0 |
| Doug Flutie, Boston College (I-A) .... | 1984 | 11 | 386 | 233 | 11 | .604 | 3,454 | 27 | 152.9 |

* Record.   † National pass-efficiency champion.

## Season Passing Efficiency
### (Minimum 15 Attempts Per Game)

| Player, Team (Division) | Year | G | Att. | Cmp. | Int. | Pct. | Yds. | TD | Pts. |
|---|---|---|---|---|---|---|---|---|---|
| Boyd Crawford, Col. of Idaho (II) ..... | †1953 | 8 | 120 | 72 | 6 | .600 | 1,462 | 21 | *210.1 |
| Chuck Green, Wittenberg (II) .......... | †1963 | 9 | 182 | 114 | 8 | .626 | 2,181 | 19 | 189.0 |
| Jim Feeley, Johns Hopkins (II) ........ | †1967 | 7 | 110 | 69 | 5 | .627 | 1,264 | 12 | 186.2 |
| John Charles, Portland St. (II) ........ | 1991 | 11 | 247 | 147 | 7 | .595 | 2,619 | 32 | 185.5 |
| Steve Smith, Western St. (II) ......... | †1992 | 10 | 271 | 180 | 5 | .664 | 2,719 | 30 | 183.5 |
| Mitch Sanders, Bridgeport (III) ........ | †1973 | 10 | 151 | 84 | 7 | .556 | 1,551 | 23 | 182.9 |
| Jim Peterson, Hanover (II) ........... | †1948 | 8 | 125 | 81 | 12 | .648 | 1,571 | 12 | 182.9 |
| John Wristen, Southern Colo. (II) ..... | †1982 | 8 | 121 | 68 | 2 | .562 | 1,358 | 13 | 182.5 |
| Michael Payton, Marshall (I-AA) ...... | †1991 | 9 | 216 | 143 | 5 | .622 | 2,333 | 19 | 181.3 |
| Pat Mayew, St. John's (Minn.) (III) ... | †1991 | 9 | 247 | 154 | 4 | .623 | 2,408 | 30 | 181.0 |
| Richard Basil, Savannah St. (II) ....... | †1989 | 9 | 211 | 120 | 7 | .568 | 2,148 | 29 | 180.9 |
| Jim Cahoon, Ripon (II).............. | †1964 | 8 | 127 | 74 | 7 | .583 | 1,206 | 19 | 176.4 |
| Ken Suhl, New Haven (II) ............. | 1992 | 10 | 239 | 148 | 6 | .619 | 2,336 | 26 | 175.7 |
| Jimbo Fisher, Samford (III) ........... | †1987 | 10 | 252 | 139 | 5 | .551 | 2,394 | 34 | 175.7 |
| Gary Collier, Emory & Henry (III) ..... | 1987 | 11 | 249 | 152 | 10 | .610 | 2,317 | 33 | 174.8 |
| James Grant, Ramapo (III) ........... | 1989 | 9 | 147 | 91 | 7 | .619 | 1,441 | 17 | 172.7 |
| Tony Aliucci, Indiana (Pa.) (II) ........ | †1990 | 10 | 181 | 111 | 10 | .613 | 1,801 | 21 | 172.0 |
| Frank Baur, Lafayette (I-AA) .......... | †1988 | 10 | 256 | 164 | 11 | .641 | 2,621 | 23 | 171.1 |
| Bobby Lamb, Furman (I-AA) .......... | †1985 | 11 | 181 | 106 | 6 | .586 | 1,856 | 18 | 170.9 |
| Gary Urwiler, Eureka (III).............. | 1991 | 10 | 171 | 103 | 5 | .602 | 1,656 | 18 | 170.3 |
| John Costello, Widener (II) ........... | †1956 | 9 | 149 | 74 | 10 | .497 | 1,702 | 17 | 169.8 |
| Kurt Coduti, Michigan Tech (II) ....... | 1992 | 9 | 155 | 92 | 3 | .594 | 1,518 | 15 | 169.7 |
| Chris Petersen, UC Davis (II) ........ | †1985 | 10 | 242 | 167 | 8 | .690 | 2,366 | 17 | 169.4 |
| Jay Fiedler, Dartmouth (I-AA) ........ | †1992 | 10 | 273 | 175 | 13 | .641 | 2,748 | 25 | 169.4 |

* Record.   † National pass-efficiency champion.

## Career Yards

| Player, Team (Division[s]) | Years | Att. | Cmp. | Int. | Pct. | Yds. | TD |
|---|---|---|---|---|---|---|---|
| Ty Detmer, Brigham Young (I-A) .............. | 1988-91 | 1,530 | *958 | 65 | .626 | *15,031 | 121 |
| Neil Lomax, Portland St. (II; I-AA) ............ | 1977; 78-80 | 1,606 | 938 | 55 | .584 | 13,220 | 106 |
| Kirk Baumgartner, Wis.-Stevens Point (III) .... | 1986-89 | *1,696 | 883 | 57 | .521 | 13,028 | 110 |
| Willie Totten, Mississippi Val. (I-AA) .......... | 1982-85 | 1,555 | 907 | *75 | .583 | 12,711 | *139 |
| Jamie Martin, Weber St. (I-AA) .............. | 1989-92 | 1,544 | 934 | 56 | .605 | 12,207 | 87 |
| Todd Santos, San Diego St. (I-A) ........... | 1984-87 | 1,484 | 910 | 57 | .613 | 11,425 | 70 |
| Alex Van Pelt, Pittsburgh (I-A) .............. | 1989-92 | 1,463 | 845 | 59 | .578 | 10,913 | 64 |
| John Friesz, Idaho (I-AA) .................. | 1986-89 | 1,350 | 801 | 40 | .593 | 10,697 | 77 |
| Greg Wyatt, Northern Ariz. (I-AA) ........... | 1986-89 | 1,510 | 926 | 49 | .613 | 10,697 | 70 |
| Sean Payton, Eastern Ill. (I-AA) ............. | 1983-86 | 1,408 | 756 | 55 | .537 | 10,655 | 75 |

*Individual Collegiate Records*

## Player, Team (Division[s])

| Player, Team (Division[s]) | Years | Att. | Cmp. | Int. | Pct. | Yds. | TD |
|---|---|---|---|---|---|---|---|
| Kevin Sweeney, Fresno St. (I-A) | $1982-86 | 1,336 | 731 | 48 | .547 | 10,623 | 66 |
| Earl Harvey, N.C. Central (II) | 1985-88 | 1,442 | 690 | 81 | .479 | 10,621 | 86 |
| Doug Flutie, Boston College (I-A) | 1981-84 | 1,270 | 677 | 54 | .533 | 10,579 | 67 |
| Tom Ehrhardt, LIU-C.W. Post (II); R. I. (I-AA) | 1981-82; 84-85 | 1,489 | 833 | 63 | .559 | 10,325 | 92 |
| Brian McClure, Bowling Green (I-A) | 1982-85 | 1,427 | 900 | 58 | .631 | 10,280 | 63 |
| Troy Kopp, Pacific (Cal.) (I-A) | 1989-92 | 1,374 | 798 | 47 | .581 | 10,258 | 87 |
| Jeff Wiley, Holy Cross (I-AA) | 1985-88 | 1,208 | 723 | 63 | .599 | 9,698 | 71 |
| Ben Bennett, Duke (I-A) | 1980-83 | 1,375 | 820 | 57 | .596 | 9,614 | 53 |
| Keith Bishop, Ill. Wes./Wheaton (Ill.) (III) | 1981, 83-85 | 1,311 | 772 | 65 | .589 | 9,579 | 71 |
| Robbie Justino, Liberty (I-AA) | 1989-92 | 1,267 | 769 | 51 | .607 | 9,548 | 64 |
| Dennis Bogacz, Wis.-Oshkosh/ Wis.-Whitewater (III) | 1988-89, 90-91 | 1,275 | 654 | 59 | .513 | 9,536 | 66 |
| Jim McMahon, Brigham Young (I-A) | 1977-78, 80-81 | 1,060 | 653 | 34 | .616 | 9,536 | 84 |
| Todd Ellis, South Caro. (I-A) | 1986-89 | 1,266 | 704 | 66 | .556 | 9,519 | 97 |
| Dave Geissler, Wis.-Stevens Point (III) | 1982-85 | 1,346 | 789 | 57 | .586 | 9,518 | 65 |
| David Klingler, Houston (I-A) | 1988-91 | 1,261 | 726 | 38 | .576 | 9,430 | 91 |
| Erik Wilhelm, Oregon St. (I-A) | 1985-88 | 1,480 | 870 | 61 | .588 | 9,393 | 52 |
| Jeremy Leach, New Mexico (I-A) | 1988-91 | 1,432 | 735 | 62 | .513 | 9,382 | 50 |
| John Elway, Stanford (I-A) | 1979-82 | 1,246 | 774 | 39 | .621 | 9,349 | 77 |
| T. J. Rubley, Tulsa (I-A) | 1987-89, 91 | 1,336 | 682 | 54 | .510 | 9,324 | 73 |
| Kirk Schulz, Villanova (I-AA) | 1986-89 | 1,297 | 774 | 70 | .597 | 9,305 | 70 |
| Ken Hobart, Idaho (I-AA) | 1980-83 | 1,219 | 629 | 42 | .516 | 9,300 | 79 |

* Record.  $ See page 8 for explanation.

## Career Yards Per Game
### (Minimum 20 Games)

| Player, Team (Division[s]) | Years | G | Att. | Cmp. | Int. | Pct. | Yds. | TD | Yd. PG |
|---|---|---|---|---|---|---|---|---|---|
| Ty Detmer, Brigham Young (I-A) | 1988-91 | 46 | 1,530 | *958 | 65 | .626 | *15,031 | 121 | *326.8 |
| Willie Totten, Mississippi Val. (I-AA) | 1982-85 | 40 | 1,555 | 907 | *75 | .583 | 12,711 | *139 | 317.8 |
| Kirk Baumgartner, Wis.-Stevens Pt. (III) | 1986-89 | 41 | *1,696 | 883 | 57 | .521 | 13,028 | 110 | 317.8 |
| Neil Lomax, Portland St. (II; I-AA) | 77;78-80 | 42 | 1,606 | 938 | 55 | .584 | 13,220 | 106 | 314.8 |
| Mike Perez, San Jose St. (I-A) | 1986-87 | 20 | 792 | 471 | 30 | .595 | 6,194 | 36 | 309.7 |
| Keith Bishop, Ill. Wes./Wheaton (Ill.) (III) | 81,83-85 | 31 | 1,311 | 772 | 65 | .589 | 9,579 | 71 | 309.0 |
| Doug Gaynor, Long Beach St. (I-A) | 1984-85 | 22 | 837 | 569 | 35 | .680 | 6,793 | 35 | 308.8 |
| John Friesz, Idaho (I-AA) | 1986-89 | 35 | 1,350 | 801 | 40 | .593 | 10,697 | 77 | 305.6 |
| Tony Eason, Illinois (I-A) | 1981-82 | 22 | 856 | 526 | 29 | .615 | 6,608 | 37 | 300.4 |

* Record.

## Career Touchdown Passes

| Player, Team (Division[s]) | Years | Att. | Cmp. | Int. | Pct. | Yds. | TD |
|---|---|---|---|---|---|---|---|
| Willie Totten, Mississippi Val. (I-AA) | 1982-85 | 1,555 | 907 | *75 | .583 | 12,711 | *139 |
| Ty Detmer, Brigham Young (I-A) | 1988-91 | 1,530 | *958 | 65 | .626 | *15,031 | 121 |
| Kirk Baumgartner, Wis.-Stevens Point (III) | 1986-89 | *1,696 | 883 | 57 | .521 | 13,028 | 110 |
| Neil Lomax, Portland St. (II; I-AA) | 1977; 78-80 | 1,606 | 938 | 55 | .584 | 13,220 | 106 |
| Matt Jozokos, Plymouth St. (III) | 1987-90 | 1,003 | 527 | 39 | .525 | 7,658 | 95 |
| Doug Williams, Grambling (II; I-A); Rhode Island (I-AA) | 1974-76; 77 | 1,009 | 484 | 52 | .480 | 8,411 | 93 |
| Tom Ehrhardt, LIU-C. W. Post (II); Rhode Island (II); | 1981-82; 84-85 | 1,489 | 833 | 63 | .559 | 10,325 | 92 |
| David Klingler, Houston (I-A) | 1988-91 | 1,261 | 726 | 38 | .576 | 9,430 | 91 |
| Troy Kopp, Pacific (Cal.) (I-A) | 1989-92 | 1,374 | 798 | 47 | .581 | 10,258 | 87 |
| Jamie Martin, Weber St. (I-AA) | 1989-92 | 1,544 | 934 | 56 | .605 | 12,207 | 87 |
| Andy Breault, Kutztown (II) | 1989-92 | 1,259 | 733 | 63 | .582 | 9,086 | 86 |
| Earl Harvey, N. C. Central (II) | 1985-88 | 1,442 | 690 | 81 | .479 | 10,621 | 86 |
| Jim McMahon, Brigham Young (I-A) | 1977-78, 80-81 | 1,060 | 653 | 34 | .616 | 9,536 | 84 |
| Joe Adams, Tennessee St. (I-AA) | 1977-80 | 1,100 | 604 | 60 | .549 | 8,649 | 81 |
| Gary Collier, Emory & Henry (III) | 1984-87 | 738 | 386 | 33 | .523 | 6,103 | 80 |
| Ken Hobart, Idaho (I-AA) | 1980-83 | 1,219 | 629 | 42 | .516 | 9,300 | 79 |

* Record.

## Season Yards

| Player, Team (Division) | Year | G | Att. | Cmp. | Int. | Pct. | Yds. | TD |
|---|---|---|---|---|---|---|---|---|
| Ty Detmer, Brigham Young (I-A) | †1990 | 12 | 562 | 361 | 28 | .642 | *5,188 | 41 |
| David Klingler, Houston (I-A) | 1990 | 11 | *643 | *374 | 20 | .582 | 5,140 | 54 |
| Andre Ware, Houston (I-A) | †1989 | 11 | 578 | 365 | 15 | .631 | 4,699 | 46 |
| Jim McMahon, Brigham Young (I-A) | †1980 | 12 | 445 | 284 | 18 | .638 | 4,571 | 47 |
| Ty Detmer, Brigham Young (I-A) | 1989 | 12 | 412 | 265 | 15 | .643 | 4,560 | 32 |

*1993 NCAA FOOTBALL*

| Player, Team (Division) | Year | G | Att. | Cmp. | Int. | Pct. | Yds. | TD |
|---|---|---|---|---|---|---|---|---|
| Willie Totten, Mississippi Val. (I-AA) .......... | †1984 | 10 | 518 | 324 | 22 | .626 | 4,557 | *56 |
| Scott Mitchell, Utah (I-A)...................... | 1988 | 11 | 533 | 323 | 15 | .606 | 4,322 | 29 |
| Robbie Bosco, Brigham Young (I-A) ......... | 1985 | 13 | 511 | 338 | 24 | .661 | 4,257 | 30 |
| Jamie Martin, Weber St. (I-AA)............... | 1991 | 11 | 500 | 310 | 17 | .620 | 4,125 | 35 |
| Neil Lomax, Portland St. (I-AA) ............... | 1980 | 11 | 473 | 296 | 12 | .626 | 4,094 | 37 |
| John Friesz, Idaho (I-AA) .................... | †1989 | 11 | 425 | 260 | 8 | .612 | 4,041 | 31 |
| Ty Detmer, Brigham Young (I-A) ............. | 1991 | 12 | 403 | 249 | 12 | .618 | 4,031 | 35 |
| Neil Lomax, Portland St. (I-AA) .............. | 1979 | 11 | 516 | 299 | 16 | .579 | 3,950 | 26 |
| Todd Santos, San Diego St. (I-A) ........... | 1987 | 12 | 492 | 306 | 15 | .622 | 3,932 | 26 |
| Todd Hammel, Stephen F. Austin (I-AA) ..... | 1989 | 11 | 401 | 238 | 13 | .594 | 3,914 | 34 |
| Steve Young, Brigham Young (I-A).......... | †1983 | 11 | 429 | 306 | 10 | *.713 | 3,902 | 33 |
| Robbie Bosco, Brigham Young (I-A) ......... | 1984 | 12 | 458 | 283 | 11 | .618 | 3,875 | 33 |
| Sean Payton, Eastern Ill. (I-AA) ............. | 1984 | 11 | 473 | 270 | 15 | .571 | 3,843 | 28 |
| Dan McGwire, San Diego St. (I-A) .......... | 1990 | 11 | 449 | 270 | 7 | .601 | 3,833 | 27 |
| Kirk Baumgartner, Wis.-Stevens Point (III) ... | 1988 | 11 | 527 | 276 | 16 | .524 | 3,828 | 25 |
| Anthony Dilweg, Duke (I-A)................... | 1988 | 11 | 484 | 287 | 18 | .593 | 3,824 | 24 |
| Jimmy Klingler, Houston (I-A) ................ | 1992 | 11 | 504 | 303 | 18 | .601 | 3,818 | 32 |
| Sam King, Nevada-Las Vegas (I-A) .......... | 1981 | 12 | 433 | 255 | 19 | .589 | 3,778 | 18 |
| Troy Kopp, Pacific (Cal.) (I-A)............... | 1991 | 12 | 449 | 275 | 16 | .612 | 3,767 | 37 |
| Kirk Baumgartner, Wis.-Stevens Point (III) ... | 1987 | 11 | 466 | 243 | 22 | .521 | 3,755 | 31 |
| Chris Hegg, Northeast Mo. St. (II) .......... | 1985 | 11 | 503 | 284 | 20 | .565 | 3,741 | 32 |
| Marc Wilson, Brigham Young (I-A)........... | 1979 | 12 | 427 | 250 | 15 | .585 | 3,720 | 29 |

*Record.   † National pass-efficiency champion.*

## Season Yards Per Game

| Player, Team (Division) | Year | G | Att. | Cmp. | Int. | Pct. | Yds. | TD | Yd. PG |
|---|---|---|---|---|---|---|---|---|---|
| David Klingler, Houston (I-A) ......... | 1990 | 11 | *643 | *374 | 20 | .582 | 5,140 | 54 | *467.3 |
| Willie Totten, Mississippi Val. (I-AA) ... | 1984 | 10 | 518 | 324 | 22 | .626 | 4,557 | *56 | 455.7 |
| Ty Detmer, Brigham Young (I-A) ...... | 1990 | 12 | 562 | 361 | 28 | .642 | *5,188 | 41 | 432.3 |
| Andre Ware, Houston (I-A)............ | 1989 | 11 | 578 | 365 | 15 | .631 | 4,699 | 46 | 427.2 |
| Scott Mitchell, Utah (I-A)............. | 1988 | 11 | 533 | 323 | 15 | .606 | 4,322 | 29 | 392.9 |
| Jim McMahon, Brigham Young (I-A) .. | 1980 | 12 | 445 | 284 | 18 | .638 | 4,571 | 47 | 380.9 |
| Ty Detmer, Brigham Young (I-A) ...... | 1989 | 12 | 412 | 265 | 15 | .643 | 4,560 | 32 | 380.0 |

*Record.*

## Season Touchdown Passes

| Player, Team (Division) | Year | Att. | Cmp. | Int. | Pct. | Yds. | TD |
|---|---|---|---|---|---|---|---|
| Willie Totten, Mississippi Val. (I-AA) .......... | 1984 | 518 | 324 | 22 | .626 | 4,557 | *56 |
| David Klingler, Houston (I-A) ................... | 1990 | *643 | *374 | 20 | .582 | 5,140 | 54 |
| Jim McMahon, Brigham Young (I-A) ........... | 1980 | 445 | 284 | 18 | .638 | 4,571 | 47 |
| Andre Ware, Houston (I-A)..................... | 1989 | 578 | 365 | 15 | .631 | 4,699 | 46 |
| Bob Toledo, San Fran. St. (II) ................. | 1967 | 396 | 211 | 24 | .533 | 3,513 | 45 |
| Ty Detmer, Brigham Young (I-A) ............... | 1990 | 562 | 361 | 28 | .642 | *5,188 | 41 |
| Kirk Baumgartner, Wis.-Stevens Point (III) .... | 1989 | 455 | 247 | 9 | .542 | 3,692 | 39 |
| Willie Totten, Mississippi Val. (I-AA) .......... | 1985 | 492 | 295 | 29 | .600 | 3,698 | 39 |
| Dennis Shaw, San Diego St. (I-A) ............. | 1969 | 335 | 199 | 26 | .594 | 3,185 | 39 |
| Doug Williams, Grambling (I-A)............... | 1977 | 352 | 181 | 18 | .514 | 3,286 | 38 |
| Andy Breault, Kutztown (II) ................... | 1991 | 360 | 225 | 20 | .625 | 2,927 | 37 |
| Troy Kopp, Pacific (Cal.) (I-A) ................ | 1991 | 449 | 275 | 16 | .613 | 3,767 | 37 |
| Neil Lomax, Portland St. (I-AA) ............... | 1980 | 473 | 296 | 12 | .626 | 4,094 | 37 |
| Jayson Merrill, Western (II) .................... | 1991 | 309 | 195 | 11 | .631 | 3,484 | 35 |
| Ty Detmer, Brigham Young (I-A) ............... | 1991 | 403 | 249 | 12 | .618 | 4,031 | 35 |
| Jamie Martin, Weber St. (I-AA) ............... | 1991 | 500 | 310 | 17 | .620 | 4,125 | 35 |
| Tom Ehrhardt, Rhode Island (I-AA) ........... | 1985 | 497 | 283 | 19 | .569 | 3,542 | 35 |

*Record.*

## Single-Game Yards

| Yds. | Div. | Player, Team (Opponent) | Date |
|---|---|---|---|
| 716 | I-A | David Klingler, Houston (Arizona St.)................................... | Dec. 2, 1990 |
| 690 | I-A | Matt Vogler, Texas Christian (Houston) ................................ | Nov. 3, 1990 |
| 631 | I-A | Scott Mitchell, Utah (Air Force)........................................ | Oct. 15, 1988 |
| 624 | I-AA | Jamie Martin, Weber St. (Idaho St.) ................................... | Nov. 23, 1991 |
| 622 | I-A | Jeremy Leach, New Mexico (Utah) .................................... | Nov. 11, 1989 |
| 621 | I-A | Dave Wilson, Illinois (Ohio St.) ........................................ | Nov. 8, 1980 |
| 619 | I-AA | Doug Pederson, Northeast La. (Stephen F. Austin)...................... | Nov. 11, 1989 |
| 613 | I-A | Jimmy Klingler, Houston (Rice).......................................... | Nov. 28, 1992 |
| 599 | I-A | Ty Detmer, Brigham Young (San Diego St.) ............................ | Nov. 16, 1991 |
| 599 | I-AA | Willie Totten, Mississippi Val. (Prairie View) ........................... | Oct. 27, 1984 |

*Individual Collegiate Records*                                      289

| Yds. | Div. | Player, Team (Opponent) | Date |
|---|---|---|---|
| 592 | II | John Charles, Portland St. (Cal Poly SLO) | Nov. 16, 1991 |
| 589 | I-AA | Vern Harris, Idaho St. (Montana) | Oct. 12, 1985 |
| 585 | III | Tim Lynch, Hofstra (Fordham) | Oct. 19, 1991 |
| 585 | I-A | Robbie Bosco, Brigham Young (New Mexico) | Oct. 19, 1985 |
| 572 | I-A | David Klingler, Houston (Eastern Wash.) | Nov. 17, 1990 |
| 571 | I-AA | Todd Hammel, Stephen F. Austin (Northeast La.) | Nov. 11, 1989 |
| 571 | I-A | Marc Wilson, Brigham Young (Utah) | Nov. 5, 1977 |
| 568 | I-A | David Lowery, San Diego St. (Brigham Young) | Nov. 16, 1991 |
| 568 | II | Bob Toledo, San Fran. St. (Cal St. Hayward) | Oct. 21, 1967 |
| 566 | I-AA | Tom Ehrhardt, Rhode Island (Connecticut) | Nov. 16, 1985 |
| 565 | I-A | Jim McMahon, Brigham Young (Utah) | Nov. 21, 1981 |
| 564 | I-A | Troy Kopp, Pacific, Cal. (New Mexico St.) | Oct. 20, 1990 |
| 563 | I-A | David Klingler, Houston (Texas Christian) | Nov. 3, 1990 |
| 561 | I-A | Tony Adams, Utah St. (Utah) | Nov. 11, 1972 |

### Single-Game Attempts

| Atts. | Div. | Player, Team (Opponent) | Date |
|---|---|---|---|
| 81 | III | Jordan Poznick, Principia (Blackburn) | Oct. 10, 1992 |
| 79 | I-A | Matt Vogler, Texas Christian (Houston) | Nov. 3, 1990 |
| 79 | III | Mike Wallace, Ohio Wesleyan (Denison) | Oct. 3, 1981 |
| 77 | I-AA | Neil Lomax, Portland St. (Northern Colo.) | Oct. 20, 1979 |
| 76 | I-A | David Klingler, Houston (Southern Methodist) | Oct. 20, 1990 |
| 75 | I-A | Chris Vargas, Nevada (McNeese St.) | Sept. 19, 1992 |
| 74 | I-AA | Paul Peterson, Idaho St. (Nevada) | Oct. 1, 1983 |
| 73 | I-A | Jeff Handy, Missouri (Oklahoma St.) | Oct. 17, 1992 |
| 73 | I-A | Troy Kopp, Pacific, Cal. (Hawaii) | Oct. 27, 1990 |
| 73 | I-A | Shane Montgomery, North Caro. St. (Duke) | Nov. 11, 1989 |
| 72 | I-A | Matt Vogler, Texas Christian (Texas Tech) | Nov. 10, 1990 |
| 72 | II | Kurt Otto, North Dak. (Texas A&I) | Sept. 13, 1986 |
| 72 | III | Bob Lockhart, Millikin (Franklin) | Nov. 12, 1977 |
| 72 | II | Kaipo Spencer, Santa Clara (Portland St.) | Oct. 11, 1975 |
| 72 | II | Joe Stetser, Cal St. Chico (Oregon Tech) | Sept. 23, 1967 |

### Single-Game Completions

| Cmp. | Div. | Player, Team (Opponent) | Date |
|---|---|---|---|
| 50 | III | Tim Lynch, Hofstra (Fordham) | Oct. 19, 1991 |
| 48 | III | Jordan Poznick, Principia (Blackburn) | Oct. 10, 1992 |
| 48 | I-A | David Klingler, Houston (Southern Methodist) | Oct. 20, 1990 |
| 47 | I-AA | Jamie Martin, Weber St. (Idaho St.) | Nov. 23, 1991 |
| 47 | III | Mike Wallace, Ohio Wesleyan (Denison) | Oct. 3, 1981 |
| 46 | I-A | Jimmy Klingler, Houston (Rice) | Nov. 28, 1992 |
| 46 | I-AA | Doug Pederson, Northeast La. (Stephen F. Austin) | Nov. 11, 1989 |
| 46 | I-AA | Willie Totten, Mississippi Val. (Southern–B.R.) | Sept. 29, 1984 |
| 45 | I-AA | Willie Totten, Mississippi Val. (Prairie View) | Oct. 27, 1984 |
| 45 | I-A | Sandy Schwab, Northwestern (Michigan) | Oct. 23, 1982 |
| 44 | I-A | Matt Vogler, Texas Christian (Houston) | Nov. 3, 1990 |
| 44 | I-A | Chuck Hartlieb, Iowa (Indiana) | Oct. 29, 1988 |
| 44 | II | Tom Bonds, Cal Lutheran (St. Mary's, Cal.) | Nov. 22, 1986 |
| 44 | I-A | Jim McMahon, Brigham Young (Colorado St.) | Nov. 7, 1981 |
| 44 | I-AA | Neil Lomax, Portland St. (Northern Colo.) | Oct. 20, 1979 |
| 43 | I-A | Jeff Handy, Missouri (Oklahoma St.) | Oct. 17, 1992 |
| 43 | I-A | Chris Vargas, Nevada (McNeese St.) | Sept. 19, 1992 |
| 43 | I-A | Gary Schofield, Wake Forest (Maryland) | Oct. 17, 1981 |
| 43 | I-A | Dave Wilson, Illinois (Ohio St.) | Nov. 8, 1980 |
| 43 | I-A | Rich Campbell, California (Florida) | Sept. 13, 1980 |
| 43 | II | George Bork, Northern Ill. (Central Mich.) | Nov. 9, 1963 |

## RECEIVING
### Career Catches

| Player, Team (Division[s]) | Years | Catches | Yards | Avg. | TD |
|---|---|---|---|---|---|
| Jerry Rice, Mississippi Val. (I-AA) | 1981-84 | *301 | *4,693 | 15.6 | *50 |
| Kasey Dunn, Idaho (I-AA) | 1988-91 | 268 | 3,847 | 14.4 | 25 |
| Aaron Turner, Pacific (Cal.) (I-A) | 1989-92 | 266 | 4,345 | 16.3 | 43 |
| Terance Mathis, New Mexico (I-A) | 1985-87, 89 | 263 | 4,254 | 16.2 | 36 |
| Mark Templeton, Long Beach St. (I-A) (RB) | 1983-86 | ¢262 | 1,969 | 7.5 | 11 |
| Howard Twilley, Tulsa (I-A) | 1963-65 | 261 | 3,343 | 12.8 | 32 |
| Bill Stromberg, Johns Hopkins (III) | 1978-81 | 258 | 3,776 | 14.6 | 39 |
| Chris Myers, Kenyon (II) | 1967-70 | 253 | 3,897 | 15.4 | 33 |
| Brian Forster, Rhode Island (I-AA) (TE) | 1983-85, 87 | #245 | #3,410 | 13.9 | 31 |
| David Williams, Illinois (I-A) | 1983-85 | 245 | 3,195 | 13.0 | 22 |

Aaron Turner finished his career at Pacific (California) last season high on several all-time collegiate receiving lists, including career catches (266, third), career touchdown receptions (43, fifth) and career yards (4,345, third).

| Player, Team (Division[s]) | Years | Catches | Yards | Avg. | TD |
|---|---|---|---|---|---|
| Bruce Cerone, Yankton/Emporia St. (II) ....... | 1966-67, 68-69 | 241 | 4,354 | 18.1 | 49 |
| Mark Didio, Connecticut (I-AA) ................ | 1988-91 | 239 | 3,535 | 14.8 | 21 |
| Rennie Benn, Lehigh (I-AA).................... | 1982-85 | 237 | 3,662 | 15.5 | 44 |
| Marc Zeno, Tulane (I-A)........................ | 1984-87 | 236 | 3,725 | 15.8 | 25 |
| Jason Wolf, Southern Methodist (I-A) .......... | 1989-92 | 235 | 2,232 | 9.5 | 17 |
| Dale Amos, Frank. & Marsh. (III) | 1986-89 | 233 | 3,846 | 16.5 | 35 |
| Scott Fredrickson, Wis.-Stout (III) ............. | 1986-89 | 233 | 3,390 | 14.5 | 23 |
| Harold "Red" Roberts, Austin Peay (II) ........ | 1967-70 | 232 | 3,005 | 13.0 | 31 |
| Mike Whitehouse, St. Norbert (III) ............ | 1986-89 | 230 | 3,480 | 15.1 | 37 |
| Jerry Hendren, Idaho (II; I-A) ................. | 1967-68; 69 | 230 | 3,435 | 14.9 | 27 |

* Record.  ¢ Record for a running back.  # Record for a tight end.

### Career Catches Per Game
### (Minimum 18 Games)

| Player, Team (Division[s]) | Years | G | Catches | Yds. | TD | Ct. PG |
|---|---|---|---|---|---|---|
| Manny Hazard, Houston (I-A)............... | 1989-90 | 21 | 220 | 2,635 | 31 | *10.5 |
| Howard Twilley, Tulsa (I-A)................. | 1963-65 | 26 | 261 | 3,343 | 32 | 10.0 |
| Jason Phillips, Houston (I-A) .............. | 1987-88 | 22 | 207 | 2,319 | 18 | 9.4 |
| Ed Bell, Idaho St. (II) ...................... | 1968-69 | 19 | 163 | 2,608 | 30 | 8.6 |
| Jerry Hendren, Idaho (II).................... | 1967-69 | 30 | 230 | 3,435 | 27 | 7.7 |
| Neal Sweeney, Tulsa (I-A) ................. | 1965-66 | 18 | 134 | 1,623 | 11 | 7.4 |
| David Williams, Illinois (I-A) ............... | 1983-85 | 33 | 245 | 3,195 | 22 | 7.4 |
| Gary Garrison, San Diego St. (II) .......... | 1964-65 | 20 | 148 | 2,188 | 26 | 7.4 |
| Jerry Rice, Mississippi Val. (I-AA) .......... | 1981-84 | 41 | *301 | *4,693 | *50 | 7.3 |
| James Dixon, Houston (I-A) ............... | 1987-88 | 22 | 161 | 1,762 | 14 | 7.3 |

* Record.

### Career Touchdown Receptions

| Player, Team (Division[s]) | Years | Games | TD |
|---|---|---|---|
| Chris Bisaillon, Ill. Wesleyan (III) ........................... | 1989-92 | 36 | *55 |
| Jerry Rice, Mississippi Val. (I-AA) ........................... | 1981-84 | 41 | 50 |
| Bruce Cerone, Yankton/Emporia St. (II) .................... | 1966-67, 68-69 | 42 | 49 |
| Rennie Benn, Lehigh (I-AA)................................. | 1982-85 | 41 | 44 |
| Aaron Turner, Pacific (Cal.) (I-A) ........................... | 1989-92 | 44 | 43 |

| Player, Team (Division[s]) | Years | Games | TD |
|---|---|---|---|
| Shannon Sharpe, Savannah St. (II) .................... | 1986-89 | 42 | 40 |
| John Aromando, Trenton St. (III) ........................ | 1981-84 | 40 | 39 |
| Bill Stromberg, Johns Hopkins (III) ..................... | 1978-81 | 40 | 39 |
| Clarkston Hines, Duke (I-A)............................. | 1986-89 | 44 | 38 |
| Roy Banks, Eastern Ill. (I-AA) ......................... | 1983-86 | 38 | 38 |
| Robert Clark, N. C. Central (II)......................... | 1983-86 | 40 | 38 |
| Mike Jones, Tennessee St. (I-AA) ...................... | 1979-82 | 42 | 38 |
| Chris Holder, Tuskegee (II)............................. | 1988-91 | 40 | 37 |
| Mike Whitehouse, St. Norbert (III) ...................... | 1986-89 | 38 | 37 |
| Terance Mathis, New Mexico (I-A) ...................... | 1985-87, 89 | 44 | 36 |
| Mike Cottle, Juniata (III) ............................... | 1985-88 | 37 | 36 |
| Joe Thomas, Mississippi Val. (I-AA)..................... | 1982-85 | 41 | 36 |
| Willie Richardson, Jackson St. (II) ...................... | 1959-62 | 38 | 36 |

* Record.

## Season Catches

| Player, Team (Division) | Year | G | Catches | Yards | TD |
|---|---|---|---|---|---|
| Manny Hazard, Houston (I-A) ...................... | †1989 | 11 | *142 | 1,689 | 22 |
| Howard Twilley, Tulsa (I-A) ......................... | †1965 | 10 | 134 | 1,779 | 16 |
| Brian Forster, Rhode Island (I-AA) (TE) ............. | †1985 | 10 | 115 | 1,617 | 12 |
| Fred Gilbert, Houston (I-A) ......................... | †1991 | 11 | 106 | 957 | 7 |
| Barry Wagner, Alabama A&M (II) ................... | †1989 | 11 | 106 | *1,812 | 17 |
| Theo Blanco, Wis.-Stevens Point (III) (RB) ......... | 1987 | 11 | #106 | #1,616 | 8 |
| Sherman Smith, Houston (I-A) ...................... | †1992 | 11 | 103 | 923 | 6 |
| Jerry Rice, Mississippi Val. (I-AA) .................. | †1984 | 10 | 103 | 1,682 | *27 |
| Jerry Rice, Mississippi Val. (I-AA) .................. | †1983 | 10 | 102 | 1,450 | 14 |
| Mike Healey, Valparaiso (II) ....................... | †1985 | 10 | 101 | 1,279 | 11 |
| David Williams, Illinois (I-A) ........................ | †1984 | 11 | 101 | 1,278 | 8 |
| Jay Miller, Brigham Young (I-A) ..................... | †1973 | 11 | 100 | 1,181 | 8 |
| Jason Phillips, Houston (I-A) ....................... | †1987 | 11 | 99 | 875 | 3 |
| Mark Templeton, Long Beach St. (I-A) (RB) ........ | †1986 | 11 | 99 | 688 | 2 |
| Matt Newton, Principia (III) ........................ | †1992 | 8 | 98 | 1,487 | 14 |
| Rodney Carter, Purdue (I-A) ....................... | †1985 | 11 | 98 | 1,099 | 4 |
| Keith Edwards, Vanderbilt (I-A) ..................... | †1983 | 11 | 97 | 909 | 0 |

* Record.  † National champion.  # Record for a running back.

## Season Catches Per Game

| Player, Team (Division) | Year | G | Catches | Yds. | TD | Ct. PG |
|---|---|---|---|---|---|---|
| Howard Twilley, Tulsa (I-A) .................. | †1965 | 10 | 134 | 1,779 | 16 | *13.4 |
| Manny Hazard, Houston (I-A) .............. | †1989 | 11 | *142 | 1,689 | 22 | 12.9 |
| Matt Newton, Principia (III) ................ | †1992 | 8 | 98 | 1,487 | 14 | 12.3 |
| Brian Forster, Rhode Island (I-AA) (TE) ..... | †1985 | 10 | 115 | 1,617 | 12 | 11.5 |
| Sean Munroe, Mass.-Boston (III) ........... | 1992 | 9 | 95 | 1,693 | 17 | 10.6 |
| Jerry Rice, Mississippi Val. (I-AA) ......... | †1984 | 10 | 103 | 1,682 | *27 | 10.3 |
| Scott Faessler, Framingham St. (III) ........ | †1990 | 9 | 92 | 916 | 5 | 10.2 |
| Jerry Rice, Mississippi Val. (I-AA) ......... | †1983 | 10 | 102 | 1,450 | 14 | 10.2 |
| Bruce Cerone, Emporia St. (II) ............. | †1968 | 9 | 91 | 1,479 | 15 | 10.1 |
| Mike Healy, Valparaiso (II) ................ | †1985 | 10 | 101 | 1,279 | 11 | 10.1 |
| Stuart Gaussoin, Portland St. (I-AA) ........ | †1979 | 9 | 90 | 1,132 | 8 | 10.0 |

* Record.  † National champion.

## Single-Game Catches

| No. | Div. | Player, Team (Opponent) | Date |
|---|---|---|---|
| 24 | I-AA | Jerry Rice, Mississippi Val. (Southern-B.R.)............................Oct. 1, 1983 | |
| 23 | III | Sean Munroe, Mass.-Boston (Mass. Maritime).........................Oct. 10, 1992 | |
| 23 | II | Barry Wagner, Alabama A&M (Clark Atlanta)............................Nov. 4, 1989 | |
| 22 | I-AA | Marvin Walker, North Texas (Tulsa) ..................................Nov. 20, 1987 | |
| 22 | I-A | Jay Miller, Brigham Young (New Mexico) ..............................Nov. 3, 1973 | |
| 21# | I-AA | David Pandt, Montana St. (Eastern Wash.) ............................Sept. 21, 1985 | |
| 20 | III | Rich Johnson, Pace (Fordham) .......................................Nov. 7, 1987 | |
| 20 | III | Pete Thompson, Carroll, Wis. (Augustana, Ill.) ........................Nov. 4, 1978 | |
| 20 | II | Harold "Red" Roberts, Austin Peay (Murray St.).......................Nov. 8, 1969 | |
| 20 | I-A | Rick Eber, Tulsa (Idaho St.) .........................................Oct. 7, 1967 | |

# Record for a running back.

## Career Yards

| Player, Team (Division[s]) | Years | Catches | Yards | Avg. | TD |
|---|---|---|---|---|---|
| Jerry Rice, Mississippi Val. (I-AA) .......... | 1981-84 | *301 | *4,693 | 15.6 | 50 |
| Bruce Cerone, Yankton/Emporia St. (II) .... | 1966-67, 68-69 | 241 | 4,354 | 18.1 | 49 |
| Aaron Turner, Pacific (Cal.) (I-A) ........... | 1989-92 | 266 | 4,345 | 16.3 | 43 |
| Terance Mathis, New Mexico (I-A) ......... | 1985-87, 89 | 263 | 4,254 | 16.2 | 36 |
| Robert Clark, N.C. Central (II) .............. | 1983-86 | 210 | 4,231 | ‡20.1 | 38 |
| Chris Myers, Kenyon (II) .................. | 1967-70 | 253 | 3,897 | 15.4 | 33 |
| Kasey Dunn, Idaho (I-AA) ................. | 1988-91 | 268 | 3,847 | 14.4 | 25 |
| Dale Amos, Frank. & Marsh. (III) .......... | 1986-89 | 233 | 3,846 | 16.5 | 35 |
| Bill Stromberg, Johns Hopkins (III) ........ | 1978-81 | 258 | 3,776 | 14.6 | 39 |
| Shannon Sharpe, Savannah St. (II) ........ | 1986-89 | 192 | 3,744 | 19.5 | 40 |
| Marc Zeno, Tulane (I-A).................... | 1984-87 | 236 | 3,725 | 15.8 | 25 |
| Jim Bradford, Carleton (III) ................ | 1988-91 | 212 | 3,719 | 17.5 | 32 |
| Chris Bisaillon, Ill. Wesleyan (III) ........... | 1989-92 | 223 | 3,670 | 16.5 | *55 |
| Rennie Benn, Lehigh (I-AA)................ | 1982-85 | 237 | 3,662 | 15.5 | 44 |
| Jeff Tiefenthaler, South Dak. St. (II) ........ | 1983-86 | 173 | 3,621 | 20.9 | 31 |
| Willie Richardson, Jackson St. (II) ......... | 1959-62 | 166 | 3,616 | 21.8 | 36 |
| Ron Sellers, Florida St. (I-A) ............... | 1966-68 | 212 | 3,598 | 17.0 | 23 |

* Record.  ‡ Record for minimum of 180 catches.

## Season Yards

| Player, Team (Division) | Year | Catches | Yards | Avg. | TD |
|---|---|---|---|---|---|
| Barry Wagner, Alabama A&M (II) ......... | †1989 | 106 | *1,812 | 17.1 | 17 |
| Howard Twilley, Tulsa (I-A)................ | †1965 | 134 | 1,779 | 13.3 | 16 |
| Sean Munroe, Mass.-Boston (III) .......... | †1992 | 95 | 1,693 | 17.8 | 17 |
| Manny Hazard, Houston (I-A)............. | †1989 | *142 | 1,689 | 11.9 | 22 |
| Jerry Rice, Mississippi Val. (I-AA) ......... | †1984 | 103 | 1,682 | 16.3 | *27 |
| Brian Forster, Rhode Island (I-AA) (TE) ... | †1985 | 115 | 1,617 | 14.1 | 12 |
| Theo Blanco, Wis.-Stevens Point (III) (RB) | 1987 | #106 | #1,616 | 15.2 | 8 |
| Aaron Turner, Pacific (Cal.) (I-A) ......... | †1991 | 92 | 1,604 | 17.4 | 18 |
| Dan Fulton, Nebraska-Omaha (II) .......... | 1976 | 67 | 1,581 | 23.6 | 16 |
| Jeff Tiefenthaler, South Dak. St. (II) ....... | 1986 | 73 | 1,534 | 21.0 | 11 |
| Ed Bell, Idaho St. (II) ..................... | †1969 | 96 | 1,522 | 15.9 | 20 |
| Chuck Hughes, UTEP (I-A) .............. | 1965 | 80 | 1,519 | 19.0 | 12 |
| Henry Ellard, Fresno St. (I-A) ............. | 1982 | 62 | 1,510 | ††24.4 | 15 |
| Rodney Richardson, Gardner-Webb (II) .. | †1992 | 89 | 1,496 | 16.8 | 16 |
| Ron Sellers, Florida St. (I-A) .............. | †1968 | 86 | 1,496 | 17.4 | 12 |

* Record.  † National champion.  †† Record for minimum of 55 catches.  # Record for a running back.

## Season Touchdown Receptions

| Player, Team (Division) | Year | Games | TD |
|---|---|---|---|
| Jerry Rice, Mississippi Val. (I-AA) ................................. | 1984 | 10 | *27 |
| Manny Hazard, Houston (I-A) ..................................... | 1989 | 11 | 22 |
| John Aromando, Trenton St. (III) .................................. | 1983 | 10 | 20 |
| Ed Bell, Idaho St. (II) ............................................. | 1969 | 10 | 20 |
| Desmond Howard, Michigan (I-A) ................................. | 1991 | 11 | 19 |
| Aaron Turner, Pacific (Cal.) (I-A) ................................. | 1991 | 11 | 18 |
| Dennis Smith, Utah (I-A)........................................... | 1989 | 12 | 18 |
| Tom Reynolds, San Diego St. (I-A) ................................ | 1971 | 10 | 18 |
| Sean Munroe, Mass.-Boston (III) .................................. | 1992 | 9 | 17 |
| Chris Bisaillon, Ill. Wesleyan (III) ................................. | 1991 | 9 | 17 |
| Mario Bailey, Washington (I-A) .................................... | 1991 | 11 | 17 |
| Clarkston Hines, Duke (I-A) ....................................... | 1989 | 11 | 17 |
| Barry Wagner, Alabama A&M (II) ................................. | 1989 | 11 | 17 |
| Dameon Reilly, Rhode Island (I-AA) ............................... | 1985 | 11 | 17 |
| Rodney Richardson, Gardner-Webb (II) ........................... | 1992 | 11 | 16 |
| Evan Elkington, Worcester Tech (III) .............................. | 1989 | 10 | 16 |
| Dan Bitson, Tulsa (I-A) ............................................ | 1989 | 11 | 16 |
| Dan Fulton, Nebraska-Omaha (II)................................. | 1976 | 10 | 16 |
| Howard Twilley, Tulsa (I-A)........................................ | 1965 | 10 | 16 |

* Record.

## Single-Game Yards

| Yds. | Div. | Player, Team (Opponent) | Date |
|---|---|---|---|
| 370 | I-AA | Michael Lerch, Princeton (Brown) ..................................... | Oct. 12, 1991 |
| 370 | II | Barry Wagner, Alabama A&M (Clark Atlanta)........................... | Nov. 4, 1989 |
| 363 | II | Tom Nettles, San Diego St. (Southern Miss.) ........................... | Nov. 9, 1968 |
| 354 | II | Robert Clark, N.C. Central (Jackson St.)................................ | Aug. 30, 1986 |
| 349 | I-A | Chuck Hughes, UTEP (North Texas) ................................... | Sept. 18, 1965 |

*Individual Collegiate Records*  293

| Yds. | Div. | Player, Team (Opponent) | Date |
|------|------|-------------------------|------|
| 332 | III | Sean Munroe, Mass.-Boston (Mass. Maritime) | Oct. 10, 1992 |
| 330 | I-AA | Nate Singleton, Grambling (Virginia Union) | Sept. 14, 1991 |
| 327@ | I-AA | Brian Forster, Rhode Island (Brown) | Sept. 28, 1985 |
| 325 | II | Paul Zaeske, North Park (North Central) | Oct. 12, 1968 |
| 322 | I-A | Rick Eber, Tulsa (Idaho St.) | Oct. 7, 1967 |
| 319 | I-AA | Jason Cristino, Lehigh (Lafayette) | Nov. 21, 1992 |
| 318 | I-A | Harry Wood, Tulsa (Idaho St.) | Oct. 7, 1967 |
| 317 | II | Dan Fulton, Nebraska-Omaha (South Dak.) | Sept. 4, 1976 |
| 316 | I-A | Jeff Evans, New Mexico St. (Southern Ill.) | Sept. 30, 1978 |
| 310 | II | Mike Collodi, Colorado Mines (Westminster, Utah) | Oct. 3, 1970 |
| 309 | III | Dale Amos, Frank. & Marsh. (Western Md.) | Oct. 24, 1987 |

@ *Record for a tight end.*

# INTERCEPTIONS

## Career Interceptions

| Player, Team (Division[s]) | Years | No. | Yards | Avg. |
|----------------------------|-------|-----|-------|------|
| Tom Collins, Indianapolis (II) | 1982-85 | *37 | 390 | 10.5 |
| Ralph Gebhardt, Rochester (III) | 1972-75 | 34 | 406 | 11.9 |
| Dean Diaz, Humboldt St. (II) | 1980-83 | 31 | 328 | 10.6 |
| Scott Wiedeman, Adams St. (II) | 1988-91 | 31 | 289 | 9.3 |
| Eugene Hunter, Fort Valley St. (III) | 1972-74 | 29 | 479 | 16.5 |
| Al Brosky, Illinois (I-A) | 1950-52 | 29 | 356 | 12.3 |
| Bill Grantham, Missouri-Rolla (II) | 1977-80 | 29 | 263 | 9.1 |
| Brian Fetterolf, Aurora (III) | 1986-89 | 28 | 390 | 13.9 |
| Dave Murphy, Holy Cross (I-AA) | 1986-89 | 28 | 309 | 11.0 |
| Rick Bealer, Lycoming (III) | 1987-90 | 28 | 279 | 10.0 |
| John Provost, Holy Cross (I-A) | 1972-74 | 27 | 470 | 17.4 |
| Martin Bayless, Bowling Green (I-A) | 1980-83 | 27 | 266 | 9.9 |
| Tim Lennon, Curry (III) | 1986-89 | 27 | 190 | 7.0 |
| Mike Hintz, Wis.-Platteville (III) | 1983-86 | 27 | 183 | 6.8 |
| Cory Mabry, Susquehanna (III) | 1988-91 | 26 | 400 | 15.4 |
| Jeff Hughes, Ripon (III) | 1975-78 | 26 | 333 | 12.8 |
| Buster West, Gust. Adolphus (II) | 1967-70 | 26 | 192 | 7.4 |
| Tony Woods, Bloomsburg (II) | 1982-85 | 26 | 105 | 4.0 |

* *Record.*

## Season Interceptions

| Player, Team (Division) | Year | No. | Yards |
|-------------------------|------|-----|-------|
| Mark Dorner, Juniata (III) | †1987 | *15 | 202 |
| Eugene Hunter, Fort Valley St. (II) | †1972 | 14 | 211 |
| Jim Blackwell, Southern-B.R. (II) | †1970 | 14 | 196 |
| Tom Rezzuti, Northeastern (II) | †1971 | 14 | 153 |
| Al Worley, Washington (I-A) | †1968 | 14 | 130 |
| Luther Howard, Delaware St. (II) | †1972 | 14 | 99 |
| Carl Ray Harris, Fresno St. (II) | †1970 | 14 | 98 |

* *Record.*  † *National champion.*

# PUNT RETURNS

## Career Average
### (Minimum 1.2 Returns Per Game)

| Player, Team (Division[s]) | Years | No. | Yards | Avg. |
|----------------------------|-------|-----|-------|------|
| Billy Johnson, Widener (II; III) | 1971-72; 73 | 40 | 989 | *24.7 |
| Jack Mitchell, Oklahoma (I-A) | 1946-48 | 39 | 922 | 23.6 |
| Keith Winston, Knoxville (III) | 1986-87 | 30 | 686 | 22.9 |
| Robert Middlebrook, Knoxville (III) | 1984-85 | 21 | 473 | 22.5 |
| Kevin Doherty, Mass. Maritime (III) | 1976-78, 80 | 45 | 939 | 20.9 |
| Chuck Downey, Stony Brook (III) | 1984-87 | 59 | 1,198 | **20.3 |
| Mike Askew, Kean (III) | 1980-81 | 28 | 555 | 19.8 |
| Eddie Macon, Pacific (Cal.) (I-A) | 1949-51 | 48 | 907 | 18.9 |
| Willie Canady, Fort Valley St. (III) | 1979-82 | 41 | 772 | 18.8 |
| Jackie Robinson, UCLA (I-A) | 1939-40 | 37 | 694 | 18.8 |

* *Record.*  ** *Record for minimum of 50 returns.*

## Season Average
### (Minimum 1.2 Returns Per Game)

| Player, Team (Division) | Year | No. | Yards | Avg. |
|---|---|---|---|---|
| Billy Johnson, Widener (II) | †1972 | 15 | 511 | *34.1 |
| Chuck Downey, Stony Brook (III) | †1986 | 17 | 530 | 31.2 |
| Kevin Doherty, Mass. Maritime (III) | †1976 | 11 | 332 | 30.2 |
| Dennis Robinson, Wesleyan (III) | †1978 | 9 | 263 | 29.2 |
| Robert Middlebrook, Knoxville (III) | †1984 | 9 | 260 | 28.9 |
| Joe Troise, Kean (III) | †1974 | 12 | 342 | 28.5 |
| William Williams, Livingstone (II) | †1976 | 16 | 453 | 28.3 |
| Terry Egerdahl, Minn.-Duluth (II) | †1975 | 13 | 360 | 27.7 |
| Melvin Dillard, Ferrum (III) | †1990 | 25 | 688 | 27.5 |
| Bill Blackstock, Tennessee (I-A) | 1951 | 12 | 311 | 25.9 |
| Ennis Thomas, Bishop (II) | †1971 | 18 | 450 | 25.0 |
| George Sims, Baylor (I-A) | 1948 | 15 | 375 | 25.0 |

* Record.  † National champion.

# KICKOFF RETURNS

## Career Average
### (Minimum 1.2 Returns Per Game)

| Player, Team (Division[s]) | Years | No. | Yards | Avg. |
|---|---|---|---|---|
| Forrest Hall, San Francisco (I-A) | 1946-47 | 22 | 796 | *36.2 |
| Anthony Davis, Southern Cal (I-A) | 1972-74 | 37 | 1,299 | 35.1 |
| Glen Printers, Southern Colo. (II) | 1973-74 | 25 | 851 | 34.0 |
| Overton Curtis, Utah St. (I-A) | 1957-58 | 32 | 991 | 31.0 |
| Fred Montgomery, New Mexico St. (I-A) | 1991-92 | 39 | 1,191 | 30.5 |
| Karl Evans, Mo. Southern St. (II) | 1991-92 | 32 | 959 | 30.0 |
| Troy Brown, Marshall (I-AA) | 1991-92 | 32 | 950 | 29.7 |
| Charles Swann, Indiana St. (I-AA) | 1989-91 | 45 | 1,319 | 29.3 |
| Altie Taylor, Utah St. (I-A) | 1966-68 | 40 | 1,170 | 29.3 |
| Daryl Brown, Tufts (III) | 1974-76 | 38 | 1,111 | 29.2 |
| Stan Brown, Purdue (I-A) | 1968-70 | 49 | 1,412 | 28.8 |
| Henry White, Colgate (I-A) | 1974-77 | 41 | 1,180 | 28.8 |
| Donald Dennis, West Tex. St. (I-A) | 1964-65 | 27 | 777 | 28.8 |
| Bobby Ward, Memphis St. (I-A) | 1973-74 | 27 | 770 | 28.5 |
| Craig Richardson, Eastern Wash. (I-AA) | 1983-86 | 71 | 2,021 | 28.5 |

* Record.

## Season Average
### (Minimum 1.2 Returns Per Game)

| Player, Team (Division) | Year | No. | Yards | Avg. |
|---|---|---|---|---|
| Paul Allen, Brigham Young (I-A) | 1961 | 12 | 481 | *40.1 |
| Jason Martin, Coe (III) | †1992 | 11 | 438 | 39.8 |
| Danny Lee, Jacksonville St. (II) | †1992 | 12 | 473 | 39.4 |
| Forrest Hall, San Francisco (I-A) | 1946 | 15 | 573 | @38.2 |
| Nate Kirtman, Pomona-Pitzer (III) | †1990 | 14 | 515 | 36.8 |
| Tom Myers, Coe (III) | †1983 | 11 | 401 | 36.5 |
| Tony Ball, Tenn.-Chatt. (I-A) | †1977 | 13 | 473 | 36.4 |
| Ron Scott, Occidental (III) | 1983 | 10 | 363 | 36.3 |
| Alan Hill, DePauw (III) | 1980 | 12 | 434 | 36.2 |
| Roscoe Word, Jackson St. (II) | †1973 | 18 | 650 | 36.1 |
| Steve Levenseller, Puget Sound (II) | †1978 | 17 | 610 | 35.9 |
| George Marinkov, North Caro. St. (I-A) | 1954 | 13 | 465 | 35.8 |

* Record.  † National champion.  @ Record for minimum of 1.5 returns per game.

# FIELD GOALS

*(One-inch tees were permitted in 1949, two-inch tees were permitted in 1965, and use of tees was eliminated before 1989 season. The goal posts were widened from 18 feet, 6 inches to 23 feet, 4 inches in 1959 and were narrowed back to 18 feet, 6 inches before 1991 season.)*

## Career Field Goals

| Player, Team (Division[s]) | Years | FGM | FGA | Pct. |
|---|---|---|---|---|
| Jeff Jaeger, Washington (S) (I-A) | 1983-86 | *80 | 99 | .808 |
| John Lee, UCLA (S) (I-A) | 1982-85 | 79 | 92 | *.859 |
| Philip Doyle, Alabama (S) (I-A) | 1987-90 | 78 | **105 | .743 |
| Luis Zendejas, Arizona St. (S) (I-A) | 1981-84 | 78 | **105 | .743 |
| Kevin Butler, Georgia (S) (I-A) | 1981-84 | 77 | 98 | .786 |

| Player, Team (Division[s]) | Years | FGM | FGA | Pct. |
|---|---|---|---|---|
| Max Zendejas, Arizona (S) (I-A) .................... | 1982-85 | 77 | 104 | .740 |
| Carlos Huerta, Miami (Fla.) (S) (I-A) ............. | 1988-91 | 73 | 91 | .802 |
| Derek Schmidt, Florida St. (S) (I-A) .............. | 1984-87 | 73 | 104 | .702 |
| Marty Zendejas, Nevada (S) (I-AA) ............... | 1984-87 | 72 | 90 | .800 |
| Fuad Reveiz, Tennessee (S) (I-A) ................. | 1981-84 | 71 | 95 | .747 |
| Kirk Roach, Western Caro. (S) (I-AA) ............. | 1984-87 | 71 | 102 | .696 |
| Tony Zendejas, Nevada (S) (I-AA) ................ | 1981-83 | 70 | 86 | .814 |
| Barry Belli, Fresno St. (S) (I-A)..................... | 1984-87 | 70 | 99 | .707 |
| Roman Anderson, Houston (S) (I-A) .............. | 1988-91 | 70 | 101 | .693 |
| Collin Mackie, South Caro. (S) (I-A) .............. | 1987-90 | 69 | 95 | .726 |
| Gary Gussman, Miami (Ohio) (S) (I-A)............ | 1984-87 | 68 | 94 | .723 |
| Larry Roach, Oklahoma St. (S) (I-A) .............. | 1981-84 | 68 | 101 | .673 |
| Paul Woodside, West Va. (S) (I-A)................. | 1981-84 | 65 | 81 | .802 |

*Record.   ** Record tied.   (S) Soccer-style kicker.*

## Season Field Goals

| Player, Team (Division) | Year | FGM | FGA | Pct. |
|---|---|---|---|---|
| John Lee, UCLA (S) (I-A) ........................... | 1984 | *29 | 33 | .879 |
| Paul Woodside, West Va. (S) (I-A) ................ | 1982 | 28 | 31 | .903 |
| Luis Zendejas, Arizona St. (S) (I-A) ............... | 1983 | 28 | 37 | .757 |
| Fuad Reveiz, Tennessee (S) (I-A) ................. | 1982 | 27 | 31 | .871 |
| Brian Mitchell, Northern Iowa (S) (I-AA) ........... | 1990 | 26 | 27 | *.963 |
| Tony Zendejas, Nevada (S) (I-AA) ................ | 1982 | 26 | 33 | .788 |
| Chuck Nelson, Washington (S) (I-A) ............... | 1982 | 25 | 26 | .962 |
| Chris Jacke, UTEP (S) (I-A)....................... | 1988 | 25 | 27 | .926 |
| John Diettrich, Ball St. (S) (I-A) ................... | 1985 | 25 | 29 | .862 |
| Kendall Trainor, Arkansas (S) (I-A) ................ | 1988 | 24 | 27 | .889 |
| Kirk Roach, Western Caro. (S) (I-AA) ............. | 1986 | 24 | 28 | .857 |
| Carlos Reveiz, Tennessee (S) (I-A) ................ | 1985 | 24 | 28 | .857 |
| Chris White, Illinois (S) (I-A) ..................... | 1984 | 24 | 28 | .857 |
| Philip Doyle, Alabama (S) (I-A) ................... | 1990 | 24 | 29 | .828 |
| Bruce Kallmeyer, Kansas (S) (I-A) ................ | 1983 | 24 | 29 | .828 |
| Mike Prindle, Western Mich. (S) (I-A) .............. | 1984 | 24 | 30 | .800 |
| George Benyola, Louisiana Tech (S) (I-AA) ........ | 1985 | 24 | 31 | .774 |

*Record.   (S) Soccer-style kicker.*

*(Record for attempts is 38)*

## Longest Field Goals

| Yards | Div. | Player, Team (Opponent) | Year |
|---|---|---|---|
| 67 | II | Tom Odle, Fort Hays St. (Washburn) .............................................1988 |  |
| 67 | I-A | Joe Williams, Wichita St. (Southern Ill.) .........................................1978 |  |
| 67 | I-A | Steve Little, Arkansas (Texas) ..................................................1977 |  |
| 67 | I-A | Russell Erxleben, Texas (Rice) ..................................................1977 |  |
| 65 | I-A | Tony Franklin, Texas A&M (Baylor) ..............................................1976 |  |
| 64 | I-A | Russell Erxleben, Texas (Oklahoma) .............................................1977 |  |
| 64 | I-A | Tony Franklin, Texas A&M (Baylor) ..............................................1976 |  |
| 63 | I-AA | Scott Roper, Arkansas St. (North Texas) .........................................1987 |  |
| 63 | I-AA | Tim Foley, Ga. Southern (James Madison) .........................................1987 |  |
| 63 | I-A | Morten Andersen, Michigan St. (Ohio St.) .........................................1981 |  |
| 63 | I-A | Clark Kemble, Colorado St. (Arizona) ............................................1975 |  |
| 63 | II | Joe Duren, Arkansas St. (McNeese St.) ..........................................1974 |  |
| 62* | I-A | Jason Hanson, Washington St. (Nevada-Las Vegas) ...............................1991 |  |
| 62 | I-A | John Diettrich, Ball St. (Ohio) ...................................................1986 |  |
| 62 | I-AA | Paul Hickert, Murray St. (Eastern Ky.) ...........................................1986 |  |
| 62 | I-A | Chip Lohmiller, Minnesota (Iowa) ................................................1986 |  |
| 62 | I-A | Tom Whelihan, Missouri (Colorado)...............................................1986 |  |
| 62 | I-A | Dan Christopulos, Wyoming (Colorado St.) ........................................1977 |  |
| 62 | I-A | Iseed Khoury, North Texas (Richmond) ...........................................1977 |  |
| 62 | III | Dom Antonini, Rowan (Salisbury St.) .............................................1976 |  |
| 62 | I-A | Dave Lawson, Air Force (Iowa St.) ...............................................1975 |  |
| 62 | II | Mike Flater, Colorado Mines (Western St.) ........................................1973 |  |

*Longest collegiate field goal without use of a tee.*

**Special Reference:** Ove Johannson, Abilene Christian (not an NCAA-member college at the time), kicked a 69-yard field goal against East Tex. St., Oct. 16, 1976.

*1993 NCAA FOOTBALL*

# PUNTING

### Career Punting Average
### (Minimum 150 Punts)

| Player, Team (Division[s]) | Years | No. | Yards | Avg. |
|---|---|---|---|---|
| Reggie Roby, Iowa (I-A) | 1979-82 | 172 | 7,849 | *45.6 |
| Greg Montgomery, Michigan St. (I-A) | 1985-87 | 170 | 7,721 | 45.4 |
| Tom Tupa, Ohio St. (I-A) | 1984-87 | 196 | 8,854 | 45.2 |
| Barry Helton, Colorado (I-A) | 1984-87 | 153 | 6,873 | 44.9 |
| Ray Guy, Southern Miss. (I-A) | 1970-72 | 200 | 8,934 | 44.7 |
| Bucky Scribner, Kansas (I-A) | 1980-82 | 217 | 9,670 | 44.6 |
| Greg Horne, Arkansas (I-A) | 1983-86 | 180 | 8,002 | 44.5 |
| Ray Criswell, Florida (I-A) | 1982-85 | 161 | 7,153 | 44.4 |
| Pumpy Tudors, Tenn.-Chatt. (I-AA) | 1988-91 | 181 | 8,041 | 44.4 |
| Bill Smith, Mississippi (I-A) | 1983-86 | 254 | 11,260 | 44.3 |
| Tim Baer, Colorado Mines (II) | 1986-89 | 235 | 10,406 | 44.3 |
| Russell Erxleben, Texas (I-A) | 1975-78 | 214 | 9,467 | 44.2 |
| Mark Simon, Air Force (I-A) | 1984-86 | 156 | 6,898 | 44.2 |
| Johnny Evans, North Caro. St. (I-A) | 1974-77 | 185 | 8,143 | 44.0 |
| Chuck Ramsey, Wake Forest (I-A) | 1971-73 | 205 | 9,010 | 44.0 |

* Record.

### Season Punting Average
### (Qualifiers for the Championship)

| Player, Team (Division) | Year | No. | Yards | Avg. |
|---|---|---|---|---|
| Reggie Roby, Iowa (I-A) | †1981 | 44 | 2,193 | *49.8 |
| Kirk Wilson, UCLA (I-A) | †1956 | 30 | 1,479 | 49.3 |
| Steve Ecker, Shippensburg (II) | †1965 | 32 | 1,570 | 49.1 |
| Zack Jordan, Colorado (I-A) | †1950 | 38 | 1,830 | 48.2 |
| Ricky Anderson, Vanderbilt (I-A) | †1984 | 58 | 2,793 | 48.2 |
| Reggie Roby, Iowa (I-A) | †1982 | 52 | 2,501 | 48.1 |
| Marv Bateman, Utah (I-A) | †1971 | 68 | 3,269 | 48.1 |
| Don Cockroft, Adams St. (II) | †1966 | 36 | 1,728 | 48.0 |
| Owen Price, UTEP (I-A) | †1940 | 30 | 1,440 | 48.0 |
| Jack Jacobs, Oklahoma (I-A) | 1940 | 31 | 1,483 | 47.8 |
| Bill Smith, Mississippi (I-A) | 1984 | 44 | 2,099 | 47.7 |

* Record. † National champion.

### Longest Punts

| Yards | Div. | Player, Team (Opponent) | Year |
|---|---|---|---|
| 99 | I-A | Pat Brady, Nevada (Loyola, Cal.) | 1950 |
| 97 | II | Earl Hurst, Emporia St. (Central Mo. St.) | 1964 |
| 96 | II | Gary Frens, Hope (Olivet) | 1966 |
| 96 | II | Jim Jarrett, North Dak. (South Dak.) | 1957 |
| 96 | I-A | George O'Brien, Wisconsin (Iowa) | 1952 |
| 94 | I-A | John Hadl, Kansas (Oklahoma) | 1959 |
| 94 | I-A | Carl Knox, Texas Christian (Oklahoma St.) | 1947 |
| 94 | I-A | Preston Johnson, Southern Methodist (Pittsburgh) | 1940 |
| 93 | II | Elliot Mills, Carleton (Monmouth, Ill.) | 1970 |
| 93 | II | Kasper Fitins, Taylor (Georgetown, Ky.) | 1966 |
| 93 | II | Leeroy Sweeney, Pomona-Pitzer (UC Riverside) | 1960 |
| 93 | I-A | Bob Handke, Drake (Wichita St.) | 1949 |

# ALL-PURPOSE RUNNING

### Career Yards

| Player, Team (Division[s]) | Years | Rush | Rcv | PR | KO | Yds. |
|---|---|---|---|---|---|---|
| Johnny Bailey, Texas A&I (II) | 1986-89 | *6,320 | 452 | 20 | 1,011 | *7,803 |
| Kenny Gamble, Colgate (I-AA) | 1984-87 | 5,220 | 536 | 104 | 1,763 | 7,623 |
| Howard Stevens, Rand.-Macon (II); Louisville (I-A) | 1968-69; 71-72 | 5,297 | 738 | 781 | 748 | 7,564 |
| Napoleon McCallum, Navy (I-A) | $1981-85 | 4,179 | 796 | 858 | 1,339 | 7,172 |
| Albert Fann, Cal St. Northridge (II) | 1987-90 | 4,090 | 803 | 0 | 2,141 | 7,032 |
| Curtis Delgardo, Portland St. (II) | $1986-90 | 4,178 | 1,258 | 318 | 1,188 | 6,942 |
| Darrin Nelson, Stanford (I-A) | 1977-78, 80-81 | 4,033 | 2,368 | 471 | 13 | 6,885 |
| Eric Frees, Western Md. (III) | 1988-91 | 5,281 | 392 | 47 | 1,158 | 6,878 |
| Steve Roberts, Butler (II) | 1986-89 | 4,623 | 1,201 | 272 | 578 | 6,674 |
| Tony Dorsett, Pittsburgh (I-A) | 1973-76 | 6,082 | 406 | 0 | 127 | 6,615 |

| Player, Team (Division[s]) | Years | Rush | Rcv | PR | KO | Yds. |
|---|---|---|---|---|---|---|
| Paul Palmer, Temple (I-A) | 1983-86 | 4,895 | 705 | 0 | 997 | 6,609 |
| Charles White, Southern Cal (I-A) | 1976-79 | 5,598 | 507 | 0 | 440 | 6,545 |
| Trevor Cobb, Rice (I-A) | 1989-92 | 4,948 | 892 | 21 | 651 | 6,512 |
| Joe Dudek, Plymouth St. (III) | 1982-85 | 5,570 | 348 | 0 | 243 | 6,509 |
| Glyn Milburn, Oklahoma/Stanford (I-A) | 1988, 90-92 | 2,302 | 1,495 | 1,145 | 1,246 | 6,188 |
| Chris Cobb, Eastern Ill. (II) | 1976-79 | 5,042 | 520 | 37 | 478 | 6,077 |
| Don Aleksiewicz, Hobart (II) | 1969-72 | 4,525 | 470 | 320 | 748 | 6,063 |
| Gary Trettel, St. Thomas (Minn.) (III) | 1988-90 | 3,724 | 853 | 0 | 1,467 | 6,044 |
| Archie Griffin, Ohio St. (I-A) | 1972-75 | 5,177 | 286 | 0 | 540 | 6,003 |
| Ron "Po" James, New Mexico St. (I-A) | 1968-71 | 3,884 | 217 | 8 | 1,870 | 5,979 |
| Eric Wilkerson, Kent (I-A) | 1985-88 | 3,830 | 506 | 0 | 1,638 | 5,974 |

* Record.   $ See page 8 for explanation.

## Career Yards Per Game
### (Minimum 18 Games)

| Player, Team (Division[s]) | Years | G | Rush | Rcv | PR | KO | Yds. | Yd. PG |
|---|---|---|---|---|---|---|---|---|
| Ryan Benjamin, Pacific (Cal.) (I-A) | 1990-92 | 24 | 3,119 | 1,063 | 100 | 1,424 | 5,706 | *237.8 |
| Sheldon Canley, San Jose St. (I-A) | 1988-90 | 25 | 2,513 | 828 | 5 | 1,800 | 5,146 | 205.8 |
| Johnny Bailey, Texas A&I (II) | 1986-89 | 39 | *6,320 | 452 | 20 | 1,011 | *7,803 | 200.1 |
| Howard Stevens, Randolph Macon (II); Louisville (I-A) | 1968-69; 71-72 | 38 | 5,297 | 738 | 781 | 748 | 7,564 | 199.1 |
| Gary Trettel, St. Thomas (Minn.) (III) | 1988-90 | 29 | 3,483 | 834 | 0 | 1,407 | 5,724 | 197.4 |
| Billy Johnson, Widener (II; III) | 1971-72; 73 | 28 | 3,737 | 27 | 43 | 989 | 5,404 | 193.0 |
| O. J. Simpson, Southern Cal (I-A) | 1967-68 | 19 | 3,124 | 235 | 0 | 307 | 3,666 | 192.9 |
| Dave Meggett, Towson St. (I-AA) | 1987-88 | 18 | 1,658 | 788 | 212 | 745 | 3,403 | 189.1 |

* Record.

## Season Yards

| Player, Team (Division) | Year | Rush | Rcv | PR | KO | Yds. |
|---|---|---|---|---|---|---|
| Barry Sanders, Oklahoma St. (I-A) | †1988 | *2,628 | 106 | 95 | 421 | *3,250 |
| Ryan Benjamin, Pacific (Cal.) (I-A) | †1991 | 1,581 | 612 | 4 | 798 | 2,995 |
| Mike Pringle, Cal St. Fullerton (I-A) | †1989 | 1,727 | 249 | 0 | 714 | 2,690 |
| Steve Roberts, Butler (II) | †1989 | 1,450 | 532 | 272 | 415 | 2,669 |
| Paul Palmer, Temple (I-A) | †1986 | 1,866 | 110 | 0 | 657 | 2,633 |
| Ryan Benjamin, Pacific (Cal.) (I-A) | †1992 | 1,441 | 434 | 96 | 626 | 2,597 |
| Marcus Allen, Southern Cal (I-A) | †1981 | 2,342 | 217 | 0 | 0 | 2,559 |
| Sheldon Canley, San Jose St. (I-A) | 1989 | 1,201 | 353 | 0 | 959 | 2,513 |
| Mike Rozier, Nebraska (I-A) | 1983 | 2,148 | 106 | 0 | 232 | 2,486 |
| Johnny Bailey, Texas A&I (II) | †1986 | 2,011 | 54 | 20 | 340 | 2,425 |
| Kenny Gamble, Colgate (I-AA) | †1986 | 1,816 | 198 | 40 | 391 | 2,425 |
| Theo Blanco, Wis.-Stevens Point (III) | 1987 | 454 | 1,616 | 245 | 103 | 2,418 |
| Rick Wegher, South Dak. St. (II) | 1984 | 1,317 | 264 | 0 | 824 | 2,405 |
| Chuck Weatherspoon, Houston (I-A) | 1989 | 1,146 | 735 | 415 | 95 | 2,391 |
| Anthony Thompson, Indiana (I-A) | 1989 | 1,793 | 201 | 0 | 394 | 2,388 |
| Ricky Gales, Simpson (III) | †1989 | 2,035 | 102 | 0 | 248 | 2,385 |
| Napoleon McCallum, Navy (I-A) | †1983 | 1,587 | 166 | 272 | 360 | 2,385 |
| Gary Trettel, St. Thomas (Minn.) (III) | 1989 | 1,502 | 337 | 0 | 496 | 2,335 |
| Michael Clemons, William & Mary (I-AA) | 1986 | 1,065 | 516 | 330 | 423 | 2,334 |
| Napoleon McCallum, Navy (I-A) | †1985 | 1,327 | 358 | 157 | 488 | 2,330 |
| Gary Trettel, St. Thomas (Minn.) (III) | 1990 | 1,620 | 388 | 0 | 319 | 2,327 |
| Keith Byars, Ohio St. (I-A) | †1984 | 1,655 | 453 | 0 | 176 | 2,284 |

* Record.   † National champion.

## Season Yards Per Game

| Player, Team (Division) | Year | G | Rush | Rcv | PR | KO | Yds. | Yd. PG |
|---|---|---|---|---|---|---|---|---|
| Barry Sanders, Oklahoma St. (I-A) | †1988 | 11 | *2,628 | 106 | 0 | 95 | *3,250 | *295.5 |
| Steve Roberts, Butler (II) | †1989 | 10 | 1,450 | 532 | 272 | 415 | 2,669 | 266.9 |
| Billy Johnson, Widener (II) | †1972 | 9 | 1,556 | 40 | 511 | 115 | %2,265 | 251.7 |
| Ryan Benjamin, Pacific (Cal.) (I-A) | †1991 | 12 | 1,581 | 612 | 4 | 798 | 2,995 | 249.6 |
| Byron "Whizzer" White, Colorado (I-A) | †1937 | 8 | 1,121 | 0 | 587 | 159 | $1,970 | 246.3 |
| Mike Pringle, Cal St. Fullerton (I-A) | †1989 | 11 | 1,727 | 249 | 0 | 714 | 2,690 | 244.6 |
| Paul Palmer, Temple (I-A) | †1986 | 11 | 1,866 | 110 | 0 | 657 | 2,633 | 239.4 |
| Ricky Gales, Simpson (III) | †1989 | 10 | 2,035 | 102 | 0 | 248 | 2,385 | 238.5 |
| Ryan Benjamin, Pacific (Cal.) (I-A) | †1992 | 11 | 1,441 | 434 | 96 | 626 | 2,597 | 236.1 |
| Gary Trettel, St. Thomas (Minn.) (III) | 1989 | 10 | 1,502 | 337 | 0 | 496 | 2,335 | 233.5 |
| Gary Trettel, St. Thomas (Minn.) (III) | 1990 | 10 | 1,620 | 388 | 0 | 319 | 2,327 | 232.7 |

* Record.   † National champion.   % Also includes 43 yards in interception returns.   $ Also includes 103 yards in interception returns.

*1993 NCAA FOOTBALL*

# SCORING

## Career Points

| Player, Team (Division[s]) | Years | TD | XPt. | FG | Pts. |
|---|---|---|---|---|---|
| Joe Dudek, Plymouth St. (III) | 1982-85 | *79 | 0 | 0 | *474 |
| Walter Payton, Jackson St. (II) | 1971-74 | 66 | 53 | 5 | 464 |
| Shawn Graves, Wofford (QB) (II) | 1989-92 | 72 | 3 | 0 | 438 |
| Johnny Bailey, Texas A&I (II) | 1986-89 | 70 | 3 | 0 | 426 |
| Roman Anderson, Houston (I-A) | 1988-91 | 0 | *213 | 70 | 423 |
| Howard Stevens, Randolph-Macon (II); Louisville (I-A) | 1968-69; 71-72 | 69 | 4 | 0 | 418 |
| Dale Mills, Northeast Mo. St. (II) | 1957-60 | 64 | 23 | 0 | 407 |
| Carlos Huerta, Miami (Fla.) (I-A) | 1988-91 | 0 | 178 | 73 | 397 |
| Jason Elam, Hawaii (I-A) | $1988-92 | 0 | 158 | 79 | 395 |
| Anthony Thompson, Indiana (I-A) | 1986-89 | 65 | 4 | 0 | 394 |
| Garney Henley, Huron (II) | 1956-59 | 63 | 16 | 0 | 394 |
| Derek Schmidt, Florida St. (I-A) | 1984-87 | 0 | 174 | 73 | 393 |
| Steve Roberts, Butler (II) | 1986-89 | 63 | 4 | 0 | 386 |
| Jeff Bentrim, North Dak. St. (QB) (II) | 1983-86 | 64 | 2 | 0 | 386 |
| Marty Zendejas, Nevada (I-AA) | 1984-87 | 0 | 169 | 72 | 385 |
| Leo Lewis, Lincoln (Mo.) (II) | 1951-54 | 64 | 0 | 0 | 384 |
| Chris Bisaillon, Ill. Wesleyan (III) | 1989-92 | 61 | 12 | 0 | 378 |
| Heath Sherman, Texas A&I (II) | 1985-88 | 63 | 0 | 0 | 378 |
| Chris Babirad, Wash. & Jeff. (III) | 1989-92 | 62 | 2 | 0 | 374 |
| Billy Johnson, Widener (II; III) | 1971-72; 73 | 62 | 0 | 0 | 372 |
| Tank Younger, Grambling (II) | 1945-48 | 60 | 9 | 0 | 369 |
| Luis Zendejas, Arizona St. (I-A) | 1981-84 | 0 | 134 | 78 | 368 |
| Bill Cooper, Muskingum (II) | 1957-60 | 54 | 37 | 1 | 364 |
| Charvez Foger, Nevada (I-AA) | 1985-88 | 60 | 2 | 0 | 362 |
| Ole Gunderson, St. Olaf (II) | 1969-71 | 60 | 2 | 0 | 362 |
| Jeff Jaeger, Washington (I-A) | 1983-86 | 0 | 118 | *80 | 358 |
| Tony Dorsett, Pittsburgh (I-A) | 1973-76 | 59 | 2 | 0 | 356 |
| Glenn Davis, Army (I-A) | 1943-46 | 59 | 0 | 0 | 354 |

* Record.   $ See page 8 for explanation.

## Career Points Per Game
### (Minimum 18 Games)

| Player, Team (Division[s]) | Years | G | TD | XPt. | FG | Pts. | Pt.PG |
|---|---|---|---|---|---|---|---|
| Ole Gunderson, St. Olaf (II) | 1969-71 | 27 | 60 | 2 | 0 | 362 | *13.4 |
| Billy Johnson, Widener (II; III) | 1971-72; 73 | 28 | 62 | 0 | 0 | 372 | 13.3 |
| Leon Burns, Long Beach St. (II) | 1969-70 | 22 | 47 | 2 | 0 | 284 | 12.9 |
| Ed Marinaro, Cornell (I-A) | 1969-71 | 27 | 52 | 6 | 0 | 318 | 11.8 |
| Joe Dudek, Plymouth St. (III) | 1982-85 | 41 | *79 | 0 | 0 | *474 | 11.6 |
| Bill Burnett, Arkansas (I-A) | 1968-70 | 26 | 49 | 0 | 0 | 294 | 11.3 |
| Dale Mills, Northeast Mo. St. (II) | 1957-60 | 36 | 64 | 23 | 0 | 407 | 11.3 |
| Steve Owens, Oklahoma (I-A) | 1967-69 | 30 | 56 | 0 | 0 | 336 | 11.2 |
| Walter Payton, Jackson St. (II) | 1971-74 | 42 | 66 | 53 | 5 | 464 | 11.0 |
| Steve Roberts, Butler (II) | 1986-89 | 35 | 63 | 4 | 0 | 386 | 11.0 |
| Jeff Bentrim, North Dak. St. (II) | 1983-86 | 35 | 64 | 2 | 0 | 386 | 11.0 |
| Shawn Graves, Wofford (II) | 1989-92 | 40 | 72 | 3 | 0 | 438 | 11.0 |
| Johnny Bailey, Texas A&I (II) | 1986-89 | 39 | 70 | 3 | 0 | 426 | 10.9 |
| Eddie Talboom, Wyoming (I-A) | 1948-50 | 28 | 34 | 99 | 0 | 303 | 10.8 |
| Chris Babirad, Wash. & Jeff. (III) | 1989-92 | 35 | 62 | 2 | 0 | 374 | 10.7 |

* Record.

## Season Points

| Player, Team (Division) | Year | TD | XPt. | FG | Pts. |
|---|---|---|---|---|---|
| Barry Sanders, Oklahoma St. (I-A) | †1988 | *39 | 0 | 0 | *234 |
| Terry Metcalf, Long Beach St. (II) | 1971 | 29 | 4 | 0 | 178 |
| Mike Rozier, Nebraska (I-A) | †1983 | 29 | 0 | 0 | 174 |
| Lydell Mitchell, Penn St. (I-A) | 1971 | 29 | 0 | 0 | 174 |
| Geoff Mitchell, Weber St. (I-AA) | †1991 | 28 | 1 | 0 | 170 |
| Stanley Drayton, Allegheny (III) | †1991 | 28 | 0 | 0 | 168 |
| Jim Switzer, Col. of Emporia (II) | †1963 | 28 | 0 | 0 | 168 |
| Carl Herakovich, Rose-Hulman (II) | †1958 | 25 | 18 | 0 | 168 |
| Ted Scown, Sul Ross St. (II) | †1948 | 28 | 0 | 0 | 168 |
| Ronald Moore, Pittsburg St. (II) | 1992 | 27 | 4 | 0 | 166 |
| Ricky Gales, Simpson (III) | †1989 | 26 | 10 | 0 | 166 |
| Art Luppino, Arizona (I-A) | †1954 | 24 | 22 | 0 | 166 |
| Leon Burns, Long Beach St. (II) | †1969 | 27 | 2 | 0 | 164 |
| Jerry Rice, Mississippi Val. (I-AA) | †1984 | 27 | 0 | 0 | 162 |
| Billy Johnson, Widener (II) | †1972 | 27 | 0 | 0 | 162 |

| Player, Team (Division) | Year | TD | XPt. | FG | Pts. |
|---|---|---|---|---|---|
| Mike Deutsch, North Dak. (II) | 1972 | 27 | 0 | 0 | 162 |
| Bobby Reynolds, Nebraska (I-A) | †1950 | 22 | 25 | 0 | 157 |

\* *Record.* † *National champion.*

## Season Points Per Game

| Player, Team (Division) | Year | G | TD | XPt. | FG | Pts. | Pt.PG |
|---|---|---|---|---|---|---|---|
| Barry Sanders, Oklahoma St. (I-A) | †1988 | 11 | *39 | 0 | 0 | *234 | 21.3 |
| Carl Herakovich, Rose-Hulman (II) | †1958 | 8 | 25 | 18 | 0 | 168 | 21.0 |
| Jim Switzer, Col. of Emporia (II) | †1963 | 9 | 28 | 0 | 0 | 168 | 18.7 |
| Billy Johnson, Widener (II) | †1972 | 9 | 27 | 0 | 0 | 162 | 18.0 |
| Carl Garrett, N. M. Highlands (II) | †1966 | 9 | 26 | 2 | 0 | 158 | 17.6 |
| Bobby Reynolds, Nebraska (I-A) | †1950 | 9 | 22 | 25 | 0 | 157 | 17.4 |
| Stanley Drayton, Allegheny (III) | †1991 | 10 | 28 | 0 | 0 | 168 | 16.8 |
| Ted Scown, Sul Ross St. (II) | †1948 | 10 | 28 | 0 | 0 | 168 | 16.8 |
| Ricky Gales, Simpson (III) | †1989 | 10 | 26 | 10 | 0 | 166 | 16.6 |
| Art Luppino, Arizona (I-A) | †1954 | 10 | 24 | 22 | 0 | 166 | 16.6 |
| Ed Marinaro, Cornell (I-A) | †1971 | 9 | 24 | 4 | 0 | 148 | 16.4 |
| Jerry Rice, Mississippi Val. (I-AA) | †1984 | 10 | 27 | 0 | 0 | 162 | 16.2 |
| Chris Babirad, Wash. & Jeff. (III) | †1992 | 9 | 24 | 0 | 0 | 144 | 16.0 |
| Larry Ras, Michigan Tech (II) | †1971 | 9 | 24 | 0 | 0 | 144 | 16.0 |
| Trent Nauholz, Simpson (III) | †1992 | 8 | 21 | 2 | 0 | 128 | 16.0 |
| Lydell Mitchell, Penn St. (I-A) | 1971 | 11 | 29 | 0 | 0 | 174 | 15.8 |
| Marshall Faulk, San Diego St. (I-A) | †1991 | 9 | 23 | 2 | 0 | 140 | 15.6 |

\* *Record.* † *National champion.*

## Single-Game Points

| Pts. | Div. | Player, Team (Opponent) | Date |
|---|---|---|---|
| 48 | I-A | Howard Griffith, Illinois (Southern Ill.) | Sept. 22, 1990 |
| 48 | II | Paul Zaeske, North Park (North Central) | Oct. 12, 1968 |
| 48 | II | Junior Wolf, Panhandle St. (St. Mary, Kan.) | Nov. 8, 1958 |
| 44 | I-A | Marshall Faulk, San Diego St. (Pacific, Cal.) | Sept. 14, 1991 |
| 43 | I-A | Jim Brown, Syracuse (Colgate) | Nov. 17, 1956 |
| 42 | I-A | Arnold "Showboat" Boykin, Mississippi (Mississippi St.) | Dec. 1, 1951 |
| 42 | I-A | Fred Wendt, UTEP (New Mexico St.) | Nov. 25, 1948 |

*1993 NCAA FOOTBALL*

# AWARD WINNERS

The 1993 Heisman Trophy presentation will be the 25th since O.J. Simpson earned the prestigious award in 1968. Simpson was the second of four Southern Cal halfbacks to win the award from 1965

# CONSENSUS ALL-AMERICA SELECTIONS
## 104 Years of All-Americans, 1889-1992

In 1950, the National Collegiate Athletic Bureau (the NCAA's service bureau) compiled the first official comprehensive roster of all-time all-americans.

The compilation of the all-American roster was supervised by a panel of analysts working in large part with the historical records contained in the files of the Dr. Baker Football Information Service.

The roster consists of only those players who were **first-team** selections on one or more of the all-America teams that were selected for the national audience and received nationwide circulation.

Not included are the thousands of players who received mention on all-America second or third teams, nor the numerous others who were selected by newspapers or agencies with circulations that were not primarily national and with viewpoints, therefore, that were not normally nationwide in scope.

Listed on the following pages are the consensus all-Americans (i.e., the players who were accorded a majority of votes at their positions by the selectors). (Included are the selections of 1889-97, 1909-12 and 1922 when there was only one selector.)

### Symbols for Selectors

AA—All-America Board
AP—Associated Press
C—Walter Camp (published in Harper's Weekly 1897; in Collier's Magazine 1898-1924)
COL—Collier's Magazine (selections by Grantland Rice 1925-47; published American Football Coaches Association teams 1948-56, listed under FC)
CP—Central Press
FBW—Football World Magazine
FC—American Football Coaches Association (published in Saturday Evening Post Magazine 1945-47; in Collier's Magazine 1948-56; sponsored by General Mills 1957-59 and by Eastman Kodak from 1960)
FN—Football News
FW—Football Writers Association of America (published in Look Magazine 1946-70)
INS—International News Service (merged with United Press in 1958 to form UPI)
L—Look Magazine (published Football Writers Association of America teams, 1946-70, listed under FW)
LIB—Liberty Magazine
M—Frank Menke Syndicate
NM—Newsweek Magazine
NANA—North American Newspaper Alliance
NEA—Newspaper Enterprise Association
SN—Sporting News
UP—United Press (merged with International News Service in 1958 to form UPI)
UPI—United Press International
W—Caspar Whitney (published in The Week's Sport in association with Walter Camp 1889-90; published in Harper's Weekly 1891-96 and in Outing Magazine, which he owned, 1898-1908; Walter Camp substituted for Whitney, who was on a world sports tour, and selected Harper's Weekly's team for 1897)
WCF—Walter Camp Foundation

### All-America Selections

#### 1889-1899

| Yr. | W | C |
|-----|---|---|
| 89 | X | |
| 90 | X | |
| 91 | X | |
| 92 | X | |
| 93 | X | |
| 94 | X | |
| 95 | X | |
| 96 | X | |
| 97 | X | |
| 98 | X | X |
| 99 | X | X |

#### 1900-1912

| Yr. | W | C |
|-----|---|---|
| 00 | X | X |
| 01 | X | X |
| 02 | X | X |
| 03 | X | X |
| 04 | X | X |
| 05 | X | X |
| 06 | X | X |
| 07 | X | X |
| 08 | X | |
| 09 | | X |
| 10 | | X |
| 11 | | X |
| 12 | | X |

#### 1913-1923

| Yr. | C | INS | M | NEA | FBW |
|-----|---|-----|---|-----|-----|
| 13 | X | X | | | |
| 14 | X | X | | | |
| 15 | X | X | | | |
| 16 | X | X | X | | |
| 17 | (*) | X | X | X | |
| 18 | X | | X | | |
| 19 | X | | X | | |
| 20 | X | X | X | | |
| 21 | X | | | | X |
| 22 | X | | | | |
| 23 | X | | | | X |

**1924-1934**

| Yr. | C | INS | NEA | FBW | AA | LIB | AP | COL | UP | NANA | SN |
|---|---|---|---|---|---|---|---|---|---|---|---|
| 24 | X | X | X | X | X | X | | | | | |
| 25 | | X | X | X | X | X | X | X | X | | |
| 26 | | X | X | | X | | X | X | X | | |
| 27 | | X | X | | X | | X | X | X | X | |
| 28 | | X | X | | X | | X | X | X | X | |
| 29 | | X | X | | X | | X | X | X | X | |
| 30 | | X | X | | X | | X | X | X | X | |
| 31 | | X | X | | X | X | X | X | X | | |
| 32 | | X | X | | X | X | X | X | X | X | |
| 33 | | X | X | | X | X | X | X | X | X | |
| 34 | | X | X | | X | X | X | X | X | X | X |

**1935-1936**

| Yr. | C | INS | NEA | FBW | AA | LIB | AP | COL | UP | NANA | SN |
|---|---|---|---|---|---|---|---|---|---|---|---|
| 35 | | X | X | | X | X | X | X | X | X | X |
| 36 | | X | X | | X | X | X | X | X | X | X |

**1937-1941**

| Yr. | INS | NEA | AA | LIB | AP | COL | UP | NANA | SN | N |
|---|---|---|---|---|---|---|---|---|---|---|
| 37 | X | X | X | X | X | X | X | X | X | X |
| 38 | X | X | X | X | X | X | X | | X | X |
| 39 | X | X | X | X | X | X | X | | X | X |
| 40 | X | X | X | X | X | X | X | | X | X |
| 41 | X | X | X | X | X | X | X | | X | X |

**1942-1957**

| Yr. | INS | NEA | AA | AP | COL | UP | SN | N | L | FBN | FW | FC |
|---|---|---|---|---|---|---|---|---|---|---|---|---|
| 42 | X | X | X | X | X | X | X | X | X | | | |
| 43 | X | | X | X | X | X | X | | X | X | | |
| 44 | X | X | X | X | X | X | X | | X | X | | |
| 45 | X | X | X | X | X | X | X | | X | | X | |
| 46 | X | X | X | X | X | X | X | | (†) | | X | X |
| 47 | X | X | | X | X | X | X | | | | X | X |
| 48 | (#)X | X | | X | (‡) | X | X | | | | X | X |
| 49 | X | X | X | X | | X | X | | | | X | X |
| 50 | X | X | X | X | | X | X | | | | X | X |
| 51 | X | X | X | X | | X | X | | | | X | X |
| 52 | X | X | X | X | | X | X | | | | X | X |
| 53 | X | X | X | X | | X | X | | | | X | X |
| 54 | X | X | X | X | | X | X | | | | X | X |
| 55 | X | X | X | X | | X | X | | | | X | X |
| 56 | X | X | | X | | X | X | | | | X | X |
| 57 | X | X | | X | | X | X | | | | X | X |

**1958-1962**

| Yr. | NEA | AP | UPI | SN | FW | FC |
|---|---|---|---|---|---|---|
| 58 | X | X | X | X | X | X |
| 59 | X | X | X | X | X | X |
| 60 | X | X | X | X | X | X |
| 61 | X | X | X | X | X | X |
| 62 | X | X | X | X | X | X |

**1963-1971**

| Yr. | NEA | AP | UPI | SN | FW | FC | CP |
|---|---|---|---|---|---|---|---|
| 63 | X | X | X | X | X | X | X |
| 64 | X | X | X | | X | X | X |
| 65 | X | X | X | | X | X | X |
| 66 | X | X | X | | X | X | X |
| 67 | X | X | X | | X | X | X |
| 68 | X | X | X | | X | X | X |
| 69 | X | X | X | | X | X | X |
| 70 | X | X | X | | X | X | X |
| 71 | X | X | X | | X | X | |

**1972-1974**

| Yr. | NEA | AP | UPI | FW | FC | WCF |
|---|---|---|---|---|---|---|
| 72 | X | X | X | X | X | X |
| 73 | X | X | X | X | X | X |
| 74 | | X | X | X | X | X |

**1975-1982**

| Yr. | AP | UPI | FW | FC |
|---|---|---|---|---|
| 75 | X | X | X | X |
| 76 | X | X | X | X |
| 77 | X | X | X | X |
| 78 | X | X | X | X |
| 79 | X | X | X | X |
| 80 | X | X | X | X |
| 81 | X | X | X | X |
| 82 | X | X | X | X |

*Consensus All-America Selections*

| Yr. | AP | 1983-1992 UPI | FW | FC | WCF |
|-----|----|----|----|----|-----|
| 83 | X | X | X | X | X |
| 84 | X | X | X | X | X |
| 85 | X | X | X | X | X |
| 86 | X | X | X | X | X |
| 87 | X | X | X | X | X |
| 88 | X | X | X | X | X |
| 89 | X | X | X | X | X |
| 90 | X | X | X | X | X |
| 91 | X | X | X | X | X |
| 92 | X | X | X | X | X |

*In 1917, Walter Camp selected an all-Service, all-America team composed of military personnel. † During 1946-70, Look Magazine published the Football Writers Association of America's selections, listed under FW. ‡ During 1948-56, Collier's Magazine published the American Football Coaches Association's selections, listed under FC. # International News Service was the first to select offensive and defensive teams.*

## 1889

E—Amos Alonzo Stagg, Yale; Arthur Cumnock, Harvard; T—Hector Cowan, Princeton; Charles Gill, Yale; G—Pudge Heffelfinger, Yale; John Cranston, Harvard; C—William George, Princeton; B—Edgar Allan Poe, Princeton; Roscoe Channing, Princeton; Knowlton Ames, Princeton; James Lee, Harvard.

## 1890

E—Frank Hallowell, Harvard; Ralph Warren, Princeton; T—Marshall Newell, Harvard; William Rhodes, Yale; G—Pudge Heffelfinger, Yale; Jesse Riggs, Princeton; C—John Cranston, Harvard; B— Thomas McClung, Yale; Sheppard Homans, Princeton; Dudley Dean, Harvard; John Corbett, Harvard.

## 1891

E—Frank Hinkey, Yale; John Hartwell, Yale; T—Wallace Winter, Yale; Marshall Newell, Harvard; G—Pudge Heffelfinger, Yale; Jesse Riggs, Princeton; C—John Adams, Pennsylvania; B—Philip King, Princeton; Everett Lake, Harvard; Thomas McClung, Yale; Sheppard Homans, Princeton.

## 1892

E—Frank Hinkey, Yale; Frank Hallowell, Harvard; T—Marshall Newell, Harvard; A. Hamilton Wallis, Yale; G—Arthur Wheeler, Princeton; Bertram Waters, Harvard; C—William Lewis, Harvard; B—Charles Brewer, Harvard; Vance McCormick, Yale; Philip King, Princeton; Harry Thayer, Pennsylvania.

## 1893

E—Frank Hinkey, Yale; Thomas Trenchard, Princeton; T—Langdon Lea, Princeton; Marshall Newell, Harvard; G—Arthur Wheeler, Princeton; William Hickok, Yale; C—William Lewis, Harvard; B—Philip King, Princeton; Charles Brewer, Harvard; Franklin Morse, Princeton; Frank Butterworth, Yale.

## 1894

E—Frank Hinkey, Yale; Charles Gelbert, Pennsylvania; T—Bertram Waters, Harvard; Langdon Lea, Princeton; G—Arthur Wheeler, Princeton; William Hickok, Yale; C—Philip Stillman, Yale; B—George Adee, Yale; Arthur Knipe, Pennsylvania; George Brooke, Pennsylvania; Frank Butterworth, Yale.

## 1895

E—Norman Cabot, Harvard; Charles Gelbert, Pennsylvania; T—Langdon Lea, Princeton; Fred Murphy, Yale; G—Charles Wharton, Pennsylvania; Dudley Riggs, Princeton; C—Alfred Bull, Pennsylvania; B—Clinton Wyckoff, Cornell; Samuel Thorne, Yale; Charles Brewer, Harvard; George Brooke, Pennsylvania.

## 1896

E—Norman Cabot, Harvard; Charles Gelbert, Pennsylvania; T—William Church, Princeton; Fred Murphy, Yale; G—Charles Wharton, Pennsylvania; Wylie Woodruff, Pennsylvania; C—Robert Gailey, Princeton; B—Clarence Fincke, Yale; Edgar Wrightington, Harvard; Addison Kelly, Princeton; John Baird, Princeton.

## 1897

E—Garrett Cochran, Princeton; John Hall, Yale; T—Burr Chamberlain, Yale; John Outland, Pennsylvania; G—T. Truxton Hare, Pennsylvania; Gordon Brown, Yale; C—Alan Doucette, Harvard; B— Charles DeSaulles, Yale; Benjamin Dibblee, Harvard; Addison Kelly, Princeton; John Minds, Pennsylvania.

## 1898

E—Lew Palmer, Princeton; John Hallowell, Harvard; T—Arthur Hillebrand, Princeton; Burr Chamberlain, Yale; G—T. Truxton Hare, Pennsylvania; Gordon Brown, Yale; Walter Boal, Harvard; C—Pete Overfield, Pennsylvania; William Cunningham, Michigan; B—Charles Daly, Harvard; Benjamin Dibblee, Harvard; John Outland, Pennsylvania; Clarence Herschberger, Chicago; Malcolm McBride, Yale; Charles Romeyn, Army.

## 1899

E—David Campbell, Harvard; Arthur Poe, Princeton; T—Arthur Hillebrand, Princeton; George Stillman, Yale; G—T. Truxton Hare, Pennsylvania; Gordon Brown, Yale; C—Pete Overfield, Pennsylvania; B—Charles Daly, Harvard; Josiah McCracken, Pennsylvania; Malcolm McBride, Yale; Isaac Seneca, Carlisle; Albert Sharpe, Yale; Howard Reiter, Princeton.

## 1900

E—John Hallowell, Harvard; David Campbell, Harvard; William Smith, Army; T—George Stillman, Yale; James Bloomer, Yale; G—Gordon Brown, Yale; T. Truxton Hare, Pennsylvania; C—Herman Olcott, Yale; Walter Bachman, Lafayette; B—Bill Morley, Columbia; George Chadwick, Yale; Perry Hale, Yale; William Fincke, Yale; Charles Daly, Harvard; Raymond Starbuck, Cornell.

## 1901

E—David Campbell, Harvard; Ralph Davis, Princeton; Edward Bowditch, Harvard; Neil Snow, Michigan; T—Oliver Cutts, Harvard; Paul Bunker, Army; Crawford Blagden, Harvard; G—William Warner, Cornell; William Lee, Harvard; Charles Barnard, Harvard; Sanford Hunt, Cornell; C—Henry Holt, Yale; Walter Bachman, Lafayette; B—Robert Kernan, Harvard; Charles Daly, Army; Thomas Graydon, Harvard; Harold Weekes, Columbia; Bill Morley, Columbia.

## 1902

E—Thomas Shevlin, Yale; Edward Bowditch, Harvard; T—Ralph Kinney, Yale; James Hogan, Yale; Paul Bunker, Army; G—Edgar Glass, Yale; John DeWitt, Princeton; William Warner, Cornell; C—Henry Holt, Yale; Robert Boyers, Army; B—Foster Rockwell, Yale; George Chadwick, Yale; Thomas Graydon, Harvard; Thomas Barry, Brown.

## 1903

E—Howard Henry, Princeton; Charles Rafferty, Yale; T—Daniel Knowlton, Harvard; James Hogan, Yale; Fred Schacht, Minnesota; G—John DeWitt, Princeton; Andrew Marshall, Harvard; James Bloomer, Yale; C—Henry Hooper, Dartmouth; B—Willie Heston, Michigan; J. Dana Kafer, Princeton; James Johnson, Carlisle; Richard Smith, Columbia; Myron Witham, Dartmouth; W. Ledyard Mitchell, Yale.

## 1904

E—Thomas Shevlin, Yale; Fred Speik, Chicago; T—James Hogan, Yale; James Cooney, Princeton; G—Frank Piekarski, Pennsylvania; Joseph Gilman, Dartmouth; Ralph Kinney, Yale; C—Arthur Tipton, Army; B—Daniel Hurley, Harvard; Walter Eckersall, Chicago; Vincent Stevenson, Pennsylvania; Willie Heston, Michigan; Andrew Smith, Pennsylvania; Foster Rockwell, Yale; Henry Torney, Army.

## 1905

E—Thomas Shevlin, Yale; Ralph Glaze, Dartmouth; Mark Catlin, Chicago; T—Otis Lamson, Pennsylvania; Beaton Squires, Harvard; Karl Brill, Harvard; G—Roswell Tripp, Yale; Francis Burr, Harvard; C—Robert Torrey, Pennsylvania; B—Walter Eckersall, Chicago; Howard Roome, Yale; John Hubbard, Amherst; James McCormick, Princeton; Guy Hutchinson, Yale; Daniel Hurley, Harvard; Henry Torney, Army.

## 1906

E—Robert Forbes, Yale; L. Casper Wister, Princeton; T—L. Horatio Biglow, Yale; James Cooney, Princeton; Charles Osborne, Harvard; G—Francis Burr, Harvard; Elmer Thompson, Cornell; August Ziegler, Pennsylvania; C—William Dunn, Penn St.; William Newman, Cornell; B—Walter Eckersall, Chicago; Hugh Knox, Yale; Edward Dillon, Princeton; John Mayhew, Brown; William Hollenback, Pennsylvania; Paul Veeder, Yale.

## 1907

E—Bill Dague, Navy; Clarence Alcott, Yale; Albert Exendine, Carlisle; L. Casper Wister, Princeton; T—Dexter Draper, Pennsylvania; L. Horatio Biglow, Yale; G—August Ziegler, Pennsylvania; William Erwin, Army; C—Adolph Schulz, Michigan; Patrick Grant, Harvard; B—John Wendell, Harvard; Thomas A. D. Jones, Yale; Edwin Harlan, Princeton; James McCormick, Princeton; Edward Coy, Yale; Peter Hauser, Carlisle.

## 1908

E—Hunter Scarlett, Pennsylvania; George Schildmiller, Dartmouth; T—Hamilton Fish, Harvard; Frank Horr, Syracuse; Percy Northcroft, Navy; G—Clark Tobin, Dartmouth; William Goebel, Yale; Hamlin Andrus, Yale; Bernard O'Rourke, Cornell; C—Charles Nourse, Harvard; B—Edward Coy, Yale; Frederick Tibbott, Princeton; William Hollenback, Pennsylvania; Walter Steffen, Chicago; Ed Lange, Navy; Hamilton Corbett, Harvard.

## 1909

E—Adrian Regnier, Brown; John Kilpatrick, Yale; T—Hamilton Fish, Harvard; Henry Hobbs, Yale; G—Albert Benbrook, Michigan; Hamlin Andrus, Yale; C—Carroll Cooney, Yale; B—Edward Coy, Yale; John McGovern, Minnesota; Stephen Philbin, Yale; Wayland Minot, Harvard.

## 1910

E—John Kilpatrick, Yale; Stanfield Wells, Michigan; T—Robert McKay, Harvard; James Walker, Minnesota; G—Robert Fisher, Harvard; Albert Benbrook, Michigan; C—Ernest Cozens, Pennsylvania; B—E. LeRoy Mercer, Pennsylvania; Percy Wendell, Harvard; Earl Sprackling, Brown; Talbot Pendleton, Princeton.

## 1911

E—Douglass Bomeisler, Yale; Sanford White, Princeton; T—Edward Hart, Princeton; Leland Devore, Army; G—Robert Fisher, Harvard; Joseph Duff, Princeton; C—Henry Ketcham, Yale; B—Jim Thorpe, Carlisle; Percy Wendell, Harvard; Arthur Howe, Yale; Jack Dalton, Navy.

## 1912

E—Samuel Felton, Harvard; Douglass Bomeisler, Yale; T—Wesley Englehorn, Dartmouth; Robert Butler, Wisconsin; G—Stanley Pennock, Harvard; John Logan, Princeton; C—Henry Ketcham, Yale; B—Charles Brickley, Harvard; Jim Thorpe, Carlisle; George Crowther, Brown; E. LeRoy Mercer, Pennsylvania.

## 1913

E—Robert Hogsett, Dartmouth; Louis Merrillat, Army; T—Harold Ballin, Princeton; Nelson Talbott, Yale; Miller Pontius, Michigan; Harvey Hitchcock, Harvard; G—John Brown, Navy; Stanley Pennock, Harvard; Ray Keeler, Wisconsin; C—Paul Des Jardien, Chicago; B—Charles Brickley, Harvard; Edward Mahan, Harvard; Jim Craig, Michigan; Ellery Huntington, Colgate; Gus Dorais, Notre Dame.

## 1914

E—Huntington Hardwick, Harvard; John O'Hearn, Cornell; Perry Graves, Illinois; T—Harold Ballin, Princeton; Walter Trumbull, Harvard; G—Stanley Pennock, Harvard; Ralph Chapman, Illinois; Clarence Spears, Dartmouth; C—John McEwan, Army; B—John Maulbetsch, Michigan; Edward Mahan, Harvard; Charles Barrett, Cornell; John Spiegel, Wash. & Jeff.; Harry LeGore, Yale.

## 1915

E—Murray Shelton, Cornell; Guy Chamberlin, Nebraska; T—Joseph Gilman, Harvard; Howard Buck, Wisconsin; G—Clarence Spears, Dartmouth; Harold White, Syracuse; C—Robert Peck, Pittsburgh; B—Charles Barrett, Cornell; Edward Mahan, Harvard; Richard King, Harvard; Bart Macomber, Illinois; Eugene Mayer, Virginia; Neno Jerry DaProto, Michigan St.

## 1916

E—Bert Baston, Minnesota; James Herron, Pittsburgh; T—Clarence Horning, Colgate; D. Belford West, Colgate; G—Clinton Black, Yale; Harrie Dadmun, Harvard; Frank Hogg, Princeton; C—Robert Peck, Pittsburgh; B—Elmer Oliphant, Army; Oscar Anderson, Colgate; Fritz Pollard, Brown; Charles Harley, Ohio St.

## 1917

E—Charles Bolen, Ohio St.; Paul Robeson, Rutgers; Henry Miller, Pennsylvania; T—Alfred Cobb, Syracuse; George Hauser, Minnesota; G—Dale Seis, Pittsburgh; John Sutherland, Pittsburgh; Eugene Neely, Dartmouth; C—Frank Rydzewski, Notre Dame; B—Elmer Oliphant, Army; Ben Boynton, Williams; Everett Strupper, Georgia Tech; Charles Harley, Ohio St.

## 1918

E—Paul Robeson, Rutgers; Bill Fincher, Georgia Tech; T—Wilbur Henry, Wash. & Jeff.; Leonard Hilty, Pittsburgh; Lou Usher, Syracuse; Joe Guyon, Georgia Tech; G—Joe Alexander, Syracuse; Lyman Perry, Navy; C—Ashel Day, Georgia Tech; John Depler, Illinois; B—Frank Murrey, Princeton; Tom Davies, Pittsburgh; Wolcott Roberts, Navy; George McLaren, Pittsburgh.

## 1919

E—Bob Higgins, Penn St.; Henry Miller, Pennsylvania; Lester Belding, Iowa; T—Wilbur Henry, Wash. & Jeff.; D. Belford West, Colgate; G—Joe Alexander, Syracuse; Adolph Youngstrom, Dartmouth; C—James Weaver, Centre; Charles Carpenter, Wisconsin; B—Charles Harley, Ohio St.; Ira Rodgers, West Va.; Edward Casey, Harvard; Bo McMillin, Centre; Ben Boynton, Williams.

## 1920

E—Luke Urban, Boston College; Charles Carney, Illinois; Bill Fincher, Georgia Tech; T—Stan Keck, Princeton; Ralph Scott, Wisconsin; G—Tim Callahan, Yale; Tom Woods, Harvard; Iolas Huffman, Ohio St.; C—Herb Stein, Pittsburgh; B—George Gipp, Notre Dame; Donold Lourie, Princeton; Gaylord Stinchcomb, Ohio St.; Charles Way, Penn St.

## 1921

E—Brick Muller, California; Eddie Anderson, Notre Dame; T—Dan McMillan, California; Iolas Huffman, Ohio St.; G—Frank Schwab, Lafayette; John Brown, Harvard; Stan Keck, Princeton; C—Herb Stein, Pittsburgh; B—Aubrey Devine, Iowa; Glenn Killinger, Penn St.; Bo McMillin, Centre; Malcolm Aldrich, Yale; Edgar Kaw, Cornell.

## 1922

E—Brick Muller, California; Wendell Taylor, Navy; T—C. Herbert Treat, Princeton; John Thurman, Pennsylvania; G—Frank Schwab, Lafayette; Charles Hubbard, Harvard; C—Ed Garbisch, Army; B—Harry Kipke, Michigan; Gordon Locke, Iowa; John Thomas, Chicago; Edgar Kaw, Cornell.

## 1923

E—Pete McRae, Syracuse; Ray Ecklund, Minnesota; Lynn Bomar, Vanderbilt; T—Century Milstead, Yale; Marty Below, Wisconsin; G—Charles Hubbard, Harvard; James McMillen, Illinois; C—Jack Blott, Michigan; B—George Pfann, Cornell; Red Grange, Illinois; William Mallory, Yale; Harry Wilson, Penn St.

*Beginning in 1924, unanimous selections are indicated by (*).*

## 1924

E—Jim Lawson, Stanford, 5-11, 190, Long Beach, Calif.; (tie) E—Dick Luman, Yale, 6-1, 176, Pinedale, Wyo.; E—Henry Wakefield, Vanderbilt, 5-10, 160, Petersburg,Tenn.; T—Ed McGinley, Pennsylvania, 5-11, 185, Swarthmore, Pa.; T—Ed Weir, Nebraska, 6-1, 194, Superior, Neb.; G—Joe Pondelik, Chicago, 5-11, 215, Cicero, Ill.; G—Carl Diehl, Dartmouth, 6-1, 205, Chicago, Ill.; C—Edwin Horrell, California, 5-11, 185, Pasadena, Calif.; B—*Red Grange, Illinois, 5-10, 170, Wheaton, Ill.; B—Harry Stuhldreher, Notre Dame, 5-7, 151, Massillon, Ohio; B—Jimmy Crowley, Notre Dame, 5-11, 162, Green Bay, Wis.; B—Elmer Layden, Notre Dame, 6-0, 162, Davenport, Iowa.

## 1925

E—Bennie Oosterbaan, Michigan, 6-0, 180, Muskegon, Mich.; E—George Tully, Dartmouth, 5-10, 175, Orange, N.J.; T—*Ed Weir, Nebraska, 6-1, 194, Superior, Neb.; T—Ralph Chase, Pittsburgh, 6-3, 202, Easton, Pa.; G—Carl Diehl, Dartmouth, 6-1, 205, Chicago, Ill.; G—Ed Hess, Ohio St., 6-1, 190, Cincinnati, Ohio; C—Ed McMillan, Princeton, 6-0, 208, Pittsburgh, Pa.; B—*Andy Oberlander, Dartmouth, 6-0, 197, Everett, Mass.; B—Red Grange, Illinois, 5-10, 170, Wheaton, Ill.; B—Ernie Nevers, Stanford, 6-0, 200, Superior, Wis.; (tie) B—Benny Friedman, Michigan, 5-8, 170, Cleveland, Ohio; B—George Wilson, Washington, 5-11, 190, Everett, Wash.

## 1926

E—Bennie Oosterbaan, Michigan, 6-0, 186, Muskegon, Mich.; E—Vic Hanson, Syracuse, 5-10, 174, Syracuse, N.Y.; T—*Frank Wickhorst, Navy, 6-0, 218, Oak Park, Ill.; T—Bud Sprague, Army, 6-2, 210, Dallas, Texas; G—Harry Connaughton, Georgetown, 6-2, 275, Philadelphia, Pa.; G—Bernie Shively, Illinois, 6-4, 208, Oliver, Ill.; C—Bud Boeringer, Notre Dame, 6-1, 186, St. Paul, Minn.; B—Benny Friedman, Michigan, 5-8, 172, Cleveland, Ohio; B—Mort Kaer, Southern Cal, 5-11, 167, Red Bluff, Calif.; B—Ralph Baker, Northwestern, 5-10, 172, Rockford, Ill.; B—Herb Joesting, Minnesota, 6-1, 192, Owatonna, Minn.

## 1927

E—*Bennie Oosterbaan, Michigan, 6-0, 186, Muskegon, Mich.; E—Tom Nash, Georgia, 6-3, 200, Washington, Ga.; T—Jesse Hibbs, Southern Cal, 5-11, 185, Glendale, Calif.; T—Ed Hake, Pennsylvania, 6-0, 190, Philadelphia, Pa.; G—Bill Webster, Yale, 6-0, 200, Shelton, Conn.; G—John Smith, Notre Dame, 5-9, 164, Hartford, Conn.; (tie) C—Larry Bettencourt, St. Mary's (Cal.), 5-10, 187, Centerville, Calif.; C—John Charlesworth, Yale, 5-11, 198, North Adams, Mass.; B—*Gibby Welch, Pittsburgh, 5-11, 170, Parkersburg, W. Va.; B—Morley Drury, Southern Cal, 6-0, 185, Long Beach, Calif.; B—Red Cagle, Army, 5-9, 167, Merryville, La.; B—Herb Joesting, Minnesota, 6-1, 192, Owatonna, Minn.

## 1928

E—Irv Phillips, California, 6-1, 188, Salinas, Calif.; E—Wes Fesler, Ohio St., 6-0, 173, Youngstown, Ohio; T—Otto Pommerening, Michigan, 6-0, 178, Ann Arbor, Mich.; T—Mike Getto, Pittsburgh, 6-2, 198, Jeannette, Pa.; G—Seraphim Post, Stanford, 6-0, 190, Berkeley, Calif.; (tie) Don Robesky, Stanford, 5-11, 198, Bakersfield, Calif.; G—Edward Burke, Navy, 6-0, 180, Larksville, Pa.; C—Pete Pund, Georgia Tech, 6-0, 195, Augusta, Ga.; B—*Red Cagle, Army, 5-9, 167, Merryville, La.; B—Paul Scull, Pennsylvania, 5-8, 187, Bala, Pa.; B—Ken Strong, New York U., 6-0, 201, West Haven, Conn.; (tie) Howard Harpster, Carnegie Mellon, 6-1, 160, Akron, Ohio; B—Charles Carroll, Washington, 6-0, 190, Seattle, Wash.

## 1929

E—*Joe Donchess, Pittsburgh, 6-0, 175, Youngstown, Ohio; E—Wes Fesler, Ohio St., 6-0, 183, Youngstown, Ohio; T—Bronko Nagurski, Minnesota, 6-2, 217, International Falls, Minn.; T—Elmer Sleight, Purdue, 6-2, 193, Morris, Ill.; G—Jack Cannon, Notre Dame, 5-11, 193, Columbus, Ohio; G—Ray Montgomery, Pittsburgh, 6-1, 188, Wheeling, W. Va.; C—Ben Ticknor, Harvard, 6-2, 193, New York, N.Y.; B—*Frank Carideo, Notre Dame, 5-7, 175, Mount Vernon, N.Y.; B—Ralph Welch, Purdue, 6-1, 189, Whitesboro, Texas; B—Red Cagle, Army, 5-9, 167, Merryville, La.; B—Gene McEver, Tennessee, 5-10, 185, Bristol, Va.

## 1930

E—*Wes Fesler, Ohio St., 6-0, 185, Youngstown, Ohio; E—Frank Baker, Northwestern, 6-2, 175, Cedar Rapids, Iowa; T—*Fred Sington, Alabama, 6-2, 215, Birmingham, Ala.; T—Milo Lubratovich, Wisconsin, 6-2, 216, Duluth, Minn.; G—Ted Beckett, California, 6-1, 190, Oroville, Calif.; G—Barton Koch, Baylor, 5-10, 195, Temple, Texas; C—*Ben Ticknor, Harvard, 6-2, 193, New York, N.Y.; B—*Frank Carideo, Notre Dame, 5-7, 175, Mount Vernon, N.Y.; B—Marchy Schwartz, Notre Dame, 5-11, 172, Bay St. Louis, Miss.; B—Erny Pinckert, Southern Cal, 6-0, 189, San Bernardino, Calif.; B—Leonard Macaluso, Colgate, 6-2, 210, East Aurora, N.Y.

## 1931

E—*Jerry Dalrymple, Tulane, 5-10, 175, Arkadelphia, Ark.; E—Vernon Smith, Georgia, 6-2, 190, Macon, Ga.; T—Jesse Quatse, Pittsburgh, 5-8, 198, Greensburg, Pa.; (tie) T—Jack Riley, Northwestern, 6-2, 218, Wilmette, Ill.; T—Dallas Marvil, Northwestern, 6-3, 227, Laurel, Del.; G—Biggie Munn, Minnesota, 5-10, 217, Minneapolis, Minn.; G—John Baker, Southern Cal, 5-10, 185, Kingsburg, Calif.; C—Tommy Yarr, Notre Dame, 5-11, 197, Chimacum, Wash.; B—Gus Shaver, Southern Cal, 5-11, 185, Covina, Calif.; B—Marchy Schwartz, Notre Dame, 5-11, 178, Bay St. Louis, Miss.; B—Pug Rentner, Northwestern, 6-1, 185, Joliet, Ill.; B—Barry Wood, Harvard, 6-1, 173, Milton, Mass.

## 1932

E—*Paul Moss, Purdue, 6-2, 185, Terre Haute, Ind.; E—Joe Skladany, Pittsburgh, 5-10, 185, Larksville, Pa.; T—*Joe Kurth, Notre Dame, 6-2, 204, Madison, Wis.; T—*Ernie Smith, Southern Cal, 6-2, 215, Los Angeles, Calif.; G—Milt Summerfelt, Army, 6-0, 181, Benton Harbor, Mich.; G—Bill Corbus, Stanford, 5-11, 188, Vallejo, Calif.; G—Pete Gracey, Vanderbilt, 6-0, 188, Franklin, Tenn.; B—*Harry Newman, Michigan, 5-7, 175, Detroit, Mich.; B—*Warren Heller, Pittsburgh, 6-0, 170, Steelton, Pa.; B—Don Zimmerman, Tulane, 5-10, 190, Lake Charles, La.; B—Jimmy Hitchcock, Auburn, 5-11, 172, Union Springs, Ala.

## 1933

E—Joe Skladany, Pittsburgh, 5-10, 190, Larksville, Pa.; E—Paul Geisler, Centenary, 6-2, 189, Berwick, La.; T—Fred Crawford, Duke, 6-2, 195, Waynesville, N.C.; T—Francis Wistert, Michigan, 6-3, 212, Chicago, Ill.; G—Bill Corbus, Stanford, 5-11, 195, Vallejo, Calif.; G—Aaron Rosenberg, Southern Cal, 6-0, 210, Los Angeles, Calif.; C—*Chuck Bernard, Michigan, 6-2, 215, Benton Harbor, Mich.; B—*Cotton Warburton, Southern Cal, 5-7, 147, San Diego, Calif.; B—George Sauer, Nebraska, 6-2, 195, Lincoln, Neb.; B—Beattie Feathers, Tennessee, 5-10, 180, Bristol, Va.; B—Duane Purvis, Purdue, 6-1, 190, Mattoon, Ill.

## 1934

E—Don Hutson, Alabama, 6-1, 185, Pine Bluff, Ark.; E—Frank Larson, Minnesota, 6-3, 190, Duluth, Minn.; T—Bill Lee, Alabama, 6-2, 225, Eutaw, Ala.; T—Bob Reynolds, Stanford, 6-4, 220, Okmulgee, Okla.; G—Chuck Hartwig, Pittsburgh, 6-0, 190, Benwood, W. Va.; G—Bill Bevan, Minnesota, 5-11, 194, St. Paul, Minn.; C—Jack Robinson, Notre Dame, 6-3, 195, Huntington, N.Y.; B—Bobby Grayson, Stanford, 5-11, 186, Portland, Ore.; B—Pug Lund, Minnesota, 5-11, 185, Rice Lake, Wis.; B—Dixie Howell, Alabama, 5-10, 164, Hartford, Ala.; B—Fred Borries, Navy, 6-0, 175, Louisville, Ky.

## 1935

E—Wayne Millner, Notre Dame, 6-0, 184, Salem, Mass.; (tie) E—James Moscrip, Stanford, 6-0, 186, Adena, Ohio; E—Gaynell Tinsley, Louisiana St., 6-0, 188, Homer, La.; T—Ed Widseth, Minnesota, 6-2, 220, McIntosh, Minn.; T—Larry Lutz, California, 6-0, 201, Santa Ana, Calif.; T—John Weller, Princeton, 6-0, 195, Wynnewood, Pa.; (tie) G—Sidney Wagner, Michigan St., 5-11, 186, Lansing, Mich.; G—J. C. Wetsel, Southern Methodist, 5-10, 185, Dallas, Texas; (tie) C—Gomer Jones, Ohio St., 5-8, 210, Cleveland, Ohio; C—Darrell Lester, Texas Christian, 6-4, 218, Jacksboro, Texas; B—*Jay Berwanger, Chicago, 6-0, 195, Dubuque, Iowa; B—*Bobby Grayson, Stanford, 5-11, 190, Portland, Ore.; B—Bobby Wilson, Southern Methodist, 5-10, 147, Corsicana, Texas; B—Riley Smith, Alabama, 6-1, 195, Columbus, Miss.

## 1936

E—*Larry Kelley, Yale, 6-1, 190, Williamsport, Pa.; E—*Gaynell Tinsley, Louisiana St., 6-0, 196, Homer,

---

*Consensus All-America Selections*

307

La.; T—*Ed Widseth, Minnesota, 6-2, 220, McIntosh, Minn.; T—Averell Daniell, Pittsburgh, 6-3, 200, Mt. Lebanon, Pa.; G—Steve Reid, Northwestern, 5-9, 192, Chicago, Ill.; G—Max Starcevich, Washington, 5-10, 198, Duluth, Minn.; (tie) C—Alex Wojciechowicz, Fordham, 6-0, 192, South River, N.J.; C—Mike Basrak, Duquesne, 6-1, 210, Bellaire, Ohio; B—Sammy Baugh, Texas Christian, 6-2, 180, Sweetwater, Texas; B—Ace Parker, Duke, 5-11, 175, Portsmouth, Va.; B—Ray Buivid, Marquette, 6-1, 193, Port Washington, Wis.; B—Sam Francis, Nebraska, 6-1, 207, Oberlin, Kan.

## 1937

E—Chuck Sweeney, Notre Dame, 6-0, 190, Bloomington, Ill.; E—Andy Bershak, North Caro., 6-0, 190, Clairton, Pa.; T—Ed Franco, Fordham, 5-8, 196, Jersey City, N.J.; T—Tony Matisi, Pittsburgh, 6-0, 224, Endicott, N.Y.; G—Joe Routt, Texas A&M, 6-0, 193, Chappel Hill, Texas; G—Leroy Monsky, Alabama, 6-0, 198, Montgomery, Ala.; C—Alex Wojciechowicz, Fordham, 6-0, 196, South River, N.J.; B—*Clint Frank, Yale, 5-10, 190, Evanston, Ill.; B—Marshall Goldberg, Pittsburgh, 5-11, 185, Elkins, W. Va.; B—Byron "Whizzer" White, Colorado, 6-1, 185, Wellington, Colo.; B—Sam Chapman, California, 6-0, 190, Tiburon, Calif.

## 1938

E—Waddy Young, Oklahoma, 6-2, 203, Ponca City, Okla.; (tie) E—Brud Holland, Cornell, 6-1, 205, Auburn, N.Y.; E—Bowden Wyatt, Tennessee, 6-1, 190, Kingston, Tenn.; T—*Ed Beinor, Notre Dame, 6-2, 207, Harvey, Ill.; T—Alvord Wolff, Santa Clara, 6-2, 220, San Francisco, Calif.; G—*Ralph Heikkinen, Michigan, 5-10, 185, Ramsey, Mich.; G—Ed Bock, Iowa St., 6-0, 202, Fort Dodge, Iowa; C—Ki Aldrich, Texas Christian, 5-11, 195, Temple, Texas; B—*Davey O'Brien, Texas Christian, 5-7, 150, Dallas, Texas; B—*Marshall Goldberg, Pittsburgh, 6-0, 190, Elkins, W. Va.; B—Bob MacLeod, Dartmouth, 6-0, 190, Glen Ellyn, Ill.; B—Vic Bottari, California, 5-9, 182, Vallejo, Calif.

## 1939

E—Esco Sarkkinen, Ohio St., 6-0, 192, Fairport Harbor, Ohio; E—Ken Kavanaugh, Louisiana St., 6-3, 203, Little Rock, Ark.; T—Nick Drahos, Cornell, 6-3, 200, Cedarhurst, N.Y.; T—Harley McCollum, Tulane, 6-4, 235, Wagoner, Okla.; G—*Harry Smith, Southern Cal, 5-11, 218, Ontario, Calif.; G—Ed Molinski, Tennessee, 5-10, 190, Massillon, Ohio; C—John Schiechl, Santa Clara, 6-2, 220, San Francisco, Calif.; B—Nile Kinnick, Iowa, 5-8, 167, Omaha, Neb.; B—Tom Harmon, Michigan, 6-0, 195, Gary, Ind.; B—John Kimbrough, Texas A&M, 6-2, 210, Haskell, Texas; B—George Cafego, Tennessee, 6-0, 174, Scarbro, W. Va.

## 1940

E—Gene Goodreault, Boston College, 5-10, 184, Haverhill, Mass.; E—Dave Rankin, Purdue, 6-1, 190, Warsaw, Ind.; T—Nick Drahos, Cornell, 6-3, 212, Cedarhurst, N.Y.; (tie) T—Alf Bauman, Northwestern, 6-1, 210, Chicago, Ill.; T—Urban Odson, Minnesota, 6-3, 247, Clark, S. D.; G—*Bob Suffridge, Tennessee, 6-0, 190, Knoxville, Tenn.; G—Marshall Robnett, Texas A&M, 6-1, 205, Klondike, Texas; C—Rudy Mucha, Washington, 6-2, 210, Chicago, Ill.; B—*Tom Harmon, Michigan, 6-0, 195, Gary, Ind.; B—*John Kimbrough, Texas A&M, 6-2, 221, Haskell, Texas; B—Frank Albert, Stanford, 5-9, 170, Glendale, Calif.; B—George Franck, Minnesota, 6-0, 175, Davenport, Iowa.

## 1941

E—Holt Rast, Alabama, 6-1, 185, Birmingham, Ala.; E—Bob Dove, Notre Dame, 6-2, 195, Youngstown, Ohio; T—Dick Wildung, Minnesota, 6-0, 210, Luverne, Minn.; T—Ernie Blandin, Tulane, 6-3, 245, Keighley, Kan.; G—*Endicott Peabody, Harvard, 6-0, 181, Syracuse, N.Y.; G—Ray Frankowski, Washington, 5-10, 210, Hammond, Ind.; C—Darold Jenkins, Missouri, 6-0, 195, Higginsville, Mo.; B—Bob Westfall, Michigan, 5-8, 190, Ann Arbor, Mich.; B—Bruce Smith, Minnesota, 6-0, 193, Faribault, Minn.; B—Frank Albert, Stanford, 5-9, 173, Glendale, Calif.; (tie) B—Bill Dudley, Virginia, 5-10, 175, Bluefield, Va.; B—Frank Sinkwich, Georgia, 5-8, 180, Youngstown, Ohio.

## 1942

E—*Dave Schreiner, Wisconsin, 6-2, 198, Lancaster, Wis.; E—Bob Dove, Notre Dame, 6-2, 195, Youngstown, Ohio; T—Dick Wildung, Minnesota, 6-0, 215, Luverne, Minn.; T—Albert Wistert, Michigan, 6-2, 205, Chicago, Ill.; G—Chuck Taylor, Stanford, 5-11, 200, San Jose, Calif.; (tie) G—Harvey Hardy, Georgia Tech, 5-10, 185, Thomaston, Ga.; G—Julie Franks, Michigan, 6-0, 187, Hamtramck, Mich.; C—Joe Domnanovich, Alabama, 6-1, 200, South Bend, Ind.; B—*Frank Sinkwich, Georgia, 5-8, 185, Youngstown, Ohio; B—Paul Governali, Columbia, 5-11, 186, New York, N.Y.; B—Mike Holovak, Boston College, 6-2, 214, Lansford, Pa.; B—Billy Hillenbrand, Indiana, 6-0, 195, Evansville, Ind.

## 1943

E—Ralph Heywood, Southern Cal, 6-2, 195, Huntington Park, Calif.; E—John Yonakor, Notre Dame, 6-4, 220, Dorchester, Mass.; T—Jim White, Notre Dame, 6-2, 210, Edgewater, N.J.; T—Don Whitmire, Navy, 5-11, 215, Decatur, Ala.; G—Alex Agase, Purdue, 5-10, 190, Evanston, Ill.; G—Pat Filley, Notre Dame, 5-8, 175, South Bend, Ind.; C—*Casimir Myslinski, Army, 5-11, 186, Steubenville, Ohio; B—*Bill Daley, Michigan, 6-2, 206, St. Cloud, Minn.; B—Angelo Bertelli, Notre Dame, 6-1, 173, West Springfield, Mass.; B—Creighton Miller, Notre Dame, 6-0, 185, Wilmington, Del.; B—Bob Odell, Pennsylvania, 5-11, 182, Sioux City, Iowa.

## 1944

E—Phil Tinsley, Georgia Tech, 6-1, 188, Bessemer, Ala.; (tie) E—Paul Walker, Yale, 6-3, 203, Oak Park, Ill.; E—Jack Dugger, Ohio St., 6-3, 210, Canton, Ohio; T—*Don Whitmire, Navy, 5-11, 215, Decatur, Ala.; T—John Ferraro, Southern Cal, 6-3, 235, Maywood, Calif.; G—Bill Hackett, Ohio St., 5-9, 191, London, Ohio; G—Ben Chase, Navy, 6-1, 195, San Diego, Calif.; C—John Tavener, Indiana, 6-0, 220, Granville,

Ohio; B—*Les Horvath, Ohio St., 5-10, 167, Parma, Ohio; B—Glenn Davis, Army, 5-9, 170, Claremont, Calif.; B—Doc Blanchard, Army, 6-0, 205, Bishopville, S. C.; B—Bob Jenkins, Navy, 6-1, 195, Talladega, Ala.

## 1945

E—Dick Duden, Navy, 6-2, 203, New York, N.Y.; E—(tie) Hubert Bechtol, Texas, 6-2, 190, Lubbock, Texas; E—Bob Ravensberg, Indiana, 6-1, 180, Bellevue, Ky.; E—Max Morris, Northwestern, 6-2, 195, West Frankfort, Ill.; T—Tex Coulter, Army, 6-3, 220, Fort Worth, Texas; T—George Savitsky, Pennsylvania, 6-3, 250, Camden, N.J.; G—*Warren Amling, Ohio St., 6-0, 197, Pana, Ill.; G—John Green, Army, 5-11, 190, Shelbyville, Ky.; C—Vaughn Mancha, Alabama, 6-0, 235, Birmingham, Ala.; B—*Glenn Davis, Army, 5-9, 170, Claremont, Calif.; B—*Doc Blanchard, Army, 6-0, 205, Bishopville, S.C.; B—*Herman Wedemeyer, St. Mary's (Cal.), 5-10, 173, Honolulu, Hawaii; B—Bob Fenimore, Oklahoma St., 6-2, 188, Woodward, Okla.

## 1946

E—*Burr Baldwin, UCLA, 6-1, 196, Bakersfield, Calif.; E—(tie) Hubert Bechtol, Texas, 6-2, 201, Lubbock, Texas; E—Hank Foldberg, Army, 6-1, 200, Dallas, Texas; T—George Connor, Notre Dame, 6-3, 225, Chicago, Ill.; (tie) T—Warren Amling, Ohio St., 6-0, 197, Pana, Ill.; T—Dick Huffman, Tennessee, 6-2, 230, Charleston, W. Va.; G—Alex Agase, Illinois, 5-10, 191, Evanston, Ill.; G—Weldon Humble, Rice, 6-1, 214, San Antonio, Texas; C—Paul Duke, Georgia Tech, 6-1, 210, Atlanta, Ga.; B—*John Lujack, Notre Dame, 6-0, 180, Connellsville, Pa.; B—*Charley Trippi, Georgia, 5-11, 185, Pittston, Pa.; B—*Glenn Davis, Army, 5-9, 170, Claremont, Calif.; B—*Doc Blanchard, Army, 6-0, 205, Bishopville, S.C.

## 1947

E—Paul Cleary, Southern Cal, 6-1, 195, Santa Ana, Calif.; E—Bill Swiacki, Columbia, 6-2, 198, Southbridge, Mass.; T—Bob Davis, Georgia Tech, 6-4, 220, Columbus, Ga.; T—George Connor, Notre Dame, 6-3, 225, Chicago, Ill.; G—Joe Steffy, Army, 5-11, 190, Chattanooga, Tenn.; G—Bill Fischer, Notre Dame, 6-2, 230, Chicago, Ill.; C—Chuck Bednarik, Pennsylvania, 6-3, 220, Bethlehem, Pa.; B—*John Lujack, Notre Dame, 6-0, 180, Connellsville, Pa.; B—*Bob Chappuis, Michigan, 6-0, 180, Toledo, Ohio; B—Doak Walker, Southern Methodist, 5-11, 170, Dallas, Texas; (tie) B—Charley Conerly, Mississippi, 6-0, 184, Clarksdale, Miss.; B—Bobby Layne, Texas, 6-0, 191, Dallas, Texas.

## 1948

E—Dick Rifenburg, Michigan, 6-3, 197, Saginaw, Mich.; E—Leon Hart, Notre Dame, 6-4, 225, Turtle Creek, Pa.; T—Leo Nomellini, Minnesota, 6-2, 248, Chicago, Ill.; T—Alvin Wistert, Michigan, 6-3, 218, Chicago, Ill.; G—Buddy Burris, Oklahoma, 5-11, 214, Muskogee, Okla.; G—Bill Fischer, Notre Dame, 6-2, 233, Chicago, Ill.; C—Chuck Bednarik, Pennsylvania, 6-3, 220, Bethlehem, Pa.; B—*Doak Walker, Southern Methodist, 5-11, 168, Dallas, Texas; B—Charlie Justice, North Caro., 5-10, 165, Asheville, N.C.; B—Jackie Jensen, California, 5-11, 195, Oakland, Calif.; (tie) B—Emil Sitko, Notre Dame, 5-8, 180, Fort Wayne, Ind.; B—Clyde Scott, Arkansas, 6-0, 175, Smackover, Ark.

## 1949

E—*Leon Hart, Notre Dame, 6-5, 260, Turtle Creek, Pa.; E—James Williams, Rice, 6-0, 197, Waco, Texas; T—Leo Nomellini, Minnesota, 6-2, 255, Chicago, Ill.; T—Alvin Wistert, Michigan, 6-3, 223, Chicago, Ill.; G—*Rod Franz, California, 6-1, 198, San Francisco, Calif.; G—Ed Bagdon, Michigan St., 5-10, 200, Dearborn, Mich.; C—*Clayton Tonnemaker, Minnesota, 6-3, 240, Minneapolis, Minn.; B—*Emil Sitko, Notre Dame, 5-8, 180, Fort Wayne, Ind.; B—Doak Walker, Southern Methodist, 5-11, 170, Dallas, Texas; B—Arnold Galiffa, Army, 6-2, 190, Donora, Pa.; B—Bob Williams, Notre Dame, 6-1, 180, Baltimore, Md.

## 1950

E—*Dan Foldberg, Army, 6-1, 185, Dallas, Texas; E—Bill McColl, Stanford, 6-4, 225, San Diego, Calif.; T—Bob Gain, Kentucky, 6-3, 230, Weirton, W. Va.; T—Jim Weatherall, Oklahoma, 6-4, 220, White Deer, Texas; G—Bud McFadin, Texas, 6-3, 225, Iraan, Texas; G—Les Richter, California, 6-2, 220, Fresno, Calif.; C—Jerry Groom, Notre Dame, 6-3, 215, Des Moines, Iowa; B—*Vic Janowicz, Ohio St., 5-9, 189, Elyria, Ohio; B—Kyle Rote, Southern Methodist, 6-0, 190, San Antonio, Texas; B—Babe Parilli, Kentucky, 6-1, 183, Rochester, Pa.; B—Leon Heath, Oklahoma, 6-1, 195, Hollis, Okla.

## 1951

E—*Bill McColl, Stanford, 6-4, 225, San Diego, Calif.; E—Bob Carey, Michigan St., 6-5, 215, Charlevoix, Mich.; T—*Don Coleman, Michigan St., 5-10, 185, Flint, Mich.; T—*Jim Weatherall, Oklahoma, 6-4, 230, White Deer, Texas; G—*Bob Ward, Maryland, 5-10, 185, Elizabeth, N.J.; G—Les Richter, California, 6-2, 230, Fresno, Calif.; C—Dick Hightower, Southern Methodist, 6-1, 215, Tyler, Texas; B—*Dick Kazmaier, Princeton, 5-11, 171, Maumee, Ohio; B—*Hank Lauricella, Tennessee, 5-10, 169, New Orleans, La.; B—Babe Parilli, Kentucky, 6-1, 188, Rochester, Pa.; B—Johnny Karras, Illinois, 5-11, 171, Argo, Ill.

## 1952

E—Frank McPhee, Princeton, 6-3, 203, Youngstown, Ohio; E—Bernie Flowers, Purdue, 6-1, 189, Erie, Pa.; T—Dick Modzelewski, Maryland, 6-0, 235, West Natrona, Pa.; T—Hal Miller, Georgia Tech, 6-4, 235, Kingsport, Tenn.; G—John Michels, Tennessee, 6-1, 195, Philadelphia, Pa.; G—Elmer Wilhoite, Southern Cal, 6-2, 216, Winton, Calif.; C—Donn Moomaw, UCLA, 6-4, 220, Santa Ana, Calif.; B—*Jack Scarbath, Maryland, 6-1, 190, Baltimore, Md.; B—*Johnny Lattner, Notre Dame, 6-1, 190, Chicago, Ill.; B—Billy Vessels, Oklahoma, 6-0, 185, Cleveland, Okla.; B—Jim Sears, Southern Cal, 5-9, 167, Inglewood, Calif.

*Consensus All-America Selections*

## 1953

E—Don Dohoney, Michigan St., 6-1, 193, Ann Arbor, Mich.; E—Carlton Massey, Texas, 6-4, 210, Rockwall, Texas; T—*Stan Jones, Maryland, 6-0, 235, Lemoyne, Pa.; T—Art Hunter, Notre Dame, 6-2, 226, Akron, Ohio; G—J. D. Roberts, Oklahoma, 5-10, 210, Dallas, Texas; G—Crawford Mims, Mississippi, 5-10, 200, Greenwood, Miss.; C—Larry Morris, Georgia Tech, 6-0, 205, Decatur, Ga.; B—*Johnny Lattner, Notre Dame, 6-1, 190, Chicago, Ill.; B—*Paul Giel, Minnesota, 5-11, 185, Winona, Minn.; B—Paul Cameron, UCLA, 6-0, 185, Burbank, Calif.; B—J. C. Caroline, Illinois, 6-0, 184, Columbia, S.C.

## 1954

E—Max Boydston, Oklahoma, 6-2, 207, Muskogee, Okla.; E—Ron Beagle, Navy, 6-0, 185, Covington, Ky.; T—Jack Ellena, UCLA, 6-3, 214, Susanville, Calif.; T—Sid Fournet, Louisiana St., 5-11, 225, Baton Rouge, La.; G—*Bud Brooks, Arkansas, 5-11, 200, Wynne, Ark.; G—Calvin Jones, Iowa, 6-0, 200, Steubenville, Ohio; C—Kurt Burris, Oklahoma, 6-1, 209, Muskogee, Okla.; B—*Ralph Guglielmi, Notre Dame, 6-0, 185, Columbus, Ohio; B—*Howard Cassady, Ohio St., 5-10, 177, Columbus, Ohio; B—*Alan Ameche, Wisconsin, 6-0, 215, Kenosha, Wis.; B—Dicky Maegle, Rice, 6-0, 175, Taylor, Texas.

## 1955

E—*Ron Beagle, Navy, 6-0, 186, Covington, Ky.; E—Ron Kramer, Michigan, 6-3, 218, East Detroit, Mich.; T—Norman Masters, Michigan St., 6-2, 225, Detroit, Mich.; T—Bruce Bosley, West Va., 6-2, 225, Green Bank, W. Va.; G—Bo Bolinger, Oklahoma, 5-10, 206, Muskogee, Okla.; (tie) G—Calvin Jones, Iowa, 6-0, 220, Steubenville, Ohio; G—Hardiman Cureton, UCLA, 6-0, 213, Duarte, Calif.; C—*Bob Pellegrini, Maryland, 6-2, 225, Yatesboro, Pa.; B—*Howard Cassady, Ohio St., 5-10, 172, Columbus, Ohio; B—*Jim Swink, Texas Christian, 6-1, 180, Rusk, Texas; B—Earl Morrall, Michigan St., 6-1, 180, Muskegon, Mich.; B—Paul Hornung, Notre Dame, 6-2, 205, Louisville, Ky.

## 1956

E—*Joe Walton, Pittsburgh, 5-11, 205, Beaver Falls, Pa.; E—*Ron Kramer, Michigan, 6-3, 220, East Detroit, Mich.; T—John Witte, Oregon St., 6-2, 232, Klamath Falls, Ore.; T—Lou Michaels, Kentucky, 6-2, 229, Swoyersville, Pa.; G—*Jim Parker, Ohio St., 6-2, 251, Toledo, Ohio; G—*Bill Glass, Baylor, 6-4, 220, Corpus Christi, Texas; C—*Jerry Tubbs, Oklahoma, 6-2, 205, Breckenridge, Texas; B—*Jim Brown, Syracuse, 6-2, 212, Manhasset, N.Y.; B—*John Majors, Tennessee, 5-10, 162, Huntland, Tenn.; B—Tommy McDonald, Oklahoma, 5-9, 169, Albuquerque, N.M.; B—John Brodie, Stanford, 6-1, 190, Oakland, Calif.

## 1957

E—*Jimmy Phillips, Auburn, 6-2, 205, Alexander City, Ala.; E—Dick Wallen, UCLA, 6-0, 185, Alhambra, Calif.; T—Lou Michaels, Kentucky, 6-2, 235, Swoyersville, Pa.; T—Alex Karras, Iowa, 6-2, 233, Gary, Ind.; G—Bill Krisher, Oklahoma, 6-1, 213, Midwest City, Okla.; G—Al Ecuyer, Notre Dame, 5-10, 190, New Orleans, La.; C—Dan Currie, Michigan St., 6-3, 225, Detroit, Mich.; B—*John David Crow, Texas A&M, 6-2, 214, Springhill, La.; B—Walt Kowalczyk, Michigan St., 6-0, 205, Westfield, Mass.; B—Bob Anderson, Army, 6-2, 200, Cocoa, Fla.; B—Clendon Thomas, Oklahoma, 6-2, 188, Oklahoma City, Okla.

## 1958

E—Buddy Dial, Rice, 6-1, 185, Magnolia, Texas; E—Sam Williams, Michigan St., 6-5, 225, Dansville, Mich.; T—Ted Bates, Oregon St., 6-2, 215, Los Angeles, Calif.; T—Brock Strom, Air Force, 6-0, 217, Ironwood, Mich.; G—John Guzik, Pittsburgh, 6-3, 223, Lawrence, Pa.; (tie) G—Zeke Smith, Auburn, 6-2, 210, Uniontown, Ala.; G—George Deiderich, Vanderbilt, 6-1, 198, Toronto, Ohio; C—Bob Harrison, Oklahoma, 6-2, 206, Stamford, Texas; B—*Randy Duncan, Iowa, 6-0, 180, Des Moines, Iowa; B—*Pete Dawkins, Army, 6-1, 197, Royal Oak, Mich.; B—*Billy Cannon, Louisiana St., 6-1, 200, Baton Rouge, La.; B—Bob White, Ohio St., 6-2, 212, Covington, Ky.

## 1959

E—Bill Carpenter, Army, 6-2, 210, Springfield, Pa.; E—Monty Stickles, Notre Dame, 6-4, 225, Poughkeepsie, N.Y.; T—*Dan Lanphear, Wisconsin, 6-2, 214, Madison, Wis.; T—Don Floyd, Texas Christian, 6-3, 215, Midlothian, Texas; G—*Roger Davis, Syracuse, 6-2, 228, Solon, Ohio; G—Bill Burrell, Illinois, 6-0, 210, Chebanse, Ill.; C—Maxie Baughan, Georgia Tech, 6-1, 212, Bessemer, Ala.; B—Richie Lucas, Penn St., 6-1, 185, Glassport, Pa.; B—Billy Cannon, Louisiana St., 6-1, 208, Baton Rouge, La.; B—Charlie Flowers, Mississippi, 6-0, 198, Marianna, Ark.; B—Ron Burton, Northwestern, 5-9, 185, Springfield, Ohio.

## 1960

E—*Mike Ditka, Pittsburgh, 6-3, 215, Aliquippa, Pa.; E—*Danny LaRose, Missouri, 6-4, 220, Crystal City, Mo.; T—*Bob Lilly, Texas Christian, 6-5, 250, Throckmorton, Texas; T—Ken Rice, Auburn, 6-3, 250, Bainbridge, Ga.; G—*Tom Brown, Minnesota, 6-0, 225, Minneapolis, Minn.; G—Joe Romig, Colorado, 5-10, 197, Lakewood, Colo.; C—E. J. Holub, Texas Tech, 6-4, 215, Lubbock, Texas; B—*Jake Gibbs, Mississippi, 6-0, 185, Grenada, Miss.; B—*Joe Bellino, Navy, 5-9, 181, Winchester, Mass.; B—*Bob Ferguson, Ohio St., 6-0, 217, Troy, Ohio; B—Ernie Davis, Syracuse, 6-2, 205, Elmira, N.Y.

## 1961

E—Gary Collins, Maryland, 6-3, 205, Williamstown, Pa.; E—Bill Miller, Miami (Fla.), 6-0, 188, McKeesport, Pa.; T—*Billy Neighbors, Alabama, 5-11, 229, Tuscaloosa, Ala.; T—Merlin Olsen, Utah St., 6-5, 265, Logan, Utah; G—*Roy Winston, Louisiana St., 6-1, 225, Baton Rouge, La.; G—Joe Romig, Colorado, 5-10, 199, Lakewood, Colo.; C—Alex Kroll, Rutgers, 6-2, 228, Leechburg, Pa.; B—*Ernie Davis, Syracuse, 6-2, 210, Elmira, N.Y.; B—*Bob Ferguson, Ohio St., 6-0, 217, Troy, Ohio; B—*Jimmy Saxton, Texas, 5-11, 160, Palestine, Texas; B—Sandy Stephens, Minnesota, 6-0, 215, Uniontown, Pa.

## 1962

E—Hal Bedsole, Southern Cal, 6-5, 225, Northridge, Calif.; E—Pat Richter, Wisconsin, 6-5, 229, Madison, Wis.; T—*Bobby Bell, Minnesota, 6-4, 214, Shelby, N.C.; T—Jim Dunaway, Mississippi, 6-4, 260, Columbia, Miss.; G—*Johnny Treadwell, Texas, 6-1, 194, Austin, Texas; G—Jack Cvercko, Northwestern, 6-0, 230, Campbell, Ohio; C—*Lee Roy Jordan, Alabama, 6-2, 207, Monroeville, Ala.; B—*Terry Baker, Oregon St., 6-3, 191, Portland, Ore.; B—*Jerry Stovall, Louisiana St., 6-2, 195, West Monroe, La.; B—Mel Renfro, Oregon, 5-11, 190, Portland, Ore.; B—George Saimes, Michigan St., 5-10, 186, Canton, Ohio.

## 1963

E—Vern Burke, Oregon St., 6-4, 195, Bakersfield, Calif.; E—Lawrence Elkins, Baylor, 6-1, 187, Brownwood, Texas; T—*Scott Appleton, Texas, 6-3, 235, Brady, Texas; T—Carl Eller, Minnesota, 6-6, 241, Winston-Salem, N.C.; G—*Bob Brown, Nebraska, 6-5, 259, Cleveland, Ohio; G—Rick Redman, Washington, 5-11, 210, Seattle, Wash.; C—*Dick Butkus, Illinois, 6-3, 234, Chicago, Ill.; B—*Roger Staubach, Navy, 6-2, 190, Cincinnati, Ohio; B—Sherman Lewis, Michigan St., 5-8, 154, Louisville, Ky.; B—Jim Grisham, Oklahoma, 6-2, 205, Olney, Texas; (tie) B—Gale Sayers, Kansas, 6-0, 196, Omaha, Neb.; B—Paul Martha, Pittsburgh, 6-1, 180, Wilkinsburg, Pa.

## 1964

E—Jack Snow, Notre Dame, 6-2, 210, Long Beach, Calif.; E—Fred Biletnikoff, Florida St., 6-1, 186, Erie, Pa.; T—*Larry Kramer, Nebraska, 6-2, 240, Austin, Minn.; T—Ralph Neely, Oklahoma, 6-5, 243, Farmington, N.M.; G—Rick Redman, Washington, 5-11, 215, Seattle, Wash.; G—Glenn Ressler, Penn St., 6-2, 230, Dornsife, Pa.; C—Dick Butkus, Illinois, 6-3, 237, Chicago, Ill.; B—John Huarte, Notre Dame, 6-0, 180, Anaheim, Calif.; B—Gale Sayers, Kansas, 6-0, 194, Omaha, Neb.; B—Lawrence Elkins, Baylor, 6-1, 187, Brownwood, Texas; B—Tucker Frederickson, Auburn, 6-2, 210, Hollywood, Fla.

*Beginning in 1965, offense and defense selected.*

## 1965
### Offense

E—*Howard Twilley, Tulsa, 5-10, 180, Galena Park, Texas; E—Freeman White, Nebraska, 6-5, 220, Detroit, Mich.; T—Sam Ball, Kentucky, 6-4, 241, Henderson, Ky.; T—Glen Ray Hines, Arkansas, 6-5, 235, El Dorado, Ark.; G—*Dick Arrington, Notre Dame, 5-11, 232, Erie, Pa.; G—Stas Maliszewski, Princeton, 6-1, 215, Davenport, Iowa; C—Paul Crane, Alabama, 6-2, 188, Prichard, Ala.; B—*Mike Garrett, Southern Cal, 5-9, 185, Los Angeles, Calif.; B—*Jim Grabowski, Illinois, 6-2, 211, Chicago, Ill.; B—Bob Griese, Purdue, 6-1, 185, Evansville, Ind.; B—Donny Anderson, Texas Tech, 6-3, 210, Stinnett, Texas.

### Defense

E—Aaron Brown, Minnesota, 6-4, 230, Port Arthur, Texas; E—Bubba Smith, Michigan St., 6-7, 268, Beaumont, Texas; T—Walt Barnes, Nebraska, 6-3, 235, Chicago, Ill.; T—Loyd Phillips, Arkansas, 6-3, 221, Longview, Texas; T—Bill Yearby, Michigan, 6-3, 222, Detroit, Mich.; LB—Carl McAdams, Oklahoma, 6-3, 215, White Deer, Texas; LB—Tommy Nobis, Texas, 6-2, 230, San Antonio, Texas; LB—Frank Emanuel, Tennessee, 6-3, 228, Newport News, Va.; B—George Webster, Michigan St., 6-4, 204, Anderson, S.C.; B—Johnny Roland, Missouri, 6-2, 198, Corpus Christi, Texas; B—Nick Rassas, Notre Dame, 6-0, 185, Winnetka, Ill.

## 1966
### Offense

E—*Jack Clancy, Michigan, 6-1, 192, Detroit, Mich.; E—Ray Perkins, Alabama, 6-0, 184, Petal, Miss.; T—*Cecil Dowdy, Alabama, 6-0, 206, Cherokee, Ala.; T—Ron Yary, Southern Cal, 6-6, 265, Bellflower, Calif.; G—Tom Regner, Notre Dame, 6-1, 245, Kenosha, Wis.; G—LaVerne Allers, Nebraska, 6-0, 209, Davenport, Iowa; C—Jim Breland, Georgia Tech, 6-2, 223, Blacksburg, Va.; B—*Steve Spurrier, Florida, 6-2, 203, Johnson City, Tenn.; B—*Nick Eddy, Notre Dame, 6-0, 195, Lafayette, Calif.; B—Mel Farr, UCLA, 6-2, 208, Beaumont, Texas; B—Clint Jones, Michigan St., 6-0, 206, Cleveland, Ohio.

### Defense

E—*Bubba Smith, Michigan St., 6-7, 283, Beaumont, Texas; E—Alan Page, Notre Dame, 6-5, 238, Canton, Ohio; T—*Loyd Phillips, Arkansas, 6-3, 230, Longview, Texas; T—Tom Greenlee, Washington, 6-0, 195, Seattle, Wash.; MG—Wayne Meylan, Nebraska, 6-0, 239, Bay City, Mich.; MG—John LaGrone, Southern Methodist, 5-10, 232, Borger, Texas; LB—*Jim Lynch, Notre Dame, 6-1, 225, Lima, Ohio; LB—Paul Naumoff, Tennessee, 6-1, 209, Columbus, Ohio; B—*George Webster, Michigan St., 6-4, 218, Anderson, S.C.; B—Tom Beier, Miami (Fla.), 5-11, 197, Fremont, Ohio; B—Nate Shaw, Southern Cal, 6-2, 205, San Diego, Calif.

## 1967
### Offense

E—Dennis Homan, Alabama, 6-0, 182, Muscle Shoals, Ala.; E—Ron Sellers, Florida St., 6-4, 187, Jacksonville, Fla.; T—*Ron Yary, Southern Cal, 6-6, 245, Bellflower, Calif.; T—Ed Chandler, Georgia, 6-2, 222, Cedartown, Ga.; G—Harry Olszewski, Clemson, 5-11, 237, Baltimore, Md.; G—Rich Stotter, Houston, 5-11, 225, Shaker Heights, Ohio; C—*Bob Johnson, Tennessee, 6-4, 232, Cleveland, Tenn.; B—Gary Beban, UCLA, 6-0, 191, Redwood City, Calif.; B—*Leroy Keyes, Purdue, 6-3, 199, Newport News, Va.; B—*O. J. Simpson, Southern Cal, 6-2, 205, San Francisco, Calif.; B—*Larry Csonka, Syracuse, 6-3, 230, Stow, Ohio.

## Defense

E—*Ted Hendricks, Miami (Fla.), 6-8, 222, Miami Springs, Fla.; E—Tim Rossovich, Southern Cal, 6-5, 235, Mountain View, Calif.; T—Dennis Byrd, North Caro. St., 6-4, 250, Lincolnton, N.C.; MG—*Granville Liggins, Oklahoma, 5-11, 216, Tulsa, Okla.; MG—Wayne Meylan, Nebraska, 6-0, 231, Bay City, Mich.; LB—Adrian Young, Southern Cal, 6-1, 210, La Puente, Calif.; LB—Don Manning, UCLA, 6-2, 204, Culver City, Calif.; B—Tom Schoen, Notre Dame, 5-11, 178, Euclid, Ohio; B—Frank Loria, Virginia Tech, 5-9, 174, Clarksburg, W. Va.; B—Bobby Johns, Alabama, 6-1, 180, Birmingham, Ala.; B—Dick Anderson, Colorado, 6-2, 204, Boulder, Colo.

## 1968
## Offense

E—*Ted Kwalick, Penn St., 6-4, 230, McKees Rocks, Pa.; E—Jerry LeVias, Southern Methodist, 5-10, 170, Beaumont, Texas; T—*Dave Foley, Ohio St., 6-5, 246, Cincinnati, Ohio; T—George Kunz, Notre Dame, 6-5, 240, Arcadia, Calif.; G—*Charles Rosenfelder, Tennessee, 6-1, 220, Humboldt, Tenn.; (tie) G—Jim Barnes, Arkansas, 6-4, 227, Pine Bluff, Ark.; G—Mike Montler, Colorado, 6-4, 235, Columbus, Ohio; C—*John Didion, Oregon St., 6-4, 242, Woodland, Calif.; B—*O. J. Simpson, Southern Cal, 6-2, 205, San Francisco, Calif.; B—*Leroy Keyes, Purdue, 6-3, 205, Newport News, Va.; B—Terry Hanratty, Notre Dame, 6-1, 200, Butler, Pa.; B—Chris Gilbert, Texas, 5-11, 176, Spring, Texas.

## Defense

E—*Ted Hendricks, Miami (Fla.), 6-8, 222, Miami Springs, Fla.; E—John Zook, Kansas, 6-4, 230, Larned, Kan.; T—Bill Stanfill, Georgia, 6-5, 245, Cairo, Ga.; T—Joe Greene, North Texas, 6-4, 274, Temple, Texas; MG—Ed White, California, 6-3, 245, Palm Desert, Calif.; MG—Chuck Kyle, Purdue, 6-1, 225, Fort Thomas, Ky.; LB—Steve Kiner, Tennessee, 6-1, 205, Tampa, Fla.; LB—Dennis Onkotz, Penn St., 6-2, 205, Northampton, Pa.; B—Jake Scott, Georgia, 6-1, 188, Arlington, Va.; B—Roger Wehrli, Missouri, 6-0, 184, King City, Mo.; B—Al Worley, Washington, 6-0, 175, Wenatchee, Wash.

## 1969
## Offense

E—Jim Mandich, Michigan, 6-3, 222, Solon, Ohio; (tie) E—Walker Gillette, Richmond, 6-5, 200, Capron, Va.; E—Carlos Alvarez, Florida, 5-11, 180, Miami, Fla.; T—Bob McKay, Texas, 6-6, 245, Crane, Texas; T—John Ward, Oklahoma St., 6-5, 248, Tulsa, Okla.; G—Chip Kell, Tennessee, 6-0, 255, Decatur, Ga.; G—Bill Bridges, Houston, 6-2, 230, Carrollton, Texas; G—Rodney Brand, Arkansas, 6-2, 218, Newport, Ark.; B—*Mike Phipps, Purdue, 6-3, 206, Columbus, Ind.; B—*Steve Owens, Oklahoma, 6-2, 215, Miami, Okla.; B—Jim Otis, Ohio St., 6-0, 214, Celina, Ohio; B—Bob Anderson, Colorado, 6-0, 208, Boulder, Colo.

## Defense

E—Jim Gunn, Southern Cal, 6-1, 210, San Diego, Calif.; E—Phil Olsen, Utah St., 6-5, 255, Logan, Utah; T—*Mike Reid, Penn St., 6-3, 240, Altoona, Pa.; T—*Mike McCoy, Notre Dame, 6-5, 274, Erie, Pa.; MG—Jim Stillwagon, Ohio St., 6-0, 216, Mount Vernon, Ohio; LB—*Steve Kiner, Tennessee, 6-1, 215, Tampa, Fla.; LB—Dennis Onkotz, Penn St., 6-2, 212, Northampton, Pa.; LB—Mike Ballou, UCLA, 6-3, 230, Los Angeles, Calif.; B—Jack Tatum, Ohio St., 6-0, 204, Passaic, N.J.; B—Buddy McClinton, Auburn, 5-11, 190, Montgomery, Ala.; B—Tom Curtis, Michigan, 6-1, 190, Aurora, Ohio.

## 1970
## Offense

E—Tom Gatewood, Notre Dame, 6-2, 208, Baltimore, Md.; E—Ernie Jennings, Air Force, 6-0, 172, Kansas City, Mo.; E—Elmo Wright, Houston, 6-0, 195, Brazoria, Texas; T—Dan Dierdorf, Michigan, 6-4, 250, Canton, Ohio; (tie) T—Bobby Wuensch, Texas, 6-3, 230, Houston, Texas; T—Bob Newton, Nebraska, 6-4, 248, LaMirada, Calif.; G—*Chip Kell, Tennessee, 6-0, 240, Decatur, Ga.; G—Larry DiNardo, Notre Dame, 6-1, 235, New York, N.Y.; C—Don Popplewell, Colorado, 6-2, 240, Raytown, Mo.; QB—Jim Plunkett, Stanford, 6-3, 204, San Jose, Calif.; RB—Steve Worster, Texas, 6-0, 210, Bridge City, Texas; RB—Don McCauley, North Caro., 6-0, 211, Garden City, N.Y.

## Defense

E—Bill Atessis, Texas, 6-3, 255, Houston, Texas; E—Charlie Weaver, Southern Cal, 6-2, 214, Richmond, Calif.; T—Rock Perdoni, Georgia Tech, 5-11, 236, Wellesley, Mass.; T—Dick Bumpas, Arkansas, 6-1, 225, Fort Smith, Ark.; MG—*Jim Stillwagon, Ohio St., 6-0, 220, Mount Vernon, Ohio; LB—Jack Ham, Penn St., 6-3, 212, Johnstown, Pa.; LB—Mike Anderson, Louisiana St., 6-3, 225, Baton Rouge, La.; B—*Jack Tatum, Ohio St., 6-0, 208, Passaic, N.J.; B—Larry Willingham, Auburn, 6-1, 185, Birmingham, Ala.; B—Dave Elmendorf, Texas A&M, 6-1, 190, Houston, Texas; B—Tommy Casanova, Louisiana St., 6-1, 191, Crowley, La.

## 1971
## Offense

E—*Terry Beasley, Auburn, 5-11, 184, Montgomery, Ala.; E—Johnny Rodgers, Nebraska, 5-10, 171, Omaha, Neb.; T—*Jerry Sisemore, Texas, 6-4, 255, Plainview, Texas; T—Dave Joyner, Penn St., 6-0, 235, State College, Pa.; G—*Royce Smith, Georgia, 6-3, 240, Savannah, Ga.; G—Reggie McKenzie, Michigan, 6-4, 232, Highland Park, Mich.; C—Tom Brahaney, Oklahoma, 6-2, 231, Midland, Texas; QB—*Pat Sullivan, Auburn, 6-0, 191, Birmingham, Ala.; RB—*Ed Marinaro, Cornell, 6-3, 210, New Milford, N.J.; RB—*Greg Pruitt, Oklahoma, 5-9, 176, Houston, Texas; RB—Johnny Musso, Alabama, 5-11, 194, Birmingham, Ala.

## Defense

E—*Walt Patulski, Notre Dame, 6-5, 235, Liverpool, N.Y.; E—Willie Harper, Nebraska, 6-3, 207, Toledo, Ohio; T—Larry Jacobson, Nebraska, 6-6, 250, Sioux Falls, S.D.; T—Mel Long, Toledo, 6-1, 230, Toledo, Ohio; T—Sherman White, California, 6-5, 250, Portsmouth, N.H.; LB—*Mike Taylor, Michigan, 6-2, 224, Detroit, Mich.; LB—Jeff Siemon, Stanford, 6-2, 225, Bakersfield, Calif.; B—*Bobby Majors, Tennessee, 6-1, 197, Sewanee, Tenn.; B—Clarence Ellis, Notre Dame, 6-0, 178, Grand Rapids, Mich.; B—Ernie Jackson, Duke, 5-10, 170, Hopkins, S.C.; B—Tommy Casanova, Louisiana St., 6-2, 195, Crowley, La.

## 1972
## Offense

WR—*Johnny Rodgers, Nebraska, 5-9, 173, Omaha, Neb.; TE—*Charles Young, Southern Cal, 6-4, 228, Fresno, Calif.; T—*Jerry Sisemore, Texas, 6-4, 260, Plainview, Texas; T—Paul Seymour, Michigan, 6-5, 250, Berkley, Mich.; G—*John Hannah, Alabama, 6-3, 282, Albertville, Ala.; G—Ron Rusnak, North Caro., 6-1, 223, Prince George, Va.; C—Tom Brahaney, Oklahoma, 6-2, 227, Midland, Texas; QB—Bert Jones, Louisiana St., 6-3, 205, Ruston, La.; RB—*Greg Pruitt, Oklahoma, 5-9, 177, Houston, Texas; RB—Otis Armstrong, Purdue, 5-11, 197, Chicago, Ill.; RB—Woody Green, Arizona St., 6-1, 190, Portland, Ore.

## Defense

E—Willie Harper, Nebraska, 6-2, 207, Toledo, Ohio; E—Bruce Bannon, Penn St., 6-3, 224, Rockaway, N.J.; T—*Greg Marx, Notre Dame, 6-5, 265, Redford, Mich.; T—Dave Butz, Purdue, 6-7, 279, Park Ridge, Ill.; MG—*Rich Glover, Nebraska, 6-1, 234, Jersey City, N.J.; LB—Randy Gradishar, Ohio St., 6-3, 232, Champion, Ohio; LB—John Skorupan, Penn St., 6-2, 208, Beaver, Pa.; B—*Brad VanPelt, Michigan St., 6-5, 221, Owosso, Mich.; B—Cullen Bryant, Colorado, 6-2, 215, Colo. Springs, Colo.; B—Robert Popelka, Southern Methodist, 6-1, 190, Temple, Texas; B—Randy Logan, Michigan, 6-2, 192, Detroit, Mich.

## 1973
## Offense

WR—Lynn Swann, Southern Cal, 6-0, 180, Foster City, Calif.; TE—Dave Casper, Notre Dame, 6-3, 252, Chilton, Wis.; T—*John Hicks, Ohio St., 6-3, 258, Cleveland, Ohio; T—Booker Brown, Southern Cal, 6-3, 270, Santa Barbara, Calif.; G—Buddy Brown, Alabama, 6-2, 242, Tallahassee, Fla.; G—Bill Yoest, North Caro. St., 6-0, 235, Pittsburgh, Pa.; C—Bill Wyman, Texas, 6-2, 235, Spring, Texas; QB—Dave Jaynes, Kansas, 6-2, 212, Bonner Springs, Kan.; RB—*John Cappelletti, Penn St., 6-1, 206, Upper Darby, Pa.; RB—Roosevelt Leaks, Texas, 5-11, 209, Brenham, Texas; RB—Woody Green, Arizona St., 6-1, 202, Portland, Ore.; RB—Kermit Johnson, UCLA, 6-0, 185, Los Angeles, Calif.

## Defense

L—*John Dutton, Nebraska, 6-7, 248, Rapid City, S.D.; L—Dave Gallagher, Michigan, 6-4, 245, Piqua, Ohio; L—*Lucious Selmon, Oklahoma, 5-11, 236, Eufaula, Okla.; L—Tony Cristiani, Miami (Fla.), 5-10, 215, Brandon, Fla.; LB—*Randy Gradishar, Ohio St., 6-3, 236, Champion, Ohio; LB—Rod Shoate, Oklahoma, 6-1, 214, Spiro, Okla.; LB—Richard Wood, Southern Cal, 6-2, 217, Elizabeth, N.J.; B—Mike Townsend, Notre Dame, 6-3, 183, Hamilton, Ohio; B—Artimus Parker, Southern Cal, 6-3, 215, Sacramento, Calif.; B—Dave Brown, Michigan, 6-1, 188, Akron, Ohio; B—Randy Rhino, Georgia Tech, 5-10, 179, Charlotte, N.C.

## 1974
## Offense

WR—Pete Demmerle, Notre Dame, 6-1, 190, New Canaan, Conn.; TE—Bennie Cunningham, Clemson, 6-5, 252, Seneca, S.C.; T—Kurt Schumacher, Ohio St., 6-4, 250, Lorain, Ohio; T—Marvin Crenshaw, Nebraska, 6-6, 240, Toledo, Ohio; G—Ken Huff, North Caro., 6-4, 261, Coronado, Calif.; G—John Roush, Oklahoma, 6-0, 252, Arvada, Colo.; G—Gerry DiNardo, Notre Dame, 6-1, 237, New York, N.Y.; C—Steve Myers, Ohio St., 6-2, 244, Kent, Ohio; QB—Steve Bartkowski, California, 6-4, 215, Santa Clara, Calif.; RB—*Archie Griffin, Ohio St., 5-9, 184, Columbus, Ohio; RB—*Joe Washington, Oklahoma, 5-10, 178, Port Arthur, Texas; RB—*Anthony Davis, Southern Cal, 5-9, 183, San Fernando, Calif.

## Defense

L—*Randy White, Maryland, 6-4, 238, Wilmington, Del.; L—Mike Hartenstine, Penn St., 6-4, 233, Bethlehem, Pa.; L—Pat Donovan, Stanford, 6-5, 240, Helena, Mont.; L—Jimmy Webb, Mississippi St., 6-5, 245, Florence, Miss.; L—Leroy Cook, Alabama, 6-4, 205, Abbeville, Ala.; MG—Louie Kelcher, Southern Methodist, 6-5, 275, Beaumont, Texas; MG—Rubin Carter, Miami (Fla.), 6-3, 260, Ft. Lauderdale, Fla.; LB—*Rod Shoate, Oklahoma, 6-1, 213, Spiro, Okla.; LB—Richard Wood, Southern Cal, 6-2, 213, Elizabeth, N.J.; LB—Ken Bernich, Auburn, 6-2, 240, Gretna, La.; LB—Woodrow Lowe, Alabama, 6-0, 211, Phenix City, Ala.; B—*Dave Brown, Michigan, 6-1, 188, Akron, Ohio; B—Pat Thomas, Texas A&M, 5-9, 180, Plano, Texas; B—John Provost, Holy Cross, 5-10, 180, Quincy, Mass.

## 1975
## Offense

E—Steve Rivera, California, 6-0, 185, Wilmington, Calif.; E—Larry Seivers, Tennessee, 6-4, 198, Clinton, Tenn.; T—Bob Simmons, Texas, 6-5, 245, Temple, Texas; T—Dennis Lick, Wisconsin, 6-3, 262, Chicago, Ill.; G—Randy Johnson, Georgia, 6-2, 250, Rome, Ga.; G—Ted Smith, Ohio St., 6-1, 242, Gibsonburg, Ohio; C—*Rik Bonness, Nebraska, 6-4, 223, Bellevue, Neb.; QB—John Sciarra, UCLA, 5-10, 178, Alhambra, Calif.; RB—*Archie Griffin, Ohio St., 5-9, 182, Columbus, Ohio; RB—*Ricky Bell,

Southern Cal, 6-2, 215, Los Angeles, Calif.; RB—Chuck Muncie, California, 6-3, 220, Uniontown, Pa.

## Defense

E—*Leroy Cook, Alabama, 6-4, 205, Abbeville, Ala.; E—Jimbo Elrod, Oklahoma, 6-0, 210, Tulsa, Okla.; T—*Lee Roy Selmon, Oklahoma, 6-2, 256, Eufaula, Okla.; T—*Steve Niehaus, Notre Dame, 6-5, 260, Cincinnati, Ohio; MG—Dewey Selmon, Oklahoma, 6-1, 257, Eufaula, Okla.; LB—*Ed Simonini, Texas A&M, 6-0, 215, Las Vegas, Nev.; LB—Greg Buttle, Penn St., 6-3, 220, Linwood, N.J.; LB—Sammy Green, Florida, 6-2, 228, Ft. Meade, Fla.; B—*Chet Moeller, Navy, 6-0, 189, Kettering, Ohio; B—Tim Fox, Ohio St., 6-0, 186, Canton, Ohio; B—Pat Thomas, Texas A&M, 5-10, 180, Plano, Texas.

## 1976
## Offense

TE—Ken MacAfee, Notre Dame, 6-4, 251, Brockton, Mass.; SE—Larry Seivers, Tennessee, 6-4, 200, Clinton, Tenn.; T—Mike Vaughan, Oklahoma, 6-5, 275, Ada, Okla.; T—Chris Ward, Ohio St., 6-4, 274, Dayton, Ohio; G—Joel Parrish, Georgia, 6-3, 232, Douglas, Ga.; G—Mark Donahue, Michigan, 6-3, 245, Oak Lawn, Ill.; C—Derrel Gofourth, Oklahoma St., 6-2, 250, Parsons, Kan.; QB—Tommy Kramer, Rice, 6-2, 190, San Antonio, Texas; RB—*Tony Dorsett, Pittsburgh, 5-11, 192, Aliquippa, Pa.; RB—*Ricky Bell, Southern Cal, 6-2, 218, Los Angeles, Calif.; RB—Rob Lytle, Michigan, 6-1, 195, Fremont, Ohio; PK—Tony Franklin, Texas A&M, 5-10, 170, Fort Worth, Texas.

## Defense

E—*Ross Browner, Notre Dame, 6-3, 248, Warren, Ohio; E—Bob Brudzinski, Ohio St., 6-4, 228, Fremont, Ohio; T—Wilson Whitley, Houston, 6-3, 268, Brenham, Texas; T—Gary Jeter, Southern Cal, 6-5, 255, Cleveland, Ohio; T—Joe Campbell, Maryland, 6-6, 255, Wilmington, Del.; MG—Al Romano, Pittsburgh, 6-3, 230, Solvay, N.Y.; LB—*Robert Jackson, Texas A&M, 6-2, 228, Houston, Texas; LB—Jerry Robinson, UCLA, 6-3, 208, Santa Rosa, Calif.; B—*Bill Armstrong, Wake Forest, 6-4, 205, Randolph, N.J.; B—Gary Green, Baylor, 5-11, 182, San Antonio, Texas; B—Dennis Thurman, Southern Cal, 5-11, 170, Santa Monica, Calif.; B—Dave Butterfield, Nebraska, 5-10, 182, Kersey, Colo.

## 1977
## Offense

TE—*Ken MacAfee, Notre Dame, 6-4, 250, Brockton, Mass.; WR—John Jefferson, Arizona St., 6-1, 184, Dallas, Texas; WR—Ozzie Newsome, Alabama, 6-4, 210, Leighton, Ala.; T—*Chris Ward, Ohio St., 6-4, 272, Dayton, Ohio; T—Dan Irons, Texas Tech, 6-7, 260, Lubbock, Texas; G—*Mark Donahue, Michigan, 6-3, 245, Oak Lawn, Ill.; G—Leotis Harris, Arkansas, 6-1, 254, Little Rock, Ark.; C—Tom Brzoza, Pittsburgh, 6-3, 240, New Castle, Pa.; QB—Guy Benjamin, Stanford, 6-4, 202, Sepulveda, Calif.; RB—*Earl Campbell, Texas, 6-1, 220, Tyler, Texas; RB—*Terry Miller, Oklahoma St., 6-0, 196, Colorado Springs, Colo.; RB—Charles Alexander, Louisiana St., 6-1, 215, Galveston, Texas; K—Steve Little, Arkansas, 6-0, 179, Overland Park, Kan.

## Defense

L—*Ross Browner, Notre Dame, 6-3, 247, Warren, Ohio; L—*Art Still, Kentucky, 6-8, 247, Camden, N.J.; L—*Brad Shearer, Texas, 6-4, 255, Austin, Texas; L—Randy Holloway, Pittsburgh, 6-6, 228, Sharon, Pa.; L—Dee Hardison, North Caro., 6-4, 252, Newton Grove, N.C.; LB—*Jerry Robinson, UCLA, 6-3, 208, Santa Rosa, Calif.; LB—Tom Cousineau, Ohio St., 6-3, 228, Fairview Park, Ohio; LB—Gary Spani, Kansas St., 6-2, 222, Manhattan, Kan.; B—*Dennis Thurman, Southern Cal, 5-11, 173, Santa Monica, Calif.; B—*Zac Henderson, Oklahoma, 6-1, 184, Burkburnett, Texas; B—Luther Bradley, Notre Dame, 6-2, 204, Muncie, Ind.; B—Bob Jury, Pittsburgh, 6-0, 190, Library, Pa.

## 1978
## Offense

TE—Kellen Winslow, Missouri, 6-6, 235, East St. Louis, Ill.; WR—Emanuel Tolbert, Southern Methodist, 5-10, 180, Little Rock, Ark.; T—*Keith Dorney, Penn St., 6-5, 257, Allentown, Pa.; T—Kelvin Clark, Nebraska, 6-4, 275, Odessa, Texas; G—*Pat Howell, Southern Cal, 6-6, 255, Fresno, Calif.; G—*Greg Roberts, Oklahoma, 6-3, 238, Nacogdoches, Texas; C—Dave Huffman, Notre Dame, 6-5, 245, Dallas, Texas; C—Jim Ritcher, North Caro. St., 6-3, 242, Hinckley, Ohio; QB—*Chuck Fusina, Penn St., 6-1, 195, McKees Rocks, Pa.; RB—*Billy Sims, Oklahoma, 6-0, 205, Hooks, Texas; RB—*Charles White, Southern Cal, 5-11, 183, San Fernando, Calif.; RB—Ted Brown, North Caro. St., 5-10, 195, High Point, N.C.; RB—Charles Alexander, Louisiana St., 6-1, 214, Galveston, Texas.

## Defense

L—*Al Harris, Arizona St., 6-5, 240, Wheeler AFB, Hawaii; L—*Bruce Clark, Penn St., 6-3, 246, New Castle, Pa.; L—Hugh Green, Pittsburgh, 6-2, 215, Natchez, Miss.; L—Mike Bell, Colorado St., 6-5, 265, Wichita, Kan.; L—Marty Lyons, Alabama, 6-6, 250, St. Petersburg, Fla.; LB—*Bob Golic, Notre Dame, 6-3, 244, Willowick, Ohio; LB—*Jerry Robinson, UCLA, 6-3, 209, Santa Rosa, Calif.; LB—Tom Cousineau, Ohio St., 6-3, 227, Fairview Park, Ohio; B—*Johnnie Johnson, Texas, 6-2, 183, LaGrange, Texas; B—Kenny Easley, UCLA, 6-2, 202, Chesapeake, Va.; B—Jeff Nixon, Richmond, 6-4, 195, Glendale, Ariz.

## 1979
## Offense

TE—*Junior Miller, Nebraska, 6-4, 222, Midland, Texas; WR—Ken Margerum, Stanford, 6-1, 175, Fountain Valley, Calif.; T—*Greg Kolenda, Arkansas, 6-1, 258, Kansas City, Kan.; T—Jim Bunch, Alabama, 6-2, 240, Mechanicsville, Va.; G—*Brad Budde, Southern Cal, 6-5, 253, Kansas City, Mo.; G—Ken Fritz, Ohio St., 6-3, 238, Ironton, Ohio; C—*Jim Ritcher, North Caro. St., 6-3, 245, Hinckley, Ohio;

*1993 NCAA FOOTBALL*

QB—*Marc Wilson, Brigham Young, 6-5, 204, Seattle, Wash.; RB—*Charles White, Southern Cal, 6-0, 185, San Fernando, Calif.; RB—*Billy Sims, Oklahoma, 6-0, 205, Hooks, Texas; RB—Vagas Ferguson, Notre Dame, 6-1, 194, Richmond, Ind.; PK—Dale Castro, Maryland, 6-1, 170, Shady Side, Md.

## Defense

L—*Hugh Green, Pittsburgh, 6-2, 220, Natchez, Miss.; L—*Steve McMichael, Texas, 6-2, 250, Freer, Texas; L—Bruce Clark, Penn St., 6-3, 255, New Castle, Pa.; L—*Jim Stuckey, Clemson, 6-5, 241, Cayce, S.C.; MG—Ron Simmons, Florida St., 6-1, 235, Warner Robins, Ga.; LB—*George Cumby, Oklahoma, 6-0, 205, Tyler, Texas; LB—Ron Simpkins, Michigan, 6-2, 220, Detroit, Mich.; LB—Mike Singletary, Baylor, 6-1, 224, Houston, Texas; B—*Kenny Easley, UCLA, 6-3, 204, Chesapeake, Va.; B—*Johnnie Johnson, Texas, 6-2, 190, LaGrange, Texas; B—Roland James, Tennessee, 6-2, 182, Jamestown, Ohio; P—Jim Miller, Mississippi, 5-11, 183, Ripley, Miss.

## 1980
## Offense

WR—*Ken Margerum, Stanford, 6-1, 175, Fountain Valley, Calif.; TE—*Dave Young, Purdue, 6-6, 242, Akron, Ohio; L—*Mark May, Pittsburgh, 6-6, 282, Oneonta, N.Y.; L—Keith Van Horne, Southern Cal, 6-7, 265, Fullerton, Calif.; L—Nick Eyre, Brigham Young, 6-5, 276, Las Vegas, Nev.; L—Louis Oubre, Oklahoma, 6-4, 262, New Orleans, La.; L—Randy Schleusener, Nebraska, 6-7, 242, Rapid City, S.D.; C—*John Scully, Notre Dame, 6-5, 255, Huntington, N.Y.; QB—*Mark Herrmann, Purdue, 6-4, 187, Carmel, Ind.; RB—*George Rogers, South Caro., 6-2, 220, Duluth, Ga.; RB—*Herschel Walker, Georgia, 6-2, 220, Wrightsville, Ga.; RB—Jarvis Redwine, Nebraska, 5-11, 204, Inglewood, Calif.

## Defense

L—*Hugh Green, Pittsburgh, 6-2, 222, Natchez, Miss.; L—*E. J. Junior, Alabama, 6-3, 227, Nashville, Tenn.; L—Kenneth Sims, Texas, 6-6, 265, Groesbeck, Texas; L—Leonard Mitchell, Houston, 6-7, 270, Houston, Texas; MG—Ron Simmons, Florida St., 6-1, 230, Warner Robins, Ga.; LB—*Mike Singletary, Baylor, 6-1, 232, Houston, Texas; LB—*Lawrence Taylor, North Caro., 6-3, 237, Williamsburg, Va.; LB—David Little, Florida, 6-1, 228, Miami, Fla.; LB—Bob Crable, Notre Dame, 6-3, 222, Cincinnati, Ohio; B—*Kenny Easley, UCLA, 6-3, 206, Chesapeake, Va.; B—*Ronnie Lott, Southern Cal, 6-2, 200, Rialto, Calif.; B—John Simmons, Southern Methodist, 5-11, 188, Little Rock, Ark.

## 1981
## Offense

WR—*Anthony Carter, Michigan, 5-11, 161, Riviera Beach, Fla.; TE—*Tim Wrightman, UCLA, 6-3, 237, San Pedro, Calif.; L—*Sean Farrell, Penn St., 6-3, 266, Westhampton Beach, N.Y.; L—Roy Foster, Southern Cal, 6-4, 265, Overland Park, Kan.; L—Terry Crouch, Oklahoma, 6-1, 275, Dallas, Texas; L—Ed Muransky, Michigan, 6-7, 275, Youngstown, Ohio; L—Terry Tausch, Texas, 6-4, 265, New Braunfels, Texas; L—Kurt Becker, Michigan, 6-6, 260, Aurora, Ill.; C—*Dave Rimington, Nebraska, 6-3, 275, Omaha, Neb.; QB—*Jim McMahon, Brigham Young, 6-0, 185, Roy, Utah; RB—*Marcus Allen, Southern Cal, 6-2, 202, San Diego, Calif.; RB—*Herschel Walker, Georgia, 6-2, 222, Wrightsville, Ga.

## Defense

L—*Billy Ray Smith, Arkansas, 6-4, 228, Plano, Texas; L—*Kenneth Sims, Texas, 6-6, 265, Groesbeck, Texas; L—Andre Tippett, Iowa, 6-4, 235, Newark, N.J.; L—Tim Krumrie, Wisconsin, 6-3, 237, Mondovi, Wis.; LB—Bob Crable, Notre Dame, 6-3, 225, Cincinnati, Ohio; LB—Jeff Davis, Clemson, 6-0, 223, Greensboro, N.C.; LB—Sal Sunseri, Pittsburgh, 6-0, 220, Pittsburgh, Pa.; DB—Tommy Wilcox, Alabama, 5-11, 187, Harahan, La.; DB—Mike Richardson, Arizona St., 6-1, 192, Compton, Calif.; DB—Terry Kinard, Clemson, 6-1, 183, Sumter, S.C.; DB—Fred Marion, Miami (Fla.), 6-3, 194, Gainesville, Fla.; P—Reggie Roby, Iowa, 6-3, 215, Waterloo, Iowa.

## 1982
## Offense

WR—*Anthony Carter, Michigan, 5-11, 161, Riviera Beach, Fla.; TE—*Gordon Hudson, Brigham Young, 6-4, 224, Salt Lake City, Utah; L—*Don Mosebar, Southern Cal, 6-7, 270, Visalia, Calif.; L—*Steve Korte, Arkansas, 6-2, 270, Littleton, Colo.; L—Jimbo Covert, Pittsburgh, 6-5, 279, Conway, Pa.; L—Bruce Matthews, Southern Cal, 6-5, 265, Arcadia, Calif.; C—*Dave Rimington, Nebraska, 6-3, 290, Omaha, Neb.; QB—*John Elway, Stanford, 6-4, 202, Northridge, Calif.; RB—*Herschel Walker, Georgia, 6-2, 222, Wrightsville, Ga.; RB—*Eric Dickerson, Southern Methodist, 6-2, 215, Sealy, Texas; RB—Mike Rozier, Nebraska, 5-11, 210, Camden, N.J.; PK—*Chuck Nelson, Washington, 5-11, 178, Everett, Wash.

## Defense

L—*Billy Ray Smith, Arkansas, 6-3, 228, Plano, Texas; L—Vernon Maxwell, Arizona St., 6-2, 225, Carson, Calif.; L—Mike Pitts, Alabama, 6-5, 255, Baltimore, Md.; L—Wilber Marshall, Florida, 6-1, 230, Titusville, Fla.; L—Gabriel Rivera, Texas Tech, 6-3, 270, San Antonio, Texas; L—Rick Bryan, Oklahoma, 6-4, 260, Coweta, Okla.; MG—George Achica, Southern Cal, 6-5, 260, San Jose, Calif.; LB—*Darryl Talley, West Va., 6-4, 210, East Cleveland, Ohio; LB—Ricky Hunley, Arizona, 6-1, 230, Petersburg, Va.; LB—Marcus Marek, Ohio St., 6-2, 224, Masury, Ohio; DB—*Terry Kinard, Clemson, 6-1, 189, Sumter, S.C.; DB—Mike Richardson, Arizona St., 6-0, 190, Compton, Calif.; DB—Terry Hoage, Georgia, 6-3, 196, Huntsville, Texas; P—*Jim Arnold, Vanderbilt, 6-3, 205, Dalton, Ga.

## 1983
## Offense

WR—*Irving Fryar, Nebraska, 6-0, 200, Mount Holly, N.J.; TE—*Gordon Hudson, Brigham Young, 6-

4, 231, Salt Lake City, Utah; L—*Bill Fralic, Pittsburgh, 6-5, 270, Penn Hills, Pa.; L—Terry Long, East Caro., 6-0, 280, Columbia, S.C.; L—Dean Steinkuhler, Nebraska, 6-3, 270, Burr, Neb.; L—Doug Dawson, Texas, 6-3, 263, Houston, Texas; C—Tony Slaton, Southern Cal, 6-4, 260, Merced, Calif.; QB—*Steve Young, Brigham Young, 6-1, 198, Greenwich, Conn.; RB—*Mike Rozier, Nebraska, 5-11, 210, Camden, N.J.; RB—Bo Jackson, Auburn, 6-1, 222, Bessemer, Ala.; RB—Greg Allen, Florida St., 6-0, 200, Milton, Fla.; RB—Napoleon McCallum, Navy, 6-2, 208, Milford, Ohio; PK—Luis Zendejas, Arizona St., 5-9, 186, Chino, Calif.

### Defense

L—*Rick Bryan, Oklahoma, 6-4, 260, Coweta, Okla.; L—*Reggie White, Tennessee, 6-5, 264, Chattanooga, Tenn.; L—William Perry, Clemson, 6-3, 320, Aiken, S.C.; L—William Fuller, North Caro., 6-4, 250, Chesapeake, Va.; LB—*Ricky Hunley, Arizona, 6-2, 230, Petersburg, Va.; LB—Wilber Marshall, Florida, 6-1, 230, Titusville, Fla.; LB—Ron Rivera, California, 6-3, 225, Monterey, Calif.; LB—Jeff Leiding, Texas, 6-4, 240, Tulsa, Okla.; DB—*Russell Carter, Southern Methodist, 6-3, 193, Ardmore, Pa.; DB—Jerry Gray, Texas, 6-1, 183, Lubbock, Texas; DB—Terry Hoage, Georgia, 6-3, 196, Huntsville, Texas; DB—Don Rogers, UCLA, 6-2, 208, Sacramento, Calif.; P—Jack Weil, Wyoming, 5-11, 171, Northglenn, Colo.

## 1984
### Offense

WR—*David Williams, Illinois, 6-3, 195, Los Angeles, Calif.; WR—Eddie Brown, Miami (Fla.), 6-0, 185, Miami, Fla.; TE—Jay Novacek, Wyoming, 6-4, 211, Gothenburg, Neb.; T—*Bill Fralic, Pittsburgh, 6-5, 285, Penn Hills, Pa.; T—Lomas Brown, Florida, 6-5, 277, Miami, Fla.; G—Del Wilkes, South Caro., 6-3, 255, Columbia, S.C.; G—Jim Lachey, Ohio St., 6-6, 274, St. Henry, Ohio; G—Bill Mayo, Tennessee, 6-3, 280, Dalton, Ga.; C—*Mark Traynowicz, Nebraska, 6-6, 265, Bellevue, Neb.; QB—*Doug Flutie, Boston College, 5-9, 177, Natick, Mass.; RB—*Keith Byars, Ohio St., 6-2, 233, Dayton, Ohio; RB—*Kenneth Davis, Texas Christian, 5-11, 205, Temple, Texas; RB—Rueben Mayes, Washington St., 6-0, 200, North Battleford, Saskatchewan, Canada; PK—Kevin Butler, Georgia, 6-1, 190, Stone Mountain, Ga.

### Defense

DL—Bruce Smith, Virginia Tech, 6-4, 275, Norfolk, Va.; DL—Tony Degrate, Texas, 6-4, 280, Snyder, Texas; DL—Ron Holmes, Washington, 6-4, 255, Lacey, Wash.; DL—Tony Casillas, Oklahoma, 6-3, 272, Tulsa, Okla.; LB—Gregg Carr, Auburn, 6-2, 215, Birmingham, Ala.; LB—Jack Del Rio, Southern Cal, 6-4, 235, Hayward, Calif.; LB—Larry Station, Iowa, 5-11, 233, Omaha, Neb.; DB—*Jerry Gray, Texas, 6-1, 183, Lubbock, Texas; DB—Tony Thurman, Boston College, 6-0, 179, Lynn, Mass.; DB—Jeff Sanchez, Georgia, 6-0, 183, Yorba Linda, Calif.; DB—David Fulcher, Arizona St., 6-3, 220, Los Angeles, Calif.; DB—Rod Brown, Oklahoma St., 6-3, 188, Gainesville, Texas; P—*Ricky Anderson, Vanderbilt, 6-2, 190, St. Petersburg, Fla.

## 1985
### Offense

WR—*David Williams, Illinois, 6-3, 195, Los Angeles, Calif.; WR—Tim McGee, Tennessee, 5-10, 181, Cleveland, Ohio; TE—Willie Smith, Miami (Fla.), 6-2, 230, Jacksonville, Fla.; L—*Jim Dombrowski, Virginia, 6-5, 290, Williamsville, N.Y.; L—Jeff Bregel, Southern Cal, 6-4, 280, Granada Hills, Calif.; L—Brian Jozwiak, West Va., 6-6, 290, Catonsville, Md.; L—John Rienstra, Temple, 6-4, 280, Colorado Springs, Colo.; L—J. D. Maarleveld, Maryland, 6-5, 300, Rutherford, N.J.; L—Jamie Dukes, Florida St., 6-0, 272, Orlando, Fla.; C—Pete Anderson, Georgia, 6-3, 264, Glen Ridge, N.J.; QB—*Chuck Long, Iowa, 6-4, 213, Wheaton, Ill.; RB—*Bo Jackson, Auburn, 6-1, 222, Bessemer, Ala.; RB—*Lorenzo White, Michigan St., 5-11, 205, Fort Lauderdale, Fla.; RB—Thurman Thomas, Oklahoma St., 5-11, 186, Missouri City, Texas; RB—Reggie Dupard, Southern Methodist, 6-0, 201, New Orleans, La.; RB—Napoleon McCallum, Navy, 6-2, 214, Milford, Ohio; PK—*John Lee, UCLA, 5-11, 187, Downey, Calif.

### Defense

L—*Tim Green, Syracuse, 6-2, 246, Liverpool, N.Y.; L—*Leslie O'Neal, Oklahoma St., 6-3, 245, Little Rock, Ark.; L—Tony Casillas, Oklahoma, 6-3, 280, Tulsa, Okla.; L—Mike Ruth, Boston College, 6-2, 250, Norristown, Pa.; L—Mike Hammerstein, Michigan, 6-4, 240, Wapakoneta, Ohio; LB—*Brian Bosworth, Oklahoma, 6-2, 234, Irving, Texas; LB—*Larry Station, Iowa, 5-11, 227, Omaha, Neb.; LB—Johnny Holland, Texas A&M, 6-2, 219, Hempstead, Texas; DB—David Fulcher, Arizona St., 6-3, 228, Los Angeles, Calif.; DB—Brad Cochran, Michigan, 6-3, 219, Royal Oak, Mich.; DB—Scott Thomas, Air Force, 6-0, 185, San Antonio, Texas; P—Barry Helton, Colorado, 6-3, 195, Simla, Colo.

## 1986
### Offense

WR—Cris Carter, Ohio St., 6-3, 194, Middletown, Ohio; TE—*Keith Jackson, Oklahoma, 6-3, 241, Little Rock, Ark.; L—Jeff Bregel, Southern Cal, 6-4, 280, Granada Hills, Calif.; L—Randy Dixon, Pittsburgh, 6-4, 286, Clewiston, Fla.; L—Danny Villa, Arizona St., 6-5, 284, Nogales, Ariz.; L—John Clay, Missouri, 6-5, 285, St. Louis, Mo.; C—*Ben Tamburello, Auburn, 6-3, 268, Birmingham, Ala.; QB—*Vinny Testaverde, Miami (Fla.), 6-5, 218, Elmont, N.Y.; RB—*Brent Fullwood, Auburn, 5-11, 209, St. Cloud, Fla.; RB—*Paul Palmer, Temple, 5-10, 180, Potomac, Md.; RB—Terrence Flagler, Clemson, 6-1, 200, Fernandina Beach, Fla.; RB—Brad Muster, Stanford, 6-3, 226, Novato, Calif.; RB—D. J. Dozier, Penn St., 6-1, 204, Virginia Beach, Va.; PK—Jeff Jaeger, Washington, 5-11, 191, Kent, Wash.

### Defense

L—*Jerome Brown, Miami (Fla.), 6-2, 285, Brooksville, Fla.; L—*Danny Noonan, Nebraska, 6-4, 280,

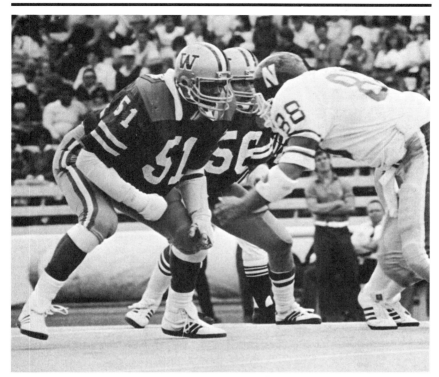

**Washington's Reggie Rogers was a consensus all-American defensive lineman in 1986.**

Lincoln, Neb.; L—Tony Woods, Pittsburgh, 6-4, 240, Newark, N.J.; L—Jason Buck, Brigham Young, 6-6, 270, St. Anthony, Idaho; L—Reggie Rogers, Washington, 6-6, 260, Sacramento, Calif.; LB—*Cornelius Bennett, Alabama, 6-4, 235, Birmingham, Ala.; LB—Shane Conlan, Penn St., 6-3, 225, Frewsburg, N.Y.; LB—Brian Bosworth, Oklahoma, 6-2, 240, Irving, Texas; LB—Chris Spielman, Ohio St., 6-2, 227, Massillon, Ohio; DB—*Thomas Everett, Baylor, 5-9, 180, Daingerfield, Texas; DB—Tim McDonald, Southern Cal, 6-3, 205, Fresno, Calif.; DB—Bennie Blades, Miami (Fla.), 6-0, 207, Ft. Lauderdale, Fla.; DB—Rod Woodson, Purdue, 6-0, 195, Fort Wayne, Ind.; DB—Garland Rivers, Michigan, 6-1, 187, Canton, Ohio; P—Barry Helton, Colorado, 6-4, 200, Simla, Colo.

## 1987
### Offense

WR—*Tim Brown, Notre Dame, 6-0, 195, Dallas, Texas; WR—Wendell Davis, Louisiana St., 6-0, 186, Shreveport, La.; TE—*Keith Jackson, Oklahoma, 6-3, 248, Little Rock, Ark.; L—*Mark Hutson, Oklahoma, 6-4, 282, Fort Smith, Ark.; L—Dave Cadigan, Southern Cal, 6-5, 280, Newport Beach, Calif.; L—John Elliott, Michigan, 6-7, 306, Lake Ronkonkoma, N.Y.; L—Randall McDaniel, Arizona St., 6-5, 261, Avondale, Ariz.; C—*Nacho Albergamo, Louisiana St., 6-2, 257, Marrera, La.; QB—*Don McPherson, Syracuse, 6-0, 182, West Hempstead, N.Y.; RB—Lorenzo White, Michigan St., 5-11, 211, Fort Lauderdale, Fla.; RB—Craig Heyward, Pittsburgh, 6-0, 260, Passaic, N.J.; PK—David Treadwell, Clemson, 6-1, 165, Jacksonville, Fla.

### Defense

L—*Daniel Stubbs, Miami (Fla.), 6-4, 250, Red Bank, N.J.; L—*Chad Hennings, Air Force, 6-5, 260, Elboron, Iowa; L—Tracy Rocker, Auburn, 6-3, 258, Atlanta, Ga.; L—Ted Gregory, Syracuse, 6-1, 260, East Islip, N.Y.; L—John Roper, Texas A&M, 6-2, 215, Houston, Texas; LB—*Chris Spielman, Ohio St., 6-2, 236, Massillon, Ohio; LB—Aundray Bruce, Auburn, 6-6, 236, Montgomery, Ala.; LB—Dante Jones, Oklahoma, 6-2, 235, Dallas, Texas; DB—*Bennie Blades, Miami (Fla.), 6-0, 215, Fort Lauderdale, Fla.; DB—*Deion Sanders, Florida St., 6-0, 192, Fort Myers, Fla.; DB—Rickey Dixon, Oklahoma, 5-10, 184,

Dallas, Texas; DB—Chuck Cecil, Arizona, 6-0, 185, Red Bluff, Calif.; P—*Tom Tupa, Ohio St., 6-5, 215, Brecksville, Ohio.

## 1988
### Offense
WR—Jason Phillips, Houston, 5-9, 175, Houston, Texas; WR—Hart Lee Dykes, Oklahoma St., 6-4, 220, Bay City, Texas; TE—Marv Cook, Iowa, 6-4, 243, West Branch, Iowa; L—*Tony Mandarich, Michigan St., 6-6, 315, Oakville, Ontario, Canada; L—*Anthony Phillips, Oklahoma, 6-3, 286, Tulsa, Okla.; L—Mike Utley, Washington St., 6-6, 302, Seattle, Wash.; L—Mark Stepnoski, Pittsburgh, 6-3, 265, Erie, Pa.; C—Jake Young, Nebraska, 6-5, 260, Midland, Texas; QB—John Vitale, Michigan, 6-1, 273, Detroit, Mich.; QB—Steve Walsh, Miami (Fla.), 6-3, 195, St. Paul, Minn.; QB—Troy Aikman, UCLA, 6-4, 217, Henryetta, Okla.; RB—*Barry Sanders, Oklahoma St., 5-8, 197, Wichita, Kan.; RB—Anthony Thompson, Indiana, 6-0, 205, Terre Haute, Ind.; RB—Tim Worley, Georgia, 6-2, 216, Lumberton, N.C.; PK—Kendall Trainor, Arkansas, 6-2, 205, Fredonia, Kan.

### Defense
L—*Mark Messner, Michigan, 6-3, 244, Hartland, Mich.; L—*Tracy Rocker, Auburn, 6-3, 278, Atlanta, Ga.; L—Wayne Martin, Arkansas, 6-5, 263, Cherry Valley, Ark.; L—Frank Stams, Notre Dame, 6-4, 237, Akron, Ohio; L—Bill Hawkins, Miami (Fla.), 6-6, 260, Hollywood, Fla.; LB—*Derrick Thomas, Alabama, 6-4, 230, Miami, Fla.; LB—*Broderick Thomas, Nebraska, 6-3, 235, Houston, Texas; LB—Michael Stonebreaker, Notre Dame, 6-1, 228, River Ridge, La.; DB—*Deion Sanders, Florida St., 6-0, 195, Fort Myers, Fla.; DB—Donnell Woolford, Clemson, 5-10, 195, Fayetteville, N.C.; DB—Louis Oliver, Florida, 6-2, 222, Bell Glade, Fla.; DB—Darryl Henley, UCLA, 5-10, 165, Ontario, Calif.; P—Keith English, Colorado, 6-3, 215, Greeley, Colo.

## 1989
### Offense
WR—*Clarkston Hines, Duke, 6-1, 170, Chapel Hill, N.C.; WR—Terance Mathis, New Mexico, 5-9, 167, Stone Mountain, Ga.; TE—Mike Busch, Iowa St., 6-5, 252, Donahue, Iowa; L—Jim Mabry, Arkansas, 6-4, 262, Memphis, Tenn.; L—Bob Kula, Michigan St., 6-4, 282, West Bloomfield, Mich.; L—Mohammed Elewonibi, Brigham Young, 6-5, 290, Kamloops, British Columbia, Canada; L—Joe Garten, Colorado, 6-3, 280, Placentia, Calif.; L—*Eric Still, Tennessee, 6-3, 283, Germantown, Tenn.; C—Jake Young, Nebraska, 6-4, 270, Midland, Texas; QB—Andre Ware, Houston, 6-2, 205, Dickinson, Texas; RB—*Anthony Thompson, Indiana, 6-0, 209, Terre Haute, Ind.; RB—*Emmitt Smith, Florida, 5-10, 201, Pensacola, Fla.; PK—*Jason Hanson, Washington St., 6-0, 164, Spokane, Wash.

### Defense
L—Chris Zorich, Notre Dame, 6-1, 268, Chicago, Ill.; L—Greg Mark, Miami (Fla.), 6-4, 255, Pennsauken, N.J.; L—Tim Ryan, Southern Cal, 6-5, 260, San Jose, Calif.; L—*Moe Gardner, Illinois, 6-2, 250, Indianapolis, Ind.; LB—*Percy Snow, Michigan St., 6-3, 240, Canton, Ohio; LB—*Keith McCants, Alabama, 6-5, 256, Mobile, Ala.; LB—Alfred Williams, Colorado, 6-6, 230, Houston, Texas; DB—*Todd Lyght, Notre Dame, 6-1, 181, Flint, Mich.; DB—*Mark Carrier, Southern Cal, 6-1, 185, Long Beach, Calif.; DB—*Tripp Welborne, Michigan, 6-1, 193, Greensboro, N.C.; DB—LeRoy Butler, Florida St., 6-0, 194, Jacksonville, Fla.; P—Tom Rouen, Colorado, 6-3, 220, Littleton, Colo.

## 1990
### Offense
WR—*Raghib Ismail, Notre Dame, 5-10, 175, Wilkes-Barre, Pa.; WR—Herman Moore, Virginia, 6-5, 197, Danville, Va.; TE—*Chris Smith, Brigham Young, 6-4, 230, La Canada, Calif.; OL—*Antone Davis, Tennessee, 6-4, 310, Fort Valley, Ga.; OL—*Joe Garten, Colorado, 6-3, 280, Placentia, Calif.; OL—*Ed King, Auburn, 6-4, 284, Phenix City, Ala.; OL—Stacy Long, Clemson, 6-2, 275, Griffin, Ga.; C—John Flannery, Syracuse, 6-4, 301, Pottsville, Pa.; QB—Ty Detmer, Brigham Young, 6-0, 175, San Antonio, Texas; RB—*Eric Bieniemy, Colorado, 5-7, 195, West Covina, Calif.; RB—Darren Lewis, Texas A&M, 6-0, 220, Dallas, Texas; PK—*Philip Doyle, Alabama, 6-1, 190, Birmingham, Ala.

### Defense
DL—*Russell Maryland, Miami (Fla.), 6-2, 273, Chicago, Ill.; DL—*Chris Zorich, Notre Dame, 6-1, 266, Chicago, Ill.; DL—Moe Gardner, Illinois, 6-2, 258, Indianapolis, Ind.; DL—David Rocker, Auburn, 6-4, 264, Atlanta, Ga.; LB—*Alfred Williams, Colorado, 6-6, 236, Houston, Texas; LB—*Michael Stonebreaker, Notre Dame, 6-1, 228, River Ridge, La.; LB—Maurice Crum, Miami (Fla.), 6-0, 222, Tampa, Fla.; DB—*Tripp Welborne, Michigan, 6-1, 201, Greensboro, N.C.; DB—*Darryll Lewis, Arizona, 5-9, 186, West Covina, Calif.; DB—*Ken Swilling, Georgia Tech, 6-3, 230, Toccoa, Ga.; DB—Todd Lyght, Notre Dame, 6-1, 184, Flint, Mich.; P—Brian Greenfield, Pittsburgh, 6-1, 210, Sherman Oaks, Calif.

## 1991
### Offense
WR—*Desmond Howard, Michigan, 5-9, 176, Cleveland, Ohio; WR—Mario Bailey, Washington, 5-9, 167, Seattle, Wash.; TE—Kelly Blackwell, Texas Christian, 6-2, 242, Fort Worth, Texas; OL—*Greg Skrepenak, Michigan, 6-8, 322, Wilkes-Barre, Pa.; OL—Bob Whitfield, Stanford, 6-7, 300, Carson, Calif.; OL—Jeb Flesch, Clemson, 6-3, 266, Morrow, Ga.; OL—(tie) Jerry Ostroski, Tulsa, 6-4, 305, Collegeville, Pa.; Mirko Jurkovic, Notre Dame, 6-4, 289, Calumet City, Ill.; C—*Jay Leeuwenburg, Colorado, 6-3, 265, Kirkwood, Mo.; QB—Ty Detmer, Brigham Young, 6-0, 175, San Antonio, Texas; RB—*Vaughn Dunbar, Indiana, 6-0, 207, Fort Wayne, Ind.; RB—(tie) Trevor Cobb, Rice, 5-9, 180, Houston, Texas; Russell White, California, 6-0, 210, Van Nuys, Calif.; PK—Carlos Huerta, Miami (Fla.), 5-9, 186, Miami, Fla.

318    *1993 NCAA FOOTBALL*

## Defense

DL—*Steve Emtman, Washington, 6-4, 280, Cheney, Wash.; DL—*Santana Dotson, Baylor, 6-5, 264, Houston, Texas; DL—Brad Culpepper, Florida, 6-2, 263, Tallahassee, Fla.; DL—Leroy Smith, Iowa, 6-2, 214, Sicklerville, N. J.; LB—*Robert Jones, East Caro., 6-3, 234, Blackstone, Va.; LB—Marvin Jones, Florida St., 6-2, 220, Miami, Fla.; LB—Levon Kirkland, Clemson, 6-2, 245, Lamar, S.C.; DB—*Terrell Buckley, Florida St., 5-10, 175, Pascagoula, Miss.; DB—Dale Carter, Tennessee, 6-2, 182, Oxford, Ga.; DB—Kevin Smith, Texas A&M, 6-0, 180, Orange, Texas; DB—Darryl Williams, Miami (Fla.), 6-2, 190, Miami, Fla.; P—*Mark Bounds, Texas Tech, 5-11, 185, Stamford, Texas.

## 1992
### Offense

WR—O. J. McDuffie, Penn St., 5-11, 185, Warrensville Heights, Ohio; WR—Sean Dawkins, California, 6-4, 205, Sunnyvale, Calif.; TE—*Chris Gedney, Syracuse, 6-5, 256, Liverpool, N.Y.; OL—*Lincoln Kennedy, Washington, 6-7, 325, San Diego, Calif.; OL—*Will Shields, Nebraska, 6-1, 305, Lawton, Okla.; OL—Aaron Taylor, Notre Dame, 6-4, 294, Concord, Calif.; OL—(tie) Willie Roaf, Louisiana Tech, 6-5, 300, Pine Bluff, Ark.; Everett Lindsay, Mississippi, 6-5, 290, Raleigh, N. C.; C—Mike Compton, West Va., 6-7, 289, Richlands, Va.; QB—*Gino Torretta, Miami (Fla.), 6-3, 205, Pinole, Calif.; RB—*Marshall Faulk, San Diego St., 5-10, 200, New Orleans, La.; RB—*Garrison Hearst, Georgia, 5-11, 202, Lincolnton, Ga.; PK—Joe Allison, Memphis St., 6-0, 184, Atlanta, Ga.

### Defense

DL—Eric Curry, Alabama, 6-6, 265, Thomasville, Ga.; DL—John Copeland, Alabama, 6-3, 261, Lanett, Ala.; DL—Chris Slade, Virginia, 6-5, 235, Tabb, Va.; DL—Rob Waldrop, Arizona, 6-2, 265, Phoenix, Ariz.; LB—*Marcus Buckley, Texas A&M, 6-4, 230, Fort Worth, Texas; LB—*Marvin Jones, Florida St., 6-2, 235, Miami, Fla.; LB—Micheal Barrow, Miami (Fla.), 6-2, 230, Homestead, Fla.; DB—*Carlton McDonald, Air Force, 6-0, 185, Jacksonville, Fla.; DB—Carlton Gray, UCLA, 6-0, 194, Cincinnati, Ohio; DB—Deon Figures, Colorado, 6-1, 195, Compton, Calif.; DB—Ryan McNeil, Miami (Fla.), 6-2, 185, Fort Pierce, Fla.; P—Sean Snyder, Kansas St., 6-1, 190, Greenville, Texas.

**(1992 Selectors: Associated Press, United Press International, Football Writers Association of America, American Football Coaches Association and Walter Camp Foundation.)**

*Indicates unanimous selection.*

# CONSENSUS ALL-AMERICANS BY COLLEGE
### Beginning in 1924, unanimous selections are indicated by (*).

**AIR FORCE**
58— Brock Strom, T
70— Ernie Jennings, E
85— Scott Thomas, DB
87—*Chad Hennings, DL
92—*Carlton McDonald, DB

**ALABAMA**
30—*Fred Sington, T
34— Don Hutson, E
Bill Lee, T
Dixie Howell, B
35— Riley Smith, B
37— Leroy Monsky, G
41— Holt Rast, E
42— Joe Domnanovich, C
45— Vaughn Mancha, C
61—*Billy Neighbors, T
62—*Lee Roy Jordan, C
65— Paul Crane, C
66— Ray Perkins, E
*Cecil Dowdy, T
67— Dennis Homan, E
Bobby Johns, DB
71— Johnny Musso, B
72—*John Hannah, G
73— Buddy Brown, G
74— Leroy Cook, DL
Woodrow Lowe, LB
75—*Leroy Cook, DE
77— Ozzie Newsome, WR
78— Marty Lyons, DL
79— Jim Bunch, T
80—*E.J. Junior, DL
81— Tommy Wilcox, DB
82— Mike Pitts, DL
86—*Cornelius Bennett, LB
88—*Derrick Thomas, LB

89—*Keith McCants, LB
90—*Philip Doyle, PK
92— John Copeland, DL
Eric Curry, DL

**AMHERST**
05— John Hubbard, B

**ARIZONA**
82—*Ricky Hunley, LB
83—*Ricky Hunley, LB
87— Chuck Cecil, DB
90—*Darryll Lewis, DB
92— Rob Waldrop, DL

**ARIZONA ST.**
72— Woody Green, B
73— Woody Green, B
77— John Jefferson, WR
78—*Al Harris, DL
81— Mike Richardson, DB
82— Mike Richardson, DB
Vernon Maxwell, DL
83— Luis Zendejas, PK
84— David Fulcher, DB
85— David Fulcher, DB
86— Danny Villa, OL
87— Randall McDaniel, OL

**ARKANSAS**
48— Clyde Scott, B
54—*Bud Brooks, G
65— Glen Ray Hines, T
Loyd Phillips, DT
66—*Loyd Phillips, DT
68— Jim Barnes, G
69— Rodney Brand, C
70— Dick Bumpas, DT
77— Leotis Harris, G
Steve Little, K

79—*Greg Kolenda, T
81—*Billy Ray Smith, DL
82—*Billy Ray Smith, DL
*Steve Korte, OL
88— Kendall Trainor, PK
Wayne Martin, DL
89— Jim Mabry, OL

**ARMY**
98— Charles Romeyn, B
00— William Smith, E
01— Paul Bunker, T
Charles Daly, B
02— Paul Bunker, T-B
Robert Boyers, C
04— Arthur Tipton, C
Henry Torney, B
05— Henry Torney, B
07— William Erwin, G
11— Leland Devore, T
13— Louis Merillat, E
14— John McEwan, C
16— Elmer Oliphant, B
17— Elmer Oliphant, B
22— Ed Garbisch, C
26— Bud Sprague, T
27— Red Cagle, B
28—*Red Cagle, B
29— Red Cagle, B
32— Milt Summerfelt, G
43—*C. Myslinski, C
44— Glenn Davis, B
Doc Blanchard, B
45— Tex Coulter, T
John Green, G
*Glenn Davis, B
*Doc Blanchard, B
46— Hank Foldberg, E

*Glenn Davis, B
*Doc Blanchard, B
47— Joe Steffy, G
49— Arnold Galiffa, B
50—*Dan Foldberg, E
57— Bob Anderson, B
58—*Pete Dawkins, B
59— Bill Carpenter, E

**AUBURN**
32— Jimmy Hitchcock, B
57—*Jimmy Phillips, E
58— Zeke Smith, G
60— Ken Rice, T
64— T. Frederickson, B
69— B. McClinton, DB
70— L. Willingham, DB
71—*Pat Sullivan, QB
*Terry Beasley, E
74— Ken Bernich, LB
83— Bo Jackson, RB
84— Gregg Carr, LB
85—*Bo Jackson, RB
86—*Ben Tamburello, C
*Brent Fullwood, RB
87— Tracy Rocker, DL
Aundray Bruce, LB
88—*Tracy Rocker, DL
90—*Ed King, OL
David Rocker, DL

**BAYLOR**
30— Barton Koch, G
56—*Bill Glass, G
63— Lawrence Elkins, E
64— Lawrence Elkins, B
76— Gary Green, DB
79— Mike Singletary, LB
80—*Mike Singletary, LB
86—*Thomas Everett, DB
91—*Santana Dotson, DL

**BOSTON COLLEGE**
20— Luke Urban, E
40— Gene Goodreault, E
42— Mike Holovak, B
84—*Doug Flutie, QB
Tony Thurman, DB
85— Mike Ruth, DL

**BRIGHAM YOUNG**
79—*Marc Wilson, QB
80— Nick Eyre, OL
81—*Jim McMahon, QB
82—*Gordon Hudson, TE
83—*Gordon Hudson, TE
*Steve Young, QB
86— Jason Buck, DL
89— M. Elewonibi, OL
90— Ty Detmer, QB
*Chris Smith, TE
91— Ty Detmer, QB

**BROWN**
02— Thomas Barry, B
06— John Mayhew, B
09— Adrian Regnier, E
10— Earl Sprackling, B
12— George Crowther, B
16— Fritz Pollard, B

**CALIFORNIA**
21— Brick Muller, E
Dan McMillan, T
22— Brick Muller, E
24— Edwin Horrell, C
28— Irv Phillips, E
30— Ted Beckett, G
35— Larry Lutz, T

37— Sam Chapman, B
38— Vic Bottari, B
48— Jackie Jensen, B
49—*Rod Franz, G
50— Les Richter, G
51— Les Richter, G
68— Ed White, MG
71— Sherman White, DT
74— Steve Bartkowski, QB
75— Chuck Muncie, RB
Steve Rivera, E
83— Ron Rivera, LB
91— Russell White, RB
92— Sean Dawkins, WR

**CARLISLE**
99— Isaac Seneca, B
03— James Johnson, B
07— Albert Exendine, E
Peter Hauser, B
11— Jim Thorpe, B
12— Jim Thorpe, B

**CARNEGIE MELLON**
28— Howard Harpster, B

**CENTENARY**
33— Paul Geisler, E

**CENTRE**
19— James Weaver, C
Bo McMillin, B
21— Bo McMillin, B

**CHICAGO**
98— C. Herschberger, B
04— Fred Speik, E
Walter Eckersall, B
05— Mark Catlin, E
Walter Eckersall, B
06— Walter Eckersall, B
08— Walter Steffen, B
13— Paul Des Jardien, C
22— John Thomas, B
24— Joe Pondelik, G
35—*Jay Berwanger, B

**CLEMSON**
67— Harry Olszewski, G
74— B. Cunningham, TE
79— Jim Stuckey, DL
81— Jeff Davis, LB
Terry Kinard, DB
82—*Terry Kinard, DB
83— William Perry, DL
86— Terrence Flagler, RB
87— David Treadwell, PK
88— Donnell Woolford, DB
90— Stacy Long, OL
91— Jeb Flesch, OL
Levon Kirkland, LB

**COLGATE**
13— Ellery Huntington, B
16— Clarence Horning, T
D. Belford West, T
Oscar Anderson, B
19— D. Belford West, T
30— L. Macaluso, B

**COLORADO**
37— Byron White, B
60— Joe Romig, G
61— Joe Romig, G
67— Dick Anderson, DB
68— Mike Montler, G
69— Bob Anderson, B
70— Don Popplewell, C
72— Cullen Bryant, DB
85— Barry Helton, P

86— Barry Helton, P
88— Keith English, P
89— Joe Garten, OL
Alfred Williams, LB
Tom Rouen, P
90—*Eric Bieniemy, RB
*Joe Garten, OL
*Alfred Williams, LB
91—*Jay Leeuwenburg, OL
92— Deon Figures, DB

**COLORADO ST.**
78— Mike Bell, DL

**COLUMBIA**
00— Bill Morley, B
01— Harold Weekes, B
Bill Morley, B
03— Richard Smith, B
42— Paul Governali, B
47— Bill Swiacki, E

**CORNELL**
95— Clinton Wyckoff, B
00— R. Starbuck, B
01— William Warner, G
Sanford Hunt, G
02— William Warner, G
06— Elmer Thompson, G
William Newman, C
08— B. O'Rourke, G
14— John O'Hearn, E
Charles Barrett, B
15— Murray Shelton, E
Charles Barrett, B
21— Edgar Kaw, B
22— Edgar Kaw, B
23— George Pfann, B
38— Brud Holland, E
39— Nick Drahos, T
40— Nick Drahos, T
71—*Ed Marinaro, B

**DARTMOUTH**
03— Henry Hooper, C
Myron Witham, B
04— Joseph Gilman, G
05— Ralph Glaze, E
08— Geo. Schildmiller, E
Clark Tobin, G
12— W. Englehorn, T
13— Robert Hogsett, E
14— Clarence Spears, G
15— Clarence Spears, G
17— Eugene Neely, G
19— A. Youngstrom, G
24— Carl Diehl, G
25— Carl Diehl, G
George Tully, E
*A. Oberlander, B
38— Bob MacLeod, B

**DUKE**
33— Fred Crawford, T
36— Ace Parker, B
71— Ernie Jackson, DB
89—*Clarkston Hines, WR

**DUQUESNE**
36— Mike Basrak, C

**EAST CARO.**
83— Terry Long, OL
91—*Robert Jones, LB

**FLORIDA**
66—*Steve Spurrier, B
69— Carlos Alvarez, E
75— Sammy Green, LB
80— David Little, LB

82— Wilber Marshall, DL
83— Wilber Marshall, DL
84— Lomas Brown, OT
88— Louis Oliver, DB
89— *Emmitt Smith, RB
91— Brad Culpepper, DL

**FLORIDA ST.**
64— Fred Biletnikoff, E
67— Ron Sellers, E
79— Ron Simmons, MG
80— Ron Simmons, MG
83— Greg Allen, RB
85— Jamie Dukes, OL
87— *Deion Sanders, DB
88— *Deion Sanders, DB
89— LeRoy Butler, DB
91— *Terrell Buckley, DB
　　Marvin Jones, LB
92— *Marvin Jones, LB

**FORDHAM**
36— A. Wojciechowicz, C
37— Ed Franco, T
　　A. Wojciechowicz, C

**GEORGETOWN**
26— H. Connaughton, G

**GEORGIA**
27— Tom Nash, E
31— Vernon Smith, E
41— Frank Sinkwich, B
42— *Frank Sinkwich, B
46— *Charley Trippi, B
67— Ed Chandler, T
68— Bill Stanfill, DT
　　Jake Scott, DB
71— *Royce Smith, G
75— Randy Johnson, G
76— Joel Parrish, G
80— *Herschel Walker, RB
81— *Herschel Walker, RB
82— *Herschel Walker, RB
　　Terry Hoage, DB
83— Terry Hoage, DB
84— Kevin Butler, PK
　　Jeff Sanchez, DB
85— Pete Anderson, C
88— Tim Worley, RB
92— *Garrison Hearst, RB

**GEORGIA TECH**
17— Everett Strupper, B
18— Bill Fincher, E
　　Joe Guyon, T
　　Ashel Day, C
20— Bill Fincher, E
28— Pete Pund, C
42— Harvey Hardy, G
44— Phil Tinsley, E
46— Paul Duke, C
47— Bob Davis, T
52— Hal Miller, T
53— Larry Morris, C
59— Maxie Baughan, C
66— Jim Breland, C
70— Rock Perdoni, DT
73— Randy Rhino, DB
90— *Ken Swilling, DB

**HARVARD**
89— Arthur Cumnock, E
　　John Cranston, G
　　James Lee, B
90— Frank Hallowell, E
　　Marshall Newell, T
　　John Cranston, C
　　Dudley Dean, B
　　John Corbett, B
91— Marshall Newell, T
　　Everett Lake, B
92— Frank Hallowell, E
　　Marshall Newell, T
　　Bertram Waters, G
　　William Lewis, C
　　Charles Brewer, B
93— Marshall Newell, T
　　William Lewis, C
　　Charles Brewer, B
94— Bertram Waters, T
95— Norman Cabot, E
　　Charles Brewer, B
96— Norman Cabot, E
　　E. Wrightington, B
97— Alan Doucette, C
　　Benjamin Dibblee, B
98— John Hallowell, E
　　Walter Boal, G
　　Charles Daly, B
　　Benjamin Dibblee, B
99— David Campbell, E
　　Charles Daly, B
00— John Hallowell, E
　　David Campbell, E
　　Charles Daly, B
01— David Campbell, E
　　Edward Bowditch, E
　　Oliver Cutts, T
　　Crawford Blagden, T
　　William Lee, G
　　Charles Barnard, G
　　Robert Kernan, B
　　Thomas Graydon, B
02— Edward Bowditch, E
　　Thomas Graydon, B
03— Daniel Knowlton, T
　　Andrew Marshall, G
04— Daniel Hurley, B
05— Beaton Squires, T
　　Karl Brill, T
　　Francis Burr, G
　　Daniel Hurley, B
06— Charles Osborne, T
　　Francis Burr, B
07— Patrick Grant, C
　　John Wendell, B
08— Hamilton Fish, T
　　Charles Nourse, C
　　Hamilton Corbett, B
09— Hamilton Fish, T
　　Wayland Minot, B
10— Robert McKay, T
　　Robert Fisher, G
　　Percy Wendell, B
11— Robert Fisher, G
　　Percy Wendell, B
12— Samuel Felton, E
　　Stanley Pennock, G
　　Charles Brickley, B
13— Harvey Hitchcock, T
　　Stanley Pennock, G
　　Charles Brickley, B
　　Edward Mahan, B
14— H. Hardwick, E
　　Walter Trumbull, T
　　Stanley Pennock, G
　　Edward Mahan, B
15— Joseph Gilman, T
　　Edward Mahan, B
　　Richard King, B
16— Harrie Dadmun, G

19— Edward Casey, B
20— Tom Woods, G
21— John Brown, G
22— Charles Hubbard, G
23— Charles Hubbard, G
29— Ben Ticknor, C
30— *Ben Ticknor, C
31— Barry Wood, B
41— *E. Peabody, G

**HOLY CROSS**
74— John Provost, DB

**HOUSTON**
67— Rich Stotter, G
69— Bill Bridges, G
70— Elmo Wright, E
76— Wilson Whitley, DT
80— Leonard Mitchell, DL
88— Jason Phillips, WR
89— Andre Ware, QB

**ILLINOIS**
14— Perry Graves, E
　　Ralph Chapman, G
15— Bart Macomber, B
18— John Depler, C
20— Charles Carney, E
23— James McMillen, G
　　Red Grange, B
24— *Red Grange, B
25— Red Grange, B
26— Bernie Shively, G
46— Alex Agase, G
51— Johnny Karras, B
53— J. C. Caroline, B
59— Bill Burrell, G
63— *Dick Butkus, C
64— Dick Butkus, C
65— *Jim Grabowski, B
84— *David Williams, WR
85— *David Williams, WR
89— *Moe Gardner, DL
90— Moe Gardner, DL

**INDIANA**
42— Billy Hillenbrand, B
44— John Tavener, C
45— Bob Ravensberg, E
88— Anthony Thompson, RB
89— *Anthony Thompson, RB
91— *Vaughn Dunbar, RB

**IOWA**
19— Lester Belding, E
21— Aubrey Devine, B
22— Gordon Locke, B
39— Nile Kinnick, B
54— Calvin Jones, G
55— Calvin Jones, G
57— Alex Karras, T
58— *Randy Duncan, B
81— Andre Tippett, DL
　　Reggie Roby, P
84— Larry Station, LB
85— *Chuck Long, QB
　　*Larry Station, LB
88— Marv Cook, TE
91— Leroy Smith, DL

**IOWA ST.**
38— Ed Bock, G
89— Mike Busch, TE

**KANSAS**
63— Gale Sayers, B
64— Gale Sayers, B
68— John Zook, DE
73— David Jaynes, QB

**KANSAS ST.**
77— Gary Spani, LB
92— Sean Snyder, P
**KENTUCKY**
50— Bob Gain, T
      Babe Parilli, B
51— Babe Parilli, B
56— Lou Michaels, T
57— Lou Michaels, T
65— Sam Ball, T
77—*Art Still, DL
**LAFAYETTE**
00— Walter Bachman, C
01— Walter Bachman, C
21— Frank Schwab, G
22— Frank Schwab, G
**LOUISIANA ST.**
35— Gaynell Tinsley, E
36—*Gaynell Tinsley, E
39— Ken Kavanaugh, E
54— Sid Fournet, T
58—*Billy Cannon, B
59—*Billy Cannon, B
61—*Roy Winston, G
62—*Jerry Stovall, B
70— Mike Anderson, LB
      T. Casanova, DB
71— T. Casanova, DB
72— Bert Jones, QB
77— C. Alexander, RB
78— C. Alexander, RB
87— Wendell Davis, WR
      *Nacho Albergamo, C
**LOUISIANA TECH**
92— Willie Roaf, OL
**MARQUETTE**
36— Ray Buivid, B
**MARYLAND**
51—*Bob Ward, G
52— Dick Modzelewski, T
      *Jack Scarbath, B
53—*Stan Jones, T
55—*Bob Pellegrini, C
61— Gary Collins, E
74—*Randy White, DL
76— Joe Campbell, DT
79— Dale Castro, PK
85— J.D. Maarleveld, OL
**MEMPHIS ST.**
92— Joe Allison, PK
**MIAMI (FLA.)**
61— Bill Miller, E
66— Tom Beier, DB
67—*Ted Hendricks, DE
68—*Ted Hendricks, DE
73— Tony Cristiani, DL
74— Rubin Carter, MG
81— Fred Marion, DB
84— Eddie Brown, WR
85— Willie Smith, TE
86—*Vinny Testaverde, QB
      *Jerome Brown, DL
      Bennie Blades, DB
87—*Daniel Stubbs, DL
      *Bennie Blades, DB
88— Steve Walsh, QB
      Bill Hawkins, DL
89— Greg Mark, DL
90— Maurice Crum, LB
      *Russell Maryland, DL
91— Carlos Huerta, PK
      Darryl Williams, DB
92—*Gino Torretta, QB

Micheal Barrow, LB
Ryan McNeil, DB
**MICHIGAN**
98— W. Cunningham, C
01— Neil Snow, E
03— Willie Heston, B
04— Willie Heston, B
07— Adolph Schulz, C
09— Albert Benbrook, G
10— Stanfield Wells, E
      Albert Benbrook, G
13— Miller Pontius, T
      Jim Craig, B
14— John Maulbetsch, B
22— Harry Kipke, B
23— Jack Blott, C
25— B. Oosterbaan, E
      Benny Friedman, B
26— B. Oosterbaan, E
      Benny Friedman, B
27—*B. Oosterbaan, E
28— O. Pommerening, T
32—*Harry Newman, B
33— Francis Wistert, T
      *Chuck Bernard, C
38—*Ralph Heikkinen, G
39— Tom Harmon, B
40—*Tom Harmon, B
41— Bob Westfall, B
42— Albert Wistert, T
      Julie Franks, G
43—*Bill Daley, B
47—*Bob Chappuis, B
48— Dick Rifenburg, E
      Alvin Wistert, T
49— Alvin Wistert, T
55— Ron Kramer, E
56—*Ron Kramer, E
65— Bill Yearby, DT
66—*Jack Clancy, E
69—*Jim Mandich, E
      Tom Curtis, DB
70— Dan Dierdorf, T
71— Reggie McKenzie, G
      *Mike Taylor, LB
72— Paul Seymour, T
      Randy Logan, DB
73— Dave Gallagher, DL
      Dave Brown, DB
74—*Dave Brown, DB
76— Rob Lytle, RB
      Mark Donahue, G
77—*Mark Donahue, G
79— Ron Simpkins, LB
81—*Anthony Carter, WR
      Ed Muransky, OL
      Kurt Becker, OL
82—*Anthony Carter, WR
85— Mike Hammerstein, DL
      Brad Cochran, DB
86— Garland Rivers, DB
87— John Elliott, OL
88— John Vitale, C
      *Mark Messner, DL
89—*Tripp Welborne, DB
90—*Tripp Welborne, DB
91—*Desmond Howard, WR
      *Greg Skrepenak, OL
**MICHIGAN ST.**
15— N. Jerry DaPrato, B
35— Sidney Wagner, G
49— Ed Bagdon, G
51— Bob Carey, E
      *Don Coleman, T

53— Don Dohoney, E
55— Norman Masters, T
      Earl Morrall, B
57— Dan Currie, C
      Walt Kowalczyk, B
58— Sam Williams, E
62— George Saimes, B
63— Sherman Lewis, B
65— Bubba Smith, DE
      *George Webster, DB
66— Clint Jones, B
      *Bubba Smith, DE
      *George Webster, DB
72—*Brad VanPelt, DB
85—*Lorenzo White, RB
87— Lorenzo White, RB
88— Tony Mandarich, OL
89—*Percy Snow, LB
      Bob Kula, OL
**MINNESOTA**
03— Fred Schacht, T
09— John McGovern, B
10— James Walker, T
16— Bert Baston, E
17— George Hauser, T
23— Ray Ecklund, E
26— Herb Joesting, B
27— Herb Joesting, B
29— Bronko Nagurski, T
31— Biggie Munn, G
34— Frank Larson, E
      Bill Bevan, G
      Pug Lund, B
35— Ed Widseth, T
36—*Ed Widseth, T
40— Urban Odson, T
      George Franck, B
41— Dick Wildung, T
      Bruce Smith, B
42— Dick Wildung, T
48— Leo Nomellini, T
49— Leo Nomellini, T
      *C. Tonnemaker, C
53—*Paul Giel, B
60—*Tom Brown, G
61— Sandy Stephens, B
62—*Bobby Bell, T
63— Carl Eller, T
65— Aaron Brown, DE
**MISSISSIPPI**
47— Charley Conerly, B
53— Crawford Mims, G
59— Charlie Flowers, B
60—*Jake Gibbs, B
62— Jim Dunaway, T
79— Jim Miller, P
92— Everett Lindsay, OL
**MISSISSIPPI ST.**
74— Jimmy Webb, DL
**MISSOURI**
41— Darold Jenkins, C
60—*Danny LaRose, E
65— Johnny Roland, DB
68— Roger Wehrli, DB
78— Kellen Winslow, TE
86— John Clay, OL
**NAVY**
07— Bill Dague, E
08— Percy Northcroft, T
      Ed Lange, B
11— Jack Dalton, B
13— John Brown, G
18— Lyman Perry, G
      Wolcott Roberts, B

22— Wendell Taylor, T
26— *Frank Wickhorst, T
28— Edward Burke, G
34— Fred Borries, B
43— Don Whitmire, T
44— *Don Whitmire, T
  Ben Chase, G
  Bob Jenkins, B
45— Dick Duden, E
54— Ron Beagle, E
55— *Ron Beagle, E
60— *Joe Bellino, B
63— *Roger Staubach, B
75— *Chet Moeller, DB
83— Napoleon McCallum, RB
85— Napoleon McCallum, RB

**NEBRASKA**
15— Guy Chamberlin, E
24— Ed Weir, T
25— *Ed Weir, T
33— George Sauer, B
36— Sam Francis, B
63— *Bob Brown, G
64— *Larry Kramer, T
65— Freeman White, E
  Walt Barnes, DT
66— LaVerne Allers, G
  Wayne Meylan, MG
67— Wayne Meylan, MG
70— Bob Newton, T
71— Johnny Rodgers, FL
  Willie Harper, DE
  Larry Jacobson, DT
72— *Johnny Rodgers, FL
  Willie Harper, DE
  *Rich Glover, MG
73— *John Dutton, DL
74— M. Crenshaw, OT
75— *Rik Bonness, C
76— Dave Butterfield, DB
78— Kelvin Clark, OT
79— *Junior Miller, TE
80— R. Schleusener, OL
  Jarvis Redwine, RB
81— *Dave Rimington, C
82— *Dave Rimington, C
  Mike Rozier, RB
83— *Irving Fryar, WR
  Dean Steinkuhler, OL
  *Mike Rozier, RB
84— *Mark Traynowicz, C
86— *Danny Noonan, DL
88— Jake Young, C
  *Broderick Thomas, LB
89— Jake Young, C
92— *Will Shields, OL

**NEW MEXICO**
89— Terance Mathis, WR

**NEW YORK U.**
28— Ken Strong, B

**NORTH CARO.**
37— Andy Bershak, E
48— Charlie Justice, B
70— Don McCauley, B
72— Ron Rusnak, G
74— Ken Huff, G
77— Dee Hardison, DL
80— *Lawrence Taylor, LB
83— William Fuller, DL

**NORTH CARO. ST.**
67— Dennis Byrd, DT
73— Bill Yoest, G
78— Jim Ritcher, C
  Ted Brown, RB

79— *Jim Ritcher, C

**NORTH TEXAS**
68— Joe Greene, DT

**NORTHWESTERN**
26— Ralph Baker, B
30— Frank Baker, E
31— Jack Riley, T
  Dallas Marvil, T
  Pug Rentner, B
36— Steve Reid, G
40— Alf Bauman, T
45— Max Morris, E
59— Ron Burton, B
62— Jack Cvercko, G

**NOTRE DAME**
13— Gus Dorais, B
17— Frank Rydzewski, C
20— George Gipp, B
21— Eddie Anderson, E
24— Harry Stuhldreher, B
  Jimmy Crowley, B
  Emer Layden, B
26— Bud Boeringer, C
27— John Smith, G
29— Jack Cannon, G
  *Frank Carideo, B
30— *Frank Carideo, B
  Marchy Schwartz, B
31— Tommy Yarr, C
  Marchy Schwartz, B
32— *Joe Kurth, T
34— Jack Robinson, C
35— Wayne Millner, E
37— Chuck Sweeney, E
38— *Ed Beinor, T
41— Bob Dove, E
42— Bob Dove, E
43— John Yonakor, E
  Jim White, T
  Pat Filley, G
  Angelo Bertelli, B
  Creighton Miller, B
46— George Connor, T
  *John Lujack, B
47— George Connor, T
  Bill Fischer, G
  *John Lujack, B
48— Leon Hart, E
  Bill Fischer, G
  Emil Sitko, B
49— *Leon Hart, E
  *Emil Sitko, B
  Bob Williams, B
50— Jerry Groom, C
52— *Johnny Lattner, B
53— Art Hunter, T
  *Johnny Lattner, B
54— *Ralph Guglielmi, B
55— Paul Hornung, B
57— Al Ecuyer, G
59— Monty Stickles, E
64— Jack Snow, E
  John Huarte, B
65— *Dick Arrington, G
  Nick Rassas, B
66— Tom Regner, G
  *Nick Eddy, B
  Alan Page, DE
  *Jim Lynch, LB
67— Tom Schoen, DB
68— George Kunz, T
  Terry Hanratty, QB
69— *Mike McCoy, DT
70— Tom Gatewood, E

  Larry DiNardo, G
71— *Walt Patulski, DE
  Clarence Ellis, DB
72— *Greg Marx, DT
73— *Dave Casper, TE
  Mike Townsend, DB
74— Pete Demmerle, WR
  Gerry DiNardo, G
75— *Steve Niehaus, DT
76— *Ken MacAfee, TE
  *Ross Browner, DE
77— *Ken MacAfee, TE
  *Ross Browner, DL
  Luther Bradley, DB
78— Dave Huffman, C
  *Bob Golic, LB
79— Vagas Ferguson, RB
80— *John Scully, C
  Bob Crable, LB
81— Bob Crable, LB
87— *Tim Brown, WR
88— Frank Stams, DL
  Michael Stonebreaker, LB
89— *Todd Lyght, DB
  Chris Zorich, DL
90— *Raghib Ismail, WR/RB
  Todd Lyght, DB
  *Michael Stonebreaker, LB
  *Chris Zorich, DL
91— Mirko Jurkovic, OL
92— Aaron Taylor, OL

**OHIO ST.**
16— Charles Harley, B
17— Charles Bolen, E
  Charles Harley, B
19— Charles Harley, B
20— Iolas Huffman, G
  G. Stinchcomb, B
21— Iolas Huffman, T
25— Ed Hess, G
28— Wes Fesler, E
29— Wes Fesler, E
30— *Wes Fesler, E
35— Gomer Jones, C
39— Esco Sarkkinen, E
44— Jack Dugger, E
  Bill Hackett, G
  *Les Horvath, B
45— *Warren Amling, G
46— *Warren Amling, T
50— *Vic Janowicz, B
54— *Howard Cassady, B
55— *Howard Cassady, B
56— *Jim Parker, G
58— Bob White, B
60— *Bob Ferguson, B
61— *Bob Ferguson, B
68— *Dave Foley, T
69— Jim Otis, B
  Jim Stillwagon, MG
  Jack Tatum, DB
70— *Jim Stillwagon, MG
  *Jack Tatum, DB
72— Randy Gradishar, LB
73— *John Hicks, OT
  *Randy Gradishar, LB
74— K. Schumacher, OT
  Steve Myers, C
  *Archie Griffin, RB
75— *Archie Griffin, RB
  Ted Smith, G
  Tim Fox, DB
76— Chris Ward, T
  Bob Brudzinski, DE
77— *Chris Ward, T

Tom Cousineau, LB
78— Tom Cousineau, LB
79— Ken Fritz, G
82— Marcus Marek, LB
84— Jim Lachey, OG
   *Keith Byars, RB
86— Cris Carter, WR
   Chris Spielman, LB
87— *Chris Spielman, LB
   *Tom Tupa, P

## OKLAHOMA
38— Waddy Young, E
48— Buddy Burris, G
50— Jim Weatherall, T
   Leon Heath, B
51— *Jim Weatherall, T
52— Billy Vessels, B
53— J. D. Roberts, G
54— Max Boydston, E
   Kurt Burris, C
55— Bo Bolinger, G
56— *Jerry Tubbs, C
   Tommy McDonald, B
57— Bill Krisher, G
   Clendon Thomas, B
58— Bob Harrison, C
63— Jim Grisham, B
64— Ralph Neely, T
65— Carl McAdams, LB
67— *G. Liggins, MG
69— *Steve Owens, B
71— *Greg Pruitt, B
   Tom Brahaney, C
72— *Greg Pruitt, B
   Tom Brahaney, C
73— *Lucious Selmon, DL
   Rod Shoate, LB
74— John Roush, G
   *Joe Washington, RB
   *Rod Shoate, LB
75— *Lee Roy Selmon, DT
   Dewey Selmon, MG
   Jimbo Elrod, DE
76— *Mike Vaughan, OT
77— *Zac Henderson, DB
78— *Greg Roberts, G
   *Billy Sims, RB
79— *Billy Sims, RB
   *George Cumby, LB
80— Louis Oubre, OL
81— Terry Crouch, OL
82— Rick Bryan, DL
83— *Rick Bryan, DL
84— Tony Casillas, DL
85— Tony Casillas, DL
   *Brian Bosworth, LB
86— *Keith Jackson, TE
   *Brian Bosworth, LB
87— *Keith Jackson, TE
   *Mark Hutson, OL
   Dante Jones, LB
   Rickey Dixon, DB
88— *Anthony Phillips, OL

## OKLAHOMA ST.
45— Bob Fenimore, B
69— John Ward, T
76— Derrel Gofourth, C
77— *Terry Miller, RB
84— Rod Brown, DB
85— Thurman Thomas, RB
   *Leslie O'Neal, DL
88— Hart Lee Dykes, WR
   *Barry Sanders, RB

## OREGON
62— Mel Renfro, B

## OREGON ST.
56— John Witte, T
58— Ted Bates, T
62— *Terry Baker, B
63— Vern Burke, E
68— *John Didion, C

## PENN ST.
06— William Dunn, C
19— Bob Higgins, E
20— Charles Way, B
21— Glenn Killinger, B
23— Harry Wilson, B
59— Richie Lucas, B
64— Glenn Ressler, G
68— *Ted Kwalick, E
   Dennis Onkotz, LB
69— *Mike Reid, DT
   Dennis Onkotz, LB
70— Jack Ham, LB
71— Dave Joyner, T
72— Bruce Bannon, DE
   John Skorupan, LB
73— *John Cappelletti, B
74— M. Hartenstine, DL
75— Greg Buttle, LB
78— *Keith Dorney, OT
   *Chuck Fusina, QB
   *Bruce Clark, DL
79— *Bruce Clark, DL
81— *Sean Farrell, OL
86— D. J. Dozier, RB
   Shane Conlan, LB
92— O. J. McDuffie, WR

## PENNSYLVANIA
91— John Adams, C
92— Harry Thayer, B
94— Charles Gelbert, E
   Arthur Knipe, B
   George Brooke, B
95— Charles Gelbert, E
   Charles Wharton, G
   Alfred Bull, C
   George Brooke, B
96— Charles Gelbert, E
   Charles Wharton, G
   Wylie Woodruff, G
97— John Outland, T
   T. Truxton Hare, G
   John Minds, B
98— T. Truxton Hare, G
   Pete Overfield, C
   John Outland, T
99— T. Truxton Hare, G
   Pete Overfield, C
   Josiah McCracken, B
00— T. Truxton Hare, G
04— Frank Piekarski, C
   V. Stevenson, B
   Andrew Smith, B
05— Otis Lamson, T
   Robert Torrey, C
06— August Ziegler, G
   Wm. Hollenback, B
07— Dexter Draper, T
   August Ziegler, G
08— Hunter Scarlett, E
   Wm. Hollenback, B
10— Ernest Cozens, C
   E. LeRoy Mercer, B
12— E. LeRoy Mercer, B
17— Henry Miller, E
19— Henry Miller, E

22— John Thurman, T
24— Ed McGinley, T
27— Ed Hake, T
28— Paul Scull, B
43— Bob Odell, B
45— George Savitsky, T
47— Chuck Bednarik, C
48— Chuck Bednarik, C

## PITTSBURGH
15— Robert Peck, C
16— James Herron, E
   Robert Peck, C
17— Dale Seis, G
   John Sutherland, G
18— Leonard Hilty, T
   Tom Davies, B
   George McLaren, B
20— Herb Stein, C
21— Herb Stein, C
25— Ralph Chase, T
27— *Gibby Welch, B
28— Mike Getto, T
29— *Joe Donchess, E
   Ray Montgomery, G
31— Jesse Quatse, T
32— Joe Skladany, E
   *Warren Heller, B
33— Joe Skladany, E
34— Chuck Hartwig, G
36— Averell Daniell, T
37— Tony Matisi, T
   Marshall Goldberg, B
38— *Marshall Goldberg, B
56— *Joe Walton, E
58— John Guzik, G
60— *Mike Ditka, E
63— Paul Martha, B
76— *Tony Dorsett, RB
   Al Romano, MG
77— Tom Brzoza, C
   Randy Holloway, DL
   Bob Jury, DB
78— Hugh Green, DL
79— *Hugh Green, DL
80— *Hugh Green, DL
   *Mark May, OL
81— Sal Sunseri, LB
82— Jimbo Covert, OL
83— *Bill Fralic, OL
84— *Bill Fralic, OT
86— Randy Dixon, OL
   Tony Woods, DL
87— Craig Heyward, RB
88— Mark Stepnoski, OL
90— Brian Greenfield, P

## PRINCETON
89— Hector Cowan, T
   William George, C
   Edgar Allan Poe, B
   Roscoe Channing, B
   Knowlton Ames, B
90— Ralph Warren, E
   Jesse Riggs, G
   Sheppard Homans, B
91— Jesse Riggs, G
   Philip King, B
   Sheppard Homans, B
92— Arthur Wheeler, G
   Philip King, B
93— Thomas Trenchard, E
   Langdon Lea, T
   Arthur Wheeler, G
   Philip King, B
   Franklin Morse, B

94— Langdon Lea, T
    Arthur Wheeler, G
95— Langdon Lea, T
    Dudley Riggs, G
96— William Church, T
    Robert Gailey, C
    Addison Kelly, B
    John Baird, B
97— Garrett Cochran, E
    Addison Kelly, B
98— Lew Palmer, E
    Arthur Hillebrand, T
99— Arthur Hillebrand, T
    Arthur Poe, E
    Howard Reiter, B
01— Ralph Davis, E
02— John DeWitt, G
03— Howard Henry, E
    John DeWitt, G
    J. Dana Kafer, B
04— James Cooney, T
05— James McCormick, B
06— L. Casper Wister, E
    James Cooney, T
    Edward Dillon, B
07— L. Casper Wister, E
    Edwin Harlan, B
    James McCormick, B
08— Frederick Tibbott, B
10— Talbot Pendleton, B
11— Sanford White, E
    Edward Hart, T
    Joseph Duff, G
12— John Logan, G
13— Harold Ballin, T
14— Harold Ballin, T
16— Frank Hogg, G
18— Frank Murrey, B
20— Stan Keck, T
    Donold Lourie, B
21— Stan Keck, G
22— C. Herbert Treat, T
25— Ed McMillan, C
35— John Weller, G
51— *Dick Kazmaier, B
52— Frank McPhee, E
65— Stas Maliszewski, G

**PURDUE**
29— Elmer Sleight, T
    Ralph Welch, B
32— *Paul Moss, E
33— Duane Purvis, B
40— Dave Rankin, E
43— Alex Agase, G
52— Bernie Flowers, E
65— Bob Griese, QB
67— *Leroy Keyes, B
68— *Leroy Keyes, B
    Chuck Kyle, MG
69— *Mike Phipps, QB
72— Otis Armstrong, B
    Dave Butz, DT
80— *Dave Young, TE
    *Mark Herrmann, QB
86— Rod Woodson, DB

**RICE**
46— Weldon Humble, G
49— James Williams, E
54— Dicky Maegle, B
58— Buddy Dial, E
76— Tommy Kramer, QB
91— Trevor Cobb, RB

**RICHMOND**
69— Walker Gillette, E

78— Jeff Nixon, DB

**RUTGERS**
17— Paul Robeson, E
18— Paul Robeson, E
61— Alex Kroll, C

**SAN DIEGO ST.**
92— *Marshall Faulk, RB

**SANTA CLARA**
38— Alvord Wolff, T
39— John Schiechl, C

**SOUTH CARO.**
80— *George Rogers, RB
84— Del Wilkes, OG

**SOUTHERN CAL**
26— Mort Kaer, B
27— Jesse Hibbs, T
    Morley Drury, B
30— Erny Pinckert, B
31— John Baker, G
    Gus Shaver, B
32— *Ernie Smith, T
33— Aaron Rosenberg, G
    *C. Warburton, B
39— *Harry Smith, G
43— Ralph Heywood, E
44— John Ferraro, T
47— Paul Cleary, E
52— Elmer Willhoite, G
    Jim Sears, B
62— Hal Bedsole, E
65— *Mike Garrett, B
66— Ron Yary, T
    Nate Shaw, DB
67— *Ron Yary, T
    *O. J. Simpson, B
    Tim Rossovich, DE
    Adrian Young, LB
68— *O. J. Simpson, B
69— Jim Gunn, DE
70— Charlie Weaver, DE
72— *Charles Young, TE
73— Lynn Swann, WR
    Booker Brown, OT
    Richard Wood, LB
    Artimus Parker, DB
74— *Anthony Davis, RB
    Richard Wood, LB
75— *Ricky Bell, RB
76— *Ricky Bell, RB
    Gary Jeter, DT
    Dennis Thurman, DB
77— *Dennis Thurman, DB
78— *Pat Howell, G
    *Charles White, RB
79— *Brad Budde, G
    *Charles White, RB
80— Keith Van Horne, OL
    *Ronnie Lott, DB
81— Roy Foster, OL
    *Marcus Allen, RB
82— *Don Mosebar, OL
    Bruce Matthews, OL
    George Achica, MG
83— Tony Slaton, C
84— Jack Del Rio, LB
85— Jeff Bregel, OL
86— Jeff Bregel, OL
    Tim McDonald, DB
87— Dave Cadigan, OL
89— *Mark Carrier, DB
    Tim Ryan, DL

**SOUTHERN METHODIST**
35— J. C. Wetsel, G

Bobby Wilson, B
47— Doak Walker, B
48— *Doak Walker, B
49— *Doak Walker, B
50— Kyle Rote, B
51— Dick Hightower, C
66— John LaGrone, MG
68— Jerry LeVias, E
72— Robert Popelka, DB
74— Louie Kelcher, G
78— Emanuel Tolbert, WR
80— John Simmons, DB
82— *Eric Dickerson, RB
83— *Russell Carter, DB
85— Reggie Dupard, RB

**ST. MARY'S (CAL.)**
27— Larry Bettencourt, C
45— *H.Wedemeyer, B

**STANFORD**
24— Jim Lawson, E
25— Ernie Nevers, B
28— Seraphim Post, G
    Don Robesky, G
32— Bill Corbus, G
33— Bill Corbus, G
34— Bob Reynolds, T
    Bobby Grayson, B
35— James Moscrip, E
    *Bobby Grayson, B
40— Frank Albert, B
41— Frank Albert, B
42— Chuck Taylor, G
50— Bill McColl, E
51— *Bill McColl, E
56— John Brodie, QB
70— Jim Plunkett, QB
71— Jeff Siemon, LB
74— Pat Donovan, DL
77— Guy Benjamin, QB
79— Ken Margerum, WR
80— *Ken Margerum, WR
82— *John Elway, QB
86— Brad Muster, RB
91— Bob Whitfield, OL

**SYRACUSE**
08— Frank Horr, T
15— Harold White, T
17— Alfred Cobb, T
18— Lou Usher, T
    Joe Alexander, G
19— Joe Alexander, G
23— Pete McRae, E
26— Vic Hanson, E
56— *Jim Brown, B
59— *Roger Davis, G
60— Ernie Davis, B
61— *Ernie Davis, B
67— *Larry Csonka, B
85— *Tim Green, DL
87— *Don McPherson, QB
    Ted Gregory, DL
90— John Flannery, C
92— *Chris Gedney, TE

**TEMPLE**
85— John Rienstra, OL
86— *Paul Palmer, RB

**TENNESSEE**
29— Gene McEver, B
33— Beattie Feathers, B
38— Bowden Wyatt, E
39— Ed Molinski, G
    George Cafego, B
40— *Bob Suffridge, G

46— Dick Huffman, T
51—*Hank Lauricella, B
52— John Michels, G
56—*John Majors, B
65— Frank Emanuel, LB
66— Paul Naumoff, LB
67—*Bob Johnson, C
68—*C. Rosenfelder, G
        Steve Kiner, LB
69— Chip Kell, G
        *Steve Kiner, LB
70—*Chip Kell, G
71—*Bobby Majors, DB
75— Larry Seivers, E
76— Larry Seivers, SE
79— Roland James, DB
83—*Reggie White, DL
84— Bill Mayo, OG
85— Tim McGee, WR
89—*Eric Still, OL
90—*Antone Davis, OL
91— Dale Carter, DB

**TEXAS**
45— Hubert Bechtol, E
46— Hubert Bechtol, E
47— Bobby Layne, B
50—*Bud McFadin, G
53— Carlton Massey, E
61—*Jimmy Saxton, B
62—*J. Treadwell, G
63—*Scott Appleton, T
65— Tommy Nobis, LB
68— Chris Gilbert, B
69— Bob McKay, T
70— Bobby Wuensch, T
        Steve Worster, B
        Bill Atessis, DE
71—*Jerry Sisemore, T
72—*Jerry Sisemore, T
73—*Bill Wyman, C
        Roosevelt Leaks, B
75— Bob Simmons, T
77—*Earl Campbell, RB
        *Brad Shearer, DL
78—*Johnnie Johnson, DB
79—*Steve McMichael, DL
        *Johnnie Johnson, DB
80— Kenneth Sims, DL
81— Terry Tausch, OL
        *Kenneth Sims, DL
83— Doug Dawson, OL
        Jeff Leiding, LB
        Jerry Gray, DB
84— Tony Degrate, DL
        *Jerry Gray, DB

**TEXAS A&M**
37— Joe Routt, G
39— John Kimbrough, B
40— Marshall Robnett, G
        *John Kimbrough, B
57—*John D. Crow, B
70— Dave Elmendorf, DB
74— Pat Thomas, DB
75—*Ed Simonini, LB
        Pat Thomas, DB
76— Tony Franklin, PK
        *Robert Jackson, LB
85—*Johnny Holland, LB
87— John Roper, DL
90— Darren Lewis, RB
91— Kevin Smith, DB
92—*Marcus Buckley, LB

**TEXAS CHRISTIAN**
35— Darrell Lester, C

36— Sammy Baugh, B
38— Ki Aldrich, C
        *Davey O'Brien, B
55—*Jim Swink, B
59— Don Floyd, T
60—*Bob Lilly, T
84—*Kenneth Davis, RB
91— Kelly Blackwell, TE

**TEXAS TECH**
60— E. J. Holub, C
65— Donny Anderson, B
77— Dan Irons, T
82— Gabriel Rivera, DL
91—*Mark Bounds, P

**TOLEDO**
71— Mel Long, DT

**TULANE**
31—*Jerry Dalrymple, E
32— Don Zimmerman, B
39— Harley McCollum, T
41— Ernie Blandin, T

**TULSA**
65—*Howard Twilley, E
91— Jerry Ostroski, OL

**UCLA**
46—*Burr Baldwin, E
52— Donn Moomaw, C
53— Paul Cameron, B
54— Jack Ellena, T
55— H. Cureton, G
57— Dick Wallen, E
66— Mel Farr, B
67—*Gary Beban, B
        Don Manning, LB
69— Mike Ballou, LB
73— Kermit Johnson, B
75— John Sciarra, QB
76—*Jerry Robinson, LB
77—*Jerry Robinson, LB
78—*Jerry Robinson, LB
        Kenny Easley, DB
79—*Kenny Easley, DB
80—*Kenny Easley, DB
81—*Tim Wrightman, TE
83— Don Rogers, DB
85—*John Lee, PK
88— Troy Aikman, QB
        Darryl Henley, DB
92—*Carlton Gray, DB

**UTAH ST.**
61— Merlin Olsen, T
69— Phil Olsen, DE

**VANDERBILT**
23— Lynn Bomar, E
24— Henry Wakefield, E
32— Pete Gracey, C
58— George Deiderich, G
82—*Jim Arnold, P
84—*Ricky Anderson, P

**VIRGINIA**
15— Eugene Mayer, B
41— Bill Dudley, B
85—*Jim Dombrowski, OL
90— Herman Moore, WR
92— Chris Slade, DL

**VIRGINIA TECH**
67— Frank Loria, DB
84— Bruce Smith, DL

**WAKE FOREST**
76—*Bill Armstrong, DB

**WASH. & JEFF.**
14— John Spiegel, B

18— Wilbur Henry, T
19— Wilbur Henry, T

**WASHINGTON**
25— George Wilson, B
28— Charles Carroll, B
36— Max Starcevich, G
40— Rudy Mucha, C
41— Ray Frankowski, G
63— Rick Redman, G
64— Rick Redman, G
66— Tom Greenlee, DT
68— Al Worley, DB
82—*Chuck Nelson, PK
84— Ron Holmes, DL
86— Jeff Jaeger, PK
        Reggie Rogers, DL
91—*Steve Emtman, DL
        Mario Bailey, WR
92—*Lincoln Kennedy, OL

**WASHINGTON ST.**
84— Rueben Mayes, RB
88— Mike Utley, OL
89—*Jason Hanson, PK

**WEST VA.**
19— Ira Rodgers, B
55— Bruce Bosley, T
82—*Darryl Talley, LB
85— Brian Jozwiak, OL
92— Mike Compton, C

**WILLIAMS**
17— Ben Boynton, B
19— Ben Boynton, B

**WISCONSIN**
12— Robert Butler, T
13— Ray Keeler, G
15— Howard Buck, T
19— C. Carpenter, C
20— Ralph Scott, T
23— Marty Below, T
30— Milo Lubratovich, T
42—*Dave Schreiner, E
54—*Alan Ameche, B
59—*Dan Lanphear, T
62— Pat Richter, E
75— Dennis Lick, T
81— Tim Krumrie, DL

**WYOMING**
83— Jack Weil, P
84— Jay Novacek, TE

**YALE**
89— Amos A. Stagg, E
        Charles Gill, T
        P. Heffelfinger, G
90— William Rhodes, T
        P. Heffelfinger, G
        Thomas McClung, B
91— Frank Hinkey, E
        John Hartwell, E
        Wallace Winter, T
        P. Heffelfinger, G
        Thomas McClung, B
92— Frank Hinkey, E
        A. H. Wallis, T
        V. McCormick, B
93— Frank Hinkey, E
        William Hickok, G
        Frank Butterworth, B
94— Frank Hinkey, E
        William Hickok, G
        Philip Stillman, C
        George Adee, B
        Frank Butterworth, B
95— Fred Murphy, T

96— Samuel Thorne, B
Fred Murphy, T
Clarence Fincke, B
97— John Hall, E
Burr Chamberlin, T
Gordon Brown, G
C. DeSaulles, B
98— Burr Chamberlin, T
Gordon Brown, G
Malcolm McBride, B
99— George Stillman, T
Gordon Brown, G
Malcolm McBride, B
Albert Sharpe, B
00— George Stillman, T
James Bloomer, T
Gordon Brown, G
Herman Olcott, C
George Chadwick, B
Perry Hale, B
William Fincke, B
01— Henry Holt, C
02— Thomas Shevlin, E
Ralph Kinney, T
James Hogan, T
Edgar Glass, G

Henry Holt, C
Foster Rockwell, B
George Chadwick, B
03— Charles Rafferty, E
James Hogan, T
James Bloomer, G
W. L. Mitchell, B
04— Thomas Shevlin, E
James Hogan, T
Ralph Kinney, G
Foster Rockwell, B
05— Thomas Shevlin, E
Roswell Tripp, G
Howard Roome, B
Guy Hutchinson, B
06— Robert Forbes, E
L. Horatio Biglow, T
Hugh Knox, B
Paul Veeder, B
07— Clarence Alcott, E
L. Horatio Biglow, T
T. A. D. Jones, B
Edward Coy, B
08— William Goebel, G
Hamlin Andrus, G
Edward Coy, B

09— John Kilpatrick, E
Henry Hobbs, T
Hamlin Andrus, G
Carroll Cooney, C
Edward Coy, B
Stephen Philbin, B
10— John Kilpatrick, E
11— D. Bomeisler, E
Henry Ketcham, C
Arthur Howe, B
12— D. Bomeisler, E
Henry Ketcham, C
13— Nelson Talbott, T
14— Harry LeGore, B
16— Clinton Black, G
20— Tim Callahan, G
21— Malcolm Aldrich, B
23— Century Milstead, T
William Mallory, B
24— Dick Luman, E
27— Bill Webster, E
J. Charlesworth, C
36— Larry Kelley, E
37—*Clint Frank, B
44— Paul Walker, E

# TEAM LEADERS IN CONSENSUS ALL-AMERICANS

*(Ranked on total number of selections)*

| Team | No. | Players | Team | No. | Players |
|---|---|---|---|---|---|
| Yale | 100 | 69 | Texas A&M | 16 | 14 |
| Notre Dame | 90 | 75 | Louisiana St. | 16 | 12 |
| Harvard | 89 | 59 | Iowa | 15 | 13 |
| Michigan | 65 | 53 | Wisconsin | 13 | 13 |
| Princeton | 65 | 49 | Clemson | 13 | 12 |
| Southern Cal | 57 | 50 | Arizona St. | 12 | 9 |
| Ohio St. | 53 | 38 | Florida St. | 12 | 9 |
| Oklahoma | 52 | 43 | Brigham Young | 11 | 9 |
| Pittsburgh | 46 | 39 | Chicago | 11 | 9 |
| Pennsylvania | 46 | 32 | Maryland | 10 | 10 |
| Nebraska | 38 | 31 | Northwestern | 10 | 10 |
| Army | 37 | 28 | Florida | 10 | 9 |
| Alabama | 34 | 33 | Oklahoma St. | 9 | 9 |
| Texas | 32 | 28 | Texas Christian | 9 | 9 |
| Minnesota | 29 | 25 | Baylor | 9 | 7 |
| Tennessee | 28 | 25 | North Caro. | 8 | 8 |
| Penn St. | 26 | 24 | Houston | 7 | 7 |
| Stanford | 25 | 20 | Mississippi | 7 | 7 |
| Miami (Fla.) | 24 | 22 | Kentucky | 7 | 5 |
| Michigan St. | 24 | 21 | Boston College | 6 | 6 |
| UCLA | 24 | 20 | Brown | 6 | 6 |
| Navy | 23 | 20 | Missouri | 6 | 6 |
| California | 21 | 19 | Rice | 6 | 6 |
| Georgia | 21 | 17 | Vanderbilt | 6 | 6 |
| Illinois | 21 | 16 | Carlisle | 6 | 5 |
| Auburn | 20 | 18 | Colgate | 6 | 5 |
| Colorado | 19 | 15 | Columbia | 6 | 5 |
| Cornell | 19 | 15 | Indiana | 6 | 5 |
| Syracuse | 18 | 16 | Air Force | 5 | 5 |
| Georgia Tech | 17 | 16 | Oregon St. | 5 | 5 |
| Purdue | 17 | 16 | Texas Tech | 5 | 5 |
| Arkansas | 17 | 15 | Virginia | 5 | 5 |
| Dartmouth | 17 | 15 | West Va. | 5 | 5 |
| Washington | 16 | 15 | Arizona | 5 | 4 |
| Southern Methodist | 16 | 14 | North Caro. St. | 5 | 4 |

*Consensus All-America Selections*

# 1992 FIRST-TEAM ALL-AMERICA FOOTBALL TEAMS

## ASSOCIATED PRESS
### Offense
QB—Gino Torretta, Miami (Fla.); RB—Marshall Faulk, San Diego St.; RB—Garrison Hearst, Georgia; WR—Sean Dawkins, California; WR—O. J. McDuffie, Penn St.; TE—Chris Gedney, Syracuse; OC—Mike Compton, West Va.; OG—Will Shields, Nebraska; OG—Aaron Taylor, Notre Dame; OT—Lincoln Kennedy, Washington; OT—Everett Lindsay, Mississippi; PK—Joe Allison, Memphis St.; AP*—Glyn Milburn, Stanford.

### Defense
DL—Eric Curry, Alabama; DL—John Copeland, Alabama; DL—Rob Waldrop, Arizona; DL—Chris Slade, Virginia; LB—Marvin Jones, Florida St.; LB—Micheal Barrow, Miami (Fla.); LB—Marcus Buckley, Texas A&M; DB—Ryan McNeil, Miami (Fla.); DB—Carlton McDonald, Air Force; DB—Deon Figures, Colorado; DB—Carlton Gray, UCLA; P—Sean Snyder, Kansas St.

* *All-Purpose.*

## KODAK
### (American Football Coaches Association)
### Offense
QB—Gino Torretta, Miami (Fla.); RB—Marshall Faulk, San Diego St.; RB—Garrison Hearst, Georgia; WR—O. J. McDuffie, Penn St.; WR—Lloyd Hill, Texas Tech; TE—Chris Gedney, Syracuse; OL—Lincoln Kennedy, Washington; OL—Will Shields, Nebraska; OL—Ben Coleman, Wake Forest; OL—Mike Compton, West Va.; OL—Mike Devlin, Iowa; PK—Jason Elam, Hawaii.

### Defense
DL—Eric Curry, Alabama; DL—Marcus Buckley, Texas A&M; DL—Chris Hutchinson, Michigan; DL—John Copeland, Alabama; DL—Travis Hill, Nebraska; LB—Marvin Jones, Florida St.; LB—Dave Hoffmann, Washington; LB—Steve Tovar, Ohio St.; DB—Carlton Gray, UCLA; DB—Ryan McNeil, Miami (Fla.); DB—Carlton McDonald, Air Force; P—Sean Snyder, Kansas St.

## FOOTBALL NEWS
### Offense
QB—Gino Torretta, Miami (Fla.); RB—Marshall Faulk, San Diego St.; RB—Garrison Hearst, Georgia; WR—Lloyd Hill, Texas Tech; WR—O. J. McDuffie, Penn St.; TE—Chris Gedney, Syracuse; OC—Mike Compton, West Va.; OG—Will Shields, Nebraska; OG—Aaron Taylor, Notre Dame; OT—Lincoln Kennedy, Washington; OT—Tom Scott, East Caro.; PK—Joe Allison, Memphis St.

### Defense
DL—John Copeland, Alabama; DL—Chris Slade, Virginia; LB—Micheal Barrow, Miami (Fla.); LB—Marvin Jones, Florida St.; LB—Marcus Buckley, Texas A&M; LB—Ron George, Stanford; DB—Deon Figures, Colorado; DB—Carlton Gray, UCLA; DB—Ryan McNeil, Miami (Fla.); DB—Lance Gunn, Texas; P—Ed Bunn, UTEP.

## FOOTBALL WRITERS ASSOCIATION OF AMERICA
### Offense
QB—Gino Torretta, Miami (Fla.); RB—Marshall Faulk, San Diego St.; RB—Garrison Hearst, Georgia; WR—Sean Dawkins, California; WR—Ryan Yarborough, Wyoming; TE—Chris Gedney, Syracuse; OL—Lincoln Kennedy, Washington; OL—Will Shields, Nebraska; OL—Everett Lindsay, Mississippi; OL—Willie Roaf, Louisiana Tech; PK—Joe Allison, Memphis St.; KR-WR—Curtis Conway, Southern Cal.

### Defense
DL—Chris Hutchinson, Michigan; DL—Rob Waldrop, Arizona; DE—John Copeland, Alabama; DE—Chris Slade, Virginia; LB—Marvin Jones, Florida St.; LB—Micheal Barrow, Miami (Fla.); LB—Marcus Buckley, Texas A&M; DB—Carlton McDonald, Air Force; DB—Patrick Bates, Texas A&M; DB—Deon Figures, Colorado; DB—Lance Gunn, Texas; P—Josh Miller, Arizona.

## THE SPORTING NEWS
### Offense
QB—Gino Torretta, Miami (Fla.); RB—Marshall Faulk, San Diego St.; RB—Garrison Hearst, Georgia; WR—Sean Dawkins, California; WR—Lloyd Hill, Texas Tech; TE—Chris Gedney, Syracuse; OC—Mike Compton, West Va.; OG—Will Shields, Nebraska; OG—Aaron Taylor, Notre Dame; OT—Lincoln Kennedy, Washington; OT—Tom Scott, East Caro.; PK—Joe Allison, Memphis St.; KR*—Tamarick Vanover, Florida St.

### Defense
DL—John Copeland, Alabama; DL—Chris Slade, Virginia; DL—Coleman Rudolph, Georgia Tech; DL—Eric Curry, Alabama; LB—Marvin Jones, Florida St.; LB—Micheal Barrow, Miami (Fla.); LB—Marcus Buckley, Texas A&M; DB—Deon Figures, Colorado; DB—Carlton McDonald, Air Force; DB—Carlton Gray, UCLA; DB—Patrick Bates, Texas A&M; P—Josh Miller, Arizona.

* *Kick Returner.*

## UNITED PRESS INTERNATIONAL
### Offense
QB—Gino Torretta, Miami (Fla.); RB—Marshall Faulk, San Diego St.; RB—Garrison Hearst, Georgia; WR—Lloyd Hill, Texas Tech; WR—O. J. McDuffie, Penn St.; TE—Chris Gedney, Syracuse; OL—Mike Compton, West Va.; OL—Lincoln Kennedy, Washington; OL—Willie Roaf, Louisiana Tech; OL—Will Shields, Nebraska; OL—Aaron Taylor, Notre Dame; PK—Joe Allison, Memphis St.

### Defense
DL—Eric Curry, Alabama; DL—Chris Slade, Virginia; DL—Rob Waldrop, Arizona; LB—Micheal Barrow, Miami (Fla.); LB—Marcus Buckley, Texas A&M; LB—Marvin Jones, Florida St.; LB—Darrin Smith, Miami (Fla.); DB—Patrick Bates, Texas A&M; DB—Deon Figures, Colorado; DB—Carlton Gray, UCLA; DB—Carlton McDonald, Air Force; P—Mitch Berger, Colorado.

## WALTER CAMP
### Offense
QB—Gino Torretta, Miami (Fla.); RB—Marshall Faulk, San Diego St.; RB—Garrison Hearst, Georgia; WR—O. J. McDuffie, Penn St.; WR—Sean Dawkins, California; TE—Chris Gedney, Syracuse; OC—Mike Compton, West Va.; OG—Will Shields, Nebraska; OG—Aaron Taylor, Notre Dame; OT—Lincoln Kennedy, Washington; OT—Tony Boscelli, Southern Cal; PK—Scott Sisson, Georgia Tech.

### Defense
DL—Eric Curry, Alabama; DL—Coleman Rudolph, Georgia Tech; DL—Chris Slade, Virginia; DL—John Copeland, Alabama; LB—Marvin Jones, Florida St.; LB—Micheal Barrow, Miami (Fla.); LB—Marcus Buckley, Texas A&M; DB—Carlton Gray, UCLA; DB—Carlton McDonald, Air Force; DB—Deon Figures, Colorado; DB—Ryan McNeil, Miami (Fla.); P—Ed Bunn, UTEP.

# SPECIAL AWARDS

## HEISMAN MEMORIAL TROPHY

Originally presented in 1935 as the DAC Trophy by the Downtown Athletic Club of New York City to the best college player east of the Mississippi River. In 1936, players across the country were eligible and the award was renamed the Heisman Memorial Trophy to honor former college coach and DAC athletics director John W. Heisman. The award now goes to the outstanding college football player in the United States.

| Year | Player, College, Pos. | Year | Player, College, Pos. |
|------|----------------------|------|----------------------|
| 1935 | Jay Berwanger, Chicago, HB | 1965 | Mike Garrett, Southern Cal, HB |
| 1936 | Larry Kelley, Yale, E | 1966 | Steve Spurrier, Florida, QB |
| 1937 | Clint Frank, Yale, HB | 1967 | Gary Beban, UCLA, QB |
| 1938 | Davey O'Brien, Texas Christian, QB | 1968 | O. J. Simpson, Southern Cal, HB |
| 1939 | Nile Kinnick, Iowa, HB | 1969 | Steve Owens, Oklahoma, HB |
| 1940 | Tom Harmon, Michigan, HB | 1970 | Jim Plunkett, Stanford, QB |
| 1941 | Bruce Smith, Minnesota, HB | 1971 | Pat Sullivan, Auburn, QB |
| 1942 | Frank Sinkwich, Georgia, HB | 1972 | Johnny Rodgers, Nebraska, FL |
| 1943 | Angelo Bertelli, Notre Dame, QB | 1973 | John Cappelletti, Penn St., HB |
| 1944 | Les Horvath, Ohio St., QB | 1974 | *Archie Griffin, Ohio St., HB |
| 1945 | *Doc Blanchard, Army, FB | 1975 | Archie Griffin, Ohio St., HB |
| 1946 | Glenn Davis, Army, HB | 1976 | Tony Dorsett, Pittsburgh, HB |
| 1947 | John Lujack, Notre Dame, QB | 1977 | Earl Campbell, Texas, HB |
| 1948 | *Doak Walker, Southern Methodist, HB | 1978 | *Billy Sims, Oklahoma, HB |
| 1949 | Leon Hart, Notre Dame, E | 1979 | Charles White, Southern Cal, HB |
| 1950 | *Vic Janowicz, Ohio St., HB | 1980 | George Rogers, South Caro., HB |
| 1951 | Dick Kazmaier, Princeton, HB | 1981 | Marcus Allen, Southern Cal, HB |
| 1952 | Billy Vessels, Oklahoma, HB | 1982 | *Herschel Walker, Georgia, HB |
| 1953 | John Lattner, Notre Dame, HB | 1983 | Mike Rozier, Nebraska, HB |
| 1954 | Alan Ameche, Wisconsin, FB | 1984 | Doug Flutie, Boston College, QB |
| 1955 | Howard Cassady, Ohio St., HB | 1985 | Bo Jackson, Auburn, HB |
| 1956 | Paul Hornung, Notre Dame, QB | 1986 | Vinny Testaverde, Miami (Fla.), QB |
| 1957 | John David Crow, Texas A&M, HB | 1987 | Tim Brown, Notre Dame, WR |
| 1958 | Pete Dawkins, Army, HB | 1988 | *Barry Sanders, Oklahoma St., RB |
| 1959 | Billy Cannon, Louisiana St., HB | 1989 | *Andre Ware, Houston, QB |
| 1960 | Joe Bellino, Navy, HB | 1990 | *Ty Detmer, Brigham Young, QB |
| 1961 | Ernie Davis, Syracuse, HB | 1991 | #Desmond Howard, Michigan, WR |
| 1962 | Terry Baker, Oregon St., QB | 1992 | Gino Torretta, Miami (Fla.), QB |
| 1963 | *Roger Staubach, Navy, QB | | |
| 1964 | John Huarte, Notre Dame, QB | | |

* Juniors (all others seniors).   # Had one year of eligibility remaining.

*First-Team All-America Football Teams*

## 1992 HEISMAN VOTING

| | | 1st | 2nd | 3rd | Total |
|---|---|---|---|---|---|
| 1. | Gino Torretta, QB, Miami (Fla.) | 310 | 179 | 112 | 1,400 |
| 2. | ¢Marshall Faulk, RB, San Diego St. | 164 | 207 | 174 | 1,080 |
| 3. | *Garrison Hearst, RB, Georgia | 140 | 196 | 170 | 982 |
| 4. | *Marvin Jones, LB, Florida St. | 81 | 51 | 47 | 392 |
| 5. | Reggie Brooks, RB, Notre Dame | 42 | 53 | 63 | 294 |
| 6. | *Charlie Ward, QB, Florida St. | 18 | 18 | 36 | 126 |
| 7. | Micheal Barrow, LB, Miami (Fla.) | 10 | 10 | 14 | 64 |
| 8. | *Drew Bledsoe, QB, Washington St. | 6 | 8 | 14 | 48 |
| 9. | Glyn Milburn, RB, Stanford | 5 | 11 | 10 | 47 |
| | Eric Curry, DL, Alabama | 3 | 13 | 12 | 47 |

\* *Junior, ¢ Sophomore (all others seniors).*

## OUTLAND TROPHY

Honoring the outstanding interior lineman in the nation, first presented in 1946 by the Football Writers Association of America. The award is named for its benefactor, Dr. John H. Outland.

| Year | Player, College, Pos. |
|---|---|
| 1946 | George Connor, Notre Dame, T |
| 1947 | Joe Steffy, Army, G |
| 1948 | Bill Fischer, Notre Dame, G |
| 1949 | Ed Bagdon, Michigan St., G |
| 1950 | Bob Gain, Kentucky, T |
| 1951 | Jim Weatherall, Oklahoma, T |
| 1952 | Dick Modzelewski, Maryland, T |
| 1953 | J. D. Roberts, Oklahoma, G |
| 1954 | Bill Brooks, Arkansas, G |
| 1955 | Calvin Jones, Iowa, G |
| 1956 | Jim Parker, Ohio St., G |
| 1957 | Alex Karras, Iowa, T |
| 1958 | Zeke Smith, Auburn, G |
| 1959 | Mike McGee, Duke, T |
| 1960 | Tom Brown, Minnesota, G |
| 1961 | Merlin Olsen, Utah St., T |
| 1962 | Bobby Bell, Minnesota, T |
| 1963 | Scott Appleton, Texas, T |
| 1964 | Steve DeLong, Tennessee, T |
| 1965 | Tommy Nobis, Texas, G |
| 1966 | Loyd Phillips, Arkansas, T |
| 1967 | Ron Yary, Southern Cal, T |
| 1968 | Bill Stanfill, Georgia, T |
| 1969 | Mike Reid, Penn St., DT |
| 1970 | Jim Stillwagon, Ohio St., MG |
| 1971 | Larry Jacobson, Nebraska, DT |
| 1972 | Rich Glover, Nebraska, MG |
| 1973 | John Hicks, Ohio St., OT |
| 1974 | Randy White, Maryland, DE |
| 1975 | Lee Roy Selmon, Oklahoma, DT |
| 1976 | *Ross Browner, Notre Dame, DE |
| 1977 | Brad Shearer, Texas, DT |
| 1978 | Greg Roberts, Oklahoma, G |
| 1979 | Jim Ritcher, North Caro. St., C |
| 1980 | Mark May, Pittsburgh, OT |
| 1981 | *Dave Rimington, Nebraska, C |
| 1982 | Dave Rimington, Nebraska, C |
| 1983 | Dean Steinkuhler, Nebraska, G |
| 1984 | Bruce Smith, Virginia Tech, DT |

| Year | Player, College, Pos. |
|---|---|
| 1985 | Mike Ruth, Boston College, NG |
| 1986 | Jason Buck, Brigham Young, DT |
| 1987 | Chad Hennings, Air Force, DT |
| 1988 | Tracy Rocker, Auburn, DT |
| 1989 | Mohammed Elewonibi, Brigham Young, G |
| 1990 | Russell Maryland, Miami (Fla.), DT |
| 1991 | *Steve Emtman, Washington, DT |
| 1992 | Will Shields, Nebraska, G |

\* *Juniors (all others seniors).*

**Maryland's Randy White won the Outland Trophy as the nation's most outstanding interior lineman in 1974.**

## VINCE LOMBARDI/ROTARY AWARD

Honoring the outstanding college lineman of the year, first presented in 1970 by the Rotary Club of Houston, Texas. The award is named after professional football coach Vince Lombardi, a member of the legendary "Seven Blocks of Granite" at Fordham in the 1930s.

| Year | Player, College, Pos. |
|---|---|
| 1970 | Jim Stillwagon, Ohio St., MG |
| 1971 | Walt Patulski, Notre Dame, DE |
| 1972 | Rich Glover, Nebraska, MG |
| 1973 | John Hicks, Ohio St., OT |
| 1974 | Randy White, Maryland, DT |

| Year | Player, College, Pos. |
|---|---|
| 1975 | Lee Roy Selmon, Oklahoma, DT |
| 1976 | Wilson Whitley, Houston, DT |
| 1977 | Ross Browner, Notre Dame, DE |
| 1978 | Bruce Clark, Penn St., DT |
| 1979 | Brad Budde, Southern Cal, G |

| Year | Player, College, Pos. | Year | Player, College, Pos. |
|------|----------------------|------|----------------------|
| 1980 | Hugh Green, Pittsburgh, DE | 1987 | Chris Spielman, Ohio St., LB |
| 1981 | Kenneth Sims, Texas, DT | 1988 | Tracy Rocker, Auburn, DT |
| 1982 | Dave Rimington, Nebraska, C | 1989 | Percy Snow, Michigan St., LB |
| 1983 | Dean Steinkuhler, Nebraska, G | 1990 | Chris Zorich, Notre Dame, NT |
| 1984 | Tony Degrate, Texas, DT | 1991 | Steve Emtman, Washington, DT |
| 1985 | Tony Casillas, Oklahoma, NG | 1992 | Marvin Jones, Florida St., LB |
| 1986 | Cornelius Bennett, Alabama, LB | | |

## MAXWELL AWARD

Honoring the nation's outstanding college football player, first presented in 1937 by the Maxwell Memorial Football Club of Philadelphia. The award is named after Robert "Tiny" Maxwell, a Philadelphia native who played at the University of Chicago as a lineman near the turn of the century.

| Year | Player, College, Pos. | Year | Player, College, Pos. |
|------|----------------------|------|----------------------|
| 1937 | Clint Frank, Yale, HB | 1967 | Gary Beban, UCLA, QB |
| 1938 | Davey O'Brien, Texas Christian, QB | 1968 | O. J. Simpson, Southern Cal, RB |
| 1939 | Nile Kinnick, Iowa, HB | 1969 | Mike Reid, Penn St., DT |
| 1940 | Tom Harmon, Michigan, HB | 1970 | Jim Plunkett, Stanford, QB |
| 1941 | Bill Dudley, Virginia, HB | 1971 | Ed Marinaro, Cornell, RB |
| 1942 | Paul Governali, Columbia, QB | 1972 | Brad VanPelt, Michigan St., DB |
| 1943 | Bob Odell, Pennsylvania, HB | 1973 | John Cappelletti, Penn St., RB |
| 1944 | Glenn Davis, Army, HB | 1974 | Steve Joachim, Temple, QB |
| 1945 | Doc Blanchard, Army, FB | 1975 | Archie Griffin, Ohio St., RB |
| 1946 | Charley Trippi, Georgia, HB | 1976 | Tony Dorsett, Pittsburgh, RB |
| 1947 | Doak Walker, Southern Methodist, HB | 1977 | Ross Browner, Notre Dame, DE |
| 1948 | Chuck Bednarik, Pennsylvania, C | 1978 | Chuck Fusina, Penn St., QB |
| 1949 | Leon Hart, Notre Dame, E | 1979 | Charles White, Southern Cal, RB |
| 1950 | Reds Bagnell, Pennsylvania, HB | 1980 | Hugh Green, Pittsburgh, DE |
| 1951 | Dick Kazmaier, Princeton, HB | 1981 | Marcus Allen, Southern Cal, RB |
| 1952 | John Lattner, Notre Dame, HB | 1982 | Herschel Walker, Georgia, RB |
| 1953 | John Lattner, Notre Dame, HB | 1983 | Mike Rozier, Nebraska, RB |
| 1954 | Ron Beagle, Navy, E | 1984 | Doug Flutie, Boston College, QB |
| 1955 | Howard Cassady, Ohio St., HB | 1985 | Chuck Long, Iowa, QB |
| 1956 | Tommy McDonald, Oklahoma, HB | 1986 | Vinny Testaverde, Miami (Fla.), QB |
| 1957 | Bob Reifsnyder, Navy, T | 1987 | Don McPherson, Syracuse, QB |
| 1958 | Pete Dawkins, Army, HB | 1988 | Barry Sanders, Oklahoma St., RB |
| 1959 | Rich Lucas, Penn St., QB | 1989 | Anthony Thompson, Indiana, RB |
| 1960 | Joe Bellino, Navy, HB | 1990 | Ty Detmer, Brigham Young, QB |
| 1961 | Bob Ferguson, Ohio St., FB | 1991 | Desmond Howard, Michigan, WR |
| 1962 | Terry Baker, Oregon St., QB | 1992 | Gino Torretta, Miami (Fla.), QB |
| 1963 | Roger Staubach, Navy, QB | | |
| 1964 | Glenn Ressler, Penn St., C | | |
| 1965 | Tommy Nobis, Texas, LB | | |
| 1966 | Jim Lynch, Notre Dame, LB | | |

## BUTKUS AWARD

First presented in 1985 to honor the nation's best collegiate linebacker by the Downtown Athletic Club of Orlando, Fla. The award is named after Dick Butkus, two-time consensus all-American at Illinois and six-time all-pro linebacker with the Chicago Bears.

| Year | Player, College | Year | Player, College |
|------|----------------|------|----------------|
| 1985 | Brian Bosworth, Oklahoma | 1989 | Percy Snow, Michigan St. |
| 1986 | Brian Bosworth, Oklahoma | 1990 | Alfred Williams, Colorado |
| 1987 | Paul McGowan, Florida St. | 1991 | Erick Anderson, Michigan |
| 1988 | Derrick Thomas, Alabama | 1992 | Marvin Jones, Florida St. |

## JIM THORPE AWARD

First presented in 1986 to honor the nation's best defensive back by the Jim Thorpe Athletic Club of Oklahoma City. The award is named after Jim Thorpe, Olympic champion, two-time consensus all-American halfback at Carlisle, and professional football player.

| Year | Player, College | Year | Player, College |
|------|----------------|------|----------------|
| 1986 | Thomas Everett, Baylor | 1989 | Mark Carrier, Southern Cal |
| 1987 | (tie) Bennie Blades, Miami (Fla.) | 1990 | Darryll Lewis, Arizona |
| | Rickey Dixon, Oklahoma | 1991 | Terrell Buckley, Florida St. |
| 1988 | Deion Sanders, Florida St. | 1992 | Deon Figures, Colorado |

## DAVEY O'BRIEN NATIONAL QUARTERBACK AWARD

First presented in 1977 as the O'Brien Memorial Trophy, the award went to the outstanding player in the Southwest. In 1981, the Davey O'Brien Educational and Charitable Trust of Fort Worth, Texas, renamed the award the Davey O'Brien National Quarterback Award, and it now honors the nation's best quarterback.

Memorial Trophy

| Year | Player, College, Position | Year | Player, College, Position |
|------|---------------------------|------|---------------------------|
| 1977 | Earl Campbell, Texas, RB | 1979 | Mike Singletary, Baylor, LB |
| 1978 | Billy Sims, Oklahoma, RB | 1980 | Mike Singletary, Baylor, LB |

## National QB Award

| Year | Player, College | Year | Player, College |
|------|-----------------|------|-----------------|
| 1981 | Jim McMahon, Brigham Young | 1987 | Don McPherson, Syracuse |
| 1982 | Todd Blackledge, Penn St. | 1988 | Troy Aikman, UCLA |
| 1983 | Steve Young, Brigham Young | 1989 | Andre Ware, Houston |
| 1984 | Doug Flutie, Boston College | 1990 | Ty Detmer, Brigham Young |
| 1985 | Chuck Long, Iowa | 1991 | Ty Detmer, Brigham Young |
| 1986 | Vinny Testaverde, Miami (Fla.) | 1992 | Gino Torretta, Miami (Fla.) |

# DOAK WALKER NATIONAL RUNNING BACK AWARD

Presented for the first time in 1990 to honor the nation's best running back among Division I-A juniors or seniors who combine outstanding achievements on the field, in the classroom and in the community. Sponsored by the GTE/Southern Methodist Athletic Forum in Dallas, Texas, a $10,000 scholarship is donated to the recipient's university in his name. It is voted on by a 16-member panel of media and former college football standouts. The award is named after Doak Walker, Southern Methodist's three-time consensus all-American halfback and 1948 Heisman Trophy winner.

| Year | Player, College |
|------|-----------------|
| 1990 | Greg Lewis, Washington |
| 1991 | Trevor Cobb, Rice |
| 1992 | Garrison Hearst, Georgia |

# LOU GROZA COLLEGIATE PLACE-KICKER AWARD

Presented for the first time in 1992 to honor the nation's top collegiate place-kicker. Sponsored by the Palm Beach County Sports Authority in conjunction with the Orange Bowl Committee. The award is named after NFL Hall of Fame kicker Lou Groza.

| Year | Player, College |
|------|-----------------|
| 1992 | Joe Allison, Memphis St. |

# WALTER PAYTON PLAYER OF THE YEAR AWARD

First presented in 1987 to honor the top Division I-AA football player by the Sports Network and voted on by Division I-AA sports information directors. The award is named after Walter Payton, former Jackson St. player and the National Football League's all-time leading rusher.

| Year | Player, College, Position | Year | Player, College, Position |
|------|---------------------------|------|---------------------------|
| 1987 | Kenny Gamble, Colgate, RB | 1990 | Walter Dean, Grambling, RB |
| 1988 | Dave Meggett, Towson St., RB | 1991 | Jamie Martin, Weber St., QB |
| 1989 | John Friesz, Idaho, QB | 1992 | Michael Payton, Marshall, QB |

# HARLON HILL TROPHY

First presented in 1986 to honor the best Division II player by Division II sports information directors. The award is named after Harlon Hill, former receiver at North Alabama and the National Football League's most valuable player for the Chicago Bears in 1955.

| Year | Player, College, Position | Year | Player, College, Position |
|------|---------------------------|------|---------------------------|
| 1986 | Jeff Bentrim, North Dak. St., QB | 1990 | Chris Simdorn, North Dak. St., QB |
| 1987 | Johnny Bailey, Texas A&I, RB | 1991 | Ronnie West, Pittsburg St., WR |
| 1988 | Johnny Bailey, Texas A&I, RB | 1992 | Ronald Moore, Pittsburg St., RB |
| 1989 | Johnny Bailey, Texas A&I, RB | | |

# COLLEGE FOOTBALL HALL OF FAME

**Established:** In 1947, by the National Football Foundation and College Hall of Fame, Inc. The first class of enshrinees was inducted in 1951. **Eligibility:** A nominated player must be out of college at least 10 years and a first-team all-America selection by a major selector during his career. Coaches must be retired three years. The voting is done by a 12-member panel made up of athletics directors, conference and bowl officials, and media representatives.

**Class of 1993** (to be inducted at the National Football Foundation and College Hall of Fame awards dinner, December 7, in New York City): Players—S Dick Anderson, Colorado (1965-67); OG-LB Bob Brown, Nebraska (1961-63); RB John Cappelletti, Penn St. (1971-73); OG Steve DeLong, Tennessee (1962-64); E Buddy Dial, Rice (1956-58); HB Harry Gilmer, Alabama (1944-47); †FB Pat Harder, Wisconsin (1941-42); OT Dick Modzelewski, Maryland (1950-52); DE Alan Page, Notre Dame (1964-66); OG J. D. Roberts, Oklahoma (1951-53); WR Lynn Swann, Southern Cal (1971-73). Coaches—†Bobby Dodd, Georgia Tech (1945-66); Glenn "Bo" Schembechler, Michigan and Miami (Ohio) (1963-89).

Member players are listed with final year they played in college, and member coaches are listed with year of induction. (†) Indicates deceased members.

**Hall Facts:** Only two individuals are enshrined in the College Football Hall of Fame as both a player and a coach. Amos Alonzo Stagg was an all-American at Yale (1889) and was inducted as a coach in 1951. The other two-time inductee is Bobby Dodd, who played at Tennessee (1930) and will be inducted as a coach this year.

## PLAYERS

| Player, College | Year | Player, College | Year |
|---|---|---|---|
| †Earl Abell, Colgate | 1915 | †Paul Bunker, Army | 1902 |
| Alex Agase, Purdue/Illinois | 1946 | Ron Burton, Northwestern | 1959 |
| †Harry Agganis, Boston U. | 1952 | Dick Butkus, Illinois | 1964 |
| Frank Albert, Stanford | 1941 | †Robert Butler, Wisconsin | 1912 |
| †Ki Aldrich, Texas Christian | 1938 | George Cafego, Tennessee | 1939 |
| †Malcolm Aldrich, Yale | 1921 | †Red Cagle, Southwestern La./Army | 1929 |
| †Joe Alexander, Syracuse | 1920 | †John Cain, Alabama | 1932 |
| Lance Alworth, Arkansas | 1961 | Ed Cameron, Wash. & Lee | 1924 |
| †Alan Ameche, Wisconsin | 1954 | †David Campbell, Harvard | 1901 |
| †Knowlton Ames, Princeton | 1889 | Earl Campbell, Texas | 1977 |
| Warren Amling, Ohio St. | 1946 | †Jack Cannon, Notre Dame | 1929 |
| Donny Anderson, Texas Tech | 1966 | †Frank Carideo, Notre Dame | 1930 |
| †Hunk Anderson, Notre Dame | 1921 | †Charles Carney, Illinois | 1921 |
| Doug Atkins, Tennessee | 1952 | J. C. Caroline, Illinois | 1954 |
| †Everett Bacon, Wesleyan | 1912 | Bill Carpenter, Army | 1959 |
| Reds Bagnell, Pennsylvania | 1950 | †Hunter Carpenter, Virginia Tech | 1905 |
| †Hobey Baker, Princeton | 1913 | Charles Carroll, Washington | 1928 |
| †John Baker, Southern Cal | 1931 | †Edward Casey, Harvard | 1919 |
| †Moon Baker, Northwestern | 1926 | Howard Cassady, Ohio St. | 1955 |
| Terry Baker, Oregon St. | 1962 | †Guy Chamberlin, Nebraska | 1915 |
| †Harold Ballin, Princeton | 1914 | Sam Chapman, California | 1938 |
| †Bill Banker, Tulane | 1929 | Bob Chappuis, Michigan | 1947 |
| Vince Banonis, Detroit Mercy | 1941 | †Paul Christman, Missouri | 1940 |
| †Stan Barnes, California | 1921 | †Dutch Clark, Colorado Col. | 1929 |
| †Charles Barrett, Cornell | 1915 | Paul Cleary, Southern Cal | 1947 |
| †Bert Baston, Minnesota | 1916 | †Zora Clevenger, Indiana | 1903 |
| †Cliff Battles, West Va. Wesleyan | 1931 | Jack Cloud, William & Mary | 1948 |
| Sammy Baugh, Texas Christian | 1936 | †Gary Cochran, Princeton | 1897 |
| Maxie Baughan, Georgia Tech | 1959 | †Josh Cody, Vanderbilt | 1919 |
| †James Bausch, Kansas | 1930 | Don Coleman, Michigan St. | 1951 |
| Ron Beagle, Navy | 1955 | Charlie Conerly, Mississippi | 1947 |
| Gary Beban, UCLA | 1967 | George Connor, Holy Cross/Notre Dame | 1947 |
| Hub Bechtol, Texas | 1946 | †William Corbin, Yale | 1888 |
| †John Beckett, Oregon | 1916 | William Corbus, Stanford | 1933 |
| Chuck Bednarik, Pennsylvania | 1948 | †Hector Cowan, Princeton | 1889 |
| Forrest Behm, Nebraska | 1940 | †Edward (Tad) Coy, Yale | 1909 |
| Bobby Bell, Minnesota | 1962 | †Fred Crawford, Duke | 1933 |
| Joe Bellino, Navy | 1960 | John David Crow, Texas A&M | 1957 |
| †Marty Below, Wisconsin | 1923 | †Jim Crowley, Notre Dame | 1924 |
| †Al Benbrook, Michigan | 1910 | Larry Csonka, Syracuse | 1967 |
| †Charlie Berry, Lafayette | 1924 | Slade Cutter, Navy | 1934 |
| Angelo Bertelli, Notre Dame | 1943 | †Ziggie Czarobski, Notre Dame | 1947 |
| Jay Berwanger, Chicago | 1935 | Carroll Dale, Virginia Tech | 1959 |
| †Lawrence Bettencourt, St. Mary's (Cal.) | 1927 | †Gerald Dalrymple, Tulane | 1931 |
| Fred Biletnikoff, Florida St. | 1964 | †John Dalton, Navy | 1911 |
| Doc Blanchard, Army | 1946 | †Charles Daly, Harvard/Army | 1902 |
| †Al Blozis, Georgetown | 1942 | Averell Daniell, Pittsburgh | 1936 |
| Ed Bock, Iowa St. | 1938 | †James Daniell, Ohio St. | 1941 |
| †Lynn Bomar, Vanderbilt | 1924 | †Tom Davies, Pittsburgh | 1921 |
| †Douglass Bomeisler, Yale | 1913 | †Ernie Davis, Syracuse | 1961 |
| †Albie Booth, Yale | 1931 | Glenn Davis, Army | 1946 |
| †Fred Borries, Navy | 1934 | Robert Davis, Georgia Tech | 1947 |
| Bruce Bosely, West Va. | 1955 | Pete Dawkins, Army | 1958 |
| Don Bosseler, Miami (Fla.) | 1956 | Al DeRogatis, Duke | 1948 |
| Vic Bottari, California | 1938 | †Paul DesJardien, Chicago | 1914 |
| †Ben Boynton, Williams | 1920 | †Aubrey Devine, Iowa | 1921 |
| †Charles Brewer, Harvard | 1895 | †John DeWitt, Princeton | 1903 |
| †Johnny Bright, Drake | 1951 | Mike Ditka, Pittsburgh | 1960 |
| John Brodie, Stanford | 1956 | Glenn Dobbs, Tulsa | 1942 |
| †George Brooke, Pennsylvania | 1895 | †Bobby Dodd, Tennessee | 1930 |
| George Brown, Navy/San Diego St. | 1947 | Holland Donan, Princeton | 1950 |
| †Gordon Brown, Yale | 1900 | †Joseph Donchess, Pittsburgh | 1929 |
| †John Brown Jr., Navy | 1913 | †Nathan Dougherty, Tennessee | 1909 |
| †Johnny Mack Brown, Alabama | 1925 | Nick Drahos, Cornell | 1940 |
| Tay Brown, Southern Cal | 1932 | †Paddy Driscoll, Northwestern | 1917 |

| Player, College | Year |
|---|---|
| †Morley Drury, Southern Cal | 1927 |
| Bill Dudley, Virginia | 1941 |
| Kenny Easley, UCLA | 1980 |
| †Walter Eckersall, Chicago | 1906 |
| †Turk Edwards, Washington St. | 1931 |
| †William Edwards, Princeton | 1899 |
| †Ray Eichenlaub, Notre Dame | 1914 |
| Bump Elliott, Michigan/Purdue | 1947 |
| Ray Evans, Kansas | 1947 |
| †Albert Exendine, Carlisle | 1907 |
| †Nello Falaschi, Santa Clara | 1936 |
| Tom Fears, Santa Clara/UCLA | 1947 |
| †Beattie Feathers, Tennessee | 1933 |
| Bob Fenimore, Oklahoma St. | 1946 |
| †Doc Fenton, Louisiana St. | 1909 |
| John Ferraro, Southern Cal | 1944 |
| †Wes Fesler, Ohio St. | 1930 |
| †Bill Fincher, Georgia Tech | 1920 |
| Bill Fischer, Notre Dame | 1948 |
| †Hamilton Fish, Harvard | 1909 |
| †Robert Fisher, Harvard | 1911 |
| †Allen Flowers, Georgia Tech | 1920 |
| Danny Fortmann, Colgate | 1935 |
| Sam Francis, Nebraska | 1936 |
| Ed Franco, Fordham | 1937 |
| †Clint Frank, Yale | 1937 |
| Rodney Franz, California | 1949 |
| †Benny Friedman, Michigan | 1926 |
| Roman Gabriel, North Caro. St. | 1961 |
| Bob Gain, Kentucky | 1950 |
| †Arnold Galiffa, Army | 1949 |
| Hugh Gallarneau, Stanford | 1940 |
| †Edgar Garbisch, Wash. & Jeff./Army | 1924 |
| Mike Garrett, Southern Cal | 1965 |
| †Charles Gelbert, Pennsylvania | 1896 |
| †Forest Geyer, Oklahoma | 1915 |
| Paul Giel, Minnesota | 1953 |
| Frank Gifford, Southern Cal | 1951 |
| †Walter Gilbert, Auburn | 1936 |
| †George Gipp, Notre Dame | 1920 |
| †Chet Gladchuk, Boston College | 1940 |
| Bill Glass, Baylor | 1956 |
| Marshall Goldberg, Pittsburgh | 1938 |
| Gene Goodreault, Boston College | 1940 |
| †Walter Gordon, California | 1918 |
| †Paul Governali, Columbia | 1942 |
| Otto Graham, Northwestern | 1943 |
| †Red Grange, Illinois | 1925 |
| †Bobby Grayson, Stanford | 1935 |
| †Jack Green, Tulane/Army | 1945 |
| Joe Greene, North Texas | 1968 |
| Bob Griese, Purdue | 1966 |
| Archie Griffin, Ohio St. | 1975 |
| †Merle Gulick, Toledo/Hobart | 1929 |
| †Joe Guyon, Georgia Tech | 1918 |
| †Edwin Hale, Mississippi Col. | 1921 |
| L. Parker Hall, Mississippi | 1938 |
| Jack Ham, Penn St. | 1970 |
| Bob Hamilton, Stanford | 1935 |
| Tom Hamilton, Navy | 1926 |
| †Vic Hanson, Syracuse | 1926 |
| †Tack Hardwick, Harvard | 1914 |
| †T. Truxton Hare, Pennsylvania | 1900 |
| †Chick Harley, Ohio St. | 1919 |
| †Tom Harmon, Michigan | 1940 |
| †Howard Harpster, Carnegie Mellon | 1928 |
| †Edward Hart, Princeton | 1911 |
| Leon Hart, Notre Dame | 1949 |
| Bill Hartman, Georgia | 1937 |
| †Homer Hazel, Rutgers | 1924 |

| Player, College | Year |
|---|---|
| †Matt Hazeltine, California | 1954 |
| †Ed Healey, Dartmouth | 1916 |
| †Pudge Heffelfinger, Yale | 1891 |
| †Mel Hein, Washington St. | 1930 |
| †Don Heinrich, Washington | 1952 |
| Ted Hendricks, Miami (Fla.) | 1968 |
| †Wilbur Henry, Wash. & Jeff. | 1919 |
| †C. Herschberger, Chicago | 1898 |
| †Robert Herwig, California | 1937 |
| †Willie Heston, Michigan | 1904 |
| †Herman Hickman, Tennessee | 1931 |
| †William Hickok, Yale | 1894 |
| †Dan Hill, Duke | 1938 |
| †Art Hillebrand, Princeton | 1899 |
| †Frank Hinkey, Yale | 1894 |
| †Carl Hinkle, Vanderbilt | 1937 |
| Clarke Hinkle, Bucknell | 1931 |
| Elroy Hirsch, Wisconsin/Michigan | 1943 |
| †James Hitchcock, Auburn | 1932 |
| Frank Hoffmann, Notre Dame | 1931 |
| †James J. Hogan, Yale | 1904 |
| †Brud Holland, Cornell | 1938 |
| †Don Holleder, Army | 1955 |
| †Bill Hollenback, Pennsylvania | 1908 |
| Mike Holovak, Boston College | 1942 |
| E. J. Holub, Texas Tech | 1960 |
| Paul Hornung, Notre Dame | 1956 |
| Edwin Horrell, California | 1924 |
| Les Horvath, Ohio St. | 1944 |
| †Arthur Howe, Yale | 1911 |
| †Dixie Howell, Alabama | 1934 |
| †Cal Hubbard, Centenary | 1926 |
| †John Hubbard, Amherst | 1906 |
| †Pooley Hubert, Alabama | 1925 |
| Sam Huff, West Va. | 1955 |
| Weldon Humble, Rice | 1946 |
| †Joel Hunt, Texas A&M | 1927 |
| †Ellery Huntington, Colgate | 1914 |
| Don Hutson, Alabama | 1934 |
| †Jonas Ingram, Navy | 1906 |
| †Cecil Isbell, Purdue | 1937 |
| †J. Jablonsky, Army/Washington | 1933 |
| Vic Janowicz, Ohio St. | 1951 |
| †Darold Jenkins, Missouri | 1941 |
| †Jackie Jensen, California | 1948 |
| †Herbert Joesting, Minnesota | 1927 |
| Bob Johnson, Tennessee | 1967 |
| †Jimmie Johnson, Carlisle/Northwestern | 1903 |
| Ron Johnson, Michigan | 1968 |
| †Calvin Jones, Iowa | 1955 |
| †Gomer Jones, Ohio St. | 1935 |
| Lee Roy Jordan, Alabama | 1962 |
| †Frank Juhan, Sewanee | 1910 |
| Charlie Justice, North Caro. | 1949 |
| †Mort Kaer, Southern Cal | 1926 |
| Alex Karras, Iowa | 1957 |
| Ken Kavanaugh, Louisiana St. | 1939 |
| †Edgar Kaw, Cornell | 1922 |
| Dick Kazmaier, Princeton | 1951 |
| †James Keck, Princeton | 1921 |
| Larry Kelley, Yale | 1936 |
| †Wild Bill Kelly, Montana | 1926 |
| Doug Kenna, Army | 1944 |
| †George Kerr, Boston College | 1941 |
| †Henry Ketcham, Yale | 1913 |
| Leroy Keyes, Purdue | 1968 |
| †Glenn Killinger, Penn St. | 1921 |
| †John Kilpatrick, Yale | 1910 |
| John Kimbrough, Texas A&M | 1940 |
| †Frank Kinard, Mississippi | 1937 |

| Player, College | Year |
|---|---|
| †Phillip King, Princeton | 1893 |
| †Nile Kinnick, Iowa | 1939 |
| †Harry Kipke, Michigan | 1923 |
| †John Kitzmiller, Oregon | 1930 |
| †Barton Koch, Baylor | 1931 |
| †Walt Koppisch, Columbia | 1924 |
| Ron Kramer, Michigan | 1956 |
| Charlie Krueger, Texas A&M | 1957 |
| Malcolm Kutner, Texas | 1941 |
| Ted Kwalick, Penn St. | 1968 |
| †Steve Lach, Duke | 1941 |
| †Myles Lane, Dartmouth | 1927 |
| Johnny Lattner, Notre Dame | 1953 |
| Hank Lauricella, Tennessee | 1952 |
| †Lester Lautenschlaeger, Tulane | 1925 |
| †Elmer Layden, Notre Dame | 1924 |
| †Bobby Layne, Texas | 1947 |
| †Langdon Lea, Princeton | 1895 |
| Eddie LeBaron, Pacific (Cal.) | 1949 |
| †James Leech, Va. Military | 1920 |
| Darrell Lester, Texas Christian | 1935 |
| Bob Lilly, Texas Christian | 1960 |
| †Augie Lio, Georgetown | 1940 |
| Floyd Little, Syracuse | 1966 |
| †Gordon Locke, Iowa | 1922 |
| Don Lourie, Princeton | 1921 |
| Richie Lucas, Penn St. | 1959 |
| Sid Luckman, Columbia | 1938 |
| Johnny Lujack, Notre Dame | 1947 |
| Pug Lund, Minnesota | 1934 |
| Jim Lynch, Notre Dame | 1966 |
| Robert MacLeod, Dartmouth | 1938 |
| †Bart Macomber, Illinois | 1915 |
| Dicky Maegle, Rice | 1954 |
| †Ned Mahon, Harvard | 1915 |
| Johnny Majors, Tennessee | 1956 |
| †William Mallory, Yale | 1923 |
| Vaughn Mancha, Alabama | 1947 |
| †Gerald Mann, Southern Methodist | 1927 |
| Archie Manning, Mississippi | 1970 |
| Edgar Manske, Northwestern | 1933 |
| Ed Marinaro, Cornell | 1971 |
| Vic Markov, Washington | 1937 |
| †Bobby Marshall, Minnesota | 1906 |
| Ollie Matson, San Francisco | 1952 |
| Ray Matthews, Texas Christian | 1927 |
| †John Maulbetsch, Michigan | 1914 |
| †Pete Mauthe, Penn St. | 1912 |
| †Robert Maxwell, Chicago/Swarthmore | 1906 |
| George McAfee, Duke | 1939 |
| †Thomas McClung, Yale | 1891 |
| Bill McColl, Stanford | 1951 |
| †Jim McCormick, Princeton | 1907 |
| Tommy McDonald, Oklahoma | 1956 |
| †Jack McDowall, North Caro. St. | 1927 |
| Hugh McElhenny, Washington | 1951 |
| †Gene McEver, Tennessee | 1931 |
| †John McEwan, Army | 1916 |
| Banks McFadden, Clemson | 1939 |
| Bud McFadin, Texas | 1950 |
| Mike McGee, Duke | 1959 |
| †Edward McGinley, Pennsylvania | 1924 |
| †John McGovern, Minnesota | 1910 |
| Thurman McGraw, Colorado St. | 1949 |
| †Mike McKeever, Southern Cal | 1960 |
| †George McLaren, Pittsburgh | 1918 |
| †Dan McMillan, Southern Cal/California | 1922 |
| †Bo McMillin, Centre | 1921 |
| †Bob McWhorter, Georgia | 1913 |
| †LeRoy Mercer, Pennsylvania | 1912 |

| Player, College | Year |
|---|---|
| Don Meredith, Southern Methodist | 1959 |
| †Bert Metzger, Notre Dame | 1930 |
| †Wayne Meylan, Nebraska | 1967 |
| Lou Michaels, Kentucky | 1957 |
| Abe Mickal, Louisiana St. | 1935 |
| Creighton Miller, Notre Dame | 1943 |
| †Don Miller, Notre Dame | 1924 |
| †Eugene Miller, Penn St. | 1913 |
| †Fred Miller, Notre Dame | 1928 |
| †Rip Miller, Notre Dame | 1924 |
| †Wayne Millner, Notre Dame | 1935 |
| †C. A. Milstead, Wabash/Yale | 1923 |
| †John Minds, Pennsylvania | 1897 |
| Skip Minisi, Pennsylvania/Navy | 1947 |
| †Alex Moffat, Princeton | 1883 |
| †Ed Molinski, Tennessee | 1940 |
| Cliff Montgomery, Columbia | 1933 |
| Donn Moomaw, UCLA | 1952 |
| †William Morley, Columbia | 1902 |
| George Morris, Georgia Tech | 1952 |
| Larry Morris, Georgia Tech | 1954 |
| †Bill Morton, Dartmouth | 1931 |
| Craig Morton, California | 1964 |
| †Monk Moscrip, Stanford | 1935 |
| †Brick Muller, California | 1922 |
| †Bronko Nagurski, Minnesota | 1929 |
| †Ernie Nevers, Stanford | 1925 |
| †Marshall Newell, Harvard | 1893 |
| Harry Newman, Michigan | 1932 |
| Tommy Nobis, Texas | 1965 |
| Leo Nomellini, Minnesota | 1949 |
| †Andrew Oberlander, Dartmouth | 1925 |
| †Davey O'Brien, Texas Christian | 1938 |
| †Pat O'Dea, Wisconsin | 1899 |
| Bob Odell, Pennsylvania | 1943 |
| †Jack O'Hearn, Cornell | 1915 |
| Robin Olds, Army | 1942 |
| †Elmer Oliphant, Army/Purdue | 1917 |
| Merlin Olsen, Utah St. | 1961 |
| †Bennie Oosterbaan, Michigan | 1927 |
| Charles O'Rourke, Boston College | 1940 |
| †John Orsi, Colgate | 1931 |
| †Win Osgood, Cornell | 1892 |
| Bill Osmanski, Holy Cross | 1938 |
| †George Owen, Harvard | 1922 |
| Jim Owens, Oklahoma | 1949 |
| Steve Owens, Oklahoma | 1969 |
| Jack Pardee, Texas A&M | 1956 |
| Babe Parilli, Kentucky | 1951 |
| Ace Parker, Duke | 1936 |
| Jackie Parker, Mississippi St. | 1953 |
| Jim Parker, Ohio St. | 1956 |
| †Vince Pazzetti, Lehigh | 1912 |
| Chub Peabody, Harvard | 1941 |
| †Robert Peck, Pittsburgh | 1916 |
| †Stan Pennock, Harvard | 1914 |
| George Pfann, Cornell | 1923 |
| †H. D. Phillips, Sewanee | 1904 |
| Loyd Phillips, Arkansas | 1966 |
| Pete Pihos, Indiana | 1946 |
| †Erny Pinckert, Southern Cal | 1931 |
| John Pingel, Michigan St. | 1938 |
| Jim Plunkett, Stanford | 1970 |
| †Arthur Poe, Princeton | 1899 |
| †Fritz Pollard, Brown | 1916 |
| B. Poole, Miss./North Caro./Army | 1947 |
| Merv Pregulman, Michigan | 1943 |
| †Eddie Price, Tulane | 1949 |
| †Peter Pund, Georgia Tech | 1928 |
| Garrard Ramsey, William & Mary | 1942 |

*Special Awards*

335

| Player, College | Year | Player, College | Year |
|---|---|---|---|
| †Claude Reeds, Oklahoma | 1913 | †Mal Stevens, Yale | 1923 |
| Mike Reid, Penn St. | 1969 | †Vincent Stevenson, Pennsylvania | 1905 |
| Steve Reid, Northwestern | 1936 | Jim Stillwagon, Ohio St. | 1970 |
| †William Reid, Harvard | 1899 | †Pete Stinchcomb, Ohio St. | 1920 |
| Mel Renfro, Oregon | 1963 | Brock Strom, Air Force | 1959 |
| †Pug Rentner, Northwestern | 1932 | †Ken Strong, New York U. | 1928 |
| Bob Reynolds, Stanford | 1935 | †George Strupper, Georgia Tech | 1917 |
| †Bobby Reynolds, Nebraska | 1952 | †Harry Stuhldreher, Notre Dame | 1924 |
| Les Richter, California | 1951 | †Herb Sturhan, Yale | 1926 |
| †Jack Riley, Northwestern | 1931 | †Joe Stydahar, West Va. | 1935 |
| †Charles Rinehart, Lafayette | 1897 | †Bob Suffridge, Tennessee | 1940 |
| †Ira Rodgers, West Va. | 1919 | †Steve Suhey, Penn St. | 1947 |
| †Edward Rogers, Carlisle/Minnesota | 1903 | Pat Sullivan, Auburn | 1971 |
| Joe Romig, Colorado | 1961 | †Frank Sundstrom, Cornell | 1923 |
| †Aaron Rosenberg, Southern Cal | 1933 | †Clarence Swanson, Nebraska | 1921 |
| Kyle Rote, Southern Methodist | 1950 | †Bill Swiacki, Columbia | 1947 |
| †Joe Routt, Texas A&M | 1937 | Jim Swink, Texas Christian | 1956 |
| †Red Salmon, Notre Dame | 1903 | George Taliaferro, Indiana | 1948 |
| George Sauer, Nebraska | 1933 | Fran Tarkenton, Georgia | 1960 |
| George Savitsky, Pennsylvania | 1947 | John Tavener, Indiana | 1944 |
| Gale Sayers, Kansas | 1964 | | |
| Jack Scarbath, Maryland | 1952 | | |
| †Hunter Scarlett, Pennsylvania | 1908 | | |
| Bob Schloredt, Washington | 1960 | | |
| †Wear Schoonover, Arkansas | 1929 | | |
| †Dave Schreiner, Wisconsin | 1942 | | |
| †Germany Schultz, Michigan | 1908 | | |
| †Dutch Schwab, Lafayette | 1922 | | |
| †Marchy Schwartz, Notre Dame | 1931 | | |
| †Paul Schwegler, Washington | 1931 | | |
| Clyde Scott, Arkansas | 1948 | | |
| Richard Scott, Navy | 1947 | | |
| Tom Scott, Virginia | 1953 | | |
| †Henry Seibels, Sewanee | 1899 | | |
| Ron Sellers, Florida St. | 1968 | | |
| Lee Roy Selmon, Oklahoma | 1975 | | |
| †Bill Shakespeare, Notre Dame | 1935 | | |
| †Murray Shelton, Cornell | 1915 | | |
| †Tom Shevlin, Yale | 1905 | | |
| †Bernie Shively, Illinois | 1926 | | |
| †Monk Simons, Tulane | 1934 | | |
| O. J. Simpson, Southern Cal | 1968 | | |
| Fred Sington, Alabama | 1930 | | |
| †Frank Sinkwich, Georgia | 1942 | | |
| †Emil Sitko, Notre Dame | 1949 | | |
| †Joe Skladany, Pittsburgh | 1933 | | |
| †Duke Slater, Iowa | 1921 | | |
| †Bruce Smith, Minnesota | 1941 | | |
| Bubba Smith, Michigan St. | 1966 | | |
| †Clipper Smith, Notre Dame | 1927 | | |
| †Ernie Smith, Southern Cal | 1932 | | |
| Harry Smith, Southern Cal | 1939 | | |
| Jim Ray Smith, Baylor | 1954 | | |
| Riley Smith, Alabama | 1935 | | |
| †Vernon Smith, Georgia | 1931 | | |
| †Neil Snow, Michigan | 1901 | | |
| Al Sparlis, UCLA | 1945 | | |
| †Clarence Spears, Dartmouth | 1915 | | |
| W. D. Spears, Vanderbilt | 1927 | | |
| †William Sprackling, Brown | 1911 | | |
| †Bud Sprague, Army/Texas | 1928 | | |
| Steve Spurrier, Florida | 1966 | | |
| Harrison Stafford, Texas | 1932 | | |
| †Amos Alonzo Stagg, Yale | 1889 | | |
| †Max Starcevich, Washington | 1936 | | |
| Roger Staubach, Navy | 1964 | | |
| †Walter Steffen, Chicago | 1908 | | |
| Joe Steffy, Tennessee/Army | 1947 | | |
| †Herbert Stein, Pittsburgh | 1921 | | |
| Bob Steuber, Missouri | 1943 | | |

**Before moving on to a distinguished pro career, Fran Tarkenton starred as Georgia's quarterback from 1958 to 1960. In his senior year, Tarkenton was named to The Associated Press' all-American team. He is a member of the College Football Hall of Fame.**

| | | | |
|---|---|---|---|
| Chuck Taylor, Stanford | 1942 | | |
| Aurelius Thomas, Ohio St. | 1957 | | |
| †Joe Thompson, Pittsburgh | 1907 | | |
| †Samuel Thorne, Yale | 1895 | | |
| †Jim Thorpe, Carlisle | 1912 | | |
| †Ben Ticknor, Harvard | 1930 | | |
| †John Tigert, Vanderbilt | 1904 | | |
| Gaynell Tinsley, Louisiana St. | 1936 | | |
| Eric Tipton, Duke | 1938 | | |
| Clayton Tonnemaker, Minnesota | 1949 | | |
| †Bob Torrey, Pennsylvania | 1905 | | |
| †Brick Travis, Missouri | 1920 | | |
| Charley Trippi, Georgia | 1946 | | |
| †Edward Tryon, Colgate | 1925 | | |
| Bulldog Turner, Hardin-Simmons | 1939 | | |

| Player, College | Year |
|---|---|
| Howard Twilley, Tulsa | 1965 |
| †Joe Utay, Texas A&M | 1907 |
| †Norm Van Brocklin, Oregon | 1948 |
| †Dale Van Sickel, Florida | 1929 |
| †H. Van Surdam, Wesleyan | 1905 |
| †Dexter Very, Penn St. | 1912 |
| Billy Vessels, Oklahoma | 1952 |
| †Ernie Vick, Michigan | 1921 |
| †Hube Wagner, Pittsburgh | 1913 |
| Doak Walker, Southern Methodist | 1949 |
| †Bill Wallace, Rice | 1935 |
| †Adam Walsh, Notre Dame | 1924 |
| †Cotton Warburton, Southern Cal | 1934 |
| Bob Ward, Maryland | 1951 |
| †William Warner, Cornell | 1904 |
| †Kenny Washington, UCLA | 1939 |
| †Jim Weatherall, Oklahoma | 1951 |
| George Webster, Michigan St. | 1966 |
| H. Wedemeyer, St. Mary's (Cal.) | 1947 |
| †Harold Weekes, Columbia | 1902 |
| Art Weiner, North Caro. | 1949 |
| †Ed Weir, Nebraska | 1925 |
| †Gus Welch, Carlisle | 1914 |
| †John Weller, Princeton | 1935 |
| †Percy Wendell, Harvard | 1912 |
| †Belford West, Colgate | 1919 |
| †Bob Westfall, Michigan | 1941 |
| †Babe Weyand, Army | 1915 |
| †Buck Wharton, Pennsylvania | 1896 |
| †Arthur Wheeler, Princeton | 1894 |

| Player, College | Year |
|---|---|
| Byron White, Colorado | 1938 |
| †Don Whitmire, Navy/Alabama | 1944 |
| †Frank Wickhorst, Navy | 1926 |
| Ed Widseth, Minnesota | 1936 |
| †Dick Wildung, Minnesota | 1942 |
| Bob Williams, Notre Dame | 1950 |
| Froggie Williams, Rice | 1949 |
| Bill Willis, Ohio St. | 1944 |
| Bobby Wilson, Southern Methodist | 1935 |
| †George Wilson, Washington | 1925 |
| †Harry Wilson, Army/Penn St. | 1926 |
| Mike Wilson, Lafayette | 1928 |
| Albert Wistert, Michigan | 1942 |
| Alvin Wistert, Michigan | 1949 |
| †Whitey Wistert, Michigan | 1933 |
| †Alex Wojciechowicz, Fordham | 1937 |
| †Barry Wood, Harvard | 1931 |
| †Andy Wyant, Chicago | 1894 |
| †Bowden Wyatt, Tennessee | 1938 |
| †Clint Wyckoff, Cornell | 1895 |
| †Tommy Yarr, Notre Dame | 1931 |
| Ron Yary, Southern Cal | 1967 |
| †Lloyd Yoder, Carnegie Mellon | 1926 |
| †Buddy Young, Illinois | 1946 |
| †Harry Young, Wash. & Lee | 1916 |
| †Waddy Young, Oklahoma | 1938 |
| Jack Youngblood, Florida | 1970 |
| Gust Zarnas, Ohio St. | 1937 |

## COACHES

| Coach | Year |
|---|---|
| †Joe Aillet | 1989 |
| †Bill Alexander | 1951 |
| †Ed Anderson | 1971 |
| †Ike Armstrong | 1957 |
| †Charlie Bachman | 1978 |
| Earl Banks | 1992 |
| †Harry Baujan | 1990 |
| †Matty Bell | 1955 |
| †Hugo Bezdek | 1954 |
| †Dana X. Bible | 1951 |
| †Bernie Bierman | 1955 |
| Bob Blackman | 1987 |
| †Earl (Red) Blaik | 1965 |
| Frank Broyles | 1983 |
| †Paul (Bear) Bryant | 1986 |
| †Charlie Caldwell | 1961 |
| †Walter Camp | 1951 |
| Len Casanova | 1977 |
| †Frank Cavanaugh | 1954 |
| †Dick Colman | 1990 |
| †Fritz Crisler | 1954 |
| †Duffy Daugherty | 1984 |
| Bob Devaney | 1981 |
| Dan Devine | 1985 |
| †Gil Dobie | 1951 |
| †Michael Donohue | 1951 |
| †Gus Dorais | 1954 |
| †Bill Edwards | 1986 |
| †Rip Engle | 1973 |
| Don Faurot | 1961 |
| Jake Gaither | 1973 |
| Sid Gillman | 1989 |
| †Ernest Godfrey | 1972 |
| Ray Graves | 1990 |
| †Andy Gustafson | 1985 |

| Coach | Year |
|---|---|
| †Edward Hall | 1951 |
| †Jack Harding | 1980 |
| †Richard Harlow | 1954 |
| †Harvey Harman | 1981 |
| †Jesse Harper | 1971 |
| †Percy Haughton | 1951 |
| †Woody Hayes | 1983 |
| †John W. Heisman | 1954 |
| †Robert Higgins | 1954 |
| †Babe Hollingberry | 1979 |
| Frank Howard | 1989 |
| †Bill Ingram | 1973 |
| †Morley Jennings | 1973 |
| †Biff Jones | 1954 |
| †Howard Jones | 1951 |
| †Tad Jones | 1958 |
| †Lloyd Jordan | 1978 |
| †Ralph (Shug) Jordan | 1982 |
| †Andy Kerr | 1951 |
| †Frank Leahy | 1970 |
| †George Little | 1955 |
| †Lou Little | 1960 |
| †Slip Madigan | 1974 |
| Dave Maurer | 1991 |
| Charlie McClendon | 1986 |
| Herb McCracken | 1973 |
| †Dan McGugin | 1951 |
| John McKay | 1988 |
| Allyn McKeen | 1991 |
| †Tuss McLaughry | 1962 |
| †Dutch Meyer | 1956 |
| †Jack Mollenkopf | 1988 |
| †Bernie Moore | 1954 |
| †Scrappy Moore | 1980 |
| †Ray Morrison | 1954 |

| Coach | Year | Coach | Year |
|---|---|---|---|
| †George Munger | 1976 | †Clark Shaughnessy | 1968 |
| †Clarence (Biggie) Munn | 1959 | †Buck Shaw | 1972 |
| †Bill Murray | 1974 | †Andy Smith | 1951 |
| †Frank Murray | 1983 | †Carl Snavely | 1965 |
| †Ed (Hooks) Mylin | 1974 | †Amos Alonzo Stagg | 1951 |
| †Earle (Greasy) Neale | 1967 | †Jock Sutherland | 1951 |
| †Jess Neely | 1971 | †Jim Tatum | 1984 |
| †David Nelson | 1987 | †Frank Thomas | 1951 |
| †Robert Neyland | 1956 | †Thad Vann | 1987 |
| †Homer Norton | 1971 | Johnny Vaught | 1979 |
| †Frank (Buck) O'Neill | 1951 | †Wallace Wade | 1955 |
| †Bennie Owen | 1951 | †Lynn (Pappy) Waldorf | 1966 |
| Ara Parseghian | 1980 | †Glenn (Pop) Warner | 1951 |
| †Doyt Perry | 1988 | †E. E. (Tad) Wieman | 1956 |
| †Jimmy Phelan | 1973 | †John Wilce | 1954 |
| Tommy Prothro | 1991 | Bud Wilkinson | 1969 |
| John Ralston | 1992 | †Henry Williams | 1951 |
| †E. N. Robinson | 1955 | †George Woodruff | 1963 |
| †Knute Rockne | 1951 | Warren Woodson | 1989 |
| †Dick Romney | 1954 | †Fielding (Hurry Up) Yost | 1951 |
| †Bill Roper | 1951 | †Bob Zuppke | 1951 |
| Darrell Royal | 1983 | | |
| †George Sanford | 1971 | | |
| †Francis Schmidt | 1971 | | |
| †Ben Schwartzwalder | 1982 | | |

# FIRST-TEAM ALL-AMERICANS BELOW DIVISION I-A

## (Selected by the Associated Press and the American Football Coaches Association)

Selection of Associated Press Little All-America Teams began in 1934. Early AP selectors were not bound by NCAA statistical classifications; therefore, 30 current Division I-A teams are included in this list.

The American Football Coaches Association began selecting all-America teams below Division I-A in 1967 for two College-Division classifications. Its College-Division I team includes NCAA Division II and National Association of Intercollegiate Athletics (NAIA) Division I players. The AFCA College-Division II team includes NCAA Division III and NAIA Division II players. The AFCA added a Division I-AA team in 1979; AP began selecting a Division I-AA team in 1982, and these players are included. In 1990, the Champion USA Division III team was added, selected by a panel of 25 sports information directors.

Nonmembers of the NCAA are included in this list, as are colleges that no longer play varsity football.

Players selected to a Division I-AA all-America team are indicated by (†). Current members of Division I-A are indicated by (*).

All-Americans are listed by college, year selected and position.

**ABILENE CHRISTIAN (16)**
48— V. T. Smith, B
51— Lester Wheeler, OT
52— Wallace Bullington, DB
65— Larry Cox, OT
69— Chip Bennett, LB
70— Jim Lindsey, QB
73— Wilbert Montgomery, RB
74— Chip Martin, DL
77— Chuck Sitton, DB
82— Grant Feasel, C
83— Mark Wilson, DB
84— Dan Remsberg, OT
87— Richard Van Druten, OT
89— John Layfield, OG
90— Dennis Brown, PK
91— Jay Jones, LB

**ADAMS ST. (3)**
79— Ronald Johnson, DB
84— Bill Stone, RB
87— Dave Humann, DB

**AKRON* (9)**
69— John Travis, OG
71— Michael Hatch, DB
76— Mark Van Horn, OG
      Steve Cockerham, LB
77— Steve Cockerham, LB
80—†Brad Reece, LB
81—†Brad Reece, LB
85—†Wayne Grant, DL
86—†Mike Clark, RB

**ALABAMA A&M (3)**
87— Howard Ballard, OL

88— Fred Garner, DB
89— Barry Wagner, WR

**ALABAMA ST. (3)**
90—†Eddie Robinson, LB
91—†Patrick Johnson, OL
      †Eddie Robinson, LB

**ALBANY (N.Y.) (1)**
92— Scott Turrin, OL

**ALBANY ST. (GA.) (1)**
72— Harold Little, DE

**ALBION (6)**
40— Walter Ptak, G
58— Tom Taylor, E
76— Steve Spencer, DL
86— Joe Felton, OG
      Mike Grant, DB

91— Hank Wineman, RB

**ALBRIGHT (3)**
36— Richard Riffle, B
37— Richard Riffle, B
75— Chris Simcic, OL

**ALCORN ST. (11)**
69— David Hadley, DB
70— Fred Carter, DT
71— Harry Gooden, LB
72— Alex Price, DT
73— Leonard Fairley, DB
74— Jerry Dismuke, OG
75— Lawrence Pillers, DE
76— Augusta Lee, RB
    Larry Warren, DT
79—†Leslie Frazier, DB
84—†Issiac Holt, DB

**ALFRED (7)**
51— Ralph DiMicco, B
52— Ralph DiMicco, B
55— Charles Schultz, E
56— Charles Schultz, E
75— Joseph Van Cura, DE
82— Brian O'Neil, DB
92— Mark Obuszewski, DB

**ALLEGHENY (11)**
75— Charles Slater, OL
87— Mike Mates, OL
88— Mike Parker, DL
90— Jeff Filkovski, QB
    David LaCarte, DB
    John Marzca, C
91— Ron Bendekovic, OT
    Stanley Drayton, RB
    Tony Bifulco, DB
92— Ron Bendekovic, OT
    Stanley Drayton, RB

**AMERICAN INT'L (10)**
71— Bruce Laird, RB
80— Ed Cebula, C
82— Paul Thompson, DT
85— Keith Barry, OL
86— Jon Provost, OL
87— Jon Provost, OL
88— Greg Doherty, OL
89— Lamont Cato, DB
90— George Patterson, DL
91— Gabe Mokwuah, DL

**AMHERST (3)**
42— Adrian Hasse, E
72— Richard Murphy, QB
73— Fred Scott, FL

**ANGELO ST. (11)**
75— James Cross, DB
78— Jerry Aldridge, RB
    Kelvin Smith, LB
81— Clay Weishuhn, LB
82— Mike Elarms, WR
83— Mike Thomas, K
85— Henry Jackson, LB
86— Pierce Holt, DL
87— Pierce Holt, DL
88— Henry Alsbrooks, LB
92— Jimmy Morris, P

**APPALACHIAN ST. (10)**
48— John Caskey, E
63— Greg Van Orden, G
85—†Dino Hackett, LB
87—†Anthony Downs, DE
88—†Bjorn Nittmo, PK
89—†Derrick Graham, OL
    †Keith Collins, DB
91—†Harold Alexander, P

92—†Avery Hall, DL
    †Harold Alexander, P

**ARIZONA\* (1)**
41— Henry Stanton, E

**ARKANSAS ST.\* (17)**
53— Richard Woit, B
64— Dan Summers, OG
65— Dan Summers, OG
68— Bill Bergey, LB
69— Dan Buckley, C
    Clovis Swinney, DT
70— Bill Phillips, OG
    Calvin Harrell, RB
71— Calvin Harrell, RB
    Dennis Meyer, DB
    Wayne Dorton, OG
73— Doug Lowrey, OG
84—†Carter Crawford, DL
85—†Carter Crawford, DL
86—†Randy Barnhill, OG
87—†Jim Wiseman, C
    †Charlie Fredrick, DT

**ARKANSAS TECH (2)**
58— Edward Meador, B
61— Powell McClellan, E

**ASHLAND (7)**
70— Len Pettigrew, LB
78— Keith Dare, OL
85— Jeff Penko, OL
86— Vince Mazza, PK
89— Douglas Powell, DB
90— Morris Furman, LB
91— Ron Greer, LB

**AUGUSTANA (ILL.) (10)**
72— Willie Van, DT
73— Robert Martin, OT
83— Kurt Kapischke, OL
84— Greg King, C
86— Lynn Thomsen, DL
87— Carlton Beasley, DL
88— John Bothe, OL
90— Barry Reade, PK
91— Mike Hesler, OL
92— George Annang, DL

**AUGUSTANA (S.D.) (3)**
60— John Simko, E
87— Tony Adkins, DL
88— Pete Jaros, DB

**AUSTIN (9)**
37— Wallace Johnson, C
79— Price Clifford, LB
80— Chris Luper, DB
81— Larry Shillings, QB
83— Ed Holt, DL
84— Jeff Timmons, PK
87— Otis Amy, WR
88— Otis Amy, WR
90— Jeff Cordell, DB

**AUSTIN PEAY (8)**
65— Tim Chilcutt, DB
66— John Ogles, FB
70— Harold Roberts, OE
77— Bob Bible, LB
78— Mike Betts, DB
80— Brett Williams, DE
82— Charlie Tucker, OL
92—†Richard Darden, DL

**AZUSA PACIFIC (1)**
86— Christian Okoye, RB

**BAKER (3)**
83— Chris Brown, LB
85— Kevin Alewine, RB

90— John Campbell, OL

**BALDWIN-WALLACE (9)**
50— Norbert Hecker, E
68— Bob Quackenbush, DT
78— Jeff Jenkins, OL
80— Dan Delfino, DE
82— Pete Primeau, DL
83— Steve Varga, K
89— Doug Halbert, DL
91— John Koz, QB
    Jim Clardy, LB

**BALL ST.\* (4)**
67— Oscar Lubke, OT
68— Amos Van Pelt, HB
72— Douglas Bell, C
73— Terry Schmidt, DB

**BATES (1)**
81— Larry DiGammarino, WR

**BEMIDJI ST. (1)**
83— Bruce Ecklund, TE

**BENEDICTINE (1)**
36— Leo Deutsch, E

**BETHANY (W. VA.) (1)**
77— Scott Lanz, P

**BETHEL (KAN.) (1)**
80— David Morford, C

**BETHUNE-COOKMAN (2)**
75— Willie Lee, DE
81— Booker Reese, DE

**BIRMINGHAM-
SOUTHERN (1)**
37— Walter Riddle, T

**BISHOP (1)**
81— Carlton Nelson, DL

**BLOOMSBURG (7)**
79— Mike Morucci, RB
82— Mike Blake, TE
83— Frank Sheptock, LB
84— Frank Sheptock, LB
85— Frank Sheptock, LB
    Tony Woods, DB
91— Eric Jonassen, OL

**BOISE ST. (21)**
72— Al Marshall, OE
73— Don Hutt, WR
74— Jim McMillan, QB
75— John Smith, FL
77— Chris Malmgren, DT
    Terry Hutt, WR
    Harold Cotton, OT
79—†Joe Aliotti, QB
    †Doug Scott, DT
80—†Randy Trautman, DT
81—†Randy Trautman, DT
    †Rick Woods, DB
82—†John Rade, DL
    †Carl Keever, LB
84—†Carl Keever, LB
85—†Marcus Koch, DL
87—†Tom DeWitz, OG
    †Pete Kwiatkowski, DT
90—†Erik Helgeson, DL
91—†Frank Robinson, DB
92—†Michael Dodd, PK

**BOSTON U. (14)**
67— Dick Farley, DB
68— Bruce Taylor, DB
69— Bruce Taylor, DB
79—†Mal Najarian, RB
    †Tom Pierzga, DL
81—†Bob Speight, OT

†Gregg Drew, RB
82—†Mike Mastrogiacomo, OG
83—†Paul Lewis, RB
84—†Paul Lewis, RB
86—†Kevin Murphy, DT
87—†Mark Seals, DB
88—†Mark Seals, DB
89—†Daren Altieri, WR

**BOWDOIN (1)**
77— Steve McCabe, OL

**BOWIE ST. (2)**
80— Victor Jackson, CB
81— Marco Tongue, DB

**BOWLING GREEN* (2)**
59— Bob Zimpfer, T
82—†Andre Young, DL

**BRADLEY (1)**
38— Ted Panish, B

**BRANDEIS (2)**
54— William McKenna, E
56— James Stehlin, B

**BRIDGEPORT (1)**
72— Dennis Paldin, DB

**BRIDGEWATER (VA.) (1)**
75— C. J. DeWitt, SE

**BRI'WATER (MASS.) (1)**
92— Erik Arthur, DL

**BROCKPORT ST. (1)**
90— Ed Smart, TE

**BUCKNELL (7)**
51— George Young, DT
60— Paul Terhes, B
64— Tom Mitchell, OE
65— Tom Mitchell, OE
74— Larry Schoenberger, LB
80— Mike McDonald, OT
90—†Mike Augsberger, DB

**BUENA VISTA (4)**
72— Joe Kotval, OG
73— Joe Kotval, OG
76— Keith Kerkhoff, DL
87— Jim Higley, LB

**BUFFALO (2)**
84— Gerry Quinlivan, LB
87— Steve Wojciechowski, LB

**BUTLER (1)**
88— Steve Roberts, RB

**CAL LUTHERAN (2)**
72— Brian Kelley, LB
79— Mike Hagen, SE

**CAL POLY SLO (13)**
53— Stan Sheriff, C
58— Charles Gonzales, G
66— David Edmondson, C
72— Mike Amos, DB
73— Fred Stewart, OG
78— Louis Jackson, RB
80— Louis Jackson, RB
    Robbie Martin, FL
81— Charles Daum, OL
84— Nick Frost, DB
89— Robert Morris, DL
90— Pat Moore, DL
91— Doug O'Neill, P

**CAL ST. CHICO (1)**
87— Chris Verhulst, TE

**CAL ST. HAYWARD (3)**
75— Greg Blankenship, LB
84— Ed Lively, DT

86— Fred Williams, OL

**CAL ST. NORTHRIDGE (5)**
75— Mel Wilson, DB
82— Pat Hauser, OT
83— Pat Hauser, OT
87— Kip Dukes, DB
91— Don Goodman, OL

**CAL ST. SACRAMENTO (4)**
64— William Fuller, OT
91— Troy Mills, RB
    Jim Crouch, PK
92— Jon Kirksey, DL

**CALIF. (PA.) (1)**
83— Perry Kemp, WR

**CANISIUS (2)**
87— Tom Doctor, LB
88— Marty Hurley, DB

**CAPITAL (3)**
74— Greg Arnold, OG
80— John Phillips, DL
    Steve Wigton, C

**CARLETON (1)**
90— Jim Bradford, WR

**CARNEGIE MELLON (3)**
81— Ken Murawski, LB
85— Robert Butts, OL
91— Chuck Jackson, OT

**CARROLL (MONT.) (5)**
76— Richard Dale, DB
79— Don Diggins, DL
87— Jeff Beaudry, DB
88— Paul Petrino, QB
89— Suitoa Keleti, OL

**CARROLL (WIS.) (2)**
74— Robert Helf, TE
90— Bill Nolan, P

**CARSON-NEWMAN (5)**
78— Tank Marr, FL
80— Brad Payne, SAF
83— Dwight Wilson, OL
90— Robert Hardy, RB
92— Darryl Gooden, LB

**CASE RESERVE (4)**
41— Mike Yurcheshen, E
52— Al Feeny, DE
84— Fred Manley, DE
85— Mark Raiff, OL

**CATAWBA (5)**
34— Charles Garland, T
35— Charles Garland, T
45— Carroll Bowen, B
72— David Taylor, OT
74— Mike McDonald, LB

**CATHOLIC (1)**
84— Chris McMahon, DB

**CENTRAL ARK. (3)**
80— Otis Chandler, MG
84— David Burnette, DT
91— David Henson, DL

**CENTRAL CONN. ST. (4)**
74— Mike Walton, C
84— Sal Cintorino, LB
88— Doug Magazu, DL
89— Doug Magazu, DL

**CENTRAL FLA. (2)**
87— Bernard Ford, WR
    Ed O'Brien, PK

**CENTRAL (IOWA) (9)**
70— Vernon Den Herder, DT
74— Al Dorenkamp, LB

77— Donald Taylor, RB
84— Scott Froehle, DB
85— Rich Thomas, DL
88— Mike Stumberg, DL
89— Mike Estes, DL
    Kris Reis, LB
92— Bill Maulder, LB

**CENTRAL MICH.* (4)**
42— Warren Schmakel, G
59— Walter Beach, B
62— Ralph Soffredine, G
74— Rick Newsome, DL

**CENTRAL MO. ST. (4)**
68— Jim Urczyk, OT
85— Steve Huff, PK
88— Jeff Wright, DL
92— Bart Woods, DL

**CENTRAL OKLA. (2)**
65— Jerome Bell, OE
78— Gary Smith, TE

**CENTRAL ST. (OHIO) (7)**
83— Mark Corbin, RB
84— Dave Dunham, OT
85— Mark Corbin, RB
86— Terry Morrow, RB
89— Kenneth Vines, OG
90— Eric Williams, OL
92— Marvin Coleman, DB

**CENTRAL WASH. (4)**
48— Robert Osgood, G
50— Jack Hawkins, G
88— Mike Estes, DL
91— Eric Lamphere, OL

**CENTRE (6)**
55— Gene Scott, B
84— Teel Bruner, DB
85— Teel Bruner, DB
86— Jeff Leonard, OL
88— John Gohmann, DL
89— Jeff Bezold, LB

**CHADRON ST. (3)**
74— Dennis Fitzgerald, DB
78— Rick Mastey, OL
90— David Jones, RB

**CHICAGO (2)**
91— Neal Cawi, DE
    Jeff Stolte, P

**CITADEL (8)**
82— Jim Ettari, DL
84— Jim Gabrish, OL
85— Jim Gabrish, OL
86— Scott Thompson, DT
88—†Carlos Avalos, OL
90—†DeRhon Robinson, OL
92—†Corey Cash, OL
    †Lester Smith, DB

**CLARION (7)**
78— Jeff Langhans, OL
80— Steve Scillitani, MG
    Gary McCauley, TE
81— Gary McCauley, TE
83— Elton Brown, RB
85— Chuck Duffy, OL
87— Lou Weiers, DL

**CLARK ATLANTA (1)**
79— Curtis Smith, OL

**COAST GUARD (2)**
90— Ron Davies, DB
91— Ron Davies, DB

**COE (4)**
74— Dan Schmidt, OG

76— Paul Wagner, OT
85— Mike Matzen, P
90— Richard Matthews, DB

**COLGATE (7)**
82—†Dave Wolf, LB
83—†Rich Erenberg, RB
84—†Tom Stenglein, WR
85—†Tom Stenglein, WR
86—†Kenny Gamble, RB
87—†Kenny Gamble, RB
†Greg Manusky, LB

**COLLEGE OF EMPORIA (1)**
51— William Chai, OG

**COLLEGE OF IDAHO (2)**
53— Norman Hayes, T
54— R. C. Owens, E

**COLORADO COL. (3)**
72— Ed Smith, DE
73— Darryl Crawford, DB
82— Ray Bridges, DL

**COLORADO MINES (5)**
39— Lloyd Madden, B
41— Dick Moe, T
59— Vince Tesone, B
72— Roger Cirimotich, DB
86— Tim Baer, P

**CONCORD (2)**
86— Kevin Johnson, LB
92— Chris Hairston, RB

**CONCORDIA-M'HEAD (3)**
77— Barry Bennett, DT
90— Mike Gindorff, DT
Shayne Lindsay, NG

**CONNECTICUT (7)**
45— Walter Trojanowski, B
73— Richard Foye, C
80—†Reggie Eccleston, WR
83—†John Dorsey, LB
88—†Glenn Antrum, WR
89—†Troy Ashley, LB
91—†Mark Didio, WR

**CORNELL (2)**
82—†Dan Suren, TE
86—†Tom McHale, DE

**CORNELL COLLEGE (2)**
82— John Ward, WR
92— Brent Sands, DB

**CORTLAND ST. (5)**
67— Rodney Verkey, DE
89— Jim Cook, OL
90— Chris Lafferty, OG
Vinny Swanda, LB
91— Vinny Swanda, LB

**CUMBERLAND (KY.) (2)**
87— David Carmichael, DB
89— Ralph McWilliams, OL

**DAKOTA WESLEYAN (1)**
45— Robert Kirkman, T

**DARTMOUTH (2)**
91—†Al Rosier, RB
92—†Dennis Durkin, PK

**DAVIDSON (1)**
34— John Mackorell, B

**DAYTON (9)**
36— Ralph Niehaus, T
78— Rick Chamberlin, LB
81— Chris Chaney, DB
84— David Kemp, LB
86— Gerry Meyer, OL
89— Mike Duvic, PK

90— Steve Harder, OL
91— Brian Olson, OG
92— Andy Pellegrino, OL

**DELAWARE (28)**
42— Hugh Bogovich, G
46— Tony Stalloni, T
54— Don Miller, B
63— Mike Brown, B
66— Herb Slattery, OT
69— John Favero, LB
70— Conway Hayman, OG
71— Gardy Kahoe, RB
72— Joe Carbone, DE
Dennis Johnson, DT
73— Jeff Cannon, DT
74— Ed Clark, LB
Ray Sweeney, OG
75— Sam Miller, DE
76— Robert Pietuszka, DB
78— Jeff Komlo, QB
79—†Herb Beck, OG
†Scott Brunner, QB
80—†Gary Kuhlman, OT
81—†Gary Kuhlman, OL
82—†George Schmitt, DB
85—†Jeff Rosen, OL
86—†Darrell Booker, LB
87—†James Anderson, WR
88—†Mike Renna, DL
89—†Mike Renna, DL
91—†Warren McIntire, DB
92—†Matt Morrill, DL

**DELAWARE ST. (4)**
84— Gene Lake, RB
86— Joe Burton, DB
91—†Rod Milstead, OL
92—†LeRoy Thompson, DL

**DELTA ST. (1)**
67— Leland Hughes, OG

**DENISON (5)**
47— William Hart, E
48— William Wehr, C
75— Dennis Thome, DL
79— Clay Sampson, RB
86— Dan Holland, DL

**DePAUW (1)**
63— Richard Dean, C

**DETROIT TECH (1)**
39— Mike Kostiuk, T

**DICKINSON (1)**
92— Brian Ridgway, DL

**DICKINSON ST. (3)**
81— Tony Moore, DL
91— Shaughn White, DB
92— Rory Farstveet, OL

**DOANE (1)**
66— Fred Davis, OT

**DRAKE (3)**
72— Mike Samples, DT
82— Pat Dunsmore, TE
Craig Wederquist, OT

**DREXEL (2)**
55— Vincent Vidas, T
56— Vincent Vidas, T

**EAST CARO.* (1)**
64— Bill Cline, HB

**EAST CENTRAL (1)**
84— Don Wilson, C

**EAST STROUDSBURG (6)**
65— Barry Roach, DB
75— William Stem, DB

79— Ronald Yakavonis, DL
83— Mike Reichenbach, LB
84— Andy Baranek, QB
91— Curtis Bunch, DB

**EAST TENN. ST. (5)**
53— Hal Morrison, E
68— Ron Overbay, DB
70— William Casey, DB
85— George Cimadevilla, P
86— George Cimadevilla, P

**EAST TEX. ST. (15)**
38— Darrell Tully, B
53— Bruno Ashley, G
58— Sam McCord, B
59— Sam McCord, B
68— Chad Brown, OT
70— William Lewis, C
72— Curtis Wester, OG
73— Autry Beamon, DB
84— Alan Veingrad, OG
88— Kim Morton, DL
90— Terry Bagsby, DL
91— Eric Turner, DB
Dwayne Phorne, OL
92— Eric Turner, DB
Pat Williams, DB

**EASTERN ILL. (16)**
72— Nate Anderson, RB
76— Ted Petersen, C
78— James Warring, WR
79— Chris Cobb, RB
Pete Catan, DE
80— Pete Catan, DE
81— †Kevin Grey, DB
82—†Robert Williams, DB
†Bob Norris, OG
83—†Robert Williams, DB
†Chris Nicholson, DT
84—†Jerry Wright, WR
86—†Roy Banks, WR
88—†John Jurkovic, DL
89—†John Jurkovic, DL
90—†Tim Lance, DB

**EASTERN KY. (22)**
69— Teddy Taylor, MG
74— Everett Talbert, RB
75— Junior Hardin, MG
76— Roosevelt Kelly, OL
79—†Bob McIntyre, LB
80—†George Floyd, DB
81—†George Floyd, DB
†Kevin Greve, OG
82—†Steve Bird, WR
83—†Chris Sullivan, OL
84—†Chris Sullivan, C
85—†Joe Spadafino, OL
86—†Fred Harvey, LB
87—†Aaron Jones, DL
88—†Elroy Harris, RB
†Jessie Small, DL
89—†Al Jacevicius, OL
90—†Kelly Blount, LB
†Al Jacevicius, OL
91—†Carl Satterly, OL
†Ernest Thompson, DL
92—†Markus Thomas, RB

**EASTERN MICH.* (5)**
68— John Schmidt, C
69— Robert Lints, MG
70— Dave Pureifory, DT
71— Dave Pureifory, DT
73— Jim Pietrzak, OT

**EASTERN N. MEX. (5)**
81— Brad Beck, RB
83— Kevin Kott, QB
87— Earl Jones, OL
89— Murray Garrett, DL
90— Anthony Pertile, DB

**EASTERN WASH. (7)**
57— Richard Huston, C
65— Mel Stanton, HB
73— Scott Garske, TE
81— John Tighe, OL
86— Ed Simmons, OT
87—†Eric Stein, P
91—†Kevin Sargent, OL

**EDINBORO (3)**
82— Rick Ruszkiewicz, K
89— Elbert Cole, RB
90— Ernest Priester, WR

**ELMHURST (1)**
82— Lindsay Barich, OL

**ELON (9)**
50— Sal Gero, T
68— Richard McGeorge, OE
69— Richard McGeorge, OE
73— Glenn Ellis, DT
76— Ricky Locklear, DT
    Dan Bass, OL
77— Dan Bass, OL
80— Bobby Hedrick, RB
86— Ricky Sigmon, OL

**EMORY & HENRY (14)**
50— Robert Miller, B
51— Robert Miller, B
56— William Earp, C
68— Sonny Wade, B
85— Keith Furr, DB
    Rob McMillen, DL
86— Sandy Rogers, RB
87— Gary Collier, QB
88— Steve Bowman, DL
89— Doug Reavis, DB
90— Billy Salyers, OL
91— Jason Grooms, DL
92— Pat Buchanan, OL
    Scott Pruner, DL

**EMPORIA ST. (5)**
35— James Fraley, B
37— Harry Klein, E
68— Bruce Cerone, OE
69— Bruce Cerone, OE
91— Quincy Tillmon, RB

**EVANSVILLE (1)**
46— Robert Hawkins, T

**FAIRMONT ST. (3)**
67— Dave Williams, DT
84— Ed Coleman, WR
88— Lou Mabin, OL

**FAYETTEVILLE ST. (1)**
90— Terrence Smith, LB

**FDU-MADISON (3)**
84— Ira Epstein, DL
86— Eric Brey, DB
87— Frank Illidge, DL

**FERRIS ST. (2)**
76— Charles Evans, RB
92— Monty Brown, LB

**FERRUM (5)**
87— Dave Harper, LB
88— Dave Harper, LB
89— Chris Warron, RB
90— Melvin Dillard, DB/KR
91— John Sheets, OG

**FINDLAY (4)**
65— Allen Smith, HB
80— Nelson Bolden, FB
85— Dana Wright, RB
90— Tim Russ, OL

**FLORIDA A&M (12)**
61— Curtis Miranda, C
62— Robert Paremore, B
67— Major Hazelton, DB
    John Eason, OE
73— Henry Lawrence, OT
75— Frank Poole, LB
77— Tyrone McGriff, OG
78— Tyrone McGriff, OG
79—†Tyrone McGriff, OG
    †Kiser Lewis, C
80—†Gifford Ramsey, DB
83—†Ray Alexander, WR

**FLORIDA ST.\* (1)**
51— William Dawkins, OG

**FORT LEWIS (2)**
89— Eric Fadness, P
92— Johnny Cox, WR

**FORT VALLEY ST. (5)**
74— Fred Harris, OT
80— Willie Canady, DB
81— Willie Canady, DB
83— Tugwan Taylor, DB
92— Joseph Best, DB

**FRANK. & MARSH. (8)**
35— Woodrow Sponaugle, C
38— Sam Roeder, B
40— Alex Schibanoff, T
47— William Iannicelli, E
50— Charles Cope, T
81— Vin Carioscia, OL
82— Vin Carioscia, OL
89— Dale Amos, WR

**FRANKLIN (1)**
82— Joe Chester, WR

**FRESNO ST.\* (5)**
39— Jack Mulkey, E
40— Jack Mulkey, E
60— Douglas Brown, G
68— Tom McCall, LB
    Erv Hunt, DB

**FROSTBURG ST. (7)**
80— Terry Beamer, LB
82— Steve Forsythe, WR
83— Kevin Walsh, DL
85— Bill Bagley, WR
86— Marcus Wooley, LB
88— Ken Boyd, DB
89— Ken Boyd, DB

**FURMAN (10)**
82—†Ernest Gibson, DB
83—†Ernest Gibson, DB
84—†Rock Hurst, LB
85—†Gene Reeder, C
88—†Jeff Blankenship, LB
89—†Kelly Fletcher, DL
90—†Steve Duggan, C
    †Kevin Kendrick, LB
91—†Eric Walter, OL
92—†Kota Suttle, LB

**GA. SOUTHERN (14)**
85—†Vance Pike, OL
    †Tim Foley, PK
86—†Fred Stokes, OT
    †Tracy Ham, QB
87—†Flint Matthews, LB
    †Dennis Franklin, C

†Tim Foley, PK
88—†Dennis Franklin, C
    †Darren Alford, DL
89—†Joe Ross, RB
    †Giff Smith, DL
90—†Giff Smith, DL
91—†Rodney Oglesby, DB
92—†Alex Mash, DL

**GA. SOUTHWESTERN (2)**
85— Roger Glover, LB
86— Roger Glover, LB

**GALLAUDET (1)**
87— Shannon Simon, OL

**GARDNER-WEBB (3)**
73— Richard Grissom, LB
87— Jeff Parker, PK
92— Rodney Robinson, WR

**GEORGETOWN (3)**
73— Robert Morris, DE
74— Robert Morris, DE
91— Chris Murphy, DE

**GEORGETOWN (KY.) (8)**
74— Charles Pierson, DL
78— John Martinelli, OL
85— Rob McCrary, RB
87— Chris Reed, C
88— Chris Reed, DL
89— Steve Blankenbaker, DL
91— Chris Hogan, DL
92— Chris Hogan, DL

**GETTYSBURG (4)**
66— Joseph Egresitz, DE
83— Ray Condren, RB
84— Ray Condren, RB
85— Brian Barr, DB

**GLASSBORO ST. (1)**
78— Dino Hall, RB

**GLENVILLE ST. (3)**
73— Scotty Hamilton, DB
83— Byron Brooks, RB
84— Mike Payne, DB

**GONZAGA (2)**
34— Ike Peterson, B
39— Tony Canadeo, B

**GRAMBLING (27)**
62— Junious Buchanan, T
64— Alphonse Dotson, OT
65— Willie Young, OG
    Frank Cornish, DT
69— Billy Manning, C
70— Richard Harris, DE
    Charles Roundtree, DT
71— Solomon Freelon, OG
    John Mendenhall, DE
72— Steve Dennis, DB
    Gary Johnson, DT
73— Gary Johnson, DT
    Willie Bryant, DB
74— Gary Johnson, DT
75— Sammie White, WR
    James Hunter, DB
79—†Joe Gordon, DT
    †Aldrich Allen, LB
    †Robert Salters, DB
80—†Trumaine Johnson, WR
    †Mike Barker, DT
81—†Andre Robinson, LB
82—†Trumaine Johnson, WR
83—†Robert Smith, DL
85—†James Harris, LB
90—†Walter Dean, RB
    †Jake Reed, WR

**GRAND VALLEY ST. (3)**
79— Ronald Essink, OL
89— Todd Tracey, DL
91— Chris Tiede, C

**GROVE CITY (1)**
87— Doug Hart, PK

**GUILFORD (2)**
75— Steve Musulin, OT
91— Rodney Alexander, DE

**GUST. ADOLPHUS (7)**
37— Wendell Butcher, B
50— Calvin Roberts, T
51— Haldo Norman, OE
52— Calvin Roberts, DT
54— Gene Nei, G
67— Richard Jaeger, LB
84— Kurt Ploeger, DL

**HAMILTON (2)**
86— Joe Gilbert, OL
91— Eric Grey, RB

**HAMLINE (4)**
55— Dick Donlin, E
84— Kevin Graslewicz, WR
85— Ed Hitchcock, OL
89— Jon Voss, TE

**HAMPDEN-SYDNEY (8)**
48— Lynn Chewning, B
54— Stokeley Fulton, C
72— Michael Leidy, LB
74— Ed Kelley, DE
75— Ed Kelley, DE
77— Robert Wilson, OL
78— Tim Smith, DL
86— Jimmy Hondroulis, PK

**HAMPTON (2)**
84— Ike Readon, MG
85— Ike Readon, DL

**HANOVER (2)**
86— Jon Pinnick, QB
88— Mike Luker, WR

**HARDIN-SIMMONS (5)**
37— Burns McKinney, B
39— Clyde Turner, C
40— Owen Goodnight, B
42— Rudy Mobley, B
46— Rudy Mobley, B

**HARDING (2)**
74— Barney Crawford, DL
91— Pat Gill, LB

**HARVARD (2)**
82—†Mike Corbat, OL
84—†Roger Caron, OL

**HASTINGS (1)**
84— Dennis Sullivan, OL

**HAWAII* (2)**
41— Nolle Smith, B
68— Tim Buchanan, LB

**HENDERSON ST. (1)**
90— Todd Jones, OL

**HILLSDALE (9)**
49— William Young, B
55— Nate Clark, B
56— Nate Clark, B
75— Mark Law, OG
81— Mike Broome, OG
82— Ron Gladnick, DE
86— Al Huge, DL
87— Al Huge, DL
88— Rodney Patterson, LB

**HOBART (3)**
72— Don Aleksiewicz, RB
75— Rich Kowalski, RB
86— Brian Verdon, DB

**HOFSTRA (4)**
83— Chuck Choinski, DL
86— Tom Salamone, P
88— Tom Salamone, DB
90— George Tischler, LB

**HOLY CROSS (12)**
83—†Bruce Kozerski, OT
     Steve Raquet, DL
84—†Bill McGovern, DB
     Kevin Garvey, OG
85—†Gil Fenerty, RB
86—†Gordie Lockbaum, RB-DB
87—†Jeff Wiley, QB
    †Gordie Lockbaum, WR-SP
88—†Dennis Golden, OL
89—†Dave Murphy, DB
90—†Craig Callahan, LB
91—†Jerome Fuller, RB

**HOPE (2)**
79— Craig Groendyk, OL
82— Kurt Brinks, C

**HOWARD (2)**
75— Ben Harris, DL
87—†Harvey Reed, RB

**HOWARD PAYNE (4)**
61— Ray Jacobs, T
72— Robert Woods, LB
73— Robert Woods, LB
92— Scott Lichner, QB

**HUMBOLDT ST. (5)**
61— Drew Roberts, E
62— Drew Roberts, E
76— Michael Gooing, OL
82— David Rush, MG
83— Dean Diaz, DB

**HURON (1)**
76— John Aldridge, OL

**IDAHO (9)**
83—†Ken Hobart, QB
85—†Eric Yarber, WR
88—†John Friesz, QB
89—†John Friesz, QB
    †Lee Allen, WR
90—†Kasey Dunn, WR
91—†Kasey Dunn, WR
92—†Yo Murphy, WR
    †Jeff Robinson, DL

**IDAHO ST. (6)**
69— Ed Bell, OE
77— Ray Allred, MG
81—†Case de Bruijn, P
    †Mike Machurek, QB
83—†Jeff Kaiser, P
84—†Steve Anderson, DL

**ILL. BENEDICTINE (2)**
72— Mike Rogowski, LB
92— Bob McMillen, TE

**ILL. WESLEYAN (4)**
34— Tony Blazine, T
74— Caesar Douglas, OT
91— Chris Bisaillon, WR
92— Chris Bisaillon, WR

**ILLINOIS COLL. (1)**
81— Joe Aiello, DL

**ILLINOIS ST. (4)**
68— Denny Nelson, OT
85—†Jim Meyer, OL
86—†Brian Gant, LB
88—†Mike McCabe, P

**INDIANA (PA.) (12)**
75— Lynn Hieber, QB
76— Jim Haslett, DE
77— Jim Haslett, DE
78— Jim Haslett, DE
79— Terrence Skelley, OE
80— Joe Cuigari, DT
84— Gregg Brenner, WR
86— Jim Angelo, OL
87— Troy Jackson, LB
88— Dean Cottrill, LB
90— Andrew Hill, WR
91— Tony Aliucci, QB

**INDIANA ST. (7)**
69— Jeff Keller, DE
75— Chris Hicks, OL
     Vince Allen, RB
83—†Ed Martin, DE
84—†Wayne Davis, DB
85—†Vencie Glenn, DB
86—†Mike Simmonds, OL

**INDIANAPOLIS (6)**
83— Mark Bless, DL
84— Paul Loggan, DB
85— Tom Collins, DB
86— Dan Jester, TE
87— Thurman Montgomery, DL
91— Greg Matheis, DL

**IOWA WESLEYAN (1)**
87— Mike Wiggins, P

**ITHACA (11)**
72— Robert Wojnar, OT
74— David Remick, RB
75— Larry Czarnecki, DT
79— John Laper, LB
80— Bob Ferrigno, HB
84— Bill Sheerin, DL
85— Tim Torrey, LB
90— Jeff Wittman, FB
91— Jeff Wittman, FB
92— Jeff Wittman, FB
     Dave Brumfield, OL

**JACKSON ST. (17)**
62— Willie Richardson, E
69— Joe Stephens, OG
71— Jerome Barkum, OE
74— Walter Payton, RB
     Robert Brazile, LB
78— Robert Hardy, DT
80—†Larry Werts, LB
81— Mike Fields, OT
85—†Jackie Walker, LB
86—†Kevin Dent, DB
87—†Kevin Dent, DB
88—†Lewis Tillman, RB
    †Kevin Dent, DB
89—†Darion Conner, LB
90—†Robert Turner, DB
91—†Deltrich Lockridge, OL
92—†Lester Holmes, OL

**JACKSONVILLE ST. (8)**
52— Jodie Connell, OG
66— Ray Vinson, DB
70— Jimmy Champion, C
77— Jesse Baker, DT
78— Jesse Baker, DT
82— Ed Lett, QB

86— Joe Billingsley, OT
88— Joe Billingsley, OT

**JAMES MADISON (6)**
77— Woody Bergeria, DT
78— Rick Booth, OL
85—†Charles Haley, LB
86—†Carlo Bianchini, OG
89—†Steve Bates, DL
90—†Eupton Jackson, DB

**JAMESTOWN (2)**
76— Brent Tischer, OL
81— Ron Hausauer, OL

**JOHN CARROLL (2)**
50— Carl Taseff, B
74— Tim Barrett, RB

**JOHNS HOPKINS (2)**
80— Bill Stromberg, WR
81— Bill Stromberg, WR

**JOHNSON SMITH (2)**
82— Dan Beauford, DE
88— Ronald Capers, LB

**JUNIATA (3)**
54— Joe Veto, T
86— Steve Yerger, OL
87— Mark Dorner, DB

**KANSAS WESLEYAN (2)**
35— Virgil Baker, G
56— Larry Houdek, B

**KEAN (1)**
87— Kevin McGuirl, TE

**KENTUCKY ST. (1)**
72— Wiley Epps, LB

**KENYON (1)**
74— Jim Myers, WR

**KNOX (2)**
86— Rich Schiele, TE
87— Chris Vogel, WR

**KNOXVILLE (1)**
77— Dwight Treadwell, OL

**KUTZTOWN (1)**
77— Steve Head, OG

**LA SALLE (2)**
38— George Somers, T
39— Frank Loughney, G

**LA VERNE (2)**
72— Dana Coleman, DT
91— Willie Reyna, QB

**LAFAYETTE (5)**
79—†Rich Smith, TE
81—†Joe Skladany, LB
82—†Tony Green, DL
88—†Frank Baur, QB
92—†Edward Hudak, OL

**LAKELAND (1)**
89— Jeff Ogiego, P

**LAMAR (5)**
57— Dudley Meredith, T
61— Bobby Jancik, B
67— Spergon Wynn, OG
83—†Eugene Seale, LB
85—†Burton Murchison, RB

**LANE (1)**
73— Edward Taylor, DT

**LANGSTON (1)**
73— Thomas Henderson, DE

**LAWRENCE (9)**
49— Claude Radtke, E
67— Charles McKee, QB
77— Frank Bouressa, C

78— Frank Bouressa, C
80— Scott Reppert, HB
81— Scott Reppert, HB
82— Scott Reppert, RB
83— Murray McDonough, DB
86— Dan Galante, DL

**LEHIGH (16)**
49— Robert Numbers, C
50— Dick Doyne, B
57— Dan Nolan, B
59— Walter Meincke, T
69— Thad Jamula, OT
71— John Hill, C
73— Kim McQuilken, QB
75— Joe Sterrett, QB
77— Steve Kreider, WR
     Mike Reiker, QB
79—†Dave Melone, OT
     †Jim McCormick, DL
80—†Bruce Rarig, LB
83—†John Shigo, LB
85—†Rennie Benn, WR
90—†Keith Petzold, OL

**LENOIR-RHYNE (4)**
52— Steve Trudnak, B
62— Richard Kemp, B
67— Eddie Joyner, OT
92— Jason Monday, PK

**LEWIS & CLARK (2)**
68— Bill Bailey, DT
91— Dan Ruhl, RB

**LIBERTY (2)**
82— John Sanders, LB
86— Mark Mathis, DB

**LINCOLN (MO.) (2)**
53— Leo Lewis, B
54— Leo Lewis, B

**LINFIELD (8)**
57— Howard Morris, G
64— Norman Musser, C
72— Bernard Peterson, OE
75— Ken Cutcher, OL
78— Paul Dombroski, DB
80— Alan Schmidlin, QB
83— Steve Lopes, OL
84— Steve Boyea, OL

**LIU-C. W. POST (5)**
71— Gary Wichard, QB
77— John Mohring, DE
78— John Mohring, DE
81— Tom DeBona, WR
89— John Levelis, DL

**LIVINGSTON (3)**
82— Charles Martin, DT
84— Andrew Fields, WR
87— Ronnie Glanton, DL

**LIVINGSTONE (1)**
84— Jo Jo White, RB

**LOCK HAVEN (1)**
45— Robert Eyer, E

**LONG BEACH ST. (4)**
68— Bill Parks, OE
69— Leon Burns, FB
70— Leon Burns, RB
71— Terry Metcalf, RB

**LORAS (2)**
47— Robert Hanlon, B
84— James Drew, P

**LOS ANGELES ST. (1)**
64— Walter Johnson, OG

**LOUISIANA COLLEGE (1)**
50— Bernard Calendar, E

**LOUISIANA TECH* (15)**
41— Garland Gregory, G
46— Mike Reed, G
68— Terry Bradshaw, QB
69— Terry Bradshaw, QB
72— Roger Carr, WR
73— Roger Carr, FL
74— Mike Barber, TE
     Fred Dean, DT
82—†Matt Dunigan, QB
84—†Doug Landry, LB
     †Walter Johnson, DE
85—†Doug Landry, LB
86—†Walter Johnson, LB-DE
87—†Glenell Sanders, LB
88—†Glenell Sanders, LB

**LOUISVILLE* (1)**
57— Leonard Lyles, B

**LOYOLA (CAL.) (1)**
42— Vince Pacewic, B

**LOYOLA (ILL.) (2)**
35— Billy Roy, B
37— Clay Calhoun, B

**LUTHER (1)**
57— Bruce Hartman, T

**LYCOMING (7)**
83— John Whalen, OL
85— Walt Zataveski, OL
89— Rick Bealer, DB
90— Rick Bealer, DB
91— Darrin Kenney, OT
     Don Kinney, DL
     Bill Small, LB

**MAINE (6)**
65— John Huard, LB
66— John Huard, LB
80—†Lorenzo Bouier, RB
89—†Carl Smith, RB
     †Scott Hough, OL
90—†Claude Pettaway, DB

**MAINE MARITIME (1)**
92— Kirk Matthieu, RB

**MANKATO ST. (3)**
73— Marty Kranz, DB
87— Duane Goldammer, OG
91— John Kelling, DB

**MARS HILL (3)**
78— Alan Rice, OL
79— Steven Campbell, DB
87— Lee Marchman, LB

**MARSHALL (12)**
37— William Smith, E
40— Jackie Hunt, B
41— Jackie Hunt, B
87—†Sean Doctor, TE
     †Mike Barber, WR
88—†Mike Barber, WR
     †Sean Doctor, TE
90—†Eric Ihnat, TE
91—†Phil Ratliff, OL
92—†Michael Payton, QB
     †Troy Brown, WR
     †Phil Ratliff, OL

**MARYVILLE (TENN.) (4)**
67— Steve Dockery, DB
73— Earl McMahon, OG
77— Wayne Dunn, LB
92— Tom Smith, OL

**MASS.-BOSTON (1)**
92— Sean Munroe, WR

**MASSACHUSETTS (19)**
52— Tony Chambers, OE
63— Paul Graham, T
64— Milt Morin, DE
67— Greg Landry, QB
71— William DeFlavio, MG
72— Steve Schubert, OE
73— Tim Berra, OE
75— Ned Deane, OL
76— Ron Harris, DB
77— Kevin Cummings, TE
        Bruce Kimball, OL
78— Bruce Kimball, OG
80—†Bob Manning, DB
81—†Garry Pearson, RB
82—†Garry Pearson, RB
85—†Mike Dwyer, DL
88—†John McKeown, LB
90—†Paul Mayberry, OL
92—†Don Caparotti, DB

**McMURRY (6)**
49— Brad Rowland, B
50— Brad Rowland, B
58— Charles Davis, G
68— Telly Windham, DE
74— Randy Roemisch, OT
80— Rick Nolly, OL

**McNEESE ST. (6)**
52— Charles Kuehn, DE
69— Glenn Kidder, OG
72— James Moore, TE
74— James Files, OT
82—†Leonard Smith, DB
92—†Terry Irving, LB

**MD.-EAST. SHORE (2)**
64— John Smith, DT
68— Bill Thompson, DB

**MEMPHIS ST.* (1)**
54— Robert Patterson, G

**MERCHANT MARINE (3)**
52— Robert Wiechard, LB
69— Harvey Adams, DE
90— Harold Krebs, DB

**MESA ST. (8)**
82— Dean Haugum, DT
83— Dean Haugum, DL
84— Don Holmes, DB
85— Mike Berk, OL
86— Mike Berk, OL
88— Tracy Bennett, PK
89— Jeff Russell, OT
90— Brian Johnson, LB

**MIAMI (FLA.)* (2)**
45— Ed Cameron, G
        William Levitt, C

**MIAMI (OHIO)* (1)**
82—†Brian Pillman, MG

**MICHIGAN TECH (1)**
76— Jim VanWagner, RB

**MIDDLE TENN. ST. (10)**
64— Jimbo Pearson, S
65— Keith Atchley, LB
83—†Robert Carroll, OL
84—†Kelly Potter, PK
85—†Don Griffin, DB
88—†Don Thomas, LB
90—†Joe Campbell, RB
91—†Steve McAdoo, OL
        †Joe Campbell, RB
92—†Steve McAdoo, OL

**MIDDLEBURY (2)**
36— George Anderson, G
83— Jonathan Good, DL

**MIDLAND LUTHERAN (2)**
76— Dave Marreel, DE
79— Scott Englehardt, OL

**MILLERSVILLE (4)**
76— Robert Parr, DB
80— Rob Riddick, RB
81— Mark Udovich, C
86— Jeff Hannis, DL

**MILLIKIN (2)**
42— Virgil Wagner, B
92— Mike Hall, KR

**MILLSAPS (10)**
72— Rowan Torrey, DB
73— Michael Reams, LB
76— Rickie Haygood, QB
78— David Culpepper, LB
79— David Culpepper, LB
83— Edmond Donald, RB
85— Tommy Powell, LB
90— Sean Brewer, DL
91— Sean Brewer, DL
92— Sean Brewer, DL

**MINN.-DULUTH (4)**
74— Mark Johnson, DB
75— Terry Egerdahl, RB
76— Ted McKnight, RB
82— Gary Birkholz, OG

**MISSISSIPPI COL. (10)**
72— Ricky Herzog, FL
79— Calvin Howard, RB
80— Bert Lyles, DE
82— Major Everett, RB
83— Wayne Frazier, OL
85— Earl Conway, DL
88— Terry Fleming, DL
89— Terry Fleming, DL
90— Fred McAfee, RB
92— Johnny Poole, OL

**MISSISSIPPI VAL. (6)**
79—†Carl White, OG
83—†Jerry Rice, WR
84—†Jerry Rice, WR
        †Willie Totten, QB
87—†Vincent Brown, LB
91—†Ashley Ambrose, DB

**MISSOURI-ROLLA (4)**
41— Ed Kromka, T
69— Frank Winfield, OG
74— Merle Dillow, TE
80— Bill Grantham, SAF

**MISSOURI VALLEY (3)**
47— James Nelson, G
48— James Nelson, G
49— Herbert McKinney, T

**MONMOUTH (ILL.) (1)**
75— Ron Baker, RB

**MONTANA (10)**
67— Bob Beers, LB
70— Ron Stein, DB
76— Greg Anderson, DB
79—†Jim Hard, DL
83—†Brian Salonen, TE
85—†Mike Rice, P
87—†Larry Clarkson, OL
88—†Tim Hauck, DB
89—†Kirk Scafford, OL
        †Tim Hauck, DB

**MONTANA ST. (10)**
66— Don Hass, HB
67— Don Hass, HB
70— Gary Gustafson, LB
73— Bill Kollar, DT
75— Steve Kracher, RB
76— Lester Leininger, DL
78— Jon Borchardt, OT
81—†Larry Rubens, OL
84—†Mark Fellows, LB
        †Dirk Nelson, P

**MONTANA TECH (3)**
73— James Persons, OT
80— Steve Hossler, HB
81— Craig Opatz, OL

**MONTCLAIR ST. (11)**
75— Barry Giblin, DB
77— Mario Benimeo, DT
79— Tom Morton, OL
80— Sam Mills, LB
81— Terrance Porter, WR
82— Mark Casale, QB
84— Jim Rennae, OL
85— Dan Zakashefski, DL
86— Dan Zakashefski, DL
89— Paul Cioffi, LB
90— Paul Cioffi, LB

**MOORHEAD ST. (2)**
76— Rocky Gullickson, OG
84— Randy Sullivan, DB

**MOREHEAD ST. (5)**
38— John Horton, C
42— Vincent Zachem, C
69— Dave Haverdick, DT
82—†John Christopher, P
86—†Randy Poe, OG

**MORGAN ST. (7)**
65— Willie Lanier, LB
67— Jeff Queen, DE
70— Willie Germany, DB
72— Stan Cherry, LB
73— Eugene Simms, LB
78— Joe Fowlkes, DB
80— Mike Holston, WR

**MORNINGSIDE (2)**
49— Connie Callahan, B
91— Jorge Diaz, PK

**MOUNT UNION (7)**
84— Troy Starr, LB
87— Russ Kring, RB
90— Ken Edelman, PK
        Dave Lasecki, LB
92— Mike Elder, OL
        Jim Ballard, QB
        Chris Dattilio, LB

**MUHLENBERG (2)**
46— George Bibighaus, E
47— Harold Bell, B

**MURRAY ST. (4)**
37— Elmer Cochran, G
73— Don Clayton, RB
79—†Terry Love, DB
86—†Charley Wiles, OL

**MUSKINGUM (4)**
40— Dave Evans, T
60— Bill Cooper, B
66— Mark DeVilling, DT
75— Jeff Heacock, DB

**N.C. CENTRAL (4)**
68— Doug Wilkerson, MG
69— Doug Wilkerson, OT
74— Charles Smith, DE

88— Earl Harvey, QB

**N'EASTERN OKLA. ST. (4)**
69— Manuel Britto, HB
71— Roosevelt Manning, DT
74— Kevin Goodlet, DB
82— Cedric Mack, WR

**NEB.-KEARNEY (2)**
76— Dale Mitchell Johnson, DB
78— Doug Peterson, DL

**NEB. WESLEYAN (3)**
90— Brad Bohn, DB
91— Darren Stohlmann, TE
92— Darren Stohlmann, TE

**NEBRASKA-OMAHA (9)**
64— Gerald Allen, HB
68— Dan Klepper, OG
76— Dan Fulton, WR
77— Dan Fulton, OE
80— Tom Sutko, LB
82— John Walker, DT
83— Tim Carlson, LB
84— Ron Petersen, OT
86— Keith Coleman, LB

**NEVADA* (23)**
52— Neil Garrett, DB
74— Greg Grouwinkel, DB
78— James Curry, MG
    Frank Hawkins, RB
79—†Frank Hawkins, RB
    †Lee Fobbs, DB
80—†Frank Hawkins, RB
    †Bubba Puha, DL
81—†John Ramatici, LB
    †Tony Zendejas, K
82—†Tony Zendejas, K
    †Charles Mann, DT
83—†Tony Zendejas, K
    †Jim Werbeckes, OG
    †Tony Shaw, DB
85—†Greg Rea, OL
    †Marty Zendejas, PK
    †Pat Hunter, DB
86—†Henry Rolling, DE-LB
88—†Bernard Ellison, DB
90—†Bernard Ellison, DB
    †Treamelle Taylor, KR
91—†Matt Clafton, LB

**NEVADA-LAS VEGAS* (3)**
73— Mike Thomas, RB
74— Mike Thomas, RB
75— Joseph Ingersoll, DL

**NEW HAMPSHIRE (10)**
50— Ed Douglas, G
68— Al Whittman, DT
75— Kevin Martell, C
76— Bill Burnham, RB
77— Bill Burnham, RB
    Grady Vigneau, OT
85—†Paul Dufault, OL
87—†John Driscoll, OL
91—†Barry Bourassa, RB
    †Dwayne Sabb, LB

**NEW HAVEN (6)**
85— David Haubner, OL
87— Erik Lesinski, LB
88— Rob Thompson, OL
90— Jay McLucas, QB
92— Scott Emmert, OL
    Roger Graham, RB

**NEWBERRY (2)**
40— Dominic Collangelo, B
81— Stan Stanton, DL

**NICHOLLS ST. (6)**
76— Gerald Butler, OE
77— Rusty Rebowe, LB
81—†Dwight Walker, WR
82—†Clint Conque, LB
84—†Dewayne Harrison, TE
86—†Mark Carrier, WR

**NICHOLS (1)**
81— Ed Zywien, LB

**N.M. HIGHLANDS (6)**
66— Carl Garrett, HB
67— Carl Garrett, HB
68— Carl Garrett, HB
81— Jay Lewis, DL
85— Neil Windham, LB
86— Tim Salz, PK

**NORFOLK ST. (2)**
79— Mike Ellis, DB
89— Arthur Jimmerson, LB

**NORTH ALA. (6)**
82— Don Smith, C
84— Daryl Smith, DB
85— Bruce Jones, DB
90— James Davis, LB
    Mike Nord, OL
92— Harvey Summerhill, DB

**NORTH CARO. A&T (5)**
69— Merl Code, DB
70— Melvin Holmes, OT
81—†Mike West, OL
86—†Ernest Riddick, NG
88—†Demetrius Harrison, LB

**NORTH DAK. (14)**
55— Steve Myhra, G
56— Steve Myhra, G
63— Neil Reuter, T
65— Dave Lince, DE
66— Roger Bonk, LB
71— Jim LeClair, LB
    Dan Martinsen, DB
72— Mike Deutsch, RB
75— Bill Deutsch, RB
79— Paul Muckenhirn, TE
80— Todd Thomas, OT
81— Milson Jones, RB
89— Cory Solberg, PK
91— Shannon Burnell, RB

**NORTH DAK. ST. (25)**
34— Melvin Hanson, B
46— Cliff Rothrock, C
66— Walt Odegaard, MG
67— Jim Ferge, LB
68— Jim Ferge, DT
    Paul Hatchett, B
69— Paul Hatchett, HB
    Joe Cichy, DB
70— Joe Cichy, DB
74— Jerry Dahl, DE
76— Rick Budde, LB
77— Lew Curry, OL
81— Wayne Schluchter, DB
82— Cliff Carmody, OG
    Steve Garske, LB
83— Mike Whetstone, OG
84— Greg Hagfors, C
86— Jeff Bentrim, QB
    Jim Dick, LB
87— Mike Favor, C
88— Matt Tracy, OL
    Mike Favor, C

    Yorrick Byers, LB
90— Phil Hansen, DL
    Chris Simdorn, QB

**NORTH PARK (2)**
72— Greg Nugent, OE
90— John Love, QB

**NORTH TEXAS (6)**
47— Frank Whitlow, T
51— Ray Renfro, DB
83—†Ronnie Hickman, DE
    †Rayford Cooks, DL
88—†Rex Johnson, DL
90—†Mike Davis, DL

**NORTHEAST LA. (18)**
67— Vic Bender, C
70— Joe Profit, RB
72— Jimmy Edwards, RB
73— Glenn Fleming, MG
74— Glenn Fleming, MG
77— Steve Powell, RB
82—†Arthur Christophe, C
    †Bruce Daigle, DB
83—†Mike Grantham, OG
84—†Mike Grantham, OG
85—†Mike Turner, DB
87—†John Clement, OT
    †Claude Brumfield, DT
88—†Cyril Crutchfield, DB
89—†Jackie Harris, E
92—†Jeff Blackshear, OL
    †Vic Zordan, OL
    †Roosevelt Potts, RB

**NORTHEAST MO. ST. (3)**
60— Dale Mills, B
65— Richard Rhodes, OT
85— Chris Hegg, QB

**NORTHEASTERN (2)**
72— Tom Rezzuti, DB
78— Dan Ross, TE

**NORTHERN ARIZ. (12)**
66— Rick Ries, LB
67— Bill Hanna, DE
68— Larry Small, OG
77— Larry Friedrichs, OL
    Tom Jurich, K
78— Jerry Lumpkin, LB
79—†Ed Judie, LB
82—†Pete Mandley, WR
83—†Pete Mandley, WR
    †James Gee, DT
86—†Goran Lingmerth, PK
89—†Darrell Jordan, LB

**NORTHERN COLO. (8)**
68— Jack O'Brien, DB
80— Todd Volkart, DT
81— Brad Wimmer, OL
82— Mark Mostek, OG
    Kevin Jelden, PK
89— Vance Lechman, DB
90— Frank Wainwright, TE
92— David Oliver, OL

**NORTHERN ILL.* (2)**
62— George Bork, B
63— George Bork, B

**NORTHERN IOWA (13)**
52— Lou Bohnsack, C
60— George Asleson, G
61— Wendell Williams, G
64— Randy Schultz, FB
65— Randy Schultz, FB
67— Ray Pedersen, MG
75— Mike Timmermans, OT

85— Joe Fuller, DB
87—†Carl Boyd, RB
90—†Brian Mitchell, PK
91—†Brian Mitchell, PK
92—†Kenny Shedd, WR
　　†William Freeney, LB
**NORTHERN MICH. (6)**
75— Daniel Stencil, OL
76— Maurice Mitchell, FL
77— Joseph Stemo, DB
82— George Works, RB
87— Jerry Woods, DB
88— Jerry Woods, DB
**NORTHERN ST. (1)**
76— Larry Kolbo, DL
**NORTHWEST MO. ST. (3)**
39— Marion Rogers, G
84— Steve Hansley, WR
89— Jason Agee, DB
**NORTHWESTERN (LA.) (11)**
66— Al Dodd, DB
80—†Warren Griffith, C
　　†Joe Delaney, RB
81—†Gary Reasons, LB
82—†Gary Reasons, LB
83—†Gary Reasons, LB
84—†Arthur Berry, DT
87—†John Kulakowski, DE
91—†Andre Carron, LB
92—†Adrian Hardy, DB
　　†Marcus Spears, OL
**NORTHWOOD (2)**
73— Bill Chandler, DT
74— Bill Chandler, DT
**NORWICH (3)**
79— Milt Williams, RB
84— Beau Almodobar, WR
85— Mike Norman, OL
**N'WESTERN (IOWA) (1)**
71— Kevin Korvor, DE
**OBERLIN (1)**
45— James Boswell, B
**OCCIDENTAL (6)**
76— Rick Fry, FL
77— Rick Fry, SE
82— Dan Osborn, P
83— Ron Scott, DB
89— David Hodges, LB
90— Peter Tucker, OL
**OHIO\* (2)**
35— Art Lewis, T
60— Dick Grecni, C
**OHIO WESLEYAN (7)**
34— John Turley, B
51— Dale Bruce, OE
71— Steve Dutton, DE
83— Eric DiMartino, LB
90— Jeff Court, OG
　　Neil Ringers, DL
91— Kevin Rucker, DL
**OTTERBEIN (3)**
82— Jim Hoyle, K
90— Ron Severance, WR
91— Ron Severance, WR
**OUACHITA BAPTIST (1)**
79— Ezekiel Vaughn, LB
**PACIFIC (CAL.)\* (4)**
34— Cris Kjeldsen, G
47— Eddie LeBaron, B
48— Eddie LeBaron, B
49— Eddie LeBaron, B

**PACIFIC LUTHERAN (9)**
40— Marv Tommervik, B
41— Marv Tommervik, B
47— Dan D'Andrea, C
52— Ron Billings, DB
65— Marvin Peterson, C
78— John Zamberlin, LB
85— Mark Foege, PK
　　Tim Shannon, DL
88— Jon Kral, DL
**PANHANDLE ST. (2)**
82— Tom Rollison, DB
83— Tom Rollison, DB
**PENNSYLVANIA (3)**
86—†Marty Peterson, OL
88—†John Zinser, OL
90—†Joe Valerio, OL
**PEPPERDINE (2)**
47— Darwin Horn, B
55— Wixie Robinson, G
**PERU ST. (4)**
52— Robert Lade, OT
53— Robert Lade, T
81— Alvin Holder, RB
91— Tim Herman, DL
**PILLSBURY (1)**
85— Calvin Addison, RB
**PITTSBURG ST. (8)**
61— Gary Snadon, B
70— Mike Potchard, OT
78— Brian Byers, OL
88— Jesse Wall, OL
89— John Roderique, LB
90— Ron West, WR
91— Ron West, WR
92— Ronald Moore, RB
**PLYMOUTH ST. (6)**
74— Robert Gibson, DB
82— Mark Barrows, LB
83— Joe Dudek, RB
84— Joe Dudek, RB
85— Joe Dudek, RB
91— Scott Allen, LB
**POMONA-PITZER (1)**
74— Larry Cenotto, QB
**PORTLAND ST. (11)**
76— June Jones, QB
77— Dave Stief, OE
79—†Stuart Gaussoin, SE
　　†Kurt Ijanoff, OT
80—†Neil Lomax, QB
84—†Doug Mikolas, DL
88— Bary Naone, TE
　　Chris Crawford, QB
89—†Darren Del'Andrae, QB
91— James Fuller, DB
92— John Charles, QB
**PRAIRIE VIEW (2)**
64— Otis Taylor, OE
70— Bivian Lee, DB
**PRESBYTERIAN (8)**
45— Andy Kavounis, G
46— Hank Caver, B
52— Joe Kirven, G
68— Dan Eckstein, DB
71— Robert Norris, LB
78— Roy Walker, OL
79— Roy Walker, OL
83— Jimmie Turner, LB
**PRINCETON (3)**
87—†Dean Cain, DB

89—†Judd Garrett, RB
92—†Keith Elias, RB
**PUGET SOUND (9)**
56— Robert Mitchell, G
63— Ralph Bauman, G
66— Joseph Peyton, OE
75— Bill Linnenkohl, LB
76— Dan Kuehl, G
81— Bob Jackson, MG
82— Mike Bos, WR
83— Larry Smith, DB
87— Mike Oliphant, RB
**RANDOLPH-MACON (6)**
47— Albert Oley, G
57— Dave Young, G
79— Rick Eades, DL
80— Rick Eades, DL
84— Cody Dearing, QB
88— Aaron Boston, OL
**REDLANDS (2)**
77— Randy Van Horn, OL
92— James Shields, DL
**RHODE ISLAND (8)**
55— Charles Gibbons, T
82—†Richard Pelzer, OL
83—†Tony DeLuca, DL
84—†Brian Forster, TE
85—†Brian Forster, TE
　　†Tom Ehrhardt, QB
90—†Kevin Smith, DB
92—†Darren Rizzi, TE
**RHODES (5)**
36— Henry Hammond, E
38— Gaylon Smith, B
76— Conrad Bradburn, DB
85— Jim Hever, PK
88— Larry Hayes, OL
**RICHMOND (1)**
84—†Eddie Martin, OL
**RIPON (5)**
57— Peter Kasson, E
75— Dick Rehbein, C
76— Dick Rehbein, OL
79— Art Pelke, TE
82— Bob Wallner, OL
**ROANOKE (1)**
38— Kenneth Moore, E
**ROCHESTER (6)**
51— Jack Wilson, DE
52— Donald Bardell, DG
67— Dave Ragusa, LB
75— Ralph Gebhardt, DB
90— Craig Chodak, P
92— Brian Laudadio, DL
**ROCKHURST (1)**
41— Joe Kiernan, T
**ROLLINS (1)**
40— Charles Lingerfelt, E
**ROSE-HULMAN (2)**
77— Gary Ellis, DB
92— Todd Holthaus, PK
**SAGINAW VALLEY (4)**
81— Eugene Marve, LB
84— Joe Rice, DL
90— David Cook, DB
92— Bill Schafer, TE
**SALISBURY ST. (4)**
82— Mark Lagowski, LB
84— Joe Mammano, OL
85— Robb Disbennett, QB
86— Tom Kress, DL

*First-Team All-Americans Below Division I-A*　　　　　　　347

Kicker Todd Holthaus of Rose-Hulman led Division III with 13 field goals in 19 attempts (68.4 percent, 1.3 per game) to earn first-team honors on Champion USA's Division III all-American squad in 1992.

**SAM HOUSTON ST. (3)**
49— Charles Williams, E
52— Don Gottlob, B
91—†Michael Bankston, DL

**SAMFORD (1)**
36— Norman Cooper, C

**SAN DIEGO (3)**
73— Bob Dulich, QB
81— Dan Herbert, DB
92— Robert Ray, P

**SAN DIEGO ST.\* (6)**
35— John Butler, G
66— Don Horn, QB
67— Steve Duich, OT
      Haven Moses, OE
68— Fred Dryer, DE
      Lloyd Edwards, B

**SAN FRAN. ST. (7)**
51— Robert Williamson, OT
60— Charles Fuller, B
67— Joe Koontz, OE
76— Forest Hancock, LB
78— Frank Duncan, DB
82— Poncho James, RB
84— Jim Jones, TE

**SAN FRANCISCO (1)**
42— John Sanchez, T

**SAN JOSE ST.\* (2)**
38— Lloyd Thomas, E
39— LeRoy Zimmerman, B

**SANTA CLARA (8)**
64— Lou Pastorini, LB

71— Ronald Sani, C
79— Jim Leonard, C
80— Brian Sullivan, K
82— Gary Hoffman, OT
83— Alex Vlahos, C
      Mike Rosselli, LB
85— Brent Jones, TE

**SAVANNAH ST. (2)**
79— Timothy Walker, DL
89— Shannon Sharpe, TE

**SEWANEE (8)**
63— Martin Agnew, B
73— Mike Lumpkin, DE
77— Nino Austin, DB
79— John Hill, DB
80— Mallory Nimocs, TE
81— Greg Worsowicz, DB
86— Mark Kent, WR
90— Ray McGowan, DL

**SHIPPENSBURG (2)**
53— Robert Adams, G
91— Jeff Fickes, DB

**SIMON FRASER (1)**
90— Nick Mazzoli, WR

**SIMPSON (1)**
89— Ricky Gales, RB

**SLIPPERY ROCK (6)**
74— Ed O'Reilly, RB
75— Jerry Skocik, TE
76— Chris Thull, LB
77— Bob Schrantz, TE
78— Bob Schrantz, TE

85— Jeff Williams, P

**SONOMA ST. (2)**
86— Mike Henry, LB
92— Larry Allen, OL

**SOUTH CARO. ST. (18)**
67— Tyrone Caldwell, DE
71— James Evans, LB
72— Barney Chavous, DE
73— Donnie Shell, DB
75— Harry Carson, DE
76— Robert Sims, DL
77— Ricky Anderson, RB
79—†Phillip Murphy, DL
80—†Edwin Bailey, OG
81—†Anthony Reed, FB
      †Dwayne Jackson, DL
82—†Dwayne Jackson, DE
      †Anthony Reed, RB
      †Ralph Green, OT
      †John Courtney, DT
83—†Ralph Green, OT
89—†Eric Douglas, OL
91—†Robert Porcher, DL

**SOUTH DAK. (10)**
68— John Kohler, OT
69— John Kohler, OT
71— Gene Macken, OG
72— Gary Kipling, OG
78— Bill Moats, DB
79— Benjamin Long, LB
83— Kurt Seibel, K
86— Jerry Glinsky, C
      Todd Salat, DB
88— Doug VanderEsch, LB

**SOUTH DAK. ST. (10)**
67— Darwin Gonnerman, HB
68— Darwin Gonnerman, FB
74— Lynn Boden, OT
77— Bill Matthews, DE
79— Charles Loewen, OL
84— Rick Wegher, RB
85— Jeff Tiefenthaler, WR
86— Jeff Tiefenthaler, WR
91— Kevin Tetzlaff, DL
92— Doug Miller, LB

**SOUTH DAK. TECH (1)**
73— Charles Waite, DB

**SOUTHEAST MO. ST. (1)**
37— Wayne Goddard, T

**SOUTHEASTERN LA. (3)**
70— Ronnie Hornsby, LB
83—†Bret Wright, P
85—†Willie Shepherd, DL

**SOUTHERN ARK. (2)**
84— Greg Stuman, LB
85— Greg Stuman, LB

**SOUTHERN-B.R. (5)**
70— Isiah Robertson, LB
72— James Wright, OG
73— Godwin Turk, LB
79—†Ken Times, DL
87—†Gerald Perry, OT

**SOUTHERN CONN. ST. (6)**
82— Mike Marshall, DB
83— Kevin Gray, OL
84— William Sixsmith, LB
86— Rick Atkinson, DB
91— Ron Lecointe, OL
92— Steve Lawrence, LB

**SOUTHERN ILL. (4)**
70— Lionel Antoine, OE
71— Lionel Antoine, OE

*1993 NCAA FOOTBALL*

83—†Donnell Daniel, DB
　†Terry Taylor, DB

**SOUTHERN MISS.* (4)**
53— Hugh Pepper, B
56— Don Owens, T
58— Robert Yencho, E
59— Hugh McInnis, E

**SOUTHERN ORE. ST. (1)**
75— Dennis Webber, LB

**SOUTHERN UTAH (4)**
79— Lane Martino, DL
87— Jeff McComb, P
89— Randy Bostic, C
90— Randy Bostic, C

**SOUTHWEST MO. ST. (5)**
66— William Stringer, OG
87—†Matt Soraghan, LB
89—†Mark Christenson, OL
90—†DeAndre Smith, QB
91—†Bill Walter, DL

**SOUTHWEST ST. (2)**
87— James Ashley, WR
91— Wayne Hawkins, DE

**SOUTHWEST TEX. ST. (10)**
53— Pence Dacus, B
63— Jerry Cole, E
64— Jerry Cole, DB
72— Bob Daigle, C
75— Bobby Kotzur, DT
82— Tim Staskus, LB
83— Tim Staskus, LB
84—†Scott Forester, C
90—†Reggie Rivers, RB
91—†Ervin Thomas, C

**SOUTHWESTERN LA.* (1)**
69— Glenn LaFleur, LB

**SPRINGFIELD (11)**
68— Dick Dobbert, C
70— John Curtis, OE
76— Roy Samuelsen, MG
78— Jack Quinn, DB
79— Jack Quinn, DB
80— Steve Foster, OT
81— Jon Richardson, LB
83— Wally Case, DT
　Ed Meachum, TE
85— Jim Anderson, LB
91— Fran Papasedero, DL

**ST. AMBROSE (4)**
40— Nick Kerasiotis, G
51— Robert Flanagan, B
58— Robert Webb, B
87— Jerry Klosterman, DL

**ST. BONAVENTURE (2)**
46— Phil Colella, B
48— Frank LoVuola, E

**ST. CLOUD ST. (1)**
85— Mike Lambrecht, DL

**ST. JOHN'S (MINN.) (5)**
65— Pat Whalin, DB
79— Ernie England, MG
82— Rick Bell, RB
83— Chris Biggins, TE
91— Pat Mayew, QB

**ST. JOHN'S (N.Y.) (1)**
83— Todd Jamison, QB

**ST. LAWRENCE (2)**
51— Ken Spencer, LB
77— Mitch Brown, DB

**ST. MARY (KAN.) (1)**
86— Joe Brinson, RB

**ST. MARY'S (CAL.) (4)**
79— Fran McDermott, DB
80— Fran McDermott, DB
88— Jon Braff, TE
92— Mike Estrella, PK

**ST. MARY'S (TEX.) (1)**
36— Douglas Locke, B

**ST. NORBERT (2)**
57— Norm Jarock, B
64— Dave Jauquet, DE

**ST. OLAF (3)**
53— John Gustafson, E
78— John Nahorniak, LB
80— Jon Anderson, DL

**ST. THOMAS (MINN.) (6)**
45— Theodore Molitor, E
48— Jack Salscheider, B
84— Neal Guggemos, DB
85— Neal Guggemos, DB
90— Gary Trettel, QB
91— Kevin DeVore, OL

**STEPHEN F. AUSTIN (6)**
51— James Terry, DE
79— Ronald Haynes, DL
85— James Noble, WR
86—†Darrell Harkless, DB
88—†Eric Lokey, LB
89—†David Whitmore, DB

**STONY BROOK (2)**
87— Chuck Downey, DB
88— David Lewis, P

**SUL ROSS ST. (2)**
65— Tom Nelson, DE
88— Francis Jones, DB

**SUSQUEHANNA (3)**
51— James Hazlett, C
90— Keith Henry, DL
92— Andy Watkins, LB

**SWARTHMORE (1)**
89— Marshall Happer, OL

**S'WESTERN (KAN.) (2)**
82— Tom Audley, DL
84— Jackie Jenson, RB

**S'WESTERN OKLA.
ST. (2)**
77— Louis Blanton, DB
82— Richard Lockman, LB

**TAMPA (5)**
65— John Perry, DB
68— Ron Brown, MG
70— Leon McQuay, RB
71— Ron Mikolajczyk, OT
　Sammy Gellerstedt, MG

**TENN.-CHATT. (22)**
35— Robert Klein, E
38— Robert Sutton, G
39— Jack Gregory, T
45— Thomas Stewart, T
46— Gene Roberts, B
48— Ralph Hutchinson, T
49— Vincent Sarratore, G
51— Chester LaGod, DT
52— Chester LaGod, DT
54— Richard Young, B
57— Howard Clark, E
58— John Green, B
60— Charles Long, T
64— Jerry Harris, S
66— Harry Sorrell, OG
76— Tim Collins, LB
86—†Mike Makins, DL
89—†Pumpy Tudors, P

　†Junior Jackson, LB
90—†Troy Boeck, DL
　†Tony Hill, DL
　†Pumpy Tudors, P

**TENN.-MARTIN (3)**
68— Julian Nunnamaker, OG
88— Emanuel McNeil, DL
91— Oscar Bunch, TE

**TENN. WESLEYAN (1)**
92— Derrick Scott, PK

**TENNESSEE ST. (16)**
67— Claude Humphrey, DT
68— Jim Marsalis, DB
69— Joe Jones, DE
70— Vernon Holland, OT
71— Cliff Brooks, DB
　Joe Gilliam, QB
72— Robert Woods, OT
　Waymond Bryant, LB
73— Waymond Bryant, LB
　Ed Jones, DE
74— Cleveland Elam, DE
81—†Mike Jones, WR
　†Malcolm Taylor, DT
82—†Walter Tate, OL
86—†Onzy Elam, LB
90—†Colin Godfrey, P

**TENNESSEE TECH (10)**
52— Tom Fann, OT
59— Tom Hackler, E
60— Tom Hackler, E
61— David Baxter, T
69— Larry Schreiber, HB
71— Jim Youngblood, LB
72— Jim Youngblood, LB
74— Elois Grooms, DE
76— Ed Burns, OG
89—†Ryan Weeks, PK

**TEXAS A&I (41)**
40— Stuart Clarkson, C
41— Stuart Clarkson, C
59— Gerald Lambert, G
60— William Crafts, T
62— Douglas Harvey, C
63— Sid Banks, B
65— Randy Johnson, QB
66— Dwayne Nix, OE
67— Dwayne Nix, OE
68— Dwayne Nix, OE
　Ray Hickl, OG
70— Dwight Harrison, DB
　Margarito Guerrero, MG
71— Eldridge Small, OE
　Levi Johnson, DB
72— Ernest Price, DE
74— Don Hardeman, RB
75— David Hill, TE
76— Richard Ritchie, QB
　Larry Grunewald, LB
77— Larry Collins, RB
　John Barefield, DE
78— Billy John, OT
79— Andy Hawkins, LB
80— Don Washington, CB
81— Durwood Roquemore, DB
82— Darrell Green, DB
83— Loyd Lewis, OG
84— Neal Lattue, PK
85— Charles Smith, C
86— Johnny Bailey, RB
　Moses Horn, OG
87— Johnny Bailey, RB
　Moses Horn, OG
88— Rod Mounts, OL

*First-Team All-Americans Below Division I-A*　　　　　349

Johnny Bailey, RB
John Randle, DL
89— Johnny Bailey, RB
90— Keithen DeGrate, OL
91— Brian Nielsen, OL
92— Earl Dotson, OL

**TEXAS-ARLINGTON (5)**
66— Ken Ozee, DT
67— Robert Diem, OG
Robert Willbanks, S
83—†Mark Cannon, C
84—†Bruce Collie, OL

**TEXAS LUTHERAN (3)**
73— David Wehmeyer, RB
74— D. W. Rutledge, LB
75— Jerry Ellis, OL

**TEXAS SOUTHERN (3)**
70— Nathaniel Allen, DB
76— Freddie Dean, OL
92—†Michael Strahan, DL

**TEXAS TECH* (2)**
35— Herschel Ramsey, E
45— Walter Schlinkman, B

**TOLEDO* (1)**
38— Dan Buckwick, G

**TOWSON ST. (9)**
75— Dan Dullea, QB
76— Skip Chase, OE
77— Randy Bielski, DB
78— Ken Snoots, SE
82— Sean Landeta, P
83— Gary Rubeling, DB
84— Terry Brooks, OG
85— Stan Eisentooth, OL
86— David Haden, LB

**TRENTON ST. (3)**
74— Eric Hamilton, C
83— John Aromando, WR
91— Chris Shaw, C

**TRINITY (CONN.) (6)**
35— Mickey Kobrosky, B
36— Mickey Kobrosky, B
55— Charles Sticka, B
59— Roger LeClerc, C
70— David Kiarsis, HB
78— Pat McNamara, FL

**TRINITY (TEX.) (4)**
54— Alvin Beal, B
55— Hubert Cook, C
56— Milton Robichaux, E
67— Marvin Upshaw, DT

**TROY ST. (10)**
39— Sherrill Busby, E
73— Mark King, C
74— Mark King, C
76— Perry Griggs, OE
78— Tim Tucker, LB
80— Willie Tullis, QB
84— Mitch Geier, OG
86— Freddie Thomas, DB
87— Mike Turk, QB
Freddie Thomas, QB

**TUFTS (6)**
34— William Grinnell, E
76— Tim Whelan, RB
78— Mark Buben, DL
79— Chris Connors, QB
80— Mike Brown, OL
86— Bob Patz, DL

**TULSA* (1)**
34— Rudy Prochaska, C

**UC DAVIS (10)**
72— Bob Biggs, QB
David Roberts, OT
76— Andrew Gagnon, OL
77— Chuck Fomasi, DT
78— Casey Merrill, DL
79— Jeffrey Allen, DB
82— Ken O'Brien, QB
83— Bo Eason, DB
84— Scott Barry, QB
85— Mike Wise, DL

**UC RIVERSIDE (1)**
75— Michael Johnson, SE

**UC SANTA BARB. (3)**
36— Douglas Oldershaw, G
37— Douglas Oldershaw, G
67— Paul Vallerga, DB

**UNION (N.Y.) (8)**
39— Sam Hammerstrom, B
82— Steve Bodmer, DL
83— Tim Howell, LB
84— Brian Cox, DE
85— Anthony Valente, DL
86— Rich Romer, DL
87— Rich Romer, DL
91— Greg Harrison, PK

**UNION (TENN.) (2)**
41— James Jones, B
42— James Jones, B

**UPSALA (1)**
64— Dick Giessuebel, LB

**U.S. INT'L (2)**
72— Jerry Robinson, DB
75— Steve Matson, FL

**VA. MILITARY (1)**
88—†Mark Stock, WR

**VALDOSTA ST. (4)**
82— Mark Catano, OL
86— Jessie Tuggle, LB
89— Randy Fisher, WR
90— Deon Searcy, DB

**VALPARAISO (5)**
51— Joe Pahr, B
71— Gary Puetz, OT
72— Gary Puetz, OT
76— John Belskis, DB
85— Mike Healey, WR

**VILLANOVA (4)**
88—†Paul Berardelli, OL
89—†Bryan Russo, OL
91—†Curtis Eller, LB
92—†Curtis Eller, LB

**VIRGINIA ST. (3)**
71— Larry Brooks, DT
84— John Greene, LB
85— James Ward, DL

**VIRGINIA UNION (12)**
73— Herb Scott, OG
74— Herb Scott, OG
75— Anthony Leonard, DB
77— Frank Dark, DB
79— Plummer Bullock, DE
80— William Dillon, DB
81— William Dillon, DB
82— William Dillon, DB
83— Larry Curtis, DT
88— Leroy Gause, LB
91— Paul DeBerry, DB
Kevin Williams, LB

**WABASH (5)**
76— Jimmy Parker, DB

77— David Harvey, QB
81— Pete Metzelaars, TE
88— Tim Pliske, PK
89— Mike Funk, WR

**WAGNER (9)**
67— John Gloistein, OT
80— Phil Theis, OL
81— Alonzo Patterson, RB
82— Alonzo Patterson, RB
83— Selwyn Davis, OT
86— Charles Stinson, DL
87— Rich Negrin, OT
88— Terry Underwood, RB
91— Walter Lopez, PK

**WASH. & JEFF. (7)**
84— Ed Kusko, OL
87— A. J. Pagano, RB
91— Chris Babirad, RB
Gilbert Floyd, DB
92— Chris Babirad, RB
Todd Pivnick, OL
Kevin Pintar, OL

**WASH. & LEE (4)**
76— Tony Perry, OE
81— Mike Pressler, DL
83— Glenn Kirschner, OL
86— John Packett, OL

**WASHBURN (2)**
64— Robert Hardy, DB
88— Troy Slusser, WR

**WASHINGTON (MO.) (4)**
72— Shelby Jordan, LB
73— Stu Watkins, OE
74— Marion Stallings, DB
88— Paul Matthews, TE

**WAYNE ST. (NEB.) (2)**
84— Herve Roussel, PK
85— Ruben Mendoza, OL

**WAYNESBURG (1)**
41— Nick George, G

**WEBER ST. (13)**
66— Ronald McCall, DE
67— Lee White, FB
Jim Schmedding, OG
69— Carter Campbell, DE
70— Henry Reed, DE
71— David Taylor, OT
77— Dennis Duncanson, DB
78— Dennis Duncanson, DB
Randy Jordan, WR
80—†Mike Humiston, LB
89—†Peter Macon, WR
91—†Jamie Martin, QB
†Alfred Pupunu, WR

**WESLEY (1)**
91— Fran Naselli, KR

**WESLEYAN (6)**
46— Bert VanderClute, G
48— Jack Geary, T
72— Robert Heller, C
73— Robert Heller, C
76— John McVicar, DL
77— John McVicar, DL

**WEST CHESTER (9)**
52— Charles Weber, DG
58— Richard Emerich, T
61— Joe Iacone, B
62— Joe Iacone, B
72— Tim Pierantozzi, QB
76— William Blystone, RB
87— Ralph Tamm, OL
88— Bill Hess, WR

92— Lee Woodall, DL

**WEST TEX. ST. (2)**
86— Stan Carraway, WR
90— Mark Bounds, P

**WEST VA.\* (1)**
34— Tod Goodwin, E

**WEST VA. TECH (3)**
82— Elliott Washington, DB
86— Calvin Wallace, DL
89— Phil Hudson, WR

**WEST VA. WESLEYAN (2)**
36— George Mike, T
82— Jerry Free, T

**WESTERN CARO. (12)**
49— Arthur Byrd, G
71— Steve Williams, DT
73— Mark Ferguson, OT
74— Jerry Gaines, SE
     Steve Yates, LB
84—†Louis Cooper, DL
     †Kirk Roach, PK
     †Steve Kornegay, P
85—†Clyde Simmons, DL
86—†Alonzo Carmichael, TE
     †Kirk Roach, PK
87—†Kirk Roach, PK

**WESTERN ILL. (14)**
59— Bill Larson, B
61— Leroy Jackson, B
74— John Passananti, OT
76— Scott Levenhagen, TE
     Greg Lee, DB
77— Craig Phalen, DT
78— Bill Huskisson, DL
80— Mike Maher, TE
     Don Greco, OG
83—†Chris Gunderson, MG
84—†Chris Gunderson, T
86—†Frank Winters, C
     †Todd Auer, DL
88—†Marlin Williams, DL

**WESTERN KY. (15)**
64— Dale Lindsey, LB
70— Lawrence Brame, DE
73— Mike McKoy, DB
74— John Bushong, DL
     Virgil Livers, DB
75— Rick Green, LB
77— Chip Carpenter, OL
80—†Pete Walters, OG
     †Tim Ford, DL
81—†Donnie Evans, DE
82—†Paul Gray, LB
83—†Paul Gray, LB
87—†James Edwards, DB
88—†Dean Tiebout, OL
     †Joe Arnold, RB

**WESTERN MD. (3)**
51— Victor Makovitch, DG
78— Ricci Bonaccorsy, DL
79— Ricci Bonaccorsy, DL

**WESTERN MICH.\* (1)**
82—†Matt Meares, OL

**WESTERN NEW MEX. (2)**
83— Jay Ogle, WR
88— Pat Maxwell, P

**WESTERN ST. (5)**
56— Bill Rhodes, B
78— Bill Campbell, DB
80— Justin Cross, OT
84— Jeff Guy, P
92— Reggie Alexander, WR

**WESTERN WASH. (2)**
51— Norman Hash, DB
79— Patrick Locker, RB

**WESTMINSTER (PA.) (10)**
73— Robert Pontius, DB
77— Rex Macey, FL
82— Gary DeGruttola, LB
83— Scott Higgins, DB
86— Joe Keaney, LB
88— Kevin Myers, LB
89— Joe Micchia, QB
90— Brad Tokar, RB
91— Brian DeLorenzo, DL
92— Matt Raich, LB

**WHEATON (ILL.) (5)**
55— Dave Burnham, B
58— Robert Bakke, T
77— Larry Wagner, LB
78— Scott Hall, QB
83— Keith Bishop, QB

**WHITTIER (3)**
38— Myron Claxton, T
62— Richard Peter, T
77— Michael Ciacci, DB

**WHITWORTH (4)**
52— Pete Swanson, OG
54— Larry Paradis, T
85— Wayne Ralph, WR
86— Wayne Ralph, WR

**WIDENER (10)**
72— Billy Johnson, RB
73— Billy Johnson, RB
75— John Warrington, DB
76— Al Senni, OL
77— Chip Zawoiski, RB
79— Tom Deery, DB
80— Tom Deery, DB
81— Tom Deery, DB
82— Tony Stefanoni, DL
88— Dave Duffy, DL

**WILKES (1)**
73— Jeff Grandinetti, DT

**WILLAMETTE (11)'**
34— Loren Grannis, G
35— John Oravec, B
36— Richard Weisgerber, B
46— Marvin Goodman, E
58— William Long, C
59— Marvin Cisneros, G
64— Robert Burles, DT
65— Robert Burles, DT
69— Calvin Lee, LB
75— Gary Johnson, DL
82— Richard Milroy, DB

**WILLIAM & MARY (4)**
83—†Mario Shaffer, OL
86—†Michael Clemons, RB
89—†Steve Christie, P
90—†Pat Crowley, DL

**WILLIAM JEWELL (4)**
52— Al Conway, B
73— John Strada, OE
81— Guy Weber, DL
83— Mark Mundel, OL

**WILLIAM PENN (1)**
72— Bruce Polen, DB

**WILLIAMS (5)**
51— Charles Salmon, DG
69— Jack Maitland, HB
74— John Chandler, LB
78— Greg McAleenan, DB
90— George Rogers, DL

**WILMINGTON (1)**
72— William Roll, OG

**WINGATE (1)**
89— Jimmy Sutton, OT

**WINONA ST. (1)**
92— Dave Ludy, AP

**WINSTON-SALEM (4)**
77— Cornelius Washington, DB
78— Tim Newsome, RB
84— Danny Moore, OG
87— Barry Turner, G

**WIS.-EAU CLAIRE (1)**
81— Roger Vann, RB

**WIS.-LA CROSSE (10)**
52— Ted Levanhagen, LB
72— Bryon Buelow, DB
78— Joel Williams, LB
83— Jim Byrne, DL
85— Tom Newberry, OL
88— Ted Pretasky, RB
89— Terry Strouf, OL
91— Jon Lauscher, LB
92— Norris Thomas, DB
     Mike Breit, LB

**WIS.-MILWAUKEE (1)**
70— Pete Papara, LB

**WIS.-PLATTEVILLE (2)**
73— William Vander Velden, DE
86— Mike Hintz, DB

**WIS.-RIVER FALLS (3)**
80— Gerald Sonsalla, OG
82— Roland Hall, LB
87— Greg Corning, RB

**WIS.-STEVENS POINT (3)**
77— Reed Giordana, QB
81— Chuck Braun, WR
92— Randy Simpson, DB

**WIS.-STOUT (1)**
79— Joseph Bullis, DL

**WIS.-SUPERIOR (3)**
66— Mel Thake, DB
83— Larry Banks, MG
85— Phil Eiting, LB

**WIS.-WHITEWATER (4)**
75— William Barwick, OL
79— Jerry Young, WR
82— Daryl Schleim, DE
90— Reggie White, OL

**WITTENBERG (18)**
62— Donald Hunt, G
63— Bob Cherry, E
64— Chuck Green, QB
68— Jim Felts, DE
73— Steve Drongowski, OT
74— Arthur Thomas, LB
75— Robert Foster, LB
76— Dean Caven, DL
78— Dave Merritt, RB
79— Joe Govern, DL
80— Mike Dowds, DE
81— Bill Beach, DB
83— Bryant Lemon, DL
87— Eric Horstman, OL
88— Ken Bonner, OT
     Eric Horstman, OL
90— Jon Warga, RB
92— Taver Johnson, LB

**WM. PATERSON (1)**
92— Craig Paskas, DB

**WOFFORD (10)**
42— Aubrey Faust, E

47— Ken Dubard, T
49— Elbert Hammett, T
51— Jack Beeler, DB
57— Charles Bradshaw, B
61— Dan Lewis, G
70— Sterling Allen, OG
79— Keith Kinard, OL
90— David Wiley, OL
91— Tom Cotter, OL
**WOOSTER (1)**
79— Blake Moore, C

**WORCESTER ST. (1)**
92— Chris Butts, DB
**XAVIER (OHIO) (1)**
51— Tito Carinci, LB
**YALE (1)**
84—†John Zanieski, DL
**YOUNGSTOWN ST. (13)**
74— Don Calloway, DB
75— Don Calloway, DB
78— Ed McGlasson, OL

79— James Ferranti, OE
      Jeff Lear, OT
80— Jeff Gergel, LB
81—†Paris Wicks, RB
82—†Paris Wicks, RB
88—†Jim Zdelar, OL
89—†Paul Soltis, LB
90—†Tony Bowens, DL
91—†Pat Danko, DL
92—†Dave Roberts, DB

# NCAA POSTGRADUATE SCHOLARSHIP WINNERS

Following are football players who are NCAA postgraduate scholarship winners, whether or not they were able to accept the grant, plus all alternates indicated by (*) who accepted grants. The program began with the 1964 season. (Those who played in 1964 are listed as 1965 winners, those who played in 1965 as 1966 winners, etc.) To qualify, student-athletes must maintain a 3.000 grade-point average (on a 4.000 scale) during their collegiate careers and perform with distinction in varsity football.

**ABILENE CHRISTIAN**
71— James Lindsey
83— *Grant Feasel
85— Daniel Remsberg
86— *James Embry
      Craig Huff
90— William Clayton
**AIR FORCE**
65— Edward Fausti
67— James Hogarty
68— Kenneth Zagzebski
69— *Richard Rivers Jr.
70— Charles Longnecker
      *Alfred Wurglitz
71— Ernest Jennings
      Robert Parker Jr.
72— Darryl Haas
73— Mark Prill
75— *Joseph Debes
84— Jeffrey Kubiak
86— Derek Brown
88— Chad Hennings
89— David Hlatky
90— Steven Wilson
91— Christopher Howard
92— Ronald James
93— Scott Hufford
**ALABAMA**
69— Donald Sutton
72— John Musso Jr.
75— Randy Hall
80— Steadman Shealy
**ALABAMA ST.**
92— Edward Robinson Jr.
**ALBANY (N.Y.)**
88— *Thomas Higgins
**ALBION**
81— Joel Manby
**ALBRIGHT**
67— *Paul Chaiet
**ALLEGHENY**
65— David Wion
92— Darren Hadlock
**ALMA**
67— Keith Bird Jr.

79— Todd Friesner
**AMHERST**
66— David Greenblatt
76— Geoffrey Miller
85— Raymond Nurme
**APPALACHIAN ST.**
78— Gill Beck
93— D. J. Campbell
**ARIZONA**
69— William Michael Moody
78— Jon Abbott
80— Jeffrey Whitton
88— Charles Cecil
**ARIZONA ST.**
78— John Harris
90— Mark Tingstad
**ARKANSAS**
70— Terry Stewart
71— William Burnett
79— William Bradford Shoup
85— *Mark Lee
**ARKANSAS ST.**
72— John Meyer
77— Thomas Humphreys
**ARMY**
66— Samuel Champi Jr.
68— Bohdan Neswiacheny
69— James McCall Jr.
      Thomas Wheelock
70— Theodore Shadid Jr.
78— Curtis Downs
81— *Stanley March
86— Donald Smith
      Douglas Black
88— William Conner
90— Michael Thorson
93— Michael McElrath
**ASHLAND**
78— Daniel Bogden
88— David Biondo
90— Douglas Powell
**AUBURN**
66— John Cochran
69— *Roger Giffin
85— Gregg Carr

90— James Lyle IV
**AUGSBURG**
90— Terry Mackenthun
**AUGUSTANA (ILL.)**
69— *Jeffrey Maurus
71— Kenneth Anderson
77— Joe Thompson
86— Steven Sanders
**AUGUSTANA (S.D.)**
72— Michael Olson
75— David Zelinsky
77— James Clemens
78— Dee Donlin
      Roger Goebel
90— *David Gubbrud
91— Scott Boyens
**BALL ST.**
67— *John Hostrawser
73— Gregory Mack
77— Arthur Yaroch
84— Richard Chitwood
88— Ronald Duncan
90— Theodore Ashburn
93— Troy Hoffer
**BATES**
79— Christopher Howard
**BAYLOR**
65— Michael Kennedy
66— Edward Whiddon
**BOISE ST.**
72— Brent McIver
76— *Glenn Sparks
79— Samuel Miller
82— Kip Bedard
92— Larry Stayner
93— David Tingstad
**BOSTON COLLEGE**
66— *Lawrence Marzetti
67— Michael O'Neill
69— Gary Andrachik
70— Robert Bouley
78— Richard Scudellari
87— Michael Degnan
**BOSTON U.**
69— Suren Donabedian Jr.

81— David Bengtson

**BOWDOIN**
65— Steven Ingram
67— Thomas Allen

**BOWIE ST.**
92— Mark Fitzgerald

**BOWLING GREEN**
77— Richard Preston
78— Mark Miller
91— Patrick Jackson

**BRIDGEPORT**
70— Terry Sparker

**BRIGHAM YOUNG**
67— Virgil Carter
76— Orrin Olsen
77—*Stephen Miller
78— Gifford Nielsen
80— Marc Wilson
82— Daniel Plater
83— Bart Oates
84— Steve Young
85— Marvin Allen
89— Charles Cutler

**BROWN**
65— John Kelly Jr.
70— James Lukens
74— Douglas Jost
75— William Taylor
77— Scott Nelson
78— Louis Cole
79— Robert Forster
82— Travis Holcombe

**BUCKNELL**
71—*Kenneth Donahue
74— John Dailey
75— Steve Leskinen
77— Lawrence Brunt
85— David Kucera
93— David Berardinelli

**BUENA VISTA**
77— Steven Trost
87— Michael Habben

**BUFFALO ST.**
87— James Dunbar

**BUTLER**
72— George Yearsich
78— William Ginn
85— Stephen Kollias

**CAL LUTHERAN**
90—*Gregory Maw

**CAL POLY SLO**
69— William Creighton

**CAL TECH**
67— William Mitchell
68— John Frazzini
74— Frank Hobbs Jr.

**CALIFORNIA**
66— William Krum
67— John Schmidt
68— Robert Crittenden
70— James Calkins
71— Robert Richards
83— Harvey Salem

**CANISIUS**
84— Thomas Schott

**CAPITAL**
84—*Michael Linton

**CARLETON**
67— Robert Paarlberg
73— Mark Williams

83— Paul Vaaler
93— Arthur Gilliland

**CARNEGIE MELLON**
80— Gusty Sunseri
91— Robert O'Toole

**CARROLL (WIS.)**
77— Stephen Thompson

**CARTHAGE**
70— William Radakovitz

**CASE RESERVE**
89— Christopher Nutter
91— James Meek

**CENTRAL (IOWA)**
71— Vernon Den Herder
87— Scott Lindell
89— Eric Perry
92— Richard Kacmarynski

**CENTRAL MICH.**
77— John Wunderlich
80—*Michael Ball
85— Kevin Egnatuk
88— Robert Stebbins
92— Jeffrey Bender

**CENTRAL WASH.**
70— Danny Collins

**CENTRE**
69— Glenn Shearer
86— Casteel "Teel" Bruner II
88—*Robert Clark
90—*James Ellington

**CHEYNEY**
76— Steven Anderson

**CHICAGO**
86—*Bruce Montella
89— Paul Haar

**CINCINNATI**
71—*Earl Willson

**CITADEL**
74— Thomas Leitner
79— Kenneth Caldwell
84—*William West IV

**CLAREMONT-M-S**
68— Craig Dodel
70—*Gregory Long
71— Stephen Endemano
73— Christopher Stecher
74— Samuel Reece

**CLEMSON**
65— James Bell Jr.
68— James Addison
73— Benjamin Anderson
79— Stephen Fuller

**COAST GUARD**
73— Rodney Leis
74— Leonard Kelly
81— Bruce Hensel
89—*Ty Rinoski
    *Jeffery Peters
90— Richard Schachner
91— John Freda

**COE**
67— Lynn Harris

**COLBY**
71— Ronald Lupton
    Frank Apantaku

**COLGATE**
73— Kenneth Nelson
80— Angelo Colosimo
89— Donald Charney

**COLORADO**
93— James Hansen

**COLORADO COL.**
69— Steven Ehrhart
72— Randy Bobier
75— Bruce Kolbezen
84— Herman Motz III

**COLORADO MINES**
66— Stuart Bennett
67— Michael Greensburg
    Charles Kirby
75— David Chambers

**COLORADO ST.**
65— Russel Mowrer
76— Mark Driscoll
87— Stephan Bartalo
88— Joseph Brookhart
93— Gregory Primus

**COLUMBIA**
72— John Sefcik
80— Mario Biaggi Jr.

**CONNECTICUT**
77—*Bernard Palmer

**CORNELL**
68— Ronald Kipicki
72— Thomas Albright
84— Derrick Harmon

**CORNELL COLLEGE**
65— Steven Miller
72— David Hilmers
73— Robert Ash
79— Brian Farrell
79— Thomas Zinkula
81—*Timothy Garry
83— John Ward
93— Brent Sands

**DARTMOUTH**
66— Anthony Yezer
68— Henry Paulson Jr.
69— Randolph Wallick
71— Willie Bogan
73— Frederick Radke
74— Thomas Csatari
    *Robert Funk
77— Patrick Sullivan
89— Paul Sorensen

**DAVIDSON**
66— Stephen Smith
71— Rick Lyon
72— Robert Norris
86—*Louis Krempel

**DAYTON**
73— Timothy Quinn
76— Roy Gordon III
83—*Michael Pignatiello
91— Daniel Sharley

**DELAWARE**
86— Brian Farrell

**DELAWARE VALLEY**
85— Daniel Glowatski

**DELTA ST.**
76— William Hood

**DENISON**
70— Richard Trumball
73— Steven Smiljanich
76—*Dennis Thome
78— David Holcombe
86— Brian Gearinger
88— Grant Jones
92— Jonathan Fortkamp

**DePAUW**
68— Bruce Montgomerie
78— Mark Frazer
81— Jay True
85— Richard Bonaccorsi
86— Anthony deNicola
92— Thomas Beaulieu

**DICKINSON**
66— Robert Averback
71— *John West
75— *Gerald Urich

**DOANE**
68— John Lothrop
70— Richard Held

**DRAKE**
73— Joseph Worobec

**DREXEL**
72— Blake Lynn Ferguson

**DUBUQUE**
82— Timothy Finn

**DUKE**
68— Robert Lasky
71— *Curt Rawley

**EAST CARO.**
92— Keith Arnold

**EAST TENN. ST.**
82— Jay Patterson

**EASTERN KY.**
78— Steven Frommeyer

**EASTERN N. MEX.**
66— Richard James

**ELIZABETH CITY ST.**
73— Darnell Johnson
80— David Nickelson

**ELMHURST**
80— Richard Green

**EMORY & HENRY**
82— Thomas Browder Jr.

**EVANSVILLE**
75— David Mattingly
76— Charles Uhde Jr.
79— *Neil Saunders

**FERRIS ST.**
79— Robert Williams
93— Monty Brown

**FLORIDA**
72— Carlos Alvarez
77— Darrell Carpenter
85— Garrison Rolle
87— Bret Wiechmann
90— *Cedric Smith
91— Huey Richardson

**FLORIDA ST.**
88— David Palmer
91— David Roberts

**FORDHAM**
91— Eric Schweiker

**FRANK. & MARSH.**
69— Frank deGenova
83— *Robert Shepardson

**FRESNO ST.**
70— *Henry Corda
74— Dwayne Westphal
83— William Griever Jr.

**FURMAN**
77— Thomas Holcomb III
82— Charles Anderson
84— Ernest Gibson
86— *David Jager

87— Stephen Squire
90— Christopher Roper
92— Paul Siffri
Eric Von Walter

**GEORGETOWN**
75— James Chesley Jr.

**GEORGIA**
68— Thomas Lawhorne Jr.
69— William Payne
71— Thomas Lyons
72— Thomas Nash Jr.
Raleigh Mixon Robinson
78— Jeffrey Lewis
80— Jeffrey Pyburn
81— Christopher Welton
84— Terrell Hoage
88— Kim Stephens
89— Richard Tardits

**GEORGIA TECH**
68— William Eastman
75— James Robinson
81— Sheldon Fox
83— Ellis Gardner
86— John Ivemeyer

**GETTYSBURG**
70— *Herbert Ruby III
80— Richard Swartz

**GRAMBLING**
73— Stephen Dennis

**GRINNELL**
72— Edward Hirsch
80— *Derek Muehrcke

**GUST. ADOLPHUS**
74— James Goodwin
81— *David Najarian

**HAMLINE**
85— Kyle Aug
91— Robert Hackney

**HAMPDEN-SYDNEY**
78— *Wilson Newell
80— Timothy Maxa

**HARVARD**
68— Alan Bersin
71— *Richard Frisbie
75— Patrick McInally
76— William Emper
81— Charles Durst
85— Brian Bergstrom
87— Scott Collins

**HAWAII**
68— James Roberts
73— *Don Satterlee

**HIRAM**
68— Sherman
Riemenschneider
74— Donald Brunetti

**HOLY CROSS**
84— *Bruce Kozerski
89— Jeffrey Wiley
91— John Lavalette

**HOPE**
74— Ronald Posthuma
80— Craig Groendyk
83— Kurt Brinks
85— *Scott Jecmen

**HOUSTON**
86— Gary Schoppe
87— Robert Brezina

**IDAHO**
67— Michael Lavens

67— Joseph McCollum Jr.
84— Boyce Bailey

**IDAHO ST.**
76— Richard Rodgers
92— Steven Boyenger

**ILL. BENEDICTINE**
70— David Cyr
71— Thomas Danaher

**ILL. WESLEYAN**
93— Christopher Bisaillon

**ILLINOIS**
72— Robert Bucklin
73— Laurence McCarren Jr.
91— Curtis Lovelace
92— Michael Hopkins
93— John Wright

**INDIANA**
73— Glenn Scolnik
79— David Abrams
81— Kevin Speer

**INDIANA (PA.)**
78— *John Mihota
84— Kenneth Moore

**INDIANA ST.**
86— Jeffrey Miller

**INDIANAPOLIS**
76— Rodney Pawlik

**IONA**
81— Neal Kurtti
82— *Paul Rupp

**IOWA**
69— Michael Miller
76— Robert Elliott
78— Rodney Sears
86— Larry Station Jr.
88— Michael Flagg
89— Charles Hartlieb

**IOWA ST.**
70— William Bliss

**JACKSON ST.**
80— *Lester Walls

**JACKSONVILLE ST.**
79— Dewey Barker

**JAMES MADISON**
79— Warren Coleman
90— Mark Kiefer

**JOHNS HOPKINS**
73— Joseph Ouslander
74— Gunter Glocker

**JUNIATA**
72— Maurice Taylor
87— Robert Crossey

**KANSAS**
65— Ronald Oelschlager
69— David Morgan
72— Michael McCoy
73— John Schroll
78— Tom Fitch
87— Mark Henderson

**KANSAS ST.**
66— *Larry Anderson
83— James Gale
88— Matthew Garver

**KENTUCKY**
76— Thomas Ranieri
79— James Kovach
84— *Keith Martin

**KENTUCKY ST.**
68— James Jackson

354

**KENYON**
75— Patrick Clements
**KNOX**
88— Robert Monroe
**LAFAYETTE**
71— William Sprecher
76— Michael Kline
78— Victor Angeline III
**LAMAR**
73—*Richard Kubiak
**LAWRENCE**
68— Charles McKee
83— Christopher Matheus
**LEBANON VALLEY**
74—*Alan Shortell
**LEHIGH**
66— Robert Adelaar
68— Richard Miller
73—*Thomas Benfield
75— James Addonizio
76—*Robert Liptak
77—*Michael Yaszemski
80— David Melone
**LIU-C. W. POST**
79— John Luchsinger
**LONG BEACH ST.**
84— Joseph Donohue
**LOUISIANA ST.**
79— Robert Dugas
83— James Britt
88— Ignazio Albergamo
91— Solomon Graves
**LUTHER**
67— Thomas Altemeier
78—*Mark Larson
85— Larry Bonney
**MANKATO ST.**
70— Bernard Maczuga
**MARYLAND**
78— Jonathan Claiborne
**MARYVILLE (TENN.)**
67— Frank Eggers II
**McNEESE ST.**
81— Daryl Burckel
86— Ross Leger
**MEMPHIS ST.**
77—*James Mincey Jr.
**MERCHANT MARINE**
70— Robert Lavinia
76—*John Castagna
**MIAMI (FLA.)**
90— Robert Chudzinski
91— Michael Sullivan
**MICHIGAN**
67— David Fisher
74— David Gallagher
81—*John Wangler
82— Norm Betts
84— Stefan Humphries
84— Thomas Dixon
86— Clayton Miller
87— Kenneth Higgins
93— Christopher Hutchinson
**MICHIGAN ST.**
69— Allen Brenner
70— Donald Baird
**MICHIGAN TECH**
72— Larry Ras
74— Bruce Trusock
75— Daniel Rhude

**MIDDLE TENN. ST.**
73—*Edwin Zaunbrecher
**MIDDLEBURY**
79— Franklin Kettle
**MIDLAND LUTHERAN**
76— Thomas Hale
**MILLERSVILLE**
92— Thomas Burns III
**MILLIKIN**
90—*Charles Martin
**MILLSAPS**
67— Edward Weller
73—*Russell Gill
92— David Harrison Jr.
**MINNESOTA**
69— Robert Stein
71— Barry Mayer
73— Douglas Kingsriter
78— Robert Weber
**MISSISSIPPI**
66— Stanley Hindman
69— Steve Hindman
81— Kenneth Toler Jr.
86— Richard Austin
87— Jeffrey Noblin
88— Daniel Hoskins
89— Charles Walls
91— Todd Sandroni
**MISSISSIPPI COL.**
80— Stephen Johnson
**MISSISSIPPI ST.**
69— William Nelson
73— Frank Dowsing Jr.
75— James Webb
77— William Coltharp
93— Daniel Boyd
**MISSOURI**
66— Thomas Lynn
67— James Whitaker
69—*Charles Weber
71— John Weisenfels
79— Christopher Garlich
82— Van Darkow
**MISSOURI-ROLLA**
69— Robert Nicodemus
73— Kim Colter
81— Paul Janke
**MIT**
91— Darcy Prather
92— Rodrigo Rubiano
93— Roderick Tranum
**MONMOUTH (ILL.)**
72— Dale Brooks
90— Brent Thurness
**MONTANA**
75— Rock Svennungsen
79— Steven Fisher
84— Brian Salonen
91— Michael McGowan
**MONTANA ST.**
65— Gene Carlson
68— Russell Dodge
71— Jay Groepper
77— Bert Markovich
79— Jon Borchardt
    James Mickelson
90— Derrick Isackson
92— Travis Annette
**MORAVIAN**
73— Daniel Joseph

**MOREHEAD ST.**
92— James Appel
**MORNINGSIDE**
65— Larry White
**MORRIS BROWN**
83— Arthur Knight Jr.
**MOUNT UNION**
89— Paul Hrics
**MUHLENBERG**
73— Edward Salo
76— Eric Butler
78— Mark Stull
81— Arthur Scavone
91— Michael Hoffman
**MURRAY ST.**
71— Matthew Haug
78— Edward McFarland
81—*Kris Robbins
90— Eric Crigler
**NAVY**
65— William Donnelly
69— William Newton
70— Daniel Pike
75—*Timothy Harden
76— Chester Moeller II
81— Theodore Dumbauld
**N.C. CENTRAL**
91— Anthony Cooley
**NEBRASKA**
70— Randall Reeves
71—*John Decker
72— Larry Jacobson
73— David Mason
74— Daniel Anderson
76— Thomas Heiser
77— Vince Ferragamo
78— Ted Harvey
79— James Pillen
80— Timothy Smith
81— Randy Schleusener
    Jeffrey Finn
82— Eric Lindquist
85— Scott Strasburger
88— Jeffrey Jamrog
89— Mark Blazek
90— Gerald Gdowski
    Jacob Young III
91— David Edeal
    Patrick Tyrance Jr.
92— Patrick Engelbert
93— Michael Stigge
**NEBRASKA-OMAHA**
84— Kirk Hutton
84— Clark Toner
**NEW HAMPSHIRE**
85— Richard Leclerc
**NEW MEXICO**
72— Roderick Long
76— Robert Berg
79— Robert Rumbaugh
83— George Parks
**NEW MEXICO ST.**
76— Ralph Jackson
77—*Joseph Fox
**NORTH ALA.**
82—*Warren Moore
**NORTH CARO.**
75— Christopher Kupec
81— William Donnalley
83— David Drechsler
91— Kevin Donnalley

*NCAA Postgraduate Scholarship Winners*

**NORTH CARO. ST.**
75— Justus Everett
82—*Calvin Warren Jr.

**NORTH DAK.**
79— Dale Lian
81— Douglas Moen
82— Paul Franzmeier
85— Glen Kucera
88— Kurt Otto
89— Matthew Gulseth
93— Timothy Gelinske

**NORTH DAK. ST.**
66— James Schindler
69—*Stephen Stephens
71— Joseph Cichy
75— Paul Cichy
84— Doug Hushka
89— Charles Stock

**NORTH TEXAS**
68— Ruben Draper
77— Peter Morris

**NORTHEAST LA.**
93— Darren Rimmer

**NORTHEAST MO. ST.**
83— Roy Pettibone

**NORTHERN ARIZ.**
78— Larry Friedrichs

**NORTHERN COLO.**
76— Robert Bliss
91— Thomas Langer

**NORTHERN IOWA**
81— Owen Dockter

**NORTHERN MICH.**
73— Guy Falkenhagen
81— Phil Kessel
86— Keith Nelsen

**NORTHWEST MO. ST.**
82— Robert Gregory

**NORTHWESTERN**
70—*Bruce Hubbard
74— Steven Craig
77— Randolph Dean
81— Charles Kern

**NORWICH**
68— Richard Starbuck
74— Matthew Hincks

**NOTRE DAME**
67— Frederick Schnurr
68— James Smithberger
69— George Kunz
70— Michael Oriard
71— Lawrence DiNardo
72— Thomas Gatewood
73— Gregory Marx
74— David Casper
75— Peter Demmerle
75— Reggie Barnett
79— Joseph Restic
81— Thomas Gibbons
82— John Krimm Jr.
86— Gregory Dingens
89— Reginald Ho

**OCCIDENTAL**
66— James Wanless
67— Richard Verry
69— John St. John
78— Richard Fry
80—*Timothy Bond
89—*Curtis Page

**OHIO**
78—*Robert Weidaw

80— Mark Geisler

**OHIO NORTHERN**
79— Mark Palmer
82— Larry Egbert

**OHIO ST.**
65— Arnold Chonko
66— Donald Unverferth
67— Ray Pryor
69— David Foley
71— Rex Kern
74— Randolph Gradishar
76— Brian Baschnagel
77— William Lukens
80— James Laughlin
84— John Frank
85— David Crecelius
86— Michael Lanese

**OKLAHOMA**
72— Larry Jack Mildren Jr.
73— Joe Wylie
81— Jay Jimerson
89— Anthony Phillips
91— Michael Sawatzky

**OKLAHOMA ST.**
83—*Doug Freeman

**OLIVET**
75— William Ziem

**OREGON**
79—*Willie Blasher Jr.
91— William Musgrave

**OREGON ST.**
69— William Enyart
69—*Jerry Belcher

**PACIFIC (CAL.)**
72—*Byron Cosgrove
78— Brian Peets
80— Bruce Filarsky

**PENN ST.**
66— Joseph Bellas
67— John Runnells III
71— Robert Holuba
72— David Joyner
73— Bruce Bannon
74— Mark Markovich
75— John Baiorunos
79—*Charles Correal
80—*Michael Guman
81— John Walsh
84— Harry Hamilton
85— Douglas Strange
87— Brian Silverling
90— Roger Thomas Duffy

**PENNSYLVANIA**
68— Ben Mortensen

**PITTSBURGH**
79— Jeff Delaney
86— Robert Schilken
89— Mark Stepnoski

**POMONA-PITZER**
69—*Lee Piatek
77— Scott Borg
83—*Calvin Oishi
85—*Derek Watanabe
88— Edward Irick
93— Torin Cunningham

**PORTLAND ST.**
79— John Urness

**PRINCETON**
67— Charles Peters
69— Richard Sandler
70— Keith Mauney

76— Ronald Beible
81— Mark Bailey
83— Brent Woods
86— James Petrucci
87— John Hammond

**PUGET SOUND**
68— Stephen Doolittle
79—*Patrick O'Loughlin
83—*Anthony Threlkeld

**PURDUE**
70— Michael Phipps
74— Robert Hoftiezer
75— Lawrence Burton

**REDLANDS**
65— Robert Jones

**RENSSELAER**
67— Robert Darnall
69— John Contento

**RHODES**
71— John Churchill
79—*Philip Mischke
81— Jeffrey Lane
83—*Russell Ashford
85—*John Foropoulos
89— James Augustine

**RICE**
81—*Lamont Jefferson
91— Donald Hollas

**RICHMOND**
86— Leland Melvin

**RIPON**
65— Phillip Steans
69— Steven Thompson
80— Thomas Klofta

**RUTGERS**
90— Steven Tardy

**SANTA CLARA**
72— Ronald Sani
77— Mark Tiernan
81—*David Alfaro
85— Alexis Vlahos
87— Patrick Sende

**SEWANEE**
65— Frank Stubblefield
66— Douglas Paschall
69— James Beene
71— John Popham IV
77— Dudley West
82— Gregory Worsowicz
82— Domenick Reina
83— Michael York
84— Michael Jordan
93— Jason Forrester

**SHIPPENSBURG**
77— Anthony Winter

**SIMPSON**
71— Richard Clogg
74— Hugh Lickiss
90— Roger Grover

**SOUTH CARO.**
67— Steven Stanley Juk Jr.

**SOUTH DAK.**
79— Michael Schurrer
87— Todd Salat
93— Jason Seurer

**SOUTH DAK. ST.**
80— Charles Loewen
81— Paul Kippley
88— Daniel Sonnek

**SOUTHEASTERN LA.**
74— William Percy Jr.

356

**SOUTHERN-B.R.**
70— Alden Roche

**SOUTHERN CAL**
66— Charles Arrobio
69— Steven Sogge
70— Harry Khasigian
       Steve Lehmer
74— Monte Doris
75— Patrick Haden
76— Kevin Bruce
78— Gary Bethel
80— Brad Budde
       Paul McDonald
81— Gordon Adams
       *Jeffrey Fisher
85— Duane Bickett
86— Anthony Colorito
       *Matthew Koart
87— Jeffrey Bregel
90— John Jackson

**SOUTHERN COLO.**
70— Gregory Smith
73— Collon Kennedy III

**SOUTHERN METHODIST**
83—*Brian O'Meara
85—*Monte Goen
87— David Adamson
93— Cary Brabham

**SOUTHERN MISS.**
83— Richard Thompson
84— Stephen Carmody

**SOUTHERN UTAH**
92— Stephen McDowell

**SOUTHWEST MO. ST.**
80— Richard Suchenski
       Mitchel Ware
85— Michael Armentrout

**SOUTHWEST TEX. ST.**
82— Michael Miller

**SOUTHWESTERN LA.**
71—*George Coussa

**ST. CLOUD ST.**
90— Richard Rodgers

**ST. FRANCIS (PA.)**
87— Christopher Tantlinger

**ST. JOHN'S (MINN.)**
92— Denis McDonough

**ST. JOSEPH'S (IND.)**
80— Michael Bettinger

**ST. NORBERT**
66— Michael Ryan
88— Matthew Lang

**ST. PAUL'S**
80— Gerald Hicks

**ST. THOMAS (MINN.)**
75— Mark Dienhart

**STANFORD**
65—*Joe Neal
66—*Terry DeSylvia
68—*John Root
71— John Sande III
72— Jackie Brown
74— Randall Poltl
75—*Keith Rowen
76— Gerald Wilson
77— Duncan McColl
81— Milton McColl
84— John Bergren
85— Scott Carpenter
86— Matthew Soderlund
87— Brian Morris

88— Douglas Robison

**STONEHILL**
93— Kevin Broderick

**SUSQUEHANNA**
77— Gerald Huesken
82— Daniel Distasio

**SWARTHMORE**
72— Christopher Leinberger
83—*John Walsh

**SYRACUSE**
78—*Robert Avery
86— Timothy Green

**TEMPLE**
74— Dwight Fulton

**TENN.-CHATT.**
67— Harvey Ouzts
72—*Frank Webb
74— John McBrayer
76— Russell Gardner

**TENNESSEE**
71— Donald Denbo
       Timothy Priest
77— Michael Mauck
81— Timothy Irwin

**TEXAS**
69— Corbin Robertson Jr.
71— Willie Zapalac Jr.
73—*Michael Bayer
74— Patrick Kelly
75— Wade Johnston
76— Robert Simmons
77— William Hamilton

**TEXAS A&M**
69— Edward Hargett
71— David Elmendorf
72— Stephen Luebbehusen
88— Kip Corrington

**TEXAS-ARLINGTON**
69— Michael Baylor

**TEXAS CHRISTIAN**
67— John Richards
68— Eldon Gresham Jr.
73— Scott Walker
75— Terry Drennan
88— J. Clinton Hailey

**TEXAS SOUTHERN**
65— Leon Hardy

**TEXAS TECH**
65— James Ellis Jr.
68— John Scovell
75— Jeffrey Jobe
78—*Richard Arledge
85—*Bradford White
90— Thomas Mathiasmeier

**TOLEDO**
82— Tad Wampfler
89— Kenneth Moyer

**TRINITY (CONN.)**
67—*Howard Wrzosek
68— Keith Miles

**TRINITY (TEX.)**
84—*Peter Broderick

**TROY ST.**
75— Mark King

**TUFTS**
65— Peter Smith
70— Robert Bass
79—*Don Leach
80—*James Ford
82—*Brian Gallagher

87— Robert Patz
92— Paulo Oliveira

**TULSA**
67—*Larry Williams
75— James Mack Lancaster II

**TUSKEGEE**
68— James Greene

**UC DAVIS**
76— Daniel Carmazzi
       David Gellerman
77— Rolf Benirschke
79— Mark Markel
86— Robert Hagenau
90—*James Tomasin
92— Robert Kincade
       Michael Shepard
93— Brian Andersen

**UC RIVERSIDE**
72— Tyrone Hooks
74— Gary Van Jandegian

**UCLA**
67—*Raymond Armstrong
       Dallas Grider
70— Gregory Jones
74— Steven Klosterman
76— John Sciarra
77— Jeffrey Dankworth
78— John Fowler Jr.
83— Cormac Carney
84— Richard Neuheisel
86— Michael Hartmeier
90— Richard Meyer
93— Carlton Gray

**UNION (N.Y.)**
88— Richard Romer

**UTAH**
81— James Baldwin
93— Steven Young

**UTAH ST.**
67— Ronnie Edwards
68— Garth Hall
70— Gary Anderson
76— Randall Stockham

**UTEP**
80— Eddie Forkerway
89— Patrick Hegarty
92— Robert Sesich

**VA. MILITARY**
79— Robert Bookmiller
80— Richard Craig Jones

**VALPARAISO**
75—*Richard Seall

**VANDERBILT**
73— Barrett Sutton Jr.
75— Douglas Martin

**VILLANOVA**
77— David Graziano
89— Richard Spugnardi

**VIRGINIA**
67— Frederick Jones
83— Patrick Chester

**VIRGINIA TECH**
73— Thomas Carpenito

**WABASH**
74—*Mark Nicolini
81—*Melvin Gore
83— David Broecker
87— James Herrmann
92— William Padgett

**WAKE FOREST**
70— Joseph Dobner
74—*Daniel Stroup
76— Thomas Fehring
78—*Michael McGlamry
83— Philip Denfeld
87— Toby Cole Jr.

**WARTBURG**
75— Conrad Mandsager
76— James Charles Peterson
82—*Rod Feddersen

**WASH. & JEFF.**
70— Edward Guna
82— Max Regula
91— David Conn
93— Raymond Cross Jr.

**WASH. & LEE**
70— Michael Thornton
74— William Wallace Jr.
78— Jeffrey Slatcoff
79— Richard Wiles
80—*Scott Smith
81— Lonnie Nunley III
89— Michael Magoline

**WASHINGTON**
65— William Douglas
67— Michael Ryan
72—*James Krieg
73— John Brady
77— Scott Phillips
78— Blair Bush
80— Bruce Harrell
82— Mark Jerue
83— Charles Nelson
        Mark Stewart
88— David Rill
92— Edward Cunningham

**WASHINGTON ST.**
67— Richard Sheron
68— A. Douglas Flansburg
83— Gregory Porter
84— Patrick Lynch Jr.

85— Daniel Lynch
**WAYNE ST. (MICH.)**
76— Edward Skowneski Jr.
81— Phillip Emery

**WEBER ST.**
68— Phillip Tuckett
74—*Douglas Smith
92— David Hall

**WESLEYAN**
67— John Dwyer
69— Stuart Blackburn
71— James Lynch
78— John McVicar

**WEST TEX. ST.**
75—*Ben Bentley
82— Kevin Dennis

**WEST VA.**
74— Ade Dillion
74—*Daniel Larcamp
82— Oliver Luck

**WESTERN ILL.**
89— Paul Singer

**WESTERN KY.**
72— Jimmy Barber
80— Charles DeLacey

**WESTERN MICH.**
68— Martin Barski
71— Jonathan Bull

**WESTERN N. MEX.**
68— Richard Mahoney

**WHEATON (ILL.)**
89— David Lauber
93— Bart Moseman

**WHITTIER**
76— John Getz
79— Mark Deven
87—*Timothy Younger

**WILLAMETTE**
87—*Gerry Preston

**WILLIAM & MARY**
78— G. Kenneth Smith
80— Clarence Gaines
85— Mark Kelso

**WILLIAM JEWELL**
66— Charles Scrogin
70— Thomas Dunn
        John Johnston

**WILLIAMS**
65— Jerry Jones
72— John Murray

**WINSTON-SALEM**
84— Eddie Sauls

**WIS.-PLATTEVILLE**
87— Michael Hintz

**WISCONSIN**
66— David Fronek
80— Thomas Stauss
82—*David Mohapp
83— Mathew Vanden Boom

**WITTENBERG**
82— William Beach

**WOOSTER**
80— Edward Blake Moore

**WYOMING**
74— Steven Cockreham
85— Bob Gustafson
89— Randall Welniak

**XAVIER (OHIO)**
65— William Eastlake

**YALE**
66—*James Groninger
67— Howard Hilgendorf Jr.
69— Frederick Morris
71— Thomas Neville
72— David Bliss
75— John Burkus
77—*Stone Phillips
79— William Crowley
82— Richard Diana
91— Vincent Mooney

# ACADEMIC ALL-AMERICA HALL OF FAME

Since its inception in 1988, 22 former NCAA football players have been inducted into the GTE Academic All-America Hall of Fame. They were selected from among nominees by the College Sports Information Directors of America (CoSIDA) from past academic all-Americans of the 1950s, '60s and '70s. Following are the selections by the year selected and each player's team, position and last year played:

**1988**
Pete Dawkins, Army, HB, 1958
Pat Haden, Southern Cal, QB, 1974
Rev. Donn Moomaw, UCLA, LB, 1953
Merlin Olsen, Utah St., T, 1961
**1989**
Carlos Alvarez, Florida, WR, 1971
Willie Bogan, Dartmouth, DB, 1970
Steve Bramwell, Washington, DB, 1965
Joe Romig, Colorado, G, 1961

Jim Swink, Texas Christian, B, 1956
John Wilson, Michigan St., DB, 1952
**1990**
Joe Theismann, Notre Dame, QB, 1970
Howard Twilley, Tulsa, TE, 1965
**1991**
Terry Baker, Oregon St., QB, 1962
Joe Holland, Cornell, RB, 1978
David Joyner, Penn St., OT, 1971
Brock Strom, Air Force, T, 1958

**1992**
Alan Ameche, Wisconsin, RB, 1954
Stephen Eisenhauer, Navy, G, 1953
Randy Gradishar, Ohio St., LB, 1973
**1993**
Raymond Berry, Southern Methodist, E, 1954
Dave Casper, Notre Dame, E, 1973
Jim Grabowski, Illinois, FB, 1965

Two-time academic all-American and 1954 Heisman Trophy winner Alan Ameche of Wisconsin is one of 19 former college football players who have been inducted into the GTE Academic All-America Hall of Fame.

# ACADEMIC ALL-AMERICANS BY SCHOOL

Since 1952, academic all-America teams have been selected by the College Sports Information Directors of America. To be eligible, student-athletes must be regular performers and have at least a 3.200 grade-point average (on a 4.000 scale) during their college careers. University division teams (I-A and I-AA) are complete in this list, but college division teams (II, III, NAIA) before 1970 are missing from CoSIDA archives, with few exceptions. Following are all known first-team selections:

**ABILENE CHRISTIAN**
63—Jack Griggs, LB
70—Jim Lindsey, QB
74—Greg Stirman, E
76—Bill Curbo, T
77—Bill Curbo, T
87—Bill Clayton, DL
88—Bill Clayton, DL
89—Bill Clayton, DL
90—Sean Grady, WR

**ADRIAN**
84—Steve Dembowski, QB

**AIR FORCE**
58—Brock Strom, T
59—Rich Mayo, B

60—Rich Mayo, B
70—Ernie Jennings, E
71—Darryl Haas, LB/K
72—Bob Homburg, DE
  Mark Prill, LB
73—Joe Debes, OT
74—Joe Debes, OT
78—Steve Hoog, WR
81—Mike France, LB
83—Jeff Kubiak, P
86—Chad Hennings, DL
87—Chad Hennings, DL
88—David Hlatky, OL
90—Chris Howard, RB
92—Grant Johnson, LB

**AKRON**
80—Andy Graham, PK

**ALABAMA**
61—Tommy Brooker, E
  Pat Trammell, B
64—Gaylon McCollough, C
65—Steve Sloan, QB
  Dennis Homan, HB
67—Steve Davis, K
  Bob Childs, LB
70—Johnny Musso, HB
71—Johnny Musso, HB
73—Randy Hall, DT
74—Randy Hall, DT
75—Danny Ridgeway, KS

79—Major Ogilvie, RB

**ALABAMA A&M**
89—Tracy Kendall, QB
90—Tracy Kendall, QB

**ALBANY (N.Y.)**
86—Thomas Higgins, OT
87—Thomas Higgins, OT

**ALBION**
82—Bruce Drogosch, LB
86—Michael Grant, DB
90—Scott Bissell, DB

**ALFRED**
89—Mark Szynkowski, OL

**ALLEGHENY**
81—Kevin Baird, P
91—Adam Lechman, OL
Darren Hadlock, LB

**ALMA**
86—Greg Luczak, TE

**AMERICAN INT'L**
81—Todd Scyocurka, LB

**APPALACHIAN ST.**
77—Gill Beck, C
92—D. J. Campbell, QB

**ARIZONA**
68—Mike Moody, OG
75—Jon Abbott, LB
76—Jon Abbott, T/LB
77—Jon Abbott, T/LB
79—Jeffrey Whitton, DL
87—Charles Cecil, DB

**ARIZONA ST.**
66—Ken Dyer, OE
88—Mark Tingstad, LB

**ARKANSAS**
57—Gerald Nesbitt, FB
61—Lance Alworth, B
64—Ken Hatfield, B
65—Randy Stewart, C
Jim Lindsey, HB
Jack Brasuell, DB
68—Bob White, K
69—Bill Burnett, HB
Terry Stewart, DB
78—Brad Shoup, DB

**ARKANSAS-MONTICELLO**
85—Ray Howard, OG
88—Sean Rochelle, QB

**ARKANSAS ST.**
59—Larry Zabrowski, OT
61—Jim McMurray, QB

**ARKANSAS TECH**
90—Karl Kuhn, TE
91—Karl Kuhn, TE

**ARMY**
55—Ralph Chesnauskas, E
57—James Kernan, C
Pete Dawkins, HB
58—Pete Dawkins, HB
59—Don Usry, E
65—Sam Champi, DE
67—Bud Neswiacheny, DE
69—Theodore Shadid, C
89—Michael Thorson, DB
92—Mike McElrath, DB

**ASHLAND**
73—Mark Gulling, DB
74—Ron Brown, LB
76—Dan Bogden, E
77—Bruce Niehm, LB
81—Mark Braun, C

91—Thomas Shiban, RB

**AUBURN**
57—Jimmy Phillips, E
59—Jackie Burkett, C
60—Ed Dyas, B
65—Bill Cody, LB
69—Buddy McClinton, DB
74—Bobby Davis, LB
75—Chuck Fletcher, DT
76—Chris Vacarella, RB
84—Gregg Carr, LB

**AUGSBURG**
81—Paul Elliott, DL

**AUGUSTANA (ILL.)**
75—George Wesbey, T
80—Bill Dannehl, WR
84—Steve Sanders, OT
85—Steve Sanders, OT

**AUGUSTANA (S.D.)**
72—Pat McNerney, T
73—Pat McNerney, T
74—Jim Clemens, G
75—Jim Clemens, C
77—Stan Biondi, K
86—David Gubbrud, DL
87—David Gubbrud, DL
88—David Gubbrud, LB
89—David Gubbrud, LB

**AUSTIN**
81—Gene Branum, PK

**AUSTIN PEAY**
74—Gregory Johnson, G

**BAKER**
61—John Jacobs, B

**BALDWIN-WALLACE**
70—Earl Stolberg, DB
72—John Yezerski, G
78—Roger Andrachik, RB
Greg Monda, LB
81—Chuck Krajacic, OG
88—Shawn Gorman, P
91—Tom Serdinak, P

**BALL ST.**
83—Rich Chitwood, C
85—Ron Duncan, TE
86—Ron Duncan, TE
87—Ron Duncan, TE
88—Ted Ashburn, OL
Greg Shackelford, DL
89—Ted Ashburn, OL
David Haugh, DL
91—Troy Hoffer, DB
92—Troy Hoffer, DB

**BATES**
82—Neal Davidson, DB

**BAYLOR**
61—Ronnie Bull, RB
62—Don Trull, QB
63—Don Trull, QB
76—Cris Quinn, DE
89—Mike Welch, DB
90—Mike Welch, DB

**BELOIT**
90—Shane Stadler, RB

**BETHANY (KAN.)**
86—Wade Gaeddert, DB

**BLOOMSBURG**
83—Dave Pepper, DL

**BOISE ST.**
71—Brent McIver, IL
73—Glenn Sparks, G

78—Sam Miller, DB

**BOSTON COLLEGE**
77—Richard Scudellari, LB
86—Michael Degnan, DL

**BOSTON U.**
83—Steve Shapiro, K
85—Brad Hokin, DB

**BOWDOIN**
84—Mike Siegel, P

**BOWLING GREEN**
75—John Boles, DE
89—Pat Jackson, LB
90—Pat Jackson, TE

**BRIGHAM YOUNG**
73—Steve Stratton, RB
80—Scott Phillips, RB
81—Dan Plater, WR
87—Chuck Cutler, WR
88—Chuck Cutler, WR
Tim Clark, DL
89—Fred Whittingham, RB
90—Andy Boyce, WR

**BROWN**
81—Travis Holcombe, OG
82—Dave Folsom, DB
86—Marty Edwards, C
87—John Cuozzo, C

**BUCKNELL**
72—Douglas Nauman, T
John Ondrasik, DB
73—John Dailey, LB
74—Steve Leskinen, T
75—Larry Brunt, E
76—Larry Brunt, E
84—Rob Masonis, RB
Jim Reilly, TE
86—Mike Morrow, WR
91—David Berardinelli, WR
92—David Berardinelli, WR

**BUFFALO**
63—Gerry Philbin, T
84—Gerry Quinlivan, LB
85—James Dunbar, C
86—James Dunbar, C

**BUFFALO ST.**
87—Clint Morano, OT

**BUTLER**
84—Steve Kollias, L

**CAL LUTHERAN**
81—John Walsh, OT

**CALIFORNIA**
67—Bob Crittenden, DG
70—Robert Richards, OT
82—Harvey Salem, OT

**CANISIUS**
82—Tom Schott, WR
83—Tom Schott, TE
86—Mike Panepinto, RB

**CAPITAL**
70—Ed Coy, E
83—Mike Linton, G
85—Kevin Sheets, WR

**CARLETON**
92—Scott Hanks, TE

**CARNEGIE MELLON**
76—Rick Lackner, LB
Dave Nackoul, E
84—Roger Roble, WR
87—Bryan Roessler, DL
Chris Haupt, LB

89—Robert O'Toole, LB
90—Frank Bellante, RB
Robert O'Toole, LB
**CARROLL (WIS.)**
76—Stephen Thompson, QB
**CARSON-NEWMAN**
61—David Dale, E
**CARTHAGE**
61—Bob Halsey, B
77—Mark Phelps, QB
**CASE RESERVE**
75—John Kosko, T
82—Jim Donnelly, RB
83—Jim Donnelly, RB
84—Jim Donnelly, RB
88—Chris Hutter, TE
90—Michael Bissler, DB
**CENTRAL (IOWA)**
79—Chris Adkins, LB
85—Scott Lindrell, LB
86—Scott Lindrell, LB
91—Rich Kacmarynski, RB
**CENTRAL MICH.**
70—Ralph Burde, DL
74—Mike Franckowiak, QB
John Wunderlich, T
79—Mike Ball, WR
84—John DeBoer, WR
91—Jeff Bender, QB
**CENTRE**
84—Teel Bruner, DB
85—Teel Bruner, DB
89—Bryan Ellington, DB
91—Eric Horstmeyer, WR
**CHADRON ST.**
73—Jerry Sutton, LB
75—Bob Lacey, KS
79—Jerry Carder, TE
**CHEYNEY**
75—Steve Anderson, G
**CHICAGO**
87—Paul Haar, OG
88—Paul Haar, OL
**CINCINNATI**
81—Kari Yli-Renko, OT
90—Kyle Stroh, DL
91—Kris Bjorson, TE
**CITADEL**
63—Vince Petno, E
76—Kenny Caldwell, LB
77—Kenny Caldwell, LB
78—Kenny Caldwell, LB
87—Thomas Frooman, RB
89—Thomas Frooman, RB
**CLEMSON**
59—Lou Cordileone, T
78—Steve Fuller, QB
**COAST GUARD**
70—Charles Pike, LB
71—Bruce Melnick, DB
81—Mark Butt, DB
**COLGATE**
78—Angelo Colosimo, RB
79—Angelo Colosimo, RB
85—Tom Stenglein, WR
89—Jeremy Garvey, TE
**COLORADO**
60—Joe Romig, G
61—Joe Romig, G
67—Kirk Tracy, OG
70—Jim Cooch, DB

73—Rick Stearns, LB
74—Rick Stearns, LB
75—Steve Young, DT
87—Eric McCarty, LB
90—Jim Hansen, OL
91—Jim Hansen, OL
92—Jim Hansen, OL
**COLORADO MINES**
72—Dave Chambers, RB
83—Charles Lane, T
**COLORADO ST.**
55—Gary Glick, B
69—Tom French, OT
86—Steve Bartalo, RB
**COLUMBIA**
52—Mitch Price, B
53—John Gasella, T
56—Claude Benham, B
71—John Sefcik, HB
**CORNELL**
77—Joseph Holland, RB
78—Joseph Holland, RB
82—Derrick Harmon, RB
83—Derrick Harmon, RB
85—Dave Van Metre, DL
**CORNELL COLLEGE**
72—Rob Ash, QB
Dewey Birkhofer, S
76—Joe Lauterbach, G
Tom Zinkula, DT
77—Tom Zinkula, DT
78—Tom Zinkula, DL
82—John Ward, WR
91—Bruce Feldmann, QB
92—Brent Sands, DB
**DARTMOUTH**
70—Willie Bogan, DB
83—Michael Patsis, DB
87—Paul Sorensen, LB
88—Paul Sorensen, LB
90—Brad Preble, DB
91—Mike Bobo, WR
Tom Morrow, LB
92—Russ Torres, RB
**DAYTON**
71—Tim Quinn, LB
72—Tim Quinn, DT
79—Scott Terry, QB
84—Greg French, K
David Kemp, LB
Jeff Slayback, L
85—Greg French, K
86—Gerry Meyer, OT
91—Brett Cuthbert, DB
Dan Rosenbaum, DB
92—Steve Lochow, DL
Dan Rosenbaum, DB
**DEFIANCE**
80—Jill Bailey, OT
Mark Bockelman, TE
**DELAWARE**
70—Yancey Phillips, T
71—Robert Depew, DE
72—Robert Depew, DE
**DELAWARE VALLEY**
84—Dan Glowatski, WR
**DELTA ST.**
70—Hal Posey, RB
74—Billy Hood, E
Ricky Lewis, LB
Larry Miller, RB
75—Billy Hood, E

78—Terry Moody, DB
79—Charles Stavley, G
**DENISON**
75—Dennis Thome, LB
87—Grant Jones, DB
**DePAUW**
70—Jim Ceaser, LB
71—Jim Ceaser, LB
73—Neil Oslos, RB
80—Jay True, WR
85—Tony deNicola, QB
87—Michael Sherman, DB
90—Tom Beaulieu, DL
91—Tom Beaulieu, DL
Matt Nelson, LB
**DICKINSON**
74—Gerald Urich, RB
79—Scott Mumma, RB
**DRAKE**
74—Todd Gaffney, KS
83—Tom Holt, RB
**DREXEL**
70—Lynn Ferguson, S
**DUBUQUE**
80—Tim Finn, RB
**DUKE**
66—Roger Hayes, DE
67—Bob Lasky, DT
70—Curt Rawley, DT
86—Mike Diminick, DB
87—Mike Diminick, DB
88—Mike Diminick, DB
89—Doug Key, DL
**EAST STROUDSBURG**
84—Ernie Siegrist, TE
**EAST TENN. ST.**
71—Ken Oster, DB
**EAST TEX. ST.**
77—Mike Hall, OT
**EASTERN KY.**
77—Steve Frommeyer, S
**EASTERN N. MEX.**
80—Tom Sager, DL
81—Tom Sager, DL
**ELON**
73—John Rascoe, E
79—Bryan Burney, DB
**EMORY & HENRY**
71—Tom Wilson, LB
**EMPORIA ST.**
79—Tom Lingg, DL
**EVANSVILLE**
74—David Mattingly, S
76—Michael Pociask, C
87—Jeffery Willman, TE
**FERRIS ST.**
81—Vic Trecha, OT
92—Monty Brown, LB
**FLORIDA**
65—Charles Casey, E
69—Carlos Alvarez, WR
71—Carlos Alvarez, WR
76—David Posey, KS
77—Wes Chandler, RB
80—Cris Collinsworth, WR
91—Brad Culpepper, DL
**FLORIDA A&M**
90—Irvin Clark, DL

**FLORIDA ST.**
72—Gary Huff, QB
79—William Jones, DB
Phil Williams, WR
80—William Jones, DB
81—Rohn Stark, P
**FORDHAM**
90—Eric Schweiker, OL
**FORT HAYS ST.**
75—Greg Custer, RB
82—Ron Johnson, P
85—Paul Nelson, DL
86—Paul Nelson, DL
89—Dean Gengler, OL
**FORT LEWIS**
72—Dee Tennison, E
**FRANK. & MARSH.**
77—Joe Fry, DB
78—Joe Fry, DB
**FURMAN**
76—Jeff Holcomb, T
85—Brian Jager, RB
88—Kelly Fletcher, DL
89—Kelly Fletcher, DL
Chris Roper, LB
91—Eric Walter, OL
**GA. SOUTHWESTERN**
87—Gregory Slappery, RB
**GEORGETOWN**
71—Gerry O'Dowd, HB
86—Andrew Phelan, OG
**GEORGETOWN (KY.)**
89—Eric Chumbley, OL
92—Bobby Wasson, PK
**GEORGIA**
60—Francis Tarkenton, QB
65—Bob Etter, K
66—Bob Etter, K
Lynn Hughes, DB
68—Bill Stanfill, DT
71—Tom Nash, OT
Mixon Robinson, DE
77—Jeff Lewis, LB
82—Terry Hoage, DB
83—Terry Hoage, DB
92—Todd Peterson, PK
**GEORGIA TECH**
52—Ed Gossage, T
Cecil Trainer, DE
Larry Morris, LB
55—Wade Mitchell, B
56—Allen Ecker, G
66—Jim Breland, C
W. J. Blaine, LB
Bill Eastman, DB
67—Bill Eastman, DB
80—Sheldon Fox, LB
90—Stefen Scotton, RB
**GETTYSBURG**
79—Richard Swartz, LB
**GRAMBLING**
72—Floyd Harvey, RB
**GRAND VALLEY ST.**
91—Mark Smith, OL
Todd Wood, DB
**GRINNELL**
71—Edward Hirsch, E
81—David Smiley, TE
**GROVE CITY**
74—Pat McCoy, LB
89—Travis Croll, P

**GUST. ADOLPHUS**
80—Dave Najarian, DL
81—Dave Najarian, LB
**HAMLINE**
73—Thomas Dufresne, E
89—Jon Voss, TE
**HAMPDEN-SYDNEY**
82—John Dickinson, OG
90—W. R. Jones, OL
91—David Brickhill, PK
**HARVARD**
84—Brian Bergstrom, DB
**HEIDELBERG**
82—Jeff Kurtzman, DL
**HILLSDALE**
61—James Richendollar, T
72—John Cervini, G
81—Mark Kellogg, LB
**HOLY CROSS**
83—Bruce Kozerski, T
85—Kevin Reilly, OT
87—Jeff Wiley, QB
91—Pete Dankert, DL
**HOPE**
73—Ronald Posthuma, T
79—Craig Groendyk, T
80—Greg Bekius, PK
82—Kurt Brinks, C
84—Scott Jecmen, DB
86—Timothy Chase, OG
**HOUSTON**
64—Horst Paul, E
76—Mark Mohr, DB
Kevin Rollwage, OT
77—Kevin Rollwage, OT
**IDAHO**
70—Bruce Langmeade, T
**IDAHO ST.**
84—Brent Koetter, DB
91—Steve Boyenger, DB
**ILL. WESLEYAN**
71—Keith Ihlanfeldt, DE
80—Jim Eaton, DL
Rick Hanna, DL
Mike Watson, DB
81—Mike Watson, DB
91—Chris Bisaillon, WR
92—Chris Udovich, DL
**ILLINOIS**
52—Bob Lenzini, DT
64—Jim Grabowski, FB
65—Jim Grabowski, FB
66—John Wright, E
70—Jim Rucks, DE
71—Bob Bucklin, DE
80—Dan Gregus, DL
81—Dan Gregus, DL
82—Dan Gregus, DL
91—Mike Hopkins, DB
92—John Wright Jr., WR
**ILLINOIS COL.**
80—Jay Wessler, RB
**ILLINOIS ST.**
76—Tony Barnes, C
80—Jeff Hembrough, DL
89—Dan Hackman, OL
**INDIANA**
67—Harry Gonso, HB
72—Glenn Scolnik, RB
80—Kevin Speer, C

**INDIANA (PA.)**
82—Kenny Moore, DB
83—Kenny Moore, DB
**INDIANA ST.**
71—Gary Brown, E
72—Michael Eads, E
**INDIANAPOLIS**
76—William Willan, E
**IONA**
80—Neal Kurtti, DL
**IOWA**
52—Bill Fenton, DE
53—Bill Fenton, DE
75—Bob Elliott, DB
85—Larry Station, LB
**IOWA ST.**
52—Max Burkett, DB
82—Mark Carlson, LB
**ITHACA**
72—Dana Hallenbeck, LB
85—Brian Dougherty, DB
89—Peter Burns, OL
**JACKSONVILLE ST.**
77—Dewey Barker, E
78—Dewey Barker, TE
**JAMES MADISON**
78—Warren Coleman, OT
**JOHN CARROLL**
83—Nick D'Angelo, LB
Jim Sferra, DL
85—Joe Burrello, LB
86—Joe Burrello, LB
**JOHNS HOPKINS**
77—Charles Hauck, DT
**JUNIATA**
70—Ray Grabiak, DL
71—Ray Grabiak, DE
71—Maurice Taylor, IL
**KALAMAZOO**
92—Sean Mullendore, LB
**KANSAS**
64—Fred Elder, T
67—Mike Sweatman, LB
68—Dave Morgan, LB
71—Mike McCoy, C
76—Tom Fitch, S
**KANSAS ST.**
74—Don Lareau, LB
77—Floyd Dorsey, OG
81—Darren Gale, DB
82—Darren Gale, DB
Mark Hundley, RB
85—Troy Faunce, P
**KENT**
72—Mark Reiheld, DB
91—Brad Smith, RB
**KENTUCKY**
74—Tom Ranieri, LB
78—Mark Keene, C
Jim Kovach, LB
85—Ken Pietrowiak, C
**KENYON**
77—Robert Jennings, RB
85—Dan Waldeck, TE
**LA VERNE**
82—Scott Shier, OT
**LAFAYETTE**
70—William Sprecher, T
74—Mike Kline, DB
79—Ed Rogusky, RB

80—Ed Rogusky, RB
**LAWRENCE**
81—Chris Matheus, DL
    Scott Reppert, RB
82—Chris Matheus, DL
**LEHIGH**
90—Shon Harker, DB
**LEWIS & CLARK**
61—Pat Clock, G
81—Dan Jones, WR
**LIU-C.W. POST**
70—Art Canario, T
75—Frank Prochilo, RB
84—Bob Jahelka, DB
**LONG BEACH ST.**
83—Joe Donohue, LB
**LORAS**
84—John Coyle, DL
    Pete Kovatsis, DB
85—John Coyle, DL
91—Mark Goedken, DL
**LOUISIANA ST.**
59—Mickey Mangham, E
60—Charles Strange, C
61—Billy Booth, T
71—Jay Michaelson, KS
73—Tyler Lafauci, OG
    Joe Winkler, DB
74—Brad Davis, RB
77—Robert Dugas, OT
84—Juan Carlos Betanzos, PK
**LUTHER**
83—Larry Bonney, DL
84—Larry Bonney, DL
89—Larry Anderson, RB
90—Joel Nerem, DL
91—Joel Nerem, DL
**LYCOMING**
74—Thomas Vanaskie, DB
85—Mike Kern, DL
**MACALESTER**
82—Lee Schaefer, OG
**MANKATO ST.**
74—Dan Miller, C
**MANSFIELD**
83—John Delate, DB
**MARIETTA**
83—Matt Wurtzbacher, DL
**MARS HILL**
92—Brent Taylor, DL
**MARYLAND**
53—Bernie Faloney, B
75—Kim Hoover, DE
78—Joe Muffler, DL
**MASS.-LOWELL**
85—Don Williams, RB
**McGILL**
87—Bruno Pietrobon, WR
**McNEESE ST.**
78—Jim Downing, OT
79—Jim Downing, OT
90—David Easterling, DB
**MEMPHIS ST.**
92—Pat Jansen, DL
**MIAMI (FLA.)**
59—Fran Curci, B
84—Bernie Kosar, QB
**MIAMI (OHIO)**
73—Andy Pederzolli, DB

**MICHIGAN**
52—Dick Balzhiser, B
55—Jim Orwig, T
57—Jim Orwig, T
64—Bob Timberlake, QB
66—Dave Fisher, FB
    Dick Vidmer, FB
69—Jim Mandich, OE
70—Phil Seymour, DE
71—Bruce Elliott, DB
72—Bill Hart, OG
74—Kirk Lewis, OG
75—Dan Jilek, DE
81—Norm Betts, TE
82—Stefan Humphries, OG
    Robert Thompson, LB
83—Stefan Humphries, OG
85—Clay Miller, OT
86—Kenneth Higgins, WR
**MICHIGAN ST.**
52—John Wilson, DB
53—Don Dohoney, E
55—Buck Nystrom, G
57—Blanche Martin, HB
65—Don Bierowicz, DT
    Don Japinga, DB
66—Pat Gallinagh, DT
68—Al Brenner, E/DB
69—Ron Saul, OG
    Rich Saul, DE
73—John Shinsky, DT
79—Alan Davis, DB
85—Dean Altobelli, DB
86—Dean Altobelli, DB
86—Shane Bullough, LB
92—Steve Wasylk, DB
**MICHIGAN TECH**
71—Larry Ras, HB
73—Bruce Trusock, C
76—Jim Van Wagner, RB
92—Kurt Coduti, QB
**MILLERSVILLE**
91—Tom Burns, OL
**MILLIKIN**
61—Gerald Domesick, B
75—Frank Stone, G
78—Charlie Sammis, K
79—Eric Stevens, WR
83—Marc Knowles, WR
84—Tom Kreller, RB
85—Cary Bottorff, LB
    Tom Kreller, RB
90—Tim Eimermann, PK
**MINNESOTA**
56—Bob Hobert, T
60—Frank Brixius, T
68—Bob Stein, DE
70—Barry Mayer, RB
89—Brent Herbel, P
**MISSISSIPPI**
54—Harold Easterwood, C
59—Robert Khayat, T
    Charlie Flowers, B
61—Doug Elmore, B
65—Stan Hindman, G
68—Steve Hindman, HB
69—Julius Fagan, K
74—Greg Markow, DE
77—Robert Fabris, OE
    George Plasketes, DE
80—Ken Toler, WR
86—Danny Hoskins, OG
87—Danny Hoskins, OG
88—Wesley Walls, TE

89—Todd Sandroni, DB
**MISSISSIPPI COL.**
75—Anthony Saway, S
78—Steve Johnson, OT
79—Steve Johnson, OT
83—Wayne Frazier, C
**MISSISSIPPI ST.**
53—Jackie Parker, B
56—Ron Bennett, E
72—Frank Dowsing, DB
73—Jimmy Webb, DE
76—Will Coltharp, DE
89—Stacy Russell, DB
**MISSOURI**
62—Tom Hertz, G
66—Dan Schuppan, DE
    Bill Powell, DT
68—Carl Garber, MG
70—John Weisenfels, LB
72—Greg Hill, KS
81—Van Darkow, LB
**MISSOURI-ROLLA**
72—Kim Colter, DB
80—Paul Janke, OG
86—Tom Reed, RB
87—Jim Pfeiffer, OT
88—Jim Pfeiffer, OL
91—Don Huff, DB
92—Don Huff, DB
**MIT**
89—Anthony Lapes, WR
90—Darcy Prather, LB
91—Rodrigo Rubiano, DL
92—Roderick Tranum, WR
**MO. SOUTHERN ST.**
85—Mike Testman, DB
**MONMOUTH (ILL.)**
83—Robb Long, QB
**MONTANA**
77—Steve Fisher, DE
79—Ed Cerkovnik, DB
88—Michael McGowan, LB
89—Michael McGowan, LB
90—Michael McGowan, LB
**MONTANA ST.**
84—Dirk Nelson, P
88—Anders Larsson, PK
**MONTCLAIR ST.**
70—Bill Trimmer, DL
82—Daniel Deneher, KS
**MOORHEAD ST.**
88—Brad Shamla, DL
**MORAVIAN**
87—Jeff Pollock, WR
**MOREHEAD ST.**
74—Don Russell, KS
90—James Appel, OL
91—James Appel, OL
**MOUNT UNION**
71—Dennis Montgomery, QB
84—Rick Marabito, L
86—Scott Gindlesberger, QB
87—Paul Hrics, C
**MUHLENBERG**
70—Edward Salo, G
71—Edward Salo, IL
72—Edward Salo, C
75—Keith Ordemann, LB
80—Arthur Scavone, OT
89—Joe Zeszotarski, DL
90—Mike Hoffman, DB

*Academic All-Americans by School*            

**MURRAY ST.**
76—Eddie McFarland, DB
**MUSKINGUM**
78—Dan Radalia, DL
79—Dan Radalia, DL
**NAVY**
53—Steve Eisenhauer, G
57—Tom Forrestal, QB
58—Joe Tranchini, B
69—Dan Pike, RB
80—Ted Dumbauld, LB
**NEB.-KEARNEY**
70—John Makovicka, RB
75—Tim Brodahl, E
**NEB. WESLEYAN**
87—Pat Sweeney, DB
88—Pat Sweeney, DB
Mike Surls, LB
89—Scott Shaffer, RB
Scott Shipman, DB
**NEBRASKA**
62—James Huge, E
63—Dennis Calridge, B
66—Marv Mueller, DB
69—Randy Reeves, DB
71—Larry Jacobson, DT
Jeff Kinney, HB
73—Frosty Anderson, E
75—Rik Bonness, C
Tom Heiser, RB
76—Vince Ferragamo, QB
Ted Harvey, DB
77—Ted Harvey, DB
78—George Andrews, DL
James Pillen, DB
79—Rod Horn, DL
Kelly Saalfeld, C
Randy Schleusener, OG
80—Jeff Finn, TE
Randy Schleusener, OG
81—Eric Lindquist, DB
David Rimington, C
Randy Theiss, OT
82—David Rimington, C
83—Scott Strasburger, DL
Rob Stuckey, DL
84—Scott Strasburger, DL
Rob Stuckey, DL
Mark Traynowicz, C
86—Dale Klein, K
Thomas Welter, OT
87—Jeffrey Jamrog, DL
Mark Blazek, DB
88—Mark Blazek, DB
John Kroeger, P
89—Gerry Gdowski, QB
Jake Young, OL
90—David Edeal, OL
Pat Tyrance, LB
Jim Wanek, OL
91—Pat Engelbert, DL
Mike Stigge, P
92—Mike Stigge, P
**NEBRASKA-OMAHA**
82—Kirk Hutton, DB
Clark Toner, LB
83—Kirk Hutton, DB
84—Jerry Kripal, QB
**NEVADA**
82—David Heppe, P
**NEW HAMPSHIRE**
52—John Driscoll, T
84—Dave Morton, OL

**NEW MEXICO**
75—Bob Johnson, S
77—Robert Rumbaugh, DT
78—Robert Rumbaugh, DL
**NEW MEXICO ST.**
66—Jim Bohl, B
74—Ralph Jackson, OG
75—Ralph Jackson, OG
85—Andy Weiler, KS
92—Todd Cutler, TE
Shane Hackney, OL
Tim Mauck, LB
**NICHOLS**
89—David Kane, DB
**NORTH CARO.**
64—Ken Willard, QB
85—Kevin Anthony, QB
**NORTH CARO. ST.**
60—Roman Gabriel, QB
63—Joe Scarpati, B
67—Steve Warren, OT
71—Craig John, OG
73—Justus Everett, C
Stan Fritts, RB
74—Justus Everett, C
80—Calvin Warren, P
**NORTH DAK.**
87—Kurt Otto, QB
88—Chuck Clairmont, OL
Matt Gulseth, DB
92—Tim Gelinske, WR
Mark Ewen, LB
**NORTH DAK. ST.**
71—Tomm Smail, DT
**NORTH PARK**
83—Mike Lilgegren, DB
85—Scott Love, WR
86—Todd Love, WR
87—Todd Love, WR
**NORTH TEXAS**
75—Pete Morris, LB
76—Pete Morris, LB
**NORTHEAST LA.**
70—Tom Miller, KS
74—Mike Bialas, T
**NORTHEAST MO. ST.**
73—Tom Roberts, T
78—Keith Driscoll, LB
79—Keith Driscoll, LB
92—K. C. Conaway, P
**NORTHEASTERN**
85—Shawn O'Malley, LB
**NORTHERN ARIZ.**
89—Chris Baniszewski, WR
**NORTHERN COLO.**
71—Charles Putnik, OG
81—Duane Hirsch, DL
Ray Sperger, DB
82—Jim Bright, RB
89—Mike Yonkovich, DL
Tom Langer, LB
90—Tom Langer, LB
**NORTHERN MICH.**
83—Bob Stefanski, WR
**NORTHWEST MO. ST.**
81—Robert "Chip" Gregory, LB
**NORTHWESTERN**
56—Al Viola, G
58—Andy Cvercko, T
61—Larry Onesti, C

62—Paul Flatley, B
63—George Burman, E
70—Joe Zigulich, OG
76—Randolph Dean, E
80—Jim Ford, OT
86—Michael Baum, OT
Bob Dirkes, DL
Todd Krehbiel, DB
87—Mike Baum, OL
88—Mike Baum, OL
90—Ira Adler, PK
**NORTHWESTERN (LA.)**
92—Guy Hedrick, RB
**NORWICH**
70—Gary Fry, RB
**NOTRE DAME**
52—Joe Heap, B
53—Joe Heap, B
54—Joe Heap, B
55—Don Schaefer, B
58—Bob Wetoska, E
63—Bob Lehmann, G
66—Tom Regner, OG
Jim Lynch, LB
67—Jim Smithberger, DB
68—George Kunz, OT
69—Jim Reilly, OT
70—Tom Gatewood, E
Larry DiNardo, OG
Joe Theismann, QB
71—Greg Marx, DT
Tom Gatewood, E
72—Michael Creaney, E
Greg Marx, OT
73—David Casper, E
Gary Potempa, LB
Robert Thomas, KS
74—Reggie Barnett, DB
Pete Demmerle, E
77—Ken MacAfee, E
Joe Restic, S
Dave Vinson, OG
78—Joe Restic, DB
80—Bob Burger, OG
Tom Gibbons, DB
81—John Krimm, DB
85—Greg Dingens, DL
87—Ted Gradel, PK
Vince Phelan, P
92—Tim Ruddy, OL
**N'WESTERN (IOWA)**
83—Mark Muilenberg, RB
92—Joel Bundt, C
**N'WESTERN (OKLA.)**
61—Stewart Arthurs, B
**OCCIDENTAL**
88—Curtis Page, DL
**OHIO**
71—John Rousch, HB
**OHIO NORTHERN**
76—Jeff McFarlin, S
79—Robert Coll, WR
86—David Myers, DL
90—Chad Hummell, OL
**OHIO ST.**
52—John Borton, B
54—Dick Hilinski, T
58—Bob White, B
61—Tom Perdue, E
65—Bill Ridder, MG
66—Dave Foley, OT
68—Dave Foley, OT

Mark Stier, LB
69 — Bill Urbanik, DT
71 — Rick Simon, OG
73 — Randy Gradishar, LB
74 — Brian Baschnagel, RB
75 — Brian Baschnagel, RB
76 — Pete Johnson, RB
Bill Lukens, OG
77 — Jeff Logan, RB
80 — Marcus Marek, LB
82 — John Frank, TE
Joseph Smith, OT
83 — John Frank, TE
84 — David Crecelius, DL
Michael Lanese, WR
85 — Michael Lanese, WR
89 — Joseph Staysniak, OL
92 — Leonard Hartman, OL
Gregory Smith, DL

**OHIO WESLEYAN**
70 — Tony Heald, LB
Tom Liller, E
81 — Ric Kinnan, WR
85 — Kevin Connell, OG

**OKLAHOMA**
52 — Tom Catlin, C
54 — Carl Allison, E
56 — Jerry Tubbs, C
57 — Doyle Jenning, T
58 — Ross Coyle, E
62 — Wayne Lee, C
63 — Newt Burton, G
64 — Newt Burton, G
66 — Ron Shotts, HB
67 — Ron Shotts, HB
68 — Eddie Hinton, DB
70 — Joe Wylie, RB
71 — Jack Mildren, QB
72 — Joe Wylie, RB
74 — Randy Hughes, S
75 — Dewey Selmon, LB
Lee Roy Selmon, DT
80 — Jay Jimerson, DB
86 — Brian Bosworth, LB

**OKLAHOMA ST.**
54 — Dale Meinert, G
72 — Tom Wolf, OT
73 — Doug Tarrant, LB
74 — Tom Wolf, OT
77 — Joe Avanzini, DE

**OREGON**
62 — Steve Barnett, T
65 — Tim Casey, LB
86 — Mike Preacher, P
90 — Bill Musgrave, QB

**OREGON ST.**
62 — Terry Baker, B
67 — Bill Enyart, FB
68 — Bill Enyart, FB

**OUACHITA BAPTIST**
78 — David Cowling, OG

**PACIFIC (CAL.)**
78 — Bruce Filarsky, OG
79 — Bruce Filarsky, DL

**PACIFIC LUTHERAN**
82 — Curt Rodin, TE

**PANHANDLE ST.**
76 — Larry Johnson, G

**PENN ST.**
65 — Joe Bellas, T
John Runnells, LB
66 — John Runnells, LB

67 — Rich Buzin, OT
69 — Charlie Pittman, HB
Dennis Onkotz, LB
71 — Dave Joyner, OT
72 — Bruce Bannon, DE
73 — Mark Markovich, OG
76 — Chuck Benjamin, OT
78 — Keith Dorney, OT
82 — Todd Blackledge, QB
Harry Hamilton, DB
Scott Radicec, LB
83 — Harry Hamilton, LB
84 — Lance Hamilton, DB
Carmen Masciantonio, LB
85 — Lance Hamilton, DB
86 — John Shaffer, QB

**PENNSYLVANIA**
86 — Rich Comizio, RB

**PITTSBURG ST.**
72 — Jay Sperry, RB
89 — Brett Potts, DL
91 — Mike Brockel, OL
92 — Mike Brockel, OL

**PITTSBURGH**
52 — Dick Deitrick, DT
54 — Lou Palatella, T
56 — Joe Walton, E
58 — John Guzik, G
76 — Jeff Delaney, LB
80 — Greg Meisner, DL
81 — Rob Fada, OG
82 — Rob Fada, OG
J. C. Pelusi, DL
88 — Mark Stepnoski, OL

**PORTLAND ST.**
72 — Bill Dials, T
77 — John Urness, WR
78 — John Urness, WR

**PRINCETON**
68 — Dick Sandler, DT
76 — Kevin Fox, OG
82 — Kevin Guthrie, WR
83 — Kevin Guthrie, WR

**PUGET SOUND**
82 — Buster Crook, DB

**PURDUE**
56 — Len Dawson, QB
60 — Jerry Beabout, T
65 — Sal Ciampi, G
67 — Jim Beirne, E
Lance Olssen, DT
68 — Tim Foley, DB
69 — Tim Foley, DB
Mike Phipps, QB
Bill Yanchar, DT
73 — Bob Hoftiezer, DE
79 — Ken Loushin, G
80 — Tim Seneff, DB
81 — Tim Seneff, DB
89 — Bruce Brineman, OL

**RHODE ISLAND**
76 — Richard Moser, RB
77 — Richard Moser, RB

**RHODES**
90 — Robert Heck, DL

**RICE**
52 — Richard Chapman, DG
53 — Richard Chapman, DG
54 — Dicky Maegle, B
69 — Steve Bradshaw, DG
79 — LaMont Jefferson, LB
83 — Brian Patterson, DB

**ROCHESTER**
82 — Bob Cordaro, LB
92 — Jeremy Hurd, RB

**ROSE-HULMAN**
78 — Rick Matovich, DL
79 — Scott Lindner, DL
80 — Scott Lindner, DL
Jim Novacek, P
83 — Jack Grote, LB
84 — Jack Grote, LB
88 — Greg Kremer, LB
Shawn Ferron, PK
89 — Shawn Ferron, PK
90 — Ed Huonden, WR
92 — Greg Hubbard, OL

**SAM HOUSTON ST.**
72 — Walter Anderson, KS
73 — Walter Anderson, KS

**SAN DIEGO**
87 — Bryan Day, DB
88 — Bryan Day, DB

**SAN JOSE ST.**
75 — Tim Toews, OG

**SANTA CLARA**
71 — Ron Sani, IL
73 — Alex Damascus, RB
74 — Steve Lagorio, LB
75 — Mark Tiernan, LB
76 — Lou Marengo, KS
Mark Tiernan, LB
80 — Dave Alfaro, QB

**SHIPPENSBURG**
76 — Tony Winter, LB
82 — Dave Butler, DL

**SOUTH CARO.**
87 — Mark Fryer, OL
88 — Mark Fryer, OL
91 — Joe Reeves, LB

**SOUTH DAK.**
78 — Scott Pollock, QB
82 — Jerus Campbell, DL
83 — Jeff Sime, T
87 — Dan Sonnek, RB

**SOUTH DAK. ST.**
74 — Bob Gissler, E
75 — Bill Matthews, T
77 — Bill Matthews, DE
79 — Tony Harris, PK
Paul Kippley, DB

**SOUTHERN CAL**
52 — Dick Nunis, DB
59 — Mike McKeever, G
60 — Mike McKeever, G
Marlin McKeever, E
65 — Charles Arrobio, T
67 — Steve Sogge, QB
68 — Steve Sogge, QB
69 — Harry Khasigian, OG
73 — Pat Haden, QB
74 — Pat Haden, QB
78 — Rich Dimler, DL
79 — Brad Budde, OG
Paul McDonald, QB
Keith Van Horne, T
84 — Duane Bickett, LB
85 — Matt Koart, DL
86 — Jeffrey Bregel, OG
88 — John Jackson, WR
89 — John Jackson, WR

**SOUTHERN COLO.**
83 — Dan DeRose, LB

**SOUTHERN CONN. ST.**
84—Gerald Carbonaro, OL
**SOUTHERN ILL.**
70—Sam Finocchio, G
88—Charles Harmke, RB
91—Dwayne Summers, DL
Jon Manley, LB
**SOUTHERN METHODIST**
52—Dave Powell, E
53—Darrell Lafitte, G
54—Raymond Berry, E
55—David Hawk, G
57—Tom Koenig, G
58—Tom Koenig, G
62—Raymond Schoenke, T
66—John LaGrone, MG
Lynn Thornhill, OG
68—Jerry LeVias, OE
72—Cleve Whitener, LB
83—Brian O'Meara, T
**SOUTHERN MISS.**
92—James Singleton, DL
**SOUTHERN UTAH**
88—Jim Andrus, RB
90—Steve McDowell, P
**SOUTHWEST MO. ST.**
73—Kent Stringer, QB
75—Kent Stringer, QB
78—Steve Newbold, WR
**SOUTHWEST ST.**
88—Bruce Saugstad, DB
**SOUTHWEST TEX. ST.**
72—Jimmy Jowers, LB
73—Jimmy Jowers, LB
78—Mike Ferris, OG
79—Mike Ferris, G
Allen Kiesling, DL
81—Mike Miller, QB
**SPRINGFIELD**
71—Bruce Rupert, LB
84—Sean Flanders, DL
85—Sean Flanders, DL
**ST. CLOUD ST.**
88—Rick Rodgers, DB
89—Rick Rodgers, DB
**ST. JOHN'S (MINN.)**
72—Jim Kruzich, E
79—Terry Geraghty, DB
**ST. JOSEPH'S (IND.)**
77—Mike Bettinger, DB
78—Mike Bettinger, DB
79—Mike Bettinger, DB
85—Ralph Laura, OT
88—Keith Woodason, OL
89—Jeff Fairchild, P
**ST. NORBERT**
86—Matthew Lang, LB
Karl Zacharias, P
87—Karl Zacharias, PK
Matthew Lang, LB
88—Mike Whitehouse, WR
89—Mike Whitehouse, WR
**ST. OLAF**
61—Dave Hindermann, T
**ST. THOMAS (MINN.)**
73—Mark Dienhart, T
74—Mark Dienhart, T
77—Tom Kelly, OG
80—Doug Groebner, C
**STANFORD**
70—John Sande, C

Terry Ewing, DB
75—Don Stevenson, RB
76—Don Stevenson, RB
77—Guy Benjamin, QB
78—Vince Mulroy, WR
Jim Stephens, OG
79—Pat Bowe, TE
Milt McColl, LB
Joe St. Geme, DB
81—John Bergren, DL
Darrin Nelson, RB
82—John Bergren, DL
83—John Bergren, DL
85—Matt Soderlund, LB
87—Brad Muster, RB
90—Ed McCaffrey, WR
91—Tommy Vardell, RB
**SUL ROSS ST.**
73—Archie Nexon, RB
**SUSQUEHANNA**
75—Gerry Huesken, T
76—Gerry Huesken, T
80—Dan Distasio, LB
**SYRACUSE**
60—Fred Mautino, E
71—Howard Goodman, LB
83—Tony Romano, LB
84—Tim Green, DL
85—Tim Green, DL
**TARLETON ST.**
81—Ricky Bush, RB
90—Mike Loveless, OL
**TENN.-MARTIN**
74—Randy West, E
**TENNESSEE**
56—Charles Rader, T
57—Bill Johnson, G
65—Mack Gentry, DT
67—Bob Johnson, C
70—Tim Priest, DB
80—Timothy Irwin, OT
82—Mike Terry, DL
**TENNESSEE TECH**
87—Andy Rittenhouse, DL
**TEXAS**
59—Maurice Doke, G
61—Johnny Treadwell, G
62—Johnny Treadwell, G
Pat Culpepper, B
63—Duke Carlisle, B
66—Gene Bledsoe, OT
67—Mike Perrin, DE
Corby Robertson, LB
68—Corby Robertson, LB
Scott Henderson, LB
69—Scott Henderson, LB
Bill Zapalac, DE
70—Bill Zapalac, LB
Scott Henderson, LB
72—Mike Bayer, DB
Tommy Keel, S
Steve Oxley, T
73—Tommy Keel, S
83—Doug Dawson, G
88—Lee Brockman, DL
**TEXAS A&I**
72—Floyd Goodwin, T
73—Johnny Jackson, E
76—Wade Whitmer, DL
77—Joe Henke, LB
Wade Whitmer, DL
78—Wade Whitmer, DL

**TEXAS A&M**
56—Jack Pardee, B
71—Steve Luebbehusen, LB
76—Kevin Monk, LB
77—Kevin Monk, LB
85—Kip Corrington, DB
86—Kip Corrington, DB
87—Kip Corrington, DB
**TEXAS CHRISTIAN**
52—Marshall Harris, T
55—Hugh Pitts, C
Jim Swink, B
56—Jim Swink, B
57—John Nikkel, E
68—Jim Ray, G
72—Scott Walker, C
74—Terry Drennan, DB
80—John McClean, DL
**TEXAS TECH**
72—Jeff Jobe, E
79—Maury Buford, P
83—Chuck Alexander, DB
**TOLEDO**
83—Michael Matz, DL
**TRINITY (TEX.)**
92—Jeff Bryan, OL
**TUFTS**
70—Bruce Zinsmeister, DL
81—Brian Gallagher, OG
83—Richard Guiunta, G
**TULANE**
71—David Hebert, DB
**TULSA**
64—Howard Twilley, E
65—Howard Twilley, E
74—Mack Lancaster, T
**UC DAVIS**
72—Steve Algeo, LB
75—Dave Gellerman, LB
90—Mike Shepard, DL
**UC RIVERSIDE**
71—Tyrone Hooks, HB
**UCLA**
52—Ed Flynn, G
Donn Moomaw, LB
53—Ira Pauly, C
54—Sam Boghosian, G
66—Ray Armstrong, E
75—John Sciarra, QB
77—John Fowler, LB
81—Cormac Carney, WR
Tim Wrightman, TE
82—Cormac Carney, WR
85—Mike Hartmeier, OG
92—Carlton Gray, DB
**UNION (N.Y.)**
71—Tom Anacher, LB
73—Dave Ricks, DB
87—Richard Romer, DL
**URSINUS**
86—Chuck Odgers, DB
87—Chuck Odgers, LB
**UTAH**
64—Mel Carpenter, T
71—Scott Robbins, DB
73—Steve Odom, RB
76—Dick Graham, E
**UTAH ST.**
61—Merlin Olsen, T
69—Gary Anderson, LB
74—Randy Stockham, DE

75—Randy Stockham, DE
**UTEP**
88—Pat Hegarty, QB
**VA. MILITARY**
78—Craig Jones, PK
79—Craig Jones, PK
84—David Twillie, OL
86—Dan Young, DL
88—Anthony McIntosh, DB
**VANDERBILT**
58—Don Donnell, C
68—Jim Burns, DB
74—Doug Martin, E
75—Damon Regen, LB
77—Greg Martin, K
83—Phil Roach, WR
**VILLANOVA**
86—Ron Sency, RB
88—Peter Lombardi, RB
92—Tim Matas, DL
**VIRGINIA**
72—Tom Kennedy, OG
75—Bob Meade, DT
92—Tom Burns, LB
**VIRGINIA TECH**
67—Frank Loria, DB
72—Tommy Carpenito, LB
**WABASH**
70—Roscoe Fouts, DB
71—Kendrick Shelburne, DT
82—Dave Broecker, QB
**WARTBURG**
75—James Charles Peterson, DB
76—Randy Groth, DB
77—Neil Mandsager, LB
90—Jerrod Staack, OL
**WASH. & JEFF.**
92—Raymond Cross, DL
**WASH. & LEE**
75—John Cocklereece, DB
78—George Ballantyne, LB
92—Evans Edwards, OL
**WASHINGTON**
55—Jim Houston, E
63—Mike Briggs, T
64—Rick Redman, G
65—Steve Bramwell, DB
79—Bruce Harrell, LB
81—Mark Jerue, LB
Chuck Nelson, PK
82—Chuck Nelson, PK
86—David Rill, LB
87—David Rill, LB
91—Ed Cunningham, OL
**WASHINGTON ST.**
89—Jason Hanson, PK
90—Lee Tilleman, DL
Jason Hanson, PK
91—Jason Hanson, PK
**WAYNE ST. (MICH.)**
71—Gary Schultz, DB

72—Walt Stasinski, DB
**WAYNESBURG**
77—John Culp, RB
78—John Culp, RB
89—Andrew Barrish, OL
90—Andrew Barrish, OL
91—Karl Petrof, OL
**WEST CHESTER**
83—Eric Wentling, K
86—Gerald Desmond, K
**WEST VA.**
52—Paul Bischoff, E
54—Fred Wyant, B
55—Sam Huff, T
70—Kim West, K
80—Oliver Luck, QB
81—Oliver Luck, QB
83—Jeff Hostetler, QB
92—Mike Compton, OL
**WESTERN CARO.**
75—Mike Wade, E
76—Mike Wade, LB
84—Eddie Maddox, RB
**WESTERN ILL.**
61—Jerry Blew, G
85—Jeff McKinney, RB
91—David Fierke, OL
**WESTERN KY.**
71—James Barber, LB
81—Tim Ford, DL
84—Mark Fatkin, OL
85—Mark Fatkin, OG
**WESTERN MD.**
73—Chip Chaney, S
**WESTERN MICH.**
70—Jon Bull, OT
**WESTERN OREGON**
61—Francis Tresler, C
**WESTERN ST.**
78—Bill Campbell, DB
88—Damon Lockhart, RB
**WESTMINSTER (PA.)**
73—Bob Clark, G
77—Scott McLuckey, LB
**WHEATON (ILL.)**
73—Bill Hyer, E
75—Eugene Campbell, RB
76—Eugene Campbell, RB
88—Paul Sternenberg, DL
92—Bart Moseman, DB
**WHITTIER**
86—Brent Kane, DL
**WILKES**
70—Al Kenney, C
**WILLAMETTE**
61—Stuart Hall
**WILLIAM & MARY**
74—John Gerdelman, RB
75—Ken Smith, DB
77—Ken Smith, DB
78—Robert Muscalus, TE

84—Mark Kelso, DB
88—Chris Gessner, DB
90—Jeff Nielsen, LB
**WIS.-EAU CLAIRE**
74—Mark Anderson, RB
80—Mike Zeihen, DB
**WIS.-PLATTEVILLE**
85—Mark Hintz, DB
Mark Rae, P
86—Mike Hintz, QB
87—Mark Rae, P
**WIS.-RIVER FALLS**
91—Mike Olson, LB
**WISCONSIN**
52—Bob Kennedy, DG
53—Alan Ameche, B
54—Alan Ameche, B
58—Jon Hobbs, B
59—Dale Hackbart, B
62—Pat Richter, E
63—Ken Bowman, C
72—Rufus Ferguson, RB
82—Kyle Borland, LB
87—Don Davey, DL
88—Don Davey, DL
89—Don Davey, DL
90—Don Davey, DL
**WITTENBERG**
80—Bill Beach, DB
81—Bill Beach, DB
82—Tom Jones, OT
88—Paul Kungl, WR
90—Victor Terebuh, DB
**WM. PATERSON**
92—John Trust, RB
**WOOSTER**
73—Dave Foy, LB
77—Blake Moore, C
78—Blake Moore, C
79—Blake Moore, C
80—Dale Fortner, DB
John Weisensell, OG
**WYOMING**
65—Bob Dinges, DE
67—George Mills, OG
73—Mike Lopiccolo, OT
84—Bob Gustafson, OT
87—Patrick Arndt, OG
**YALE**
68—Fred Morris, C
70—Tom Neville, DT
78—William Crowley, LB
81—Rich Diana, RB
Frederick Leone, DL
89—Glover Lawrence, DL
91—Scott Wagner, DB

# COLLEGE FOOTBALL ASSOCIATION SCHOLAR-ATHLETE TEAM

Following are football players acknowledged by the College Football Association for successfully balancing athletics and academics. The team was chosen for the first time in 1991 by a panel that included faculty members, athletics administrators, football coaches, academic advisers and sports information directors. The criteria included a cumulative grade-point average between 3.000 and 4.000 (4.000 scale), standing as at least a junior athletically, completion of 50 percent of degree requirements, completion of at least one year at the nominating institution, and playing time as a starter or significant reserve.

**AIR FORCE**
92—Grant Johnson, LB
**ARKANSAS**
91—Mick Thomas, LB
92—Owen Kelly, DL
**ARMY**
91—Michael McElrath, DB
92—Michael McElrath, DB
**BAYLOR**
92—J. J. Joe, QB
**CINCINNATI**
91—Kris Bjorson, WR
**CLEMSON**
91—Bruce Batton, OL
**COLORADO**
91—James Hansen, OL
92—James Hansen, OL
**COLORADO ST.**
92—Greg Primus, WR
**FLORIDA**
91—Cal Dixon, OL
    Brad Culpepper, DL
**GEORGIA**
92—Alec Millen, OL
**HAWAII**
92—Travis Sims, RB
**KANSAS ST.**
92—Brooks Barta, LB

**KENTUCKY**
91—Greg Lahr, OL
92—Doug Pelfrey, PK
    Dean Wells, LB
**LOUISIANA ST.**
91—Scott Wharton, DL
**LOUISVILLE**
91—Eric Watts, QB
**MEMPHIS ST.**
92—Jeremy Williams, DB
**MIAMI (FLA.)**
91—Carlos Huerta, PK
92—Darrin Smith, LB
    Gino Torretta, QB
**MISSISSIPPI**
91—James Singleton, DL
**MISSISSIPPI ST.**
91—Daniel Boyd, LB
92—Daniel Boyd, LB
**NEBRASKA**
91—Pat Engelbert, DL
    Mike Stigge, P
92—Jim Scott, OL
    Mike Stigge, P
**NEW MEXICO**
92—Justin Hall, OL

**NORTH CARO.**
92—Corey Holliday, WR
**OKLAHOMA ST.**
91—Stacey Satterwhite, DL
**PITTSBURGH**
91—Dave Moore, WR
**RICE**
91—Howard Teichelman, OL
92—Joey Wheeler, LB
**SOUTH CARO.**
91—Joe Reaves, LB
**SOUTHERN METHODIST**
91—Cary Brabham, DB
92—Cary Brabham, DB
**SOUTHERN MISS.**
92—James Singleton, DL
**TEMPLE**
91—Tony Schmitz, DB
**VIRGINIA TECH**
91—Will Furrer, QB
**WEST VA.**
91—Alex Shook, WR
92—Mike Compton, OL
**WYOMING**
91—Tom Corontzos, QB

# BOWL/ALL-STAR
## GAME RESULTS

*Alabama defensive back George Teague prances into the end zone with a 31-yard interception return that gave the Crimson Tide a 27-6 third-quarter lead and virtually sealed its victory over Miami (Florida) in the Sugar Bowl to claim last season's mythical national*

# 1993-94 BOWL SCHEDULE

**(All starting times Eastern)**

**ALAMO BOWL**
December 31, 1993—9 p.m.
Alamodome (cap. 65,000)
San Antonio, Texas
Televising Network: Raycom

**FEDERAL EXPRESS ORANGE BOWL**
January 1, 1994—8 p.m.
Orange Bowl Stadium (cap. 74,712)
Miami, Florida
Televising Network: NBC

**COMPUSA FLORIDA CITRUS BOWL**
January 1, 1994—1 p.m.
Florida Citrus Bowl—Orange County
    Stadium (cap. 70,000)
Orlando, Florida
Televising Network: ABC

**FREEDOM BOWL**
December 30, 1993—9 p.m.
Anaheim Stadium (cap. 70,962)
Anaheim, California
Televising Network: Raycom

**HALL OF FAME BOWL**
January 1, 1994—11 a.m.
Tampa Stadium (cap. 74,350)
Tampa, Florida
Televising Network: ESPN

**IBM OS/2 FIESTA BOWL**
January 1, 1994—4:30 p.m.
Sun Devil Stadium (cap. 74,783)
Tempe, Arizona
Televising Network: NBC

**JEEP EAGLE ALOHA BOWL**
December 25, 1993—3:30 p.m.
Aloha Stadium (cap. 50,000)
Honolulu, Hawaii
Televising Network: ABC

**JOHN HANCOCK BOWL**
December 30, 1993—2:30 p.m.
Sun Bowl Stadium (cap. 51,270)
El Paso, Texas
Televising Network: CBS

**LAS VEGAS BOWL**
December 17, 1993—9 p.m.
Sam Boyd Silver Bowl (cap. 31,000)
Las Vegas, Nevada
Televising Network: ESPN

**MOBIL COTTON BOWL**
January 1, 1994—1 p.m.
Cotton Bowl (cap. 71,615)
Dallas, Texas
Televising Network: NBC

**OUTBACK STEAKHOUSE GATOR BOWL**
December 31, 1993—6:30 p.m.
Gator Bowl (cap. 80,129)
Jacksonville, Florida
Televising Network: TBS

**PEACH BOWL**
December 31, 1993—7:30 p.m.
Georgia Dome (cap. 71,596)
Atlanta, Georgia
Televising Network: ESPN

**POULAN/WEED EATER
INDEPENDENCE BOWL**
December 31, 1993—12:30 p.m.
Independence Stadium (cap. 50,459)
Shreveport, Louisiana
Televising Network: ESPN

**ROSE BOWL**
January 1, 1994—5 p.m.
Rose Bowl (cap. 99,563)
Pasadena, California
Televising Network: ABC

**ST. JUDE LIBERTY BOWL**
December 28, 1993—8 p.m.
Liberty Bowl Stadium (cap. 62,425)
Memphis, Tennessee
Televising Network: ESPN

**SUNSHINE FOOTBALL CLASSIC**
January 1, 1994—1:30 p.m.
Joe Robbie Stadium (cap. 73,000)
Miami, Florida
Televising Network: CBS

**THRIFTY CAR RENTAL HOLIDAY BOWL**
December 30, 1993—7:30 or 8 p.m.
San Diego Jack Murphy Stadium
    (cap. 62,809)
San Diego, California
Televising Network: ESPN

**USF&G SUGAR BOWL**
January 1, 1994—8:30 p.m.
Louisiana Superdome (cap. 72,704)
New Orleans, Louisiana
Televising Network: ABC

**WEISER LOCK COPPER BOWL**
December 29, 1993—9:30 p.m.
Arizona Stadium (cap. 58,000)
Tucson, Arizona
Televising Network: ESPN

# 1992-93 BOWL RESULTS

## GAME-BY-GAME SCORES

| Bowl | Date | Score | Attendance |
|---|---|---|---|
| Las Vegas | Dec. 18 | Bowling Green 35, Nevada 34 | 15,476 |
| Jeep Eagle Aloha | Dec. 25 | Kansas 23, Brigham Young 20 | 42,933 |
| Weiser Lock Copper | Dec. 29 | Washington St. 31, Utah 28 | 40,876 |
| Freedom | Dec. 29 | Fresno St. 24, Southern Cal 7 | 50,745 |
| Thrifty Car Rental Holiday | Dec. 30 | Hawaii 27, Illinois 17 | 44,457 |
| Poulan/Weed Eater Independence | Dec. 31 | Wake Forest 39, Oregon 35 | 31,337 |
| John Hancock | Dec. 31 | Baylor 20, Arizona 15 | 41,622 |
| Outback Steakhouse Gator | Dec. 31 | Florida 27, North Caro. St. 10 | 71,233 |
| Liberty | Dec. 31 | Mississippi 13, Air Force 0 | 32,107 |
| Hall of Fame | Jan. 1 | Tennessee 38, Boston College 23 | 52,056 |
| Florida Citrus | Jan. 1 | Georgia 21, Ohio St. 14 | 65,861 |
| Mobil Cotton | Jan. 1 | Notre Dame 28, Texas A&M 3 | 71,615 |
| Blockbuster | Jan. 1 | Stanford 24, Penn St. 3 | 45,554 |
| Fiesta | Jan. 1 | Syracuse 26, Colorado 22 | 70,224 |
| Rose | Jan. 1 | Michigan 38, Washington 31 | 94,236 |
| Federal Express Orange | Jan. 1 | Florida St. 27, Nebraska 14 | 57,324 |
| USF&G Sugar | Jan. 1 | Alabama 34, Miami (Fla.) 13 | 76,789 |
| Peach | Jan. 2 | North Caro. 21, Mississippi St. 17 | 69,125 |
| **Other All-Star Games:** | | | |
| Kelly Tire Blue-Gray | Dec. 25 | Gray 27, Blue 17 (Montgomery, Ala.) | 20,500 |
| Japan Bowl | Jan. 10 | East 27, West 13 (Tokyo, Japan) | 46,000 |
| Kodak Hula Bowl | Jan. 16 | West 13, East 10 (Honolulu, Hawaii) | 25,479 |
| Senior Bowl | Jan. 16 | NFC 21, AFC 6 (Mobile, Ala.) | 37,124 |
| East-West Shrine Game | Jan. 24 | East 31, West 17 (Stanford, Calif.) | 84,000 |

**Special Note:** Grambling defeated Florida A&M, 45-15, in the second annual Heritage Bowl on Saturday, Jan. 2, at Bragg Memorial Stadium in Tallahassee, Fla. The game, the second bowl game for the historically black schools, drew 11,273 fans. The game matched the winners of the Southwestern Athletic Conference and the Mid-Eastern Athletic Conference.

## GAME-BY-GAME SUMMARIES

### LAS VEGAS BOWL
**December 18, 1992**
**Las Vegas, Nev.**

**Synopsis:** Erik White completed a two-yard touch-down pass to Dave Hankins on fourth down with 22 seconds remaining, giving Bowling Green a 35-34 triumph over Nevada in the inaugural Las Vegas Bowl.

| | | | | | |
|---|---|---|---|---|---|
| **Nevada** | 3 | 0 | 21 | 10 | —34 |
| **Bowling Green** | 14 | 14 | 0 | 7 | —35 |

BG—Smith 10 pass from White (Leaver kick)
NV—Terelak 30 field goal
BG—Jackson 4 run (Leaver kick)
BG—White 8 pass from Smith (Leaver kick)
BG—Jackson 17 run (Leaver kick)
NV—Senior 5 pass from Vargas (Terelak kick)
NV—Holmes 5 run (Terelak kick)
NV—Matter 3 pass from Vargas (Terelak kick)
NV—Reeves 3 run (Terelak kick)
NV—Terelak 19 field goal
BG—Hankins 3 pass from White (Leaver kick)

#### Game Statistics

| | NV | BG |
|---|---|---|
| First Downs | 21 | 25 |
| Rushes-Yards | 35-94 | 41-157 |
| Passing Yards | 344 | 253 |
| Comp-Att-Int | 29-49-0 | 25-41-0 |
| Punts-Avg | 4-17 | 5-23 |
| Fumbles-Lost | 3-2 | 0-0 |
| Penalties-Yards | 3-10 | 5-56 |
| Time of Possession | 26:25 | 33:35 |

Attendance: 15,476

### JEEP EAGLE ALOHA BOWL
**December 25, 1992**
**Honolulu, Hawaii**

**Synopsis:** Dan Eichloff kicked a 48-yard field goal with 2:57 left and Dana Stubblefield led a furious defensive assault to pace Kansas to a 23-20 victory over Brigham Young in the Aloha Bowl.

| | | | | | |
|---|---|---|---|---|---|
| **Kansas** | 9 | 3 | 0 | 11 | —23 |
| **Brigham Young** | 7 | 7 | 6 | 0 | —20 |

BY—Heimuli 94 kickoff return (Lauder kick)
KS—Harris 74 pass from Gay (Eichloff kick)
KS—Safety, Willis tackled in end zone
BY—Willis 29 run (Lauder kick)
KS—Eichloff 42 field goal
BY—Sterling 10 pass from Young (pass failed)
KS—Hilleary 1 run (Hilleary run)
KS—Eichloff 48 field goal

#### Game Statistics

| | KS | BY |
|---|---|---|
| First Downs | 18 | 19 |
| Rushes-Yards | 49-172 | 32-142 |
| Passing Yards | 200 | 262 |
| Comp-Att-Int | 12-24-0 | 15-31-1 |
| Punts-Avg | 8-48 | 4-48 |
| Fumbles-Lost | 0-0 | 1-0 |
| Penalties-Yards | 7-55 | 7-73 |
| Time of Possession | 33:23 | 26:37 |

Attendance: 42,933

## WEISER LOCK COPPER BOWL
### December 29, 1992
### Tucson, Ariz.

**Synopsis:** Drew Bledsoe passed for a Washington State-record 476 yards and Aaron Price kicked his second game-winning field goal this season at Arizona Stadium as the No. 18 Cougars withstood Utah's second-half comeback for a 31-28 Copper Bowl victory.

| | | | | | |
|---|---|---|---|---|---|
| **Utah** | 0 | 14 | 14 | 0 | —28 |
| **Washington St.** | 21 | 7 | 0 | 3 | —31 |

WS—Wright-Fair 3 run (Price kick)
WS—Bobo 87 pass from Bledsoe (Price kick)
WS—Wright-Fair 3 run (Price kick)
UT—S. Williams 10 pass from Dolce (Yergensen kick)
UT—K. Williams 25 run (Yergensen kick)
WS—Bobo 48 pass from Bledsoe (Price kick)
UT—Lusk 49 pass from Dolce (kick blocked)
UT—Jones 8 run (Murry pass from Dolce)
WS—Price 22 field goal

### Game Statistics

| | UT | WS |
|---|---|---|
| First Downs | 20 | 28 |
| Rushes-Yards | 39-179 | 41-144 |
| Passing Yards | 316 | 492 |
| Comp-Att-Int | 21-40-0 | 32-48-1 |
| Punts-Avg | 6-43 | 6-37 |
| Fumbles-Lost | 3-1 | 4-2 |
| Penalties-Yards | 7-55 | 18-136 |
| Time of Possession | 30:08 | 29:52 |
| Attendance: 40,876 | | |

## FREEDOM BOWL
### December 29, 1992
### Anaheim, Calif.

**Synopsis:** Ron Rivers rushed for 104 yards and a touchdown as Fresno State rattled off 24 unanswered points to post a 24-7 upset victory over Southern California in the Freedom Bowl. The Trojans were held to 183 total yards by the tough Bulldog defense.

| | | | | | |
|---|---|---|---|---|---|
| **Fresno St.** | 0 | 7 | 3 | 14 | —24 |
| **Southern Cal** | 0 | 7 | 0 | 0 | — 7 |

SC—Strother 1 run (Ford kick)
FS—Neal 1 run (Mahoney kick)
FS—Mahoney 43 field goal
FS—Daigle 2 run (Mahoney kick)
FS—Rivers 5 run (Mahoney kick)

### Game Statistics

| | FS | SC |
|---|---|---|
| First Downs | 24 | 14 |
| Rushes-Yards | 56-241 | 32-88 |
| Passing Yards | 164 | 95 |
| Comp-Att-Int | 13-28-0 | 7-18-3 |
| Punts-Avg | 5-40 | 5-43 |
| Fumbles-Lost | 1-0 | 1-1 |
| Penalties-Yards | 9-61 | 7-35 |
| Time of Possession | 37:32 | 22:28 |
| Attendance: 50,745 | | |

## THRIFTY CAR RENTAL HOLIDAY BOWL
### December 30, 1992
### San Diego, Calif.

**Synopsis:** Hawaii's Travis Sims hammered for 113 yards and two touchdowns to lead the Rainbows to a 27-17 victory over Illinois in the Holiday Bowl. It was Illinois' third consecutive bowl loss.

| | | | | | |
|---|---|---|---|---|---|
| **Illinois** | 7 | 3 | 0 | 7 | —17 |
| **Hawaii** | 0 | 7 | 10 | 10 | —27 |

IL—Wright 14 pass from Verduzco (Richardson kick)
HA—Sims 6 run (Elam kick)
IL—Richardson 19 field goal
HA—Sims 1 run (Elam kick)
HA—Elam 45 field goal
HA—Elam 37 field goal
HA—Branch 53 pass from Carter (Elam kick)
IL—Wright 18 pass from Verduzco (Richardson kick)

### Game Statistics

| | IL | HA |
|---|---|---|
| First Downs | 23 | 23 |
| Rushes-Yards | 32-99 | 59-287 |
| Passing Yards | 248 | 115 |
| Comp-Att-Int | 26-34-1 | 6-17-2 |
| Punts-Avg | 3-46 | 2-41 |
| Fumbles-Lost | 2-1 | 2-0 |
| Penalties-Yards | 3-25 | 3-26 |
| Time of Possession | 27:27 | 32:33 |
| Attendance: 44,457 | | |

## POULAN/WEED EATER INDEPENDENCE BOWL
### December 31, 1992
### Shreveport, La.

**Synopsis:** Wake Forest fought back from a 22-10 half-time deficit behind the passing of Keith West and the receiving of Todd Dixon to defeat Oregon, 39-35, in the Independence Bowl. West hit 15 of 27 passes for 262 yards and Dixon caught five passes for 166 yards and two scores.

| | | | | | |
|---|---|---|---|---|---|
| **Oregon** | 13 | 9 | 7 | 6 | —35 |
| **Wake Forest** | 7 | 3 | 14 | 15 | —39 |

WF—Leach 1 run (Green kick)
OR—Burwell 40 run (Thompson kick)
OR—O'Berry 24 fumble return (pass failed)
WF—Green 38 field goal
OR—Ferry 4 pass from O'Neil (kick failed)
OR—Thompson 48 field goal
OR—Molden 8 interception return (Thompson kick)
WF—Moultrie 1 run (Green kick)
WF—Dixon 30 pass from West (Green kick)
WF—Dixon 61 pass from Jones (Leach pass from West)
WF—Leach 6 run (Green kick)
OR—Harris 10 pass from O'Neil (kick failed)

### Game Statistics

| | OR | WF |
|---|---|---|
| First Downs | 23 | 18 |
| Rushes-Yards | 32-83 | 49-193 |
| Passing Yards | 227 | 323 |
| Comp-Att-Int | 24-41-1 | 16-29-3 |
| Punts-Avg | 7-36 | 4-40 |
| Fumbles-Lost | 0-0 | 3-3 |
| Penalties-Yards | 6-55 | 11-108 |
| Time of Possession | 29:25 | 30:35 |
| Attendance: 31,337 | | |

## JOHN HANCOCK BOWL
### December 31, 1992
### El Paso, Texas

**Synopsis:** Melvin Bonner caught two long touchdown passes as Baylor coach Grant Teaff closed out his career with a 20-15 John Hancock Bowl victory over Arizona. Bonner had five catches for 166 yards and scored on 69- and 61-yard bombs.

| | | | | | |
|---|---|---|---|---|---|
| **Arizona** | 3 | 10 | 0 | 2 | —15 |
| **Baylor** | 0 | 7 | 7 | 6 | —20 |

AR—McLaughlin 22 field goal
AR—Malauulu 7 run (McLaughlin kick)

BA—Bonner 61 pass from Jackson (Weir kick)
AR—McLaughlin 20 field goal
BA—Bonner 69 pass from Joe (Weir kick)
BA—Weir 32 field goal
BA—Weir 35 field goal
AR—Safety, Delaney ran out of end zone

### Game Statistics

|  | AR | BA |
|---|---|---|
| First Downs | 23 | 12 |
| Rushes-Yards | 44-136 | 43-47 |
| Passing Yards | 292 | 202 |
| Comp-Att-Int | 20-30-0 | 8-24-0 |
| Punts-Avg | 5-34 | 6-40 |
| Fumbles-Lost | 2-2 | 4-0 |
| Penalties-Yards | 8-91 | 8-30 |
| Time of Possession | 32:22 | 27:38 |
| Attendance: 41,622 | | |

## OUTBACK STEAKHOUSE GATOR BOWL
### December 31, 1992
### Jacksonville, Fla.

**Synopsis:** Errict Rhett rushed for 182 yards and Shane Matthews passed for two touchdowns and rushed for another as Florida shut down North Carolina State, 27-10, in the Gator Bowl. The Gator defense allowed the Wolfpack only 54 yards rushing.

| North Caro. St. | 0 | 0 | 3 | 7 | —10 |
|---|---|---|---|---|---|
| Florida | 0 | 10 | 10 | 7 | —27 |

FL—Davis 26 field goal
FL—Matthews 1 run (Davis kick)
FL—W. Jackson 17 pass from Matthews (Davis kick)
NC—Videtich 23 field goal
FL—Davis 42 field goal
NC—Shaw 11 pass from Jordan (Videtich kick)
FL—Houston 34 pass from Matthews (Davis kick)

### Game Statistics

|  | NC | FL |
|---|---|---|
| First Downs | 13 | 26 |
| Rushes-Yards | 25-54 | 50-198 |
| Passing Yards | 213 | 247 |
| Comp-Att-Int | 22-42-2 | 19-38-0 |
| Punts-Avg | 11-39 | 5-41 |
| Fumbles-Lost | 2-1 | 3-2 |
| Penalties-Yards | 1-10 | 6-44 |
| Time of Possession | 26:17 | 33:43 |
| Attendance: 71,233 | | |

## LIBERTY BOWL
### December 31, 1992
### Memphis, Tenn.

**Synopsis:** Mississippi held Air Force's vaunted ground attack in check allowing only 104 yards rushing and blanked the Falcons, 13-0, in the Liberty Bowl.

| Mississippi | 7 | 3 | 0 | 3 | —13 |
|---|---|---|---|---|---|
| Air Force | 0 | 0 | 0 | 0 | — 0 |

MS—Innocent 5 run (Lee kick)
MS—Lee 24 field goal
MS—Lee 29 field goal

### Game Statistics

|  | MS | AF |
|---|---|---|
| First Downs | 13 | 13 |
| Rushes-Yards | 42-168 | 47-104 |
| Passing Yards | 163 | 81 |
| Comp-Att-Int | 9-19-0 | 10-17-0 |
| Punts-Avg | 5-20 | 7-33 |
| Fumbles-Lost | 2-1 | 2-1 |

|  | MS | AF |
|---|---|---|
| Penalties-Yards | 7-57 | 6-53 |
| Time of Possession | 27:56 | 32:04 |
| Attendance: 32,107 | | |

## HALL OF FAME BOWL
### January 1, 1993
### Tampa, Fla.

**Synopsis:** Tennessee, playing without long-time coach Johnny Majors, built a 31-7 lead and coasted to a 38-23 victory over Boston College in the Hall of Fame Bowl. Volunteer quarterback Heath Shuler threw for two touchdowns and scored twice on the ground himself.

| Boston College | 0 | 7 | 0 | 16 | —23 |
|---|---|---|---|---|---|
| Tennessee | 14 | 0 | 17 | 7 | —38 |

TN—Shuler 1 run (Becksvoort kick)
TN—Fleming 27 pass from Shuler (Becksvoort kick)
BC—Mitchell 12 pass from Foley (Gordon kick)
TN—Shuler 14 run (Becksvoort kick)
TN—Becksvoort 25 field goal
TN—Phillips 69 pass from Shuler (Becksvoort kick)
TN—Fleming 28 pass from Colquitt (Becksvoort kick)
BC—Mitchell 17 pass from Foley (Mitchell pass from Foley)
BC—D. Campbell 7 run (I. Boyd pass from Foley)

### Game Statistics

|  | BC | TN |
|---|---|---|
| First Downs | 22 | 20 |
| Rushes-Yards | 33-103 | 39-157 |
| Passing Yards | 268 | 293 |
| Comp-Att-Int | 23-47-1 | 19-26-0 |
| Punts-Avg | 5-37 | 4-41 |
| Fumbles-Lost | 1-0 | 1-1 |
| Penalties-Yards | 5-25 | 5-40 |
| Time of Possession | 30:29 | 29:31 |
| Attendance: 52,056 | | |

## FLORIDA CITRUS BOWL
### January 1, 1993
### Orlando, Fla.

**Synopsis:** Georgia rode the legs of Garrison Hearst and the arm of Eric Zeier as the eighth-ranked Bulldogs downed Ohio State, 21-14, in the Florida Citrus Bowl. Hearst rushed for 163 yards and two scores and Zeier completed 21 of 31 passes for 242 yards.

| Georgia | 7 | 0 | 7 | 7 | —21 |
|---|---|---|---|---|---|
| Ohio St. | 0 | 7 | 7 | 0 | —14 |

GA—Hearst 1 run (Peterson kick)
OS—R. Smith 1 run (T. Williams kick)
GA—Hearst 5 run (Peterson kick)
OS—R. Smith 5 run (T. Williams kick)
GA—Harvey 1 run (Peterson kick)

### Game Statistics

|  | GA | OS |
|---|---|---|
| First Downs | 26 | 18 |
| Rushes-Yards | 49-202 | 47-179 |
| Passing Yards | 242 | 110 |
| Comp-Att-Int | 21-31-0 | 8-24-1 |
| Punts-Avg | 6-39 | 8-37 |
| Fumbles-Lost | 2-2 | 1-1 |
| Penalties-Yards | 3-30 | 5-35 |
| Time of Possession | 31:01 | 28:59 |
| Attendance: 65,861 | | |

## MOBIL COTTON BOWL
### January 1, 1993
### Dallas, Texas

**Synopsis:** Notre Dame rolled up 439 yards on Texas A&M's sticky defense and kept the Aggie offense out of the end zone to post a lopsided 28-3 victory in the Cotton Bowl. The Fighting Irish defense allowed Texas A&M only 165 total yards.

| | | | | | |
|---|---|---|---|---|---|
| **Notre Dame** | 0 | 7 | 14 | 7 | —28 |
| **Texas A&M** | 0 | 0 | 0 | 3 | — 3 |

ND—Dawson 40 pass from Mirer (Hentrich kick)
ND—Bettis 26 pass from Mirer (Hentrich kick)
ND—Bettis 1 run (Hentrich kick)
TX—Venetoulias 41 field goal
ND—Bettis 4 run (Hentrich kick)

### Game Statistics

| | ND | TX |
|---|---|---|
| First Downs | 28 | 11 |
| Rushes-Yards | 64-290 | 33-78 |
| Passing Yards | 149 | 87 |
| Comp-Att-Int | 9-18-0 | 7-18-0 |
| Punts-Avg | 4-38 | 6-41 |
| Fumbles-Lost | 3-3 | 2-2 |
| Penalties-Yards | 3-30 | 7-42 |
| Time of Possession | 38:01 | 21:59 |
| Attendance: 71,615 | | |

## BLOCKBUSTER BOWL
### January 1, 1993
### Miami, Fla.

**Synopsis:** Stanford's unheralded defense took control of Penn State's offense and quarterback Steve Stenstrom passed for two touchdowns as the Cardinal cruised to a 24-3 Blockbuster Bowl victory over the Nittany Lions.

| | | | | | |
|---|---|---|---|---|---|
| **Stanford** | 7 | 7 | 10 | 0 | —24 |
| **Penn St.** | 3 | 0 | 0 | 0 | — 3 |

ST—Wetnight 2 pass from Stenstrom (Abrams kick)
PS—Muscillo 33 field goal
ST—Lasley 5 run (Abrams kick)
ST—Abrams 28 field goal
ST—Milburn 40 pass from Stenstrom (Abrams kick)

### Game Statistics

| | ST | PS |
|---|---|---|
| First Downs | 16 | 12 |
| Rushes-Yards | 42-155 | 35-107 |
| Passing Yards | 210 | 156 |
| Comp-Att-Int | 17-30-2 | 13-40-2 |
| Punts-Avg | 7-42 | 11-38 |
| Fumbles-Lost | 2-1 | 0-0 |
| Penalties-Yards | 5-41 | 3-25 |
| Time of Possession | 32:27 | 27:33 |
| Attendance: 45,554 | | |

## FIESTA BOWL
### January 1, 1993
### Tempe, Ariz.

**Synopsis:** Syracuse scored 20 third-quarter points, including Kirby Dar Dar's 100-yard kickoff return, to break open a close game and edge Colorado, 26-22, in the Fiesta Bowl. The Orangemen trailed 7-6 at half time.

| | | | | | |
|---|---|---|---|---|---|
| **Syracuse** | 3 | 3 | 20 | 0 | —26 |
| **Colorado** | 0 | 7 | 9 | 6 | —22 |

SY—Biskup 46 field goal
SY—Biskup 34 field goal
CO—Embree 7 pass from Stewart (Berger kick)
SY—Walker 13 run (pass failed)
CO—Berger 38 field goal

SY—Graves 28 run (Biskup kick)
CO—C. Johnson 16 pass from Stewart (kick failed)
SY—Dar Dar 100 kickoff return (Biskup kick)
CO—Warren 6 run (kick failed)

### Game Statistics

| | SY | CO |
|---|---|---|
| First Downs | 15 | 19 |
| Rushes-Yards | 44-201 | 31-153 |
| Passing Yards | 64 | 217 |
| Comp-Att-Int | 5-12-1 | 17-43-3 |
| Punts-Avg | 5-45 | 3-48 |
| Fumbles-Lost | 0-0 | 0-0 |
| Penalties-Yards | 5-30 | 8-37 |
| Time of Possession | 30:37 | 29:23 |
| Attendance: 70,224 | | |

## ROSE BOWL
### January 1, 1993
### Pasadena, Calif.

**Synopsis:** Tailback Tyrone Wheatley rushed for 235 yards and scored three touchdowns to lead Michigan to a 38-31 win over Washington in the Rose Bowl. Wheatley had a Rose Bowl-record 88-yarder to go with 56- and 24-yard scores.

| | | | | | |
|---|---|---|---|---|---|
| **Michigan** | 10 | 7 | 14 | 7 | —38 |
| **Washington** | 7 | 14 | 10 | 0 | —31 |

MI—Elezovic 41 field goal
WA—Turner 1 run (Hanson kick)
MI—McGee 49 pass from Grbac (Elezovic kick)
MI—Wheatley 56 run (Elezovic kick)
WA—Shelley 64 pass from Brunell (Hanson kick)
WA—Bruener 18 pass from Brunell (Hanson kick)
MI—Wheatley 88 run (Elezovic kick)
WA—Kaufman 1 run (Hanson kick)
WA—Hanson 44 field goal
MI—Wheatley 24 run (Elezovic kick)
MI—McGee 15 pass from Grbac (Elezovic kick)

### Game Statistics

| | MI | WA |
|---|---|---|
| First Downs | 16 | 19 |
| Rushes-Yards | 36-308 | 43-105 |
| Passing Yards | 175 | 308 |
| Comp-Att-Int | 17-30-0 | 18-31-0 |
| Punts-Avg | 6-37 | 5-39 |
| Fumbles-Lost | 1-0 | 1-1 |
| Penalties-Yards | 8-72 | 5-43 |
| Time of Possession | 28:12 | 31:48 |
| Attendance: 94,236 | | |

## FEDERAL EXPRESS ORANGE BOWL
### January 1, 1993
### Miami, Fla.

**Synopsis:** Florida State cruised to a 20-0 advantage behind quarterback Charlie Ward and never let Nebraska get off the mat in an easy 27-14 win in the Orange Bowl. Ward, a starter on the Seminoles' basketball team, threw two touchdown passes.

| | | | | | |
|---|---|---|---|---|---|
| **Florida St.** | 7 | 13 | 7 | 0 | —27 |
| **Nebraska** | 0 | 7 | 0 | 7 | —14 |

FS—Vanover 25 pass from Ward (Mowrey kick)
FS—Mowrey 40 field goal
FS—McCorvey 4 pass from Ward (Mowrey kick)
FS—Mowrey 24 field goal
NE—Dixon 41 pass from Frazier (Bennett kick)
FS—Jackson 11 run (Mowrey kick)
NE—Armstrong 1 pass from Frazier (Bennett kick)

## Game Statistics

| | FS | NE |
|---|---|---|
| First Downs | 23 | 13 |
| Rushes-Yards | 48-221 | 34-144 |
| Passing Yards | 215 | 146 |
| Comp-Att-Int | 16-31-1 | 10-22-2 |
| Punts-Avg | 6-36 | 4-45 |
| Fumbles-Lost | 3-0 | 5-1 |
| Penalties-Yards | 6-71 | 6-50 |
| Time of Possession | 36:53 | 23:07 |
| Attendance: 57,324 | | |

### USF&G SUGAR BOWL
#### January 1, 1993
#### New Orleans, La.

**Synopsis:** This was the Bowl Coalition's No. 1 vs. No. 2 matchup for the national championship and Alabama dominated Miami (Florida), 34-13, to take the big prize. The Crimson Tide won all phases of the game and running back Derrick Lassic gained 135 yards.

| | | | | | |
|---|---|---|---|---|---|
| Miami (Fla.) | 3 | 3 | 0 | 7 | —13 |
| Alabama | 3 | 10 | 14 | 7 | —34 |

AL—Proctor 19 field goal
MI—Prewitt 49 field goal
AL—Proctor 23 field goal
AL—S. Williams 2 run (Proctor kick)
MI—Prewitt 42 field goal
AL—Lassic 1 run (Proctor kick)
AL—Teague 31 interception return (Proctor kick)
MI—K. Williams 78 punt return (Prewitt kick)
AL—Lassic 4 run (Proctor kick)

### Game Statistics

| | MI | AL |
|---|---|---|
| First Downs | 16 | 15 |
| Rushes-Yards | 18-48 | 60-267 |
| Passing Yards | 278 | 18 |

| | MI | AL |
|---|---|---|
| Comp-Att-Int | 24-56-3 | 4-13-2 |
| Punts-Avg | 5-42 | 6-45 |
| Fumbles-Lost | 4-1 | 0-0 |
| Penalties-Yards | 6-37 | 7-46 |
| Time of Possession | 23:56 | 36:04 |
| Attendance: 76,789 | | |

### PEACH BOWL
#### January 2, 1993
#### Atlanta, Ga.

**Synopsis:** North Carolina rode the turnover train with a pass interception for a touchdown and two blocked punts offsetting 440 yards by Mississippi State to win the Peach Bowl, 21-17, in the inaugural bowl game in the Georgia Dome.

| | | | | | |
|---|---|---|---|---|---|
| Mississippi St. | 14 | 0 | 0 | 3 | —17 |
| North Caro. | 0 | 0 | 14 | 7 | —21 |

MS—Truitt 2 pass from Plump (Gardner kick)
MS—Roberts 22 run (Gardner kick)
NC—Means 1 run (Pignetti kick)
NC—Walker 24 blocked punt return (Pignetti kick)
NC—Baskerville 44 interception return (Pignetti kick)
MS—Gardner 46 field goal

### Game Statistics

| | MS | NC |
|---|---|---|
| First Downs | 24 | 13 |
| Rushes-Yards | 41-144 | 36-149 |
| Passing Yards | 296 | 106 |
| Comp-Att-Int | 25-45-2 | 7-17-2 |
| Punts-Avg | 3-37 | 6-38 |
| Fumbles-Lost | 1-0 | 1-1 |
| Penalties-Yards | 9-87 | 4-36 |
| Time of Possession | 34:33 | 25:27 |
| Attendance: 69,125 | | |

# ALL-TIME BOWL GAME RESULTS

## MAJOR BOWL GAMES

### ROSE BOWL

**Present Site:** Pasadena, Calif.
**Stadium (Capacity):** Rose Bowl (99,563)
**Playing Surface:** Grass
**Playing Sites:** Tournament Park, Pasadena (1902, 1916-22); Rose Bowl, Pasadena (1923-41); Duke Stadium, Durham, N.C. (1942); Rose Bowl (since 1943)

1-1-02—Michigan 49, Stanford 0
1-1-16—Washington St. 14, Brown 0
1-1-17—Oregon 14, Pennsylvania 0
1-1-18—Mare Island 19, Camp Lewis 7
1-1-19—Great Lakes 17, Mare Island 0

1-1-20—Harvard 7, Oregon 6
1-1-21—California 28, Ohio St. 0
1-2-22—Wash. & Jeff. 0, California 0
1-1-23—Southern Cal 14, Penn St. 3
1-1-24—Navy 14, Washington 14

1-1-25—Notre Dame 27, Stanford 10
1-1-26—Alabama 20, Washington 19
1-1-27—Alabama 7, Stanford 7
1-2-28—Stanford 7, Pittsburgh 6
1-1-29—Georgia Tech 8, California 7

1-1-30—Southern Cal 47, Pittsburgh 14
1-1-31—Alabama 24, Washington St. 0
1-1-32—Southern Cal 21, Tulane 12
1-2-33—Southern Cal 35, Pittsburgh 0
1-1-34—Columbia 7, Stanford 0

1-1-35—Alabama 29, Stanford 13
1-1-36—Stanford 7, Southern Methodist 0
1-1-37—Pittsburgh 21, Washington 0
1-1-38—California 13, Alabama 0
1-2-39—Southern Cal 7, Duke 3

1-1-40—Southern Cal 14, Tennessee 0
1-1-41—Stanford 21, Nebraska 13
1-1-42—Oregon St. 20, Duke 16 (at Durham)
1-1-43—Georgia 9, UCLA 0
1-1-44—Southern Cal 29, Washington 0

1-1-45—Southern Cal 25, Tennessee 0
1-1-46—Alabama 34, Southern Cal 14
1-1-47—Illinois 45, UCLA 14
1-1-48—Michigan 49, Southern Cal 0
1-1-49—Northwestern 20, California 14

1-2-50—Ohio St. 17, California 14
1-1-51—Michigan 14, California 6
1-1-52—Illinois 40, Stanford 7
1-1-53—Southern Cal 7, Wisconsin 0
1-1-54—Michigan St. 28, UCLA 20

1-1-55—Ohio St. 20, Southern Cal 7
1-2-56—Michigan St. 17, UCLA 14
1-1-57—Iowa 35, Oregon St. 19
1-1-58—Ohio St. 10, Oregon 7
1-1-59—Iowa 38, California 12
1-1-60—Washington 44, Wisconsin 8
1-2-61—Washington 17, Minnesota 7
1-1-62—Minnesota 21, UCLA 3
1-1-63—Southern Cal 42, Wisconsin 37
1-1-64—Illinois 17, Washington 7
1-1-65—Michigan 34, Oregon St. 7
1-1-66—UCLA 14, Michigan St. 12
1-2-67—Purdue 14, Southern Cal 13
1-1-68—Southern Cal 14, Indiana 3
1-1-69—Ohio St. 27, Southern Cal 16
1-1-70—Southern Cal 10, Michigan 3
1-1-71—Stanford 27, Ohio St. 17
1-1-72—Stanford 13, Michigan 12
1-1-73—Southern Cal 42, Ohio St. 17
1-1-74—Ohio St. 42, Southern Cal 21

1-1-75—Southern Cal 18, Ohio St. 17
1-1-76—UCLA 23, Ohio St. 10
1-1-77—Southern Cal 14, Michigan 6
1-2-78—Washington 27, Michigan 20
1-1-79—Southern Cal 17, Michigan 10
1-1-80—Southern Cal 17, Ohio St. 16
1-1-81—Michigan 23, Washington 6
1-1-82—Washington 28, Iowa 0
1-1-83—UCLA 24, Michigan 14
1-2-84—UCLA 45, Illinois 9
1-1-85—Southern Cal 20, Ohio St. 17
1-1-86—UCLA 45, Iowa 28
1-1-87—Arizona St. 22, Michigan 15
1-1-88—Michigan St. 20, Southern Cal 17
1-2-89—Michigan 22, Southern Cal 14
1-1-90—Southern Cal 17, Michigan 10
1-1-91—Washington 46, Iowa 34
1-1-92—Washington 34, Michigan 14
1-1-93—Michigan 38, Washington 31

## ORANGE BOWL

**Present Site:** Miami, Fla.
**Stadium (Capacity):** Orange Bowl (74,712)
**Playing Surface:** Grass
**Name Changes:** Orange Bowl (1935-88); Federal Express Orange Bowl (since 1989)
**Playing Sites:** Miami Field Stadium (1935-37); Orange Bowl (since 1938)

1-1-35—Bucknell 26, Miami (Fla.) 0
1-1-36—Catholic 20, Mississippi 19
1-1-37—Duquesne 13, Mississippi St. 12
1-1-38—Auburn 6, Michigan St. 0
1-2-39—Tennessee 17, Oklahoma 0
1-1-40—Georgia Tech 21, Missouri 7
1-1-41—Mississippi St. 14, Georgetown 7
1-1-42—Georgia 40, Texas Christian 26
1-1-43—Alabama 37, Boston College 21
1-1-44—Louisiana St. 19, Texas A&M 14
1-1-45—Tulsa 26, Georgia Tech 12
1-1-46—Miami (Fla.) 13, Holy Cross 6
1-1-47—Rice 8, Tennessee 0
1-1-48—Georgia Tech 20, Kansas 14
1-1-49—Texas 41, Georgia 28
1-2-50—Santa Clara 21, Kentucky 13
1-1-51—Clemson 15, Miami (Fla.) 14
1-1-52—Georgia Tech 17, Baylor 14
1-1-53—Alabama 61, Syracuse 6
1-1-54—Oklahoma 7, Maryland 0
1-1-55—Duke 34, Nebraska 7
1-2-56—Oklahoma 20, Maryland 6
1-1-57—Colorado 27, Clemson 21
1-1-58—Oklahoma 48, Duke 21
1-1-59—Oklahoma 21, Syracuse 6
1-1-60—Georgia 14, Missouri 0
1-2-61—Missouri 21, Navy 14
1-1-62—Louisiana St. 25, Colorado 7
1-1-63—Alabama 17, Oklahoma 0
1-1-64—Nebraska 13, Auburn 7

1-1-65—Texas 21, Alabama 17
1-1-66—Alabama 39, Nebraska 28
1-2-67—Florida 27, Georgia Tech 12
1-1-68—Oklahoma 26, Tennessee 24
1-1-69—Penn St. 15, Kansas 14
1-1-70—Penn St. 10, Missouri 3
1-1-71—Nebraska 17, Louisiana St. 12
1-1-72—Nebraska 38, Alabama 6
1-1-73—Nebraska 40, Notre Dame 6
1-1-74—Penn St. 16, Louisiana St. 9
1-1-75—Notre Dame 13, Alabama 11
1-1-76—Oklahoma 14, Michigan 6
1-1-77—Ohio St. 27, Colorado 10
1-2-78—Arkansas 31, Oklahoma 6
1-1-79—Oklahoma 31, Nebraska 24
1-1-80—Oklahoma 24, Florida St. 7
1-1-81—Oklahoma 18, Florida St. 17
1-1-82—Clemson 22, Nebraska 15
1-1-83—Nebraska 21, Louisiana St. 20
1-2-84—Miami (Fla.) 31, Nebraska 30
1-1-85—Washington 28, Oklahoma 17
1-1-86—Oklahoma 25, Penn St. 10
1-1-87—Oklahoma 42, Arkansas 8
1-1-88—Miami (Fla.) 20, Oklahoma 14
1-2-89—Miami (Fla.) 23, Nebraska 3
1-1-90—Notre Dame 21, Colorado 6
1-1-91—Colorado 10, Notre Dame 9
1-1-92—Miami (Fla.) 22, Nebraska 0
1-1-93—Florida St. 27, Nebraska 14

## SUGAR BOWL

**Present Site:** New Orleans, La.
**Stadium (Capacity):** Louisiana Superdome (72,704)
**Playing Surface:** AstroTurf
**Name Changes:** Sugar Bowl (1935-87); USF&G Sugar Bowl (since 1988)
**Playing Sites:** Tulane Stadium, New Orleans (1935-74); Louisiana Superdome (since 1975)

1-1-35—Tulane 20, Temple 14
1-1-36—Texas Christian 3, Louisiana St. 2
1-1-37—Santa Clara 21, Louisiana St. 14
1-1-38—Santa Clara 6, Louisiana St. 0
1-2-39—Texas Christian 15, Carnegie Mellon 7

1-1-40—Texas A&M 14, Tulane 13
1-1-41—Boston College 19, Tennessee 13
1-1-42—Fordham 2, Missouri 0
1-1-43—Tennessee 14, Tulsa 7
1-1-44—Georgia Tech 20, Tulsa 18

*1993 NCAA FOOTBALL*

1-1-45—Duke 29, Alabama 26
1-1-46—Oklahoma St. 33, St. Mary's (Cal.) 13
1-1-47—Georgia 20, North Caro. 10
1-1-48—Texas 27, Alabama 7
1-1-49—Oklahoma 14, North Caro. 6
1-2-50—Oklahoma 35, Louisiana St. 0
1-1-51—Kentucky 13, Oklahoma 7
1-1-52—Maryland 28, Tennessee 13
1-1-53—Georgia Tech 24, Mississippi 7
1-1-54—Georgia Tech 42, West Va. 19
1-1-55—Navy 21, Mississippi 0
1-2-56—Georgia Tech 7, Pittsburgh 0
1-1-57—Baylor 13, Tennessee 7
1-1-58—Mississippi 39, Texas 7
1-1-59—Louisiana St. 7, Clemson 0
1-1-60—Mississippi 21, Louisiana St. 0
1-2-61—Mississippi 14, Rice 6
1-1-62—Alabama 10, Arkansas 3
1-1-63—Mississippi 17, Arkansas 13
1-1-64—Alabama 12, Mississippi 7
1-1-65—Louisiana St. 13, Syracuse 10
1-1-66—Missouri 20, Florida 18
1-2-67—Alabama 34, Nebraska 7
1-1-68—Louisiana St. 20, Wyoming 13
1-1-69—Arkansas 16, Georgia 2

1-1-70—Mississippi 27, Arkansas 22
1-1-71—Tennessee 34, Air Force 13
1-1-72—Oklahoma 40, Auburn 22
12-31-72—Oklahoma 14, Penn St. 0
12-31-73—Notre Dame 24, Alabama 23
12-31-74—Nebraska 13, Florida 10
12-31-75—Alabama 13, Penn St. 6
1-1-77—Pittsburgh 27, Georgia 3
1-2-78—Alabama 35, Ohio St. 6
1-1-79—Alabama 14, Penn St. 7
1-1-80—Alabama 24, Arkansas 9
1-1-81—Georgia 17, Notre Dame 10
1-1-82—Pittsburgh 24, Georgia 20
1-1-83—Penn St. 27, Georgia 23
1-2-84—Auburn 9, Michigan 7
1-1-85—Nebraska 28, Louisiana St. 10
1-1-86—Tennessee 35, Miami (Fla.) 7
1-1-87—Nebraska 30, Louisiana St. 15
1-1-88—Syracuse 16, Auburn 16
1-2-89—Florida St. 13, Auburn 7
1-1-90—Miami (Fla.) 33, Alabama 25
1-1-91—Tennessee 23, Virginia 22
1-1-92—Notre Dame 39, Florida 28
1-1-93—Alabama 34, Miami (Fla.) 13

## COTTON BOWL

**Present Site:** Dallas, Texas
**Stadium (Capacity):** Cotton Bowl (71,615)
**Playing Surface:** AstroTurf
**Name Changes:** Cotton Bowl (1937-88); Mobil Cotton Bowl (since 1989)
**Playing Sites:** Fair Park Stadium, Dallas (1937); Cotton Bowl (since 1938)

1-1-37—Texas Christian 16, Marquette 6
1-1-38—Rice 28, Colorado 14
1-2-39—St. Mary's (Cal.) 20, Texas Tech 13
1-1-40—Clemson 6, Boston College 3
1-1-41—Texas A&M 13, Fordham 12
1-1-42—Alabama 29, Texas A&M 21
1-1-43—Texas 14, Georgia Tech 7
1-1-44—Texas 7, Randolph Field 7
1-1-45—Oklahoma St. 34, Texas Christian 0
1-1-46—Texas 40, Missouri 27
1-1-47—Arkansas 0, Louisiana St. 0
1-1-48—Southern Methodist 13, Penn St. 13
1-1-49—Southern Methodist 21, Oregon 13
1-2-50—Rice 27, North Caro. 13
1-1-51—Tennessee 20, Texas 14
1-1-52—Kentucky 20, Texas Christian 7
1-1-53—Texas 16, Tennessee 0
1-1-54—Rice 28, Alabama 6
1-1-55—Georgia Tech 14, Arkansas 6
1-2-56—Mississippi 14, Texas Christian 13
1-1-57—Texas Christian 28, Syracuse 27
1-1-58—Navy 20, Rice 7
1-1-59—Texas Christian 0, Air Force 0
1-1-60—Syracuse 23, Texas 14
1-2-61—Duke 7, Arkansas 6
1-1-62—Texas 12, Mississippi 7
1-1-63—Louisiana St. 13, Texas 0
1-1-64—Texas 28, Navy 6
1-1-65—Arkansas 10, Nebraska 7
1-1-66—Louisiana St. 14, Arkansas 7

12-31-66—Georgia 24, Southern Methodist 9
1-1-68—Texas A&M 20, Alabama 16
1-1-69—Texas 36, Tennessee 13
1-1-70—Texas 21, Notre Dame 17
1-1-71—Notre Dame 24, Texas 11
1-1-72—Penn St. 30, Texas 6
1-1-73—Texas 17, Alabama 13
1-1-74—Nebraska 19, Texas 3
1-1-75—Penn St. 41, Baylor 20
1-1-76—Arkansas 31, Georgia 10
1-1-77—Houston 30, Maryland 21
1-2-78—Notre Dame 38, Texas 10
1-1-79—Notre Dame 35, Houston 34
1-1-80—Houston 17, Nebraska 14
1-1-81—Alabama 30, Baylor 2
1-1-82—Texas 14, Alabama 12
1-1-83—Southern Methodist 7, Pittsburgh 3
1-2-84—Georgia 10, Texas 9
1-1-85—Boston College 45, Houston 28
1-1-86—Texas A&M 36, Auburn 16
1-1-87—Ohio St. 28, Texas A&M 12
1-1-88—Texas A&M 35, Notre Dame 10
1-2-89—UCLA 17, Arkansas 3
1-1-90—Tennessee 31, Arkansas 27
1-1-91—Miami (Fla.) 46, Texas 3
1-1-92—Florida St. 10, Texas A&M 2
1-1-93—Notre Dame 28, Texas A&M 3

## JOHN HANCOCK BOWL

**Present Site:** El Paso, Texas
**Stadium (Capacity):** Sun Bowl (51,270)
**Playing Surface:** AstroTurf
**Name Changes:** Sun Bowl (1936-86); John Hancock Sun Bowl (1987-88); John Hancock Bowl (since 1989)
**Playing Sites:** Kidd Field, UTEP, El Paso (1936-62); Sun Bowl Stadium (since 1963)

1-1-36—Hardin-Simmons 14, New Mexico St. 14
1-1-37—Hardin-Simmons 34, UTEP 6
1-1-38—West Va. 7, Texas Tech 6
1-2-39—Utah 26, New Mexico 0 ɩ
1-1-40—Catholic 0, Arizona St. 0
1-1-41—Case Reserve 26, Arizona St. 13
1-1-42—Tulsa 6, Texas Tech 0
1-1-43—Second Air Force 13, Hardin-Simmons 7
1-1-44—Southwestern (Tex.) 7, New Mexico 0
1-1-45—Southwestern (Tex.) 35, U. of Mexico 0
1-1-46—New Mexico 34, Denver 24
1-1-47—Cincinnati 18, Virginia Tech 6
1-1-48—Miami (Ohio) 13, Texas Tech 12
1-1-49—West Va. 21, UTEP 12
1-2-50—UTEP 33, Georgetown 20
1-1-51—West Tex. St. 14, Cincinnati 13
1-1-52—Texas Tech 25, Pacific (Cal.) 14
1-1-53—Pacific (Cal.) 26, Southern Miss. 7
1-1-54—UTEP 37, Southern Miss. 14
1-1-55—UTEP 47, Florida St. 20
1-2-56—Wyoming 21, Texas Tech 14
1-1-57—Geo. Washington 13, UTEP 0
1-1-58—Louisville 34, Drake 20
12-31-58—Wyoming 14, Hardin-Simmons 6
12-31-59—New Mexico St. 28, North Texas 8
12-31-60—New Mexico St. 20, Utah St. 13
12-30-61—Villanova 17, Wichita St. 9
12-31-62—West Tex. St. 15, Ohio 14
12-31-63—Oregon 21, Southern Methodist 14
12-26-64—Georgia 7, Texas Tech 0

12-31-65—UTEP 13, Texas Christian 12
12-24-66—Wyoming 28, Florida St. 20
12-30-67—UTEP 14, Mississippi 7
12-28-68—Auburn 34, Arizona 10
12-20-69—Nebraska 45, Georgia 6
12-19-70—Georgia Tech 17, Texas Tech 9
12-18-71—Louisiana St. 33, Iowa St. 15
12-30-72—North Caro. 32, Texas Tech 28
12-29-73—Missouri 34, Auburn 17
12-28-74—Mississippi St. 26, North Caro. 24
12-26-75—Pittsburgh 33, Kansas 19
1-2-77—Texas A&M 37, Florida 14
12-31-77—Stanford 24, Louisiana St. 14
12-23-78—Texas 42, Maryland 0
12-22-79—Washington 14, Texas 7
12-27-80—Nebraska 31, Mississippi St. 17
12-26-81—Oklahoma 40, Houston 14
12-25-82—North Caro. 26, Texas 10
12-24-83—Alabama 28, Southern Methodist 7
12-22-84—Maryland 28, Tennessee 27
12-28-85—Georgia 13, Arizona 13
12-25-86—Alabama 28, Washington 6
12-25-87—Oklahoma 35, West Va. 33
12-24-88—Alabama 29, Army 28
12-30-89—Pittsburgh 31, Texas A&M 28
12-31-90—Michigan St. 17, Southern Cal 16
12-31-91—UCLA 6, Illinois 3
12-31-92—Baylor 20, Arizona 15

## GATOR BOWL

**Present Site:** Jacksonville, Fla.
**Stadium (Capacity):** Gator Bowl (80,129)
**Playing Surface:** Grass
**Name Changes:** Gator Bowl (1946-89); Mazda Gator Bowl (1991); Outback Steakhouse Gator Bowl (since 1992)
**Playing Sites:** Gator Bowl (since 1946)

1-1-46—Wake Forest 26, South Caro. 14
1-1-47—Oklahoma 34, North Caro. St. 13
1-1-48—Maryland 20, Georgia 20
1-1-49—Clemson 24, Missouri 23
1-2-50—Maryland 20, Missouri 7
1-1-51—Wyoming 20, Wash. & Lee 7
1-1-52—Miami (Fla.) 14, Clemson 0
1-1-53—Florida 14, Tulsa 13
1-1-54—Texas Tech 35, Auburn 13
12-31-54—Auburn 33, Baylor 13
12-31-55—Vanderbilt 25, Auburn 13
12-29-56—Georgia Tech 21, Pittsburgh 14
12-28-57—Tennessee 3, Texas A&M 0
12-27-58—Mississippi 7, Florida 3
1-2-60—Arkansas 14, Georgia Tech 7
12-31-60—Florida 13, Baylor 12
12-30-61—Penn St. 30, Georgia Tech 15
12-29-62—Florida 17, Penn St. 7
12-28-63—North Caro. 35, Air Force 0
1-2-65—Florida St. 36, Oklahoma 19
12-31-65—Georgia Tech 31, Texas Tech 21
12-31-66—Tennessee 18, Syracuse 12
12-30-67—Penn St. 17, Florida St. 17
12-28-68—Missouri 35, Alabama 10
12-27-69—Florida 14, Tennessee 13

1-2-71—Auburn 35, Mississippi 28
12-31-71—Georgia 7, North Caro. 3
12-30-72—Auburn 24, Colorado 3
12-29-73—Texas Tech 28, Tennessee 19
12-30-74—Auburn 27, Texas 3
12-29-75—Maryland 13, Florida 0
12-27-76—Notre Dame 20, Penn St. 9
12-30-77—Pittsburgh 34, Clemson 3
12-29-78—Clemson 17, Ohio St. 15
12-28-79—North Caro. 17, Michigan 15
12-29-80—Pittsburgh 37, South Caro. 9
12-28-81—North Caro. 31, Arkansas 27
12-30-82—Florida St. 31, West Va. 12
12-30-83—Florida 14, Iowa 6
12-28-84—Oklahoma St. 21, South Caro. 14
12-30-85—Florida St. 34, Oklahoma St. 23
12-27-86—Clemson 27, Stanford 21
12-31-87—Louisiana St. 30, South Caro. 13
1-1-89—Georgia 34, Michigan St. 27
12-30-89—Clemson 27, West Va. 7
1-1-91—Michigan 35, Mississippi 3
12-29-91—Oklahoma 48, Virginia 14
12-31-92—Florida 27, North Caro. St. 10

## FLORIDA CITRUS BOWL

**Present Site:** Orlando, Fla.
**Stadium (Capacity):** Florida Citrus Bowl-Orange County (70,000)
**Playing Surface:** Grass
**Name Changes:** Tangerine Bowl (1947-82); Florida Citrus Bowl (1983-93); CompUSA Florida Citrus Bowl (since 1994)

*1993 NCAA FOOTBALL*

**Playing Sites:** Tangerine Bowl, Orlando (1947-72); Florida Field, Gainesville (1973); Tangerine Bowl (now Florida Citrus Bowl) (1974-82); Orlando Stadium (now Florida Citrus Bowl) (1983-85); Florida Citrus Bowl-Orange County (since 1986)

1-1-47 — Catawba 31, Maryville (Tenn.) 6
1-1-48 — Catawba 7, Marshall 0
1-1-49 — Murray St. 21, Sul Ross St. 21
1-2-50 — St. Vincent 7, Emory & Henry 6
1-1-51 — Morris Harvey 35, Emory & Henry 14
1-1-52 — Stetson 35, Arkansas St. 20
1-1-53 — East Tex. St. 33, Tennessee Tech 0
1-1-54 — East Tex. St. 7, Arkansas St. 7
1-1-55 — Nebraska-Omaha 7, Eastern Ky. 6
1-2-56 — Juniata 6, Missouri Valley 6
1-1-57 — West Tex. St. 20, Southern Miss. 13
1-1-58 — East Tex. St. 10, Southern Miss. 9
12-27-58 — East Tex. St. 26, Missouri Valley 7
1-1-60 — Middle Tenn. St. 21, Presbyterian 12
12-30-60 — Citadel 27, Tennessee Tech 0
12-29-61 — Lamar 21, Middle Tenn. St. 14
12-22-62 — Houston 49, Miami (Ohio) 21
12-28-63 — Western Ky. 27, Coast Guard 0
12-12-64 — East Caro. 14, Massachusetts 13
12-11-65 — East Caro. 31, Maine 0
12-10-66 — Morgan St. 14, West Chester 6
12-16-67 — Tenn.-Martin 25, West Chester 8
12-27-68 — Richmond 49, Ohio 42
12-26-69 — Toledo 56, Davidson 33
12-28-70 — Toledo 40, William & Mary 12

12-28-71 — Toledo 28, Richmond 3
12-29-72 — Tampa 21, Kent 18
12-22-73 — Miami (Ohio) 16, Florida 7
12-21-74 — Miami (Ohio) 21, Georgia 10
12-20-75 — Miami (Ohio) 20, South Caro. 7
12-18-76 — Oklahoma St. 49, Brigham Young 21
12-23-77 — Florida St. 40, Texas Tech 17
12-23-78 — North Caro. St. 30, Pittsburgh 17
12-22-79 — Louisiana St. 34, Wake Forest 10
12-20-80 — Florida 35, Maryland 20
12-19-81 — Missouri 19, Southern Miss. 17
12-18-82 — Auburn 33, Boston College 26
12-17-83 — Tennessee 30, Maryland 23
12-22-84 — Georgia 17, Florida St. 17
12-28-85 — Ohio St. 10, Brigham Young 7
1-1-87 — Auburn 16, Southern Cal 7
1-1-88 — Clemson 35, Penn St. 10
1-2-89 — Clemson 13, Oklahoma 6
1-1-90 — Illinois 31, Virginia 21
1-1-91 — Georgia Tech 45, Nebraska 21
1-1-92 — California 37, Clemson 13
1-1-93 — Georgia 21, Ohio St. 14

Note: No classified major teams participated in games from January 1, 1947, through December 30, 1960, or in 1961 and 1963 through 1967.

## LIBERTY BOWL

**Present Site:** Memphis, Tenn.
**Stadium (Capacity):** Liberty Bowl Memorial (62,425)
**Playing Surface:** Grass
**Name Changes:** Liberty Bowl (1959-92); St. Jude Liberty Bowl (since 1993)
**Playing Sites:** Municipal Stadium, Philadelphia (1959-63); Convention Hall, Atlantic City, N.J. (1964); Liberty Bowl Memorial (since 1965)

12-19-59 — Penn St. 7, Alabama 0
12-17-60 — Penn St. 41, Oregon 12
12-16-61 — Syracuse 15, Miami (Fla.) 14
12-15-62 — Oregon St. 6, Villanova 0
12-21-63 — Mississippi St. 16, North Caro. St. 12
12-19-64 — Utah 32, West Va. 6
12-18-65 — Mississippi 13, Auburn 7
12-10-66 — Miami (Fla.) 14, Virginia Tech 7
12-16-67 — North Caro. St. 14, Georgia 7
12-14-68 — Mississippi 34, Virginia Tech 17
12-13-69 — Colorado 47, Alabama 33
12-12-70 — Tulane 17, Colorado 3
12-20-71 — Tennessee 14, Arkansas 13
12-18-72 — Georgia Tech 31, Iowa St. 30
12-17-73 — North Caro. St. 31, Kansas 18
12-16-74 — Tennessee 7, Maryland 3
12-22-75 — Southern Cal 20, Texas A&M 0
12-20-76 — Alabama 36, UCLA 6
12-19-77 — Nebraska 21, North Caro. 17
12-23-78 — Missouri 20, Louisiana St. 15

12-22-79 — Penn St. 9, Tulane 6
12-27-80 — Purdue 28, Missouri 25
12-30-81 — Ohio St. 31, Navy 28
12-29-82 — Alabama 21, Illinois 15
12-29-83 — Notre Dame 19, Boston College 18
12-27-84 — Auburn 21, Arkansas 15
12-27-85 — Baylor 21, Louisiana St. 7
12-29-86 — Tennessee 21, Minnesota 14
12-29-87 — Georgia 20, Arkansas 17
12-28-88 — Indiana 34, South Caro. 10
12-28-89 — Mississippi 42, Air Force 29
12-27-90 — Air Force 23, Ohio St. 11
12-29-91 — Air Force 38, Mississippi St. 15
12-31-92 — Mississippi 13, Air Force 0

## PEACH BOWL

**Present Site:** Atlanta, Ga.
**Stadium (Capacity):** Georgia Dome (71,596)
**Playing Surface:** Turf
**Playing Sites:** Grant Field, Atlanta (1968-70); Atlanta/Fulton County (1971-92); Georgia Dome (since 1993)

12-30-68 — Louisiana St. 31, Florida St. 27
12-30-69 — West Va. 14, South Caro. 3
12-30-70 — Arizona St. 48, North Caro. 26
12-30-71 — Mississippi 41, Georgia Tech 18
12-29-72 — North Caro. St. 49, West Va. 13

12-28-73 — Georgia 17, Maryland 16
12-28-74 — Vanderbilt 6, Texas Tech 6
12-31-75 — West Va. 13, North Caro. St. 10
12-31-76 — Kentucky 21, North Caro. 0
12-31-77 — North Caro. St. 24, Iowa St. 14

*All-Time Bowl Game Results*

12-25-78—Purdue 41, Georgia Tech 21
12-31-79—Baylor 24, Clemson 18
1-2-81—Miami (Fla.) 20, Virginia Tech 10
12-31-81—West Va. 26, Florida 6
12-31-82—Iowa 28, Tennessee 22

12-30-83—Florida St. 28, North Caro. 3
12-31-84—Virginia 27, Purdue 24
12-31-85—Army 31, Illinois 29
12-31-86—Virginia Tech 25, North Caro. St. 24
1-2-88—Tennessee 27, Indiana 22

12-31-88—North Caro. St. 28, Iowa 23
12-30-89—Syracuse 19, Georgia 18
12-29-90—Auburn 27, Indiana 23
1-1-92—East Caro. 37, North Caro. St. 34
1-2-93—North Caro. 21, Mississippi St. 17

## FIESTA BOWL

**Present Site:** Tempe, Ariz.
**Stadium (Capacity):** Sun Devil (74,783)
**Playing Surface:** Grass
**Name Changes:** Fiesta Bowl (1971-88); Sunkist Fiesta Bowl (1989-90); Fiesta Bowl (1991-93); IBM OS/2 Fiesta Bowl (since 1994)
**Playing Sites:** Sun Devil Stadium (since 1971)

12-27-71—Arizona St. 45, Florida St. 38
12-23-72—Arizona St. 49, Missouri 35
12-21-73—Arizona St. 28, Pittsburgh 7
12-28-74—Oklahoma St. 16, Brigham Young 6
12-26-75—Arizona St. 17, Nebraska 14

12-25-76—Oklahoma 41, Wyoming 7
12-25-77—Penn St. 42, Arizona St. 30
12-25-78—Arkansas 10, UCLA 10
12-25-79—Pittsburgh 16, Arizona 10
12-26-80—Penn St. 31, Ohio St. 19

1-1-82—Penn St. 26, Southern Cal 10
1-1-83—Arizona St. 32, Oklahoma 21
1-2-84—Ohio St. 28, Pittsburgh 23
1-1-85—UCLA 39, Miami (Fla.) 37
1-1-86—Michigan 27, Nebraska 23

1-2-87—Penn St. 14, Miami (Fla.) 10
1-1-88—Florida St. 31, Nebraska 28
1-2-89—Notre Dame 34, West Va. 21
1-1-90—Florida St. 41, Nebraska 17
1-1-91—Louisville 34, Alabama 7
1-1-92—Penn St. 42, Tennessee 17
1-1-93—Syracuse 26, Colorado 22

## INDEPENDENCE BOWL

**Present Site:** Shreveport, La.
**Stadium (Capacity):** Independence (50,459)
**Playing Surface:** Grass
**Name Changes:** Independence Bowl (1976-89); Poulan Independence Bowl (1990); Poulan/Weed Eater Independence Bowl (since 1991)
**Playing Sites:** Independence Stadium (since 1976)

12-13-76—McNeese St. 20, Tulsa 16
12-17-77—Louisiana Tech 24, Louisville 14
12-16-78—East Caro. 35, Louisiana Tech 13
12-15-79—Syracuse 31, McNeese St. 7
12-13-80—Southern Miss. 16, McNeese St. 14

12-12-81—Texas A&M 33, Oklahoma St. 16
12-11-82—Wisconsin 14, Kansas St. 3
12-10-83—Air Force 9, Mississippi 3
12-15-84—Air Force 23, Virginia Tech 7
12-21-85—Minnesota 20, Clemson 13

12-20-86—Mississippi 20, Texas Tech 17
12-19-87—Washington 24, Tulane 12
12-23-88—Southern Miss. 38, UTEP 18
12-16-89—Oregon 27, Tulsa 24
12-15-90—Louisiana Tech 34, Maryland 34
12-29-91—Georgia 24, Arkansas 15
12-31-92—Wake Forest 39, Oregon 35

## HOLIDAY BOWL

**Present Site:** San Diego, Calif.
**Stadium (Capacity):** San Diego Jack Murphy (62,809)
**Playing Surface:** Grass
**Name Changes:** Sea World Holiday Bowl (1978-90); Thrifty Car Rental Holiday Bowl (since 1991)
**Playing Sites:** San Diego Jack Murphy Stadium (since 1978)

12-22-78—Navy 23, Brigham Young 16
12-21-79—Indiana 38, Brigham Young 37
12-19-80—Brigham Young 46, Southern Methodist 45
12-18-81—Brigham Young 38, Washington St. 36
12-17-82—Ohio St. 47, Brigham Young 17

12-23-83—Brigham Young 21, Missouri 17
12-21-84—Brigham Young 24, Michigan 17
12-22-85—Arkansas 18, Arizona St. 17
12-30-86—Iowa 39, San Diego St. 38
12-30-87—Iowa 20, Wyoming 19

12-30-88—Oklahoma St. 62, Wyoming 14
12-29-89—Penn St. 50, Brigham Young 39
12-29-90—Texas A&M 65, Brigham Young 14
12-30-91—Iowa 13, Brigham Young 13
12-30-92—Hawaii 27, Illinois 17

# ALOHA BOWL

**Present Site:** Honolulu, Hawaii
**Stadium (Capacity):** Aloha (50,000)
**Playing Surface:** AstroTurf
**Name Changes:** Aloha Bowl (1982-89); Eagle Aloha Bowl (1990); Jeep Eagle Aloha Bowl (since 1991)
**Playing Sites:** Aloha Stadium (since 1982)

12-25-82—Washington 21, Maryland 20
12-26-83—Penn St. 13, Washington 10
12-29-84—Southern Methodist 27, Notre Dame 20
12-28-85—Alabama 24, Southern Cal 3
12-27-86—Arizona 30, North Caro. 21

12-25-87—UCLA 20, Florida 16
12-25-88—Washington St. 24, Houston 22
12-25-89—Michigan St. 33, Hawaii 13
12-25-90—Syracuse 28, Arizona 0
12-25-91—Georgia Tech 18, Stanford 17
12-25-92—Kansas 23, Brigham Young 20

# FREEDOM BOWL

**Present Site:** Anaheim, Calif.
**Stadium (Capacity):** Anaheim (70,962)
**Playing Surface:** Grass
**Name Changes:** Anaheim Freedom Bowl (1984-90); Freedom Bowl (since 1991)
**Playing Sites:** Anaheim Stadium (since 1984)

12-26-84—Iowa 55, Texas 17
12-30-85—Washington 20, Colorado 17
12-30-86—UCLA 31, Brigham Young 10
12-30-87—Arizona St. 33, Air Force 28
12-29-88—Brigham Young 20, Colorado 17

12-30-89—Washington 34, Florida 7
12-29-90—Colorado St. 32, Oregon 31
12-30-91—Tulsa 28, San Diego St. 17
12-29-92—Fresno St. 24, Southern Cal 7

# HALL OF FAME BOWL

**Present Site:** Tampa, Fla.
**Stadium (Capacity):** Tampa (74,350)
**Playing Surface:** Grass
**Playing Sites:** Tampa Stadium (since 1986)

12-23-86—Boston College 27, Georgia 24
1-2-88—Michigan 28, Alabama 24
1-2-89—Syracuse 23, Louisiana St. 10
1-1-90—Auburn 31, Ohio St. 14
1-1-91—Clemson 30, Illinois 0

1-1-92—Syracuse 24, Ohio St. 17
1-1-93—Tennessee 38, Boston College 23

# COPPER BOWL

**Present Site:** Tucson, Ariz.
**Stadium (Capacity):** Arizona Wildcats (58,000)
**Playing Surface:** Grass
**Name Changes:** Domino's Pizza Copper Bowl (1989-91); Weiser Lock Copper Bowl (since 1992)
**Playing Sites:** Arizona Wildcats Stadium (since 1989)

12-31-89—Arizona 17, North Caro. St. 10
12-30-90—California 17, Wyoming 15

12-31-91—Indiana 24, Baylor 0
12-29-92—Washington St. 31, Utah 28

# SUNSHINE FOOTBALL CLASSIC

**Present Site:** Miami, Fla.
**Stadium (Capacity):** Joe Robbie (73,000)
**Playing Surface:** Grass
**Name Changes:** Blockbuster Bowl (1990-93); Sunshine Football Classic (since 1993)
**Playing Sites:** Joe Robbie Stadium (since 1990)

12-28-90—Florida St. 24, Penn St. 17
12-28-91—Alabama 30, Colorado 25

1-1-93—Stanford 24, Penn St. 3

# LAS VEGAS BOWL

**Present Site:** Las Vegas, Nev.
**Stadium (Capacity):** Sam Boyd Silver Bowl (31,000)
**Playing Surface:** Turf
**Playing Sites:** Sam Boyd Silver Bowl (since 1992)

12-18-92—Bowling Green 35, Nevada 34

*All-Time Bowl Game Results*

# 26 FORMER MAJOR BOWL GAMES
## (Games in which at least one team was classified major that season.)

**Alamo (San Antonio, Texas):** 1-4-47—Hardin-Simmons 20, Denver 0

**All-American (Birmingham, Ala.):** 12-22-77—Maryland 17, Minnesota 17; 12-20-78—Texas A&M 28, Iowa St. 12; 12-29-79—Missouri 24, South Caro. 14; 12-27-80—Arkansas 34, Tulane 15; 12-31-81—Mississippi St. 10, Kansas 0; 12-31-82—Air Force 36, Vanderbilt 28; 12-22-83—West Va. 20, Kentucky 16; 12-29-84—Kentucky 20, Wisconsin 19; 12-31-85—Georgia Tech 17, Michigan St. 14; 12-31-86—Florida St. 27, Indiana 13; 12-22-87—Virginia 22, Brigham Young 16; 12-29-88—Florida 14, Illinois 10; 12-28-89—Texas Tech 49, Duke 21; 12-28-90—North Caro. St. 31, Southern Miss. 27

**Aviation (Dayton, Ohio):** 12-9-61—New Mexico 28, Western Mich. 12

**Bacardi (Cuban National Sports Festival at Havana):** 1-1-37—Auburn 7, Villanova 7

**Bluebonnet (Houston, Texas):** 12-19-59—Clemson 23, Texas Christian 7; 12-17-60—Texas 3, Alabama 3; 12-16-61—Kansas 33, Rice 7; 12-22-62—Missouri 14, Georgia Tech 10; 12-21-63—Baylor 14, Louisiana St. 7; 12-19-64—Tulsa 14, Mississippi 7; 12-18-65—Tennessee 27, Tulsa 6; 12-17-66—Texas 19, Mississippi 0; 12-23-67—Colorado 31, Miami (Fla.) 21; 12-31-68—Southern Methodist 28, Oklahoma 27; 12-31-69—Houston 36, Auburn 7; 12-31-70—Alabama 24, Oklahoma 24; 12-31-71—Colorado 29, Houston 17; 12-30-72—Tennessee 24, Louisiana St. 17; 12-29-73—Houston 47, Tulane 7; 12-23-74—North Caro. St. 31, Houston 31; 12-27-75—Texas 38, Colorado 21; 12-31-76—Nebraska 27, Texas Tech 24; 12-31-77—Southern Cal 47, Texas A&M 28; 12-31-78—Stanford 25, Georgia 22; 12-31-79—Purdue 27, Tennessee 22; 12-31-80—North Caro. 16, Texas 7; 12-31-81—Michigan 33, UCLA 14; 12-31-82—Arkansas 28, Florida 24; 12-31-83—Oklahoma St. 24, Baylor 14; 12-31-84—West Va. 31, Texas Christian 14; 12-31-85—Air Force 24, Texas 16; 12-31-86—Baylor 21, Colorado 9; 12-31-87—Texas 32, Pittsburgh 27

**Bluegrass (Louisville, Ky.):** 12-13-58—Oklahoma St. 15, Florida St. 6

**California (Fresno, Calif.):** 12-19-81—Toledo 27, San Jose St. 25; 12-18-82—Fresno St. 29, Bowling Green 28; 12-17-83—Northern Ill. 20, Cal St. Fullerton 13; 12-15-84—Nevada-Las Vegas 30, *Toledo 13; 12-14-85—Fresno St. 51, Bowling Green 7; 12-13-86—San Jose St. 37, Miami (Ohio) 7; 12-12-87—Eastern Mich. 30, San Jose St. 27; 12-10-88—Fresno St. 35, Western Mich. 30; 12-9-89—Fresno St. 27, Ball St. 6; 12-8-90—San Jose St. 48, Central Mich. 24; 12-14-91—Bowling Green 28, Fresno St. 21

*Won by forfeit.

**Camellia (Lafayette, La.):** 12-30-48—Hardin-Simmons 49, Wichita St. 12

**Cherry (Pontiac, Mich.):** 12-22-84—Army 10, Michigan St. 6; 12-21-85—Maryland 35, Syracuse 18

**Delta (Memphis, Tenn.):** 1-1-48—Mississippi 13, Texas Christian 9; 1-1-49—William & Mary 20, Oklahoma St. 0

**Dixie (Birmingham, Ala.):** 1-1-48—Arkansas 21, William & Mary 19; 1-1-49—Baylor 20, Wake Forest 7

**Dixie Classic (Dallas, Texas):** 1-2-22—Texas A&M 22, Centre 14; 1-1-25—West Va. Wesleyan 9, Southern Methodist 7; 1-1-34—Arkansas 7, Centenary 7

**Fort Worth Classic (Fort Worth, Texas):** 1-1-21—Centre 63, Texas Christian 7

**Garden State (East Rutherford, N.J.):** 12-16-78—Arizona St. 34, Rutgers 18; 12-15-79—Temple 28, California 17; 12-14-80—Houston 35, Navy 0; 12-13-81—Tennessee 28, Wisconsin 21

**Gotham (New York, N.Y.):** 12-9-61—Baylor 24, Utah St. 9; 12-15-62—Nebraska 36, Miami (Fla.) 34

**Great Lakes (Cleveland, Ohio):** 12-6-47—Kentucky 24, Villanova 14

**Harbor (San Diego, Calif.):** 1-1-47—New Mexico 13, Montana St. 13; 1-1-48—Hardin-Simmons 53, San Diego St. 0; 1-1-49—Villanova 27, Nevada 7

**Los Angeles Christmas (Los Angeles, Calif.):** 12-25-24—Southern Cal 20, Missouri 7

**Mercy (Los Angeles, Calif.):** 11-23-61—Fresno St. 36, Bowling Green 6

**Oil (Houston, Texas):** 1-1-46—Georgia 20, Tulsa 6; 1-1-47—Georgia Tech 41, St. Mary's (Calif.) 19

**Pasadena (called Junior Rose in 1967) (Pasadena, Calif.):** 12-2-67—West Tex. St. 35, Cal St. Northridge 13; 12-6-69—San Diego St. 28, Boston U. 7; 12-19-70—Louisville 24, Long Beach St. 24; 12-18-71—Memphis St. 28, San Jose St. 9

**Presidential Cup (College Park, Md.):** 12-9-50—Texas A&M 40, Georgia 20

**Raisin (Fresno, Calif.):** 1-1-46—Drake 13, Fresno St. 12; 1-1-47—San Jose St. 20, Utah St. 0; 1-1-48—Pacific (Cal.) 26, Wichita St. 14; 1-1-49—Occidental 21, Colorado St. 20; 12-31-49— San Jose St. 20, Texas Tech 13

**Salad (Phoenix, Ariz.):** 1-1-48—Nevada 13, North Texas 6; 1-1-49—Drake 14, Arizona 13; 1-1-50—Xavier (Ohio) 33, Arizona St. 21; 1-1-51—Miami (Ohio) 34, Arizona St. 21; 1-1-52—Houston 26, Dayton 21

**San Diego East-West Christmas Classic (San Diego, Calif.):** 12-26-21—Centre 38, Arizona 0; 12-25-22—West Va. 21, Gonzaga 13

**Shrine (Little Rock, Ark.):** 12-18-48—Hardin-Simmons 40, Ouachita Baptist 12

# OTHER MAJOR POSTSEASON GAMES

There was a proliferation of postseason benefit games specially scheduled at the conclusion of the regular season during the Great Depression (principally in 1931) to raise money for relief of the unemployed in response to the President's Committee on Mobilization of Relief Resources and for other charitable causes.

The exact number of these games is unknown, but it is estimated that more than 100 college games were played nationwide during this period, often irrespective of the competing teams' records. Proceeds went to the benefit of the emergency relief for unemployment and numerous charities.

Most notable among these postseason games were the Tennessee-New York U. game of 1931 and the Army-Navy contests of 1930 and 1931 (the two academies had severed athletics relations during 1928-31 and did not meet in regular-season play). All three games were played before huge crowds in New York City's Yankee Stadium.

Following is a list of the principal postseason benefit and charity games involving at least one major college. Not included (nor included in all-time team won-lost records) are several special feature, same-day double-header tournaments in 1931 in which four participating teams were paired to play halves or modified quarters.

| Date | Site | Opposing Teams |
|---|---|---|
| 12-6-30 | New York | Colgate 7, New York U. 0 |
| 12-13-30 | New York | Army 6, Navy 0 |
| 11-28-31 | Kansas City | Temple 38, Missouri 6 |
| 11-28-31 | Chicago | Purdue 7, Northwestern 0 |
| 11-28-31 | Minneapolis | Minnesota 19, Ohio St. 7 |
| 11-28-31 | Ann Arbor | Michigan 16, Wisconsin 0 |
| 11-28-31 | Philadelphia | Penn St. 31, Lehigh 0 |
| 12-2-31 | Chattanooga | Alabama 49, Tenn.-Chatt. 0 |
| 12-3-31 | Brooklyn | Manhattan 7, Rutgers 6 |
| 12-5-31 | Denver | Nebraska 20, Colorado St. 7 |
| 12-5-31 | Pittsburgh | Carnegie Mellon 0, Duquesne 0 |
| 12-5-31 | New York | Tennessee 13, New York U. 0 |
| 12-5-31 | St. Louis | St. Louis 31, Missouri 6 |
| 12-5-31 | Topeka | Kansas 6, Washburn 0 |
| 12-5-31 | Wichita | Kansas St. 20, Wichita St. 6 |
| 12-5-31 | Columbia | Centre 9, South Caro. 7 |
| 12-5-31 | Norman | Oklahoma City 6, Oklahoma 0 |
| 12-12-31 | New York | Army 17, Navy 7 |
| 12-12-31 | Tulsa | Oklahoma 20, Tulsa 7 |
| 1-2-33 | El Paso | Southern Methodist 26, UTEP 0 |
| 12-8-34 | St. Louis | Southern Methodist 7, Washington (Mo.) 0 |

# TEAM-BY-TEAM BOWL RESULTS

## ALL-TIME BOWL-GAME RECORDS

This list includes all bowls played by a current major team, providing its opponent was classified major that season or it was a major team then. The list excludes games in which a home team served as a predetermined, preseason host regardless of its record and/or games scheduled before the season, thus eliminating the old Pineapple, Glass and Palm Festival. Following is the alphabetical list showing the record of each current major team in all major bowls.

| Team | W | L | T | Team | W | L | T |
|---|---|---|---|---|---|---|---|
| Air Force | 6 | 5 | 1 | Georgia Tech | 17 | 8 | 0 |
| Alabama | 25 | 17 | 3 | Hawaii | 1 | 1 | 0 |
| Arizona | 2 | 6 | 1 | Houston | 7 | 5 | 1 |
| Arizona St. | 9 | 5 | 1 | Illinois | 4 | 7 | 0 |
| Arkansas | 9 | 15 | 3 | Indiana | 3 | 4 | 0 |
| Army | 2 | 1 | 0 | Iowa | 6 | 5 | 1 |
| Auburn | 12 | 9 | 2 | Iowa St. | 0 | 4 | 0 |
| Ball St. | 0 | 1 | 0 | Kansas | 2 | 5 | 0 |
| Baylor | 8 | 7 | 0 | Kansas St. | 0 | 1 | 0 |
| Boston College | 3 | 5 | 0 | Kent | 0 | 1 | 0 |
| Bowling Green | 2 | 3 | 0 | Kentucky | 5 | 2 | 0 |
| Brigham Young | 5 | 11 | 1 | Louisiana St. | 11 | 16 | 1 |
| California | 4 | 6 | 1 | Louisiana Tech | 0 | 0 | 1 |
| Central Mich. | 0 | 1 | 0 | Louisville | 2 | 1 | 1 |
| Cincinnati | 1 | 1 | 0 | Maryland | 6 | 9 | 2 |
| Clemson | 11 | 7 | 0 | Memphis St. | 1 | 0 | 0 |
| Colorado | 5 | 12 | 0 | Miami (Fla.) | 10 | 9 | 0 |
| Colorado St. | 1 | 1 | 0 | Miami (Ohio) | 5 | 2 | 0 |
| Duke | 3 | 4 | 0 | Michigan | 11 | 13 | 0 |
| East Caro. | 2 | 0 | 0 | Michigan St. | 5 | 5 | 0 |
| Eastern Mich. | 1 | 0 | 0 | Minnesota | 2 | 3 | 0 |
| Florida | 9 | 11 | 0 | Mississippi | 14 | 11 | 0 |
| Florida St. | 12 | 7 | 2 | Mississippi St. | 4 | 4 | 0 |
| Fresno St. | 6 | 2 | 0 | Missouri | 8 | 11 | 0 |
| Georgia | 15 | 13 | 3 | Navy | 3 | 4 | 1 |

| Team | W | L | T | Team | W | L | T |
|---|---|---|---|---|---|---|---|
| Nebraska | 14 | 17 | 0 | Temple | 1 | 1 | 0 |
| Nevada | 1 | 2 | 0 | Tennessee | 18 | 15 | 0 |
| Nevada-Las Vegas | #1 | 0 | 0 | Texas | 16 | 16 | 2 |
| New Mexico | 2 | 2 | 1 | Texas A&M | 11 | 9 | 0 |
| New Mexico St. | 2 | 0 | 1 | Texas Christian | 4 | 9 | 1 |
| North Caro. | 7 | 10 | 0 | Texas Tech | 4 | 13 | 1 |
| North Caro. St. | 7 | 7 | 1 | Toledo | 4 | 1 | 0 |
| Northern Ill. | 1 | 0 | 0 | Tulane | 2 | 6 | 0 |
| Northwestern | 1 | 0 | 0 | Tulsa | 4 | 7 | 0 |
| Notre Dame | 12 | 6 | 0 | UCLA | 10 | 7 | 1 |
| Ohio | 0 | 2 | 0 | Utah | 2 | 1 | 0 |
| Ohio St. | 11 | 14 | 0 | Utah St. | 0 | 3 | 0 |
| Oklahoma | 19 | 10 | 1 | UTEP | 5 | 4 | 0 |
| Oklahoma St. | 9 | 3 | 0 | Vanderbilt | 1 | 1 | 0 |
| Oregon | 3 | 6 | 0 | Virginia | 2 | 3 | 0 |
| Oregon St. | 2 | 2 | 0 | Virginia Tech | 1 | 5 | 0 |
| Pacific (Cal.) | 2 | 1 | 0 | Wake Forest | 2 | 2 | 0 |
| Penn St. | 17 | 10 | 2 | Washington | 12 | 8 | 1 |
| Pittsburgh | 8 | 10 | 0 | Washington St. | 3 | 2 | 0 |
| Purdue | 4 | 1 | 0 | West Va. | 8 | 7 | 0 |
| Rice | 4 | 3 | 0 | Western Mich. | 0 | 2 | 0 |
| Rutgers | 0 | 1 | 0 | Wisconsin | 1 | 5 | 0 |
| San Diego St. | 1 | 3 | 0 | Wyoming | 4 | 5 | 0 |
| San Jose St. | 4 | 3 | 0 | | | | |
| South Caro. | 0 | 8 | 0 | | | | |
| Southern Cal | 22 | 13 | 0 | | | | |
| Southern Methodist | 4 | 6 | 1 | | | | |
| Southern Miss. | 2 | 4 | 0 | | | | |
| Stanford | 8 | 7 | 1 | | | | |
| Syracuse | 8 | 6 | 1 | | | | |

# Later lost game by forfeit.

The following current Division I-A teams have not played in a major bowl game: Akron, Arkansas St. and Southwestern La.

## MAJOR BOWL-GAME RECORDS OF NON-DIVISION I-A TEAMS

Boston U. 0-1-0; Brown 0-1-0; Bucknell 1-0-0; Cal St. Fullerton 0-1-0; Cal St. Northridge 0-1-0; Carnegie Mellon 0-1-0; Case Reserve 1-0-0; Catholic 1-0-1; Centenary 0-0-1; Centre 2-1-0; Citadel 1-0-0; Columbia 1-0-0; Davidson 0-1-0; Dayton 0-1-0; Denver 0-1-0; Drake 2-1-0; Duquesne 1-0-0; Fordham 1-1-0; Geo. Washington 1-0-0; Georgetown 0-2-0; Gonzaga 0-1-0; Hardin-Simmons 5-2-1; Harvard 1-0-0; Holy Cross 0-1-0; Long Beach St. 0-0-1; Marquette 0-1-0; McNeese St. 1-2-0; Montana St. 0-0-1; North Texas 0-2-0; Occidental 1-0-0; Ouachita Baptist 0-1-0; Pennsylvania 0-1-0; Randolph Field 0-0-1; Richmond 1-1-0; Santa Clara 3-0-0; Second Air Force 1-0-0; Southwestern (Tex.) 2-0-0; St. Mary's (Cal.) 1-2-0; Tampa 1-0-0; Tennessee Tech 0-1-0; U. of Mexico 0-1-0; Villanova 2-2-1; Wash. & Jeff. 0-0-1; Wash. & Lee 0-1-0; West Tex. St. 3-0-0; West Va. Wesleyan 1-0-0; Wichita St. 0-3-0; William & Mary 1-2-0; Xavier (Ohio) 1-0-0. **TOTALS: 37-38-8**

## ALL-TIME BOWL APPEARANCES

(Must be classified as a major bowl game where one team was considered a major college at the time)

| Team | Appearances | Team | Appearances |
|---|---|---|---|
| Alabama | 45 | Florida St. | 21 |
| Southern Cal | 35 | Washington | 21 |
| Texas | 34 | Florida | 20 |
| Tennessee | 33 | Texas A&M | 20 |
| Georgia | 31 | Miami (Fla.) | 19 |
| Nebraska | 31 | Missouri | 19 |
| Oklahoma | 30 | Clemson | 18 |
| Penn St. | 29 | Notre Dame | 18 |
| Louisiana St. | 28 | Pittsburgh | 18 |
| Arkansas | 27 | Texas Tech | 18 |
| Georgia Tech | 25 | UCLA | 18 |
| Mississippi | 25 | Brigham Young | 17 |
| Ohio St. | 25 | Colorado | 17 |
| Michigan | 24 | Maryland | 17 |
| Auburn | 23 | North Caro. | 17 |

# ALL-TIME BOWL VICTORIES
### (Includes bowls where at least one team was classified a major college at the time)

| Team | Victories | Team | Victories |
|------|-----------|------|-----------|
| Alabama | 25 | UCLA | 10 |
| Southern Cal | 22 | Arizona St. | 9 |
| Oklahoma | 19 | Arkansas | 9 |
| Tennessee | 18 | Florida | 9 |
| Georgia Tech | 17 | Oklahoma St. | 9 |
| Penn St. | 17 | Baylor | 8 |
| Texas | 16 | Missouri | 8 |
| Georgia | 15 | Pittsburgh | 8 |
| Mississippi | 14 | Stanford | 8 |
| Nebraska | 14 | Syracuse | 8 |
| Auburn | 12 | West Va. | 8 |
| Florida St. | 12 | | |
| Notre Dame | 12 | | |
| Washington | 12 | | |
| Clemson | 11 | | |
| Louisiana St. | 11 | | |
| Michigan | 11 | | |
| Ohio St. | 11 | | |
| Texas A&M | 11 | | |
| Miami (Fla.) | 10 | | |

# TEAM-BY-TEAM MAJOR BOWL SCORES
# WITH COACH OF EACH BOWL TEAM

Listed below are the 103 I-A teams that have participated in history's 633 major bowl games (the term "major bowl" is defined above the alphabetical list of team bowl records). The teams are listed alphabetically, with each coach listed along with the bowl participated in, date played, opponent, score and team's all-time bowl-game record. Following the I-A list is a group of 49 teams that played in a major bowl game or games but are no longer classified as I-A.

## AIR FORCE

| | Bowl | Date | Opponent | Score |
|---|------|------|----------|-------|
| Ben Martin | Cotton | 1-1-59 | Texas Christian | 0-0 |
| Ben Martin | Gator | 12-28-63 | North Caro. | 0-35 |
| Ben Martin | Sugar | 1-1-71 | Tennessee | 13-34 |
| Ken Hatfield | Hall of Fame | 12-31-82 | Vanderbilt | 36-28 |
| Ken Hatfield | Independence | 12-10-83 | Mississippi | 9-3 |
| Fisher DeBerry | Independence | 12-15-84 | Virginia Tech | 23-7 |
| Fisher DeBerry | Bluebonnet | 12-31-85 | Texas | 24-16 |
| Fisher DeBerry | Freedom | 12-30-87 | Arizona St. | 28-33 |
| Fisher DeBerry | Liberty | 12-28-89 | Mississippi | 29-42 |
| Fisher DeBerry | Liberty | 12-27-90 | Ohio St. | 23-11 |
| Fisher DeBerry | Liberty | 12-29-91 | Mississippi St. | 38-15 |
| Fisher DeBerry | Liberty | 12-31-92 | Mississippi | 0-13 |

All bowls 6-5-1

## ALABAMA

| | Bowl | Date | Opponent | Score |
|---|------|------|----------|-------|
| Wallace Wade | Rose | 1-1-26 | Washington | 20-19 |
| Wallace Wade | Rose | 1-1-27 | Stanford | 7-7 |
| Wallace Wade | Rose | 1-1-31 | Washington St. | 24-0 |
| Frank Thomas | Rose | 1-1-35 | Stanford | 29-13 |
| Frank Thomas | Rose | 1-1-38 | California | 0-13 |
| Frank Thomas | Cotton | 1-1-42 | Texas A&M | 29-21 |
| Frank Thomas | Orange | 1-1-43 | Boston College | 37-21 |
| Frank Thomas | Sugar | 1-1-45 | Duke | 26-29 |
| Frank Thomas | Rose | 1-1-46 | Southern Cal | 34-14 |
| Harold "Red" Drew | Sugar | 1-1-48 | Texas | 7-27 |
| Harold "Red" Drew | Orange | 1-1-53 | Syracuse | 61-6 |
| Harold "Red" Drew | Cotton | 1-1-54 | Rice | 6-28 |
| Paul "Bear" Bryant | Liberty | 12-19-59 | Penn St. | 0-7 |
| Paul "Bear" Bryant | Bluebonnet | 12-17-60 | Texas | 3-3 |
| Paul "Bear" Bryant | Sugar | 1-1-62 | Arkansas | 10-3 |
| Paul "Bear" Bryant | Orange | 1-1-63 | Oklahoma | 17-0 |
| Paul "Bear" Bryant | Sugar | 1-1-64 | Mississippi | 12-7 |
| Paul "Bear" Bryant | Orange | 1-1-65 | Texas | 17-21 |
| Paul "Bear" Bryant | Orange | 1-1-66 | Nebraska | 39-28 |
| Paul "Bear" Bryant | Sugar | 1-2-67 | Nebraska | 34-7 |

*Team-by-Team Bowl Results*

The legendary Paul "Bear" Bryant coached Alabama to 24 of the Crimson Tide's 45 bowl appearances, the most of any school. Alabama also holds the all-time lead in bowl-game victories (25).

| | | | | |
|---|---|---|---|---|
| Paul "Bear" Bryant | Cotton | 1-1-68 | Texas A&M | 16-20 |
| Paul "Bear" Bryant | Gator | 12-28-68 | Missouri | 10-35 |
| Paul "Bear" Bryant | Liberty | 12-13-69 | Colorado | 33-47 |
| Paul "Bear" Bryant | Bluebonnet | 12-31-70 | Oklahoma | 24-24 |
| Paul "Bear" Bryant | Orange | 1-1-72 | Nebraska | 6-38 |
| Paul "Bear" Bryant | Cotton | 1-1-73 | Texas | 13-17 |
| Paul "Bear" Bryant | Sugar | 12-31-73 | Notre Dame | 23-24 |
| Paul "Bear" Bryant | Orange | 1-1-75 | Notre Dame | 11-13 |
| Paul "Bear" Bryant | Sugar | 12-31-75 | Penn St. | 13-6 |
| Paul "Bear" Bryant | Liberty | 12-20-76 | UCLA | 36-6 |
| Paul "Bear" Bryant | Sugar | 1-2-78 | Ohio St. | 35-6 |
| Paul "Bear" Bryant | Sugar | 1-1-79 | Penn St. | 14-7 |
| Paul "Bear" Bryant | Sugar | 1-1-80 | Arkansas | 24-9 |
| Paul "Bear" Bryant | Cotton | 1-1-81 | Baylor | 30-2 |
| Paul "Bear" Bryant | Cotton | 1-1-82 | Texas | 12-14 |
| Paul "Bear" Bryant | Liberty | 12-29-82 | Illinois | 21-15 |
| Ray Perkins | Sun | 12-24-83 | Southern Methodist | 28-7 |
| Ray Perkins | Aloha | 12-28-85 | Southern Cal | 24-3 |
| Ray Perkins | Sun | 12-25-86 | Washington | 28-6 |
| Bill Curry | Hall of Fame | 1-2-88 | Michigan | 24-28 |
| Bill Curry | Sun | 12-24-88 | Army | 29-28 |
| Bill Curry | Sugar | 1-1-90 | Miami (Fla.) | 25-33 |
| Gene Stallings | Fiesta | 1-1-91 | Louisville | 7-34 |
| Gene Stallings | Blockbuster | 12-28-91 | Colorado | 30-25 |
| Gene Stallings | Sugar | 1-1-93 | Miami (Fla.) | 34-13 |

All bowls 25-17-3

| ARIZONA | Bowl | Date | Opponent | Score |
|---|---|---|---|---|
| J. F. "Pop" McKale | San Diego E-W Christmas Classic | 12-26-21 | Centre | 0-38 |
| Miles Casteel | Salad | 1-1-49 | Drake | 13-14 |
| Darrell Mudra | Sun | 12-28-68 | Auburn | 10-34 |
| Tony Mason | Fiesta | 12-25-79 | Pittsburgh | 10-16 |
| Larry Smith | Sun | 12-28-85 | Georgia | 13-13 |
| Larry Smith | Aloha | 12-27-86 | North Caro. | 30-21 |
| Dick Tomey | Copper | 12-31-89 | North Caro. St. | 17-10 |
| Dick Tomey | Aloha | 12-25-90 | Syracuse | 0-28 |
| Dick Tomey | John Hancock | 12-31-92 | Baylor | 15-20 |

All bowls 2-6-1

| ARIZONA ST. | Bowl | Date | Opponent | Score |
|---|---|---|---|---|
| Millard "Dixie" Howell | Sun | 1-1-40 | Catholic | 0-0 |
| Millard "Dixie" Howell | Sun | 1-1-41 | Case Reserve | 13-26 |
| Ed Doherty | Salad | 1-1-50 | Xavier (Ohio) | 21-33 |
| Ed Doherty | Salad | 1-1-51 | Miami (Ohio) | 21-34 |
| Frank Kush | Peach | 12-30-70 | North Caro. | 48-26 |
| Frank Kush | Fiesta | 12-27-71 | Florida St. | 45-38 |
| Frank Kush | Fiesta | 12-23-72 | Missouri | 49-35 |
| Frank Kush | Fiesta | 12-21-73 | Pittsburgh | 28-7 |
| Frank Kush | Fiesta | 12-26-75 | Nebraska | 17-14 |
| Frank Kush | Fiesta | 12-25-77 | Penn St. | 30-42 |
| Frank Kush | Garden State | 12-16-78 | Rutgers | 34-18 |
| Darryl Rogers | Fiesta | 1-1-83 | Oklahoma | 32-21 |
| John Cooper | Holiday | 12-22-85 | Arkansas | 17-18 |
| John Cooper | Rose | 1-1-87 | Michigan | 22-15 |
| John Cooper | Freedom | 12-30-87 | Air Force | 33-28 |

All bowls 9-5-1

| ARKANSAS | Bowl | Date | Opponent | Score |
|---|---|---|---|---|
| Fred Thomsen | Dixie Classic | 1-1-34 | Centenary | 7-7 |
| John Barnhill | Cotton | 1-1-47 | Louisiana St. | 0-0 |
| John Barnhill | Dixie | 1-1-48 | William & Mary | 21-19 |
| Bowden Wyatt | Cotton | 1-1-55 | Georgia Tech | 6-14 |
| Frank Broyles | Gator | 1-2-60 | Georgia Tech | 14-7 |
| Frank Broyles | Cotton | 1-2-61 | Duke | 6-7 |
| Frank Broyles | Sugar | 1-1-62 | Alabama | 3-10 |
| Frank Broyles | Sugar | 1-1-63 | Mississippi | 13-17 |
| Frank Broyles | Cotton | 1-1-65 | Nebraska | 10-7 |
| Frank Broyles | Cotton | 1-1-66 | Louisiana St. | 7-14 |
| Frank Broyles | Sugar | 1-1-69 | Georgia | 16-2 |
| Frank Broyles | Sugar | 1-1-70 | Mississippi | 22-27 |
| Frank Broyles | Liberty | 12-20-71 | Tennessee | 13-14 |
| Frank Broyles | Cotton | 1-1-76 | Georgia | 31-10 |
| Lou Holtz | Orange | 1-2-78 | Oklahoma | 31-6 |
| Lou Holtz | Fiesta | 12-25-78 | UCLA | 10-10 |
| Lou Holtz | Sugar | 1-1-80 | Alabama | 9-24 |
| Lou Holtz | Hall of Fame | 12-27-80 | Tulane | 34-15 |
| Lou Holtz | Gator | 12-28-81 | North Caro. | 27-31 |
| Lou Holtz | Bluebonnet | 12-31-82 | Florida | 28-24 |
| Ken Hatfield | Liberty | 12-27-84 | Auburn | 15-21 |
| Ken Hatfield | Holiday | 12-22-85 | Arizona St. | 18-17 |
| Ken Hatfield | Orange | 1-1-87 | Oklahoma | 8-42 |
| Ken Hatfield | Liberty | 12-29-87 | Georgia | 17-20 |
| Ken Hatfield | Cotton | 1-2-89 | UCLA | 3-17 |
| Ken Hatfield | Cotton | 1-1-90 | Tennessee | 27-31 |
| Jack Crowe | Independence | 12-29-91 | Georgia | 15-24 |

All bowls 9-15-3

| ARMY | Bowl | Date | Opponent | Score |
|---|---|---|---|---|
| Jim Young | Cherry | 12-22-84 | Michigan St. | 10-6 |
| Jim Young | Peach | 12-31-85 | Illinois | 31-29 |
| Jim Young | Sun | 12-24-88 | Alabama | 28-29 |

All bowls 2-1-0

| AUBURN | Bowl | Date | Opponent | Score |
|---|---|---|---|---|
| Jack Meagher | Bacardi, Cuba | 1-1-37 | Villanova | 7-7 |
| Jack Meagher | Orange | 1-1-38 | Michigan St. | 6-0 |
| Ralph "Shug" Jordan | Gator | 1-1-54 | Texas Tech | 13-35 |
| Ralph "Shug" Jordan | Gator | 12-31-54 | Baylor | 33-13 |
| Ralph "Shug" Jordan | Gator | 12-31-55 | Vanderbilt | 13-25 |

*Team-by-Team Bowl Results*

387

| | | | | |
|---|---|---|---|---|
| Ralph "Shug" Jordan ............. | Orange | 1-1-64 | Nebraska | 7-13 |
| Ralph "Shug" Jordan ............. | Liberty | 12-18-65 | Mississippi | 7-13 |
| Ralph "Shug" Jordan ............. | Sun | 12-28-68 | Arizona | 34-10 |
| Ralph "Shug" Jordan ............. | Bluebonnet | 12-31-69 | Houston | 7-36 |
| Ralph "Shug" Jordan ............. | Gator | 1-2-71 | Mississippi | 35-28 |
| Ralph "Shug" Jordan ............. | Sugar | 1-1-72 | Oklahoma | 22-40 |
| Ralph "Shug" Jordan ............. | Gator | 12-30-72 | Colorado | 24-3 |
| Ralph "Shug" Jordan ............. | Sun | 12-29-73 | Missouri | 17-34 |
| Ralph "Shug" Jordan ............. | Gator | 12-30-74 | Texas | 27-3 |
| Pat Dye ........................ | Tangerine | 12-18-82 | Boston College | 33-26 |
| Pat Dye ........................ | Sugar | 1-2-84 | Michigan | 9-7 |
| Pat Dye ........................ | Liberty | 12-27-84 | Arkansas | 21-15 |
| Pat Dye ........................ | Cotton | 1-1-86 | Texas A&M | 16-36 |
| Pat Dye ........................ | Florida Citrus | 1-1-87 | Southern Cal | 16-7 |
| Pat Dye ........................ | Sugar | 1-1-88 | Syracuse | 16-16 |
| Pat Dye ........................ | Sugar | 1-2-89 | Florida St. | 7-13 |
| Pat Dye ........................ | Hall of Fame | 1-1-90 | Ohio St. | 31-24 |
| Pat Dye ........................ | Peach | 12-29-90 | Indiana | 27-23 |

All bowls 12-9-2

### BALL ST.
| | Bowl | Date | Opponent | Score |
|---|---|---|---|---|
| Paul Schudel.................... | California | 12-9-89 | Fresno St. | 6-27 |

All bowls 0-1-0

### BAYLOR
| | Bowl | Date | Opponent | Score |
|---|---|---|---|---|
| Bob Woodruff .................... | Dixie | 1-1-49 | Wake Forest | 20-7 |
| George Sauer .................... | Orange | 1-1-52 | Georgia Tech | 14-17 |
| George Sauer .................... | Gator | 12-31-54 | Auburn | 13-33 |
| Sam Boyd........................ | Sugar | 1-1-57 | Tennessee | 13-7 |
| John Bridgers ................... | Gator | 12-31-60 | Florida | 12-13 |
| John Bridgers ................... | Gotham | 12-9-61 | Utah St. | 24-9 |
| John Bridgers ................... | Bluebonnet | 12-21-63 | Louisiana St. | 14-7 |
| Grant Teaff ..................... | Cotton | 1-1-75 | Penn St. | 20-41 |
| Grant Teaff ..................... | Peach | 12-31-79 | Clemson | 24-18 |
| Grant Teaff ..................... | Cotton | 1-1-81 | Alabama | 2-30 |
| Grant Teaff ..................... | Bluebonnet | 12-31-83 | Oklahoma St. | 14-24 |
| Grant Teaff ..................... | Liberty | 12-27-85 | Louisiana St. | 21-7 |
| Grant Teaff ..................... | Bluebonnet | 12-31-86 | Colorado | 21-9 |
| Grant Teaff ..................... | Copper | 12-31-91 | Indiana | 0-24 |
| Grant Teaff ..................... | John Hancock | 12-31-92 | Arizona | 20-15 |

All bowls 8-7-0

### BOSTON COLLEGE
| | Bowl | Date | Opponent | Score |
|---|---|---|---|---|
| Frank Leahy ..................... | Cotton | 1-1-40 | Clemson | 3-6 |
| Frank Leahy ..................... | Sugar | 1-1-41 | Tennessee | 19-13 |
| Denny Myers..................... | Orange | 1-1-43 | Alabama | 21-37 |
| Jack Bicknell.................... | Tangerine | 12-18-82 | Auburn | 26-33 |
| Jack Bicknell.................... | Liberty | 12-29-83 | Notre Dame | 18-19 |
| Jack Bicknell.................... | Cotton | 1-1-85 | Houston | 45-28 |
| Jack Bicknell.................... | Hall of Fame | 12-23-86 | Georgia | 27-24 |
| Tom Coughlin.................... | Hall of Fame | 1-1-93 | Tennessee | 23-38 |

All bowls 3-5-0

### BOWLING GREEN
| | Bowl | Date | Opponent | Score |
|---|---|---|---|---|
| Doyt Perry ...................... | Mercy | 11-23-61 | Fresno St. | 6-36 |
| Denny Stolz..................... | California | 12-18-82 | Fresno St. | 28-29 |
| Denny Stolz..................... | California | 12-14-85 | Fresno St. | 7-51 |
| Gary Blackney .................. | California | 12-14-91 | Fresno St. | 28-21 |
| Gary Blackney .................. | Las Vegas | 12-18-92 | Nevada | 35-34 |

All bowls 2-3-0

### BRIGHAM YOUNG
| | Bowl | Date | Opponent | Score |
|---|---|---|---|---|
| LaVell Edwards .................. | Fiesta | 12-28-74 | Oklahoma St. | 6-16 |
| LaVell Edwards .................. | Tangerine | 12-18-76 | Oklahoma St. | 21-49 |
| LaVell Edwards .................. | Holiday | 12-22-78 | Navy | 16-23 |
| LaVell Edwards .................. | Holiday | 12-21-79 | Indiana | 37-38 |
| LaVell Edwards .................. | Holiday | 12-19-80 | Southern Methodist | 46-45 |
| LaVell Edwards .................. | Holiday | 12-18-81 | Washington St. | 38-36 |
| LaVell Edwards .................. | Holiday | 12-17-82 | Ohio St. | 17-47 |
| LaVell Edwards .................. | Holiday | 12-23-83 | Missouri | 21-17 |
| LaVell Edwards .................. | Holiday | 12-21-84 | Michigan | 24-17 |
| LaVell Edwards .................. | Florida Citrus | 12-28-85 | Ohio St. | 7-10 |

| LaVell Edwards | Freedom | 12-30-86 | UCLA | 10-31 |
| LaVell Edwards | All-American | 12-22-87 | Virginia | 16-22 |
| LaVell Edwards | Freedom | 12-29-88 | Colorado | 20-17 |
| LaVell Edwards | Holiday | 12-29-89 | Penn St. | 39-50 |
| LaVell Edwards | Holiday | 12-29-90 | Texas A&M | 14-65 |
| LaVell Edwards | Holiday | 12-30-91 | Iowa | 13-13 |
| LaVell Edwards | Aloha | 12-25-92 | Kansas | 20-23 |

All bowls 5-11-1

## CALIFORNIA

| | Bowl | Date | Opponent | Score |
| --- | --- | --- | --- | --- |
| Andy Smith | Rose | 1-1-21 | Ohio St. | 28-0 |
| Andy Smith | Rose | 1-2-22 | Wash. & Jeff. | 0-0 |
| Clarence "Nibs" Price | Rose | 1-1-29 | Georgia Tech | 7-8 |
| Leonard "Stub" Allison | Rose | 1-1-38 | Alabama | 13-0 |
| Lynn "Pappy" Waldorf | Rose | 1-1-49 | Northwestern | 14-20 |
| Lynn "Pappy" Waldorf | Rose | 1-2-50 | Ohio St. | 14-17 |
| Lynn "Pappy" Waldorf | Rose | 1-1-51 | Michigan | 6-14 |
| Pete Elliott | Rose | 1-1-59 | Iowa | 12-38 |
| Roger Theder | Garden State | 12-15-79 | Temple | 17-28 |
| Bruce Snyder | Copper | 12-31-90 | Wyoming | 17-15 |
| Bruce Snyder | Florida Citrus | 1-1-92 | Clemson | 37-13 |

All bowls 4-6-1

## CENTRAL MICH.

| | Bowl | Date | Opponent | Score |
| --- | --- | --- | --- | --- |
| Herb Deromedi | California | 12-8-90 | San Jose St. | 24-48 |

All bowls 0-1-0

## CINCINNATI

| | Bowl | Date | Opponent | Score |
| --- | --- | --- | --- | --- |
| Ray Nolting | Sun | 1-1-47 | Virginia Tech | 18-6 |
| Sid Gillman | Sun | 1-1-51 | West Tex. St. | 13-14 |

All bowls 1-1-0

## CLEMSON

| | Bowl | Date | Opponent | Score |
| --- | --- | --- | --- | --- |
| Jess Neely | Cotton | 1-1-40 | Boston College | 6-3 |
| Frank Howard | Gator | 1-1-49 | Missouri | 24-23 |
| Frank Howard | Orange | 1-1-51 | Miami (Fla.) | 15-14 |
| Frank Howard | Gator | 1-1-52 | Miami (Fla.) | 0-14 |
| Frank Howard | Orange | 1-1-57 | Colorado | 21-27 |
| Frank Howard | Sugar | 1-1-59 | Louisiana St. | 0-7 |
| Frank Howard | Bluebonnet | 12-19-59 | Texas Christian | 23-7 |
| Charley Pell | Gator | 12-30-77 | Pittsburgh | 3-34 |
| Danny Ford | Gator | 12-29-78 | Ohio St. | 17-15 |
| Danny Ford | Peach | 12-31-79 | Baylor | 18-24 |
| Danny Ford | Orange | 1-1-82 | Nebraska | 22-15 |
| Danny Ford | Independence | 12-21-85 | Minnesota | 13-20 |
| Danny Ford | Gator | 12-27-86 | Stanford | 27-21 |
| Danny Ford | Florida Citrus | 1-1-88 | Penn St. | 35-10 |
| Danny Ford | Florida Citrus | 1-2-89 | Oklahoma | 23-6 |
| Danny Ford | Gator | 12-30-89 | West Va. | 27-7 |
| Ken Hatfield | Hall of Fame | 1-1-91 | Illinois | 30-0 |
| Ken Hatfield | Florida Citrus | 1-1-92 | California | 13-37 |

All bowls 11-7-0

## COLORADO

| | Bowl | Date | Opponent | Score |
| --- | --- | --- | --- | --- |
| Bernard "Bunnie" Oaks | Cotton | 1-1-38 | Rice | 14-28 |
| Dallas Ward | Orange | 1-1-57 | Clemson | 27-21 |
| Sonny Grandelius | Orange | 1-1-62 | Louisiana St. | 7-25 |
| Eddie Crowder | Bluebonnet | 12-23-67 | Miami (Fla.) | 31-21 |
| Eddie Crowder | Liberty | 12-13-69 | Alabama | 47-33 |
| Eddie Crowder | Liberty | 12-12-70 | Tulane | 3-17 |
| Eddie Crowder | Bluebonnet | 12-31-71 | Houston | 29-17 |
| Eddie Crowder | Gator | 12-30-72 | Auburn | 3-24 |
| Bill Mallory | Bluebonnet | 12-27-75 | Texas | 21-38 |
| Bill Mallory | Orange | 1-1-77 | Ohio St. | 10-27 |
| Bill McCartney | Freedom | 12-30-85 | Washington | 17-20 |
| Bill McCartney | Bluebonnet | 12-31-86 | Baylor | 9-21 |
| Bill McCartney | Freedom | 12-29-88 | Brigham Young | 17-20 |
| Bill McCartney | Orange | 1-1-90 | Notre Dame | 6-21 |
| Bill McCartney | Orange | 1-1-91 | Notre Dame | 10-9 |
| Bill McCartney | Blockbuster | 12-28-91 | Alabama | 25-30 |
| Bill McCartney | Fiesta | 1-1-93 | Syracuse | 22-26 |

All bowls 5-12-0

## COLORADO ST.

| | Bowl | Date | Opponent | Score |
|---|---|---|---|---|
| Bob Davis........................ | Raisin | 1-1-49 | Occidental | 20-21 |
| Earle Bruce ..................... | Freedom | 12-24-90 | Oregon | 32-31 |

All bowls 1-1-0

## DUKE

| | Bowl | Date | Opponent | Score |
|---|---|---|---|---|
| Wallace Wade ................... | Rose | 1-2-39 | Southern Cal | 3-7 |
| Wallace Wade ................... | Rose | 1-1-42 | Oregon St. | 16-20 |
| Eddie Cameron .................. | Sugar | 1-1-45 | Alabama | 29-26 |
| Bill Murray ...................... | Orange | 1-1-55 | Nebraska | 34-7 |
| Bill Murray ...................... | Orange | 1-1-58 | Oklahoma | 21-48 |
| Bill Murray ...................... | Cotton | 1-2-61 | Arkansas | 7-6 |
| Steve Spurrier................... | All-American | 12-28-89 | Texas Tech | 21-49 |

All bowls 3-4-0

## EAST CARO.

| | Bowl | Date | Opponent | Score |
|---|---|---|---|---|
| Pat Dye .......................... | Independence | 12-16-78 | Louisiana Tech | 35-13 |
| Bill Lewis........................ | Peach | 1-1-92 | North Caro. St. | 37-34 |

All bowls 2-0-0

## EASTERN MICH.

| | Bowl | Date | Opponent | Score |
|---|---|---|---|---|
| Jim Harkema..................... | California | 12-12-87 | San Jose St. | 30-27 |

All bowls 1-0-0

## FLORIDA

| | Bowl | Date | Opponent | Score |
|---|---|---|---|---|
| Bob Woodruff ................... | Gator | 1-1-53 | Tulsa | 14-13 |
| Bob Woodruff ................... | Gator | 12-27-58 | Mississippi | 3-7 |
| Ray Graves ..................... | Gator | 12-31-60 | Baylor | 13-12 |
| Ray Graves ..................... | Gator | 12-29-62 | Penn St. | 17-7 |
| Ray Graves ..................... | Sugar | 1-1-66 | Missouri | 18-20 |
| Ray Graves ..................... | Orange | 1-2-67 | Georgia Tech | 27-12 |
| Ray Graves ..................... | Gator | 12-27-69 | Tennessee | 14-13 |
| Doug Dickey..................... | Tangerine | 12-22-73 | Miami (Ohio) | 7-16 |
| Doug Dickey..................... | Sugar | 12-31-74 | Nebraska | 10-13 |
| Doug Dickey..................... | Gator | 12-29-75 | Maryland | 0-13 |
| Doug Dickey..................... | Sun | 1-2-77 | Texas A&M | 14-37 |
| Charley Pell..................... | Tangerine | 12-20-80 | Maryland | 35-20 |
| Charley Pell..................... | Peach | 12-31-81 | West Va. | 6-26 |
| Charley Pell..................... | Bluebonnet | 12-31-82 | Arkansas | 24-28 |
| Charley Pell..................... | Gator | 12-30-83 | Iowa | 14-6 |
| Galen Hall ...................... | Aloha | 12-25-87 | UCLA | 16-20 |
| Galen Hall ...................... | All-American | 12-29-88 | Illinois | 14-10 |
| Gary Darnell .................... | Freedom | 12-30-89 | Washington | 7-34 |
| Steve Spurrier................... | Sugar | 1-1-92 | Notre Dame | 28-39 |
| Steve Spurrier................... | Gator | 12-31-92 | North Caro. St. | 27-10 |

All bowls 9-11-0

## FLORIDA ST.

| | Bowl | Date | Opponent | Score |
|---|---|---|---|---|
| Tom Nugent...................... | Sun | 1-1-55 | UTEP | 20-47 |
| Tom Nugent...................... | Bluegrass | 12-13-58 | Oklahoma St. | 6-15 |
| Bill Peterson .................... | Gator | 1-2-65 | Oklahoma | 36-19 |
| Bill Peterson .................... | Sun | 12-24-66 | Wyoming | 20-28 |
| Bill Peterson .................... | Gator | 12-30-67 | Penn St. | 17-17 |
| Bill Peterson .................... | Peach | 12-30-68 | Louisiana St. | 27-31 |
| Larry Jones ..................... | Fiesta | 12-27-71 | Arizona St. | 38-45 |
| Bobby Bowden .................. | Tangerine | 12-23-77 | Texas Tech | 40-17 |
| Bobby Bowden .................. | Orange | 1-1-80 | Oklahoma | 7-24 |
| Bobby Bowden .................. | Orange | 1-1-81 | Oklahoma | 17-18 |
| Bobby Bowden .................. | Gator | 12-30-82 | West Va. | 31-12 |
| Bobby Bowden .................. | Peach | 12-30-83 | North Caro. | 28-3 |
| Bobby Bowden .................. | Florida Citrus | 12-22-84 | Georgia | 17-17 |
| Bobby Bowden .................. | Gator | 12-30-85 | Oklahoma St. | 34-23 |
| Bobby Bowden .................. | All-American | 12-31-86 | Indiana | 27-13 |
| Bobby Bowden .................. | Fiesta | 1-1-88 | Nebraska | 31-28 |
| Bobby Bowden .................. | Sugar | 1-2-89 | Auburn | 13-7 |
| Bobby Bowden .................. | Fiesta | 1-1-90 | Nebraska | 41-17 |
| Bobby Bowden .................. | Blockbuster | 12-28-90 | Penn St. | 24-17 |
| Bobby Bowden .................. | Cotton | 1-1-92 | Texas A&M | 10-2 |
| Bobby Bowden .................. | Orange | 1-1-93 | Nebraska | 27-14 |

All bowls 12-7-2

| FRESNO ST. | Bowl | Date | Opponent | Score |
|---|---|---|---|---|
| Alvin "Pix" Pierson ............... | Raisin | 1-1-46 | Drake | 12-13 |
| Cecil Coleman ................... | Mercy | 11-23-61 | Bowling Green | 36-6 |
| Jim Sweeney..................... | California | 12-18-82 | Bowling Green | 29-28 |
| Jim Sweeney..................... | California | 12-14-85 | Bowling Green | 51-7 |
| Jim Sweeney..................... | California | 12-10-88 | Western Mich. | 35-30 |
| Jim Sweeney..................... | California | 12-9-89 | Ball St. | 27-6 |
| Jim Sweeney..................... | California | 12-14-91 | Bowling Green | 21-28 |
| Jim Sweeney..................... | Freedom | 12-29-92 | Southern Cal | 24-7 |
| All bowls 6-2-0 | | | | |
| **GEORGIA** | Bowl | Date | Opponent | Score |
| Wally Butts....................... | Orange | 1-1-42 | Texas Christian | 40-26 |
| Wally Butts....................... | Rose | 1-1-43 | UCLA | 9-0 |
| Wally Butts....................... | Oil | 1-1-46 | Tulsa | 20-6 |
| Wally Butts....................... | Sugar | 1-1-47 | North Caro. | 20-10 |
| Wally Butts....................... | Gator | 1-1-48 | Maryland | 20-20 |
| Wally Butts....................... | Orange | 1-1-49 | Texas | 28-41 |
| Wally Butts....................... | Presidential | 12-9-50 | Texas A&M | 20-40 |
| Wally Butts....................... | Orange | 1-1-60 | Missouri | 14-0 |
| Vince Dooley..................... | Sun | 12-26-64 | Texas Tech | 7-0 |
| Vince Dooley..................... | Cotton | 12-31-66 | Southern Methodist | 24-9 |
| Vince Dooley..................... | Liberty | 12-16-67 | North Caro. St. | 7-14 |
| Vince Dooley..................... | Sugar | 1-1-69 | Arkansas | 2-16 |
| Vince Dooley..................... | Sun | 12-20-69 | Nebraska | 6-45 |
| Vince Dooley..................... | Gator | 12-31-71 | North Caro. | 7-3 |
| Vince Dooley..................... | Peach | 12-28-73 | Maryland | 17-16 |
| Vince Dooley..................... | Tangerine | 12-21-74 | Miami (Ohio) | 10-21 |
| Vince Dooley..................... | Cotton | 1-1-76 | Arkansas | 10-31 |
| Vince Dooley..................... | Sugar | 1-1-77 | Pittsburgh | 3-27 |
| Vince Dooley..................... | Bluebonnet | 12-31-78 | Stanford | 22-25 |
| Vince Dooley..................... | Sugar | 1-1-81 | Notre Dame | 17-10 |
| Vince Dooley..................... | Sugar | 1-1-82 | Pittsburgh | 20-24 |
| Vince Dooley..................... | Sugar | 1-1-83 | Penn St. | 23-27 |
| Vince Dooley..................... | Cotton | 1-2-84 | Texas | 10-9 |
| Vince Dooley..................... | Florida Citrus | 12-22-84 | Florida St. | 17-17 |
| Vince Dooley..................... | Sun | 12-28-85 | Arizona | 13-13 |
| Vince Dooley..................... | Hall of Fame | 12-23-86 | Boston College | 24-27 |
| Vince Dooley..................... | Liberty | 12-29-87 | Arkansas | 20-17 |
| Vince Dooley..................... | Gator | 1-1-89 | Michigan St. | 34-27 |
| Ray Goff ......................... | Peach | 12-30-89 | Syracuse | 18-19 |
| Ray Goff ......................... | Independence | 12-29-91 | Arkansas | 24-15 |
| Ray Goff ......................... | Florida Citrus | 1-1-93 | Ohio St. | 21-14 |
| All bowls 15-13-3 | | | | |
| **GEORGIA TECH** | Bowl | Date | Opponent | Score |
| Bill Alexander .................... | Rose | 1-1-29 | California | 8-7 |
| Bill Alexander .................... | Orange | 1-1-40 | Missouri | 21-7 |
| Bill Alexander .................... | Cotton | 1-1-43 | Texas | 7-14 |
| Bill Alexander .................... | Sugar | 1-1-44 | Tulsa | 20-18 |
| Bill Alexander .................... | Orange | 1-1-45 | Tulsa | 12-26 |
| Bobby Dodd ..................... | Oil | 1-1-47 | St. Mary's (Cal.) | 41-19 |
| Bobby Dodd ..................... | Orange | 1-1-48 | Kansas | 20-14 |
| Bobby Dodd ..................... | Orange | 1-1-52 | Baylor | 17-14 |
| Bobby Dodd ..................... | Sugar | 1-1-53 | Mississippi | 24-7 |
| Bobby Dodd ..................... | Sugar | 1-1-54 | West Va. | 42-19 |
| Bobby Dodd ..................... | Cotton | 1-1-55 | Arkansas | 14-6 |
| Bobby Dodd ..................... | Sugar | 1-2-56 | Pittsburgh | 7-0 |
| Bobby Dodd ..................... | Gator | 12-29-56 | Pittsburgh | 21-14 |
| Bobby Dodd ..................... | Gator | 1-2-60 | Arkansas | 7-14 |
| Bobby Dodd ..................... | Gator | 12-30-61 | Penn St. | 15-30 |
| Bobby Dodd ..................... | Bluebonnet | 12-22-62 | Missouri | 10-14 |
| Bobby Dodd ..................... | Gator | 12-31-65 | Texas Tech | 31-21 |
| Bobby Dodd ..................... | Orange | 1-2-67 | Florida | 12-27 |
| Bud Carson ...................... | Sun | 12-19-70 | Texas Tech | 17-9 |
| Bud Carson ...................... | Peach | 12-30-71 | Mississippi | 18-41 |
| Bill Fulcher....................... | Liberty | 12-18-72 | Iowa St. | 31-30 |
| Pepper Rodgers.................. | Peach | 12-25-78 | Purdue | 21-41 |
| Bill Curry......................... | All-American | 12-31-85 | Michigan St. | 17-14 |
| Bobby Ross...................... | Florida Citrus | 1-1-91 | Nebraska | 45-21 |
| Bobby Ross...................... | Aloha | 12-25-91 | Stanford | 18-17 |
| All bowls 17-8-0 | | | | |

*Team-by-Team Bowl Results*

| HAWAII | Bowl | Date | Opponent | Score |
|---|---|---|---|---|
| Bob Wagner | Aloha | 12-25-89 | Michigan St. | 13-33 |
| Bob Wagner | Holiday | 12-30-92 | Illinois | 27-17 |
| All bowls 1-1-0 | | | | |

| HOUSTON | Bowl | Date | Opponent | Score |
|---|---|---|---|---|
| Clyde Lee | Salad | 1-1-52 | Dayton | 26-21 |
| Bill Yeoman | Tangerine | 12-22-62 | Miami (Ohio) | 49-21 |
| Bill Yeoman | Bluebonnet | 12-31-69 | Auburn | 36-7 |
| Bill Yeoman | Bluebonnet | 12-31-71 | Colorado | 17-29 |
| Bill Yeoman | Bluebonnet | 12-29-73 | Tulane | 47-7 |
| Bill Yeoman | Bluebonnet | 12-23-74 | North Caro. St. | 31-31 |
| Bill Yeoman | Cotton | 1-1-77 | Maryland | 30-21 |
| Bill Yeoman | Cotton | 1-1-79 | Notre Dame | 34-35 |
| Bill Yeoman | Cotton | 1-1-80 | Nebraska | 17-14 |
| Bill Yeoman | Garden State | 12-14-80 | Navy | 35-0 |
| Bill Yeoman | Sun | 12-26-81 | Oklahoma | 14-40 |
| Bill Yeoman | Cotton | 1-1-85 | Boston College | 28-45 |
| Jack Pardee | Aloha | 12-25-88 | Washington St. | 22-24 |
| All bowls 7-5-1 | | | | |

| ILLINOIS | Bowl | Date | Opponent | Score |
|---|---|---|---|---|
| Ray Eliot | Rose | 1-1-47 | UCLA | 45-14 |
| Ray Eliot | Rose | 1-1-52 | Stanford | 40-7 |
| Pete Elliott | Rose | 1-1-64 | Washington | 17-7 |
| Mike White | Liberty | 12-29-82 | Alabama | 15-21 |
| Mike White | Rose | 1-2-84 | UCLA | 9-45 |
| Mike White | Peach | 12-31-85 | Army | 29-31 |
| John Mackovic | All-American | 12-29-88 | Florida | 10-14 |
| John Mackovic | Florida Citrus | 1-1-90 | Virginia | 31-21 |
| John Mackovic | Hall of Fame | 1-1-91 | Clemson | 0-30 |
| Lou Tepper | John Hancock | 12-31-91 | UCLA | 3-6 |
| Lou Tepper | Holiday | 12-30-92 | Hawaii | 17-27 |
| All bowls 4-7-0 | | | | |

| INDIANA | Bowl | Date | Opponent | Score |
|---|---|---|---|---|
| John Pont | Rose | 1-1-68 | Southern Cal | 3-14 |
| Lee Corso | Holiday | 12-21-79 | Brigham Young | 38-37 |
| Bill Mallory | All-American | 12-31-86 | Florida St. | 13-27 |
| Bill Mallory | Peach | 1-2-88 | Tennessee | 22-27 |
| Bill Mallory | Liberty | 12-28-88 | South Caro. | 34-10 |
| Bill Mallory | Peach | 12-29-90 | Auburn | 23-27 |
| Bill Mallory | Copper | 12-31-91 | Baylor | 24-0 |
| All bowls 3-4-0 | | | | |

| IOWA | Bowl | Date | Opponent | Score |
|---|---|---|---|---|
| Forest Evashevski | Rose | 1-1-57 | Oregon St. | 35-19 |
| Forest Evashevski | Rose | 1-1-59 | California | 38-12 |
| Hayden Fry | Rose | 1-1-82 | Washington | 0-28 |
| Hayden Fry | Peach | 12-31-82 | Tennessee | 28-22 |
| Hayden Fry | Gator | 12-30-83 | Florida | 6-14 |
| Hayden Fry | Freedom | 12-26-84 | Texas | 55-17 |
| Hayden Fry | Rose | 1-1-86 | UCLA | 28-45 |
| Hayden Fry | Holiday | 12-30-86 | San Diego St. | 39-38 |
| Hayden Fry | Holiday | 12-30-87 | Wyoming | 20-19 |
| Hayden Fry | Peach | 12-31-88 | North Caro. St. | 23-28 |
| Hayden Fry | Rose | 1-1-91 | Washington | 34-46 |
| Hayden Fry | Holiday | 12-30-91 | Brigham Young | 13-13 |
| All bowls 6-5-1 | | | | |

| IOWA ST. | Bowl | Date | Opponent | Score |
|---|---|---|---|---|
| Johnny Majors | Sun | 12-18-71 | Louisiana St. | 15-33 |
| Johnny Majors | Liberty | 12-18-72 | Georgia Tech | 30-31 |
| Earle Bruce | Peach | 12-31-77 | North Caro. St. | 14-24 |
| Earle Bruce | Hall of Fame | 12-20-78 | Texas A&M | 12-28 |
| All bowls 0-4-0 | | | | |

| KANSAS | Bowl | Date | Opponent | Score |
|---|---|---|---|---|
| George Sauer | Orange | 1-1-48 | Georgia Tech | 14-20 |
| Jack Mitchell | Bluebonnet | 12-16-61 | Rice | 33-7 |
| Pepper Rodgers | Orange | 1-1-69 | Penn St. | 14-15 |
| Don Fambrough | Liberty | 12-17-73 | North Caro. St. | 18-31 |
| Bud Moore | Sun | 12-26-75 | Pittsburgh | 19-33 |
| Don Fambrough | Hall of Fame | 12-31-81 | Mississippi St. | 0-10 |
| Glen Mason | Aloha | 12-25-92 | Brigham Young | 23-20 |

All bowls 2-5-0

## KANSAS ST.

| | Bowl | Date | Opponent | Score |
|---|---|---|---|---|
| Jim Dickey | Independence | 12-11-82 | Wisconsin | 3-14 |

All bowls 0-1-0

## KENT

| | Bowl | Date | Opponent | Score |
|---|---|---|---|---|
| Don James | Tangerine | 12-29-72 | Tampa | 18-21 |

All bowls 0-1-0

## KENTUCKY

| | Bowl | Date | Opponent | Score |
|---|---|---|---|---|
| Paul "Bear" Bryant | Great Lakes | 12- 6-47 | Villanova | 24-14 |
| Paul "Bear" Bryant | Orange | 1-2-50 | Santa Clara | 13-21 |
| Paul "Bear" Bryant | Sugar | 1-1-51 | Oklahoma | 13-7 |
| Paul "Bear" Bryant | Cotton | 1-1-52 | Texas Christian | 20-7 |
| Fran Curci | Peach | 12-31-76 | North Caro. | 21-0 |
| Jerry Claiborne | Hall of Fame | 12-22-83 | West Va. | 16-20 |
| Jerry Claiborne | Hall of Fame | 12-29-84 | Wisconsin | 20-19 |

All bowls 5-2-0

## LOUISIANA ST.

| | Bowl | Date | Opponent | Score |
|---|---|---|---|---|
| Bernie Moore | Sugar | 1-1-36 | Texas Christian | 2-3 |
| Bernie Moore | Sugar | 1-1-37 | Santa Clara | 14-21 |
| Bernie Moore | Sugar | 1-1-38 | Santa Clara | 0-6 |
| Bernie Moore | Orange | 1-1-44 | Texas A&M | 19-14 |
| Bernie Moore | Cotton | 1-1-47 | Arkansas | 0-0 |
| Gaynell Tinsley | Sugar | 1-2-50 | Oklahoma | 0-35 |
| Paul Dietzel | Sugar | 1-1-59 | Clemson | 7-0 |
| Paul Dietzel | Sugar | 1-1-60 | Mississippi | 0-21 |
| Paul Dietzel | Orange | 1-1-62 | Colorado | 25-7 |
| Charlie McClendon | Cotton | 1-1-63 | Texas | 13-0 |
| Charlie McClendon | Bluebonnet | 12-21-63 | Baylor | 7-14 |
| Charlie McClendon | Sugar | 1-1-65 | Syracuse | 13-10 |
| Charlie McClendon | Cotton | 1-1-66 | Arkansas | 14-7 |
| Charlie McClendon | Sugar | 1-1-68 | Wyoming | 20-13 |
| Charlie McClendon | Peach | 12-30-68 | Florida St. | 31-27 |
| Charlie McClendon | Orange | 1-1-71 | Nebraska | 12-17 |
| Charlie McClendon | Sun | 12-18-71 | Iowa St. | 33-15 |
| Charlie McClendon | Bluebonnet | 12-30-72 | Tennessee | 17-24 |
| Charlie McClendon | Orange | 1-1-74 | Penn St. | 9-16 |
| Charlie McClendon | Sun | 12-31-77 | Stanford | 14-24 |
| Charlie McClendon | Liberty | 12-23-78 | Missouri | 15-20 |
| Charlie McClendon | Tangerine | 12-22-79 | Wake Forest | 34-10 |
| Jerry Stovall | Orange | 1-1-83 | Nebraska | 20-21 |
| Bill Arnsparger | Sugar | 1-1-85 | Nebraska | 10-28 |
| Bill Arnsparger | Liberty | 12-27-85 | Baylor | 7-21 |
| Bill Arnsparger | Sugar | 1-1-87 | Nebraska | 15-30 |
| Mike Archer | Gator | 12-31-87 | South Caro. | 30-13 |
| Mike Archer | Hall of Fame | 1-2-89 | Syracuse | 10-23 |

All bowls 11-16-1

## LOUISIANA TECH

| | Bowl | Date | Opponent | Score |
|---|---|---|---|---|
| Maxie Lambright | Independence | 12-17-77 | Louisville | 24-14 |
| Maxie Lambright | Independence | 12-16-78 | East Caro. | 13-35 |
| Joe Raymond Peace | Independence | 12-15-90 | Maryland | 34-34 |

All bowls 1-1-1

## LOUISVILLE

| | Bowl | Date | Opponent | Score |
|---|---|---|---|---|
| Frank Camp | Sun | 1-1-58 | Drake | 34-20 |
| Lee Corso | Pasadena | 12-19-70 | Long Beach St. | 24-24 |
| Vince Gibson | Independence | 12-17-77 | Louisiana Tech | 14-24 |
| Howard Schnellenberger | Fiesta | 1-1-91 | Alabama | 34-7 |

All bowls 2-1-1

## MARYLAND

| | Bowl | Date | Opponent | Score |
|---|---|---|---|---|
| Jim Tatum | Gator | 1-1-48 | Georgia | 20-20 |
| Jim Tatum | Gator | 1-2-50 | Missouri | 20-7 |
| Jim Tatum | Sugar | 1-1-52 | Tennessee | 28-13 |
| Jim Tatum | Orange | 1-1-54 | Oklahoma | 0-7 |
| Jim Tatum | Orange | 1-2-56 | Oklahoma | 6-20 |
| Jerry Claiborne | Peach | 12-28-73 | Georgia | 16-17 |
| Jerry Claiborne | Liberty | 12-16-74 | Tennessee | 3-7 |
| Jerry Claiborne | Gator | 12-29-75 | Florida | 13-0 |
| Jerry Claiborne | Cotton | 1-1-77 | Houston | 21-30 |
| Jerry Claiborne | Hall of Fame | 12-22-77 | Minnesota | 17-7 |

*Team-by-Team Bowl Results*

| | Bowl | Date | Opponent | Score |
|---|---|---|---|---|
| Jerry Claiborne ................... | Sun | 12-23-78 | Texas | 0-42 |
| Jerry Claiborne ................... | Tangerine | 12-20-80 | Florida | 20-35 |
| Bobby Ross ....................... | Aloha | 12-25-82 | Washington | 20-21 |
| Bobby Ross ....................... | Florida Citrus | 12-17-83 | Tennessee | 23-30 |
| Bobby Ross ....................... | Sun | 12-22-84 | Tennessee | 27-26 |
| Bobby Ross ....................... | Cherry | 12-21-85 | Syracuse | 35-18 |
| Joe Krivak ....................... | Independence | 12-15-90 | Louisiana Tech | 34-34 |

All bowls 6-9-2

| **MEMPHIS ST.** | **Bowl** | **Date** | **Opponent** | **Score** |
|---|---|---|---|---|
| Billy Murphy ..................... | Pasadena | 12-18-71 | San Jose St. | 28-9 |

All bowls 1-0-0

| **MIAMI (FLA.)** | **Bowl** | **Date** | **Opponent** | **Score** |
|---|---|---|---|---|
| Tom McCann ..................... | Orange | 1-1-35 | Bucknell | 0-26 |
| Jack Harding..................... | Orange | 1-1-46 | Holy Cross | 13-6 |
| Andy Gustafson.................. | Orange | 1-1-51 | Clemson | 14-15 |
| Andy Gustafson.................. | Gator | 1-1-52 | Clemson | 14-0 |
| Andy Gustafson.................. | Liberty | 12-16-61 | Syracuse | 14-15 |
| Andy Gustafson.................. | Gotham | 12-15-62 | Nebraska | 34-36 |
| Charlie Tate ..................... | Liberty | 12-10-66 | Virginia Tech | 14-7 |
| Charlie Tate ..................... | Bluebonnet | 12-31-67 | Colorado | 21-31 |
| Howard Schnellenberger ......... | Peach | 1-2-81 | Virginia Tech | 20-10 |
| Howard Schnellenberger ......... | Orange | 1-2-84 | Nebraska | 31-30 |
| Jimmy Johnson .................. | Fiesta | 1-1-85 | UCLA | 37-39 |
| Jimmy Johnson .................. | Sugar | 1-1-86 | Tennessee | 7-35 |
| Jimmy Johnson .................. | Fiesta | 1-2-87 | Penn St. | 10-14 |
| Jimmy Johnson .................. | Orange | 1-1-88 | Oklahoma | 20-14 |
| Jimmy Johnson .................. | Orange | 1-2-89 | Nebraska | 23-3 |
| Dennis Erickson ................. | Sugar | 1-1-90 | Alabama | 33-25 |
| Dennis Erickson ................. | Cotton | 1-1-91 | Texas | 46-3 |
| Dennis Erickson ................. | Orange | 1-1-92 | Nebraska | 22-0 |
| Dennis Erickson ................. | Sugar | 1-1-93 | Alabama | 13-34 |

All bowls 10-9-0

| **MIAMI (OHIO)** | **Bowl** | **Date** | **Opponent** | **Score** |
|---|---|---|---|---|
| Sid Gillman ...................... | Sun | 1-1-48 | Texas Tech | 13-12 |
| Woody Hayes .................... | Salad | 1-1-51 | Arizona St. | 34-21 |
| John Pont........................ | Tangerine | 12-22-62 | Houston | 21-49 |
| Bill Mallory...................... | Tangerine | 12-22-73 | Florida | 16-7 |
| Dick Crum ....................... | Tangerine | 12-21-74 | Georgia | 21-10 |
| Dick Crum ....................... | Tangerine | 12-20-75 | South Caro. | 20-7 |
| Tim Rose........................ | California | 12-13-86 | San Jose St. | 7-37 |

All bowls 5-2-0

| **MICHIGAN** | **Bowl** | **Date** | **Opponent** | **Score** |
|---|---|---|---|---|
| Fielding "Hurry Up" Yost .......... | Rose | 1-1-02 | Stanford | 49-0 |
| H.O. "Fritz" Crisler .............. | Rose | 1-1-48 | Southern Cal | 49-0 |
| Bennie Oosterbaan ............... | Rose | 1-1-51 | California | 14-6 |
| Chalmers "Bump" Elliott .......... | Rose | 1-1-65 | Oregon St. | 34-7 |
| Glenn "Bo" Schembechler ........ | Rose | 1-1-70 | Southern Cal | 3-10 |
| Glenn "Bo" Schembechler ........ | Rose | 1-1-72 | Stanford | 12-13 |
| Glenn "Bo" Schembechler ........ | Orange | 1-1-76 | Oklahoma | 6-14 |
| Glenn "Bo" Schembechler ........ | Rose | 1-1-77 | Southern Cal | 6-14 |
| Glenn "Bo" Schembechler ........ | Rose | 1-2-78 | Washington | 20-27 |
| Glenn "Bo" Schembechler ........ | Rose | 1-1-79 | Southern Cal | 10-17 |
| Glenn "Bo" Schembechler ........ | Gator | 12-28-79 | North Caro. | 15-17 |
| Glenn "Bo" Schembechler ........ | Rose | 1-1-81 | Washington | 23-6 |
| Glenn "Bo" Schembechler ........ | Bluebonnet | 12-31-81 | UCLA | 33-14 |
| Glenn "Bo" Schembechler ........ | Rose | 1-1-83 | UCLA | 14-24 |
| Glenn "Bo" Schembechler ........ | Sugar | 1-2-84 | Auburn | 7-9 |
| Glenn "Bo" Schembechler ........ | Holiday | 12-21-84 | Brigham Young | 17-24 |
| Glenn "Bo" Schembechler ........ | Fiesta | 1-1-86 | Nebraska | 27-23 |
| Glenn "Bo" Schembechler ........ | Rose | 1-1-87 | Arizona St. | 15-22 |
| Glenn "Bo" Schembechler ........ | Hall of Fame | 1-2-88 | Alabama | 28-24 |
| Glenn "Bo" Schembechler ........ | Rose | 1-2-89 | Southern Cal | 22-14 |
| Glenn "Bo" Schembechler ........ | Rose | 1-1-90 | Southern Cal | 10-17 |
| Gary Moeller ..................... | Gator | 1-1-91 | Mississippi | 35-3 |
| Gary Moeller ..................... | Rose | 1-1-92 | Washington | 14-34 |
| Gary Moeller ..................... | Rose | 1-1-93 | Washington | 38-31 |

All bowls 11-13-0

## MICHIGAN ST.

| | Bowl | Date | Opponent | Score |
|---|---|---|---|---|
| Charlie Bachman | Orange | 1-1-38 | Auburn | 0-6 |
| Clarence "Biggie" Munn | Rose | 1-1-54 | UCLA | 28-20 |
| Duffy Daugherty | Rose | 1-2-56 | UCLA | 17-14 |
| Duffy Daugherty | Rose | 1-1-66 | UCLA | 12-14 |
| George Perles | Cherry | 12-22-84 | Army | 6-10 |
| George Perles | All-American | 12-31-85 | Georgia Tech | 14-17 |
| George Perles | Rose | 1-1-88 | Southern Cal | 20-17 |
| George Perles | Gator | 1-1-89 | Georgia | 27-34 |
| George Perles | Aloha | 12-25-89 | Hawaii | 33-13 |
| George Perles | John Hancock | 12-31-90 | Southern Cal | 17-6 |

All bowls 5-5-0

## MINNESOTA

| | Bowl | Date | Opponent | Score |
|---|---|---|---|---|
| Murray Warmath | Rose | 1-2-61 | Washington | 7-17 |
| Murray Warmath | Rose | 1-1-62 | UCLA | 21-3 |
| Cal Stoll | Hall of Fame | 12-22-77 | Maryland | 7-17 |
| John Gutekunst | Independence | 12-21-85 | Clemson | 20-13 |
| John Gutekunst | Liberty | 12-29-86 | Tennessee | 14-21 |

All bowls 2-3-0

## MISSISSIPPI

| | Bowl | Date | Opponent | Score |
|---|---|---|---|---|
| Ed Walker | Orange | 1-1-36 | Catholic | 19-20 |
| John Vaught | Delta | 1-1-48 | Texas Christian | 13-9 |
| John Vaught | Sugar | 1-1-53 | Georgia Tech | 7-24 |
| John Vaught | Sugar | 1-1-55 | Navy | 0-21 |
| John Vaught | Cotton | 1-2-56 | Texas Christian | 14-13 |
| John Vaught | Sugar | 1-1-58 | Texas | 39-7 |
| John Vaught | Gator | 12-27-58 | Florida | 7-3 |
| John Vaught | Sugar | 1-1-60 | Louisiana St. | 21-0 |
| John Vaught | Sugar | 1-2-61 | Rice | 14-6 |
| John Vaught | Cotton | 1-1-62 | Texas | 7-12 |
| John Vaught | Sugar | 1-1-63 | Arkansas | 17-13 |
| John Vaught | Sugar | 1-1-64 | Alabama | 7-12 |
| John Vaught | Bluebonnet | 12-19-64 | Tulsa | 7-14 |
| John Vaught | Liberty | 12-18-65 | Auburn | 13-7 |
| John Vaught | Bluebonnet | 12-17-66 | Texas | 0-19 |
| John Vaught | Sun | 12-30-67 | UTEP | 7-14 |
| John Vaught | Liberty | 12-14-68 | Virginia Tech | 34-17 |
| John Vaught | Sugar | 1-1-70 | Arkansas | 27-22 |
| John Vaught | Gator | 1-2-71 | Auburn | 28-35 |
| Billy Kinard | Peach | 12-30-71 | Georgia Tech | 41-18 |
| Billy Brewer | Independence | 12-10-83 | Air Force | 3-9 |
| Billy Brewer | Independence | 12-20-86 | Texas Tech | 20-17 |
| Billy Brewer | Liberty | 12-28-89 | Air Force | 42-29 |
| Billy Brewer | Gator | 1-1-91 | Michigan | 3-35 |
| Billy Brewer | Liberty | 12-31-92 | Air Force | 13-0 |

All bowls 14-11-0

## MISSISSIPPI ST.

| | Bowl | Date | Opponent | Score |
|---|---|---|---|---|
| Ralph Sasse | Orange | 1-1-37 | Duquesne | 12-13 |
| Allyn McKeen | Orange | 1-1-41 | Georgetown | 14-7 |
| Paul Davis | Liberty | 12-21-63 | North Caro. St. | 16-12 |
| Bob Tyler | Sun | 12-28-74 | North Caro. | 26-24 |
| Emory Bellard | Sun | 12-27-80 | Nebraska | 17-31 |
| Emory Bellard | Hall of Fame | 12-31-81 | Kansas | 10-0 |
| Jackie Sherrill | Liberty | 12-29-91 | Air Force | 15-38 |
| Jackie Sherrill | Peach | 1-2-93 | North Caro. | 17-21 |

All bowls 4-4-0

## MISSOURI

| | Bowl | Date | Opponent | Score |
|---|---|---|---|---|
| Gwinn Henry | Los Angeles Christmas Festival | 12-25-24 | Southern Cal | 7-20 |
| Don Faurot | Orange | 1-1-40 | Georgia Tech | 7-21 |
| Don Faurot | Sugar | 1-1-42 | Fordham | 0-2 |
| Chauncey Simpson | Cotton | 1-1-46 | Texas | 27-40 |
| Don Faurot | Gator | 1-1-49 | Clemson | 23-24 |
| Don Faurot | Gator | 1-2-50 | Maryland | 7-20 |
| Dan Devine | Orange | 1-1-60 | Georgia | 0-40 |
| Dan Devine | Orange | 1-2-61 | Navy | 21-14 |
| Dan Devine | Bluebonnet | 12-22-62 | Georgia Tech | 14-10 |
| Dan Devine | Sugar | 1-1-66 | Florida | 20-18 |

| | | | | |
|---|---|---|---|---|
| Dan Devine | Gator | 12-28-68 | Alabama | 35-10 |
| Dan Devine | Orange | 1-1-70 | Penn St. | 3-10 |
| Al Onofrio | Fiesta | 12-23-72 | Arizona St. | 35-49 |
| Al Onofrio | Sun | 12-29-73 | Auburn | 34-17 |
| Warren Powers | Liberty | 12-23-78 | Louisiana St. | 20-15 |
| Warren Powers | Hall of Fame | 12-29-79 | South Caro. | 24-14 |
| Warren Powers | Liberty | 12-27-80 | Purdue | 25-28 |
| Warren Powers | Tangerine | 12-19-81 | Southern Miss. | 19-17 |
| Warren Powers | Holiday | 12-23-83 | Brigham Young | 17-21 |

All bowls 8-11-0

| NAVY | Bowl | Date | Opponent | Score |
|---|---|---|---|---|
| Bob Folwell | Rose | 1-1-24 | Washington | 14-14 |
| Eddie Erdelatz | Sugar | 1-1-55 | Mississippi | 21-0 |
| Eddie Erdelatz | Cotton | 1-1-58 | Rice | 20-7 |
| Wayne Hardin | Orange | 1-1-61 | Missouri | 14-21 |
| Wayne Hardin | Cotton | 1-1-64 | Texas | 6-28 |
| George Welsh | Holiday | 12-22-78 | Brigham Young | 23-16 |
| George Welsh | Garden State | 12-14-80 | Houston | 0-35 |
| George Welsh | Liberty | 12-30-81 | Ohio St. | 28-31 |

All bowls 3-4-1

| NEBRASKA | Bowl | Date | Opponent | Score |
|---|---|---|---|---|
| Lawrence McC. "Biff" Jones | Rose | 1-1-41 | Stanford | 13-21 |
| Bill Glassford | Orange | 1-1-55 | Duke | 7-34 |
| Bob Devaney | Gotham | 12-15-62 | Miami (Fla.) | 36-34 |
| Bob Devaney | Orange | 1-1-64 | Auburn | 13-7 |
| Bob Devaney | Cotton | 1-1-65 | Arkansas | 7-10 |
| Bob Devaney | Orange | 1-1-66 | Alabama | 28-39 |
| Bob Devaney | Sugar | 1-2-67 | Alabama | 7-34 |
| Bob Devaney | Sun | 12-20-69 | Georgia | 45-6 |
| Bob Devaney | Orange | 1-1-71 | Louisiana St. | 17-12 |
| Bob Devaney | Orange | 1-1-72 | Alabama | 38-6 |
| Bob Devaney | Orange | 1-1-73 | Notre Dame | 40-6 |
| Tom Osborne | Cotton | 1-1-74 | Texas | 19-3 |
| Tom Osborne | Sugar | 12-31-74 | Florida | 13-10 |
| Tom Osborne | Fiesta | 12-26-75 | Arizona St. | 14-17 |
| Tom Osborne | Bluebonnet | 12-31-76 | Texas Tech | 27-24 |
| Tom Osborne | Liberty | 12-19-77 | North Caro. | 21-17 |
| Tom Osborne | Orange | 1-1-79 | Oklahoma | 24-31 |
| Tom Osborne | Cotton | 1-1-80 | Houston | 14-17 |
| Tom Osborne | Sun | 12-27-80 | Mississippi St. | 31-17 |
| Tom Osborne | Orange | 1-1-82 | Clemson | 15-22 |
| Tom Osborne | Orange | 1-1-83 | Louisiana St. | 21-20 |
| Tom Osborne | Orange | 1-2-84 | Miami (Fla.) | 30-31 |
| Tom Osborne | Sugar | 1-1-85 | Louisiana St. | 28-10 |
| Tom Osborne | Fiesta | 1-1-86 | Michigan | 23-27 |
| Tom Osborne | Sugar | 1-1-87 | Louisiana St. | 30-15 |
| Tom Osborne | Fiesta | 1-1-88 | Florida St. | 28-31 |
| Tom Osborne | Orange | 1-2-89 | Miami (Fla.) | 3-23 |
| Tom Osborne | Fiesta | 1-1-90 | Florida St. | 17-41 |
| Tom Osborne | Florida Citrus | 1-1-91 | Georgia Tech | 21-45 |
| Tom Osborne | Orange | 1-1-92 | Miami (Fla.) | 0-22 |
| Tom Osborne | Orange | 1-1-93 | Florida St. | 14-27 |

All bowls 14-17-0

| NEVADA | Bowl | Date | Opponent | Score |
|---|---|---|---|---|
| Joe Sheeketski | Salad | 1-1-48 | North Texas | 13-6 |
| Joe Sheeketski | Harbor | 1-1-49 | Villanova | 7-27 |
| Chris Ault | Las Vegas | 12-18-92 | Bowling Green | 34-35 |

All bowls 1-2-0

| NEVADA-LAS VEGAS | Bowl | Date | Opponent | Score |
|---|---|---|---|---|
| Harvey Hyde | California | 12-15-84 | Toledo | 30-13 |

All bowls 1-0-0

| NEW MEXICO | Bowl | Date | Opponent | Score |
|---|---|---|---|---|
| Ted Shipkey | Sun | 1-2-39 | Utah | 0-26 |
| Willis Barnes | Sun | 1-1-44 | Southwestern (Tex.) | 0-7 |
| Willis Barnes | Sun | 1-1-46 | Denver | 34-24 |
| Willis Barnes | Harbor | 1-1-47 | Montana St. | 13-13 |
| Bill Weeks | Aviation | 12-9-61 | Western Mich. | 28-12 |

All bowls 2-2-1

**NEW MEXICO ST.**

| | Bowl | Date | Bowl | Date |
|---|---|---|---|---|
| Jerry Hines | Sun | 1-1-36 | Hardin-Simmons | 14-14 |
| Warren Woodson | Sun | 12-31-59 | North Texas | 28-8 |
| Warren Woodson | Sun | 12-31-60 | Utah St. | 20-13 |
| All bowls 2-0-1 | | | | |

**NORTH CARO.**

| | Bowl | Date | Opponent | Score |
|---|---|---|---|---|
| Carl Snavely | Sugar | 1-1-47 | Georgia | 10-20 |
| Carl Snavely | Sugar | 1-1-49 | Oklahoma | 6-14 |
| Carl Snavely | Cotton | 1-2-50 | Rice | 13-27 |
| Jim Hickey | Gator | 12-28-63 | Air Force | 35-0 |
| Bill Dooley | Peach | 12-30-70 | Arizona St. | 26-48 |
| Bill Dooley | Gator | 12-31-71 | Georgia | 3-7 |
| Bill Dooley | Sun | 12-30-72 | Texas Tech | 32-28 |
| Bill Dooley | Sun | 12-28-74 | Mississippi St. | 24-26 |
| Bill Dooley | Peach | 12-31-76 | Kentucky | 0-21 |
| Bill Dooley | Liberty | 12-19-77 | Nebraska | 17-21 |
| Dick Crum | Gator | 12-28-79 | Michigan | 17-15 |
| Dick Crum | Bluebonnet | 12-31-80 | Texas | 16-7 |
| Dick Crum | Gator | 12-28-81 | Arkansas | 31-27 |
| Dick Crum | Sun | 12-25-82 | Texas | 26-10 |
| Dick Crum | Peach | 12-30-83 | Florida St. | 3-28 |
| Dick Crum | Aloha | 12-27-86 | Arizona | 21-30 |
| Mack Brown | Peach | 1-2-93 | Mississippi St. | 21-17 |
| All bowls 7-10-0 | | | | |

**NORTH CARO. ST.**

| | Bowl | Date | Opponent | Score |
|---|---|---|---|---|
| Beattie Feathers | Gator | 1-1-47 | Oklahoma | 13-34 |
| Earle Edwards | Liberty | 12-21-63 | Mississippi St. | 12-16 |
| Earle Edwards | Liberty | 12-16-67 | Georgia | 14-7 |
| Lou Holtz | Peach | 12-29-72 | West Va. | 49-13 |
| Lou Holtz | Liberty | 12-17-73 | Kansas | 31-18 |
| Lou Holtz | Bluebonnet | 12-23-74 | Houston | 31-31 |
| Lou Holtz | Peach | 12-31-75 | West Va. | 10-13 |
| Bo Rein | Peach | 12-31-77 | Iowa St. | 24-14 |
| Bo Rein | Tangerine | 12-23-78 | Pittsburgh | 30-17 |
| Dick Sheridan | Peach | 12-31-86 | Virginia Tech | 24-25 |
| Dick Sheridan | Peach | 12-31-88 | Iowa | 28-23 |
| Dick Sheridan | Copper | 12-31-89 | Arizona | 10-17 |
| Dick Sheridan | All-American | 12-28-90 | Southern Miss. | 31-27 |
| Dick Sheridan | Peach | 1-1-92 | East Caro. | 34-37 |
| Dick Sheridan | Gator | 12-31-92 | Florida | 10-27 |
| All bowls 7-7-1 | | | | |

**NORTHERN ILL.**

| | Bowl | Date | Opponent | Score |
|---|---|---|---|---|
| Bill Mallory | California | 12-17-83 | Cal St. Fullerton | 20-13 |
| All bowls 1-0-0 | | | | |

**NORTHWESTERN**

| | Bowl | Date | Opponent | Score |
|---|---|---|---|---|
| Bob Voigts | Rose | 1-1-49 | California | 20-14 |
| All bowls 1-0-0 | | | | |

**NOTRE DAME**

| | Bowl | Date | Opponent | Score |
|---|---|---|---|---|
| Knute Rockne | Rose | 1-1-25 | Stanford | 27-10 |
| Ara Parseghian | Cotton | 1-1-70 | Texas | 17-21 |
| Ara Parseghian | Cotton | 1-1-71 | Texas | 24-11 |
| Ara Parseghian | Orange | 1-1-73 | Nebraska | 6-40 |
| Ara Parseghian | Sugar | 12-31-73 | Alabama | 24-23 |
| Ara Parseghian | Orange | 1-1-75 | Alabama | 13-11 |
| Dan Devine | Gator | 12-27-76 | Penn St. | 20-9 |
| Dan Devine | Cotton | 1-2-78 | Texas | 38-10 |
| Dan Devine | Cotton | 1-1-79 | Houston | 35-34 |
| Dan Devine | Sugar | 1-1-81 | Georgia | 10-17 |
| Gerry Faust | Liberty | 12-29-83 | Boston College | 19-18 |
| Gerry Faust | Aloha | 12-29-84 | Southern Methodist | 20-27 |
| Lou Holtz | Cotton | 1-1-88 | Texas A&M | 10-35 |
| Lou Holtz | Fiesta | 1-2-89 | West Va. | 34-21 |
| Lou Holtz | Orange | 1-1-90 | Colorado | 21-6 |
| Lou Holtz | Orange | 1-1-91 | Colorado | 9-10 |
| Lou Holtz | Sugar | 1-1-92 | Florida | 39-28 |
| Lou Holtz | Cotton | 1-1-93 | Texas A&M | 28-3 |
| All bowls 12-6-0 | | | | |

*Team-by-Team Bowl Results*

| OHIO | Bowl | Date | Opponent | Score |
|------|------|------|----------|-------|
| Bill Hess .......................... | Sun | 12-31-62 | West Tex. St. | 14-15 |
| Bill Hess .......................... | Tangerine | 12-27-68 | Richmond | 42-49 |
| All bowls 0-2-0 | | | | |

| OHIO ST. | Bowl | Date | Opponent | Score |
|----------|------|------|----------|-------|
| John Wilce ....................... | Rose | 1-1-21 | California | 0-28 |
| Wes Fesler ....................... | Rose | 1-2-50 | California | 17-14 |
| Woody Hayes ..................... | Rose | 1-1-55 | Southern Cal | 20-7 |
| Woody Hayes ..................... | Rose | 1-1-58 | Oregon | 10-7 |
| Woody Hayes ..................... | Rose | 1-1-69 | Southern Cal | 27-16 |
| Woody Hayes ..................... | Rose | 1-1-71 | Stanford | 17-27 |
| Woody Hayes ..................... | Rose | 1-1-73 | Southern Cal | 17-42 |
| Woody Hayes ..................... | Rose | 1-1-74 | Southern Cal | 42-21 |
| Woody Hayes ..................... | Rose | 1-1-75 | Southern Cal | 17-18 |
| Woody Hayes ..................... | Rose | 1-1-76 | UCLA | 10-23 |
| Woody Hayes ..................... | Orange | 1-1-77 | Colorado | 27-10 |
| Woody Hayes ..................... | Sugar | 1-2-78 | Alabama | 6-35 |
| Woody Hayes ..................... | Gator | 12-29-78 | Clemson | 15-17 |
| Earle Bruce ...................... | Rose | 1-1-80 | Southern Cal | 16-17 |
| Earle Bruce ...................... | Fiesta | 12-26-80 | Penn St. | 19-31 |
| Earle Bruce ...................... | Liberty | 12-30-81 | Navy | 31-28 |
| Earle Bruce ...................... | Holiday | 12-17-82 | Brigham Young | 47-17 |
| Earle Bruce ...................... | Fiesta | 1-2-84 | Pittsburgh | 28-23 |
| Earle Bruce ...................... | Rose | 1-1-85 | Southern Cal | 17-20 |
| Earle Bruce ...................... | Florida Citrus | 12-28-85 | Brigham Young | 10-7 |
| Earle Bruce ...................... | Cotton | 1-1-87 | Texas A&M | 28-12 |
| John Cooper...................... | Hall of Fame | 1-1-90 | Auburn | 14-31 |
| John Cooper...................... | Liberty | 12-27-90 | Air Force | 11-23 |
| John Cooper...................... | Hall of Fame | 1-1-92 | Syracuse | 17-24 |
| John Cooper...................... | Florida Citrus | 1-1-93 | Georgia | 14-21 |
| All bowls 11-14-0 | | | | |

| OKLAHOMA | Bowl | Date | Opponent | Score |
|----------|------|------|----------|-------|
| Tom Stidham...................... | Orange | 1-2-39 | Tennessee | 0-17 |
| Jim Tatum........................ | Gator | 1-1-47 | North Caro. St. | 34-13 |
| Bud Wilkinson .................... | Sugar | 1-1-49 | North Caro. | 14-6 |
| Bud Wilkinson .................... | Sugar | 1-2-50 | Louisiana St. | 35-0 |
| Bud Wilkinson .................... | Sugar | 1-1-51 | Kentucky | 7-13 |
| Bud Wilkinson .................... | Orange | 1-1-54 | Maryland | 7-0 |
| Bud Wilkinson .................... | Orange | 1-2-56 | Maryland | 20-6 |
| Bud Wilkinson .................... | Orange | 1-1-58 | Duke | 48-21 |
| Bud Wilkinson .................... | Orange | 1-1-59 | Syracuse | 21-6 |
| Bud Wilkinson .................... | Orange | 1-1-63 | Alabama | 0-17 |
| Gomer Jones ..................... | Gator | 1-2-65 | Florida St. | 19-36 |
| Chuck Fairbanks.................. | Orange | 1-1-68 | Tennessee | 26-24 |
| Chuck Fairbanks.................. | Bluebonnet | 12-31-68 | Southern Methodist | 27-28 |
| Chuck Fairbanks.................. | Bluebonnet | 12-31-70 | Alabama | 24-24 |
| Chuck Fairbanks.................. | Sugar | 1-1-72 | Auburn | 40-22 |
| Chuck Fairbanks.................. | Sugar | 12-31-72 | Penn St. | 14-0 |
| Barry Switzer ..................... | Orange | 1-1-76 | Michigan | 14-6 |
| Barry Switzer ..................... | Fiesta | 12-25-76 | Wyoming | 41-7 |
| Barry Switzer ..................... | Orange | 1-2-78 | Arkansas | 6-31 |
| Barry Switzer ..................... | Orange | 1-1-79 | Nebraska | 31-24 |
| Barry Switzer ..................... | Orange | 1-1-80 | Florida St. | 24-7 |
| Barry Switzer ..................... | Orange | 1-1-81 | Florida St. | 18-17 |
| Barry Switzer ..................... | Sun | 12-26-81 | Houston | 40-14 |
| Barry Switzer ..................... | Fiesta | 1-1-83 | Arizona St. | 21-32 |
| Barry Switzer ..................... | Orange | 1-1-85 | Washington | 17-28 |
| Barry Switzer ..................... | Orange | 1-1-86 | Penn St. | 25-10 |
| Barry Switzer ..................... | Orange | 1-1-87 | Arkansas | 42-8 |
| Barry Switzer ..................... | Orange | 1-1-88 | Miami (Fla.) | 14-20 |
| Barry Switzer ..................... | Florida Citrus | 1-2-89 | Clemson | 6-13 |
| Gary Gibbs ....................... | Gator | 12-29-91 | Virginia | 48-14 |
| All bowls 19-10-1 | | | | |

| OKLAHOMA ST. | Bowl | Date | Opponent | Score |
|--------------|------|------|----------|-------|
| Jim Lookabaugh .................. | Cotton | 1-1-45 | Texas Christian | 34-0 |
| Jim Lookabaugh .................. | Sugar | 1-1-46 | St. Mary's (Cal.) | 33-13 |
| Jim Lookabaugh .................. | Delta | 1-1-49 | William & Mary | 0-20 |
| Cliff Speegle ..................... | Bluegrass | 12-13-58 | Florida St. | 15-6 |
| Jim Stanley ...................... | Fiesta | 12-28-74 | Brigham Young | 16-6 |

| | | | | |
|---|---|---|---|---|
| Jim Stanley ........................ | Tangerine | 12-18-76 | Brigham Young | 49-12 |
| Jimmy Johnson .................... | Independence | 12-12-81 | Texas A&M | 16-33 |
| Jimmy Johnson .................... | Bluebonnet | 12-31-83 | Baylor | 24-14 |
| Pat Jones .......................... | Gator | 12-28-84 | South Caro. | 21-14 |
| Pat Jones .......................... | Gator | 12-30-85 | Florida St. | 23-34 |
| Pat Jones .......................... | Sun | 12-25-87 | West Va. | 35-33 |
| Pat Jones .......................... | Holiday | 12-30-88 | Wyoming | 62-14 |
| All bowls 9-3-0 | | | | |

| **OREGON** | **Bowl** | **Date** | **Opponent** | **Score** |
|---|---|---|---|---|
| Hugo Bezdek ...................... | Rose | 1-1-17 | Pennsylvania | 14-0 |
| Charles "Shy" Huntington ......... | Rose | 1-1-20 | Harvard | 6-7 |
| Jim Aiken .......................... | Cotton | 1-1-49 | Southern Methodist | 13-21 |
| Len Casanova ..................... | Rose | 1-1-58 | Ohio St. | 7-10 |
| Len Casanova ..................... | Liberty | 12-17-60 | Penn St. | 12-41 |
| Len Casanova ..................... | Sun | 12-31-63 | Southern Methodist | 21-14 |
| Rich Brooks ....................... | Independence | 12-16-89 | Tulsa | 27-24 |
| Rich Brooks ....................... | Freedom | 12-29-90 | Colorado St. | 31-32 |
| Rich Brooks ....................... | Independence | 12-31-92 | Wake Forest | 35-39 |
| All bowls 3-6-0 | | | | |

| **OREGON ST.** | **Bowl** | **Date** | **Opponent** | **Score** |
|---|---|---|---|---|
| Don Stiner ........................ | Rose | 1-1-42 | Duke | 20-16 |
| Tommy Prothro ................... | Rose | 1-1-57 | Iowa | 19-35 |
| Tommy Prothro ................... | Liberty | 12-15-62 | Villanova | 6-0 |
| Tommy Prothro ................... | Rose | 1-1-65 | Michigan | 7-34 |
| All bowls 2-2-0 | | | | |

| **PACIFIC (CAL.)** | **Bowl** | **Date** | **Opponent** | **Score** |
|---|---|---|---|---|
| Larry Siemering ................... | Raisin | 1-1-48 | Wichita St. | 26-14 |
| Ernie Jorge ....................... | Sun | 1-1-52 | Texas Tech | 14-25 |
| Ernie Jorge ....................... | Sun | 1-1-53 | Southern Miss. | 26-7 |
| All bowls 2-1-0 | | | | |

| **PENN ST.** | **Bowl** | **Date** | **Opponent** | **Score** |
|---|---|---|---|---|
| Hugo Bezdek ...................... | Rose | 1-1-23 | Southern Cal | 3-14 |
| Bob Higgins ....................... | Cotton | 1-1-48 | Southern Methodist | 13-13 |
| Charles "Rip" Engle ............... | Liberty | 12-19-59 | Alabama | 7-0 |
| Charles "Rip" Engle ............... | Liberty | 12-17-60 | Oregon | 41-12 |
| Charles "Rip" Engle ............... | Gator | 12-30-61 | Georgia Tech | 30-15 |
| Charles "Rip" Engle ............... | Gator | 12-29-62 | Florida | 7-17 |
| Joe Paterno ....................... | Gator | 12-30-67 | Florida St. | 17-17 |
| Joe Paterno ....................... | Orange | 1-1-69 | Kansas | 15-14 |
| Joe Paterno ....................... | Orange | 1-1-70 | Missouri | 10-3 |
| Joe Paterno ....................... | Cotton | 1-1-72 | Texas | 30-6 |
| Joe Paterno ....................... | Sugar | 12-31-72 | Oklahoma | 0-14 |
| Joe Paterno ....................... | Orange | 1-1-74 | Louisiana St. | 16-9 |
| Joe Paterno ....................... | Cotton | 1-1-75 | Baylor | 41-20 |
| Joe Paterno ....................... | Sugar | 12-31-75 | Alabama | 6-13 |
| Joe Paterno ....................... | Gator | 12-27-76 | Notre Dame | 9-20 |
| Joe Paterno ....................... | Fiesta | 12-25-77 | Arizona St. | 42-30 |
| Joe Paterno ....................... | Sugar | 1-1-79 | Alabama | 7-14 |
| Joe Paterno ....................... | Liberty | 12-22-79 | Tulane | 9-6 |
| Joe Paterno ....................... | Fiesta | 12-26-80 | Ohio St. | 31-19 |
| Joe Paterno ....................... | Fiesta | 1-1-82 | Southern Cal | 26-10 |
| Joe Paterno ....................... | Sugar | 1-1-83 | Georgia | 27-23 |
| Joe Paterno ....................... | Aloha | 12-26-83 | Washington | 13-10 |
| Joe Paterno ....................... | Orange | 1-1-86 | Oklahoma | 10-25 |
| Joe Paterno ....................... | Fiesta | 1-2-87 | Miami (Fla.) | 14-10 |
| Joe Paterno ....................... | Florida Citrus | 1-1-88 | Clemson | 10-35 |
| Joe Paterno ....................... | Holiday | 12-29-89 | Brigham Young | 50-39 |
| Joe Paterno ....................... | Blockbuster | 12-28-90 | Florida St. | 17-24 |
| Joe Paterno ....................... | Fiesta | 1-1-92 | Tennessee | 42-17 |
| Joe Paterno ....................... | Blockbuster | 1-1-93 | Stanford | 3-24 |
| All bowls 17-10-2 | | | | |

| **PITTSBURGH** | **Bowl** | **Date** | **Opponent** | **Score** |
|---|---|---|---|---|
| Jock Sutherland .................. | Rose | 1-2-28 | Stanford | 6-7 |
| Jock Sutherland .................. | Rose | 1-1-30 | Southern Cal | 14-47 |
| Jock Sutherland .................. | Rose | 1-2-33 | Southern Cal | 0-35 |
| Jock Sutherland .................. | Rose | 1-1-37 | Washington | 21-0 |
| John Michelosen .................. | Sugar | 1-2-56 | Georgia Tech | 0-7 |

| | | | | |
|---|---|---|---|---|
| John Michelosen | Gator | 12-29-56 | Georgia Tech | 14-21 |
| Johnny Majors | Fiesta | 12-21-73 | Arizona St. | 7-28 |
| Johnny Majors | Sun | 12-26-75 | Kansas | 33-19 |
| Johnny Majors | Sugar | 1-1-77 | Georgia | 27-3 |
| Jackie Sherrill | Gator | 12-30-77 | Clemson | 34-3 |
| Jackie Sherrill | Tangerine | 12-23-78 | North Caro. St. | 17-30 |
| Jackie Sherrill | Fiesta | 12-25-79 | Arizona | 16-10 |
| Jackie Sherrill | Gator | 12-29-80 | South Caro. | 37-9 |
| Jackie Sherrill | Sugar | 1-1-82 | Georgia | 24-20 |
| Foge Fazio | Cotton | 1-1-83 | Southern Methodist | 3-7 |
| Foge Fazio | Fiesta | 1-2-84 | Ohio St. | 23-28 |
| Mike Gottfried | Bluebonnet | 12-31-87 | Texas | 27-32 |
| Paul Hackett | John Hancock | 12-30-89 | Texas A&M | 31-28 |

All bowls 8-10-0

| PURDUE | Bowl | Date | Opponent | Score |
|---|---|---|---|---|
| Jack Mollenkopf | Rose | 1-2-67 | Southern Cal | 14-13 |
| Jim Young | Peach | 12-25-78 | Georgia Tech | 41-21 |
| Jim Young | Bluebonnet | 12-31-79 | Tennessee | 27-22 |
| Jim Young | Liberty | 12-27-80 | Missouri | 28-25 |
| Leon Burtnett | Peach | 12-31-84 | Virginia | 24-27 |

All bowls 4-1-0

| RICE | Bowl | Date | Opponent | Score |
|---|---|---|---|---|
| Jimmy Kitts | Cotton | 1-1-38 | Colorado | 28-14 |
| Jess Neely | Orange | 1-1-47 | Tennessee | 8-0 |
| Jess Neely | Cotton | 1-2-50 | North Caro. | 27-13 |
| Jess Neely | Cotton | 1-1-54 | Alabama | 28-6 |
| Jess Neely | Cotton | 1-1-58 | Navy | 7-20 |
| Jess Neely | Sugar | 1-2-61 | Mississippi | 6-14 |
| Jess Neely | Bluebonnet | 12-16-61 | Kansas | 7-33 |

All bowls 4-3-0

| RUTGERS | Bowl | Date | Opponent | Score |
|---|---|---|---|---|
| Frank Burns | Garden State | 12-16-78 | Arizona St. | 18-34 |

All bowls 0-1-0

| SAN DIEGO ST. | Bowl | Date | Opponent | Score |
|---|---|---|---|---|
| Bill Schutte | Harbor | 1-1-48 | Hardin-Simmons | 0-53 |
| Don Coryell | Pasadena | 12- 6-69 | Boston U. | 28-7 |
| Denny Stolz | Holiday | 12-30-86 | Iowa | 38-39 |
| Al Luginbill | Freedom | 12-30-91 | Tulsa | 17-28 |

All bowls 1-3-0

| SAN JOSE ST. | Bowl | Date | Opponent | Score |
|---|---|---|---|---|
| Bill Hubbard | Raisin | 1-1-47 | Utah St. | 20-0 |
| Bill Hubbard | Raisin | 12-31-49 | Texas Tech | 20-13 |
| Dewey King | Pasadena | 12-18-71 | Memphis St. | 9-28 |
| Jack Elway | California | 12-19-81 | Toledo | 25-27 |
| Claude Gilbert | California | 12-31-86 | Miami (Ohio) | 37-7 |
| Claude Gilbert | California | 12-12-87 | Eastern Mich. | 27-30 |
| Terry Shea | California | 12- 8-90 | Central Mich. | 48-24 |

All bowls 4-3-0

| SOUTH CARO. | Bowl | Date | Opponent | Score |
|---|---|---|---|---|
| Johnny McMillan | Gator | 1-1-46 | Wake Forest | 14-26 |
| Paul Dietzel | Peach | 12-30-69 | West Va. | 3-14 |
| Jim Carlen | Tangerine | 12-20-75 | Miami (Ohio) | 7-20 |
| Jim Carlen | Hall of Fame | 12-29-79 | Missouri | 14-24 |
| Jim Carlen | Gator | 12-29-80 | Pittsburgh | 9-37 |
| Joe Morrison | Gator | 12-28-84 | Oklahoma St. | 14-21 |
| Joe Morrison | Gator | 12-31-87 | Louisiana St. | 13-30 |
| Joe Morrison | Liberty | 12-28-88 | Indiana | 10-34 |

All bowls 0-8-0

| SOUTHERN CAL | Bowl | Date | Opponent | Score |
|---|---|---|---|---|
| Elmer "Gus" Henderson | Rose | 1-1-23 | Penn St. | 14-3 |
| Elmer "Gus" Henderson | Los Angeles Christmas Festival | 12-25-24 | Missouri | 20-7 |
| Howard Jones | Rose | 1-1-30 | Pittsburgh | 47-14 |
| Howard Jones | Rose | 1-1-32 | Tulane | 21-12 |
| Howard Jones | Rose | 1-2-33 | Pittsburgh | 35-0 |

Southern Cal broke open a 7-7 game at halftime as Anthony Davis (above) ran for 157 yards to pace the Trojans to a 42-17 victory over Ohio State in the 1973 Rose Bowl, one of Southern Cal's 22 victories in 35 bowl appearances.

| | | | | |
|---|---|---|---|---|
| Howard Jones | Rose | 1-2-39 | Duke | 7-3 |
| Howard Jones | Rose | 1-1-40 | Tennessee | 14-0 |
| Jeff Cravath | Rose | 1-1-44 | Washington | 29-0 |
| Jeff Cravath | Rose | 1-1-45 | Tennessee | 25-0 |
| Jeff Cravath | Rose | 1-1-46 | Alabama | 14-34 |
| Jeff Cravath | Rose | 1-1-48 | Michigan | 0-49 |
| Jess Hill | Rose | 1-1-53 | Wisconsin | 7-0 |
| Jess Hill | Rose | 1-1-55 | Ohio St. | 7-20 |
| John McKay | Rose | 1-1-63 | Wisconsin | 42-37 |
| John McKay | Rose | 1-2-67 | Purdue | 13-14 |
| John McKay | Rose | 1-1-68 | Indiana | 14-3 |
| John McKay | Rose | 1-1-69 | Ohio St. | 16-27 |
| John McKay | Rose | 1-1-70 | Michigan | 10-3 |
| John McKay | Rose | 1-1-73 | Ohio St. | 42-17 |
| John McKay | Rose | 1-1-74 | Ohio St. | 21-42 |
| John McKay | Rose | 1-1-75 | Ohio St. | 18-17 |
| John McKay | Liberty | 12-22-75 | Texas A&M | 20-0 |
| John Robinson | Rose | 1-1-77 | Michigan | 14-6 |
| John Robinson | Bluebonnet | 12-31-77 | Texas A&M | 47-28 |
| John Robinson | Rose | 1-1-79 | Michigan | 17-10 |
| John Robinson | Rose | 1-1-80 | Ohio St. | 17-16 |
| John Robinson | Fiesta | 1-1-82 | Penn St. | 10-26 |
| Ted Tollner | Rose | 1-1-85 | Ohio St. | 20-17 |
| Ted Tollner | Aloha | 12-28-85 | Alabama | 3-24 |
| Ted Tollner | Florida Citrus | 1-1-87 | Auburn | 7-16 |
| Larry Smith | Rose | 1-1-88 | Michigan St. | 17-20 |
| Larry Smith | Rose | 1-2-89 | Michigan | 14-22 |
| Larry Smith | Rose | 1-1-90 | Michigan | 17-10 |
| Larry Smith | John Hancock | 12-31-90 | Michigan St. | 16-17 |
| Larry Smith | Freedom | 12-29-92 | Fresno St. | 7-24 |

All bowls 22-13-0

| SOUTHERN METHODIST | Bowl | Date | Opponent | Score |
|---|---|---|---|---|
| Ray Morrison | Dixie Classic | 1-1-25 | West Va. Wesleyan | 7-9 |
| Matty Bell | Rose | 1-1-36 | Stanford | 0-7 |
| Matty Bell | Cotton | 1-1-48 | Penn St. | 13-13 |
| Matty Bell | Cotton | 1-1-49 | Oregon | 21-13 |
| Hayden Fry | Sun | 12-31-63 | Oregon | 14-21 |
| Hayden Fry | Cotton | 12-31-66 | Georgia | 9-24 |
| Hayden Fry | Bluebonnet | 12-31-68 | Oklahoma | 28-27 |
| Ron Meyer | Holiday | 12-19-80 | Brigham Young | 45-46 |
| Bobby Collins | Cotton | 1-1-83 | Pittsburgh | 7-3 |
| Bobby Collins | Sun | 12-24-83 | Alabama | 7-28 |
| Bobby Collins | Aloha | 12-29-84 | Notre Dame | 27-20 |
| All bowls 4-6-1 | | | | |

| SOUTHERN MISS. | Bowl | Date | Opponent | Score |
|---|---|---|---|---|
| Thad "Pie" Vann | Sun | 1-1-53 | Pacific (Cal.) | 7-26 |
| Thad "Pie" Vann | Sun | 1-1-54 | UTEP | 14-37 |
| Bobby Collins | Independence | 12-13-80 | McNeese St. | 16-14 |
| Bobby Collins | Tangerine | 12-19-81 | Missouri | 17-19 |
| Curley Hallman | Independence | 12-23-88 | UTEP | 38-18 |
| Jeff Bower | All-American | 12-28-90 | North Caro. St. | 27-31 |
| All bowls 2-4-0 | | | | |

| STANFORD | Bowl | Date | Opponent | Score |
|---|---|---|---|---|
| Charlie Fickert | Rose | 1-1-02 | Michigan | 0-49 |
| Glenn "Pop" Warner | Rose | 1-1-25 | Notre Dame | 10-27 |
| Glenn "Pop" Warner | Rose | 1-1-27 | Alabama | 7-7 |
| Glenn "Pop" Warner | Rose | 1-2-28 | Pittsburgh | 7-6 |
| Claude "Tiny" Thornhill | Rose | 1-1-34 | Columbia | 0-7 |
| Claude "Tiny" Thornhill | Rose | 1-1-35 | Alabama | 13-29 |
| Claude "Tiny" Thornhill | Rose | 1-1-36 | Southern Methodist | 7-0 |
| Clark Shaughnessy | Rose | 1-1-41 | Nebraska | 21-13 |
| Chuck Taylor | Rose | 1-1-52 | Illinois | 7-40 |
| John Ralston | Rose | 1-1-71 | Ohio St. | 27-17 |
| John Ralston | Rose | 1-1-72 | Michigan | 13-12 |
| Bill Walsh | Sun | 12-31-77 | Louisiana St. | 24-14 |
| Bill Walsh | Bluebonnet | 12-31-78 | Georgia | 25-22 |
| Jack Elway | Gator | 12-27-86 | Clemson | 21-27 |
| Dennis Green | Aloha | 12-25-91 | Georgia Tech | 17-18 |
| Bill Walsh | Blockbuster | 1-1-93 | Penn St. | 24-3 |
| All bowls 8-7-1 | | | | |

| SYRACUSE | Bowl | Date | Opponent | Score |
|---|---|---|---|---|
| Ben Schwartzwalder | Orange | 1-1-53 | Alabama | 6-61 |
| Ben Schwartzwalder | Cotton | 1-1-57 | Texas Christian | 27-28 |
| Ben Schwartzwalder | Orange | 1-1-59 | Oklahoma | 6-21 |
| Ben Schwartzwalder | Cotton | 1-1-60 | Texas | 23-14 |
| Ben Schwartzwalder | Liberty | 12-16-61 | Miami (Fla.) | 15-14 |
| Ben Schwartzwalder | Sugar | 1-1-65 | Louisiana St. | 10-13 |
| Ben Schwartzwalder | Gator | 12-31-66 | Tennessee | 12-18 |
| Frank Maloney | Independence | 12-15-79 | McNeese St. | 31-7 |
| Dick MacPherson | Cherry | 12-21-85 | Maryland | 18-35 |
| Dick MacPherson | Sugar | 1-1-88 | Auburn | 16-16 |
| Dick MacPherson | Hall of Fame | 1-2-89 | Louisiana St. | 23-10 |
| Dick MacPherson | Peach | 12-30-89 | Georgia | 19-18 |
| Dick MacPherson | Aloha | 12-25-90 | Arizona | 28-0 |
| Paul Pasqualoni | Hall of Fame | 1-1-92 | Ohio St. | 24-17 |
| Paul Pasqualoni | Fiesta | 1-1-93 | Colorado | 26-22 |
| All bowls 8-6-1 | | | | |

| TEMPLE | Bowl | Date | Opponent | Score |
|---|---|---|---|---|
| Glenn "Pop" Warner | Sugar | 1-1-35 | Tulane | 14-20 |
| Wayne Hardin | Garden State | 12-15-79 | California | 28-17 |
| All bowls 1-1-0 | | | | |

| TENNESSEE | Bowl | Date | Opponent | Score |
|---|---|---|---|---|
| Bob Neyland | Orange | 1-2-39 | Oklahoma | 17-0 |
| Bob Neyland | Rose | 1-1-40 | Southern Cal | 0-14 |
| Bob Neyland | Sugar | 1-1-41 | Boston College | 13-19 |
| John Barnhill | Sugar | 1-1-43 | Tulsa | 14-7 |
| John Barnhill | Rose | 1-1-45 | Southern Cal | 0-25 |

| | | | | |
|---|---|---|---|---|
| Bob Neyland | Orange | 1-1-47 | Rice | 0-8 |
| Bob Neyland | Cotton | 1-1-51 | Texas | 20-14 |
| Bob Neyland | Sugar | 1-1-52 | Baylor | 7-13 |
| Bob Neyland | Cotton | 1-1-53 | Texas | 0-16 |
| Bowden Wyatt | Sugar | 1-1-57 | Maryland | 13-28 |
| Bowden Wyatt | Gator | 12-28-57 | Texas A&M | 3-0 |
| Doug Dickey | Bluebonnet | 12-18-65 | Tulsa | 27-6 |
| Doug Dickey | Gator | 12-31-66 | Syracuse | 18-12 |
| Doug Dickey | Orange | 1-1-68 | Oklahoma | 24-26 |
| Doug Dickey | Cotton | 1-1-69 | Texas | 13-36 |
| Doug Dickey | Gator | 12-27-69 | Florida | 13-14 |
| Bill Battle | Sugar | 1-1-71 | Air Force | 34-13 |
| Bill Battle | Liberty | 12-20-71 | Arkansas | 14-13 |
| Bill Battle | Bluebonnet | 12-30-72 | Louisiana St. | 24-17 |
| Bill Battle | Gator | 12-29-73 | Texas Tech | 19-28 |
| Bill Battle | Liberty | 12-16-74 | Maryland | 7-3 |
| Johnny Majors | Bluebonnet | 12-31-79 | Purdue | 22-27 |
| Johnny Majors | Garden State | 12-13-81 | Wisconsin | 28-21 |
| Johnny Majors | Peach | 12-31-82 | Iowa | 22-28 |
| Johnny Majors | Florida Citrus | 12-17-83 | Maryland | 30-23 |
| Johnny Majors | Sun | 12-24-84 | Maryland | 26-27 |
| Johnny Majors | Sugar | 1-1-86 | Miami (Fla.) | 35-7 |
| Johnny Majors | Liberty | 12-29-86 | Minnesota | 21-14 |
| Johnny Majors | Peach | 1-2-88 | Indiana | 27-22 |
| Johnny Majors | Cotton | 1-1-90 | Arkansas | 31-27 |
| Johnny Majors | Sugar | 1-1-91 | Virginia | 23-22 |
| Johnny Majors | Fiesta | 1-1-92 | Penn St. | 17-42 |
| Phillip Fulmer | Hall of Fame | 1-1-93 | Boston College | 38-23 |

All bowls 18-15-0

| TEXAS | Bowl | Date | Opponent | Score |
|---|---|---|---|---|
| Dana Bible | Cotton | 1-1-43 | Georgia Tech | 14-7 |
| Dana Bible | Cotton | 1-1-44 | Randolph Field | 7-7 |
| Dana Bible | Cotton | 1-1-46 | Missouri | 40-27 |
| Blair Cherry | Sugar | 1-1-48 | Alabama | 27-7 |
| Blair Cherry | Orange | 1-1-49 | Georgia | 41-28 |
| Blair Cherry | Cotton | 1-1-51 | Tennessee | 14-20 |
| Ed Price | Cotton | 1-1-53 | Tennessee | 16-0 |
| Darrell Royal | Sugar | 1-1-58 | Mississippi | 7-39 |
| Darrell Royal | Cotton | 1-1-60 | Syracuse | 14-23 |
| Darrell Royal | Bluebonnet | 12-17-60 | Alabama | 3-3 |
| Darrell Royal | Cotton | 1-1-62 | Mississippi | 12-7 |
| Darrell Royal | Cotton | 1-1-63 | Louisiana St. | 0-13 |
| Darrell Royal | Cotton | 1-1-64 | Navy | 28-6 |
| Darrell Royal | Orange | 1-1-65 | Alabama | 21-17 |
| Darrell Royal | Bluebonnet | 12-17-66 | Mississippi | 19-0 |
| Darrell Royal | Cotton | 1-1-69 | Tennessee | 36-13 |
| Darrell Royal | Cotton | 1-1-70 | Notre Dame | 21-17 |
| Darrell Royal | Cotton | 1-1-71 | Notre Dame | 11-24 |
| Darrell Royal | Cotton | 1-1-72 | Penn St. | 6-30 |
| Darrell Royal | Cotton | 1-1-73 | Alabama | 17-13 |
| Darrell Royal | Cotton | 1-1-74 | Nebraska | 3-19 |
| Darrell Royal | Gator | 12-30-74 | Auburn | 3-27 |
| Darrell Royal | Bluebonnet | 12-27-75 | Colorado | 38-21 |
| Fred Akers | Cotton | 1-2-78 | Notre Dame | 10-38 |
| Fred Akers | Sun | 12-23-78 | Maryland | 42-0 |
| Fred Akers | Sun | 12-22-79 | Washington | 7-14 |
| Fred Akers | Bluebonnet | 12-31-80 | North Caro. | 7-16 |
| Fred Akers | Cotton | 1-1-82 | Alabama | 14-12 |
| Fred Akers | Sun | 12-25-82 | North Caro. | 10-26 |
| Fred Akers | Cotton | 1-2-84 | Georgia | 9-10 |
| Fred Akers | Freedom | 12-26-84 | Iowa | 17-55 |
| Fred Akers | Bluebonnet | 12-31-85 | Air Force | 16-24 |
| David McWilliams | Bluebonnet | 12-31-87 | Pittsburgh | 32-27 |
| David McWilliams | Cotton | 1-1-91 | Miami (Fla.) | 3-46 |

All bowls 16-16-2

*Team-by-Team Bowl Results*

| TEXAS A&M | Bowl | Date | Opponent | Score |
|---|---|---|---|---|
| Dana Bible | Dixie Classic | 1-2-22 | Centre | 22-14 |
| Homer Norton | Sugar | 1-1-40 | Tulane | 14-13 |
| Homer Norton | Cotton | 1-1-41 | Fordham | 13-12 |
| Homer Norton | Cotton | 1-1-42 | Alabama | 21-29 |
| Homer Norton | Orange | 1-1-44 | Louisiana St. | 14-19 |
| Harry Stiteler | Presidential | 12-9-50 | Georgia | 40-20 |
| Paul "Bear" Bryant | Gator | 12-28-57 | Tennessee | 0-3 |
| Gene Stallings | Cotton | 1-1-68 | Alabama | 20-16 |
| Emory Bellard | Liberty | 12-22-75 | Southern Cal | 0-20 |
| Emory Bellard | Sun | 1-2-77 | Florida | 37-14 |
| Emory Bellard | Bluebonnet | 12-31-77 | Southern Cal | 28-47 |
| Tom Wilson | Hall of Fame | 12-20-78 | Iowa St. | 28-12 |
| Tom Wilson | Independence | 12-12-81 | Oklahoma St. | 33-16 |
| Jackie Sherrill | Cotton | 1-1-86 | Auburn | 36-16 |
| Jackie Sherrill | Cotton | 1-1-87 | Ohio St. | 12-28 |
| Jackie Sherrill | Cotton | 1-1-88 | Notre Dame | 35-10 |
| R. C. Slocum | John Hancock | 12-30-89 | Pittsburgh | 28-31 |
| R. C. Slocum | Holiday | 12-29-90 | Brigham Young | 65-14 |
| R. C. Slocum | Cotton | 1-1-92 | Florida St. | 2-10 |
| R. C. Slocum | Cotton | 1-1-93 | Notre Dame | 3-28 |

All bowls 11-9-0

| TEXAS CHRISTIAN | Bowl | Date | Opponent | Score |
|---|---|---|---|---|
| Bill Driver | Fort Worth Classic | 1-1-21 | Centre | 7-63 |
| Leo "Dutch" Meyer | Sugar | 1-1-36 | Louisiana St. | 3-2 |
| Leo "Dutch" Meyer | Cotton | 1-1-37 | Marquette | 16-6 |
| Leo "Dutch" Meyer | Sugar | 1-2-39 | Carnegie Mellon | 15-7 |
| Leo "Dutch" Meyer | Orange | 1-1-42 | Georgia | 26-40 |
| Leo "Dutch" Meyer | Cotton | 1-1-45 | Oklahoma St. | 0-34 |
| Leo "Dutch" Meyer | Delta | 1-1-48 | Mississippi | 9-13 |
| Leo "Dutch" Meyer | Cotton | 1-1-52 | Kentucky | 7-20 |
| Abe Martin | Cotton | 1-2-56 | Mississippi | 13-14 |
| Abe Martin | Cotton | 1-1-57 | Syracuse | 28-27 |
| Abe Martin | Cotton | 1-1-59 | Air Force | 0-0 |
| Abe Martin | Bluebonnet | 12-19-59 | Clemson | 7-23 |
| Abe Martin | Sun | 12-31-65 | UTEP | 12-13 |
| Jim Wacker | Bluebonnet | 12-31-84 | West Va. | 14-31 |

All bowls 4-9-1

| TEXAS TECH | Bowl | Date | Opponent | Score |
|---|---|---|---|---|
| Pete Cawthon | Sun | 1-1-38 | West Va. | 6-7 |
| Pete Cawthon | Cotton | 1-2-39 | St. Mary's (Cal.) | 13-20 |
| Dell Morgan | Sun | 1-1-42 | Tulsa | 0-6 |
| Dell Morgan | Sun | 1-1-48 | Miami (Ohio) | 12-13 |
| Dell Morgan | Raisin | 12-31-49 | San Jose St. | 13-20 |
| DeWitt Weaver | Sun | 1-1-52 | Pacific (Cal.) | 25-14 |
| DeWitt Weaver | Gator | 1-1-54 | Auburn | 35-13 |
| DeWitt Weaver | Sun | 1-2-56 | Wyoming | 14-21 |
| J. T. King | Sun | 12-26-64 | Georgia | 0-7 |
| J. T. King | Gator | 12-31-65 | Georgia Tech | 21-31 |
| Jim Carlen | Sun | 12-19-70 | Georgia Tech | 9-17 |
| Jim Carlen | Sun | 12-30-72 | North Caro. | 28-32 |
| Jim Carlen | Gator | 12-29-73 | Tennessee | 28-19 |
| Jim Carlen | Peach | 12-28-74 | Vanderbilt | 6-6 |
| Steve Sloan | Bluebonnet | 12-31-76 | Nebraska | 24-27 |
| Steve Sloan | Tangerine | 12-23-77 | Florida St. | 17-40 |
| Spike Dykes | Independence | 12-20-86 | Mississippi | 17-20 |
| Spike Dykes | All-American | 12-28-89 | Duke | 49-21 |

All bowls 4-13-1

| TOLEDO | Bowl | Date | Opponent | Score |
|---|---|---|---|---|
| Frank Lauterbur | Tangerine | 12-26-69 | Davidson | 56-33 |
| Frank Lauterbur | Tangerine | 12-28-70 | William & Mary | 40-12 |
| Jack Murphy | Tangerine | 12-28-71 | Richmond | 28-3 |
| Chuck Stobart | California | 12-19-81 | San Jose St. | 27-25 |
| Dan Simrell | California | 12-15-84 | Nevada-Las Vegas | 13-30 |

All bowls 4-1-0

| TULANE | Bowl | Date | Opponent | Score |
|---|---|---|---|---|
| Bernie Bierman ................... | Rose | 1-1-32 | Southern Cal | 12-21 |
| Ted Cox ............................ | Sugar | 1-1-35 | Temple | 20-14 |
| Lowell "Red" Dawson ............. | Sugar | 1-1-40 | Texas A&M | 13-14 |
| Jim Pittman ....................... | Liberty | 12-12-70 | Colorado | 17-3 |
| Bennie Ellender ................... | Bluebonnet | 12-29-73 | Houston | 7-47 |
| Larry Smith ....................... | Liberty | 12-22-79 | Penn St. | 6-9 |
| Vince Gibson ..................... | Hall of Fame | 12-27-80 | Arkansas | 15-34 |
| Mack Brown ...................... | Independence | 12-19-87 | Washington | 12-24 |
| All bowls 2-6-0 | | | | |

| TULSA | Bowl | Date | Opponent | Score |
|---|---|---|---|---|
| Henry Frnka ...................... | Sun | 1-1-42 | Texas Tech | 6-0 |
| Henry Frnka ...................... | Sugar | 1-1-43 | Tennessee | 7-14 |
| Henry Frnka ...................... | Sugar | 1-1-44 | Georgia Tech | 18-20 |
| Henry Frnka ...................... | Orange | 1-1-45 | Georgia Tech | 26-12 |
| Henry Frnka ...................... | Oil | 1-1-46 | Georgia | 6-20 |
| J. O. "Buddy" Brothers ............ | Gator | 1-1-53 | Florida | 13-14 |
| Glenn Dobbs...................... | Bluebonnet | 12-19-64 | Mississippi | 14-7 |
| Glenn Dobbs...................... | Bluebonnet | 12-18-65 | Tennessee | 6-27 |
| F. A. Dry.......................... | Independence | 12-13-76 | McNeese St. | 16-20 |
| Dave Rader ...................... | Independence | 12-16-89 | Oregon | 24-27 |
| Dave Rader ...................... | Freedom | 12-30-91 | San Diego St. | 28-17 |
| All bowls 4-7-0 | | | | |

| UCLA | Bowl | Date | Opponent | Score |
|---|---|---|---|---|
| Edwin "Babe" Horrell ............. | Rose | 1-1-43 | Georgia | 0-9 |
| Bert LaBrucherie................... | Rose | 1-1-47 | Illinois | 14-45 |
| Henry "Red" Sanders ............. | Rose | 1-1-54 | Michigan St. | 20-28 |
| Henry "Red" Sanders ............. | Rose | 1-2-56 | Michigan St. | 14-17 |
| Bill Barnes ....................... | Rose | 1-1-62 | Minnesota | 3-21 |
| Tommy Prothro ................... | Rose | 1-1-66 | Michigan St. | 14-12 |
| Dick Vermeil ..................... | Rose | 1-1-76 | Ohio St. | 23-10 |
| Terry Donahue ................... | Liberty | 12-20-76 | Alabama | 6-36 |
| Terry Donahue ................... | Fiesta | 12-25-78 | Arkansas | 10-10 |
| Terry Donahue ................... | Bluebonnet | 12-31-81 | Michigan | 14-33 |
| Terry Donahue ................... | Rose | 1-1-83 | Michigan | 24-14 |
| Terry Donahue ................... | Rose | 1-2-84 | Illinois | 45-9 |
| Terry Donahue ................... | Fiesta | 1-1-85 | Miami (Fla.) | 39-37 |
| Terry Donahue ................... | Rose | 1-1-86 | Iowa | 45-28 |
| Terry Donahue ................... | Freedom | 12-30-86 | Brigham Young | 31-10 |
| Terry Donahue ................... | Aloha | 12-25-87 | Florida | 20-16 |
| Terry Donahue ................... | Cotton | 1-1-89 | Arkansas | 17-3 |
| Terry Donahue ................... | John Hancock | 12-31-91 | Illinois | 6-3 |
| All bowls 10-7-1 | | | | |

| UTAH | Bowl | Date | Opponent | Score |
|---|---|---|---|---|
| Ike Armstrong..................... | Sun | 1-2-39 | New Mexico | 26-0 |
| Ray Nagel......................... | Liberty | 12-19-64 | West Va. | 32-6 |
| Ron McBride ..................... | Copper | 12-29-92 | Washington St. | 28-31 |
| All bowls 2-1-0 | | | | |

| UTAH ST. | Bowl | Date | Opponent | Score |
|---|---|---|---|---|
| E. L. "Dick" Romney .............. | Raisin | 1-1-47 | San Jose St. | 0-20 |
| John Ralston ...................... | Sun | 12-31-60 | New Mexico St. | 13-20 |
| John Ralston...................... | Gotham | 12-9-61 | Baylor | 9-24 |
| All bowls 0-3-0 | | | | |

| UTEP | Bowl | Date | Opponent | Score |
|---|---|---|---|---|
| Mack Saxon....................... | Sun | 1-1-37 | Hardin-Simmons | 6-34 |
| Jack "Cactus Jack" Curtice ....... | Sun | 1-1-49 | West Va. | 12-21 |
| Jack "Cactus Jack" Curtice ....... | Sun | 1-2-50 | Georgetown | 33-20 |
| Mike Brumbelow .................. | Sun | 1-1-54 | Southern Miss. | 37-14 |
| Mike Brumbelow .................. | Sun | 1-1-55 | Florida St. | 47-20 |
| Mike Brumbelow .................. | Sun | 1-1-57 | Geo. Washington | 0-13 |
| Bobby Dobbs ..................... | Sun | 12-31-65 | Texas Christian | 13-12 |
| Bobby Dobbs ..................... | Sun | 12-30-67 | Mississippi | 14-7 |
| Bob Stull ......................... | Independence | 12-23-88 | Southern Miss. | 18-38 |
| All bowls 5-4-0 | | | | |

| VANDERBILT | Bowl | Date | Opponent | Score |
|---|---|---|---|---|
| Art Guepe........................ | Gator | 12-31-55 | Auburn | 25-13 |
| Steve Sloan ...................... | Peach | 12-28-74 | Texas Tech | 6-6 |
| George MacIntyre................. | Hall of Fame | 12-31-82 | Air Force | 28-36 |
| All bowls 1-1-1 | | | | |

*Team-by-Team Bowl Results*

| VIRGINIA | Bowl | Date | Opponent | Score |
|---|---|---|---|---|
| George Welsh | Peach | 12-31-84 | Purdue | 27-24 |
| George Welsh | All-American | 12-22-87 | Brigham Young | 22-16 |
| George Welsh | Florida Citrus | 1-1-90 | Illinois | 21-31 |
| George Welsh | Sugar | 1-1-91 | Tennessee | 22-23 |
| George Welsh | Gator | 12-29-91 | Oklahoma | 14-48 |
| All bowls 2-3-0 | | | | |
| VIRGINIA TECH | Bowl | Date | Opponent | Score |
| Jimmy Kitts | Sun | 1-1-47 | Cincinnati | 6-18 |
| Jerry Claiborne | Liberty | 12-10-66 | Miami (Fla.) | 7-14 |
| Jerry Claiborne | Liberty | 12-14-68 | Mississippi | 17-34 |
| Bill Dooley | Peach | 1-2-81 | Miami (Fla.) | 10-20 |
| Bill Dooley | Independence | 12-15-84 | Air Force | 7-23 |
| Bill Dooley | Peach | 12-31-86 | North Caro. St. | 25-24 |
| All bowls 1-5-0 | | | | |
| WAKE FOREST | Bowl | Date | Opponent | Score |
| D. C. "Peahead" Walker | Gator | 1-1-46 | South Caro. | 26-14 |
| D. C. "Peahead" Walker | Dixie | 1-1-49 | Baylor | 7-20 |
| John Mackovic | Tangerine | 12-22-79 | Louisiana St. | 10-34 |
| Bill Dooley | Independence | 12-31-92 | Oregon | 39-35 |
| All bowls 2-2-0 | | | | |
| WASHINGTON | Bowl | Date | Opponent | Score |
| Enoch Bagshaw | Rose | 1-1-24 | Navy | 14-14 |
| Enoch Bagshaw | Rose | 1-1-26 | Alabama | 19-20 |
| Jimmy Phelan | Rose | 1-1-37 | Pittsburgh | 0-21 |
| Ralph "Pest" Welch | Rose | 1-1-44 | Southern Cal | 0-29 |
| Jim Owens | Rose | 1-1-60 | Wisconsin | 44-8 |
| Jim Owens | Rose | 1-2-61 | Minnesota | 17-7 |
| Jim Owens | Rose | 1-1-64 | Illinois | 7-17 |
| Don James | Rose | 1-2-78 | Michigan | 27-20 |
| Don James | Sun | 12-22-79 | Texas | 14-7 |
| Don James | Rose | 1-1-81 | Michigan | 6-23 |
| Don James | Rose | 1-1-82 | Iowa | 28-0 |
| Don James | Aloha | 12-25-82 | Maryland | 21-20 |
| Don James | Aloha | 12-26-83 | Penn St. | 10-13 |
| Don James | Orange | 1-1-85 | Oklahoma | 28-17 |
| Don James | Freedom | 12-30-85 | Colorado | 20-17 |
| Don James | Sun | 12-25-86 | Alabama | 6-28 |
| Don James | Independence | 12-19-87 | Tulane | 24-12 |
| Don James | Freedom | 12-30-89 | Florida | 34-7 |
| Don James | Rose | 1-1-91 | Iowa | 46-34 |
| Don James | Rose | 1-1-92 | Michigan | 34-14 |
| Don James | Rose | 1-1-93 | Michigan | 31-38 |
| All bowls 12-8-1 | | | | |
| WASHINGTON ST. | Bowl | Date | Opponent | Score |
| Bill "Lone Star" Dietz | Rose | 1-1-16 | Brown | 14-0 |
| Orin "Babe" Hollingbery | Rose | 1-1-31 | Alabama | 0-24 |
| Jim Walden | Holiday | 12-18-81 | Brigham Young | 36-38 |
| Dennis Erickson | Aloha | 12-25-88 | Houston | 24-22 |
| Mike Price | Copper | 12-29-92 | Utah | 31-28 |
| All bowls 3-2-0 | | | | |
| WEST VA. | Bowl | Date | Opponent | Score |
| Clarence "Doc" Spears | San Diego E-W Christmas Classic | 12-25-22 | Gonzaga | 21-13 |
| Marshall "Little Sleepy" Glenn | Sun | 1-1-38 | Texas Tech | 7-6 |
| Dud DeGroot | Sun | 1-1-49 | UTEP | 21-12 |
| Art Lewis | Sugar | 1-1-54 | Georgia Tech | 19-42 |
| Gene Corum | Liberty | 12-19-64 | Utah | 6-32 |
| Jim Carlen | Peach | 12-30-69 | South Caro. | 14-3 |
| Bobby Bowden | Peach | 12-29-72 | North Caro. St. | 13-49 |
| Bobby Bowden | Peach | 12-31-75 | North Caro. St. | 13-10 |
| Don Nehlen | Peach | 12-31-81 | Florida | 26-6 |
| Don Nehlen | Gator | 12-30-82 | Florida St. | 12-31 |
| Don Nehlen | Hall of Fame | 12-22-83 | Kentucky | 20-16 |
| Don Nehlen | Bluebonnet | 12-31-84 | Texas Christian | 31-14 |
| Don Nehlen | Sun | 12-25-87 | Oklahoma St. | 33-35 |
| Don Nehlen | Fiesta | 1-2-89 | Notre Dame | 21-34 |
| Don Nehlen | Gator | 12-30-89 | Clemson | 7-27 |
| All bowls 8-7-0 | | | | |

| WESTERN MICH. | Bowl | Date | Opponent | Score |
|---|---|---|---|---|
| Merle Schlosser | Aviation | 12-9-61 | New Mexico | 12-28 |
| Al Molde | California | 12-10-88 | Fresno St. | 30-35 |
| All bowls 0-2-0 | | | | |
| **WISCONSIN** | **Bowl** | **Date** | **Opponent** | **Score** |
| Ivy Williamson | Rose | 1-1-53 | Southern Cal | 0-7 |
| Milt Bruhn | Rose | 1-1-60 | Washington | 8-44 |
| Milt Bruhn | Rose | 1-2-63 | Southern Cal | 37-42 |
| Dave McClain | Garden State | 12-13-81 | Tennessee | 21-28 |
| Dave McClain | Independence | 12-11-82 | Kansas St. | 14-3 |
| Dave McClain | Hall of Fame | 12-22-83 | Kentucky | 19-20 |
| All bowls 1-5-0 | | | | |
| **WYOMING** | **Bowl** | **Date** | **Opponent** | **Score** |
| Bowden Wyatt | Gator | 1-1-51 | Wash. & Lee | 20-7 |
| Phil Dickens | Sun | 1-2-56 | Texas Tech | 21-14 |
| Bob Devaney | Sun | 12-31-58 | Hardin-Simmons | 14-6 |
| Lloyd Eaton | Sun | 12-24-66 | Florida St. | 28-20 |
| Lloyd Eaton | Sugar | 1-1-68 | Louisiana St. | 13-20 |
| Fred Akers | Fiesta | 12-25-76 | Oklahoma | 7-41 |
| Paul Roach | Holiday | 12-30-87 | Iowa | 19-20 |
| Paul Roach | Holiday | 12-30-88 | Oklahoma St. | 14-62 |
| Paul Roach | Copper | 12-31-90 | California | 15-17 |
| All bowls 4-5-0 | | | | |

# PLAYED IN MAJOR BOWL—NO LONGER I-A

| BOSTON U. | Bowl | Date | Opponent | Score |
|---|---|---|---|---|
| Larry Naviaux | Pasadena | 12-6-69 | San Diego St. | 7-28 |
| All bowls 0-1-0 | | | | |
| **BROWN** | **Bowl** | **Date** | **Opponent** | **Score** |
| Ed Robinson | Rose | 1-1-16 | Washington St. | 0-14 |
| All bowls 0-1-0 | | | | |
| **BUCKNELL** | **Bowl** | **Date** | **Opponent** | **Score** |
| Edward "Hook" Mylin | Orange | 1-1-35 | Miami (Fla.) | 26-0 |
| All bowls 1-0-0 | | | | |
| **CAL ST. FULLERTON** | **Bowl** | **Date** | **Opponent** | **Score** |
| Gene Murphy | California | 12-17-83 | Northern Ill. | 13-20 |
| All bowls 0-1-0 | | | | |
| **CAL ST. NORTHRIDGE** | **Bowl** | **Date** | **Opponent** | **Score** |
| Sam Winningham | Pasadena | 12-2-67 | West Tex. St. | 13-35 |
| All bowls 0-1-0 | | | | |
| **CARNEGIE MELLON** | **Bowl** | **Date** | **Opponent** | **Score** |
| Bill Kern | Sugar | 1-2-39 | Texas Christian | 7-15 |
| All bowls 0-1-0 | | | | |
| **CASE RESERVE** | **Bowl** | **Date** | **Opponent** | **Score** |
| Bill Edwards | Sun | 1-1-41 | Arizona St. | 26-13 |
| All bowls 1-0-0 | | | | |
| **CATHOLIC** | **Bowl** | **Date** | **Opponent** | **Score** |
| Arthur "Dutch" Bergman | Orange | 1-1-36 | Mississippi | 20-19 |
| Arthur "Dutch" Bergman | Sun | 1-1-40 | Arizona St. | 0-0 |
| All bowls 1-0-1 | | | | |
| **CENTENARY** | **Bowl** | **Date** | **Opponent** | **Score** |
| Homer Norton | Dixie Classic | 1-1-34 | Arkansas | 7-7 |
| All bowls 0-0-1 | | | | |
| **CENTRE** | **Bowl** | **Date** | **Opponent** | **Score** |
| Charley Moran | Fort Worth Classic | 1-1-21 | Texas Christian | 63-7 |
| Charley Moran | San Diego E-W Christmas Classic | 12-26-21 | Arizona | 38-0 |
| Charley Moran | Dixie Classic | 1-2-22 | Texas A&M | 14-22 |
| All bowls 2-1-0 | | | | |
| **CITADEL** | **Bowl** | **Date** | **Opponent** | **Score** |
| Eddie Teague | Tangerine | 12-30-60 | Tennessee Tech | 27-0 |
| All bowls 1-0-0 | | | | |
| **COLUMBIA** | **Bowl** | **Date** | **Opponent** | **Score** |
| Lou Little | Rose | 1-1-34 | Stanford | 7-0 |
| All bowls 1-0-0 | | | | |

*Team-by-Team Bowl Results*

| DAVIDSON | Bowl | Date | Opponent | Score |
|---|---|---|---|---|
| Homer Smith..................... | Tangerine | 12-26-69 | Toledo | 33-56 |
| All bowls 0-1-0 | | | | |
| **DAYTON** | **Bowl** | **Date** | **Opponent** | **Score** |
| Joe Gavin ........................ | Salad | 1-1-52 | Houston | 21-26 |
| All bowls 0-1-0 | | | | |
| **DENVER** | **Bowl** | **Date** | **Opponent** | **Score** |
| Clyde "Cac" Hubbard ............ | Sun | 1-1-46 | New Mexico | 24-34 |
| Clyde "Cac" Hubbard ............ | Alamo | 1-4-47 | Hardin-Simmons | 0-20 |
| All bowls 0-2-0 | | | | |
| **DRAKE** | **Bowl** | **Date** | **Opponent** | **Score** |
| Vee Green....................... | Raisin | 1-1-46 | Fresno St. | 13-12 |
| Al Kawal ........................ | Salad | 1-1-49 | Arizona | 14-13 |
| Warren Gaer ..................... | Sun | 1-1-58 | Louisville | 20-34 |
| All bowls 2-1-0 | | | | |
| **DUQUESNE** | **Bowl** | **Date** | **Opponent** | **Score** |
| John "Little Clipper" Smith ........ | Orange | 1-1-37 | Mississippi St. | 13-12 |
| All bowls 1-0-0 | | | | |
| **FORDHAM** | **Bowl** | **Date** | **Opponent** | **Score** |
| Jim Crowley ..................... | Cotton | 1-1-41 | Texas A&M | 12-13 |
| Jim Crowley ..................... | Sugar | 1-1-42 | Missouri | 2-0 |
| All bowls 1-1-0 | | | | |
| **GEO. WASHINGTON** | **Bowl** | **Date** | **Opponent** | **Score** |
| Eugene "Bo" Sherman ............ | Sun | 1-1-57 | UTEP | 13-0 |
| All bowls 1-0-0 | | | | |
| **GEORGETOWN** | **Bowl** | **Date** | **Opponent** | **Score** |
| Jack Hagerty..................... | Orange | 1-1-41 | Mississippi St. | 7-14 |
| Bob Margarita.................... | Sun | 1-2-50 | UTEP | 20-33 |
| All bowls 0-2-0 | | | | |
| **GONZAGA** | **Bowl** | **Date** | **Opponent** | **Score** |
| Charles "Gus" Dorais ............ | San Diego E-W Christmas Classic | 12-15-22 | West Va. | 13-21 |
| All bowls 0-1-0 | | | | |
| **HARDIN-SIMMONS** | **Bowl** | **Date** | **Opponent** | **Score** |
| Frank Kimbrough ................ | Sun | 1-1-36 | New Mexico St. | 14-14 |
| Frank Kimbrough ................ | Sun | 1-1-37 | UTEP | 34-6 |
| Warren Woodson ................ | Sun | 1-1-43 | Second Air Force | 7-13 |
| Warren Woodson ................ | Alamo | 1-4-47 | Denver | 20-6 |
| Warren Woodson ................ | Harbor | 1-1-48 | San Diego St. | 53-0 |
| Warren Woodson ................ | Shrine | 12-18-48 | Ouachita Baptist | 40-12 |
| Warren Woodson ................ | Camellia | 12-30-48 | Wichita St. | 29-12 |
| Sammy Baugh .................... | Sun | 12-31-58 | Wyoming | 6-14 |
| All bowls 5-2-1 | | | | |
| **HARVARD** | **Bowl** | **Date** | **Opponent** | **Score** |
| Robert Fisher .................... | Rose | 1-1-20 | Oregon | 7-6 |
| All bowls 1-0-0 | | | | |
| **HOLY CROSS** | **Bowl** | **Date** | **Opponent** | **Score** |
| John "Ox" Da Grosa .............. | Orange | 1-1-46 | Miami (Fla.) | 6-13 |
| All bowls 0-1-0 | | | | |
| **LONG BEACH ST.** | **Bowl** | **Date** | **Opponent** | **Score** |
| Jim Stangeland ................... | Pasadena | 12-19-70 | Louisville | 24-24 |
| All bowls 0-0-1 | | | | |
| **MARQUETTE** | **Bowl** | **Date** | **Opponent** | **Score** |
| Frank Murray .................... | Cotton | 1-1-37 | Texas Christian | 6-16 |
| All bowls 0-1-0 | | | | |
| **McNEESE ST.** | **Bowl** | **Date** | **Opponent** | **Score** |
| Jack Doland ..................... | Independence | 12-13-76 | Tulsa | 20-16 |
| Ernie Duplechin.................. | Independence | 12-15-79 | Syracuse | 7-31 |
| Ernie Duplechin.................. | Independence | 12-13-80 | Southern Miss. | 14-16 |
| All bowls 1-2-0 | | | | |
| **MONTANA ST.** | **Bowl** | **Date** | **Opponent** | **Score** |
| Clyde Carpenter ................. | Harbor | 1-1-47 | New Mexico | 13-13 |
| All bowls 0-0-1 | | | | |
| **NORTH TEXAS** | **Bowl** | **Date** | **Opponent** | **Score** |
| Odus Mitchell .................... | Salad | 1-1-48 | Nevada | 6-13 |
| Odus Mitchell .................... | Sun | 12-31-59 | New Mexico St. | 8-28 |
| All bowls 0-2-0 | | | | |

*1993 NCAA FOOTBALL*

| OCCIDENTAL | Bowl | Date | Opponent | Score |
|---|---|---|---|---|
| Roy Dennis ..................... | Raisin | 1-1-49 | Colorado St. | 21-20 |
| All bowls 1-0-0 | | | | |

| OUACHITA BAPTIST | Bowl | Date | Opponent | Score |
|---|---|---|---|---|
| Wesley Bradshaw ................ | Shrine | 12-18-48 | Hardin-Simmons | 12-40 |
| All bowls 0-1-0 | | | | |

| PENNSYLVANIA | Bowl | Date | Opponent | Score |
|---|---|---|---|---|
| Bob Folwell ..................... | Rose | 1-1-17 | Oregon | 0-14 |
| All bowls 0-1-0 | | | | |

| RANDOLPH FIELD | Bowl | Date | Opponent | Score |
|---|---|---|---|---|
| Frank Tritico ................... | Cotton | 1-1-44 | Texas | 7-7 |
| All bowls 0-0-1 | | | | |

| RICHMOND | Bowl | Date | Opponent | Score |
|---|---|---|---|---|
| Frank Jones..................... | Tangerine | 12-27-68 | Ohio | 49-42 |
| Frank Jones..................... | Tangerine | 12-28-71 | Toledo | 3-28 |
| All bowls 1-1-0 | | | | |

| SANTA CLARA | Bowl | Date | Opponent | Date |
|---|---|---|---|---|
| Lawrence "Buck" Shaw .......... | Sugar | 1-1-37 | Louisiana St. | 21-14 |
| Lawrence "Buck" Shaw .......... | Sugar | 1-1-38 | Louisiana St. | 6-0 |
| Len Casanova................... | Orange | 1-2-50 | Kentucky | 21-13 |
| All bowls 3-0-0 | | | | |

| SECOND AIR FORCE | Bowl | Date | Opponent | Score |
|---|---|---|---|---|
| Red Reese ..................... | Sun | 1-1-43 | Hardin-Simmons | 13-7 |
| All bowls 1-0-0 | | | | |

| SOUTHWESTERN (TEX.) | Bowl | Date | Opponent | Score |
|---|---|---|---|---|
| Randolph R. M. Medley .......... | Sun | 1-1-44 | New Mexico | 7-0 |
| Randolph R. M. Medley .......... | Sun | 1-1-45 | U. of Mexico | 35-0 |
| All bowls 2-0-0 | | | | |

| ST. MARY'S (CAL.) | Bowl | Date | Opponent | Score |
|---|---|---|---|---|
| Edward "Slip" Madigan .......... | Cotton | 1-2-39 | Texas Tech | 20-13 |
| Jimmy Phelan................... | Sugar | 1-1-46 | Oklahoma St. | 13-33 |
| Jimmy Phelan................... | Oil | 1-1-47 | Georgia Tech | 19-41 |
| All bowls 1-2-0 | | | | |

| TAMPA | Bowl | Date | Opponent | Score |
|---|---|---|---|---|
| Earle Bruce .................... | Tangerine | 12-29-72 | Kent | 21-18 |
| All bowls 1-0-0 | | | | |

| TENNESSEE TECH | Bowl | Date | Opponent | Score |
|---|---|---|---|---|
| Wilburn Tucker.................. | Tangerine | 12-30-60 | Citadel | 0-27 |
| All bowls 0-1-0 | | | | |

| U. OF MEXICO | Bowl | Date | Opponent | Score |
|---|---|---|---|---|
| Bernard A. Hoban................ | Sun | 1-1-45 | Southwestern (Tex.) | 0-35 |
| All bowls 0-1-0 | | | | |

| VILLANOVA | Bowl | Date | Opponent | Score |
|---|---|---|---|---|
| Maurice "Clipper" Smith ......... | Bacardi, Cuba | 1-1-37 | Auburn | 7-7 |
| Jordan Olivar ................... | Great Lakes | 12-6-47 | Kentucky | 14-24 |
| Jordan Olivar ................... | Harbor | 1-1-49 | Nevada | 27-7 |
| Alex Bell ....................... | Sun | 12-30-61 | Wichita St. | 17-9 |
| Alex Bell ....................... | Liberty | 12-15-62 | Oregon St. | 0-6 |
| All bowls 2-2-1 | | | | |

| WASH. & JEFF. | Bowl | Date | Opponent | Score |
|---|---|---|---|---|
| Earle "Greasy" Neale............. | Rose | 1-2-22 | California | 0-0 |
| All bowls 0-0-1 | | | | |

| WASH. & LEE | Bowl | Date | Opponent | Score |
|---|---|---|---|---|
| George Barclay ................. | Gator | 1-1-51 | Wyoming | 7-20 |
| All bowls 0-1-0 | | | | |

| WEST TEX. ST. | Bowl | Date | Opponent | Score |
|---|---|---|---|---|
| Frank Kimbrough ................ | Sun | 1-1-51 | Cincinnati | 14-13 |
| Joe Kerbel ...................... | Sun | 12-31-62 | Ohio | 15-14 |
| Joe Kerbel ...................... | Pasadena | 12-2-67 | Cal St. Northridge | 35-13 |
| All bowls 3-0-0 | | | | |

| WEST VA. WESLEYAN | Bowl | Date | Opponent | Score |
|---|---|---|---|---|
| Bob Higgins ................... | Dixie Classic | 1-1-25 | Southern Methodist | 9-7 |
| All bowls 1-0-0 | | | | |

| WICHITA ST. | Bowl | Date | Opponent | Score |
|---|---|---|---|---|
| Ralph Graham ................... | Raisin | 1-1-48 | Pacific (Cal.) | 14-26 |
| Jim Trimble .................... | Camellia | 12-30-48 | Hardin-Simmons | 12-49 |
| Hank Foldberg .................. | Sun | 12-30-61 | Villanova | 9-17 |
| All bowls 0-3-0 | | | | |

*Team-by-Team Bowl Results*

| WILLIAM & MARY | Bowl | Date | Opponent | Score |
|---|---|---|---|---|
| Rube McCray ..................... | Dixie | 1-1-48 | Arkansas | 19-21 |
| Rube McCray ..................... | Delta | 1-1-49 | Oklahoma St. | 20-0 |
| Lou Holtz ........................ | Tangerine | 12-28-70 | Toledo | 12-40 |
| All bowls 1-2-0 | | | | |
| **XAVIER (OHIO)** | **Bowl** | **Date** | **Opponent** | **Score** |
| Ed Kluska ........................ | Salad | 1-1-50 | Arizona St. | 33-21 |
| All bowls 1-0-0 | | | | |

# MAJOR BOWL GAME ATTENDANCE

### (Current site in parentheses.)

(For participating teams, refer to pages 375-382)

## ROSE BOWL

(Rose Bowl Stadium, Pasadena, Calif.; Capacity: 99,563)

| Date | | Date | | Date | | Date | |
|---|---|---|---|---|---|---|---|
| 1-1-02 | 8,000 | 1-1-37 | 87,196 | 1-1-57 | 97,126 | 1-1-77 | 106,182 |
| 1-1-16 | 7,000 | 1-1-38 | 90,000 | 1-1-58 | 98,202 | 1-2-78 | 105,312 |
| 1-1-17 | 26,000 | 1-2-39 | 89,452 | 1-1-59 | 98,297 | 1-1-79 | 105,629 |
| 1-1-20 | 30,000 | 1-1-40 | 92,200 | 1-1-60 | 100,809 | 1-1-80 | 105,526 |
| 1-1-21 | 42,000 | 1-1-41 | 91,500 | 1-2-61 | 97,314 | 1-1-81 | 104,863 |
| 1-2-22 | 40,000 | 1-1-42# | 56,000 | 1-1-62 | 98,214 | 1-1-82 | 105,611 |
| 1-1-23 | 43,000 | 1-1-43 | 93,000 | 1-1-63 | 98,698 | 1-1-83 | 104,991 |
| 1-1-24 | 40,000 | 1-1-44 | 68,000 | 1-1-64 | 96,957 | 1-2-84 | 103,217 |
| 1-1-25 | 53,000 | 1-1-45 | 91,000 | 1-1-65 | 100,423 | 1-1-85 | 102,594 |
| 1-1-26 | 50,000 | 1-1-46 | 93,000 | 1-1-66 | 100,087 | 1-1-86 | 103,292 |
| 1-1-27 | 57,417 | 1-1-47 | 90,000 | 1-2-67 | 100,807 | 1-1-87 | 103,168 |
| 1-2-28 | 65,000 | 1-1-48 | 93,000 | 1-1-68 | 102,946 | 1-1-88 | 103,847 |
| 1-1-29 | 66,604 | 1-1-49 | 93,000 | 1-1-69 | 102,063 | 1-2-89 | 101,688 |
| 1-1-30 | 72,000 | 1-2-50 | 100,963 | 1-1-70 | 103,878 | 1-1-90 | 103,450 |
| 1-1-31 | 60,000 | 1-1-51 | 98,939 | 1-1-71 | 103,839 | 1-1-91 | 101,273 |
| 1-1-32 | 75,562 | 1-1-52 | 96,825 | 1-1-72 | 103,154 | 1-1-92 | 103,566 |
| 1-2-33 | 78,874 | 1-1-53 | 101,500 | 1-1-73 | *106,869 | 1-1-93 | 94,236 |
| 1-1-34 | 35,000 | 1-1-54 | 101,000 | 1-1-74 | 105,267 | | |
| 1-1-35 | 84,474 | 1-1-55 | 89,191 | 1-1-75 | 106,721 | | |
| 1-1-36 | 84,474 | 1-2-56 | 100,809 | 1-1-76 | 105,464 | | |

* *Record attendance.*   # *Game held at Duke, Durham, N.C., due to war-time West Coast restrictions.*

## ORANGE BOWL

(Orange Bowl Stadium, Miami, Fla.; Capacity: 74,712)

| Date | | Date | | Date | | Date | |
|---|---|---|---|---|---|---|---|
| 1-1-35 | 5,134 | 1-2-50 | 64,816 | 1-1-65 | 72,647 | 1-1-80 | 66,714 |
| 1-1-36 | 6,568 | 1-1-51 | 65,181 | 1-1-66 | 72,214 | 1-1-81 | 71,043 |
| 1-1-37 | 9,210 | 1-1-52 | 65,839 | 1-2-67 | 72,426 | 1-1-82 | 72,748 |
| 1-1-38 | 18,972 | 1-1-53 | 66,280 | 1-1-68 | 77,993 | 1-1-83 | 68,713 |
| 1-2-39 | 32,191 | 1-1-54 | 68,640 | 1-1-69 | 77,719 | 1-2-84 | 72,549 |
| 1-1-40 | 29,278 | 1-1-55 | 68,750 | 1-1-70 | 77,282 | 1-1-85 | 56,294 |
| 1-1-41 | 29,554 | 1-2-56 | 76,561 | 1-1-71 | 80,699 | 1-1-86 | 74,178 |
| 1-1-42 | 35,786 | 1-1-57 | 73,280 | 1-1-72 | 78,151 | 1-1-87 | 52,717 |
| 1-1-43 | 25,166 | 1-1-58 | 76,561 | 1-1-73 | 80,010 | 1-1-88 | 74,760 |
| 1-1-44 | 25,203 | 1-1-59 | 75,281 | 1-1-74 | 60,477 | 1-2-89 | 79,480 |
| 1-1-45 | 23,279 | 1-1-60 | 72,186 | 1-1-75 | 71,801 | 1-1-90 | *81,190 |
| 1-1-46 | 35,709 | 1-2-61 | 72,212 | 1-1-76 | 76,799 | 1-1-91 | 77,062 |
| 1-1-47 | 36,152 | 1-1-62 | 68,150 | 1-1-77 | 65,537 | 1-1-92 | 77,747 |
| 1-1-48 | 59,578 | 1-1-63 | 72,880 | 1-2-78 | 60,987 | 1-1-93 | 57,324 |
| 1-1-49 | 60,523 | 1-1-64 | 72,647 | 1-1-79 | 66,365 | | |

* *Record attendance.*

## SUGAR BOWL

(Louisiana Superdome, New Orleans, La.; Capacity: 72,704)

| Date | | Date | | Date | | Date | |
|---|---|---|---|---|---|---|---|
| 1-1-35 | 22,026 | 1-1-40 | 73,000 | 1-1-45 | 72,000 | 1-2-50 | 82,470 |
| 1-1-36 | 35,000 | 1-1-41 | 73,181 | 1-1-46 | 75,000 | 1-1-51 | 82,000 |
| 1-1-37 | 41,000 | 1-1-42 | 72,000 | 1-1-47 | 73,300 | 1-1-52 | 82,000 |
| 1-1-38 | 45,000 | 1-1-43 | 70,000 | 1-1-48 | 72,000 | 1-1-53 | 82,000 |
| 1-2-39 | 50,000 | 1-1-44 | 69,000 | 1-1-49 | 82,000 | 1-1-54 | 76,000 |

*1993 NCAA FOOTBALL*

| Date | | Date | | Date | | Date | |
|---|---|---|---|---|---|---|---|
| 1-1-55 | 82,000 | 1-1-65 | 65,000 | 12-31-74 | 67,890 | 1-1-85 | 75,608 |
| 1-2-56 | 80,175 | 1-1-66 | 67,421 | 12-31-75 | 75,212 | 1-1-86 | 77,432 |
| 1-1-57 | 81,000 | 1-2-67 | 82,000 | 1-1-77 | 76,117 | 1-1-87 | 76,234 |
| 1-1-58 | 82,000 | 1-1-68 | 78,963 | 1-2-78 | 76,811 | 1-1-88 | 75,495 |
| 1-1-59 | 82,000 | 1-1-69 | 82,113 | 1-1-79 | 76,824 | 1-2-89 | 61,934 |
| 1-1-60 | 83,000 | 1-1-70 | 82,500 | 1-1-80 | 77,486 | 1-1-90 | 77,452 |
| 1-2-61 | 82,851 | 1-1-71 | 78,655 | 1-1-81 | 77,895 | 1-1-91 | 75,132 |
| 1-1-62 | 82,910 | 1-1-72 | 84,031 | 1-1-82 | 77,224 | 1-1-92 | 76,447 |
| 1-1-63 | 82,900 | 12-31-72 | 80,123 | 1-1-83 | 78,124 | 1-1-93 | 76,789 |
| 1-1-64 | 80,785 | 12-31-73 | *85,161 | 1-2-84 | 77,893 | | |

* Record attendance.

## COTTON BOWL
(Cotton Bowl Stadium, Dallas, Texas; Capacity: 71,615)

| Date | | Date | | Date | | Date | |
|---|---|---|---|---|---|---|---|
| 1-1-37 | 17,000 | 1-1-52 | 75,347 | 12-31-66 | 75,400 | 1-1-82 | 73,243 |
| 1-1-38 | 37,000 | 1-1-53 | 75,504 | 1-1-68 | 75,504 | 1-1-83 | 60,359 |
| 1-2-39 | 40,000 | 1-1-54 | 75,504 | 1-1-69 | 72,000 | 1-2-84 | 67,891 |
| 1-1-40 | 20,000 | 1-1-55 | 75,504 | 1-1-70 | 73,000 | 1-1-85 | 56,522 |
| 1-1-41 | 45,500 | 1-2-56 | 75,504 | 1-1-71 | 72,000 | 1-1-86 | 73,137 |
| 1-1-42 | 38,000 | 1-1-57 | 68,000 | 1-1-72 | 72,000 | 1-1-87 | 74,188 |
| 1-1-43 | 36,000 | 1-1-58 | 75,504 | 1-1-73 | 72,000 | 1-1-88 | 73,006 |
| 1-1-44 | 15,000 | 1-1-59 | 75,504 | 1-1-74 | 67,500 | 1-2-89 | 74,304 |
| 1-1-45 | 37,000 | 1-1-60 | 75,504 | 1-1-75 | 67,500 | 1-1-90 | 74,358 |
| 1-1-46 | 45,000 | 1-2-61 | 74,000 | 1-1-76 | 74,500 | 1-1-91 | 73,521 |
| 1-1-47 | 38,000 | 1-1-62 | 75,504 | 1-1-77 | 54,500 | 1-1-92 | 73,728 |
| 1-1-48 | 43,000 | 1-1-63 | 75,504 | 1-2-78 | *76,601 | 1-1-93 | 71,615 |
| 1-1-49 | 69,000 | 1-1-64 | 75,504 | 1-1-79 | 32,500 | | |
| 1-2-50 | 75,347 | 1-1-65 | 75,504 | 1-1-80 | 72,032 | | |
| 1-1-51 | 75,349 | 1-1-66 | 76,200 | 1-1-81 | 74,281 | | |

* Record attendance.

## JOHN HANCOCK BOWL#
(Sun Bowl Stadium, El Paso, Texas; Capacity: 51,270)

| Date | | Date | | Date | | Date | |
|---|---|---|---|---|---|---|---|
| 1-1-36 | 11,000 | 1-1-51 | 16,000 | 12-31-65 | 27,450 | 12-27-80 | 34,723 |
| 1-1-37 | 10,000 | 1-1-52 | 17,000 | 12-24-66 | 24,381 | 12-26-81 | 33,816 |
| 1-1-38 | 12,000 | 1-1-53 | 11,000 | 12-30-67 | 34,685 | 12-25-82 | 31,359 |
| 1-2-39 | 13,000 | 1-1-54 | 9,500 | 12-28-68 | 32,307 | 12-24-83 | 41,412 |
| 1-1-40 | 12,000 | 1-1-55 | 14,000 | 12-20-69 | 29,723 | 12-22-84 | 50,126 |
| 1-1-41 | 14,000 | 1-2-56 | 14,500 | 12-19-70 | 30,512 | 12-28-85 | *52,203 |
| 1-1-42 | 14,000 | 1-1-57 | 13,500 | 12-18-71 | 33,503 | 12-25-86 | 48,722 |
| 1-1-43 | 16,000 | 1-1-58 | 12,000 | 12-30-72 | 31,312 | 12-25-87 | 43,240 |
| 1-1-44 | 18,000 | 12-31-58 | 13,000 | 12-29-73 | 30,127 | 12-24-88 | 48,719 |
| 1-1-45 | 13,000 | 12-31-59 | 14,000 | 12-28-74 | 30,131 | 12-30-89 | 44,887 |
| 1-1-46 | 15,000 | 12-31-60 | 16,000 | 12-26-75 | 33,240 | 12-31-90 | 50,562 |
| 1-1-47 | 10,000 | 12-30-61 | 15,000 | 1-2-77 | 33,252 | 12-31-91 | 42,821 |
| 1-1-48 | 18,000 | 12-31-62 | 16,000 | 12-31-77 | 31,318 | 12-31-92 | 41,622 |
| 1-1-49 | 13,000 | 12-31-63 | 26,500 | 12-23-78 | 33,122 | | |
| 1-2-50 | 15,000 | 12-26-64 | 28,500 | 12-22-79 | 33,412 | | |

* Record attendance.    # Named Sun Bowl before 1989.

## GATOR BOWL
(Gator Bowl Stadium, Jacksonville, Fla.; Capacity: 80,129)

| Date | | Date | | Date | | Date | |
|---|---|---|---|---|---|---|---|
| 1-2-46 | 7,362 | 12-31-60 | 50,112 | 12-29-75 | 64,012 | 12-30-85 | 79,417 |
| 1-1-47 | 10,134 | 12-30-61 | 50,202 | 12-27-76 | 67,827 | 12-27-86 | 80,104 |
| 1-1-48 | 16,666 | 12-29-62 | 50,026 | 12-30-77 | 72,289 | 12-31-87 | 82,119 |
| 1-1-49 | 32,939 | 12-28-63 | 50,018 | 12-29-78 | 72,011 | 1-1-89 | 76,236 |
| 1-2-50 | 18,409 | 1-2-65 | 50,408 | 12-28-79 | 70,407 | 12-30-89 | *82,911 |
| 1-1-51 | 19,834 | 12-31-65 | 60,127 | 12-29-80 | 72,297 | 1-1-91 | 68,927 |
| 1-1-52 | 34,577 | 12-31-66 | 60,312 | 12-28-81 | 71,009 | 12-29-91 | 62,003 |
| 1-1-53 | 30,015 | 12-30-67 | 68,019 | 12-30-82 | 80,913 | 12-31-92 | 71,233 |
| 1-1-54 | 28,641 | 12-28-68 | 68,011 | 12-30-83 | 81,293 | | |
| 12-31-54 | 28,426 | 12-27-69 | 72,248 | 12-28-84 | 82,138 | | |
| 12-31-55 | 32,174 | 1-2-71 | 71,136 | | | | |
| 12-29-56 | 36,256 | 12-31-71 | 71,208 | | | | |
| 12-28-57 | 41,160 | 12-30-72 | 71,114 | | | | |
| 12-27-58 | 41,312 | 12-29-73 | 62,109 | | | | |
| 1-2-60 | 45,104 | 12-30-74 | 63,811 | | | | |

* Record attendance.

## LIBERTY BOWL †

(Liberty Bowl Memorial Stadium, Memphis, Tenn.; Capacity: 62,425)

| Date | | Date | | Date | | Date | |
|------|------|------|------|------|------|------|------|
| 12-19-59 | 36,211 | 12-13-69 | 50,042 | 12-22-79 | 50,021 | 12-28-89 | 60,128 |
| 12-17-60 | 16,624 | 12-12-70 | 44,640 | 12-27-80 | 53,667 | 12-27-90 | 13,144 |
| 12-16-61 | 15,712 | 12-20-71 | 51,410 | 12-30-81 | 43,216 | 12-29-91 | *61,497 |
| 12-15-62 | 17,048 | 12-18-72 | 50,021 | 12-29-82 | 54,123 | 12-31-92 | 32,107 |
| 12-31-63 | 8,309 | 12-17-73 | 50,011 | 12-29-83 | 38,229 | | |
| 12-19-64 | 6,059 | 12-16-74 | 51,284 | 12-27-84 | 50,108 | | |
| 12-18-65 | 38,607 | 12-22-75 | 52,129 | 12-27-85 | 40,186 | | |
| 12-10-66 | 39,101 | 12-20-76 | 52,736 | 12-29-86 | 51,327 | | |
| 12-16-67 | 35,045 | 12-19-77 | 49,456 | 12-29-87 | 53,249 | | |
| 12-14-68 | 46,206 | 12-23-78 | 53,064 | 12-28-88 | 39,210 | | |

*Record attendance.*   † *Played at Philadelphia, 1959-63; Atlantic City, 1964; Memphis, from 1965.*

## FLORIDA CITRUS BOWL #

(Florida Citrus Bowl—Orange County Stadium, Orlando, Fla.; Capacity: 70,000)

| Date | | Date | | Date | | Date | |
|------|------|------|------|------|------|------|------|
| 12-30-60 | 13,000 | 12-18-76 | 37,812 | 1-1-87 | 51,113 | 1-1-92 | 64,192 |
| 12-22-62 | 7,500 | 12-23-77 | 44,502 | 1-1-88 | 53,152 | 1-1-93 | 65,861 |
| 12-27-68 | 16,114 | 12-23-78 | 31,356 | 1-2-89 | 53,571 | | |
| 12-26-69 | 16,311 | 12-22-79 | 38,666 | 1-1-90 | 60,016 | | |
| 12-28-70 | 15,164 | 12-20-80 | 52,541 | 1-1-91 | *72,328 | | |
| 12-28-71 | 16,750 | 12-19-81 | 50,045 | | | | |
| 12-29-72 | 20,062 | 12-18-82 | 51,296 | | | | |
| 12-22-73 | @37,234 | 12-17-83 | 50,183 | | | | |
| 12-21-74 | 20,246 | 12-22-84 | 51,821 | | | | |
| 12-20-75 | 20,247 | 12-28-85 | 50,920 | | | | |

*Record attendance.*   # *Named Tangerine Bowl before 1982. The first 14 games in the Tangerine Bowl, through 1-1-60, are not listed because no major teams were involved. The same is true for those games played in December 1961, 1963, 1964, 1965, 1966 and 1967.*   @ *Played at Gainesville, Fla.*

## PEACH BOWL

(Georgia Dome, Atlanta, Ga.; Capacity: 71,596)

| Date | | Date | | Date | | Date | |
|------|------|------|------|------|------|------|------|
| 12-30-68 | 35,545 | 12-25-78 | 20,277 | 12-30-83 | 25,648 | 12-31-88 | 44,635 |
| 12-30-69 | 48,452 | 12-31-79 | 57,371 | 12-31-84 | 41,107 | 12-30-89 | 44,991 |
| 12-30-70 | 52,126 | 1-2-81 | 45,384 | 12-31-85 | 29,857 | 12-29-90 | 38,912 |
| 12-30-71 | 36,771 | 12-31-81 | 37,582 | 12-31-86 | 53,668 | 1-1-92 | 59,322 |
| 12-29-72 | 52,671 | 12-31-82 | 50,134 | 1-2-88 | 58,737 | 1-2-93 | *69,125 |
| 12-28-73 | 38,107 | | | | | | |
| 12-28-74 | 31,695 | | | | | | |
| 12-31-75 | 45,134 | | | | | | |
| 12-31-76 | 54,132 | | | | | | |
| 12-31-77 | 36,733 | | | | | | |

*Record attendance.*

## FIESTA BOWL

(Sun Devil Stadium, Tempe, Ariz.; Capacity: 74,783)

| Date | | Date | | Date | | Date | |
|------|------|------|------|------|------|------|------|
| 12-27-71 | 51,089 | 1-1-82 | 71,053 | 1-2-87 | 73,098 | 1-1-92 | 71,133 |
| 12-23-72 | 51,318 | 1-1-83 | 70,533 | 1-1-88 | 72,112 | 1-1-93 | 70,224 |
| 12-21-73 | 50,878 | 1-2-84 | 66,484 | 1-2-89 | *74,911 | | |
| 12-28-74 | 50,878 | 1-1-85 | 60,310 | 1-1-90 | 73,953 | | |
| 12-26-75 | 51,396 | 1-1-86 | 72,454 | 1-1-91 | 69,098 | | |
| 12-25-76 | 48,174 | | | | | | |
| 12-25-77 | 57,727 | | | | | | |
| 12-25-78 | 55,227 | | | | | | |
| 12-25-79 | 55,347 | | | | | | |
| 12-26-80 | 66,738 | | | | | | |

*Record attendance.*

## INDEPENDENCE BOWL

(Independence Stadium, Shreveport, La.; Capacity: 50,459)

| Date | | Date | | Date | | Date | |
|------|------|------|------|------|------|------|------|
| 12-13-76 | 15,542 | 12-12-81 | 47,300 | 12-20-86 | 46,369 | 12-29-91 | 46,932 |
| 12-17-77 | 18,500 | 12-11-82 | *49,503 | 12-19-87 | 41,683 | 12-31-92 | 31,337 |
| 12-16-78 | 18,200 | 12-10-83 | 41,274 | 12-23-88 | 20,242 | | |
| 12-15-79 | 27,234 | 12-15-84 | 41,000 | 12-16-89 | 30,333 | | |
| 12-13-80 | 45,000 | 12-21-85 | 42,800 | 12-15-90 | 48,325 | | |

*Record attendance.*

# HOLIDAY BOWL

(San Diego Jack Murphy Stadium, San Diego, Calif.; Capacity: 62,809)

| Date | | Date | | Date | | Date | |
|---|---|---|---|---|---|---|---|
| 12-28-78 | 52,500 | 12-23-83 | 51,480 | 12-30-88 | 60,718 | 12-30-91 | 60,646 |
| 12-21-79 | 52,200 | 12-21-84 | 61,243 | 12-29-89 | 61,113 | 12-30-92 | 44,457 |
| 12-19-80 | 50,214 | 12-22-85 | 42,324 | 12-29-90 | 61,441 | | |
| 12-18-81 | 52,419 | 12-30-86 | 59,473 | | | | |
| 12-17-82 | 52,533 | 12-30-87 | *61,892 | | | | |

* Record attendance.

# ALOHA BOWL

(Aloha Stadium, Honolulu, Hawaii; Capacity: 50,000)

| Date | | Date | | Date | | Date | |
|---|---|---|---|---|---|---|---|
| 12-25-82 | 30,055 | 12-28-85 | 35,183 | 12-25-88 | 35,132 | 12-25-91 | 34,433 |
| 12-26-83 | 37,212 | 12-27-86 | 26,743 | 12-25-89 | *50,000 | 12-25-92 | 42,933 |
| 12-29-84 | 41,777 | 12-25-87 | 24,839 | 12-25-90 | 14,185 | | |

* Record attendance.

# FREEDOM BOWL

(Anaheim Stadium, Anaheim, Calif.; Capacity: 70,962)

| Date | | Date | | Date | | Date | |
|---|---|---|---|---|---|---|---|
| 12-26-84 | 24,093 | 12-30-87 | 33,261 | 12-30-89 | 33,858 | 12-30-91 | 34,217 |
| 12-30-85 | 30,961 | 12-29-88 | 35,941 | 12-29-90 | 41,450 | 12-29-92 | 50,745 |
| 12-30-86 | *55,422 | | | | | | |

* Record attendance.

# HALL OF FAME BOWL

(Tampa Stadium, Tampa, Fla.; Capacity: 74,350)

| Date | | Date | | Date | | Date | |
|---|---|---|---|---|---|---|---|
| 12-23-86 | 25,368 | 1-2-89 | 51,112 | 1-1-91 | *63,154 | 1-1-93 | 52,056 |
| 1-2-88 | 60,156 | 1-1-90 | 52,535 | 1-1-92 | 57,789 | | |

* Record attendance.

# COPPER BOWL

(Arizona Wildcats Stadium, Tucson, Ariz.; Capacity: 58,000)

| Date | | Date | | Date | |
|---|---|---|---|---|---|
| 12-31-89 | 37,237 | 12-31-91 | 35,752 | 12-29-92 | *40,876 |
| 12-31-90 | 36,340 | | | | |

* Record attendance.

# SUNSHINE FOOTBALL CLASSIC#

(Joe Robbie Stadium, Miami, Fla.; Capacity: 73,000)

| Date | | Date | |
|---|---|---|---|
| 12-28-90 | *74,021 | 1-1-93 | 45,554 |
| 12-28-91 | 52,644 | | |

* Record attendance.   # Named Blockbuster Bowl before 1993.

# LAS VEGAS BOWL

(Silver Bowl, Las Vegas, Nev.; Capacity: 31,000)

| Date | |
|---|---|
| 12-18-92 | 15,476 |

# FORMER MAJOR BOWL GAMES

**ALAMO** (San Antonio, Texas): 1-4-47 (3,730)

**ALL-AMERICAN** (Birmingham, Ala., named Hall of Fame Classic until 1985 and then discontinued after 1990 game; played at Legion Field, capacity 75,952) 12-22-77 (47,000); 12-20-78 (41,500); 12-29-79 (62,785); 12-27-80 (30,000); 12-31-81 (41,672); 12-31-82 (75,000); 12-22-83 (42,000); 12-29-84 (47,300); 12-31-85 (45,000); 12-31-86 (30,000); 12-22-87 (37,000); 12-29-88 (48,218); 12-31-89 (47,750); 12-28-90 (44,000)

**AVIATION** (Dayton, Ohio): 12-9-61 (3,694)

**BACARDI** (Havana, Cuba): 1-1-37 (12,000)

**BLUEBONNET** (Houston, Texas, played at Rice Stadium 1959-67 and 1985, Astrodome 1968-84 and from 1986; Astrodome capacity 60,000): 12-19-59 (55,000); 12-17-60 (68,000); 12-16-61 (52,000); 12-22-62 (55,000); 12-21-63 (50,000); 12-19-64 (50,000); 12-18-65 (40,000); 12-17-66 (67,000); 12-23-67 (30,156); 12-31-68 (53,543); 12-31-69 (55,203); 12-31-70 (53,829); 12-31-71 (54,720); 12-30-72 (52,960); 12-29-73 (44,358); 12-23-74 (35,122); 12-27-75 (52,748); 12-31-76 (48,618); 12-31-77 (52,842); 12-31-78 (34,084); 12-31-79 (40,542); 12-31-80 (36,667); 12-31-81 (40,309); 12-31-82 (31,557); 12-31-83 (50,090); 12-31-84 (43,260); 12-31-85 (42,000); 12-31-86 (40,476); 12-31-87 (23,282)

**BLUEGRASS** (Louisville, Ky.): 12-13-58 (7,000)

**CALIFORNIA** (Fresno, Calif.): 12-19-81 (15,565); 12-18-82 (30,000); 12-17-83 (20,464); 12-15-84 (21,741); 12-14-85 (32,554); 12-13-86 (10,743); 12-12-87 (24,000); 12-10-88 (31,272); 12-9-89 (31,610); 12-8-90 (25,431); 12-14-91 (34,825)
**CAMELLIA** (Lafayette, La.): 12-30-48 (4,500)
**CHERRY** (Pontiac, Mich.): 12-22-84 (70,332); 12-21-85 (51,858)
**DELTA** (Memphis, Tenn.): 1-1-48 (28,120); 1-1-49 (15,069)
**DIXIE BOWL** (Birmingham, Ala.): 1-1-48 (22,000); 1-1-49 (20,000)
**DIXIE CLASSIC** (Dallas, Texas): 1-2-22 (12,000); 1-1-25 (7,000); 1-1-34 (12,000)
**FORT WORTH CLASSIC** (Fort Worth, Texas): 1-1-21 (9,000)
**GARDEN STATE** (East Rutherford, N.J.): 12-16-78 (33,402); 12-15-79 (55,493); 12-14-80 (41,417); 12-13-81 (38,782)
**GOTHAM** (New York City): 12-9-61 (15,123); 12-15-62 (6,166)

**GREAT LAKES** (Cleveland, Ohio): 12-6-47 (14,908)
**HARBOR** (San Diego, Calif.): 1-1-47 (7,000); 1-1-48 (12,000); 1-1-49 (20,000)
**LOS ANGELES CHRISTMAS FESTIVAL** (Los Angeles, Calif.): 12-25-24 (47,000)
**MERCY** (Los Angeles, Calif.): 11-23-41 (33,145)
**OIL** (Houston, Texas): 1-1-46 (27,000); 1-1-47 (23,000)

**PASADENA** (Pasadena, Calif.): 12-2-67 (28,802); 12-6-69 (41,276); 12-19-70 (20,472); 12-18-71 (15,244)
**PRESIDENTIAL CUP** (College Park, Md.): 12-9-50 (12,245)
**RAISIN** (Fresno, Calif.): 1-1-46 (10,000); 1-1-47 (13,000); 1-1-48 (13,000); 1-1-49 (10,000); 12-31-49 (9,000)
**SALAD** (Phoenix, Ariz.): 1-1-48 (12,500); 1-1-49 (17,500); 1-1-50 (18,500); 1-1-51 (23,000); 1-1-52 (17,000)
**SAN DIEGO EAST-WEST CHRISTMAS CLASSIC** (San Diego, Calif.): 12-26-21 (5,000); 12-25-22 (5,000)
**SHRINE** (Little Rock, Ark.): 12-18-48 (5,000)

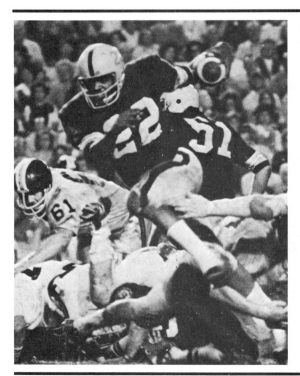

Arizona State running backs Woody Green (pictured) and Brent McClanahan combined for 373 rushing yards in a 49-35 victory over Missouri in the 1972 Fiesta Bowl. It was the most yardage gained by two teammates in bowl history.

# BOWL GAME RECORDS

Only official records after 1937 are included. Prior records are included if able to be substantiated. Each team's score is in parentheses after the team name. The year listed is the actual (calendar) year the game was played. The list also includes discontinued bowls, marked with (D). Bowls are listed by the name of the bowl at the time it was played: The Florida Citrus Bowl was the Tangerine Bowl in 1947-82; the first Hall of Fame Bowl (1977-85) was called the All-American Bowl in 1986-90; the current Hall of Fame Bowl is played in Tampa, Fla., and started in 1986; the John Hancock Bowl was called the Sun Bowl in 1936-86 and the John Hancock Sun Bowl in 1987-88; and the Blockbuster Bowl changed its name to Sunshine Football Classic in 1993. The NCAA Statistics Service thanks former staff member Steve Boda for his valuable assistance in compiling these records.

## SINGLE GAME—INDIVIDUAL

### TOTAL OFFENSE

**Most Total Plays**
74 (D)—Tony Kimbrough, Western Mich. (30) vs. Fresno St. (35) (California, 1988) (431 yards)

**Most Total Yards**
594—Ty Detmer, Brigham Young (39) vs. Penn St. (50) (Holiday, 1989) (576 passing yards, 67 plays)

**Highest Average Per Play (Min. 10 Plays)**
24.1—Dicky Maegle, Rice (28) vs. Alabama (6) (Cotton, 1954) (11 for 265)

**Most Touchdowns Responsible For (TDs Scored & Passed For)**
6—Chuck Long, Iowa (55) vs. Texas (17) (Freedom, 1984) (6 pass); Bobby Layne, Texas (40) vs. Missouri (27) (Cotton, 1946) (3 rush, 2 pass, 1 catch)

### RUSHING

**Most Rushing Attempts**
46—Ron Jackson, Tulsa (28) vs. San Diego St. (17) (Freedom, 1991) (211 yards)

**Most Net Rushing Yards**
280 (D)—James Gray, Texas Tech (49) vs. Duke (21) (All-American, 1989) (33 carries)

**Most Net Rushing Yards by a Quarterback**
180 (D)—Mike Mosley, Texas A&M (28) vs. Southern Cal (47) (Bluebonnet, 1977) (20 carries)

**Highest Average Per Rush (Min. 9 Carries)**
24.1—Dicky Maegle, Rice (28) vs. Alabama (6) (Cotton, 1954) (11 for 265)

**Most Net Rushing Yards by Two Rushers, Same Team, Over 100 Yards Rushing Each**
373—Woody Green (202) & Brent McClanahan (171), Arizona St. (49) vs. Missouri (35) (Fiesta, 1972)

**Most Rushing Touchdowns**
5—Barry Sanders, Oklahoma St. (62) vs. Wyoming (14) (Holiday, 1988) (runs of 33, 2, 67, 1, 10 yards); Neil Snow, Michigan (49) vs. Stanford (0) (Rose, 1902) (touchdowns counted as five-point scores)

### PASSING

**Most Pass Attempts**
62 (D)—Steve Clarkson, San Jose St. (25) vs. Toledo (27) (California, 1981) (completed 43)

**Most Pass Completions**
43 (D)—Steve Clarkson, San Jose St. (25) vs. Toledo (27) (California, 1981) (attempted 62)

**Most Consecutive Pass Completions**
10—Rick Neuheisel, UCLA (45) vs. Illinois (9) (Rose, 1984) (22 of 31 for 298 yards and 4 touchdowns)

**Most Net Passing Yards**
576—Ty Detmer, Brigham Young (39) vs. Penn St. (50) (Holiday, 1989) (42 of 59 with 2 interceptions)

**Most Net Passing Yards, One Quarter**
223—Browning Nagle, Louisville (34) vs. Alabama (7) (Fiesta, 1991) (1st quarter, 9 of 16)

**Most Touchdown Passes Thrown**
6—Chuck Long, Iowa (55) vs. Texas (17) (Freedom, 1984) (29 of 39 with no interceptions)

(touchdown passes of 6, 11, 33, 49, 4, 15 yards)

**Most Passes Had Intercepted**
6—Bruce Lee, Arizona (10) vs. Auburn (34) (Sun, 1968) (6 of 24)

**Highest Completion Percentage (Min. 10 Attempts)**
.917—Bobby Layne, Texas (40) vs. Missouri (27) (Cotton, 1946) (11 of 12 with no interceptions)

**Most Yards Per Pass Attempt (Min. 10 Attempts)**
19.4—Tony Rice, Notre Dame (34) vs. West Va. (21) (Fiesta, 1989) (11 for 213 yards)

**Most Yards Per Pass Completion (Min. 7 Completions)**
30.4—Tony Rice, Notre Dame (34) vs. West Va. (21) (Fiesta, 1989) (7 for 213 yards); Duke Carlisle, Texas (28) vs. Navy (6) (Cotton, 1964) (7 for 213 yards)

*Bowl Game Records*

# RECEIVING

**Most Pass Receptions**
20—(D) Norman Jordan, Vanderbilt (28) vs. Air Force (36) (Hall of Fame, 1982) (173 yards); Walker Gillette, Richmond (49) vs. Ohio (42) (Tangerine, 1968) (242 yards)

**Most Pass Receiving Yards**
252—Andre Rison, Michigan St. (27) vs. Georgia (34) (Gator, 1989) (9 catches)

**Highest Average Per Catch (Min. 3 Receptions)**
52.3—Phil Harris, Texas (28) vs. Navy (6) (Cotton, 1964) (3 for 157 yards)

**Most Touchdowns Receiving**
4—Fred Biletnikoff, Florida St. (36) vs. Oklahoma (19) (Gator, 1965) (13 catches); (D) Bob McChesney, Hardin-Simmons (49) vs. Wichita St. (12) (Camellia, 1948) (8 catches)

# SCORING

**Most Points Scored**
30—(D) Sheldon Canley, San Jose St. (48) vs. Central Mich. (24) (California, 1990) (5 touchdowns); Barry Sanders, Oklahoma St. (62) vs. Wyoming (14) (Holiday, 1988) (5 touchdowns)

**Most Points Responsible For (TDs Scored & Passed For, Extra Points and FGs)**
40—Bobby Layne, Texas (40) vs. Missouri (27) (Cotton, 1946) (18 rushing, 12 passing, 6 receiving and 4 PATs)

**Most Touchdowns Scored**
5—(D) Sheldon Canley, San Jose St. (48) vs. Central Mich. (24) (California, 1990) (4 rushing, 1 receiving); Barry Sanders, Oklahoma St. (62) vs. Wyoming (14) (Holiday, 1988) (5 rushing); Neil Snow, Michigan (49) vs. Stanford (0) (Rose, 1902) (5 rushing five-point TDs)

**Most Two-Point Conversions**
2—Ernie Davis, Syracuse (23) vs. Texas (14) (Cotton, 1960) (2 receptions)

# KICKING

**Most Field Goals Attempted**
5—Arden Czyzewski, Florida (28) vs. Notre Dame (39) (Sugar, 1992) (5 made); Jess Atkinson, Maryland (23) vs. Tennessee (30) (Florida Citrus, 1983) (5 made); Bob White, Arkansas (16) vs. Georgia (2) (Sugar, 1969) (3 made); Tim Davis, Alabama (12) vs. Mississippi (7) (Sugar, 1964) (4 made)

**Most Field Goals Made**
5—Arden Czyzewski, Florida (28) vs. Notre Dame (39) (Sugar, 1992) (26, 24, 36, 37, 24 yards); Jess Atkinson, Maryland (23) vs. Tennessee (30) (Florida Citrus, 1983) (18, 48, 31, 22, 26 yards)

**Most Extra-Point Kick Attempts**
9—Layne Talbot, Texas A&M (65) vs. Brigham Young (14) (Holiday, 1990) (9 made); Bobby Luna, Alabama (61) vs. Syracuse (6) (Orange, 1953) (7 made); (D) James Weaver, Centre (63) vs. Texas Christian (7) (Fort Worth Classic, 1921) (9 made)

**Most Extra-Point Kicks Made**
9—Layne Talbot, Texas A&M (65) vs. Brigham Young (14) (Holiday, 1990) (9 attempts); (D) James Weaver, Centre (63) vs. Texas Christian (7) (Fort Worth Classic, 1921) (9 attempts)

**Most Points By a Kicker**
16—Arden Czyzewski, Florida (28) vs. Notre Dame (39) (Sugar, 1992) (5 FGs, 1 PAT)

# PUNTING

**Most Punts**
21—Everett Sweeney, Michigan (49) vs. Stanford (0) (Rose, 1902)

**Highest Average Per Punt (Min. 5 Punts)**
52.7—Des Koch, Southern Cal (7) vs. Wisconsin (0) (Rose, 1953) (7 for 369 yards)

# PUNT RETURNS

**Most Punt Returns**
9—Buzy Rosenberg, Georgia (7) vs. North Caro. (3) (Gator, 1971) (54 yards); Paddy Driscoll, Great Lakes (17) vs. Mare Island (0) (Rose, 1919) (115 yards)

**Most Punt Return Yards**
136—Johnny Rodgers, Nebraska (38) vs. Alabama (6) (Orange, 1972) (6 returns)

**Highest Punt Return Average (Min. 3 Returns)**
40.7—George Fleming, Washington (44) vs. Wisconsin (8) (Rose, 1960) (3 for 122 yards)

**Most Touchdowns on Punt Returns**
2—James Henry, Southern Miss. (38) vs. UTEP (18) (Independence, 1988) (65 and 45 yards)

# KICKOFF RETURNS

**Most Kickoff Returns**
7—Dale Carter, Tennessee (17) vs. Penn St. (42) (Fiesta, 1992) (132 yards); Jeff Sydner, Hawaii (13) vs. Michigan St. (33) (Aloha, 1989) (174 yards); Homer Jones, Brigham Young (37) vs. Indiana (38) (Holiday, 1979) (126 yards)

**Most Kickoff Return Yards**
203—Mike Fink, Missouri (35) vs. Arizona St. (49) (Fiesta, 1972) (6 returns)

**Highest Kickoff Return Average (Min. 2 Returns)**
60.5—(D) Bob Smith, Texas A&M (40) vs.

Georgia (20) (Presidential Cup, 1950) (2 for 121 yards)

**Most Touchdowns on Kickoff Returns**
1—Many players tied

# INTERCEPTIONS

**Most Interceptions Made**
4—Jim Dooley, Miami (Fla.) (14) vs. Clemson (0) (Gator, 1952); (D) Manuel Aja, Arizona St. (21) vs. Xavier (Ohio) (33) (Salad, 1950)

**Most Interception Return Yardage**
148—Elmer Layden, Notre Dame (27) vs. Stanford (10) (Rose, 1925) (2 interceptions)

# ALL-PURPOSE

**(Includes all runs from scrimmage, pass receptions and all returns)**

**Most All-Purpose Plays**
**(Must Have at Least One Reception or Return)**
47—Ron Jackson, Tulsa (28) vs. San Diego St. (17) (Freedom, 1991) (46 rushes, 1 reception)

**Most All-Purpose Yards Gained**
**(Must Have at Least One Reception or Return)**
303 (D) Michael Stewart, Bob Smith, Texas A&M (40) vs. Georgia (20) (Presidential Cup, 1950) (160 rushing, 22 receiving, 121 kickoff returns)

# DEFENSIVE STATISTICS

**Most Total Tackles Made (Includes Assists)**
31—Lee Roy Jordan, Alabama (17) vs. Oklahoma (0) (Orange, 1963)

**Most Unassisted Tackles**
18—Rod Smith, Notre Dame (39) vs. Florida (28) (Sugar, 1992)

**Most Tackles Made for Losses**
5—Michael Jones, Colorado (17) vs. Brigham Young (20) (Freedom, 1988) (20 yards in losses); Jimmy Walker, Arkansas (10) vs. UCLA (10) (Fiesta, 1978)

**Most Quarterback Sacks**
4—Rusty Medearis, Miami (Fla.) (22) vs. Nebraska (0) (Orange, 1992); Bobby Bell, Missouri (17) vs. Brigham Young (21) (Holiday, 1983)

**Fumble Recoveries**
2—(D) Michael Stewart, Fresno St. (51) vs. Bowling Green (7) (California, 1985); Rod Kirby, Pittsburgh (7) vs. Arizona St. (28) (Fiesta, 1973)

**Blocked Kicks**
2—Carlton Williams, Pittsburgh (7) vs. Arizona St. (28) (Fiesta, 1973)

**Passes Broken Up**
3—Demouy Williams, Washington (24) vs. Tulane (12) (Independence, 1987)

# SINGLE GAME—TEAM

**(Totals for each team in both-team records are in brackets after the team's score)**

## TOTAL OFFENSE

**Most Total Plays**
96—North Caro. St. (10) vs. Arizona (17) (Copper, 1989) (310 yards)

**Most Total Plays, Both Teams**
171—Auburn (34) [82] & Arizona (10) [89] (Sun, 1968) (537 yards)

**Most Yards Gained**
718—Arizona St. (49) vs. Missouri (35) (Fiesta, 1972) (452 rush, 266 pass)

**Most Yards Gained, Both Teams**
1,143 (D)—Southern Cal (47) [624] & Texas A&M (28) [519] (Bluebonnet, 1977) (148 plays)

**Highest Average Gained Per Play**
9.5—Louisville (34) vs. Alabama (7) (Fiesta, 1991) (60 plays for 571 yards)

**Fewest Plays**
35—Tennessee (0) vs. Texas (16) (Cotton, 1953) (29 rush, 6 pass)

**Fewest Plays, Both Teams**
107—Texas Christian (16) [54] & Marquette (6) [53] (Cotton, 1937)

**Fewest Yards**
Minus 21—U. of Mexico (0) vs. Southwestern (Tex.) (35) (Sun, 1945) (29 rush, -50 pass)

**Fewest Yards, Both Teams**
260—Randolph Field (7) [150] & Texas (7) [110] (Cotton, 1944)

**Lowest Average Per Play**
0.9—Tennessee (0) vs. Texas (16) (Cotton, 1953) (35 plays for 32 yards)

## RUSHING

**Most Rushing Attempts**
87—Oklahoma (40) vs. Auburn (22) (Sugar, 1972) (439 yards)

**Most Rushing Attempts, Both Teams**
122—(D) Southern Cal (47) [50] & Texas A&M (28) [72] (Bluebonnet, 1977) (864 yards); Mississippi St. (26) [68] & North Caro. (24) [54] (Sun, 1974) (732 yards)

**Most Net Rushing Yards**
486 (D)—Texas A&M (28) vs. Southern Cal (47) (Bluebonnet, 1977) (72 attempts)

**Most Net Rushing Yards, Both Teams**
864 (D)—Southern Cal (47) [378] & Texas A&M (28) [486] (Bluebonnet, 1977) (122 attempts)

**Highest Rushing Average (Min. 30 Attempts)**
8.6—UCLA (31) vs. Brigham Young (10) (Freedom, 1986) (49 for 423 yards)

**Fewest Rushing Attempts**
12 (D)—Vanderbilt (28) vs. Air Force (36) (Hall of Fame, 1982) (35 yards)

**Fewest Rushing Attempts, Both Teams**
57—Iowa (20) [36] & Wyoming (19) [21] (Holiday, 1987)

**Fewest Rushing Yards**
Minus 45—Alabama (10) vs. Missouri (35) (Gator, 1968) (29 attempts)

**Fewest Rushing Yards, Both Teams**
74—Tennessee (34) [86] & Air Force (13) [-12] (Sugar, 1971)

**Lowest Rushing Average (Min. 20 Attempts)**
Minus 1.6—Alabama (10) vs. Missouri (35) (Gator, 1968) (29 for -45 yards)

**Rushing Defense, Fewest Yards Allowed**
Minus 45—Missouri (35) vs. Alabama (10) (Gator, 1968) (29 attempts)

# PASSING

**Most Pass Attempts**
63 (D)—San Jose St. (25) vs. Toledo (27) (California, 1981) (43 completions, 5 interceptions, 467 yards)

**Most Pass Attempts, Both Teams**
92—Air Force (13) [46] & Tennessee (34) [46] (Sugar, 1971) (47 completions)

**Most Pass Completions**
43 (D)—San Jose St. (25) vs. Toledo (27) (California, 1981) (63 attempts, 5 interceptions, 467 yards)

**Most Pass Completions, Both Teams**
56—Richmond (49) [39] & Ohio (42) [17] (Tangerine, 1968) (91 attempts)

**Most Passing Yards**
576—Brigham Young (39) vs. Penn St. (50) (Holiday, 1989) (42 completions, 59 attempts, 2 interceptions)

**Most Passing Yards, Both Teams**
808—Washington St. (31) [492] & Utah (28) [316] (Copper, 1992) (88 attempts)

**Most Passes Had Intercepted**
8—Arizona (10) vs. Auburn (34) (Sun, 1968)

**Most Passes Had Intercepted, Both Teams**
12—Arizona (10) [8] & Auburn (34) [4] (Sun, 1968)

**Most Passes Attempted Without an Interception**
57 (D)—Western Mich. (30) vs. Fresno St. (35) (California, 1988) (24 completions)

**Most Passes Attempted by Both Teams Without an Interception**
90—Bowling Green (35) [49] & Nevada (34) [41] (Las Vegas, 1992) (54 completions)

**Highest Completion Percentage (Min. 10 Attempts)**
.929—Texas (40) vs. Missouri (27) (Cotton, 1946) (13 of 14, no interceptions, 234 yards)

**Most Yards Per Attempt (Min. 10 Attempts)**
21.7—Southern Cal (47) vs. Pittsburgh (14) (Rose, 1930) (13 for 282 yards)

**Most Yards Per Completion (Min. 8 Completions)**
35.2—Southern Cal (47) vs. Pittsburgh (14) (Rose, 1930) (8 for 282 yards)

**Fewest Pass Attempts**
2—Air Force (38) vs. Mississippi St. (15) (Liberty, 1991) (1 completion); (D) Army (10) vs. Michigan St. (6) (Cherry, 1984) (1 completion); West Va. (14) vs. South Caro. (3) (Peach, 1969) (1 completion)

**Fewest Pass Attempts, Both Teams**
9—Fordham (2) [4] & Missouri (0) [5] (Sugar, 1942)

**Fewest Pass Completions**
0—13 teams tied (see Team Record Lists)

**Fewest Pass Completions, Both Teams**
3—Arizona St. (0) [0] & Catholic (0) [3] (Sun, 1940)

**Fewest Passing Yards**
Minus 50—U. of Mexico (0) vs. Southwestern (Tex.) (35) (Sun, 1945) (2 completions, 9 attempts, 3 interceptions)

**Fewest Passing Yards, Both Teams**
15—Rice (8) [-17] & Tennessee (0) [32] (Orange, 1947)

**Lowest Completion Percentage**
.000—13 teams tied (see Team Record Lists)

**Fewest Yards Per Pass Attempt**
Minus 5.6—U. of Mexico (0) vs. Southwestern (Tex.) (35) (Sun, 1945) (9 for -50 yards)

**Fewest Yards Per Pass Completion (Min. 1 Completion)**
Minus 25.0—U. of Mexico (0) vs. Southwestern (Tex.) (35) (Sun, 1945) (2 for -50 yards)

# SCORING

**Most Touchdowns**
9—Texas A&M (65) vs. Brigham Young (14) (Holiday, 1990) (5 rush, 4 pass); Alabama (61) vs. Syracuse (6) (Orange, 1953) (4 rush, 3 pass, 1 punt return, 1 interception return); (D) Centre (63) vs. Texas Christian (7) (Fort Worth Classic, 1921) (8 rush, 1 blocked punt recovery in end zone)

**Most Touchdowns, Both Teams**
13—Richmond (49) [7] & Ohio (42) [6] (Tangerine, 1968)

**Most Touchdowns Rushing**
8 (D)—Centre (63) vs. Texas Christian (7) (Fort Worth Classic, 1921)

**Most Touchdowns Rushing, Both Teams**
9—Arizona St. (48) [6] & North Caro. (26) [3] (Peach, 1970)

**Most Touchdowns Passing**
6—Iowa (55) vs. Texas (17) (Freedom, 1984)

**Most Touchdowns Passing, Both Teams**
8—Iowa (55) [6] & Texas (17) [2] (Freedom, 1984); Richmond (49) [4] & Ohio (42) [4] (Tangerine, 1968)

**Most Field Goals Made**
5—Florida (28) vs. Notre Dame (39) (Sugar, 1992) (26, 24, 36, 37, 24 yards); Maryland (23) vs. Tennessee (30) (Florida Citrus, 1983) (18, 48, 31, 22, 26 yards)

**Most Field Goals Made, Both Teams**
6—Notre Dame (39) [1] & Florida (28) [5] (Sugar, 1992); Syracuse (16) [3] & Auburn (16) [3] (Sugar, 1988); Maryland (23) [5] & Tennessee (30) [1] (Florida Citrus, 1983)

**Most Points, Winning Team**
65—Texas A&M vs. Brigham Young (14) (Holiday, 1990)

**Most Points, Losing Team**
45—Southern Methodist vs. Brigham Young (46) (Holiday, 1980)

**Most Points, Both Teams**
91—Brigham Young (46) & Southern Methodist (45) (Holiday, 1980); Richmond (49) & Ohio (42) (Tangerine, 1968)

**Largest Margin of Victory**
55—Alabama (61) vs. Syracuse (6) (Orange, 1953)

**Fewest Points, Winning Team**
2—Fordham vs. Missouri (0) (Sugar, 1942)

**Fewest Points, Losing Team**
0—By many teams

**Fewest Points, Both Teams**
0—Texas Christian (0) & Air Force (0) (Cotton, 1959); Arkansas (0) & Louisiana St. (0) (Cotton, 1947); Arizona St. (0) & Catholic (0) (Sun, 1940); California (0) & Wash. & Jeff. (0) (Rose, 1922)

**Most Points Scored in First Half**
42—Toledo (56) vs. Davidson (33) (Tangerine, 1969)

**Most Points Scored in Second Half**
45—Oklahoma St. (62) vs. Wyoming (14) (Holiday, 1988)

**Most Points Scored in First Half, Both Teams**
49—Arizona St. (45) [21] & Florida St. (38) [28] (Fiesta, 1971); Toledo (56) [42] & Davidson (33) [7] (Tangerine, 1969)

**Most Points Scored in Second Half, Both Teams**
64—Penn St. (50) [38] & Brigham Young (39) [26] (Holiday, 1989)

**Most Points Scored Each Quarter**
*1st:* 25—Louisville (34) vs. Alabama (7) (Fiesta, 1991)
*2nd:* 28—Missouri (34) vs. Auburn (17) (Sun, 1973); Mississippi (41) vs. Georgia Tech (18) (Peach, 1971); Toledo (56) vs. Davidson (33) (Tangerine, 1969); Houston (49) vs. Miami (Ohio) (21) (Tangerine, 1962)
*3rd:* 31—Iowa (55) vs. Texas (17) (Freedom, 1984)
*4th:* 30—Oklahoma (40) vs. Houston (14) (Sun, 1981)

**Most Points Scored Each Quarter, Both Teams**
*1st:* 28—Indiana (38) [14] & Brigham Young (37) [14] (Holiday, 1979); Louisiana Tech (24) [21] & Louisville (14) [7] (Independence, 1977)
*2nd:* 40—Arizona St. (48) [14] & North Caro. (26) [26] (Peach, 1970)
*3rd:* 35—Oklahoma St. (62) [28] & Wyoming (14) [7] (Holiday, 1988)
*4th:* 37—Oklahoma (40) [30] & Houston (14) [7] (Sun, 1981)

# FIRST DOWNS

**Most First Downs**
36—Oklahoma (48) vs. Virginia (14) (Gator, 1991) (16 rush, 18 pass, 2 penalty)

**Most First Downs, Both Teams**
61—Penn St. (50) [26] & Brigham Young (39) [35] (Holiday, 1989)

**Most First Downs Rushing**
26—Oklahoma (40) vs. Auburn (22) (Sugar, 1972)

**Most First Downs Rushing, Both Teams**
36—Miami (Fla.) (46) [16] & Texas (3) [20] (Cotton, 1991); Colorado (47) [24] & Alabama (33) [12] (Liberty, 1969)

**Most First Downs Passing**
27—Brigham Young (39) vs. Penn St. (50) (Holiday, 1989)

**Most First Downs Passing, Both Teams**
30—(D) Fresno St. (29) [21] & Bowling Green (28) [9] (California, 1982); Richmond (49) [24] & Ohio (42) [6] (Tangerine, 1968)

**Most First Downs by Penalty**
6—Texas (3) vs. Miami (Fla.) (46) (Cotton, 1991)

**Most First Downs by Penalty, Both Teams**
8—Miami (Fla.) (46) [2] & Texas (3) [6] (Cotton, 1991)

**Fewest First Downs**
1—Alabama (29) vs. Texas A&M (21) (Cotton, 1942) (1 pass); Arkansas (0) vs. Louisiana St. (0) (Cotton, 1947) (1 rush)

**Fewest First Downs, Both Teams**
10—Randolph Field (7) [7] & Texas (7) [3] (Cotton, 1944)

**Fewest First Downs Rushing**
0—Florida (18) vs. Missouri (20) (Sugar, 1966); Navy (6) vs. Texas (28) (Cotton, 1964); Alabama (29) vs. Texas A&M (21) (Cotton, 1942)

**Fewest First Downs Rushing, Both Teams**
3—Texas A&M (21) [3] & Alabama (29) [0] (Cotton, 1942)

**Fewest First Downs Passing**
0—By 13 teams (see Team Record Lists)

**Fewest First Downs Passing, Both Teams**
1—Alabama (10) [0] & Arkansas (3) [1] (Sugar, 1962)

# PUNTING

**Most Punts**
17—Duke (3) vs. Southern Cal (7) (Rose, 1939)

**Most Punts, Both Teams**
28—Rice (8) [13] & Tennessee (0) [15] (Orange, 1947); Santa Clara (6) [14] & Louisiana St. (0) [14] (Sugar, 1938)

**Highest Punting Average (Min. 5 Punts)**
53.9—Southern Cal (7) vs. Wisconsin (0) (Rose, 1953) (8 for 431)

**Fewest Punts**
0—Oklahoma St. (62) vs. Wyoming (14) (Holiday, 1988); Oklahoma (41) vs. Wyoming (7) (Fiesta, 1976)

**Lowest Punting Average (Min. 3 Punts)**
17.0—Nevada (34) vs. Bowling Green (35) (Las Vegas, 1992) (4 for 68 yards)

**Most Punts Blocked by One Team**
2—North Caro. St. (14) vs. Georgia (7) (Liberty, 1967)

# PUNT RETURNS

**Most Punt Returns**
9—Georgia (7) vs. North Caro. (3) (Gator, 1971) (6.8 average)

**Most Punt Return Yards**
136—Nebraska (38) vs. Alabama (6) (Orange, 1972) (6 returns)

**Highest Punt Return Average (Min. 3 Returns)**
33.0—Kent (18) vs. Tampa (21) (Tangerine, 1972) (3 for 99 yards)

# KICKOFF RETURNS

**Most Kickoff Returns**
10—Wyoming (14) vs. Oklahoma St. (62) (Holiday, 1988) (20.5 average)

**Most Kickoff Return Yards**
259—UCLA (14) vs. Illinois (45) (Rose, 1947) (8 returns)

**Highest Kickoff Return Average (Min. 3 Returns)**
42.5—Tennessee (27) vs. Maryland (28) (Sun, 1984) (4 for 170 yards)

# FUMBLES

**Most Fumbles**
11—Mississippi (7) vs. Alabama (12) (Sugar, 1964) (lost 6)

**Most Fumbles, Both Teams**
17—Mississippi (7) [11] & Alabama (12) [6] (Sugar, 1964) (lost 9)

**Most Fumbles Lost**
6—By five teams (see Team Record Lists)

**Most Fumbles Lost, Both Teams**
9—Mississippi (7) [6] & Alabama (12) [3] (Sugar, 1964) (17 fumbles)

# PENALTIES

**Most Penalties**
20 (D)—Fresno St. (35) vs. Western Mich. (30) (California, 1988) (166 yards)

**Most Penalties, Both Teams**
29—McNeese St. (20) [13] & Tulsa (16) [16] (Independence, 1976) (205 yards)

**Most Yards Penalized**
202—Miami (Fla.) (46) vs. Texas (3) (Cotton, 1991) (16 penalties)

**Most Yards Penalized, Both Teams**
270—Miami (Fla.) (46) [202] & Texas (3) [68] (Cotton, 1991)

**Fewest Penalties**
0—By eight teams (see Team Record Lists)

**Fewest Penalties, Both Teams**
3—In five games (see Team Record Lists)

**Fewest Yards Penalized**
0—By eight teams (see Team Record Lists)

**Fewest Yards Penalized, Both Teams**
10—Mississippi St. (12) [5] & Duquesne (13) [5] (Orange, 1937)

# INDIVIDUAL RECORD LISTS

Only official records after 1937 are included. Prior records are included if able to be substantiated. Each team's score is in parentheses after the team name. The year listed is the actual (calendar) year the game was played. The list also includes discontinued bowls, marked with (D). Bowls are listed by the name of the bowl at the time it was played: The Florida Citrus Bowl was the Tangerine Bowl in 1947-82; the first Hall of Fame Bowl (1977-85) was called the All-American Bowl in 1986-90; the current Hall of Fame Bowl is played in Tampa, Fla., and started in 1986; the John Hancock Bowl was called the Sun Bowl in 1936-86 and the John Hancock Sun Bowl in 1987-88; and the Blockbuster Bowl changed its name to Sunshine Football Classic in 1993.

## TOTAL OFFENSE

**Most Plays**
74 (D)—Tony Kimbrough, Western Mich. (30) vs. Fresno St. (35) (California, 1988)
67—Ty Detmer, Brigham Young (39) vs. Penn St. (50) (Holiday, 1989)
65—Shane Matthews, Florida (28) vs. Notre Dame (39) (Sugar, 1992)
65—Tony Eason, Illinois (15) vs. Alabama (21) (Liberty, 1982)
65—Buster O'Brien, Richmond (49) vs. Ohio (42) (Tangerine, 1968)
63 (D)—Steve Clarkson, San Jose St. (25) vs. Toledo (27) (California, 1981)
62—Mark Young, Mississippi (20) vs. Texas Tech (17) (Independence, 1986)
62—Jack Trudeau, Illinois (29) vs. Army (31) (Peach, 1985)
62—Dennis Sproul, Arizona St. (30) vs. Penn St. (42) (Fiesta, 1977)
61—Jeff Blake, East Caro. (37) vs. North Caro. St. (34) (Peach, 1992)
61—Shawn Halloran, Boston College (27) vs. Georgia (24) (Hall of Fame, 1986)
61—Kim Hammond, Florida St. (17) vs. Penn St. (17) (Gator, 1967)
59—Vinny Testaverde, Miami (Fla.) (10) vs. Penn St. (14) (Fiesta, 1987)
59—Jim McMahon, Brigham Young (46) vs. Southern Methodist (45) (Holiday, 1980)
58—Terrence Jones, Tulane (12) vs. Washington (24) (Independence, 1987)
58 (D)—Jerry Rhome, Tulsa (14) vs. Mississippi (7) (Bluebonnet, 1964)

## Most Total Yards
594—Ty Detmer, Brigham Young (39) vs. Penn St. (50) (Holiday, 1989) (576 pass)
486—Buster O'Brien, Richmond (49) vs. Ohio (42) (Tangerine, 1968) (447 pass)
481—Chuck Long, Iowa (55) vs. Texas (17) (Freedom, 1984) (461 pass)
464 (D)—Steve Clarkson, San Jose St. (25) vs. Toledo (27) (California, 1981) (467 pass)
446 (D)—Whit Taylor, Vanderbilt (28) vs. Air Force (36) (Hall of Fame, 1982) (452 pass)
446—Jim McMahon, Brigham Young (46) vs. Southern Methodist (45) (Holiday, 1980) (446 pass)
431—Browning Nagle, Louisville (34) vs. Alabama (7) (Fiesta, 1991) (451 pass)
431 (D)—Tony Kimbrough, Western Mich. (30) vs. Fresno St. (35) (California, 1988) (366 pass)
420 (D)—Ralph Martini, San Jose St. (48) vs. Central Mich. (24) (California, 1990) (404 pass)
414—Peter Tom Willis, Florida St. (41) vs. Nebraska (17) (Fiesta, 1990) (422 pass)
413—Tony Eason, Illinois (15) vs. Alabama (21) (Liberty, 1982) (423 pass)
412—David Smith, Alabama (29) vs. Army (28) (John Hancock Sun, 1988) (412 pass)
410—Chuck Hartlieb, Iowa (23) vs. North Caro. St. (28) (Peach, 1988) (428 pass)
408—Marc Wilson, Brigham Young (37) vs. Indiana (38) (Holiday, 1979) (380 pass)
407—Jack Trudeau, Illinois (29) vs. Army (31) (Peach, 1985) (401 pass)

## Highest Average Per Play (Min. 10 Plays)
24.1—Dicky Maegle, Rice (28) vs. Alabama (6) (Cotton, 1954) (11 for 265 yards)
14.1—Marcus Dupree, Oklahoma (21) vs. Arizona St. (32) (Fiesta, 1983) (17 for 239 yards)
14.0—Bucky Richardson, Texas A&M (65) vs. Brigham Young (14) (Holiday, 1990) (23 for 322 yards)
12.2—Ger Schwedes, Syracuse (23) vs. Texas (14) (Cotton, 1960) (10 for 122 yards)
12.0—Tony Rice, Notre Dame (34) vs. West Va. (21) (Fiesta, 1989) (24 for 288 yards)
11.2 (D)—Dwight Ford, Southern Cal (47) vs. Texas A&M (28) (Bluebonnet, 1977) (14 for 157 yards)
11.1—Browning Nagle, Louisville (34) vs. Alabama (7) (Fiesta, 1991) (39 for 431 yards)
10.8—Danny White, Arizona St. (49) vs. Missouri (35) (Fiesta, 1972) (27 for 291 yards)
10.8 (D)—Ralph Martini, San Jose St. (48) vs. Central Mich. (24) (California, 1990) (39 for 420 yards)
10.5—Chuck Long, Iowa (55) vs. Texas (17) (Freedom, 1984) (46 for 481 yards)
10.4—Frank Sinkwich, Georgia (40) vs. Texas Christian (26) (Orange, 1942) (35 for 365 yards)
10.3—Chuck Curtis, Texas Christian (28) vs. Syracuse (27) (Cotton, 1957) (18 for 185 yards)

## Most Touchdowns Responsible For (TDs Scored & Passed For)
6—Chuck Long, Iowa (55) vs. Texas (17) (Freedom, 1984) (6 pass)
6—Bobby Layne, Texas (40) vs. Missouri (27) (Cotton, 1946) (3 rush, 2 pass, 1 catch)
5—Jeff Blake, East Caro. (37) vs. North Caro. St. (34) (Peach, 1992) (4 pass, 1 rush)
5—Peter Tom Willis, Florida St. (41) vs. Nebraska (17) (Fiesta, 1990) (5 pass)
5 (D)—Sheldon Canley, San Jose St. (48) vs. Central Mich. (24) (California, 1990) (4 rush, 1 pass)
5—Buster O'Brien, Richmond (49) vs. Ohio (42) (Tangerine, 1968) (4 pass, 1 rush)
5—Steve Tensi, Florida St. (36) vs. Oklahoma (19) (Gator, 1965) (5 pass)
5—Neil Snow, Michigan (49) vs. Stanford (0) (Rose, 1902) (5 rush)

# RUSHING

## Most Rushing Attempts
46—Ron Jackson, Tulsa (28) vs. San Diego St. (17) (Freedom, 1991) (211 yards)
41—Blake Ezor, Michigan St. (33) vs. Hawaii (13) (Aloha, 1989) (179 yards)
39—Errict Rhett, Florida (27) vs. North Caro. St. (10) (Gator, 1992) (182 yards)
39—Charlie Wysocki, Maryland (20) vs. Florida (35) (Tangerine, 1980) (159 yards)
39—Charles White, Southern Cal (17) vs. Ohio St. (16) (Rose, 1980) (247 yards)
37 (D)—Charles Davis, Colorado (29) vs. Houston (17) (Bluebonnet, 1971) (202 yards)
36—Herschel Walker, Georgia (17) vs. Notre Dame (10) (Sugar, 1981) (150 yards)
36—Don McCauley, North Caro. (26) vs. Arizona St. (48) (Peach, 1970) (143 yards)
35—Blair Thomas, Penn St. (50) vs. Brigham Young (39) (Holiday, 1989) (186 yards)
35—Lorenzo White, Michigan St. (20) vs. Southern Cal (17) (Rose, 1988) (113 yards)
35 (D)—Robert Newhouse, Houston (17) vs. Colorado (29) (Bluebonnet, 1971) (168 yards)
35—Ed Williams, West Va. (14) vs. South Caro. (3) (Peach, 1969) (208 yards)
35—Bob Anderson, Colorado (47) vs. Alabama (33) (Liberty, 1969) (254 yards)
34—Curtis Dickey, Texas A&M (28) vs. Iowa St. (12) (Hall of Fame, 1978) (276 yards)
34—Vic Bottari, California (13) vs. Alabama (0) (Rose, 1938) (137 yards)
34—Ernie Nevers, Stanford (10) vs. Notre Dame (27) (Rose, 1925) (114 yards)

## Most Net Rushing Yards
280 (D)—James Gray, Texas Tech (49) vs. Duke (21) (All-American, 1989) (33 carries)
276—Curtis Dickey, Texas A&M (28) vs. Iowa St. (12) (Hall of Fame, 1978) (34 carries)
266—Gaston Green, UCLA (31) vs. Brigham Young (10) (Freedom, 1986) (33 carries)
265—Dicky Maegle, Rice (28) vs. Alabama (6) (Cotton, 1954) (11 carries)
254—Bob Anderson, Colorado (47) vs. Alabama (33) (Liberty, 1969) (35 carries)
250—Chuck Webb, Tennessee (31) vs. Arkansas (27) (Cotton, 1990) (26 carries)
247—Charles White, Southern Cal (17) vs. Ohio St. (16) (Rose, 1980) (39 carries)
239—Marcus Dupree, Oklahoma (21) vs. Arizona St. (32) (Fiesta, 1983) (17 carries)
235—Tyrone Wheatley, Michigan (38) vs. Washington (31) (Rose, 1993) (15 carries)
234—Jamie Morris, Michigan (28) vs. Alabama (24) (Hall of Fame, 1988) (23 carries)

227—Eric Ball, UCLA (45) vs. Iowa (28) (Rose, 1986) (22 carries)
225—Craig James, Southern Methodist (45) vs. Brigham Young (46) (Holiday, 1980) (23 carries)
222—Barry Sanders, Oklahoma St. (62) vs. Wyoming (14) (Holiday, 1988) (29 carries)
216—Floyd Little, Syracuse (12) vs. Tennessee (18) (Gator, 1966) (29 carries)
211—Ron Jackson, Tulsa (28) vs. San Diego St. (17) (Freedom, 1991) (46 carries)

208—Ed Williams, West Va. (14) vs. South Caro. (3) (Peach, 1969) (35 carries)
205 (D)—Sammie Smith, Florida St. (27) vs. Indiana (13) (All-American, 1986) (25 carries)
205—Roland Sales, Arkansas (31) vs. Oklahoma (6) (Orange, 1978) (22 carries)
202—Tony Dorsett, Pittsburgh (27) vs. Georgia (3) (Sugar, 1977) (32 carries)
202—Woody Green, Arizona St. (49) vs. Missouri (35) (Fiesta, 1972) (25 carries)

202 (D)—Charles Davis, Colorado (29) vs. Houston (17) (Bluebonnet, 1971) (37 carries)

**Most Net Rushing Yards by a Quarterback**
180 (D)—Mike Mosley, Texas A&M (28) vs. Southern Cal (47) (Bluebonnet, 1977) (20 carries)
164—Eddie Phillips, Texas (11) vs. Notre Dame (24) (Cotton, 1971) (23 carries)
136 (D)—Nate Sassaman, Army (10) vs. Michigan St. (6) (Cherry, 1984) (28 carries)
133 (D)—Eddie Wolgast, Arizona (13) vs. Drake (14) (Salad, 1949) (22 carries) (listed in newspaper
  accounts as halfback but also attempted 15 passes in game)
129—Rex Kern, Ohio St. (17) vs. Stanford (27) (Rose, 1971) (20 carries)

127—J. C. Watts, Oklahoma (24) vs. Florida St. (7) (Orange, 1980) (12 carries)
119—Bucky Richardson, Texas A&M (65) vs. Brigham Young (14) (Holiday, 1990) (12 carries)
113—Harry Gilmer, Alabama (34) vs. Southern Cal (14) (Rose, 1946)
107—Darrell Shepard, Oklahoma (40) vs. Houston (14) (Sun, 1981) (12 carries)
103—Major Harris, West Va. (33) vs. Oklahoma St. (35) (John Hancock Sun, 1987)

**Highest Average Per Rush (Min. 9 Carries)**
24.1—Dicky Maegle, Rice (28) vs. Alabama (6) (Cotton, 1954) (11 for 265 yards)
21.6—Bob Jeter, Iowa (38) vs. California (12) (Rose, 1959) (9 for 194 yards)
15.7—Tyrone Wheatley, Michigan (38) vs. Washington (31) (Rose, 1993) (15 for 235 yards)
14.2 (D)—Gary Anderson, Arkansas (34) vs. Tulane (15) (Hall of Fame, 1980) (11 for 156 yards)
14.1—Mike Holovak, Boston College (21) vs. Alabama (37) (Orange, 1943) (10 for 141 yards)

14.1—Marcus Dupree, Oklahoma (21) vs. Arizona St. (32) (Fiesta, 1983) (17 for 239 yards)
12.6—Randy Baldwin, Mississippi (42) vs. Air Force (29) (Liberty, 1989) (14 for 177 yards)
12.6—Ben Barnett, Army (28) vs. Alabama (29) (John Hancock Sun, 1988) (14 for 177 yards)
12.3—George Smith, Texas Tech (28) vs. North Caro. (32) (Sun, 1972) (14 for 172 yards)
11.2 (D)—Dwight Ford, Southern Cal (47) vs. Texas A&M (28) (Bluebonnet, 1977) (14 for 157 yards)

11.2—Elliott Walker, Pittsburgh (33) vs. Kansas (19) (Sun, 1975) (11 for 123 yards)
10.9—Rodney Hampton, Georgia (34) vs. Michigan St. (27) (Gator, 1989) (10 for 109 yards)
10.8—Bobby Cavazos, Texas Tech (35) vs. Auburn (13) (Gator, 1954) (13 for 141 yards)
10.6—J. C. Watts, Oklahoma (24) vs. Florida St. (7) (Orange, 1980) (12 for 127 yards)
10.5—Ray Brown, Mississippi (39) vs. Texas (7) (Sugar, 1958) (15 for 157 yards)

10.3—Eric Ball, UCLA (45) vs. Iowa (28) (Rose, 1986) (22 for 227 yards)
10.2 (D)—Bill Tobin, Missouri (14) vs. Georgia Tech (10) (Bluebonnet, 1962) (11 for 112 yards)
10.2—Jamie Morris, Michigan (28) vs. Alabama (24) (Hall of Fame, 1988) (23 for 234 yards)

**Three Rushers, Same Team, Over 100 Yards**
366—Tony Dorsett (142), Elliott Walker (123) & Robert Haygood (QB) (101), Pittsburgh (33) vs.
  Kansas (19) (Sun, 1975)

**Two Rushers, Same Team, Over 100 Yards**
373—Woody Green (202) & Brent McClanahan (171), Arizona St. (49) vs. Missouri (35) (Fiesta, 1972)
365 (D)—George Woodard (185) & Mike Mosley (QB) (180), Texas A&M (28) vs. Southern Cal (47)
  (Bluebonnet, 1977)
365—Bob Anderson (254) & Jim Bratten (111), Colorado (47) vs. Alabama (33) (Liberty, 1969)
347—Walter Packer (183) & Terry Vitrano (164), Mississippi St. (26) vs. North Caro. (24) (Sun, 1974)
343 (D)—Charles White (186) & Dwight Ford (157), Southern Cal (47) vs. Texas A&M (28)
  (Bluebonnet, 1977)
330—Floyd Little (216) & Larry Csonka (114), Syracuse (12) vs. Tennessee (18) (Gator, 1966)
297—Monroe Eley (173) & Bob Thomas (124), Arizona St. (48) vs. North Caro. (26) (Peach, 1970)
292—Kelvin Bryant (148) & Ethan Horton (144), North Caro. (31) vs. Arkansas (27) (Gator, 1981)
291—Billy Sims (164) & J. C. Watts (QB) (127), Oklahoma (24) vs. Florida St. (7) (Orange, 1980)
288—Billy Sims (181) & Darrell Shepard (QB) (107), Oklahoma (40) vs. Houston (14) (Sun, 1981)
277—Willie Heston (170) & Neil Snow (107), Michigan (49) vs. Stanford (0) (Rose, 1902)
270—Anthony Brown (167) & Major Harris (QB) (103), West Va. (33) vs. Oklahoma St. (35) (John
  Hancock Sun, 1987)
253—Alois Blackwell (149) & Dyral Thomas (104), Houston (30) vs. Maryland (21) (Cotton, 1977)
246—T. Robert Hopkins (125) & Leonard Brown (121), Missouri (27) vs. Texas (40) (Cotton, 1946)
240—Jon Vaughn (128) & Ricky Powers (112), Michigan (35) vs. Mississippi (3) (Gator, 1991)
237—James Rouse (134) & Barry Foster (103), Arkansas (27) vs. Tennessee (31) (Cotton, 1990)
237—Raymond Bybee (127) & Thomas Reamon (110), Missouri (34) vs. Auburn (17) (Sun, 1973)
230—Rex Kern (QB) (129) & John Brockington (101), Ohio St. (17) vs. Stanford (27) (Rose, 1971)
223—Bucky Richardson (QB) (119) & Darren Lewis (104), Texas A&M (65) vs. Brigham Young (14)
  (Holiday, 1990)
222 (D)—Marshall Johnson (114) & Donnie McGraw (108), Houston (47) vs. Tulane (7) (Bluebonnet,
  1973)

*1993 NCAA FOOTBALL*

218—Travis Sims (113) & Michael Carter (105), Hawaii (27) vs. Illinois (17) (Holiday, 1992)
218—Steve Giese (111) & Bob Torrey (107), Penn St. (42) vs. Arizona St. (30) (Fiesta, 1977)
215—Jeff Atkins (112) & Reggie Dupard (103), Southern Methodist (27) vs. Notre Dame (20) (Aloha, 1984)
215—Allen Pinkett (111) & Chris Smith (104), Notre Dame (19) vs. Boston College (18) (Liberty, 1983)
204—Johnny "Ham" Jones (104) & Johnny "Jam" Jones (100), Texas (42) vs. Maryland (0) (Sun, 1978)
201—Jerome Heavens (101) & Vagas Ferguson (100), Notre Dame (38) vs. Texas (10) (Cotton, 1978)

**Most Rushing Touchdowns**
5—Barry Sanders, Oklahoma St. (62) vs. Wyoming (14) (Holiday, 1988) (runs of 33, 2, 67, 1, 10)
5—Neil Snow, Michigan (49) vs. Stanford (0) (Rose, 1902) (five-point scores)
4—Ron Jackson, Tulsa (28) vs. San Diego St. (17) (Freedom, 1991) (runs of 10, 6, 3, 4)
4 (D)—Sheldon Canley, San Jose St. (48) vs. Central Mich. (24) (California, 1990) (runs of 5, 22, 59, 5)
4 (D)—James Gray, Texas Tech (49) vs. Duke (21) (All-American, 1989) (runs of 2, 54, 18, 32)
4—Thurman Thomas, Oklahoma St. (35) vs. West Va. (33) (John Hancock Sun, 1987) (runs of 5, 9, 4, 4)
4—Eric Ball, UCLA (45) vs. Iowa (28) (Rose, 1986) (runs of 30, 40, 6, 32)
4—Terry Miller, Oklahoma St. (49) vs. Brigham Young (21) (Tangerine, 1976) (runs of 3, 78, 6, 1)
4—Sam Cunningham, Southern Cal (42) vs. Ohio St. (17) (Rose, 1973) (runs of 2, 1, 1, 1)
4—Woody Green, Arizona St. (49) vs. Missouri (35) (Fiesta, 1972) (runs of 2, 12, 17, 21)
4—Charles Cole, Toledo (56) vs. Davidson (33) (Tangerine, 1969) (runs of 1, 11, 16, 1)
4 (D)—Gene Shannon, Houston (26) vs. Dayton (21) (Salad, 1952) (runs of 15, 19, 1, 10)

# PASSING

**Most Pass Attempts**
62 (D)—Steve Clarkson, San Jose St. (25) vs. Toledo (27) (California, 1981)
61 (D)—Sean Covey, Brigham Young (16) vs. Virginia (22) (All-American, 1987)
59—Ty Detmer, Brigham Young (39) vs. Penn St. (50) (Holiday, 1989)
58—Shane Matthews, Florida (28) vs. Notre Dame (39) (Sugar, 1992)
58—Buster O'Brien, Richmond (49) vs. Ohio (42) (Tangerine, 1968)
57 (D)—Tony Kimbrough, Western Mich. (30) vs. Fresno St. (35) (California, 1988)
56—Gino Torretta, Miami (Fla.) (13) vs. Alabama (34) (Sugar, 1993)
55—Jack Trudeau, Illinois (29) vs. Army (31) (Peach, 1985)
55—Tony Eason, Illinois (15) vs. Alabama (21) (Liberty, 1982)
53—Tim Cowan, Washington (21) vs. Maryland (20) (Aloha, 1982)
53—Kim Hammond, Florida St. (17) vs. Penn St. (17) (Gator, 1967)
52—David Smith, Alabama (29) vs. Army (28) (John Hancock Sun, 1988)
52—Shawn Halloran, Boston College (27) vs. Georgia (24) (Hall of Fame, 1986)
51—Jeff Blake, East Caro. (37) vs. North Caro. St. (34) (Peach, 1992)
51—Danny McManus, Florida St. (31) vs. Nebraska (28) (Fiesta, 1988)
51—Chuck Hartlieb, Iowa (23) vs. North Caro. St. (28) (Peach, 1988)
51—Craig Burnett, Wyoming (19) vs. Iowa (20) (Holiday, 1987)
51 (D)—Whit Taylor, Vanderbilt (28) vs. Air Force (36) (Hall of Fame, 1982)

**Most Pass Completions**
43 (D)—Steve Clarkson, San Jose St. (25) vs. Toledo (27) (California, 1981)
42—Ty Detmer, Brigham Young (39) vs. Penn St. (50) (Holiday, 1989)
39—Buster O'Brien, Richmond (49) vs. Ohio (42) (Tangerine, 1968)
38—Jack Trudeau, Illinois (29) vs. Army (31) (Peach, 1985)
38 (D)—Whit Taylor, Vanderbilt (28) vs. Air Force (36) (Hall of Fame, 1982)
37 (D)—Sean Covey, Brigham Young (16) vs. Virginia (22) (All-American, 1987)
37—Kim Hammond, Florida St. (17) vs. Penn St. (17) (Gator, 1967)
35—Tony Eason, Illinois (15) vs. Alabama (21) (Liberty, 1982)
33—David Smith, Alabama (29) vs. Army (28) (John Hancock Sun, 1988)
33—Tim Cowan, Washington (21) vs. Maryland (20) (Aloha, 1982)
33—Ron VanderKelen, Wisconsin (37) vs. Southern Cal (42) (Rose, 1963)
32—Jim McMahon, Brigham Young (46) vs. Southern Methodist (45) (Holiday, 1980)
31—Jeff Blake, East Caro. (37) vs. North Caro. St. (34) (Peach, 1992)
31—Stan White, Auburn (27) vs. Indiana (23) (Peach, 1990)
31—Shawn Halloran, Boston College (27) vs. Georgia (24) (Hall of Fame, 1986)
31—Mark Young, Mississippi (20) vs. Texas Tech (17) (Independence, 1986)
31—Bernie Kosar, Miami (Fla.) (37) vs. UCLA (39) (Fiesta, 1985)
31—John Congemi, Pittsburgh (23) vs. Ohio St. (28) (Fiesta, 1984)
31 (D)—Jeff Tedford, Fresno St. (29) vs. Bowling Green (28) (California, 1982)

**Most Consecutive Pass Completions**
10—Rick Neuheisel, UCLA (45) vs. Illinois (9) (Rose, 1984)
9—Bill Montgomery, Arkansas (16) vs. Georgia (2) (Sugar, 1969)
9—Glenn Dobbs, Tulsa (7) vs. Tennessee (14) (Sugar, 1943)
8—Billy Roland, Houston (49) vs. Miami (Ohio) (21) (Tangerine, 1962)
8—Bobby Layne, Texas (40) vs. Missouri (27) (Cotton, 1946)

8—Harry Gilmer, Alabama (26) vs. Duke (29) (Sugar, 1945)
7—Daniel Ford, Arizona St. (33) vs. Air Force (28) (Freedom, 1987)

## Most Net Passing Yards (followed by comp.-att.-int.)
576—Ty Detmer, Brigham Young (39) vs. Penn St. (50) (Holiday, 1989) (42-59-2)
476—Drew Bledsoe, Washington St. (31) vs. Utah (28) (Copper, 1992) (30-46-1)
467 (D)—Steve Clarkson, San Jose St. (25) vs. Toledo (27) (California, 1981) (43-62-5)
461—Chuck Long, Iowa (55) vs. Texas (17) (Freedom, 1984) (29-39-0)
452 (D)—Whit Taylor, Vanderbilt (28) vs. Air Force (36) (Hall of Fame, 1982) (38-51-3)

451—Browning Nagle, Louisville (34) vs. Alabama (7) (Fiesta, 1991) (20-33-1)
447—Buster O'Brien, Richmond (49) vs. Ohio (42) (Tangerine, 1968) (39-58-2)
446—Jim McMahon, Brigham Young (46) vs. Southern Methodist (45) (Holiday, 1980) (32-49-1)
428—Chuck Hartlieb, Iowa (23) vs. North Caro. St. (28) (Peach, 1988) (30-51-4)
423—Tony Eason, Illinois (15) vs. Alabama (21) (Liberty, 1982) (35-55-4)
422—Peter Tom Willis, Florida St. (41) vs. Nebraska (17) (Fiesta, 1990) (25-40-0)
412—David Smith, Alabama (29) vs. Army (28) (John Hancock Sun, 1988) (33-52-1)
404 (D)—Ralph Martini, San Jose St. (48) vs. Central Mich. (24) (California, 1990) (27-36-1)
401—Jack Trudeau, Illinois (29) vs. Army (31) (Peach, 1985) (38-55-2)
401—Ron VanderKelen, Wisconsin (37) vs. Southern Cal (42) (Rose, 1963) (33-48-3)

## Most Net Passing Yards, One Quarter
223—Browning Nagle, Louisville (34) vs. Alabama (7) (Fiesta, 1991) (1st, 9 of 16)
202 (D)—Bret Stafford, Texas (32) vs. Pittsburgh (27) (Bluebonnet, 1987) (1st)

## Most Touchdown Passes Thrown
6—Chuck Long, Iowa (55) vs. Texas (17) (Freedom, 1984) (29-39-0) (6, 11, 33, 49, 4, 15 yards)
5—Peter Tom Willis, Florida St. (41) vs. Nebraska (17) (Fiesta, 1990)
5—Steve Tensi, Florida St. (36) vs. Oklahoma (19) (Gator, 1965)
4—Tony Sacca, Penn St. (42) vs. Tennessee (17) (Fiesta, 1992)
4—Jeff Blake, East Caro. (37) vs. North Caro. St. (34) (Peach, 1992)

4—Elvis Grbac, Michigan (35) vs. Mississippi (3) (Gator, 1991)
4—Rick Neuheisel, UCLA (45) vs. Illinois (9) (Rose, 1984)
4—Jim McMahon, Brigham Young (46) vs. Southern Methodist (45) (Holiday, 1980)
4—Mark Herrmann, Purdue (28) vs. Missouri (25) (Liberty, 1980)
4 (D)—Rob Hertel, Southern Cal (47) vs. Texas A&M (28) (Bluebonnet, 1977)
4—Matt Kavanaugh, Pittsburgh (34) vs. Clemson (3) (Gator, 1977)
4—Gordon Slade, Davidson (33) vs. Toledo (55) (Tangerine, 1969)
4—Buster O'Brien, Richmond (49) vs. Ohio (42) (Tangerine, 1968)
4—Cleve Bryant, Ohio (42) vs. Richmond (49) (Tangerine, 1968)
4—Pete Beathard, Southern Cal (42) vs. Wisconsin (37) (Rose, 1963)

## Most Passes Had Intercepted (followed by comp.-att.-int.)
6—Bruce Lee, Arizona (10) vs. Auburn (34) (Sun, 1968) (6-24-6)
5—Wade Hill, Arkansas (15) vs. Georgia (24) (Independence, 1991) (12-31-5)
5—Kevin Murray, Texas A&M (12) vs. Ohio St. (28) (Cotton, 1987) (12-31-5)
5—Vinny Testaverde, Miami (Fla.) (10) vs. Penn St. (14) (Fiesta, 1987) (26-50-5)
5—Jeff Wickersham, Louisiana St. (10) vs. Nebraska (28) (Sugar, 1985) (20-38-5)

5 (D)—Steve Clarkson, San Jose St. (25) vs. Toledo (27) (California, 1981) (43-62-5)
5—Terry McMillan, Missouri (3) vs. Penn St. (10) (Orange, 1970) (6-28-5)
5—Paul Gilbert, Georgia (6) vs. Nebraska (45) (Sun, 1969) (10-30-5)

## Highest Completion Percentage (Min. 10 Attempts) (followed by comp.-att.-int.)
.917—Bobby Layne, Texas (40) vs. Missouri (27) (Cotton, 1946) (11-12-0)
.900—Ken Ploen, Iowa (35) vs. Oregon St. (19) (Rose, 1957) (9-10-0)
.846—Tom Sorley, Nebraska (21) vs. North Caro. (17) (Liberty, 1977) (11-13-0)
.833—Mike Gundy, Oklahoma St. (62) vs. Wyoming (14) (Holiday, 1988) (20-24-0)
.833—Richard Todd, Alabama (13) vs. Penn St. (6) (Sugar, 1975) (10-12-0)

.818—Bucky Richardson, Texas A&M (65) vs. Brigham Young (14) (Holiday, 1990) (9-11-0)
.806—Cale Gundy, Oklahoma (48) vs. Virginia (14) (Gator, 1991) (25-31-0)
.800—Art Schlichter, Ohio St. (15) vs. Clemson (17) (Gator, 1978) (16-20-1)
.800—Jim Stevens, Georgia Tech (31) vs. Iowa St. (30) (Liberty, 1972) (12-15-0)
.800—Don Altman, Duke (7) vs. Arkansas (6) (Cotton, 1961) (12-15-0)

.800—Chuck Curtis, Texas Christian (28) vs. Syracuse (27) (Cotton, 1957) (12-15-0)
.789—Charles Ortmann, Michigan (14) vs. California (6) (Rose, 1951) (15-19-0)
.786—Mark Herrmann, Purdue (28) vs. Missouri (25) (Liberty, 1980) (22-28-0)

## Most Yards Per Pass Attempt (Min. 10 Attempts)
19.4—Tony Rice, Notre Dame (34) vs. West Va. (21) (Fiesta, 1989) (11 for 213)
18.7—Frank Sinkwich, Georgia (40) vs. Texas Christian (26) (Orange, 1942) (13 for 243)
18.5—Bucky Richardson, Texas A&M (65) vs. Brigham Young (14) (Holiday, 1990) (11 for 203)
17.3—Don Rumley, New Mexico (34) vs. Denver (24) (Sun, 1946) (12 for 207)
16.4 (D)—Rob Hertel, Southern Cal (47) vs. Texas A&M (28) (Bluebonnet, 1977) (15 for 246)

15.4—James Street, Texas (36) vs. Tennessee (3) (Cotton, 1969) (13 for 200)
14.2—Danny White, Arizona St. (28) vs. Pittsburgh (24) (Fiesta, 1973) (19 for 269)
13.7—Browning Nagle, Louisville (34) vs. Alabama (7) (Fiesta, 1991) (33 for 451)
13.6—Bob Churchich, Nebraska (28) vs. Alabama (39) (Orange, 1966) (17 for 232)
13.2—Bobby Layne, Texas (40) vs. Missouri (27) (Cotton, 1946) (12 for 158)

**Most Yards Per Pass Completion (Min. 7 Completions)**
30.4—Tony Rice, Notre Dame (34) vs. West Va. (21) (Fiesta, 1989) (7 for 213)
30.4—Duke Carlisle, Texas (28) vs. Navy (6) (Cotton, 1964) (7 for 213)
28.6—James Street, Texas (36) vs. Tennessee (13) (Cotton, 1969) (7 for 200)
27.0—Frank Sinkwich, Georgia (40) vs. Texas Christian (26) (Orange, 1942) (9 for 243)

# RECEIVING

**Most Pass Receptions**
20 (D)—Norman Jordan, Vanderbilt (28) vs. Air Force (36) (Hall of Fame, 1982) (173 yards)
20—Walker Gillette, Richmond (49) vs. Ohio (42) (Tangerine, 1968) (242 yards)
18 (D)—Gerald Willhite, San Jose St. (25) vs. Toledo (27) (California, 1981) (124 yards)
15 (D)—Stephone Paige, Fresno St. (29) vs. Bowling Green (28) (California, 1982) (246 yards)
14—Ron Sellers, Florida St. (17) vs. Penn St. (17) (Gator, 1967) (145 yards)
13—Fred Biletnikoff, Florida St. (36) vs. Oklahoma (19) (Gator, 1965) (192 yards)
12—Luke Fisher, East Caro. (37) vs. North Caro. St. (34) (Peach, 1992) (144 yards)
12—Chuck Dicus, Arkansas (16) vs. Georgia (2) (Sugar, 1969) (169 yards)
12—Bill Moremen, Florida St. (17) vs. Penn St. (17) (Gator, 1967) (106 yards)
11 (D)—Mark Szlachcic, Bowling Green (28) vs. Fresno St. (21) (California, 1991) (189 yards)
11—Ronnie Harmon, Iowa (28) vs. UCLA (45) (Rose, 1986) (102 yards)
11—David Mills, Brigham Young (24) vs. Michigan (17) (Holiday, 1984) (103 yards)
11 (D)—Chip Otten, Bowling Green (28) vs. Fresno St. (29) (California, 1982) (76 yards)
11 (D)—Anthony Hancock, Tennessee (28) vs. Wisconsin (21) (Garden State, 1981) (196 yards)
11 (D)—James Ingram, Baylor (14) vs. Louisiana St. (7) (Bluebonnet, 1963) (163 yards)
11—Pat Richter, Wisconsin (37) vs. Southern Cal (42) (Rose, 1963) (163 yards)
10—Matt Bellini, Brigham Young (39) vs. Penn St. (50) (Holiday, 1989) (124 yards)
10—Hart Lee Dykes, Oklahoma St. (62) vs. Wyoming (14) (Holiday, 1988) (163 yards)
10 (D)—David Miles, Brigham Young (16) vs. Virginia (22) (All-American, 1987) (188 yards)
10—Lakei Heimuli, Brigham Young (7) vs. Ohio St. (10) (Florida Citrus, 1985)
10—Bobby Joe Edmonds, Arkansas (15) vs. Auburn (21) (Liberty, 1984)
10—David Williams, Illinois (9) vs. UCLA (45) (Rose, 1984)
10—Kelly Smith, Brigham Young (24) vs. Michigan (17) (Holiday, 1984) (88 yards)
10—Paul Skansi, Washington (21) vs. Maryland (20) (Aloha, 1982) (87 yards)
10 (D)—Tim Kearse, San Jose St. (25) vs. Toledo (27) (California, 1981) (104 yards)
10—Scott Phillips, Brigham Young (46) vs. Southern Methodist (45) (Holiday, 1980) (81 yards)
10—Gordon Jones, Pittsburgh (34) vs. Clemson (3) (Gator, 1977) (163 yards)
10—Bobby Crockett, Arkansas (7) vs. Louisiana St. (14) (Cotton, 1966)
10—Ron Stover, Oregon (7) vs. Ohio St. (10) (Rose, 1958) (144 yards)

**Most Pass Receiving Yards**
252—Andre Rison, Michigan St. (27) vs. Georgia (34) (Gator, 1989) (9 catches)
246 (D)—Stephone Paige, Fresno St. (29) vs. Bowling Green (28) (California, 1982) (15 catches)
242 (D)—Tony Jones, Texas (32) vs. Pittsburgh (27) (Bluebonnet, 1987) (8 catches)
242—Walker Gillette, Richmond (49) vs. Ohio (42) (Tangerine, 1968) (20 catches)
212—Phillip Bobo, Washington St. (31) vs. Utah (28) (Copper, 1992) (7 catches)
201 (D)—Bob McChesney, Hardin-Simmons (49) vs. Wichita St. (12) (Camellia, 1948) (8 catches)
196 (D)—Anthony Hancock, Tennessee (28) vs. Wisconsin (21) (Garden State, 1981) (11 catches)
192—Fred Biletnikoff, Florida St. (36) vs. Oklahoma (19) (Gator, 1965) (13 catches)
189 (D)—Mark Szlachcic, Bowling Green (28) vs. Fresno St. (21) (California, 1991) (11 catches)
188 (D)—David Miles, Brigham Young (16) vs. Virginia (22) (All-American, 1987) (10 catches)
186—Greg Hudson, Arizona St. (28) vs. Pittsburgh (7) (Fiesta, 1973) (8 catches)
182—Rob Turner, Indiana (34) vs. South Caro. (10) (Liberty, 1988) (5 catches)
178—Ray Perkins, Alabama (34) vs. Nebraska (7) (Sugar, 1967) (7 catches)
173 (D)—Norman Jordan, Vanderbilt (28) vs. Air Force (36) (Hall of Fame, 1982) (20 catches)
172—Cris Carter, Ohio St. (17) vs. Southern Cal (20) (Rose, 1985) (9 catches)

**Highest Average Per Catch (Min. 3 Receptions)**
52.3—Phil Harris, Texas (28) vs. Navy (6) (Cotton, 1964) (3 for 157 yards)
36.4—Rob Turner, Indiana (34) vs. South Caro. (10) (Liberty, 1988) (5 for 182 yards)
35.5—Rodney Harris, Kansas (23) vs. Brigham Young (20) (Aloha, 1992) (4 for 142 yards)
35.3—Anthony Carter, Michigan (15) vs. North Caro. (17) (Gator, 1979) (4 for 141 yards)
34.3 (D)—Andre Alexander, Fresno St. (35) vs. Western Mich. (30) (California, 1988) (3 for 103 yards)
34.3—Ron Beverly, Arizona St. (49) vs. Missouri (35) (Fiesta, 1972) (3 for 103 yards)
34.0—Jimmy Cefalo, Penn St. (41) vs. Baylor (20) (Cotton, 1975) (3 for 102 yards)
33.7—J. D. Hill, Arizona St. (48) vs. North Caro. (26) (Peach, 1970) (3 for 101 yards)
33.3—Tony Buford, Indiana (34) vs. South Caro. (10) (Liberty, 1988) (3 for 100 yards)
33.2—Melvin Bonner, Baylor (20) vs. Arizona (15) (John Hancock, 1992) (5 for 166 yards)
33.2—Todd Dixon, Wake Forest (39) vs. Oregon (35) (Independence, 1992) (5 for 166 yards)
32.2—Cotton Speyrer, Texas (36) vs. Tennessee (13) (Cotton, 1969) (5 for 161 yards)
31.0—Olanda Truitt, Pittsburgh (31) vs. Texas A&M (28) (John Hancock, 1989) (4 for 124 yards)
31.0—Clay Brown, Brigham Young (46) vs. Southern Methodist (45) (Holiday, 1980) (5 for 155 yards)

*Bowl Game Records*                                                                 425

## Most Touchdowns Receiving
4—Fred Biletnikoff, Florida St. (36) vs. Oklahoma (19) (Gator, 1965) (13 catches)
4 (D)—Bob McChesney, Hardin-Simmons (49) vs. Wichita St. (12) (Camellia, 1948) (8 catches)
3 (D)—Ken Ealy, Central Mich. (24) vs. San Jose St. (48) (California, 1990) (7 catches)
3—Wendell Davis, Louisiana St. (30) vs. South Caro. (13) (Gator, 1987) (9 catches)
3—Anthony Allen, Washington (21) vs. Maryland (20) (Aloha, 1982) (8 catches)

3 (D)—Norman Jordan, Vanderbilt (28) vs. Air Force (36) (Hall of Fame, 1982) (20 catches)
3 (D)—Dwayne Dixon, Florida (24) vs. Arkansas (28) (Bluebonnet, 1982) (8 catches)
3 (D)—Mervyn Fernandez, San Jose St. (25) vs. Toledo (27) (California, 1981) (9 catches)
3—Clay Brown, Brigham Young (46) vs. Southern Methodist (45) (Holiday, 1980) (5 catches)
3—Elliott Walker, Pittsburgh (34) vs. Clemson (3) (Gator, 1977) (6 catches)

3—Rhett Dawson, Florida St. (38) vs. Arizona St. (45) (Fiesta, 1971) (8 catches)
3—George Hannen, Davidson (33) vs. Toledo (56) (Tangerine, 1969)
3—Todd Snyder, Richmond (49) vs. Ohio (42) (Tangerine, 1968)

# SCORING

## Most Points Scored
30 (D)—Sheldon Canley, San Jose St. (48) vs. Central Mich. (24) (California, 1990) (5 TDs)
30—Barry Sanders, Oklahoma St. (62) vs. Wyoming (14) (Holiday, 1988) (5 TDs)
28—Bobby Layne, Texas (40) vs. Missouri (27) (Cotton, 1946) (4 TDs, 4 PATs)
25—Neil Snow, Michigan (49) vs. Stanford (0) (Rose, 1902) (5 five-point TDs)
24—Ron Jackson, Tulsa (28) vs. San Diego St. (17) (Freedom, 1991) (4 TDs)

24 (D)—James Gray, Texas Tech (49) vs. Duke (21) (All-American, 1989) (4 TDs)
24—Thurman Thomas, Oklahoma St. (35) vs. West Va. (33) (John Hancock Sun, 1987) (4 TDs)
24—Eric Ball, UCLA (45) vs. Iowa (28) (Rose, 1986) (4 TDs)
24—Terry Miller, Oklahoma St. (49) vs. Brigham Young (21) (Tangerine, 1976) (4 TDs)
24—Sam Cunningham, Southern Cal (42) vs. Ohio St. (17) (Rose, 1973) (4 TDs)

24—Johnny Rodgers, Nebraska (40) vs. Notre Dame (6) (Orange, 1973) (4 TDs)
24—Woody Green, Arizona St. (49) vs. Missouri (35) (Fiesta, 1972) (4 TDs)
24—Charles Cole, Toledo (56) vs. Davidson (33) (Tangerine, 1969) (4 TDs)
24—Fred Biletnikoff, Florida St. (36) vs. Oklahoma (19) (Gator, 1965) (4 TDs)
24—Joe Lopasky, Houston (49) vs. Miami (Ohio) (21) (Tangerine, 1962) (4 TDs)

24 (D)—Gene Shannon, Houston (26) vs. Dayton (21) (Salad, 1952) (4 TDs)
24 (D)—Bob McChesney, Hardin-Simmons (49) vs. Wichita St. (12) (Camellia, 1948) (4 TDs)

## Most Points Responsible For (TDs Scored & Passed For, Extra Points and FGs)
40—Bobby Layne, Texas (40) vs. Missouri (27) (Cotton, 1946) (18 rush, 12 pass, 6 receiving and 4 PATs)
36—Chuck Long, Iowa (55) vs. Texas (17) (Freedom, 1984) (36 pass)
30—Jeff Blake, East Caro. (37) vs. North Caro. St. (34) (Peach, 1992) (24 pass, 6 rush)
30 (D)—Sheldon Canley, San Jose St. (48) vs. Central Mich. (24) (California, 1990) (24 rush, 6 receiving)
30—Peter Tom Willis, Florida St. (41) vs. Nebraska (17) (Fiesta, 1990) (30 pass)
30—Barry Sanders, Oklahoma St. (62) vs. Wyoming (14) (Holiday, 1988) (30 rush)
30—Johnny Rodgers, Nebraska (40) vs. Notre Dame (6) (Orange, 1973) (18 rush, 6 pass, 6 receiving)
30—Steve Tensi, Florida St. (36) vs. Oklahoma (19) (Gator, 1965) (30 pass)

## Most Touchdowns
5 (D)—Sheldon Canley, San Jose St. (48) vs. Central Mich. (24) (California, 1990) (4 rush, 1 catch)
5—Barry Sanders, Oklahoma St. (62) vs. Wyoming (14) (Holiday, 1988) (5 rush)
5—Neil Snow, Michigan (49) vs. Stanford (0) (Rose, 1902) (5 rush five-point TDs)
4—Ron Jackson, Tulsa (28) vs. San Diego St. (17) (Freedom, 1991) (4 rush)
4 (D)—James Gray, Texas Tech (49) vs. Duke (21) (All-American, 1989) (4 rush)

4—Thurman Thomas, Oklahoma St. (35) vs. West Va. (33) (John Hancock Sun, 1987) (4 rush)
4—Eric Ball, UCLA (45) vs. Iowa (28) (Rose, 1986) (4 rush)
4—Terry Miller, Oklahoma St. (49) vs. Brigham Young (21) (Tangerine, 1976) (4 rush)
4—Sam Cunningham, Southern Cal (42) vs. Ohio St. (17) (Rose, 1973) (4 rush)
4—Johnny Rodgers, Nebraska (40) vs. Notre Dame (6) (Orange, 1973) (3 rush, 1 catch)

4—Woody Green, Arizona St. (49) vs. Missouri (35) (Fiesta, 1972) (4 rush)
4—Charles Cole, Toledo (56) vs. Davidson (33) (Tangerine, 1969) (4 rush)
4—Fred Biletnikoff, Florida St. (36) vs. Oklahoma (19) (Gator, 1965) (4 catch)
4—Joe Lopasky, Houston (49) vs. Miami (Ohio) (21) (Tangerine, 1962) (2 rush, 1 catch, 1 punt return)
4 (D)—Gene Shannon, Houston (26) vs. Dayton (21) (Salad, 1952) (4 rush)

4 (D)—Bob McChesney, Hardin-Simmons (49) vs. Wichita St. (12) (Camellia, 1948) (4 catch)
4—Bobby Layne, Texas (40) vs. Missouri (27) (Cotton, 1946) (3 rush, 1 catch)
4 (D)—Alvin McMillin, Centre (63) vs. Texas Christian (7) (Fort Worth Classic, 1921) (4 rush)

## Most Two-Point Conversions
2—Ernie Davis, Syracuse (23) vs. Texas (14) (Cotton, 1960) (2 pass receptions)

Oklahoma State running back Terry Miller scored four rushing touchdowns in the 1976 Tangerine Bowl, a 49-21 Cowboys victory over Brigham Young. Only 18 players have scored four or more touchdowns in a bowl game.

## KICKING

**Most Field Goals Attempted**
5—Arden Czyzewski, Florida (28) vs. Notre Dame (39) (Sugar, 1992) (5 made)
5—Jess Atkinson, Maryland (23) vs. Tennessee (30) (Florida Citrus, 1983) (5 made)
5—Bob White, Arkansas (16) vs. Georgia (2) (Sugar, 1969) (3 made)
5—Tim Davis, Alabama (12) vs. Mississippi (7) (Sugar, 1964) (4 made)
4—Carlos Huerta, Miami (Fla.) (22) vs. Nebraska (0) (Orange, 1992) (3 made)

4—Greg Worker, Wyoming (19) vs. Iowa (20) (Holiday, 1987) (2 made)
4—Tim Lashar, Oklahoma (25) vs. Penn St. (10) (Orange, 1986) (4 made)
4—Kent Bostrom, Arizona St. (17) vs. Arkansas (18) (Holiday, 1985) (3 made)
4 (D)—Todd Gregoire, Wisconsin (19) vs. Kentucky (20) (Hall of Fame, 1984) (4 made)
4—Bill Capece, Florida St. (17) vs. Oklahoma (18) (Orange, 1981) (1 made)

4—David Hardy, Texas A&M (33) vs. Oklahoma St. (16) (Independence, 1981)(4 made)
4—Bob Lucchesi, Missouri (19) vs. Southern Miss. (17) (Tangerine, 1981) (4 made)
4—Paul Woodside, West Va. (26) vs. Florida (6) (Peach, 1981) (4 made)
4 (D)—Fuad Reveiz, Tennessee (28) vs. Wisconsin (21) (Garden State, 1981) (2 made)
4—Dale Castro, Maryland (20) vs. Florida (35) (Tangerine, 1980) (4 made)

4—Brent Johnson, Brigham Young (37) vs. Indiana (38) (Holiday, 1979) (3 made)
4—Ricky Townsend, Tennessee (19) vs. Texas Tech (28) (Gator, 1973) (2 made)
4—Paul Rogers, Nebraska (45) vs. Georgia (6) (Sun, 1969) (4 made)

**Most Field Goals Made**
5—Arden Czyzewski, Florida (28) vs. Notre Dame (39) (Sugar, 1992) (26, 24, 36, 37, 24 yards)
5—Jess Atkinson, Maryland (23) vs. Tennessee (30) (Florida Citrus, 1983) (18, 48, 31, 22, 26 yards)
4—Tim Lashar, Oklahoma (25) vs. Penn St. (10) (Orange, 1986) (26, 31, 21, 22 yards)
4 (D)—Todd Gregoire, Wisconsin (19) vs. Kentucky (20) (Hall of Fame, 1984) (40, 27, 20, 40 yards)
4—David Hardy, Texas A&M (33) vs. Oklahoma St. (16) (Independence, 1981) (33, 32, 50, 18 yards)
4—Paul Woodside, West Va. (26) vs. Florida (6) (Peach, 1981) (35, 42, 49, 24 yards)
4—Bob Lucchesi, Missouri (19) vs. Southern Miss. (17) (Tangerine, 1981) (45, 41, 30, 28 yards)
4—Dale Castro, Maryland (20) vs. Florida (35) (Tangerine, 1980) (35, 27, 27, 43 yards)
4—Paul Rogers, Nebraska (45) vs. Georgia (6) (Sun, 1969) (50, 32, 42, 37 yards, all in 1st quarter)
4—Tim Davis, Alabama (12) vs. Mississippi (7) (Sugar, 1964) (31, 46, 22, 48 yards)

**Most Extra-Point Kick Attempts**
9—Layne Talbot, Texas A&M (65) vs. Brigham Young (14) (Holiday, 1990) (9 made)
9—Bobby Luna, Alabama (61) vs. Syracuse (6) (Orange, 1953) (7 made)
9 (D)—James Weaver, Centre (63) vs. Texas Christian (7) (Fort Worth Classic, 1921) (9 made)
8—Cary Blanchard, Oklahoma St. (62) vs. Wyoming (14) (Holiday, 1988) (8 made)
8—Ken Crots, Toledo (56) vs. Davidson (33) (Tangerine, 1969) (8 made)

7—Scott Blanton, Oklahoma (48) vs. Virginia (14) (Gator, 1991) (6 made)
7 (D)—Barry Belli, Fresno St. (51) vs. Bowling Green (7) (California, 1985) (7 made)
7—Tom Nichol, Iowa (55) vs. Texas (17) (Freedom, 1984) (7 made)
7—Juan Cruz, Arizona St. (49) vs. Missouri (35) (Fiesta, 1972) (7 made)
7—Ron Sewell, North Caro. St. (49) vs. West Va. (13) (Peach, 1972) (7 made)

7—Don Ekstrand, Arizona St. (48) vs. North Caro. (26) (Peach, 1970) (6 made)
7—Bill McMillan, Houston (49) vs. Miami (Ohio) (21) (Tangerine, 1962) (7 made)
7—Jesse Whittenton, UTEP (47) vs. Florida St. (20) (Sun, 1955) (5 made)
7—Jim Brieske, Michigan (49) vs. UCLA (0) (Rose, 1948) (7 made)
7 (D)—Pat Bailey, Hardin-Simmons (49) vs. Wichita St. (12) (Camellia, 1948) (7 made)

**Most Extra-Point Kicks Made**
9—Layne Talbot, Texas A&M (65) vs. Brigham Young (14) (Holiday, 1990) (9 attempts)
9 (D)—James Weaver, Centre (63) vs. Texas Christian (7) (Fort Worth Classic, 1921) (9 attempts)
8—Cary Blanchard, Oklahoma St. (62) vs. Wyoming (14) (Holiday, 1988) (8 attempts)
8—Ken Crots, Toledo (56) vs. Davidson (33) (Tangerine, 1969) (8 attempts)
7 (D)—Barry Belli, Fresno St. (51) vs. Bowling Green (7) (California, 1985) (7 attempts)

7—Tom Nichol, Iowa (55) vs. Texas (17) (Freedom, 1984) (7 attempts)
7—Juan Cruz, Arizona St. (49) vs. Missouri (35) (Fiesta, 1972) (7 attempts)
7—Ron Sewell, North Caro. St. (49) vs. West Va. (13) (Peach, 1972) (7 attempts)
7—Bill McMillan, Houston (49) vs. Miami (Ohio) (21) (Tangerine, 1962) (7 attempts)
7—Bobby Luna, Alabama (61) vs. Syracuse (6) (Orange, 1953) (9 attempts)

7—Jim Brieske, Michigan (49) vs. UCLA (0) (Rose, 1948) (7 attempts)
7 (D)—Pat Bailey, Hardin-Simmons (49) vs. Wichita St. (12) (Camellia, 1948) (7 attempts)

**Most Points by a Kicker**
16—Arden Czyzewski, Florida (28) vs. Notre Dame (39) (Sugar, 1992) (5 FGs, 1 PAT)
15—Jess Atkinson, Maryland (23) vs. Tennessee (30) (Florida Citrus, 1983) (5 FGs)
15—David Hardy, Texas A&M (33) vs. Oklahoma St. (16) (Independence, 1981) (4 FGs, 3 PATs)
15—Paul Rogers, Nebraska (45) vs. Georgia (6) (John Hancock, 1969) (4 FGs, 3 PATs)
14—Cary Blanchard, Oklahoma St. (62) vs. Wyoming (14) (Holiday, 1988) (2 FGs, 8 PATs)

14—Paul Woodside, West Va. (26) vs. Florida (6) (Peach, 1981) (4 FGs, 2 PATs)
13—Tim Lashar, Oklahoma (25) vs. Penn. St. (10) (Orange, 1986) (4 FGs, 1 PAT)
13—John Lee, UCLA (39) vs. Miami (Fla.) (37) (Fiesta, 1985) (3 FGs, 4 PATs)
13—Tom Nichol, Iowa (55) vs. Texas (17) (Freedom, 1984) (2 FGs, 7 PATs)
13 (D)—Todd Gregoire, Wisconsin (19) vs. Kentucky (20) (Hall of Fame, 1984) (4 FGs, 1 PAT)

13—Bob Lucchesi, Missouri (19) vs. Southern Miss. (17) (Tangerine, 1981) (4 FGs, 1 PAT)
13—Dave Johnson, Brigham Young (37) vs. Indiana (38) (Holiday, 1979) (3 FGs, 4 PATs)
12—Chris Gardocki, Clemson (30) vs. Illinois (0) (Hall of Fame, 1991) (3 FGs, 3 PATs)
12—Ray Tarasi, Penn St. (50) vs. Brigham Young (39) (Holiday, 1989) (3 FGs, 3 PATs)
12—Luis Zendejas, Arizona St. (32) vs. Oklahoma (21) (Fiesta, 1983) (3 FGs, 3 PATs)

12—Dale Castro, Maryland (20) vs. Florida (35) (Tangerine, 1980) (4 FGs)
12—Nathan Ritter, North Caro. St. (30) vs. Pittsburgh (17) (Tangerine, 1978) (3 FGs, 3 PATs)
12—Buckey Berrey, Alabama (36) vs. UCLA (6) (Liberty, 1976) (3 FGs, 3 PATs)
12—Al Vitiello, Penn St. (30) vs. Texas (6) (Cotton, 1972) (3 FGs, 3 PATs)
12—Frank Fontes, Florida St. (38) vs. Arizona St. (45) (Fiesta, 1971) (3 FGs, 3 PATs)

# PUNTING

**Most Punts**
21—Everett Sweeney, Michigan (49) vs. Stanford (0) (Rose, 1902)
16—Lem Pratt, New Mexico St. (14) vs. Hardin-Simmons (14) (Sun, 1936) (38.4 average)
14—Sammy Baugh, Texas Christian (3) vs. Louisiana St. (2) (Sugar, 1936)
13—Hugh Keeney, Rice (8) vs. Tennessee (0) (Orange, 1947)
13—N. A. Keithley, Tulsa (6) vs. Texas Tech (0) (Sun, 1942) (37.0 average)

13—Hugh McCullough, Oklahoma (0) vs. Tennessee (17) (Orange, 1939) (40.6 average)
13—Tyler, Hardin-Simmons (14) vs. New Mexico St. (14) (Sun, 1936) (45.2 average)
13 (D)—Tom Murphy, Arkansas (7) vs. Centenary (7) (Dixie Classic, 1934) (44.0 average)
12—Mitch Berger, Colorado (25) vs. Alabama (30) (Blockbuster, 1991) (41.0 average)
12—Bob Parsons, Penn St. (10) vs. Missouri (3) (Orange, 1970) (42.6 average)

12—Jim Callahan, Texas Tech (0) vs. Tulsa (6) (Sun, 1942) (43.0 average)
12—Mike Palm, Penn St. (3) vs. Southern Cal (14) (Rose, 1923)

*1993 NCAA FOOTBALL*

### Highest Average Per Punt (Min. 5 Punts)

52.7—Des Koch, Southern Cal (7) vs. Wisconsin (0) (Rose, 1953) (7 for 369 yards) (adjusted to current statistical rules)
52.4—Mike Sochko, Maryland (21) vs. Houston (30) (Cotton, 1977) (5 for 262 yards)
51.0—Chris Clauss, Penn St. (10) vs. Clemson (35) (Florida Citrus, 1988) (5 for 255 yards)
50.0—Dana Moore, Mississippi St. (17) vs. Nebraska (31) (Sun, 1980) (5 for 250 yards)
49.2 (D)—Mark Simon, Air Force (24) vs. Texas (16) (Bluebonnet, 1985) (11 for 541 yards)
49.2—Allen Meacham, Arkansas (3) vs. UCLA (17) (Cotton, 1989) (6 for 295 yards)
49.0—Jim DiGuilio, Indiana (24) vs. Baylor (0) (Copper, 1991) (6 for 294 yards)
49.0 (D)—Dana Moore, Mississippi St. (10) vs. Kansas (0) (Hall of Fame, 1981) (9 for 441 yards)
48.0—Dan Eichloff, Kansas (23) vs. Brigham Young (20) (Aloha, 1992) (8 for 384 yards)
47.9—Doug Helkowski, Penn St. (42) vs. Tennessee (17) (Fiesta, 1992) (9 for 431 yards)
47.8 (D)—Kevin Buenafe, UCLA (14) vs. Michigan (33) (Bluebonnet, 1981) (8 for 382 yards)
47.6—Todd Thomsen, Oklahoma (42) vs. Arkansas (8) (Orange, 1987) (5 for 238 yards)
47.5—Jerry Dowd, St. Mary's (Cal.) (20) vs. Texas Tech (13) (Cotton, 1939) (11 for 523 yards)
47.4—Jason Bender, Georgia Tech (18) vs. Stanford (17) (Aloha, 1991) (7 for 332 yards)
47.4 (D)—Mike Mancini, Fresno St. (51) vs. Bowling Green (7) (California, 1985) (7 for 332 yards)
47.4 (D)—Jimmy Colquitt, Tennessee (28) vs. Wisconsin (21) (Garden State, 1981) (5 for 237 yards)

## PUNT RETURNS

### Most Punt Returns

9—Buzy Rosenberg, Georgia (7) vs. North Caro. (3) (Gator, 1971) (54 yards)
9—Paddy Driscoll, Great Lakes (17) vs. Mare Island (0) (Rose, 1919) (115 yards)
6—Dale Carter, Tennessee (17) vs. Penn St. (42) (Fiesta, 1992)
6—Joey Smith, Louisville (34) vs. Alabama (7) (Fiesta, 1991) (35 yards)
6—David Palmer, Alabama (30) vs. Colorado (25) (Blockbuster, 1991) (74 yards)
6 (D)—Hesh Colar, San Jose St. (48) vs. Central Mich. (24) (California, 1990)
6—David Kintigh, Miami (Fla.) (10) vs. Penn St. (14) (Fiesta, 1987) (32 yards)
6 (D)—Eric Metcalf, Texas (16) vs. Air Force (24) (Bluebonnet, 1985) (49 yards)
6—Vai Sikahema, Brigham Young (7) vs. Ohio St. (10) (Florida Citrus, 1985)
6—Ray Horton, Washington St. (21) vs. Maryland (20) (Aloha, 1982) (28 yards)
6—Bill Gribble, Washington St. (36) vs. Brigham Young (38) (Holiday, 1981) (39 yards)
6—Johnny Rodgers, Nebraska (38) vs. Alabama (6) (Orange, 1972) (136 yards)
6—Rick Sygar, Michigan (34) vs. Oregon St. (7) (Rose, 1965) (50 yards)
6—Billy Hair, Clemson (0) vs. Miami (Fla.) (14) (Gator, 1952) (73 yards)
6—Don Zimmerman, Tulane (12) vs. Southern Cal (21) (Rose, 1932)

### Most Punt Return Yards

136—Johnny Rodgers, Nebraska (38) vs. Alabama (6) (Orange, 1972) (6 returns)
122—George Fleming, Washington (44) vs. Wisconsin (8) (Rose, 1960) (3 returns)
122—Bobby Kellogg, Tulane (13) vs. Texas A&M (14) (Sugar, 1940) (5 returns)
115—Paddy Driscoll, Great Lakes (17) vs. Mare Island (0) (Rose, 1919) (9 returns)
110—James Henry, Southern Miss. (38) vs. UTEP (18) (Independence, 1988) (2 returns, touchdowns of 65 and 45 yards)
106—Kevin Baugh, Penn St. (27) vs. Georgia (23) (Sugar, 1983) (5 returns)
106—Steve Holden, Arizona St. (45) vs. Florida St. (38) (Fiesta, 1971) (3 returns)
104—Leo Daniels, Texas A&M (21) vs. Alabama (29) (Cotton, 1942) (5 returns)
103—Jon Staggers, Missouri (3) vs. Penn St. (10) (Orange, 1970)
89—Lawrence Williams, Texas Tech (28) vs. North Caro. (32) (Sun, 1972) (5 returns)
87—Vai Sikahema, Brigham Young (46) vs. Southern Methodist (45) (Holiday, 1980) (2 returns)
86—Bobby Majors, Tennessee (34) vs. Air Force (13) (Sugar, 1971) (4 returns)
86—Aramis Dandoy, Southern Cal (7) vs. Ohio St. (20) (Rose, 1955) (1 return)
82—Willie Drewrey, West Va. (12) vs. Florida St. (31) (Gator, 1982) (1 return)
80 (D)—Gary Anderson, Arkansas (34) vs. Tulane (15) (Hall of Fame, 1980) (2 returns)
80—Cecil Ingram, Alabama (61) vs. Syracuse (6) (Orange, 1953) (1 return)

### Highest Punt Return Average (Min. 3 Returns)

40.7—George Fleming, Washington (44) vs. Wisconsin (8) (Rose, 1960) (3 for 122 yards)
35.3—Steve Holden, Arizona St. (45) vs. Florida St. (38) (Fiesta, 1971) (3 for 106 yards)
24.4—Bobby Kellogg, Tulane (13) vs. Texas A&M (14) (Sugar, 1940) (5 for 122 yards)
24.0—Shayne Wasden, Auburn (31) vs. Ohio St. (14) (Hall of Fame, 1990) (3 for 72 yards)
22.7—Johnny Rodgers, Nebraska (38) vs. Alabama (6) (Orange, 1972) (6 for 136 yards)
21.5—Bobby Majors, Tennessee (34) vs. Air Force (13) (Sugar, 1971) (4 for 86 yards)
21.0 (D)—Brian Williams, Kentucky (16) vs. West Va. (20) (Hall of Fame, 1983) (3 for 63 yards)
20.8—Leo Daniels, Texas A&M (21) vs. Alabama (29) (Cotton, 1942) (5 for 104 yards)
19.5 (D)—Zippy Morocco, Georgia (20) vs. Texas A&M (40) (Presidential Cup, 1950) (4 for 78 yards)
19.3—Dave Liegi, Nebraska (14) vs. Houston (17) (Cotton, 1980) (3 for 58 yards)
19.0—Gary Moss, Georgia (10) vs. Texas (9) (Cotton, 1984) (3 for 57 yards)

# KICKOFF RETURNS

**Most Kickoff Returns**

7—Dale Carter, Tennessee (17) vs. Penn St. (42) (Fiesta, 1992) (132 yards)
7—Jeff Sydner, Hawaii (13) vs. Michigan St. (33) (Aloha, 1989) (174 yards)
7—Homer Jones, Brigham Young (37) vs. Indiana (38) (Holiday, 1979) (126 yards)
6—Eugene Napoleon, West Va. (21) vs. Notre Dame (34) (Fiesta, 1989) (107 yards)
6—Tim Brown, Notre Dame (10) vs. Texas A&M (35) (Cotton, 1988) (129 yards)

6—Leroy Thompson, Penn St. (10) vs. Clemson (35) (Florida Citrus, 1988)
6—Anthony Roberson, Air Force (28) vs. Arizona St. (33) (Freedom, 1987) (109 yards)
6—Casey Tiumalu, Brigham Young (17) vs. Ohio St. (47) (Holiday, 1982) (116 yards)
6—Brian Nelson, Texas Tech (17) vs. Florida St. (40) (Tangerine, 1977) (143 yards)
6—Wally Henry, UCLA (6) vs. Alabama (36) (Liberty, 1976)

6—Steve Williams, Alabama (6) vs. Nebraska (38) (Orange, 1972)
6—Mike Fink, Missouri (35) vs. Arizona St. (49) (Fiesta, 1972) (203 yards)

**Most Kickoff Return Yards**

203—Mike Fink, Missouri (35) vs. Arizona St. (49) (Fiesta, 1972) (6 returns)
178—Al Hoisch, UCLA (14) vs. Illinois (45) (Rose, 1947) (4 returns)
174—Jeff Sydner, Hawaii (13) vs. Michigan St. (33) (Aloha, 1989) (7 returns)
166—Willie Jones, Iowa St. (30) vs. Georgia Tech (31) (Liberty, 1972) (4 returns)
154—Dave Lowery, Brigham Young (21) vs. Oklahoma St. (49) (Tangerine, 1976) (4 returns)

154 (D)—Martin Mitchell, Tulane (7) vs. Houston (47) (Bluebonnet, 1973) (5 returns)
148—Earl Allen, Houston (28) vs. Boston College (45) (Cotton, 1985) (4 returns)
147—Carlos Snow, Ohio St. (17) vs. Syracuse (24) (Hall of Fame, 1992) (4 returns)
144—Clint Johnson, Notre Dame (39) vs. Florida (28) (Sugar, 1992) (5 returns)
143—Barry Smith, Florida St. (38) vs. Arizona St. (45) (Fiesta, 1971) (5 returns)

143—Brian Nelson, Texas Tech (17) vs. Florida St. (40) (Tangerine, 1977) (6 returns)

**Highest Kickoff Return Average (Min. 2 Returns)**

60.5 (D)—Bob Smith, Texas A&M (40) vs. Georgia (20) (Presidential Cup, 1950) (2 for 121 yards)
57.5—Pete Panuska, Tennessee (27) vs. Maryland (28) (Sun, 1984) (2 for 115 yards)
55.5—Todd Snyder, Ohio (42) vs. Richmond (49) (Tangerine, 1968) (2 for 111 yards)
44.5—Al Hoisch, UCLA (14) vs. Illinois (45) (Rose, 1947) (4 for 178 yards)
43.7—Larry Key, Florida St. (40) vs. Texas Tech (17) (Tangerine, 1977) (3 for 131 yards)

41.5—Willie Jones, Iowa St. (30) vs. Georgia Tech (31) (Liberty, 1972) (4 for 166 yards)
41.0—Kevin Williams, Miami (Fla.) (46) vs. Texas (3) (Cotton, 1991) (2 for 82 yards)
40.3 (D)—Willie Gault, Tennessee (28) vs. Wisconsin (21) (Garden State, 1981) (3 for 121 yards)
37.0—Earl Allen, Houston (28) vs. Boston College (45) (Cotton, 1985) (4 for 148 yards)
36.8—Carlos Snow, Ohio St. (17) vs. Syracuse (24) (Hall of Fame, 1992) (4 for 147 yards)

33.8—Mike Fink, Missouri (35) vs. Arizona St. (49) (Fiesta, 1972) (6 for 203 yards)
32.0—Eric Alozie, Washington (34) vs. Florida (7) (Freedom, 1989) (2 for 64 yards)
32.0—Harry Jones, Kentucky (20) vs. Texas Christian (7) (Cotton, 1952) (2 for 64 yards)
32.0—Jim Brown, Syracuse (27) vs. Texas Christian (28) (Cotton, 1957) (3 for 96 yards)

# INTERCEPTIONS

**Most Interceptions Made**

4—Jim Dooley, Miami (Fla.) (14) vs. Clemson (0) (Gator, 1952)
4 (D)—Manuel Aja, Arizona St. (21) vs. Xavier (Ohio) (33) (Salad, 1950)
3—Michael Brooks, North Caro. St. (28) vs. Iowa (23) (Peach, 1988)
3—Bud Hebert, Oklahoma (24) vs. Florida St. (7) (Orange, 1980)
3—Louis Campbell, Arkansas (13) vs. Tennessee (14) (Liberty, 1971)

3—Bud McClinton, Auburn (34) vs. Arizona (10) (Sun, 1968)
3 (D)—Les Derrick, Texas (19) vs. Mississippi (0) (Bluebonnet, 1966)
3 (D)—Tommy Luke, Mississippi (0) vs. Texas (19) (Bluebonnet, 1966)
3—Jerry Cook, Texas (12) vs. Mississippi (7) (Cotton, 1962)
3—Ray Brown, Mississippi (39) vs. Texas (7) (Sugar, 1958)

3—Bill Paulman, Stanford (7) vs. Southern Methodist (0) (Rose, 1936)
3—Shy Huntington, Oregon (14) vs. Pennsylvania (0) (Rose, 1917)

**Most Interception Return Yardage**

148—Elmer Layden, Notre Dame (27) vs. Stanford (10) (Rose, 1925) (2 interceptions)
94—David Baker, Oklahoma (48) vs. Duke (21) (Orange, 1958) (1 interception)
90—Norm Beal, Missouri (21) vs. Navy (14) (Orange, 1961) (1 interception)
90—Charlie Brembs, South Caro. (14) vs. Wake Forest (26) (Gator, 1946) (1 interception)
89—Al Hudson, Miami (Fla.) (13) vs. Holy Cross (6) (Orange, 1946) (1 interception)

81—Gary Moss, Georgia (24) vs. Boston College (27) (Hall of Fame, 1986) (1 interception)
80 (D)—Russ Meredith, West Va. (21) vs. Gonzaga (13) (San Diego East-West Christmas Classic, 1922) (1 interception)
77—George Halas, Great Lakes (17) vs. Mare Island (0) (Rose, 1919) (1 interception)
75—Hugh Morrow, Alabama (26) vs. Duke (29) (Sugar, 1945) (1 interception)
72—Alton Montgomery, Houston (22) vs. Washington St. (24) (Aloha, 1988) (1 interception)

70—Robert Bailey, Mississippi (34) vs. Virginia Tech (17) (Liberty, 1968) (1 interception)
70 (D)—Mel McGaha, Arkansas (21) vs. William & Mary (19) (Dixie, 1948) (1 interception)
69—Howard Ehler, Florida St. (36) vs. Oklahoma (19) (Gator, Jan. 2, 1965) (1 interception)
67—John Matsock, Michigan St. (28) vs. UCLA (20) (Rose, 1954) (2 interceptions)

## ALL-PURPOSE

**(Includes all runs from scrimmage, pass receptions and all returns)**

**Most All-Purpose Plays (Must Have at Least One Reception or Return)**
47—Ron Jackson, Tulsa (28) vs. San Diego St. (17) (Freedom, 1991) (46 rush, 1 reception)
46—Errict Rhett, Florida (27) vs. North Caro. St. (10) (Gator, 1992) (39 rush, 7 receptions)
42—Blake Ezor, Michigan St. (33) vs. Hawaii (13) (Aloha, 1989) (41 rush, 1 reception)
39—Marshall Faulk, San Diego St. (17) vs. Tulsa (28) (Freedom, 1991) (30 rush, 9 receptions)
37—O. J. Simpson, Southern Cal (16) vs. Ohio St. (27) (Rose, 1969) (28 rush, 8 receptions, 1 kickoff return)
36—Thurman Thomas, Oklahoma St. (35) vs. West Va. (33) (John Hancock Sun, 1987)
36—Bob Anderson, Colorado (47) vs. Alabama (33) (Liberty, 1969) (35 rush, 1 kickoff return)
35—Ricky Ervins, Southern Cal (17) vs. Michigan (10) (Rose, 1990) (30 rush, 5 receptions)
35—Eric Bieniemy, Colorado (17) vs. Brigham Young (20) (Freedom, 1988) (33 rush, 2 receptions)
33—Shaumbe Wright-Fair, Washington St. (31) vs. Utah (28) (Copper, 1992) (27 rush, 6 receptions)
33—Greg Lewis, Washington (34) vs. Florida (7) (Freedom, 1989) (27 rush, 6 receptions)
33—Bo Jackson, Auburn (16) vs. Texas A&M (36) (Cotton, 1986) (31 rush, 2 receptions)

**Most All-Purpose Yards Gained (Must Have at Least One Reception or Return)**
303 (D)—Bob Smith, Texas A&M (40) vs. Georgia (20) (Presidential Cup, 1950) (160 rush, 22 receptions, 121 kickoff returns)
277—Bob Anderson, Colorado (47) vs. Alabama (33) (Liberty, 1969) (254 rush, 23 kickoff returns)
276—O. J. Simpson, Southern Cal (16) vs. Ohio St. (27) (Rose, 1969) (171 rush, 85 receptions, 20 kickoff returns)
247 (D)—Wilford White, Arizona St. (21) vs. Miami (Ohio) (34) (Salad, 1951) (106 rush, 87 receptions, 54 kickoff returns)
246—Ernie Jones, Indiana (22) vs. Tennessee (27) (Peach, 1987) (15 rush, 150 receiving, 81 kickoff returns)
242—Errict Rhett, Florida (27) vs. North Caro. St. (10) (Gator, 1992) (182 rush, 60 receptions)
239—Tyrone Wheatley, Michigan (38) vs. Washington (31) (Rose, 1993) (235 rush, 4 receptions)
236 (D)—Gary Anderson, Arkansas (34) vs. Tulane (15) (Hall of Fame, 1980) (156 rush, 80 punt returns)
230—Jamie Morris, Michigan (28) vs. Alabama (24) (Hall of Fame, 1987) (234 rush, minus 4 receptions)
228—Phillip Bobo, Washington St. (31) vs. Utah (28) (Copper, 1992) (16 rush, 212 receptions)
225—Ron Jackson, Tulsa (28) vs. San Diego St. (17) (Freedom, 1991) (211 rush, 14 receptions)
223—Donnie Anderson, Texas Tech (21) vs. Georgia Tech (31) (Gator, 1966) (85 rush, 138 receptions)
212—Troy Stradford, Boston College (45) vs. Houston (28) (Cotton, 1985) (196 rush, 16 receptions)
211 (D)—Charles White, Southern Cal (47) vs. Texas A&M (28) (Bluebonnet, 1977) (186 rush, 25 receptions)
208 (D)—Sheldon Canley, San Jose St. (48) vs. Central Mich. (24) (California, 1990) (164 rush, 44 receptions)

## DEFENSIVE STATISTICS

**Most Total Tackles Made (Includes Assists)**
31—Lee Roy Jordan, Alabama (17) vs. Oklahoma (0) (Orange, 1963)
22—Bubba Brown, Clemson (17) vs. Ohio St. (15) (Gator, 1978)
22—Gordy Ceresino, Stanford (24) vs. Louisiana St. (14) (Sun, 1977)
20—Vada Murray, Michigan (10) vs. Southern Cal (17) (Rose, 1990)
20 (D)—Gordy Ceresino, Stanford (25) vs. Georgia (22) (Bluebonnet, 1978)
18—Rod Smith, Notre Dame (39) vs. Florida (28) (Sugar, 1992)
18—Erick Anderson, Michigan (10) vs. Southern Cal (17) (Rose, 1990)
18 (D)—Yepi Pauu, San Jose St. (27) vs. Eastern Mich. (30) (California, 1987)
18—Garland Rivers, Michigan (17) vs. Brigham Young (24) (Holiday, 1984)
18 (D)—Terry Hubbard, Cal St. Fullerton (13) vs. Northern Ill. (20) (California, 1983)
18 (D)—Don Turner, Fresno St. (29) vs. Bowling Green (28) (California, 1982)
18—Matt Millen, Penn St. (42) vs. Arizona St. (30) (Fiesta, 1977)

**Most Unassisted Tackles**
18—Rod Smith, Notre Dame (39) vs. Florida (28) (Sugar, 1992)
17—Garland Rivers, Michigan (17) vs. Brigham Young (24) (Holiday, 1984)
15—Ken Norton Jr., UCLA (31) vs. Brigham Young (10) (Freedom, 1986)
15—Lynn Evans, Missouri (35) vs. Arizona St. (49) (Fiesta, 1972)

**Most Tackles Made for Losses**
5—Michael Jones, Colorado (17) vs. Brigham Young (20) (Freedom, 1988) (20 yards)
5—Jimmy Walker, Arkansas (10) vs. UCLA (10) (Fiesta, 1978)
4—Ken Norton Jr., UCLA (31) vs. Brigham Young (10) (Freedom, 1986) (6 yards)
3 (D)—Guy Boliaux, Wisconsin (21) vs. Tennessee (28) (Garden State, 1981)

**Most Quarterback Sacks**
4—Rusty Medearis, Miami (Fla.) (22) vs. Nebraska (0) (Orange, 1992)
4—Bobby Bell, Missouri (17) vs. Brigham Young (21) (Holiday, 1983)
3—Alfred Williams, Colorado (17) vs. Brigham Young (20) (Freedom, 1988)
3—Jim Wahler, UCLA (31) vs. Brigham Young (10) (Freedom, 1986)
3—James Mosley, Texas Tech (17) vs. Mississippi (20) (Independence, 1986)
3 (D)—Ernie Barnes, Mississippi St. (10) vs. Kansas (0) (Hall of Fame, 1981)

**Fumble Recoveries**
2 (D)—Michael Stewart, Fresno St. (51) vs. Bowling Green (7) (California, 1985)
2—Rod Kirby, Pittsburgh (7) vs. Arizona St. (28) (Fiesta, 1973)

**Blocked Kicks**
2—Carlton Williams, Pittsburgh (7) vs. Arizona St. (28) (Fiesta, 1973)

**Passes Broken Up**
3—Demouy Williams, Washington (24) vs. Tulane (12) (Independence, 1987)

# TEAM RECORD LISTS

Only official records after 1937 are included. Prior records are included if able to be substantiated. Each team's score is in parentheses after the team name. Totals for each team in both-team records are in brackets after the team's score. The year listed is the actual (calendar) year the game was played. The list also includes discontinued bowls, marked with (D). Bowls are listed by the name of the bowl at the time it was played: The Florida Citrus Bowl was the Tangerine Bowl in 1947-82; the first Hall of Fame Bowl (1977-85) was called the All-American Bowl in 1986-90; the current Hall of Fame Bowl is played in Tampa, Fla., and started in 1986; the John Hancock Bowl was called the Sun Bowl in 1936-86 and the John Hancock Sun Bowl in 1987-88; and the Blockbuster Bowl changed its name to Sunshine Football Classic in 1993.

## TOTAL OFFENSE

**Most Total Plays**
96—North Caro. St. (10) vs. Arizona (17) (Copper, 1989) (310 yards)
95—North Caro. St. (28) vs. Iowa (23) (Peach, 1988) (431 yards)
94—Arkansas (27) vs. Tennessee (31) (Cotton, 1990) (568 yards)
93—Miami (Fla.) (10) vs. Penn St. (14) (Fiesta, 1987) (445 yards)
92—Washington St. (24) vs. Houston (22) (Aloha, 1988) (460 yards)
92 (D)—Western Mich. (30) vs. Fresno St. (35) (California, 1988) (503 yards)
92 (D)—Purdue (27) vs. Tennessee (22) (Bluebonnet, 1979) (483 yards)
92—Arizona St. (30) vs. Penn St. (42) (Fiesta, 1977) (426 yards)
91—Florida (28) vs. Notre Dame (39) (Sugar, 1992) (511 yards)
91—Baylor (21) vs. Louisiana St. (7) (Liberty, 1985) (489 yards)
90—Virginia Tech (25) vs. North Caro. St. (24) (Peach, 1986) (487 yards)
90—Maryland (0) vs. Texas (42) (Sun, 1978) (248 yards)
90—Nebraska (40) vs. Notre Dame (6) (Orange, 1973) (560 yards)
90 (D)—Oklahoma (27) vs. Southern Methodist (28) (Bluebonnet, 1968)
90—Richmond (49) vs. Ohio (42) (Tangerine, 1968) (556 yards)

**Most Total Plays, Both Teams**
171—Auburn (34) [82] & Arizona (10) [89] (Sun, 1968) (537 yards)
167 (D)—Fresno St. (35) [75] & Western Mich. (30) [92] (California, 1988) (943 yards)
167—Arizona St. (45) [86] & Florida St. (38) [81] (Fiesta, 1971) (863 yards)
166—Colorado (47) [86] & Alabama (33) [80] (Liberty, 1969) (930 yards)
165—North Caro. St. (28) [95] & Iowa (23) [70] (Peach, 1988)
165—East Caro. (35) [80] & Louisiana Tech (13) [85] (Independence, 1978) (607 yards)
165—Arizona St. (30) [92] & Penn St. (42) [73] (Fiesta, 1977) (777 yards)
163—Nebraska (45) [88] & Georgia (6) [75] (Sun, 1969) (540 yards)
161—Pittsburgh (23) [83] & Ohio St. (28) [78] (Fiesta, 1984) (897 yards)
161—Auburn (35) [84] & Mississippi (28) [77] (Gator, 1971) (1,024 yards)
160—Air Force (29) [82] & Mississippi (42) [78] (Liberty, 1989) (1,047 yards)
159—Florida (28) [91] & Notre Dame (39) [68] (Sugar, 1992) (944 yards)
159—Notre Dame (38) [85] & Texas (10) [74] (Cotton, 1978) (690 yards)
159—Maryland (0) [90] & Texas (42) [69] (Sun, 1978) (517 yards)

**Most Yards Gained**
718—Arizona St. (49) vs. Missouri (35) (Fiesta, 1972) (452 rush, 266 pass)
715—Michigan (35) vs. Mississippi (3) (Gator, 1991) (324 rush, 391 pass)
698—Oklahoma St. (62) vs. Wyoming (14) (Holiday, 1988) (320 rush, 378 pass)
680—Texas A&M (65) vs. Brigham Young (14) (Holiday, 1989) (356 rush, 324 pass)
655 (D)—Houston (47) vs. Tulane (7) (Bluebonnet, 1973) (402 rush, 253 pass)
651—Brigham Young (39) vs. Penn St. (50) (Holiday, 1989) (75 rush, 576 pass)
642 (D)—San Jose St. (48) vs. Central Mich. (24) (California, 1990) (200 rush, 442 pass)
624 (D)—Southern Cal (47) vs. Texas A&M (28) (Bluebonnet, 1977) (378 rush, 246 pass)
618—Oklahoma (48) vs. Virginia (14) (Gator, 1991) (261 rush, 357 pass)
596—Alabama (61) vs. Syracuse (6) (Orange, 1953) (296 rush, 300 pass)

575—Indiana (34) vs. South Caro. (10) (Liberty, 1988) (185 rush, 390 pass)
571—Louisville (34) vs. Alabama (7) (Fiesta, 1991) (113 rush, 458 pass)
569—Florida St. (34) vs. Oklahoma St. (23) (Gator, 1985) (231 rush, 338 pass)
568—Arkansas (27) vs. Tennessee (31) (Cotton, 1990) (361 rush, 207 pass)
566—Pittsburgh (34) vs. Clemson (3) (Gator, 1977) (179 rush, 387 pass)

**Most Yards Gained, Both Teams**
1,143 (D)—Southern Cal (47) [624] & Texas A&M (28) [519] (Bluebonnet, 1977) (148 plays)
1,129—Arizona St. (49) [718] & Missouri (35) [411] (Fiesta, 1972) (134 plays)
1,115—Brigham Young (39) [651] & Penn St. (50) [464] (Holiday, 1989) (157 plays)
1,048—Michigan (35) [715] & Mississippi (3) [333] (Gator, 1991) (153 plays)
1,047—Mississippi (42) [533] & Air Force (29) [514] (Liberty, 1989) (160 plays)
1,038—Arkansas (27) [568] & Tennessee (31) [470] (Cotton, 1990) (155 plays)
1,024—Auburn (35) [559] & Mississippi (28) [465] (Gator, 1971) (161 plays)
1,007 (D)—San Jose St. (25) [521] & Toledo (27) [486] (California, 1981) (158 plays)
978—Pittsburgh (31) [530] & Texas A&M (28) [448] (John Hancock, 1989) (158 plays)
954—Arkansas (22) [527] & Mississippi (27) [427] (Sugar, 1970)
950—Texas (40) [436] & Missouri (27) [514] (Cotton, 1946)
944—Notre Dame (39) [433] & Florida (28) [511] (Sugar, 1992) (159 plays)
943 (D)—Fresno St. (35) [440] & Western Mich. (30) [503] (California, 1988) (167 plays)
939 (D)—Texas Tech (49) [523] & Duke (21) [416] (All-American, 1989) (141 plays)

**Highest Average Gained Per Play**
9.5—Louisville (34) vs. Alabama (7) (Fiesta, 1991) (60 for 571 yards)
8.7—Oklahoma St. (62) vs. Wyoming (14) (Holiday, 1988) (80 for 698 yards)
8.4—Michigan (35) vs. Mississippi (3) (Gator, 1991) (85 for 715 yards)
8.3—Texas A&M (65) vs. Brigham Young (14) (Holiday, 1990) (82 for 680 yards)
8.1—Arizona St. (49) vs. Missouri (35) (Fiesta, 1972) (89 for 718 yards)
7.9—Brigham Young (39) vs. Penn St. (50) (Holiday, 1989) (82 for 651 yards)
7.7—Alabama (61) vs. Syracuse (6) (Orange, 1953) (77 for 596 yards)
7.7 (D)—Vanderbilt (28) vs. Air Force (36) (Hall of Fame, 1982) (63 for 487 yards)
7.7—Tennessee (31) vs. Arkansas (27) (Cotton, 1990) (61 for 470 yards)
7.6—Florida St. (41) vs. Nebraska (17) (Fiesta, 1990) (65 for 494 yards)
7.5 (D)—Houston (47) vs. Tulane (7) (Bluebonnet, 1973) (87 for 655 yards)
7.5—Iowa (38) vs. California (12) (Rose, 1959) (69 for 516 yards)
7.4—UCLA (31) vs. Brigham Young (10) (Freedom, 1986) (70 for 518 yards)
7.3 (D)—Nevada-Las Vegas (30) vs. Toledo (13) (California, 1984) (56 for 409 yards)
7.3 (D)—San Jose St. (48) vs. Central Mich. (24) (California, 1990) (88 for 642 yards)

**Fewest Plays**
35—Tennessee (0) vs. Texas (16) (Cotton, 1953) (29 rush, 6 pass)
36—Arkansas (3) vs. UCLA (17) (Cotton, 1989) (22 rush, 14 pass)
37—Texas Christian (0) vs. Oklahoma St. (34) (Cotton, 1945) (27 rush, 10 pass)

**Fewest Plays, Both Teams**
107—Texas Christian (16) [54] & Marquette (6) [53] (Cotton, 1937)

**Fewest Yards**
-21—U. of Mexico (0) vs. Southwestern (Tex.) (35) (Sun, 1945) (29 rush, -50 pass)
23—Alabama (10) vs. Missouri (35) (Gator, 1968) (-45 rush, 68 pass)
28—Miami (Fla.) (0) vs. Bucknell (26) (Orange, 1935) (15 rush, 13 pass)
32—Tennessee (0) vs. Texas (16) (Cotton, 1953) (-14 rush, 46 pass)
41—Southern Cal (14) vs. Alabama (34) (Rose, 1946) (6 rush, 35 pass)
42—Arkansas (3) vs. UCLA (17) (Cotton, 1989) (21 rush, 21 pass)
48—New Mexico (0) vs. Southwestern (Tex.) (7) (Sun, 1944) (38 rush, 10 pass)
54—Arkansas (0) vs. Louisiana St. (0) (Cotton, 1947) (54 rush, 0 pass)
57—Michigan St. (0) vs. Auburn (6) (Orange, 1938) (32 rush, 25 pass)

**Fewest Yards, Both Teams**
260—Randolph Field (7) [150] & Texas (7) [110] (Cotton, 1944)
263—Louisiana St. (19) [92] & Texas A&M (14) [171] (Orange, 1944)

**Lowest Average Per Play**
0.9—Tennessee (0) vs. Texas (16) (Cotton, 1953) (35 for 32 yards)
1.2—Arkansas (3) vs. UCLA (17) (Cotton, 1989) (36 for 42 yards)

# RUSHING

**Most Rushing Attempts**
87—Oklahoma (40) vs. Auburn (22) (Sugar, 1972) (439 yards)
82—Missouri (35) vs. Alabama (10) (Gator, 1968) (402 yards)
79—West Va. (14) vs. South Caro. (3) (Peach, 1969) (356 yards)
79—Georgia Tech (31) vs. Texas Tech (21) (Gator, Dec. 31, 1965) (364 yards)
78 (D)—Houston (35) vs. Navy (0) (Garden State, 1980) (405 yards)

78—Texas (16) vs. Tennessee (0) (Cotton, 1953) (296 yards)
76—Oklahoma (14) vs. Penn St. (0) (Sugar, Dec. 31, 1972) (278 yards)
74—Oklahoma (41) vs. Wyoming (7) (Fiesta, 1976) (415 yards)
74—Michigan (12) vs. Stanford (13) (Rose, 1972) (264 yards)
74—Ohio St. (20) vs. Southern Cal (7) (Rose, 1955) (305 yards)
73—Syracuse (31) vs. McNeese St. (7) (Independence, 1979) (276 yards)
73—Penn St. (41) vs. Oregon (12) (Liberty, 1960) (301 yards)
72—Arkansas (27) vs. Tennessee (31) (Cotton, 1990) (361 yards)
72—North Caro. St. (28) vs. Iowa (23) (Peach, 1988) (236 yards)
72 (D)—Texas A&M (28) vs. Southern Cal (47) (Bluebonnet, 1977) (486 yards)

**Most Rushing Attempts, Both Teams**
122 (D)—Southern Cal (47) [50] & Texas A&M (28) [72] (Bluebonnet, 1977) (864 yards)
122—Mississippi St. (26) [68] & North Caro. (24) [54] (Sun, 1974) (732 yards)
120—Pittsburgh (33) [53] & Kansas (19) [67] (Sun, 1975) (714 yards)
117—Oklahoma (14) [65] & Michigan (6) [52] (Orange, 1976) (451 yards)
117—West Va. (14) [79] & South Caro. (3) [38] (Peach, 1969) (420 yards)

116—Oklahoma (41) [74] & Wyoming (7) [42] (Fiesta, 1976) (568 yards)
116—Colorado (47) [70] & Alabama (33) [46] (Liberty, 1969) (628 yards)
115—Wisconsin (0) [68] & Southern Cal (7) [47] (Rose, 1953) (259 yards)
113—Oklahoma (40) [54] & Houston (14) [59] (Sun, 1981) (566 yards)
113 (D)—Houston (35) [78] & Navy (0) [35] (Garden State, 1980) (540 yards)

113—Missouri (34) [71] & Auburn (17) [42] (Sun, 1973) (408 yards)
112—Arkansas (31) [65] & Georgia (10) [47] (Cotton, 1976) (426 yards)
112 (D)—Colorado (29) [62] & Houston (17) [50] (Bluebonnet, 1971) (552 yards)

**Most Net Rushing Yards**
486 (D)—Texas A&M (28) vs. Southern Cal (47) (Bluebonnet, 1977) (72 attempts)
473—Colorado (47) vs. Alabama (33) (Liberty, 1969) (70 attempts)
455—Mississippi St. (26) vs. North Caro. (24) (Sun, 1974) (68 attempts)
452—Arizona St. (49) vs. Missouri (35) (Fiesta, 1972) (65 attempts)
439—Oklahoma (40) vs. Auburn (22) (Sugar, 1972) (87 attempts)
434—Oklahoma (41) vs. Wyoming (7) (Fiesta, 1976) (74 attempts)
429—Iowa (38) vs. California (12) (Rose, 1959) (55 attempts)
423—UCLA (31) vs. Brigham Young (10) (Freedom, 1986) (49 attempts)
423—Auburn (33) vs. Baylor (13) (Gator, 1954) (48 attempts)
417—Oklahoma (21) vs. Arizona St. (32) (Fiesta, 1983) (63 attempts)
411—Oklahoma (24) vs. Florida St. (7) (Orange, 1980) (62 attempts)
409—Oklahoma (40) vs. Houston (14) (Sun, 1981) (54 attempts)
408—Missouri (27) vs. Texas (40) (Cotton, 1946)
405 (D)—Houston (35) vs. Navy (0) (Garden State, 1980) (78 attempts)
402 (D)—Houston (47) vs. Tulane (7) (Bluebonnet, 1973) (58 attempts)

**Most Net Rushing Yards, Both Teams**
864 (D)—Southern Cal (47) [378] & Texas A&M (28) [486] (Bluebonnet, 1977) (122 attempts)
732—Mississippi St. (26) [455] & North Caro. (24) [277] (Sun, 1974) (122 attempts)
714—Pittsburgh (33) [372] & Kansas (19) [342] (Sun, 1975) (120 attempts)
701—Arizona St. (49) [453] & Missouri (35) [248] (Fiesta, 1972) (109 attempts)
681—Arkansas (27) [361] & Tennessee (31) [320] (Cotton, 1990) (110 attempts)
643—Iowa (38) [429] & California (12) [214] (Rose, 1959) (108 attempts)
628—Colorado (47) [473] & Alabama (33) [155] (Liberty, 1969) (116 attempts)
616—Oklahoma (41) [434] & Wyoming (7) [182] (Fiesta, 1976) (116 attempts)
610—Missouri (27) [408] & Texas (40) [202] (Cotton, 1946)

**Highest Rushing Average (Min. 30 Attempts)**
8.6—UCLA (31) vs. Brigham Young (10) (Freedom, 1986) (49 for 423 yards)
8.6—Michigan (38) vs. Washington (31) (Rose, 1993) (36 for 308 yards)
8.4—Tennessee (31) vs. Arkansas (27) (Cotton, 1990) (38 for 320 yards)
8.0—Toledo (56) vs. Davidson (33) (Tangerine, 1969) (42 for 334 yards)
7.8—Iowa (38) vs. California (12) (Rose, 1959) (55 for 429 yards)
7.7—Texas Tech (28) vs. North Caro. (32) (Sun, 1972) (38 for 293 yards)
7.6—Oklahoma (42) vs. Arkansas (8) (Orange, 1987) (48 for 366 yards)
7.6—Oklahoma (40) vs. Houston (14) (Sun, 1981) (54 for 409 yards)
7.6 (D)—Southern Cal (47) vs. Texas A&M (28) (Bluebonnet, 1977) (50 for 378 yards)
7.4—Michigan (35) vs. Mississippi (3) (Gator, 1991) (53 for 391 yards)
7.1—Boston College (45) vs. Houston (28) (Cotton, 1985) (50 for 353 yards)
7.0—Pittsburgh (33) vs. Kansas (19) (Sun, 1975) (53 for 372 yards)
7.0—Arizona St. (49) vs. Missouri (35) (Fiesta, 1972) (65 for 453 yards)

**Fewest Rushing Attempts**
12 (D)—Vanderbilt (28) vs. Air Force (36) (Hall of Fame, 1982) (35 yards)
16—Florida (18) vs. Missouri (20) (Sugar, 1966) (-2 yards)
16—Colorado (7) vs. Louisiana St. (25) (Orange, 1962) (24 yards)
17 (D)—Duke (21) vs. Texas Tech (49) (All-American, 1989) (67 yards)
17—Illinois (9) vs. UCLA (45) (Rose, 1984) (0 yards)

*1993 NCAA FOOTBALL*

18—Brigham Young (46) vs. Southern Methodist (45) (Holiday, 1980) (-2 yards)
19—Iowa (23) vs. North Caro. St. (28) (Peach, 1988) (46 yards)
19—Baylor (13) vs. Auburn (33) (Gator, 1954) (108 yards)
20 (D)—San Jose St. (27) vs. Eastern Mich. (30) (California, 1987) (81 yards)
20—Tulane (6) vs. Penn St. (9) (Liberty, 1979) (-8 yards)
21—Brigham Young (14) vs. Texas A&M (65) (Holiday, 1990) (-12 yards)
21—Houston (22) vs. Washington St. (24) (Aloha, 1988) (68 yards)
21—Wyoming (19) vs. Iowa (20) (Holiday, 1987) (43 yards)
21 (D)—San Jose St. (25) vs. Toledo (27) (California, 1981) (54 yards)

**Fewest Rushing Attempts, Both Teams**
57—Iowa (20) [36] & Wyoming (19) [21] (Holiday, 1987)
66—Iowa (13) [33] & Brigham Young (13) [33] (Holiday, 1991)
66—Miami (Fla.) (23) [28] & Nebraska (3) [38] (Orange, 1989)
66—Texas Christian (16) [34] & Marquette (6) [32] (Cotton, 1937)
67—UCLA (6) [41] & Illinois (3) [26] (John Hancock, 1991)
67—Southern Cal (7) [39] & Duke (3) [28] (Rose, 1939)
68 (D)—Fresno St. (29) [24] & Bowling Green (28) [44] (California, 1982)
70—Florida St. (41) [24] & Nebraska (17) [46] (Fiesta, 1990)
70—Florida St. (24) [39] & Penn St. (17) [31] (Blockbuster, 1990)

**Fewest Rushing Yards**
-45—Alabama (10) vs. Missouri (35) (Gator, 1968) (29 attempts)
-30—Florida (6) vs. West Va. (26) (Peach, 1981) (34 attempts)
-21—Florida St. (20) vs. Wyoming (28) (Sun, 1966) (31 attempts)
-15—Louisiana St. (0) vs. Mississippi (20) (Sugar, 1960)
-14—Navy (6) vs. Texas (28) (Cotton, 1964) (29 attempts)
-14—Tennessee (0) vs. Texas (16) (Cotton, 1953) (29 attempts)
-12—Brigham Young (14) vs. Texas A&M (65) (Holiday, 1990) (21 attempts)
-12—Air Force (13) vs. Tennessee (34) (Sugar, 1971)
-11—Colorado (25) vs. Alabama (30) (Blockbuster, 1991) (30 attempts)
-8—Tulane (6) vs. Penn St. (9) (Liberty, 1979) (20 attempts)
-8—Navy (14) vs. Missouri (21) (Orange, 1961) (24 attempts)
-2—Brigham Young (46) vs. Southern Methodist (45) (Holiday, 1980) (24 attempts)
-2—Florida (18) vs. Missouri (20) (Sugar, 1966) (16 attempts)

**Fewest Rushing Yards, Both Teams**
74—Tennessee (34) [86] & Air Force (13) [-12] (Sugar, 1971)
137—Iowa (20) [94] & Wyoming (19) [43] (Holiday, 1987)
145—Nebraska (7) [100] & Arkansas (10) [45] (Cotton, 1965)
147 (D)—San Jose St. (37) [123] & Miami (Ohio) (7) [24] (California, 1986)

**Lowest Rushing Average (Min. 20 Attempts)**
-1.6—Alabama (10) vs. Missouri (35) (Gator, 1968) (29 for -45 yards)
-0.9—Florida (6) vs. West Va. (26) (Peach, 1981) (32 for -30 yards)
-0.7—Florida St. (20) vs. Wyoming (28) (Sun, 1966) (31 for -21 yards)
-0.6—Brigham Young (14) vs. Texas A&M (65) (Holiday, 1990) (21 for -12 yards)
-0.5—Navy (6) vs. Texas (28) (Cotton, 1964) (29 for -14 yards)
-0.5—Tennessee (0) vs. Texas (16) (Cotton, 1953) (29 for -14 yards)
-0.4—Colorado (25) vs. Alabama (30) (Blockbuster, 1991) (30 for -11 yards)
-0.3—Navy (14) vs. Missouri (21) (Orange, 1961) (24 for -8 yards)

**Rushing Defense, Fewest Yards Allowed**
-45—Missouri (35) vs. Alabama (10) (Gator, 1968) (29 attempts)
-30—West Va. (26) vs. Florida (6) (Peach, 1981) (32 attempts)
-21—Wyoming (28) vs. Florida St. (20) (Sun, 1966) (31 attempts)
-15—Mississippi (20) vs. Louisiana St. (0) (Sugar, 1960)
-14—Texas (28) vs. Navy (6) (Cotton, 1964) (29 attempts)
-14—Texas (16) vs. Tennessee (0) (Cotton, 1953) (29 attempts)
-12—Texas A&M (65) vs. Brigham Young (14) (Holiday, 1990) (21 attempts)
-12—Tennessee (34) vs. Air Force (13) (Sugar, 1971)
-11—Alabama (30) vs. Colorado (25) (Blockbuster, 1991) (30 attempts)
-8—Penn St. (9) vs. Tulane (6) (Liberty, 1979) (20 attempts)
-8—Missouri (21) vs. Navy (14) (Orange, 1961) (24 attempts)
-2—Southern Methodist (45) vs. Brigham Young (46) (Holiday, 1980) (24 attempts)
-2—Missouri (20) vs. Florida (18) (Sugar, 1966) (16 attempts)

# PASSING

**Most Pass Attempts (followed by comp.-att.-int. and yardage)**
63 (D)—San Jose St. (25) vs. Toledo (27) (California, 1981) (43-63-5, 467 yards)
61 (D)—Brigham Young (16) vs. Virginia (22) (All-American, 1987) (37-61-1, 394 yards)
59—Brigham Young (39) vs. Penn St. (50) (Holiday, 1989) (42-59-2, 576 yards)
58—Florida (28) vs. Notre Dame (39) (Sugar, 1992) (28-58-2, 370 yards)
58—Illinois (15) vs. Alabama (21) (Liberty, 1982) (35-58-7, 423 yards)

58—Richmond (49) vs. Ohio (42) (Tangerine, 1968) (39-58-2, 447 yards)
57 (D)—Western Mich. (30) vs. Fresno St. (35) (California, 1988) (24-57-0, 366 yards)
56—Miami (Fla.) (13) vs. Alabama (34) (Sugar, 1993) (24-56-3, 278 yards)
56—Washington (21) vs. Maryland (20) (Aloha, 1982) (35-56-0, 369 yards)
55—Illinois (29) vs. Army (31) (Peach, 1985) (38-55-2, 401 yards)

55—Florida St. (17) vs. Penn St. (17) (Gator, 1967) (38-55-4, 363 yards)
52—Alabama (29) vs. Army (28) (John Hancock Sun, 1988) (33-52-1, 412 yards)
52—Louisiana Tech (13) vs. East Caro. (35) (Independence, 1978) (18-52-3, 263 yards)

**Most Pass Attempts, Both Teams**
92—Air Force (13) [46] & Tennessee (34) [46] (Sugar, 1971) (47 completed)
91—Richmond (49) [58] & Ohio (42) [33] (Tangerine, 1968) (56 completed)
90—Bowling Green (35) [41] & Nevada (34) [49] (Las Vegas, 1992) (54 completed)
90—Mississippi (20) [50] & Texas Tech (17) [40] (Independence, 1986) (48 completed)
88—Washington St. (31) [48] & Utah (28) [40] (Copper, 1992) (53 completed)

88—Washington (21) [56] & Maryland (20) [32] (Aloha, 1982) (54 completed)
86 (D)—Western Mich. (30) [57] & Fresno St. (35) [29] (California, 1988) (39 completed)
86—Wyoming (19) [51] & Iowa (20) [35] (Holiday, 1987) (49 completed)
85—Ohio St. (10) [35] & Brigham Young (7) [50] (Florida Citrus, 1985) (45 completed)
85 (D)—San Jose St. (25) [63] & Toldeo (27) [22] (California, 1981) (54 completed)

83—Auburn (35) [44] & Mississippi (28) [39] (Gator, 1971) (50 completed)
82 (D)—Fresno St. (29) [50] & Bowling Green (28) [32] (California, 1982) (53 completed)
80—Brigham Young (39) [59] & Penn St. (50) [21] (Holiday, 1989) (53 completed)
80 (D)—Virginia (22) [19] & Brigham Young (16) [61] (All-American, 1987) (47 completed)
80 (D)—Miami (Ohio) (7) [41] & San Jose St. (37) [39] (California, 1986) (40 completed)

**Most Pass Completions (followed by comp.-att.-int. and yardage)**
43 (D)—San Jose St. (25) vs. Toledo (27) (California, 1981) (43-63-5, 467 yards)
42—Brigham Young (39) vs. Penn St. (50) (Holiday, 1989) (42-59-2, 576 yards)
39—Richmond (49) vs. Ohio (42) (Tangerine, 1968) (39-58-2, 447 yards)
38—Illinois (29) vs. Army (31) (Peach, 1985) (38-55-2, 401 yards)
38—Vanderbilt (28) vs. Air Force (36) (Hall of Fame, 1982) (38-51-3, 452 yards)

38—Florida St. (17) vs. Penn St. (17) (Gator, 1967) (38-55-4, 363 yards)
37 (D)—Brigham Young (16) vs. Virginia (22) (All-American, 1987) (37-61-1, 394 yards)
35—Brigham Young (24) vs. Michigan (17) (Holiday, 1984) (35-49-3, 371 yards)
35—Illinois (15) vs. Alabama (21) (Liberty, 1982) (35-58-7, 423 yards)
35—Washington (21) vs. Maryland (20) (Aloha, 1982) (35-56-0, 369 yards)

34—Wisconsin (37) vs. Southern Cal (42) (Rose, 1963) (34-49-3, 419 yards)
33—Alabama (29) vs. Army (28) (John Hancock Sun, 1988) (33-52-1, 412 yards)

**Most Pass Completions, Both Teams**
56—Richmond (49) [39] & Ohio (42) [17] (Tangerine, 1968) (91 attempted)
54—Bowling Green (35) [25] & Nevada (34) [29] (Las Vegas, 1992) (90 attempted)
54—Washington (21) [35] & Maryland (20) [19] (Aloha, 1982) (88 attempted)
54 (D)—San Jose St. (25) [43] & Toledo (27) [11] (California, 1981) (85 attempted)
53—Washington St. (31) [32] & Utah (28) [21] (Copper, 1992) (88 attempted)

53—Brigham Young (39) [42] & Penn St. (50) [11] (Holiday, 1989) (80 attempted)
53 (D)—Fresno St. (29) [31] & Bowling Green (28) [22] (California, 1982) (82 attempted)
50—Auburn (35) [27] & Mississippi (28) [23] (Gator, 1971) (83 attempted)
49—Wyoming (19) [28] & Iowa (20) [21] (Holiday, 1987) (86 attempted)
49—Miami (Fla.) (37) [31] & UCLA (39) [18] (Fiesta, 1985) (71 attempted)

49—Air Force (36) [11] & Vanderbilt (28) [38] (Hall of Fame, 1982) (68 attempted)
48—Brigham Young (13) [29] & Iowa (13) [19] (Holiday, 1991) (72 attempted)
48—Louisiana St. (30) [20] & South Caro. (13) [28] (Gator, 1987) (79 attempted)
48—Mississippi (20) [31] & Texas Tech (17) [17] (Independence, 1986) (90 attempted)

**Most Passing Yards (followed by comp.-att.-int.)**
576—Brigham Young (39) vs. Penn St. (50) (Holiday, 1989) (42-59-2)
492—Washington St. (31) vs. Utah (28) (Copper, 1992) (32-48-1)
469—Iowa (55) vs. Texas (17) (Freedom, 1984) (30-40-0)
467 (D)—San Jose St. (25) vs. Toledo (27) (California, 1981) (43-63-5)
458—Louisville (34) vs. Alabama (7) (Fiesta, 1991) (21-39-3)

455—Florida St. (40) vs. Texas Tech (17) (Tangerine, 1977) (25-35-0)
452—Vanderbilt (28) vs. Air Force (36) (Hall of Fame, 1982) (38-51-3)
447—Richmond (49) vs. Ohio (42) (Tangerine, 1968) (39-58-2)
446—Brigham Young (46) vs. Southern Methodist (45) (Holiday, 1980) (32-49-1)
442 (D)—San Jose St. (48) vs. Central Mich. (24) (California, 1990) (32-43-1)

428—Iowa (23) vs. North Caro. St. (28) (Peach, 1988) (30-51-4)
423—Illinois (15) vs. Alabama (21) (Liberty, 1982) (35-58-7)
422—Florida St. (41) vs. Nebraska (17) (Fiesta, 1990) (25-41-0)
419—Wisconsin (37) vs. Southern Cal (42) (Rose, 1963) (34-49-3)
412—Alabama (29) vs. Army (28) (John Hancock Sun, 1988) (33-52-1)

**Most Passing Yards, Both Teams**
808—Washington St. (31) [492] & Utah (28) [316] (Copper, 1992) (88 attempted)
791—Brigham Young (39) [576] & Penn St. (50) [215] (Holiday, 1989) (80 attempted)
734—Florida St. (40) [455] & Texas Tech (17) [279] (Tangerine, 1977) (63 attempted)
732 (D)—San Jose St. (25) [467] & Toledo (27) [265] (California, 1981) (85 attempted)
672—Wisconsin (37) [419] & Southern Cal (42) [253] (Rose, 1963) (69 attempted)
662 (D)—San Jose St. (48) [442] & Central Mich. (24) [220] (California, 1990) (68 attempted)
654—Iowa (55) [469] & Texas (17) [185] (Freedom, 1984) (74 attempted)
629—Florida St. (41) [422] & Nebraska (17) [207] (Fiesta, 1990) (67 attempted)
623—North Caro. St. (28) [195] & Iowa (23) [428] (Peach, 1988) (74 attempted)
620—Washington (21) [369] & Maryland (20) [251] (Aloha, 1982) (88 attempted)
619 (D)—Fresno St. (29) [373] & Bowling Green (28) [246] (California, 1982) (82 attempted)
611—Florida St. (38) [361] & Arizona St. (45) [250] (Fiesta, 1971) (77 attempted)
611—Arkansas (22) [338] & Mississippi (27) [273] (Sugar, 1970) (70 attempted)
607—Auburn (35) [351] & Mississippi (28) [256] (Gator, 1971) (83 attempted)
606 (D)—Western Mich. (30) [366] & Fresno St. (35) [240] (California, 1988) (86 attempted)

**Most Passes Had Intercepted**
8—Arizona (10) vs. Auburn (34) (Sun, 1968)
7—Illinois (15) vs. Alabama (21) (Liberty, 1982)
7—Missouri (3) vs. Penn St. (10) (Orange, 1970)
7—Texas A&M (21) vs. Alabama (29) (Cotton, 1942)
6—Georgia (6) vs. Nebraska (45) (Sun, 1969)
6—Texas Christian (26) vs. Georgia (40) (Orange, 1942)
6—Southern Methodist (0) vs. Stanford (7) (Rose, 1936)

**Most Passes Had Intercepted, Both Teams**
12—Arizona (10) [8] & Auburn (34) [4] (Sun, 1968)
10—Georgia (40) [6] & Texas Christian (26) [4] (Orange, 1942)
9—Illinois (15) [7] & Alabama (21) [2] (Liberty, 1982)
8—Texas A&M (12) [5] & Ohio St. (28) [3] (Cotton, 1987)
8—Louisiana St. (10) [5] & Nebraska (28) [3] (Sugar, 1985)
8—Penn St. (10) [1] & Missouri (3) [7] (Orange, 1970)
8—Georgia (6) [6] & Nebraska (45) [2] (Sun, 1969)
8—Mississippi (7) [5] & Texas (12) [3] (Cotton, 1962)

**Most Passes Attempted Without an Interception (followed by comp.-att.-int. and yardage)**
57 (D)—Western Mich. (30) vs. Fresno St. (35) (California, 1988) (24-57-0, 366 yards)

**Most Passes Attempted by Both Teams Without an Interception (followed by comp.-att.-int. and yardage)**
90—Bowling Green (35) [49] & Nevada (34) [41] (Las Vegas, 1992) (54-90-0, 597 yards)

**Highest Completion Percentage (Min. 10 Attempts) (followed by comp.-att.-int. and yardage)**
.929—Texas (40) vs. Missouri (27) (Cotton, 1946) (13-14-0, 234 yards)
.900—Mississippi (13) vs. Air Force (0) (Liberty, 1992) (9-10-0, 163 yards)
.889—Texas A&M (65) vs. Brigham Young (14) (Holiday, 1990) (16-18-0, 324 yards)
.833—Alabama (13) vs. Penn St. (6) (Sugar, 1975) (10-12-0, 210 yards)
.828—Oklahoma St. (62) vs. Wyoming (14) (Holiday, 1988) (24-29-0, 378 yards)
.824—Nebraska (21) vs. North Caro. (17) (Liberty, 1977) (14-17-2, 161 yards)
.813—Texas Christian (28) vs. Syracuse (27) (Cotton, 1957) (13-16-0, 202 yards)
.800—Ohio St. (15) vs. Clemson (17) (Gator, 1978) (16-20-1, 205 yards)
.800—Georgia Tech (31) vs. Iowa St. (30) (Liberty, 1972) (12-15-1, 157 yards)
.778—Tennessee (27) vs. Indiana (22) (Peach, 1987) (21-27-0, 230 yards)
.765—Illinois (17) vs. Hawaii (27) (Holiday, 1992) (26-34-1, 248 yards)
.765—Duke (7) vs. Arkansas (6) (Cotton, 1961) (13-17-1, 93 yards)
.763—Iowa (28) vs. UCLA (45) (Rose, 1986) (29-38-1, 319 yards)
.750—Oklahoma (48) vs. Virginia (14) (Gator, 1991) (27-36-0, 357 yards)
.750—Iowa (55) vs. Texas (17) (Freedom, 1984) (30-40-0, 469 yards)

**Most Yards Per Attempt (Min. 10 Attempts)**
21.7—Southern Cal (47) vs. Pittsburgh (14) (Rose, 1930) (13 for 282 yards)
18.0—Texas A&M (65) vs. Brigham Young (14) (Holiday, 1990) (18 for 324 yards)
17.5—Alabama (13) vs. Penn St. (6) (Sugar, 1975) (12 for 210 yards)
16.7—Texas (36) vs. Tennessee (13) (Cotton, 1969) (14 for 234 yards)
16.7—Texas (40) vs. Missouri (27) (Cotton, 1946) (14 for 234 yards)

**Most Yards Per Completion (Min. 8 Completions)**
35.2—Southern Cal (47) vs. Pittsburgh (14) (Rose, 1930) (8 for 282 yards)
29.3—Texas (36) vs. Tennessee (13) (Cotton, 1969) (8 for 234 yards)
29.3—Texas (28) vs. Navy (6) (Cotton, 1964) (8 for 234 yards)

**Fewest Pass Attempts**
2—Air Force (38) vs. Mississippi St. (15) (Liberty, 1991) (completed 1)
2 (D)—Army (10) vs. Michigan St. (6) (Cherry, 1984) (completed 1)
2—West Va. (14) vs. South Caro. (3) (Peach, 1969) (completed 1)
3—Air Force (23) vs. Ohio St. (11) (Liberty, 1990) (completed 1)
3—Oklahoma (31) vs. Nebraska (24) (Orange, 1979) (completed 2)

3—Georgia Tech (21) vs. Pittsburgh (14) (Gator, 1956) (completed 3)
3—Georgia Tech (7) vs. Pittsburgh (0) (Sugar, 1956) (completed 0)
3—Miami (Fla.) (14) vs. Clemson (0) (Gator, 1952) (completed 2)
3—Hardin-Simmons (7) vs. Second Air Force (13) (Sun, 1943) (completed 1)
3—Catholic (20) vs. Mississippi (19) (Orange, 1936) (completed 1)

**Fewest Pass Attempts, Both Teams**
9—Fordham (2) [4] & Missouri (0) [5] (Sugar, 1942)
13—Colorado (27) [9] & Clemson (21) [4] (Orange, 1957)
14—Texas (16) [8] & Tennessee (0) [6] (Cotton, 1953)
15—Louisiana St. (7) [11] & Clemson (0) [4] (Sugar, 1959)
15—Utah (26) [4] & New Mexico (0) [11] (Sun, 1939)

**Fewest Pass Completions (followed by comp.-att.-int.)**
0—Army (28) vs. Alabama (29) (John Hancock Sun, 1988) (0-6-1)
0—Missouri (35) vs. Alabama (10) (Gator, 1968) (0-6-2)
0 (D)—Missouri (14) vs. Georgia Tech (10) (Bluebonnet, 1962) (0-7-2)
0 (D)—New Mexico (28) vs. Western Mich. (12) (Aviation, 1961) (0-4-0)
0—Utah St. (13) vs. New Mexico St. (20) (Sun, 1960) (0-4-0)
0—Georgia Tech (7) vs. Pittsburgh (0) (Sugar, 1956) (0-3-1)
0—Arkansas (0) vs. Louisiana St. (0) (Cotton, 1947) (0-4-1)
0—Rice (8) vs. Tennessee (0) (Orange, 1947) (0-6-2)
0—Miami (Fla.) (13) vs. Holy Cross (6) (Orange, 1946) (0-10-3)
0—Fordham (2) vs. Missouri (0) (Sugar, 1942) (0-4-0)
0—Arizona St. (0) vs. Catholic (0) (Sun, 1940) (0-7-2)
0—Tulane (13) vs. Texas A&M (14) (Sugar, 1940) (0-4-0)
0—West Va. (7) vs. Texas Tech (6) (Sun, 1938) (0-7-0)

**Fewest Pass Completions, Both Teams**
3—Arizona St. (0) [0] & Catholic (0) [3] (Sun, 1940)
4—Penn St. (7) [2] & Alabama (0) [2] (Liberty, 1959)
5—Oklahoma (14) [3] & Michigan (6) [2] (Orange, 1976)
5—Kentucky (21) [2] & North Caro. (0) [3] (Peach, 1976)
5—Tennessee (0) [3] & Texas (16) [2] (Cotton, 1953)
5—Louisiana St. (0) [5] & Arkansas (0) [0] (Cotton, 1947)
5—Wake Forest (26) [1] & South Caro. (14) [4] (Gator, 1946)
5—Utah (26) [1] & New Mexico (0) [4] (Sun, 1939)

**Fewest Passing Yards (followed by comp.-att.-int.)**
-50—U. of Mexico (0) vs. Southwestern (Tex.) (35) (Sun, 1945) (2-9-3)
-17—Rice (8) vs. Tennessee (0) (Orange, 1947) (0-6-2)
-2—Oklahoma (40) vs. Houston (14) (Sun, 1981) (1-5-1)
0—Army (28) vs. Alabama (29) (John Hancock Sun, 1988) (0-6-1)
0—Missouri (35) vs. Alabama (10) (Gator, 1968) (0-6-2)
0 (D)—Missouri (14) vs. Georgia Tech (10) (Bluebonnet, 1962) (0-7-2)
0 (D)—New Mexico (28) vs. Western Mich. (12) (Aviation, 1961) (0-4-0)
0—Georgia Tech (7) vs. Pittsburgh (0) (Sugar, 1956) (0-3-1)
0—Arkansas (0) vs. Louisiana St. (0) (Cotton, 1947) (0-4-1)
0—Miami (Fla.) (13) vs. Holy Cross (6) (Orange, 1946) (0-10-3)
0—Fordham (2) vs. Missouri (0) (Sugar, 1942) (0-4-0)
0—Arizona St. (0) vs. Catholic (0) (Sun, 1940) (0-7-2)
0—West Va. (7) vs. Texas Tech (6) (Sun, 1938) (0-7-0)
0—California (0) vs. Wash. & Jeff. (0) (Rose, 1922)
0—Oregon (6) vs. Harvard (7) (Rose, 1920)

**Fewest Passing Yards, Both Teams**
15—Rice (8) [-17] & Tennessee (0) [32] (Orange, 1947)
16—Louisiana St. (0) [16] & Arkansas (0) [0] (Cotton, 1947)
16—Arizona St. (0) [0] & Catholic (0) [16] (Sun, 1940)
21—Fordham (2) [0] & Missouri (0) [21] (Sugar, 1942)
52—Colorado (27) [25] & Clemson (21) [27] (Orange, 1957)
59—Miami (Fla.) (13) [0] & Holy Cross (6) [59] (Orange, 1946)
68—Missouri (35) [0] & Alabama (10) [68] (Gator, 1968)
68—Penn St. (7) [41] & Alabama (0) [27] (Liberty, 1959)
74—Oklahoma (41) [23] & Wyoming (7) [51] (Fiesta, 1976)
75—New Mexico (0) [10] & Southwestern (Tex.) (7) [65] (Sun, 1944)
77—Utah (26) [18] & New Mexico (0) [59] (Sun, 1939)
78—Tennessee (0) [46] & Texas (16) [32] (Cotton, 1953)

**Lowest Completion Percentage (followed by comp.-att.-int.)**
.000—Army (28) vs. Alabama (29) (John Hancock Sun, 1988) (0-6-1)
.000—Missouri (35) vs. Alabama (10) (Gator, 1968) (0-6-2)
.000 (D)—Missouri (14) vs. Georgia Tech (10) (Bluebonnet, 1962) (0-7-2)
.000 (D)—New Mexico (28) vs. Western Mich. (12) (Aviation, 1961) (0-4-0)
.000—Utah St. (13) vs. New Mexico St. (20) (Sun, 1960) (0-4-0)

.000—Georgia Tech (7) vs. Pittsburgh (0) (Sugar, 1956) (0-3-1)
.000—Arkansas (0) vs. Louisiana St. (0) (Cotton, 1947) (0-4-1)
.000—Rice (8) vs. Tennessee (0) (Orange, 1947) (0-6-2)
.000—Miami (Fla.) (13) vs. Holy Cross (6) (Orange, 1946) (0-10-3)
.000—Fordham (2) vs. Missouri (0) (Sugar, 1942) (0-4-0)
.000—Arizona St. (0) vs. Catholic (0) (Sun, 1940) (0-7-2)
.000—Tulane (13) vs. Texas A&M (14) (Sugar, 1940) (0-4-0)
.000—West Va. (7) vs. Texas Tech (6) (Sun, 1938) (0-7-0)

**Fewest Yards Per Pass Attempt**
-5.6—U. of Mexico (0) vs. Southwestern (Tex.) (35) (Sun, 1945) (9 for -50 yards)
-2.8—Rice (8) vs. Tennessee (0) (Orange, 1947) (6 for -17 yards)
-0.4—Oklahoma (40) vs. Houston (14) (Sun, 1981) (5 for -2 yards)
0.0—Army (28) vs. Alabama (29) (John Hancock Sun, 1988) (6 for 0 yards)
0.0—Missouri (35) vs. Alabama (10) (Gator, 1968) (6 for 0 yards)

0.0 (D)—Missouri (14) vs. Georgia Tech (10) (Bluebonnet, 1962) (7 for 0 yards)
0.0 (D)—New Mexico (28) vs. Western Mich. (12) (Aviation, 1961) (4 for 0 yards)
0.0—Utah St. (13) vs. New Mexico St. (20) (Sun, 1960) (4 for 0 yards)
0.0—Georgia Tech (7) vs. Pittsburgh (0) (Sugar, 1956) (3 for 0 yards)
0.0—Arkansas (0) vs. Louisiana St. (0) (Cotton, 1947) (4 for 0 yards)

0.0—Miami (Fla.) (13) vs. Holy Cross (6) (Orange, 1946) (10 for 0 yards)
0.0—Fordham (2) vs. Missouri (0) (Sugar, 1942) (4 for 0 yards)
0.0—Arizona St. (0) vs. Catholic (0) (Sun, 1940) (7 for 0 yards)
0.0—Tulane (13) vs. Texas A&M (14) (Sugar, 1940) (4 for 0 yards)
0.0—West Va. (7) vs. Texas Tech (6) (Sun, 1938) (7 for 0 yards)

**Fewest Yards Per Pass Completion (Min. 1 completion)**
-25.0—U. of Mexico (0) vs. Southwestern (Tex.) (35) (Sun, 1945) (2 for -50 yards)
-2.0—Oklahoma (40) vs. Houston (14) (Sun, 1981) (1 for -2 yards)
3.0—West Va. (14) vs. South Caro. (3) (Peach, 1969) (1 for 3 yards)
3.2—Louisiana St. (0) vs. Arkansas (0) (Cotton, 1947) (5 for 16 yards)
3.3—New Mexico (0) vs. Southwestern (Tex.) (7) (Sun, 1944) (3 for 10 yards)

4.5—Alabama (34) vs. Miami (Fla.) (13) (Sugar, 1993) (4 for 18 yards)
4.6—Texas (14) vs. Georgia Tech (7) (Cotton, 1943) (5 for 23 yards)
4.8—UTEP (33) vs. Georgetown (20) (Sun, 1950) (5 for 24 yards)
5.3—Case Reserve (26) vs. Arizona St. (13) (Sun, 1941) (3 for 16 yards)
5.3—Arkansas (3) vs. UCLA (17) (Cotton, 1989) (4 for 21 yards)

# SCORING

**Most Touchdowns**
9—Texas A&M (65) vs. Brigham Young (14) (Holiday, 1990) (5 rush, 4 pass)
9—Alabama (61) vs. Syracuse (6) (Orange, 1953) (4 rush, 3 pass, 1 punt return, 1 interception return)
9 (D)—Centre (63) vs. Texas Christian (7) (Fort Worth Classic, 1921) (8 rush, 1 blocked punt recovery in end zone)
8—Oklahoma St. (62) vs. Wyoming (14) (Holiday, 1988) (6 rush, 2 pass)
8—Toledo (56) vs. Davidson (33) (Tangerine, 1969) (4 rush, 3 pass, 1 fumble return)

7—Oklahoma (48) vs. Virginia (14) (Gator, 1991) (4 rush, 2 pass, 1 blocked punt return)
7 (D)—Texas Tech (49) vs. Duke (21) (All-American, 1989) (6 rush, 1 pass)
7 (D)—Fresno St. (51) vs. Bowling Green (7) (California, 1985) (4 rush, 3 pass)
7—Iowa (55) vs. Texas (17) (Freedom, 1984) (1 rush, 6 pass)
7 (D)—Houston (47) vs. Tulane (7) (Bluebonnet, 1973) (7 rush)

7—Arizona St. (49) vs. Missouri (35) (Fiesta, 1972) (5 rush, 2 pass)
7—North Caro. St. (49) vs. West Va. (13) (Peach, 1972) (4 rush, 3 pass)
7—Arizona St. (48) vs. North Caro. (26) (Peach, 1970) (6 rush, 1 pass)
7—Houston (49) vs. Miami (Ohio) (21) (Tangerine, 1962) (4 rush, 2 pass, 1 punt return)
7—Oklahoma (48) vs. Duke (21) (Orange, 1958) (3 rush, 2 pass, 1 pass interception return, 1 intercepted lateral return)

7—UTEP (47) vs. Florida St. (20) (Sun, 1955) (4 rush, 3 pass)
7—Michigan (49) vs. Southern Cal (0) (Rose, 1948) (3 rush, 4 pass)
7—Illinois (45) vs. UCLA (14) (Rose, 1947) (5 rush, 2 pass interception returns)

**Most Touchdowns, Both Teams**
13—Richmond (49) [7] & Ohio (42) [6] (Tangerine, 1968)
11—Washington (46) [6] & Iowa (34) [5] (Rose, 1991)
11—Texas A&M (65) [9] & Brigham Young (14) [2] (Holiday, 1990)
11—Penn St. (50) [6] & Brigham Young (39) [5] (Holiday, 1989)
11—Arizona St. (49) [7] & Missouri (35) [4] (Fiesta, 1971)

11—Arizona St. (48) [7] & North Caro. (26) [4] (Peach, 1970)
11—Southern Cal (42) [6] & Wisconsin (37) [5] (Rose, 1963)
10—East Caro. (37) [5] & North Caro. St. (34) [5] (Peach, 1992)
10 (D)—Texas Tech (49) [7] & Duke (21) [3] (All-American, 1989)
10—Mississippi (42) [6] & Air Force (29) [4] (Liberty, 1989)

10—Oklahoma St. (62) [8] & Wyoming (14) [2] (Holiday, 1988)
10—Boston College (45) [6] & Houston (28) [4] (Cotton, 1985)
10—Colorado (47) [6] & Alabama (33) [4] (Liberty, 1969)
10 (D)—Nebraska (36) [5] & Miami (Fla.) (34) [5] (Gotham, 1962)
10—UTEP (47) [7] & Florida St. (20) [3] (Sun, 1955)
10—Alabama (61) [9] & Syracuse (6) [1] (Orange, 1953)

**Most Touchdowns Rushing**
8 (D)—Centre (63) vs. Texas Christian (7) (Fort Worth Classic, 1921)
7 (D)—Houston (47) vs. Tulane (7) (Bluebonnet, 1973)
6 (D)—Texas Tech (49) vs. Duke (21) (All-American, 1989)
6—Oklahoma St. (62) vs. Wyoming (14) (Holiday, 1988)
6—Oklahoma (42) vs. Arkansas (8) (Orange, 1987)
6—Ohio St. (47) vs. Brigham Young (17) (Holiday, 1982)
6—Oklahoma St. (49) vs. Brigham Young (21) (Tangerine, 1976)
6—Arizona St. (48) vs. North Caro. (26) (Peach, 1970)
6—Michigan (49) vs. Stanford (0) (Rose, 1902)

**Most Touchdowns Rushing, Both Teams**
9—Arizona St. (48) [6] & North Caro. (26) [3] (Peach, 1970)
8—Oklahoma St. (62) [6] & Wyoming (14) [2] (Holiday, 1988)
8—Colorado (47) [5] & Alabama (33) [3] (Liberty, 1969)
7—Oklahoma (42) [6] & Arkansas (8) [1] (Orange, 1987)
7—Oklahoma St. (33) [4] & West Va. (33) [3] (John Hancock Sun, 1987)
7—UCLA (45) [5] & Iowa (28) [2] (Rose, 1986)
7—Oklahoma St. (49) [6] & Brigham Young (21) [1] (Tangerine, 1976)
7—Arizona St. (49) [5] & Missouri (35) [2] (Fiesta, 1972)
7—Penn St. (41) [5] & Oregon (12) [2] (Liberty, 1960)

**Most Touchdowns Passing**
6—Iowa (55) vs. Texas (17) (Freedom, 1984)
5—Florida St. (41) vs. Nebraska (17) (Fiesta, 1990)
5—Florida St. (36) vs. Oklahoma (19) (Gator, 1965)
4—East Caro. (37) vs. North Caro. St. (34) (Peach, 1992)
4—Miami (Fla.) (46) vs. Texas (3) (Cotton, 1991)
4—Michigan (35) vs. Mississippi (3) (Gator, 1991)
4—Texas A&M (65) vs. Brigham Young (14) (Holiday, 1990)
4—UCLA (45) vs. Illinois (9) (Rose, 1984)
4—Purdue (28) vs. Missouri (25) (Liberty, 1980)
4—Pittsburgh (34) vs. Clemson (3) (Gator, 1977)
4—Florida St. (40) vs. Texas Tech (17) (Tangerine, 1977)
4—Davidson (33) vs. Toledo (56) (Tangerine, 1969)
4—Richmond (49) vs. Ohio (42) (Tangerine, 1968)
4—Ohio (42) vs. Richmond (49) (Tangerine, 1968)
4—Southern Cal (42) vs. Wisconsin (37) (Rose, 1963)
4—Michigan (49) vs. Southern Cal (0) (Rose, 1948)
4—Georgia (40) vs. Texas Christian (26) (Orange, 1942)
4—Southern Cal (47) vs. Pittsburgh (14) (Rose, 1930)

**Most Touchdowns Passing, Both Teams**
8—Iowa (55) [6] & Texas (17) [2] (Freedom, 1984)
8—Richmond (49) [4] & Ohio (42) [4] (Tangerine, 1968)
7—East Caro. (37) [4] & North Caro. St. (34) [3] (Peach, 1992)
7—Davidson (33) [4] & Toledo (56) [3] (Tangerine, 1969)
7—Georgia (40) [4] & Texas Christian (26) [3] (Orange, 1942)
6—Miami (Fla.) (33) [3] & Alabama (25) [3] (Sugar, 1990)
6—Florida St. (41) [5] & Nebraska (17) [1] (Fiesta, 1990)
6—Texas A&M (65) [4] & Brigham Young (14) [2] (Holiday, 1990)
6—Florida St. (36) [5] & Oklahoma (19) [1] (Gator, 1965)
6—Southern Cal (42) [4] & Wisconsin (37) [2] (Rose, 1963)

**Most Field Goals Made**
5—Florida (28) vs. Notre Dame (39) (Sugar, 1992) (26, 24, 36, 37, 24 yards)
5—Maryland (23) vs. Tennessee (30) (Florida Citrus, 1983) (18, 48, 31, 22, 26 yards)
4—Oklahoma (25) vs. Penn St. (10) (Orange, 1986) (26, 31, 21, 22 yards)
4—North Caro. (26) vs. Texas (10) (Sun, 1982) (53, 47, 24, 42 yards)
4—Texas A&M (33) vs. Oklahoma St. (16) (Independence, 1981) (33, 32, 50, 18 yards)
4—West Va. (26) vs. Florida (6) (Peach, 1981) (35, 42, 49, 24 yards)
4—Missouri (19) vs. Southern Miss. (17) (Tangerine, 1981) (45, 41, 30, 28 yards)
4—Nebraska (45) vs. Georgia (6) (Sun, 1969) (50, 32, 42, 37 yards)
4—Alabama (12) vs. Mississippi (7) (Sugar, 1964) (46, 31, 34, 48 yards)

**Most Field Goals Made, Both Teams**
6—Notre Dame (39) [1] & Florida (28) [5] (Sugar, 1992)
6—Syracuse (16) [3] & Auburn (16) [3] (Sugar, 1988)
6—Maryland (23) [5] & Tennessee (30) [1] (Florida Citrus, 1983)
5—Penn St. (50) [3] & Brigham Young (39) [2] (Holiday, 1989)
5—Oklahoma (25) [4] & Penn St. (10) [1] (Orange, 1986)
5—North Caro. (26) [4] & Texas (10) [1] (Sun, 1982)
5—Texas A&M (33) [4] & Oklahoma St. (16) [1] (Independence, 1981)
5—Missouri (19) [4] & Southern Miss. (17) [1] (Tangerine, 1981)
5—Penn St. (9) [3] & Tulane (6) [2] (Liberty, 1979)
5—Penn St. (30) [3] & Texas (6) [2] (Cotton, 1972)

**Most Points, Winning Team**
65—Texas A&M vs. Brigham Young (14) (Holiday, 1990)
62—Oklahoma St. vs. Wyoming (14) (Holiday, 1988)
61—Alabama vs. Syracuse (6) (Orange, 1953)
56—Toledo vs. Davidson (33) (Tangerine, 1969)
55—Iowa vs. Texas (17) (Freedom, 1984)

51 (D)—Fresno St. vs. Bowling Green (7) (California, 1985)
50—Penn St. vs. Brigham Young (39) (Holiday, 1989)
49 (D)—Texas Tech vs. Duke (21) (All-American, 1989)
49—Oklahoma St. vs. Brigham Young (21) (Tangerine, 1976)
49—North Caro. St. vs. West Va. (13) (Peach, 1972)
49—Arizona St. vs. Missouri (35) (Fiesta, 1972)
49—Richmond vs. Ohio (42) (Tangerine, 1968)
49—Michigan vs. Southern Cal (0) (Rose, 1948)

**Most Points, Losing Team**
45—Southern Methodist vs. Brigham Young (46) (Holiday, 1980)
42—Ohio vs. Richmond (49) (Tangerine, 1968)
39—Brigham Young vs. Penn St. (50) (Holiday, 1989)
38—San Diego St. vs. Iowa (39) (Holiday, 1986)
38—Florida St. vs. Arizona St. (45) (Fiesta, 1971)

37—Miami (Fla.) vs. UCLA (39) (Fiesta, 1985)
37—Brigham Young vs. Indiana (38) (Holiday, 1979)
37—Wisconsin vs. Southern Cal (42) (Rose, 1963)
36—Washington St. vs. Brigham Young (38) (Holiday, 1981)
35—Oregon vs. Wake Forest (39) (Independence, 1992)
35—Missouri vs. Arizona St. (49) (Fiesta, 1972)
34—Nevada vs. Bowling Green (35) (Las Vegas, 1992)
34—North Caro. St. vs. East Caro. (37) (Peach, 1992)
34—Iowa vs. Washington (46) (Rose, 1991)
34—Houston vs. Notre Dame (35) (Cotton, 1979)

34 (D)—Miami (Fla.) vs. Nebraska (36) (Gotham, 1962)

**Most Points, Both Teams**
91—Brigham Young (46) & Southern Methodist (45) (Holiday, 1980)
91—Richmond (49) & Ohio (42) (Tangerine, 1968)
89—Penn St. (50) & Brigham Young (39) (Holiday, 1989)
89—Toledo (56) & Davidson (33) (Tangerine, 1969)
84—Arizona St. (49) & Missouri (35) (Fiesta, 1972)

83—Arizona St. (45) & Florida St. (38) (Fiesta, 1971)
80—Washington (46) & Iowa (34) (Rose, 1991)
80—Colorado (47) & Alabama (33) (Liberty, 1969)
79—Texas A&M (65) & Brigham Young (14) (Holiday, 1990)
79—Southern Cal (42) & Wisconsin (37) (Rose, 1963)

77—Iowa (39) & San Diego St. (38) (Holiday, 1986)
76—Oklahoma St. (62) & Wyoming (14) (Holiday, 1988)
76—UCLA (39) & Miami (Fla.) (37) (Fiesta, 1985)
75—Indiana (38) & Brigham Young (37) (Holiday, 1979)
75—Houston (47) & Miami (Ohio) (28) (Tangerine, 1962)

**Largest Margin of Victory**
55—Alabama (61) vs. Syracuse (6) (Orange, 1953)
51—Texas A&M (65) vs. Brigham Young (14) (Holiday, 1990)
48—Oklahoma St. (62) vs. Wyoming (14) (Holiday, 1988)
44 (D)—Fresno St. (51) vs. Bowling Green (7) (California, 1985)
43—Miami (Fla. ) (46) vs. Texas (3) (Cotton, 1991)

42—Texas (42) vs. Maryland (0) (Sun, 1978)
40 (D)—Houston (47) vs. Tulane (7) (Bluebonnet, 1973)
39—Nebraska (45) vs. Georgia (6) (Sun, 1969)
38—Iowa (55) vs. Texas (17) (Freedom, 1984)
36—North Caro. St. (49) vs. West Va. (13) (Peach, 1972)

35 (D)—Houston (35) vs. Navy (0) (Garden State, 1980)
35—North Caro. (35) vs. Air Force (0) (Gator, 1963)
35—Oklahoma (35) vs. Louisiana St. (0) (Sugar, 1950)
35—Southwestern (Tex.) (35) vs. U. of Mexico (0) (Sun, 1945)

**Fewest Points, Winning Team**
2—Fordham vs. Missouri (0) (Sugar, 1942)
3—Tennessee vs. Texas A&M (0) (Gator, 1957)
3—Texas Christian vs. Louisiana St. (2) (Sugar, 1936)
6—UCLA vs. Illinois (3) (John Hancock, 1991)
6—Oregon St. vs. Villanova (0) (Liberty, 1962)

6—Tulsa vs. Texas Tech (0) (Sun, 1942)
6—Clemson vs. Boston College (3) (Cotton, 1940)
6—Auburn vs. Michigan St. (0) (Orange, 1938)
6—Santa Clara vs. Louisiana St. (0) (Sugar, 1938)

**Fewest Points, Losing Team**
0—By many teams

**Fewest Points, Both Teams**
0—Texas Christian (0) & Air Force (0) (Cotton, 1959)
0—Arkansas (0) & Louisiana St. (0) (Cotton, 1947)
0—Arizona St. (0) & Catholic (0) (Sun, 1940)
0—California (0) & Wash. & Jeff. (0) (Rose, 1922)

**Most Points Scored in One Half**
45—Oklahoma St. (62) vs. Wyoming (14) (Holiday, 1988) (2nd half)
42—Toledo (56) vs. Davidson (33) (Tangerine, 1969) (1st half)
40—Alabama (61) vs. Syracuse (6) (Orange, 1953) (2nd half)
38—Penn St. (50) vs. Brigham Young (39) (Holiday, 1989) (2nd half)
38—Penn St. (41) vs. Baylor (20) (Cotton, 1975) (2nd half)
38—Mississippi (41) vs. Georgia Tech (18) (Peach, 1971) (1st half)
37—Texas A&M (65) vs. Brigham Young (14) (Holiday, 1990) (1st half)
35—Penn St. (42) vs. Tennessee (17) (Fiesta, 1992) (2nd half)
35—Southern Cal (42) vs. Ohio St. (17) (Rose, 1973) (2nd half)
35—North Caro. St. (49) vs. West Va. (13) (Peach, 1972) (2nd half)
35—Houston (49) vs. Miami (Ohio) (21) (Tangerine, 1962) (1st half)
34—Oklahoma (48) vs. Virginia (14) (Gator, 1991) (1st half)
34—Purdue (41) vs. Georgia Tech (21) (Peach, 1978) (1st half)
34—Oklahoma (48) vs. Duke (21) (Orange, 1958) (2nd half)
34—UTEP (47) vs. Florida St. (20) (Sun, 1955) (1st half)

**Most Points Scored in One Half, Both Teams**
64—Penn St. (50) [38] & Brigham Young (39) [26] (Holiday, 1989) (2nd half)
52—Oklahoma St. (62) [45] & Wyoming (14) [7] (Holiday, 1988) (2nd half)
51—Penn St. (41) [38] & Baylor (20) [13] (Cotton, 1975) (2nd half)
49—Brigham Young (46) [33] & Southern Methodist (45) [16] (Holiday, 1980) (2nd half)
49 (D)—Houston (31) [28] & North Caro. St. (31) [21] (Bluebonnet, 1974) (2nd half)
49—Arizona St. (49) [21] & Missouri (35) [28] (Fiesta, 1972) (2nd half)
49—Arizona St. (45) [21] & Florida St. (38) [28] (Fiesta, 1971) (1st half)
49—Toledo (56) [42] & Davidson (33) [7] (Tangerine, 1969) (1st half)
49—Richmond (49) [28] & Ohio (42) [21] (Tangerine, 1968) (1st half)
48—Oklahoma (48) [34] & Duke (21) [14] (Orange, 1958) (2nd half)
47—Arizona St. (48) [21] & North Caro. (26) [26] (Peach, 1970) (1st half)
45—Boston College (45) [31] & Houston (28) [14] (Cotton, 1985) (1st half)
45—Southern Cal (42) [35] & Ohio St. (17) [10] (Rose, 1973) (2nd half)

**Most Points Scored in One Quarter**
31—Iowa (55) vs. Texas (17) (Freedom, 1984) (3rd quarter)
30—Oklahoma (40) vs. Houston (14) (Sun, 1981) (4th quarter)
28—Oklahoma St. (62) vs. Wyoming (14) (Holiday, 1988) (3rd quarter)
28—Missouri (34) vs. Auburn (17) (Sun, 1973) (2nd quarter)
28—Mississippi (41) vs. Georgia Tech (18) (Peach, 1971) (2nd quarter)
28—Toledo (56) vs. Davidson (33) (Tangerine, 1969) (2nd quarter)
28—Houston (49) vs. Miami (Ohio) (21) (Tangerine, 1962) (2nd quarter)
27—Oklahoma (48) vs. Virginia (14) (Gator, 1991) (2nd quarter)
27—Brigham Young (46) vs. Southern Methodist (45) (Holiday, 1980) (4th quarter)
27—Oklahoma (48) vs. Duke (21) (Orange, 1958) (4th quarter)
27—UTEP (47) vs. Florida St. (20) (Sun, 1955) (2nd quarter)
27—Illinois (40) vs. Stanford (7) (Rose, 1952) (4th quarter)
26—North Caro. (26) vs. Arizona St. (48) (Peach, 1970) (2nd quarter)
25—Louisville (34) vs. Alabama (7) (Fiesta, 1991) (1st quarter)

**Most Points Scored in One Quarter, Both Teams**
40—Arizona St. (48) [14] & North Caro. (26) [26] (Peach, 1970) (2nd quarter)
38—Missouri (34) [28] & Auburn (17) [10] (Sun, 1973) (2nd quarter)
37—Oklahoma (40) [30] & Houston (14) [7] (Sun, 1981) (4th quarter)
35—Oklahoma St. (62) [28] & Wyoming (14) [7] (Holiday, 1988) (3rd quarter)
35—Oklahoma St. (49) [21] & Brigham Young (21) [14] (Tangerine, 1976) (2nd quarter)
35 (D)—Houston (31) [21] & North Caro. St. (31) [14] (Bluebonnet, 1974) (4th quarter)
35—Arizona St. (49) [21] & Missouri (35) [14] (Fiesta, 1972) (4th quarter)
35—Richmond (49) [21] & Ohio (42) [14] (Tangerine, 1968) (2nd quarter)
34—Oklahoma (48) [27] & Virginia (14) [7] (Gator, 1991) (2nd quarter)
34—Penn St. (50) [21] & Brigham Young (39) [13] (Holiday, 1989) (4th quarter)
34—Brigham Young (46) [27] & Southern Methodist (45) [7] (Holiday, 1980) (4th quarter)
34—Penn St. (42) [18] & Arizona St. (30) [16] (Fiesta, 1977) (4th quarter)
34—Mississippi (41) [28] & Georgia Tech (18) [6] (Peach, 1971) (2nd quarter)
34—Oklahoma (48) [27] & Duke (21) [7] (Orange, 1958) (4th quarter)

# FIRST DOWNS

**Most First Downs**
36—Oklahoma (48) vs. Virginia (14) (Gator, 1991) (16 rush, 18 pass, 2 penalty)
35—Michigan (35) vs. Mississippi (3) (Gator, 1991) (20 rush, 14 pass, 1 penalty)
35—Brigham Young (39) vs. Penn St. (50) (Holiday, 1989) (8 rush, 27 pass, 0 penalty)
34—Oklahoma St. (62) vs. Wyoming (14) (Holiday, 1988) (15 rush, 17 pass, 2 penalty)
34 (D)—Miami (Fla.) (34) vs. Nebraska (36) (Gotham, 1962)
33—Arizona St. (49) vs. Missouri (35) (Fiesta, 1972) (22 rush, 11 pass, 0 penalty)
32—Brigham Young (24) vs. Michigan (17) (Holiday, 1984)
32—Richmond (49) vs. Ohio (42) (Tangerine, 1968) (8 rush, 24 pass, 0 penalty)
32—Wisconsin (37) vs. Southern Cal (42) (Rose, 1963) (7 rush, 23 pass, 2 penalty)
31—Arkansas (27) vs. Tennessee (31) (Cotton, 1990) (21 rush, 10 pass, 0 penalty)
31—Florida St. (34) vs. Oklahoma St. (23) (Gator, 1985) (10 rush, 21 pass, 0 penalty)
31—Brigham Young (37) vs. Indiana (38) (Holiday, 1979) (9 rush, 21 pass, 1 penalty)
31 (D)—Purdue (27) vs. Tennessee (22) (Bluebonnet, 1979)
31 (D)—Houston (26) vs. Dayton (21) (Salad, 1952) (25 rush, 6 pass, 0 penalty)

**Most First Downs, Both Teams**
61—Penn St. (50) [26] & Brigham Young (39) [35] (Holiday, 1989)
56—Mississippi (42) [30] & Air Force (29) [26] (Liberty, 1989)
55—Michigan (35) [35] & Mississippi (3) [20] (Gator, 1991)
54—UCLA (45) [29] & Iowa (28) [25] (Rose, 1986)
54—Florida St. (34) [31] & Oklahoma St. (23) [23] (Gator, 1985)
53—Tennessee (23) [28] & Virginia (22) [25] (Sugar, 1991)
53—Colorado (47) [29] & Alabama (33) [24] (Liberty, 1969)
52—Notre Dame (39) [23] & Florida (28) [29] (Sugar, 1991)
52—Indiana (38) [21] & Brigham Young (37) [31] (Holiday, 1979)
51 (D)—Arkansas (28) [28] & Florida (24) [23] (Bluebonnet, 1982)
50 (D)—Toledo (27) [21] & San Jose St. (25) [29] (California, 1981)
50—Texas (21) [25] & Notre Dame (17) [25] (Cotton, 1970)

**Most First Downs Rushing**
26—Oklahoma (40) vs. Auburn (22) (Sugar, 1972)
25 (D)—Houston (26) vs. Dayton (21) (Salad, 1952)
24—Colorado (47) vs. Alabama (33) (Liberty, 1969)
23—Georgia Tech (31) vs. Texas Tech (21) (Gator, 1965)
22 (D)—Arkansas (28) vs. Florida (24) (Bluebonnet, 1982)
22—Oklahoma (41) vs. Wyoming (7) (Fiesta, 1976)
22—Arizona St. (49) vs. Missouri (35) (Fiesta, 1972)
21—Arkansas (27) vs. Tennessee (31) (Cotton, 1990)
21—Florida St. (7) vs. Oklahoma (24) (Orange, 1980)
21 (D)—Houston (35) vs. Navy (0) (Garden State, 1980)
21—Mississippi St. (26) vs. North Caro. (24) (Sun, 1974)
21—Missouri (35) vs. Alabama (10) (Gator, 1968)

**Most First Downs Rushing, Both Teams**
36—Miami (Fla.) (46) [16] & Texas (3) [20] (Cotton, 1991)
36—Colorado (47) [24] & Alabama (33) [12] (Liberty, 1969)
32—Oklahoma (41) [22] & Wyoming (7) [10] (Fiesta, 1976)
32—Arizona St. (49) [22] & Missouri (35) [10] (Fiesta, 1972)
32—Texas (21) [19] & Notre Dame (17) [13] (Cotton, 1970)
32—Arkansas (27) [21] & Tennessee (31) [11] (Cotton, 1990)
31—Air Force (38) [18] & Mississippi St. (15) [13] (Liberty, 1991)

## Most First Downs Passing
27—Brigham Young (39) vs. Penn St. (50) (Holiday, 1989)
24—Richmond (49) vs. Ohio (42) (Tangerine, 1968)
23 (D)—San Jose St. (25) vs. Toledo (27) (California, 1981)
23—Wisconsin (37) vs. Southern Cal (42) (Rose, 1963)
21 (D)—Fresno St. (29) vs. Bowling Green (28) (California, 1982)

21—Brigham Young (46) vs. Southern Methodist (45) (Holiday, 1980)
21—Brigham Young (37) vs. Indiana (38) (Holiday, 1979)
20—Mississippi (20) vs. Texas Tech (17) (Independence, 1986)
20—Brigham Young (24) vs. Michigan (17) (Holiday, 1984)
20 (D)—Vanderbilt (28) vs. Air Force (36) (Hall of Fame, 1982)

19—Oregon (31) vs. Colorado St. (32) (Freedom, 1990)
19—Florida St. (31) vs. Nebraska (28) (Fiesta, 1988)
19—Florida St. (34) vs. Oklahoma (23) (Gator, 1985)
19—Illinois (29) vs. Army (31) (Peach, 1985)

## Most First Downs Passing, Both Teams
30 (D)—Fresno St. (29) [21] & Bowling Green (28) [9] (California, 1982)
30—Richmond (49) [24] & Ohio (42) [6] (Tangerine, 1968)
29—Mississippi (42) [17] & Air Force (29) [12] (Liberty, 1989)
29—Indiana (38) [8] & Brigham Young (37) [21] (Holiday, 1979)
28—Pittsburgh (23) [16] & Ohio St. (28) [12] (Fiesta, 1984)

27—Florida St. (38) [14] & Arizona St. (45) [13] (Fiesta, 1971)
26—Brigham Young (24) [20] & Michigan (17) [6] (Holiday, 1984)
26—Washington (21) [15] & Maryland (20) [11] (Aloha, 1982)
26 (D)—Air Force (36) [6] & Vanderbilt (28) [20] (Hall of Fame, 1982)
25—Oklahoma St. (62) [17] & Wyoming (14) [8] (Holiday, 1988)

25—Florida St. (31) [19] & Nebraska (28) [6] (Fiesta, 1988)
25—Miami (Fla.) (31) [15] & Nebraska (30) [10] (Orange, 1984)
25—Brigham Young (46) [21] & Southern Methodist (45) [4] (Holiday, 1980)

## Most First Downs by Penalty
6—Texas (3) vs. Miami (Fla.) (46) (Cotton, 1991)
5—West Va. (21) vs. Notre Dame (34) (Fiesta, 1989)
5—Washington (34) vs. Florida (7) (Freedom, 1989)
5 (D)—Western Mich. (30) vs. Fresno St. (35) (California, 1988)
5—Miami (Fla.) (7) vs. Tennessee (35) (Sugar, 1986)

5 (D)—Miami (Ohio) (7) vs. San Jose St. (37) (California, 1986)
4—Alabama (25) vs. Miami (Fla.) (33) (Sugar, 1990)
4—Brigham Young (14) vs. Texas A&M (65) (Holiday, 1990)
4—Georgia (10) vs. Texas (9) (Cotton, 1984)
4—Iowa (55) vs. Texas (17) (Freedom, 1984)

4 (D)—Vanderbilt (28) vs. Air Force (36) (Hall of Fame, 1982)
4—Maryland (20) vs. Florida (35) (Tangerine, 1980)
4—Baylor (20) vs. Penn St. (41) (Cotton, 1975)
4—Arkansas (13) vs. Tennessee (14) (Liberty, 1971)
4—Arizona St. (45) vs. Florida St. (38) (Fiesta, 1971)

4—Alabama (33) vs. Colorado (47) (Liberty, 1969)
4—Texas A&M (21) vs. Alabama (29) (Cotton, 1942)

## Most First Downs by Penalty, Both Teams
8—Miami (Fla.) (46) [2] & Texas (3) [6] (Cotton, 1991)
7—Washington (34) [5] & Florida (7) [2] (Freedom, 1989)
7—Tennessee (35) [2] & Miami (Fla.) (7) [5] (Sugar, 1986)
6—Miami (Fla.) (33) [2] & Alabama (25) [4] (Sugar, 1990)
5—Texas A&M (65) [1] & Brigham Young (14) [4] (Holiday, 1990)

5—West Va. (21) [5] & Notre Dame (34) [0] (Fiesta, 1989)
5—Georgia (10) [4] & Texas (9) [1] (Cotton, 1984)
5—Southern Methodist (7) [3] & Pittsburgh (3) [2] (Cotton, 1983)
5—Pittsburgh (16) [3] & Arizona (10) [2] (Fiesta, 1979)
5—Baylor (20) [4] & Penn St. (41) [1] (Cotton, 1975)

## Fewest First Downs
1—Arkansas (0) vs. Louisiana St. (0) (Cotton, 1947) (rushing)
1—Alabama (29) vs. Texas A&M (21) (Cotton, 1942) (passing)
2—Michigan St. (0) vs. Auburn (6) (Orange, 1938) (1 rushing, 1 passing)

## Fewest First Downs, Both Teams
10—Randolph Field (7) [7] & Texas (7) [3] (Cotton, 1944)
12—Texas A&M (14) [8] & Louisiana St. (19) [4] (Orange, 1944)

## Fewest First Downs Rushing
0—Florida (18) vs. Missouri (20) (Sugar, 1966)
0—Navy (6) vs. Texas (28) (Cotton, 1964)
0—Alabama (29) vs. Texas A&M (21) (Cotton, 1942)

### Fewest First Downs Rushing, Both Teams
3—Texas A&M (21) [3] & Alabama (29) [0] (Cotton, 1942)
9—Florida St. (41) [2] & Nebraska (17) [7] (Fiesta, 1990)
9—Texas (28) [9] & Navy (6) [0] (Cotton, 1964)

### Fewest First Downs Passing
0—Army (28) vs. Alabama (29) (John Hancock Sun, 1988)
0—Oklahoma (40) vs. Houston (10) (Sun, 1981)
0—West Va. (14) vs. South Caro. (3) (Peach, 1969)
0—Missouri (35) vs. Alabama (10) (Gator, 1968)
0—Virginia Tech (7) vs. Miami (Fla.) (14) (Liberty, 1966)

0—Auburn (7) vs. Mississippi (13) (Liberty, 1965)
0—Alabama (10) vs. Arkansas (3) (Sugar, 1962)
0 (D)—Missouri (14) vs. Georgia Tech (10) (Bluebonnet, 1962)
0—Utah St. (13) vs. New Mexico St. (20) (Sun, 1960)
0—Arkansas (0) vs. Louisiana St. (0) (Cotton, 1947)

0—Fordham (2) vs. Missouri (0) (Sugar, 1942)
0—Arizona St. (0) vs. Catholic (0) (Sun, 1940)
0—West Va. (7) vs. Texas Tech (6) (Sun, 1938)

### Fewest First Downs Passing, Both Teams
1—Alabama (10) [0] & Arkansas (3) [1] (Sugar, 1962)
4—Oklahoma (41) [1] & Wyoming (7) [3] (Fiesta, 1976)
4—Texas (16) [2] & Tennessee (0) [2] (Cotton, 1953)
4—Rice (28) [3] & Colorado (14) [1] (Cotton, 1938)

# PUNTING

### Most Punts
17—Duke (3) vs. Southern Cal (7) (Rose, 1939)
16—Alabama (29) vs. Texas A&M (21) (Cotton, 1942)
16—New Mexico St. (14) vs. Hardin-Simmons (14) (Sun, 1936)
15—Tennessee (0) vs. Rice (8) (Orange, 1947)
14—Tulsa (7) vs. Tennessee (14) (Sugar, 1943)

14—Santa Clara (6) vs. Louisiana St. (0) (Sugar, 1938)
14—Louisiana St. (0) vs. Santa Clara (6) (Sugar, 1938)
14—Texas Christian (3) vs. Louisiana St. (2) (Sugar, 1936)
13—Rice (8) vs. Tennessee (0) (Orange, 1947)
13—Tennessee (0) vs. Southern Cal (25) (Rose, 1945)

13—Oklahoma (0) vs. Tennessee (17) (Orange, 1939)
13—Catholic (20) vs. Mississippi (19) (Orange, 1936)
13—Louisiana St. (2) vs. Texas Christian (3) (Sugar, 1936)
13—Miami (Fla.) (0) vs. Bucknell (26) (Orange, 1935)

### Most Punts, Both Teams
28—Rice (8) [13] & Tennessee (0) [15] (Orange, 1947)
28—Santa Clara (6) [14] & Louisiana St. (0) [14] (Sugar, 1938)
27—Texas Christian (3) [14] & Louisiana St. (2) [13] (Sugar, 1936)
25—Tennessee (17) [12] & Oklahoma (0) [13] (Orange, 1939)
24—Catholic (20) [13] & Mississippi (19) [11] (Orange, 1936)

23—UTEP (14) [12] & Mississippi (7) [11] (Sun, 1967)
22—Auburn (6) [10] & Michigan St. (0) [12] (Orange, 1938)

### Highest Punting Average (Min. 5 Punts)
53.9—Southern Cal (7) vs. Wisconsin (0) (Rose, 1953) (8 for 431 yards)
51.0—Penn St. (10) vs. Clemson (35) (Florida Citrus, 1988) (5 for 255 yards)
50.0—Mississippi St. (17) vs. Nebraska (31) (Sun, 1980) (5 for 250 yards)
49.2 (D)—Air Force (24) vs. Texas (16) (Bluebonnet, 1985) (11 for 541 yards)
49.2—Arkansas (3) vs. UCLA (17) (Cotton, 1989) (6 for 295 yards)

49.0—Indiana (24) vs. Baylor (0) (Copper, 1991) (6 for 294 yards)
49.0 (D)—Mississippi St. (10) vs. Kansas (0) (Hall of Fame, 1981) (9 for 441 yards)
48.0—Kansas (23) vs. Brigham Young (20) (Aloha, 1992) (8 for 384 yards)
47.9—Penn St. (42) vs. Tennessee (17) (Fiesta, 1992) (9 for 431 yards)
47.9—Oregon St. (20) vs. Duke (16) (Rose, 1942) (7 for 335 yards)

47.6—Oklahoma (42) vs. Arkansas (8) (Orange, 1987) (5 for 238 yards)
47.5—St. Mary's (Cal.) (20) vs. Texas Tech (13) (Cotton, 1939) (11 for 523 yards)
47.4—Georgia Tech (18) vs. Stanford (17) (Aloha, 1991) (7 for 332 yards)
47.4 (D)—Fresno St. (51) vs. Bowling Green (7) (California, 1985) (7 for 332 yards)
47.4 (D)—Tennessee (28) vs. Wisconsin (21) (Garden State, 1981) (5 for 237 yards)

### Fewest Punts
0—Oklahoma St. (62) vs. Wyoming (14) (Holiday, 1988)
0—Oklahoma (41) vs. Wyoming (7) (Fiesta, 1976)
1—Brigham Young (39) vs. Penn St. (50) (Holiday, 1989)
1—Nebraska (21) vs. Louisiana St. (20) (Orange, 1983)
1—North Caro. St. (31) vs. Kansas (18) (Liberty, 1973)

1—Utah (32) vs. West Va. (6) (Liberty, 1964)
1 (D)—Miami (Fla.) (34) vs. Nebraska (36) (Gotham, 1962)
1—Georgia Tech (42) vs. West Va. (19) (Sugar, 1954)
1—West Va. (19) vs. Georgia Tech (42) (Sugar, 1954)
1—Missouri (23) vs. Clemson (24) (Gator, 1949)

**Lowest Punting Average (Min. 3 Punts)**
17.0—Nevada (34) vs. Bowling Green (35) (Las Vegas, 1992) (4 for 68 yards)
19.0—Cincinnati (18) vs. Virginia Tech (6) (Sun, 1947) (6 for 114 yards)
22.0—Mississippi St. (16) vs. North Caro. St. (12) (Liberty, 1963) (3 for 66 yards)
23.0—Bowling Green (35) vs. Nevada (34) (Las Vegas, 1992) (5 for 115 yards)
25.5—Houston (34) vs. Notre Dame (35) (Cotton, 1979) (10 for 255 yards)

26.3—Oklahoma St. (34) vs. Texas Christian (0) (Cotton, 1945) (6 for 158 yards)
26.3—Notre Dame (35) vs. Houston (34) (Cotton, 1979) (7 for 184 yards)
26.3—Rice (28) vs. Alabama (6) (Cotton, 1954) (8 for 210 yards)

**Most Punts Blocked by One Team**
2—North Caro. St. (14) vs. Georgia (7) (Liberty, 1967)

# PUNT RETURNS

**Most Punt Returns**
9—Georgia (7) vs. North Caro. (3) (Gator, 1971) (6.8 average)
8—Tennessee (34) vs. Air Force (13) (Sugar, 1971) (10.8 average)
8—Mississippi (7) vs. UTEP (14) (Sun, 1967) (9.4 average)
8—Michigan (34) vs. Oregon St. (7) (Rose, 1965) (10.6 average)
7—Louisville (34) vs. Alabama (7) (Fiesta, 1991) (7.3 average)

6—Tennessee (17) vs. Penn St. (42) (Fiesta, 1992) (8.2 average)
6—Clemson (30) vs. Illinois (0) (Hall of Fame, 1991)
6 (D)—San Jose St. (48) vs. Central Mich. (24) (California, 1990)
6—Brigham Young (7) vs. Ohio St. (10) (Florida Citrus, 1985)
6—Texas (9) vs. Georgia (10) (Cotton, 1984) (2.5 average)

6—Washington (21) vs. Maryland (20) (Aloha, 1982) (4.7 average)
6 (D)—Vanderbilt (28) vs. Air Force (36) (Hall of Fame, 1982)
6—Washington St. (36) vs. Brigham Young (38) (Holiday, 1981)
6—Nebraska (38) vs. Alabama (6) (Orange, 1972) (22.7 average)
6—Miami (Fla.) (14) vs. Syracuse (15) (Liberty, 1961) (13.0 average)

6—Air Force (0) vs. Texas Christian (0) (Cotton, 1959) (5.8 average)
6—Tulane (13) vs. Texas A&M (14) (Sugar, 1940) (21.0 average)
6—Tulane (20) vs. Temple (14) (Sugar, 1935)
6—Tulane (12) vs. Southern Cal (21) (Rose, 1932)

**Most Punt Return Yards**
136—Nebraska (38) vs. Alabama (6) (Orange, 1972) (6 returns)
128—Oklahoma (48) vs. Duke (21) (Orange, 1958)
126—Tulane (13) vs. Texas A&M (14) (Sugar, 1940) (6 returns)
124—California (37) vs. Clemson (13) (Florida Citrus, 1992) (5 returns)
124—Washington (44) vs. Wisconsin (8) (Rose, 1960) (4 returns)

108—Southern Miss. (38) vs. UTEP (18) (Independence, 1988) (2 returns)
107—Arizona St. (45) vs. Florida St. (38) (Fiesta, 1971) (5 returns)
104—Texas A&M (21) vs. Alabama (29) (Cotton, 1942) (5 returns)
99—Kent (18) vs. Tampa (21) (Tangerine, 1972) (3 returns)
98—Brigham Young (46) vs. Southern Methodist (45) (Holiday, 1980) (3 returns)

94—Denver (24) vs. New Mexico (34) (Sun, 1946)
93—Auburn (35) vs. Mississippi (28) (Gator, 1971) (4 returns)
92—Southern Cal (7) vs. Ohio St. (20) (Rose, 1955) (2 returns)
89—Nebraska (28) vs. Florida St. (31) (Fiesta, 1988) (3 returns)
88—Penn St. (42) vs. Arizona St. (30) (Fiesta, 1977) (2 returns)

**Highest Punt Return Average (Min. 3 Returns)**
33.0—Kent (18) vs. Tampa (21) (Tangerine, 1972) (3 for 99 yards)
32.7—Brigham Young (46) vs. Southern Methodist (45) (Holiday, 1980) (3 for 98 yards)
31.0—Washington (44) vs. Wisconsin (8) (Rose, 1960) (4 for 124 yards)
29.7—Nebraska (28) vs. Florida St. (31) (Fiesta, 1988) (3 for 89 yards)
24.8—California (37) vs. Clemson (13) (Florida Citrus, 1992) (5 for 124 yards)

24.0—Auburn (31) vs. Ohio St. (14) (Hall of Fame, 1990) (3 for 72 yards)
23.3—Auburn (35) vs. Mississippi (28) (Gator, 1971) (4 for 93 yards)
22.7—Nebraska (38) vs. Alabama (6) (Orange, 1972) (6 for 136 yards)
21.4—Arizona St. (45) vs. Florida St. (38) (Fiesta, 1971) (5 for 107 yards)
21.0—Arkansas (6) vs. Duke (7) (Cotton, 1961) (3 for 63 yards)

21.0—Tulane (13) vs. Texas A&M (14) (Sugar, 1940) (6 for 126 yards)
20.8—Texas A&M (21) vs. Alabama (29) (Cotton, 1942) (5 for 104 yards)
19.5 (D)—Georgia (20) vs. Texas A&M (40) (Presidential Cup, 1950) (4 for 78 yards)
19.3—Nebraska (14) vs. Houston (17) (Cotton, 1980) (3 for 58 yards)

# KICKOFF RETURNS

## Most Kickoff Returns
10—Wyoming (14) vs. Oklahoma St. (62) (Holiday, 1988) (20.5 average)
9—Brigham Young (14) vs. Texas A&M (65) (Holiday, 1990) (18.2 average)
9—Colorado (47) vs. Alabama (33) (Liberty, 1969)
8—Nebraska (21) vs. Georgia Tech (45) (Florida Citrus, 1991) (23.6 average)
8—Notre Dame (10) vs. Texas A&M (35) (Cotton, 1988) (18.9 average)
8—Texas Tech (17) vs. Florida St. (40) (Tangerine, 1977)
8—UCLA (6) vs. Alabama (36) (Liberty, 1976) (17.6 average)
8—Brigham Young (21) vs. Oklahoma St. (49) (Tangerine, 1976)
8 (D)—Tulane (7) vs. Houston (47) (Bluebonnet, 1973) (28.1 average)
8—Missouri (35) vs. Arizona St. (49) (Fiesta, 1972) (32.3 average)
8—Arizona St. (45) vs. Florida St. (38) (Fiesta, 1971)
8—Florida St. (38) vs. Arizona St. (45) (Fiesta, 1971) (23.0 average)
8—Colorado (47) vs. Alabama (33) (Liberty, 1969) (27.8 average)
8—Ohio (42) vs. Richmond (49) (Tangerine, 1968)
8—Florida St. (20) vs. UTEP (47) (Sun, 1955)
8—UCLA (14) vs. Illinois (45) (Rose, 1947) (32.4 average)

## Most Kickoff Return Yards
259—UCLA (14) vs. Illinois (45) (Rose, 1947) (8 returns)
258—Missouri (35) vs. Arizona St. (49) (Fiesta, 1972) (8 returns)
225 (D)—Tulane (7) vs. Houston (47) (Bluebonnet, 1973) (8 returns)
222—Colorado (47) vs. Alabama (33) (Liberty, 1969) (8 returns)
205—Wyoming (14) vs. Oklahoma (62) (Holiday, 1988) (10 returns)
204—Brigham Young (21) vs. Oklahoma St. (49) (Tangerine, 1976) (8 returns)
191—Houston (22) vs. Washington St. (24) (Aloha, 1988) (5 returns)
189—Nebraska (21) vs. Georgia Tech (45) (Florida Citrus, 1991) (8 returns)
187—Houston (28) vs. Boston College (45) (Cotton, 1985) (7 returns)
184—Florida St. (38) vs. Arizona St. (45) (Fiesta, 1971) (8 returns)
174—Hawaii (13) vs. Michigan St. (33) (Aloha, 1989) (7 returns)
170—Tennessee (27) vs. Maryland (28) (John Hancock, 1984) (4 returns)
169—Oregon St. (19) vs. Iowa (35) (Rose, 1957) (5 returns)
164—Brigham Young (14) vs. Texas A&M (65) (Holiday, 1990) (9 returns)

## Highest Kickoff Return Average (Min. 3 Returns)
42.5—Tennessee (27) vs. Maryland (28) (John Hancock, 1984) (4 for 170 yards)
38.3—Ohio St. (28) vs. Pittsburgh (23) (Fiesta, 1984) (4 for 153 yards)
38.2—Houston (22) vs. Washington St. (24) (Aloha, 1988) (5 for 191 yards)
37.5—Notre Dame (24) vs. Alabama (23) (Sugar, 1973) (4 for 150 yards)
36.8—Ohio St. (17) vs. Syracuse (24) (Hall of Fame, 1992) (4 for 147 yards)
33.8—Oregon St. (19) vs. Iowa (35) (Rose, 1957) (5 for 169 yards)
32.8—Florida St. (40) vs. Texas Tech (17) (Tangerine, 1977) (4 for 131 yards)
32.4—UCLA (14) vs. Illinois (45) (Rose, 1947) (8 for 259 yards)
32.3—Missouri (35) vs. Arizona St. (49) (Fiesta, 1972) (8 for 258 yards)
31.7—Penn St. (41) vs. Baylor (20) (Cotton, 1975) (3 for 95 yards)
29.0—Mississippi St. (17) vs. Nebraska (31) (Sun, 1980) (4 for 116 yards)
27.0—Arizona St. (17) vs. Arkansas (18) (Holiday, 1985) (3 for 81 yards)
26.7—Houston (28) vs. Boston College (45) (Cotton, 1985) (7 for 187 yards)

# FUMBLES

## Most Fumbles
11—Mississippi (7) vs. Alabama (12) (Sugar, 1964) (lost 6)
9—Texas (11) vs. Notre Dame (24) (Cotton, 1971) (lost 5)
8—North Caro. St. (28) vs. Iowa (23) (Peach, 1988) (lost 5)
8 (D)—Houston (35) vs. Navy (0) (Garden State, 1980) (lost 3)
8—Louisville (14) vs. Louisiana Tech (24) (Independence, 1977) (lost 3)
8—North Texas (8) vs. New Mexico St. (28) (Sun, 1959) (lost 6)
8—Texas Christian (0) vs. Air Force (0) (Cotton, 1959) (lost 3)
8—Colorado (27) vs. Clemson (21) (Orange, 1957) (lost 3)
7—Florida (7) vs. Washington (34) (Freedom, 1989) (lost 3)
7—Hawaii (13) vs. Michigan St. (33) (Aloha, 1989) (lost 4)
7 (D)—Toledo (27) vs. San Jose St. (25) (California, 1981) (lost 2)
7 (D)—Texas A&M (28) vs. Southern Cal (47) (Bluebonnet, 1977) (lost 5)
7—Auburn (27) vs. Texas (3) (Gator, 1974) (lost 5)
7—Tennessee (34) vs. Air Force (13) (Sugar, 1971) (lost 4)
7—Air Force (13) vs. Tennessee (34) (Sugar, 1971) (lost 3)
7—Georgia (2) vs. Arkansas (16) (Sugar, 1969) (lost 5)
7—Alabama (0) vs. Penn St. (7) (Liberty, 1959) (lost 4)
7—Southern Cal (7) vs. Ohio St. (20) (Rose, 1955) (lost 3)
7—Wash. & Lee (7) vs. Wyoming (20) (Gator, 1951) (lost 2)
7—Missouri (7) vs. Maryland (20) (Gator, 1950) (lost 5)

7 (D)—Georgia (20) vs. Texas A&M (40) (Presidential Cup, 1950)
7 (D)—Arizona St. (21) vs. Xavier (Ohio) (33) (Salad, 1950) (lost 6)

**Most Fumbles, Both Teams**
17—Mississippi (7) [11] & Alabama (12) [6] (Sugar, 1964) (lost 9)
14—Louisiana Tech (24) [6] & Louisville (14) [8] (Independence, 1977) (lost 6)
14—Tennessee (34) [7] & Air Force (13) [7] (Sugar, 1971) (lost 7)
13—Texas Christian (0) [8] & Air Force (0) [5] (Cotton, 1959) (lost 6)
12—North Caro. St. (28) [8] & Iowa (23) [4] (Peach, 1988) (lost 8)

12 (D)—Houston (35) [8] & Navy (0) [4] (Garden State, 1980) (lost 6)
12—North Texas (8) [8] & New Mexico St. (28) [4] (Sun, 1959) (lost 8)
11 (D)—Toledo (27) [7] & San Jose St. (25) [4] (California, 1981) (lost 3)
11—Oklahoma (41) [6] & Wyoming (7) [5] (Fiesta, 1976)
10—Alabama (30) [5] & Baylor (2) [5] (Cotton, 1981) (lost 5)

10 (D)—North Caro. St. (31) [5] & Houston (31) [5] (Bluebonnet, 1974) (lost 4)
10—Texas (11) [9] & Notre Dame (24) [1] (Cotton, 1971) (lost 6)
10—Illinois (17) [5] & Washington (7) [5] (Rose, 1964) (lost 6)
10—Rice (7) [5] & Navy (20) [5] (Cotton, 1958) (lost 8)
10—Mississippi (7) [5] & Florida (3) [5] (Gator, 1958) (lost 5)
10—Texas (16) [5] & Tennessee (0) [5] (Cotton, 1953) (lost 6)

**Most Fumbles Lost**
6—Texas A&M (2) vs. Florida St. (10) (Cotton, 1992) (6 fumbles)
6—East Caro. (31) vs. Maine (0) (Tangerine, 1965) (6 fumbles)
6—Mississippi (7) vs. Alabama (12) (Sugar, 1964) (11 fumbles)
6—North Texas (8) vs. New Mexico St. (28) (Sun, 1959) (8 fumbles)
6 (D)—Arizona St. (21) vs. Xavier (Ohio) (33) (Salad, 1950) (7 fumbles)
5—North Caro. St. (28) vs. Iowa (23) (Peach, 1988) (8 fumbles)
5—North Caro. (21) vs. Arizona (30) (Aloha, 1986) (5 fumbles)
5 (D)—Bowling Green (7) vs. Fresno St. (51) (California, 1985) (6 fumbles)
5 (D)—Georgia (22) vs. Stanford (25) (Bluebonnet, 1978) (6 fumbles)
5 (D)—Texas A&M (28) vs. Southern Cal (47) (Bluebonnet, 1977) (7 fumbles)
5—Auburn (27) vs. Texas (3) (Gator, 1974) (7 fumbles)
5—Texas (11) vs. Notre Dame (24) (Cotton, 1971) (9 fumbles)
5—Georgia (2) vs. Arkansas (16) (Sugar, 1969) (7 fumbles)
5 (D)—Utah St. (9) vs. Baylor (24) (Gotham, 1961) (5 fumbles)
5—Rice (7) vs. Navy (20) (Cotton, 1958) (5 fumbles)
5—Auburn (13) vs. Vanderbilt (25) (Gator, 1955) (5 fumbles)
5—Oklahoma (7) vs. Kentucky (13) (Sugar, 1951)
5—Missouri (7) vs. Maryland (20) (Gator, 1950) (7 fumbles)
5—Texas A&M (21) vs. Alabama (29) (Cotton, 1942) (6 fumbles)

**Most Fumbles Lost, Both Teams**
9—Mississippi (7) [6] & Alabama (12) [3] (Sugar, 1964) (17 fumbles)
8—North Caro. St. (28) [5] & Iowa (23) [3] (Peach, 1988) (12 fumbles)
8—North Texas (8) [6] & New Mexico St. (28) [2] (Sun, 1959) (12 fumbles)
8—Rice (7) [5] & Navy (20) [3] (Cotton, 1958) (10 fumbles)
7—Texas A&M (2) [6] & Florida St. (10) [1] (Cotton, 1992) (7 fumbles)
7—Florida (14) [4] & Texas A&M (37) [3] (Sun, 1977) (8 fumbles)
7—Pittsburgh (7) [4] & Arizona St. (28) [3] (Fiesta, 1973) (9 fumbles)
7—Tennessee (34) [4] & Air Force (13) [3] (Sugar, 1971) (14 fumbles)
7—Michigan St. (28) [4] & UCLA (20) [3] (Rose, 1954) (8 fumbles)

# PENALTIES

**Most Penalties**
20 (D)—Fresno St. (35) vs. Western Mich. (30) (California, 1988) (166 yards)
18—Washington St. (31) vs. Utah (28) (Copper, 1992) (136 yards)
17—Tennessee (17) vs. Oklahoma (0) (Orange, 1939) (157 yards)
16—Miami (Fla.) (46) vs. Texas (3) (Cotton, 1991) (202 yards)
16—Tulsa (16) vs. McNeese St. (20) (Independence, 1976) (100 yards)
15—Miami (Fla.) (7) vs. Tennessee (35) (Sugar, 1986) (120 yards)
15 (D)—Michigan (33) vs. UCLA (14) (Bluebonnet, 1981) (148 yards)
14 (D)—San Jose St. (37) vs. Miami (Ohio) (7) (California, 1986) (163 yards)
13—Florida St. (41) vs. Nebraska (17) (Fiesta, 1990) (135 yards)
13 (D)—San Jose St. (27) vs. Eastern Mich. (30) (California, 1987) (103 yards)
13—Washington (20) vs. Colorado (17) (Freedom, 1985) (88 yards)
13—Miami (Fla.) (31) vs. Nebraska (30) (Orange, 1984) (101 yards)
13—McNeese St. (20) vs. Tulsa (16) (Independence, 1976) (105 yards)
13—Lamar (21) vs. Middle Tenn. St. (14) (Tangerine, 1961) (140 yards)

## Most Penalties, Both Teams
29—McNeese St. (20 ) [13] & Tulsa (16) [16] (Independence, 1976) (205 yards)
28 (D)—Fresno St. (35) [20] & Western Mich. (30) [8] (California, 1988) (231 yards)
26—Tennessee (35) [11] & Miami (Fla.) (7) [15] (Sugar, 1986) (245 yards)
26—Tennessee (17) [17] & Oklahoma (0) [9] (Orange, 1939) (221 yards)
25—Washington St. (31) [18] & Utah (28) [7] (Copper, 1992) (191 yards)
24—Miami (Fla.) (46) [16] & Texas (3) [8] (Cotton, 1991) (270 yards)
24 (D)—San Jose St. (37) [14] & Miami (Ohio) (7) [10] (California, 1986) (264 yards)
24 (D)—Michigan (33) [15] & UCLA (14) [9] (Bluebonnet, 1981) (242 yards)
23 (D)—Fresno St. (51) [12] & Bowling Green (7) [11] (California, 1985) (183 yards)
22 (D)—San Jose St. (27) [14] & Eastern Mich. (30) [9] (California, 1987) (162 yards)
21—Ohio St. (47) [12] & Brigham Young (17) [9] (Holiday, 1982) (184 yards)
21—Oklahoma St. (16) [12] & Brigham Young (6) [9] (Fiesta, 1974) (150 yards)
20—Penn St. (50) [10] & Brigham Young (39) [10] (Holiday, 1989) (181 yards)
20—Washington St. (24) [11] & Houston (22) [9] (Aloha, 1988) (153 yards)
20—Brigham Young (24) [9] & Michigan (17) [11] (Holiday, 1984) (194 yards)

## Most Yards Penalized
202—Miami (Fla.) (46) vs. Texas (3) (Cotton, 1991) (16 penalties)
166 (D)—Fresno St. (35) vs. Western Mich. (30) (California, 1988) (20 penalties)
163 (D)—San Jose St. (37) vs. Miami (Ohio) (7) (California, 1986) (14 penalties)
150—Oklahoma (48) vs. Duke (21) (Orange, 1958) (12 penalties)
148 (D)—Michigan (33) vs. UCLA (14) (Bluebonnet, 1981) (15 penalties)
143—Miami (Fla.) (22) vs. Nebraska (0) (Orange, 1992) (12 penalties)
140—Lamar (21) vs. Middle Tenn. St. (14) (Tangerine, 1961) (13 penalties)
136—Washington St. (31) vs. Utah (28) (Copper, 1992) (18 penalties)
135—Florida St. (41) vs. Nebraska (17) (Fiesta, 1990) (13 penalties)
130—Louisiana St. (15) vs. Nebraska (30) (Sugar, 1987) (12 penalties)
130—Tennessee (17) vs. Oklahoma (0) (Orange, 1939)
128—Oklahoma (48) vs. Virginia (14) (Gator, 1991) (12 penalties)
126—Penn St. (42) vs. Arizona St. (30) (Fiesta, 1977) (12 penalties)
125—Tennessee (35) vs. Miami (Fla.) (7) (Sugar, 1986) (11 penalties)
122—Mississippi St. (16) vs. North Caro. St. (12) (Liberty, 1963) (11 penalties)

## Most Yards Penalized, Both Teams
270—Miami (Fla.) (46) [202] & Texas (3) [68] (Cotton, 1991)
264 (D)—San Jose St. (37) [163] & Miami (Ohio) (7) [101] (California, 1986)
245—Tennessee (35) [125] & Miami (Fla.) (7) [120] (Sugar, 1986)
242 (D)—Michigan (33) [148] & UCLA (14) [94] (Bluebonnet, 1981)
231 (D)—Fresno St. (35) [166] & Western Mich. (30) [65] (California, 1988)
221—Tennessee (17) [130] & Oklahoma (0) [91] (Orange, 1939)
205—McNeese St. (20) [105] & Tulsa (16) [100] (Independence, 1976)
194—Brigham Young (24) [82] & Michigan (17) [112] (Holiday, 1984)
191—Washington St. (31) [136] & Utah (28) [55] (Copper, 1992)
183—Florida St. (41) [135] & Nebraska (17) [48] (Fiesta, 1990)
183 (D)—Fresno St. (51) [112] & Bowling Green (7) [71] (California, 1985)
181—Penn St. (50) [93] & Brigham Young (39) [88] (Holiday, 1989)
179—Miami (Fla.) (22) [143] & Nebraska (0) [36] (Orange, 1992)
176—Oklahoma (48) [128] & Virginia (14) [48] (Gator, 1991)
175—Oklahoma (48) [150] & Duke (21) [25] (Orange, 1958)

## Fewest Penalties
0—Southern Methodist (7) vs. Alabama (28) (Sun, 1983)
0—Louisiana Tech (13) vs. East Caro. (35) (Independence, 1978)
0—Texas (17) vs. Alabama (13) (Cotton, 1973)
0 (D)—Rice (7) vs. Kansas (33) (Bluebonnet, 1961)
0—Pittsburgh (14) vs. Georgia Tech (21) (Gator, 1956)
0—Clemson (0) vs. Miami (Fla.) (14) (Gator, 1952)
0—Texas (7) vs. Randolph Field (7) (Cotton, 1944)
0—Alabama (20) vs. Washington (19) (Rose, 1926)

## Fewest Penalties, Both Teams
3—Alabama (28) [3] & Southern Methodist (7) [0] (Sun, 1983)
3—Penn St. (30) [2] & Texas (6) [1] (Cotton, 1972)
3—Notre Dame (17) [2] & Texas (21) [1] (Cotton, 1970)
3—Penn St. (15) [1] & Kansas (14) [2] (Orange, 1969)
3 (D)—Kansas (33) [3] & Rice (7) [0] (Bluebonnet, 1961)

## Fewest Yards Penalized
0—Southern Methodist (7) vs. Alabama (28) (Sun, 1983)
0—Louisiana Tech (13) vs. East Caro. (35) (Independence, 1978)
0—Texas (17) vs. Alabama (13) (Cotton, 1973)
0 (D)—Rice (7) vs. Kansas (33) (Bluebonnet, 1961)
0—Pittsburgh (14) vs. Georgia Tech (21) (Gator, 1956)

0—Clemson (0) vs. Miami (Fla.) (14) (Gator, 1952)
0—Texas (7) vs. Randolph Field (7) (Cotton, 1944)
0—Alabama (20) vs. Washington (19) (Rose, 1926)
**Fewest Yards Penalized, Both Teams**
10—Mississippi St. (12) [5] vs. Duquesne (13) [5] (Orange, 1937)
15—Notre Dame (17) [10] vs. Texas (21) [5] (Cotton, 1970)
15 (D)—Kansas (33) [15] vs. Rice (7) [0] (Bluebonnet, 1961)

## MISCELLANEOUS RECORDS

**Scoreless Ties**
1959—Texas Christian 0, Air Force 0 (Cotton)
1947—Arkansas 0, Louisiana St. 0 (Cotton)
1940—Catholic 0, Arizona St. 0 (Sun)
1922—California 0, Wash. & Jeff. 0 (Rose)

**Tie Games (Not Scoreless)**
1991—Brigham Young 13, Iowa 13 (Holiday)
1990—Louisiana Tech 34, Maryland 34 (Independence)
1988—Syracuse 16, Auburn 16 (Sugar)
1985—Georgia 13, Arizona 13 (Sun)
1984—Georgia 17, Florida St. 17 (Florida Citrus)
1978—Arkansas 10, UCLA 10 (Fiesta)
1977 (D)—Maryland 17, Minnesota 17 (Hall of Fame)
1974—Vanderbilt 6, Texas Tech 6 (Peach)
1974 (D)—Houston 31, North Caro. St. 31 (Bluebonnet)
1970 (D)—Alabama 24, Oklahoma 24 (Bluebonnet)
1970 (D)—Louisville 24, Long Beach St. 24 (Pasadena)
1967—Florida St. 17, Penn St. 17 (Gator)
1960 (D)—Texas 3, Alabama 3 (Bluebonnet)
1948—Georgia 20, Maryland 20 (Gator)
1948—Southern Methodist 13, Penn St. 13 (Cotton)
1947 (D)—New Mexico 13, Montana St. 13 (Harbor)
1944—Texas 7, Randolph Field 7 (Cotton)
1937 (D)—Auburn 7, Villanova 7 (Bacardi)
1936—Hardin-Simmons 14, New Mexico St. 14 (Sun)
1934 (D)—Arkansas 7, Centenary 7 (Dixie Classic)
1927—Stanford 7, Alabama 7 (Rose)
1924—Washington 14, Navy 14 (Rose)

**Largest Deficit Overcome to Win**
22—Brigham Young (46) vs. Southern Methodist (45) (Holiday, 1980) (trailed 35-13 in 3rd quarter and then trailed 45-25 with four minutes remaining in the game)
22—Notre Dame (35) vs. Houston (34) (Cotton, 1979) (trailed 34-12 in 4th quarter)
21 (D)—Fresno St. (29) vs. Bowling Green (28) (California, 1982) (trailed 21-0 in 2nd quarter)
19—Wake Forest (39) vs. Oregon (35) (Independence, 1992) (trailed 29-10 in 3rd quarter)
14—Rice (28) vs. Colorado (14) (Cotton, 1938) (trailed 14-0 in 2nd quarter)
13—Mississippi (14) vs. Texas Christian (13) (Cotton, 1956) (trailed 13-0 in 2nd quarter)
11—Michigan (27) vs. Nebraska (23) (Fiesta, 1986) (trailed 14-3 in 3rd quarter)

# LONGEST PLAYS

**(D) Denotes discontinued bowl**
**(Year listed is actual year bowl was played)**

## LONGEST RUNS FROM SCRIMMAGE

| Yds. | Player, Team (Score) vs. Opponent (Score) | Bowl, Year |
|---|---|---|
| 99* | Terry Baker (QB), Oregon St. (6) vs. Villanova (0) | Liberty, 1962 |
| 95*# | Dicky Maegle, Rice (28) vs. Alabama (6) | Cotton, 1954 |
| 94*(D) | Dwight Ford, Southern Cal (47) vs. Texas A&M (28) | Bluebonnet, 1977 |
| 94* | Larry Smith, Florida (27) vs. Georgia Tech (12) | Orange, 1967 |
| 94* | Hascall Henshaw, Arizona St. (13) vs. Case Reserve (26) | Sun, 1941 |

*# Famous bench-tackle play; Maegle tackled on Alabama 40-yard line by Tommy Lewis, awarded touchdown.*
*\* Scored touchdown on play.*

Oregon State quarterback Terry Baker's 99-yard touchdown scamper in the 1962 Liberty Bowl is the longest run from scrimmage in bowl history.

## LONGEST PASS PLAYS

| Yds. | Player, Team (Score) vs. Opponent (Score) | Bowl, Year |
|---|---|---|
| 95* | Ronnie Fletcher to Ben Hart, Oklahoma (19) vs. Florida St. (36) | Gator, 1965 |
| 93*(D) | Stan Heath to Tommy Kalminir, Nevada (13) vs. North Texas (6) | Salad, 1948 |
| 91*(D) | Mark Barsotti to Stephen Shelley, Fresno St. (27) vs. Ball St. (6) | California, 1989 |
| 88* | Dave Schnell to Rob Turner, Indiana (34) vs. South Caro. (10) | Liberty, 1988 |
| 87* | Drew Bledsoe to Phillip Bobo, Washington St. (31) vs. Utah (28) | Copper, 1992 |
| 87* | Randy Wright to Tim Stracka, Wisconsin (14) vs. Kansas St. (3) | Independence, 1982 |
| 87* | Ger Schwedes to Ernie Davis, Syracuse (23) vs. Texas (14) | Cotton, 1960 |

\* Scored touchdown on play.

## LONGEST FIELD GOALS

| Yds. | Player, Team (Score) vs. Opponent (Score) | Bowl, Year |
|---|---|---|
| 62 | Tony Franklin, Texas A&M (37) vs. Florida (14) | Sun, 1977 |
| 56 | Greg Cox, Miami (Fla.) (20) vs. Oklahoma (14) | Orange, 1988 |
| 55(D) | Russell Erxleben, Texas (38) vs. Colorado (21) | Bluebonnet, 1975 |
| 54 | Carlos Huerta, Miami (Fla.) (22) vs. Nebraska (0) | Orange, 1992 |
| 54 | Quin Rodriguez, Southern Cal (16) vs. Michigan St. (17) | John Hancock, 1990 |
| 54 | Luis Zendejas, Arizona St. (32) vs. Oklahoma (21) | Fiesta, 1983 |

## LONGEST PUNTS

| Yds. | Player, Team (Score) vs. Opponent (Score) | Bowl, Year |
|---|---|---|
| 84$ | Kyle Rote, Southern Methodist (21) vs. Oregon (13) | Cotton, 1949 |
| 82 | Ike Pickle, Mississippi St. (12) vs. Duquesne (13) | Orange, 1937 |
| 80 | Elmer Layden, Notre Dame (27) vs. Stanford (10) | Rose, 1925 |
| 79$ | Doak Walker, Southern Methodist (21) vs. Oregon (13) | Cotton, 1949 |
| 77 | Mike Sochko, Maryland (21) vs. Houston (30) | Cotton, 1977 |

$ Quick kick.

## LONGEST PUNT RETURNS

| Yds. | Player, Team (Score) vs. Opponent (Score) | Bowl, Year |
|---|---|---|
| 86* | Aramis Dandoy, Southern Cal (7) vs. Ohio St. (20) | Rose, 1955 |
| 83* | Vai Sikahema, Brigham Young (46) vs. Southern Methodist (45) | Holiday, 1980 |
| 82 | Willie Drewrey, West Va. (12) vs. Florida St. (31) | Gator, 1982 |
| 80*(D) | Gary Anderson, Arkansas (34) vs. Tulane (15) | All-American, 1980 |
| 80* | Cecil Ingram, Alabama (61) vs. Syracuse (6) | Orange, 1953 |

* Scored touchdown on play.

## LONGEST KICKOFF RETURNS

| Yds. | Player, Team (Score) vs. Opponent (Score) | Bowl, Year |
|---|---|---|
| 100* | Kirby Dar Dar, Syracuse (26) vs. Colorado (22) | Fiesta, 1993 |
| 100* | Pete Panuska, Tennessee (27) vs. Maryland (28) | Sun, 1984 |
| 100* | Dave Lowery, Brigham Young (21) vs. Oklahoma St. (49) | Tangerine, 1976 |
| 100* | Mike Fink, Missouri (35) vs. Arizona St. (49) | Fiesta, 1972 |
| 100*(D) | Bob Smith, Texas A&M (40) vs. Georgia (20) | Presidential Cup, 1950 |
| 100*! | Al Hoisch, UCLA (14) vs. Illinois (45) | Rose, 1947 |

! Rose Bowl records carry as 103-yard return.
* Scored touchdown on play.

## LONGEST INTERCEPTION RETURNS

| Yds. | Player, Team (Score) vs. Opponent (Score) | Bowl, Year |
|---|---|---|
| 94* | David Baker, Oklahoma (48) vs. Duke (21) | Orange, 1958 |
| 91* | Don Hoover, Ohio (14) vs. West Tex. St. (15) | Sun, 1962 |
| 90* | Norm Beal, Missouri (21) vs. Navy (14) | Orange, 1961 |
| 90* | Charlie Brembs, South Caro. (14) vs. Wake Forest (26) | Gator, 1946 |
| 90*(D) | G. P. Jackson, Texas Christian (7) vs. Centre (63) | Fort Worth Classic, 1921 |

* Scored touchdown on play.

## LONGEST MISCELLANEOUS RETURNS

| Yds. | Player, Team (Score) vs. Opponent (Score) | Bowl, Year |
|---|---|---|
| 98 | Greg Mather, Navy (14) vs. Missouri (21) (Int. Lat.) | Orange, 1961 |
| 73 | Dick Carpenter, Oklahoma (48) vs. Duke (21) (Int. Lat.) | Orange, 1958 |
| 65 | Steve Manstedt, Nebraska (19) vs. Texas (3) (Live Fum.) | Cotton, 1974 |

# BOWL COACHING RECORDS

## COACHES' ALL-TIME BOWL APPEARANCES
### (Ranked by most bowl games coached)

| Coach (Teams Taken to Bowl) | Appearances | W-L-T | Pct. |
|---|---|---|---|
| Paul "Bear" Bryant, Alabama, Texas A&M, Kentucky | 29 | 15-12-2 | .552 |
| *Joe Paterno, Penn St. | 23 | 14-8-1 | .630 |
| Vince Dooley, Georgia | 20 | 8-10-2 | .450 |
| *Tom Osborne, Nebraska | 20 | 8-12-0 | .400 |
| John Vaught, Mississippi | 18 | 10-8-0 | .556 |
| *Lou Holtz, Wm. & Mary, North Caro. St., Arkansas, Notre Dame | 17 | 9-6-2 | .588 |
| *LaVell Edwards, Brigham Young | 17 | 5-11-1 | .324 |
| Bo Schembechler, Michigan | 17 | 5-12-0 | .294 |
| *Bobby Bowden, West Va., Florida St. | 16 | 12-3-1 | .781 |
| *Johnny Majors, Iowa St., Pittsburgh, Tennessee | 16 | 9-7-0 | .563 |
| Darrell Royal, Texas | 16 | 8-7-1 | .531 |
| *Don James, Kent, Washington | 15 | 10-5-0 | .667 |
| Bobby Dodd, Georgia Tech | 13 | 9-4-0 | .692 |
| Barry Switzer, Oklahoma | 13 | 8-5-0 | .615 |
| Charlie McClendon, Louisiana St. | 13 | 7-6-0 | .538 |
| *Hayden Fry, Southern Methodist, Iowa | 13 | 5-7-1 | .423 |
| Earle Bruce, Ohio St., Colorado St. | 12 | 7-5-0 | .583 |
| Woody Hayes, Miami (Ohio), Ohio St. | 12 | 6-6-0 | .500 |
| Ralph "Shug" Jordan, Auburn | 12 | 5-7-0 | .417 |
| *Terry Donahue, UCLA | 11 | 8-2-1 | .773 |
| Bill Yeoman, Houston | 11 | 6-4-1 | .591 |
| Jerry Claiborne, Virginia Tech, Maryland, Kentucky | 11 | 3-8-0 | .273 |

* Active coach.

*1993 NCAA FOOTBALL*

# COACHES' ALL-TIME BOWL VICTORIES

| | Wins | Record | | Wins | Record |
|---|---|---|---|---|---|
| Paul "Bear" Bryant ........... | 15 | 15-12-2 | Darrell Royal ................. | 8 | 8-7-1 |
| *Joe Paterno ................. | 14 | 14-8-1 | Vince Dooley ................. | 8 | 8-10-2 |
| *Bobby Bowden .............. | 12 | 12-3-1 | *Tom Osborne ............... | 8 | 8-12 |
| *Don James.................... | 10 | 10-5 | Bob Devaney ............... | 7 | 7-3 |
| John Vaught ................. | 10 | 10-8 | Dan Devine ................. | 7 | 7-3 |
| Bobby Dodd ................. | 9 | 9-4 | Earle Bruce ................. | 7 | 7-5 |
| *Lou Holtz .................... | 9 | 9-6-2 | Charlie McClendon .......... | 7 | 7-6 |
| *Johnny Majors .............. | 9 | 9-7 | | | |
| *Terry Donahue ............... | 8 | 8-2-1 | | | |
| Barry Switzer................. | 8 | 8-5 | | | |

* Active coach.

# COACHES' ALL-TIME BOWL WINNING PERCENTAGE
## (Minimum 11 Games)

| Coach, Last Team Coached | Appearances | W-L-T | Pct. |
|---|---|---|---|
| *Bobby Bowden, Florida St.............................................. | 16 | 12-3-1 | .781 |
| *Terry Donahue, UCLA .................................................. | 11 | 8-2-1 | .773 |
| Bobby Dodd, Georgia Tech ............................................ | 13 | 9-4-0 | .692 |
| *Don James, Washington .............................................. | 15 | 10-5-0 | .667 |
| *Joe Paterno, Penn St. ................................................. | 23 | 14-8-1 | .630 |
| Barry Switzer, Oklahoma ............................................... | 13 | 8-5-0 | .615 |
| Bill Yeoman, Houston .................................................. | 11 | 6-4-1 | .591 |
| *Lou Holtz, Notre Dame ................................................ | 17 | 9-6-2 | .588 |
| Earle Bruce, Colorado St. .............................................. | 12 | 7-5-0 | .583 |
| *Johnny Majors, Pittsburgh ............................................. | 16 | 9-7-0 | .563 |
| John Vaught, Mississippi ............................................... | 18 | 10-8-0 | .556 |
| Paul "Bear" Bryant, Alabama ........................................... | 29 | 15-12-2 | .552 |
| Charlie McClendon, Louisiana St......................................... | 13 | 7-6-0 | .538 |
| Darrell Royal, Texas.................................................... | 16 | 8-7-1 | .531 |
| Woody Hayes, Ohio St. ................................................. | 12 | 6-6-0 | .500 |
| Vince Dooley, Georgia .................................................. | 20 | 8-10-2 | .450 |
| *Hayden Fry, Iowa ..................................................... | 13 | 5-7-1 | .423 |
| Ralph "Shug" Jordan, Auburn ........................................... | 12 | 5-7-0 | .417 |
| *Tom Osborne, Nebraska ............................................... | 20 | 8-12-0 | .400 |
| *LaVell Edwards, Brigham Young ........................................ | 17 | 5-11-1 | .324 |
| Bo Schembechler, Michigan ............................................ | 17 | 5-12-0 | .294 |
| Jerry Claiborne, Kentucky .............................................. | 11 | 3-8-0 | .273 |

* Active coach.

# ALL-TIME MAJOR BOWL-GAME COACHING HISTORY

A total of 396 coaches have head-coached in history's 633 major bowl games (the term "major bowl" is defined above the alphabetical list of team bowl records). Below is an alphabetical list of all 396 bowl coaches, with their alma mater and year, their birth date, and their game-by-game bowl records, with name and date of each bowl, opponent, final score (own score first) and opposing coach (in parentheses). A handful coached service teams or colleges never in the major category but are included because they coached against a major team in a major bowl.

**JIM AIKEN**, 0-1-0 (Wash. & Jeff. '22) b 5-26-99
| | | |
|---|---|---|
| Oregon .............. | Cotton 1-1-49 | Southern Methodist 12-21 (Matty Bell) |

**FRED AKERS**, 2-8-0 (Arkansas '60) b 3-17-38
| | | |
|---|---|---|
| Wyoming............. | Fiesta 12-19-76 | Oklahoma 7-41 (Barry Switzer) |
| Texas ............... | Cotton 1-2-78 | Notre Dame 10-38 (Dan Devine) |
| Texas ............... | Sun 12-23-78 | Maryland 42-0 (Jerry Claiborne) |
| Texas ............... | Sun 12-22-79 | Washington 7-14 (Don James) |
| Texas ............... | Bluebonnet 12-31-80 | North Caro. 7-16 (Dick Crum) |
| Texas ............... | Cotton 1-1-82 | Alabama 14-12 (Paul "Bear" Bryant) |
| Texas ............... | Sun 12-25-82 | North Caro. 10-26 (Dick Crum) |
| Texas ............... | Cotton 1-2-84 | Georgia 9-10 (Vince Dooley) |
| Texas ............... | Freedom 12-26-84 | Iowa 17-55 (Hayden Fry) |
| Texas ............... | Bluebonnet 12-31-85 | Air Force 16-24 (Fisher DeBerry) |

**BILL ALEXANDER**, 3-2-0 (Georgia Tech '12) b 6-6-89
| | | |
|---|---|---|
| Georgia Tech ........ | Rose 1-1-29 | California 8-7 (Clarence "Nibs" Price) |
| Georgia Tech ........ | Orange 1-1-40 | Missouri 21-7 (Don Faurot) |
| Georgia Tech ........ | Cotton 1-1-43 | Texas 7-14 (Dana Bible) |
| Georgia Tech ........ | Sugar 1-1-44 | Tulsa 20-18 (Henry Frnka) |
| Georgia Tech ........ | Orange 1-1-45 | Tulsa 12-26 (Henry Frnka) |

**LEONARD "STUB" ALLISON**, 1-0-0   (Carleton '17)   b 1892
California ............   Rose 1-1-38   Alabama 13-0 (Frank Thomas)

**MIKE ARCHER**, 1-1-0   (Miami, Fla. '75)   b 7-26-53
Louisiana St. .........   Gator 12-31-87   South Caro. 30-13 (Joe Morrison)
Louisiana St. .........   Hall of Fame 1-2-89   Syracuse 10-23 (Dick MacPherson)

**IKE ARMSTRONG**, 1-0-0   (Drake '23)   b 6-8-95
Utah .................   Sun 1-2-39   New Mexico 16-0 (Ted Shipkey)

**BILL ARNSPARGER**, 0-3-0   (Miami, Ohio '50)   b 12-16-26
Louisiana St. .........   Sugar 1-1-85   Nebraska 10-28 (Tom Osborne)
Louisiana St. .........   Liberty 12-27-85   Baylor 7-21 (Grant Teaff)
Louisiana St. .........   Sugar 1-1-87   Nebraska 15-30 (Tom Osborne)

**CHRIS AULT**, 0-1-0   (Nevada '68)   b 11-8-47
Nevada...............   Las Vegas 12-18-92   Bowling Green 34-35 (Gary Blackney)

**CHARLEY BACHMAN**, 0-1-0   (Notre Dame '17)   b 12-1-92
Michigan St. .........   Orange 1-1-38   Auburn 0-6 (Jack Meagher)

**ENOCH BAGSHAW**, 0-1-1   (Washington '08)   b 1884
Washington ..........   Rose 1-1-24   Navy 14-14 (Bob Folwell)
Washington ..........   Rose 1-1-26   Alabama 19-20 (Wallace Wade)

**GEORGE BARCLAY**, 0-1-0   (North Caro. '35)   b 5-14-11
Wash. & Lee .........   Gator 1-1-51   Wyoming 7-20 (Bowden Wyatt)

**BILL BARNES**, 0-1-0   (Tennessee '41)   b 10-20-17
UCLA ................   Rose 1-1-62   Minnesota 3-21 (Murray Warmath)

**WILLIS BARNES**, 1-1-1   (Nebraska)   b 10-22-00
New Mexico..........   Sun 1-1-44   Southwestern (Tex.) 0-7 (R. M. Medley)
New Mexico..........   Sun 1-1-46   Denver 34-24 (Clyde "Cac" Hubbard)
New Mexico..........   Harbor 1-1-47   Montana St. 13-13 (Clyde Carpenter)

**JOHN BARNHILL**, 2-1-1   (Tennessee '28)   b 2-21-03
Tennessee ..........   Sugar 1-1-43   Tulsa 14-7 (Henry Frnka)
Tennessee ..........   Rose 1-1-45   Southern Cal 0-25 (Jeff Cravath)
Arkansas .............   Cotton 1-1-47   Louisiana St. 0-0 (Bernie Moore)
Arkansas .............   Dixie 1-1-48   William & Mary 21-19 (Rube McCray)

**BILL BATTLE**, 4-1-0   (Alabama '63)   b 12-8-41
Tennessee ..........   Sugar 1-1-71   Air Force 34-13 (Ben Martin)
Tennessee ..........   Liberty 12-20-71   Arkansas 14-13 (Frank Broyles)
Tennessee ..........   Bluebonnet 12-30-72   Louisiana St. 24-17 (Charlie McClendon)
Tennessee ..........   Gator 12-29-73   Texas Tech 19-28 (Jim Carlen)
Tennessee ..........   Liberty 12-16-74   Maryland 7-3 (Jerry Claiborne)

**SAMMY BAUGH**, 0-1-0   (Texas Christian '37)   b 3-17-14
Hardin-Simmons .....   Sun 12-31-58   Wyoming 6-14 (Bob Devaney)

**ALEX BELL**, 1-1-0   (Villanova '38)   b 8-12-15
Villanova .............   Sun 12-20-61   Wichita St. 17-9 (Hank Foldberg)
Villanova .............   Liberty 12-15-62   Oregon St. 0-6 (Tommy Prothro)

**MATTY BELL**, 1-1-1   (Centre '20)   b 2-22-99
Southern Methodist ..   Rose 1-1-36   Stanford 0-7 (Claude "Tiny" Thornhill)
Southern Methodist ..   Cotton 1-1-48   Penn St. 13-13 (Bob Higgins)
Southern Methodist ..   Cotton 1-1-49   Oregon 21-13 (Jim Aiken)

**EMORY BELLARD**, 2-3-0   (Southwest Tex. St. '49)   b 12-17-27
Texas A&M...........   Liberty 12-22-75   Southern Cal 0-20 (John McKay)
Texas A&M...........   Sun 1-2-77   Florida 37-14 (Doug Dickey)
Texas A&M...........   Bluebonnet 12-31-77   Southern Cal 28-47 (John Robinson)
Mississippi St.........   Sun 12-27-80   Nebraska 17-31 (Tom Osborne)
Mississippi St.........   Hall of Fame 12-31-81   Kansas 10-0 (Don Fambrough)

**ARTHUR "DUTCH" BERGMAN**, 1-0-1   (Notre Dame '20)   b 2-23-95
Catholic..............   Orange 1-1-36   Mississippi 20-19 (Ed Walker)
Catholic..............   Sun 1-1-40   Arizona St. 0-0 (Millard "Dixie" Howell)

**HUGO BEZDEK**, 1-1-0   (Chicago '06)   b 4-1-84
Oregon ..............   Rose 1-1-17   Pennsylvania 14-0 (Bob Folwell)
Penn St..............   Rose 1-1-23   Southern Cal 3-14 (Elmer "Gus" Henderson)

**DANA BIBLE**, 3-0-1   (Carson-Newman '12)   b 10-8-91
Texas A&M...........   Dixie Classic 1-2-22   Centre 22-14 (Charley Moran)
Texas ...............   Cotton 1-1-43   Georgia Tech 14-7 (Bill Alexander)
Texas ...............   Cotton 1-1-44   Randolph Field 7-7 (Frank Tritico)
Texas ...............   Cotton 1-1-46   Missouri 40-27 (Chauncey Simpson)

**JACK BICKNELL**, 2-2-0   (Montclair St. '60)   b 2-20-38
Boston College ......   Tangerine 12-18-82   Auburn 26-33 (Pat Dye)
Boston College ......   Liberty 12-29-83   Notre Dame 18-19 (Gerry Faust)
Boston College ......   Cotton 1-1-85   Houston 45-28 (Bill Yeoman)
Boston College ......   Hall of Fame 12-23-86   Georgia 27-24 (Vince Dooley)

454

**BERNIE BIERMAN**, 0-1-0   (Minnesota '16)   b 3-11-94
Tulane . . . . . . . . . . . . . . .   Rose 1-1-32                         Southern Cal 12-21 (Howard Jones)
**GARY BLACKNEY**, 2-0-0   (Connecticut '67)   b 12-10-55
Bowling Green . . . . . . .   California 12-14-91                Fresno St. 28-21 (Jim Sweeney)
Bowling Green . . . . . . .   Las Vegas 12-18-92              Nevada 35-34 (Chris Ault)
**BOBBY BOWDEN**, 12-3-1   (Samford '53)   b 11-8-29
West Va. . . . . . . . . . . . . .   Peach 12-29-72                    North Caro. St. 13-49 (Lou Holtz)
West Va. . . . . . . . . . . . . .   Peach 12-31-75                    North Caro. St. 13-10 (Lou Holtz)
Florida St. . . . . . . . . . . .   Tangerine 12-23-77             Texas Tech 40-17 (Steve Sloan)
Florida St. . . . . . . . . . . .   Orange 1-1-80                     Oklahoma 7-24 (Barry Switzer)
Florida St. . . . . . . . . . . .   Orange 1-1-81                     Oklahoma 17-18 (Barry Switzer)
Florida St. . . . . . . . . . . .   Gator 12-30-82                    West Va. 31-12 (Don Nehlen)
Florida St. . . . . . . . . . . .   Peach 12-30-83                   North Caro. 28-3 (Dick Crum)
Florida St. . . . . . . . . . . .   Fla. Citrus 12-22-84            Georgia 17-17 (Vince Dooley)
Florida St. . . . . . . . . . . .   Gator 12-30-85                    Oklahoma St. 34-23 (Pat Jones)
Florida St. . . . . . . . . . . .   All-American 12-31-86         Indiana 27-13 (Bill Mallory)
Florida St. . . . . . . . . . . .   Fiesta 1-1-88                       Nebraska 31-28 (Tom Osborne)
Florida St. . . . . . . . . . . .   Sugar 1-2-89                       Auburn 13-7 (Pat Dye)
Florida St. . . . . . . . . . . .   Fiesta 1-1-90                       Nebraska 41-17 (Tom Osborne)
Florida St. . . . . . . . . . . .   Blockbuster 12-28-90         Penn St. 24-17 (Joe Paterno)
Florida St. . . . . . . . . . . .   Cotton 1-1-92                      Texas A&M 10-2 (R. C. Slocum)
Florida St. . . . . . . . . . . .   Orange 1-1-93                     Nebraska 27-14 (Tom Osborne)
**JEFF BOWER**, 0-1-0   (Southern Miss. '76)   b 5-28-53
Southern Miss. . . . . . . .   All-American 12-28-90          North Caro. St. 27-31 (Dick Sheridan)
**SAM BOYD**, 1-0-0   (Baylor '38)   b 8-12-15
Baylor . . . . . . . . . . . . . . .   Sugar 1-1-57                       Tennessee 13-7 (Bowden Wyatt)
**WESLEY BRADSHAW**, 0-1-0   (Baylor '23)   b 11-26-98
Ouachita Baptist . . . . .   Shrine 12-18-48                    Hardin-Simmons 12-40 (Warren Woodson)
**BILLY BREWER**, 3-2-0   (Mississippi '61)   b 10-8-35
Mississippi . . . . . . . . . . .   Independence 12-10-83        Air Force 3-9 (Ken Hatfield)
Mississippi . . . . . . . . . . .   Independence 12-20-86        Texas Tech 20-17 (Spike Dykes)
Mississippi . . . . . . . . . . .   All-American 12-29-89         Air Force 42-29 (Fisher DeBerry)
Mississippi . . . . . . . . . . .   Gator 1-1-91                        Michigan 3-35 (Gary Moeller)
Mississippi . . . . . . . . . . .   Liberty 12-31-92                 Air Force 13-0 (Fisher DeBerry)
**JOHN BRIDGERS**, 2-1-0   (Auburn '47)   b 1-13-22
Baylor . . . . . . . . . . . . . . .   Gator 12-31-60                    Florida 12-13 (Ray Graves)
Baylor . . . . . . . . . . . . . . .   Gotham 12-9-61                   Utah St. 24-9 (John Ralston)
Baylor . . . . . . . . . . . . . . .   Bluebonnet 12-21-63           Louisiana St. 14-7 (Charlie McClendon)
**RICH BROOKS**, 1-2-0   (Oregon St. '63)   b 8-20-41
Oregon  . . . . . . . . . . . . .   Independence 12-16-89        Tulsa 27-24 (Dave Rader)
Oregon  . . . . . . . . . . . . .   Freedom 12-29-90               Colorado St. 31-32 (Earle Bruce)
Oregon  . . . . . . . . . . . . .   Independence 12-31-92        Wake Forest 35-39 (Bill Dooley)
**J. O. "BUDDY" BROTHERS**, 0-1-0   (Texas Tech '31)   b 5-29-09
Tulsa . . . . . . . . . . . . . . . .   Gator 1-1-53                        Florida 13-14 (Bob Woodruff)
**MACK BROWN**, 1-1-0   (Florida St. '74)   b 8-27-51
Tulane . . . . . . . . . . . . . . .   Independence 12-19-87        Washington 12-24 (Don James)
North Caro. . . . . . . . . .   Peach 1-2-93                         Mississippi St. 21-17 (Jackie Sherrill)
**FRANK BROYLES**, 4-6-0   (Georgia Tech '47)   b 12-26-24
Arkansas . . . . . . . . . . . .   Gator 1-2-60                         Georgia Tech 14-7 (Bobby Dodd)
Arkansas . . . . . . . . . . . .   Cotton 1-2-61                        Duke 6-7 (Bill Murray)
Arkansas . . . . . . . . . . . .   Sugar 1-1-62                         Alabama 3-10 (Paul "Bear" Bryant)
Arkansas . . . . . . . . . . . .   Sugar 1-1-63                         Mississippi 13-17 (John Vaught)
Arkansas . . . . . . . . . . . .   Cotton 1-1-65                        Nebraska 10-7 (Bob Devaney)
Arkansas . . . . . . . . . . . .   Cotton 1-1-66                        Louisiana St. 7-14 (Charlie McClendon)
Arkansas . . . . . . . . . . . .   Sugar 1-1-69                         Georgia 16-2 (Vince Dooley)
Arkansas . . . . . . . . . . . .   Sugar 1-1-70                         Mississippi 22-27 (John Vaught)
Arkansas . . . . . . . . . . . .   Liberty 12-20-71                   Tennessee 13-14 (Bill Battle)
Arkansas . . . . . . . . . . . .   Cotton 1-1-76                        Georgia 31-10 (Vince Dooley)
**EARLE BRUCE**, 7-5-0   (Ohio St. '53)   b 3-8-31
Tampa  . . . . . . . . . . . . . .   Tangerine 12-29-72             Kent 21-18 (Don James)
Iowa St. . . . . . . . . . . . . .   Peach 12-31-77                    North Caro. St. 14-24 (Bo Rein)
Iowa St. . . . . . . . . . . . . .   Hall of Fame 12-20-78         Texas A&M 12-28 (Tom Wilson)
Ohio St. . . . . . . . . . . . . .   Rose 1-1-80                         Southern Cal 16-17 (John Robinson)
Ohio St. . . . . . . . . . . . . .   Fiesta 12-26-80                   Penn St. 19-31 (Joe Paterno)
Ohio St. . . . . . . . . . . . . .   Liberty 12-30-81                  Navy 31-28 (George Welsh)
Ohio St. . . . . . . . . . . . . .   Holiday 12-17-82                 Brigham Young 47-17 (LaVell Edwards)
Ohio St. . . . . . . . . . . . . .   Fiesta 1-2-84                       Pittsburgh 28-23 (Foge Fazio)
Ohio St. . . . . . . . . . . . . .   Rose 1-1-85                         Southern Cal 17-20 (Ted Tollner)
Ohio St. . . . . . . . . . . . . .   Fla. Citrus 12-28-85            Brigham Young 10-7 (LaVell Edwards)
Ohio St. . . . . . . . . . . . . .   Cotton 1-1-87                       Texas A&M 28-12 (Jackie Sherrill)
Colorado St. . . . . . . . . .   Freedom 12-29-90               Oregon 32-31 (Rich Brooks)

*Bowl Coaching Records*                                                                          455

**MILT BRUHN**, 0-2-0  (Minnesota '35)  b 7-28-12
Wisconsin . . . . . . . . . . .  Rose 1-1-60  Washington 8-44 (Jim Owens)
Wisconsin . . . . . . . . . . . .  Rose 1-2-63  Southern Cal 37-42 (John McKay)

**MIKE BRUMBELOW**, 2-1-0  (Texas Christian '30)  b 7-13-06
UTEP . . . . . . . . . . . . . . .  Sun 1-1-54  Southern Miss. 37-14 (Thad "Pie" Vann)
UTEP . . . . . . . . . . . . . . .  Sun 1-1-55  Florida St. 47-20 (Tom Nugent)
UTEP . . . . . . . . . . . . . . .  Sun 1-1-57  Geo. Washington 0-13 (Eugene "Bo" Sherman)

**PAUL "BEAR" BRYANT**, 15-12-2  (Alabama '36)  b 9-11-13
Kentucky . . . . . . . . . . . . .  Great Lakes 12-6-47  Villanova 24-14 (Jordan Oliver)
Kentucky . . . . . . . . . . . . .  Orange 1-2-50  Santa Clara 13-21 (Len Casanova)
Kentucky . . . . . . . . . . . . .  Sugar 1-1-51  Oklahoma 13-7 (Bud Wilkinson)
Kentucky . . . . . . . . . . . . .  Cotton 1-1-52  Texas Christian 20-7 (Leo "Dutch" Meyer)
Texas A&M . . . . . . . . . .  Gator 12-28-57  Tennessee 0-3 (Bowden Wyatt)
Alabama . . . . . . . . . . . .  Liberty 12-19-59  Penn St. 0-7 (Charles "Rip" Engle)
Alabama . . . . . . . . . . . .  Bluebonnet 12-17-60  Texas 3-3 (Darrell Royal)
Alabama . . . . . . . . . . . .  Sugar 1-1-62  Arkansas 10-3 (Frank Broyles)
Alabama . . . . . . . . . . . .  Orange 1-1-63  Oklahoma 17-0 (Bud Wilkinson)
Alabama . . . . . . . . . . . .  Sugar 1-1-64  Mississippi 12-7 (John Vaught)
Alabama . . . . . . . . . . . .  Orange 1-1-65  Texas 17-21 (Darrell Royal)
Alabama . . . . . . . . . . . .  Orange 1-1-66  Nebraska 39-28 (Bob Devaney)
Alabama . . . . . . . . . . . .  Sugar 1-2-67  Nebraska 34-7 (Bob Devaney)
Alabama . . . . . . . . . . . .  Cotton 1-1-68  Texas A&M 16-20 (Gene Stallings)
Alabama . . . . . . . . . . . .  Gator 12-28-68  Missouri 10-35 (Dan Devine)
Alabama . . . . . . . . . . . .  Liberty 12-13-69  Colorado 33-47 (Eddie Crowder)
Alabama . . . . . . . . . . . .  Bluebonnet 12-31-70  Oklahoma 24-24 (Chuck Fairbanks)
Alabama . . . . . . . . . . . .  Orange 1-1-72  Nebraska 6-38 (Bob Devaney)
Alabama . . . . . . . . . . . .  Cotton 1-1-73  Texas 13-17 (Darrell Royal)
Alabama . . . . . . . . . . . .  Sugar 12-31-73  Notre Dame 23-24 (Ara Parseghian)
Alabama . . . . . . . . . . . .  Orange 1-1-75  Notre Dame 11-13 (Ara Parseghian)
Alabama . . . . . . . . . . . .  Sugar 12-31-75  Penn St. 13-6 (Joe Paterno)
Alabama . . . . . . . . . . . .  Liberty 12-20-76  UCLA 36-6 (Terry Donahue)
Alabama . . . . . . . . . . . .  Sugar 1-2-78  Ohio St. 35-6 (Woody Hayes)
Alabama . . . . . . . . . . . .  Sugar 1-1-79  Penn St. 14-7 (Joe Paterno)
Alabama . . . . . . . . . . . .  Sugar 1-1-80  Arkansas 24-9 (Lou Holtz)
Alabama . . . . . . . . . . . .  Cotton 1-1-81  Baylor 30-2 (Grant Teaff)
Alabama . . . . . . . . . . . .  Cotton 1-1-82  Texas 12-14 (Fred Akers)
Alabama . . . . . . . . . . . .  Liberty 12-29-82  Illinois 21-15 (Mike White)

**FRANK BURNS**, 0-1-0  (Rutgers '49)  b 3-16-28
Rutgers . . . . . . . . . . . . .  Garden State 12-16-78  Arizona St. 18-34 (Frank Kush)

**LEON BURTNETT**, 0-1-0  (Southwestern, Kan. '65)  b 5-30-43
Purdue . . . . . . . . . . . . . .  Peach 12-31-84  Virginia 24-27 (George Welsh)

**WALLY BUTTS**, 5-2-1  (Mercer '28)  b 2-7-05
Georgia . . . . . . . . . . . . .  Orange 1-1-42  Texas Christian 40-26 (Leo "Dutch" Meyer)
Georgia . . . . . . . . . . . . .  Rose 1-1-43  UCLA 9-0 (Edwin "Babe" Horrell)
Georgia . . . . . . . . . . . . .  Oil 1-1-46  Tulsa 20-6 (Henry Frnka)
Georgia . . . . . . . . . . . . .  Sugar 1-1-47  North Caro. 20-10 (Carl Snavely)
Georgia . . . . . . . . . . . . .  Gator 1-1-48  Maryland 20-20 (Jim Tatum)
Georgia . . . . . . . . . . . . .  Orange 1-1-49  Texas 28-41 (Blair Cherry)
Georgia . . . . . . . . . . . . .  Presidential Cup 12-9-50  Texas A&M 20-40 (Harry Stiteler)
Georgia . . . . . . . . . . . . .  Orange 1-1-60  Missouri 14-0 (Dan Devine)

**EDDIE CAMERON**, 1-0-0  (Wash. & Lee '24)  b 4-22-02
Duke . . . . . . . . . . . . . . . .  Sugar 1-1-45  Alabama 29-26 (Frank Thomas)

**FRANK CAMP**, 1-0-0  (Transylvania '30)  b 12-23-05
Louisville . . . . . . . . . . . .  Sun 1-1-58  Drake 34-20 (Warren Gaer)

**JIM CARLEN**, 2-5-1  (Georgia Tech '55)  b 7-11-33
West Va. . . . . . . . . . . . . .  Peach 12-30-69  South Caro. 14-3 (Paul Dietzel)
Texas Tech . . . . . . . . . .  Sun 12-19-70  Georgia Tech 9-17 (Bud Carson)
Texas Tech . . . . . . . . . .  Sun 12-30-72  North Caro. 28-32 (Bill Dooley)
Texas Tech . . . . . . . . . .  Gator 12-29-73  Tennessee 28-19 (Bill Battle)
Texas Tech . . . . . . . . . .  Peach 12-28-74  Vanderbilt 6-6 (Steve Sloan)
South Caro. . . . . . . . . .  Tangerine 12-20-75  Miami (Ohio) 7-20 (Dick Crum)
South Caro. . . . . . . . . .  Hall of Fame 12-29-79  Missouri 14-24 (Warren Powers)
South Caro. . . . . . . . . .  Gator 12-29-80  Pittsburgh 8-37 (Jackie Sherrill)

**CLYDE CARPENTER**, 0-0-1  (Montana '32)  b 4-17-08
Montana St. . . . . . . . . . .  Harbor 1-1-47  New Mexico 13-13 (Willis Barnes)

**BUD CARSON**, 1-1-0  (North Caro. '52)  b 4-28-30
Georgia Tech . . . . . . . .  Sun 12-19-70  Texas Tech 17-9 (Jim Carlen)
Georgia Tech . . . . . . . .  Peach 12-30-71  Mississippi 18-41 (Billy Kinard)

**LEN CASANOVA**, 2-2-0  (Santa Clara '27)  b 6-12-05
Santa Clara . . . . . . . . . .  Orange 1-2-50  Kentucky 21-13 (Paul "Bear" Bryant)
Oregon . . . . . . . . . . . . . .  Rose 1-1-58  Ohio St. 7-10 (Woody Hayes)

| | | |
|---|---|---|
| Oregon ............. | Liberty 12-17-60 | Penn St. 12-41 (Charles "Rip" Engle) |
| Oregon ............. | Sun 12-31-63 | Southern Methodist 21-14 (Hayden Fry) |

**MILES CASTEEL**, 0-1-0   (Kalamazoo '25)   b 12-30-96
| | | |
|---|---|---|
| Arizona ............. | Salad 1-1-49 | Drake 13-14 (Al Kawal) |

**PETE CAWTHON**, 0-2-0   (Southwestern, Tex. '20)   b 8-24-98
| | | |
|---|---|---|
| Texas Tech .......... | Sun 1-1-38 | West Va. 6-7 (Marshall "Little Sleepy" Glenn) |
| Texas Tech .......... | Cotton 1-2-39 | St. Mary's (Cal.) 13-20 (Edward "Slip" Madigan) |

**BLAIR CHERRY**, 2-1-0   (Texas Christian '24)   b 9-7-01
| | | |
|---|---|---|
| Texas ............... | Sugar 1-1-48 | Alabama 27-7 (Harold "Red" Drew) |
| Texas ............... | Orange 1-1-49 | Georgia 41-28 (Wally Butts) |
| Texas ............... | Cotton 1-1-51 | Tennessee 14-20 (Bob Neyland) |

**JERRY CLAIBORNE**, 3-8-0   (Kentucky '50)   b 8-26-28
| | | |
|---|---|---|
| Virginia Tech ........ | Liberty 12-10-66 | Miami (Fla.) 7-14 (Charlie Tate) |
| Virginia Tech ........ | Liberty 12-14-68 | Mississippi 17-34 (John Vaught) |
| Maryland ............ | Peach 12-28-73 | Georgia 16-17 (Vince Dooley) |
| Maryland ............ | Liberty 12-16-74 | Tennessee 3-7 (Bill Battle) |
| Maryland ............ | Gator 12-29-75 | Florida 13-0 (Doug Dickey) |
| Maryland ............ | Cotton 1-1-77 | Houston 21-30 (Bill Yeoman) |
| Maryland ............ | Hall of Fame 12-22-77 | Minnesota 17-7 (Cal Stoll) |
| Maryland ............ | Sun 12-23-78 | Texas 0-42 (Fred Akers) |
| Maryland ............ | Tangerine 12-20-80 | Florida 20-35 (Charley Pell) |
| Kentucky ............ | Hall of Fame 12-22-83 | West Va. 16-20 (Don Nehlen) |
| Kentucky ............ | Hall of Fame 12-29-84 | Wisconsin 20-19 (Dave McClain) |

**CECIL COLEMAN**, 1-0-0   (Arizona St. '50)   b 4-12-26
| | | |
|---|---|---|
| Fresno St. ........... | Mercy 11-23-61 | Bowling Green 36-6 (Doyt Perry) |

**BOBBY COLLINS**, 3-2-0   (Mississippi St. '55)   b 10-25-33
| | | |
|---|---|---|
| Southern Miss. ...... | Independence 12-13-70 | McNeese St. 16-14 (Ernie Duplechin) |
| Southern Miss. ...... | Tangerine 12-19-81 | Missouri 17-19 (Warren Powers) |
| Southern Methodist .. | Cotton 1-1-83 | Pittsburgh 7-3 (Foge Fazio) |
| Southern Methodist .. | Sun 12-24-83 | Alabama 7-28 (Ray Perkins) |
| Southern Methodist .. | Aloha 12-29-84 | Notre Dame 27-20 (Gerry Faust) |

**JOHN COOPER**, 2-5-0   (Iowa St. '62)   b 7-2-37
| | | |
|---|---|---|
| Arizona St. .......... | Holiday 12-22-85 | Arkansas 17-18 (Ken Hatfield) |
| Arizona St. .......... | Rose 1-1-87 | Michigan 22-15 (Glenn "Bo" Schembechler) |
| Arizona St. .......... | Freedom 12-30-87 | Air Force 33-28 (Fisher DeBerry) |
| Ohio St. ............. | Hall of Fame 1-1-90 | Auburn 14-31 (Pat Dye) |
| Ohio St. ............. | Liberty 12-27-90 | Air Force 11-23 (Fisher DeBerry) |
| Ohio St. ............. | Hall of Fame 1-1-92 | Syracuse 17-24 (Paul Pasqualoni) |
| Ohio St. ............. | Fla. Citrus 1-1-93 | Georgia 14-21 (Ray Goff) |

**LEE CORSO**, 1-0-1   (Florida St. '57)   b 8-7-35
| | | |
|---|---|---|
| Louisville ............ | Pasadena 12-19-70 | Long Beach St. 24-24 (Jim Stangeland) |
| Indiana .............. | Holiday 12-21-79 | Brigham Young 38-37 (LaVell Edwards) |

**GENE CORUM**, 0-1-0   (West Va. '48)   b 5-29-21
| | | |
|---|---|---|
| West Va. ............ | Liberty 12-19-64 | Utah 6-32 (Ray Nagel) |

**DON CORYELL**, 1-0-0   (Washington '50)   b 10-17-24
| | | |
|---|---|---|
| San Diego St. ........ | Pasadena 12-6-69 | Boston U. 28-7 (Larry Naviaux) |

**TOM COUGHLIN**, 0-1-0   (Syracuse '68)   b 8-31-46
| | | |
|---|---|---|
| Boston College ...... | Hall of Fame 1-1-93 | Tennessee 23-38 (Phillip Fulmer) |

**TED COX**, 1-0-0   (Minnesota '26)   b 6-30-03
| | | |
|---|---|---|
| Tulane ............... | Sugar 1-1-35 | Temple 20-14 (Glenn "Pop" Warner) |

**JEFF CRAVATH**, 2-2-0   (Southern Cal '27)   b 2-5-05
| | | |
|---|---|---|
| Southern Cal ........ | Rose 1-1-44 | Washington 29-0 (Ralph "Pest" Welch) |
| Southern Cal ........ | Rose 1-1-45 | Tennessee 25-0 (John Barnhill) |
| Southern Cal ........ | Rose 1-1-46 | Alabama 14-34 (Frank Thomas) |
| Southern Cal ........ | Rose 1-1-48 | Michigan 0-49 (H. O. "Fritz" Crisler) |

**H. O. "FRITZ" CRISLER**, 1-0-0   (Chicago '22)   b 1-2-99
| | | |
|---|---|---|
| Michigan ............. | Rose 1-1-48 | Southern Cal 49-0 (Jeff Cravath) |

**EDDIE CROWDER**, 3-2-0   (Oklahoma '55)   b 8-26-31
| | | |
|---|---|---|
| Colorado ............ | Bluebonnet 12-23-67 | Miami (Fla.) 31-21 (Charlie Tate) |
| Colorado ............ | Liberty 12-13-69 | Alabama 47-33 (Paul "Bear" Bryant) |
| Colorado ............ | Liberty 12-12-70 | Tulane 3-17 (Jim Pittman) |
| Colorado ............ | Bluebonnet 12-31-71 | Houston 29-17 (Bill Yeoman) |
| Colorado ............ | Gator 12-20-72 | Auburn 3-24 (Ralph "Shug" Jordan) |

**JACK CROWE**, 0-1-0   (Ala.-Birmingham '70)   b 4-6-48
| | | |
|---|---|---|
| Arkansas ............ | Independence 12-29-91 | Georgia 15-24 (Ray Goff) |

**JIM CROWLEY**, 1-1-0   (Notre Dame '25)   b 9-10-02
| | | |
|---|---|---|
| Fordham ............. | Cotton 1-1-41 | Texas A&M 12-13 (Homer Norton) |
| Fordham ............. | Sugar 1-1-42 | Missouri 2-0 (Don Faurot) |

**DICK CRUM**, 6-2-0   (Mount Union '57)   b 4-29-34
| | | |
|---|---|---|
| Miami (Ohio) . . . . . . . . | Tangerine 12-21-74 | Georgia 21-10 (Vince Dooley) |
| Miami (Ohio) . . . . . . . . | Tangerine 12-20-75 | South Caro. 20-7 (Jim Carlen) |
| North Caro. . . . . . . . . | Gator 12-28-79 | Michigan 17-15 (Glenn "Bo" Schembechler) |
| North Caro. . . . . . . . . | Bluebonnet 12-31-80 | Texas 16-7 (Fred Akers) |
| North Caro. . . . . . . . . | Gator 12-28-81 | Arkansas 31-27 (Lou Holtz) |
| North Caro. . . . . . . . . | Sun 12-25-82 | Texas 26-10 (Fred Akers) |
| North Caro. . . . . . . . . | Peach 12-30-83 | Florida St. 3-28 (Bobby Bowden) |
| North Caro. . . . . . . . . | Aloha 12-27-86 | Arizona 21-30 (Larry Smith) |

**FRAN CURCI**, 1-0-0   (Miami, Fla. '60)   b 6-11-38
| | | |
|---|---|---|
| Kentucky . . . . . . . . . . . | Peach 12-31-76 | North Caro. 21-0 (Bill Dooley) |

**BILL CURRY**, 2-2-0   (Georgia Tech '65)   b 10-21-42
| | | |
|---|---|---|
| Georgia Tech . . . . . . . | All-American 12-31-85 | Michigan St. 17-14 (George Perles) |
| Alabama . . . . . . . . . . . | Hall of Fame 1-2-88 | Michigan 24-28 (Glenn "Bo" Schembechler) |
| Alabama . . . . . . . . . . . | Sun 12-24-88 | Army 29-28 (Jim Young) |
| Alabama . . . . . . . . . . . | Sugar 1-1-90 | Miami (Fla.) 25-33 (Dennis Erickson) |

**JACK "CACTUS JACK" CURTICE**, 1-1-0   (Transylvania '30)   b 5-24-07
| | | |
|---|---|---|
| UTEP . . . . . . . . . . . . . . | Sun 1-1-49 | West Va. 12-21 (Dud DeGroot) |
| UTEP . . . . . . . . . . . . . . | Sun 1-2-50 | Georgetown 33-20 (Bob Margarita) |

**JOHN "OX" Da GROSA**, 0-1-0   (Colgate '26)   b 2-17-02
| | | |
|---|---|---|
| Holy Cross . . . . . . . . . . | Orange 1-1-46 | Miami (Fla.) 6-13 (Jack Harding) |

**GARY DARNELL**, 0-1-0   (Oklahoma St. '71)   b 10-15-48
| | | |
|---|---|---|
| Florida . . . . . . . . . . . . . | Freedom 12-29-89 | Washington 7-34 (Don James) |

**DUFFY DAUGHERTY**, 1-1-0   (Syracuse '40)   b 9-8-15
| | | |
|---|---|---|
| Michigan St. . . . . . . . . | Rose 1-2-56 | UCLA 17-14 (Henry "Red" Sanders) |
| Michigan St. . . . . . . . . | Rose 1-1-66 | UCLA 12-14 (Tommy Prothro) |

**BOB DAVIS**, 0-1-0   (Utah '30)   b 2-13-08
| | | |
|---|---|---|
| Colorado St. . . . . . . . . | Raisin 1-1-49 | Occidental 20-21 (Roy Dennis) |

**PAUL DAVIS**, 1-0-0   (Mississippi '47)   b 2-3-22
| | | |
|---|---|---|
| Mississippi St. . . . . . . . | Liberty 12-21-63 | North Caro St. 16-12 (Earle Edwards) |

**LOWELL "RED" DAWSON**, 0-1-0   (Tulane '30)   b 12-26-06
| | | |
|---|---|---|
| Tulane . . . . . . . . . . . . . . | Sugar 1-1-40 | Texas A&M 13-14 (Homer Norton) |

**FISHER DeBERRY**, 4-3-0   (Wofford '60)   b 9-9-38
| | | |
|---|---|---|
| Air Force . . . . . . . . . . . | Independence 12-15-84 | Virginia Tech 23-7 (Bill Dooley) |
| Air Force . . . . . . . . . . . | Bluebonnet 12-31-85 | Texas 24-16 (Fred Akers) |
| Air Force . . . . . . . . . . . | Freedom 12-30-87 | Arizona St. 28-33 (John Cooper) |
| Air Force . . . . . . . . . . . | Liberty 12-29-89 | Mississippi 29-42 (Billy Brewer) |
| Air Force . . . . . . . . . . . | Liberty 12-27-90 | Ohio St. 23-11 (John Cooper) |
| Air Force . . . . . . . . . . . | Liberty 12-29-91 | Mississippi St. 38-15 (Jackie Sherrill) |
| Air Force . . . . . . . . . . . | Liberty 12-31-92 | Mississippi 0-13 (Billy Brewer) |

**DUD DeGROOT**, 1-0-0   (Stanford '24)   b 11-20-95
| | | |
|---|---|---|
| West Va. . . . . . . . . . . . . | Sun 1-1-49 | UTEP 21-12 (Jack "Cactus Jack" Curtice) |

**ROY DENNIS**, 1-0-0   (Occidental '33)   b 5-13-05
| | | |
|---|---|---|
| Occidental . . . . . . . . . . | Raisin 1-1-49 | Colorado St. 21-20 (Bob Davis) |

**HERB DEROMEDI**, 0-1-0   (Michigan '60)   b 5-26-39
| | | |
|---|---|---|
| Central Mich. . . . . . . . . | California 12-8-90 | San Jose St. 24-48 (Terry Shea) |

**BOB DEVANEY**, 7-3-0   (Alma '39)   b 4-2-15
| | | |
|---|---|---|
| Wyoming . . . . . . . . . . . . | Sun 12-31-58 | Hardin-Simmons 14-6 (Sammy Baugh) |
| Nebraska . . . . . . . . . . . | Gotham 12-15-62 | Miami (Fla.) 36-34 (Andy Gustafson) |
| Nebraska . . . . . . . . . . . | Orange 1-1-64 | Auburn 13-7 (Ralph "Shug" Jordan) |
| Nebraska . . . . . . . . . . . | Cotton 1-1-65 | Arkansas 7-10 (Frank Broyles) |
| Nebraska . . . . . . . . . . . | Orange 1-1-66 | Alabama 28-39 (Paul "Bear" Bryant) |
| Nebraska . . . . . . . . . . . | Sugar 1-2-67 | Alabama 7-34 (Paul "Bear" Bryant) |
| Nebraska . . . . . . . . . . . | Sun 12-20-69 | Georgia 45-6 (Vince Dooley) |
| Nebraska . . . . . . . . . . . | Orange 1-1-71 | Louisiana St. 17-12 (Charlie McClendon) |
| Nebraska . . . . . . . . . . . | Orange 1-1-72 | Alabama 38-6 (Paul "Bear" Bryant) |
| Nebraska . . . . . . . . . . . | Orange 1-1-73 | Notre Dame 40-6 (Ara Parseghian) |

**DAN DEVINE**, 7-3-0   (Minn.-Duluth '48)   b 12-23-24
| | | |
|---|---|---|
| Missouri . . . . . . . . . . . . | Orange 1-1-60 | Georgia 0-14 (Wally Butts) |
| Missouri . . . . . . . . . . . . | Orange 1-2-61 | Navy 21-14 (Wayne Hardin) |
| Missouri . . . . . . . . . . . . | Bluebonnet 12-22-62 | Georgia Tech 14-10 (Bobby Dodd) |
| Missouri . . . . . . . . . . . . | Sugar 1-1-66 | Florida 20-18 (Ray Graves) |
| Missouri . . . . . . . . . . . . | Gator 12-28-68 | Alabama 35-10 (Paul "Bear" Bryant) |
| Missouri . . . . . . . . . . . . | Orange 1-1-70 | Penn St. 3-10 (Joe Paterno) |
| Notre Dame . . . . . . . . . | Gator 12-27-76 | Penn St. 20-9 (Joe Paterno) |
| Notre Dame . . . . . . . . . | Cotton 1-2-78 | Texas 38-10 (Fred Akers) |
| Notre Dame . . . . . . . . . | Cotton 1-1-79 | Houston 35-34 (Bill Yeoman) |
| Notre Dame . . . . . . . . . | Sugar 1-1-81 | Georgia 10-17 (Vince Dooley) |

**PHIL DICKENS**, 1-0-0   (Tennessee '37)   b 6-29-14
| | | |
|---|---|---|
| Wyoming . . . . . . . . . . . . | Sun 1-2-56 | Texas Tech 21-14 (DeWitt Weaver) |

**DOUG DICKEY**, 2-7-0   (Florida '54)   b 6-24-32
| | | |
|---|---|---|
| Tennessee ........... | Bluebonnet 12-18-65 | Tulsa 27-6 (Glenn Dobbs) |
| Tennessee ........... | Gator 12-31-66 | Syracuse 18-12 (Ben Schwartzwalder) |
| Tennessee ........... | Orange 1-1-68 | Oklahoma 24-26 (Chuck Fairbanks) |
| Tennessee .......... | Cotton 1-1-69 | Texas 13-35 (Darrell Royal) |
| Tennessee .......... | Gator 12-27-69 | Florida 13-14 (Ray Graves) |
| Florida .............. | Tangerine 12-22-73 | Miami (Ohio) 7-16 (Bill Mallory) |
| Florida .............. | Sugar 12-31-74 | Nebraska 10-13 (Tom Osborne) |
| Florida .............. | Gator 12-29-75 | Maryland 0-13 (Jerry Claiborne) |
| Florida .............. | Sun 1-2-77 | Texas A&M 14-37 (Emory Bellard) |

**JIM DICKEY**, 0-1-0   (Houston '56)   b 3-22-34
| | | |
|---|---|---|
| Kansas St. .......... | Independence 12-11-82 | Wisconsin 3-14 (Dave McClain) |

**BILL "LONE STAR" DIETZ**, 1-0-0   (Carlisle '12)   b 8-15-85
| | | |
|---|---|---|
| Washington St........ | Rose 1-1-16 | Brown 14-0 (Ed Robinson) |

**PAUL DIETZEL**, 2-2-0   (Miami, Ohio '48)   b 9-5-24
| | | |
|---|---|---|
| Louisiana St. ......... | Sugar 1-1-59 | Clemson 7-0 (Frank Howard) |
| Louisiana St. ......... | Sugar 1-1-60 | Mississippi 0-21 (John Vaught) |
| Louisiana St. ......... | Orange 1-1-62 | Colorado 25-7 (Sonny Grandelius) |
| South Caro. .......... | Peach 12-20-69 | West Va. 3-14 (Jim Carlen) |

**BOBBY DOBBS**, 2-0-0   (Army '46)   b 10-13-22
| | | |
|---|---|---|
| UTEP ................ | Sun 12-31-65 | Texas Christian 13-12 (Abe Martin) |
| UTEP ................ | Sun 12-30-67 | Mississippi 14-7 (John Vaught) |

**GLENN DOBBS**, 1-1-0   (Tulsa '43)   b 7-12-20
| | | |
|---|---|---|
| Tulsa ................. | Bluebonnet 12-19-64 | Mississippi 14-7 (John Vaught) |
| Tulsa ................. | Bluebonnet 12-18-65 | Tennessee 6-27 (Doug Dickey) |

**BOBBY DODD**, 9-4-0   (Tennessee '31)   b 11-11-08
| | | |
|---|---|---|
| Georgia Tech ....... | Oil 1-1-47 | St. Mary's (Cal.) 41-19 (Jimmy Phelan) |
| Georgia Tech ....... | Orange 1-1-48 | Kansas 20-14 (George Sauer) |
| Georgia Tech ....... | Orange 1-1-52 | Baylor 17-14 (George Sauer) |
| Georgia Tech ....... | Sugar 1-1-53 | Mississippi 24-7 (John Vaught) |
| Georgia Tech ....... | Sugar 1-1-54 | West Va. 42-19 (Art Lewis) |
| Georgia Tech ....... | Cotton 1-1-55 | Arkansas 14-6 (Bowden Wyatt) |
| Georgia Tech ....... | Sugar 1-2-56 | Pittsburgh 7-0 (John Michelosen) |
| Georgia Tech ....... | Gator 12-29-56 | Pittsburgh 21-14 (John Michelosen) |
| Georgia Tech ....... | Gator 12-2-60 | Arkansas 7-14 (Frank Broyles) |
| Georgia Tech ....... | Gator 12-30-61 | Penn St. 15-30 (Charles "Rip" Engle) |
| Georgia Tech ....... | Bluebonnet 12-22-62 | Missouri 10-14 (Dan Devine) |
| Georgia Tech ....... | Gator 12-31-65 | Texas Tech 31-21 (J. T. King) |
| Georgia Tech ....... | Orange 1-2-67 | Florida 12-27 (Ray Graves) |

**ED DOHERTY**, 0-2-0   (Boston College '44)   b 7-25-18
| | | |
|---|---|---|
| Arizona St. .......... | Salad 1-1-50 | Xavier (Ohio) 21-33 (Ed Kluska) |
| Arizona St. .......... | Salad 1-1-51 | Miami (Ohio) 21-34 (Woody Hayes) |

**JACK DOLAND**, 1-0-0   (Tulane '50)   b 3-3-28
| | | |
|---|---|---|
| McNeese St. ........ | Independence 12-13-76 | Tulsa 20-16 (F. A. Dry) |

**TERRY DONAHUE**, 8-2-1   (UCLA '67)   b 6-24-44
| | | |
|---|---|---|
| UCLA ................ | Liberty 12-30-76 | Alabama 6-36 (Paul "Bear" Bryant) |
| UCLA ................ | Fiesta 12-25-78 | Arkansas 10-10 (Lou Holtz) |
| UCLA ................ | Bluebonnet 12-31-81 | Michigan 14-33 (Glenn "Bo" Schembechler) |
| UCLA ................ | Rose 1-1-83 | Michigan 24-14 (Glenn "Bo" Schembechler) |
| UCLA ................ | Rose 1-2-84 | Illinois 45-9 (Mike White) |
| UCLA ................ | Fiesta 1-1-85 | Miami (Fla.) 39-37 (Jimmy Johnson) |
| UCLA ................ | Rose 1-1-86 | Iowa 45-28 (Hayden Fry) |
| UCLA ................ | Freedom 12-30-86 | Brigham Young 31-10 (LaVell Edwards) |
| UCLA ................ | Aloha 12-25-87 | Florida 20-16 (Galen Hall) |
| UCLA ................ | Cotton 1-2-89 | Arkansas 17-3 (Ken Hatfield) |
| UCLA ................ | John Hancock 12-31-91 | Illinois 6-3 (Lou Tepper) |

**BILL DOOLEY**, 3-7-0   (Mississippi St. '56)   b 5-19-34
| | | |
|---|---|---|
| North Caro. ......... | Peach 12-30-70 | Arizona St. 26-48 (Frank Kush) |
| North Caro. ......... | Gator 12-31-71 | Georgia 3-7 (Vince Dooley) |
| North Caro. ......... | Sun 12-30-72 | Texas Tech 32-28 (Jim Carlen) |
| North Caro. ......... | Sun 12-28-74 | Mississippi St. 24-26 (Bob Tyler) |
| North Caro. ......... | Peach 12-31-76 | Kentucky 0-21 (Fran Curci) |
| North Caro. ......... | Liberty 12-19-77 | Nebraska 17-21 (Tom Osborne) |
| Virginia Tech ........ | Peach 1-2-81 | Miami (Fla.) 10-20 (Howard Schnellenberger) |
| Virginia Tech ........ | Independence 12-15-84 | Air Force 7-23 (Fisher DeBerry) |
| Virginia Tech ........ | Peach 12-31-86 | North Caro. St. 25-24 (Dick Sheridan) |
| Wake Forest.......... | Independence 12-31-92 | Oregon 39-35 (Rich Brooks) |

**VINCE DOOLEY**, 8-10-2   (Auburn '54)   b 9-4-32
| | | |
|---|---|---|
| Georgia .............. | Sun 12-26-64 | Texas Tech 7-0 (J. T. King) |
| Georgia .............. | Cotton 12-31-66 | Southern Methodist 24-9 (Hayden Fry) |
| Georgia .............. | Liberty 12-16-67 | North Caro. St. 7-14 (Earle Edwards) |
| Georgia .............. | Sugar 1-1-69 | Arkansas 2-16 (Frank Broyles) |

| Georgia .............. | Sun 12-20-69 | Nebraska 6-45 (Bob Devaney) |
|---|---|---|
| Georgia .............. | Gator 12-31-71 | North Caro. 7-3 (Bill Dooley) |
| Georgia .............. | Peach 12-28-73 | Maryland 17-16 (Jerry Claiborne) |
| Georgia .............. | Tangerine 12-21-74 | Miami (Ohio) 10-21 (Dick Crum) |
| Georgia .............. | Cotton 1-1-76 | Arkansas 10-31 (Frank Broyles) |
| Georgia .............. | Sugar 1-1-77 | Pittsburgh 3-27 (Johnny Majors) |
| Georgia .............. | Bluebonnet 12-31-78 | Stanford 22-25 (Bill Walsh) |
| Georgia .............. | Sugar 1-1-81 | Notre Dame 17-10 (Dan Devine) |
| Georgia .............. | Sugar 1-1-82 | Pittsburgh 20-24 (Jackie Sherrill) |
| Georgia .............. | Sugar 1-1-83 | Penn St. 23-27 (Joe Paterno) |
| Georgia .............. | Cotton 1-2-84 | Texas 10-9 (Fred Akers) |
| Georgia .............. | Fla. Citrus 12-22-84 | Florida St. 17-17 (Bobby Bowden) |
| Georgia .............. | Sun 12-28-85 | Arizona 13-13 (Larry Smith) |
| Georgia .............. | Hall of Fame 12-23-86 | Boston College 24-27 (Jack Bicknell) |
| Georgia .............. | Liberty 12-29-87 | Arkansas 20-17 (Ken Hatfield) |
| Georgia .............. | Gator 1-1-89 | Michigan St. 34-27 (George Perles) |

**CHARLES "GUS" DORAIS**, 0-1-0  (Notre Dame '14)    b 7-21-91
| Gonzaga .............. | San Diego East-West Christmas Classic 12-25-22 | West Va. 13-21 (Clarence "Doc" Spears) |
|---|---|---|

**HAROLD "RED" DREW**, 1-2-0  (Bates '16)    b 11-9-94
| Alabama .............. | Sugar 1-1-48 | Texas 7-27 (Blair Cherry) |
|---|---|---|
| Alabama .............. | Orange 1-1-53 | Syracuse 61-6 (Ben Schwartzwalder) |
| Alabama .............. | Cotton 1-1-54 | Rice 6-28 (Jess Neely) |

**BILL DRIVER**, 0-1-0  (Missouri '09)    b 11-7-83
| Texas Christian ...... | Fort Worth Classic 1-1-21 | Centre 7-63 (Charley Moran) |
|---|---|---|

**F. A. DRY**, 0-1-0  (Oklahoma St. '53)    b 9-2-31
| Tulsa ................ | Independence 12-13-76 | McNeese St. 16-20 (Jack Doland) |
|---|---|---|

**ERNIE DUPLECHIN**, 0-2-0  (Louisiana Col. '55)    b 7-19-32
| McNeese St. ......... | Independence 12-15-79 | Syracuse 7-31 (Frank Maloney) |
|---|---|---|
| McNeese St. ......... | Independence 12-13-80 | Southern Miss. 14-16 (Bobby Collins) |

**PAT DYE**, 7-2-1  (Georgia '62)    b 11-6-39
| East Caro............. | Independence 12-16-78 | Louisiana Tech 35-13 (Maxie Lambright) |
|---|---|---|
| Auburn ............... | Tangerine 12-18-82 | Boston College 33-26 (Jack Bicknell) |
| Auburn ............... | Sugar 1-2-84 | Michigan 9-7 (Glenn "Bo" Schembechler) |
| Auburn ............... | Liberty 12-27-84 | Arkansas 21-15 (Ken Hatfield) |
| Auburn ............... | Cotton 1-1-86 | Texas A&M 16-36 (Jackie Sherrill) |
| Auburn ............... | Fla. Citrus 1-1-87 | Southern Cal 16-7 (Ted Tollner) |
| Auburn ............... | Sugar 1-1-88 | Syracuse 16-16 (Dick MacPherson) |
| Auburn ............... | Sugar 1-2-89 | Florida St. 7-13 (Bobby Bowden) |
| Auburn ............... | Hall of Fame 1-1-90 | Ohio St. 31-14 (John Cooper) |
| Auburn ............... | Peach 12-29-90 | Indiana 27-23 (Bill Mallory) |

**SPIKE DYKES**, 1-1-0  (Stephen F. Austin '59)    b 4-15-38
| Texas Tech .......... | Independence 12-20-86 | Mississippi 17-20 (Billy Brewer) |
|---|---|---|
| Texas Tech .......... | All-American 12-28-89 | Duke 49-21 (Steve Spurrier) |

**LLOYD EATON**, 1-1-0  (Black Hills St. '40)    b 3-23-18
| Wyoming............. | Sun 12-24-66 | Florida St. 28-20 (Bill Peterson) |
|---|---|---|
| Wyoming............. | Sugar 1-1-68 | Louisiana St. 13-20 (Charlie McClendon) |

**BILL EDWARDS**, 1-0-0  (Wittenberg '31)    b 6-21-05
| Case Reserve ........ | Sun 1-1-41 | Arizona St. 26-13 (Millard "Dixie" Howell) |
|---|---|---|

**EARLE EDWARDS**, 1-1-0  (Penn St. '31)    b 11-10-08
| North Caro. St........ | Liberty 12-21-63 | Mississippi St. 12-16 (Paul Davis) |
|---|---|---|
| North Caro. St........ | Liberty 12-16-67 | Georgia 14-7 (Vince Dooley) |

**LaVELL EDWARDS**, 5-11-1  (Utah St. '52)    b 10-11-30
| Brigham Young ...... | Fiesta 12-28-74 | Oklahoma St. 6-16 (Jim Stanley) |
|---|---|---|
| Brigham Young ...... | Tangerine 12-18-76 | Oklahoma St. 21-49 (Jim Stanley) |
| Brigham Young ...... | Holiday 12-22-78 | Navy 16-23 (George Welsh) |
| Brigham Young ...... | Holiday 12-21-79 | Indiana 37-38 (Lee Corso) |
| Brigham Young ...... | Holiday 12-19-80 | Southern Methodist 46-45 (Ron Meyer) |
| Brigham Young ...... | Holiday 12-18-81 | Washington St. 38-36 (Jim Walden) |
| Brigham Young ...... | Holiday 12-17-82 | Ohio St. 17-47 (Earle Bruce) |
| Brigham Young ...... | Holiday 12-23-83 | Missouri 21-17 (Warren Powers) |
| Brigham Young ...... | Holiday 12-21-84 | Michigan 24-17 (Glenn "Bo" Schembechler) |
| Brigham Young ...... | Fla. Citrus 12-28-85 | Ohio St. 7-10 (Earle Bruce) |
| Brigham Young ...... | Freedom 12-30-86 | UCLA 10-31 (Terry Donahue) |
| Brigham Young ...... | All-American 12-22-87 | Virginia 16-22 (George Welsh) |
| Brigham Young ...... | Freedom 12-29-88 | Colorado 20-17 (Bill McCartney) |
| Brigham Young ...... | Holiday 12-29-89 | Penn St. 39-50 (Joe Paterno) |
| Brigham Young ...... | Holiday 12-29-90 | Texas A&M 14-65 (R. C. Slocum) |
| Brigham Young ...... | Holiday 12-30-91 | Iowa 13-13 (Hayden Fry) |
| Brigham Young ...... | Aloha 12-25-92 | Kansas 20-23 (Glen Mason) |

**RAY ELIOT**, 2-0-0   (Illinois '32)   b 6-13-05
Illinois . . . . . . . . . . . . . . .   Rose 1-1-47
Illinois . . . . . . . . . . . . . . .   Rose 1-1-52

UCLA 45-14 (Bert LaBrucherie)
Stanford 40-7 (Chuck Taylor)

**BENNIE ELLENDER**, 0-1-0   (Tulane '48)   b 3-2-25
Tulane . . . . . . . . . . . . . . .   Bluebonnet 12-29-73

Houston 7-47 (Bill Yeoman)

**CHALMERS "BUMP" ELLIOTT**, 1-0-0   (Michigan '48)   b 1-30-25
Michigan . . . . . . . . . . . .   Rose 1-1-65

Oregon St. 34-7 (Tommy Prothro)

**PETE ELLIOTT**, 1-1-0   (Michigan '49)   b 9-29-26
California . . . . . . . . . . . .   Rose 1-1-59
Illinois . . . . . . . . . . . . . . .   Rose 1-1-64

Iowa 12-38 (Forest Evashevski)
Washington 17-7 (Jim Owens)

**JACK ELWAY**, 0-2-0   (Washington St. '53)   b 5-30-31
San Jose St. . . . . . . . . .   California 12-19-81
Stanford . . . . . . . . . . . . .   Gator 12-27-86

Toledo 25-27 (Chuck Stobart)
Clemson 21-27 (Danny Ford)

**CHARLES "RIP" ENGLE**, 3-1-0   (Western Md. '30)   b 3-26-06
Penn St. . . . . . . . . . . . . .   Liberty 12-19-53
Penn St. . . . . . . . . . . . . .   Liberty 12-17-60
Penn St. . . . . . . . . . . . . .   Gator 12-30-61
Penn St. . . . . . . . . . . . . .   Gator 12-29-62

Alabama 7-0 (Paul "Bear" Bryant)
Oregon 41-12 (Len Casanova)
Georgia Tech 30-15 (Bobby Dodd)
Florida 7-17 (Ray Graves)

**EDDIE ERDELATZ**, 2-0-0   (St. Mary's, Cal. '36)   b 4-21-13
Navy . . . . . . . . . . . . . . . .   Sugar 1-1-55
Navy . . . . . . . . . . . . . . . .   Cotton 1-1-58

Mississippi 21-0 (John Vaught)
Rice 20-7 (Jess Neely)

**DENNIS ERICKSON**, 4-1-0   (Montana St. '70)   b 3-24-47
Washington St. . . . . . . .   Aloha 12-25-88
Miami (Fla.) . . . . . . . . . .   Sugar 1-1-90
Miami (Fla.) . . . . . . . . . .   Cotton 1-1-91
Miami (Fla.) . . . . . . . . . .   Orange 1-1-92
Miami (Fla.) . . . . . . . . . .   Sugar 1-1-93

Houston 24-22 (Jack Pardee)
Alabama 33-25 (Bill Curry)
Texas 46-3 (David McWilliams)
Nebraska 22-0 (Tom Osborne)
Alabama 13-34 (Gene Stallings)

**FOREST EVASHEVSKI**, 2-0-0   (Michigan '41)   b 2-19-18
Iowa . . . . . . . . . . . . . . . .   Rose 1-1-57
Iowa . . . . . . . . . . . . . . . .   Rose 1-1-59

Oregon St. 35-19 (Tommy Prothro)
California 38-12 (Pete Elliott)

**CHUCK FAIRBANKS**, 3-1-1   (Michigan St. '55)   b 6-10-33
Oklahoma . . . . . . . . . . . .   Orange 1-1-68
Oklahoma . . . . . . . . . . . .   Bluebonnet 12-31-68
Oklahoma . . . . . . . . . . . .   Bluebonnet 12-31-70
Oklahoma . . . . . . . . . . . .   Sugar 1-1-72
Oklahoma . . . . . . . . . . . .   Sugar 12-31-72

Tennessee 26-24 (Doug Dickey)
Southern Methodist 27-28 (Hayden Fry)
Alabama 24-24 (Paul "Bear" Bryant)
Auburn 40-22 (Ralph "Shug" Jordan)
Penn St. 14-0 (Joe Paterno)

**DON FAMBROUGH**, 0-2-0   (Kansas '48)   b 10-19-22
Kansas . . . . . . . . . . . . . .   Liberty 12-17-73
Kansas . . . . . . . . . . . . . .   Hall of Fame 12-31-81

North Caro. St. 18-31 (Lou Holtz)
Mississippi St. 0-10 (Emory Bellard)

**DON FAUROT**, 0-4-0   (Missouri '25)   b 6-23-02
Missouri . . . . . . . . . . . . .   Orange 1-1-40
Missouri . . . . . . . . . . . . .   Sugar 1-1-42
Missouri . . . . . . . . . . . . .   Gator 1-1-49
Missouri . . . . . . . . . . . . .   Gator 1-2-50

Georgia Tech 7-21 (Bill Alexander)
Fordham 0-2 (Jim Crowley)
Clemson 23-24 (Frank Howard)
Maryland 7-21 (Jim Tatum)

**GERRY FAUST**, 1-1-0   (Dayton '58)   b 5-21-35
Notre Dame . . . . . . . . . .   Liberty 12-29-83
Notre Dame . . . . . . . . . .   Aloha 12-29-84

Boston College 19-18 (Jack Bicknell)
Southern Methodist 20-27 (Bobby Collins)

**FOGE FAZIO**, 0-2-0   (Pittsburgh '60)   b 2-28-39
Pittsburgh . . . . . . . . . . . .   Cotton 1-1-83
Pittsburgh . . . . . . . . . . . .   Fiesta 1-2-84

Southern Methodist 3-7 (Bobby Collins)
Ohio St. 23-28 (Earle Bruce)

**BEATTIE FEATHERS**, 0-1-0   (Tennessee '34)   b 6-1-12
North Caro. St. . . . . . . .   Gator 1-1-47

Oklahoma 13-34 (Jim Tatum)

**WES FESLER**, 1-0-0   (Ohio St. '32)   b 6-29-08
Ohio St. . . . . . . . . . . . . .   Rose 1-2-50

California 17-14 (Lynn "Pappy" Waldorf)

**CHARLIE FICKERT**, 0-1-0   (Stanford '98)   b 2-23-73
Stanford . . . . . . . . . . . . .   Rose 1-1-02

Michigan 0-49 (Fielding "Hurry Up" Yost)

**ROBERT FISHER**, 1-0-0   (Harvard '12)   b 12-3-88
Harvard . . . . . . . . . . . . . .   Rose 1-1-20

Oregon 7-6 (Charles "Shy" Huntington)

**HANK FOLDBERG**, 0-1-0   (Army '48)   b 3-12-23
Wichita St. . . . . . . . . . . .   Sun 12-30-61

Villanova 9-17 (Alex Bell)

**BOB FOLWELL**, 0-1-1   (Pennsylvania '08)   b 1885
Pennsylvania . . . . . . . . .   Rose 1-1-17
Navy . . . . . . . . . . . . . . . .   Rose 1-1-24

Oregon 0-14 (Hugo Bezdek)
Washington 14-14 (Enoch Bagshaw)

**DANNY FORD**, 6-2-0   (Alabama '70)   b 4-2-48
Clemson . . . . . . . . . . . . .   Gator 12-29-78
Clemson . . . . . . . . . . . . .   Peach 12-31-79
Clemson . . . . . . . . . . . . .   Orange 1-1-82
Clemson . . . . . . . . . . . . .   Independence 12-21-85
Clemson . . . . . . . . . . . . .   Gator 12-27-86

Ohio St. 17-15 (Woody Hayes)
Baylor 18-24 (Grant Teaff)
Nebraska 22-15 (Tom Osborne)
Minnesota 13-20 (John Gutekunst)
Stanford 27-21 (Jack Elway)

*Bowl Coaching Records*

Clemson ............. Fla. Citrus 1-1-88    Penn St. 35-10 (Joe Paterno)
Clemson ............. Fla. Citrus 1-2-89    Oklahoma 23-6 (Barry Switzer)
Clemson ............. Gator 12-30-89    West Va. 27-7 (Don Nehlen)

**HENRY FRNKA**, 2-3-0 (Austin '26) b 3-16-03
Tulsa ................. Sun 1-1-42    Texas Tech 6-0 (Dell Morgan)
Tulsa ................. Sugar 1-1-43    Tennessee 7-14 (John Barnhill)
Tulsa ................. Sugar 1-1-44    Georgia Tech 18-20 (Bill Alexander)
Tulsa ................. Orange 1-1-45    Georgia Tech 26-12 (Bill Alexander)
Tulsa ................. Oil 1-1-46    Georgia 6-20 (Wally Butts)

**HAYDEN FRY**, 5-7-1 (Baylor '51) b 2-28-29
Southern Methodist .. Sun 12-31-63    Oregon 13-21 (Len Casanova)
Southern Methodist .. Cotton 12-31-66    Georgia 9-24 (Vince Dooley)
Southern Methodist .. Bluebonnet 12-31-68    Oklahoma 28-27 (Chuck Fairbanks)
Iowa ................. Rose 1-1-82    Washington 0-28 (Don James)
Iowa ................. Peach 12-31-82    Tennessee 28-22 (Johnny Majors)
Iowa ................. Gator 12-30-83    Florida 6-14 (Charley Pell)
Iowa ................. Freedom 12-26-84    Texas 55-17 (Fred Akers)
Iowa ................. Rose 1-1-86    UCLA 28-45 (Terry Donahue)
Iowa ................. Holiday 12-30-86    San Diego St. 39-38 (Denny Stolz)
Iowa ................. Holiday 12-30-87    Wyoming 20-19 (Paul Roach)
Iowa ................. Peach 12-31-88    North Caro. St. 23-29 (Dick Sheridan)
Iowa ................. Rose 1-1-91    Washington 34-46 (Don James)
Iowa ................. Holiday 12-30-91    Brigham Young 13-13 (LaVell Edwards)

**BILL FULCHER**, 1-0-0 (Georgia Tech '57) b 2-9-34
Georgia Tech ....... Liberty 12-18-72    Iowa St. 31-30 (Johnny Majors)

**PHILLIP FULMER**, 1-0-0 (Tennessee '72) b 9-1-50
Tennessee .......... Hall of Fame 1-1-93    Boston College 38-23 (Tom Coughlin)

**WARREN GAER**, 0-1-0 (Drake '35) b 2-7-12
Drake ................ Sun 1-1-58    Louisville 20-34 (Frank Camp)

**JOE GAVIN**, 0-1-0 (Notre Dame '31) b 3-20-08
Dayton .............. Salad 1-1-52    Houston 21-26 (Clyde Lee)

**GARY GIBBS**, 1-0-0 (Oklahoma '75) b 8-13-52
Oklahoma ........... Gator 12-29-91    Virginia 48-14 (George Welsh)

**VINCE GIBSON**, 0-2-0 (Florida St. '55) b 3-27-33
Louisville ............ Independence 12-17-77    Louisiana Tech 14-24 (Maxie Lambright)
Tulane............... Hall of Fame 12-27-80    Arkansas 15-34 (Lou Holtz)

**CLAUDE GILBERT**, 1-1-0 (San Jose St. '59) b 7-10-32
San Jose St. ........ California 12-13-86    Miami (Ohio) 37-7 (Tim Rose)
San Jose St. ........ California 12-12-87    Eastern Mich. 27-30 (Jim Harkema)

**SID GILLMAN**, 1-1-0 (Ohio St. '34) b 10-26-11
Miami (Ohio)........ Sun 1-1-48    Texas Tech 13-12 (Dell Morgan)
Cincinnati ........... Sun 1-1-51    West Tex. St. 13-14 (Frank Kimbrough)

**BILL GLASSFORD**, 0-1-0 (Pittsburgh '37) b 3-8-14
Nebraska............ Orange 1-1-55    Duke 7-34 (Bill Murray)

**MARSHALL "LITTLE SLEEPY" GLENN**, 1-0-0 (West Va. '31) b 4-22-08
West Va.............. Sun 1-1-38    Texas Tech 7-6 (Pete Cawthon)

**RAY GOFF**, 2-1-0 (Georgia '78) b 7-10-55
Georgia ............. Peach 12-30-89    Syracuse 18-19 (Dick MacPherson)
Georgia ............. Independence 12-29-91    Arkansas 24-15 (Jack Crowe)
Georgia ............. Fla. Citrus 1-1-93    Ohio St. 21-14 (John Cooper)

**MIKE GOTTFRIED**, 0-1-0 (Morehead St. '66) b 12-17-44
Pittsburgh ........... Bluebonnet 12-31-87    Texas 27-32 (David McWilliams)

**RALPH GRAHAM**, 0-1-0 (Kansas St. '34) b 8-16-10
Wichita St. .......... Raisin 1-1-48    Pacific (Cal.) 14-26 (Larry Siemering)

**SONNY GRANDELIUS**, 0-1-0 (Michigan St. '51) b 4-16-29
Colorado............. Orange 1-1-62    Louisiana St. 7-25 (Paul Dietzel)

**RAY GRAVES**, 4-1-0 (Tennessee '43) b 12-31-18
Florida .............. Gator 12-31-60    Baylor 13-12 (John Bridgers)
Florida .............. Gator 12-29-62    Penn St. 17-7 (Charles "Rip" Engle)
Florida .............. Sugar 1-1-66    Missouri 18-20 (Dan Devine)
Florida .............. Orange 1-2-67    Georgia Tech 27-12 (Bobby Dodd)
Florida .............. Gator 12-27-69    Tennessee 14-13 (Doug Dickey)

**DENNIS GREEN**, 0-1-0 (Iowa '71) b 2-17-49
Stanford ............. Aloha 12-25-91    Georgia Tech 17-18 (Bobby Ross)

**VEE GREEN**, 1-0-0 (Illinois '24) b 10-9-00
Drake ................ Raisin 1-1-46    Fresno St. 13-12 (Alvin "Pix" Pierson)

**ART GUEPE**, 1-0-0 (Marquette '37) b 1-28-15
Vanderbilt ........... Gator 12-31-55    Auburn 25-13 (Ralph "Shug" Jordan)

**ANDY GUSTAFSON**, 1-3-0   (Pittsburgh '26)   b 4-3-03
| | | |
|---|---|---|
| Miami (Fla.) .......... | Orange 1-1-51 | Clemson 14-15 (Frank Howard) |
| Miami (Fla.) .......... | Gator 1-1-52 | Clemson 14-0 (Frank Howard) |
| Miami (Fla.) .......... | Liberty 12-16-61 | Syracuse 14-15 (Ben Schwartzwalder) |
| Miami (Fla.) .......... | Gotham 12-15-62 | Nebraska 34-36 (Bob Devaney) |

**JOHN GUTEKUNST**, 1-1-0   (Duke '66)   b 4-13-44
| | | |
|---|---|---|
| Minnesota............ | Independence 12-21-85 | Clemson 20-13 (Danny Ford) |
| Minnesota............ | Liberty 12-29-86 | Tennessee 14-21 (Johnny Majors) |

**PAUL HACKETT**, 1-0-0   (UC Davis '69)   b 6-5-47
| | | |
|---|---|---|
| Pittsburgh ............ | John Hancock 12-30-89 | Texas A&M 31-28 (R. C. Slocum) |

**JACK HAGERTY**, 0-1-0   (Georgetown '26)   b 7-3-03
| | | |
|---|---|---|
| Georgetown ......... | Orange 1-1-41 | Mississippi St. 7-14 (Alvin McKeen) |

**GALEN HALL**, 1-1-0   (Penn St. '62)   b 8-14-40
| | | |
|---|---|---|
| Florida ............... | Aloha 12-25-87 | UCLA 16-20 (Terry Donahue) |
| Florida ............... | All-American 12-29-88 | Illinois 14-10 (John Mackovic) |

**CURLEY HALLMAN**, 1-0-0   (Texas A&M '70)   b 9-3-47
| | | |
|---|---|---|
| Southern Miss........ | Independence 12-23-88 | UTEP 38-18 (Bob Stull) |

**WAYNE HARDIN**, 1-2-0   (Pacific, Cal. '50)   b 3-23-27
| | | |
|---|---|---|
| Navy ................. | Orange 1-2-61 | Missouri 14-21 (Dan Devine) |
| Navy ................. | Cotton 1-1-64 | Texas 6-28 (Darrell Royal) |
| Temple ............... | Garden State 12-15-79 | California 28-17 (Roger Theder) |

**JACK HARDING**, 1-0-0   (Pittsburgh '26)   b 1-5-98
| | | |
|---|---|---|
| Miami (Fla.) .......... | Orange 1-1-48 | Holy Cross 13-6 (John "Ox" Da Grosa) |

**JIM HARKEMA**, 1-0-0   (Kalamazoo '64)   b 6-25-42
| | | |
|---|---|---|
| Eastern Mich. ........ | California 12-12-87 | San Jose St. 30-27 (Claude Gilbert) |

**KEN HATFIELD**, 4-6-0   (Arkansas '65)   b 6-8-43
| | | |
|---|---|---|
| Air Force ............. | Hall of Fame 12-31-82 | Vanderbilt 36-28 (George MacIntyre) |
| Air Force ............. | Independence 12-10-83 | Mississippi 9-3 (Billy Brewer) |
| Arkansas ............. | Liberty 12-27-84 | Auburn 15-21 (Pat Dye) |
| Arkansas ............. | Holiday 12-22-85 | Arizona St. 18-17 (John Cooper) |
| Arkansas ............. | Orange 1-1-87 | Oklahoma 8-42 (Barry Switzer) |
| Arkansas ............. | Liberty 12-29-87 | Georgia 17-20 (Vince Dooley) |
| Arkansas ............. | Cotton 1-2-89 | UCLA 3-17 (Terry Donahue) |
| Arkansas ............. | Cotton 1-1-90 | Tennessee 27-31 (Johnny Majors) |
| Clemson ............. | Hall of Fame 1-1-91 | Illinois 30-0 (John Mackovic) |
| Clemson ............. | Fla. Citrus 1-1-92 | California 13-37 (Bruce Snyder) |

**WOODY HAYES**, 6-6-0   (Denison '35)   b 2-14-13
| | | |
|---|---|---|
| Miami (Ohio) ......... | Salad 1-1-51 | Arizona St. 34-21 (Ed Doherty) |
| Ohio St. .............. | Rose 1-1-55 | Southern Cal 20-7 (Jess Hill) |
| Ohio St. .............. | Rose 1-1-58 | Oregon 10-7 (Len Casanova) |
| Ohio St. .............. | Rose 1-1-69 | Southern Cal 27-16 (John McKay) |
| Ohio St. .............. | Rose 1-1-71 | Stanford 17-27 (John Ralston) |
| Ohio St. .............. | Rose 1-1-73 | Southern Cal 17-42 (John McKay) |
| Ohio St. .............. | Rose 1-1-74 | Southern Cal 42-21 (John McKay) |
| Ohio St. .............. | Rose 1-1-75 | Southern Cal 17-18 (John McKay) |
| Ohio St. .............. | Rose 1-1-76 | UCLA 10-23 (Dick Vermeil) |
| Ohio St. .............. | Orange 1-1-77 | Colorado 27-10 (Bill Mallory) |
| Ohio St. .............. | Sugar 1-2-78 | Alabama 6-35 (Paul "Bear" Bryant) |
| Ohio St. .............. | Gator 12-29-78 | Clemson 15-17 (Danny Ford) |

**ELMER "GUS" HENDERSON**, 2-0-0   (Oberlin '12)   b 3-10-89
| | | |
|---|---|---|
| Southern Cal......... | Rose 1-1-23 | Penn St. 14-3 (Hugo Bezdek) |
| Southern Cal......... | L.A. Christmas Festival 12-25-24 | Missouri 20-7 (Gwinn Henry) |

**GWINN HENRY**, 0-1-0   (Howard Payne '17)   b 8-5-87
| | | |
|---|---|---|
| Missouri .............. | L.A. Christmas Festival 12-25-24 | Southern Cal 7-20 (Elmer "Gus" Henderson) |

**BILL HESS**, 0-2-0   (Ohio '47)   b 2-5-23
| | | |
|---|---|---|
| Ohio ................. | Sun 12-31-62 | West Tex. St. 14-15 (Joe Kerbel) |
| Ohio ................. | Tangerine 12-27-68 | Richmond 42-49 (Frank Jones) |

**JIM HICKEY**, 1-0-0   (William & Mary '42)   b 1-22-20
| | | |
|---|---|---|
| North Caro. .......... | Gator 12-28-63 | Air Force 35-0 (Ben Martin) |

**BOB HIGGINS**, 1-0-1   (Penn St. '20)   b 12-24-93
| | | |
|---|---|---|
| West Va. Wesleyan ... | Dixie Classic 1-1-25 | Southern Methodist 9-7 (Ray Morrison) |
| Penn St............... | Cotton 1-1-48 | Southern Methodist 13-13 (Matty Bell) |

**JESS HILL**, 1-1-0   (Southern Cal '30)   b 1-20-07
| | | |
|---|---|---|
| Southern Cal......... | Rose 1-1-53 | Wisconsin 7-0 (Ivy Williamson) |
| Southern Cal......... | Rose 1-1-55 | Ohio St. 7-20 (Woody Hayes) |

**JERRY HINES**, 0-0-1   (New Mexico St. '26)   b 10-11-03
| | | |
|---|---|---|
| New Mexico St. ...... | Sun 1-1-36 | Hardin-Simmons 14-14 (Frank Kimbrough) |

*Bowl Coaching Records*

**BERNARD A. HOBAN**, 0-1-0 (Dartmouth '12)  b 4-21-90
U. of Mexico . . . . . . . . Sun 1-1-45  Southwestern (Tex.) 0-35 (Randolph R. M. Medley)

**ORIN "BABE" HOLLINGBERY**, 0-1-0 (No college)  b 7-15-93
Washington St. . . . . . . . Rose 1-1-31  Alabama 0-24 (Wallace Wade)

**LOU HOLTZ**, 9-6-2 (Kent '59)  b 1-6-37
William & Mary . . . . . . . Tangerine 12-28-70  Toledo 12-40 (Frank Lauterbur)
North Caro. St. . . . . . . . Peach 12-29-72  West Va. 49-13 (Bobby Bowden)
North Caro. St. . . . . . . . Liberty 12-17-73  Kansas 31-18 (Don Fambrough)
North Caro. St. . . . . . . . Bluebonnet 12-23-74  Houston 31-31 (Bill Yeoman)
North Caro. St. . . . . . . . Peach 12-31-75  West Va. 10-13 (Bobby Bowden)
Arkansas . . . . . . . . . . . Orange 1-2-78  Oklahoma 31-6 (Barry Switzer)
Arkansas . . . . . . . . . . . Fiesta 12-25-78  UCLA 10-10 (Terry Donahue)
Arkansas . . . . . . . . . . . Sugar 1-1-80  Alabama 9-24 (Paul "Bear" Bryant)
Arkansas . . . . . . . . . . . Hall of Fame 12-27-80  Tulane 34-15 (Vince Gibson)
Arkansas . . . . . . . . . . . Gator 12-28-81  North Caro. 27-31 (Dick Crum)
Arkansas . . . . . . . . . . . Bluebonnet 12-31-82  Florida 28-24 (Charley Pell)
Notre Dame . . . . . . . . . Cotton 1-1-88  Texas A&M 10-35 (Jackie Sherrill)
Notre Dame . . . . . . . . . Fiesta 1-2-89  West Va. 34-21 (Don Nehlen)
Notre Dame . . . . . . . . . Orange 1-1-90  Colorado 21-6 (Bill McCartney)
Notre Dame . . . . . . . . . Orange 1-1-91  Colorado 9-10 (Bill McCartney)
Notre Dame . . . . . . . . . Sugar 1-1-92  Florida 39-28 (Steve Spurrier)
Notre Dame . . . . . . . . . Cotton 1-1-93  Texas A&M 28-3 (R. C. Slocum)

**EDWIN "BABE" HORRELL**, 0-1-0 (California '26)  b 9-29-02
UCLA . . . . . . . . . . . . . . Rose 1-1-43  Georgia 0-9 (Wally Butts)

**FRANK HOWARD**, 3-3-0 (Alabama '31)  b 3-25-09
Clemson . . . . . . . . . . . Gator 1-1-49  Missouri 24-23 (Don Faurot)
Clemson . . . . . . . . . . . Orange 1-1-51  Miami (Fla.) 15-14 (Andy Gustafson)
Clemson . . . . . . . . . . . Gator 1-1-52  Miami (Fla.) 0-14 (Andy Gustafson)
Clemson . . . . . . . . . . . Orange 1-1-57  Colorado 21-27 (Dallas Ward)
Clemson . . . . . . . . . . . Sugar 1-1-59  Louisiana St. 0-7 (Paul Dietzel)
Clemson . . . . . . . . . . . Bluebonnet 12-19-59  Texas Christian 23-7 (Abe Martin)

**MILLARD "DIXIE" HOWELL**, 0-1-1 (Alabama '35)  b 11-24-12
Arizona St. . . . . . . . . . . Sun 1-1-40  Catholic 0-0 (Arthur "Dutch" Bergman)
Arizona St. . . . . . . . . . . Sun 1-1-41  Case Reserve 13-26 (Bill Edwards)

**BILL HUBBARD**, 2-0-0 (Stanford '30)  b 2-5-07
San Jose St. . . . . . . . . Raisin 1-1-47  Utah St. 20-0 (E. L. "Dick" Romney)
San Jose St. . . . . . . . . Raisin 12-31-49  Texas Tech 20-13 (Dell Morgan)

**CLYDE "CAC" HUBBARD**, 0-2-0 (Oregon St. '21)  b 9-13-97
Denver . . . . . . . . . . . . . Sun 1-1-46  New Mexico 24-34 (Willis Barnes)
Denver . . . . . . . . . . . . . Alamo 1-4-47  Hardin-Simmons 0-20 (Warren Woodson)

**CHARLES "SHY" HUNTINGTON**, 0-1-0 (Oregon)  b 7-7-91
Oregon . . . . . . . . . . . . Rose 1-1-20  Harvard 6-7 (Robert Fisher)

**HARVEY HYDE**, 1-0-0 (Redlands '62)  b 7-13-39
Nevada-Las Vegas . . . California 12-15-84  Toledo 30-13 (Dan Simrell)

**DON JAMES**, 10-5-0 (Miami, Fla. '54)  b 12-31-32
Kent . . . . . . . . . . . . . . . Tangerine 12-29-72  Tampa 18-21 (Earle Bruce)
Washington . . . . . . . . . Rose 1-2-78  Michigan 27-20 (Glenn "Bo" Schembechler)
Washington . . . . . . . . . Sun 12-22-79  Texas 14-7 (Fred Akers)
Washington . . . . . . . . . Rose 1-1-81  Michigan 6-23 (Glenn "Bo" Schembechler)
Washington . . . . . . . . . Rose 1-1-82  Iowa 28-0 (Hayden Fry)
Washington . . . . . . . . . Aloha 12-25-82  Maryland 21-20 (Bobby Ross)
Washington . . . . . . . . . Aloha 12-26-83  Penn St. 10-13 (Joe Paterno)
Washington . . . . . . . . . Orange 1-1-85  Oklahoma 28-17 (Barry Switzer)
Washington . . . . . . . . . Freedom 12-30-85  Colorado 20-17 (Bill McCartney)
Washington . . . . . . . . . Sun 12-25-86  Alabama 6-28 (Ray Perkins)
Washington . . . . . . . . . Independence 12-18-87  Tulane 24-12 (Mack Brown)
Washington . . . . . . . . . Freedom 12-29-89  Florida 34-7 (Gary Darnell)
Washington . . . . . . . . . Rose 1-1-91  Iowa 46-34 (Hayden Fry)
Washington . . . . . . . . . Rose 1-1-92  Michigan 34-14 (Gary Moeller)
Washington . . . . . . . . . Rose 1-1-93  Michigan 31-38 (Gary Moeller)

**JIMMY JOHNSON**, 3-4-0 (Arkansas '65)  b 7-16-43
Oklahoma St. . . . . . . . . Independence 12-12-81  Texas A&M 16-33 (Tom Wilson)
Oklahoma St. . . . . . . . . Bluebonnet 12-31-83  Baylor 24-14 (Grant Teaff)
Miami (Fla.) . . . . . . . . . Fiesta 1-1-85  UCLA 37-39 (Terry Donahue)
Miami (Fla.) . . . . . . . . . Sugar 1-1-86  Tennessee 7-35 (Johnny Majors)
Miami (Fla.) . . . . . . . . . Fiesta 1-2-87  Penn St. 10-14 (Joe Paterno)
Miami (Fla.) . . . . . . . . . Orange 1-1-88  Oklahoma 20-14 (Barry Switzer)
Miami (Fla.) . . . . . . . . . Orange 1-2-89  Nebraska 23-3 (Tom Osborne)

**FRANK JONES**, 1-1-0 (North Caro. '48)  b 8-30-21
Richmond . . . . . . . . . . . Tangerine 12-27-68  Ohio 49-42 (Bill Hess)
Richmond . . . . . . . . . . . Tangerine 12-28-71  Toledo 3-28 (John Murphy)

**GOMER JONES**, 0-1-0  (Ohio St. '36)  b 2-26-14
Oklahoma . . . . . . . . . . . .  Gator 1-2-65  Florida St. 19-36 (Bill Peterson)
**HOWARD JONES**, 5-0-0  (Yale '08)  b 8-23-85
Southern Cal . . . . . . . .  Rose 1-1-30  Pittsburgh 47-14 (Jock Sutherland)
Southern Cal . . . . . . . .  Rose 1-1-32  Tulane 21-12 (Bernie Bierman)
Southern Cal . . . . . . . .  Rose 1-2-33  Pittsburgh 35-0 (Jock Sutherland)
Southern Cal . . . . . . . .  Rose 1-2-39  Duke 7-3 (Wallace Wade)
Southern Cal . . . . . . . .  Rose 1-1-40  Tennessee 14-0 (Bob Neyland)
**LARRY JONES**, 0-1-0  (Louisiana St. '54)  b 12-18-33
Florida St. . . . . . . . . . . .  Fiesta 12-27-71  Arizona St. 38–45 (Frank Kush)
**LAWRENCE McC. "BIFF" JONES**, 0-1-0  (Army '17)  b 10-8-95
Nebraska . . . . . . . . . . . .  Rose 1-1-41  Stanford 13-21 (Clark Shaughnessy)
**PAT JONES**, 3-1-0  (Arkansas '69)  b 11-4-47
Oklahoma St. . . . . . . . .  Gator 12-28-84  South Caro. 21-14 (Joe Morrison)
Oklahoma St. . . . . . . . .  Gator 12-30-85  Florida St. 23-34 (Bobby Bowden)
Oklahoma St. . . . . . . . .  Sun 12-25-87  West Va. 35-33 (Don Nehlen)
Oklahoma St. . . . . . . . .  Holiday 12-30-88  Wyoming 62-14 (Paul Roach)
**RALPH "SHUG" JORDAN**, 5-7-0  (Auburn '32)  b 9-25-10
Auburn . . . . . . . . . . . . . .  Gator 1-1-54  Texas Tech 13-35 (DeWitt Weaver)
Auburn . . . . . . . . . . . . . .  Gator 12-31-54  Baylor 33-13 (George Sauer)
Auburn . . . . . . . . . . . . . .  Gator 12-31-55  Vanderbilt 13-25 (Art Gueppe)
Auburn . . . . . . . . . . . . . .  Orange 1-1-64  Nebraska 7-13 (Bob Devaney)
Auburn . . . . . . . . . . . . . .  Liberty 12-18-65  Mississippi 7-13 (John Vaught)
Auburn . . . . . . . . . . . . . .  Sun 12-28-68  Arizona 34-10 (Darrell Mudra)
Auburn . . . . . . . . . . . . . .  Bluebonnet 12-31-69  Houston 7-36 (Bill Yeoman)
Auburn . . . . . . . . . . . . . .  Gator 1-2-71  Mississippi 35-28 (John Vaught)
Auburn . . . . . . . . . . . . . .  Sugar 1-1-72  Oklahoma 22-40 (Chuck Fairbanks)
Auburn . . . . . . . . . . . . . .  Gator 12-30-72  Colorado 24-3 (Eddie Crowder)
Auburn . . . . . . . . . . . . . .  Sun 12-29-73  Missouri 17-34 (Al Onofrio)
Auburn . . . . . . . . . . . . . .  Gator 12-30-74  Texas 27-3 (Darrell Royal)
**ERNIE JORGE**, 1-1-0  (St. Mary's, Cal. '36)  b 10-7-14
Pacific (Cal.) . . . . . . . .  Sun 1-1-52  Texas Tech 14-25 (DeWitt Weaver)
Pacific (Cal.) . . . . . . . .  Sun 1-1-53  Southern Miss. 26-7 (Thad "Pie" Vann)
**AL KAWAL**, 1-0-0  (Northwestern '35)  b 7-4-12
Drake . . . . . . . . . . . . . . .  Salad 1-1-49  Arizona 14-13 (Miles Casteel)
**JOE KERBEL**, 2-0-0  (Oklahoma '47)  b 5-3-21
West Tex. St. . . . . . . . .  Sun 12-21-62  Ohio 15-14 (Bill Hess)
West Tex. St. . . . . . . . .  Pasadena 12-2-67  Cal St. Northridge 35-13 (Sam Winningham)
**BILL KERN**, 0-1-0  (Pittsburgh '28)  b 9-2-06
Carnegie Mellon . . . . .  Sugar 1-2-39  Texas Christian 7-15 (Leo "Dutch" Meyer)
**FRANK KIMBROUGH**, 2-0-1  (Hardin-Simmons '26)  b 6-24-04
Hardin-Simmons . . . . .  Sun 1-1-36  New Mexico St. 14-14 (Jerry Hines)
Hardin-Simmons . . . . .  Sun 1-1-37  UTEP 34-6 (Max Saxon)
West Tex. St. . . . . . . . .  Sun 1-1-51  Cincinnati 14-13 (Sid Gillman)
**BILLY KINARD**, 1-0-0  (Mississippi '56)  b 12-16-33
Mississippi . . . . . . . . . .  Peach 12-30-71  Georgia Tech 41-18 (Bud Carson)
**DEWEY KING**, 0-1-0  (North Dak. '50)  b 10-1-25
San Jose St. . . . . . . . . .  Pasadena 12-18-71  Memphis St. 9-28 (Billy Murphy)
**J. T. KING**, 0-2-0  (Texas '38)  b 10-22-12
Texas Tech . . . . . . . . . .  Sun 12-26-64  Georgia 0-7 (Vince Dooley)
Texas Tech . . . . . . . . . .  Gator 12-31-65  Georgia Tech 21-31 (Bobby Dodd)
**JIMMY KITTS**, 1-1-0  (Southern Methodist)  b 6-14-00
Rice . . . . . . . . . . . . . . . . .  Cotton 1-1-38  Colorado 28-14 (Bernard "Bunnie" Oakes)
Virginia Tech . . . . . . . . .  Sun 1-1-47  Cincinnati 6-18 (Ray Nolting)
**ED KLUSKA**, 1-0-0  (Xavier, Ohio '40)  b 5-21-18
Xavier (Ohio) . . . . . . . . .  Salad 1-1-50  Arizona St. 33-21 (Ed Doherty)
**JOE KRIVAK**, 0-0-1  (Syracuse '57)  b 3-20-35
Maryland . . . . . . . . . . . .  Independence 12-15-90  Louisiana Tech 34-34 (Joe Raymond Peace)
**FRANK KUSH**, 6-1-0  (Michigan St. '53)  b 1-20-29
Arizona St. . . . . . . . . . .  Peach 12-30-70  North Caro. 48-26 (Bill Dooley)
Arizona St. . . . . . . . . . .  Fiesta 12-27-71  Florida St. 45-38 (Larry Jones)
Arizona St. . . . . . . . . . .  Fiesta 12-23-72  Missouri 49-35 (Al Onofrio)
Arizona St. . . . . . . . . . .  Fiesta 12-21-73  Pittsburgh 28-7 (Johnny Majors)
Arizona St. . . . . . . . . . .  Fiesta 12-26-75  Nebraska 17-14 (Tom Osborne)
Arizona St. . . . . . . . . . .  Fiesta 12-25-77  Penn St. 30-42 (Joe Paterno)
Arizona St. . . . . . . . . . .  Garden State 12-16-78  Rutgers 34-18 (Frank Burns)
**BERT LaBRUCHERIE**, 0-1-0  (UCLA '29)  b 1-19-05
UCLA . . . . . . . . . . . . . . .  Rose 1-1-47  Illinois 14-45 (Ray Eliot)
**MAXIE LAMBRIGHT**, 1-1-0  (Southern Miss. '49)  b 6-3-24
Louisiana Tech . . . . . . .  Independence 12-17-77  Louisville 24-14 (Vince Gibson)

Louisiana Tech . . . . . . .    Independence 12-16-78     East Caro. 13-35 (Pat Dye)

**FRANK LAUTERBUR**, 2-0-0    (Mount Union '49)    b 8-8-25
Toledo . . . . . . . . . . . . .    Tangerine 12-26-69     Davidson 56-33 (Homer Smith)
Toledo . . . . . . . . . . . . . .    Tangerine 12-28-70     William & Mary 40-12 (Lou Holtz)

**FRANK LEAHY**, 1-1-0    (Notre Dame '31)    b 8-27-08
Boston College . . . . . .    Cotton 1-1-40     Clemson 3-6 (Jess Neely)
Boston College . . . . . .    Sugar 1-1-41     Tennessee 19-13 (Bob Neyland)

**CLYDE LEE**, 1-0-0    (Centenary '32)    b 2-11-08
Houston. . . . . . . . . . . . .    Salad 1-1-52     Dayton 26-21 (Joe Gavin)

**ART LEWIS**, 0-1-0    (Ohio '36)    b 2-18-11
West Va. . . . . . . . . . . . .    Sugar 1-1-54     Georgia Tech 19-42 (Bobby Dodd)

**BILL LEWIS**, 1-0-0    (East Stroudsburg '63)    b 8-5-41
East Caro. . . . . . . . . . . .    Peach 1-1-92     North Caro. St. 37-34 (Dick Sheridan)

**LOU LITTLE**, 1-0-0    (Pennsylvania '20)    12-6-93
Columbia . . . . . . . . . . . .    Rose 1-1-34     Stanford 7-0 (Claude "Tiny" Thornhill)

**JIM LOOKABAUGH**, 2-1-0    (Oklahoma St. '25)    b 6-15-02
Oklahoma St. . . . . . . . .    Cotton 1-1-45     Texas Christian 34-0 (Leo "Dutch" Meyer)
Oklahoma St. . . . . . . . .    Sugar 1-1-46     St. Mary's (Cal.) 33-13 (Jimmy Phelan)
Oklahoma St. . . . . . . . .    Delta 1-1-49     William & Mary 0-20 (Rube McCray)

**AL LUGINBILL**, 0-1-0    (Cal Poly Pomona '67)    b 11-3-46
San Diego St. . . . . . . . .    Freedom 12-30-91     Tulsa 17-28 (Dave Rader)

**GEORGE MacINTYRE**, 0-1-0    (Miami, Fla. '61)    b 4-30-39
Vanderbilt . . . . . . . . . . .    Hall of Fame 12-31-82     Air Force 28-36 (Ken Hatfield)

**JOHN MACKOVIC**, 1-3-0    (Wake Forest '65)    b 10-1-43
Wake Forest . . . . . . . . .    Tangerine 12-22-79     Louisiana St. 10-34 (Charlie McClendon)
Illinois. . . . . . . . . . . . . . .    All-American 12-29-88     Florida 10-14 (Galen Hall)
Illinois. . . . . . . . . . . . . . .    Fla. Citrus 1-1-90     Virginia 31-21 (George Welsh)
Illinois. . . . . . . . . . . . . . .    Hall of Fame 1-1-91     Clemson 0-30 (Ken Hatfield)

**DICK MacPHERSON**, 3-1-1    (Springfield '58)    b 11-4-30
Syracuse . . . . . . . . . . .    Cherry 12-21-85     Maryland 18-35 (Bobby Ross)
Syracuse . . . . . . . . . . .    Sugar 1-1-88     Auburn 16-16 (Pat Dye)
Syracuse . . . . . . . . . . .    Hall of Fame 1-2-89     Louisiana St. 23-10 (Mike Archer)
Syracuse . . . . . . . . . . .    Peach 12-30-89     Georgia 19-18 (Ray Goff)
Syracuse . . . . . . . . . . .    Aloha 12-25-90     Arizona 28-0 (Dick Tomey)

**EDWARD "SLIP" MADIGAN**, 1-0-0    (Notre Dame '20)    b 11-18-95
St. Mary's (Cal.) . . . . . .    Cotton 1-2-39     Texas Tech 20-13 (Pete Cawthon)

**JOHNNY MAJORS**, 9-7-0    (Tennessee '57)    b 5-21-35
Iowa St. . . . . . . . . . . . .    Sun 12-18-71     Louisiana St. 15-33 (Charlie McClendon)
Iowa St. . . . . . . . . . . . .    Liberty 12-18-72     Georgia Tech 30-31 (Bill Fulcher)
Pittsburgh . . . . . . . . . . .    Fiesta 12-28-73     Arizona St. 7-28 (Frank Kush)
Pittsburgh . . . . . . . . . . .    Sun 12-26-75     Kansas 33-19 (Bud Moore)
Pittsburgh . . . . . . . . . . .    Sugar 1-1-77     Georgia 27-3 (Vince Dooley)
Tennessee . . . . . . . . . .    Bluebonnet 12-31-79     Purdue 22-27 (Jim Young)
Tennessee . . . . . . . . . .    Garden State 12-13-81     Wisconsin 28-21 (Dave McClain)
Tennessee . . . . . . . . . .    Peach 12-31-82     Iowa 22-28 (Hayden Fry)
Tennessee . . . . . . . . . .    Fla. Citrus 12-17-83     Maryland 30-23 (Bobby Ross)
Tennessee . . . . . . . . . .    Sun 12-24-84     Maryland 26-27 (Bobby Ross)
Tennessee . . . . . . . . . .    Sugar 1-1-86     Miami (Fla.) 35-7 (Jimmy Johnson)
Tennessee . . . . . . . . . .    Liberty 12-29-86     Minnesota 21-14 (John Gutekunst)
Tennessee . . . . . . . . . .    Peach 1-2-88     Indiana 27-22 (Bill Mallory)
Tennessee . . . . . . . . . .    Cotton 1-1-90     Arkansas 31-27 (Ken Hatfield)
Tennessee . . . . . . . . . .    Sugar 1-1-91     Virginia 23-22 (George Welsh)
Tennessee . . . . . . . . . .    Fiesta 1-1-92     Penn St. 17-42 (Joe Paterno)

**BILL MALLORY**, 4-5-0    (Miami, Ohio '57)    b 5-30-35
Miami (Ohio) . . . . . . . . .    Tangerine 12-22-73     Florida 16-7 (Doug Dickey)
Colorado . . . . . . . . . . . .    Bluebonnet 12-27-75     Texas 21-38 (Darrell Royal)
Colorado . . . . . . . . . . . .    Orange 1-1-77     Ohio St. 10-27 (Woody Hayes)
Northern Ill. . . . . . . . . .    California 12-17-83     Cal St. Fullerton 20-13 (Gene Murphy)
Indiana. . . . . . . . . . . . . .    All-American 12-31-86     Florida St. 13-27 (Bobby Bowden)
Indiana. . . . . . . . . . . . . .    Peach 1-2-88     Tennessee 22-27 (Johnny Majors)
Indiana. . . . . . . . . . . . . .    Liberty 12-28-88     South Caro. 34-10 (Joe Morrison)
Indiana. . . . . . . . . . . . . .    Peach 12-29-90     Auburn 23-27 (Pat Dye)
Indiana. . . . . . . . . . . . . .    Copper 12-31-91     Baylor 24-0 (Grant Teaff)

**FRANK MALONEY**, 1-0-0    (Michigan '62)    b 9-26-40
Syracuse . . . . . . . . . . .    Independence 12-15-79     McNeese St. 31-7 (Ernie Duplechin)

**BOB MARGARITA**, 0-1-0    (Brown '44)    b 11-3-20
Georgetown . . . . . . . . .    Sun 1-2-50     UTEP 20-33 (Jack "Cactus Jack" Curtice)

**ABE MARTIN**, 1-3-1    (Texas Christian '32)    b 10-8-08
Texas Christian . . . . . .    Cotton 1-2-56     Mississippi 13-14 (John Vaught)
Texas Christian . . . . . .    Cotton 1-1-57     Syracuse 28-27 (Ben Schwartzwalder)

| Texas Christian ...... | Cotton 1-1-59 | Air Force 0-0 (Ben Martin) |
|---|---|---|
| Texas Christian ...... | Bluebonnet 12-19-59 | Clemson 7-23 (Frank Howard) |
| Texas Christian ...... | Sun 12-31-65 | UTEP 12-13 (Bobby Dobbs) |

**BEN MARTIN**, 0-2-1 (Navy '46) b 6-28-21
| Air Force ............. | Cotton 1-1-59 | Texas Christian 0-0 (Abe Martin) |
|---|---|---|
| Air Force ............. | Gator 12-28-63 | North Caro. 0-35 (Jim Hickey) |
| Air Force ............. | Sugar 1-1-71 | Tennessee 13-34 (Bill Battle) |

**GLEN MASON**, 1-0-0 (Ohio St. '72) b 4-9-50
| Kansas ............... | Aloha 12-25-92 | Brigham Young 23-20 (LaVell Edwards) |
|---|---|---|

**TONY MASON**, 0-1-0 (Clarion '50) b 3-2-30
| Arizona .............. | Fiesta 12-25-79 | Pittsburgh 10-16 (Jackie Sherrill) |
|---|---|---|

**RON McBRIDE**, 0-1-0 (San Jose St. '63) b 10-14-39
| Utah ................. | Copper 12-29-92 | Washington St. 28-31 (Mike Price) |
|---|---|---|

**TOM McCANN**, 0-1-0 (Illinois '24) b 11-7-98
| Miami (Fla.) .......... | Orange 1-1-35 | Bucknell 0-26 (Edward "Hook" Mylin) |
|---|---|---|

**BILL McCARTNEY**, 1-6-0 (Missouri '62) b 8-22-40
| Colorado ............. | Freedom 12-30-85 | Washington 17-20 (Don James) |
|---|---|---|
| Colorado ............. | Bluebonnet 12-31-86 | Baylor 9-21 (Grant Teaff) |
| Colorado ............. | Freedom 12-29-88 | Brigham Young 17-20 (LaVell Edwards) |
| Colorado ............. | Orange 1-1-90 | Notre Dame 6-21 (Lou Holtz) |
| Colorado ............. | Orange 1-1-91 | Notre Dame 10-9 (Lou Holtz) |
| Colorado ............. | Blockbuster 12-28-91 | Alabama 25-30 (Gene Stallings) |
| Colorado ............. | Fiesta 1-1-93 | Syracuse 22-26 (Paul Pasqualoni) |

**DAVE McCLAIN**, 1-2-0 (Bowling Green '60) b 1-28-38
| Wisconsin ............ | Garden State 12-13-81 | Tennessee 21-28 (Johnny Majors) |
|---|---|---|
| Wisconsin ............ | Independence 12-11-82 | Kansas St. 14-3 (Jim Dickey) |
| Wisconsin ............ | Hall of Fame 12-22-83 | Kentucky 19-20 (Jerry Claiborne) |

**CHARLIE McCLENDON**, 7-6-0 (Kentucky '50) b 10-17-22
| Louisiana St. ......... | Cotton 1-1-63 | Texas 13-0 (Darrell Royal) |
|---|---|---|
| Louisiana St. ......... | Bluebonnet 12-21-63 | Baylor 7-14 (John Bridgers) |
| Louisiana St. ......... | Sugar 1-1-65 | Syracuse 13-10 (Ben Schwartzwalder) |
| Louisiana St. ......... | Cotton 1-1-66 | Arkansas 14-7 (Frank Broyles) |
| Louisiana St. ......... | Sugar 1-1-68 | Wyoming 20-13 (Lloyd Eaton) |
| Louisiana St. ......... | Peach 12-30-68 | Florida St. 31-27 (Bill Peterson) |
| Louisiana St. ......... | Orange 1-1-71 | Nebraska 12-17 (Bob Devaney) |
| Louisiana St. ......... | Sun 12-18-71 | Iowa St. 33-15 (Johnny Majors) |
| Louisiana St. ......... | Bluebonnet 12-30-72 | Tennessee 17-24 (Bill Battle) |
| Louisiana St. ......... | Orange 1-1-74 | Penn St. 9-16 (Joe Paterno) |
| Louisiana St. ......... | Sun 12-31-77 | Stanford 14-24 (Bill Walsh) |
| Louisiana St. ......... | Liberty 12-23-78 | Missouri 15-20 (Warren Powers) |
| Louisiana St. ......... | Tangerine 12-22-79 | Wake Forest 34-10 (John Mackovic) |

**RUBE McCRAY**, 1-1-0 (Ky. Wesleyan '30) b 6-13-05
| William & Mary ....... | Dixie 1-1-48 | Arkansas 19-21 (John Barnhill) |
|---|---|---|
| William & Mary ....... | Delta 1-1-49 | Oklahoma St. 20-0 (Jim Lookabaugh) |

**J. F. "POP" McKALE**, 0-1-0 (Albion '10) b 6-12-87
| Arizona .............. | San Diego East-West Christmas Classic 12-26-21 | Centre 0-38 (Charley Moran) |
|---|---|---|

**JOHN McKAY**, 6-3-0 (Oregon St. '50) b 7-5-23
| Southern Cal ........ | Rose 1-2-63 | Wisconsin 42-37 (Milt Bruhn) |
|---|---|---|
| Southern Cal ........ | Rose 1-2-67 | Purdue 13-14 (Jack Mollenkopf) |
| Southern Cal ........ | Rose 1-1-68 | Indiana 14-3 (John Pont) |
| Southern Cal ........ | Rose 1-1-69 | Ohio St. 16-27 (Woody Hayes) |
| Southern Cal ........ | Rose 1-1-70 | Michigan 10-3 (Glenn "Bo" Schembechler) |
| Southern Cal ........ | Rose 1-1-73 | Ohio St. 42-17 (Woody Hayes) |
| Southern Cal ........ | Rose 1-1-74 | Ohio St. 21-42 (Woody Hayes) |
| Southern Cal ........ | Rose 1-1-75 | Ohio St. 18-17 (Woody Hayes) |
| Southern Cal ........ | Liberty 12-22-75 | Texas A&M 20-0 (Emory Bellard) |

**ALLYN McKEEN**, 1-0-0 (Tennessee '29) b 1-26-05
| Mississippi St. ........ | Orange 1-1-41 | Georgetown 14-7 (Jack Hagerty) |
|---|---|---|

**JOHNNIE McMILLAN**, 0-1-0 (South Caro. '41) b 1-27-19
| South Caro. .......... | Gator 1-1-46 | Wake Forest 14-26 (D. C. "Peahead" Walker) |
|---|---|---|

**DAVID McWILLIAMS**, 1-1-0 (Texas '64) b 4-18-42
| Texas ............... | Bluebonnet 12-31-87 | Pittsburgh 32-27 (Mike Gottfried) |
|---|---|---|
| Texas ............... | Cotton 1-1-91 | Miami (Fla.) 3-46 (Dennis Erickson) |

**JACK MEAGHER**, 1-0-1 (Notre Dame '17) b 7-4-94
| Auburn ............... | Bacardi, Cuba 1-1-37 | Villanova 7-7 (Maurice "Clipper" Smith) |
|---|---|---|
| Auburn ............... | Orange 1-1-38 | Michigan St. 6-0 (Charlie Bachman) |

**RANDOLPH R. M. MEDLEY**, 2-0-0 (Mo. Wesleyan '21) b 9-22-98
| Southwestern (Tex.).. | Sun 1-1-44 | New Mexico 7-0 (Willis Barnes) |
|---|---|---|

Southwestern (Tex.) .. Sun 1-1-45      U. of Mexico 35-0 (Bernard A. Hoban)

**LEO "DUTCH" MEYER**, 3-4-0   (Texas Christian '22)   b 1-15-98
Texas Christian ......   Sugar 1-1-36     Louisiana St. 3-2 (Bernie Moore)
Texas Christian ......   Cotton 1-1-37     Marquette 16-6 (Frank Murray)
Texas Christian ......   Sugar 1-2-39     Carnegie Mellon 15-7 (Bill Kern)
Texas Christian ......   Orange 1-1-42     Georgia 26-40 (Wally Butts)
Texas Christian ......   Cotton 1-1-45     Oklahoma St. 0-34 (Jim Lookabaugh)
Texas Christian ......   Delta 1-1-48     Mississippi 9-13 (John Vaught)
Texas Christian ......   Cotton 1-1-52     Kentucky 7-20 (Paul "Bear" Bryant)

**RON MEYER**, 0-1-0   (Purdue '63)   b 2-17-41
Southern Methodist ..   Holiday 12-19-80     Brigham Young 45-46 (LaVell Edwards)

**JOHN MICHELOSEN**, 0-2-0   (Pittsburgh '38)   b 2-13-16
Pittsburgh ............   Sugar 1-2-56     Georgia Tech 0-7 (Bobby Dodd)
Pittsburgh ............   Gator 12-29-56     Georgia Tech 14-21 (Bobby Dodd)

**JACK MITCHELL**, 1-0-0   (Oklahoma '49)   b 12-3-24
Kansas ...............   Bluebonnet 12-16-61     Rice 33-7 (Jess Neely)

**ODUS MITCHELL**, 0-2-0   (West Tex. St. '25)   b 6-29-99
North Texas ..........   Salad 1-1-48     Nevada 6-13 (Joe Sheeketski)
North Texas ..........   Sun 12-31-59     New Mexico St. 8-28 (Warren Woodson)

**GARY MOELLER**, 2-1-0   (Ohio St. '63)   b 1-26-41
Michigan ..............   Gator 1-1-91     Mississippi 35-3 (Billy Brewer)
Michigan ..............   Rose 1-1-92     Washington 14-34 (Don James)
Michigan ..............   Rose 1-1-93     Washington 38-31 (Don James)

**AL MOLDE**, 0-1-0   (Gust. Adolphus '66)   b 11-15-43
Western Mich.........   California 12-10-88     Fresno St. 30-35 (Jim Sweeney)

**JACK MOLLENKOPF**, 1-0-0   (Bowling Green '31)   b 11-24-05
Purdue ...............   Rose 1-2-67     Southern Cal 14-13 (John McKay)

**BERNIE MOORE**, 1-3-1   (Carson-Newman '17)   b 4-30-95
Louisiana St. .........   Sugar 1-1-36     Texas Christian 2-3 (Leo "Dutch" Meyer)
Louisiana St. .........   Sugar 1-1-37     Santa Clara 14-21 (Lawrence "Buck" Shaw)
Louisiana St. .........   Sugar 1-1-38     Santa Clara 0-6 (Lawrence "Buck" Shaw)
Louisiana St. .........   Orange 1-1-44     Texas A&M 19-14 (Homer Norton)
Louisiana St. .........   Cotton 1-1-47     Arkansas 0-0 (John Barnhill)

**BUD MOORE**, 0-1-0   (Alabama '61)   b 10-16-39
Kansas ...............   Sun 12-26-75     Pittsburgh 19-33 (Johnny Majors)

**CHARLEY MORAN**, 2-1-0   (Tennessee '98)   b 2-22-78
Centre ...............   Fort Worth Classic     Texas Christian 63-7 (Bill Driver)
                      1-1-21
Centre ...............   San Diego East-West     Arizona 38-0 (J. F. "Pop" McKale)
                      Christmas Classic
                      12-26-21
Centre ...............   Dixie Classic 1-2-22     Texas A&M 14-22 (Dana Bible)

**DELL MORGAN**, 0-3-0   (Austin '25)   b 2-14-02
Texas Tech ..........   Sun 1-1-42     Tulsa 0-6 (Henry Frnka)
Texas Tech ..........   Sun 1-1-48     Miami (Ohio) 12-13 (Sid Gillman)
Texas Tech ..........   Raisin 12-31-49     San Jose St. 13-20 (Bill Hubbard)

**JOE MORRISON**, 0-3-0   (Cincinnati '59)   b 8-21-37
South Caro. ..........   Gator 12-28-84     Oklahoma St. 14-21 (Pat Jones)
South Caro. ..........   Gator 12-31-87     Louisiana St. 13-30 (Mike Archer)
South Caro. ..........   Liberty 12-28-88     Indiana 10-34 (Bill Mallory)

**RAY MORRISON**, 0-1-0   (Vanderbilt '12)   b 2-28-85
Southern Methodist ..   Dixie Classic 1-1-25     West Va. Wesleyan 7-9 (Bob Higgins)

**DARRELL MUDRA**, 0-1-0   (Peru St. '51)   b 1-4-29
Arizona ..............   Sun 12-28-68     Auburn 10-34 (Ralph "Shug" Jordan)

**CLARENCE "BIGGIE" MUNN**, 1-0-0   (Minnesota '32)   b 9-11-08
Michigan St. .........   Rose 1-1-54     UCLA 28-20 (Henry "Red" Sanders)

**BILLY MURPHY**, 1-0-0   (Mississippi St. '47)   b 1-13-21
Memphis St. .........   Pasadena 12-18-71     San Jose St. 28-9 (Dewey King)

**GENE MURPHY**, 0-1-0   (North Dak. '62)   b 8-6-39
Cal St. Fullerton ......   California 12-17-83     Northern Ill. 13-20 (Bill Mallory)

**JACK MURPHY**, 1-0-0   (Heidelberg '54)   b 8-6-32
Toledo ...............   Tangerine 12-28-71     Richmond 28-3 (Frank Jones)

**BILL MURRAY**, 2-1-0   (Duke '31)   b 9-9-08
Duke .................   Orange 1-1-55     Nebraska 34-7 (Bill Glassford)
Duke .................   Orange 1-1-58     Oklahoma 21-48 (Bud Wilkinson)
Duke .................   Cotton 1-2-61     Arkansas 7-6 (Frank Broyles)

**FRANK MURRAY**, 0-1-0   (Tufts '08)   b 2-12-85
Marquette ............   Cotton 1-1-37     Texas Christian 6-16 (Leo "Dutch" Meyer)

**DENNY MYERS**, 0-1-0   (Iowa '30)   b 11-10-05
Boston College ......   Orange 1-1-43            Alabama 21-37 (Frank Thomas)
**EDWARD "HOOK" MYLIN**, 1-0-0   (Frank. & Marsh.)   b 10-23-97
Bucknell .............   Orange 1-1-35            Miami (Fla.) 26-0 (Tom McCann)
**RAY NAGEL**, 1-0-0   (UCLA '50)   b 5-18-27
Utah ................   Liberty 12-19-64           West Va. 32-6 (Gene Corum)
**LARRY NAVIAUX**, 0-1-0   (Nebraska '59)   b 12-17-36
Boston U. ...........   Pasadena 12-6-69           San Diego St. 7-28 (Don Coryell)
**EARLE "GREASY" NEALE**, 0-0-1   (West Va. Wesleyan '14)   b 11-5-91
Wash. & Jeff. ........   Rose 1-2-22              California 0-0 (Andy Smith)
**JESS NEELY**, 4-3-0   (Vanderbilt '23)   b 1-4-98
Clemson .............   Cotton 1-1-40            Boston College 6-3 (Frank Leahy)
Rice ................   Orange 1-1-47            Tennessee 8-0 (Bob Neyland)
Rice ................   Cotton 1-2-50            North Caro. 27-13 (Carl Snavely)
Rice ................   Cotton 1-1-54            Alabama 28-6 (Harold "Red" Drew)
Rice ................   Cotton 1-1-58            Navy 7-20 (Eddie Erdelatz)
Rice ................   Sugar 1-2-61             Mississippi 6-14 (John Vaught)
Rice ................   Bluebonnet 12-16-61         Kansas 7-33 (Jack Mitchell)
**DON NEHLEN**, 3-4-0   (Bowling Green '58)   b 1-1-36
West Va. .............   Peach 12-31-81           Florida 26-6 (Charley Pell)
West Va. .............   Gator 12-30-82           Florida St. 12-31 (Bobby Bowden)
West Va. .............   Hall of Fame 12-22-83       Kentucky 20-16 (Jerry Claiborne)
West Va. .............   Bluebonnet 12-31-84         Texas Christian 31-14 (Jim Wacker)
West Va. .............   Sun 12-25-87             Oklahoma St. 33-35 (Pat Jones)
West Va. .............   Fiesta 1-2-89            Notre Dame 21-34 (Lou Holtz)
West Va. .............   Gator 12-30-89           Clemson 7-27 (Danny Ford)
**BOB NEYLAND**, 2-5-0   (Army '16)   b 2-17-92
Tennessee ...........   Orange 1-2-39            Oklahoma 17-0 (Tom Stidham)
Tennessee ...........   Rose 1-1-40             Southern Cal 0-14 (Howard Jones)
Tennessee ...........   Sugar 1-1-41            Boston College 13-19 (Frank Leahy)
Tennessee ...........   Orange 1-1-47            Rice 0-8 (Jess Neely)
Tennessee ...........   Cotton 1-1-51            Texas 20-14 (Blair Cherry)
Tennessee ...........   Sugar 1-1-52            Maryland 13-28 (Jim Tatum)
Tennessee ...........   Cotton 1-1-53            Texas 0-16 (Ed Price)
**RAY NOLTING**, 1-0-0   (Cincinnati '36)   b 11-8-13
Cincinnati ...........   Sun 1-1-47              Virginia Tech 18-6 (Jimmy Kitts)
**HOMER NORTON**, 2-2-1   (Birmingham Southern '16)   b 12-30-96
Centenary ...........   Dixie Classic 1-1-34        Arkansas 7-7 (Fred Thomsen)
Texas A&M ...........   Sugar 1-1-40            Tulane 14-13 (Lowell "Red" Dawson)
Texas A&M ...........   Cotton 1-1-41            Fordham 13-12 (Jim Crowley)
Texas A&M ...........   Cotton 1-1-42            Alabama 21-29 (Frank Thomas)
Texas A&M ...........   Orange 1-1-44            Louisiana St. 14-19 (Bernie Moore)
**TOM NUGENT**, 0-2-0   (Ithaca '36)   b 2-24-16
Florida St. ...........   Sun 1-1-55              UTEP 20-47 (Mike Brumbelow)
Florida St. ...........   Bluegrass 12-13-58         Oklahoma St. 6-15 (Cliff Speegle)
**BERNARD "BUNNIE" OAKES**, 0-1-0   (Illinois '24)   b 9-15-98
Colorado .............   Cotton 1-1-38            Rice 14-28 (Jimmy Kitts)
**JORDAN OLIVAR**, 1-1-0   (Villanova '38)   b 1-30-15
Villanova ............   Great Lakes 12-6-47        Kentucky 14-24 (Paul "Bear" Bryant)
Villanova ............   Harbor 1-1-49            Nevada 27-7 (Joe Sheeketski)
**AL ONOFRIO**, 1-1-0   (Arizona St. '43)   b 3-15-21
Missouri .............   Fiesta 12-23-72           Arizona St. 35-49 (Frank Kush)
Missouri .............   Sun 12-29-73            Auburn 34-17 (Ralph "Shug" Jordan)
**BENNIE OOSTERBAAN**, 1-0-0   (Michigan '28)   b 2-24-06
Michigan .............   Rose 1-1-51             California 14-6 (Lynn "Pappy" Waldorf)
**TOM OSBORNE**, 8-12-0   (Hastings '59)   b 2-23-37
Nebraska .............   Cotton 1-1-74            Texas 19-3 (Darrell Royal)
Nebraska .............   Sugar 12-31-74           Florida 13-10 (Doug Dickey)
Nebraska .............   Fiesta 12-26-75           Arizona St. 14-17 (Frank Kush)
Nebraska .............   Bluebonnet 12-31-76         Texas Tech 27-24 (Steve Sloan)
Nebraska .............   Liberty 12-19-77           North Caro. 21-17 (Bill Dooley)
Nebraska .............   Orange 1-1-79            Oklahoma 24-31 (Barry Switzer)
Nebraska .............   Cotton 1-1-80            Houston 14-17 (Bill Yeoman)
Nebraska .............   Sun 12-27-80            Mississippi St. 31-17 (Emory Bellard)
Nebraska .............   Orange 1-1-82            Clemson 15-22 (Danny Ford)
Nebraska .............   Orange 1-1-83            Louisiana St. 21-20 (Jerry Stovall)
Nebraska .............   Orange 1-2-84            Miami (Fla.) 30-31 (Howard Schnellenberger)
Nebraska .............   Sugar 1-1-85            Louisiana St. 28-10 (Bill Arnsparger)
Nebraska .............   Fiesta 1-1-86            Michigan 23-27 (Glenn "Bo" Schembechler)
Nebraska .............   Sugar 1-1-87            Louisiana St. 30-15 (Bill Arnsparger)
Nebraska .............   Fiesta 1-1-88            Florida St. 28-31 (Bobby Bowden)

*Bowl Coaching Records*

| Nebraska............ | Orange 1-2-89 | Miami (Fla.) 3-23 (Jimmy Johnson) |
| Nebraska............ | Fiesta 1-1-90 | Florida St. 17-41 (Bobby Bowden) |
| Nebraska............ | Fla. Citrus 1-1-91 | Georgia Tech 21-45 (Bobby Ross) |
| Nebraska............ | Orange 1-1-92 | Miami (Fla.) 0-22 (Dennis Erickson) |
| Nebraska............ | Orange 1-1-93 | Florida St. 14-27 (Bobby Bowden) |

**JIM OWENS**, 2-1-0   (Oklahoma '50)   b 3-6-27

| Washington .......... | Rose 1-1-60 | Wisconsin 44-8 (Milt Bruhn) |
| Washington .......... | Rose 1-2-61 | Minnesota 17-7 (Murray Warmath) |
| Washington .......... | Rose 1-1-64 | Illinois 7-17 (Pete Elliott) |

**JACK PARDEE**, 0-1-0   (Texas A&M '57)   b 4-9-36

| Houston.............. | Aloha 12-25-88 | Washington St. 22-24 (Dennis Erickson) |

**ARA PARSEGHIAN**, 3-2-0   (Miami, Ohio '49)   b 5-21-23

| Notre Dame ......... | Cotton 1-1-70 | Texas 17-21 (Darrell Royal) |
| Notre Dame ......... | Cotton 1-1-71 | Texas 24-11 (Darrell Royal) |
| Notre Dame ......... | Orange 1-1-73 | Nebraska 6-40 (Bob Devaney) |
| Notre Dame ......... | Sugar 12-31-73 | Alabama 24-23 (Paul "Bear" Bryant) |
| Notre Dame ......... | Orange 1-1-75 | Alabama 13-11 (Paul "Bear" Bryant) |

**PAUL PASQUALONI**, 2-0-0   (Penn St. '72)   b 8-16-49

| Syracuse ............. | Hall of Fame 1-1-92 | Ohio St. 24-17 (John Cooper) |
| Syracuse ............. | Fiesta 1-1-93 | Colorado 26-22 (Bill McCartney) |

**JOE PATERNO**, 14-8-1   (Brown '50)   b 12-21-26

| Penn St............... | Gator 12-30-67 | Florida St. 17-17 (Bill Peterson) |
| Penn St............... | Orange 1-1-69 | Kansas 15-14 (Pepper Rodgers) |
| Penn St............... | Orange 1-1-70 | Missouri 10-3 (Dan Devine) |
| Penn St............... | Cotton 1-1-72 | Texas 30-6 (Darrell Royal) |
| Penn St............... | Sugar 12-31-72 | Oklahoma 0-14 (Chuck Fairbanks) |
| Penn St............... | Orange 1-1-74 | Louisiana St. 16-9 (Charlie McClendon) |
| Penn St............... | Cotton 1-1-75 | Baylor 41-20 (Grant Teaff) |
| Penn St............... | Sugar 12-31-75 | Alabama 6-13 (Paul "Bear" Bryant) |
| Penn St............... | Gator 12-27-76 | Notre Dame 9-20 (Dan Devine) |
| Penn St............... | Fiesta 12-25-77 | Arizona St. 42-30 (Frank Kush) |
| Penn St............... | Sugar 1-1-79 | Alabama 7-14 (Paul "Bear" Bryant) |
| Penn St............... | Liberty 12-22-79 | Tulane 9-6 (Larry Smith) |
| Penn St............... | Fiesta 12-26-80 | Ohio St. 31-19 (Earle Bruce) |
| Penn St............... | Fiesta 1-1-82 | Southern Cal 26-10 (John Robinson) |
| Penn St............... | Sugar 1-1-83 | Georgia 27-23 (Vince Dooley) |
| Penn St............... | Aloha 12-26-83 | Washington 13-10 (Don James) |
| Penn St............... | Orange 1-1-86 | Oklahoma 10-25 (Barry Switzer) |
| Penn St............... | Fiesta 1-1-87 | Miami (Fla.) 14-10 (Jimmy Johnson) |
| Penn St............... | Fla. Citrus 1-1-88 | Clemson 10-35 (Danny Ford) |
| Penn St............... | Holiday 12-29-89 | Brigham Young 50-39 (LaVell Edwards) |
| Penn St............... | Blockbuster 12-28-90 | Florida St. 17-24 (Bobby Bowden) |
| Penn St............... | Fiesta 1-1-92 | Tennessee 42-17 (Johnny Majors) |
| Penn St............... | Blockbuster 1-1-93 | Stanford 3-24 (Bill Walsh) |

**JOE RAYMOND PEACE**, 0-0-1   (Louisiana Tech '68)   b 6-5-45

| Louisiana Tech ....... | Independence 12-15-90 | Maryland 34-34 (Joe Krivak) |

**CHARLEY PELL**, 2-3-0   (Alabama '64)   b 2-27-41

| Clemson ............. | Gator 12-30-77 | Pittsburgh 3-34 (Jackie Sherrill) |
| Florida .............. | Tangerine 12-20-80 | Maryland 35-20 (Jerry Claiborne) |
| Florida .............. | Peach 12-31-81 | West Va. 6-26 (Don Nehlen) |
| Florida .............. | Bluebonnet 12-31-82 | Arkansas 24-28 (Lou Holtz) |
| Florida .............. | Gator 12-30-83 | Iowa 14-6 (Hayden Fry) |

**RAY PERKINS**, 3-0-0   (Alabama '67)   b 11-6-41

| Alabama ............. | Sun 12-24-83 | Southern Methodist 28-7 (Bobby Collins) |
| Alabama ............. | Aloha 12-28-85 | Southern Cal 24-3 (Ted Tollner) |
| Alabama ............. | Sun 12-26-86 | Washington 28-6 (Don James) |

**GEORGE PERLES**, 3-3-0   (Michigan St. '60)   b 7-16-34

| Michigan St. ......... | Cherry 12-22-84 | Army 6-10 (Jim Young) |
| Michigan St. ......... | All-American 12-31-85 | Georgia Tech 14-17 (Bill Curry) |
| Michigan St. ......... | Rose 1-1-88 | Southern Cal 20-17 (Larry Smith) |
| Michigan St. ......... | Gator 1-1-89 | Georgia 27-34 (Vince Dooley) |
| Michigan St. ......... | Aloha 12-25-89 | Hawaii 33-13 (Bob Wagner) |
| Michigan St. ......... | John Hancock 12-31-90 | Southern Cal 17-16 (Larry Smith) |

**DOYT PERRY**, 0-1-0   (Bowling Green '32)   b 1-6-10

| Bowling Green ....... | Mercy 11-23-61 | Fresno St. 6-36 (Cecil Coleman) |

**BILL PETERSON**, 1-2-1   (Ohio Northern '46)   b 5-14-20

| Florida St............. | Gator 1-2-65 | Oklahoma 36-19 (Gomer Jones) |
| Florida St............. | Sun 12-24-66 | Wyoming 20-28 (Lloyd Eaton) |
| Florida St............. | Gator 12-30-67 | Penn St. 17-17 (Joe Paterno) |
| Florida St............. | Peach 12-30-68 | Louisiana St. 27-31 (Charlie McClendon) |

**JIMMY PHELAN**, 0-3-0   (Notre Dame '19)   b 12-5-92

| Washington .......... | Rose 1-1-37 | Pittsburgh 0-21 (Jock Sutherland) |

St. Mary's (Cal.) ...... Sugar 1-1-46  Oklahoma St. 12-33 (Jim Lookabaugh)
St. Mary's (Cal.) ...... Oil 1-1-47  Georgia Tech 19-41 (Bobby Dodd)
**ALVIN "PIX" PIERSON**, 0-1-0  (Nevada '22)  b 7-25-98
Fresno St. ............ Raisin 1-1-46  Drake 12-13 (Vee Green)
**JIM PITTMAN**, 1-0-0  (Mississippi St. '50)  b 8-28-25
Tulane............... Liberty 12-12-70  Colorado 17-3 (Eddie Crowder)
**JOHN PONT**, 0-2-0  (Miami, Ohio '52)  b 11-13-27
Miami (Ohio).......... Tangerine 12-22-52  Houston 21-49 (Bill Yeoman)
Indiana.............. Rose 1-1-68  Southern Cal 3-14 (John McKay)
**WARREN POWERS**, 3-2-0  (Nebraska '63)  b 2-19-41
Missouri............. Liberty 12-23-78  Louisiana St. 20-15 (Charlie McClendon)
Missouri............. Hall of Fame 12-29-79  South Caro. 24-14 (Jim Carlen)
Missouri............. Liberty 12-27-80  Purdue 25-28 (Jim Young)
Missouri............. Tangerine 12-19-81  Southern Miss. 19-17 (Bobby Collins)
Missouri............. Holiday 12-23-83  Brigham Young 17-21 (LaVell Edwards)
**CLARENCE "NIBS" PRICE**, 0-1-0  (California '14)  b 1889
California ........... Rose 1-1-29  Georgia Tech 7-8 (Bill Alexander)
**ED PRICE**, 1-0-0  (Texas '33)  b 1-12-09
Texas ............... Cotton 1-1-53  Tennessee 16-0 (Bob Neyland)
**MIKE PRICE**, 1-0-0  (Puget Sound '69)  b 4-6-46
Washington St....... Copper 12-29-92  Utah 31-28 (Ron McBride)
**TOMMY PROTHRO**, 2-2-0  (Duke '42)  b 7-20-20
Oregon St. .......... Rose 1-1-57  Iowa 19-35 (Forest Evashevski)
Oregon St. .......... Liberty 12-15-62  Villanova 6-0 (Alex Bell)
Oregon St. .......... Rose 1-1-65  Michigan 7-34 (Chalmers "Bump" Elliott)
UCLA .............. Rose 1-1-66  Michigan St. 14-12 (Duffy Daugherty)
**DAVE RADER**, 1-1-0  (Tulsa '80)  b 3-9-57
Tulsa ............... Independence 12-16-89  Oregon 24-27 (Rich Brooks)
Tulsa ............... Freedom 12-30-91  San Diego St. 28-17 (Al Luginbill)
**JOHN RALSTON**, 2-2-0  (California '54)  b 4-25-27
Utah St. ............ Sun 12-31-60  New Mexico St. 13-20 (Warren Woodson)
Utah St. ............ Gotham 12-9-61  Baylor 9-24 (John Bridgers)
Stanford ........... Rose 1-1-71  Ohio St. 27-17 (Woody Hayes)
Stanford ........... Rose 1-1-72  Michigan 13-12 (Glenn "Bo" Schembechler)
**RED REESE**, 1-0-0  (Washington St. '25)  b 3-2-99
Second Air Force .... Sun 1-1-43  Hardin-Simmons 13-7 (Warren Woodson)
**BO REIN**, 2-0-0  (Ohio St. '58)  b 7-20-45
North Caro. St....... Peach 12-31-77  Iowa St. 24-14 (Earle Bruce)
North Caro. St....... Tangerine 12-23-78  Pittsburgh 30-17 (Jackie Sherrill)
**PAUL ROACH**, 0-3-0  (Black Hills St. '52)  b 10-24-27
Wyoming............ Holiday 12-30-87  Iowa 19-20 (Hayden Fry)
Wyoming............ Holiday 12-30-88  Oklahoma St. 14-62 (Pat Jones)
Wyoming............ Copper 12-31-90  California 15-17 (Bruce Snyder)
**ED ROBINSON**, 0-1-0  (Brown '96)  b 10-15-73
Brown.............. Rose 1-1-16  Washington St. 0-14 (Bill "Lone Star" Dietz)
**JOHN ROBINSON**, 4-1-0  (Oregon '58)  b 7-25-35
Southern Cal........ Rose 1-1-77  Michigan 14-6 (Glenn "Bo" Schembechler)
Southern Cal........ Bluebonnet 12-31-77  Texas A&M 47-28 (Emory Bellard)
Southern Cal........ Rose 1-1-79  Michigan 17-10 (Glenn "Bo" Schembechler)
Southern Cal........ Rose 1-1-80  Ohio St. 17-16 (Earle Bruce)
Southern Cal........ Fiesta 1-1-82  Penn St. 10-26 (Joe Paterno)
**KNUTE ROCKNE**, 1-0-0  (Notre Dame '14)  b 3-4-88
Notre Dame.......... Rose 1-1-25  Stanford 27-10 (Glenn "Pop" Warner)
**PEPPER RODGERS**, 0-2-0  (Georgia Tech '55)  b 10-8-31
Kansas .............. Orange 1-1-69  Penn St. 14-15 (Joe Paterno)
Georgia Tech ........ Peach 12-25-78  Purdue 21-41 (Jim Young)
**DARRYL ROGERS**, 1-0-0  (Fresno St. '57)  b 5-28-34
Arizona St. .......... Fiesta 1-1-83  Oklahoma 32-21 (Barry Switzer)
**E. L. "DICK" ROMNEY**, 0-1-0  (Utah '17)  b 2-12-95
Utah St. ............. Raisin 1-1-47  San Jose St. 0-20 (Bill Hubbard)
**TIM ROSE**, 0-1-0  (Xavier, Ohio '62)  b 10-14-41
Miami (Ohio)......... California 12-13-86  San Jose St. 7-37 (Claude Gilbert)
**BOBBY ROSS**, 4-2-0  (Va. Military '59)  12-23-36
Maryland............ Aloha 12-25-82  Washington 20-21 (Don James)
Maryland............ Fla. Citrus 12-17-83  Tennessee 23-30 (Johnny Majors)
Maryland............ Sun 12-22-84  Tennessee 27-26 (Johnny Majors)
Maryland............ Cherry 12-21-85  Syracuse 35-18 (Dick MacPherson)
Georgia Tech ........ Fla. Citrus 1-1-91  Nebraska 45-21 (Tom Osborne)
Georgia Tech ........ Aloha 12-25-91  Stanford 18-17 (Dennis Green)

*Bowl Coaching Records*

**DARRELL ROYAL,** 8-7-1 (Oklahoma '50) b 7-6-24
| | | |
|---|---|---|
| Texas .............. | Sugar 1-1-58 | Mississippi 7-39 (John Vaught) |
| Texas .............. | Cotton 1-1-60 | Syracuse 14-23 (Ben Schwartzwalder) |
| Texas .............. | Bluebonnet 12-17-60 | Alabama 3-3 (Paul "Bear" Bryant) |
| Texas .............. | Cotton 1-1-62 | Mississippi 12-7 (John Vaught) |
| Texas .............. | Cotton 1-1-63 | Louisiana St. 0-13 (Charlie McClendon) |
| Texas .............. | Cotton 1-1-64 | Navy 28-6 (Wayne Hardin) |
| Texas .............. | Orange 1-1-65 | Alabama 21-17 (Paul "Bear" Bryant) |
| Texas .............. | Bluebonnet 12-17-66 | Mississippi 19-0 (John Vaught) |
| Texas .............. | Cotton 1-1-69 | Tennessee 36-13 (Doug Dickey) |
| Texas .............. | Cotton 1-1-70 | Notre Dame 21-17 (Ara Parseghian) |
| Texas .............. | Cotton 1-1-71 | Notre Dame 11-24 (Ara Parseghian) |
| Texas .............. | Cotton 1-1-72 | Penn St. 6-30 (Joe Paterno) |
| Texas .............. | Cotton 1-1-73 | Alabama 17-13 (Paul "Bear" Bryant) |
| Texas .............. | Cotton 1-1-74 | Nebraska 3-19 (Tom Osborne) |
| Texas .............. | Gator 12-30-74 | Auburn 3-27 (Ralph "Shug" Jordan) |
| Texas .............. | Bluebonnet 12-27-75 | Colorado 38-21 (Bill Mallory) |

**HENRY "RED" SANDERS,** 0-2-0 (Vanderbilt '27) b 3-7-05
| | | |
|---|---|---|
| UCLA .............. | Rose 1-1-54 | Michigan St. 20-28 (Clarence "Biggie" Munn) |
| UCLA .............. | Rose 1-2-56 | Michigan St. 14-17 (Duffy Daugherty) |

**RALPH SASSE,** 0-1-0 (Army '10) b 7-19-89
| | | |
|---|---|---|
| Mississippi St. ........ | Orange 1-1-37 | Duquesne 12-13 (John Smith) |

**GEORGE SAUER,** 0-3-0 (Nebraska '34) b 12-11-10
| | | |
|---|---|---|
| Kansas .............. | Orange 1-1-48 | Georgia Tech 14-20 (Bobby Dodd) |
| Baylor............... | Orange 1-1-52 | Georgia Tech 14-17 (Bobby Dodd) |
| Baylor............... | Gator 12-31-54 | Auburn 13-33 (Ralph "Shug" Jordan) |

**MACK SAXON,** 0-1-0 (Texas) b 1901
| | | |
|---|---|---|
| UTEP .............. | Sun 1-1-37 | Hardin-Simmons 6-34 (Frank Kimbrough) |

**GLENN "BO" SCHEMBECHLER,** 5-12-0 (Miami, Ohio '51) b 4-1-29
| | | |
|---|---|---|
| Michigan ............ | Rose 1-1-70 | Southern Cal 3-10 (John McKay) |
| Michigan ............ | Rose 1-1-72 | Stanford 12-13 (John Ralston) |
| Michigan ............ | Orange 1-1-76 | Oklahoma 6-14 (Barry Switzer) |
| Michigan ............ | Rose 1-1-77 | Southern Cal 6-14 (John Robinson) |
| Michigan ............ | Rose 1-2-78 | Washington 20-27 (Don James) |
| Michigan ............ | Rose 1-1-79 | Southern Cal 10-17 (John Robinson) |
| Michigan ............ | Gator 12-28-79 | North Caro. 15-17 (Dick Crum) |
| Michigan ............ | Rose 1-1-81 | Washington 23-6 (Don James) |
| Michigan ............ | Bluebonnet 12-31-81 | UCLA 33-14 (Terry Donahue) |
| Michigan ............ | Rose 1-1-83 | UCLA 14-24 (Terry Donahue) |
| Michigan ............ | Sugar 1-2-84 | Auburn 7-9 (Pat Dye) |
| Michigan ............ | Holiday 12-21-84 | Brigham Young 17-24 (LaVell Edwards) |
| Michigan ............ | Fiesta 1-1-86 | Nebraska 27-23 (Tom Osborne) |
| Michigan ............ | Rose 1-1-87 | Arizona St. 15-22 (John Cooper) |
| Michigan ............ | Hall of Fame 1-2-88 | Alabama 28-24 (Bill Curry) |
| Michigan ............ | Rose 1-2-89 | Southern Cal 22-14 (Larry Smith) |
| Michigan ............ | Rose 1-1-90 | Southern Cal 10-17 (Larry Smith) |

**MERLE SCHLOSSER,** 0-1-0 (Illinois '50) b 10-14-27
| | | |
|---|---|---|
| Western Mich. ........ | Aviation 12-9-61 | New Mexico 12-28 (Bill Weeks) |

**HOWARD SCHNELLENBERGER,** 3-0-0 (Kentucky '56) b 3-16-34
| | | |
|---|---|---|
| Miami (Fla.) ......... | Peach 1-2-81 | Virginia Tech 20-10 (Bill Dooley) |
| Miami (Fla.) ......... | Orange 1-2-84 | Nebraska 31-30 (Tom Osborne) |
| Louisville............ | Fiesta 1-1-91 | Alabama 34-7 (Gene Stallings) |

**PAUL SCHUDEL,** 0-1-0 (Miami, Ohio '66) b 7-2-44
| | | |
|---|---|---|
| Ball St. .............. | California 12-9-89 | Fresno St. 6-27 (Jim Sweeney) |

**BILL SCHUTTE,** 0-1-0 (Idaho '33) b 5-7-10
| | | |
|---|---|---|
| San Diego St. ........ | Harbor 1-1-48 | Hardin-Simmons 0-53 (Warren Woodson) |

**BEN SCHWARTZWALDER,** 2-5-0 (West Va. '35) b 6-2-09
| | | |
|---|---|---|
| Syracuse ............ | Orange 1-1-53 | Alabama 6-61 (Harold "Red" Drew) |
| Syracuse ............ | Cotton 1-1-57 | Texas Christian 27-28 (Abe Martin) |
| Syracuse ............ | Orange 1-1-59 | Oklahoma 6-21 (Bud Wilkinson) |
| Syracuse ............ | Cotton 1-1-60 | Texas 23-14 (Darrell Royal) |
| Syracuse ............ | Liberty 12-16-61 | Miami (Fla.) 15-14 (Andy Gustafson) |
| Syracuse ............ | Sugar 1-1-65 | Louisiana St. 10-13 (Charlie McClendon) |
| Syracuse ............ | Gator 12-31-66 | Tennessee 12-18 (Doug Dickey) |

**CLARK SHAUGHNESSY,** 1-0-0 (Minnesota '14) b 3-6-92
| | | |
|---|---|---|
| Stanford ............. | Rose 1-1-41 | Nebraska 21-13 (Lawrence McC. "Biff" Jones) |

**LAWRENCE "BUCK" SHAW,** 2-0-0 (Notre Dame '22) b 3-28-99
| | | |
|---|---|---|
| Santa Clara ......... | Sugar 1-1-37 | Louisiana St. 21-14 (Bernie Moore) |
| Santa Clara ......... | Sugar 1-1-38 | Louisiana St. 6-0 (Bernie Moore) |

**TERRY SHEA,** 1-0-0 (Oregon '68) b 6-12-46
| | | |
|---|---|---|
| San Jose St. ......... | California 12-8-90 | Central Mich. 48-24 (Herb Deromedi) |

**JOE SHEEKETSKI**, 1-1-0   (Notre Dame '33)   b 4-15-09
Nevada . . . . . . . . . . . . .    Salad 1-1-48          North Texas 13-6 (Odus Mitchell)
Nevada . . . . . . . . . . . . .    Harbor 1-1-49       Villanova 7-27 (Jordan Olivar)

**DICK SHERIDAN**, 2-4-0   (South Caro. '64)   b 8-9-41
North Caro. St. . . . . . . .    Peach 12-31-86      Virginia Tech 24-25 (Bill Dooley)
North Caro. St. . . . . . . .    Peach 12-31-88      Iowa 28-23 (Hayden Fry)
North Caro. St. . . . . . . .    Copper 12-31-89     Arizona 10-17 (Dick Tomey)
North Caro. St. . . . . . . .    All-American 12-28-90    Southern Miss. 31-27 (Jeff Bower)
North Caro. St. . . . . . . .    Peach 1-1-92        East Caro. 34-37 (Bill Lewis)
North Caro. St. . . . . . . .    Gator 12-31-92      Florida 10-27 (Steve Spurrier)

**EUGENE "BO" SHERMAN**, 1-0-0   (Henderson St. '30)   b 7-5-08
Geo. Washington . . . .    Sun 1-1-57          UTEP 13-0 (Mike Brumbelow)

**JACKIE SHERRILL**, 6-4-0   (Alabama '66)   b 11-28-43
Pittsburgh . . . . . . . . . . .    Gator 12-30-77      Clemson 34-3 (Charley Pell)
Pittsburgh . . . . . . . . . . .    Tangerine 12-23-78    North Caro. St. 17-30 (Bo Rein)
Pittsburgh . . . . . . . . . . .    Fiesta 12-25-79      Arizona 16-10 (Tony Mason)
Pittsburgh . . . . . . . . . . .    Gator 12-29-80      South Caro. 37-9 (Jim Carlen)
Pittsburgh . . . . . . . . . . .    Sugar 1-1-82        Georgia 24-20 (Vince Dooley)
Texas A&M . . . . . . . . .    Cotton 1-1-86       Auburn 36-16 (Pat Dye)
Texas A&M . . . . . . . . .    Cotton 1-1-87       Ohio St. 12-28 (Earle Bruce)
Texas A&M . . . . . . . . .    Cotton 1-1-88       Notre Dame 35-10 (Lou Holtz)
Mississippi St. . . . . . . .    Liberty 12-29-91    Air Force 15-38 (Fisher DeBerry)
Mississippi St. . . . . . . .    Peach 1-2-93        North Caro. 17-21 (Mack Brown)

**TED SHIPKEY**, 0-1-0   (Stanford '27)   b 9-28-04
New Mexico . . . . . . . . .    Sun 1-2-39          Utah 0-28 (Ike Armstrong)

**LARRY SIEMERING**, 1-0-0   (San Francisco '35)   b 11-24-10
Pacific (Cal.) . . . . . . . . .    Raisin 1-1-48       Wichita St. 26-14 (Ralph Graham)

**CHAUNCEY SIMPSON**, 0-1-0   (Missouri '25)   b 12-21-02
Missouri . . . . . . . . . . . . .    Cotton 1-1-46       Texas 27-40 (Dana Bible)

**DAN SIMRELL**, 0-1-0   (Toledo '65)   b 4-9-43
Toledo . . . . . . . . . . . . . .    California 12-15-84    Nevada-Las Vegas 13-30 (Harvey Hyde)

**STEVE SLOAN**, 0-2-1   (Alabama '66)   b 8-19-44
Vanderbilt . . . . . . . . . . .    Peach 12-28-74      Texas Tech 6-6 (Jim Carlen)
Texas Tech . . . . . . . . . .    Bluebonnet 12-31-76    Nebraska 24-27 (Tom Osborne)
Texas Tech . . . . . . . . . .    Tangerine 12-23-77    Florida St. 17-40 (Bobby Bowden)

**R. C. SLOCUM**, 1-3-0   (McNeese St. '67)   b 11-7-44
Texas A&M . . . . . . . . .    John Hancock 12-30-89    Pittsburgh 28-31 (Paul Hackett)
Texas A&M . . . . . . . . .    Holiday 12-29-90     Brigham Young 65-14 (LaVell Edwards)
Texas A&M . . . . . . . . .    Cotton 1-1-92       Florida St. 2-10 (Bobby Bowden)
Texas A&M . . . . . . . . .    Cotton 1-1-93       Notre Dame 3-28 (Lou Holtz)

**ANDY SMITH**, 1-0-1   (Pennsylvania '06)   b 9-10-83
California . . . . . . . . . . . .    Rose 1-1-21          Ohio St. 28-0 (John Wilce)
California . . . . . . . . . . . .    Rose 1-2-22          Wash. & Jeff. 0-0 (Earle "Greasy" Neale)

**HOMER SMITH**, 0-1-0   (Princeton '54)   b 10-9-31
Davidson . . . . . . . . . . . .    Tangerine 12-26-69    Toledo 33-56 (Frank Lauterbur)

**JOHN "LITTLE CLIPPER" SMITH**, 1-0-0   (Notre Dame '29)   b 12-12-04
Duquesne . . . . . . . . . . .    Orange 1-1-37       Mississippi St. 13-12 (Ralph Sasse)

**LARRY SMITH**, 2-5-1   (Bowling Green '62)   b 9-12-39
Tulane . . . . . . . . . . . . . .    Liberty 12-22-79     Penn St. 6-9 (Joe Paterno)
Arizona . . . . . . . . . . . . .    Sun 12-28-85        Georgia 13-13 (Vince Dooley)
Arizona . . . . . . . . . . . . .    Aloha 12-27-86      North Caro. 30-21 (Dick Crum)
Southern Cal . . . . . . . .    Rose 1-1-88          Michigan St. 17-20 (George Perles)
Southern Cal . . . . . . . .    Rose 1-2-89          Michigan 14-22 (Glenn "Bo" Schembechler)
Southern Cal . . . . . . . .    Rose 1-1-90          Michigan 17-10 (Glenn "Bo" Schembechler)
Southern Cal . . . . . . . .    John Hancock 12-31-90    Michigan St. 16-17 (George Perles)
Southern Cal . . . . . . . .    Freedom 12-29-92    Fresno St. 7-24 (Jim Sweeney)

**MAURICE "CLIPPER" SMITH**, 0-0-1   (Notre Dame '21)   b 10-15-98
Villanova . . . . . . . . . . . .    Bacardi, Cuba 1-1-37    Auburn 7-7 (Jack Meagher)

**CARL SNAVELY**, 0-3-0   (Lebanon Valley '15)   b 7-30-94
North Caro. . . . . . . . . .    Sugar 1-1-47        Georgia 10-20 (Wally Butts)
North Caro. . . . . . . . . .    Sugar 1-1-49        Oklahoma 6-14 (Bud Wilkinson)
North Caro. . . . . . . . . .    Cotton 1-2-50       Rice 13-27 (Jess Neely)

**BRUCE SNYDER**, 2-0-0   (Oregon '62)   b 3-14-40
California . . . . . . . . . . . .    Copper 12-31-90     Wyoming 17-15 (Paul Roach)
California . . . . . . . . . . . .    Fla. Citrus 1-1-92    Clemson 37-13 (Ken Hatfield)

**CLARENCE "DOC" SPEARS**, 1-0-0   (Dartmouth '16)   b 7-24-94
West Va. . . . . . . . . . . . .    San Diego East-West    Gonzaga 21-13 (Charles "Gus" Dorais)
                    Christmas Classic
                    12-25-22

**CLIFF SPEEGLE**, 1-0-0  (Oklahoma '41)  b 11-4-17
Oklahoma St. . . . . . . . . Bluegrass 12-13-58      Florida St. 15-6 (Tom Nugent)
**STEVE SPURRIER**, 1-2-0  (Florida '67)  b 4-20-45
Duke . . . . . . . . . . . . . . . All-American 12-28-89      Texas Tech 21-49 (Spike Dykes)
Florida . . . . . . . . . . . . . . Sugar 1-1-92      Notre Dame 28-39 (Lou Holtz)
Florida . . . . . . . . . . . . . . Gator 12-31-92      North Caro. St. 27-10 (Dick Sheridan)
**GENE STALLINGS**, 3-1-0  (Texas A&M '57)  b 3-2-35
Texas A&M . . . . . . . . . . Cotton 1-1-68      Alabama 20-16 (Paul "Bear" Bryant)
Alabama . . . . . . . . . . . . Fiesta 1-1-91      Louisville 7-34 (Howard Schnellenberger)
Alabama . . . . . . . . . . . . Blockbuster 12-28-91      Colorado 30-25 (Bill McCartney)
Alabama . . . . . . . . . . . . Sugar 1-1-93      Miami (Fla.) 34-13 (Dennis Erickson)
**JIM STANGELAND**, 0-0-1  (Arizona St. '48)  b 12-21-21
Long Beach St. . . . . . . Pasadena 12-19-70      Louisville 24-24 (Lee Corso)
**JIM STANLEY**, 2-0-0  (Texas A&M '59)  b 5-22-35
Oklahoma St. . . . . . . . . Fiesta 12-28-74      Brigham Young 16-6 (LaVell Edwards)
Oklahoma St. . . . . . . . . Tangerine 12-18-76      Brigham Young 49-12 (LaVell Edwards)
**TOM STIDHAM**, 0-1-0  (Haskell '27)  b 3-27-04
Oklahoma . . . . . . . . . . . Orange 1-2-39      Tennessee 0-17 (Bob Neyland)
**LON STINER**, 1-0-0  (Nebraska '27)  b 6-20-03
Oregon St. . . . . . . . . . . Rose 1-1-42      Duke 20-16 (Wallace Wade)
**HARRY STITELER**, 1-0-0  (Texas A&M '31)  b 9-17-09
Texas A&M . . . . . . . . . . Presidential Cup 12-9-50      Georgia 40-20 (Wally Butts)
**CHUCK STOBART**, 1-0-0  (Ohio '59)  b 10-27-34
Toledo . . . . . . . . . . . . . . California 12-19-81      San Jose St. 27-25 (Jack Elway)
**CAL STOLL**, 0-1-0  (Minnesota '50)  b 12-12-23
Minnesota . . . . . . . . . . . Hall of Fame 12-22-77      Maryland 7-17 (Jerry Claiborne)
**DENNY STOLZ**, 0-3-0  (Alma '55)  b 9-12-34
Bowling Green . . . . . . . California 12-18-82      Fresno St. 28-29 (Jim Sweeney)
Bowling Green . . . . . . . California 12-14-85      Fresno St. 7-51 (Jim Sweeney)
San Diego St. . . . . . . . . Holiday 12-30-86      Iowa 38-39 (Hayden Fry)
**JERRY STOVALL**, 0-1-0  (Louisiana St. '63)  b 4-30-41
Louisiana St. . . . . . . . . . Sugar 1-1-83      Nebraska 20-21 (Tom Osborne)
**BOB STULL**, 0-1-0  (Kansas St. '68)  b 11-21-45
UTEP . . . . . . . . . . . . . . . Independence 12-23-88      Southern Miss. 18-38 (Curley Hallman)
**JOCK SUTHERLAND**, 1-3-0  (Pittsburgh '18)  b 3-21-89
Pittsburgh . . . . . . . . . . . Rose 1-1-28      Stanford 6-7 (Glenn "Pop" Warner)
Pittsburgh . . . . . . . . . . . Rose 1-1-30      Southern Cal 14-47 (Howard Jones)
Pittsburgh . . . . . . . . . . . Rose 1-2-33      Southern Cal 0-35 (Howard Jones)
Pittsburgh . . . . . . . . . . . Rose 1-1-37      Washington 21-0 (Jimmy Phelan)
**JIM SWEENEY**, 5-1-0  (Portland '51)  b 9-1-29
Fresno St. . . . . . . . . . . . California 12-18-82      Bowling Green 29-28 (Denny Stolz)
Fresno St. . . . . . . . . . . . California 12-14-85      Bowling Green 51-7 (Denny Stolz)
Fresno St. . . . . . . . . . . . California 12-10-88      Western Mich. 35-30 (Al Molde)
Fresno St. . . . . . . . . . . . California 12-9-89      Ball St. 27-8 (Paul Schudel)
Fresno St. . . . . . . . . . . . California 12-13-91      Bowling Green 21-28 (Gary Blackney)
Fresno St. . . . . . . . . . . . Freedom 12-29-92      Southern Cal 24-7 (Larry Smith)
**BARRY SWITZER**, 8-5-0  (Arkansas '60)  b 10-5-37
Oklahoma . . . . . . . . . . . Orange 1-1-76      Michigan 14-6 (Glenn "Bo" Schembechler)
Oklahoma . . . . . . . . . . . Fiesta 12-25-76      Wyoming 41-7 (Fred Akers)
Oklahoma . . . . . . . . . . . Orange 1-2-78      Arkansas 6-31 (Lou Holtz)
Oklahoma . . . . . . . . . . . Orange 1-1-79      Nebraska 31-24 (Tom Osborne)
Oklahoma . . . . . . . . . . . Orange 1-1-80      Florida St. 24-7 (Bobby Bowden)
Oklahoma . . . . . . . . . . . Orange 1-1-81      Florida St. 18-17 (Bobby Bowden)
Oklahoma . . . . . . . . . . . Sun 12-26-81      Houston 40-14 (Bill Yeoman)
Oklahoma . . . . . . . . . . . Fiesta 1-1-83      Arizona St. 21-32 (Darryl Rogers)
Oklahoma . . . . . . . . . . . Orange 1-1-85      Washington 17-28 (Don James)
Oklahoma . . . . . . . . . . . Orange 1-1-86      Penn St. 25-10 (Joe Paterno)
Oklahoma . . . . . . . . . . . Orange 1-1-87      Arkansas 42-8 (Ken Hatfield)
Oklahoma . . . . . . . . . . . Orange 1-1-88      Miami (Fla.) 14-20 (Jimmy Johnson)
Oklahoma . . . . . . . . . . . Fla. Citrus 1-2-89      Clemson 6-13 (Danny Ford)
**CHARLIE TATE**, 1-1-0  (Florida '42)  b 2-20-21
Miami (Fla.) . . . . . . . . . Liberty 12-10-66      Virginia Tech 14-7 (Jerry Claiborne)
Miami (Fla.) . . . . . . . . . Bluebonnet 12-23-67      Colorado 21-31 (Eddie Crowder)
**JIM TATUM**, 3-2-1  (North Caro. '35)  b 7-22-13
Oklahoma . . . . . . . . . . . Gator 1-1-47      North Caro. St. 34-13 (Beattie Feathers)
Maryland . . . . . . . . . . . . Gator 1-1-48      Georgia 20-20 (Wally Butts)
Maryland . . . . . . . . . . . . Gator 1-2-50      Missouri 20-7 (Don Faurot)
Maryland . . . . . . . . . . . . Sugar 1-1-52      Tennessee 28-13 (Bob Neyland)
Maryland . . . . . . . . . . . . Orange 1-1-54      Oklahoma 0-7 (Bud Wilkinson)
Maryland . . . . . . . . . . . . Orange 1-2-56      Oklahoma 6-20 (Bud Wilkinson)

**CHUCK TAYLOR**, 0-1-0   (Stanford '43)   b 1-24-20
Stanford ............   Rose 1-1-52   Illinois 7-40 (Ray Eliot)
**GRANT TEAFF**, 4-4-0   (McMurry '56)   b 11-12-33
Baylor................   Cotton 1-1-75   Penn St. 20-41 (Joe Paterno)
Baylor................   Peach 12-31-79   Clemson 24-18 (Danny Ford)
Baylor................   Cotton 1-1-81   Alabama 2-30 (Paul "Bear" Bryant)
Baylor................   Bluebonnet 12-31-83   Oklahoma St. 14-24 (Jimmy Johnson)
Baylor................   Liberty 12-27-85   Louisiana St. 21-7 (Bill Arnsparger)
Baylor................   Bluebonnet 12-31-86   Colorado 21-9 (Bill McCartney)
Baylor................   Copper 12-31-91   Indiana 0-24 (Bill Mallory)
Baylor................   John Hancock 12-31-92   Arizona 20-15 (Dick Tomey)
**EDDIE TEAGUE**, 1-0-0   (North Caro. '44)   b 12-14-21
Citadel ..............   Tangerine 12-30-60   Tennessee Tech 27-0 (Wilburn Tucker)
**LOU TEPPER**, 0-2-0   (Rutgers '67)   b 7-21-45
Illinois...............   John Hancock 12-31-91   UCLA 3-6 (Terry Donahue)
Illinois...............   Holiday 12-30-92   Hawaii 17-27 (Bob Wagner)
**ROBERT THEDER**, 0-1-0   (Western Mich. '63)   b 9-22-39
California ...........   Garden State 12-15-79   Temple 17-28 (Wayne Hardin)
**FRANK THOMAS**, 4-2-0   (Notre Dame '23)   b 11-14-98
Alabama .............   Rose 1-1-35   Stanford 29-13 (Claude "Tiny" Thornhill)
Alabama .............   Rose 1-1-38   California 0-13 (Leonard "Stub" Allison)
Alabama .............   Cotton 1-1-42   Texas A&M 29-21 (Homer Norton)
Alabama .............   Orange 1-1-43   Boston College 37-21 (Denny Myers)
Alabama ............   Sugar 1-1-45   Duke 26-29 (Eddie Cameron)
Alabama ............   Rose 1-1-46   Southern Cal 34-14 (Jeff Cravath)
**FRED THOMSEN**, 0-0-1   (Nebraska '25)   b 4-25-97
Arkansas ............   Dixie Classic 1-1-34   Centenary 7-7 (Homer Norton)
**CLAUDE "TINY" THORNHILL**, 1-2-0   (Pittsburgh '17)   b 4-14-93
Stanford .............   Rose 1-1-34   Columbia 0-7 (Lou Little)
Stanford .............   Rose 1-1-35   Alabama 13-29 (Frank Thomas)
Stanford .............   Rose 1-1-36   Southern Methodist 7-0 (Matty Bell)
**GAYNELL TINSLEY**, 0-1-0   (Louisiana St. '37)   b 2-1-15
Louisiana St. .........   Sugar 1-2-50   Oklahoma 0-35 (Bud Wilkinson)
**TED TOLLNER**, 1-2-0   (Cal Poly SLO '62)   b 5-29-40
Southern Cal ........   Rose 1-1-85   Ohio St. 20-17 (Earle Bruce)
Southern Cal ........   Aloha 12-28-85   Alabama 3-24 (Ray Perkins)
Southern Cal ........   Fla. Citrus 1-1-87   Auburn 7-16 (Pat Dye)
**DICK TOMEY**, 1-2-0   (DePauw '61)   b 6-20-38
Arizona ..............   Copper 12-30-89   North Caro. St. 17-10 (Dick Sheridan)
Arizona ..............   Aloha 12-28-90   Syracuse 0-28 (Dick MacPherson)
Arizona ..............   John Hancock 12-31-92   Baylor 15-20 (Grant Teaff)
**JIM TRIMBLE**, 0-1-0   (Indiana '42)   b 5-29-18
Wichita St. ...........   Camellia 12-30-48   Hardin-Simmons 12-49 (Warren Woodson)
**FRANK TRITICO**, 0-0-1   (Southwestern La. '34)   b 3-25-09
Randolph Field.......   Cotton 1-1-44   Texas 7-7 (Dana Bible)
**WILBURN TUCKER**, 0-1-0   (Tennessee Tech '43)   b 8-11-20
Tennessee Tech ......   Tangerine 12-30-60   Citadel 0-27 (Eddie Teague)
**BOB TYLER**, 1-0-0   (Mississippi '58)   b 7-4-32
Mississippi St........   Sun 12-28-74   North Caro. 26-24 (Bill Dooley)
**THAD "PIE" VANN**, 0-2-0   (Mississippi '28)   b 9-22-07
Southern Miss.......   Sun 1-1-53   Pacific (Cal.) 7-26 (Ernie Jorge)
Southern Miss.......   Sun 1-1-54   UTEP 14-37 (Mike Brumbelow)
**JOHN VAUGHT**, 10-8-0   (Texas Christian '33)   b 5-6-08
Mississippi ..........   Delta 1-1-48   Texas Christian 13-9 (Leo "Dutch" Meyer)
Mississippi ..........   Sugar 1-1-53   Georgia Tech 7-24 (Bobby Dodd)
Mississippi ..........   Sugar 1-1-55   Navy 0-21 (Eddie Erdelatz)
Mississippi ..........   Cotton 1-2-56   Texas Christian 14-13 (Abe Martin)
Mississippi ..........   Sugar 1-1-58   Texas 39-7 (Darrell Royal)
Mississippi ..........   Gator 12-27-58   Florida 7-3 (Bob Woodruff)
Mississippi ..........   Sugar 1-1-60   Louisiana St. 21-0 (Paul Dietzel)
Mississippi ..........   Sugar 1-2-61   Rice 14-6 (Jess Neely)
Mississippi ..........   Cotton 1-1-62   Texas 7-12 (Darrell Royal)
Mississippi ..........   Sugar 1-1-63   Arkansas 17-13 (Frank Broyles)
Mississippi ..........   Sugar 1-1-64   Alabama 7-12 (Paul "Bear" Bryant)
Mississippi ..........   Bluebonnet 12-19-64   Tulsa 7-14 (Glenn Dobbs)
Mississippi ..........   Liberty 12-18-65   Auburn 13-7 (Ralph "Shug" Jordan)
Mississippi ..........   Bluebonnet 12-17-66   Texas 0-19 (Darrell Royal)
Mississippi ..........   Sun 12-30-67   UTEP 7-14 (Bobby Dobbs)
Mississippi ..........   Liberty 12-14-68   Virginia Tech 34-17 (Jerry Claiborne)
Mississippi ..........   Sugar 1-1-70   Arkansas 27-22 (Frank Broyles)

*Bowl Coaching Records*

| | | |
|---|---|---|
| Mississippi ........... | Gator 1-2-71 | Auburn 28-35 (Ralph "Shug" Jordan) |

**DICK VERMEIL**, 1-0-0   (San Jose St. '58)   b 10-30-36

| | | |
|---|---|---|
| UCLA ................ | Rose 1-1-76 | Ohio St. 23-10 (Woody Hayes) |

**BOB VOIGTS**, 1-0-0   (Northwestern '39)   b 3-29-16

| | | |
|---|---|---|
| Northwestern ........ | Rose 1-1-49 | California 20-14 (Lynn "Pappy" Waldorf) |

**JIM WACKER**, 0-1-0   (Valparaiso '60)   b 4-28-37

| | | |
|---|---|---|
| Texas Christian ...... | Bluebonnet 12-31-84 | West Va. 14-31 (Don Nehlen) |

**WALLACE WADE**, 2-2-1   (Brown '17)   b 6-15-92

| | | |
|---|---|---|
| Alabama ............. | Rose 1-1-26 | Washington 20-19 (Enoch Bagshaw) |
| Alabama ............. | Rose 1-1-27 | Stanford 7-7 (Glenn "Pop" Warner) |
| Alabama ............. | Rose 1-1-31 | Washington St. 24-0 (Orin "Babe" Hollingbery) |
| Duke ................. | Rose 1-2-39 | Southern Cal 3-7 (Howard Jones) |
| Duke ................. | Rose 1-1-42 | Oregon St. 16-20 (Lon Stiner) |

**BOB WAGNER**, 1-1-0   (Wittenberg '69)   b 5-16-47

| | | |
|---|---|---|
| Hawaii .............. | Aloha 12-25-89 | Michigan St. 13-33 (George Perles) |
| Hawaii .............. | Holiday 12-30-92 | Illinois 27-17 (Lou Tepper) |

**JIM WALDEN**, 0-1-0   (Wyoming '60)   b 4-10-38

| | | |
|---|---|---|
| Washington St........ | Holiday 12-18-81 | Brigham Young 36-38 (LaVell Edwards) |

**LYNN "PAPPY" WALDORF**, 0-3-0   (Syracuse '25)   b 10-3-02

| | | |
|---|---|---|
| California ........... | Rose 1-1-49 | Northwestern 14-20 (Bob Voigts) |
| California ........... | Rose 1-2-50 | Ohio St. 14-17 (Wes Fesler) |
| California ........... | Rose 1-1-51 | Michigan 6-14 (Bennie Oosterbaan) |

**D. C. "PEAHEAD" WALKER**, 1-1-0   (Samford '22)   b 2-17-00

| | | |
|---|---|---|
| Wake Forest.......... | Gator 1-1-46 | South Caro. 26-14 (Johnnie McMillan) |
| Wake Forest.......... | Dixie 1-1-49 | Baylor 7-20 (Bob Woodruff) |

**ED WALKER**, 0-1-0   (Stanford '27)   b 3-25-01

| | | |
|---|---|---|
| Mississippi ........... | Orange 1-1-36 | Catholic 19-20 (Arthur "Dutch" Bergman) |

**BILL WALSH**, 3-0-0   (San Jose St. '54)   b 11-30-31

| | | |
|---|---|---|
| Stanford ............. | Sun 12-31-77 | Louisiana St. 24-14 (Charlie McClendon) |
| Stanford ............. | Bluebonnet 12-31-78 | Georgia 25-22 (Vince Dooley) |
| Stanford ............. | Blockbuster 1-1-93 | Penn St. 24-3 (Joe Paterno) |

**DALLAS WARD**, 1-0-0   (Oregon St. '27)   b 8-11-06

| | | |
|---|---|---|
| Colorado ............ | Orange 1-1-57 | Clemson 27-21 (Frank Howard) |

**MURRAY WARMATH**, 1-1-0   (Tennessee '35)   b 12-26-13

| | | |
|---|---|---|
| Minnesota ........... | Rose 1-2-61 | Washington 7-17 (Jim Owens) |
| Minnesota ........... | Rose 1-1-62 | UCLA 21-3 (Bill Barnes) |

**GLENN "POP" WARNER**, 1-2-1   (Cornell '95)   b 4-5-71

| | | |
|---|---|---|
| Stanford ............. | Rose 1-1-25 | Notre Dame 10-27 (Knute Rockne) |
| Stanford ............. | Rose 1-1-27 | Alabama 7-7 (Wallace Wade) |
| Stanford ............. | Rose 1-2-28 | Pittsburgh 7-6 (Jock Sutherland) |
| Temple .............. | Sugar 1-1-35 | Tulane 14-20 (Ted Cox) |

**DeWITT WEAVER**, 2-1-0   (Tennessee '37)   b 5-11-12

| | | |
|---|---|---|
| Texas Tech .......... | Sun 1-1-52 | Pacific (Cal.) 25-14 (Ernie Jorge) |
| Texas Tech .......... | Gator 1-1-54 | Auburn 35-13 (Ralph "Shug" Jordan) |
| Texas Tech .......... | Sun 1-2-56 | Wyoming 14-21 (Phil Dickens) |

**BILL WEEKS**, 1-0-0   (Iowa St. '51)   b 10-20-29

| | | |
|---|---|---|
| New Mexico.......... | Aviation 12-9-61 | Western Mich. 28-12 (Merle Schlosser) |

**RALPH "PEST" WELCH**, 0-1-0   (Purdue '30)   b 8-11-07

| | | |
|---|---|---|
| Washington .......... | Rose 1-1-44 | Southern Cal 0-29 (Jeff Cravath) |

**GEORGE WELSH**, 3-5-0   (Navy '56)   b 8-26-33

| | | |
|---|---|---|
| Navy ................ | Holiday 12-22-78 | Brigham Young 23-16 (LaVell Edwards) |
| Navy ................ | Garden State 12-14-80 | Houston 0-35 (Bill Yeoman) |
| Navy ................ | Liberty 12-30-81 | Ohio St. 28-31 (Earle Bruce) |
| Virginia.............. | Peach 12-31-84 | Purdue 27-24 (Leon Burtnett) |
| Virginia.............. | All-American 12-22-87 | Brigham Young 22-16 (LaVell Edwards) |
| Virginia.............. | Fla. Citrus 1-1-90 | Illinois 21-31 (John Mackovic) |
| Virginia.............. | Sugar 1-1-91 | Tennessee 22-23 (Johnny Majors) |
| Virginia.............. | Gator 12-29-91 | Oklahoma 14-48 (Gary Gibbs) |

**MIKE WHITE**, 0-3-0   (California '58)   b 1-3-36

| | | |
|---|---|---|
| Illinois............... | Liberty 12-29-82 | Alabama 15-21 (Paul "Bear" Bryant) |
| Illinois............... | Rose 1-2-84 | UCLA 9-45 (Terry Donahue) |
| Illinois............... | Peach 12-31-85 | Army 29-31 (Jim Young) |

**JOHN WILCE**, 0-1-0   (Wisconsin '10)   b 5-12-88

| | | |
|---|---|---|
| Ohio St. .............. | Rose 1-1-21 | California 0-28 (Andy Smith) |

**BUD WILKINSON**, 6-2-0   (Minnesota '37)   b 4-12-16

| | | |
|---|---|---|
| Oklahoma............ | Sugar 1-1-49 | North Caro. 14-6 (Carl Snavely) |
| Oklahoma............ | Sugar 1-2-50 | Louisiana St. 35-0 (Gaynell Tinsley) |
| Oklahoma............ | Sugar 1-1-51 | Kentucky 7-13 (Paul "Bear" Bryant) |
| Oklahoma............ | Orange 1-1-54 | Maryland 7-0 (Jim Tatum) |

| | | |
|---|---|---|
| Oklahoma........... | Orange 1-2-56 | Maryland 20-6 (Jim Tatum) |
| Oklahoma........... | Orange 1-1-58 | Duke 48-21 (Bill Murray) |
| Oklahoma........... | Orange 1-1-59 | Syracuse 21-6 (Ben Schwartzwalder) |
| Oklahoma........... | Orange 1-1-63 | Alabama 0-17 (Paul "Bear" Bryant) |

**IVY WILLIAMSON**, 0-1-0  (Michigan '33)  b 2-4-11

| | | |
|---|---|---|
| Wisconsin........... | Rose 1-1-53 | Southern Cal 0-7 (Jess Hill) |

**TOM WILSON**, 2-0-0  (Texas Tech '66)  b 2-24-44

| | | |
|---|---|---|
| Texas A&M.......... | Hall of Fame 12-20-78 | Iowa St. 28-18 (Earle Bruce) |
| Texas A&M.......... | Independence 12-12-81 | Oklahoma St. 33-16 (Jimmy Johnson) |

**SAM WINNINGHAM**, 0-1-0  (Colorado '50)  b 10-11-26

| | | |
|---|---|---|
| Cal St. Northridge.... | Pasadena 12-2-67 | West Tex. St. 13-35 (Joe Kerbel) |

**BOB WOODRUFF**, 2-1-0  (Tennessee '39)  b 3-14-16

| | | |
|---|---|---|
| Baylor................ | Dixie 1-1-49 | Wake Forest 20-7 (D. C. "Peahead" Walker) |
| Florida .............. | Gator 1-1-53 | Tulsa 14-13 (J. O. "Buddy" Brothers) |
| Florida .............. | Gator 12-27-58 | Mississippi 3-7 (John Vaught) |

**WARREN WOODSON**, 6-1-0  (Baylor '24)  b 2-24-03

| | | |
|---|---|---|
| Hardin-Simmons..... | Sun 1-1-43 | Second Air Force 7-13 (Red Reese) |
| Hardin-Simmons..... | Alamo 1-4-47 | Denver 20-6 (Clyde "Cac" Hubbard) |
| Hardin-Simmons..... | Harbor 1-1-48 | San Diego St. 53-0 (Bill Schutte) |
| Hardin-Simmons..... | Shrine 12-18-48 | Ouachita Baptist 40-12 (Wesley Bradshaw) |
| Hardin-Simmons..... | Camellia 12-30-48 | Wichita St. 49-12 (Jim Trimble) |
| New Mexico St. ...... | Sun 12-31-59 | North Texas 28-8 (Odus Mitchell) |
| New Mexico St. ...... | Sun 12-31-60 | Utah St. 20-13 (John Ralston) |

**BOWDEN WYATT**, 2-2-0  (Tennessee '39)  b 11-3-17

| | | |
|---|---|---|
| Wyoming............ | Gator 1-1-51 | Wash. & Lee 20-7 (George Barclay) |
| Arkansas........... | Cotton 1-1-55 | Georgia Tech 6-14 (Bobby Dodd) |
| Tennessee .......... | Sugar 1-1-57 | Baylor 7-13 (Sam Boyd) |
| Tennessee .......... | Gator 12-26-57 | Texas A&M 3-0 (Paul "Bear" Bryant) |

**BILL YEOMAN**, 6-4-1  (Army '50)  b 12-26-27

| | | |
|---|---|---|
| Houston............. | Tangerine 12-22-62 | Miami (Ohio) 49-21 (John Pont) |
| Houston............. | Bluebonnet 12-31-69 | Auburn 36-7 (Ralph "Shug" Jordan) |
| Houston............. | Bluebonnet 12-31-71 | Colorado 17-29 (Eddie Crowder) |
| Houston............. | Bluebonnet 12-29-73 | Tulane 47-7 (Bennie Ellender) |
| Houston............. | Bluebonnet 12-23-74 | North Caro. St. 31-31 (Lou Holtz) |
| Houston............. | Cotton 1-1-77 | Maryland 30-21 (Jerry Claiborne) |
| Houston............. | Cotton 1-1-79 | Notre Dame 34-35 (Dan Devine) |
| Houston............. | Cotton 1-1-80 | Nebraska 17-14 (Tom Osborne) |
| Houston............. | Garden State 12-14-80 | Navy 35-0 (George Welsh) |
| Houston............. | Sun 12-26-81 | Oklahoma 14-40 (Barry Switzer) |
| Houston............. | Cotton 1-1-85 | Boston College 28-45 (Jack Bicknell) |

**FIELDING "HURRY UP" YOST**, 1-0-0  (Lafayette '97)  b 4-30-71

| | | |
|---|---|---|
| Michigan ............ | Rose 1-1-02 | Stanford 49-0 (Charlie Fickert) |

**JIM YOUNG**, 5-1-0  (Bowling Green '57)  b 4-21-35

| | | |
|---|---|---|
| Purdue .............. | Peach 12-25-78 | Georgia Tech 41-21 (Pepper Rodgers) |
| Purdue .............. | Bluebonnet 12-31-79 | Tennessee 27-22 (Johnny Majors) |
| Purdue .............. | Liberty 12-27-80 | Missouri 28-25 (Warren Powers) |
| Army ................ | Cherry 12-22-84 | Michigan St. 10-6 (George Perles) |
| Army ................ | Peach 12-31-85 | Illinois 31-29 (Mike White) |
| Army ................ | Sun 12-24-88 | Alabama 28-29 (Bill Curry) |

# COACHES WHO HAVE TAKEN MORE THAN ONE TEAM TO A BOWL GAME

**Four Teams (3)**
Earle Bruce: Tampa, Iowa St., Ohio St. & Colorado St.
*Lou Holtz: William & Mary, North Caro. St., Arkansas & Notre Dame
*Bill Mallory: Miami (Ohio), Colorado, Northern Ill. & Indiana

**Three Teams (9)**
Paul "Bear" Bryant: Kentucky, Texas A&M & Alabama
Jim Carlen: West Va., Texas Tech & South Caro.
Jerry Claiborne: Virginia Tech, Maryland & Kentucky
Bill Dooley: North Caro., Virginia Tech & Wake Forest
*Ken Hatfield: Air Force, Arkansas & Clemson
*Johnny Majors: Iowa St., Pittsburgh & Tennessee
*Jackie Sherrill: Pittsburgh, Texas A&M & Mississippi St.
Larry Smith: Tulane, Arizona & Southern Cal
Bowden Wyatt: Wyoming, Arkansas & Tennessee

*Bowl Coaching Records*

**Bill Mallory, currently head coach at Indiana, is one of only three coaches who have taken four different schools to a bowl game. He shares that distinction with Earle Bruce and current Notre Dame coach Lou Holtz.**

**Two Teams (54)**
　Fred Akers: Wyoming & Texas
　John Barnhill: Tennessee & Arkansas
　Emory Bellard: Texas A&M & Mississippi St.
　Hugo Bezdek: Oregon & Penn St.
　Dana X. Bible: Texas A&M & Texas
*Bobby Bowden: West Va. & Florida St.
　Len Casanova: Santa Clara & Oregon
　Bobby Collins: Southern Miss. & Southern Methodist
*John Cooper: Arizona St. & Ohio St.
　Lee Corso: Louisville & Indiana
　Dick Crum: Miami (Ohio) & North Caro.
*Bill Curry: Georgia Tech & Alabama
　Bob Devaney: Wyoming & Nebraska
　Dan Devine: Missouri & Notre Dame
　Doug Dickey: Tennessee & Florida
　Paul Dietzel: Louisiana St. & South Caro.
　Pat Dye: East Caro. & Auburn
　Pete Elliott: California & Illinois
　Jack Elway: San Jose St. & Stanford
*Dennis Erickson: Washington St. & Miami (Fla.)
　Bob Folwell: Pennsylvania & Navy
*Hayden Fry: Southern Methodist & Iowa
　Vince Gibson: Louisville & Tulane
　Sid Gillman: Miami (Ohio) & Cincinnati
　Wayne Hardin: Navy & Temple
　Woody Hayes: Miami (Ohio) & Ohio St.
　Bob Higgins: West Va. Wesleyan & Penn St.
*Don James: Kent & Washington
　Jimmy Johnson: Oklahoma St. & Miami (Fla.)
　Frank Kimbrough: Hardin-Simmons & West Tex. St.
　Jimmy Kitts: Rice & Virginia Tech

*John Mackovic: Wake Forest & Illinois
Jess Neely: Clemson & Rice
Homer Norton: Centenary & Texas A&M
Charley Pell: Clemson & Florida
Jimmy Phelan: Washington & St. Mary's (Cal.)
John Pont: Miami (Ohio) & Indiana
Tommy Prothro: Oregon St. & UCLA
*John Ralston: Utah St. & Stanford
Pepper Rodgers: Kansas & Georgia Tech
Bobby Ross: Maryland & Georgia Tech
George Sauer: Kansas & Baylor
*Howard Schnellenberger: Miami (Fla.) & Louisville
Steve Sloan: Vanderbilt & Texas Tech
*Steve Spurrier: Duke & Florida
*Gene Stallings: Texas A&M & Alabama
Denny Stolz: Bowling Green & San Diego St.
Jim Tatum: Oklahoma & Maryland
Wallace Wade: Alabama & Duke
Glenn "Pop" Warner: Stanford & Temple
*George Welsh: Navy & Virginia
Bob Woodruff: Baylor & Florida
Warren Woodson: Hardin-Simmons & New Mexico St.
Jim Young: Purdue & Army
* Active coach.

## COACHES WITH THE MOST YEARS TAKING
## ONE COLLEGE TO A BOWL GAME

| Coach, Team Taken | Bowls | Consecutive Years |
|---|---|---|
| Paul "Bear" Bryant, Alabama | 24 | 24 |
| *Joe Paterno, Penn St. | 23 | 13 |
| Vince Dooley, Georgia | 20 | 9 |
| *Tom Osborne, Nebraska | 20 | 20 |
| John Vaught, Mississippi | 18 | 14 |
| *LaVell Edwards, Brigham Young | 17 | 15 |
| Bo Schembechler, Michigan | 17 | 15 |
| Darrell Royal, Texas | 16 | 8 |
| *Don James, Washington | 14 | 10 |
| *Bobby Bowden, Florida St. | 13 | 13 |
| Bobby Dodd, Georgia Tech | 13 | 6 |
| Charlie McClendon, Louisiana St. | 13 | 4 |
| Barry Switzer, Oklahoma | 13 | 8 |
| Shug Jordan, Auburn | 12 | 7 |
| *Terry Donahue, UCLA | 11 | 8 |
| Woody Hayes, Ohio St. | 11 | 6 |
| *Johnny Majors, Tennessee | 11 | 7 |
| Bill Yeoman, Houston | 11 | 4 |
| Frank Broyles, Arkansas | 10 | 4 |
| *Hayden Fry, Iowa | 10 | 10 |
| Fred Akers, Texas | 9 | 9 |
| Bob Devaney, Nebraska | 9 | 5 |
| Pat Dye, Auburn | 9 | 9 |
| John McKay, Southern Cal | 9 | 4 |
| Earle Bruce, Ohio St. | 8 | 8 |
| Wally Butts, Georgia | 8 | 4 |
| *Danny Ford, Clemson | 8 | 5 |
| Grant Teaff, Baylor | 8 | 2 |
| Bud Wilkinson, Oklahoma | 8 | 3 |

* Active coach.   # Active consecutive streak.

# CONFERENCE BOWL RECORDS

## 1992-93 BOWL RECORDS BY CONFERENCE

| Conference | W-L-T | Pct. |
|---|---|---|
| Mid-American Athletic Conference | 1-0-0 | 1.000 |
| Atlantic Coast Conference | 4-1-0 | .800 |
| Southeastern Conference | 5-2-0 | .714 |
| Southwest Conference | 1-1-0 | .500 |
| Independents | 1-1-0 | .500 |

*Bowl Coaching Records*

| Conference | W-L-T | Pct. |
|---|---|---|
| Western Athletic Conference | 2-3-0 | .400 |
| Pacific-10 Conference | 2-4-0 | .333 |
| Big East Conference | 1-2-0 | .333 |
| Big Eight Conference | 1-2-0 | .333 |
| Big Ten Conference | 1-2-0 | .333 |
| Big West Conference | 0-1-0 | .000 |

# ALL-TIME CONFERENCE BOWL RECORDS

(Through 1992-93 bowls, using present conference alignments.)

## ATLANTIC COAST CONFERENCE

| Institution | Bowls | W-L-T | Pct. | Last Appearance |
|---|---|---|---|---|
| Clemson | 18 | 11- 7-0 | .611 | 1992 Florida Citrus |
| Duke | 7 | 3- 4-0 | .429 | 1989 All-American |
| Florida St. | 21 | 12- 7-2 | .619 | 1993 Orange |
| Georgia Tech | 25 | 17- 8-0 | .680 | 1991 Aloha |
| Maryland | 17 | 6- 9-2 | .412 | 1990 Independence |
| North Caro. | 17 | 7-10-0 | .412 | 1993 Peach |
| North Caro. St. | 15 | 7- 7-1 | .500 | 1992 Gator |
| Virginia | 5 | 2- 3-0 | .400 | 1991 Gator |
| Wake Forest | 4 | 2- 2-0 | .500 | 1992 Independence |
| **Current Members** | **129** | **67-57-5** | **.539** | |

## BIG EAST CONFERENCE

| Institution | Bowls | W-L-T | Pct. | Last Appearance |
|---|---|---|---|---|
| Boston College | 8 | 3- 5-0 | .375 | 1993 Hall of Fame |
| Miami (Fla.) | 19 | 10- 9-0 | .526 | 1993 Sugar |
| Pittsburgh | 18 | 8-10-0 | .444 | 1989 John Hancock |
| Rutgers | 1 | 0- 1-0 | .000 | 1978 Garden State |
| Syracuse | 15 | 8- 6-1 | .567 | 1993 Fiesta |
| Temple | 2 | 1- 1-0 | .500 | 1979 Garden State |
| Virginia Tech | 6 | 1- 5-0 | .167 | 1986 Peach |
| West Va. | 15 | 8- 7-0 | .533 | 1989 Gator |
| **Current Members** | **84** | **39-44-1** | **.470** | |

## BIG EIGHT CONFERENCE

| Institution | Bowls | W-L-T | Pct. | Last Appearance |
|---|---|---|---|---|
| Colorado | 16 | 5-11-0 | .313 | 1993 Fiesta |
| Iowa St. | 4 | 0- 4-0 | .000 | 1978 Hall of Fame |
| Kansas | 7 | 2- 5-0 | .286 | 1992 Aloha |
| Kansas St. | 1 | 0- 1-0 | .000 | 1982 Independence |
| Missouri | 18 | 8-10-0 | .444 | 1983 Holiday |
| Nebraska | 31 | 14-17-0 | .452 | 1993 Orange |
| Oklahoma | 30 | 19-10-1 | .650 | 1991 Gator |
| Oklahoma St. | 12 | 9- 3-0 | .750 | 1988 Holiday |
| **Current Members** | **119** | **57-61-1** | **.483** | |

## BIG TEN CONFERENCE

| Institution | Bowls | W-L-T | Pct. | Last Appearance |
|---|---|---|---|---|
| Illinois | 11 | 4- 7-0 | .364 | 1992 Holiday |
| Indiana | 7 | 3- 4-0 | .429 | 1991 Copper |
| Iowa | 12 | 6- 5-1 | .542 | 1991 Holiday |
| Michigan | 24 | 11-13-0 | .458 | 1993 Rose |
| Michigan St. | 10 | 5- 5-0 | .500 | 1990 John Hancock |
| Minnesota | 5 | 2- 3-0 | .400 | 1986 Liberty |
| Northwestern | 1 | 1- 0-0 | 1.000 | 1948 Rose |
| Ohio St. | 25 | 11-14-0 | .440 | 1993 Florida Citrus |
| Purdue | 5 | 4- 1-0 | .800 | 1984 Peach |
| Wisconsin | 6 | 1- 5-0 | .167 | 1984 Hall of Fame |
| **Current Members** | **106** | **48-57-1** | **.458** | |

## BIG WEST CONFERENCE

| Institution | Bowls | W-L-T | Pct. | Last Appearance |
|---|---|---|---|---|
| Cal St. Fullerton* | 1 | 0- 1-0 | .000 | 1983 California |
| Nevada | 3 | 1- 2-0 | .333 | 1992 Las Vegas |
| Nevada-Las Vegas | 1 | 1- 0-0 | 1.000 | 1984 California |
| New Mexico St. | 3 | 2- 0-1 | .833 | 1960 Sun |
| Pacific (Cal.) | 3 | 2- 1-0 | .667 | 1953 Sun |
| San Jose St. | 7 | 4- 3-0 | .571 | 1990 California |
| Utah St. | 3 | 0- 3-0 | .000 | 1961 Gotham |
| **Current Members** | **21** | **10-10-1** | **.500** | |

* Cal St. Fullerton dropped football after the 1992 season.

## MID-AMERICAN ATHLETIC CONFERENCE

| Institution | Bowls | W-L-T | Pct. | Last Appearance |
|---|---|---|---|---|
| Akron | 0 | 0- 0-0 | .000 | Has never appeared |
| Ball St. | 1 | 0- 1-0 | .000 | 1989 California |
| Bowling Green | 5 | 2- 3-0 | .400 | 1992 Las Vegas |
| Central Mich. | 1 | 0- 1-0 | .000 | 1990 California |
| Eastern Mich. | 1 | 1- 0-0 | 1.000 | 1987 California |
| Kent | 1 | 0- 1-0 | .000 | 1972 Tangerine |
| Miami (Ohio) | 7 | 5- 2-0 | .714 | 1986 California |
| Ohio | 2 | 0- 2-0 | .000 | 1968 Tangerine |
| Toledo | 5 | 4- 1-0 | .800 | 1984 California |
| Western Mich. | 2 | 0- 2-0 | .000 | 1988 California |
| **Current Members** | **25** | **12-13-0** | **.480** | |

## PACIFIC-10 CONFERENCE

| Institution | Bowls | W-L-T | Pct. | Last Appearance |
|---|---|---|---|---|
| Arizona | 9 | 2- 6-1 | .278 | 1992 John Hancock |
| Arizona St. | 15 | 9- 5-1 | .633 | 1987 Freedom |
| California | 11 | 4- 6-1 | .409 | 1992 Florida Citrus |
| Oregon | 9 | 3- 6-0 | .333 | 1992 Independence |
| Oregon St. | 4 | 2- 2-0 | .500 | 1965 Rose |
| Southern Cal | 35 | 22-13-0 | .629 | 1992 Freedom |
| Stanford | 16 | 8- 7-1 | .531 | 1993 Blockbuster |
| UCLA | 18 | 10- 7-1 | .583 | 1991 John Hancock |
| Washington | 21 | 12- 8-1 | .595 | 1993 Rose |
| Washington St. | 5 | 3- 2-0 | .600 | 1992 Copper |
| **Current Members** | **143** | **75-62-6** | **.545** | |

## SOUTHEASTERN CONFERENCE

| Institution | Bowls | W-L-T | Pct. | Last Appearance |
|---|---|---|---|---|
| Alabama | 45 | 25-17-3 | .589 | 1993 Sugar |
| Arkansas | 27 | 9-15-3 | .389 | 1991 Independence |
| Auburn | 23 | 12- 9-2 | .565 | 1990 Peach |
| Florida | 20 | 9-11-0 | .450 | 1992 Gator |
| Georgia | 31 | 15-13-3 | .532 | 1993 Florida Citrus |
| Kentucky | 7 | 5- 2-0 | .714 | 1984 Hall of Fame |
| Louisiana St. | 28 | 11-16-1 | .411 | 1989 Hall of Fame |
| Mississippi | 25 | 14-11-0 | .560 | 1992 Liberty |
| Mississippi St. | 8 | 4- 4-0 | .500 | 1993 Peach |
| South Caro. | 8 | 0- 8-0 | .000 | 1988 Liberty |
| Tennessee | 33 | 18-15-0 | .545 | 1993 Hall of Fame |
| Vanderbilt | 3 | 1- 1-1 | .500 | 1982 Hall of Fame |
| **Current Members** | **258** | **123-122-13** | **.502** | |

## SOUTHWEST CONFERENCE

| Institution | Bowls | W-L-T | Pct. | Last Appearance |
|---|---|---|---|---|
| Baylor | 15 | 8- 7-0 | .533 | 1992 John Hancock |
| Houston | 13 | 7- 5-1 | .577 | 1988 Aloha |
| Rice | 7 | 4- 3-0 | .571 | 1961 Bluebonnet |
| Southern Methodist | 11 | 4- 6-1 | .409 | 1984 Aloha |
| Texas | 34 | 16-16-2 | .500 | 1991 Cotton |
| Texas A&M | 20 | 11- 9-0 | .550 | 1992 Cotton |
| Texas Christian | 14 | 4- 9-1 | .321 | 1984 Bluebonnet |
| Texas Tech | 18 | 4-13-1 | .250 | 1989 All-American |
| **Current Members** | **132** | **58-68-6** | **.462** | |

## WESTERN ATHLETIC CONFERENCE

| Institution | Bowls | W-L-T | Pct. | Last Appearance |
|---|---|---|---|---|
| Air Force | 12 | 6- 5-1 | .542 | 1992 Liberty |
| Brigham Young | 17 | 5-11-1 | .324 | 1992 Aloha |
| Colorado St. | 2 | 1- 1-0 | .500 | 1990 Freedom |
| Fresno St. | 8 | 6- 2-0 | .750 | 1992 Freedom |
| Hawaii | 2 | 1- 1-0 | .500 | 1992 Holiday |
| New Mexico | 5 | 2- 2-1 | .500 | 1961 Aviation |
| San Diego St. | 4 | 1- 3-0 | .250 | 1991 Freedom |
| Utah | 3 | 2- 1-0 | .667 | 1992 Copper |
| UTEP | 9 | 5- 4-0 | .556 | 1988 Independence |
| Wyoming | 9 | 4- 5-0 | .444 | 1990 Copper |
| **Current Members** | **71** | **33-35-3** | **.486** | |

## INDEPENDENTS

| Institution | Bowls | W-L-T | Pct. | Last Appearance |
|---|---|---|---|---|
| Arkansas St. | 0 | 0- 0-0 | .000 | Has never appeared |
| Army | 3 | 2- 1-0 | .667 | 1988 Sun |
| Cincinnati | 2 | 1- 1-0 | .500 | 1951 Sun |
| East Caro. | 2 | 2- 0-0 | 1.000 | 1992 Peach |
| Louisiana Tech | 3 | 1- 1-1 | .500 | 1990 Independence |
| Louisville | 4 | 2- 1-1 | .625 | 1991 Fiesta |

*Conference Bowl Records*                    481

| Institution | Bowls | W-L-T | Pct. | Last Appearance |
|---|---|---|---|---|
| Memphis St. | 1 | 1- 0-0 | 1.000 | 1971 Pasadena |
| Navy | 8 | 3- 4-1 | .438 | 1981 Liberty |
| Northern Ill. | 1 | 1- 0-0 | 1.000 | 1983 California |
| Notre Dame | 18 | 12- 6-0 | .667 | 1993 Cotton |
| Penn St. | 29 | 17-10-2 | .621 | 1993 Blockbuster |
| Southern Miss. | 6 | 2- 4-0 | .333 | 1990 All-American |
| Southwestern La. | 0 | 0- 0-0 | .000 | Has never appeared |
| Tulane | 8 | 2- 6-0 | .250 | 1987 Independence |
| Tulsa | 11 | 4- 7-0 | .364 | 1991 Freedom |
| **Current Independents** | **96** | **50-41-5** | **.547** | |

# AWARD WINNERS IN BOWL GAMES

## MOST VALUABLE PLAYERS IN MAJOR BOWLS

### ALOHA BOWL

**Year** **Player, Team, Position**
1982 Offense—Tim Cowan, Washington, quarterback
Defense—Tony Caldwell, Washington, linebacker
1983 Offense—Danny Greene, Washington, wide receiver
Defense—George Reynolds, Penn St., punter
1984 Offense—Jeff Atkins, Southern Methodist, running back
Defense—Jerry Ball, Southern Methodist, nose guard
1985 Offense—Gene Jelks, Alabama, running back
Defense—Cornelius Bennett, Alabama, linebacker

**Year** **Player, Team, Position**
1986 Offense—Alfred Jenkins, Arizona, quarterback
Defense—Chuck Cecil, Arizona, safety
1987* Troy Aikman, UCLA, quarterback
Emmitt Smith, Florida, running back
1988 David Dacus, Houston, quarterback
Victor Wood, Washington St., wide receiver
1989 Blake Ezor, Michigan St., tailback
Chris Roscoe, Hawaii, wide receiver
1990 Todd Burden, Arizona, cornerback
Marvin Graves, Syracuse, quarterback
1991 Tommy Vardell, Stanford, running back
Shawn Jones, Georgia Tech, quarterback
1992 Tom Young, Brigham Young, quarterback
Dana Stubblefield, Kansas, defensive tackle

* *Began selecting one MVP for each team.*

### COPPER BOWL

**Year** **Player, Team, Position**
1989 Shane Montgomery, North Caro. St., quarterback
Scott Geyer, Arizona, defensive back
1990 Mike Pawlawski, California, quarterback
Robert Midgett, Wyoming, linebacker
1991 Vaughn Dunbar, Indiana, tailback
Mark Hagen, Indiana, linebacker

**Year** **Player, Team, Position**
1992 Drew Bledsoe, Washington St., quarterback (overall)
Phillip Bobo, Washington St., wide receiver (offense)
Kareen Leary, Utah, defensive back (defense)

### COTTON BOWL

**Year** **Player, Team, Position**
1937 Ki Aldrich, Texas Christian, center
Sammy Baugh, Texas Christian, quarterback
L. D. Meyer, Texas Christian, end
1938 Ernie Lain, Rice, back
Byron "Whizzer" White, Colorado, quarterback
1939 Jerry Dowd, St. Mary's (Tex.), center
Elmer Tarbox, Texas Tech, back
1940 Banks McFadden, Clemson, back
1941 Charles Henke, Texas A&M, guard
John Kimbrough, Texas A&M, fullback
Chip Routt, Texas A&M, tackle
Lou De Filippo, Fordham, center
Joe Ungerer, Fordham, tackle
1942 Martin Ruby, Alabama, tackle
Jimmy Nelson, Alabama, halfback
Holt Rast, Alabama, end
Don Whitmire, Alabama, tackle

**Year** **Player, Team, Position**
1943 Jack Freeman, Texas, guard
Roy McKay, Texas, fullback
Stanley Mauldin, Texas, tackle
Harvey Hardy, Georgia Tech, guard
Jack Marshall, Georgia Tech, end
1944 Joe Parker, Texas, end
Martin Ruby, Randolph Field, tackle
Glenn Dobbs, Randolph Field, quarterback
1945 Neil Armstrong, Oklahoma St., end
Bob Fenimore, Oklahoma St., back
Ralph Foster, Oklahoma St., tackle
1946 Hub Bechtol, Texas, end
Bobby Layne, Texas, back
Jim Kekeris, Missouri, tackle
1947 Alton Baldwin, Arkansas, end
Y. A. Tittle, Louisiana St., quarterback
1948 Doak Walker, Southern Methodist, back
Steve Suhey, Penn St., guard

482

| Year | Player, Team, Position | Year | Player, Team, Position |
|---|---|---|---|
| 1949 | Kyle Rote, Southern Methodist, back | 1970 | Steve Worster, Texas, fullback |
| | Doak Walker, Southern Methodist, back | | Bob Olson, Notre Dame, linebacker |
| | Brad Ecklund, Oregon, center | 1971 | Eddie Phillips, Texas, quarterback |
| | Norm Van Brocklin, Oregon, quarterback | | Clarence Ellis, Notre Dame, cornerback |
| 1950 | Billy Burkhalter, Rice, halfback | 1972 | Bruce Bannon, Penn St., defensive end |
| | Joe Watson, Rice, center | | Lydell Mitchell, Penn St., running back |
| | James "Froggie" Williams, Rice, end | 1973 | Randy Braband, Texas, linebacker |
| 1951 | Bud McFadin, Texas, guard | | Alan Lowry, Texas, quarterback |
| | Andy Kozar, Tennessee, fullback | 1974 | Wade Johnston, Texas, linebacker |
| | Hank Lauricella, Tennessee, halfback | | Tony Davis, Nebraska, tailback |
| | Horace "Bud" Sherrod, Tennessee, defensive end | 1975 | Ken Quesenberry, Baylor, safety |
| | | | Tom Shuman, Penn St., quarterback |
| 1952 | Keith Flowers, Texas Christian, fullback | 1976 | Ike Forte, Arkansas, running back |
| | Emery Clark, Kentucky, halfback | | Hal McAfee, Arkansas, linebacker |
| | Ray Correll, Kentucky, guard | 1977 | Alois Blackwell, Houston, running back |
| | Vito "Babe" Parilli, Kentucky, quarterback | | Mark Mohr, Houston, cornerback |
| 1953 | Richard Ochoa, Texas, fullback | 1978 | Vagas Ferguson, Notre Dame, running back |
| | Harley Sewell, Texas, guard | | |
| | Bob Griesbach, Tennessee, linebacker | | Bob Golic, Notre Dame, linebacker |
| 1954 | Richard Chapman, Rice, tackle | 1979 | David Hodge, Houston, linebacker |
| | Dan Hart, Rice, end | | Joe Montana, Notre Dame, quarterback |
| | Dicky Maegle, Rice, halfback | 1980 | Terry Elston, Houston, quarterback |
| 1955 | Bud Brooks, Arkansas, guard | | David Hodge, Houston, linebacker |
| | George Humphreys, Georgia Tech, fullback | 1981 | Warren Lyles, Alabama, noseguard |
| | | | Major Ogilvie, Alabama, running back |
| 1956 | Buddy Alliston, Mississippi, guard | 1982 | Robert Brewer, Texas, quarterback |
| | Eagle Day, Mississippi, quarterback | | Robbie Jones, Alabama, linebacker |
| 1957 | Norman Hamilton, Texas Christian, tackle | 1983 | Wes Hopkins, Southern Methodist, strong safety |
| | Jim Brown, Syracuse, halfback | | |
| 1958 | Tom Forrestal, Navy, quarterback | | Lance McIlhenny, Southern Methodist, quarterback |
| | Tony Stremic, Navy, guard | | |
| 1959 | Jack Spikes, Texas Christian, fullback | 1984 | Jeff Leiding, Texas, linebacker |
| | Dave Phillips, Air Force, tackle | | John Lastinger, Georgia, quarterback |
| 1960 | Maurice Doke, Texas, guard | 1985 | Bill Romanowski, Boston College, linebacker |
| | Ernie Davis, Syracuse, halfback | | |
| 1961 | Lance Alworth, Arkansas, halfback | | Steve Strachan, Boston College, fullback |
| | Dwight Bumgarner, Duke, tackle | 1986 | Domingo Bryant, Texas A&M, strong safety |
| 1962 | Mike Cotten, Texas, quarterback | | |
| | Bob Moser, Texas, end | | Bo Jackson, Auburn, tailback |
| 1963 | Johnny Treadwell, Texas, guard | 1987 | Chris Spielman, Ohio St., linebacker |
| | Lynn Amedee, Louisiana St., quarterback | | Roger Vick, Texas A&M, fullback |
| 1964 | Scott Appleton, Texas, tackle | 1988 | Adam Bob, Texas A&M, linebacker |
| | Duke Carlisle, Texas, quarterback | | Bucky Richardson, Texas A&M, quarterback |
| 1965 | Ronnie Caveness, Arkansas, linebacker | | |
| | Fred Marshall, Arkansas, quarterback | 1989 | LaSalle Harper, Arkansas, linebacker |
| 1966 | Joe Labruzzo, Louisiana St., tailback | | Troy Aikman, UCLA, quarterback |
| | David McCormick, Louisiana St., tackle | 1990 | Carl Pickens, Tennessee, free safety |
| 1966 | Kent Lawrence, Georgia, tailback | | Chuck Webb, Tennessee, tailback |
| | George Patton, Georgia, tackle | 1991 | Craig Erickson, Miami (Fla.), quarterback |
| 1968 | Grady Allen, Texas A&M, defensive end | | Russell Maryland, Miami (Fla.), defensive lineman |
| | Edd Hargett, Texas A&M, quarterback | | |
| | Bill Hobbs, Texas A&M, linebacker | 1992 | Sean Jackson, Florida St., running back |
| 1969 | Tom Campbell, Texas, linebacker | | Chris Crooms, Texas A&M, safety |
| | Charles "Cotton" Speyrer, Texas, wide receiver | 1993 | Rick Mirer, Notre Dame, quarterback |
| | James Street, Texas, quarterback | | Devon McDonald, Notre Dame, defensive end |

# FIESTA BOWL

| Year | Player, Team, Position | Year | Player, Team, Position |
|---|---|---|---|
| 1971 | Gary Huff, Florida St., quarterback | 1977 | Dennis Sproul, Arizona St., quarterback (sportsmanship award) |
| | Junior Ah You, Arizona St., defensive end | | |
| 1972 | Woody Green, Arizona St., halfback | | Matt Millen, Penn St., linebacker |
| | Mike Fink, Missouri, defensive back | 1978 | James Owens, UCLA, running back |
| 1973 | Greg Hudson, Arizona St., split end | | Jimmy Walker, Arkansas, defensive tackle |
| | Mike Haynes, Arizona St., cornerback | | Kenny Easley, UCLA, safety (sportsmanship award) |
| 1974 | Kenny Walker, Oklahoma St., running back | | |
| | | 1979 | Mark Schubert, Pittsburgh, kicker |
| | Phillip Dokes, Oklahoma St., defensive tackle | | Dave Liggins, Arizona, safety |
| | | | Dan Fidler, Pittsburgh, offensive guard (sportsmanship award) |
| 1975 | John Jefferson, Arizona St., split end | | |
| | Larry Gordon, Arizona St., linebacker | 1980 | Curt Warner, Penn St., running back |
| 1976 | Thomas Lott, Oklahoma, quarterback | | Frank Case, Penn St., defensive end (sportsmanship award) |
| | Terry Peters, Oklahoma, cornerback | | |

*Award Winners in Bowl Games*

| Year | Player, Team, Position | Year | Player, Team, Position |
|---|---|---|---|
| 1982 | Curt Warner, Penn St., running back | 1987 | D. J. Dozier, Penn St., running back |
| | Leo Wisniewski, Penn St., nose tackle | | Shane Conlan, Penn St., linebacker |
| | George Achica, Southern Cal, nose guard (sportsmanship award) | | Paul O'Connor, Miami (Fla.), offensive guard (sportsmanship award) |
| 1983 | Marcus Dupree, Oklahoma, running back | 1988 | Danny McManus, Florida St., quarterback |
| | Jim Jeffcoat, Arizona St., defensive line-man | | Neil Smith, Nebraska, defensive lineman |
| | | | Steve Forch, Nebraska, linebacker (sportsmanship award) |
| | Paul Ferrer, Oklahoma, center (sportsmanship award) | 1989 | Tony Rice, Notre Dame, quarterback |
| 1984 | John Congemi, Pittsburgh, quarterback | | Frank Stams, Notre Dame, defensive end |
| | Rowland Tatum, Ohio St., linebacker (sportsmanship award) | | Chris Parker, West Va., defensive lineman (sportsmanship award) |
| 1985 | Gaston Green, UCLA, tailback | 1990 | Peter Tom Willis, Florida St., quarterback |
| | James Washington, UCLA, defensive back | | Odell Haggins, Florida St., nose guard |
| | | | Jake Young, Nebraska, center (sports-manship award) |
| | Bruce Fleming, Miami (Fla.), linebacker (sportsmanship award) | 1991 | Browning Nagle, Louisville, quarterback |
| 1986 | Jamie Morris, Michigan, running back | | Ray Buchanan, Louisville, free safety |
| | Mark Messner, Michigan, defensive tackle | 1992 | O. J. McDuffie, Penn St., wide receiver |
| | Mike Mallory, Michigan, linebacker (sportsmanship award) | | Reggie Givens, Penn St., outside line-backer |
| | | 1993 | Marvin Graves, Syracuse, quarterback |
| | | | Kevin Mitchell, Syracuse, nose guard |

## FLORIDA CITRUS BOWL
**(Named Tangerine Bowl, 1947-82)**
**Players of the Game (Pre-1977)**

| Year | Player, Team, Position | Year | Player, Team, Position |
|---|---|---|---|
| 1949 | Dale McDaniels, Murray St. | 1965 | Dave Alexander, East Caro. |
| | Ted Scown, Sul Ross St. | 1966 | Willie Lanier, Morgan St. |
| 1950 | Don Henigan, St. Vincent | 1967 | Errol Hook, Tenn.-Martin |
| | Chick Davis, Emory & Henry | | Gordon Lambert, Tenn.-Martin |
| 1951 | Pete Anania, Morris Harvey | 1968 | Buster O'Brien, Richmond, back |
| | Charles Hubbard, Morris Harvey | | Walker Gillette, Richmond, lineman |
| 1952 | Bill Johnson, Stetson | 1969 | Chuck Ealy, Toledo, back |
| | Dave Laude, Stetson | | Dan Crockett, Toledo, lineman |
| 1953 | Marvin Brown, East Tex. St. | 1970 | Chuck Ealy, Toledo, back |
| 1954 | Billy Ray Norris, East Tex. St. | | Vince Hubler, William & Mary, lineman |
| | Bobby Spann, Arkansas St. | 1971 | Chuck Ealy, Toledo, back |
| 1955 | Bill Englehardt, Nebraska-Omaha | | Mel Long, Toledo, lineman |
| 1956 | Pat Tarquinio, Juniata | 1972 | Freddie Solomon, Tampa, back |
| 1957 | Ron Mills, West Tex. St. | | Jack Lambert, Kent, lineman |
| 1958 | Garry Berry, East Tex. St. | 1973 | Chuck Varner, Miami (Ohio), back |
| | Neal Hinson, East Tex. St. | | Brad Cousino, Miami (Ohio), lineman |
| 1958 | Sam McCord, East Tex. St. | 1974 | Sherman Smith, Miami (Ohio), back |
| 1960 | Bucky Pitts, Middle Tenn. St. | | Brad Cousino, Miami (Ohio), lineman (tie) |
| | Bob Waters, Presbyterian | | John Roudebush, Miami (Ohio), lineman (tie) |
| 1960 | Jerry Nettles, Citadel | | |
| 1961 | Win Herbert, Lamar | 1975 | Rob Carpenter, Miami (Ohio), back |
| 1962 | Joe Lopasky, Houston | | Jeff Kelly, Miami (Ohio), lineman |
| | Billy Roland, Houston | 1976 | Terry Miller, Oklahoma St., back |
| 1963 | Sharon Miller, Western Ky. | | Phillip Dokes, Oklahoma St., lineman |
| 1964 | Bill Cline, East Caro. | | |
| | Jerry Whelchel, Massachusetts | | |

### Most Valuable Player (1977-Present)

| Year | Player, Team, Position | Year | Player, Team, Position |
|---|---|---|---|
| 1977 | Jimmy Jordan, Florida St., quarterback | 1985 | Larry Kolic, Ohio St., middle guard |
| 1978 | Ted Brown, North Caro. St., running back | 1987 | Aundray Bruce, Auburn, linebacker |
| 1979 | David Woodley, Louisiana St., quarterback | 1988 | Rodney Williams, Clemson, quarterback |
| 1980 | Cris Collingsworth, Florida, wide receiver | 1989 | Terry Allen, Clemson, tailback |
| 1981 | Jeff Gaylord, Missouri, linebacker | 1990 | Jeff George, Illinois, quarterback |
| 1982 | Randy Campbell, Auburn, quarterback | 1991 | Shawn Jones, Georgia Tech, quarterback |
| 1983 | Johnnie Jones, Tennessee, running back | 1992 | Mike Pawlawski, California, quarterback |
| 1984 | James Jackson, Georgia, quarterback | 1993 | Garrison Hearst, Georgia, running back |

## FREEDOM BOWL

| Year | Player, Team, Position | Year | Player, Team, Position |
|---|---|---|---|
| 1984 | Chuck Long, Iowa, quarterback | 1986 | Gaston Green, UCLA, tailback |
| | William Harris, Texas, tight end | | Shane Shumway, Brigham Young, defensive back |
| 1985 | Chris Chandler, Washington, quarterback | 1987 | Daniel Ford, Arizona St., quarterback |
| | Barry Helton, Colorado, punter | | |

| Year | Player, Team, Position |
|------|------------------------|
|      | Chad Hennings, Air Force, defensive tackle |
| 1988 | Ty Detmer, Brigham Young, quarterback |
|      | Eric Bieniemy, Colorado, halfback |
| 1989 | Cary Conklin, Washington, quarterback |
|      | Huey Richardson, Florida, linebacker |
| 1990 | Todd Yert, Colorado St., running back |
|      | Bill Musgrave, Oregon, quarterback |

| Year | Player, Team, Position |
|------|------------------------|
| 1991 | Marshall Faulk, San Diego St., running back |
|      | Ron Jackson, Tulsa, running back |
| 1992 | Lorenzo Neal, Fresno St., fullback |
|      | Estrus Crayton, Southern Cal, tailback |

# GATOR BOWL

| Year | Player, Team |
|------|--------------|
| 1946 | Nick Sacrinty, Wake Forest |
| 1947 | Joe Golding, Oklahoma |
| 1948 | Lu Gambino, Maryland |
| 1949 | Bobby Gage, Clemson |
| 1950 | Bob Ward, Maryland |
| 1951 | Eddie Talboom, Wyoming |
| 1952 | Jim Dooley, Miami (Fla.) |
| 1953 | Marv Matuszak, Tulsa |
|      | John Hall, Florida |
| 1954 | Vince Dooley, Auburn |
|      | Bobby Cavazos, Texas Tech |
| 1954 | Billy Hooper, Baylor |
|      | Joe Childress, Auburn |
| 1955 | Joe Childress, Auburn |
|      | Don Orr, Vanderbilt |
| 1956 | Corny Salvaterra, Pittsburgh |
|      | Wade Mitchell, Georgia Tech |
| 1957 | John David Crow, Texas A&M |
|      | Bobby Gordon, Tennessee |
| 1958 | Dave Hudson, Florida |
|      | Bobby Franklin, Mississippi |
| 1960 | Maxie Baughan, Georgia Tech |
|      | Jim Mooty, Arkansas |
| 1960 | Bobby Ply, Baylor |
|      | Larry Libertore, Florida |
| 1961 | Joe Auer, Georgia Tech |
|      | Galen Hall, Penn St. |
| 1962 | Dave Robinson, Penn St. |
|      | Tom Shannon, Florida |
| 1963 | David Sicks, Air Force |
|      | Ken Willard, North Caro. |
| 1965 | Carl McAdams, Oklahoma |
|      | Fred Biletnikoff, Florida St. |
|      | Steve Tensi, Florida |
| 1965 | Donny Anderson, Texas Tech |
|      | Lenny Snow, Georgia Tech |
| 1966 | Floyd Little, Syracuse |
|      | Dewey Warren, Tennessee |
| 1967 | Tom Sherman, Penn St. |
|      | Kim Hammond, Florida St. |
| 1968 | Mike Hall, Alabama |
|      | Terry McMillan, Missouri |
| 1969 | Curt Watson, Tennessee |
|      | Mike Kelley, Florida |
| 1971 | Archie Manning, Mississippi |
|      | Pat Sullivan, Auburn |

| Year | Player, Team |
|------|--------------|
| 1971 | James Webster, North Caro. |
|      | Jimmy Poulos, Georgia |
| 1972 | Mark Cooney, Colorado |
|      | Wade Whatley, Auburn |
| 1973 | Haskell Stanback, Tennessee |
|      | Joe Barnes, Texas Tech |
| 1974 | Earl Campbell, Texas |
|      | Phil Gargis, Auburn |
| 1975 | Sammy Green, Florida |
|      | Steve Atkins, Maryland |
| 1976 | Jim Cefalo, Penn St. |
|      | Al Hunter, Notre Dame |
| 1977 | Jerry Butler, Clemson |
|      | Matt Cavanaugh, Pittsburgh |
| 1978 | Art Schlichter, Ohio St. |
|      | Steve Fuller, Clemson |
| 1979 | John Wangler, Michigan |
|      | Anthony Carter, Michigan |
|      | Matt Kupec, North Caro. |
|      | Amos Lawrence, North Caro. |
| 1980 | George Rogers, South Caro. |
|      | Rick Trocano, Pittsburgh |
| 1981 | Gary Anderson, Arkansas |
|      | Kelvin Bryant, North Caro. |
|      | Ethan Horton, North Caro. |
| 1982 | Paul Woodside, West Va. |
|      | Greg Allen, Florida St. |
| 1983 | Owen Gill, Iowa |
|      | Tony Lilly, Florida |
| 1984 | Mike Hold, South Caro. |
|      | Thurman Thomas, Oklahoma St. |
| 1985 | Thurman Thomas, Oklahoma St. |
|      | Chip Ferguson, Florida St. |
| 1986 | Brad Muster, Stanford |
|      | Rodney Williams, Clemson |
| 1987 | Harold Green, South Caro. |
|      | Wendell Davis, Louisiana St. |
| 1989 | Andre Rison, Michigan St. |
|      | Wayne Johnson, Georgia |
| 1989 | Mike Fox, West Va. |
|      | Levon Kirkland, Clemson |
| 1991 | Tyrone Ashley, Mississippi |
|      | Michigan offensive line: Tom Dohring, Matt Elliott, Steve Everitt, Dean Dingman, Greg Skrepanak |
| 1991 | Cale Gundy, Oklahoma |
|      | Tyrone Lewis, Virginia |
| 1992 | Errict Rhett, Florida |

# HALL OF FAME BOWL (Tampa Bay)

| Year | Player, Team, Position |
|------|------------------------|
| 1987 | Shawn Halloran, Boston College, quarterback |
|      | James Jackson, Georgia, quarterback |
| 1988 | Jamie Morris, Michigan, tailback |
|      | Bobby Humphrey, Alabama, tailback |
| 1989 | Robert Drummond, Syracuse, running back |

| Year | Player, Team, Position |
|------|------------------------|
| 1990 | Reggie Slack, Alabama, quarterback |
|      | Derek Isaman, Ohio St., linebacker |
| 1991 | DeChane Cameron, Clemson, quarterback |
| 1992 | Marvin Graves, Syracuse, quarterback |
| 1993 | Heath Shuler, Tennessee, quarterback |

*Award Winners in Bowl Games*

# HOLIDAY BOWL

| Year | Player, Team, Position | Year | Player, Team, Position |
|---|---|---|---|
| 1978 | Phil McConkey, Navy, wide receiver | 1986 | Todd Santos, San Diego St., quarterback (co-offensive) |
| 1979 | Marc Wilson, Brigham Young, quarterback | | Mark Vlasic, Iowa, quarterback (co-offensive) |
| | Tim Wilbur, Indiana, cornerback | | Richard Brown, San Diego St., linebacker |
| 1980 | Jim McMahon, Brigham Young, quarterback | 1987 | Craig Burnett, Wyoming, quarterback |
| | Craig James, Southern Methodist, running back | | Anthony Wright, Iowa, cornerback |
| 1981 | Jim McMahon, Brigham Young, quarterback | 1988 | Barry Sanders, Oklahoma St., running back |
| | Kyle Whittingham, Brigham Young, linebacker | | Sim Drain, Oklahoma St., linebacker |
| 1982 | Tim Spencer, Ohio St., running back | 1989 | Blair Thomas, Penn St., running back |
| | Garcia Lane, Ohio St., cornerback | | Ty Detmer, Brigham Young, quarterback |
| 1983 | Steve Young, Brigham Young, quarterback | 1990 | Bucky Richardson, Texas A&M, quarterback |
| | Bobby Bell, Missouri, defensive end | | William Thomas, Texas A&M, linebacker |
| 1984 | Robbie Bosco, Brigham Young, quarterback | 1991 | Ty Detmer, Brigham Young, quarterback |
| | Leon White, Brigham Young, linebacker | | Josh Arnold, Brigham Young, defensive back (co-defensive) |
| 1985 | Bobby Joe Edmonds, Arkansas, running back | | Carlos James, Iowa, defensive back (co-defensive) |
| | Greg Battle, Arizona St., linebacker | 1992 | Michael Carter, Hawaii, quarterback |
| | | | Junior Tagoai, Hawaii, defensive tackle |

# INDEPENDENCE BOWL

| Year | Player, Team, Position | Year | Player, Team, Position |
|---|---|---|---|
| 1976 | Terry McFarland, McNeese St., quarterback | 1984 | Bart Weiss, Air Force, quarterback |
| | Terry Clark, Tulsa, cornerback | | Scott Thomas, Air Force, safety |
| 1977 | Keith Thibodeaux, Louisiana Tech, quarterback | 1985 | Rickey Foggie, Minnesota, quarterback |
| | Otis Wilson, Louisville, linebacker | | Bruce Holmes, Minnesota, linebacker |
| 1978 | Theodore Sutton, East Caro., fullback | 1986 | Mark Young, Mississippi, quarterback |
| | Zack Valentine, East Caro., defensive end | | James Mosley, Texas Tech, defensive end |
| 1979 | Joe Morris, Syracuse, running back | 1987 | Chris Chandler, Washington, quarterback |
| | Clay Carroll, McNeese St., defensive tackle | | David Rill, Washington, linebacker |
| 1980 | Stephan Starring, McNeese St., quarterback | 1988 | James Henry, Southern Miss., punt returner/cornerback |
| | Jerald Baylis, Southern Miss., nose guard | 1989 | Bill Musgrave, Oregon, quarterback |
| 1981 | Gary Kubiak, Texas A&M, quarterback | | Chris Oldham, Oregon, defensive back |
| | Mike Green, Oklahoma St., linebacker | 1990 | Mike Richardson, Louisiana Tech, running back |
| 1982 | Randy Wright, Wisconsin, quarterback | | Lorenzo Baker, Louisiana Tech, linebacker |
| | Tim Krumrie, Wisconsin, nose guard | 1991 | Andre Hastings, Georgia, flanker |
| 1983 | Marty Louthan, Air Force, quarterback | | Torrey Evans, Georgia, linebacker |
| | Andre Townsend, Mississippi, defensive tackle | 1992 | Todd Dixon, Wake Forest, split end |

# JOHN HANCOCK BOWL

**(Named Sun Bowl, 1936-86; John Hancock Sun Bowl, 1987-88)**
**C. M. Hendricks Most Valuable Player Trophy (1954-present)**
**Jimmy Rogers Jr. Most Valuable Lineman Trophy (1961-present)**

| Year | Player, Team, Position | Year | Player, Team, Position |
|---|---|---|---|
| 1950 | Harvey Gabriel, UTEP, halfback | 1963 | Bob Berry, Oregon, quarterback |
| 1951 | Bill Cross, West Tex. St., end | | John Hughes, Southern Methodist, guard |
| 1952 | Junior Arteburn, Texas Tech, quarterback | 1964 | Preston Ridlehuber, Georgia, quarterback |
| 1953 | Tom McCormick, Pacific (Cal.), halfback | | Jim Wilson, Georgia, tackle |
| 1954 | Dick Shinaut, UTEP, quarterback | 1965 | Billy Stevens, UTEP, quarterback |
| 1955 | Jesse Whittenton, UTEP, quarterback | | Ronny Nixon, Texas Christian, tackle |
| 1956 | Jim Crawford, Wyoming, halfback | 1966 | Jim Kiick, Wyoming, tailback |
| 1957 | Claude Austin, Geo. Washington | | Jerry Durling, Wyoming, middle guard |
| 1958 | Leonard Kucewski, Wyoming, guard | 1967 | Billy Stevens, UTEP, quarterback |
| 1959 | Charley Johnson, New Mexico St., quarterback | | Fred Carr, UTEP, linebacker |
| 1960 | Charley Johnson, New Mexico St., quarterback | 1968 | Buddy McClintock, Auburn, defensive back |
| 1961 | Billy Joe, Villanova, fullback | | David Campbell, Auburn, tackle |
| | Richie Ross, Villanova, guard | 1969 | Paul Rogers, Nebraska, halfback |
| 1962 | Jerry Logan, West Tex. St., halfback | | Jerry Murtaugh, Nebraska, linebacker |
| | Don Hoovler, Ohio, guard | 1970 | Rock Perdoni, Georgia Tech, defensive tackle |

| Year | Player, Team, Position | Year | Player, Team, Position |
|---|---|---|---|
| | Bill Flowers, Georgia Tech, linebacker | 1981 | Darrell Shepard, Oklahoma, quarterback |
| 1971 | Bert Jones, Louisiana St., quarterback | | Rick Bryan, Oklahoma, defensive tackle |
| | Matt Blair, Iowa St., linebacker | 1982 | Ethan Horton, North Caro., tailback |
| 1972 | George Smith, Texas Tech, halfback | | Ronnie Mullins, Texas, defensive end |
| | Ecomet Burley, Texas Tech, defensive tackle | 1983 | Walter Lewis, Alabama, quarterback |
| 1973 | Ray Bybee, Missouri, fullback | | Wes Neighbors, Alabama, center |
| | John Kelsey, Missouri, tight end | 1984 | Rick Badanjek, Maryland, fullback |
| 1974 | Terry Vitrano, Mississippi St., fullback | | Carl Zander, Tennessee, linebacker |
| | Jimmy Webb, Mississippi St., defensive tackle | 1985 | Max Zendejas, Arizona, kicker |
| | | | Peter Anderson, Georgia, center |
| 1975 | Robert Haygood, Pittsburgh, quarterback | 1986 | Cornelius Bennett, Alabama, defensive end |
| | Al Romano, Pittsburgh, middle guard | | Steve Alvord, Washington, middle guard |
| 1977 | Tony Franklin, Texas A&M, kicker | 1987 | Thurman Thomas, Oklahoma St., running back |
| | Edgar Fields, Texas A&M, defensive tackle | | Darnell Warren, West Va., linebacker |
| 1977 | Charles Alexander, Louisiana St., tailback | 1988 | David Smith, Alabama, quarterback |
| | Gordon Ceresino, Stanford, linebacker | | Derrick Thomas, Alabama, linebacker |
| 1978 | Johnny "Ham" Jones, Texas, running back | 1989 | Alex Van Pelt, Pittsburgh, quarterback |
| | Dwight Jefferson, Texas, defensive end | 1990 | Anthony Williams, Texas A&M, linebacker |
| 1979 | Paul Skansi, Washington, flanker | | Courtney Hawkins, Michigan St., wide receiver |
| | Doug Martin, Washington, defensive tackle | | Craig Hartsuyker, Southern Cal, linebacker |
| 1980 | Jeff Quinn, Nebraska, quarterback | 1991 | Arnold Ale, UCLA, inside linebacker |
| | Jimmy Williams, Nebraska, defensive end | 1992 | Melvin Bonner, Baylor, flanker |

## LAS VEGAS BOWL

| Year | Player, Team, Position |
|---|---|
| 1992 | Erik White, Bowling Green, quarterback |

## LIBERTY BOWL

| Year | Player, Team | Year | Player, Team |
|---|---|---|---|
| 1959 | Jay Huffman, Penn St. | 1976 | Barry Krauss, Alabama |
| 1960 | Dick Hoak, Penn St. | 1977 | Matt Kupec, North Caro. |
| 1961 | Ernie Davis, Syracuse | 1978 | James Wilder, Missouri |
| 1962 | Terry Baker, Oregon St. | 1979 | Roch Hontas, Tulane |
| 1963 | Ode Burrell, Mississippi St. | 1980 | Mark Herrmann, Purdue |
| 1964 | Ernest Adler, Utah | 1981 | Eddie Meyers, Navy |
| 1965 | Tom Bryan, Auburn | 1982 | Jeremiah Castille, Alabama |
| 1966 | Jimmy Cox, Miami (Fla.) | 1983 | Doug Flutie, Boston College |
| 1967 | Jim Donnan, North Caro. St. | 1984 | Bo Jackson, Auburn |
| 1968 | Steve Hindman, Mississippi | 1985 | Cody Carlson, Baylor |
| 1969 | Bob Anderson, Colorado | 1986 | Jeff Francis, Tennessee |
| 1970 | Dave Abercrombie, Tulane | 1987 | Greg Thomas, Arkansas |
| 1971 | Joe Ferguson, Arkansas | 1988 | Dave Schnell, Indiana |
| 1972 | Jim Stevens, Georgia Tech | 1989 | Randy Baldwin, Mississippi |
| 1973 | Stan Fritts, North Caro. St. | 1990 | Rob Perez, Air Force |
| 1974 | Randy White, Maryland | 1991 | Rob Perez, Air Force |
| 1975 | Ricky Bell, Southern Cal | 1992 | Cassius Ware, Mississippi |

## ORANGE BOWL

| Year | Player, Team, Position | Year | Player, Team, Position |
|---|---|---|---|
| 1965 | Joe Namath, Alabama, quarterback | 1976 | Steve Davis, Oklahoma, quarterback |
| 1966 | Steve Sloan, Alabama, quarterback | | Lee Roy Selmon, Oklahoma, defensive tackle |
| 1967 | Larry Smith, Florida, tailback | 1977 | Rod Gerald, Ohio St., quarterback |
| 1968 | Bob Warmack, Oklahoma, quarterback | | Tom Cousineau, Ohio St., linebacker |
| 1969 | Donnie Shanklin, Kansas, halfback | 1978 | Roland Sales, Arkansas, running back |
| 1970 | Chuck Burkhart, Penn St., quarterback | | Reggie Freeman, Arkansas, nose guard |
| | Mike Reid, Penn St., defensive tackle | 1979 | Billy Sims, Oklahoma, running back |
| 1971 | Jerry Tagge, Nebraska, quarterback | | Reggie Kinlaw, Oklahoma, nose guard |
| | Willie Harper, Nebraska, defensive end | 1980 | J. C. Watts, Oklahoma, quarterback |
| 1972 | Jerry Tagge, Nebraska, quarterback | | Bud Hebert, Oklahoma, free safety |
| | Rich Glover, Nebraska, defensive guard | 1981 | J. C. Watts, Oklahoma, quarterback |
| 1973 | Johnny Rodgers, Nebraska, wingback | | Jarvis Coursey, Florida St., defensive end |
| | Rich Glover, Nebraska, defensive guard | 1982 | Homer Jordan, Clemson, quarterback |
| 1974 | Tom Shuman, Penn St., quarterback | | Jeff Davis, Clemson, linebacker |
| | Randy Crowder, Penn St., defensive tackle | 1983 | Turner Gill, Nebraska, quarterback |
| 1975 | Wayne Bullock, Notre Dame, fullback | | Dave Rimington, Nebraska, center |
| | Leroy Cook, Alabama, defensive end | | |

*Award Winners in Bowl Games*

| Year | Player, Team, Position | Year | Player, Team, Position |
|------|------------------------|------|------------------------|
| 1984 | Bernie Kosar, Miami (Fla.), quarterback | 1989 | Steve Walsh, Miami (Fla.), quarterback |
|      | Jack Fernandez, Miami (Fla.), linebacker |      | Charles Fryar, Nebraska, cornerback |
| 1985 | Jacque Robinson, Washington, tailback | 1990 | Raghib Ismail, Notre Dame, tailback/wide |
|      | Ron Holmes, Washington, defensive |      | receiver |
|      | tackle |      | Darian Hagan, Colorado, quarterback |
| 1986 | Sonny Brown, Oklahoma, defensive back | 1991 | Charles Johnson, Colorado, quarterback |
|      | Tim Lashar, Oklahoma, kicker |      | Chris Zorich, Notre Dame, nose guard |
| 1987 | Dante Jones, Oklahoma, linebacker | 1992 | Larry Jones, Miami (Fla.), running back |
|      | Spencer Tillman, Oklahoma, halfback | 1993 | Charlie Ward, Florida St., quarterback |
| 1988 | Bernard Clark, Miami (Fla.), linebacker |      | Corey Dixon, Nebraska, split end |
|      | Darrell Reed, Oklahoma, defensive end |      | |

## PEACH BOWL

| Year | Player, Team, Position | Year | Player, Team, Position |
|------|------------------------|------|------------------------|
| 1968 | Mike Hillman, Louisiana St. (offense) | 1984 | Howard Petty, Virginia (offense) |
|      | Buddy Millican, Florida St. (defense) |      | Ray Daly, Virginia (defense) |
| 1969 | Ed Williams, West Va. (offense) | 1985 | Rob Healy, Army (offense) |
|      | Carl Crennel, West Va. (defense) |      | Peel Chronister, Army (defense) |
| 1970 | Monroe Eley, Arizona St. (offense) | 1986 | Erik Kramer, North Caro. St. (offense) |
|      | Junior Ah You, Arizona St. (defense) |      | Derrick Taylor, North Caro. St. (defense) |
| 1971 | Norris Weese, Mississippi (offense) | 1987 | Reggie Cobb, Tennessee (offense) |
|      | Crowell Armstrong, Mississippi (defense) |      | Van Waiters, Indiana (defense) |
| 1972 | Dave Buckey, North Caro. St. (offense) | 1988 | Shane Montgomery, North Caro. St. (of- |
|      | George Bell, North Caro. St. (defense) |      | fense) |
| 1973 | Louis Carter, Maryland (offense) |      | Michael Brooks, North Caro. St. (defense) |
|      | Sylvester Boler, Georgia (defense) | 1989 | Michael Owens, Syracuse (offense) |
| 1974 | Larry Isaac, Texas Tech (offense) |      | Rodney Hampton, Georgia (offense) |
|      | Dennis Harrison, Vanderbilt (defense) |      | Terry Wooden, Syracuse (defense) |
| 1975 | Dan Kendra, West Va. (offense) |      | Morris Lewis, Georgia (defense) |
|      | Ray Marshall, West Va. (defense) | 1990 | Stan White, Auburn (offense) |
| 1976 | Rod Stewart, Kentucky (offense) |      | Vaughn Dunbar, Indiana (offense) |
|      | Mike Martin, Kentucky (defense) |      | Darrel Crawford, Auburn (defense) |
| 1977 | Johnny Evans, North Caro. St. (offense) |      | Mike Dumas, Indiana (defense) |
|      | Richard Carter, North Caro. St. (defense) | 1991 | Jeff Blake, East Caro. (offense) |
| 1978 | Mark Herrmann, Purdue (offense) |      | Terry Jordan, North Caro. St. (offense) |
|      | Calvin Clark, Purdue (defense) |      | Robert Jones, East Caro. (defense) |
| 1979 | Mike Brannan, Baylor (offense) |      | Billy Ray Haynes, North Caro. St. (de- |
|      | Andrew Melontree, Baylor (defense) |      | fense) |
| 1980 | Jim Kelly, Miami (Fla.) (offense) | 1993 | Natrone Means, North Caro., running |
|      | Jim Burt, Miami (Fla.) (defense) |      | back (offense) |
| 1981 | Mickey Walczak, West Va. (offense) |      | Greg Plump, Mississippi St., quarterback |
|      | Don Stemple, West Va. (defense) |      | (offense) |
| 1982 | Chuck Long, Iowa (offense) |      | Bracey Walker, North Caro., strong safety |
|      | Clay Uhlenhake, Iowa (defense) |      | (defense) |
| 1983 | Eric Thomas, Florida St. (offense) |      | Marc Woodard, Mississippi St., linebacker |
|      | Alphonso Carreker, Florida St. (defense) |      | (defense) |

## ROSE BOWL

| Year | Player, Team, Position | Year | Player, Team, Position |
|------|------------------------|------|------------------------|
| 1902 | Neil Snow, Michigan, fullback | 1935 | Millard "Dixie" Howell, Alabama, halfback |
| 1916 | Carl Dietz, Washington St., fullback | 1936 | James "Monk" Moscrip, Stanford, end |
| 1917 | John Beckett, Oregon, tackle |      | Keith Topping, Stanford, end |
| 1918 | Hollis Huntington, Mare Island, fullback | 1937 | William Daddio, Pittsburgh, end |
| 1919 | George Halas, Great Lakes, end | 1938 | Victor Bottari, California, halfback |
| 1920 | Edward Casey, Harvard, halfback | 1939 | Doyle Nave, Southern Cal, quarterback |
| 1921 | Harold "Brick" Muller, California, end |      | Alvin Krueger, Southern Cal, end |
| 1922 | Russell Stein, Wash. & Jeff., tackle | 1940 | Ambrose Schindler, Southern Cal, quar- |
| 1923 | Leo Calland, Southern Cal, guard |      | terback |
| 1924 | Ira McKee, Navy, quarterback | 1941 | Peter Kmetovic, Stanford, halfback |
| 1925 | Elmer Layden, Notre Dame, fullback | 1942 | Donald Durdan, Oregon St., halfback |
|      | Ernie Nevers, Stanford, fullback | 1943 | Charles Trippi, Georgia, halfback |
| 1926 | Johnny Mack Brown, Alabama, halfback | 1944 | Norman Verry, Southern Cal, guard |
|      | George Wilson, Washington, halfback | 1945 | James Hardy, Southern Cal, quarterback |
| 1927 | Fred Pickhard, Alabama, tackle | 1946 | Harry Gilmer, Alabama, halfback |
| 1928 | Clifford Hoffman, Stanford, fullback | 1947 | Claude "Buddy" Young, Illinois, halfback |
| 1929 | Benjamin Lom, California, halfback |      | Julius Rykovich, Illinois, halfback |
| 1930 | Russell Saunders, Southern Cal, quarter- | 1948 | Robert Chappuis, Michigan, halfback |
|      | back | 1949 | Frank Aschenbrenner, Northwestern, half- |
| 1931 | John "Monk" Campbell, Alabama, quar- |      | back |
|      | terback | 1950 | Fred Morrison, Ohio St., fullback |
| 1932 | Ernie Pinckert, Southern Cal, halfback | 1951 | Donald Dufek, Michigan, fullback |
| 1933 | Homer Griffith, Southern Cal, quarterback | 1952 | William Tate, Illinois, halfback |
| 1934 | Cliff Montgomery, Columbia, quarterback | 1953 | Rudy Bukich, Southern Cal, quarterback |

| Year | Player, Team, Position | Year | Player, Team, Position |
|---|---|---|---|
| 1954 | Billy Wells, Michigan St., halfback | 1977 | Vince Evans, Southern Cal, quarterback |
| 1955 | Dave Leggett, Ohio St., quarterback | 1978 | Warren Moon, Washington, quarterback |
| 1956 | Walter Kowalczyk, Michigan St., halfback | 1979 | Charles White, Southern Cal, tailback |
| 1957 | Kenneth Ploen, Iowa, quarterback | | Rick Leach, Michigan, quarterback |
| 1958 | Jack Crabtree, Oregon, quarterback | 1980 | Charles White, Southern Cal, tailback |
| 1959 | Bob Jeter, Iowa, halfback | 1981 | Butch Woolfolk, Michigan, running back |
| 1960 | Bob Schloredt, Washington, quarterback | 1982 | Jacque Robinson, Washington, running back |
| | George Fleming, Washington, halfback | | |
| 1961 | Bob Schloredt, Washington, quarterback | 1983 | Don Rogers, UCLA, free safety |
| 1962 | Sandy Stephens, Minnesota, quarterback | | Tom Ramsey, UCLA, quarterback |
| 1963 | Pete Beathard, Southern Cal, quarterback | 1984 | Rick Neuheisel, UCLA, quarterback |
| | Ron VanderKelen, Wisconsin, quarterback | 1985 | Tim Green, Southern Cal, quarterback |
| 1964 | Jim Grabowski, Illinois, fullback | | Jack Del Rio, Southern Cal, linebacker |
| 1965 | Mel Anthony, Michigan, fullback | 1986 | Eric Ball, UCLA, tailback |
| 1966 | Bob Stiles, UCLA, defensive back | 1987 | Jeff Van Raaphorst, Arizona St., quarterback |
| 1967 | John Charles, Purdue, halfback | | |
| 1968 | O. J. Simpson, Southern Cal, tailback | 1988 | Percy Snow, Michigan St., linebacker |
| 1969 | Rex Kern, Ohio St., quarterback | 1989 | Leroy Hoard, Michigan, fullback |
| 1970 | Bob Chandler, Southern Cal, flanker | 1990 | Ricky Ervins, Southern Cal, tailback |
| 1971 | Jim Plunkett, Stanford, quarterback | 1991 | Mark Brunell, Washington, quarterback |
| 1972 | Don Bunce, Stanford, quarterback | 1992 | Steve Emtman, Washington, defensive tackle |
| 1973 | Sam Cunningham, Southern Cal, fullback | | Billy Joe Hobert, Washington, quarterback |
| 1974 | Cornelius Greene, Ohio St., quarterback | 1993 | Tyrone Wheatley, Michigan, running back |
| 1975 | Pat Haden, Southern Cal, quarterback | | |
| | John McKay Jr., Southern Cal, split end | | |
| 1976 | John Sciarra, UCLA, quarterback | | |

## SUGAR BOWL
### Miller-Digby Memorial Trophy

| Year | Player, Team, Position | Year | Player, Team, Position |
|---|---|---|---|
| 1948 | Bobby Layne, Texas, quarterback | 1971 | Bobby Scott, Tennessee, quarterback |
| 1949 | Jack Mitchell, Oklahoma, quarterback | 1972 | Jack Mildren, Oklahoma, quarterback |
| 1950 | Leon Heath, Oklahoma, fullback | 1972 | Tinker Owens, Oklahoma, flanker |
| 1951 | Walt Yowarsky, Kentucky, tackle | 1973 | Tom Clements, Notre Dame, quarterback |
| 1952 | Ed Modzelewski, Maryland, fullback | 1974 | Tony Davis, Nebraska, fullback |
| 1953 | Leon Hardemann, Georgia Tech, halfback | 1975 | Richard Todd, Alabama, quarterback |
| 1954 | "Pepper" Rodgers, Georgia Tech, quarterback | 1977 | Matt Cavanaugh, Pittsburgh, quarterback |
| | | 1978 | Jeff Rutledge, Alabama, quarterback |
| 1955 | Joe Gattuso, Navy, fullback | 1979 | Barry Krauss, Alabama, linebacker |
| 1956 | Franklin Brooks, Georgia Tech, guard | 1980 | Major Ogilvie, Alabama, running back |
| 1957 | Del Shofner, Baylor, halfback | 1981 | Herschel Walker, Georgia, running back |
| 1958 | Raymond Brown, Mississippi, quarterback | 1982 | Dan Marino, Pittsburgh, quarterback |
| 1959 | Billy Cannon, Louisiana St., halfback | 1983 | Todd Blackledge, Penn St., quarterback |
| 1960 | Bobby Franklin, Mississippi, quarterback | 1984 | Bo Jackson, Auburn, running back |
| 1961 | Jake Gibbs, Mississippi, quarterback | 1985 | Craig Sundberg, Nebraska, quarterback |
| 1962 | Mike Fracchia, Alabama, fullback | 1986 | Daryl Dickey, Tennessee, quarterback |
| 1963 | Glynn Griffing, Mississippi, quarterback | 1987 | Steve Taylor, Nebraska, quarterback |
| 1964 | Tim Davis, Alabama, kicker | 1988 | Don McPherson, Syracuse, quarterback |
| 1965 | Doug Moreau, Louisiana St., flanker | 1989 | Sammie Smith, Florida St., running back |
| 1966 | Steve Spurrier, Florida, quarterback | 1990 | Craig Erickson, Miami (Fla.), quarterback |
| 1967 | Kenny Stabler, Alabama, quarterback | 1991 | Andy Kelly, Tennessee, quarterback |
| 1968 | Glenn Smith, Louisiana St., halfback | 1992 | Jerome Bettis, Notre Dame, fullback |
| 1969 | Chuck Dicus, Arkansas, flanker | 1993 | Derrick Lassic, Alabama, running back |
| 1970 | Archie Manning, Mississippi, quarterback | | |

## SUNSHINE FOOTBALL CLASSIC
### (Named Blockbuster Bowl, 1990-92)
### Brian Piccolo Most Valuable Player Award

| Year | Player, Team, Position | Year | Player, Team, Position |
|---|---|---|---|
| 1990 | Amp Lee, Florida St., running back | 1992 | Darrien Gordon, Stanford, cornerback |
| 1991 | David Palmer, Alabama, wide receiver | | |

# MOST VALUABLE PLAYERS IN FORMER MAJOR BOWLS
## ALL-AMERICAN BOWL
### (Known as Hall of Fame Classic, 1977-84)
### (Birmingham, Ala.; discontinued after 1990 game)

| Year | Player, Team, Position | Year | Player, Team, Position |
|---|---|---|---|
| 1977 | Chuck White, Maryland, split end | 1979 | Phil Bradley, Missouri, quarterback |
| | Charles Johnson, Maryland, defensive tackle | 1980 | Gary Anderson, Arkansas, running back |
| | | | Billy Ray Smith, Arkansas, linebacker |
| 1978 | Curtis Dickey, Texas A&M, running back | 1981 | John Bond, Mississippi St., quarterback |

| Year | Player, Team, Position |
|------|------------------------|
|      | Johnie Cooks, Mississippi St., linebacker |
| 1982 | Whit Taylor, Vanderbilt, quarterback |
|      | Carl Dieudonne, Air Force, defensive end |
| 1983 | Jeff Hostetler, West Va., quarterback |
| 1984 | Mark Logan, Kentucky, running back |
|      | Todd Gregoire, Wisconsin, placekicker |

| Year | Player, Team, Position |
|------|------------------------|
| 1985 | Mark Ingram, Michigan St., wide receiver |
| 1986 | Sammie Smith, Florida St., running back |
| 1987 | Scott Secules, Virginia, quarterback |
| 1988 | Emmitt Smith, Florida, running back |
| 1989 | Jerry Gray, Texas Tech, running back |
| 1990 | Brett Favre, Southern Miss., quarterback |

## AVIATION BOWL
### (Dayton, Ohio)

| Year | Player, Team, Position |
|------|------------------------|
| 1961 | Bobby Santiago, New Mexico, running back |
|      | Chuck Cummings, New Mexico, guard |

## BLUEBONNET BOWL
### (Houston, Texas; discontinued after 1987 game)

| Year | Player, Team |
|------|--------------|
| 1959 | Lowndes Shingles, Clemson |
|      | Bob Lilly, Texas Christian |
| 1960 | James Saxton, Texas |
|      | Lee Roy Jordan, Alabama |
| 1961 | Ken Coleman, Kansas |
|      | Elvin Basham, Kansas |
| 1962 | Bill Tobin, Missouri |
|      | Conrad Hitchler, Missouri |
| 1963 | Don Trull, Baylor |
|      | James Ingram, Baylor |
| 1964 | Jerry Rhome, Tulsa |
|      | Willy Townes, Tulsa |
| 1965 | Dewey Warren, Tennessee |
|      | Frank Emanuel, Tennessee |
| 1966 | Chris Gilbert, Texas |
|      | Fred Edwards, Texas |
| 1967 | Bob Anderson, Colorado |
|      | Ted Hendricks, Miami (Fla.) |
| 1968 | Joe Pearce, Oklahoma |
|      | Rufus Cormier, Southern Methodist |
| 1969 | Jim Strong, Houston |
|      | Jerry Drones, Houston |
| 1970 | Greg Pruitt, Oklahoma |
|      | Jeff Rouzie, Alabama |
| 1971 | Charlie Davis, Colorado |
|      | Butch Brezina, Houston |
| 1972 | Condredge Holloway, Tennessee |
|      | Carl Johnson, Tennessee |

| Year | Player, Team |
|------|--------------|
| 1973 | D. C. Nobles, Houston |
|      | Deryl McGallion, Houston |
| 1974 | John Housmann, Houston |
|      | Mack Mitchell, Houston |
| 1975 | Earl Campbell, Texas |
|      | Tim Campbell, Texas |
| 1976 | Chuck Malito, Nebraska |
|      | Rodney Allison, Texas Tech |
| 1977 | Rob Hertel, Southern Cal |
|      | Walt Underwood, Southern Cal |
| 1978 | Steve Dils, Stanford |
|      | Gordy Ceresino, Stanford |
| 1979 | Mark Herrmann, Purdue |
|      | Roland James, Tennessee |
| 1980 | Amos Lawrence, North Caro. |
|      | Steve Streater, North Caro. |
| 1981 | Butch Woolfolk, Michigan |
|      | Ben Needham, Michigan |
| 1982 | Gary Anderson, Arkansas |
|      | Dwayne Dixon, Florida |
| 1983 | Rusty Hilger, Oklahoma St. |
|      | Alfred Anderson, Baylor |
| 1984 | Willie Drewrey, West Va. |
| 1985 | Pat Evans, Air Force |
|      | James McKinney, Texas |
| 1986 | Ray Berry, Baylor |
|      | Mark Hatcher, Colorado |
| 1987 | Tony Jones, Texas |
|      | Zeke Gadson, Pittsburgh |

## BLUEGRASS BOWL
### (Louisville, Ky.)

| Year | Player, Team |
|------|--------------|
| 1958 | Forrest Campbell, Oklahoma St. |

## CALIFORNIA RAISIN BOWL
### (Beginning in 1992, Mid-American Conference and Big West Conference winners met in Las Vegas Bowl)

| Year | Player, Team, Position |
|------|------------------------|
| 1981 | Arnold Smiley, Toledo, running back |
|      | Marlin Russell, Toledo, linebacker |
| 1982 | Chip Otten, Bowling Green, tailback |
|      | Jac Tomasello, Bowling Green, defensive back |
| 1983 | Lou Wicks, Northern Ill., fullback |
|      | James Pruitt, Cal St. Fullerton, wide receiver |
| 1984 | Randall Cunningham, Nevada-Las Vegas, quarterback |
|      | Steve Morgan, Toledo, tailback |
| 1985 | Mike Mancini, Fresno St., punter |
|      | Greg Meehan, Bowling Green, flanker |
| 1986 | Mike Perez, San Jose St., quarterback |

| Year | Player, Team, Position |
|------|------------------------|
|      | Andrew Marlatt, Miami (Ohio), defensive tackle |
| 1987 | Gary Patton, Eastern Mich., tailback |
|      | Mike Perez, San Jose St., quarterback |
| 1988 | Darrell Rosette, Fresno St., running back |
|      | Tony Kimbrough, Western Mich., quarterback |
| 1989 | Ron Cox, Fresno St., linebacker |
|      | Sean Jones, Ball St., wide receiver |
| 1990 | Sheldon Canley, San Jose St., tailback |
|      | Ken Ealy, Central Mich., wide receiver |
| 1991 | Mark Szlachcic, Bowling Green, wide receiver |
|      | Mark Barsotti, Fresno St., quarterback |

## CHERRY BOWL
### (Pontiac, Mich.)

| Year | Player, Team | Year | Player, Team |
|------|-------------|------|-------------|
| 1984 | Nate Sassaman, Army | 1985 | Stan Gelbaugh, Maryland |
|      |             |      | Scott Shankweiler, Maryland |

## DELTA BOWL
### (Memphis, Tenn.)

| Year | Player, Team |
|------|-------------|
| 1948 | Charlie Conerly, Mississippi |

## GARDEN STATE BOWL
### (East Rutherford, N. J.)

| Year | Player, Team | Year | Player, Team |
|------|-------------|------|-------------|
| 1978 | John Mistler, Arizona St. | 1981 | Steve Alatorre, Tennessee |
| 1979 | Mark Bright, Temple |      | Anthony Hancock, Tennessee |
| 1980 | Terald Clark, Houston |      | Randy Wright, Wisconsin |

## GOTHAM BOWL
### (New York, N. Y.)

| Year | Player, Team | Year | Player, Team |
|------|-------------|------|-------------|
| 1961 | Don Trull, Baylor | 1962 | Willie Ross, Nebraska |
|      |             |      | George Mira, Miami (Fla.) |

## HARBOR BOWL
### (San Diego, Calif.)

| Year | Player, Team |
|------|-------------|
| 1947 | Bryan Brock, New Mexico |
|      | Bill Nelson, Montana St. |

## MERCY BOWL
### (Los Angeles, Calif.)

| Year | Player, Team |
|------|-------------|
| 1961 | Beau Carter, Fresno St. |

## PASADENA BOWL
### (Called Junior Rose Bowl in 1967)
### (Pasadena, Calif.)

| Year | Player, Team | Year | Player, Team |
|------|-------------|------|-------------|
| 1967 | Eugene "Mercury" Morris, West Tex. St. | 1970 | Leon Burns, Long Beach St. |
|      | Albie Owens, West Tex. St. |      | Paul Mattingly, Louisville |
| 1969 | John Featherstone, San Diego St. | 1971 | Tom Carlsen, Memphis St. |
|      |             |      | Dornell Harris, Memphis St. |

## PRESIDENTIAL CUP
### (College Park, Md.)

| Year | Player, Team |
|------|-------------|
| 1950 | Bob Smith, Texas A&M |
|      | Zippy Morocco, Georgia |

## SALAD BOWL
### (Phoenix, Ariz.)

| Year | Player, Team | Year | Player, Team |
|------|-------------|------|-------------|
| 1950 | Bob McQuade, Xavier (Ohio) | 1951 | Jim Bailey, Miami (Ohio) |
|      | Wilford "Whizzer" White, Arizona St. | 1952 | Gene Shannon, Houston |

# HEISMAN TROPHY WINNERS IN BOWL GAMES

## YEAR-BY-YEAR BOWL RESULTS FOR HEISMAN WINNERS
### (Includes bowl games immediately after award of Heisman Trophy)

Of the 57 winners of the 58 Heisman Trophies (Archie Griffin won twice), 33 played in bowl games after they received their prize. Of those 33 players, only 14 were on the winning team in the bowl.

Houston's Andre Ware is the only Heisman recipient to miss a bowl date since 1969. The Cougars were on probation during the 1989 season and were ineligible for selection to a bowl. Before that lapse, Oklahoma's Steve Owens in 1969 was the last Heisman awardee not to participate in a bowl game.

Only three of the first 22 Heisman Trophy winners played in bowl games after receiving the award—Texas Christian's Davey O'Brien in 1938, Georgia's Frank Sinkwich in 1942 and Southern Methodist's Doak Walker in 1948.

| Year | Heisman Winner, Team, Position | Bowl (Opponent, Result) |
|---|---|---|
| 1935 | Jay Berwanger, Chicago, HB | Did not play in bowl |
| 1936 | Larry Kelley, Yale, E | Did not play in bowl |
| 1937 | Clint Frank, Yale, HB | Did not play in bowl |
| 1938 | Davey O'Brien, Texas Christian, QB | Sugar (Carnegie Mellon, W 15-7) |
| 1939 | Nile Kinnick, Iowa, HB | Did not play in bowl |
| 1940 | Tom Harmon, Michigan, HB | Did not play in bowl |
| 1941 | Bruce Smith, Minnesota, HB | Did not play in bowl |
| 1942 | Frank Sinkwich, Georgia, HB | Rose (UCLA, W 9-0) |
| 1943 | Angelo Bertelli, Notre Dame, QB | Did not play in bowl |
| 1944 | Les Horvath, Ohio St., QB | Did not play in bowl |
| 1945 | Doc Blanchard, Army, FB | Did not play in bowl |
| 1946 | Glenn Davis, Army, HB | Did not play in bowl |
| 1947 | Johnny Lujack, Notre Dame, QB | Did not play in bowl |
| 1948 | Doak Walker, Southern Methodist, HB | Cotton (Oregon, W 21-13) |
| 1949 | Leon Hart, Notre Dame, E | Did not play in bowl |
| 1950 | Vic Janowicz, Ohio St., HB | Did not play in bowl |
| 1951 | Dick Kazmeier, Princeton, HB | Did not play in bowl |
| 1952 | Billy Vessels, Oklahoma, HB | Did not play in bowl |
| 1953 | John Lattner, Notre Dame, HB | Did not play in bowl |
| 1954 | Alan Ameche, Wisconsin, FB | Did not play in bowl |
| 1955 | Howard Cassady, Ohio St., HB | Did not play in bowl |
| 1956 | Paul Hornung, Notre Dame, QB | Did not play in bowl |
| 1957 | John David Crow, Texas A&M, HB | Gator (Tennessee, L 0-3) |
| 1958 | Pete Dawkins, Army, HB | Did not play in bowl |
| 1959 | Billy Cannon, Louisiana St., HB | Sugar (Mississippi, L 0-21) |
| 1960 | Joe Bellino, Navy, HB | Orange (Missouri, L 14-21) |
| 1961 | Ernie Davis, Syracuse, HB | Liberty (Miami, Fla., W 15-14) |
| 1962 | Terry Baker, Oregon St., QB | Liberty (Villanova, W 6-0) |
| 1963 | Roger Staubach, Navy, QB | Cotton (Texas, L 6-28) |
| 1964 | John Huarte, Notre Dame, QB | Did not play in bowl |
| 1965 | Mike Garrett, Southern Cal, HB | Did not play in bowl |
| 1966 | Steve Spurrier, Florida, QB | Orange (Georgia Tech, W 27-12) |
| 1967 | Gary Beban, UCLA, QB | Did not play in bowl |
| 1968 | O. J. Simpson, Southern Cal, HB | Rose (Ohio St., L 16-27) |
| 1969 | Steve Owens, Oklahoma, HB | Did not play in bowl |
| 1970 | Jim Plunkett, Stanford, QB | Rose (Ohio St., W 27-17) |
| 1971 | Pat Sullivan, Auburn, QB | Sugar (Oklahoma, L 22-40) |
| 1972 | Johnny Rodgers, Nebraska, FL | Orange (Notre Dame, W 40-6) |
| 1973 | John Cappelletti, Penn St., HB | Orange (Louisiana St., W 16-9) |
| 1974 | Archie Griffin, Ohio St., HB | Rose (Southern Cal, L 17-18) |
| 1975 | Archie Griffin, Ohio St., HB | Rose (UCLA, L 10-23) |
| 1976 | Tony Dorsett, Pittsburgh, HB | Sugar (Georgia, W 27-3) |
| 1977 | Earl Campbell, Texas, HB | Cotton (Notre Dame, L 10-38) |
| 1978 | Billy Sims, Oklahoma, HB | Orange (Nebraska, W 31-24) |
| 1979 | Charles White, Southern Cal, HB | Rose (Ohio St., W 17-16) |
| 1980 | George Rogers, South Caro., HB | Gator (Pittsburgh, L 9-37) |
| 1981 | Marcus Allen, Southern Cal, HB | Fiesta (Penn St., L 10-26) |
| 1982 | Herschel Walker, Georgia, HB | Sugar (Penn St., L 23-27) |
| 1983 | Mike Rozier, Nebraska, HB | Orange (Miami, Fla., L 30-31) |
| 1984 | Doug Flutie, Boston College, QB | Cotton (Houston, W 45-28) |
| 1985 | Bo Jackson, Auburn, HB | Cotton (Texas A&M, L 16-36) |
| 1986 | Vinny Testaverde, Miami (Fla.), QB | Fiesta (Penn St., L 10-14) |
| 1987 | Tim Brown, Notre Dame, WR | Cotton (Texas A&M, L 10-35) |
| 1988 | Barry Sanders, Oklahoma St., RB | Holiday (Wyoming, W 62-14) |
| 1989 | Andre Ware, Houston, QB | Did not play in bowl |
| 1990 | Ty Detmer, Brigham Young, QB | Holiday (Texas A&M, L 14-65) |
| 1991 | Desmond Howard, Michigan, WR | Rose (Washington, L 14-34) |
| 1992 | Gino Torretta, Miami (Fla.), QB | Sugar (Alabama, L 13-34) |

## TOP BOWLS FOR HEISMAN WINNERS

| Bowl | Heisman Winner Year | Heisman Winners |
|---|---|---|
| Rose | 1942, 1968, 1970, 1974, 1975, 1979, 1991 | 7 |
| Cotton | 1948, 1963, 1977, 1984, 1985, 1987 | 6 |
| Orange | 1960, 1966, 1972, 1973, 1978, 1983 | 6 |
| Sugar | 1938, 1959, 1971, 1976, 1982, 1992 | 6 |
| Fiesta | 1981, 1986 | 2 |
| Gator | 1957, 1980 | 2 |

| Bowl | Heisman Winner Year | Heisman Winners |
|------|---------------------|-----------------|
| Liberty | 1961, 1962 | 2 |
| Holiday | 1988, 1990 | 2 |

## HEISMAN TROPHY WINNERS WHO WERE BOWL-GAME MVPs

| Heisman Winner, Team (Year Won) | Bowl, Year Played |
|---------------------------------|-------------------|
| Doak Walker, Southern Methodist (1948) | Cotton, 1948 |
| Doak Walker, Southern Methodist (1948) | Cotton, 1949 |
| John David Crow, Texas A&M (1957) | Gator, 1957 |
| Billy Cannon, Louisiana St. (1959) | Sugar, 1959 |
| Ernie Davis, Syracuse (1961) | Cotton, 1960 |
| Ernie Davis, Syracuse (1961) | Liberty, 1961 |
| Terry Baker, Oregon St. (1962) | Liberty, 1962 |
| Steve Spurrier, Florida (1966) | Sugar, 1966 |
| O. J. Simpson, Southern Cal (1968) | Rose, 1968 |
| Jim Plunkett, Stanford (1970) | Rose, 1971 |
| Pat Sullivan, Auburn (1971) | Gator, 1971 |
| Johnny Rodgers, Nebraska (1972) | Orange, 1973 |
| Earl Campbell, Texas (1977) | Gator, 1974 |
| Earl Campbell, Texas (1977) | Bluebonnet, 1975* |
| Billy Sims, Oklahoma (1978) | Orange, 1979 |
| Charles White, Southern Cal (1979) | Rose, 1979 |
| Charles White, Southern Cal (1979) | Rose, 1980 |
| George Rogers, South Caro. (1980) | Gator, 1980 |
| Herschel Walker, Georgia (1982) | Sugar, 1981 |
| Doug Flutie, Boston College (1984) | Liberty, 1983 |
| Bo Jackson, Auburn (1985) | Liberty, 1984 |
| Bo Jackson, Auburn (1985) | Sugar, 1984 |
| Bo Jackson, Auburn (1985) | Cotton, 1986 |
| Barry Sanders, Oklahoma St. (1988) | Holiday, 1988 |
| Ty Detmer, Brigham Young (1990) | Freedom , 1988 |
| Ty Detmer, Brigham Young (1990) | Holiday, 1989 |
| Ty Detmer, Brigham Young (1990) | Holiday, 1991 |

\* *Discontinued bowl.*

In addition to earning the 1985 Heisman Trophy, Bo Jackson earned most-valuable-player awards in the 1984 Liberty Bowl, 1984 Sugar Bowl and 1986 Cotton Bowl. Only one other Heisman winner (Ty Detmer) has claimed three bowl MVP awards.

# BOWLS AND POLLS

## ASSOCIATED PRESS NO. 1 TEAMS DEFEATED IN BOWL GAMES

| Date | Bowl | Teams Involved | Score | New No. 1 |
|------|------|----------------|-------|-----------|
| 1-1-51 | Sugar | No. 7 Kentucky beat No. 1 Oklahoma | 13-7 | Same |
| 1-1-52 | Sugar | No. 3 Maryland beat No. 1 Tennessee | 28-13 | Same |
| 1-1-54 | Orange | No. 4 Oklahoma beat No. 1 Maryland | 7-0 | Same |
| 1-1-61 | Rose | No. 6 Washington beat No. 1 Minnesota | 17-7 | Same |
| 1-1-65 | Orange | No. 5 Texas beat No. 1 Alabama | 21-17 | Same |
| 1-1-71 | Cotton | No. 6 Notre Dame beat No. 1 Texas | 24-11 | Nebraska |
| 12-31-73 | Sugar | No. 3 Notre Dame beat No. 1 Alabama | 24-23 | Notre Dame |
| 1-1-76 | Rose | No. 11 UCLA beat No. 1 Ohio St. | 23-10 | Oklahoma |
| 1-2-78 | Cotton | No. 5 Notre Dame beat No. 1 Texas | 38-10 | Notre Dame |
| 1-1-79 | Sugar | No. 2 Alabama beat No. 1 Penn St. | 14-7 | Alabama |
| 1-1-83 | Sugar | No. 2 Penn St. beat No. 1 Georgia | 27-23 | Penn St. |
| 1-2-84 | Orange | No. 5 Miami (Fla.) beat No. 1 Nebraska | 31-30 | Miami (Fla.) |
| 1-1-86 | Orange | No. 3 Oklahoma beat No. 1 Penn St. | 25-10 | Oklahoma |
| 1-2-87 | Fiesta | No. 2 Penn St. beat No. 1 Miami (Fla.) | 14-10 | Penn St. |
| 1-1-88 | Orange | No. 2 Miami (Fla.) beat No. 1 Oklahoma | 20-14 | Miami (Fla.) |
| 1-1-90 | Orange | No. 4 Notre Dame beat No. 1 Colorado | 21-6 | Miami (Fla.) |
| 1-1-93 | Sugar | No. 2 Alabama beat No. 1 Miami (Fla.) | 34-13 | Alabama |

## ASSOCIATED PRESS NO. 1 VS. NO. 2 IN BOWL GAMES

| Date | Bowl | Teams, Score |
|------|------|--------------|
| 1-1-63 | Rose | No. 1 Southern Cal 42, No. 2 Wisconsin 37 |
| 1-1-64 | Cotton | No. 1 Texas 28, No. 2 Navy 6 |
| 1-1-69 | Rose | No. 1 Ohio St. 27, No. 2 Southern Cal 16 |
| 1-1-72 | Orange | No. 1 Nebraska 28, No. 2 Alabama 6 |
| 1-1-79 | Sugar | No. 2 Alabama 14, No. 1 Penn St. 7 |
| 1-1-83 | Sugar | No. 2 Penn St. 27, No. 1 Georgia 23 |
| 1-2-87 | Fiesta | No. 2 Penn St. 14, No. 1 Miami (Fla.) 10 |
| 1-1-88 | Orange | No. 2 Miami (Fla.) 20, No. 1 Oklahoma 14 |
| 1-1-93 | Sugar* | No. 2 Alabama 34, No. 1 Miami (Fla.) 13 |

* *Bowl Alliance matched the No.1 and No. 2 teams.*

## BOWL GAMES AND THE NATIONAL CHAMPIONSHIP

**(How the bowl games determined the national champion from 1965 to present. Year listed is the football season before the bowl games.)**

Note: The national champion was selected before the bowl games as follows: Associated Press (1936-64 and 66-67); United Press International (1950-73); Football Writers Association of America (1954), and National Football Foundation and Hall of Fame (1959-70).

**1965** The Associated Press (AP) selected Alabama as national champion after it defeated Nebraska, 39-28, in the Orange Bowl on January 1, 1966.

**1968** AP selected Ohio St. as national champion after it defeated Southern Cal, 27-16, in the Rose Bowl on January 1, 1969.

**1969** AP selected Texas as national champion after it defeated Notre Dame, 21-17, in the Cotton Bowl on January 1, 1970.

**1970** AP selected Nebraska as national champion after it defeated Louisiana St., 17-12, in the Orange Bowl on January 1, 1971.

**1971** AP selected Nebraska as national champion after it defeated Alabama, 38-6, in the Orange Bowl on January 1, 1972.

**1972** AP selected Southern Cal as national champion after it defeated Ohio St., 42-17, in the Rose Bowl on January 1, 1973.

**1973** AP selected Notre Dame as national champion after it defeated Alabama, 24-23, in the Sugar Bowl on December 31, 1973.

Beginning in 1974, all four of the national polls waited until after the bowl-game results before selecting a national champion. The following list shows how the bowl games figured in the final national championship polls for AP and UPI:

**1974** First year of the agreement between the American Football Coaches Association (AFCA) and the UPI Board of Coaches to declare any teams on NCAA probation ineligible for the poll. AP—Oklahoma (11-0-0) did not participate in a bowl game because of NCAA probation. UPI—Southern Cal (10-1-1) defeated Ohio St., 18-17, in the Rose Bowl on January 1, 1975.

**1975** AP and UPI both selected Oklahoma (11-1-0). Coach Barry Switzer's Sooners defeated Michigan, 14-6, in the Orange Bowl on January 1, 1976. Ohio St. had led the AP poll for nine consecutive weeks until a 23-10 loss to UCLA in the Rose Bowl on January 1, 1976. Oklahoma had led the AP poll for the first four weeks of the year.

**1976** AP and UPI both selected Tony Dorsett-led Pittsburgh (12-0-0). Pittsburgh whipped Georgia, 27-3, in the Sugar Bowl on January 1, 1977. Pittsburgh took over the No. 1 position from Michigan in the ninth week of the season en route to an undefeated year.

**1977** AP and UPI were in agreement again, picking Notre Dame as national titlist. The Irish crushed previously undefeated and top-ranked Texas, 38-10, in the Cotton Bowl on January 2, 1978. Notre Dame was the sixth team to be ranked No. 1 during the 1977 season in the AP poll.

**1978** This was the last time until the 1991 season that the two polls split on a national champion, with AP selecting Alabama (11-1-0) and UPI going for Southern Cal (12-1-0). Alabama, ranked No. 2 in the AP poll, upset No. 1 Penn St., 14-7, in the Sugar Bowl on January 1, 1979. Alabama had been ranked No. 1 in the first two weeks of the season until a 24-14 loss to Southern Cal.

**1979** Unbeaten Alabama (12-0-0) was the unanimous choice of both polls. Bear Bryant's Tide whipped Arkansas easily, 24-9, in the Sugar Bowl on January 1, 1980, to claim the title.

**1980** Georgia made it three No. 1s in a row for the Southeastern Conference with an undefeated season (12-0-0) to take the top spot in both polls. Vince Dooley's Bulldogs downed Notre Dame, 17-10, behind freshman phenom Herschel Walker in the Sugar Bowl on January 1, 1981.

**1981** Both polls selected unbeaten Clemson (12-0-0). The Tigers gave coach Danny Ford the first Clemson national football championship with a 22-15 victory over Nebraska in the Orange Bowl on January 1, 1982. Clemson did not take over the AP No. 1 slot until the next-to-last poll of the year.

**1982** AP and UPI both selected Penn St. (11-1-0). The Nittany Lions were No. 2 in the AP poll but knocked off No. 1 Georgia, 27-23, in the Sugar Bowl on January 1, 1983. Georgia had led the AP poll for the final five weeks of the season.

**1983** AP and UPI had no choice but to select Miami (Fla.) as the unanimous champion after the No. 2 Hurricanes downed No. 1 Nebraska, 31-30, in the Orange Bowl on January 2, 1984. Many observers felt this may have been the most exciting Orange Bowl ever played as the Cornhuskers failed on a two-point conversion attempt with 48 seconds remaining. Nebraska had led the AP poll since the first week of the season.

**1984** Unknown and a victim of the Mountain time zone, Brigham Young (13-0-0) overcame many obstacles to ascend to No. 1 in both polls. Coach LaVell Edwards' Cougars downed Michigan, 24-17, in the Holiday Bowl on December 21, 1984. BYU took over the top spot in the AP poll with three weeks left in the season after four other teams came and went as the top-rated team.

**1985** Oklahoma (11-1-0) returned as the unanimous choice of both polls. Barry Switzer's Sooners knocked off top-rated Penn St., 25-10, in the Orange Bowl on January 1, 1986, to claim the national title.

**1986** Penn St. (12-0-0) had to battle top-rated Miami (Fla.) in the Fiesta Bowl to take the top slot in both polls. Joe Paterno's No. 2 Nittany Lions upset the Hurricanes, 14-10, on January 2, 1987, to claim the championship. Miami (Fla.) had been ranked No. 1 for the final 10 weeks of the season.

**1987** Miami (Fla.) (12-0-0) bounced back to a similar scenario as Jimmy Johnson's Hurricanes played underdog and finished ranked first in both polls. The No. 2 Hurricanes beat No. 1-ranked Oklahoma, 20-14, in the Orange Bowl on January 1, 1988. The Sooners had been the top-rated AP team for 13 of the season's 15 polls.

**1988** Notre Dame (12-0-0) finished as the top team in both polls and gave the Fiesta Bowl its second national title game in three seasons. Lou Holtz's Irish whipped West Va., 34-21, on January 2, 1989, to claim their eighth AP title. Notre Dame took over the top spot in the poll from UCLA in the ninth week of the season.

**1989** Miami (Fla.) (11-1-0) claimed its second national title in three years in both polls. The Hurricanes downed Alabama, 33-25, in the Sugar Bowl on January 1, 1990, while No. 1-ranked Colorado lost to Notre Dame, 21-6, in the Orange Bowl to clear the way. Notre Dame led the AP poll for 12 of the 15 weeks.

**1990** Colorado (11-1-0) and Georgia Tech (11-0-1) split the polls for the first time since 1978 with the Buffs taking the AP vote and the Jackets the UPI. Colorado bounced back from a disappointing 1989 title march to edge Notre Dame, 10-9, in the Orange Bowl on January 1, 1991. Georgia Tech had little trouble with Nebraska, 45-21, in the Florida Citrus Bowl on January 1, 1991, to finish as Division I-A's only undefeated team.

**1991** Miami (Fla.) (12-0-0) and Washington (12-0-0) kept Division I-A playoff talk alive with a split in the national polls for the second consecutive year. The Hurricanes took the AP vote, while the Huskies took both the USA Today/CNN and UPI polls. If either had stumbled in a bowl, then the other would have been a unanimous selection. However, Washington drubbed Michigan, 34-14, in the Rose Bowl, and Miami had little trouble shutting out Nebraska, 22-0, in the Orange Bowl later that evening.

**1992** No. 2 Alabama (13-0-0) turned in a magnificent performance in the Sugar Bowl by upsetting No. 1 Miami (Fla.), 34-13, in a game dominated by the Crimson Tide. It marked the first year of the bowl coalition, and the bowlmeisters managed to match the top two teams for the national championship. It also marked the 17th time that a No. 1 team in the AP poll was knocked off in a bowl game since 1951. Alabama was named No. 1 in all polls after the January 1, 1993, matchup.

# BOWL RESULTS OF TEAMS RANKED IN THE
# ASSOCIATED PRESS POLL

The bowls and national polls have been perpetually linked since 1936, when The Associated Press introduced its weekly college football poll. The final AP poll was released at the end of the regular season until 1965, when bowl results were included for one year, dropped for two more and then added again in 1968 until the present. (Key to polls: AP, Associated Press; UPI, United Press International; FW, Football Writers; NFF, National Football Foundation and Hall of Fame; USA/CNN, USA Today/Cable News Network; UPI/NFF, United Press International/National Football Foundation and Hall of Fame.) This is a list of the key bowl games as they related to the AP poll since 1936 (with pertinent references made to other polls where applicable).

**1936**   SUGAR—No. 6 Santa Clara beat No. 2 Louisiana St., 21-14; ROSE—No. 3 Pittsburgh beat No. 5 Washington, 21-0; ORANGE—No. 14 Duquesne beat Mississippi St., 13-12; COTTON—No. 16 Texas Christian beat No. 20 Marquette, 16-6. (Minnesota selected No. 1 but did not play in a bowl)

**1937**   ROSE—No. 2 California beat No. 4 Alabama, 13-0; SUGAR—No. 9 Santa Clara beat No. 8 Louisiana St., 6-0; COTTON—No. 18 Rice beat No. 17 Colorado, 28-14. (Pittsburgh selected No. 1 but did not play in a bowl)

**1938**   SUGAR—No. 1 Texas Christian beat No. 6 Carnegie Mellon, 15-7; ORANGE—No. 2 Tennessee beat No. 4 Oklahoma, 17-0; ROSE—No. 7 Southern Cal beat No. 3 Duke, 7-3; COTTON—Unranked St. Mary's (Cal.) beat No. 11 Texas Tech, 20-13. (Texas Christian selected No. 1)

**1939**   SUGAR—No. 1 Texas A&M beat No. 5 Tulane, 14-13; ROSE—No. 3 Southern Cal beat No. 2 Tennessee, 14-0; ORANGE—No. 16 Georgia Tech beat No. 6 Missouri, 21-7; COTTON—No. 12 Clemson beat No. 11 Boston College, 6-3. (Texas A&M selected No. 1)

**1940**   ROSE—No. 2 Stanford beat No. 7 Nebraska, 21-13; SUGAR—No. 5 Boston College beat No. 4 Tennessee, 19-13; COTTON—No. 6 Texas A&M beat No. 12 Fordham, 13-12; ORANGE—No. 9 Mississippi St. beat No. 13 Georgetown, 14-7. (Minnesota selected No. 1 but did not play in a bowl)

**1941**   ROSE—No. 12 Oregon St. beat No. 2 Duke, 20-16 (played at Durham, N.C., because of World War II); SUGAR—No. 6 Fordham beat No. 7 Missouri, 2-0; COTTON—No. 20 Alabama beat No. 9 Texas A&M, 29-21; ORANGE—No. 14 Georgia beat unranked Texas Christian, 40-26. (Minnesota selected No. 1 but did not play in a bowl)

**1942**   ROSE—No. 2 Georgia beat No. 13 UCLA, 9-0; SUGAR—No. 7 Tennessee beat No. 4 Tulsa, 14-7; COTTON—No. 11 Texas beat No. 5 Georgia Tech, 14-7; ORANGE—No. 10 Alabama beat No. 8 Boston College, 37-21. (Ohio St. selected No. 1 but did not play in a bowl)

**1943**   ROSE—Unranked Southern Cal beat No. 12 Washington, 29-0; COTTON—No. 14 Texas tied unranked Randolph Field, 7-7; SUGAR—No. 13 Georgia Tech beat No. 15 Tulsa, 20-18. (Notre Dame selected No. 1 but did not play in a bowl)

**1944**   ROSE—No. 7 Southern Cal beat No. 12 Tennessee, 25-0; ORANGE—Unranked Tulsa beat No. 13 Georgia Tech, 26-12; No. 3 Randolph Field beat No. 20 Second Air Force, 13-6, in a battle of military powers. (Army selected No. 1 but did not play in a bowl)

**1945**   ROSE—No. 2 Alabama beat No. 11 Southern Cal, 34-14; COTTON—No. 10 Texas beat unranked Missouri, 40-27; ORANGE—Unranked Miami (Fla.) beat No. 16 Holy Cross, 13-6; SUGAR—No. 5 Oklahoma St. beat No. 7 St. Mary's (Cal.), 33-13. (Army selected No. 1 but did not play in a bowl)

**1946**   COTTON—No. 8 Louisiana St. tied No. 16 Arkansas, 0-0; ROSE—No. 5 Illinois beat No. 4 UCLA, 45-14; SUGAR—No. 3 Georgia beat No. 9 North Caro., 20-10; ORANGE—No. 10 Rice beat No. 7 Tennessee, 8-0. (Notre Dame selected No. 1 but did not play in a bowl)

**1947**   ORANGE—No. 10 Georgia Tech beat No. 12 Kansas, 20-14; ROSE—No. 2 Michigan beat No. 8 Southern Cal, 49-0; SUGAR—No. 5 Texas beat No. 6 Alabama, 27-7; COTTON—No. 3 Southern Methodist tied No. 4 Penn St., 13-13. (Notre Dame selected No. 1 but did not play in a bowl; Michigan also declared champion in vote after Rose Bowl victory but AP kept Notre Dame as vote of record)

**1948**   ROSE—No. 7 Northwestern beat No. 4 California, 20-14; COTTON—No. 10 Southern Methodist beat No. 9 Oregon, 21-13; SUGAR—No. 5 Oklahoma beat No. 3 North Caro., 14-6; ORANGE—Unranked Texas beat No. 8 Georgia, 41-28. (Michigan selected No. 1 but did not play in a bowl)

**1949**   ORANGE—No. 15 Santa Clara beat No. 11 Kentucky, 21-13; COTTON—No. 5 Rice beat No. 16 North Caro., 27-13; ROSE—No. 6 Ohio St. beat No. 3 California, 17-14; SUGAR—No. 2 Oklahoma beat No. 9 Louisiana St., 35-0. (Notre Dame selected No. 1 but did not play in a bowl)

**1950**   ROSE—No. 9 Michigan beat No. 5 California, 14-6; SUGAR—No. 7 Kentucky beat No. 1 Oklahoma, 13-7; ORANGE—No. 10 Clemson beat No. 15 Miami (Fla.), 15-14; COTTON—No. 4 Tennessee beat No. 3 Texas, 20-14. (Oklahoma selected No. 1 in vote before losing in Sugar Bowl)

**1951**   COTTON—No. 15 Kentucky beat No. 11 Texas Christian, 20-7; ORANGE—No. 5 Georgia Tech beat No. 9 Baylor, 17-14; ROSE—No. 4 Illinois beat No. 7 Stanford, 40-7; SUGAR—No. 3 Maryland beat No. 1 Tennessee, 28-13. (Tennessee selected No. 1 in vote before losing in Sugar Bowl)

**1952**   ROSE—No. 5 Southern Cal beat No. 11 Wisconsin, 7-0; SUGAR—No. 2 Georgia Tech beat No. 7 Mississippi, 24-7; ORANGE—No. 9 Alabama beat No. 14 Syracuse, 61-6; COTTON—No. 10 Texas beat No. 8 Tennessee, 16-0. (Michigan St. selected No. 1 but did not play in bowl)

**1953**   SUGAR—No. 8 Georgia Tech beat No. 10 West Va., 42-19; ORANGE—No. 4 Oklahoma beat No. 1 Maryland, 7-0; COTTON—No. 5 Rice beat No. 13 Alabama, 28-6; ROSE—No. 3 Michigan St. beat No. 5 UCLA, 28-20. (Maryland selected No. 1 before losing in Orange Bowl)

**1954**   ROSE—No. 1 Ohio St. beat No. 17 Southern Cal, 20-7; ORANGE—No. 14 Duke beat unranked Nebraska, 34-7; SUGAR—No. 5 Navy beat No. 6 Mississippi, 21-0; COTTON—Unranked Georgia Tech beat No. 10 Arkansas, 14-6. (Ohio St. remained No. 1 but UCLA named in UPI and FW polls)

**1955**   GATOR—Unranked Vanderbilt beat No. 8 Auburn, 25-13; ROSE—No. 2 Michigan St. beat No. 4 UCLA, 17-14; ORANGE—No. 1 Oklahoma beat No. 3 Maryland, 20-6; COTTON—No. 10

                                        *1993 NCAA FOOTBALL*

Mississippi beat No. 6 Texas Christian, 14-13; SUGAR—No. 7 Georgia Tech beat No. 11 Pittsburgh, 7-0. (Oklahoma remained No. 1)

**1956** SUGAR—No. 11 Baylor beat No. 2 Tennessee, 13-7; ORANGE—No. 20 Colorado beat No. 19 Clemson, 27-21; GATOR—No. 4 Georgia Tech beat No. 13 Pittsburgh, 21-14; ROSE—No. 3 Iowa beat No. 10 Oregon St., 35-19; COTTON—No. 14 Texas Christian beat No. 8 Syracuse, 28-27. (Oklahoma selected No. 1 but did not play in a bowl)

**1957** GATOR—No. 13 Tennessee beat No. 9 Texas A&M, 3-0; ROSE—No. 2 Ohio St. beat unranked Oregon, 10-7; COTTON—No. 5 Navy beat No. 8 Rice, 20-7; ORANGE—No. 4 Oklahoma beat No. 16 Duke, 48-21; SUGAR—No. 7 Mississippi beat No. 11 Texas, 39-7. (Auburn selected No. 1 but did not play in a bowl; Ohio St. selected No. 1 in both UPI and FW polls)

**1958** SUGAR—No. 1 Louisiana St. beat No. 12 Clemson, 7-0; COTTON—No. 6 Air Force tied No. 10 Texas Christian, 0-0; ROSE—No. 2 Iowa beat No. 16 California, 38-12; ORANGE—No. 5 Oklahoma beat No. 9 Syracuse, 21-6. (Louisiana St. remained No. 1 in AP and UPI but Iowa selected in FW poll)

**1959** COTTON—No. 1 Syracuse beat No. 4 Texas, 23-14; ROSE—No. 8 Washington beat No. 6 Wisconsin, 44-8; ORANGE—No. 5 Georgia beat No. 18 Missouri, 14-0; SUGAR—No. 2 Mississippi beat No. 3 Louisiana St., 21-0; BLUEBONNET—No. 11 Clemson beat No. 7 Texas Christian, 23-7; LIBERTY—No. 12 Penn St. beat No. 10 Alabama, 7-0; GATOR—No. 9 Arkansas beat unranked Georgia Tech, 14-7. (Syracuse selected No. 1 by all four polls)

**1960** ROSE—No. 6 Washington beat No. 1 Minnesota, 17-7; COTTON—No. 10 Duke beat No. 7 Arkansas, 7-6; SUGAR—No. 2 Mississippi beat unranked Rice, 14-6; ORANGE—No. 5 Missouri beat No. 4 Navy, 21-14; BLUEBONNET—No. 9 Alabama tied unranked Texas, 3-3. (Minnesota selected No. 1 by AP, UPI and NFF before losing in Rose Bowl; Mississippi named No. 1 in FW poll)

**1961** COTTON—No. 3 Texas beat No. 5 Mississippi, 12-7; SUGAR—No. 1 Alabama beat No. 9 Arkansas, 10-3; ORANGE—No. 4 Louisiana St. beat No. 7 Colorado, 25-7; GOTHAM—Unranked Baylor beat No. 10 Utah St., 24-9; ROSE—No. 6 Minnesota beat No. 16 UCLA, 21-3. (Alabama selected No. 1 in AP, UPI and NFF but Ohio St. picked by FW poll)

**1962** ROSE—No. 1 Southern Cal beat No. 2 Wisconsin, 42-37; SUGAR—No. 3 Mississippi beat No. 6 Arkansas, 17-13; COTTON—No. 7 Louisiana St. beat No. 4 Texas, 13-0; GATOR—Unranked Florida beat No. 9 Penn St., 17-7; ORANGE—No. 5 Alabama beat No. 8 Oklahoma, 17-0. (Southern Cal selected No. 1 by all four polls)

**1963** COTTON—No. 1 Texas beat No. 2 Navy, 28-6; ORANGE—No. 6 Nebraska beat No. 5 Auburn, 13-7; ROSE—No. 3 Illinois beat unranked Washington, 17-7; SUGAR—No. 8 Alabama beat No. 7 Mississippi, 12-7. (Texas selected No. 1 by all four polls)

**1964** ORANGE—No. 5 Texas beat No. 1 Alabama, 21-17; ROSE—No. 4 Michigan beat No. 8 Oregon St., 34-7; COTTON—No. 2 Arkansas beat No. 6 Nebraska, 10-7; SUGAR—No. 7 Louisiana St. beat unranked Syracuse, 13-10. (Alabama selected No. 1 by AP and UPI before losing in the Orange Bowl, while Arkansas No. 1 in FW poll and Notre Dame No. 1 in NFF poll)

**1965** *(First year final poll taken after bowl games)* ROSE—No. 5 UCLA beat No. 1 Michigan St., 14-12; COTTON—Unranked Louisiana St. beat No. 2 Arkansas, 14-7; SUGAR—No. 6 Missouri beat unranked Florida, 20-18; ORANGE—No. 4 Alabama beat No. 3 Nebraska, 39-28; BLUEBONNET—No. 7 Tennessee beat unranked Tulsa, 27-6; GATOR—Unranked Georgia Tech beat No. 10 Texas Tech, 31-21. (Alabama selected No. 1 in final poll but Michigan St. named by UPI and NFF polls and they tied in FW poll)

**1966** *(Returned to final poll taken before bowls)* SUGAR—No. 3 Alabama beat No. 6 Nebraska, 34-7; ROSE—No. 7 Purdue beat unranked Southern Cal, 14-13; COTTON—No. 4 Georgia beat No. 10 Southern Methodist, 24-9; ORANGE—Unranked Florida beat No. 8 Georgia Tech, 27-12; LIBERTY—No. 9 Miami (Fla.) beat unranked Virginia Tech, 14-7. (Notre Dame selected No. 1 by AP, UPI and FW polls and tied with Michigan St. in NFF poll; neither team played in a bowl game and they tied in a regular-season game)

**1967** ROSE—No. 1 Southern Cal beat No. 4 Indiana, 14-3; SUGAR—Unranked Louisiana St. beat No. 6 Wyoming, 20-13; ORANGE—No. 3 Oklahoma beat No. 2 Tennessee, 26-24; COTTON—Unranked Texas A&M beat No. 8 Alabama, 20-16; GATOR—No. 10 Penn St. tied Florida St., 17-17. (Southern Cal selected No. 1 in all four polls)

**1968** *(Returned to final poll taken after bowl games)* ROSE—No. 1 Ohio St. beat No. 2 Southern Cal, 27-16; SUGAR—No. 9 Arkansas beat No. 4 Georgia, 16-2; ORANGE—No. 3 Penn St. beat No. 6 Kansas, 15-14; COTTON—No. 5 Texas beat No. 8 Tennessee, 36-13; BLUEBONNET—No. 20 Southern Methodist beat No. 10 Oklahoma, 28-27; GATOR—No. 16 Missouri beat No. 12 Alabama, 35-10. (Ohio St. remained No. 1)

**1969** COTTON—No. 1 Texas beat No. 9 Notre Dame, 21-17; SUGAR—No. 13 Mississippi beat No. 3 Arkansas, 27-22; ORANGE—No. 2 Penn St. beat No. 6 Missouri, 10-3; ROSE—No. 5 Southern Cal beat No. 7 Michigan, 10-3. (Texas remained No. 1)

**1970** ROSE—No. 12 Stanford beat No. 2 Ohio St., 27-17; COTTON—No. 6 Notre Dame beat No. 1 Texas, 24-11; ROSE—No. 12 Stanford beat No. 2 Ohio St., 27-17; SUGAR—No. 5 Tennessee beat No. 11 Air Force, 34-13; ORANGE—No. 3 Nebraska beat No. 8 Louisiana St., 17-12; PEACH—No. 9 Arizona St. beat unranked North Caro., 48-26. (Nebraska selected No. 1 in AP and FW polls while Texas was No. 1 in UPI and tied with Ohio St. in NFF poll)

**1971** ORANGE—No. 1 Nebraska beat No. 2 Alabama, 38-6; SUGAR—No. 3 Oklahoma beat No. 5 Auburn, 40-22; ROSE—No. 16 Stanford beat No. 4 Michigan, 13-12; GATOR—No. 6 Georgia beat unranked North Caro., 7-3; COTTON—No. 10 Penn St. beat No. 12 Texas, 30-6; FIESTA—No. 8 Arizona St. beat Florida St., 45-38; BLUEBONNET—No. 7 Colorado beat No. 15 Houston, 29-17. (Nebraska remained No. 1 in all four polls)

**1972** ROSE—No. 1 Southern Cal beat No. 3 Ohio St., 42-17; COTTON—No. 7 Texas beat No. 4 Alabama, 17-13; SUGAR—No. 2 Oklahoma beat No. 5 Penn St., 14-0; ORANGE—No. 9

Nebraska beat No. 12 Notre Dame, 40-6; GATOR—No. 6 Auburn beat No. 13 Colorado, 24-3; BLUEBONNET—No. 11 Tennessee beat No. 10 Louisiana St., 24-17. (Southern Cal remained No. 1 in all four polls)

**1973**  SUGAR—No. 3 Notre Dame beat No. 1 Alabama, 24-23; ROSE—No. 4 Ohio St. beat No. 7 Southern Cal, 42-21; ORANGE—No. 6 Penn St. beat No. 13 Louisiana St., 16-9; COTTON—No. 12 Nebraska beat No. 8 Texas, 19-3; FIESTA—No. 10 Arizona St. beat unranked Pittsburgh, 28-7; BLUEBONNET—No. 14 Houston beat No. 17 Tulane, 47-7. (Notre Dame selected No. 1 in AP, FW and NFF polls, Alabama named No. 1 by UPI but No. 2 Oklahoma was on probation and could not go to a bowl game)

**1974**  ROSE—No. 5 Southern Cal beat No. 3 Ohio St., 18-17; ORANGE—No. 9 Notre Dame beat No. 2 Alabama, 13-11; GATOR—No. 6 Auburn beat No. 11 Texas, 27-3; COTTON—No. 7 Penn St. beat No. 12 Baylor, 41-20; SUGAR—No. 8 Nebraska beat No. 18 Florida, 13-10; LIBERTY—Unranked Tennessee beat No. 10 Maryland, 7-3. (Oklahoma selected No. 1 in AP poll despite being on probation and not able to participate in bowl game; Southern Cal named No. 1 by UPI, FW and NFF polls)

**1975**  ROSE—No. 11 UCLA beat No. 1 Ohio St., 23-10; ORANGE—No. 3 Oklahoma beat No. 5 Michigan, 14-6; LIBERTY—No. 17 Southern Cal beat No. 2 Texas A&M, 20-0; SUGAR—No. 4 Alabama beat No. 8 Penn St., 13-6; FIESTA—No. 7 Arizona St. beat No. 6 Nebraska, 17-14; COTTON—No. 18 Arkansas beat No. 12 Georgia, 31-10; BLUEBONNET—No. 9 Texas beat No. 10 Colorado, 38-21. (Oklahoma selected No. 1 in all four polls)

**1976**  SUGAR—No. 1 Pittsburgh beat No. 5 Georgia, 27-3; ROSE—No. 3 Southern Cal beat No. 2 Michigan, 14-6; COTTON—No. 6 Houston beat No. 4 Maryland, 30-21; LIBERTY—No. 16 Alabama beat No. 7 UCLA, 36-6; ORANGE—No. 11 Ohio St. beat No. 12 Colorado, 27-10; FIESTA—No. 8 Oklahoma beat unranked Wyoming, 41-7; SUN—No. 10 Texas A&M beat unranked Florida, 37-14; BLUEBONNET—No. 13 Nebraska beat No. 9 Texas Tech, 27-24. (Pittsburgh remained No. 1 in all four polls)

**1977**  COTTON—No. 5 Notre Dame beat No. 1 Texas, 38-10; ORANGE—No. 6 Arkansas beat No. 2 Oklahoma, 31-6; SUGAR—No. 3 Alabama beat No. 9 Ohio St., 35-6; ROSE—No. 13 Washington beat No. 4 Michigan, 27-20; FIESTA—No. 8 Penn St. beat No. 15 Arizona St., 42-30; GATOR—No. 10 Pittsburgh beat No. 11 Clemson, 34-3. (Notre Dame selected No. 1 in all four polls)

**1978**  SUGAR—No. 2 Alabama beat No. 1 Penn St., 14-7; ROSE—No. 3 Southern Cal beat No. 5 Michigan, 17-10; ORANGE—No. 4 Oklahoma beat No. 6 Nebraska, 31-24; COTTON—No. 10 Notre Dame beat No. 9 Houston, 35-34; GATOR—No. 7 Clemson beat No. 20 Ohio St., 17-15; FIESTA—No. 8 Arkansas tied with No. 15 UCLA, 10-10. (Alabama selected No. 1 in AP, FW and NFF polls while Southern Cal named in UPI)

**1979**  ROSE—No. 3 Southern Cal beat No. 1 Ohio St., 17-16; SUGAR—No. 2 Alabama beat No. 6 Arkansas, 24-9; ORANGE—No. 5 Oklahoma beat No. 4 Florida St., 24-7; COTTON—No. 8 Houston beat No. 7 Nebraska, 17-14; SUN—No. 13 Washington beat No. 11 Texas, 14-7; FIESTA—No. 10 Pittsburgh beat unranked Arizona, 16-10. (Alabama selected No. 1 in all four polls)

**1980**  SUGAR—No. 1 Georgia beat No. 7 Notre Dame, 17-10; ORANGE—No. 4 Oklahoma beat No. 2 Florida St., 18-17; ROSE—No. 5 Michigan beat No. 16 Washington, 23-6; COTTON—No. 9 Alabama beat No. 6 Baylor, 30-2; GATOR—No. 3 Pittsburgh beat No. 18 South Caro., 37-9; SUN—No. 8 Nebraska beat No. 17 Mississippi St., 31-17; FIESTA—No. 10 Penn St. beat No. 11 Ohio St., 31-19; BLUEBONNET—No. 13 North Caro. beat unranked Texas, 16-7. (Georgia remained No. 1 in all four polls)

**1981**  ORANGE—No. 1 Clemson beat No. 4 Nebraska, 22-15; SUGAR—No. 10 Pittsburgh beat No. 2 Georgia, 24-20; COTTON—No. 6 Texas beat No. 3 Alabama, 14-12; GATOR—No. 11 North Caro. beat Arkansas, 31-27; ROSE—No. 12 Washington beat No. 13 Iowa, 28-0; FIESTA—No. 7 Penn St. beat No. 8 Southern Cal, 26-10. (Clemson remained No. 1 in all four polls)

**1982**  SUGAR—No. 2 Penn St. beat No. 1 Georgia, 27-23; ORANGE—No. 3 Nebraska beat No. 13 Louisiana St., 21-20; COTTON—No. 4 Southern Methodist beat No. 6 Pittsburgh, 7-3; ROSE—No. 5 UCLA beat No. 19 Michigan, 24-14; ALOHA—No. 9 Washington beat No. 16 Maryland, 21-20; FIESTA—No. 11 Arizona St. beat No. 12 Oklahoma, 32-21; BLUEBONNET—No. 14 Arkansas beat Florida, 28-24. (Penn St. selected No. 1 in all four polls)

**1983**  ORANGE—No. 5 Miami (Fla.) beat No. 1 Nebraska, 31-30; COTTON—No. 7 Georgia beat No. 2 Texas, 10-9; SUGAR—No. 3 Auburn beat No. 8 Michigan, 9-7; ROSE—Unranked UCLA beat No. 4 Illinois, 45-9; HOLIDAY—No. 9 Brigham Young beat unranked Missouri, 21-17; GATOR—No. 11 Florida beat No. 10 Iowa, 14-6; FIESTA—No. 14 Ohio St. beat No. 15 Pittsburgh, 28-23. (Miami, Fla., selected No. 1 in all four polls)

**1984**  HOLIDAY—No. 1 Brigham Young beat unranked Michigan, 24-17; ORANGE—No. 4 Washington beat No. 2 Oklahoma, 28-17; SUGAR—No. 5 Nebraska beat No. 11 Louisiana St., 28-10; ROSE—No. 18 Southern Cal beat No. 6 Ohio St., 20-17; COTTON—No. 8 Boston College beat Houston, 45-28; GATOR—No. 9 Oklahoma St. beat No. 7 South Caro., 21-14; ALOHA—No. 10 Southern Methodist beat No. 17 Notre Dame, 27-20. (Brigham Young remained No. 1 in all four polls)

**1985**  ORANGE—No. 3 Oklahoma beat No. 1 Penn St., 25-10; SUGAR—No. 8 Tennessee beat No. 2 Miami (Fla.), 35-7; ROSE—No. 13 UCLA beat No. 4 Iowa, 45-28; COTTON—No. 11 Texas A&M beat No. 16 Auburn, 36-16; FIESTA—No. 5 Michigan beat No. 7 Nebraska, 27-23; BLUEBONNET—No. 10 Air Force beat unranked Texas, 24-16. (Oklahoma selected No. 1 in all four polls)

**1986**  FIESTA—No. 2 Penn St. beat No. 1 Miami (Fla.), 14-10; ORANGE—No. 3 Oklahoma beat No. 9 Arkansas, 42-8; ROSE—No. 7 Arizona St. beat No. 4 Michigan, 22-15; SUGAR—No. 6 Nebraska beat No. 5 Louisiana St., 30-15; COTTON—No. 11 Ohio St. beat No. 8 Texas A&M,

498                                                                                    *1993 NCAA FOOTBALL*

28-12; CITRUS—No. 10 Auburn beat unranked Southern Cal, 16-7; SUN—No. 13 Alabama beat No. 12 Washington, 28-6. (Penn St. selected No. 1 in all four polls)

**1987** ORANGE—No. 2 Miami (Fla.) beat No. 1 Oklahoma, 20-14; FIESTA—No. 3 Florida St. beat No. 5 Nebraska, 31-28; SUGAR—No. 4 Syracuse tied No. 6 Auburn, 16-16; ROSE—No. 8 Michigan St. beat No. 16 Southern Cal, 20-17; COTTON—No. 13 Texas A&M beat No. 12 Notre Dame, 35-10; GATOR—No. 7 Louisiana St. beat No. 9 South Caro., 30-13; ALOHA—No. 10 UCLA beat unranked Florida, 20-16. (Miami, Fla., selected No. 1 in all four polls)

**1988** FIESTA—No. 1 Notre Dame beat No. 3 West Va., 34-21; ORANGE—No. 2 Miami (Fla.) beat No. 6 Nebraska, 23-3; SUGAR—No. 4 Florida St. beat No. 7 Auburn, 13-7; ROSE—No. 11 Michigan beat No. 5 Southern Cal, 22-14; COTTON—No. 9 UCLA beat No. 8 Arkansas, 17-3; CITRUS—No. 13 Clemson beat No. 10 Oklahoma, 13-6. (Notre Dame selected No. 1 in all four polls)

**1989** ORANGE—No. 4 Notre Dame beat No. 1 Colorado, 21-6; SUGAR—No. 2 Miami (Fla.) beat No. 7 Alabama, 33-25; ROSE—No. 12 Southern Cal beat No. 3 Michigan, 17-10; COTTON—No. 8 Tennessee beat No. 10 Arkansas, 31-27; FIESTA—No. 5 Florida St. beat No. 6 Nebraska, 41-17; HALL OF FAME—No. 9 Auburn beat No. 21 Ohio St., 31-14; CITRUS—No. 11 Illinois beat No. 15 Virginia, 31-21. (Miami, Fla., selected No. 1 in all four polls)

**1990** ORANGE—No. 1 Colorado beat No. 5 Notre Dame, 10-9; CITRUS—No. 2 Georgia Tech beat No. 19 Nebraska, 45-21; COTTON—No. 4 Miami (Fla.) beat No. 3 Texas, 46-3; BLOCKBUS-TER—No. 6 Florida St. beat No. 7 Penn St., 24-17; ROSE—No. 8 Washington beat No. 17 Iowa, 46-34; GATOR—No. 12 Michigan beat No. 15 Mississippi, 35-3; SUGAR—No. 10 Tennessee beat unranked Virginia, 23-22. (Colorado selected No. 1 in AP, FW and NFF polls but Georgia Tech picked in UPI poll)

**1991** ORANGE—No. 1 Miami (Fla.) beat No. 11 Nebraska, 22-0; ROSE—No. 2 Washington beat No. 4 Michigan, 34-14; COTTON—No. 5 Florida St. beat No. 9 Texas A&M, 10-3; BLOCKBUSTER—No. 8 Alabama beat No. 15 Colorado, 30-25; SUGAR—No. 18 Notre Dame beat No. 3 Florida, 39-28; FIESTA—No. 6 Penn St. beat No. 10 Tennessee, 42-17; CITRUS—No. 14 California beat No. 13 Clemson, 37-13; PEACH—No. 12 East Caro. beat No. 21 North Caro. St., 37-34; HOLIDAY—No. 7 Iowa tied unranked Brigham Young, 13-13. (Miami, Fla., selected No. 1 in AP poll while Washington named in USA/CNN, NFF and FW polls)

**1992** SUGAR—No. 2 Alabama beat No. 1 Miami (Fla.), 34-13; GATOR—No. 14 Florida beat No. 12 North Caro. St., 27-10; COTTON—No. 5 Notre Dame beat No. 4 Texas A&M, 28-3; HALL OF FAME—No. 17 Tennessee beat No. 16 Boston College, 38-23; CITRUS—No. 8 Georgia beat No. 15 Ohio St., 21-14; ROSE—No. 7 Michigan beat No. 9 Washington, 38-31; ORANGE—No. 3 Florida St. beat No. 11 Nebraska, 27-14; FIESTA—No. 6 Syracuse beat No. 10 Colorado, 26-22; BLOCKBUSTER—No. 13 Stanford beat No. 21 Penn St., 24-3; PEACH—No. 19 North Caro. beat No. 24 Mississippi St., 21-17; COPPER—No. 18 Washington St. beat unranked Utah, 31-28. (Alabama selected No. 1 in all four polls)

# MOST CONSECUTIVE BOWL-GAME VICTORIES
### (Bowls do not have to be in consecutive years)

| College | Victories (Years) |
|---|---|
| Southern Cal | 9 (1923-24-30-32-33-39-40-44-45) |
| Florida St. | 8 (1985-86-88-89-90-90-92-93) |
| UCLA | 8 (1983-84-85-86-86-87-89-91) |
| Georgia Tech | 8 (1947-48-52-53-54-55-56-56) |
| Alabama | 6 (1975-76-78-79-80-81) |
| Syracuse | 5 (1989-89-90-92-93) |
| Notre Dame | 5 (1973-75-76-78-79) |
| Arizona St. | 5 (1970-71-72-73-75) |
| Air Force | 4 (1982-83-84-85) |
| Alabama | 4 (1982-83-85-86) |

# MOST CONSECUTIVE SEASONS WITH BOWL-GAME VICTORIES
### Bowl, Opponent, Score

*8 Florida St.—85 Gator, Oklahoma St. 34-23; 86 All-American, Indiana 27-13; 87 Fiesta, Nebraska 31-28; 88 Sugar, Auburn 13-7; 89 Fiesta, Nebraska 41-17; 90 Blockbuster, Penn St. 24-17; 92 Cotton, Texas A&M 10-2; 93 Orange, Nebraska 27-14. Coach: Bobby Bowden.

7 UCLA—83 Rose, Michigan 24-14; 84 Rose, Illinois 45-9; 85 Fiesta, Miami (Fla.) 39-37; 86 Rose, Iowa 45-28; 86 Freedom, Brigham Young 31-10; 87 Aloha, Florida 20-16; 89 Cotton, Arkansas, 17-3. Coach: Terry Donahue.

6 Alabama—75 Sugar, Penn St. 13-6; 76 Liberty, UCLA 36-6; 78 Sugar, Ohio St. 35-6; 79 Sugar, Penn St. 14-7; 80 Sugar, Arkansas 24-9; 81 Cotton, Baylor 30-2. Coach: Paul "Bear" Bryant.

6 Nebraska—69 Sun, Georgia 45-6; 71 Orange, Louisiana St. 17-12; 72 Orange, Alabama 38-6; 73 Orange, Notre Dame 40-6; 74 Cotton, Texas 19-3; 74 Sugar, Florida 13-10. Coaches: Bob Devaney first 4 games, Tom Osborne last 2.

6 Georgia Tech—52 Orange, Baylor 17-14; 53 Sugar, Mississippi 24-7; 54 Sugar, West Va. 42-19; 55 Cotton, Arkansas 14-6; 56 Sugar, Pittsburgh 7-0; 56 Gator, Pittsburgh 21-14. Coach: Bobby Dodd.

* Active streak.

*Bowls and Polls*

# ACTIVE CONSECUTIVE APPEARANCES IN BOWL GAMES
### (Must have appeared in 1992-93 bowls)

| Team | Appearances | Team | Appearances |
|---|---|---|---|
| Nebraska | 24 | Syracuse | 6 |
| Michigan | 18 | Illinois | 5 |
| Brigham Young | 15 | Alabama | 4 |
| Florida St. | 11 | Tennessee | 4 |
| Miami (Fla.) | 10 | Texas A&M | 4 |
| Notre Dame | 6 | Washington | 4 |

## UNDEFEATED, UNTIED TEAM MATCHUPS IN BOWL GAMES

| Bowl | Date | Winner (record going in, coach) | Loser (record going in, coach) |
|---|---|---|---|
| Rose | 1-1-21 | California 28 (8-0, Andy Smith) | Ohio St. 0 (7-0, John Wilce) |
| Rose | 1-2-22 | 0-0 tie: California (9-0, Andy Smith) Wash. & Jeff. (10-0, Earle "Greasy" Neale) | |
| Rose | 1-1-27 | 7-7 tie: Stanford (10-0, Glenn "Pop" Warner) Alabama (9-0, Wallace Wade) | |
| Rose | 1-1-31 | Alabama 24 (9-0, Wallace Wade) | Washington St. 0 (9-0, Orin "Babe" Hollingbery) |
| Orange | 1-2-39 | Tennessee 17 (10-0, Bob Neyland) | Oklahoma 0 (10-0, Tom Stidham) |
| Sugar | 1-1-41 | Boston College 19 (10-0, Frank Leahy) | Tennessee 13 (10-0, Bob Neyland) |
| Sugar | 1-1-52 | Maryland 28 (9-0, Jim Tatum) | Tennessee 13 (10-0, Bob Neyland) |
| Orange | 1-2-56 | Oklahoma 20 (10-0, Bud Wilkinson) | Maryland 6 (10-0, Jim Tatum) |
| Orange | 1-1-72 | Nebraska 38 (12-0, Bob Devaney) | Alabama 6 (11-0, Paul "Bear" Bryant) |
| Sugar | 12-31-73 | Notre Dame 24 (10-0, Ara Parseghian) | Alabama 23 (11-0, Paul "Bear" Bryant) |
| Fiesta | 1-2-87 | Penn St. 14 (11-0, Joe Paterno) | Miami (Fla.) 10 (11-0, Jimmy Johnson) |
| Orange | 1-1-88 | Miami (Fla.) 20 (11-0, Jimmy Johnson) | Oklahoma 14 (11-0, Barry Switzer) |
| Fiesta | 1-2-89 | Notre Dame 34 (11-0, Lou Holtz) | West Va. 21 (11-0, Don Nehlen) |
| Sugar | 1-1-93 | Alabama 34 (12-0, Gene Stallings) | Miami (Fla.) 13 (11-0, Dennis Erickson) |

## UNDEFEATED TEAM MATCHUPS IN BOWL GAMES
### (Both teams were undefeated but one or both was tied one or more times)

| Bowl | Date | Winner (record going in, coach) | Loser (record going in, coach) |
|---|---|---|---|
| Rose | 1-1-25 | Notre Dame 27 (9-0, Knute Rockne) | Stanford 10 (7-0-1, Glenn "Pop" Warner) |
| Rose | 1-1-26 | Alabama 20 (9-0, Wallace Wade) | Washington 19 (10-0-1, Enoch Bagshaw) |
| Rose | 1-2-33 | Southern Cal 35 (9-0, Howard Jones) | Pittsburgh 0 (8-0-2, Jock Sutherland) |
| Rose | 1-1-35 | Alabama 29 (9-0, Frank Thomas) | Stanford 13 (9-0-1, Claude "Tiny" Thornhill) |
| Rose | 1-1-38 | California 13 (9-0-1, Leonard "Stub" Allison) | Alabama 0 (9-0, Frank Thomas) |
| Rose | 1-1-40 | Southern Cal 14 (7-0-2, Howard Jones) | Tennessee 0 (10-0, Bob Neyland) |
| Sugar | 1-1-40 | Texas A&M 14 (10-0, Homer Norton) | Tulane 13 (8-0-1, Lowell "Red" Dawson) |
| Rose | 1-1-45 | Southern Cal 25 (7-0-2, Jeff Cravath) | Tennessee 0 (7-0-1, John Barnhill) |
| Cotton | 1-1-48 | 13-13 tie: Southern Methodist (9-0-1, Matty Bell) Penn St. (9-0, Bob Higgins) | |

| Bowl | Date | Winner (record going in, coach) | Loser (record going in, coach) |
|---|---|---|---|
| Orange | 1-1-51 | Clemson 15 (8-0-1, Frank Howard) | Miami (Fla.) 14 (9-0-1, Andy Gustafson) |
| Sugar | 1-1-53 | Georgia Tech 24 (11-0, Bobby Dodd) | Mississippi 7 (8-0-2, John Vaught) |
| Rose | 1-1-69 | Ohio St. 27 (9-0, Woody Hayes) | Southern Cal 16 (9-0-1, John McKay) |
| Rose | 1-1-80 | Southern Cal 17 (10-0-1, John Robinson) | Ohio St. 16 (11-0, Earle Bruce) |
| California | 12-14-85 | Fresno St. 51 (10-0-1, Jim Sweeney) | Bowling Green 7 (11-0, Denny Stolz) |

## REGULAR-SEASON MAJOR-BOWL GAME REMATCHES

| Date | Regular Season | Date | Bowl Game Rematch |
|---|---|---|---|
| 10-6-56 | Iowa 14, Oregon St. 13 | 1-1-57 | (Rose) Iowa 35, Oregon St. 19 |
| 10-31-59 | Louisiana St. 7, Mississippi 3 | 1-1-60 | (Sugar) Mississippi 21, Louisiana St. 0 |
| 9-18-65 | Michigan St. 13, UCLA 3 | 1-1-66 | (Rose) UCLA 14, Michigan St. 12 |
| 10-4-75 | Ohio St. 41, UCLA 20 | 1-1-76 | (Rose) UCLA 23, Ohio St. 10 |
| 11-11-78 | Nebraska 17, Oklahoma 14 | 1-1-79 | (Orange) Oklahoma 31, Nebraska 24 |
| 9-25-82 | UCLA 31, Michigan 27 | 1-1-83 | (Rose) UCLA 24, Michigan 14 |
| 9-7-87 | Michigan St. 27, Southern Cal 13 | 1-1-88 | (Rose) Michigan St. 20, Southern Cal 17 |

## BOWL-GAME FACTS
### THE BOWL/BASKETBALL CONNECTION

Nine times in history, a football bowl winner also won the NCAA basketball championship during the same academic year. They are as follows:

| Year | School | Bowl | Date of Bowl |
|---|---|---|---|
| 1992-93 | North Caro. | Peach | 1-2-93 |
| 1988-89 | Michigan | Rose | 1-2-89 |
| 1981-82 | North Caro. | Gator | 12-28-81 |
| 1973-74 | North Caro. St. | Liberty | 12-17-73 |
| 1965-66 | UTEP | Sun | 12-31-65 |
| 1950-51 | Kentucky | Sugar | 1-1-51 |
| 1947-48 | Kentucky | Great Lakes | 12-6-47 |
| 1945-46 | Oklahoma St. | Sugar | 1-1-46 |
| 1944-45 | Oklahoma St. | Cotton | 1-1-45 |

### ONE-TIME WONDERS

Twelve major-college teams have played in only one bowl game in their football history, and only five of those have posted victories. The winners were Eastern Mich., Memphis St., Nevada-Las Vegas, Northern Ill. and Northwestern. The one-time bowlers are as follows:

| Date | School | Bowl | Opponent (Score) |
|---|---|---|---|
| 12-9-89 | Ball St. | California | Fresno St. (6-27) |
| 12-17-83 | Cal St. Fullerton | California | Northern Ill. (13-20) |
| 12-8-90 | Central Mich. | California | San Jose St. (24-48) |
| 12-12-87 | Eastern Mich. | California | San Jose St. (30-27) |
| 12-11-82 | Kansas St. | Independence | Wisconsin (3-14) |
| 12-29-72 | Kent | Tangerine | Tampa (18-21) |
| 12-19-70 | Long Beach St. | Pasadena | Louisville (24-24) |
| 12-18-71 | Memphis St. | Pasadena | San Jose St. (28-9) |
| 12-15-84 | Nevada-Las Vegas | California | Toledo (30-13) |
| 12-17-83 | Northern Ill. | California | Cal St. Fullerton (20-13) |
| 1-1-49 | Northwestern | Rose | California (20-14) |
| 12-16-78 | Rutgers | Garden State | Arizona St. (18-34) |

### YEAR-BY-YEAR BOWL FACTS

(A note about bowl-game dates: Traditionally, bowl games have been played on January 1, but as more bowl games joined the holiday lineup, schedule adjustments were made whereby some bowl games are now played as early as mid-December. In the interest of avoiding confusion, all years referred to in bowl records are the actual calendar year in which the bowl game was played.)

**1917** Coach Hugo Bezdek led the first of three teams to the Rose Bowl from 1917 to 1923. His Oregon team beat Pennsylvania, 14-0, in 1917; his Mare Island squad defeated Camp Lewis, 19-7, in 1918, and his Penn St. team lost to Southern Cal, 14-3, in 1923. In his 1923 trip with the Nittany Lions, Bezdek almost came to blows with Southern Cal coach Elmer "Gloomy Gus" Henderson because Penn St. did not arrive for the game until an hour after the scheduled kickoff time.

*Bowls and Polls*

Henderson accused Bezdek of not taking the field until the hot California sun had gone down to give his winterized Easterners an advantage.

**1919** George Halas (yes, "Papa Bear") was the player of the game for Great Lakes Naval Training Station in Chicago as the Sailors shut out Mare Island, 17-0, in another of the wartime Rose Bowls.

**1923** The first Rose Bowl game actually played in the stadium in Pasadena saw Southern Cal defeat Penn St., 14-3.

**1926** Johnny Mack Brown, one of Hollywood's most famous movie cowboys, also was one of college football's most exciting players at Alabama. He was selected as player of the game for the Rose Bowl in the Crimson Tide's 20-19 victory over Washington.

**1927** The Rose Bowl becomes the first coast-to-coast radio broadcast of a sporting event.

**1929** The Rose Bowl game became one of the most famous in bowl history because of California player Roy Riegels' now-legendary wrong-way run. Early in the second quarter, with each team just changing directions, Georgia Tech was on its own 20. Tech halfback Stumpy Thompson broke for a seven-yard run, fumbled, and Riegels picked up the ball, momentarily headed for the Tech goal, then reversed his field and started running the wrong way. Teammate Benny Lom tried to stop him and finally did on the California one-yard line, where the dazed Riegels was pounced on by a group of Tech tacklers. Lom went back to punt on the next play and the kick was blocked out of the end zone for a safety, which decided the contest, eventually won by Tech, 8-7. Riegels died in early 1993.

**1938** The first Orange Bowl played in Miami's new stadium, which sat 22,000 at the time, saw Auburn edge Michigan St., 6-0. Also, in the second annual Cotton Bowl, Colorado's do-it-all standout Byron "Whizzer" White, the Rhodes Scholar and U.S. Supreme Court justice, passed for one score and returned a pass interception for another, but the Buffs lost to Rice, 28-14.

**1941** On December 6, 1941, Hawaii defeated Willamette, 20-6, but a second postseason game, scheduled with San Jose St. for the next week, was cancelled after the attack on Pearl Harbor.

**1942** You would think a team making only one first down and gaining only 75 yards to its opponents' 309 yards could not come out of a game a 29-21 victor, but it happened in the Cotton Bowl as Alabama downed Texas A&M. The Tide intercepted seven of A&M's 42 passes and recovered five Aggie fumbles. Also, the Rose Bowl was moved for one year to Durham, N.C., because of wartime considerations that precluded large gatherings on the West Coast, and Oregon St. downed Duke, 20-16.

**1946** The first and only bowl game decided after time expired was the Orange Bowl when Miami (Fla.) downed Holy Cross, 13-6. Time expired as Miami (Fla.) halfback Al Hudson returned an 89-yard intercepted pass for the deciding score.

**1949** A Pacific Coast team had never been allowed to play in a major bowl other than the Rose Bowl, but the conference fathers let Oregon play in the Cotton Bowl against Southern Methodist. Doak Walker and Kyle Rote led Southern Methodist to a 20-13 victory over the Ducks and quarterback Norm Van Brocklin. John McKay, later the head coach at Southern Cal, also was on the Oregon roster.

**1953** The Rose, Cotton, Sugar and Orange Bowls are televised nationally for the first time.

**1954** Dicky Maegle of Rice may be the best-remembered bowl player, not because of his 265 yards rushing and three touchdowns vs. Alabama in 1954, but because of what happened on a 95-yard scoring run. Alabama's Tommy Lewis became infamous by coming off the bench to tackle Maegle in the Cotton Bowl, won by Rice, 28-6.

**1960** In one of those pupil-vs.-teacher battles, former Georgia Tech player and assistant coach Frank Broyles led his Arkansas Razorbacks to a 14-7 Gator Bowl victory over his former coach, Bobby Dodd, and the Yellow Jackets.

**1962** Oregon St. quarterback Terry Baker turned in the longest run in bowl history with a 99-yard scamper to down Villanova, 6-0, in the Liberty Bowl. Baker, an outstanding athlete, became the only Heisman Trophy winner to play in an NCAA Final Four basketball game later that academic year (1963).

**1964** Utah and West Va. became the first teams to play a major bowl game indoors when they met in the Atlantic City Convention Hall. Utah won, 32-6, beneath the bright indoor lights.

**1965** The first Orange Bowl played under the lights in Miami saw Texas stun national champion Alabama and quarterback Joe Namath, 21-17.

**1968** It was the student beating the teacher in the Cotton Bowl as Texas A&M head coach Gene Stallings saw his Aggies hold on for a 20-16 victory over Alabama and legendary head coach Paul "Bear" Bryant. Stallings had played (at Texas A&M) and coached (at Alabama) under Bryant. The "Bear" met Stallings at midfield after the contest and lifted the 6-foot-3 Aggie coach up in admiration. Also, the Astro-Bluebonnet Bowl (also known as the Bluebonnet Bowl) became the first bowl game to be played in a domed stadium as the Astrodome served as the site of the December 31, 1968, game between Southern Methodist (28) and Oklahoma (27).

**1970** Three of the four surviving legendary Four Horsemen of Notre Dame came to Dallas to watch the Fighting Irish drop a 21-17 Cotton Bowl game to Texas. The only other time Notre Dame had played in a bowl game was the 1925 Rose Bowl, when the Four Horsemen led the Irish to a 27-10 victory over Stanford.

**1971** Notre Dame snapped the second-longest winning streak going into a bowl game by halting Texas' 30-game string, 24-11, in the Cotton Bowl. In 1951, Kentucky had stopped Oklahoma's 31-game streak in the Sugar Bowl, 13-7.

**1976** Archie Griffin started his fourth straight Rose Bowl for Ohio St. (1973-76), totaling 412 yards on 79 carries in the four games. The Buckeyes, under legendary head coach Woody Hayes, won only the 1974 contest, but Griffin is the only collegiate player to win two Heisman Trophies (1974-75).

## POSTSEASON GAMES

### OTHER OR UNSANCTIONED BOWLS

The following bowl games were unsanctioned by the NCAA or otherwise had no team classified as major college at the time of the bowl. In many cases, statistics are not available and the scores are listed only to provide a historical reference. Attendance for the game, if known, is listed in parentheses after the score.

**Bluegrass Bowl (Louisville, Ky.):** 12-13-58—Oklahoma St. 15, Florida St. 6 (7,000)

**Grape Bowl (Lodi, Calif.):** 12-13-47—Pacific (Cal.) 35, Utah St. 21 (12,000); 12-11-48—Pacific (Cal.) 35, Hardin-Simmons 35 (11,000)

**New Year's Classic (Honolulu, Hawaii):** 1-1-34—Santa Clara 26, Hawaii 7; 1-1-35—Hawaii 14, California 0 (later called Poi Bowl)

**Optimist Bowl (Houston, Texas):** 12-21-46—North Texas 14, Pacific (Cal.) 13 (10,000)

**Palm Festival (Miami, Fla.):** 1-1-33—Miami (Fla.) 7, Manhattan 0 (6,000); 1-1-34—Duquesne 33, Miami (Fla.) 7 (3,500) (forerunner to Orange Bowl)

**Pineapple Bowl (Honolulu, Hawaii):** 1-1-40—Oregon St. 39, Hawaii 6; 1-1-41—Fresno St. 3, Hawaii 0; 1-1-47—Hawaii 19, Utah 16; 1-1-48—Hawaii 33, Redlands 32; 1-1-49—Oregon St. 47, Hawaii 27 (15,000); 1-2-50—Stanford 74, Hawaii 20; 1-1-51—Hawaii 28, Denver 27; 1-1-52—San Diego St. 34, Hawaii 13

**Poi Bowl (Honolulu, Hawaii):** 1-1-36—Southern Cal 38, Hawaii 6; 1-2-37—Hawaii 18, Honolulu All-Stars 12; 1-1-38—Washington 53, Hawaii 13; 1-2-39—UCLA 32, Hawaii 7 (later called Pineapple Bowl)

### POSTSEASON BOWL INVOLVING NON-I-A TEAMS
#### HERITAGE BOWL

**Site:** Tallahassee, Fla.
**Stadium (Capacity):** Bragg Memorial (25,500)
**Name Changes:** Alamo Heritage Bowl (1991); Heritage Bowl (1993)
**Playing Surface:** Grass
**Playing Sites:** Joe Robbie Stadium, Miami (1991); Bragg Memorial Stadium, Tallahassee (since 1993)

| Date | Score (Attendance) |
|---|---|
| 12-21-91 | Alabama St. 36, North Caro. A&T 13 (7,724) |
| 1-2-93 | Grambling 45, Florida A&M 15 (11,273) |

### NCAA-CERTIFIED ALL-STAR GAMES
#### EAST-WEST SHRINE CLASSIC

**Present Site:** Palo Alto, Calif.
**Stadium (Capacity):** Stanford (85,500)
**Playing Surface:** Grass
**Playing Sites:** Ewing Field, San Francisco (1925); Kezar Stadium, San Francisco (1927-41); Sugar Bowl, New Orleans (1942); Kezar Stadium, San Francisco (1943-66); Candlestick Park, San Francisco (1967-68); Stanford Stadium, Palo Alto (1969); Oakland Coliseum (1971); Candlestick Park, San Francisco (1971-73); Stanford Stadium, Palo Alto (since 1974)

| Date | Score (Attendance) | Date | Score (Attendance) | Date | Score (Attendance) |
|---|---|---|---|---|---|
| 12-26-25 | West 6-0 (20,000) | 1-1-46 | Tie 7-7 (60,000) | 12-31-65 | West 22-7 (47,000) |
| 1-1-27 | West 7-3 (15,000) | 1-1-47 | West 13-9 (60,000) | 12-31-66 | East 45-22 (46,000) |
| 12-26-27 | West 16-6 (27,500) | 1-1-48 | East 40-9 (60,000) | 12-30-67 | East 16-14 (29,000) |
| 12-29-28 | East 20-0 (55,000) | 1-1-49 | East 14-12 (60,000) | 12-28-68 | West 18-7 (29,000) |
| 1-1-30 | East 19-7 (58,000) | 12-31-49 | East 28-6 (60,000) | 12-27-69 | West 15-0 (70,000) |
| 12-27-30 | West 3-0 (40,000) | 12-30-50 | West 16-7 (60,000) | 1-2-71 | West 17-13 (50,000) |
| 1-1-32 | East 6-0 (45,000) | 12-29-51 | East 15-14 (60,000) | 12-31-71 | West 17-13 (35,000) |
| 1-2-33 | West 21-13 (45,000) | 12-27-52 | East 21-20 (60,000) | 12-30-72 | East 9-3 (37,000) |
| 1-1-34 | West 12-0 (35,000) | 1-2-54 | West 31-7 (60,000) | 12-29-73 | East 35-7 (30,000) |
| 1-1-35 | West 19-13 (52,000) | 1-1-55 | East 13-12 (60,000) | 12-28-74 | East 16-14 (35,000) |
| 1-1-36 | East 19-3 (55,000) | 12-31-55 | East 29-6 (60,000) | 1-3-76 | West 21-14 (75,000) |
| 1-1-37 | East 3-0 (38,000) | 12-29-56 | West 7-6 (60,000) | 1-2-77 | West 30-14 (45,000) |
| 1-1-38 | Tie 0-0 (55,000) | 12-28-57 | West 27-13 (60,000) | 12-31-77 | West 23-3 (65,000) |
| 1-2-39 | West 14-0 (60,000) | 12-27-58 | East 26-14 (60,000) | 1-6-79 | East 56-17 (72,000) |
| 1-1-40 | West 28-11 (60,000) | 1-2-60 | West 21-14 (60,000) | 1-5-80 | West 20-10 (75,000) |
| 1-1-41 | West 20-14 (60,000) | 12-31-60 | East 7-0 (60,000) | 1-10-81 | East 21-3 (76,000) |
| 1-3-42 | Tie 6-6 (35,000) | 12-30-61 | West 21-8 (60,000) | 1-9-82 | West 20-13 (75,000) |
| 1-1-43 | East 13-12 (57,000) | 12-29-62 | East 25-19 (60,000) | 1-15-83 | East 26-25 (72,999) |
| 1-1-44 | Tie 13-13 (55,000) | 12-28-63 | Tie 6-6 (60,000) | 1-7-84 | East 27-19 (77,000) |
| 1-1-45 | West 13-7 (60,000) | 1-2-65 | West 11-7 (60,000) | 1-5-85 | West 21-10 (72,000) |

| Date | Score (Attendance) | Date | Score (Attendance) |
|---|---|---|---|
| 1-11-86 | East 18-7 (77,000) | 1-24-91 | West 24-21 (70,000) |
| 1-10-87 | West 24-21 (74,000) | 1-19-92 | West 14-6 (83,000) |
| 1-16-88 | West 16-13 (62,000) | 1-24-93 | East 31-17 (84,000) |
| 1-16-89 | East 24-6 (76,000) | | |
| 1-21-90 | West 22-21 (78,000) | | |

Series record: West won 35, East 28, 5 ties.

## BLUE-GRAY ALL-STAR CLASSIC

**Present Site:** Montgomery, Ala.
**Stadium (Capacity):** Cramton Bowl (24,600)
**Playing Surface:** Grass
**Playing Sites:** Cramton Bowl, Montgomery (since 1939)

| Date | Score (Attendance) | Date | Score (Attendance) | Date | Score (Attendance) |
|---|---|---|---|---|---|
| 1-2-39 | Blue 7-0 (8,000) | 12-27-58 | Blue 16-0 (16,000) | 12-29-78 | Gray 28-24 (18,380) |
| 12-30-39 | Gray 33-20 (10,000) | 12-26-59 | Blue 20-8 (20,000) | 12-25-79 | Blue 22-13 (18,312) |
| 12-28-40 | Blue 14-12 (14,000) | 12-31-60 | Blue 35-7 (18,000) | 12-25-80 | Blue 24-23 (25,000) |
| 12-27-41 | Gray 16-0 (15,571) | 12-30-61 | Gray 9-7 (18,000) | 12-25-81 | Blue 21-9 (19,000) |
| 12-26-42 | Gray 24-0 (16,000) | 12-29-62 | Blue 10-6 (20,000) | 12-25-82 | Gray 20-10 (21,000) |
| 1943 | No Game | 12-28-63 | Gray 21-14 (20,000) | 12-25-83 | Gray 17-13 (2,000) |
| 12-30-44 | Gray 24-7 (16,000) | 12-26-64 | Blue 10-6 (16,000) | 12-25-84 | Gray 33-6 (24,080) |
| 12-29-45 | Blue 26-0 (20,000) | 12-25-65 | Gray 23-19 (18,000) | 12-25-85 | Blue 27-20 (18,500) |
| 12-28-46 | Gray 20-13 (22,500) | 12-24-66 | Blue 14-9 (18,000) | 12-25-86 | Blue 31-7 (18,500) |
| 12-27-47 | Gray 33-6 (22,500) | 12-30-67 | Blue 22-16 (23,350) | 12-25-87 | Gray 12-10 (20,300) |
| 12-25-48 | Blue 19-13 (15,000) | 12-28-68 | Gray 28-7 (18,000) | 12-25-88 | Blue 22-21 (20,000) |
| 12-31-49 | Gray 27-13 (21,500) | 12-27-69 | Tie 6-6 (21,500) | 12-25-89 | Gray 28-10 (16,000) |
| 12-30-50 | Gray 31-6 (21,000) | 12-28-70 | Gray 38-7 (23,000) | 12-25-90 | Blue 17-14 (17,500) |
| 12-29-51 | Gray 20-14 (22,000) | 12-28-71 | Gray 9-0 (24,000) | 12-25-91 | Gray 20-12 (21,000) |
| 12-27-52 | Gray 28-7 (22,000) | 12-27-72 | Gray 27-15 (20,000) | 12-25-92 | Gray 27-17 (20,500) |
| 12-26-53 | Gray 40-20 (18,500) | 12-18-73 | Blue 20-14 (21,000) | | |
| 12-25-54 | Blue 14-7 (18,000) | 12-17-74 | Blue 29-24 (12,000) | | |
| 12-31-55 | Gray 20-19 (19,000) | 12-19-75 | Blue 14-13 (10,000) | | |
| 12-29-56 | Blue 14-0 (21,000) | 12-24-76 | Gray 31-10 (16,000) | | |
| 12-28-57 | Gray 21-20 (16,000) | 12-30-77 | Blue 20-16 (5,000) | | |

Series record: Gray won 29, Blue 24, 1 tie.

## HULA BOWL

**Present Site:** Honolulu, Hawaii
**Stadium (Capacity):** Aloha (50,000)
**Playing Surface:** AstroTurf
**Format:** From 1947 through 1950, the College All-Stars played the Hawaii All-Stars. Beginning in 1951, the Hawaiian team was augmented by players from the National Football League. This format, however, was changed to an all-collegiate contest—first between the East and West, then between North and South (in 1963), and then back to East and West in 1974. The results reflect the all-collegiate format only.
**Playing Sites:** Honolulu Stadium (1960-74); Aloha Stadium (since 1975)

| Date | Score (Attendance) | Date | Score (Attendance) | Date | Score (Attendance) |
|---|---|---|---|---|---|
| 1-10-60 | East 34-8 (23,000) | 1-4-75 | East 34-25 (22,000) | 1-5-85 | East 34-14 (30,767) |
| 1-8-61 | East 14-7 (17,017) | 1-10-76 | East 16-0 (45,458) | 1-11-86 | West 23-10 (29,564) |
| 1-7-62 | Tie 7-7 (20,598) | 1-8-77 | West 20-17 (45,579) | 1-10-87 | West 16-14 (17,775) |
| 1-6-63 | North 20-13 (20,000) | 1-7-78 | West 42-22 (48,197) | 1-16-88 | West 20-18 (26,737) |
| 1-4-64 | North 20-13 (18,177) | 1-6-79 | East 29-24 (49,132) | 1-7-89 | East 21-10 (25,000) |
| 1-9-65 | South 16-14 (22,100) | 1-5-80 | East 17-10 (47,096) | 1-13-90 | West 21-13 (28,742) |
| 1-8-66 | North 27-26 (25,000) | 1-10-81 | West 24-17 (39,010) | 1-19-91 | East 23-10 (21,926) |
| 1-7-67 | North 28-27 (23,500) | 1-9-82 | West 26-23 (43,002) | 1-11-92 | West 27-20 (23,112) |
| 1-6-68 | North 50-6 (21,000) | 1-15-83 | East 30-14 (39,456) | 1-16-93 | West 13-10 (25,479) |
| 1-4-69 | North 13-7 (23,000) | 1-7-84 | West 21-16 (34,216) | | |
| 1-10-70 | South 35-13 (25,000) | | | | |
| 1-9-71 | North 42-32 (23,500) | | | | |
| 1-8-72 | North 24-7 (23,000) | | | | |
| 1-6-73 | South 17-3 (23,000) | | | | |
| 1-5-74 | East 24-14 (23,000) | | | | |

Series records: North-South (1963-73)—North won 8, South 3. East-West (1960-62 and 1974 to date)—East won 11, West 11, 1 tie.

*1993 NCAA FOOTBALL*

# JAPAN BOWL

**Present Site:** Yokohama, Japan
**Stadium (Capacity):** Yokohama (30,000)
**Playing Surface:** Grass
**Playing Sites:** Tokyo Stadium (1976-79); Yokohama Stadium (since 1980)

| Date | Score (Attendance) | Date | Score (Attendance) | Date | Score (Attendance) |
|---|---|---|---|---|---|
| 1-18-76 | West 27-18 (68,000) | 1-11-86 | East 31-14 (30,000) | 1-12-91 | West 20-14 (30,000) |
| 1-16-77 | West 21-10 (58,000) | 1-11-87 | West 24-17 (30,000) | 1-11-92 | East 14-13 (50,000) |
| 1-15-78 | East 26-10 (32,500) | 1-10-88 | West 17-3 (30,000) | 1-9-93 | East 27-13 (46,000) |
| 1-14-79 | East 33-14 (55,000) | 1-15-89 | East 30-7 (29,000) | | |
| 1-13-80 | West 28-17 (27,000) | 1-13-90 | East 24-10 (27,000) | | |
| 1-17-81 | West 25-13 (30,000) | | | | |
| 1-16-82 | West 28-17 (28,000) | | | | |
| 1-23-83 | West 30-21 (30,000) | | | | |
| 1-15-84 | West 26-21 (26,000) | | | | |
| 1-13-85 | West 28-14 (30,000) | | | | |

Series record: West won 11, East 7.

## CHICAGO COLLEGE ALL-STAR FOOTBALL GAME
### (Discontinued after 1976 game)

An all-star team composed of the top senior collegiate players would meet the National Football League champions (1933-66) or the Super Bowl champions (1967-75) from the previous season, beginning in 1934. The only times the all-stars did not play the league champions were in 1935 and 1946. All games were played at Soldier Field, Chicago, Ill.

| Date | Score (Attendance) |
|---|---|
| 8-31-34 | (Tie) Chicago Bears 0-0 (79,432) |
| 8-29-35 | Chicago Bears 5, All-Stars 0 (77,450) |
| 9-3-36 | (Tie) Detroit 7-7 (76,000) |
| 9-1-37 | All-Stars 6, Green Bay 0 (84,560) |
| 8-31-38 | All-Stars 28, Washington 16 (74,250) |
| 8-30-39 | New York Giants 9, All-Stars 0 (81,456) |
| 8-29-40 | Green Bay 45, All-Stars 28 (84,567) |
| 8-28-41 | Chicago Bears 37, All-Stars 13 (98,203) |
| 8-28-42 | Chicago Bears 21, All-Stars 0 (101,100) |
| 8-25-43 | All-Stars 27, Washington 7 (48,471) |
| 8-30-44 | Chicago Bears 24, All-Stars 21 (48,769) |
| 8-30-45 | Green Bay 19, All-Stars 7 (92,753) |
| 8-23-46 | All-Stars 16, Los Angeles 0 (97,380) |
| 8-22-47 | All-Stars 16, Chicago Bears 0 (105,840) |
| 8-20-48 | Chicago Cardinals 28, All-Stars 0 (101,220) |
| 8-12-49 | Philadelphia 38, All-Stars 0 (93,780) |
| 8-11-50 | All-Stars 17, Philadelphia 7 (88,885) |
| 8-17-51 | Cleveland 33, All-Stars 0 (92,180) |
| 8-15-52 | Los Angeles 10, All-Stars 7 (88,316) |
| 8-14-53 | Detroit 24, All-Stars 10 (93,818) |
| 8-13-54 | Detroit 31, All-Stars 6 (93,470) |
| 8-12-55 | All-Stars 30, Cleveland 27 (75,000) |
| 8-10-56 | Cleveland 26, All-Stars 0 (75,000) |
| 8-9-57 | New York Giants 22, All-Stars 12 (75,000) |
| 8-15-58 | All-Stars 35, Detroit 19 (70,000) |
| 8-14-59 | Baltimore 29, All-Stars 0 (70,000) |
| 8-12-60 | Baltimore 32, All-Stars 7 (70,000) |
| 8-4-61 | Philadelphia 28, All-Stars 14 (66,000) |
| 8-3-62 | Green Bay 42, All-Stars 20 (65,000) |
| 8-2-63 | All-Stars 20, Green Bay 17 (65,000) |
| 8-7-64 | Chicago Bears 28, All-Stars 17 (65,000) |
| 8-6-65 | Cleveland 24, All-Stars 16 (68,000) |
| 8-5-66 | Green Bay 38, All-Stars 0 (72,000) |
| 8-4-67 | Green Bay 27, All-Stars 0 (70,934) |
| 8-2-68 | Green Bay 34, All-Stars 17 (69,917) |
| 8-1-69 | New York Jets 26, All-Stars 24 (74,208) |
| 7-31-70 | Kansas City 24, All-Stars 3 (69,940) |
| 7-30-71 | Baltimore 24, All-Stars 17 (52,289) |
| 7-28-72 | Dallas 20, All-Stars 7 (54,162) |
| 7-27-73 | Miami 14, All-Stars 3 (54,103) |
| 1974 | No game played |
| 8-1-75 | Pittsburgh 21, All-Stars 14 (54,103) |
| 7-23-76 | *Pittsburgh 24, All-Stars 0 (52,895) |

* *Game was not completed due to thunderstorms.*

# DISCONTINUED ALL-STAR FOOTBALL GAMES

Many of these games were identified without complete information such as scores, teams, sites or dates. Please send any updates or additional information to: NCAA Statistics Service, 6201 College Boulevard, Overland Park, Kansas 66211-2422.

## All-America/Canadian-American Bowl (1969-79)
### Tampa, Fla.

## Black College All-Star Bowl (1980-81)

| Date | Score, Location (Attendance) |
|---|---|
| 1-5-80 | West 27, East 21 at New Orleans, La. |
| 1-17-81 | West 19, East 10 at Jackson, Miss. (7,500) |

## Camp Football Foundation Bowl (1974)
## Challenge Bowl (1962-63)
### Corpus Christi, Texas

| Date | Score |
|---|---|
| 1-4-63 | National 66, Southwest 14 |

## Challenge Bowl (1977-78)
### Seattle, Wash.

## Coaches All-American Game (1961-75)
### Lubbock, Texas

| Year | Score | Year | Score | Year | Score |
|---|---|---|---|---|---|
| 1961 | West 30, East 20 | 1966 | West 24, East 7 | 1971 | West 33, East 28 |
| 1962 | East 13, West 8 | 1967 | East 12, West 9 | 1972 | East 42, West 20 |
| 1963 | West 22, East 21 | 1968 | West 34, East 20 | 1973 | West 20, East 6 |
| 1964 | East 18, West 15 | 1969 | West 14, East 10 | 1974 | West 36, East 6 |
| 1965 | East 24, West 14 | 1970 | East 34, West 27 | 1975 | East 23, West 21 |

## Cocoanut Bowl (1942)
### Miami, Fla.

| Date | Score (Attendance) |
|---|---|
| 1-1-42 | Florida Normal 0, Miami All-Stars 0 (9,000) |

## College All-Star Game (1940-41)
### New York City

## Copper Bowl (1959-60)
### Tempe, Ariz.

| Date | Score (Attendance) | Date | Score (Attendance) |
|---|---|---|---|
| 12-31-59 | National All-Stars 21, Southwest All-Stars 6 (16,000) | 12-31-60 | National All-Stars 27, Southwest All-Stars 7 (8,000) |

## Dallas All-Star Game (1938-39)
### Dallas, Texas

## Freedom Bowl All-Star Classic (1984-86)
### Southwestern Athletic Conference vs. Mid-Eastern Athletic Conference
### Atlanta, Ga.

| Date | Score (Attendance) |
|---|---|
| 1-14-84 | SWAC 36, MEAC 22 (16,097) |
| 1-12-85 | SWAC 14, MEAC 0 (18,352) |
| 1-11-86 | SWAC 16, MEAC 14 (10,200) |

## Lions American Bowl Game (1969-1976)
### Tampa, Fla.

| Year | Score | Year | Score | Year | Score |
|---|---|---|---|---|---|
| 1969 | North 21, South 15 | 1972 | North 27, South 8 | 1975 | South 28, North 22 |
| 1970 | South 24, North 23 | 1973 | North 10, South 6 | 1976 | North 21, South 14 |
| 1971 | North 39, South 2 | 1974 | North 28, South 7 | | |

## Martin Luther King All-American Bowl (1990-91)
### San Francisco, Calif.

## North-South Shrine Game
### Montgomery, Ala. (1939)/Miami, Fla. (1958-61, 1964-65)

| Date | Score (Attendance) | Date | Score (Attendance) |
|---|---|---|---|
| 1-2-39 | North 7, South 0 (8,000) | 12-25-61 | South 35, North 16 (18,892) |
| 12-27-58 | South 49, North 20 (35,519) | 12-25-64 | North 37, South 30 (29,194) |
| 12-26-59 | North 27, South 17 (35,185) | 12-25-65 | South 21, North 14 (25,640) |
| 12-26-60 | North 41, South 14 (26,146) | | |

## Olympia Gold Bowl (1982)
### San Diego, Calif.

| Date | Score |
|---|---|
| 1-16-82 | National 30, American 21 |

**Optimist Bowl (1958-59)**
**Tucson, Ariz.**

**Pelican Bowl (1973, 75-76)**
**New Orleans, La.**

| Year | Score |
|------|-------|
| 1973 | Grambling 56, N. C. Central 6 |
| 1975 | Grambling 28, South Caro. St. 7 |
| 1976 | Southern-B. R. 15, South Caro. St. 12 |

**Salad Bowl All-Star Game (1955)**
**Phoenix, Ariz.**

| Date | Score (Attendance) |
|------|---------------------|
| 1-1-55 | Skyline Conference All-Stars 20, Border Conference All-Stars 13 (8,000) |

**Smoke Bowl (1941)**
**Richmond, Va.**

| Date | Score (Attendance) |
|------|---------------------|
| 1-1-41 | Norfolk All-Stars 16, Richmond All-Stars 2 (5,000) |

**Southwest Challenge Bowl (1962)**

**Steel Bowl (1941-42)**
**Birmingham, Ala.**

| Date | Score |
|------|-------|
| 1-1-42 | Southern All-Stars 26, Nashville Pros 13 |

**Sun Bowl (1958)**
**Phoenix, Ariz.**

**Vulcan Bowl (1942)**
**Birmingham, Ala.**

| Year | Score (Attendance) |
|------|---------------------|
| 1942 | Langston 13, Morris Brown 0 (9,000) |

# SPECIAL REGULAR-SEASON GAMES

## KICKOFF CLASSIC

**Present Site:** East Rutherford, N.J.
**Stadium (Capacity):** Giants (76,000)
**Playing Surface:** AstroTurf
**Sponsor:** National Association of Collegiate Directors of Athletics (NACDA). It is a permitted 12th regular-season game.
**Playing Sites:** Giants Stadium (since 1983)

| Date | Teams, Score (Attendance) |
|------|----------------------------|
| 8-29-83 | Nebraska 44, Penn St. 6 (71,123) |
| 8-27-84 | Miami (Fla.) 20, Auburn 18 (51,131) |
| 8-29-85 | Brigham Young 28, Boston Collge 14 (51,227) |
| 8-27-86 | Alabama 16, Ohio St. 10 (68,296) |
| 8-30-87 | Tennessee 23, Iowa 22 (54,681) |
| 8-27-88 | Nebraska 23, Texas A&M 14 (58,172) |
| 8-31-89 | Notre Dame 36, Virginia 13 (77,323) |
| 8-31-90 | Southern Cal 34, Syracuse 16 (57,293) |
| 8-28-91 | Penn St. 34, Georgia Tech 22 (77,409) |
| 8-29-92 | North Caro. St. 24, Iowa 14 (46,251) |
| 8-28-93 | Florida St. vs. Kansas |

## PIGSKIN CLASSIC

**Present Site:** Anaheim, Calif.
**Stadium (Capacity):** Anaheim (70,962)
**Playing Surface:** Grass
**Sponsor:** Disneyland. It is a permitted 12th regular-season game.
**Playing Sites:** Anaheim Stadium (since 1990)

| Date | Teams, Score (Attendance) |
|------|----------------------------|
| 8-26-90 | Tennessee 31, Colorado 31 (33,458) |
| 8-29-91 | Florida St. 44, Brigham Young 28 (38,363) |
| 8-26-92 | Texas A&M 10, Stanford 7 (35,240) |
| 8-29-93 | North Caro. vs. Southern Cal |

*Special Regular- and Postseason Games*

## SOUTHEASTERN CONFERENCE CHAMPIONSHIP

**Present Site:** Birmingham, Ala.
**Stadium (Capacity):** Legion Field (83,091)
**Playing Surface:** AstroTurf
**Playing Sites:** Legion Field (since 1992)

**Date          Teams, Score (Attendance)**
12-5-92       Alabama (Western Div.) 28, Florida (Eastern Div.) 21 (83,091)

# REGULAR-SEASON GAMES PLAYED IN FOREIGN COUNTRIES
## TOKYO, JAPAN

(Called Mirage Bowl 1976-85, Coca-Cola Classic from 1986. Played at Tokyo Olympic Memorial Stadium 1976-87, Tokyo Dome from 1988.)

**Date          Teams, Score (Attendance)**
9-4-76        Grambling 42, Morgan St. 16 (50,000)
12-11-77      Grambling 35, Temple 32 (50,000)
12-10-78      Temple 28, Boston College 24 (55,000)
11-24-79      Notre Dame 40, Miami (Fla.) 15 (62,574)
11-30-80      UCLA 34, Oregon St. 3 (86,000)

11-28-81      Air Force 21, San Diego St. 16 (80,000)
11-27-82      Clemson 21, Wake Forest 17 (64,700)
11-26-83      Southern Methodist 34, Houston 12 (70,000)
11-17-84      Army 45, Montana 31 (60,000)
11-30-85      Southern Cal 20, Oregon 6 (65,000)

11-30-86      Stanford 29, Arizona 24 (55,000)
11-28-87      California 17, Washington St. 17 (45,000)
12-3-88       Oklahoma St. 45, Texas Tech 42 (56,000)
12-4-89       Syracuse 24, Louisville 13 (50,000)
12-2-90       Houston 62, Arizona St. 45 (50,000)

11-30-91      Clemson 33, Duke 21 (50,000)
12-6-92       Nebraska 38, Kansas St. 24 (50,000)
12-4-93       Michigan St. vs. Wisconsin

## MELBOURNE, AUSTRALIA

**Date          Teams, Score (Attendance)**
12-6-85*      Wyoming 24, UTEP 21 (22,000)
12-4-87†      Brigham Young 30, Colorado St. 26 (76,652)
*  *Played at V.F.L. Park.*    †  *Played at Princes Park.*

## YOKOHAMA, JAPAN

**Date          Teams, Score (Attendance)**
12-2-78       Brigham Young 28, Nevada-Las Vegas 24 (27,500)

## OSAKA, JAPAN

**Date          Teams, Score (Attendance)**
9-3-78        Utah St. 10, Idaho St. 0 (15,000)

## DUBLIN, IRELAND

(Called Emerald Isle Classic. Played at Lansdowne Road Stadium.)

**Date          Teams, Score (Attendance)**
11-19-88      Boston College 38, Army 24 (45,525)
12-2-89       Pittsburgh 46, Rutgers 29 (19,800)

## LONDON, ENGLAND

**Date          Teams, Score (Attendance)**
10-16-88      Richmond 20, Boston U. 17 (6,000)

## MILAN, ITALY

(Played at The Arena.)

**Date          Teams, Score (Attendance)**
10-28-89      Villanova 28, Rhode Island 25 (5,000)

## LIMERICK, IRELAND

(Wild Geese Classic. Played at Limerick Gaelic Grounds.)

**Date          Teams, Score (Attendance)**
11-16-91      Holy Cross 24, Fordham 19 (17,411)
10-9-93       Massachusetts vs. Rhode Island

*1993 NCAA FOOTBALL*

## FRANKFURT, GERMANY
(Played at Wald Stadium.)

| Date | Teams, Score (Attendance) |
|------|---------------------------|
| 9-19-92 | Heidelberg 7, Otterbein 7 (4,351) |

## GALWAY, IRELAND
(Called Christopher Columbus Classic.)

| Date | Teams, Score (Attendance) |
|------|---------------------------|
| 11-29-92 | Bowdoin 7, Tufts 6 (2,500) |

## HAMILTON, BERMUDA

| Date | Teams |
|------|-------|
| 11-20-93 | Georgetown vs. Wash. & Lee |

## COLLEGE FOOTBALL TROPHY GAMES

Following is a list of the current college football trophy games. The games are listed alphabetically by the trophy-object name. The date refers to the season the trophy was first exchanged and is not necessarily the start of competition between the participants. A game involving interdivision teams is listed in the higher-division classification.

### DIVISION I-A

| Trophy | Date | Colleges |
|--------|------|----------|
| Anniversary Award | 1985 | Bowling Green-Kent |
| Apple Cup | 1962 | Washington-Washington St. |
| Axe | 1933 | California-Stanford |
| Bayou Bucket | 1974 | Houston-Rice |
| Beehive Boot | 1971 | Brigham Young, Utah, Weber St. |
| Beer Barrel | 1925 | Kentucky-Tennessee |
| Bell | 1927 | Missouri-Nebraska |
| Bell Clapper | 1931 | Oklahoma-Oklahoma St. |
| Big Game | 1953 | Arizona-Arizona St. |
| Blue Key Victory Bell | 1940 | Ball St.-Indiana St. |
| Bourbon Barrel | 1967 | Indiana-Kentucky |
| Brass Spittoon | 1950 | Indiana-Michigan St. |
| Brass Spittoon | 1981 | New Mexico St.-UTEP |
| Bronze Boot | 1968 | Colorado St.-Wyoming |
| Cannon | 1943 | Illinois-Purdue |
| Commander In Chief's | 1972 | Air Force, Army, Navy |
| Cy-Hawk | 1977 | Iowa-Iowa St. |
| Floyd of Rosedale | 1935 | Iowa-Minnesota |
| Foy-O.D.K. | 1948 | Alabama-Auburn |
| Fremont Cannon | 1970 | Nevada — Nevada-Las Vegas |
| Golden Egg | 1927 | Mississippi-Mississippi St. |
| Golden Hat | 1941 | Oklahoma-Texas |
| Governor's | 1969 | Kansas-Kansas St. |
| Governor's Cup | 1958 | Florida-Florida St. |
| Governor's Cup | 1983 | Colorado-Colorado St. |
| Illibuck | 1925 | Illinois-Ohio St. |
| Indian War Drum | 1935 | Kansas-Missouri |
| Iron Bowl | 1983 | Alabama-Auburn |
| Keg of Nails | 1950 | Cincinnati-Louisville |
| Kit Carson Rifle | 1938 | Arizona-New Mexico |
| Little Brown Jug | 1909 | Michigan-Minnesota |
| Megaphone | 1949 | Michigan St.-Notre Dame |
| Old Oaken Bucket | 1925 | Indiana-Purdue |
| Old Wagon Wheel | 1948 | Brigham Young-Utah St. |
| Paniolo Trophy | 1979 | Hawaii-Wyoming |
| Paul Bunyan Axe | 1948 | Minnesota-Wisconsin |
| Paul Bunyan-Governor of Michigan | 1953 | Michigan-Michigan St. |
| Peace Pipe | 1929 | Missouri-Oklahoma |
| Peace Pipe | 1955 | Miami (Ohio)-Western Mich. |
| Peace Pipe | 1980 | Bowling Green-Toledo |
| Ram-Falcon | 1980 | Air Force-Colorado St. |
| Sabine Shoe | 1937 | Lamar-Southwestern La. |
| Shillelagh | 1952 | Notre Dame-Southern Cal |
| Shillelagh | 1958 | Notre Dame-Purdue |
| Silver Spade | 1955 | New Mexico St.-UTEP |

*Special Regular- and Postseason Games*

| Trophy | Date | Colleges |
|---|---|---|
| Steel Tire | 1976 | Akron-Youngstown St. |
| Telephone | 1960 | Iowa St.-Missouri |
| Textile Bowl | 1981 | Clemson-North Caro. St. |
| Tomahawk | 1945 | Illinois-Northwestern |
| Victory Bell | 1942 | Southern Cal-UCLA |
| Victory Bell | 1948 | Cincinnati-Miami (Ohio) |
| Victory Bell | 1948 | Duke-North Caro. |
| Wagon Wheel | 1946 | Akron-Kent |

## DIVISION I-AA

| Trophy | Date | Colleges |
|---|---|---|
| Bill Knight | 1986 | Massachusetts-New Hampshire |
| Brice-Colwell Musket | 1946 | Maine-New Hampshire |
| Chief Caddo | 1962 | Northwestern (La.)-Stephen F. Austin |
| Gem State | 1978 | Boise St., Idaho, Idaho St. |
| Governor's Cup | 1972 | Brown-Rhode Island |
| Governor's Cup | 1975 | Dartmouth-Princeton |
| Governor's Cup | 1984 | Eastern Wash.-Idaho |
| Harvey—Shin-A-Ninny Totem Pole | 1961 | Middle Tenn. St.-Tennessee Tech |
| Little Brown Stein | 1938 | Idaho-Montana |
| Mare's | 1987 | Murray St.—Tenn.-Martin |
| Mayor's Cup | 1981 | Bethune-Cookman—Central Fla. |
| Ol' Mountain Jug | 1937 | Appalachian St.-Western Caro. |
| Painting Grizzly-Bobcat | 1984 | Montana-Montana St. |
| Red Belt | 1978 | Murray St.-Western Ky. |
| Ron Rogerson Memorial | 1988 | Maine-Rhode Island |
| Silver Shako | 1976 | Citadel-Va. Military |
| Team of Game's MVP | 1960 | Lafayette-Lehigh |

## DIVISION II

| Trophy | Date | Colleges |
|---|---|---|
| Axe | 1946 | Cal St. Chico-Humboldt St. |
| Axe Bowl | 1975 | Northwood-Saginaw Valley |
| Backyard Bowl | 1987 | Cheyney-West Chester |
| Battle Axe | 1948 | Bemidji St.-Moorhead St. |
| Battle of the Ravine | 1976 | Henderson St.-Ouachita Baptist |
| Bell (Little Big Game) | 1947 | Santa Clara-St. Mary's (Cal.) |
| Bishop's | 1970 | Lenoir-Rhyne—Newberry |
| Board of Trustees | 1987 | Central Conn. St.-Western Conn. St. |
| Bronze Derby | 1946 | Newberry-Presbyterian |
| Eagle-Rock | 1980 | Black Hills St.-Chadron St. |
| East Meets West | 1987 | Chadron St.-Peru St. |
| Elm City | 1983 | New Haven-Southern Conn. St. |
| Governor's | 1979 | Central Conn. St.-Southern Conn. St. |
| Heritage Bell | 1979 | Delta St.-Mississippi Col. |
| Miner's Bowl | 1986 | Mo. Southern St.-Pittsburg St. |
| Nickel | 1938 | North Dak.-North Dak. St. |
| Ol' School Bell | 1988 | Jacksonville St.-Troy St. |
| Old Hickory Stick | 1931 | Northeast Mo. St.-Northwest Mo. St. |
| Old Settler's Musket | 1975 | Adams St.-Fort Lewis St. |
| Sitting Bull | 1953 | North Dak.-South Dak. |
| Springfield Mayor's | 1941 | American Int'l-Springfield |
| Textile | 1960 | Clark Atlanta-Fort Valley St. |
| Top Dog | 1971 | Butler-Indianapolis |
| Traveling | 1976 | Ashland-Hillsdale |
| Victory Carriage | 1960 | Cal St. Sacramento-UC Davis |
| Wagon Wheel | 1986 | Eastern N. Mex.-West Tex. St. |
| Wooden Shoes | 1977 | Grand Valley St.-Wayne St. (Mich.) |

## DIVISION III

| Trophy | Date | Colleges |
|---|---|---|
| Academic Bowl | 1986 | Carnegie Mellon-Case Reserve |
| Admiral's Cup | 1980 | Maine Maritime-Mass. Maritime |
| Baird Bros. Golden Stringer | 1984 | Case Reserve-Wooster |
| Bell | *1931 | Franklin-Hanover |
| Bill Edwards Trophy | 1989 | Case Reserve-Wittenberg |
| Bronze Turkey | 1929 | Knox-Monmouth (Ill.) |
| CBB | 1966 | Bates, Bowdoin, Colby |
| Conestoga Wagon | 1963 | Dickinson-Frank. & Marsh. |
| Cortaca Jug | 1959 | Cortland St.-Ithaca |
| Cranberry Bowl | 1979 | Bri'water (Mass.)-Mass. Maritime |
| Doehling-Heselton Helmet | 1988 | Lawrence-Ripon |
| Drum | 1940 | Occidental—Pomona-Pitzer |
| Dutchman's Shoes | 1950 | Rensselaer-Union (N.Y.) |

| Trophy | Date | Colleges |
|---|---|---|
| Edmund Orgill | 1954 | Rhodes-Sewanee |
| Field Cup | 1983 | Evansville-Ky. Wesleyan |
| Founder's | 1987 | Chicago-Washington (Mo.) |
| Goal Post | 1953 | Juniata-Susquehanna |
| Goat | 1931 | Carleton-St. Olaf |
| Golden Circle | 1988 | Drake-Simpson |
| John Wesley | 1984 | Ky. Wesleyan-Union (Ky.) |
| Keystone Cup | 1981 | Delaware Valley-Widener |
| Little Brass Bell | 1947 | North Central-Wheaton (Ill.) |
| Little Brown Bucket | 1938 | Dickinson-Gettysburg |
| Little Three | 1971 | Amherst, Wesleyan, Williams |
| Mercer County Cup | 1984 | Grove City-Thiel |
| Monon Bell | 1932 | DePauw-Wabash |
| Mug | 1931 | Coast Guard-Norwich |
| Old Goal Post | 1953 | Juniata-Susquehanna |
| Old Musket | 1964 | Carroll (Wis.)-Carthage |
| Old Rocking Chair | 1980 | Hamilton-Middlebury |
| Old Tin Cup | 1954 | Gettysburg-Muhlenberg |
| Old Water Bucket | 1989 | Maranatha-N'western Col. (Wis.) |
| Paint Bucket | 1965 | Hamline-Macalester |
| Pella Corporation Classic | 1988 | Central (Iowa)—William Penn |
| President's Cup | 1971 | Case Reserve-John Carroll |
| Secretary's Cup | 1981 | Coast Guard-Merchant Marine |
| Shoes | 1946 | Occidental-Whittier |
| Shot Glass | 1938 | Coast Guard-Rensselaer |
| Steve Dean Memorial | 1976 | Catholic-Georgetown |
| Transit | 1980 | Rensselaer-Worcester Tech |
| Victory Bell | 1946 | Loras-St. Thomas (Minn.) |
| Victory Bell | 1949 | Upper Iowa-Wartburg |
| Wadsworth | 1977 | Middlebury-Norwich |
| Wilson Brothers Cup | 1986 | Hamline-St. Thomas (Minn.) |
| Wooden Shoes | 1946 | Hope-Kalamazoo |

### NON-NCAA MEMBERS

| Trophy | Date | Colleges |
|---|---|---|
| Baptist Bible Bowl | 1982 | Maranatha-Pillsbury |
| Home Stake-Gold Mine | 1950 | Black Hills St.-South Dak. Tech |
| KTEN Savage-Tiger | 1979 | East Central Okla.-Southeastern Okla. |
| Paint Bucket | 1961 | Jamestown-Valley City St. |
| Wagon Wheel | 1957 | Lewis & Clark-Willamette |

* Was reinstated in 1988 after a 17-year lapse.

# COACHES' RECORDS

As if one wasn't enough to handle, Division I-A teams will have to contend with two Bowden-coached opponents in 1993. After a successful stint at Division I-AA Samford, Terry Bowden (right) will take over at Auburn and try to build a resume as impressive as that of his father, Bobby, who is seventh on the all-time Division I-A coaching victory list with 227 in 27 seasons.

# WINNINGEST ALL-TIME DIVISION I-A COACHES

## (By Percentage)

Minimum 10 years as head coach at Division I institutions; record at four-year colleges only; bowl games included; ties computed as half won, half lost. Active coaches indicated by (*). Hall of Fame members indicated by (†).

| Coach (Alma Mater, Colleges Coached, Tenure) | Years | Won | Lost | Tied | Pct. |
|---|---|---|---|---|---|
| Knute K. Rockne (Notre Dame '14)† ........................... | 13 | 105 | 12 | 5 | .881 |
| (Notre Dame 1918-30) | | | | | |
| Frank W. Leahy (Notre Dame '31)† ........................... | 13 | 107 | 13 | 9 | .864 |
| (Boston College 1939-40; Notre Dame 1941-43, 1946-53) | | | | | |
| George W. Woodruff (Yale '89)† ........................... | 12 | 142 | 25 | 2 | .846 |
| (Pennsylvania 1892-01; Illinois 1903; Carlisle 1905) | | | | | |
| Barry Switzer (Arkansas '60) ................................... | 16 | 157 | 29 | 4 | .837 |
| (Oklahoma 1973-88) | | | | | |
| Percy D. Haughton (Harvard '99)† ........................... | 13 | 96 | 17 | 6 | .832 |
| (Cornell 1899-00; Harvard 1908-16; Columbia 1923-24) | | | | | |
| Robert R. "Bob" Neyland (Army '16)† ........................... | 21 | 173 | 31 | 12 | .829 |
| (Tennessee 1926-34, 1936-40, 1946-52) | | | | | |
| Fielding H. "Hurry Up" Yost (Lafayette '97)† ................... | 29 | 196 | 36 | 12 | .828 |
| (Ohio Wesleyan 1897; Nebraska 1898; Kansas 1899; Stanford 1900; Michigan 1901-23, 1925-26) | | | | | |
| Charles "Bud" Wilkinson (Minnesota '37)† ..................... | 17 | 145 | 29 | 4 | .826 |
| (Oklahoma 1947-63) | | | | | |
| John B. "Jock" Sutherland (Pittsburgh '18)† ................... | 20 | 144 | 28 | 14 | .812 |
| (Lafayette 1919-23; Pittsburgh 1924-38) | | | | | |
| Robert S. "Bob" Devaney (Alma '39)† ........................... | 16 | 136 | 30 | 7 | .806 |
| (Wyoming 1957-61; Nebraska 1962-72) | | | | | |
| *Thomas W. "Tom" Osborne (Hastings '59) ..................... | 20 | 195 | 46 | 3 | .805 |
| (Nebraska 1973—) | | | | | |
| Frank W. Thomas (Notre Dame '23)† ........................... | 19 | 141 | 33 | 9 | .795 |
| (Chattanooga 1925-28; Alabama 1931-42, 1944-46) | | | | | |
| Henry L. Williams (Yale '91)† ................................... | 23 | 141 | 34 | 12 | .786 |
| (Army 1891; Minnesota 1900-21) | | | | | |
| *Joseph V. "Joe" Paterno (Brown '50) ........................... | 27 | 247 | 67 | 3 | .784 |
| (Penn St. 1966—) | | | | | |
| Gilmour "Gloomy Gil" Dobie (Minnesota '02)† ................. | 33 | 180 | 45 | 15 | .781 |
| (North Dak. St. 1906-07; Washington 1908-16; Navy 1917-19; Cornell 1920-35; Boston College 1936-38) | | | | | |
| Paul W. "Bear" Bryant (Alabama '36)† ........................... | 38 | 323 | 85 | 17 | .780 |
| (Maryland 1945; Kentucky 1946-53; Texas A&M 1954-57; Alabama 1958-82) | | | | | |
| Fred Folsom (Dartmouth '95) ................................... | 19 | 106 | 28 | 6 | .779 |
| (Colorado 1895-99, 1901-02; Dartmouth 1903-06; Colorado 1908-15) | | | | | |
| Glenn "Bo" Schembechler (Miami, Ohio '51)† ................. | 27 | 234 | 65 | 8 | .775 |
| (Miami, Ohio 1963-68; Michigan 1969-89) | | | | | |
| Herbert O. "Fritz" Crisler (Chicago '22)† ..................... | 18 | 116 | 32 | 9 | .768 |
| (Minnesota 1930-31; Princeton 1932-37; Michigan 1938-47) | | | | | |
| Charles B. "Charley" Moran (Tennessee '98) ................... | 18 | 122 | 33 | 12 | .766 |
| (Texas A&M 1909-14; Centre 1919-23; Bucknell 1924-26; Catawba 1930-33) | | | | | |
| William Wallace Wade (Brown '17)† ........................... | 24 | 171 | 49 | 10 | .765 |
| (Alabama 1923-30; Duke 1931-41, 1946-50) | | | | | |
| Frank Kush (Michigan St. '53) ................................... | 22 | 176 | 54 | 1 | .764 |
| (Arizona St. 1958-1979) | | | | | |
| Daniel E. "Dan" McGugin (Michigan '04)† ..................... | 30 | 197 | 55 | 19 | .762 |
| (Vanderbilt 1904-17, 1919-34) | | | | | |
| James "Jimmy" Crowley (Notre Dame '25)# ................... | 13 | 78 | 21 | 10 | .761 |
| (Michigan St. 1929-32; Fordham 1933-41) | | | | | |
| Andrew L. "Andy" Smith (Penn St., Pennsylvania '05)† ......... | 17 | 116 | 32 | 13 | .761 |
| (Pennsylvania 1909-12; Purdue 1913-15; California 1916-25) | | | | | |
| *Danny L. Ford (Alabama '70) ................................... | ‡12 | 96 | 29 | 4 | .760 |
| (Clemson 1978-89) | | | | | |
| Wayne Woodrow "Woody" Hayes (Denison '35)† ............... | 33 | 238 | 72 | 10 | .759 |
| (Denison 1946-48; Miami, Ohio 1949-50; Ohio St. 1951-78) | | | | | |
| Earl H. "Red" Blaik (Miami, Ohio '18; Army '20)† ............... | 25 | 166 | 48 | 14 | .759 |
| (Dartmouth 1934-40; Army 1941-58) | | | | | |
| Darrell Royal (Oklahoma '50)† ................................... | 23 | 184 | 60 | 5 | .749 |
| (Mississippi St. 1954-55; Washington 1956; Texas 1957-76) | | | | | |
| John McKay (Oregon '50)† ................................... | 16 | 127 | 40 | 8 | .749 |
| (Southern Cal 1960-75) | | | | | |

| Coach (Alma Mater, Colleges Coached, Tenure) | Years | Won | Lost | Tied | Pct. |
|---|---|---|---|---|---|
| John H. Vaught (Texas Christian '33)† .......................... | 25 | 190 | 61 | 12 | .745 |
| (Mississippi 1947-70, 1973) | | | | | |
| *Robert "Bobby" Bowden (Samford '53)✓ ..................... | 27 | 227 | 77 | 3 | .744 |
| (Samford 1959-62; West Va. 1970-75; Florida St. 1976—) | | | | | |
| Daniel J. "Dan" Devine (Minn.-Duluth '48)† ................... | 22 | 172 | 57 | 9 | .742 |
| (Arizona St. 1955-57; Missouri 1958-70; Notre Dame 1975-80) | | | | | |
| Elmer C. "Gus" Henderson (Oberlin '12) ....................... | 20 | 126 | 42 | 7 | .740 |
| (Southern Cal 1919-24; Tulsa 1925-35; Occidental 1940-42) | | | | | |
| Ara Parseghian (Miami, Ohio '49)† ............................. | 24 | 170 | 58 | 6 | .739 |
| (Miami, Ohio 1951-55; Northwestern 1956-63; Notre Dame 1964-74) | | | | | |
| *LaVell Edwards (Utah St. '52) ................................. | 21 | 191 | 67 | 3 | .738 |
| (Brigham Young 1972—) | | | | | |
| Elmer F. Layden (Notre Dame '25)# ........................... | 16 | 103 | 34 | 11 | .733 |
| (Loras 1925-26; Duquesne 1927-33; Notre Dame 1934-40) | | | | | |
| Howard H. Jones (Yale '08)† .................................. | 29 | 194 | 64 | 21 | .733 |
| (Syracuse 1908; Yale 1909; Ohio St. 1910; Yale 1913; Iowa 1916-23; Duke 1924; Southern Cal 1925-40) | | | | | |
| Frank W. Cavanaugh (Dartmouth '97)† ......................... | 24 | 145 | 48 | 17 | .731 |
| (Cincinnati 1898; Holy Cross 1903-05; Dartmouth 1911-16; Boston College 1919-26; Fordham 1927-32) | | | | | |
| Glenn S. "Pop" Warner (Cornell '95)† .......................... | 44 | 313 | 106 | 32 | .729 |
| (Georgia 1895-96; Cornell 1897-98; Carlisle 1899-1903; Cornell 1904-06; Carlisle 1907-14; Pittsburgh 1915-23; Stanford 1924-32; Temple 1933-38) | | | | | |
| James M. "Jim" Tatum (North Caro. '35)† ...................... | 14 | 100 | 35 | 7 | .729 |
| (North Caro. 1942; Oklahoma 1946; Maryland 1947-55; North Caro. 1956-58) | | | | | |
| Francis A. Schmidt (Nebraska '14)† ............................ | 24 | 158 | 57 | 11 | .723 |
| (Tulsa 1919-21; Arkansas 1922-28; Texas Christian 1929-33; Ohio St. 1934-40; Idaho 1941-42) | | | | | |
| William W. "Bill" Roper (Princeton '03)† ........................ | 22 | 112 | 37 | 19 | .723 |
| (Va. Military 1903-04; Princeton 1906-08; Missouri 1909; Princeton 1910-11; Swarthmore 1915-16; Princeton 1919-30) | | | | | |
| Albert R. "Doc" Kennedy (Kansas & Pennsylvania '03) ......... | 13 | 85 | 31 | 7 | .720 |
| (Kansas 1904-10; Haskell 1911-16) | | | | | |
| T. A. Dwight "Tad" Jones (Yale '08)† .......................... | 11 | 66 | 24 | 6 | .719 |
| (Syracuse 1909-10; Yale 1916, 1920-27) | | | | | |
| Vincent J. "Vince" Dooley (Auburn '54) ........................ | 25 | 201 | 77 | 10 | .715 |
| (Georgia 1964-88) | | | | | |
| Dana X. Bible (Carson-Newman '12)† ........................... | 33 | 198 | 72 | 23 | .715 |
| (Mississippi Col. 1913-15; Louisiana St. 1916; Texas A&M 1917, 1919-28; Nebraska 1929-36; Texas 1937-46) | | | | | |
| Robert L. "Bobby" Dodd (Tennessee '31)†# ................... | 22 | 165 | 64 | 8 | .713 |
| (Georgia Tech 1945-66) | | | | | |
| John W. Heisman (Brown '90, Pennsylvania '92)† .............. | 36 | 185 | 70 | 17 | .711 |
| (Oberlin 1892; Akron 1893; Oberlin 1894; Auburn 1895-99; Clemson 1900-03; Georgia Tech 1904-19; Pennsylvania 1920-22; Wash. & Jeff. 1923; Rice 1924-27) | | | | | |
| Ewald O. "Jumbo" Stiehm (Wisconsin '09) ..................... | 12 | 59 | 23 | 4 | .709 |
| (Ripon 1910; Nebraska 1911-15; Indiana 1916-21) | | | | | |
| Henry R. "Red" Sanders (Vanderbilt '27) ...................... | 15 | 102 | 41 | 3 | .709 |
| (Vanderbilt 1940-42, 1946-48; UCLA 1949-57) | | | | | |
| Patrick F. "Pat" Dye (Georgia '62) ............................ | 19 | 153 | 62 | 5 | .707 |
| (East Caro. 1974-79; Wyoming 1980; Auburn 1981-92) | | | | | |
| John F. "Chick" Meehan (Syracuse '18) ....................... | 18 | 115 | 44 | 14 | .705 |
| (Syracuse 1920-24; New York U. 1925-31; Manhattan 1932-37) | | | | | |
| John J. McEwan (Army '17) ................................... | 10 | 59 | 23 | 6 | .705 |
| (Army 1923-25; Oregon 1926-29; Holy Cross 1930-32) | | | | | |
| Benjamin G. "Bennie" Owen (Kansas '00)† ..................... | 27 | 155 | 60 | 19 | .703 |
| (Washburn 1900; Bethany, Kan. 1901-04; Oklahoma 1905-26) | | | | | |
| Ike J. Armstrong (Drake '23)† ................................. | 25 | 140 | 55 | 15 | .702 |
| (Utah 1925-49) | | | | | |
| Frank Broyles (Georgia Tech '47)† ............................. | 20 | 149 | 62 | 6 | .700 |
| (Missouri 1957; Arkansas 1958-76) | | | | | |
| Lawrence McC. "Biff" Jones (Army '17)† ....................... | 14 | 87 | 33 | 15 | .700 |
| (Army 1926-29; Louisiana St. 1932-34; Oklahoma 1935-36; Nebraska 1937-41) | | | | | |

# Member of College Football Hall of Fame as a player.   ‡ Last game of 1978 season counted as full season.   ✓ Includes games forfeited, team and/or individual statistics abrogated, and coaching records changed by action of the NCAA Council under the restitution provisions of Bylaw 19.6 of the Official

*Coaches' Records*

*Procedure Governing the NCAA Enforcement Program (adopted by the NCAA membership at the 69th annual Convention in January 1975). The restitution provisions may be applied by the Council when a student-athlete has been permitted to participate while ineligible as a result of a court order against his institution or the NCAA, if the court order subsequently is overturned.*

## ALL-TIME DIVISION I-A COACHING VICTORIES

Minimum 10 years as head coach at Division I institutions; record at four-year colleges only; bowl games included. After each coach's name is his alma mater, year graduated, total years coached, won-lost record and percentage, tenure at each college coached, and won-lost record there. Active coaches are denoted by an asterisk (*).

### (Minimum 150 Victories)

323 Paul "Bear" Bryant (Born 9-11-13 Moro Bottoms, Ark.; Died 1-26-83)
Alabama 1936 (38: 323-85-17 .780)
Maryland 1945 (6-2-1); Kentucky 1946-53 (60-23-5); Texas A&M 1954-57 (25-14-2); Alabama 1958-82 (232-46-9)

314 Amos Alonzo Stagg (Born 8-16-1862 West Orange, N.J.; Died 3-17-65)
Yale 1888 (57: 314-199-35 .605)
Springfield 1890-91 (10-11-1); Chicago 1892-1932 (244-111-27); Pacific (Cal.) 1933-46 (60-77-7)

313 Glenn "Pop" Warner (Born 4-5-1871 Springville, N.Y.; Died 9-7-54)
Cornell 1895 (44: 313-106-32 .729)
Georgia 1895-96 (7-4-0); Cornell 1897-98, 1904-06 (36-13-3); Carlisle 1899-1903, 1907-14 (109-42-8); Pittsburgh 1915-23 (59-12-4); Stanford 1924-32 (71-17-8); Temple 1933-38 (31-18-9)

247 *Joe Paterno (Born 12-21-26 Brooklyn, N.Y.)
Brown 1951 (27: 247-67-3 .784)
Penn St. 1966-92 (247-67-3)

238 Wayne Woodrow "Woody" Hayes (Born 2-13-14 Clifton, Ohio; Died 3-12-87)
Denison 1935 (33: 238-72-10 .759)
Denison 1946-48 (19-6-0); Miami (Ohio) 1949-50 (14-5-0); Ohio St. 1951-78 (205-61-10)

234 Glenn "Bo" Schembechler (Born 9-1-29 Barberton, Ohio)
Miami (Ohio) 1951 (27: 234-65-8 .775)
Miami (Ohio) 1963-68 (40-17-3); Michigan 1969-89 (194-48-5)

227 *Bobby Bowden (Born 11-8-29 Birmingham, Ala.)
Samford 1953 (✓27: 227-77-3 .744)
Samford 1959-62 (31-6-0); West Va. 1970-75 (✓42-26-0); Florida St. 1976-92 (154-45-3)

207 Jess Neely (Born 1-4-1898 Smyrna, Tenn.; Died 4-9-83)
Vanderbilt 1924 (40: 207-176-19 .539)
Rhodes 1924-27 (20-17-2); Clemson 1931-39 (43-35-7); Rice 1940-66 (144-124-10)

203 Warren Woodson (Born 2-24-03 Fort Worth, Texas)
Baylor 1924 (31: 203-95-14 .673)
Central Ark. 1935-39 (40-8-3); Hardin-Simmons 1941-42, 1946-51 (58-24-6); Arizona 1952-56 (26-22-2); New Mexico St. 1958-67 (63-36-3); Trinity (Tex.) 1972-73 (16-5-0)

201 Vince Dooley (Born 9-4-32 Mobile, Ala.)
Auburn 1954 (25: 201-77-10 .715)
Georgia 1964-88 (201-77-10)

201 Eddie Anderson (Born 11-13-1900 Mason City, Iowa; Died 4-26-74)
Notre Dame 1922 (39: 201-128-15 .606)
Loras 1922-24 (16-6-2); DePaul 1925-31 (21-22-3); Holy Cross 1933-38, 1950-64 (129-67-8); Iowa 1939-42, 1946-49 (35-33-2)

198 Dana Bible (Born 10-8-1891 Jefferson City, Tenn.; Died 1-19-80)
Carson-Newman 1912 (33: 198-72-23 .715)
Mississippi Col. 1913-15 (12-7-2); Louisiana St. 1916 (1-0-2); Texas A&M 1917, 1919-28 (72-19-9); Nebraska 1929-36 (50-15-7); Texas 1937-46 (63-31-3)

197 Dan McGugin (Born 7-29-1879 Tingley, Iowa; Died 1-19-36)
Michigan 1904 (30: 197-55-19 .762)
Vanderbilt 1904-17, 1919-34 (197-55-19)

196 Fielding "Hurry Up" Yost (Born 4-30-1871 Fairview, W. Va.; Died 8-20-46)
Lafayette 1897 (29: 196-36-12 .828)
Ohio Wesleyan 1897 (7-1-1); Nebraska 1898 (7-4-0); Kansas 1899 (10-0-0); Stanford 1900 (7-2-1); Michigan 1901-23, 1925-26 (165-29-10)

195 *Tom Osborne (Born 2-23-37 Hastings, Neb.)
Hastings 1959 (20: 195-46-3 .805)
Nebraska 1973-92 (195-46-3)

194 Howard Jones (Born 8-23-1885 Excello, Ohio; Died 7-27-41)
Yale 1908 (29: 194-64-21 .733)
Syracuse 1908 (6-3-1); Yale 1909, 1913 (15-2-3); Ohio St. 1910 (6-1-3); Iowa 1916-23 (42-17-1); Duke 1924 (4-5-0); Southern Cal 1925-40 (121-36-13)

194 *Hayden Fry (Born 2-28-29 Odessa, Texas)
Baylor 1951 (✓31: 194-147-9 .567)
Southern Methodist 1962-72 (49-66-1); North Texas 1973-78 (✓40-23-3); Iowa 1979-92 (105-58-5)

191 *LaVell Edwards (Born 10-11-30 Provo, Utah)
　　Utah St. 1952 (21: 191-67-3 .738)
　　Brigham Young 1972-92 (191-67-3)
190 John Vaught (Born 5-6-08 Olney, Texas)
　　Texas Christian 1933 (25: 190-61-12 .745)
　　Mississippi 1947-70, 1973 (190-61-12)
185 John Heisman (Born 10-23-1869 Cleveland, Ohio; Died 10-3-36)
　　Brown 1890 (36: 185-70-17 .711)
　　Oberlin 1892, 1894 (11-3-1); Akron 1893 (5-2-0); Auburn 1895-99 (12-4-2); Clemson 1900-03
　　(19-3-2); Georgia Tech 1904-19 (102-29-6); Pennsylvania 1920-22 (16-10-2); Wash. & Jeff.
　　1923 (6-1-1); Rice 1924-27 (14-18-3)
184 Darrell Royal (Born 7-6-24 Hollis, Okla.)
　　Oklahoma 1950 (23: 184-60-5 .749)
　　Mississippi St. 1954-55 (12-8-0); Washington 1956 (5-5-0); Texas 1957-76 (167-47-5)
182 *Lou Holtz (Born 1-6-37 Follansbee, W. Va.)
　　Kent 1959 (23: 182-83-6 .683)
　　William & Mary 1969-71 (13-20-0); North Caro. St. 1972-75 (33-12-3); Arkansas 1977-83 (60-
　　21-2); Minnesota 1984-85 (10-12-0); Notre Dame 1986-92 (66-18-1)
180 Gil Dobie (Born 1-31-1879 Hastings, Minn.; Died 12-24-48)
　　Minnesota 1902 (33: 180-45-15 .781)
　　North Dak. St. 1906-07 (7-0-0); Washington 1908-16 (58-0-3); Navy 1917-19 (17-3-0); Cornell
　　1920-35 (82-36-7); Boston College 1936-38 (16-6-5)
180 Carl Snavely (Born 7-30-1894 Omaha, Neb.; Died 7-12-75)
　　Lebanon Valley 1915 (32: 180-96-16 .644)
　　Bucknell 1927-33 (42-16-8); North Caro. 1934-35, 1945-52 (59-35-5); Cornell 1936-44 (46-26-
　　3); Washington (Mo.) 1953-58 (33-19-0)
179 Jerry Claiborne (Born 8-26-28 Hopkinsville, Ky.)
　　Kentucky 1950 (28: 179-122-8 .592)
　　Virginia Tech 1961-70 (61-39-2); Maryland 1972-81 (77-37-3); Kentucky 1982-89 (36-40-3)
178 Ben Schwartzwalder (Born 6-2-09 Point Pleasant, W. Va.; Died 4-28-93)
　　West Va. 1933 (28: 178-96-3 .648)
　　Muhlenberg 1946-48 (25-5-0); Syracuse 1949-73 (153-91-3)
178 *Jim Sweeney (Born 9-1-29 Butte, Mont.)
　　Portland 1951 (28: 178-129-3 .579)
　　Montana St. 1963-67 (31-20-0); Washington St. 1968-75 (26-59-1); Fresno St. 1976-92 (121-
　　50-2)
176 Frank Kush (Born 1-20-29 Windber, Pa.)
　　Michigan St. 1953 (22: 176-54-1 .764)
　　Arizona St. 1958-79 (176-54-1)
176 *Don James (Born 12-31-32 Massillon, Ohio)
　　Miami (Fla.) 1954 (22: 176-78-3 .691)
　　Kent 1971-74 (25-19-1); Washington 1975-92 (151-59-2)
176 Ralph Jordan (Born 9-25-10 Selma, Ala.; Died 7-17-80)
　　Auburn 1932 (✓25: 176-83-6 .675)
　　Auburn 1951-75 (✓176-83-6)
174 Lynn "Pappy" Waldorf (Born 10-3-02 Clifton Springs, N.Y.; Died 8-15-81)
　　Syracuse 1925 (31: 174-100-22 .625)
　　Oklahoma City 1925-27 (17-11-3); Oklahoma St. 1929-33 (34-10-7); Kansas St. 1934 (7-2-1);
　　Northwestern 1935-46 (49-45-7); California 1947-56 (67-32-4)
173 Bob Neyland (Born 2-17-92 Greenville, Texas; Died 3-28-62)
　　Army 1916 (21: 173-31-12 .829)
　　Tennessee 1926-34, 1936-40, 1946-52 (173-31-12)
173 *Johnny Majors (Born 5-21-35 Lynchburg, Tenn.)
　　Tennessee 1957 (25: 173-105-10 .618)
　　Iowa St. 1968-72 (24-30-1); Pittsburgh 1973-76 (33-13-1); Tennessee 1977-92 (116-62-8)
172 Dan Devine (Born 12-23-24 Augusta, Wis.)
　　Minn.-Duluth 1948 (22: 172-57-9 .742)
　　Arizona St. 1955-57 (27-3-1); Missouri 1958-70 (92-38-7); Notre Dame 1975-80 (53-16-1)
171 Wallace Wade (Born 6-15-1892 Trenton, Tenn.; Died 10-7-86)
　　Brown 1917 (24: 171-49-10 .765)
　　Alabama 1923-30 (61-13-3); Duke 1931-41, 1946-50 (110-36-7)
170 Ara Parseghian (Born 5-21-23 Akron, Ohio)
　　Miami (Ohio) 1949 (24: 170-58-6 .739)
　　Miami (Ohio) 1951-55 (39-6-1); Northwestern 1956-63 (36-35-1); Notre Dame 1964-74 (95-17-
　　4)
170 Grant Teaff (Born 11-12-33 Hermleigh, Texas)
　　McMurry 1956 (30: 170-151-8 .529)
　　McMurry 1960-65 (23-35-2); Angelo St. 1969-71 (19-11-0); Baylor 1972-92 (128-105-6)
168 Bob Blackman (Born 7-7-18 De Soto, Iowa)
　　Southern Cal 1941 (30: 168-112-7 .598)
　　Denver 1953-54 (12-6-2); Dartmouth 1955-70 (104-37-3); Illinois 1971-76 (29-36-1); Cornell
　　1977-82 (23-33-1)
166 Earl "Red" Blaik (Born 2-17-1897 Detroit, Mich.; Died 5-6-89)
　　Miami (Ohio) 1918; Army 1920 (25: 166-48-14 .759)
　　Dartmouth 1934-40 (45-15-4); Army 1941-58 (121-33-10)

| | |
|---|---|
| 165 | Bobby Dodd (Born 11-11-08 Galax, Va.; Died 6-21-88) |
| | Tennessee 1931 (22: 165-64-8 .713) |
| | Georgia Tech 1945-66 (165-64-8) |
| 165 | Frank Howard (Born 3-25-09 Barlow Ben, Ala.) |
| | Alabama 1931 (30: 165-118-12 .580) |
| | Clemson 1940-69 (165-118-12) |
| 163 | Don Faurot (Born 6-23-02 Mountain Grove, Mo.) |
| | Missouri 1925 (28: 163-93-13 .630) |
| | Northeast Mo. St. 1926-34 (63-13-3); Missouri 1935-42, 1946-56 (100-80-10) |
| 162 | Ossie Solem (Born 12-13-1891 Minneapolis, Minn.; Died 10-26-70) |
| | Minnesota 1915 (37: 162-117-20 .575) |
| | Luther 1920 (5-1-1); Drake 1921-31 (54-35-2); Iowa 1932-36 (15-21-4); Syracuse 1937-45 (30-27-6); Springfield 1946-57 (58-33-7) |
| 161 | Bill Dooley (Born 5-19-34 Mobile, Ala.) |
| | Mississippi St. 1956 (26: 161-127-5 .558) |
| | North Caro. 1967-77 (69-53-2); Virginia Tech 1978-86 (64-37-1); Wake Forest 1987-92 (29-36-2) |
| 160 | Bill Yeoman (Born 12-26-27 Elnora, Ind.) |
| | Army 1949 (25: 160-108-8 .595) |
| | Houston 1962-86 (160-108-8) |
| 158 | Francis Schmidt (Born 12-3-1885 Downs, Kan.; Died 9-19-44) |
| | Nebraska 1914 (24: 158-57-11 .723) |
| | Tulsa 1919-21 (24-3-2); Arkansas 1922-28 (42-20-3); Texas Christian 1929-33 (46-6-5); Ohio St. 1934-40 (39-16-1); Idaho 1941-42 (7-12-0) |
| 157 | Barry Switzer (Born 10-5-37 Crossett, Ark.) |
| | Arkansas 1960 (16: 157-29-4 .837) |
| | Oklahoma 1973-88 (157-29-4) |
| 157 | Edward Robinson (Born 10-15-1873 Lynn, Miss.; Died 3-10-45) |
| | Brown 1896 (27: 157-88-13 .632) |
| | Nebraska 1896-97 (11-4-1); Brown 1898-1901, 1904-07, 1910-1925 (140-82-12); Maine 1902 (6-2-0) |
| 155 | Bennie Owen (Born 7-24-1875 Chicago, Ill.; Died 2-9-70) |
| | Kansas 1900 (27: 155-60-19 .703) |
| | Washburn 1900 (6-2-0); Bethany (Kan.) 1901-04 (27-4-3); Oklahoma 1905-26 (122-54-16) |
| 155 | Ray Morrison (Born 2-28-1885 Switzerland Co., Ind.; Died 11-19-82) |
| | Vanderbilt 1912 (34: 155-130-33 .539) |
| | Southern Methodist 1915-16, 1922-34 (84-44-22); Vanderbilt 1918, 1935-39 (29-22-2); Temple 1940-48 (31-38-9); Austin 1949-52 (11-26-0) |
| 154 | Earle Bruce (Born 3-8-31 Massillon, Ohio) |
| | Ohio St. 1953 (21: 154-90-2 .630) |
| | Tampa 1972 (10-2-0); Iowa St. 1973-78 (36-32-0); Ohio St. 1979-87 (81-26-1); Northern Iowa 1988 (5-6-0); Colorado St. 1989-92 (22-24-1) |
| 153 | Patrick F. "Pat" Dye (Born 11-6-39 Augusta, Ga.) |
| | Georgia 1962 (19: 153-62-5 .707) |
| | East Caro. 1974-79 (48-18-1); Wyoming 1980 (6-5-0); Auburn 1981-92 (99-39-4) |
| 153 | Morley Jennings (Born 1-23-1885 Holland, Mich.; Died 5-13-85) |
| | Mississippi St. 1912 (29: 153-75-18 .658) |
| | Ouachita Baptist 1912-25 (70-15-12); Baylor 1926-40 (83-60-6) |
| 153 | Matty Bell (Born 2-22-1899 Baylor Co., Texas; Died 6-30-83) |
| | Centre 1920 (26: 153-87-16 .630) |
| | Haskell 1920-21 (13-6-0); Carroll (Wis.) 1922 (4-3-0); Texas Christian 1923-28 (33-17-5); Texas A&M 1929-33 (24-21-3); Southern Methodist 1935-41, 1945-49 (79-40-8) |
| 151 | Lou Little (Born 12-6-1893 Leominster, Pa.; Died 5-28-79) |
| | Pennsylvania 1920 (33: 151-128-13 .539) |
| | Georgetown 1924-29 (41-12-3); Columbia 1930-56 (110-116-10) |

✓ Includes games forfeited, team and/or individual statistics abrogated, and coaching records changed by action of the NCAA Council under the restitution provisions of Bylaw 19.6 of the Official Procedure Governing the NCAA Enforcement Program (adopted by the NCAA membership at the 69th annual Convention in January 1975). The restitution provisions may be applied by the Council when a student-athlete has been permitted to participate while ineligible as a result of a court order against his institution or the NCAA, if the court order subsequently is overturned.

## COACHES WITH 200 OR MORE CAREER VICTORIES

This list includes all coaches in NCAA history who have won at least 200 games at four-year colleges (regardless of whether the college was an NCAA member at the time). Bowl and playoff games included.

| Coach (Alma Mater, Colleges Coached, Tenure) | Years | Won | Lost | Tied | Pct. |
|---|---|---|---|---|---|
| #Eddie Robinson (Leland '41) ................................... | †50 | 381 | 136 | 15 | .730 |
| (Grambling 1941-42, 1945—) | | | | | |
| Paul "Bear" Bryant (Alabama '36) ............................ | 38 | 323 | 85 | 17 | .780 |
| (Maryland 1945; Kentucky 1946-53; Texas A&M 1954-57; Alabama 1958-82) | | | | | |

| Coach (Alma Mater, Colleges Coached, Tenure) | Years | Won | Lost | Tied | Pct. |
|---|---|---|---|---|---|
| Amos Alonzo Stagg (Yale '88).................................<br>(Springfield 1890-91; Chicago 1892-1932; Pacific, Cal., 1933-46) | 57 | 314 | 199 | 35 | .605 |
| Glenn S. "Pop" Warner (Cornell '95) ......................<br>(Georgia 1895-96; Cornell 1897-98; Carlisle 1899-1903; Cornell 1904-06; Carlisle 1907-14; Pittsburgh 1915-23; Stanford 1924-32; Temple 1933-38) | 44 | 313 | 106 | 32 | .729 |
| #John Gagliardi (Colorado Col. '49) ......................<br>(Carroll, Mont. 1949-52; St. John's, Minn. 1953—) | †44 | 294 | 95 | 10 | .749 |
| #Ron Schipper (Hope '52) ......................................<br>(Central, Iowa 1961—) | †32 | 252 | 61 | 3 | .802 |
| #Joe Paterno (Brown '50) ......................................<br>(Penn St. 1966—) | 27 | 247 | 67 | 3 | .784 |
| #Roy Kidd (Eastern Ky. '54) ...................................<br>(Eastern Ky. 1964—) | †29 | 239 | 84 | 8 | .734 |
| Wayne Woodrow "Woody" Hayes (Denison '35)...............<br>(Denison 1946-48; Miami, Ohio 1949-50; Ohio St. 1951-78) | 33 | 238 | 72 | 10 | .759 |
| Glenn "Bo" Schembechler (Miami, Ohio '51)....................<br>(Miami, Ohio 1963-68; Michigan 1969-89) | 27 | 234 | 65 | 8 | .775 |
| Arnett Mumford (Wilberforce '24).............................<br>(Jarvis 1924-26; Bishop 1927-29; Texas College 1931-35; Southern-B.R. 1936-42, 1944-61) | †36 | 233 | 85 | 23 | .717 |
| ††John Merritt (Kentucky St. '50) .............................<br>(Jackson St. 1953-62; Tennessee St. 1963-83) | †31 | 232 | 65 | 11 | .771 |
| #Bobby Bowden (Samford '53) ...............................<br>(Samford 1959-62; West Va. 1970-75; Florida St. 1976—) | 27 | 227 | 77 | 3 | .744 |
| Fred Long (Millikin '18) .........................................<br>(Paul Quinn 1921-22; Wiley 1923-47; Prairie View 1948; Texas College 1949-55; Wiley 1956-65) | †45 | 227 | 151 | 31 | .593 |
| #Tubby Raymond (Michigan '50).............................<br>(Delaware 1966—) | †27 | 223 | 88 | 2 | .716 |
| #Jim Malosky (Minnesota '51) ...............................<br>(Minn.-Duluth 1958—) | †35 | 223 | 104 | 12 | .676 |
| #Fred Martinelli (Otterbein '51)...............................<br>(Ashland 1959—) | †34 | 208 | 117 | 12 | .635 |
| Jess Neely (Vanderbilt '24)....................................<br>(Southwestern, Tenn. 1924-27; Clemson 1931-39; Rice 1940-66) | 40 | 207 | 176 | 19 | .539 |
| Jake Gaither (Knoxville '27) ..................................<br>(Florida A&M 1945-69) | †25 | 203 | 36 | 4 | .844 |
| Warren Woodson (Baylor '24) ................................<br>(Conway St. 1935-40; Hardin-Simmons 1941-42, 1946-51; Arizona 1952-56; New Mexico St. 1958-67; Trinity, Tex. 1972-73) | 31 | 203 | 95 | 14 | .673 |
| Vince Dooley (Auburn '54) ....................................<br>(Georgia 1964-88) | 25 | 201 | 77 | 10 | .715 |
| Eddie Anderson (Notre Dame '22) ..........................<br>(Loras 1922-24; DePaul 1925-31; Holy Cross 1933-38; Iowa 1939-42, 1946-49; Holy Cross 1950-64) | 39 | 201 | 128 | 15 | .606 |
| #Jim Butterfield (Maine '53) ..................................<br>(Ithaca 1967—) | †26 | 200 | 67 | 1 | .748 |
| Darrell Mudra (Peru St. '51) ..................................<br>(Adams St. 1959-62; North Dak. St. 1963-65; Arizona 1967-68; Western Ill. 1969-73; Florida St. 1974-75; Eastern Ill. 1978-82; Northern Iowa 1983-87) | †26 | 200 | 81 | 4 | .709 |

† Zero to nine years in Division I-A.   †† Tennessee State's participation in 1981 and 1982 Division I-AA championships (1-2 record) voided.   # Active coach.

## COACHES WITH 200 OR MORE VICTORIES AT ONE COLLEGE

### (Bowl and Playoff Games Included)

| Coach (College, Tenure) | Years | Won | Lost | Tied | Pct. |
|---|---|---|---|---|---|
| #Eddie Robinson (Grambling 1941-42, 1945—) ................ | †50 | 381 | 136 | 15 | .730 |
| #John Gagliardi (St. John's, Minn. 1953—) .................... | †40 | 273 | 89 | 9 | .748 |
| #Ron Schipper (Central, Iowa 1961—) ......................... | †32 | 252 | 61 | 3 | .802 |
| #Joe Paterno (Penn St. 1966—)................................. | 27 | 247 | 67 | 3 | .784 |
| Amos Alonzo Stagg (Chicago 1892-1932) ..................... | 41 | 244 | 111 | 27 | .674 |
| #Roy Kidd (Eastern Ky. 1964—) ................................ | †29 | 239 | 84 | 8 | .734 |
| Paul "Bear" Bryant (Alabama 1958-82) ........................ | 25 | 232 | 46 | 9 | .824 |

*Coaches' Records*

| Coach (College, Tenure) | Years | Won | Lost | Tied | Pct. |
|---|---|---|---|---|---|
| #Tubby Raymond (Delaware 1966—) ........................ | †27 | 223 | 88 | 2 | .716 |
| #Jim Malosky (Minn.-Duluth 1958—) ...................... | †35 | 223 | 104 | 12 | .676 |
| #Fred Martinelli (Ashland 1959—) ........................ | †34 | 208 | 117 | 12 | .635 |
| Wayne Woodrow "Woody" Hayes (Ohio St. 1951-78) ........... | 28 | 205 | 61 | 10 | .761 |
| Jake Gaither (Florida A&M 1945-69) ...................... | †25 | 203 | 36 | 4 | .844 |
| Vince Dooley (Georgia 1964-88) .......................... | 25 | 201 | 77 | 10 | .715 |
| #Jim Butterfield (Ithaca 1967—) ......................... | †26 | 200 | 67 | 1 | .748 |

† Zero to nine years in Division I-A.   # Active coach.

## MATCH-UPS OF COACHES EACH WITH 200 VICTORIES

| Date | Coaches, Team (Victories Going In) | Winner (Score) |
|---|---|---|
| 11-11-61 | Arnett Mumford, Southern-B.R. (232) | |
| | Fred Long, Wiley (215) | Wiley (21-19) |
| 1-1-78 | Paul "Bear" Bryant, Alabama (272) | Alabama (35-6) |
| Sugar Bowl | "Woody" Hayes, Ohio St. (231) | |
| 10-11-80 | Eddie Robinson, Grambling (284) | Grambling (52-27) |
| | John Merritt, Tennessee St. (200) | |
| 10-10-81 | Eddie Robinson, Grambling (294) | |
| | John Merritt, Tennessee St. (209) | Tennessee St. (14-10) |
| 10-9-82 | Eddie Robinson, Grambling (301) | |
| | John Merritt, Tennessee St. (218) | Tennessee St. (22-8) |
| 10-8-83 | Eddie Robinson, Grambling (308) | |
| | John Merritt, Tennessee St. (228) | Tie (7-7) |
| 11-28-87 | John Gagliardi, St. John's (Minn.) (251) | |
| | Ron Schipper, Central (Iowa) (202) | Central (Iowa) (13-3) |
| 11-25-89 | John Gagliardi, St. John's (Minn.) (268) | St. John's (Minn.) (27-24) |
| | Ron Schipper, Central (Iowa) (224) | |
| 12-28-90 | Joe Paterno, Penn St. (229) | |
| Blockbuster | Bobby Bowden, Florida St. (204) | Florida St. (24-17) |
| Bowl | | |

## COACHES WITH CAREER WINNING
## PERCENTAGE OF .800 OR BETTER

This list includes all coaches in history with a winning percentage of at least .800 over a career of at least 10 seasons at four-year colleges (regardless of division or association). Bowl and playoff games included.

| Coach (Alma Mater, Colleges Coached, Tenure) | Years | Won | Lost | Tied | Pct. |
|---|---|---|---|---|---|
| Knute Rockne (Notre Dame '14) ............................... | 13 | 105 | 12 | 5 | .881 |
| (Notre Dame 1918-30) | | | | | |
| #Bob Reade (Cornell College '54).............................. | †14 | 131 | 19 | 1 | .871 |
| (Augustana, Ill. 1979—) | | | | | |
| Frank Leahy (Notre Dame '31) ............................... | 13 | 107 | 13 | 9 | .864 |
| (Boston College 1939-40; Notre Dame 1941-43, 1946-53) | | | | | |
| Doyt Perry (Bowling Green '32) .............................. | †10 | 77 | 11 | 5 | .855 |
| (Bowling Green 1955-64) | | | | | |
| George Woodruff (Yale '89) ................................. | 12 | 142 | 25 | 2 | .846 |
| (Pennsylvania 1892-1901; Illinois 1903; Carlisle 1905) | | | | | |
| Jake Gaither (Knoxville '27) .................................. | †25 | 203 | 36 | 4 | .844 |
| (Florida A&M 1945-69) | | | | | |
| Dave Maurer (Denison '54)................................... | †15 | 129 | 23 | 3 | .842 |
| (Wittenberg 1969-83) | | | | | |
| #Mike Kelly (Manchester '70) ................................ | †12 | 119 | 22 | 1 | .842 |
| (Dayton 1981—) | | | | | |
| Paul Hoereman (Heidelberg '38) ............................ | †14 | 102 | 18 | 4 | .839 |
| (Heidelberg 1946-59) | | | | | |
| Barry Switzer (Arkansas '60) ............................... | 16 | 157 | 29 | 4 | .837 |
| (Oklahoma 1973-88) | | | | | |
| Don Coryell (Washington '50)................................ | †15 | 127 | 24 | 3 | .834 |
| (Whittier 1957-59; San Diego St. 1961-72) | | | | | |
| Percy Haughton (Harvard '99) .............................. | 13 | 96 | 17 | 6 | .832 |
| (Cornell 1899-1900; Harvard 1908-16; Columbia 1923-24) | | | | | |
| Robert "Bob" Neyland (Army '16) ........................... | 21 | 173 | 31 | 12 | .829 |
| (Tennessee 1926-34, 1936-40, 1946-52) | | | | | |
| Fielding "Hurry Up" Yost (Lafayette '97)....................... | 29 | 196 | 36 | 12 | .828 |
| (Ohio Wesleyan 1897; Nebraska 1898; Kansas 1899; Stanford 1900; Michigan 1901-23, 1925-26) | | | | | |

| Coach (Alma Mater, Colleges Coached, Tenure) | Years | Won | Lost | Tied | Pct. |
|---|---|---|---|---|---|
| Charles "Bud" Wilkinson (Minnesota '37) ........................ <br> (Oklahoma 1947-63) | 17 | 145 | 29 | 4 | .826 |
| Charles "Chuck" Klausing (Slippery Rock '48) .................. <br> (Indiana, Pa. 1964-69; Carnegie Mellon 1976-85) | †16 | 123 | 26 | 2 | .821 |
| Vernon McCain (Langston '31) ................................. <br> (Md.-East. Shore 1948-63) | †16 | 102 | 21 | 5 | .816 |
| John "Jock" Sutherland (Pittsburgh '18) ........................ <br> (Lafayette 1919-23; Pittsburgh 1924-38) | 20 | 144 | 28 | 14 | .812 |
| #Al Bagnoli (Central Conn. St. '74) ............................. <br> (Union, N.Y. 1982-91; Pennsylvania 1992) | †11 | 93 | 22 | 0 | .809 |
| Bob Devaney (Alma '39) ...................................... <br> (Wyoming 1957-61; Nebraska 1962-72) | 16 | 136 | 30 | 7 | .806 |
| #Tom Osborne (Hastings '59) ................................. <br> (Nebraska 1973—) | 20 | 195 | 46 | 3 | .805 |
| Sid Gillman (Ohio St. '34) ...................................... <br> (Miami, Ohio 1944-47; Cincinnati 1949-54) | †10 | 81 | 19 | 2 | .804 |
| #Ron Schipper (Hope '52) ..................................... <br> (Central, Iowa 1961—) | †32 | 252 | 61 | 3 | .802 |

†Zero to nine years in Division I-A.   #Active coach.

# ALL-TIME DIVISION I
# COACHING LONGEVITY RECORDS
**(Minimum 10 Head-Coaching Seasons in Division I; Bowl Games Included)**

## MOST GAMES

| Games | Coach, School(s) and Years |
|---|---|
| 548 | Amos Alonzo Stagg, Springfield 1890-91, Chicago 1892-1932, Pacific (Cal.) 1933-46 |
| 451 | Glenn "Pop" Warner, Georgia 1895-96, Cornell 1897-98 and 1904-06, Carlisle 1899-1903 and 1907-14, Pittsburgh 1915-23, Stanford 1924-32, Temple 1933-38 |
| 425 | Paul "Bear" Bryant, Maryland 1945, Kentucky 1946-53, Texas A&M 1954-57, Alabama 1958-82 |
| 402 | Jess Neely, Rhodes 1924-27, Clemson 1931-39, Rice 1940-66 |
| 350 | *Hayden Fry, Southern Methodist 1962-72, North Texas 1973-78, Iowa 1979-92 |
| 344 | Eddie Anderson, Loras 1922-24, DePaul 1925-31, Holy Cross 1933-38 and 1950-64, Iowa 1939-42 and 1946-49 |
| 329 | Grant Teaff, McMurry 1960-65, Angelo St. 1969-71, Baylor 1972-92 |
| 320 | Wayne Woodrow "Woody" Hayes, Denison 1946-48, Miami (Ohio) 1949-50, Ohio St. 1951-78 |
| 318 | Ray Morrison, Southern Methodist 1915-16 and 1922-34, Vanderbilt 1918 and 1935-39, Temple 1940-48, Austin 1949-52 |
| 317 | *Joe Paterno, Penn St. 1966-92 |
| 312 | Warren Woodson, Central Ark. 1935-39, Hardin-Simmons 1941-42 and 1946-51, Arizona 1952-56, New Mexico St. 1958-67, Trinity (Tex.) 1972-73 |
| 310 | *Jim Sweeney, Montana St. 1963-67, Washington St. 1968-75, Fresno St. 1976-77 and 1980-92 |
| 309 | Jerry Claiborne, Virginia Tech 1961-70, Maryland 1972-81, Kentucky 1982-89 |
| 307 | *Bobby Bowden, Samford 1959-62, West Va. 1970-75, Florida St. 1976-92 |
| 307 | Glenn "Bo" Schembechler, Miami (Ohio) 1963-68, Michigan 1969-89 |
| 299 | Ossie Solem, Luther 1920, Drake 1921-31, Iowa 1932-36, Syracuse 1937-45, Springfield 1946-57 |
| 296 | DeOrmond "Tuss" McLaughry, Westminster 1916, 1918 and 1921, Amherst 1922-25, Brown 1926-40, Dartmouth 1941-54 |
| 296 | Lynn "Pappy" Waldorf, Oklahoma City 1925-27, Oklahoma St. 1929-33, Kansas St. 1934, Northwestern 1935-46, California 1947-56 |
| 295 | Frank Howard, Clemson 1940-69 |
| 293 | Dana Bible, Mississippi Col. 1913-15, Louisiana St. 1916, Texas A&M 1917 and 1919-28, Nebraska 1929-36, Texas 1937-46 |
| 293 | Bill Dooley, North Caro. 1967-77, Virginia Tech 1978-86, Wake Forest 1987-92 |
| 292 | Lou Little, Georgetown 1924-29, Columbia 1930-56 |
| 292 | Carl Snavely, Bucknell 1927-33, North Caro. 1934-35 and 1945-52, Cornell 1936-44, Washington (Mo.) 1953-58 |
| 288 | Vince Dooley, Georgia 1964-88 |
| 288 | *Johnny Majors, Iowa St. 1968-72, Pittsburgh 1973-76, Tennessee 1977-92 |
| 287 | Bob Blackman, Denver 1953-54, Dartmouth 1955-70, Illinois 1971-76, Cornell 1977-82 |
| 282 | Clark Shaughnessy, Tulane 1915-20 and 1922-26, Loyola (La.) 1927-32, Chicago 1933-39, Stanford 1940-41, Maryland 1942 and 1946, Pittsburgh 1943-45, Hawaii 1965 |
| 279 | Howard Jones, Syracuse 1908, Yale 1909 and 1913, Ohio St. 1910, Iowa 1916-23, Duke 1924, Southern Cal 1925-40 |
| 277 | Ben Schwartzwalder, Muhlenberg 1946-48, Syracuse 1949-73 |

| Games | Coach, School(s) and Years |
|---|---|
| 276 | Bill Yeoman, Houston 1962-86 |
| 272 | John Heisman, Oberlin 1892 and 1894, Akron 1893, Auburn 1895-99, Clemson 1900-03, Georgia Tech 1904-19, Pennsylvania 1920-22, Wash. & Jeff. 1923, Rice 1924-27 |
| 271 | *Lou Holtz, William & Mary 1969-71, North Caro. St. 1972-75, Arkansas 1977-83, Minnesota 1984-85, Notre Dame 1986-92 |
| 271 | Dan McGugin, Vanderbilt 1904-17 and 1919-34 |
| 269 | Don Faurot, Northeast Mo. St. 1926-34, Missouri 1935-42 and 1946-56 |
| 265 | Ralph "Shug" Jordan, Auburn 1951-75 |
| 263 | John Vaught, Mississippi 1947-70 and 1973 |
| 261 | *LaVell Edwards, Brigham Young, 1972-92 |
| 260 | Jack Curtice, West Tex. St. 1940-41, UTEP 1946-49, Utah 1950-57, Stanford 1958-61, UC Santa Barb. 1962-69 |
| 258 | Edward Robinson, Nebraska 1896-97, Brown 1898-1901, 1904-07 and 1910-25 |
| 257 | *Don James, Kent 1971-74, Washington 1975-92 |
| 256 | Matty Bell, Haskell 1920-21, Carroll (Wis.) 1922, Texas Christian 1923-28, Texas A&M 1929-33, Southern Methodist 1935-41 and 1945-49 |
| 256 | *Bill Mallory, Miami (Ohio) 1969-73, Colorado 1974-78, Northern Ill. 1980-83, Indiana 1984-92 |
| 252 | Harvey Harman, Haverford 1922-29, Sewanee 1930, Pennsylvania 1931-37, Rutgers 1938-55 |

* Active.

## MOST YEARS

| Years | Coach, School(s) and Years |
|---|---|
| 57 | Amos Alonzo Stagg, Springfield 1890-91, Chicago 1892-1932, Pacific (Cal.) 1933-46 |
| 44 | Glenn "Pop" Warner, Georgia 1895-96, Cornell 1897-98 and 1904-06, Carlisle 1899-1903 and 1907-14, Pittsburgh 1915-23, Stanford 1924-32, Temple 1933-38 |
| 40 | Jess Neely, Rhodes 1924-27, Clemson 1931-39, Rice 1940-66 |
| 39 | Eddie Anderson, Loras 1922-24, DePaul 1925-31, Holy Cross 1933-38 and 1950-54, Iowa 1939-42 and 1946-49 |
| 38 | Paul "Bear" Bryant, Maryland 1945, Kentucky 1946-53, Texas A&M 1954-57, Alabama 1958-82 |
| 37 | Ossie Solem, Luther 1920, Drake 1921-31, Iowa 1932-36, Syracuse 1937-45, Springfield 1946-57 |
| 36 | John Heisman, Oberlin 1892 and 1894, Akron 1893, Auburn 1895-99, Clemson 1900-03, Georgia Tech 1904-19, Pennsylvania 1920-22, Wash. & Jeff. 1923, Rice 1924-27 |
| 34 | DeOrmond "Tuss" McLaughry, Westminster 1916, 1918 and 1921, Amherst 1922-25, Brown 1926-40, Dartmouth 1941-54 |
| 34 | Ray Morrison, Southern Methodist 1915-16 and 1922-34, Vanderbilt 1918 and 1935-39, Temple 1940-48, Austin 1949-52 |
| 33 | Dana Bible, Mississippi Col. 1913-15, Louisiana St. 1916, Texas A&M 1917 and 1919-28, Nebraska 1929-36, Texas 1937-46 |
| 33 | Gil Dobie, North Dak. St. 1906-07, Washington 1908-16, Navy 1917-19, Cornell 1920-35, Boston College 1936-38 |
| 33 | Wayne Woodrow "Woody" Hayes, Denison 1946-48, Miami (Ohio) 1949-50, Ohio St. 1951-78 |
| 33 | Lou Little, Georgetown 1924-29, Columbia 1930-56 |
| 32 | Clark Shaughnessy, Tulane 1915-20 and 1922-26, Loyola (La.) 1927-32, Chicago 1933-39, Stanford 1940-41, Maryland 1942 and 1946, Pittsburgh 1943-45, Hawaii 1965 |
| 32 | Carl Snavely, Bucknell 1927-33, North Caro. 1934-35 and 1945-52, Cornell 1936-44, Washington (Mo.) 1953-58 |
| 31 | *Hayden Fry, Southern Methodist 1962-72, North Texas 1973-78, Iowa 1979-92 |
| 31 | Lynn "Pappy" Waldorf, Oklahoma City 1925-27, Oklahoma St. 1929-33, Kansas St. 1934, Northwestern 1935-46, California 1947-56 |
| 31 | Warren Woodson, Central Ark. 1935-39, Hardin-Simmons 1941-42 and 1946-51, Arizona 1952-56, New Mexico St. 1958-67, Trinity (Tex.) 1972-73 |
| 30 | Bob Blackman, Denver 1953-54, Dartmouth 1955-70, Illinois 1971-76, Cornell 1977-82 |
| 30 | Harvey Harman, Haverford 1922-29, Sewanee 1930, Pennsylvania 1931-37, Rutgers 1938-55 |
| 30 | Frank Howard, Clemson 1940-69 |
| 30 | Dan McGugin, Vanderbilt 1904-17 and 1919-34 |
| 30 | Grant Teaff, McMurry 1960-65, Angelo St. 1969-71, Baylor 1972-92 |

* Active.

## MOST SCHOOLS

**(Must Have Coached at Least One Division I or Major-College Team)**

| Schools | Coach, Schools and Years |
|---|---|
| 8 | John Heisman, Oberlin 1892 and 1894, Akron 1893, Auburn 1895-99, Clemson 1900-03, Georgia Tech 1904-19, Pennsylvania 1920-22, Wash. & Jeff. 1923, Rice 1924-27 |
| 7 | Darrell Mudra, Adams St. 1959-62, North Dak. St. 1963-65, Arizona 1967-68, Western Ill. 1969-73, Florida St. 1974-75, Eastern Ill. 1978-82, Northern Iowa 1983-87 |
| 7 | Lou Saban, Case Reserve 1950-52, Northwestern 1955, Western Ill. 1957-59, Maryland 1966, Miami (Fla.) 1977-78, Army 1979, Central Fla. 1983-84 |
| 7 | Clark Shaughnessy, Tulane 1915-20 and 1922-26, Loyola (La.) 1927-32, Chicago 1933-39, Stanford 1940-41, Maryland 1942 and 1946, Pittsburgh 1943-45, Hawaii 1965 |

| Schools | Coach, Schools and Years |
|---|---|
| 6 | Howard Jones, Syracuse 1908, Yale 1909 and 1913, Ohio St. 1910, Iowa 1916-23, Duke 1924, Southern Cal 1925-40 |
| 6 | Chuck Mills, Cal Poly Pomona 1959-61, Indiana (Pa.) 1962-63, King's Point 1964, Utah St. 1967-72, Wake Forest 1973-77, Southern Ore. 1980-83 |
| 6 | Glenn "Pop" Warner, Georgia 1895-96, Cornell 1897-98 and 1904-06, Carlisle 1899-1903 and 1907-14, Pittsburgh 1915-23, Stanford 1924-32, Temple 1933-38 |
| 5 | Matty Bell, Haskell 1920-21, Carroll (Wis.) 1922, Texas Christian 1923-28, Texas A&M 1929-33, Southern Methodist 1935-41 and 1945-49 |
| 5 | Dana Bible, Mississippi Col. 1913-15, Louisiana St. 1916, Texas A&M 1917 and 1919-28, Nebraska 1929-36, Texas 1937-46 |
| 5 | Earle Bruce, Tampa 1972, Iowa St. 1973-78, Ohio St. 1979-87, Northern Iowa 1988, Colorado St. 1989-92 |
| 5 | Frank Cavanaugh, Cincinnati 1898, Holy Cross 1903-05, Dartmouth 1911-16, Boston College 1919-26, Fordham 1927-32 |
| 5 | Jack Curtice, West Tex. St. 1940-41, UTEP 1946-49, Utah 1950-57, Stanford 1958-61, UC Santa Barb. 1962-69 |
| 5 | Gil Dobie, North Dak. St. 1906-07, Washington 1908-16, Navy 1917-19, Cornell 1920-35, Boston College 1936-38 |
| 5 | Ed Doherty, Arizona St. 1947-50, Rhode Island 1951, Arizona 1957-58, Xavier (Ohio) 1959-61, Holy Cross 1971-75 |
| 5 | Harold "Red" Drew, Trinity (Conn.) 1921-23, Birmingham So. 1924-27, Tenn.-Chatt. 1929-30, Mississippi 1946, Alabama 1947-54 |
| 5 | Stuart Holcomb, Findlay 1932-35, Muskingum 1936-40, Wash. & Jeff. 1941, Miami (Ohio) 1942-43, Purdue 1947-55 |
| 5 | *Lou Holtz, William & Mary 1969-71, North Caro. St. 1972-75, Arkansas 1977-83, Minnesota 1984-85, Notre Dame 1986-92 |
| 5 | *Al Molde, Sioux Falls 1971-72, Minn.-Morris 1973-79, Central Mo. St. 1980-82, Eastern Ill. 1983-86, Western Mich. 1987-92 |
| 5 | Darryl Rogers, Cal St. Hayward 1965, Fresno St. 1966-72, San Jose St. 1973-75, Michigan St. 1976-79, Arizona St. 1980-84 |
| 5 | John Rowland, Henderson St. 1925-30, Ouachita Baptist 1931, Citadel 1940-42, Oklahoma City 1946-47, Geo. Washington 1948-51 |
| 5 | Francis Schmidt, Tulsa 1919-21, Arkansas 1922-28, Texas Christian 1929-33, Ohio St. 1934-40, Idaho 1941-42 |
| 5 | Maurice "Clipper" Smith, Gonzaga 1925-28, Santa Clara 1929-35, Villanova 1936-42, San Francisco 1946, Lafayette 1949-51 |
| 5 | Carl Snavely, Bucknell 1927-33, North Caro. 1934-35 and 1945-52, Cornell 1936-44, Washington (Mo.) 1953-58 |
| 5 | Ossie Solem, Luther 1920, Drake 1921-31, Iowa 1932-36, Syracuse 1937-45, Springfield 1946-57 |
| 5 | J. Neil "Skip" Stahley, Delaware 1934, Brown 1941-43, Geo. Washington 1946-47, Toledo 1948-49, Idaho 1954-60 |
| 5 | *Jim Wacker, Texas Lutheran 1971-75, North Dak. St. 1976-78, Southwest Tex. St. 1979-82, Texas Christian 1983-91, Minnesota 1992 |
| 5 | Lynn "Pappy" Waldorf, Oklahoma City 1925-27, Oklahoma St. 1929-33, Kansas St. 1934, Northwestern 1935-46, California 1947-56 |
| 5 | Warren Woodson, Central Ark. 1935-39, Hardin-Simmons 1941-42, Arizona 1952-56, New Mexico St. 1958-67, Trinity (Tex.) 1972-73 |
| 5 | Fielding "Hurry Up" Yost, Ohio Wesleyan 1897, Nebraska 1898, Kansas 1899, Stanford 1900, Michigan 1901-23 and 1925-26 |
| 4 | Eddie Anderson, Loras 1922-24, DePaul 1925-31, Holy Cross 1933-38 and 1950-64, Iowa 1939-42 and 1946-49 |
| 4 | Jerry Berndt, DePauw 1979-80, Pennsylvania 1981-85, Rice 1986-88, Temple 1989-92 |
| 4 | Bob Blackman, Denver 1953-54, Dartmouth 1955-70, Illinois 1971-76, Cornell 1977-82 |
| 4 | Watson Brown, Austin Peay 1979-80, Cincinnati 1983, Rice 1984-85, Vanderbilt 1986-90 |
| 4 | Paul "Bear" Bryant, Maryland 1945, Kentucky 1946-53, Texas A&M 1954-57, Alabama 1958-82 |
| 4 | Dudley DeGroot, UC Santa Barb. 1926-31, San Jose St. 1932-43, West Va. 1948-49, New Mexico 1950-52 |
| 4 | Pete Elliott, Nebraska 1956, California 1957-59, Illinois 1960-66, Miami (Fla.) 1973-74 |
| 4 | *Dennis Erickson, Idaho 1982-85, Wyoming 1986, Washington St. 1987-88, Miami (Fla.) 1989-92 |
| 4 | Wesley Fesler, Wesleyan 1941-42, Pittsburgh 1946, Ohio St. 1947-50, Minnesota 1951-53 |
| 4 | *Dennis Franchione, S'western (Kan.) 1981-82, Pittsburg St. 1985-89, Southwest Tex. St. 1990-91, New Mexico St. 1992 |
| 4 | Mike Gottfried, Murray St. 1978-80, Cincinnati 1981-82, Kansas 1983-85, Pittsburgh 1986-89 |
| 4 | Harvey Harman, Haverford 1922-29, Sewanee 1930, Pennsylvania 1931-37, Rutgers 1938-55 |
| 4 | *Bill Mallory, Miami (Ohio) 1969-73, Colorado 1974-78, Northern Ill. 1980-83, Indiana 1984-92 |
| 4 | DeOrmond "Tuss" McLaughry, Westminster 1916, 1918 and 1921, Amherst 1922-25, Brown 1926-40, Dartmouth 1941-54 |
| 4 | Joe McMullen, Stetson 1950-51, Wash. & Jeff. 1952-53, Akron 1954-60, San Jose St. 1969-70 |

*Coaches' Records*

| Schools | Coach, Schools and Years |
|---|---|
| 4 | Bill Meek, Kansas St. 1951-54, Houston 1955-56, Southern Methodist 1957-61, Utah 1968-73 |
| 4 | Charley Moran, Texas A&M 1909-14, Centre 1919-23, Bucknell 1924-26, Catawba 1930-31 |
| 4 | Ray Morrison, Southern Methodist 1915-16 and 1922-34, Vanderbilt 1918 and 1935-39, Temple 1940-48, Austin 1949-52 |
| 4 | Frank Navarro, Williams 1963-67, Columbia 1968-73, Wabash 1974-77, Princeton 1978-84 |
| 4 | John Pont, Miami (Ohio) 1956-62, Yale 1963-64, Indiana 1965-72, Northwestern 1973-77 |
| 4 | Bill Roper, Va. Military 1903-04, Princeton 1906-08, 1910-11 and 1919-30, Missouri 1909, Swarthmore 1915-16 |
| 4 | Philip Sarboe, Central Wash. 1941-42, Washington St. 1945-49, Humboldt St. 1951-65, Hawaii 1966 |
| 4 | George Sauer, New Hampshire 1937-41, Kansas 1946-47, Navy 1948-49, Baylor 1950-55 |
| 4 | *Jackie Sherrill, Washington St. 1976, Pittsburgh 1977-81, Texas A&M 1982-88, Mississippi St. 1991-92 |
| 4 | Steve Sloan, Vanderbilt 1973-74, Texas Tech 1975-77, Mississippi 1978-82, Duke 1983-86 |
| 4 | Denny Stolz, Alma 1965-70, Michigan St. 1973-75, Bowling Green 1977-85, San Diego St. 1986-88 |

\* *Active.*

# MOST YEARS COACHED FOOTBALL AT ONE DIVISION I-A COLLEGE
## (Minimum 15 Years)

| Coach, College (Years) | Years | School W-L-T | Overall W-L-T |
|---|---|---|---|
| Amos Alonzo Stagg, Chicago (1892-32) | 41 | 244-111-27 | 314-199-35 |
| Frank Howard, Clemson (1940-69) | 30# | 165-118-12 | 165-118-12 |
| Dan McGugin, Vanderbilt (1904-17, 1919-34) | 30# | 197-55-19 | 197-55-19 |
| Wayne Woodrow "Woody" Hayes, Ohio St. (1951-78) | 28 | 205-61-10 | 238-72-10 |
| Lou Little, Columbia (1930-56) | 27 | 110-116-10 | 151-128-13 |
| Jess Neely, Rice (1940-66) | 27 | 144-124-10 | 207-176-19 |
| *Joe Paterno, Penn St. (1966-92) | 27# | 247-67-3 | 247-67-3 |
| Ike Armstrong, Utah (1925-49) | 25# | 140-55-15 | 140-55-15 |
| Paul "Bear" Bryant, Alabama (1958-82) | 25 | 232-46-9 | 323-85-17 |
| Vince Dooley, Georgia (1964-88) | 25# | 201-77-10 | 201-77-10 |
| Ralph Jordan, Auburn (1951-75) | 25# | 176-83-6 | 176-83-6 |
| Ben Schwartzwalder, Syracuse (1949-73) | 25 | 153-91-3 | 178-96-3 |
| John Vaught, Mississippi (1947-70, 1973) | 25# | 190-61-12 | 190-61-12 |
| Bill Yeoman, Houston (1962-86) | 25# | 160-108-8 | 160-108-8 |
| Fielding "Hurry Up" Yost, Michigan (1901-23, 1925-26) | 25 | 165-29-10 | 196-36-12 |
| Frank Camp, Louisville (1946-68) | 23# | 118-96-2 | 118-96-2 |
| Edward Robinson, Brown (1898-1901, 1904-07, 1910-25) | 23 | 140-82-12 | 157-88-13 |
| Bobby Dodd, Georgia Tech (1945-66) | 22# | 165-64-8 | 165-64-8 |
| Frank Kush, Arizona St. (1958-79) | 22# | 176-54-1 | 176-54-1 |
| Bennie Owen, Oklahoma (1905-26) | 22 | 122-54-16 | 155-60-19 |
| Henry Williams, Minnesota (1900-21) | 22 | 140-33-11 | 141-34-12 |
| Eddie Anderson, Holy Cross (1933-38, 1950-64) | 21 | 129-67-8 | 201-128-15 |
| *LaVell Edwards, Brigham Young (1972-92) | 21# | 191-67-3 | 191-67-3 |
| Bob Neyland, Tennessee (1926-34, 1936-40, 1946-50) | 21# | 173-31-12 | 173-31-12 |
| Bo Schembechler, Michigan (1969-89) | 21 | 194-48-5 | 234-65-8 |
| Grant Teaff, Baylor (1972-92) | 21 | 128-105-6 | 170-151-8 |
| Bill Hess, Ohio (1958-77) | 20# | 107-92-4 | 107-92-4 |
| Ben Martin, Air Force (1958-77) | 20 | 96-103-9 | 102-116-10 |
| *Tom Osborne, Nebraska (1973-92) | 20# | 195-46-3 | 195-46-3 |
| Darrell Royal, Texas (1957-76) | 20 | 167-47-5 | 184-60-5 |
| Thad "Pie" Vann, Southern Miss. (1949-68) | 20# | 139-59-2 | 139-59-2 |
| Frank Broyles, Arkansas (1958-76) | 19 | 144-58-5 | 149-62-6 |
| Earl "Red" Blaik, Army (1941-58) | 18 | 121-33-10 | 166-48-14 |
| Ray Eliot, Illinois (1942-59) | 18 | 83-73-11 | 102-82-13 |
| *Don James, Washington (1975-92) | 18 | 151-59-2 | 176-78-3 |
| Charlie McClendon, Louisiana St. (1962-79) | 18# | 137-59-7 | 137-59-7 |
| Jim Owens, Washington (1957-74) | 18# | 99-82-6 | 99-82-6 |
| Murray Warmath, Minnesota (1954-71) | 18 | 87-78-7 | 97-84-10 |
| *Chris Ault, Nevada (1976-92) | 17# | 145-58-1 | 145-58-1 |
| *Bobby Bowden, Florida St. (1976-92) | 17 | 154-45-3 | 227-77-3 |
| *Terry Donahue, UCLA (1976-92) | 17# | 131-59-8 | 131-59-8 |
| Earle Edwards, North Caro. St. (1954-70) | 17 | 77-88-8 | 77-88-8 |
| Bud Wilkinson, Oklahoma (1947-63) | 17# | 145-29-4 | 145-29-4 |
| Bob Blackman, Dartmouth (1955-70) | 16 | 104-37-3 | 168-112-7 |
| *Rich Brooks, Oregon (1977-92) | 16# | 77-99-4 | 77-99-4 |

| Coach, College (Years) | Years | School W-L-T | Overall W-L-T |
|---|---|---|---|
| Len Casanova, Oregon (1951-66) .................................. | 16 | 82-73-8 | 104-94-11 |
| Gil Dobie, Cornell (1920-35) ...................................... | 16 | 82-36-7 | 180-45-15 |
| Rip Engle, Penn St. (1950-65) .................................... | 16 | 104-48-4 | 132-68-8 |
| Andy Gustafson, Miami (Fla.) (1948-63) ......................... | 16 | 93-65-3 | 115-78-4 |
| John Heisman, Georgia Tech (1904-19) ........................... | 16 | 102-29-6 | 185-70-17 |
| Howard Jones, Southern Cal (1925-40) ........................... | 16 | 121-36-13 | 194-64-21 |
| *Johnny Majors, Tennessee (1977-92) ............................ | 16 | 116-62-8 | 173-105-10 |
| John McKay, Southern Cal (1960-75) ............................. | 16# | 127-40-8 | 127-40-8 |
| Barry Switzer, Oklahoma (1973-88) ............................... | 16# | 157-29-4 | 157-29-4 |
| Wallace Wade, Duke (1931-41, 1946-50) .......................... | 16 | 110-36-7 | 171-49-10 |
| *Herb Deromedi, Central Mich. (1978-92) ........................ | 15# | 105-49-10 | 105-49-10 |
| Rex Enright, South Caro. (1938-42, 1946-55) ..................... | 15# | 64-69-7 | 64-69-7 |
| Morley Jennings, Baylor (1926-40) ................................. | 15 | 83-60-6 | 153-75-18 |
| Ray Morrison, Southern Methodist (1915-16, 1922-34) ........... | 15 | 84-44-22 | 155-130-33 |
| William Murray, Duke (1951-65) ................................... | 15 | 83-51-9 | 142-67-11 |
| Jock Sutherland, Pittsburgh (1924-38) ............................ | 15 | 111-20-12 | 144-28-14 |
| *Jim Sweeney, Fresno St. (1976-77, 1980-92) .................... | 15 | 121-50-2 | 178-129-3 |
| Frank Thomas, Alabama (1931-42, 1944-46) ...................... | 15 | 115-24-7 | 141-33-9 |

*Active coach.  # Never coached at any other college.

# ACTIVE COACHING LONGEVITY RECORDS
(Through 1992 season; minimum five years as a Division I-A head coach; includes bowl games)

## MOST GAMES

| Games | Coach, School(s) and Years |
|---|---|
| 350 | Hayden Fry, Southern Methodist 1962-72, North Texas 1973-78, Iowa 1979-92 |
| 317 | Joe Paterno, Penn St., 1966-92 |
| 310 | Jim Sweeney, Montana St. 1963-67, Washington St. 1968-75, Fresno St. 1976-77 and 1980-92 |
| 307 | Bobby Bowden, Samford 1959-62, West Va. 1970-75, Florida St. 1976-92 |
| 288 | Johnny Majors, Iowa St. 1968-72, Pittsburgh 1973-76, Tennessee 1977-92 |
| 271 | Lou Holtz, William & Mary 1969-71, North Caro. St. 1972-75, Arkansas 1977-83, Minnesota 1984-85, Notre Dame 1986-92 |
| 261 | LaVell Edwards, Brigham Young 1972-92 |
| 257 | Don James, Kent 1971-74, Washington 1975-92 |
| 256 | Bill Mallory, Miami (Ohio) 1969-73, Colorado 1974-78, Northern Ill. 1980-83, Indiana 1984-92 |
| 249 | Jim Wacker, Texas Lutheran 1971-75, North Dak. St. 1976-78, Southwest Tex. St. 1979-82, Texas Christian 1983-91, Minnesota 1992 |
| 244 | Tom Osborne, Nebraska 1973-92 |
| 243 | Don Nehlen, Bowling Green 1968-76, West Va. 1980-92 |
| 229 | George Welsh, Navy 1973-81, Virginia 1982-92 |
| 214 | Billy Brewer, Southeastern La. 1974-79, Louisiana Tech 1980-82, Mississippi 1983-92 |

## MOST YEARS

| Years | Coach, School(s) and Years |
|---|---|
| 31 | Hayden Fry, Southern Methodist 1962-72, North Texas 1973-78, Iowa 1979-92 |
| 28 | Jim Sweeney, Montana St. 1963-67, Washington St. 1968-75, Fresno St. 1976-77 and 1980-92 |
| 27 | Bobby Bowden, Samford 1959-62, West Va. 1970-75, Florida St. 1976-92 |
| 27 | Joe Paterno, Penn St. 1966-92 |
| 25 | Johnny Majors, Iowa St. 1968-72, Pittsburgh 1973-76, Tennessee 1977-92 |
| 23 | Lou Holtz, William & Mary 1969-71, North Caro. St. 1972-75, Arkansas 1977-83, Minnesota 1984-85, Notre Dame 1986-92 |
| 23 | Bill Mallory, Miami (Ohio) 1969-73, Colorado 1974-78, Northern Ill. 1980-83, Indiana 1984-92 |
| 22 | Don James, Kent 1971-74, Washington 1975-92 |
| 22 | Al Molde, Sioux Falls 1971-72, Minn.-Morris 1973-79, Central Mo. St. 1980-82, Eastern Ill. 1983-86, Western Mich. 1987-92 |
| 22 | Don Nehlen, Bowling Green 1968-76, West Va. 1980-92 |
| 22 | Jim Wacker, Texas Lutheran 1971-75, North Dak. St. 1976-78, Southwest Tex. St. 1979-82, Texas Christian 1983-91, Minnesota 1992 |
| 21 | LaVell Edwards, Brigham Young 1972-92 |
| 20 | Tom Osborne, Nebraska 1973-92 |
| 20 | George Welsh, Navy 1973-81, Virginia 1982-92 |
| 19 | Billy Brewer, Southeastern La. 1974-79, Louisiana Tech 1980-82, Mississippi 1983-92 |
| 17 | Terry Donahue, UCLA 1976-92 |
| 16 | Rich Brooks, Oregon 1977-92 |
| 16 | John Cooper, Tulsa 1977-84, Arizona 1985-87, Ohio St. 1988-92 |
| 16 | Chuck Shelton, Drake 1977-85, Utah St. 1986-91, Pacific (Cal.) 1992 |
| 16 | Dick Tomey, Hawaii 1977-86, Arizona 1987-92 |

*Coaches' Records*

| Years | Coach, School(s) and Years |
|---|---|
| 15 | Herb Deromedi, Central Mich. 1978-92 |
| 15 | Dick Sheridan, Furman 1978-85, North Caro. St. 1986-92 |
| 15 | Jackie Sherrill, Washington St. 1976, Pittsburgh 1977-81, Texas A&M 1982-88, Mississippi St. 1991-92 |
| 15 | Jim Walden, Washington St. 1978-86, Iowa St. 1987-92 |

**Less Than 5 Years as Division I-A Head Coach:**

| | |
|---|---|
| 18 | Jim Hess, Angelo St. 1974-81, Stephen F. Austin 1982-88, New Mexico St. 1990-92 |

## MOST YEARS AT CURRENT SCHOOL

| Years | Coach, School and Years |
|---|---|
| 27 | Joe Paterno, Penn St. 1966-92 |
| 21 | LaVell Edwards, Brigham Young 1972-92 |
| 20 | Tom Osborne, Nebraska 1973-92 |
| 18 | Don James, Washington 1975-92 |
| 17 | Bobby Bowden, Florida St. 1976-92 |
| 17 | Terry Donahue, UCLA 1976-92 |
| 16 | Rich Brooks, Oregon 1977-92 |
| 15 | Herb Deromedi, Central Mich. 1978-92 |
| 15 | Jim Sweeney, Fresno St. 1976-77, 1980-92 |
| 14 | Hayden Fry, Iowa 1979-92 |
| 13 | Don Nehlen, West Va. 1980-92 |
| 11 | Bill McCartney, Colorado 1982-92 |
| 11 | George Welsh, Virginia 1982-92 |
| 10 | Billy Brewer, Mississippi 1983-92 |
| 10 | George Perles, Michigan St. 1983-92 |

## MOST SCHOOLS

| Schools | Coach, Schools and Years |
|---|---|
| 5 | Lou Holtz, William & Mary 1969-71, North Caro. St. 1972-75, Arkansas 1977-83, Minnesota 1984-85, Notre Dame 1986-92 |
| 5 | Al Molde, Sioux Falls 1971-72, Minn.-Morris 1973-79, Central Mo. St. 1980-82, Eastern Ill. 1983-86, Western Mich. 1987-92 |
| 5 | Jim Wacker, Texas Lutheran 1971-75, North Dak. St. 1976-78, Southwest Tex. St. 1979-82, Texas Christian 1983-91, Minnesota 1992 |
| 4 | Dennis Erickson, Idaho 1982-85, Wyoming 1986, Washington St. 1987-88, Miami (Fla.) 1989-92 |
| 4 | Bill Mallory, Miami (Ohio) 1969-73, Colorado 1974-78, Northern Ill. 1980-83, Indiana 1984-92 |
| 4 | Jackie Sherrill, Washington St. 1976, Pittsburgh 1977-81, Texas A&M 1982-88, Mississippi St. 1991-92 |
| 3 | Bobby Bowden, Samford 1959-62, West Va. 1970-75, Florida St. 1976-92 |
| 3 | Billy Brewer, Southeastern La. 1974-79, Louisiana Tech 1980-82, Mississippi 1983-92 |
| 3 | Mack Brown, Appalachian St. 1983, Tulane 1985-87, North Caro. 1988-92 |
| 3 | George Chaump, Indiana (Pa.) 1982-85, Marshall 1986-89, Navy 1990-92 |
| 3 | John Cooper, Tulsa 1977-84, Arizona St. 1985-87, Ohio St. 1988-92 |
| 3 | Bill Curry, Georgia Tech 1980-86, Alabama 1987-89, Kentucky 1990-92 |
| 3 | Hayden Fry, Southern Methodist 1962-72, North Texas 1973-78, Iowa 1979-92 |
| 3 | Ken Hatfield, Air Force 1979-83, Arkansas 1984-89, Clemson 1990-92 |
| 3 | Bill Lewis, Wyoming 1977-79, East Caro. 1989-91, Georgia Tech 1992 |
| 3 | John Mackovic, Wake Forest 1978-80, Illinois 1988-91, Texas 1992 |
| 3 | Johnny Majors, Iowa St. 1968-72, Pittsburgh 1973-76, Tennessee 1977-92 |
| 3 | Chuck Shelton, Drake 1977-85, Utah St. 1986-91, Pacific (Cal.) 1992 |
| 3 | Bruce Snyder, Utah St. 1976-82, California 1987-91, Arizona St. 1992 |
| 3 | Chuck Stobart, Toledo 1977-81, Utah 1982-84, Memphis St. 1989-92 |
| 3 | Bob Stull, Massachusetts 1984-85, UTEP 1986-88, Missouri 1989-92 |
| 3 | Jim Sweeney, Montana St. 1963-67, Washington St. 1968-75, Fresno St. 1976-77 and 1980-92 |

**Less Than 5 Years as Division I-A Head Coach:**

| | |
|---|---|
| 4 | Dennis Franchione, S'western (Kan.) 1981-82, Pittsburg St. 1985-89, Southwest Tex. St. 1990-91, New Mexico St. 1992 |
| 3 | Terry Bowden, Salem (W. Va.) 1984-86, Samford 1987-92, Auburn 1993 |
| 3 | Jim Hess, Angelo St. 1974-81, Stephen F. Austin 1982-88, New Mexico St. 1990-92 |
| 3 | Tom Lichtenberg, Morehead St. 1979-80, Maine 1989, Ohio 1990-92 |
| 3 | Buddy Teevens, Maine 1985-86, Dartmouth 1987-91, Tulane 1992 |

# MAJOR-COLLEGE BROTHER VS. BROTHER
# COACHING MATCHUPS
### (Each brother's victories in parentheses)

Bump Elliott, Michigan (6), vs. Pete, Illinois (1), 1960-66
Howard Jones, Yale 1909 and Iowa 1922 (2), vs. Tad, Syracuse 1909 and Yale 1922 (0)
Mack Brown, Tulane (2), vs. Watson, Vanderbilt (0), 1986-87
Vince Dooley, Georgia (1), vs. Bill, North Caro. (0), 1971 Gator Bowl

After leading Alabama to a perfect record in 1992 and a victory over Miami (Florida) in the Sugar Bowl to claim the national championship, Gene Stallings was the coach-of-the-year choice of both the American Football Coaches Association and the Football Writers Association of America.

## COACH-OF-THE-YEAR AWARD
**(Selected by the American Football Coaches Association and the Football Writers Association of America)**

### AFCA

| | |
|---|---|
| 1935 | Lynn Waldorf, Northwestern |
| 1936 | Dick Harlow, Harvard |
| 1937 | Edward Mylin, Lafayette |
| 1938 | Bill Kern, Carnegie Mellon |
| 1939 | Eddie Anderson, Iowa |
| 1940 | Clark Shaughnessy, Stanford |
| 1941 | Frank Leahy, Notre Dame |
| 1942 | Bill Alexander, Georgia Tech |
| 1943 | Amos Alonzo Stagg, Pacific (Cal.) |
| 1944 | Carroll Widdoes, Ohio St. |
| 1945 | Bo McMillin, Indiana |
| 1946 | Earl "Red" Blaik, Army |
| 1947 | Fritz Crisler, Michigan |
| 1948 | Bennie Oosterbaan, Michigan |
| 1949 | Bud Wilkinson, Oklahoma |
| 1950 | Charlie Caldwell, Princeton |
| 1951 | Chuck Taylor, Stanford |
| 1952 | Biggie Munn, Michigan St. |
| 1953 | Jim Tatum, Maryland |
| 1954 | Henry "Red" Sanders, UCLA |
| 1955 | Duffy Daugherty, Michigan St. |
| 1956 | Bowden Wyatt, Tennessee |

| Year | AFCA | FWAA |
|---|---|---|
| 1957 | "Woody" Hayes, Ohio St. | "Woody" Hayes, Ohio St. |
| 1958 | Paul Dietzel, Louisiana St. | Paul Dietzel, Louisiana St. |
| 1959 | Ben Schwartzwalder, Syracuse | Ben Schwartzwalder, Syracuse |
| 1960 | Murray Warmath, Minnesota | Murray Warmath, Minnesota |
| 1961 | Paul "Bear" Bryant, Alabama | Darrell Royal, Texas |
| 1962 | John McKay, Southern Cal | John McKay, Southern Cal |
| 1963 | Darrell Royal, Texas | Darrell Royal, Texas |
| 1964 | Frank Broyles, Arkansas, and Ara Parseghian, Notre Dame | Ara Parseghian, Notre Dame |
| 1965 | Tommy Prothro, UCLA | Duffy Daugherty, Michigan St. |
| 1966 | Tom Cahill, Army | Tom Cahill, Army |
| 1967 | John Pont, Indiana | John Pont, Indiana |
| 1968 | Joe Paterno, Penn St. | "Woody" Hayes, Ohio St. |
| 1969 | "Bo" Schembechler, Michigan | "Bo" Schembechler, Michigan |
| 1970 | Charles McClendon, Louisiana St., and Darrell Royal, Texas | Alex Agase, Northwestern |
| 1971 | Paul "Bear" Bryant, Alabama | Bob Devaney, Nebraska |

*Coaches' Records*

|  | AFCA | FWAA |
|---|---|---|
| 1972 | John McKay, Southern Cal | John McKay, Southern Cal |
| 1973 | Paul "Bear" Bryant, Alabama | Johnny Majors, Pittsburgh |
| 1974 | Grant Teaff, Baylor | Grant Teaff, Baylor |
| 1975 | Frank Kush, Arizona St. | "Woody" Hayes, Ohio St. |
| 1976 | Johnny Majors, Pittsburgh | Johnny Majors, Pittsburgh |
| 1977 | Don James, Washington | Lou Holtz, Arkansas |
| 1978 | Joe Paterno, Penn St. | Joe Paterno, Penn St. |
| 1979 | Earle Bruce, Ohio St. | Earle Bruce, Ohio St. |
| 1980 | Vince Dooley, Georgia | Vince Dooley, Georgia |
| 1981 | Danny Ford, Clemson | Danny Ford, Clemson |
| 1982 | Joe Paterno, Penn St. | Joe Paterno, Penn St. |
| 1983 | Ken Hatfield, Air Force | Howard Schnellenberger, Miami (Fla.) |
| 1984 | LaVell Edwards, Brigham Young | LaVell Edwards, Brigham Young |
| 1985 | Fisher DeBerry, Air Force | Fisher DeBerry, Air Force |
| 1986 | Joe Paterno, Penn St. | Joe Paterno, Penn St. |
| 1987 | Dick MacPherson, Syracuse | Dick MacPherson, Syracuse |
| 1988 | Don Nehlen, West Va. | Lou Holtz, Notre Dame |
| 1989 | Bill McCartney, Colorado | Bill McCartney, Colorado |
| 1990 | Bobby Ross, Georgia Tech | Bobby Ross, Georgia Tech |
| 1991 | Bill Lewis, East Caro. | Don James, Washington |
| 1992 | Gene Stallings, Alabama | Gene Stallings, Alabama |

## WINNINGEST ACTIVE DIVISION I-A COACHES

(Minimum five years as Division I-A head coach; record at four-year colleges only.)

### BY PERCENTAGE

| Coach, College | Years | Won | Lost | Tied | *Pct. | BOWLS W | L | T |
|---|---|---|---|---|---|---|---|---|
| John Robinson, Southern Cal | 7 | 67 | 14 | 2 | .819 | 4 | 1 | 0 |
| Tom Osborne, Nebraska | 20 | 195 | 46 | 3 | .805 | 8 | 12 | 0 |
| Joe Paterno, Penn St. | 27 | 247 | 67 | 3 | .784 | 14 | 8 | 1 |
| Danny Ford, Arkansas@ | 12 | 96 | 29 | 4 | .760 | 6 | 2 | 0 |
| Bobby Bowden, Florida St. | 27 | 227 | 77 | 3 | .744 | 12 | 3 | 1 |
| LaVell Edwards, Brigham Young | 21 | 191 | 67 | 3 | .738 | 5 | 11 | 1 |
| Dennis Erickson, Miami (Fla.) | 11 | 94 | 35 | 1 | .727 | %4 | 1 | 0 |
| Dick Sheridan, North Caro. St. | 15 | 121 | 52 | 5 | .694 | %5 | 7 | 0 |
| Steve Spurrier, Florida | 6 | 48 | 21 | 1 | .693 | 1 | 2 | 0 |
| Don James, Washington | 22 | 176 | 78 | 3 | .691 | 10 | 5 | 0 |
| Lou Holtz, Notre Dame | 23 | 182 | 83 | 6 | .683 | 9 | 6 | 2 |
| Terry Donahue, UCLA | 17 | 131 | 59 | 8 | .682 | 8 | 2 | 1 |
| Jackie Sherrill, Mississippi St. | 15 | 119 | 55 | 2 | .682 | 6 | 4 | 0 |
| Herb Deromedi, Central Mich. | 15 | 105 | 49 | 10 | .671 | 0 | 1 | 0 |
| Fisher DeBerry, Air Force | 9 | 72 | 38 | 1 | .653 | 4 | 3 | 0 |
| John Cooper, Ohio St. | 16 | 116 | 62 | 5 | .648 | 2 | 5 | 0 |
| John Ralston, San Jose St. | 13 | 86 | 47 | 4 | .642 | 2 | 2 | 0 |
| Ken Hatfield, Clemson | 14 | 105 | 59 | 3 | .638 | 4 | 6 | 0 |
| Al Molde, Western Mich. | 22 | 145 | 84 | 7 | .629 | %3 | 6 | 0 |
| Bob Wagner, Hawaii | 6 | 45 | 27 | 2 | .622 | 1 | 1 | 0 |
| Johnny Majors, Pittsburgh | 25 | 173 | 105 | 10 | .618 | 9 | 7 | 0 |
| Don Nehlen, West Va. | 22 | 145 | 90 | 8 | .613 | 3 | 4 | 0 |
| Jim Wacker, Minnesota | 22 | 146 | 100 | 3 | .592 | %13 | 2 | 0 |
| Bill Mallory, Indiana | 23 | 148 | 104 | 4 | .586 | 4 | 5 | 0 |
| Joe Raymond Peace, Louisiana Tech | 5 | 30 | 21 | 4 | .582 | 0 | 0 | 1 |
| Jim Sweeney, Fresno St. | 28 | 178 | 129 | 4 | .579 | 5 | 1 | 0 |
| Bill McCartney, Colorado | 11 | 74 | 51 | 4 | .576 | 1 | 6 | 0 |
| Billy Brewer, Mississippi | 19 | 119 | 89 | 6 | .570 | %4 | 3 | 0 |
| George Welsh, Virginia | 20 | 128 | 97 | 4 | .568 | 3 | 5 | 0 |
| Hayden Fry, Iowa | 31 | 194 | 147 | 9 | .567 | 5 | 7 | 1 |
| Dick Tomey, Arizona | 16 | 99 | 75 | 7 | .566 | 1 | 2 | 0 |
| Howard Schnellenberger, Louisville | 13 | 80 | 64 | 2 | .555 | 3 | 0 | 0 |
| Pat Jones, Oklahoma St. | 9 | 56 | 45 | 2 | .553 | 3 | 1 | 0 |
| George Perles, Michigan St. | 10 | 62 | 50 | 4 | .552 | 3 | 3 | 0 |
| John Mackovic, Texas | 8 | 50 | 41 | 1 | .549 | 1 | 3 | 0 |
| Paul Schudel, Ball St. | 8 | 47 | 40 | 2 | .539 | 0 | 1 | 0 |
| Gary Moeller, Michigan | 6 | 34 | 29 | 6 | .536 | 2 | 1 | 0 |
| Curley Hallman, Louisiana St. | 5 | 30 | 26 | 0 | .536 | 1 | 0 | 0 |
| Gene Stallings, Alabama | 10 | 58 | 51 | 1 | .532 | 3 | 1 | 0 |
| Spike Dykes, Texas Tech# | 7 | 35 | 32 | 1 | .522 | 1 | 1 | 0 |

| Coach, College | Years | Won | Lost | Tied | *Pct. | BOWLS W | L | T |
|---|---|---|---|---|---|---|---|---|
| Bruce Snyder, Arizona St. | 13 | 72 | 67 | 6 | .517 | 2 | 0 | 0 |
| Gerry Faust, Akron | 12 | 67 | 63 | 4 | .515 | 1 | 1 | 0 |
| Frank Beamer, Virginia Tech | 12 | 66 | 63 | 4 | .511 | %0 | 1 | 0 |
| Bill Lewis, Georgia Tech | 7 | 39 | 39 | 2 | .500 | 1 | 0 | 0 |
| Bill Curry, Kentucky | 13 | 68 | 75 | 4 | .476 | 2 | 2 | 0 |
| Dave Rader, Tulsa | 5 | 27 | 30 | 0 | .474 | 1 | 1 | 0 |
| Nelson Stokley, Southwestern La. | 7 | 34 | 42 | 1 | .448 | 0 | 0 | 0 |
| Glen Mason, Kansas | 7 | 34 | 43 | 1 | .442 | 1 | 0 | 0 |
| Rich Brooks, Oregon | 16 | 77 | 99 | 4 | .439 | 1 | 2 | 0 |
| Chuck Stobart, Memphis St. | 12 | 57 | 74 | 3 | .437 | 1 | 0 | 0 |
| Bob Stull, Missouri | 9 | 43 | 58 | 1 | .426 | 0 | 1 | 0 |
| Jim Walden, Iowa St. | 15 | 66 | 94 | 6 | .416 | 0 | 1 | 0 |
| Mack Brown, North Caro. | 9 | 41 | 59 | 1 | .411 | 1 | 1 | 0 |
| Jerry Pettibone, Oregon St. | 8 | 35 | 51 | 2 | .409 | 0 | 0 | 0 |
| Chuck Shelton, Pacific (Cal.) | 16 | 69 | 106 | 1 | .395 | 0 | 0 | 0 |
| Tim Murphy, Cincinnati | 6 | 24 | 42 | 1 | .366 | 0 | 0 | 0 |
| Jim Colletto, Purdue | 7 | 25 | 52 | 1 | .327 | 0 | 0 | 0 |

**Less Than 5 Years in Division I-A**
**(school followed by years in I-A)**
**(includes record at all four-year colleges)**

| Coach, College | Years | Won | Lost | Tied | *Pct. | BOWLS W | L | T |
|---|---|---|---|---|---|---|---|---|
| Mark Duffner, Maryland (1) | 7 | 63 | 13 | 1 | .825 | 0 | 0 | 0 |
| Dennis Franchione, New Mexico (1) | 10 | 83 | 27 | 2 | .750 | %6 | 5 | 0 |
| Paul Pasqualoni, Syracuse (2) | 7 | 54 | 21 | 0 | .720 | %2 | 1 | 0 |
| Terry Bowden, Auburn (0) | 9 | 64 | 36 | 1 | .639 | %2 | 4 | 0 |
| Jim Hess, New Mexico St. (3) | 18 | 121 | 77 | 5 | .608 | %5 | 3 | 0 |
| Sparky Woods, Appalachian St. (4) | 9 | 58 | 40 | 5 | .587 | %2 | 2 | 0 |
| George Chaump, Navy (3) | 11 | 63 | 59 | 2 | .516 | %4 | 2 | 0 |
| Buddy Teevens, Tulane (1) | 8 | 41 | 40 | 2 | .506 | 0 | 0 | 0 |
| Mike Price, Washington St. (4) | 12 | 68 | 67 | 0 | .504 | %2 | 1 | 0 |
| Fred Goldsmith, Rice (4) | 5 | 19 | 33 | 1 | .368 | 0 | 0 | 0 |
| Tom Lichtenberg, Ohio (3) | 6 | 22 | 41 | 3 | .356 | %0 | 1 | 0 |

* *Ties computed as half won and half lost. Overall record includes bowl and playoff games.  % Includes record in NCAA and/or NAIA championships.  @ Win in Gator Bowl in first game.  # Loss in Independence Bowl in first game.*

## BY VICTORIES
### (Minimum 100 victories)

| Coach, College, Winning Percentage | Won |
|---|---|
| Joe Paterno, Penn St. .784 | 247 |
| Bobby Bowden, Florida St. .744 | 227 |
| Tom Osborne, Nebraska .805 | 195 |
| Hayden Fry, Iowa .567 | 194 |
| LaVell Edwards, Brigham Young .738 | 191 |
| Lou Holtz, Notre Dame .683 | 182 |
| Jim Sweeney, Fresno St. .579 | 178 |
| Don James, Washington .691 | 176 |
| Johnny Majors, Pittsburgh .618 | 173 |
| Bill Mallory, Indiana .586 | 148 |
| Jim Wacker, Minnesota .592 | 146 |
| Al Molde, Western Mich. .629 | 145 |
| Don Nehlen, West Va. .613 | 145 |

| Coach, College, Winning Percentage | Won |
|---|---|
| Terry Donahue, UCLA .682 | 131 |
| George Welsh, Virginia .568 | 128 |
| Dick Sheridan, North Caro. St. .694 | 121 |
| Jackie Sherrill, Mississippi St. .682 | 119 |
| Billy Brewer, Mississippi .570 | 119 |
| John Cooper, Ohio St. .648 | 116 |
| Herb Deromedi, Central Mich. .671 | 105 |
| Ken Hatfield, Clemson .638 | 105 |

**Less Than 5 Years in Division I-A**
**(includes record at all four-year colleges)**

| Coach, College, Winning Percentage | Won |
|---|---|
| Jim Hess, New Mexico St. .608 | 121 |

## ANNUAL DIVISION I-A HEAD-COACHING CHANGES

| Year | Changes | Teams | Pct. | Year | Changes | Teams | Pct. |
|---|---|---|---|---|---|---|---|
| 1947 | 27 | 125 | .216 | 1962 | 20 | 119 | .168 |
| 1948 | 24 | 121 | .198 | 1963 | 12 | 118 | .102 |
| 1949 | 22 | 114 | .193 | 1964 | 14 | 116 | .121 |
| 1950 | 23 | 119 | .193 | 1965 | 16 | 114 | .140 |
| 1951 | 23 | 115 | .200 | 1966 | 16 | 116 | .138 |
| 1952 | 15 | 113 | .133 | 1967 | 21 | 114 | .184 |
| 1953 | 18 | 111 | .162 | 1968 | 14 | 114 | .123 |
| 1954 | 14 | 103 | .136 | 1969 | 22 | 118 | .186 |
| 1955 | 23 | 103 | .223 | 1970 | 13 | 118 | .110 |
| 1956 | 19 | 105 | .181 | 1971 | 27 | 119 | .227 |
| 1957 | 22 | 108 | .204 | 1972 | 17 | 121 | .140 |
| 1958 | 18 | 109 | .165 | 1973 | 36 | 126 | †.286 |
| 1959 | 18 | 110 | .164 | 1974 | 28 | 128 | .219 |
| 1960 | 18 | 114 | .158 | 1975 | 18 | 134 | .134 |
| 1961 | 11 | 112 | .098 | 1976 | 23 | 137 | .168 |

| Year | Changes | Teams | Pct. | Year | Changes | Teams | Pct. |
|---|---|---|---|---|---|---|---|
| 1977 | 27 | 144 | .188 | 1987 | 24 | 104 | .231 |
| 1978 | 27 | 139 | .194 | 1988 | 9 | 104 | *.087 |
| 1979 | 26 | 139 | .187 | 1989 | 19 | 106 | .179 |
| 1980 | 27 | 139 | .194 | 1990 | 20 | 106 | .189 |
| 1981 | 17 | 137 | .123 | 1991 | 16 | 106 | .151 |
| 1982 | 17 | 97 | .175 | 1992 | 16 | 107 | .150 |
| 1983 | 22 | 105 | .210 | 1993 | 15 | 106 | .142 |
| 1984 | 16 | 105 | .152 | | | | |
| 1985 | 15 | 105 | .143 | | | | |
| 1986 | 22 | 105 | .210 | | | | |

* Record low.   † Record high.

# RECORDS OF DIVISION I-A FIRST-YEAR HEAD COACHES

(Coaches with no previous head-coaching experience at a four-year college.)

| | | | | | | Bowl | Team's Previous Season Record | | | | Bowl |
|---|---|---|---|---|---|---|---|---|---|---|---|
| Year | No. | Won | Lost | Tied | Pct. | Record | Won | Lost | Tied | Pct. | Record |
| 1948 | 14 | 56 | 68 | 7 | .454 | 0-1 | 76 | 52 | 8 | .588 | 2-1 |
| 1949 | 8 | 26 | 49 | 3 | .353 | 0-1 | 35 | 41 | 4 | .463 | 0-0 |
| 1950 | 10 | 37 | 56 | 4 | .402 | 0-0 | 49 | 42 | 6 | .536 | 2-0 |
| 1951 | 13 | 60 | 67 | 4 | .473 | 1-2 | 39 | 88 | 7 | .317 | 1-1 |
| 1952 | 8 | 31 | 42 | 3 | .428 | 0-0 | 38 | 40 | 0 | .487 | 0-0 |
| 1953 | 8 | 29 | 45 | 5 | .399 | 0-0 | 48 | 28 | 7 | .620 | 1-2 |
| 1954 | 8 | 31 | 43 | 4 | .423 | 0-0 | 40 | 33 | 7 | .543 | 1-0 |
| 1955 | 9 | 36 | 50 | 4 | .422 | 0-1 | 36 | 52 | 1 | .410 | 0-0 |
| 1956 | 14 | 47 | 80 | 11 | .380 | 1-0 | 61 | 68 | 6 | .474 | 0-1 |
| 1957 | 9 | 32 | 50 | 6 | .398 | 0-0 | 44 | 42 | 2 | .511 | 0-0 |
| 1958 | 7 | 26 | 44 | 0 | .371 | 0-0 | 37 | 31 | 2 | .543 | 0-0 |
| 1959 | 8 | 34 | 43 | 2 | .443 | 0-0 | 41 | 35 | 2 | .538 | 0-1 |
| 1960 | 14 | 54 | 80 | 5 | .406 | 1-0 | 57 | 78 | 2 | .423 | 0-0 |
| 1961 | 8 | 26 | 50 | 0 | .342 | 0-0 | 38 | 38 | 2 | .500 | 0-0 |
| 1962 | 12 | 40 | 74 | 4 | .356 | 2-0 | 52 | 66 | 2 | .442 | 1-1 |
| 1963 | 8 | 23 | 49 | 6 | .333 | 0-0 | 32 | 46 | 1 | .411 | 0-1 |
| 1964 | 12 | 45 | 67 | 7 | .408 | 1-1 | 42 | 71 | 4 | .376 | 0-0 |
| 1965 | 8 | 28 | 47 | 2 | .377 | 0-0 | 36 | 42 | 1 | .462 | 0-0 |
| 1966 | 10 | 46 | 50 | 3 | .480 | 0-0 | 38 | 56 | 5 | .409 | 0-0 |
| 1967 | 18 | 58 | 114 | 5 | .342 | 1-0 | 60 | 116 | 4 | .344 | 0-1 |
| 1968 | 6 | 19 | 40 | 1 | .325 | 0-0 | 20 | 38 | 2 | .350 | 0-0 |
| 1969 | 15 | 49 | 90 | 1 | .353 | 0-0 | 62 | 85 | 3 | .423 | 0-1 |
| 1970 | 10 | 45 | 61 | 1 | .425 | 1-0 | 46 | 54 | 0 | .460 | 0-2 |
| 1971 | 12 | 57 | 72 | 0 | .442 | 1-1 | 64 | 61 | 0 | .512 | 0-1 |
| 1972 | 11 | 57 | 64 | 1 | .471 | 1-0 | 53 | 64 | 2 | .454 | 1-0 |
| 1973 | 14 | 84 | 63 | 8 | .568 | 1-0 | 83 | 71 | 2 | .538 | 3-0 |
| 1974 | 17 | 63 | 116 | 5 | .356 | 1-0 | 78 | 105 | 1 | .427 | 1-0 |
| 1975 | 10 | 38 | 72 | 0 | .345 | 0-1 | 43 | 67 | 0 | .391 | 0-0 |
| 1976 | 15 | 57 | 109 | 2 | .345 | 3-1 | 72 | 91 | 5 | .443 | 3-1 |
| 1977 | 14 | 55 | 94 | 5 | .373 | 1-0 | 66 | 88 | 3 | .430 | 0-2 |
| 1978 | 16 | 68 | 104 | 3 | .397 | 0-0 | 77 | 96 | 3 | .446 | 0-1 |
| 1979 | 11 | 53 | 66 | 3 | .447 | 0-0 | 66 | 57 | 1 | .536 | 2-2 |
| 1980 | 12 | 54 | 75 | 2 | .420 | 0-0 | 60 | 68 | 3 | .469 | 1-0 |
| 1981 | 6 | 25 | 40 | 0 | .385 | 0-0 | 31 | 35 | 1 | .470 | 0-1 |
| 1982 | 10 | 51 | 59 | 1 | .464 | 0-1 | 58 | 57 | 2 | .504 | 2-2 |
| 1983 | 12 | 51 | 82 | 2 | .385 | 1-0 | 60 | 73 | 1 | .451 | 1-1 |
| 1984 | 7 | 47 | 28 | 1 | *.625 | 2-1 | 45 | 35 | 1 | .562 | 3-0 |
| 1985 | 5 | 19 | 37 | 0 | .339 | 0-0 | 20 | 32 | 4 | .393 | 0-0 |
| 1986 | 12 | 53 | 81 | 0 | .396 | 0-1 | 56 | 76 | 3 | .426 | 1-1 |
| 1987 | 9 | 51 | 49 | 3 | .510 | 1-1 | 52 | 50 | 1 | .510 | 0-2 |
| 1988 | 4 | 25 | 20 | 0 | .556 | 1-0 | 22 | 23 | 1 | .489 | 1-1 |
| 1989 | 7 | 32 | 49 | 1 | .396 | 0-2 | 39 | 43 | 0 | .476 | 1-2 |
| 1990 | 9 | 46 | 42 | 2 | .522 | 1-1 | 41 | 48 | 1 | .461 | 0-1 |
| 1991 | 10 | 38 | 72 | 1 | .347 | 1-0 | 46 | 64 | 2 | .420 | 0-2 |
| 1992 | 4 | 15 | 20 | 1 | .431 | 0-0 | 32 | 14 | 0 | .696 | 1-1 |

* Record percentage for first-year coaches. 1984 coaches and their records, with bowl game indicated by an asterisk (*): Pat Jones, Oklahoma St. (*10-2-0); Galen Hall, Florida (8-0-0, took over from Charley Pell after three games); Bill Arnsparger, Louisiana St. (8-*3-1); Fisher DeBerry, Air Force (*8-4-0); Dick Anderson, Rutgers (7-3-0); Mike Sheppard, Long Beach St. (4-7-0); Ron Chismar, Wichita St. (2-9-0).

*1993 NCAA FOOTBALL*

## MOST VICTORIES BY FIRST-YEAR HEAD COACHES

| Coach, College, Year | W | L | T |
|---|---|---|---|
| Gary Blackney, Bowling Green, 1991 | *11 | 1 | 0 |
| John Robinson, Southern Cal, 1976 | *11 | 1 | 0 |
| Bill Battle, Tennessee, 1970 | *11 | 1 | 0 |
| Dick Crum, Miami (Ohio), 1974 | *10 | 0 | 1 |
| Barry Switzer, Oklahoma, 1973 | 10 | 0 | 1 |
| John Jenkins, Houston, 1990 | 10 | 1 | 0 |
| Dwight Wallace, Ball St., 1978 | 10 | 1 | 0 |
| Chuck Fairbanks, Oklahoma, 1967 | 10 | 1 | 0 |
| Mike Archer, Louisiana St., 1987 | *10 | 1 | 0 |
| Curley Hallman, Southern Miss., 1988 | *10 | 1 | 1 |
| Pat Jones, Oklahoma St., 1984 | *10 | 2 | 0 |
| Earle Bruce, Tampa, 1972 | *10 | 2 | 0 |
| Billy Kinard, Mississippi, 1971 | *10 | 2 | 0 |

* Bowl game victory included.
Only first-year coach to win a national championship: Bennie Oosterbaan, Michigan, 1948 (9-0-0).

## WINNINGEST ACTIVE DIVISION I-AA COACHES

(Minimum five years as a Division I-A and/or Division I-AA head coach;
record at four-year colleges only.)

### BY PERCENTAGE

| Coach, College | Years | Won | Lost | Tied | *Pct. | PLAYOFFS# W | L | T |
|---|---|---|---|---|---|---|---|---|
| Roy Kidd, Eastern Ky. | 29 | 239 | 84 | 8 | .734 | 16 | 12 | 0 |
| Eddie Robinson, Grambling | 50 | 381 | 136 | 15 | .730 | 10 | 7 | 0 |
| Tubby Raymond, Delaware | 27 | 223 | 88 | 2 | .716 | 16 | 10 | 0 |
| Jimmy Satterfield, Furman | 7 | 61 | 24 | 2 | .713 | 7 | 3 | 0 |
| Houston Markham, Alabama St. | 6 | 44 | 19 | 3 | .689 | 1 | 0 | 0 |
| Andy Talley, Villanova | 13 | 84 | 42 | 2 | .664 | 1 | 4 | 0 |
| Bill Davis, Tennessee St. | 14 | 100 | 51 | 1 | .662 | 3 | 3 | 0 |
| Bill Hayes, North Caro. A&T | 17 | 123 | 63 | 2 | .660 | 1 | 5 | 0 |
| William Collick, Delaware St. | 8 | 56 | 29 | 0 | .659 | 0 | 0 | 0 |
| James Donnelly, Middle Tenn. St. | 16 | 119 | 64 | 1 | .649 | 6 | 6 | 0 |
| Jim Tressel, Youngstown St. | 7 | 57 | 31 | 1 | .646 | 8 | 4 | 0 |
| Steve Tosches, Princeton | 6 | 38 | 21 | 1 | .642 | 0 | 0 | 0 |
| Carmen Cozza, Yale | 28 | 166 | 92 | 5 | .641 | 0 | 0 | 0 |
| Bill Bowes, New Hampshire | 21 | 136 | 78 | 5 | .632 | 1 | 3 | 0 |
| Charlie Taaffe, Citadel | 6 | 42 | 27 | 1 | .607 | 1 | 3 | 0 |
| Ron Randleman, Sam Houston St. | 24 | 151 | 98 | 6 | .604 | 3 | 5 | 1 |
| Willie Jeffries, South Caro. St. | 20 | 124 | 88 | 6 | .583 | 2 | 3 | 0 |
| Jesse Branch, Southwest Mo. St. | 7 | 44 | 33 | 1 | .571 | 1 | 2 | 0 |
| Ken Riley, Florida A&M | 7 | 43 | 33 | 2 | .564 | 0 | 1 | 0 |
| Bill Russo, Lafayette | 15 | 89 | 69 | 1 | .563 | 0 | 1 | 0 |
| Jimmye Laycock, William & Mary | 13 | 81 | 64 | 2 | .558 | 1 | 3 | 0 |
| Joe Restic, Harvard | 22 | 114 | 90 | 6 | .557 | 0 | 0 | 0 |
| Dick Zornes, Eastern Wash. | 14 | 79 | 63 | 2 | .556 | 1 | 2 | 0 |
| Dave Roberts, Northeast La. | 9 | 54 | 47 | 3 | .534 | 2 | 4 | 0 |
| Hank Small, Lehigh | 7 | 40 | 36 | 1 | .526 | 0 | 0 | 0 |
| Tom Jackson, Connecticut | 10 | 56 | 52 | 0 | .519 | 0 | 0 | 0 |
| Sam Goodwin, Northwestern (La.) | 12 | 66 | 63 | 4 | .511 | 1 | 1 | 0 |
| Don Read, Montana | 23 | 120 | 120 | 1 | .500 | 2 | 2 | 0 |
| Bob Spoo, Eastern Ill. | 6 | 33 | 35 | 0 | .485 | 1 | 1 | 0 |
| Dennis Raetz, Indiana St. | 13 | 68 | 76 | 1 | .472 | 1 | 2 | 0 |
| Jerry Moore, Appalachian St. | 11 | 57 | 65 | 2 | .468 | 0 | 3 | 0 |
| Jack Harbaugh, Western Ky. | 9 | 40 | 54 | 3 | .428 | 0 | 0 | 0 |
| Jim Heacock, Illinois St. | 5 | 21 | 34 | 0 | .382 | 0 | 0 | 0 |
| Jim Ragland, Tennessee Tech | 7 | 25 | 50 | 0 | .333 | 0 | 0 | 0 |

**Less Than 5 Years as Division I-A and/or Division I-AA Head Coach
(school followed by years in I-A or I-AA)
(includes record at all four-year colleges)**

| | | | | | | | | |
|---|---|---|---|---|---|---|---|---|
| Mike Kelly, Dayton (0) | 12 | 119 | 22 | 1 | .842 | 13 | 8 | 0 |
| Al Bagnoli, Pennsylvania (1) | 11 | 93 | 22 | 0 | .809 | 7 | 6 | 0 |
| Walt Hameline, Wagner (0) | 12 | 95 | 30 | 2 | .756 | 4 | 2 | 0 |
| Pete Richardson, Southern-B. R. (0) | 5 | 41 | 14 | 1 | .741 | 0 | 3 | 0 |
| Ed Sweeney, Colgate (0) | 8 | 56 | 22 | 3 | .710 | 0 | 2 | 0 |
| Pokey Allen, Boise St. (0) | 7 | 63 | 26 | 2 | .703 | 10 | 5 | 0 |
| Robin Cooper, Evansville (0) | 5 | 31 | 14 | 0 | .689 | 0 | 0 | 0 |
| Peter Vaas, Holy Cross (1) | 5 | 35 | 16 | 1 | .683 | 0 | 1 | 0 |
| Bob Ricca, St. John's (N. Y.) (0) | 15 | 91 | 59 | 1 | .606 | 0 | 0 | 0 |
| Mike Cavan, East Tenn. St. (0) | 7 | 42 | 28 | 2 | .597 | 0 | 0 | 0 |

*Coaches' Records*

| Coach, College | Years | Won | Lost | Tied | *Pct. | PLAYOFFS# W | L | T |
|---|---|---|---|---|---|---|---|---|
| Gene McDowell, Central Fla. (3) .............. | 8 | 54 | 37 | 0 | .593 | 3 | 2 | 0 |
| Rob Ash, Drake (0) ........................... | 13 | 75 | 51 | 4 | .592 | 0 | 0 | 0 |
| Jack Bishop, Southern Utah (0) ............... | 12 | 71 | 51 | 3 | .580 | 0 | 0 | 0 |
| Mickey Kwiatkowski, Brown (3) ............... | 12 | 71 | 54 | 0 | .568 | 0 | 5 | 0 |
| Bob Burt, Cal St. Northridge (0) ............. | 8 | 48 | 37 | 0 | .565 | 0 | 1 | 0 |
| Brian Fogerty, San Diego (0) ................. | 10 | 50 | 41 | 3 | .548 | 0 | 0 | 0 |
| Barry Mynter, Canisius (0) ................... | 17 | 78 | 84 | 3 | .482 | 0 | 0 | 0 |
| Don McLeary, Tenn.-Martin (1)................ | 9 | 43 | 54 | 0 | .443 | 1 | 1 | 0 |
| Roy Miller, St. Peter's (0) ................... | 9 | 38 | 48 | 0 | .442 | 0 | 0 | 0 |
| Harold Crocker, Iona (0) ..................... | 8 | 33 | 46 | 1 | .419 | 0 | 0 | 0 |
| Larry Glueck, Fordham (4) ................... | 7 | 29 | 41 | 1 | .415 | 1 | 2 | 0 |
| Bob Smith, Southern Ill. (4) ................. | 8 | 32 | 55 | 1 | .369 | 0 | 0 | 0 |
| Dave Fagg, Davidson (1) ..................... | 7 | 22 | 45 | 1 | .331 | 0 | 0 | 0 |
| Ray Tellier, Columbia (4) .................... | 9 | 27 | 60 | 1 | .313 | 0 | 1 | 0 |
| Jack Dubois, Siena (0) ....................... | 6 | 13 | 39 | 0 | .250 | 0 | 0 | 0 |

* Ties computed as half won and half lost. Overall record includes bowl and playoff games.   # Playoffs includes all divisional championships as well as bowl games and NAIA playoffs.

## BY VICTORIES
### (Minimum 100 victories)

| Coach, College, Winning Percentage | Won |
|---|---|
| Eddie Robinson, Grambling .730 ............ | 381 |
| Roy Kidd, Eastern Ky. .734 ................. | 239 |
| Tubby Raymond, Delaware .716 ............. | 223 |
| Carmen Cozza, Yale .641 ................... | 166 |
| Ron Randleman, Sam Houston St. .604 ..... | 151 |
| Bill Bowes, New Hampshire .632 ............ | 136 |
| Willie Jeffries, South Caro. St. .583 ........ | 124 |
| Bill Hayes, North Caro. A&T .660 ........... | 123 |

| Coach, College, Winning Percentage | Won |
|---|---|
| Don Read, Montana .500 ................... | 120 |
| James Donnelly, Middle Tenn. St. .649 ..... | 119 |
| Joe Restic, Harvard .557 ................... | 114 |
| Bill Davis, Tennessee St. .662 ............. | 100 |

**Less Than 5 Yrs. as a I-A/I-AA Head Coach**
Mike Kelly, Dayton .842..................... | 119

## ANNUAL DIVISION I-AA HEAD-COACHING CHANGES
(From the 1982 reorganization of the division for parallel comparisons)

| Year | Changes | Teams | Pct. | Year | Changes | Teams | Pct. |
|---|---|---|---|---|---|---|---|
| 1982 | 7 | 92 | .076 | 1988 | 12 | 88 | .136 |
| 1983 | 17 | 84 | .202 | 1989 | 21 | 89 | †.236 |
| 1984 | 14 | 87 | .161 | 1990 | 16 | 89 | .180 |
| 1985 | 11 | 87 | .126 | 1991 | 6 | 87 | *.069 |
| 1986 | 18 | 86 | .209 | 1992 | 14 | 89 | .157 |
| 1987 | 13 | 87 | .149 | 1993 | 13 | #115 | .113 |

* Record low.   † Record high.   # Twenty-seven teams switched from Divisions II & III to I-AA.

## DIVISION I-AA COACH-OF-THE-YEAR AWARD
(Selected by the American Football Coaches Association)

| | | | |
|---|---|---|---|
| 1983 | Rey Dempsey, Southern Ill. | 1988 | Jimmy Satterfield, Furman |
| 1984 | Dave Arnold, Montana St. | 1989 | Erk Russell, Ga. Southern |
| 1985 | Dick Sheridan, Furman | 1990 | Tim Stowers, Ga. Southern |
| 1986 | Erk Russell, Ga. Southern | 1991 | Mark Duffner, Holy Cross |
| 1987 | Mark Duffner, Holy Cross | 1992 | Charlie Taafe, Citadel |

## DIVISION I-AA CHAMPIONSHIP COACHES

All coaches who have coached teams in the Division I-AA championship playoffs since 1978 are listed below with their playoff record, alma mater and year graduated, team, year coached, opponent, and score.

**Terry Allen (3-3) (Northern Iowa '79)**
| Northern Iowa .............90 | Boise St. 3-20 |
|---|---|
| Northern Iowa .............91 | Weber St. 38-21 |
| Northern Iowa .............91 | Marshall 13-41 |
| Northern Iowa .............92 | Eastern Wash. 17-14 |
| Northern Iowa .............92 | McNeese St. 29-7 |
| Northern Iowa .............92 | Youngstown St. 7-19 |

**Dave Arnold (3-0) (Drake '67)**
| Montana St. .................84 | Arkansas St. 31-24 |
|---|---|
| Montana St. .................84 | Rhode Island 32-20 |
| Montana St. .................84* | Louisiana Tech 19-6 |

**Dave Arslanian (0-1) (Weber St. '72)**
| Weber St. ...................91 | Northern Iowa 21-38 |
|---|---|

**Chris Ault (9-7) (Nevada '68)**

| | | |
|---|---|---|
| Nevada | 78 | Massachusetts 21-44 |
| Nevada | 79 | Eastern Ky. 30-33 |
| Nevada | 83 | Idaho St. 27-20 |
| Nevada | 83 | North Texas 20-17 (OT) |
| Nevada | 83 | Southern Ill. 7-23 |
| Nevada | 85 | Arkansas St. 24-23 |
| Nevada | 85 | Furman 12-35 |
| Nevada | 86 | Idaho 27-7 |
| Nevada | 86 | Tennessee St. 33-6 |
| Nevada | 86 | Ga. Southern 38-48 |
| Nevada | 90 | Northeast La. 27-14 |
| Nevada | 90 | Furman 42-35 (3 OT) |
| Nevada | 90 | Boise St. 59-52 (3 OT) |
| Nevada | 90 | Ga. Southern 13-36 |
| Nevada | 91 | McNeese St. 22-16 |
| Nevada | 91 | Youngstown St. 28-30 |

**Randy Ball (0-1) (Northeast Mo. St. '73)**

| | | |
|---|---|---|
| Western Ill. | 91 | Marshall 17-20 (OT) |

**Frank Beamer (0-1) (Virginia Tech '69)**

| | | |
|---|---|---|
| Murray St. | 86 | Eastern Ill. 21-28 |

**Terry Bowden (2-2) (West Va. '78)**

| | | |
|---|---|---|
| Samford | 91 | New Hampshire 29-13 |
| Samford | 91 | James Madison 24-21 |
| Samford | 91 | Youngstown St. 0-10 |
| Samford | 92 | Delaware 21-56 |

**Bill Bowes (0-1) (Penn St. '65)**

| | | |
|---|---|---|
| New Hampshire | 91 | Samford 13-29 |

**Jesse Branch (1-2) (Arkansas '64)**

| | | |
|---|---|---|
| Southwest Mo. St. | 89 | Maine 38-35 |
| Southwest Mo. St. | 89 | Stephen F. Austin 25-55 |
| Southwest Mo. St. | 90 | Idaho 35-41 |

**Billy Brewer (1-1) (Mississippi '61)**

| | | |
|---|---|---|
| Louisiana Tech | 82 | South Caro. St. 38-3 |
| Louisiana Tech | 82 | Delaware 0-17 |

**Rick Carter (0-1) (Earlham '65)**

| | | |
|---|---|---|
| Holy Cross | 83 | Western Caro. 21-28 |

**Marino Casem (0-1) (Xavier, La. '56)**

| | | |
|---|---|---|
| Alcorn St. | 84 | Louisiana Tech 21-44 |

**George Chaump (4-2) (Bloomsburg '58)**

| | | |
|---|---|---|
| Marshall | 87 | James Madison 41-12 |
| Marshall | 87 | Weber St. 51-23 |
| Marshall | 87 | Appalachian St. 24-10 |
| Marshall | 87 | Northeast La. 42-43 |
| Marshall | 88 | North Texas 7-0 |
| Marshall | 88 | Furman 9-13 |

**Pat Collins (4-0) (Louisiana Tech '63)**

| | | |
|---|---|---|
| Northeast La. | 87 | North Texas 30-9 |
| Northeast La. | 87 | Eastern Ky. 33-32 |
| Northeast La. | 87 | Northern Iowa 44-41 (OT) |
| Northeast La. | 87* | Marshall 43-42 |

**Archie Cooley Jr. (0-1) (Jackson St. '62)**

| | | |
|---|---|---|
| Mississippi Val. | 84 | Louisiana Tech 19-66 |

**Bruce Craddock (0-1) (Northeast Mo. St. '66)**

| | | |
|---|---|---|
| Western Ill. | 88 | Western Ky. 32-35 |

**Jim Criner (3-1) (Cal Poly Pomona '61)**

| | | |
|---|---|---|
| Boise St. | 80 | Grambling 14-9 |
| Boise St. | 80* | Eastern Ky. 31-29 |
| Boise St. | 81 | Jackson St. 19-7 |
| Boise St. | 81 | Eastern Ky. 17-23 |

**Bill Davis (2-2) (Johnson Smith '65)**

| | | |
|---|---|---|
| South Caro. St. | 81 | Tennessee St. 26-25 |
| South Caro. St. | 81 | Idaho St. 12-41 |
| South Caro. St. | 82 | Furman 17-0 |
| South Caro. St. | 82 | Louisiana Tech 3-38 |

**Rey Dempsey (3-0) (Geneva '58)**

| | | |
|---|---|---|
| Southern Ill. | 83 | Indiana St. 23-7 |
| Southern Ill. | 83 | Nevada 23-7 |
| Southern Ill. | 83* | Western Caro. 43-7 |

*Coaches' Records*

**Jim Dennison (0-1) (Wooster '60)**
Akron . . . . . . . . . . . . . . . . . . . . . .85          Rhode Island 27-35

**Jim Donnan (7-1) (North Caro. St. '67)**
Marshall . . . . . . . . . . . . . . . . . . . .91          Western Ill. 20-17 (OT)
Marshall . . . . . . . . . . . . . . . . . . . .91          Northern Iowa 41-13
Marshall . . . . . . . . . . . . . . . . . . . .91          Eastern Ky. 14-7
Marshall . . . . . . . . . . . . . . . . . . . .91          Youngstown St. 17-25
Marshall . . . . . . . . . . . . . . . . . . . .92          Eastern Ky. 44-0
Marshall . . . . . . . . . . . . . . . . . . . .92          Middle Tenn. St. 35-21
Marshall . . . . . . . . . . . . . . . . . . . .92          Delaware 28-7
Marshall . . . . . . . . . . . . . . . . . . . .92*         Youngstown St. 31-28

**James "Boots" Donnelly (6-6) (Middle Tenn. St. '65)**
Middle Tenn. St. . . . . . . . . . . . . .84          Eastern Ky. 27-10
Middle Tenn. St. . . . . . . . . . . . . .84          Indiana St. 42-41 (3 OT)
Middle Tenn. St. . . . . . . . . . . . . .84          Louisiana Tech 13-21
Middle Tenn. St. . . . . . . . . . . . . .85          Ga. Southern 21-28
Middle Tenn. St. . . . . . . . . . . . . .89          Appalachian St. 24-21
Middle Tenn. St. . . . . . . . . . . . . .89          Ga. Southern 3-45
Middle Tenn. St. . . . . . . . . . . . . .90          Jackson St. 28-7
Middle Tenn. St. . . . . . . . . . . . . .90          Boise St. 13-20
Middle Tenn. St. . . . . . . . . . . . . .91          Sam Houston St. 20-19 (OT)
Middle Tenn. St. . . . . . . . . . . . . .91          Eastern Ky. 13-23
Middle Tenn. St. . . . . . . . . . . . . .92          Appalachian St. 35-10
Middle Tenn. St. . . . . . . . . . . . . .92          Marshall 21-35

**Larry Donovan (0-1) (Nebraska '64)**
Montana . . . . . . . . . . . . . . . . . . . .82          Idaho 7-21

**Fred Dunlap (1-2) (Colgate '50)**
Colgate . . . . . . . . . . . . . . . . . . . . .82          Boston U. 21-7
Colgate . . . . . . . . . . . . . . . . . . . . .82          Delaware 13-20
Colgate . . . . . . . . . . . . . . . . . . . . .83          Western Caro. 23-24

**Dennis Erickson (1-2) (Montana St. '70)**
Idaho . . . . . . . . . . . . . . . . . . . . . .82          Montana 21-7
Idaho . . . . . . . . . . . . . . . . . . . . . .82          Eastern Ky. 30-38
Idaho . . . . . . . . . . . . . . . . . . . . . .85          Eastern Wash. 38-42

**Maurice "Mo" Forte (0-1) (Minnesota '71)**
North Caro. A&T . . . . . . . . . . . .86          Ga. Southern 21-52

**Keith Gilbertson (2-3) (Central Wash. '71)**
Idaho . . . . . . . . . . . . . . . . . . . . . .86          Nevada 7-27
Idaho . . . . . . . . . . . . . . . . . . . . . .87          Weber St. 30-59
Idaho . . . . . . . . . . . . . . . . . . . . . .88          Montana 38-19
Idaho . . . . . . . . . . . . . . . . . . . . . .88          Northwestern (La.) 38-30
Idaho . . . . . . . . . . . . . . . . . . . . . .88          Furman 7-38

**Sam Goodwin (1-1) (Henderson St. '66)**
Northwestern (La.) . . . . . . . . . .88          Boise St. 22-13
Northwestern (La.) . . . . . . . . . .88          Idaho 30-38

**W. C. Gorden (0-9) (Tennessee St. '52)**
Jackson St. . . . . . . . . . . . . . . . . .78          Florida A&M 10-15
Jackson St. . . . . . . . . . . . . . . . . .81          Boise St. 7-19
Jackson St. . . . . . . . . . . . . . . . . .82          Eastern Ill. 13-16 (OT)
Jackson St. . . . . . . . . . . . . . . . . .85          Ga. Southern 0-27
Jackson St. . . . . . . . . . . . . . . . . .86          Tennessee St. 23-32
Jackson St. . . . . . . . . . . . . . . . . .87          Arkansas St. 32-35
Jackson St. . . . . . . . . . . . . . . . . .88          Stephen F. Austin 0-24
Jackson St. . . . . . . . . . . . . . . . . .89          Montana 7-48
Jackson St. . . . . . . . . . . . . . . . . .90          Middle Tenn. St. 7-28

**Mike Gottfried (0-1) (Morehead St. '66)**
Murray St. . . . . . . . . . . . . . . . . . . .79          Lehigh 9-28

**Lynn Graves (3-1) %(Stephen F. Austin '65)**
Stephen F. Austin . . . . . . . . . . .89%         Grambling 59-56
Stephen F. Austin . . . . . . . . . . .89%         Southwest Mo. St. 55-25
Stephen F. Austin . . . . . . . . . . .89%         Furman 21-19
Stephen F. Austin . . . . . . . . . . .89%         Ga. Southern 34-37

**Bob Griffin (2-3) (Southern Conn. St. '63)**
Rhode Island . . . . . . . . . . . . . . . .81          Idaho St. 0-51
Rhode Island . . . . . . . . . . . . . . . .84          Richmond 23-17
Rhode Island . . . . . . . . . . . . . . . .84          Montana St. 20-32
Rhode Island . . . . . . . . . . . . . . . .85          Akron 35-27
Rhode Island . . . . . . . . . . . . . . . .85          Furman 15-59

**Skip Hall (2-2) (Concordia-M'head '66)**
Boise St. . . . . . . . . . . . . . . . . . . . .88          Northwestern (La.) 13-22

Boise St. . . . . . . . . . . . . . . . . . .90      Northern Iowa 20-3  
Boise St. . . . . . . . . . . . . . . . . . .90      Middle Tenn. St. 20-13  
Boise St. . . . . . . . . . . . . . . . . . .90      Nevada 52-59 (3 OT)  

**Bill Hayes (0-1) (N.C. Central '64)**  
North Caro. A&T . . . . . . . . . .92      Citadel 0-44  

**Jim Hess (1-1) (Southeastern Okla. '59)**  
Stephen F. Austin . . . . . . . . . .88      Jackson St. 24-0  
Stephen F. Austin . . . . . . . . . .88      Ga. Southern 6-27  

**Rudy Hubbard (2-0) (Ohio St. '68)**  
Florida A&M . . . . . . . . . . . . . . .78      Jackson St. 15-10  
Florida A&M . . . . . . . . . . . . . . .78*      Massachusetts 35-28  

**Sonny Jackson (1-1) (Nicholls St. '63)**  
Nicholls St. . . . . . . . . . . . . . . . .86      Appalachian St. 28-26  
Nicholls St. . . . . . . . . . . . . . . . .86      Ga. Southern 31-55  

**Cardell Jones (0-1) (Alcorn St. '65)**  
Alcorn St. . . . . . . . . . . . . . . . . .92      Northeast La. 27-78  

**Bobby Keasler (1-2) (Northeast La. '70)**  
McNeese St. . . . . . . . . . . . . . .91      Nevada 16-22  
McNeese St. . . . . . . . . . . . . . .92      Idaho 23-20  
McNeese St. . . . . . . . . . . . . . .92      Northern Iowa 7-29  

**Roy Kidd (15-11) (Eastern Ky. '54)**  
Eastern Ky. . . . . . . . . . . . . . . . .79      Nevada 33-30  
Eastern Ky. . . . . . . . . . . . . . . . .79*      Lehigh 30-7  
Eastern Ky. . . . . . . . . . . . . . . . .80      Lehigh 23-20  
Eastern Ky. . . . . . . . . . . . . . . . .80      Boise St. 29-31  
Eastern Ky. . . . . . . . . . . . . . . . .81      Delaware 35-28  

Eastern Ky. . . . . . . . . . . . . . . . .81      Boise St. 23-17  
Eastern Ky. . . . . . . . . . . . . . . . .81      Idaho St. 23-34  
Eastern Ky. . . . . . . . . . . . . . . . .82      Idaho St. 38-30  
Eastern Ky. . . . . . . . . . . . . . . . .82      Tennessee St. 13-7  
Eastern Ky. . . . . . . . . . . . . . . . .82*      Delaware 17-14  

Eastern Ky. . . . . . . . . . . . . . . . .83      Boston U. 20-24  
Eastern Ky. . . . . . . . . . . . . . . . .84      Middle Tenn. St. 10-27  
Eastern Ky. . . . . . . . . . . . . . . . .86      Furman 23-10  
Eastern Ky. . . . . . . . . . . . . . . . .86      Eastern Ill. 24-22  
Eastern Ky. . . . . . . . . . . . . . . . .86      Arkansas St. 10-24  

Eastern Ky. . . . . . . . . . . . . . . . .87      Western Ky. 40-17  
Eastern Ky. . . . . . . . . . . . . . . . .87      Northeast La. 32-33  
Eastern Ky. . . . . . . . . . . . . . . . .88      Massachusetts 28-17  
Eastern Ky. . . . . . . . . . . . . . . . .88      Western Ky. 41-24  
Eastern Ky. . . . . . . . . . . . . . . . .88      Ga. Southern 17-21  

Eastern Ky. . . . . . . . . . . . . . . . .89      Youngstown St. 24-28  
Eastern Ky. . . . . . . . . . . . . . . . .90      Furman 17-45  
Eastern Ky. . . . . . . . . . . . . . . . .91      Appalachian St. 14-3  
Eastern Ky. . . . . . . . . . . . . . . . .91      Middle Tenn. St. 23-13  
Eastern Ky. . . . . . . . . . . . . . . . .91      Marshall 7-14  
Eastern Ky. . . . . . . . . . . . . . . . .92      Marshall 0-44  

**Jim Koetter (0-1) (Idaho St. '61)**  
Idaho St. . . . . . . . . . . . . . . . . . .83      Nevada 20-27  

**Dave Kragthorpe (3-0) (Utah St. '55)**  
Idaho St. . . . . . . . . . . . . . . . . . .81      Rhode Island 51-0  
Idaho St. . . . . . . . . . . . . . . . . . .81      South Caro. St. 41-12  
Idaho St. . . . . . . . . . . . . . . . . . .81*      Eastern Ky. 34-23  

**Larry Lacewell (6-4) (Ark.-Monticello '59)**  
Arkansas St. . . . . . . . . . . . . . .84      Tenn.-Chatt. 37-10  
Arkansas St. . . . . . . . . . . . . . .84      Montana St. 14-31  
Arkansas St. . . . . . . . . . . . . . .85      Grambling 10-7  
Arkansas St. . . . . . . . . . . . . . .85      Nevada 23-24  
Arkansas St. . . . . . . . . . . . . . .86      Sam Houston St. 48-7  

Arkansas St. . . . . . . . . . . . . . .86      Delaware 55-14  
Arkansas St. . . . . . . . . . . . . . .86      Eastern Ky. 24-10  
Arkansas St. . . . . . . . . . . . . . .86      Ga. Southern 21-48  
Arkansas St. . . . . . . . . . . . . . .87      Jackson St. 35-32  
Arkansas St. . . . . . . . . . . . . . .87      Northern Iowa 28-49  

**Jimmye Laycock (1-3) (William & Mary '70)**  
William & Mary . . . . . . . . . . . . .86      Delaware 17-51  
William & Mary . . . . . . . . . . . . .89      Furman 10-24  
William & Mary . . . . . . . . . . . . .90      Massachusetts 38-0  
William & Mary . . . . . . . . . . . . .90      Central Fla. 38-52

**Tom Lichtenberg (0-1) (Louisville '62)**
Maine . . . . . . . . . . . . . . . . . . . . . 89          Southwest Mo. St. 35-38

**Gene McDowell (2-1) (Florida St. '63)**
Central Fla. . . . . . . . . . . . . . . . . 90          Youngstown St. 20-17
Central Fla. . . . . . . . . . . . . . . . . 90          William & Mary 52-38
Central Fla. . . . . . . . . . . . . . . . . 90          Ga. Southern 7-44

**John Merritt (1-2)† (Kentucky St. '50)**
Tennessee St. . . . . . . . . . . . . . . 81†          South Caro. St. 25-26 (OT)
Tennessee St. . . . . . . . . . . . . . . 82†          Eastern Ill. 20-19
Tennessee St. . . . . . . . . . . . . . . 82†          Eastern Ky. 7-13

**Al Molde (1-2) (Gust. Adolphus '66)**
Eastern Ill. . . . . . . . . . . . . . . . . . 83          Indiana St. 13-16 (2 OT)
Eastern Ill. . . . . . . . . . . . . . . . . . 86          Murray St. 28-21
Eastern Ill. . . . . . . . . . . . . . . . . . 86          Eastern Ky. 22-24

**Jerry Moore (0-3) (Baylor '61)**
Appalachian St. . . . . . . . . . . . . 89          Middle Tenn. St. 21-24
Appalachian St. . . . . . . . . . . . . 91          Eastern Ky. 3-14
Appalachian St. . . . . . . . . . . . . 92          Middle Tenn. St. 10-35

**Darrell Mudra (4-3) (Peru St. '51)**
Eastern Ill. . . . . . . . . . . . . . . . . . 82          Jackson St. 16-13 (OT)
Eastern Ill. . . . . . . . . . . . . . . . . . 82          Tennessee St. 19-20
Northern Iowa . . . . . . . . . . . . . 85          Eastern Wash. 17-14
Northern Iowa . . . . . . . . . . . . . 85          Ga. Southern 33-40
Northern Iowa . . . . . . . . . . . . . 87          Youngstown St. 31-28
Northern Iowa . . . . . . . . . . . . . 87          Arkansas St. 49-28
Northern Iowa . . . . . . . . . . . . . 87          Northeast La. 41-44 (OT)

**Tim Murphy (0-1) (Springfield '78)**
Maine . . . . . . . . . . . . . . . . . . . . . 87          Ga. Southern 28-31 (OT)

**Corky Nelson (0-3) (Southwest Tex. St. '64)**
North Texas . . . . . . . . . . . . . . . 83          Nevada 17-20 (OT)
North Texas . . . . . . . . . . . . . . . 87          Northeast La. 9-30
North Texas . . . . . . . . . . . . . . . 88          Marshall 0-7

**Buddy Nix (0-1) (Livingston '61)**
Tenn.-Chatt. . . . . . . . . . . . . . . . 84          Arkansas St. 10-37

**Bob Pickett (1-1) (Maine '59)**
Massachusetts . . . . . . . . . . . . . 78          Nevada 44-21
Massachusetts . . . . . . . . . . . . . 78          Florida A&M 28-35

**Mike Price (1-1) (Puget Sound '69)**
Weber St. . . . . . . . . . . . . . . . . . 87          Idaho 59-30
Weber St. . . . . . . . . . . . . . . . . . 87          Marshall 23-51

**Joe Purzycki (0-1) (Delaware '71)**
James Madison . . . . . . . . . . . . 87          Marshall 12-41

**Dennis Raetz (1-2) (Nebraska '68)**
Indiana St. . . . . . . . . . . . . . . . . 83          Eastern Ill. 16-13 (2 OT)
Indiana St. . . . . . . . . . . . . . . . . 83          Southern Ill. 7-23
Indiana St. . . . . . . . . . . . . . . . . 84          Middle Tenn. St. 41-42 (3 OT)

**Ron Randleman (0-2) (William Penn '64)**
Sam Houston St. . . . . . . . . . . . 86          Arkansas St. 7-48
Sam Houston St. . . . . . . . . . . . 91          Middle Tenn. St. 19-20 (OT)

**Harold "Tubby" Raymond (5-6) (Michigan '50)**
Delaware . . . . . . . . . . . . . . . . . . 81          Eastern Ky. 28-35
Delaware . . . . . . . . . . . . . . . . . . 82          Colgate 20-13
Delaware . . . . . . . . . . . . . . . . . . 82          Louisiana Tech 17-0
Delaware . . . . . . . . . . . . . . . . . . 82          Eastern Ky. 14-17
Delaware . . . . . . . . . . . . . . . . . . 86          William & Mary 51-17
Delaware . . . . . . . . . . . . . . . . . . 86          Arkansas St. 14-55
Delaware . . . . . . . . . . . . . . . . . . 88          Furman 7-21
Delaware . . . . . . . . . . . . . . . . . . 91          James Madison 35-42 (2 OT)
Delaware . . . . . . . . . . . . . . . . . . 92          Samford 56-21
Delaware . . . . . . . . . . . . . . . . . . 92          Northeast La. 41-18
Delaware . . . . . . . . . . . . . . . . . . 92          Marshall 7-28

**Don Read (2-2) (Cal St. Sacramento '59)**
Montana . . . . . . . . . . . . . . . . . . 88          Idaho 19-38
Montana . . . . . . . . . . . . . . . . . . 89          Jackson St. 48-7
Montana . . . . . . . . . . . . . . . . . . 89          Eastern Ill. 25-19
Montana . . . . . . . . . . . . . . . . . . 89          Ga. Southern 15-45

**Jim Reid (0-2) (Maine '73)**
Massachusetts . . . . . . . . . . . . . 88          Eastern Ky. 17-28
Massachusetts . . . . . . . . . . . . . 90          William & Mary 0-38

**Dave Roberts (2-4) (Western Caro. '68)**

| | |
|---|---|
| Western Ky. | 87 | Eastern Ky. 17-40 |
| Western Ky. | 88 | Western Ill. 35-32 |
| Western Ky. | 88 | Eastern Ky. 24-41 |
| Northeast La. | 90 | Nevada 14-27 |
| Northeast La. | 92 | Alcorn St. 78-27 |
| Northeast La. | 92 | Delaware 18-41 |

**Eddie Robinson (0-3) (Leland '41)**

| | |
|---|---|
| Grambling | 80 | Boise St. 9-14 |
| Grambling | 85 | Arkansas St. 7-10 |
| Grambling | 89 | Stephen F. Austin 56-59 |

**Erk Russell (16-2) (Auburn '49)**

| | |
|---|---|
| Ga. Southern | 85 | Jackson St. 27-0 |
| Ga. Southern | 85 | Middle Tenn. St. 28-21 |
| Ga. Southern | 85 | Northern Iowa 40-33 |
| Ga. Southern | 85* | Furman 44-42 |
| Ga. Southern | 86 | North Caro. A&T 52-21 |
| Ga. Southern | 86 | Nicholls St. 55-31 |
| Ga. Southern | 86 | Nevada 48-38 |
| Ga. Southern | 86* | Arkansas St. 48-21 |
| Ga. Southern | 87 | Maine 31-28 (OT) |
| Ga. Southern | 87 | Appalachian St. 0-19 |
| Ga. Southern | 88 | Citadel 38-20 |
| Ga. Southern | 88 | Stephen F. Austin 27-6 |
| Ga. Southern | 88 | Eastern Ky. 21-17 |
| Ga. Southern | 88 | Furman 12-17 |
| Ga. Southern | 89 | Villanova 52-36 |
| Ga. Southern | 89 | Middle Tenn. St. 45-3 |
| Ga. Southern | 89 | Montana 45-15 |
| Ga. Southern | 89* | Stephen F. Austin 37-34 |

**Jimmy Satterfield (7-3) (South Caro. '62)**

| | |
|---|---|
| Furman | 86 | Eastern Ky. 10-23 |
| Furman | 88 | Delaware 21-7 |
| Furman | 88 | Marshall 13-9 |
| Furman | 88 | Idaho 38-7 |
| Furman | 88* | Ga. Southern 17-12 |
| Furman | 89 | William & Mary 24-10 |
| Furman | 89 | Youngstown St. 42-23 |
| Furman | 89 | Stephen F. Austin 19-21 |
| Furman | 90 | Eastern Ky. 45-17 |
| Furman | 90 | Nevada 35-42 (3 OT) |

**Rip Scherer (1-1) (William & Mary '74)**

| | |
|---|---|
| James Madison | 91 | Delaware 42-35 (2 OT) |
| James Madison | 91 | Samford 21-24 |

**Dal Shealy (1-2) (Carson-Newman '60)**

| | |
|---|---|
| Richmond | 84 | Boston U. 35-33 |
| Richmond | 84 | Rhode Island 17-23 |
| Richmond | 87 | Appalachian St. 3-20 |

**Dick Sheridan (3-3) (South Caro. '64)**

| | |
|---|---|
| Furman | 82 | South Caro. St. 0-17 |
| Furman | 83 | Boston U. 35-16 |
| Furman | 83 | Western Caro. 7-14 |
| Furman | 85 | Rhode Island 59-15 |
| Furman | 85 | Nevada 35-12 |
| Furman | 85 | Ga. Southern 42-44 |

**John L. Smith (1-3) (Weber St. '71)**

| | |
|---|---|
| Idaho | 89 | Eastern Ill. 21-38 |
| Idaho | 90 | Southwest Mo. St. 41-35 |
| Idaho | 90 | Ga. Southern 27-28 |
| Idaho | 92 | McNeese St. 20-23 |

**Bob Spoo (1-1) (Purdue '60)**

| | |
|---|---|
| Eastern Ill. | 89 | Idaho 38-21 |
| Eastern Ill. | 89 | Montana 19-25 |

**Tim Stowers (4-0) (Auburn '79)**

| | |
|---|---|
| Ga. Southern | 90 | Citadel 31-0 |
| Ga. Southern | 90 | Idaho 28-27 |
| Ga. Southern | 90 | Central Fla. 44-7 |
| Ga. Southern | 90* | Nevada 36-13 |

**Charlie Taaffe (1-3) (Siena '73)**

| | |
|---|---|
| Citadel | 88 | Ga. Southern 20-38 |

*Coaches' Records*

| Citadel . . . . . . . . . . . . . . . . . . . . . 90 | Ga. Southern 0-31 |
| Citadel . . . . . . . . . . . . . . . . . . . . . 92 | North Caro. A&T 44-0 |
| Citadel . . . . . . . . . . . . . . . . . . . . . 92 | Youngstown St. 17-42 |

**Andy Talley (0-3) (Southern Conn. St. '67)**

| Villanova . . . . . . . . . . . . . . . . . . . . 89 | Ga. Southern 36-52 |
| Villanova . . . . . . . . . . . . . . . . . . . . 91 | Youngstown St. 16-17 |
| Villanova . . . . . . . . . . . . . . . . . . . . 92 | Youngstown St. 20-23 |

**Rick Taylor (1-3) (Gettysburg '64)**

| Boston U. . . . . . . . . . . . . . . . . . . . . 82 | Colgate 7-21 |
| Boston U. . . . . . . . . . . . . . . . . . . . . 83 | Eastern Ky. 24-20 |
| Boston U. . . . . . . . . . . . . . . . . . . . . 83 | Furman 16-35 |
| Boston U. . . . . . . . . . . . . . . . . . . . . 84 | Richmond 33-35 |

**Bill Thomas (1-1) (Tennessee St. '71)**

| Tennessee St. . . . . . . . . . . . . . . . 86 | Jackson St. 32-23 |
| Tennessee St. . . . . . . . . . . . . . . . 86 | Nevada 6-33 |

**Jim Tressel (8-4) (Baldwin-Wallace '75)**

| Youngstown St. . . . . . . . . . . . . . 87 | Northern Iowa 28-31 |
| Youngstown St. . . . . . . . . . . . . . 89 | Eastern Ky. 28-24 |
| Youngstown St. . . . . . . . . . . . . . 89 | Furman 23-42 |
| Youngstown St. . . . . . . . . . . . . . 90 | Central Fla. 17-20 |
| Youngstown St. . . . . . . . . . . . . . 91 | Villanova 17-16 |
| Youngstown St. . . . . . . . . . . . . . 91 | Nevada 30-28 |
| Youngstown St. . . . . . . . . . . . . . 91 | Samford 10-0 |
| Youngstown St. . . . . . . . . . . . . . 91* | Marshall 25-17 |
| Youngstown St. . . . . . . . . . . . . . 92 | Villanova 23-20 |
| Youngstown St. . . . . . . . . . . . . . 92 | Citadel 42-17 |
| Youngstown St. . . . . . . . . . . . . . 92 | Northern Iowa 19-7 |
| Youngstown St. . . . . . . . . . . . . . 92 | Marshall 28-31 |

**Bob Waters (3-1) (Presbyterian '60)**

| Western Caro. . . . . . . . . . . . . . . 83 | Colgate 24-23 |
| Western Caro. . . . . . . . . . . . . . . 83 | Holy Cross 28-21 |
| Western Caro. . . . . . . . . . . . . . . 83 | Furman 14-7 |
| Western Caro. . . . . . . . . . . . . . . 83 | Southern Ill. 7-43 |

**John Whitehead (1-2) (East Stroudsburg '50)**

| Lehigh . . . . . . . . . . . . . . . . . . . . . 79 | Murray St. 28-9 |
| Lehigh . . . . . . . . . . . . . . . . . . . . . 79 | Eastern Ky. 7-30 |
| Lehigh . . . . . . . . . . . . . . . . . . . . . 80 | Eastern Ky. 20-23 |

**A. L. Williams (3-1) (Louisiana Tech '57)**

| Louisiana Tech . . . . . . . . . . . . . . 84 | Mississippi Val. 66-19 |
| Louisiana Tech . . . . . . . . . . . . . . 84 | Alcorn St. 44-21 |
| Louisiana Tech . . . . . . . . . . . . . . 84 | Middle Tenn. St. 21-13 |
| Louisiana Tech . . . . . . . . . . . . . . 84 | Montana St. 6-19 |

**Sparky Woods (2-2) (Carson-Newman '76)**

| Appalachian St. . . . . . . . . . . . . . 86 | Nicholls St. 26-28 |
| Appalachian St. . . . . . . . . . . . . . 87 | Richmond 20-3 |
| Appalachian St. . . . . . . . . . . . . . 87 | Ga. Southern 19-0 |
| Appalachian St. . . . . . . . . . . . . . 87 | Marshall 10-24 |

**Dick Zornes (1-2) (Eastern Wash. '68)**

| Eastern Wash. . . . . . . . . . . . . . . 85 | Idaho 42-38 |
| Eastern Wash. . . . . . . . . . . . . . . 85 | Northern Iowa 14-17 |
| Eastern Wash. . . . . . . . . . . . . . . 92 | Northern Iowa 14-17 |

*\* National championship.   † Tennessee State's participation voided.   % Stephen F. Austin's participation voided.*

# WINNINGEST ACTIVE DIVISION II COACHES

(Minimum five years as a college head coach; record at four-year colleges only.)

## BY PERCENTAGE

| Coach, College | Years | Won | Lost | Tied | *Pct. | #Playoffs W-L-T |
|---|---|---|---|---|---|---|
| Rocky Hager, North Dak. St. . . . . . . . . . . . . . . . . . . . . . . . . . | 6 | 59 | 12 | 1 | .826 | 10-3-0 |
| Ken Sparks, Carson-Newman . . . . . . . . . . . . . . . . . . . . . . . | 13 | 119 | 37 | 1 | .761 | 0-0-0 |
| Danny Hale, Bloomsburg . . . . . . . . . . . . . . . . . . . . . . . . . . | 5 | 40 | 13 | 0 | .755 | 0-1-0 |
| Bob Cortese, Fort Hays St. . . . . . . . . . . . . . . . . . . . . . . . . . | 13 | 106 | 34 | 3 | .752 | 0-0-0 |
| Bill Burgess, Jacksonville St. . . . . . . . . . . . . . . . . . . . . . . . | 8 | 69 | 22 | 4 | .747 | 12-4-0 |
| Dick Lowry, Hillsdale . . . . . . . . . . . . . . . . . . . . . . . . . . . . . | 19 | 145 | 59 | 2 | .709 | 0-0-0 |
| Mark Whipple, New Haven . . . . . . . . . . . . . . . . . . . . . . . . . | 5 | 37 | 16 | 0 | .698 | 2-1-0 |
| Gene Carpenter, Millersville . . . . . . . . . . . . . . . . . . . . . . . . | 24 | 159 | 69 | 5 | .693 | 1-1-0 |
| Tom Hollman, Edinboro . . . . . . . . . . . . . . . . . . . . . . . . . . . | 9 | 61 | 27 | 3 | .687 | 1-3-0 |
| Joe Taylor, Hampton . . . . . . . . . . . . . . . . . . . . . . . . . . . . . | 10 | 70 | 31 | 4 | .686 | 0-4-0 |

| Coach, College | Years | Won | Lost | Tied | *Pct. | #Playoffs W-L-T |
|---|---|---|---|---|---|---|
| Frank Cignetti, Indiana (Pa.) | 11 | 86 | 41 | 1 | .676 | 7-5-0 |
| Jim Malosky, Minn.-Duluth | 35 | 223 | 104 | 12 | .676 | 0-0-0 |
| Kevin Donley, Calif. (Pa.) | 15 | 103 | 52 | 1 | .663 | 0-0-0 |
| Dennis Miller, Northern St. | 7 | 51 | 26 | 0 | .662 | 0-0-0 |
| Jerry Vandergriff, Angelo St. | 11 | 77 | 42 | 1 | .646 | 2-2-0 |
| Carl Iverson, Western St. | 9 | 62 | 35 | 1 | .638 | 0-1-0 |
| Ron Harms, Texas A&I | 24 | 156 | 88 | 4 | .637 | 3-3-0 |
| Fred Martinelli, Ashland | 34 | 208 | 117 | 12 | .635 | 0-1-0 |
| Claire Boroff, Neb.-Kearney | 21 | 129 | 74 | 4 | .633 | 0-0-0 |
| Rocky Rees, Shippensburg | 8 | 54 | 31 | 2 | .632 | 1-1-0 |
| Archie Cooley Jr., Norfolk St. | 11 | 68 | 40 | 5 | .624 | 0-0-0 |
| Gordie Gillespie, St. Francis (Ill.) | 7 | 43 | 27 | 0 | .614 | 0-0-0 |
| Dick Mannini, San Fran. St. | 8 | 48 | 30 | 1 | .614 | 0-0-0 |
| Dennis Douds, East Stroudsburg | 19 | 117 | 74 | 2 | .611 | 0-1-0 |
| Jon Lantz, Mo. Southern St. | 7 | 43 | 27 | 2 | .611 | 0-0-0 |
| Brad Smith, Chadron St. | 6 | 35 | 23 | 1 | .602 | 0-0-0 |
| Douglas Porter, Fort Valley St. | 23 | 135 | 89 | 4 | .601 | 0-1-0 |
| Jeff Geiser, Adams St. | 9 | 53 | 37 | 1 | .588 | 0-0-0 |
| Joe Glenn, Northern Colo. | 8 | 48 | 34 | 1 | .584 | 0-2-0 |
| Stan McGarvey, Mo. Western St. | 8 | 49 | 35 | 2 | .581 | 0-0-0 |
| Woody Fish, Gardner-Webb | 9 | 58 | 43 | 1 | .574 | 0-0-0 |
| George Ihler, Saginaw Valley | 10 | 58 | 44 | 1 | .568 | 0-0-0 |
| Monte Cater, Shepherd | 12 | 66 | 50 | 2 | .568 | 0-0-0 |
| Lyle Setencich, Cal Poly SLO | 10 | 59 | 45 | 2 | .566 | 1-1-0 |
| George Mihalik, Slippery Rock | 5 | 27 | 21 | 4 | .558 | 0-0-0 |
| Henry Lattimore, Virginia Union | 14 | 81 | 64 | 4 | .557 | 1-2-0 |
| Hampton Smith, Albany St. (Ga.) | 17 | 93 | 74 | 4 | .556 | 0-1-0 |
| Gary Howard, Central Okla. | 16 | 88 | 70 | 5 | .555 | 0-0-0 |
| Denny Creehan, South Dak. | 8 | 45 | 36 | 1 | .555 | 0-0-0 |
| Bill Bless, Indianapolis | 21 | 112 | 90 | 9 | .552 | 0-0-0 |
| Noel Martin, St. Cloud St. | 10 | 60 | 49 | 0 | .550 | 1-1-0 |
| Gene Sobolewski, Clarion | 10 | 55 | 46 | 0 | .545 | 0-0-0 |
| Larry Kramer, Emporia St. | 22 | 116 | 101 | 6 | .534 | 0-0-0 |
| Eddie Vowell, East Tex. St. | 7 | 42 | 37 | 1 | .531 | 2-2-0 |
| Alex Rotsko, American Int'l | 10 | 52 | 46 | 3 | .530 | 0-0-0 |
| Dennis Moller, Augustana (S. D.) | 7 | 36 | 32 | 0 | .529 | 0-0-0 |
| Terry Noland, Central Mo. St. | 10 | 56 | 50 | 1 | .528 | 0-0-0 |
| Bud Elliott, Northwest Mo. St. | 25 | 134 | 122 | 7 | .523 | 0-1-0 |
| Mike Ayers, Wofford | 8 | 46 | 42 | 1 | .522 | 0-2-0 |
| Keith Otterbein, Ferris St. | 7 | 40 | 37 | 1 | .519 | 1-1-0 |
| Bernie Anderson, Michigan Tech | 6 | 29 | 28 | 0 | .509 | 0-0-0 |
| Mike DeLong, Springfield | 11 | 52 | 51 | 2 | .505 | 0-0-0 |
| James Martin, Tuskegee | 9 | 43 | 43 | 2 | .500 | 0-0-0 |
| Jim Paronto, Mesa St. | 7 | 36 | 36 | 0 | .500 | 0-0-0 |

\* *Ties computed as half won and half lost; bowl and postseason games included.* # *NCAA Division II playoff games.*

## BY VICTORIES
### (Minimum 80 victories)

| Coach, College, Winning Percentage | Won | Coach, College, Winning Percentage | Won |
|---|---|---|---|
| Jim Malosky, Minn.-Duluth .676 | 223 | Dennis Douds, East Stroudsburg .611 | 117 |
| Fred Martinelli, Ashland .635 | 208 | Larry Kramer, Emporia St. .525 | 116 |
| Gene Carpenter, Millersville .693 | 159 | Bill Bless, Indianapolis .552 | 112 |
| Ron Harms, Texas A&I .637 | 156 | Bob Cortese, Fort Hays St. .752 | 106 |
| Dick Lowry, Hillsdale .709 | 145 | Kevin Donley, Calif. (Pa.) .663 | 103 |
| Douglas Porter, Fort Valley St. .601 | 135 | Hampton Smith, Albany St. (Ga.) .556 | 93 |
| Bud Elliott, Northwest Mo. St. .523 | 134 | Gary Howard, Central Okla. .555 | 88 |
| Claire Boroff, Neb.-Kearney .633 | 129 | Frank Cignetti, Indiana (Pa.) .676 | 86 |
| Ken Sparks, Carson-Newman .761 | 119 | Henry Lattimore, Virginia Union .557 | 81 |

## DIVISION II CHAMPIONSHIP COACHES

All coaches who have coached teams in the Division II championship playoffs since 1973 are listed below with their playoff record, alma mater and year graduated, team, year coached, opponent, and score.

**Phil Albert (1-3) (Arizona '66)**

| Towson St. | 83 | North Dak. St. 17-24 |
|---|---|---|
| Towson St. | 84 | Norfolk St. 31-21 |
| Towson St. | 84 | Troy St. 3-45 |
| Towson St. | 86 | Central St. (Ohio) 0-31 |

*Coaches' Records*

**Pokey Allen (10-5) (Utah '65)**

| | | |
|---|---|---|
| Portland St. | 87 | Mankato St. 27-21 |
| Portland St. | 87 | Northern Mich. 13-7 |
| Portland St. | 87 | Troy St. 17-31 |
| Portland St. | 88 | Bowie St. 34-17 |
| Portland St. | 88 | Jacksonville St. 20-13 |
| Portland St. | 88 | Texas A&I 35-27 |
| Portland St. | 88 | North Dak. St. 21-35 |
| Portland St. | 89 | West Chester 56-50 (3 OT) |
| Portland St. | 89 | Indiana (Pa.) 0-17 |
| Portland St. | 91 | Northern Colo. 28-24 |
| Portland St. | 91 | Mankato St. 37-27 |
| Portland St. | 91 | Pittsburg St. 21-53 |
| Portland St. | 92 | UC Davis 42-28 |
| Portland St. | 92 | Texas A&I 35-30 |
| Portland St. | 92 | Pittsburg St. 38-41 |

**Mike Ayers (0-2) (Georgetown, Ky. '74)**

| | | |
|---|---|---|
| Wofford | 90 | Mississippi Col. 19-70 |
| Wofford | 91 | Mississippi Col. 15-28 |

**Willard Bailey (0-6) (Norfolk St. '62)**

| | | |
|---|---|---|
| Virginia Union | 79 | Delaware 28-58 |
| Virginia Union | 80 | North Ala. 8-17 |
| Virginia Union | 81 | Shippensburg 27-40 |
| Virginia Union | 82 | North Dak. St. 20-21 |
| Virginia Union | 83 | North Ala. 14-16 |
| Norfolk St. | 84 | Towson St. 21-31 |

**Bob Bartolomeo (0-1) (Butler '77)**

| | | |
|---|---|---|
| Butler | 91 | Pittsburg St. 16-26 |

**Tom Beck (0-2) (Northern Ill. '61)**

| | | |
|---|---|---|
| Grand Valley St. | 89 | Indiana (Pa.) 24-34 |
| Grand Valley St. | 90 | East Tex. St. 14-20 |

**Bob Blasi (0-1) (Colorado St. '53)**

| | | |
|---|---|---|
| Northern Colo. | 80 | Eastern Ill. 14-21 |

**Bill Bowes (1-2) (Penn St. '65)**

| | | |
|---|---|---|
| New Hampshire | 75 | Lehigh 35-21 |
| New Hampshire | 75 | Western Ky. 3-14 |
| New Hampshire | 76 | Montana St. 16-17 |

**Chuck Broyles (9-2) (Pittsburg St. '70)**

| | | |
|---|---|---|
| Pittsburg St. | 90 | Northeast Mo. St. 59-3 |
| Pittsburg St. | 90 | East Tex. St. 60-28 |
| Pittsburg St. | 90 | North Dak. St. 29-39 |
| Pittsburg St. | 91 | Butler 26-16 |
| Pittsburg St. | 91 | East Tex. St. 38-28 |
| Pittsburg St. | 91 | Portland St. 53-21 |
| Pittsburg St. | 91* | Jacksonville St. 23-6 |
| Pittsburg St. | 92 | North Dak. 26-21 |
| Pittsburg St. | 92 | North Dak. St. 38-37 (OT) |
| Pittsburg St. | 92 | Portland St. 41-38 |
| Pittsburg St. | 92 | Jacksonville St. 13-17 |

**Sandy Buda (1-2) (Kansas '67)**

| | | |
|---|---|---|
| Nebraska-Omaha | 78 | Youngstown St. 14-21 |
| Nebraska-Omaha | 84 | Northwest Mo. St. 28-15 |
| Nebraska-Omaha | 84 | North Dak. St. 14-25 |

**Bill Burgess (12-4) (Auburn '63)**

| | | |
|---|---|---|
| Jacksonville St. | 88 | West Chester 63-24 |
| Jacksonville St. | 88 | Portland St. 13-20 |
| Jacksonville St. | 89 | Alabama A&M 33-9 |
| Jacksonville St. | 89 | North Dak. St. 21-17 |
| Jacksonville St. | 89 | Angelo St. 34-16 |
| Jacksonville St. | 89 | Mississippi Col. 0-3 |
| Jacksonville St. | 90 | North Ala. 38-14 |
| Jacksonville St. | 90 | Mississippi Col. 7-14 |
| Jacksonville St. | 91 | Winston-Salem 49-24 |
| Jacksonville St. | 91 | Mississippi Col. 35-7 |
| Jacksonville St. | 91 | Indiana (Pa.) 27-20 |
| Jacksonville St. | 91 | Pittsburg St. 6-23 |
| Jacksonville St. | 92 | Savannah St. 41-16 |
| Jacksonville St. | 92 | North Ala. 14-12 |
| Jacksonville St. | 92 | New Haven 46-35 |
| Jacksonville St. | 92* | Pittsburg St. 17-13 |

After coaching Jacksonville State in championship-game losses in 1989 and 1991, Bill Burgess and his Gamecocks finally captured the Division II title in 1992 with a 17-13 victory over defending champion Pittsburg State. For his efforts, Burgess was named College Division I coach of the year by the AFCA.

**Bob Burt (0-1) (Cal St. Los Angeles '62)**
Cal St. Northridge...........90          Cal Poly SLO 7-14

**Gene Carpenter (1-1) (Huron '63)**
Millersville...................88          Indiana (Pa.) 27-24
Millersville...................88          North Dak. St. 26-36

**Marino Casem (0-1) (Xavier, La. '56)**
Alcorn St. ..................74          Nevada-Las Vegas 22-35

**Frank Cignetti (7-5) (Indiana, Pa. '60)**
Indiana (Pa.) ..............87          Central Fla. 10-12
Indiana (Pa.) ..............88          Millersville 24-27
Indiana (Pa.) ..............89          Grand Valley St. 34-24
Indiana (Pa.) ..............89          Portland St. 17-0
Indiana (Pa.) ..............89          Mississippi Col. 14-26
Indiana (Pa.) ..............90          Winston-Salem 48-0
Indiana (Pa.) ..............90          Edinboro 14-7
Indiana (Pa.) ..............90          Mississippi Col. 27-8
Indiana (Pa.) ..............90          North Dak. St. 11-51
Indiana (Pa.) ..............91          Virginia Union 56-7
Indiana (Pa.) ..............91          Shippensburg 52-7
Indiana (Pa.) ..............91          Jacksonville St. 20-27

**Bruce Craddock (0-1) (Northeast Mo. St. '66)**
Northeast Mo. St. ..........82          Jacksonville St. 21-34

**Rick Daniels (0-2) (West Chester '75)**
West Chester...............89          Portland St. 50-56 (3 OT)
West Chester...............92          New Haven 26-38

**Bill Davis (0-1) (Johnson Smith '65)**
Savannah St.................92          Jacksonville St. 16-41

**Rey Dempsey (0-1) (Geneva '58)**
Youngstown St. ............74          Delaware 14-35

**Jim Dennison (2-1) (Wooster '60)**
Akron ........................76        Nevada-Las Vegas 26-6
Akron ........................76        Northern Mich. 29-26
Akron ........................76        Montana St. 13-24

**Dennis Douds (0-1) (Slippery Rock '63)**
East Stroudsburg ...........91        Shippensburg 33-34

**Fred Dunlap (0-2) (Colgate '50)**
Lehigh ......................73        Western Ky. 16-25
Lehigh ......................75        New Hampshire 21-35

**Bud Elliott (0-1) (Baker '53)**
Northwest Mo. St. ...........89        Pittsburg St. 7-28

**Jimmy Feix (4-2) (Western Ky. '53)**
Western Ky. .................73        Lehigh 25-16
Western Ky. .................73        Grambling 28-20
Western Ky. .................73        Louisiana Tech 0-34
Western Ky. .................75        Northern Iowa 14-12
Western Ky. .................75        New Hampshire 14-3
Western Ky. .................75        Northern Mich. 14-16

**Bob Foster (0-2) (UC Davis '62)**
UC Davis.....................89        Angelo St. 23-28
UC Davis.....................92        Portland St. 28-42

**Dennis Franchione (1-1) (Pittsburg St. '73)**
Pittsburg St..................89        Northwest Mo. St. 28-7
Pittsburg St..................89        Angelo St. 21-24

**Fred Freeman (0-1) (Mississippi Val. '66)**
Hampton .....................85        Bloomsburg 28-38

**Jim Fuller (3-5) (Alabama '67)**
Jacksonville St. .............77        Northern Ariz. 35-0
Jacksonville St. .............77        North Dak. St. 31-7
Jacksonville St. .............77        Lehigh 0-33
Jacksonville St. .............78        Delaware 27-42
Jacksonville St. .............80        Cal Poly SLO 0-15

Jacksonville St. .............81        Southwest Tex. St. 22-38
Jacksonville St. .............82        Northeast Mo. St. 34-21
Jacksonville St. .............82        Southwest Tex. St. 14-19

**Chan Gailey (3-0) (Florida '74)**
Troy St. ....................84        Central St. (Ohio) 31-21
Troy St. ....................84        Towson St. 45-3
Troy St. ....................84*       North Dak. St. 18-17

**Joe Glenn (0-2) (South Dak. '71)**
Northern Colo. ..............90        North Dak. St. 7-17
Northern Colo. ..............91        Portland St. 24-28

**Ray Greene (1-1) (Akron '63)**
Alabama A&M ...............79        Morgan St. 27-7
Alabama A&M ...............79        Youngstown St. 0-52

**John Gregory (0-1) (Northern Iowa '61)**
South Dak. St. ..............79        Youngstown St. 7-50

**Herb Grenke (1-1) (Wis.-Milwaukee '63)**
Northern Mich...............87        Angelo St. 23-20 (OT)
Northern Mich...............87        Portland St. 7-13

**Wayne Grubb (4-3) (Tennessee '61)**
North Ala. ..................80        Virginia Union 17-8
North Ala. ..................80        Eastern Ill. 31-56
North Ala. ..................83        Virginia Union 16-14
North Ala. ..................83        Central St. (Ohio) 24-27
North Ala. ..................85        Fort Valley St. 14-7

North Ala. ..................85        Bloomsburg 34-0
North Ala. ..................85        North Dak. St. 7-35

**Rocky Hager (10-3) (Minot St. '74)**
North Dak. St................88        Augustana (S.D.) 49-7
North Dak. St................88        Millersville 36-26
North Dak. St................88        Cal St. Sacramento 42-20
North Dak. St................88*       Portland St. 35-21
North Dak. St................89        Edinboro 45-32

North Dak. St................89        Jacksonville St. 17-21
North Dak. St................90        Northern Colo. 17-7
North Dak. St................90        Cal Poly SLO 47-0
North Dak. St................90        Pittsburg St. 39-29
North Dak. St................90*       Indiana (Pa.) 51-11

North Dak. St. . . . . . . . . . . . . . . 91    Mankato St. 7-27
North Dak. St. . . . . . . . . . . . . . . 92    Northeast Mo. St. 42-7
North Dak. St. . . . . . . . . . . . . . . 92    Pittsburg St. 37-38 (OT)

**Danny Hale (0-1) (West Chester '68)**
West Chester . . . . . . . . . . . . . . . 88    Jacksonville St. 24-63

**Ron Harms (3-3) (Valparaiso '59)**
Texas A&I . . . . . . . . . . . . . . . . . 88    Mississippi Col. 39-15
Texas A&I . . . . . . . . . . . . . . . . . 88    Tenn.-Martin 34-0
Texas A&I . . . . . . . . . . . . . . . . . 88    Portland St. 27-35
Texas A&I . . . . . . . . . . . . . . . . . 89    Mississippi Col. 19-34
Texas A&I . . . . . . . . . . . . . . . . . 92    Western St. 22-13
Texas A&I . . . . . . . . . . . . . . . . . 92    Portland St. 30-35

**Joe Harper (3-1) (UCLA '59)**
Cal Poly SLO . . . . . . . . . . . . . . 78    Winston-Salem 0-17
Cal Poly SLO . . . . . . . . . . . . . . 80    Jacksonville St. 15-0
Cal Poly SLO . . . . . . . . . . . . . . 80    Santa Clara 38-14
Cal Poly SLO . . . . . . . . . . . . . . 80*    Eastern Ill. 21-13

**Bill Hayes (1-2) (N. C. Central '64)**
Winston-Salem . . . . . . . . . . . . . 78    Cal Poly SLO 17-0
Winston-Salem . . . . . . . . . . . . . 78    Delaware 0-41
Winston-Salem . . . . . . . . . . . . . 87    Troy St. 14-45

**Jim Heinitz (0-2) (South Dak. St. '72)**
Augustana (S. D.) . . . . . . . . . . 88    North Dak. St. 7-49
Augustana (S. D.) . . . . . . . . . . 89    St. Cloud St. 20-27

**Andy Hinson (0-1) (Bethune-Cookman '53)**
Bethune-Cookman . . . . . . . . . . 77    UC Davis 16-34

**Sonny Holland (3-0) (Montana St. '60)**
Montana St. . . . . . . . . . . . . . . . 76    New Hampshire 17-16
Montana St. . . . . . . . . . . . . . . . 76    North Dak. St. 10-3
Montana St. . . . . . . . . . . . . . . . 76*    Akron 24-13

**Tom Hollman (1-3) (Ohio Northern '68)**
Edinboro . . . . . . . . . . . . . . . . . . 89    North Dak. St. 32-45
Edinboro . . . . . . . . . . . . . . . . . . 90    Virginia Union 38-14
Edinboro . . . . . . . . . . . . . . . . . . 90    Indiana (Pa.) 7-14
Edinboro . . . . . . . . . . . . . . . . . . 92    Ferris St. 15-19

**Eric Holm (0-2) (Northeast Mo. St. '81)**
Northeast Mo. St. . . . . . . . . . . 90    Pittsburg St. 3-59
Northeast Mo. St. . . . . . . . . . . 92    North Dak. St. 7-42

**Carl Iverson (0-1) (Whitman '62)**
Western St. . . . . . . . . . . . . . . . . 92    Texas A&I 13-22

**Billy Joe (3-4) (Cheyney '70)**
Central St. (Ohio) . . . . . . . . . . 83    Southwest Tex. St. 24-16
Central St. (Ohio) . . . . . . . . . . 83    North Ala. 27-24
Central St. (Ohio) . . . . . . . . . . 83    North Dak. St. 21-41
Central St. (Ohio) . . . . . . . . . . 84    Troy St. 21-31
Central St. (Ohio) . . . . . . . . . . 85    South Dak. 10-13 (2 OT)
Central St. (Ohio) . . . . . . . . . . 86    Towson St. 31-0
Central St. (Ohio) . . . . . . . . . . 86    North Dak. St. 12-35

**Brian Kelly (0-1) (Assumption '83)**
Grand Valley St. . . . . . . . . . . . . 91    East Tex. St. 15-36

**Roy Kidd (0-1) (Eastern Ky. '54)**
Eastern Ky. . . . . . . . . . . . . . . . . 76    North Dak. St. 7-10

**Jim King (1-1)**
Livingston . . . . . . . . . . . . . . . . . 75    North Dak. 34-14
Livingston . . . . . . . . . . . . . . . . . 75    Northern Mich. 26-28

**Tony Knap (1-4) (Idaho '39)**
Boise St. . . . . . . . . . . . . . . . . . . 73    South Dak. 53-10
Boise St. . . . . . . . . . . . . . . . . . . 73    Louisiana Tech 34-38
Boise St. . . . . . . . . . . . . . . . . . . 74    Central Mich. 6-20
Boise St. . . . . . . . . . . . . . . . . . . 75    Northern Mich. 21-24
Nevada-Las Vegas . . . . . . . . . . 76    Akron 6-26

**Roy Kramer (3-0) (Maryville, Tenn. '53)**
Central Mich. . . . . . . . . . . . . . . 74    Boise St. 20-6
Central Mich. . . . . . . . . . . . . . . 74    Louisiana Tech 35-14
Central Mich. . . . . . . . . . . . . . . 74*    Delaware 54-14

**Gil Krueger (4-2) (Marquette '52)**
Northern Mich. . . . . . . . . . . . . . 75    Boise St. 24-21
Northern Mich. . . . . . . . . . . . . . 75    Livingston 28-26
Northern Mich. . . . . . . . . . . . . . 75*    Western Ky. 16-14

Northern Mich. . . . . . . . . . . . . .76        Delaware 28-17
Northern Mich. . . . . . . . . . . . . .76        Akron 26-29
Northern Mich. . . . . . . . . . . . . .77        North Dak. St. 6-20

**Maxie Lambright (4-1) (Southern Miss. '49)**
Louisiana Tech . . . . . . . . . . . . .73        Western Ill. 18-13
Louisiana Tech . . . . . . . . . . . . .73        Boise St. 38-34
Louisiana Tech . . . . . . . . . . . . .73*       Western Ky. 34-0
Louisiana Tech . . . . . . . . . . . . .74        Western Caro. 10-7
Louisiana Tech . . . . . . . . . . . . .74        Central Mich. 14-35

**George Landis (1-1) (Penn St. '71)**
Bloomsburg. . . . . . . . . . . . . . . .85        Hampton 38-28
Bloomsburg. . . . . . . . . . . . . . . .85        North Ala. 0-34

**Henry Lattimore (1-1) (Jackson St. '57)**
N. C. Central . . . . . . . . . . . . . . .88       Winston-Salem 31-16
N. C. Central . . . . . . . . . . . . . . .88       Cal St. Sacramento 7-56

**Bill Lynch (0-1) (Butler '77)**
Butler . . . . . . . . . . . . . . . . . . . . . .88    Tenn.-Martin 6-23

**Dick MacPherson (0-1) (Springfield '58)**
Massachusetts . . . . . . . . . . . . . .77        Lehigh 23-30

**Pat Malley (1-1) (Santa Clara '53)**
Santa Clara . . . . . . . . . . . . . . . .80       Northern Mich. 27-26
Santa Clara . . . . . . . . . . . . . . . .80       Cal Poly SLO 14-38

**Noel Martin (1-1) (Nebraska '63)**
St. Cloud St. . . . . . . . . . . . . . . .89       Augustana (S.D.) 27-20
St. Cloud St. . . . . . . . . . . . . . . .89       Mississippi Col. 24-55

**Fred Martinelli (0-1) (Otterbein '51)**
Ashland . . . . . . . . . . . . . . . . . . .86      North Dak. St. 0-50

**Bob Mattos (2-1) (Cal St. Sacramento '64)**
Cal St. Sacramento . . . . . . . . .88            UC Davis 35-14
Cal St. Sacramento . . . . . . . . .88            N. C. Central 56-7
Cal St. Sacramento . . . . . . . . .88            North Dak. St. 20-42

**Gene McDowell (1-1) (Florida St. '65)**
Central Fla. . . . . . . . . . . . . . . . .87      Indiana (Pa.) 12-10
Central Fla. . . . . . . . . . . . . . . . .87      Troy St. 10-31

**Don McLeary (1-1) (Tennessee '70)**
Tenn.-Martin . . . . . . . . . . . . . . .88       Butler 23-6
Tenn.-Martin . . . . . . . . . . . . . . .88       Texas A&I 0-34

**Terry McMillan (1-1) (Southern Miss. '69)**
Mississippi Col. . . . . . . . . . . . . .91       Wofford 28-15
Mississippi Col. . . . . . . . . . . . . .91       Jacksonville St. 7-35

**Ron Meyer (1-1) (Purdue '63)**
Nevada-Las Vegas . . . . . . . . . .74            Alcorn St. 35-22
Nevada-Las Vegas . . . . . . . . . .74            Delaware 11-49

**Don Morton (8-3) (Augustana, Ill. '69)**
North Dak. St. . . . . . . . . . . . . . .81       Puget Sound 24-10
North Dak. St. . . . . . . . . . . . . . .81       Shippensburg 18-6
North Dak. St. . . . . . . . . . . . . . .81       Southwest Tex. St. 13-42
North Dak. St. . . . . . . . . . . . . . .82       Virginia Union 21-20
North Dak. St. . . . . . . . . . . . . . .82       UC Davis 14-19

North Dak. St. . . . . . . . . . . . . . .83       Towson St. 24-17
North Dak. St. . . . . . . . . . . . . . .83       UC Davis 26-17
North Dak. St. . . . . . . . . . . . . . .83*      Central St. (Ohio) 41-21
North Dak. St. . . . . . . . . . . . . . .84       UC Davis 31-23
North Dak. St. . . . . . . . . . . . . . .84       Nebraska-Omaha 25-14

North Dak. St. . . . . . . . . . . . . . .84       Troy St. 17-18

**Darrell Mudra (5-2) (Peru St. '51)**
Western Ill. . . . . . . . . . . . . . . . .73      Louisiana Tech 13-18
Eastern Ill. . . . . . . . . . . . . . . . . .78     UC Davis 35-31
Eastern Ill. . . . . . . . . . . . . . . . . .78     Youngstown St. 26-22
Eastern Ill. . . . . . . . . . . . . . . . . .78*    Delaware 10-9
Eastern Ill. . . . . . . . . . . . . . . . . .80     Northern Colo. 21-14

Eastern Ill. . . . . . . . . . . . . . . . . .80     North Ala. 56-31
Eastern Ill. . . . . . . . . . . . . . . . . .80     Cal Poly SLO 13-21

**Gene Murphy (0-1) (North Dak. '62)**
North Dak. . . . . . . . . . . . . . . . . .79      Mississippi Col. 15-35

**Bill Narduzzi (3-2) (Miami, Ohio '59)**
Youngstown St. . . . . . . . . . . . . .78          Nebraska-Omaha 21-14
Youngstown St. . . . . . . . . . . . . .78          Eastern Ill. 22-26
Youngstown St. . . . . . . . . . . . . .79          South Dak. St. 50-7

Youngstown St. . . . . . . . . . . . 79     Alabama A&M 52-0
Youngstown St. . . . . . . . . . . . 79     Delaware 21-38

**John O'Hara (0-1) (Panhandle St. '67)**
Southwest Tex. St. . . . . . . . . . 83     Central St. (Ohio) 16-24

**Jerry Olson (0-1) (Valley City St. '55)**
North Dak. . . . . . . . . . . . . . . . 75     Livingston 14-34

**Keith Otterbein (1-1) (Ferris St. '79)**
Ferris St. . . . . . . . . . . . . . . . . 92     Edinboro 19-15
Ferris St. . . . . . . . . . . . . . . . . 92     New Haven 13-35

**Doug Porter (0-1) (Xavier, La. '52)**
Fort Valley St. . . . . . . . . . . . . 82     Southwest Tex. St. 6-27

**George Pugh (0-1) (Alabama '76)**
Alabama A&M . . . . . . . . . . . . 89     Jacksonville St. 9-33

**Bill Rademacher (1-3) (Northern Mich. '63)**
Northern Mich. . . . . . . . . . . . 80     Santa Clara 26-27
Northern Mich. . . . . . . . . . . . 81     Elizabeth City St. 55-6
Northern Mich. . . . . . . . . . . . 81     Southwest Tex. St. 0-62
Northern Mich. . . . . . . . . . . . 82     UC Davis 21-42

**Vito Ragazzo (1-1) (William & Mary '51)**
Shippensburg . . . . . . . . . . . . 81     Virginia Union 40-27
Shippensburg . . . . . . . . . . . . 81     North Dak. St. 6-18

**Harold "Tubby" Raymond (7-4) (Michigan '50)**
Delaware . . . . . . . . . . . . . . . . 73     Grambling 8-17
Delaware . . . . . . . . . . . . . . . . 74     Youngstown St. 35-14
Delaware . . . . . . . . . . . . . . . . 74     Nevada-Las Vegas 49-11
Delaware . . . . . . . . . . . . . . . . 74     Central Mich. 14-54
Delaware . . . . . . . . . . . . . . . . 76     Northern Mich. 17-28
Delaware . . . . . . . . . . . . . . . . 78     Jacksonville St. 42-27
Delaware . . . . . . . . . . . . . . . . 78     Winston-Salem 41-0
Delaware . . . . . . . . . . . . . . . . 78     Eastern Ill. 9-10
Delaware . . . . . . . . . . . . . . . . 79     Virginia Union 58-28
Delaware . . . . . . . . . . . . . . . . 79     Mississippi Col. 60-10
Delaware . . . . . . . . . . . . . . . . 79*    Youngstown St. 38-21

**Rocky Rees (1-1) (West Chester '71)**
Shippensburg . . . . . . . . . . . . 91     East Stroudsburg 34-33
Shippensburg . . . . . . . . . . . . 91     Indiana (Pa.) 7-52

**Rick Rhodes (4-1)**
Troy St. . . . . . . . . . . . . . . . . . 86     Virginia Union 31-7
Troy St. . . . . . . . . . . . . . . . . . 86     South Dak. 28-42
Troy St. . . . . . . . . . . . . . . . . . 87     Winston-Salem 45-14
Troy St. . . . . . . . . . . . . . . . . . 87     Central Fla. 31-10
Troy St. . . . . . . . . . . . . . . . . . 87*    Portland St. 31-17

**Pete Richardson (0-3) (Dayton '68)**
Winston-Salem . . . . . . . . . . . 88     N. C. Central 16-31
Winston-Salem . . . . . . . . . . . 90     Indiana (Pa.) 0-48
Winston-Salem . . . . . . . . . . . 91     Jacksonville St. 24-49

**Eddie Robinson (1-1) (Leland '41)**
Grambling . . . . . . . . . . . . . . . 73     Delaware 17-8
Grambling . . . . . . . . . . . . . . . 73     Western Ky. 20-28

**Dan Runkle (1-2) (Illinois Col. '68)**
Mankato St. . . . . . . . . . . . . . . 87     Portland St. 21-27
Mankato St. . . . . . . . . . . . . . . 91     North Dak. St. 27-7
Mankato St. . . . . . . . . . . . . . . 91     Portland St. 27-37

**Joe Salem (0-2) (Minnesota '61)**
South Dak. . . . . . . . . . . . . . . . 73     Boise St. 10-53
Northern Ariz. . . . . . . . . . . . . 77     Jacksonville St. 0-35

**Lyle Setencich (1-1) (Fresno St. '68)**
Cal Poly SLO . . . . . . . . . . . . . 90     Cal St. Northridge 14-7
Cal Poly SLO . . . . . . . . . . . . . 90     North Dak. St. 0-47

**Stan Sheriff (0-1) (Cal Poly SLO '54)**
Northern Iowa . . . . . . . . . . . . 75     Western Ky. 12-14

**Sanders Shiver (0-1) (Carson-Newman '76)**
Bowie St. . . . . . . . . . . . . . . . . 88     Portland St. 17-34

**Ron Simonson (0-1) (Portland St. '65)**
Puget Sound . . . . . . . . . . . . . 81     North Dak. St. 10-24

**Jim Sochor (4-8) (San Fran. St. '60)**
UC Davis . . . . . . . . . . . . . . . . 77     Bethune-Cookman 34-16
UC Davis . . . . . . . . . . . . . . . . 77     Lehigh 30-39
UC Davis . . . . . . . . . . . . . . . . 78     Eastern Ill. 31-35

*Coaches' Records*                                                    545

| | | |
|---|---|---|
| UC Davis | 82 | Northern Mich. 42-21 |
| UC Davis | 82 | North Dak. St. 19-14 |
| UC Davis | 82 | Southwest Tex. St. 9-34 |
| UC Davis | 83 | Butler 25-6 |
| UC Davis | 83 | North Dak. St. 17-26 |
| UC Davis | 84 | North Dak. St. 23-31 |
| UC Davis | 85 | North Dak. St. 12-31 |
| UC Davis | 86 | South Dak. 23-26 |
| UC Davis | 88 | Cal St. Sacramento 14-35 |

**Earle Solomonson (6-0) (Augsburg '69)**

| | | |
|---|---|---|
| North Dak. St. | 85 | UC Davis 31-12 |
| North Dak. St. | 85 | South Dak. 16-7 |
| North Dak. St. | 85* | North Ala. 35-7 |
| North Dak. St. | 86 | Ashland 50-0 |
| North Dak. St. | 86 | Central St. (Ohio) 35-12 |
| North Dak. St. | 86* | South Dak. 27-7 |

**Bill Sylvester (0-1) (Butler '50)**

| | | |
|---|---|---|
| Butler | 83 | UC Davis 6-25 |

**Joe Taylor (0-4) (Western Ill. '72)**

| | | |
|---|---|---|
| Virginia Union | 86 | Troy St. 7-31 |
| Virginia Union | 90 | Edinboro 14-38 |
| Virginia Union | 91 | Indiana (Pa.) 7-56 |
| Hampton | 92 | North Ala. 21-33 |

**Clarence Thomas (0-1)**

| | | |
|---|---|---|
| Morgan St. | 79 | Alabama A&M 7-27 |

**Roger Thomas (0-1) (Augustana, Ill. '69)**

| | | |
|---|---|---|
| North Dak. | 92 | Pittsburg St. 21-26 |

**Vern Thomsen (0-1) (Peru St. '61)**

| | | |
|---|---|---|
| Northwest Mo. St. | 84 | Nebraska-Omaha 15-28 |

**Dave Triplett (3-2) (Iowa '72)**

| | | |
|---|---|---|
| South Dak. | 85 | Central St. (Ohio) 13-10 (2 OT) |
| South Dak. | 85 | North Dak. St. 7-16 |
| South Dak. | 86 | UC Davis 26-23 |
| South Dak. | 86 | Troy St. 42-28 |
| South Dak. | 86 | North Dak. St. 7-27 |

**Jerry Vandergriff (2-2) (Corpus Christi '65)**

| | | |
|---|---|---|
| Angelo St. | 87 | Northern Mich. 20-23 (OT) |
| Angelo St. | 89 | UC Davis 28-23 |
| Angelo St. | 89 | Pittsburg St. 24-21 |
| Angelo St. | 89 | Jacksonville St. 16-34 |

**Eddie Vowell (2-2) (S'western Okla. '69)**

| | | |
|---|---|---|
| East Tex. St. | 90 | Grand Valley St. 20-14 |
| East Tex. St. | 90 | Pittsburg St. 28-60 |
| East Tex. St. | 91 | Grand Valley St. 36-15 |
| East Tex. St. | 91 | Pittsburg St. 28-38 |

**Jim Wacker (8-2) (Valparaiso '60)**

| | | |
|---|---|---|
| North Dak. St. | 76 | Eastern Ky. 10-7 |
| North Dak. St. | 76 | Montana St. 3-10 |
| North Dak. St. | 77 | Northern Mich. 20-6 |
| North Dak. St. | 77 | Jacksonville St. 7-31 |
| Southwest Tex. St. | 81 | Jacksonville St. 38-22 |
| Southwest Tex. St. | 81 | Northern Mich. 62-0 |
| Southwest Tex. St. | 81* | North Dak. 42-13 |
| Southwest Tex. St. | 82 | Fort Valley St. 27-6 |
| Southwest Tex. St. | 82 | Jacksonville St. 19-14 |
| Southwest Tex. St. | 82* | UC Davis 34-9 |

**Gerald Walker (0-1) (Lincoln, Mo. '62)**

| | | |
|---|---|---|
| Fort Valley St. | 85 | North Ala. 7-14 |

**Bobby Wallace (1-2) (Mississippi St. '76)**

| | | |
|---|---|---|
| North Ala. | 90 | Jacksonville St. 14-38 |
| North Ala. | 92 | Hampton 33-21 |
| North Ala. | 92 | Jacksonville St. 12-14 |

**Johnnie Walton (0-1) (Elizabeth City St. '69)**

| | | |
|---|---|---|
| Elizabeth City St. | 81 | Northern Mich. 6-55 |

**Bob Waters (0-1) (Presbyterian '60)**

| | | |
|---|---|---|
| Western Caro. | 74 | Louisiana Tech 7-10 |

**Mark Whipple (2-1) (Brown '79)**

| | | |
|---|---|---|
| New Haven | 92 | West Chester 38-26 |
| New Haven | 92 | Ferris St. 35-13 |
| New Haven | 92 | Jacksonville St. 35-46 |

**John Whitehead (3-0) (East Stroudsburg '50)**

| | | | |
|---|---|---|---|
| Lehigh | 77 | Massachusetts 30-23 | |
| Lehigh | 77 | UC Davis 39-30 | |
| Lehigh | 77* | Jacksonville St. 33-0 | |

**John Williams (7-3) (Mississippi Col. '57)**

| | | | |
|---|---|---|---|
| Mississippi Col. | 79 | North Dak. 35-15 | |
| Mississippi Col. | 79 | Delaware 10-60 | |
| Mississippi Col. | 88 | Texas A&I 15-39 | |
| Mississippi Col. | 89 | Texas A&I 34-19 | |
| Mississippi Col. | 89 | St. Cloud St. 55-24 | |
| Mississippi Col. | 89 | Indiana (Pa.) 26-14 | |
| Mississippi Col. | 89* | Jacksonville St. 3-0 | |
| Mississippi Col. | 90 | Wofford 70-19 | |
| Mississippi Col. | 90 | Jacksonville St. 14-7 | |
| Mississippi Col. | 90 | Indiana (Pa.) 8-27 | |

\* *National championship.*

# WINNINGEST ACTIVE DIVISION III COACHES
(Minimum five years as a college head coach; record at four-year colleges only.)

## BY PERCENTAGE

| Coach, College | Years | Won | Lost | Tied | *Pct. | #Playoffs W-L-T |
|---|---|---|---|---|---|---|
| Bob Reade, Augustana (Ill.) | 14 | 131 | 19 | 1 | .871 | 19-5-0 |
| Dick Farley, Williams | 6 | 38 | 8 | 2 | .813 | 0-0-0 |
| Larry Kehres, Mount Union | 7 | 60 | 13 | 3 | .809 | 3-3-0 |
| Ron Schipper, Central (Iowa) | 32 | 252 | 61 | 3 | .802 | 16-9-0 |
| Lou Desloges, Plymouth St. | 7 | 55 | 14 | 3 | .785 | 0-0-0 |
| John Luckhardt, Wash. & Jeff. | 11 | 86 | 24 | 2 | .777 | 6-7-0 |
| Jack Siedlecki, Amherst | 5 | 36 | 10 | 1 | .777 | 0-1-0 |
| Bob Packard, Baldwin-Wallace | 12 | 93 | 27 | 2 | .770 | 0-2-0 |
| Roger Harring, Wis.-La Crosse | 24 | 199 | 59 | 7 | .764 | 6-2-0 |
| Bill Manlove, Delaware Valley | 24 | 185 | 60 | 1 | .754 | 9-5-0 |
| Rich Lackner, Carnegie Mellon | 7 | 51 | 16 | 2 | .754 | 0-1-0 |
| John Gagliardi, St. John's (Minn.) | 44 | 294 | 95 | 10 | .749 | 8-5-0 |
| Jim Butterfield, Ithaca | 26 | 200 | 67 | 1 | .748 | 21-8-0 |
| Rick Giancola, Montclair St. | 10 | 77 | 26 | 2 | .743 | 3-3-0 |
| Frank Girardi, Lycoming | 21 | 150 | 51 | 5 | .740 | 5-5-0 |
| Jim Svoboda, Neb. Wesleyan | 6 | 45 | 16 | 0 | .738 | 0-0-0 |
| Mike Clary, Rhodes | 9 | 58 | 20 | 5 | .729 | 0-1-0 |
| Tony DeCarlo, John Carroll | 6 | 42 | 15 | 2 | .729 | 0-1-0 |
| Pete Schmidt, Albion | 10 | 64 | 24 | 4 | .717 | 0-2-0 |
| Tom Gilburg, Frank. & Marsh. | 18 | 122 | 49 | 2 | .711 | 0-0-0 |
| Carl Poelker, Millikin | 11 | 71 | 29 | 1 | .708 | 1-1-0 |
| Jim Christopherson, Concordia-M'head | 24 | 169 | 69 | 6 | .705 | 7-2-1 |
| Lou Wacker, Emory & Henry | 11 | 82 | 36 | 0 | .695 | 3-3-0 |
| Scot Dapp, Moravian | 6 | 43 | 19 | 0 | .694 | 1-1-0 |
| Dale Widolff, Occidental | 11 | 71 | 31 | 2 | .692 | 1-3-0 |
| Greg Carlson, Wabash | 10 | 63 | 28 | 2 | .688 | 0-0-0 |
| D. J. LeRoy, Coe | 10 | 73 | 33 | 2 | .685 | 3-2-1 |
| Don Miller, Trinity (Conn.) | 26 | 140 | 63 | 5 | .685 | 0-0-0 |
| Ray Smith, Hope | 23 | 138 | 62 | 8 | .683 | 0-1-0 |
| Mike Maynard, Redlands | 5 | 32 | 15 | 0 | .681 | 0-2-0 |
| Nick Mourouzis, DePauw | 12 | 79 | 36 | 4 | .681 | 0-0-0 |
| Hank Norton, Ferrum | 8 | 58 | 27 | 1 | .680 | 4-4-0 |
| Peter Yetten, Bentley | 5 | 28 | 13 | 1 | .679 | 0-0-0 |
| C. Wayne Perry, Hanover | 11 | 71 | 35 | 2 | .667 | 0-0-0 |
| John Miech, Wis.-Stevens Point | 5 | 32 | 16 | 2 | .660 | 0-0-0 |
| Jim Scott, Aurora | 7 | 39 | 20 | 1 | .658 | 0-1-0 |
| Kelly Kane, Monmouth (Ill.) | 9 | 55 | 29 | 0 | .655 | 0-0-0 |
| Jim Williams, Simpson | 7 | 45 | 24 | 1 | .650 | 0-3-0 |
| Rich Parrinello, Rochester | 5 | 31 | 17 | 0 | .646 | 0-0-0 |
| Bob Berezowitz, Wis.-Whitewater | 8 | 53 | 29 | 4 | .640 | 1-2-0 |
| Scott Duncan, Rose-Hulman | 7 | 44 | 25 | 1 | .636 | 0-0-0 |
| Norm Eash, Ill. Wesleyan | 6 | 35 | 20 | 1 | .634 | 1-1-0 |
| Jim Moretti, Alfred | 8 | 50 | 29 | 2 | .630 | 0-0-0 |
| Eric Hamilton, Trenton St. | 16 | 98 | 57 | 4 | .629 | 1-1-0 |
| Duane Ford, Tufts | 8 | 38 | 23 | 3 | .617 | 0-0-0 |
| Mike McGlinchey, Frostburg St. | 11 | 67 | 41 | 5 | .615 | 5-3-0 |
| J. R. Bishop, Wheaton (Ill.) | 11 | 60 | 38 | 1 | .611 | 0-0-0 |
| John Huard, Maine Maritime | 11 | 59 | 38 | 0 | .608 | 0-0-0 |
| Bob Bierie, Loras | 13 | 80 | 51 | 4 | .607 | 0-0-0 |
| Joe Harper, Cal Lutheran | 20 | 118 | 82 | 3 | .589 | 3-2-0 |

*Coaches' Records*

| Coach, College | Years | Won | Lost | Tied | *Pct. | #Playoffs W-L-T |
|---|---|---|---|---|---|---|
| Steve Frank, Hamilton | 8 | 37 | 26 | 1 | .586 | 0-0-0 |
| Dick Tressel, Hamline | 15 | 85 | 60 | 2 | .585 | 0-0-0 |
| Bill Samko, Sewanee | 6 | 31 | 22 | 1 | .583 | 0-0-0 |
| Malen Luke, Defiance | 5 | 28 | 20 | 0 | .583 | 0-0-0 |
| Barry Streeter, Gettysburg | 15 | 87 | 62 | 4 | .582 | 2-1-0 |
| Don Canfield, St. Olaf | 20 | 108 | 79 | 1 | .577 | 0-1-0 |
| Dennis Riccio, St. Lawrence | 6 | 34 | 25 | 0 | .576 | 0-0-0 |
| Joe Bush, Hampden-Sydney | 8 | 45 | 33 | 1 | .576 | 0-0-0 |
| Mickey Heinecken, Middlebury | 20 | 91 | 67 | 2 | .575 | 0-0-0 |
| Craig Rundle, Colorado Col. | 7 | 39 | 29 | 0 | .574 | 0-0-0 |
| Don Ruggeri, Mass. Maritime | 20 | 101 | 75 | 1 | .573 | 0-0-0 |
| Bob Sullivan, Carleton | 14 | 77 | 58 | 0 | .570 | 0-1-0 |
| Don LaViolette, St. Norbert | 10 | 53 | 40 | 1 | .569 | 0-1-0 |
| Joe McDaniel, Centre | 27 | 138 | 104 | 4 | .569 | 0-3-0 |
| Mike Hollway, Ohio Wesleyan | 10 | 55 | 42 | 2 | .566 | 0-0-0 |
| Robert Ford, Albany (N.Y.) | 24 | 126 | 100 | 1 | .557 | 1-1-0 |
| Jeff Heacock, Muskingum | 12 | 64 | 51 | 2 | .556 | 0-0-0 |
| Bob Naslund, Luther | 15 | 78 | 63 | 0 | .553 | 0-0-0 |
| Steve Miller, Cornell College | 14 | 68 | 58 | 3 | .539 | 0-1-0 |
| Peter Mazzaferro, Bri'water (Mass.) | 29 | 134 | 114 | 11 | .539 | 0-0-0 |
| Ed DeGeorge, Beloit | 16 | 76 | 69 | 1 | .524 | 0-0-0 |
| Tim Keating, Western Md. | 5 | 25 | 23 | 0 | .521 | 0-0-0 |
| Tom Marshall, LIU-C. W. Post | 10 | 48 | 46 | 2 | .510 | 0-0-0 |
| Steve Byrne, Gust. Adolphus | 5 | 25 | 24 | 0 | .510 | 0-0-0 |
| Ray Solari, Menlo | 7 | 32 | 31 | 1 | .508 | 0-1-0 |
| Larry Kindbom, Washington (Mo.) | 10 | 49 | 48 | 1 | .505 | 0-0-0 |
| Joe Kimball, Mercyhurst | 8 | 37 | 37 | 1 | .500 | 0-0-0 |
| Dominic Livedoti, Olivet | 5 | 21 | 21 | 3 | .500 | 0-0-0 |

* *Ties computed as half won and half lost; bowl and postseason games included.*   # *NCAA Division III playoff games.*

## BY VICTORIES
### (Minimum 100 victories)

| Coach, College, Winning Percentage | Won | Coach, College, Winning Percentage | Won |
|---|---|---|---|
| John Gagliardi, St. John's (Minn.) .749 | 294 | Peter Mazzaferro, Bri'water (Mass.) .539 | 134 |
| Ron Schipper, Central (Iowa) .802 | 252 | Bob Reade, Augustana (Ill.) .871 | 131 |
| Jim Butterfield, Ithaca .748 | 200 | Robert Ford, Albany (N. Y.) .557 | 126 |
| Roger Harring, Wis.-La Crosse .764 | 199 | Tom Gilburg, Frank. & Marsh. .711 | 122 |
| Bill Manlove, Delaware Valley .754 | 185 | Joe Harper, Cal Lutheran .589 | 118 |
| Jim Christopherson, Con.-M'head .705 | 169 | Don Canfield, St. Olaf .577 | 108 |
| Frank Girardi, Lycoming .740 | 150 | Don Ruggeri, Mass. Maritime .573 | 101 |
| Don Miller, Trinity (Conn.) .685 | 140 | | |
| Ray Smith, Hope .683 | 138 | | |
| Joe McDaniel, Centre .569 | 138 | | |

## DIVISION III CHAMPIONSHIP COACHES

All coaches who have coached teams in the Division III championship playoffs since 1973 are listed below with their playoff record, alma mater and year graduated, team, year coached, opponent, and score.

**Phil Albert (2-1) (Arizona '66)**

| Towson St. | 76 | LIU-C. W. Post 14-10 |
|---|---|---|
| Towson St. | 76 | St. Lawrence 38-36 |
| Towson St. | 76 | St. John's (Minn.) 28-31 |

**Dom Anile (0-1) (LIU-C. W. Post '59)**

| LIU-C. W. Post | 76 | Towson St. 10-14 |
|---|---|---|

**Don Ault (0-1) (West Liberty St. '52)**

| Bethany (W. Va.) | 80 | Widener 12-43 |
|---|---|---|

**Al Bagnoli (7-6) (Central Conn. St. '74)**

| Union (N. Y.) | 83 | Hofstra 51-19 |
|---|---|---|
| Union (N. Y.) | 83 | Salisbury St. 23-21 |
| Union (N. Y.) | 83 | Augustana (Ill.) 17-21 |
| Union (N. Y.) | 84 | Plymouth St. 26-14 |
| Union (N. Y.) | 84 | Augustana (Ill.) 6-23 |
| Union (N. Y.) | 85 | Ithaca 12-13 |
| Union (N. Y.) | 86 | Ithaca 17-24 (OT) |
| Union (N. Y.) | 89 | Cortland St. 42-14 |
| Union (N. Y.) | 89 | Montclair St. 45-6 |
| Union (N. Y.) | 89 | Ferrum 37-21 |
| Union (N. Y.) | 89 | Dayton 7-17 |

Union (N. Y.) . . . . . . . . . . . . . . .91    Mass.-Lowell 55-16
Union (N. Y.) . . . . . . . . . . . . . . .91    Ithaca 23-35

**Bob Berezowitz (1-2) (Wis.-Whitewater '67)**
Wis.-Whitewater . . . . . . . . . . . .88    Simpson 29-27
Wis.-Whitewater . . . . . . . . . . . .88    Central (Iowa) 13-16
Wis.-Whitewater . . . . . . . . . . . .90    St. Thomas (Minn.) 23-24

**Don Birmingham (0-2) (Westmar '62)**
Dubuque . . . . . . . . . . . . . . . . . . .79    Ithaca 7-27
Dubuque . . . . . . . . . . . . . . . . . . .80    Minn.-Morris 35-41

**Jim Blackburn (0-1) (Virginia '71)**
Randolph-Macon . . . . . . . . . . .84    Wash. & Jeff. 21-22

**Bill Bless (0-1) (Indianapolis '63)**
Indianapolis . . . . . . . . . . . . . . . .75    Wittenberg 13-17

**Jerry Boyes (1-1) (Ithaca '76)**
Buffalo St. . . . . . . . . . . . . . . . . . .92    Ithaca 28-26
Buffalo St. . . . . . . . . . . . . . . . . . .92    Rowan 19-28

**Steve Briggs (2-1) (Springfield '84)**
Susquehanna . . . . . . . . . . . . . . .91    Dickinson 21-20
Susquehanna . . . . . . . . . . . . . . .91    Lycoming 31-24
Susquehanna . . . . . . . . . . . . . . .91    Ithaca 13-49

**John Bunting (2-2) (North Caro. '72)**
Rowan . . . . . . . . . . . . . . . . . . . . .91    Ithaca 10-31
Rowan . . . . . . . . . . . . . . . . . . . . .92    Worcester Tech 41-14
Rowan . . . . . . . . . . . . . . . . . . . . .92    Buffalo St. 28-19
Rowan . . . . . . . . . . . . . . . . . . . . .92    Wash. & Jeff. 13-18

**Jim Butterfield (21-8) (Maine '53)**
Ithaca . . . . . . . . . . . . . . . . . . . . .74    Slippery Rock 27-14
Ithaca . . . . . . . . . . . . . . . . . . . . .74    Central (Iowa) 8-10
Ithaca . . . . . . . . . . . . . . . . . . . . .75    Fort Valley St. 41-12
Ithaca . . . . . . . . . . . . . . . . . . . . .75    Widener 23-14
Ithaca . . . . . . . . . . . . . . . . . . . . .75    Wittenberg 0-28
Ithaca . . . . . . . . . . . . . . . . . . . . .78    Wittenberg 3-6
Ithaca . . . . . . . . . . . . . . . . . . . . .79    Dubuque 27-7
Ithaca . . . . . . . . . . . . . . . . . . . . .79    Carnegie Mellon 15-6
Ithaca . . . . . . . . . . . . . . . . . . . . .79*    Wittenberg 14-10
Ithaca . . . . . . . . . . . . . . . . . . . . .80    Wagner 41-13
Ithaca . . . . . . . . . . . . . . . . . . . . .80    Minn.-Morris 36-0
Ithaca . . . . . . . . . . . . . . . . . . . . .80    Dayton 0-63
Ithaca . . . . . . . . . . . . . . . . . . . . .85    Union (N. Y.) 13-12
Ithaca . . . . . . . . . . . . . . . . . . . . .85    Montclair St. 50-28
Ithaca . . . . . . . . . . . . . . . . . . . . .85    Gettysburg 34-0
Ithaca . . . . . . . . . . . . . . . . . . . . .85    Augustana (Ill.) 7-20
Ithaca . . . . . . . . . . . . . . . . . . . . .86    Union (N. Y.) 24-17 (OT)
Ithaca . . . . . . . . . . . . . . . . . . . . .86    Montclair St. 29-15
Ithaca . . . . . . . . . . . . . . . . . . . . .86    Salisbury St. 40-44
Ithaca . . . . . . . . . . . . . . . . . . . . .88    Wagner 34-31 (OT)
Ithaca . . . . . . . . . . . . . . . . . . . . .88    Cortland St. 24-17
Ithaca . . . . . . . . . . . . . . . . . . . . .88    Ferrum 62-28
Ithaca . . . . . . . . . . . . . . . . . . . . .88*    Central (Iowa) 39-24
Ithaca . . . . . . . . . . . . . . . . . . . . .90    Trenton St. 14-24
Ithaca . . . . . . . . . . . . . . . . . . . . .91    Rowan 31-10
Ithaca . . . . . . . . . . . . . . . . . . . . .91    Union (N. Y.) 35-23
Ithaca . . . . . . . . . . . . . . . . . . . . .91    Susquehanna 49-13
Ithaca . . . . . . . . . . . . . . . . . . . . .91*    Dayton 34-20
Ithaca . . . . . . . . . . . . . . . . . . . . .92    Buffalo St. 26-28

**Jim Byers (0-1) (Michigan '59)**
Evansville . . . . . . . . . . . . . . . . . .74    Central (Iowa) 16-17

**Don Canfield (0-1)**
Wartburg . . . . . . . . . . . . . . . . . . .82    Bishop 7-32

**Jerry Carle (0-1) (Northwestern '48)**
Colorado Col. . . . . . . . . . . . . . . .75    Millsaps 21-28

**Gene Carpenter (0-1) (Huron '63)**
Millersville . . . . . . . . . . . . . . . . . .79    Wittenberg 14-21

**Rick Carter (3-1) (Earlham '65)**
Dayton . . . . . . . . . . . . . . . . . . . . .78    Carnegie Mellon 21-24
Dayton . . . . . . . . . . . . . . . . . . . . .80    Baldwin-Wallace 34-0
Dayton . . . . . . . . . . . . . . . . . . . . .80    Widener 28-24
Dayton . . . . . . . . . . . . . . . . . . . . .80*    Ithaca 63-0

**Don Charlton (0-1) (Lock Haven '65)**
Hiram . . . . . . . . . . . . . . . . . . . . . .87    Augustana (Ill.) 0-53

*Coaches' Records*        549

**Jim Christopherson (2-2) (Concordia-M'head '60)**
Concordia-M'head .......... 86    Wis.-Stevens Point 24-15
Concordia-M'head .......... 86    Central (Iowa) 17-14
Concordia-M'head .......... 86    Augustana (Ill.) 7-41
Concordia-M'head .......... 88    Central (Iowa) 0-7

**Vic Clark (0-1) (Indiana St. '71)**
Thomas More .............. 92    Emory & Henry 0-17

**Mike Clary (0-1) (Rhodes '77)**
Rhodes .................... 88    Ferrum 10-35

**Jay Cottone (0-1) (Norwich '71)**
Plymouth St. .............. 84    Union (N. Y.) 14-26

**Scot Dapp (1-1) (West Chester '73)**
Moravian ................... 88    Widener 17-7
Moravian ................... 88    Ferrum 28-49

**Harper Davis (1-1) (Mississippi St. '49)**
Millsaps .................... 75    Colorado Col. 28-21
Millsaps .................... 75    Wittenberg 22-55

**Tony DeCarlo (0-1) (Kent '62)**
John Carroll ............... 89    Dayton 10-35

**Bob Di Spirito (0-1) (Rhode Island '53)**
Slippery Rock .............. 74    Ithaca 14-27

**Norm Eash (1-1) (Ill. Wesleyan '75)**
Ill. Wesleyan ............... 92    Aurora 21-12
Ill. Wesleyan ............... 92    Mount Union 27-49

**Ed Farrell (0-1) (Rutgers '56)**
Bridgeport ................. 73    Juniata 14-35

**Bob Ford (1-1) (Springfield '59)**
Albany (N. Y.) .............. 77    Hampden-Sydney 51-45
Albany (N. Y.) .............. 77    Widener 15-33

**Stokeley Fulton (0-1) (Hampden-Sydney '55)**
Hampden-Sydney ........... 77    Albany (N. Y.) 45-51

**John Gagliardi (8-5) (Colorado Col. '49)**
St. John's (Minn.) .......... 76    Augustana (Ill.) 46-7
St. John's (Minn.) .......... 76    Buena Vista 61-0
St. John's (Minn.) .......... 76*    Towson St. 31-28
St. John's (Minn.) .......... 77    Wabash 9-20
St. John's (Minn.) .......... 85    Occidental 10-28

St. John's (Minn.) .......... 87    Gust. Adolphus 7-3
St. John's (Minn.) .......... 87    Central (Iowa) 3-13
St. John's (Minn.) .......... 89    Simpson 42-35
St. John's (Minn.) .......... 89    Central (Iowa) 27-24
St. John's (Minn.) .......... 89    Dayton 0-28

St. John's (Minn.) .......... 91    Coe 75-2
St. John's (Minn.) .......... 91    Wis.-La Crosse 29-10
St. John's (Minn.) .......... 91    Dayton 7-19

**Joe Gardi (2-1) (Maryland '60)**
Hofstra ..................... 90    Cortland St. 35-9
Hofstra ..................... 90    Trenton St. 38-3
Hofstra ..................... 90    Lycoming 10-20

**Rick Giancola (3-3) (Rowan '68)**
Montclair St. ............... 85    Western Conn. St. 28-0
Montclair St. ............... 85    Ithaca 28-50
Montclair St. ............... 86    Hofstra 24-21
Montclair St. ............... 86    Ithaca 15-29
Montclair St. ............... 89    Hofstra 23-6

Montclair St. ............... 89    Union (N. Y.) 6-45

**Frank Girardi (5-5) (West Chester '61)**
Lycoming .................. 85    Gettysburg 10-14
Lycoming .................. 89    Dickinson 21-0
Lycoming .................. 89    Ferrum 24-49
Lycoming .................. 90    Carnegie Mellon 17-7
Lycoming .................. 90    Wash. & Jeff. 24-0

Lycoming .................. 90    Hofstra 20-10
Lycoming .................. 90    Allegheny 14-21 (OT)
Lycoming .................. 91    Wash. & Jeff. 18-16
Lycoming .................. 91    Susquehanna 24-31
Lycoming .................. 92    Wash. & Jeff. 0-33

**Larry Glueck (1-1) (Villanova '63)**
Fordham ................... 87    Hofstra 41-6
Fordham ................... 87    Wagner 0-21

**Walt Hameline (4-2) (Brockport St. '75)**

| | | |
|---|---|---|
| Wagner | 82 | St. Lawrence 34-43 |
| Wagner | 87 | Rochester 38-14 |
| Wagner | 87 | Fordham 21-0 |
| Wagner | 87 | Emory & Henry 20-15 |
| Wagner | 87* | Dayton 19-3 |
| Wagner | 88 | Ithaca 31-34 (OT) |

**Eric Hamilton (1-1) (Trenton St. '75)**

| | | |
|---|---|---|
| Trenton St. | 90 | Ithaca 24-14 |
| Trenton St. | 90 | Hofstra 3-38 |

**Roger Harring (6-2) (Wis.-La Crosse '58)**

| | | |
|---|---|---|
| Wis.-La Crosse | 83 | Occidental 43-42 |
| Wis.-La Crosse | 83 | Augustana (Ill.) 15-21 |
| Wis.-La Crosse | 91 | Simpson 28-13 |
| Wis.-La Crosse | 91 | St. John's (Minn.) 10-29 |
| Wis.-La Crosse | 92 | Redlands 47-26 |
| Wis.-La Crosse | 92 | Central (Iowa) 34-9 |
| Wis.-La Crosse | 92 | Mount Union 29-24 |
| Wis.-La Crosse | 92* | Wash. & Jeff. 16-12 |

**Jim Hershberger (1-2) (Northern Iowa '57)**

| | | |
|---|---|---|
| Buena Vista | 76 | Carroll (Wis.) 20-14 (OT) |
| Buena Vista | 76 | St. John's (Minn.) 0-61 |
| Buena Vista | 86 | Central (Iowa) 0-37 |

**Fred Hill (1-1) (Upsala '57)**

| | | |
|---|---|---|
| Montclair St. | 81 | Alfred 13-12 |
| Montclair St. | 81 | Widener 12-23 |

**James Jones (1-1) (Bishop '49)**

| | | |
|---|---|---|
| Bishop | 82 | Wartburg 32-7 |
| Bishop | 82 | West Ga. 6-27 |

**Frank Joranko (0-1) (Albion '52)**

| | | |
|---|---|---|
| Albion | 77 | Minn.-Morris 10-13 |

**Dennis Kayser (1-2) (Ithaca '74)**

| | | |
|---|---|---|
| Cortland St. | 88 | Hofstra 32-27 |
| Cortland St. | 88 | Ithaca 17-24 |
| Cortland St. | 89 | Union (N. Y.) 14-42 |

**Larry Kehres (3-3) (Mount Union '71)**

| | | |
|---|---|---|
| Mount Union | 86 | Dayton 42-36 |
| Mount Union | 86 | Augustana (Ill.) 7-16 |
| Mount Union | 90 | Allegheny 15-26 |
| Mount Union | 92 | Dayton 27-10 |
| Mount Union | 92 | Ill. Wesleyan 49-27 |
| Mount Union | 92 | Wis.-La Crosse 24-29 |

**Mike Kelly (13-8) (Manchester '70)**

| | | |
|---|---|---|
| Dayton | 81 | Augustana (Ill.) 19-7 |
| Dayton | 81 | Lawrence 38-0 |
| Dayton | 81 | Widener 10-17 |
| Dayton | 84 | Augustana (Ill.) 13-14 |
| Dayton | 86 | Mount Union 36-42 |
| Dayton | 87 | Capital 52-28 |
| Dayton | 87 | Augustana (Ill.) 38-36 |
| Dayton | 87 | Central (Iowa) 34-0 |
| Dayton | 87 | Wagner 3-19 |
| Dayton | 88 | Wittenberg 28-35 (2 OT) |
| Dayton | 89 | John Carroll 35-10 |
| Dayton | 89 | Millikin 28-16 |
| Dayton | 89 | St. John's (Minn.) 28-0 |
| Dayton | 89* | Union (N. Y.) 17-7 |
| Dayton | 90 | Augustana (Ill.) 24-14 |
| Dayton | 90 | Allegheny 23-31 |
| Dayton | 91 | Baldwin-Wallace 27-10 |
| Dayton | 91 | Allegheny 28-25 (OT) |
| Dayton | 91 | St. John's (Minn.) 19-7 |
| Dayton | 91 | Ithaca 20-34 |
| Dayton | 92 | Mount Union 10-27 |

**Chuck Klausing (2-4) (Slippery Rock '48)**

| | | |
|---|---|---|
| Carnegie Mellon | 78 | Dayton 24-21 |
| Carnegie Mellon | 78 | Baldwin-Wallace 6-31 |
| Carnegie Mellon | 79 | Minn.-Morris 31-25 |
| Carnegie Mellon | 79 | Ithaca 6-15 |
| Carnegie Mellon | 83 | Salisbury St. 14-16 |

| Carnegie Mellon | 85 | Salisbury St. 22-35 |

**Mickey Kwiatkowski (0-5) (Delaware '70)**
| Hofstra | 83 | Union (N. Y.) 19-51 |
| Hofstra | 86 | Montclair St. 21-24 |
| Hofstra | 87 | Fordham 6-41 |
| Hofstra | 88 | Cortland St. 27-32 |
| Hofstra | 89 | Montclair St. 6-23 |

**Ron Labadie (0-2) (Adrian '71)**
| Adrian | 83 | Augustana (Ill.) 21-22 |
| Adrian | 88 | Augustana (Ill.) 7-25 |

**Rich Lackner (0-1) (Carnegie Mellon '79)**
| Carnegie Mellon | 90 | Lycoming 7-17 |

**Don LaViolette (0-1) (St. Norbert '54)**
| St. Norbert | 89 | Central (Iowa) 7-55 |

**D. J. LeRoy (0-2) (Wis.-Eau Claire '79)**
| Wis.-Stevens Point | 86 | Concordia-M'head 15-24 |
| Coe | 91 | St. John's (Minn.) 2-75 |

**Leon Lomax (0-1) (Fort Valley St. '43)**
| Fort Valley St. | 75 | Ithaca 12-41 |

**John Luckhardt (6-7) (Purdue '67)**
| Wash. & Jeff. | 84 | Randolph-Macon 22-21 |
| Wash. & Jeff. | 84 | Central (Iowa) 0-20 |
| Wash. & Jeff. | 86 | Susquehanna 20-28 |
| Wash. & Jeff. | 87 | Allegheny 23-17 (OT) |
| Wash. & Jeff. | 87 | Emory & Henry 16-23 |
| Wash. & Jeff. | 89 | Ferrum 7-41 |
| Wash. & Jeff. | 90 | Ferrum 10-7 |
| Wash. & Jeff. | 90 | Lycoming 0-24 |
| Wash. & Jeff. | 91 | Lycoming 16-18 |
| Wash. & Jeff. | 92 | Lycoming 33-0 |
| Wash. & Jeff. | 92 | Emory & Henry 51-15 |
| Wash. & Jeff. | 92 | Rowan 18-13 |
| Wash. & Jeff. | 92 | Wis.-La Crosse 12-16 |

**Bill Manlove (9-5) (Temple '58)**
| Widener | 75 | Albright 14-6 |
| Widener | 75 | Ithaca 14-23 |
| Widener | 77 | Central (Iowa) 19-0 |
| Widener | 77 | Albany (N. Y.) 33-15 |
| Widener | 77* | Wabash 39-36 |
| Widener | 79 | Baldwin-Wallace 29-8 |
| Widener | 79 | Wittenberg 14-17 |
| Widener | 80 | Bethany (W. Va.) 43-12 |
| Widener | 80 | Dayton 24-28 |
| Widener | 81 | West Ga. 10-3 |
| Widener | 81 | Montclair St. 23-12 |
| Widener | 81* | Dayton 17-10 |
| Widener | 82 | West Ga. 24-31 (3 OT) |
| Widener | 88 | Moravian 7-17 |

**Dave Maurer (9-2) (Denison '54)**
| Wittenberg | 73 | San Diego 21-14 |
| Wittenberg | 73* | Juniata 41-0 |
| Wittenberg | 75 | Indianapolis 17-13 |
| Wittenberg | 75 | Millsaps 55-22 |
| Wittenberg | 75* | Ithaca 28-0 |
| Wittenberg | 78 | Ithaca 6-3 |
| Wittenberg | 78 | Minn.-Morris 35-14 |
| Wittenberg | 78 | Baldwin-Wallace 10-24 |
| Wittenberg | 79 | Millersville 21-14 |
| Wittenberg | 79 | Widener 17-14 |
| Wittenberg | 79 | Ithaca 10-14 |

**Mike Maynard (0-2) (Ill. Wesleyan '80)**
| Redlands | 90 | Central (Iowa) 14-24 |
| Redlands | 92 | Wis.-La Crosse 26-47 |

**Mike McGlinchey (5-3) (Delaware '67)**
| Salisbury St. | 83 | Carnegie Mellon 16-14 |
| Salisbury St. | 83 | Union (N. Y.) 21-23 |
| Salisbury St. | 85 | Carnegie Mellon 35-22 |
| Salisbury St. | 85 | Gettysburg 6-22 |
| Salisbury St. | 86 | Emory & Henry 34-20 |
| Salisbury St. | 86 | Susquehanna 31-17 |

Salisbury St. . . . . . . . . . . . . . . 86      Ithaca 44-40
Salisbury St. . . . . . . . . . . . . . . 86      Augustana (III.) 3-31

**Steve Miller (0-1) (Cornell College '65)**
Carroll (Wis.) . . . . . . . . . . . . . . 76      Buena Vista 14-20 (OT)

**Al Molde (2-3) (Gust. Adolphus '66)**
Minn.-Morris . . . . . . . . . . . . . . 77      Albion 13-10
Minn.-Morris . . . . . . . . . . . . . . 77      Wabash 21-37
Minn.-Morris . . . . . . . . . . . . . . 78      St. Olaf 23-10
Minn.-Morris . . . . . . . . . . . . . . 78      Wittenberg 14-35
Minn.-Morris . . . . . . . . . . . . . . 79      Carnegie Mellon 25-31

**Ron Murphy (1-1)**
Wittenberg . . . . . . . . . . . . . . . . 88      Dayton 35-28 (2 OT)
Wittenberg . . . . . . . . . . . . . . . . 88      Augustana (III.) 14-28

**Dave Murray (0-1) (Springfield '81)**
Cortland St. . . . . . . . . . . . . . . . . 90      Hofstra 9-35

**Walt Nadzak (1-1) (Denison '57)**
Juniata . . . . . . . . . . . . . . . . . . . . 73      Bridgeport 35-14
Juniata . . . . . . . . . . . . . . . . . . . . 73      Wittenberg 0-41

**Frank Navarro (2-1) (Maryland '53)**
Wabash . . . . . . . . . . . . . . . . . . . 77      St. John's (Minn.) 20-9
Wabash . . . . . . . . . . . . . . . . . . . 77      Minn.-Morris 37-21
Wabash . . . . . . . . . . . . . . . . . . . 77      Widener 36-39

**Ben Newcomb (0-1)**
Augustana (III.) . . . . . . . . . . . . . 76      St. John's (Minn.) 7-46

**Hank Norton (4-4) (Lynchburg '51)**
Ferrum . . . . . . . . . . . . . . . . . . . . 87      Emory & Henry 7-49
Ferrum . . . . . . . . . . . . . . . . . . . . 88      Rhodes 35-10
Ferrum . . . . . . . . . . . . . . . . . . . . 88      Moravian 49-28
Ferrum . . . . . . . . . . . . . . . . . . . . 88      Ithaca 28-62
Ferrum . . . . . . . . . . . . . . . . . . . . 89      Wash. & Jeff. 41-7
Ferrum . . . . . . . . . . . . . . . . . . . . 89      Lycoming 49-24
Ferrum . . . . . . . . . . . . . . . . . . . . 89      Union (N. Y.) 21-37
Ferrum . . . . . . . . . . . . . . . . . . . . 90      Wash. & Jeff. 7-10

**Ken O'Keefe (5-1) (John Carroll '75)**
Allegheny . . . . . . . . . . . . . . . . . 90      Mount Union 26-15
Allegheny . . . . . . . . . . . . . . . . . 90      Dayton 31-23
Allegheny . . . . . . . . . . . . . . . . . 90      Central (Iowa) 24-7
Allegheny . . . . . . . . . . . . . . . . . 90*      Lycoming 21-14 (OT)
Allegheny . . . . . . . . . . . . . . . . . 91      Albion 24-21 (OT)
Allegheny . . . . . . . . . . . . . . . . . 91      Dayton 25-28 (OT)

**Bob Packard (0-2) (Baldwin-Wallace '65)**
Baldwin-Wallace . . . . . . . . . . . 82      Augustana (III.) 22-28
Baldwin-Wallace . . . . . . . . . . . 91      Dayton 10-27

**Paul Pasqualoni (0-1) (Penn St. '72)**
Western Conn. St. . . . . . . . . . . 85      Montclair St. 0-28

**Bobby Pate (3-1) (Georgia '63)**
West Ga. . . . . . . . . . . . . . . . . . . 81      Widener 3-10
West Ga. . . . . . . . . . . . . . . . . . . 82      Widener 31-24 (3 OT)
West Ga. . . . . . . . . . . . . . . . . . . 82      Bishop 27-6
West Ga. . . . . . . . . . . . . . . . . . . 82*      Augustana (III.) 14-0

**Keith Piper (0-1) (Baldwin-Wallace '48)**
Denison . . . . . . . . . . . . . . . . . . . 85      Mount Union 3-35

**Carl Poelker (1-1) (Millikin '68)**
Millikin . . . . . . . . . . . . . . . . . . . . 89      Augustana (III.) 21-12
Millikin . . . . . . . . . . . . . . . . . . . . 89      Dayton 16-28

**Tom Porter (0-1) (St. Olaf '51)**
St. Olaf . . . . . . . . . . . . . . . . . . . . 78      Minn.-Morris 10-23

**John Potsklan (0-2) (Penn St. '49)**
Albright . . . . . . . . . . . . . . . . . . . . 75      Widener 6-14
Albright . . . . . . . . . . . . . . . . . . . . 76      St. Lawrence 7-26

**Steve Raarup (0-1) (Gust. Adolphus '53)**
Gust. Adolphus . . . . . . . . . . . . 87      St. John's (Minn.) 3-7

**Bob Reade (19-6) (Cornell College '54)**
Augustana (III.) . . . . . . . . . . . . . 81      Dayton 7-19
Augustana (III.) . . . . . . . . . . . . . 82      Baldwin-Wallace 28-22
Augustana (III.) . . . . . . . . . . . . . 82      St. Lawrence 14-0
Augustana (III.) . . . . . . . . . . . . . 82      West Ga. 0-14
Augustana (III.) . . . . . . . . . . . . . 83      Adrian 22-21
Augustana (III.) . . . . . . . . . . . . . 83      Wis.-La Crosse 21-15

| | | |
|---|---|---|
| Augustana (Ill.) | 83* | Union (N. Y.) 21-17 |
| Augustana (Ill.) | 84 | Dayton 14-13 |
| Augustana (Ill.) | 84 | Union (N. Y.) 23-6 |
| Augustana (Ill.) | 84* | Central (Iowa) 21-12 |
| Augustana (Ill.) | 85 | Albion 26-10 |
| Augustana (Ill.) | 85 | Mount Union 21-14 |
| Augustana (Ill.) | 85 | Central (Iowa) 14-7 |
| Augustana (Ill.) | 85* | Ithaca 20-7 |
| Augustana (Ill.) | 86 | Hope 34-10 |
| Augustana (Ill.) | 86 | Mount Union 16-7 |
| Augustana (Ill.) | 86 | Concordia-M'head 41-7 |
| Augustana (Ill.) | 86* | Salisbury St. 31-3 |
| Augustana (Ill.) | 87 | Hiram 53-0 |
| Augustana (Ill.) | 87 | Dayton 36-38 |
| Augustana (Ill.) | 88 | Adrian 25-7 |
| Augustana (Ill.) | 88 | Wittenberg 28-14 |
| Augustana (Ill.) | 88 | Central (Iowa) 17-23 (2 OT) |
| Augustana (Ill.) | 89 | Millikin 12-21 |
| Augustana (Ill.) | 90 | Dayton 14-24 |

**Rocky Rees (1-1) (West Chester '71)**

| | | |
|---|---|---|
| Susquehanna | 86 | Wash. & Jeff. 28-20 |
| Susquehanna | 86 | Salisbury St. 17-31 |

**Ron Roberts (1-1) (Wisconsin '54)**

| | | |
|---|---|---|
| Lawrence | 81 | Minn.-Morris 21-14 (OT) |
| Lawrence | 81 | Dayton 0-38 |

**Bill Russo (0-1)**

| | | |
|---|---|---|
| Wagner | 80 | Ithaca 13-41 |

**Sam Sanders (0-1) (Buffalo '60)**

| | | |
|---|---|---|
| Alfred | 81 | Montclair St. 12-13 |

**Dennis Scannell (0-1) (Villanova '74)**

| | | |
|---|---|---|
| Mass.-Lowell | 91 | Union (N. Y.) 16-55 |

**Ron Schipper (16-9) (Hope '52)**

| | | |
|---|---|---|
| Central (Iowa) | 74 | Evansville 17-16 |
| Central (Iowa) | 74* | Ithaca 10-8 |
| Central (Iowa) | 77 | Widener 0-19 |
| Central (Iowa) | 84 | Occidental 23-22 |
| Central (Iowa) | 84 | Wash. & Jeff. 20-0 |
| Central (Iowa) | 84 | Augustana (Ill.) 12-21 |
| Central (Iowa) | 85 | Coe 27-7 |
| Central (Iowa) | 85 | Occidental 71-0 |
| Central (Iowa) | 85 | Augustana (Ill.) 7-14 |
| Central (Iowa) | 86 | Buena Vista 37-0 |
| Central (Iowa) | 86 | Concordia-M'head 14-17 |
| Central (Iowa) | 87 | Menlo 17-0 |
| Central (Iowa) | 87 | St. John's (Minn.) 13-3 |
| Central (Iowa) | 87 | Dayton 0-34 |
| Central (Iowa) | 88 | Concordia-M'head 7-0 |
| Central (Iowa) | 88 | Wis.-Whitewater 16-13 |
| Central (Iowa) | 88 | Augustana (Ill.) 23-17 (2 OT) |
| Central (Iowa) | 88 | Ithaca 24-39 |
| Central (Iowa) | 89 | St. Norbert 55-7 |
| Central (Iowa) | 89 | St. John's (Minn.) 24-27 |
| Central (Iowa) | 90 | Redlands 24-14 |
| Central (Iowa) | 90 | St. Thomas (Minn.) 33-32 |
| Central (Iowa) | 90 | Allegheny 7-24 |
| Central (Iowa) | 92 | Carleton 20-8 |
| Central (Iowa) | 92 | Wis.-La Crosse 9-34 |

**Pete Schmidt (0-2) (Alma '70)**

| | | |
|---|---|---|
| Albion | 85 | Augustana (Ill.) 10-26 |
| Albion | 91 | Allegheny 21-24 (OT) |

**Jim Scott (0-1) (Luther '61)**

| | | |
|---|---|---|
| Aurora | 92 | Ill. Wesleyan 12-21 |

**Jack Siedlecki (0-1) (Union, N.Y. '73)**

| | | |
|---|---|---|
| Worcester Tech | 92 | Rowan 14-41 |

**Dick Smith (1-2) (Coe '68)**

| | | |
|---|---|---|
| Minn.-Morris | 80 | Dubuque 41-35 |
| Minn.-Morris | 80 | Ithaca 0-36 |
| Minn.-Morris | 81 | Lawrence 14-21 (OT) |

**Ray Smith (0-1) (UCLA '61)**

| | | |
|---|---|---|
| Hope | 86 | Augustana (Ill.) 10-34 |

**Ray Solari (0-1) (California '51)**
Menlo ........................87          Central (Iowa) 0-17
**Ted Stratford (1-2) (St. Lawrence '57)**
St. Lawrence ................76          Albright 26-7
St. Lawrence ................76          Towson St. 36-38
St. Lawrence ................78          Baldwin-Wallace 7-71
**Barry Streeter (2-1) (Lebanon Valley '71)**
Gettysburg .................85          Lycoming 14-10
Gettysburg .................85          Salisbury St. 22-6
Gettysburg .................85          Ithaca 0-34
**Bob Sullivan (0-1) (St. John's, Minn. '59)**
Carleton ....................92          Central (Iowa) 8-20
**Ed Sweeney (0-2) (LIU-C. W. Post '71)**
Dickinson ...................89          Lycoming 0-21
Dickinson ...................91          Susquehanna 20-21
**Andy Talley (1-1) (Southern Conn. St. '67)**
St. Lawrence ................82          Wagner 43-34
St. Lawrence ................82          Augustana (Ill.) 0-14
**Ray Tellier (0-1) (Connecticut '73)**
Rochester ...................87          Wagner 14-38
**Bob Thurness (0-1) (Coe '62)**
Coe .........................85          Central (Iowa) 7-27
**Lee Tressel (3-2) (Baldwin-Wallace '48)**
Baldwin-Wallace ............78          St. Lawrence 71-7
Baldwin-Wallace ............78          Carnegie Mellon 31-6
Baldwin-Wallace ............78*         Wittenberg 24-10
Baldwin-Wallace ............79          Widener 8-29
Baldwin-Wallace ............80          Dayton 0-34
**Peter Vaas (0-1) (Holy Cross '74)**
Allegheny ...................87          Wash. & Jeff. 17-23 (OT)
**Andy Vinci (0-1) (Cal St. Los Angeles '63)**
San Diego...................73          Wittenberg 14-21
**Ken Wable (1-1) (Muskingum '52)**
Mount Union ...............85          Denison 35-3
Mount Union ...............85          Augustana (Ill.) 14-21
**Lou Wacker (3-3) (Richmond '56)**
Emory & Henry ............86          Salisbury St. 20-34
Emory & Henry ............87          Ferrum 49-7
Emory & Henry ............87          Wash. & Jeff. 23-16
Emory & Henry ............87          Wagner 15-20
Emory & Henry ............92          Thomas More 17-0
Emory & Henry ............92          Wash. & Jeff. 15-51
**Vic Wallace (1-1) (Cornell College '65)**
St. Thomas (Minn.) ........90          Wis.-Whitewater 24-23
St. Thomas (Minn.) ........90          Central (Iowa) 32-33
**Roger Welsh (0-1) (Muskingum '64)**
Capital .....................87          Dayton 28-52
**Dale Widolff (1-3) (Indiana Central '75)**
Occidental .................83          Wis.-La Crosse 42-43
Occidental .................84          Central (Iowa) 22-23
Occidental .................85          St. John's (Minn.) 28-10
Occidental .................85          Central (Iowa) 0-71
**Jim Williams (0-3) (Northern Iowa '60)**
Simpson ....................88          Wis.-Whitewater 27-29
Simpson ....................89          St. John's (Minn.) 35-42
Simpson ....................91          Wis.-La Crosse 13-28
* National championship.


# COACH-OF-THE-YEAR AWARDS
(Selected by the American Football Coaches Association)
## COLLEGE DIVISION

| 1960 | Warren Woodson, New Mexico St. | 1965 | Jack Curtice, UC Santa Barb. |
|------|-------------------------------|------|------------------------------|
| 1961 | Jake Gaither, Florida A&M | 1966 | Dan Jessee, Trinity (Conn.) |
| 1962 | Bill Edwards, Wittenberg | 1967 | A. C. "Scrappy" Moore, Tenn.-Chatt. |
| 1963 | Bill Edwards, Wittenberg | 1968 | Jim Root, New Hampshire |
| 1964 | Clarence Stasavich, East Caro. | 1969 | Larry Naviaux, Boston U. |

| 1970 | Bennie Ellender, Arkansas St. | 1977 | Bill Manlove, Widener |
|------|------------------------------|------|-----------------------|
| 1971 | Harold "Tubby" Raymond, Delaware | 1978 | Lee Tressel, Baldwin-Wallace |
| 1972 | Harold "Tubby" Raymond, Delaware | 1979 | Bill Narduzzi, Youngstown St. |
| 1973 | Dave Maurer, Wittenberg | 1980 | Rick Carter, Dayton |
| 1974 | Roy Kramer, Central Mich. | 1981 | Vito Ragazzo, Shippensburg |
| 1975 | Dave Maurer, Wittenberg | 1982 | Jim Wacker, Southwest Tex. St. |
| 1976 | Jim Dennison, Akron | | |

## COLLEGE DIVISION I
### (NCAA Division II and NAIA Division I)

## COLLEGE DIVISION II
### (NCAA Division III and NAIA Division II)

| 1983 | Don Morton, North Dak. St. | 1983 | Bob Reade, Augustana (Ill.) |
|------|----------------------------|------|------------------------------|
| 1984 | Chan Gailey, Troy St. | 1984 | Bob Reade, Augustana (Ill.) |
| 1985 | George Landis, Bloomsburg | 1985 | Bob Reade, Augustana (Ill.) |
| 1986 | Earle Solomonson, North Dak. St. | 1986 | Bob Reade, Augustana (Ill.) |
| 1987 | Rick Rhoades, Troy St. | 1987 | Walt Hameline, Wagner |
| 1988 | Rocky Hager, North Dak. St. | 1988 | Jim Butterfield, Ithaca |
| 1989 | John Williams, Mississippi Col. | 1989 | Mike Kelly, Dayton |
| 1990 | Rocky Hager, North Dak. St. | 1990 | Ken O'Keefe, Allegheny |
| 1991 | Frank Cignetti, Indiana (Pa.) | 1991 | Mike Kelly, Dayton |
| 1992 | Bill Burgess, Jacksonville St. | 1992 | John Luckhardt, Wash. & Jeff. |

*1993 NCAA FOOTBALL*

# ADDED OR RESUMED PROGRAMS

*Quarterback John Whitcomb threw for 1,377 yards and 10 touch-downs to help Alabama-Birmingham post a 7-3 record in 1992. Since becoming a Division III varsity team in 1991, the Blazers have*

# NATIONALLY PROMINENT TEAMS THAT PERMANENTLY DROPPED FOOTBALL

Listed alphabetically below are the all-time records of teams formerly classified as major college that permanently discontinued football. Also included are those teams that, retroactively, are considered to have been major college (before the advent of official classification in 1937) by virtue of their schedules (i.e., at least half of their games versus other major-college opponents). All schools listed were classified as major college, or considered to have been, for a minimum of 10 consecutive seasons.

| Team | Inclusive Seasons | Years | Won | Lost | Tied | Pct.† |
|------|-------------------|-------|-----|------|------|-------|
| Cal St. Fullerton | 1970-1992 | 23 | 107 | 150 | 3 | .417 |
| Carlisle Indian School | 1893-1917 | 25 | 167 | 88 | 13 | .647 |
| Centenary | 1894-1947 | 36 | 148 | 100 | 21 | .589 |
| Creighton | 1900-1942 | 43 | 183 | 139 | 27 | .563 |
| Denver | 1885-1960 | 73 | 273 | 262 | 40 | .510 |
| Detroit Mercy | 1896-1964 | 64 | 305 | 200 | 25 | .599 |
| Geo. Washington | 1890-1966 | 58 | 209 | 240 | 34 | .468 |
| Gonzaga | 1892-1941 | 39 | 130 | 99 | 20 | .562 |
| Haskell Institute | 1896-1938 | 43 | 199 | 166 | 18 | .543 |
| Lamar | 1951-1989 | 39 | 171 | 225 | 9 | .433 |
| Long Beach St. | 1955-1991 | 37 | 199 | 183 | 4 | .521 |
| Manhattan | 1923-1942 | 20 | 77 | 75 | 11 | .506 |
| Marquette | 1892-1960 | 68 | 273 | 220 | 38 | .550 |
| New York U. | 1873-1952 | 66 | 201 | 231 | 32 | .468 |
| San Francisco | *1924-1951; 1959-1971 | 38 | 133 | 169 | 20 | .444 |
| St. Louis | 1899-1949 | 49 | 235 | 179 | 33 | .563 |
| Texas-Arlington | 1959-1985 | 27 | 129 | 150 | 2 | .463 |
| Wichita St. | 1897-1986 | 89 | 375 | 402 | 47 | .484 |
| Xavier (Ohio) | 1900-1973 | 61 | 302 | 223 | 21 | .572 |

† Ties computed as half won and half lost.
* Discontinued football during 1952 after having been classified major college. Resumed at the Division II level during 1959-71, when it was discontinued again.

## SENIOR COLLEGES THAT HAVE ADDED OR RESUMED VARSITY FOOTBALL SINCE 1968

### NCAA MEMBER COLLEGES

**1968 (4)**
Boise St.; *Chicago; Jersey City St.; Nevada-Las Vegas.

**1969 (2)**
*Adelphi (dropped 1972); Towson St.

**1970 (6)**
Cal St. Fullerton (dropped 1993); *Fordham; *Georgetown; Plattsburgh St. (dropped 1979); Plymouth St.; *St. Mary's (Cal.).

**1971 (6)**
Boston St. (dropped 1982); D.C. Teachers (dropped 1974); Federal City (dropped 1975); *New England Col. (dropped 1973); Rochester Tech (dropped 1978); St. Peter's (suspended after one game 1984, resumed 1985, dropped 1988, resumed 1989).

**1972 (6)**
Kean; *Lake Forest; Nicholls St.; Salisbury St.; *San Diego; Wm. Paterson.

**1973 (7)**
Albany St. (N.Y.); *Benedictine; Bowie St.; James Madison; New Haven; New York Tech (dropped 1984); Seton Hall (dropped 1982).

**1974 (2)**
FDU-Madison; Framingham St.

**1975 (2)**
*Brooklyn (dropped 1991); *Canisius.

**1976 (1)**
Oswego St. (dropped 1977).

**1977 (2)**
*Catholic; *Mankato St.

**1978 (7)**
*Buffalo; Dist. Columbia; Iona; Marist; Pace; *St. Francis (Pa.); *St. John's (N.Y.).

**1979 (2)**
Central Fla.; *Duquesne.

**1980 (5)**
*Loras; Mass.-Lowell; *Miles (dropped 1989, resumed 1990); Ramapo (dropped 1993); *Sonoma St.

**1981 (4)**
Buffalo St.; Mercyhurst; *West Ga.; Western New Eng.

**1982 (2)**
Valdosta St.; Westfield St.

**1983 (2)**
*Ky. Wesleyan; Stony Brook.

**1984 (3)**
Fitchburg St.; *Ga. Southern; *Samford.

**1985 (6)**
Ferrum; MacMurray; N.Y. Maritime (dropped 1986, resumed 1987, dropped 1989); *St. Peter's (dropped 1988, resumed 1989); *Villanova; Worcester St.

**1986 (4)**
Menlo; *Quincy; *UC Santa Barb.; Wesley.

**1987 (5)**
*Aurora; *Drake; Gallaudet; *N.Y. Maritime

(dropped 1989); St. John Fisher.

**1988 (7)**
Assumption; Bentley; Mass.-Boston; Mass.-Dartmouth; *MIT (last team was in 1901); Siena; Stonehill.

**1989 (5)**
*Gannon; Merrimack; Methodist; *Southern Methodist; *St. Peter's.

* Previously dropped football.

**1990 (3)**
*Hardin-Simmons; *Miles; Thomas More.

**1991 (3)**
Ala.-Birmingham; Charleston So.; Sacred Heart.

**1992 (1)**
*West Tex. St.

**1993 (0)**

## NON-NCAA COLLEGES

**1968 (2)**
#Mo. Southern St.; #Southwest St.

**1970 (1)**
#Mo. Western St.

**1971 (3)**
Concordia-St. Paul (Minn.); #Gardner-Webb; #Grand Valley St.

**1972 (5)**
Dr. Martin Luther; #Mars Hill; N'western (Minn.); Pillsbury; #Western Conn. St.

**1973 (2)**
#Liberty; #Mass. Maritime.

**1974 (3)**
#*N.M. Highlands; #Northeastern Ill. (dropped 1988); #Saginaw Valley.

**1976 (2)**
Maranatha; #Mesa St.

**1977 (2)**
Evangel; Olivet Nazarene.

**1978 (3)**
*Baptist Christian (dropped 1983); *St. Ambrose; *Yankton (dropped 1984).

**1979 (2)**
Fort Lauderdale (dropped 1982); Lubbock Christian (dropped 1983).

**1980 (1)**
Mid-America Nazarene.

**1983 (2)**
Ga. Southwestern (dropped 1989); #Loras.

**1984 (3)**
#Southwest Baptist; St. Paul Bible; *Union (Ky.).

**1985 (4)**
*Cumberland (Ky.); *Lambuth; *Tenn. Wesleyan; Tiffin.

**1986 (4)**
St. Francis (Ill.); Trinity Bible (N.D.); Urbana; #Wingate.

**1987 (1)**
Greenville.

**1988 (5)**
Campbellsville; Mary; Midwestern St.; Trinity (Ill.); *Western Mont.

**1990 (2)**
Lindenwood; Mt. St. Joseph (Ohio).

**1991 (3)**
Clinch Valley; Lees-McRae; Tusculum.

**1993 (1)**
Chowan.

* Previously dropped football.   # Now NCAA member.

# SENIOR COLLEGES THAT DISCONTINUED
# FOOTBALL SINCE 1950

(Includes NCAA member colleges and nonmember colleges; also colleges that closed or merged with other institutions.)

**1950 (9)**
Alliance; Canisius (resumed 1975); Huntington; Oklahoma City; *Portland; Rio Grande; Rollins; *St. Louis; Steubenville.

**1951 (38)**
Arkansas Col.; Atlantic Christian; Canterbury; Catholic (resumed 1977); CCNY; Corpus Christi (resumed 1954, dropped 1967); Daniel Baker; Detroit Tech; *Duquesne (resumed 1979); East Tex. Baptist; Gannon (resumed 1989); *Georgetown (resumed 1970); Glassboro St. (resumed 1964 — name changed to Rowan in 1992); Hartwick; High Point; LeMoyne-Owen; Lowell Textile; Lycoming (resumed 1954); McKendree; Milligan; Mt. St. Mary's (Md.); Nevada (resumed 1952); New Bedford Textile; New England Col. (resumed 1971, dropped 1973); Niagara; Northern Idaho; Panzer; Shurtleff (resumed 1953, dropped 1954); Southern Idaho; Southwestern (Tenn.) (resumed 1952 — name changed to Rhodes in 1986); Southwestern (Tex.); St. Mary's (Cal.) (resumed 1970); St. Michael's (N.M.); Tillotson; Tusculum (resumed 1991); Washington (Md.); West Va. Wesleyan (resumed 1953); William Penn (resumed 1953).

**1952 (13)**
Aquinas; Clarkson; Erskine; Louisville Municipal; *Loyola (Cal.); Nebraska Central; Rider; Samuel Huston; *San Francisco (resumed 1959, dropped 1972); Shaw (resumed 1953, dropped 1979); St. Bonaventure; St. Martin's; Teikyo Westmar (resumed 1953).

**1953 (10)**
Arnold; Aurora; Bethel (Tenn.); Cedarville; Champlain; Davis & Elkins (resumed 1955, dropped 1962); Georgetown (Ky.) (resumed 1955); *New York U.; *Santa Clara (resumed 1959, dropped 1993); Union (Tenn.).

**1954 (8)**
Adelphi (resumed 1969, dropped 1972); Case Tech (resumed 1955); Quincy (resumed 1986); Shurtleff; St. Francis (Pa.) (resumed 1978); St. Michael's (Vt.); *Wash. & Lee (resumed 1955); York (Neb.).

**1955 (2)**
*Fordham (resumed 1970); St. Mary's (Minn.).

**1956 (4)**
Brooklyn (resumed 1975, dropped 1991); Hendrix

(resumed 1957, dropped 1961); William Carey; Wisconsin Extension.

**1957 (4)**
Lewis; Midwestern (Iowa) (resumed 1966); Morris Harvey; Stetson.

**1959 (2)**
Florida N&I; West Ga. (resumed 1981).

**1960 (5)**
Brandeis; Leland; Loras (resumed 1980); St. Ambrose (resumed 1978); Xavier (La.).

**1961 (9)**
*Denver; Hawaii (resumed 1962); Hendrix; Lincoln (Pa.); *Marquette; Paul Quinn; Scranton; Texas College; Tougaloo.

**1962 (5)**
Azusa Pacific (resumed 1965); Davis & Elkins; San Diego (resumed 1972); Southern Cal Col.; Westminster (Utah) (resumed 1965, dropped 1979).

**1963 (3)**
Benedictine (resumed 1973); *Hardin-Simmons (resumed 1990); St. Vincent (Pa.).

**1964 (2)**
King's (Pa.); Paine.

**1965 (7)**
Claflin; *Detroit Mercy; Dillard; Miss. Industrial; Morris; Philander Smith; Rust.

**1966 (1)**
St. Augustine's.

**1967 (6)**
Benedict; Corpus Christi; *Geo. Washington; Jarvis Christian; Ozarks; South Caro. Trade.

**1968 (2)**
Edward Waters; Frederick.

**1969 (6)**
Allen; Case Tech and Western Reserve merged to form Case Western Reserve; George Fox; Louisiana Col.; UC San Diego; Wiley.

**1971 (5)**
Bradley; *Buffalo (resumed 1978); Hiram Scott; Lake Forest (resumed 1972); Parsons.

**1972 (8)**
Adelphi; Haverford; North Dak.-Ellendale; Northern Mont.; Northwood (Tex.); San Francisco; Sonoma St. (resumed 1980); UC Santa Barb. (resumed 1986).

**1973 (2)**
New England Col.; N.M. Highlands (resumed 1974).

**1974 (6)**
Col. of Emporia; D.C. Teachers; Drexel; Ill.-Chicago; Samford (resumed 1984); *Xavier (Ohio).

**1975 (6)**
Baptist Christian (resumed 1978, dropped 1983);

Bridgeport; Federal City; *Tampa; Vermont; Wis.-Milwaukee.

**1976 (3)**
Mankato St. (resumed 1977); Northland; UC Riverside.

**1977 (4)**
Cal Tech; Oswego St.; Whitman; Yankton (resumed 1978, dropped 1984).

**1978 (3)**
Cal St. Los Angeles; Col. of Idaho; Rochester Tech.

**1979 (5)**
Eastern Mont.; Miles (resumed 1980); Plattsburgh St.; Shaw; Westminster (Utah).

**1980 (3)**
†Gallaudet; Md.-East. Shore; U.S. Int'l.

**1981 (2)**
Bluefield St.; *Villanova (resumed 1985).

**1982 (4)**
Boston St.; Fort Lauderdale; Milton; Seton Hall.

**1983 (3)**
Baptist Christian; Cal Poly Pomona; Lubbock Christian.

**1984 (5)**
Fisk; New York Tech; So. Dak.-Springfield; St. Peter's (suspended after one game, resumed 1985, dropped 1988, resumed 1989); Yankton.

**1985 (1)**
Southern Colo.

**1986 (4)**
Drake (resumed 1987); N.Y. Maritime (resumed 1987, dropped 1989); Southeastern La.; *Texas-Arlington.

**1987 (4)**
Bishop; *Southern Methodist (resumed 1989); Western Mont. (resumed 1988); *Wichita St.

**1988 (4)**
Northeastern Ill.; St. Paul's; St. Peter's (resumed 1989); Texas Lutheran.

**1989 (3)**
Ga. Southwestern; Miles (resumed 1990); N.Y. Maritime.

**1990 (1)**
*Lamar.

**1991 (3)**
Brooklyn; Tarkio; West Tex. St. (resumed 1992).

**1992 (3)**
*Long Beach St.; Pacific (Ore.); St. Mary of the Plains.

**1993 (5)**
*Cal St. Fullerton; Cameron; Ramapo; Santa Clara; Wis.-Superior.

* *Classified major college previous year.*
† *Did not play a 7-game varsity schedule, 1980-86.*

# CHAMPIONSHIP RESULTS

*Defensive end Tim Berg (left) and his Wisconsin-La Crosse team-mates kept Washington & Jefferson quarterback Bob Strope on the run throughout the 1992 Division III championship game. The Eagles allowed Strope to complete just 13 of 35 passes and cap-tured their first title with a 16-12 victory.*

# 1992 DIVISION I-AA CHAMPIONSHIP

## MARSHALL UNIVERSITY STADIUM, HUNTINGTON, W. VA.; DECEMBER 19, 1992

|  | Youngstown St. | Marshall |
|---|---|---|
| First Downs | 17 | 26 |
| Rushes-Net Yardage | 34-116 | 42-185 |
| Passing Yardage | 256 | 270 |
| Return Yardage (Punts, Int. & Fum.) | 35 | 70 |
| Passes (Comp.-Att.-Int.) | 18-31-2 | 25-40-1 |
| Punts (Number-Average) | 6-41.6 | 5-39.8 |
| Fumbles (Number-Lost) | 1-1 | 0-0 |
| Penalties (Number-Yards) | 3-20 | 7-40 |

| | | | | | |
|---|---|---|---|---|---|
| Youngstown St. | 0 | 0 | 14 | 14 | —28 |
| Marshall | 0 | 14 | 14 | 3 | —31 |

Game Conditions: Temperature, 54 degrees; Wind, 10-15 variable; Weather, partly sunny. Attendance: 31,304.

### Second Quarter
Marshall—Mike Bartrum 6 pass from Michael Payton (Willy Merrick kick) (80 yards in 10 plays, 10:33 left)

Marshall—Orlando Hatchett 5 run (Merrick kick) (28 yards in 7 plays, 3:30 left)

### Third Quarter
Marshall—Glenn Pedro 1 run (Merrick kick) (78 yards in 9 plays, 10:13 left)

Marshall—Hatchett 22 pass from Payton (Merrick kick) (22 yards in 1 play, 5:46 left)

Youngstown St.—Herb Williams 30 pass from Nick Cochran (Jeff Wilkins kick) (57 yards in 6 plays, 3:41 left)

Youngstown St.—Tamron Smith 4 run (Wilkins kick) (65 yards in 4 plays, 0:16 left)

### Fourth Quarter
Youngstown St.—Smith 1 run (Wilkins kick) (49 yards in 4 plays, 12:04 left)

Youngstown St.—Smith 10 run (Wilkins kick) (89 yards in 10 plays, 2:28 left)

Marshall—Merrick 22 field goal (81 yards in 14 plays, 0:10 left)

### Individual Leaders
Rushing—Youngstown St.: Smith, 82 yards on 20 carries; Marshall: Hatchett, 112 yards on 15 carries.

Passing—Youngstown St.: Cochran, 18 of 31 for 256 yards; Marshall: Payton, 25 of 39 for 270 yards.

Receiving—Youngstown St.: Williams, 5 catches for 104 yards; Marshall: Troy Brown, 10 catches for 115 yards.

## NCAA I-AA FOOTBALL CHAMPIONSHIP HISTORY

1978    At the 72nd NCAA Convention in Atlanta, Ga., the membership voted to establish the Division I-AA Football Championship and a statistics program for the division. The format for the first I-AA championship, held in Wichita Falls, Texas, was a single-elimination, four-team tournament. Florida A&M defeated Massachusetts, 35-28, in the title game. The game was televised by ABC.

1981    The championship expanded to include eight teams in a single-elimination championship.

1982    The championship expanded to include 12 teams. Eight teams played first-round games at campus sites, and the top four teams—seeded by the Division I-AA Football Committee—received byes.

1986    The championship field expanded to its current format of 16 teams, with each team playing a first-round game.

1992    The I-AA championship provided for a maximum field of 16 teams. Six member conferences (Big Sky, Gateway, Ohio Valley, Southern, Southland and Yankee) were granted automatic qualification for their respective champions. The remaining 10 teams were selected at large by the committee.

## DIVISION I-AA ALL-TIME CHAMPIONSHIP RESULTS

| Year | Champion | Coach | Score | Runner-Up | Site |
|---|---|---|---|---|---|
| 1978 | Florida A&M | Rudy Hubbard | 35-28 | Massachusetts | Wichita Falls, Texas |
| 1979 | Eastern Ky. | Roy Kidd | 30-7 | Lehigh | Orlando, Fla. |
| 1980 | Boise St. | Jim Criner | 31-29 | Eastern Ky. | Sacramento, Calif. |
| 1981 | Idaho St. | Dave Kragthorpe | 34-23 | Eastern Ky. | Wichita Falls, Texas |
| 1982 | Eastern Ky. | Roy Kidd | 17-14 | Delaware | Wichita Falls, Texas |
| 1983 | Southern Ill. | Rey Dempsey | 43-7 | Western Caro. | Charleston, S.C. |
| 1984 | Montana St. | Dave Arnold | 19-6 | Louisiana Tech | Charleston, S.C. |
| 1985 | Ga. Southern | Erk Russell | 44-42 | Furman | Tacoma, Wash. |
| 1986 | Ga. Southern | Erk Russell | 48-21 | Arkansas St. | Tacoma, Wash. |
| 1987 | Northeast La. | Pat Collins | 43-42 | Marshall | Pocatello, Idaho |
| 1988 | Furman | Jimmy Satterfield | 17-12 | Ga. Southern | Pocatello, Idaho |
| 1989 | Ga. Southern | Erk Russell | 37-34 | Vacated | Statesboro, Ga. |
| 1990 | Ga. Southern | Tim Stowers | 36-13 | Nevada | Statesboro, Ga. |
| 1991 | Youngstown St. | Jim Tressel | 25-17 | Marshall | Statesboro, Ga. |
| 1992 | Marshall | Jim Donnan | 31-28 | Youngstown St. | Huntington, W. Va. |

# 1992 DIVISION I-AA CHAMPIONSHIP RESULTS

**First Round**
Northeast La. 78, Alcorn St. 27
Delaware 56, Samford 21
Middle Tenn. St. 35, Appalachian St. 10
Marshall 44, Eastern Ky. 0
Citadel 44, North Caro. A&T 0
Youngstown St. 23, Villanova 20
Northern Iowa 17, Eastern Wash. 14
McNeese St. 23, Idaho 20

**Quarterfinals**
Delaware 41, Northeast La. 18
Marshall 35, Middle Tenn. St. 21
Youngstown St. 42, Citadel 17
Northern Iowa 29, McNeese St. 7

**Semifinals**
Marshall 28, Delaware 7
Youngstown St. 19, Northern Iowa 7

**Championship**
Marshall 31, Youngstown St. 28

# 1992 DIVISION I-AA GAME SUMMARIES

**FIRST-ROUND GAMES (Nov. 28)**

**Northeast La. 78, Alcorn St. 27**
at Monroe, La.

| | | | | |
|---|---|---|---|---|
| Alcorn St. | 0 | 20 | 0 | 7—27 |
| Northeast La. | 17 | 20 | 27 | 14—78 |

N—Potts 17 rush (Tallent kick)
N—Tallent 32 field goal
N—Robinson 16 rush (Tallent kick)
A—Brown 1 rush (Bowden kick)
N—Potts 1 rush (Tallent kick)
A—Price 11 pass from McNair (Bowden kick)
N—Robinson 1 run (kick failed)
N—Potts 6 rush (Tallent kick)
A—McNair 17 rush (pass failed)
N—Pederson 5 pass from Liles (Tallent kick)
N—Robinson 4 rush (kick failed)
N—Williams 86 pass from Liles (Tallent kick)
N—Williams 32 pass from Liles (Tallent kick)
N—Jackson 16 rush (Tallent kick)
A—Evans 20 pass from McNair (Bowden kick)
N—Fudge 20 rush (Tallent kick)
A—14,416

**Delaware 56, Samford 21**
at Newark, Del.

| | | | | |
|---|---|---|---|---|
| Samford | 0 | 7 | 7 | 7—21 |
| Delaware | 7 | 21 | 21 | 7—56 |

D—Lewis 53 pass from Vergantino (Leo kick)
D—Organ 1 rush (Leo kick)
D—Vergantino 5 rush (Leo kick)
S—Wiggins 1 rush (O'Neal kick)
D—Cooper 2 pass from Vergantino (Leo kick)
S—Edwards 1 rush (O'Neal kick)
D—Johnson 3 rush (Leo kick)
D—Johnson 31 pass from Vergantino (Leo kick)
D—Brown 43 rush (Leo kick)
D—Brown 4 rush (Leo kick)
S—McFadden 8 pass from Hackbarth (O'Neal kick)
A—11,364

**Middle Tenn. St. 35, Appalachian St. 10**
at Murfreesboro, Tenn.

| | | | | |
|---|---|---|---|---|
| Appalachian St. | 0 | 0 | 7 | 3—10 |
| Middle Tenn. St. | 14 | 14 | 0 | 7—35 |

M—Crowder 15 rush (Petrilli kick)
M—Lyons 14 rush (Petrilli kick)
M—Lyons 2 rush (Petrilli kick)
M—Simpson 44 pass from Holcomb (Petrilli kick)
A—Hooks 4 pass from Campbell (Millson kick)
A—Millson 27 field goal
M—Crowder 32 rush (Petrilli kick)
A—4,000

**Marshall 44, Eastern Ky. 0**
at Huntington, W. Va.

| | | | | |
|---|---|---|---|---|
| Eastern Ky. | 0 | 0 | 0 | 0— 0 |
| Marshall | 10 | 24 | 7 | 3—44 |

M—Hatchett 2 rush (D. Merrick kick)
M—D. Merrick 34 field goal
M—Brown 37 pass from Payton (D. Merrick kick)
M—Brown 71 punt return (D. Merrick kick)
M—McKee 1 rush (D. Merrick kick)

M—D. Merrick 33 field goal
M—Brown 44 pass from Payton (D. Merrick kick)
M—D. Merrick 24 field goal
A—16,598

**Citadel 44, North Caro. A&T 0**
at Charleston, S.C.

| | | | | |
|---|---|---|---|---|
| North Caro. A&T | 0 | 0 | 0 | 0— 0 |
| Citadel | 7 | 13 | 7 | 17—44 |

C—Douglas 2 rush (Cahill kick)
C—Sims 2 rush (kick failed)
C—Lair 65 fumble return (Cahill kick)
C—Sims 3 rush (Cahill kick)
C—Trinh 30 field goal
C—Smith 66 punt return (Cahill kick)
C—Mitchem 24 rush (Cahill kick)
A—12,300

**Youngstown St. 23, Villanova 20**
at Youngstown, Ohio

| | | | | |
|---|---|---|---|---|
| Villanova | 7 | 3 | 3 | 7—20 |
| Youngstown St. | 0 | 13 | 3 | 7—23 |

V—Mosley 2 rush (Hoffman kick)
Y—Clark 32 rush (Wilkins kick)
V—Hoffman 22 field goal
Y—Smith 1 rush (kick failed)
V—Hoffman 26 field goal
Y—Wilkins 23 field goal
Y—Smith 1 rush (Wilkins kick)
V—Hart 11 pass from Columbo (Hoffman kick)
A—9,465

**Northern Iowa 17, Eastern Wash. 14**
at Cedar Falls, Iowa

| | | | | |
|---|---|---|---|---|
| Eastern Wash. | 0 | 7 | 0 | 7—14 |
| Northern Iowa | 0 | 17 | 0 | 0—17 |

N—Obermeier 41 field goal
N—Mosley 17 pass from Johnson (Obermeier kick)
E—Wright 1 rush (Lacson kick)
N—Shedd 19 pass from Johnson (Obermeier kick)
E—Major 89 blocked field goal return (Lacson kick)
A—13,149

**McNeese St. 23, Idaho 20**
at Moscow, Idaho

| | | | | |
|---|---|---|---|---|
| McNeese St. | 3 | 7 | 7 | 6—23 |
| Idaho | 0 | 14 | 6 | 0—20 |

M—Larios 42 field goal
M—Fields 68 rush (Larios kick)
I—Saunders 17 pass from Nussmeier (Hollis kick)
I—Murphy 19 pass from Nussmeier (Hollis kick)
M—Foster 2 rush (Larios kick)
I—Hollis 36 field goal
I—Hollis 37 field goal
M—Fields 1 rush (kick failed)
A—6,000

## QUARTERFINAL GAMES (Dec. 5)

**Delaware 41, Northeast La. 18**
at Monroe, La.

| | | | | |
|---|---|---|---|---|
| Delaware | 7 | 14 | 7 | 13—41 |
| Northeast La. | 7 | 3 | 0 | 8—18 |

N—Potts 2 rush (Tallent kick)
D—Johnson 3 rush (Leo kick)
D—Vergantino 4 rush (Leo Kick)
D—Quigg 37 interception return (Leo kick)
N—Tallent 20 field goal
D—Vergantino 2 rush (Leo kick)
N—Brisby 4 pass from Cobb (Potts pass from Cobb)
D—Johnson 42 rush (Leo kick)
D—Brown 3 rush (kick failed)
A—10,172

**Marshall 35, Middle Tenn. St. 21**
at Huntington, W. Va.

| | | | | |
|---|---|---|---|---|
| Middle Tenn. St. | 7 | 0 | 0 | 14—21 |
| Marshall | 7 | 14 | 7 | 7—35 |

M—Payton 6 rush (D. Merrick kick)
MT—Lyons 81 rush (Petrilli kick)

M—Pedro 3 rush (D. Merrick kick)
M—Brown 45 pass from Donnan (D. Merrick kick)
M—Brown 13 pass from Donnan (D. Merrick kick)
MT—Dark 31 pass from Holcomb (kick failed)
M—Brown 5 pass from Donnan (D. Merrick kick)
MT—Dunson 1 rush (Lyons pass from Holcomb)
A—14,011

**Youngstown St. 42, Citadel 17**
at Charleston, S.C.

| | | | | |
|---|---|---|---|---|
| Youngstown St. | 14 | 7 | 0 | 21—42 |
| Citadel | 0 | 7 | 7 | 3—17 |

Y—Clark 2 rush (Wilkins kick)
Y—Zwisler 39 pass from Cochran (Wilkins kick)
Y—Smith 1 rush (Wilkins kick)
C—Douglas 9 rush (Cahill kick)
C—Sands 13 rush (Cahill kick)
C—Trinh 32 field goal
Y—Smith 3 rush (Wilkins kick)
Y—Clark 4 rush (Wilkins kick)
Y—Jones 5 rush (Wilkins kick)
A—NA

**Northern Iowa 29, McNeese St. 7**
at Cedar Falls, Iowa

| | | | | |
|---|---|---|---|---|
| McNeese St. | 0 | 0 | 7 | 0— 7 |
| Northern Iowa | 7 | 15 | 7 | 0—29 |

N—Freeney 1 rush (Obermeier kick)
N—Mosley 31 pass from Johnson (Obermeier kick)
N—Punt blocked out of end zone for safety
N—Shedd 11 pass from Johnson (pass failed)
M—Fontenette 100 kickoff return (Larios kick)
N—Mosley 12 pass from Johnson (Obermeier kick)
A—13,375

**SEMIFINAL GAMES (Dec. 12)**

**Marshall 28, Delaware 7**
at Huntington, W. Va.

| | | | | |
|---|---|---|---|---|
| Delaware | 7 | 0 | 0 | 0— 7 |
| Marshall | 0 | 7 | 7 | 14—28 |

D—Vergantino 1 rush (Leo kick)
M—McKee 1 rush (D. Merrick kick)
M—Pedro 31 pass from Payton (D. Merrick kick)
M—Payton 4 rush (D. Merrick kick)
M—Johnson 79 interception return (D. Merrick kick)
A—16,323

**Youngstown St. 19, Northern Iowa 7**
at Cedar Falls, Iowa

| | | | | |
|---|---|---|---|---|
| Youngstown St. | 7 | 6 | 0 | 6—19 |
| Northern Iowa | 0 | 0 | 7 | 0— 7 |

Y—Roberts 71 punt return (Wilkins kick)
Y—Wilkins 54 field goal
Y—Wilkins 35 field goal
N—Johnson 1 rush (Obermeier kick)
Y—Wilkins 29 field goal
Y—Wilkins 33 field goal
A—14,682

# CHAMPIONSHIP RECORDS
## INDIVIDUAL: SINGLE GAME

**Net Yards Rushing**
250—Greg Robinson, Northeast La. (78) vs. Alcorn St. (27), 11-28-92.

**Rushes Attempted**
46—Tamron Smith, Youngstown St. (10) vs. Samford (0), 12-14-91.

**Touchdowns by Rushing**
6—Sean Sanders, Weber St. (59) vs. Idaho (30), 11-28-87.

**Net Yards Passing**
517—Todd Hammel, Stephen F. Austin (59) vs. Grambling (56), 11-25-89.

**Passes Attempted**
78—Tom Ehrhardt, Rhode Island (15) vs. Furman (59), 12-7-85.

**Passes Completed**
44—Willie Totten, Mississippi Val. (19) vs. Louisiana Tech (66), 11-24-84.

**Passes Had Intercepted**
7—Jeff Gilbert, Western Caro. (7) vs. Southern Ill. (43), 12-17-83.

**Touchdown Passes Completed**
6—Mike Smith, Northern Iowa (41) vs. Northeast La. (44), 12-12-87; Clemente Gordon, Grambling (56) vs. Stephen F. Austin (59), 11-25-89.

**Completion Percentage (Min. 15 Attempts)**
.792—Bill Vergantino, Delaware (35) vs. James Madison (42), 2 OT, 11-30-91 (19 of 24).

**Net Yards Rushing and Passing**
539—Todd Hammel, Stephen F. Austin (59) vs. Grambling (56), 11-25-89 (517 passing, 22 rushing).

**Number of Rushing and Passing Plays**
80—Willie Totten, Mississippi Val. (19) vs. Louisiana Tech (66), 11-24-84; Tom Ehrhardt, Rhode Island (15) vs. Furman (59), 12-7-85.

**Punting Average (Min. 3 Punts)**
50.3—Steve Rowe, Eastern Ky. (38) vs. Idaho (30), 12-4-82.

**Number of Punts**
14—Fred McRae, Jackson St. (0) vs. Stephen F. Austin (24), 11-26-88.

**Passes Caught**
18—Brian Forster, Rhode Island (23) vs. Richmond (17), 12-1-84.

**Net Yards Receiving**
264—Winky White, Boise St. (52) vs. Nevada (59), 3OT, 12-8-90 (11 catches).

**Touchdown Passes Caught**
4—Tony DiMaggio, Rhode Island (35) vs. Akron (27), 11-30-85.

**Passes Intercepted**
4—Greg Shipp, Southern Ill. (43) vs. Western Caro. (7), 12-17-83.

**Yards Gained on Interception Returns**
117—Kevin Sullivan, Massachusetts (44) vs. Nevada (21), 12-9-78.

**Yards Gained on Punt Returns**
95—Troy Brown, Marshall (44) vs. Eastern Ky. (0), 11-28-92.

**Yards Gained on Kickoff Returns**
232—Mike Cadore, Eastern Ky. (32) vs. Northeast La. (33), 12-5-87, 6 returns, 1 for 99-yard TD.

**Yards Gained on Fumble Returns**
65—Todd Lair, Citadel (44) vs. North Caro. A&T (0), 11-28-92.

**Points**
36—Sean Sanders, Weber St. (59) vs. Idaho (30), 11-28-87.

**Touchdowns**
6—Sean Sanders, Weber St. (59) vs. Idaho (30), 11-28-87.

**Extra Points**
9—George Benyola, Louisiana Tech (66) vs. Mississippi Val. (19), 11-24-84; Rob Tallent, Northeast La. (78) vs. Alcorn St. (27), 11-28-92.

**Field Goals**
4—Jeff Wilkins, Youngstown St. (19) vs. Northern Iowa (7), 12-12-92.

# INDIVIDUAL: TOURNAMENT

**Net Yards Rushing**
661—Tracy Ham, Ga. Southern, 1986 (128 vs. North Caro. A&T, 191 vs. Nicholls St., 162 vs. Nevada, 180 vs. Arkansas St.).

**Rushes Attempted**
123—Ray Whalen, Nevada, 1990 (21 vs. Northeast La., 34 vs. Furman, 44 vs. Boise St., 24 vs. Ga. Southern).

**Net Yards Passing**
1,449—Todd Hammel, Stephen F. Austin, 1989 (517 vs. Grambling, 405 vs. Southwest Mo. St., 224 vs. Furman, 303 vs. Ga. Southern).

**Passes Attempted**
177—Jeff Gilbert, Western Caro., 1983 (47 vs. Colgate, 52 vs. Holy Cross, 45 vs. Furman, 33 vs. Southern Ill.).

**Passes Completed**
94—Stan Humphries, Northeast La., 1987 (19 vs. North Texas, 33 vs. Eastern Ky., 16 vs. Northern Iowa, 26 vs. Marshall).

**Touchdown Passes Completed**
14—Todd Hammel, Stephen F. Austin, 1989 (5 vs. Grambling, 4 vs. Southwest Mo. St., 2 vs. Furman, 3 vs. Ga. Southern).

**Completion Percentage (Min. 2 Games)**
.667—Steve Nolan, Idaho, 1990, 56 of 84 (24-41 vs. Southwest Mo. St., 32-43 vs. Ga. Southern); Michael Payton, Marshall, 1992, 68 of 102 (26-35 vs. Eastern Ky., 3-5 vs. Middle Tenn. St., 14-23 vs. Delaware, 25-39 vs. Youngstown St.).

**Passes Had Intercepted**
11—Todd Hammel, Stephen F. Austin, 1989 (0 vs. Grambling, 4 vs. Southwest Mo. St., 2 vs. Furman, 5 vs. Ga. Southern).

**Passes Caught**
36—Ross Ortega, Nevada, 1990 (1 vs. Northeast La., 15 vs. Furman, 10 vs. Boise St., 10 vs. Ga. Southern).

**Net Yards Receiving**
545—Troy Brown, Marshall, 1992 (188 vs. Eastern Ky., 189 vs. Middle Tenn. St., 53 vs. Delaware, 115 vs. Youngstown St.).

**Touchdown Passes Caught**
6—Keith Baxter, Marshall, 1987 (1 vs. James Madison, 3 vs. Weber St., 0 vs. Appalachian St., 2 vs. Northeast La.).

**Points**
66—Gerald Harris, Ga. Southern, 1986 (30 vs. North Caro. A&T, 18 vs. Nicholls St., 12 vs. Nevada, 6 vs. Arkansas St.).

**Touchdowns**
11—Gerald Harris, Ga. Southern, 1986 (5 vs. North Caro. A&T, 3 vs. Nicholls St., 2 vs. Nevada, 1 vs. Arkansas St.).

# INDIVIDUAL: LONGEST PLAYS

**Longest Rush**
81—Brigham Lyons, Middle Tenn. St. (21) vs. Marshall (35), 12-5-92, TD.

**Longest Pass (Including Run)**
90—Paul Singer 22 pass to Derek Swanson and 68 fumble recovery advancement by Steve Williams, Western Ill. (32) vs. Western Ky. (35), 11-26-88.

**Longest Field Goal**
56—Tony Zendejas, Nevada (27) vs. Idaho St. (20), 11-26-83.

**Longest Punt**
88—Mike Cassidy, Rhode Island (20) vs. Montana St. (32), 12-8-84.

**Longest Punt Return**
84—Rob Friese, Eastern Wash. (14) vs. Northern Iowa (17), 12-7-85, TD.

**Longest Kickoff Return**
100—Chris Fontenette, McNeese St. (7) vs. Northern Iowa (29), 12-5-92, TD.

**Longest Fumble Return**
65—Todd Lair, Citadel (44) vs. North Caro. A&T (0), 11-28-92, TD.

**Longest Interception Return**
99—Dwayne Hans, Montana (19) vs. Idaho (38), 11-26-88, TD.

## TEAM: SINGLE GAME

**First Downs**
36—Northeast La. (78) vs. Alcorn St. (27), 11-28-92.

**First Downs by Rushing**
26—Northeast La. (78) vs. Alcorn St. (27), 11-28-92.

**First Downs by Passing**
28—Rhode Island (35) vs. Akron (27), 11-30-85.

**Rushes Attempted**
81—Youngstown St. (10) vs. Samford (0), 12-14-91.

**Net Yards Rushing**
518—Arkansas St. (55) vs. Delaware (14), 12-6-86.

**Net Yards Passing**
532—Rhode Island (15) vs. Furman (59), 12-7-85.

**Passes Attempted**
90—Rhode Island (15) vs. Furman (59), 12-7-85.

**Passes Completed**
45—Mississippi Val. (19) vs. Louisiana Tech (66), 11-24-84; Rhode Island (15) vs. Furman (59), 12-7-85.

**Completion Percentage (Min. 10 Attempts)**
.792—Delaware (35) vs. James Madison (42), 2 OT, 11-30-91 (19 of 24).

**Passes Had Intercepted**
7—Western Caro. (7) vs. Southern Ill. (43), 12-17-83; Rhode Island (15) vs. Furman (59), 12-7-85; Weber St. (23) vs. Marshall (51), 12-5-87.

**Net Yards Rushing and Passing**
742—Northeast La. (78) vs. Alcorn St. (27), 11-28-92.

**Rushing and Passing Plays**
114—Nevada (42) vs. Furman (35), 3OT, 12-1-90 (47 rushing, 67 passing).

**Punting Average**
50.2—Montana St. (32) vs. Rhode Island (20), 12-8-84.

**Number of Punts**
14—Jackson St. (0) vs. Stephen F. Austin (24), 11-26-88.

**Punts Had Blocked**
2—Florida A&M (35) vs. Massachusetts (28), 12-16-78; Boise St. (14) vs. Grambling (9), 12-13-80.

**Yards Gained on Punt Returns**
115—Youngstown St. (19) vs. Northern Iowa (7), 12-12-92.

**Yards Gained on Kickoff Returns**
232—Eastern Ky. (32) vs. Northeast La. (33), 12-5-87.

**Yards Gained on Interception Returns**
164—Marshall (51) vs. Weber St. (23), 12-5-87.

**Yards Penalized**
172—Tennessee St. (32) vs. Jackson St. (23), 11-29-86.

**Fumbles Lost**
6—South Caro. St. (12) vs. Idaho St. (41), 12-12-81; Idaho (38) vs. Eastern Wash. (42), 11-30-85.

**Points**
78—Northeast La. vs. Alcorn St. (27), 11-28-92.

## TEAM: TOURNAMENT

**First Downs**
105—Northeast La., 1987 (22 vs. North Texas, 31 vs. Eastern Ky., 24 vs. Northern Iowa, 28 vs. Marshall).

**Net Yards Rushing**
1,522—Ga. Southern, 1986 (442 vs. North Caro. A&T, 317 vs. Nicholls St., 466 vs. Nevada, 297 vs. Arkansas St.).

**Net Yards Passing**
1,449—Stephen F. Austin, 1989 (517 vs. Grambling, 405 vs. Southwest Mo. St., 224 vs. Furman, 303 vs. Ga. Southern).

**Net Yards Rushing and Passing**
2,241—Ga. Southern, 1986 (541 vs. North Caro. A&T, 484 vs. Nicholls St., 613 vs. Nevada, 603 vs. Arkansas St.).

**Passes Attempted**
185—Nevada, 1990 (29 vs. Northeast La., 67 vs. Furman, 36 vs. Boise St., 53 vs. Ga. Southern).

**Passes Completed**
98—Nevada, 1990 (12 vs. Northeast La., 39 vs. Furman, 20 vs. Boise St., 27 vs. Ga. Southern).

**Passes Had Intercepted**
11—Stephen F. Austin, 1989 (0 vs. Grambling, 4 vs. Southwest Mo. St., 2 vs. Furman, 5 vs. Ga. Southern).

**Number of Punts**
29—Northern Iowa, 1992 (11 vs. Eastern Wash., 10 vs. McNeese St., 8 vs. Youngstown St.).

**Yards Penalized**
350—Ga. Southern, 1986 (106 vs. North Caro. A&T, 104 vs. Nicholls St., 75 vs. Nevada, 65 vs. Arkansas St.).

**Fumbles Lost**
9—Nevada, 1983 (3 vs. Idaho St., 4 vs. North Texas, 2 vs. Southern Ill.); Youngstown St., 1991 (3 vs. Villanova, 1 vs. Nevada, 4 vs. Samford, 1 vs. Marshall).

**Points**
203—Ga. Southern, 1986 (52 vs. North Caro. A&T, 55 vs. Nicholls St., 48 vs. Nevada, 48 vs. Arkansas St.).

## INDIVIDUAL: CHAMPIONSHIP GAME

**Net Yards Rushing**
207—Mike Solomon, Florida A&M (35) vs. Massachusetts (28), 1978 (27 carries).

**Rushes Attempted**
31—Joe Ross, Ga. Southern (37) vs. Stephen F. Austin (34), 1989 (152 yards); Raymond

Gross, Ga. Southern (36) vs. Nevada (13), 1990 (145 yards).

**Touchdowns by Rushing**
4—John Bagwell, Furman (42) vs. Ga. Southern (44), 1985.

**Net Yards Passing**
474—Tony Peterson, Marshall (42) vs. Northeast La. (43), 1987 (28 of 54).

**Passes Attempted**
57—Kelly Bradley, Montana St. (19) vs. Louisiana Tech (6), 1984 (32 completions).

**Passes Completed**
32—Kelly Bradley, Montana St. (19) vs. Louisiana Tech (6), 1984 (57 attempts).

**Passes Had Intercepted**
7—Jeff Gilbert, Western Caro. (7) vs. Southern Ill. (43), 1983.

**Touchdown Passes Completed**
4—Tracy Ham, Ga. Southern (44) vs. Furman (42), 1985; Tony Peterson, Marshall (42) vs. Northeast La. (43), 1987.

**Completion Percentage (Min. 8 Attempts)**
.760—Rick Johnson, Southern Ill. (43) vs. Western Caro. (7), 1983 (19 of 25).

**Net Yards Rushing and Passing**
509—Tracy Ham, Ga. Southern (44) vs. Furman (42), 1985 (56 plays).

**Number of Rushing and Passing Plays**
65—Kelly Bradley, Montana St. (19) vs. Louisiana Tech (6), 1984 (309 yards).

**Punting Average (Min. 3 Punts)**
48.3—Todd Fugate, Marshall (42) vs. Northeast La. (43), 1987 (3 punts).

**Number of Punts**
10—Rick Titus, Delaware (14) vs. Eastern Ky. (17), 1982 (41.6 average).

**Passes Caught**
11—David Booze, Eastern Ky. (29) vs. Boise St. (31), 1980 (212 yards).

**Net Yards Receiving**
212—David Booze, Eastern Ky. (29) vs. Boise St. (31), 1980 (11 catches).

**Touchdown Passes Caught**
2—Steve Bird, Eastern Ky. (23) vs. Idaho St. (34), 1981; Joseph Bignell, Montana St. (19) vs. Louisiana Tech (6), 1984; Frank Johnson, Ga. Southern (44) vs. Furman (42), 1985; Keith Baxter, Marshall (42) vs. Northeast La. (43), 1987; Larry Centers, Stephen F. Austin (34) vs. Ga. Southern (37), 1989.

**Passes Intercepted**
4—Greg Shipp, Southern Ill. (43) vs. Western Caro. (7), 1983.

**Yards Gained on Interception Returns**
52—George Thomas, Marshall (31) vs. Youngstown St. (28), 1992 (1 interception).

**Yards Gained on Punt Returns**
67—Rodney Oglesby, Ga. Southern (36) vs. Nevada (13), 1990 (6 returns).

**Yards Gained on Kickoff Returns**
207—Eric Rasheed, Western Caro. (7) vs. Southern Ill. (43), 1983 (6 returns).

**Points**
24—John Bagwell, Furman (42) vs. Ga. Southern (44), 1985.

**Touchdowns**
4—John Bagwell, Furman (42) vs. Ga. Southern (44), 1985.

**Extra Points**
6—Keven Esval, Furman (42) vs. Ga. Southern (44), 1985.

**Field Goals**
4—Tim Foley, Ga. Southern (48) vs. Arkansas St. (21), 1986.

**Longest Rush**
58—Dale Patton, Eastern Ky. (30) vs. Lehigh (7), 1979.

**Longest Pass Completion**
79—Tracy Ham to Ricky Harris, Ga. Southern (48) vs. Arkansas St. (21), 1986.

**Longest Field Goal**
55—David Cool, Ga. Southern (12) vs. Furman (17), 1988.

**Longest Punt**
72—Rick Titus, Delaware (14) vs. Eastern Ky. (17), 1982.

# TEAM: CHAMPIONSHIP GAME

**First Downs**
28—Furman (42) vs. Ga. Southern (44), 1985; Ga. Southern (48) vs. Arkansas St. (21), 1986; Northeast La. (43) vs. Marshall (42), 1987.

**First Downs by Rushing**
19—Florida A&M (35) vs. Massachusetts (28), 1978.

**First Downs by Passing**
19—Marshall (42) vs. Northeast La. (43), 1987.

**First Downs by Penalty**
3—Eastern Ky. (23) vs. Idaho St. (34), 1981; Furman (42) vs. Ga. Southern (44), 1985; Northeast La. (43) vs. Marshall (42), 1987.

**Net Yards Rushing**
470—Florida A&M (35) vs. Massachusetts (28), 1978 (76 attempts).

**Rushes Attempted**
76—Florida A&M (35) vs. Massachusetts (28), 1978 (470 yards).

**Net Yards Passing**
474—Marshall (42) vs. Northeast La. (43), 1987 (28 of 54).

**Passes Attempted**
57—Montana St. (19) vs. Louisiana Tech (6), 1984 (32 completions).

**Passes Completed**
32—Montana St. (19) vs. Louisiana Tech (6), 1984 (57 attempts).

**Completion Percentage (Min. 10 Attempts)**
.760—Southern Ill. (43) vs. Western Caro. (7), 1983 (19 of 25).

**Passes Had Intercepted**
7—Western Caro. (7) vs. Southern Ill. (43), 1983.

**Net Yards Rushing and Passing**
640—Ga. Southern (44) vs. Furman (42), 1985 (77 plays).

**Rushing and Passing Plays**
86—Boise St. (31) vs. Eastern Ky. (29), 1980 (510 yards); Nevada (13) vs. Ga. Southern (36), 1990 (321 yards).

**Punting Average (Min. 3 Punts)**
48.3—Marshall (42) vs. Northeast La. (43), 1987 (3 punts).

**Number of Punts**
10—Delaware (14) vs. Eastern Ky. (17), 1982 (41.6 average).

**Yards Gained on Punt Returns**
67—Ga. Southern (36) vs. Nevada (13), 1990 (6 returns).

**Yards Gained on Kickoff Returns**
229—Western Caro. (7) vs. Southern Ill. (43), 1983 (8 returns).

**Yards Gained on Interception Returns**
70—Marshall (31) vs. Youngstown St. (28), 1992 (2 interceptions).

**Yards Penalized**
162—Idaho St. (34) vs. Eastern Ky. (23), 1981 (12 penalties).

**Fumbles**
5—Eastern Ky. (17) vs. Delaware (14), 1982; Western Caro. (7) vs. Southern Ill. (43), 1983; Louisiana Tech (6) vs. Montana St. (19), 1984; Northeast La. (43) vs. Marshall (42), 1987; Ga. Southern (12) vs. Furman (17), 1988; Ga. Southern (36) vs. Nevada (13), 1990.

**Fumbles Lost**
4—Northeast La. (43) vs. Marshall (42), 1987; Ga. Southern (36) vs. Nevada (13), 1990.

**Points**
48—Ga. Southern vs. Arkansas St. (21), 1986.

**Attendance**
31,304—Marshall University Stadium, Huntington, W. Va., 1992.

## YEAR-BY-YEAR DIVISION I-AA CHAMPIONSHIP RESULTS

| Year (Number of Teams) | Coach | Record | Result |
|---|---|---|---|
| **1978 (4)** | | | |
| Florida A&M | Rudy Hubbard | 2-0 | Champion |
| Massachusetts | Bob Pickett | 1-1 | Second |
| Jackson St. | W. C. Gorden | 0-1 | Lost 1st Round |
| Nevada | Chris Ault | 0-1 | Lost 1st Round |
| **1979 (4)** | | | |
| Eastern Ky. | Roy Kidd | 2-0 | Champion |
| Lehigh | John Whitehead | 1-1 | Second |
| Murray St. | Mike Gottfried | 0-1 | Lost 1st Round |
| Nevada | Chris Ault | 0-1 | Lost 1st Round |
| **1980 (4)** | | | |
| Boise St. | Jim Criner | 2-0 | Champion |
| Eastern Ky. | Roy Kidd | 1-1 | Second |
| Grambling | Eddie Robinson | 0-1 | Lost 1st Round |
| Lehigh | John Whitehead | 0-1 | Lost 1st Round |
| **1981 (8)** | | | |
| Idaho St. | Dave Kragthorpe | 3-0 | Champion |
| Eastern Ky. | Roy Kidd | 2-1 | Second |
| Boise St. | Jim Criner | 1-1 | Semifinalist |
| South Caro. St. | Bill Davis | 1-1 | Semifinalist |
| Delaware | Tubby Raymond | 0-1 | Lost 1st Round |
| Jackson St. | W. C. Gorden | 0-1 | Lost 1st Round |
| Rhode Island | Bob Griffin | 0-1 | Lost 1st Round |
| *Tennessee St. | John Merritt | 0-1 | Vacated |
| **1982 (12)** | | | |
| Eastern Ky. | Roy Kidd | 3-0 | Champion |
| Delaware | Tubby Raymond | 2-1 | Second |
| Louisiana Tech | Billy Brewer | 1-1 | Semifinalist |
| *Tennessee St. | John Merritt | 1-1 | Vacated |
| Colgate | Fred Dunlap | 1-1 | Quarterfinalist |
| Eastern Ill. | Darrell Mudra | 1-1 | Quarterfinalist |
| Idaho | Dennis Erickson | 1-1 | Quarterfinalist |
| South Caro. St. | Bill Davis | 1-1 | Quarterfinalist |
| Boston U. | Rick Taylor | 0-1 | Lost 1st Round |
| Furman | Dick Sheridan | 0-1 | Lost 1st Round |
| Jackson St. | W. C. Gorden | 0-1 | Lost 1st Round |
| Montana | Larry Donovan | 0-1 | Lost 1st Round |
| **1983 (12)** | | | |
| Southern Ill. | Rey Dempsey | 3-0 | Champion |
| Western Caro. | Bob Waters | 3-1 | Second |
| Furman | Dick Sheridan | 1-1 | Semifinalist |
| Nevada | Chris Ault | 2-1 | Semifinalist |
| Boston U. | Rick Taylor | 1-1 | Quarterfinalist |
| Holy Cross | Rick Carter | 0-1 | Quarterfinalist |
| Indiana St. | Dennis Raetz | 1-1 | Quarterfinalist |
| North Texas | Corky Nelson | 0-1 | Quarterfinalist |
| Colgate | Fred Dunlap | 0-1 | Lost 1st Round |
| Eastern Ill. | Al Molde | 0-1 | Lost 1st Round |
| Eastern Ky. | Roy Kidd | 0-1 | Lost 1st Round |
| Idaho St. | Jim Koetter | 0-1 | Lost 1st Round |

*Division I-AA Championship Results, Records*

| Year (Number of Teams) | Coach | Record | Result |
|---|---|---|---|
| **1984 (12)** | | | |
| Montana St. | Dave Arnold | 3-0 | Champion |
| Louisiana Tech | A. L. Williams | 3-1 | Second |
| Middle Tenn. St. | James Donnelly | 2-1 | Semifinalist |
| Rhode Island | Bob Griffin | 1-1 | Semifinalist |
| Alcorn St. | Marino Casem | 0-1 | Quarterfinalist |
| Arkansas St. | Larry Lacewell | 1-1 | Quarterfinalist |
| Indiana St. | Dennis Raetz | 0-1 | Quarterfinalist |
| Richmond | Dal Shealy | 1-1 | Quarterfinalist |
| Boston U. | Rick Taylor | 0-1 | Lost 1st Round |
| Eastern Ky. | Roy Kidd | 0-1 | Lost 1st Round |
| Mississippi Val. | Archie Cooley Jr. | 0-1 | Lost 1st Round |
| Tenn.-Chatt. | Buddy Nix | 0-1 | Lost 1st Round |
| **1985 (12)** | | | |
| Ga. Southern | Erk Russell | 4-0 | Champion |
| Furman | Dick Sheridan | 2-1 | Second |
| Nevada | Chris Ault | 1-1 | Semifinalist |
| Northern Iowa | Darrell Mudra | 1-1 | Semifinalist |
| Arkansas St. | Larry Lacewell | 1-1 | Quarterfinalist |
| Eastern Wash. | Dick Zornes | 1-1 | Quarterfinalist |
| Middle Tenn. St. | James Donnelly | 0-1 | Quarterfinalist |
| Rhode Island | Bob Griffin | 1-1 | Quarterfinalist |
| Akron | Jim Dennison | 0-1 | Lost 1st Round |
| Grambling | Eddie Robinson | 0-1 | Lost 1st Round |
| Idaho | Dennis Erickson | 0-1 | Lost 1st Round |
| Jackson St. | W. C. Gorden | 0-1 | Lost 1st Round |
| **1986 (16)** | | | |
| Ga. Southern | Erk Russell | 4-0 | Champion |
| Arkansas St. | Larry Lacewell | 3-1 | Second |
| Eastern Ky. | Roy Kidd | 2-1 | Semifinalist |
| Nevada | Chris Ault | 2-1 | Semifinalist |
| Delaware | Tubby Raymond | 1-1 | Quarterfinalist |
| Eastern Ill. | Al Molde | 1-1 | Quarterfinalist |
| Nicholls St. | Sonny Jackson | 1-1 | Quarterfinalist |
| Tennessee St. | William Thomas | 1-1 | Quarterfinalist |
| Appalachian St. | Sparky Woods | 0-1 | Lost 1st Round |
| Furman | Jimmy Satterfield | 0-1 | Lost 1st Round |
| Idaho | Keith Gilbertson | 0-1 | Lost 1st Round |
| Jackson St. | W. C. Gorden | 0-1 | Lost 1st Round |
| Murray St. | Frank Beamer | 0-1 | Lost 1st Round |
| North Caro. A&T | Maurice Forte | 0-1 | Lost 1st Round |
| Sam Houston St. | Ron Randleman | 0-1 | Lost 1st Round |
| William & Mary | Jimmye Laycock | 0-1 | Lost 1st Round |
| **1987 (16)** | | | |
| Northeast La. | Pat Collins | 4-0 | Champion |
| Marshall | George Chaump | 3-1 | Second |
| Appalachian St. | Sparky Woods | 2-1 | Semifinalist |
| Northern Iowa | Darrell Mudra | 2-1 | Semifinalist |
| Arkansas St. | Larry Lacewell | 1-1 | Quarterfinalist |
| Eastern Ky. | Roy Kidd | 1-1 | Quarterfinalist |
| Ga. Southern | Erk Russell | 1-1 | Quarterfinalist |
| Weber St. | Mike Price | 1-1 | Quarterfinalist |
| Idaho | Keith Gilbertson | 0-1 | Lost 1st Round |
| Jackson St. | W. C. Gorden | 0-1 | Lost 1st Round |
| James Madison | Joe Purzycki | 0-1 | Lost 1st Round |
| Maine | Tim Murphy | 0-1 | Lost 1st Round |
| North Texas | Corky Nelson | 0-1 | Lost 1st Round |
| Richmond | Dal Shealy | 0-1 | Lost 1st Round |
| Western Ky. | Dave Roberts | 0-1 | Lost 1st Round |
| Youngstown St. | Jim Tressel | 0-1 | Lost 1st Round |
| **1988 (16)** | | | |
| Furman | Jimmy Satterfield | 4-0 | Champion |
| Ga. Southern | Erk Russell | 3-1 | Second |
| Eastern Ky. | Roy Kidd | 2-1 | Semifinalist |
| Idaho | Keith Gilbertson | 2-1 | Semifinalist |
| Marshall | George Chaump | 1-1 | Quarterfinalist |
| Northwestern (La.) | Sam Goodwin | 1-1 | Quarterfinalist |
| Stephen F. Austin | Jim Hess | 1-1 | Quarterfinalist |
| Western Ky. | Dave Roberts | 1-1 | Quarterfinalist |
| Boise St. | Skip Hall | 0-1 | Lost 1st Round |
| Citadel | Charlie Taaffe | 0-1 | Lost 1st Round |

570

| Year (Number of Teams) | Coach | Record | Result |
|---|---|---|---|
| Delaware | Tubby Raymond | 0-1 | Lost 1st Round |
| Jackson St. | W. C. Gorden | 0-1 | Lost 1st Round |
| Massachusetts | Jim Reid | 0-1 | Lost 1st Round |
| Montana | Don Read | 0-1 | Lost 1st Round |
| North Texas | Corky Nelson | 0-1 | Lost 1st Round |
| Western Ill. | Bruce Craddock | 0-1 | Lost 1st Round |
| **1989 (16)** | | | |
| Ga. Southern | Erk Russell | 4-0 | Champion |
| *Stephen F. Austin | Lynn Graves | 3-1 | Vacated |
| Furman | Jimmy Satterfield | 2-1 | Semifinalist |
| Montana | Don Read | 2-1 | Semifinalist |
| Eastern Ill. | Bob Spoo | 1-1 | Quarterfinalist |
| Middle Tenn. St. | James Donnelly | 1-1 | Quarterfinalist |
| Southwest Mo. St. | Jesse Branch | 1-1 | Quarterfinalist |
| Youngstown St. | Jim Tressel | 1-1 | Quarterfinalist |
| Appalachian St. | Jerry Moore | 0-1 | Lost 1st Round |
| Eastern Ky. | Roy Kidd | 0-1 | Lost 1st Round |
| Grambling | Eddie Robinson | 0-1 | Lost 1st Round |
| Idaho | John L. Smith | 0-1 | Lost 1st Round |
| Jackson St. | W. C. Gorden | 0-1 | Lost 1st Round |
| Maine | Tom Lichtenberg | 0-1 | Lost 1st Round |
| Villanova | Andy Talley | 0-1 | Lost 1st Round |
| William & Mary | Jimmye Laycock | 0-1 | Lost 1st Round |
| **1990 (16)** | | | |
| Ga. Southern | Tim Stowers | 4-0 | Champion |
| Nevada | Chris Ault | 3-1 | Second |
| Boise St. | Skip Hall | 2-1 | Semifinalist |
| Central Fla. | Gene McDowell | 2-1 | Semifinalist |
| Furman | Jimmy Satterfield | 1-1 | Quarterfinalist |
| Idaho | John L. Smith | 1-1 | Quarterfinalist |
| Middle Tenn. St. | James Donnelly | 1-1 | Quarterfinalist |
| William & Mary | Jimmye Laycock | 1-1 | Quarterfinalist |
| Citadel | Charlie Taaffe | 0-1 | Lost 1st Round |
| Eastern Ky. | Roy Kidd | 0-1 | Lost 1st Round |
| Jackson St. | W. C. Gorden | 0-1 | Lost 1st Round |
| Massachusetts | Jim Reid | 0-1 | Lost 1st Round |
| Northeast La. | Dave Roberts | 0-1 | Lost 1st Round |
| Northern Iowa | Terry Allen | 0-1 | Lost 1st Round |
| Southwest Mo. St. | Jesse Branch | 0-1 | Lost 1st Round |
| Youngstown St. | Jim Tressel | 0-1 | Lost 1st Round |
| **1991 (16)** | | | |
| Youngstown St. | Jim Tressel | 4-0 | Champion |
| Marshall | Jim Donnan | 3-1 | Second |
| Eastern Ky. | Roy Kidd | 2-1 | Semifinalist |
| Samford | Terry Bowden | 2-1 | Semifinalist |
| James Madison | Rip Scherer | 1-1 | Quarterfinalist |
| Middle Tenn. St. | James Donnelly | 1-1 | Quarterfinalist |
| Nevada | Chris Ault | 1-1 | Quarterfinalist |
| Northern Iowa | Terry Allen | 1-1 | Quarterfinalist |
| Appalachian St. | Jerry Moore | 0-1 | Lost 1st Round |
| Delaware | Tubby Raymond | 0-1 | Lost 1st Round |
| McNeese St. | Bobby Keasler | 0-1 | Lost 1st Round |
| New Hampshire | Bill Bowes | 0-1 | Lost 1st Round |
| Sam Houston St. | Ron Randleman | 0-1 | Lost 1st Round |
| Villanova | Andy Talley | 0-1 | Lost 1st Round |
| Weber St. | Dave Arslanian | 0-1 | Lost 1st Round |
| Western Ill. | Randy Ball | 0-1 | Lost 1st Round |
| **1992 (16)** | | | |
| Marshall | Jim Donnan | 4-0 | Champion |
| Youngstown St. | Jim Tressel | 3-1 | Second |
| Delaware | Tubby Raymond | 2-1 | Semifinalist |
| Northern Iowa | Terry Allen | 2-1 | Semifinalist |
| Citadel | Charlie Taaffe | 1-1 | Quarterfinalist |
| McNeese St. | Bobby Keasler | 1-1 | Quarterfinalist |
| Middle Tenn. St. | James Donnelly | 1-1 | Quarterfinalist |
| Northeast La. | Dave Roberts | 1-1 | Quarterfinalist |
| Alcorn St. | Cardell Jones | 0-1 | Lost 1st Round |
| Appalachian St. | Jerry Moore | 0-1 | Lost 1st Round |

*Division I-AA Championship Results, Records*

| Team | Coach | Record | Result |
|------|-------|--------|--------|
| Eastern Ky. ........................... | Roy Kidd | 0-1 | Lost 1st Round |
| Eastern Wash. ....................... | Dick Zornes | 0-1 | Lost 1st Round |
| Idaho ................................... | John L. Smith | 0-1 | Lost 1st Round |
| North Caro. A&T ..................... | Bill Hayes | 0-1 | Lost 1st Round |
| Samford ............................... | Terry Bowden | 0-1 | Lost 1st Round |
| Villanova ............................. | Andy Talley | 0-1 | Lost 1st Round |

* Competition in championship vacated by the NCAA.

## DIVISION I-AA CHAMPIONSHIP
## ALL-TIME RECORD OF EACH COLLEGE
## COACH-BY-COACH, 1978-92 (59 Colleges)

| | Yrs | Won | Lost | CH | 2D |
|---|---|---|---|---|---|
| **AKRON** | | | | | |
| Jim Dennison (Wooster '60) 85 ..................... | 1 | 0 | 1 | 0 | 0 |
| **ALCORN ST.** | | | | | |
| Marino Casem (Xavier, La. '56) 84 .................. | 1 | 0 | 1 | 0 | 0 |
| Cardell Jones (Alcorn St. '65) 92 ................... | 1 | 0 | 1 | 0 | 0 |
| TOTAL | 2 | 0 | 2 | 0 | 0 |
| **APPALACHIAN ST.** | | | | | |
| Sparky Woods (Carson-Newman '76) 86, 87 ......... | 2 | 2 | 2 | 0 | 0 |
| Jerry Moore (Baylor '61) 89, 91, 92 ................. | 3 | 0 | 3 | 0 | 0 |
| TOTAL | 5 | 2 | 5 | 0 | 0 |
| **ARKANSAS ST.** | | | | | |
| Larry Lacewell (Ark.-Monticello '59) 84, 85, 86-2D, 87 ......................................... | 4 | 6 | 4 | 0 | 1 |
| **BOISE ST.** | | | | | |
| Jim Criner (Cal Poly Pomona '61) 80-CH, 81 ........ | 2 | 3 | 1 | 1 | 0 |
| Skip Hall (Concordia-M'head '66) 88, 90 ............ | 2 | 2 | 2 | 0 | 0 |
| TOTAL | 4 | 5 | 3 | 1 | 0 |
| **BOSTON U.** | | | | | |
| Rick Taylor (Gettysburg '64) 82, 83, 84 .............. | 3 | 1 | 3 | 0 | 0 |
| **CENTRAL FLA.** | | | | | |
| Gene McDowell (Florida St. '63) 90 ................. | 1 | 2 | 1 | 0 | 0 |
| **CITADEL** | | | | | |
| Charlie Taaffe (Siena '73) 88, 90, 92 ............... | 3 | 1 | 3 | 0 | 0 |
| **COLGATE** | | | | | |
| Fred Dunlap (Colgate '50) 82, 83 ................... | 2 | 1 | 2 | 0 | 0 |
| **DELAWARE** | | | | | |
| Harold "Tubby" Raymond (Michigan '50) 81, 82-2D, 86, 87, 91, 92 .................................... | 6 | 5 | 6 | 0 | 1 |
| **EASTERN ILL.** | | | | | |
| Darrell Mudra (Peru St. '51) 82 .................... | 1 | 1 | 1 | 0 | 0 |
| Al Molde (Gust. Adolphus '66) 83, 86 ............... | 2 | 1 | 2 | 0 | 0 |
| Bob Spoo (Purdue '60) 89 ......................... | 1 | 1 | 1 | 0 | 0 |
| TOTAL | 4 | 3 | 4 | 0 | 0 |
| **EASTERN KY.** | | | | | |
| Roy Kidd (Eastern Ky. '54) 79-CH, 80-2D, 81-2D, 82-CH, 83, 84, 86, 87, 88, 89, 90, 91, 92 ..... | 13 | 15 | 11 | 2 | 2 |
| **EASTERN WASH.** | | | | | |
| Dick Zornes (Eastern Wash. '68) 85, 92 ............. | 2 | 1 | 2 | 0 | 0 |
| **FLORIDA A&M** | | | | | |
| Rudy Hubbard (Ohio St. '68) 78-CH ................ | 1 | 2 | 0 | 1 | 0 |
| **FURMAN** | | | | | |
| Dick Sheridan (South Caro. '64) 82, 83, 85-2D ....... | 3 | 3 | 3 | 0 | 1 |
| Jimmy Satterfield (South Caro. '62) 86, 88-CH, 89, 90 | 4 | 7 | 3 | 1 | 0 |
| TOTAL | 7 | 10 | 6 | 1 | 1 |
| **GA. SOUTHERN** | | | | | |
| Erk Russell (Auburn '49) 85-CH, 86-CH, 87, 88-2D, 89-CH.......................................... | 5 | 16 | 2 | 3 | 1 |
| Tim Stowers (Auburn '79) 90-CH ................... | 1 | 4 | 0 | 1 | 0 |
| TOTAL | 6 | 20 | 2 | 4 | 1 |
| **GRAMBLING** | | | | | |
| Eddie Robinson (Leland '41) 80, 85, 89 ............. | 3 | 0 | 3 | 0 | 0 |
| **HOLY CROSS** | | | | | |
| Rick Carter (Earlham '65) 83 ...................... | 1 | 0 | 1 | 0 | 0 |

| | Yrs | Won | Lost | CH | 2D |
|---|---|---|---|---|---|
| **IDAHO** | | | | | |
| Dennis Erickson (Montana St. '70) 82, 85 ........... | 2 | 1 | 2 | 0 | 0 |
| Keith Gilbertson (Central Wash. '71) 86, 87, 88 ....... | 3 | 2 | 3 | 0 | 0 |
| John L. Smith (Weber St. '71) 89, 90, 92 ............ | 3 | 1 | 3 | 0 | 0 |
| TOTAL | 8 | 4 | 8 | 0 | 0 |
| **IDAHO ST.** | | | | | |
| Dave Kragthorpe (Utah St. '55) 81-CH .............. | 1 | 3 | 0 | 1 | 0 |
| Jim Koetter (Idaho St. '61) 83 ..................... | 1 | 0 | 1 | 0 | 0 |
| TOTAL | 2 | 3 | 1 | 1 | 0 |
| **INDIANA ST.** | | | | | |
| Dennis Raetz (Nebraska '68) 83, 84 ................ | 2 | 1 | 2 | 0 | 0 |
| **JACKSON ST.** | | | | | |
| W. C. Gorden (Tennessee St. '52) 78, 81, 82, 85, 86, 87, 88, 89, 90 ................................... | 9 | 0 | 9 | 0 | 0 |
| **JAMES MADISON** | | | | | |
| Joe Purzycki (Delaware '71) 87 .................... | 1 | 0 | 1 | 0 | 0 |
| Rip Scherer (William & Mary '74) 91 ................ | 1 | 1 | 1 | 0 | 0 |
| TOTAL | 2 | 1 | 2 | 0 | 0 |
| **LEHIGH** | | | | | |
| John Whitehead (East Stroudsburg '50) 79-2D, 80 ... | 2 | 1 | 2 | 0 | 1 |
| **LOUISIANA TECH** | | | | | |
| Billy Brewer (Mississippi '61) 82 ................... | 1 | 1 | 1 | 0 | 0 |
| A. L. Williams (Louisiana Tech '57) 84-2D ........... | 1 | 3 | 1 | 0 | 1 |
| TOTAL | 2 | 4 | 2 | 0 | 1 |
| **MAINE** | | | | | |
| Tim Murphy (Springfield '78) 87 ................... | 1 | 0 | 1 | 0 | 0 |
| Tom Lichtenberg (Louisville '62) 89 ................ | 1 | 0 | 1 | 0 | 0 |
| TOTAL | 2 | 0 | 2 | 0 | 0 |
| **MARSHALL** | | | | | |
| George Chaump (Bloomsburg '58) 87-2D, 88 ....... | 2 | 4 | 2 | 0 | 1 |
| Jim Donnan (North Caro. St. '67) 91-2D, 92-CH ..... | 2 | 7 | 1 | 1 | 1 |
| TOTAL | 4 | 11 | 3 | 1 | 2 |
| **MASSACHUSETTS** | | | | | |
| Bob Pickett (Maine '59) 78-2D ..................... | 1 | 1 | 1 | 0 | 1 |
| Jim Reid (Maine '73) 88, 90 ....................... | 2 | 0 | 2 | 0 | 0 |
| TOTAL | 3 | 1 | 3 | 0 | 1 |
| **McNEESE ST.** | | | | | |
| Bobby Keasler (Northeast La. '70) 91, 92 ............ | 2 | 1 | 2 | 0 | 0 |
| **MIDDLE TENN. ST.** | | | | | |
| James "Boots" Donnelly (Middle Tenn. St. '65) 84, 85, 89, 90, 91, 92 ................................. | 6 | 6 | 6 | 0 | 0 |
| **MISSISSIPPI VAL.** | | | | | |
| Archie Cooley Jr. (Jackson St. '62) 84 .............. | 1 | 0 | 1 | 0 | 0 |
| **MONTANA** | | | | | |
| Larry Donovan (Nebraska '64) 82 .................. | 1 | 0 | 1 | 0 | 0 |
| Don Read (Cal St. Sacramento '59) 88, 89 .......... | 2 | 2 | 2 | 0 | 0 |
| TOTAL | 3 | 2 | 3 | 0 | 0 |
| **MONTANA ST.** | | | | | |
| Dave Arnold (Drake '67) 84-CH .................... | 1 | 3 | 0 | 1 | 0 |
| **MURRAY ST.** | | | | | |
| Mike Gottfried (Morehead St. '66) 79 .............. | 1 | 0 | 1 | 0 | 0 |
| Frank Beamer (Virginia Tech '69) 86 ................ | 1 | 0 | 1 | 0 | 0 |
| TOTAL | 2 | 0 | 2 | 0 | 0 |
| **NEVADA** | | | | | |
| Chris Ault (Nevada '68) 78, 79, 83, 85, 86, 90-2D, 91 .. | 7 | 9 | 7 | 0 | 1 |
| **NEW HAMPSHIRE** | | | | | |
| Bill Bowes (Penn St. '65) 91 ...................... | 1 | 0 | 1 | 0 | 0 |
| **NICHOLLS ST.** | | | | | |
| Sonny Jackson (Nicholls St. '63) 86 ................ | 1 | 1 | 1 | 0 | 0 |
| **NORTH CARO. A&T** | | | | | |
| Maurice "Mo" Forte (Minnesota '71) 86 .............. | 1 | 0 | 1 | 0 | 0 |
| Bill Hayes (N.C. Central '64) 92 .................... | 1 | 0 | 1 | 0 | 0 |
| TOTAL | 2 | 0 | 2 | 0 | 0 |
| **NORTH TEXAS** | | | | | |
| Corky Nelson (Southwest Tex. St. '64) 83, 87, 88 ..... | 3 | 0 | 3 | 0 | 0 |

*Division I-AA Championship Results, Records*

| | Yrs | Won | Lost | CH | 2D |
|---|---|---|---|---|---|
| **NORTHEAST LA.** | | | | | |
| Pat Collins (Louisiana Tech '63) 87-CH ............. | 1 | 4 | 0 | 1 | 0 |
| Dave Roberts (Western Caro. '68) 90, 92 ............ | 2 | 1 | 2 | 0 | 0 |
| TOTAL | 3 | 5 | 2 | 1 | 0 |
| **NORTHERN IOWA** | | | | | |
| Darrell Mudra (Peru St. '51) 85, 87 ................ | 2 | 3 | 2 | 0 | 0 |
| Terry Allen (Northern Iowa '79) 90, 91, 92 ........... | 3 | 3 | 3 | 0 | 0 |
| TOTAL | 5 | 6 | 5 | 0 | 0 |
| **NORTHWESTERN (LA.)** | | | | | |
| Sam Goodwin (Henderson St. '66) 88 ............. | 1 | 1 | 1 | 0 | 0 |
| **RHODE ISLAND** | | | | | |
| Bob Griffin (Southern Conn. St. '63) 81, 84, 85....... | 3 | 2 | 3 | 0 | 0 |
| **RICHMOND** | | | | | |
| Dal Shealy (Carson-Newman '60) 84, 87 ............ | 2 | 1 | 2 | 0 | 0 |
| **SAM HOUSTON ST.** | | | | | |
| Ron Randleman (William Penn '64) 86, 91 ........... | 2 | 0 | 2 | 0 | 0 |
| **SAMFORD** | | | | | |
| Terry Bowden (West Va. '78) 91, 92................. | 2 | 2 | 2 | 0 | 0 |
| **SOUTH CARO. ST.** | | | | | |
| Bill Davis (Johnson Smith '65) 81, 82 .............. | 2 | 2 | 2 | 0 | 0 |
| **SOUTHERN ILL.** | | | | | |
| Rey Dempsey (Geneva '58) 83-CH ................ | 1 | 3 | 0 | 1 | 0 |
| **SOUTHWEST MO. ST.** | | | | | |
| Jesse Branch (Arkansas '64) 89, 90 ............... | 2 | 1 | 2 | 0 | 0 |
| **STEPHEN F. AUSTIN¢** | | | | | |
| Jim Hess (S'eastern Okla. '59) 88 ................ | 1 | 1 | 1 | 0 | 0 |
| Lynn Graves (Stephen F. Austin '65) 89-2D ......... | 1 | 3 | 1 | 0 | 1 |
| TOTAL | 2 | 4 | 2 | 0 | 1 |
| **TENN.-CHATT.** | | | | | |
| Buddy Nix (Livingston '61) 84 .................... | 1 | 0 | 1 | 0 | 0 |
| **TENNESSEE ST.*** | | | | | |
| John Merritt (Kentucky St. '50) 81, 82 ............. | 2 | 1 | 2 | 0 | 0 |
| Bill Thomas (Tennessee St. '71) 86 ................ | 1 | 1 | 1 | 0 | 0 |
| TOTAL | 3 | 2 | 3 | 0 | 0 |
| **VILLANOVA** | | | | | |
| Andy Talley (Southern Conn. St. '67) 89, 91, 92 ...... | 3 | 0 | 3 | 0 | 0 |
| **WEBER ST.** | | | | | |
| Mike Price (Puget Sound '69) 87 .................. | 1 | 1 | 1 | 0 | 0 |
| Dave Arslanian (Weber St. '72) 91 ................. | 1 | 0 | 1 | 0 | 0 |
| TOTAL | 2 | 1 | 2 | 0 | 0 |
| **WESTERN CARO.** | | | | | |
| Bob Waters (Presbyterian '60) 83-2D .............. | 1 | 3 | 1 | 0 | 1 |
| **WESTERN ILL.** | | | | | |
| Bruce Craddock (Northeast Mo. St. '66) 88 ......... | 1 | 0 | 1 | 0 | 0 |
| Randy Ball (Northeast Mo. St. '73) 91............... | 1 | 0 | 1 | 0 | 0 |
| TOTAL | 2 | 0 | 2 | 0 | 0 |
| **WESTERN KY.** | | | | | |
| Dave Roberts (Western Caro. '68) 87, 88 ........... | 2 | 1 | 2 | 0 | 0 |
| **WILLIAM & MARY** | | | | | |
| Jimmye Laycock (William & Mary '70) 86, 89, 90 ..... | 3 | 1 | 3 | 0 | 0 |
| **YOUNGSTOWN ST.** | | | | | |
| Jim Tressel (Baldwin-Wallace '75) 87, 89, 90, 91-CH, 92-2D ........................................ | 5 | 8 | 4 | 1 | 1 |

*Tennessee State's competition in the 1981 and 1982 Division I-AA championships was vacated by the NCAA (official record is 1-1). ¢ Stephen F. Austin's competition in the 1989 Division I-AA championship was vacated by the NCAA (official record is 1-1).*

## ALL-TIME RESULTS

**1978 First Round:** Florida A&M 15, Jackson St. 10; Massachusetts 44, Nevada 21. **Championship:** Florida A&M 35, Massachusetts 28.

**1979 First Round:** Lehigh 28, Murray St. 9; Eastern Ky. 33, Nevada 30 (2 OT). **Championship:** Eastern Ky. 30, Lehigh 7.

**1980 First Round:** Eastern Ky. 23, Lehigh 20; Boise St. 14, Grambling 9. **Championship:** Boise St. 31, Eastern Ky. 29.

**1981 First Round:** Eastern Ky. 35, Delaware 28; Boise St. 19, Jackson St. 7; Idaho St. 51, Rhode Island 0; South Caro. St. 26, *Tennessee St. 25 (OT). **Semifinals:** Eastern Ky. 23, Boise St. 17; Idaho St. 41, South Caro. St. 12. **Championship:**

Idaho St. 34, Eastern Ky. 23.

* *Tennessee State's participation in 1981 playoff vacated.*

**1982 First Round:** Idaho 21, Montana 7; Eastern Ill. 16, Jackson St. 13 (OT); South Caro. St. 17, Furman 0; Colgate 21, Boston U. 7. **Quarterfinals:** Eastern Ky. 38, Idaho 30; *Tennessee St. 20, Eastern Ill. 19; Louisiana Tech 38, South Caro. St. 3; Delaware 20, Colgate 13. **Semifinals:** Eastern Ky. 13, *Tennessee St. 7; Delaware 17, Louisiana Tech 0. **Championship:** Eastern Ky. 17, Delaware 14.

* *Tennessee State's participation in 1982 playoff vacated.*

**1983 First Round:** Indiana St. 16, Eastern Ill. 13 (2 OT); Nevada 27, Idaho St. 20; Western Caro. 24, Colgate 23; Boston U. 24, Eastern Ky. 20. **Quarterfinals:** Southern Ill. 23, Indiana St. 7; Nevada 20, North Texas 17 (OT); Western Caro. 28, Holy Cross 21; Furman 35, Boston U. 16. **Semifinals:** Southern Ill. 23, Nevada 7; Western Caro. 14, Furman 7. **Championship:** Southern Ill. 43, Western Caro. 7.

**1984 First Round:** Louisiana Tech 66, Mississippi Val. 19; Middle Tenn. St. 27, Eastern Ky. 10; Richmond 35, Boston U. 33; Arkansas St. 37, Tenn.-Chatt. 10. **Quarterfinals:** Louisiana Tech 44, Alcorn St. 21; Middle Tenn. St. 42, Indiana St. 41 (3 OT); Rhode Island 23, Richmond 17; Montana St. 31, Arkansas St. 14. **Semifinals:** Louisiana Tech 21, Middle Tenn. St. 13; Montana St. 32, Rhode Island 20. **Championship:** Montana St. 19, Louisiana Tech 6.

**1985 First Round:** Ga. Southern 27, Jackson St. 0; Eastern Wash. 42, Idaho 38; Rhode Island 35, Akron 27; Arkansas St. 10, Grambling 7. **Quarterfinals:** Ga. Southern 28, Middle Tenn. St. 21; Northern Iowa 17, Eastern Wash. 14; Furman 59, Rhode Island 15; Nevada 24, Arkansas St. 23. **Semifinals:** Ga. Southern 40, Northern Iowa 33; Furman 35, Nevada 12. **Championship:** Ga. Southern 44, Furman 42.

**1986 First Round:** Nevada 27, Idaho 7; Tennessee St. 32, Jackson St. 23; Ga. Southern 52, North Caro. A&T 21; Nicholls St. 28, Appalachian St. 26; Arkansas St. 48, Sam Houston St. 7; Delaware 51, William & Mary 17; Eastern Ill. 28, Murray St. 21; Eastern Ky. 23, Furman 10. **Quarterfinals:** Nevada 33, Tennessee St. 6; Ga. Southern 55, Nicholls St. 31; Arkansas St. 55, Delaware 24; Eastern Ky. 24, Eastern Ill. 22. **Semifinals:** Ga. Southern 48, Nevada 38; Arkansas St. 24, Eastern Ky. 10. **Championship:** Ga. Southern 48, Arkansas St. 21.

**1987 First Round:** Appalachian St. 20, Richmond 3; Ga. Southern 31, Maine 28 (OT); Weber St. 59, Idaho 30; Marshall 41, James Madison 12; Northeast La. 30, North Texas 9; Eastern Ky. 40, Western Ky. 17; Northern Iowa 31, Youngstown St. 28; Arkansas St. 35, Jackson St. 32. **Quarterfinals:** Appalachian St. 19, Ga. Southern 0; Marshall 51, Weber St. 23; Northeast La. 33, Eastern Ky. 32; Northern Iowa 49, Arkansas St. 28. **Semifinals:** Marshall 24, Appalachian St. 10; Northeast La. 44, Northern Iowa 41 (2 OT). **Championship:** Northeast La. 43, Marshall 42.

**1988 First Round:** Idaho 38, Montana 19; Northwestern (La.) 22, Boise St. 13; Furman 21, Delaware 7; Marshall 7, North Texas 0; Ga. Southern 38, Citadel 20; Stephen F. Austin 24, Jackson St. 0; Western Ky. 35, Western Ill. 32; Eastern Ky. 28, Massachusetts 17. **Quarterfinals:** Idaho 38, North-

western (La.) 30; Furman 13, Marshall 9; Ga. Southern 27, Stephen F. Austin 6; Eastern Ky. 41, Western Ky. 24. **Semifinals:** Furman 38, Idaho 7; Ga. Southern 21, Eastern Ky. 17. **Championship:** Furman 17, Ga. Southern 12.

**1989 First Round:** Ga. Southern 52, Villanova 36; Middle Tenn. St. 24, Appalachian St. 21; Eastern Ill. 38, Idaho 21; Montana 48, Jackson St. 7; Furman 24, William & Mary 10; Youngstown St. 28, Eastern Ky. 24; ¢Stephen F. Austin 59, Grambling 56; Southwest Mo. St. 38, Maine 35. **Quarterfinals:** Ga. Southern 45, Middle Tenn. St. 3; Montana 25, Eastern Ill. 19; Furman 42, Youngstown St. 23; ¢Stephen F. Austin 55, Southwest Mo. St. 25. **Semifinals:** Ga. Southern 45, Montana 15; ¢Stephen F. Austin 21, Furman 19. **Championship:** Ga. Southern 37, ¢Stephen F. Austin 34.

¢ *Stephen F. Austin's participation in 1989 playoff vacated.*

**1990 First Round:** Middle Tenn. St. 28, Jackson St. 7; Boise St. 20, Northern Iowa 3; Nevada 27, Northeast La. 14; Furman 45, Eastern Ky. 17; Central Fla. 20, Youngstown St. 17; William & Mary 38, Massachusetts 0; Ga. Southern 31, Citadel 0; Idaho 41, Southwest Mo. St. 35. **Quarterfinals:** Boise St. 20, Middle Tenn. St. 13; Nevada 42, Furman 35 (3 OT); Central Fla. 52, William &

**Marshall back-up kicker Willy Merrick (17) watches the first and only field-goal attempt of his collegiate career sail through the uprights with 10 seconds left in the game to give the Thundering Herd a 31-28 victory over Youngstown State in the 1992 Division I-AA Football Championship title game.**

*Division I-AA Championship Results, Records*

Mary 38; Ga. Southern 28, Idaho 27. **Semifinals:** Nevada 59, Boise St. 52 (3 OT); Ga. Southern 44, Central Fla. 7. **Championship:** Ga. Southern 36, Nevada 13.

**1991 First Round:** Nevada 22, McNeese St. 16; Youngstown St. 17, Villanova 16; James Madison 42, Delaware 35 (2 OT); Samford 29, New Hampshire 13; Eastern Ky. 14, Appalachian St. 3; Middle Tenn. St. 20, Sam Houston St. 19 (OT); Northern Iowa 38, Weber St. 21; Marshall 20, Western Ill. 17 (OT). **Quarterfinals:** Youngstown St. 30, Nevada 28; Samford 24, James Madison 21; Eastern Ky. 23, Middle Tenn. St. 13; Marshall 41, Northern Iowa 13. **Semifinals:** Youngstown St. 10, Samford 0; Marshall 14, Eastern Ky. 7. **Championship:** Youngstown St. 25, Marshall 17.

**1992 First Round:** Northeast La. 78, Alcorn St. 27; Delaware 56, Samford 21; Middle Tenn. St. 35, Appalachian St. 10; Marshall 44, Eastern Ky. 0; Citadel 44, North Caro. A&T 0; Youngstown St. 23, Villanova 20; Northern Iowa 17, Eastern Wash. 14; McNeese St. 23, Idaho 20. **Quarterfinals:** Delaware 41, Northeast La. 18; Marshall 35, Middle Tenn. St. 21; Youngstown St. 42, Citadel 17; Northern Iowa 29, McNeese St. 7. **Semifinals:** Marshall 28, Delaware 7; Youngstown St. 19, Northern Iowa 7. **Championship:** Marshall 31, Youngstown St. 28.

## 1992 DIVISION II CHAMPIONSHIP

### BRALY MUNICIPAL STADIUM, FLORENCE, ALA.; DECEMBER 12, 1992

|  | Jacksonville St. | Pittsburg St. |
|---|---|---|
| First Downs | 24 | 14 |
| Rushes-Net Yardage | 76-390 | 41-156 |
| Passing Yardage | 5 | 98 |
| Return Yardage (Punts, Int. & Fum.) | 32 | 0 |
| Passes (Comp.-Att.-Int.) | 2-4-1 | 7-15-1 |
| Punts (Number-Average) | 3-35.3 | 4-32.2 |
| Fumbles (Number-Lost) | 0-0 | 0-0 |
| Penalties (Number-Yards) | 5-35 | 2-20 |

Jacksonville St. ...................................... 0   10   7   0—17
Pittsburg St. ........................................ 6   7   0   0—13

Game Conditions: Temperature, 47 degrees; Wind, 5-10 from north; Weather, sunny and fair. Attendance: 11,733.

**First Quarter**

Pittsburg St.—Ronald Moore 99 kickoff return (try for two failed) (99 yards in 1 play, 14:47 left)

**Second Quarter**

Jacksonville St.—Slade Stinnett 42 field goal (38 yards in 10 plays, 12:35 left)
Pittsburg St.—Ray Staten 21 pass from Brian Hutchins (Jeff Wood kick) (52 yards in 7 plays, 9:14 left)
Jacksonville St.—Danny Lee 8 run (Stinnett kick) (78 yards in 15 plays, 2:23 left)

**Third Quarter**

Jacksonville St.—Sean Richardson 5 run (Stinnett kick) (71 yards in 8 plays, 11:13 left)

**Individual Leaders**

Rushing—Jacksonville St.: Chuck Robinson, 110 yards on 15 carries, and Richardson, 106 yards on 23 carries; Pittsburg St.: Moore, 83 yards on 20 carries.
Passing—Jacksonville St.: Robinson, 2 of 4 for 5 yards; Pittsburg St.: Hutchins, 7 of 15 for 98 yards.
Receiving—Jacksonville St.: Lee, 2 catches for 5 yards; Pittsburg St.: Staten, 3 catches for 47 yards.

### DIVISION II ALL-TIME CHAMPIONSHIP RESULTS

| Year | Champion | Coach | Score | Runner-Up | Site |
|---|---|---|---|---|---|
| 1973 | Louisiana Tech | Maxie Lambright | 34-0 | Western Ky. | Sacramento, Calif. |
| 1974 | Central Mich. | Roy Kramer | 54-14 | Delaware | Sacramento, Calif. |
| 1975 | Northern Mich. | Gil Krueger | 16-14 | Western Ky. | Sacramento, Calif. |
| 1976 | Montana St. | Sonny Holland | 24-13 | Akron | Wichita Falls, Texas |
| 1977 | Lehigh | John Whitehead | 33-0 | Jacksonville St. | Wichita Falls, Texas |
| 1978 | Eastern Ill. | Darrell Mudra | 10-9 | Delaware | Longview, Texas |
| 1979 | Delaware | Tubby Raymond | 38-21 | Youngstown St. | Albuquerque, N. M. |
| 1980 | Cal Poly SLO | Joe Harper | 21-13 | Eastern Ill. | Albuquerque, N. M. |
| 1981 | Southwest Tex. St. | Jim Wacker | 42-13 | North Dak. St. | McAllen, Texas |
| 1982 | Southwest Tex. St. | Jim Wacker | 34-9 | UC Davis | McAllen, Texas |
| 1983 | North Dak. St. | Don Morton | 41-21 | Central St. (Ohio) | McAllen, Texas |
| 1984 | Troy St. | Chan Gailey | 18-17 | North Dak. St. | McAllen, Texas |
| 1985 | North Dak. St. | Earle Solomonson | 35-7 | North Ala. | McAllen, Texas |
| 1986 | North Dak. St. | Earle Solomonson | 27-7 | South Dak. | Florence, Ala. |
| 1987 | Troy St. | Rick Rhoades | 31-17 | Portland St. | Florence, Ala. |

| Year | Champion | Coach | Score | Runner-Up | Site |
|---|---|---|---|---|---|
| 1988 | North Dak. St. | Rocky Hager | 35-21 | Portland St. | Florence, Ala. |
| 1989 | Mississippi Col. | John Williams | 3-0 | Jacksonville St. | Florence, Ala. |
| 1990 | North Dak. St. | Rocky Hager | 51-11 | Indiana (Pa.) | Florence, Ala. |
| 1991 | Pittsburg St. | Chuck Broyles | 23-6 | Jacksonville St. | Florence, Ala. |
| 1992 | Jacksonville St. | Bill Burgess | 17-13 | Pittsburg St. | Florence, Ala. |

## REGIONAL CHAMPIONSHIP RESULTS

Before 1973, there was no Division II Football Championship. Instead, four regional bowl games were played in order to provide postseason action for what then were called NCAA College Division member institutions. Following are the results of those bowl games:

### EAST (Tangerine Bowl)

| Year | Champion | Coach | Score | Runner-Up | Site |
|---|---|---|---|---|---|
| 1964 | East Caro. | Clarence Stasavich | 14-13 | Massachusetts | Orlando, Fla. |
| 1965 | East Caro. | Clarence Stasavich | 31-0 | Maine | Orlando, Fla. |
| 1966 | Morgan St. | Earl Banks | 14-6 | West Chester | Orlando, Fla. |
| 1967 | Tenn.-Martin | Robert Carroll | 25-8 | West Chester | Orlando, Fla. |

### EAST (Boardwalk Bowl)

| Year | Champion | Coach | Score | Runner-Up | Site |
|---|---|---|---|---|---|
| 1968 | Delaware | Tubby Raymond | 31-24 | Indiana (Pa.) | Atlantic City, N. J. |
| 1969 | Delaware | Tubby Raymond | 31-13 | N. C. Central | Atlantic City, N. J. |
| 1970 | Delaware | Tubby Raymond | 38-23 | Morgan St. | Atlantic City, N. J. |
| 1971 | Delaware | Tubby Raymond | 72-22 | LIU-C. W. Post | Atlantic City, N. J. |
| 1972 | Massachusetts | Dick MacPherson | 35-14 | UC Davis | Atlantic City, N. J. |

### MIDEAST (Grantland Rice Bowl)

| Year | Champion | Coach | Score | Runner-Up | Site |
|---|---|---|---|---|---|
| 1964 | Middle Tenn. St. | Charles Murphy | 20-0 | Muskingum | Murfreesboro, Tenn. |
| 1965 | Ball St. | Ray Louthen | 14-14 | — | Murfreesboro, Tenn. |
| | Tennessee St. | John Merritt | | | |
| 1966 | Tennessee St. | John Merritt | 34-7 | Muskingum | Murfreesboro, Tenn. |
| 1967 | Eastern Ky. | Roy Kidd | 27-13 | Ball St. | Murfreesboro, Tenn. |
| 1968 | Louisiana Tech | Maxie Lambright | 33-13 | Akron | Murfreesboro, Tenn. |
| 1969 | East Tenn. St. | John Bell | 34-14 | Louisiana Tech | Baton Rouge, La. |
| 1970 | Tennessee St. | John Merritt | 26-25 | Southwestern La. | Baton Rouge, La. |
| 1971 | Tennessee St. | John Merritt | 26-23 | McNeese St. | Baton Rouge, La. |
| 1972 | Louisiana Tech | Maxie Lambright | 35-0 | Tennessee Tech | Baton Rouge, La. |

### MIDWEST (Pecan Bowl)

| Year | Champion | Coach | Score | Runner-Up | Site |
|---|---|---|---|---|---|
| 1964 | Northern Iowa | Stan Sheriff | 19-17 | Lamar | Abilene, Texas |
| 1965 | North Dak. St. | Darrell Mudra | 20-7 | Grambling | Abilene, Texas |
| 1966 | North Dak. | Marv Helling | 42-24 | Parsons | Abilene, Texas |
| 1967 | Texas-Arlington | Burley Bearden | 13-0 | North Dak. St. | Abilene, Texas |
| 1968 | North Dak. St. | Ron Erhardt | 23-14 | Arkansas St. | Arlington, Texas |
| 1969 | Arkansas St. | Bennie Ellender | 29-21 | Drake | Arlington, Texas |
| 1970 | Arkansas St. | Bennie Ellender | 38-21 | Central Mo. St. | Arlington, Texas |

### MIDWEST (Pioneer Bowl)

| Year | Champion | Coach | Score | Runner-Up | Site |
|---|---|---|---|---|---|
| 1971 | Louisiana Tech | Maxie Lambright | 14-3 | Eastern Mich. | Wichita Falls, Texas |
| 1972 | Tennessee St. | John Merritt | 29-7 | Drake | Wichita Falls, Texas |

### WEST (Camellia Bowl)

| Year | Champion | Coach | Score | Runner-Up | Site |
|---|---|---|---|---|---|
| 1964 | Montana St. | Jim Sweeney | 28-7 | Cal St. Sacramento | Sacramento, Calif. |
| 1965 | Cal St. Los Angeles | Homer Beatty | 18-10 | UC Santa Barb. | Sacramento, Calif. |
| 1966 | San Diego St. | Don Coryell | 28-7 | Montana St. | Sacramento, Calif. |
| 1967 | San Diego St. | Don Coryell | 27-6 | San Fran. St. | Sacramento, Calif. |
| 1968 | Humboldt St. | Frank VanDeren | 29-14 | Fresno St. | Sacramento, Calif. |
| 1969 | North Dak. St. | Ron Erhardt | 30-3 | Montana | Sacramento, Calif. |
| 1970 | North Dak. St. | Ron Erhardt | 31-16 | Montana | Sacramento, Calif. |
| 1971 | Boise St. | Tony Knap | 32-28 | Cal St. Chico | Sacramento, Calif. |
| 1972 | North Dak. | Jerry Olson | 38-21 | Cal Poly SLO | Sacramento, Calif. |

## 1992 DIVISION II CHAMPIONSHIP RESULTS

**First Round**
Ferris St. 19, Edinboro 15
New Haven 38, West Chester 26
Jacksonville St. 41, Savannah St. 16
North Ala. 33, Hampton 21
Texas A&I 22, Western St. 13
Portland St. 42, UC Davis 28
Pittsburg St. 26, North Dak. 21
North Dak. St. 42, Northeast Mo. St. 7

**Quarterfinals**
New Haven 35, Ferris St. 13
Jacksonville St. 14, North Ala. 12
Portland St. 35, Texas A&I 30
Pittsburg St. 38, North Dak. St. 37 (OT)

**Semifinals**
Jacksonville St. 46, New Haven 35
Pittsburg St. 41, Portland St. 38

**Championship**
Jacksonville St. 17, Pittsburg St. 13

*Division II Championship Results, Records*

# 1992 DIVISION II GAME SUMMARIES

**FIRST-ROUND GAMES (Nov. 21)**

**Ferris St. 19, Edinboro 15**
at Big Rapids, Mich.

| | | | | |
|---|---|---|---|---|
| Edinboro | 3 | 6 | 6 | 0—15 |
| Ferris St. | 3 | 9 | 7 | 0—19 |

FS—Lipke 37 field goal
ED—Joyce 32 field goal
FS—Lipke 28 field goal
ED—Stone fumble recovery in end zone (pass failed)
FS—Pettit 10 pass from Arnold (kick failed)
FS—Diggins 1 run (Lipke kick)
ED—Snyder 1 run (pass failed)
A—825

**New Haven 38, West Chester 26**
at West Chester, Pa.

| | | | | |
|---|---|---|---|---|
| New Haven | 13 | 6 | 13 | 6—38 |
| West Chester | 0 | 14 | 6 | 6—26 |

NH—Joyner-Brown 18 pass from Suhl (Capuano kick)
NH—Willis 46 pass from Suhl (kick failed)
WC—Weaver 22 pass from MacDonald (Smink kick)
NH—Livingston 1 run (kick failed)
WC—Weaver 25 pass from MacDonald (Smink kick)
NH—Livingston 9 run (pass failed)
NH—Joyner-Brown 6 pass from Suhl (Capuano kick)
WC—Goodwin 1 run (pass failed)
WC—Little 4 run (pass failed)
NH—Graham 45 run (pass failed)
A—6,350

**Jacksonville St. 41, Savannah St. 16**
at Jacksonville, Ala.

| | | | | |
|---|---|---|---|---|
| Savannah St. | 0 | 3 | 0 | 13—16 |
| Jacksonville St. | 21 | 10 | 7 | 3—41 |

JS—Robinson 3 run (kick failed)
JS—Bowens 1 run (Bowens run)
JS—Richardson 2 run (Stinnett kick)
SS—Schewe 29 field goal
JS—Stinnett 37 field goal
JS—Gordon 22 run (Stinnett kick)
JS—Lee 37 pass from Robinson (Stinnett kick)
JS—Stinnett 36 field goal
SS—D. Smith 10 pass from Leverett (Schewe kick)
SS—Grant 19 pass from Alexander (kick failed)
A—6,128

**North Ala. 33, Hampton 21**
at Hampton, Va.

| | | | | |
|---|---|---|---|---|
| North Ala. | 6 | 14 | 0 | 13—33 |
| Hampton | 0 | 0 | 7 | 14—21 |

NA—Rush 20 run (kick blocked)
NA—Gross 27 run (run failed)
NA—Satterfield 1 run (Hayes pass from Gross)
HU—Rainy 5 pass from Montgomery (Pitts kick)
NA—Gross 1 run (Scroggins kick)
HU—Harvey 1 run (Pitts kick)
HU—Rainy 11 pass from Montgomery (Pitts kick)
NA—Gross 2 run (run failed)
A—NA

**Texas A&I 22, Western St. 13**
at Kingsville, Texas

| | | | | |
|---|---|---|---|---|
| Western St. | 0 | 13 | 0 | 0—13 |
| Texas A&I | 0 | 7 | 9 | 6—22 |

A&I—Deese 7 run (Cortez kick)
WS—Selanders 33 pass from Smith (Mattingly kick)
WS—Mattingly 19 field goal
WS—Mattingly 22 field goal
A&I—Safety, Thenell stepped out of end zone
A&I—Deese 4 run (Cortez kick)
A&I—Deese 27 run (kick failed)
A—7,000

**Portland St. 42, UC Davis 28**
at Portland, Ore.

| | | | | |
|---|---|---|---|---|
| UC Davis | 7 | 7 | 7 | 7—28 |
| Portland St. | 21 | 14 | 7 | 0—42 |

PS—Palomino 19 pass from Matos (Eberhardt kick)
PS—Hicks 21 pass from Matos (Eberhardt kick)
UCD—Jones 54 run (Fernandez kick)
PS—Aho 26 run (Eberhardt kick)
PS—Palomino 8 pass from Matos (Eberhardt kick)
UCD—Hasson 1 run (Fernandez kick)
PS—Newson 8 pass from Matos (Eberhardt kick)
UCD—Hasson 1 run (Fernandez kick)
PS—Aho 10 run (Eberhardt kick)
UCD—Ichiyama 5 run (Fernandez kick)
A—7,316

**Pittsburg St. 26, North Dak. 21**
at Pittsburg, Kan.

| | | | | |
|---|---|---|---|---|
| **North Dak.** | 6 | 8 | 0 | 7—21 |
| **Pittsburg St.** | 13 | 0 | 6 | 7—26 |

PS—Moore 1 run (Wood kick)
ND—Burnell 2 run (kick failed)
PS—Hutchins 13 run (run failed)
ND—Burnell 2 run (Schumacher pass from Wahl)
PS—Moore 1 run (pass failed)
PS—Moore 3 run (Wood kick)
ND—Gelinske 40 pass from Wahl (Dahlem kick)
A—4,000

**North Dak. St. 42, Northeast Mo. St. 7**
at Fargo, N. D.

| | | | | |
|---|---|---|---|---|
| **Northeast Mo. St.** | 0 | 0 | 7 | 0— 7 |
| **North Dak. St.** | 14 | 14 | 0 | 14—42 |

NDS—Erickson 12 run (Millfors kick)
NDS—Hansen 9 run (Millfors kick)
NDS—Beachy 12 run (Millfors kick)
NDS—Hansen 44 run (Millfors kick)
NEM—Walker 32 pass from Thompson (Rudel kick)
NDS—McDonald 16 pass from Beachy (Millfors kick)
NDS—Sanchez 29 run (Millfors kick)
A—6,230

**QUARTERFINAL GAMES (Nov. 28)**

**New Haven 35, Ferris St. 13**
at New Haven, Conn.

| | | | | |
|---|---|---|---|---|
| **Ferris St.** | 0 | 6 | 0 | 7—13 |
| **New Haven** | 7 | 0 | 21 | 7—35 |

NH—Graham 52 run (Capuano kick)
FS—Lipke 24 field goal
FS—Lipke 38 field goal
NH—Livingston 1 run (Capuano kick)
NH—Raba 4 run (Capuano kick)
NH—Davis 53 pass from Willis (Capuano kick)
FS—Koutsopoulos 34 pass from Morgan (Lipke kick)
NH—Willis 99 pass from Suhl (Capuano kick)
A—8,712

**Jacksonville St. 14, North Ala. 12**
at Florence, Ala.

| | | | | |
|---|---|---|---|---|
| **Jacksonville St.** | 7 | 7 | 0 | 0—14 |
| **North Ala.** | 6 | 0 | 0 | 6—12 |

NA—Satterfield 1 run (kick blocked)
JS—Bowens 1 run (Stinnett kick)
JS—Robinson 1 run (Stinnett kick)
NA—Gross 4 run (run failed)
A—5,784

**Portland St. 35, Texas A&I 30**
at Portland, Ore.

| | | | | |
|---|---|---|---|---|
| **Texas A&I** | 3 | 7 | 13 | 7—30 |
| **Portland St.** | 21 | 7 | 0 | 7—35 |

PS—Aho 10 run (Eberhardt kick)
A&I—Cortez 29 field goal
PS—Newson 30 pass from Matos (Eberhardt kick)
PS—James 24 pass from Matos (Eberhardt kick)
A&I—Rodgers 77 fumble return (Cortez kick)
PS—Aho 1 run (Eberhardt kick)
A&I—Deese 1 run (Cortez kick)
A&I—Alexander 6 run (run failed)
PS—Newson 20 pass from Matos (Eberhardt kick)
A&I—Alexander 2 run (Cortez kick)
A—12,657

*Division II Championship Results, Records*

**Pittsburg St. 38, North Dak. St. 37 (OT)**
at Pittsburg, Kan.

| | | | | | |
|---|---|---|---|---|---|
| North Dak. St. | 7 | 7 | 10 | 7 | 6—37 |
| Pittsburg St. | 7 | 7 | 6 | 11 | 7—38 |

NDS—Erickson 4 run (Millfors kick)
PS—Moore 2 run (Wood kick)
PS—Moore 1 run (Wood kick)
NDS—Beachy 3 run (Millfors kick)
NDS—Carlson 30 run (Millfors kick)
NDS—Millfors 26 field goal
PS—Moore 1 run (kick failed)
NDS—Carlson 18 run (Millfors kick)
PS—Moore 13 run (Moore run)
PS—Wood 39 field goal
PS—Moore 1 run (Wood kick)
NDS—Geren 26 pass from Beachy (run failed)
A—5,200

**SEMIFINAL GAMES (Dec. 5)**
**Jacksonville St. 46, New Haven 35**
at Jacksonville, Ala.

| | | | | | |
|---|---|---|---|---|---|
| New Haven | 0 | 14 | 7 | 14—35 |
| Jacksonville St. | 0 | 21 | 7 | 18—46 |

JS—Lee 82 punt return (Stinnett kick)
JS—Richardson 1 run (Stinnett kick)
JS—Lee 90 pass from Robinson (Stinnett kick)
NH—Joyner-Brown 13 pass from Suhl (Capuano kick)
NH—Graham 11 run (Capuano kick)
JS—Richardson 1 run (Stinnett kick)
NH—Willis 13 pass from Suhl (Capuano kick)
NH—Joyner-Brown 12 pass from Suhl (Capuano kick)
JS—Lee 13 run (kick failed)
NH—Graham 9 run (Capuano kick)
JS—Lee 39 run (run failed)
JS—Richardson 35 run (run failed)
A—5,804

**Pittsburg St. 41, Portland St. 38**
at Portland Ore.

| | | | | | |
|---|---|---|---|---|---|
| Pittsburg St. | 13 | 6 | 7 | 15—41 |
| Portland St. | 21 | 10 | 7 | 0—38 |

PIT—Tobin 78 run (Wood kick)
POR—Bledsoe 2 run (Eberhardt kick)
POR—Aho 37 pass from Matos (Eberhardt kick)
POR—James 14 run (Eberhardt kick)
PIT—Moore 80 run (pass failed)
POR—Aho 1 run (Eberhardt kick)
PIT—Moore 36 run (run failed)
POR—Eberhardt 32 field goal
PIT—Moore 1 run (Wood kick)
POR—Palomino 18 pass from Matos (Eberhardt kick)
PIT—Moore 2 run (Wood kick)
PIT—Moore 93 run (Moore run)
A—13,180

# CHAMPIONSHIP RECORDS
## INDIVIDUAL: SINGLE GAME

**Net Yards Rushing**
379—Ronald Moore, Pittsburg St. (41) vs. Portland St. (38), 12-5-92.

**Rushes Attempted**
51—Terry Morrow, Central St. (Ohio) (31) vs. Towson St. (0), 11-28-86.

**Touchdowns by Rushing**
5—Ronald Moore, Pittsburg St. (38) vs. North Dak. St. (37), OT, 11-28-92; Ronald Moore, Pittsburg St. (41) vs. Portland St. (38), 12-5-92.

**Net Yards Passing**
443—Tom Bertoldi, Northern Mich. (55) vs. Elizabeth City St. (6), 11-28-81.

**Passes Attempted**
59—Bob Biggs, UC Davis (14) vs. Massachusetts (35), 12-9-72.

**Passes Completed**
32—Darren Del'Andrae, Portland St. (56) vs. West Chester (50), 3 OT, 11-18-89.

**Passes Had Intercepted**
7—George Coussan, Southwestern La. (25) vs. Tennessee St. (26), 12-12-70.

**Touchdown Passes Completed**
6—Darren Del'Andrae, Portland St. (56) vs. West Chester (50), 3 OT, 11-18-89.

**Completion Percentage (Min. 8 Attempts)**
.833—Tony Aliucci, Indiana (Pa.) (56) vs. Virginia Union (7), 11-23-91 (10 of 12).

**Net Yards Rushing and Passing**
444—Tom Bertoldi, Northern Mich. (55) vs. Elizabeth City St. (6), 11-28-81.

**Number of Rushing and Passing Plays**
63—Bob Biggs, UC Davis (14) vs. Massachusetts (35), 12-9-72.

**Punting Average (Min. 3 Punts)**
53.7—Chris Humes, UC Davis (23) vs. Angelo St. (28), 11-18-89.

**Number of Punts**
12—Dan Gentry, Tennessee Tech (0) vs. Louisiana Tech (35), 12-9-72.

**Passes Caught**
14—Don Hutt, Boise St. (34) vs. Louisiana Tech (38), 12-8-73.

**Net Yards Receiving**
220—Steve Hansley, Northwest Mo. St. (15) vs. Nebraska-Omaha (28), 11-24-84.

**Touchdown Passes Caught**
4—Steve Kreider, Lehigh (30) vs. Massachusetts (23), 11-26-77; Scott Asman, West Chester (50) vs. Portland St. (56), 3 OT, 11-18-89.

**Passes Intercepted**
5—Don Pinson, Tennessee St. (26) vs. Southwestern La. (25), 12-12-70.

**Yards Gained on Interception Returns**
113—Darren Ryals, Millersville (27) vs. Indiana (Pa.) (24), 2 returns for 53- and 60-yard TDs,

11-19-88.

**Yards Gained on Punt Returns**
138—Rick Caswell, Western Ky. (14) vs. New Hampshire (3), 12-6-75.

**Yards Gained on Kickoff Returns**
182—Larry Anderson, LIU-C. W. Post (22) vs. Delaware (72), 12-11-71.

**Points**
32—Ronald Moore, Pittsburg St. (38) vs. North Dak. St. (37), OT, 11-28-92; Ronald Moore, Pittsburg St. (41) vs. Portland St. (38), 12-5-92.

**Touchdowns**
5—Ronald Moore, Pittsburg St. (38) vs. North Dak. St. (37), OT, 11-28-92; Ronald Moore, Pittsburg St. (41) vs. Portland St. (38), 12-5-92.

**Extra Points**
10—Larry Washington, Delaware (72) vs. LIU-C. W. Post (22), 12-11-71.

**Field Goals**
4—Mario Ferretti, Northern Mich. (55) vs. Elizabeth City St. (6), 11-28-81; Ken Kubisz, North Dak. St. (26) vs. UC Davis (17), 12-3-83.

## INDIVIDUAL: TOURNAMENT

**Net Yards Rushing**
721—Ronald Moore, Pittsburg St., 1992 (108 vs. North Dak., 151 vs. North Dak. St., 379 vs. Portland St., 83 vs. Jacksonville St.).

**Rushes Attempted**
117—Ronald Moore, Pittsburg St., 1992 (29 vs. North Dak., 31 vs. North Dak. St., 37 vs. Portland St., 20 vs. Jacksonville St.).

**Net Yards Passing**
1,226—Chris Crawford, Portland St., 1988 (248 vs. Bowie St., 375 vs. Jacksonville St., 270 vs. Texas A&I, 333 vs. North Dak. St.).

**Passes Attempted**
139—Chris Crawford, Portland St., 1988 (31 vs. Bowie St., 41 vs. Jacksonville St., 32 vs. Texas A&I, 35 vs. North Dak. St.).

**Passes Completed**
94—Chris Crawford, Portland St., 1988 (20 vs. Bowie St., 27 vs. Jacksonville St., 25 vs. Texas A&I, 22 vs. North Dak. St.).

**Touchdown Passes Completed**
10—Chris Crawford, Portland St., 1988 (2 vs. Bowie St., 2 vs. Jacksonville St., 3 vs. Texas A&I, 3 vs. North Dak. St.).

**Completion Percentage (Min. 2 Games)**
.824—Mike Turk, Troy St., 1984, 14 of 17 (4-5

vs. Central St., Ohio, 5-5 vs. Towson St., 5-7 vs. North Dak. St.).

**Passes Had Intercepted**
9—Dennis Tomek, Western Ky., 1973 (0 vs. Lehigh, 6 vs. Grambling, 3 vs. Louisiana Tech).

**Passes Caught**
27—Don Hutt, Boise St., 1973 (13 vs. South Dak., 14 vs. Louisiana Tech).

**Net Yards Receiving**
452—Henry Newson, Portland St., 1991 (94 vs. Northern Colo., 209 vs. Mankato St., 149 vs. Pittsburg St.).

**Touchdown Passes Caught**
7—Steve Kreider, Lehigh, 1977 (4 vs. Massachusetts, 1 vs. UC Davis, 2 vs. Jacksonville St.).

**Points**
88—Ronald Moore, Pittsburg St., 1992 (18 vs. North Dak., 32 vs. North Dak. St., 32 vs. Portland St., 6 vs. Jacksonville St.).

**Touchdowns**
14—Ronald Moore, Pittsburg St., 1992 (3 vs. North Dak., 5 vs. North Dak. St., 5 vs. Portland St., 1 vs. Jacksonville St.).

## INDIVIDUAL: LONGEST PLAYS

**Longest Rush**
93—Ronald Moore, Pittsburg St. (41) vs. Portland St. (38), 12-5-92, TD.

**Longest Pass Completion**
99—Ken Suhl to Tony Willis, New Haven (35) vs. Ferris St. (13), 11-28-92, TD.

**Longest Field Goal**
50—Ted Clem, Troy St. (18) vs. North Dak. St. (17), 12-8-84.

**Longest Punt**
76—Chris Humes, UC Davis (23) vs. Angelo St. (28), 11-18-89.

**Longest Punt Return**
91—Winford Wilborn, Louisiana Tech (14) vs. Eastern Mich. (3), 12-11-71, TD.

**Longest Kickoff Return**
100—Ken Bowles, Nevada-Las Vegas (6) vs. Akron (26), 11-26-76, TD.

**Longest Interception Return**
100—Charles Harris, Jacksonville St. (34) vs. Northeast Mo. St. (21), 11-27-82, TD.

**Longest Fumble Return**
93—Ray Neal, Middle Tenn. St. (20) vs. Muskingum (0), 12-12-64, TD.

# TEAM: SINGLE GAME

**First Downs**
34—Delaware (72) vs. LIU-C. W. Post (22), 12-11-71; Delaware (60) vs. Mississippi Col. (10), 12-1-79; Cal St. Sacramento (56) vs. N. C. Central (7), 11-26-88.

**First Downs by Rushing**
27—Delaware (72) vs. LIU-C. W. Post (22), 12-11-71.

**First Downs by Passing**
23—Central Fla. (10) vs. Troy St. (31), 12-5-87; Portland St. (56) vs. West Chester (50), 3 OT, 11-18-89.

**Net Yards Rushing**
566—Jacksonville St. (63) vs. West Chester (24), 11-19-88.

**Rushes Attempted**
84—Southwest Tex. St. (34) vs. UC Davis (9), 12-11-82.

**Net Yards Passing**
464—Northern Mich. (55) vs. Elizabeth City St. (6), 11-28-81.

**Passes Attempted**
60—San Fran. St. (6) vs. San Diego St. (27), 12-9-67; Central Fla. (10) vs. Troy St. (31), 12-5-87.

**Passes Completed**
36—Central Fla. (10) vs. Troy St. (31), 12-5-87.

**Completion Percentage (Min. 10 Attempts)**
.813—Delaware (60) vs. Mississippi Col. (10), 12-1-79 (13 of 16).

**Passes Had Intercepted**
8—Southwestern La. (25) vs. Tennessee St. (26), 12-12-70.

**Net Yards Rushing and Passing**
695—Northern Mich. (55) vs. Elizabeth City St. (6), 11-28-81.

**Rushing and Passing Plays**
98—Northern Mich. (55) vs. Elizabeth City St. (6), 11-28-81.

**Punting Average**
53.7—UC Davis (23) vs. Angelo St. (28), 11-18-89.

**Number of Punts**
12—Tennessee Tech (0) vs. Louisiana Tech (35), 12-9-72; Delaware (8) vs. Grambling (17), 12-1-73; Western Ky. (0) vs. Louisiana Tech (34), 12-15-73.

**Punts Had Blocked**
2—Delaware (31) vs. Indiana (Pa.) (24), 12-14-68; Humboldt St. (29) vs. Fresno St. (14), 12-14-68; Northeast Mo. St. (21) vs. Jacksonville St. (34), 11-27-82.

**Yards Gained on Punt Returns**
140—Southwest Tex. St. (62) vs. Northern Mich. (0), 12-5-81.

**Yards Gained on Kickoff Returns**
251—LIU-C. W. Post (22) vs. Delaware (72), 12-11-71.

**Yards Gained on Interception Returns**
131—Millersville (27) vs. Indiana (Pa.) (24), 11-19-88.

**Yards Penalized**
166—San Diego St. (27) vs. San Fran. St. (6), 12-9-67.

**Number of Penalties**
21—San Diego St. (27) vs. San Fran. St. (6), 12-9-67.

**Fumbles**
10—Winston-Salem (0) vs. Delaware (41), 12-2-78.

**Fumbles Lost**
7—Louisiana Tech (10) vs. Western Caro. (7), 11-30-74.

**Points**
72—Delaware vs. LIU-C. W. Post (22), 12-11-72.

# TEAM: TOURNAMENT

**First Downs**
98—North Dak. St., 1990 (27 vs. Northern Colo., 23 vs. Cal Poly SLO, 25 vs. Pittsburg St., 23 vs. Indiana, Pa.).

**Net Yards Rushing**
1,660—North Dak. St., 1988 (474 vs. Augustana, S.D., 434 vs. Millersville, 413 vs. Cal St. Sacramento, 339 vs. Portland St.).

**Net Yards Passing**
1,226—Portland St., 1988 (248 vs. Bowie St., 375 vs. Jacksonville St., 270 vs. Texas A&I, 333 vs. North Dak. St.).

**Net Yards Rushing and Passing**
1,969—North Dak. St., 1990 (455 vs. Northern Colo., 463 vs. Cal Poly SLO, 424 vs. Pittsburg St., 627 vs. Indiana, Pa.).

**Passes Attempted**
139—Portland St., 1988 (31 vs. Bowie St., 41 vs. Jacksonville St., 32 vs. Texas A&I, 35 vs. North Dak. St.).

**Passes Completed**
94—Portland St., 1988 (20 vs. Bowie St., 27 vs. Jacksonville St., 25 vs. Texas A&I, 22 vs. North Dak. St.).

**Passes Had Intercepted**
10—Western Ky., 1973 (0 vs. Lehigh, 6 vs. Grambling, 4 vs. Louisiana Tech).

**Number of Punts**
29—Western Ky., 1973 (6 vs. Lehigh, 11 vs. Grambling, 12 vs. Louisiana Tech).

**Yards Penalized**
355—New Haven, 1992 (114 vs. West Chester, 146 vs. Ferris St., 95 vs. Jacksonville St.).

**Fumbles**
16—Delaware, 1978 (8 vs. Jacksonville St., 2 vs. Winston-Salem, 6 vs. Eastern Ill.).

**Fumbles Lost**
12—Delaware, 1978 (6 vs. Jacksonville St., 2 vs. Winston-Salem, 4 vs. Eastern Ill.).

**Points**
162—North Dak. St., 1988 (49 vs. Augustana, S.D., 36 vs. Millersville, 42 vs. Cal St. Sacramento, 35 vs. Portland St.).

# YEAR-BY-YEAR DIVISION II CHAMPIONSHIP RESULTS

| Year (Number of Teams) | Coach | Record | Result |
|---|---|---|---|
| **1973 (8)** | | | |
| Louisiana Tech.................. | Maxie Lambright | 3-0 | Champion |
| Western Ky..................... | Jimmy Feix | 2-1 | Second |
| Boise St....................... | Tony Knap | 1-1 | Semifinalist |
| Grambling...................... | Eddie Robinson | 1-1 | Semifinalist |
| Delaware....................... | Tubby Raymond | 0-1 | Lost 1st Round |
| Lehigh......................... | Fred Dunlap | 0-1 | Lost 1st Round |
| South Dak...................... | Joe Salem | 0-1 | Lost 1st Round |
| Western Ill.................... | Darrell Mudra | 0-1 | Lost 1st Round |
| **1974 (8)** | | | |
| Central Mich................... | Roy Kramer | 3-0 | Champion |
| Delaware....................... | Tubby Raymond | 2-1 | Second |
| Louisiana Tech................. | Maxie Lambright | 1-1 | Semifinalist |
| Nevada-Las Vegas............... | Ron Meyer | 1-1 | Semifinalist |
| Alcorn St...................... | Marino Casem | 0-1 | Lost 1st Round |
| Boise St....................... | Tony Knap | 0-1 | Lost 1st Round |
| Western Caro................... | Bob Waters | 0-1 | Lost 1st Round |
| Youngstown St.................. | Rey Dempsey | 0-1 | Lost 1st Round |
| **1975 (8)** | | | |
| Northern Mich.................. | Gil Krueger | 3-0 | Champion |
| Western Ky..................... | Jimmy Feix | 2-1 | Second |
| Livingston..................... | Jim King | 1-1 | Semifinalist |
| New Hampshire.................. | Bill Bowes | 1-1 | Semifinalist |
| Boise St....................... | Tony Knap | 0-1 | Lost 1st Round |
| Lehigh......................... | Fred Dunlap | 0-1 | Lost 1st Round |
| North Dak...................... | Jerry Olson | 0-1 | Lost 1st Round |
| Northern Iowa.................. | Stan Sheriff | 0-1 | Lost 1st Round |
| **1976 (8)** | | | |
| Montana St..................... | Sonny Holland | 3-0 | Champion |
| Akron.......................... | Jim Dennison | 2-1 | Second |
| North Dak. St.................. | Jim Wacker | 1-1 | Semifinalist |
| Northern Mich.................. | Gil Krueger | 1-1 | Semifinalist |
| Delaware....................... | Tubby Raymond | 0-1 | Lost 1st Round |
| Eastern Ky..................... | Roy Kidd | 0-1 | Lost 1st Round |
| Nevada-Las Vegas............... | Tony Knap | 0-1 | Lost 1st Round |
| New Hampshire.................. | Bill Bowes | 0-1 | Lost 1st Round |
| **1977 (8)** | | | |
| Lehigh......................... | John Whitehead | 3-0 | Champion |
| Jacksonville St................ | Jim Fuller | 2-1 | Second |
| North Dak. St.................. | Jim Wacker | 1-1 | Semifinalist |
| UC Davis....................... | Jim Sochor | 1-1 | Semifinalist |
| Bethune-Cookman................ | Andy Hinson | 0-1 | Lost 1st Round |
| Massachusetts.................. | Dick MacPherson | 0-1 | Lost 1st Round |
| Northern Ariz.................. | Joe Salem | 0-1 | Lost 1st Round |
| Northern Mich.................. | Gil Krueger | 0-1 | Lost 1st Round |
| **1978 (8)** | | | |
| Eastern Ill.................... | Darrell Mudra | 3-0 | Champion |
| Delaware....................... | Tubby Raymond | 2-1 | Second |
| Winston-Salem.................. | Bill Hayes | 1-1 | Semifinalist |
| Youngstown St.................. | Bill Narduzzi | 1-1 | Semifinalist |
| Cal Poly SLO .................. | Joe Harper | 0-1 | Lost 1st Round |
| Jacksonville St................ | Jim Fuller | 0-1 | Lost 1st Round |
| Nebraska-Omaha................. | Sandy Buda | 0-1 | Lost 1st Round |
| UC Davis....................... | Jim Sochor | 0-1 | Lost 1st Round |
| **1979 (8)** | | | |
| Delaware....................... | Tubby Raymond | 3-0 | Champion |
| Youngstown St.................. | Bill Narduzzi | 2-1 | Second |
| Alabama A&M.................... | Ray Greene | 1-1 | Semifinalist |
| Mississippi Col................ | John Williams | 1-1 | Semifinalist |
| Morgan St...................... | Clarence Thomas | 0-1 | Lost 1st Round |
| North Dak...................... | Gene Murphy | 0-1 | Lost 1st Round |
| South Dak. St.................. | John Gregory | 0-1 | Lost 1st Round |
| Virginia Union................. | Willard Bailey | 0-1 | Lost 1st Round |
| **1980 (8)** | | | |
| Cal Poly SLO .................. | Joe Harper | 3-0 | Champion |
| Eastern Ill.................... | Darrell Mudra | 2-1 | Second |
| North Ala...................... | Wayne Grubb | 1-1 | Semifinalist |
| Santa Clara.................... | Pat Malley | 1-1 | Semifinalist |

*Division II Championship Results, Records*

| Year (Number of Teams) | Coach | Record | Result |
|---|---|---|---|
| Jacksonville St................ | Jim Fuller | 0-1 | Lost 1st Round |
| Northern Colo................ | Bob Blasi | 0-1 | Lost 1st Round |
| Northern Mich................ | Bill Rademacher | 0-1 | Lost 1st Round |
| Virginia Union................ | Willard Bailey | 0-1 | Lost 1st Round |
| **1981 (8)** | | | |
| Southwest Tex. St............. | Jim Wacker | 3-0 | Champion |
| North Dak. St................. | Don Morton | 2-1 | Second |
| Northern Mich................ | Bill Rademacher | 1-1 | Semifinalist |
| Shippensburg................. | Vito Ragazzo | 1-1 | Semifinalist |
| Elizabeth City St.............. | Johnnie Walton | 0-1 | Lost 1st Round |
| Jacksonville St................ | Jim Fuller | 0-1 | Lost 1st Round |
| Puget Sound.................. | Ron Simonson | 0-1 | Lost 1st Round |
| Virginia Union................ | Willard Bailey | 0-1 | Lost 1st Round |
| **1982 (8)** | | | |
| Southwest Tex. St............. | Jim Wacker | 3-0 | Champion |
| UC Davis..................... | Jim Sochor | 2-1 | Second |
| Jacksonville St................ | Jim Fuller | 1-1 | Semifinalist |
| North Dak. St................. | Don Morton | 1-1 | Semifinalist |
| Fort Valley St................. | Doug Porter | 0-1 | Lost 1st Round |
| Northeast Mo. St.............. | Bruce Craddock | 0-1 | Lost 1st Round |
| Northern Mich................ | Bill Rademacher | 0-1 | Lost 1st Round |
| Virginia Union................ | Willard Bailey | 0-1 | Lost 1st Round |
| **1983 (8)** | | | |
| North Dak. St................. | Don Morton | 3-0 | Champion |
| Central St. (Ohio)............. | Billy Joe | 2-1 | Second |
| North Ala..................... | Wayne Grubb | 1-1 | Semifinalist |
| UC Davis..................... | Jim Sochor | 1-1 | Semifinalist |
| Butler........................ | Bill Sylvester | 0-1 | Lost 1st Round |
| Southwest Tex. St............. | John O'Hara | 0-1 | Lost 1st Round |
| Towson St.................... | Phil Albert | 0-1 | Lost 1st Round |
| Virginia Union................ | Willard Bailey | 0-1 | Lost 1st Round |
| **1984 (8)** | | | |
| Troy St....................... | Chan Gailey | 3-0 | Champion |
| North Dak. St................. | Don Morton | 2-1 | Second |
| Nebraska-Omaha.............. | Sandy Buda | 1-1 | Semifinalist |
| Towson St.................... | Phil Albert | 1-1 | Semifinalist |
| Central St. (Ohio)............. | Billy Joe | 0-1 | Lost 1st Round |
| Norfolk St..................... | Willard Bailey | 0-1 | Lost 1st Round |
| Northwest Mo. St.............. | Vern Thomsen | 0-1 | Lost 1st Round |
| UC Davis..................... | Jim Sochor | 0-1 | Lost 1st Round |
| **1985 (8)** | | | |
| North Dak. St................. | Earle Solomonson | 3-0 | Champion |
| North Ala..................... | Wayne Grubb | 2-1 | Second |
| Bloomsburg.................. | George Landis | 1-1 | Semifinalist |
| South Dak.................... | Dave Triplett | 1-1 | Semifinalist |
| Central St. (Ohio)............. | Billy Joe | 0-1 | Lost 1st Round |
| Fort Valley St................. | Gerald Walker | 0-1 | Lost 1st Round |
| Hampton...................... | Fred Freeman | 0-1 | Lost 1st Round |
| UC Davis..................... | Jim Sochor | 0-1 | Lost 1st Round |
| **1986 (8)** | | | |
| North Dak. St................. | Earle Solomonson | 3-0 | Champion |
| South Dak.................... | Dave Triplett | 2-1 | Second |
| Central St. (Ohio)............. | Billy Joe | 1-1 | Semifinalist |
| Troy St....................... | Rick Rhodes | 1-1 | Semifinalist |
| Ashland...................... | Fred Martinelli | 0-1 | Lost 1st Round |
| Towson St.................... | Phil Albert | 0-1 | Lost 1st Round |
| UC Davis..................... | Jim Sochor | 0-1 | Lost 1st Round |
| Virginia Union................ | Joe Taylor | 0-1 | Lost 1st Round |
| **1987 (8)** | | | |
| Troy St....................... | Rick Rhodes | 3-0 | Champion |
| Portland St................... | Pokey Allen | 2-1 | Second |
| Central Fla................... | Gene McDowell | 1-1 | Semifinalist |
| Northern Mich................ | Herb Grenke | 1-1 | Semifinalist |
| Angelo St..................... | Jerry Vandergriff | 0-1 | Lost 1st Round |
| Indiana (Pa.)................. | Frank Cignetti | 0-1 | Lost 1st Round |
| Mankato St................... | Dan Runkle | 0-1 | Lost 1st Round |
| Winston-Salem............... | Bill Hayes | 0-1 | Lost 1st Round |
| **1988 (16)** | | | |
| North Dak. St................. | Rocky Hager | 4-0 | Champion |

| Year (Number of Teams) | Coach | Record | Result |
|---|---|---|---|
| Portland St. | Pokey Allen | 3-1 | Second |
| Cal St. Sacramento | Bob Mattos | 2-1 | Semifinalist |
| Texas A&I | Ron Harms | 2-1 | Semifinalist |
| Jacksonville St. | Bill Burgess | 1-1 | Quarterfinalist |
| Millersville | Gene Carpenter | 1-1 | Quarterfinalist |
| N. C. Central | Henry Lattimore | 1-1 | Quarterfinalist |
| Tenn.-Martin | Don McLeary | 1-1 | Quarterfinalist |
| Augustana (S. D.) | Jim Heinitz | 0-1 | Lost 1st Round |
| Bowie St. | Sanders Shiver | 0-1 | Lost 1st Round |
| Butler | Bill Lynch | 0-1 | Lost 1st Round |
| Indiana (Pa.) | Frank Cignetti | 0-1 | Lost 1st Round |
| Mississippi Col. | John Williams | 0-1 | Lost 1st Round |
| UC Davis | Jim Sochor | 0-1 | Lost 1st Round |
| West Chester | Danny Hale | 0-1 | Lost 1st Round |
| Winston-Salem | Pete Richardson | 0-1 | Lost 1st Round |
| **1989 (16)** | | | |
| Mississippi Col. | John Williams | 4-0 | Champion |
| Jacksonville St. | Bill Burgess | 3-1 | Second |
| Angelo St. | Jerry Vandergriff | 2-1 | Semifinalist |
| Indiana (Pa.) | Frank Cignetti | 2-1 | Semifinalist |
| North Dak. St. | Rocky Hager | 1-1 | Quarterfinalist |
| Pittsburg St. | Dennis Franchione | 1-1 | Quarterfinalist |
| Portland St. | Pokey Allen | 1-1 | Quarterfinalist |
| St. Cloud St. | Noel Martin | 1-1 | Quarterfinalist |
| Alabama A&M | George Pugh | 0-1 | Lost 1st Round |
| Augustana (S. D.) | Jim Heinitz | 0-1 | Lost 1st Round |
| Edinboro | Tom Hollman | 0-1 | Lost 1st Round |
| Grand Valley St. | Tom Beck | 0-1 | Lost 1st Round |
| Northwest Mo. St. | Bud Elliott | 0-1 | Lost 1st Round |
| Texas A&I | Ron Harms | 0-1 | Lost 1st Round |
| UC Davis | Bob Foster | 0-1 | Lost 1st Round |
| West Chester | Rick Daniels | 0-1 | Lost 1st Round |
| **1990 (16)** | | | |
| North Dak. St. | Rocky Hager | 4-0 | Champion |
| Indiana (Pa.) | Frank Cignetti | 3-1 | Second |
| Mississippi Col. | John Williams | 2-1 | Semifinalist |
| Pittsburg St. | Chuck Broyles | 2-1 | Semifinalist |
| Cal Poly SLO | Lyle Setencich | 1-1 | Quarterfinalist |
| East Tex. St. | Eddie Vowell | 1-1 | Quarterfinalist |
| Edinboro | Tom Hollman | 1-1 | Quarterfinalist |
| Jacksonville St. | Bill Burgess | 1-1 | Quarterfinalist |
| Cal St. Northridge | Bob Burt | 0-1 | Lost 1st Round |
| Grand Valley St. | Tom Beck | 0-1 | Lost 1st Round |
| North Ala. | Bobby Wallace | 0-1 | Lost 1st Round |
| Northeast Mo. St. | Eric Holm | 0-1 | Lost 1st Round |
| Northern Colo. | Joe Glenn | 0-1 | Lost 1st Round |
| Virginia Union | Joe Taylor | 0-1 | Lost 1st Round |
| Winston-Salem | Pete Richardson | 0-1 | Lost 1st Round |
| Wofford | Mike Ayers | 0-1 | Lost 1st Round |
| **1991 (16)** | | | |
| Pittsburg St. | Chuck Broyles | 4-0 | Champion |
| Jacksonville St. | Bill Burgess | 3-1 | Second |
| Indiana (Pa.) | Frank Cignetti | 2-1 | Semifinalist |
| Portland St. | Pokey Allen | 2-1 | Semifinalist |
| East Tex. St. | Eddie Vowell | 1-1 | Quarterfinalist |
| Mankato St. | Dan Runkle | 1-1 | Quarterfinalist |
| Mississippi Col. | Terry McMillan | 1-1 | Quarterfinalist |
| Shippensburg | Rocky Rees | 1-1 | Quarterfinalist |
| Butler | Bob Bartolomeo | 0-1 | Lost 1st Round |
| East Stroudsburg | Dennis Douds | 0-1 | Lost 1st Round |
| Grand Valley St. | Brian Kelly | 0-1 | Lost 1st Round |
| North Dak. St. | Rocky Hager | 0-1 | Lost 1st Round |
| Northern Colo. | Joe Glenn | 0-1 | Lost 1st Round |
| Virginia Union | Joe Taylor | 0-1 | Lost 1st Round |
| Winston-Salem | Pete Richardson | 0-1 | Lost 1st Round |
| Wofford | Mike Ayers | 0-1 | Lost 1st Round |
| **1992 (16)** | | | |
| Jacksonville St. | Bill Burgess | 4-0 | Champion |
| Pittsburg St. | Chuck Broyles | 3-1 | Second |

*Division II Championship Results, Records*                                      585

| Team | Coach | Record | Result |
|------|-------|--------|--------|
| New Haven................... | Mark Whipple | 2-1 | Semifinalist |
| Portland St..................... | Pokey Allen | 2-1 | Semifinalist |
| Ferris St....................... | Keith Otterbein | 1-1 | Quarterfinalist |
| North Ala..................... | Bobby Wallace | 1-1 | Quarterfinalist |
| North Dak. St.................. | Rocky Hager | 1-1 | Quarterfinalist |
| Texas A&I..................... | Ron Harms | 1-1 | Quarterfinalist |
| Edinboro...................... | Tom Hollman | 0-1 | Lost 1st Round |
| Hampton...................... | Joe Taylor | 0-1 | Lost 1st Round |
| North Dak..................... | Roger Thomas | 0-1 | Lost 1st Round |
| Northeast Mo. St.............. | Eric Holm | 0-1 | Lost 1st Round |
| Savannah St................... | Bill Davis | 0-1 | Lost 1st Round |
| UC Davis..................... | Bob Foster | 0-1 | Lost 1st Round |
| West Chester................. | Rick Daniels | 0-1 | Lost 1st Round |
| Western St.................... | Carl Iverson | 0-1 | Lost 1st Round |

## DIVISION II CHAMPIONSHIP
## ALL-TIME RECORD OF EACH COLLEGE
## COACH-BY-COACH, 1973-92 (79 Colleges)

| | Yrs | Won | Lost | CH | 2D |
|---|---|---|---|---|---|
| **AKRON** | | | | | |
| Jim Dennison (Wooster '60) 76-2D................ | 1 | 2 | 1 | 0 | 1 |
| **ALABAMA A&M** | | | | | |
| Ray Greene (Akron '63) 79....................... | 1 | 1 | 1 | 0 | 0 |
| George Pugh (Alabama '76) 89................... | 1 | 0 | 1 | 0 | 0 |
| TOTAL | 2 | 1 | 2 | 0 | 0 |
| **ALCORN ST.** | | | | | |
| Marino Casem (Xavier, La. '56) 74................ | 1 | 0 | 1 | 0 | 0 |
| **ANGELO ST.** | | | | | |
| Jerry Vandergriff (Corpus Christi '65) 87, 89........ | 2 | 2 | 2 | 0 | 0 |
| **ASHLAND** | | | | | |
| Fred Martinelli (Otterbein '51) 86................... | 1 | 0 | 1 | 0 | 0 |
| **AUGUSTANA (S. D.)** | | | | | |
| Jim Heinitz (South Dak. St. '72) 88, 89............. | 2 | 0 | 2 | 0 | 0 |
| **BETHUNE-COOKMAN** | | | | | |
| Andy Hinson (Bethune-Cookman '53) 77........... | 1 | 0 | 1 | 0 | 0 |
| **BLOOMSBURG** | | | | | |
| George Landis (Penn St. '71) 85.................. | 1 | 1 | 1 | 0 | 0 |
| **BOISE ST.** | | | | | |
| Tony Knap (Idaho '39) 73, 74, 75................. | 3 | 1 | 3 | 0 | 0 |
| **BOWIE ST.** | | | | | |
| Sanders Shiver (Carson-Newman '76) 88........... | 1 | 0 | 1 | 0 | 0 |
| **BUTLER** | | | | | |
| Bill Sylvester (Butler '50) 83..................... | 1 | 0 | 1 | 0 | 0 |
| Bill Lynch (Butler '77) 88........................ | 1 | 0 | 1 | 0 | 0 |
| Bob Bartolomeo (Butler '77) 91................... | 1 | 0 | 1 | 0 | 0 |
| TOTAL | 3 | 0 | 3 | 0 | 0 |
| **CAL POLY SLO** | | | | | |
| Joe Harper (UCLA '59) 78, 80-CH................. | 2 | 3 | 1 | 1 | 0 |
| Lyle Setencich (Fresno St. '68) 90................. | 1 | 1 | 1 | 0 | 0 |
| TOTAL | 3 | 4 | 2 | 1 | 0 |
| **CAL ST. NORTHRIDGE** | | | | | |
| Bob Burt (Cal St. Los Angeles '62) 90.............. | 1 | 0 | 1 | 0 | 0 |
| **CAL ST. SACRAMENTO** | | | | | |
| Bob Mattos (Cal St. Sacramento '64) 88........... | 1 | 2 | 1 | 0 | 0 |
| **CENTRAL FLA.** | | | | | |
| Gene McDowell (Florida St. '65) 87............... | 1 | 1 | 1 | 0 | 0 |
| **CENTRAL MICH.** | | | | | |
| Roy Kramer (Maryville, Tenn. '53) 74-CH........... | 1 | 3 | 0 | 1 | 0 |
| **CENTRAL ST. (OHIO)** | | | | | |
| Billy Joe (Cheyney '70) 83-2D, 84, 85, 86........... | 4 | 3 | 4 | 0 | 1 |
| **DELAWARE** | | | | | |
| Harold "Tubby" Raymond (Michigan '50) 73, 74-2D, 76, 78-2D, 79-CH.............................. | 5 | 7 | 4 | 1 | 2 |
| **EAST STROUDSBURG** | | | | | |
| Dennis Douds (Slippery Rock '63) 91.............. | 1 | 0 | 1 | 0 | 0 |

| | Yrs | Won | Lost | CH | 2D |
|---|---|---|---|---|---|
| **EAST TEX. ST.** | | | | | |
| Eddie Vowell (S'western Okla. '69) 90, 91 . . . . . . . . . . | 2 | 2 | 2 | 0 | 0 |
| **EASTERN ILL.** | | | | | |
| Darrell Mudra (Peru St. '51) 78-CH, 80-2D . . . . . . . . . | 2 | 5 | 1 | 1 | 1 |
| **EASTERN KY.** | | | | | |
| Roy Kidd (Eastern Ky. '54) 76 . . . . . . . . . . . . . . . . . . . . | 1 | 0 | 1 | 0 | 0 |
| **EDINBORO** | | | | | |
| Tom Hollman (Ohio Northern '68) 89, 90, 92 . . . . . . . . | 3 | 1 | 3 | 0 | 0 |
| **ELIZABETH CITY ST.** | | | | | |
| Johnnie Walton (Elizabeth City St. '69) 81 . . . . . . . . . . | 1 | 0 | 1 | 0 | 0 |
| **FERRIS ST.** | | | | | |
| Keith Otterbein (Ferris St. '79) 92 . . . . . . . . . . . . . . . . | 1 | 1 | 1 | 0 | 0 |
| **FORT VALLEY ST.** | | | | | |
| Doug Porter (Xavier, La. '52) 82 . . . . . . . . . . . . . . . . . . | 1 | 0 | 1 | 0 | 0 |
| Gerald Walker (Lincoln, Mo. '62) 85 . . . . . . . . . . . . . . | 1 | 0 | 1 | 0 | 0 |
| TOTAL | 2 | 0 | 2 | 0 | 0 |
| **GRAMBLING** | | | | | |
| Eddie Robinson (Leland '41) 73 . . . . . . . . . . . . . . . . . . | 1 | 1 | 1 | 0 | 0 |
| **GRAND VALLEY ST.** | | | | | |
| Tom Beck (Northern Ill. '61) 89, 90 . . . . . . . . . . . . . . . . | 2 | 0 | 2 | 0 | 0 |
| Brian Kelly (Assumption '83) 91 . . . . . . . . . . . . . . . . . . | 1 | 0 | 1 | 0 | 0 |
| TOTAL | 3 | 0 | 3 | 0 | 0 |
| **HAMPTON** | | | | | |
| Fred Freeman (Mississippi Val. '66) 85 . . . . . . . . . . . . | 1 | 0 | 1 | 0 | 0 |
| Joe Taylor (Western Ill. '72) 92 . . . . . . . . . . . . . . . . . . . | 1 | 0 | 1 | 0 | 0 |
| TOTAL | 2 | 0 | 2 | 0 | 0 |
| **INDIANA (PA.)** | | | | | |
| Frank Cignetti (Indiana, Pa. '60) 87, 88, 89, 90-2D, 91.. | 5 | 7 | 5 | 0 | 1 |
| **JACKSONVILLE ST.** | | | | | |
| Jim Fuller (Alabama '67) 77-2D, 78, 80, 81, 82 . . . . . . . | 5 | 3 | 5 | 0 | 1 |
| Bill Burgess (Auburn '63) 88, 89-2D, 90, 91-2D, 92-CH | 5 | 12 | 4 | 1 | 2 |
| TOTAL | 10 | 15 | 9 | 1 | 3 |
| **LEHIGH** | | | | | |
| Fred Dunlap (Colgate '50) 73, 75 . . . . . . . . . . . . . . . . . . | 2 | 0 | 2 | 0 | 0 |
| John Whitehead (East Stroudsburg '50) 77-CH . . . . . . | 1 | 3 | 0 | 1 | 0 |
| TOTAL | 3 | 3 | 2 | 1 | 0 |
| **LIVINGSTON** | | | | | |
| Jim King 75 . . . . . . . . . . . . . . . . . . . . . . . . . . . . . . . . . . . . | 1 | 1 | 1 | 0 | 0 |
| **LOUISIANA TECH** | | | | | |
| Maxie Lambright (Southern Miss. '49) 73-CH, 74 . . . . . | 2 | 4 | 1 | 1 | 0 |
| **MANKATO ST.** | | | | | |
| Dan Runkle (Illinois Col. '68) 87, 91 . . . . . . . . . . . . . . . | 2 | 1 | 2 | 0 | 0 |
| **MASSACHUSETTS** | | | | | |
| Dick MacPherson (Springfield '58) 77 . . . . . . . . . . . . . | 1 | 0 | 1 | 0 | 0 |
| **MILLERSVILLE** | | | | | |
| Gene Carpenter (Huron '63) 88 . . . . . . . . . . . . . . . . . . . | 1 | 1 | 1 | 0 | 0 |
| **MISSISSIPPI COL.** | | | | | |
| John Williams (Mississippi Col. '57) 79, 88, 89-CH, 90 . . . . . . . . . . . . . . . . . . . . . . . . . . . . . . . . . . . . . . . . . | 4 | 7 | 3 | 1 | 0 |
| Terry McMillan (Southern Miss. '69) 91 . . . . . . . . . . . . | 1 | 1 | 1 | 0 | 0 |
| TOTAL | 5 | 8 | 4 | 1 | 0 |
| **MONTANA ST.** | | | | | |
| Sonny Holland (Montana St. '60) 76-CH . . . . . . . . . . . . | 1 | 3 | 0 | 1 | 0 |
| **MORGAN ST.** | | | | | |
| Clarence Thomas 79 . . . . . . . . . . . . . . . . . . . . . . . . . . . . | 1 | 0 | 1 | 0 | 0 |
| **N. C. CENTRAL** | | | | | |
| Henry Lattimore (Jackson St. '57) 88 . . . . . . . . . . . . . . | 1 | 1 | 1 | 0 | 0 |
| **NEBRASKA-OMAHA** | | | | | |
| Sandy Buda (Kansas '67) 78, 84 . . . . . . . . . . . . . . . . . . | 2 | 1 | 2 | 0 | 0 |
| **NEVADA-LAS VEGAS** | | | | | |
| Ron Meyer (Purdue '63) 74 . . . . . . . . . . . . . . . . . . . . . . . | 1 | 1 | 1 | 0 | 0 |
| Tony Knap (Idaho '39) 76 . . . . . . . . . . . . . . . . . . . . . . . . | 1 | 0 | 1 | 0 | 0 |
| TOTAL | 2 | 1 | 2 | 0 | 0 |

*Division II Championship Results, Records*

| | Yrs | Won | Lost | CH | 2D |
|---|---|---|---|---|---|
| **NEW HAMPSHIRE** | | | | | |
| Bill Bowes (Penn St. '65) 75, 76.................... | 2 | 1 | 2 | 0 | 0 |
| **NEW HAVEN** | | | | | |
| Mark Whipple (Brown '79) 92...................... | 1 | 2 | 1 | 0 | 0 |
| **NORFOLK ST.** | | | | | |
| Willard Bailey (Norfolk St. '62) 84.................. | 1 | 0 | 1 | 0 | 0 |
| **NORTH ALA.** | | | | | |
| Wayne Grubb (Tennessee '61) 80, 83, 85-2D......... | 3 | 4 | 3 | 0 | 1 |
| Bobby Wallace (Mississippi St. '76) 90, 92........... | 2 | 1 | 2 | 0 | 0 |
| TOTAL | 5 | 5 | 5 | 0 | 1 |
| **NORTH DAK.** | | | | | |
| Jerry Olson (Valley City St. '55) 75................. | 1 | 0 | 1 | 0 | 0 |
| Gene Murphy (North Dak. '62) 79.................... | 1 | 0 | 1 | 0 | 0 |
| Roger Thomas (Augustana, Ill. '69) 92.............. | 1 | 0 | 1 | 0 | 0 |
| TOTAL | 3 | 0 | 3 | 0 | 0 |
| **NORTH DAK. ST.** | | | | | |
| Jim Wacker (Valparaiso '60) 76, 77................. | 2 | 2 | 2 | 0 | 0 |
| Don Morton (Augustana, Ill. '69) 81-2D, 82, 83-CH, 84-2D.......................................... | 4 | 8 | 3 | 1 | 2 |
| Earle Solomonson (Augsburg '69) 85-CH, 86-CH..... | 2 | 6 | 0 | 2 | 0 |
| Rocky Hager (Minot St. '74) 88-CH, 89, 90-CH, 91, 92........................................... | 5 | 10 | 3 | 2 | 0 |
| TOTAL | 13 | 26 | 8 | 5 | 2 |
| **NORTHEAST MO. ST.** | | | | | |
| Bruce Craddock (Northeast Mo. St. '66) 82.......... | 1 | 0 | 1 | 0 | 0 |
| Eric Holm (Northeast Mo. St. '81) 90, 92............ | 2 | 0 | 2 | 0 | 0 |
| TOTAL | 3 | 0 | 3 | 0 | 0 |
| **NORTHERN ARIZ.** | | | | | |
| Joe Salem (Minnesota '61) 77..................... | 1 | 0 | 1 | 0 | 0 |
| **NORTHERN COLO.** | | | | | |
| Bob Blasi (Colorado St. '53) 80.................... | 1 | 0 | 1 | 0 | 0 |
| Joe Glenn (South Dak. '71) 90, 91................. | 2 | 0 | 2 | 0 | 0 |
| TOTAL | 3 | 0 | 3 | 0 | 0 |
| **NORTHERN IOWA** | | | | | |
| Stan Sheriff (Cal Poly SLO '54) 75................. | 1 | 0 | 1 | 0 | 0 |
| **NORTHERN MICH.** | | | | | |
| Gil Krueger (Marquette '52) 75-CH, 76, 77........... | 3 | 4 | 2 | 1 | 0 |
| Bill Rademacher (Northern Mich. '63) 80, 81, 82...... | 3 | 1 | 3 | 0 | 0 |
| Herb Grenke (Wis.-Milwaukee '63) 87.............. | 1 | 1 | 1 | 0 | 0 |
| TOTAL | 7 | 6 | 6 | 1 | 0 |
| **NORTHWEST MO. ST.** | | | | | |
| Vern Thomsen (Peru St. '61) 84.................... | 1 | 0 | 1 | 0 | 0 |
| Bud Elliott (Baker '53) 89......................... | 1 | 0 | 1 | 0 | 0 |
| TOTAL | 2 | 0 | 2 | 0 | 0 |
| **PITTSBURG ST.** | | | | | |
| Dennis Franchione (Pittsburg St. '73) 89............ | 1 | 1 | 1 | 0 | 0 |
| Chuck Broyles (Pittsburg St. '70) 90, 91-CH, 92-2D... | 3 | 9 | 2 | 1 | 1 |
| TOTAL | 4 | 10 | 3 | 1 | 1 |
| **PORTLAND ST.** | | | | | |
| Pokey Allen (Utah '65) 87-2D, 88-2D, 89, 91, 92...... | 5 | 10 | 5 | 0 | 2 |
| **PUGET SOUND** | | | | | |
| Ron Simonson (Portland St. '65) 81................. | 1 | 0 | 1 | 0 | 0 |
| **SANTA CLARA** | | | | | |
| Pat Malley (Santa Clara '53) 80.................... | 1 | 1 | 1 | 0 | 0 |
| **SAVANNAH ST.** | | | | | |
| Bill Davis (Johnson Smith '65) 92.................. | 1 | 0 | 1 | 0 | 0 |
| **SHIPPENSBURG** | | | | | |
| Vito Ragazzo (William & Mary '51) 81............... | 1 | 1 | 1 | 0 | 0 |
| Rocky Rees (West Chester '71) 91.................. | 1 | 1 | 1 | 0 | 0 |
| TOTAL | 2 | 2 | 2 | 0 | 0 |
| **SOUTH DAK.** | | | | | |
| Joe Salem (Minnesota '61) 73...................... | 1 | 0 | 1 | 0 | 0 |
| Dave Triplett (Iowa '72) 85, 86-2D................. | 2 | 3 | 2 | 0 | 1 |
| TOTAL | 3 | 3 | 3 | 0 | 1 |

| | Yrs | Won | Lost | CH | 2D |
|---|---|---|---|---|---|
| **SOUTH DAK. ST.** | | | | | |
| John Gregory (Northern Iowa '61) 79.............. | 1 | 0 | 1 | 0 | 0 |
| **SOUTHWEST TEX. ST.** | | | | | |
| Jim Wacker (Valparaiso '60) 81-CH, 82-CH.......... | 2 | 6 | 0 | 2 | 0 |
| John O'Hara (Panhandle St. '67) 83................ | 1 | 0 | 1 | 0 | 0 |
| TOTAL | 3 | 6 | 1 | 2 | 0 |
| **ST. CLOUD ST.** | | | | | |
| Noel Martin (Nebraska '63) 89..................... | 1 | 1 | 1 | 0 | 0 |
| **TEXAS A&I** | | | | | |
| Ron Harms (Valparaiso '59) 88, 89, 92.............. | 3 | 3 | 3 | 0 | 0 |
| **TENN.-MARTIN** | | | | | |
| Don McLeary (Tennessee '70) 88................... | 1 | 1 | 1 | 0 | 0 |
| **TOWSON ST.** | | | | | |
| Phil Albert (Arizona '66) 83, 84, 86................. | 3 | 1 | 3 | 0 | 0 |
| **TROY ST.** | | | | | |
| Chan Gailey (Florida '74) 84-CH.................... | 1 | 3 | 0 | 1 | 0 |
| Rick Rhodes 86, 87-CH........................... | 2 | 4 | 1 | 1 | 0 |
| TOTAL | 3 | 7 | 1 | 2 | 0 |
| **UC DAVIS** | | | | | |
| Jim Sochor (San Fran. St. '60) 77, 78, 82-2D, 83, 84, 85, 86, 88......................... | 8 | 4 | 8 | 0 | 1 |
| Bob Foster (UC Davis '62) 89, 92.................. | 2 | 0 | 2 | 0 | 0 |
| TOTAL | 10 | 4 | 10 | 0 | 1 |
| **VIRGINIA UNION** | | | | | |
| Willard Bailey (Norfolk St. '62) 79, 80, 81, 82, 83...... | 5 | 0 | 5 | 0 | 0 |
| Joe Taylor (Western Ill. '72) 86, 90, 91.............. | 3 | 0 | 3 | 0 | 0 |
| TOTAL | 8 | 0 | 8 | 0 | 0 |
| **WEST CHESTER** | | | | | |
| Danny Hale (West Chester '68) 88................. | 1 | 0 | 1 | 0 | 0 |
| Rick Daniels (West Chester '75) 89, 92.............. | 2 | 0 | 2 | 0 | 0 |
| TOTAL | 3 | 0 | 3 | 0 | 0 |
| **WESTERN CARO.** | | | | | |
| Bob Waters (Presbyterian '60) 74.................. | 1 | 0 | 1 | 0 | 0 |
| **WESTERN ILL.** | | | | | |
| Darrell Mudra (Peru St. '51) 73.................... | 1 | 0 | 1 | 0 | 0 |
| **WESTERN KY.** | | | | | |
| Jimmy Feix (Western Ky. '53) 73-2D, 75-2D.......... | 2 | 4 | 2 | 0 | 2 |
| **WESTERN ST.** | | | | | |
| Carl Iverson (Whitman '62) 92..................... | 1 | 0 | 1 | 0 | 0 |
| **WINSTON-SALEM** | | | | | |
| Bill Hayes (N. C. Central '64) 78, 87................ | 2 | 1 | 2 | 0 | 0 |
| Pete Richardson (Dayton '68) 88, 90, 91............. | 3 | 0 | 3 | 0 | 0 |
| TOTAL | 5 | 1 | 5 | 0 | 0 |
| **WOFFORD** | | | | | |
| Mike Ayers (Georgetown, Ky. '74) 90, 91............ | 2 | 0 | 2 | 0 | 0 |
| **YOUNGSTOWN ST.** | | | | | |
| Rey Dempsey (Geneva '58) 74..................... | 1 | 0 | 1 | 0 | 0 |
| Bill Narduzzi (Miami, Ohio '59) 78, 79-2D........... | 2 | 3 | 2 | 0 | 1 |
| TOTAL | 3 | 3 | 3 | 0 | 1 |

## ALL-TIME RESULTS

**1973 First Round:** Grambling 17, Delaware 8; Western Ky. 25, Lehigh 16; Louisiana Tech 18, Western Ill. 13; Boise St. 53, South Dak. 10. **Semifinals:** Western Ky. 28, Grambling 20; Louisiana Tech 38, Boise St. 34. **Championship:** Louisiana Tech 34, Western Ky. 0.

**1974 First Round:** Central Mich. 20, Boise St. 6; Louisiana Tech 10, Western Caro. 7; Nevada-Las Vegas 35, Alcorn St. 22; Delaware 35, Youngstown St. 14. **Semifinals:** Central Mich. 35, Louisiana Tech 14; Delaware 49, Nevada-Las Vegas 11. **Championship:** Central Mich. 54, Delaware 14.

**1975 First Round:** Northern Mich. 24, Boise St. 21; Livingston 34, North Dak. 14; Western Ky. 14, Northern Iowa 12; New Hampshire 35, Lehigh 21. **Semifinals:** Northern Mich. 28, Livingston 26; Western Ky. 14, New Hampshire 3. **Championship:** Northern Mich. 16, Western Ky. 14.

**1976 First Round:** Akron 26, Nevada-Las Vegas 6; Northern Mich. 28, Delaware 17; North Dak. St. 10, Eastern Ky. 7; Montana St. 17, New Hampshire 16. **Semifinals:** Akron 28, Northern Mich. 26; Montana St. 10, North Dak. St. 3. **Championship:** Montana St. 24, Akron 13.

**1977 First Round:** UC Davis 34, Bethune-Cookman 16; Lehigh 30, Massachusetts 23; North Dak.

St. 20, Northern Mich. 6; Jacksonville St. 35, Northern Ariz. 0. **Semifinals:** Lehigh 39, UC Davis 30; Jacksonville St. 31, North Dak. St. 7. **Championship:** Lehigh 33, Jacksonville St. 0.

**1978 First Round:** Winston-Salem 17, Cal Poly SLO 0; Delaware 42, Jacksonville St. 27; Youngstown St. 21, Nebraska-Omaha 14; Eastern Ill. 35, UC Davis 31. **Semifinals:** Delaware 41, Winston-Salem 0; Eastern Ill. 26, Youngstown St. 22. **Championship:** Eastern Ill. 10, Delaware 9.

**1979 First Round:** Delaware 58, Virginia Union 28; Mississippi Col. 35, North Dak. 15; Youngstown St. 50, South Dak. St. 7; Alabama A&M 27, Morgan St. 7. **Semifinals:** Delaware 60, Mississippi Col. 10; Youngstown St. 52, Alabama A&M 0. **Championship:** Delaware 38, Youngstown St. 21.

**1980 First Round:** Eastern Ill. 21, Northern Colo. 14; North Ala. 17, Virginia Union 8; Santa Clara 27, Northern Mich. 26; Cal Poly SLO 15, Jacksonville St. 0. **Semifinals:** Eastern Ill. 56, North Ala. 31; Cal Poly SLO 38, Santa Clara 14. **Championship:** Cal Poly SLO 21, Eastern Ill. 13.

**1981 First Round:** Northern Mich. 55, Elizabeth City St. 6; Southwest Tex. St. 38, Jacksonville St. 22; North Dak. St. 24, Puget Sound 10; Shippensburg 40, Virginia Union 27. **Semifinals:** Southwest Tex. St. 62, Northern Mich. 0; North Dak. St. 18, Shippensburg 6. **Championship:** Southwest Tex. St. 42, North Dak. St. 13.

**1982 First Round:** Southwest Tex. St. 27, Fort Valley St. 6; Jacksonville St. 34, Northeast Mo. St. 21; North Dak. St. 21, Virginia Union 20; UC Davis 42, Northern Mich. 21. **Semifinals:** Southwest Tex. St. 19, Jacksonville St. 14; UC Davis 19, North Dak. St. 14. **Championship:** Southwest Tex. St. 34, UC Davis 9.

**1983 First Round:** UC Davis 25, Butler 6; North Dak. St. 24, Towson St. 17; North Ala. 16, Virginia Union 14; Central St. (Ohio) 24, Southwest Tex. St. 16. **Semifinals:** North Dak. St. 26, UC Davis 17; Central St. (Ohio) 27, North Ala. 24. **Championship:** North Dak. St. 41, Central St. (Ohio) 21.

**1984 First Round:** North Dak. St. 31, UC Davis 23; Nebraska-Omaha 28, Northwest Mo. St. 15; Troy

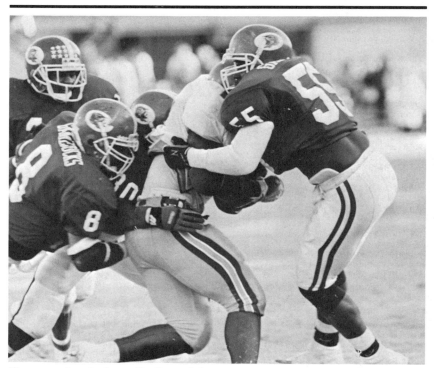

**The swarming Jacksonville State defense was out in full force during the 1992 Division II Football Championship title game. The Gamecocks held the high-powered Pittsburg State offense, which had averaged 35 points and 345 yards rushing in three previous playoff games, to just 156 yards on the ground en route to a 17-13 victory.**

St. 31, Central St. (Ohio) 21; Towson St. 31, Norfolk St. 21. **Semifinals:** North Dak. St. 25, Nebraska-Omaha 14; Troy St. 45, Towson St. 3. **Championship:** Troy St. 18, North Dak. St. 17.

**1985 First Round:** North Dak. St. 31, UC Davis 12; South Dak. 13, Central St. (Ohio) 10 (2 OT); Bloomsburg 38, Hampton 28; North Ala. 14, Fort Valley St. 7. **Semifinals:** North Dak. St. 16, South Dak. 7; North Ala. 34, Bloomsburg 0. **Championship:** North Dak. St. 35, North Ala. 0.

**1986 First Round:** North Dak. St. 50, Ashland 0; Central St. (Ohio) 31, Towson St. 0; Troy St. 31, Virginia Union 7; South Dak. 26, UC Davis 23. **Semifinals:** North Dak. St. 35, Central St. (Ohio) 12; South Dak. 42, Troy St. 28. **Championship:** North Dak. St. 27, South Dak. 7.

**1987 First Round:** Portland St. 27, Mankato St. 21; Northern Mich. 23, Angelo St. 20 (OT); Central Fla. 12, Indiana (Pa.) 10; Troy St. 45, Winston-Salem 14. **Semifinals:** Portland St. 13, Northern Mich. 7; Troy St. 31, Central Fla. 10. **Championship:** Troy St. 31, Portland St. 17.

**1988 First Round:** North Dak. St. 49, Augustana (S.D.) 7; Millersville 27, Indiana (Pa.) 24; Cal St. Sacramento 35, UC Davis 14; N.C. Central 31, Winston-Salem 16; Texas A&I 39, Mississippi Col. 15; Tenn.-Martin 23, Butler 6; Portland St. 34, Bowie St. 17; Jacksonville St. 63, West Chester 24. **Quarterfinals:** North Dak. St. 36, Millersville 26; Cal St. Sacramento 56, N.C. Central 7; Texas A&I 34, Tenn.-Martin 0; Portland St. 20, Jacksonville St. 13. **Semifinals:** North Dak. St. 42, Cal St. Sacramento 20; Portland St. 35, Texas A&I 27. **Championship:** North Dak. St. 35, Portland St. 21.

**1989 First Round:** Mississippi Col. 34, Texas A&I 19; St. Cloud St. 27, Augustana (S.D.) 20; Portland St. 56, West Chester 50 (3 OT); Indiana (Pa.) 34, Grand Valley St. 24; Pittsburg St. 28, Northwest Mo. St. 7; Angelo St. 28, UC Davis 23; North Dak. St. 45, Edinboro 32; Jacksonville St. 33, Alabama A&M 9. **Quarterfinals:** Mississippi Col. 55, St. Cloud St. 24; Indiana (Pa.) 17, Portland St. 0;

Angelo St. 24, Pittsburg St. 21; Jacksonville St. 21, North Dak. St. 17. **Semifinals:** Mississippi Col. 26, Indiana (Pa.) 14; Jacksonville St. 34, Angelo St. 16. **Championship:** Mississippi Col. 3, Jacksonville St. 0.

**1990 First Round:** Mississippi Col. 70, Wofford 19; Jacksonville St. 38, North Ala. 14; Indiana (Pa.) 48, Winston-Salem 0; Edinboro 38, Virginia Union 14; North Dak. St. 17, Northern Colo. 7; Cal Poly SLO 14, Cal St. Northridge 7; Pittsburg St. 59, Northeast Mo. St. 3; East Tex. St. 20, Grand Valley St. 14. **Quarterfinals:** Mississippi Col. 14, Jacksonville St. 7; Indiana (Pa.) 8; North Dak. St. 47, Cal Poly SLO 0; Pittsburg St. 60, East Tex. St. 28. **Semifinals:** Indiana (Pa.) 27, Mississippi Col. 8; North Dak. St. 39, Pittsburg St. 29. **Championship:** North Dak. St. 51, Indiana (Pa.) 11.

**1991 First Round:** Pittsburg St. 26, Butler 16; East Tex. St. 36, Grand Valley St. 15; Portland St. 28, Northern Colo. 24; Mankato St. 27, North Dak. St. 7; Jacksonville St. 49, Winston-Salem 24; Mississippi Col. 28, Wofford 15; Indiana (Pa.) 56, Virginia Union 7; Shippensburg 34, East Stroudsburg 33 (OT). **Quarterfinals:** Pittsburg St. 38, East Tex. St. 28; Portland St. 37, Mankato St. 7; Jacksonville St. 35, Mississippi Col. 7; Indiana (Pa.) 52, Shippensburg 7. **Semifinals:** Pittsburg St. 53, Portland St. 21; Jacksonville St. 27, Indiana (Pa.) 20. **Championship:** Pittsburg St. 23, Jacksonville St. 6.

**1992 First Round:** Ferris St. 19, Edinboro 15; New Haven 38, West Chester 26; Jacksonville St. 41, Savannah St. 16; North Ala. 33, Hampton 21; Texas A&I 22, Western St. 13; Portland St. 42, UC Davis 28; Pittsburg St. 26, North Dak. 21; North Dak. St. 42, Northeast Mo. St. 7. **Quarterfinals:** New Haven 35, Ferris St. 13; Jacksonville St. 14, North Ala. 12; Portland St. 35, Texas A&I 30; Pittsburg St. 38, North Dak. St. 37 (OT). **Semifinals:** Jacksonville St. 46, New Haven 35; Pittsburg St. 41, Portland St. 38. **Championship:** Jacksonville St. 17, Pittsburg St. 13.

# 1992 DIVISION III CHAMPIONSHIP

## AMOS ALONZO STAGG BOWL, HAWKINS STADIUM, BRADENTON, FLA.; DECEMBER 12, 1992

|  | Wis.-La Crosse | Wash. & Jeff. |
|---|---|---|
| First Downs | 14 | 14 |
| Rushes-Net Yardage | 53-189 | 32-109 |
| Passing Yardage | 91 | 149 |
| Return Yardage (Punts, Int. & Fum.) | 47 | 40 |
| Passes (Comp.-Att.-Int.) | 7-17-1 | 13-36-4 |
| Punts (Number-Average) | 9-38.3 | 6-41.8 |
| Fumbles (Number-Lost) | 2-2 | 0-0 |
| Penalties (Number-Yards) | 5-54 | 1-5 |

| | | | | |
|---|---|---|---|---|
| Wis.-La Crosse | 0 | 14 | 2 | 0—16 |
| Wash. & Jeff. | 0 | 0 | 12 | 0—12 |

Game Conditions: Temperature, 70 degrees; Wind, slight; Weather, sunny and clear. Attendance: 5,329.

**Second Quarter**
Wis.-La Crosse—Paul Kling 25 pass from Jason Gonnion (Matt Anderson kick) (73 yards in 8 plays, 14:14 left)
Wis.-La Crosse—Gonnion 1 run (Anderson kick) (85 yards in 14 plays, 4:26 left)

**Third Quarter**
Wash. & Jeff.—Mike Speca 20 pass from Bob Strope (kick blocked) (42 yards in 5 plays, 6:09 left)
Wis.-La Crosse—Norris Thomas 86 blocked extra-point return (6:09 left)
Wash. & Jeff.—Chris Babirad 9 run (kick blocked) (15 yards in 3 plays, 0:30 left)

**Individual Leaders**

Rushing—Wis.-La Crosse: John Janke, 119 yards on 24 carries; Wash. & Jeff.: Babirad, 104 yards on 25 carries.
Passing—Wis.-La Crosse: Gonnion, 7 of 17 for 91 yards; Wash. & Jeff.: Strope, 13 of 35 for 149 yards.
Receiving—Wis.-La Crosse: Jason Janke, 4 catches for 31 yards; Wash. & Jeff.: Doug Yarabinetz, 4 catches for 38 yards.

## DIVISION III ALL-TIME CHAMPIONSHIP RESULTS

| Year | Champion | Coach | Score | Runner-Up | Site |
|------|----------|-------|-------|-----------|------|
| 1973 | Wittenberg | Dave Maurer | 41-0 | Juniata | Phenix City, Ala. |
| 1974 | Central (Iowa) | Ron Schipper | 10-8 | Ithaca | Phenix City, Ala. |
| 1975 | Wittenberg | Dave Maurer | 28-0 | Ithaca | Phenix City, Ala. |
| 1976 | St. John's (Minn.) | John Gagliardi | 31-28 | Towson St. | Phenix City, Ala. |
| 1977 | Widener | Bill Manlove | 39-36 | Wabash | Phenix City, Ala. |
| 1978 | Baldwin-Wallace | Lee Tressel | 24-10 | Wittenberg | Phenix City, Ala. |
| 1979 | Ithaca | Jim Butterfield | 14-10 | Wittenberg | Phenix City, Ala. |
| 1980 | Dayton | Rick Carter | 63-0 | Ithaca | Phenix City, Ala. |
| 1981 | Widener | Bill Manlove | 17-10 | Dayton | Phenix City, Ala. |
| 1982 | West Ga. | Bobby Pate | 14-0 | Augustana (Ill.) | Phenix City, Ala. |
| 1983 | Augustana (Ill.) | Bob Reade | 21-17 | Union (N.Y.) | Kings Island, Ohio |
| 1984 | Augustana (Ill.) | Bob Reade | 21-12 | Central (Iowa) | Kings Island, Ohio |
| 1985 | Augustana (Ill.) | Bob Reade | 20-7 | Ithaca | Phenix City, Ala. |
| 1986 | Augustana (Ill.) | Bob Reade | 31-3 | Salisbury St. | Phenix City, Ala. |
| 1987 | Wagner | Walt Hameline | 19-3 | Dayton | Phenix City, Ala. |
| 1988 | Ithaca | Jim Butterfield | 39-24 | Central (Iowa) | Phenix City, Ala. |
| 1989 | Dayton | Mike Kelly | 17-7 | Union (N.Y.) | Phenix City, Ala. |
| 1990 | Allegheny | Ken O'Keefe | 21-14 (OT) | Lycoming | Bradenton, Fla. |
| 1991 | Ithaca | Jim Butterfield | 34-20 | Dayton | Bradenton, Fla. |
| 1992 | Wis.-La Crosse | Roger Harring | 16-12 | Wash. & Jeff. | Bradenton, Fla. |

## REGIONAL CHAMPIONSHIP RESULTS
### (Before Division III Championship)
### EAST (Knute Rockne Bowl)

| Year | Champion | Coach | Score | Runner-Up | Site |
|------|----------|-------|-------|-----------|------|
| 1969 | Randolph-Macon | Ted Keller | 47-28 | Bridgeport | Bridgeport, Conn. |
| 1970 | Montclair St. | Clary Anderson | 7-6 | Hampden-Sydney | Atlantic City, N. J. |
| 1971 | Bridgeport | Ed Farrell | 17-12 | Hampden-Sydney | Atlantic City, N. J. |
| 1972 | Bridgeport | Ed Farrell | 27-22 | Slippery Rock | Atlantic City, N. J. |

### WEST (Amos Alonzo Stagg Bowl)

| Year | Champion | Coach | Score | Runner-Up | Site |
|------|----------|-------|-------|-----------|------|
| 1969 | Wittenberg | Dave Maurer | 27-21 | William Jewell | Springfield, Ohio |
| 1970 | Capital | Gene Slaughter | 34-21 | Luther | Columbus, Ohio |
| 1971 | Vacated | | 20-10 | Ohio Wesleyan | Phenix City, Ala. |
| 1972 | Heidelberg | Pete Riesen | 28-16 | Fort Valley St. | Phenix City, Ala. |

## 1992 DIVISION III CHAMPIONSHIP RESULTS

**Regionals**
Mount Union 27, Dayton 10
Ill. Wesleyan 21, Aurora 12
Central (Iowa) 20, Carleton 8
Wis.-La Crosse 47, Redlands 26
Emory & Henry 17, Thomas More 0
Wash. & Jeff. 33, Lycoming 0
Rowan 41, Worcester Tech 14
Buffalo St. 28, Ithaca 26

**Quarterfinals**
Mount Union 49, Ill. Wesleyan 27
Wis.-La Crosse 34, Central (Iowa) 9
Wash. & Jeff. 51, Emory & Henry 15
Rowan 28, Buffalo St. 19

**Semifinals**
Wis.-La Crosse 29, Mount Union 24
Wash. & Jeff. 18, Rowan 13

**Championship**
Wis.-La Crosse 16, Wash. & Jeff. 12

## 1992 DIVISION III GAME SUMMARIES

**FIRST-ROUND GAMES (Nov. 21)**

**Mount Union 27, Dayton 10**
at Dayton, Ohio

| | | | | |
|---|---|---|---|---|
| Mount Union | 3 | 14 | 7 | 3—27 |
| Dayton | 3 | 7 | 0 | 0—10 |

D—Duvic 24 field goal
MU—Dreslinski 23 field goal
D—Hofacre 1 run (Duvic kick)
MU—Sirianni 21 pass from Ballard (Dreslinski kick)
MU—Gresko 2 run (Dreslinski kick)
MU—Huss 3 run (Dreslinski kick)
MU—Dreslinski 20 field goal
A—2,546

**Ill. Wesleyan 21, Aurora 12**
at Bloomington, Ill.

| | | | | |
|---|---|---|---|---|
| Aurora | 0 | 6 | 0 | 6—12 |
| Ill. Wesleyan | 0 | 14 | 7 | 0—21 |

IW—McLeod 18 pass from Monken (Blaskovich kick)
A—Robertson 15 pass from Deming (kick failed)
IW—Bisaillon 27 pass from Monken (Blaskovich kick)
IW—Houston 10 pass from Monken (Blaskovich kick)
A—McBride 10 pass from Deming (pass failed)
A—3,500

**Central (Iowa) 20, Carleton 8**
at Pella, Iowa

| | | | | |
|---|---|---|---|---|
| Carleton | 0 | 6 | 0 | 2— 8 |
| Central (Iowa) | 3 | 7 | 3 | 7—20 |

CI—Sanger 21 field goal
CI—Hugunin 26 run (Sanger kick)
CA—Hanks 16 pass from Kluender (kick blocked)
CI—Sanger 28 field goal
CI—Kacmarynski 14 run (Sanger kick)
CA—Safety, Sandquist tackled in end zone
A—1,000

**Wis.-La Crosse 47, Redlands 26**
at La Crosse, Wis.

| | | | | |
|---|---|---|---|---|
| Redlands | 7 | 7 | 0 | 12—26 |
| Wis.-La Crosse | 0 | 21 | 13 | 13—47 |

RD—Cheatham 1 run (Skipper kick)
LC—Tabor 18 pass from Gonnion (Anderson kick)
LC—Richards 9 run (Anderson kick)
RD—Bruich 19 pass from Harmon (Skipper kick)
LC—Ja. Janke 5 pass from Gonnion (Anderson kick)
LC—Gonnion 1 run (Anderson kick)
LC—Jo. Janke 2 run (kick blocked)
LC—Jo. Janke 1 run (Anderson kick)
LC—Davis 16 run (pass failed)
RD—Schulenberg 16 pass from Harmon (pass failed)
RD—Cheatham 2 run (pass failed)
A—1,178

**Emory & Henry 17, Thomas More 0**
at Emory, Va.

| | | | | |
|---|---|---|---|---|
| Thomas More | 0 | 0 | 0 | 0— 0 |
| Emory & Henry | 0 | 7 | 7 | 3—17 |

EH—Cole 5 run (Garnett kick)
EH—Cox 74 fumble return (Garnett kick)
EH—Garnett 35 field goal
A—NA

**Wash. & Jeff. 33, Lycoming 0**
at Williamsport, Pa.

| | | | | |
|---|---|---|---|---|
| Wash. & Jeff. | 6 | 13 | 14 | 0—33 |
| Lycoming | 0 | 0 | 0 | 0— 0 |

WJ—Babirad 5 run (kick blocked)
WJ—Babirad 23 run (run failed)
WJ—Speca 22 pass from Strope (Lautner kick)
WJ—Wass 2 run (Lautner kick)
WJ—Babirad 2 run (Lautner kick)
A—2,700

**Rowan 41, Worcester Tech 14**
at Glassboro, N. J.

| | | | | |
|---|---|---|---|---|
| Worcester Tech | 0 | 7 | 7 | 0—14 |
| Rowan | 14 | 13 | 7 | 7—41 |

R—Trent 64 pass from Hesson (Leone kick)
R—Johnson 20 pass from Hesson (Leone kick)
R—Perry 1 run (Leone kick)
R—Marshall 19 run (kick failed)
WT—Padula 9 run (Harvey kick)
WT—Swedick 5 pass from Ceppetelli (Harvey kick)
R—Fox 28 pass from Hesson (Leone kick)
R—Anderson 20 run (Leone kick)
A—3,800

**Buffalo St. 28, Ithaca 26**
at Ithaca, N. Y.

| | | | | |
|---|---|---|---|---|
| Buffalo St. | 14 | 7 | 7 | 0—28 |
| Ithaca | 0 | 14 | 3 | 9—26 |

BS—Fisher 8 pass from Weigel (Frey kick)

*Division III Championship Results, Records*

BS—Otremba 36 pass from Weigel (Frey kick)
BS—Miceli 9 pass from Weigel (Frey kick)
ITH—Adams 1 run (Mahoney kick)
ITH—Wittman 5 run (Mahoney kick)
ITH—Mahoney 25 field goal
BS—Miceli 17 pass from Bacon (Frey kick)
ITH—Mahoney 30 field goal
ITH—Cahill 9 pass from Fitzgerald (pass failed)
A—1,327

## QUARTERFINAL GAMES (Nov. 28)

### Mount Union 49, Ill. Wesleyan 27
at Alliance, Ohio

| | | | | |
|---|---|---|---|---|
| Ill. Wesleyan | 0 | 14 | 6 | 7—27 |
| Mount Union | 21 | 21 | 0 | 7—49 |

MU—Atwood 13 pass from Ballard (Dreslinski kick)
MU—Sirianni 31 pass from Ballard (Dreslinski kick)
MU—Gresko 2 pass from Ballard (Dreslinski kick)
IW—Liesimer 12 pass from Monken (Blaskovich kick)
MU—McCrate 40 pass from Ballard (Dreslinski kick)
IW—Liesimer 34 pass from Monken (Blaskovich kick)
MU—Gresko 1 run (Dreslinski kick)
MU—Gresko 2 run (Dreslinski kick)
IW—Liesimer 1 pass from Monken (kick failed)
MU—Gresko 30 pass from Ballard (Dreslinski kick)
IW—Liesimer 6 pass from Monken (Blaskovich kick)
A—5,800

### Wis.-La Crosse 34, Central (Iowa) 9
at Ames, Iowa

| | | | | |
|---|---|---|---|---|
| Wis.-La Crosse | 0 | 14 | 7 | 13—34 |
| Central (Iowa) | 0 | 3 | 0 | 6— 9 |

CI—Sanger 36 field goal
LC—Ja. Janke 4 pass from Gonnion (Anderson kick)
LC—Berg 47 interception return (Anderson kick)
LC—Ja. Janke 26 pass from Gonnion (Anderson kick)
CI—Arendt 16 pass from Flynn (pass failed)
LC—Schaefer 1 pass from Gonnion (kick failed)
LC—Murray 4 run (Anderson kick)
A—NA

### Wash. & Jeff. 51, Emory & Henry 15
at Washington, Pa.

| | | | | |
|---|---|---|---|---|
| Emory & Henry | 7 | 0 | 8 | 0—15 |
| Wash. & Jeff. | 9 | 21 | 14 | 7—51 |

WJ—Babirad 17 run (kick failed)
EH—Buchanan 12 pass from Perkins (Garnett kick)
WJ—Lautner 32 field goal
WJ—Babirad 21 run (Lautner kick)
WJ—Babirad 17 run (Lautner kick)
WJ—Babirad 58 run (Lautner kick)
WJ—Fields 16 pass from Strope (Lautner kick)
WJ—Yarabinetz 9 pass from Strope (Lautner kick)
EH—Turner 32 pass from Perkins (Woodall pass from Perkins)
WJ—Bandes 1 run (Lautner kick)
A—NA

### Rowan 28, Buffalo St. 19
at Buffalo, N. Y.

| | | | | |
|---|---|---|---|---|
| Rowan | 7 | 0 | 14 | 7—28 |
| Buffalo St. | 7 | 6 | 0 | 6—19 |

BS—Rogowski 3 run (Frey kick)
R—Trent 80 pass from Hesson (Leone kick)
BS—Rogowski 2 run (kick blocked)
R—Perry 1 run (Leone kick)
R—Fox 59 pass from Hesson (Leone kick)
BS—Miceli 27 pass from Bacon (two-point attempt failed)
R—Trent 38 onside-kick return (Leone kick)
A—4,228

## SEMIFINAL GAMES (Dec. 5)

### Wis.-La Crosse 29, Mount Union 24
at La Crosse, Wis.

| | | | | |
|---|---|---|---|---|
| Mount Union | 0 | 10 | 7 | 7—24 |
| Wis.-La Crosse | 7 | 7 | 0 | 15—29 |

LC—Schaaf 67 interception return (Anderson kick)
MU—Atwood 28 pass from Ballard (Dreslinski kick)
MU—Dreslinski 22 field goal

LC—Gonnion 3 run (Anderson kick)
MU—Ballard 4 run (Dreslinski kick)
LC—Safety, Ballard tackled in end zone
LC—Richards 15 run (pass failed)
LC—Gonnion 1 run (Anderson kick)
MU—Huss 5 pass from Ballard (Dreslinski kick)
A—3,733

**Wash. & Jeff. 18, Rowan 13**
at Glassboro, N. J.

| | | | | | |
|---|---|---|---|---|---|
| **Wash. & Jeff.** | 0 | 0 | 6 | 12 | 18 |
| **Rowan** | 0 | 7 | 0 | 6 | 13 |

R—Johnson 15 pass from Hesson (Leone kick)
WJ—McGee 7 interception return (kick failed)
WJ—Babirad 21 run (pass failed)
R—Hyde 3 run (two-point attempt failed)
WJ—Babirad 80 run (two-point attempt failed)
A—5,100

# CHAMPIONSHIP RECORDS

## INDIVIDUAL: SINGLE GAME

**Net Yards Rushing**
389—Ricky Gales, Simpson (35) vs. St. John's (Minn.) (42), 11-18-89.

**Rushes Attempted**
51—Ricky Gales, Simpson (35) vs. St. John's (Minn.) (42), 11-18-89.

**Touchdowns by Rushing**
5—Jeff Norman, St. John's (Minn.) (46) vs. Augustana (Ill.) (7), 11-20-76; Mike Coppa, Salisbury St. (44) vs. Ithaca (40), 12-6-86; Paul Parker, Ithaca (62) vs. Ferrum (28), 12-3-88; Kevin Hofacre, Dayton (35) vs. John Carroll (10), 11-18-89.

**Net Yards Passing**
461—Jim Ballard, Mount Union (24) vs. Wis.-La Crosse (29), 12-5-92.

**Passes Attempted**
53—Walter Briggs, Montclair St. (28) vs. Ithaca (50), 11-30-85.

**Passes Completed**
32—Tim Lynch, Hofstra (10) vs. Lycoming (20), 12-1-90.

**Passes Had Intercepted**
7—Rick Steil, Dubuque (7) vs. Ithaca (27), 11-17-79.

**Touchdown Passes Completed**
5—Pat Mayew, St. John's (Minn.) (75) vs. Coe (2), 11-23-91; Jim Ballard, Mount Union (49) vs. Ill. Wesleyan (27), 11-28-92.

**Completion Percentage (Min. 8 Attempts)**
.900—Robb Disbennett, Salisbury St. (16) vs. Carnegie Mellon (14), 11-19-83 (18 of 20).

**Net Yards Rushing and Passing**
480—Jim Ballard, Mount Union (24) vs. Wis.-La Crosse (29), 12-5-92.

**Number of Rushing and Passing Plays**
66—Steve Thompson, Carroll (Wis.) (14) vs. Buena Vista (20), 11-20-76.

**Punting Average (Min. 3 Punts)**
48.5—Phil Macken, Minn.-Morris (25) vs. Carnegie Mellon (31), 11-17-79.

**Number of Punts**
14—Tim Flynn, Gettysburg (14) vs. Lycoming (10), 11-23-85.

**Passes Caught**
13—Keith Willike, Capital (28) vs. Dayton (52), 11-21-87.

**Net Yards Receiving**
253—Eric Welgat, Augustana (Ill.) (36) vs. Dayton (38), 11-28-87.

**Touchdown Passes Caught**
4—Kirk Liesimer, Ill. Wesleyan (27) vs. Mount Union (49), 11-28-92.

**Passes Intercepted**
3—By seven players. Most recent: Tom Knapp, Ithaca (31) vs. Central (Iowa) (24), 12-10-88.

**Yards Gained on Interception Returns**
100—Jay Zunic, Ithaca (31) vs. Rowan (10), 11-23-91 (2 interceptions, 1 for 100-yard TD).

**Yards Gained on Punt Returns**
98—Leroy Horn, Montclair St. (28) vs. Western Conn. St. (0), 11-23-85.

**Yards Gained on Kickoff Returns**
190—George Day, Susquehanna (31) vs. Lycoming (24), 11-30-91.

**Points**
36—Mike Coppa, Salisbury St. (44) vs. Ithaca (40), 12-6-86.

**Touchdowns**
6—Mike Coppa, Salisbury St. (44) vs. Ithaca (40), 12-6-86.

**Extra Points**
9—Tim Robinson, Baldwin-Wallace (71) vs. St. Lawrence (7), 11-18-78.

## INDIVIDUAL: TOURNAMENT

**Net Yards Rushing**
882—Chris Babirad, Wash. & Jeff., 1992 (285 vs. Lycoming, 286 vs. Emory & Henry, 207 vs. Rowan, 104 vs. Wis.-La Crosse).

**Rushes Attempted**
129—Chris Babirad, Wash. & Jeff., 1992 (37 vs. Lycoming, 31 vs. Emory & Henry, 36 vs. Rowan, 25 vs. Wis.-La Crosse).

**Net Yards Passing**
1,247—Jim Ballard, Mount Union, 1992 (332 vs. Dayton, 454 vs. Ill. Wesleyan, 461 vs. Wis.-La Crosse).

**Passes Attempted**
141—Brett Russ, Union (N.Y.), 1989 (23 vs. Cortland St., 37 vs. Montclair St., 38 vs. Ferrum, 43 vs. Dayton).

*Division III Championship Results, Records*

595

**Passes Completed**
80 — Brett Russ, Union (N.Y.), 1989 (13 vs. Cortland St., 22 vs. Montclair St., 23 vs. Ferrum, 22 vs. Dayton).

**Touchdown Passes Completed**
8 — Brett Russ, Union (N.Y.), 1989 (3 vs. Cortland St., 3 vs. Montclair St., 2 vs. Ferrum, 0 vs. Dayton); Jim Ballard, Mount Union, 1992 (1 vs. Dayton, 5 vs. Ill. Wesleyan, 2 vs. Wis.-La Crosse).

**Completion Percentage (Min. 2 Games)**
.667 — Greg Thomas, Central (Iowa), 1989, 10 of 15 (5-7 vs. St. Norbert, 5-8 vs. St. John's, Minn.).

**Passes Had Intercepted**
9 — Rollie Wiebers, Buena Vista, 1976 (4 vs. Carroll, Wis., 5 vs. St. John's, Minn.).

**Passes Caught**
39 — Nick Ismailoff, Ithaca, 1991 (12 vs. Rowan, 6 vs. Union, N.Y., 11 vs. Susquehanna, 10 vs. Dayton).

**Net Yards Receiving**
599 — Nick Ismailoff, Ithaca, 1991 (179 vs. Rowan, 122 vs. Union, N.Y., 105 vs. Susquehanna, 193 vs. Dayton).

**Touchdown Passes Caught**
5 — Nick Ismailoff, Ithaca, 1991 (1 vs. Rowan, 1 vs. Union, N.Y., 1 vs. Susquehanna, 2 vs. Dayton).

**Points**
60 — By four players. Most recent: Chris Babirad, Wash. & Jeff., 1992 (18 vs. Lycoming, 24 vs. Emory & Henry, 12 vs. Rowan, 6 vs. Wis.-La Crosse).

**Touchdowns**
10 — Brad Price, Augustana (Ill.), 1986 (4 vs. Hope, 1 vs. Mount Union, 2 vs. Concordia-M'head, 3 vs. Salisbury St.); Mike Coppa, Salisbury St., 1986 (1 vs. Emory & Henry, 3 vs. Susquehanna, 6 vs. Ithaca, 0 vs. Augustana, Ill.); Chris Babirad, Wash. & Jeff., 1992 (3 vs. Lycoming, 4 vs. Emory & Henry, 2 vs. Rowan, 1 vs. Wis.-La Crosse).

## INDIVIDUAL: LONGEST PLAYS

**Longest Rush**
93 — Rick Papke, Augustana (Ill.) (17) vs. Central (Iowa) (23), 12-3-88, TD.

**Longest Pass Completion**
96 — Mark Blom to Tom McDonald, Central (Iowa) (37) vs. Buena Vista (0), 11-22-86, TD.

**Longest Field Goal**
52 — Rod Vesling, St. Lawrence (43) vs. Wagner (34), 11-20-82.

**Longest Punt**
79 — Tom Hansen, Ithaca (3) vs. Wittenberg (6), 11-18-78.

**Longest Punt Return**
78 — Pete Minturn, Ithaca (34) vs. Gettysburg (0), 12-7-85, TD.

**Longest Kickoff Return**
100 — Tom Deery, Widener (23) vs. Montclair St. (12), 11-30-81, TD.

**Longest Interception Return**
100 — Jay Zunic, Ithaca (31) vs. Rowan (10), 11-23-91, TD.

## TEAM: SINGLE GAME

**First Downs**
35 — Central (Iowa) (71) vs. Occidental (0), 12-7-85.

**First Downs by Rushing**
30 — Central (Iowa) (71) vs. Occidental (0), 12-7-85.

**First Downs by Passing**
20 — Rowan (10) vs. Ithaca (31), 11-23-91.

**Net Yards Rushing**
530 — St. John's (Minn.) (46) vs. Augustana (Ill.) (7), 11-20-76.

**Rushes Attempted**
83 — Capital (34) vs. Luther (21), 11-28-70; Baldwin-Wallace (31) vs. Carnegie Mellon (6), 11-25-78.

**Net Yards Passing**
461 — Mount Union (24) vs. Wis.-La Crosse (29), 12-5-92.

**Passes Attempted**
59 — Montclair St. (28) vs. Ithaca (50), 11-30-85.

**Passes Completed**
32 — Hofstra (10) vs. Lycoming (20), 12-1-90.

**Completion Percentage (Min. 10 Attempts)**
.857 — Salisbury St. (16) vs. Carnegie Mellon (14), 11-19-83 (18 of 21).

**Passes Had Intercepted**
9 — Dubuque (7) vs. Ithaca (27), 11-17-79.

**Net Yards Rushing and Passing**
607 — Ferrum (49) vs. Moravian (28), 11-26-88.

**Rushing and Passing Plays**
101 — Union (N.Y.) (45) vs. Montclair St. (6), 11-25-89.

**Punting Average**
48.5 — Minn.-Morris (25) vs. Carnegie Mellon (31), 11-17-79.

**Number of Punts**
14 — Gettysburg (14) vs. Lycoming (10), 11-23-85.

**Yards Gained on Punt Returns**
100 — Gettysburg (22) vs. Salisbury St. (6), 11-30-85.

**Yards Gained on Kickoff Returns**
234 — Ithaca (40) vs. Salisbury St. (44), 12-6-86.

**Yards Gained on Interception Returns**
176 — Augustana (Ill.) (14) vs. St. Lawrence (0), 11-27-82.

**Yards Penalized**
166 — Ferrum (49) vs. Moravian (28), 11-26-88.

**Fumbles Lost**
6 — Albright (7) vs. St. Lawrence (26), 11-20-76; St. John's (Minn.) (7) vs. Dayton (19), 12-7-91.

**Points**
75 — St. John's (Minn.) vs. Coe (2), 11-23-91.

# TEAM: TOURNAMENT

**First Downs**
94—Ithaca, 1991 (22 vs. Rowan, 15 vs. Union, N.Y., 28 vs. Susquehanna, 29 vs. Dayton).

**Net Yards Rushing**
1,377—Ithaca, 1988 (251 vs. Wagner, 293 vs. Cortland St., 425 vs. Ferrum, 408 vs. Central, Iowa).

**Net Yards Passing**
1,247—Mount Union, 1992 (332 vs. Dayton, 454 vs. Ill. Wesleyan, 461 vs. Wis.-La Crosse).

**Net Yards Rushing and Passing**
1,867—Ithaca, 1991 (486 vs. Rowan, 350 vs. Union, N.Y., 473 vs. Susquehanna, 558 vs. Dayton).

**Passes Attempted**
150—Hofstra, 1990 (51 vs. Cortland St., 50 vs. Trenton St., 49 vs. Lycoming).

**Passes Completed**
87—Hofstra, 1990 (31 vs. Cortland St., 24 vs. Trenton St., 32 vs. Lycoming).

**Passes Had Intercepted**
11—Hofstra, 1990 (5 vs. Cortland St., 3 vs. Trenton St., 3 vs. Lycoming).

**Number of Punts**
30—Central (Iowa), 1988 (12 vs. Concordia-M'head, 8 vs. Wis.-Whitewater, 5 vs. Augustana, Ill., 5 vs. Ithaca).

**Yards Penalized**
331—Wagner, 1987 (61 vs. Rochester, 80 vs. Fordham, 87 vs. Emory & Henry, 103 vs. Dayton).

**Fumbles Lost**
10—Wittenberg, 1978 (4 vs. Ithaca, 2 vs. Minn.-Morris, 4 vs. Baldwin-Wallace).

**Points**
159—Ithaca, 1988 (34 vs. Wagner, 24 vs. Cortland St., 62 vs. Ferrum, 39 vs. Central, Iowa).

## YEAR-BY-YEAR DIVISION III CHAMPIONSHIP RESULTS

| Year (Number of Teams) | Coach | Record | Result |
|---|---|---|---|
| **1973 (4)** | | | |
| Wittenberg | Dave Maurer | 2-0 | Champion |
| Juniata | Walt Nadzak | 1-1 | Second |
| Bridgeport | Ed Farrell | 0-1 | Semifinalist |
| San Diego | Andy Vinci | 0-1 | Semifinalist |
| **1974 (4)** | | | |
| Central (Iowa) | Ron Schipper | 2-0 | Champion |
| Ithaca | Jim Butterfield | 1-1 | Second |
| Evansville | Jim Byers | 0-1 | Semifinalist |
| Slippery Rock | Bob Di Spirito | 0-1 | Semifinalist |
| **1975 (8)** | | | |
| Wittenberg | Dave Maurer | 3-0 | Champion |
| Ithaca | Jim Butterfield | 2-1 | Second |
| Millsaps | Harper Davis | 1-1 | Semifinalist |
| Widener | Bill Manlove | 1-1 | Semifinalist |
| Albright | John Potsklan | 0-1 | Lost 1st Round |
| Colorado Col. | Jerry Carle | 0-1 | Lost 1st Round |
| Fort Valley St. | Leon Lomax | 0-1 | Lost 1st Round |
| Indianapolis | Bill Bless | 0-1 | Lost 1st Round |
| **1976 (8)** | | | |
| St. John's (Minn.) | John Gagliardi | 3-0 | Champion |
| Towson St. | Phil Albert | 2-1 | Second |
| Buena Vista | Jim Hershberger | 1-1 | Semifinalist |
| St. Lawrence | Ted Stratford | 1-1 | Semifinalist |
| Albright | John Potsklan | 0-1 | Lost 1st Round |
| Augustana (Ill.) | Ben Newcomb | 0-1 | Lost 1st Round |
| Carroll (Wis.) | Steve Miller | 0-1 | Lost 1st Round |
| LIU-C. W. Post | Dom Anile | 0-1 | Lost 1st Round |
| **1977 (8)** | | | |
| Widener | Bill Manlove | 3-0 | Champion |
| Wabash | Frank Navarro | 2-1 | Second |
| Albany (N.Y.) | Bob Ford | 1-1 | Semifinalist |
| Minn.-Morris | Al Molde | 1-1 | Semifinalist |
| Albion | Frank Joranko | 0-1 | Lost 1st Round |
| Central (Iowa) | Ron Schipper | 0-1 | Lost 1st Round |
| Hampden-Sydney | Stokeley Fulton | 0-1 | Lost 1st Round |
| St. John's (Minn.) | John Gagliardi | 0-1 | Lost 1st Round |
| **1978 (8)** | | | |
| Baldwin-Wallace | Lee Tressel | 3-0 | Champion |
| Wittenberg | Dave Maurer | 2-1 | Second |
| Carnegie Mellon | Chuck Klausing | 1-1 | Semifinalist |
| Minn.-Morris | Al Molde | 1-1 | Semifinalist |
| Dayton | Rick Carter | 0-1 | Lost 1st Round |
| Ithaca | Jim Butterfield | 0-1 | Lost 1st Round |
| St. Lawrence | Ted Stratford | 0-1 | Lost 1st Round |
| St. Olaf | Tom Porter | 0-1 | Lost 1st Round |

| Year (Number of Teams) | Coach | Record | Result |
|---|---|---|---|
| **1979 (8)** | | | |
| Ithaca | Jim Butterfield | 3-0 | Champion |
| Wittenberg | Dave Maurer | 2-1 | Second |
| Carnegie Mellon | Chuck Klausing | 1-1 | Semifinalist |
| Widener | Bill Manlove | 1-1 | Semifinalist |
| Baldwin-Wallace | Lee Tressel | 0-1 | Lost 1st Round |
| Dubuque | Don Birmingham | 0-1 | Lost 1st Round |
| Millersville | Gene Carpenter | 0-1 | Lost 1st Round |
| Minn.-Morris | Al Molde | 0-1 | Lost 1st Round |
| **1980 (8)** | | | |
| Dayton | Rick Carter | 3-0 | Champion |
| Ithaca | Jim Butterfield | 2-1 | Second |
| Minn.-Morris | Dick Smith | 1-1 | Semifinalist |
| Widener | Bill Manlove | 1-1 | Semifinalist |
| Baldwin-Wallace | Lee Tressel | 0-1 | Lost 1st Round |
| Bethany (W. Va.) | Don Ault | 0-1 | Lost 1st Round |
| Dubuque | Don Birmingham | 0-1 | Lost 1st Round |
| Wagner | Bill Russo | 0-1 | Lost 1st Round |
| **1981 (8)** | | | |
| Widener | Bill Manlove | 3-0 | Champion |
| Dayton | Mike Kelly | 2-1 | Second |
| Lawrence | Ron Roberts | 1-1 | Semifinalist |
| Montclair St. | Fred Hill | 1-1 | Semifinalist |
| Alfred | Sam Sanders | 0-1 | Lost 1st Round |
| Augustana (Ill.) | Bob Reade | 0-1 | Lost 1st Round |
| Minn.-Morris | Dick Smith | 0-1 | Lost 1st Round |
| West Ga. | Bobby Pate | 0-1 | Lost 1st Round |
| **1982 (8)** | | | |
| West Ga. | Bobby Pate | 3-0 | Champion |
| Augustana (Ill.) | Bob Reade | 2-1 | Second |
| Bishop | James Jones | 1-1 | Semifinalist |
| St. Lawrence | Andy Talley | 1-1 | Semifinalist |
| Baldwin-Wallace | Bob Packard | 0-1 | Lost 1st Round |
| Wagner | Walt Hameline | 0-1 | Lost 1st Round |
| Wartburg | Don Canfield | 0-1 | Lost 1st Round |
| Widener | Bill Manlove | 0-1 | Lost 1st Round |
| **1983 (8)** | | | |
| Augustana (Ill.) | Bob Reade | 3-0 | Champion |
| Union (N. Y.) | Al Bagnoli | 2-1 | Second |
| Salisbury St. | Mike McGlinchey | 1-1 | Semifinalist |
| Wis.-La Crosse | Roger Harring | 1-1 | Semifinalist |
| Adrian | Ron Labadie | 0-1 | Lost 1st Round |
| Carnegie Mellon | Chuck Klausing | 0-1 | Lost 1st Round |
| Hofstra | Mickey Kwiatkowski | 0-1 | Lost 1st Round |
| Occidental | Dale Widolff | 0-1 | Lost 1st Round |
| **1984 (8)** | | | |
| Augustana (Ill.) | Bob Reade | 3-0 | Champion |
| Central (Iowa) | Ron Schipper | 2-1 | Second |
| Union (N.Y.) | Al Bagnoli | 1-1 | Semifinalist |
| Wash. & Jeff. | John Luckhardt | 1-1 | Semifinalist |
| Dayton | Mike Kelly | 0-1 | Lost 1st Round |
| Occidental | Dale Widolff | 0-1 | Lost 1st Round |
| Plymouth St. | Jay Cottone | 0-1 | Lost 1st Round |
| Randolph-Macon | Jim Blackburn | 0-1 | Lost 1st Round |
| **1985 (16)** | | | |
| Augustana (Ill.) | Bob Reade | 4-0 | Champion |
| Ithaca | Jim Butterfield | 3-1 | Second |
| Central (Iowa) | Ron Schipper | 2-1 | Semifinalist |
| Gettysburg | Barry Streeter | 2-1 | Semifinalist |
| Montclair St. | Rick Giancola | 1-1 | Quarterfinalist |
| Mount Union | Ken Wable | 1-1 | Quarterfinalist |
| Occidental | Dale Widolff | 1-1 | Quarterfinalist |
| Salisbury St. | Mike McGlinchey | 1-1 | Quarterfinalist |
| Albion | Pete Schmidt | 0-1 | Lost 1st Round |
| Carnegie Mellon | Chuck Klausing | 0-1 | Lost 1st Round |
| Coe | Bob Thurness | 0-1 | Lost 1st Round |
| Denison | Keith Piper | 0-1 | Lost 1st Round |
| Lycoming | Frank Girardi | 0-1 | Lost 1st Round |
| St. John's (Minn.) | John Gagliardi | 0-1 | Lost 1st Round |
| Union (N.Y.) | Al Bagnoli | 0-1 | Lost 1st Round |

| Year (Number of Teams) | Coach | Record | Result |
|---|---|---|---|
| Western Conn. St............... | Paul Pasqualoni | 0-1 | Lost 1st Round |
| **1986 (16)** | | | |
| Augustana (III.)................. | Bob Reade | 4-0 | Champion |
| Salisbury St.................... | Mike McGlinchey | 3-1 | Second |
| Concordia-M'head.............. | Jim Christopherson | 2-1 | Semifinalist |
| Ithaca........................ | Jim Butterfield | 2-1 | Semifinalist |
| Central (Iowa)................. | Ron Schipper | 1-1 | Quarterfinalist |
| Montclair St................... | Rick Giancola | 1-1 | Quarterfinalist |
| Mount Union................... | Larry Kehres | 1-1 | Quarterfinalist |
| Susquehanna.................. | Rocky Rees | 1-1 | Quarterfinalist |
| Buena Vista................... | Jim Hershberger | 0-1 | Lost 1st Round |
| Dayton....................... | Mike Kelly | 0-1 | Lost 1st Round |
| Emory & Henry................ | Lou Wacker | 0-1 | Lost 1st Round |
| Hofstra....................... | Mickey Kwiatkowski | 0-1 | Lost 1st Round |
| Hope......................... | Ray Smith | 0-1 | Lost 1st Round |
| Union (N.Y.).................. | Al Bagnoli | 0-1 | Lost 1st Round |
| Wash. & Jeff.................. | John Luckhardt | 0-1 | Lost 1st Round |
| Wis.-Stevens Point............. | D. J. LeRoy | 0-1 | Lost 1st Round |
| **1987 (16)** | | | |
| Wagner....................... | Walt Hameline | 4-0 | Champion |
| Dayton....................... | Mike Kelly | 3-1 | Second |
| Central (Iowa)................. | Ron Schipper | 2-1 | Semifinalist |
| Emory & Henry................ | Lou Wacker | 2-1 | Semifinalist |
| Augustana (III.)................. | Bob Reade | 1-1 | Quarterfinalist |
| Fordham...................... | Larry Glueck | 1-1 | Quarterfinalist |
| St. John's (Minn.).............. | John Gagliardi | 1-1 | Quarterfinalist |
| Wash. & Jeff.................. | John Luckhardt | 1-1 | Quarterfinalist |
| Allegheny..................... | Peter Vaas | 0-1 | Lost 1st Round |
| Capital....................... | Roger Welsh | 0-1 | Lost 1st Round |
| Ferrum....................... | Hank Norton | 0-1 | Lost 1st Round |
| Gust. Adolphus............... | Steve Raarup | 0-1 | Lost 1st Round |
| Hiram........................ | Don Charlton | 0-1 | Lost 1st Round |
| Hofstra....................... | Mickey Kwiatkowski | 0-1 | Lost 1st Round |
| Menlo........................ | Ray Solari | 0-1 | Lost 1st Round |
| Rochester.................... | Ray Tellier | 0-1 | Lost 1st Round |
| **1988 (16)** | | | |
| Ithaca........................ | Jim Butterfield | 4-0 | Champion |
| Central (Iowa)................. | Ron Schipper | 3-1 | Second |
| Augustana (III.)................. | Bob Reade | 2-1 | Semifinalist |
| Ferrum....................... | Hank Norton | 2-1 | Semifinalist |
| Cortland St.................... | Dennis Kayser | 1-1 | Quarterfinalist |
| Moravian..................... | Scot Dapp | 1-1 | Quarterfinalist |
| Wis.-Whitewater............... | Bob Berezowitz | 1-1 | Quarterfinalist |
| Wittenberg.................... | Ron Murphy | 1-1 | Quarterfinalist |
| Adrian........................ | Ron Labadie | 0-1 | Lost Regionals |
| Concordia-M'head.............. | Jim Christopherson | 0-1 | Lost Regionals |
| Dayton....................... | Mike Kelly | 0-1 | Lost Regionals |
| Hofstra....................... | Mickey Kwiatkowski | 0-1 | Lost Regionals |
| Rhodes....................... | Mike Clary | 0-1 | Lost Regionals |
| Simpson...................... | Jim Williams | 0-1 | Lost Regionals |
| Wagner....................... | Walt Hameline | 0-1 | Lost Regionals |
| Widener...................... | Bill Manlove | 0-1 | Lost Regionals |
| **1989 (16)** | | | |
| Dayton....................... | Mike Kelly | 4-0 | Champion |
| Union (N.Y.).................. | Al Bagnoli | 3-1 | Second |
| Ferrum....................... | Hank Norton | 2-1 | Semifinalist |
| St. John's (Minn.).............. | John Gagliardi | 2-1 | Semifinalist |
| Central (Iowa)................. | Ron Schipper | 1-1 | Quarterfinalist |
| Lycoming..................... | Frank Girardi | 1-1 | Quarterfinalist |
| Millikin....................... | Carl Poelker | 1-1 | Quarterfinalist |
| Montclair St................... | Rick Giancola | 1-1 | Quarterfinalist |
| Augustana (III.)................. | Bob Reade | 0-1 | Lost Regionals |
| Cortland St.................... | Dennis Kayser | 0-1 | Lost Regionals |
| Dickinson..................... | Ed Sweeney | 0-1 | Lost Regionals |
| Hofstra....................... | Mickey Kwiatkowski | 0-1 | Lost Regionals |
| John Carroll................... | Tony DeCarlo | 0-1 | Lost Regionals |
| Simpson...................... | Jim Williams | 0-1 | Lost Regionals |
| St. Norbert................... | Don LaViolette | 0-1 | Lost Regionals |
| Wash. & Jeff.................. | John Luckhardt | 0-1 | Lost Regionals |

| Year (Number of Teams) | Coach | Record | Result |
|---|---|---|---|
| **1990 (16)** | | | |
| Allegheny..................... | Ken O'Keefe | 4-0 | Champion |
| Lycoming..................... | Frank Girardi | 3-1 | Second |
| Central (Iowa)................. | Ron Schipper | 2-1 | Semifinalist |
| Hofstra...................... | Joe Gardi | 2-1 | Semifinalist |
| Dayton...................... | Mike Kelly | 1-1 | Quarterfinalist |
| St. Thomas (Minn.)............ | Vic Wallace | 1-1 | Quarterfinalist |
| Trenton St.................... | Eric Hamilton | 1-1 | Quarterfinalist |
| Wash. & Jeff.................. | John Luckhardt | 1-1 | Quarterfinalist |
| Augustana (Ill.)............... | Bob Reade | 0-1 | Lost Regionals |
| Carnegie Mellon.............. | Rich Lackner | 0-1 | Lost Regionals |
| Cortland St................... | Dave Murray | 0-1 | Lost Regionals |
| Ferrum...................... | Hank Norton | 0-1 | Lost Regionals |
| Ithaca...................... | Jim Butterfield | 0-1 | Lost Regionals |
| Mount Union................. | Larry Kehres | 0-1 | Lost Regionals |
| Redlands.................... | Mike Maynard | 0-1 | Lost Regionals |
| Wis.-Whitewater.............. | Bob Berezowitz | 0-1 | Lost Regionals |
| **1991 (16)** | | | |
| Ithaca...................... | Jim Butterfield | 4-0 | Champion |
| Dayton...................... | Mike Kelly | 3-1 | Second |
| St. John's (Minn.)............. | John Gagliardi | 2-1 | Semifinalist |
| Susquehanna................. | Steve Briggs | 2-1 | Semifinalist |
| Allegheny................... | Ken O'Keefe | 1-1 | Quarterfinalist |
| Lycoming................... | Frank Girardi | 1-1 | Quarterfinalist |
| Union (N. Y.)................. | Al Bagnoli | 1-1 | Quarterfinalist |
| Wis.-La Crosse............... | Roger Harring | 1-1 | Quarterfinalist |
| Albion...................... | Pete Schmidt | 0-1 | Lost Regionals |
| Baldwin-Wallace.............. | Bob Packard | 0-1 | Lost Regionals |
| Coe........................ | D. J. LeRoy | 0-1 | Lost Regionals |
| Dickinson................... | Ed Sweeney | 0-1 | Lost Regionals |
| Mass.-Lowell................. | Dennis Scannell | 0-1 | Lost Regionals |
| Rowan...................... | John Bunting | 0-1 | Lost Regionals |
| Simpson..................... | Jim Williams | 0-1 | Lost Regionals |
| Wash. & Jeff................. | John Luckhardt | 0-1 | Lost Regionals |
| **1992 (16)** | | | |
| Wis.-La Crosse................ | Roger Harring | 4-0 | Champion |
| Wash. & Jeff................. | John Luckhardt | 3-1 | Second |
| Mount Union................. | Larry Kehres | 2-1 | Semifinalist |
| Rowan...................... | John Bunting | 2-1 | Semifinalist |
| Buffalo St.................... | Jerry Boyes | 1-1 | Quarterfinalist |
| Central (Iowa)................. | Ron Schipper | 1-1 | Quarterfinalist |
| Emory & Henry............... | Lou Wacker | 1-1 | Quarterfinalist |
| Ill. Wesleyan................. | Norm Eash | 1-1 | Quarterfinalist |
| Aurora...................... | Jim Scott | 0-1 | Lost Regionals |
| Carleton.................... | Bob Sullivan | 0-1 | Lost Regionals |
| Dayton...................... | Mike Kelly | 0-1 | Lost Regionals |
| Ithaca...................... | Jim Butterfield | 0-1 | Lost Regionals |
| Lycoming................... | Frank Girardi | 0-1 | Lost Regionals |
| Redlands.................... | Mike Maynard | 0-1 | Lost Regionals |
| Thomas More................ | Vic Clark | 0-1 | Lost Regionals |
| Worcester Tech............... | Jack Siedlecki | 0-1 | Lost Regionals |

### DIVISION III CHAMPIONSHIP
### ALL-TIME RECORD OF EACH COLLEGE
### COACH-BY-COACH, 1973-92 (88 Colleges)

| | Yrs | Won | Lost | CH | 2D |
|---|---|---|---|---|---|
| **ADRIAN** | | | | | |
| Ron Labadie (Adrian '71) 83, 88.................. | 2 | 0 | 2 | 0 | 0 |
| **ALBANY (N.Y.)** | | | | | |
| Bob Ford (Springfield '59) 77..................... | 1 | 1 | 1 | 0 | 0 |
| **ALBION** | | | | | |
| Frank Joranko (Albion '52) 77.................... | 1 | 0 | 1 | 0 | 0 |
| Pete Schmidt (Alma '70) 85, 91.................. | 2 | 0 | 2 | 0 | 0 |
| TOTAL | 3 | 0 | 3 | 0 | 0 |
| **ALBRIGHT** | | | | | |
| John Potsklan (Penn St. '49) 75, 76................ | 2 | 0 | 2 | 0 | 0 |
| **ALFRED** | | | | | |
| Sam Sanders (Buffalo '60) 81..................... | 1 | 0 | 1 | 0 | 0 |

*1993 NCAA FOOTBALL*

| | Yrs | Won | Lost | CH | 2D |
|---|---|---|---|---|---|
| **ALLEGHENY** | | | | | |
| Peter Vaas (Holy Cross '74) 87 . . . . . . . . . . . . . . . . . . . . . | 1 | 0 | 1 | 0 | 0 |
| Ken O'Keefe (John Carroll '75) 90-CH, 91 . . . . . . . . . . | 2 | 5 | 1 | 1 | 0 |
| TOTAL | 3 | 5 | 2 | 1 | 0 |
| **AUGUSTANA (ILL.)** | | | | | |
| Ben Newcomb 76 . . . . . . . . . . . . . . . . . . . . . . . . . . . . . | 1 | 0 | 1 | 0 | 0 |
| Bob Reade (Cornell College '54) 81, 82-2D, 83-CH, | | | | | |
| 84-CH, 85-CH, 86-CH, 87, 88, 89, 90 . . . . . . . . . . . . . | 10 | 19 | 6 | 4 | 1 |
| TOTAL | 11 | 19 | 7 | 4 | 1 |
| **AURORA** | | | | | |
| Jim Scott (Luther '61) 92 . . . . . . . . . . . . . . . . . . . . . . . . | 1 | 0 | 1 | 0 | 0 |
| **BALDWIN-WALLACE** | | | | | |
| Lee Tressel (Baldwin-Wallace '48) 78-CH, 79, 80 . . . . . . | 3 | 3 | 2 | 1 | 0 |
| Bob Packard (Baldwin-Wallace '65) 82, 91 . . . . . . . . . . | 2 | 0 | 2 | 0 | 0 |
| TOTAL | 5 | 3 | 4 | 1 | 0 |
| **BETHANY (W. VA.)** | | | | | |
| Don Ault (West Liberty St. '52) 80 . . . . . . . . . . . . . . . . . | 1 | 0 | 1 | 0 | 0 |
| **BISHOP** | | | | | |
| James Jones (Bishop '49) 82 . . . . . . . . . . . . . . . . . . . . . | 1 | 1 | 1 | 0 | 0 |
| **BRIDGEPORT** | | | | | |
| Ed Farrell (Rutgers '56) 73 . . . . . . . . . . . . . . . . . . . . . . | 1 | 0 | 1 | 0 | 0 |
| **BUENA VISTA** | | | | | |
| Jim Hershberger (Northern Iowa '57) 76, 86 . . . . . . . . . | 2 | 1 | 2 | 0 | 0 |
| **BUFFALO ST.** | | | | | |
| Jerry Boyes (Ithaca '76) 92 . . . . . . . . . . . . . . . . . . . . . . | 1 | 1 | 1 | 0 | 0 |
| **CAPITAL** | | | | | |
| Roger Welsh (Muskingum '64) 87 . . . . . . . . . . . . . . . . . | 1 | 0 | 1 | 0 | 0 |
| **CARLETON** | | | | | |
| Bob Sullivan (St. John's, Minn. '59) 92 . . . . . . . . . . . . . | 1 | 0 | 1 | 0 | 0 |
| **CARNEGIE MELLON** | | | | | |
| Chuck Klausing (Slippery Rock '48) 78, 79, 83, 85 . . . . | 4 | 2 | 4 | 0 | 0 |
| Rich Lackner (Carnegie Mellon '79) 90 . . . . . . . . . . . . . | 1 | 0 | 1 | 0 | 0 |
| TOTAL | 5 | 2 | 5 | 0 | 0 |
| **CARROLL (WIS.)** | | | | | |
| Steve Miller (Cornell College '65) 76 . . . . . . . . . . . . . . . | 1 | 0 | 1 | 0 | 0 |
| **CENTRAL (IOWA)** | | | | | |
| Ron Schipper (Hope '52) 74-CH, 77, 84-2D, 85, 86, | | | | | |
| 87, 88-2D, 89, 90, 92 . . . . . . . . . . . . . . . . . . . . . . . . | 10 | 16 | 9 | 1 | 2 |
| **COE** | | | | | |
| Bob Thurness (Coe '62) 85 . . . . . . . . . . . . . . . . . . . . . . | 1 | 0 | 1 | 0 | 0 |
| D. J. LeRoy (Wis.-Eau Claire '79) 91 . . . . . . . . . . . . . . . | 1 | 0 | 1 | 0 | 0 |
| TOTAL | 2 | 0 | 2 | 0 | 0 |
| **COLORADO COL.** | | | | | |
| Jerry Carle (Northwestern '48) 75 . . . . . . . . . . . . . . . . . | 1 | 0 | 1 | 0 | 0 |
| **CONCORDIA-M'HEAD** | | | | | |
| Jim Christopherson (Concordia-M'head '60) 86, | | | | | |
| 88 . . . . . . . . . . . . . . . . . . . . . . . . . . . . . . . . . . . . . . . . . | 2 | 2 | 2 | 0 | 0 |
| **CORTLAND ST.** | | | | | |
| Dennis Kayser (Ithaca '74) 88, 89 . . . . . . . . . . . . . . . . . | 2 | 1 | 2 | 0 | 0 |
| Dave Murray (Springfield '81) 90 . . . . . . . . . . . . . . . . . | 1 | 0 | 1 | 0 | 0 |
| TOTAL | 3 | 1 | 3 | 0 | 0 |
| **DAYTON** | | | | | |
| Rick Carter (Earlham '65) 78, 80-CH . . . . . . . . . . . . . . | 2 | 3 | 1 | 1 | 0 |
| Mike Kelly (Manchester '70) 81-2D, 84, 86, 87-2D, | | | | | |
| 88, 89-CH, 90, 91-2D, 92 . . . . . . . . . . . . . . . . . . . . . . . | 9 | 13 | 8 | 1 | 3 |
| TOTAL | 11 | 16 | 9 | 2 | 3 |
| **DENISON** | | | | | |
| Keith Piper (Baldwin-Wallace '48) 85 . . . . . . . . . . . . . . | 1 | 0 | 1 | 0 | 0 |
| **DICKINSON** | | | | | |
| Ed Sweeney (LIU-C. W. Post '71) 89, 91 . . . . . . . . . . . . | 2 | 0 | 2 | 0 | 0 |
| **DUBUQUE** | | | | | |
| Don Birmingham (Westmar '62) 79, 80 . . . . . . . . . . . . . | 2 | 0 | 2 | 0 | 0 |
| **EMORY & HENRY** | | | | | |
| Lou Wacker (Richmond '56) 86, 87, 92 . . . . . . . . . . . . . | 3 | 3 | 3 | 0 | 0 |

*Division III Championship Results, Records*

| | Yrs | Won | Lost | CH | 2D |
|---|---|---|---|---|---|
| **EVANSVILLE** | | | | | |
| Jim Byers (Michigan '59) 74...................... | 1 | 0 | 1 | 0 | 0 |
| **FERRUM** | | | | | |
| Hank Norton (Lynchburg '51) 87, 88, 89, 90......... | 4 | 4 | 4 | 0 | 0 |
| **FORDHAM** | | | | | |
| Larry Glueck (Villanova '63) 87.................... | 1 | 1 | 1 | 0 | 0 |
| **FORT VALLEY ST.** | | | | | |
| Leon Lomax (Fort Valley St. '43) 75................ | 1 | 0 | 1 | 0 | 0 |
| **GETTYSBURG** | | | | | |
| Barry Streeter (Lebanon Valley '71) 85.............. | 1 | 2 | 1 | 0 | 0 |
| **GUST. ADOLPHUS** | | | | | |
| Steve Raarup (Gust. Adolphus '53) 87............... | 1 | 0 | 1 | 0 | 0 |
| **HAMPDEN-SYDNEY** | | | | | |
| Stokeley Fulton (Hampden-Sydney '55) 77.......... | 1 | 0 | 1 | 0 | 0 |
| **HIRAM** | | | | | |
| Don Charlton (Lock Haven '65) 87.................. | 1 | 0 | 1 | 0 | 0 |
| **HOFSTRA** | | | | | |
| Mickey Kwiatkowski (Delaware '70) 83, 86, 87, 88, | | | | | |
| 89............................................ | 5 | 0 | 5 | 0 | 0 |
| Joe Gardi (Maryland '60) 90....................... | 1 | 2 | 1 | 0 | 0 |
| TOTAL | 6 | 2 | 6 | 0 | 0 |
| **HOPE** | | | | | |
| Ray Smith (UCLA '61) 86.......................... | 1 | 0 | 1 | 0 | 0 |
| **ILL. WESLEYAN** | | | | | |
| Norm Eash (Ill. Wesleyan '75) 92.................. | 1 | 1 | 1 | 0 | 0 |
| **INDIANAPOLIS** | | | | | |
| Bill Bless (Indianapolis '63) 75.................... | 1 | 0 | 1 | 0 | 0 |
| **ITHACA** | | | | | |
| Jim Butterfield (Maine '53) 74-2D, 75-2D, 78, 79-CH, | | | | | |
| 80-2D, 85-2D, 86, 88-CH, 90, 91-CH, 92........... | 11 | 21 | 8 | 3 | 4 |
| **JOHN CARROLL** | | | | | |
| Tony DeCarlo (Kent '62) 89....................... | 1 | 0 | 1 | 0 | 0 |
| **JUNIATA** | | | | | |
| Walt Nadzak (Denison '57) 73-2D.................. | 1 | 1 | 1 | 0 | 1 |
| **LAWRENCE** | | | | | |
| Ron Roberts (Wisconsin '54) 81.................... | 1 | 1 | 1 | 0 | 0 |
| **LIU-C. W. POST** | | | | | |
| Dom Anile (LIU-C. W. Post '59) 76................. | 1 | 0 | 1 | 0 | 0 |
| **LYCOMING** | | | | | |
| Frank Girardi (West Chester '61) 85, 89, 90-2D, 91, 92 | 5 | 5 | 5 | 0 | 1 |
| **MASS.-LOWELL** | | | | | |
| Dennis Scannell (Villanova '74) 91................. | 1 | 0 | 1 | 0 | 0 |
| **MENLO** | | | | | |
| Ray Solari (California '51) 87...................... | 1 | 0 | 1 | 0 | 0 |
| **MILLERSVILLE** | | | | | |
| Gene Carpenter (Huron '63) 79.................... | 1 | 0 | 1 | 0 | 0 |
| **MILLIKIN** | | | | | |
| Carl Poelker (Millikin '68) 89...................... | 1 | 1 | 1 | 0 | 0 |
| **MILLSAPS** | | | | | |
| Harper Davis (Mississippi St. '49) 75................ | 1 | 1 | 1 | 0 | 0 |
| **MINN.-MORRIS** | | | | | |
| Al Molde (Gust. Adolphus '66) 77, 78, 79........... | 3 | 2 | 3 | 0 | 0 |
| Dick Smith (Coe '68) 80, 81...................... | 2 | 1 | 2 | 0 | 0 |
| TOTAL | 5 | 3 | 5 | 0 | 0 |
| **MONTCLAIR AT.** | | | | | |
| Fred Hill (Upsala '57) 81.......................... | 1 | 1 | 1 | 0 | 0 |
| Rick Giancola (Rowan '68) 85, 86, 89.............. | 3 | 3 | 3 | 0 | 0 |
| TOTAL | 4 | 4 | 4 | 0 | 0 |
| **MORAVIAN** | | | | | |
| Scot Dapp (West Chester '73) 88.................. | 1 | 1 | 1 | 0 | 0 |
| **MOUNT UNION** | | | | | |
| Ken Wable (Muskingum '52) 85..................... | 1 | 1 | 1 | 0 | 0 |
| Larry Kehres (Mount Union '71) 86, 90, 92.......... | 3 | 3 | 3 | 0 | 0 |
| TOTAL | 4 | 4 | 4 | 0 | 0 |

*1993 NCAA FOOTBALL*

| | Yrs | Won | Lost | CH | 2D |
|---|---|---|---|---|---|
| **OCCIDENTAL**<br>Dale Widolff (Indiana Central '75) 83, 84, 85 . . . . . . . . | 3 | 1 | 3 | 0 | 0 |
| **PLYMOUTH ST.**<br>Jay Cottone (Norwich '71) 84 . . . . . . . . . . . . . . . . . . . . | 1 | 0 | 1 | 0 | 0 |
| **RANDOLPH-MACON**<br>Jim Blackburn (Virginia '71) 84 . . . . . . . . . . . . . . . . . . | 1 | 0 | 1 | 0 | 0 |
| **REDLANDS**<br>Mike Maynard (Ill. Wesleyan '80) 90, 92 . . . . . . . . . . . . | 2 | 0 | 2 | 0 | 0 |
| **RHODES**<br>Mike Clary (Rhodes '77) 88 . . . . . . . . . . . . . . . . . . . . . . | 1 | 0 | 1 | 0 | 0 |
| **ROCHESTER**<br>Ray Tellier (Connecticut '73) 87 . . . . . . . . . . . . . . . . . . . | 1 | 0 | 1 | 0 | 0 |
| **ROWAN**<br>John Bunting (North Caro. '72) 91, 92 . . . . . . . . . . . . . . | 2 | 2 | 2 | 0 | 0 |
| **SALISBURY ST.**<br>Mike McGlinchey (Delaware '67) 83, 85, 86-2D . . . . . . . | 3 | 5 | 3 | 0 | 1 |
| **SAN DIEGO**<br>Andy Vinci (Cal St. Los Angeles '63) 73 . . . . . . . . . . . . | 1 | 0 | 1 | 0 | 0 |
| **SIMPSON**<br>Jim Williams (Northern Iowa '60) 88, 89, 91 . . . . . . . . . . | 3 | 0 | 3 | 0 | 0 |
| **SLIPPERY ROCK**<br>Bob Di Spirito (Rhode Island '53) 74 . . . . . . . . . . . . . . | 1 | 0 | 1 | 0 | 0 |
| **ST. JOHN'S (MINN.)**<br>John Gagliardi (Colorado Col. '49) 76-CH, 77, 85,<br>87, 89, 91 . . . . . . . . . . . . . . . . . . . . . . . . . . . . . . . . . . | 6 | 8 | 5 | 1 | 0 |
| **ST. LAWRENCE**<br>Ted Stratford (St. Lawrence '57) 76, 78 . . . . . . . . . . . . | 2 | 1 | 2 | 0 | 0 |
| Andy Talley (Southern Conn. St. '67) 82 . . . . . . . . . . . | 1 | 1 | 1 | 0 | 0 |
| TOTAL | 3 | 2 | 3 | 0 | 0 |
| **ST. NORBERT**<br>Don LaViolette (St. Norbert '54) 89 . . . . . . . . . . . . . . . . | 1 | 0 | 1 | 0 | 0 |
| **ST. OLAF**<br>Tom Porter (St. Olaf '51) 78 . . . . . . . . . . . . . . . . . . . . . . | 1 | 0 | 1 | 0 | 0 |
| **ST. THOMAS (MINN.)**<br>Vic Wallace (Cornell College '65) 90 . . . . . . . . . . . . . . . | 1 | 1 | 1 | 0 | 0 |
| **SUSQUEHANNA**<br>Rocky Rees (West Chester '71) 86 . . . . . . . . . . . . . . . . . | 1 | 1 | 1 | 0 | 0 |
| Steve Briggs (Springfield '84) 91 . . . . . . . . . . . . . . . . . . | 1 | 2 | 1 | 0 | 0 |
| TOTAL | 2 | 3 | 2 | 0 | 0 |
| **THOMAS MORE**<br>Vic Clark (Indiana St. '71) 92 . . . . . . . . . . . . . . . . . . . . . | 1 | 0 | 1 | 0 | 0 |
| **TOWSON ST.**<br>Phil Albert (Arizona '66) 76-2D . . . . . . . . . . . . . . . . . . . | 1 | 2 | 1 | 0 | 1 |
| **TRENTON ST.**<br>Eric Hamilton (Trenton St. '75) 90 . . . . . . . . . . . . . . . . | 1 | 1 | 1 | 0 | 0 |
| **UNION (N.Y.)**<br>Al Bagnoli (Central Conn. St. '74) 83-2D, 84, 85,<br>86, 89-2D, 91 . . . . . . . . . . . . . . . . . . . . . . . . . . . . . . . | 6 | 7 | 6 | 0 | 2 |
| **WABASH**<br>Frank Navarro (Maryland '53) 77-2D . . . . . . . . . . . . . . | 1 | 2 | 1 | 0 | 1 |
| **WAGNER**<br>Bill Russo 80 . . . . . . . . . . . . . . . . . . . . . . . . . . . . . . . . . . | 1 | 0 | 1 | 0 | 0 |
| Walt Hameline (Brockport St. '75) 82, 87-CH, 88 . . . . . . | 3 | 4 | 2 | 1 | 0 |
| TOTAL | 4 | 4 | 3 | 1 | 0 |
| **WARTBURG**<br>Don Canfield 82 . . . . . . . . . . . . . . . . . . . . . . . . . . . . . . . | 1 | 0 | 1 | 0 | 0 |
| **WASH. & JEFF.**<br>John Luckhardt (Purdue '67) 84, 86, 87, 89, 90, 91<br>92-2D . . . . . . . . . . . . . . . . . . . . . . . . . . . . . . . . . . . . . . | 7 | 6 | 7 | 0 | 1 |
| **WESTERN CONN. ST.**<br>Paul Pasqualoni (Penn St. '72) 85 . . . . . . . . . . . . . . . . . | 1 | 0 | 1 | 0 | 0 |
| **WEST GA.**<br>Bobby Pate (Georgia '63) 81, 82-CH . . . . . . . . . . . . . . | 2 | 3 | 1 | 1 | 0 |

| | Yrs | Won | Lost | CH | 2D |
|---|---|---|---|---|---|
| **WIDENER** | | | | | |
| Bill Manlove (Temple '58) 75, 77-CH, 79, 80, 81-CH, 82, 88 | 7 | 9 | 5 | 2 | 0 |
| **WIS.-LA CROSSE** | | | | | |
| Roger Harring (Wis.-La Crosse '58) 83, 91, 92-CH | 3 | 6 | 2 | 1 | 0 |
| **WIS.-STEVENS POINT** | | | | | |
| D. J. LeRoy (Wis.-Eau Claire '79) 86 | 1 | 0 | 1 | 0 | 0 |
| **WIS.-WHITEWATER** | | | | | |
| Bob Berezowitz (Wis.-Whitewater '67) 88, 90 | 2 | 1 | 2 | 0 | 0 |
| **WITTENBERG** | | | | | |
| Dave Maurer (Denison '54) 73-CH, 75-CH, 78-2D, 79-2D | 4 | 9 | 2 | 2 | 2 |
| Ron Murphy 88 | 1 | 1 | 1 | 0 | 0 |
| TOTAL | 5 | 10 | 3 | 2 | 2 |
| **WORCESTER TECH** | | | | | |
| Jack Siedlecki (Union, N.Y. '73) 92 | 1 | 0 | 1 | 0 | 0 |

## ALL-TIME RESULTS

**1973 Semifinals:** Juniata 35, Bridgeport 14; Wittenberg 21, San Diego 14. **Championship:** Wittenberg 41, Juniata 0.

**1974 Semifinals:** Central (Iowa) 17, Evansville 16; Ithaca 27, Slippery Rock 14. **Championship:** Central (Iowa) 10, Ithaca 8.

**1975 First Round:** Widener 14, Albright 6; Ithaca 41, Fort Valley St. 12; Wittenberg 17, Indianapolis 13; Millsaps 28, Colorado Col. 21. **Semifinals:** Ithaca 23, Widener 14; Wittenberg 55, Millsaps 22. **Championship:** Wittenberg 28, Ithaca 0.

**1976 First Round:** St. John's (Minn.) 46, Augustana (Ill.) 7; Buena Vista 20, Carroll (Wis.) 14 (OT); St. Lawrence 26, Albright 7; Towson St. 14, LIU-C.W. Post 10. **Semifinals:** St. John's (Minn.) 61, Buena Vista 0; Towson St. 38, St. Lawrence 36. **Championship:** St. John's (Minn.) 31, Towson St. 28.

**1977 First Round:** Minn.-Morris 13, Albion 12; Wabash 20, St. John's (Minn.) 9; Widener 19, Central (Iowa) 0; Albany (N.Y.) 51, Hampden-Sydney 45. **Semifinals:** Wabash 37, Minn.-Morris 21; Widener 33, Albany (N.Y.) 15. **Championship:** Widener 39, Wabash 36.

**1978 First Round:** Minn.-Morris 23, St. Olaf 10; Wittenberg 6, Ithaca 3; Carnegie Mellon 24, Dayton 21; Baldwin-Wallace 71, St. Lawrence 7. **Semifinals:** Wittenberg 35, Minn.-Morris 14; Baldwin-Wallace 31, Carnegie Mellon 6. **Championship:** Baldwin-Wallace 24, Wittenberg 10.

**1979 First Round:** Wittenberg 21, Millersville 14; Widener 29, Baldwin-Wallace 8; Carnegie Mellon 31, Minn.-Morris 25; Ithaca 27, Dubuque 7. **Semifinals:** Wittenberg 17, Widener 14; Ithaca 15, Carnegie Mellon 6. **Championship:** Ithaca 14, Wittenberg 10.

**1980 First Round:** Ithaca 41, Wagner 13; Minn.-Morris 41, Dubuque 35; Dayton 34, Baldwin-Wallace 0; Widener 43, Bethany (W. Va.) 12. **Semifinals:** Ithaca 36, Minn.-Morris 0; Dayton 28, Widener 24. **Championship:** Dayton 63, Ithaca 0.

**1981 First Round:** Dayton 19, Augustana (Ill.) 7; Lawrence 21, Minn.-Morris 14 (OT); Montclair St. 13, Alfred 12; Widener 10, West Ga. 3. **Semifinals:** Dayton 38, Lawrence 0; Widener 23, Montclair St. 12. **Championship:** Widener 17, Dayton 10.

**1982 First Round:** Augustana (Ill.) 28, Baldwin-Wallace 22; St. Lawrence 43, Wagner 34; Bishop 32, Wartburg 7; West Ga. 31, Widener 24 (3 OT). **Semifinals:** Augustana (Ill.) 14, St. Lawrence 0;

West Ga. 27, Bishop 6. **Championship:** West Ga. 14, Augustana (Ill.) 0.

**1983 First Round:** Union (N.Y.) 51, Hofstra 19; Salisbury St. 16, Carnegie Mellon 14; Augustana (Ill.) 22, Adrian 21; Wis.-La Crosse 43, Occidental 42. **Semifinals:** Union (N.Y.) 23, Salisbury St. 21; Augustana (Ill.) 21, Wis.-La Crosse 15. **Championship:** Augustana (Ill.) 21, Union (N.Y.) 17.

**1984 First Round:** Union (N.Y.) 26, Plymouth St. 14; Augustana (Ill.) 14, Dayton 13; Wash. & Jeff. 22, Randolph-Macon 21; Central (Iowa) 23, Occidental 22. **Semifinals:** Augustana (Ill.) 23, Union (N.Y.) 6; Central (Iowa) 20, Wash. & Jeff. 0. **Championship:** Augustana (Ill.) 21, Central (Iowa) 12.

**1985 First Round:** Ithaca 13, Union (N.Y.) 12; Montclair St. 28, Western Conn. St. 0; Salisbury St. 35, Carnegie Mellon 22; Gettysburg 14, Lycoming 10; Augustana (Ill.) 26, Albion 10; Mount Union 35, Denison 3; Central (Iowa) 27, Coe 7; Occidental 28, St. John's (Minn.) 10. **Quarterfinals:** Ithaca 50, Montclair St. 28; Gettysburg 22, Salisbury St. 6; Augustana (Ill.) 21, Mount Union 14; Central (Iowa) 71, Occidental 0. **Semifinals:** Ithaca 34, Gettysburg 0; Augustana (Ill.) 14, Central (Iowa) 7. **Championship:** Augustana (Ill.) 20, Ithaca 7.

**1986 First Round:** Ithaca 24, Union (N.Y.) 17 (OT); Montclair St. 24, Hofstra 21; Susquehanna 28, Wash. & Jeff. 20; Salisbury St. 34, Emory & Henry 20; Mount Union 42, Dayton 36; Augustana (Ill.) 34, Hope 10; Central (Iowa) 37, Buena Vista 0; Concordia-M'head 17, Wis.-Stevens Point 15. **Quarterfinals:** Ithaca 29, Montclair St. 15; Salisbury St. 31, Susquehanna 17; Augustana (Ill.) 16, Mount Union 7; Concordia-M'head 17, Central (Iowa) 14. **Semifinals:** Salisbury St. 44, Ithaca 40; Augustana (Ill.) 41, Concordia-M'head 7. **Championship:** Augustana (Ill.) 31, Salisbury St. 3.

**1987 First Round:** Wagner 38, Rochester 14; Fordham 41, Hofstra 6; Wash. & Jeff. 23, Allegheny 17 (OT); Emory & Henry 49, Ferrum 7; Dayton 52, Capital 28; Augustana (Ill.) 53, Hiram 0; St. John's (Minn.) 7, Gust. Adolphus 3; Central (Iowa) 17, Menlo 0. **Quarterfinals:** Wagner 21, Fordham 0; Emory & Henry 23, Wash. & Jeff. 16; Dayton 38, Augustana (Ill.) 36; Central (Iowa) 13, St. John's (Minn.) 3. **Semifinals:** Wagner 20, Emory & Henry 15; Dayton 34, Central (Iowa) 0. **Championship:** Wagner 19, Dayton 3.

*1993 NCAA FOOTBALL*

**1988 Regionals:** Cortland St. 32, Hofstra 27; Ithaca 34, Wagner 31 (OT); Ferrum 35, Rhodes 10; Moravian 17, Widener 7; Wittenberg 35, Dayton 28 (2 OT); Augustana (Ill.) 25, Adrian 7; Central (Iowa) 7, Concordia-M'head 0; Wis.-Whitewater 29, Simpson 27. **Quarterfinals:** Ithaca 24, Cortland St. 17; Ferrum 49, Moravian 28; Augustana (Ill.) 28, Wittenberg 14; Central (Iowa) 16, Wis.-Whitewater 13. **Semifinals:** Ithaca 62, Ferrum 28; Central (Iowa) 23, Augustana 17 (2 OT). **Championship:** Ithaca 39, Central (Iowa) 24.

**1989 Regionals:** Union (N.Y.) 42, Cortland St. 14; Montclair St. 23, Hofstra 6; Lycoming 21, Dickinson 0; Ferrum 41, Wash. & Jeff. 7; Dayton 35, John Carroll 10; Millikin 21, Augustana (Ill.) 12; Central (Iowa) 55, St. Norbert 7; St. John's (Minn.) 42, Simpson 35. **Quarterfinals:** Union (N.Y.) 45, Montclair St. 6; Ferrum 49, Lycoming 24; Dayton 28, Millikin 16; St. John's (Minn.) 27, Central (Iowa) 24. **Semifinals:** Union (N.Y.) 37, Ferrum 21; Dayton 28, St. John's (Minn.) 0. **Championship:** Dayton 17, Union (N.Y.) 7.

**1990 Regionals:** Hofstra 35, Cortland St. 9; Trenton St. 24, Ithaca 14; Wash. & Jeff. 10, Lycoming 17, Carnegie Mellon 7; Dayton 24, Augustana (Ill.) 14; Allegheny 26, Mount Union 15; St. Thomas (Minn.) 24, Wis.-Whitewater 23; Central (Iowa) 24, Redlands 14. **Quarterfinals:** Hofstra 38, Trenton St. 3; Lycoming 24, Wash. & Jeff. 0; Allegheny 31, Dayton 23; Central (Iowa) 33, St. Thomas (Minn.) 32. **Semifinals:** Lycoming 20, Hofstra 10; Allegheny 24, Central (Iowa) 7. **Championship:** Allegheny 21, Lycoming 14 (OT).

**1991 Regionals:** St. John's (Minn.) 75, Coe 2; Wis.-La Crosse 28, Simpson 13; Allegheny 24, Albion 21 (OT); Dayton 27, Baldwin-Wallace 10; Ithaca 31, Rowan 10; Union (N.Y.) 55, Mass.-Lowell 16; Lycoming 18, Wash. & Jeff. 16; Susquehanna 21, Dickinson 20. **Quarterfinals:** St. John's (Minn.) 29, Wis.-La Crosse 10; Dayton 28, Allegheny 25 (OT); Ithaca 35, Union (N.Y.) 23; Susquehanna 31, Lycoming 24. **Semifinals:** Dayton 19, St. John's (Minn.) 7; Ithaca 49, Susquehanna 13. **Championship:** Ithaca 34, Dayton 20.

**1992 Regionals:** Mount Union 27, Dayton 10; Ill. Wesleyan 21, Aurora 12; Central (Iowa) 20, Carleton 8; Wis.-La Crosse 47, Redlands 26; Emory & Henry 17, Thomas More 0; Wash. & Jeff. 33, Lycoming 0; Rowan 41, Worcester Tech 14; Buffalo St. 28, Ithaca 26. **Quarterfinals:** Mount Union 49, Ill. Wesleyan 27; Wis.-La Crosse 34, Central (Iowa) 9; Wash. & Jeff. 51, Emory & Henry 15; Rowan 28, Buffalo St. 19. **Semifinals:** Wis.-La Crosse 29, Mount Union 24; Wash. & Jeff. 18, Rowan 13. **Championship:** Wis.-La Crosse 16, Wash. & Jeff. 12.

# COLLEGE FOOTBALL
# ATTENDANCE RECORDS

News about college football attendance was mixed in 1992. Although total attendance topped 36 million for the fourth year in a row and the 10th time in the past 11 years, the average game was attended by 153 fewer fans than in 1991 and the per-game average

## ANNUAL TOTAL ATTENDANCE
### (Includes all divisions and non-NCAA teams)

| Year | No. Teams | Games | Total Attendance | Avg. | Yearly Change Total | Percent |
|---|---|---|---|---|---|---|
| 1948 | 685 | — | 19,134,159 | — | — | — |
| 1949 | 682 | — | 19,651,995 | — | Up 517,836 | 2.71 |
| 1950 | 674 | — | 18,961,688 | — | Down 690,307 | 3.51 |
| 1951 | 635 | — | 17,480,533 | — | Down 1,481,155 | 7.81 |
| 1952 | 625 | — | 17,288,062 | — | Down 192,471 | 1.10 |
| 1953 | 618 | — | 16,681,731 | — | Down 606,331 | 3.51 |
| 1954 | 614 | — | 17,048,603 | — | Up 366,872 | 2.20 |
| 1955 | 621 | — | 17,266,556 | — | Up 217,953 | 1.28 |
| 1956 | 618 | — | 18,031,805 | — | Up 765,249 | 4.43 |
| 1957 | 618 | 2,586 | 18,290,724 | 7,073 | Up 258,919 | 1.44 |
| 1958 | 618 | 2,673 | 19,280,709 | 7,213 | Up 989,985 | 5.41 |
| 1959 | 623 | 2,695 | 19,615,344 | 7,278 | Up 334,635 | 1.74 |
| 1960 | 620 | 2,711 | 20,403,409 | 7,526 | Up 788,065 | 4.02 |
| 1961 | 616 | 2,697 | 20,677,604 | 7,667 | Up 274,195 | 1.34 |
| 1962 | 610 | 2,679 | 21,227,162 | 7,924 | Up 549,558 | 2.66 |
| 1963 | 616 | 2,686 | 22,237,094 | 8,279 | Up 1,009,932 | 4.76 |
| 1964 | 622 | 2,745 | 23,354,477 | 8,508 | Up 1,117,383 | 5.02 |
| 1965 | 616 | 2,749 | 24,682,572 | 8,979 | Up 1,328,095 | 5.69 |
| 1966 | 616 | 2,768 | 25,275,899 | 9,131 | Up 593,327 | 2.40 |
| 1967 | 610 | 2,764 | 26,430,639 | 9,562 | Up 1,154,740 | 4.57 |
| 1968 | 612 | 2,786 | 27,025,846 | 9,701 | Up 595,207 | 2.25 |
| 1969 | 615 | 2,820 | 27,626,160 | 9,797 | Up 600,314 | 2.22 |
| 1970 | 617 | 2,895 | 29,465,604 | 10,178 | *Up 1,839,444 | *6.66 |
| 1971 | 618 | 2,955 | 30,455,442 | 10,306 | Up 989,838 | 3.36 |
| 1972 | 620 | 2,997 | 30,828,802 | 10,287 | Up 373,360 | 1.23 |
| 1973 | 630 | 3,062 | 31,282,540 | 10,216 | Up 453,738 | 1.47 |
| 1974 | 634 | 3,101 | 31,234,855 | 10,073 | Down 47,685 | 0.15 |
| 1975 | 634 | 3,089 | 31,687,847 | 10,258 | Up 452,992 | 1.45 |
| 1976 | 637 | 3,108 | 32,012,008 | 10,299 | Up 324,161 | 1.02 |
| 1977 | 638 | 3,145 | 32,905,178 | 10,463 | Up 893,170 | 2.79 |
| 1978 | 643 | 3,163 | 34,251,606 | 10,829 | Up 1,346,428 | 4.09 |
| 1979 | 643 | 3,174 | 35,020,284 | 11,033 | Up 768,678 | 2.24 |
| 1980 | 642 | 3,196 | 35,540,975 | 11,120 | Up 520,691 | 1.49 |
| 1981 | 648 | 3,217 | 35,807,040 | 11,131 | Up 266,065 | 0.75 |
| 1982 | 649 | 3,224 | 36,538,637 | *11,333 | Up 731,597 | 2.04 |
| 1983 | 651 | 3,250 | 36,301,877 | 11,170 | Down 236,760 | 0.65 |
| 1984 | 654 | 3,270 | *36,652,179 | 11,209 | Up 350,302 | 0.96 |
| 1985 | 661 | 3,309 | 36,312,022 | 10,974 | Down 340,157 | 0.93 |
| 1986 | 666 | 3,339 | 36,387,905 | 10,898 | Up 75,883 | 0.21 |
| 1987 | 667 | 3,353 | 36,462,671 | 10,875 | Up 74,766 | 0.21 |
| 1988 | 680 | 3,360 | 35,581,790 | 10,590 | Down 880,881 | 2.42 |
| 1989 | 673 | 3,360 | 36,406,297 | 10,790 | Up 824,507 | 2.32 |
| 1990 | 673 | 3,374 | 36,626,547 | 10,846 | Up 220,250 | 0.60 |
| 1991 | 681 | 3,378 | 36,565,880 | 10,825 | Down 60,667 | 0.17 |
| 1992 | 674 | 3,392 | 36,198,508 | 10,672 | Down 367,372 | 1.00 |

*Record*

## ANNUAL DIVISION I-A ATTENDANCE

| Year | Teams | Games | Attendance | Avg. | Year | Teams | Games | Attendance | Avg. |
|---|---|---|---|---|---|---|---|---|---|
| 1976 | 137 | 796 | 23,917,522 | 30,047 | 1986 | 105 | 611 | 25,692,095 | 42,049 |
| 1977 | 144 | 799 | 24,613,285 | 30,805 | 1987 | 104 | 607 | 25,471,744 | 41,963 |
| 1978 | 139 | 772 | 25,017,915 | 32,407 | 1988 | 104 | 605 | 25,079,490 | 41,454 |
| 1979 | 139 | 774 | 25,862,801 | 33,414 | 1989 | 106 | 603 | 25,307,915 | 41,970 |
| 1980 | 139 | 776 | 26,499,022 | 34,148 | 1990 | 106 | 615 | 25,513,098 | 41,485 |
| 1981 | 137 | 768 | *26,588,688 | 34,621 | 1991 | 106 | 610 | 25,646,067 | 42,043 |
| 1982 | 97 | 567 | 24,771,855 | *43,689 | 1992 | 107 | 617 | 25,402,046 | 41,170 |
| 1983 | 105 | 602 | 25,381,761 | 42,162 | | | | | |
| 1984 | 105 | 606 | 25,783,807 | 42,548 | | | | | |
| 1985 | 105 | 605 | 25,434,412 | 42,040 | | | | | |

*Record.*

# ANNUAL DIVISION I-AA ATTENDANCE

| Year | Teams | Games | Attendance | Avg. | Year | Teams | Games | Attendance | Avg. |
|------|-------|-------|------------|------|------|-------|-------|------------|------|
| 1978 | 38 | 201 | 2,032,766 | 10,113 | 1986 | 86 | 456 | 5,044,992 | 11,064 |
| 1979 | 39 | 211 | 2,073,890 | 9,829 | 1987 | 87 | 460 | 5,129,250 | 11,151 |
| 1980 | 46 | 251 | 2,617,932 | 10,430 | 1988 | 88 | 465 | 4,801,637 | 10,326 |
| 1981 | 50 | 270 | 2,950,156 | 10,927 | 1989 | 89 | 471 | 5,278,520 | 11,020 |
| 1982 | 92 | 483 | *5,655,519 | *11,709 | 1990 | 87 | 473 | 5,328,477 | 11,265 |
| 1983 | 84 | 450 | 4,879,709 | 10,844 | 1991 | 89 | 490 | 5,386,425 | 10,993 |
| 1984 | 87 | 465 | 5,061,480 | 10,885 | 1992 | 88 | 485 | 5,057,955 | 10,429 |
| 1985 | 87 | 471 | 5,143,077 | 10,919 | | | | | |

* Record.

# ANNUAL DIVISION II ATTENDANCE

| Year | Teams | Games | Attendance | Avg. | Year | Teams | Games | Attendance | Avg. |
|------|-------|-------|------------|------|------|-------|-------|------------|------|
| 1978 | 103 | 518 | *2,871,683 | *5,544 | 1986 | 111 | 551 | 2,404,852 | 4,365 |
| 1979 | 105 | 526 | 2,775,569 | 5,277 | 1987 | 107 | 541 | 2,424,041 | 4,481 |
| 1980 | 111 | 546 | 2,584,765 | 4,734 | 1988 | 117 | 580 | 2,570,964 | 4,493 |
| 1981 | 121 | 589 | 2,726,537 | 4,629 | 1989 | 116 | 579 | 2,572,496 | 4,428 |
| 1982 | 126 | 618 | 2,745,964 | 4,443 | 1990 | 120 | 580 | 2,472,811 | 4,263 |
| 1983 | 122 | 611 | 2,705,892 | 4,429 | 1991 | 128 | 622 | 2,490,929 | 4,005 |
| 1984 | 114 | 568 | 2,413,947 | 4,250 | 1992 | 129 | 643 | 2,733,094 | 4,251 |
| 1985 | 114 | 569 | 2,475,325 | 4,350 | | | | | |

* Record.

# ANNUAL DIVISION III ATTENDANCE

| Year | Teams | Games | Attendance | Avg. | Year | Teams | Games | Attendance | Avg. |
|------|-------|-------|------------|------|------|-------|-------|------------|------|
| 1978 | 204 | 931 | *2,447,366 | *2,629 | 1986 | 208 | 987 | 1,888,963 | 1,914 |
| 1979 | 195 | 870 | 2,162,495 | 2,486 | 1987 | 209 | 981 | 1,982,506 | 2,021 |
| 1980 | 189 | 878 | 2,006,053 | 2,285 | 1988 | 215 | 994 | 1,871,751 | 1,883 |
| 1981 | 189 | 878 | 1,965,090 | 2,238 | 1989 | 213 | 977 | 1,957,257 | 1,948 |
| 1982 | 195 | 901 | 2,002,857 | 2,223 | 1990 | 220 | 1,036 | 2,015,560 | 1,946 |
| 1983 | 194 | 894 | 1,849,902 | 2,069 | 1991 | 225 | 1,054 | 2,004,799 | 1,902 |
| 1984 | 195 | 903 | 1,951,842 | 2,162 | 1992 | 228 | 1,079 | 2,032,336 | 1,884 |
| 1985 | 203 | 954 | 1,898,734 | 1,990 | | | | | |

* Record.

# ANNUAL NON-NCAA ATTENDANCE

| Year | Teams | Games | Attendance | Avg. | Year | Teams | Games | Attendance | Avg. |
|------|-------|-------|------------|------|------|-------|-------|------------|------|
| 1978 | 159 | 741 | 1,881,876 | 2,540 | 1986 | 156 | 734 | 1,357,003 | 1,849 |
| 1979 | 165 | 793 | *2,145,529 | *2,706 | 1987 | 160 | 764 | 1,455,130 | 1,905 |
| 1980 | 157 | 745 | 1,833,203 | 2,461 | 1988 | 156 | 716 | 1,257,948 | 1,757 |
| 1981 | 151 | 712 | 1,576,569 | 2,214 | 1989 | 149 | 723 | 1,333,328 | 1,899 |
| 1982 | 139 | 655 | 1,362,442 | 2,080 | 1990 | 140 | 673 | 1,296,601 | 1,927 |
| 1983 | 146 | 693 | 1,484,613 | 2,142 | 1991 | 133 | 602 | 1,037,660 | 1,724 |
| 1984 | 153 | 728 | 1,441,103 | 1,980 | 1992 | 122 | 568 | 973,077 | 1,713 |
| 1985 | 152 | 710 | 1,360,474 | 1,916 | | | | | |

* Record.

# LARGE REGULAR-SEASON CROWDS

THE 14 LARGEST REGULAR-SEASON COLLEGE-FOOTBALL CROWDS IN THE 45 SEASONS THAT OFFICIAL NATIONAL ATTENDANCE RECORDS HAVE BEEN MAINTAINED:

| Crowd | Date | Home | Visitor |
|-------|------|------|---------|
| 106,788 | 10-10-92 | Michigan 35, Michigan St. 10 | |
| 106,579 | 10-24-92 | Michigan 63, Minnesota 13 | |
| 106,481 | 11-14-92 | Michigan 22, Illinois 22 | |
| 106,255 | 11-17-79 | Michigan 15, Ohio St. 18 | |
| 106,208 | 10-8-88 | Michigan 17, Michigan St. 3 | |
| 106,188 | 10-13-90 | Michigan 27, Michigan St. 28 | |
| 106,156 | 11-23-91 | Michigan 31, Ohio St. 3 | |
| 106,145 | 9-28-91 | Michigan 31, Florida St. 51 | |
| 106,141 | 10-11-86 | Michigan 27, Michigan St. 6 | |
| 106,138 | 9-14-91 | Michigan 24, Notre Dame 14 | |
| 106,137 | 11-25-89 | Michigan 28, Ohio St. 18 | |
| 106,132 | 10-3-92 | Michigan 52, Iowa 28 | |
| 106,115 | 11-19-83 | Michigan 24, Ohio St. 21 | |
| 106,113 | 10-9-82 | Michigan 31, Michigan St. 17 | |

HIGHEST WEEKS OF THE WEEKLY TOP-10 ATTENDED GAMES:

| Total | Date |
|-------|------|
| 857,115 | 10-10-92 |
| 833,285 | 10-22-83 |
| 827,232 | 9-16-89 |
| 825,455 | 9-22-84 |
| 820,668 | 11-18-89 |
| 819,980 | 10-18-86 |
| 816,954 | 9-14-91 |
| 816,618 | 9-28-91 |
| 816,458 | 10-13-84 |
| 815,853 | 11-10-90 |
| 815,423 | 11-5-88 |

*College Football Attendance Records*

## THE 25 LARGEST REGULAR-SEASON COLLEGE-FOOTBALL CROWDS
### FOR GAMES NOT PLAYED AT MICHIGAN:

| Attendance | Date | Score (Home Team in Boldface) | Site |
|---|---|---|---|
| 97,731 | 9-28-91 | **Tennessee** 30, Auburn 21 | Knoxville, Tenn. |
| 97,388 | 10-17-92 | Alabama 17, **Tennessee** 10 | Knoxville, Tenn. |
| 97,372 | 11-30-85 | **Tennessee** 30, Vanderbilt 0 | Knoxville, Tenn. |
| 97,137 | 9-19-92 | **Tennessee** 31, Florida 14 | Knoxville, Tenn. |
| 97,123 | 11-11-90 | Notre Dame 34, **Tennessee** 29 | Knoxville, Tenn. |
| 97,117 | 9-14-91 | **Tennessee** 30, UCLA 16 | Knoxville, Tenn. |
| 96,874 | 10-13-90 | **Tennessee** 45, Florida 3 | Knoxville, Tenn. |
| 96,748 | 10-18-80 | Alabama 27, **Tennessee** 0 | Knoxville, Tenn. |
| 96,732 | 10-20-90 | Alabama 9, **Tennessee** 6 | Knoxville, Tenn. |
| 96,704 | 10-10-92 | Miami (Fla.) 17, **Penn St.** 14 | University Park, Pa. |
| 96,672 | 11-16-91 | **Penn St.** 35, Notre Dame 13 | University Park, Pa. |
| 96,664 | 11-2-91 | **Tennessee** 52, Memphis St. 24 | Knoxville, Tenn. |
| 96,597 | 9-26-92 | **Tennessee** 40, Cincinnati 0 | Knoxville, Tenn. |
| 96,445 | 10-26-91 | **Penn St.** 51, West Va. 6 | University Park, Pa. |
| 96,304 | 9-21-91 | **Penn St.** 33, Brigham Young 7 | University Park, Pa. |
| 96,130 | 10-17-92 | Boston College 35, **Penn St.** 32 | University Park, Pa. |
| 96,058 | 10-7-89 | **Tennessee** 17, Georgia 14 | Knoxville, Tenn. |
| 95,974 | 9-21-91 | **Tennessee** 26, Mississippi St. 24 | Knoxville, Tenn. |
| 95,937 | 11-16-91 | **Tennessee** 36, Mississippi 25 | Knoxville, Tenn. |
| 95,927 | 9-28-91 | **Penn St.** 28, Boston College 21 | University Park, Pa. |
| 95,891 | 9-26-92 | **Penn St.** 49, Maryland 13 | University Park, Pa. |
| 95,824 | 9-3-83 | Pittsburgh 13, **Tennessee** 3 | Knoxville, Tenn. |
| 95,729 | 10-19-91 | **Penn St.** 37, Rutgers 17 | University Park, Pa. |
| 95,585 | 11-12-83 | Mississippi 13, **Tennessee** 10 | Knoxville, Tenn. |
| 95,422 | 10-20-84 | **Tennessee** 28, Alabama 27 | Knoxville, Tenn. |

### †PRE-1948 REGULAR-SEASON AND
### NON-MICHIGAN CROWDS IN EXCESS OF 100,000

| Crowd | Date | Site | Opponents, Score |
|---|---|---|---|
| 120,000* | 11-26-27 | Soldier Field, Chicago | Notre Dame 7, Southern Cal 6 |
| 120,000* | 10-13-28 | Soldier Field, Chicago | Notre Dame 7, Navy 0 |
| 112,912 | 11-16-29 | Soldier Field, Chicago | Notre Dame 13, Southern Cal 12 |
| 110,000* | 11-27-26 | Soldier Field, Chicago | Army 21, Navy 21 |
| 110,000* | 11-29-30 | Soldier Field, Chicago | Notre Dame 7, Army 6 |
| 104,953 | 12-6-47 | Los Angeles | Notre Dame 38, Southern Cal 7 |
| 101,799 | 11-30-68 | Philadelphia | Army 21, Navy 14 |
| 100,428 | 12-2-67 | Philadelphia | Navy 19, Army 14 |

*Estimated attendance; others are audited figures.*

*† Since 1956, when Michigan Stadium's capacity was increased to 101,000, there have been 127 100,000-plus crowds at Michigan. The 14 largest crowds are listed on page 609. Therefore, there has been a total of 135 regular-season crowds in excess of 100,000.*

## ADDITIONAL RECORDS
**Highest Average Attendance Per Home Game:** 105,867, Michigan, 1992 (635,201 in 6)
**Highest Total Home Attendance:** 731,281, Michigan, 1987 (7 games)
**Highest Total Attendance, Home and Away:** 1,005,195, Michigan, 1986 (12 games)
**Highest Bowl Game Attendance:** 106,869, 1973 Rose Bowl (Southern Cal 42, Ohio St. 17)
**Most Consecutive Home Sellout Crowds:** 187, Nebraska (current, from Nov. 3, 1962)
**Most Consecutive 100,000-Plus Crowds:** 109, Michigan (current, from Nov. 8, 1975)

## 1992 ATTENDANCE
### LEADING DIVISION I-A TEAMS IN
### 1992 HOME ATTENDANCE

| | G | Attend. | Avg. | Change | | | G | Attend. | Avg. | Change | |
|---|---|---|---|---|---|---|---|---|---|---|---|
| 1. Michigan | 6 | 635,201 | 105,867 | Up | 530 | 11. Washington | 7 | 504,500 | 72,071 | Down | 213 |
| 2. Tennessee | 6 | 575,544 | 95,924 | Down | 474 | 12. Texas | 5 | 340,758 | 68,152 | Down | 942 |
| 3. Penn St. | 6 | 569,195 | 94,866 | Down | 980 | 13. Louisiana St. | 7 | 469,195 | 67,028 | Down | 1,718 |
| 4. Ohio St. | 6 | 555,900 | 92,650 | Up | 3,958 | 14. Iowa | 7 | 466,485 | 66,641 | Down | 3,430 |
| 5. Florida | 7 | 586,626 | 83,804 | Down | 651 | 15. Brigham Young | 6 | 390,476 | 65,079 | Up | 3,173 |
| 6. Georgia | 6 | 499,162 | 83,194 | Up | 634 | 16. Oklahoma | 7 | 449,161 | 64,166 | Down | 4,890 |
| 7. Clemson | 6 | 460,732 | 76,789 | Up | 3,373 | 17. South Caro. | 6 | 382,368 | 63,728 | Down | 1,551 |
| 8. Alabama | 7 | 537,264 | 76,752 | Up | 1,236 | 18. Florida St. | 6 | 376,784 | 62,797 | Up | 1,491 |
| 9. Nebraska | 6 | 457,124 | 76,187 | Down | 58 | 19. Wisconsin | 6 | 368,269 | 61,378 | Up | 11,702 |
| 10. Auburn | 7 | 510,549 | 72,936 | Down | 5,943 | 20. Michigan St. | 6 | 358,886 | 59,814 | Down | 10,391 |

| | G | Attend. | Avg. | Change | |
|---|---|---|---|---|---|
| 21. Southern Cal . | 5 | 298,769 | 59,754 | Down | 4,450 |
| 22. Notre Dame ... | 6 | 354,450 | 59,075 | None | — |
| 23. California .... | 5 | 280,162 | 56,032 | Up | 6,532 |
| 24. Miami (Fla.).... | 6 | 334,052 | 55,675 | Down | 2,289 |
| 25. Texas A&M ... | 7 | 387,846 | 55,407 | Down | 7,911 |
| 26. Kentucky ...... | 6 | 324,875 | 54,146 | Down | 396 |
| 27. Stanford ...... | 6 | 312,401 | 52,067 | Down | 368 |
| 28. Illinois ........ | 6 | 301,216 | 50,203 | Down | 5,404 |
| 29. Colorado ...... | 6 | 298,149 | 49,692 | Down | 2,218 |
| 30. Syracuse ..... | 6 | 295,910 | 49,318 | Up | 5,819 |
| 31. West Va........ | 7 | 344,989 | 49,284 | Up | 600 |
| 32. UCLA ......... | 6 | 295,561 | 49,260 | Up | 108 |
| 33. Arizona St. .... | 6 | 293,365 | 48,894 | Down | 6,821 |
| 34. North Caro..... | 6 | 283,025 | 47,171 | Up | 814 |
| 35. North Caro. St.. | 6 | 282,942 | 47,157 | Up | 3,661 |
| 36. Arizona ...... | 6 | 282,127 | 47,021 | Up | 1,590 |
| 37. Arkansas ...... | 6 | 276,196 | 46,033 | Down | 110 |
| 38. San Diego St... | 6 | 274,347 | 45,725 | Up | 12,579 |
| 39. Virginia Tech... | 6 | 270,613 | 45,102 | Up | 1,414 |
| 40. Hawaii ........ | 7 | 311,022 | 44,432 | Up | 982 |
| 41. Indiana ....... | 6 | 260,799 | 43,467 | Down | 3,829 |
| 42. Georgia Tech .. | 6 | 259,066 | 43,178 | Down | 4,446 |
| 43. Virginia ....... | 6 | 258,400 | 43,067 | Up | 1,481 |
| 44. Kansas ........ | 6 | 251,500 | 41,917 | Up | 11,985 |
| 45. Air Force ...... | 7 | 284,371 | 40,624 | Down | 3,498 |

| | G | Attend. | Avg. | Change | |
|---|---|---|---|---|---|
| 46. Mississippi St.. | 5 | 197,099 | 39,420 | Down | 915 |
| 47. Northwestern .. | 5 | 196,835 | 39,367 | Up | 4,530 |
| 48. Texas Tech .... | 6 | 233,894 | 38,982 | Up | 1,178 |
| 49. Missouri ...... | 6 | 233,833 | 38,972 | Down | 841 |
| 50. Oklahoma St... | 5 | 193,783 | 38,757 | Up | 11,631 |
| 51. Purdue ........ | 6 | 229,373 | 38,229 | Down | 943 |
| 52. Vanderbilt .... | 6 | 229,070 | 38,178 | Up | 2,372 |
| 53. Minnesota ..... | 6 | 227,446 | 37,908 | Up | 1,538 |
| 54. Iowa St. ...... | 6 | 225,490 | 37,582 | Down | 4,753 |
| 55. Memphis St... | 6 | 224,449 | 37,408 | Up | 5,425 |
| 56. Mississippi .... | 7 | 256,066 | 36,581 | Down | 2,179 |
| 57. Fresno St...... | 8 | 211,352 | 35,225 | Up | 1,326 |
| 58. Navy .......... | 7 | 245,764 | 35,109 | Up | 10,012 |
| 59. Army ......... | 7 | 244,041 | 34,863 | Down | 5,242 |
| 60. Oregon ....... | 7 | 236,584 | 33,798 | Down | 7,716 |
| 61. East Caro..... | 5 | 164,068 | 32,814 | Up | 772 |
| 62. Louisville .... | 5 | 161,913 | 32,383 | Down | 4,113 |
| 63. Baylor ........ | 7 | 226,512 | 32,359 | Down | 5,661 |
| 64. UTEP ......... | 5 | 158,962 | 31,792 | Up | 2,433 |
| 65. Pittsburgh .... | 6 | 190,316 | 31,719 | Down | 4,793 |
| 66. Boston College. | 6 | 179,095 | 29,849 | Up | 1,177 |
| 67. Utah .......... | 5 | 149,034 | 29,807 | Up | 3,542 |
| 68. Rutgers ...... | 6 | 174,817 | 29,136 | Up | 7,263 |
| 69. Tulane ........ | 5 | 142,323 | 28,465 | Up | 3,048 |
| 70. Oregon St. .... | 6 | 168,704 | 28,117 | Up | 3,148 |

*Designated home team at off-campus neutral sites (total included in averages above): Florida 1g Jacksonville 82,439 (avg. 84,031 six home games); Alabama 3g Birmingham 243,804; Iowa 1g East Rutherford 46,251 (average 70,039 six home games—ranked 12th); Oklahoma 1g Dallas 75,587; Texas A&M 1g Anaheim 35,240 (average 58,768 six home games—ranked 23rd); Arkansas 3g Little Rock 151,178; Northwestern 1g Chicago 64,877; Mississippi 1g Jackson 47,133; Navy 1g Philadelphia 65,207, 1g East Rutherford 50,941; Rutgers 2g East Rutherford 90,471.*

## OTHER DIVISIONAL LEADERS IN 1992 HOME ATTENDANCE

### DIVISION I-AA

| | G | Attend. | Avg. | Change | |
|---|---|---|---|---|---|
| 1. Southern-B.R. . | 7 | 202,344 | 28,906 | Up | 13,745 |
| 2. Jackson St. .... | 4 | 99,000 | 24,750 | Up | 1,584 |
| 3. Alabama St. ... | 7 | 164,859 | 23,551 | Up | 1,122 |
| 4. Marshall ...... | 6 | 138,910 | 23,152 | Up | 1,191 |
| 5. Florida A&M .. | 6 | 132,396 | 22,066 | Down | 3,141 |
| 6. Tennessee St.. . | 6 | 130,574 | 21,762 | Up | 13,134 |
| 7. Grambling ..... | 6 | 129,547 | 21,591 | Down | 5,590 |
| 8. Alcorn St. ..... | 4 | 79,715 | 19,929 | Up | 8,126 |
| 9. Citadel ........ | 6 | 116,156 | 19,359 | Up | 864 |
| 10. Boise St. ...... | 6 | 114,807 | 19,135 | Down | 636 |
| 11. Appalachian St. | 5 | 93,189 | 18,638 | Up | 3,076 |
| 12. Delaware ...... | 6 | 107,090 | 17,848 | Down | 1,952 |
| 13. Northeast La. .. | 5 | 87,360 | 17,472 | Up | 1,903 |
| 14. South Caro. St. | 7 | 120,764 | 17,252 | Up | 2,985 |
| 15. McNeese St. .. | 5 | 85,191 | 17,038 | Up | 4,034 |

| | G | Attend. | Avg. | Change | |
|---|---|---|---|---|---|
| 16. Mississippi Val.. | 4 | 66,412 | 16,603 | Down | 1,394 |
| 17. Ga. Southern .. | 8 | 118,562 | 14,820 | Down | 1,884 |
| 18. North Caro. A&T | 5 | 71,673 | 14,335 | Down | 20 |
| 19. Richmond ..... | 6 | 85,386 | 14,231 | Up | 4,330 |
| 20. Northern Iowa . | 6 | 85,263 | 14,211 | Up | 3,174 |
| 21. Texas Southern | 4 | 55,500 | 13,875 | Up | 2,946 |
| 22. Harvard ...... | 5 | 68,840 | 13,768 | Up | 2,061 |
| 23. Pennsylvania .. | 5 | 67,004 | 13,401 | Down | 3,473 |
| 24. Furman ...... | 6 | 80,104 | 13,351 | Up | 845 |
| 25. Eastern Ky. .... | 5 | 64,300 | 12,860 | Down | 2,307 |
| 26. Princeton...... | 5 | 63,799 | 12,760 | Up | 1,635 |
| 27. Prairie View... | 6 | 76,395 | 12,733 | Up | 6,180 |
| 28. Yale .......... | 5 | 60,744 | 12,149 | Down | 8,421 |
| 29. Southwest Mo. St.. | 5 | 60,639 | 12,128 | Up | 407 |
| 30. William & Mary. | 5 | 60,484 | 12,097 | Down | 687 |

*Designated home team at off-campus neutral sites (total included in averages above): Southern-B.R. 1g New Orleans 71,282, 1g Shreveport 27,132; Alabama St. 1g Mobile 10,261, 1g Birmingham 43,275, 1g Indianapolis 62,109; Florida A&M 1g Orlando 21,610, 1g Tampa 40,741; Tennessee St. 1g Nashville 23,578, 1g Memphis 37,437, 1g Atlanta 43,211; Grambling 1g Pontiac 26,000, 1g East Rutherford 40,848; South Caro. St. 1g Columbus 25,200, 1g Atlanta 55,296, 1g Summerville 8,500; Mississippi Val. 1g Chicago 43,692; Prairie View 1g Dallas 54,307.*

### DIVISION II

| | G | Attend. | Avg. | Change | |
|---|---|---|---|---|---|
| 1. Norfolk St...... | 5 | 70,978 | 14,196 | Down | 2,583 |
| 2. Tuskegee ...... | 6 | 80,218 | 13,370 | Up | 2,661 |
| 3. Jacksonville St. | 5 | 61,950 | 12,390 | Down | 1,890 |
| 4. Portland St. .... | 6 | 74,226 | 12,371 | Up | 2,209 |
| 5. North Dak. St... | 5 | 59,126 | 11,825 | Down | 78 |
| 6. Morehouse .... | 5 | 52,966 | 10,593 | Up | 2,264 |
| 7. Virginia St...... | 5 | 49,720 | 9,944 | Up | 5,649 |
| 8. Texas A&I ..... | 5 | 49,000 | 9,800 | Up | 140 |

| | G | Attend. | Avg. | Change | |
|---|---|---|---|---|---|
| 9. Hampton ...... | 5 | 43,123 | 8,625 | Up | 3,275 |
| 10. N.C. Central ... | 5 | 41,574 | 8,315 | Up | 4,290 |
| 11. Winston-Salem . | 5 | 41,439 | 8,288 | Down | 4,363 |
| 12. UC Davis ...... | 5 | 40,350 | 8,070 | Up | 3,170 |
| 13. Troy St. ....... | 4 | 31,200 | 7,800 | Up | 1,675 |
| 14. North Dak. .... | 5 | 38,667 | 7,733 | Up | 2,887 |
| 15. Morris Brown .. | 5 | 37,687 | 7,537 | Down | 213 |

### DIVISION III

| | G | Attend. | Avg. | Change | |
|---|---|---|---|---|---|
| 1. Dayton ........ | 7 | 42,687 | 6,098 | Down | 1,559 |
| 2. Ala.-Birmingham . | 5 | 29,909 | 5,982 | Up | 1,737 |
| 3. Emory & Henry | 5 | 25,495 | 5,099 | Up | 475 |
| 4. Trenton St. .... | 5 | 25,485 | 5,097 | Up | 1,977 |
| 5. Hampden-Sydney ..... | 6 | 30,068 | 5,011 | Up | 1,469 |

| | G | Attend. | Avg. | Change | |
|---|---|---|---|---|---|
| 6. St. John's (Minn.) ...... | 5 | 24,456 | 4,891 | Down | 209 |
| 7. Williams ........ | 4 | 19,120 | 4,780 | Down | 1,149 |
| 8. Baldwin-Wallace ..... | 5 | 23,200 | 4,640 | Down | 1,377 |
| 9. Lycoming ...... | 5 | 23,106 | 4,621 | Up | 1,721 |
| 10. Cortland St. ... | 4 | 18,100 | 4,525 | Up | 1,383 |

### NON-NCAA

| | G | Attend. | Avg. | Change | |
|---|---|---|---|---|---|
| 1. Central St. (Ohio) ...... | 7 | 44,000 | 6,286 | Up | 3,086 |
| 2. Arkansas Tech . | 4 | 20,036 | 5,009 | Up | 1,025 |

| | G | Attend. | Avg. | Change | |
|---|---|---|---|---|---|
| 3. Northeastern Okla......... | 5 | 24,100 | 4,820 | Up | 320 |

*College Football Attendance Records*

## DIVISIONS I-A AND I-AA CONFERENCES AND INDEPENDENT GROUPS

| | Total Teams | Games | 1992 Attendance | Avg. PG | Change† in Avg. | | Change† in Total | |
|---|---|---|---|---|---|---|---|---|
| Southeastern (I-A)# | 12 | 76 | *4,844,014 | 63,737 | Down | 838 | Up | 874 |
| Big Ten (I-A) | 10 | 60 | 3,600,410 | 60,007 | Down | 233 | Down | 74,244 |
| Big Eight (I-A) | 8 | 47 | 2,247,907 | 47,828 | Up | 721 | Down | 60,331 |
| Pacific-10 (I-A) | 10 | 60 | 2,825,401 | 47,090 | Down | 1,249 | Down | 26,590 |
| Atlantic Coast (I-A)# | 9 | 53 | *2,332,674 | 44,013 | Down | 2,044 | Down | 292,572 |
| Big East (I-A) | 8 | 48 | *1,847,269 | *38,485 | Up | 429 | Up | 58,658 |
| Southwest (I-A)# | 8 | 47 | 1,697,152 | 36,110 | Down | 4,339 | Down | 42,159 |
| Western Athletic (I-A)# | 10 | 60 | *2,111,587 | 35,193 | Up | 976 | Up | 24,332 |
| I-A Independents# | 15 | 81 | 2,676,108 | 33,038 | Down | 524 | Down | 109,537 |
| Southwestern (I-AA) | 8 | 42 | *873,772 | *20,804 | Up | 2,581 | Up | 17,281 |
| Mid-American (I-A)# | 10 | 49 | 704,233 | 14,372 | Up | 807 | Up | 26,004 |
| Big West (I-A)# | 7 | 36 | 515,291 | 14,314 | Up | 684 | Down | 2,666 |
| Southern (I-AA)# | 9 | 55 | *700,613 | *12,738 | Down | 156 | Up | 43,035 |
| Mid-Eastern (I-AA) | 7 | 38 | 450,962 | 11,867 | Down | 2,593 | Down | 127,450 |
| Ivy Group (I-AA) | 8 | 40 | 401,980 | 10,050 | Down | 1,923 | Down | 64,948 |
| Southland (I-AA) | 8 | 45 | 429,971 | 9,555 | Down | 18 | Up | 37,458 |
| Big Sky (I-AA)# | 8 | 46 | 437,592 | 9,513 | Up | 126 | Up | 34,715 |
| Yankee (I-AA) | 9 | 53 | 461,366 | 8,705 | Up | 285 | Up | 29,844 |
| Gateway (I-AA) | 7 | 40 | 345,823 | 8,646 | Down | 104 | Up | 13,341 |
| Ohio Valley (I-AA)# | 9 | 49 | 395,264 | 8,067 | Up | 666 | Up | 54,838 |
| I-AA Independents# | 9 | 46 | 358,425 | 7,792 | Down | 129 | Down | 37,647 |
| Patriot League (I-AA) | 6 | 31 | 202,187 | 6,522 | Down | 702 | Down | 28,968 |
| DIVISION I-A# | 107 | 617 | 25,402,046 | 41,170 | Down | 403 | Down | 498,231 |
| DIVISION I-AA# | 88 | 485 | 5,057,955 | 10,429 | Down | 290 | Down | 97,931 |
| I-A & I-AA Combined | 195 | 1,102 | 30,460,001 | 27,641 | Down | 490 | Down | 596,162 |
| NCAA DIVISION II# | 129 | 643 | 2,733,094 | 4,251 | Up | 273 | Up | 219,002 |
| NCAA DIVISION III# | 228 | 1,079 | 2,032,336 | 1,884 | Down | 15 | Down | 5,351 |
| ALL NON-NCAA# | 122 | 568 | 973,077 | 1,713 | Up | 29 | Up | 15,139 |
| ALL VARSITY TEAMS | 674 | 3,392 | 36,198,508 | 10,672 | Down | 153 | Down | 367,372 |

By Percentage of Capacity:

Div. I-A 77.27 percent—Southeastern 93.54, Atlantic Coast 89.88, Big Ten 82.44, Big Eight 82.25, Western Athletic 77.55, Div. I-A Independents 72.12, Pacific-10 70.83, Big East 70.68, Southwest 64.10, Mid-American 54.50, Big West 50.39.

Div. I-AA 52.53 percent—Southern 76.49, Big Sky 62.82, Southwestern 62.15, Mid-Eastern 59.48, Southland 56.57, Yankee 56.49, Gateway 54.18, Ohio Valley 50.19, Patriot 44.16, I-AA Independents 40.31, Ivy 26.77.

* Record high for this conference.   † The 1992 figures used for comparison reflect changes in conference, division and association lineups to provide parallel, valid comparisons (i.e., 1992 lineups vs. same teams in 1991, whether members or not); conferences and independent groups and divisions marked (#) did not have the same lineups in 1992 as in 1991.

## LEADING CONFERENCES AND INDEPENDENT GROUPS
## BELOW DIVISION I-AA

| | Total Teams | Games | 1992 Attendance | Avg. PG | Change† in Avg. | | Change† in Total | |
|---|---|---|---|---|---|---|---|---|
| Southern Intercollegiate | 9 | 46 | 344,504 | 7,489 | Up | 1,114 | Up | 134,132 |
| Central Intercollegiate | 11 | 53 | 386,465 | 7,292 | Up | 689 | Up | 36,503 |
| Western Football# | 5 | 25 | 149,211 | 5,968 | Up | 28 | Up | 12,587 |
| Gulf South | 7 | 35 | 182,545 | 5,216 | Down | 140 | Down | 10,281 |
| Lone Star | 7 | 32 | 156,847 | 4,901 | Up | 626 | Up | 2,964 |
| North Central | 10 | 53 | 249,684 | 4,711 | Up | 17 | Up | 15,000 |
| Pennsylvania | 14 | 72 | 295,454 | 4,104 | Down | 115 | Up | 12,753 |
| South Atlantic | 8 | 40 | 145,527 | 3,638 | Up | 565 | Up | 19,523 |
| Mid-American Intercollegiate | 10 | 54 | 192,830 | 3,571 | Up | 292 | Up | 22,326 |
| Arkansas Intercollegiate | 7 | 33 | 114,864 | 3,481 | Up | 101 | Down | 3,426 |
| Oklahoma Intercollegiate | 6 | 27 | 90,600 | 3,356 | Up | 363 | Up | 3,800 |
| Old Dominion Athletic | 6 | 30 | 100,132 | 3,338 | Up | 55 | Down | 1,642 |
| Northern California | 6 | 29 | 96,218 | 3,318 | Up | 956 | Up | 18,267 |
| Div. II Independents# | 16 | 71 | 212,370 | 2,991 | Up | 279 | Up | 22,514 |
| Midwest Intercollegiate | 11 | 59 | 167,512 | 2,839 | Down | 356 | Up | 14,624 |
| New England Small College | 10 | 40 | 112,912 | 2,823 | Down | 135 | Down | 5,416 |
| Middle Atlantic | 9 | 45 | 112,006 | 2,489 | Down | 70 | Up | 1,971 |
| Ohio Athletic | 10 | 51 | 124,607 | 2,443 | Down | 41 | Up | 2,903 |
| New Jersey Athletic | 7 | 34 | 82,428 | 2,424 | Up | 317 | Up | 4,470 |
| Wisconsin State University | 9 | 37 | 89,184 | 2,410 | Up | 602 | Up | 9,613 |
| Minnesota Intercollegiate | 10 | 48 | 114,781 | 2,391 | Down | 152 | Down | 2,186 |
| Michigan Intercollegiate | 6 | 27 | 64,414 | 2,386 | Down | 39 | Down | 3,480 |
| Texas Intercollegiate | 6 | 29 | 66,879 | 2,306 | Down | 219 | Down | 16,439 |

*1993 NCAA FOOTBALL*

| | Total Teams | Games | 1992 Attendance | Avg. PG | Change† in Avg. | | Change† in Total | |
|---|---|---|---|---|---|---|---|---|
| Centennial Football ........... | 8 | 38 | 82,879 | 2,181 | Up | 198 | Up | 1,570 |
| University Athletic ............ | 4 | 19 | 38,421 | 2,022 | Up | 238 | Up | 957 |

† The 1992 figures used for comparison reflect changes in conference, division and association lineups to provide parallel, valid comparisons (i.e., 1992 lineups vs. same teams in 1991, whether members or not); conferences and independent groups marked (#) did not have the same lineups in 1992 as in 1991.

# ANNUAL LEADING DIVISION I-A TEAMS IN PER-GAME HOME ATTENDANCE

| Team | G | Attendance | Average | Team | G | Attendance | Average |
|---|---|---|---|---|---|---|---|
| **1949** | | | | **1963** | | | |
| Michigan ...............6 | | 563,363 | 93,894 | Ohio St. ................5 | | 416,023 | 83,205 |
| Ohio St. ................5 | | 382,146 | 76,429 | Louisiana St. ...........6 | | 396,846 | 66,141 |
| Southern Methodist ....8 | | 484,000 | 60,500 | Michigan St. ...........5 | | 326,597 | 65,319 |
| **1950** | | | | **1964** | | | |
| Michigan ...............6 | | 493,924 | 82,321 | Ohio St. ................7 | | 583,740 | 83,391 |
| Ohio St. ................5 | | 368,021 | 73,604 | Michigan St. ...........4 | | 284,933 | 71,233 |
| Southern Methodist ....5 | | 309,000 | 61,800 | Michigan ...............6 | | 388,829 | 64,805 |
| **1951** | | | | **1965** | | | |
| Ohio St. ................6 | | 455,737 | 75,956 | Ohio St. ................5 | | 416,282 | 83,256 |
| Michigan ...............6 | | 445,635 | 74,273 | Michigan ...............6 | | 480,487 | 80,081 |
| Illinois .................4 | | 237,035 | 59,259 | Michigan St. ...........5 | | 346,296 | 69,259 |
| **1952** | | | | **1966** | | | |
| Ohio St. ................6 | | 453,911 | 75,652 | Ohio St. ................6 | | 488,399 | 81,400 |
| Michigan ...............6 | | 395,907 | 65,985 | Michigan St. ...........6 | | 426,750 | 71,125 |
| Texas .................#5 | | 311,160 | 62,232 | Michigan ...............6 | | 413,599 | 68,933 |
| **1953** | | | | **1967** | | | |
| Ohio St. ................5 | | 397,998 | 79,600 | Ohio St. ................5 | | 383,502 | 76,700 |
| Southern Cal ..........6 | | 413,617 | 68,936 | Michigan ...............6 | | 447,289 | 74,548 |
| Michigan ...............6 | | 353,860 | 58,977 | Michigan St. ...........6 | | 411,916 | 68,653 |
| **1954** | | | | **1968** | | | |
| Ohio St. ................6 | | 479,840 | 79,973 | Ohio St. ................6 | | 482,564 | 80,427 |
| Michigan ...............6 | | 409,454 | 68,242 | Southern Cal ..........5 | | 354,945 | 70,989 |
| UCLA .................5 | | 318,371 | 63,674 | Michigan St. ...........6 | | 414,177 | 69,030 |
| **1955** | | | | **1969** | | | |
| Michigan ...............7 | | 544,838 | 77,834 | Ohio St. ................5 | | 431,175 | 86,235 |
| Ohio St. ................7 | | 493,178 | 70,454 | Michigan ...............6 | | 428,780 | 71,463 |
| Southern Cal ..........7 | | 467,085 | 66,726 | Michigan St. ...........5 | | 352,123 | 70,425 |
| **1956** | | | | **1970** | | | |
| Ohio St. ................6 | | 494,575 | 82,429 | Ohio St. ................5 | | 432,451 | 86,490 |
| Michigan ...............7 | | 566,145 | 80,878 | Michigan ...............6 | | 476,164 | 79,361 |
| Minnesota .............6 | | 375,407 | 62,568 | Purdue .................5 | | 340,090 | 68,018 |
| **1957** | | | | **1971** | | | |
| Michigan ...............6 | | 504,954 | 84,159 | Ohio St. ................6 | | 506,699 | 84,450 |
| Ohio St. ................6 | | 484,118 | 80,686 | Michigan ...............7 | | 564,376 | 80,625 |
| Minnesota .............5 | | 319,942 | 63,988 | Wisconsin ..............6 | | 408,885 | 68,148 |
| **1958** | | | | **1972** | | | |
| Ohio St. ................6 | | 499,352 | 82,225 | Michigan ...............6 | | 513,398 | 85,566 |
| Michigan ...............6 | | 405,115 | 67,519 | Ohio St. ................6 | | 509,420 | 84,903 |
| Louisiana St. ...........5 | | 296,576 | 59,315 | Nebraska ..............6 | | 456,859 | 76,143 |
| **1959** | | | | **1973** | | | |
| Ohio St. ................6 | | 495,536 | 82,589 | Ohio St. ................6 | | 523,369 | 87,228 |
| Michigan ...............6 | | 456,385 | 76,064 | Michigan ...............7 | | 595,171 | 85,024 |
| Louisiana St. ...........7 | | 408,727 | 58,390 | Nebraska ..............6 | | 456,726 | 76,121 |
| **1960** | | | | **1974** | | | |
| Ohio St. ................5 | | 413,583 | 82,717 | Michigan ...............6 | | 562,105 | 93,684 |
| Michigan St. ...........4 | | 274,367 | 68,592 | Ohio St. ................6 | | 525,314 | 87,552 |
| Michigan ...............6 | | 374,682 | 62,447 | Nebraska ..............7 | | 534,388 | 76,341 |
| **1961** | | | | **1975** | | | |
| Ohio St. ................5 | | 414,712 | 82,942 | Michigan ...............7 | | 689,146 | 98,449 |
| Michigan ...............7 | | 514,924 | 73,561 | Ohio St. ................6 | | 527,141 | 87,856 |
| Louisiana St. ...........6 | | 381,409 | 63,651 | Nebraska ..............7 | | 533,368 | 76,195 |
| **1962** | | | | **1976** | | | |
| Ohio St. ................6 | | 497,644 | 82,941 | Michigan ...............7 | | 722,113 | 103,159 |
| Michigan St. ...........4 | | 272,568 | 68,142 | Ohio St. ................6 | | 526,216 | 87,702 |
| Louisiana St. ...........6 | | 397,701 | 66,284 | Tennessee .............7 | | 564,922 | 80,703 |

*College Football Attendance Records*

| Team | G | Attendance | Average | Team | G | Attendance | Average |
|---|---|---|---|---|---|---|---|
| **1977** | | | | **1985** | | | |
| Michigan | 7 | 729,418 | 104,203 | Michigan | 6 | 633,530 | 105,588 |
| Ohio St. | 6 | 525,535 | 87,589 | Tennessee | 7 | 658,690 | 94,099 |
| Tennessee | 7 | 582,979 | 83,283 | Ohio St. | 6 | 535,284 | 89,214 |
| **1978** | | | | **1986** | | | |
| Michigan | 6 | 629,690 | 104,948 | Michigan | 6 | 631,261 | 105,210 |
| Ohio St. | 7 | 614,881 | 87,840 | Tennessee | 7 | 643,317 | 91,902 |
| Tennessee | †8 | 627,381 | 78,422 | Ohio St. | 6 | 536,210 | 89,368 |
| **1979** | | | | **1987** | | | |
| Michigan | 7 | 730,315 | 104,331 | Michigan | 7 | *731,281 | 104,469 |
| Ohio St. | 7 | 611,794 | 87,399 | Tennessee | ‡8 | 705,434 | 88,179 |
| Tennessee | 6 | 512,139 | 85,357 | Ohio St. | 6 | 511,772 | 85,295 |
| **1980** | | | | **1988** | | | |
| Michigan | 6 | 625,750 | 104,292 | Michigan | 6 | 628,807 | 104,801 |
| Tennessee | †8 | 709,193 | 88,649 | Tennessee | 6 | 551,677 | 91,946 |
| Ohio St. | 7 | 615,476 | 87,925 | Ohio St. | 6 | 516,972 | 86,162 |
| **1981** | | | | **1989** | | | |
| Michigan | 6 | 632,990 | 105,498 | Michigan | 6 | 632,136 | 105,356 |
| Tennessee | 6 | 558,996 | 93,166 | Tennessee | 6 | 563,502 | 93,917 |
| Ohio St. | 6 | 521,760 | 86,960 | Ohio St. | 6 | 511,812 | 85,302 |
| **1982** | | | | **1990** | | | |
| Michigan | 6 | 631,743 | 105,291 | Michigan | 6 | 627,046 | 104,508 |
| Tennessee | 6 | 561,102 | 93,517 | Tennessee | 7 | 666,540 | 95,220 |
| Ohio St. | 7 | 623,152 | 89,022 | Ohio St. | 6 | 536,297 | 89,383 |
| **1983** | | | | **1991** | | | |
| Michigan | 6 | 626,916 | 104,486 | Michigan | 6 | 632,024 | 105,337 |
| Ohio St. | 6 | 534,110 | 89,018 | Tennessee | 6 | 578,389 | 96,398 |
| Tennessee | †8 | 679,420 | 84,928 | Penn St. | 6 | 575,077 | 95,846 |
| **1984** | | | | **1992** | | | |
| Michigan | 7 | 726,734 | 103,819 | Michigan | 6 | 635,201 | *105,867 |
| Tennessee | 7 | 654,602 | 93,515 | Tennessee | 6 | 575,544 | 95,924 |
| Ohio St. | 6 | 536,691 | 89,449 | Penn St. | 6 | 569,195 | 94,866 |

*Record. # Includes neutral-site game (Oklahoma) at Dallas counted as a home game (75,500). † Includes neutral-site game at Memphis counted as a home game. Attendance: 1978 (40,879), 1980 (50,003), 1983 (20,135). ‡ Includes neutral-site game at East Rutherford (54,681).

## ANNUAL LEADING DIVISION I-AA TEAMS IN PER-GAME HOME ATTENDANCE

| Year | | Avg. | Year | | Avg. |
|---|---|---|---|---|---|
| 1978 | Southern-B.R. | 28,333 | 1988 | Jackson St. | 26,500 |
| 1979 | Grambling | 29,900 | 1989 | Jackson St. | 32,269 |
| 1980 | Southern-B.R. | 29,708 | 1990 | Grambling | 30,152 |
| 1981 | Grambling | 30,835 | 1991 | Grambling | 27,181 |
| 1982 | Southern-B.R. | 32,265 | 1992 | Southern-B.R. | 28,906 |
| 1983 | Jackson St. | 29,117 | | | |
| 1984 | Jackson St. | 29,215 | | | |
| 1985 | Yale | 29,347 | | | |
| 1986 | Jackson St. | 25,177 | | | |
| 1987 | Jackson St. | *32,734 | | | |

* Record.

## ANNUAL LEADING DIVISION II TEAMS IN PER-GAME HOME ATTENDANCE

| Year | | Avg. | Year | | Avg. |
|---|---|---|---|---|---|
| 1958 | Southern Miss. | 11,998 | 1968 | San Diego St. | 36,969 |
| 1959 | Southern Miss. | 13,964 | 1969 | Grambling | 27,680 |
| 1960 | Florida A&M | 12,083 | 1970 | Tampa | 24,204 |
| 1961 | Akron | 12,988 | 1971 | Grambling | 29,341 |
| 1962 | Mississippi Col. | 13,125 | 1972 | Grambling | 22,663 |
| 1963 | San Diego St. | 14,200 | 1973 | Morgan St. | 22,371 |
| 1964 | Southern-B.R. | 12,633 | 1974 | Southern-B.R. | 33,563 |
| 1965 | San Diego St. | 15,227 | 1975 | Texas Southern | 22,800 |
| 1966 | San Diego St. | 15,972 | 1976 | Southern-B.R. | 25,864 |
| 1967 | San Diego St. | *41,030 | 1977 | Florida A&M | 21,376 |

| Year | | Avg. | Year | | Avg. |
|------|------|------|------|------|------|
| 1978 | Delaware | 18,981 | 1988 | Central Fla. | 21,905 |
| 1979 | Delaware | 19,644 | 1989 | North Dak. St. | 16,833 |
| 1980 | Alabama A&M | 15,820 | 1990 | Norfolk St. | 14,904 |
| 1981 | Norfolk St. | 19,750 | 1991 | Norfolk St. | 16,779 |
| 1982 | Norfolk St. | 16,183 | 1992 | Norfolk St. | 14,196 |
| 1983 | Norfolk St. | 15,417 | | | |
| 1984 | Norfolk St. | 18,500 | | | |
| 1985 | Norfolk St. | 18,430 | | | |
| 1986 | Norfolk St. | 13,836 | | | |
| 1987 | North Dak. St. | 14,120 | | | |

* Record.

## ANNUAL LEADING DIVISION III TEAMS IN PER-GAME HOME ATTENDANCE

| Year | | Avg. | Year | | Avg. |
|------|------|------|------|------|------|
| 1974 | Albany St. (Ga.) | 9,380 | 1984 | Dayton | 8,332 |
| 1975 | Wittenberg | 7,000 | 1985 | Villanova | 11,740 |
| 1976 | Morehouse | 11,600 | 1986 | Villanova | *11,883 |
| 1977 | Dayton | 10,315 | 1987 | Trinity (Conn.) | 6,254 |
| 1978 | Dayton | 9,827 | 1988 | St. John's (Minn.) | 5,788 |
| 1979 | Central Fla. | 11,240 | 1989 | Dayton | 5,962 |
| 1980 | Central Fla. | 10,450 | 1990 | Dayton | 6,185 |
| 1981 | Dayton | 10,025 | 1991 | Dayton | 7,657 |
| 1982 | Dayton | 7,906 | 1992 | Dayton | 6,098 |
| 1983 | Dayton | 6,542 | | | |

* Record.

## ANNUAL LEADING NON-NCAA TEAMS IN PER-GAME HOME ATTENDANCE

| Year | | Avg. | Year | | Avg. |
|------|------|------|------|------|------|
| 1974 | Texas A&I | 12,000 | 1984 | Elon | 6,100 |
| 1975 | Texas A&I | 11,000 | 1985 | Emporia St. | 5,120 |
| 1976 | Texas A&I | 12,000 | 1986 | Elon | 5,833 |
| 1977 | Texas A&I | *14,400 | 1987 | Ark.-Pine Bluff | 9,172 |
| 1978 | Angelo St. | 12,391 | 1988 | Ark.-Pine Bluff | 7,214 |
| 1979 | Texas A&I | 11,667 | 1989 | Ark.-Pine Bluff | 13,920 |
| 1980 | Angelo St. | 8,099 | 1990 | Ark.-Pine Bluff | 12,356 |
| 1981 | Presbyterian | 8,000 | 1991 | Central Ark. | 5,902 |
| 1982 | Lenoir-Rhyne | 6,040 | 1992 | Central St. (Ohio) | 6,286 |
| 1983 | Northeastern Okla. | 7,575 | | | |

* Record.

*Running back Garrison Hearst brought back memories of Herschel Walker for Georgia fans in 1992 by leading Division I-A in scoring (126 points) and touchdowns (21) and finishing second in rushing (140.6 yards per game). The junior finished third in the voting for*

# 1992 DIVISION I-A INDIVIDUAL LEADERS

## RUSHING

| | 1992 Class | Games | Car. | Yards | Avg. | TD | Yds.PG |
|---|---|---|---|---|---|---|---|
| Marshall Faulk, San Diego St. | So | 10 | 265 | 1630 | 6.2 | 15 | 163.00 |
| Garrison Hearst, Georgia | Jr | 11 | 228 | 1547 | 6.8 | 19 | 140.64 |
| Ryan Benjamin, Pacific (Cal.) | Sr | 11 | 231 | 1441 | 6.2 | 13 | 131.00 |
| Chuckie Dukes, Boston College | Sr | 11 | 238 | 1387 | 5.8 | 10 | 126.09 |
| Trevor Cobb, Rice | Sr | 11 | 279 | 1386 | 5.0 | 11 | 126.00 |
| Travis Sims, Hawaii | Sr | 12 | 220 | 1498 | 6.8 | 9 | 124.83 |
| Reggie Brooks, Notre Dame | Sr | 11 | 167 | 1343 | 8.0 | 13 | 122.09 |
| LeShon Johnson, Northern Ill. | Jr | 11 | 265 | 1338 | 5.0 | 6 | 121.64 |
| Byron Morris, Texas Tech | So | 11 | 242 | 1279 | 5.3 | 10 | 116.27 |
| Deland McCullough, Miami (Ohio) | Fr | 9 | 227 | 1026 | 4.5 | 6 | 114.00 |
| Nathan DuPree, San Jose St. | Jr | 11 | 237 | 1239 | 5.2 | 11 | 112.64 |
| Tyrone Wheatley, Michigan | So | 10 | 170 | 1122 | 6.6 | 10 | 112.20 |
| Greg Hill, Texas A&M | So | 12 | 267 | 1339 | 5.0 | 15 | 111.58 |
| Calvin Jones, Nebraska | So | 11 | 168 | 1210 | 7.2 | 14 | 110.00 |
| Shaumbe Wright-Fair, Washington St. | Sr | 11 | 237 | 1207 | 5.1 | 11 | 109.73 |
| Natrone Means, North Caro. | Jr | 11 | 235 | 1195 | 5.1 | 13 | 108.64 |
| Russell White, California | Sr | 10 | 206 | 1069 | 5.2 | 9 | 106.90 |
| Winslow Oliver, New Mexico | Fr | 10 | 245 | 1063 | 4.3 | 3 | 106.30 |
| Corey Croom, Ball St. | Sr | 11 | 301 | 1157 | 3.8 | 6 | 105.18 |
| Adrian Murrell, West Va. | Sr | 11 | 222 | 1145 | 5.2 | 6 | 104.09 |
| Derek Brown, Nebraska | Jr | 10 | 170 | 1015 | 6.0 | 4 | 101.50 |
| Anthony Barbour, North Caro. St. | Sr | 12 | 199 | 1204 | 6.1 | 8 | 100.33 |
| Napoleon Kaufman, Washington | So | 11 | 162 | 1045 | 6.5 | 6 | 95.00 |
| Junior Smith, East Caro. | So | 11 | 186 | 1037 | 5.6 | 9 | 94.27 |
| Casey McBeth, Toledo | Jr | 11 | 223 | 1037 | 4.7 | 10 | 94.27 |

## PASSING EFFICIENCY

| (Min. 15 att. per game) | 1992 Class | Gms. | Att. | Cmp. | Cmp. Pct. | Int. | Int. Pct. | Yards | Yds./ Att. | TD | TD Pct. | Rating Points |
|---|---|---|---|---|---|---|---|---|---|---|---|---|
| Elvis Grbac, Michigan | Sr | 9 | 169 | 112 | 66.27 | 12 | 7.10 | 1465 | 8.67 | 15 | 8.88 | 154.2 |
| Marvin Graves, Syracuse | Jr | 11 | 242 | 146 | 60.33 | 12 | 4.96 | 2296 | 9.49 | 14 | 5.79 | 149.2 |
| Ryan Hancock, Brigham Young | So | 9 | 288 | 165 | 57.29 | 13 | 4.51 | 2635 | 9.15 | 17 | 5.90 | 144.6 |
| Bert Emanuel, Rice | Jr | 11 | 179 | 94 | 52.51 | 6 | 3.35 | 1558 | 8.70 | 11 | 6.15 | 139.2 |
| Kordell Stewart, Colorado | So | 9 | 252 | 151 | 59.92 | 9 | 3.57 | 2109 | 8.37 | 12 | 4.76 | 138.8 |
| Eric Zeier, Georgia | So | 11 | 258 | 151 | 58.53 | 12 | 4.65 | 2248 | 8.71 | 12 | 4.65 | 137.8 |
| Jimmy Klingler, Houston | So | 11 | 504 | 303 | 60.12 | 18 | 3.57 | 3818 | 7.58 | 32 | 6.35 | 137.6 |
| Bobby Goodman, Virginia | Sr | 11 | 232 | 130 | 56.03 | 12 | 5.17 | 1707 | 7.36 | 21 | 9.05 | 137.4 |
| Joe Youngblood, Central Mich. | Jr | 11 | 278 | 161 | 57.91 | 13 | 4.68 | 2209 | 7.95 | 18 | 6.47 | 136.7 |
| Trent Dilfer, Fresno St. | So | 12 | 331 | 174 | 52.57 | 14 | 4.23 | 2828 | 8.54 | 20 | 6.04 | 135.8 |
| J. J. Joe, Baylor | Jr | 11 | 189 | 88 | 46.56 | 13 | 6.88 | 1765 | 9.34 | 14 | 7.41 | 135.7 |
| Glenn Foley, Boston College | Jr | 11 | 265 | 146 | 55.09 | 12 | 4.53 | 2231 | 8.42 | 15 | 5.66 | 135.4 |
| Steve Matthews, Memphis St. | Jr | 11 | 286 | 175 | 61.19 | 12 | 4.20 | 2084 | 7.29 | 18 | 6.29 | 134.8 |
| Rick Mirer, Notre Dame | Sr | 11 | 234 | 120 | 51.28 | 6 | 2.56 | 1876 | 8.02 | 15 | 6.41 | 134.7 |
| Terry Jordan, North Caro. St. | Sr | 12 | 256 | 164 | 64.06 | 8 | 3.13 | 1963 | 7.67 | 9 | 3.52 | 133.8 |
| Grady Benton, Arizona St. | Fr | 10 | 225 | 149 | 66.22 | 9 | 4.00 | 1707 | 7.59 | 8 | 3.56 | 133.7 |
| Heath Shuler, Tennessee | So | 11 | 224 | 130 | 58.04 | 4 | 1.79 | 1712 | 7.64 | 10 | 4.46 | 133.4 |
| Alex Van Pelt, Pittsburgh | Sr | 12 | 407 | 245 | 60.20 | 17 | 4.18 | 3163 | 7.77 | 20 | 4.91 | 133.3 |
| Gino Torretta, Miami (Fla.) | Sr | 11 | 402 | 228 | 56.72 | 7 | 1.74 | 3060 | 7.61 | 19 | 4.73 | 132.8 |
| Len Williams, Northwestern | Sr | 11 | 286 | 181 | 63.29 | 9 | 3.15 | 2110 | 7.38 | 11 | 3.85 | 131.7 |

## TOTAL OFFENSE

| | RUSHING | | | PASSING | | TOTAL OFFENSE | | | | |
|---|---|---|---|---|---|---|---|---|---|---|
| | Car. | Gain | Loss | Net | Att. | Yards | Plays | Yards | Avg. | TDR* | Yds.PG |
| Jimmy Klingler, Houston | 40 | 94 | 144 | -50 | 504 | 3818 | 544 | 3768 | 6.93 | 32 | 342.55 |
| John Kaleo, Maryland | 106 | 320 | 240 | 80 | 482 | 3392 | 588 | 3472 | 5.90 | 22 | 315.64 |
| Ryan Hancock, Brigham Young | 33 | 79 | 128 | -49 | 288 | 2635 | 321 | 2586 | 8.06 | 17 | 287.33 |
| Charlie Ward, Florida St. | 100 | 648 | 144 | 504 | 365 | 2647 | 465 | 3151 | 6.78 | 28 | 286.45 |
| Gino Torretta, Miami (Fla.) | 34 | 95 | 119 | -24 | 402 | 3060 | 436 | 3036 | 6.96 | 19 | 276.00 |
| Shane Matthews, Florida | 73 | 162 | 191 | -29 | 463 | 3205 | 536 | 3176 | 5.93 | 25 | 264.67 |
| Frank Dolce, Utah | 60 | 161 | 156 | 5 | 322 | 2369 | 382 | 2374 | 6.21 | 22 | 263.78 |
| Alex Van Pelt, Pittsburgh | 27 | 103 | 103 | 0 | 407 | 3163 | 434 | 3163 | 7.29 | 20 | 263.58 |
| Drew Bledsoe, Washington St. | 78 | 192 | 245 | -53 | 386 | 2770 | 464 | 2717 | 5.86 | 22 | 247.00 |
| Trent Dilfer, Fresno St. | 73 | 280 | 198 | 82 | 331 | 2828 | 404 | 2910 | 7.20 | 22 | 242.50 |
| Michael Anderson, East Caro. | 43 | 56 | 135 | -79 | 398 | 2486 | 441 | 2407 | 5.46 | 22 | 240.70 |
| Jeff Garcia, San Jose St. | 94 | 411 | 188 | 223 | 371 | 2418 | 465 | 2641 | 5.68 | 22 | 240.09 |
| Charles Puleri, New Mexico St. | 63 | 112 | 269 | -157 | 349 | 2788 | 412 | 2631 | 6.39 | 19 | 239.18 |
| Jeff Handy, Missouri | 23 | 38 | 110 | -72 | 329 | 2463 | 352 | 2391 | 6.79 | 14 | 239.10 |
| Joe Hughes, Wyoming | 113 | 367 | 230 | 137 | 373 | 2706 | 486 | 2843 | 5.85 | 21 | 236.92 |
| Tony Calvillo, Utah St. | 65 | 281 | 197 | 84 | 360 | 2494 | 425 | 2578 | 6.07 | 20 | 234.36 |
| David Lowery, San Diego St. | 47 | 71 | 142 | -71 | 366 | 2632 | 413 | 2561 | 6.20 | 21 | 232.82 |
| Stoney Case, New Mexico | 114 | 511 | 241 | 270 | 308 | 2289 | 422 | 2559 | 6.06 | 22 | 232.64 |
| Kordell Stewart, Colorado | 60 | 206 | 224 | -18 | 252 | 2109 | 312 | 2091 | 6.70 | 13 | 232.33 |
| Marquel Fleetwood, Minnesota | 116 | 562 | 243 | 319 | 385 | 2168 | 501 | 2487 | 4.96 | 12 | 226.09 |

* Touchdowns responsible for are players' TDs scored and passed for.

## RECEPTIONS PER GAME

| | 1992 Class | Games | Catches | Yards | TD | Ct.PG |
|---|---|---|---|---|---|---|
| Sherman Smith, Houston | Jr | 11 | 103 | 923 | 6 | 9.36 |
| Bryan Reeves, Nevada | Jr | 11 | 81 | 1114 | 10 | 7.36 |
| Aaron Turner, Pacific (Cal.) | Sr | 11 | 79 | 1171 | 11 | 7.18 |
| Ryan Yarborough, Wyoming | Jr | 12 | 86 | 1351 | 12 | 7.17 |
| Lloyd Hill, Texas Tech | Jr | 11 | 76 | 1261 | 12 | 6.91 |
| Michael Westbrook, Colorado | So | 11 | 76 | 1060 | 8 | 6.91 |
| Marcus Badgett, Maryland | Sr | 11 | 75 | 1240 | 9 | 6.82 |
| Victor Bailey, Missouri | Sr | 11 | 75 | 1210 | 6 | 6.82 |
| Darnay Scott, San Diego St. | So | 11 | 68 | 1150 | 9 | 6.18 |
| Lee Gissendaner, Northwestern | Jr | 11 | 68 | 846 | 6 | 6.18 |
| Sean Dawkins, California | Jr | 11 | 65 | 1070 | 14 | 5.91 |
| Corey Parham, Louisiana Tech | Sr | 11 | 65 | 741 | 1 | 5.91 |
| Korey Beard, Southern Methodist | Sr | 11 | 64 | 813 | 6 | 5.82 |
| O. J. McDuffie, Penn St. | Sr | 11 | 63 | 977 | 9 | 5.73 |

## RECEIVING YARDS PER GAME

| | 1992 Class | Games | Catches | Yards | TD | Yds.PG |
|---|---|---|---|---|---|---|
| Lloyd Hill, Texas Tech | Jr | 11 | 76 | 1261 | 12 | 114.64 |
| Marcus Badgett, Maryland | Sr | 11 | 75 | 1240 | 9 | 112.73 |
| Ryan Yarborough, Wyoming | Jr | 12 | 86 | 1351 | 12 | 112.58 |
| Victor Bailey, Missouri | Sr | 11 | 75 | 1210 | 6 | 110.00 |
| Aaron Turner, Pacific (Cal.) | Sr | 11 | 79 | 1171 | 11 | 106.45 |
| Darnay Scott, San Diego St. | So | 11 | 68 | 1150 | 9 | 104.55 |
| Charles Johnson, Colorado | Jr | 11 | 57 | 1149 | 5 | 104.45 |
| Bryan Reeves, Nevada | Jr | 11 | 81 | 1114 | 10 | 101.27 |
| Sean Dawkins, California | Jr | 11 | 65 | 1070 | 14 | 97.27 |
| Michael Westbrook, Colorado | So | 11 | 76 | 1060 | 8 | 96.36 |
| Eric Drage, Brigham Young | Jr | 12 | 56 | 1093 | 12 | 91.08 |
| Dietrich Jells, Pittsburgh | So | 12 | 55 | 1091 | 8 | 90.92 |
| Marlon Pearce, Cincinnati | Jr | 10 | 56 | 891 | 5 | 89.10 |
| O. J. McDuffie, Penn St. | Sr | 11 | 63 | 977 | 9 | 88.82 |
| Greg Primus, Colorado St. | Sr | 12 | 60 | 1007 | 6 | 83.92 |
| Sherman Smith, Houston | Jr | 11 | 103 | 923 | 6 | 83.91 |
| Demond Thompkins, Nevada-Las Vegas | So | 11 | 54 | 919 | 6 | 83.55 |
| Malcolm Seabron, Fresno St. | Jr | 12 | 41 | 974 | 9 | 81.17 |
| C. J. Davis, Washington St. | Sr | 11 | 55 | 890 | 5 | 80.91 |
| Andre Hastings, Georgia | Jr | 11 | 52 | 860 | 5 | 78.18 |

## INTERCEPTIONS

| | 1992 Class | Games | Int. | Yards | TD | Int.PG |
|---|---|---|---|---|---|---|
| Carlton McDonald, Air Force | Sr | 11 | 8 | 109 | 1 | .73 |
| C. J. Masters, Kansas St. | Sr | 11 | 7 | 152 | 2 | .64 |
| T. Drakeford, Virginia Tech | Jr | 11 | 7 | 121 | 1 | .64 |
| Greg Evans, Texas Christian | Jr | 11 | 7 | 121 | 0 | .64 |
| Joe Bair, Bowling Green | Jr | 11 | 7 | 51 | 0 | .64 |
| Chris Owens, Akron | Sr | 11 | 7 | 49 | 0 | .64 |
| Corey Sawyer, Florida St. | So | 11 | 7 | 0 | 0 | .64 |
| Deon Figures, Colorado | Sr | 10 | 6 | 21 | 0 | .60 |
| Herman O'Berry, Oregon | So | 10 | 6 | 3 | 0 | .60 |
| Terryl Ulmer, Southern Miss. | Jr | 11 | 6 | 132 | 0 | .55 |
| Rico Wesley, Texas Christian | Jr | 11 | 6 | 125 | 0 | .55 |
| Jaime Mendez, Kansas St. | Jr | 11 | 6 | 121 | 0 | .55 |
| Greg Grandison, East Caro. | Sr | 11 | 6 | 104 | 0 | .55 |
| Charlie Brennan, Boston College | Sr | 11 | 6 | 88 | 0 | .55 |
| Victor Green, Akron | Sr | 11 | 6 | 69 | 1 | .55 |
| Stephen Harris, Houston | Sr | 11 | 6 | 53 | 0 | .55 |
| Greg Myers, Colorado St. | Fr | 11 | 6 | 51 | 0 | .55 |
| Bob Grosvenor, Syracuse | Jr | 11 | 6 | 38 | 0 | .55 |
| Cary Brabham, Southern Methodist | Sr | 11 | 6 | 30 | 0 | .55 |
| Donald Toomer, Utah St. | So | 11 | 6 | 21 | 0 | .55 |

## SCORING

| | 1992 Class | Games | TD | XP | FG | Points | Pts.PG |
|---|---|---|---|---|---|---|---|
| Garrison Hearst, Georgia | Jr | 11 | 21 | 0 | 0 | 126 | 11.45 |
| Richie Anderson, Penn St. | Sr | 11 | 19 | 2 | 0 | 116 | 10.55 |
| Marshall Faulk, San Diego St. | So | 10 | 15 | 2 | 0 | 92 | 9.20 |
| Joe Allison, Memphis St. | Jr | 11 | 0 | 32 | 23 | 101 | 9.18 |
| Greg Hill, Texas A&M | So | 12 | 17 | 0 | 0 | 102 | 8.50 |
| Tyrone Wheatley, Michigan | So | 10 | 14 | 0 | 0 | 84 | 8.40 |
| Trevor Cobb, Rice | Sr | 11 | 15 | 2 | 0 | 92 | 8.36 |
| Calvin Jones, Nebraska | So | 11 | 15 | 0 | 0 | 90 | 8.18 |
| Craig Thomas, Michigan St. | Jr | 11 | 15 | 0 | 0 | 90 | 8.18 |
| Rusty Hanna, Toledo | Sr | 11 | 0 | 26 | 21 | 89 | 8.09 |

| | 1992 Class | Games | TD | XP | FG | Points | Pts.PG |
|---|---|---|---|---|---|---|---|
| Nelson Welch, Clemson | So | 11 | 0 | 23 | 22 | 89 | 8.09 |
| Anthony Daigle, Fresno St. | Jr | 12 | 16 | 0 | 0 | 96 | 8.00 |
| Michael Proctor, Alabama | Fr | 12 | 0 | 37 | 19 | 94 | 7.83 |
| Reggie Brooks, Notre Dame | Sr | 11 | 14 | 2 | 0 | 86 | 7.82 |
| Dan Eichloff, Kansas | Jr | 11 | 0 | 38 | 16 | 86 | 7.82 |
| Scott Ethridge, Auburn | So | 11 | 0 | 20 | 22 | 86 | 7.82 |
| Jason Elam, Hawaii | Sr | 12 | 0 | 44 | 16 | 92 | 7.67 |
| Derrick Alexander, Michigan | Sr | 11 | 14 | 0 | 0 | 84 | 7.64 |
| Sean Dawkins, California | Jr | 11 | 14 | 0 | 0 | 84 | 7.64 |
| John Becksvoort, Tennessee | So | 11 | 0 | 35 | 16 | 83 | 7.55 |
| Sean Jones, Utah St. | Sr | 11 | 0 | 28 | 18 | 82 | 7.45 |
| Rich Thompson, Wisconsin | Sr | 11 | 0 | 16 | 22 | 82 | 7.45 |
| John Biskup, Syracuse | Sr | 11 | 0 | 33 | 16 | 81 | 7.36 |
| Dan Mowrey, Florida St. | So | 11 | 0 | 51 | 10 | 81 | 7.36 |
| Derek Mahoney, Fresno St. | Jr | 12 | 0 | 58 | 10 | 88 | 7.33 |
| Lamar Smith, Houston | Jr | 9 | 11 | 0 | 0 | 66 | 7.33 |

## ALL-PURPOSE RUNNERS

| | 1992 Class | Games | Rush | Rec. | PR | KOR | Yards | Total Yds.PG |
|---|---|---|---|---|---|---|---|---|
| Ryan Benjamin, Pacific (Cal.) | Sr | 11 | 1441 | 434 | 96 | 626 | 2597 | 236.09 |
| Glyn Milburn, Stanford | Sr | 12 | 851 | 405 | 573 | 292 | 2121 | 176.75 |
| Marshall Faulk, San Diego St. | So | 10 | 1630 | 128 | 0 | 0 | 1758 | 175.80 |
| Garrison Hearst, Georgia | Jr | 11 | 1547 | 324 | 0 | 39 | 1910 | 173.64 |
| Henry Bailey, Nevada-Las Vegas | So | 11 | 15 | 832 | 219 | 817 | 1883 | 171.18 |
| O. J. McDuffie, Penn St. | Sr | 11 | 133 | 977 | 398 | 323 | 1831 | 166.45 |
| Chuckie Dukes, Boston College | Sr | 11 | 1387 | 194 | 0 | 225 | 1806 | 164.18 |
| Curtis Conway, Southern Cal | Jr | 11 | 37 | 764 | 324 | 652 | 1777 | 161.55 |
| Tyrone Wheatley, Michigan | So | 10 | 1122 | 141 | 0 | 260 | 1523 | 152.30 |
| Trevor Cobb, Rice | Sr | 11 | 1386 | 283 | 0 | 0 | 1669 | 151.73 |
| Darnay Scott, San Diego St. | So | 11 | 20 | 1150 | 0 | 499 | 1669 | 151.73 |
| Morris Letcher, East Caro. | Jr | 11 | 35 | 557 | 263 | 771 | 1626 | 147.82 |
| Lee Gissendaner, Northwestern | Jr | 11 | 10 | 846 | 327 | 381 | 1564 | 142.18 |
| Tony Jackson, Vanderbilt | Jr | 11 | 652 | 114 | 0 | 794 | 1560 | 141.82 |
| Corey Croom, Ball St. | Sr | 11 | 1157 | 161 | 0 | 237 | 1555 | 141.36 |
| Anthony Barbour, North Caro. St. | Sr | 12 | 1204 | 166 | 0 | 306 | 1676 | 139.67 |
| Bruce Presley, Rutgers | Fr | 11 | 817 | 263 | 0 | 452 | 1532 | 139.27 |
| Nathan DuPree, San Jose St. | Jr | 11 | 1239 | 191 | 0 | 73 | 1503 | 136.64 |
| Terrance Strickland, Tulane | Sr | 9 | 311 | 51 | 82 | 775 | 1219 | 135.44 |
| Andre Hastings, Georgia | Jr | 11 | 22 | 860 | 298 | 294 | 1474 | 134.00 |

## PUNT RETURNS

| (Min. 1.2 per game) | 1992 Class | No. | Yds. | TD | Avg. | (Min. 1.2 per game) | 1992 Class | No. | Yds. | TD | Avg. |
|---|---|---|---|---|---|---|---|---|---|---|---|
| L. Gissendaner, Northwestern | Jr | 15 | 327 | 1 | 21.80 | C. Thompson, Eastern Mich. | Jr | 15 | 193 | 0 | 12.87 |
| James McMillion, Iowa St. | Jr | 23 | 435 | 3 | 18.91 | Gary Voelker, Illinois | Jr | 17 | 214 | 0 | 12.59 |
| Glyn Milburn, Stanford | Sr | 31 | 573 | 3 | 18.48 | Jeff Brothers, Vanderbilt | Jr | 20 | 246 | 0 | 12.30 |
| Jamie Mouton, Houston | Sr | 18 | 278 | 1 | 15.44 | Donald Allen, Rice | Sr | 21 | 252 | 0 | 12.00 |
| Corey Sawyer, Florida St. | So | 33 | 488 | 1 | 14.79 | Morris Letcher, East Caro. | Jr | 22 | 263 | 0 | 11.95 |
| H. Bailey, Nev.-Las Vegas | So | 15 | 219 | 1 | 14.60 | Ezell Brown, New Mexico St. | Sr | 14 | 167 | 0 | 11.93 |
| N. Kaufman, Washington | So | 19 | 269 | 0 | 14.16 | Courtney Burton, Ohio | Jr | 24 | 283 | 0 | 11.79 |
| Marc Baxter, Temple | Fr | 12 | 167 | 0 | 13.92 | Darrick Branch, Hawaii | Sr | 26 | 305 | 1 | 11.73 |
| Derrick Alexander, Michigan | Sr | 25 | 343 | 2 | 13.72 | Dwayne Owens, Oregon St. | Sr | 18 | 211 | 1 | 11.72 |
| O. J. McDuffie, Penn St. | Sr | 30 | 398 | 0 | 13.27 | Deon Figures, Colorado | Sr | 42 | 479 | 0 | 11.40 |

## KICKOFF RETURNS

| (Min. 1.2 per game) | 1992 Class | No. | Yds. | TD | Avg. | (Min. 1.2 per game) | 1992 Class | No. | Yds. | TD | Avg. |
|---|---|---|---|---|---|---|---|---|---|---|---|
| F. Montgomery, N. Mex. St. | Sr | 14 | 457 | 0 | 32.64 | C. Thompson, Eastern Mich. | Jr | 18 | 490 | 1 | 27.22 |
| Leroy Gallman, Duke | Sr | 14 | 433 | 0 | 30.93 | N. Banks, Cal St. Fullerton | Jr | 14 | 370 | 0 | 26.43 |
| Lew Lawhorn, Temple | So | 20 | 600 | 2 | 30.00 | John Lewis, Minnesota | Sr | 29 | 755 | 1 | 26.03 |
| Chris Singleton, Nevada | Jr | 17 | 497 | 0 | 29.24 | Courtney Burton, Ohio | Jr | 21 | 545 | 1 | 25.95 |
| Brad Breedlove, Duke | Sr | 15 | 438 | 0 | 29.20 | E. Redmon, Louisiana Tech | So | 12 | 310 | 0 | 25.83 |

## PUNTING

| (Min. 3.6 per game) | 1992 Class | No. | Avg. | (Min. 3.6 per game) | 1992 Class | No. | Avg. |
|---|---|---|---|---|---|---|---|
| Ed Bunn, UTEP | Sr | 41 | 47.68 | Daron Alcorn, Akron | Sr | 60 | 43.58 |
| Mitch Berger, Colorado | Jr | 53 | 47.04 | Mike Stigge, Nebraska | Sr | 53 | 43.21 |
| Brian Parvin, Nevada-Las Vegas | Sr | 57 | 46.26 | Pete Raether, Arkansas | Sr | 68 | 43.21 |
| Sean Snyder, Kansas St. | Sr | 80 | 44.65 | Mike Thomas, North Caro. | Fr | 56 | 43.13 |
| Jeff Buffaloe, Memphis St. | Sr | 52 | 44.56 | Lee Myhre, San Jose St. | Jr | 54 | 42.89 |
| Jason Elam, Hawaii | Sr | 49 | 44.47 | Josh Miller, Arizona | Sr | 74 | 42.69 |
| Todd Sauerbrun, West Va. | So | 53 | 44.30 | Terry Daniel, Auburn | So | 65 | 42.63 |
| Jim DiGuilio, Indiana | So | 53 | 44.28 | Chris Noonan, California | Sr | 60 | 42.62 |
| David Davis, Texas A&M | Sr | 70 | 43.81 | Robert King, Texas Tech | Jr | 53 | 42.57 |
| Todd Jordan, Mississippi St. | Jr | 52 | 43.60 | Tommy Thompson, Oregon | Jr | 54 | 42.13 |

## FIELD GOALS

| | 1992 Class | Games | FGA | FG | Pct. | FGPG |
|---|---|---|---|---|---|---|
| Joe Allison, Memphis St. | Jr | 11 | 25 | 23 | .920 | 2.09 |
| Scott Ethridge, Auburn | So | 11 | 28 | 22 | .786 | 2.00 |
| Nelson Welch, Clemson | So | 11 | 28 | 22 | .786 | 2.00 |
| Rich Thompson, Wisconsin | Sr | 11 | 32 | 22 | .688 | 2.00 |
| Rusty Hanna, Toledo | Sr | 11 | 29 | 21 | .724 | 1.91 |
| Tommy Thompson, Oregon | Jr | 11 | 31 | 20 | .645 | 1.82 |
| Eric Lange, Tulsa | Sr | 11 | 23 | 19 | .826 | 1.73 |
| Scott Sisson, Georgia Tech | Sr | 11 | 24 | 19 | .792 | 1.73 |
| Sean Jones, Utah St. | Sr | 11 | 24 | 18 | .750 | 1.64 |
| Daron Alcorn, Akron | Sr | 11 | 26 | 18 | .692 | 1.64 |
| Michael Proctor, Alabama | Fr | 12 | 27 | 19 | .704 | 1.58 |
| Todd Wright, Arkansas | Sr | 11 | 25 | 17 | .680 | 1.55 |
| Aaron Piepkorn, Minnesota | Sr | 11 | 29 | 17 | .586 | 1.55 |
| Joe O'Leary, Purdue | Sr | 10 | 19 | 15 | .789 | 1.50 |
| Scott Blanton, Oklahoma | So | 11 | 18 | 16 | .889 | 1.45 |
| Doug Brien, California | Jr | 11 | 18 | 16 | .889 | 1.45 |
| Eric Abrams, Stanford | Fr | 11 | 20 | 16 | .800 | 1.45 |
| Dan Eichloff, Kansas | Jr | 11 | 20 | 16 | .800 | 1.45 |
| Scott Szeredy, Texas | Jr | 11 | 21 | 16 | .762 | 1.45 |
| John Becksvoort, Tennessee | So | 11 | 23 | 16 | .696 | 1.45 |
| John Biskup, Syracuse | Sr | 11 | 24 | 16 | .667 | 1.45 |
| Jeff Jacke, Missouri | Sr | 11 | 24 | 16 | .667 | 1.45 |
| Tim Williams, Ohio St. | Sr | 11 | 29 | 16 | .552 | 1.45 |

# 1992 DIVISION I-A TEAM LEADERS

## TOTAL OFFENSE

| | Games | Plays | Yds. | Avg. | TD* | Yds.PG | | Games | Plays | Yds. | Avg. | TD* | Yds.PG |
|---|---|---|---|---|---|---|---|---|---|---|---|---|---|
| Houston | 11 | 842 | 5714 | 6.8 | 48 | 519.45 | Nebraska | 11 | 817 | 4820 | 5.9 | 55 | 438.18 |
| Fresno St. | 12 | 881 | 5791 | 6.6 | 61 | 482.58 | Miami (Fla.) | 11 | 838 | 4801 | 5.7 | 41 | 436.45 |
| Notre Dame | 11 | 808 | 5174 | 6.4 | 52 | 470.36 | San Diego St. | 11 | 807 | 4776 | 5.9 | 40 | 434.18 |
| Maryland | 11 | 945 | 5131 | 5.4 | 37 | 466.45 | Syracuse | 11 | 804 | 4769 | 5.9 | 36 | 433.55 |
| Michigan | 11 | 806 | 5120 | 6.4 | 51 | 465.45 | Penn St. | 11 | 820 | 4751 | 5.8 | 49 | 431.91 |
| Florida St. | 11 | 851 | 5080 | 6.0 | 49 | 461.82 | Nevada | 11 | 906 | 4739 | 5.2 | 33 | 430.82 |
| Brigham Young | 12 | 879 | 5517 | 6.3 | 44 | 459.75 | Texas Tech | 11 | 872 | 4660 | 5.3 | 34 | 423.64 |
| Pittsburgh | 12 | 919 | 5429 | 5.9 | 35 | 452.42 | East Caro. | 11 | 824 | 4632 | 5.6 | 36 | 421.09 |
| Georgia | 11 | 732 | 4954 | 6.8 | 41 | 450.36 | Utah | 11 | 834 | 4576 | 5.5 | 33 | 416.00 |
| Boston College | 11 | 817 | 4822 | 5.9 | 41 | 438.36 | West Va. | 11 | 811 | 4488 | 5.5 | 34 | 408.00 |

* Touchdowns scored by rushing-passing only.

## TOTAL DEFENSE

| | Games | Plays | Yds. | Avg. | TD* | Yds.PG | | Games | Plays | Yds. | Avg. | TD* | Yds.PG |
|---|---|---|---|---|---|---|---|---|---|---|---|---|---|
| Alabama | 12 | 725 | 2330 | 3.2 | 11 | 194.2 | Toledo | 11 | 791 | 3128 | 4.0 | 15 | 284.4 |
| Arizona | 11 | 747 | 2783 | 3.7 | 9 | 253.0 | Florida St. | 11 | 786 | 3217 | 4.1 | 18 | 292.5 |
| Memphis St. | 11 | 766 | 2788 | 3.6 | 20 | 253.5 | Western Mich. | 11 | 739 | 3223 | 4.4 | 23 | 293.0 |
| Louisiana Tech | 11 | 698 | 2822 | 4.0 | 15 | 256.5 | Michigan | 11 | 733 | 3251 | 4.4 | 15 | 295.5 |
| Auburn | 11 | 699 | 2837 | 4.1 | 20 | 257.9 | Oregon | 11 | 710 | 3251 | 4.6 | 21 | 295.5 |
| Mississippi | 11 | 775 | 2909 | 3.8 | 20 | 264.5 | UCLA | 11 | 754 | 3266 | 4.3 | 21 | 296.9 |
| Arizona St. | 11 | 734 | 2957 | 4.0 | 18 | 268.8 | Ohio St. | 11 | 731 | 3295 | 4.5 | 16 | 299.5 |
| Miami (Fla.) | 11 | 764 | 2979 | 3.9 | 14 | 270.8 | Washington St. | 11 | 786 | 3297 | 4.2 | 26 | 299.7 |
| Colorado | 11 | 731 | 3058 | 4.2 | 19 | 278.0 | California | 11 | 739 | 3303 | 4.5 | 32 | 300.3 |
| Stanford | 12 | 821 | 3369 | 4.1 | 23 | 280.8 | Oklahoma | 11 | 748 | 3328 | 4.4 | 21 | 302.5 |

* Touchdowns scored by rushing-passing only.

## RUSHING OFFENSE

| | Games | Car. | Yds. | Avg. | TD | Yds.PG | | Games | Car. | Yds. | Avg. | TD | Yds.PG |
|---|---|---|---|---|---|---|---|---|---|---|---|---|---|
| Nebraska | 11 | 618 | 3610 | 5.8 | 40 | 328.2 | Georgia | 11 | 458 | 2584 | 5.6 | 28 | 234.9 |
| Hawaii | 12 | 630 | 3519 | 5.6 | 32 | 293.3 | Boston College | 11 | 548 | 2568 | 4.7 | 26 | 233.5 |
| Notre Dame | 11 | 555 | 3090 | 5.6 | 34 | 280.9 | Kansas | 11 | 563 | 2553 | 4.5 | 27 | 232.1 |
| Army | 11 | 667 | 2934 | 4.4 | 20 | 266.7 | West Va. | 11 | 532 | 2522 | 4.7 | 19 | 229.3 |
| Michigan | 11 | 531 | 2909 | 5.5 | 28 | 264.5 | Texas A&M | 12 | 570 | 2734 | 4.8 | 31 | 227.8 |
| Clemson | 11 | 580 | 2828 | 4.9 | 21 | 257.1 | Fresno St. | 12 | 535 | 2725 | 5.1 | 38 | 227.1 |
| Air Force | 11 | 610 | 2665 | 4.4 | 26 | 242.3 | Oregon St. | 11 | 620 | 2452 | 4.0 | 20 | 222.9 |
| Baylor | 11 | 570 | 2641 | 4.6 | 24 | 240.1 | North Caro. | 11 | 534 | 2439 | 4.6 | 23 | 221.7 |
| Colorado St. | 12 | 571 | 2881 | 5.0 | 25 | 240.1 | Vanderbilt | 11 | 578 | 2435 | 4.2 | 21 | 221.4 |
| Virginia | 11 | 513 | 2589 | 5.0 | 19 | 235.4 | Syracuse | 11 | 552 | 2426 | 4.4 | 21 | 220.5 |

* Touchdowns scored by rushing-passing only.

## RUSHING DEFENSE

| | Games | Car. | Yds. | Avg. | TD | Yds.PG | | Games | Car. | Yds. | Avg. | TD | Yds.PG |
|---|---|---|---|---|---|---|---|---|---|---|---|---|---|
| Alabama | 12 | 395 | 660 | 1.7 | 5 | 55.0 | Auburn | 11 | 429 | 1272 | 3.0 | 10 | 115.6 |
| Arizona | 11 | 384 | 716 | 1.9 | 4 | 65.1 | Texas A&M | 12 | 429 | 1412 | 3.3 | 8 | 117.7 |
| Mississippi | 11 | 413 | 895 | 2.2 | 10 | 81.4 | Clemson | 11 | 413 | 1321 | 3.2 | 6 | 120.1 |
| Michigan | 11 | 369 | 985 | 2.7 | 6 | 89.5 | Arizona St. | 11 | 434 | 1323 | 3.0 | 11 | 120.3 |
| Syracuse | 11 | 339 | 1007 | 3.0 | 10 | 91.5 | Southern Cal | 11 | 405 | 1323 | 3.3 | 10 | 120.3 |
| Florida St. | 11 | 400 | 1103 | 2.8 | 3 | 100.3 | Ohio St. | 11 | 399 | 1340 | 3.4 | 11 | 121.8 |
| Memphis St. | 11 | 447 | 1107 | 2.5 | 9 | 100.6 | Wisconsin | 11 | 451 | 1348 | 3.0 | 11 | 122.5 |
| Miami (Fla.) | 11 | 406 | 1118 | 2.8 | 4 | 101.6 | Oregon | 11 | 432 | 1350 | 3.1 | 8 | 122.7 |
| Notre Dame | 11 | 399 | 1222 | 3.1 | 9 | 111.1 | Stanford | 12 | 467 | 1500 | 3.2 | 13 | 125.0 |
| Toledo | 11 | 466 | 1248 | 2.7 | 8 | 113.5 | Kansas | 11 | 463 | 1383 | 3.0 | 16 | 125.7 |

## SCORING OFFENSE

| | Games | Pts. | Avg. | | Games | Pts. | Avg. |
|---|---|---|---|---|---|---|---|
| Fresno St. | 12 | 486 | 40.5 | Kansas | 11 | 350 | 31.8 |
| Nebraska | 11 | 427 | 38.8 | Rutgers | 11 | 341 | 31.0 |
| Florida St. | 11 | 419 | 38.1 | Virginia | 11 | 341 | 31.0 |
| Notre Dame | 11 | 409 | 37.2 | San Diego St. | 11 | 334 | 30.4 |
| Michigan | 11 | 393 | 35.7 | San Jose St. | 11 | 330 | 30.0 |
| Penn St. | 11 | 388 | 35.3 | Brigham Young | 12 | 355 | 29.6 |
| Houston | 11 | 378 | 34.4 | Baylor | 11 | 324 | 29.5 |
| Hawaii | 12 | 394 | 32.8 | Texas A&M | 12 | 349 | 29.1 |
| Miami (Fla.) | 11 | 356 | 32.4 | Colorado | 11 | 318 | 28.9 |
| Georgia | 11 | 352 | 32.0 | Syracuse | 11 | 314 | 28.5 |

## SCORING DEFENSE

| | Games | Pts. | Avg. | | Games | Pts. | Avg. |
|---|---|---|---|---|---|---|---|
| Arizona | 11 | 98 | 8.9 | North Caro. St. | 12 | 184 | 15.3 |
| Alabama | 12 | 109 | 9.1 | Central Mich. | 11 | 170 | 15.5 |
| Miami (Fla.) | 11 | 127 | 11.5 | Florida St. | 11 | 172 | 15.6 |
| Ohio St. | 11 | 137 | 12.5 | Nebraska | 11 | 172 | 15.6 |
| Michigan | 11 | 140 | 12.7 | Tennessee | 11 | 173 | 15.7 |
| Georgia | 11 | 141 | 12.8 | Mississippi | 11 | 174 | 15.8 |
| Washington | 11 | 148 | 13.5 | Mississippi St. | 11 | 176 | 16.0 |
| Toledo | 11 | 153 | 13.9 | Stanford | 12 | 193 | 16.1 |
| Texas A&M | 12 | 168 | 14.0 | Western Mich. | 11 | 177 | 16.1 |
| Louisiana Tech | 11 | 167 | 15.2 | Notre Dame | 11 | 178 | 16.2 |

## PASSING OFFENSE

| | Games | Att. | Cmp. | Int. | Pct. | Yards | Yds./Att. | TD | Yds.PG |
|---|---|---|---|---|---|---|---|---|---|
| Houston | 11 | 619 | 368 | 24 | 59.5 | 4478 | 7.2 | 36 | 407.1 |
| Maryland | 11 | 514 | 304 | 23 | 59.1 | 3628 | 7.1 | 18 | 329.8 |
| Miami (Fla.) | 11 | 457 | 259 | 7 | 56.7 | 3476 | 7.6 | 23 | 316.0 |
| Nevada | 11 | 497 | 268 | 27 | 53.9 | 3328 | 6.7 | 23 | 302.5 |
| Brigham Young | 12 | 405 | 222 | 19 | 54.8 | 3575 | 8.8 | 27 | 297.9 |
| Colorado | 11 | 398 | 232 | 20 | 58.3 | 3271 | 8.2 | 22 | 297.4 |
| Missouri | 11 | 442 | 258 | 12 | 58.4 | 3223 | 7.3 | 13 | 293.0 |
| Pittsburgh | 12 | 455 | 266 | 20 | 58.5 | 3483 | 7.7 | 23 | 290.3 |
| Florida | 12 | 503 | 290 | 18 | 57.7 | 3440 | 6.8 | 25 | 286.7 |
| East Caro. | 11 | 497 | 272 | 27 | 54.7 | 3085 | 6.2 | 27 | 280.5 |
| Washington St. | 11 | 409 | 227 | 15 | 55.5 | 2986 | 7.3 | 20 | 271.5 |
| Pacific (Cal.) | 11 | 441 | 243 | 19 | 55.1 | 2984 | 6.8 | 18 | 271.3 |
| Southern Methodist | 11 | 452 | 255 | 13 | 56.4 | 2893 | 6.4 | 16 | 263.0 |
| Utah | 11 | 407 | 236 | 12 | 58.0 | 2878 | 7.1 | 14 | 261.6 |
| Florida St. | 11 | 387 | 214 | 17 | 55.3 | 2828 | 7.3 | 23 | 257.1 |
| Fresno St. | 12 | 346 | 184 | 14 | 53.2 | 3066 | 8.9 | 23 | 255.5 |
| Wyoming | 12 | 434 | 244 | 22 | 56.2 | 3065 | 7.1 | 17 | 255.4 |
| New Mexico St. | 11 | 349 | 189 | 15 | 54.2 | 2788 | 8.0 | 16 | 253.5 |
| Utah St. | 11 | 427 | 232 | 14 | 54.3 | 2786 | 6.5 | 16 | 253.3 |
| San Diego St. | 11 | 386 | 201 | 11 | 52.1 | 2764 | 7.2 | 22 | 251.3 |

## PASS-EFFICIENCY DEFENSE

| | Games | Att. | Cmp. | Cmp. Pct. | Int. | Int. Pct. | Yards | Yds./Att. | TD | TD Pct. | Rating Points |
|---|---|---|---|---|---|---|---|---|---|---|---|
| Western Mich. | 11 | 283 | 121 | 42.76 | 15 | 5.30 | 1522 | 5.38 | 5 | 1.77 | 83.16 |
| Alabama | 12 | 330 | 164 | 49.70 | 22 | 6.67 | 1670 | 5.06 | 6 | 1.82 | 84.87 |
| Colorado | 11 | 257 | 105 | 40.86 | 18 | 7.00 | 1461 | 5.68 | 8 | 3.11 | 84.87 |
| Stanford | 12 | 354 | 161 | 45.48 | 18 | 5.08 | 1869 | 5.28 | 10 | 2.82 | 88.98 |
| Miami (Fla.) | 11 | 358 | 173 | 48.32 | 18 | 5.03 | 1861 | 5.20 | 10 | 2.79 | 91.15 |
| Auburn | 11 | 270 | 117 | 43.33 | 16 | 5.93 | 1565 | 5.80 | 10 | 3.70 | 92.39 |
| Mississippi | 11 | 362 | 169 | 46.69 | 17 | 4.70 | 2014 | 5.56 | 10 | 2.76 | 93.14 |
| Southern Miss. | 11 | 297 | 143 | 48.15 | 19 | 6.40 | 1692 | 5.70 | 9 | 3.03 | 93.21 |
| Toledo | 11 | 325 | 148 | 45.54 | 13 | 4.00 | 1880 | 5.78 | 7 | 2.15 | 93.24 |
| Georgia | 11 | 302 | 151 | 50.00 | 12 | 3.97 | 1699 | 5.63 | 5 | 1.66 | 94.77 |

| | Games | Att. | Cmp. | Cmp. Pct. | Int. | Int. Pct. | Yards | Yds./ Att. | TD | TD Pct. | Rating Points |
|---|---|---|---|---|---|---|---|---|---|---|---|
| Memphis St. | 11 | 319 | 152 | 47.65 | 13 | 4.08 | 1681 | 5.27 | 11 | 3.45 | 95.14 |
| Arizona | 11 | 363 | 188 | 51.79 | 16 | 4.41 | 2067 | 5.69 | 5 | 1.38 | 95.35 |
| Ohio St. | 11 | 332 | 178 | 53.61 | 19 | 5.72 | 1955 | 5.89 | 5 | 1.51 | 96.60 |
| Florida St. | 11 | 386 | 182 | 47.15 | 18 | 4.66 | 2114 | 5.48 | 15 | 3.89 | 96.65 |
| Arizona St. | 11 | 300 | 153 | 51.00 | 11 | 3.67 | 1634 | 5.45 | 7 | 2.33 | 97.12 |
| Akron | 11 | 299 | 153 | 51.17 | 24 | 8.03 | 1871 | 6.26 | 9 | 3.01 | 97.61 |
| Bowling Green | 11 | 359 | 182 | 50.70 | 19 | 5.29 | 2071 | 5.77 | 9 | 3.06 | 98.68 |
| Texas A&M | 12 | 379 | 184 | 48.55 | 16 | 4.22 | 2230 | 5.88 | 11 | 2.90 | 99.11 |
| Northern Ill. | 11 | 331 | 178 | 53.78 | 11 | 3.32 | 1775 | 5.36 | 7 | 2.11 | 99.15 |
| Washington St. | 11 | 317 | 147 | 46.37 | 14 | 4.42 | 1905 | 6.01 | 11 | 3.47 | 99.47 |

## NET PUNTING

| | Punts | Avg. | No. Ret. | Yds. Ret. | Net Avg. | | Punts | Avg. | No. Ret. | Yds. Ret. | Net Avg. |
|---|---|---|---|---|---|---|---|---|---|---|---|
| Nebraska | 53 | 43.2 | 20 | 81 | 41.7 | Air Force | 59 | 41.6 | 29 | 200 | 38.2 |
| Colorado | 54 | 46.2 | 33 | 243 | 41.7 | North Caro. | 60 | 42.3 | 29 | 255 | 38.0 |
| Arizona | 80 | 41.8 | 25 | 83 | 40.8 | Oklahoma | 49 | 41.9 | 21 | 206 | 37.7 |
| Notre Dame | 40 | 41.7 | 9 | 82 | 39.6 | Southern Miss. | 67 | 39.6 | 29 | 123 | 37.7 |
| Auburn | 67 | 42.4 | 35 | 214 | 39.2 | Tulsa | 52 | 39.4 | 18 | 97 | 37.5 |
| Mississippi St. | 53 | 42.8 | 25 | 199 | 39.0 | Memphis St. | 57 | 43.3 | 32 | 331 | 37.5 |
| Texas A&M | 72 | 43.4 | 33 | 316 | 39.0 | Akron | 60 | 43.6 | 35 | 366 | 37.5 |
| Syracuse | 38 | 40.7 | 15 | 78 | 38.7 | Kansas | 55 | 40.6 | 23 | 173 | 37.5 |
| West Va. | 53 | 44.3 | 28 | 305 | 38.5 | Louisville | 61 | 41.0 | 33 | 220 | 37.4 |
| Boston College | 46 | 40.8 | 22 | 120 | 38.2 | Hawaii | 50 | 43.6 | 24 | 315 | 37.3 |

## PUNT RETURNS

| | Games | No. | Yds. | TD | Avg. | | Games | No. | Yds. | TD | Avg. |
|---|---|---|---|---|---|---|---|---|---|---|---|
| Northwestern | 11 | 15 | 327 | 1 | 21.8 | Nevada-Las Vegas | 11 | 22 | 289 | 2 | 13.1 |
| Iowa St. | 11 | 28 | 497 | 3 | 17.8 | Michigan | 11 | 35 | 439 | 2 | 12.5 |
| Stanford | 12 | 36 | 597 | 3 | 16.6 | Hawaii | 12 | 30 | 368 | 2 | 12.3 |
| Penn St. | 11 | 33 | 497 | 1 | 15.1 | Tennessee | 11 | 35 | 410 | 1 | 11.7 |
| East Caro. | 11 | 24 | 358 | 1 | 14.9 | Michigan St. | 11 | 16 | 187 | 0 | 11.7 |
| Florida St. | 11 | 35 | 516 | 2 | 14.7 | Colorado | 11 | 50 | 579 | 0 | 11.6 |
| Fresno St. | 12 | 24 | 343 | 2 | 14.3 | Illinois | 11 | 19 | 219 | 0 | 11.5 |
| Rice | 11 | 26 | 358 | 1 | 13.8 | Washington | 11 | 29 | 332 | 0 | 11.4 |
| Houston | 11 | 28 | 374 | 1 | 13.4 | Ohio | 11 | 25 | 286 | 0 | 11.4 |
| Vanderbilt | 11 | 21 | 278 | 0 | 13.2 | Nebraska | 11 | 31 | 353 | 0 | 11.4 |

## KICKOFF RETURNS

| | Games | No. | Yds. | TD | Avg. | | Games | No. | Yds. | TD | Avg. |
|---|---|---|---|---|---|---|---|---|---|---|---|
| Florida St. | 11 | 27 | 819 | 3 | 30.3 | Duke | 11 | 55 | 1,271 | 0 | 23.1 |
| Arkansas | 11 | 29 | 739 | 1 | 25.5 | New Mexico | 11 | 32 | 739 | 0 | 23.1 |
| Texas A&M | 12 | 26 | 644 | 0 | 24.8 | Washington St. | 11 | 34 | 781 | 1 | 23.0 |
| New Mexico St. | 11 | 40 | 990 | 1 | 24.8 | Notre Dame | 11 | 26 | 591 | 0 | 22.7 |
| Mississippi | 11 | 29 | 716 | 0 | 24.7 | Louisiana Tech | 11 | 28 | 634 | 0 | 22.6 |
| Memphis St. | 11 | 31 | 737 | 0 | 23.8 | Ohio St. | 11 | 21 | 475 | 0 | 22.6 |
| Nevada | 11 | 42 | 997 | 0 | 23.7 | South Caro. | 11 | 36 | 812 | 0 | 22.6 |
| West Va. | 11 | 34 | 797 | 0 | 23.4 | Minnesota | 11 | 51 | 1,139 | 1 | 22.3 |
| Louisville | 11 | 37 | 863 | 1 | 23.3 | Miami (Fla.) | 11 | 18 | 399 | 0 | 22.2 |
| Oregon | 11 | 26 | 602 | 0 | 23.2 | Southern Methodist | 11 | 37 | 820 | 0 | 22.2 |

## TURNOVER MARGIN

| | TURNOVERS GAINED | | | TURNOVERS LOST | | | Margin/ Game |
|---|---|---|---|---|---|---|---|
| | Fum. | Int. | Total | Fum. | Int. | Total | |
| Nebraska | 14 | 16 | 30 | 5 | 7 | 12 | 1.64 |
| Akron | 10 | 24 | 34 | 7 | 11 | 18 | 1.45 |
| Miami (Fla.) | 11 | 18 | 29 | 6 | 7 | 13 | 1.45 |
| Alabama | 15 | 22 | 37 | 10 | 10 | 20 | 1.42 |
| Rice | 12 | 18 | 30 | 8 | 8 | 16 | 1.27 |
| Southern Miss. | 11 | 19 | 30 | 6 | 10 | 16 | 1.27 |
| Tennessee | 14 | 11 | 25 | 7 | 4 | 11 | 1.27 |
| Wake Forest | 15 | 13 | 28 | 7 | 9 | 16 | 1.09 |
| Stanford | 16 | 18 | 34 | 12 | 9 | 21 | 1.08 |
| Arizona | 10 | 16 | 26 | 8 | 7 | 15 | 1.00 |
| Ohio St. | 5 | 19 | 24 | 8 | 6 | 14 | .91 |
| Washington | 13 | 14 | 27 | 10 | 7 | 17 | .91 |
| Hawaii | 20 | 14 | 34 | 18 | 6 | 24 | .83 |
| Texas Christian | 13 | 21 | 34 | 10 | 15 | 25 | .82 |
| Iowa | 14 | 18 | 32 | 10 | 13 | 23 | .75 |

| | TURNOVERS GAINED | | | TURNOVERS LOST | | | Margin/ |
| --- | --- | --- | --- | --- | --- | --- | --- |
| | Fum. | Int. | Total | Fum. | Int. | Total | Game |
| Texas A&M | 10 | 16 | 26 | 12 | 5 | 17 | .75 |
| Miami (Ohio) | 17 | 13 | 30 | 13 | 9 | 22 | .73 |
| Utah St. | 13 | 20 | 33 | 11 | 14 | 25 | .73 |
| Fresno St. | 14 | 16 | 30 | 8 | 14 | 22 | .67 |
| Boston College | 8 | 15 | 23 | 4 | 12 | 16 | .64 |
| Kansas St. | 8 | 21 | 29 | 9 | 13 | 22 | .64 |
| Louisville | 9 | 20 | 29 | 10 | 12 | 22 | .64 |
| Mississippi St. | 15 | 18 | 33 | 13 | 13 | 26 | .64 |
| Penn St. | 7 | 13 | 20 | 8 | 5 | 13 | .64 |
| Syracuse | 5 | 24 | 29 | 10 | 12 | 22 | .64 |

# LONGEST DIVISION I-A PLAYS OF 1992

## RUSHING

| Player, Team (Opponent) | Yards |
| --- | --- |
| Calvin Jones, Nebraska (Oklahoma St.) | 90 |
| Sean Jackson, Florida St. (Wake Forest) | 88 |
| Adrian Walker, Texas (Houston) | 88 |
| LeShon Johnson, Northern Ill. (Southern Miss.) | 85 |
| Rodney Thomas, Texas A&M (Baylor) | 84 |
| Clyde Allen, Florida St. (Maryland) | *84 |
| Tyrone Wheatley, Michigan (Iowa) | 82 |
| Craig Thomas, Michigan St. (Purdue) | *82 |

* Did not score.

## PASSING

| Passer-Receiver, Team (Opponent) | Yards |
| --- | --- |
| Marquel Fleetwood-John Lewis, Minnesota (Michigan) | 94 |
| Koy Detmer-Charles Johnson, Colorado (Oklahoma) | 92 |
| Alex Van Pelt-Dietrich Jells, Pittsburgh (Rutgers) | 91 |
| John Barnes-J. J. Stokes, UCLA (Southern Cal) | 90 |
| Marcus Wilson-Clarence Sevillian, Vanderbilt (Tennessee) | 88 |
| Brian Fortay-Bruce Presley, Rutgers (Cincinnati) | 84 |
| Brad Tayles-John Morton, Western Mich. (Ball St.) | 84 |
| Bob Utter-Lamont Hill, Iowa St. (Ohio) | 83 |
| Treg Koel-Antonio Freeman, Virginia Tech (West Va.) | 83 |
| Jimmy Klingler-Ron Peters, Houston (Texas) | 82 |

## INTERCEPTION RETURNS

| Player, Team (Opponent) | Yards |
| --- | --- |
| Aaron Glenn, Texas A&M (Texas) | 95 |
| Hank Cooper, East Caro. (Cincinnati) | 95 |
| Leon Fowler, Florida St. (Duke) | 94 |
| Dexter Seigler, Miami, Fla. (Temple) | 89 |
| Gary Adams, Arkansas (Auburn) | 85 |
| Sean Thomas, Duke (East Caro.) | 84 |
| C. J. Masters, Kansas St. (Kansas) | 80 |
| Carlton McDonald, Air Force (Wyoming) | 78 |
| Anthony Bridges, Louisville (Pittsburgh) | 77 |
| Barry Minter, Tulsa (Southern Miss.) | 74 |

## PUNT RETURNS

| Player, Team (Opponent) | Yards |
| --- | --- |
| Dwayne Owens, Oregon St. (UCLA) | 97 |
| Derrek Batson, East Caro. (West Va.) | 97 |
| Curtis Conway, Southern Cal (Oregon) | 96 |
| James McMillion, Iowa St. (Oklahoma St.) | 91 |
| Ray Peterson, San Diego St. (Fresno St.) | 91 |

| Player, Team (Opponent) | Yards |
|---|---|
| Eric Guliford, Arizona St. (California) | 89 |
| Ron Harris, Oregon (Nevada-Las Vegas) | 87 |
| James McMillion, Iowa St. (Tulane) | 87 |
| Orlando Watters, Arkansas (South Caro.) | 87 |
| Tommy Jones, Fresno St. (Hawaii) | 86 |

## KICKOFF RETURNS

| Player, Team (Opponent) | Yards |
|---|---|
| Tyrone Wheatley, Michigan (Houston) | 99 |
| Oscar Malone, Arkansas (Memphis St.) | 99 |
| Deron Pointer, Washington St. (UCLA) | 98 |
| Craig Thompson, Eastern Mich. (Army) | 98 |
| Derrick Cullors, Texas Christian (Southern Methodist) | 97 |
| Tony Jackson, Vanderbilt (Duke) | 97 |
| Matthew Harding, Hawaii (Fresno St.) | 97 |
| Brian Pizula, New Mexico St. (Nevada) | 97 |
| Jerrod Washington, Virginia (Georgia Tech) | 96 |
| Tamarick Vanover, Florida St. (Wake Forest) | 96 |

## FIELD GOALS

| Player, Team (Opponent) | Yards |
|---|---|
| Dan Eichloff, Kansas (Ball St.) | 61 |
| Joe Nedney, San Jose St. (Wyoming) | 60 |
| Daron Alcorn, Akron (Toledo) | 56 |
| Jason Elam, Hawaii (Brigham Young) | 56 |
| Tommy Thompson, Oregon (Washington) | 56 |
| Dan Eichloff, Kansas (Ball St.) | 55 |
| Peter Rantzau, Colorado St. (Air Force) | 55 |
| Jason Elam, Hawaii (UTEP) | 55 |
| Sean Jones, Utah St. (New Mexico St.) | 54 |
| Eric Lange, Tulsa (Houston) | 53 |
| John Becksvoort, Tennessee (Arkansas) | 53 |
| Mitch Berger, Colorado (Oklahoma) | 53 |
| Chris MacInnis, Air Force (Utah) | 53 |

## PUNTS

| Player, Team (Opponent) | Yards |
|---|---|
| Mike Stigge, Nebraska (Oklahoma St.) | 87 |
| Jim DiGuilio, Indiana (Wisconsin) | 86 |
| Marty Simpson, South Caro. (Vanderbilt) | 79 |
| Robert King, Texas Tech (Rice) | 77 |
| Shayne Edge, Florida (Vanderbilt) | 76 |
| Tommy Thompson, Oregon (California) | 76 |
| Eric Estes, Southern Miss. (Tulsa) | 76 |
| Lee Myhre, San Jose St. (Wyoming) | 75 |
| Robert King, Texas Tech (Wyoming) | 75 |
| Mitch Berger, Colorado (Iowa St.) | 74 |
| Daryl Altic, Louisiana Tech (Mississippi) | 74 |

## FUMBLE RETURNS

| Player, Team (Opponent) | Yards |
|---|---|
| Ernie Lewis, East Caro. (West Va.) | 97 |
| Jeff Arneson, Illinois (Ohio St.) | 96 |
| Michael Barber, Clemson (Tenn.-Chatt.) | 91 |
| Cassius Ware, Mississippi (Auburn) | 91 |
| Keith Caldwell, Baylor (Texas Christian) | 86 |
| George Coghill, Wake Forest (Vanderbilt) | 83 |
| Brad Armstead, Kentucky (Vanderbilt) | 70 |

*1992 Statistical Leaders*

# 1992 DIVISION I-AA INDIVIDUAL LEADERS

## RUSHING

| | 1992 Class | Games | Car. | Yards | Avg. | TD | Yds.PG |
|---|---|---|---|---|---|---|---|
| Keith Elias, Princeton | Jr | 10 | 245 | 1575 | 6.4 | 18 | 157.50 |
| Toby Davis, Illinois St. | Sr | 11 | 341 | 1561 | 4.6 | 20 | 141.91 |
| Carl Tremble, Furman | Sr | 11 | 228 | 1555 | 6.8 | 13 | 141.36 |
| Kelvin Anderson, Southeast Mo. St. | So | 10 | 205 | 1371 | 6.7 | 13 | 137.10 |
| Erik Marsh, Lafayette | So | 10 | 284 | 1365 | 4.8 | 10 | 136.50 |
| Markus Thomas, Eastern Ky. | Sr | 11 | 238 | 1498 | 6.3 | 17 | 136.18 |
| Tony Vinson, Towson St. | Jr | 8 | 191 | 1042 | 5.5 | 6 | 130.25 |
| Kenny Sims, James Madison | Sr | 9 | 191 | 1157 | 6.1 | 14 | 128.56 |
| Surkano Edwards, Samford | Sr | 10 | 187 | 1270 | 6.8 | 13 | 127.00 |
| James Johnson, Jackson St. | Sr | 11 | 221 | 1324 | 6.0 | 15 | 120.36 |
| Uly Scott, Richmond | So | 11 | 299 | 1318 | 4.4 | 13 | 119.82 |
| Everette Sands, Citadel | Jr | 11 | 218 | 1313 | 6.0 | 11 | 119.36 |
| David Wright, Indiana St. | Fr | 11 | 219 | 1313 | 6.0 | 10 | 119.36 |
| Eric Gant, Grambling | Jr | 11 | 209 | 1289 | 6.2 | 16 | 117.18 |
| Keith Price, Yale | Jr | 10 | 245 | 1141 | 4.7 | 10 | 114.10 |
| Gerod Davis, Central Fla. | Fr | 10 | 183 | 1134 | 6.2 | 10 | 113.40 |
| Willie Queen, Tennessee Tech | So | 11 | 219 | 1228 | 5.6 | 8 | 111.64 |
| Ben Sirmans, Maine | Sr | 11 | 264 | 1214 | 4.6 | 10 | 110.36 |
| Sundiata Rush, Pennsylvania | Sr | 9 | 190 | 960 | 5.1 | 10 | 106.67 |
| Sherriden May, Idaho | So | 11 | 237 | 1111 | 4.7 | 21 | 101.00 |

## PASSING EFFICIENCY

| (Min. 15 att. per game) | 1992 Class | Gms. | Att. | Cmp. | Cmp. Pct. | Int. | Int. Pct. | Yards | Yds./ Att. | TD | TD Pct. | Rating Points |
|---|---|---|---|---|---|---|---|---|---|---|---|---|
| Jay Fiedler, Dartmouth | Jr | 10 | 273 | 175 | 64.10 | 13 | 4.76 | 2748 | 10.07 | 25 | 9.16 | 169.4 |
| Lonnie Galloway, Western Caro. | Jr | 11 | 211 | 128 | 60.66 | 12 | 5.69 | 2181 | 10.34 | 20 | 9.48 | 167.4 |
| Wendal Lowrey, Northeast La. | Sr | 11 | 227 | 147 | 64.76 | 9 | 3.96 | 2190 | 9.65 | 16 | 7.05 | 161.1 |
| Donny Simmons, Western Ill. | Sr | 11 | 281 | 182 | 64.77 | 11 | 3.91 | 2496 | 8.88 | 25 | 8.90 | 160.9 |
| Michael Payton, Marshall | Sr | 11 | 313 | 200 | 63.90 | 11 | 3.51 | 2788 | 8.91 | 26 | 8.31 | 159.1 |
| Shawn Knight, William & Mary | Jr | 11 | 195 | 124 | 63.59 | 5 | 2.56 | 1892 | 9.70 | 11 | 5.64 | 158.6 |
| Ricky Jordan, Jackson St. | Jr | 11 | 215 | 119 | 55.35 | 9 | 4.19 | 2124 | 9.88 | 18 | 8.37 | 157.6 |
| Greg Lilly, Richmond | Jr | 11 | 275 | 162 | 58.91 | 10 | 3.64 | 2704 | 9.83 | 19 | 6.91 | 157.0 |
| Doug Nussmeier, Idaho | Jr | 11 | 333 | 206 | 61.86 | 9 | 2.70 | 3028 | 9.09 | 22 | 6.61 | 154.6 |
| Jay Johnson, Northern Iowa | Sr | 11 | 223 | 115 | 51.57 | 11 | 4.93 | 2255 | 10.11 | 18 | 8.07 | 153.3 |
| Tom Kirchhoff, Lafayette | Sr | 11 | 296 | 180 | 60.81 | 9 | 3.04 | 2350 | 7.94 | 26 | 8.78 | 150.4 |
| Nick Cochran, Youngstown St. | Sr | 11 | 172 | 99 | 57.56 | 6 | 3.49 | 1533 | 8.91 | 10 | 5.81 | 144.6 |
| Mark Tenneson, Eastern Wash. | So | 10 | 295 | 179 | 60.68 | 12 | 4.07 | 2489 | 8.44 | 18 | 6.10 | 143.6 |
| Bill Vergantino, Delaware | Sr | 11 | 192 | 99 | 51.56 | 9 | 4.69 | 1720 | 8.96 | 15 | 7.81 | 143.2 |
| Eriq Williams, James Madison | Sr | 11 | 231 | 134 | 58.01 | 12 | 5.19 | 1949 | 8.44 | 17 | 7.36 | 142.8 |
| Steve McNair, Alcorn St. | So | 10 | 427 | 231 | 54.10 | 11 | 2.58 | 3541 | 8.29 | 29 | 6.79 | 141.0 |
| Scott Gabbert, Southern Ill. | Sr | 11 | 305 | 172 | 56.39 | 12 | 3.93 | 2463 | 8.08 | 22 | 7.21 | 140.2 |
| Darin Hinshaw, Central Fla. | So | 10 | 303 | 161 | 53.14 | 16 | 5.28 | 2505 | 8.27 | 24 | 7.92 | 138.2 |
| Kelly Holcomb, Middle Tenn. St. | So | 10 | 168 | 92 | 54.76 | 6 | 3.57 | 1409 | 8.39 | 9 | 5.36 | 135.7 |
| Scott Semptimphelter, Lehigh | Jr | 11 | 405 | 241 | 59.51 | 13 | 3.21 | 3190 | 7.88 | 19 | 4.69 | 134.7 |

## TOTAL OFFENSE

| | RUSHING | | | | PASSING | | TOTAL OFFENSE | | | | |
|---|---|---|---|---|---|---|---|---|---|---|---|
| | Car. | Gain | Loss | Net | Att. | Yards | Plays | Yards | Avg. | TDR* | Yds.PG |
| Steve McNair, Alcorn St. | 92 | 633 | 117 | 516 | 427 | 3541 | 519 | 4057 | 7.82 | 39 | 405.70 |
| Doug Nussmeier, Idaho | 97 | 620 | 211 | 409 | 333 | 3028 | 430 | 3437 | 7.99 | 28 | 312.45 |
| Jay Fiedler, Dartmouth | 80 | 326 | 140 | 186 | 273 | 2748 | 353 | 2934 | 8.31 | 31 | 293.40 |
| Scott Semptimphelter, Lehigh | 107 | 272 | 288 | -16 | 405 | 3190 | 512 | 3174 | 6.20 | 20 | 288.55 |
| Jamie Martin, Weber St. | 86 | 200 | 278 | -78 | 463 | 3207 | 549 | 3129 | 5.70 | 22 | 284.45 |
| Michael Payton, Marshall | 67 | 292 | 184 | 108 | 313 | 2788 | 380 | 2896 | 7.62 | 28 | 263.27 |
| Ralph Barone, Northeastern | 111 | 732 | 203 | 529 | 355 | 2285 | 466 | 2814 | 6.04 | 25 | 255.82 |
| Travis Stuart, Boise St. | 87 | 412 | 159 | 253 | 356 | 2207 | 443 | 2460 | 5.55 | 13 | 246.00 |
| Darin Hinshaw, Central Fla. | 38 | 70 | 125 | -55 | 303 | 2505 | 341 | 2450 | 7.18 | 25 | 245.00 |
| Mark Tenneson, Eastern Wash. | 75 | 215 | 265 | -50 | 295 | 2489 | 370 | 2439 | 6.59 | 21 | 243.90 |
| Greg Lilly, Richmond | 83 | 175 | 262 | -87 | 275 | 2704 | 358 | 2617 | 7.31 | 22 | 237.91 |
| Bill Lazor, Cornell | 77 | 291 | 117 | 174 | 328 | 2205 | 405 | 2379 | 5.87 | 16 | 237.90 |
| James Wade, Tennessee St. | 116 | 328 | 268 | 60 | 308 | 2541 | 424 | 2601 | 6.13 | 18 | 236.45 |
| Orlando Persell, Morgan St. | 95 | 312 | 188 | 124 | 248 | 1992 | 343 | 2116 | 6.17 | 13 | 235.11 |
| Jim Stayer, New Hampshire | 67 | 106 | 191 | -85 | 286 | 2200 | 353 | 2115 | 5.99 | 11 | 235.00 |
| Brad Lebo, Montana | 79 | 163 | 244 | -81 | 378 | 2646 | 457 | 2565 | 5.61 | 19 | 233.18 |
| Donny Simmons, Western Ill. | 121 | 376 | 323 | 53 | 281 | 2496 | 402 | 2549 | 6.34 | 30 | 231.73 |
| Dan Crowley, Towson St. | 23 | 73 | 88 | -15 | 330 | 2322 | 353 | 2307 | 6.54 | 14 | 230.70 |
| Eriq Williams, James Madison | 166 | 761 | 187 | 574 | 231 | 1949 | 397 | 2523 | 6.36 | 25 | 229.36 |
| Scott Gabbert, Southern Ill. | 46 | 151 | 95 | 56 | 305 | 2463 | 351 | 2519 | 7.18 | 24 | 229.00 |

* Touchdowns responsible for are players' TDs scored and passed for.

## RECEPTIONS PER GAME

| | 1992 Class | Games | Catches | Yards | TD | Ct.PG |
|---|---|---|---|---|---|---|
| Glenn Krupa, Southeast Mo. St. | Sr | 11 | 77 | 773 | 4 | 7.00 |
| Mike Wilson, Boise St. | Jr | 11 | 76 | 913 | 2 | 6.91 |
| Darren Rizzi, Rhode Island | Sr | 11 | 74 | 1102 | 6 | 6.73 |
| Yo Murphy, Idaho | Sr | 11 | 68 | 1156 | 9 | 6.18 |
| Troy Brown, Marshall | Sr | 11 | 67 | 1109 | 11 | 6.09 |
| Mike Sardo, Columbia | Sr | 10 | 60 | 571 | 4 | 6.00 |
| Jason Cristino, Lehigh | Sr | 11 | 65 | 1282 | 9 | 5.91 |
| Kevin Howard, Towson St. | Jr | 10 | 59 | 693 | 3 | 5.90 |
| Vincent Brisby, Northeast La. | Sr | 10 | 56 | 1050 | 9 | 5.60 |
| Jess Humphrey, Morgan St. | Jr | 10 | 56 | 995 | 6 | 5.60 |
| James McKnight, Liberty | Jr | 9 | 50 | 711 | 5 | 5.56 |
| Tom Garlick, Fordham | Sr | 10 | 55 | 738 | 8 | 5.50 |
| Matt Brzica, Dartmouth | Sr | 10 | 53 | 965 | 8 | 5.30 |
| David McLeod, James Madison | Jr | 11 | 58 | 933 | 7 | 5.27 |
| Steve Decker, Western Ill. | Sr | 11 | 58 | 764 | 9 | 5.27 |
| Alex Davis, Connecticut | Sr | 11 | 57 | 760 | 8 | 5.18 |
| David Rhodes, Central Fla. | So | 10 | 51 | 1002 | 5 | 5.10 |
| Tony Price, Alcorn St. | Sr | 10 | 51 | 842 | 4 | 5.10 |
| Nate Taylor, Brown | Sr | 10 | 51 | 647 | 7 | 5.10 |
| Demeris Johnson, Western Ill. | Sr | 11 | 55 | 998 | 12 | 5.00 |
| Scott Mallory, Boston U. | Sr | 11 | 55 | 585 | 5 | 5.00 |
| Trevor Shaw, Weber St. | Jr | 10 | 50 | 457 | 4 | 5.00 |

## RECEIVING YARDS PER GAME

| | 1992 Class | Games | Catches | Yards | TD | Yds.PG |
|---|---|---|---|---|---|---|
| Jason Cristino, Lehigh | Sr | 11 | 65 | 1282 | 9 | 116.55 |
| Yo Murphy, Idaho | Sr | 11 | 68 | 1156 | 9 | 105.09 |
| Vincent Brisby, Northeast La. | Sr | 10 | 56 | 1050 | 9 | 105.00 |
| Rod Boothes, Richmond | Jr | 11 | 47 | 1115 | 10 | 101.36 |
| Troy Brown, Marshall | Sr | 11 | 67 | 1109 | 11 | 100.82 |
| David Rhodes, Central Fla. | So | 10 | 51 | 1002 | 5 | 100.20 |
| Darren Rizzi, Rhode Island | Sr | 11 | 74 | 1102 | 6 | 100.18 |
| Jess Humphrey, Morgan St. | Jr | 10 | 56 | 995 | 6 | 99.50 |
| Matt Brzica, Dartmouth | Sr | 10 | 53 | 965 | 8 | 96.50 |
| Demeris Johnson, Western Ill. | Sr | 11 | 55 | 998 | 12 | 90.73 |
| Herb Williams, Youngstown St. | Sr | 11 | 54 | 977 | 8 | 88.82 |
| Tony Brooks, Eastern Wash. | Jr | 10 | 45 | 862 | 10 | 86.20 |
| Craig Aiken, Western Caro. | So | 11 | 44 | 942 | 6 | 85.64 |
| David McLeod, James Madison | Jr | 11 | 58 | 933 | 7 | 84.82 |
| Tony Price, Alcorn St. | Sr | 10 | 51 | 842 | 4 | 84.20 |
| Kenny Shedd, Northern Iowa | Sr | 11 | 25 | 926 | 9 | 84.18 |
| Mike Wilson, Boise St. | Jr | 11 | 76 | 913 | 2 | 83.00 |
| Terry Mickens, Florida A&M | Jr | 11 | 52 | 900 | 6 | 81.82 |
| Antonious Kimbrough, Jackson St. | Sr | 11 | 35 | 900 | 6 | 81.82 |
| Kerry Hayes, Western Caro. | So | 11 | 40 | 896 | 8 | 81.45 |

## INTERCEPTIONS

| | 1992 Class | Games | Int. | Yards | TD | Int.PG |
|---|---|---|---|---|---|---|
| Dave Roberts, Youngstown St. | Sr | 11 | 9 | 39 | 0 | .82 |
| Mark Chapman, Connecticut | Sr | 11 | 8 | 67 | 0 | .73 |
| Don Caparotti, Massachusetts | Sr | 10 | 7 | 15 | 0 | .70 |
| Torrence Forney, Citadel | Sr | 11 | 7 | 71 | 1 | .64 |
| Bob Jordan, New Hampshire | Jr | 11 | 7 | 35 | 0 | .64 |
| Randy Fuller, Tennessee St. | Jr | 10 | 6 | 70 | 0 | .60 |
| Jackie Kellogg, Eastern Wash. | Jr | 10 | 6 | 52 | 0 | .60 |
| Lecorey Harvest, Alabama St. | Jr | 11 | 6 | 116 | 1 | .55 |
| Lance Guidry, McNeese St. | Jr | 11 | 6 | 106 | 2 | .55 |
| Cedric Walker, Stephen F. Austin | Jr | 11 | 6 | 71 | 0 | .55 |
| Ken McKelvey, Boise St. | Sr | 11 | 6 | 63 | 0 | .55 |
| Reggie Carthon, Montana St. | Jr | 11 | 6 | 61 | 0 | .55 |
| Brian Randall, Delaware St. | Jr | 11 | 6 | 51 | 0 | .55 |
| Todd Ericson, Montana | Jr | 11 | 6 | 47 | 1 | .55 |
| Chris Parrott, James Madison | Sr | 11 | 6 | 34 | 0 | .55 |
| Morgan Ryan, Montana St. | Jr | 11 | 6 | 26 | 0 | .55 |
| Donnie Ellis, Texas Southern | Sr | 11 | 6 | 21 | 0 | .55 |
| Kirk Pointer, Austin Peay | Fr | 11 | 6 | 0 | 0 | .55 |

## SCORING

| | 1992 Class | Games | TD | XP | FG | Points | Pts.PG |
|---|---|---|---|---|---|---|---|
| Sherriden May, Idaho | So | 11 | 25 | 0 | 0 | 150 | 13.64 |
| Keith Elias, Princeton | Jr | 10 | 18 | 2 | 0 | 110 | 11.00 |
| Toby Davis, Illinois St. | Sr | 11 | 20 | 0 | 0 | 120 | 10.91 |
| Markus Thomas, Eastern Ky. | Sr | 11 | 18 | 0 | 0 | 108 | 9.82 |
| Harry Brown, Alcorn St. | Jr | 9 | 14 | 0 | 0 | 84 | 9.33 |

| | 1992 Class | Games | TD | XP | FG | Points | Pts.PG |
|---|---|---|---|---|---|---|---|
| Kenny Sims, James Madison | Sr | 9 | 14 | 0 | 0 | 84 | 9.33 |
| Eric Gant, Grambling | Jr | 11 | 17 | 0 | 0 | 102 | 9.27 |
| Bret Cooper, Central Fla. | Sr | 10 | 15 | 0 | 0 | 90 | 9.00 |
| Surkano Edwards, Samford | Sr | 10 | 15 | 0 | 0 | 90 | 9.00 |
| Kelvin Anderson, Southeast Mo. St. | So | 10 | 14 | 0 | 0 | 84 | 8.40 |
| Ron Dyson, Grambling | So | 11 | 15 | 0 | 0 | 90 | 8.18 |
| Mike Hollis, Idaho | Jr | 11 | 0 | 54 | 12 | 90 | 8.18 |
| James Johnson, Jackson St. | Sr | 11 | 15 | 0 | 0 | 90 | 8.18 |
| Scott Obermeier, Northern Iowa | Fr | 11 | 0 | 37 | 17 | 88 | 8.00 |
| Greg Robinson, Northeast La. | Sr | 11 | 14 | 0 | 0 | 84 | 7.64 |
| Tamron Smith, Youngstown St. | Jr | 11 | 14 | 0 | 0 | 84 | 7.64 |
| Dennis Durkin, Dartmouth | Sr | 10 | 0 | 37 | 13 | 76 | 7.60 |
| Mike Dodd, Boise St. | Sr | 11 | 0 | 16 | 22 | 82 | 7.45 |
| Bill Sparacio, Colgate | Jr | 9 | 11 | 0 | 0 | 66 | 7.33 |
| David Merrick, Marshall | So | 11 | 0 | 53 | 9 | 80 | 7.27 |

## ALL-PURPOSE RUNNERS

| | 1992 Class | Games | Rush | Rec. | PR | KOR | Total Yards | Yds.PG |
|---|---|---|---|---|---|---|---|---|
| David Wright, Indiana St. | Fr | 11 | 1313 | 108 | 0 | 593 | 2014 | 183.09 |
| Kelvin Anderson, Southeast Mo. St. | So | 10 | 1371 | 171 | 0 | 253 | 1795 | 179.50 |
| Troy Brown, Marshall | Sr | 11 | 152 | 1109 | 101 | 482 | 1844 | 167.64 |
| Keith Elias, Princeton | Jr | 10 | 1575 | 98 | 0 | 0 | 1673 | 167.30 |
| Patrick Robinson, Tennessee St. | Sr | 10 | 0 | 803 | 150 | 665 | 1618 | 161.80 |
| Tony Vinson, Towson St. | Jr | 8 | 1042 | 252 | 0 | 0 | 1294 | 161.75 |
| Toby Davis, Illinois St. | Sr | 11 | 1561 | 87 | 0 | 114 | 1762 | 160.18 |
| Surkano Edwards, Samford | Sr | 10 | 1270 | 164 | 0 | 155 | 1589 | 158.90 |
| Kenny Shedd, Northern Iowa | Sr | 11 | 0 | 926 | 477 | 342 | 1745 | 158.64 |
| Jerry Ellison, Tenn.-Chatt. | Jr | 11 | 814 | 118 | 0 | 755 | 1687 | 153.36 |
| Kerry Hayes, Western Caro. | So | 11 | 4 | 896 | 231 | 545 | 1676 | 152.36 |
| Erik Marsh, Lafayette | So | 10 | 1365 | 143 | 0 | 2 | 1510 | 151.00 |
| Sherriden May, Idaho | So | 11 | 1111 | 362 | 0 | 147 | 1620 | 147.27 |
| Tony Phillips, Morgan St. | Jr | 10 | 736 | 213 | 0 | 518 | 1467 | 146.70 |
| Carl Tremble, Furman | Sr | 11 | 1555 | 54 | 0 | 0 | 1609 | 146.27 |
| Steve Decker, Western Ill. | Sr | 11 | 27 | 764 | 251 | 548 | 1590 | 144.55 |
| Matt Walsh, Bucknell | Sr | 11 | 839 | 232 | 55 | 458 | 1584 | 144.00 |
| Barry Bourassa, New Hampshire | Sr | 10 | 816 | 283 | 173 | 131 | 1403 | 140.30 |
| Markus Thomas, Eastern Ky. | Sr | 11 | 1498 | 38 | 0 | 0 | 1536 | 139.64 |
| Kenny Sims, James Madison | Sr | 9 | 1157 | 77 | 0 | 0 | 1234 | 137.11 |

## PUNT RETURNS

| (Min. 1.2 per game) | 1992 Class | No. | Yds. | TD | Avg. | (Min. 1.2 per game) | 1992 Class | No. | Yds. | TD | Avg. |
|---|---|---|---|---|---|---|---|---|---|---|---|
| Q. Miller, South Caro. St. | Jr | 17 | 311 | 0 | 18.29 | D. Mimms, Middle Tenn. St. | So | 28 | 367 | 1 | 13.11 |
| Kerry Lawyer, Boise St. | So | 18 | 325 | 2 | 18.06 | Brian Randall, Delaware St. | Jr | 29 | 378 | 2 | 13.03 |
| Kenny Shedd, Northern Iowa | Sr | 27 | 477 | 4 | 17.67 | C. Johnson, Southern-B.R. | Sr | 28 | 358 | 1 | 12.79 |
| Michael Lerch, Princeton | Sr | 12 | 180 | 1 | 15.00 | M. Stewart, Tennessee Tech | Jr | 26 | 328 | 1 | 12.62 |
| Kerry Hayes, Western Caro. | So | 16 | 231 | 1 | 14.44 | Ernest Pate, Jackson St. | Jr | 25 | 309 | 0 | 12.36 |
| Andre Worrell, Furman | Jr | 22 | 309 | 2 | 14.05 | Eric Alden, Idaho St. | Jr | 19 | 233 | 0 | 12.26 |
| D. Faust, Southwest Tex. St. | Sr | 21 | 287 | 0 | 13.67 | P. Scarritt, William & Mary | Sr | 34 | 415 | 0 | 12.21 |
| D. Adams, N'western (La.) | Sr | 21 | 284 | 1 | 13.52 | Ron Ransom, Colgate | Sr | 19 | 216 | 1 | 11.37 |
| A. Smith, Appalachian St. | Sr | 20 | 269 | 1 | 13.45 | Walter Saunders, Idaho | Sr | 22 | 249 | 0 | 11.32 |
| Garrett Shine, Lafayette | Fr | 15 | 201 | 1 | 13.40 | Michael High, North Texas | So | 14 | 155 | 0 | 11.07 |

## KICKOFF RETURNS

| (Min. 1.2 per game) | 1992 Class | No. | Yds. | TD | Avg. | (Min. 1.2 per game) | 1992 Class | No. | Yds. | TD | Avg. |
|---|---|---|---|---|---|---|---|---|---|---|---|
| Marcus Durgin, Samford | Jr | 15 | 499 | 0 | 33.27 | Chris Wright, Ga. Southern | So | 15 | 410 | 1 | 27.33 |
| Robert Johnson, Idaho St. | Fr | 14 | 416 | 0 | 29.71 | Kerry Hayes, Western Caro. | So | 20 | 545 | 2 | 27.25 |
| Timmy Bland, Murray St. | So | 22 | 644 | 1 | 29.27 | David Wright, Indiana St. | Fr | 22 | 593 | 0 | 26.95 |
| Ako Mott, Pennsylvania | Sr | 19 | 545 | 0 | 28.68 | D. Robinson, James Madison | So | 17 | 447 | 0 | 26.29 |
| M. Henderson, S. F. Austin | So | 20 | 551 | 0 | 27.55 | B. Rodman, North Caro. A&T | So | 22 | 571 | 2 | 25.95 |

## PUNTING

| (Min. 3.6 per game) | 1992 Class | No. | Avg. | (Min. 3.6 per game) | 1992 Class | No. | Avg. |
|---|---|---|---|---|---|---|---|
| Harold Alexander, Appalachian St. | Sr | 55 | 44.45 | Pat Neck, McNeese St. | Jr | 71 | 40.37 |
| Terry Belden, Northern Ariz. | Jr | 59 | 44.31 | Jim Kantowski, East Tenn. St. | Sr | 63 | 40.14 |
| Rob Sims, Pennsylvania | Sr | 67 | 43.43 | Chad McCarty, Northeast La. | Sr | 44 | 40.00 |
| Colin Godfrey, Tennessee St. | Sr | 54 | 42.20 | Tim McNamee, Eastern Ky. | So | 55 | 39.91 |
| Tim Mosley, Northern Iowa | Jr | 50 | 42.04 | Holloman, North Caro A&T | Sr | 50 | 39.38 |
| Leo Araguz, Stephen F. Austin | Sr | 54 | 42.04 | Cedric Rawls, Howard | Sr | 54 | 39.31 |
| Ross Schulte, Western Ill. | So | 51 | 41.59 | Chad Brummitt, Tennessee Tech | Sr | 59 | 39.27 |
| Scott Frazier, James Madison | Jr | 42 | 40.64 | Eric Colvard, Liberty | Fr | 61 | 39.25 |
| Chris Schrock, Boston U. | Sr | 66 | 40.64 | Rick Boeckmann, Western Ky. | So | 57 | 39.19 |
| Jason Caldwell, Eastern Ill. | Sr | 58 | 40.55 | Chuck Poplos, Delaware St. | So | 56 | 39.11 |

*1993 NCAA FOOTBALL*

## FIELD GOALS

| | 1992 Class | Games | FGA | FG | Pct. | FGPG |
|---|---|---|---|---|---|---|
| Mike Dodd, Boise St. | Sr | 11 | 31 | 22 | .710 | 2.00 |
| Scott Obermeier, Northern Iowa | Fr | 11 | 19 | 17 | .895 | 1.55 |
| Terry Belden, Northern Ariz. | Jr | 11 | 24 | 15 | .625 | 1.36 |
| Dennis Durkin, Dartmouth | Sr | 10 | 13 | 13 | 1.000 | 1.30 |
| Mike Cochrane, Cornell | Sr | 10 | 22 | 13 | .591 | 1.30 |
| Richard Defelice, North Texas | Jr | 11 | 16 | 13 | .813 | 1.18 |
| C. Fontana, Stephen F. Austin | Jr | 11 | 21 | 13 | .619 | 1.18 |
| Daniel Whitehead, Liberty | So | 11 | 14 | 12 | .857 | 1.09 |
| Jeff Wilkins, Youngstown St. | Jr | 11 | 15 | 12 | .800 | 1.09 |
| Richard Grote, Southwest Mo. St. | Sr | 11 | 17 | 12 | .706 | 1.09 |
| Mike Hollis, Idaho | Jr | 11 | 20 | 12 | .600 | 1.09 |
| Ray Whitehead, Southwest Tex. St. | So | 11 | 13 | 11 | .846 | 1.00 |
| Jose Larios, McNeese St. | Fr | 11 | 16 | 11 | .688 | 1.00 |
| Rob Tallent, Northeast La. | Sr | 11 | 17 | 11 | .647 | 1.00 |
| Bill Hoffman, Villanova | Jr | 11 | 20 | 11 | .550 | 1.00 |

# 1992 DIVISION I-AA TEAM LEADERS

## TOTAL OFFENSE

| | Games | Plays | Yds. | Avg. | TD* | Yds.PG |
|---|---|---|---|---|---|---|
| Alcorn St. | 10 | 728 | 5029 | 6.9 | 57 | 502.90 |
| Marshall | 11 | 796 | 5397 | 6.8 | 62 | 490.64 |
| Idaho | 11 | 856 | 5390 | 6.3 | 56 | 490.00 |
| Central Fla. | 10 | 708 | 4768 | 6.7 | 49 | 476.80 |
| Dartmouth | 10 | 751 | 4740 | 6.3 | 45 | 474.00 |
| Southern Ill. | 11 | 815 | 5057 | 6.2 | 47 | 459.73 |
| Grambling | 11 | 749 | 4995 | 6.7 | 57 | 454.09 |
| Northeast La. | 11 | 793 | 4946 | 6.2 | 49 | 449.64 |
| Towson St. | 10 | 766 | 4383 | 5.7 | 33 | 438.30 |
| Lafayette | 11 | 848 | 4795 | 5.7 | 48 | 435.91 |
| Richmond | 11 | 844 | 4761 | 5.6 | 45 | 432.82 |
| Jackson St. | 11 | 734 | 4634 | 6.3 | 47 | 421.27 |
| Delaware | 11 | 789 | 4600 | 5.8 | 53 | 418.18 |
| Western Caro. | 11 | 723 | 4567 | 6.3 | 39 | 415.18 |
| Citadel | 11 | 750 | 4560 | 6.1 | 37 | 414.55 |
| New Hampshire | 11 | 801 | 4532 | 5.7 | 34 | 412.00 |
| James Madison | 11 | 773 | 4525 | 5.9 | 45 | 411.36 |
| Eastern Wash. | 10 | 732 | 4113 | 5.6 | 35 | 411.30 |
| Morgan St. | 10 | 789 | 4079 | 5.2 | 31 | 407.90 |
| Weber St. | 11 | 865 | 4480 | 5.2 | 36 | 407.27 |

* Touchdowns scored by rushing-passing only.

## TOTAL DEFENSE

| | Games | Plays | Yds. | Avg. | TD* | Yds.PG |
|---|---|---|---|---|---|---|
| South Caro. St. | 11 | 691 | 2760 | 4.0 | 20 | 250.9 |
| Massachusetts | 10 | 699 | 2705 | 3.9 | 20 | 270.5 |
| Holy Cross | 11 | 798 | 3026 | 3.8 | 20 | 275.1 |
| Villanova | 11 | 750 | 3055 | 4.1 | 18 | 277.7 |
| North Caro. A&T | 11 | 713 | 3085 | 4.3 | 26 | 280.5 |
| Pennsylvania | 10 | 684 | 2807 | 4.1 | 18 | 280.7 |
| Tennessee Tech | 11 | 722 | 3236 | 4.5 | 27 | 294.2 |
| Middle Tenn. St. | 11 | 788 | 3240 | 4.1 | 18 | 294.5 |
| Northern Iowa | 11 | 766 | 3262 | 4.3 | 19 | 296.5 |
| Princeton | 10 | 676 | 3011 | 4.5 | 23 | 301.1 |
| Southern-B.R. | 11 | 719 | 3327 | 4.6 | 26 | 302.5 |
| Samford | 11 | 740 | 3356 | 4.5 | 25 | 305.1 |
| Jackson St. | 11 | 722 | 3368 | 4.7 | 26 | 306.2 |
| Mississippi Val. | 9 | 538 | 2771 | 5.2 | 28 | 307.9 |
| Alcorn St. | 10 | 686 | 3102 | 4.5 | 29 | 310.2 |
| Furman | 11 | 712 | 3419 | 4.8 | 24 | 310.8 |
| Ga. Southern | 11 | 737 | 3434 | 4.7 | 19 | 312.2 |
| Citadel | 11 | 654 | 3440 | 5.3 | 18 | 312.7 |
| Morehead St. | 11 | 672 | 3450 | 5.1 | 43 | 313.6 |
| Fordham | 10 | 726 | 3155 | 4.3 | 27 | 315.5 |

* Touchdowns scored by rushing-passing only.

## RUSHING OFFENSE

| | Games | Car. | Yds. | Avg. | TD | Yds.PG |
|---|---|---|---|---|---|---|
| Citadel | 11 | 672 | 3800 | 5.7 | 33 | 345.5 |
| Western Ky. | 10 | 592 | 2871 | 4.8 | 26 | 287.1 |
| Delaware St. | 11 | 618 | 3099 | 5.0 | 31 | 281.7 |
| Southwest Mo. St. | 11 | 646 | 3037 | 4.7 | 30 | 276.1 |
| Indiana St. | 11 | 578 | 3029 | 5.2 | 33 | 275.4 |
| Grambling | 11 | 496 | 2989 | 6.0 | 30 | 271.7 |
| Princeton | 10 | 532 | 2591 | 4.9 | 26 | 259.1 |
| Delaware | 11 | 588 | 2827 | 4.8 | 38 | 257.0 |
| South Caro. St. | 11 | 590 | 2783 | 4.7 | 26 | 253.0 |
| Southwest Tex. St. | 11 | 585 | 2782 | 4.8 | 21 | 252.9 |
| Eastern Ky. | 11 | 524 | 2713 | 5.2 | 31 | 246.6 |
| Va. Military | 11 | 598 | 2708 | 4.5 | 24 | 246.2 |
| Austin Peay | 11 | 581 | 2696 | 4.6 | 17 | 245.1 |
| Furman | 11 | 513 | 2691 | 5.2 | 24 | 244.6 |
| Southern Ill. | 11 | 502 | 2532 | 5.0 | 25 | 230.2 |
| James Madison | 11 | 527 | 2490 | 4.7 | 28 | 226.4 |
| Northwestern (La.) | 11 | 538 | 2445 | 4.5 | 28 | 222.3 |
| Middle Tenn. St. | 11 | 469 | 2438 | 5.2 | 33 | 221.6 |
| North Caro. A&T | 11 | 517 | 2423 | 4.7 | 24 | 220.3 |
| Youngstown St. | 11 | 567 | 2398 | 4.2 | 30 | 218.0 |

## RUSHING DEFENSE

| | Games | Car. | Yds. | Avg. | TD | Yds.PG |
|---|---|---|---|---|---|---|
| Villanova | 11 | 401 | 856 | 2.1 | 9 | 77.8 |
| Eastern Wash. | 10 | 340 | 830 | 2.4 | 11 | 83.0 |
| Montana | 11 | 417 | 1086 | 2.6 | 11 | 98.7 |
| Princeton | 10 | 398 | 1011 | 2.5 | 10 | 101.1 |
| Fordham | 10 | 415 | 1067 | 2.6 | 16 | 106.7 |
| McNeese St. | 11 | 428 | 1230 | 2.9 | 10 | 111.8 |
| Idaho | 11 | 393 | 1243 | 3.2 | 14 | 113.0 |
| Maine | 11 | 381 | 1256 | 3.3 | 11 | 114.2 |
| Mississippi Val. | 9 | 336 | 1075 | 3.2 | 12 | 119.4 |
| Jackson St. | 11 | 414 | 1333 | 3.2 | 12 | 121.2 |
| South Caro. St. | 11 | 432 | 1337 | 3.1 | 10 | 121.5 |
| Holy Cross | 11 | 512 | 1396 | 2.7 | 10 | 126.9 |
| New Hampshire | 11 | 471 | 1448 | 3.1 | 15 | 131.6 |
| Samford | 11 | 418 | 1449 | 3.5 | 15 | 131.7 |
| Northern Iowa | 11 | 499 | 1457 | 2.9 | 9 | 132.5 |
| Florida A&M | 11 | 480 | 1472 | 3.1 | 17 | 133.8 |
| Massachusetts | 10 | 457 | 1342 | 2.9 | 9 | 134.2 |
| Dartmouth | 10 | 376 | 1345 | 3.6 | 20 | 134.5 |
| Pennsylvania | 10 | 415 | 1354 | 3.3 | 11 | 135.4 |
| Montana St. | 11 | 451 | 1497 | 3.3 | 11 | 136.1 |

## SCORING OFFENSE

| | Games | Pts. | Avg. | | Games | Pts. | Avg. |
|---|---|---|---|---|---|---|---|
| Marshall | 11 | 466 | 42.4 | Howard | 11 | 366 | 33.3 |
| Idaho | 11 | 446 | 40.5 | Jackson St. | 11 | 361 | 32.8 |
| Grambling | 11 | 438 | 39.8 | Middle Tenn. St. | 11 | 361 | 32.8 |
| Alcorn St. | 10 | 398 | 39.8 | Northern Iowa | 11 | 352 | 32.0 |
| Central Fla. | 10 | 373 | 37.3 | Southern Ill. | 11 | 350 | 31.8 |
| Dartmouth | 10 | 364 | 36.4 | Western Ill. | 11 | 348 | 31.6 |
| Delaware | 11 | 399 | 36.3 | Richmond | 11 | 338 | 30.7 |
| Northeast La. | 11 | 394 | 35.8 | Youngstown St. | 11 | 336 | 30.5 |
| Lafayette | 11 | 382 | 34.7 | James Madison | 11 | 333 | 30.3 |
| Samford | 11 | 379 | 34.5 | Western Caro. | 11 | 332 | 30.2 |

## SCORING DEFENSE

| | Games | Pts. | Avg. | | Games | Pts. | Avg. |
|---|---|---|---|---|---|---|---|
| Citadel | 11 | 143 | 13.0 | Southwest Tex. St. | 11 | 190 | 17.3 |
| Middle Tenn. St. | 11 | 144 | 13.1 | Princeton | 10 | 175 | 17.5 |
| Ga. Southern | 11 | 151 | 13.7 | Eastern Ky. | 11 | 200 | 18.2 |
| Villanova | 11 | 153 | 13.9 | Delaware | 11 | 201 | 18.3 |
| Pennsylvania | 10 | 144 | 14.4 | Samford | 11 | 201 | 18.3 |
| Northern Iowa | 11 | 162 | 14.7 | Cornell | 10 | 183 | 18.3 |
| Massachusetts | 10 | 151 | 15.1 | Appalachian St. | 11 | 202 | 18.4 |
| Holy Cross | 11 | 175 | 15.9 | William & Mary | 11 | 205 | 18.6 |
| Howard | 11 | 178 | 16.2 | North Caro. A&T | 11 | 205 | 18.6 |
| South Caro. St. | 11 | 180 | 16.4 | | | | |

## PASSING OFFENSE

| | Games | Att. | Cmp. | Int. | Pct. | Yards | Yds./Att. | TD | Yds.PG |
|---|---|---|---|---|---|---|---|---|---|
| Alcorn St. | 10 | 436 | 236 | 13 | 54.1 | 3605 | 8.3 | 30 | 360.5 |
| Montana | 11 | 503 | 283 | 20 | 56.3 | 3582 | 7.1 | 22 | 325.6 |
| Morgan St. | 10 | 394 | 207 | 25 | 52.5 | 2985 | 7.6 | 19 | 298.5 |
| Weber St. | 11 | 476 | 286 | 16 | 60.1 | 3271 | 6.9 | 21 | 297.4 |
| Central Fla. | 10 | 359 | 190 | 19 | 52.9 | 2973 | 8.3 | 29 | 297.3 |
| Marshall | 11 | 372 | 234 | 14 | 62.9 | 3245 | 8.7 | 29 | 295.0 |
| Lehigh | 11 | 408 | 241 | 14 | 59.1 | 3190 | 7.8 | 19 | 290.0 |
| Idaho | 11 | 341 | 211 | 9 | 61.9 | 3093 | 9.1 | 22 | 281.2 |
| Dartmouth | 10 | 276 | 176 | 13 | 63.8 | 2755 | 10.0 | 25 | 275.5 |
| Tennessee St. | 11 | 357 | 189 | 16 | 52.9 | 2963 | 8.3 | 13 | 269.4 |
| New Hampshire | 11 | 385 | 218 | 19 | 56.6 | 2854 | 7.4 | 13 | 259.5 |
| Richmond | 11 | 286 | 171 | 12 | 59.8 | 2817 | 9.8 | 19 | 256.1 |
| Eastern Wash. | 10 | 301 | 182 | 12 | 60.5 | 2544 | 8.5 | 18 | 254.4 |
| Northeast La. | 11 | 315 | 198 | 11 | 62.9 | 2748 | 8.7 | 21 | 249.8 |
| Howard | 11 | 364 | 176 | 12 | 48.4 | 2738 | 7.5 | 23 | 248.9 |
| Towson St. | 10 | 363 | 182 | 22 | 50.1 | 2488 | 6.9 | 15 | 248.8 |
| Rhode Island | 11 | 447 | 207 | 28 | 46.3 | 2722 | 6.1 | 16 | 247.5 |
| Western Ill. | 11 | 302 | 194 | 12 | 64.2 | 2698 | 8.9 | 28 | 245.3 |
| Boise St. | 11 | 449 | 235 | 20 | 52.3 | 2692 | 6.0 | 10 | 244.7 |
| Lafayette | 11 | 327 | 199 | 9 | 60.9 | 2630 | 8.0 | 29 | 239.1 |

## PASS-EFFICIENCY DEFENSE

| | Games | Att. | Cmp. | Cmp. Pct. | Int. | Int. Pct. | Yards | Yds./Att. | TD | TD Pct. | Rating Points |
|---|---|---|---|---|---|---|---|---|---|---|---|
| Middle Tenn. St. | 11 | 254 | 107 | 42.13 | 17 | 6.69 | 1300 | 5.12 | 4 | 1.57 | 76.93 |
| South Caro. St. | 11 | 259 | 106 | 40.93 | 19 | 7.34 | 1423 | 5.49 | 10 | 3.86 | 85.15 |
| Pennsylvania | 10 | 269 | 126 | 46.84 | 14 | 5.20 | 1453 | 5.40 | 7 | 2.60 | 90.39 |
| Sam Houston St. | 11 | 306 | 140 | 45.75 | 17 | 5.56 | 1840 | 6.01 | 6 | 1.96 | 91.62 |
| Howard | 11 | 264 | 117 | 44.32 | 23 | 8.71 | 1660 | 6.29 | 10 | 3.79 | 92.21 |
| Citadel | 11 | 218 | 110 | 50.46 | 15 | 6.88 | 1281 | 5.88 | 5 | 2.29 | 93.63 |
| Massachusetts | 10 | 242 | 117 | 48.35 | 19 | 7.85 | 1363 | 5.63 | 11 | 4.55 | 94.96 |
| Alcorn St. | 10 | 246 | 94 | 38.21 | 13 | 5.28 | 1463 | 5.95 | 13 | 5.28 | 95.04 |
| Tennessee Tech | 11 | 256 | 127 | 49.61 | 15 | 5.86 | 1453 | 5.68 | 8 | 3.13 | 95.88 |
| Dartmouth | 10 | 308 | 150 | 48.70 | 15 | 4.87 | 1821 | 5.91 | 8 | 2.60 | 97.20 |
| Samford | 11 | 322 | 158 | 49.07 | 19 | 5.90 | 1907 | 5.92 | 10 | 3.11 | 97.26 |
| Southern-B.R. | 11 | 238 | 97 | 40.76 | 11 | 4.62 | 1472 | 6.18 | 10 | 4.20 | 97.33 |
| Jackson St. | 11 | 308 | 120 | 38.96 | 18 | 5.84 | 2035 | 6.61 | 14 | 4.55 | 97.77 |
| William & Mary | 11 | 323 | 174 | 53.87 | 15 | 4.64 | 1829 | 5.66 | 6 | 1.86 | 98.28 |
| Villanova | 11 | 349 | 169 | 48.42 | 17 | 4.87 | 2199 | 6.30 | 10 | 2.87 | 101.06 |
| Delaware | 11 | 378 | 189 | 50.00 | 20 | 5.29 | 2322 | 6.14 | 12 | 3.17 | 101.49 |
| Montana | 11 | 450 | 211 | 46.89 | 18 | 4.00 | 2742 | 6.09 | 16 | 3.56 | 101.81 |
| Tennessee St. | 11 | 234 | 109 | 46.58 | 18 | 7.69 | 1505 | 6.43 | 12 | 5.13 | 102.15 |
| North Caro. A&T | 11 | 248 | 114 | 45.97 | 10 | 4.03 | 1553 | 6.26 | 9 | 3.63 | 102.48 |
| Grambling | 11 | 290 | 133 | 45.86 | 23 | 7.93 | 1895 | 6.53 | 16 | 5.52 | 103.10 |

## NET PUNTING

| | Punts | Avg. | No. Ret. | Yds. Ret. | Net Avg. | | Punts | Avg. | No. Ret. | Yds. Ret. | Net Avg. |
|---|---|---|---|---|---|---|---|---|---|---|---|
| Stephen F. Austin | 65 | 41.2 | 28 | 189 | 38.2 | Northern Ariz. | 61 | 42.9 | 28 | 351 | 37.1 |
| Marshall | 27 | 40.6 | 10 | 76 | 37.8 | James Madison | 42 | 40.6 | 28 | 160 | 36.8 |
| North Caro. A&T | 51 | 39.5 | 19 | 91 | 37.7 | Pennsylvania | 68 | 43.0 | 45 | 427 | 36.7 |
| McNeese St. | 72 | 40.5 | 35 | 217 | 37.5 | Western Caro. | 40 | 40.9 | 18 | 172 | 36.6 |
| Appalachian St. | 56 | 44.1 | 30 | 370 | 37.5 | Indiana St. | 41 | 41.6 | 16 | 213 | 36.4 |

| | Punts | Avg. | No. Ret. | Yds. Ret. | Net Avg. | | Punts | Avg. | No. Ret. | Yds. Ret. | Net Avg. |
|---|---|---|---|---|---|---|---|---|---|---|---|
| Western Ill. | 51 | 41.6 | 24 | 269 | 36.3 | Eastern Ill. | 60 | 39.4 | 26 | 245 | 35.3 |
| Howard | 54 | 39.3 | 23 | 164 | 36.3 | Central Fla. | 46 | 39.1 | 14 | 187 | 35.0 |
| Delaware St. | 58 | 39.2 | 29 | 186 | 35.9 | Tenn.-Martin | 79 | 37.0 | 32 | 174 | 34.8 |
| Citadel | 36 | 37.1 | 10 | 46 | 35.9 | Richmond | 47 | 38.0 | 19 | 155 | 34.7 |
| Va. Military | 45 | 38.4 | 15 | 130 | 35.5 | Northern Iowa | 56 | 40.7 | 34 | 339 | 34.7 |

## PUNT RETURNS

| | Games | No. | Yds. | TD | Avg. | | Games | No. | Yds. | TD | Avg. |
|---|---|---|---|---|---|---|---|---|---|---|---|
| South Caro. St. | 11 | 30 | 538 | 2 | 17.9 | Delaware St. | 11 | 34 | 439 | 2 | 12.9 |
| Northern Iowa | 11 | 35 | 561 | 4 | 16.0 | Northwestern (La.) | 11 | 22 | 284 | 1 | 12.9 |
| Morgan St. | 10 | 13 | 203 | 2 | 15.6 | Western Caro. | 11 | 21 | 267 | 1 | 12.7 |
| Furman | 11 | 27 | 395 | 3 | 14.6 | William & Mary | 11 | 34 | 415 | 0 | 12.2 |
| Southwest Tex. St. | 11 | 28 | 408 | 0 | 14.6 | Prairie View | 11 | 18 | 219 | 0 | 12.2 |
| Middle Tenn. St. | 11 | 36 | 523 | 3 | 14.5 | Montana St. | 11 | 28 | 339 | 2 | 12.1 |
| Lafayette | 11 | 20 | 280 | 1 | 14.0 | Southeast Mo. St. | 11 | 21 | 252 | 2 | 12.0 |
| Idaho St. | 11 | 30 | 414 | 1 | 13.8 | Jackson St. | 11 | 32 | 380 | 0 | 11.9 |
| Appalachian St. | 11 | 23 | 314 | 2 | 13.7 | Southern B.R. | 11 | 41 | 482 | 1 | 11.8 |
| Boise St. | 11 | 33 | 430 | 2 | 13.0 | Austin Peay | 11 | 22 | 255 | 1 | 11.6 |

## KICKOFF RETURNS

| | Games | No. | Yds. | TD | Avg. | | Games | No. | Yds. | TD | Avg. |
|---|---|---|---|---|---|---|---|---|---|---|---|
| Pennsylvania | 10 | 29 | 726 | 0 | 25.0 | Murray St. | 11 | 52 | 1,152 | 1 | 22.2 |
| Samford | 11 | 29 | 723 | 0 | 24.9 | Western Caro. | 11 | 36 | 792 | 3 | 22.0 |
| Indiana St. | 11 | 51 | 1,247 | 0 | 24.5 | Eastern Ky. | 11 | 34 | 742 | 2 | 21.8 |
| Northwestern (La.) | 11 | 38 | 888 | 1 | 23.4 | North Texas | 11 | 35 | 758 | 0 | 21.7 |
| North Caro. A&T | 11 | 37 | 864 | 2 | 23.4 | Western Ill. | 11 | 44 | 951 | 0 | 21.6 |
| Montana | 11 | 38 | 878 | 0 | 23.1 | Northern Ariz. | 11 | 36 | 778 | 1 | 21.6 |
| Idaho St. | 11 | 47 | 1,077 | 1 | 22.9 | James Madison | 11 | 48 | 1,037 | 0 | 21.6 |
| Stephen F. Austin | 11 | 39 | 871 | 0 | 22.3 | Northeast La. | 11 | 37 | 795 | 0 | 21.5 |
| Eastern Wash. | 10 | 33 | 735 | 0 | 22.3 | Tenn.-Chatt. | 11 | 57 | 1,211 | 3 | 21.2 |
| Ga. Southern | 11 | 27 | 601 | 1 | 22.3 | Grambling | 11 | 42 | 890 | 1 | 21.2 |

## TURNOVER MARGIN

| | TURNOVERS GAINED | | | TURNOVERS LOST | | | Margin/ |
|---|---|---|---|---|---|---|---|
| | Fum. | Int. | Total | Fum. | Int. | Total | Game |
| Howard | 20 | 23 | 43 | 13 | 12 | 25 | 1.64 |
| Youngstown St. | 9 | 21 | 30 | 6 | 6 | 12 | 1.64 |
| Grambling | 18 | 23 | 41 | 14 | 10 | 24 | 1.55 |
| Montana St. | 11 | 20 | 31 | 5 | 10 | 15 | 1.45 |
| Cornell | 13 | 13 | 26 | 8 | 4 | 12 | 1.40 |
| Connecticut | 11 | 25 | 36 | 10 | 11 | 21 | 1.36 |
| Massachusetts | 21 | 19 | 40 | 16 | 12 | 28 | 1.20 |
| Richmond | 19 | 16 | 35 | 10 | 12 | 22 | 1.18 |
| Samford | 19 | 19 | 38 | 16 | 10 | 26 | 1.09 |
| Southwest Mo. St. | 11 | 16 | 27 | 10 | 6 | 16 | 1.00 |
| Delaware | 13 | 20 | 33 | 14 | 9 | 23 | .91 |
| Lafayette | 17 | 10 | 27 | 8 | 9 | 17 | .91 |
| Middle Tenn. St. | 17 | 17 | 34 | 16 | 8 | 24 | .91 |
| South Caro. St. | 16 | 19 | 35 | 20 | 5 | 25 | .91 |
| Fordham | 12 | 19 | 31 | 9 | 13 | 22 | .90 |
| Jackson St. | 18 | 18 | 36 | 15 | 12 | 27 | .82 |
| Tenn.-Martin | 13 | 10 | 23 | 5 | 9 | 14 | .82 |
| Idaho | 8 | 18 | 26 | 9 | 9 | 18 | .73 |
| McNeese St. | 16 | 19 | 35 | 16 | 11 | 27 | .73 |
| Princeton | 14 | 7 | 21 | 11 | 3 | 14 | .70 |

# LONGEST DIVISION I-AA PLAYS OF 1992

## RUSHING

| Player, Team (Opponent) | Yards |
|---|---|
| Norman Bradford, Grambling (Prairie View) | 97 |
| Kelvin Anderson, Southeast Mo. St. (Murray St.) | 96 |
| Jerry Ellison, Tenn.-Chatt. (Boise St.) | 95 |
| Cornelius Turner, Mississippi Val. (Alabama St.) | 89 |
| Chris Parker, Marshall (Eastern Ill.) | 89 |
| Shundell Hicks, Rhode Island (Northeastern) | 87 |
| Brigham Lyons, Middle Tenn. St. (Murray St.) | 87 |
| Robert Johnson, Idaho St. (Weber St.) | 86 |
| Walter Dunson, Middle Tenn. St. (Murray St.) | 85 |
| Brigham Lyons, Middle Tenn. St. (Murray St.) | 85 |

# PASSING

| Passer-Receiver, Team (Opponent) | Yards |
|---|---|
| Tom Kirchhoff-Jamal Jordan, Lafayette (Fordham) | 95 |
| Stacey Moore-Joe Rogers, Texas Southern (Southwest Tex. St.) | 87 |
| Philly Jones-Billy Whitley, Furman (Western Caro.) | 86 |
| Lonnie Galloway-Kerry Hayes, Western Caro. (East Tenn. St.) | 86 |
| Emilio Colon-Tony Szydlowski, Maine (Connecticut) | 84 |
| Jay Johnson-Kenny Shedd, Northern Iowa (Idaho) | 84 |
| Shawn Knight-Mike Tomlin, William & Mary (Colgate) | 84 |
| Tom Kirchhoff-Jamal Jordan, Lafayette (Lehigh) | 84 |
| Scott Gabbert-Lavance Banks, Southern Ill. (Indiana St.) | 84 |
| Don Simmons-Demeris Johnson, Western Ill. (Morgan St.) | 83 |
| Rob Glus-Brad Bernardini, Bucknell (Colgate) | 83 |

# INTERCEPTION RETURNS

| Player, Team (Opponent) | Yards |
|---|---|
| Rick Hamilton, Central Fla. (Western Ill.) | 97 |
| Lamar Thomas, McNeese St. (Weber St.) | 92 |
| James Daniels, Pennsylvania (Columbia) | 91 |
| Ray Lyons, New Hampshire (Rhode Island) | 87 |
| Sean Hill, Montana St. (Eastern Wash.) | 80 |
| Richard Grice, Western Ky. (Murray St.) | 80 |
| Des Werthman, Columbia (Fordham) | 76 |
| Bill Curry, Maine (Liberty) | 74 |
| Lawrence Gore, Morehead St. (Tenn.-Martin) | 70 |

# PUNT RETURNS

| Player, Team (Opponent) | Yards |
|---|---|
| Darius Adams, Northwestern, La. (Troy St.) | 89 |
| Kerry Hayes, Western Caro. (East Tenn. St.) | 83 |
| Dennis Mimms, Middle Tenn. St. (Northern Ill.) | 83 |
| Michael Lerch, Princeton (Harvard) | 82 |
| Anthony Smith, Appalachian St. (Wake Forest) | 81 |
| Shalon Baker, Montana (Hofstra) | *78 |
| Kenny Shedd, Northern Iowa (Western Ky.) | 77 |
| Joel Pelagio-Williams, Weber St. (Southern Utah) | 73 |
| Jarrett Shine, Lafayette (Princeton) | 72 |
| Mike Stewart, Tennessee Tech (Southeast Mo. St.) | 72 |

* Did not score.

# KICKOFF RETURNS

| Player, Team (Opponent) | Yards |
|---|---|
| Leon Brown, Eastern Ky. (Western Ky.) | 100 |
| Leon Brown, Eastern Ky. (Northeast La.) | 98 |
| Brian Rodman, North Caro. A&T (South Caro. St.) | 97 |
| Kevin Robinson, Columbia (Harvard) | *96 |
| Sherriden May, Idaho (Northern Ariz.) | 95 |
| Chris Wright, Ga. Southern (Furman) | 94 |
| Rod Boothes, Richmond (Villanova) | 94 |
| Kerry Hayes, Western Caro. (Va. Military) | 94 |
| Tobe Taylor, Tenn.-Chatt. (Tenn.-Martin) | 92 |
| Len Raney, Northern Ariz. (Southern Utah) | 90 |
| Jerry Ellison, Tenn.-Chatt. (Tenn.-Martin) | 90 |
| Kerry Hayes, Western Caro. (Va. Military) | 90 |

* Did not score.

# FIELD GOALS

| Player, Team (Opponent) | Yards |
|---|---|
| Terry Belden, Northern Ariz. (Montana St.) | 56 |
| Garth Petrilli, Middle Tenn. St. (Murray St.) | 54 |
| Steve Leo, Delaware (Navy) | 54 |
| Reed Haley, Ga. Southern (Jacksonville St.) | 53 |
| Steve Largent, Eastern Ill. (Southwest Mo. St.) | 53 |
| Phil Shirley, Western Caro. (East Tenn. St.) | 53 |
| Reed Haley, Ga. Southern (Youngstown St.) | 53 |
| Terry Belden, Northern Ariz. (Montana) | 52 |
| Mike Hollis, Idaho (Northern Iowa) | 52 |

*1993 NCAA FOOTBALL*

## PUNTS

| Player, Team (Opponent) | Yards |
|---|---|
| Terry Belden, Northern Ariz. (Northeastern) | 81 |
| Harold Alexander, Appalachian St. (Citadel) | 78 |
| Rob Sims, Pennsylvania (Cornell) | 76 |
| Steve Krieger, Indiana St. (Eastern Ill.) | 72 |
| Todd Barton, Richmond (Rhode Island) | 71 |
| Chuck Poplos, Delaware St. (Liberty) | 70 |
| Danny Weeks, Boise St. (Pacific, Cal.) | 68 |

## FUMBLE RETURNS

| Player, Team (Opponent) | Yards |
|---|---|
| Brian Randall, Delaware St. (Morgan St.) | 95 |
| Eric Ward, Alcorn St. (Texas Southern) | 86 |
| Wesley McConnell, Liberty (Delaware St.) | 85 |
| Maceo Grant, Pennsylvania (William & Mary) | 79 |
| Tim Jacobs, Delaware (Maine) | 76 |
| Todd Ericson, Montana (Weber St.) | 74 |
| Miles McLean, Northeastern (Lehigh) | 72 |

# 1992 DIVISION II INDIVIDUAL LEADERS

## RUSHING

| | 1992 Class | Games | Car. | Yards | TD | Yds.PG |
|---|---|---|---|---|---|---|
| Roger Graham, New Haven | So | 10 | 200 | 1717 | 22 | 171.7 |
| Ronald Moore, Pittsburg St. | Sr | 11 | 239 | 1864 | 26 | 169.5 |
| Karl Evans, Mo. Southern St. | Sr | 10 | 327 | 1586 | 14 | 158.6 |
| Thelbert Withers, N.M. Highlands | Jr | 11 | 240 | 1621 | 15 | 147.4 |
| Scott Schulte, Hillsdale | Jr | 11 | 271 | 1582 | 16 | 143.8 |
| Rob Clodfelter, Livingstone | Jr | 10 | 272 | 1425 | 11 | 142.5 |
| David McCartney, Chadron St. | Jr | 10 | 267 | 1359 | 25 | 135.9 |
| Quincy Tillmon, Emporia St. | Jr | 9 | 240 | 1219 | 11 | 135.4 |
| Preston Jackson, UC Davis | Jr | 10 | 209 | 1334 | 15 | 133.4 |
| Chad Guthrie, Northeast Mo. St. | Sr | 11 | 276 | 1458 | 19 | 132.5 |
| Leonard Davis, Lenoir-Rhyne | Jr | 10 | 242 | 1308 | 13 | 130.8 |
| Kelly Yancy, Morningside | Jr | 11 | 250 | 1396 | 12 | 126.9 |
| Joe Gough, Wayne St. (Mich.) | So | 11 | 285 | 1340 | 8 | 121.8 |
| Carlos Fleeks, Hampton | Jr | 11 | 209 | 1312 | 15 | 119.3 |
| Kevin Kimble, Butler | Sr | 10 | 275 | 1190 | 11 | 119.0 |
| Jeremy Monroe, Michigan Tech | Jr | 9 | 152 | 1061 | 17 | 117.9 |
| Hosea Knowlton, Central Ark. | Jr | 10 | 221 | 1171 | 10 | 117.1 |
| Larry Jackson, Edinboro | So | 10 | 198 | 1154 | 17 | 115.4 |
| Rais Aho, Portland St. | Sr | 9 | 222 | 1030 | 12 | 114.4 |
| Jamarl Eiland, Grand Valley St. | Sr | 9 | 204 | 1029 | 15 | 114.3 |
| Aron Wise, Santa Clara | Sr | 10 | 227 | 1140 | 13 | 114.0 |
| Tyrone Rush, North Ala. | Jr | 10 | 181 | 1136 | 5 | 113.6 |
| Joseph Johnson, Northwest Mo. St. | Sr | 11 | 205 | 1241 | 11 | 112.8 |
| Lucius Cole, Savannah St. | Sr | 11 | 165 | 1213 | 13 | 110.3 |
| Shawn Graves, Wofford | Sr | 9 | 160 | 990 | 11 | 110.0 |

## PASSING EFFICIENCY

| (Min. 15 att. per game) | 1992 Class | Games | Att. | Cmp. | Pct. | Int. | Yards | TD | Rating Points |
|---|---|---|---|---|---|---|---|---|---|
| Steve Smith, Western St. | Sr | 10 | 271 | 180 | 66.4 | 5 | 2719 | 30 | 183.5 |
| John Charles, Portland St. | Sr | 8 | 263 | 179 | 68.0 | 7 | 2770 | 24 | 181.3 |
| Ken Suhl, New Haven | Sr | 10 | 239 | 148 | 61.9 | 5 | 2336 | 26 | 175.7 |
| Kurt Coduti, Michigan Tech | Sr | 9 | 155 | 92 | 59.3 | 3 | 1518 | 15 | 169.7 |
| Rovell McMillien, Winston-Salem | Jr | 11 | 165 | 83 | 50.3 | 5 | 1532 | 14 | 150.2 |
| Scott Woods, Indiana (Pa.) | Jr | 10 | 288 | 171 | 59.3 | 14 | 2580 | 20 | 147.8 |
| Jermaine Whitaker, N.M. Highlands | So | 11 | 326 | 176 | 53.9 | 9 | 2836 | 25 | 146.9 |
| Matt Montgomery, Hampton | So | 11 | 252 | 136 | 53.9 | 9 | 2000 | 25 | 146.3 |
| Daryl Fortenberry, Sonoma St. | Sr | 10 | 271 | 138 | 50.9 | 8 | 2311 | 24 | 145.9 |
| Khari Jones, UC Davis | Jr | 10 | 275 | 154 | 56.0 | 9 | 2342 | 20 | 145.0 |
| Mark Ramstack, Mo. Western St. | Sr | 11 | 301 | 170 | 56.4 | 11 | 2440 | 24 | 143.6 |
| John Craven, Gardner-Webb | So | 11 | 423 | 240 | 56.7 | 16 | 3320 | 32 | 140.1 |
| Dave McDonald, West Chester | So | 10 | 323 | 176 | 54.4 | 14 | 2759 | 22 | 140.0 |
| Joe Stochmal, Southern Conn. St. | Sr | 9 | 195 | 106 | 54.3 | 6 | 1683 | 11 | 139.3 |
| Kent Sikora, Saginaw Valley | Fr | 11 | 182 | 90 | 49.4 | 5 | 1580 | 12 | 138.6 |
| Brad Bretz, Cal St. Hayward | Jr | 10 | 293 | 180 | 61.4 | 13 | 2339 | 17 | 137.6 |
| John Linhart, Slippery Rock | Sr | 10 | 262 | 146 | 55.7 | 16 | 2110 | 21 | 137.6 |
| Trevor Spradley, Southwest Baptist | Sr | 10 | 295 | 189 | 64.0 | 10 | 2414 | 10 | 137.2 |
| Kory Wahl, North Dak. | Sr | 10 | 247 | 144 | 58.3 | 9 | 1889 | 15 | 135.3 |
| Gary Clayton, Tuskegee | Jr | 10 | 248 | 130 | 52.4 | 9 | 2174 | 12 | 134.8 |

*1992 Statistical Leaders*

## TOTAL OFFENSE

| | 1992 Class | Games | Plays | Yards | Yds.PG |
|---|---|---|---|---|---|
| John Charles, Portland St. | Sr | 8 | 303 | 2708 | 338.5 |
| Thad Trujillo, Fort Lewis | So | 10 | 477 | 3047 | 304.7 |
| John Craven, Gardner-Webb | So | 11 | 453 | 3216 | 292.4 |
| Vernon Buck, Wingate | So | 10 | 504 | 2838 | 283.8 |
| Steve Smith, Western St. | Sr | 10 | 296 | 2771 | 277.1 |
| Dave McDonald, West Chester | So | 10 | 362 | 2771 | 277.1 |
| Ken Suhl, New Haven | Sr | 10 | 332 | 2759 | 275.9 |
| Jermaine Whitaker, N.M. Highlands | So | 11 | 422 | 3009 | 273.5 |
| Khari Jones, UC Davis | Jr | 10 | 371 | 2629 | 262.9 |
| Scott Woods, Indiana (Pa.) | Jr | 10 | 325 | 2541 | 254.1 |
| Don Catlett, Kentucky St. | Sr | 10 | 364 | 2529 | 252.9 |
| Chris Hatcher, Valdosta St. | So | 10 | 424 | 2493 | 249.3 |
| Trevor Spradley, Southwest Baptist | Sr | 10 | 431 | 2476 | 247.6 |
| Brad Bretz, Cal St. Hayward | Jr | 10 | 369 | 2472 | 247.2 |
| Andy Breault, Kutztown | Sr | 10 | 389 | 2454 | 245.4 |
| Daryl Fortenberry, Sonoma St. | Sr | 10 | 320 | 2402 | 240.2 |
| Troy Mott, Wayne St. (Neb.) | Sr | 10 | 429 | 2390 | 239.0 |
| Gary Clayton, Tuskegee | Jr | 10 | 351 | 2369 | 236.9 |
| Tim Meyers, Clarion | Sr | 10 | 357 | 2369 | 236.9 |
| Tim Johnson, Elizabeth City St. | Sr | 10 | 378 | 2358 | 235.8 |
| Chris Teal, West Ga. | Jr | 11 | 396 | 2551 | 231.9 |
| Marty Washington, Livingston | Jr | 9 | 320 | 2066 | 229.6 |
| Dustin McEwen, Fort Hays St. | So | 11 | 481 | 2507 | 227.9 |
| Mark Ramstack, Mo. Western St. | Sr | 11 | 358 | 2433 | 221.2 |
| Arden Beachy, North Dak. St. | Jr | 9 | 277 | 1966 | 218.4 |

## RECEPTIONS PER GAME

| | 1992 Class | Games | Catches | Yards | TD | Ct.PG |
|---|---|---|---|---|---|---|
| Randy Bartosh, Southwest Baptist | Sr | 8 | 65 | 860 | 2 | 8.1 |
| Rodney Robinson, Gardner-Webb | Sr | 11 | 89 | 1496 | 16 | 8.1 |
| Troy Walker, Cal St. Chico | Jr | 10 | 79 | 874 | 5 | 7.9 |
| Matt Carman, Livingston | Jr | 9 | 66 | 759 | 3 | 7.3 |
| Calvin Walker, Valdosta St. | Jr | 10 | 71 | 867 | 8 | 7.1 |
| Damon Thomas, Wayne St. (Neb.) | Jr | 10 | 71 | 821 | 3 | 7.1 |
| Johnny Cox, Fort Lewis | Jr | 10 | 65 | 1331 | 12 | 6.5 |
| Lawrence Samuels, Livingston | Sr | 9 | 58 | 898 | 5 | 6.4 |
| Charles Guy, Sonoma St. | Sr | 10 | 64 | 1260 | 12 | 6.4 |
| Eric Jennings, Cal St. Hayward | Jr | 9 | 55 | 764 | 8 | 6.1 |
| Mike Key, Southern Utah | Sr | 11 | 67 | 955 | 5 | 6.1 |
| Tim Brown, Clarion | Jr | 10 | 60 | 614 | 4 | 6.0 |
| Derrick Sharpe, Mars Hill | Jr | 11 | 64 | 923 | 2 | 5.8 |
| Mike Ragin, Wingate | Jr | 10 | 57 | 892 | 4 | 5.7 |
| Brad Bailey, West Tex. St. | So | 10 | 57 | 642 | 2 | 5.7 |

## RECEIVING YARDS PER GAME

| | 1992 Class | Games | Catches | Yards | TD | Yds.PG |
|---|---|---|---|---|---|---|
| Rodney Robinson, Gardner-Webb | Sr | 11 | 89 | 1496 | 16 | 136.0 |
| Johnny Cox, Fort Lewis | Jr | 10 | 65 | 1331 | 12 | 133.1 |
| Charles Guy, Sonoma St. | Sr | 10 | 64 | 1260 | 12 | 126.0 |
| Randy Bartosh, Southwest Baptist | Sr | 8 | 65 | 860 | 2 | 107.5 |
| Steve Weaver, West Chester | Sr | 10 | 53 | 1037 | 11 | 103.7 |
| Tony Willis, New Haven | Jr | 10 | 51 | 1030 | 10 | 103.0 |
| Reggie Alexander, Western St. | Sr | 10 | 56 | 1013 | 11 | 101.3 |
| Terren Adams, Mo. Western St. | Sr | 11 | 62 | 1112 | 14 | 101.1 |
| Lawrence Samuels, Livingston | Sr | 9 | 58 | 898 | 5 | 99.8 |
| Bill Schafer, Saginaw Valley | Sr | 11 | 53 | 1089 | 10 | 99.0 |
| Rus Bailey, N.M. Highlands | Jr | 11 | 57 | 1063 | 12 | 96.6 |
| Clint Primm, Cal St. Sacramento | Jr | 10 | 50 | 951 | 8 | 95.1 |
| Sean Stevenson, Kentucky St. | So | 11 | 60 | 1028 | 9 | 93.5 |
| Mike Ragin, Wingate | Jr | 10 | 57 | 892 | 4 | 89.2 |
| Randy Montoya, N.M. Highlands | Sr | 11 | 58 | 963 | 10 | 87.5 |
| Troy Walker, Cal St. Chico | Jr | 10 | 79 | 874 | 5 | 87.4 |
| Matt James, Portland St. | So | 9 | 44 | 786 | 9 | 87.3 |
| Ed Minogue, Shippensburg | Sr | 11 | 52 | 958 | 6 | 87.1 |
| Mike Key, Southern Utah | Sr | 11 | 67 | 955 | 5 | 86.8 |
| Calvin Walker, Valdosta St. | Jr | 10 | 71 | 867 | 8 | 86.7 |
| Adrian Webber, Southern Conn. St. | Sr | 10 | 46 | 860 | 9 | 86.0 |
| James Roe, Norfolk St. | Fr | 10 | 46 | 850 | 9 | 85.0 |
| Eric Jennings, Cal St. Hayward | Jr | 9 | 55 | 764 | 8 | 84.9 |
| Tyrone Johnson, Western St. | Jr | 10 | 41 | 848 | 10 | 84.8 |
| Matt Carman, Livingston | Jr | 9 | 66 | 759 | 3 | 84.3 |

## SCORING

| | 1992 Class | Games | TD | XP | FG | Points | Pts.PG |
|---|---|---|---|---|---|---|---|
| David McCartney, Chadron St. | Jr | 10 | 25 | 4 | 0 | 154 | 15.4 |
| Ronald Moore, Pittsburg St. | Sr | 11 | 27 | 4 | 0 | 166 | 15.1 |
| Roger Graham, New Haven | So | 10 | 22 | 0 | 0 | 132 | 13.2 |

| | 1992 Class | Games | TD | XP | FG | Points | Pts.PG |
|---|---|---|---|---|---|---|---|
| Chad Guthrie, Northeast Mo. St. | Sr | 11 | 22 | 2 | 0 | 134 | 12.2 |
| Larry Jackson, Edinboro | So | 10 | 19 | 0 | 0 | 114 | 11.4 |
| A. J. Livingston, New Haven | Jr | 10 | 19 | 0 | 0 | 114 | 11.4 |
| Greg Marshall, Colorado Mines | Sr | 10 | 18 | 6 | 0 | 114 | 11.4 |
| Jamarl Eiland, Grand Valley St. | Sr | 9 | 17 | 0 | 0 | 102 | 11.3 |
| Jeremy Monroe, Michigan Tech | Jr | 9 | 17 | 0 | 0 | 102 | 11.3 |
| Carlos Fleeks, Hampton | Jr | 11 | 18 | 0 | 0 | 108 | 9.8 |
| Andre Nelson, Elizabeth City St. | Jr | 10 | 15 | 6 | 0 | 96 | 9.6 |
| Thelbert Withers, N.M. Highlands | Jr | 11 | 15 | 12 | 0 | 102 | 9.3 |
| Preston Jackson, UC Davis | Jr | 10 | 15 | 2 | 0 | 92 | 9.2 |
| Rus Bailey, N.M. Highlands | Jr | 11 | 12 | 27 | 0 | 99 | 9.0 |
| Karl Evans, Mo. Southern St. | Sr | 10 | 15 | 0 | 0 | 90 | 9.0 |
| Aron Wise, Santa Clara | Sr | 10 | 15 | 0 | 0 | 90 | 9.0 |
| Scott Schulte, Hillsdale | Jr | 11 | 16 | 2 | 0 | 98 | 8.9 |
| Richard Huntley, Winston-Salem | Fr | 10 | 14 | 4 | 0 | 88 | 8.8 |
| Doug Grant, Savannah St. | Jr | 11 | 16 | 0 | 0 | 96 | 8.7 |
| Rodney Robinson, Gardner-Webb | Sr | 11 | 16 | 0 | 0 | 96 | 8.7 |
| Rais Aho, Portland St. | Sr | 9 | 13 | 0 | 0 | 78 | 8.7 |
| Johnny Cox, Fort Lewis | Jr | 10 | 14 | 0 | 0 | 84 | 8.4 |
| Leonard Davis, Lenoir-Rhyne | Jr | 10 | 14 | 0 | 0 | 84 | 8.4 |
| Terren Adams, Mo. Western St. | Sr | 11 | 15 | 0 | 0 | 90 | 8.2 |
| Lucius Cole, Savannah St. | Sr | 11 | 15 | 0 | 0 | 90 | 8.2 |

## FIELD GOALS

| | 1992 Class | Games | FGA | FG | Pct. | FGPG |
|---|---|---|---|---|---|---|
| Mike Estrella, St. Mary's (Cal.) | Jr | 9 | 27 | 15 | 55.6 | 1.67 |
| Roy Miller, Fort Hays St. | Sr | 11 | 21 | 15 | 71.4 | 1.36 |
| Billy Watkins, East Tex. St. | Jr | 11 | 26 | 15 | 57.7 | 1.36 |
| Jason Monday, Lenoir-Rhyne | Sr | 10 | 15 | 13 | 86.7 | 1.30 |
| Ed Detwiler, East Stroudsburg | Sr | 10 | 25 | 13 | 52.0 | 1.30 |
| Brad Heim, Millersville | Jr | 10 | 16 | 12 | 75.0 | 1.20 |
| Kevin Houston, N.C. Central | Fr | 11 | 23 | 13 | 56.5 | 1.18 |
| Jason Tebeaux, Angelo St. | So | 7 | 12 | 8 | 66.7 | 1.14 |
| Chris Pyatt, Central Mo. St. | Jr | 10 | 18 | 11 | 61.1 | 1.10 |
| J. J. Phair, Fort Lewis | Jr | 10 | 20 | 11 | 55.0 | 1.10 |
| Jason Lipke, Ferris St. | Fr | 11 | 18 | 12 | 66.7 | 1.09 |
| Troy Ford, Elon | Sr | 10 | 12 | 10 | 83.3 | 1.00 |
| Joel Yohn, Shippensburg | Fr | 11 | 15 | 11 | 73.3 | 1.00 |
| Paul Cramer, Clarion | So | 10 | 14 | 10 | 71.4 | 1.00 |
| Mike Rowen, Neb.-Kearney | Fr | 9 | 13 | 9 | 69.2 | 1.00 |
| Angel Ronguillo, Eastern N. Mex. | So | 9 | 14 | 9 | 64.3 | 1.00 |
| Bryan Seward, Ashland | Jr | 11 | 18 | 11 | 61.1 | 1.00 |

## ALL-PURPOSE RUNNERS

| | 1992 Class | Games | Rush | Rec. | PR | KOR | Yards | Total Yds. PG |
|---|---|---|---|---|---|---|---|---|
| Johnny Cox, Fort Lewis | Jr | 10 | 95 | 1,331 | 80 | 679 | 2,185 | 218.50 |
| Ronald Moore, Pittsburg St. | Sr | 11 | 1,864 | 141 | 0 | 388 | 2,393 | 217.55 |
| Karl Evans, Mo. Southern St. | Sr | 10 | 1,586 | 10 | 0 | 571 | 2,167 | 216.70 |
| Bobby Phillips, Virginia Union | So | 9 | 881 | 156 | 0 | 584 | 1,621 | 180.11 |
| Dave Ludy, Winona St. | So | 10 | 737 | 166 | 0 | 881 | 1,784 | 178.40 |
| Roger Graham, New Haven | So | 10 | 1,717 | 47 | 0 | 8 | 1,772 | 177.20 |
| Craig Harris, American Int'l | So | 10 | 979 | 193 | 40 | 538 | 1,750 | 175.00 |
| Rob Clodfelter, Livingstone | Jr | 10 | 1,425 | 311 | 0 | 0 | 1,736 | 173.60 |
| Mike Key, Southern Utah | Sr | 11 | 74 | 955 | 555 | 265 | 1,849 | 168.09 |
| Greg Marshall, Colorado Mines | Sr | 10 | 828 | 182 | 3 | 634 | 1,647 | 164.70 |
| Thelbert Withers, N.M. Highlands | Jr | 11 | 1,621 | 136 | 0 | 7 | 1,764 | 160.36 |
| Mike Ragin, Wingate | Jr | 10 | 0 | 892 | 0 | 689 | 1,581 | 158.10 |
| Chad Guthrie, Northeast Mo. St. | Sr | 11 | 1,458 | 216 | 52 | 0 | 1,726 | 156.91 |
| Larry Jackson, Edinboro | So | 10 | 1,154 | 72 | 0 | 331 | 1,557 | 155.70 |
| Scott Schulte, Hillsdale | Jr | 11 | 1,582 | 112 | 0 | 0 | 1,694 | 154.00 |
| Tyrone Rush, North Ala. | Jr | 10 | 1,136 | 0 | 0 | 350 | 1,486 | 148.60 |
| Anthony Brooks, East Tex. St. | Sr | 11 | 65 | 738 | 294 | 537 | 1,634 | 148.55 |
| Carlos Fleeks, Hampton | Jr | 11 | 1,312 | 286 | 0 | 24 | 1,622 | 147.45 |
| Jamarl Eiland, Grand Valley St. | Sr | 9 | 1,029 | 283 | 0 | 0 | 1,312 | 145.78 |
| Quincy Tillmon, Emporia St. | Jr | 9 | 1,219 | 80 | 0 | 0 | 1,299 | 144.33 |

## PUNT RETURNS

| [Min. 1.2 per game] | 1992 Class | Ret. | Yds. | Avg. | [Min. 1.2 per game] | 1992 Class | Ret. | Yds. | Avg. |
|---|---|---|---|---|---|---|---|---|---|
| Doug Grant, Savannah St. | Jr | 15 | 366 | 24.4 | Cleveland Phillips, Central Okla. | Jr | 25 | 338 | 13.5 |
| Reece Brown, Indiana (Pa.) | Sr | 12 | 196 | 16.3 | L. Townsend, St. Mary's (Cal.) | So | 23 | 308 | 13.4 |
| Maurice Dix, Morris Brown | Jr | 19 | 301 | 15.8 | Randy Montoya, N.M. Highlands | Sr | 14 | 186 | 13.3 |
| Daryl Owens, Texas A&I | Jr | 27 | 409 | 15.1 | Derrick Miller, Virginia St. | Jr | 22 | 290 | 13.2 |
| Reggie Alexander, Western St. | Sr | 15 | 227 | 15.1 | Gerald Dockery, Eastern N. Mex. | Sr | 14 | 178 | 12.7 |
| Tyrone Poole, Fort Valley St. | So | 24 | 354 | 14.8 | Tom Jackson, Central Mo. St. | So | 13 | 162 | 12.5 |
| Tyree Davis, Central Ark. | Sr | 28 | 404 | 14.4 | Mike Key, Southern Utah | Sr | 45 | 555 | 12.3 |
| Mike Ichiyama, UC Davis | So | 17 | 245 | 14.4 | Marlon Worthy, Clarion | So | 21 | 254 | 12.1 |
| William Covington, Troy St. | Sr | 23 | 318 | 13.8 | Chad Zeigler, San Fran. St. | Sr | 16 | 192 | 12.0 |
| Tim Singleton, Newberry | Sr | 17 | 235 | 13.8 | Sean Francisco, Wayne St. (Neb.) | So | 24 | 287 | 12.0 |

# KICKOFF RETURNS

| (Min. 1.2 per game) | 1992 Class | Ret. | Yds. | Avg. | (Min. 1.2 per game) | 1992 Class | Ret. | Yds. | Avg. |
|---|---|---|---|---|---|---|---|---|---|
| Danny Lee, Jacksonville St. | Sr | 12 | 473 | 39.4 | Anthony Jefferson, Sonoma St. | Jr | 18 | 495 | 27.5 |
| Dave Ludy, Winona St. | So | 25 | 881 | 35.2 | B. R. Thompson, Eastern N. Mex. | Sr | 13 | 357 | 27.5 |
| Karl Evans, Mo. Southern St. | Sr | 18 | 571 | 31.7 | Anthony Cowins, Emporia St. | Sr | 20 | 537 | 26.9 |
| Johnny Cox, Fort Lewis | Jr | 22 | 679 | 30.9 | Rod Clark, Elon | So | 14 | 375 | 26.8 |
| Duane Joubert, West Tex. St. | Fr | 25 | 756 | 30.2 | Damon Wright, Carson-Newman | Jr | 13 | 347 | 26.7 |
| Daniel Harris, Southern Utah | Jr | 11 | 323 | 29.4 | John Raba, New Haven | Sr | 19 | 504 | 26.5 |
| David Richmond, Saginaw Valley | Sr | 15 | 425 | 28.3 | Pedro Lewis, Cal St. Sacramento | So | 12 | 313 | 26.1 |
| Ronald Moore, Pittsburg St. | Sr | 14 | 388 | 27.7 | Kevin Cannon, Millersville | Fr | 17 | 443 | 26.1 |
| Dennis McWhite, East Stroudsburg | So | 13 | 360 | 27.7 | Mike Gillock, Indianapolis | Jr | 22 | 573 | 26.0 |
| Dwayne Zackery, Bowie St. | So | 20 | 552 | 27.6 | Chris Smith, Cal Poly SLO | Jr | 21 | 544 | 25.9 |

# PUNTING

| (Min. 3.6 per game) | 1992 Class | No. | Avg. | (Min. 3.6 per game) | 1992 Class | No. | Avg. |
|---|---|---|---|---|---|---|---|
| Jimmy Morris, Angelo St. | So | 45 | 44.5 | Shane Boyd, Eastern N. Mex. | Jr | 56 | 40.6 |
| Eric Fadness, Fort Lewis | Sr | 43 | 43.9 | Gary Lhotsky, Edinboro | Jr | 41 | 40.6 |
| Chris Carter, Henderson St. | Jr | 57 | 43.6 | Chris Humes, UC Davis | Sr | 39 | 40.6 |
| Alex Campbell, Morris Brown | Fr | 54 | 42.6 | Jason Curcio, Adams St. | Sr | 42 | 40.3 |
| Jon Waugh, Sonoma St. | Jr | 46 | 42.5 | Adam Vinatieri, South Dak. St. | So | 58 | 40.1 |
| Pat Hogelin, Colorado Mines | So | 38 | 42.1 | Eric Lang, Mars Hill | Fr | 71 | 40.0 |
| Barry Gillingwater, East Tex. St. | Jr | 52 | 42.0 | Richie Ambrose, Gardner-Webb | Jr | 52 | 39.8 |
| Matt Gordon, Southern Utah | Jr | 61 | 41.8 | John Ruder, Fort Hays St. | Sr | 55 | 39.7 |
| John Crittenden, North Ala. | Sr | 41 | 41.2 | Ed Detwiler, East Stroudsburg | Sr | 51 | 39.6 |
| Chris Afarian, Santa Clara | Jr | 54 | 41.2 | Doug Strange, Central Ark. | Sr | 54 | 39.6 |

# INTERCEPTIONS

| | 1992 Class | G | No. | Yds. | Int.PG | | 1992 Class | G | No. | Yds. | Int.PG |
|---|---|---|---|---|---|---|---|---|---|---|---|
| Pat Williams, East Tex. St. | Jr | 11 | 13 | 145 | 1.2 | Cody Gamble, Chadron St. | So | 10 | 8 | 107 | .8 |
| Joseph Best, Fort Valley St. | Jr | 11 | 12 | 129 | 1.1 | Maurice Davenport, Central Okla. | Sr | 10 | 8 | 67 | .8 |
| Tom McKenney, West Liberty St. | So | 10 | 10 | 59 | 1.0 | Gerald Mitchell, Angelo St. | Sr | 9 | 7 | 78 | .8 |
| Jason Johnson, Shepherd | So | 10 | 9 | 66 | .9 | Melvin Crawford, Hampton | So | 11 | 8 | 83 | .7 |
| James Harbinson, Gardner-Webb | Jr | 11 | 9 | 159 | .8 | Tim Sudduth, Jacksonville St. | So | 10 | 7 | 70 | .7 |
| Duke Palmer, Pittsburg St. | Sr | 11 | 9 | 134 | .8 | David Healea, Central Ark. | Sr | 10 | 7 | 54 | .7 |
| Jason Bryant, Morehouse | Jr | 10 | 8 | 196 | .8 | Johnnie Stewart, Indianapolis | Sr | 10 | 7 | 0 | .7 |
| Roger Straub, East Stroudsburg | Sr | 10 | 8 | 119 | .8 | | | | | | |

**Fort Lewis wide receiver Johnny Cox led Division II in all-purpose yardage (218.5 yards per game) in 1992 and finished second in receiving yards per game (133.1) and seventh in receptions per game (6.5).**

# 1992 DIVISION II TEAM LEADERS

## TOTAL OFFENSE

| | Games | Plays | Yds. | Yds.PG | | Games | Plays | Yds. | Yds.PG |
|---|---|---|---|---|---|---|---|---|---|
| New Haven | 10 | 741 | 5877 | 587.7 | West Chester | 10 | 752 | 4292 | 429.2 |
| Western St. | 10 | 770 | 5644 | 564.4 | Wayne St. (Neb.) | 10 | 788 | 4239 | 423.9 |
| N.M. Highlands | 11 | 818 | 5394 | 490.4 | Southern Conn. St. | 10 | 664 | 4212 | 421.2 |
| Portland St. | 9 | 562 | 4403 | 489.2 | Colorado Mines | 10 | 728 | 4205 | 420.5 |
| Gardner-Webb | 11 | 854 | 5311 | 482.8 | Indiana (Pa.) | 10 | 691 | 4185 | 418.5 |
| Pittsburg St. | 11 | 813 | 5222 | 474.7 | Fort Lewis | 10 | 754 | 4162 | 416.2 |
| Hampton | 11 | 810 | 5069 | 460.8 | Chadron St. | 10 | 764 | 4130 | 413.0 |
| Michigan Tech | 9 | 653 | 4135 | 459.4 | Tuskegee | 10 | 670 | 4115 | 411.5 |
| UC Davis | 10 | 680 | 4546 | 454.6 | Northwest Mo. St. | 11 | 770 | 4518 | 410.7 |
| Wofford | 11 | 721 | 4737 | 430.6 | Edinboro | 10 | 717 | 4090 | 409.0 |

## TOTAL DEFENSE

| | Games | Plays | Yds. | Yds.PG | | Games | Plays | Yds. | Yds.PG |
|---|---|---|---|---|---|---|---|---|---|
| Ashland | 11 | 705 | 2326 | 211.5 | Texas A&I | 10 | 683 | 2498 | 249.8 |
| Eastern N. Mex. | 10 | 663 | 2227 | 222.7 | Butler | 10 | 699 | 2555 | 255.5 |
| East Tex. St. | 11 | 718 | 2450 | 222.7 | Angelo St. | 9 | 612 | 2314 | 257.1 |
| Central Ark. | 10 | 634 | 2293 | 229.3 | Elon | 10 | 643 | 2620 | 262.0 |
| Augustana (S.D.) | 11 | 743 | 2539 | 230.8 | Hampton | 11 | 685 | 2895 | 263.2 |
| Ferris St. | 11 | 721 | 2550 | 231.8 | Saginaw Valley | 11 | 736 | 2897 | 263.4 |
| Fort Valley St. | 11 | 656 | 2580 | 234.5 | Cal St. Sacramento | 10 | 641 | 2634 | 263.4 |
| North Dak. St. | 10 | 612 | 2397 | 239.7 | St. Cloud St. | 11 | 655 | 2923 | 265.7 |
| Central Mo. St. | 10 | 697 | 2464 | 246.4 | Wayne St. (Neb.) | 10 | 693 | 2685 | 268.5 |
| Hillsdale | 11 | 696 | 2722 | 247.5 | Carson-Newman | 10 | 653 | 2691 | 269.1 |

## RUSHING OFFENSE

| | Games | Car. | Yds. | Yds.PG | | Games | Plays | Yds. | Yds.PG |
|---|---|---|---|---|---|---|---|---|---|
| Pittsburg St. | 11 | 651 | 3892 | 353.8 | Texas A&I | 10 | 510 | 2625 | 262.5 |
| Northwest Mo. St. | 11 | 653 | 3775 | 343.2 | North Dak. St. | 10 | 537 | 2621 | 262.1 |
| New Haven | 10 | 487 | 3397 | 339.7 | Carson-Newman | 10 | 552 | 2558 | 255.8 |
| Wofford | 11 | 616 | 3606 | 327.8 | Springfield | 9 | 530 | 2270 | 252.2 |
| North Ala. | 10 | 573 | 2989 | 298.9 | Jacksonville St. | 10 | 533 | 2508 | 250.8 |
| Elon | 10 | 568 | 2889 | 288.9 | Henderson St. | 11 | 596 | 2730 | 248.2 |
| Colorado Mines | 10 | 521 | 2871 | 287.1 | Minn.-Duluth | 11 | 602 | 2725 | 247.7 |
| Michigan Tech | 9 | 490 | 2576 | 286.2 | Edinboro | 10 | 485 | 2362 | 236.2 |
| Troy St. | 11 | 579 | 3114 | 283.1 | Adams St. | 10 | 487 | 2360 | 236.0 |
| Hampton | 11 | 551 | 3051 | 277.4 | Central Ark. | 10 | 576 | 2302 | 230.2 |

## RUSHING DEFENSE

| | Games | Car. | Yds. | Yds.PG | | Games | Car. | Yds. | Yds.PG |
|---|---|---|---|---|---|---|---|---|---|
| Ashland | 11 | 407 | 708 | 64.4 | Cal St. Sacramento | 10 | 343 | 872 | 87.2 |
| Humboldt St. | 11 | 369 | 772 | 70.2 | Texas A&I | 10 | 417 | 887 | 88.7 |
| Wayne St. (Neb.) | 10 | 380 | 704 | 70.4 | Jacksonville St. | 10 | 350 | 935 | 93.5 |
| Slippery Rock | 11 | 323 | 804 | 73.1 | North Dak. St. | 10 | 359 | 953 | 95.3 |
| Carson-Newman | 10 | 333 | 782 | 78.2 | St. Mary's (Cal.) | 9 | 329 | 873 | 97.0 |
| Ferris St. | 11 | 414 | 901 | 81.9 | Shepherd | 10 | 331 | 999 | 99.9 |
| West Liberty St. | 10 | 337 | 831 | 83.1 | Albany St. (Ga.) | 10 | 372 | 1001 | 100.1 |
| Hampton | 11 | 353 | 932 | 84.7 | Augustana (S.D.) | 11 | 436 | 1114 | 101.3 |
| Millersville | 10 | 327 | 860 | 86.0 | West Chester | 10 | 367 | 1022 | 102.2 |
| Eastern N. Mex. | 10 | 403 | 868 | 86.8 | St. Cloud St. | 11 | 377 | 1142 | 103.8 |

## SCORING OFFENSE

| | Games | TD | XP | 2XP | DXP | FG | Saf. | Pts. | Avg. |
|---|---|---|---|---|---|---|---|---|---|
| New Haven | 10 | 72 | 65 | 1 | 0 | 2 | 0 | 505 | 50.5 |
| Western St. | 10 | 65 | 54 | 3 | 0 | 7 | 0 | 471 | 47.1 |
| Gardner-Webb | 11 | 68 | 61 | 0 | 0 | 9 | 1 | 498 | 45.3 |
| Hampton | 11 | 66 | 46 | 8 | 0 | 5 | 1 | 475 | 43.2 |
| Michigan Tech | 9 | 50 | 35 | 2 | 0 | 4 | 1 | 353 | 39.2 |
| Pittsburg St. | 11 | 56 | 40 | 7 | 0 | 10 | 0 | 420 | 38.2 |
| Portland St. | 9 | 46 | 36 | 1 | 0 | 6 | 0 | 332 | 36.9 |
| UC Davis | 10 | 50 | 41 | 3 | 0 | 6 | 1 | 367 | 36.7 |
| Savannah St. | 11 | 53 | 44 | 3 | 0 | 4 | 1 | 382 | 34.7 |
| N.M. Highlands | 11 | 56 | 21 | 11 | 0 | 0 | 1 | 381 | 34.6 |
| Indiana (Pa.) | 10 | 47 | 39 | 0 | 0 | 5 | 0 | 336 | 33.6 |
| Northeast Mo. St. | 11 | 50 | 39 | 2 | 0 | 6 | 0 | 361 | 32.8 |
| Wofford | 11 | 51 | 44 | 1 | 0 | 3 | 0 | 361 | 32.8 |
| Edinboro | 10 | 44 | 33 | 1 | 0 | 6 | 2 | 321 | 32.1 |
| Colorado Mines | 10 | 44 | 30 | 5 | 0 | 4 | 1 | 318 | 31.8 |
| Texas A&I | 10 | 42 | 32 | 5 | 0 | 5 | 4 | 317 | 31.7 |
| North Dak. St. | 10 | 42 | 30 | 3 | 0 | 7 | 1 | 311 | 31.1 |
| West Ga. | 11 | 46 | 40 | 1 | 0 | 7 | 0 | 339 | 30.8 |
| Emporia St. | 10 | 41 | 37 | 2 | 0 | 5 | 0 | 302 | 30.2 |
| Southern Conn. St. | 10 | 42 | 38 | 0 | 0 | 3 | 1 | 301 | 30.1 |

## SCORING DEFENSE

| | Games | TD | XP | 2XP | DXP | FG | Saf. | Pts. | Avg. |
|---|---|---|---|---|---|---|---|---|---|
| Ferris St. | 11 | 14 | 9 | 1 | 0 | 6 | 1 | 115 | 10.5 |
| Troy St. | 11 | 12 | 10 | 0 | 0 | 12 | 0 | 118 | 10.7 |
| Central Mo. St. | 10 | 14 | 12 | 0 | 0 | 4 | 0 | 108 | 10.8 |
| Edinboro | 10 | 15 | 10 | 0 | 0 | 4 | 0 | 112 | 11.2 |
| Ashland | 11 | 18 | 15 | 0 | 0 | 5 | 0 | 138 | 12.5 |
| Butler | 10 | 18 | 13 | 0 | 0 | 1 | 1 | 126 | 12.6 |
| Elon | 10 | 17 | 16 | 0 | 0 | 3 | 0 | 127 | 12.7 |
| North Ala. | 10 | 16 | 14 | 0 | 0 | 6 | 0 | 128 | 12.8 |
| Central Ark. | 10 | 17 | 17 | 0 | 0 | 4 | 0 | 131 | 13.1 |
| Angelo St. | 9 | 13 | 12 | 0 | 0 | 10 | 0 | 120 | 13.3 |
| Hillsdale | 11 | 19 | 18 | 0 | 0 | 5 | 0 | 147 | 13.4 |
| Saginaw Valley | 11 | 18 | 14 | 0 | 0 | 8 | 1 | 148 | 13.5 |
| North Dak. St. | 10 | 15 | 12 | 1 | 1 | 9 | 1 | 135 | 13.5 |
| Albany St. (Ga.) | 10 | 18 | 17 | 0 | 0 | 4 | 0 | 137 | 13.7 |
| North Dak. | 10 | 17 | 12 | 2 | 0 | 7 | 0 | 139 | 13.9 |
| Northeast Mo. St. | 11 | 22 | 18 | 0 | 0 | 2 | 1 | 158 | 14.4 |
| St. Cloud St. | 11 | 22 | 13 | 1 | 0 | 3 | 1 | 158 | 14.4 |
| East Tex. St. | 11 | 20 | 11 | 2 | 0 | 8 | 0 | 159 | 14.5 |
| Cal St. Sacramento | 10 | 20 | 18 | 0 | 0 | 3 | 1 | 149 | 14.9 |
| Carson-Newman | 10 | 18 | 9 | 1 | 0 | 10 | 0 | 149 | 14.9 |
| Texas A&I | 10 | 20 | 10 | 2 | 0 | 5 | 0 | 149 | 14.9 |

## PASSING OFFENSE

| | Games | Att. | Cmp. | Pct. | Int. | Yards | Yds.PG |
|---|---|---|---|---|---|---|---|
| Gardner-Webb | 11 | 501 | 282 | 56.3 | 19 | 4046 | 367.8 |
| Portland St. | 9 | 318 | 216 | 67.9 | 7 | 3250 | 361.1 |
| Western St. | 10 | 348 | 223 | 64.1 | 7 | 3460 | 346.0 |
| Fort Lewis | 10 | 433 | 227 | 52.4 | 14 | 3200 | 320.0 |
| Livingston | 9 | 443 | 237 | 53.5 | 16 | 2824 | 313.8 |
| Kutztown | 10 | 376 | 219 | 58.2 | 18 | 2923 | 292.3 |
| West Chester | 10 | 330 | 179 | 54.2 | 14 | 2809 | 280.9 |
| Sonoma St. | 10 | 347 | 174 | 50.1 | 12 | 2786 | 278.6 |
| Indiana (Pa.) | 10 | 303 | 180 | 59.4 | 14 | 2721 | 272.1 |
| Cal St. Sacramento | 10 | 332 | 178 | 53.6 | 13 | 2687 | 268.7 |
| St. Mary's (Cal.) | 9 | 318 | 155 | 48.7 | 11 | 2376 | 264.0 |
| N.M. Highlands | 11 | 339 | 181 | 53.4 | 11 | 2894 | 263.1 |
| Cal St. Chico | 10 | 468 | 227 | 48.5 | 20 | 2622 | 262.2 |
| Kentucky St. | 11 | 362 | 169 | 46.7 | 18 | 2864 | 260.4 |
| Valdosta St. | 10 | 416 | 273 | 65.6 | 15 | 2586 | 258.6 |
| Tuskegee | 10 | 307 | 162 | 52.8 | 11 | 2544 | 254.4 |
| Wingate | 10 | 391 | 206 | 52.7 | 17 | 2537 | 253.7 |
| Southwest Baptist | 10 | 315 | 199 | 63.2 | 11 | 2534 | 253.4 |
| UC Davis | 10 | 294 | 164 | 55.8 | 9 | 2492 | 249.2 |
| New Haven | 10 | 244 | 152 | 62.3 | 6 | 2483 | 248.3 |

## PASS-EFFICIENCY DEFENSE

| | Games | Att. | Cmp. | Pct. | Int. | Yards | TD | Rating Points |
|---|---|---|---|---|---|---|---|---|
| East Tex. St. | 11 | 260 | 89 | 34.2 | 26 | 1276 | 5 | 61.8 |
| Fort Valley St. | 11 | 266 | 96 | 36.0 | 28 | 1267 | 13 | 71.2 |
| Central Mo. St. | 10 | 181 | 72 | 39.7 | 12 | 789 | 6 | 74.1 |
| Gardner-Webb | 11 | 335 | 140 | 41.7 | 35 | 1848 | 11 | 78.1 |
| Central Ark. | 10 | 256 | 109 | 42.5 | 17 | 1197 | 8 | 78.9 |
| Augustana (S.D.) | 11 | 307 | 132 | 43.0 | 18 | 1425 | 11 | 82.1 |
| Hillsdale | 11 | 275 | 113 | 41.0 | 29 | 1572 | 12 | 82.4 |
| Ferris St. | 11 | 307 | 132 | 43.0 | 17 | 1649 | 6 | 83.5 |
| Presbyterian | 11 | 263 | 129 | 49.0 | 17 | 1488 | 2 | 86.2 |
| Michigan Tech | 9 | 266 | 119 | 44.7 | 15 | 1434 | 6 | 86.2 |
| Angelo St. | 9 | 261 | 127 | 48.6 | 15 | 1337 | 5 | 86.5 |
| Hampton | 11 | 332 | 135 | 40.6 | 24 | 1963 | 11 | 86.8 |
| Savannah St. | 11 | 264 | 119 | 45.0 | 14 | 1344 | 8 | 87.2 |
| East Stroudsburg | 10 | 332 | 150 | 45.1 | 25 | 2092 | 8 | 88.0 |
| Edinboro | 10 | 275 | 116 | 42.1 | 14 | 1623 | 6 | 88.8 |
| Butler | 10 | 290 | 143 | 49.3 | 11 | 1481 | 4 | 89.2 |
| Central Okla. | 10 | 274 | 113 | 41.2 | 22 | 1737 | 9 | 89.3 |
| Millersville | 10 | 345 | 154 | 44.6 | 20 | 1988 | 10 | 91.0 |
| Saginaw Valley | 11 | 305 | 144 | 47.2 | 13 | 1555 | 9 | 91.3 |
| North Dak. St. | 10 | 253 | 115 | 45.4 | 14 | 1444 | 7 | 91.5 |

## NET PUNTING

| | Punts | Avg. | No. Ret. | Yds. Ret. | Net Avg. | | Punts | Avg. | No. Ret. | Yds. Ret. | Net Avg. |
|---|---|---|---|---|---|---|---|---|---|---|---|
| Fort Lewis | 43 | 43.86 | 23 | 255 | 37.93 | Catawba | 55 | 38.21 | 23 | 67 | 37.00 |
| East Tex. St. | 53 | 41.18 | 22 | 177 | 37.84 | North Dak. | 55 | 38.94 | 19 | 110 | 36.94 |
| Edinboro | 41 | 40.60 | 18 | 118 | 37.73 | Michigan Tech | 28 | 40.07 | 7 | 94 | 36.71 |
| Savannah St. | 40 | 39.35 | 12 | 69 | 37.62 | Fort Hays St. | 69 | 39.63 | 28 | 211 | 36.57 |
| Sonoma St. | 46 | 42.50 | 20 | 238 | 37.32 | Emporia St. | 56 | 38.12 | 22 | 90 | 36.51 |

| | Punts | Avg. | No. Ret. | Yds. Ret. | Net Avg. | | Punts | Avg. | No. Ret. | Yds. Ret. | Net Avg. |
|---|---|---|---|---|---|---|---|---|---|---|---|
| North Ala. | 45 | 40.15 | 23 | 176 | 36.24 | UC Davis | 40 | 39.55 | 19 | 149 | 35.82 |
| Central Okla. | 65 | 41.93 | 29 | 372 | 36.21 | South Dak. | 57 | 37.84 | 22 | 116 | 35.80 |
| Jacksonville St. | 64 | 39.14 | 29 | 190 | 36.17 | Shepherd | 56 | 37.50 | 17 | 98 | 35.75 |
| Mansfield | 48 | 38.56 | 20 | 118 | 36.10 | Morris Brown | 54 | 42.61 | 33 | 375 | 35.66 |
| Carson-Newman | 45 | 38.26 | 19 | 109 | 35.84 | Portland St. | 25 | 37.24 | 5 | 41 | 35.60 |

## PUNT RETURNS

| | Games | No. | Yds. | TD | Avg. | | Games | No. | Yds. | TD | Avg. |
|---|---|---|---|---|---|---|---|---|---|---|---|
| Savannah St. | 11 | 22 | 467 | 2 | 21.22 | Central Ark. | 10 | 34 | 438 | 4 | 12.88 |
| Texas A&I | 10 | 32 | 591 | 4 | 18.46 | Central Okla. | 10 | 32 | 411 | 3 | 12.84 |
| Eastern N. Mex. | 10 | 20 | 307 | 2 | 15.35 | Norfolk St. | 10 | 20 | 252 | 4 | 12.60 |
| UC Davis | 10 | 17 | 245 | 0 | 14.41 | Clarion | 10 | 24 | 299 | 1 | 12.45 |
| Morris Brown | 10 | 25 | 351 | 1 | 14.04 | N. M. Highlands | 11 | 15 | 186 | 0 | 12.40 |
| Fort Valley St. | 11 | 26 | 363 | 1 | 13.96 | Indiana (Pa.) | 10 | 21 | 260 | 1 | 12.38 |
| Delta St. | 10 | 12 | 167 | 1 | 13.91 | Southern Utah | 11 | 47 | 567 | 2 | 12.06 |
| St. Mary's (Cal.) | 9 | 25 | 345 | 1 | 13.80 | Bowie St. | 11 | 24 | 289 | 0 | 12.04 |
| Troy St. | 11 | 24 | 329 | 1 | 13.70 | South Dak. | 11 | 28 | 329 | 0 | 11.75 |
| Mesa St. | 11 | 19 | 255 | 0 | 13.42 | Jacksonville St. | 10 | 20 | 234 | 1 | 11.70 |

## KICKOFF RETURNS

| | Games | No. | Yds. | TD | Avg. | | Games | No. | Yds. | TD | Avg. |
|---|---|---|---|---|---|---|---|---|---|---|---|
| Jacksonville St. | 10 | 28 | 951 | 5 | 33.96 | Central Okla. | 10 | 24 | 550 | 1 | 22.91 |
| Winona St. | 10 | 36 | 1,083 | 3 | 30.08 | Carson-Newman | 10 | 31 | 710 | 1 | 22.90 |
| Clark Atlanta | 10 | 30 | 854 | 2 | 28.46 | Saginaw Valley | 11 | 33 | 753 | 1 | 22.81 |
| West Tex. St. | 10 | 52 | 1,308 | 2 | 25.15 | Augustana (S.D.) | 11 | 25 | 570 | 0 | 22.80 |
| Portland St. | 9 | 33 | 824 | 0 | 24.96 | Angelo St. | 9 | 19 | 433 | 0 | 22.78 |
| Mo. Southern St. | 10 | 38 | 944 | 1 | 24.84 | Shepherd | 10 | 42 | 957 | 2 | 22.78 |
| North Dak. St. | 10 | 24 | 567 | 1 | 23.62 | Indianapolis | 10 | 54 | 1,226 | 0 | 22.70 |
| Cal Poly SLO | 10 | 40 | 938 | 0 | 23.45 | Eastern N. Mex. | 10 | 23 | 522 | 1 | 22.69 |
| Elon | 10 | 24 | 554 | 2 | 23.08 | Troy St. | 11 | 29 | 656 | 1 | 22.62 |
| East Tex. St. | 11 | 33 | 757 | 1 | 22.93 | Bowie St. | 11 | 48 | 1,083 | 1 | 22.56 |

## TURNOVER MARGIN

| | TURNOVERS GAINED | | | TURNOVERS LOST | | | Margin/ |
|---|---|---|---|---|---|---|---|
| | Fum. | Int. | Total | Fum. | Int. | Total | Game |
| Hillsdale | 17 | 29 | 46 | 12 | 10 | 22 | 2.18 |
| Gardner-Webb | 21 | 35 | 56 | 16 | 19 | 35 | 1.90 |
| Neb.-Kearney | 20 | 18 | 38 | 7 | 13 | 20 | 1.80 |
| Pittsburg St. | 16 | 23 | 39 | 15 | 6 | 21 | 1.63 |
| Michigan Tech | 14 | 15 | 29 | 12 | 3 | 15 | 1.55 |
| Fort Hays St. | 22 | 18 | 40 | 10 | 13 | 23 | 1.54 |
| Fort Valley St. | 16 | 28 | 44 | 12 | 15 | 27 | 1.54 |
| Elon | 21 | 14 | 35 | 15 | 5 | 20 | 1.50 |
| Hampton | 15 | 24 | 39 | 14 | 9 | 23 | 1.45 |
| Winston-Salem | 12 | 25 | 37 | 14 | 7 | 21 | 1.45 |
| Central Okla. | 13 | 22 | 35 | 8 | 13 | 21 | 1.40 |
| Jacksonville St. | 15 | 16 | 31 | 14 | 4 | 18 | 1.30 |
| Western St. | 17 | 12 | 29 | 9 | 7 | 16 | 1.30 |
| Cal St. Sacramento | 17 | 13 | 30 | 5 | 13 | 18 | 1.20 |
| Central Mo. St. | 18 | 12 | 30 | 15 | 3 | 18 | 1.20 |
| Chadron St. | 13 | 18 | 31 | 7 | 12 | 19 | 1.20 |
| Ferris St. | 13 | 17 | 30 | 6 | 11 | 17 | 1.18 |
| Slippery Rock | 16 | 26 | 42 | 11 | 18 | 29 | 1.18 |
| Central Ark. | 10 | 17 | 27 | 8 | 8 | 16 | 1.10 |
| North Dak. | 9 | 16 | 25 | 5 | 9 | 14 | 1.10 |

# LONGEST DIVISION II PLAYS OF 1992

## RUSHING

| Player, Team (Opponent) | Yards |
|---|---|
| Thelbert Withers, N.M. Highlands (Fort Lewis) | 99 |
| Dedrick Young, Morehouse (Albany St., Ga.) | 98 |
| Lance Dunn, Mankato St. (Nebraska-Omaha) | 95 |
| Shawn Graves, Wofford (Catawba) | 93 |
| Roger Graham, New Haven (Buffalo) | 90 |
| Shawn Graves, Wofford (Lenoir-Rhyne) | 90 |
| Roger Graham, New Haven (American Int'l) | 89 |
| Ron Porter, Millersville (Cheyney) | 88 |
| Joe Gough, Wayne St., Mich. (St. Joseph's, Ind.) | 86 |
| Brett Mullins, Saginaw Valley (Grand Valley St.) | 86 |

# PASSING

| Passer-Receiver, Team (Opponent) | Yards |
|---|---|
| Rob Rayl-John Unger, Valparaiso (Hillsdale) | 99 |
| Ken Terry-Doug Russell, Neb.-Kearney (Mesa St.) | 98 |
| Donnie Catlett-Eric Alford, Kentucky St. (Findlay) | 97 |
| Troy Mott-Damon Thomas, Wayne St., Neb. (Mayville St.) | 97 |
| Andre Savage-Remus James, Virginia St. (Virginia Union) | 94 |
| Chad Alexander-Doug Grant, Savannah St. (Morehouse) | 88 |
| Bobby Fresques-Clint Primm, Cal St. Sacramento (Cal St. Chico) | 87 |
| Dave MacDonald-Steve Weaver, West Chester (Cheyney) | 86 |
| Chad Alexander-Dedric Smith, Savannah St. (Tuskegee) | 85 |
| Kent Sikora-Bill Schafer, Saginaw Valley (Ashland) | 85 |

# INTERCEPTION RETURNS

| Player, Team (Opponent) | Yards |
|---|---|
| Michael Robinson, Hampton (Virginia St.) | 98 |
| Steve Smith, Bowie St. (Elizabeth City St.) | 95 |
| Roger Straub, East Stroudsburg (Kutztown) | 94 |
| John Stuart, Indiana, Pa. (Lock Haven) | 91 |

# PUNT RETURNS

| Player, Team (Opponent) | Yards |
|---|---|
| William Covington, Troy St. (Central Fla.) | 89 |
| Vance Kinney, Ashland (Grand Valley St.) | 89 |
| Rod Clark, Elon (Mars Hill) | 88 |
| Tom Jackson, Central Mo. St. (Mo. Western St.) | 87 |
| Tyree Davis, Central Ark. (Ark.-Monticello) | 85 |
| Reece Brown, Indiana, Pa. (East Stroudsburg) | 83 |
| Tyrone Poole, Fort Valley St. (Miles) | 81 |
| James Roe, Norfolk St. (Bowie St.) | 81 |

# KICKOFF RETURNS

| Player, Team (Opponent) | Yards |
|---|---|
| Karl Evans, Mo. Southern St. (Northwest Mo. St.) | 100 |
| Danny Lee, Jacksonville St. (Delta St.) | 100 |
| Billy Ray Thompson, Eastern N. Mex. (Western St.) | 100 |
| Damon Wright, Carson-Newman (Wingate) | 100 |
| William Covington, Troy St. (Samford) | 99 |
| Jeff McLeod, Central Conn. St. (Southern Conn. St.) | 99 |
| Rick Starling, Wayne St., Neb. (Michigan Tech) | 98 |
| Joe Pierce, N.M. Highlands (Fort Lewis) | 97 |
| Chris Phillips, Adams St. (Colorado Mines) | 96 |
| Jason Johnson, Shepherd (Fairmont) | 95 |
| Duane Joubert, West Tex. St. (Fort Lewis) | 95 |
| Dave Ludy, Winona St. (Bemidji St.) | 95 |
| Glenn Starks, Central Okla. (Eastern N. Mex.) | 95 |

# FIELD GOALS

| Player, Team (Opponent) | Yards |
|---|---|
| Roy Miller, Fort Hays St. (N.M. Highlands) | 55 |
| Scott Doyle, Chadron St. (Adams St.) | 52 |
| Paul Tocco, Northern Mich. (Wayne St., Mich.) | 52 |
| Paul Tocco, Northern Mich. (Saginaw Valley) | 52 |
| Adam Vinatieri, South Dak. St. (North Dak.) | 51 |
| John Cortez, Texas A&I (East Tex. St.) | 50 |
| Tim Hatcher, Sonoma St. (Portland St.) | 50 |

# PUNTS

| Player, Team (Opponent) | Yards |
|---|---|
| Branton Dawson, Mo. Southern St. (Emporia St.) | 84 |
| Barry Gillingwater, East Tex. St. (Abilene Christian) | 84 |
| Rus Bailey, N.M. Highlands (Western St.) | 79 |
| George Moeke, Michigan Tech (Minn.-Morris) | 78 |
| Casey Anderson, Neb.-Kearney (Wayne St., Neb.) | 75 |
| Alex Campbell, Morris Brown (Cheyney) | 75 |
| Alex Campbell, Morris Brown (Morehouse) | 74 |
| Jud Heldreth, Wofford (Newberry) | 74 |
| Paul Irland, Central Okla. (Southern Utah) | 71 |
| Chris Shreve, West Liberty St. (Fairmont) | 71 |

# 1992 DIVISION III INDIVIDUAL LEADERS

## RUSHING

| | 1992 Class | Games | Car. | Yards | TD | Yds.PG |
|---|---|---|---|---|---|---|
| Kirk Matthieu, Maine Maritime | Jr | 9 | 327 | 1733 | 16 | 192.6 |
| Chris Babirad, Wash. & Jeff. | Sr | 9 | 243 | 1589 | 22 | 176.6 |
| Wes Stearns, Merchant Marine | Sr | 9 | 247 | 1477 | 12 | 164.1 |
| Trent Nauholz, Simpson | Jr | 8 | 254 | 1302 | 21 | 162.8 |
| Rob Johnson, Western Md. | Jr | 10 | 330 | 1560 | 18 | 156.0 |
| Kevin Piecewicz, Mass. Maritime | Jr | 9 | 200 | 1339 | 12 | 148.8 |
| Derrick Harris, Eureka | Jr | 10 | 328 | 1485 | 14 | 148.5 |
| Anthony Russo, St. John's (N.Y.) | Jr | 10 | 278 | 1479 | 15 | 147.9 |
| Dwayne Marcus, Gettysburg | So | 10 | 243 | 1476 | 11 | 147.6 |
| Stanley Drayton, Allegheny | Sr | 9 | 207 | 1255 | 19 | 139.4 |
| Steve Dixon, Beloit | Jr | 10 | 268 | 1388 | 13 | 138.8 |
| Greg Novarro, Bentley | Sr | 10 | 280 | 1384 | 23 | 138.4 |
| Sean Cheatham, Redlands | Jr | 9 | 203 | 1236 | 13 | 137.3 |
| Derek Tieman, Aurora | Sr | 9 | 207 | 1233 | 13 | 137.0 |
| Mike Haines, Duquesne | Jr | 9 | 238 | 1230 | 10 | 136.7 |
| Jeremy Hurd, Rochester | Jr | 9 | 262 | 1210 | 15 | 134.4 |
| Chris Wiens, Bethel (Minn.) | So | 10 | 270 | 1330 | 6 | 133.0 |
| Jeff Wittman, Ithaca | Sr | 10 | 207 | 1301 | 19 | 130.1 |
| Craig Woodard, Mercyhurst | Fr | 9 | 176 | 1166 | 8 | 129.6 |
| Steve Harris, Carroll (Wis.) | So | 9 | 191 | 1150 | 12 | 127.8 |

## PASSING EFFICIENCY

| (Min. 15 att. per game) | 1992 Class | Games | Att. | Cmp. | Pct. | Int. | Yards | TD | Rating Points |
|---|---|---|---|---|---|---|---|---|---|
| Steve Keller, Dayton | Sr | 10 | 153 | 99 | 64.7 | 5 | 1350 | 17 | 168.9 |
| Jim Ballard, Mount Union | Jr | 10 | 292 | 186 | 63.7 | 8 | 2656 | 29 | 167.4 |
| Tom Miles, Grove City | Jr | 9 | 192 | 113 | 58.8 | 9 | 1767 | 15 | 152.5 |
| Jason Gonnion, Wis.-La Crosse | Jr | 9 | 219 | 127 | 57.9 | 5 | 1904 | 17 | 152.0 |
| John Koz, Baldwin-Wallace | Jr | 10 | 293 | 182 | 62.1 | 6 | 2382 | 22 | 151.1 |
| Guy Simons, Coe | Jr | 9 | 169 | 86 | 50.8 | 10 | 1580 | 16 | 148.8 |
| Willie Reyna, La Verne | Sr | 9 | 275 | 176 | 64.0 | 13 | 2169 | 21 | 146.0 |
| Ed Smith, Ill. Benedictine | Jr | 10 | 320 | 184 | 57.5 | 16 | 2770 | 25 | 146.0 |
| Michael Bennett, San Diego | Sr | 10 | 181 | 102 | 56.3 | 4 | 1387 | 16 | 145.4 |
| Kenton Carr, Eureka | Sr | 10 | 203 | 119 | 58.6 | 10 | 1648 | 17 | 144.6 |
| Bob Strope, Wash. & Jeff. | Sr | 9 | 186 | 113 | 60.7 | 8 | 1474 | 14 | 143.5 |
| Paul Broderick, Trinity (Conn.) | Sr | 8 | 187 | 105 | 56.1 | 4 | 1411 | 16 | 143.5 |
| Tom Monken, Ill. Wesleyan | Sr | 9 | 257 | 139 | 54.0 | 8 | 2091 | 24 | 143.2 |
| John Smith, Defiance | Jr | 10 | 172 | 101 | 58.7 | 9 | 1500 | 11 | 142.6 |
| Shad Flynn, Central (Iowa) | Jr | 9 | 168 | 103 | 61.3 | 5 | 1263 | 12 | 142.1 |
| Scott Isphording, Hanover | Jr | 10 | 359 | 207 | 57.6 | 19 | 3098 | 24 | 141.7 |
| Wade Labatte, St. John's (Minn.) | Sr | 10 | 219 | 112 | 51.1 | 9 | 1746 | 21 | 141.5 |
| Mike Montico, Albion | Jr | 9 | 202 | 122 | 60.4 | 9 | 1613 | 14 | 141.5 |
| Chris Delmonaco, Gannon | Jr | 10 | 176 | 94 | 53.4 | 8 | 1429 | 15 | 140.6 |
| Kevin Magee, St. Francis (Pa.) | Jr | 10 | 249 | 143 | 57.4 | 13 | 1986 | 19 | 139.2 |

## TOTAL OFFENSE

| | 1992 Class | Games | Plays | Yards | Yds.PG |
|---|---|---|---|---|---|
| Jordan Poznick, Principia | Jr | 8 | 519 | 2747 | 343.4 |
| Steve Austin, Mass.-Boston | Sr | 9 | 466 | 3003 | 333.7 |
| Scott Isphording, Hanover | Jr | 10 | 484 | 3150 | 315.0 |
| Chip Chevalier, Swarthmore | Sr | 9 | 408 | 2564 | 284.9 |
| Leroy Williams, Upsala | So | 10 | 476 | 2822 | 282.2 |
| Ed Smith, Ill. Benedictine | Jr | 10 | 336 | 2736 | 273.6 |
| Jeff Roth, Upper Iowa | Sr | 10 | 439 | 2725 | 272.5 |
| Chris Ings, Wabash | Fr | 9 | 369 | 2446 | 271.8 |
| Jim Ballard, Mount Union | Jr | 10 | 322 | 2636 | 263.6 |
| Willie Reyna, La Verne | Sr | 9 | 331 | 2363 | 262.6 |
| Cliff Scott, Buffalo | So | 10 | 435 | 2546 | 254.6 |
| Tom Monken, Ill. Wesleyan | Sr | 9 | 321 | 2248 | 249.8 |
| Bill Meekings, Frank. & Marsh. | Jr | 10 | 462 | 2440 | 244.0 |
| Drew Robison, Rhodes | Sr | 10 | 474 | 2426 | 242.6 |
| John Koz, Baldwin-Wallace | Jr | 10 | 333 | 2388 | 238.8 |
| Adam Hacker, Cal Lutheran | So | 9 | 295 | 2074 | 230.4 |
| Kyle Farnham, Catholic | Sr | 9 | 328 | 2037 | 226.3 |
| Willie Rivera, Manchester | So | 10 | 373 | 2259 | 225.9 |
| Chad Hohne, Evansville | Sr | 7 | 277 | 1555 | 222.1 |
| Paul Laundry, Plymouth St. | Sr | 8 | 328 | 1765 | 220.6 |
| Jason Gonnion, Wis.-La Crosse | Jr | 9 | 299 | 1972 | 219.1 |
| Bill Hyland, Iona | Sr | 8 | 340 | 1732 | 216.5 |
| Brian Wild, Cortland St. | Sr | 10 | 361 | 2161 | 216.1 |
| Tom Miles, Grove City | Jr | 9 | 269 | 1929 | 214.3 |
| Aley Demarest, Georgetown | So | 8 | 307 | 1703 | 212.9 |

## RECEPTIONS PER GAME

| | 1992 Class | Games | Catches | Yards | TD | CLPG |
|---|---|---|---|---|---|---|
| Matt Newton, Principia | Jr | 8 | 98 | 1487 | 14 | 12.3 |
| Sean Munroe, Mass.-Boston | Sr | 9 | 95 | 1693 | 17 | 10.6 |
| Matt Hess, Ripon | Jr | 9 | 71 | 1208 | 16 | 7.9 |
| Brian Vandegrift, Rhodes | Jr | 10 | 78 | 881 | 4 | 7.8 |
| Rod Tranum, MIT | Sr | 8 | 61 | 745 | 5 | 7.6 |
| Josh Drake, Swarthmore | Jr | 9 | 67 | 1042 | 9 | 7.4 |
| Eric Green, Ill. Benedictine | Sr | 10 | 74 | 1189 | 12 | 7.4 |
| Chris Murphy, Georgetown | Sr | 10 | 74 | 904 | 13 | 7.4 |
| Kendall Griffin, Loras | Jr | 10 | 73 | 1138 | 7 | 7.3 |
| Ed Sullivan, Catholic | Sr | 10 | 73 | 1119 | 13 | 7.3 |
| Charlie Whalen, Salisbury St. | Jr | 9 | 63 | 547 | 4 | 7.0 |
| Rick Sems, Grove City | Sr | 9 | 62 | 1006 | 6 | 6.9 |
| Darren Stohlmann, Neb. Wesleyan | Sr | 9 | 61 | 708 | 11 | 6.8 |
| Hanz Hoag, Evansville | So | 9 | 61 | 536 | 4 | 6.8 |
| Tom Bradley, Mass.-Lowell | Sr | 9 | 59 | 893 | 5 | 6.6 |
| Demetri Patikas, Rhodes | Sr | 8 | 52 | 735 | 5 | 6.5 |
| Ted Brockman, Kenyon | Jr | 8 | 52 | 569 | 7 | 6.5 |

## RECEIVING YARDS PER GAME

| | 1992 Class | Games | Catches | Yards | TD | Yds.PG |
|---|---|---|---|---|---|---|
| Sean Munroe, Mass.-Boston | Sr | 9 | 95 | 1693 | 17 | 188.1 |
| Matt Newton, Principia | Jr | 8 | 98 | 1487 | 14 | 185.9 |
| Matt Hess, Ripon | Jr | 9 | 71 | 1208 | 16 | 134.2 |
| Eric Green, Ill. Benedictine | Sr | 10 | 74 | 1189 | 12 | 118.9 |
| Josh Drake, Swarthmore | Jr | 9 | 67 | 1042 | 9 | 115.8 |
| Kendall Griffin, Loras | Jr | 10 | 73 | 1138 | 7 | 113.8 |
| Ed Sullivan, Catholic | Sr | 10 | 73 | 1119 | 13 | 111.9 |
| Bob McMillen, Ill. Benedictine | Sr | 10 | 63 | 1119 | 10 | 111.9 |
| Rick Sems, Grove City | Sr | 9 | 62 | 1006 | 6 | 111.8 |
| Chris Bisaillon, Ill. Wesleyan | Sr | 9 | 54 | 979 | 12 | 108.8 |
| Doc Smith, Buffalo | Jr | 10 | 47 | 996 | 10 | 99.6 |
| Eric Stouch, Lebanon Valley | Sr | 10 | 62 | 993 | 11 | 99.3 |
| Tom Bradley, Mass.-Lowell | Sr | 9 | 59 | 893 | 5 | 99.2 |
| Chris Wiesehan, Wabash | Jr | 9 | 51 | 873 | 9 | 97.0 |
| Brian Glesing, Hanover | Sr | 10 | 57 | 952 | 10 | 95.2 |
| Rod Tranum, MIT | Sr | 8 | 61 | 745 | 5 | 93.1 |
| Matt Baker, Juniata | Jr | 10 | 52 | 927 | 9 | 92.7 |
| Demetri Patikas, Rhodes | Sr | 8 | 52 | 735 | 5 | 91.9 |
| Terence Brody, Kean | Sr | 10 | 44 | 907 | 8 | 90.7 |
| Chris Murphy, Georgetown | Sr | 10 | 74 | 904 | 13 | 90.4 |
| Eric Frink, Pace | Sr | 10 | 54 | 895 | 6 | 89.5 |
| Jason Janke, Wis.-La Crosse | Sr | 9 | 52 | 800 | 7 | 88.9 |
| Brian Vandegrift, Rhodes | Jr | 10 | 78 | 881 | 4 | 88.1 |
| Greg Lehrer, Heidelberg | Jr | 10 | 54 | 881 | 6 | 88.1 |
| Jason Keston, Upper Iowa | Sr | 10 | 64 | 880 | 11 | 88.0 |

## SCORING

| | 1992 Class | Games | TD | XP | FG | Points | Pts.PG |
|---|---|---|---|---|---|---|---|
| Chris Babirad, Wash. & Jeff. | Sr | 9 | 24 | 0 | 0 | 144 | 16.0 |
| Trent Nauholz, Simpson | Jr | 8 | 21 | 2 | 0 | 128 | 16.0 |
| Greg Novarro, Bentley | Sr | 10 | 25 | 0 | 0 | 150 | 15.0 |
| Carey Bender, Coe | Jr | 9 | 21 | 4 | 0 | 130 | 14.4 |
| Stanley Drayton, Allegheny | Sr | 9 | 20 | 0 | 0 | 120 | 13.3 |
| Thomas Lee, Anderson | So | 10 | 22 | 0 | 0 | 132 | 13.2 |
| Steve Harris, Carroll (Wis.) | So | 9 | 16 | 10 | 0 | 106 | 11.8 |
| Rob Johnson, Western Md. | Jr | 10 | 18 | 8 | 0 | 116 | 11.6 |
| Jeff Wittman, Ithaca | Sr | 10 | 19 | 0 | 0 | 114 | 11.4 |
| Sean Munroe, Mass.-Boston | Sr | 9 | 17 | 0 | 0 | 102 | 11.3 |
| Mike Muraca, Wesleyan | Sr | 8 | 15 | 0 | 0 | 90 | 11.3 |
| Eric LaPlaca, Bowdoin | Sr | 6 | 11 | 0 | 0 | 66 | 11.0 |
| Jim Gresko, Mount Union | Jr | 10 | 18 | 0 | 2 | 110 | 11.0 |
| Matt Hess, Ripon | Jr | 9 | 16 | 2 | 0 | 98 | 10.9 |
| Heath Butler, N'western (Wis.) | Jr | 7 | 12 | 0 | 4 | 76 | 10.9 |
| Von Cummings, Defiance | Sr | 10 | 18 | 0 | 0 | 108 | 10.8 |
| Matt Newton, Principia | Jr | 8 | 14 | 2 | 0 | 86 | 10.8 |
| Derek Tieman, Aurora | Sr | 9 | 16 | 0 | 0 | 96 | 10.7 |
| Kirk Matthieu, Maine Maritime | Jr | 9 | 16 | 0 | 0 | 96 | 10.7 |
| Jeremy Hurd, Rochester | Jr | 9 | 16 | 0 | 0 | 96 | 10.7 |

*1993 NCAA FOOTBALL*

# FIELD GOALS

| | 1992 Class | Games | FGA | FG | Pct. | FGPG |
|---|---|---|---|---|---|---|
| Todd Holthaus, Rose-Hulman | Jr | 10 | 19 | 13 | 68.4 | 1.30 |
| T. J. Robles, Catholic | So | 10 | 26 | 12 | 46.2 | 1.20 |
| Scott Rubinetti, Montclair St. | Fr | 9 | 14 | 10 | 71.4 | 1.11 |
| Tim Dreslinski, Mount Union | So | 10 | 17 | 11 | 64.7 | 1.10 |
| Joop De Groot, Blackburn | Sr | 9 | 12 | 9 | 75.0 | 1.00 |
| Chris DiMaggio, Alfred | Sr | 10 | 15 | 10 | 66.7 | 1.00 |
| Garret Skipper, Redlands | So | 9 | 14 | 9 | 64.3 | 1.00 |
| Todd Van Orden, Delaware Valley | So | 10 | 11 | 9 | 81.8 | .90 |
| George Paydock, Mercyhurst | So | 10 | 12 | 9 | 75.0 | .90 |
| Jim Cowper, Iona | Sr | 10 | 12 | 8 | 66.7 | .80 |
| Pat Bell, Carleton | Sr | 10 | 13 | 8 | 61.5 | .80 |
| Kevin Thomason, Ala.-Birmingham | Sr | 10 | 14 | 8 | 57.1 | .80 |
| Matt Wooden, Defiance | So | 10 | 14 | 8 | 57.1 | .80 |
| Anthony DeGuzman, Georgetown | Sr | 10 | 16 | 8 | 50.0 | .80 |
| Robby Robertson, Ky. Wesleyan | So | 10 | 18 | 8 | 44.4 | .80 |

# ALL-PURPOSE RUNNERS

| | 1992 Class | Games | Rush | Rec. | PR | KOR | Yards | Total Yds. PG |
|---|---|---|---|---|---|---|---|---|
| Kirk Matthieu, Maine Maritime | Jr | 9 | 1,733 | 91 | 56 | 308 | 2,188 | 243.11 |
| Eric Green, Ill. Benedictine | Sr | 10 | 17 | 1,189 | 247 | 755 | 2,208 | 220.80 |
| Matt Newton, Principia | Jr | 8 | 37 | 1,487 | 28 | 202 | 1,754 | 219.25 |
| Trent Nauholz, Simpson | Jr | 8 | 1,302 | 38 | 0 | 345 | 1,685 | 210.63 |
| Ryan Reynolds, Thomas More | So | 9 | 1,042 | 210 | 103 | 473 | 1,828 | 203.11 |
| Chris Babirad, Wash. & Jeff. | Sr | 9 | 1,589 | 161 | 17 | 11 | 1,778 | 197.56 |
| Rob Johnson, Western Md. | Jr | 10 | 1,560 | 78 | 0 | 334 | 1,972 | 197.20 |
| Carey Bender, Coe | Jr | 9 | 1,139 | 618 | 0 | 0 | 1,757 | 195.22 |
| Adam Henry, Carleton | Jr | 10 | 1,194 | 146 | 92 | 482 | 1,914 | 191.40 |
| Sean Munroe, Mass.-Boston | Sr | 9 | 0 | 1,693 | 0 | 0 | 1,693 | 188.11 |
| Dave Keenan, St. Olaf | Jr | 10 | 592 | 611 | 119 | 552 | 1,874 | 187.40 |
| Steve Harris, Carroll (Wis.) | So | 9 | 1,150 | 239 | 0 | 296 | 1,685 | 187.22 |
| Kevin Piecewicz, Mass. Maritime | Jr | 9 | 1,339 | 15 | 24 | 303 | 1,681 | 186.78 |
| Wes Stearns, Merchant Marine | Sr | 9 | 1,477 | 176 | 0 | 0 | 1,653 | 183.67 |
| Jody Stoldt, Muskingum | Jr | 10 | 1,243 | 259 | 0 | 273 | 1,775 | 177.50 |
| Derrick Harris, Eureka | Jr | 10 | 1,485 | 146 | 0 | 124 | 1,755 | 175.50 |
| Chad Blunt, Case Reserve | Sr | 10 | 947 | 235 | 41 | 499 | 1,722 | 172.20 |
| Chris Wiesehan, Wabash | Jr | 9 | 0 | 873 | 141 | 535 | 1,549 | 172.11 |
| Stanley Drayton, Allegheny | Sr | 9 | 1,255 | 225 | 0 | 21 | 1,501 | 166.78 |
| Mike Hall, Millikin | Sr | 9 | 122 | 543 | 134 | 698 | 1,497 | 166.33 |

# PUNT RETURNS

| (Min. 1.2 per game) | 1992 Class | Ret. | Yds. | Avg. | (Min. 1.2 per game) | 1992 Class | Ret. | Yds. | Avg. |
|---|---|---|---|---|---|---|---|---|---|
| Vic Moncato, FDU-Madison | So | 10 | 243 | 24.3 | Eric Green, Ill. Benedictine | Sr | 17 | 247 | 14.5 |
| Andrew Wind, Occidental | Jr | 23 | 430 | 18.7 | Ted Mason, Waynesburg | Jr | 12 | 169 | 14.1 |
| Rich Jinnette, Methodist | Sr | 15 | 274 | 18.3 | Paul Rogers, Rose-Hulman | So | 24 | 326 | 13.6 |
| Sammy Williams, Defiance | So | 23 | 417 | 18.1 | Scott Tumilty, Augustana (Ill.) | Jr | 15 | 203 | 13.5 |
| John Beutz, St. John's (Minn.) | Sr | 15 | 241 | 16.1 | Mike Tisdale, Blackburn | Jr | 17 | 226 | 13.3 |
| Todd Konick, Ithaca | Jr | 12 | 191 | 15.9 | Steve Anderson, Rowan | Fr | 27 | 357 | 13.2 |
| James Spriggs, Sewanee | Fr | 24 | 380 | 15.8 | Cedric Buchannon, Ala.-Birm. | So | 21 | 276 | 13.1 |
| Jimmy Carter, Frostburg St. | Sr | 21 | 315 | 15.0 | Chris Bisaillon, Ill. Wesleyan | Sr | 30 | 389 | 13.0 |
| Jim Fischer, Brockport St. | So | 17 | 255 | 15.0 | Greg Lehrer, Heidelberg | Jr | 14 | 170 | 12.1 |
| Doug Wrecke, Carroll (Wis.) | Jr | 12 | 177 | 14.8 | Mark Fink, Swarthmore | So | 15 | 181 | 12.1 |

# KICKOFF RETURNS

| (Min. 1.2 per game) | 1992 Class | Ret. | Yds. | Avg. | (Min. 1.2 per game) | 1992 Class | Ret. | Yds. | Avg. |
|---|---|---|---|---|---|---|---|---|---|
| Jason Martin, Coe | So | 11 | 438 | 39.8 | Linwood Jones, Ferrum | Sr | 20 | 556 | 27.8 |
| Rich Jinnette, Methodist | Sr | 15 | 514 | 34.3 | Steve Anderson, Rowan | Fr | 15 | 413 | 27.5 |
| Ryan Reynolds, Thomas More | So | 14 | 473 | 33.8 | Vince Richardson, Illinois Col. | Jr | 11 | 301 | 27.4 |
| Mike Hall, Millikin | Sr | 21 | 698 | 33.2 | Todd Konick, Ithaca | Jr | 12 | 328 | 27.3 |
| Chad Briley, Drake | Jr | 17 | 545 | 32.1 | Calvin Newman, MIT | Fr | 18 | 492 | 27.3 |
| Chris Wiesehan, Wabash | Jr | 18 | 535 | 29.7 | Charlie Whalen, Salisbury St. | Jr | 17 | 464 | 27.3 |
| George Day, Susquehanna | Jr | 13 | 384 | 29.5 | Kirk Rathjen, Central (Iowa) | Fr | 13 | 353 | 27.2 |
| Ronnie Howard, Bridgewater (Va.) | Jr | 14 | 411 | 29.4 | Tom Pastore, Mercyhurst | Sr | 14 | 378 | 27.0 |
| C. J. Brantner, Wis.-Eau Claire | So | 24 | 687 | 28.6 | Eric Green, Ill. Benedictine | Sr | 28 | 755 | 27.0 |
| Fred Miller, Thiel | Fr | 10 | 279 | 27.9 | Chad Klunder, Wartburg | So | 17 | 458 | 26.9 |

# PUNTING

| (Min. 3.6 per game) | 1992 Class | No. | Avg. | (Min. 3.6 per game) | 1992 Class | No. | Avg. |
|---|---|---|---|---|---|---|---|
| Robert Ray, San Diego | So | 44 | 42.3 | Mark Middleton, Emory & Henry | So | 39 | 40.0 |
| Joel Blackerby, Ferrum | Sr | 45 | 41.0 | Pete Pistone, Cal Lutheran | Sr | 43 | 39.7 |
| Bob Ehret, Wash. & Lee | Sr | 54 | 40.7 | Mitch Holloway, Millsaps | Jr | 60 | 39.6 |
| Andy Mahle, Otterbein | So | 59 | 40.1 | Don Siler, Earlham | So | 54 | 39.2 |
| Ryan Haley, John Carroll | Jr | 51 | 40.1 | Tim Schwartz, N'western (Wis.) | So | 35 | 39.1 |

*1992 Statistical Leaders*

| (Min. 3.6 per game) | 1992 Class | No. | Avg. | (Min. 3.6 per game) | 1992 Class | No. | Avg. |
|---|---|---|---|---|---|---|---|
| R. C. Freedman, Mercyhurst | Sr | 51 | 39.1 | Jim Wark, Widener | Jr | 57 | 38.8 |
| A. J. Fratoni, Kean | Sr | 54 | 39.1 | Joe Jeckel, Mount Union | So | 37 | 38.7 |
| Matt Anderson, Wis.-La Crosse | So | 37 | 38.9 | Josh Vitt, Colorado Col. | So | 55 | 38.4 |
| Jon Hardy, Wesley | Jr | 47 | 38.9 | Chris Maye, Ala.-Birmingham | So | 45 | 38.3 |
| Michael Manzella, LIU-C. W. Post | Sr | 53 | 38.8 | Jason Houchins, Olivet | Jr | 47 | 38.2 |

## INTERCEPTIONS

| | 1992 Class | G | No. | Yds. | Int.PG | | 1992 Class | G | No. | Yds. | Int.PG |
|---|---|---|---|---|---|---|---|---|---|---|---|
| Chris Butts, Worcester St. | Jr | 9 | 12 | 109 | 1.3 | Marty James, Simpson | Sr | 9 | 8 | 91 | .9 |
| Randy Simpson, Wis.-Stevens Point | So | 8 | 8 | 127 | 1.0 | Rob Taylor, Rensselaer | Fr | 9 | 8 | 73 | .9 |
| Andrew Ostrand, Carroll (Wis.) | Sr | 9 | 9 | 91 | 1.0 | Jeff Devanney, Trinity (Conn.) | Sr | 8 | 7 | 134 | .9 |
| Brent Sands, Cornell College | Sr | 10 | 9 | 163 | .9 | Todd Romboli, Tufts | Sr | 8 | 7 | 18 | .9 |
| Greg Thoma, St. John's (Minn.) | Jr | 10 | 9 | 149 | .9 | Rob Ferraro, Mass.-Boston | Sr | 7 | 6 | 56 | .9 |
| Curtis Turner, Hampden-Sydney | So | 10 | 9 | 109 | .9 | Sean McKenna, Tufts | Sr | 7 | 6 | 38 | .9 |
| Rickey Williams, Wash. & Jeff. | Jr | 9 | 8 | 119 | .9 | Ryan Davis, Ky. Wesleyan | So | 10 | 8 | 151 | .8 |
| | | | | | | Bob Thomas, Trenton St. | Sr | 10 | 8 | 10 | .8 |

# 1992 DIVISION III TEAM LEADERS

## TOTAL OFFENSE

| | Games | Plays | Yds. | Yds.PG | | Games | Plays | Yds. | Yds.PG |
|---|---|---|---|---|---|---|---|---|---|
| Mount Union | 10 | 752 | 4637 | 463.7 | Ithaca | 10 | 723 | 4199 | 419.9 |
| Upper Iowa | 10 | 763 | 4568 | 456.8 | Dayton | 10 | 709 | 4172 | 417.2 |
| Hanover | 10 | 731 | 4492 | 449.2 | Ohio Northern | 10 | 791 | 4167 | 416.7 |
| Wash. & Jeff. | 9 | 660 | 4004 | 444.9 | LIU-C. W. Post | 10 | 712 | 4155 | 415.5 |
| Ill. Wesleyan | 9 | 682 | 3997 | 444.1 | Central (Iowa) | 9 | 666 | 3696 | 410.7 |
| Ill. Benedictine | 10 | 674 | 4435 | 443.5 | Bentley | 10 | 793 | 4105 | 410.5 |
| Coe | 9 | 598 | 3970 | 441.1 | Merchant Marine | 9 | 670 | 3694 | 410.4 |
| Simpson | 9 | 755 | 3956 | 439.6 | Mass.-Boston | 9 | 689 | 3691 | 410.1 |
| Wabash | 9 | 673 | 3838 | 426.4 | Drake | 10 | 692 | 4098 | 409.8 |
| Wis.-La Crosse | 9 | 675 | 3813 | 423.7 | Ohio Wesleyan | 10 | 743 | 4081 | 408.1 |

## TOTAL DEFENSE

| | Games | Plays | Yds. | Yds.PG | | Games | Plays | Yds. | Yds.PG |
|---|---|---|---|---|---|---|---|---|---|
| Bentley | 10 | 592 | 1845 | 184.5 | Central (Iowa) | 9 | 591 | 1901 | 211.2 |
| Defiance | 10 | 614 | 1856 | 185.6 | John Carroll | 10 | 645 | 2145 | 214.5 |
| St. Peter's | 9 | 581 | 1681 | 186.8 | Rochester | 9 | 598 | 1940 | 215.6 |
| Bri'water (Mass.) | 10 | 609 | 1928 | 192.8 | Merchant Marine | 9 | 508 | 1946 | 216.2 |
| Dayton | 10 | 587 | 2013 | 201.3 | Wash. & Jeff. | 9 | 543 | 1987 | 220.8 |
| Stonehill | 9 | 556 | 1838 | 204.2 | Tufts | 8 | 543 | 1807 | 225.9 |
| St. John's (Minn.) | 10 | 691 | 2049 | 204.9 | Nichols | 9 | 590 | 2042 | 226.9 |
| Emory & Henry | 10 | 665 | 2052 | 205.2 | Frostburg St. | 10 | 599 | 2280 | 228.0 |
| Middlebury | 8 | 516 | 1667 | 208.4 | Augustana (Ill.) | 9 | 577 | 2073 | 230.3 |
| Lycoming | 9 | 573 | 1895 | 210.6 | Albion | 9 | 554 | 2081 | 231.2 |

## RUSHING OFFENSE

| | Games | Car. | Yds. | Yds.PG | | Games | Car. | Yds. | Yds.PG |
|---|---|---|---|---|---|---|---|---|---|
| Wis.-River Falls | 9 | 516 | 2840 | 315.6 | Rochester | 9 | 593 | 2497 | 277.4 |
| Chicago | 10 | 560 | 3083 | 308.3 | Dickinson | 10 | 586 | 2756 | 275.6 |
| Ithaca | 10 | 561 | 3065 | 306.5 | Wm. Paterson | 10 | 548 | 2622 | 262.2 |
| Simpson | 9 | 558 | 2622 | 291.3 | Dayton | 10 | 526 | 2567 | 256.7 |
| Occidental | 9 | 485 | 2619 | 291.0 | Concordia-M'head | 10 | 596 | 2553 | 255.3 |
| Augustana (Ill.) | 9 | 534 | 2613 | 290.3 | Emory & Henry | 10 | 550 | 2523 | 252.3 |
| Redlands | 9 | 470 | 2603 | 289.2 | John Carroll | 10 | 535 | 2511 | 251.1 |
| Bentley | 10 | 617 | 2892 | 289.2 | Cornell College | 10 | 537 | 2497 | 249.7 |
| Aurora | 9 | 495 | 2600 | 288.9 | Gettysburg | 10 | 542 | 2481 | 248.1 |
| Ohio Wesleyan | 10 | 552 | 2831 | 283.1 | Mass. Maritime | 9 | 453 | 2177 | 241.9 |

## RUSHING DEFENSE

| | Games | Car. | Yds. | Yds.PG | | Games | Car. | Yds. | Yds.PG |
|---|---|---|---|---|---|---|---|---|---|
| Bri'water (Mass.) | 10 | 343 | 432 | 43.2 | Dickinson | 10 | 352 | 799 | 79.9 |
| Defiance | 10 | 373 | 594 | 59.4 | Wm. Paterson | 10 | 341 | 812 | 81.2 |
| Merchant Marine | 9 | 260 | 582 | 64.7 | Ohio Northern | 10 | 371 | 817 | 81.7 |
| Wis.-River Falls | 9 | 300 | 587 | 65.2 | Rowan | 10 | 346 | 829 | 82.9 |
| Bentley | 10 | 350 | 669 | 66.9 | Susquehanna | 10 | 389 | 847 | 84.7 |
| Wagner | 10 | 311 | 703 | 70.3 | Middlebury | 8 | 315 | 707 | 88.4 |
| Wabash | 9 | 303 | 633 | 70.3 | Mount Union | 10 | 309 | 891 | 89.1 |
| Central (Iowa) | 9 | 340 | 658 | 73.1 | Albion | 9 | 334 | 831 | 92.3 |
| Wittenberg | 9 | 332 | 666 | 74.0 | Rose-Hulman | 10 | 349 | 930 | 93.0 |
| Lycoming | 9 | 328 | 683 | 75.9 | Dayton | 10 | 376 | 930 | 93.0 |
| DePauw | 10 | 369 | 794 | 79.4 | | | | | |

## SCORING OFFENSE

| | Games | TD | XP | 2XP | DXP | FG | Saf. | Pts. | Avg. |
|---|---|---|---|---|---|---|---|---|---|
| Coe | 9 | 59 | 43 | 4 | 1 | 3 | 1 | 418 | 46.4 |
| Central (Iowa) | 9 | 52 | 33 | 2 | 0 | 7 | 4 | 378 | 42.0 |
| Wash. & Jeff. | 9 | 53 | 47 | 1 | 0 | 2 | 0 | 373 | 41.4 |
| Dayton | 10 | 57 | 48 | 0 | 0 | 6 | 0 | 408 | 40.8 |
| Ithaca | 10 | 54 | 48 | 1 | 1 | 7 | 1 | 399 | 39.9 |
| Allegheny | 10 | 54 | 45 | 0 | 0 | 5 | 0 | 384 | 38.4 |
| St. John's (Minn.) | 10 | 54 | 31 | 7 | 0 | 1 | 1 | 374 | 37.4 |
| Bentley | 10 | 51 | 37 | 2 | 0 | 6 | 1 | 367 | 36.7 |
| Mount Union | 10 | 48 | 40 | 2 | 0 | 11 | 0 | 365 | 36.5 |
| John Carroll | 10 | 49 | 45 | 1 | 0 | 5 | 1 | 358 | 35.8 |
| Ill. Wesleyan | 9 | 43 | 35 | 5 | 1 | 4 | 0 | 317 | 35.2 |
| Baldwin-Wallace | 10 | 50 | 42 | 1 | 0 | 1 | 0 | 347 | 34.7 |
| Defiance | 10 | 46 | 38 | 2 | 0 | 8 | 1 | 344 | 34.4 |
| Cornell College | 10 | 49 | 39 | 1 | 0 | 1 | 2 | 342 | 34.2 |
| Wis.-River Falls | 9 | 42 | 29 | 6 | 0 | 4 | 0 | 305 | 33.9 |
| Drake | 10 | 44 | 35 | 4 | 0 | 9 | 0 | 334 | 33.4 |
| Rowan | 10 | 46 | 37 | 0 | 0 | 6 | 1 | 333 | 33.3 |
| Worcester Tech | 10 | 45 | 36 | 2 | 0 | 6 | 1 | 330 | 33.0 |
| Upper Iowa | 10 | 47 | 30 | 4 | 0 | 2 | 0 | 326 | 32.6 |
| Carnegie Mellon | 9 | 40 | 33 | 3 | 0 | 2 | 2 | 289 | 32.1 |

## SCORING DEFENSE

| | Games | TD | XP | 2XP | DXP | FG | Saf. | Pts. | Avg. |
|---|---|---|---|---|---|---|---|---|---|
| Dayton | 10 | 9 | 3 | 2 | 0 | 2 | 0 | 67 | 6.7 |
| Dickinson | 10 | 9 | 7 | 0 | 0 | 5 | 0 | 76 | 7.6 |
| Emory & Henry | 10 | 11 | 7 | 0 | 0 | 1 | 0 | 76 | 7.6 |
| St. John's (Minn.) | 10 | 11 | 6 | 3 | 0 | 1 | 0 | 81 | 8.1 |
| Aurora | 9 | 11 | 5 | 1 | 0 | 1 | 0 | 76 | 8.4 |
| Wittenberg | 9 | 10 | 5 | 1 | 0 | 5 | 0 | 82 | 9.1 |
| Defiance | 10 | 13 | 10 | 1 | 0 | 2 | 0 | 96 | 9.6 |
| Mass.-Dartmouth | 9 | 12 | 8 | 0 | 0 | 3 | 0 | 89 | 9.9 |
| Mount Union | 10 | 15 | 9 | 0 | 0 | 0 | 0 | 99 | 9.9 |
| Bentley | 10 | 15 | 9 | 1 | 0 | 0 | 0 | 101 | 10.1 |
| St. Peter's | 9 | 10 | 3 | 1 | 0 | 9 | 0 | 92 | 10.2 |
| John Carroll | 10 | 14 | 9 | 0 | 0 | 4 | 0 | 105 | 10.5 |
| Bri'water (Mass.) | 10 | 16 | 9 | 0 | 0 | 1 | 0 | 108 | 10.8 |
| Merchant Marine | 9 | 13 | 8 | 3 | 0 | 2 | 0 | 98 | 10.9 |
| Tufts | 8 | 13 | 8 | 0 | 0 | 1 | 0 | 89 | 11.1 |
| Central (Iowa) | 9 | 14 | 12 | 1 | 0 | 1 | 0 | 101 | 11.2 |
| Rochester | 9 | 14 | 9 | 1 | 0 | 2 | 0 | 101 | 11.2 |
| Wash. & Jeff. | 9 | 13 | 7 | 1 | 0 | 5 | 0 | 102 | 11.3 |
| Nichols | 9 | 15 | 9 | 1 | 0 | 1 | 0 | 104 | 11.6 |
| Frostburg St. | 10 | 15 | 9 | 2 | 0 | 4 | 1 | 117 | 11.7 |

## PASSING OFFENSE

| | Games | Att. | Cmp. | Pct. | Int. | Yards | Yds.PG |
|---|---|---|---|---|---|---|---|
| Mass.-Boston | 9 | 402 | 184 | 45.8 | 27 | 3033 | 337.0 |
| Principia | 8 | 454 | 242 | 53.3 | 13 | 2633 | 329.1 |
| Hanover | 10 | 375 | 212 | 56.5 | 20 | 3181 | 318.1 |
| Upper Iowa | 10 | 399 | 243 | 60.9 | 13 | 2879 | 287.9 |
| Mount Union | 10 | 323 | 205 | 63.5 | 8 | 2875 | 287.5 |
| Ill. Benedictine | 10 | 333 | 191 | 57.4 | 17 | 2854 | 285.4 |
| Iona | 10 | 445 | 228 | 51.2 | 20 | 2826 | 282.6 |
| LIU-C. W. Post | 10 | 393 | 201 | 51.1 | 21 | 2748 | 274.8 |
| Swarthmore | 9 | 292 | 160 | 54.8 | 7 | 2371 | 263.4 |
| Franklin | 10 | 481 | 235 | 48.9 | 22 | 2621 | 262.1 |
| Rhodes | 10 | 422 | 221 | 52.4 | 12 | 2509 | 250.9 |
| Upsala | 10 | 389 | 178 | 45.8 | 20 | 2481 | 248.1 |
| Coe | 9 | 232 | 122 | 52.6 | 14 | 2221 | 246.8 |
| Baldwin-Wallace | 10 | 317 | 189 | 59.6 | 8 | 2429 | 242.9 |
| La Verne | 9 | 283 | 180 | 63.6 | 14 | 2181 | 242.3 |
| DePauw | 10 | 341 | 168 | 49.3 | 17 | 2384 | 238.4 |
| Cal Lutheran | 9 | 282 | 173 | 61.3 | 9 | 2140 | 237.8 |
| Pace | 10 | 492 | 187 | 38.0 | 27 | 2348 | 234.8 |
| Ill. Wesleyan | 9 | 263 | 141 | 53.6 | 9 | 2113 | 234.8 |
| Wabash | 9 | 272 | 150 | 55.1 | 13 | 2095 | 232.8 |

## PASS-EFFICIENCY DEFENSE

| | Games | Att. | Cmp. | Pct. | Int. | Yards | TD | Rating Points |
|---|---|---|---|---|---|---|---|---|
| St. Peter's | 9 | 223 | 83 | 37.2 | 21 | 766 | 3 | 51.7 |
| Mass.-Boston | 9 | 194 | 74 | 38.1 | 20 | 899 | 4 | 63.2 |
| Emory & Henry | 10 | 254 | 96 | 37.8 | 20 | 1076 | 5 | 64.2 |
| Rochester | 9 | 230 | 82 | 35.6 | 15 | 944 | 5 | 64.2 |
| Cornell College | 10 | 235 | 94 | 40.0 | 21 | 929 | 8 | 66.5 |

| | Games | Att. | Cmp. | Pct. | Int. | Yards | TD | Rating Points |
|---|---|---|---|---|---|---|---|---|
| St. John's (Minn.) | 10 | 247 | 95 | 38.4 | 22 | 1156 | 5 | 66.6 |
| Nichols | 9 | 197 | 87 | 44.1 | 15 | 836 | 5 | 72.9 |
| Aurora | 9 | 205 | 81 | 39.5 | 13 | 995 | 4 | 74.0 |
| Frostburg St. | 10 | 215 | 89 | 41.4 | 12 | 1005 | 3 | 74.1 |
| Wash. & Jeff. | 9 | 200 | 82 | 41.0 | 20 | 993 | 7 | 74.3 |
| Tufts | 8 | 183 | 78 | 42.6 | 20 | 1010 | 4 | 74.4 |
| Mount Union | 10 | 340 | 160 | 47.0 | 33 | 1564 | 9 | 75.0 |
| Dickinson | 10 | 318 | 147 | 46.2 | 28 | 1568 | 5 | 75.2 |
| Defiance | 10 | 241 | 98 | 40.6 | 19 | 1262 | 5 | 75.8 |
| Bentley | 10 | 242 | 94 | 38.8 | 19 | 1176 | 9 | 76.2 |
| Concordia-M'head | 10 | 277 | 106 | 38.2 | 19 | 1389 | 9 | 77.4 |
| Rensselaer | 9 | 243 | 103 | 42.3 | 22 | 1262 | 9 | 77.4 |
| Coe | 9 | 272 | 105 | 38.6 | 22 | 1372 | 11 | 78.1 |
| Eureka | 10 | 209 | 87 | 41.6 | 11 | 977 | 5 | 78.2 |
| Middlebury | 8 | 201 | 89 | 44.2 | 17 | 960 | 7 | 79.0 |

## NET PUNTING

| | Punts | Avg. | No. Ret. | Yds. Ret. | Net Avg. | | Punts | Avg. | No. Ret. | Yds. Ret. | Net Avg. |
|---|---|---|---|---|---|---|---|---|---|---|---|
| San Diego | 44 | 42.27 | 24 | 136 | 39.18 | Widener | 59 | 38.23 | 29 | 129 | 36.05 |
| Redlands | 28 | 40.75 | 10 | 49 | 39.00 | Allegheny | 51 | 37.11 | 16 | 64 | 35.86 |
| John Carroll | 51 | 40.05 | 22 | 150 | 37.11 | Mount Union | 38 | 38.18 | 18 | 90 | 35.81 |
| N'western (Wis.) | 42 | 37.83 | 12 | 34 | 37.02 | Cal Lutheran | 44 | 38.84 | 26 | 141 | 35.63 |
| Central (Iowa) | 32 | 38.81 | 13 | 63 | 36.84 | Dayton | 36 | 37.16 | 11 | 60 | 35.50 |
| Ithaca | 25 | 37.92 | 6 | 29 | 36.76 | Rowan | 37 | 37.45 | 17 | 77 | 35.37 |
| LIU-C. W. Post | 53 | 38.84 | 24 | 119 | 36.60 | Earlham | 54 | 39.18 | 23 | 216 | 35.18 |
| Wash. & Lee | 54 | 40.72 | 30 | 230 | 36.46 | Baldwin-Wallace | 53 | 36.98 | 21 | 96 | 35.16 |
| Wis.-Stout | 44 | 38.20 | 14 | 77 | 36.45 | Mercyhurst | 51 | 39.09 | 30 | 210 | 34.98 |
| Emory & Henry | 54 | 38.12 | 14 | 100 | 36.27 | Wis.-La Crosse | 38 | 37.94 | 18 | 122 | 34.73 |

## PUNT RETURNS

| | Games | No. | Yds. | TD | Avg. | | Games | No. | Yds. | TD | Avg. |
|---|---|---|---|---|---|---|---|---|---|---|---|
| Occidental | 9 | 23 | 430 | 2 | 18.69 | Rose-Hulman | 10 | 25 | 326 | 0 | 13.04 |
| Methodist | 10 | 15 | 274 | 2 | 18.26 | Wabash | 9 | 12 | 153 | 1 | 12.75 |
| Millikin | 9 | 13 | 213 | 1 | 16.38 | Ill. Wesleyan | 9 | 32 | 394 | 1 | 12.31 |
| Sewanee | 9 | 24 | 380 | 2 | 15.83 | Rowan | 10 | 36 | 438 | 0 | 12.16 |
| William Penn | 10 | 14 | 214 | 1 | 15.28 | Frostburg St. | 10 | 42 | 484 | 2 | 11.52 |
| Defiance | 10 | 38 | 573 | 2 | 15.07 | St. John's (Minn.) | 10 | 41 | 470 | 1 | 11.46 |
| Brockport St. | 10 | 20 | 296 | 3 | 14.80 | N'western (Wis.) | 8 | 14 | 159 | 0 | 11.35 |
| Dayton | 10 | 36 | 531 | 1 | 14.75 | Concordia (Ill.) | 10 | 26 | 295 | 1 | 11.34 |
| Ill. Benedictine | 10 | 18 | 254 | 0 | 14.11 | Ala.-Birmingham | 10 | 36 | 408 | 3 | 11.33 |
| Blackburn | 9 | 17 | 226 | 1 | 13.29 | Augustana (Ill.) | 9 | 41 | 462 | 0 | 11.26 |

## KICKOFF RETURNS

| | Games | No. | Yds. | TD | Avg. | | Games | No. | Yds. | TD | Avg. |
|---|---|---|---|---|---|---|---|---|---|---|---|
| Thomas More | 10 | 26 | 719 | 1 | 27.65 | Wabash | 9 | 32 | 763 | 0 | 23.84 |
| Merchant Marine | 9 | 19 | 508 | 2 | 26.73 | Susquehanna | 10 | 33 | 783 | 1 | 23.72 |
| Millikin | 9 | 33 | 873 | 3 | 26.45 | Central (Iowa) | 9 | 26 | 615 | 0 | 23.65 |
| Methodist | 10 | 34 | 885 | 1 | 26.02 | Wis.-Eau Claire | 9 | 40 | 933 | 0 | 23.32 |
| Carroll (Wis.) | 9 | 21 | 535 | 2 | 25.47 | St. John's (Minn.) | 10 | 21 | 487 | 0 | 23.19 |
| Aurora | 9 | 19 | 480 | 2 | 25.26 | Rensselaer | 9 | 26 | 591 | 1 | 22.73 |
| Colorado Col. | 9 | 24 | 604 | 0 | 25.16 | Sewanee | 9 | 30 | 679 | 0 | 22.63 |
| Coe | 9 | 28 | 678 | 1 | 24.21 | Anderson | 10 | 41 | 927 | 1 | 22.60 |
| Drake | 10 | 34 | 823 | 2 | 24.20 | Rowan | 10 | 26 | 587 | 0 | 22.57 |
| Wesley | 10 | 35 | 836 | 1 | 23.88 | Mercyhurst | 10 | 31 | 698 | 1 | 22.51 |

## TURNOVER MARGIN

| | TURNOVERS GAINED | | | TURNOVERS LOST | | | Margin/ Game |
|---|---|---|---|---|---|---|---|
| | Fum. | Int. | Total | Fum. | Int. | Total | |
| Illinois Col. | 23 | 11 | 34 | 6 | 6 | 12 | 2.44 |
| Buffalo St. | 15 | 23 | 38 | 10 | 7 | 17 | 2.33 |
| Baldwin-Wallace | 14 | 24 | 38 | 7 | 8 | 15 | 2.30 |
| Trinity (Conn.) | 8 | 22 | 30 | 9 | 4 | 13 | 2.12 |
| Mount Union | 5 | 33 | 38 | 9 | 8 | 17 | 2.10 |
| Dayton | 11 | 21 | 32 | 7 | 5 | 12 | 2.00 |
| Dickinson | 13 | 28 | 41 | 14 | 7 | 21 | 2.00 |
| Thomas More | 15 | 13 | 28 | 6 | 3 | 9 | 1.90 |
| Luther | 17 | 15 | 32 | 6 | 8 | 14 | 1.80 |
| San Diego | 16 | 13 | 29 | 7 | 4 | 11 | 1.80 |
| Wesley | 17 | 21 | 38 | 11 | 9 | 20 | 1.80 |
| Adrian | 17 | 13 | 30 | 10 | 4 | 14 | 1.77 |
| Wittenberg | 16 | 10 | 26 | 6 | 4 | 10 | 1.77 |
| Carnegie Mellon | 12 | 17 | 29 | 7 | 7 | 14 | 1.66 |
| Ohio Wesleyan | 15 | 15 | 30 | 10 | 5 | 15 | 1.50 |

| | TURNOVERS GAINED | | | TURNOVERS LOST | | | Margin/ |
|---|---|---|---|---|---|---|---|
| | Fum. | Int. | Total | Fum. | Int. | Total | Game |
| Rowan | 13 | 18 | 31 | 6 | 10 | 16 | 1.50 |
| III. Wesleyan | 12 | 26 | 38 | 16 | 9 | 25 | 1.44 |
| Lycoming | 11 | 20 | 31 | 7 | 11 | 18 | 1.44 |
| Drake | 19 | 16 | 35 | 10 | 11 | 21 | 1.40 |
| Ripon | 18 | 16 | 34 | 13 | 9 | 22 | 1.33 |
| Sewanee | 14 | 14 | 28 | 6 | 10 | 16 | 1.33 |

# LONGEST DIVISION III PLAYS OF 1992

## RUSHING

| Player, Team (Opponent) | Yards |
|---|---|
| Arnie Boigner, Ohio Northern (Muskingum) | 99 |
| Rich Vargas, Wis.-Stout (Wis.-Oshkosh) | 98 |
| John Rivers, Coast Guard (Plymouth St.) | 97 |
| Marty Alger, Augsburg (St. Thomas, Minn.) | 95 |
| Craig Woodard, Mercyhurst (Canisius) | 94 |
| Frank Baker, Chicago (Lawrence) | 92 |
| Thomas Lee, Anderson (Franklin) | 91 |
| Howard Lindsay, Wesleyan (Bates) | 89 |
| Brian Willis, Ohio Wesleyan (Wilmington, Ohio) | 88 |
| Dave Allard, Trinity, Conn. (Bates) | 87 |
| Don Dawson, Ripon (N'western, Minn.) | 86 |
| Gary Smiddy, Bluffton (Wilmington, Ohio) | 85 |
| Eric LaPlaca, Bowdoin (Trinity, Conn.) | 85 |
| Ben Alston, Albany, N.Y. (St. Lawrence) | 83 |
| Mike Muraca, Wesleyan (Bates) | 82 |

## PASSING

| Passer-Receiver, Team (Opponent) | Yards |
|---|---|
| Marc Klausner-Eric Frink, Pace (Hobart) | 99 |
| Erik Holm-Sean Armbruster, Fitchburg St. (Framingham St.) | 96 |
| Alix Sgouros-Rod Tranum, MIT (Westfield St.) | 96 |
| John Smith-Sammy Williams, Defiance (Kalamazoo) | 95 |
| Charlie Vannieuwenhoven-Aaron Robinson, N'western, Wis. (Maranatha) | 95 |
| Pete Kutches-Jeff Kaeppe, Augsburg (St. Olaf) | 90 |
| Frank Plefka-Vic Moncato, FDU-Madison (St. John's, N.Y.) | 90 |
| Brian Ganser-Mike Hall, Millikin (Elmhurst) | 89 |
| Derek Scavnicky-Brian Dickman, Bethany, W. Va. (Thiel) | 88 |
| Michael Ferraro-Glen Fields, LIU-C. W. Post (Alfred) | 88 |
| Derek Gagnon-Todd Greenfield, Mass. Maritime (Bri'water, Mass.) | 87 |
| Guy Simons-Darrell Gordon, Coe (William Penn) | 86 |
| Wade Kurzinger-Matt Baker, Juniata (Lycoming) | 85 |
| Chris Hare-Matt Hess, Ripon (Knox) | 85 |
| Len Annetta-Shawn Powell, Salisbury St. (Frostburg St.) | 85 |

## INTERCEPTION RETURNS

| Player, Team (Opponent) | Yards |
|---|---|
| Scott Schuster, Stony Brook (Pace) | 100 |
| Aaron Peterson, Coe (William Penn) | 99 |
| Robert Pitts, Montclair St. (Ithaca) | 99 |
| Dan Thobe, Dayton (Mt. St. Joseph) | 93 |
| Rich Kozlowski, III. Wesleyan (Carthage) | 90 |

## PUNT RETURNS

| Player, Team (Opponent) | Yards |
|---|---|
| Brian Sarver, William Penn (Dubuque) | 95 |
| Vic Moncato, FDU-Madison (Iona) | 94 |
| Jimmy Carter, Frostburg St. (Bridgewater, Va.) | 93 |
| James Spriggs, Sewanee (Ky. Wesleyan) | 86 |
| Cedric Buchannon, Ala.-Birmingham (Lindenwood) | 84 |
| Chris Wiesehan, Wabash (Anderson) | 80 |

## KICKOFF RETURNS

| Player, Team (Opponent) | Yards |
|---|---|
| Eric Green, Ill. Benedictine (Carthage) | 100 |
| Craig Stewart, La Verne (Redlands) | 98 |
| Ronnie Howard, Bridgewater, Va. (Emory & Henry) | 97 |
| Fred Miller, Thiel (Gannon) | 95 |
| Fran DeFalco, Assumption (Siena) | 94 |
| Chad Briley, Drake (Simpson) | 94 |
| Steve Anderson, Rowan (Salisbury St.) | 94 |
| Sunni Muqqddim, Wis.-Whitewater (Wis.-Stout) | 94 |
| Chad Briley, Drake (Aurora) | 93 |
| Calvin Newman, MIT (Mass.-Boston) | 92 |
| Mike Hall, Millikin (Ill. Benedictine) | 92 |
| Brian Simpson, Merchant Marine (Muhlenberg) | 91 |
| Mike Hall, Millikin (Carthage) | 91 |

## FIELD GOALS

| Player, Team (Opponent) | Yards |
|---|---|
| Scott Rubinetti, Montclair St. (Ramapo) | 50 |

*No other player with a successful field goal of at least 50 yards.*

## PUNTS

| Player, Team (Opponent) | Yards |
|---|---|
| Geoff Hansen, Gust. Adolphus (Augustana, S.D.) | 83 |
| Mike Gabrielson, Wartburg (Simpson) | 79 |
| Tim Gargasz, Wooster (Oberlin) | 73 |
| Kris Theriault, Fitchburg St. (Bri'water, Mass.) | 72 |
| Greg Martin, Hobart (St. Lawrence) | 72 |
| Marty Thompson, Trinity, Tex. (Austin) | 72 |
| Bob Ehret, Wash. & Lee (Guilford) | 72 |
| Kris Theriault, Fitchburg St. (Mass. Martime) | 71 |
| Erick Renshaw, Loras (Simpson) | 71 |
| Mitch Holloway, Millsaps (Rhodes) | 71 |
| Josh Vitt, Colorado Col. (Washington, Mo.) | 70 |
| Chris Gabriel, Curry (Stonehill) | 70 |
| Marty Engel, St. Thomas, Minn. (Augsburg) | 70 |
| Robert Ray, San Diego (La Verne) | 70 |

# 1992 CONFERENCE STANDINGS

*Idaho running back Sherriden May scores one of the 25 touchdowns that earned him the 1992 Division I-AA scoring title and helped the Vandals finish 9-2 and claim their fifth Big Sky Conference title in the past eight years.*

# 1992 CONFERENCE STANDINGS

### (Full-Season Records Do Not Include Postseason Play)

## DIVISION I-A

### ATLANTIC COAST CONFERENCE

| Team | CONFERENCE | | | | FULL SEASON | | | |
|---|---|---|---|---|---|---|---|---|
| | W | L | T | Pct. | W | L | T | Pct. |
| Florida St.......... | 8 | 0 | 0 | 1.000 | 10 | 1 | 0 | .909 |
| North Caro. St...... | 6 | 2 | 0 | .750 | 9 | 2 | 1 | .792 |
| North Caro........ | 5 | 3 | 0 | .625 | 8 | 3 | 0 | .727 |
| Virginia*......... | 4 | 4 | 0 | .500 | 7 | 4 | 0 | .636 |
| Wake Forest*...... | 4 | 4 | 0 | .500 | 7 | 4 | 0 | .636 |
| Georgia Tech....... | 4 | 4 | 0 | .500 | 5 | 6 | 0 | .454 |
| Clemson.......... | 3 | 5 | 0 | .375 | 5 | 6 | 0 | .454 |
| Maryland.......... | 2 | 6 | 0 | .250 | 3 | 8 | 0 | .273 |
| Duke............. | 0 | 8 | 0 | .000 | 2 | 9 | 0 | .182 |

* Virginia defeated Wake Forest, 31-17, on October 3.

**Bowl Games (3-1-0):** Florida St. (defeated Nebraska, 27-14, in Orange); North Caro. (defeated Mississippi St., 21-17, in Peach); North Caro. St. (lost to Florida, 27-10, in Gator); Wake Forest (defeated Oregon, 39-35, in Independence)

### BIG EAST CONFERENCE

| Team | CONFERENCE | | | | FULL SEASON | | | |
|---|---|---|---|---|---|---|---|---|
| | W | L | T | Pct. | W | L | T | Pct. |
| Miami (Fla.)....... | 4 | 0 | 0 | 1.000 | 11 | 0 | 0 | 1.000 |
| Syracuse.......... | 6 | 1 | 0 | .857 | 9 | 2 | 0 | .818 |
| Rutgers........... | 4 | 2 | 0 | .667 | 7 | 4 | 0 | .636 |
| Boston College..... | 2 | 1 | 1 | .625 | 8 | 2 | 1 | .773 |
| West Va........... | 2 | 3 | 1 | .417 | 5 | 4 | 2 | .545 |
| Pittsburgh........ | 1 | 3 | 0 | .250 | 3 | 9 | 0 | .250 |
| Virginia Tech...... | 1 | 4 | 0 | .200 | 2 | 8 | 1 | .227 |
| Temple........... | 0 | 6 | 0 | .000 | 1 | 10 | 0 | .091 |

As in 1991, the Big East Conference football champion was the team ranked the highest in the CNN/USA Today College Football Poll. Selected Division I-A football coaches participate in the poll. Beginning in 1993, the Big East will have a full round-robin schedule to determine its champion.

**Bowl Games (1-2-0):** Boston College (lost to Tennessee, 38-23, in Hall of Fame); Miami (Fla.) (lost to Alabama, 34-13, in Sugar); Syracuse (defeated Colorado, 26-22, in Fiesta)

### BIG EIGHT CONFERENCE

| Team | CONFERENCE | | | | FULL SEASON | | | |
|---|---|---|---|---|---|---|---|---|
| | W | L | T | Pct. | W | L | T | Pct. |
| Nebraska.......... | 6 | 1 | 0 | .857 | 9 | 2 | 0 | .818 |
| Colorado.......... | 5 | 1 | 1 | .786 | 9 | 1 | 1 | .864 |
| Kansas........... | 4 | 3 | 0 | .571 | 7 | 4 | 0 | .636 |
| Oklahoma........ | 3 | 2 | 2 | .571 | 5 | 4 | 2 | .545 |
| Oklahoma St....... | 2 | 4 | 1 | .357 | 4 | 6 | 1 | .409 |
| Kansas St.......... | 2 | 5 | 0 | .286 | 5 | 6 | 0 | .455 |
| Iowa St........... | 2 | 5 | 0 | .286 | 4 | 7 | 0 | .364 |
| Missouri.......... | 2 | 5 | 0 | .286 | 3 | 8 | 0 | .273 |

**Bowl Games (1-2-0):** Colorado (lost to Syracuse, 26-22, in Fiesta); Kansas (defeated Brigham Young, 23-20, in Aloha); Nebraska (lost to Florida St., 27-14, in Orange)

### BIG TEN CONFERENCE

| Team | CONFERENCE | | | | FULL SEASON | | | |
|---|---|---|---|---|---|---|---|---|
| | W | L | T | Pct. | W | L | T | Pct. |
| Michigan.......... | 6 | 0 | 2 | .875 | 8 | 0 | 3 | .864 |
| Ohio St........... | 5 | 2 | 1 | .688 | 8 | 2 | 1 | .773 |
| Michigan St....... | 5 | 3 | 0 | .625 | 5 | 6 | 0 | .455 |
| Illinois........... | 4 | 3 | 1 | .563 | 6 | 4 | 1 | .591 |
| Iowa............ | 4 | 4 | 0 | .500 | 5 | 7 | 0 | .417 |
| Indiana*.......... | 3 | 5 | 0 | .375 | 5 | 6 | 0 | .455 |
| Wisconsin*........ | 3 | 5 | 0 | .375 | 5 | 6 | 0 | .455 |
| Purdue........... | 3 | 5 | 0 | .375 | 4 | 7 | 0 | .364 |
| Northwestern...... | 3 | 5 | 0 | .375 | 3 | 8 | 0 | .273 |
| Minnesota........ | 2 | 6 | 0 | .250 | 2 | 9 | 0 | .182 |

* Indiana defeated Wisconsin, 10-3, on October 24.

**Bowl Games (1-2-0):** Illinois (lost to Hawaii, 27-17, in Holiday); Michigan (defeated Washington, 38-31, in Rose); Ohio St. (lost to Georgia, 21-14, in Florida Citrus)

### BIG WEST CONFERENCE

| Team | CONFERENCE | | | | FULL SEASON | | | |
|---|---|---|---|---|---|---|---|---|
| | W | L | T | Pct. | W | L | T | Pct. |
| Nevada........... | 5 | 1 | 0 | .833 | 7 | 4 | 0 | .636 |
| San Jose St........ | 4 | 2 | 0 | .667 | 7 | 4 | 0 | .636 |
| Utah St............ | 4 | 2 | 0 | .667 | 5 | 6 | 0 | .455 |
| New Mexico St.*.... | 3 | 3 | 0 | .500 | 6 | 5 | 0 | .545 |
| Nev.-Las Vegas*.... | 3 | 3 | 0 | .500 | 6 | 5 | 0 | .545 |
| Pacific (Cal.)....... | 2 | 4 | 0 | .333 | 3 | 8 | 0 | .273 |
| Cal St. Fullerton†... | 0 | 6 | 0 | .000 | 2 | 9 | 0 | .182 |

† Dropped football program after 1992 season. * New Mexico St. defeated Nevada-Las Vegas, 40-10, on October 10.

**Bowl Games (0-1-0):** Nevada (lost to Bowling Green, 35-34, in Las Vegas)

### MID-AMERICAN ATHLETIC CONFERENCE

| Team | CONFERENCE | | | | FULL SEASON | | | |
|---|---|---|---|---|---|---|---|---|
| | W | L | T | Pct. | W | L | T | Pct. |
| Bowling Green...... | 8 | 0 | 0 | 1.000 | 9 | 2 | 0 | .818 |
| Western Mich...... | 6 | 3 | 0 | .667 | 7 | 3 | 1 | .682 |
| Toledo........... | 5 | 3 | 0 | .625 | 8 | 3 | 0 | .727 |
| Akron............ | 5 | 3 | 0 | .625 | 7 | 3 | 1 | .682 |
| Miami (Ohio)....... | 5 | 3 | 0 | .625 | 6 | 4 | 1 | .591 |
| Ball St........... | 5 | 4 | 0 | .556 | 5 | 6 | 0 | .455 |
| Central Mich....... | 4 | 5 | 0 | .444 | 5 | 6 | 0 | .455 |
| Kent............. | 2 | 7 | 0 | .222 | 2 | 9 | 0 | .182 |
| Eastern Mich.*..... | 1 | 7 | 0 | .125 | 1 | 10 | 0 | .091 |
| Ohio*............ | 1 | 7 | 0 | .125 | 1 | 10 | 0 | .091 |

* Eastern Mich. defeated Ohio, 7-6, on October 24.

**Bowl Games (1-0-0):** Bowling Green (defeated Nevada, 35-34, in Las Vegas)

### PACIFIC-10 CONFERENCE

| Team | CONFERENCE | | | | FULL SEASON | | | |
|---|---|---|---|---|---|---|---|---|
| | W | L | T | Pct. | W | L | T | Pct. |
| Washington*....... | 6 | 2 | 0 | .750 | 9 | 2 | 0 | .818 |
| Stanford*......... | 6 | 2 | 0 | .750 | 9 | 3 | 0 | .750 |
| Washington St...... | 5 | 3 | 0 | .625 | 8 | 3 | 0 | .727 |
| Southern Cal....... | 5 | 3 | 0 | .625 | 6 | 4 | 1 | .591 |
| Arizona.......... | 4 | 3 | 1 | .563 | 6 | 4 | 1 | .591 |
| Oregon @......... | 4 | 4 | 0 | .500 | 6 | 5 | 0 | .545 |
| Arizona St. @...... | 4 | 4 | 0 | .500 | 6 | 5 | 0 | .545 |
| UCLA............ | 3 | 5 | 0 | .375 | 6 | 5 | 0 | .545 |
| California......... | 2 | 6 | 0 | .250 | 4 | 7 | 0 | .364 |
| Oregon St......... | 0 | 7 | 1 | .063 | 1 | 9 | 1 | .136 |

* Washington defeated Stanford, 41-7, on October 31. @ Oregon defeated Arizona St., 30-20, on October 3.

**Bowl Games (2-4-0):** Arizona (lost to Baylor, 20-15, in John Hancock); Oregon (lost to Wake Forest, 39-35, in Independence); Southern Cal (lost to Fresno St., 24-7, in Freedom); Stanford (defeated Penn St., 24-3, in Blockbuster); Washington (lost to Michigan, 38-31, in Rose); Washington St. (defeated Utah, 31-28, in Copper)

> **Michigan was undefeated in 1992 but had three ties, becoming just the second Big Ten team since 1956 to tie that many.** Ⓜ®

## SOUTHEASTERN CONFERENCE

| Team | CONFERENCE | | | | FULL SEASON | | | |
|------|---|---|---|---|---|---|---|---|
| | W | L | T | Pct. | W | L | T | Pct. |
| **East** | | | | | | | | |
| Florida†*......... | 6 | 2 | 0 | .750 | 8 | 4 | 0 | .667 |
| Georgia*......... | 6 | 2 | 0 | .750 | 9 | 2 | 0 | .818 |
| Tennessee........ | 5 | 3 | 0 | .625 | 8 | 3 | 0 | .727 |
| South Caro........ | 3 | 5 | 0 | .375 | 5 | 6 | 0 | .455 |
| Vanderbilt @..... | 2 | 6 | 0 | .250 | 4 | 7 | 0 | .364 |
| Kentucky @....... | 2 | 6 | 0 | .250 | 4 | 7 | 0 | .364 |
| **West** | | | | | | | | |
| Alabama†........ | 8 | 0 | 0 | 1.000 | 12 | 0 | 0 | 1.000 |
| Mississippi....... | 5 | 3 | 0 | .625 | 8 | 3 | 0 | .727 |
| Mississippi St..... | 4 | 4 | 0 | .500 | 7 | 4 | 0 | .636 |
| Arkansas......... | 3 | 4 | 1 | .438 | 3 | 7 | 1 | .318 |
| Auburn........... | 2 | 5 | 1 | .313 | 5 | 5 | 1 | .500 |
| Louisiana St....... | 1 | 7 | 0 | .125 | 2 | 9 | 0 | .182 |

† *Overall record includes first SEC championship game, as Alabama defeated Florida, 28-21, on December 5.* *Florida defeated Georgia, 26-24, on October 31.* @ *Vanderbilt defeated Kentucky, 20-7, on November 7.*

**Bowl Games (5-1-0):** Alabama (defeated Miami, Fla., 34-13, in Sugar); Florida (defeated North Caro. St., 27-10, in Gator); Georgia (defeated Ohio St., 21-14, in Florida Citrus); Mississippi (defeated Air Force, 13-0, in Liberty); Mississippi St. (lost to North Caro., 21-17, in Peach); Tennessee (defeated Boston College, 38-23, in Hall of Fame)

## SOUTHWEST CONFERENCE

| Team | CONFERENCE | | | | FULL SEASON | | | |
|------|---|---|---|---|---|---|---|---|
| | W | L | T | Pct. | W | L | T | Pct. |
| Texas A&M..... | 7 | 0 | 0 | 1.000 | 12 | 0 | 0 | 1.000 |
| Baylor*.......... | 4 | 3 | 0 | .571 | 6 | 5 | 0 | .545 |
| Rice*............ | 4 | 3 | 0 | .571 | 6 | 5 | 0 | .545 |
| Texas*........... | 4 | 3 | 0 | .571 | 6 | 5 | 0 | .545 |
| Texas Tech...... | 4 | 3 | 0 | .571 | 5 | 6 | 0 | .455 |
| Southern Methodist. | 2 | 5 | 0 | .286 | 5 | 6 | 0 | .455 |
| Houston.......... | 2 | 5 | 0 | .286 | 4 | 7 | 0 | .364 |
| Texas Christian.... | 1 | 6 | 0 | .143 | 2 | 8 | 1 | .227 |

* *Baylor defeated Texas, 21-20, on November 21; Rice defeated Baylor, 34-31, on November 14; Texas defeated Rice, 23-21, on October 3.*

**Bowl Games (1-1-0):** Baylor (defeated Arizona, 20-15, in John Hancock); Texas A&M (lost to Notre Dame, 28-3, in Cotton)

## WESTERN ATHLETIC CONFERENCE

| Team | CONFERENCE | | | | FULL SEASON | | | |
|------|---|---|---|---|---|---|---|---|
| | W | L | T | Pct. | W | L | T | Pct. |
| Hawaii*.......... | 6 | 2 | 0 | .778 | 10 | 2 | 0 | .833 |
| Brigham Young*.... | 6 | 2 | 0 | .750 | 8 | 4 | 0 | .667 |
| Fresno St.*....... | 6 | 2 | 0 | .750 | 8 | 4 | 0 | .667 |
| San Diego St....... | 5 | 3 | 0 | .625 | 5 | 5 | 1 | .500 |
| Air Force......... | 4 | 4 | 0 | .500 | 7 | 4 | 0 | .636 |
| Utah............. | 4 | 4 | 0 | .500 | 6 | 5 | 0 | .545 |
| Wyoming @........ | 3 | 5 | 0 | .375 | 5 | 7 | 0 | .417 |
| Colorado St.@..... | 3 | 5 | 0 | .375 | 5 | 7 | 0 | .417 |
| New Mexico...... | 2 | 6 | 0 | .250 | 3 | 8 | 0 | .273 |
| UTEP............. | 1 | 7 | 0 | .125 | 1 | 10 | 0 | .091 |

* *Hawaii defeated Brigham Young, 36-32, on September 26 and defeated Fresno St., 47-45, on October 17; Brigham Young defeated Fresno St., 36-24, on October 10.* @ *Wyoming defeated Colorado St., 31-14, on October 24.*

**Bowl Games (2-3-0):** Air Force (lost to Mississippi, 13-0, in Liberty); Brigham Young (lost to Kansas, 23-20, in Aloha); Fresno St. (defeated Southern Cal, 24-7, in Freedom); Hawaii (defeated Illinois, 27-17, in Holiday); Utah (lost to Washington St., 31-28, in Copper)

## DIVISION I-A INDEPENDENTS

| Team | FULL SEASON | | | |
|------|---|---|---|---|
| | W | L | T | Pct. |
| Notre Dame..................... | 9 | 1 | 1 | .864 |
| Penn St......................... | 7 | 4 | 0 | .636 |
| Southern Miss.................. | 7 | 4 | 0 | .636 |
| Memphis St..................... | 6 | 5 | 0 | .545 |
| Army........................... | 5 | 6 | 0 | .455 |
| East Caro....................... | 5 | 6 | 0 | .455 |
| Louisiana Tech.................. | 5 | 6 | 0 | .455 |
| Louisville....................... | 5 | 6 | 0 | .455 |
| Northern Ill.................... | 5 | 6 | 0 | .455 |
| Tulsa........................... | 4 | 7 | 0 | .364 |
| Cincinnati...................... | 3 | 8 | 0 | .273 |
| Arkansas St..................... | 2 | 9 | 0 | .182 |
| Southwestern La................. | 2 | 9 | 0 | .182 |
| Tulane......................... | 2 | 9 | 0 | .182 |
| Navy........................... | 1 | 10 | 0 | .091 |

**Bowl Games (1-1-0):** Notre Dame (defeated Texas A&M, 28-3, in Cotton); Penn St. (lost to Stanford, 24-3, in Blockbuster)

Southeastern Conference teams dominated the 1992-93 postseason bowl games, winning five – including Alabama's defeat of Miami (Fla.) in the Sugar Bowl for the national championship – and losing just one.

# DIVISION I-AA

## BIG SKY CONFERENCE

| Team | CONFERENCE | | | | FULL SEASON | | | |
|------|---|---|---|---|---|---|---|---|
| | W | L | T | Pct. | W | L | T | Pct. |
| Idaho*........... | 6 | 1 | 0 | .857 | 9 | 2 | 0 | .818 |
| Eastern Wash.*..... | 6 | 1 | 0 | .857 | 7 | 3 | 0 | .700 |
| Weber St. @........ | 4 | 3 | 0 | .571 | 6 | 5 | 0 | .545 |
| Montana @........ | 4 | 3 | 0 | .571 | 6 | 5 | 0 | .545 |
| Boise St.......... | 3 | 4 | 0 | .429 | 5 | 6 | 0 | .455 |
| Northern Ariz. ‡..... | 2 | 5 | 0 | .286 | 4 | 7 | 0 | .364 |
| Montana St.‡..... | 2 | 5 | 0 | .286 | 4 | 7 | 0 | .364 |
| Idaho St......... | 1 | 6 | 0 | .143 | 3 | 8 | 0 | .273 |

* *Idaho defeated Eastern Wash., 38-21, on October 17.* @ *Weber St. defeated Montana, 24-7, on October 10.* ‡ *Northern Ariz. defeated Montana St., 13-9, on October 3.*

**Division I-AA Playoffs (0-2-0):** Idaho (0-1, lost in first round to McNeese St., 23-20); Eastern Wash. (0-1, lost in first round to Northern Iowa, 17-14)

## GATEWAY COLLEGIATE ATHLETIC CONFERENCE

| Team | CONFERENCE | | | | FULL SEASON | | | |
|------|---|---|---|---|---|---|---|---|
| | W | L | T | Pct. | W | L | T | Pct. |
| Northern Iowa...... | 5 | 1 | 0 | .833 | 10 | 1 | 0 | .909 |
| Western Ill........ | 4 | 2 | 0 | .667 | 7 | 4 | 0 | .636 |
| Southwest Mo. St.... | 4 | 2 | 0 | .667 | 6 | 5 | 0 | .545 |
| Illinois St.*....... | 2 | 4 | 0 | .333 | 5 | 6 | 0 | .455 |
| Eastern Ill.*........ | 2 | 4 | 0 | .333 | 5 | 6 | 0 | .455 |
| Southern Ill. @...... | 2 | 4 | 0 | .333 | 4 | 7 | 0 | .364 |
| Indiana St.@....... | 2 | 4 | 0 | .333 | 4 | 7 | 0 | .364 |

* *Illinois St. defeated Eastern Ill., 48-7, on September 26.* @ *Southern Ill. defeated Indiana St., 42-35, on November 21.*

**Division I-AA Playoffs (2-1-0):** Northern Iowa (2-1; defeated Eastern Wash., 17-14, in first round; defeated McNeese St., 29-7, in quarterfinals; lost to Youngstown St., 19-7, in semifinals)

## IVY GROUP

| Team | CONFERENCE | | | | FULL SEASON | | | |
|---|---|---|---|---|---|---|---|---|
| | W | L | T | Pct. | W | L | T | Pct. |
| Dartmouth* | 6 | 1 | 0 | .857 | 8 | 2 | 0 | .800 |
| Princeton* | 6 | 1 | 0 | .857 | 8 | 2 | 0 | .800 |
| Pennsylvania | 5 | 2 | 0 | .714 | 7 | 3 | 0 | .700 |
| Cornell | 4 | 3 | 0 | .571 | 7 | 3 | 0 | .700 |
| Harvard | 3 | 4 | 0 | .429 | 3 | 7 | 0 | .300 |
| Yale | 2 | 5 | 0 | .286 | 4 | 6 | 0 | .400 |
| Columbia | 2 | 5 | 0 | .286 | 3 | 7 | 0 | .300 |
| Brown | 0 | 7 | 0 | .000 | 0 | 10 | 0 | .000 |

* Dartmouth defeated Princeton, 34-20, on November 21.

*Ivy Group teams do not participate in postseason games.*

## MID-EASTERN ATHLETIC CONFERENCE

| Team | CONFERENCE | | | | FULL SEASON | | | |
|---|---|---|---|---|---|---|---|---|
| | W | L | T | Pct. | W | L | T | Pct. |
| North Caro. A&T | 5 | 1 | 0 | .833 | 9 | 2 | 0 | .818 |
| Florida A&M* | 4 | 2 | 0 | .667 | 7 | 4 | 0 | .636 |
| South Caro. St.* | 4 | 2 | 0 | .667 | 7 | 4 | 0 | .636 |
| Howard | 3 | 3 | 0 | .500 | 7 | 4 | 0 | .636 |
| Delaware St. | 3 | 3 | 0 | .500 | 6 | 5 | 0 | .545 |
| Bethune-Cookman | 2 | 4 | 0 | .333 | 3 | 7 | 0 | .300 |
| Morgan St. | 0 | 6 | 0 | .000 | 2 | 8 | 0 | .200 |

* Florida A&M defeated South Caro. St., 33-20, on September 12.

**Division I-AA Playoffs (0-1-0):** North Caro. A&T (0-1, lost in first round to Citadel, 44-0).

**Postseason Game (0-1-0):** Florida A&M (0-1, lost to Grambling, 45-15, in second Heritage Bowl, January 2, at Tallahassee, Fla.)

## OHIO VALLEY CONFERENCE

| Team | CONFERENCE | | | | FULL SEASON | | | |
|---|---|---|---|---|---|---|---|---|
| | W | L | T | Pct. | W | L | T | Pct. |
| Middle Tenn. St. | 8 | 0 | 0 | 1.000 | 9 | 2 | 0 | .818 |
| Eastern Ky. | 7 | 1 | 0 | .875 | 9 | 2 | 0 | .818 |
| Tennessee Tech | 6 | 2 | 0 | .750 | 7 | 4 | 0 | .636 |
| Tennessee St. | 5 | 3 | 0 | .625 | 5 | 6 | 0 | .455 |
| Morehead St. | 3 | 5 | 0 | .375 | 3 | 8 | 0 | .273 |
| Austin Peay* | 2 | 6 | 0 | .250 | 3 | 8 | 0 | .273 |
| Tenn.-Martin* | 2 | 6 | 0 | .250 | 3 | 8 | 0 | .273 |
| Southeast Mo. St. | 2 | 6 | 0 | .250 | 2 | 9 | 0 | .182 |
| Murray St. | 1 | 7 | 0 | .125 | 2 | 9 | 0 | .182 |

* Austin Peay defeated Tenn.-Martin, 32-18, on November 21.

**Division I-AA Playoffs (1-2-0):** Eastern Ky. (0-1, lost in first round to Marshall, 44-0); Middle Tenn. St. (1-1; defeated Appalachian St., 35-10, in first round; lost to Marshall, 35-21, in quarterfinals)

## PATRIOT LEAGUE

| Team | CONFERENCE | | | | FULL SEASON | | | |
|---|---|---|---|---|---|---|---|---|
| | W | L | T | Pct. | W | L | T | Pct. |
| Lafayette | 5 | 0 | 0 | 1.000 | 8 | 3 | 0 | .727 |
| Holy Cross | 4 | 1 | 0 | .800 | 6 | 5 | 0 | .545 |
| Colgate | 2 | 3 | 0 | .400 | 4 | 7 | 0 | .364 |
| Lehigh | 2 | 3 | 0 | .400 | 3 | 8 | 0 | .273 |
| Bucknell | 1 | 4 | 0 | .200 | 4 | 7 | 0 | .364 |
| Fordham | 1 | 4 | 0 | .200 | 1 | 9 | 0 | .100 |

*Patriot League teams do not participate in postseason games.*

> For the first time since 1988, there were no undefeated, untied teams in Division I-AA last season.

## SOUTHERN CONFERENCE

| Team | CONFERENCE | | | | FULL SEASON | | | |
|---|---|---|---|---|---|---|---|---|
| | W | L | T | Pct. | W | L | T | Pct. |
| Citadel | 6 | 1 | 0 | .857 | 10 | 1 | 0 | .909 |
| Marshall | 5 | 2 | 0 | .714 | 8 | 3 | 0 | .727 |
| Appalachian St.* | 5 | 2 | 0 | .714 | 7 | 4 | 0 | .636 |
| Western Caro.* | 5 | 2 | 0 | .714 | 7 | 4 | 0 | .636 |
| Furman | 4 | 3 | 0 | .571 | 6 | 5 | 0 | .545 |
| East Tenn. St. | 2 | 5 | 0 | .286 | 5 | 6 | 0 | .455 |
| Va. Military | 1 | 6 | 0 | .143 | 3 | 8 | 0 | .273 |
| Tenn.-Chatt. | 0 | 7 | 0 | .000 | 2 | 9 | 0 | .182 |
| Ga. Southern# | — | — | — | — | 7 | 4 | 0 | .636 |

* Appalachian St. defeated Western Caro., 14-12, on November 21. # Ga. Southern did not compete for conference title in 1992.

**Division I-AA Playoffs (5-2-0):** Appalachian St. (0-1, lost in first round to Middle Tenn. St., 35-10); Citadel (1-1; defeated North Caro. A&T, 44-0, in first round; lost to Youngstown St., 42-17, in quarterfinals); Marshall (4-0; defeated Eastern Ky., 44-0, in first round; defeated Middle Tenn. St., 35-21, in quarterfinals; defeated Delaware, 28-7, in semifinals; defeated Youngstown St., 31-28, in championship game)

## SOUTHLAND CONFERENCE

| Team | CONFERENCE | | | | FULL SEASON | | | |
|---|---|---|---|---|---|---|---|---|
| | W | L | T | Pct. | W | L | T | Pct. |
| Northeast La. | 7 | 0 | 0 | 1.000 | 9 | 2 | 0 | .818 |
| McNeese St. | 6 | 1 | 0 | .857 | 8 | 3 | 0 | .727 |
| Sam Houston St.* | 3 | 2 | 2 | .571 | 6 | 3 | 2 | .636 |
| Northwestern (La.)* | 4 | 3 | 0 | .571 | 7 | 4 | 0 | .636 |
| North Texas | 3 | 4 | 0 | .429 | 4 | 7 | 0 | .364 |
| Southwest Tex. St. | 2 | 4 | 1 | .357 | 5 | 5 | 1 | .500 |
| Stephen F. Austin | 1 | 6 | 0 | .143 | 3 | 8 | 0 | .273 |
| Nicholls St. | 0 | 6 | 1 | .071 | 1 | 9 | 1 | .136 |

* Sam Houston St. defeated Northwestern (La.), 42-19, on November 7.

**Division I-AA Playoffs (2-2-0):** McNeese St. (1-1; defeated Idaho, 23-20, in first round; lost to Northern Iowa, 29-7, in quarterfinals); Northeast La. (1-1; defeated Alcorn St., 78-27, in first round; lost to Delaware, 41-18, in quarterfinals)

## SOUTHWESTERN ATHLETIC CONFERENCE

| Team | CONFERENCE | | | | FULL SEASON | | | |
|---|---|---|---|---|---|---|---|---|
| | W | L | T | Pct. | W | L | T | Pct. |
| Alcorn St. | 7 | 0 | 0 | 1.000 | 7 | 3 | 0 | .700 |
| Grambling | 6 | 1 | 0 | .857 | 9 | 2 | 0 | .818 |
| Jackson St. | 4 | 3 | 0 | .571 | 7 | 4 | 0 | .636 |
| Alabama St.* | 3 | 4 | 0 | .429 | 5 | 6 | 0 | .455 |
| Southern-B.R.* | 3 | 4 | 0 | .429 | 5 | 6 | 0 | .455 |
| Texas Southern* | 3 | 4 | 0 | .429 | 5 | 6 | 0 | .455 |
| Mississippi Val. | 2 | 5 | 0 | .286 | 4 | 5 | 0 | .444 |
| Prairie View | 0 | 7 | 0 | .000 | 0 | 11 | 0 | .000 |

* Alabama St. defeated Southern-B.R., 30-10, on September 12; Texas Southern defeated Alabama St., 30-28, on October 17; Southern-B.R. defeated Texas Southern, 34-6, on November 14.

**Division I-AA Playoffs (0-1-0):** Alcorn St. (0-1, lost in first round to Northeast La., 78-27).

**Postseason Game (1-0-0):** Grambling (1-0, defeated Florida A&M, 45-15, in second Heritage Bowl, January 2, at Tallahassee, Fla.)

## YANKEE CONFERENCE

| Team | CONFERENCE | | | | FULL SEASON | | | |
|---|---|---|---|---|---|---|---|---|
| | W | L | T | Pct. | W | L | T | Pct. |
| Delaware | 7 | 1 | 0 | .875 | 9 | 2 | 0 | .818 |
| Villanova | 6 | 2 | 0 | .750 | 9 | 2 | 0 | .818 |
| Massachusetts | 5 | 3 | 0 | .625 | 7 | 3 | 0 | .700 |
| Richmond | 5 | 3 | 0 | .625 | 7 | 4 | 0 | .636 |
| Maine | 4 | 4 | 0 | .500 | 6 | 5 | 0 | .545 |
| Connecticut | 4 | 4 | 0 | .500 | 5 | 6 | 0 | .455 |
| New Hampshire | 3 | 5 | 0 | .375 | 5 | 5 | 1 | .500 |
| Boston U. | 2 | 6 | 0 | .250 | 3 | 8 | 0 | .273 |
| Rhode Island | 0 | 8 | 0 | .000 | 1 | 10 | 0 | .091 |

**Division I-AA Playoffs (2-2-0):** Delaware (2-1; defeated Samford, 56-21, in first round; defeated Northeast La., 41-18, in quarterfinals; lost to Marshall, 28-7, in semifinals); Villanova (0-1, lost in first round to Youngstown St., 23-20)

## DIVISION I-AA INDEPENDENTS

| Team | FULL SEASON | | | |
|------|---|---|---|---|
| | W | L | T | Pct. |
| Samford | 9 | 2 | 0 | .818 |
| William & Mary | 9 | 2 | 0 | .818 |
| Youngstown St. | 8 | 2 | 1 | .773 |
| Liberty | 7 | 4 | 0 | .636 |
| Central Fla. | 6 | 4 | 0 | .600 |
| Towson St.* | 5 | 5 | 0 | .500 |
| Northeastern* | 5 | 5 | 1 | .500 |
| Western Ky. | 4 | 6 | 0 | .400 |
| James Madison | 4 | 7 | 0 | .364 |

* Towson St. defeated Northeastern, 33-32, on November 14.

**Division I-AA Playoffs (3-2-0):** Samford (0-1, lost in first round to Delaware, 56-21); Youngstown St. (3-1; defeated Villanova, 23-20, in first round; defeated Citadel, 42-17, in quarterfinals; defeated Northern Iowa, 19-7, in semifinals; lost to Marshall, 31-28, in championship game)

The top three independents – Samford, William & Mary, and Youngstown State – combined for more victories (26) than the top three teams in any Division I-AA conference. Youngstown State won three more games on its way to a runner-up finish in the playoffs.

# DIVISION II

## CENTRAL INTERCOLLEGIATE ATHLETIC ASSOCIATION

| Team | CONFERENCE | | | | FULL SEASON | | | |
|------|---|---|---|---|---|---|---|---|
| | W | L | T | Pct. | W | L | T | Pct. |
| Hampton | 5 | 0 | 1 | .917 | 9 | 1 | 1 | .864 |
| Winston-Salem | 5 | 1 | 0 | .833 | 7 | 4 | 0 | .636 |
| Fayetteville St. | 3 | 2 | 1 | .583 | 5 | 4 | 1 | .550 |
| Virginia Union | 3 | 2 | 1 | .583 | 3 | 5 | 1 | .389 |
| Johnson Smith | 3 | 3 | 0 | .500 | 5 | 5 | 0 | .500 |
| Virginia St. | 3 | 3 | 0 | .500 | 3 | 7 | 0 | .300 |
| Elizabeth City St. | 2 | 3 | 1 | .417 | 3 | 6 | 1 | .350 |
| Livingstone | 2 | 4 | 0 | .333 | 3 | 7 | 0 | .300 |
| Norfolk St. | 2 | 4 | 0 | .333 | 3 | 7 | 0 | .300 |
| N. C. Central | 2 | 4 | 0 | .333 | 3 | 8 | 0 | .273 |
| Bowie St. | 1 | 5 | 0 | .167 | 1 | 10 | 0 | .091 |

Designated conference game: Grambling defeated Virginia Union, 54-7, on September 12.

**Division II Playoffs (0-1-0):** Hampton (0-1, lost in first round to North Ala., 33-21)

## GULF SOUTH CONFERENCE

| Team | CONFERENCE | | | | FULL SEASON | | | |
|------|---|---|---|---|---|---|---|---|
| | W | L | T | Pct. | W | L | T | Pct. |
| Jacksonville St. | 5 | 0 | 1 | .917 | 8 | 1 | 1 | .850 |
| North Ala. | 3 | 2 | 1 | .583 | 6 | 3 | 1 | .650 |
| Valdosta St. | 3 | 2 | 1 | .583 | 5 | 4 | 1 | .550 |
| Mississippi Col. | 2 | 3 | 1 | .417 | 4 | 5 | 1 | .450 |
| Livingston | 2 | 4 | 0 | .333 | 5 | 4 | 0 | .556 |
| West Ga. | 2 | 4 | 0 | .333 | 5 | 6 | 0 | .455 |
| Delta St. | 2 | 4 | 0 | .333 | 3 | 6 | 1 | .350 |

**Division II Playoffs (5-1-0):** Jacksonville St. (4-0; defeated Savannah St., 41-16, in first round; defeated North Ala., 14-12, in quarterfinals; defeated New Haven, 46-35, in semifinals; defeated Pittsburg St., 17-13, in championship game); North Ala. (1-1; defeated Hampton, 33-21, in first round; lost to Jacksonville St., 14-12, in quarterfinals)

## LONE STAR CONFERENCE

| Team | CONFERENCE | | | | FULL SEASON | | | |
|------|---|---|---|---|---|---|---|---|
| | W | L | T | Pct. | W | L | T | Pct. |
| Texas A&I | 6 | 0 | 0 | 1.000 | 8 | 2 | 0 | .800 |
| East Tex. St. | 5 | 1 | 0 | .833 | 8 | 3 | 0 | .727 |
| Eastern N. Mex.* | 3 | 3 | 0 | .500 | 5 | 5 | 0 | .500 |
| Angelo St.* | 3 | 3 | 0 | .500 | 5 | 5 | 0 | .500 |
| Central Okla. | 2 | 4 | 0 | .333 | 6 | 4 | 0 | .600 |
| Abilene Christian | 2 | 4 | 0 | .333 | 3 | 6 | 0 | .333 |
| Cameron† | 0 | 6 | 0 | .000 | 1 | 9 | 0 | .100 |

† Dropped football program after 1992 season.
* Eastern N. Mex. defeated Angelo St., 26-25, on October 10.

**Division II Playoffs (1-1-0):** Texas A&I (1-1; defeated Western St., 22-13, in first round; lost to Portland St., 35-30, in quarterfinals)

## MID-AMERICA INTERCOLLEGIATE ATHLETIC ASSOCIATION

| Team | CONFERENCE | | | | FULL SEASON | | | |
|------|---|---|---|---|---|---|---|---|
| | W | L | T | Pct. | W | L | T | Pct. |
| Pittsburg St. | 9 | 0 | 0 | 1.000 | 11 | 0 | 0 | 1.000 |
| Northeast Mo. St. | 7 | 2 | 0 | .778 | 9 | 2 | 0 | .818 |
| Emporia St. | 6 | 3 | 0 | .667 | 7 | 3 | 0 | .700 |
| Central Mo. St. | 6 | 3 | 0 | .667 | 6 | 4 | 0 | .600 |
| Northwest Mo. St. | 6 | 3 | 0 | .667 | 6 | 5 | 0 | .545 |
| Mo. Western St. | 4 | 5 | 0 | .444 | 5 | 6 | 0 | .455 |
| Mo. Southern St. | 3 | 6 | 0 | .333 | 4 | 6 | 0 | .400 |
| Washburn | 2 | 7 | 0 | .222 | 2 | 8 | 0 | .200 |
| Southwest Baptist. | 1 | 8 | 0 | .111 | 2 | 8 | 0 | .200 |
| Missouri-Rolla | 1 | 8 | 0 | .111 | 2 | 9 | 0 | .182 |

**Division II Playoffs (3-2-0):** Northeast Mo. St. (0-1, lost in first round to North Dak. St., 42-7); Pittsburg St. (3-1; defeated North Dak., 26-21, in first round; defeated North Dak. St., 38-37 in overtime, in quarterfinals; defeated Portland St., 41-38, in semifinals; lost to Jacksonville St., 17-13, in championship game)

## MIDWEST INTERCOLLEGIATE FOOTBALL CONFERENCE

| Team | CONFERENCE | | | | FULL SEASON | | | |
|------|---|---|---|---|---|---|---|---|
| | W | L | T | Pct. | W | L | T | Pct. |
| Hillsdale* | 8 | 2 | 0 | .800 | 9 | 2 | 0 | .818 |
| Ferris St.* | 8 | 2 | 0 | .800 | 9 | 2 | 0 | .818 |
| Butler | 8 | 2 | 0 | .800 | 8 | 2 | 0 | .800 |
| Grand Valley St. | 8 | 2 | 0 | .800 | 8 | 3 | 0 | .727 |
| Ashland | 7 | 3 | 0 | .700 | 8 | 3 | 0 | .727 |
| Saginaw Valley | 4 | 6 | 0 | .400 | 7 | 4 | 0 | .636 |
| Wayne St. (Mich.) | 3 | 7 | 0 | .300 | 4 | 7 | 0 | .364 |
| Valparaiso | 3 | 7 | 0 | .300 | 3 | 8 | 0 | .273 |
| Indianapolis @ | 1 | 8 | 1 | .150 | 1 | 8 | 1 | .150 |
| St. Joseph's (Ind.) @ | 1 | 8 | 1 | .150 | 1 | 8 | 1 | .150 |
| Northern Mich. | 1 | 9 | 0 | .100 | 1 | 9 | 0 | .100 |

* Hillsdale defeated Ferris St., 36-14, on September 19. @ Indianapolis and St. Joseph's (Ind.) tied, 24-24, on September 19.

**Division II Playoffs (1-1-0):** Ferris St. (1-1; defeated Edinboro, 19-15, in first round; lost to New Haven, 35-13, in quarterfinals)

Pittsburg State (11-0-0) and New Haven (10-0-0) were the only Division II teams with perfect regular-season records in 1992.

## NORTH CENTRAL INTERCOLLEGIATE ATHLETIC CONFERENCE

| Team | CONFERENCE | | | | FULL SEASON | | | |
|------|---|---|---|---|---|---|---|---|
| | W | L | T | Pct. | W | L | T | Pct. |
| North Dak. St. | 8 | 1 | 0 | .889 | 9 | 1 | 0 | .900 |
| North Dak. | 6 | 2 | 1 | .722 | 6 | 3 | 1 | .650 |
| Augustana (S.D.) | 6 | 3 | 0 | .667 | 8 | 3 | 0 | .727 |
| St. Cloud St. | 6 | 3 | 0 | .667 | 7 | 4 | 0 | .636 |
| South Dak. St. | 5 | 4 | 0 | .556 | 6 | 4 | 0 | .600 |
| Morningside | 4 | 4 | 1 | .500 | 5 | 5 | 1 | .500 |
| Mankato St.* | 4 | 5 | 0 | .444 | 6 | 5 | 0 | .545 |
| Northern Colo.* | 4 | 5 | 0 | .444 | 6 | 5 | 0 | .545 |
| South Dak. | 1 | 8 | 0 | .111 | 2 | 9 | 0 | .182 |
| Nebraska-Omaha | 0 | 9 | 0 | .000 | 2 | 9 | 0 | .182 |

*Mankato St. defeated Northern Colo., 14-0, on September 19.

**Division II Playoffs (1-2-0):** North Dak. (0-1, lost in first round to Pittsburg St., 26-21); North Dak. St. (1-1; defeated Northeast Mo. St., 42-7, in first round; lost to Pittsburg St., 38-37, in overtime, in quarterfinals)

## NORTHERN CALIFORNIA ATHLETIC CONFERENCE

| Team | CONFERENCE | | | | FULL SEASON | | | |
|------|---|---|---|---|---|---|---|---|
| | W | L | T | Pct. | W | L | T | Pct. |
| UC Davis | 5 | 0 | 0 | 1.000 | 8 | 1 | 1 | .850 |
| Sonoma St. | 3 | 2 | 0 | .600 | 7 | 3 | 0 | .700 |
| Humboldt St. | 3 | 2 | 0 | .600 | 7 | 4 | 0 | .636 |
| Cal St. Hayward | 3 | 2 | 0 | .600 | 5 | 5 | 0 | .500 |
| San Fran. St.† | 1 | 4 | 0 | .200 | 2 | 7 | 0 | .222 |
| Cal St. Chico | 0 | 5 | 0 | .000 | 1 | 9 | 0 | .100 |

†Does not include 28-0 victory over Amsterdam.

**Division II Playoffs (0-1-0):** UC Davis (0-1, lost in first round to Portland St., 42-28)

## PENNSYLVANIA STATE ATHLETIC CONFERENCE

| Team | CONFERENCE | | | | FULL SEASON | | | |
|------|---|---|---|---|---|---|---|---|
| | W | L | T | Pct. | W | L | T | Pct. |
| **Western Division** | | | | | | | | |
| Clarion | 5 | 1 | 0 | .833 | 6 | 4 | 0 | .600 |
| Edinboro | 4 | 1 | 1 | .750 | 8 | 1 | 1 | .850 |
| Indiana (Pa.) | 4 | 1 | 1 | .750 | 7 | 2 | 1 | .750 |
| Slippery Rock | 4 | 2 | 0 | .667 | 8 | 3 | 0 | .727 |
| Shippensburg | 1 | 4 | 1 | .250 | 3 | 7 | 1 | .318 |
| Calif. (Pa.) | 1 | 5 | 0 | .167 | 3 | 7 | 1 | .318 |
| Lock Haven | 0 | 5 | 1 | .083 | 2 | 8 | 1 | .227 |
| **Eastern Division** | | | | | | | | |
| West Chester | 6 | 0 | 0 | 1.000 | 9 | 1 | 0 | .900 |
| East Stroudsburg | 5 | 1 | 0 | .833 | 8 | 2 | 0 | .800 |
| Millersville | 4 | 2 | 0 | .667 | 7 | 3 | 0 | .700 |
| Mansfield | 3 | 3 | 0 | .500 | 5 | 6 | 0 | .455 |
| Kutztown | 2 | 4 | 0 | .333 | 4 | 5 | 1 | .450 |
| Bloomsburg | 1 | 5 | 0 | .167 | 1 | 9 | 0 | .100 |
| Cheyney | 0 | 6 | 0 | .000 | 0 | 11 | 0 | .000 |

**Division II Playoffs (0-2-0):** Edinboro (0-1, lost in first round to Ferris St., 19-15); West Chester (0-1, lost in first round to New Haven, 38-26)

## ROCKY MOUNTAIN ATHLETIC CONFERENCE

| Team | CONFERENCE | | | | FULL SEASON | | | |
|------|---|---|---|---|---|---|---|---|
| | W | L | T | Pct. | W | L | T | Pct. |
| Western St. | 7 | 0 | 0 | 1.000 | 9 | 1 | 0 | .900 |
| Fort Hays St. | 6 | 1 | 0 | .857 | 6 | 5 | 0 | .545 |
| Chadron St. | 5 | 2 | 0 | .714 | 7 | 3 | 0 | .700 |
| N. M. Highlands | 4 | 3 | 0 | .571 | 7 | 3 | 1 | .682 |
| Mesa St. | 3 | 4 | 0 | .429 | 3 | 8 | 0 | .273 |
| Colorado Mines | 2 | 5 | 0 | .286 | 4 | 6 | 0 | .400 |
| Adams St. | 1 | 6 | 0 | .143 | 3 | 7 | 0 | .300 |
| Fort Lewis | 0 | 7 | 0 | .000 | 1 | 9 | 0 | .100 |

**Division II Playoffs (0-1-0):** Western St. (0-1, lost in first round to Texas A&I, 22-13)

## SOUTH ATLANTIC CONFERENCE

| Team | CONFERENCE | | | | FULL SEASON | | | |
|------|---|---|---|---|---|---|---|---|
| | W | L | T | Pct. | W | L | T | Pct. |
| Gardner-Webb | 7 | 0 | 0 | 1.000 | 10 | 1 | 0 | .909 |
| Carson-Newman | 6 | 1 | 0 | .857 | 8 | 2 | 0 | .800 |
| Elon | 5 | 2 | 0 | .714 | 8 | 2 | 0 | .800 |
| Catawba | 3 | 4 | 0 | .429 | 4 | 6 | 0 | .400 |
| Presbyterian | 3 | 4 | 0 | .429 | 4 | 7 | 0 | .364 |
| Lenoir-Rhyne | 2 | 5 | 0 | .286 | 5 | 5 | 0 | .500 |
| Mars Hill | 1 | 6 | 0 | .143 | 2 | 8 | 1 | .227 |
| Wingate | 1 | 6 | 0 | .143 | 1 | 9 | 0 | .100 |

**NAIA Division I Playoffs (2-2-0):** Carson-Newman (0-1, lost in first round to Shepherd, 6-3); Gardner-Webb (2-1; defeated Concord, W. Va., 28-21, in first round; defeated Shepherd, 22-7, in semifinals; lost to Central St., Ohio, 19-16, in the championship game)

## SOUTHERN INTERCOLLEGIATE ATHLETIC CONFERENCE

| Team | CONFERENCE | | | | FULL SEASON | | | |
|------|---|---|---|---|---|---|---|---|
| | W | L | T | Pct. | W | L | T | Pct. |
| Fort Valley St. | 6 | 1 | 0 | .857 | 7 | 4 | 0 | .636 |
| Albany St. (Ga.) | 5 | 1 | 1 | .786 | 6 | 1 | 1 | .650 |
| Savannah St. | 5 | 2 | 0 | .714 | 8 | 3 | 0 | .727 |
| Morehouse | 4 | 3 | 0 | .571 | 6 | 5 | 0 | .545 |
| Clark Atlanta | 3 | 4 | 0 | .429 | 5 | 5 | 0 | .500 |
| Tuskegee | 2 | 4 | 1 | .357 | 3 | 6 | 1 | .350 |
| Alabama A&M‡ | 2 | 4 | 0 | .333 | 3 | 8 | 0 | .273 |
| Morris Brown | 2 | 5 | 0 | .286 | 4 | 6 | 0 | .400 |
| Miles‡ | 0 | 6 | 0 | .000 | 0 | 10 | 0 | .000 |

‡ Not eligible for conference title. Did not play each other during season.

**Division II Playoffs (0-1-0):** Savannah St. (0-1, lost in first round to Jacksonville St., 41-16)

## WESTERN FOOTBALL CONFERENCE

| Team | CONFERENCE | | | | FULL SEASON | | | |
|------|---|---|---|---|---|---|---|---|
| | W | L | T | Pct. | W | L | T | Pct. |
| Portland St. | 3 | 1 | 0 | .750 | 6 | 3 | 0 | .667 |
| Cal St. Sacramento | 2 | 2 | 0 | .500 | 7 | 3 | 0 | .700 |
| Southern Utah | 2 | 2 | 0 | .500 | 6 | 5 | 0 | .545 |
| Cal St. Northridge | 2 | 2 | 0 | .500 | 5 | 5 | 0 | .500 |
| Cal Poly SLO | 1 | 3 | 0 | .250 | 4 | 5 | 1 | .450 |

**Division II Playoffs (2-1-0):** Portland St. (2-1; defeated UC Davis, 42-28, in first round; defeated Texas A&I, 35-30, in quarterfinals; lost to Pittsburg St., 41-38, in semifinals)

North Central Conference rivals North Dakota State and North Dakota have the longest-running series in Division II (97 games). North Dakota State claimed its 42nd win in the rivalry in 1992 en route to its third straight conference title.

## DIVISION II INDEPENDENTS

| Team | FULL SEASON W | L | T | Pct. |
|---|---|---|---|---|
| New Haven | 10 | 0 | 0 | 1.000 |
| Troy St. | 10 | 1 | 0 | .909 |
| Michigan Tech | 8 | 1 | 0 | .889 |
| Central Ark. | 8 | 1 | 1 | .850 |
| Neb.-Kearney | 7 | 3 | 0 | .700 |
| Shepherd # | 7 | 3 | 0 | .700 |
| Southern Conn. St. | 6 | 4 | 0 | .600 |
| St. Mary's (Cal.) | 5 | 4 | 0 | .556 |
| Wayne St. (Neb.) | 5 | 4 | 1 | .550 |
| Wofford | 6 | 5 | 0 | .545 |
| Minn.-Duluth | 5 | 5 | 1 | .500 |
| Newberry | 5 | 6 | 0 | .455 |
| Henderson St. | 4 | 6 | 1 | .409 |
| American Int'l | 4 | 6 | 0 | .400 |
| Santa Clara* | 4 | 6 | 0 | .400 |
| Kentucky St. | 4 | 7 | 0 | .364 |
| Springfield | 3 | 6 | 0 | .333 |
| West Liberty St. | 3 | 7 | 0 | .300 |
| Bemidji St. | 2 | 8 | 0 | .200 |
| Winona St. | 2 | 8 | 0 | .200 |
| Central Conn. St. | 1 | 8 | 0 | .111 |
| West Tex. St. | 1 | 9 | 0 | .100 |
| Northwood | 0 | 9 | 0 | .000 |

*Dropped football program after 1992 season.*
*# Does not include forfeit win over Shippensburg for ineligible player.*

**NAIA Division I Playoffs (2-2-0):** Central Ark. (1-1; defeated Southwestern Okla., 14-2, in first round; lost to Central St., Ohio, 30-23, in semifinals); Shepherd (1-1; defeated Carson-Newman, 6-3, in first round; lost to Gardner-Webb, 22-7, in semifinals)

**Division II Playoffs (2-1-0):** New Haven (2-1; defeated West Chester, 38-26, in first round; defeated Ferris St., 35-13, in quarterfinals; lost to Jacksonville St., 46-35, in semifinals)

**Chadron State's David McCartney scores one of his 25 touchdowns, helping his team to a 7-3 record in 1992 and earning him the Division II scoring title (15.4 points per game).**

# DIVISION III

## ASSOCIATION OF MIDEAST COLLEGES

| Team | CONFERENCE W | L | T | Pct. | FULL SEASON W | L | T | Pct. |
|---|---|---|---|---|---|---|---|---|
| Thomas More | 3 | 0 | 0 | 1.000 | 9 | 1 | 0 | .900 |
| Defiance | 2 | 1 | 0 | .667 | 9 | 1 | 0 | .900 |
| Bluffton | 1 | 2 | 0 | .333 | 1 | 8 | 0 | .111 |
| Wilmington (Ohio) | 0 | 3 | 0 | .000 | 2 | 8 | 0 | .200 |

**Division III Playoffs (0-1-0):** Thomas More (0-1, lost in first round to Emory & Henry, 17-0)

## CENTENNIAL FOOTBALL CONFERENCE

| Team | CONFERENCE W | L | T | Pct. | FULL SEASON W | L | T | Pct. |
|---|---|---|---|---|---|---|---|---|
| Dickinson† | 5 | 1 | 1 | .786 | 8 | 1 | 1 | .850 |
| Swarthmore | 4 | 2 | 1 | .643 | 5 | 3 | 1 | .611 |
| Gettysburg* | 4 | 3 | 0 | .571 | 6 | 4 | 0 | .600 |
| Johns Hopkins* | 4 | 3 | 0 | .571 | 6 | 4 | 0 | .600 |
| Western Md. | 4 | 3 | 0 | .571 | 5 | 5 | 0 | .500 |
| Frank. & Marsh. | 3 | 4 | 0 | .429 | 5 | 5 | 0 | .500 |
| Ursinus | 2 | 5 | 0 | .286 | 4 | 6 | 0 | .400 |
| Muhlenberg | 1 | 6 | 0 | .143 | 1 | 8 | 1 | .150 |

*† Does not include 20-13 loss to Merchant Marine in ECAC Southwest playoff game. * Gettysburg defeated Johns Hopkins, 13-10, on October 2.*

## COLLEGE CONFERENCE OF ILLINOIS AND WISCONSIN

| Team | CONFERENCE W | L | T | Pct. | FULL SEASON W | L | T | Pct. |
|---|---|---|---|---|---|---|---|---|
| Ill. Wesleyan | 7 | 0 | 0 | 1.000 | 9 | 0 | 0 | 1.000 |
| Augustana (Ill.) | 6 | 1 | 0 | .857 | 6 | 3 | 0 | .667 |
| Wheaton (Ill.) | 5 | 2 | 0 | .714 | 6 | 3 | 0 | .667 |
| Millikin | 4 | 3 | 0 | .571 | 4 | 5 | 0 | .444 |
| Elmhurst | 2 | 4 | 1 | .357 | 2 | 6 | 1 | .278 |
| North Park | 1 | 4 | 2 | .286 | 1 | 6 | 2 | .222 |
| North Central | 1 | 5 | 1 | .214 | 1 | 7 | 1 | .167 |
| Carthage | 0 | 7 | 0 | .000 | 0 | 9 | 0 | .000 |

**Division III Playoffs (1-1-0):** Ill. Wesleyan (1-1; defeated Aurora, 21-12, in first round; lost to Mount Union, 49-27, in quarterfinals)

## EASTERN COLLEGIATE FOOTBALL CONFERENCE

| Team | CONFERENCE W | L | T | Pct. | FULL SEASON W | L | T | Pct. |
|---|---|---|---|---|---|---|---|---|
| Bentley† | 6 | 0 | 0 | 1.000 | 9 | 1 | 0 | .900 |
| Nichols | 4 | 1 | 1 | .750 | 7 | 1 | 1 | .833 |
| Stonehill | 4 | 1 | 1 | .750 | 6 | 2 | 1 | .722 |
| Assumption | 3 | 3 | 0 | .500 | 5 | 5 | 0 | .500 |
| Western New Eng. | 1 | 5 | 0 | .167 | 4 | 6 | 0 | .400 |
| Curry | 1 | 5 | 0 | .167 | 2 | 6 | 0 | .250 |
| MIT | 1 | 5 | 0 | .167 | 1 | 7 | 0 | .125 |

*† Does not include 38-20 loss to Cortland St. in ECAC Northwest playoff game.*

## FREEDOM FOOTBALL CONFERENCE

| Team | CONFERENCE W | L | T | Pct. | FULL SEASON W | L | T | Pct. |
|---|---|---|---|---|---|---|---|---|
| Worcester Tech | 5 | 0 | 0 | 1.000 | 9 | 1 | 0 | .900 |
| Merchant Marine† | 4 | 1 | 0 | .800 | 7 | 1 | 1 | .833 |
| Plymouth St. | 4 | 1 | 1 | .750 | 4 | 4 | 1 | .500 |
| Mass.-Lowell | 2 | 3 | 1 | .417 | 4 | 4 | 1 | .500 |
| Stony Brook | 2 | 3 | 0 | .400 | 5 | 5 | 0 | .500 |
| Norwich | 2 | 4 | 0 | .333 | 3 | 6 | 0 | .333 |
| Western Conn. St. | 2 | 4 | 0 | .333 | 2 | 8 | 0 | .200 |
| Coast Guard | 1 | 6 | 0 | .143 | 1 | 8 | 0 | .111 |

*† Does not include 20-13 win over Dickinson in ECAC Southwest playoff game.*

**Division III Playoffs (0-1-0):** Worcester Tech (0-1, lost in first round to Rowan, 41-14)

## INDIANA COLLEGIATE ATHLETIC CONFERENCE

| Team | CONFERENCE W | L | T | Pct. | FULL SEASON W | L | T | Pct. |
|---|---|---|---|---|---|---|---|---|
| Wabash | 5 | 0 | 1 | .917 | 6 | 2 | 1 | .722 |
| Hanover | 4 | 2 | 0 | .667 | 6 | 4 | 0 | .600 |
| DePauw | 3 | 1 | 2 | .667 | 4 | 4 | 2 | .500 |
| Anderson | 3 | 3 | 0 | .500 | 5 | 5 | 0 | .500 |
| Manchester | 2 | 4 | 0 | .333 | 5 | 5 | 0 | .500 |
| Rose-Hulman | 2 | 4 | 0 | .333 | 4 | 6 | 0 | .400 |
| Franklin | 0 | 5 | 1 | .083 | 0 | 9 | 1 | .050 |

## IOWA INTERCOLLEGIATE ATHLETIC CONFERENCE

| Team | CONFERENCE | | | | FULL SEASON | | | |
|------|---|---|---|------|---|---|---|------|
| | W | L | T | Pct. | W | L | T | Pct. |
| Central (Iowa) ..... | 8 | 0 | 0 | 1.000 | 9 | 0 | 0 | 1.000 |
| Simpson .......... | 6 | 2 | 0 | .750 | 6 | 2 | 1 | .722 |
| Loras............ | 5 | 3 | 0 | .625 | 7 | 3 | 0 | .700 |
| Upper Iowa........ | 5 | 3 | 0 | .625 | 6 | 4 | 0 | .600 |
| Wartburg ......... | 5 | 3 | 0 | .625 | 5 | 5 | 0 | .500 |
| Luther .......... | 4 | 4 | 0 | .500 | 6 | 4 | 0 | .600 |
| Buena Vista ...... | 2 | 6 | 0 | .333 | 2 | 7 | 0 | .222 |
| William Penn ...... | 1 | 7 | 0 | .125 | 1 | 9 | 0 | .100 |
| Dubuque .......... | 0 | 8 | 0 | .000 | 1 | 9 | 0 | .100 |

**Division III Playoffs (1-1-0):** Central (Iowa) (1-1; defeated Carleton, 20-8, in first round; lost to Wis.-La Crosse, 34-9, in quarterfinals)

## LIBERTY FOOTBALL CONFERENCE

| Team | CONFERENCE | | | | FULL SEASON | | | |
|------|---|---|---|------|---|---|---|------|
| | W | L | T | Pct. | W | L | T | Pct. |
| Wagner† .......... | 5 | 0 | 0 | 1.000 | 8 | 2 | 0 | .800 |
| St. John's (N.Y.) .... | 3 | 2 | 0 | .600 | 5 | 5 | 0 | .500 |
| LIU-C.W. Post ...... | 2 | 2 | 1 | .500 | 6 | 3 | 1 | .650 |
| Marist ............ | 2 | 2 | 1 | .500 | 4 | 5 | 1 | .450 |
| Iona .............. | 2 | 3 | 0 | .400 | 5 | 5 | 0 | .500 |
| Pace .............. | 0 | 5 | 0 | .000 | 1 | 9 | 0 | .100 |

† Does not include 48-6 win over St. Francis (Pa.) in ECAC Southeast playoff game.

## MICHIGAN INTERCOLLEGIATE ATHLETIC ASSOCIATION

| Team | CONFERENCE | | | | FULL SEASON | | | |
|------|---|---|---|------|---|---|---|------|
| | W | L | T | Pct. | W | L | T | Pct. |
| Albion ............ | 5 | 0 | 0 | 1.000 | 8 | 1 | 0 | .889 |
| Hope ............. | 4 | 1 | 0 | .800 | 6 | 3 | 0 | .667 |
| Olivet ............ | 2 | 3 | 0 | .400 | 2 | 6 | 1 | .278 |
| Adrian ............ | 2 | 3 | 0 | .400 | 2 | 7 | 0 | .222 |
| Alma* ............ | 1 | 4 | 0 | .200 | 3 | 6 | 0 | .333 |
| Kalamazoo* ........ | 1 | 4 | 0 | .200 | 3 | 6 | 0 | .333 |

* Alma defeated Kalamazoo, 17-7, on October 24.

## MIDDLE ATLANTIC STATES COLLEGIATE ATHLETIC CONFERENCE

| Team | CONFERENCE | | | | FULL SEASON | | | |
|------|---|---|---|------|---|---|---|------|
| | W | L | T | Pct. | W | L | T | Pct. |
| Lycoming ......... | 7 | 0 | 1 | .938 | 8 | 0 | 1 | .944 |
| Susquehanna ...... | 7 | 1 | 0 | .875 | 9 | 1 | 0 | .900 |
| Lebanon Valley .... | 5 | 3 | 0 | .625 | 7 | 3 | 0 | .700 |
| Moravian ......... | 4 | 4 | 0 | .500 | 6 | 4 | 0 | .600 |
| Wilkes ........... | 3 | 4 | 1 | .438 | 5 | 4 | 1 | .550 |
| Juniata* .......... | 3 | 4 | 1 | .438 | 3 | 6 | 1 | .350 |
| Widener* ......... | 3 | 4 | 1 | .438 | 3 | 6 | 1 | .350 |
| Delaware Valley .... | 2 | 6 | 0 | .250 | 3 | 7 | 0 | .300 |
| Albright........... | 0 | 8 | 0 | .000 | 0 | 10 | 0 | .000 |

* Juniata defeated Widener, 13-7, on October 3.

**Division III Playoffs (0-1-0):** Lycoming (0-1, lost in first round to Wash. & Jeff., 33-0)

## MIDWEST COLLEGIATE ATHLETIC CONFERENCE

| Team | CONFERENCE | | | | FULL SEASON | | | |
|------|---|---|---|------|---|---|---|------|
| | W | L | T | Pct. | W | L | T | Pct. |
| **North Division** | | | | | | | | |
| Beloit*† .......... | 4 | 1 | 0 | .800 | 6 | 4 | 0 | .600 |
| Carroll (Wis.)* .... | 4 | 1 | 0 | .800 | 8 | 1 | 0 | .889 |
| St. Norbert ....... | 3 | 2 | 0 | .600 | 4 | 5 | 0 | .444 |
| Ripon............. | 2 | 3 | 0 | .400 | 5 | 4 | 0 | .556 |
| Lake Forest ....... | 1 | 4 | 0 | .200 | 3 | 6 | 0 | .333 |
| Lawrence ......... | 1 | 4 | 0 | .200 | 2 | 7 | 0 | .222 |
| **South Division** | | | | | | | | |
| Cornell College† .... | 5 | 0 | 0 | 1.000 | 10 | 0 | 0 | 1.000 |
| Coe .............. | 4 | 1 | 0 | .800 | 8 | 1 | 0 | .889 |
| Monmouth (III.) .... | 3 | 2 | 0 | .600 | 5 | 4 | 0 | .556 |
| Illinois Col. ....... | 2 | 3 | 0 | .400 | 5 | 4 | 0 | .556 |
| Knox ............. | 1 | 4 | 0 | .200 | 2 | 7 | 0 | .222 |
| Grinnell .......... | 0 | 5 | 0 | .000 | 0 | 9 | 0 | .000 |

* Beloit defeated Carroll (Wis.), 6-3, on October 17.   † Cornell College defeated Beloit, 40-14, on November 14.

## MINNESOTA INTERCOLLEGIATE ATHLETIC CONFERENCE

| Team | CONFERENCE | | | | FULL SEASON | | | |
|------|---|---|---|------|---|---|---|------|
| | W | L | T | Pct. | W | L | T | Pct. |
| Carleton .......... | 8 | 1 | 0 | .889 | 9 | 1 | 0 | .900 |
| St. John's (Minn.) ... | 7 | 1 | 1 | .833 | 8 | 1 | 1 | .850 |
| Concordia-M'head .. | 6 | 2 | 1 | .722 | 7 | 2 | 1 | .750 |
| Hamline .......... | 5 | 4 | 0 | .556 | 6 | 4 | 0 | .600 |
| Bethel (Minn.)...... | 5 | 4 | 0 | .556 | 5 | 5 | 0 | .500 |
| Gust. Adolphus* .... | 4 | 5 | 0 | .444 | 4 | 6 | 0 | .400 |
| St. Olaf* ......... | 4 | 5 | 0 | .444 | 4 | 6 | 0 | .400 |
| St. Thomas (Minn.) . | 3 | 6 | 0 | .333 | 3 | 7 | 0 | .300 |
| Augsburg ......... | 2 | 7 | 0 | .222 | 3 | 7 | 0 | .300 |
| Macalester ........ | 0 | 9 | 0 | .000 | 0 | 10 | 0 | .000 |

* Gust. Adolphus defeated St. Olaf, 14-9, on October 10.

**Division III Playoffs (0-1-0):** Carleton (0-1, lost in first round to Central, Iowa, 20-8)

## NEW ENGLAND FOOTBALL CONFERENCE

| Team | CONFERENCE | | | | FULL SEASON | | | |
|------|---|---|---|------|---|---|---|------|
| | W | L | T | Pct. | W | L | T | Pct. |
| Bri'water (Mass.)† .. | 8 | 0 | 0 | 1.000 | 9 | 0 | 1 | .950 |
| Mass. Maritime .... | 6 | 2 | 0 | .750 | 6 | 3 | 0 | .667 |
| Westfield St.* ...... | 5 | 3 | 0 | .625 | 6 | 3 | 0 | .667 |
| Maine Maritime* ... | 5 | 3 | 0 | .625 | 6 | 3 | 0 | .667 |
| Mass.-Dartmouth ... | 4 | 4 | 0 | .500 | 5 | 4 | 0 | .556 |
| Mass.-Boston ...... | 4 | 4 | 0 | .500 | 5 | 4 | 0 | .556 |
| Framingham St..... | 3 | 5 | 0 | .375 | 4 | 5 | 0 | .444 |
| Worcester St. ..... | 1 | 7 | 0 | .125 | 1 | 9 | 0 | .100 |
| Fitchburg St. ...... | 0 | 8 | 0 | .000 | 0 | 9 | 0 | .000 |

† Does not include 28-25 loss to Rensselaer in ECAC Northeast playoff game.   * Westfield St. defeated Maine Maritime, 22-13, on November 14.

## NEW JERSEY ATHLETIC CONFERENCE

| Team | CONFERENCE | | | | FULL SEASON | | | |
|------|---|---|---|------|---|---|---|------|
| | W | L | T | Pct. | W | L | T | Pct. |
| Rowan ............ | 6 | 0 | 0 | 1.000 | 10 | 0 | 0 | 1.000 |
| Montclair St. ...... | 5 | 1 | 0 | .833 | 6 | 3 | 0 | .667 |
| Wm. Paterson ..... | 4 | 2 | 0 | .667 | 8 | 2 | 0 | .800 |
| Kean ............. | 3 | 3 | 0 | .500 | 6 | 3 | 1 | .650 |
| Trenton St. ........ | 2 | 4 | 0 | .333 | 3 | 7 | 0 | .300 |
| Ramapo* .......... | 1 | 5 | 0 | .167 | 1 | 8 | 0 | .111 |
| Jersey City St. ..... | 0 | 6 | 0 | .000 | 0 | 10 | 0 | .000 |

* Dropped football program after 1992 season.

**Division III Playoffs (2-1-0):** Rowan (2-1; defeated Worcester Tech, 41-14, in first round; defeated Buffalo St., 28-19, in quarterfinals; lost to Wash. & Jeff., 18-13, in semifinals)

## NORTH COAST ATHLETIC CONFERENCE#

| Team | CONFERENCE | | | | FULL SEASON | | | |
|------|---|---|---|------|---|---|---|------|
| | W | L | T | Pct. | W | L | T | Pct. |
| Wittenberg* ....... | 7 | 0 | 0 | 1.000 | 7 | 1 | 1 | .833 |
| Allegheny ......... | 7 | 1 | 0 | .875 | 8 | 2 | 0 | .800 |
| Ohio Wesleyan ..... | 6 | 2 | 0 | .750 | 8 | 2 | 0 | .800 |
| Denison .......... | 2 | 4 | 2 | .375 | 3 | 5 | 2 | .400 |
| Wooster .......... | 2 | 4 | 1 | .357 | 3 | 6 | 1 | .350 |
| Case Reserve ...... | 1 | 3 | 2 | .333 | 2 | 6 | 2 | .300 |
| Kenyon ........... | 2 | 5 | 1 | .313 | 2 | 6 | 2 | .300 |
| Earlham .......... | 2 | 5 | 0 | .286 | 5 | 5 | 0 | .500 |
| Oberlin* .......... | 1 | 6 | 0 | .125 | 1 | 8 | 0 | .111 |

# North Coast Athletic Conference teams do not play the same number of conference games. Standings are determined by winning percentage (there are no designated conference games).   * Records do not include Oberlin forfeit to Wittenberg.

---

Eight Division III teams – including Dayton, which will move to Division I-AA in 1993 – had perfect (undefeated, untied) records in the 1992 regular season.

---

656

## OHIO ATHLETIC CONFERENCE

| Team | CONFERENCE W | L | T | Pct. | FULL SEASON W | L | T | Pct. |
|------|---|---|---|------|---|---|---|------|
| Mount Union | 9 | 0 | 0 | 1.000 | 10 | 0 | 0 | 1.000 |
| Baldwin-Wallace* | 7 | 2 | 0 | .778 | 8 | 2 | 0 | .800 |
| John Carroll* | 7 | 2 | 0 | .778 | 8 | 2 | 0 | .800 |
| Ohio Northern | 5 | 4 | 0 | .556 | 6 | 4 | 0 | .600 |
| Heidelberg | 4 | 4 | 1 | .500 | 5 | 4 | 1 | .550 |
| Otterbein | 3 | 4 | 2 | .444 | 3 | 5 | 2 | .400 |
| Muskingum | 3 | 6 | 0 | .333 | 4 | 6 | 0 | .400 |
| Marietta | 3 | 6 | 0 | .333 | 3 | 6 | 1 | .350 |
| Capital | 1 | 7 | 1 | .167 | 2 | 7 | 1 | .250 |
| Hiram | 1 | 8 | 0 | .111 | 1 | 9 | 0 | .100 |

* Baldwin-Wallace defeated John Carroll, 27-17, on November 14.

**Division III Playoffs (2-1-0):** Mount Union (2-1; defeated Dayton, 27-10, in first round; defeated Ill. Wesleyan, 49-27, in quarterfinals; lost to Wis.-La Crosse, 29-24, in semifinals)

## OLD DOMINION ATHLETIC CONFERENCE

| Team | CONFERENCE W | L | T | Pct. | FULL SEASON W | L | T | Pct. |
|------|---|---|---|------|---|---|---|------|
| Emory & Henry | 5 | 0 | 0 | 1.000 | 10 | 0 | 0 | 1.000 |
| Hampden-Sydney | 3 | 2 | 0 | .600 | 6 | 4 | 0 | .600 |
| Wash. & Lee | 2 | 3 | 0 | .400 | 5 | 4 | 0 | .556 |
| Randolph-Macon | 2 | 3 | 0 | .400 | 4 | 6 | 0 | .400 |
| Bridgewater (Va.) | 2 | 3 | 0 | .400 | 3 | 7 | 0 | .300 |
| Guilford | 1 | 4 | 0 | .200 | 2 | 8 | 0 | .200 |

**Division III Playoffs (1-1-0):** Emory & Henry (1-1; defeated Thomas More, 17-0, in first round; lost to Wash. & Jeff., 51-15, in quarterfinals)

## PRESIDENTS' ATHLETIC CONFERENCE

| Team | CONFERENCE W | L | T | Pct. | FULL SEASON W | L | T | Pct. |
|------|---|---|---|------|---|---|---|------|
| Wash. & Jeff. | 4 | 0 | 0 | 1.000 | 8 | 1 | 0 | .889 |
| Grove City | 3 | 1 | 0 | .750 | 5 | 4 | 0 | .556 |
| Bethany (W. Va.) | 2 | 2 | 0 | .500 | 3 | 6 | 0 | .333 |
| Waynesburg | 1 | 3 | 0 | .250 | 2 | 7 | 0 | .222 |
| Thiel | 0 | 4 | 0 | .000 | 1 | 8 | 0 | .111 |

**Division III Playoffs (3-1-0):** Wash. & Jeff. (3-1; defeated Lycoming, 33-0, in first round; defeated Emory & Henry, 51-15, in quarterfinals; defeated Rowan, 18-13, in semifinals; lost to Wis.-La Crosse, 16-12, in championship game)

## SOUTHERN CALIFORNIA INTERCOLLEGIATE ATHLETIC CONFERENCE

| Team | CONFERENCE W | L | T | Pct. | FULL SEASON W | L | T | Pct. |
|------|---|---|---|------|---|---|---|------|
| Redlands | 6 | 0 | 0 | 1.000 | 8 | 1 | 0 | .889 |
| La Verne | 5 | 1 | 0 | .833 | 7 | 1 | 0 | .833 |
| Occidental | 3 | 3 | 0 | .500 | 5 | 4 | 0 | .556 |
| Pomona-Pitzer | 3 | 3 | 0 | .500 | 4 | 4 | 0 | .500 |
| Whittier* | 2 | 4 | 0 | .333 | 3 | 6 | 0 | .333 |
| Cal Lutheran* | 2 | 4 | 0 | .333 | 3 | 6 | 0 | .333 |
| Claremont-M-S | 0 | 6 | 0 | .000 | 0 | 9 | 0 | .000 |

* Whittier defeated Cal Lutheran, 33-30, on November 14.

**Division III Playoffs (0-1-0):** Redlands (0-1, lost in first round to Wis.-La Crosse, 47-26)

## SOUTHERN COLLEGIATE ATHLETIC CONFERENCE

| Team | CONFERENCE W | L | T | Pct. | FULL SEASON W | L | T | Pct. |
|------|---|---|---|------|---|---|---|------|
| Sewanee | 4 | 0 | 0 | 1.000 | 8 | 1 | 0 | .889 |
| Millsaps | 2 | 1 | 1 | .625 | 5 | 4 | 1 | .550 |
| Centre | 2 | 2 | 0 | .500 | 3 | 6 | 0 | .333 |
| Rhodes | 1 | 2 | 1 | .375 | 5 | 4 | 1 | .550 |
| Trinity (Tex.) | 0 | 4 | 0 | .000 | 2 | 8 | 0 | .200 |

## UNIVERSITY ATHLETIC ASSOCIATION

| Team | CONFERENCE W | L | T | Pct. | FULL SEASON W | L | T | Pct. |
|------|---|---|---|------|---|---|---|------|
| Rochester | 4 | 0 | 0 | 1.000 | 8 | 1 | 0 | .889 |
| Carnegie Mellon | 3 | 1 | 0 | .750 | 7 | 2 | 0 | .778 |
| Washington (Mo.) | 1 | 3 | 0 | .250 | 4 | 6 | 0 | .400 |
| Case Reserve | 1 | 3 | 0 | .250 | 2 | 6 | 2 | .300 |
| Chicago | 1 | 3 | 0 | .250 | 3 | 7 | 0 | .300 |

## WISCONSIN STATE UNIVERSITY CONFERENCE

| Team | CONFERENCE W | L | T | Pct. | FULL SEASON W | L | T | Pct. |
|------|---|---|---|------|---|---|---|------|
| Wis.-La Crosse | 6 | 0 | 1 | .929 | 8 | 0 | 1 | .944 |
| Wis.-Whitewater | 5 | 2 | 0 | .714 | 8 | 2 | 0 | .800 |
| Wis.-River Falls | 4 | 2 | 1 | .643 | 6 | 2 | 1 | .722 |
| Wis.-Stevens Pt.* | 4 | 3 | 0 | .571 | 5 | 4 | 0 | .556 |
| Wis.-Platteville* | 4 | 3 | 0 | .571 | 5 | 4 | 0 | .556 |
| Wis.-Eau Claire | 3 | 4 | 0 | .429 | 4 | 5 | 0 | .444 |
| Wis.-Stout | 1 | 6 | 0 | .143 | 2 | 7 | 0 | .222 |
| Wis.-Oshkosh | 0 | 7 | 0 | .000 | 1 | 8 | 0 | .111 |
| Wis.-Superior# | — | — | — | — | 1 | 1 | 0 | .500 |

* Wis.-Stevens Point defeated Wis.-Platteville, 31-7, on October 31.   # Wis.-Superior suspended season after two nonconference games, later discontinued program.

**Division III Playoffs (4-0-0):** Wis.-La Crosse (4-0; defeated Redlands, 47-26, in first round; defeated Central, Iowa, 34-9, in quarterfinals; defeated Mount Union, 29-24, in semifinals; defeated Wash. & Jeff., 16-12, in championship game)

## DIVISION III INDEPENDENTS

| Team | FULL SEASON W | L | T | Pct. |
|------|---|---|---|------|
| Dayton | 10 | 0 | 0 | 1.000 |
| Aurora | 9 | 0 | 0 | 1.000 |
| Hardin-Simmons | 9 | 1 | 0 | .900 |
| Ithaca | 9 | 1 | 0 | .900 |
| Middlebury‡ | 7 | 1 | 0 | .875 |
| St. Francis (Pa.)# | 8 | 1 | 1 | .850 |
| Buffalo St. | 7 | 2 | 0 | .778 |
| Evansville | 7 | 2 | 0 | .778 |
| Rensselaer @ | 7 | 2 | 0 | .778 |
| St. Peter's | 7 | 2 | 1 | .750 |
| Drake | 7 | 2 | 1 | .750 |
| San Diego | 7 | 2 | 1 | .750 |
| Trinity (Conn.)‡ | 6 | 2 | 0 | .750 |
| Ala.-Birmingham | 7 | 3 | 0 | .700 |
| Ill. Benedictine | 7 | 3 | 0 | .700 |
| Wesley | 7 | 3 | 0 | .700 |
| Williams‡ | 5 | 2 | 1 | .688 |
| Neb. Wesleyan | 6 | 3 | 0 | .667 |
| Union (N.Y.) | 6 | 3 | 0 | .667 |
| Frostburg St. | 6 | 3 | 1 | .650 |
| Gannon | 6 | 3 | 1 | .650 |
| Colby‡ | 5 | 3 | 0 | .625 |
| Hamilton‡ | 5 | 3 | 0 | .625 |
| Albany (N.Y.) | 6 | 4 | 0 | .600 |
| Cortland St.% | 6 | 4 | 0 | .600 |
| Duquesne | 5 | 4 | 0 | .556 |
| Mercyhurst | 5 | 4 | 1 | .550 |
| Concordia (Ill.) | 5 | 5 | 0 | .500 |
| Davidson | 5 | 5 | 0 | .500 |
| Eureka | 5 | 5 | 0 | .500 |
| Maryville (Tenn.) | 5 | 5 | 0 | .500 |
| Bowdoin‡ | 4 | 4 | 0 | .500 |
| N'western (Wis.) | 4 | 4 | 0 | .500 |
| Wesleyan‡ | 4 | 4 | 0 | .500 |
| FDU-Madison | 4 | 5 | 0 | .444 |
| Ferrum | 4 | 5 | 0 | .444 |
| Quincy | 4 | 5 | 0 | .444 |
| Tufts‡ | 3 | 4 | 1 | .438 |
| Alfred | 4 | 6 | 0 | .400 |
| Buffalo | 4 | 6 | 0 | .400 |
| Catholic | 4 | 6 | 0 | .400 |
| Georgetown | 4 | 6 | 0 | .400 |
| Hobart | 4 | 6 | 0 | .400 |
| Hofstra | 4 | 6 | 0 | .400 |
| St. John Fisher | 4 | 6 | 0 | .400 |
| Upsala | 4 | 6 | 0 | .400 |
| Canisius | 3 | 6 | 1 | .350 |
| Colorado Col. | 3 | 6 | 0 | .333 |
| Menlo | 3 | 6 | 0 | .333 |
| St. Lawrence | 3 | 6 | 0 | .333 |

| Team | FULL SEASON | | | |
|---|---|---|---|---|
| | W | L | T | Pct. |
| Brockport St. ..................... | 3 | 7 | 0 | .300 |
| Ky. Wesleyan ................... | 3 | 7 | 0 | .300 |
| MacMurray..................... | 3 | 7 | 0 | .300 |
| Principia ....................... | 2 | 6 | 0 | .250 |
| Blackburn ...................... | 2 | 7 | 0 | .222 |
| Charleston So. ................. | 2 | 7 | 0 | .222 |
| Salisbury St. .................. | 2 | 7 | 0 | .222 |
| Siena.......................... | 2 | 7 | 0 | .222 |
| Hartwick....................... | 1 | 7 | 0 | .125 |
| Amherst‡ ...................... | 0 | 8 | 0 | .000 |
| Bates‡ ........................ | 0 | 8 | 0 | .000 |
| Gallaudet ...................... | 0 | 9 | 0 | .000 |
| Sacred Heart ................... | 0 | 9 | 0 | .000 |
| Methodist ...................... | 0 | 10 | 0 | .000 |

#Does not include 48-6 loss to Wagner in ECAC Southeast playoff game.  @ Does not include 28-25 win over Bri'water (Mass.) in ECAC Northeast playoff game.  % Does not include 38-20 win over Bentley in ECAC Northwest playoff game.  ‡ Member of New England Small College Athletic Conference but league does not keep standings.

**NAIA Division II Playoffs (1-1-0):** Hardin-Simmons (1-1; defeated Howard Payne, 42-28, in first round; lost to Minot St., 21-14, in quarterfinals)

**Division III Playoffs (1-4-0):** Aurora (0-1, lost in first round to Ill. Wesleyan, 21-12); Buffalo St. (1-1; defeated Ithaca, 28-26, in first round; lost to Rowan, 28-19, in quarterfinals); Dayton (0-1, lost in first round to Mount Union, 27-10); Ithaca (0-1, lost in first round to Buffalo St., 28-26)

# 1993 SCHEDULES
# 1992 RESULTS

*In 1993, players from 27 Divisions II and III schools will be jumping, like Dayton's Keith Miller, to Division I-AA. Miller was the leading rusher for Dayton in 1992, its last season as a Division III team.*

# 1993 DIVISIONS I-A & I-AA SCHEDULES

Listed alphabetically in this section are 1993 schedules and 1992 records of all teams classified Division I-A and Division I-AA in football. The division designation for each school is indicated to the right of the school name.

Coaching records (below head coaches' names) are for all seasons as the head coach at any four-year collegiate institution.

**Game dates and starting times are subject to change.**

---

## AIR FORCE . . . Air Force Academy, Colo.  80840                    I-A

Coach: Fisher DeBerry, Wofford '60
Record: 9 yrs., W-72, L-38, T-1
1993 SCHEDULE

| | |
|---|---|
| Indiana St. ■ | Sep 4 |
| Colorado St. | Sep 11 |
| San Diego St. ■ | Sep 18 |
| Brigham Young | Sep 25 |
| Wyoming ■ | Oct 2 |
| Navy | Oct 9 |
| Fresno St. | Oct 16* |
| Citadel ■ | Oct 23 |
| UTEP ■ | Oct 30 |
| Army ■ | Nov 6 |
| Utah | Nov 13 |
| Hawaii | Nov 20* |

1992 RECORD

| | | | | |
|---|---|---|---|---|
| 30 | Rice | 21 | 13 | Utah | 20 |
| 3 | Hawaii | 6 | 7 | Army | 3 |
| 42 | Wyoming | 28 | 7 | Brigham Young | 28 |
| 33 | New Mexico | 32 | | | |
| 28 | UTEP | 22 | 229 | (7-4-0) | 225 |
| 18 | Navy | 16 | | **Liberty Bowl** | |
| 28 | Colorado St. | 32 | 0 | Mississippi | 13 |
| 20 | San Diego St. | 17 | | | |

Conference: Western Athl. Conf.  Enrollment: 4,400.  Colors: Blue & Silver.
Nickname: Falcons.  Stadium: Falcon (1962), 53,533 capacity.  Natural turf.
1992 home attendance: 284,371 in 7 games.
Director of Athletics: Col. Ken Schweitzer.
Sports Info. Director: Dave Kellogg  719-472-2313

---

## AKRON . . . Akron, Ohio  44325                    I-A

Coach: Gerry Faust, Dayton '58
Record: 12 yrs., W-67, L-63, T-4
1993 SCHEDULE

| | |
|---|---|
| Central Mich. | Sep 2* |
| Kent ■ | Sep 11* |
| Western Mich. | Sep 18 |
| Army | Oct 2 |
| Miami (Ohio) ■ | Oct 9* |
| Bowling Green | Oct 16 |
| Temple | Oct 23 |
| Ohio | Oct 30 |
| Eastern Mich. ■ | Nov 6 |
| Ball St. ■ | Nov 13 |
| Youngstown St. ■ | Nov 20 |

1992 RECORD

| | | | | |
|---|---|---|---|---|
| 27 | Eastern Mich. | 9 | 29 | Temple | 15 |
| 23 | Toledo | 20 | 10 | Youngstown St. | 10 |
| 20 | Western Mich. | 24 | 24 | Cincinnati | 22 |
| 13 | Ohio | 0 | | | |
| 16 | Kent | 20 | 218 | (7-3-1) | 186 |
| 22 | Ball St. | 14 | | | |
| 3 | Bowling Green | 24 | | | |
| 31 | Central Mich. | 28 | | | |

Conference: Mid-American Conf.  Enrollment: 29,779.  Colors: Blue & Gold.
Nickname: Zips.  Stadium: Rubber Bowl (1940), 35,482 capacity.  Artificial turf.
1992 home attendance: 61,242 in 5 games.
Director of Athletics: Richard Aynes.
Sports Info. Director: Mac Yates  216-972-7468

---

## ALABAMA . . . University, Ala.  35486                    I-A

Coach: Gene Stallings, Texas A&M '57
Record: 10 yrs., W-58, L-51, T-1
1993 SCHEDULE

| | |
|---|---|
| Tulane [Birmingham, Ala.] | Sep 4 |
| Vanderbilt | Sep 11* |
| Arkansas ■ | Sep 18 |
| Louisiana Tech [Birmingham, Ala.] | Sep 25 |
| South Caro. | Oct 2* |
| Tennessee [Birmingham, Ala.] | Oct 16 |
| Mississippi | Oct 23 |
| Southern Miss. ■ | Oct 30 |
| Louisiana St. | Nov 6 |
| Mississippi St. ■ | Nov 13 |
| Auburn | Nov 20 |

1992 RECORD

| | | | | |
|---|---|---|---|---|
| 25 | Vanderbilt | 8 | 30 | Mississippi St. | 21 |
| 17 | Southern Miss. | 10 | 17 | Auburn | 0 |
| 38 | Arkansas | 11 | | **SEC Championship** | |
| 13 | Louisiana Tech | 0 | 28 | Florida | 21 |
| 48 | South Caro. | 7 | | | |
| 37 | Tulane | 0 | 332 | (12-0-0) | 109 |
| 17 | Tennessee | 10 | | **Sugar Bowl** | |
| 31 | Mississippi | 10 | 34 | Miami (Fla.) | 13 |
| 31 | Louisiana St. | 11 | | | |

Conference: Southeastern Conf.  Enrollment: 20,000.  Colors: Crimson & White.
Nickname: Crimson Tide.  Stadium: Bryant-Denny (1929), 70,123 capacity.  Natural turf.
1992 home attendance: 537,264 in 7 games.
Director of Athletics: Hootie Ingram.
Sports Info. Director: Larry White  205-348-6084

---

## ALABAMA-BIRMINGHAM . . . Birmingham, Ala.  35294                    I-AA

Coach: Jim Hilyer, Stetson '57
Record: 2 yrs., W-11, L-6, T-2
1993 SCHEDULE

| | |
|---|---|
| Troy St. ■ | Sep 6 |
| Morehead St. ■ | Sep 11 |
| Western Ky. | Sep 25* |
| Miles | Oct 2 |
| Lambuth ■ | Oct 9 |
| Mississippi Val. | Oct 16 |
| Charleston So. | Oct 23 |
| Wofford | Oct 30* |
| Butler | Nov 6 |
| Dayton ■ | Nov 13 |
| Prairie View ■ | Nov 20 |

1992 RECORD

| | | | | |
|---|---|---|---|---|
| 17 | Millsaps | 0 | 41 | Lindenwood | 12 |
| 44 | Gallaudet | 6 | 41 | Clinch Valley | 30 |
| 26 | Lane | 6 | | | |
| 12 | Tenn. Wesleyan | 16 | 270 | (7-3-0) | 163 |
| 30 | Miles | 6 | | | |
| 39 | Charleston So. | 7 | | | |
| 17 | Ferrum | 31 | | | |
| 3 | Samford | 49 | | | |

Conference: I-AA Independents.  Enrollment: 16,000.  Colors: Green, Gold & White.
Nickname: Blazers.  Stadium: Legion Field (1927), 83,091 capacity.  Artificial turf.
1992 home attendance: 29,909 in 5 games.
Director of Athletics: Gene Bartow.
Sports Info. Director: Grant Shingleton  205-934-0722

---

■ Home games on each schedule [neutral sites shown in brackets].   *Night Games.

*1993 NCAA FOOTBALL*

## ALABAMA STATE . . . Montgomery, Ala   36195   I-AA

Coach: Houston Markham, Alcorn State '65
Record: 6 yrs., W-44, L-19, T-3
### 1993 SCHEDULE
Southern-B.R. .......................... Sep 11*
Alcorn St. ■ .......................... Sep 18*
Troy St. ■ .............................. Sep 25*
Jackson St. ............................ Oct  9*
Texas Southern ........................ Oct 16
Prairie View ........................... Oct 23
Alabama A&M [Birmingham, Ala.] ....... Oct 30
Grambling ■ ........................... Nov  6*
Mississippi Val. ....................... Nov 13

### 1992 RECORD
| | | | | | |
|---|---|---|---|---|---|
| 30 | Southern-B.R. | 10 | 19 | Grambling | 44 |
| 7 | Alcorn St. | 32 | 35 | Mississippi Val. | 19 |
| 14 | Troy St. | 31 | 17 | Fayetteville St. | 14 |
| 13 | Central St. (Ohio) | 34 | | | |
| 7 | Jackson St. | 21 | 228 | (5-6-0) | 252 |
| 28 | Texas Southern | 30 | | | |
| 44 | Prairie View | 6 | | | |
| 14 | Alabama A&M | 11 | | | |

Conference: Southwestern.  Enrollment: 4,200.  Colors: Black & Gold.
Nickname: Hornets.  Stadium: Cramton, 24,600 capacity.  Natural turf.
1992 home attendance: 164,859 in 7 games.
Director of Athletics: Arthur Barnett.
Sports Info. Director: Jack Jeffery  205-240-6857

---

## ALCORN STATE . . . Lorman, Miss.   39096   I-AA

Coach: Cardell Jones, Alcorn St. '65
Record: 2 yrs., W-14, L-6, T-1
### 1993 SCHEDULE
Grambling ■ ........................... Sep  4
Texas Southern [Jackson, Miss.] ....... Sep 11*
Alabama St. ........................... Sep 18*
Howard [St. Louis, Mo.] ............... Sep 25
Sam Houston St. ■ ..................... Oct  2
Prairie View ■ ........................ Oct 16
Southern-B.R. ......................... Oct 23*
Jacksonville St. ■ ..................... Oct 30
Mississippi Val. ■ ..................... Nov  6
Troy St. ............................... Nov 13
Jackson St. ........................... Nov 20

### 1992 RECORD
| | | | | | |
|---|---|---|---|---|---|
| 35 | Grambling | 33 | 31 | Mississippi Val. | 0 |
| 32 | Alabama St. | 7 | 42 | Jackson St. | 35 |
| 42 | Howard | 48 | | | |
| 27 | Sam Houston St. | 28 | 398 | (7-3-0) | 259 |
| 46 | Texas Southern | 36 | | I-AA Championship | |
| 63 | Prairie View | 0 | 27 | Northeast La. | 78 |
| 35 | Southern-B.R. | 13 | | | |
| 45 | Jacksonville St. | 59 | | | |

Conference: Southwestern.  Enrollment: 3,100.  Colors: Purple & Gold.
Nickname: Braves.  Stadium: Jack Spinks (1993), 25,000 capacity.  Natural turf.
1992 home attendance: 79,715 in 4 games.
Director of Athletics: Cardell Jones.
Sports Info. Director: Gus Howard  601-877-6466

---

## APPALACHIAN STATE . . . Boone, N.C.   28608   I-AA

Coach: Jerry Moore, Baylor '61
Record: 11 yrs., W-57, L-65, T-2
### 1993 SCHEDULE
North Caro. A&T ........................ Sep  4
Liberty ■ .............................. Sep 11
Wake Forest ........................... Sep 18*
Citadel ■ .............................. Sep 25*
East Tenn. St. ■ ....................... Oct  2
Furman ................................ Oct  9
Ga. Southern ■ ........................ Oct 16
Marshall .............................. Oct 23*
Tenn.-Chatt. ■ ........................ Oct 30
Western Caro. ■ ....................... Nov 13
Va. Military .......................... Nov 20

### 1992 RECORD
| | | | | | |
|---|---|---|---|---|---|
| 10 | North Caro. St. | 35 | 37 | Marshall | 34 |
| 7 | Wake Forest | 10 | 42 | North Caro. A&T | 6 |
| 38 | East Tenn. St. | 14 | 14 | Western Caro. | 12 |
| 0 | Citadel | 25 | | | |
| 27 | James Madison | 21 | 252 | (7-4-0) | 202 |
| 27 | Va. Military | 12 | | I-AA Championship | |
| 13 | Furman | 16 | 10 | Middle Tenn. St. | 35 |
| 37 | Tenn.-Chatt. | 17 | | | |

Conference: Southern Conf.  Enrollment: 11,501.  Colors: Black & Gold.
Nickname: Mountaineers.  Stadium: Kidd Brewer (1962), 18,000 capacity.  Artificial turf.
1992 home attendance: 93,189 in 5 games.
Director of Athletics: Roachel Laney.
Sports Info. Director: Rick Covington  704-262-3080

---

## ARIZONA . . . Tucson, Ariz.   85721   I-A

Coach: Dick Tomey, De Pauw '61
Record: 16 yrs., W-99, L-75, T-7
### 1993 SCHEDULE
UTEP ■ ................................. Sep  4*
Pacific (Cal.) ■ ....................... Sep 11
Illinois .............................. Sep 18
Oregon St. ............................ Sep 25
Southern Cal ■ ........................ Oct  2
Stanford ■ ............................ Oct 16*
Washington St. ■ ...................... Oct 23*
UCLA .................................. Oct 30
Oregon ■ .............................. Nov  6*
California ............................ Nov 13
Arizona St. ........................... Nov 26*

### 1992 RECORD
| | | | | | |
|---|---|---|---|---|---|
| 49 | Utah St. | 3 | 16 | Washington | 3 |
| 20 | Washington St. | 23 | 7 | Southern Cal | 14 |
| 14 | Oregon St. | 14 | 6 | Arizona St. | 7 |
| 7 | Miami (Fla.) | 8 | | | |
| 23 | UCLA | 3 | 217 | (6-4-1) | 98 |
| 21 | Stanford | 6 | | John Hancock Bowl | |
| 24 | California | 17 | 15 | Baylor | 20 |
| 30 | New Mexico St. | 0 | | | |

Conference: Pacific-10.  Enrollment: 35,647.  Colors: Cardinal & Navy.
Nickname: Wildcats.  Stadium: Arizona (1928), 56,167 capacity.  Natural turf.
1992 home attendance: 282,127 in 6 games.
Director of Athletics: Cedric Dempsey.
Sports Info. Director: Butch Henry  602-621-4163

---

## ARIZONA STATE . . . Tempe, Ariz.   85287   I-A

Coach: Bruce Snyder, Oregon '63
Record: 13 yrs., W-72, L-67, T-6
### 1993 SCHEDULE
Utah ■ ................................ Sep  4*
Louisville ............................ Sep 18
Oklahoma St. ■ ........................ Sep 25*
Oregon St. ............................ Oct  2
Washington St. ........................ Oct  9
Oregon ■ .............................. Oct 16*
Stanford .............................. Oct 23
Washington ■ .......................... Oct 30*
California ............................ Nov  6*
UCLA .................................. Nov 13
Arizona ■ ............................. Nov 26*

### 1992 RECORD
| | | | | | |
|---|---|---|---|---|---|
| 7 | Washington | 31 | 18 | Washington St. | 20 |
| 19 | Louisville | 0 | 28 | California | 12 |
| 24 | Nebraska | 45 | 7 | Arizona | 6 |
| 20 | Oregon | 30 | | | |
| 39 | Pacific (Cal.) | 5 | 235 | (6-5-0) | 185 |
| 40 | Oregon St. | 13 | | | |
| 20 | UCLA | 0 | | | |
| 13 | Southern Cal | 23 | | | |

Conference: Pacific-10.  Enrollment: 42,626.  Colors: Maroon & Gold.
Nickname: Sun Devils.  Stadium: Sun Devil (1958), 74,783 capacity.  Natural turf.
1992 home attendance: 293,365 in 6 games.
Director of Athletics: Charles S. Harris.
Sports Info. Director: Mark Brand  602-965-6592

---

■ Home games on each schedule [neutral sites shown in brackets].   *Night Games.

## ARKANSAS . . . Fayetteville, Ark.   72701   I-A

Coach: Danny Ford, Alabama '70
Record: 12 yrs., W-96, L-29, T-4
1993 SCHEDULE

Southern Methodist ..................... Sep 4*
South Caro. ■ ......................... Sep 11
Alabama ............................... Sep 18
Memphis St. [Little Rock, Ark.] ......... Sep 25
Georgia ............................... Oct 2
Tennessee [Little Rock, Ark.] ........... Oct 9
Mississippi [Jackson, Miss.] ............ Oct 16*
Auburn ■ .............................. Oct 30
Mississippi St. [Little Rock, Ark.] ...... Nov 6
Tulsa ■ ............................... Nov 13
Louisiana St. .......................... Nov 27*

1992 RECORD

| | | | | |
|---|---|---|---|---|
| 3 | Citadel | 10 | 3 Mississippi St. | 10 |
| 45 | South Caro. | 7 | 19 Southern Methodist | 24 |
| 11 | Alabama | 38 | 30 Louisiana St. | 6 |
| 6 | Memphis St. | 22 | | |
| 3 | Georgia | 27 | 172       (3-7-1) | 209 |
| 25 | Tennessee | 24 | | |
| 3 | Mississippi | 17 | | |
| 24 | Auburn | 24 | | |

Conference: Southeastern Conf.   Enrollment: 14,000.   Colors: Cardinal & White.
Nickname: Razorbacks.   Stadium: Razorback (1938), 51,000 capacity.   Artificial turf.
1992 home attendance: 276,196 in 6 games.
Director of Athletics: Frank Broyles.
Sports Info. Director: Rick Schaeffer  501-575-2751

## ARKANSAS STATE . . . State University, Ark.   72467   I-A

Coach: John Bobo, Maryville (Tenn.) '80
Record: First year as head coach
1993 SCHEDULE

Florida ............................... Sep 4*
New Mexico St. ■ ...................... Sep 11*
Northern Ill. .......................... Sep 18*
Southern Ill. ■ ........................ Sep 25*
Louisiana Tech ........................ Oct 2*
Memphis St. ........................... Oct 9
Southwestern La. ■ .................... Oct 16*
Mississippi St. ........................ Oct 23
Northeast La. ■ ....................... Nov 6
Pacific (Cal.) ......................... Nov 13
Nevada ■ ............................. Nov 20

1992 RECORD

| | | | | |
|---|---|---|---|---|
| 0 | Toledo | 49 | 0 Louisiana Tech | 23 |
| 0 | Oklahoma | 61 | 18 East Caro. | 35 |
| 0 | Northern Ill. | 31 | 20 Southwestern La. | 7 |
| 42 | Southern Ill. | 38 | | |
| 18 | Northwestern (La.) | 24 | 118       (2-9-0) | 402 |
| 7 | Troy St. | 41 | | |
| 7 | Memphis St. | 37 | | |
| 6 | Mississippi St. | 56 | | |

Conference: Big West.   Enrollment: 10,300.   Colors: Scarlet & Black.
Nickname: Indians.   Stadium: Indian (1974), 33,410 capacity.   Natural turf.
1992 home attendance: 44,500 in 4 games.
Director of Athletics: Brad Hovious.
Sports Info. Director: Jerry Schaeffer  501-972-2541

## ARMY . . . West Point, N.Y.   10996   I-A

Coach: Bob Sutton, Eastern Mich. '74
Record: 2 yrs., W-9, L-13, T-0
1993 SCHEDULE

Colgate ■ ............................. Sep 11
Duke ................................. Sep 18*
Va. Military ■ ......................... Sep 25
Akron ■ .............................. Oct 2
Temple ............................... Oct 9
Rutgers ■ ............................ Oct 16
Boston College ........................ Oct 23
Western Mich. ■ ...................... Oct 30
Air Force ............................. Nov 6
Lafayette ............................. Nov 13
Navy [East Rutherford, N.J.] ........... Dec 4

1992 RECORD

| | | | | |
|---|---|---|---|---|
| 17 | Holy Cross | 7 | 21 Northern Ill. | 14 |
| 9 | North Caro. | 22 | 24 Boston College | 41 |
| 14 | Citadel | 15 | 25 Navy | 24 |
| 38 | Lafayette | 36 | | |
| 10 | Rutgers | 45 | 225       (5-6-0) | 251 |
| 7 | Wake Forest | 23 | | |
| 57 | Eastern Mich. | 17 | | |
| 3 | Air Force | 7 | | |

Conference: I-A Independents.   Enrollment: 4,200.   Colors: Black, Gold, Gray.
Nickname: Cadets, Black Knights.   Stadium: Michie (1924), 39,929 capacity.   Artificial turf.
1992 home attendance: 244,041 in 7 games.
Director of Athletics: Al Vanderbush.
Sports Info. Director: Robert Kinney  914-938-3303

## AUBURN . . . Auburn, Ala.   36830   I-A

Coach: Terry Bowden, West Va. '78
Record: 9 yrs., W-64, L-36, T-1
1993 SCHEDULE

Mississippi ■ ......................... Sep 2*
Samford ■ ............................ Sep 11*
Louisiana St. ■ ....................... Sep 18*
Southern Miss. ■ ..................... Sep 25
Vanderbilt ............................ Oct 2*
Mississippi St. ■ ..................... Oct 9
Florida ■ ............................ Oct 16
Arkansas ............................. Oct 30
New Mexico St. ■ ..................... Nov 6
Georgia .............................. Nov 13
Alabama ■ ........................... Nov 20

1992 RECORD

| | | | | |
|---|---|---|---|---|
| 21 | Mississippi | 45 | 24 Arkansas | 24 |
| 55 | Samford | 0 | 10 Georgia | 14 |
| 30 | Louisiana St. | 28 | 0 Alabama | 17 |
| 16 | Southern Miss. | 8 | | |
| 31 | Vanderbilt | 7 | 228       (5-5-1) | 205 |
| 7 | Mississippi St. | 14 | | |
| 9 | Florida | 24 | | |
| 25 | Southwestern La. | 24 | | |

Conference: Southeastern Conf.   Enrollment: 21,551.   Colors: Burnt Orange & Navy Blue.
Nickname: Tigers.   Stadium: Jordan-Hare (1939), 85,214 capacity.   Natural turf.
1992 home attendance: 510,549 in 7 games.
Director of Athletics: Mike Lude.
Sports Info. Director: David Housel  205-844-4750

## AUSTIN PEAY STATE . . . Clarksville, Tenn.   37044   I-AA

Coach: Roy Gregory, Tenn.-Chatt. '68
Record: 2 yrs., W-8, L-14, T-0
1993 SCHEDULE

Cincinnati ............................ Sep 4*
Knoxville ■ ........................... Sep 11*
Western Ky. ■ ........................ Sep 18*
Eastern Ky. .......................... Sep 25*
Tennessee Tech ■ .................... Oct 2*
Murray St. ........................... Oct 9
Tennessee St. ■ ..................... Oct 16*
Morehead St. ......................... Oct 23
Southeast Mo. St. ■ .................. Oct 30
Middle Tenn. St. ...................... Nov 6
Tenn.-Martin ■ ....................... Nov 20

1992 RECORD

| | | | | |
|---|---|---|---|---|
| 9 | Eastern Ill. | 14 | 34 Morehead St. | 41 |
| 31 | Knoxville | 7 | 14 Eastern Ky. | 45 |
| 7 | Southern Ill. | 37 | 32 Tenn.-Martin | 18 |
| 21 | Southeast Mo. St. | 16 | | |
| 10 | Murray St. | 27 | 182       (3-8-0) | 299 |
| 10 | Middle Tenn. St. | 49 | | |
| 0 | Tennessee Tech | 10 | | |
| 14 | Tennessee St. | 35 | | |

Conference: Ohio Valley Conf.   Enrollment: 7,400.   Colors: Red & White.
Nickname: Governors.   Stadium: Municipal (1946), 10,000 capacity.   Artificial turf.
1992 home attendance: 18,926 in 6 games.
Director of Athletics: Tim Weiser.
Sports Info. Director: Brad Kirtley  615-648-7561

■ Home games on each schedule [neutral sites shown in brackets].   *Night Games.

## BALL STATE . . . Muncie, Ind.   47306                                   I-A

Coach: Paul Schudel, Miami (Ohio) '66
Record: 8 yrs., W-47, L-40, T-2

### 1993 SCHEDULE

| | |
|---|---|
| Syracuse | Sep  4* |
| Illinois St. ■ | Sep 11 |
| Ohio | Sep 18 |
| Central Mich. | Oct  2 |
| Toledo ■ | Oct  9 |
| Cincinnati | Oct 16* |
| Bowling Green ■ | Oct 23 |
| Eastern Mich. | Oct 30 |
| Miami (Ohio) ■ | Nov  6 |
| Akron | Nov 13 |
| Kent ■ | Nov 20 |

### 1992 RECORD

| | | | | | |
|---|---|---|---|---|---|
| 10 | Clemson | 24 | 24 | Ohio | 21 |
| 10 | Kansas | 62 | 9 | Toledo | 10 |
| 10 | Kent | 6 | 6 | Bowling Green | 38 |
| 19 | Miami (Ohio) | 9 | | | |
| 14 | Western Mich. | 21 | 171 | (5-6-0) | 243 |
| 31 | Eastern Mich. | 7 | | | |
| 14 | Akron | 22 | | | |
| 24 | Central Mich. | 23 | | | |

Conference: Mid-American Conf.   Enrollment: 20,333.   Colors: Cardinal & White.
Nickname: Cardinals.   Stadium: Ball State (1967), 16,319 capacity.   Natural turf.
1992 home attendance: 47,111 in 5 games.
Director of Athletics: Don Purvis.
Sports Info. Director: Joe Hernandez   317-285-8242

---

## BAYLOR . . . Waco, Texas   76706                                   I-A

Coach: Chuck Reedy, Appalachian St. '71
Record: First year as head coach

### 1993 SCHEDULE

| | |
|---|---|
| Fresno St. ■ | Sep  4* |
| Colorado | Sep 11 |
| Utah St. | Sep 18 |
| Texas Tech ■ | Sep 25* |
| Houston | Oct  2 |
| Southern Methodist | Oct  9 |
| Texas A&M ■ | Oct 16* |
| Texas Christian ■ | Oct 23 |
| Georgia Tech | Nov  6 |
| Rice ■ | Nov 13 |
| Texas | Nov 27 |

### 1992 RECORD

| | | | | | |
|---|---|---|---|---|---|
| 9 | Louisiana Tech | 10 | 31 | Georgia Tech | 27 |
| 38 | Colorado | 57 | 31 | Rice | 34 |
| 45 | Utah St. | 10 | 21 | Texas | 20 |
| 17 | Texas Tech | 36 | | | |
| 49 | Southern Methodist | 7 | 324 | (6-5-0) | 263 |
| 41 | Texas Christian | 20 | | **John Hancock Bowl** | |
| 29 | Houston | 23 | 20 | Arizona | 15 |
| 13 | Texas A&M | 19 | | | |

Conference: Southwest Conf.   Enrollment: 12,000.   Colors: Green & Gold.
Nickname: Bears.   Stadium: Floyd Casey (1950), 48,500 capacity.   Artificial turf.
1992 home attendance: 226,512 in 7 games.
Director of Athletics: Grant Teaff.
Sports Info. Director: Maxey Parrish   817-755-1234

---

## BETHUNE-COOKMAN . . . Daytona Beach, Fla.   32015                   I-AA

Coach: Sylvester Collins, Jackson St. '72
Record: 1 yr., W-3, L-7, T-0

### 1993 SCHEDULE

| | |
|---|---|
| Knoxville [Jacksonville, Fla.] | Sep  4* |
| Morgan St. ■ | Sep 11 |
| Johnson Smith ■ | Sep 18 |
| Samford ■ | Sep 25* |
| Delaware St. | Oct  2 |
| Howard ■ | Oct  9 |
| South Caro. St. ■ | Oct 16 |
| Central Fla. ■ | Oct 23 |
| North Caro. A&T ■ | Oct 30 |
| Norfolk St. | Nov 13 |
| Florida A&M [Tampa, Fla.] | Nov 27 |

### 1992 RECORD

| | | | | | |
|---|---|---|---|---|---|
| 21 | Savannah St. | 31 | 35 | Norfolk St. | 26 |
| 3 | Central Fla. | 28 | 35 | Florida A&M | 21 |
| 17 | Delaware St. | 31 | | | |
| 13 | Samford | 42 | 170 | (3-7-0) | 277 |
| 7 | Howard | 26 | | | |
| 7 | South Caro. St. | 35 | | | |
| 14 | Albany St. (Ga.) | 7 | | | |
| 22 | North Caro. A&T | 30 | | | |

Conference: Mid-Eastern.   Enrollment: 2,300.   Colors: Maroon & Gold.
Nickname: Wildcats.   Stadium: Municipal, 10,000 capacity.   Natural turf.
1992 home attendance: 24,044 in 5 games.
Director of Athletics: Lynn Thompson.
Sports Info. Director: W. Earl Kitchings   904-255-1401

---

## BOISE STATE . . . Boise, Idaho   83725                              I-AA

Coach: Pokey Allen, Utah '65
Record: 7 yrs., W-62, L-26, T-2

### 1993 SCHEDULE

| | |
|---|---|
| Rhode Island ■ | Sep  4* |
| Nevada | Sep 11 |
| Northeastern ■ | Sep 18* |
| Stephen F. Austin ■ | Sep 25* |
| Montana | Oct  2 |
| Northern Ariz. ■ | Oct  9* |
| Weber St. | Oct 16* |
| Idaho St. ■ | Oct 23* |
| Montana St. ■ | Oct 30 |
| Eastern Wash. ■ | Nov 13 |
| Idaho | Nov 20 |

### 1992 RECORD

| | | | | | |
|---|---|---|---|---|---|
| 20 | Tenn.-Chatt. | 35 | 13 | Montana St. | 17 |
| 20 | Idaho St. | 24 | 13 | Eastern Wash. | 14 |
| 17 | Pacific (Cal.) | 7 | 16 | Idaho | 62 |
| 24 | Stephen F. Austin | 20 | | | |
| 27 | Montana | 21 | 220 | (5-6-0) | 286 |
| 20 | Northern Ariz. | 14 | | | |
| 24 | Weber St. | 21 | | | |
| 26 | Portland St. | 51 | | | |

Conference: Big Sky Conf.   Enrollment: 14,254.   Colors: Orange & Blue.
Nickname: Broncos.   Stadium: Bronco (1970), 22,600 capacity.   Artificial blue turf.
1992 home attendance: 114,807 in 6 games.
Director of Athletics: Gene Bleymaier.
Sports Info. Director: Max Corbet   208-385-1515

---

## BOSTON COLLEGE . . . Chestnut Hill, Mass.   02167                   I-A

Coach: Tom Coughlin, Syracuse '68
Record: 4 yrs., W-19, L-20, T-2

### 1993 SCHEDULE

| | |
|---|---|
| Miami (Fla.) ■ | Sep  4 |
| Northwestern | Sep 18 |
| Temple ■ | Sep 25 |
| Syracuse | Oct  2 |
| Rutgers | Oct  9 |
| Army ■ | Oct 23 |
| Tulane ■ | Oct 30 |
| Virginia Tech ■ | Nov  6 |
| Pittsburgh | Nov 13 |
| Notre Dame | Nov 20 |
| West Va. ■ | Nov 26 |

### 1992 RECORD

| | | | | | |
|---|---|---|---|---|---|
| 37 | Rutgers | 20 | 7 | Notre Dame | 54 |
| 49 | Northwestern | 0 | 10 | Syracuse | 27 |
| 28 | Navy | 0 | 41 | Army | 24 |
| 14 | Michigan St. | 0 | | | |
| 24 | West Va. | 24 | 307 | (8-2-1) | 200 |
| 35 | Penn St. | 32 | | **Hall of Fame Bowl** | |
| 17 | Tulane | 13 | 23 | Tennessee | 38 |
| 45 | Temple | 6 | | | |

Conference: Big East Conference.   Enrollment: 9,040.   Colors: Maroon & Gold.
Nickname: Eagles.   Stadium: Alumni (1957), 32,000 capacity.   Artificial turf.
1992 home attendance: 179,095 in 6 games.
Director of Athletics: Chet Gladchuk.
Sports Info. Director: Reid Oslin   617-552-3004

---

■ Home games on each schedule [neutral sites shown in brackets].   *Night Games.

## BOSTON U. . . . Boston, Mass.  02215      I-AA

Coach: Dan Allen, Hanover '78
Record: 3 yrs., W-12, L-21, T-0

**1993 SCHEDULE**

| | |
|---|---|
| Maine ■ | Sep 11 |
| Holy Cross | Sep 18 |
| Massachusetts ■ | Sep 25 |
| Villanova ■ | Oct 2 |
| Northeastern | Oct 9 |
| Richmond | Oct 16 |
| Rhode Island ■ | Oct 23 |
| New Hampshire | Oct 30 |
| Buffalo ■ | Nov 6 |
| Connecticut | Nov 13 |
| James Madison | Nov 20 |

**1992 RECORD**

| | | | | |
|---|---|---|---|---|
| 0 | Temple | 35 | 11 Maine | 40 |
| 21 | William & Mary | 31 | 30 Connecticut | 25 |
| 28 | Massachusetts | 30 | 25 Northeastern | 19 |
| 14 | Villanova | 22 | | |
| 14 | Delaware | 49 | 218    (3-8-0) | 352 |
| 27 | Richmond | 37 | | |
| 34 | Rhode Island | 21 | | |
| 14 | New Hampshire | 43 | | |

Conference: Yankee.  Enrollment: 13,663.  Colors: Scarlet & White.
Nickname: Terriers.  Stadium: Nickerson Field (1930), 17,369 capacity.  Artificial turf.
1992 home attendance: 20,209 in 5 games.
Director of Athletics: Gary Strickler.
Sports Info. Director: Ed Carpenter  617-353-2872

---

## BOWLING GREEN . . . Bowling Green, Ohio  43403      I-A

Coach: Gary Blackney, Connecticut '67
Record: 2 yrs., W-21, L-3, T-0

**1993 SCHEDULE**

| | |
|---|---|
| Virginia Tech | Sep 4 |
| Cincinnati ■ | Sep 11 |
| Navy | Sep 25 |
| Toledo ■ | Oct 2 |
| Ohio | Oct 9 |
| Akron ■ | Oct 16 |
| Ball St. | Oct 23 |
| Miami (Ohio) | Oct 30 |
| Kent ■ | Nov 6 |
| Central Mich. | Nov 13 |
| Western Mich. ■ | Nov 20 |

**1992 RECORD**

| | | | | |
|---|---|---|---|---|
| 29 | Western Mich. | 19 | 44 Miami (Ohio) | 24 |
| 6 | Ohio St. | 17 | 28 Kent | 22 |
| 18 | Wisconsin | 39 | 38 Ball St. | 6 |
| 44 | East Caro. | 34 | | |
| 17 | Central Mich. | 14 | 289    (9-2-0) | 201 |
| 31 | Ohio | 14 | **Las Vegas Bowl** | |
| 10 | Toledo | 9 | 35 Nevada | 34 |
| 24 | Akron | 3 | | |

Conference: Mid-American Conf.  Enrollment: 17,600.  Colors: Orange & Brown.
Nickname: Falcons.  Stadium: Doyt Perry (1966), 30,599 capacity.  Natural turf.
1992 home attendance: 69,093 in 5 games.
Director of Athletics: Jack Gregory.
Sports Info. Director: Steve Barr  419-372-7076

---

## BRIGHAM YOUNG . . . Provo, Utah  84602      I-A

Coach: LaVell Edwards, Utah State '52
Record: 21 yrs., W-191, L-67, T-3

**1993 SCHEDULE**

| | |
|---|---|
| New Mexico | Sep 4* |
| Hawaii ■ | Sep 11 |
| Colorado St. | Sep 18 |
| Air Force ■ | Sep 25 |
| UCLA | Oct 9* |
| Notre Dame ■ | Oct 16 |
| Fresno St. ■ | Oct 23 |
| Utah St. | Oct 30 |
| San Diego St. | Nov 11* |
| Utah ■ | Nov 20 |
| UTEP ■ | Nov 27 |

**1992 RECORD**

| | | | | |
|---|---|---|---|---|
| 38 | UTEP | 28 | 30 Penn St. | 17 |
| 38 | San Diego St. | 45 | 35 New Mexico | 0 |
| 10 | UCLA | 17 | 28 Air Force | 7 |
| 32 | Hawaii | 36 | 31 Utah | 22 |
| 30 | Utah St. | 9 | | |
| 36 | Fresno St. | 24 | 355    (8-4-0) | 275 |
| 31 | Wyoming | 28 | **Aloha Bowl** | |
| 16 | Notre Dame | 42 | 20 Kansas | 23 |

Conference: Western Athl. Conf.  Enrollment: 27,000.  Colors: Royal Blue & White.
Nickname: Cougars.  Stadium: B Y U (1964), 65,000 capacity.  Natural turf.
1992 home attendance: 390,476 in 6 games.
Director of Athletics: Clayne Jensen.
Sports Info. Director: Ralph Zobell  801-378-4911

---

## BROWN . . . Providence, R.I.  02912      I-AA

Coach: Mickey Kwiatkowski, Delaware '70
Record: 12 yrs., W-71, L-54, T-0

**1993 SCHEDULE**

| | |
|---|---|
| Yale | Sep 18 |
| Lehigh | Sep 25 |
| Rhode Island ■ | Oct 2 |
| Princeton ■ | Oct 9 |
| Bucknell ■ | Oct 16 |
| Pennsylvania | Oct 23 |
| Cornell ■ | Oct 30 |
| Harvard ■ | Nov 6 |
| Dartmouth | Nov 13 |
| Columbia ■ | Nov 20 |

**1992 RECORD**

| | | | | |
|---|---|---|---|---|
| 17 | Yale | 22 | 28 Dartmouth | 51 |
| 14 | Bucknell | 33 | 28 Columbia | 34 |
| 6 | William & Mary | 51 | | |
| 14 | Princeton | 28 | 156    (0-10-0) | 333 |
| 24 | Lehigh | 31 | | |
| 0 | Pennsylvania | 38 | | |
| 6 | Cornell | 16 | | |
| 19 | Harvard | 29 | | |

Conference: Ivy League.  Enrollment: 5,519.  Colors: Seal Brown, Cardinal & White.
Nickname: Bears.  Stadium: Brown (1925), 20,000 capacity.  Natural turf.
1992 home attendance: 30,750 in 4 games.
Director of Athletics: David Roach.
Sports Info. Director: Christopher Humm  401-863-2219

---

## BUCKNELL . . . Lewisburg, Pa.  17837      I-AA

Coach: Lou Maranzana, Dartmouth '70
Record: 4 yrs., W-17, L-25, T-0

**1993 SCHEDULE**

| | |
|---|---|
| Bloomsburg ■ | Sep 4 |
| Lafayette | Sep 11 |
| Pennsylvania ■ | Sep 25 |
| Dartmouth ■ | Oct 2 |
| Hofstra | Oct 9 |
| Brown | Oct 16 |
| Holy Cross ■ | Oct 23 |
| Fordham | Oct 30 |
| Lehigh ■ | Nov 6 |
| Towson St. | Nov 13 |
| Colgate | Nov 20 |

**1992 RECORD**

| | | | | |
|---|---|---|---|---|
| 41 | Bloomsburg | 24 | 16 Lehigh | 38 |
| 0 | Villanova | 34 | 7 Lafayette | 49 |
| 21 | Towson St. | 24 | 28 Colgate | 21 |
| 33 | Brown | 14 | | |
| 14 | Dartmouth | 44 | 201    (4-7-0) | 318 |
| 29 | Columbia | 22 | | |
| 12 | Holy Cross | 27 | | |
| 0 | Fordham | 21 | | |

Conference: Patriot League.  Enrollment: 3,400.  Colors: Orange & Blue.
Nickname: Bison.  Stadium: Christy Mathewson (1924), 13,100 capacity.  Natural turf.
1992 home attendance: 20,897 in 5 games.
Director of Athletics: Rick Hartzell.
Sports Info. Director: Bo Smolka  717-524-1227

---

■ Home games on each schedule [neutral sites shown in brackets].  *Night Games.

## BUFFALO . . . Buffalo, N.Y.   14260                                I-AA

Coach: Jim Ward, Md-East. Shore '68
Record: 1 yr., W-4, L-6, T-0

**1993 SCHEDULE**

| | |
|---|---|
| Maine ■ | Sep 4* |
| New Haven ■ | Sep 11* |
| Lafayette ■ | Sep 18* |
| Edinboro ■ | Sep 25* |
| Hofstra | Oct 2* |
| Fordham | Oct 9 |
| Buffalo St. ■ | Oct 16 |
| Towson St. | Oct 23 |
| Youngstown St. | Oct 30 |
| Boston U. | Nov 6 |
| Central Fla. | Nov 13 |

**1992 RECORD**

| | | | | |
|---|---|---|---|---|
| 13 | Edinboro | 35 | 60 Central Conn. St. | 27 |
| 48 | New Haven | 69 | 21 Central Fla. | 63 |
| 28 | Lafayette | 49 | | |
| 56 | Mansfield | 42 | 319 | (4-6-0) | 395 |
| 27 | Morgan St. | 45 | | |
| 21 | Colgate | 35 | | |
| 19 | Buffalo St. | 15 | | |
| 26 | Hofstra | 15 | | |

Conference: I-AA Independents.   Enrollment: 18,000.   Colors: Buffalo Blue, White & Red.
Nickname: Bulls.   Stadium: UB Stadium (1993), 16,500 capacity.   Natural turf.
1992 home attendance: 12,800 in 4 games.
Director of Athletics: Nelson E. Townsend.
Sports Info. Director: Mike Rowland   716-645-3178

---

## BUTLER . . . Indianapolis, Ind.   46208                               I-AA

Coach: Ken LaRose, Butler '80
Record: 1 yr., W-8, L-2, T-0

**1993 SCHEDULE**

| | |
|---|---|
| Hofstra | Sep 4* |
| Georgetown (Ky.) | Sep 18 |
| Drake ■ | Sep 25 |
| Hillsdale ■ | Oct 2 |
| Valparaiso ■ | Oct 9 |
| Dayton | Oct 16 |
| San Diego | Oct 23* |
| Evansville | Oct 30 |
| Ala.-Birmingham ■ | Nov 6 |
| Indianapolis | Nov 13 |

**1992 RECORD**

| | | | | |
|---|---|---|---|---|
| 14 | Northern Mich. | 0 | 28 Hillsdale | 17 |
| 33 | St. Joseph's (Ind.) | 7 | 37 Saginaw Valley | 0 |
| 10 | Grand Valley St. | 21 | | |
| 28 | Indianapolis | 6 | 254 | (8-2-0) | 126 |
| 31 | Wayne St. (Mich.) | 6 | | |
| 42 | Valparaiso | 13 | | |
| 7 | Ferris St. | 35 | | |
| 24 | Ashland | 21 | | |

Conference: Pioneer Football League.   Enrollment: 4,150.   Colors: Blue & White.
Nickname: Bulldogs.   Stadium: Butler Bowl (1927), 19,000 capacity.   Natural turf.
1992 home attendance: 20,298 in 5 games.
Director of Athletics: John Parry.
Sports Info. Director: Jim McGrath   317-283-9375

---

## CAL STATE NORTHRIDGE . . . Northridge, Calif.   91330               I-AA

Coach: Bob Burt, Cal St. Los Angeles '62
Record: 8 yrs., W-48, L-37, T-0

**1993 SCHEDULE**

| | |
|---|---|
| San Diego St. | Sep 4* |
| Weber St. | Sep 11* |
| Northern Ariz. | Sep 18* |
| Sonoma St. ■ | Sep 25* |
| Nevada-Las Vegas | Oct 9* |
| Cal St. Sacramento ■ | Oct 16* |
| UC Davis | Oct 23* |
| Cal St. Chico ■ | Oct 30* |
| Cal Poly SLO | Nov 6* |
| Southern Utah ■ | Nov 13* |

**1992 RECORD**

| | | | | |
|---|---|---|---|---|
| 7 | Cal St. Fullerton | 28 | 10 Portland St. | 35 |
| 16 | UC Davis | 14 | 23 Cal St. Sacramento | 17 |
| 22 | San Fran. St. | 6 | | |
| 0 | Central Okla. | 14 | 161 | (5-5-0) | 224 |
| 7 | Idaho | 30 | | |
| 42 | Santa Clara | 18 | | |
| 14 | Cal Poly SLO | 13 | | |
| 20 | Southern Utah | 49 | | |

Conference: American West.   Enrollment: 31,000.   Colors: Red, White & Black.
Nickname: Matadors.   Stadium: North Campus (1971), 6,000 capacity.   Natural turf.
1992 home attendance: 17,438 in 5 games.
Director of Athletics: Bob Hiegert.
Sports Info. Director: Barry Smith   818-885-3243

---

## CAL STATE SACRAMENTO . . . Sacramento, Calif.   95819             I-AA

Coach: Mike Clemons, Cal St. Sac. '69
Record: First year as head coach

**1993 SCHEDULE**

| | |
|---|---|
| Cal St. Hayward ■ | Sep 4* |
| San Fran. St. | Sep 11 |
| Eastern Wash. ■ | Sep 18* |
| Pacific (Cal.) | Sep 25* |
| St. Mary's (Cal.) ■ | Oct 9* |
| Cal St. Northridge | Oct 16* |
| Cal Poly SLO | Oct 23 |
| Montana | Oct 30 |
| UC Davis ■ | Nov 13* |
| Southern Utah | Nov 20* |

**1992 RECORD**

| | | | | |
|---|---|---|---|---|
| 10 | Montana St. | 7 | 32 Santa Clara | 21 |
| 57 | Abilene Christian | 9 | 17 Cal St. Northridge | 23 |
| 29 | Cal St. Fullerton | 3 | | |
| 14 | UC Davis | 21 | 268 | (7-3-0) | 149 |
| 36 | Cal St. Chico | 20 | | |
| 24 | Cal Poly SLO | 0 | | |
| 14 | Southern Utah | 17 | | |
| 35 | Portland St. | 28 | | |

Conference: American West.   Enrollment: 25,000.   Colors: Green & Gold.
Nickname: Hornets.   Stadium: Hornet, 26,000 capacity.   Natural turf.
1992 home attendance: 17,865 in 5 games.
Director of Athletics: Lee McElroy.
Sports Info. Director: Jeff Minahan   916-278-6896

---

## CALIFORNIA . . . Berkeley, Calif.   94720                             I-A

Coach: Keith Gilbertson, Central Wash. '71
Record: 4 yrs., W-32, L-16, T-0

**1993 SCHEDULE**

| | |
|---|---|
| UCLA | Sep 4* |
| San Diego St. ■ | Sep 11 |
| Temple | Sep 18 |
| San Jose St. ■ | Sep 25 |
| Oregon ■ | Oct 2 |
| Washington ■ | Oct 9 |
| Washington St. | Oct 16 |
| Southern Cal ■ | Oct 30 |
| Arizona St. | Nov 6* |
| Arizona ■ | Nov 13 |
| Stanford ■ | Nov 20 |
| Hawaii | Nov 27* |

**1992 RECORD**

| | | | | |
|---|---|---|---|---|
| 46 | San Jose St. | 16 | 17 Oregon | 37 |
| 14 | Purdue | 41 | 12 Arizona St. | 28 |
| 27 | Kansas | 23 | 21 Stanford | 41 |
| 42 | Oregon St. | 0 | | |
| 16 | Washington | 35 | 284 | (4-7-0) | 284 |
| 24 | Southern Cal | 27 | | |
| 17 | Arizona | 24 | | |
| 48 | UCLA | 12 | | |

Conference: Pacific-10.   Enrollment: 32,000.   Colors: Blue & Gold.
Nickname: Golden Bears.   Stadium: Memorial (1923), 75,662 capacity.   Artificial turf.
1992 home attendance: 280,162 in 5 games.
Director of Athletics: Robert L. Bockrath.
Sports Info. Director: Kevin Reneau   510-642-5363

---

■ Home games on each schedule [neutral sites shown in brackets].   *Night Games.

*Divisions I-A & I-AA 1993 Schedules and 1992 Results*                      665

## CANISIUS . . . Buffalo, N.Y.   14208                                      I-AA

Coach: Barry Mynter, St. Lawrence '58
Record: 17 yrs., W-78, L-84, T-3

### 1993 SCHEDULE

| | |
|---|---|
| Duquesne | Sep 11* |
| Buffalo St. | Sep 18 |
| Gannon ■ | Sep 25* |
| Mercyhurst ■ | Oct 2 |
| Iona ■ | Oct 9 |
| St. John's (N.Y.) | Oct 16 |
| St. Peter's | Oct 23 |
| St. Francis (Pa.) ■ | Oct 30 |
| Siena | Nov 6 |
| Georgetown ■ | Nov 13 |

**1992 RECORD**

| | | | | | |
|---|---|---|---|---|---|
| 14 | St. Francis (Pa.) | 17 | 27 | Alfred | 23 |
| 7 | Buffalo St. | 14 | 14 | Marist | 10 |
| 27 | St. Lawrence | 45 | | | |
| 13 | Mercyhurst | 34 | 150 | (3-6-1) | 210 |
| 14 | St. John Fisher | 12 | | | |
| 14 | Frostburg St. | 14 | | | |
| 6 | Hobart | 13 | | | |
| 14 | Duquesne | 28 | | | |

Conference: Metro Atlantic Ath. Conf.   Enrollment: 4,600.   Colors: Blue & Gold.
Nickname: Golden Griffins.   Stadium: Demske Sports Complex (1989), 1,000
    capacity.   Artificial turf.
1992 home attendance: 2,966 in 5 games.
Director of Athletics: Daniel P. Starr.
Sports Info. Director: John Maddock   716-888-2977

## CENTRAL CONNECTICUT STATE . . . New Britain, Conn.   06050        I-AA

Coach: Sal Cintorio, Cent. Conn. St. '86
Record: 1 yr., W-1, L-8, T-0

### 1993 SCHEDULE

| | |
|---|---|
| Towson St. | Sep 11 |
| Iona | Sep 18 |
| Wagner ■ | Sep 25 |
| St. Francis (Pa.) | Oct 2 |
| Marist ■ | Oct 9 |
| Springfield ■ | Oct 16 |
| LIU-C.W. Post ■ | Oct 23 |
| Southern Conn. St. | Oct 30 |
| St. Peter's ■ | Nov 6 |
| Duquesne ■ | Nov 13 |

**1992 RECORD**

| | | | | | |
|---|---|---|---|---|---|
| 7 | Hofstra | 14 | 19 | Wm. Paterson | 27 |
| 14 | Trenton St. | 6 | | | |
| 13 | Rowan | 14 | 142 | (1-8-0) | 292 |
| 12 | American Int'l | 40 | | | |
| 21 | New Haven | 55 | | | |
| 9 | Springfield | 34 | | | |
| 27 | Buffalo | 60 | | | |
| 20 | Southern Conn. St. | 42 | | | |

Conference: I-AA Independents.   Enrollment: 14,000.   Colors: Blue & White.
Nickname: Blue Devils.   Stadium: Arute Field (1969), 5,000 capacity.   Natural turf.
1992 home attendance: 5,700 in 4 games.
Director of Athletics: Judith Davidson.
Sports Info. Director: Brent Rutkowski   203-827-7824

## CENTRAL FLORIDA . . . Orlando, Fla.   32816                          I-AA

Coach: Gene McDowell, Florida St. '63
Record: 8 yrs., W-54, L-37, T-0

### 1993 SCHEDULE

| | |
|---|---|
| Valdosta St. ■ | Sep 11 |
| East Caro. | Sep 18 |
| McNeese St. ■ | Sep 25 |
| Yale ■ | Oct 2 |
| Samford ■ | Oct 9 |
| Western Ill. | Oct 16 |
| Bethune-Cookman | Oct 23 |
| Troy St. | Oct 30 |
| Liberty ■ | Nov 6 |
| Buffalo ■ | Nov 13 |
| Louisiana Tech | Nov 20* |

**1992 RECORD**

| | | | | | |
|---|---|---|---|---|---|
| 71 | Gardner-Webb | 21 | 41 | James Madison | 37 |
| 28 | Bethune-Cookman | 3 | 13 | Samford | 20 |
| 16 | Troy St. | 20 | | | |
| 35 | Western Ill. | 22 | 373 | (6-4-0) | 243 |
| 42 | Nicholls St. | 18 | | | |
| 36 | Western Ky. | 50 | | | |
| 28 | Liberty | 31 | | | |
| 63 | Buffalo | 21 | | | |

Conference: I-AA Independents.   Enrollment: 22,000.   Colors: Black & Gold.
Nickname: Knights.   Stadium: Florida Citrus Bowl (1936), 70,000 capacity.   Natural turf.
1992 home attendance: 53,941 in 6 games.
Director of Athletics: Gene McDowell.
Sports Info. Director: Bob Cefalo   407-823-2464

## CENTRAL MICHIGAN . . . Mt. Pleasant, Mich.   48859                    I-A

Coach: Herb Deromedi, Michigan '60
Record: 15 yrs., W-105, L-49, T-10

### 1993 SCHEDULE

| | |
|---|---|
| Akron ■ | Sep 2* |
| Ohio ■ | Sep 11 |
| Nevada-Las Vegas | Sep 18* |
| Michigan St. | Sep 25 |
| Ball St. ■ | Oct 2 |
| Western Mich. | Oct 9 |
| Eastern Mich. ■ | Oct 16 |
| Kent | Oct 23 |
| Toledo | Nov 6 |
| Bowling Green ■ | Nov 13 |
| Miami (Ohio) | Nov 20 |

**1992 RECORD**

| | | | | | |
|---|---|---|---|---|---|
| 14 | Kentucky | 21 | 28 | Akron | 31 |
| 24 | Michigan St. | 20 | 30 | Eastern Mich. | 13 |
| 24 | Ohio | 0 | 14 | Western Mich. | 19 |
| 28 | Toledo | 9 | | | |
| 14 | Bowling Green | 17 | 247 | (5-6-0) | 170 |
| 13 | Miami (Ohio) | 16 | | | |
| 35 | Kent | 0 | | | |
| 23 | Ball St. | 24 | | | |

Conference: Mid-American Conf.   Enrollment: 16,367.   Colors: Maroon & Gold.
Nickname: Chippewas.   Stadium: Kelly-Shorts (1972), 20,086 capacity.   Artificial turf.
1992 home attendance: 95,637 in 5 games.
Director of Athletics: Dave Keilitz.
Sports Info. Director: Fred Stabley Jr.   517-774-3277

## CHARLESTON SOUTHERN . . . Charleston, S. C.   29411                   I-AA

Coach: David Dowd, Guilford '76
Record: 2 yrs., W-5, L-14, T-0

### 1993 SCHEDULE

| | |
|---|---|
| Morgan St. | Sep 4 |
| Presbyterian ■ | Sep 11 |
| South Caro. St. | Sep 18* |
| Towson St. | Sep 25 |
| Troy St. | Oct 2 |
| Newberry | Oct 9 |
| Lees-McRae ■ | Oct 16 |
| Ala.-Birmingham ■ | Oct 23 |
| Liberty | Oct 30 |
| Newport News App. | Nov 6 |
| Wofford ■ | Nov 13 |

**1992 RECORD**

| | | | | | |
|---|---|---|---|---|---|
| 20 | Methodist | 19 | 0 | South Caro. St. | 32 |
| 0 | Gardner-Webb | 56 | | | |
| 7 | Newport News App. | 28 | 110 | (2-7-0) | 309 |
| 37 | Guilford | 13 | | | |
| 12 | Newberry | 28 | | | |
| 0 | East Tenn. St. | 62 | | | |
| 7 | Ala.-Birmingham | 39 | | | |
| 27 | Davidson | 32 | | | |

Conference: I-AA Independents.   Enrollment: 2,491.   Colors: Blue & Gold.
Nickname: Buccaneers.   Stadium: CSU Field, 1,500 capacity.   Natural turf.
1992 home attendance: 4,833 in 5 games.
Director of Athletics: Howard Bagwell.
Sports Info. Director: Michael Meyer   803-863-7688

---

■ Home games on each schedule [neutral sites shown in brackets].   *Night Games.

## CINCINNATI . . . Cincinnati, Ohio  45221 — I-A

Coach: Tim Murphy, Springfield '78
Record: 6 yrs., W-24, L-42, T-1

**1993 SCHEDULE**

| | |
|---|---|
| Austin Peay ■ | Sep 4* |
| Bowling Green | Sep 11 |
| Miami (Ohio) ■ | Sep 18* |
| Syracuse | Sep 25* |
| Tulsa | Oct 2 |
| Vanderbilt | Oct 9* |
| Ball St. ■ | Oct 16* |
| Toledo | Oct 23 |
| Memphis St. ■ | Oct 30 |
| Houston | Nov 13 |
| East Caro. ■ | Nov 20 |

**1992 RECORD**

| | | | | |
|---|---|---|---|---|
| 20 | Penn St. | 24 | 26 Rutgers | 24 |
| 14 | Miami (Ohio) | 17 | 17 Kentucky | 13 |
| 0 | Tennessee | 40 | 22 Akron | 24 |
| 31 | Kent | 0 | | |
| 14 | Memphis St. | 34 | 199 (3-8-0) | 276 |
| 21 | East Caro. | 42 | | |
| 17 | Southern Miss. | 31 | | |
| 17 | Louisville | 27 | | |

Conference: I-A Independents.  Enrollment: 36,000.  Colors: Red & Black.
Nickname: Bearcats.  Stadium: Nippert (1916), 35,000 capacity.  Artificial turf.
1992 home attendance: 109,812 in 6 games.
Director of Athletics: Rick Taylor.
Sports Info. Director: Tom Hathaway  513-556-5191

## CITADEL . . . Charleston, S.C.  29409 — I-AA

Coach: Charlie Taaffe, Siena '73
Record: 6 yrs., W-42, L-27, T-1

**1993 SCHEDULE**

| | |
|---|---|
| Wofford ■ | Sep 4* |
| Ga. Southern | Sep 11 |
| Western Caro. | Sep 18 |
| Appalachian St. ■ | Sep 25* |
| Lees-McRae ■ | Oct 2* |
| East Tenn. St. | Oct 9* |
| Furman ■ | Oct 16 |
| Air Force | Oct 23 |
| Marshall ■ | Oct 30 |
| Tenn.-Chatt. | Nov 6 |
| Va. Military ■ | Nov 13 |

**1992 RECORD**

| | | | | |
|---|---|---|---|---|
| 10 | Arkansas | 3 | 32 Newberry | 14 |
| 30 | Wofford | 13 | 50 Va. Military | 0 |
| 28 | East Tenn. St. | 7 | 20 Furman | 14 |
| 15 | Army | 14 | | |
| 25 | Appalachian St. | 0 | 292 (10-1-0) | 143 |
| 33 | Tenn.-Chatt. | 13 | **I-AA Championship** | |
| 13 | Marshall | 34 | 44 North Caro. A&T | 0 |
| 36 | Western Caro. | 31 | 17 Youngstown St. | 42 |

Conference: Southern Conf.  Enrollment: 2,000.  Colors: Blue & White.
Nickname: Bulldogs.  Stadium: Johnson Hagood (1948), 22,500 capacity.  Natural turf.
1992 home attendance: 116,156 in 6 games.
Director of Athletics: Walt Nadzak.
Sports Info. Director: Josh Baker  803-792-5120

## CLEMSON . . . Clemson, S.C.  29633 — I-A

Coach: Ken Hatfield, Arkansas '65
Record: 14 yrs., W-105, L-59, T-3

**1993 SCHEDULE**

| | |
|---|---|
| Nevada-Las Vegas ■ | Sep 4 |
| Florida St. | Sep 11 |
| Georgia Tech ■ | Sep 25 |
| North Caro. St. ■ | Oct 2 |
| Duke | Oct 9 |
| Wake Forest ■ | Oct 16 |
| East Tenn. St. ■ | Oct 23 |
| Maryland ■ | Oct 30 |
| North Caro. | Nov 6 |
| Virginia ■ | Nov 13 |
| South Caro. | Nov 20 |

**1992 RECORD**

| | | | | |
|---|---|---|---|---|
| 24 | Ball St. | 10 | 40 North Caro. | 7 |
| 20 | Florida St. | 24 | 23 Maryland | 53 |
| 16 | Georgia Tech | 20 | 13 South Caro. | 24 |
| 54 | Tenn.-Chatt. | 3 | | |
| 29 | Virginia | 28 | 261 (5-6-0) | 213 |
| 21 | Duke | 6 | | |
| 6 | North Caro. St. | 20 | | |
| 15 | Wake Forest | 18 | | |

Conference: Atlantic Coast Conf.  Enrollment: 17,295.  Colors: Orange & Purple.
Nickname: Tigers.  Stadium: Memorial (1942), 81,473 capacity.  Natural turf.
1992 home attendance: 460,732 in 6 games.
Director of Athletics: Bobby Robinson.
Sports Info. Director: Tim Bourret  803-656-2114

## COLGATE . . . Hamilton, N.Y.  13346 — I-AA

Coach: Ed Sweeney, LIU-C. W. Post '71
Record: 8 yrs., W-56, L-22, T-3

**1993 SCHEDULE**

| | |
|---|---|
| Rutgers | Sep 4* |
| Army | Sep 11 |
| Cornell | Sep 25* |
| Columbia ■ | Oct 2 |
| Pennsylvania ■ | Oct 9 |
| Navy | Oct 16 |
| Lehigh | Oct 23 |
| Lafayette | Oct 30 |
| Fordham | Nov 6 |
| Holy Cross | Nov 13 |
| Bucknell ■ | Nov 20 |

**1992 RECORD**

| | | | | |
|---|---|---|---|---|
| 0 | Rutgers | 41 | 26 William & Mary | 44 |
| 17 | Fordham | 7 | 17 Holy Cross | 18 |
| 0 | Pennsylvania | 24 | 21 Bucknell | 28 |
| 34 | Columbia | 29 | | |
| 35 | Buffalo | 21 | 199 (4-7-0) | 287 |
| 7 | Cornell | 25 | | |
| 14 | Lehigh | 13 | | |
| 28 | Lafayette | 37 | | |

Conference: Patriot League.  Enrollment: 2,700.  Colors: Maroon.
Nickname: Red Raiders.  Stadium: Andy Kerr (1937), 10,221 capacity.  Natural turf.
1992 home attendance: 12,350 in 5 games.
Director of Athletics: Mark Murphy.
Sports Info. Director: Bob Cornell  315-824-7616

## COLORADO . . . Boulder, Colo.  80309 — I-A

Coach: Bill McCartney, Missouri '62
Record: 11 yrs., W-74, L-51, T-4

**1993 SCHEDULE**

| | |
|---|---|
| Texas ■ | Sep 4 |
| Baylor ■ | Sep 11 |
| Stanford | Sep 18* |
| Miami (Fla.) ■ | Sep 25 |
| Missouri ■ | Oct 9 |
| Oklahoma | Oct 16 |
| Kansas St. | Oct 23 |
| Nebraska ■ | Oct 30 |
| Oklahoma St. | Nov 6 |
| Kansas ■ | Nov 13 |
| Iowa St. | Nov 20 |

**1992 RECORD**

| | | | | |
|---|---|---|---|---|
| 37 | Colorado St. | 17 | 28 Oklahoma St. | 0 |
| 57 | Baylor | 38 | 25 Kansas | 18 |
| 21 | Minnesota | 20 | 31 Iowa St. | 10 |
| 28 | Iowa | 12 | | |
| 6 | Missouri | 0 | 318 (9-1-1) | 198 |
| 24 | Oklahoma | 24 | **Fiesta Bowl** | |
| 54 | Kansas St. | 7 | 22 Syracuse | 26 |
| 7 | Nebraska | 52 | | |

Conference: Big Eight Conf.  Enrollment: 25,176.  Colors: Silver, Gold & Black.
Nickname: Buffaloes.  Stadium: Folsom (1924), 51,748 capacity.  Artificial turf.
1992 home attendance: 298,149 in 6 games.
Director of Athletics: Bill Marolt.
Sports Info. Director: David Plati  303-492-5626

■ Home games on each schedule [neutral sites shown in brackets].  *Night Games.

*Divisions I-A & I-AA 1993 Schedules and 1992 Results*

## COLORADO STATE . . . Fort Collins, Colo.  80523    I-A

Coach: Sonny Lubick, Western Mont. '60
Record: 4 yrs., W-21, L-19, T-0

**1993 SCHEDULE**

| | |
|---|---|
| Oregon ■ | Sep 4 |
| Air Force ■ | Sep 11 |
| Brigham Young ■ | Sep 18 |
| Nebraska | Sep 25 |
| Kansas | Oct 2 |
| Fresno St. ■ | Oct 9 |
| San Diego St. | Oct 16* |
| Utah | Oct 23 |
| New Mexico ■ | Oct 30 |
| UTEP | Nov 13* |
| Wyoming | Nov 20 |

**1992 RECORD**

| | | | | | |
|---|---|---|---|---|---|
| 17 | Colorado | 37 | 13 | San Diego St. | 20 |
| 34 | Idaho | 37 | 13 | Hawaii | 24 |
| 21 | Fresno St. | 52 | 35 | Ohio | 24 |
| 17 | Louisiana St. | 14 | 14 | New Mexico | 10 |
| 29 | Utah | 33 | | | |
| 42 | UTEP | 24 | 281 | (5-7-0) | 334 |
| 32 | Air Force | 28 | | | |
| 14 | Wyoming | 31 | | | |

Conference: Western Athl. Conf. Enrollment: 20,600. Colors: Green & Gold.
Nickname: Rams. Stadium: Hughes (1968), 30,000 capacity. Natural turf.
1992 home attendance: 109,520 in 6 games.
Director of Athletics: Corey Johnson.
Sports Info. Director: Gary Ozzello 303-491-5067

## COLUMBIA . . . New York, N.Y.  10027    I-AA

Coach: Ray Tellier, Connecticut '73
Record: 9 yrs., W-27, L-60, T-1

**1993 SCHEDULE**

| | |
|---|---|
| Harvard | Sep 18 |
| Fordham ■ | Sep 25 |
| Colgate | Oct 2 |
| Lafayette ■ | Oct 9 |
| Pennsylvania ■ | Oct 16 |
| Yale ■ | Oct 23 |
| Princeton | Oct 30 |
| Dartmouth ■ | Nov 6 |
| Cornell | Nov 13 |
| Brown | Nov 20 |

**1992 RECORD**

| | | | | | |
|---|---|---|---|---|---|
| 20 | Harvard | 27 | 35 | Cornell | 30 |
| 18 | Fordham | 9 | 34 | Brown | 28 |
| 29 | Colgate | 34 | | | |
| 22 | Bucknell | 29 | 205 | (3-7-0) | 286 |
| 21 | Pennsylvania | 34 | | | |
| 0 | Yale | 23 | | | |
| 7 | Princeton | 34 | | | |
| 19 | Dartmouth | 38 | | | |

Conference: Ivy League. Enrollment: 4,000. Colors: Columbia Blue & White.
Nickname: Lions. Stadium: Lawrence A. Wien (1984), 17,000 capacity. Natural turf.
1992 home attendance: 34,670 in 6 games.
Director of Athletics: John Reeves.
Sports Info. Director: Bill Steinman 212-854-2534

## CONNECTICUT . . . Storrs, Conn.  06269    I-AA

Coach: Tom Jackson, Penn St. '70
Record: 10 yrs., W-56, L-52, T-0

**1993 SCHEDULE**

| | |
|---|---|
| Furman | Sep 4 |
| New Hampshire ■ | Sep 11 |
| James Madison ■ | Sep 18 |
| Yale | Sep 25 |
| Towson St. ■ | Oct 2 |
| Villanova | Oct 9 |
| Massachusetts ■ | Oct 16 |
| Maine | Oct 23 |
| Richmond | Oct 30 |
| Rhode Island | Nov 6 |
| Boston U. ■ | Nov 13 |

**1992 RECORD**

| | | | | | |
|---|---|---|---|---|---|
| 13 | New Haven | 14 | 7 | Delaware | 33 |
| 24 | New Hampshire | 21 | 25 | Boston U. | 30 |
| 13 | Northeastern | 16 | 38 | Rhode Island | 0 |
| 40 | Yale | 20 | | | |
| 20 | Villanova | 27 | 254 | (5-6-0) | 239 |
| 7 | Massachusetts | 20 | | | |
| 37 | Maine | 30 | | | |
| 30 | Richmond | 28 | | | |

Conference: Yankee. Enrollment: 13,128. Colors: National Flag Blue & White.
Nickname: Huskies. Stadium: Memorial (1953), 16,200 capacity. Natural turf.
1992 home attendance: 45,596 in 6 games.
Director of Athletics: Lew Perkins.
Sports Info. Director: Tim Tolokan 203-486-3531

## CORNELL . . . Ithaca, N.Y.  14853    I-AA

Coach: Jim Hofher, Cornell '79
Record: 3 yrs., W-19, L-11, T-0

**1993 SCHEDULE**

| | |
|---|---|
| Princeton | Sep 18 |
| Colgate ■ | Sep 25* |
| Lehigh | Oct 2 |
| Harvard ■ | Oct 9 |
| Fordham ■ | Oct 16 |
| Dartmouth | Oct 23 |
| Brown | Oct 30 |
| Yale ■ | Nov 6 |
| Columbia ■ | Nov 13 |
| Pennsylvania | Nov 20 |

**1992 RECORD**

| | | | | | |
|---|---|---|---|---|---|
| 20 | Princeton | 22 | 30 | Columbia | 35 |
| 29 | Lehigh | 23 | 7 | Pennsylvania | 14 |
| 44 | Lafayette | 33 | | | |
| 31 | Harvard | 13 | 263 | (7-3-0) | 183 |
| 25 | Colgate | 7 | | | |
| 26 | Dartmouth | 16 | | | |
| 16 | Brown | 6 | | | |
| 35 | Yale | 14 | | | |

Conference: Ivy League. Enrollment: 12,900. Colors: Carnelian & White.
Nickname: Big Red. Stadium: Schoellkopf (1915), 27,000 capacity. Artificial turf.
1992 home attendance: 47,480 in 6 games.
Director of Athletics: Laing Kennedy.
Sports Info. Director: Dave Wohlhueter 607-255-3753

## DARTMOUTH . . . Hanover, N.H.  03755    I-AA

Coach: John Lyons, Pennsylvania '74
Record: 1 yr., W-8, L-2, T-0

**1993 SCHEDULE**

| | |
|---|---|
| Pennsylvania | Sep 18 |
| Holy Cross ■ | Sep 25 |
| Bucknell | Oct 2 |
| New Hampshire ■ | Oct 9 |
| Yale | Oct 16 |
| Cornell ■ | Oct 23 |
| Harvard ■ | Oct 30 |
| Columbia | Nov 6 |
| Brown | Nov 13 |
| Princeton ■ | Nov 20 |

**1992 RECORD**

| | | | | | |
|---|---|---|---|---|---|
| 36 | Pennsylvania | 17 | 51 | Brown | 28 |
| 27 | New Hampshire | 45 | 34 | Princeton | 20 |
| 44 | Bucknell | 14 | | | |
| 48 | Holy Cross | 0 | 364 | (8-2-0) | 203 |
| 39 | Yale | 27 | | | |
| 16 | Cornell | 26 | | | |
| 31 | Harvard | 7 | | | |
| 38 | Columbia | 19 | | | |

Conference: Ivy League. Enrollment: 4,000. Colors: Dartmouth Green & White.
Nickname: Big Green. Stadium: Memorial Field (1923), 20,416 capacity. Natural turf.
1992 home attendance: 28,693 in 4 games.
Director of Athletics: Dick Jaeger.
Sports Info. Director: Kathy Slattery 603-646-2468

---

■ Home games on each schedule [neutral sites shown in brackets].   *Night Games.

*1993 NCAA FOOTBALL*

## DAVIDSON . . . Davidson, N.C.   28036                               I-AA

Coach: Tim Landis, Randolph-Macon '86
Record: First year as head coach

### 1993 SCHEDULE
| | |
|---|---|
| Sewanee | Sep 11 |
| Rhodes ■ | Sep 18 |
| Emory & Henry | Sep 25 |
| Guilford | Oct 2 |
| Wash. & Lee | Oct 9 |
| Methodist ■ | Oct 16 |
| Randolph-Macon ■ | Oct 23 |
| Hampden-Sydney ■ | Oct 30 |
| Centre | Nov 6 |
| Bridgewater (Va.) ■ | Nov 13 |

### 1992 RECORD
| 18 | Guilford | 3 | 10 | Centre | 3 |
|---|---|---|---|---|---|
| 20 | Sewanee | 37 | 28 | Bridgewater (Va.) | 13 |
| 6 | Rhodes | 31 | | | |
| 7 | Emory & Henry | 36 | 178 | (5-5-0) | 218 |
| 12 | Wash. & Lee | 27 | | | |
| 27 | Methodist | 6 | | | |
| 32 | Charleston So. | 27 | | | |
| 18 | Hampden-Sydney | 35 | | | |

Conference: I-AA Independents.   Enrollment: 1,500.   Colors: Red & Black.
Nickname: Wildcats.   Stadium: Richardson Field (1924), 5,200 capacity.   Natural turf.
1992 home attendance: 10,260 in 5 games.
Director of Athletics: Terry Holland.
Sports Info. Director: Emil Parker  704-892-2374

## DAYTON . . . Dayton, Ohio   45469                               I-AA

Coach: Mike Kelly, Manchester '70
Record: 12 yrs., W-119, L-22, T-1

### 1993 SCHEDULE
| | |
|---|---|
| Wis.-Platteville ■ | Sep 11* |
| Wheaton (Ill.) ■ | Sep 18* |
| San Diego ■ | Sep 25 |
| Mt. St. Joseph | Oct 2 |
| Evansville | Oct 9 |
| Butler ■ | Oct 16 |
| Drake | Oct 23 |
| Valparaiso ■ | Oct 30 |
| Urbana ■ | Nov 6 |
| Ala.-Birmingham | Nov 13 |

### 1992 RECORD
| 48 | Wis.-Platteville | 0 | 24 | Hofstra | 13 |
|---|---|---|---|---|---|
| 44 | Wheaton (Ill.) | 3 | 62 | Mt. Senario | 6 |
| 45 | Urbana | 0 | | | |
| 47 | Mt. St. Joseph | 0 | 408 | (10-0-0) | 67 |
| 42 | Mercyhurst | 14 | | III Championship | |
| 38 | Drake | 9 | 10 | Mount Union | 27 |
| 18 | Thomas More | 7 | | | |
| 40 | Evansville | 15 | | | |

Conference: Pioneer Football League.   Enrollment: 6,500.   Colors: Red & Blue.
Nickname: Flyers.   Stadium: Welcome (1949), 11,000 capacity.   Artificial turf.
1992 home attendance: 42,687 in 7 games. .
Director of Athletics: Ted Kissell.
Sports Info. Director: Doug Hauschild  513-229-4460

## DELAWARE . . . Newark, Del.   19716                               I-AA

Coach: Harold Raymond, Michigan '50
Record: 27 yrs., W-223, L-88, T-2

### 1993 SCHEDULE
| | |
|---|---|
| Lehigh ■ | Sep 4 |
| William & Mary ■ | Sep 11 |
| Rhode Island | Sep 18 |
| West Chester ■ | Sep 25 |
| James Madison | Oct 9 |
| Villanova ■ | Oct 16 |
| Massachusetts | Oct 23 |
| Maine ■ | Oct 30 |
| Towson St. ■ | Nov 6 |
| Richmond ■ | Nov 13 |
| Northeastern | Nov 20 |

### 1992 RECORD
| 33 | Massachusetts | 13 | 21 | Richmond | 29 |
|---|---|---|---|---|---|
| 31 | Rhode Island | 14 | 55 | Towson St. | 27 |
| 20 | West Chester | 21 | | | |
| 42 | New Hampshire | 22 | 399 | (9-2-0) | 201 |
| 49 | Boston U. | 14 | | I-AA Championship | |
| 21 | Villanova | 20 | 56 | Samford | 21 |
| 37 | Navy | 21 | 41 | Northeast La. | 18 |
| 57 | Maine | 13 | 7 | Marshall | 28 |
| 33 | Connecticut | 7 | | | |

Conference: Yankee.   Enrollment: 15,248.   Colors: Blue & Gold.
Nickname: Fightin' Blue Hens.   Stadium: Delaware (1952), 23,000 capacity.   Natural turf.
1992 home attendance: 107,090 in 6 games.
Director of Athletics: Edgar Johnson.
Sports Info. Director: Scott Selheimer  302-831-2186

## DELAWARE STATE . . . Dover, Del.   19901                               I-AA

Coach: William Collick, Delaware '74
Record: 8 yrs., W-56, L-29, T-0

### 1993 SCHEDULE
| | |
|---|---|
| Fayetteville St. [Wilmington, Del.] | Sep 4 |
| Cheyney ■ | Sep 11 |
| Towson St. | Sep 18 |
| Bethune-Cookman ■ | Oct 2 |
| Youngstown St. | Oct 9 |
| Florida A&M | Oct 16 |
| Morgan St. ■ | Oct 23 |
| South Caro. St. | Oct 30 |
| North Caro. A&T | Nov 6 |
| Liberty ■ | Nov 13 |
| Howard ■ | Nov 20 |

### 1992 RECORD
| 54 | Cheyney | 0 | 10 | North Caro. A&T | 24 |
|---|---|---|---|---|---|
| 20 | Youngstown St. | 42 | 27 | Liberty | 49 |
| 31 | Bethune-Cookman | 17 | 28 | Howard | 31 |
| 45 | Grambling | 42 | | | |
| 27 | Towson St. | 13 | 305 | (6-5-0) | 282 |
| 22 | Florida A&M | 20 | | | |
| 34 | Morgan St. | 16 | | | |
| 7 | South Caro. St. | 28 | | | |

Conference: Mid-Eastern.   Enrollment: 3,000.   Colors: Red & Blue.
Nickname: Hornets.   Stadium: Alumni Field (1957), 5,000 capacity.   Natural turf.
1992 home attendance: 23,040 in 5 games.
Director of Athletics: John Martin.
Sports Info. Director: Craig Cotton  302-739-4926

## DRAKE . . . Des Moines, Iowa   50311                               I-AA

Coach: Rob Ash, Cornell College '73
Record: 13 yrs., W-75, L-51, T-4

### 1993 SCHEDULE
| | |
|---|---|
| Simpson ■ | Sep 11 |
| Augustana (Ill.) | Sep 18 |
| Butler ■ | Sep 25 |
| Aurora ■ | Oct 2 |
| Chicago | Oct 9 |
| Valparaiso | Oct 16 |
| Dayton ■ | Oct 23 |
| Ill. Benedictine ■ | Oct 30 |
| San Diego | Nov 6 |
| Evansville ■ | Nov 13 |

### 1992 RECORD
| 20 | Simpson | 20 | 50 | Olivet Nazarene | 14 |
|---|---|---|---|---|---|
| 39 | Augustana (Ill.) | 19 | 17 | Evansville | 7 |
| 30 | Millikin | 12 | | | |
| 20 | Aurora | 30 | 334 | (7-2-1) | 172 |
| 31 | Chicago | 19 | | | |
| 9 | Dayton | 38 | | | |
| 59 | Quincy | 7 | | | |
| 59 | Ill. Benedictine | 6 | | | |

Conference: Pioneer Football League.   Enrollment: 4,000.   Colors: Blue & White.
Nickname: Bulldogs.   Stadium: Drake (1925), 18,000 capacity.   Natural turf.
1992 home attendance: 14,771 in 5 games.
Director of Athletics: Lynn King.
Sports Info. Director: Mike Mahon  515-271-3012

■ Home games on each schedule [neutral sites shown in brackets].   *Night Games.

## DUKE . . . Durham, N.C.  27706     I-A

Coach: Barry Wilson, Georgia '65
Record: 3 yrs., W-10, L-22, T-1
### 1993 SCHEDULE
| | |
|---|---|
| Florida St. ■ | Sep  4* |
| Rutgers | Sep 11* |
| Army ■ | Sep 18* |
| Virginia | Sep 25 |
| Tennessee | Oct  2 |
| Clemson ■ | Oct  9 |
| Maryland | Oct 16 |
| Wake Forest | Oct 23 |
| Georgia Tech ■ | Oct 30 |
| North Caro. St. ■ | Nov  6 |
| North Caro. | Nov 26 |

### 1992 RECORD
| | | | | |
|---|---|---|---|---|
| 21 | Florida St. | 48 | 14 Wake Forest | 28 |
| 37 | Vanderbilt | 42 | 27 North Caro. St. | 45 |
| 17 | Rice | 12 | 28 North Caro. | 31 |
| 28 | Virginia | 55 | | |
| 45 | East Caro. | 14 | 265    (2-9-0) | 343 |
| 6 | Clemson | 21 | | |
| 25 | Maryland | 27 | | |
| 17 | Georgia Tech | 20 | | |

Conference: Atlantic Coast Conf.  Enrollment: 6,095.  Colors: Royal Blue & White.
Nickname: Blue Devils.  Stadium: Wallace Wade (1929), 33,941 capacity.  Natural turf.
1992 home attendance: 150,030 in 6 games.
Director of Athletics: Tom Butters.
Sports Info. Director: Mike Cragg  919-684-2633

## DUQUESNE . . . Pittsburgh, Pa.  15282     I-AA

Coach: Greg Gattuso, Penn St. '83
Record: First year as head coach
### 1993 SCHEDULE
| | |
|---|---|
| Canisius ■ | Sep 11* |
| Bethany (W.Va.) ■ | Sep 18* |
| Thiel | Sep 25 |
| Gannon | Oct  2 |
| Wagner ■ | Oct  9 |
| Marist | Oct 16 |
| Mercyhurst ■ | Oct 23* |
| St. John's (N.Y.) ■ | Oct 30 |
| St. Francis (Pa.) | Nov  6 |
| Central Conn. St. | Nov 13 |

### 1992 RECORD
| | | | | |
|---|---|---|---|---|
| 27 | Grove City | 26 | 6 Wagner | 31 |
| 7 | Bethany (W.Va.) | 20 | | |
| 22 | Thiel | 0 | 170    (5-4-0) | 159 |
| 17 | Gannon | 21 | | |
| 23 | Catholic | 3 | | |
| 27 | St. John's (N.Y.) | 21 | | |
| 28 | Canisius | 14 | | |
| 13 | St. Francis (Pa.) | 23 | | |

Conference: I-AA Independents.  Enrollment: 8,500.  Colors: Red & Blue.
Nickname: Dukes.  Stadium: South High, 7,000 capacity.  Artificial turf.
1992 home attendance: 8,362 in 4 games.
Director of Athletics: Brian Colleary.
Sports Info. Director: Sue Ryan  412-396-5861

## EAST CAROLINA . . . Greenville, N.C.  27834     I-A

Coach: Steve Logan, Tulsa '75
Record: 1 yr., W-5, L-6, T-0
### 1993 SCHEDULE
| | |
|---|---|
| Syracuse ■ | Sep  9* |
| Central Fla. ■ | Sep 18 |
| Washington | Sep 25 |
| Memphis St. ■ | Oct  2 |
| South Caro. | Oct  9 |
| Louisiana Tech ■ | Oct 16 |
| Southern Miss. | Oct 23 |
| Virginia Tech | Oct 30 |
| Tulsa ■ | Nov  6 |
| Kentucky | Nov 13 |
| Cincinnati | Nov 20 |

### 1992 RECORD
| | | | | |
|---|---|---|---|---|
| 21 | Syracuse | 42 | 28 West Va. | 41 |
| 30 | Virginia Tech | 27 | 35 Arkansas St. | 18 |
| 20 | South Caro. | 18 | 7 Memphis St. | 42 |
| 34 | Bowling Green | 44 | | |
| 14 | Duke | 45 | 289    (5-6-0) | 367 |
| 42 | Cincinnati | 21 | | |
| 37 | Pittsburgh | 31 | | |
| 21 | Southern Miss. | 38 | | |

Conference: I-A Independents.  Enrollment: 16,423.  Colors: Purple & Gold.
Nickname: Pirates.  Stadium: Ficklen (1963), 35,000 capacity.  Natural turf.
1992 home attendance: 164,068 in 5 games.
Director of Athletics: Dave Hart.
Sports Info. Director: Charles Bloom  919-757-4522

## EAST TENNESSEE STATE . . . Johnson City, Tenn.  37614     I-AA

Coach: Mike Cavan, Georgia '72
Record: 7 yrs., W-42, L-28, T-2
### 1993 SCHEDULE
| | |
|---|---|
| Wingate ■ | Sep  4* |
| Mars Hill ■ | Sep 11* |
| Va. Military | Sep 18 |
| Furman | Sep 25 |
| Appalachian St. | Oct  2 |
| Citadel ■ | Oct  9* |
| Western Caro. ■ | Oct 16 |
| Clemson | Oct 23 |
| Marshall | Nov  6 |
| Tenn.-Chatt. ■ | Nov 13 |
| Ga. Southern ■ | Nov 20 |

### 1992 RECORD
| | | | | |
|---|---|---|---|---|
| 18 | Va. Military | 16 | 27 Tenn.-Chatt. | 24 |
| 21 | Mars Hill | 0 | 12 Western Caro. | 41 |
| 7 | Citadel | 28 | 10 Marshall | 49 |
| 14 | Appalachian St. | 38 | | |
| 27 | Morehead St. | 7 | 219    (5-6-0) | 313 |
| 62 | Charleston So. | 0 | | |
| 7 | Louisiana Tech | 65 | | |
| 14 | Furman | 45 | | |

Conference: Southern Conf.  Enrollment: 12,000.  Colors: Blue & Gold.
Nickname: Buccaneers.  Stadium: Memorial (1977), 12,000 capacity.  Artificial turf.
1992 home attendance: 29,970 in 6 games.
Director of Athletics: Janice Shelton.
Sports Info. Director: John Cathey  615-929-4220

## EASTERN ILLINOIS . . . Charleston, Ill.  61920     I-AA

Coach: Bob Spoo, Purdue '60
Record: 6 yrs., W-33, L-35, T-0
### 1993 SCHEDULE
| | |
|---|---|
| Murray St. | Sep  2* |
| McNeese St. | Sep 11* |
| Navy | Sep 18* |
| Western Ill. ■ | Sep 25* |
| Indiana St. | Oct  2 |
| Northern Iowa | Oct 16* |
| Illinois St. | Oct 23 |
| Southwest Mo. St. ■ | Oct 30 |
| Northwestern (La.) ■ | Nov  6 |
| Western Ky. | Nov 13 |
| Southern Ill. | Nov 20 |

### 1992 RECORD
| | | | | |
|---|---|---|---|---|
| 14 | Austin Peay | 9 | 19 Youngstown St. | 28 |
| 28 | Marshall | 63 | 21 Northern Iowa | 15 |
| 48 | Murray St. | 9 | 28 Western Ky. | 7 |
| 7 | Illinois St. | 48 | | |
| 46 | Southern Ill. | 47 | 276    (5-6-0) | 295 |
| 31 | Indiana St. | 28 | | |
| 24 | Western Ill. | 28 | | |
| 10 | Southwest Mo. St. | 13 | | |

Conference: Gateway.  Enrollment: 10,000.  Colors: Blue & Gray.
Nickname: Panthers.  Stadium: O'Brien (1970), 10,000 capacity.  Natural turf.
1992 home attendance: 31,212 in 5 games.
Director of Athletics: Mike Ryan.
Sports Info. Director: Dave Kidwell  217-581-6408

■ Home games on each schedule [neutral sites shown in brackets].  *Night Games.

*1993 NCAA FOOTBALL*

## EASTERN KENTUCKY ... Richmond, Ky.  40475     I-AA

Coach: Roy Kidd, Eastern Ky. '54
Record: 29 yrs., W-239, L-84, T-8
### 1993 SCHEDULE
| | |
|---|---|
| Western Ky. ■ | Sep  2* |
| Northeast La. | Sep 11* |
| Austin Peay ■ | Sep 25* |
| Youngstown St. ■ | Oct  2* |
| Tennessee St. [Louisville, Ky.] | Oct  9 |
| Murray St. | Oct 16* |
| Tennessee Tech ■ | Oct 23 |
| Tenn.-Martin ■ | Oct 30 |
| Southeast Mo. St. | Nov  6 |
| Middle Tenn. St. ■ | Nov 13 |
| Morehead St. | Nov 20 |

### 1992 RECORD
| | | | | | |
|---|---|---|---|---|---|
| 21 | Western Ky. | 7 | 21 | Murray St. | 18 |
| 26 | Northeast La. | 21 | 45 | Austin Peay | 14 |
| 35 | Tennessee Tech | 0 | 37 | Morehead St. | 9 |
| 20 | Southeast Mo. St. | 10 | | | |
| 14 | Samford | 46 | 310 | (9-2-0) | 200 |
| 7 | Middle Tenn. St. | 38 | | **I-AA Championship** | |
| 35 | Tenn.-Martin | 9 | 0 | Marshall | 44 |
| 49 | Tennessee St. | 28 | | | |

Conference: Ohio Valley Conf.  Enrollment: 16,866.  Colors: Maroon & White.
Nickname: Colonels.  Stadium: Roy Kidd (1969), 20,000 capacity.  Natural turf.
1992 home attendance: 64,300 in 5 games.
Director of Athletics: Roy Kidd.
Sports Info. Director: Karl Park  606-622-1253

## EASTERN MICHIGAN ... Ypsilanti, Mich.  48197     I-A

Coach: Ron Cooper, Jacksonville St. '83
Record: First year as head coach
### 1993 SCHEDULE
| | |
|---|---|
| West Va. | Sep  4 |
| Temple ■ | Sep  9* |
| Western Ill. ■ | Sep 18* |
| Miami (Ohio) | Oct  2 |
| Kent ■ | Oct  9* |
| Central Mich. | Oct 16 |
| Western Mich. ■ | Oct 23* |
| Ball St. ■ | Oct 30 |
| Akron ■ | Nov  6 |
| Ohio ■ | Nov 13 |
| Toledo | Nov 19* |

### 1992 RECORD
| | | | | | |
|---|---|---|---|---|---|
| 9 | Akron | 27 | 17 | Army | 57 |
| 17 | Louisiana Tech | 31 | 13 | Central Mich. | 30 |
| 7 | Penn St. | 52 | 0 | Toledo | 41 |
| 14 | Kent | 17 | | | |
| 7 | Miami (Ohio) | 24 | 117 | (1-10-0) | 336 |
| 7 | Ball St. | 31 | | | |
| 19 | Western Mich. | 20 | | | |
| 7 | Ohio | 6 | | | |

Conference: Mid-American Conf.  Enrollment: 25,836.  Colors: Dark Green & White.
Nickname: Eagles.  Stadium: Rynearson (1969), 30,200 capacity.  Artificial turf.
1992 home attendance: 63,405 in 4 games.
Director of Athletics: Gene Smith.
Sports Info. Director: Jim Streeter  313-487-0317

## EASTERN WASHINGTON ... Cheney, Wash.  99004     I-AA

Coach: Dick Zornes, Eastern Wash. '68
Record: 14 yrs., W-79, L-63, T-2
### 1993 SCHEDULE
| | |
|---|---|
| Northeast La. | Sep  4 |
| Cal St. Sacramento | Sep 18* |
| Montana ■ | Sep 25 |
| Weber St. | Oct  2* |
| Portland St. ■ | Oct  9 |
| Idaho | Oct 16 |
| Northern Ariz. ■ | Oct 23 |
| Idaho St. ■ | Oct 30 |
| Montana St. | Nov  6 |
| Boise St. | Nov 13 |

### 1992 RECORD
| | | | | | |
|---|---|---|---|---|---|
| 21 | Portland St. | 24 | 31 | Northeast La. | 41 |
| 45 | Sonoma St. | 14 | 14 | Boise St. | 13 |
| 27 | Montana | 21 | | | |
| 32 | Weber St. | 14 | 266 | (7-3-0) | 194 |
| 23 | Montana St. | 17 | | **I-AA Championship** | |
| 21 | Idaho | 38 | 14 | Northern Iowa | 17 |
| 15 | Northern Ariz. | 9 | | | |
| 37 | Idaho St. | 3 | | | |

Conference: Big Sky Conf.  Enrollment: 8,000.  Colors: Red & White.
Nickname: Eagles.  Stadium: Woodward (1967), 6,000 capacity.  Natural turf.
1992 home attendance: 23,160 in 5 games.
Director of Athletics: John Johnson.
Sports Info. Director: Dave Cook  509-359-6334

## EVANSVILLE ... Evansville, Ind. 47722

Coach: Robin Cooper, Ill. Wesleyan '75
Record: 5 yrs., W-31, L-14, T-0
### 1993 SCHEDULE
| | |
|---|---|
| Franklin | Sep 11 |
| Ky. Wesleyan ■ | Sep 18 |
| Rose-Hulman ■ | Sep 25 |
| Adrian | Oct  2 |
| Dayton ■ | Oct  9 |
| San Diego ■ | Oct 16 |
| Valparaiso | Oct 23 |
| Butler ■ | Oct 30 |
| Cumberland (Tenn.) ■ | Nov  6 |
| Drake | Nov 13 |

### 1992 RECORD
| | | | | | |
|---|---|---|---|---|---|
| 24 | Franklin | 20 | 7 | Drake | 17 |
| 38 | Ky. Wesleyan | 6 | | | |
| 19 | Rose-Hulman | 13 | 199 | (7-2-0) | 127 |
| 43 | Adrian | 12 | | | |
| 26 | Lambuth | 7 | | | |
| 13 | Tusculum | 12 | | | |
| 15 | Dayton | 40 | | | |
| 14 | Cumberland (Tenn.) | 0 | | | |

Conference: Pioneer Football League.  Enrollment: 2,200.  Colors: Purple & White.
Nickname: Purple Aces.  Stadium: Arad McCutchan (1985), 3,000 capacity.  Natural turf.
1992 home attendance: 5,330 in 4 games.
Director of Athletics: Jim Byers.
Sports Info. Director: Bob Boxell  812-479-2350

## FLORIDA ... Gainesville, Fla.  32604     I-A

Coach: Steve Spurrier, Florida '67
Record: 6 yrs., W-48, L-21, T-1
### 1993 SCHEDULE
| | |
|---|---|
| Arkansas St. ■ | Sep  4* |
| Kentucky | Sep 11* |
| Tennessee ■ | Sep 18 |
| Mississippi St. ■ | Oct  2 |
| Louisiana St. | Oct  9* |
| Auburn | Oct 16 |
| Georgia [Jacksonville, Fla.] | Oct 30 |
| Southwestern La. ■ | Nov  6 |
| South Caro. | Nov 13 |
| Vanderbilt ■ | Nov 20 |
| Florida St. ■ | Nov 27 |

### 1992 RECORD
| | | | | | |
|---|---|---|---|---|---|
| 35 | Kentucky | 19 | 41 | Vanderbilt | 21 |
| 14 | Tennessee | 31 | 24 | Florida St. | 45 |
| 6 | Mississippi St. | 30 | | **SEC Championship** | |
| 28 | Louisiana St. | 21 | 21 | Alabama | 28 |
| 24 | Auburn | 9 | | | |
| 31 | Louisville | 17 | 288 | (8-4-0) | 274 |
| 26 | Georgia | 24 | | **Gator Bowl** | |
| 24 | Southern Miss. | 20 | 27 | North Caro. St. | 10 |
| 14 | South Caro. | 9 | | | |

Conference: Southeastern Conf.  Enrollment: 34,500.  Colors: Blue & Orange.
Nickname: Gators.  Stadium: Florida Field (1929), 83,000 capacity.  Natural turf.
1992 home attendance: 586,626 in 7 games.
Director of Athletics: Jeremy Foley.
Sports Info. Director: John Humenik  904-375-4683

■ Home games on each schedule [neutral sites shown in brackets].  *Night Games.

## FLORIDA A&M . . . Tallahassee, Fla.   32307   I-AA

Coach: Ken Riley, Florida A&M '69
Record: 7 yrs., W-43, L-33, T-2

### 1993 SCHEDULE

| | |
|---|---|
| Tennessee St. ■ | Sep 4 |
| South Caro. St. [Columbia, S.C.] | Sep 11 |
| Jackson St. ■ | Sep 18* |
| Howard | Oct 2 |
| North Caro. A&T | Oct 9 |
| Delaware St. ■ | Oct 16 |
| Albany St. (Ga.) ■ | Oct 23* |
| Morgan St. [Orlando, Fla.] | Oct 30* |
| Southern-B.R. ■ | Nov 6 |
| Grambling | Nov 13 |
| Bethune-Cookman [Tampa, Fla.] | Nov 27 |

### 1992 RECORD

| | | | | | |
|---|---|---|---|---|---|
| 28 | Ga. Southern | 17 | 16 | Southern-B.R. | 6 |
| 33 | South Caro. St. | 20 | 10 | Grambling | 27 |
| 0 | Miami (Fla.) | 38 | 21 | Bethune-Cookman | 35 |
| 20 | Tennessee St. | 12 | | | |
| 10 | Howard | 3 | 221 | (7-4-0) | 219 |
| 21 | North Caro. A&T | 7 | | **Heritage Bowl** | |
| 20 | Delaware St. | 22 | 15 | Grambling | 45 |
| 42 | Morgan St. | 32 | | | |

Conference: Mid-Eastern.   Enrollment: 8,300.   Colors: Orange & Green.
Nickname: Rattlers.   Stadium: Bragg Memorial (1957), 25,500 capacity.   Natural turf.
1992 home attendance: 132,396 in 6 games.
Director of Athletics: Walter Reed.
Sports Info. Director: Alvin Hollins   904-599-3200

---

## FLORIDA STATE . . . Tallahassee, Fla.   32306   I-A

Coach: Bobby Bowden, Samford '53
Record: 27 yrs., W-227, L-77, T-3

### 1993 SCHEDULE

| | |
|---|---|
| Kansas [East Rutherford, N.J.] | Aug 28 |
| Duke | Sep 4* |
| Clemson ■ | Sep 11 |
| North Caro. | Sep 18 |
| Georgia Tech ■ | Oct 2* |
| Miami (Fla.) ■ | Oct 9 |
| Virginia ■ | Oct 16 |
| Wake Forest ■ | Oct 30 |
| Maryland | Nov 6 |
| Notre Dame | Nov 13 |
| North Caro. St. ■ | Nov 20 |
| Florida | Nov 27 |

### 1992 RECORD

| | | | | | |
|---|---|---|---|---|---|
| 48 | Duke | 21 | 69 | Maryland | 21 |
| 24 | Clemson | 20 | 70 | Tulane | 7 |
| 34 | North Caro. St. | 13 | 45 | Florida | 24 |
| 35 | Wake Forest | 7 | | | |
| 16 | Miami (Fla.) | 19 | 419 | (10-1-0) | 172 |
| 36 | North Caro. | 13 | | **Orange Bowl** | |
| 29 | Georgia Tech | 24 | 27 | Nebraska | 14 |
| 13 | Virginia | 3 | | | |

Conference: Atlantic Coast Conf.   Enrollment: 28,077.   Colors: Garnet & Gold.
Nickname: Seminoles.   Stadium: Doak S. Campbell (1950), 72,000 capacity.   Natural turf.
1992 home attendance: 376,784 in 6 games.
Director of Athletics: Bob Goin.
Sports Info. Director: Donna Turner   904-644-1403

---

## FORDHAM . . . New York, N.Y.   10458   I-AA

Coach: Larry Glueck, Villanova '63
Record: 7 yrs., W-29, L-41, T-1

### 1993 SCHEDULE

| | |
|---|---|
| Lehigh ■ | Sep 11 |
| Villanova | Sep 18 |
| Columbia | Sep 25 |
| Pennsylvania | Oct 2 |
| Buffalo ■ | Oct 9 |
| Cornell | Oct 16 |
| Lafayette | Oct 23 |
| Bucknell ■ | Oct 30 |
| Colgate | Nov 6 |
| Hofstra ■ | Nov 13 |
| Holy Cross | Nov 20 |

### 1992 RECORD

| | | | | | |
|---|---|---|---|---|---|
| 14 | Lehigh | 16 | 14 | Villanova | 31 |
| 7 | Colgate | 17 | 13 | Holy Cross | 21 |
| 9 | Columbia | 18 | | | |
| 10 | Pennsylvania | 13 | 141 | (1-9-0) | 222 |
| 12 | Yale | 31 | | | |
| 20 | Hofstra | 31 | | | |
| 21 | Lafayette | 44 | | | |
| 21 | Bucknell | 0 | | | |

Conference: Patriot League.   Enrollment: 6,500.   Colors: Maroon & White.
Nickname: Rams.   Stadium: Jack Coffey Field (1930), 7,000 capacity.   Natural turf.
1992 home attendance: 16,939 in 4 games.
Director of Athletics: Frank McLaughlin.
Sports Info. Director: Joe Favorito   718-579-2445

---

## FRESNO STATE . . . Fresno, Calif.   93740   I-A

Coach: Jim Sweeney, Portland '51
Record: 28 yrs., W-178, L-129, T-3

### 1993 SCHEDULE

| | |
|---|---|
| Baylor | Sep 4* |
| Oregon St. ■ | Sep 11* |
| New Mexico | Sep 18* |
| Utah St. ■ | Sep 25* |
| Colorado St. | Oct 9 |
| Air Force ■ | Oct 16* |
| Brigham Young | Oct 23 |
| Wyoming | Oct 30 |
| UTEP ■ | Nov 6* |
| Hawaii | Nov 13* |
| San Diego St. ■ | Nov 20* |

### 1992 RECORD

| | | | | | |
|---|---|---|---|---|---|
| 42 | Pacific (Cal.) | 21 | 42 | Wyoming | 31 |
| 36 | Oregon St. | 46 | 41 | Utah | 15 |
| 52 | Colorado St. | 21 | 45 | San Diego St. | 41 |
| 37 | Washington St. | 39 | 43 | UTEP | 18 |
| 48 | Louisiana Tech | 14 | | | |
| 24 | Brigham Young | 36 | 486 | (8-4-0) | 357 |
| 45 | Hawaii | 47 | | **Freedom Bowl** | |
| 31 | New Mexico | 28 | 24 | Southern Cal | 7 |

Conference: Western Athl. Conf.   Enrollment: 19,586.   Colors: Cardinal & Blue.
Nickname: Bulldogs.   Stadium: Bulldog (1981), 41,031 capacity.   Natural turf.
1992 home attendance: 211,352 in 6 games.
Director of Athletics: Gary Cunningham.
Sports Info. Director: Scott Johnson   209-278-2509

---

## FURMAN . . . Greenville, S.C.   29613   I-AA

Coach: Jimmy Satterfield, South Carolina '62
Record: 7 yrs., W-61, L-24, T-2

### 1993 SCHEDULE

| | |
|---|---|
| Connecticut ■ | Sep 4 |
| Georgia Tech | Sep 11 |
| Wofford ■ | Sep 18 |
| East Tenn. St. ■ | Sep 25 |
| Western Caro. | Oct 2 |
| Appalachian St. ■ | Oct 9 |
| Citadel | Oct 16 |
| Va. Military ■ | Oct 30 |
| Ga. Southern | Nov 6 |
| Marshall ■ | Nov 13 |
| Tenn.-Chatt. | Nov 20 |

### 1992 RECORD

| | | | | | |
|---|---|---|---|---|---|
| 31 | Liberty | 13 | 27 | Western Caro. | 29 |
| 0 | North Caro. | 28 | 35 | Tenn.-Chatt. | 0 |
| 43 | Presbyterian | 7 | 14 | Citadel | 20 |
| 0 | Ga. Southern | 21 | | | |
| 41 | Va. Military | 13 | 258 | (6-5-0) | 206 |
| 6 | Marshall | 48 | | | |
| 16 | Appalachian St. | 13 | | | |
| 45 | East Tenn. St. | 14 | | | |

Conference: Southern Conf.   Enrollment: 2,500.   Colors: Purple & White.
Nickname: Paladins.   Stadium: Paladin (1981), 16,000 capacity.   Natural turf.
1992 home attendance: 80,104 in 6 games.
Director of Athletics: Ray Parlier.
Sports Info. Director: Hunter Reid   803-294-2061

---

■ Home games on each schedule [neutral sites shown in brackets].   *Night Games.

*1993 NCAA FOOTBALL*

## GEORGETOWN . . . Washington, D.C.  20057     I-AA

Coach: Bob Benson, Vermont '86
Record: First year as head coach

### 1993 SCHEDULE

| | |
|---|---|
| Iona | Sep 25 |
| Siena | Oct  2 |
| St. Peter's | Oct  9* |
| Frank. & Marsh. ■ | Oct 16 |
| Johns Hopkins | Oct 22* |
| Catholic ■ | Oct 30 |
| St. John's (N.Y.) ■ | Nov  6 |
| Canisius | Nov 13 |
| Wash. & Lee [Hamilton, Bermuda] | Nov 20 |

### 1992 RECORD

| | | | | |
|---|---|---|---|---|
| 16 | Ursinus | 23 | 33 St. John's (N.Y.) | 49 |
| 52 | Gallaudet | 20 | 27 Wash. & Lee | 19 |
| 14 | Dickinson | 20 | | |
| 19 | Frank. & Marsh. | 34 | 220 | 246 |
| 12 | St. Peter's | 21 | | |
| 28 | Swarthmore | 27 | (4-6-0) | |
| 0 | Johns Hopkins | 17 | | |
| 19 | Catholic | 16 | | |

Conference: Metro Atlantic Ath. Conf.   Enrollment: 6,229.   Colors: Blue & Gray.
Nickname: Hoyas.   Stadium: Kehoe Field, 2,400 capacity.   Artificial turf.
1992 home attendance: 5,431 in 4 games.
Director of Athletics: Francis X. Rienzo.
Sports Info. Director: Bill Hurd  202-687-2492

## GEORGIA . . . Athens, Ga.  30602

Coach: Ray Goff, Georgia '78
Record: 4 yrs., W-29, L-18, T-0

### 1993 SCHEDULE

| | |
|---|---|
| South Caro. ■ | Sep  4 |
| Tennessee | Sep 11 |
| Texas Tech ■ | Sep 18 |
| Mississippi | Sep 25* |
| Arkansas ■ | Oct  2 |
| Southern Miss. ■ | Oct  9 |
| Vanderbilt | Oct 16 |
| Kentucky ■ | Oct 23 |
| Florida [Jacksonville, Fla.] | Oct 30 |
| Auburn ■ | Nov 13 |
| Georgia Tech | Nov 25 |

### 1992 RECORD

| | | | | |
|---|---|---|---|---|
| 28 | South Caro. | 6 | 24 Florida | 26 |
| 31 | Tennessee | 34 | 14 Auburn | 10 |
| 56 | Cal St. Fullerton | 0 | 31 Georgia Tech | 17 |
| 37 | Mississippi | 11 | | |
| 27 | Arkansas | 3 | 352 | 141 |
| 34 | Ga. Southern | 7 | (9-2-0) | |
| 30 | Vanderbilt | 20 | **Florida Citrus Bowl** | |
| 40 | Kentucky | 7 | 21 Ohio St. | 14 |

Conference: Southeastern Conf.   Enrollment: 28,395.   Colors: Red & Black.
Nickname: Bulldogs.   Stadium: Sanford (1929), 85,434 capacity.   Natural turf.
1992 home attendance: 499,162 in 6 games.
Director of Athletics: Vince Dooley.
Sports Info. Director: Claude Felton  706-542-1621

## GEORGIA SOUTHERN . . . Statesboro, Ga.  30460     I-AA

Coach: Tim Stowers, Auburn '80
Record: 3 yrs., W-26, L-11, T-0

### 1993 SCHEDULE

| | |
|---|---|
| Savannah St. ■ | Sep  4 |
| Citadel ■ | Sep 11 |
| Marshall | Sep 18* |
| Tenn.-Chatt. ■ | Sep 25 |
| Miami (Fla.) ■ | Oct  2 |
| Western Caro. ■ | Oct  9 |
| Appalachian ■ | Oct 16 |
| Va. Military | Oct 23 |
| Furman ■ | Nov  6 |
| Concord (W. Va.) ■ | Nov 13 |
| East Tenn. St. | Nov 20 |

### 1992 RECORD

| | | | | |
|---|---|---|---|---|
| 17 | Florida A&M | 28 | 30 Mississippi Col. | 0 |
| 24 | Valdosta St. | 13 | 0 Troy St. | 21 |
| 21 | Furman | 0 | 10 Youngstown St. | 21 |
| 21 | Savannah St. | 7 | | |
| 7 | Georgia | 34 | 177 | 151 |
| 24 | James Madison | 17 | (7-4-0) | |
| 10 | Jacksonville St. | 0 | | |
| 13 | Middle Tenn. St. | 10 | | |

Conference: Southern Conf.   Enrollment: 14,030.   Colors: Blue & White.
Nickname: Eagles.   Stadium: Paulson (1984), 18,000 capacity.   Natural turf.
1992 home attendance: 118,562 in 8 games.
Director of Athletics: David Wagner.
Sports Info. Director: Matt Rogers  912-681-5239

## GEORGIA TECH . . . Atlanta, Ga.  30332     I-A

Coach: Bill Lewis, East Stroudsburg '63
Record: 7 yrs., W-39, L-39, T-2

### 1993 SCHEDULE

| | |
|---|---|
| Furman ■ | Sep 11 |
| Virginia ■ | Sep 16* |
| Clemson ■ | Sep 25 |
| Florida St. | Oct  2* |
| Maryland ■ | Oct  9 |
| North Caro. | Oct 16 |
| North Caro. St. | Oct 23 |
| Duke | Oct 30 |
| Baylor ■ | Nov  6 |
| Wake Forest | Nov 13 |
| Georgia ■ | Nov 25 |

### 1992 RECORD

| | | | | |
|---|---|---|---|---|
| 37 | Western Caro. | 19 | 27 Baylor | 31 |
| 24 | Virginia | 55 | 10 Wake Forest | 23 |
| 20 | Clemson | 16 | 17 Georgia | 31 |
| 16 | North Caro. St. | 13 | | |
| 28 | Maryland | 26 | 237 | 286 |
| 24 | Florida St. | 29 | (5-6-0) | |
| 14 | North Caro. | 26 | | |
| 20 | Duke | 17 | | |

Conference: Atlantic Coast Conf.   Enrollment: 12,800.   Colors: Old Gold & White.
Nickname: Yellow Jackets.   Stadium: Bobby Dodd/Grant Field (1914),
   46,000 capacity.   Artificial turf.
1992 home attendance: 259,066 in 6 games.
Director of Athletics: Homer Rice.
Sports Info. Director: Mike Finn  404-894-5445

## GRAMBLING . . . Grambling, La.  71245     I-AA

Coach: Eddie Robinson, Leland '41
Record: 50 yrs., W-381, L-136, T-15

### 1993 SCHEDULE

| | |
|---|---|
| Alcorn St. ■ | Sep  4 |
| Tennessee St. [Memphis, Tenn.] | Sep 18* |
| Hampton [East Rutherford, N.J.] | Sep 25* |
| Prairie View [Dallas, Texas] | Oct  2* |
| Mississippi Val. ■ | Oct  9* |
| Ark.-Pine Bluff ■ | Oct 16 |
| Jackson St. | Oct 23* |
| Texas Southern ■ | Oct 30 |
| Alabama St. | Nov  6* |
| Florida A&M ■ | Nov 13 |
| Southern-B.R. | Nov 27 |

### 1992 RECORD

| | | | | |
|---|---|---|---|---|
| 33 | Alcorn St. | 35 | 44 Alabama St. | 19 |
| 54 | Virginia Union | 6 | 27 Florida A&M | 10 |
| 38 | Tennessee St. | 28 | 30 Southern-B.R. | 27 |
| 42 | Delaware St. | 45 | | |
| 63 | Prairie View | 3 | 438 | 227 |
| 49 | Mississippi Val. | 6 | (9-2-0) | |
| 34 | Jackson St. | 31 | **Heritage Bowl** | |
| 24 | Texas Southern | 17 | 45 Florida A&M | 15 |

Conference: Southwestern.   Enrollment: 7,533.   Colors: Black & Gold.
Nickname: Tigers.   Stadium: Robinson (1983), 22,000 capacity.   Natural turf.
1992 home attendance: 129,547 in 6 games.
Director of Athletics: Eddie Robinson.
Sports Info. Director: Stanley Lewis  318-274-2761

■ Home games on each schedule [neutral sites shown in brackets].   *Night Games.

## HARVARD . . . Cambridge, Mass.   02138                                          I-AA

Coach: Joseph Restic, Villanova '52
Record: 22 yrs., W-114, L-90, T-6

### 1993 SCHEDULE

| | |
|---|---|
| Columbia ■ | Sep 18 |
| William & Mary | Sep 25 |
| Lafayette ■ | Oct 2 |
| Cornell ■ | Oct 9 |
| Holy Cross ■ | Oct 16 |
| Princeton ■ | Oct 23 |
| Dartmouth | Oct 30 |
| Brown | Nov 6 |
| Pennsylvania ■ | Nov 13 |
| Yale | Nov 20 |

**1992 RECORD**

| | | | | | |
|---|---|---|---|---|---|
| 27 | Columbia | 20 | 19 | Pennsylvania | 21 |
| 16 | William & Mary | 36 | 14 | Yale | 0 |
| 7 | Holy Cross | 30 | | | |
| 13 | Cornell | 31 | 167 | (3-7-0) | 240 |
| 29 | Lafayette | 31 | | | |
| 6 | Princeton | 21 | | | |
| 7 | Dartmouth | 31 | | | |
| 29 | Brown | 19 | | | |

Conference: Ivy League.   Enrollment: 6,677.   Colors: Crimson, Black & White.
Nickname: Crimson.   Stadium: Harvard (1903), 37,967 capacity.   Natural turf.
1992 home attendance: 68,840 in 5 games.
Director of Athletics: William Cleary Jr.
Sports Info. Director: John Veneziano   617-495-2206

---

## HAWAII . . . Honolulu, Hawaii   96822                                          I-A

Coach: Bob Wagner, Wittenberg '69
Record: 6 yrs., W-45, L-27, T-2

### 1993 SCHEDULE

| | |
|---|---|
| Middle Tenn. St. ■ | Sep 4* |
| Brigham Young | Sep 11 |
| Kent ■ | Sep 18* |
| UTEP ■ | Sep 25* |
| New Mexico | Oct 2* |
| San Diego St. ■ | Oct 9* |
| Wyoming | Oct 23 |
| Utah ■ | Nov 6* |
| Fresno St. | Nov 13* |
| Air Force ■ | Nov 20* |
| California ■ | Nov 27* |
| Tulane ■ | Dec 4* |

**1992 RECORD**

| | | | | | |
|---|---|---|---|---|---|
| 24 | Oregon | 21 | 28 | San Diego St. | 52 |
| 6 | Air Force | 3 | 42 | Wyoming | 18 |
| 36 | Brigham Young | 32 | 38 | Tulsa | 9 |
| 17 | Utah | 38 | 36 | Pittsburgh | 23 |
| 47 | Fresno St. | 45 | | | |
| 55 | Nevada-Las Vegas | 25 | 394 | (10-2-0) | 300 |
| 41 | UTEP | 21 | | **Holiday Bowl** | |
| 24 | Colorado St. | 13 | 27 | Illinois | 17 |

Conference: Western Athl. Conf.   Enrollment: 19,810.   Colors: Green & White.
Nickname: Rainbow Warriors.   Stadium: Aloha (1975), 50,000 capacity.   Artificial turf.
1992 home attendance: 311,022 in 7 games.
Director of Athletics: To be named.
Sports Info. Director: Eddie Inouye   808-956-7523

---

## HOFSTRA . . . Hempstead, N.Y.   11550                                          I-AA

Coach: Joe Gardi, Maryland '60
Record: 3 yrs., W-24, L-9, T-0

### 1993 SCHEDULE

| | |
|---|---|
| Butler ■ | Sep 4* |
| Rhode Island | Sep 11 |
| Lehigh | Sep 18 |
| Illinois St. ■ | Sep 25* |
| Buffalo ■ | Oct 2* |
| Bucknell ■ | Oct 9 |
| Lafayette | Oct 16 |
| Towson St. ■ | Oct 30* |
| Fordham | Nov 13 |
| Maine | Nov 20 |

**1992 RECORD**

| | | | | | |
|---|---|---|---|---|---|
| 14 | Central Conn. St. | 7 | 13 | Dayton | 24 |
| 14 | Lafayette | 21 | 6 | Montana | 50 |
| 6 | James Madison | 38 | | | |
| 18 | Towson St. | 37 | 177 | (4-6-0) | 261 |
| 28 | Rhode Island | 18 | | | |
| 32 | Southern Conn. St. | 20 | | | |
| 31 | Fordham | 20 | | | |
| 15 | Buffalo | 26 | | | |

Conference: I-AA Independents.   Enrollment: 12,000.   Colors: Blue, Gold & White.
Nickname: Flying Dutchmen.   Stadium: Hofstra (1963), 7,500 capacity.   Artificial turf.
1992 home attendance: 18,430 in 5 games.
Director of Athletics: James Garvey.
Sports Info. Director: Jim Sheehan   516-463-6764

---

## HOLY CROSS . . . Worcester, Mass.   01610                                          I-AA

Coach: Peter Vaas, Holy Cross '74
Record: 5 yrs., W-35, L-16, T-1

### 1993 SCHEDULE

| | |
|---|---|
| Massachusetts | Sep 11 |
| Boston U. ■ | Sep 18 |
| Dartmouth | Sep 25 |
| Princeton | Oct 2 |
| Yale ■ | Oct 9 |
| Harvard | Oct 16 |
| Bucknell | Oct 23 |
| Lehigh | Oct 30 |
| Lafayette ■ | Nov 6 |
| Colgate ■ | Nov 13 |
| Fordham | Nov 20 |

**1992 RECORD**

| | | | | | |
|---|---|---|---|---|---|
| 7 | Army | 17 | 6 | Lafayette | 15 |
| 3 | Massachusetts | 7 | 18 | Colgate | 17 |
| 3 | Yale | 7 | 21 | Fordham | 13 |
| 30 | Harvard | 7 | | | |
| 0 | Dartmouth | 48 | 153 | (6-5-0) | 175 |
| 10 | Princeton | 7 | | | |
| 27 | Bucknell | 12 | | | |
| 28 | Lehigh | 25 | | | |

Conference: Patriot League.   Enrollment: 2,600.   Colors: Royal Purple.
Nickname: Crusaders.   Stadium: Fitton Field (1924), 23,500 capacity.   Natural turf.
1992 home attendance: 61,632 in 7 games.
Director of Athletics: Ron Perry.
Sports Info. Director: Jeff Nelson   508-793-2583

---

## HOUSTON . . . Houston, Texas   77004                                          I-A

Coach: Kim Helton, Florida '70
Record: First year as head coach

### 1993 SCHEDULE

| | |
|---|---|
| Southern Cal | Sep 4 |
| Tulsa ■ | Sep 11 |
| Michigan | Sep 25 |
| Baylor ■ | Oct 2 |
| Texas A&M | Oct 9 |
| Southern Methodist ■ | Oct 16 |
| Texas Christian | Oct 30 |
| Texas ■ | Nov 4* |
| Cincinnati ■ | Nov 13 |
| Texas Tech [San Antonio, Texas] | Nov 20* |
| Rice | Nov 26 |

**1992 RECORD**

| | | | | | |
|---|---|---|---|---|---|
| 25 | Tulsa | 28 | 30 | Texas A&M | 38 |
| 31 | Illinois | 13 | 35 | Texas Tech | 44 |
| 7 | Michigan | 61 | 61 | Rice | 34 |
| 63 | Southwestern La. | 7 | | | |
| 23 | Baylor | 29 | 378 | (4-7-0) | 386 |
| 38 | Texas | 45 | | | |
| 49 | Texas Christian | 46 | | | |
| 16 | Southern Methodist | 41 | | | |

Conference: Southwest Conf.   Enrollment: 34,000.   Colors: Scarlet & White.
Nickname: Cougars.   Stadium: Astrodome (1965), 60,000 capacity.   Artificial turf.
1992 home attendance: 111,830 in 5 games.
Director of Athletics: Bill Carr.
Sports Info. Director: Ted Nance   713-743-9404

---

■ Home games on each schedule [neutral sites shown in brackets].   *Night Games.

## HOWARD . . . Washington, D.C.   20059   I-AA

Coach: Steve Wilson, Howard '79
Record: 4 yrs., W-23, L-21, T-0

**1993 SCHEDULE**

| | |
|---|---|
| Virginia Union ■ | Sep 4 |
| Winston-Salem ■ | Sep 18 |
| Alcorn St. [St. Louis, Mo.] | Sep 25 |
| Florida A&M ■ | Oct 2 |
| Bethune-Cookman | Oct 9 |
| Towson St. | Oct 16 |
| North Caro. A&T | Oct 23 |
| Morehouse ■ | Oct 30 |
| South Caro. St. ■ | Nov 6 |
| Morgan St. | Nov 13 |
| Delaware St. | Nov 20 |

**1992 RECORD**

| | | | | |
|---|---|---|---|---|
| 0 | Morehouse | 7 | 18 South Caro. St. | 28 |
| 28 | Alabama A&M | 7 | 68 Morgan St. | 21 |
| 75 | Cheyney | 6 | 31 Delaware St. | 28 |
| 48 | Alcorn St. | 42 | | |
| 3 | Florida A&M | 10 | 366 | 178 |
| 26 | Bethune-Cookman | 7 | (7-4-0) | |
| 14 | North Caro. A&T | 16 | | |
| 55 | Bowie St. | 6 | | |

Conference: Mid-Eastern.  Enrollment: 12,000.  Colors: Blue & White.
Nickname: Bison.  Stadium: Greene (1986), 7,500 capacity.  Artificial turf.
1992 home attendance: 52,546 in 7 games.
Director of Athletics: David C. Simmons.
Sports Info. Director: Edward Hill   202-806-7182

## IDAHO . . . Moscow, Idaho   83843   I-AA

Coach: John L. Smith, Weber St. '71
Record: 4 yrs., W-33, L-15, T-0

**1993 SCHEDULE**

| | |
|---|---|
| Stephen F. Austin | Sep 2* |
| Southwest Tex. St. ■ | Sep 11 |
| Weber St. ■ | Sep 18* |
| Utah | Oct 2* |
| Idaho St. | Oct 9 |
| Eastern Wash. ■ | Oct 16 |
| Montana St. | Oct 23 |
| Northern Ariz. | Oct 30* |
| Montana ■ | Nov 6 |
| Lehigh ■ | Nov 13 |
| Boise St. ■ | Nov 20 |

**1992 RECORD**

| | | | | |
|---|---|---|---|---|
| 42 | St. Cloud St. | 9 | 29 Montana | 47 |
| 37 | Colorado St. | 34 | 28 Montana St. | 7 |
| 52 | Weber St. | 24 | 62 Boise St. | 16 |
| 30 | Cal St. Northridge | 7 | | |
| 49 | Idaho St. | 18 | 446 | 224 |
| 38 | Eastern Wash. | 21 | (9-2-0) | |
| 26 | Northern Iowa | 27 | **I-AA Championship** | |
| 53 | Northern Ariz. | 14 | 20 McNeese St. | 23 |

Conference: Big Sky Conf.  Enrollment: 14,202.  Colors: Silver & Gold.
Nickname: Vandals.  Stadium: Kibbie (1975), 16,000 capacity.  Artificial turf.
1992 home attendance: 58,650 in 6 games.
Director of Athletics: Pete Liske.
Sports Info. Director: Rance Pugmire   208-885-0211

## IDAHO STATE . . . Pocatello, Idaho   83209   I-AA

Coach: Brian McNeely, Wichita St. '79
Record: 1 yr., W-3, L-8, T-0

**1993 SCHEDULE**

| | |
|---|---|
| Chadron St. ■ | Sep 4* |
| Portland St. | Sep 11* |
| Montana | Sep 18 |
| Northern Ariz. ■ | Sep 25* |
| Mesa St. ■ | Oct 2* |
| Idaho ■ | Oct 9 |
| Montana St. ■ | Oct 16* |
| Boise St. | Oct 23* |
| Eastern Wash. | Oct 30 |
| New Mexico | Nov 6 |
| Weber St. ■ | Nov 13* |

**1992 RECORD**

| | | | | |
|---|---|---|---|---|
| 52 | Mesa St. | 17 | 3 Eastern Wash. | 37 |
| 24 | Boise St. | 20 | 28 Southern Utah | 29 |
| 11 | Northern Iowa | 49 | 14 Montana | 21 |
| 12 | Northern Ariz. | 27 | | |
| 38 | Central Wash. | 26 | 218 | 316 |
| 18 | Idaho | 49 | (3-8-0) | |
| 7 | Montana St. | 14 | | |
| 11 | Weber St. | 27 | | |

Conference: Big Sky Conf.  Enrollment: 11,155.  Colors: Orange & Black.
Nickname: Bengals.  Stadium: Holt Arena (1970), 12,000 capacity.  Artificial turf.
1992 home attendance: 42,000 in 6 games.
Director of Athletics: Randy Hoffman.
Sports Info. Director: Glenn Alford   208-236-3651

## ILLINOIS . . . Champaign, Ill.   61820   I-A

Coach: Lou Tepper, Rutgers '67
Record: 2 yrs., W-6, L-6, T-1

**1993 SCHEDULE**

| | |
|---|---|
| Missouri | Sep 11 |
| Arizona ■ | Sep 18 |
| Oregon ■ | Sep 25 |
| Purdue | Oct 2 |
| Ohio St. ■ | Oct 9 |
| Iowa | Oct 16 |
| Michigan | Oct 23 |
| Northwestern ■ | Oct 30 |
| Minnesota ■ | Nov 6 |
| Penn St. | Nov 13 |
| Wisconsin ■ | Nov 20 |

**1992 RECORD**

| | | | | |
|---|---|---|---|---|
| 30 | Northern Ill. | 14 | 20 Purdue | 17 |
| 24 | Missouri | 17 | 22 Michigan | 22 |
| 13 | Houston | 31 | 14 Michigan St. | 10 |
| 17 | Minnesota | 18 | | |
| 18 | Ohio St. | 16 | 211 | 208 |
| 14 | Iowa | 24 | (6-4-1) | |
| 26 | Northwestern | 27 | **Holiday Bowl** | |
| 13 | Wisconsin | 12 | 17 Hawaii | 27 |

Conference: Big Ten Conf.  Enrollment: 35,766.  Colors: Orange & Blue.
Nickname: Fighting Illini.  Stadium: Memorial (1923), 69,200 capacity.  Artificial turf.
1992 home attendance: 301,216 in 6 games.
Director of Athletics: Ron Guenther.
Sports Info. Director: Mike Pearson   217-333-1390

## ILLINOIS STATE . . . Normal, Ill.   61761   I-AA

Coach: Jim Heacock, Muskingum '70
Record: 5 yrs., W-21, L-34, T-0

**1993 SCHEDULE**

| | |
|---|---|
| Tennessee Tech | Sep 4* |
| Ball St. | Sep 11 |
| McNeese St. ■ | Sep 18* |
| Hofstra | Sep 25* |
| Western Ill. ■ | Oct 2 |
| Southwest Mo. St. | Oct 9 |
| Indiana St. ■ | Oct 16 |
| Eastern Ill. | Oct 23 |
| Northern Iowa ■ | Oct 30 |
| Southern Ill. | Nov 6 |
| Youngstown St. ■ | Nov 13 |

**1992 RECORD**

| | | | | |
|---|---|---|---|---|
| 51 | Southwest St. | 12 | 9 Western Ill. | 37 |
| 19 | Northern Ill. | 26 | 23 Western Ky. | 7 |
| 7 | Indiana St. | 12 | 52 Southeast Mo. St. | 33 |
| 48 | Eastern Ill. | 7 | | |
| 14 | Northern Iowa | 41 | 289 | 244 |
| 10 | Youngstown St. | 34 | (5-6-0) | |
| 21 | Southwest Mo. St. | 24 | | |
| 35 | Southern Ill. | 11 | | |

Conference: Gateway.  Enrollment: 20,000.  Colors: Red & White.
Nickname: Redbirds.  Stadium: Hancock (1963), 15,000 capacity.  Artificial turf.
1992 home attendance: 44,696 in 5 games.
Director of Athletics: Rick Greenspan.
Sports Info. Director: Kenny Mossman   309-438-3825

■ Home games on each schedule [neutral sites shown in brackets].   *Night Games.

## INDIANA ... Bloomington, Ind.  47405  I-A

Coach: Bill Mallory, Miami (Ohio) '57
Record: 23 yrs., W-148, L-104, T-4

**1993 SCHEDULE**

| | |
|---|---|
| Toledo ■ | Sep 4* |
| Northern Ill. ■ | Sep 11 |
| Kentucky ■ | Sep 18 |
| Wisconsin ■ | Sep 25 |
| Minnesota | Oct 2* |
| Iowa ■ | Oct 9 |
| Northwestern | Oct 23 |
| Michigan St. ■ | Oct 30 |
| Penn St. | Nov 6 |
| Ohio St. | Nov 13 |
| Purdue ■ | Nov 20 |

**1992 RECORD**

| | | | | | |
|---|---|---|---|---|---|
| 16 | Miami (Ohio) | 0 | 0 | Iowa | 14 |
| 25 | Kentucky | 37 | 10 | Ohio St. | 27 |
| 20 | Missouri | 10 | 10 | Purdue | 13 |
| 31 | Michigan St. | 42 | | | |
| 28 | Northwestern | 3 | 177 | (5-6-0) | 197 |
| 3 | Michigan | 31 | | | |
| 10 | Wisconsin | 3 | | | |
| 24 | Minnesota | 17 | | | |

Conference: Big Ten Conf.  Enrollment: 36,000.  Colors: Cream & Crimson.
Nickname: Hoosiers.  Stadium: Memorial (1960), 52,354 capacity.  Artificial turf.
1992 home attendance: 260,799 in 6 games.
Director of Athletics: Clarence Doninger.
Sports Info. Director: Kit Klingelhoffer  812-855-2421

---

## INDIANA STATE ... Terre Haute, Ind.  47809  I-AA

Coach: Dennis Raetz, Nebraska '68
Record: 13 yrs., W-68, L-76, T-1

**1993 SCHEDULE**

| | |
|---|---|
| Air Force | Sep 4 |
| Minnesota | Sep 11* |
| Southwest Mo. St. | Sep 25* |
| Eastern Ill. ■ | Oct 2 |
| Northern Iowa | Oct 9 |
| Illinois St. | Oct 16 |
| Western Ky. ■ | Oct 23 |
| Southern Ill. ■ | Oct 30 |
| Youngstown St. | Nov 6 |
| West Va. Tech ■ | Nov 13 |
| Western Ill. ■ | Nov 20 |

**1992 RECORD**

| | | | | | |
|---|---|---|---|---|---|
| 3 | Oklahoma St. | 35 | 13 | Northern Iowa | 34 |
| 14 | Western Ky. | 34 | 31 | Southwest Mo. St. | 28 |
| 12 | Illinois St. | 7 | 35 | Southern Ill. | 42 |
| 66 | Lock Haven | 13 | | | |
| 24 | Youngstown St. | 30 | 319 | (4-7-0) | 345 |
| 28 | Eastern Ill. | 31 | | | |
| 63 | Glenville St. | 49 | | | |
| 30 | Western Ill. | 42 | | | |

Conference: Gateway.  Enrollment: 12,271.  Colors: Blue & White.
Nickname: Sycamores.  Stadium: Memorial (1970), 20,500 capacity.  Artificial turf.
1992 home attendance: 26,850 in 6 games.
Director of Athletics: Brian Faison.
Sports Info. Director: Eric Ruden  812-237-4161

---

## IONA ... New Rochelle, N.Y.  10801  I-AA

Coach: Harold Crocker, Central Conn. St. '74
Record: 8 yrs., W-33, L-46, T-1

**1993 SCHEDULE**

| | |
|---|---|
| Sacred Heart | Sep 11 |
| Central Conn. St. ■ | Sep 18 |
| Georgetown ■ | Sep 25 |
| Wagner | Oct 2 |
| Canisius | Oct 9 |
| St. Peter's | Oct 16* |
| Pace ■ | Oct 23 |
| Siena | Oct 30 |
| Marist ■ | Nov 6 |
| St. John's (N.Y.) | Nov 12* |

**1992 RECORD**

| | | | | | |
|---|---|---|---|---|---|
| 30 | St. John's (N.Y.) | 33 | 26 | Merchant Marine | 32 |
| 32 | Siena | 7 | 10 | FDU-Madison | 14 |
| 28 | Catholic | 13 | | | |
| 21 | Marist | 20 | 242 | (5-5-0) | 209 |
| 20 | Wagner | 27 | | | |
| 0 | LIU-C.W. Post | 24 | | | |
| 41 | Pace | 24 | | | |
| 34 | Sacred Heart | 15 | | | |

Conference: Metro Atlantic Ath. Conf.  Enrollment: 7,500.  Colors: Maroon & Gold.
Nickname: Gaels.  Stadium: Mazzella Field (1989), 1,200 capacity.  Artificial turf.
1992 home attendance: 4,800 in 5 games.
Director of Athletics: Rich Petriccione.
Sports Info. Director: Dave Torromeo  914-633-2334

---

## IOWA ... Iowa City, Iowa  52242  I-A

Coach: Hayden Fry, Baylor '51
Record: 31 yrs., W-194, L-147, T-9

**1993 SCHEDULE**

| | |
|---|---|
| Tulsa ■ | Sep 4 |
| Iowa St. | Sep 11 |
| Penn St. ■ | Sep 18 |
| Michigan | Oct 2 |
| Indiana | Oct 9 |
| Illinois ■ | Oct 16 |
| Michigan St. | Oct 23 |
| Purdue ■ | Oct 30 |
| Northern Ill. ■ | Nov 6 |
| Northwestern | Nov 13 |
| Minnesota ■ | Nov 20 |

**1992 RECORD**

| | | | | | |
|---|---|---|---|---|---|
| 14 | North Caro. St. | 24 | 15 | Ohio St. | 38 |
| 7 | Miami (Fla.) | 24 | 14 | Indiana | 0 |
| 21 | Iowa St. | 7 | 56 | Northwestern | 14 |
| 12 | Colorado | 28 | 13 | Minnesota | 28 |
| 28 | Michigan | 52 | | | |
| 23 | Wisconsin | 22 | 243 | (5-7-0) | 278 |
| 24 | Illinois | 14 | | | |
| 16 | Purdue | 27 | | | |

Conference: Big Ten Conf.  Enrollment: 28,000.  Colors: Old Gold & Black.
Nickname: Hawkeyes.  Stadium: Kinnick (1929), 70,311 capacity.  Natural turf.
1992 home attendance: 466,485 in 7 games.
Director of Athletics: Bob Bowlsby.
Sports Info. Director: To be named  319-335-9411

---

## IOWA STATE ... Ames, Iowa  50011  I-A

Coach: Jim Walden, Wyoming '60
Record: 15 yrs., W-66, L-94, T-6

**1993 SCHEDULE**

| | |
|---|---|
| Northern Ill. ■ | Sep 2* |
| Iowa ■ | Sep 11 |
| Wisconsin | Sep 18 |
| Rice | Sep 25 |
| Oklahoma ■ | Oct 2 |
| Kansas | Oct 16 |
| Oklahoma St. ■ | Oct 23 |
| Missouri | Oct 30 |
| Kansas St. ■ | Nov 6 |
| Nebraska | Nov 13 |
| Colorado ■ | Nov 20 |

**1992 RECORD**

| | | | | | |
|---|---|---|---|---|---|
| 35 | Ohio | 9 | 13 | Kansas St. | 22 |
| 7 | Iowa | 21 | 19 | Nebraska | 10 |
| 38 | Tulane | 14 | 10 | Colorado | 31 |
| 10 | Northern Iowa | 27 | | | |
| 3 | Oklahoma | 17 | 231 | (4-7-0) | 242 |
| 47 | Kansas | 50 | | | |
| 21 | Oklahoma St. | 27 | | | |
| 28 | Missouri | 14 | | | |

Conference: Big Eight Conf.  Enrollment: 25,263.  Colors: Cardinal & Gold.
Nickname: Cyclones.  Stadium: Cyclone-Jack Trice (1975), 50,000 capacity.  Artificial turf.
1992 home attendance: 225,490 in 6 games.
Director of Athletics: Eugene Smith.
Sports Info. Director: Dave Starr  515-294-3372

---

■ Home games on each schedule [neutral sites shown in brackets].  *Night Games.

*1993 NCAA FOOTBALL*

## JACKSON STATE . . . Jackson, Miss.   39217   I-AA

Coach: James Carson, Jackson St. '63
Record: 1 yr., W-7, L-4, T-0
1993 SCHEDULE

| | |
|---|---|
| Tuskegee ■ | Sep  4 |
| Tennessee St. [Chicago, Ill.] | Sep 11* |
| Florida A&M ■ | Sep 18* |
| Mississippi Val. | Sep 25* |
| South Caro. St. [Indianapolis, Ind.] | Oct  2 |
| Alabama St. ■ | Oct  9* |
| Southern-B.R. ■ | Oct 16* |
| Grambling ■ | Oct 23* |
| Texas Southern ■ | Nov  6* |
| Prairie View | Nov 13 |
| Alcorn St. ■ | Nov 20 |

1992 RECORD

| | | | | |
|---|---|---|---|---|
| 30 | Tuskegee | 0 | 26 Texas Southern | 27 |
| 38 | Tennessee St. | 18 | 46 Prairie View | 0 |
| 26 | Stephen F. Austin | 41 | 35 Alcorn St. | 42 |
| 42 | Mississippi Val. | 14 | | |
| 41 | South Caro. St. | 3 | 361      (7-4-0) | 210 |
| 21 | Alabama St. | 7 | | |
| 25 | Southern-B.R. | 24 | | |
| 31 | Grambling | 34 | | |

Conference: Southwestern.   Enrollment: 6,699.   Colors: Blue & White.
Nickname: Tigers.   Stadium: Mississippi Memorial (1949), 62,512 capacity.   Natural turf.
1992 home attendance: 99,000 in 4 games.
Director of Athletics: W. C. Gorden.
Sports Info. Director: Samuel Jefferson  601-968-2273

## JAMES MADISON . . . Harrisonburg, Va.   22807   I-AA

Coach: William "Rip" Scherer, William & Mary '74
Record: 2 yrs., W-13, L-11, T-0
1993 SCHEDULE

| | |
|---|---|
| Lock Haven ■ | Sep  4* |
| Richmond ■ | Sep 11 |
| Connecticut | Sep 18 |
| Jacksonville St. ■ | Sep 25 |
| Massachusetts | Oct  2 |
| Delaware ■ | Oct  9 |
| New Hampshire ■ | Oct 16 |
| William & Mary | Oct 30 |
| Northeastern | Nov  6 |
| Villanova | Nov 13 |
| Boston U. ■ | Nov 20 |

1992 RECORD

| | | | | |
|---|---|---|---|---|
| 20 | Virginia Tech | 49 | 21 William & Mary | 14 |
| 40 | Richmond | 49 | 31 Liberty | 34 |
| 38 | Hofstra | 6 | 37 Central Fla. | 41 |
| 52 | Youngstown St. | 49 | | |
| 35 | Northeastern | 34 | 333      (4-7-0) | 355 |
| 21 | Appalachian St. | 27 | | |
| 17 | Ga. Southern | 24 | | |
| 21 | Towson St. | 28 | | |

Conference: Yankee.   Enrollment: 11,200.   Colors: Purple & Gold.
Nickname: Dukes.   Stadium: Bridgeforth (1975), 12,800 capacity.   Artificial turf.
1992 home attendance: 49,050 in 5 games.
Director of Athletics: Dean Ehlers.
Sports Info. Director: Gary Michael   703-568-6154

## KANSAS . . . Lawrence, Kan.   66045   I-A

Coach: Glen Mason, Ohio St. '72
Record: 7 yrs., W-34, L-43, T-1
1993 SCHEDULE

| | |
|---|---|
| Florida St. [East Rutherford, N.J.] | Aug 28 |
| Western Caro. ■ | Sep  4 |
| Michigan St. | Sep 11 |
| Utah ■ | Sep 18 |
| Colorado St. ■ | Oct  2 |
| Kansas St. | Oct  9 |
| Iowa St. ■ | Oct 16 |
| Oklahoma | Oct 23 |
| Oklahoma St. | Oct 30 |
| Nebraska ■ | Nov  6 |
| Colorado | Nov 13 |
| Missouri ■ | Nov 20 |

1992 RECORD

| | | | | |
|---|---|---|---|---|
| 49 | Oregon St. | 20 | 7 Nebraska | 49 |
| 62 | Ball St. | 10 | 18 Colorado | 25 |
| 40 | Tulsa | 7 | 17 Missouri | 22 |
| 23 | California | 27 | | |
| 31 | Kansas St. | 7 | 350      (7-4-0) | 242 |
| 50 | Iowa St. | 47 | Aloha Bowl | |
| 27 | Oklahoma | 10 | 23 Brigham Young | 20 |
| 26 | Oklahoma St. | 18 | | |

Conference: Big Eight Conf.   Enrollment: 29,160.   Colors: Crimson & Blue.
Nickname: Jayhawks.   Stadium: Memorial (1921), 50,250 capacity.   Artificial turf.
1992 home attendance: 251,500 in 6 games.
Director of Athletics: Bob Frederick.
Sports Info. Director: Doug Vance  913-864-3417

## KANSAS STATE . . . Manhattan, Kan.   66506   I-A

Coach: Bill Snyder, William Jewell '63
Record: 4 yrs., W-18, L-26, T-0
1993 SCHEDULE

| | |
|---|---|
| New Mexico St. ■ | Sep  4 |
| Western Ky. ■ | Sep 11 |
| Minnesota | Sep 18* |
| Nevada-Las Vegas ■ | Sep 25 |
| Kansas ■ | Oct  9 |
| Nebraska | Oct 16 |
| Colorado ■ | Oct 23 |
| Oklahoma ■ | Oct 30 |
| Iowa St. | Nov  6 |
| Missouri ■ | Nov 13 |
| Oklahoma St. | Nov 20 |

1992 RECORD

| | | | | |
|---|---|---|---|---|
| 27 | Montana | 12 | 14 Missouri | 27 |
| 35 | Temple | 14 | 10 Oklahoma St. | 0 |
| 19 | New Mexico St. | 0 | 24 Nebraska | 38 |
| 7 | Kansas | 31 | | |
| 16 | Utah St. | 28 | 195      (5-6-0) | 233 |
| 7 | Colorado | 54 | | |
| 14 | Oklahoma | 16 | | |
| 22 | Iowa St. | 13 | | |

Conference: Big Eight Conf.   Enrollment: 21,112.   Colors: Purple & White.
Nickname: Wildcats.   Stadium: K S U (1968), 42,000 capacity.   Artificial turf.
1992 home attendance: 138,867 in 5 games.
Director of Athletics: To be named.
Sports Info. Director: Ben Boyle  913-532-6735

## KENT . . . Kent, Ohio   44242   I-A

Coach: Pete Cordelli, North Caro. St. '76
Record: 2 yrs., W-3, L-19, T-0
1993 SCHEDULE

| | |
|---|---|
| Kentucky | Sep  4* |
| Akron | Sep 11* |
| Hawaii | Sep 18* |
| Western Mich. ■ | Oct  2 |
| Eastern Mich. | Oct  9* |
| Ohio | Oct 16 |
| Central Mich. ■ | Oct 23 |
| Toledo ■ | Oct 30 |
| Bowling Green | Nov  6 |
| Miami (Ohio) ■ | Nov 13 |
| Ball St. | Nov 20 |

1992 RECORD

| | | | | |
|---|---|---|---|---|
| 10 | Pittsburgh | 51 | 17 Toledo | 32 |
| 14 | Ohio | 27 | 22 Bowling Green | 28 |
| 6 | Ball St. | 10 | 14 Miami (Ohio) | 31 |
| 17 | Eastern Mich. | 14 | | |
| 0 | Cincinnati | 31 | 133      (2-9-0) | 301 |
| 20 | Akron | 16 | | |
| 0 | Central Mich. | 35 | | |
| 13 | Western Mich. | 26 | | |

Conference: Mid-American Conf.   Enrollment: 33,468.   Colors: Navy Blue & Gold.
Nickname: Golden Flashes.   Stadium: Dix (1969), 30,520 capacity.   Natural turf.
1992 home attendance: 34,183 in 5 games.
Director of Athletics: Paul Amodio.
Sports Info. Director: Dale Gallagher  216-672-2110

■ Home games on each schedule [neutral sites shown in brackets].   *Night Games.

## KENTUCKY . . . Lexington, Ky.  40506     I-A

Coach: Bill Curry, Georgia Tech '65
Record: 13 yrs., W-68, L-75, T-4

**1993 SCHEDULE**

| | |
|---|---|
| Kent ■ | Sep 4* |
| Florida ■ | Sep 11* |
| Indiana | Sep 18 |
| South Caro. | Sep 23* |
| Mississippi ■ | Oct 2* |
| Louisiana St. ■ | Oct 16* |
| Georgia | Oct 23 |
| Mississippi St. | Oct 30 |
| Vanderbilt | Nov 6 |
| East Caro. ■ | Nov 13 |
| Tennessee ■ | Nov 20 |

**1992 RECORD**

| | | | | | |
|---|---|---:|---|---|---:|
| 21 | Central Mich. | 14 | 7 | Vanderbilt | 20 |
| 19 | Florida | 35 | 13 | Cincinnati | 17 |
| 37 | Indiana | 25 | 13 | Tennessee | 34 |
| 13 | South Caro. | 9 | | | |
| 14 | Mississippi | 24 | 207 | (4-7-0) | 280 |
| 27 | Louisiana St. | 25 | | | |
| 7 | Georgia | 40 | | | |
| 36 | Mississippi St. | 37 | | | |

Conference: Southeastern Conf.   Enrollment: 24,000.   Colors: Blue & White.
Nickname: Wildcats.   Stadium: Commonwealth (1973), 58,000 capacity.   Natural turf.
1992 home attendance: 324,875 in 6 games.
Director of Athletics: C. M. Newton.
Sports Info. Director: To be named   606-257-3838

## LAFAYETTE . . . Easton, Pa.  18042     I-AA

Coach: Bill Russo, Brown '69
Record: 15 yrs., W-89, L-69, T-1

**1993 SCHEDULE**

| | |
|---|---|
| Bucknell ■ | Sep 11 |
| Buffalo | Sep 18* |
| Princeton ■ | Sep 25 |
| Harvard | Oct 2 |
| Columbia | Oct 9 |
| Hofstra ■ | Oct 16 |
| Fordham | Oct 23 |
| Colgate ■ | Oct 30 |
| Holy Cross | Nov 6 |
| Army | Nov 13 |
| Lehigh | Nov 20 |

**1992 RECORD**

| | | | | | |
|---|---|---:|---|---|---:|
| 21 | Hofstra | 14 | 15 | Holy Cross | 6 |
| 49 | Buffalo | 28 | 49 | Bucknell | 7 |
| 35 | Princeton | 38 | 32 | Lehigh | 29 |
| 33 | Cornell | 44 | | | |
| 36 | Army | 38 | 382 | (8-3-0) | 282 |
| 31 | Harvard | 29 | | | |
| 44 | Fordham | 21 | | | |
| 37 | Colgate | 28 | | | |

Conference: Patriot League.   Enrollment: 2,000.   Colors: Maroon & White.
Nickname: Leopards.   Stadium: Fisher Field (1926), 13,750 capacity.   Natural turf.
1992 home attendance: 38,311 in 5 games.
Director of Athletics: Eve Atkinson.
Sports Info. Director: Steve Pulver   215-250-5122

## LEHIGH . . . Bethlehem, Pa.  18015     I-AA

Coach: Hank Small, Gettysburg '69
Record: 7 yrs., W-40, L-36, T-1

**1993 SCHEDULE**

| | |
|---|---|
| Delaware | Sep 4 |
| Fordham | Sep 11 |
| Hofstra ■ | Sep 18 |
| Brown ■ | Sep 25 |
| Cornell ■ | Oct 2 |
| Princeton | Oct 16 |
| Colgate | Oct 23 |
| Holy Cross ■ | Oct 30 |
| Bucknell | Nov 6 |
| Idaho | Nov 13 |
| Lafayette ■ | Nov 20 |

**1992 RECORD**

| | | | | | |
|---|---|---:|---|---|---:|
| 16 | Fordham | 14 | 38 | Bucknell | 16 |
| 14 | New Hampshire | 28 | 13 | William & Mary | 26 |
| 23 | Cornell | 29 | 29 | Lafayette | 32 |
| 28 | Princeton | 38 | | | |
| 28 | Northeastern | 42 | 258 | (3-8-0) | 291 |
| 31 | Brown | 24 | | | |
| 13 | Colgate | 14 | | | |
| 25 | Holy Cross | 28 | | | |

Conference: Patriot League.   Enrollment: 4,500.   Colors: Brown & White.
Nickname: Engineers.   Stadium: Goodman (1988), 16,000 capacity.   Natural turf.
1992 home attendance: 52,058 in 5 games.
Director of Athletics: Joseph D. Sterrett.
Sports Info. Director: Glenn Hofmann   215-758-3174

## LIBERTY . . . Lynchburg, Va.  24506     I-AA

Coach: Sam Rutigliano, Tulsa '56
Record: 4 yrs., W-25, L-18, T-0

**1993 SCHEDULE**

| | |
|---|---|
| Concord (W. Va.) ■ | Sep 4* |
| Appalachian St. | Sep 11 |
| Southwest Tex. St. | Sep 18 |
| Indiana (Pa.) ■ | Sep 25 |
| North Caro. A&T ■ | Oct 2* |
| Troy St. | Oct 9 |
| Youngstown St. | Oct 16 |
| Charleston So. ■ | Oct 30 |
| Central Fla. | Nov 6 |
| Delaware St. | Nov 13 |
| Villanova ■ | Nov 20 |

**1992 RECORD**

| | | | | | |
|---|---|---:|---|---|---:|
| 13 | Furman | 31 | 31 | Central Fla. | 28 |
| 55 | Morgan St. | 27 | 34 | James Madison | 31 |
| 26 | Concord (W. Va.) | 8 | 49 | Delaware St. | 27 |
| 32 | North Caro. A&T | 35 | | | |
| 16 | Towson St. | 14 | 306 | (7-4-0) | 277 |
| 20 | Maine | 42 | | | |
| 9 | Troy St. | 7 | | | |
| 21 | Northern Ill. | 27 | | | |

Conference: I-AA Independents.   Enrollment: 10,000.   Colors: Red, White & Blue.
Nickname: Flames.   Stadium: Liberty (1989), 12,000 capacity.   Artificial turf.
1992 home attendance: 26,073 in 5 games.
Director of Athletics: Chuck Burch.
Sports Info. Director: Mitch Goodman   804-582-2292

## LOUISIANA STATE . . . Baton Rouge, La.  70893     I-A

Coach: Curley Hallman, Texas A&M '70
Record: 5 yrs., W-30, L-26, T-0

**1993 SCHEDULE**

| | |
|---|---|
| Texas A&M | Sep 4* |
| Mississippi St. | Sep 11* |
| Auburn ■ | Sep 18* |
| Tennessee | Sep 25 |
| Utah St. ■ | Oct 2* |
| Florida ■ | Oct 9* |
| Kentucky | Oct 16* |
| Mississippi ■ | Oct 30* |
| Alabama | Nov 6 |
| Tulane ■ | Nov 20* |
| Arkansas ■ | Nov 27* |

**1992 RECORD**

| | | | | | |
|---|---|---:|---|---|---:|
| 22 | Texas A&M | 31 | 11 | Alabama | 31 |
| 24 | Mississippi St. | 3 | 24 | Tulane | 12 |
| 28 | Auburn | 30 | 6 | Arkansas | 30 |
| 14 | Colorado St. | 17 | | | |
| 0 | Tennessee | 20 | 175 | (2-9-0) | 261 |
| 21 | Florida | 28 | | | |
| 25 | Kentucky | 27 | | | |
| 0 | Mississippi | 32 | | | |

Conference: Southeastern Conf.   Enrollment: 24,753.   Colors: Purple & Gold.
Nickname: Fighting Tigers.   Stadium: Tiger (1924), 80,150 capacity.   Natural turf.
1992 home attendance: 469,195 in 7 games.
Director of Athletics: Joe Dean.
Sports Info. Director: Herb Vincent   504-388-8226

---

■ Home games on each schedule [neutral sites shown in brackets].   *Night Games.

*1993 NCAA FOOTBALL*

## LOUISIANA TECH . . . Ruston, La.   71272                    I-A

Coach: Joe Raymond Peace, Louisiana Tech '68
Record: 5 yrs., W-30, L-21, T-4
### 1993 SCHEDULE
| | |
|---|---|
| Tennessee | Sep  4 |
| South Caro. [Birmingham, Ala.] | Sep 18* |
| Alabama [Birmingham, Ala.] | Sep 25 |
| Arkansas St. ■ | Oct  2* |
| East Caro. | Oct 16* |
| San Jose St. | Oct 23 |
| Northern Ill. ■ | Oct 30 |
| Nevada-Las Vegas ■ | Nov  6 |
| Utah St. | Nov 13 |
| Central Fla. ■ | Nov 20* |
| Southwestern La. | Nov 27* |

### 1992 RECORD
| | | | | | |
|---|---|---|---|---|---|
| 10 | Baylor | 9 | 13 | South Caro. | 14 |
| 31 | Eastern Mich. | 17 | 6 | Mississippi | 13 |
| 13 | Southern Miss. | 16 | 3 | West Va. | 23 |
| 0 | Alabama | 13 | | | |
| 14 | Fresno St. | 48 | 199 | (5-6-0) | 167 |
| 21 | Southwestern La. | 7 | | | |
| 65 | East Tenn. St. | 7 | | | |
| 23 | Arkansas St. | 0 | | | |

Conference: Big West.   Enrollment: 10,380.   Colors: Red & Blue.
Nickname: Bulldogs.   Stadium: Joe Aillet (1968), 30,600 capacity.   Natural turf.
1992 home attendance: 70,450 in 4 games.
Director of Athletics: Jerry Stovall.
Sports Info. Director: Keith Prince   318-257-3144

## LOUISVILLE . . . Louisville, Ky.   40292                    I-A

Coach: Howard Schnellenberger, Kentucky '56
Record: 13 yrs., W-80, L-64, T-2
### 1993 SCHEDULE
| | |
|---|---|
| San Jose St. ■ | Sep  4 |
| Memphis St. | Sep 11* |
| Arizona St. ■ | Sep 18 |
| Texas ■ | Sep 25 |
| Pittsburgh | Oct  2* |
| West Va. | Oct  9 |
| Southern Miss. ■ | Oct 16 |
| Navy ■ | Oct 23 |
| Tennessee | Nov  6 |
| Texas A&M | Nov 13 |
| Tulsa | Nov 25 |

### 1992 RECORD
| | | | | | |
|---|---|---|---|---|---|
| 19 | Ohio St. | 20 | 27 | Cincinnati | 17 |
| 16 | Memphis St. | 15 | 18 | Texas A&M | 40 |
| 0 | Arizona St. | 19 | 31 | Pittsburgh | 16 |
| 24 | Wyoming | 26 | | | |
| 9 | Syracuse | 15 | 214 | (5-6-0) | 243 |
| 21 | Virginia Tech | 17 | | | |
| 32 | Tulsa | 27 | | | |
| 17 | Florida | 31 | | | |

Conference: I-A Independents.   Enrollment: 23,000.   Colors: Red, Black & White.
Nickname: Cardinals.   Stadium: Cardinal (1956), 35,500 capacity.   Artificial turf.
1992 home attendance: 161,913 in 5 games.
Director of Athletics: William Olsen.
Sports Info. Director: Kenny Klein   502-588-6581

## MAINE . . . Orono, Maine   04469                    I-AA

Coach: Jack Cosgrove, Maine '78
Record: First year as head coach
### 1993 SCHEDULE
| | |
|---|---|
| Buffalo | Sep  4* |
| Boston U. | Sep 11 |
| Massachusetts ■ | Sep 18 |
| New Hampshire | Sep 25 |
| Richmond [Portland, Maine] | Oct  9 |
| Rhode Island | Oct 16 |
| Connecticut ■ | Oct 23 |
| Delaware | Oct 30 |
| William & Mary ■ | Nov  6 |
| Northeastern ■ | Nov 13 |
| Hofstra ■ | Nov 20 |

### 1992 RECORD
| | | | | | |
|---|---|---|---|---|---|
| 27 | New Hampshire | 24 | 40 | Boston U. | 11 |
| 10 | Kutztown | 0 | 21 | Massachusetts | 13 |
| 36 | Northeastern | 47 | 8 | Villanova | 28 |
| 6 | Richmond | 28 | | | |
| 42 | Liberty | 20 | 254 | (6-5-0) | 274 |
| 21 | Rhode Island | 9 | | | |
| 30 | Connecticut | 37 | | | |
| 13 | Delaware | 57 | | | |

Conference: Yankee.   Enrollment: 12,165.   Colors: Blue & White.
Nickname: Black Bears.   Stadium: Alumni (1942), 10,000 capacity.   Natural turf.
1992 home attendance: 45,013 in 7 games.
Director of Athletics: Michael Ploszek.
Sports Info. Director: Matt Bourque   207-581-1086

## MARIST . . . Poughkeepsie, N.Y.   12601                    I-AA

Coach: Jim Parady, Maine '84
Record: 1 yr., W-4, L-5, T-1
### 1993 SCHEDULE
| | |
|---|---|
| St. Francis (Pa.) | Sep 11 |
| Pace ■ | Sep 18 |
| LIU-C.W. Post ■ | Sep 25 |
| St. John's (N.Y.) | Sep 30* |
| Central Conn. St. | Oct  9 |
| Duquesne ■ | Oct 16 |
| Rensselaer ■ | Oct 23 |
| Wagner ■ | Oct 30 |
| Iona | Nov  6 |
| Siena ■ | Nov 13 |

### 1992 RECORD
| | | | | | |
|---|---|---|---|---|---|
| 28 | Siena | 12 | 28 | FDU-Madison | 21 |
| 18 | Pace | 13 | 10 | Canisius | 14 |
| 12 | LIU-C.W. Post | 12 | | | |
| 20 | Iona | 21 | 177 | (4-5-1) | 218 |
| 14 | St. Francis (Pa.) | 42 | | | |
| 7 | Wagner | 42 | | | |
| 17 | Rensselaer | 26 | | | |
| 23 | St. John's (N.Y.) | 15 | | | |

Conference: I-AA Independents.   Enrollment: 3,200.   Colors: Black, Red & White.
Nickname: Red Foxes.   Stadium: Leonidoff Field (1972), 2,500 capacity.   Natural turf.
1992 home attendance: 6,247 in 4 games.
Director of Athletics: Eugene Doris.
Sports Info. Director: Dan Sullivan   914-575-2322

## MARSHALL . . . Huntington, W. Va.   25715                    I-AA

Coach: Jim Donnan, North Caro. St. '67
Record: 3 yrs., W-29, L-12, T-0
### 1993 SCHEDULE
| | |
|---|---|
| Morehead St. ■ | Sep  4* |
| Murray St. ■ | Sep 11* |
| Ga. Southern ■ | Sep 18* |
| Tenn.-Chatt. | Oct  2* |
| Va. Military ■ | Oct  9* |
| North Caro. | Oct 16 |
| Appalachian St. ■ | Oct 23* |
| Citadel | Oct 30 |
| East Tenn. St. ■ | Nov  6 |
| Furman | Nov 13 |
| Western Caro. ■ | Nov 20 |

### 1992 RECORD
| | | | | | |
|---|---|---|---|---|---|
| 49 | Morehead St. | 7 | 52 | Tennessee Tech | 14 |
| 63 | Eastern Ill. | 28 | 49 | East Tenn. St. | 10 |
| 34 | Va. Military | 16 | | | |
| 21 | Missouri | 44 | 466 | (8-3-0) | 236 |
| 48 | Furman | 6 | | **I-AA Championship** | |
| 34 | Citadel | 13 | 44 | Eastern Ky. | 0 |
| 52 | Tenn.-Chatt. | 23 | 35 | Middle Tenn. St. | 21 |
| 30 | Western Caro. | 38 | 28 | Delaware | 7 |
| 34 | Appalachian St. | 37 | 31 | Youngstown St. | 28 |

Conference: Southern Conf.   Enrollment: 12,000.   Colors: Green & White.
Nickname: Thundering Herd.   Stadium: Marshall University (1992), 28,000 capacity.   Artificial turf.
1992 home attendance: 138,910 in 6 games.
Director of Athletics: William Lee Moon.
Sports Info. Director: Gary Richter   304-696-5275

■ Home games on each schedule [neutral sites shown in brackets].   *Night Games.

*Divisions I-A & I-AA 1993 Schedules and 1992 Results*                    679

## MARYLAND ... College Park, Md.  20740  I-A

Coach: Mark Duffner, William & Mary '75
Record: 7 yrs., W-63, L-13, T-1
### 1993 SCHEDULE
Virginia ■ .............................. Sep 4
North Caro. ............................ Sep 11
West Va. ■ ............................. Sep 18
Virginia Tech .......................... Sep 25
Penn St. ■ ............................. Oct 2
Georgia Tech .......................... Oct 9
Duke ■ ................................ Oct 16
Clemson ............................... Oct 30
Florida St. ■ ........................... Nov 6
North Caro. St. ........................ Nov 13
Wake Forest ........................... Nov 20

#### 1992 RECORD
| | | | | | |
|---|---|--:|---|---|--:|
| 15 | Virginia | 28 | 24 | North Caro. | 31 |
| 10 | North Caro. St. | 14 | 21 | Florida St. | 69 |
| 33 | West Va. | 34 | 53 | Clemson | 23 |
| 13 | Penn St. | 49 | | | |
| 47 | Pittsburgh | 34 | 292 | (3-8-0) | 365 |
| 26 | Georgia Tech | 28 | | | |
| 23 | Wake Forest | 30 | | | |
| 27 | Duke | 25 | | | |

Conference: Atlantic Coast Conf.  Enrollment: 21,799.  Colors: Red, White, Black & Gold.
Nickname: Terps.  Stadium: Byrd (1950), 45,000 capacity.  Natural turf.
1992 home attendance: 168,145 in 6 games.
Director of Athletics: Andy Geiger.
Sports Info. Director: Herb Hartnett  301-314-7064

## MASSACHUSETTS ... Amherst, Mass.  01003  I-AA

Coach: Mike Hodges, Maine '67
Record: 1 yr., W-7, L-3, T-0
### 1993 SCHEDULE
Holy Cross ■ ........................... Sep 11
Maine ................................. Sep 18
Boston U. .............................. Sep 25
James Madison ■ ...................... Oct 2
Rhode Island [Killarney, Ireland] ........ Oct 9
Connecticut ........................... Oct 16
Delaware ■ ............................ Oct 23
Northeastern .......................... Oct 30
Richmond ■ ........................... Nov 6
William & Mary ■ ...................... Nov 13
New Hampshire ■ ...................... Nov 20

#### 1992 RECORD
| | | | | | |
|---|---|--:|---|---|--:|
| 13 | Delaware | 33 | 13 | Maine | 21 |
| 7 | Holy Cross | 3 | 13 | New Hampshire | 20 |
| 30 | Boston U. | 28 | | | |
| 32 | Rhode Island | 7 | 180 | (7-3-0) | 151 |
| 20 | Connecticut | 7 | | | |
| 13 | Villanova | 9 | | | |
| 22 | Northeastern | 10 | | | |
| 17 | Richmond | 13 | | | |

Conference: Yankee.  Enrollment: 17,091.  Colors: Maroon & White.
Nickname: Minutemen.  Stadium: Warren McGuirk (1965), 16,000 capacity.  Natural turf.
1992 home attendance: 34,698 in 5 games.
Director of Athletics: Bob Marcum.
Sports Info. Director: To be named  413-545-2439

## McNEESE STATE ... Lake Charles, La.  70601  I-AA

Coach: Bobby Keasler, Northeast La. '70
Record: 3 yrs., W-20, L-14, T-2
### 1993 SCHEDULE
Northern Iowa ......................... Sep 4*
Eastern Ill. ■ .......................... Sep 11*
Illinois St. ............................ Sep 18*
Central Fla. ........................... Sep 25
Northeast La. .......................... Oct 9*
North Texas ■ ......................... Oct 16*
Sam Houston St. ■ ..................... Oct 23*
Stephen F. Austin ...................... Oct 30
Southwest Tex. St. ..................... Nov 6*
Northwestern (La.) ..................... Nov 13
Nicholls St. ■ .......................... Nov 20*

#### 1992 RECORD
| | | | | | |
|---|---|--:|---|---|--:|
| 16 | Southwest Mo. St. | 13 | 28 | Stephen F. Austin | 3 |
| 18 | Northern Iowa | 21 | 37 | Sam Houston St. | 14 |
| 21 | Nevada | 31 | 23 | Weber St. | 22 |
| 21 | Nicholls St. | 17 | | | |
| 35 | Northeast La. | 52 | 271 | (8-3-0) | 211 |
| 29 | Northwestern (La.) | 0 | | I-AA Championship | |
| 17 | Southwest Tex. St. | 13 | 23 | Idaho | 20 |
| 26 | North Texas | 25 | 7 | Northern Iowa | 29 |

Conference: Southland Conf.  Enrollment: 8,400.  Colors: Blue & Gold.
Nickname: Cowboys.  Stadium: Cowboy (1965), 20,000 capacity.  Natural turf.
1992 home attendance: 85,191 in 5 games.
Director of Athletics: Bob Hayes.
Sports Info. Director: Louis Bonnette  318-475-5207

## MEMPHIS STATE ... Memphis, Tenn.  38152  I-A

Coach: Chuck Stobart, Ohio '59
Record: 12 yrs., W-57, L-74, T-3
### 1993 SCHEDULE
Mississippi St. ......................... Sep 4*
Louisville ■ ........................... Sep 11*
Southwestern La. ...................... Sep 18*
Arkansas [Little Rock, Ark.] ............ Sep 25
East Caro. ............................ Oct 2
Arkansas St. ■ ........................ Oct 9
Tulsa ■ ............................... Oct 16
Cincinnati ............................. Oct 30
Mississippi ■ .......................... Nov 6
Southern Miss. ■ ...................... Nov 13
Miami (Fla.) ........................... Nov 27

#### 1992 RECORD
| | | | | | |
|---|---|--:|---|---|--:|
| 21 | Southern Miss. | 23 | 12 | Mississippi | 17 |
| 15 | Louisville | 16 | 21 | Tennessee | 26 |
| 16 | Mississippi St. | 20 | 42 | East Caro. | 7 |
| 22 | Arkansas | 6 | | | |
| 34 | Cincinnati | 14 | 312 | (6-5-0) | 181 |
| 37 | Arkansas St. | 7 | | | |
| 30 | Tulsa | 25 | | | |
| 62 | Tulane | 20 | | | |

Conference: I-A Independents.  Enrollment: 21,500.  Colors: Blue & Gray.
Nickname: Tigers.  Stadium: Liberty Bowl (1965), 62,425 capacity.  Natural turf.
1992 home attendance: 224,449 in 6 games.
Director of Athletics: Charles Cavagnaro.
Sports Info. Director: Bob Winn  901-678-2337

## MIAMI (FLORIDA) ... Coral Gables, Fla.  33124  I-A

Coach: Dennis Erickson, Montana St. '70
Record: 11 yrs., W-94, L-35, T-1
### 1993 SCHEDULE
Boston College ........................ Sep 4
Virginia Tech ■ ........................ Sep 18
Colorado .............................. Sep 25
Ga. Southern ■ ........................ Oct 2
Florida St. ............................ Oct 9
Syracuse .............................. Oct 23
Temple ■ .............................. Oct 30
Pittsburgh ............................. Nov 6
Rutgers ■ ............................. Nov 13
West Va. .............................. Nov 20
Memphis St. ■ ......................... Nov 27

#### 1992 RECORD
| | | | | | |
|---|---|--:|---|---|--:|
| 24 | Iowa | 7 | 48 | Temple | 0 |
| 38 | Florida A&M | 0 | 16 | Syracuse | 10 |
| 8 | Arizona | 7 | 63 | San Diego St. | 17 |
| 19 | Florida St. | 16 | | | |
| 17 | Penn St. | 14 | 356 | (11-0-0) | 127 |
| 45 | Texas Christian | 10 | | Sugar Bowl | |
| 43 | Virginia Tech | 23 | 13 | Alabama | 34 |
| 35 | West Va. | 23 | | | |

Conference: Big East Conference.  Enrollment: 13,153.  Colors: Orange, Green, White.
Nickname: Hurricanes.  Stadium: Orange Bowl (1935), 74,712 capacity.  Natural turf.
1992 home attendance: 334,052 in 6 games.
Director of Athletics: Dave Maggard.
Sports Info. Director: Linda Venzon  305-284-3244

■ Home games on each schedule [neutral sites shown in brackets].  *Night Games.

## MIAMI (OHIO) . . . Oxford, Ohio   45056   I-A

Coach: Randy Walker, Miami (Ohio) '76
Record: 3 yrs., W-17, L-13, T-3
1993 SCHEDULE

| | |
|---|---|
| Southwestern La. ■ | Sep 11* |
| Cincinnati | Sep 18* |
| Western Mich. | Sep 25 |
| Eastern Mich. ■ | Oct 2 |
| Akron | Oct 9* |
| Toledo | Oct 16* |
| Ohio | Oct 23 |
| Bowling Green ■ | Oct 30 |
| Ball St. | Nov 6 |
| Kent | Nov 13 |
| Central Mich. ■ | Nov 20 |

1992 RECORD

| | | | | | |
|---|---|---|---|---|---|
| 29 | West Va. | 29 | 24 | Bowling Green | 44 |
| 0 | Indiana | 16 | 20 | Western Mich. | 7 |
| 17 | Cincinnati | 14 | 31 | Kent | 14 |
| 9 | Ball St. | 19 | | | |
| 24 | Eastern Mich. | 7 | 210 | (6-4-1) | 204 |
| 16 | Central Mich. | 13 | | | |
| 23 | Ohio | 21 | | | |
| 17 | Toledo | 20 | | | |

Conference: Mid-American Conf.   Enrollment: 16,000.   Colors: Red & White.
Nickname: Redskins.   Stadium: Fred C. Yager (1983), 25,183 capacity.   Natural turf.
1992 home attendance: 94,105 in 5 games.
Director of Athletics: R. C. Johnson.
Sports Info. Director: Brian Teter   513-529-4327

---

## MICHIGAN . . . Ann Arbor, Mich.   48109   I-A

Coach: Gary Moeller, Ohio St. '63
Record: 6 yrs., W-34, L-29, T-6
1993 SCHEDULE

| | |
|---|---|
| Washington St. ■ | Sep 4 |
| Notre Dame ■ | Sep 11 |
| Houston ■ | Sep 25 |
| Iowa ■ | Oct 2 |
| Michigan St. | Oct 9 |
| Penn St. | Oct 16 |
| Illinois ■ | Oct 23 |
| Wisconsin | Oct 30 |
| Purdue ■ | Nov 6 |
| Minnesota | Nov 13* |
| Ohio St. ■ | Nov 20 |

1992 RECORD

| | | | | | |
|---|---|---|---|---|---|
| 17 | Notre Dame | 17 | 40 | Northwestern | 7 |
| 35 | Oklahoma St. | 3 | 22 | Illinois | 22 |
| 61 | Houston | 7 | 13 | Ohio St. | 13 |
| 52 | Iowa | 28 | | | |
| 35 | Michigan St. | 10 | 393 | (8-0-3) | 140 |
| 31 | Indiana | 3 | | Rose Bowl | |
| 63 | Minnesota | 13 | 38 | Washington | 31 |
| 24 | Purdue | 17 | | | |

Conference: Big Ten Conf.   Enrollment: 36,375.   Colors: Maize & Blue.
Nickname: Wolverines.   Stadium: Michigan (1927), 102,501 capacity.   Natural turf.
1992 home attendance: 635,201 in 6 games.
Director of Athletics: To be named.
Sports Info. Director: Bruce Madej   313-763-4423

---

## MICHIGAN STATE . . . East Lansing, Mich.   48824   I-A

Coach: George Perles, Michigan St. '60
Record: 10 yrs., W-62, L-50, T-4
1993 SCHEDULE

| | |
|---|---|
| Kansas ■ | Sep 11 |
| Notre Dame | Sep 18 |
| Central Mich. ■ | Sep 25 |
| Michigan ■ | Oct 9 |
| Ohio St. | Oct 16 |
| Iowa ■ | Oct 23 |
| Indiana | Oct 30 |
| Northwestern ■ | Nov 6 |
| Purdue | Nov 13 |
| Penn St. ■ | Nov 27 |
| Wisconsin [Tokyo, Japan] | Dec 5* |

1992 RECORD

| | | | | | |
|---|---|---|---|---|---|
| 20 | Central Mich. | 24 | 26 | Wisconsin | 10 |
| 31 | Notre Dame | 52 | 35 | Purdue | 13 |
| 0 | Boston College | 14 | 10 | Illinois | 14 |
| 42 | Indiana | 31 | | | |
| 10 | Michigan | 35 | 238 | (5-6-0) | 261 |
| 20 | Minnesota | 15 | | | |
| 17 | Ohio St. | 27 | | | |
| 27 | Northwestern | 26 | | | |

Conference: Big Ten Conf.   Enrollment: 40,047.   Colors: Green & White.
Nickname: Spartans.   Stadium: Spartan (1957), 76,000 capacity.   Artificial turf.
1992 home attendance: 358,886 in 6 games.
Director of Athletics: Merrily Baker.
Sports Info. Director: Ken Hoffman   517-355-2271

---

## MIDDLE TENNESSEE STATE . . . Murfreesboro, Tenn.   37132   I-AA

Coach: Boots Donnelly, Middle Tenn. St. '65
Record: 16 yrs., W-119, L-64, T-1
1993 SCHEDULE

| | |
|---|---|
| Hawaii | Sep 4* |
| Campbellsville ■ | Sep 18* |
| Murray St. ■ | Sep 25* |
| Tennessee St. | Oct 3 |
| Tenn.-Martin | Oct 9* |
| Morehead St. | Oct 16 |
| Southeast Mo. St. ■ | Oct 23 |
| Tulsa | Oct 30 |
| Austin Peay ■ | Nov 6 |
| Eastern Ky. | Nov 13 |
| Tennessee Tech | Nov 20 |

1992 RECORD

| | | | | | |
|---|---|---|---|---|---|
| 35 | Tennessee St. | 31 | 14 | Tenn.-Martin | 0 |
| 7 | Nebraska | 48 | 70 | Morehead St. | 0 |
| 66 | Murray St. | 6 | 21 | Tennessee Tech | 0 |
| 21 | Northern Ill. | 13 | | | |
| 49 | Austin Peay | 10 | 361 | (9-2-0) | 144 |
| 38 | Eastern Ky. | 7 | | I-AA Championship | |
| 30 | Southeast Mo. St. | 16 | 35 | Appalachian St. | 10 |
| 10 | Ga. Southern | 13 | 21 | Marshall | 35 |

Conference: Ohio Valley Conf.   Enrollment: 16,787.   Colors: Blue & White.
Nickname: Blue Raiders.   Stadium: Johnny Floyd (1969), 15,000 capacity.   Artificial turf.
1992 home attendance: 42,800 in 4 games.
Director of Athletics: John Stanford.
Sports Info. Director: Ed Given   615-898-2450

---

## MINNESOTA . . . Minneapolis, Minn.   55455   I-A

Coach: Jim Wacker, Valparaiso '60
Record: 22 yrs., W-146, L-100, T-3
1993 SCHEDULE

| | |
|---|---|
| Penn St. | Sep 4 |
| Indiana St. ■ | Sep 11* |
| Kansas St. ■ | Sep 18* |
| San Diego St. ■ | Sep 25* |
| Indiana ■ | Oct 2* |
| Purdue | Oct 9* |
| Northwestern | Oct 16 |
| Wisconsin ■ | Oct 23* |
| Illinois | Nov 6 |
| Michigan ■ | Nov 13* |
| Iowa | Nov 20 |

1992 RECORD

| | | | | | |
|---|---|---|---|---|---|
| 30 | San Jose St. | 39 | 0 | Ohio St. | 17 |
| 20 | Colorado | 21 | 6 | Wisconsin | 34 |
| 33 | Pittsburgh | 41 | 28 | Iowa | 13 |
| 18 | Illinois | 17 | | | |
| 20 | Purdue | 24 | 200 | (2-9-0) | 313 |
| 15 | Michigan St. | 20 | | | |
| 13 | Michigan | 63 | | | |
| 17 | Indiana | 24 | | | |

Conference: Big Ten Conf.   Enrollment: 39,000.   Colors: Maroon & Gold.
Nickname: Golden Gophers.   Stadium: Metrodome (1982), 62,345 capacity.   Artificial turf.
1992 home attendance: 227,446 in 6 games.
Director of Athletics: McKinley Boston.
Sports Info. Director: Robert Peterson   612-625-4090

---

■ Home games on each schedule [neutral sites shown in brackets].   *Night Games.

*Divisions I-A & I-AA 1993 Schedules and 1992 Results*   681

## MISSISSIPPI . . . University, Miss.   38677   I-A

Coach: Billy Brewer, Mississippi '61
Record: 19 yrs., W-119, L-89, T-6

### 1993 SCHEDULE

| | |
|---|---|
| Auburn | Sep 2* |
| Tenn.-Chatt. ■ | Sep 11* |
| Vanderbilt ■ | Sep 18* |
| Georgia ■ | Sep 25* |
| Kentucky | Oct 2* |
| Arkansas [Jackson, Miss.] | Oct 16* |
| Alabama ■ | Oct 23 |
| Louisiana St. | Oct 30* |
| Memphis St. | Nov 6 |
| Northern Ill. ■ | Nov 13 |
| Mississippi St. | Nov 27 |

1992 RECORD

| | | | | |
|---|---|---|---|---|
| 45 | Auburn | 21 | 17 Memphis St. | 12 |
| 35 | Tulane | 9 | 13 Louisiana Tech | 6 |
| 9 | Vanderbilt | 31 | 17 Mississippi St. | 10 |
| 11 | Georgia | 37 | | |
| 24 | Kentucky | 14 | 230 (8-3-0) | 174 |
| 17 | Arkansas | 3 | **Liberty Bowl** | |
| 10 | Alabama | 31 | 13 Air Force | 0 |
| 32 | Louisiana St. | 0 | | |

Conference: Southeastern Conf.   Enrollment: 11,033.   Colors: Cardinal Red & Navy Blue.
Nickname: Rebels.   Stadium: Vaught-Hemingway (1941), 42,577 capacity.   Natural turf.
1992 home attendance: 256,066 in 7 games.
Director of Athletics: Warner Alford.
Sports Info. Director: Langston Rogers   601-232-7522

## MISSISSIPPI STATE . . . Mississippi State, Miss.   39762   I-A

Coach: Jackie Sherrill, Alabama '66
Record: 15 yrs., W-119, L-55, T-2

### 1993 SCHEDULE

| | |
|---|---|
| Memphis St. ■ | Sep 4* |
| Louisiana St. ■ | Sep 11* |
| Tulane | Sep 25* |
| Florida | Oct 2 |
| Auburn | Oct 9 |
| South Caro. ■ | Oct 16* |
| Arkansas St. ■ | Oct 23 |
| Kentucky ■ | Oct 30 |
| Arkansas [Little Rock, Ark.] | Nov 6 |
| Alabama | Nov 13 |
| Mississippi ■ | Nov 27 |

1992 RECORD

| | | | | |
|---|---|---|---|---|
| 28 | Texas | 10 | 10 Arkansas | 3 |
| 3 | Louisiana St. | 24 | 21 Alabama | 30 |
| 20 | Memphis St. | 16 | 10 Mississippi | 17 |
| 30 | Florida | 6 | | |
| 14 | Auburn | 7 | 235 (7-4-0) | 176 |
| 6 | South Caro. | 21 | **Peach Bowl** | |
| 56 | Arkansas St. | 6 | 17 North Caro. | 21 |
| 37 | Kentucky | 36 | | |

Conference: Southeastern Conf.   Enrollment: 13,741.   Colors: Maroon & White.
Nickname: Bulldogs.   Stadium: Scott Field (1935), 40,656 capacity.   Natural turf.
1992 home attendance: 197,099 in 5 games.
Director of Athletics: Larry Templeton.
Sports Info. Director: Mike Nemeth   601-325-2703

## MISSISSIPPI VALLEY . . . Itta Bena, Miss.   38941   I-AA

Coach: Larry Dorsey, Tennessee St. '76
Record: 3 yrs., W-16, L-14, T-1

### 1993 SCHEDULE

| | |
|---|---|
| Ark.-Pine Bluff ■ | Sep 4* |
| Lane | Sep 11* |
| Jackson St. ■ | Sep 25* |
| Southern-B.R. ■ | Oct 2* |
| Grambling | Oct 9* |
| Ala.-Birmingham ■ | Oct 16 |
| Prairie View | Oct 30 |
| Alcorn St. | Nov 6 |
| Alabama St. ■ | Nov 13 |
| Texas Southern ■ | Nov 20 |

1992 RECORD

| | | | | |
|---|---|---|---|---|
| 30 | Lane | 0 | 19 Alabama St. | 35 |
| 19 | Miles | 6 | | |
| 14 | Jackson St. | 42 | 158 (4-5-0) | 203 |
| 10 | Southern-B.R. | 13 | | |
| 6 | Grambling | 49 | | |
| 25 | Texas Southern | 13 | | |
| 35 | Prairie View | 14 | | |
| 0 | Alcorn St. | 31 | | |

Conference: Southwestern.   Enrollment: 2,340.   Colors: Green & White.
Nickname: Delta Devils.   Stadium: Magnolia (1958), 10,500 capacity.   Natural turf.
1992 home attendance: 66,412 in 4 games.
Director of Athletics: Chuck Prophet.
Sports Info. Director: Chuck Prophet   601-254-9041

## MISSOURI . . . Columbia, Mo.   65201   I-A

Coach: Bob Stull, Kansas St. '68
Record: 9 yrs., W-43, L-58, T-1

### 1993 SCHEDULE

| | |
|---|---|
| Illinois ■ | Sep 11 |
| Texas A&M | Sep 18* |
| West Va. | Sep 25 |
| Southern Methodist ■ | Oct 2 |
| Colorado | Oct 9 |
| Oklahoma St. ■ | Oct 16 |
| Nebraska | Oct 23 |
| Iowa St. ■ | Oct 30 |
| Oklahoma ■ | Nov 6 |
| Kansas St. | Nov 13 |
| Kansas | Nov 20 |

1992 RECORD

| | | | | |
|---|---|---|---|---|
| 17 | Illinois | 24 | 17 Oklahoma | 51 |
| 13 | Texas A&M | 26 | 27 Kansas St. | 14 |
| 10 | Indiana | 20 | 22 Kansas | 17 |
| 44 | Marshall | 21 | | |
| 0 | Colorado | 6 | 214 (3-8-0) | 269 |
| 26 | Oklahoma St. | 28 | | |
| 24 | Nebraska | 34 | | |
| 14 | Iowa St. | 28 | | |

Conference: Big Eight Conf.   Enrollment: 23,346.   Colors: Old Gold & Black.
Nickname: Tigers.   Stadium: Faurot Field (1926), 62,000 capacity.   Artificial turf.
1992 home attendance: 233,833 in 6 games.
Director of Athletics: Dan Devine.
Sports Info. Director: Bob Brendel   314-882-0712

## MONTANA . . . Missoula, Mont.   59812   I-AA

Coach: Don Read, Cal St. Sacramento '59
Record: 23 yrs., W-120, L-120, T-1

### 1993 SCHEDULE

| | |
|---|---|
| South Dak. St. ■ | Sep 4 |
| Oregon | Sep 11 |
| Idaho St. ■ | Sep 18 |
| Eastern Wash. | Sep 25 |
| Boise St. ■ | Oct 2 |
| Weber St. ■ | Oct 9 |
| Northern Ariz. | Oct 16* |
| Jacksonville St. ■ | Oct 23 |
| Cal St. Sacramento ■ | Oct 30 |
| Idaho | Nov 6 |
| Montana St. | Nov 13 |

1992 RECORD

| | | | | |
|---|---|---|---|---|
| 13 | Washington St. | 25 | 47 Idaho | 29 |
| 41 | Cal St. Chico | 0 | 50 Hofstra | 6 |
| 12 | Kansas St. | 27 | 21 Idaho St. | 14 |
| 21 | Eastern Wash. | 27 | | |
| 21 | Boise St. | 27 | 290 (6-5-0) | 223 |
| 7 | Weber St. | 24 | | |
| 28 | Northern Ariz. | 27 | | |
| 29 | Montana St. | 17 | | |

Conference: Big Sky Conf.   Enrollment: 10,400.   Colors: Copper, Silver & Gold.
Nickname: Grizzlies.   Stadium: Washington-Grizzly (1986), 14,000 capacity.   Natural turf.
1992 home attendance: 69,476 in 6 games.
Director of Athletics: Bill Moos.
Sports Info. Director: Dave Guffey   406-243-6899

---

■ Home games on each schedule [neutral sites shown in brackets].   *Night Games.

## MONTANA STATE . . . Bozeman, Mont.  59717    I-AA

Coach: Cliff Hysell, Montana St. '66
Record: 1 yr., W-4, L-7, T-0
1993 SCHEDULE

| | |
|---|---|
| Western Ill. | Sep  4* |
| Washington St. | Sep 11 |
| Fort Lewis ■ | Sep 18 |
| Weber St. ■ | Sep 25 |
| Northern Ariz. | Oct  2* |
| Southern Utah ■ | Oct  9 |
| Idaho St. | Oct 16* |
| Idaho ■ | Oct 23 |
| Boise St. | Oct 30 |
| Eastern Wash. ■ | Nov  6 |
| Montana ■ | Nov 13 |

1992 RECORD

| | | | | | |
|---|---|---|---|---|---|
| 7 | Cal St. Sacramento | 10 | 17 | Boise St. | 13 |
| 13 | Stephen F. Austin | 6 | 7 | Idaho | 28 |
| 43 | Mesa St. | 0 | 7 | Nevada-Las Vegas | 36 |
| 19 | Weber St. | 47 | | | |
| 9 | Northern Ariz. | 13 | 170 | (4-7-0) | 212 |
| 17 | Eastern Wash. | 23 | | | |
| 14 | Idaho St. | 7 | | | |
| 17 | Montana | 29 | | | |

Conference: Big Sky Conf.   Enrollment: 10,100.   Colors: Blue & Gold.
Nickname: Bobcats.   Stadium: Reno H. Sales (1973), 15,197 capacity.   Natural turf.
1992 home attendance: 37,484 in 5 games.
Director of Athletics: Doug Fullerton.
Sports Info. Director: Bill Lamberty  406-994-5133

## MOREHEAD STATE . . . Morehead, Ky.  40351    I-AA

Coach: Cole Proctor, Morehead St. '68
Record: 3 yrs., W-12, L-21, T-0
1993 SCHEDULE

| | |
|---|---|
| Marshall | Sep  4* |
| Ala.-Birmingham | Sep 11 |
| West Va. Tech ■ | Sep 18* |
| Tennessee Tech | Sep 25 |
| Southeast Mo. St. | Oct  2* |
| Middle Tenn. St. ■ | Oct 16 |
| Austin Peay ■ | Oct 23 |
| Tennessee St. | Oct 30* |
| Murray St. | Nov  6 |
| Tenn.-Martin ■ | Nov 13 |
| Eastern Ky. ■ | Nov 20 |

1992 RECORD

| | | | | | |
|---|---|---|---|---|---|
| 7 | Marshall | 49 | 20 | Southeast Mo. St. | 17 |
| 0 | West Va. St. | 22 | 0 | Middle Tenn. St. | 70 |
| 7 | Tenn.-Martin | 20 | 9 | Eastern Ky. | 37 |
| 7 | East Tenn. St. | 27 | | | |
| 14 | Tennessee St. | 24 | 148 | (3-8-0) | 338 |
| 31 | Murray St. | 7 | | | |
| 12 | Tennessee Tech | 31 | | | |
| 41 | Austin Peay | 34 | | | |

Conference: Ohio Valley Conf.   Enrollment: 9,170.   Colors: Blue & Gold.
Nickname: Eagles.   Stadium: Jayne (1964), 10,000 capacity.   Artificial turf.
1992 home attendance: 28,800 in 5 games.
Director of Athletics: Steve Hamilton.
Sports Info. Director: Randy Stacy  606-783-2500

## MORGAN STATE . . . Baltimore, Md.  21239    I-AA

Coach: Ricky Diggs, Shippensburg '75
Record: 2 yrs., W-3, L-19, T-0
1993 SCHEDULE

| | |
|---|---|
| Charleston So. ■ | Sep  4 |
| Bethune-Cookman | Sep 11 |
| Youngstown St. | Sep 18 |
| South Caro. St. ■ | Oct  9 |
| North Caro. A&T ■ | Oct 16 |
| Delaware St. | Oct 23 |
| Florida A&M [Orlando, Fla.] | Oct 30* |
| Knoxville | Nov  5 |
| Howard ■ | Nov 13 |
| Towson St. ■ | Nov 20 |

1992 RECORD

| | | | | | |
|---|---|---|---|---|---|
| 27 | Liberty | 55 | 13 | Western Ill. | 63 |
| 23 | North Caro. A&T | 52 | 21 | Howard | 68 |
| 25 | Johnson Smith | 21 | | | |
| 45 | Buffalo | 27 | 245 | (2-8-0) | 444 |
| 14 | South Caro. St. | 31 | | | |
| 29 | Central St. (Ohio) | 51 | | | |
| 16 | Delaware St. | 34 | | | |
| 32 | Florida A&M | 42 | | | |

Conference: Mid-Eastern.   Enrollment: 4,750.   Colors: Blue & Orange.
Nickname: Bears.   Stadium: Hughes, 10,000 capacity.   Natural turf.
1992 home attendance: 26,499 in 3 games.
Director of Athletics: Ken McBride.
Sports Info. Director: Joe McIver  410-319-3831

## MURRAY STATE . . . Murray, Ky.  42071    I-AA

Coach: Houston Nutt, Oklahoma St. '81
Record: First year as head coach
1993 SCHEDULE

| | |
|---|---|
| Eastern Ill. ■ | Sep  2* |
| Marshall ■ | Sep 11* |
| Southeast Mo. St. ■ | Sep 18* |
| Middle Tenn. St. | Sep 25* |
| Tenn.-Martin | Oct  2* |
| Austin Peay ■ | Oct  9 |
| Eastern Ky. ■ | Oct 16* |
| Tennessee Tech | Oct 30 |
| Morehead St. ■ | Nov  6 |
| Tennessee St. | Nov 13 |
| Western Ky. | Nov 20 |

1992 RECORD

| | | | | | |
|---|---|---|---|---|---|
| 21 | Southeast Mo. St. | 27 | 18 | Eastern Ky. | 21 |
| 36 | Missouri-Rolla | 0 | 10 | Tennessee St. | 19 |
| 9 | Eastern Ill. | 48 | 15 | Western Ky. | 47 |
| 6 | Middle Tenn. St. | 66 | | | |
| 27 | Austin Peay | 10 | 166 | (2-9-0) | 317 |
| 7 | Tenn.-Martin | 13 | | | |
| 7 | Morehead St. | 31 | | | |
| 10 | Tennessee Tech | 35 | | | |

Conference: Ohio Valley Conf.   Enrollment: 8,190.   Colors: Blue & Gold.
Nickname: Racers.   Stadium: Stewart (1973), 16,800 capacity.   Artificial turf.
1992 home attendance: 13,314 in 6 games.
Director of Athletics: Mike Strickland.
Sports Info. Director: Tim Tucker  502-762-4270

## NAVY . . . Annapolis, Md.  21402    I-A

Coach: George Chaump, Bloomsburg '58
Record: 11 yrs., W-63, L-59, T-2
1993 SCHEDULE

| | |
|---|---|
| Virginia | Sep 11 |
| Eastern Ill. ■ | Sep 18* |
| Bowling Green ■ | Sep 25 |
| Tulane | Oct  2* |
| Air Force ■ | Oct  9 |
| Colgate ■ | Oct 16 |
| Louisville | Oct 23 |
| Notre Dame [Philadelphia, Pa.] | Oct 30 |
| Vanderbilt | Nov 13 |
| Southern Methodist ■ | Nov 20 |
| Army [East Rutherford, N.J.] | Dec  4 |

1992 RECORD

| | | | | | |
|---|---|---|---|---|---|
| 0 | Virginia | 53 | 7 | Vanderbilt | 27 |
| 0 | Boston College | 28 | 22 | Rice | 27 |
| 0 | Rutgers | 40 | 24 | Army | 25 |
| 14 | North Caro. | 28 | | | |
| 16 | Air Force | 18 | 131 | (1-10-0) | 338 |
| 21 | Delaware | 37 | | | |
| 7 | Notre Dame | 38 | | | |
| 20 | Tulane | 17 | | | |

Conference: I-A Independents.   Enrollment: 4,200.   Colors: Navy Blue & Gold.
Nickname: Midshipmen.   Stadium: Navy-Marine Corps Mem. (1959),
  30,000 capacity.   Natural turf.
1992 home attendance: 245,764 in 7 games.
Director of Athletics: Jack Lengyel.
Sports Info. Director: Tom Bates  410-268-6226

■ Home games on each schedule [neutral sites shown in brackets].   *Night Games.

## NEBRASKA . . . Lincoln, Neb.   68588     I-A

Coach: Tom Osborne, Hastings '59
Record: 20 yrs., W-195, L-46, T-3
1993 SCHEDULE

| | |
|---|---|
| North Texas ■ | Sep 4 |
| Texas Tech ■ | Sep 11 |
| UCLA | Sep 18 |
| Colorado St. ■ | Sep 25 |
| Oklahoma St. | Oct 7* |
| Kansas St. ■ | Oct 16 |
| Missouri ■ | Oct 23 |
| Colorado | Oct 30 |
| Kansas | Nov 6 |
| Iowa St. ■ | Nov 13 |
| Oklahoma ■ | Nov 26 |

### 1992 RECORD

| | | | | |
|---|---|---|---|---|
| 49 | Utah | 22 | 10 Iowa St. | 19 |
| 48 | Middle Tenn. St. | 7 | 33 Oklahoma | 9 |
| 14 | Washington | 29 | 38 Kansas St. | 24 |
| 45 | Arizona St. | 24 | | |
| 55 | Oklahoma St. | 0 | 427 (9-2-0) | 172 |
| 34 | Missouri | 24 | **Orange Bowl** | |
| 52 | Colorado | 7 | 14 Florida St. | 27 |
| 49 | Kansas | 7 | | |

Conference: Big Eight Conf.  Enrollment: 24,000.  Colors: Scarlet & Cream.
Nickname: Cornhuskers.  Stadium: Memorial (1923), 73,650 capacity.  Artificial turf.
1992 home attendance: 457,124 in 6 games.
Director of Athletics: Bill Byrne.
Sports Info. Director: Chris Anderson  402-472-2263

## NEVADA . . . Reno, Nev.   89557     I-A

Coach: Jeff Horton, Nevada '81
Record: First year as head coach
1993 SCHEDULE

| | |
|---|---|
| Wisconsin | Sep 4 |
| Boise St. ■ | Sep 11 |
| Texas Southern ■ | Sep 18 |
| Northern Ill. ■ | Sep 25 |
| Nevada-Las Vegas ■ | Oct 2 |
| Utah St. | Oct 16* |
| Weber St. ■ | Oct 23 |
| Pacific (Cal.) | Oct 30 |
| San Jose St. ■ | Nov 6 |
| New Mexico St. | Nov 13 |
| Arkansas St. | Nov 20 |

### 1992 RECORD

| | | | | |
|---|---|---|---|---|
| 6 | Wyoming | 25 | 35 San Jose St. | 39 |
| 20 | Pacific (Cal.) | 14 | 48 Utah St. | 47 |
| 31 | McNeese St. | 21 | 38 Texas Southern | 14 |
| 17 | Tulane | 34 | | |
| 19 | Cal St. Fullerton | 0 | 284 (7-4-0) | 248 |
| 14 | Nevada-Las Vegas | 10 | **Las Vegas Bowl** | |
| 35 | New Mexico St. | 21 | 34 Bowling Green | 35 |
| 21 | Weber St. | 23 | | |

Conference: Big West.  Enrollment: 12,000.  Colors: Silver & Blue.
Nickname: Wolf Pack.  Stadium: Mackay (1965), 31,545 capacity.  Natural turf.
1992 home attendance: 132,115 in 6 games.
Director of Athletics: Chris Ault.
Sports Info. Director: Paul Stuart  702-784-4600

## NEVADA-LAS VEGAS . . . Las Vegas, Nev.   89154     I-A

Coach: Jim Strong, Mo. Southern St. '76
Record: 3 yrs., W-14, L-19, T-0
1993 SCHEDULE

| | |
|---|---|
| Clemson | Sep 4 |
| UTEP | Sep 11* |
| Central Mich. ■ | Sep 18* |
| Kansas St. ■ | Sep 25 |
| Nevada | Oct 2 |
| Cal St. Northridge ■ | Oct 9* |
| Utah St. ■ | Oct 23* |
| New Mexico St. ■ | Oct 30* |
| Louisiana Tech | Nov 6 |
| San Jose St. | Nov 13* |
| Southwestern La. ■ | Nov 20 |

### 1992 RECORD

| | | | | |
|---|---|---|---|---|
| 19 | UTEP | 17 | 8 Utah St. | 48 |
| 40 | Northern Ariz. | 7 | 36 Montana St. | 7 |
| 6 | Oregon | 59 | 33 Cal St. Fullerton | 16 |
| 21 | Pacific (Cal.) | 17 | | |
| 10 | New Mexico St. | 40 | 243 (6-5-0) | 311 |
| 10 | Nevada | 14 | | |
| 25 | Hawaii | 55 | | |
| 35 | San Jose St. | 31 | | |

Conference: Big West.  Enrollment: 19,561.  Colors: Scarlet & Gray.
Nickname: Rebels.  Stadium: Sam Boyd Silver Bowl (1971), 32,000 capacity.  Artificial turf.
1992 home attendance: 78,492 in 6 games.
Director of Athletics: Jim Weaver.
Sports Info. Director: Tommy Sheppard  702-895-3764

## NEW HAMPSHIRE . . . Durham, N.H.   03824     I-AA

Coach: Bill Bowes, Penn St. '65
Record: 21 yrs., W-136, L-78, T-5
1993 SCHEDULE

| | |
|---|---|
| William & Mary | Sep 4 |
| Connecticut | Sep 11 |
| Richmond ■ | Sep 18 |
| Maine ■ | Sep 25 |
| Dartmouth | Oct 9 |
| James Madison | Oct 16 |
| Northeastern ■ | Oct 23 |
| Boston U. ■ | Oct 30 |
| Villanova | Nov 6 |
| Rhode Island ■ | Nov 13 |
| Massachusetts | Nov 20 |

### 1992 RECORD

| | | | | |
|---|---|---|---|---|
| 24 | Maine | 27 | 21 Villanova | 27 |
| 21 | Connecticut | 24 | 20 Rhode Island | 13 |
| 28 | Lehigh | 14 | 20 Massachusetts | 13 |
| 45 | Dartmouth | 27 | | |
| 22 | Delaware | 42 | 261 (5-5-1) | 226 |
| 7 | Richmond | 15 | | |
| 10 | Northeastern | 10 | | |
| 43 | Boston U. | 14 | | |

Conference: Yankee.  Enrollment: 11,500.  Colors: Blue & White.
Nickname: Wildcats.  Stadium: Cowell (1936), 9,571 capacity.  Natural turf.
1992 home attendance: 42,410 in 6 games.
Director of Athletics: Gilbert Chapman.
Sports Info. Director: Pete Dauphinais  603-862-2585

## NEW MEXICO . . . Albuquerque, N.M.   87131     I-A

Coach: Dennis Franchione, Pittsburg St. '73
Record: 10 yrs., W-83, L-27, T-2
1993 SCHEDULE

| | |
|---|---|
| Brigham Young ■ | Sep 4* |
| Texas Christian | Sep 11* |
| Fresno St. ■ | Sep 18* |
| New Mexico St. ■ | Sep 25* |
| Hawaii ■ | Oct 2* |
| Utah | Oct 9* |
| San Diego St. | Oct 23* |
| Colorado St. | Oct 30 |
| Idaho St. ■ | Nov 6 |
| Wyoming ■ | Nov 13 |
| UTEP | Nov 20 |

### 1992 RECORD

| | | | | |
|---|---|---|---|---|
| 24 | Texas Christian | 7 | 0 Brigham Young | 35 |
| 39 | New Mexico St. | 42 | 35 UTEP | 14 |
| 13 | Southern Methodist | 20 | 10 Colorado St. | 14 |
| 32 | Air Force | 33 | | |
| 21 | San Diego St. | 49 | 247 (3-8-0) | 287 |
| 21 | Wyoming | 35 | | |
| 24 | Utah | 7 | | |
| 28 | Fresno St. | 31 | | |

Conference: Western Athl. Conf.  Enrollment: 24,194.  Colors: Cherry & Silver.
Nickname: Lobos.  Stadium: University (1960), 30,646 capacity.  Natural turf.
1992 home attendance: 115,539 in 6 games.
Director of Athletics: Rudy Davalos.
Sports Info. Director: Greg Remington  505-277-2026

■ Home games on each schedule [neutral sites shown in brackets].   *Night Games.

## NEW MEXICO STATE . . . Las Cruces, N.M.  88003

**I-A**

Coach: Jim Hess, Southeast Okla. '59
Record: 18 yrs., W-121, L-77, T-5

### 1993 SCHEDULE

| | |
|---|---|
| Kansas St. | Sep 4 |
| Arkansas St. | Sep 11* |
| UTEP ■ | Sep 18* |
| New Mexico | Sep 25* |
| Northern Ill. ■ | Oct 9 |
| San Jose St. ■ | Oct 16 |
| Pacific (Cal.) | Oct 23* |
| Nevada-Las Vegas | Oct 30* |
| Auburn | Nov 6 |
| Nevada ■ | Nov 13 |
| Utah St. ■ | Nov 20 |

### 1992 RECORD

| | | | | | |
|---|---|---|---|---|---|
| 37 | Weber St. | 21 | 0 | Arizona | 30 |
| 42 | New Mexico | 39 | 44 | Cal St. Fullerton | 31 |
| 30 | UTEP | 24 | 34 | San Jose St. | 24 |
| 21 | Utah St. | 48 | | | |
| 0 | Kansas St. | 19 | 286 | (6-5-0) | 330 |
| 40 | Nevada-Las Vegas | 10 | | | |
| 17 | Pacific (Cal.) | 49 | | | |
| 21 | Nevada | 35 | | | |

Conference: Big West.  Enrollment: 15,494.  Colors: Crimson & White.
Nickname: Aggies.  Stadium: Aggie Memorial (1978), 30,300 capacity.  Natural turf.
1992 home attendance: 98,824 in 5 games.
Director of Athletics: Al Gonzales.
Sports Info. Director: Steve Shutt  505-646-3929

## NICHOLLS STATE . . . Thibodaux, La.  70301

**I-AA**

Coach: Rick Rhoades, Central Mo. St. '70
Record: 4 yrs., W-32, L-14, T-1

### 1993 SCHEDULE

| | |
|---|---|
| Livingston | Sep 11* |
| Troy St. ■ | Sep 18* |
| Northeast La. ■ | Sep 25* |
| Samford ■ | Oct 2* |
| Northwestern (La.) | Oct 9 |
| Stephen F. Austin | Oct 16 |
| Southwest Tex. St. ■ | Oct 23 |
| Southern-B.R. | Oct 30* |
| Sam Houston St. ■ | Nov 6* |
| North Texas | Nov 13 |
| McNeese St. | Nov 20* |

### 1992 RECORD

| | | | | | |
|---|---|---|---|---|---|
| 10 | Northeast La. | 38 | 3 | North Texas | 31 |
| 12 | Texas A&I. | 50 | 6 | Northwestern (La.) | 44 |
| 17 | McNeese St. | 21 | 0 | Troy St. | 21 |
| 13 | Southwest Tex. St. | 38 | | | |
| 19 | Sam Houston St. | 19 | 131 | (1-9-1) | 349 |
| 18 | Central Fla. | 42 | | | |
| 6 | Stephen F. Austin | 21 | | | |
| 27 | Southern-B.R. | 24 | | | |

Conference: Southland Conf.  Enrollment: 7,605.  Colors: Red & Gray.
Nickname: Colonels.  Stadium: John L. Guidry (1972), 12,800 capacity.  Natural turf.
1992 home attendance: 23,442 in 5 games.
Director of Athletics: Phil Greco.
Sports Info. Director: Ron Mears  504-448-4282

## NORTH CAROLINA . . . Chapel Hill, N.C.  27514

**I-A**

Coach: Mack Brown, Florida St. '74
Record: 9 yrs., W-41, L-59, T-1

### 1993 SCHEDULE

| | |
|---|---|
| Southern Cal [Anaheim, Calif.] | Aug 29* |
| Ohio ■ | Sep 4* |
| Maryland ■ | Sep 11 |
| Florida St. ■ | Sep 18 |
| North Caro. St. | Sep 25 |
| UTEP ■ | Oct 2 |
| Wake Forest ■ | Oct 9 |
| Georgia Tech | Oct 16 |
| Virginia | Oct 23 |
| Clemson ■ | Nov 6 |
| Tulane | Nov 13* |
| Duke ■ | Nov 26 |

### 1992 RECORD

| | | | | | |
|---|---|---|---|---|---|
| 35 | Wake Forest | 17 | 31 | Maryland | 24 |
| 28 | Furman | 0 | 7 | Clemson | 40 |
| 22 | Army | 9 | 31 | Duke | 28 |
| 20 | North Caro. St. | 27 | | | |
| 28 | Navy | 14 | 268 | | 216 |
| 13 | Florida St. | 36 | | **Peach Bowl** | |
| 27 | Virginia | 7 | 21 | Mississippi St. | 17 |
| 26 | Georgia Tech | 14 | | | |

Conference: Atlantic Coast Conf.  Enrollment: 23,852.  Colors: Blue & White.
Nickname: Tar Heels.  Stadium: Kenan (1927), 52,000 capacity.  Natural turf.
1992 home attendance: 283,025 in 6 games.
Director of Athletics: John Swofford.
Sports Info. Director: Rick Brewer  919-962-2123

## NORTH CAROLINA A&T . . . Greensboro, N.C.  27411

**I-AA**

Coach: Bill Hayes, N. C. Central '65
Record: 17 yrs., W-123, L-63, T-2

### 1993 SCHEDULE

| | |
|---|---|
| Appalachian St. ■ | Sep 4 |
| Winston-Salem | Sep 11* |
| Western Caro. | Sep 25 |
| Liberty | Oct 2* |
| Florida A&M ■ | Oct 9 |
| Morgan St. | Oct 16 |
| Howard ■ | Oct 23 |
| Bethune-Cookman | Oct 30 |
| Delaware St. ■ | Nov 6 |
| Johnson Smith ■ | Nov 13 |
| South Caro. St. | Nov 20 |

### 1992 RECORD

| | | | | | |
|---|---|---|---|---|---|
| 49 | N.C. Central | 7 | 24 | Delaware St. | 10 |
| 21 | Winston-Salem | 7 | 6 | Appalachian St. | 42 |
| 52 | Morgan St. | 23 | 24 | South Caro. St. | 21 |
| 35 | Liberty | 32 | | | |
| 35 | Norfolk St. | 6 | 299 | (9-2-0) | 205 |
| 7 | Florida A&M | 21 | | **I-AA Championship** | |
| 16 | Howard | 14 | 0 | Citadel | 44 |
| 30 | Bethune-Cookman | 22 | | | |

Conference: Mid-Eastern.  Enrollment: 7,600.  Colors: Blue & Gold.
Nickname: Aggies.  Stadium: Aggie (1981), 17,500 capacity.  Natural turf.
1992 home attendance: 71,673 in 5 games.
Director of Athletics: Willie J. Burden.
Sports Info. Director: Charles E. Mooney  919-334-7582

## NORTH CAROLINA STATE . . . Raleigh, N.C.  27695

**I-A**

Coach: Dick Sheridan, South Caro. '64
Record: 15 yrs., W-121, L-52, T-5

### 1993 SCHEDULE

| | |
|---|---|
| Purdue ■ | Sep 4 |
| Wake Forest | Sep 11* |
| North Caro. ■ | Sep 25 |
| Clemson | Oct 2 |
| Texas Tech | Oct 9* |
| Marshall ■ | Oct 16 |
| Georgia Tech ■ | Oct 23 |
| Virginia ■ | Oct 30 |
| Duke | Nov 6 |
| Maryland ■ | Nov 13 |
| Florida St. | Nov 20 |

### 1992 RECORD

| | | | | | |
|---|---|---|---|---|---|
| 24 | Iowa | 14 | 20 | Clemson | 6 |
| 35 | Appalachian St. | 10 | 31 | Virginia | 7 |
| 14 | Maryland | 10 | 45 | Duke | 27 |
| 13 | Florida St. | 34 | 42 | Wake Forest | 14 |
| 27 | North Caro. | 20 | | | |
| 13 | Georgia Tech | 16 | 325 | (9-2-1) | 184 |
| 48 | Texas Tech | 13 | | **Gator Bowl** | |
| 13 | Virginia Tech | 13 | 10 | Florida | 27 |

Conference: Atlantic Coast Conf.  Enrollment: 26,683.  Colors: Red & White.
Nickname: Wolfpack.  Stadium: Carter-Finley (1966), 47,000 capacity.  Natural turf.
1992 home attendance: 282,942 in 6 games.
Director of Athletics: Todd Turner.
Sports Info. Director: Mark Bockelman  919-515-2102

■ Home games on each schedule [neutral sites shown in brackets].  *Night Games.

*Divisions I-A & I-AA 1993 Schedules and 1992 Results*

## NORTH TEXAS . . . Denton, Texas   76203   I-AA

Coach: Dennis Parker, Southeast Okla.'72
Record: 2 yrs., W-7, L-14, T-1

**1993 SCHEDULE**

| | |
|---|---|
| Nebraska | Sep  4 |
| Northern Ariz. | Sep 11* |
| Southwest Mo. St. ■ | Sep 18* |
| Abilene Christian ■ | Sep 25* |
| Southwest Tex. St. ■ | Oct  9 |
| McNeese St. | Oct 16* |
| Northwestern (La.) ■ | Oct 23 |
| Sam Houston St. | Oct 30 |
| Stephen F. Austin ■ | Nov  6 |
| Nicholls St. ■ | Nov 13 |
| Northeast La. | Nov 20* |

**1992 RECORD**

| | | | | | |
|---|---|---|---|---|---|
| 41 | Abilene Christian | 0 | 31 | Nicholls St. | 3 |
| 14 | Southern Methodist | 28 | 13 | Southwest Tex. St. | 10 |
| 10 | Southwest Mo. St. | 35 | 25 | Northeast La. | 47 |
| 15 | Texas | 33 | | | |
| 34 | Northwestern (La.) | 37 | 243 | (4-7-0) | 264 |
| 21 | Stephen F. Austin | 11 | | | |
| 14 | Sam Houston St. | 34 | | | |
| 25 | McNeese St. | 26 | | | |

Conference: Southland Conf.   Enrollment: 27,108.   Colors: Green & White.
Nickname: Mean Green, Eagles.   Stadium: Fouts Field (1952), 20,000 capacity.   Artificial turf.
1992 home attendance: 34,728 in 5 games.
Director of Athletics: Steve Sloan.
Sports Info. Director: Brian Briscoe   817-565-2664

---

## NORTHEAST LOUISIANA . . . Monroe, La.   71209   I-AA

Coach: Dave Roberts, Western Caro. '68
Record: 9 yrs., W-54, L-47, T-3

**1993 SCHEDULE**

| | |
|---|---|
| Eastern Wash. | Sep  4 |
| Eastern Ky. ■ | Sep 11* |
| Southern Miss. | Sep 18 |
| Nicholls St. | Sep 25* |
| Northwestern (La.) ■ | Oct  2* |
| McNeese St. ■ | Oct  9* |
| Southwest Tex. St. | Oct 16* |
| Stephen F. Austin ■ | Oct 23* |
| Arkansas St. | Nov  6 |
| Sam Houston St. | Nov 13 |
| North Texas ■ | Nov 20* |

**1992 RECORD**

| | | | | | |
|---|---|---|---|---|---|
| 38 | Nicholls St. | 10 | 41 | Eastern Wash. | 31 |
| 23 | Southwestern La. | 31 | 41 | Stephen F. Austin | 22 |
| 21 | Eastern Ky. | 26 | 47 | North Texas | 25 |
| 13 | Southwest Tex. St. | 6 | | | |
| 52 | Delta St. | 13 | 394 | (9-2-0) | 227 |
| 52 | McNeese St. | 35 | | **I-AA Championship** | |
| 38 | Sam Houston St. | 10 | 78 | Alcorn St. | 27 |
| 28 | Northwestern (La.) | 18 | 18 | Delaware | 41 |

Conference: Southland Conf.   Enrollment: 11,732.   Colors: Maroon & Gold.
Nickname: Indians.   Stadium: Malone (1978), 23,277 capacity.   Natural turf.
1992 home attendance: 87,360 in 5 games.
Director of Athletics: Benny Hollis.
Sports Info. Director: Bob Anderson   318-342-5460

---

## NORTHEASTERN . . . Boston, Mass.   02115   I-AA

Coach: Barry Gallup, Boston College '69
Record: 2 yrs., W-9, L-12, T-1

**1993 SCHEDULE**

| | |
|---|---|
| Villanova | Sep 10* |
| Boise St. | Sep 18* |
| Rhode Island | Sep 25 |
| Richmond | Oct  2 |
| Boston U. ■ | Oct  9 |
| William & Mary ■ | Oct 16 |
| New Hampshire | Oct 23 |
| Massachusetts ■ | Oct 30 |
| James Madison ■ | Nov  6 |
| Maine | Nov 13 |
| Delaware ■ | Nov 20 |

**1992 RECORD**

| | | | | | |
|---|---|---|---|---|---|
| 14 | Northern Ariz. | 21 | 35 | Rhode Island | 26 |
| 47 | Maine | 36 | 32 | Towson St. | 33 |
| 16 | Connecticut | 13 | 19 | Boston U. | 25 |
| 34 | James Madison | 35 | | | |
| 42 | Lehigh | 28 | 287 | (5-5-1) | 272 |
| 28 | Youngstown St. | 23 | | | |
| 10 | New Hampshire | 10 | | | |
| 10 | Massachusetts | 22 | | | |

Conference: Yankee.   Enrollment: 12,000.   Colors: Red & Black.
Nickname: Huskies.   Stadium: E.S. Parsons (1933), 7,000 capacity.   Artificial turf.
1992 home attendance: 20,700 in 4 games.
Director of Athletics: Irwin Cohen.
Sports Info. Director: Jack Grinold   617-437-2691

---

## NORTHERN ARIZONA . . . Flagstaff, Ariz.   86011   I-AA

Coach: Steve Axman, LIU-C. W. Post '69
Record: 3 yrs., W-12, L-21, T-0

**1993 SCHEDULE**

| | |
|---|---|
| Southern Utah | Sep  4* |
| North Texas ■ | Sep 11* |
| Cal St. Northridge ■ | Sep 18* |
| Idaho St. | Sep 25* |
| Montana St. ■ | Oct  2* |
| Boise St. | Oct  9* |
| Montana ■ | Oct 16* |
| Eastern Wash. | Oct 23 |
| Idaho ■ | Oct 30* |
| Weber St. | Nov  6 |
| Valparaiso ■ | Nov 13* |

**1992 RECORD**

| | | | | | |
|---|---|---|---|---|---|
| 17 | Southern Utah | 20 | 14 | Idaho | 53 |
| 21 | Northeastern | 14 | 19 | Weber St. | 25 |
| 7 | Nevada-Las Vegas | 40 | 31 | Minn.-Duluth | 22 |
| 27 | Idaho St. | 12 | | | |
| 13 | Montana St. | 9 | 199 | (4-7-0) | 258 |
| 14 | Boise St. | 20 | | | |
| 27 | Montana | 28 | | | |
| 9 | Eastern Wash. | 15 | | | |

Conference: Big Sky Conf.   Enrollment: 17,698.   Colors: Blue & Gold.
Nickname: Lumberjacks.   Stadium: Walkup Skydome (1977), 15,300 capacity.   Artificial turf.
1992 home attendance: 49,829 in 7 games.
Director of Athletics: Tom Jurich.
Sports Info. Director: Chris Burkhalter   602-523-6791

---

## NORTHERN ILLINOIS . . . De Kalb, Ill.   60115   I-A

Coach: Charlie Sadler, Northeast Okla. '71
Record: 2 yrs., W-7, L-15, T-0

**1993 SCHEDULE**

| | |
|---|---|
| Iowa St. | Sep  2* |
| Indiana | Sep 11 |
| Arkansas St. ■ | Sep 18* |
| Nevada | Sep 25 |
| Southern Ill. ■ | Oct  2 |
| New Mexico St. | Oct  9 |
| Pacific (Cal.) ■ | Oct 16 |
| Southwestern La. ■ | Oct 23 |
| Louisiana Tech | Oct 30 |
| Iowa | Nov  6 |
| Mississippi | Nov 13 |

**1992 RECORD**

| | | | | | |
|---|---|---|---|---|---|
| 14 | Illinois | 30 | 23 | Southwestern La. | 15 |
| 26 | Illinois St. | 19 | 14 | Army | 21 |
| 31 | Arkansas St. | 0 | 8 | Toledo | 25 |
| 17 | Wisconsin | 18 | | | |
| 13 | Middle Tenn. St. | 21 | 203 | (5-6-0) | 193 |
| 23 | Southern Miss. | 10 | | | |
| 27 | Liberty | 21 | | | |
| 7 | Western Mich. | 13 | | | |

Conference: Big West.   Enrollment: 24,052.   Colors: Cardinal & Black.
Nickname: Huskies.   Stadium: Huskie (1965), 30,998 capacity.   Artificial turf.
1992 home attendance: 56,474 in 5 games.
Director of Athletics: Gerald K. O'Dell.
Sports Info. Director: Mike Korcek   815-753-1706

---

■ Home games on each schedule [neutral sites shown in brackets].   *Night Games.

*1993 NCAA FOOTBALL*

## NORTHERN IOWA . . . Cedar Falls, Iowa   50613   I-AA

Coach: Terry Allen, Northern Iowa '79
Record: 4 yrs., W-39, L-11, T-0
1993 SCHEDULE

| | |
|---|---|
| McNeese St. | Sep 4* |
| Wyoming | Sep 11 |
| Jacksonville St. ■ | Sep 18* |
| Southwest Tex. St. ■ | Sep 25* |
| Southwest Mo. St. | Oct 2* |
| Indiana St. ■ | Oct 9 |
| Eastern Ill. ■ | Oct 16* |
| Western Ill. | Oct 23 |
| Illinois St. | Oct 30 |
| Moorhead St. ■ | Nov 6* |
| Southern Ill. ■ | Nov 13* |

1992 RECORD

| | | | |
|---|---|---|---|
| 21 McNeese St. | 18 | 37 Western Ill. | 6 |
| 49 Idaho St. | 11 | 37 Southwest Mo. St. | 12 |
| 27 Iowa St. | 10 | | |
| 41 Illinois St. | 14 | 352  (10-1-0) | 162 |
| 34 Western Ky. | 6 | **I-AA Championship** | |
| 30 Southern Ill. | 25 | 17 Eastern Wash. | 14 |
| 27 Idaho | 26 | 29 McNeese St. | 7 |
| 34 Indiana St. | 13 | 7 Youngstown St. | 19 |
| 15 Eastern Ill. | 21 | | |

Conference: Gateway.  Enrollment: 13,100.  Colors: Purple & Old Gold.
Nickname: Panthers.  Stadium: UNI-Dome (1976), 16,400 capacity.  Artificial turf.
1992 home attendance: 85,263 in 6 games.
Director of Athletics: Christopher Ritrievi.
Sports Info. Director: Nancy Justis  319-273-6354

## NORTHWESTERN . . . Evanston, Ill.   60208   I-A

Coach: Gary Barnett, Missouri '69
Record: 3 yrs., W-11, L-19, T-1
1993 SCHEDULE

| | |
|---|---|
| Notre Dame | Sep 4 |
| Boston College ■ | Sep 18 |
| Wake Forest ■ | Sep 25 |
| Ohio St. | Oct 2 |
| Wisconsin | Oct 9 |
| Minnesota ■ | Oct 16 |
| Indiana ■ | Oct 23 |
| Illinois | Oct 30 |
| Michigan St. | Nov 6 |
| Iowa ■ | Nov 13 |
| Penn St. ■ | Nov 20 |

1992 RECORD

| | | | |
|---|---|---|---|
| 7 Notre Dame | 42 | 7 Michigan | 40 |
| 0 Boston College | 49 | 14 Iowa | 56 |
| 24 Stanford | 35 | 27 Wisconsin | 25 |
| 28 Purdue | 14 | | |
| 3 Indiana | 28 | 170  (3-8-0) | 373 |
| 7 Ohio St. | 31 | | |
| 27 Illinois | 26 | | |
| 26 Michigan St. | 27 | | |

Conference: Big Ten Conf.  Enrollment: 7,400.  Colors: Purple & White.
Nickname: Wildcats.  Stadium: Dyche (1926), 49,256 capacity.  Artificial turf.
1992 home attendance: 196,835 in 5 games.
Director of Athletics: Bill Foster.
Sports Info. Director: To be named  708-491-7503

## NORTHWESTERN STATE (LOUISIANA) . . . Natchitoches, La.   71497   I-AA

Coach: Sam Goodwin, Henderson St. '66
Record: 12 yrs., W-66, L-63, T-4
1993 SCHEDULE

| | |
|---|---|
| Southern-B.R. [New Orleans, La.] | Sep 4 |
| Troy St. ■ | Sep 11* |
| East Tex. St. ■ | Sep 25* |
| Northeast La. | Oct 2* |
| Nicholls St. ■ | Oct 9 |
| Sam Houston St. | Oct 16 |
| North Texas | Oct 23 |
| Southwest Tex. St. ■ | Oct 30* |
| Eastern Ill. | Nov 6 |
| McNeese St. ■ | Nov 13 |
| Stephen F. Austin ■ | Nov 20 |

1992 RECORD

| | | | |
|---|---|---|---|
| 27 Mississippi Col. | 6 | 19 Sam Houston St. | 42 |
| 19 Troy St. | 38 | 44 Nicholls St. | 6 |
| 20 East Tex. St. | 0 | 24 Stephen F. Austin | 10 |
| 24 Arkansas St. | 18 | | |
| 37 North Texas | 34 | 252  (7-4-0) | 228 |
| 0 McNeese St. | 29 | | |
| 18 Northeast La. | 28 | | |
| 20 Southwest Tex. St. | 17 | | |

Conference: Southland Conf.  Enrollment: 8,412.  Colors: Purple & White.
Nickname: Demons.  Stadium: Turpin (1976), 16,522 capacity.  Artificial turf.
1992 home attendance: 46,350 in 6 games.
Director of Athletics: Tynes Hildebrand.
Sports Info. Director: Doug Ireland  318-357-6467

## NOTRE DAME . . . Notre Dame, Ind.   46556   I-A

Coach: Lou Holtz, Kent '59
Record: 23 yrs., W-182, L-83, T-6
1993 SCHEDULE

| | |
|---|---|
| Northwestern ■ | Sep 4 |
| Michigan | Sep 11 |
| Michigan St. ■ | Sep 18 |
| Purdue | Sep 25 |
| Stanford | Oct 2 |
| Pittsburgh ■ | Oct 9 |
| Brigham Young | Oct 16 |
| Southern Cal ■ | Oct 23 |
| Navy [Philadelphia, Pa.] | Oct 30 |
| Florida St. ■ | Nov 13 |
| Boston College ■ | Nov 20 |

1992 RECORD

| | | | |
|---|---|---|---|
| 42 Northwestern | 7 | 54 Boston College | 7 |
| 17 Michigan | 17 | 17 Penn St. | 16 |
| 52 Michigan St. | 31 | 31 Southern Cal | 23 |
| 48 Purdue | 0 | | |
| 16 Stanford | 33 | 409  (9-1-1) | 178 |
| 52 Pittsburgh | 21 | **Cotton Bowl** | |
| 42 Brigham Young | 16 | 28 Texas A&M | 3 |
| 38 Navy | 7 | | |

Conference: I-A Independents.  Enrollment: 10,085.  Colors: Gold & Blue.
Nickname: Fighting Irish.  Stadium: Notre Dame (1930), 59,075 capacity.  Natural turf.
1992 home attendance: 354,450 in 6 games.
Director of Athletics: Dick Rosenthal.
Sports Info. Director: John Heisler  219-631-7516

## OHIO . . . Athens, Ohio   45701   I-A

Coach: Tom Lichtenberg, Louisville '62
Record: 6 yrs., W-22, L-41, T-3
1993 SCHEDULE

| | |
|---|---|
| North Caro. | Sep 4* |
| Central Mich. | Sep 11 |
| Ball St. ■ | Sep 18 |
| Toledo | Sep 25* |
| Virginia | Oct 2 |
| Bowling Green ■ | Oct 9 |
| Kent ■ | Oct 16 |
| Miami (Ohio) | Oct 23 |
| Akron ■ | Oct 30 |
| Western Mich. ■ | Nov 6 |
| Eastern Mich. | Nov 13 |

1992 RECORD

| | | | |
|---|---|---|---|
| 9 Iowa St. | 35 | 21 Ball St. | 24 |
| 27 Kent | 14 | 20 Youngstown St. | 28 |
| 0 Central Mich. | 24 | 24 Colorado St. | 35 |
| 3 Western Mich. | 19 | | |
| 0 Akron | 13 | 145  (1-10-0) | 253 |
| 14 Bowling Green | 31 | | |
| 21 Miami (Ohio) | 23 | | |
| 6 Eastern Mich. | 7 | | |

Conference: Mid-American Conf.  Enrollment: 18,600.  Colors: Kelly Green & White.
Nickname: Bobcats.  Stadium: Peden (1929), 20,000 capacity.  Natural turf.
1992 home attendance: 61,859 in 5 games.
Director of Athletics: Harold McElhaney.
Sports Info. Director: To be named  614-593-1299

■ Home games on each schedule [neutral sites shown in brackets].  *Night Games.

*Divisions I-A & I-AA 1993 Schedules and 1992 Results*   687

## OHIO STATE . . . Columbus, Ohio   43210     I-A

Coach: John Cooper, Iowa St. '62
Record: 16 yrs., W-116, L-62, T-5

**1993 SCHEDULE**

| | |
|---|---|
| Rice ■ | Sep 4 |
| Washington ■ | Sep 11* |
| Pittsburgh | Sep 18 |
| Northwestern ■ | Oct 2 |
| Illinois | Oct 9 |
| Michigan St. ■ | Oct 16 |
| Purdue ■ | Oct 23 |
| Penn St. ■ | Oct 30 |
| Wisconsin | Nov 6 |
| Indiana ■ | Nov 13 |
| Michigan | Nov 20 |

**1992 RECORD**

| | | | | |
|---|---|---|---|---|
| 20 | Louisville | 19 | 17 Minnesota | 0 |
| 17 | Bowling Green | 6 | 27 Indiana | 10 |
| 35 | Syracuse | 12 | 13 Michigan | 13 |
| 16 | Wisconsin | 20 | | |
| 16 | Illinois | 18 | 257 (8-2-1) | 137 |
| 31 | Northwestern | 7 | **Florida Citrus Bowl** | |
| 27 | Michigan St. | 17 | 14 Georgia | 21 |
| 38 | Iowa | 15 | | |

Conference: Big Ten Conf.   Enrollment: 54,000.   Colors: Scarlet & Gray.
Nickname: Buckeyes.   Stadium: Ohio (1922), 91,470 capacity.   Natural turf.
1992 home attendance: 555,900 in 6 games.
Director of Athletics: James L. Jones.
Sports Info. Director: Steve Snapp   614-292-6861

## OKLAHOMA . . . Norman, Okla.   73019     I-A

Coach: Gary Gibbs, Oklahoma '75
Record: 4 yrs., W-29, L-14, T-2

**1993 SCHEDULE**

| | |
|---|---|
| Texas Christian | Sep 4* |
| Texas A&M ■ | Sep 11 |
| Tulsa ■ | Sep 25 |
| Iowa St. | Oct 2 |
| Texas [Dallas, Texas] | Oct 9 |
| Colorado ■ | Oct 16 |
| Kansas ■ | Oct 23 |
| Kansas St. | Oct 30 |
| Missouri | Nov 6 |
| Oklahoma St. ■ | Nov 13 |
| Nebraska | Nov 26 |

**1992 RECORD**

| | | | | |
|---|---|---|---|---|
| 34 | Texas Tech | 9 | 51 Missouri | 17 |
| 61 | Arkansas St. | 0 | 15 Oklahoma St. | 15 |
| 10 | Southern Cal | 20 | 9 Nebraska | 33 |
| 17 | Iowa St. | 3 | | |
| 24 | Texas | 34 | 271 (5-4-2) | 196 |
| 24 | Colorado | 24 | | |
| 10 | Kansas | 27 | | |
| 16 | Kansas St. | 14 | | |

Conference: Big Eight Conf.   Enrollment: 21,500.   Colors: Crimson & Cream.
Nickname: Sooners.   Stadium: Owen Field (1924), 75,004 capacity.   Artificial turf.
1992 home attendance: 449,161 in 7 games.
Director of Athletics: Donnie Duncan.
Sports Info. Director: Mike Prusinski   405-325-8228

## OKLAHOMA STATE . . . Stillwater, Okla.   74078     I-A

Coach: Pat Jones, Arkansas '69
Record: 9 yrs., W-56, L-45, T-2

**1993 SCHEDULE**

| | |
|---|---|
| Southwest Mo. St. ■ | Sep 11* |
| Tulsa | Sep 18* |
| Arizona St. | Sep 25* |
| Texas Christian ■ | Oct 2* |
| Nebraska ■ | Oct 7* |
| Missouri | Oct 16 |
| Iowa St. | Oct 23 |
| Kansas | Oct 30 |
| Colorado ■ | Nov 6 |
| Oklahoma | Nov 13 |
| Kansas St. ■ | Nov 20 |

**1992 RECORD**

| | | | | |
|---|---|---|---|---|
| 35 | Indiana St. | 3 | 0 Colorado | 28 |
| 3 | Michigan | 35 | 15 Oklahoma | 15 |
| 24 | Tulsa | 19 | 0 Kansas St. | 10 |
| 11 | Texas Christian | 13 | | |
| 0 | Nebraska | 55 | 161 (4-6-1) | 251 |
| 28 | Missouri | 26 | | |
| 27 | Iowa St. | 21 | | |
| 18 | Kansas | 26 | | |

Conference: Big Eight Conf.   Enrollment: 18,500.   Colors: Orange & Black.
Nickname: Cowboys.   Stadium: Lewis (1920), 50,614 capacity.   Artificial turf.
1992 home attendance: 193,783 in 5 games.
Director of Athletics: Jim Garner.
Sports Info. Director: Steve Buzzard   405-744-5749

## OREGON . . . Eugene, Ore.   97401     I-A

Coach: Rich Brooks, Oregon St. '63
Record: 16 yrs., W-77, L-99, T-4

**1993 SCHEDULE**

| | |
|---|---|
| Colorado St. | Sep 4 |
| Montana ■ | Sep 11 |
| Illinois | Sep 25 |
| California | Oct 2 |
| Southern Cal ■ | Oct 9 |
| Arizona St. | Oct 16* |
| Washington | Oct 23 |
| Washington St. ■ | Oct 30 |
| Arizona | Nov 6* |
| Stanford | Nov 13 |
| Oregon St. ■ | Nov 20 |

**1992 RECORD**

| | | | | |
|---|---|---|---|---|
| 21 | Hawaii | 24 | 37 California | 17 |
| 7 | Stanford | 21 | 6 UCLA | 9 |
| 16 | Texas Tech | 13 | 7 Oregon St. | 0 |
| 59 | Nevada-Las Vegas | 6 | | |
| 30 | Arizona St. | 20 | 230 (6-5-0) | 183 |
| 10 | Southern Cal | 32 | **Independence Bowl** | |
| 3 | Washington | 24 | 35 Wake Forest | 39 |
| 34 | Washington St. | 17 | | |

Conference: Pacific-10.   Enrollment: 16,500.   Colors: Green & Yellow.
Nickname: Ducks.   Stadium: Autzen (1967), 41,678 capacity.   Artificial turf.
1992 home attendance: 236,584 in 7 games.
Director of Athletics: Rich Brooks.
Sports Info. Director: Steve Hellyer   503-346-5488

## OREGON STATE . . . Corvallis, Ore.   97331     I-A

Coach: Jerry Pettibone, Oklahoma '63
Record: 8 yrs., W-35, L-51, T-2

**1993 SCHEDULE**

| | |
|---|---|
| Wyoming | Sep 4 |
| Fresno St. | Sep 11* |
| Washington St. | Sep 18 |
| Arizona ■ | Sep 25 |
| Arizona St. ■ | Oct 2 |
| Pacific (Cal.) ■ | Oct 9 |
| Southern Cal | Oct 16 |
| UCLA ■ | Oct 23 |
| Stanford | Oct 30 |
| Washington ■ | Nov 6 |
| Oregon | Nov 20 |

**1992 RECORD**

| | | | | |
|---|---|---|---|---|
| 20 | Kansas | 49 | 14 UCLA | 26 |
| 46 | Fresno St. | 36 | 16 Washington | 45 |
| 14 | Arizona | 14 | 0 Oregon | 7 |
| 9 | Utah | 42 | | |
| 0 | California | 42 | 163 (1-9-1) | 363 |
| 10 | Washington St. | 35 | | |
| 13 | Arizona St. | 40 | | |
| 21 | Stanford | 27 | | |

Conference: Pacific-10.   Enrollment: 15,500.   Colors: Orange & Black.
Nickname: Beavers.   Stadium: Parker (1953), 35,547 capacity.   Artificial turf.
1992 home attendance: 168,704 in 6 games.
Director of Athletics: Dutch Baughman.
Sports Info. Director: Hal Cowan   503-737-3720

■ Home games on each schedule [neutral sites shown in brackets].   *Night Games.

*1993 NCAA FOOTBALL*

## PACIFIC (CALIFORNIA) ... Stockton, Calif.   95211    I-A

Coach: Chuck Shelton, Pittsburg St. '61
Record: 16 yrs., W-69, L-106, T-1

**1993 SCHEDULE**

| | |
|---|---|
| Texas Tech | Sep 4* |
| Arizona | Sep 11 |
| Cal St. Sacramento ■ | Sep 25* |
| Washington St. ■ | Oct 2* |
| Oregon St. | Oct 9 |
| Northern Ill. | Oct 16 |
| New Mexico St. ■ | Oct 23* |
| Nevada ■ | Oct 30 |
| Utah St. | Nov 6 |
| Arkansas St. ■ | Nov 13 |
| San Jose St. | Nov 20* |

**1992 RECORD**

| | | | | |
|---|---|---|---|---|
| 21 | Fresno St. | 42 | 23 Cal St. Fullerton | 20 |
| 14 | Nevada | 20 | 27 San Jose St. | 28 |
| 7 | Boise St. | 17 | 35 Utah St. | 38 |
| 48 | Southwest Mo. St. | 14 | | |
| 17 | Nevada-Las Vegas | 21 | 253    (3-8-0) | 287 |
| 5 | Arizona St. | 39 | | |
| 49 | New Mexico St. | 17 | | |
| 7 | Washington | 31 | | |

Conference: Big West.   Enrollment: 3,800.   Colors: Orange & Black.
Nickname: Tigers.   Stadium: Amos Alonzo Stagg (1950), 30,000 capacity.   Natural turf.
1992 home attendance: 62,490 in 6 games.
Director of Athletics: Bob Lee.
Sports Info. Director: Kevin Messenger   209-946-2479

## PENN STATE ... University Park, Pa.   16802    I-A

Coach: Joe Paterno, Brown '50
Record: 27 yrs., W-247, L-67, T-3

**1993 SCHEDULE**

| | |
|---|---|
| Minnesota ■ | Sep 4 |
| Southern Cal ■ | Sep 11 |
| Iowa | Sep 18 |
| Rutgers ■ | Sep 25 |
| Maryland | Oct 2 |
| Michigan ■ | Oct 16 |
| Ohio St. | Oct 30 |
| Indiana ■ | Nov 6 |
| Illinois ■ | Nov 13 |
| Northwestern | Nov 20 |
| Michigan St. | Nov 27 |

**1992 RECORD**

| | | | | |
|---|---|---|---|---|
| 24 | Cincinnati | 20 | 17 Brigham Young | 30 |
| 49 | Temple | 8 | 16 Notre Dame | 17 |
| 52 | Eastern Mich. | 7 | 57 Pittsburgh | 13 |
| 49 | Maryland | 13 | | |
| 38 | Rutgers | 24 | 388    (7-4-0) | 210 |
| 14 | Miami (Fla.) | 17 | **Blockbuster Bowl** | |
| 32 | Boston College | 35 | 3 Stanford | 24 |
| 40 | West Va. | 26 | | |

Conference: Big Ten Conf.   Enrollment: 38,373.   Colors: Blue & White.
Nickname: Nittany Lions.   Stadium: Beaver (1960), 93,967 capacity.   Natural turf.
1992 home attendance: 569,195 in 6 games.
Director of Athletics: Jim Tarman.
Sports Info. Director: Budd Thalman   814-865-1757

## PENNSYLVANIA ... Philadelphia, Pa.   19104    I-AA

Coach: Al Bagnoli, Central Conn. St. '74
Record: 11 yrs., W-93, L-22, T-0

**1993 SCHEDULE**

| | |
|---|---|
| Dartmouth ■ | Sep 18 |
| Bucknell ■ | Sep 25 |
| Fordham ■ | Oct 2 |
| Colgate | Oct 9 |
| Columbia | Oct 16 |
| Brown ■ | Oct 23 |
| Yale | Oct 30 |
| Princeton ■ | Nov 6 |
| Harvard | Nov 13 |
| Cornell ■ | Nov 20 |

**1992 RECORD**

| | | | | |
|---|---|---|---|---|
| 17 | Dartmouth | 36 | 21 Harvard | 19 |
| 24 | Colgate | 0 | 14 Cornell | 7 |
| 13 | Fordham | 10 | | |
| 19 | William & Mary | 21 | 207    (7-3-0) | 144 |
| 34 | Columbia | 21 | | |
| 38 | Brown | 0 | | |
| 13 | Yale | 10 | | |
| 14 | Princeton | 20 | | |

Conference: Ivy League.   Enrollment: 9,300.   Colors: Red & Blue.
Nickname: Red & Blue, Quakers.   Stadium: Franklin Field (1895),
  60,546 capacity.   Artificial turf.
1992 home attendance: 67,004 in 5 games.
Director of Athletics: Paul Rubincam.
Sports Info. Director: B. Hurlbut & G. Stasulli   215-898-6128

## PITTSBURGH ... Pittsburgh, Pa.   15213    I-A

Coach: Johnny Majors, Tennessee '57
Record: 25 yrs., W-173, L-105, T-10

**1993 SCHEDULE**

| | |
|---|---|
| Southern Miss. | Sep 4 |
| Virginia Tech ■ | Sep 11* |
| Ohio St. | Sep 18 |
| Louisville ■ | Oct 2* |
| Notre Dame | Oct 9 |
| Syracuse | Oct 16 |
| West Va. | Oct 23 |
| Rutgers | Oct 28* |
| Miami (Fla.) ■ | Nov 6 |
| Boston College ■ | Nov 13 |
| Temple | Nov 20 |

**1992 RECORD**

| | | | | |
|---|---|---|---|---|
| 51 | Kent | 10 | 10 Syracuse | 41 |
| 6 | West Va. | 44 | 16 Louisville | 31 |
| 16 | Rutgers | 21 | 13 Penn St. | 57 |
| 41 | Minnesota | 33 | 23 Hawaii | 36 |
| 34 | Maryland | 47 | | |
| 21 | Notre Dame | 52 | 289    (3-9-0) | 429 |
| 27 | Temple | 20 | | |
| 31 | East Caro. | 37 | | |

Conference: Big East Conference.   Enrollment: 13,500.   Colors: Blue & Gold.
Nickname: Panthers.   Stadium: Pitt (1925), 56,500 capacity.   Artificial turf.
1992 home attendance: 190,315 in 6 games.
Director of Athletics: L. Oval Jaynes.
Sports Info. Director: Ron Wahl   412-648-8240

## PRAIRIE VIEW A&M ... Prairie View, Texas   77445    I-AA

Coach: Ronald Beard, Eastern Mich. '74
Record: 2 yrs., W-0, L-22, T-0

**1993 SCHEDULE**

| | |
|---|---|
| Texas Southern | Sep 4* |
| Langston | Sep 11* |
| Southern-B.R. | Sep 18* |
| Grambling [Dallas, Texas] | Oct 2* |
| West Tex. St. ■ | Oct 9 |
| Alcorn St. | Oct 16 |
| Alabama St. ■ | Oct 23 |
| Mississippi Val. ■ | Oct 30 |
| Ark.-Pine Bluff ■ | Nov 6 |
| Jackson St. ■ | Nov 13 |
| Ala.-Birmingham | Nov 20 |

**1992 RECORD**

| | | | | |
|---|---|---|---|---|
| 0 | Texas Southern | 35 | 7 Southwest Tex. St. | 56 |
| 3 | Angelo St. | 33 | 0 Jackson St. | 46 |
| 0 | Langston | 33 | 7 Southern-B.R. | 12 |
| 3 | Grambling | 63 | | |
| 15 | West Tex. St. | 21 | 55    (0-11-0) | 441 |
| 0 | Alcorn St. | 63 | | |
| 6 | Alabama St. | 44 | | |
| 14 | Mississippi Val. | 35 | | |

Conference: Southwestern.   Enrollment: 6,300.   Colors: Purple & Gold.
Nickname: Panthers.   Stadium: Blackshear (1960), 6,600 capacity.   Natural turf.
1992 home attendance: 76,395 in 6 games.
Director of Athletics: Barbara Jacket.
Sports Info. Director: Jacqueline Davis   409-857-2114

---

■ Home games on each schedule [neutral sites shown in brackets].    *Night Games.

*Divisions I-A & I-AA 1993 Schedules and 1992 Results*      

## PRINCETON ... Princeton, N.J.  08544                     I-AA

Coach: Steve Tosches, Rhode Island '79
Record: 6 yrs., W-38, L-21, T-1

### 1993 SCHEDULE

| | |
|---|---|
| Cornell ■ | Sep 18 |
| Lafayette | Sep 25 |
| Holy Cross ■ | Oct 2 |
| Brown | Oct 9 |
| Lehigh ■ | Oct 16 |
| Harvard | Oct 23 |
| Columbia ■ | Oct 30 |
| Pennsylvania | Nov 6 |
| Yale ■ | Nov 13 |
| Dartmouth | Nov 20 |

**1992 RECORD**

| | | | | |
|---|---|---|---|---|
| 22 | Cornell | 20 | 36 Yale | 7 |
| 38 | Lafayette | 35 | 20 Dartmouth | 34 |
| 38 | Lehigh | 28 | | |
| 28 | Brown | 14 | 264 (8-2-0) | 175 |
| 7 | Holy Cross | 10 | | |
| 21 | Harvard | 6 | | |
| 34 | Columbia | 7 | | |
| 20 | Pennsylvania | 14 | | |

Conference: Ivy League.  Enrollment: 4,500.  Colors: Orange & Black.
Nickname: Tigers.  Stadium: Palmer (1914), 45,725 capacity.  Natural turf.
1992 home attendance: 63,799 in 5 games.
Director of Athletics: Robert Myslik.
Sports Info. Director: Mark Panus  609-258-3568

---

## PURDUE ... West Lafayette, Ind.  47907                     I-A

Coach: Jim Colletto, UCLA '67
Record: 7 yrs., W-25, L-52, T-1

### 1993 SCHEDULE

| | |
|---|---|
| North Caro. St. | Sep 4 |
| Western Mich. ■ | Sep 11 |
| Notre Dame ■ | Sep 25 |
| Illinois ■ | Oct 2 |
| Minnesota | Oct 9* |
| Wisconsin ■ | Oct 16 |
| Ohio St. ■ | Oct 23 |
| Iowa | Oct 30 |
| Michigan | Nov 6 |
| Michigan St. ■ | Nov 13 |
| Indiana | Nov 20 |

**1992 RECORD**

| | | | | |
|---|---|---|---|---|
| 41 | California | 14 | 17 Illinois | 20 |
| 29 | Toledo | 33 | 13 Michigan St. | 35 |
| 0 | Notre Dame | 48 | 13 Indiana | 10 |
| 14 | Northwestern | 28 | | |
| 24 | Minnesota | 20 | 211 (4-7-0) | 267 |
| 16 | Wisconsin | 19 | | |
| 27 | Iowa | 16 | | |
| 17 | Michigan | 24 | | |

Conference: Big Ten Conf.  Enrollment: 35,833.  Colors: Old Gold & Black.
Nickname: Boilermakers.  Stadium: Ross-Ade (1924), 67,861 capacity.  Natural turf.
1992 home attendance: 229,373 in 6 games.
Director of Athletics: Morgan Burke.
Sports Info. Director: Mark Adams  317-494-3197

---

## RHODE ISLAND ... Kingston, R.I.  02881                     I-AA

Coach: Floyd Keith, Ohio Northern '70
Record: 4 yrs., W-23, L-17, T-2

### 1993 SCHEDULE

| | |
|---|---|
| Boise St. | Sep 4* |
| Hofstra ■ | Sep 11 |
| Delaware ■ | Sep 18 |
| Northeastern ■ | Sep 25 |
| Brown | Oct 2 |
| Massachusetts [Killarney, Ireland] | Oct 9 |
| Maine ■ | Oct 16 |
| Boston U. | Oct 23 |
| Villanova | Oct 30 |
| Connecticut ■ | Nov 6 |
| New Hampshire | Nov 13 |

**1992 RECORD**

| | | | | |
|---|---|---|---|---|
| 36 | Towson St. | 19 | 26 Northeastern | 35 |
| 14 | Delaware | 31 | 13 New Hampshire | 20 |
| 14 | Richmond | 46 | 0 Connecticut | 38 |
| 18 | Hofstra | 28 | | |
| 7 | Massachusetts | 32 | 161 (1-10-0) | 338 |
| 9 | Maine | 21 | | |
| 21 | Boston U. | 34 | | |
| 3 | Villanova | 34 | | |

Conference: Yankee.  Enrollment: 12,500.  Colors: Blue & White.
Nickname: Rams.  Stadium: Meade Stadium (1928), 10,000 capacity.  Natural turf.
1992 home attendance: 24,003 in 5 games.
Director of Athletics: Ronald J. Petro.
Sports Info. Director: Jim Norman  401-792-2409

---

## RICE ... Houston, Texas  77251                     I-A

Coach: Fred Goldsmith, Florida '67
Record: 5 yrs., W-19, L-33, T-1

### 1993 SCHEDULE

| | |
|---|---|
| Ohio St. | Sep 4 |
| Tulane | Sep 11 |
| Sam Houston St. ■ | Sep 18 |
| Iowa St. ■ | Sep 25 |
| Texas | Oct 2* |
| Texas Christian ■ | Oct 9 |
| Texas Tech | Oct 16* |
| Texas A&M ■ | Oct 23 |
| Southern Methodist | Nov 6 |
| Baylor | Nov 13 |
| Houston ■ | Nov 26 |

**1992 RECORD**

| | | | | |
|---|---|---|---|---|
| 21 | Air Force | 30 | 34 Baylor | 31 |
| 12 | Duke | 17 | 27 Navy | 22 |
| 45 | Sam Houston St. | 14 | 34 Houston | 61 |
| 21 | Texas | 23 | | |
| 28 | Southern Methodist | 13 | 294 (6-5-0) | 261 |
| 9 | Texas A&M | 35 | | |
| 29 | Texas Christian | 12 | | |
| 34 | Texas Tech | 3 | | |

Conference: Southwest Conf.  Enrollment: 2,600.  Colors: Blue & Gray.
Nickname: Owls.  Stadium: Rice (1950), 70,000 capacity.  Artificial turf.
1992 home attendance: 143,100 in 6 games.
Director of Athletics: J. R. "Bobby" May.
Sports Info. Director: Bill Cousins  713-527-4034

---

## RICHMOND ... Richmond, Va.  23173                     I-AA

Coach: Jim Marshall, Tenn.-Martin '69
Record: 4 yrs., W-11, L-33, T-0

### 1993 SCHEDULE

| | |
|---|---|
| Va. Military ■ | Sep 4 |
| James Madison | Sep 11 |
| New Hampshire | Sep 18 |
| Villanova ■ | Sep 25 |
| Northeastern ■ | Oct 2 |
| Maine [Portland, Maine] | Oct 9 |
| Boston U. ■ | Oct 16 |
| Connecticut ■ | Oct 30 |
| Massachusetts | Nov 6 |
| Delaware | Nov 13 |
| William & Mary | Nov 20 |

**1992 RECORD**

| | | | | |
|---|---|---|---|---|
| 49 | James Madison | 40 | 13 Massachusetts | 17 |
| 33 | Villanova | 36 | 29 Delaware | 21 |
| 46 | Rhode Island | 14 | 19 William & Mary | 34 |
| 28 | Maine | 6 | | |
| 15 | New Hampshire | 7 | 338 (7-4-0) | 250 |
| 37 | Boston U. | 27 | | |
| 41 | Va. Military | 18 | | |
| 28 | Connecticut | 30 | | |

Conference: Yankee.  Enrollment: 2,800.  Colors: Red & Blue.
Nickname: Spiders.  Stadium: Richmond (1929), 22,611 capacity.  Artificial turf.
1992 home attendance: 85,386 in 6 games.
Director of Athletics: Chuck Boone.
Sports Info. Director: Phil Stanton  804-289-8320

---

■ Home games on each schedule [neutral sites shown in brackets].   *Night Games.

## RUTGERS . . . New Brunswick, N.J.   08903                               I-A

Coach: Doug Graber, Wayne St. (Mich.) '66
Record: 4 yrs., W-22, L-22, T-0

**1993 SCHEDULE**

| | |
|---|---|
| Colgate ■ | Sep  4* |
| Duke ■ | Sep 11* |
| Penn St. | Sep 25 |
| Temple ■ | Oct  2* |
| Boston College ■ | Oct  9 |
| Army | Oct 16 |
| Virginia Tech | Oct 23 |
| Pittsburgh ■ | Oct 28* |
| West Va. | Nov  6 |
| Miami (Fla.) | Nov 13 |
| Syracuse ■ | Nov 26 |

**1992 RECORD**

| | | | | | |
|---|---|---|---|---|---|
| 20 | Boston College | 37 | 24 | Cincinnati | 26 |
| 41 | Colgate | 0 | 13 | West Va. | 9 |
| 21 | Pittsburgh | 16 | 35 | Temple | 10 |
| 40 | Navy | 0 | | | |
| 24 | Penn St. | 38 | 341 | (7-4-0) | 245 |
| 28 | Syracuse | 50 | | | |
| 45 | Army | 10 | | | |
| 50 | Virginia Tech | 49 | | | |

Conference: Big East Conference.   Enrollment: 22,000.   Colors: Scarlet.
Nickname: Scarlet Knights.   Stadium: Rutgers (1938), 25,000 capacity.   Natural turf.
1992 home attendance: 174,817 in 6 games.
Director of Athletics: Fred E. Gruninger.
Sports Info. Director: Peter Kowalski   908-932-4200

## SAM HOUSTON STATE . . . Huntsville, Texas   77341                          I-AA

Coach: Ron Randleman, William Penn '64
Record: 24 yrs., W-151, L-98, T-6

**1993 SCHEDULE**

| | |
|---|---|
| Southeast Mo. St. | Sep 11* |
| Rice | Sep 18 |
| Texas A&I ■ | Sep 25* |
| Alcorn St. | Oct  2 |
| Stephen F. Austin ■ | Oct  9 |
| Northwestern (La.) ■ | Oct 16 |
| McNeese St. | Oct 23* |
| North Texas ■ | Oct 30 |
| Nicholls St. | Nov  6* |
| Northeast La. ■ | Nov 13 |
| Southwest Tex. St. | Nov 20 |

**1992 RECORD**

| | | | | | |
|---|---|---|---|---|---|
| 19 | Western Ill. | 14 | 42 | Northwestern (La.) | 19 |
| 20 | Angelo St. | 0 | 14 | McNeese St. | 37 |
| 14 | Rice | 45 | 22 | Southwest Tex. St. | 22 |
| 28 | Alcorn St. | 27 | | | |
| 19 | Nicholls St. | 19 | 256 | (6-3-2) | 258 |
| 10 | Northeast La. | 38 | | | |
| 34 | North Texas | 14 | | | |
| 34 | Stephen F. Austin | 23 | | | |

Conference: Southland Conf.   Enrollment: 13,252.   Colors: Orange & White with Blue Trim.
Nickname: Bearkats.   Stadium: Elliott T. Bowers (1986), 14,000 capacity.   Artificial turf.
1992 home attendance: 48,457 in 6 games.
Director of Athletics: Ronnie Choate.
Sports Info. Director: Paul Ridings Jr.   409-294-1764

## SAMFORD . . . Birmingham, Ala.   35229                                    I-AA

Coach: Chan Gailey, Florida '74
Record: 2 yrs., W-19, L-5, T-0

**1993 SCHEDULE**

| | |
|---|---|
| Glenville St. ■ | Sep  4* |
| Auburn | Sep 11* |
| Tennessee Tech ■ | Sep 18* |
| Bethune-Cookman ■ | Sep 25* |
| Nicholls St. | Oct  2* |
| Central Fla. | Oct  9 |
| Mississippi Col. ■ | Oct 16 |
| Youngstown St. | Oct 23 |
| Tenn.-Martin ■ | Nov  6 |
| Southwest Mo. St. | Nov 13 |
| Troy St. ■ | Nov 20 |

**1992 RECORD**

| | | | | | |
|---|---|---|---|---|---|
| 44 | West Ga. | 16 | 24 | Troy St. | 29 |
| 0 | Auburn | 55 | 42 | Tenn.-Martin | 25 |
| 37 | Tennessee Tech | 13 | 20 | Central Fla. | 13 |
| 42 | Bethune-Cookman | 13 | | | |
| 30 | Western Caro. | 6 | 379 | (9-2-0) | 201 |
| 46 | Eastern Ky. | 14 | | **I-AA Championship** | |
| 45 | Southeast Mo. St. | 14 | 21 | Delaware | 56 |
| 49 | Ala.-Birmingham | 3 | | | |

Conference: I-AA Independents.   Enrollment: 4,341.   Colors: Crimson & Blue.
Nickname: Bulldogs.   Stadium: Seibert (1960), 6,700 capacity.   Natural turf.
1992 home attendance: 28,735 in 5 games.
Director of Athletics: Steve Allgood.
Sports Info. Director: Riley Adair   205-870-2799

## SAN DIEGO . . . San Diego, Calif.   92110                                 I-AA

Coach: Brian Fogarty, Cal St. LA '75
Record: 10 yrs., W-50, L-41, T-3

**1993 SCHEDULE**

| | |
|---|---|
| Menlo ■ | Sep  4* |
| La Verne ■ | Sep 11* |
| Dayton | Sep 25 |
| Valparaiso | Oct  2 |
| Cal Lutheran | Oct  9 |
| Evansville | Oct 16 |
| Butler ■ | Oct 23* |
| Azusa Pacific ■ | Oct 30* |
| Drake ■ | Nov  6 |
| Wagner ■ | Nov 13* |

**1992 RECORD**

| | | | | | |
|---|---|---|---|---|---|
| 14 | Cal St. Hayward | 13 | 33 | Pomona-Pitzer | 28 |
| 21 | La Verne | 21 | 36 | Menlo | 6 |
| 7 | Redlands | 28 | | | |
| 42 | Claremont-M-S | 13 | 284 | (7-2-1) | 233 |
| 21 | Cal Lutheran | 20 | | | |
| 33 | Whittier | 21 | | | |
| 42 | Azusa Pacific | 35 | | | |
| 35 | Occidental | 48 | | | |

Conference: Pioneer Football League.   Enrollment: 6,000.   Colors: Columbia Blue, Navy & White.
Nickname: Toreros.   Stadium: USD Torero, 4,000 capacity.   Natural turf.
1992 home attendance: 15,754 in 5 games.
Director of Athletics: Tom Iannacone.
Sports Info. Director: Ted Gosen   619-260-4745

## SAN DIEGO STATE . . . San Diego, Calif.   92182                           I-A

Coach: Al Luginbill, Cal Poly Pomona '67
Record: 4 yrs., W-25, L-19, T-3

**1993 SCHEDULE**

| | |
|---|---|
| Cal St. Northridge ■ | Sep  4* |
| California | Sep 11 |
| Air Force | Sep 18 |
| Minnesota ■ | Sep 25* |
| UCLA ■ | Sep 30* |
| Hawaii | Oct  9* |
| Colorado St. ■ | Oct 16* |
| New Mexico ■ | Oct 23* |
| Utah | Oct 30 |
| Brigham Young ■ | Nov 11* |
| Fresno St. ■ | Nov 20* |
| Wyoming ■ | Nov 27* |

**1992 RECORD**

| | | | | | |
|---|---|---|---|---|---|
| 31 | Southern Cal | 31 | 52 | Hawaii | 28 |
| 45 | Brigham Young | 38 | 41 | Fresno St. | 45 |
| 7 | UCLA | 35 | 17 | Miami (Fla.) | 63 |
| 49 | New Mexico | 21 | | | |
| 49 | UTEP | 27 | 334 | (5-5-1) | 338 |
| 17 | Air Force | 20 | | | |
| 20 | Colorado St. | 13 | | | |
| 6 | Wyoming | 17 | | | |

Conference: Western Athl. Conf.   Enrollment: 29,000.   Colors: Scarlet & Black.
Nickname: Aztecs.   Stadium: Jack Murphy (1967), 62,809 capacity.   Natural turf.
1992 home attendance: 274,347 in 6 games.
Director of Athletics: Fred Miller.
Sports Info. Director: John Rosenthal   619-594-5547

■ Home games on each schedule [neutral sites shown in brackets].   *Night Games.

*Divisions I-A & I-AA 1993 Schedules and 1992 Results*

## SAN JOSE STATE . . . San Jose, Calif.   95192   I-A

Coach: John Ralston, California '51
Record: 13 yrs., W-86, L-47, T-4
1993 SCHEDULE

| | |
|---|---|
| Louisville | Sep 4 |
| Stanford | Sep 11 |
| Wyoming ■ | Sep 18* |
| California | Sep 25 |
| Washington | Oct 2 |
| New Mexico St. ■ | Oct 16 |
| Louisiana Tech ■ | Oct 23* |
| Southwestern La. | Oct 30 |
| Nevada | Nov 6 |
| Nevada-Las Vegas ■ | Nov 13* |
| Pacific (Cal.) ■ | Nov 20* |

1992 RECORD

| | | | | | |
|---|---|---:|---|---|---:|
| 16 | California | 46 | 39 | Nevada | 35 |
| 39 | Minnesota | 30 | 28 | Pacific (Cal.) | 27 |
| 38 | Southwestern La. | 13 | 24 | New Mexico St. | 34 |
| 13 | Stanford | 37 | | | |
| 26 | Wyoming | 24 | 330 | (7-4-0) | 309 |
| 49 | Cal St. Fullerton | 3 | | | |
| 27 | Utah St. | 25 | | | |
| 31 | Nevada-Las Vegas | 35 | | | |

Conference: Big West.   Enrollment: 30,000.   Colors: Gold, White & Blue.
Nickname: Spartans.   Stadium: Spartan (1932), 31,218 capacity.   Natural turf.
1992 home attendance: 55,132 in 4 games.
Director of Athletics: Thomas Brennan.
Sports Info. Director: Lawrence Fan   408-924-1217

---

## SIENA . . . Loudonville, N.Y.   12211   I-AA

Coach: Jack DuBois, Oneonta St. '58
Record: 6 yrs., W-13, L-39, T-0
1993 SCHEDULE

| | |
|---|---|
| Assumption | Sep 11 |
| St. Peter's ■ | Sep 18 |
| St. John's (N.Y.) ■ | Sep 25 |
| Georgetown ■ | Oct 2 |
| Rensselaer | Oct 9 |
| Bentley | Oct 16 |
| Stonehill | Oct 23 |
| Iona ■ | Oct 30 |
| Canisius ■ | Nov 6 |
| Marist | Nov 13 |

1992 RECORD

| | | | | | |
|---|---|---:|---|---|---:|
| 12 | Marist | 28 | 0 | Western New Eng. | 22 |
| 7 | Iona | 32 | | | |
| 31 | Hartwick | 12 | 92 | (2-7-0) | 235 |
| 6 | Rensselaer | 26 | | | |
| 0 | Bentley | 24 | | | |
| 0 | Stonehill | 40 | | | |
| 21 | Assumption | 12 | | | |
| 15 | St. Peter's | 39 | | | |

Conference: Metro Atlantic Ath. Conf.   Enrollment: 2,700.   Colors: Green & Gold.
Nickname: Saints.   Stadium: Siena Field, 500 capacity.   Natural turf.
1992 home attendance: 3,150 in 4 games.
Director of Athletics: John D'Argenio.
Sports Info. Director: Meg Culhane   518-783-2450

---

## SOUTH CAROLINA . . . Columbia, S.C.   29208   I-A

Coach: Sparky Woods, Carson-Newman '76
Record: 9 yrs., W-58, L-40, T-5
1993 SCHEDULE

| | |
|---|---|
| Georgia | Sep 4 |
| Arkansas | Sep 11 |
| Louisiana Tech ■ | Sep 18* |
| Kentucky ■ | Sep 23* |
| Alabama ■ | Oct 2* |
| East Caro. ■ | Oct 9 |
| Mississippi St. | Oct 16* |
| Vanderbilt ■ | Oct 23 |
| Tennessee | Oct 30 |
| Florida | Nov 13 |
| Clemson ■ | Nov 20 |

1992 RECORD

| | | | | | |
|---|---|---:|---|---|---:|
| 6 | Georgia | 28 | 14 | Louisiana Tech | 13 |
| 7 | Arkansas | 45 | 9 | Florida | 14 |
| 18 | East Caro. | 20 | 24 | Clemson | 13 |
| 9 | Kentucky | 13 | | | |
| 7 | Alabama | 48 | 160 | (5-6-0) | 240 |
| 21 | Mississippi St. | 6 | | | |
| 21 | Vanderbilt | 17 | | | |
| 24 | Tennessee | 23 | | | |

Conference: Southeastern Conf.   Enrollment: 25,613.   Colors: Garnet & Black.
Nickname: Fighting Gamecocks.   Stadium: Williams-Brice (1934), 72,400 capacity.   Natural turf.
1992 home attendance: 382,368 in 6 games.
Director of Athletics: Mike McGee.
Sports Info. Director: Kerry Tharp   803-777-5204

---

## SOUTH CAROLINA STATE . . . Orangeburg, S.C.   29117   I-AA

Coach: Willie Jeffries, South Caro. St. '60
Record: 20 yrs., W-124, L-88, T-6
1993 SCHEDULE

| | |
|---|---|
| Newberry | Sep 4* |
| Florida A&M [Columbia, S.C.] | Sep 11 |
| Charleston So. ■ | Sep 18* |
| Southern-B.R. [Atlanta, Ga.] | Sep 25 |
| Jackson St. [Indianapolis, Ind.] | Oct 2 |
| Morgan St. | Oct 9 |
| Bethune-Cookman | Oct 16 |
| N.C. Central ■ | Oct 23 |
| Delaware St. ■ | Oct 30 |
| Howard | Nov 6 |
| North Caro. A&T ■ | Nov 20 |

1992 RECORD

| | | | | | |
|---|---|---:|---|---|---:|
| 42 | Newberry | 17 | 28 | Howard | 18 |
| 20 | Florida A&M | 33 | 32 | Charleston So. | 0 |
| 18 | Southern-B.R. | 19 | 21 | North Caro. A&T | 24 |
| 3 | Jackson St. | 41 | | | |
| 31 | Morgan St. | 14 | 327 | (7-4-0) | 180 |
| 35 | Bethune-Cookman | 7 | | | |
| 69 | N.C. Central | 0 | | | |
| 28 | Delaware St. | 7 | | | |

Conference: Mid-Eastern.   Enrollment: 5,000.   Colors: Garnet & Blue.
Nickname: Bulldogs.   Stadium: Dawson Bulldog (1955), 14,000 capacity.   Natural turf.
1992 home attendance: 120,764 in 7 games.
Director of Athletics: Charlene M. Johnson.
Sports Info. Director: Bill Hamilton   803-536-7060

---

## SOUTHEAST MISSOURI STATE . . . Cape Girardeau, Mo.   63701   I-AA

Coach: John Mumford, Pittsburg St. '79
Record: 3 yrs., W-12, L-20, T-0
1993 SCHEDULE

| | |
|---|---|
| Southwest Mo. St. | Sep 4* |
| Sam Houston St. ■ | Sep 11* |
| Murray St. | Sep 18* |
| Tenn.-Martin | Sep 25* |
| Morehead St. ■ | Oct 2* |
| Tennessee Tech ■ | Oct 9 |
| Middle Tenn. St. | Oct 23 |
| Austin Peay | Oct 30 |
| Eastern Ky. ■ | Nov 6 |
| Kentucky St. ■ | Nov 13 |
| Tennessee St. ■ | Nov 20 |

1992 RECORD

| | | | | | |
|---|---|---:|---|---|---:|
| 27 | Murray St. | 21 | 17 | Morehead St. | 20 |
| 35 | Southern Ill. | 44 | 33 | Illinois St. | 52 |
| 16 | Austin Peay | 21 | 27 | Tennessee St. | 37 |
| 10 | Eastern Ky. | 20 | | | |
| 14 | Tennessee Tech | 49 | 246 | (2-9-0) | 352 |
| 14 | Samford | 45 | | | |
| 16 | Middle Tenn. St. | 30 | | | |
| 37 | Tenn.-Martin | 13 | | | |

Conference: Ohio Valley Conf.   Enrollment: 9,000.   Colors: Red & Black.
Nickname: Indians.   Stadium: Houck (1930), 10,000 capacity.   Natural turf.
1992 home attendance: 33,199 in 5 games.
Director of Athletics: Richard McDuffie.
Sports Info. Director: Ron Hines   314-651-2294

---

■ Home games on each schedule [neutral sites shown in brackets].   *Night Games.

*1993 NCAA FOOTBALL*

## SOUTHERN-BATON ROUGE . . . Baton Rouge, La.   70813   I-AA

Coach: Pete Richardson, Dayton '68
Record: 5 yrs., W-41, L-14, T-1

### 1993 SCHEDULE
Northwestern (La.) [New Orleans, La.] . . . Sep  4
Alabama St. ....................................... Sep 11*
Prairie View ■ ................................... Sep 18*
South Caro. St. [Atlanta, Ga.] ............. Sep 25
Mississippi Val. .................................. Oct  2*
Texas Southern ................................. Oct  9*
Jackson St. ........................................ Oct 16*
Alcorn St. ■ ....................................... Oct 23*
Nicholls St. ■ ..................................... Oct 30*
Florida A&M ...................................... Nov  6
Grambling [New Orleans, La.] ........... Nov 27

### 1992 RECORD
| | | | | |
|---|---|---|---|---|
| 10 | Alabama St. | 30 | 34 | Texas Southern | 6 |
| 19 | South Caro. St. | 18 | 12 | Prairie View | 7 |
| 13 | Mississippi Val. | 10 | 27 | Grambling | 30 |
| 47 | Winston-Salem | 14 | | | |
| 24 | Jackson St. | 25 | 229 | (5-6-0) | 218 |
| 13 | Alcorn St. | 35 | | | |
| 24 | Nicholls St. | 27 | | | |
| 6 | Florida A&M | 16 | | | |

Conference: Southwestern.  Enrollment: 9,914.  Colors: Blue & Gold.
Nickname: Jaguars.  Stadium: A.W. Mumford (1928), 24,000 capacity.  Natural turf.
1992 home attendance: 202,344 in 7 games.
Director of Athletics: Marino Casem.
Sports Info. Director: Rodney Lockett  504-771-4142

## SOUTHERN CALIFORNIA . . . Los Angeles, Calif.   90089   I-A

Coach: John Robinson, Oregon '58
Record: 7 yrs., W-67, L-14, T-2

### 1993 SCHEDULE
North Caro. [Anaheim, Calif.] ............. Aug 29*
Houston ■ ........................................ Sep  4
Penn St. ........................................... Sep 11
Washington St. ■ ............................... Sep 25
Arizona ............................................. Oct  2
Oregon ............................................. Oct  9
Oregon St. ■ ..................................... Oct 16
Notre Dame ...................................... Oct 23
California .......................................... Oct 30
Stanford ■ ........................................ Nov  6
Washington ....................................... Nov 13
UCLA ■ ............................................ Nov 20

### 1992 RECORD
| | | | | |
|---|---|---|---|---|
| 31 | San Diego St. | 31 | 14 | Arizona | 7 |
| 20 | Oklahoma | 10 | 37 | UCLA | 38 |
| 10 | Washington | 17 | 23 | Notre Dame | 31 |
| 32 | Oregon | 10 | | | |
| 27 | California | 24 | 257 | (6-4-1) | 225 |
| 31 | Washington St. | 21 | | **Freedom Bowl** | |
| 23 | Arizona St. | 13 | 7 | Fresno St. | 24 |
| 9 | Stanford | 23 | | | |

Conference: Pacific-10.  Enrollment: 28,374.  Colors: Cardinal & Gold.
Nickname: Trojans.  Stadium: L.A. Coliseum (1923), 92,516 capacity.  Natural turf.
1992 home attendance: 298,769 in 5 games.
Director of Athletics: Mike Garrett.
Sports Info. Director: Tim Tessalone  213-740-8480

## SOUTHERN ILLINOIS . . . Carbondale, Ill.   62901   I-AA

Coach: Bob Smith, Bradley '62
Record: 8 yrs., W-32, L-55, T-1

### 1993 SCHEDULE
Washburn ■ ...................................... Sep 11
Toledo .............................................. Sep 18*
Arkansas St. ...................................... Sep 25*
Northern Ill. ...................................... Oct  2
Western Ill. ....................................... Oct  9
Western Ky. ■ ................................... Oct 16
Southwest Mo. St. ■ .......................... Oct 23
Indiana St. ........................................ Oct 30
Illinois St. ■ ...................................... Nov  6
Northern Iowa ................................... Nov 13*
Eastern Ill. ■ ..................................... Nov 20

### 1992 RECORD
| | | | | |
|---|---|---|---|---|
| 13 | Troy St. | 37 | 39 | Western Ky. | 41 |
| 44 | Southeast Mo. St. | 35 | 12 | Southwest Mo. St. | 51 |
| 37 | Austin Peay | 7 | 42 | Indiana St. | 35 |
| 38 | Arkansas St. | 42 | | | |
| 47 | Eastern Ill. | 46 | 350 | (4-7-0) | 409 |
| 42 | Western Ill. | 50 | | | |
| 25 | Northern Iowa | 30 | | | |
| 11 | Illinois St. | 35 | | | |

Conference: Gateway.  Enrollment: 24,325.  Colors: Maroon & White.
Nickname: Salukis.  Stadium: McAndrew (1975), 17,324 capacity.  Artificial turf.
1992 home attendance: 49,900 in 6 games.
Director of Athletics: Jim Hart.
Sports Info. Director: Fred Huff  618-453-7235

## SOUTHERN METHODIST . . . Dallas, Texas   75275   I-A

Coach: Tom Rossley, Cincinnati '69
Record: 2 yrs., W-6, L-16, T-0

### 1993 SCHEDULE
Arkansas ........................................... Sep  4*
Wisconsin ■ ...................................... Sep 11*
Texas Christian ................................. Sep 25*
Missouri ............................................ Oct  2
Baylor ■ ........................................... Oct  9
Houston ............................................ Oct 16
Texas [San Antonio, Texas] ............... Oct 23*
Texas A&M ....................................... Oct 30
Rice ■ .............................................. Nov  6
Texas Tech ■ .................................... Nov 13
Navy ................................................. Nov 20

### 1992 RECORD
| | | | | |
|---|---|---|---|---|
| 12 | Tulane | 13 | 41 | Houston | 16 |
| 28 | North Texas | 14 | 14 | Texas | 35 |
| 20 | New Mexico | 13 | 24 | Arkansas | 19 |
| 21 | Texas Christian | 9 | | | |
| 7 | Baylor | 49 | 212 | (5-6-0) | 276 |
| 13 | Rice | 28 | | | |
| 25 | Texas Tech | 39 | | | |
| 7 | Texas A&M | 41 | | | |

Conference: Southwest Conf.  Enrollment: 8,978.  Colors: Red & Blue.
Nickname: Mustangs.  Stadium: Ownby (1926), 23,783 capacity.  Artificial turf.
1992 home attendance: 99,090 in 5 games.
Director of Athletics: Forrest Gregg.
Sports Info. Director: Ed Wisneski  214-768-2883

## SOUTHERN MISSISSIPPI . . . Hattiesburg, Miss.   39406   I-A

Coach: Jeff Bower, Southern Miss. '76
Record: 3 yrs., W-11, L-12, T-0

### 1993 SCHEDULE
Pittsburgh ■ ..................................... Sep  4
Northeast La. ■ ................................. Sep 18
Auburn ............................................. Sep 25
Southwestern La. .............................. Oct  2*
Georgia ............................................ Oct  9
Louisville .......................................... Oct 16
East Caro. ■ ..................................... Oct 23
Alabama ........................................... Oct 30
Tulane ■ ........................................... Nov  6
Memphis St. ...................................... Nov 13
Tulsa ................................................ Nov 20

### 1992 RECORD
| | | | | |
|---|---|---|---|---|
| 23 | Memphis St. | 21 | 38 | East Caro. | 21 |
| 10 | Alabama | 17 | 20 | Florida | 24 |
| 16 | Louisiana Tech | 13 | 13 | Virginia Tech | 12 |
| 8 | Auburn | 16 | | | |
| 33 | Tulsa | 24 | 219 | (7-4-0) | 195 |
| 10 | Northern Ill. | 23 | | | |
| 17 | Tulane | 7 | | | |
| 31 | Cincinnati | 17 | | | |

Conference: I-A Independents.  Enrollment: 13,500.  Colors: Black & Gold.
Nickname: Golden Eagles.  Stadium: Roberts (1976), 33,000 capacity.  Natural turf.
1992 home attendance: 61,991 in 4 games.
Director of Athletics: Bill McLellan.
Sports Info. Director: M.R. Napier  601-266-4503

■ Home games on each schedule [neutral sites shown in brackets].   *Night Games.

*Divisions I-A & I-AA 1993 Schedules and 1992 Results*                693

## SOUTHERN UTAH . . . Cedar City, Utah  84720        I-AA

Coach: Jack Bishop, Southern Utah '69
Record: 12 yrs., W-71, L-51, T-3

### 1993 SCHEDULE

| | |
|---|---|
| Northern Ariz. ■ | Sep 4* |
| Angelo St. | Sep 11* |
| Central Okla. | Sep 18 |
| UC Davis ■ | Sep 25* |
| Montana St. | Oct 9 |
| Cal Poly SLO ■ | Oct 16 |
| St. Mary's (Cal.) | Oct 23 |
| Weber St. | Oct 30 |
| Portland St. ■ | Nov 6 |
| Cal St. Northridge | Nov 13* |
| Cal St. Sacramento | Nov 20* |

**1992 RECORD**

| | | | | |
|---|---|---|---|---|
| 20 | Northern Ariz. | 17 | 49 Cal St. Northridge | 20 |
| 24 | Weber St. | 35 | 14 Cal Poly SLO | 17 |
| 20 | Central Okla. | 21 | 29 Idaho St. | 28 |
| 17 | Angelo St. | 10 | | |
| 18 | Portland St. | 35 | 259  (6-5-0) | 225 |
| 25 | Santa Clara | 28 | | |
| 26 | St. Mary's (Cal.) | 0 | | |
| 17 | Cal St. Sacramento | 14 | | |

Conference: American West. Enrollment: 4,500. Colors: Scarlet, Royal Blue & White.
Nickname: Thunderbirds. Stadium: Coliseum of Southern Utah (1967), 6,500 capacity. Natural turf.
1992 home attendance: 19,701 in 5 games.
Director of Athletics: Jack Bishop.
Sports Info. Director: Neil Gardner 801-586-7753

## SOUTHWEST MISSOURI STATE . . . Springfield, Mo.  65804        I-AA

Coach: Jesse Branch, Arkansas '64
Record: 7 yrs., W-44, L-33, T-1

### 1993 SCHEDULE

| | |
|---|---|
| Southeast Mo. St. ■ | Sep 4* |
| Oklahoma St. | Sep 11* |
| North Texas | Sep 18* |
| Indiana St. ■ | Sep 25* |
| Northern Iowa ■ | Oct 2* |
| Illinois St. ■ | Oct 9 |
| Jacksonville St. ■ | Oct 16 |
| Southern Ill. | Oct 23 |
| Eastern Ill. | Oct 30 |
| Western Ill. | Nov 6 |
| Samford ■ | Nov 13 |

**1992 RECORD**

| | | | | |
|---|---|---|---|---|
| 13 | McNeese St. | 16 | 51 Southern Ill. | 12 |
| 66 | Washburn | 15 | 28 Indiana St. | 31 |
| 35 | North Texas | 10 | 12 Northern Iowa | 37 |
| 14 | Pacific (Cal.) | 48 | | |
| 16 | Western Ill. | 13 | 286  (6-5-0) | 230 |
| 14 | Tulsa | 17 | | |
| 24 | Illinois St. | 21 | | |
| 13 | Eastern Ill. | 10 | | |

Conference: Gateway. Enrollment: 20,236. Colors: Maroon & White.
Nickname: Bears. Stadium: Plaster Field (1941), 16,600 capacity. Artificial turf.
1992 home attendance: 60,639 in 5 games.
Director of Athletics: Bill Rowe.
Sports Info. Director: Mark Stillwell 417-836-5402

## SOUTHWEST TEXAS STATE . . . San Marcos, Texas  78666        I-AA

Coach: Jim Bob Helduser, Texas Lutheran '79
Record: 1 yr., W-5, L-5, T-1

### 1993 SCHEDULE

| | |
|---|---|
| Texas A&I ■ | Sep 4* |
| Idaho | Sep 11 |
| Liberty ■ | Sep 18 |
| Northern Iowa | Sep 25* |
| North Texas | Oct 9 |
| Northeast La. ■ | Oct 16* |
| Nicholls St. | Oct 23 |
| Northwestern (La.) | Oct 30* |
| McNeese St. ■ | Nov 6* |
| Stephen F. Austin | Nov 13 |
| Sam Houston St. ■ | Nov 20 |

**1992 RECORD**

| | | | | |
|---|---|---|---|---|
| 15 | Texas A&I | 14 | 56 Prairie View | 7 |
| 39 | Texas Southern | 34 | 10 North Texas | 13 |
| 20 | Youngstown St. | 23 | 22 Sam Houston St. | 22 |
| 6 | Northeast La. | 13 | | |
| 38 | Nicholls St. | 13 | 253  (5-5-1) | 190 |
| 17 | Stephen F. Austin | 14 | | |
| 13 | McNeese St. | 17 | | |
| 17 | Northwestern (La.) | 20 | | |

Conference: Southland Conf. Enrollment: 21,475. Colors: Maroon & Gold.
Nickname: Bobcats. Stadium: Bobcat (1981), 14,104 capacity. Natural turf.
1992 home attendance: 47,815 in 6 games.
Director of Athletics: Richard Hannan.
Sports Info. Director: Tony Brubaker 512-245-2966

## SOUTHWESTERN LOUISIANA . . . Lafayette, La.  70506        I-A

Coach: Nelson Stokley, Louisiana St. '68
Record: 7 yrs., W-34, L-42, T-1

### 1993 SCHEDULE

| | |
|---|---|
| Utah St. ■ | Sep 4* |
| Miami (Ohio) | Sep 11* |
| Memphis St. ■ | Sep 18* |
| Southern Miss. ■ | Oct 2* |
| Tulane | Oct 9* |
| Arkansas St. | Oct 16* |
| Northern Ill. | Oct 23 |
| San Jose St. ■ | Oct 30 |
| Florida | Nov 6 |
| Nevada-Las Vegas | Nov 20 |
| Louisiana Tech ■ | Nov 27* |

**1992 RECORD**

| | | | | |
|---|---|---|---|---|
| 3 | Tennessee | 38 | 9 Tulsa | 27 |
| 31 | Northeast La. | 23 | 15 Northern Ill. | 23 |
| 13 | San Jose St. | 38 | 7 Arkansas St. | 20 |
| 17 | Western Ky. | 14 | | |
| 7 | Houston | 63 | 143  (2-9-0) | 306 |
| 7 | Louisiana Tech | 21 | | |
| 10 | Cal St. Fullerton | 14 | | |
| 24 | Auburn | 25 | | |

Conference: Big West. Enrollment: 17,000. Colors: Vermilion & White.
Nickname: Ragin' Cajuns. Stadium: Cajun Field (1971), 31,000 capacity. Natural turf.
1992 home attendance: 92,111 in 5 games.
Director of Athletics: Nelson Schexnayder.
Sports Info. Director: Dan McDonald 318-231-6331

## ST. FRANCIS (PENNSYLVANIA) . . . Loretto, Pa.  15940        I-AA

Coach: Frank Pergolizzi, Williams '78
Record: 4 yrs., W-20, L-19, T-1

### 1993 SCHEDULE

| | |
|---|---|
| Gannon ■ | Sep 4 |
| Marist ■ | Sep 11 |
| Sacred Heart | Sep 18 |
| St. Peter's | Sep 25* |
| Central Conn. St. ■ | Oct 2 |
| Monmouth (N. J.) ■ | Oct 16 |
| Wagner | Oct 23 |
| Canisius | Oct 30 |
| Duquesne ■ | Nov 6 |
| Mercyhurst ■ | Nov 13 |

**1992 RECORD**

| | | | | |
|---|---|---|---|---|
| 20 | Gannon | 20 | 18 St. John Fisher | 0 |
| 17 | Canisius | 14 | 23 Duquesne | 13 |
| 21 | Wagner | 18 | | |
| 13 | Mercyhurst | 38 | 238  (8-1-1) | 127 |
| 33 | Gallaudet | 7 | **ECAC Southeast** | |
| 42 | Marist | 14 | 6 Wagner | 48 |
| 15 | St. Peter's | 3 | | |
| 36 | Hartwick | 0 | | |

Conference: I-AA Independents. Enrollment: 1,100. Colors: Red & White.
Nickname: Red Flash. Stadium: Pine Bowl, 1,500 capacity. Natural turf.
1992 home attendance: 3,711 in 5 games.
Director of Athletics: Frank Pergolizzi.
Sports Info. Director: Kevin Southard 814-472-3128

---

■ Home games on each schedule [neutral sites shown in brackets].  *Night Games.

## ST. JOHN'S (NEW YORK) . . . Jamaica, N.Y.  11439          I-AA

Coach: Bob Ricca, LIU-C.W. Post '69
Record: 15 yrs., W-91, L-59, T-1
1993 SCHEDULE

| | |
|---|---|
| St. Peter's ■ | Sep  9* |
| Wagner | Sep 18 |
| Siena | Sep 25 |
| Marist ■ | Sep 30* |
| Pace | Oct  9 |
| Canisius ■ | Oct 16 |
| Sacred Heart ■ | Oct 23* |
| Duquesne | Oct 30 |
| Georgetown | Nov  6 |
| Iona ■ | Nov 12* |
| Stony Brook ■ | Nov 25 |

1992 RECORD

| | | | |
|---|---|---|---|
| 33 | Iona | 30 | |
| 39 | Sacred Heart | 16 | |
| 0 | Wagner | 27 | |
| 14 | FDU-Madison | 15 | |
| 41 | Pace | 21 | |
| 21 | Duquesne | 27 | |
| 45 | LIU-C.W. Post | 29 | |
| 15 | Marist | 23 | |

| | | |
|---|---|---|
| 49 | Georgetown | 33 |
| 28 | Bentley | 48 |
| 285 | (5-5-0) | 269 |

Conference: Metro Atlantic Ath. Conf.  Enrollment: 20,000.  Colors: Red & White.
Nickname: Redmen.  Stadium: Redmen Field (1961), 3,000 capacity.  Artificial turf.
1992 home attendance: 6,483 in 5 games.
Director of Athletics: John Kaiser.
Sports Info. Director: Frank Racaniello  718-990-6367

## ST. MARY'S (CALIFORNIA) . . . Moraga, Calif.  94575          I-AA

Coach: Mike Rasmussen, Michigan St. '72
Record: 3 yrs., W-18, L-12, T-0
1993 SCHEDULE

| | |
|---|---|
| San Fran. St. | Sep  4 |
| Cal St. Hayward ■ | Sep 11 |
| Sonoma St. | Sep 18 |
| Humboldt St. | Sep 25* |
| Cal St. Chico ■ | Oct  2 |
| Cal St. Sacramento | Oct  9* |
| Southern Utah ■ | Oct 23 |
| UC Davis ■ | Oct 30 |
| Western N. Mex. | Nov  6 |
| Cal Poly SLO ■ | Nov 13 |

1992 RECORD

| | | | |
|---|---|---|---|
| 17 | San Fran. St. | 14 | |
| 10 | Cal St. Hayward | 6 | |
| 43 | Humboldt St. | 6 | |
| 26 | UC Davis | 30 | |
| 21 | Cal St. Chico | 28 | |
| 21 | Sonoma St. | 26 | |
| 0 | Southern Utah | 26 | |
| 52 | Western N. Mex. | 39 | |

| | | |
|---|---|---|
| 55 | Santa Clara | 22 |
| 245 | (5-4-0) | 197 |

Conference: I-AA Independents.  Enrollment: 2,200.  Colors: Red & Blue.
Nickname: Gaels.  Stadium: St. Mary's Field (1976), 3,500 capacity.  Natural turf.
1992 home attendance: 15,472 in 5 games.
Director of Athletics: Rick Mazzuto.
Sports Info. Director: Steve Janisch  510-631-4402

## ST. PETER'S . . . Jersey City, N.J.  07306          I-AA

Coach: Roy Miller, Jersey City St. '74
Record: 9 yrs., W-38, L-48, T-0
1993 SCHEDULE

| | |
|---|---|
| St. John's (N.Y.) | Sep  9* |
| Siena | Sep 18 |
| St. Francis (Pa.) ■ | Sep 25* |
| Monmouth (N. J.) | Oct  2 |
| Georgetown ■ | Oct  9* |
| Iona ■ | Oct 16* |
| Canisius ■ | Oct 23 |
| Assumption | Oct 30 |
| Central Conn. St. | Nov  6 |
| Jersey City St. ■ | Nov 13 |

1992 RECORD

| | | | |
|---|---|---|---|
| 14 | Assumption | 21 | |
| 29 | Hartwick | 0 | |
| 13 | Sacred Heart | 6 | |
| 19 | Western New Eng. | 3 | |
| 21 | Georgetown | 12 | |
| 3 | St. Francis (Pa.) | 15 | |
| 27 | Gallaudet | 6 | |
| 39 | Siena | 15 | |

| | | |
|---|---|---|
| 20 | Jersey City St. | 14 |
| 185 | (7-2-0) | 92 |

Conference: Metro Atlantic Ath. Conf.  Enrollment: 3,600.  Colors: Blue & White.
Nickname: Peacocks.  Stadium: JFK Stadium (1990), 4,000 capacity.  Artificial turf.
1992 home attendance: 6,615 in 5 games.
Director of Athletics: William Stein.
Sports Info. Director: Tim Camp  201-915-9101

## STANFORD . . . Stanford, Calif.  94305          I-A

Coach: Bill Walsh, San Jose St. '59
Record: 3 yrs., W-27, L-10, T-0
1993 SCHEDULE

| | |
|---|---|
| Washington | Sep  4 |
| San Jose St. ■ | Sep 11 |
| Colorado ■ | Sep 18* |
| UCLA ■ | Sep 25 |
| Notre Dame ■ | Oct  2 |
| Arizona | Oct 16* |
| Arizona St. ■ | Oct 23 |
| Oregon St. ■ | Oct 30 |
| Southern Cal | Nov  6 |
| Oregon | Nov 13 |
| California ■ | Nov 20 |

1992 RECORD

| | | | |
|---|---|---|---|
| 7 | Texas A&M | 10 | |
| 21 | Oregon | 7 | |
| 35 | Northwestern | 24 | |
| 37 | San Jose St. | 13 | |
| 33 | Notre Dame | 16 | |
| 19 | UCLA | 7 | |
| 6 | Arizona | 21 | |
| 27 | Oregon St. | 21 | |

| | | |
|---|---|---|
| 7 | Washington | 41 |
| 23 | Southern Cal | 9 |
| 40 | Washington St. | 3 |
| 41 | California | 21 |
| 296 | (9-3-0) | 193 |
| | **Blockbuster Bowl** | |
| 24 | Penn St. | 3 |

Conference: Pacific-10.  Enrollment: 6,556.  Colors: Cardinal & White.
Nickname: Cardinal.  Stadium: Stanford (1921), 85,500 capacity.  Natural turf.
1992 home attendance: 312,401 in 6 games.
Director of Athletics: Ted Leland.
Sports Info. Director: Gary Migdol  415-723-4418

## STEPHEN F. AUSTIN . . . Nacogdoches, Texas  75962          I-AA

Coach: John Pearce, East Tex. St. '70
Record: 1 yr., W-3, L-8, T-0
1993 SCHEDULE

| | |
|---|---|
| Idaho ■ | Sep  2* |
| Youngstown St. ■ | Sep 11* |
| Livingston ■ | Sep 18* |
| Boise St. ■ | Sep 25* |
| Sam Houston St. | Oct  9 |
| Nicholls St. ■ | Oct 16 |
| Northeast La. | Oct 23* |
| McNeese St. ■ | Oct 30 |
| North Texas | Nov  6 |
| Southwest Tex. St. ■ | Nov 13 |
| Northwestern (La.) | Nov 20 |

1992 RECORD

| | | | |
|---|---|---|---|
| 24 | Ark.-Monticello | 6 | |
| 6 | Montana St. | 13 | |
| 41 | Jackson St. | 26 | |
| 20 | Boise St. | 24 | |
| 14 | Southwest Tex. St. | 17 | |
| 11 | North Texas | 21 | |
| 21 | Nicholls St. | 6 | |
| 23 | Sam Houston St. | 34 | |

| | | |
|---|---|---|
| 3 | McNeese St. | 28 |
| 22 | Northeast La. | 41 |
| 10 | Northwestern (La.) | 24 |
| 195 | (3-8-0) | 240 |

Conference: Southland Conf.  Enrollment: 12,800.  Colors: Purple & White.
Nickname: Lumberjacks.  Stadium: Homer Bryce (1973), 14,575 capacity.  Artificial turf.
1992 home attendance: 56,628 in 7 games.
Director of Athletics: Steve McCarty.
Sports Info. Director: Gregg Fort  409-568-2606

■ Home games on each schedule [neutral sites shown in brackets].  *Night Games.

*Divisions I-A & I-AA 1993 Schedules and 1992 Results*          695

## SYRACUSE . . . Syracuse, N.Y.   13244   I-A

Coach: Paul Pasqualoni, Penn St. '72
Record: 7 yrs., W-54, L-21, T-0

### 1993 SCHEDULE

| | |
|---|---|
| Ball St. ■ | Sep 4* |
| East Caro. | Sep 9* |
| Texas | Sep 18* |
| Cincinnati ■ | Sep 25* |
| Boston College ■ | Oct 2 |
| Pittsburgh | Oct 16 |
| Miami (Fla.) | Oct 23 |
| West Va. ■ | Oct 30 |
| Temple ■ | Nov 6 |
| Virginia Tech | Nov 13 |
| Rutgers | Nov 26 |

### 1992 RECORD

| | | | | | |
|---|---|---|---|---|---|
| 42 | East Caro. | 21 | 28 | Virginia Tech | 9 |
| 31 | Texas | 21 | 27 | Boston College | 10 |
| 12 | Ohio St. | 35 | 10 | Miami (Fla.) | 16 |
| 15 | Louisville | 9 | | | |
| 50 | Rutgers | 28 | 314 | (9-2-0) | 183 |
| 20 | West Va. | 17 | | **Fiesta Bowl** | |
| 38 | Temple | 7 | 26 | Colorado | 22 |
| 41 | Pittsburgh | 10 | | | |

Conference: Big East Conference.   Enrollment: 10,500.   Colors: Orange.
Nickname: Orangemen.   Stadium: Carrier Dome (1980), 50,000 capacity.   Artificial turf.
1992 home attendance: 295,910 in 6 games.
Director of Athletics: Jake Crouthamel.
Sports Info. Director: Larry Kimball   315-443-2608

---

## TEMPLE . . . Philadelphia, Pa.   19122   I-A

Coach: Ron Dickerson, Kansas St. '71
Record: First year as head coach

### 1993 SCHEDULE

| | |
|---|---|
| Eastern Mich. ■ | Sep 9* |
| California ■ | Sep 18 |
| Boston College | Sep 25 |
| Rutgers | Oct 2* |
| Army ■ | Oct 9 |
| Virginia Tech | Oct 16 |
| Akron | Oct 23 |
| Miami (Fla.) | Oct 30 |
| Syracuse | Nov 6 |
| West Va. ■ | Nov 13 |
| Pittsburgh ■ | Nov 20 |

### 1992 RECORD

| | | | | | |
|---|---|---|---|---|---|
| 35 | Boston U. | 0 | 15 | Akron | 29 |
| 8 | Penn St. | 49 | 0 | Miami (Fla.) | 48 |
| 7 | Virginia Tech | 26 | 10 | Rutgers | 35 |
| 14 | Kansas St. | 35 | | | |
| 10 | Washington St. | 51 | 132 | (1-10-0) | 383 |
| 20 | Pittsburgh | 27 | | | |
| 7 | Syracuse | 38 | | | |
| 6 | Boston College | 45 | | | |

Conference: Big East Conference.   Enrollment: 33,000.   Colors: Cherry & White.
Nickname: Owls.   Stadium: Veterans (1971), 66,592 capacity.   Artificial turf.
1992 home attendance: 57,477 in 5 games.
Director of Athletics: Charles Theokas.
Sports Info. Director: Al Shrier   215-204-7445

---

## TENNESSEE . . . Knoxville, Tenn.   37996   I-A

Coach: Phillip Fulmer, Tennessee '72
Record: 1 yr., W-4, L-0, T-0

### 1993 SCHEDULE

| | |
|---|---|
| Louisiana Tech ■ | Sep 4 |
| Georgia ■ | Sep 11 |
| Florida | Sep 18 |
| Louisiana St. ■ | Sep 25 |
| Duke ■ | Oct 2 |
| Arkansas [Little Rock, Ark.] | Oct 9 |
| Alabama [Birmingham, Ala.] | Oct 16 |
| South Caro. ■ | Oct 30 |
| Louisville ■ | Nov 6 |
| Kentucky | Nov 20 |
| Vanderbilt ■ | Nov 27 |

### 1992 RECORD

| | | | | | |
|---|---|---|---|---|---|
| 38 | Southwestern La. | 3 | 26 | Memphis St. | 21 |
| 34 | Georgia | 31 | 34 | Kentucky | 13 |
| 31 | Florida | 14 | 29 | Vanderbilt | 25 |
| 40 | Cincinnati | 0 | | | |
| 20 | Louisiana St. | 0 | 309 | (8-3-0) | 173 |
| 24 | Arkansas | 25 | | **Hall of Fame Bowl** | |
| 10 | Alabama | 17 | 38 | Boston College | 23 |
| 23 | South Caro. | 24 | | | |

Conference: Southeastern Conf.   Enrollment: 26,579.   Colors: Orange & White.
Nickname: Volunteers.   Stadium: Neyland (1921), 91,902 capacity.   Artificial turf.
1992 home attendance: 575,544 in 6 games.
Director of Athletics: Doug Dickey.
Sports Info. Director: Bud Ford   615-974-1212

---

## TENNESSEE-CHATTANOOGA . . . Chattanooga, Tenn.   37402   I-AA

Coach: Tommy West, Tennessee '75
Record: First year as head coach

### 1993 SCHEDULE

| | |
|---|---|
| Tenn.-Martin | Sep 2* |
| Mississippi | Sep 11* |
| Gardner-Webb ■ | Sep 18* |
| Ga. Southern | Sep 25 |
| Marshall ■ | Oct 2* |
| Va. Military ■ | Oct 16 |
| Western Caro. ■ | Oct 23 |
| Appalachian St. | Oct 30 |
| Citadel ■ | Nov 6 |
| East Tenn. St. | Nov 13 |
| Furman ■ | Nov 20 |

### 1992 RECORD

| | | | | | |
|---|---|---|---|---|---|
| 35 | Boise St. | 20 | 24 | East Tenn. St. | 27 |
| 37 | Tenn.-Martin | 28 | 0 | Furman | 35 |
| 17 | Central Ark. | 24 | 34 | Va. Military | 37 |
| 3 | Clemson | 54 | | | |
| 13 | Citadel | 33 | 216 | (2-9-0) | 391 |
| 13 | Western Caro. | 44 | | | |
| 23 | Marshall | 52 | | | |
| 17 | Appalachian St. | 37 | | | |

Conference: Southern Conf.   Enrollment: 8,200.   Colors: Navy Blue & Gold.
Nickname: Moccasins.   Stadium: Chamberlain Field (1947), 10,501 capacity.   Natural turf.
1992 home attendance: 29,397 in 6 games.
Director of Athletics: Ed Farrell.
Sports Info. Director: Neil Magnussen   615-755-4618

---

## TENNESSEE-MARTIN . . . Martin, Tenn.   38238   I-AA

Coach: Don McLeary, Tennessee '70
Record: 9 yrs., W-43, L-54, T-0

### 1993 SCHEDULE

| | |
|---|---|
| Tenn.-Chatt. ■ | Sep 2* |
| West Ga. ■ | Sep 11* |
| Southeast Mo. St. ■ | Sep 25* |
| Murray St. ■ | Oct 2* |
| Middle Tenn. St. ■ | Oct 9* |
| Tennessee Tech | Oct 16 |
| Tennessee St. ■ | Oct 23 |
| Eastern Ky. | Oct 30 |
| Samford | Nov 6 |
| Morehead St. | Nov 13 |
| Austin Peay | Nov 20 |

### 1992 RECORD

| | | | | | |
|---|---|---|---|---|---|
| 24 | Delta St. | 0 | 0 | Middle Tenn. St. | 14 |
| 28 | Tenn.-Chatt. | 37 | 25 | Samford | 42 |
| 20 | Morehead St. | 7 | 18 | Austin Peay | 32 |
| 13 | Tennessee Tech | 17 | | | |
| 13 | Murray St. | 7 | 178 | (3-8-0) | 251 |
| 15 | Tennessee St. | 23 | | | |
| 9 | Eastern Ky. | 35 | | | |
| 13 | Southeast Mo. St. | 37 | | | |

Conference: Ohio Valley Conf.   Enrollment: 5,594.   Colors: Orange, White & Royal Blue.
Nickname: Pacers.   Stadium: Pacer (1964), 7,500 capacity.   Natural turf.
1992 home attendance: 30,428 in 6 games.
Director of Athletics: Don McLeary.
Sports Info. Director: Lee Wilmot   901-587-7630

---

■ Home games on each schedule [neutral sites shown in brackets].   *Night Games.

*1993 NCAA FOOTBALL*

## TENNESSEE STATE . . . Nashville, Tenn.   37203   I-AA

Coach: Bill Davis, Johnson Smith '65
Record: 14 yrs., W-100, L-51, T-1

### 1993 SCHEDULE

| | |
|---|---|
| Florida A&M | Sep 4 |
| Jackson St. [Chicago, Ill.] | Sep 11* |
| Grambling [Memphis, Tenn.] | Sep 18* |
| Middle Tenn. St. ■ | Oct 3 |
| Eastern Ky. [Louisville, Ky.] | Oct 9 |
| Austin Peay | Oct 16* |
| Tenn.-Martin | Oct 23 |
| Morehead St. ■ | Oct 30* |
| Tennessee Tech ■ | Nov 6* |
| Murray St. ■ | Nov 13 |
| Southeast Mo. St. | Nov 20 |

### 1992 RECORD

| | | | |
|---|---|---|---|
| 31 | Middle Tenn. St. | 35 |  |
| 18 | Jackson St. | 38 |  |
| 28 | Grambling | 38 |  |
| 12 | Florida A&M | 20 |  |
| 24 | Morehead St. | 14 |  |
| 23 | Tenn.-Martin | 15 |  |
| 35 | Austin Peay | 14 |  |
| 28 | Eastern Ky. | 49 |  |
| 15 | Tennessee Tech | 26 |  |
| 19 | Murray St. | 10 |  |
| 37 | Southeast Mo. St. | 27 |  |
| 270 | | (5-6-0) | 286 |

Conference: Ohio Valley Conf.   Enrollment: 8,000.   Colors: Blue & White.
Nickname: Tigers.   Stadium: W.J. Hale (1953), 16,000 capacity.   Natural turf.
1992 home attendance: 130,574 in 6 games.
Director of Athletics: William A. Thomas.
Sports Info. Director: Johnny M. Franks   615-320-3596

---

## TENNESSEE TECH . . . Cookeville, Tenn.   38505   I-AA

Coach: Jim Ragland, Tennessee Tech '64
Record: 7 yrs., W-25, L-39, T-0

### 1993 SCHEDULE

| | |
|---|---|
| Illinois St. ■ | Sep 4* |
| Lock Haven ■ | Sep 11* |
| Samford ■ | Sep 18* |
| Morehead St. ■ | Sep 25 |
| Austin Peay | Oct 2* |
| Southeast Mo. St. | Oct 9 |
| Tenn.-Martin ■ | Oct 16 |
| Eastern Ky. | Oct 23 |
| Murray St. ■ | Oct 30 |
| Tennessee St. | Nov 6* |
| Middle Tenn. St. ■ | Nov 20 |

### 1992 RECORD

| | | | |
|---|---|---|---|
| 31 | Lock Haven | 21 |  |
| 13 | Samford | 37 |  |
| 0 | Eastern Ky. | 35 |  |
| 17 | Tenn.-Martin | 13 |  |
| 49 | Southeast Mo. St. | 14 |  |
| 10 | Austin Peay | 0 |  |
| 31 | Morehead St. | 12 |  |
| 35 | Murray St. | 10 |  |
| 26 | Tennessee St. | 15 |  |
| 14 | Marshall | 52 |  |
| 0 | Middle Tenn. St. | 21 |  |
| 226 | | (7-4-0) | 230 |

Conference: Ohio Valley Conf.   Enrollment: 8,240.   Colors: Purple & Gold.
Nickname: Golden Eagles.   Stadium: Tucker (1966), 16,500 capacity.   Artificial turf.
1992 home attendance: 32,923 in 6 games.
Director of Athletics: David Larimore.
Sports Info. Director: Rob Schabert   615-372-3088

---

## TEXAS . . . Austin, Texas   78712   I-A

Coach: John Mackovic, Wake Forest '65
Record: 8 yrs., W-50, L-41, T-1

### 1993 SCHEDULE

| | |
|---|---|
| Colorado | Sep 4 |
| Syracuse ■ | Sep 18* |
| Louisville ■ | Sep 25 |
| Rice ■ | Oct 2* |
| Oklahoma [Dallas, Texas] | Oct 9 |
| Southern Methodist [San Antonio, Texas] | Oct 23* |
| Texas Tech ■ | Oct 30 |
| Houston | Nov 4* |
| Texas Christian ■ | Nov 13 |
| Baylor ■ | Nov 20 |
| Texas A&M | Nov 25* |

### 1992 RECORD

| | | | |
|---|---|---|---|
| 10 | Mississippi St. | 28 |  |
| 21 | Syracuse | 31 |  |
| 33 | North Texas | 15 |  |
| 23 | Rice | 21 |  |
| 34 | Oklahoma | 24 |  |
| 45 | Houston | 38 |  |
| 44 | Texas Tech | 33 |  |
| 14 | Texas Christian | 23 |  |
| 35 | Southern Methodist | 14 |  |
| 20 | Baylor | 21 |  |
| 13 | Texas A&M | 34 |  |
| 292 | | (6-5-0) | 282 |

Conference: Southwest Conf.   Enrollment: 49,253.   Colors: Burnt Orange & White.
Nickname: Longhorns.   Stadium: Memorial (1924), 77,809 capacity.   Artificial turf.
1992 home attendance: 340,758 in 5 games.
Director of Athletics: DeLoss Dodds.
Sports Info. Director: Bill Little   512-471-7437

---

## TEXAS A&M . . . College Station, Texas   77843   I-A

Coach: R. C. Slocum, McNeese St. '67
Record: 4 yrs., W-39, L-10, T-1

### 1993 SCHEDULE

| | |
|---|---|
| Louisiana St. ■ | Sep 4* |
| Oklahoma | Sep 11 |
| Missouri ■ | Sep 18* |
| Texas Tech | Oct 2* |
| Houston ■ | Oct 9 |
| Baylor | Oct 16* |
| Rice | Oct 23 |
| Southern Methodist ■ | Oct 30 |
| Louisville ■ | Nov 13 |
| Texas Christian | Nov 20 |
| Texas ■ | Nov 25* |

### 1992 RECORD

| | | | |
|---|---|---|---|
| 10 | Stanford | 7 |  |
| 31 | Louisiana St. | 22 |  |
| 19 | Tulsa | 9 |  |
| 26 | Missouri | 13 |  |
| 19 | Texas Tech | 17 |  |
| 35 | Rice | 9 |  |
| 19 | Baylor | 13 |  |
| 41 | Southern Methodist | 7 |  |
| 40 | Louisville | 18 |  |
| 38 | Houston | 30 |  |
| 37 | Texas Christian | 10 |  |
| 34 | Texas | 13 |  |
| 349 | | (12-0-0) | 168 |
|  | | **Cotton Bowl** |  |
| 3 | Notre Dame | 28 |  |

Conference: Southwest Conf.   Enrollment: 42,988.   Colors: Maroon & White.
Nickname: Aggies.   Stadium: Kyle Field (1925), 70,210 capacity.   Artificial turf.
1992 home attendance: 387,846 in 7 games.
Director of Athletics: Wally Groff (Interim).
Sports Info. Director: Alan Cannon   409-845-5725

---

## TEXAS CHRISTIAN . . . Fort Worth, Texas   76129   I-A

Coach: Pat Sullivan, Auburn '72
Record: 1 yr., W-2, L-8, T-1

### 1993 SCHEDULE

| | |
|---|---|
| Oklahoma ■ | Sep 4* |
| New Mexico ■ | Sep 11* |
| Southern Methodist ■ | Sep 25* |
| Oklahoma St. | Oct 2 |
| Rice | Oct 9 |
| Tulane ■ | Oct 16 |
| Baylor | Oct 23 |
| Houston ■ | Oct 30 |
| Texas Tech | Nov 6 |
| Texas | Nov 13 |
| Texas A&M ■ | Nov 20 |

### 1992 RECORD

| | | | |
|---|---|---|---|
| 7 | New Mexico | 24 |  |
| 17 | Western Mich. | 17 |  |
| 9 | Southern Methodist | 21 |  |
| 13 | Oklahoma St. | 11 |  |
| 20 | Baylor | 41 |  |
| 10 | Miami (Fla.) | 45 |  |
| 12 | Rice | 29 |  |
| 46 | Houston | 49 |  |
| 23 | Texas | 14 |  |
| 28 | Texas Tech | 31 |  |
| 10 | Texas A&M | 37 |  |
| 195 | | (2-8-1) | 319 |

Conference: Southwest Conf.   Enrollment: 6,900.   Colors: Purple & White.
Nickname: Horned Frogs.   Stadium: Amon G. Carter (1929), 46,000 capacity.   Natural turf.
1992 home attendance: 154,122 in 6 games.
Director of Athletics: Frank Windegger.
Sports Info. Director: Glen Stone   817-921-7969

---

■ Home games on each schedule [neutral sites shown in brackets].   *Night Games.

*Divisions I-A & I-AA 1993 Schedules and 1992 Results*

## TEXAS SOUTHERN . . . Houston, Texas  77004    I-AA

Coach: Walter Highsmith, Florida A&M '64
Record: 4 yrs., W-17, L-25, T-2
1993 SCHEDULE

| | |
|---|---|
| Prairie View ■ | Sep 4* |
| Alcorn St. [Jackson, Miss.] | Sep 11* |
| Nevada | Sep 18 |
| Central St. (Ohio) | Sep 25 |
| Knoxville ■ | Oct 2 |
| Southern-B.R. ■ | Oct 9* |
| Alabama St. ■ | Oct 16 |
| Grambling | Oct 30 |
| Jackson St. | Nov 6* |
| East Tex. St. | Nov 13 |
| Mississippi Val. | Nov 20 |

1992 RECORD

| | | | |
|---|---|---|---|
| 35 | Prairie View | 0 | 27 Jackson St. ... 26 |
| 34 | Southwest Tex. St. | 39 | 6 Southern-B.R. ... 34 |
| 30 | Central St. (Ohio) | 17 | 14 Nevada ... 38 |
| 39 | Knoxville | 22 | |
| 36 | Alcorn St. | 46 | 281   (5-6-0)   299 |
| 30 | Alabama St. | 28 | |
| 13 | Mississippi Val. | 25 | |
| 17 | Grambling | 24 | |

Conference: Southwestern.  Enrollment: 10,000.  Colors: Maroon & Gray.
Nickname: Tigers.  Stadium: Robertson (1965), 25,000 capacity.  Natural turf.
1992 home attendance: 55,500 in 4 games.
Director of Athletics: Curtis Williams.
Sports Info. Director: Andre Smith  713-527-7270

## TEXAS TECH . . . Lubbock, Texas  79409    I-A

Coach: Spike Dykes, Stephen F. Austin '59
Record: 7 yrs., W-35, L-32, T-1
1993 SCHEDULE

| | |
|---|---|
| Pacific (Cal.) ■ | Sep 4* |
| Nebraska | Sep 11 |
| Georgia | Sep 18 |
| Baylor | Sep 25* |
| Texas A&M ■ | Oct 2* |
| North Caro. St. ■ | Oct 9* |
| Rice ■ | Oct 16* |
| Texas | Oct 30 |
| Texas Christian ■ | Nov 6 |
| Southern Methodist | Nov 13 |
| Houston [San Antonio, Texas] | Nov 20* |

1992 RECORD

| | | | |
|---|---|---|---|
| 9 | Oklahoma | 34 | 3 Rice ... 34 |
| 49 | Wyoming | 32 | 31 Texas Christian ... 28 |
| 13 | Oregon | 16 | 44 Houston ... 35 |
| 36 | Baylor | 17 | |
| 17 | Texas A&M | 19 | 287   (5-6-0)   332 |
| 13 | North Caro. St. | 48 | |
| 39 | Southern Methodist | 25 | |
| 33 | Texas | 44 | |

Conference: Southwest Conf.  Enrollment: 24,285.  Colors: Scarlet & Black.
Nickname: Red Raiders.  Stadium: Jones (1947), 50,500 capacity.  Artificial turf.
1992 home attendance: 233,894 in 6 games.
Director of Athletics: To be named.
Sports Info. Director: Joe Hornaday  806-742-2770

## TOLEDO . . . Toledo, Ohio  43606    I-A

Coach: Gary Pinkel, Kent '75
Record: 2 yrs., W-13, L-8, T-1
1993 SCHEDULE

| | |
|---|---|
| Indiana | Sep 4* |
| Southern Ill. ■ | Sep 18* |
| Ohio ■ | Sep 25* |
| Bowling Green | Oct 2 |
| Ball St. | Oct 9 |
| Miami (Ohio) ■ | Oct 16* |
| Cincinnati ■ | Oct 23 |
| Kent | Oct 30 |
| Central Mich. ■ | Nov 6 |
| Western Mich. | Nov 13 |
| Eastern Mich. | Nov 19* |

1992 RECORD

| | | | |
|---|---|---|---|
| 49 | Arkansas St. | 0 | 10 Ball St. ... 9 |
| 20 | Akron | 23 | 41 Eastern Mich. ... 0 |
| 33 | Purdue | 29 | 25 Northern Ill. ... 8 |
| 9 | Central Mich. | 28 | |
| 21 | Western Mich. | 12 | 269   (8-3-0)   153 |
| 9 | Bowling Green | 10 | |
| 20 | Miami (Ohio) | 17 | |
| 32 | Kent | 17 | |

Conference: Mid-American Conf.  Enrollment: 24,781.  Colors: Blue & Gold.
Nickname: Rockets.  Stadium: Glass Bowl (1937), 26,248 capacity.  Artificial turf.
1992 home attendance: 102,771 in 5 games.
Director of Athletics: Allen R. Bohl.
Sports Info. Director: Rod Brandt  419-537-3790

## TOWSON STATE . . . Towson, Md.  21204    I-AA

Coach: Gordy Combs, Towson St. '72
Record: 1 yr., W-5, L-5, T-0
1993 SCHEDULE

| | |
|---|---|
| Central Conn. St. ■ | Sep 11 |
| Delaware St. ■ | Sep 18 |
| Charleston So. ■ | Sep 25 |
| Connecticut | Oct 2 |
| Howard ■ | Oct 16 |
| Buffalo | Oct 23 |
| Hofstra | Oct 30* |
| Delaware | Nov 6 |
| Bucknell ■ | Nov 13 |
| Morgan St. | Nov 20 |

1992 RECORD

| | | | |
|---|---|---|---|
| 19 | Rhode Island | 36 | 33 Northeastern ... 32 |
| 24 | Bucknell | 21 | 27 Delaware ... 55 |
| 37 | Hofstra | 18 | |
| 14 | Liberty | 16 | 245   (5-5-0)   302 |
| 13 | Delaware St. | 27 | |
| 15 | William & Mary | 43 | |
| 28 | James Madison | 21 | |
| 35 | Indiana (Pa.) | 33 | |

Conference: I-AA Independents.  Enrollment: 15,400.  Colors: Gold & White.
Nickname: Tigers.  Stadium: Minnegan Stadium (1978), 5,000 capacity.  Natural turf.
1992 home attendance: 11,883 in 5 games.
Director of Athletics: Bill Hunter.
Sports Info. Director: Peter Schlehr  410-830-2232

## TROY STATE . . . Troy, Ala.  36081    I-AA

Coach: Larry Blakeney, Auburn '70
Record: 2 yrs., W-15, L-7, T-0
1993 SCHEDULE

| | |
|---|---|
| Ala.-Birmingham | Sep 6 |
| Northwestern (La.) | Sep 11* |
| Nicholls St. ■ | Sep 18* |
| Alabama St. | Sep 25* |
| Charleston So. ■ | Oct 2 |
| Liberty ■ | Oct 9 |
| Central St. (Ohio) ■ | Oct 23 |
| Central Fla. ■ | Oct 30 |
| Western Ky. ■ | Nov 6 |
| Alcorn St. ■ | Nov 13 |
| Samford | Nov 20 |

1992 RECORD

| | | | |
|---|---|---|---|
| 37 | Southern Ill. | 13 | 29 Samford ... 24 |
| 38 | Northwestern (La.) | 19 | 21 Ga. Southern ... 0 |
| 20 | Central Fla. | 16 | 21 Nicholls St. ... 0 |
| 31 | Alabama St. | 14 | |
| 26 | Valdosta St. | 10 | 295   (10-1-0)   122 |
| 41 | Arkansas St. | 7 | |
| 7 | Liberty | 9 | |
| 24 | North Ala. | 10 | |

Conference: I-AA Independents.  Enrollment: 5,000.  Colors: Cardinal, Grey & Black.
Nickname: Trojans.  Stadium: Memorial (1949), 12,000 capacity.  Natural turf.
1992 home attendance: 24,500 in 4 games.
Director of Athletics: Kenneth Blankenship.
Sports Info. Director: Tom Ensey  205-670-3480

■ Home games on each schedule [neutral sites shown in brackets].  *Night Games.

## TULANE . . . New Orleans, La.   70118    I-A

Coach: Buddy Teevens, Dartmouth '79
Record: 8 yrs., W-41, L-40, T-2
1993 SCHEDULE

| | |
|---|---|
| Alabama [Birmingham, Ala.] | Sep 4 |
| Rice | Sep 11 |
| William & Mary ■ | Sep 18* |
| Mississippi St. ■ | Sep 25* |
| Navy ■ | Oct 2* |
| Southwestern La. ■ | Oct 9* |
| Texas Christian | Oct 16 |
| Boston College | Oct 30 |
| Southern Miss. | Nov 6 |
| North Caro. ■ | Nov 13* |
| Louisiana St. | Nov 20* |
| Hawaii | Dec 4* |

1992 RECORD

| | | | | | |
|---|---|---|---|---|---|
| 13 | Southern Methodist | 12 | 17 | Navy | 20 |
| 9 | Mississippi | 35 | 7 | Florida St. | 70 |
| 14 | Iowa St. | 38 | 12 | Louisiana St. | 24 |
| 34 | Nevada | 17 | | | |
| 0 | Alabama | 37 | 146 | (2-9-0) | 349 |
| 7 | Southern Miss. | 17 | | | |
| 13 | Boston College | 17 | | | |
| 20 | Memphis St. | 62 | | | |

Conference: I-A Independents.   Enrollment: 11,049.   Colors: Olive Green & Sky Blue.
Nickname: Green Wave.   Stadium: Superdome (1975), 72,704 capacity.   Artificial turf.
1992 home attendance: 142,323 in 5 games.
Director of Athletics: Kevin White.
Sports Info. Director: Lenny Vangilder   504-865-5506

---

## TULSA . . . Tulsa, Okla.   74104    I-A

Coach: David Rader, Tulsa '80
Record: 5 yrs., W-27, L-30, T-0
1993 SCHEDULE

| | |
|---|---|
| Iowa | Sep 4 |
| Houston | Sep 11 |
| Oklahoma St. ■ | Sep 18* |
| Oklahoma | Sep 25 |
| Cincinnati ■ | Oct 2 |
| Memphis St. | Oct 16 |
| Middle Tenn. St. ■ | Oct 30 |
| East Caro. | Nov 6 |
| Arkansas | Nov 13 |
| Southern Miss. ■ | Nov 20 |
| Louisville ■ | Nov 25 |

1992 RECORD

| | | | | | |
|---|---|---|---|---|---|
| 28 | Houston | 25 | 27 | Southwestern La. | 9 |
| 9 | Texas A&M | 19 | 48 | UTEP | 39 |
| 7 | Kansas | 40 | 9 | Hawaii | 38 |
| 19 | Oklahoma St. | 24 | | | |
| 24 | Southern Miss. | 33 | 240 | (4-7-0) | 303 |
| 17 | Southwest Mo. St. | 14 | | | |
| 27 | Louisville | 32 | | | |
| 25 | Memphis St. | 30 | | | |

Conference: I-A Independents.   Enrollment: 4,922.   Colors: Blue & Gold.
Nickname: Golden Hurricane.   Stadium: Skelly (1930), 40,385 capacity.   Artificial turf.
1992 home attendance: 134,567 in 6 games.
Director of Athletics: Rick Dickson.
Sports Info. Director: Don Tomkalski   918-631-2395

---

## UCLA . . . Los Angeles, Calif.   90024    I-A

Coach: Terry Donahue, UCLA '67
Record: 17 yrs., W-131, L-59, T-8
1993 SCHEDULE

| | |
|---|---|
| California ■ | Sep 4* |
| Nebraska ■ | Sep 18 |
| Stanford | Sep 25 |
| San Diego St. | Sep 30* |
| Brigham Young ■ | Oct 9* |
| Washington ■ | Oct 16 |
| Oregon St. | Oct 23 |
| Arizona ■ | Oct 30 |
| Washington St. | Nov 6 |
| Arizona St. ■ | Nov 13 |
| Southern Cal | Nov 20 |

1992 RECORD

| | | | | | |
|---|---|---|---|---|---|
| 37 | Cal St. Fullerton | 14 | 26 | Oregon St. | 14 |
| 17 | Brigham Young | 10 | 9 | Oregon | 6 |
| 35 | San Diego St. | 7 | 38 | Southern Cal | 37 |
| 3 | Arizona | 23 | | | |
| 7 | Stanford | 19 | 201 | (6-5-0) | 228 |
| 17 | Washington St. | 30 | | | |
| 0 | Arizona St. | 20 | | | |
| 12 | California | 48 | | | |

Conference: Pacific-10.   Enrollment: 33,770.   Colors: Blue & Gold.
Nickname: Bruins.   Stadium: Rose Bowl (1922), 99,563 capacity.   Natural turf.
1992 home attendance: 295,561 in 6 games.
Director of Athletics: Peter Dalis.
Sports Info. Director: Marc Dellins   310-206-6831

---

## UTAH . . . Salt Lake City, Utah   84112    I-A

Coach: Ron McBride, San Jose St. '63
Record: 3 yrs., W-17, L-18, T-0
1993 SCHEDULE

| | |
|---|---|
| Arizona St. | Sep 4* |
| Utah St. ■ | Sep 11* |
| Kansas | Sep 18 |
| Wyoming | Sep 25 |
| Idaho ■ | Oct 2* |
| New Mexico ■ | Oct 9* |
| UTEP | Oct 16* |
| Colorado St. ■ | Oct 23 |
| San Diego St. ■ | Oct 30 |
| Hawaii | Nov 6* |
| Air Force ■ | Nov 13 |
| Brigham Young | Nov 20 |

1992 RECORD

| | | | | | |
|---|---|---|---|---|---|
| 22 | Nebraska | 49 | 15 | Fresno St. | 41 |
| 42 | Utah St. | 18 | 38 | Wyoming | 7 |
| 42 | Oregon St. | 9 | 22 | Brigham Young | 31 |
| 33 | Colorado St. | 29 | | | |
| 38 | Hawaii | 17 | 292 | (6-5-0) | 258 |
| 7 | New Mexico | 24 | | | |
| 13 | UTEP | 20 | | **Copper Bowl** | |
| 20 | Air Force | 13 | 28 | Washington St. | 31 |

Conference: Western Athl. Conf.   Enrollment: 26,600.   Colors: Crimson & White.
Nickname: Utes.   Stadium: Robert Rice (1927), 35,000 capacity.   Artificial turf.
1992 home attendance: 149,034 in 5 games.
Director of Athletics: Chris Hill.
Sports Info. Director: Liz Abel   801-581-3510

---

## UTAH STATE . . . Logan, Utah   84322    I-A

Coach: Charlie Weatherbie, Oklahoma St. '77
Record: 1 yr., W-5, L-6, T-0
1993 SCHEDULE

| | |
|---|---|
| Southwestern La. | Sep 4* |
| Utah | Sep 11* |
| Baylor ■ | Sep 18 |
| Fresno St. | Sep 25* |
| Louisiana St. | Oct 2* |
| Nevada ■ | Oct 16* |
| Nevada-Las Vegas | Oct 23* |
| Brigham Young ■ | Oct 30 |
| Pacific (Cal.) ■ | Nov 6 |
| Louisiana Tech ■ | Nov 13 |
| New Mexico St. | Nov 20 |

1992 RECORD

| | | | | | |
|---|---|---|---|---|---|
| 3 | Arizona | 49 | 48 | Nevada-Las Vegas | 8 |
| 18 | Utah | 42 | 47 | Nevada | 48 |
| 10 | Baylor | 45 | 38 | Pacific (Cal.) | 35 |
| 48 | New Mexico St. | 21 | | | |
| 9 | Brigham Young | 30 | 300 | (5-6-0) | 328 |
| 28 | Kansas St. | 16 | | | |
| 25 | San Jose St. | 27 | | | |
| 26 | Cal St. Fullerton | 7 | | | |

Conference: Big West.   Enrollment: 15,572.   Colors: Navy Blue & White.
Nickname: Aggies.   Stadium: E.L. Romney (1968), 30,257 capacity.   Natural turf.
1992 home attendance: 73,596 in 5 games.
Director of Athletics: Chuck Bell.
Sports Info. Director: Craig Hislop   801-750-1361

---

■ Home games on each schedule [neutral sites shown in brackets].   *Night Games.

## UTEP . . . El Paso, Texas   79968 — I-A

Coach: David Lee, Vanderbilt '75
Record: 4 yrs., W-10, L-35, T-1
### 1993 SCHEDULE

| | |
|---|---|
| Arizona | Sep  4* |
| Nevada-Las Vegas ■ | Sep 11* |
| New Mexico St. | Sep 18* |
| Hawaii | Sep 25* |
| North Caro. | Oct  2 |
| Wyoming ■ | Oct  9* |
| Utah ■ | Oct 16* |
| Air Force | Oct 30 |
| Fresno St. | Nov  6* |
| Colorado St. ■ | Nov 13* |
| New Mexico ■ | Nov 20 |
| Brigham Young ■ | Nov 27 |

1992 RECORD

| | | | | | |
|---|---|---|---|---|---|
| 28 | Brigham Young | 38 | 39 | Tulsa | 48 |
| 17 | Nevada-Las Vegas | 19 | 14 | New Mexico | 35 |
| 24 | New Mexico St. | 30 | 18 | Fresno St. | 43 |
| 22 | Air Force | 28 | | | |
| 24 | Colorado St. | 42 | 254 | (1-10-0) | 386 |
| 27 | San Diego St. | 49 | | | |
| 20 | Utah | 13 | | | |
| 21 | Hawaii | 41 | | | |

Conference: Western Athl. Conf.  Enrollment: 17,200.  Colors: Orange, White & Blue.
Nickname: Miners.  Stadium: Sun Bowl (1963), 51,270 capacity.  Artificial turf.
1992 home attendance: 158,962 in 5 games.
Director of Athletics: To be named.
Sports Info. Director: Eddie Mullens  915-747-5330

## VALPARAISO . . . Valparaiso, Ind.   46383 — I-AA

Coach: Tom Horne, Wis.-La Crosse '76
Record: 7 yrs., W-22, L-48, T-2
### 1993 SCHEDULE

| | |
|---|---|
| St. Ambrose | Sep  4 |
| St. Xavier (Ill.) ■ | Sep 11 |
| Millikin | Sep 18 |
| San Diego ■ | Oct  2 |
| Butler | Oct  9 |
| Drake ■ | Oct 16 |
| Evansville ■ | Oct 23 |
| Dayton | Oct 30 |
| Michigan Tech ■ | Nov  6 |
| Northern Ariz. | Nov 13* |

1992 RECORD

| | | | | | |
|---|---|---|---|---|---|
| 7 | Ashland | 34 | 3 | Saginaw Valley | 34 |
| 7 | Hillsdale | 45 | 31 | Michigan Tech | 38 |
| 23 | Wayne St. (Mich.) | 10 | 14 | Grand Valley St. | 45 |
| 3 | Northern Mich. | 35 | | | |
| 16 | St. Joseph's (Ind.) | 14 | 130 | (3-8-0) | 344 |
| 3 | Ferris St. | 33 | | | |
| 13 | Butler | 42 | | | |
| 20 | Indianapolis | 14 | | | |

Conference: Pioneer Football League.  Enrollment: 3,800.  Colors: Brown & Gold.
Nickname: Crusaders.  Stadium: Brown Field (1947), 5,000 capacity.  Natural turf.
1992 home attendance: 10,945 in 5 games.
Director of Athletics: William Steinbrecher.
Sports Info. Director: Bill Rogers  219-464-5232

## VANDERBILT . . . Nashville, Tenn.   37212 — I-A

Coach: Gerry DiNardo, Notre Dame '75
Record: 2 yrs., W-9, L-13, T-0
### 1993 SCHEDULE

| | |
|---|---|
| Wake Forest ■ | Sep  4* |
| Alabama ■ | Sep 11* |
| Mississippi | Sep 18* |
| Auburn ■ | Oct  2* |
| Cincinnati ■ | Oct  9* |
| Georgia ■ | Oct 16 |
| South Caro. | Oct 23 |
| Kentucky ■ | Nov  6 |
| Navy ■ | Nov 13 |
| Florida | Nov 20 |
| Tennessee | Nov 27 |

1992 RECORD

| | | | | | |
|---|---|---|---|---|---|
| 8 | Alabama | 25 | 27 | Navy | 7 |
| 42 | Duke | 37 | 21 | Florida | 41 |
| 31 | Mississippi | 9 | 25 | Tennessee | 29 |
| 7 | Auburn | 31 | | | |
| 6 | Wake Forest | 40 | 224 | (4-7-0) | 277 |
| 20 | Georgia | 30 | | | |
| 17 | South Caro. | 21 | | | |
| 20 | Kentucky | 7 | | | |

Conference: Southeastern Conf.  Enrollment: 9,302.  Colors: Black & Gold.
Nickname: Commodores.  Stadium: Vanderbilt Stadium (1981), 41,000 capacity.  Artificial turf.
1992 home attendance: 229,070 in 6 games.
Director of Athletics: Paul Hoolahan.
Sports Info. Director: Tony Neely  615-322-4121

## VILLANOVA . . . Villanova, Pa.   19085 — I-AA

Coach: Andy Talley, Southern Conn. St. '67
Record: 13 yrs., W-84, L-42, T-2
### 1993 SCHEDULE

| | |
|---|---|
| Northeastern ■ | Sep 10* |
| Fordham ■ | Sep 18 |
| Richmond | Sep 25 |
| Boston U. | Oct  2 |
| Connecticut ■ | Oct  9 |
| Delaware | Oct 16 |
| William & Mary | Oct 23 |
| Rhode Island ■ | Oct 30 |
| New Hampshire ■ | Nov  6 |
| James Madison ■ | Nov 13 |
| Liberty | Nov 20 |

1992 RECORD

| | | | | | |
|---|---|---|---|---|---|
| 26 | West Chester | 6 | 27 | New Hampshire | 21 |
| 34 | Bucknell | 0 | 31 | Fordham | 14 |
| 36 | Richmond | 33 | 28 | Maine | 8 |
| 22 | Boston U. | 14 | | | |
| 27 | Connecticut | 20 | 294 | (9-2-0) | 153 |
| 20 | Delaware | 21 | | I-AA Championship | |
| 9 | Massachusetts | 13 | 20 | Youngstown St. | 23 |
| 34 | Rhode Island | 3 | | | |

Conference: Yankee.  Enrollment: 6,500.  Colors: Blue & White.
Nickname: Wildcats.  Stadium: Villanova (1927), 12,000 capacity.  Artificial turf.
1992 home attendance: 56,961 in 7 games.
Director of Athletics: To be named.
Sports Info. Director: James H. DeLorenzo  215-645-4120

## VIRGINIA . . . Charlottesville, Va.   22903 — I-A

Coach: George Welsh, Navy '56
Record: 20 yrs., W-128, L-97, T-4
### 1993 SCHEDULE

| | |
|---|---|
| Maryland | Sep  4 |
| Navy ■ | Sep 11 |
| Georgia Tech | Sep 16* |
| Duke ■ | Sep 25 |
| Ohio ■ | Oct  2 |
| Florida St. | Oct 16 |
| North Caro. ■ | Oct 23 |
| North Caro. St. | Oct 30 |
| Wake Forest ■ | Nov  6 |
| Clemson | Nov 13 |
| Virginia Tech ■ | Nov 20 |

1992 RECORD

| | | | | | |
|---|---|---|---|---|---|
| 28 | Maryland | 15 | 3 | Florida St. | 13 |
| 53 | Navy | 0 | 7 | North Caro. St. | 31 |
| 55 | Georgia Tech | 24 | 41 | Virginia Tech | 38 |
| 55 | Duke | 28 | | | |
| 31 | Wake Forest | 17 | 341 | (7-4-0) | 229 |
| 28 | Clemson | 29 | | | |
| 7 | North Caro. | 27 | | | |
| 33 | William & Mary | 7 | | | |

Conference: Atlantic Coast Conf.  Enrollment: 18,000.  Colors: Orange & Blue.
Nickname: Cavaliers.  Stadium: Scott (1931), 42,000 capacity.  Artificial turf.
1992 home attendance: 258,400 in 6 games.
Director of Athletics: Jim Copeland.
Sports Info. Director: Rich Murray  804-982-5500

■ Home games on each schedule [neutral sites shown in brackets].   *Night Games.

## VIRGINIA MILITARY . . . Lexington, Va.  24450  I-AA

Coach: Jim Shuck, Indiana '76
Record: 4 yrs., W-13, L-30, T-1

### 1993 SCHEDULE

| | |
|---|---|
| Richmond | Sep 4 |
| East Tenn. St. ■ | Sep 18 |
| Army | Sep 25 |
| William & Mary [Norfolk, Va.] | Oct 2 |
| Marshall | Oct 9* |
| Tenn.-Chatt. ■ | Oct 16 |
| Ga. Southern ■ | Oct 23 |
| Furman | Oct 30 |
| Western Caro. | Nov 6 |
| Citadel | Nov 13 |
| Appalachian St. ■ | Nov 20 |

### 1992 RECORD

| | | | |
|---|---|---|---|
| 16 | East Tenn. St. | | 18 |
| 16 | William & Mary | | 21 |
| 16 | Marshall | | 34 |
| 48 | West Va. Tech | | 8 |
| 13 | Furman | | 41 |
| 25 | Western Caro. | | 28 |
| 12 | Appalachian St. | | 27 |
| 18 | Richmond | | 41 |

| | | |
|---|---|---|
| 44 | Wofford | 13 |
| 0 | Citadel | 50 |
| 37 | Tenn.-Chatt. | 34 |
| 245 | (3-8-0) | 315 |

Conference: Southern Conf.   Enrollment: 1,300.   Colors: Red, White & Yellow.
Nickname: Keydets.   Stadium: Alumni Field (1962), 10,000 capacity.   Natural turf.
1992 home attendance: 42,021 in 6 games.
Director of Athletics: Davis Babb.
Sports Info. Director: Wade Branner   703-464-7253

## VIRGINIA TECH . . . Blacksburg, Va.  24061  I-A

Coach: Frank Beamer, Virginia Tech '69
Record: 12 yrs., W-66, L-63, T-4

### 1993 SCHEDULE

| | |
|---|---|
| Bowling Green ■ | Sep 4 |
| Pittsburgh | Sep 11* |
| Miami (Fla.) | Sep 18 |
| Maryland ■ | Sep 25 |
| West Va. | Oct 2 |
| Temple ■ | Oct 16 |
| Rutgers ■ | Oct 23 |
| East Caro. ■ | Oct 30 |
| Boston College | Nov 6 |
| Syracuse ■ | Nov 13 |
| Virginia | Nov 20 |

### 1992 RECORD

| | | | |
|---|---|---|---|
| 49 | James Madison | | 20 |
| 27 | East Caro. | | 30 |
| 26 | Temple | | 7 |
| 7 | West Va. | | 16 |
| 17 | Louisville | | 21 |
| 13 | North Caro. St. | | 13 |
| 23 | Miami (Fla.) | | 43 |
| 49 | Rutgers | | 50 |

| | | |
|---|---|---|
| 9 | Syracuse | 28 |
| 12 | Southern Miss. | 13 |
| 38 | Virginia | 41 |
| 270 | (2-8-1) | 282 |

Conference: Big East Conference.   Enrollment: 23,000.   Colors: Orange & Maroon.
Nickname: Gobblers, Hokies.   Stadium: Lane (1965), 51,000 capacity.   Natural turf.
1992 home attendance: 270,613 in 6 games.
Director of Athletics: Dave Braine.
Sports Info. Director: Dave Smith   703-231-6726

## WAGNER . . . Staten Island, N.Y.  10301  I-AA

Coach: Walt Hameline, Brockport St. '75
Record: 12 yrs., W-95, L-30, T-2

### 1993 SCHEDULE

| | |
|---|---|
| LIU-C.W. Post ■ | Sep 11 |
| St. John's (N.Y.) ■ | Sep 18 |
| Central Conn. St. ■ | Sep 25 |
| Iona ■ | Oct 2 |
| Duquesne | Oct 9 |
| Pace | Oct 16 |
| St. Francis (Pa.) ■ | Oct 23 |
| Marist | Oct 30 |
| Monmouth (N. J.) | Nov 6 |
| San Diego | Nov 13* |

### 1992 RECORD

| | | | |
|---|---|---|---|
| 12 | Delaware Valley | | 0 |
| 18 | St. Francis (Pa.) | | 21 |
| 27 | St. John's (N.Y.) | | 0 |
| 20 | Newport News App. | | 17 |
| 27 | Iona | | 20 |
| 42 | Marist | | 7 |
| 30 | Rowan | | 59 |
| 28 | LIU-C.W. Post | | 26 |

| | | |
|---|---|---|
| 48 | Pace | 6 |
| 31 | Duquesne | 6 |
| 283 | (8-2-0) | 162 |
| | **ECAC Southeast** | |
| 48 | St. Francis (Pa.) | 6 |

Conference: I-AA Independents.   Enrollment: 1,250.   Colors: Green & White.
Nickname: Seahawks.   Stadium: Fischer Memorial Field, 5,000 capacity.   Natural turf.
1992 home attendance: 11,443 in 4 games.
Director of Athletics: Walt Hameline.
Sports Info. Director: Scott Morse   718-390-3227

## WAKE FOREST . . . Winston-Salem, N.C.  27109  I-A

Coach: Jim Caldwell, Iowa '77
Record: First year as head coach

### 1993 SCHEDULE

| | |
|---|---|
| Vanderbilt ■ | Sep 4* |
| North Caro. St. ■ | Sep 11* |
| Appalachian St. ■ | Sep 18* |
| Northwestern | Sep 25 |
| North Caro. | Oct 2 |
| Clemson | Oct 16 |
| Duke ■ | Oct 23 |
| Florida St. | Oct 30 |
| Virginia | Nov 6 |
| Georgia Tech ■ | Nov 13 |
| Maryland ■ | Nov 20 |

### 1992 RECORD

| | | | |
|---|---|---|---|
| 17 | North Caro. | | 35 |
| 10 | Appalachian St. | | 7 |
| 7 | Florida St. | | 35 |
| 17 | Virginia | | 31 |
| 40 | Vanderbilt | | 6 |
| 30 | Maryland | | 23 |
| 23 | Army | | 7 |
| 18 | Clemson | | 15 |

| | | |
|---|---|---|
| 28 | Duke | 14 |
| 23 | Georgia Tech | 10 |
| 14 | North Caro. St. | 42 |
| 227 | (7-4-0) | 225 |
| | **Independence Bowl** | |
| 39 | Oregon | 35 |

Conference: Atlantic Coast Conf.   Enrollment: 3,600.   Colors: Old Gold & Black.
Nickname: Demon Deacons.   Stadium: Groves (1968), 31,500 capacity.   Natural turf.
1992 home attendance: 93,550 in 5 games.
Director of Athletics: Ron Wellman.
Sports Info. Director: John Justus   919-759-5640

## WASHINGTON . . . Seattle, Wash.  98195  I-A

Coach: Don James, Miami (Fla.) '54
Record: 22 yrs., W-176, L-78, T-3

### 1993 SCHEDULE

| | |
|---|---|
| Stanford ■ | Sep 4 |
| Ohio St. | Sep 11* |
| East Caro. ■ | Sep 25 |
| San Jose St. ■ | Oct 2 |
| California | Oct 9 |
| UCLA | Oct 16 |
| Oregon ■ | Oct 23 |
| Arizona St. | Oct 30* |
| Oregon St. | Nov 6 |
| Southern Cal ■ | Nov 13 |
| Washington St. ■ | Nov 20 |

### 1992 RECORD

| | | | |
|---|---|---|---|
| 31 | Arizona St. | | 7 |
| 27 | Wisconsin | | 10 |
| 29 | Nebraska | | 14 |
| 17 | Southern Cal | | 10 |
| 35 | California | | 16 |
| 24 | Oregon | | 3 |
| 31 | Pacific (Cal.) | | 7 |
| 41 | Stanford | | 7 |

| | | |
|---|---|---|
| 3 | Arizona | 16 |
| 45 | Oregon St. | 16 |
| 23 | Washington St. | 42 |
| 306 | (9-2-0) | 148 |
| | **Rose Bowl** | |
| 31 | Michigan | 38 |

Conference: Pacific-10.   Enrollment: 34,000.   Colors: Purple & Gold.
Nickname: Huskies.   Stadium: Husky (1920), 72,500 capacity.   Artificial turf.
1992 home attendance: 504,500 in 7 games.
Director of Athletics: Barbara Hedges.
Sports Info. Director: Jim Daves   206-543-8333

■ Home games on each schedule [neutral sites shown in brackets].   *Night Games.

*Divisions I-A & I-AA 1993 Schedules and 1992 Results*

## WASHINGTON STATE . . . Pullman, Wash.   99164   I-A

Coach: Mike Price, Puget Sound '69
Record: 12 yrs., W-68, L-67, T-0
1993 SCHEDULE

| | |
|---|---|
| Michigan | Sep 4 |
| Montana St. ■ | Sep 11 |
| Oregon St. ■ | Sep 18 |
| Southern Cal | Sep 25 |
| Pacific (Cal.) | Oct 2* |
| Arizona St. ■ | Oct 9 |
| California | Oct 16 |
| Arizona | Oct 23* |
| Oregon | Oct 30 |
| UCLA ■ | Nov 6 |
| Washington | Nov 20 |

1992 RECORD

| | | | | |
|---|---|---|---|---|
| 25 | Montana | 13 | 20 Arizona St. | 18 |
| 23 | Arizona | 20 | 3 Stanford | 40 |
| 39 | Fresno St. | 37 | 42 Washington | 23 |
| 51 | Temple | 10 | | |
| 35 | Oregon St. | 10 | 306 | 253 |
| 30 | UCLA | 17 | Copper Bowl | |
| 21 | Southern Cal | 31 | 31 Utah | 28 |
| 17 | Oregon | 34 | | |

Conference: Pacific-10.  Enrollment: 17,500.  Colors: Crimson & Gray.
Nickname: Cougars.  Stadium: Clarence D. Martin (1972), 40,000 capacity.  Artificial turf.
1992 home attendance: 153,228 in 6 games.
Director of Athletics: Jim Livengood.
Sports Info. Director: Rod Commons  509-335-0270

---

## WEBER STATE . . . Ogden, Utah   84408   I-AA

Coach: Dave Arslanian, Weber St. '72
Record: 4 yrs., W-22, L-23, T-0
1993 SCHEDULE

| | |
|---|---|
| Sonoma St. ■ | Sep 4* |
| Cal St. Northridge ■ | Sep 11* |
| Idaho ■ | Sep 18* |
| Montana St. | Sep 25 |
| Eastern Wash. ■ | Oct 2* |
| Montana | Oct 9 |
| Boise St. ■ | Oct 16* |
| Nevada | Oct 23 |
| Southern Utah ■ | Oct 30 |
| Northern Ariz. ■ | Nov 6 |
| Idaho St. | Nov 13* |

1992 RECORD

| | | | | |
|---|---|---|---|---|
| 21 | New Mexico St. | 37 | 23 Nevada | 21 |
| 35 | Southern Utah | 24 | 25 Northern Ariz. | 19 |
| 24 | Idaho | 52 | 22 McNeese St. | 23 |
| 47 | Montana St. | 19 | | |
| 14 | Eastern Wash. | 32 | 283 | 269 |
| 24 | Montana | 7 | (6-5-0) | |
| 21 | Boise St. | 24 | | |
| 27 | Idaho St. | 11 | | |

Conference: Big Sky Conf.  Enrollment: 14,500.  Colors: Royal Purple & White.
Nickname: Wildcats.  Stadium: Wildcat (1966), 17,500 capacity.  Natural turf.
1992 home attendance: 42,186 in 5 games.
Director of Athletics: Tom Stewart.
Sports Info. Director: Brad Larsen  801-626-6010

---

## WEST VIRGINIA . . . Morgantown, W.Va.   26505   I-A

Coach: Don Nehlen, Bowling Green '58
Record: 22 yrs., W-145, L-90, T-8
1993 SCHEDULE

| | |
|---|---|
| Eastern Mich. ■ | Sep 4 |
| Maryland | Sep 18 |
| Missouri ■ | Sep 25 |
| Virginia Tech ■ | Oct 2 |
| Louisville ■ | Oct 9 |
| Pittsburgh ■ | Oct 23 |
| Syracuse | Oct 30 |
| Rutgers ■ | Nov 6 |
| Temple | Nov 13 |
| Miami (Fla.) ■ | Nov 20 |
| Boston College | Nov 26 |

1992 RECORD

| | | | | |
|---|---|---|---|---|
| 29 | Miami (Ohio) | 29 | 41 East Caro. | 28 |
| 44 | Pittsburgh | 6 | 9 Rutgers | 13 |
| 34 | Maryland | 33 | 23 Louisiana Tech | 3 |
| 16 | Virginia Tech | 7 | | |
| 24 | Boston College | 24 | 286 | 238 |
| 17 | Syracuse | 20 | (5-4-2) | |
| 26 | Penn St. | 40 | | |
| 23 | Miami (Fla.) | 35 | | |

Conference: Big East Conference.  Enrollment: 20,000.  Colors: Old Gold & Blue.
Nickname: Mountaineers.  Stadium: Mountaineer Field (1980), 63,500 capacity.  Artificial turf.
1992 home attendance: 344,989 in 7 games.
Director of Athletics: Ed Pastilong.
Sports Info. Director: Shelly Poe  304-293-2821

---

## WESTERN CAROLINA . . . Cullowhee, N.C.   28723   I-AA

Coach: Steve Hodgin, North Caro. '71
Record: 3 yrs., W-12, L-21, T-0
1993 SCHEDULE

| | |
|---|---|
| Kansas | Sep 4 |
| Citadel ■ | Sep 18 |
| North Caro. A&T ■ | Sep 25 |
| Furman ■ | Oct 2 |
| Ga. Southern | Oct 9 |
| East Tenn. St. | Oct 16 |
| Tenn.-Chatt. | Oct 23 |
| Newberry ■ | Oct 30 |
| Va. Military ■ | Nov 6 |
| Appalachian St. | Nov 13 |
| Marshall | Nov 20 |

1992 RECORD

| | | | | |
|---|---|---|---|---|
| 42 | Mars Hill | 6 | 29 Furman | 27 |
| 19 | Georgia Tech | 37 | 41 East Tenn. St. | 12 |
| 42 | Ferrum | 0 | 12 Appalachian St. | 14 |
| 6 | Samford | 30 | | |
| 28 | Va. Military | 25 | 332 | 230 |
| 44 | Tenn.-Chatt. | 13 | (7-4-0) | |
| 31 | Citadel | 36 | | |
| 38 | Marshall | 30 | | |

Conference: Southern Conf.  Enrollment: 6,500.  Colors: Purple & Gold.
Nickname: Catamounts.  Stadium: E.J. Whitmire (1974), 12,000 capacity.  Artificial turf.
1992 home attendance: 52,304 in 6 games.
Director of Athletics: Larry B. Travis.
Sports Info. Director: Steve White  704-227-7171

---

## WESTERN ILLINOIS . . . Macomb, III.   61455   I-AA

Coach: Randy Ball, Northeast Mo. St. '73
Record: 3 yrs., W-17, L-16, T-1
1993 SCHEDULE

| | |
|---|---|
| Montana St. ■ | Sep 4* |
| Eastern Mich. | Sep 18* |
| Eastern III. ■ | Sep 25* |
| Illinois St. | Oct 2 |
| Southern III. ■ | Oct 9 |
| Central Fla. | Oct 16 |
| Northern Iowa ■ | Oct 23 |
| Western Ky. | Oct 30 |
| Southwest Mo. St. ■ | Nov 6 |
| St. Ambrose ■ | Nov 13 |
| Indiana St. | Nov 20 |

1992 RECORD

| | | | | |
|---|---|---|---|---|
| 42 | Mo. Western St. | 7 | 37 Illinois St. | 9 |
| 14 | Sam Houston St. | 19 | 63 Morgan St. | 13 |
| 31 | Western Ky. | 30 | 6 Northern Iowa | 37 |
| 22 | Central Fla. | 35 | | |
| 13 | Southwest Mo. St. | 16 | 348 | 262 |
| 50 | Southern III. | 42 | (7-4-0) | |
| 28 | Eastern III. | 24 | | |
| 42 | Indiana St. | 30 | | |

Conference: Gateway.  Enrollment: 13,750.  Colors: Purple & Gold.
Nickname: Leathernecks.  Stadium: Hanson Field (1948), 15,000 capacity.  Natural turf.
1992 home attendance: 47,263 in 7 games.
Director of Athletics: Gil Peterson.
Sports Info. Director: Larry Heimburger  309-298-1133

---

■ Home games on each schedule [neutral sites shown in brackets].   *Night Games.

*1993 NCAA FOOTBALL*

## WESTERN KENTUCKY . . . Bowling Green, Ky.  42101  I-AA

Coach: Jack Harbaugh, Bowling Green '61
Record: 9 yrs., W-40, L-54, T-3

**1993 SCHEDULE**

| | |
|---|---|
| Eastern Ky. | Sep 2* |
| Kansas St. | Sep 11 |
| Austin Peay | Sep 18* |
| Ala.-Birmingham ■ | Sep 25* |
| Jacksonville St. ■ | Oct 2 |
| Southern Ill. | Oct 16 |
| Indiana St. | Oct 23 |
| Western Ill. ■ | Oct 30 |
| Troy St. | Nov 6 |
| Eastern Ill. ■ | Nov 13 |
| Murray St. ■ | Nov 20 |

**1992 RECORD**

| | | | | |
|---|---|---|---|---|
| 7 | Eastern Ky. | 21 | 7 Eastern Ill. | 28 |
| 34 | Indiana St. | 14 | 47 Murray St. | 15 |
| 30 | Western Ill. | 31 | | |
| 14 | Southwestern La. | 17 | 243 (4-6-0) | 258 |
| 6 | Northern Iowa | 34 | | |
| 50 | Central Fla. | 36 | | |
| 41 | Southern Ill. | 39 | | |
| 7 | Illinois St. | 23 | | |

Conference: I-AA Independents.  Enrollment: 15,750.  Colors: Red & White.
Nickname: Hilltoppers.  Stadium: L.T. Smith (1968), 17,500 capacity.  Natural turf.
1992 home attendance: 39,884 in 4 games.
Director of Athletics: Lou Marciani.
Sports Info. Director: Paul Just  502-745-4298

## WESTERN MICHIGAN . . . Kalamazoo, Mich.  49008  I-A

Coach: Al Molde, Gust. Adolphus '66
Record: 22 yrs., W-145, L-84, T-7

**1993 SCHEDULE**

| | |
|---|---|
| Youngstown St. ■ | Sep 2* |
| Purdue | Sep 11 |
| Akron ■ | Sep 18 |
| Miami (Ohio) ■ | Sep 25 |
| Kent | Oct 2 |
| Central Mich. ■ | Oct 9 |
| Eastern Mich. | Oct 23* |
| Army | Oct 30 |
| Ohio | Nov 6 |
| Toledo ■ | Nov 13 |
| Bowling Green | Nov 20 |

**1992 RECORD**

| | | | | |
|---|---|---|---|---|
| 19 | Bowling Green | 29 | 13 Northern Ill. | 7 |
| 17 | Texas Christian | 17 | 7 Miami (Ohio) | 20 |
| 24 | Akron | 20 | 19 Central Mich. | 14 |
| 19 | Ohio | 3 | | |
| 21 | Ball St. | 14 | 197 (7-3-1) | 177 |
| 12 | Toledo | 21 | | |
| 20 | Eastern Mich. | 19 | | |
| 26 | Kent | 13 | | |

Conference: Mid-American Conf.  Enrollment: 27,708.  Colors: Brown & Gold.
Nickname: Broncos.  Stadium: Waldo (1939), 30,000 capacity.  Natural turf.
1992 home attendance: 74,827 in 5 games.
Director of Athletics: To be named.
Sports Info. Director: John Beatty  616-387-4104

## WILLIAM AND MARY . . . Williamsburg, Va.  23185  I-AA

Coach: Jimmye Laycock, Wm. & Mary '70
Record: 13 yrs., W-81, L-64, T-2

**1993 SCHEDULE**

| | |
|---|---|
| New Hampshire ■ | Sep 4 |
| Delaware | Sep 11 |
| Tulane | Sep 18* |
| Harvard ■ | Sep 25 |
| Va. Military [Norfolk, Va.] | Oct 2 |
| Northeastern | Oct 16 |
| Villanova ■ | Oct 23 |
| James Madison ■ | Oct 30 |
| Maine | Nov 6 |
| Massachusetts | Nov 13 |
| Richmond ■ | Nov 20 |

**1992 RECORD**

| | | | | |
|---|---|---|---|---|
| 21 | Va. Military | 16 | 44 Colgate | 26 |
| 31 | Boston U. | 21 | 26 Lehigh | 13 |
| 36 | Harvard | 16 | 34 Richmond | 19 |
| 51 | Brown | 6 | | |
| 21 | Pennsylvania | 19 | 328 (9-2-0) | 205 |
| 43 | Towson St. | 15 | | |
| 7 | Virginia | 33 | | |
| 14 | James Madison | 21 | | |

Conference: Yankee.  Enrollment: 5,500.  Colors: Green, Gold & Silver.
Nickname: Indians, Tribe.  Stadium: Walter Zable (1935), 15,000 capacity.  Natural turf.
1992 home attendance: 60,484 in 5 games.
Director of Athletics: John Randolph.
Sports Info. Director: Jean Elliott  804-221-3368

## WISCONSIN . . . Madison, Wis.  53711  I-A

Coach: Barry Alvarez, Nebraska '69
Record: 3 yrs., W-11, L-22, T-0

**1993 SCHEDULE**

| | |
|---|---|
| Nevada ■ | Sep 4 |
| Southern Methodist | Sep 11* |
| Iowa St. ■ | Sep 18 |
| Indiana ■ | Sep 25 |
| Northwestern ■ | Oct 9 |
| Purdue | Oct 16 |
| Minnesota | Oct 23* |
| Michigan ■ | Oct 30 |
| Ohio St. ■ | Nov 6 |
| Illinois | Nov 20 |
| Michigan St. [Tokyo, Japan] | Dec 5* |

**1992 RECORD**

| | | | | |
|---|---|---|---|---|
| 10 | Washington | 27 | 10 Michigan St. | 26 |
| 39 | Bowling Green | 18 | 34 Minnesota | 6 |
| 18 | Northern Ill. | 17 | 25 Northwestern | 27 |
| 20 | Ohio St. | 16 | | |
| 22 | Iowa | 23 | 212 (5-6-0) | 199 |
| 19 | Purdue | 16 | | |
| 3 | Indiana | 10 | | |
| 12 | Illinois | 13 | | |

Conference: Big Ten Conf.  Enrollment: 43,000.  Colors: Cardinal & White.
Nickname: Badgers.  Stadium: Camp Randall (1917), 77,745 capacity.  Artificial turf.
1992 home attendance: 368,269 in 6 games.
Director of Athletics: Pat Richter.
Sports Info. Director: Steve Malchow  608-262-1811

## WYOMING . . . Laramie, Wyo.  82071  I-A

Coach: Joe Tiller, Montana St. '65
Record: 2 yrs., W-9, L-13, T-1

**1993 SCHEDULE**

| | |
|---|---|
| Oregon St. ■ | Sep 4 |
| Northern Iowa ■ | Sep 11 |
| San Jose St. ■ | Sep 18* |
| Utah ■ | Sep 25 |
| Air Force | Oct 2 |
| UTEP | Oct 9* |
| Hawaii | Oct 23 |
| Fresno St. ■ | Oct 30 |
| New Mexico | Nov 13 |
| Colorado St. ■ | Nov 20 |
| San Diego St. | Nov 27 |

**1992 RECORD**

| | | | | |
|---|---|---|---|---|
| 25 | Nevada | 6 | 31 Fresno St. | 42 |
| 32 | Texas Tech | 49 | 17 San Diego St. | 6 |
| 28 | Air Force | 42 | 7 Utah | 38 |
| 26 | Louisville | 24 | 18 Hawaii | 42 |
| 24 | San Jose St. | 26 | | |
| 35 | New Mexico | 21 | 302 (5-7-0) | 341 |
| 28 | Brigham Young | 31 | | |
| 31 | Colorado St. | 14 | | |

Conference: Western Athl. Conf.  Enrollment: 10,000.  Colors: Brown & Yellow.
Nickname: Cowboys.  Stadium: War Memorial (1950), 33,500 capacity.  Natural turf.
1992 home attendance: 106,964 in 6 games.
Director of Athletics: Paul Roach.
Sports Info. Director: Kevin McKinney  307-766-2256

■ Home games on each schedule [neutral sites shown in brackets].   *Night Games.

*Divisions I-A & I-AA 1993 Schedules and 1992 Results*                     703

## YALE . . . New Haven, Conn.   06520                                            I-AA

Coach: Carmen Cozza, Miami (Ohio) '52
Record: 28 yrs., W-166, L-92, T-5
**1993 SCHEDULE**

| | |
|---|---|
| Brown ■ | Sep 18 |
| Connecticut ■ | Sep 25 |
| Central Fla. | Oct 2 |
| Holy Cross | Oct 9 |
| Dartmouth ■ | Oct 16 |
| Columbia | Oct 23 |
| Pennsylvania ■ | Oct 30 |
| Cornell | Nov 6 |
| Princeton | Nov 13 |
| Harvard ■ | Nov 20 |

**1992 RECORD**

| | | | | | |
|---|---|---|---|---|---|
| 22 | Brown | 17 | 7 | Princeton | 36 |
| 7 | Holy Cross | 3 | 0 | Harvard | 14 |
| 20 | Connecticut | 40 | | | |
| 31 | Fordham | 12 | 161 | (4-6-0) | 209 |
| 27 | Dartmouth | 39 | | | |
| 23 | Columbia | 0 | | | |
| 10 | Pennsylvania | 13 | | | |
| 14 | Cornell | 35 | | | |

Conference: Ivy League.   Enrollment: 5,200.   Colors: Yale Blue and White.
Nickname: Elis, Bulldogs.   Stadium: Yale Bowl (1914), 70,896 capacity.   Natural turf.
1992 home attendance: 60,744 in 5 games.
Director of Athletics: Harold E. Woodsum Jr.
Sports Info. Director: Steve Conn   203-432-1456

---

## YOUNGSTOWN STATE . . . Youngstown, Ohio   44555                      I-AA

Coach: Jim Tressel, Baldwin-Wallace '75
Record: 7 yrs., W-57, L-31, T-1
**1993 SCHEDULE**

| | |
|---|---|
| Western Mich. | Sep 2* |
| Stephen F. Austin | Sep 11* |
| Morgan St. ■ | Sep 18 |
| Eastern Ky. | Oct 2* |
| Delaware St. ■ | Oct 9 |
| Liberty ■ | Oct 16 |
| Samford ■ | Oct 23 |
| Buffalo ■ | Oct 30 |
| Indiana St. ■ | Nov 6 |
| Illinois St. | Nov 13 |
| Akron | Nov 20 |

**1992 RECORD**

| | | | | | |
|---|---|---|---|---|---|
| 48 | Clarion | 7 | 10 | Akron | 10 |
| 42 | Delaware St. | 20 | 21 | Ga. Southern | 10 |
| 23 | Southwest Tex. St. | 20 | | | |
| 49 | James Madison | 52 | 336 | (8-2-1) | 220 |
| 30 | Indiana St. | 24 | | **I-AA Championship** | |
| 34 | Illinois St. | 10 | 23 | Villanova | 20 |
| 23 | Northeastern | 28 | 42 | Citadel | 17 |
| 28 | Eastern Ill. | 19 | 19 | Northern Iowa | 7 |
| 28 | Ohio | 20 | 28 | Marshall | 31 |

Conference: I-AA Independents.   Enrollment: 14,822.   Colors: Scarlet & White.
Nickname: Penguins.   Stadium: Arnold D. Stambaugh (1982), 16,000 capacity.   Artificial turf.
1992 home attendance: 67,665 in 6 games.
Director of Athletics: Joe Malmisur.
Sports Info. Director: Greg Gulas   216-742-3192

---

# Discontinued Division I-A Program

## CAL STATE FULLERTON . . . Fullerton, Calif.   92634                   I-A

**1992 RECORD**

| | | | | | |
|---|---|---|---|---|---|
| 28 | Cal St. Northridge | 7 | 7 | Utah St. | 26 |
| 14 | UCLA | 37 | 20 | Pacific (Cal.) | 23 |
| 0 | Georgia | 56 | 31 | New Mexico St. | 44 |
| 3 | Cal St. Sacramento | 29 | 16 | Nevada-Las Vegas | 33 |
| 0 | Nevada | 19 | | | |
| 3 | San Jose St. | 49 | 136 | (2-9-0) | 333 |
| 14 | Southwestern La. | 10 | | | |

Conference: Big West.   Enrollment: 25,000.   Colors: Blue, Orange & White.
Nickname: Titans.   Stadium: Titan (1992), 10,000 capacity.   Natural turf.
1992 home attendance: 14,642 in 4 games.
Director of Athletics: Bill Shumard.
Sports Info. Director: Mel Franks   714-773-3970

---

■ Home games on each schedule [neutral sites shown in brackets].   *Night Games.

# 1993 SCHEDULES BY DATE

This listing by dates includes all 1993-season games involving Divisions I-A and I-AA teams, as of printing deadline.

Neutral sites, indicated by footnote numbers, are listed at the end of each date. Asterisks (*) indicate night games.

**Game dates and starting times are subject to change.**

| HOME | OPPONENT |
|---|---|
| **Saturday** | |
| **August 28** | |
| Florida St. | Kansas(1) |
| (1) East Rutherford, N.J. | |
| | |
| **Sunday** | |
| **August 29** | |
| Southern Cal | North Caro.(1)* |
| (1) Anaheim, Calif. | |
| | |
| **Thursday** | |
| **September 2** | |
| Auburn | Mississippi* |
| Central Mich. | Akron* |
| Eastern Ky. | Western Ky.* |
| Iowa St. | Northern Ill.* |
| Murray St. | Eastern Ill.* |
| Stephen F. Austin | Idaho* |
| Tenn.-Martin | Tenn.-Chatt.* |
| Western Mich. | Youngstown St.* |
| | |
| **Saturday** | |
| **September 4** | |
| Air Force | Indiana St. |
| Alabama | Tulane(1) |
| Alcorn St. | Grambling |
| Arizona | UTEP* |
| Arizona St. | Utah* |
| Baylor | Fresno St.* |
| Bethune-Cookman | Knoxville(2)* |
| Boise St. | Rhode Island* |
| Boston College | Miami (Fla.) |
| Bucknell | Bloomsburg |
| Buffalo | Maine* |
| Cal St. Sacramento | Cal St. Hayward* |
| Cincinnati | Austin Peay* |
| Citadel | Wofford* |
| Clemson | Nevada-Las Vegas |
| Colorado | Texas |
| Colorado St. | Oregon |
| Delaware | Lehigh |
| Delaware St. | Fayetteville St.(3) |
| Duke | Florida St.* |
| East Tenn. St. | Wingate* |
| Eastern Wash. | Northeast La. |
| Florida | Arkansas St.* |
| Florida A&M | Tennessee St. |
| Furman | Connecticut |
| Georgia | South Caro. |
| Ga. Southern | Savannah St. |
| Hawaii | Middle Tenn. St.* |
| Hofstra | Butler* |
| Howard | Virginia Union |
| Idaho St. | Chadron St.* |
| Indiana | Toledo* |
| Iowa | Tulsa |
| Jackson St. | Tuskegee |
| James Madison | Lock Haven* |

| HOME | OPPONENT |
|---|---|
| Kansas | Western Caro. |
| Kansas St. | New Mexico St. |
| Kentucky | Kent* |
| Liberty | Concord (W. Va.)* |
| Louisville | San Jose St. |
| Marshall | Morehead St.* |
| Maryland | Virginia |
| McNeese St. | Northern Iowa* |
| Michigan | Washington St. |
| Mississippi St. | Memphis St.* |
| Mississippi Val. | Ark.-Pine Bluff* |
| Montana | South Dak. St. |
| Morgan St. | Charleston So. |
| Nebraska | North Texas |
| New Mexico | Brigham Young* |
| Newberry | South Caro. St.* |
| North Caro. | Ohio* |
| North Caro. A&T | Appalachian St. |
| North Caro. St. | Purdue |
| Notre Dame | Northwestern |
| Ohio St. | Rice |
| Penn St. | Minnesota |
| Richmond | Va. Military |
| Rutgers | Colgate* |
| St. Ambrose | Valparaiso |
| St. Francis (Pa.) | Gannon |
| Samford | Glenville St.* |
| San Diego | Menlo* |
| San Diego St. | Cal St. Northridge* |
| San Fran. St. | St. Mary's (Cal.) |
| Southern Cal | Houston |
| Southern Methodist | Arkansas* |
| Southern Miss. | Pittsburgh |
| Southern-B.R. | Northwestern (La.)(4) |
| Southern Utah | Northern Ariz.* |
| Southwestern La. | Utah St.* |
| Southwest Mo. St. | Southeast Mo. St.* |
| Southwest Tex. St. | Texas A&I* |
| Syracuse | Ball St.* |
| Tennessee | Louisiana Tech |
| Tennessee Tech | Illinois St.* |
| Texas A&M | Louisiana St.* |
| Texas Christian | Oklahoma* |
| Texas Southern | Prairie View* |
| Texas Tech | Pacific (Cal.)* |
| UCLA | California* |
| Virginia Tech | Bowling Green |
| Wake Forest | Vanderbilt* |
| Washington | Stanford |
| Weber St. | Sonoma St.* |
| West Va. | Eastern Mich. |
| Western Ill. | Montana St.* |
| William & Mary | New Hampshire |
| Wisconsin | Nevada |
| Wyoming | Oregon St. |
| (1) Birmingham, Ala. | |
| (2) Jacksonville, Fla. | |
| (3) Wilmington, Del. | |
| (4) New Orleans, La. | |
| | |
| **Monday** | |
| **September 6** | |
| Ala.-Birmingham | Troy St. |

| HOME | OPPONENT |
|---|---|
| **Thursday** | |
| **September 9** | |
| East Caro. | Syracuse* |
| Eastern Mich. | Temple* |
| St. John's (N.Y.) | St. Peter's* |
| | |
| **Friday** | |
| **September 10** | |
| Villanova | Northeastern* |
| | |
| **Saturday** | |
| **September 11** | |
| Akron | Kent* |
| Ala.-Birmingham | Morehead St. |
| Alabama St. | Southern-B.R.* |
| Alcorn St. | Texas Southern(1)* |
| Angelo St. | Southern Utah* |
| Appalachian St. | Liberty |
| Arizona | Pacific (Cal.) |
| Arkansas | South Caro. |
| Arkansas St. | New Mexico St.* |
| Army | Colgate |
| Assumption | Siena |
| Auburn | Samford* |
| Austin Peay | Knoxville* |
| Ball St. | Illinois St. |
| Bethune-Cookman | Morgan St. |
| Boston U. | Maine |
| Bowling Green | Cincinnati |
| Brigham Young | Hawaii |
| Buffalo | New Haven* |
| California | San Diego St. |
| Central Fla. | Valdosta St. |
| Central Mich. | Ohio |
| Charleston So. | Presbyterian |
| Colorado | Baylor |
| Colorado St. | Air Force |
| Connecticut | New Hampshire |
| Dayton | Wis.-Platteville* |
| Delaware | William & Mary |
| Delaware St. | Cheyney |
| Drake | Simpson |
| Duquesne | Canisius* |
| East Tenn. St. | Mars Hill* |
| Florida St. | Clemson |
| Fordham | Lehigh |
| Franklin | Evansville |
| Fresno St. | Oregon St.* |
| Ga. Southern | Citadel |
| Georgia Tech | Furman |
| Houston | Tulsa |
| Idaho | Southwest Tex. St. |
| Indiana | Northern Ill. |
| Iowa St. | |
| Jackson St. | Tennessee St.(2)* |
| James Madison | Richmond |
| Kansas St. | Western Ky. |
| Kentucky | Florida* |
| Lafayette | Bucknell |

| HOME | OPPONENT |
|---|---|
| Lane | Mississippi Val.* |
| Langston | Prairie View* |
| Livingston | Nicholls St.* |
| Marshall | Murray St.* |
| Massachusetts | Holy Cross |
| McNeese St. | Eastern Ill.* |
| Memphis St. | Louisville* |
| Miami (Ohio) | Southwestern La.* |
| Michigan | Notre Dame |
| Michigan St. | Kansas |
| Minnesota | Indiana St.* |
| Mississippi | Tenn.-Chatt.* |
| Mississippi St. | Louisiana St.* |
| Missouri | Illinois |
| Nebraska | Texas Tech |
| Nevada | Boise St. |
| North Caro. | Maryland |
| Northeast La. | Eastern Ky.* |
| Northern Ariz. | North Texas* |
| Northwestern (La.) | Troy St.* |
| Ohio St. | Washington* |
| Oklahoma | Texas A&M |
| Oklahoma St. | Southwest Mo. St.* |
| Oregon | Montana |
| Penn St. | Southern Cal |
| Pittsburgh | Virginia Tech* |
| Portland St. | Idaho St.* |
| Purdue | Western Mich. |
| Rhode Island | Hofstra |
| Rice | Tulane |
| Rutgers | Duke* |
| Sacred Heart | Iona |
| St. Francis (Pa.) | Marist |
| St. Mary's (Cal.) | Cal St. Hayward |
| San Diego | La Verne* |
| San Fran. St. | Cal St. Sacramento |
| Sewanee | Davidson |
| South Caro. St. | Florida A&M(3) |
| Southeast Mo. St. | Sam Houston St.* |
| Southern Ill. | Washburn |
| Southern Methodist | Wisconsin* |
| Stanford | San Jose St. |
| Stephen F. Austin | Youngstown St.* |
| Tennessee | Georgia |
| Tenn.-Martin | West Ga.* |
| Tennessee Tech | Lock Haven* |
| Texas Christian | New Mexico* |
| Towson St. | Central Conn. St. |
| Utah | Utah St.* |
| UTEP | Nevada-Las Vegas* |
| Valparaiso | St. Xavier (Ill.) |
| Vanderbilt | Alabama* |
| Virginia | Navy |
| Wagner | LIU-C.W. Post |
| Wake Forest | North Caro. St.* |
| Washington St. | Montana St. |
| Weber St. | Cal St. Northridge* |
| Winston-Salem | North Caro. A&T* |
| Wyoming | Northern Iowa |

(1) Jackson, Miss.
(2) Chicago, Ill.
(3) Columbia, S.C.

## Thursday
## September 16
Georgia Tech .................. Virginia*

## Saturday
## September 18

| HOME | OPPONENT |
|---|---|
| Air Force | San Diego St. |
| Alabama | Arkansas |
| Alabama St. | Alcorn St.* |
| Augustana (Ill.) | Drake |
| Austin Peay | Western Ky.* |
| Bethune-Cookman | Johnson Smith |

| HOME | OPPONENT |
|---|---|
| Boise St. | Northeastern* |
| Buffalo | Lafayette* |
| Buffalo St. | Canisius |
| Cal St. Sacramento | Eastern Wash.* |
| Central Okla. | Southern Utah |
| Cincinnati | Miami (Ohio)* |
| Colorado St. | Brigham Young |
| Connecticut | James Madison |
| Davidson | Rhodes |
| Dayton | Wheaton (Ill.)* |
| Duke | Army* |
| Duquesne | Bethany (W.Va.)* |
| East Caro. | Central Fla. |
| Eastern Mich. | Western Ill.* |
| Evansville | Ky. Wesleyan |
| Florida | Tennessee |
| Florida A&M | Jackson St.* |
| Furman | Wofford |
| Georgetown (Ky.) | Butler |
| Georgia | Texas Tech |
| Harvard | Columbia |
| Hawaii | Kent* |
| Holy Cross | Boston U. |
| Howard | Winston-Salem |
| Illinois | Arizona |
| Illinois St. | McNeese St.* |
| Indiana | Kentucky |
| Iona | Central Conn. St. |
| Iowa | Penn St. |
| Kansas | Utah |
| Lehigh | Hofstra |
| Louisiana St. | Auburn* |
| Louisville | Arizona St. |
| Maine | Massachusetts |
| Marist | Pace |
| Marshall | Ga. Southern* |
| Maryland | West Va. |
| Miami (Fla.) | Virginia Tech |
| Middle Tenn. St. | Campbellsville* |
| Millikin | Valparaiso |
| Minnesota | Kansas St. |
| Mississippi | Vanderbilt* |
| Montana | Idaho St. |
| Montana St. | Fort Lewis |
| Morehead St. | West Va. Tech* |
| Murray St. | Southeast Mo. St.* |
| Navy | Eastern Ill.* |
| Nevada-Las Vegas | Central Mich.* |
| Nevada | Texas Southern |
| New Hampshire | Richmond |
| New Mexico | Fresno St.* |
| New Mexico St. | UTEP* |
| Nicholls St. | Troy St.* |
| North Caro. | Florida St. |
| North Texas | Southwest Mo. St.* |
| Northern Ariz. | Cal St. Northridge* |
| Northern Ill. | Arkansas St.* |
| Northern Iowa | Jacksonville St.* |
| Northwestern | Boston College |
| Notre Dame | Michigan St. |
| Ohio | Ball St. |
| Pennsylvania | Dartmouth |
| Pittsburgh | Ohio St. |
| Princeton | Cornell |
| Rhode Island | Delaware |
| Rice | Sam Houston St. |
| Sacred Heart | St. Francis (Pa.) |
| Samford | Tennessee Tech* |
| San Jose St. | Wyoming* |
| Siena | St. Peter's |
| Sonoma St. | St. Mary's (Cal.) |
| South Caro. | Louisiana Tech* |
| South Caro. St. | Charleston So.* |
| Southern Miss. | Northeast La. |
| Southern-B.R. | Prairie View* |
| Southwestern La. | Memphis St.* |
| Southwest Tex. St. | Liberty |
| Stanford | Colorado* |

| HOME | OPPONENT |
|---|---|
| Stephen F. Austin | Livingston* |
| Temple | California |
| Tenn.-Chatt. | Gardner-Webb* |
| Tennessee St. | Grambling(1)* |
| Texas | Syracuse* |
| Texas A&M | Missouri* |
| Toledo | Southern Ill.* |
| Towson St. | Delaware St. |
| Tulane | William & Mary* |
| Tulsa | Oklahoma St.* |
| UCLA | Nebraska |
| Utah St. | Baylor |
| Villanova | Fordham |
| Va. Military | East Tenn. St. |
| Wagner | St. John's (N.Y.) |
| Wake Forest | Appalachian St.* |
| Washington St. | Oregon St. |
| Weber St. | Idaho* |
| Western Caro. | Citadel |
| Western Mich. | Akron |
| Wisconsin | Iowa St. |
| Yale | Brown |
| Youngstown St. | Morgan St. |

(1) Memphis, Tenn.

## Thursday
## September 23
South Caro. .................. Kentucky*

## Saturday
## September 25

| HOME | OPPONENT |
|---|---|
| Alabama | Louisiana Tech(1) |
| Alabama St. | Troy St.* |
| Alcorn St. | Howard(2) |
| Arizona St. | Oklahoma St.* |
| Arkansas | Memphis St.(3) |
| Arkansas St. | Southern Ill.* |
| Army | Va. Military |
| Auburn | Southern Miss. |
| Baylor | Texas Tech* |
| Boise St. | Stephen F. Austin* |
| Boston College | Temple |
| Boston U. | Massachusetts |
| Brigham Young | Air Force |
| Bucknell | Pennsylvania |
| Buffalo | Edinboro* |
| Butler | Drake |
| Cal St. Northridge | Sonoma St.* |
| California | San Jose St. |
| Canisius | Gannon* |
| Central Fla. | McNeese St. |
| Central St. (Ohio) | Texas Southern |
| Citadel | Appalachian St.* |
| Clemson | Georgia Tech |
| Colorado | Miami (Fla.) |
| Columbia | Fordham |
| Cornell | Colgate* |
| Dartmouth | Holy Cross |
| Dayton | San Diego |
| Delaware | West Chester |
| Eastern Ill. | Western Ill.* |
| Eastern Ky. | Austin Peay* |
| Eastern Wash. | Montana |
| Emory & Henry | Davidson |
| Evansville | Rose-Hulman |
| Fresno St. | Utah St.* |
| Furman | East Tenn. St. |
| Ga. Southern | Tenn.-Chatt. |
| Grambling | Hampton(4)* |
| Hawaii | UTEP* |
| Hofstra | Illinois St.* |
| Humboldt St. | St. Mary's (Cal.)* |
| Idaho St. | Northern Ariz.* |
| Illinois | Oregon |
| Indiana | Wisconsin |

| HOME | OPPONENT |
|---|---|
| Iona | Georgetown |
| James Madison | Jacksonville St. |
| Kansas St. | Nevada-Las Vegas |
| Lafayette | Princeton |
| Lehigh | Brown |
| Liberty | Indiana (Pa.) |
| Louisville | Texas |
| Marist | LIU-C.W. Post |
| Michigan | Houston |
| Michigan St. | Central Mich. |
| Middle Tenn. St. | Murray St.* |
| Mississippi | Georgia* |
| Mississippi Val. | Jackson St.* |
| Montana St. | Weber St. |
| Navy | Bowling Green |
| Nebraska | Colorado St. |
| Nevada | Northern Ill. |
| New Hampshire | Maine |
| New Mexico | New Mexico St.* |
| Nicholls St. | Northeast La.* |
| North Caro. St. | North Caro. |
| North Texas | Abilene Christian* |
| Northern Iowa | Southwest Tex. St.* |
| Northwestern | Wake Forest |
| Northwestern (La.) | East Tex. St.* |
| Oklahoma | Tulsa |
| Oregon St. | Arizona |
| Pacific (Cal.) | Cal St. Sacramento* |
| Penn St. | Rutgers |
| Purdue | Notre Dame |
| Rhode Island | Northeastern |
| Rice | Iowa St. |
| Richmond | Villanova |
| St. Peter's | St. Francis (Pa.)* |
| Sam Houston St. | Texas A&I* |
| Samford | Bethune-Cookman* |
| San Diego St. | Minnesota* |
| Siena | St. John's (N.Y.) |
| South Caro. St. | Southern-B.R.(5) |
| Southern Cal | Washington St. |
| Southern Utah | UC Davis* |
| Southwest Mo. St. | Indiana St.* |
| Stanford | UCLA |
| Syracuse | Cincinnati* |
| Tennessee | Louisiana St. |
| Tenn.-Martin | Southeast Mo. St.* |
| Tennessee Tech | Morehead St.* |
| Texas Christian | Southern Methodist* |
| Thiel | Duquesne |
| Toledo | Ohio* |
| Towson St. | Charleston So. |
| Tulane | Mississippi St.* |
| Virginia | Duke |
| Virginia Tech | Maryland |
| Wagner | Central Conn. St. |
| Washington | East Caro. |
| West Va. | Missouri |
| Western Caro. | North Caro. A&T |
| Western Ky. | Ala.-Birmingham* |
| Western Mich. | Miami (Ohio) |
| William & Mary | Harvard |
| Wyoming | Utah |
| Yale | Connecticut |

(1) Birmingham, Ala.
(2) St. Louis, Mo.
(3) Little Rock, Ark.
(4) East Rutherford, N.J.
(5) Atlanta, Ga.

## Thursday
## September 30

| HOME | OPPONENT |
|---|---|
| St. John's (N.Y.) | Marist* |
| San Diego St. | UCLA* |

## Saturday
## October 2

| HOME | OPPONENT |
|---|---|
| Adrian | Evansville |
| Air Force | Wyoming |
| Alcorn St. | Sam Houston St. |
| Appalachian St. | East Tenn. St. |
| Arizona | Southern Cal |
| Army | Akron |
| Austin Peay | Tennessee Tech* |
| Boston U. | Villanova |
| Bowling Green | Toledo |
| Brown | Rhode Island |
| Bucknell | Dartmouth |
| Butler | Hillsdale |
| California | Oregon |
| Canisius | Mercyhurst |
| Central Fla. | Yale |
| Central Mich. | Ball St. |
| Citadel | Lees-McRae* |
| Clemson | North Caro. St. |
| Colgate | Columbia |
| Connecticut | Towson St. |
| Delaware St. | Bethune-Cookman |
| Drake | Aurora |
| East Caro. | Memphis St. |
| Eastern Ky. | Youngstown St.* |
| Florida | Mississippi St. |
| Florida St. | Georgia Tech* |
| Gannon | Duquesne |
| Georgia | Arkansas |
| Grambling | Prairie View(1)* |
| Guilford | Davidson |
| Harvard | Lafayette |
| Hofstra | Buffalo* |
| Houston | Baylor |
| Howard | Florida A&M |
| Idaho St. | Mesa St.* |
| Illinois St. | Western Ill. |
| Indiana St. | Eastern Ill. |
| Iowa St. | Oklahoma |
| Jackson St. | South Caro. St.(2) |
| Kansas | Colorado St. |
| Kent | Western Mich. |
| Kentucky | Mississippi* |
| Lehigh | Cornell |
| Liberty | North Caro. A&T* |
| Louisiana St. | Utah St.* |
| Louisiana Tech | Arkansas St.* |
| Maryland | Penn St. |
| Massachusetts | James Madison |
| Miami (Fla.) | Ga. Southern |
| Miami (Ohio) | Eastern Mich. |
| Michigan | Iowa |
| Miles | Ala.-Birmingham |
| Minnesota | Indiana* |
| Mississippi Val. | Southern-B.R.* |
| Missouri | Southern Methodist |
| Monmouth (N. J.) | St. Peter's |
| Montana | Boise St. |
| Mt. St. Joseph | Dayton |
| Nevada | Nevada-Las Vegas |
| New Mexico | Hawaii* |
| Nicholls St. | Samford* |
| North Caro. | UTEP |
| Northeast La. | Northwestern (La.)* |
| Northern Ariz. | Montana St.* |
| Northern Ill. | Southern Ill. |
| Ohio St. | Northwestern |
| Oklahoma St. | Texas Christian |
| Oregon St. | Arizona St. |
| Pacific (Cal.) | Washington St.* |
| Pennsylvania | Fordham |
| Pittsburgh | Louisville* |
| Princeton | Holy Cross |
| Purdue | Illinois |
| Richmond | Northeastern |
| Rutgers | Temple* |

| HOME | OPPONENT |
|---|---|
| St. Francis (Pa.) | Central Conn. St. |
| St. Mary's (Cal.) | Cal St. Chico |
| Siena | Georgetown |
| South Caro. | Alabama* |
| Southeast Mo. St. | Morehead St.* |
| Southwestern La. | Southern Miss.* |
| Southwest Mo. St. | Northern Iowa* |
| Stanford | Notre Dame |
| Syracuse | Boston College |
| Tennessee | Duke |
| Tenn.-Chatt. | Marshall* |
| Tenn.-Martin | Murray St.* |
| Texas | Rice* |
| Texas Southern | Knoxville |
| Texas Tech | Texas A&M* |
| Troy St. | Charleston So. |
| Tulane | Navy* |
| Tulsa | Cincinnati |
| Utah | Idaho* |
| Valparaiso | San Diego |
| Vanderbilt | Auburn* |
| Virginia | Ohio |
| Va. Military | William & Mary(3) |
| Wagner | Iona |
| Washington | San Jose St. |
| Weber St. | Eastern Wash.* |
| West Va. | Virginia Tech |
| Western Caro. | Furman |
| Western Ky. | Jacksonville St. |

(1) Dallas, Texas
(2) Indianapolis, Ind.
(3) Norfolk, Va.

## Sunday
## October 3

| HOME | OPPONENT |
|---|---|
| Tennessee St. | Middle Tenn. St. |

## Thursday
## October 7

| HOME | OPPONENT |
|---|---|
| Oklahoma St. | Nebraska* |

## Saturday
## October 9

| HOME | OPPONENT |
|---|---|
| Akron | Miami (Ohio)* |
| Ala.-Birmingham | Lambuth |
| Arkansas | Tennessee(1) |
| Auburn | Mississippi St. |
| Ball St. | Toledo |
| Bethune-Cookman | Howard |
| Boise St. | Northern Ariz.* |
| Brown | Princeton |
| Butler | Valparaiso |
| California | Washington |
| Cal Lutheran | San Diego |
| Cal St. Sacramento | St. Mary's (Cal.)* |
| Canisius | Iona |
| Central Conn. St. | Marist |
| Central Fla. | Samford |
| Chicago | Drake |
| Colgate | Pennsylvania |
| Colorado | Missouri |
| Colorado St. | Fresno St. |
| Columbia | Lafayette |
| Cornell | Harvard |
| Dartmouth | New Hampshire |
| Duke | Clemson |
| Duquesne | Wagner |
| East Tenn. St. | Citadel* |
| Eastern Ky. | Tennessee St.(2) |
| Eastern Mich. | Kent* |
| Eastern Wash. | Portland St. |
| Evansville | Dayton |
| Florida St. | Miami (Fla.) |
| Fordham | Buffalo |

| HOME | OPPONENT |
|---|---|
| Furman | Appalachian St. |
| Georgia | Southern Miss. |
| Ga. Southern | Western Caro. |
| Georgia Tech | Maryland |
| Grambling | Mississippi Val.* |
| Hawaii | San Diego St.* |
| Hofstra | Bucknell |
| Holy Cross | Yale |
| Idaho St. | Idaho |
| Illinois | Ohio St. |
| Indiana | Iowa |
| Jackson St. | Alabama St.* |
| James Madison | Delaware |
| Kansas St. | Kansas |
| Louisiana St. | Florida* |
| Maine | Richmond(3) |
| Marshall | Va. Military* |
| Memphis St. | Arkansas St. |
| Michigan St. | Michigan |
| Minnesota | Purdue* |
| Montana | Weber St. |
| Montana St. | Southern Utah |
| Morgan St. | South Caro. St. |
| Murray St. | Austin Peay |
| Navy | Air Force |
| Nevada-Las Vegas | Cal St. Northridge* |
| New Mexico St. | Northern Ill. |
| Newberry | Charleston So. |
| North Caro. | Wake Forest |
| North Caro. A&T | Florida A&M |
| North Texas | Southwest Tex. St. |
| Northeastern | Boston U. |
| Northeast La. | McNeese St.* |
| Northern Iowa | Indiana St. |
| Northwestern (La.) | Nicholls St. |
| Notre Dame | Pittsburgh |
| Ohio | Bowling Green |
| Oregon | Southern Cal |
| Oregon St. | Pacific (Cal.) |
| Pace | St. John's (N.Y.) |
| Prairie View | West Tex. St. |
| Rensselaer | Siena |
| Rhode Island | Massachusetts(4) |
| Rice | Texas Christian |
| Rutgers | Boston College |
| St. Peter's | Georgetown* |
| Sam Houston St. | Stephen F. Austin |
| South Caro. | East Caro. |
| Southeast Mo. St. | Tennessee Tech |
| Southern Methodist | Baylor |
| Southwest Mo. St. | Illinois St. |
| Temple | Army |
| Tenn.-Martin | Middle Tenn. St.* |
| Texas | Oklahoma(5) |
| Texas A&M | Houston |
| Texas Southern | Southern-B.R.* |
| Texas Tech | North Caro. St.* |
| Troy St. | Liberty |
| Tulane | Southwestern La.* |
| UCLA | Brigham Young* |
| Utah | New Mexico* |
| UTEP | Wyoming* |
| Vanderbilt | Cincinnati* |
| Villanova | Connecticut |
| Wash. & Lee | Davidson |
| Washington St. | Arizona St. |
| West Va. | Louisville |
| Western Ill. | Southern Ill. |
| Western Mich. | Central Mich. |
| Wisconsin | Northwestern |
| Youngstown St. | Delaware St. |

(1) Little Rock, Ark.
(2) Louisville, Ky.
(3) Portland, Maine
(4) Killarney, Ireland
(5) Dallas, Texas

| HOME | OPPONENT |
|---|---|

## Saturday
## October 16

| Alabama | Tennessee(1) |
|---|---|
| Alcorn St. | Prairie View |
| Appalachian St. | Ga. Southern |
| Arizona | Stanford* |
| Arizona St. | Oregon* |
| Arkansas St. | Southwestern La.* |
| Army | Rutgers |
| Auburn | Florida |
| Austin Peay | Tennessee St.* |
| Baylor | Texas A&M* |
| Bentley | Siena |
| Bethune-Cookman | South Caro. St. |
| Bowling Green | Akron |
| Brigham Young | Notre Dame |
| Brown | Bucknell |
| Buffalo | Buffalo St. |
| Cal St. Northridge | Cal St. Sacramento* |
| Central Conn. St. | Springfield |
| Central Fla. | Western Ill. |
| Central Mich. | Eastern Mich. |
| Charleston So. | Lees-McRae |
| Cincinnati | Ball St.* |
| Citadel | Furman |
| Clemson | Wake Forest |
| Columbia | Pennsylvania |
| Connecticut | Massachusetts |
| Cornell | Fordham |
| Davidson | Methodist |
| Dayton | Butler |
| Delaware | Villanova |
| East Caro. | Louisiana Tech |
| East Tenn. St. | Western Caro. |
| Evansville | San Diego |
| Florida A&M | Delaware St. |
| Florida St. | Virginia |
| Fresno St. | Air Force* |
| Georgetown | Frank. & Marsh. |
| Georgia Tech | North Caro. |
| Grambling | Ark.-Pine Bluff(2) |
| Harvard | Holy Cross |
| Houston | Southern Methodist |
| Idaho | Eastern Wash. |
| Idaho St. | Montana St.* |
| Illinois St. | Indiana St. |
| Iowa | Illinois |
| Jackson St. | Southern-B.R.* |
| James Madison | New Hampshire |
| Kansas | Iowa St. |
| Kentucky | Louisiana St.* |
| Lafayette | Hofstra |
| Louisville | Southern Miss. |
| Marist | Duquesne |
| Maryland | Duke |
| McNeese St. | North Texas* |
| Memphis St. | Tulsa |
| Mississippi | Arkansas(3)* |
| Mississippi St. | South Caro.* |
| Mississippi Val. | Ala.-Birmingham |
| Missouri | Oklahoma St. |
| Morehead St. | Middle Tenn. St. |
| Morgan St. | North Caro. A&T |
| Murray St. | Eastern Ky.* |
| Navy | Colgate |
| Nebraska | Kansas St. |
| New Mexico St. | San Jose St. |
| North Caro. St. | Marshall |
| Northeastern | William & Mary |
| Northern Ariz. | Montana* |
| Northern Ill. | Pacific (Cal.) |
| Northern Iowa | Eastern Ill.* |
| Northwestern | Minnesota |
| Ohio | Kent |
| Ohio St. | Michigan St. |
| Oklahoma | Colorado |
| Pace | Wagner |

| HOME | OPPONENT |
|---|---|
| Penn St. | Michigan |
| Pittsburgh | Syracuse |
| Princeton | Lehigh |
| Purdue | Wisconsin |
| Rhode Island | Maine |
| Richmond | Boston U. |
| St. Francis (Pa.) | Monmouth (N. J.) |
| St. John's (N.Y.) | Canisius |
| St. Peter's | Iona* |
| Sam Houston St. | Northwestern (La.) |
| Samford | Mississippi Col. |
| San Diego St. | Colorado St.* |
| San Jose St. | New Mexico St. |
| Southern Cal | Oregon St. |
| Southern Ill. | Western Ky. |
| Southern Utah | Cal Poly SLO |
| Southwest Mo. St. | Jacksonville St. |
| Southwest Tex. St. | Northeast La.* |
| Stephen F. Austin | Nicholls St. |
| Tennessee Tech | Tenn.-Martin |
| Texas Christian | Tulane |
| Texas Southern | Alabama St. |
| Texas Tech | Rice* |
| Toledo | Miami (Ohio)* |
| Towson St. | Howard |
| UCLA | Washington |
| Utah St. | Nevada* |
| UTEP | Utah* |
| Valparaiso | Drake |
| Vanderbilt | Georgia |
| Va. Military | Tenn.-Chatt. |
| Virginia Tech | Temple |
| Washington St. | California |
| Weber St. | Boise St.* |
| Yale | Dartmouth |
| Youngstown St. | Liberty |

(1) Birmingham, Ala.
(2) Shreveport, La.
(3) Jackson, Miss.

## Friday
## October 22

| Johns Hopkins | Georgetown* |
|---|---|

## Saturday
## October 23

| Air Force | Citadel |
|---|---|
| Arizona | Washington St.* |
| Ball St. | Bowling Green |
| Baylor | Texas Christian |
| Bethune-Cookman | Central Fla. |
| Boise St. | Idaho St.* |
| Boston College | Army |
| Boston U. | Rhode Island |
| Brigham Young | Fresno St. |
| Bucknell | Holy Cross |
| Buffalo | Towson St. |
| UC Davis | Cal St. Northridge* |
| Cal Poly SLO | Cal St. Sacramento |
| Central Conn. St. | LIU-C.W. Post |
| Charleston So. | Ala.-Birmingham |
| Clemson | East Tenn. St. |
| Colgate | Lehigh |
| Columbia | Yale |
| Dartmouth | Cornell |
| Davidson | Randolph-Macon |
| Delaware St. | Morgan St. |
| Drake | Dayton |
| Duquesne | Mercyhurst* |
| Eastern Ill. | Illinois St. |
| Eastern Ky. | Tennessee Tech |
| Eastern Mich. | Western Mich.* |
| Eastern Wash. | Northern Ariz. |
| Florida A&M | Albany St. (Ga.)* |
| Georgia | Kentucky |

| HOME | OPPONENT |
|---|---|
| Harvard | Princeton |
| Indiana St. | Western Ky. |
| Iona | Pace |
| Iowa St. | Oklahoma St. |
| Jackson St. | Grambling* |
| Kansas St. | Colorado |
| Kent | Central Mich. |
| Lafayette | Fordham |
| Louisville | Navy |
| Maine | Connecticut |
| Marist | Rensselaer |
| Marshall | Appalachian St.* |
| Massachusetts | Delaware |
| McNeese St. | Sam Houston St. |
| Miami (Fla.) | Syracuse |
| Miami (Ohio) | Ohio |
| Michigan | Illinois |
| Michigan St. | Iowa |
| Middle Tenn. St. | Southeast Mo. St. |
| Minnesota | Wisconsin* |
| Mississippi | Alabama |
| Mississippi St. | Arkansas St. |
| Montana | Jacksonville St. |
| Montana St. | Idaho |
| Morehead St. | Austin Peay |
| Nebraska | Missouri |
| Nevada-Las Vegas | Utah St.* |
| Nevada | Weber St. |
| New Hampshire | Northeastern |
| Nicholls St. | Southwest Tex. St. |
| North Caro. A&T | Howard |
| North Caro. St. | Georgia Tech |
| North Texas | Northwestern (La.) |
| Northeast La. | Stephen F. Austin* |
| Northern Ill. | Southwestern La. |
| Northwestern | Indiana |
| Notre Dame | Southern Cal |
| Oklahoma | Kansas |
| Oregon St. | UCLA |
| Pacific (Cal.) | New Mexico St.* |
| Pennsylvania | Brown |
| Prairie View | Alabama St. |
| Purdue | Ohio St. |
| Rice | Texas A&M |
| St. John's (N.Y.) | Sacred Heart* |
| St. Mary's (Cal.) | Southern Utah |
| St. Peter's | Canisius |
| San Diego | Butler* |
| San Diego St. | New Mexico* |
| San Jose St. | Louisiana Tech* |
| South Caro. | Vanderbilt |
| South Caro. St. | N.C. Central |
| Southern Ill. | Southwest Mo. St. |
| Southern Methodist | Texas(1)* |
| Southern Miss. | East Caro. |
| Southern-B.R. | Alcorn St.* |
| Stanford | Arizona St. |
| Stonehill | Siena |
| Temple | Akron |
| Tenn.-Chatt. | Western Caro. |
| Tenn.-Martin | Tennessee St. |
| Toledo | Cincinnati |
| Troy St. | Central St. (Ohio) |
| Utah | Colorado St. |
| Valparaiso | Evansville |
| Virginia | North Caro. |
| Va. Military | Ga. Southern |
| Virginia Tech | Rutgers |
| Wagner | St. Francis (Pa.) |
| Wake Forest | Duke |
| Washington | Oregon |
| West Va. | Pittsburgh |
| Western Iowa | Northern Iowa |
| William & Mary | Villanova |
| Wyoming | Hawaii |
| Youngstown St. | Samford |
| (1) San Antonio, Texas | |

## Thursday
## October 28

| HOME | OPPONENT |
|---|---|
| Rutgers | Pittsburgh* |

## Saturday
## October 30

| HOME | OPPONENT |
|---|---|
| Air Force | UTEP |
| Alabama | Southern Miss. |
| Alabama A&M | Alabama St.(1) |
| Alcorn St. | Jacksonville St. |
| Appalachian St. | Tenn.-Chatt. |
| Arizona St. | Washington* |
| Arkansas | Auburn |
| Army | Western Mich. |
| Assumption | St. Peter's |
| Austin Peay | Southeast Mo. St. |
| Bethune-Cookman | North Caro. A&T |
| Boise St. | Montana St. |
| Boston College | Tulane |
| Brown | Cornell |
| Cal St. Northridge | Cal St. Chico* |
| California | Southern Cal |
| Canisius | St. Francis (Pa.) |
| Cincinnati | Memphis St. |
| Citadel | Marshall |
| Clemson | Maryland |
| Colorado | Nebraska |
| Colorado St. | New Mexico |
| Dartmouth | Harvard |
| Davidson | Hampden-Sydney |
| Dayton | Valparaiso |
| Delaware | Maine |
| Drake | Ill. Benedictine |
| Duke | Georgia Tech |
| Duquesne | St. John's (N.Y.) |
| Eastern Ill. | Southwest Mo. St. |
| Eastern Ky. | Tenn.-Martin |
| Eastern Mich. | Ball St. |
| Eastern Wash. | Idaho St. |
| Evansville | Butler |
| Florida | Georgia(2) |
| Florida A&M | Morgan St.(3)* |
| Florida St. | Wake Forest |
| Fordham | Bucknell |
| Furman | Va. Military |
| Georgetown | Catholic |
| Grambling | Texas Southern |
| Hofstra | Towson St.* |
| Howard | Morehouse |
| Illinois | Northwestern |
| Illinois St. | Northern Iowa |
| Indiana | Michigan St. |
| Indiana St. | Southern Ill. |
| Iowa | Purdue |
| Kansas St. | Oklahoma |
| Kent | Toledo |
| Lafayette | Colgate |
| Lehigh | Holy Cross |
| Liberty | Charleston So. |
| Louisiana St. | Mississippi* |
| Louisiana Tech | Northern Ill. |
| Marist | Wagner |
| Miami (Fla.) | Temple |
| Miami (Ohio) | Bowling Green |
| Mississippi St. | Kentucky |
| Missouri | Iowa St. |
| Montana | Cal St. Sacramento |
| Navy | Notre Dame(4) |
| Nevada-Las Vegas | New Mexico St.* |
| New Hampshire | Boston U. |
| North Caro. St. | Virginia |
| Northeastern | Massachusetts |
| Northern Ariz. | Idaho* |
| Northwestern (La.) | Southwest Tex. St.* |
| Ohio | Akron |
| Ohio St. | Penn St. |

## HOME OPPONENT

| HOME | OPPONENT |
|---|---|
| Oklahoma St. | Kansas |
| Oregon | Washington St. |
| Pacific (Cal.) | Nevada |
| Prairie View | Mississippi Val. |
| Princeton | Columbia |
| Richmond | Connecticut |
| St. Mary's (Cal.) | UC Davis |
| Sam Houston St. | North Texas |
| San Diego | Azusa Pacific* |
| Siena | Iona |
| South Caro. St. | Delaware St. |
| Southern Conn. St. | Central Conn. St. |
| Southern-B.R. | Nicholls St.* |
| Southwestern La. | San Jose St. |
| Stanford | Oregon St. |
| Stephen F. Austin | McNeese St. |
| Syracuse | West Va. |
| Tennessee | South Caro. |
| Tennessee St. | Morehead St. |
| Tennessee Tech | Murray St. |
| Texas | Texas Tech |
| Texas A&M | Southern Methodist |
| Texas Christian | Houston |
| Troy St. | Central Fla. |
| Tulsa | Middle Tenn. St. |
| UCLA | Arizona |
| Utah | San Diego St. |
| Utah St. | Brigham Young |
| Villanova | Rhode Island |
| Virginia Tech | East Caro. |
| Weber St. | Southern Utah |
| Western Caro. | Newberry |
| Western Ky. | Western Ill. |
| William & Mary | James Madison |
| Wisconsin | Michigan |
| Wofford | Ala.-Birmingham* |
| Wyoming | Fresno St. |
| Yale | Pennsylvania |
| Youngstown St. | Buffalo |
| (1) Birmingham, Ala. | |
| (2) Jacksonville, Fla. | |
| (3) Orlando, Fla. | |
| (4) Philadelphia, Pa. | |

## Thursday
## November 4

| HOME | OPPONENT |
|---|---|
| Houston | Texas* |

## Friday
## November 5

| HOME | OPPONENT |
|---|---|
| Knoxville | Morgan St. |

## Saturday
## November 6

| HOME | OPPONENT |
|---|---|
| Air Force | Army |
| Akron | Eastern Mich. |
| Alabama | Louisiana St. |
| Alabama St. | Grambling* |
| Alcorn St. | Mississippi Val. |
| Arizona | Oregon* |
| Arizona St. | California* |
| Arkansas | Mississippi St.(1) |
| Arkansas St. | Northeast La. |
| Auburn | New Mexico St. |
| Ball St. | Miami (Ohio) |
| Boston College | Virginia Tech |
| Boston U. | Buffalo |
| Bowling Green | Kent |
| Brown | Harvard |
| Bucknell | Lehigh |
| Butler | Ala.-Birmingham |
| Cal Poly SLO | Cal St. Northridge* |
| Central Conn. St. | St. Peter's |
| Central Fla. | Liberty |

| HOME | OPPONENT |
|---|---|
| Centre | Davidson |
| Columbia | Dartmouth |
| Cornell | Yale |
| Dayton | Urbana |
| Delaware | Towson St. |
| Duke | North Caro. St. |
| East Caro. | Tulsa |
| Eastern Ill. | Northwestern (La.) |
| Evansville | Cumberland (Tenn.) |
| Florida | Southwestern La. |
| Florida A&M | Southern-B.R. |
| Fordham | Colgate |
| Fresno St. | UTEP* |
| Georgetown | St. John's (N.Y.) |
| Ga. Southern | Furman |
| Georgia Tech | Baylor |
| Hawaii | Utah* |
| Holy Cross | Lafayette |
| Howard | South Caro. St. |
| Idaho | Montana |
| Illinois | Minnesota |
| Iona | Marist |
| Iowa | Northern Ill. |
| Iowa St. | Kansas St. |
| Jackson St. | Texas Southern* |
| Kansas | Nebraska |
| Louisiana Tech | Nevada-Las Vegas |
| Maine | William & Mary |
| Marshall | East Tenn. St. |
| Maryland | Florida St. |
| Massachusetts | Richmond |
| Memphis St. | Mississippi |
| Michigan | Purdue |
| Michigan St. | Northwestern |
| Middle Tenn. St. | Austin Peay |
| Missouri | Oklahoma |
| Monmouth (N. J.) | Wagner |
| Montana St. | Eastern Wash. |
| Murray St. | Morehead St. |
| Nevada | San Jose St. |
| New Mexico | Idaho St. |
| Newport News App. | Charleston So. |
| Nicholls St. | Sam Houston St.* |
| North Caro. | Clemson |
| North Caro. A&T | Delaware St. |
| North Texas | Stephen F. Austin |
| Northeastern | James Madison |
| Northern Iowa | Moorhead St.* |
| Ohio | Western Mich. |
| Oklahoma St. | Colorado |
| Oregon St. | Washington |
| Penn St. | Indiana |
| Pennsylvania | Princeton |
| Pittsburgh | Miami (Fla.) |
| Prairie View | Ark.-Pine Bluff |
| Rhode Island | Connecticut |
| St. Francis (Pa.) | Duquesne |
| Samford | Tenn.-Martin |
| San Diego | Drake |
| Siena | Canisius |
| Southeast Mo. St. | Eastern Ky. |
| Southern Cal | Stanford |
| Southern Ill. | Illinois St. |
| Southern Methodist | Rice |
| Southern Miss. | Tulane |
| Southern Utah | Portland St. |
| Southwest Tex. St. | McNeese St.* |
| Syracuse | Temple |
| Tennessee | Louisville |
| Tenn.-Chatt. | Citadel |
| Tennessee St. | Tennessee Tech* |
| Texas Tech | Texas Christian |
| Toledo | Central Mich. |
| Troy St. | Western Ky. |
| Utah St. | Pacific (Cal.) |
| Valparaiso | Michigan Tech |
| Vanderbilt | Kentucky |
| Villanova | New Hampshire |

| HOME | OPPONENT |
|---|---|
| Virginia | Wake Forest |
| Washington St. | UCLA |
| Weber St. | Northern Ariz. |
| West Va. | Rutgers |
| Western Caro. | Va. Military |
| Western Ill. | Southwest Mo. St. |
| Western N. Mex. | St. Mary's (Cal.) |
| Wisconsin | Ohio St. |
| Youngstown St. | Indiana St. |
| (1) Little Rock, Ark. | |

## Thursday
## November 11

| San Diego St. | Brigham Young* |
|---|---|

## Friday
## November 12

| St. John's (N.Y.) | Iona* |
|---|---|

## Saturday
## November 13

| HOME | OPPONENT |
|---|---|
| Akron | Ball St. |
| Alabama | Mississippi St. |
| Ala.-Birmingham | Dayton |
| Appalachian St. | Western Caro. |
| Arkansas | Tulsa |
| Army | Lafayette |
| Baylor | Rice |
| Boise St. | Eastern Wash. |
| Cal St. Northridge | Southern Utah* |
| California | Arizona |
| Canisius | Georgetown |
| Central Conn. St. | Duquesne |
| Central Fla. | Buffalo |
| Central Mich. | Bowling Green |
| Charleston So. | Wofford |
| Citadel | Va. Military |
| Clemson | Virginia |
| Colorado | Kansas |
| Connecticut | Boston U. |
| Cornell | Columbia |
| Dartmouth | Brown |
| Davidson | Bridgewater (Va.) |
| Delaware | Richmond |
| Delaware St. | Liberty |
| Drake | Evansville |
| East Tenn. St. | Tenn.-Chatt. |
| East Tex. St. | Texas Southern |
| Eastern Ky. | Middle Tenn. St. |
| Eastern Mich. | Ohio |
| Fordham | Hofstra |
| Fresno St. | Hawaii* |
| Furman | Marshall |
| Georgia | Auburn |
| Ga. Southern | Concord (W. Va.) |
| Grambling | Florida A&M |
| Harvard | Pennsylvania |
| Holy Cross | Colgate |
| Houston | Cincinnati |
| Idaho | Lehigh |
| Idaho St. | Weber St.* |
| Illinois St. | Youngstown St. |
| Indianapolis | Butler |
| Indiana St. | West Va. Tech |
| Kansas St. | Missouri |
| Kent | Miami (Ohio) |
| Kentucky | East Caro. |
| Maine | Northeastern |
| Marist | Siena |
| Massachusetts | William & Mary |
| Memphis St. | Southern Miss. |
| Mercyhurst | St. Francis (Pa.) |
| Miami (Fla.) | Rutgers |
| Minnesota | Michigan* |

| HOME | OPPONENT |
|---|---|
| Mississippi | Northern Ill. |
| Mississippi Val. | Alabama St. |
| Montana St. | Montana |
| Morehead St. | Tenn.-Martin |
| Morgan St. | Howard |
| Nebraska | Iowa St. |
| New Hampshire | Rhode Island |
| New Mexico | Wyoming |
| New Mexico St. | Nevada |
| Norfolk St. | Bethune-Cookman |
| North Caro. A&T | Johnson Smith |
| North Caro. St. | Maryland |
| North Texas | Nicholls St. |
| Northern Ariz. | Valparaiso* |
| Northern Iowa | Southern Ill.* |
| Northwestern | Iowa |
| Northwestern (La.) | McNeese St. |
| Notre Dame | Florida St. |
| Ohio St. | Indiana |
| Oklahoma | Oklahoma St. |
| Oregon | Stanford |
| Pacific (Cal.) | Arkansas St. |
| Penn St. | Illinois |
| Pittsburgh | Boston College |
| Prairie View | Jackson St. |
| Princeton | Yale |
| Purdue | Michigan St. |
| Cal St. Sacramento | UC Davis* |
| St. Mary's (Cal.) | Cal Poly SLO |
| St. Peter's | Jersey City St. |
| Sam Houston St. | Northeast La. |
| San Diego | Wagner* |
| San Jose St. | Nevada-Las Vegas* |
| South Caro. | Florida |
| Southeast Mo. St. | Kentucky St. |
| Southern Methodist | Texas Tech |
| Southwest Mo. St. | Samford |
| Stephen F. Austin | Southwest Tex. St. |
| Temple | West Va. |
| Tennessee St. | Murray St. |
| Texas | Texas Christian |
| Texas A&M | Louisville |
| Towson St. | Bucknell |
| Troy St. | Alcorn St. |
| Tulane | North Caro.* |
| UCLA | Arizona St. |
| Utah | Air Force |
| Utah St. | Louisiana Tech |
| UTEP | Colorado St.* |
| Vanderbilt | Navy |
| Villanova | James Madison |
| Virginia Tech | Syracuse |
| Wake Forest | Georgia Tech |
| Washington | Southern Cal |
| Western Ill. | St. Ambrose |
| Western Ky. | Eastern Ill. |
| Western Mich. | Toledo |

## Friday
## November 19

| Toledo | Eastern Mich.* |
|---|---|

## Saturday
## November 20

| HOME | OPPONENT |
|---|---|
| Akron | Youngstown St. |
| Ala.-Birmingham | Prairie View |
| Arkansas St. | Nevada |
| Auburn | Alabama |
| Austin Peay | Tenn.-Martin |
| Ball St. | Kent |
| Bowling Green | Western Mich. |
| Brigham Young | Utah |
| Brown | Columbia |
| Cincinnati | East Caro. |
| Colgate | Bucknell |

| HOME | OPPONENT |
|---|---|
| Dartmouth | Princeton |
| Delaware St. | Howard |
| East Tenn. St. | Ga. Southern |
| Florida | Vanderbilt |
| Florida St. | North Caro. St. |
| Fresno St. | San Diego St.* |
| Georgetown | Wash. & Lee(1) |
| Hawaii | Air Force* |
| Holy Cross | Fordham |
| Houston | Texas Tech(2)* |
| Idaho | Boise St. |
| Illinois | Wisconsin |
| Indiana | Purdue |
| Indiana St. | Western Ill. |
| Iowa | Minnesota |
| Iowa St. | Colorado |
| Jackson St. | Alcorn St. |
| James Madison | Boston U. |
| Kansas | Missouri |
| Kentucky | Tennessee |
| Lehigh | Lafayette |
| Liberty | Villanova |
| Louisiana St. | Tulane* |
| Louisiana Tech | Central Fla.* |
| Maine | Hofstra |
| Marshall | Western Caro. |
| Massachusetts | New Hampshire |
| McNeese St. | Nicholls St.* |
| Miami (Ohio) | Central Mich. |
| Michigan | Ohio St. |
| Mississippi Val. | Texas Southern |
| Morehead St. | Eastern Ky. |
| Morgan St. | Towson St. |
| Navy | Southern Methodist |
| Nevada-Las Vegas | Southwestern La. |
| New Mexico St. | Utah St. |
| Northeastern | Delaware |
| Northeast La. | North Texas* |
| Northwestern | Penn St. |
| Northwestern (La.) | Stephen F. Austin |
| Notre Dame | Boston College |
| Oklahoma St. | Kansas St. |

| HOME | OPPONENT |
|---|---|
| Oregon | Oregon St. |
| Pennsylvania | Cornell |
| Cal St. Sacramento | Southern Utah* |
| Samford | Troy St. |
| San Jose St. | Pacific (Cal.)* |
| South Caro. | Clemson |
| South Caro. St. | North Caro. A&T |
| Southeast Mo. St. | Tennessee St. |
| Southern Cal | UCLA |
| Southern Ill. | Eastern Ill. |
| Southwest Tex. St. | Sam Houston St. |
| Stanford | California |
| Temple | Pittsburgh |
| Tenn.-Chatt. | Furman |
| Tennessee Tech | Middle Tenn. St. |
| Texas | Baylor |
| Texas Christian | Texas A&M |
| Tulsa | Southern Miss. |
| UTEP | New Mexico |
| Virginia | Virginia Tech |
| Va. Military | Appalachian St. |
| Wake Forest | Maryland |
| Washington | Washington St. |
| West Va. | Miami (Fla.) |
| Western Ky. | Murray St. |
| William & Mary | Richmond |
| Wyoming | Colorado St. |
| Yale | Harvard |
| (1) Hamilton, Bermuda | |
| (2) San Antonio, Texas | |

## Thursday
## November 25

| | |
|---|---|
| Georgia Tech | Georgia |
| St. John's (N.Y.) | Stony Brook |
| Texas A&M | Texas* |
| Tulsa | Louisville |

| HOME | OPPONENT |
|---|---|

## Friday
## November 26

| | |
|---|---|
| Arizona St. | Arizona* |
| Boston College | West Va. |
| Nebraska | Oklahoma |
| North Caro. | Duke |
| Rice | Houston |
| Rutgers | Syracuse |

## Saturday
## November 27

| | |
|---|---|
| Bethune-Cookman | Florida A&M(1) |
| Brigham Young | UTEP |
| Florida | Florida St. |
| Grambling | Southern-B.R.(2) |
| Hawaii | California* |
| Louisiana St. | Arkansas* |
| Miami (Fla.) | Memphis St. |
| Michigan St. | Penn St. |
| Mississippi St. | Mississippi |
| San Diego St. | Wyoming |
| Southwestern La. | Louisiana Tech* |
| Tennessee | Vanderbilt |
| UTEP | Brigham Young |
| (1) Tampa, Fla. | |
| (2) New Orleans, La. | |

## Saturday
## December 4

| | |
|---|---|
| Army | Navy(1) |
| Hawaii | Tulane* |
| (1) East Rutherford, N.J. | |

## Sunday
## December 5

| | |
|---|---|
| Wisconsin | Michigan St.(1)* |

# 1993 NCAA Divisions II & III Schedules

Below each school's name and location is the name of its 1993 head coach and his won-lost-tied record for all seasons as a college head coach.

Schedules for 1993 are on the left, with 1992 records on the right.

Home games on each schedule are indicated by a square (■) and night games are indicated by an asterisk (*). Neutral sites are designated by symbol (†).

**Game dates and starting times are subject to change.**

## ABILENE CHRISTIAN .............. Abilene, TX 79699
*Bob Strader (1st yr. as head coach)*

| 1993 Opponent | Date | 1992 Pts | 1992 Opponent | Opp Pts |
|---|---|---|---|---|
| Western N. Mex. † | S 4* | 0 | North Texas | 41 |
| Midwestern St. | S11 | 9 | Cal St. Sacramento | 57 |
| Adams St. ■ | S18* | 24 | Midwestern St. | 10 |
| North Texas | S25* | 6 | Eastern N. Mex. | 30 |
| Eastern N. Mex. ■ | O 2 | 35 | Central Okla. | 31 |
| Central Okla. ■ | O 9 | 7 | Angelo St. | 48 |
| Angelo St. ■ | O16* | 12 | Cameron | 7 |
| Tarleton St. | O23 | 10 | East Tex. St. | 52 |
| East Tex. St. ■ | O30 | 14 | Texas A&I | 38 |
| Texas A&I ■ | N 6 | | | |

Colors: Purple & White. Nickname: Wildcats. II

## ADAMS STATE ................... Alamosa, CO 81102
*Jeff Geiser (9 yrs., 53-37-1)*

| 1993 Opponent | Date | 1992 Pts | 1992 Opponent | Opp Pts |
|---|---|---|---|---|
| Southwestern Okla. ■ | S11 | 25 | Northwestern Okla. | 15 |
| Abilene Christian | S18* | 10 | Southwestern Okla. | 21 |
| Northwestern Okla. | S25* | 31 | Western St. | 64 |
| Chadron St. ■ | O 2 | 28 | Chadron St. | 38 |
| Colorado Mines ■ | O 9 | 36 | Colorado Mines | 46 |
| Fort Hays St. ■ | O16 | 17 | Fort Hays St. | 31 |
| Fort Lewis | O23 | 60 | Fort Lewis | 36 |
| Mesa St. ■ | O30 | 10 | Mesa St. | 21 |
| N.M. Highlands | N 6 | 21 | N.M. Highlands | 41 |
| Western St. ■ | N13 | 30 | Western N. Mex. | 21 |

Colors: Green & White. Nickname: Indians. II

## ADRIAN ........................ Adrian, MI 49221
*Jim Lyall (3 yrs., 10-16-1)*

| 1993 Opponent | Date | 1992 Pts | 1992 Opponent | Opp Pts |
|---|---|---|---|---|
| Mount Union ■ | S11 | 12 | Mount Union | 21 |
| Defiance | S18 | 14 | Defiance | 17 |
| Ill. Wesleyan | S25 | 20 | Ill. Wesleyan | 24 |
| Evansville ■ | O 2 | 12 | Evansville | 43 |
| Albion ■ | O 9 | 42 | Olivet | 7 |
| Kalamazoo | O16 | 20 | Alma | 6 |
| Olivet | O23 | 14 | Hope | 19 |
| Hope ■ | O30 | 10 | Albion | 21 |
| Alma | N 6 | 16 | Kalamazoo | 18 |

Colors: Gold & Black. Nickname: Bulldogs. III

## ALABAMA A&M .................... Normal, AL 35762
*Raymond Bonner (2 yrs., 5-11-0)*

| 1993 Opponent | Date | 1992 Pts | 1992 Opponent | Opp Pts |
|---|---|---|---|---|
| Miles | S 4 | 6 | Jacksonville St. | 7 |
| Jacksonville St. | S11 | 7 | Howard | 28 |
| North Ala. ■ | S18* | 7 | North Ala. | 15 |
| Savannah St. ■ | S25* | 14 | Savannah St. | 31 |
| Morris Brown ■ | O 2 | 9 | Morris Brown | 10 |
| Morehouse† | O 9 | 20 | Morehouse | 9 |
| Albany St. (Ga.) † | O16 | 3 | Albany St. (Ga.) | 10 |
| Fort Valley St. ■ | O23 | 0 | Fort Valley St. | 16 |
| Alabama St.† | O30 | 11 | Alabama St. | 14 |
| Clark Atlanta | N 6 | 29 | Clark Atlanta | 21 |
| Tuskegee ■ | N13 | 26 | Tuskegee | 14 |

Colors: Maroon & White. Nickname: Bulldogs. II

## ALBANY (NEW YORK) .............. Albany, NY 12222
*Robert Ford (24 yrs., 126-100-1)*

| 1993 Opponent | Date | 1992 Pts | 1992 Opponent | Opp Pts |
|---|---|---|---|---|
| Ithaca | S11 | 7 | Ithaca | 51 |
| St. Lawrence ■ | S18 | 14 | Springfield | 28 |
| Brockport St. ■ | S25* | 41 | Brockport St. | 33 |
| Alfred | O 2 | 49 | Alfred | 21 |
| Union (N.Y.) | O 9 | 23 | Union (N.Y.) | 17 |
| Cortland St. | O16 | 0 | Cortland St. | 35 |
| Norwich | O23 | 35 | Norwich | 32 |
| Salisbury St. | O30 | 48 | Salisbury St. | 7 |
| Western Conn. St. ■ | N 6 | 50 | Western Conn. St. | 0 |
| Wm. Paterson ■ | N13* | 19 | St. Lawrence | 24 |

Colors: Purple & Gold. Nickname: Great Danes. III

## ALBANY STATE (GEORGIA) ........ Albany, GA 31705
*Hampton Smith (17 yrs., 93-74-4)*

| 1993 Opponent | Date | 1992 Pts | 1992 Opponent | Opp Pts |
|---|---|---|---|---|
| Livingston | S 4* | 70 | Miles | 6 |
| Miles | S11 | 36 | Livingston | 42 |
| West Ga. | S18 | 10 | Morehouse | 17 |
| Morehouse ■ | S25 | 14 | Tuskegee | 14 |
| Tuskegee | O 2 | 33 | Savannah St. | 24 |
| Savannah St. | O 9 | 10 | Alabama A&M | 3 |
| Alabama A&M† | O16 | 7 | Bethune-Cookman | 14 |
| Florida A&M | O23* | 41 | Clark Atlanta | 7 |
| Clark Atlanta | O30 | 34 | Morris Brown | 0 |
| Morris Brown ■ | N 6 | 29 | Fort Valley St. | 10 |
| Fort Valley St.† | N13 | | | |

Colors: Blue & Gold. Nickname: Golden Rams. II

## ALBION ........................ Albion, MI 49224
*Pete Schmidt (10 yrs., 64-24-4)*

| 1993 Opponent | Date | 1992 Pts | 1992 Opponent | Opp Pts |
|---|---|---|---|---|
| Thiel ■ | S 4 | 20 | Thiel | 0 |
| Ohio Wesleyan | S11 | 17 | Ohio Wesleyan | 21 |
| Wabash ■ | S18 | 25 | Wabash | 24 |
| DePauw | S25 | 45 | DePauw | 20 |
| Adrian | O 9 | 49 | Kalamazoo | 12 |
| Olivet ■ | O16 | 37 | Hope | 0 |
| Hope | O23 | 35 | Olivet | 20 |
| Alma ■ | O30 | 21 | Adrian | 10 |
| Kalamazoo ■ | N 6 | 31 | Alma | 7 |

Colors: Purple & Gold. Nickname: Britons. III

## ALBRIGHT ...................... Reading, PA 19612
*Kevin Kiesel (1st yr. as head coach)*

| 1993 Opponent | Date | 1992 Pts | 1992 Opponent | Opp Pts |
|---|---|---|---|---|
| King's (Pa.) ■ | S11 | 0 | Western Md. | 28 |
| Juniata | S18 | 10 | Wilkes | 19 |
| Lycoming | S25 | 35 | Lebanon Valley | 41 |
| Susquehanna ■ | O 2 | 11 | Delaware Valley | 40 |
| FDU-Madison | O 9 | 22 | Merchant Marine | 49 |
| Widener ■ | O16 | 33 | Widener | 35 |
| Moravian | O23 | 21 | Juniata | 33 |
| Lebanon Valley | O30 | 30 | Lycoming | 33 |
| Delaware Valley ■ | N 6 | 20 | Moravian | 28 |
| Monmouth (N. J.) ■ | N13 | 16 | Susquehanna | 47 |

Colors: Cardinal & White. Nickname: Lions. III

## ALFRED ........................ Alfred, NY 14802
*Jim Moretti (8 yrs., 50-29-2)*

| 1993 Opponent | Date | 1992 Pts | 1992 Opponent | Opp Pts |
|---|---|---|---|---|
| Denison | S 4 | 24 | St. John Fisher | 6 |
| Frostburg St. ■ | S11 | 15 | Brockport St. | 14 |
| Brockport St. | S18 | 15 | Ithaca | 45 |
| Ithaca ■ | S25 | 21 | Albany (N.Y.) | 49 |
| Albany (N.Y.) | O 2 | 36 | St. Lawrence | 26 |
| St. Lawrence ■ | O 9 | 17 | Hobart | 28 |
| Hobart ■ | O23 | 13 | Mercyhurst | 9 |
| Union (N.Y.) | O30 | 13 | Buffalo St. | 44 |
| Merchant Marine | N 6 | 23 | Canisius | 27 |
| LIU-C.W. Post ■ | N13 | 21 | LIU-C.W. Post | 43 |

Colors: Purple & Gold. Nickname: Saxons. III

## ALLEGHENY ..................... Meadville, PA 16335
*Ken O'Keefe (3 yrs., 32-3-1)*

| 1993 Opponent | Date | 1992 Pts | 1992 Opponent | Opp Pts |
|---|---|---|---|---|
| Westminster (Pa.) ■ | S11 | 0 | Westminster (Pa.) | 20 |
| Wooster ■ | S18 | 56 | Wooster | 7 |
| Case Reserve | S25 | 32 | Case Reserve | 0 |
| Carnegie Mellon | O 2 | 35 | Carnegie Mellon | 21 |
| Wittenberg ■ | O 9 | 12 | Wittenberg | 17 |
| Kenyon | O16 | 41 | Kenyon | 14 |
| Oberlin ■ | O23 | 56 | Oberlin | 0 |
| Denison | O30 | 52 | Denison | 13 |
| Ohio Wesleyan ■ | N 6 | 32 | Ohio Wesleyan | 25 |
| Earlham | N13 | 68 | Earlham | 6 |

Colors: Blue & Gold. Nickname: Gators. III

■ Home games on each schedule.   *Night Games.

## ALMA ........................ Alma, MI 48801
*Jim Cole (2 yrs., 7-11-0)*

| 1993 Opponent | Date | Pts | 1992 Opponent | Opp |
|---|---|---|---|---|
| John Carroll | S 11 | 3 | John Carroll | 28 |
| Franklin | S 18 | 31 | Franklin | 18 |
| Wis.-River Falls ■ | S 25 | 42 | Bluffton | 6 |
| Ill. Benedictine ■ | O 2 | 26 | Ill. Benedictine | 47 |
| Olivet | O 9 | 6 | Hope | 35 |
| Hope ■ | O16 | 6 | Adrian | 20 |
| Kalamazoo ■ | O23 | 17 | Kalamazoo | 7 |
| Albion | O30 | 7 | Olivet | 33 |
| Adrian ■ | N 6 | 7 | Albion | 31 |

Colors: Maroon & Cream.   Nickname: Scots.   **III**

## AMERICAN INTERNATIONAL ... Springfield, MA 01109
*Alex Rotsko (10 yrs., 52-46-3)*

| 1993 Opponent | Date | Pts | 1992 Opponent | Opp |
|---|---|---|---|---|
| Springfield | S 11 | 37 | Springfield | 13 |
| Millersville ■ | S 18 | 6 | Millersville | 31 |
| Bloomsburg | S 25 | 40 | Central Conn. St. | 12 |
| Southern Conn. St. ■ | O 2 | 32 | Southern Conn. St. | 47 |
| Ithaca | O 9 | 13 | Ithaca | 31 |
| Wayne St. (Mich.) ■ | O16 | 7 | New Haven | 66 |
| Portland St. ■ | O23* | 21 | Valdosta St. | 31 |
| New Haven ■ | O30 | 27 | East Stroudsburg | 28 |
| East Stroudsburg | N 6 | 17 | Bowie St. | 15 |
| Springfield | N13 | 13 | Springfield | 10 |

Colors: Gold & White.   Nickname: Yellow Jackets.   **II**

## AMHERST ........................ Amherst, MA 01002
*Jack Siedlecki (5 yrs., 36-11-1)*

| 1993 Opponent | Date | Pts | 1992 Opponent | Opp |
|---|---|---|---|---|
| Hamilton | S 26 | 0 | Hamilton | 41 |
| Bowdoin ■ | O 2 | 0 | Bowdoin | 41 |
| Middlebury ■ | O 9 | 13 | Middlebury | 24 |
| Colby | O16 | 14 | Colby | 28 |
| Wesleyan ■ | O23 | 14 | Wesleyan | 46 |
| Tufts | O30 | 0 | Tufts | 23 |
| Trinity (Conn.) ■ | N 6 | 21 | Trinity (Conn.) | 44 |
| Williams | N13 | 6 | Williams | 41 |

Colors: Purple & White.   Nickname: Lord Jeffs.   **III**

## ANDERSON ........................ Anderson, IN 46012
*Mike Manley (11 yrs., 37-66-3)*

| 1993 Opponent | Date | Pts | 1992 Opponent | Opp |
|---|---|---|---|---|
| Aurora | S 11 | 6 | Aurora | 24 |
| Carthage ■ | S 18 | 35 | Carthage | 18 |
| Geneva ■ | S 25 | 13 | Geneva | 28 |
| Franklin | O 2 | 42 | Franklin | 18 |
| Hanover | O 9 | 19 | Hanover | 38 |
| Manchester ■ | O16 | 20 | Manchester | 17 |
| Wabash | O23 | 21 | Wabash | 42 |
| DePauw ■ | O30 | 24 | DePauw | 8 |
| Rose-Hulman ■ | N 6 | 14 | Rose-Hulman | 23 |
| Taylor | N13 | 47 | Taylor | 18 |

Colors: Orange & Black.   Nickname: Ravens.   **III**

## ANGELO STATE ............... San Angelo, TX 76909
*Jerry Vandergriff (11 yrs., 77-42-1)*

| 1993 Opponent | Date | Pts | 1992 Opponent | Opp |
|---|---|---|---|---|
| Portland St. | S 4* | 24 | Henderson St. | 7 |
| Southern Utah ■ | S 11* | 33 | Prairie View | 3 |
| N.M. Highlands ■ | S 18* | 0 | Sam Houston St. | 20 |
| Southern Ark. | S 25* | 10 | Southern Utah | 17 |
| Fort Lewis ■ | O 2* | 25 | Eastern N. Mex. | 26 |
| Eastern N. Mex. | O 9 | 48 | Abilene Christian | 7 |
| Abilene Christian ■ | O16* | 27 | Central Okla. | 6 |
| Central Okla. | O23* | 20 | Cameron | 7 |
| East Tex. St. ■ | N 6 | 11 | East Tex. St. | 25 |
| Texas A&I | N13* | 6 | Texas A&I | 9 |

Colors: Blue & Gold.   Nickname: Rams.   **II**

## ASHLAND ........................ Ashland, OH 44805
*Fred Martinelli (34 yrs., 208-117-12)*

| 1993 Opponent | Date | Pts | 1992 Opponent | Opp |
|---|---|---|---|---|
| St. Francis (Ill.) ■ | S 4 | 34 | Valparaiso | 7 |
| Ferris St. | S 11 | 15 | Ferris St. | 7 |
| Slippery Rock | S 18 | 37 | Slippery Rock | 31 |
| Hillsdale ■ | S 25* | 21 | Hillsdale | 24 |
| Wayne St. (Mich.) | O 2 | 14 | Wayne St. (Mich.) | 0 |
| Saginaw Valley | O 9 | 7 | Saginaw Valley | 16 |
| St. Joseph's (Ind.) | O16 | 21 | St. Joseph's (Ind.) | 7 |
| Grand Valley St. ■ | O23 | 27 | Grand Valley St. | 10 |
| Northwood ■ | O30 | 21 | Butler | 24 |
| Indianapolis ■ | N 6 | 45 | Indianapolis | 12 |
| Northern Mich. | N13* | 22 | Northern Mich. | 0 |

Colors: Purple & Gold.   Nickname: Eagles.   **II**

## ASSUMPTION ................... Worcester, MA 01615
*Bernie Gaughan (5 yrs., 13-29-1)*

| 1993 Opponent | Date | Pts | 1992 Opponent | Opp |
|---|---|---|---|---|
| Siena ■ | S 11 | 21 | St. Peter's | 14 |
| MIT | S 18 | 27 | MIT | 7 |
| Stonehill ■ | S 25 | 0 | Stonehill | 32 |
| Nichols | O 2 | 14 | Nichols | 19 |
| Bentley ■ | O 9 | 6 | Bentley | 45 |
| Sacred Heart | O16 | 13 | Western New Eng. | 6 |
| Curry | O23 | 40 | Curry | 14 |
| St. Peter's ■ | O30 | 12 | Siena | 21 |
| Mass.-Lowell | N 6 | 27 | Mass.-Lowell | 32 |
| Western New Eng. ■ | N13 | 35 | Sacred Heart | 18 |

Colors: Royal Blue & White.   Nickname: Grayhounds.   **III**

## AUGSBURG ................... Minneapolis, MN 55454
*Jack Osberg (2 yrs., 5-14-0)*

| 1993 Opponent | Date | Pts | 1992 Opponent | Opp |
|---|---|---|---|---|
| Huron ■ | S 11 | 31 | Wis.-Superior | 3 |
| St. John's (Minn.) | S 18 | 0 | St. John's (Minn.) | 58 |
| Gust. Adolphus ■ | S 25* | 12 | Gust. Adolphus | 28 |
| Hamline | O 2 | 9 | Hamline | 25 |
| Bethel (Minn.) ■ | O 9 | 9 | Bethel (Minn.) | 24 |
| St. Thomas (Minn.) | O16 | 37 | St. Thomas (Minn.) | 7 |
| Macalester | O23 | 42 | Macalester | 17 |
| Carleton | O30 | 28 | Carleton | 38 |
| Concordia-M'head† | N 6 | 0 | Concordia-M'head | 62 |
| St. Olaf ■ | N13 | 18 | St. Olaf | 20 |

Colors: Maroon & Gray.   Nickname: Auggies.   **III**

## AUGUSTANA (ILLINOIS) ........ Rock Island, IL 61201
*Bob Reade (14 yrs., 131-19-1)*

| 1993 Opponent | Date | Pts | 1992 Opponent | Opp |
|---|---|---|---|---|
| Loras ■ | S 11 | 7 | Loras | 10 |
| Drake ■ | S 18 | 19 | Drake | 39 |
| North Park | O 2 | 35 | North Park | 10 |
| North Central ■ | O 9 | 21 | North Central | 0 |
| Ill. Wesleyan ■ | O16 | 0 | Ill. Wesleyan | 21 |
| Elmhurst | O23 | 46 | Elmhurst | 14 |
| Millikin ■ | O30 | 13 | Millikin | 3 |
| Carthage | N 6 | 67 | Carthage | 6 |
| Wheaton (Ill.) | N13 | 20 | Wheaton (Ill.) | 15 |

Colors: Gold & Blue.   Nickname: Vikings.   **III**

## AUGUSTANA (SOUTH DAKOTA) . Sioux Falls, SD 57197
*Dennis Moller (1st yr. as head coach)*

| 1993 Opponent | Date | Pts | 1992 Opponent | Opp |
|---|---|---|---|---|
| Neb.-Kearney ■ | S 4 | 33 | Neb.-Kearney | 14 |
| Gust. Adolphus ■ | S 11 | 34 | Gust. Adolphus | 0 |
| Northern Colo. | S 18 | 17 | North Dak. St. | 21 |
| Mankato St. ■ | S 25 | 36 | Nebraska-Omaha | 28 |
| South Dak. | O 2 | 27 | Northern Colo. | 20 |
| St. Cloud St. | O 9 | 9 | St. Cloud St. | 14 |
| North Dak. ■ | O16 | 24 | North Dak. | 20 |
| Morningside | O23 | 20 | South Dak. | 7 |
| South Dak. St. | O30 | 20 | South Dak. St. | 14 |
| Nebraska-Omaha | N 6 | 14 | Morningside | 31 |
| North Dak. St. ■ | N13 | 38 | Mankato St. | 28 |

Colors: Blue & Yellow.   Nickname: Vikings.   **II**

## AURORA ........................ Aurora, IL 60506
*Jim Scott (7 yrs., 39-20-1)*

| 1993 Opponent | Date | Pts | 1992 Opponent | Opp |
|---|---|---|---|---|
| Anderson ■ | S 11 | 24 | Anderson | 6 |
| Trinity (Ill.) ■ | S 18 | 23 | Trinity (Ill.) | 0 |
| Elmhurst | S 25 | 27 | Elmhurst | 0 |
| Drake | O 2 | 30 | Drake | 20 |
| Olivet Nazarene ■ | O 9 | 27 | Olivet Nazarene | 14 |
| MacMurray | O16 | 37 | MacMurray | 0 |
| Ill. Benedictine | O23 | 28 | Ill. Benedictine | 16 |
| Chicago ■ | O30 | 28 | Chicago | 6 |
| Wartburg | N 6 | 21 | Wartburg | 14 |
| **III Championship** | | | | |
| | | 12 | Ill. Wesleyan | 21 |

Colors: Royal Blue & White.   Nickname: Spartans.   **III**

## BALDWIN-WALLACE ................. Berea, OH 44017
*Bob Packard (12 yrs., 93-27-2)*

| 1993 Opponent | Date | Pts | 1992 Opponent | Opp |
|---|---|---|---|---|
| Moravian ■ | S 11 | 20 | Wittenberg | 0 |
| Hiram ■ | S 18* | 61 | Hiram | 0 |
| Muskingum ■ | S 25 | 35 | Muskingum | 18 |
| Mount Union ■ | O 2 | 14 | Mount Union | 23 |
| Otterbein | O 9 | 38 | Otterbein | 15 |
| Capital | O16 | 50 | Capital | 0 |
| Marietta ■ | O23 | 35 | Marietta | 7 |
| Heidelberg | O30 | 39 | Heidelberg | 20 |
| Ohio Northern ■ | N 6 | 28 | Ohio Northern | 29 |
| John Carroll | N13 | 27 | John Carroll | 17 |

Colors: Brown & Gold.   Nickname: Yellow Jackets.   **III**

■ Home games on each schedule.          *Night Games.

## BATES................Lewiston, ME 04240
*Rick Pardy (4 yrs., 17-19-2)*

| Opponent | Date | Pts | Opponent | Pts |
|---|---|---|---|---|
| Trinity (Conn.) ■ | S25 | 0 | Trinity (Conn.) | 42 |
| Tufts ■ | O 2 | 12 | Tufts | 42 |
| Williams | O 9 | 6 | Williams | 39 |
| Wesleyan | O16 | 6 | Wesleyan | 49 |
| Middlebury ■ | O23 | 0 | Middlebury | 49 |
| Colby | O30 | 6 | Colby | 52 |
| Bowdoin ■ | N 6 | 14 | Bowdoin | 35 |
| Hamilton | N13 | 6 | Hamilton | 47 |

Colors: Garnet. Nickname: Bobcats.　III

## BELOIT.........................Beloit, WI 53511
*Ed DeGeorge (16 yrs., 76-69-1)*

| Opponent | Date | Pts | Opponent | Pts |
|---|---|---|---|---|
| Concordia (Wis.) ■ | S11 | 26 | Concordia (Wis.) | 8 |
| Cornell College | S18 | 6 | Cornell College | 20 |
| Knox | S25 | 21 | Knox | 14 |
| Coe ■ | O 2 | 13 | Coe | 37 |
| Ripon | O 9 | 39 | Ripon | 12 |
| Carroll (Wis.) | O16 | 6 | Carroll (Wis.) | 3 |
| Lawrence | O23 | 32 | Lawrence | 14 |
| St. Norbert ■ | O30 | 6 | St. Norbert | 21 |
| Lake Forest | N 6 | 27 | Lake Forest | 13 |
|  |  | 14 | Cornell College | 40 |

Colors: Gold & Blue. Nickname: Buccaneers.　III

## BEMIDJI STATE...............Bemidji, MN 56601
*Kris Diaz (4 yrs., 9-30-0)*

| Opponent | Date | Pts | Opponent | Pts |
|---|---|---|---|---|
| South Dak. | S11 | 8 | St. John's (Minn.) | 35 |
| Wayne St. (Neb.) | S18 | 7 | Wayne St. (Neb.) | 44 |
| Michigan Tech ■ | S25 | 7 | Michigan Tech | 47 |
| Minn.-Duluth | O 2 | 13 | Minn.-Duluth | 22 |
| Southwest St. (Minn.) ■ | O 9 | 39 | Southwest St. (Minn.) | 53 |
| Moorhead St. | O16 | 28 | Moorhead St. | 27 |
| Winona St. | O23 | 12 | Winona St. | 14 |
| Minn.-Morris | O30 | 34 | Minn.-Morris | 7 |
| Northern St. (S.D.) ■ | N 6 | 10 | Northern St. (S.D.) | 17 |
| Neb.-Kearney† | N13 | 21 | Neb.-Kearney | 31 |

Colors: Kelly Green & White. Nickname: Beavers.　II

## BENTLEY.....................Waltham, MA 02154
*Peter Yetten (5 yrs., 28-13-1)*

| Opponent | Date | Pts | Opponent | Pts |
|---|---|---|---|---|
| Mass.-Lowell ■ | S10* | 47 | Curry | 7 |
| Mass. Maritime ■ | S18 | 12 | Stony Brook | 27 |
| Nichols | S25 | 30 | Nichols | 0 |
| Curry | O 2 | 43 | MIT | 14 |
| Assumption | O 9 | 45 | Assumption | 6 |
| Siena ■ | O16 | 24 | Siena | 6 |
| Western New Eng. ■ | O23 | 34 | Western New Eng. | 6 |
| Sacred Heart ■ | O30 | 42 | Stonehill | 0 |
| MIT | N 6 | 42 | Upsala | 13 |
| Stonehill ■ | N13 | 48 | St. John's (N.Y.) | 28 |
| **ECAC Northwest** |  |  |  |  |
|  |  | 20 | Cortland St. | 38 |

Colors: Blue & Gold. Nickname: Falcons.　III

## BETHANY (WEST VIRGINIA).......Bethany, WV 26032
*Steve Campos (1st yr. as head coach)*

| Opponent | Date | Pts | Opponent | Pts |
|---|---|---|---|---|
| Malone ■ | S 4 | 12 | Mercyhurst | 47 |
| Capital ■ | S11 | 10 | Capital | 35 |
| Duquesne | S18* | 20 | Duquesne | 7 |
| Wash. & Jeff. | S25 | 14 | Wash. & Jeff. | 62 |
| Thiel | O 2 | 31 | Thiel | 7 |
| Grove City | O 9 | 8 | Grove City | 58 |
| Waynesburg ■ | O16 | 27 | Waynesburg | 16 |
| Gannon ■ | O23 | 16 | Gannon | 31 |
| Clinch Valley ■ | N 6 | 14 | Clinch Valley | 45 |

Colors: Green & White. Nickname: Bison.　III

## BETHEL (MINNESOTA)...........St. Paul, MN 55112
*Steve Johnson (4 yrs., 21-17-1)*

| Opponent | Date | Pts | Opponent | Pts |
|---|---|---|---|---|
| Central (Iowa) ■ | S11 | 7 | Central (Iowa) | 40 |
| Macalester ■ | S18 | 40 | Macalester | 15 |
| Carleton | S25 | 14 | Carleton | 24 |
| Concordia-M'head ■ | O 2 | 7 | Concordia-M'head | 33 |
| Augsburg | O 9 | 24 | Augsburg | 9 |
| St. John's (Minn.) ■ | O16 | 12 | St. John's (Minn.) | 34 |
| Gust. Adolphus | O23 | 44 | Gust. Adolphus | 13 |
| Hamline | O30 | 10 | Hamline | 10 |
| St. Olaf | N 5* | 20 | St. Olaf | 27 |
| St. Thomas (Minn.) | N13 | 21 | St. Thomas (Minn.) | 10 |

Colors: Royal Blue & Gold. Nickname: Royals.　III

## BLACKBURN...................Carlinville, IL 62626
*Don Flowers (2 yrs., 2-16-0)*

| Opponent | Date | Pts | Opponent | Pts |
|---|---|---|---|---|
| Chicago ■ | S 4 | 27 | Chicago | 26 |
| Maranatha | S11 | 13 | Maranatha | 27 |
| Illinois Col. ■ | S18 | 7 | Illinois Col. | 19 |
| North Park ■ | S25 | 17 | North Park | 13 |
| Ky. Wesleyan | O 2 | 0 | Ky. Wesleyan | 34 |
| Principia | O 9 | 27 | Principia | 28 |
| MacMurray ■ | O23 | 7 | MacMurray | 26 |
| Crown | O30 | 16 | Crown | 22 |
| Concordia (Ill.) | N13 | 3 | Concordia (Ill.) | 34 |

Colors: Scarlet & Black. Nickname: Beavers.　III

## BLOOMSBURG...............Bloomsburg, PA 17815
*Danny Hale (5 yrs., 40-13-0)*

| Opponent | Date | Pts | Opponent | Pts |
|---|---|---|---|---|
| Bucknell | S 4 | 24 | Bucknell | 41 |
| Shippensburg ■ | S11 | 14 | Shippensburg | 20 |
| Lock Haven | S18 | 33 | Lock Haven | 38 |
| American Int'l ■ | S25 | 17 | East Stroudsburg | 42 |
| Millersville ■ | O 2 | 12 | Millersville | 48 |
| Clarion | O 9 | 20 | Clarion | 23 |
| Kutztown | O16 | 10 | Kutztown | 17 |
| West Chester ■ | O23 | 2 | West Chester | 34 |
| East Stroudsburg | O30 | 30 | Cheyney | 7 |
| Cheyney ■ | N 6 | 24 | Mansfield | 30 |
| Mansfield | N13 |  |  |  |

Colors: Maroon & Gold. Nickname: Huskies.　II

## BLUFFTON....................Bluffton, OH 45817
*Carlin Carpenter (14 yrs., 55-72-1)*

| Opponent | Date | Pts | Opponent | Pts |
|---|---|---|---|---|
| Ohio Northern ■ | S11 | 0 | Ohio Northern | 39 |
| Hanover | S18 | 49 | Hanover | 56 |
| Malone ■ | S25 | 6 | Alma | 42 |
| Grove City ■ | O 2 | 10 | Grove City | 35 |
| Manchester | O 9 | 14 | Urbana | 20 |
| Urbana ■ | O16 | 0 | Mt. St. Joseph | 41 |
| Mt. St. Joseph ■ | O23 | 40 | Wilmington (Ohio) | 21 |
| Wilmington (Ohio) | O30 | 14 | Defiance | 24 |
| Defiance | N 6 | 7 | Thomas More | 33 |
| Thomas More | N13 |  |  |  |

Colors: Purple & White. Nickname: Beavers.　III

## BOWDOIN....................Brunswick, ME 04011
*Howard Vandersea (17 yrs., 69-78-2)*

| Opponent | Date | Pts | Opponent | Pts |
|---|---|---|---|---|
| Middlebury ■ | S25 | 14 | Middlebury | 18 |
| Amherst | O 2 | 41 | Amherst | 0 |
| Tufts | O 9 | 25 | Hamilton | 28 |
| Hamilton ■ | O16 | 14 | Trinity (Conn.) | 3 |
| Trinity (Conn.) | O23 | 6 | Wesleyan | 40 |
| Wesleyan ■ | O30 | 35 | Bates | 14 |
| Bates | N 6 | 18 | Colby | 26 |
| Colby ■ | N13 | 7 | Tufts | 6 |

Colors: White. Nickname: Polar Bears.　III

## BOWIE STATE....................Bowie, MD 20715
*To be named*

| Opponent | Date | Pts | Opponent | Pts |
|---|---|---|---|---|
| N.C. Central | S 4* | 13 | Livingstone | 21 |
| Hampton ■ | S11 | 7 | Hampton | 58 |
| Southern Conn. St. ■ | S18 | 0 | N.C. Central | 9 |
| Virginia St. | S25 | 28 | Virginia St. | 14 |
| Virginia Union | O 2 | 6 | Virginia Union | 26 |
| Livingstone ■ | O 9 | 7 | Norfolk St. | 24 |
| Elizabeth City St. | O16 | 16 | Elizabeth City St. | 20 |
| Winston-Salem ■ | O23 | 0 | Winston-Salem | 29 |
| Fayetteville St. ■ | O30 | 6 | Howard | 55 |
| New Haven | N 6 | 15 | American Int'l | 17 |
|  |  | 22 | Wofford | 24 |

Colors: Black & Gold. Nickname: Bulldogs.　II

## BRIDGEWATER STATE (Mass.) Bridgewater, MA 02324
*Peter Mazzaferro (29 yrs., 134-114-11)*

| Opponent | Date | Pts | Opponent | Pts |
|---|---|---|---|---|
| Kean | S11 | 20 | Kean | 20 |
| Maine Maritime ■ | S18 | 27 | Maine Maritime | 7 |
| Mass.-Boston | S25 | 47 | Mass.-Boston | 21 |
| Fitchburg St. ■ | O 2 | 14 | Fitchburg St. | 0 |
| Framingham St. | O 9 | 48 | Framingham St. | 7 |
| Westfield St. ■ | O16 | 22 | Westfield St. | 10 |
| Plymouth St. ■ | O23 | 24 | Plymouth St. | 6 |
| Worcester St. | O30 | 24 | Worcester St. | 12 |
| Mass. Maritime ■ | N 6 | 34 | Mass. Maritime | 13 |
| Mass.-Dartmouth | N13 | 30 | Mass.-Dartmouth | 12 |
| **ECAC Northeast** |  |  |  |  |
|  |  | 25 | Rensselaer | 28 |

Colors: Crimson & White. Nickname: Bears.　III

■ Home games on each schedule.　　　*Night Games.

## BRIDGEWATER (VIRGINIA) .... Bridgewater, VA 22812
*Max Lowe (1 yr., 3-7-0)*

| 1993 Opponent | Date | 1992 | Opponent | Opp |
|---|---|---|---|---|
| Wesley ■ | S11 | 14 | Clinch Valley | 17 |
| Emory & Henry ■ | S18 | 6 | Emory & Henry | 51 |
| Clinch Valley | S25 | 13 | Wesley | 26 |
| Hampden-Sydney | O 2 | 10 | Hampden-Sydney | 16 |
| Methodist | O 9 | 27 | Methodist | 0 |
| Guilford ■ | O16 | 9 | Guilford | 7 |
| Frostburg St. ■ | O23 | 2 | Frostburg St. | 37 |
| Wash. & Lee | O30 | 20 | Wash. & Lee | 12 |
| Randolph-Macon ■ | N 6 | 0 | Randolph-Macon | 28 |
| Davidson | N13 | 13 | Davidson | 28 |

Colors: Crimson & Gold. Nickname: Eagles. III

## BROCKPORT STATE ............ Brockport, NY 14420
*Ed Matejkovic (7 yrs., 25-44-0)*

| 1993 Opponent | Date | 1992 | Opponent | Opp |
|---|---|---|---|---|
| Jersey City St. ■ | S11 | 21 | Denison | 28 |
| Alfred ■ | S18 | 42 | Jersey City St. | 6 |
| Albany (N.Y.) | S25* | 14 | Alfred | 15 |
| Buffalo St. | O 2 | 33 | Albany (N.Y.) | 41 |
| Cortland St. ■ | O 9 | 14 | Buffalo St. | 40 |
| Norwich | O16 | 12 | Cortland St. | 62 |
| St. John Fisher ■ | O23 | 8 | Norwich | 21 |
| Frostburg St. ■ | O30 | 26 | St. John Fisher | 21 |
| Kean | N 6 | 31 | Frostburg St. | 17 |
| St. Lawrence | N13 | 8 | Mercyhurst | 38 |

Colors: Green & Gold. Nickname: Golden Eagles. III

## BUENA VISTA ................. Storm Lake, IA 50588
*Kevin Twait (3 yrs., 4-25-0)*

| 1993 Opponent | Date | 1992 | Opponent | Opp |
|---|---|---|---|---|
| Cornell College ■ | S11 | 21 | Cornell College | 31 |
| Loras | S18 | 0 | Loras | 14 |
| Simpson ■ | S25 | 15 | Simpson | 37 |
| Central (Iowa) | O 2 | 7 | Central (Iowa) | 62 |
| Upper Iowa ■ | O16 | 24 | Upper Iowa | 42 |
| Wartburg | O23 | 7 | Wartburg | 28 |
| William Penn ■ | O30 | 17 | William Penn | 0 |
| Dubuque ■ | N 6 | 28 | Dubuque | 21 |
| Luther | N13 | 10 | Luther | 17 |

Colors: Navy Blue & Gold. Nickname: Beavers. III

## BUFFALO STATE ................. Buffalo, NY 14222
*Jerry Boyes (7 yrs., 27-39-0)*

| 1993 Opponent | Date | 1992 | Opponent | Opp |
|---|---|---|---|---|
| Mansfield | S11 | 21 | Mansfield | 17 |
| Canisius ■ | S18 | 14 | Canisius | 7 |
| Cortland St. | S25 | 30 | Cortland St. | 21 |
| Brockport St. ■ | O 2 | 40 | Brockport St. | 14 |
| Mercyhurst | O 9 | 15 | Buffalo | 19 |
| Buffalo | O16 | 13 | Ithaca | 21 |
| Ithaca ■ | O23 | 44 | Alfred | 13 |
| Hobart | N 6 | 33 | Hobart | 0 |
| Westminster (Pa.) | N13 | 14 | Gannon | 6 |
| | | | **III Championship** | |
| | | 28 | Ithaca | 26 |
| | | 19 | Rowan | 28 |

Colors: Orange & Black. Nickname: Bengals. III

## CAL LUTHERAN ........... Thousand Oaks, CA 91360
*Joe Harper (20 yrs., 118-82-3)*

| 1993 Opponent | Date | 1992 | Opponent | Opp |
|---|---|---|---|---|
| Azusa Pacific ■ | S11 | 21 | Pomona-Pitzer | 27 |
| Whittier ■ | S18 | 33 | Azusa Pacific | 34 |
| La Verne | S25 | 20 | San Diego | 21 |
| Menlo | O 2 | 41 | Claremont-M-S | 7 |
| San Diego | O 9 | 17 | Occidental | 14 |
| Pomona-Pitzer | O23 | 19 | Menlo | 7 |
| Redlands ■ | O30 | 24 | Redlands | 56 |
| Occidental | N 6* | 37 | La Verne | 55 |
| Claremont-M-S ■ | N13 | 30 | Whittier | 33 |

Colors: Purple & Gold. Nickname: Kingsmen. III

## CAL POLY SLO ........... San Luis Obispo, CA 93407
*Lyle Setencich (10 yrs., 59-45-2)*

| 1993 Opponent | Date | 1992 | Opponent | Opp |
|---|---|---|---|---|
| UC Davis | S11* | 10 | North Dak. St. | 26 |
| Humboldt St. ■ | S18* | 41 | Cal St. Chico | 10 |
| Cal St. Chico ■ | S25* | 35 | Cal St. Hayward | 3 |
| Sonoma St. | O 2 | 35 | Sonoma St. | 36 |
| San Fran. St. ■ | O 9* | 31 | UC Davis | 31 |
| Southern Utah ■ | O16 | 0 | Cal St. Sacramento | 24 |
| Cal St. Sacramento ■ | O23 | 13 | Cal St. Northridge | 14 |
| Portland St. | O30* | 40 | Santa Clara | 14 |
| Cal St. Northridge ■ | N 6* | 17 | Southern Utah | 14 |
| St. Mary's (Cal.) | N13 | 31 | Portland St. | 45 |

Colors: Green & Gold. Nickname: Mustangs. II

## CAL STATE CHICO ................... Chico, CA 95929
*Gary Houser (4 yrs., 15-25-0)*

| 1993 Opponent | Date | 1992 | Opponent | Opp |
|---|---|---|---|---|
| Whittier ■ | S11* | 25 | Santa Clara | 35 |
| Cal Poly SLO | S25* | 0 | Montana | 41 |
| St. Mary's (Cal.) | O 2 | 10 | Cal Poly SLO | 41 |
| UC Davis ■ | O 9* | 28 | St. Mary's (Cal.) | 21 |
| Cal St. Hayward | O16 | 20 | Cal St. Sacramento | 36 |
| San Fran. St. ■ | O23 | 21 | Cal St. Hayward | 24 |
| Cal St. Northridge | O30* | 28 | San Fran. St. | 43 |
| Sonoma St. | N 6 | 37 | UC Davis | 44 |
| Humboldt St. ■ | N13* | 23 | Sonoma St. | 41 |
| | | 7 | Humboldt St. | 27 |

Colors: Cardinal & White. Nickname: Wildcats. II

## CAL STATE HAYWARD........... Hayward, CA 94542
*Tim Tierney (18 yrs., 74-103-5)*

| 1993 Opponent | Date | 1992 | Opponent | Opp |
|---|---|---|---|---|
| Cal St. Sacramento | S 4* | 13 | San Diego | 14 |
| St. Mary's (Cal.) | S11 | 6 | St. Mary's (Cal.) | 10 |
| UC Davis | S18* | 33 | Azusa Pacific | 25 |
| Redlands ■ | S25 | 3 | Cal Poly SLO | 35 |
| Azusa Pacific | O 2 | 22 | Redlands | 8 |
| Cal St. Chico ■ | O16 | 24 | Cal St. Chico | 21 |
| Sonoma St. ■ | O23 | 20 | Sonoma St. | 37 |
| San Fran. St. | O30 | 41 | San Fran. St. | 22 |
| Humboldt St. ■ | N 6 | 38 | Humboldt St. | 36 |
| | | 27 | UC Davis | 38 |

Colors: Red, Black & White. Nickname: Pioneers. II

## CALIFORNIA (PENNSYLVANIA)... California, PA 15419
*Kevin Donley (15 yrs., 103-52-1)*

| 1993 Opponent | Date | 1992 | Opponent | Opp |
|---|---|---|---|---|
| West Liberty St. | S 4 | 21 | West Liberty St. | 9 |
| West Va. Wesleyan ■ | S11 | 12 | West Va. Wesleyan | 14 |
| Fairmont St. ■ | S18 | 14 | Fairmont St. | 7 |
| Kutztown | S25 | 30 | Kutztown | 30 |
| East Stroudsburg ■ | O 2 | 13 | East Stroudsburg | 40 |
| Slippery Rock | O 9 | 15 | Slippery Rock | 23 |
| Indiana (Pa.) ■ | O16 | 20 | Indiana (Pa.) | 36 |
| Edinboro | O23 | 13 | Edinboro | 33 |
| Clarion | O30 | 18 | Clarion | 23 |
| Lock Haven | N 6 | 20 | Lock Haven | 7 |
| Shippensburg ■ | N13 | 8 | Shippensburg | 17 |

Colors: Red & Black. Nickname: Vulcans. II

## CAMERON .................... Lawton, OK 73505
*Dropped program after 1992.*

| 1992 | Opponent | Opp |
|---|---|---|
| 7 | Mo. Southern St. | 59 |
| 6 | Tarleton St. | 17 |
| 15 | East Central (Okla.) | 27 |
| 44 | West Tex. St. | 10 |
| 0 | Texas A&I | 50 |
| 7 | Eastern N. Mex. | 45 |
| 7 | Abilene Christian | 12 |
| 7 | Angelo St. | 20 |
| 6 | Central Okla. | 44 |
| 3 | East Tex. St. | 40 |

Colors: Black & Gold. Nickname: Aggies. II

## CAPITAL ....................... Columbus, OH 43209
*Roger Welsh (7 yrs., 32-34-4)*

| 1993 Opponent | Date | 1992 | Opponent | Opp |
|---|---|---|---|---|
| Bethany (W.Va.) | S11 | 35 | Bethany (W.Va.) | 10 |
| John Carroll | S18 | 10 | John Carroll | 51 |
| Hiram ■ | S25 | 33 | Hiram | 36 |
| Marietta ■ | O 2 | 0 | Marietta | 20 |
| Heidelberg | O 9 | 10 | Heidelberg | 26 |
| Baldwin-Wallace ■ | O16 | 0 | Baldwin-Wallace | 50 |
| Muskingum | O23 | 7 | Muskingum | 41 |
| Ohio Northern | O30 | 21 | Ohio Northern | 9 |
| Mount Union ■ | N 6 | 0 | Mount Union | 44 |
| Otterbein | N13 | 17 | Otterbein | 17 |

Colors: Purple & White. Nickname: Crusaders. III

## CARLETON ..................... Northfield, MN 55057
*Bob Sullivan (14 yrs., 77-58-0)*

| 1993 Opponent | Date | 1992 | Opponent | Opp |
|---|---|---|---|---|
| Northwestern Minn. | S11 | 49 | Northwestern Minn. | 3 |
| Hamline | S18 | 36 | Hamline | 0 |
| Bethel (Minn.) ■ | S25 | 24 | Bethel (Minn.) | 14 |
| St. Thomas (Minn.) | O 2 | 25 | St. Thomas (Minn.) | 20 |
| Macalester | O 9 | 32 | Macalester | 6 |
| St. Olaf ■ | O16 | 9 | St. Olaf | 9 |
| Concordia-M'head | O23 | 26 | Concordia-M'head | 24 |
| Augsburg | O30 | 38 | Augsburg | 28 |
| St. John's (Minn.)† | N 6 | 7 | St. John's (Minn.) | 70 |
| Gust. Adolphus ■ | N13 | 21 | Gust. Adolphus | 20 |
| | | | **III Championship** | |
| | | 8 | Central (Iowa) | 20 |

Colors: Maize & Blue. Nickname: Knights. III

■ Home games on each schedule.    *Night Games.

### CARNEGIE MELLON ............. Pittsburgh, PA 15213
*Rich Lackner (7 yrs., 51-16-2)*

| Opponent | Date | Pts | Opponent | Pts |
|---|---|---|---|---|
| Frank. & Marsh. ■ | S 4 | 34 | Juniata | 0 |
| Washington (Mo.) ■ | S11 | 31 | Washington (Mo.) | 7 |
| Rochester | S18 | 10 | Rochester | 16 |
| Juniata | S25 | 21 | Allegheny | 35 |
| Allegheny ■ | O 2 | 42 | Trinity (Tex.) | 17 |
| Trinity (Tex.) ■ | O 9 | 55 | Chicago | 12 |
| Chicago | O16 | 35 | Grove City | 14 |
| Grove City | O30 | 28 | Catholic | 12 |
| Catholic ■ | N 6* | 33 | Case Reserve | 14 |
| Case Reserve ■ | N13 | | | |

Colors: Cardinal, White & Gray. Nickname: Tartans.    III

### CARROLL (WISCONSIN) ........ Waukesha, WI 53186
*Merle Masonholder (11 yrs., 44-54-0)*

| Opponent | Date | Pts | Opponent | Pts |
|---|---|---|---|---|
| North Central ■ | S11* | 34 | North Central | 18 |
| Kalamazoo ■ | S18 | 14 | Kalamazoo | 10 |
| Illinois Col. | S25 | 20 | Illinois Col. | 6 |
| Monmouth (Ill.) | O 2 | 40 | Monmouth (Ill.) | 21 |
| Lawrence | O 9 | 47 | Lawrence | 6 |
| Beloit ■ | O16 | 3 | Beloit | 6 |
| Lake Forest | O23 | 40 | Lake Forest | 6 |
| Ripon ■ | O30 | 35 | Ripon | 20 |
| St. Norbert | N 6 | 40 | St. Norbert | 7 |

Colors: Orange & White. Nickname: Pioneers.    III

### CARSON-NEWMAN ........ Jefferson City, TN 37760
*Ken Sparks (13 yrs., 119-37-1)*

| Opponent | Date | Pts | Opponent | Pts |
|---|---|---|---|---|
| Central St. (Ohio) ■ | S 2* | 20 | Western N. Mex. | 7 |
| Catawba ■ | S11* | 17 | Howard Payne | 12 |
| Elon ■ | S25 | 17 | Elon | 13 |
| New Haven | O 2 | 14 | Catawba | 6 |
| Wingate | O 9 | 36 | Wingate | 28 |
| Mars Hill ■ | O16 | 27 | Mars Hill | 0 |
| Gardner-Webb | O23 | 6 | Gardner-Webb | 25 |
| Lenoir-Rhyne ■ | O30 | 39 | Lenoir-Rhyne | 27 |
| Howard Payne | N 6 | 0 | New Haven | 14 |
| Presbyterian | N13 | 34 | Presbyterian | 17 |
| | **NAIA I Championship** | | | |
| | | 3 | Shepherd | 6 |

Colors: Orange & Blue. Nickname: Eagles.    II

### CARTHAGE ...................... Kenosha, WI 53140
*Mike Larry (1 yr., 0-9-0)*

| Opponent | Date | Pts | Opponent | Pts |
|---|---|---|---|---|
| Anderson | S18 | 18 | Anderson | 35 |
| Ill. Benedictine ■ | S25 | 17 | Ill. Benedictine | 41 |
| Elmhurst ■ | O 2 | 10 | Elmhurst | 35 |
| Millikin | O 9 | 0 | Millikin | 61 |
| Wheaton (Ill.) | O16 | 0 | Wheaton (Ill.) | 28 |
| Ill. Wesleyan ■ | O23 | 8 | Ill. Wesleyan | 63 |
| North Park | O30 | 0 | North Park | 17 |
| Augustana (Ill.) ■ | N 6 | 6 | Augustana (Ill.) | 67 |
| North Central | N13 | 14 | North Central | 51 |

Colors: Red & White. Nickname: Redmen.    III

### CASE RESERVE ................. Cleveland, OH 44106
*Ron Stuckey (6 yrs., 27-30-2)*

| Opponent | Date | Pts | Opponent | Pts |
|---|---|---|---|---|
| Rochester ■ | S11 | 10 | Rochester | 24 |
| Washington (Mo.) ■ | S18 | 9 | Washington (Mo.) | 21 |
| Allegheny ■ | S25 | 0 | Allegheny | 32 |
| Wittenberg | O 2 | 10 | Wittenberg | 42 |
| Kenyon ■ | O 9 | 14 | Kenyon | 14 |
| Oberlin | O16 | 14 | Oberlin | 3 |
| Denison ■ | O23 | 14 | Denison | 14 |
| Ohio Wesleyan | O30 | 7 | Ohio Wesleyan | 14 |
| Chicago | N 6 | 23 | Chicago | 14 |
| Carnegie Mellon | N13 | 14 | Carnegie Mellon | 33 |

Colors: Blue, Gray & White. Nickname: Spartans.    III

### CATAWBA ...................... Salisbury, NC 28144
*J. D. Haglan (2 yrs., 11-9-0)*

| Opponent | Date | Pts | Opponent | Pts |
|---|---|---|---|---|
| Carson-Newman ■ | S11* | 38 | Lees-McRae | 13 |
| Mars Hill ■ | S18 | 14 | Mars Hill | 21 |
| Wofford ■ | S25* | 17 | Wofford | 42 |
| Newberry ■ | O 2 | 6 | Carson-Newman | 14 |
| Presbyterian | O 9 | 28 | Presbyterian | 14 |
| Gardner-Webb ■ | O16 | 17 | Gardner-Webb | 34 |
| Elon | O23 | 7 | Elon | 15 |
| West Va. St. | O30 | 0 | Newberry | 20 |
| Wingate | N 6 | 27 | Wingate | 24 |
| Lenoir-Rhyne | N13 | 24 | Lenoir-Rhyne | 22 |

Colors: Blue & White. Nickname: Indians.    II

### CATHOLIC .................... Washington, DC 20064
*Rick Novak (3 yrs., 14-16-0)*

| Opponent | Date | Pts | Opponent | Pts |
|---|---|---|---|---|
| Gettysburg ■ | S11 | 15 | St. John Fisher | 17 |
| Randolph-Macon | S18 | 14 | Swarthmore | 27 |
| Merchant Marine ■ | S25 | 30 | Randolph-Macon | 14 |
| St. John Fisher ■ | O 2 | 13 | Iona | 28 |
| Coast Guard | O 9* | 27 | Methodist | 21 |
| Gallaudet | O16 | 3 | Duquesne | 23 |
| Hampden-Sydney ■ | O23 | 44 | Gallaudet | 11 |
| Georgetown | O30 | 16 | Sacred Heart | 2 |
| Carnegie Mellon | N 6* | 16 | Georgetown | 19 |
| Wash. & Lee | N13 | 12 | Carnegie Mellon | 28 |

Colors: Cardinal & Black. Nickname: Cardinals.    III

### CENTRAL ARKANSAS ............. Conway, AR 72032
*Mike Isom (3 yrs., 26-8-3)*

| Opponent | Date | Pts | Opponent | Pts |
|---|---|---|---|---|
| East Tex. St. | S 4* | 18 | East Tex. St. | 30 |
| Mo. Southern St. | S11* | 14 | Delta St. | 14 |
| Fort Hays St. ■ | S18* | 21 | Fort Hays St. | 14 |
| West Ga. | S25* | 24 | Tenn.-Chatt. | 17 |
| Delta St. | O 2* | 34 | Ouachita Baptist | 7 |
| Ark.-Pine Bluff ■ | O 9 | 18 | Harding | 10 |
| Livingston ■ | O16* | 45 | Ark.-Monticello | 14 |
| North Ala. ■ | O23 | 18 | Henderson St. | 10 |
| Henderson St. ■ | O30 | 34 | Southern Ark. | 0 |
| Mississippi Col. | N 6* | 40 | Arkansas Tech | 9 |
| Portland St. | N13* | | **NAIA I Championship** | |
| | | 14 | Southwestern Okla. | 2 |
| | | 23 | Central St. (Ohio) | 30 |

Colors: Purple & Gray. Nickname: Bears.    II

### CENTRAL (IOWA) ................... Pella, IA 50219
*Ron Schipper (32 yrs., 252-61-3)*

| Opponent | Date | Pts | Opponent | Pts |
|---|---|---|---|---|
| Bethel (Minn.) | S11 | 40 | Bethel (Minn.) | 7 |
| Dubuque | S18 | 54 | Dubuque | 7 |
| Wartburg | S25 | 31 | Wartburg | 21 |
| Buena Vista ■ | O 2 | 62 | Buena Vista | 7 |
| William Penn | O 9 | 55 | William Penn | 0 |
| Simpson ■ | O16 | 16 | Simpson | 7 |
| Loras | O23 | 42 | Loras | 21 |
| Upper Iowa | O30 | 45 | Upper Iowa | 20 |
| Luther ■ | N 6 | 33 | Luther | 11 |
| | **III Championship** | | | |
| | | 20 | Carleton | 8 |
| | | 9 | Wis.-La Crosse | 34 |

Colors: Red & White. Nickname: Flying Dutchmen.    III

### CENTRAL MISSOURI STATE .. Warrensburg, MO 64093
*Terry Noland (10 yrs., 56-50-1)*

| Opponent | Date | Pts | Opponent | Pts |
|---|---|---|---|---|
| Wis.-Whitewater | S 4* | 16 | North Ala. | 17 |
| Northeast Mo. St. | S18 | 10 | Mo. Southern St. | 7 |
| Washburn ■ | S25 | 29 | Southwest Baptist | 10 |
| Mo. Western St. | O 2* | 9 | Emporia St. | 7 |
| Southwest Baptist ■ | O 9 | 10 | Northwest Mo. St. | 7 |
| Mo. Southern St. ■ | O16 | 10 | Washburn | 13 |
| Pittsburg St. | O23 | 6 | Northeast Mo. St. | 24 |
| Emporia St. | O30 | 17 | Missouri-Rolla | 0 |
| Northwest Mo. St. ■ | N 6 | 38 | Mo. Western St. | 3 |
| Missouri-Rolla | N13 | 10 | Pittsburg St. | 20 |

Colors: Cardinal & Black. Nickname: Mules.    II

### CENTRAL OKLAHOMA ............ Edmond, OK 73034
*Gary Howard (16 yrs., 88-70-5)*

| Opponent | Date | Pts | Opponent | Pts |
|---|---|---|---|---|
| Mesa St. | S 4* | 27 | Northwest Mo. St. | 9 |
| Fort Hays St. ■ | S11* | 17 | Fort Hays St. | 15 |
| Southern Utah ■ | S18 | 21 | Southern Utah | 20 |
| Langston | S25* | 14 | Cal St. Northridge | 0 |
| East Tex. St. | O 2 | 9 | East Tex. St. | 26 |
| Abilene Christian | O 9 | 31 | Abilene Christian | 35 |
| Texas A&I ■ | O16* | 12 | Texas A&I | 36 |
| Angelo St. | O23* | 6 | Angelo St. | 27 |
| Neb.-Kearney ■ | N 6 | 44 | Cameron | 6 |
| Eastern N. Mex. | N13 | 35 | Eastern N. Mex. | 13 |

Colors: Bronze & Blue. Nickname: Bronchos.    II

### CENTRE ...................... Danville, KY 40422
*Joe McDaniel (27 yrs., 138-104-4)*

| Opponent | Date | Pts | Opponent | Pts |
|---|---|---|---|---|
| Denison ■ | S11 | 7 | Hampden-Sydney | 21 |
| Maryville (Tenn.) | S18 | 17 | Maryville (Tenn.) | 21 |
| Wash. & Lee | S25 | 22 | Wash. & Lee | 32 |
| Sewanee | O 2 | 21 | Sewanee | 26 |
| Millsaps ■ | O 9 | 10 | Millsaps | 21 |
| Trinity (Tex.) | O23* | 17 | Trinity (Tex.) | 7 |
| Ky. Wesleyan | O30 | 42 | Ky. Wesleyan | 26 |
| Davidson ■ | N 6 | 3 | Davidson | 10 |
| Rhodes ■ | N13 | 21 | Rhodes | 18 |

Colors: Gold & White. Nickname: Colonels.    III

■ Home games on each schedule.    *Night Games.

### CHADRON STATE .............. Chadron, NE 69337
*Brad Smith (6 yrs., 35-23-1)*

| 1993 Opponent | Date | | Pts | 1992 Opponent | Pts |
|---|---|---|---|---|---|
| Idaho St. | S 4* | | 44 | South Dak. Tech | 30 |
| South Dak. Tech ■ | S11 | | 26 | Black Hills St. | 22 |
| Black Hills St. ■ | S18 | | 23 | Peru St. | 27 |
| Peru St.† | S25* | | 38 | Adams St. | 28 |
| Adams St. ■ | O 2 | | 38 | N.M. Highlands | 0 |
| N.M. Highlands | O 9 | | 35 | Colorado Mines | 30 |
| Colorado Mines | O16 | | 21 | Western St. | 49 |
| Western St. ■ | O23 | | 0 | Fort Hays St. | 10 |
| Fort Hays St. | O30 | | 29 | Fort Lewis | 22 |
| Fort Lewis ■ | N 6 | | 37 | Mesa St. | 24 |
| Mesa St. | N13 | | | | |

Colors: Cardinal & White. Nickname: Eagles.  II

### CHEYNEY ....................... Cheyney, PA 19319
*Chris Roulhac (1 yr., 0-11-0)*

| 1993 Opponent | Date | | Pts | 1992 Opponent | Pts |
|---|---|---|---|---|---|
| Southern Conn. St. ■ | S 4 | | 0 | Delaware St. | 54 |
| Delaware St. | S11 | | 21 | Morris Brown | 28 |
| West Va. St.† | S18 | | 6 | Howard | 75 |
| Fayetteville St. ■ | S25 | | 0 | Hampton | 72 |
| West Chester | O 1* | | 7 | West Chester | 48 |
| East Stroudsburg ■ | O 9 | | 6 | East Stroudsburg | 48 |
| Slippery Rock | O16 | | 27 | Slippery Rock | 43 |
| Mansfield | O23 | | 16 | Mansfield | 37 |
| Millersville ■ | O30 | | 0 | Millersville | 38 |
| Bloomsburg | N 6 | | 7 | Bloomsburg | 30 |
| Kutztown ■ | N13 | | 6 | Kutztown | 63 |

Colors: Blue & White. Nickname: Wolves.  II

### CHICAGO...................... Chicago, IL 60637
*Greg Quick (4 yrs., 6-33-0)*

| 1993 Opponent | Date | | Pts | 1992 Opponent | Pts |
|---|---|---|---|---|---|
| Blackburn | S 4 | | 26 | Blackburn | 27 |
| Concordia (Ill.) ■ | S11 | | 21 | Concordia (Ill.) | 3 |
| Lawrence | S18 | | 37 | Lawrence | 0 |
| Kalamazoo ■ | S25 | | 13 | Kalamazoo | 21 |
| Rochester | O 2 | | 13 | Rochester | 41 |
| Drake ■ | O 9 | | 19 | Drake | 31 |
| Carnegie Mellon ■ | O16 | | 12 | Carnegie Mellon | 55 |
| Washington (Mo.) | O23 | | 24 | Washington (Mo.) | 23 |
| Aurora | O30 | | 6 | Aurora | 28 |
| Case Reserve ■ | N 6 | | 14 | Case Reserve | 23 |

Colors: White & Maroon. Nickname: Maroons.  III

### CLAREMONT-MUDD-SCRIPPS... Claremont, CA 91711
*John Zinda (24 yrs., 87-121-3)*

| 1993 Opponent | Date | | Pts | 1992 Opponent | Pts |
|---|---|---|---|---|---|
| Trinity (Tex.) | S11 | | 0 | Rhodes | 21 |
| La Verne | S18 | | 13 | San Diego | 42 |
| Redlands ■ | O 2 | | 17 | Menlo | 33 |
| Menlo | O16 | | 7 | Cal Lutheran | 41 |
| Whittier | O23 | | 6 | Redlands | 48 |
| Occidental ■ | O30 | | 20 | Pomona-Pitzer | 33 |
| Pomona-Pitzer ■ | N 6 | | 19 | Whittier | 42 |
| Cal Lutheran | N13 | | 3 | Occidental | 42 |
| | | | 6 | La Verne | 28 |

Colors: Maroon, Gold & White. Nickname: Stags.  III

### CLARION .......................... Clarion, PA 16214
*Gene Sobolewski (10 yrs., 55-46-0)*

| 1993 Opponent | Date | | Pts | 1992 Opponent | Pts |
|---|---|---|---|---|---|
| West Chester ■ | S11 | | 7 | Youngstown St. | 48 |
| New Haven | S18 | | 47 | New Haven | 48 |
| Westminster (Pa.) | S25 | | 11 | Westminster (Pa.) | 21 |
| Edinboro ■ | O 2 | | 17 | Edinboro | 26 |
| Bloomsburg ■ | O 9 | | 23 | Bloomsburg | 20 |
| Lock Haven | O16 | | 42 | Lock Haven | 14 |
| Shippensburg ■ | O23 | | 23 | Shippensburg | 20 |
| Calif. (Pa.) | O30 | | 23 | Calif. (Pa.) | 18 |
| Slippery Rock ■ | N 6 | | 49 | Slippery Rock | 37 |
| Indiana (Pa.) ■ | N13 | | 35 | Indiana (Pa.) | 26 |

Colors: Blue & Gold. Nickname: Golden Eagles.  II

### CLARK ATLANTA.................. Atlanta, GA 30314
*Willie Hunter (2 yrs., 15-14-1)*

| 1993 Opponent | Date | | Pts | 1992 Opponent | Pts |
|---|---|---|---|---|---|
| Morris Brown ■ | S 6 | | 28 | Morris Brown | 20 |
| Valdosta St. | S25* | | 7 | Savannah St. | 21 |
| Fort Valley St.† | O 2* | | 28 | West Ga. | 26 |
| Tuskegee | O 9 | | 17 | Fort Valley St. | 42 |
| Kentucky St. | O16 | | 30 | Tuskegee | 19 |
| Miles ■ | O23 | | 24 | Kentucky St. | 14 |
| Albany St. (Ga.) ■ | O30 | | 14 | Miles | 13 |
| Alabama A&M ■ | N 6 | | 17 | Albany St. (Ga.) | 41 |
| Morehouse | N13 | | 21 | Alabama A&M | 29 |
| | | | 14 | Morehouse | 33 |

Colors: Red, Black & Gray. Nickname: Panthers.  II

### COAST GUARD............... New London, CT 06320
*Bill Schmitz (1st yr. as head coach)*

| 1993 Opponent | Date | | Pts | 1992 Opponent | Pts |
|---|---|---|---|---|---|
| Rensselaer | S18 | | 20 | Mass.-Lowell | 0 |
| Stony Brook | S25 | | 15 | Rensselaer | 14 |
| Norwich ■ | O 2 | | 19 | Stony Brook | 24 |
| Catholic ■ | O 9* | | 13 | Norwich | 14 |
| Western Conn. St. | O16 | | 6 | Western Conn. St. | 8 |
| Union (N.Y.) ■ | O23 | | 9 | Union (N.Y.) | 21 |
| Plymouth St. | O30 | | 13 | Plymouth St. | 20 |
| Worcester Tech ■ | N 6 | | 10 | Worcester Tech | 28 |
| Merchant Marine ■ | N13 | | 0 | Merchant Marine | 42 |

Colors: Blue, White & Orange. Nickname: Cadets, Bears.  III

### COE........................... Cedar Rapids, IA 52402
*D. J. LeRoy (10 yrs., 73-33-2)*

| 1993 Opponent | Date | | Pts | 1992 Opponent | Pts |
|---|---|---|---|---|---|
| Wartburg | S11 | | 20 | Wartburg | 16 |
| William Penn | S18 | | 79 | William Penn | 23 |
| Ripon ■ | S25 | | 39 | Ripon | 32 |
| Beloit | O 2 | | 37 | Beloit | 13 |
| Grinnell | O 9 | | 68 | Grinnell | 0 |
| Illinois Col. ■ | O16 | | 34 | Illinois Col. | 0 |
| Monmouth (Ill.) | O23 | | 62 | Monmouth (Ill.) | 21 |
| Knox ■ | O30 | | 59 | Knox | 7 |
| Cornell College | N 6 | | 20 | Cornell College | 37 |

Colors: Crimson & Gold. Nickname: Kohawks.  III

### COLBY.......................... Waterville, ME 04901
*Tom Austin (7 yrs., 22-34-0)*

| 1993 Opponent | Date | | Pts | 1992 Opponent | Pts |
|---|---|---|---|---|---|
| Williams ■ | S25 | | 6 | Williams | 10 |
| Middlebury | O 2 | | 23 | Middlebury | 24 |
| Wesleyan | O 9 | | 28 | Wesleyan | 21 |
| Amherst ■ | O16 | | 28 | Amherst | 14 |
| Hamilton | O23 | | 27 | Hamilton | 19 |
| Bates ■ | O30 | | 52 | Bates | 0 |
| Tufts ■ | N 6 | | 13 | Tufts | 23 |
| Bowdoin | N13 | | 26 | Bowdoin | 18 |

Colors: Blue & Gray. Nickname: White Mules.  III

### COLORADO COLLEGE .... Colorado Springs, CO 80903
*Craig Rundle (7 yrs., 39-29-0)*

| 1993 Opponent | Date | | Pts | 1992 Opponent | Pts |
|---|---|---|---|---|---|
| Grinnell | S11 | | 75 | Grinnell | 7 |
| Pomona-Pitzer | S25 | | 7 | Pomona-Pitzer | 8 |
| Rhodes ■ | O 2 | | 21 | Greenville | 30 |
| Austin | O 9 | | 9 | Austin | 30 |
| Trinity (Tex.) ■ | O16 | | 20 | Trinity (Tex.) | 6 |
| Millsaps | O23 | | 0 | Millsaps | 15 |
| Hardin-Simmons ■ | O30 | | 10 | Hardin-Simmons | 16 |
| Washington (Mo.) | N 6 | | 26 | Washington (Mo.) | 27 |
| Hastings ■ | N13 | | 14 | Hastings | 28 |

Colors: Black & Gold. Nickname: Tigers.  III

### COLORADO SCHOOL OF MINES ..... Golden, CO 80401
*Marvin Kay (24 yrs., 78-145-4)*

| 1993 Opponent | Date | | Pts | 1992 Opponent | Pts |
|---|---|---|---|---|---|
| Doane ■ | S11 | | 21 | Midland Lutheran | 17 |
| Hastings | S18 | | 26 | Doane | 13 |
| Eastern N. Mex. ■ | S25 | | 33 | Hastings | 28 |
| Western St. | O 2 | | 32 | Western St. | 39 |
| Adams St. | O 9 | | 46 | Adams St. | 36 |
| Chadron St. ■ | O16 | | 30 | Chadron St. | 35 |
| Fort Hays St. ■ | O23 | | 14 | Fort Hays St. | 54 |
| Fort Lewis | O30 | | 53 | Fort Lewis | 19 |
| Mesa St. ■ | N 6 | | 21 | Mesa St. | 24 |
| N.M. Highlands ■ | N13 | | 42 | N.M. Highlands | 49 |

Colors: Silver & Blue. Nickname: Orediggers.  II

### CONCORD .......................... Athens, WV 24712
*Bob Mullett (4 yrs., 28-11-2)*

| 1993 Opponent | Date | | Pts | 1992 Opponent | Pts |
|---|---|---|---|---|---|
| Liberty | S 4* | | 47 | Lees-McRae | 13 |
| Elon ■ | S18 | | 8 | Liberty | 26 |
| West Va. St. ■ | S25 | | 16 | West Va. Wesleyan | 14 |
| Fairmont St. | O 2 | | 0 | Mars Hill | 13 |
| West Va. Tech ■ | O 9 | | 24 | Fairmont St. | 13 |
| Shepherd ■ | O16 | | 17 | West Va. Tech | 19 |
| West Liberty St. | O23 | | 17 | Shepherd | 24 |
| Glenville St. | O30 | | 16 | West Liberty St. | 13 |
| West Va. Wesleyan ■ | N 6 | | 30 | Glenville St. | 24 |
| Ga. Southern | N13 | | 25 | West Va. St. | 6 |
| | | | 21 | Gardner-Webb | 28 |

Colors: Maroon & Gray. Nickname: Mountain Lions.  II

---

■ Home games on each schedule.          *Night Games.

## CONCORDIA (ILLINOIS).........River Forest, IL 60305
*Jim Braun (14 yrs., 54-68-3)*

| Chicago | S 11 | 3 | Chicago | 21 |
|---|---|---|---|---|
| N'western (Wis.) ■ | S 18 | 13 | N'western (Wis.) | 11 |
| Maranatha ■ | S 25 | 13 | Maranatha | 20 |
| Lakeland ■ | O 2 | 10 | Lakeland | 15 |
| Eureka | O 9 | 15 | Eureka | 13 |
| Concordia (Wis.) ■ | O 16 | 18 | Concordia (Wis.) | 28 |
| Greenville | O 23 | 28 | Greenville | 40 |
| MacMurray | O 30 | 18 | MacMurray | 12 |
| Principia ■ | N 6 | 44 | Principia | 30 |
| Blackburn ■ | N 13 | 34 | Blackburn | 3 |

Colors: Maroon & Gold.  Nickname: Cougars.  III

## CONCORDIA (MOORHEAD)......Moorhead, MN 56560
*Jim Christopherson (24 yrs., 169-69-6)*

| Moorhead St. ■ | S 11 | 13 | Moorhead St. | 12 |
|---|---|---|---|---|
| Gust. Adolphus | S 18 | 41 | Gust. Adolphus | 31 |
| Hamline ■ | S 25 | 10 | Hamline | 0 |
| Bethel (Minn.) | O 2 | 33 | Bethel (Minn.) | 7 |
| St. Thomas (Minn.) ■ | O 9 | 7 | St. Thomas (Minn.) | 10 |
| Macalester | O 16 | 55 | Macalester | 12 |
| Carleton | O 23 | 24 | Carleton | 26 |
| St. Olaf | O 30 | 45 | St. Olaf | 21 |
| Augsburg† | N 6 | 62 | Augsburg | 0 |
| St. John's (Minn.) ■ | N 13 | 18 | St. John's (Minn.) | 18 |

Colors: Maroon & Gold.  Nickname: Cobbers.  III

## CORNELL COLLEGE.............Mt. Vernon, IA 52314
*Steve Miller (14 yrs., 68-58-3)*

| Buena Vista | S 11 | 31 | Buena Vista | 21 |
|---|---|---|---|---|
| Beloit ■ | S 18 | 20 | Beloit | 6 |
| St. Norbert | S 25 | 28 | St. Norbert | 15 |
| Lake Forest ■ | O 2 | 36 | Lake Forest | 0 |
| Knox | O 9 | 33 | Knox | 0 |
| Monmouth (Ill.) ■ | O 16 | 28 | Monmouth (Ill.) | 18 |
| Grinnell | O 23 | 63 | Grinnell | 20 |
| Illinois Col. | O 30 | 26 | Illinois Col. | 17 |
| Coe ■ | N 6 | 37 | Coe | 20 |
| | | 40 | Beloit | 14 |

Colors: Purple & White.  Nickname: Rams.  III

## CORTLAND STATE................Cortland, NY 13045
*Dave Murray (3 yrs., 23-9-0)*

| Mansfield ■ | S 4 | 21 | Ferrum | 10 |
|---|---|---|---|---|
| Montclair St. ■ | S 11 | 23 | Montclair St. | 17 |
| Ferrum | S 18 | 10 | Mansfield | 24 |
| Buffalo St. ■ | S 25 | 21 | Buffalo St. | 30 |
| Brockport St. | O 9 | 62 | Brockport St. | 12 |
| Albany (N.Y.) ■ | O 16 | 35 | Albany (N.Y.) | 0 |
| Springfield | O 23 | 26 | Springfield | 6 |
| Wash. & Jeff. ■ | O 30 | 6 | Wash. & Jeff. | 31 |
| Ithaca | N 6 | 22 | Ithaca | 20 |
| Southern Conn. St. | N 13 | 17 | Southern Conn. St. | 28 |
| | | | **ECAC Northwest** | |
| | | 38 | Bentley | 20 |

Colors: Red & White.  Nickname: Red Dragons.  III

## CURRY..............................Milton, MA 02186
*Jerry Varnum (1st yr. as head coach)*

| Western New Eng. | S 18 | 7 | Bentley | 47 |
|---|---|---|---|---|
| Framingham St. | S 25 | 22 | Western New Eng. | 25 |
| Bentley ■ | O 2 | 14 | Framingham St. | 33 |
| Nichols | O 9 | 6 | Stonehill | 40 |
| MIT ■ | O 16 | 6 | Nichols | 27 |
| Assumption ■ | O 23 | 14 | Assumption | 40 |
| Stonehill ■ | O 30 | 32 | Hartwick | 13 |
| Salve Regina ■ | N 6 | 13 | MIT | 12 |
| Hartwick | N 13 | | | |

Colors: Purple & White.  Nickname: Colonels.  III

## DEFIANCE......................Defiance, OH 43512
*Malen Luke (5 yrs., 28-20-0)*

| Hanover ■ | S 4 | 35 | Hanover | 14 |
|---|---|---|---|---|
| Olivet Nazarene | S 11 | 17 | Adrian | 14 |
| Adrian ■ | S 18 | 30 | Olivet | 16 |
| Olivet ■ | S 25 | 30 | Kalamazoo | 0 |
| Kalamazoo | O 2 | 32 | Mt. St. Joseph | 3 |
| Mt. St. Joseph | O 9 | 45 | Wilmington (Ohio) | 7 |
| Wilmington (Ohio) | O 16 | 59 | Urbana | 7 |
| Urbana | O 23 | 10 | Thomas More | 21 |
| Thomas More ■ | O 30 | 24 | Bluffton | 14 |
| Bluffton ■ | N 6 | 62 | Wooster | 0 |

Colors: Purple & Gold.  Nickname: Yellow Jackets.  III

## DELAWARE VALLEY...........Doylestown, PA 18901
*Bill Manlove (24 yrs., 185-60-1)*

| FDU-Madison | S 11* | 0 | Wagner | 12 |
|---|---|---|---|---|
| Moravian ■ | S 18 | 16 | Juniata | 20 |
| Lebanon Valley ■ | S 25 | 9 | Lycoming | 20 |
| Wilkes | O 2 | 40 | Albright | 11 |
| Widener | O 9 | 21 | Susquehanna | 25 |
| King's (Pa.) ■ | O 16 | 13 | Wilkes | 17 |
| Susquehanna ■ | O 23 | 17 | Lebanon Valley | 14 |
| Upsala | O 30 | 14 | Moravian | 28 |
| Albright | N 6 | 30 | Wesley | 29 |
| Lycoming ■ | N 13 | 16 | Widener | 31 |

Colors: Green & Gold.  Nickname: Aggies.  III

## DELTA STATE....................Cleveland, MS 38733
*Todd Knight (1st yr. as head coach)*

| Southwest Baptist | S 11* | 0 | Tenn.-Martin | 24 |
|---|---|---|---|---|
| Harding ■ | S 18* | 14 | Central Ark. | 14 |
| North Ala. | S 25* | 18 | Henderson St. | 17 |
| Central Ark. ■ | O 2* | 14 | North Ala. | 10 |
| Henderson St. | O 9* | 13 | Northeast La. | 52 |
| East Tex. St. | O 16* | 10 | Jacksonville St. | 38 |
| Livingston | O 23 | 24 | Livingston | 30 |
| Valdosta St. ■ | O 30* | 36 | West Ga. | 35 |
| West Ga. | N 6 | 7 | Valdosta St. | 34 |
| Mississippi Col. ■ | N 13 | 23 | Mississippi Col. | 34 |

Colors: Green & White.  Nickname: Statesmen.  II

## DENISON.......................Granville, OH 43023
*Bill Wentworth (1st yr. as head coach)*

| Alfred ■ | S 4 | 28 | Brockport St. | 21 |
|---|---|---|---|---|
| Centre | S 11 | 18 | Muskingum | 42 |
| Oberlin | S 18 | 48 | Oberlin | 9 |
| Ohio Wesleyan ■ | O 2 | 7 | Ohio Wesleyan ■ | 25 |
| Earlham | O 9 | 29 | Earlham | 24 |
| Wooster ■ | O 16 | 14 | Wooster | 14 |
| Case Reserve | O 23 | 14 | Case Reserve | 14 |
| Allegheny ■ | O 30 | 13 | Allegheny | 52 |
| Wittenberg | N 6 | 0 | Wittenberg | 36 |
| Kenyon ■ | N 13 | 20 | Kenyon | 23 |

Colors: Red & White.  Nickname: Big Red.  III

## DePAUW..........................Greencastle, IN 46135
*Nick Mourouzis (12 yrs., 79-36-4)*

| Hope ■ | S 11 | 6 | Hope | 0 |
|---|---|---|---|---|
| Millsaps | S 18 | 14 | Millsaps | 21 |
| Albion ■ | S 25 | 20 | Albion | 45 |
| Hanover ■ | O 2 | 31 | Hanover | 15 |
| Rose-Hulman | O 9 | 27 | Rose-Hulman | 15 |
| Taylor ■ | O 16 | 21 | Taylor | 34 |
| Manchester | O 23 | 52 | Manchester | 34 |
| Anderson | O 30 | 8 | Anderson | 4 |
| Franklin ■ | N 6 | 13 | Franklin | 13 |
| Wabash ■ | N 13 | 17 | Wabash | 17 |

Colors: Old Gold & Black.  Nickname: Tigers.  III

## DICKINSON........................Carlisle, PA 17013
*Darwin Breaux (1st yr. as head coach)*

| Hobart ■ | S 11 | 14 | Hobart | 10 |
|---|---|---|---|---|
| Muhlenberg | S 18 | 32 | Muhlenberg | 0 |
| Mercyhurst | S 25 | 20 | Georgetown | 14 |
| Union (N.Y.) | O 2 | 27 | Union (N.Y.) | 3 |
| Frank. & Marsh. | O 9 | 20 | Frank. & Marsh. | 0 |
| Western Md. ■ | O 16 | 14 | Western Md. | 17 |
| Swarthmore | O 23 | 26 | Swarthmore | 26 |
| Johns Hopkins ■ | O 30 | 32 | Johns Hopkins | 0 |
| Gettysburg ■ | N 6 | 41 | Gettysburg | 6 |
| Ursinus ■ | N 13 | 21 | Ursinus | 0 |
| | | | **ECAC Southwest** | |
| | | 13 | Merchant Marine | 20 |

Colors: Red & White.  Nickname: Red Devils.  III

## DUBUQUE.........................Dubuque, IA 52001
*Mike Messer (3 yrs., 4-24-0)*

| Graceland | S 11 | 19 | Graceland | 6 |
|---|---|---|---|---|
| Central (Iowa) ■ | S 18 | 7 | Central (Iowa) | 54 |
| Eureka ■ | S 25 | 7 | Eureka | 14 |
| Luther | O 2 | 6 | Luther | 54 |
| Upper Iowa | O 9 | 12 | Upper Iowa | 54 |
| Loras ■ | O 16 | 0 | Loras | 35 |
| Simpson | O 23 | 3 | Simpson | 35 |
| Wartburg ■ | O 30 | 6 | Wartburg | 55 |
| Buena Vista | N 6 | 21 | Buena Vista | 28 |
| William Penn ■ | N 13 | 26 | William Penn | 28 |

Colors: Blue & White.  Nickname: Spartans.  III

■ Home games on each schedule.          *Night Games.

## EARLHAM .......................Richmond, IN 47374
*Frank Carr (8 yrs., 14-61-0)*

| Opponent | Date | Pts | Opponent | Opp |
|---|---|---|---|---|
| Manchester ■ | S 4 | 28 | Manchester | 12 |
| Otterbein | S11* | 20 | Otterbein | 14 |
| Wittenberg | S18* | 3 | Wittenberg | 35 |
| Kenyon ■ | S25 | 29 | Kenyon | 21 |
| Oberlin | O 2 | 21 | Oberlin | 6 |
| Denison ■ | O 9 | 24 | Denison | 29 |
| Ohio Wesleyan | O16 | 8 | Ohio Wesleyan | 37 |
| Principia | O23 | 61 | Principia | 35 |
| Wooster ■ | O30 | 21 | Wooster | 28 |
| Allegheny ■ | N13 | 6 | Allegheny | 68 |

Colors: Maroon & White.   Nickname: Hustlin' Quakers.   III

## EAST STROUDSBURG ....East Stroudsburg, PA 18301
*Dennis Douds (19 yrs., 117-74-2)*

| Opponent | Date | Pts | Opponent | Opp |
|---|---|---|---|---|
| Kutztown | S11 | 21 | Southern Conn. St. | 16 |
| Springfield ■ | S18 | 12 | Indiana (Pa.) | 31 |
| Southern Conn. St. | S25 | 42 | Bloomsburg | 17 |
| Calif. (Pa.) | O 2 | 40 | Calif. (Pa.) | 13 |
| Cheyney | O 9 | 48 | Cheyney | 6 |
| Mansfield ■ | O16 | 20 | Mansfield | 6 |
| Millersville | O23 | 20 | Millersville | 13 |
| Bloomsburg ■ | O30 | 28 | American Int'l | 27 |
| American Int'l ■ | N 6 | 27 | Kutztown | 21 |
| West Chester ■ | N13 | 0 | West Chester | 3 |

Colors: Red & Black.   Nickname: Warriors.   II

## EAST TEXAS STATE............Commerce, TX 75428
*Eddie Vowell (7 yrs., 42-37-1)*

| Opponent | Date | Pts | Opponent | Opp |
|---|---|---|---|---|
| Central Ark. ■ | S 4* | 30 | Central Ark. | 18 |
| Northwest Mo. St. | S11 | 13 | Pittsburg St. | 27 |
| Henderson St. | S18* | 31 | Southern Ark. | 16 |
| Northwestern (La.) | S25* | 0 | Northwestern (La.) | 20 |
| Central Okla. ■ | O 2 | 26 | Central Okla. | 9 |
| Texas A&I | O 9* | 10 | Texas A&I | 17 |
| Delta St. ■ | O16* | 57 | Iowa Wesleyan | 7 |
| Eastern N. Mex. | O23 | 30 | Eastern N. Mex. | 21 |
| Abilene Christian ■ | O30 | 52 | Abilene Christian | 10 |
| Angelo St. | N 6 | 25 | Angelo St. | 11 |
| Texas Southern ■ | N13 | 40 | Cameron | 3 |

Colors: Blue & Gold.   Nickname: Lions.   II

## EASTERN NEW MEXICO..........Portales, NM 88130
*Howard Stearns (1 yr., 5-5-0)*

| Opponent | Date | Pts | Opponent | Opp |
|---|---|---|---|---|
| N.M. Highlands ■ | S 4* | 9 | N.M. Highlands | 21 |
| Western St. ■ | S11* | 14 | Western St. | 57 |
| Western N. Mex. | S18* | 27 | Western N. Mex. | 13 |
| Colorado Mines | S25 | 30 | Abilene Christian | 6 |
| Abilene Christian | O 2 | 26 | Angelo St. | 25 |
| Angelo St. | O 9 | 45 | Cameron | 7 |
| East Tex. St. | O23 | 21 | East Tex. St. | 30 |
| Texas A&I | O30* | 0 | Texas A&I | 26 |
| West Tex. St. ■ | N 6 | 56 | West Tex. St. | 0 |
| Central Okla. | N13 | 13 | Central Okla. | 35 |

Colors: Silver & Green.   Nickname: Grayhounds.   II

## EDINBORO .......................Edinboro, PA 16444
*Tom Hollman (9 yrs., 61-27-3)*

| Opponent | Date | Pts | Opponent | Opp |
|---|---|---|---|---|
| Ferris St. ■ | S 4 | 35 | Buffalo | 13 |
| Elizabeth City St. | S18 | 37 | Northwood | 13 |
| Buffalo | S25* | 41 | Southern Conn. St. | 0 |
| Clarion | O 2 | 26 | Clarion | 17 |
| Lock Haven ■ | O 9 | 38 | Lock Haven | 10 |
| Shippensburg | O16 | 47 | Shippensburg | 3 |
| Calif. (Pa.) ■ | O23 | 33 | Calif. (Pa.) | 13 |
| Slippery Rock | O30 | 7 | Slippery Rock | 10 |
| Indiana (Pa.) ■ | N 6 | 21 | Indiana (Pa.) | 21 |
| Millersville | N13 | 36 | Millersville | 12 |
| | | | **II Championship** | |
| | | 15 | Ferris St. | 19 |

Colors: Red & White.   Nickname: Fighting Scots.   II

## ELIZABETH CITY STATE .....Elizabeth City, NC 27909
*Alvin T. Kelley (2 yrs., 10-8-1)*

| Opponent | Date | Pts | Opponent | Opp |
|---|---|---|---|---|
| Winston-Salem ■ | S 4 | 18 | Winston-Salem | 27 |
| Fayetteville St. | S11* | 0 | Fayetteville St. | 0 |
| Edinboro ■ | S18 | 10 | Central St. (Ohio) | 24 |
| Norfolk St. | S25* | 45 | Norfolk St. | 46 |
| N.C. Central ■ | O 2* | 42 | N.C. Central | 24 |
| Virginia Union | O 9 | 38 | Virginia Union | 6 |
| Bowie St. ■ | O16 | 20 | Bowie St. | 16 |
| Virginia St. | O23 | 27 | Virginia St. | 28 |
| Hampton | O30 | 22 | Hampton | 30 |
| Lane ■ | N13 | 40 | Kentucky St. | 41 |

Colors: Royal Blue & White.   Nickname: Vikings.   II

## ELMHURST........................Elmhurst, IL 60126
*Bob Fabrizio (1st yr. as head coach)*

| Opponent | Date | Pts | Opponent | Opp |
|---|---|---|---|---|
| III. Benedictine | S18 | 20 | III. Benedictine | 49 |
| Aurora ■ | S25 | 0 | Aurora | 27 |
| Carthage | O 2 | 35 | Carthage | 10 |
| North Park ■ | O 9 | 20 | North Park | 20 |
| North Central | O16* | 30 | North Central | 28 |
| Augustana (III.) ■ | O23 | 14 | Augustana (III.) | 46 |
| III. Wesleyan | O30 | 14 | III. Wesleyan | 42 |
| Wheaton (III.) ■ | N 6 | 6 | Wheaton (III.) | 30 |
| Millikin | N13 | 28 | Millikin | 33 |

Colors: Blue & White.   Nickname: Bluejays.   III

## ELON ..........................Elon College, NC 27244
*Leon Hart (4 yrs., 20-22-0)*

| Opponent | Date | Pts | Opponent | Opp |
|---|---|---|---|---|
| West Ga. ■ | S 4* | 41 | Wofford | 27 |
| West Va. St. ■ | S11* | 13 | Carson-Newman | 17 |
| Concord (W. Va.) | S18 | 42 | Newberry | 10 |
| Carson-Newman | S25 | 10 | Lenoir-Rhyne | 7 |
| Lenoir-Rhyne ■ | O 2 | 23 | Mars Hill | 3 |
| Mars Hill ■ | O 9 | 21 | Presbyterian | 0 |
| Presbyterian | O16 | 15 | Catawba | 7 |
| Catawba ■ | O23 | 23 | Gardner-Webb | 28 |
| Gardner-Webb | O30 | 40 | Lees-McRae | 7 |
| Wofford ■ | N 6 | 55 | Wingate | 21 |
| Wingate ■ | N13 | | | |

Colors: Maroon & Gold.   Nickname: Fightin' Christians.   II

## EMORY AND HENRY.................Emory, VA 24327
*Lou Wacker (11 yrs., 82-36-0)*

| Opponent | Date | Pts | Opponent | Opp |
|---|---|---|---|---|
| Cumberland (Ky.) | S 4 | 49 | Cumberland (Ky.) | 6 |
| Wash. & Lee ■ | S11 | 41 | Wash. & Lee | 13 |
| Bridgewater (Va.) | S18 | 51 | Bridgewater (Va.) | 6 |
| Davidson ■ | S25 | 36 | Davidson | 7 |
| Millsaps | O 2 | 17 | Millsaps | 6 |
| Hampden-Sydney | O 9 | 13 | Hampden-Sydney | 7 |
| Randolph-Macon | O16 | 21 | Randolph-Macon | 3 |
| Guilford ■ | O23 | 41 | Guilford | 0 |
| Ferrum ■ | N 6 | 21 | Ferrum | 14 |
| Maryville (Tenn.) | N13 | 24 | Maryville (Tenn.) | 14 |
| | | | **III Championship** | |
| | | 17 | Thomas More | 0 |
| | | 15 | Wash. & Jeff. | 51 |

Colors: Blue & Gold.   Nickname: Wasps.   III

## EMPORIA STATE .................Emporia, KS 66801
*Larry Kramer (22 yrs., 116-101-6)*

| Opponent | Date | Pts | Opponent | Opp |
|---|---|---|---|---|
| Fort Hays St. ■ | S 4* | 24 | Fort Hays St. | 17 |
| Southwest Baptist ■ | S18* | 28 | Mo. Southern St. | 7 |
| Missouri-Rolla | S25 | 35 | Mo. Western St. | 30 |
| Northwest Mo. St. ■ | O 2 | 24 | Northeast Mo. St. | 7 |
| Northeast Mo. St. | O 9 | 7 | Central Mo. St. | 9 |
| Mo. Western St. ■ | O16 | 25 | Washburn | 18 |
| Mo. Southern St. | O23 | 35 | Missouri-Rolla | 6 |
| Central Mo. St. ■ | O30 | 45 | Southwest Baptist | 6 |
| Washburn ■ | N 6 | 38 | Pittsburg St. | 49 |
| Pittsburg St. | N13 | 41 | Northwest Mo. St. | 54 |

Colors: Black & Old Gold.   Nickname: Hornets.   II

## EUREKA..........................Eureka, IL 61530
*John Tully (3 yrs., 20-11-0)*

| Opponent | Date | Pts | Opponent | Opp |
|---|---|---|---|---|
| MacMurray ■ | S 4 | 30 | MacMurray | 15 |
| Monmouth (III.) | S11 | 15 | Monmouth (III.) | 26 |
| North Central ■ | S18 | 32 | North Central | 14 |
| Dubuque | S25 | 7 | Dubuque | 7 |
| Quincy ■ | O 2 | 26 | Quincy | 28 |
| Concordia (III.) ■ | O 9 | 13 | Concordia (III.) | 15 |
| Lakeland | O16 | 28 | Lakeland | 7 |
| Ky. Wesleyan ■ | O23 | 6 | Ky. Wesleyan | 28 |
| Concordia (Wis.) ■ | O30 | 27 | Concordia (Wis.) | 0 |
| Greenville | N 6 | 46 | Greenville | 56 |

Colors: Maroon & Gold.   Nickname: Red Devils.   III

## FAIRLEIGH DICKINSON-MADISON . Madison, NJ 07940
*Bill Klika (19 yrs., 45-117-1)*

| Opponent | Date | Pts | Opponent | Opp |
|---|---|---|---|---|
| Delaware Valley ■ | S11* | 19 | Jersey City St. | 14 |
| Lycoming | S18 | 0 | Johns Hopkins | 7 |
| Johns Hopkins ■ | S24* | 15 | St. John's (N.Y.) | 14 |
| Montclair St. | O 2 | 0 | Trenton St. | 15 |
| Albright ■ | O 9 | 12 | Frank. & Marsh. | 22 |
| Wilkes | O16 | 0 | Ursinus | 14 |
| Ursinus ■ | O23 | 22 | Upsala | 16 |
| King's (Pa.) | O30 | 21 | Marist | 28 |
| Widener ■ | N 5* | 14 | Iona | 10 |
| Upsala ■ | N12* | | | |

Colors: Columbia, Navy & White.   Nickname: Jersey Devils.   III

---

■ Home games on each schedule.            *Night Games.

## FAIRMONT STATE ............. Fairmont, WV 26554
### Doug Sams (2 yrs., 9-11-0)

| Opponent | Date | | Result |
|---|---|---|---|
| Presbyterian | S 4 | 12 | Presbyterian ...10 |
| Slippery Rock ■ | S11 | 0 | Slippery Rock ...24 |
| Calif. (Pa.) | S18 | 7 | Calif. (Pa.) ...14 |
| West Va. Wesleyan ■ | S25 | 16 | West Va. Wesleyan ...14 |
| Concord (W. Va.) ■ | O 2 | 12 | Concord (W. Va.) ...24 |
| West Va. St. | O 9 | 14 | West Va. St. ...40 |
| West Va. Tech | O16 | 40 | West Va. Tech ...26 |
| Glenville St. ■ | O23 | 13 | Glenville St. ...34 |
| Shepherd ■ | O30 | 14 | Shepherd ...24 |
| West Liberty St. | N 6 | 12 | West Liberty St. ...10 |

Colors: Maroon & White.  Nickname: Falcons.    II

## FAYETTEVILLE STATE ........ Fayetteville, NC 28301
### Jerome Harper (1 yr., 5-4-1)

| Opponent | Date | | Result |
|---|---|---|---|
| Delaware St.† | S 4 | 28 | Miles ... 8 |
| Elizabeth City St. ■ | S11* | 0 | Elizabeth City St. ... 0 |
| Norfolk St. ■ | S18* | 32 | Norfolk St. ...23 |
| Cheyney | S25 | 8 | Winston-Salem ...34 |
| Winston-Salem ■ | O 2* | 13 | N.C. Central ... 3 |
| N.C. Central | O 9 | 35 | Virginia St. ...15 |
| Virginia St. | O16 | 6 | Johnson Smith ...24 |
| Johnson Smith ■ | O23 | 26 | Livingstone ...20 |
| Bowie St. | O30 | 12 | Newberry ...35 |
| Livingstone | N 7 | 14 | Alabama St. ...17 |
| Newberry ■ | N13 | | |

Colors: White & Royal Blue.  Nickname: Broncos.    II

## FERRIS STATE ................. Big Rapids, MI 49307
### Keith Otterbein (7 yrs., 40-37-1)

| Opponent | Date | | Result |
|---|---|---|---|
| Edinboro | S 4 | 33 | Northwood ...10 |
| Ashland ■ | S11 | 7 | Ashland ...15 |
| Hillsdale | S18* | 14 | Hillsdale ...36 |
| Wayne St. (Mich.) ■ | S25 | 21 | Wayne St. (Mich.) ... 3 |
| Northern Mich. | O 2* | 23 | Northern Mich. ...12 |
| St. Francis (Ill.) ■ | O 9 | 33 | Valparaiso ... 3 |
| Grand Valley St. | O16 | 23 | Grand Valley St. ... 0 |
| Northwood | O23 | 35 | Butler ... 7 |
| Indianapolis ■ | O30 | 54 | Indianapolis ...13 |
| Saginaw Valley | N 6 | 10 | Saginaw Valley ... 9 |
| St. Joseph's (Ind.) | N13 | 23 | St. Joseph's (Ind.) ... 7 |
| **II Championship** | | | |
| | | 19 | Edinboro ...15 |
| | | 13 | New Haven ...35 |

Colors: Crimson & Gold.  Nickname: Bulldogs.    II

## FERRUM ........................... Ferrum, VA 24088
### Hank Norton (8 yrs., 58-27-1)

| Opponent | Date | | Result |
|---|---|---|---|
| Thomas More | S 4 | 10 | Cortland St. ...21 |
| Cortland St. ■ | S18 | 29 | Ramapo ...22 |
| Lees-McRae | S25 | 0 | Western Caro. ...42 |
| Westminster (Pa.) | O 2 | 14 | Westminster (Pa.) ...21 |
| Newport News App. ■ | O 9 | 34 | Guilford ... 4 |
| Chowan | O16 | 49 | Newport News App. ...20 |
| Montclair St. ■ | O23 | 31 | Ala.-Birmingham ...17 |
| Mansfield ■ | O30 | 28 | Mansfield ...41 |
| Emory & Henry | N 6 | 14 | Emory & Henry ...21 |

Colors: Black & Gold.  Nickname: Panthers.    III

## FITCHBURG STATE ............. Fitchburg, MA 01420
### Mike Woessner (1st yr. as head coach)

| Opponent | Date | | Result |
|---|---|---|---|
| Western New Eng. ■ | S11 | 14 | Western New Eng. ...28 |
| Framingham St. | S18 | 14 | Framingham St. ...35 |
| Westfield St. | S25 | 0 | Westfield St. ...41 |
| Bri'water (Mass.) | O 2 | 0 | Bri'water (Mass.) ...14 |
| Worcester St. ■ | O 9 | 0 | Worcester St. ...45 |
| Mass. Maritime | O16 | 0 | Mass. Maritime ...33 |
| Mass.-Dartmouth ■ | O23 | 0 | Mass.-Dartmouth ...26 |
| Maine Maritime | O30 | 6 | Maine Maritime ...25 |
| Mass.-Boston ■ | N 6 | 18 | Mass.-Boston ...32 |

Colors: Green, Gold & White.  Nickname: Falcons.    III

## FORT HAYS STATE.................. Hays, KS 67601
### Bob Cortese (13 yrs., 106-34-3)

| Opponent | Date | | Result |
|---|---|---|---|
| Emporia St. ■ | S 4* | 17 | Emporia St. ...24 |
| Central Okla. | S11* | 15 | Central Okla. ...17 |
| Central Ark. | S18* | 14 | Central Ark. ...21 |
| N.M. Highlands ■ | S25 | 13 | Neb.-Kearney ...17 |
| Neb.-Kearney | O 2* | 28 | N.M. Highlands ...28 |
| Mesa St. | O 9 | 38 | Mesa St. ...17 |
| Adams St. | O16 | 31 | Adams St. ...17 |
| Colorado Mines | O23 | 54 | Colorado Mines ...14 |
| Chadron St. ■ | O30 | 0 | Chadron St. ... 0 |
| Western St. | N 6 | 10 | Western St. ...35 |
| Fort Lewis | N13 | 49 | Fort Lewis ...25 |

Colors: Black & Gold.  Nickname: Tigers.    II

## FORT LEWIS ...................... Durango, CO 81301
### Kevin Donnalley (1 yr., 1-9-0)

| Opponent | Date | | Result |
|---|---|---|---|
| West Tex. St. | S11* | 46 | West Tex. St. ...35 |
| Montana St. | S18 | 28 | Montana Tech ...51 |
| Mesa St. | S25* | 23 | Western N. Mex. ...52 |
| Angelo St. | O 2* | 27 | Mesa St. ...38 |
| Western St. ■ | O 9 | 16 | Western St. ...69 |
| N.M. Highlands | O16 | 55 | N.M. Highlands ...60 |
| Adams St. ■ | O23 | 36 | Adams St. ...60 |
| Colorado Mines ■ | O30 | 19 | Colorado Mines ...53 |
| Chadron St. | N 6 | 22 | Chadron St. ...29 |
| Fort Hays St. ■ | N13 | 25 | Fort Hays St. ...49 |

Colors: Blue & Gold.  Nickname: Raiders.    II

## FORT VALLEY STATE .......... Fort Valley, GA 31030
### Douglas Porter (23 yrs., 135-89-4)

| Opponent | Date | | Result |
|---|---|---|---|
| North Ala. | S 4* | 0 | Central St. (Ohio) ...33 |
| Morehouse | S11 | 13 | Morehouse ... 0 |
| Valdosta St. ■ | S18* | 17 | Valdosta St. ...24 |
| Morris Brown† | S25* | 32 | Morris Brown ... 6 |
| Clark Atlanta† | O 2* | 42 | Clark Atlanta ...17 |
| Jacksonville St. | O 9 | 7 | North Ala. ...41 |
| Miles ■ | O16 | 38 | Miles ... 0 |
| Alabama A&M | O23 | 16 | Alabama A&M ... 0 |
| Tuskegee | O30 | 38 | Tuskegee ... 6 |
| Savannah St. | N 6 | 22 | Savannah St. ...13 |
| Albany St. (Ga.)† | N13 | 10 | Albany St. (Ga.) ...29 |

Colors: Royal Blue & Old Gold.  Nickname: Wildcats.    II

## FRAMINGHAM STATE ........ Framingham, MA 01701
### Thomas Raeke (8 yrs., 27-44-0)

| Opponent | Date | | Result |
|---|---|---|---|
| Fitchburg St. ■ | S18 | 35 | Fitchburg St. ...14 |
| Curry ■ | S25 | 33 | Curry ...14 |
| Westfield St. | O 2 | 6 | Westfield St. ...24 |
| Bri'water (Mass.) ■ | O 9 | 7 | Bri'water (Mass.) ...48 |
| Worcester St. | O16 | 14 | Worcester St. ... 0 |
| Mass. Maritime ■ | O23 | 28 | Mass. Maritime ...42 |
| Mass.-Dartmouth | O30 | 6 | Mass.-Dartmouth ... 3 |
| Maine Maritime ■ | N 6 | 0 | Maine Maritime ...36 |
| Mass.-Boston | N13 | 28 | Mass.-Boston ...53 |

Colors: Black & Gold.  Nickname: Rams.    III

## FRANKLIN .......................... Franklin, IN 46131
### Mike McClure (4 yrs., 12-27-1)

| Opponent | Date | | Result |
|---|---|---|---|
| Evansville ■ | S11 | 20 | Evansville ...24 |
| Alma | S18 | 18 | Alma ...31 |
| Thomas More | S25 | 14 | Thomas More ...42 |
| Anderson ■ | O 2 | 18 | Anderson ...46 |
| Wabash | O 9 | 14 | Wabash ...16 |
| Rose-Hulman | O16 | 7 | Rose-Hulman ...27 |
| Manchester | O30 | 33 | Taylor ...34 |
| DePauw | N 6 | 20 | Manchester ...21 |
| Hanover ■ | N13 | 13 | DePauw ...13 |
| | | 7 | Hanover ...31 |

Colors: Old Gold & Navy Blue.  Nickname: Grizzlies.    III

## FRANKLIN AND MARSHALL..... Lancaster, PA 17604
### Tom Gilburg (18 yrs., 122-49-2)

| Opponent | Date | | Result |
|---|---|---|---|
| Carnegie Mellon | S 4 | 7 | Moravian ...14 |
| Wash. & Jeff. ■ | S11 | 13 | Ursinus ... 6 |
| Ursinus | S18 | 6 | Muhlenberg ... 9 |
| Muhlenberg ■ | S25 | 34 | Georgetown ...19 |
| Dickinson ■ | O 9 | 0 | Dickinson ...20 |
| Georgetown | O16 | 28 | FDU-Madison ...12 |
| Western Md. | O23 | 41 | Western Md. ...26 |
| Swarthmore ■ | O30 | 21 | Swarthmore ...28 |
| Johns Hopkins | N 6 | 44 | Johns Hopkins ...14 |
| Gettysburg | N13 | 13 | Gettysburg ...26 |

Colors: Blue & White.  Nickname: Diplomats.    III

## FROSTBURG STATE ............ Frostburg, MD 21532
### Mike McGlinchey (11 yrs., 67-41-5)

| Opponent | Date | | Result |
|---|---|---|---|
| Alfred | S11 | 6 | Lycoming ...13 |
| Thiel ■ | S18 | 44 | Thiel ... 0 |
| Salisbury St. | S25 | 31 | Salisbury St. ...14 |
| Chowan ■ | O 2 | 17 | Wesley ... 0 |
| Trenton St. ■ | O 9 | 7 | Geneva ...22 |
| Wesley ■ | O16 | 14 | Canisius ...14 |
| Bridgewater (Va.) | O23 | 37 | Bridgewater (Va.) ... 2 |
| Brockport St. | O30 | 17 | Brockport St. ...31 |
| Waynesburg ■ | N 6 | 14 | Waynesburg ... 0 |
| Methodist | N13 | 35 | Methodist ...14 |

Colors: Red, White & Black.  Nickname: Bobcats.    III

■ Home games on each schedule.    *Night Games.

## GALLAUDET ... Washington, DC 20785
*Geoffrey Ciniero (1st yr. as head coach)*

| 1993 Opponent | Date | Pts | 1992 Opponent | Opp |
|---|---|---|---|---|
| Chowan | S11 | 6 | Ala.-Birmingham | 44 |
| Salve Regina | S18 | 20 | Georgetown | 52 |
| Stevens Tech ■ | S25 | 6 | Stevens Tech | 34 |
| Hartwick | O 2 | 7 | St. Francis (Pa.) | 33 |
| Catholic ■ | O16 | 14 | Wesley | 47 |
| Methodist ■ | O23 | 11 | Catholic | 44 |
| Newport News App. | O30 | 6 | St. Peter's | 27 |
| Williamson ■ | N 6 | 7 | Newport News App. | 24 |
| St. John Fisher | N13 | 10 | St. John Fisher | 35 |

Colors: Buff & Blue.  Nickname: Bison.  III

## GANNON ... Erie, PA 16541
*Tom Herman (4 yrs., 15-20-1)*

| 1993 Opponent | Date | Pts | 1992 Opponent | Opp |
|---|---|---|---|---|
| St. Francis (Pa.) | S 4 | 20 | St. Francis (Pa.) | 20 |
| Waynesburg ■ | S11 | 34 | Waynesburg | 3 |
| Mercyhurst ■ | S18 | 24 | Mercyhurst | 21 |
| Canisius | S25* | 21 | Duquesne | 17 |
| Duquesne ■ | O 2 | 14 | LIU-C.W. Post | 21 |
| LIU-C.W. Post | O 9 | 16 | Wash. & Jeff. | 49 |
| Wash. & Jeff. ■ | O16 | 31 | Bethany (W.Va.) | 16 |
| Bethany (W.Va.) | O23 | 34 | Thiel | 26 |
| Thiel | O30 | 33 | Grove City | 20 |
| Grove City ■ | N 6 | 6 | Buffalo St. | 14 |

Colors: Maroon & Gold.  Nickname: Golden Knights.  III

## GARDNER-WEBB ... Boiling Springs, NC 28017
*Woody Fish (9 yrs., 58-43-1)*

| 1993 Opponent | Date | Pts | 1992 Opponent | Opp |
|---|---|---|---|---|
| Lees-McRae | S11 | 21 | Central Fla. | 71 |
| Tenn.-Chatt. | S18* | 56 | Charleston So. | 0 |
| Newberry ■ | S25 | 65 | Newberry | 16 |
| Wingate | O 2 | 57 | Lees-McRae | 6 |
| Lenoir-Rhyne ■ | O 9 | 69 | Wingate | 33 |
| Catawba | O16 | 52 | Lenoir-Rhyne | 17 |
| Carson-Newman ■ | O23 | 34 | Catawba | 17 |
| Elon ■ | O30 | 25 | Carson-Newman | 6 |
| Presbyterian ■ | N 6 | 28 | Elon | 23 |
| Mars Hill | N13 | 46 | Presbyterian | 13 |
| | | 45 | Mars Hill | 13 |
| **NAIA I Championship** | | | | |
| | | 28 | Concord (W. Va.) | 21 |
| | | 22 | Shepherd | 7 |
| | | 16 | Central St. (Ohio) | 19 |

Colors: Scarlet, White & Black.  Nickname: Bulldogs.  II

## GETTYSBURG ... Gettysburg, PA 17325
*Barry Streeter (15 yrs., 87-62-4)*

| 1993 Opponent | Date | Pts | 1992 Opponent | Opp |
|---|---|---|---|---|
| Catholic ■ | S11 | 40 | Widener | 6 |
| Western Md. ■ | S18 | 13 | Western Md. | 38 |
| Swarthmore | S25 | 45 | Swarthmore | 34 |
| Johns Hopkins ■ | O 2 | 13 | Johns Hopkins | 10 |
| Stony Brook | O 9 | 15 | Stony Brook | 12 |
| Ursinus | O16 | 6 | Ursinus | 28 |
| Muhlenberg ■ | O23 | 18 | Muhlenberg | 7 |
| Merchant Marine ■ | O30 | 7 | Union (N.Y.) | 43 |
| Dickinson ■ | N 6 | 6 | Dickinson | 41 |
| Frank. & Marsh. | N13 | 26 | Frank. & Marsh. | 13 |

Colors: Orange & Blue.  Nickname: Bullets.  III

## GLENVILLE STATE ... Glenville, WV 26351
*Rich Rodriguez (4 yrs., 13-24-2)*

| 1993 Opponent | Date | Pts | 1992 Opponent | Opp |
|---|---|---|---|---|
| Samford | S 4* | 34 | Geneva | 15 |
| Johnson Smith ■ | S11 | 20 | Shepherd | 23 |
| Shepherd | S25 | 35 | West Va. St. | 6 |
| West Va. St. | O 2 | 28 | West Liberty St. | 23 |
| West Liberty St. ■ | O 9 | 10 | Johnson Smith | 13 |
| West Va. Wesleyan ■ | O16 | 49 | Indiana St. | 63 |
| Fairmont St. | O23 | 30 | West Va. Wesleyan | 6 |
| Concord (W. Va.) ■ | O30 | 34 | Fairmont St. | 13 |
| West Va. Tech | N 6 | 24 | Concord (W. Va.) | 30 |
| | | 70 | West Va. Tech | 7 |

Colors: Blue & White.  Nickname: Pioneers.  II

## GRAND VALLEY STATE ... Allendale, MI 49401
*Brian Kelly (2 yrs., 17-6-0)*

| 1993 Opponent | Date | Pts | 1992 Opponent | Opp |
|---|---|---|---|---|
| St. Joseph's (Ind.) ■ | S 4 | 28 | St. Joseph's (Ind.) | 18 |
| Indiana (Pa.) | S11 | 27 | Indiana (Pa.) | 45 |
| Northwood | S18 | 21 | Butler | 10 |
| Indianapolis ■ | S25 | 21 | Indianapolis | 7 |
| Saginaw Valley ■ | O 2 | 24 | Saginaw Valley | 20 |
| Northern Mich. ■ | O 9 | 23 | Northern Mich. | 20 |
| Ferris St. | O16 | 0 | Ferris St. | 23 |
| Ashland | O23 | 10 | Ashland | 27 |
| Hillsdale ■ | O30 | 34 | Hillsdale | 7 |
| Wayne St. (Mich.) | N 6 | 16 | Wayne St. (Mich.) | 14 |
| St. Francis (Ill.) ■ | N13 | 45 | Valparaiso | 14 |

Colors: Blue, Black & White.  Nickname: Lakers.  II

## GRINNELL ... Grinnell, IA 50112
*Greg Wallace (5 yrs., 7-36-1)*

| 1993 Opponent | Date | Pts | 1992 Opponent | Opp |
|---|---|---|---|---|
| Colorado Col. ■ | S11 | 7 | Colorado Col. | 75 |
| Principia | S18 | 13 | Principia | 38 |
| Lake Forest | S25 | 14 | Lake Forest | 27 |
| St. Norbert ■ | O 2 | 12 | St. Norbert | 44 |
| Coe | O 9 | 0 | Coe | 68 |
| Knox ■ | O16 | 7 | Knox | 21 |
| Cornell College | O23 | 20 | Cornell College | 63 |
| Monmouth (Ill.) | O30 | 0 | Monmouth (Ill.) | 72 |
| Illinois Col. ■ | N 7 | 13 | Illinois Col. | 60 |

Colors: Scarlet & Black.  Nickname: Pioneers.  III

## GROVE CITY ... Grove City, PA 16127
*Christopher Smith (9 yrs., 30-49-2)*

| 1993 Opponent | Date | Pts | 1992 Opponent | Opp |
|---|---|---|---|---|
| Hiram | S11 | 26 | Duquesne | 27 |
| Waynesburg ■ | S25 | 23 | Waynesburg | 3 |
| Bluffton | O 2 | 35 | Bluffton | 10 |
| Bethany (W.Va.) ■ | O 9 | 58 | Bethany (W.Va.) | 8 |
| Thiel | O16 | 41 | Thiel | 6 |
| Wash. & Jeff. ■ | O23 | 13 | Wash. & Jeff. | 34 |
| Carnegie Mellon ■ | O30 | 14 | Carnegie Mellon | 35 |
| Gannon | N 6 | 20 | Gannon | 33 |
| Oberlin | N13 | 34 | Oberlin | 0 |

Colors: Crimson & White.  Nickname: Wolverines.  III

## GUILFORD ... Greensboro, NC 27410
*Mike Ketchum (2 yrs., 10-10-0)*

| 1993 Opponent | Date | Pts | 1992 Opponent | Opp |
|---|---|---|---|---|
| Lenoir-Rhyne | S 4* | 3 | Davidson | 18 |
| Methodist ■ | S11 | 38 | Methodist | 7 |
| Chowan ■ | S18 | 6 | Hampden-Sydney | 10 |
| Hampden-Sydney ■ | S25 | 13 | Charleston So. | 37 |
| Davidson ■ | O 2 | 10 | Salisbury St. | 14 |
| Bridgewater (Va.) | O16 | 4 | Ferrum | 34 |
| Emory & Henry | O23 | 7 | Bridgewater (Va.) | 9 |
| Randolph-Macon ■† | O30 | 0 | Emory & Henry | 41 |
| Wash. & Lee | N 6 | 21 | Randolph-Macon | 20 |
| Salisbury St. | N13 | 0 | Wash. & Lee | 21 |

Colors: Crimson & Gray.  Nickname: Quakers.  III

## GUSTAVUS ADOLPHUS ... St. Peter, MN 56082
*Steve Byrne (5 yrs., 25-24-0)*

| 1993 Opponent | Date | Pts | 1992 Opponent | Opp |
|---|---|---|---|---|
| Augustana (S.D.) | S11 | 0 | Augustana (S.D.) | 34 |
| Concordia-M'head ■ | S18 | 31 | Concordia-M'head | 41 |
| Augsburg | S25* | 28 | Augsburg | 12 |
| St. John's (Minn.) ■ | O 2 | 7 | St. John's (Minn.) | 35 |
| St. Olaf | O 9 | 14 | St. Olaf | 9 |
| Hamline | O16 | 24 | Hamline | 34 |
| Bethel (Minn.) ■ | O23 | 13 | Bethel (Minn.) | 44 |
| St. Thomas (Minn.) | O30 | 16 | St. Thomas (Minn.) | 10 |
| Macalester† | N 5* | 32 | Macalester | 12 |
| Carleton | N13 | 20 | Carleton | 21 |

Colors: Black & Gold.  Nickname: Golden Gusties.  III

## HAMILTON ... Clinton, NY 13323
*Steve Frank (8 yrs., 37-26-1)*

| 1993 Opponent | Date | Pts | 1992 Opponent | Opp |
|---|---|---|---|---|
| Amherst ■ | S26 | 41 | Amherst | 0 |
| Wesleyan ■ | O 2 | 24 | Wesleyan | 14 |
| Trinity (Conn.) | O 9 | 17 | Trinity (Conn.) | 21 |
| Bowdoin | O16 | 28 | Bowdoin | 25 |
| Colby ■ | O23 | 19 | Colby | 27 |
| Williams | O30 | 34 | Williams | 33 |
| Middlebury ■ | N 6 | 9 | Middlebury | 17 |
| Bates | N13 | 47 | Bates | 6 |

Colors: Buff & Blue.  Nickname: Continentals.  III

## HAMLINE ... St. Paul, MN 55104
*Dick Tressel (15 yrs., 85-60-2)*

| 1993 Opponent | Date | Pts | 1992 Opponent | Opp |
|---|---|---|---|---|
| Mt. Senario ■ | S11 | 38 | Mt. Senario | 0 |
| Carleton | S18 | 0 | Carleton | 36 |
| Concordia-M'head | S25 | 0 | Concordia-M'head | 10 |
| Augsburg ■ | O 2 | 25 | Augsburg | 9 |
| St. John's (Minn.) | O 9 | 7 | St. John's (Minn.) | 21 |
| Gust. Adolphus ■ | O16 | 34 | Gust. Adolphus | 24 |
| St. Olaf | O23 | 17 | St. Olaf | 14 |
| Bethel (Minn.) | O30 | 10 | Bethel (Minn.) | 13 |
| St. Thomas (Minn.)† | N 6 | 14 | St. Thomas (Minn.) | 6 |
| Macalester | N13 | 44 | Macalester | 0 |

Colors: Red & Gray.  Nickname: Pipers.  III

■ Home games on each schedule.     *Night Games.

## HAMPDEN-SYDNEY ..... Hampden-Sydney, VA 23943
*Joe Bush (8 yrs., 45-33-1)*

| Opponent | Date | Pts | Opponent | Pts |
|---|---|---|---|---|
| Muhlenberg ■ | S11 | 21 | Centre | 7 |
| Clinch Valley ■ | S18 | 10 | Guilford | 6 |
| Guilford | S25 | 23 | Union (Ky.) | 24 |
| Bridgewater (Va.) ■ | O 2 | 16 | Bridgewater (Va.) | 10 |
| Emory & Henry | O 9 | 7 | Emory & Henry | 13 |
| Wash. & Lee ■ | O16 | 21 | Wash. & Lee | 24 |
| Catholic | O23 | 23 | Wesley | 33 |
| Davidson | O30 | 35 | Davidson | 18 |
| Methodist ■ | N 6 | 17 | Methodist | 3 |
| Randolph-Macon | N13 | 26 | Randolph-Macon | 22 |

Colors: Garnet & Gray.  Nickname: Tigers.  III

## HAMPTON ...... Hampton, VA 23668
*Joe Taylor (10 yrs., 70-31-4)*

| Opponent | Date | Pts | Opponent | Pts |
|---|---|---|---|---|
| Livingstone | S 4 | 48 | Johnson Smith | 6 |
| Bowie St. | S11 | 58 | Bowie St. | 7 |
| Virginia Union ■ | S18* | 20 | Virginia Union | 20 |
| Grambling† | S25* | 72 | Cheyney | 0 |
| Johnson Smith | O 2 | 46 | Morehouse | 19 |
| Virginia St. | O 9 | 55 | Virginia St. | 23 |
| Norfolk St. | O16 | 60 | Norfolk St. | 0 |
| Tuskegee ■ | O23 | 28 | Tuskegee | 41 |
| Elizabeth City St. ■ | O30 | 30 | Elizabeth City St. | 22 |
| Morris Brown | N13 | 27 | Winston-Salem | 14 |
| | | 31 | N.C. Central | 19 |
| | | **II Championship** | | |
| | | 21 | North Ala. | 33 |

Colors: Royal Blue & White.  Nickname: Pirates.  II

## HANOVER ..... Hanover, IN 47243
*C. Wayne Perry (11 yrs., 71-35-2)*

| Opponent | Date | Pts | Opponent | Pts |
|---|---|---|---|---|
| Defiance | S 4 | 14 | Defiance | 35 |
| Thomas More ■ | S11 | 30 | Thomas More | 42 |
| Bluffton ■ | S18 | 56 | Bluffton | 49 |
| DePauw | O 2 | 15 | DePauw | 31 |
| Anderson ■ | O 9 | 38 | Anderson | 19 |
| Wabash | O16 | 33 | Wabash | 38 |
| Rose-Hulman ■ | O23 | 17 | Rose-Hulman | 16 |
| Taylor | O30 | 49 | Taylor | 21 |
| Manchester ■ | N 6 | 28 | Manchester | 21 |
| Franklin | N13 | 31 | Franklin | 7 |

Colors: Red & Blue.  Nickname: Panthers.  III

## HARDIN-SIMMONS ..... Abilene, TX 79698
*Jimmie Keeling (3 yrs., 13-18-0)*

| Opponent | Date | Pts | Opponent | Pts |
|---|---|---|---|---|
| Panhandle St. ■ | S11 | 29 | Panhandle St. | 13 |
| Colorado Col. | O30 | 38 | Sul Ross St. | 7 |
| Sul Ross St. ■ | S18 | 21 | Millsaps | 13 |
| Millsaps ■ | S25 | 23 | Howard Payne | 39 |
| Howard Payne | O 2 | 48 | McMurry | 16 |
| McMurry | O 9* | 24 | Tarleton St. | 14 |
| Tarleton St. | O16* | 28 | Sul Ross St. | 22 |
| Sul Ross St. ■ | O23 | 16 | Colorado Col. | 10 |
| Colorado Col. | O30 | 42 | Midwestern St. | 35 |
| Midwestern St. ■ | N 6 | 28 | Austin | 9 |
| Austin | N13 | **NAIA II Championship** | | |
| | | 42 | Howard Payne | 28 |
| | | 14 | Minot St. | 21 |

Colors: Purple & Gold.  Nickname: Cowboys.  III

## HARTWICK ..... Oneonta, NY 13820
*Steve Stetson (7 yrs., 20-44-1)*

| Opponent | Date | Pts | Opponent | Pts |
|---|---|---|---|---|
| St. Lawrence | S 4 | 17 | King's (Pa.) | 20 |
| Westfield St. ■ | S11* | 0 | St. Peter's | 29 |
| St. John Fisher ■ | S25* | 12 | St. John Fisher | 37 |
| Gallaudet ■ | O 2 | 12 | Siena | 31 |
| Salve Regina | O 9* | 0 | St. Francis (Pa.) | 36 |
| Monmouth (N. J.) | O23 | 13 | Curry | 32 |
| Western New Eng. | N 6 | 7 | Western New Eng. | 9 |
| Curry ■ | N13 | 14 | Pace | 0 |

Colors: Royal Blue & White.  Nickname: Warriors.  III

## HEIDELBERG ..... Tiffin, OH 44883
*Dick West (9 yrs., 41-47-2)*

| Opponent | Date | Pts | Opponent | Pts |
|---|---|---|---|---|
| Olivet | S11 | 14 | Olivet | 13 |
| Otterbein ■ | S18 | 7 | Otterbein | 7 |
| John Carroll ■ | S25 | 6 | John Carroll | 49 |
| Muskingum | O 2 | 6 | Muskingum | 28 |
| Capital ■ | O 9 | 26 | Capital | 10 |
| Mount Union ■ | O16 | 7 | Mount Union | 48 |
| Hiram | O23 | 32 | Hiram | 13 |
| Baldwin-Wallace ■ | O30 | 20 | Baldwin-Wallace | 39 |
| Marietta | N 6 | 21 | Marietta | 14 |
| Ohio Northern | N13 | 14 | Ohio Northern | 14 |

Colors: Red, Orange & Black.  Nickname: Student Princes.  III

## HENDERSON STATE ......... Arkadelphia, AR 71923
*Ken Turner (3 yrs., 13-15-3)*

| Opponent | Date | Pts | Opponent | Pts |
|---|---|---|---|---|
| Ark.-Monticello ■ | S11* | 7 | Angelo St. | 24 |
| East Tex. St. ■ | S18* | 21 | East Central (Okla.) | 10 |
| Ark.-Pine Bluff | S25* | 17 | Delta St. | 18 |
| Mississippi Col. ■ | O 2* | 12 | Mississippi Col. | 24 |
| Delta St. ■ | O 9* | 14 | Northeastern Okla. | 14 |
| North Ala. | O16* | 21 | Southern Ark. | 14 |
| Central Ark. | O30 | 12 | Arkansas Tech | 10 |
| Livingston | N 6 | 10 | Central Ark. | 18 |
| Valdosta St. ■ | N13 | 35 | Ouachita Baptist | 23 |
| | | 10 | Harding | 29 |
| | | 38 | Ark.-Monticello | 55 |

Colors: Red & Gray.  Nickname: Reddies.  II

## HILLSDALE ..... Hillsdale, MI 49242
*Dick Lowry (19 yrs., 145-59-2)*

| Opponent | Date | Pts | Opponent | Pts |
|---|---|---|---|---|
| Saginaw Valley ■ | S 4* | 21 | Saginaw Valley | 0 |
| St. Francis (Ill.) | S11 | 45 | Valparaiso | 7 |
| Ferris St. ■ | S18* | 36 | Ferris St. | 14 |
| Ashland | S25* | 24 | Ashland | 21 |
| Butler | O 2 | 24 | Northwood | 7 |
| Indianapolis ■ | O 9 | 36 | Indianapolis | 10 |
| Northern Mich. | O16 | 32 | Northern Mich. | 14 |
| St. Joseph's (Ind.) ■ | O23 | 14 | St. Joseph's (Ind.) | 6 |
| Grand Valley St. | O30 | 21 | Grand Valley St. | 34 |
| Northwood ■ | N 6 | 17 | Butler | 28 |
| Wayne St. (Mich.) | N13 | 41 | Wayne St. (Mich.) | 14 |

Colors: Royal Blue & White.  Nickname: Chargers.  II

## HIRAM ..... Hiram, OH 44234
*Bobby Thomas (1 yr., 1-9-0)*

| Opponent | Date | Pts | Opponent | Pts |
|---|---|---|---|---|
| Grove City ■ | S11 | 6 | Wash. & Jeff. | 61 |
| Baldwin-Wallace ■ | S18* | 0 | Baldwin-Wallace | 61 |
| Capital | S25 | 36 | Capital | 33 |
| Otterbein ■ | O 2 | 15 | Otterbein | 27 |
| Marietta ■ | O 9 | 0 | Marietta | 13 |
| Ohio Northern | O16 | 35 | Ohio Northern | 42 |
| Heidelberg ■ | O23 | 13 | Heidelberg | 32 |
| Muskingum ■ | O30 | 22 | Muskingum | 44 |
| John Carroll ■ | N 6 | 0 | John Carroll | 44 |
| Mount Union | N13 | 13 | Mount Union | 55 |

Colors: Red & Columbia Blue.  Nickname: Terriers.  III

## HOBART ..... Geneva, NY 14456
*William Maxwell (2 yrs., 7-13-0)*

| Opponent | Date | Pts | Opponent | Pts |
|---|---|---|---|---|
| Dickinson | S11 | 10 | Dickinson | 14 |
| St. John Fisher ■ | S18 | 14 | St. John Fisher | 3 |
| Union (N.Y.) ■ | S25 | 3 | Union (N.Y.) | 24 |
| St. Lawrence | O 2 | 13 | St. Lawrence | 0 |
| Rochester | O 9 | 0 | Rochester | 31 |
| Swarthmore ■ | O16 | 28 | Alfred | 17 |
| Alfred | O23 | 13 | Canisius | 6 |
| Pace ■ | O30 | 12 | Pace | 23 |
| Buffalo St. | N 6 | 0 | Buffalo St. | 33 |
| Rensselaer | N13 | 0 | Rensselaer | 28 |

Colors: Orange & Purple.  Nickname: Statesmen.  III

## HOPE ..... Holland, MI 49423
*Ray Smith (23 yrs., 138-62-8)*

| Opponent | Date | Pts | Opponent | Pts |
|---|---|---|---|---|
| DePauw | S11 | 0 | DePauw | 6 |
| Ill. Wesleyan ■ | S18 | 20 | Ill. Wesleyan | 33 |
| Wabash | S25 | 19 | Wabash | 0 |
| Trinity (Ill.) ■ | O 2 | 12 | Trinity (Ill.) | 0 |
| Kalamazoo ■ | O 9 | 35 | Alma | 6 |
| Alma | O16 | 0 | Albion | 37 |
| Albion ■ | O23 | 19 | Adrian | 14 |
| Adrian | O30 | 26 | Kalamazoo | 6 |
| Olivet | N 6 | 21 | Olivet | 17 |

Colors: Orange & Blue.  Nickname: Flying Dutchmen.  III

## HUMBOLDT STATE ..... Arcata, CA 95521
*Fred Whitmire (2 yrs., 12-9-0)*

| Opponent | Date | Pts | Opponent | Pts |
|---|---|---|---|---|
| Rocky Mountain ■ | S 4* | 24 | Azusa Pacific | 7 |
| Western Mont. ■ | S11* | 41 | Western Mont. | 21 |
| Cal Poly SLO ■ | S18* | 6 | St. Mary's (Cal.) | 43 |
| St. Mary's (Cal.) ■ | S25* | 36 | Southern Ore. | 16 |
| UC Davis | O 2* | 10 | Santa Clara | 14 |
| Azusa Pacific ■ | O 9* | 38 | Whitworth | 36 |
| San Fran. St. ■ | O16 | 24 | San Fran. St. | 14 |
| Western N. Mex. | O23* | 31 | UC Davis | 58 |
| Sonoma St. ■ | O30* | 19 | Sonoma St. | 7 |
| Cal St. Hayward | N 6 | 36 | Cal St. Hayward | 38 |
| Cal St. Chico ■ | N13* | 27 | Cal St. Chico | 14 |

Colors: Green & Gold.  Nickname: Lumberjacks.  II

■ Home games on each schedule.          *Night Games.

## ILLINOIS BENEDICTINE .............. Lisle, IL 60532
*John Welty (3 yrs., 10-19-0)*

| Opponent | Date | Pts | Opponent | Pts |
|---|---|---|---|---|
| Loras ■ | S 4 | 9 | Loras | 38 |
| Millikin | S11 | 25 | Millikin | 24 |
| Elmhurst ■ | S18 | 49 | Elmhurst | 20 |
| Carthage | S25 | 41 | Carthage | 17 |
| Alma | O 2 | 47 | Alma | 26 |
| Quincy ■ | O 9 | 40 | Quincy | 28 |
| Olivet Nazarene | O16 | 34 | Olivet Nazarene | 24 |
| Aurora ■ | O23 | 16 | Aurora | 28 |
| Drake | O30 | 6 | Drake | 59 |
| Trinity (Ill.) ■ | N 6 | 51 | Trinity (Ill.) | 30 |

Colors: Cardinal & White.  Nickname: Eagles.  III

## ILLINOIS COLLEGE ............. Jacksonville, IL 62650
*Bill Anderson (15 yrs., 38-97-0)*

| Opponent | Date | Pts | Opponent | Pts |
|---|---|---|---|---|
| Principia ■ | S11 | 30 | Principia | 7 |
| Blackburn | S18 | 19 | Blackburn | 7 |
| Carroll (Wis.) | S25 | 6 | Carroll (Wis.) | 20 |
| Lawrence | O 2 | 21 | Lawrence | 7 |
| Monmouth (Ill.) ■ | O 9 | 6 | Monmouth (Ill.) | 14 |
| Coe | O16 | 0 | Coe | 34 |
| Knox | O23 | 6 | Knox | 0 |
| Cornell College ■ | O30 | 17 | Cornell College | 26 |
| Grinnell | N 7 | 60 | Grinnell | 13 |

Colors: Royal Blue & White.  Nickname: Blueboys.  III

## ILLINOIS WESLEYAN ......... Bloomington, IL 61701
*Norm Eash (6 yrs., 35-20-1)*

| Opponent | Date | Pts | Opponent | Pts |
|---|---|---|---|---|
| Hope | S18 | 33 | Hope | 20 |
| Adrian | S25 | 24 | Adrian | 20 |
| North Central | O 2* | 35 | North Central | 20 |
| Wheaton (Ill.) ■ | O 9 | 33 | Wheaton (Ill.) | 19 |
| Augustana (Ill.) | O16 | 21 | Augustana (Ill.) | 0 |
| Carthage | O23 | 63 | Carthage | 8 |
| Elmhurst ■ | O30 | 42 | Elmhurst | 14 |
| Millikin | N 6 | 24 | Millikin | 13 |
| North Park ■ | N13 | 42 | North Park | 0 |
| | | **III Championship** | | |
| | | 21 | Aurora | 12 |
| | | 27 | Mount Union | 49 |

Colors: Green & White.  Nickname: Titans.  III

## INDIANA (PENNSYLVANIA) ........ Indiana, PA 15705
*Frank Cignetti (11 yrs., 86-41-1)*

| Opponent | Date | Pts | Opponent | Pts |
|---|---|---|---|---|
| Kutztown ■ | S 4 | 31 | North Dak. | 13 |
| Grand Valley St. ■ | S11 | 45 | Grand Valley St. | 27 |
| West Chester ■ | S18 | 31 | East Stroudsburg | 12 |
| Liberty | S25 | 44 | Lock Haven | 0 |
| Lock Haven | O 2 | 35 | Shippensburg | 16 |
| Shippensburg ■ | O 9 | 36 | Calif. (PA) | 20 |
| Calif. (PA) | O16 | 34 | Slippery Rock | 17 |
| Slippery Rock ■ | O23 | 33 | Towson St. | 35 |
| Edinboro | N 6 | 21 | Edinboro | 21 |
| Clarion ■ | N13 | 26 | Clarion | 35 |

Colors: Crimson & Gray.  Nickname: Indians.  II

## INDIANAPOLIS ............... Indianapolis, IN 46227
*Bill Bless (21 yrs., 112-90-9)*

| Opponent | Date | Pts | Opponent | Pts |
|---|---|---|---|---|
| Wayne St. (Mich.) ■ | S 4 | 26 | Wayne St. (Mich.) | 31 |
| Northern Mich. ■ | S11 | 32 | Northern Mich. | 10 |
| St. Joseph's (Ind.) ■ | S18 | 24 | St. Joseph's (Ind.) | 24 |
| Grand Valley St. | S25 | 7 | Grand Valley St. | 21 |
| Northwood ■ | O 2 | 6 | Butler | 28 |
| Hillsdale | O 9 | 10 | Hillsdale | 36 |
| Saginaw Valley | O16 | 0 | Saginaw Valley | 42 |
| St. Francis (Ill.) ■ | O23 | 14 | Valparaiso | 20 |
| Ferris St. | O30 | 13 | Ferris St. | 54 |
| Ashland ■ | N 6 | 12 | Ashland | 45 |
| Butler ■ | N13 | | | |

Colors: Crimson & Gray.  Nickname: Grayhounds.  II

## ITHACA ............................ Ithaca, NY 14850
*Jim Butterfield (26 yrs., 200-67-1)*

| Opponent | Date | Pts | Opponent | Pts |
|---|---|---|---|---|
| Albany (N.Y.) ■ | S11 | 51 | Albany (N.Y.) | 7 |
| Montclair St. | S18 | 49 | Montclair St. | 19 |
| Alfred ■ | S25 | 45 | Alfred | 15 |
| Springfield | O 2 | 31 | Springfield | 7 |
| American Int'l ■ | O 9 | 31 | American Int'l | 13 |
| St. Lawrence ■ | O16 | 56 | St. Lawrence | 14 |
| Buffalo St. | O23 | 21 | Buffalo St. | 13 |
| Mercyhurst | O30 | 48 | Mercyhurst | 7 |
| Cortland St. ■ | N 6 | 20 | Cortland St. | 22 |
| Wash. & Jeff. | N13 | 47 | Wash. & Jeff. | 28 |
| | | **III Championship** | | |
| | | 26 | Buffalo St. | 28 |

Colors: Blue & Gold.  Nickname: Bombers.  III

## JACKSONVILLE STATE ........ Jacksonville, AL 36265
*Bill Burgess (8 yrs., 69-22-4)*

| Opponent | Date | Pts | Opponent | Pts |
|---|---|---|---|---|
| Alabama A&M ■ | S11 | 7 | Alabama A&M | 6 |
| Northern Iowa | S18* | 17 | West Ga. | 10 |
| James Madison | S25 | 20 | Valdosta St. | 6 |
| Western Ky. | O 2 | 14 | Mississippi Col. | 14 |
| Fort Valley St. ■ | O 9 | 38 | Delta St. | 10 |
| Southwest Mo. St. | O16 | 10 | North Ala. | 6 |
| Montana | O23 | 0 | Ga. Southern | 10 |
| Alcorn St. | O30 | 59 | Alcorn St. | 45 |
| Central St. (Ohio) ■ | N13 | 54 | Livingston | 27 |
| | | 63 | Kentucky St. | 21 |
| | | **II Championship** | | |
| | | 41 | Savannah St. | 16 |
| | | 14 | North Ala. | 12 |
| | | 46 | New Haven | 35 |
| | | 17 | Pittsburg St. | 13 |

Colors: Red & White.  Nickname: Gamecocks.  II

## JERSEY CITY STATE ........... Jersey City, NJ 07305
*Bill Olear (1 yr., 0-10-0)*

| Opponent | Date | Pts | Opponent | Pts |
|---|---|---|---|---|
| Brockport St. | S11 | 7 | Brockport St. | 42 |
| Stony Brook ■ | S18 | 14 | FDU-Madison | 19 |
| Rowan ■ | S25 | 0 | Rowan | 29 |
| Upsala | O 2 | 6 | Upsala | 19 |
| Kean | O16 | 7 | Ramapo | 21 |
| Trenton St. ■ | O23 | 19 | Kean | 27 |
| Wm. Paterson ■ | O30 | 7 | Trenton St. | 54 |
| Montclair St. | N 6 | 20 | Wm. Paterson | 43 |
| St. Peter's | N13 | 0 | Montclair St. | 15 |
| | | 14 | St. Peter's | 20 |

Colors: Green & Gold.  Nickname: Gothic Knights.  III

## JOHN CARROLL ................. Cleveland, OH 44118
*Tony DeCarlo (6 yrs., 42-15-2)*

| Opponent | Date | Pts | Opponent | Pts |
|---|---|---|---|---|
| Alma ■ | S11 | 28 | Alma | 3 |
| Capital ■ | S18 | 51 | Capital | 10 |
| Heidelberg | S25 | 49 | Heidelberg | 6 |
| Ohio Northern ■ | O 2 | 30 | Ohio Northern | 6 |
| Mount Union | O 9 | 14 | Mount Union | 24 |
| Muskingum | O16 | 27 | Muskingum | 3 |
| Otterbein ■ | O23 | 56 | Otterbein | 20 |
| Marietta | O30 | 42 | Marietta | 6 |
| Hiram | N 6 | 44 | Hiram | 0 |
| Baldwin-Wallace ■ | N13 | 17 | Baldwin-Wallace | 27 |

Colors: Blue & Gold.  Nickname: Blue Streaks.  III

## JOHNS HOPKINS ............... Baltimore, MD 21218
*Jim Margraff (3 yrs., 16-12-2)*

| Opponent | Date | Pts | Opponent | Pts |
|---|---|---|---|---|
| Lebanon Valley ■ | S10* | 14 | Lebanon Valley | 33 |
| Swarthmore ■ | S17* | 30 | Swarthmore | 20 |
| FDU-Madison ■ | S24* | 7 | FDU-Madison | 0 |
| Gettysburg | O 2 | 10 | Gettysburg | 13 |
| Ursinus ■ | O 9 | 35 | Ursinus | 34 |
| Muhlenberg | O16 | 30 | Muhlenberg | 8 |
| Georgetown ■ | O22* | 17 | Georgetown | 0 |
| Dickinson | O30 | 0 | Dickinson | 32 |
| Frank. & Marsh. ■ | N 6 | 26 | Frank. & Marsh. | 44 |
| Western Md. | N13 | 21 | Western Md. | 9 |

Colors: Blue & Black.  Nickname: Blue Jays.  III

## JOHNSON C. SMITH .............. Charlotte, NC 28216
*Ray Lee (1 yr., 5-5-0)*

| Opponent | Date | Pts | Opponent | Pts |
|---|---|---|---|---|
| Morehouse | S 4 | 6 | Hampton | 48 |
| Glenville St. | S11 | 7 | Norfolk St. | 0 |
| Bethune-Cookman | S18 | 17 | Morehouse | 21 |
| N.C. Central ■ | S25* | 21 | Morgan St. | 25 |
| Hampton ■ | O 2 | 13 | Winston-Salem | 40 |
| Kentucky St. ■ | O 9 | 13 | Glenville St. | 10 |
| Livingstone ■ | O16 | 14 | Livingstone | 6 |
| Fayetteville St. | O23 | 24 | Fayetteville St. | 6 |
| Winston-Salem | O30 | 28 | Morris Brown | 26 |
| Norfolk St. ■ | N 6 | 12 | N.C. Central | 13 |
| North Caro. A&T | N13 | | | |

Colors: Blue & Gold.  Nickname: Golden Bulls.  II

## JUNIATA ...................... Huntingdon, PA 16652
*Chris Coller (1 yr., 3-6-1)*

| Opponent | Date | Pts | Opponent | Pts |
|---|---|---|---|---|
| Western Md. ■ | S11 | 0 | Carnegie Mellon | 34 |
| Albright ■ | S18 | 20 | Delaware Valley | 16 |
| Carnegie Mellon ■ | S25 | 0 | Randolph-Macon | 27 |
| Widener | O 2 | 13 | Widener | 7 |
| Wilkes | O 9 | 14 | Moravian | 31 |
| Lebanon Valley | O16 | 14 | Lycoming | 14 |
| King's (PA) | O23 | 23 | Albright | 21 |
| Moravian ■ | O30 | 7 | Susquehanna | 35 |
| Lycoming ■ | N 6 | 6 | Wilkes | 13 |
| Susquehanna ■ | N13 | 13 | Lebanon Valley | 14 |

Colors: Yale Blue & Old Gold.  Nickname: To be named.  III

■ Home games on each schedule.    *Night Games.

## KALAMAZOO .................. Kalamazoo, MI 49007
*Dave Warmack (3 yrs., 11-15-1)*

| Opponent | Date | Score | Opponent | Score |
|---|---|---|---|---|
| Wooster ■ | S11 | 27 | Wooster | 17 |
| Carroll (Wis.) | S18 | 10 | Carroll (Wis.) | 14 |
| Chicago | S25 | 21 | Chicago | 13 |
| Defiance ■ | O 2 | 0 | Defiance | 30 |
| Hope | O 9 | 12 | Albion | 49 |
| Adrian ■ | O16 | 18 | Olivet | 19 |
| Alma | O23 | 7 | Alma | 17 |
| Olivet ■ | O30 | 6 | Hope | 26 |
| Albion | N 6 | 18 | Adrian | 16 |

Colors: Orange & Black.   Nickname: Hornets.   III

## KUTZTOWN ..................... Kutztown, PA 19530
*Al Leonzi (1 yr., 2-7-1)*

| Opponent | Date | Score | Opponent | Score |
|---|---|---|---|---|
| Indiana (PA) | S 4 | 0 | Maine | 10 |
| East Stroudsburg ■ | S11 | 16 | Shippensburg | 3 |
| Shippensburg | S18 | 30 | Calif. (PA) | 30 |
| Calif. (PA) ■ | S25 | 27 | Mansfield | 30 |
| Mansfield ■ | O 2 | 21 | Millersville | 23 |
| Millersville | O 9 | 17 | Bloomsburg | 10 |
| Bloomsburg ■ | O16 | 48 | Lock Haven | 13 |
| Lock Haven | O23 | 34 | West Chester | 35 |
| West Chester | O30 | 21 | East Stroudsburg | 27 |
| Southern Conn. St. ■ | N 6 | 63 | Cheyney | 6 |
| Cheyney | N13 | | | |

Colors: Maroon & Gold.   Nickname: Golden Bears.   II

## KEAN .............................. Union, NJ 07083
*Brian Carlson (1 yr., 6-3-1)*

| Opponent | Date | Score | Opponent | Score |
|---|---|---|---|---|
| Western Conn. St. | S 4* | 16 | Western Conn. St. | 14 |
| Bri'water (Mass.) ■ | S11 | 20 | Bri'water (Mass.) | 20 |
| Upsala | S18 | 59 | Upsala | 20 |
| Wm. Paterson ■ | O 2 | 7 | Ramapo | 0 |
| Montclair St. | O 9 | 21 | Wm. Paterson | 26 |
| Jersey City St. ■ | O16 | 3 | Montclair St. | 16 |
| Rowan | O30 | 27 | Jersey City St. | 19 |
| Brockport St. ■ | N 6 | 7 | Rowan | 27 |
| Trenton St. ■ | N13 | 12 | Trenton St. | 6 |
| | | 70 | Salisbury St. | 6 |

Colors: Royal Blue & Silver.   Nickname: Cougars.   III

## LA VERNE ....................... La Verne, CA 91750
*Rex Huigens (2 yrs., 14-3-1)*

| Opponent | Date | Score | Opponent | Score |
|---|---|---|---|---|
| San Diego | S11* | 21 | San Diego | 21 |
| Claremont-M-S ■ | S18 | 21 | Whittier | 18 |
| Cal Lutheran ■ | S25 | 48 | Pomona-Pitzer | 9 |
| Occidental | O 2* | 34 | Azusa Pacific | 7 |
| Menlo | O 9 | 30 | Menlo | 7 |
| Azusa Pacific ■ | O16 | 13 | Redlands | 20 |
| Pomona-Pitzer | O30 | 31 | Occidental | 21 |
| Redlands | N 6* | 55 | Cal Lutheran | 37 |
| Whittier ■ | N13 | 28 | Claremont-M-S | 6 |

Colors: Orange & Green.   Nickname: Leopards.   III

## KENTUCKY STATE ............... Frankfort, KY 40601
*Maurice Hunt (1 yr., 4-7-0)*

| Opponent | Date | Score | Opponent | Score |
|---|---|---|---|---|
| Findlay | S 4* | 13 | Findlay | 23 |
| Central St. (Ohio) ■ | S11* | 35 | Wingate | 33 |
| Knoxville ■ | S18* | 0 | Knoxville | 22 |
| Lane | S25* | 32 | N.C. Central | 26 |
| Mars Hill ■ | O 2* | 34 | Lane | 0 |
| Johnson Smith | O 9 | 0 | Central St. (Ohio) | 83 |
| Clark Atlanta ■ | O16 | 14 | Clark Atlanta | 24 |
| Ark.-Pine Bluff ■ | O23 | 22 | St. Francis (Ill.) | 62 |
| Norfolk St. ■ | O30 | 0 | Norfolk St. | 23 |
| N.C. Central | N 6 | 41 | Elizabeth City St. | 40 |
| Southeast Mo. St. | N13 | 21 | Jacksonville St. | 63 |

Colors: Green & Gold.   Nickname: Thorobreds.   II

## KENTUCKY WESLEYAN ........ Owensboro, KY 42301
*Randy Awrey (3 yrs., 5-25-0)*

| Opponent | Date | Score | Opponent | Score |
|---|---|---|---|---|
| Quincy ■ | S 4 | 19 | Mt. Senario | 29 |
| Maryville (Tenn.) | S11 | 10 | Tenn. Wesleyan | 35 |
| Evansville | S18 | 6 | Evansville | 38 |
| Rhodes ■ | S25 | 22 | Rhodes | 35 |
| Blackburn ■ | O 2 | 34 | Blackburn | 0 |
| Bethel (Tenn.) | O 9 | 7 | Lakeland | 8 |
| Principia ■ | O16 | 48 | Principia | 28 |
| Eureka | O23 | 28 | Eureka | 6 |
| Centre ■ | O30 | 26 | Centre | 42 |
| Mt. Senario ■ | N13 | 19 | Sewanee | 26 |

Colors: Purple & White.   Nickname: Panthers.   III

## LAKE FOREST ................. Lake Forest, IL 60045
*Maury Waugh (12 yrs., 39-68-2)*

| Opponent | Date | Score | Opponent | Score |
|---|---|---|---|---|
| Wheaton (Ill.) ■ | S11 | 0 | Wheaton (Ill.) | 29 |
| North Park | S18 | 9 | North Park | 7 |
| Grinnell ■ | S25 | 27 | Grinnell | 14 |
| Cornell College | O 2 | 0 | Cornell College | 36 |
| St. Norbert | O 9 | 14 | St. Norbert | 21 |
| Ripon ■ | O16 | 8 | Ripon | 15 |
| Carroll (Wis.) ■ | O23 | 6 | Carroll (Wis.) | 40 |
| Lawrence | O30 | 14 | Lawrence | 13 |
| Beloit ■ | N 6 | 13 | Beloit | 27 |

Colors: Red & Black.   Nickname: Foresters.   III

## KENYON ...................... Gambier, OH 43022
*Jim Meyer (4 yrs., 18-19-3)*

| Opponent | Date | Score | Opponent | Score |
|---|---|---|---|---|
| Marietta ■ | S11 | 7 | Marietta | 7 |
| Ohio Wesleyan ■ | S18 | 7 | Ohio Wesleyan | 24 |
| Earlham | S25 | 21 | Earlham | 29 |
| Wooster ■ | O 2 | 35 | Wooster | 29 |
| Case Reserve | O 9 | 14 | Case Reserve | 14 |
| Allegheny ■ | O16 | 14 | Allegheny | 41 |
| Wittenberg | O23 | 7 | Wittenberg | 51 |
| Waynesburg | O30 | 21 | Waynesburg | 26 |
| Oberlin ■ | N 6 | 8 | Oberlin | 14 |
| Denison | N13 | 23 | Denison | 20 |

Colors: Purple & White.   Nickname: Lords.   III

## LANE ............................ Jackson, TN 38301
*Lee Henry Triplett (1st yr. as head coach)*

| Opponent | Date | | |
|---|---|---|---|
| Georgetown (Ky.) | S 4 | 1992 results not available. | |
| Mississippi Val. ■ | S11* | | |
| Kentucky St. ■ | S25* | | |
| Norfolk St. | O 2 | | |
| Langston ■ | O 9 | | |
| Knoxville ■ | O23 | | |
| Ark.-Pine Bluff | O30 | | |
| Virginia St. | N 6 | | |
| Elizabeth City St. | N13 | | |

Colors: Blue & Red.   Nickname: Dragons.   II

## LAWRENCE ..................... Appleton, WI 54911
*Rick Coles (1st yr. as head coach)*

| Opponent | Date | Score | Opponent | Score |
|---|---|---|---|---|
| N'western (Wis.) | S11 | 31 | N'western (Wis.) | 22 |
| Chicago ■ | S18 | 0 | Chicago | 37 |
| Monmouth (Ill.) ■ | S25 | 30 | Monmouth (Ill.) | 35 |
| Illinois Col. | O 2 | 7 | Illinois Col. | 21 |
| Carroll (Wis.) ■ | O 9 | 22 | Carroll (Wis.) | 47 |
| St. Norbert | O16 | 27 | St. Norbert | 26 |
| Beloit | O23 | 14 | Beloit | 32 |
| Lake Forest ■ | O30 | 13 | Lake Forest | 14 |
| Ripon | N 6 | 7 | Ripon | 34 |

Colors: Navy & White.   Nickname: Vikings.   III

## KNOX .............................. Galesburg, IL 61401
*Randy Oberembt (8 yrs., 27-44-1)*

| Opponent | Date | Score | Opponent | Score |
|---|---|---|---|---|
| Rose-Hulman | S11 | 14 | Rose-Hulman | 34 |
| Concordia (St. Paul) ■ | S18 | 17 | Concordia (St. Paul) | 6 |
| Beloit ■ | S25 | 14 | Beloit | 21 |
| Ripon | O 2 | 7 | Ripon | 28 |
| Cornell College ■ | O 9 | 21 | Cornell College | 33 |
| Grinnell | O16 | 21 | Grinnell | 7 |
| Illinois Col. ■ | O23 | 0 | Illinois Col. | 6 |
| Coe | O30 | 7 | Coe | 59 |
| Monmouth (Ill.) ■ | N 6 | 20 | Monmouth (Ill.) | 34 |

Colors: Purple & Gold.   Nickname: To be named.   III

## LEBANON VALLEY ................. Annville, PA 17003
*James Monos (7 yrs., 30-38-2)*

| Opponent | Date | Score | Opponent | Score |
|---|---|---|---|---|
| Johns Hopkins | S10* | 33 | Johns Hopkins | 14 |
| Wilkes ■ | S18 | 17 | Lycoming | 35 |
| Delaware Valley ■ | S25 | 41 | Albright | 20 |
| Moravian ■ | O 2 | 21 | Susquehanna | 27 |
| Susquehanna | O 9 | 26 | Wilkes | 7 |
| Juniata ■ | O16 | 14 | Moravian | 13 |
| Lycoming | O23 | 14 | Delaware Valley | 17 |
| Albright ■ | O30 | 22 | Western Md. | 20 |
| Upsala | N 6 | 30 | Widener | 3 |
| Widener | N13 | 14 | Juniata | 13 |

Colors: Royal Blue & White.   Nickname: Flying Dutchmen.   III

---

■ Home games on each schedule.          *Night Games.

## LENOIR-RHYNE...............Hickory, NC 28603
*Charles Forbes (17 yrs., 79-83-3)*

| Opponent | Date | | Opponent (1992) | |
|---|---|---|---|---|
| Guilford ■ | S 4* | 26 | Newberry | 11 |
| Newberry | S11* | 35 | Wofford | 28 |
| Presbyterian ■ | S25* | 25 | Presbyterian | 14 |
| Elon | O 2 | 7 | Elon | 10 |
| Gardner-Webb | O 9 | 17 | Gardner-Webb | 52 |
| Wingate ■ | O16* | 49 | Wingate | 7 |
| Wofford ■ | O23 | 41 | West Liberty St. | 29 |
| Carson-Newman | O30 | 27 | Carson-Newman | 39 |
| Mars Hill | N 6 | 28 | Mars Hill | 7 |
| Catawba ■ | N13 | 22 | Catawba | 24 |

Colors: Red & Black. Nickname: Bears.    II

## LUTHER..............................Decorah, IA 52101
*Bob Naslund (15 yrs., 78-63-0)*

| Opponent | Date | | Opponent (1992) | |
|---|---|---|---|---|
| St. Olaf | S11 | 31 | St. Olaf | 13 |
| Simpson | S18 | 21 | Simpson | 35 |
| Upper Iowa ■ | S25 | 28 | Upper Iowa | 20 |
| Dubuque | O 2 | 24 | Dubuque | 6 |
| Wartburg ■ | O 9 | 28 | Wartburg | 56 |
| Trinity (Ill.) | O16 | 35 | Trinity (Ill.) | 12 |
| William Penn | O23 | 42 | William Penn | 7 |
| Loras ■ | O30 | 16 | Loras | 17 |
| Central (Iowa) | N 6 | 11 | Central (Iowa) | 33 |
| Buena Vista ■ | N13 | 17 | Buena Vista | 10 |

Colors: Blue & White. Nickname: Norse.    III

## LIVINGSTON....................Livingston, AL 35470
*Lloyd Sisco (2 yrs., 11-9-0)*

| Opponent | Date | | Opponent (1992) | |
|---|---|---|---|---|
| Albany St. (Ga.) ■ | S 4* | 22 | Knoxville | 12 |
| Nicholls St. ■ | S11* | 13 | Ark.-Monticello | 10 |
| Stephen F. Austin | S18* | 42 | Albany St. (Ga.) | 36 |
| Mississippi Col. | S25* | 13 | West Ga. | 47 |
| Valdosta St. | O 2* | 15 | Valdosta St. | 42 |
| West Ga. ■ | O 9* | 37 | Mississippi Col. | 32 |
| Central Ark. | O16* | 30 | Delta St. | 24 |
| Delta St. ■ | O23 | 13 | North Ala. | 20 |
| North Ala. | O30 | 27 | Jacksonville St. | 54 |
| Henderson St. ■ | N 6 | | | |

Colors: Red & White. Nickname: Tigers.    II

## LYCOMING..................Williamsport, PA 17701
*Frank Girardi (21 yrs., 150-51-5)*

| Opponent | Date | | Opponent (1992) | |
|---|---|---|---|---|
| Susquehanna | S11 | 13 | Frostburg St. | 6 |
| FDU-Madison ■ | S18 | 35 | Lebanon Valley | 17 |
| Albright ■ | S25 | 20 | Delaware Valley | 9 |
| King's (PA) | O 2 | 28 | Widener | 16 |
| Moravian | O 9 | 14 | Juniata | 14 |
| Upsala ■ | O16 | 27 | Moravian | 7 |
| Lebanon Valley ■ | O23 | 33 | Albright | 30 |
| Wilkes | O30 | 23 | Susquehanna | 19 |
| Juniata ■ | N 6 | 33 | Wilkes | 0 |
| Delaware Valley | N13 | | III Championship | |
| | | 0 | Wash. & Jeff. | 33 |

Colors: Blue & Gold. Nickname: Warriors.    III

## LIVINGSTONE....................Salisbury, NC 28144
*Delano Tucker (3 yrs., 11-18-0)*

| Opponent | Date | | Opponent (1992) | |
|---|---|---|---|---|
| Hampton ■ | S 4 | 21 | Bowie St. | 13 |
| Virginia Union ■ | S11 | 12 | West Ga. | 18 |
| Central St. (Ohio) | S18 | 32 | Lees-McRae | 14 |
| Winston-Salem | S25 | 0 | Wis.-Whitewater | 9 |
| Virginia St. ■ | O 2 | 19 | Virginia St. | 35 |
| Bowie St. | O 9 | 6 | Johnson Smith | 14 |
| Johnson Smith | O16 | 21 | Savannah St. | 63 |
| Savannah St. ■ | O23 | 40 | N.C. Central | 29 |
| N.C. Central | O31 | 20 | Fayetteville St. | 26 |
| Fayetteville St. ■ | N 7 | 12 | Winston-Salem | 49 |
| Knoxville | N13 | | | |

Colors: Blue & Black. Nickname: Fighting Bears.    II

## MACALESTER.....................St. Paul, MN 55105
*Gary Etcheverry (3 yrs., 2-27-0)*

| Opponent | Date | | Opponent (1992) | |
|---|---|---|---|---|
| Pomona-Pitzer ■ | S11* | 0 | Huron | 26 |
| Bethel (Minn.) | S18 | 15 | Bethel (Minn.) | 40 |
| St. Thomas (Minn.) ■ | S25* | 6 | St. Thomas (Minn.) | 21 |
| St. Olaf ■ | O 2* | 0 | St. Olaf | 47 |
| Carleton | O 9 | 6 | Carleton | 32 |
| Concordia-M'head ■ | O16 | 12 | Concordia-M'head | 55 |
| Augsburg | O23 | 17 | Augsburg | 42 |
| St. John's (Minn.) ■ | O30* | 0 | St. John's (Minn.) | 41 |
| Gust. Adolphus† | N 5* | 12 | Gust. Adolphus | 32 |
| Hamline ■ | N13 | 0 | Hamline | 44 |

Colors: Orange & Blue. Nickname: Scots.    III

## LOCK HAVEN .................Lock Haven, PA 17745
*Dennis Therrell (3 yrs., 7-25-1)*

| Opponent | Date | | Opponent (1992) | |
|---|---|---|---|---|
| James Madison | S 4* | 32 | Mansfield | 26 |
| Tennessee Tech | S11* | 21 | Tennessee Tech | 31 |
| Bloomsburg ■ | S18 | 38 | Bloomsburg | 33 |
| Mansfield | S25 | 13 | Indiana St. | 66 |
| Indiana (PA) ■ | O 2 | 0 | Indiana (PA) | 44 |
| Edinboro | O 9 | 10 | Edinboro | 38 |
| Clarion ■ | O16 | 14 | Clarion | 42 |
| Kutztown ■ | O23 | 13 | Kutztown | 48 |
| Shippensburg | O30 | 28 | Shippensburg | 28 |
| Calif. (PA) ■ | N 6 | 7 | Calif. (PA) | 20 |
| Slippery Rock | N13 | 17 | Slippery Rock | 41 |

Colors: Crimson & White. Nickname: Bald Eagles.    II

## MacMURRAY..................Jacksonville, IL 62650
*Michael Hensley (6 yrs., 22-37-1)*

| Opponent | Date | | Opponent (1992) | |
|---|---|---|---|---|
| Eureka ■ | S 4 | 15 | Eureka | 30 |
| Manchester | S11 | 8 | Manchester | 11 |
| Monmouth (Ill.) ■ | S18 | 21 | Monmouth (Ill.) | 13 |
| Quincy | S25 | 13 | Quincy | 24 |
| Concordia (Wis.) ■ | O 2 | 14 | Concordia (Wis.) | 28 |
| Greenville | O 9 | 25 | Greenville | 41 |
| Aurora | O16 | 0 | Aurora | 37 |
| Blackburn | O23 | 26 | Blackburn | 7 |
| Concordia (Ill.) ■ | O30 | 12 | Concordia (Ill.) | 18 |
| Lakeland | N 6 | 28 | Lakeland | 14 |

Colors: Navy & Scarlet. Nickname: Fighting Highlanders.    III

## LONG ISLAND-C.W. POST .......Brookville, NY 11548
*Tom Marshall (10 yrs., 48-46-2)*

| Opponent | Date | | Opponent (1992) | |
|---|---|---|---|---|
| Wagner | S11 | 53 | Salisbury St. | 25 |
| Rowan ■ | S18 | 17 | Ramapo | 3 |
| Marist | S25 | 12 | Marist | 12 |
| Pace ■ | O 2 | 51 | Pace | 7 |
| Gannon ■ | O 9 | 21 | Gannon | 14 |
| Trenton St. | O16 | 24 | Iona | 0 |
| Central Conn. St. | O23 | 29 | St. John's (N.Y.) | 45 |
| Springfield ■ | O30 | 26 | Wagner | 28 |
| Salisbury St. ■ | N 6 | 22 | Springfield | 43 |
| Alfred | N13 | 43 | Alfred | 21 |

Colors: Green & Gold. Nickname: Pioneers.    III

## MAINE MARITIME .................Castine, ME 04420
*John Huard (11 yrs., 59-38-0)*

| Opponent | Date | | Opponent (1992) | |
|---|---|---|---|---|
| Bri'water (Mass.) | S18 | 7 | Bri'water (Mass.) | 27 |
| Worcester St. ■ | S25 | 20 | Worcester St. | 14 |
| Mass. Maritime | O 3 | 20 | Mass. Maritime | 25 |
| Mass.-Dartmouth ■ | O 9 | 17 | Mass.-Dartmouth | 14 |
| Plymouth St. ■ | O16 | 25 | Plymouth St. | 12 |
| Mass.-Boston | O23 | 26 | Mass.-Boston | 14 |
| Fitchburg St. ■ | O30 | 25 | Fitchburg St. | 6 |
| Framingham St. | N 6 | 36 | Framingham St. | 0 |
| Westfield St. ■ | N13 | 13 | Westfield St. | 22 |

Colors: Royal Blue & Gold. Nickname: Mariners.    III

## LORAS..............................Dubuque, IA 52001
*Bob Bierie (13 yrs., 80-51-4)*

| Opponent | Date | | Opponent (1992) | |
|---|---|---|---|---|
| Ill. Benedictine | S 4 | 38 | Ill. Benedictine | 9 |
| Augustana (Ill.) ■ | S11 | 10 | Augustana (Ill.) | 7 |
| Buena Vista ■ | S18 | 14 | Buena Vista | 0 |
| William Penn | S25 | 63 | William Penn | 14 |
| Simpson ■ | O 9 | 14 | Simpson | 20 |
| Dubuque | O16 | 24 | Dubuque | 0 |
| Central (Iowa) ■ | O23 | 21 | Central (Iowa) | 42 |
| Luther | O30 | 17 | Luther | 16 |
| Upper Iowa ■ | N 6 | 38 | Upper Iowa | 57 |
| Wartburg | N13 | 33 | Wartburg | 22 |

Colors: Purple & Gold. Nickname: Duhawks.    III

## MANCHESTER ..........North Manchester, IN 46962
*Dale Liston (10 yrs., 40-52-0)*

| Opponent | Date | | Opponent (1992) | |
|---|---|---|---|---|
| Earlham | S 4 | 12 | Earlham | 28 |
| MacMurray ■ | S11 | 11 | MacMurray | 8 |
| Urbana ■ | S18 | 33 | Clinch Valley | 23 |
| Wabash ■ | O 2 | 8 | Wabash | 40 |
| Bluffton ■ | O 9 | 38 | Taylor | 34 |
| Anderson | O16 | 17 | Anderson | 7 |
| DePauw ■ | O23 | 34 | DePauw | 52 |
| Franklin ■ | O30 | 21 | Franklin | 20 |
| Hanover | N 6 | 21 | Hanover | 28 |
| Rose-Hulman | N13 | 21 | Rose-Hulman | 7 |

Colors: Black & Old Gold. Nickname: Spartans.    III

■ Home games on each schedule.     *Night Games.

# MANKATO STATE ............... Mankato, MN 56001
*Dan Runkle (12 yrs., 62-69-2)*

| Opponent | | Opponent | |
|---|---|---|---|
| Northwest Mo. St. ■ ........S 4* | 24 | St. Francis (Ill.) ...........13 |
| Northeast Mo. St. .........S11* | 27 | Northwest Mo. St. .........13 |
| South Dak. ..................S18 | 14 | Northern Colo. ..............0 |
| Augustana (S.D.) ...........S25 | 31 | Morningside ...............24 |
| North Dak. St. ■ ..........O 2 | 0 | St. Cloud St. ...............7 |
| North Dak. .................O 9 | 37 | Nebraska-Omaha ..........7 |
| Morningside ■ ............O16 | 10 | North Dak. St. .............28 |
| Northern Colo. ■ .........O23 | 7 | North Dak. .................16 |
| St. Cloud St. ..............O30 | 22 | South Dak. .................15 |
| South Dak. St. ■ .........N 6 | 30 | South Dak. St. .............34 |
| Nebraska-Omaha ■ ........N13 | 28 | Augustana (S.D.) ...........38 |

Colors: Purple & Gold.   Nickname: Mavericks.   II

# MANSFIELD .................... Mansfield, PA 16933
*Tom Elsasser (10 yrs., 40-58-6)*

| Opponent | | Opponent | |
|---|---|---|---|
| Cortland St. .................S 4 | 26 | Lock Haven ................32 |
| Buffalo St. ■ ...............S11 | 17 | Buffalo St. .................21 |
| Lock Haven ■ .............S25 | 24 | Cortland St. ................10 |
| Kutztown ...................O 2 | 42 | Buffalo .....................56 |
| West Chester ■ ...........O 9 | 30 | Kutztown ...................27 |
| East Stroudsburg .........O16 | 13 | West Chester ..............39 |
| Cheyney ■ .................O23 | 6 | East Stroudsburg ..........20 |
| Ferrum .....................O30 | 37 | Cheyney ....................16 |
| Millersville .................N 6 | 41 | Ferrum .....................28 |
| Bloomsburg ■ .............N13 | 14 | Millersville .................27 |
| | 30 | Bloomsburg .................24 |

Colors: Red & Black.   Nickname: Mountaineers.   II

# MARIETTA ...................... Marietta, OH 45750
*Gene Epley (6 yrs., 21-38-2)*

| Opponent | | Opponent | |
|---|---|---|---|
| Kenyon .....................S11 | 7 | Kenyon ......................7 |
| Ohio Northern ■ ..........S18* | 0 | Ohio Northern ..............21 |
| Mount Union ■ ...........S25* | 0 | Mount Union ...............31 |
| Capital ......................O 2 | 20 | Capital ......................0 |
| Hiram .......................O 9 | 13 | Hiram .......................0 |
| Otterbein ■ ...............O16 | 16 | Otterbein ...................28 |
| Baldwin-Wallace ..........O23 | 7 | Baldwin-Wallace ............35 |
| John Carroll ■ .............O30 | 6 | John Carroll ................42 |
| Heidelberg .................N 6 | 14 | Heidelberg ..................21 |
| Muskingum ■ .............N13 | 21 | Muskingum ..................0 |

Colors: Navy Blue & White.   Nickname: Pioneers.   III

# MARS HILL ...................... Mars Hill, NC 28754
*Tim Clifton (1st yr. as head coach)*

| Opponent | | Opponent | |
|---|---|---|---|
| Tusculum ....................S 4 | 6 | Western Caro. ..............42 |
| East Tenn. St. .............S11* | 0 | East Tenn. St. ..............21 |
| Catawba ....................S18 | 21 | Catawba ....................14 |
| Wingate .....................S25 | 16 | Wingate .....................19 |
| Kentucky St. ..............O 2* | 13 | Concord (W. Va.) ...........13 |
| Elon .........................O 9 | 3 | Elon .........................23 |
| Carson-Newman ..........O16 | 0 | Carson-Newman ............27 |
| Presbyterian ...............O23 | 6 | Presbyterian ................19 |
| Lenoir-Rhyne ■ ...........N 6 | 22 | Lees-McRae ................7 |
| Gardner-Webb ■ ..........N13 | 7 | Lenoir-Rhyne ...............28 |
| | 13 | Gardner-Webb ..............45 |

Colors: Blue & Gold.   Nickname: Lions.   II

# MARYVILLE (TENNESSEE) ........ Maryville, TN 37801
*Phil Wilks (5 yrs., 23-26-0)*

| Opponent | | Opponent | |
|---|---|---|---|
| Ky. Wesleyan ■ ...........S11 | 0 | Tenn. Wesleyan ............17 |
| Centre ■ ....................S18 | 10 | Mercyhurst .................14 |
| Sewanee ....................S25 | 21 | Centre ......................17 |
| Cumberland (Tenn.) ■ ....O 2 | 15 | Sewanee ....................18 |
| Tenn. Wesleyan ...........O 9 | 29 | Clinch Valley ................19 |
| Clinch Valley ...............O16 | 23 | Cumberland (Tenn.) ........21 |
| Rhodes .....................O23 | 49 | Rhodes .....................27 |
| Methodist ..................O30 | 34 | Methodist ...................6 |
| Tusculum ■ ................N 6 | 19 | Tusculum ...................26 |
| Emory & Henry ■ .........N13 | 14 | Emory & Henry .............24 |

Colors: Orange & Garnet.   Nickname: Scots.   III

# MASSACHUSETTS-BOSTON ........ Boston, MA 02125
*Jim Kent (5 yrs., 17-27-1)*

| Opponent | | Opponent | |
|---|---|---|---|
| Westfield St. ...............S17* | 34 | Westfield St. ................20 |
| Bri'water (Mass.) ■ ......S25 | 21 | Bri'water (Mass.) ...........47 |
| Worcester St. ..............O 2 | 32 | Worcester St. ...............27 |
| Mass. Maritime ■ .........O 9 | 28 | Mass. Maritime .............32 |
| Mass.-Dartmouth ..........O16 | 7 | Mass.-Dartmouth ...........26 |
| Maine Maritime ■ .........O23 | 14 | Maine Maritime .............26 |
| MIT ..........................O30 | 40 | MIT ..........................13 |
| Fitchburg St. ...............N 6 | 32 | Fitchburg St. ................18 |
| Framingham St. ■ .........N13 | 53 | Framingham St. .............28 |

Colors: Blue & White.   Nickname: Beacons.   III

# MASS.-DARTMOUTH ..... North Dartmouth, MA 02747
*William Kavanaugh (3 yrs., 12-15-0)*

| Opponent | | Opponent | |
|---|---|---|---|
| Worcester St. ...............S18 | 9 | Stonehill ....................0 |
| Mass. Maritime ■ ..........S26 | 47 | Worcester St. ...............0 |
| Western Conn. St. .........O 2* | 6 | Mass. Maritime .............9 |
| Maine Maritime ............O 9 | 14 | Maine Maritime .............17 |
| Mass.-Boston ■ ...........O16 | 26 | Mass.-Boston ...............7 |
| Fitchburg St. ...............O23 | 26 | Fitchburg St. ................0 |
| Framingham St. ■ .........O30 | 3 | Framingham St. .............6 |
| Westfield St. ...............N 5* | 21 | Westfield St. ................14 |
| Bri'water (Mass.) ■ ......N13 | 12 | Bri'water (Mass.) ...........30 |

Colors: Gold & Blue.   Nickname: Corsairs.   III

# MASSACHUSETTS-LOWELL ........ Lowell, MA 01854
*Tom Radulski (1st yr. as head coach)*

| Opponent | | Opponent | |
|---|---|---|---|
| Bentley .....................S10* | 0 | Coast Guard ................20 |
| Norwich .....................S18 | 20 | Norwich .....................8 |
| Pace ........................S25 | 9 | Worcester Tech .............13 |
| Plymouth St. ■ ...........O 2* | 20 | Plymouth St. ................21 |
| Sacred Heart ■ ...........O 9* | 19 | Sacred Heart ...............0 |
| Stonehill ....................O16 | 18 | Susquehanna ...............35 |
| Western Conn. St. .........O23 | 41 | Western Conn. St. ..........17 |
| Worcester Tech ............O30 | 32 | Assumption .................26 |
| Assumption ■ ..............N 6 | 27 | Stony Brook ................31 |
| Stony Brook ■ .............N13 | | |

Colors: Red, White & Blue.   Nickname: Chiefs.   III

# MASSACHUSETTS MARITIME   Buzzards Bay, MA 02532
*Don Ruggeri (20 yrs., 101-75-1)*

| Opponent | | Opponent | |
|---|---|---|---|
| Nichols ......................S11 | 14 | Nichols ......................31 |
| Bentley ■ ...................S18 | 9 | Mass.-Dartmouth ...........6 |
| Mass.-Dartmouth .........S26 | 25 | Maine Maritime .............20 |
| Maine Maritime ■ .........O 3 | 32 | Mass.-Boston ...............28 |
| Mass.-Boston ..............O 9 | 33 | Fitchburg St. ................0 |
| Fitchburg St. ■ ............O16 | 42 | Framingham St. .............28 |
| Framingham St. ............O23 | 10 | Westfield St. ................13 |
| Westfield St. ■ ............O30 | 13 | Bri'water (Mass.) ...........34 |
| Bri'water (Mass.) ..........N 6 | 23 | Worcester St. ...............6 |
| Worcester St. ■ ...........N13 | | |

Colors: Blue & Gold.   Nickname: Buccaneers.   III

# MENLO ........................ Menlo Park, CA 94025
*Ray Solari (7 yrs., 32-31-1)*

| Opponent | | Opponent | |
|---|---|---|---|
| San Diego ..................S 4* | 16 | Redlands ....................21 |
| Redlands ...................S11* | 20 | Occidental ..................19 |
| San Fran. St. ■ ...........S18 | 34 | Whittier .....................24 |
| Cal Lutheran ■ ...........O 2 | 33 | Claremont-M-S .............17 |
| La Verne ...................O 9 | 7 | San Fran. St. ...............14 |
| Claremont-M-S ■ .........O16 | 7 | La Verne ....................30 |
| Occidental .................O23* | 7 | Cal Lutheran ...............19 |
| Whittier .....................O30 | 6 | San Diego ..................36 |
| Azusa Pacific ..............N13 | 22 | Azusa Pacific ...............25 |

Colors: Blue & White.   Nickname: Oaks.   III

# MERCHANT MARINE .......... Kings Point, NY 11024
*Charlie Pravata (2 yrs., 9-7-2)*

| Opponent | | Opponent | |
|---|---|---|---|
| Norwich ■ ..................S11 | 27 | Norwich .....................0 |
| Western Conn. St. .......S18 | 37 | Western Conn. St. .........14 |
| Catholic .....................S25 | 45 | Pace ........................6 |
| St. John Fisher .............O 9 | 49 | Albright .....................22 |
| Worcester Tech ............O16 | 15 | Worcester Tech .............14 |
| Stony Brook ■ ............O23 | 28 | Stony Brook ................7 |
| Gettysburg .................O30 | 6 | Muhlenberg .................6 |
| Alfred ■ .....................N 6 | 32 | Iona .........................26 |
| Coast Guard ...............N13 | 42 | Coast Guard ................0 |
| | **ECAC Southwest** | |
| | 20 | Dickinson ...................13 |

Colors: Blue & Gray.   Nickname: Mariners.   III

# MERCYHURST .................... Erie, PA 16546
*Joe Kimball (8 yrs., 37-37-1)*

| Opponent | | Opponent | |
|---|---|---|---|
| Gannon .....................S18 | 47 | Bethany (W.Va.) ............12 |
| Dickinson ■ ...............S25 | 21 | Maryville (Tenn.) ...........10 |
| Canisius ....................O 2 | 21 | Gannon .....................24 |
| Buffalo St. ■ ..............O 9 | 38 | St. Francis (PA) .............13 |
| Wittenberg .................O16 | 34 | Canisius ....................13 |
| Duquesne ..................O23* | 14 | Dayton ......................13 |
| Ithaca ■ ....................O30 | 20 | Wittenberg ..................20 |
| Pace .........................N 6 | 9 | Alfred .......................14 |
| St. Francis (PA) ■ ........N13 | 7 | Ithaca .......................48 |
| | 38 | Brockport St. ...............8 |

Colors: Blue & Green.   Nickname: Lakers.   III

---

■ Home games on each schedule.          *Night Games.

## MESA STATE .............. Grand Junction, CO 81501
*Jim Paronto (7 yrs., 36-36-0)*

| | | | | |
|---|---|---|---|---|
| Central Okla. ■ | .............S 4* | 17 | Idaho St. .................. | 52 |
| Northern Colo. .............. | S 11 | 0 | Northern Colo. ............ | 27 |
| Fort Lewis ■ | .................S 25* | 0 | Montana St. .............. | 43 |
| Idaho St. ■ | .................0 2* | 3 | N.M. Highlands ............ | 52 |
| Fort Hays St. ............... | 0 9 | 38 | Fort Lewis ................ | 27 |
| Western St. ................. | 0 16 | 17 | Fort Hays St. .............. | 38 |
| N.M. Highlands ■ | .........0 23* | 3 | Western St. ................ | 30 |
| Adams St. ................. | 0 30 | 14 | Neb.-Kearney .............. | 38 |
| Colorado Mines .............N 6 | | 21 | Adams St. .................. | 10 |
| Chadron St. ■ | ..............N 13 | 24 | Colorado Mines ............ | 21 |
| | | 24 | Chadron St. .............. | 37 |

Colors: Maroon, White & Gold.   Nickname: Mavericks.   II

## METHODIST ................. Fayetteville, NC 28311
*Jim Sypult (1 yr., 0-10-0)*

| | | | | |
|---|---|---|---|---|
| Chowan ■ | .................S 4 | 19 | Charleston So. .............. | 20 |
| Guilford ...................... | S 11 | 7 | Guilford .................. | 38 |
| Salisbury St. ............... | S 18 | 14 | Salisbury St. .............. | 37 |
| Newport News App. ■ | .......0 2 | 0 | Newport News App. ........ | 49 |
| Bridgewater (Va.) ■ | .........0 9 | 21 | Catholic .................. | 27 |
| Davidson ................. | 0 16 | 0 | Bridgewater (Va.) .......... | 27 |
| Gallaudet ................. | 0 23 | 6 | Davidson .................. | 27 |
| Maryville (Tenn.) ■ | .........0 30 | 6 | Maryville (Tenn.) .......... | 34 |
| Hampden-Sydney .............N 6 | | 3 | Hampden-Sydney .......... | 17 |
| Frostburg St. ■ | ..............N 13 | 14 | Frostburg St. .............. | 35 |

Colors: Green & Gold.   Nickname: Monarchs.   III

## MICHIGAN TECH ................. Houghton, MI 49931
*Bernie Anderson (6 yrs., 29-28-0)*

| | | | | |
|---|---|---|---|---|
| Wis.-Stevens Point .........S 4 | | 25 | Wis.-Stevens Point ........ | 13 |
| Northern St. (S.D.) .......S 11 | | 42 | Northern St. (S.D.) ........ | 26 |
| Minn.-Morris ■ | .............S 18 | 40 | Minn.-Morris .............. | 7 |
| Bemidji St. ................. | S 25 | 47 | Bemidji St. ................ | 7 |
| Winona St. ■ | .................0 2 | 38 | Winona St. ................ | 19 |
| Minn.-Duluth ................ | 0 9 | 40 | Minn.-Duluth .............. | 20 |
| Saginaw Valley .............. | 0 23 | 48 | Wayne St. (Neb.) .......... | 38 |
| Wayne St. (Neb.) ■ | .........0 30 | 38 | Valparaiso ................ | 21 |
| Valparaiso .................N 6 | | 35 | Moorhead St. .............. | 36 |
| Southwest St. (Minn.)† ......N 12* | | | | |

Colors: Silver & Gold.   Nickname: Huskies.   II

## MIDDLEBURY ................. Middlebury, VT 05753
*Mickey Heinecken (20 yrs., 91-67-2)*

| | | | | |
|---|---|---|---|---|
| Bowdoin ................... | S 25 | 18 | Bowdoin .................. | 14 |
| Colby ■ | ..................0 2 | 24 | Colby .................... | 23 |
| Amherst ................. | 0 9 | 24 | Amherst .................. | 13 |
| Williams ■ | .................0 16 | 3 | Williams .................. | 0 |
| Bates ■ | ...................0 23 | 49 | Bates .................... | 0 |
| Trinity (Conn.) ■ | ..........0 30 | 0 | Trinity (Conn.) ............ | 43 |
| Hamilton ■ | .................N 6 | 17 | Hamilton .................. | 9 |
| Tufts ...................... | N 13 | 19 | Tufts .................... | 7 |

Colors: Blue & White.   Nickname: Panthers.   III

## MILES ....................... Birmingham, AL 35208
*Theophilus Danzy (1st yr. as head coach)*

| | | | | |
|---|---|---|---|---|
| Alabama A&M ■ | ...........S 4 | 8 | Fayetteville St. ............ | 28 |
| Albany St. (Ga.) ■ | .........S 11 | 6 | Albany St. (Ga.) .......... | 70 |
| Morehouse .................S 18 | | 6 | Mississippi Val. ............ | 19 |
| Tuskegee ■ | .................S 25 | 7 | Morris Brown .............. | 13 |
| Ala.-Birmingham ■ | .........0 2 | 6 | Ala.-Birmingham .......... | 30 |
| Morris Brown ................ | 0 9 | 0 | Fort Valley St. ............ | 38 |
| Fort Valley St. .............. | 0 16 | 13 | Clark Atlanta .............. | 14 |
| Clark Atlanta ............... | 0 23 | 20 | Morehouse ................ | 28 |
| Knoxville .................. | 0 30 | 6 | Tuskegee .................. | 40 |
| Savannah St. ■ | ..............N 13 | 6 | Savannah St. .............. | 73 |

Colors: Purple & Gold.   Nickname: Golden Bears.   II

## MILLERSVILLE ................. Millersville, PA 17551
*Gene Carpenter (24 yrs., 159-69-5)*

| | | | | |
|---|---|---|---|---|
| Shepherd ..................S 11* | | 17 | Shepherd .................. | 9 |
| American Int'l ............... | S 18 | 31 | American Int'l .............. | 6 |
| Shippensburg ■ | .............S 25* | 35 | Shippensburg .............. | 10 |
| Bloomsburg ................ | 0 2 | 48 | Bloomsburg .............. | 12 |
| Kutztown ................. | 0 9 | 23 | Kutztown .................. | 21 |
| West Chester ............... | 0 16 | 14 | West Chester .............. | 38 |
| East Stroudsburg ■ | .........0 23 | 13 | East Stroudsburg .......... | 20 |
| Cheyney ................. | 0 30 | 38 | Cheyney .................. | 9 |
| Mansfield ■ | .................N 6 | 27 | Mansfield ................ | 14 |
| Edinboro ..................N 13 | | 12 | Edinboro .................. | 36 |

Colors: Black & Gold.   Nickname: Marauders.   II

## MILLIKIN ..................... Decatur, IL 62522
*Carl Poelker (11 yrs., 71-29-1)*

| | | | | |
|---|---|---|---|---|
| Ill. Benedictine ■ | ...........S 11 | 24 | Ill. Benedictine ............ | 25 |
| Valparaiso ■ | .................S 18 | 12 | Drake .................... | 30 |
| Wheaton (Ill.) ............... | 0 2 | 6 | Wheaton (Ill.) .............. | 21 |
| Carthage ■ | .................0 9 | 61 | Carthage .................. | 0 |
| North Park ................. | 0 16 | 49 | North Park ................ | 0 |
| North Central ■ | .............0 23 | 35 | North Central .............. | 21 |
| Augustana (Ill.) ............. | 0 30 | 3 | Augustana (Ill.) ............ | 13 |
| Ill. Wesleyan ................ | N 6 | 13 | Ill. Wesleyan .............. | 24 |
| Elmhurst ..................N 13 | | 33 | Elmhurst .................. | 28 |

Colors: Royal Blue & White.   Nickname: Big Blue.   III

## MILLSAPS ......................... Jackson, MS 39210
*Tommy Ranager (4 yrs., 21-14-2)*

| | | | | |
|---|---|---|---|---|
| Austin ...................... | S 11 | 0 | Ala.-Birmingham .......... | 17 |
| DePauw ■ | ..................S 18 | 27 | Greenville ................ | 21 |
| Hardin-Simmons ■ | .........S 25 | 21 | DePauw .................. | 14 |
| Emory & Henry ■ | ..........0 2 | 13 | Hardin-Simmons .......... | 21 |
| Centre ■ | ...................0 9 | 6 | Emory & Henry ............ | 17 |
| Colorado Col. ............... | 0 23 | 21 | Centre .................. | 10 |
| Sewanee ................. | 0 30 | 15 | Colorado Col. .............. | 0 |
| Rhodes ■ | ...................N 6 | 14 | Sewanee .................. | 33 |
| Trinity (Tex.) ............... | N 13* | 14 | Rhodes .................. | 14 |
| | | 40 | Trinity (Tex.) .............. | 17 |

Colors: Purple & White.   Nickname: Majors.   III

## MINNESOTA-DULUTH ............. Duluth, MN 55812
*James Malosky (35 yrs., 223-104-12)*

| | | | | |
|---|---|---|---|---|
| Wis.-Eau Claire .............S 4* | | 17 | Wis.-Eau Claire ............ | 6 |
| St. Cloud St. ................ | S 11 | 0 | St. Cloud St. .............. | 33 |
| Wis.-Stout ■ | .................S 18 | 17 | St. Francis (Ill.) ............ | 42 |
| Northern St. (S.D.) .........S 25 | | 9 | Northern St. (S.D.) ........ | 0 |
| Bemidji St. ................. | 0 2 | 22 | Bemidji St. ................ | 13 |
| Michigan Tech ■ | .............0 9 | 20 | Michigan Tech ............ | 40 |
| Southwest St. (Minn.) .......0 16 | | 18 | Southwest St. (Minn.) ...... | 18 |
| Moorhead St. ............... | 0 23 | 6 | Moorhead St. .............. | 21 |
| Winona St. ................. | 0 30 | 21 | Winona St. ................ | 0 |
| Minn.-Morris ■ | .............N 6 | 41 | Minn.-Morris .............. | 22 |
| Wayne St. (Neb.)† ..........N 13 | | 22 | Northern Ariz. .............. | 31 |

Colors: Maroon & Gold.   Nickname: Bulldogs.   II

## MINNESOTA-MORRIS .............. Morris, MN 56267
*Jay Mills (1st yr. as head coach)*

| | | | | |
|---|---|---|---|---|
| Wis.-River Falls ..............S 4 | | 20 | Wis.-River Falls ............ | 42 |
| Wis.-Stevens Point ..........S 11 | | 12 | Wis.-Stevens Point ........ | 42 |
| Michigan Tech ■ | .............S 18 | 7 | Michigan Tech ............ | 40 |
| Southwest St. (Minn.) ■ | .....S 25 | 0 | Southwest St. (Minn.) ...... | 50 |
| Moorhead St. ................ | 0 2 | 17 | Moorhead St. .............. | 24 |
| Winona St. ■ | .................0 9 | 7 | Winona St. ................ | 44 |
| Teikyo Westmar ■ | ..........0 16 | 30 | Teikyo Westmar ............ | 12 |
| Northern St. (S.D.) .........0 23 | | 28 | Northern St. (S.D.) ........ | 48 |
| Bemidji St. ■ | .................0 30 | 7 | Bemidji St. ................ | 34 |
| Minn.-Duluth ................ | N 6 | 22 | Minn.-Duluth .............. | 41 |
| Northern St. (S.D.)† .........N 12 | | 14 | Lindenwood ................ | 13 |

Colors: Maroon & Gold.   Nickname: Cougars.   II

## MISSISSIPPI COLLEGE ............. Clinton, MS 39058
*Terry McMillan (2 yrs., 11-9-2)*

| | | | | |
|---|---|---|---|---|
| Ark.-Monticello ■ | ...........S 4* | 6 | Northwestern (La.) ........ | 27 |
| Texas A&I ..................S 11* | | 6 | North Ala. ................ | 14 |
| Livingston ■ | .................S 25* | 24 | Henderson St. ............ | 12 |
| Henderson St. ............... | 0 2* | 14 | Jacksonville St. ............ | 14 |
| North Ala. ■ | .................0 9 | 45 | West Ga. .................. | 38 |
| Samford ................. | 0 16 | 32 | Livingston ................ | 37 |
| Valdosta St. ............... | 0 23 | 37 | Texas A&I ................ | 33 |
| West Ga. ■ | ..................0 30* | 14 | Valdosta St. .............. | 28 |
| Central Ark. ■ | ...............N 6* | 0 | Ga. Southern .............. | 30 |
| Delta St. ................. | N 13 | 34 | Delta St. .................. | 23 |

Colors: Blue & Gold.   Nickname: Choctaws.   II

## MISSOURI-ROLLA ..................... Rolla, MO 65401
*Jim Anderson (1 yr., 2-9-0)*

| | | | | |
|---|---|---|---|---|
| Iowa Wesleyan ■ | ...........S 11 | 27 | Iowa Wesleyan ............ | 26 |
| Washburn ................. | S 18* | 0 | Murray St. ................ | 36 |
| Emporia St. ■ | .................S 25 | 14 | Northwest Mo. St. .......... | 29 |
| Southwest Baptist ■ | .........0 2 | 3 | Pittsburg St. .............. | 45 |
| Pittsburg St. ................ | 0 9* | 21 | Mo. Western St. ............ | 28 |
| Northwest Mo. St. ........... | 0 16 | 13 | Mo. Southern St. .......... | 33 |
| Northeast Mo. St. ........... | 0 23 | 6 | Emporia St. ................ | 35 |
| Mo. Western St. ■ | .........0 30 | 26 | Washburn ................ | 21 |
| Mo. Southern St. ............ | N 6 | 0 | Central Mo. St. ............ | 17 |
| Central Mo. St. ■ | .............N 13 | 7 | Southwest Baptist .......... | 17 |
| | | 14 | Northeast Mo. St. .......... | 36 |

Colors: Silver & Gold.   Nickname: Miners.   II

---

■ Home games on each schedule.        *Night Games.

## MISSOURI SOUTHERN STATE ......Joplin, MO 64801
*Jon Lantz (7 yrs., 43-27-2)*

| | | | | |
|---|---|---|---|---|
| Central Ark. ■ | .........S 11* | 59 | Cameron .................... | 7 |
| Pittsburg St. ■ | .........S 18* | 7 | Emporia St. .................. | 28 |
| Southwest Baptist | .........S 25 | 7 | Central Mo. St. ............. | 10 |
| Northeast Mo. St. ■ | ......O 2 | 24 | Mo. Western St. ............ | 28 |
| Mo. Western St. | .........O 9* | 44 | Washburn ................... | 14 |
| Central Mo. St. | .........O 16 | 33 | Missouri-Rolla .............. | 13 |
| Emporia St. ■ | ..........O 23 | 28 | Southwest Baptist ......... | 27 |
| Washburn | .............O 30 | 13 | Pittsburg St. ................ | 42 |
| Missouri-Rolla ■ | ..........N 6 | 27 | Northwest Mo. St. .......... | 35 |
| Northwest Mo. St. | .......N 13 | 6 | Northeast Mo. St. .......... | 52 |

Colors: Green & Gold.   Nickname: Lions.          **II**

## MISSOURI WESTERN STATE....St. Joseph, MO 64507
*Stan McGarvey (8 yrs., 49-35-2)*

| | | | | |
|---|---|---|---|---|
| Southwest St. (Minn.) | ......S 4 | 7 | Western Ill. .................. | 42 |
| Friends ■ | .............S 11* | 54 | Peru St. ...................... | 6 |
| Northwest Mo. St. ■ | ......S 18* | 30 | Emporia St. .................. | 35 |
| Pittsburg St. | .........S 25* | 28 | Mo. Southern St. ........... | 24 |
| Central Mo. St. ■ | .......O 2* | 34 | Missouri-Rolla .............. | 21 |
| Mo. Southern St. ■ | ......O 9* | 34 | Southwest Baptist ......... | 24 |
| Emporia St. ■ | ...........O 16 | 28 | Pittsburg St. ................ | 31 |
| Washburn ■ | ..........O 23 | 26 | Northwest Mo. St. .......... | 43 |
| Missouri-Rolla | ..........O 30 | 7 | Northeast Mo. St. .......... | 41 |
| Southwest Baptist ■ | .....N 6 | 3 | Central Mo. St. ............. | 38 |
| Northeast Mo. St. | .........N 13 | 41 | Washburn ................... | 17 |

Colors: Black & Gold.   Nickname: Griffons.          **II**

## MIT ............................Cambridge, MA 02139
*Dwight Smith (5 yrs., 11-25-1)*

| | | | | |
|---|---|---|---|---|
| Assumption ■ | .............S 18 | 7 | Assumption ................ | 27 |
| Western New Eng. | .......S 25 | 27 | Western New Eng. ......... | 9 |
| Stonehill ■ | .............O 2 | 14 | Bentley ...................... | 43 |
| Westfield St. | .............O 9 | 12 | Westfield St. ................ | 31 |
| Curry | ...............O 16 | 19 | Stonehill .................... | 21 |
| Nichols ■ | ..............O 23 | 0 | Nichols ..................... | 19 |
| Mass.-Boston | .............O 30 | 13 | Mass.-Boston .............. | 40 |
| Bentley ■ | ..............N 6 | 12 | Curry ........................ | 13 |

Colors: Cardinal & Gray.   Nickname: Beavers.          **III**

## MONMOUTH (ILLINOIS).........Monmouth, IL 61462
*Kelly Kane (9 yrs., 55-29-0)*

| | | | | |
|---|---|---|---|---|
| Eureka ■ | .............S 11 | 26 | Eureka ....................... | 15 |
| MacMurray | .............S 18 | 13 | MacMurray .................. | 21 |
| Lawrence | .............S 25 | 35 | Lawrence .................... | 30 |
| Carroll (Wis.) ■ | .........O 2 | 21 | Carroll (Wis.) ............... | 40 |
| Illinois Col. | .............O 9 | 14 | Illinois Col. ................. | 6 |
| Cornell College | ..........O 16 | 18 | Cornell College ............ | 28 |
| Coe ■ | ...............O 23 | 21 | Coe .......................... | 62 |
| Grinnell ■ | ..............O 30 | 72 | Grinnell ..................... | 0 |
| Knox | ..................N 6 | 34 | Knox ......................... | 20 |

Colors: Crimson & White.   Nickname: Fighting Scots.          **III**

## MONTCLAIR STATE .......Upper Montclair, NJ 07043
*Rick Giancola (11 yrs., 77-26-2)*

| | | | | |
|---|---|---|---|---|
| Cortland St. | .............S 11 | 17 | Cortland St. ................. | 23 |
| Ithaca ■ | .............S 18 | 19 | Ithaca ....................... | 49 |
| FDU-Madison ■ | ........O 2 | 27 | Ramapo ..................... | 7 |
| Kean ■ | ...............O 9 | 16 | Kean ......................... | 3 |
| Wm. Paterson | ..........O 16 | 24 | Wm. Paterson .............. | 19 |
| Ferrum | .............O 23 | 21 | Salisbury St. ............... | 12 |
| Trenton St. | .............O 30 | 17 | Trenton St. ................. | 5 |
| Jersey City St. ■ | .........N 6 | 15 | Jersey City St. ............. | 0 |
| Rowan | ..............N 13 | 17 | Rowan ...................... | 49 |

Colors: Scarlet & White.   Nickname: Red Hawks.          **III**

## MOORHEAD STATE .............Moorhead, MN 56560
*Ralph Micheli (10 yrs., 29-63-0)*

| | | | | |
|---|---|---|---|---|
| Concordia-M'head | ..........S 11 | 12 | Concordia-M'head .......... | 13 |
| Neb.-Kearney | .............S 18 | 0 | Neb.-Kearney ............... | 26 |
| Winona St. | .............S 25 | 38 | Winona St. .................. | 13 |
| Minn.-Morris ■ | .........O 2 | 40 | Minn.-Morris ............... | 17 |
| Northern St. (S.D.) | ......O 9 | 34 | Northern St. (S.D.) ......... | 35 |
| Bemidji St. ■ | ...........O 16 | 7 | Bemidji St. .................. | 28 |
| Minn.-Duluth | ..........O 23 | 21 | Minn.-Duluth ............... | 6 |
| Southwest St. (Minn.) ■ | ......O 30 | 19 | Southwest St. (Minn.) ...... | 23 |
| Northern Iowa | .......N 6* | 30 | Michigan Tech .............. | 35 |
| Winona St.† | ...............N 12 | | | |

Colors: Scarlet & White.   Nickname: Dragons.          **II**

## MORAVIAN ......................Bethlehem, PA 18018
*Scot Dapp (6 yrs., 43-19-0)*

| | | | | |
|---|---|---|---|---|
| Baldwin-Wallace ■ | ..........S 11 | 14 | Frank. & Marsh. ............ | 7 |
| Delaware Valley | ..........S 18 | 12 | Susquehanna ............... | 20 |
| Widener ■ | .............S 25 | 7 | Widener ..................... | 16 |
| Lebanon Valley | .............O 2 | 28 | Wilkes ....................... | 14 |
| Lycoming ■ | .............O 9 | 31 | Juniata ...................... | 14 |
| Susquehanna | ..........O 16 | 13 | Lebanon Valley ............. | 18 |
| Albright ■ | ..............O 23 | 7 | Lycoming .................... | 27 |
| Juniata | ...............O 30 | 28 | Delaware Valley ............ | 14 |
| King's (PA) ■ | ..............N 6 | 28 | Albright ..................... | 20 |
| Muhlenberg | .............N 13 | 35 | Muhlenberg ................ | 14 |

Colors: Blue & Gray.   Nickname: Grayhounds.          **III**

## MOREHOUSE......................Atlanta, GA 30314
*Craig Cason (2 yrs., 12-9-0)*

| | | | | |
|---|---|---|---|---|
| Johnson Smith ■ | .........S 4 | 7 | Howard ...................... | 0 |
| Fort Valley St. ■ | .........S 11 | 0 | Fort Valley St. .............. | 13 |
| Miles ■ | ...............S 18 | 21 | Johnson Smith ............. | 17 |
| Albany St. (Ga.) | .........S 25 | 17 | Albany St. (Ga.) ............ | 10 |
| Alabama A&M† | .........O 9 | 19 | Hampton .................... | 46 |
| Tuskegee† | ...............O 16* | 9 | Alabama A&M ............... | 20 |
| Morris Brown | ...........O 23 | 12 | Tuskegee .................... | 9 |
| Howard | .............O 30 | 20 | Morris Brown ............... | 21 |
| Clark Atlanta ■ | .........N 13 | 0 | Savannah St. ............... | 54 |
| | | 28 | Miles ........................ | 20 |
| | | 33 | Clark Atlanta ............... | 14 |

Colors: Maroon & White.   Nickname: Maroon Tigers/Tigers.          **II**

## MORNINGSIDE ...................Sioux City, IA 51106
*Greg Lees (1st yr. as head coach)*

| | | | | |
|---|---|---|---|---|
| Northwestern Ia. | ........S 4 | 21 | Northeast Mo. St. .......... | 25 |
| Wayne St. (Neb.) | .........S 11* | 24 | Wayne St. (Neb.) ........... | 7 |
| North Dak. | .............S 18 | 31 | South Dak. .................. | 8 |
| North Dak. St. | .........S 25* | 24 | Mankato St. ................. | 31 |
| South Dak. St. ■ | .........O 2 | 24 | North Dak. .................. | 24 |
| Nebraska-Omaha ■ | ......O 9 | 9 | Northern Colo. .............. | 21 |
| Mankato St. | ...........O 16 | 6 | South Dak. St. .............. | 2 |
| Augustana (S.D.) | .........O 23 | 35 | Nebraska-Omaha .......... | 18 |
| South Dak. ■ | ..........O 30 | 31 | Augustana (S.D.) ........... | 14 |
| St. Cloud St. | ..............N 6 | 14 | North Dak. St. .............. | 24 |
| Northern Colo. | .........N 13 | 6 | St. Cloud St. ................ | 23 |

Colors: Maroon & White.   Nickname: Chiefs.          **II**

## MORRIS BROWN ...................Atlanta, GA 30314
*Greg Thompson (12 yrs., 49-61-4)*

| | | | | |
|---|---|---|---|---|
| Clark Atlanta | ..............S 6 | 20 | Clark Atlanta ............... | 28 |
| Tuskegee ■ | .............S 18 | 28 | Cheyney ..................... | 21 |
| Fort Valley St.† | .........S 25* | 20 | Tuskegee .................... | 25 |
| Alabama A&M | .............O 2 | 6 | Fort Valley St. .............. | 32 |
| Miles ■ | ...............O 9 | 10 | Alabama A&M ............... | 9 |
| Savannah St. | ...........O 16 | 13 | Miles ........................ | 7 |
| Morehouse ■ | ..........O 23 | 15 | Savannah St. ............... | 30 |
| Albany St. (Ga.) | ..........N 6 | 21 | Morehouse .................. | 20 |
| Hampton ■ | .............N 13 | 26 | Johnson Smith ............. | 28 |
| | | 0 | Albany St. (Ga.) ............ | 34 |

Colors: Purple & Black.   Nickname: Wolverines.          **II**

## MOUNT UNION ...................Alliance, OH 44601
*Larry Kehres (7 yrs., 60-13-3)*

| | | | | |
|---|---|---|---|---|
| Adrian | ...............S 11 | 21 | Adrian ....................... | 12 |
| Muskingum ■ | .............S 18* | 31 | Muskingum .................. | 13 |
| Marietta | .............S 25* | 31 | Marietta ..................... | 0 |
| Baldwin-Wallace | .........O 2 | 23 | Baldwin-Wallace ........... | 14 |
| John Carroll ■ | .........O 9 | 24 | John Carroll ................ | 7 |
| Heidelberg | ...........O 16 | 48 | Heidelberg .................. | 7 |
| Ohio Northern ■ | .........O 23 | 34 | Ohio Northern .............. | 13 |
| Otterbein | .............O 30 | 54 | Otterbein .................... | 13 |
| Capital | ...............N 6 | 44 | Capital ...................... | 0 |
| Hiram ■ | .............N 13 | 55 | Hiram ....................... | 13 |

|   | **III Championship** | |
|---|---|---|
| 27 | Dayton ...................... | 10 |
| 49 | Ill. Wesleyan ............... | 27 |
| 24 | Wis.-La Crosse ............ | 29 |

Colors: Purple & White.   Nickname: Purple Raiders.          **III**

## MUHLENBERG......................Allentown, PA 18104
*Fran Meagher (8 yrs., 23-54-1)*

| | | | | |
|---|---|---|---|---|
| Hampden-Sydney ■ | .........S 11 | 11 | Susquehanna ............... | 35 |
| Dickinson | .............S 18 | 0 | Dickinson ................... | 32 |
| Frank. & Marsh. | .........S 25 | 9 | Frank. & Marsh. ............ | 6 |
| Western Md. ■ | .........O 2 | 0 | Western Md. ................ | 39 |
| Swarthmore | .............O 9 | 14 | Swarthmore ................. | 21 |
| Johns Hopkins ■ | .........O 16 | 8 | Johns Hopkins ............. | 30 |
| Gettysburg | ..........O 23 | 7 | Gettysburg .................. | 18 |
| Ursinus ■ | ..............N 6 | 6 | Merchant Marine ........... | 6 |
| Moravian ■ | .............N 13 | 3 | Ursinus ..................... | 6 |
| | | 14 | Moravian .................... | 35 |

Colors: Cardinal & Gray.   Nickname: Mules.          **III**

---

■ Home games on each schedule.          *Night Games.

## MUSKINGUM . . . . . . . . . . . . . . . New Concord, OH 43762
### Jeff Heacock (12 yrs., 64-51-2)
| | | | | |
|---|---|---|---|---|
| Wittenberg ■ | S 11 | 42 | Denison | 18 |
| Mount Union | S 18* | 13 | Mount Union | 31 |
| Baldwin-Wallace ■ | S 25 | 18 | Baldwin-Wallace | 35 |
| Heidelberg ■ | O 2 | 28 | Heidelberg | 6 |
| Ohio Northern | O 9 | 20 | Ohio Northern | 48 |
| John Carroll ■ | O 16 | 3 | John Carroll | 27 |
| Capital | O 23 | 41 | Capital | 7 |
| Hiram ■ | O 30 | 44 | Hiram | 22 |
| Otterbein ■ | N 6 | 40 | Otterbein | 41 |
| Marietta | N 13 | 0 | Marietta | 21 |

Colors: Black & Magenta.    Nickname: Fighting Muskies.    III

## NEBRASKA-KEARNEY . . . . . . . . . . . . Kearney, NE 68849
### Claire Boroff (21 yrs., 129-74-4)
| | | | | |
|---|---|---|---|---|
| Augustana (S.D.) | S 4 | 14 | Augustana (S.D.) | 33 |
| Nebraska-Omaha ■ | S 11* | 3 | Nebraska-Omaha | 17 |
| Moorhead St. ■ | S 18 | 26 | Moorhead St. | 0 |
| Western St. | S 25 | 17 | Fort Hays St. | 13 |
| Fort Hays St. | O 2* | 7 | Wayne St. (Neb.) | 2 |
| Wayne St. (Neb.) ■ | O 9 | 0 | Portland St. | 44 |
| Portland St. ■ | O 16 | 30 | St. Francis (Ill.) | 6 |
| Northern St. (S.D.) ■ | O 30 | 38 | Mesa St. | 14 |
| Central Okla. ■ | N 6 | 20 | Northern St. (S.D.) | 18 |
| Bemidji St.† | N 13 | 31 | Bemidji St. | 21 |

Colors: Royal Blue & Old Gold.    Nickname: Antelopes.    II

## NEBRASKA-OMAHA . . . . . . . . . . . . . . Omaha, NE 68182
### Tom Mueller (3 yrs., 10-22-0)
| | | | | |
|---|---|---|---|---|
| Wayne St. (Neb.) ■ | S 4 | 20 | Wayne St. (Neb.) | 18 |
| Neb.-Kearney | S 11* | 17 | Neb.-Kearney | 3 |
| North Dak. St. | S 18* | 13 | St. Cloud St. | 31 |
| South Dak. ■ | S 25* | 28 | Augustana (S.D.) | 36 |
| St. Cloud St. ■ | O 2* | 0 | South Dak. St. | 21 |
| Morningside | O 9 | 7 | Mankato St. | 37 |
| South Dak. St. | O 16 | 14 | Northern Colo. | 24 |
| North Dak. ■ | O 23* | 18 | Morningside | 35 |
| Northern Colo. | O 30 | 16 | North Dak. St. | 50 |
| Augustana (S.D.) ■ | N 6 | 0 | North Dak. | 52 |
| Mankato St. | N 13 | 22 | South Dak. | 25 |

Colors: Black & Crimson.    Nickname: Mavericks.    II

## NEBRASKA WESLEYAN . . . . . . . . . . . Lincoln, NE 68504
### Jim Svoboda (6 yrs., 45-16-0)
| | | | | |
|---|---|---|---|---|
| Austin | S 4* | 29 | Austin | 28 |
| Kan. Wesleyan ■ | S 10 | 49 | Kan. Wesleyan | 3 |
| Carroll (Mont.) ■ | S 18 | 8 | Northwestern Ia. | 34 |
| Northwestern Ia. ■ | S 25 | 22 | Hastings | 30 |
| Hastings | O 2 | 31 | Dana | 20 |
| Dana ■ | O 9 | 16 | Doane | 14 |
| Doane ■ | O 23 | 48 | Midland Lutheran | 16 |
| Midland Lutheran | O 30 | 34 | Concordia (Neb.) | 21 |
| Concordia (Neb.) ■ | N 6 | 6 | Peru St. | 54 |
| Peru St. ■ | N 13 | | | |

Colors: Yellow & Brown.    Nickname: Plainsmen.    III

## NEW HAVEN . . . . . . . . . . . . . . . . West Haven, CT 06516
### Mark Whipple (5 yrs., 37-16-0)
| | | | | |
|---|---|---|---|---|
| West Chester ■ | S 4 | 14 | Connecticut | 13 |
| Buffalo | S 11* | 69 | Buffalo | 48 |
| Clarion ■ | S 18 | 48 | Clarion | 47 |
| Springfield | S 24* | 80 | Virginia Union | 26 |
| Carson-Newman | O 2 | 55 | Central Conn. St. | 21 |
| Virginia Union ■ | O 16 | 66 | American Int'l | 7 |
| Southern Conn. St. | O 22* | 56 | Southern Conn. St. | 13 |
| American Int'l | O 30 | 54 | Springfield | 6 |
| Bowie St. ■ | N 6 | 14 | Carson-Newman | 0 |
| Shepherd | N 13 | 49 | Shepherd | 23 |
| | | | **II Championship** | |
| | | 38 | West Chester | 26 |
| | | 35 | Ferris St. | 13 |
| | | 35 | Jacksonville St. | 46 |

Colors: Blue & Gold.    Nickname: Chargers.    II

## NEW MEXICO HIGHLANDS . . . . . . Las Vegas, NM 87701
### Jim Ewan (1 yr., 7-3-1)
| | | | | |
|---|---|---|---|---|
| Eastern N. Mex. | S 4* | 21 | Eastern N. Mex. | 9 |
| Western N. Mex. ■ | S 11* | 45 | Western N. Mex. | 23 |
| Angelo St. | S 18* | 18 | Northwestern Okla. | 18 |
| Fort Hays St. | S 25 | 52 | Mesa St. | 3 |
| Chadron St. ■ | O 9 | 28 | Fort Hays St. | 51 |
| Fort Lewis | O 16 | 0 | Chadron St. | 38 |
| Mesa St. ■ | O 23* | 70 | Fort Lewis | 55 |
| Western St. | O 30 | 42 | West Tex. St. | 14 |
| Adams St. ■ | N 6 | 15 | Western St. | 43 |
| Colorado Mines | N 13 | 41 | Adams St. | 21 |
| | | 49 | Colorado Mines | 42 |

Colors: Purple & White.    Nickname: Cowboys.    II

## NEWBERRY . . . . . . . . . . . . . . . . . . Newberry, NC 29108
### Mike Taylor (1 yr., 5-6-0)
| | | | | |
|---|---|---|---|---|
| South Caro. St. ■ | S 4* | 17 | South Caro. St. | 42 |
| Lenoir-Rhyne ■ | S 11* | 11 | Lenoir-Rhyne | 26 |
| Presbyterian ■ | S 18* | 16 | Gardner-Webb | 65 |
| Gardner-Webb | S 25 | 10 | Elon | 42 |
| Catawba | O 2 | 28 | Charleston So. | 12 |
| Charleston So. ■ | O 9 | 16 | Wofford | 34 |
| Wofford | O 16* | 41 | Lees-McRae | 18 |
| Western Caro. | O 30 | 20 | Catawba | 0 |
| Lees-McRae ■ | N 6 | 14 | Citadel | 32 |
| Fayetteville St. | N 13 | 35 | Fayetteville St. | 12 |
| | | 14 | Presbyterian | 0 |

Colors: Scarlet & Gray.    Nickname: Indians.    II

## NICHOLS . . . . . . . . . . . . . . . . . . . . . . Dudley, MA 01570
### Jim Crowley/Rene Langevin (1st yr. as head coach)
| | | | | |
|---|---|---|---|---|
| Mass. Maritime ■ | S 11 | 31 | Mass. Maritime | 14 |
| Stonehill | S 18 | 14 | Stonehill | 14 |
| Bentley ■ | S 25 | 0 | Bentley | 30 |
| Assumption ■ | O 2 | 19 | Assumption | 14 |
| Curry ■ | O 9 | 27 | Curry | 6 |
| Salve Regina ■ | O 16 | 27 | Sacred Heart | 6 |
| MIT | O 23 | 19 | MIT | 0 |
| Western New Eng. | O 30 | 35 | Western New Eng. | 7 |
| Worcester St. | N 6 | 19 | Worcester St. | 13 |

Colors: Black & Green.    Nickname: Bison.    III

## NORFOLK STATE . . . . . . . . . . . . . . . Norfolk, VA 23504
### Archie Cooley Jr. (11 yrs., 68-40-5)
| | | | | |
|---|---|---|---|---|
| Virginia St. ■ | S 4* | 21 | Virginia St. | 28 |
| N.C. Central | S 11* | 0 | Johnson Smith | 7 |
| Fayetteville St. | S 18* | 23 | Fayetteville St. | 32 |
| Elizabeth City St. ■ | S 25* | 46 | Elizabeth City St. | 45 |
| Lane ■ | O 2 | 6 | North Caro. A&T | 35 |
| Winston-Salem | O 9* | 24 | Bowie St. | 7 |
| Hampton ■ | O 16 | 0 | Hampton | 60 |
| Virginia Union | O 23 | 38 | Virginia Union | 41 |
| Kentucky St. | O 30 | 23 | Kentucky St. | 6 |
| Johnson Smith ■ | N 6 | 26 | Bethune-Cookman | 31 |
| Bethune-Cookman ■ | N 13 | | | |

Colors: Green & Gold.    Nickname: Spartans.    II

## NORTH ALABAMA . . . . . . . . . . . . . . Florence, AL 35630
### Bobby Wallace (5 yrs., 26-27-1)
| | | | | |
|---|---|---|---|---|
| Fort Valley St. ■ | S 4* | 17 | Central Mo. St. | 16 |
| Alabama A&M ■ | S 18* | 14 | Mississippi Col. | 6 |
| Delta St. ■ | S 25* | 15 | Alabama A&M | 7 |
| Portland St. | O 2* | 10 | Delta St. | 14 |
| Mississippi Col. | O 9 | 41 | Fort Valley St. | 7 |
| Henderson St. ■ | O 16* | 6 | Jacksonville St. | 10 |
| Central Ark. | O 23 | 10 | Troy St. | 24 |
| Livingston ■ | O 30 | 20 | Livingston | 13 |
| Valdosta St. | N 6* | 19 | West Ga. | 7 |
| West Ga. ■ | N 13 | 24 | Valdosta St. | 24 |
| | | | **II Championship** | |
| | | 33 | Hampton | 21 |
| | | 12 | Jacksonville St. | 14 |

Colors: Purple & Gold.    Nickname: Lions.    II

## NORTH CAROLINA CENTRAL . . . . . . Durham, NC 27707
### Larry Little (9 yrs., 42-50-1)
| | | | | |
|---|---|---|---|---|
| Bowie St. ■ | S 4* | 7 | North Caro. A&T | 49 |
| Norfolk St. ■ | S 11* | 31 | Virginia St. | 7 |
| Virginia St. | S 18 | 9 | Bowie St. | 0 |
| Johnson Smith | S 25* | 26 | Kentucky St. | 32 |
| Elizabeth City St. ■ | O 2* | 24 | Elizabeth City St. | 42 |
| Fayetteville St. ■ | O 9 | 3 | Fayetteville St. | 13 |
| Winston-Salem | O 16* | 30 | Winston-Salem | 48 |
| South Caro. St. | O 23 | 0 | South Caro. St. | 69 |
| Livingstone ■ | O 31 | 29 | Livingstone | 40 |
| Kentucky St. ■ | N 6 | 13 | Johnson Smith | 12 |
| Virginia Union | N 13 | 19 | Hampton | 31 |

Colors: Maroon & Gray.    Nickname: Eagles.    II

## NORTH CENTRAL . . . . . . . . . . . . . . Naperville, IL 60540
### Bill Mack (1st yr. as head coach)
| | | | | |
|---|---|---|---|---|
| Carroll (Wis.) ■ | S 11* | 18 | Carroll (Wis.) | 34 |
| Eureka | S 18 | 14 | Eureka | 6 |
| Ill. Wesleyan ■ | O 2* | 20 | Ill. Wesleyan | 35 |
| Augustana (Ill.) | O 9 | 0 | Augustana (Ill.) | 21 |
| Elmhurst ■ | O 16* | 28 | Elmhurst | 30 |
| Millikin | O 23 | 24 | Millikin | 35 |
| Wheaton (Ill.) ■ | O 30* | 6 | Wheaton (Ill.) | 33 |
| North Park ■ | N 6 | 20 | North Park | 20 |
| Carthage | N 13 | 51 | Carthage | 14 |

Colors: Cardinal & White.    Nickname: Cardinals.    III

---

■ Home games on each schedule.        *Night Games.

*Divisions II and III 1993 Schedules and 1992 Results*      **729**

## NORTH DAKOTA .............. Grand Forks, ND 58202
*Roger Thomas (9 yrs., 39-50-2)*

| Opponent | Date | Pts | Opponent | Pts |
|---|---|---|---|---|
| Southern Conn. St. ■ | S11 | 13 | Indiana (PA) | 31 |
| Morningside ■ | S18 | 14 | South Dak. St. | 3 |
| St. Cloud St. | S25 | 52 | South Dak. | 3 |
| Northern Colo. | O 2 | 24 | Morningside | 24 |
| Mankato St. ■ | O 9 | 20 | Augustana (S.D.) | 24 |
| Augustana (S.D.) | O16 | 22 | St. Cloud St. | 13 |
| Nebraska-Omaha | O23* | 16 | Mankato St. | 7 |
| North Dak. St. ■ | O30 | 21 | Northern Colo. | 14 |
| South Dak. ■ | N 6 | 52 | Nebraska-Omaha | 0 |
| South Dak. St. | N13 | 19 | North Dak. St. | 20 |
| **II Championship** | | | | |
| | | 21 | Pittsburg St. | 26 |

Colors: Kelly Green & White.  Nickname: Sioux.   II

## NORTH DAKOTA STATE.............. Fargo, ND 58105
*Rocky Hager (6 yrs., 59-12-1)*

| Opponent | Date | Pts | Opponent | Pts |
|---|---|---|---|---|
| Pittsburg St. ■ | S 4* | 26 | Cal Poly SLO | 10 |
| Nebraska-Omaha ■ | S18* | 21 | Augustana (S.D.) | 17 |
| Morningside ■ | S25* | 47 | South Dak. St. | 10 |
| Mankato St. | O 2 | 39 | South Dak. | 20 |
| South Dak. St. ■ | O 9 | 21 | St. Cloud St. | 23 |
| South Dak. ■ | O16 | 28 | Mankato St. | 10 |
| St. Cloud St. | O23 | 35 | Northern Colo. | 3 |
| North Dak. | O30 | 50 | Nebraska-Omaha | 16 |
| Northern Colo. ■ | N 6* | 24 | Morningside | 7 |
| Augustana (S.D.) | N13 | 20 | North Dak. | 19 |
| **II Championship** | | | | |
| | | 42 | Northeast Mo. St. | 7 |
| | | 37 | Pittsburg St. | 38 |

Colors: Yellow & Green.  Nickname: Bison.   II

## NORTH PARK ...................... Chicago, IL 60625
*Tim Rucks (3 yrs., 2-23-2)*

| Opponent | Date | Pts | Opponent | Pts |
|---|---|---|---|---|
| Lake Forest ■ | S18 | 7 | Lake Forest | 9 |
| Blackburn | S25 | 13 | Blackburn | 17 |
| Augustana (Ill.) ■ | O 2 | 10 | Augustana (Ill.) | 35 |
| Elmhurst | O 9 | 20 | Elmhurst | 20 |
| Millikin ■ | O16 | 0 | Millikin | 49 |
| Wheaton (Ill.) | O23 | 0 | Wheaton (Ill.) | 24 |
| Carthage ■ | O30 | 17 | Carthage | 0 |
| North Central | N 6 | 20 | North Central | 20 |
| Ill. Wesleyan | N13 | 0 | Ill. Wesleyan | 42 |

Colors: Blue & Gold.  Nickname: Vikings.   III

## NORTHEAST MISSOURI STATE... Kirksville, MO 63501
*Eric Holm (3 yrs., 23-11-0)*

| Opponent | Date | Pts | Opponent | Pts |
|---|---|---|---|---|
| Iowa Wesleyan | S 4* | 25 | Morningside | 21 |
| Mankato St. ■ | S11* | 37 | Iowa Wesleyan | 7 |
| Central Mo. St. ■ | S18 | 42 | Washburn | 8 |
| Northwest Mo. St. | S25 | 7 | Emporia St. | 24 |
| Mo. Southern St. | O 2 | 48 | Southwest Baptist | 10 |
| Emporia St. ■ | O 9 | 21 | Pittsburg St. | 35 |
| Washburn ■ | O16 | 28 | Northwest Mo. St. | 20 |
| Missouri-Rolla | O23 | 24 | Central Mo. St. | 6 |
| Southwest Baptist | O30 | 41 | Mo. Western St. | 7 |
| Pittsburg St. ■ | N 6 | 52 | Mo. Southern St. | 6 |
| Mo. Western St. ■ | N13 | 36 | Missouri-Rolla | 14 |
| **II Championship** | | | | |
| | | 7 | North Dak. St. | 42 |

Colors: Purple & White.  Nickname: Bulldogs.   II

## NORTHERN COLORADO ........... Greeley, CO 80639
*Joe Glenn (8 yrs., 48-34-1)*

| Opponent | Date | Pts | Opponent | Pts |
|---|---|---|---|---|
| Western St. | S 4 | 30 | Western St. | 27 |
| Mesa St. ■ | S11 | 27 | Mesa St. | 0 |
| Augustana (S.D.) ■ | S18 | 0 | Mankato St. | 14 |
| South Dak. St. ■ | S25 | 15 | St. Cloud St. | 9 |
| North Dak. | O 2 | 20 | Augustana (S.D.) | 27 |
| South Dak. | O 9 | 21 | Morningside | 14 |
| St. Cloud St. ■ | O16 | 24 | Nebraska-Omaha | 14 |
| Mankato St. | O23 | 3 | North Dak. St. | 35 |
| Nebraska-Omaha ■ | O30 | 14 | North Dak. | 21 |
| North Dak. St. ■ | N 6* | 21 | South Dak. | 10 |
| Morningside ■ | N13 | 20 | South Dak. St. | 24 |

Colors: Navy & Gold.  Nickname: Bears.   II

## NORTHERN MICHIGAN ......... Marquette, MI 49855
*Mark Marana (2 yrs., 4-15-1)*

| Opponent | Date | Pts | Opponent | Pts |
|---|---|---|---|---|
| Northwood | S 4 | 0 | Butler | 14 |
| Indianapolis ■ | S11 | 10 | Indianapolis | 32 |
| Saginaw Valley | S18 | 3 | Saginaw Valley | 17 |
| St. Francis (Ill.) | S25* | 35 | Valparaiso | 3 |
| Ferris St. ■ | O 2* | 12 | Ferris St. | 23 |
| Grand Valley St. | O 9 | 20 | Grand Valley St. | 23 |
| Hillsdale ■ | O16 | 6 | Hillsdale | 32 |
| Wayne St. (Mich.) | O23 | 24 | Wayne St. (Mich.) | 27 |
| St. Joseph's (Ind.) ■ | N 6 | 14 | St. Joseph's (Ind.) | 44 |
| Ashland | N13* | 0 | Ashland | 22 |

Colors: Old Gold & Olive Green.  Nickname: Wildcats.   II

## NORTHERN STATE .............. Aberdeen, SD 57401
*Dennis Miller (7 yrs., 51-26-0)*

| Opponent | Date | Pts | Opponent | Pts |
|---|---|---|---|---|
| South Dak. | S 4 | 14 | South Dak. | 47 |
| Michigan Tech | S11 | 26 | Michigan Tech | 42 |
| Minot St. ■ | S18 | 18 | Minot St. | 55 |
| Minn.-Duluth ■ | S25 | 0 | Minn.-Duluth | 9 |
| Southwest St. (Minn.) | O 2 | 35 | Southwest St. (Minn.) | 26 |
| Moorhead St. ■ | O 9 | 35 | Moorhead St. | 34 |
| Winona St. | O16 | 21 | Winona St. | 16 |
| Minn.-Morris | O23 | 48 | Minn.-Morris | 28 |
| Neb.-Kearney ■ | O30 | 18 | Neb.-Kearney | 20 |
| Bemidji St. | N 6 | 17 | Bemidji St. | 10 |
| Minn.-Morris† | N12 | 14 | Winona St. | 8 |

Colors: Maroon and Gold.  Nickname: Wolves.   II

## NORTHWEST MISSOURI STATE .. Maryville, MO 64468
*Bud Elliott (25 yrs., 134-122-7)*

| Opponent | Date | Pts | Opponent | Pts |
|---|---|---|---|---|
| Mankato St. | S 4* | 9 | Central Okla. | 27 |
| East Tex. St. ■ | S11 | 13 | Mankato St. | 27 |
| Mo. Western St. ■ | S18* | 29 | Missouri-Rolla | 14 |
| Northeast Mo. St. ■ | S25 | 22 | Washburn | 21 |
| Emporia St. | O 2 | 14 | Pittsburg St. | 31 |
| Washburn ■ | O 9 | 7 | Central Mo. St. | 10 |
| Missouri-Rolla | O16 | 20 | Northeast Mo. St. | 28 |
| Southwest Baptist ■ | O23 | 43 | Mo. Western St. | 26 |
| Pittsburg St. | O30* | 35 | Mo. Southern St. | 27 |
| Central Mo. St. ■ | N 6 | 54 | Emporia St. | 41 |
| Mo. Southern St. ■ | N13 | 35 | Southwest Baptist | 28 |

Colors: Green & White.  Nickname: Bearcats.   II

## NORTHWESTERN (WISCONSIN) . Watertown, WI 53094
*Dennis Gorsline (22 yrs., 76-84-0)*

| Opponent | Date | Pts | Opponent | Pts |
|---|---|---|---|---|
| Lawrence ■ | S11 | 22 | Lawrence | 31 |
| Concordia (Ill.) | S18 | 11 | Concordia (Ill.) | 13 |
| Principia | S25 | 14 | Principia | 7 |
| Maranatha | O 2 | 30 | Maranatha | 36 |
| Concordia (St. Paul) ■ | O 9 | 34 | Concordia (St. Paul) | 27 |
| Northwestern Minn. | O16 | 18 | Northwestern Minn. | 6 |
| Dr. Martin Luther ■ | O23 | 35 | Dr. Martin Luther | 7 |
| Mt. Senario ■ | O30 | 26 | Mt. Senario | 48 |

Colors: Black & Red.  Nickname: Trojans.   III

## NORTHWOOD ..................... Midland, MI 48640
*Pat Riepma (1st yr. as head coach)*

| Opponent | Date | Pts | Opponent | Pts |
|---|---|---|---|---|
| Northern Mich. | S 4 | 10 | Ferris St. | 33 |
| St. Joseph's (Ind.) | S11 | 13 | Edinboro | 37 |
| Grand Valley St. | S18 | 7 | Westminster (PA) | 21 |
| Findlay | S25 | 21 | Slippery Rock | 35 |
| Indianapolis | O 2 | 7 | Hillsdale | 24 |
| Wayne St. (Mich.) ■ | O 9 | 0 | Wayne St. (Mich.) | 21 |
| St. Francis (Ill.) | O16 | 12 | Saginaw Valley | 31 |
| Ferris St. ■ | O23 | 6 | St. Francis (Ill.) | 10 |
| Ashland | O30 | 6 | Findlay | 21 |
| Hillsdale | N 6 | | | |
| Saginaw Valley | N13 | | | |

Colors: Columbia Blue & White.  Nickname: Northmen.   II

## NORWICH ..................... Northfield, VT 05663
*Steve Hackett (2 yrs., 5-14-0)*

| Opponent | Date | Pts | Opponent | Pts |
|---|---|---|---|---|
| Merchant Marine | S11 | 0 | Merchant Marine | 27 |
| Mass.-Lowell ■ | S18 | 8 | Mass.-Lowell | 20 |
| Plymouth St. ■ | S25 | 13 | Plymouth St. | 14 |
| Coast Guard | O 2 | 14 | Coast Guard | 13 |
| Worcester Tech ■ | O 9 | 6 | Worcester Tech | 56 |
| Brockport St. ■ | O16 | 21 | Brockport St. | 8 |
| Albany (N.Y.) ■ | O23 | 32 | Albany (N.Y.) | 35 |
| St. Lawrence | O30 | 32 | St. Lawrence | 46 |
| Western Conn. St. ■ | N13 | 36 | Western Conn. St. | 21 |

Colors: Maroon & Gold.  Nickname: Cadets.   III

■ Home games on each schedule.     *Night Games.

## OBERLIN ............ Oberlin, OH 44074
*Tony Pierce (1 yr., 1-8-0)*

| Opponent | Date | Pts | Opponent | Pts |
|---|---|---|---|---|
| Thiel | S11 | 0 | Thiel | 7 |
| Denison ■ | S18 | 9 | Denison | 48 |
| Ohio Wesleyan | S25 | 7 | Ohio Wesleyan | 62 |
| Earlham ■ | O 2 | 6 | Earlham | 21 |
| Wooster | O 9 | 14 | Wooster | 45 |
| Case Reserve ■ | O16 | 3 | Case Reserve | 14 |
| Allegheny | O23 | 0 | Allegheny | 56 |
| Wittenberg ■ | O30 | 14 | Kenyon | 8 |
| Kenyon | N 6 | 0 | Grove City | 34 |
| Grove City ■ | N13 | | | |

Colors: Crimson & Gold. Nickname: Yeomen. III

## OCCIDENTAL ............ Los Angeles, CA 90041
*Dale Widolff (11 yrs., 71-31-2)*

| Opponent | Date | Pts | Opponent | Pts |
|---|---|---|---|---|
| Azusa Pacific ■ | S18* | 19 | Menlo | 20 |
| Trinity (Tex.) ■ | S25* | 39 | Trinity (Tex.) | 0 |
| La Verne ■ | O 2* | 34 | Whittier | 6 |
| Whittier | O 9* | 34 | Pomona-Pitzer | 20 |
| Pomona-Pitzer | O16 | 14 | Cal Lutheran | 17 |
| Menlo ■ | O23* | 48 | San Diego | 35 |
| Claremont-M-S | O30 | 21 | La Verne | 31 |
| Cal Lutheran ■ | N 6* | 42 | Claremont-M-S | 3 |
| Redlands ■ | N13* | 6 | Redlands | 35 |

Colors: Orange and Black. Nickname: Tigers. III

## OHIO NORTHERN ............ Ada, OH 45810
*Tom Kaczkowski (7 yrs., 24-44-1)*

| Opponent | Date | Pts | Opponent | Pts |
|---|---|---|---|---|
| Bluffton | S11 | 39 | Bluffton | 0 |
| Marietta | S18* | 21 | Marietta | 0 |
| Otterbein ■ | S25 | 43 | Otterbein | 0 |
| John Carroll | O 2 | 6 | John Carroll | 30 |
| Muskingum ■ | O 9 | 48 | Muskingum | 20 |
| Hiram ■ | O16 | 42 | Hiram | 35 |
| Mount Union | O23 | 13 | Mount Union | 34 |
| Capital ■ | O30 | 9 | Capital | 21 |
| Baldwin-Wallace | N 6 | 29 | Baldwin-Wallace | 28 |
| Heidelberg ■ | N13 | 14 | Heidelberg | 21 |

Colors: Orange & Black. Nickname: Polar Bears. III

## OHIO WESLEYAN ............ Delaware, OH 43015
*Mike Hollway (10 yrs., 55-42-2)*

| Opponent | Date | Pts | Opponent | Pts |
|---|---|---|---|---|
| Albion ■ | S11 | 21 | Albion | 17 |
| Kenyon | S18 | 24 | Kenyon | 7 |
| Oberlin ■ | S25 | 62 | Oberlin | 7 |
| Denison | O 2 | 25 | Denison | 7 |
| Wilmington (Ohio) | O 9 | 50 | Wilmington (Ohio) | 14 |
| Earlham ■ | O16 | 37 | Earlham | 8 |
| Wooster | O23 | 41 | Wooster | 12 |
| Case Reserve ■ | O30 | 23 | Case Reserve | 7 |
| Allegheny | N 6 | 25 | Allegheny | 32 |
| Wittenberg ■ | N13 | 7 | Wittenberg | 14 |

Colors: Red & Black. Nickname: Battling Bishops. III

## OLIVET ............ Olivet, MI 49076
*Dominic Livedoti (5 yrs., 21-21-3)*

| Opponent | Date | Pts | Opponent | Pts |
|---|---|---|---|---|
| Heidelberg ■ | S11 | 13 | Heidelberg | 14 |
| Taylor ■ | S18 | 31 | Taylor | 31 |
| Defiance | S25 | 16 | Defiance | 30 |
| Wilmington (Ohio) | O 2 | 21 | Wilmington (Ohio) | 27 |
| Alma | O 9 | 7 | Adrian | 42 |
| Albion | O16 | 19 | Kalamazoo | 18 |
| Adrian ■ | O23 | 20 | Albion | 35 |
| Kalamazoo | O30 | 33 | Alma | 7 |
| Hope | N 6 | 17 | Hope | 21 |

Colors: Red & White. Nickname: Comets. III

## OTTERBEIN ............ Westerville, OH 43081
*John Hussey (2 yrs., 5-13-2)*

| Opponent | Date | Pts | Opponent | Pts |
|---|---|---|---|---|
| Earlham ■ | S11* | 14 | Earlham | 20 |
| Heidelberg ■ | S18 | 7 | Heidelberg | 7 |
| Ohio Northern | S25 | 0 | Ohio Northern | 43 |
| Hiram | O 2 | 27 | Hiram | 15 |
| Baldwin-Wallace ■ | O 9 | 15 | Baldwin-Wallace | 38 |
| Marietta | O16 | 28 | Marietta | 16 |
| John Carroll | O23 | 20 | John Carroll | 56 |
| Mount Union ■ | O30 | 13 | Mount Union | 54 |
| Muskingum | N 6 | 41 | Muskingum | 40 |
| Capital ■ | N13 | 17 | Capital | 17 |

Colors: Tan & Cardinal. Nickname: Cardinals. III

## PACE ............ Pleasantville, NY 10570
*Douglas Bieling (1 yr., 1-9-0)*

| Opponent | Date | Pts | Opponent | Pts |
|---|---|---|---|---|
| Stony Brook ■ | S11 | 0 | Stony Brook | 28 |
| Marist | S18 | 13 | Marist | 18 |
| Mass.-Lowell ■ | S25 | 6 | Merchant Marine | 45 |
| LIU-C.W. Post | O 2 | 7 | LIU-C.W. Post | 51 |
| St. John's (N.Y.) | O 9 | 21 | St. John's (N.Y.) | 41 |
| Wagner ■ | O16 | 20 | Upsala | 37 |
| Iona | O23 | 24 | Iona | 41 |
| Hobart | O30 | 23 | Hobart | 12 |
| Mercyhurst ■ | N 6 | 6 | Wagner | 48 |
| Sacred Heart | N13 | 0 | Hartwick | 14 |

Colors: Blue & Gold. Nickname: Setters. III

## PITTSBURG STATE ............ Pittsburg, KS 66762
*Chuck Broyles (3 yrs., 39-3-1)*

| Opponent | Date | Pts | Opponent | Pts |
|---|---|---|---|---|
| North Dak. St. | S 4* | 61 | Friends | 0 |
| Mo. Southern St. | S18* | 27 | East Tex. St. | 13 |
| Mo. Western St. ■ | S25* | 31 | Southwest Baptist | 28 |
| Washburn | O 2* | 45 | Missouri-Rolla | 3 |
| Missouri-Rolla ■ | O 9* | 31 | Northwest Mo. St. | 14 |
| Southwest Baptist | O16 | 35 | Northeast Mo. St. | 21 |
| Central Mo. St. ■ | O23 | 31 | Mo. Western St. | 28 |
| Northwest Mo. St. ■ | O30* | 42 | Mo. Southern St. | 13 |
| Northeast Mo. St. | N 6 | 49 | Emporia St. | 38 |
| Emporia St. ■ | N13 | 20 | Washburn | 29 |
| | | 20 | Central Mo. St. | 10 |
| **II Championship** | | | | |
| | | 26 | North Dak. | 21 |
| | | 38 | North Dak. St. | 37 |
| | | 41 | Portland St. | 38 |
| | | 13 | Jacksonville St. | 17 |

Colors: Crimson & Gold. Nickname: Gorillas. II

## PLYMOUTH STATE ............ Plymouth, NH 03264
*Don Brown (1st yr. as head coach)*

| Opponent | Date | Pts | Opponent | Pts |
|---|---|---|---|---|
| Wilkes ■ | S11 | 24 | Wilkes | 35 |
| Norwich | S25 | 14 | Norwich | 13 |
| Mass.-Lowell ■ | O 2* | 20 | Mass.-Lowell | 20 |
| Western Conn. St. ■ | O 9 | 39 | Western Conn. St. | 35 |
| Maine Maritime | O16 | 12 | Maine Maritime | 25 |
| Bri'water (Mass.) | O23 | 6 | Bri'water (Mass.) | 14 |
| Coast Guard ■ | O30 | 20 | Coast Guard | 13 |
| Stony Brook ■ | N 6 | 21 | Stony Brook | 10 |
| Worcester Tech | N13 | 20 | Worcester Tech | 43 |

Colors: Green & White. Nickname: Panthers. III

## POMONA-PITZER ............ Claremont, CA 91711
*Clarence Thomas (16 yrs., 50-89-3)*

| Opponent | Date | Pts | Opponent | Pts |
|---|---|---|---|---|
| Macalester | S11* | 27 | Cal Lutheran | 21 |
| Redlands | S18* | 8 | Colorado Col. | 7 |
| Colorado Col. ■ | S25 | 7 | Redlands | 27 |
| Whittier | O 2* | 9 | La Verne | 48 |
| Occidental | O16 | 20 | Occidental | 34 |
| Cal Lutheran | O23 | 23 | Whittier | 21 |
| La Verne ■ | O30 | 33 | Claremont-M-S | 20 |
| Claremont-M-S | N 6 | 28 | San Diego | 33 |

Colors: Blue, White & Orange. Nickname: Sagehens. III

## PORTLAND STATE ............ Portland, OR 97201
*Tim Walsh (4 yrs., 27-14-0)*

| Opponent | Date | Pts | Opponent | Pts |
|---|---|---|---|---|
| Angelo St. ■ | S 4* | 24 | Eastern Wash. | 21 |
| Idaho St. ■ | S11* | 43 | Texas A&I | 44 |
| Texas A&I | S18* | 27 | Sonoma St. | 37 |
| North Ala. ■ | O 2* | 35 | Southern Utah | 18 |
| Eastern Wash. | O 9 | 44 | Neb.-Kearney | 0 |
| Neb.-Kearney | O16 | 20 | Boise St. | 26 |
| American Int'l ■ | O23* | 28 | Cal St. Sacramento | 35 |
| Cal Poly SLO ■ | O30* | 35 | Cal St. Northridge | 10 |
| Southern Utah | N 6 | 45 | Cal Poly SLO | 31 |
| Central Ark. ■ | N13* | | | |
| **II Championship** | | | | |
| | | 24 | UC Davis | 28 |
| | | 35 | Texas A&I | 30 |
| | | 38 | Pittsburg St. | 41 |

Colors: Green & White. Nickname: Vikings. II

■ Home games on each schedule.  *Night Games.

## PRESBYTERIAN .................. Clinton, SC 29325
*John Perry (9 yrs., 43-56-0)*

| Opponent | Date | | Opponent | Score |
|---|---|---|---|---|
| Fairmont St. ■ | S 4 | 10 | Fairmont St. | 12 |
| Charleston So. | S11 | 7 | Furman | 43 |
| Newberry | S18* | 14 | Lenoir-Rhyne | 8 |
| Lenoir-Rhyne | S25* | 41 | Wofford | 27 |
| Wofford ■ | O 2 | 24 | Catawba | 28 |
| Catawba | O 9 | 0 | Elon | 21 |
| Elon ■ | O16 | 19 | Mars Hill | 6 |
| Mars Hill ■ | O23 | 34 | Wingate | 13 |
| Wingate | O30 | 13 | Gardner-Webb | 46 |
| Gardner-Webb | N 6 | 17 | Carson-Newman | 34 |
| Carson-Newman ■ | N13 | 0 | Newberry | 14 |

Colors: Garnet & Blue.   Nickname: Blue Hose.   II

## PRINCIPIA ...................... Elsah, IL 62028
*Michael Barthelmess (3 yrs., 4-20-1)*

| Opponent | Date | | Opponent | Score |
|---|---|---|---|---|
| Illinois Col. | S11 | 7 | Illinois Col. | 30 |
| Grinnell ■ | S18 | 38 | Grinnell | 13 |
| N'western (Wis.) ■ | S25 | 7 | N'western (Wis.) | 14 |
| Blackburn | O 9 | 28 | Blackburn | 27 |
| Ky. Wesleyan | O16 | 28 | Ky. Wesleyan | 48 |
| Earlham ■ | O23 | 35 | Earlham | 61 |
| Washington (Mo.) ■ | O30 | 27 | Washington (Mo.) | 34 |
| Concordia (Ill.) | N 6 | 30 | Concordia (Ill.) | 44 |

Colors: Navy Blue & Gold.   Nickname: Panthers.   III

## QUINCY ............................ Quincy, IL 62301
*Ron Taylor (4 yrs., 26-14-2)*

| Opponent | Date | | Opponent | Score |
|---|---|---|---|---|
| Ky. Wesleyan ■ | S 4 | 13 | Benedictine | 38 |
| Central Meth. ■ | S18 | 20 | Central Meth. | 21 |
| MacMurray ■ | S25 | 24 | MacMurray | 13 |
| Eureka | O 2 | 28 | Eureka | 26 |
| Ill. Benedictine | O 9 | 28 | Ill. Benedictine | 40 |
| Greenville ■ | O16 | 49 | Greenville | 50 |
| Lakeland | O23 | 7 | Drake | 59 |
| Concordia (Wis.) ■ | N 6 | 38 | Concordia (Wis.) | 35 |
| Culver-Stockton | N13 | 7 | Culver-Stockton | 6 |

Colors: Brown & White.   Nickname: Hawks.   III

## RAMAPO .......................... Mahwah, NJ 07430
*Dropped program after 1992.*

| | Opponent | Score |
|---|---|---|
| 22 | Ferrum | 29 |
| 3 | LIU-C.W. Post | 17 |
| 0 | Kean | 7 |
| 7 | Montclair St. | 27 |
| 21 | Jersey City St. | 7 |
| 0 | Rowan | 33 |
| 0 | Wm. Paterson | 23 |
| 12 | Southern Conn. St. | 49 |
| 7 | Trenton St. | 30 |

Colors: Red & Gold.   Nickname: Roadrunners.   III

## RANDOLPH-MACON ............. Ashland, VA 23005
*Joe Riccio (2 yrs., 8-12-0)*

| Opponent | Date | | Opponent | Score |
|---|---|---|---|---|
| Swarthmore ■ | S11 | 20 | Wesley | 32 |
| Catholic ■ | S18 | 14 | Catholic | 30 |
| Wesley | S25 | 27 | Juniata | 0 |
| Wash. & Lee ■ | O 2 | 31 | Wash. & Lee | 9 |
| Western Md. | O 9 | 48 | Western Md. | 30 |
| Emory & Henry ■ | O16 | 3 | Emory & Henry | 21 |
| Davidson | O23 | 7 | Worcester Tech | 45 |
| Guilford | O30 | 20 | Guilford | 21 |
| Bridgewater (Va.) | N 6 | 28 | Bridgewater (Va.) | 0 |
| Hampden-Sydney ■ | N13 | 22 | Hampden-Sydney | 26 |

Colors: Lemon & Black.   Nickname: Yellow Jackets.   III

## REDLANDS ...................... Redlands, CA 92373
*Mike Maynard (5 yrs., 32-15-0)*

| Opponent | Date | | Opponent | Score |
|---|---|---|---|---|
| Menlo ■ | S11* | 21 | Menlo | 16 |
| Pomona-Pitzer ■ | S18* | 28 | San Diego | 7 |
| Cal St. Hayward | S25 | 27 | Pomona-Pitzer | 7 |
| Claremont-M-S | O 2 | 8 | Cal St. Hayward | 22 |
| Whittier ■ | O16* | 48 | Claremont-M-S | 0 |
| Azusa Pacific | O23 | 20 | La Verne | 13 |
| Cal Lutheran | O30 | 56 | Cal Lutheran | 24 |
| La Verne ■ | N 6* | 45 | Whittier | 14 |
| Occidental | N13* | 35 | Occidental | 6 |
| III Championship | | | | |
| | | 26 | Wis.-La Crosse | 47 |

Colors: Maroon & Gray.   Nickname: Bulldogs.   III

## RENSSELAER ..................... Troy, NY 12180
*Joe King (4 yrs., 20-14-2)*

| Opponent | Date | | Opponent | Score |
|---|---|---|---|---|
| St. John Fisher | S11 | 14 | Coast Guard | 12 |
| Coast Guard ■ | S18 | 31 | Upsala | 8 |
| Worcester Tech | O 2 | 14 | Worcester Tech | 28 |
| Siena | O 9 | 26 | Siena | 6 |
| Union (N.Y.) ■ | O16 | 23 | Union (N.Y.) | 8 |
| Marist | O23 | 26 | Marist | 17 |
| Rochester | O30 | 21 | Rochester | 38 |
| St. Lawrence | N 6 | 33 | St. Lawrence | 7 |
| Hobart ■ | N13 | 28 | Hobart | 0 |
| ECAC Northeast | | | | |
| | | 28 | Bri'water (Mass.) | 25 |

Colors: Cherry & White.   Nickname: Engineers.   III

## RHODES ...................... Memphis, TN 38112
*Mike Clary (9 yrs., 58-20-5)*

| Opponent | Date | | Opponent | Score |
|---|---|---|---|---|
| Lambuth ■ | S11 | 21 | Claremont-M-S | 0 |
| Davidson | S18 | 31 | Davidson | 6 |
| Ky. Wesleyan | S25 | 35 | Ky. Wesleyan | 22 |
| Colorado Col. | O 2 | 10 | Lambuth | 17 |
| Washington (Mo.) | O 9* | 26 | Washington (Mo.) | 19 |
| Sewanee ■ | O16 | 17 | Sewanee | 27 |
| Maryville (Tenn.) ■ | O23 | 27 | Maryville (Tenn.) | 49 |
| Trinity (Tex.) ■ | O30 | 31 | Trinity (Tex.) | 19 |
| Millsaps | N 6 | 14 | Millsaps | 14 |
| Centre | N13 | 18 | Centre | 21 |

Colors: Cardinal & Black.   Nickname: Lynx.   III

## RIPON ............................ Ripon, WI 54971
*Ron Ernst (2 yrs., 10-8-0)*

| Opponent | Date | | Opponent | Score |
|---|---|---|---|---|
| Lakeland | S11 | 34 | Lakeland | 20 |
| Northwestern Minn. ■ | S18 | 43 | Northwestern Minn. | 25 |
| Coe | S25 | 32 | Coe | 39 |
| Knox ■ | O 2 | 29 | Knox | 7 |
| Beloit ■ | O 9 | 12 | Beloit | 39 |
| Lake Forest | O16 | 15 | Lake Forest | 8 |
| St. Norbert ■ | O23 | 14 | St. Norbert | 16 |
| Carroll (Wis.) | O30 | 20 | Carroll (Wis.) | 7 |
| Lawrence ■ | N 6 | 34 | Lawrence | 7 |

Colors: Crimson & White.   Nickname: Red.   III

## ROCHESTER..................... Rochester, NY 14627
*Rich Parrinello (5 yrs., 31-17-0)*

| Opponent | Date | | Opponent | Score |
|---|---|---|---|---|
| Case Reserve | S11 | 24 | Case Reserve | 10 |
| Carnegie Mellon ■ | S18 | 16 | Carnegie Mellon | 10 |
| Washington (Mo.) | S25 | 42 | Washington (Mo.) | 6 |
| Chicago ■ | O 2 | 41 | Chicago | 13 |
| Hobart ■ | O 9 | 31 | Hobart | 0 |
| St. John Fisher | O16 | 33 | St. John Fisher | 14 |
| St. Lawrence ■ | O23 | 41 | St. Lawrence | 21 |
| Rensselaer | O30 | 38 | Rensselaer | 21 |
| Union (N.Y.) | N 6 | 10 | Union (N.Y.) | 14 |

Colors: Yellow & Blue.   Nickname: Yellowjackets.   III

## ROSE-HULMAN................. Terre Haute, IN 47803
*Scott Duncan (7 yrs., 44-25-1)*

| Opponent | Date | | Opponent | Score |
|---|---|---|---|---|
| Washington (Mo.) | S 4* | 13 | Washington (Mo.) | 15 |
| Knox ■ | S11 | 34 | Knox | 14 |
| Evansville | S25 | 13 | Evansville | 19 |
| Greenville ■ | O 2 | 45 | Taylor | 21 |
| DePauw ■ | O 9 | 15 | DePauw | 27 |
| Franklin ■ | O16 | 27 | Franklin | 7 |
| Hanover | O23 | 16 | Hanover | 17 |
| Wabash ■ | O30 | 13 | Wabash | 40 |
| Anderson | N 6 | 23 | Anderson | 21 |
| Manchester ■ | N13 | 7 | Manchester | 21 |

Colors: Red & White.   Nickname: Fightin' Engineers.   III

## ROWAN .......................... Glassboro, NJ 08028
*K. C. Keeler (1st yr. as head coach)*

| Opponent | Date | | Opponent | Score |
|---|---|---|---|---|
| Newport News App. | S11 | 30 | Newport News App. | 28 |
| LIU-C.W. Post | S18 | 14 | Central Conn. | 13 |
| Jersey City St. | S25 | 29 | Jersey City St. | 0 |
| Trenton St. ■ | O 2* | 26 | Trenton St. | 10 |
| Salisbury St. ■ | O 9 | 43 | Salisbury St. | 18 |
| Southern Conn. St. ■ | O16 | 33 | Ramapo | 0 |
| Kean ■ | O30 | 59 | Wagner | 30 |
| Wm. Paterson | N 5* | 27 | Kean | 7 |
| Montclair St. ■ | N13 | 30 | Wm. Paterson | 7 |
| | | 42 | Montclair St. | 17 |
| III Championship | | | | |
| | | 41 | Worcester Tech | 14 |
| | | 28 | Buffalo St. | 19 |
| | | 13 | Wash. & Jeff. | 18 |

Colors: Brown & Gold.   Nickname: Profs.   III

■ Home games on each schedule.        *Night Games.

## SACRED HEART .................. Fairfield, CT 06432
*Gary Reho (2 yrs., 5-13-0)*

| Opponent | Date | Pts | Opponent | Pts |
|---|---|---|---|---|
| Iona ■ | S11 | 16 | St. John's (N.Y.) | 39 |
| St. Francis (PA) ■ | S18 | 6 | St. Peter's | 13 |
| Monmouth (N. J.) | S25 | 0 | Stony Brook | 20 |
| Stony Brook ■ | O 2 | 0 | Mass.-Lowell | 19 |
| Mass.-Lowell | O 9* | 6 | Nichols | 27 |
| Assumption ■ | O16 | 2 | Catholic | 16 |
| St. John's (N.Y.) | O 23* | 15 | Iona | 34 |
| Bentley | O30 | 12 | Stonehill | 25 |
| Stonehill | N 6 | 18 | Assumption | 35 |
| Pace ■ | N13 | | | |

Colors: Red & White. Nickname: Pioneers.    III

## SAGINAW VALLEY STATE University Center, MI 48710
*George Ihler (10 yrs., 58-44-1)*

| Opponent | Date | Pts | Opponent | Pts |
|---|---|---|---|---|
| Hillsdale | S 4* | 0 | Hillsdale | 21 |
| Wayne St. (Mich.) ■ | S11 | 32 | Wayne St. (Mich.) | 13 |
| Northern Mich. | S18 | 17 | Northern Mich. | 3 |
| St. Joseph's (Ind.) | S25 | 20 | St. Joseph's (Ind.) | 18 |
| Grand Valley St. ■ | O 2 | 20 | Grand Valley St. | 24 |
| Ashland | O 9 | 16 | Ashland | 7 |
| Indianapolis | O16 | 42 | Indianapolis | 0 |
| Michigan Tech ■ | O23 | 31 | Northwood | 12 |
| St. Francis (Ill.) | O30 | 34 | Valparaiso | 3 |
| Ferris St. ■ | N 6 | 9 | Ferris St. | 10 |
| Northwood | N13 | 0 | Butler | 37 |

Colors: Red, White & Blue. Nickname: Cardinals.    II

## SALISBURY STATE ............. Salisbury, MD 21801
*Joe Rotellini (3 yrs., 4-24-0)*

| Opponent | Date | Pts | Opponent | Pts |
|---|---|---|---|---|
| Trenton St. | S10* | 25 | LIU-C.W. Post | 53 |
| Methodist ■ | S18 | 37 | Methodist | 14 |
| Frostburg St. ■ | S25 | 14 | Frostburg St. | 31 |
| Rowan | O 9 | 14 | Guilford | 10 |
| Newport News App. | O16 | 18 | Rowan | 43 |
| Wesley | O23 | 12 | Montclair St. | 21 |
| Albany (N.Y.) | O30 | 7 | Albany (N.Y.) | 48 |
| LIU-C.W. Post | N 6 | 14 | Newport News App. | 20 |
| Guilford ■ | N13 | 6 | Kean | 70 |

Colors: Maroon & Gold. Nickname: Sea Gulls.    III

## SAN FRANCISCO STATE ..... San Francisco, CA 94132
*Dick Mannini (8 yrs., 48-30-1)*

| Opponent | Date | Pts | Opponent | Pts |
|---|---|---|---|---|
| St. Mary's (Cal.) ■ | S 4 | 14 | St. Mary's (Cal.) | 17 |
| Cal St. Sacramento ■ | S11 | 6 | Cal St. Northridge | 22 |
| Menlo | S18 | 30 | Santa Clara | 42 |
| Western N. Mex. ■ | S25 | 14 | Menlo | 7 |
| Cal Poly SLO | O 9* | 14 | Humboldt St. | 24 |
| Humboldt St. | O16 | 43 | Cal St. Chico | 28 |
| Cal St. Chico | O23 | 22 | Cal St. Hayward | 41 |
| Cal St. Hayward ■ | O30 | 14 | UC Davis | 42 |
| UC Davis | N 6* | 28 | Sonoma St. | 33 |
| Sonoma St. ■ | N13 | | | |

Colors: Purple & Gold. Nickname: Gators.    II

## SANTA CLARA ................ Santa Clara, CA 95053
*Dropped program after 1992.*

| Pts | Opponent | Pts |
|---|---|---|
| 35 | Cal St. Chico | 25 |
| 7 | Sonoma St. | 27 |
| 44 | UC Davis | 48 |
| 42 | San Fran. St. | 30 |
| 14 | Humboldt St. | 10 |
| 28 | Southern Utah | 25 |
| 18 | Cal St. Northridge | 42 |
| 14 | Cal Poly SLO | 40 |
| 21 | Cal St. Sacramento | 32 |
| 22 | St. Mary's (Cal.) | 55 |

Colors: Bronco Red & White. Nickname: Broncos.    II

## SAVANNAH STATE ............. Savannah, GA 31404
*To be named*

| Opponent | Date | Pts | Opponent | Pts |
|---|---|---|---|---|
| Ga. Southern | S 4 | 31 | Bethune-Cookman | 21 |
| Tuskegee | S11 | 35 | Tuskegee | 24 |
| Alabama A&M ■ | S25* | 21 | Clark Atlanta | 7 |
| Morehouse | O 2 | 31 | Alabama A&M | 14 |
| Albany St. (Ga.) ■ | O 9 | 7 | Ga. Southern | 21 |
| Morris Brown | O16 | 24 | Albany St. (Ga.) | 33 |
| Livingstone | O23 | 30 | Morris Brown | 15 |
| Fort Valley St. | N 6 | 63 | Livingstone | 21 |
| Miles | N13 | 54 | Morehouse | 0 |
| | | 13 | Fort Valley St. | 22 |
| | | 73 | Miles | 6 |
| | | *II Championship* | | |
| | | 16 | Jacksonville St. | 41 |

Colors: Blue & Orange. Nickname: Tigers.    II

## SEWANEE (UNIV. of the SOUTH) .. Sewanee, TN 37375
*Bill Samko (6 yrs., 31-22-1)*

| Opponent | Date | Pts | Opponent | Pts |
|---|---|---|---|---|
| Davidson ■ | S11 | 37 | Davidson | 20 |
| Tenn. Wesleyan ■ | S18 | 12 | Tenn. Wesleyan | 0 |
| Maryville (Tenn.) ■ | S25 | 18 | Maryville (Tenn.) | 15 |
| Centre | O 2 | 26 | Centre | 21 |
| Cumberland (Tenn.) | O 9 | 27 | Rhodes | 17 |
| Rhodes | O16 | 16 | Wash. & Lee | 17 |
| Wash. & Lee ■ | O23 | 33 | Millsaps | 14 |
| Millsaps | O30 | 15 | Trinity (Tex.) | 12 |
| Trinity (Tex.) ■ | N 6 | 26 | Ky. Wesleyan | 19 |

Colors: Purple & White. Nickname: Tigers.    III

## SHEPHERD ................ Shepherdstown, WV 25443
*Monte Cater (12 yrs., 66-50-2)*

| Opponent | Date | Pts | Opponent | Pts |
|---|---|---|---|---|
| Shippensburg ■ | S 4 | 7 | Shippensburg | 21 |
| Millersville | S11* | 9 | Millersville | 17 |
| Glenville St. ■ | S25 | 23 | Glenville St. | 20 |
| West Liberty St. | O 2 | 35 | West Liberty St. | 29 |
| West Va. Wesleyan | O 9 | 19 | West Va. St. | 0 |
| Concord (W. Va.) | O16 | 19 | West Va. Wesleyan | 13 |
| West Va. Tech | O23 | 24 | Concord (W. Va.) | 17 |
| Fairmont St. | O30 | 40 | West Va. Tech | 15 |
| West Va. St. ■ | N 6 | 24 | Fairmont St. | 14 |
| New Haven | N13 | 23 | New Haven | 49 |
| | | *NAIA I Championship* | | |
| | | 6 | Carson-Newman | 3 |
| | | 7 | Gardner-Webb | 22 |

Colors: Blue & Gold. Nickname: Rams.    II

## SHIPPENSBURG ............. Shippensburg, PA 17257
*Rocky Rees (8 yrs., 54-31-2)*

| Opponent | Date | Pts | Opponent | Pts |
|---|---|---|---|---|
| Shepherd | S 4 | 21 | Shepherd | 7 |
| Bloomsburg | S11 | 20 | Bloomsburg | 14 |
| Kutztown ■ | S18 | 3 | Kutztown | 16 |
| Millersville | S 25* | 10 | Millersville | 35 |
| Slippery Rock ■ | O 2 | 5 | Slippery Rock | 20 |
| Indiana (PA) | O 9 | 16 | Indiana (PA) | 35 |
| Edinboro ■ | O16 | 3 | Edinboro | 47 |
| Clarion | O23 | 20 | Clarion | 23 |
| Lock Haven ■ | O30 | 28 | Lock Haven | 28 |
| West Chester ■ | N 6 | 31 | West Chester | 35 |
| Calif. (PA) | N13 | 17 | Calif. (PA) | 8 |

Colors: Red & Blue. Nickname: Red Raiders.    II

## SIMPSON ......................... Indianola, IA 50125
*Jim Williams (7 yrs., 45-24-1)*

| Opponent | Date | Pts | Opponent | Pts |
|---|---|---|---|---|
| Drake | S11 | 20 | Drake | 20 |
| Luther ■ | S18 | 35 | Luther | 21 |
| Buena Vista | S25 | 37 | Buena Vista | 15 |
| Wartburg ■ | O 2 | 48 | Wartburg | 26 |
| Loras | O 9 | 20 | Loras | 14 |
| Central (Iowa) | O16 | 7 | Central (Iowa) | 16 |
| Dubuque ■ | O23 | 35 | Dubuque | 3 |
| Wis.-La Crosse ■ | O30 | 66 | William Penn | 21 |
| William Penn | N 6 | 20 | Upper Iowa | 28 |
| Upper Iowa ■ | N13 | | | |

Colors: Red & Gold. Nickname: Storm.    III

## SLIPPERY ROCK ............. Slippery Rock, PA 16057
*George Mihalik (5 yrs., 27-21-4)*

| Opponent | Date | Pts | Opponent | Pts |
|---|---|---|---|---|
| West Va. Wesleyan | S 4 | 45 | West Va. Wesleyan | 7 |
| Fairmont St. | S11 | 24 | Fairmont St. | 0 |
| Ashland ■ | S18 | 31 | Ashland | 37 |
| Shippensburg | O 2 | 35 | Northwood | 21 |
| Calif. (PA) ■ | O 9 | 20 | Shippensburg | 3 |
| Cheyney | O16 | 23 | Calif. (PA) | 15 |
| Indiana (PA) | O23 | 43 | Cheyney | 27 |
| Edinboro ■ | O30 | 17 | Indiana (PA) | 34 |
| Clarion | N 6 | 10 | Edinboro | 7 |
| Lock Haven ■ | N13 | 37 | Clarion | 49 |
| | | 41 | Lock Haven | 17 |

Colors: Green & White. Nickname: Rockets, The Rock.    II

## SONOMA STATE ............. Rohnert Park, CA 94928
*Frank Scalercio (1st yr. as head coach)*

| Opponent | Date | Pts | Opponent | Pts |
|---|---|---|---|---|
| Weber St. | S 4* | 27 | Santa Clara | 7 |
| St. Mary's (Cal.) ■ | S18 | 14 | Eastern Wash. | 45 |
| Cal St. Northridge ■ | S 25* | 37 | Portland St. | 27 |
| Cal Poly SLO ■ | O 2 | 36 | Cal Poly SLO | 35 |
| UC Davis ■ | O16 | 26 | St. Mary's (Cal.) | 21 |
| Cal St. Hayward | O23 | 38 | UC Davis | 41 |
| Humboldt St. | O 30* | 37 | Cal St. Hayward | 20 |
| Cal St. Chico ■ | N 6 | 7 | Humboldt St. | 19 |
| San Fran. St. | N13 | 41 | Cal St. Chico | 23 |
| | | 33 | San Fran. St. | 28 |

Colors: Navy Blue & White. Nickname: Cossacks.    II

■ Home games on each schedule.    *Night Games.

## SOUTH DAKOTA................Vermillion, SD 57069
*Dennis Creehan (8 yrs., 45-36-1)*

| Opponent | Date | | Opponent | |
|---|---|---|---|---|
| Northern St. (S.D.) ■ | S 4 | 47 | Northern St. (S.D.) | 14 |
| Bemidji St. ■ | S 11 | 0 | South Dak. St. | 13 |
| Mankato St. ■ | S 18 | 8 | Morningside | 31 |
| Nebraska-Omaha | S 25* | 3 | North Dak. | 52 |
| Augustana (S.D.) ■ | O 2 | 20 | North Dak. St. | 39 |
| Northern Colo. ■ | O 9 | 21 | South Dak. St. | 31 |
| North Dak. | O 16 | 7 | Augustana (S.D.) | 27 |
| South Dak. St. | O 23 | 16 | St. Cloud St. | 29 |
| Morningside | O 30 | 15 | Mankato St. | 22 |
| North Dak. | N 6 | 10 | Northern Colo. | 21 |
| St. Cloud St. ■ | N 13 | 25 | Nebraska-Omaha | 22 |

Colors: Red & White.  Nickname: Coyotes.  II

## SOUTH DAKOTA STATE.........Brookings, SD 57007
*Mike Daly (2 yrs., 13-7-0)*

| Opponent | Date | | Opponent | |
|---|---|---|---|---|
| Montana | S 4 | 13 | South Dak. | 0 |
| Southwest St. (Minn.) ■ | S 11 | 3 | North Dak. | 14 |
| St. Cloud St. ■ | S 18 | 10 | North Dak. St. | 47 |
| Northern Colo. | S 25 | 21 | Nebraska-Omaha | 0 |
| Morningside | O 2 | 31 | South Dak. | 21 |
| North Dak. St. ■ | O 9 | 2 | Morningside | 6 |
| Nebraska-Omaha ■ | O 16 | 14 | Augustana (S.D.) | 20 |
| South Dak. | O 23 | 14 | St. Cloud St. | 6 |
| Augustana (S.D.) ■ | O 30 | 34 | Mankato St. | 30 |
| Mankato St. ■ | N 6 | 24 | Northern Colo. | 20 |
| North Dak. ■ | N 13 | | | |

Colors: Yellow & Blue.  Nickname: Jackrabbits.  II

## SOUTHERN CONNECTICUT STATE  New Haven, CT 06515
*Richard Cavanaugh (8 yrs., 32-46-0)*

| Opponent | Date | | Opponent | |
|---|---|---|---|---|
| Cheyney | S 4 | 16 | East Stroudsburg | 21 |
| North Dak. | S 11 | 0 | Edinboro | 41 |
| Bowie St. ■ | S 18 | 27 | Springfield | 14 |
| East Stroudsburg ■ | S 25 | 47 | American Int'l | 32 |
| American Int'l | O 2 | 32 | Hofstra | 32 |
| Springfield ■ | O 8* | 59 | Trenton St. | 12 |
| Rowan ■ | O 16* | 13 | New Haven | 56 |
| New Haven ■ | O 22* | 49 | Ramapo | 12 |
| Central Conn. St. ■ | O 30 | 42 | Central Conn. St. | 20 |
| Kutztown | N 6 | 28 | Cortland St. | 17 |
| Cortland St. ■ | N 13 | | | |

Colors: Blue & White.  Nickname: Owls.  II

## SOUTHWEST BAPTIST ............Bolivar, MO 65613
*Wayne Haynes (1st yr. as head coach)*

| Opponent | Date | | Opponent | |
|---|---|---|---|---|
| Ouachita Baptist ■ | S 4 | 37 | Ouachita Baptist | 27 |
| Delta St. | S 11* | 28 | Pittsburg St. | 31 |
| Emporia St. ■ | S 18* | 10 | Central Mo. St. | 29 |
| Mo. Southern St. ■ | S 25 | 10 | Northeast Mo. St. | 48 |
| Missouri-Rolla | O 2 | 24 | Mo. Western St. | 34 |
| Central Mo. St. | O 9 | 27 | Mo. Southern St. | 28 |
| Pittsburg St. ■ | O 16 | 6 | Emporia St. | 45 |
| Northwest Mo. St. | O 23 | 17 | Washburn | 21 |
| Northeast Mo. St. ■ | O 30 | 17 | Missouri-Rolla | 7 |
| Mo. Western St. | N 6 | 28 | Northwest Mo. St. | 35 |
| Washburn ■ | N 13 | | | |

Colors: Purple & White.  Nickname: Bearcats.  II

## SOUTHWEST STATE..............Marshall, MN 56258
*Brent Jeffers (1st yr. as head coach)*

| Opponent | Date | | Opponent | |
|---|---|---|---|---|
| Mo. Western St. ■ | S 4 | 12 | Illinois St. | 51 |
| South Dak. St. | S 11 | 69 | Lindenwood | 9 |
| Minn.-Morris | S 25 | 50 | Minn.-Morris | 0 |
| Northern St. (S.D.) ■ | O 2 | 26 | Northern St. (S.D.) | 35 |
| Bemidji St. | O 9 | 53 | Bemidji St. | 39 |
| Minn.-Duluth ■ | O 16 | 18 | Minn.-Duluth | 18 |
| Wayne St. (Neb.) ■ | O 23 | 29 | Wayne St. (Neb.) | 49 |
| Moorhead St. | O 30 | 23 | Moorhead St. | 19 |
| Winona St. ■ | N 6 | 20 | Winona St. | 17 |
| Michigan Tech† | N 12* | 38 | St. Francis (Ill.) | 28 |

Colors: Brown & Gold.  Nickname: Golden Mustangs.  II

## SPRINGFIELD...............Springfield, MA 01109
*Mike DeLong (11 yrs., 52-51-2)*

| Opponent | Date | | Opponent | |
|---|---|---|---|---|
| American Int'l | S 11 | 13 | American Int'l | 37 |
| East Stroudsburg | S 18 | 28 | Albany (N.Y.) | 14 |
| New Haven ■ | S 24* | 14 | Southern Conn. St. | 27 |
| Ithaca ■ | O 2 | 7 | Ithaca | 31 |
| Southern Conn. St. | O 8* | 34 | Central Conn. St. | 9 |
| Central Conn. St. | O 16 | 14 | Cortland St. | 26 |
| Cortland St. ■ | O 23 | 6 | New Haven | 54 |
| Trenton St. ■ | O 30 | 43 | LIU-C.W. Post | 22 |
| LIU-C.W. Post | N 6 | 10 | American Int'l | 13 |
| American Int'l ■ | N 13 | | | |

Colors: Maroon & White.  Nickname: Chiefs.  II

## ST. CLOUD STATE ...............St. Cloud, MN 56301
*Noel Martin (10 yrs., 60-49-0)*

| Opponent | Date | | Opponent | |
|---|---|---|---|---|
| Minn.-Duluth | S 11 | 9 | Idaho | 42 |
| South Dak. St. | S 18 | 33 | Minn.-Duluth | 0 |
| North Dak. | S 25 | 31 | Nebraska-Omaha | 13 |
| Nebraska-Omaha | O 2* | 10 | Northern Colo. | 15 |
| Augustana (S.D.) ■ | O 9 | 7 | Mankato St. | 0 |
| Northern Colo. | O 16 | 23 | North Dak. St. | 21 |
| North Dak. St. ■ | O 23 | 13 | North Dak. | 22 |
| Mankato St. ■ | O 30 | 29 | South Dak. | 16 |
| Morningside | N 6 | 6 | South Dak. St. | 14 |
| South Dak. | N 13 | 14 | Augustana (S.D.) | 9 |
| | | 23 | Morningside | 6 |

Colors: Cardinal & Black.  Nickname: Huskies.  II

## ST. FRANCIS (ILLINOIS)...............Joliet, IL 60435
*Gordie Gillespie (7 yrs., 43-27-0)*

| Opponent | Date | | Opponent | |
|---|---|---|---|---|
| Ashland | S 4 | 13 | Wayne St. (Mich.) | 24 |
| Hillsdale ■ | S 11 | 3 | Central St. (Ohio) | 7 |
| Wayne St. (Mich.) | S 18 | 42 | Minn.-Duluth | 17 |
| Northern Mich. ■ | S 25* | 41 | Iowa Wesleyan | 25 |
| St. Joseph's (Ind.) ■ | O 2 | 21 | Wayne St. (Neb.) | 35 |
| Ferris St. | O 9 | 6 | Neb.-Kearney | 30 |
| Northwood ■ | O 16 | 62 | Kentucky St. | 22 |
| Indianapolis | O 23 | 10 | Northwood | 6 |
| Saginaw Valley ■ | O 30 | 28 | Southwest St. (Minn.) | 38 |
| Central St. (Ohio) ■ | N 6 | | | |
| Grand Valley St. | N 13 | | | |

Colors: Brown & Gold.  Nickname: Fighting Saints.  II

## ST. JOHN FISHER ...............Rochester, NY 14618
*Paul Vosburgh (2 yrs., 4-15-0)*

| Opponent | Date | | Opponent | |
|---|---|---|---|---|
| Rensselaer ■ | S 11 | 17 | Catholic | 15 |
| Hobart | S 18 | 6 | Alfred | 24 |
| Hartwick ■ | S 25* | 3 | Hobart | 14 |
| Catholic | O 2 | 37 | Hartwick | 12 |
| Merchant Marine ■ | O 9 | 35 | Salve Regina | 7 |
| Rochester ■ | O 16 | 12 | Canisius | 14 |
| Brockport St. | O 23 | 14 | Rochester | 33 |
| Salve Regina ■ | O 30* | 21 | Brockport St. | 26 |
| Gallaudet ■ | N 13 | 0 | St. Francis (PA) | 18 |
| | | 35 | Gallaudet | 10 |

Colors: Cardinal & Gold.  Nickname: Cardinals.  III

## ST. JOHN'S (MINNESOTA).....Collegeville, MN 56321
*John Gagliardi (44 yrs., 294-95-10)*

| Opponent | Date | | Opponent | |
|---|---|---|---|---|
| Mayville St. ■ | S 11 | 35 | Bemidji St. | 8 |
| Augsburg ■ | S 18 | 58 | Augsburg | 0 |
| St. Olaf | S 25 | 62 | St. Olaf | 7 |
| Gust. Adolphus | O 2 | 35 | Gust. Adolphus | 7 |
| Hamline ■ | O 9 | 21 | Hamline | 7 |
| Bethel (Minn.) | O 16 | 34 | Bethel (Minn.) | 12 |
| St. Thomas (Minn.) ■ | O 23 | 12 | St. Thomas (Minn.) | 15 |
| Macalester | O 30* | 41 | Macalester | 0 |
| Carleton† | N 6 | 70 | Carleton | 7 |
| Concordia-M'head | N 13 | 18 | Concordia-M'head | 18 |

Colors: Red & White.  Nickname: Johnnies.  III

## ST. JOSEPH'S (INDIANA).......Rensselaer, IN 47978
*Bill Reagan (8 yrs., 29-49-2)*

| Opponent | Date | | Opponent | |
|---|---|---|---|---|
| Grand Valley St. | S 4 | 18 | Grand Valley St. | 28 |
| Northwood ■ | S 11 | 7 | Butler | 33 |
| Indianapolis | S 18 | 24 | Indianapolis | 24 |
| Saginaw Valley ■ | S 25 | 18 | Saginaw Valley | 20 |
| St. Francis (Ill.) | O 2 | 14 | Valparaiso | 16 |
| Ashland ■ | O 16 | 7 | Ashland | 21 |
| Hillsdale | O 23 | 6 | Hillsdale | 24 |
| Wayne St. (Mich.) ■ | O 30 | 6 | Wayne St. (Mich.) | 27 |
| Northern Mich. | N 6 | 44 | Northern Mich. | 0 |
| Ferris St. ■ | N 13 | 7 | Ferris St. | 23 |

Colors: Cardinal & Purple.  Nickname: Pumas.  II

## ST. LAWRENCE................Canton, NY 13617
*Dennis Riccio (7 yrs., 34-25-0)*

| Opponent | Date | | Opponent | |
|---|---|---|---|---|
| Hartwick ■ | S 4 | 14 | Union (N.Y.) | 41 |
| Union (N.Y.) ■ | S 11 | 45 | Canisius | 27 |
| Albany (N.Y.) ■ | S 18 | 0 | Hobart | 13 |
| Hobart ■ | O 2 | 26 | Alfred | 36 |
| Alfred | O 9 | 14 | Ithaca | 56 |
| Ithaca | O 16 | 13 | Rochester | 47 |
| Rochester | O 30 | 46 | Norwich | 32 |
| Norwich | N 6 | 7 | Rensselaer | 33 |
| Rensselaer ■ | N 6 | 24 | Albany (N.Y.) | 19 |
| Brockport St. ■ | N 13 | | | |

Colors: Scarlet & Brown.  Nickname: Saints.  III

---

■ Home games on each schedule.        *Night Games.

*1993 NCAA FOOTBALL*

### ST. NORBERT — DePere, WI 54115
*Don La Violette (10 yrs., 53-40-1)*

| 1993 Opponent | Date | Score | 1992 Opponent | Score |
|---|---|---|---|---|
| Wis.-Oshkosh ■ | S11* | 14 | Wis.-Oshkosh | 20 |
| Concordia (Wis.) | S18 | 13 | Concordia (Wis.) | 14 |
| Cornell College ■ | S25 | 15 | Cornell College | 28 |
| Grinnell | O 2 | 44 | Grinnell | 12 |
| Lake Forest ■ | O 9 | 21 | Lake Forest | 14 |
| Lawrence ■ | O16 | 26 | Lawrence | 27 |
| Ripon | O23 | 16 | Ripon | 14 |
| Beloit | O30 | 21 | Beloit | 6 |
| Carroll (Wis.) ■ | N 6 | 7 | Carroll (Wis.) | 40 |

Colors: Green & Gold. Nickname: Green Knights.   III

### SWARTHMORE — Swarthmore, PA 19081
*Karl Miran (3 yrs., 14-13-1)*

| 1993 Opponent | Date | Score | 1992 Opponent | Score |
|---|---|---|---|---|
| Randolph-Macon | S11 | 27 | Catholic | 14 |
| Johns Hopkins | S17* | 20 | Johns Hopkins | 30 |
| Gettysburg ■ | S25 | 34 | Gettysburg | 45 |
| Ursinus | O 2 | 34 | Ursinus | 32 |
| Muhlenberg ■ | O 9 | 21 | Muhlenberg | 14 |
| Hobart | O16 | 27 | Georgetown | 28 |
| Dickinson | O23 | 26 | Dickinson | 26 |
| Frank. & Marsh. | O30 | 28 | Frank. & Marsh. | 21 |
| Western Md. ■ | N 6 | 25 | Western Md. | 20 |

Colors: Garnet & White. Nickname: Garnet.   III

### ST. OLAF — Northfield, MN 55057
*Don Canfield (20 yrs., 108-79-1)*

| 1993 Opponent | Date | Score | 1992 Opponent | Score |
|---|---|---|---|---|
| Luther ■ | S11 | 13 | Luther | 31 |
| St. Thomas (Minn.) | S18 | 14 | St. Thomas (Minn.) | 7 |
| St. John's (Minn.) ■ | S25 | 7 | St. John's (Minn.) | 62 |
| Macalester | O 2* | 47 | Macalester | 0 |
| Gust. Adolphus ■ | O 9 | 9 | Gust. Adolphus | 14 |
| Carleton | O16 | 9 | Carleton | 21 |
| Hamline | O23 | 14 | Hamline | 17 |
| Concordia-M'head | O30 | 21 | Concordia-M'head | 45 |
| Bethel (Minn.) ■ | N 5* | 27 | Bethel (Minn.) | 20 |
| Augsburg | N13 | 20 | Augsburg | 18 |

Colors: Black & Old Gold. Nickname: Oles.   III

### TEXAS A&I — Kingsville, TX 78363
*Ron Harms (24 yrs., 156-88-4)*

| 1993 Opponent | Date | Score | 1992 Opponent | Score |
|---|---|---|---|---|
| Southwest Tex. St. ■ | S 4* | 14 | Southwest Tex. St. | 15 |
| Mississippi Col. ■ | S11* | 50 | Nicholls St. | 12 |
| Portland St. ■ | S18* | 44 | Portland St. | 43 |
| Sam Houston St. | S25* | 50 | Cameron | 0 |
| Central St. (Ohio) | O 2 | 17 | East Tex. St. | 10 |
| East Tex. St. ■ | O 9* | 36 | Central Okla. | 12 |
| Central Okla. | O16* | 33 | Mississippi Col. | 37 |
| Eastern N. Mex. ■ | O30* | 26 | Eastern N. Mex. | 0 |
| Abilene Christian ■ | N 6 | 38 | Abilene Christian | 14 |
| Angelo St. | N13* | 9 | Angelo St. | 6 |
| *II Championship* | | | | |
| | | 22 | Western St. | 13 |
| | | 30 | Portland St. | 35 |

Colors: Blue & Gold. Nickname: Javelinas.   II

### ST. THOMAS (MINNESOTA) — St. Paul, MN 55105
*Mal Scanlan (1st yr. as head coach)*

| 1993 Opponent | Date | Score | 1992 Opponent | Score |
|---|---|---|---|---|
| Wis.-River Falls | S11 | 14 | Wis.-River Falls | 36 |
| St. Olaf ■ | S18 | 7 | St. Olaf | 14 |
| Macalester | S25* | 21 | Macalester | 6 |
| Carleton ■ | O 2 | 20 | Carleton | 25 |
| Concordia-M'head | O 9 | 10 | Concordia-M'head | 7 |
| Augsburg | O16 | 7 | Augsburg | 37 |
| St. John's (Minn.) | O23 | 15 | St. John's (Minn.) | 12 |
| Gust. Adolphus | O30 | 10 | Gust. Adolphus | 16 |
| Hamline† | N 6 | 6 | Hamline | 14 |
| Bethel (Minn.) ■ | N13 | 10 | Bethel (Minn.) | 21 |

Colors: Purple & Gray. Nickname: Tommies.   III

### THIEL — Greenville, PA 16125
*Charles Giangrosso (4 yrs., 19-19-0)*

| 1993 Opponent | Date | Score | 1992 Opponent | Score |
|---|---|---|---|---|
| Albion | S 4 | 0 | Albion | 20 |
| Oberlin ■ | S11 | 7 | Oberlin | 0 |
| Frostburg St. | S18 | 7 | Frostburg St. | 44 |
| Duquesne ■ | S25 | 0 | Duquesne | 22 |
| Bethany (W.Va.) ■ | O 2 | 7 | Bethany (W.Va.) | 31 |
| Wash. & Jeff. | O 9 | 0 | Wash. & Jeff. | 38 |
| Grove City | O16 | 6 | Grove City | 41 |
| Waynesburg | O23 | 0 | Waynesburg | 19 |
| Gannon ■ | O30 | 26 | Gannon | 34 |

Colors: Blue & Gold. Nickname: Tomcats.   III

### STONEHILL — North Easton, MA 02356
*Connie Driscoll (1st yr. as head coach)*

| 1993 Opponent | Date | Score | 1992 Opponent | Score |
|---|---|---|---|---|
| Monmouth (N. J.) ■ | S11 | 6 | Mass.-Dartmouth | 9 |
| Nichols | S18 | 14 | Nichols | 14 |
| Assumption | S25 | 32 | Assumption | |
| MIT | O 2 | 40 | Curry | 0 |
| Western New Eng. | O 9 | 54 | Western New Eng. | 21 |
| Mass.-Lowell ■ | O16 | 21 | MIT | 19 |
| Siena ■ | O23 | 40 | Siena | |
| Curry | O30 | 0 | Bentley | 42 |
| Sacred Heart ■ | N 6 | 25 | Sacred Heart | 12 |
| Bentley | N13 | | | |

Colors: Purple & White. Nickname: Chieftains.   III

### THOMAS MORE — Crestview Hills, KY 41017
*Vic Clark (3 yrs., 22-8-0)*

| 1993 Opponent | Date | Score | 1992 Opponent | Score |
|---|---|---|---|---|
| Ferrum ■ | S 4 | 36 | Cumberland (Tenn.) | 21 |
| Hanover | S11 | 42 | Hanover | 30 |
| Wilmington (Ohio) ■ | S18 | 52 | Wilmington (Ohio) | 21 |
| Franklin ■ | S25 | 24 | Franklin | 14 |
| Wesley ■ | O 2 | 10 | Waynesburg | 0 |
| Waynesburg | O 9 | 28 | Tenn. Wesleyan | 7 |
| Wis.-Stevens Point | O16 | 7 | Dayton | 18 |
| Defiance | O30 | 21 | Defiance | 10 |
| Mt. St. Joseph ■ | N 6 | 41 | Mt. St. Joseph | 3 |
| Bluffton | N13 | 33 | Bluffton | 7 |
| *III Championship* | | | | |
| | | 0 | Emory & Henry | 17 |

Colors: Royal Blue & White. Nickname: Blue Rebels.   III

### STONY BROOK — Stony Brook, NY 11794
*Sam Kornhauser (9 yrs., 37-46-1)*

| 1993 Opponent | Date | Score | 1992 Opponent | Score |
|---|---|---|---|---|
| Pace | S11 | 28 | Pace | 0 |
| Jersey City St. | S18 | 27 | Bentley | 12 |
| Coast Guard ■ | S25 | 24 | Coast Guard | 19 |
| Sacred Heart | O 2 | 20 | Sacred Heart | 0 |
| Gettysburg ■ | O 9 | 12 | Gettysburg | 15 |
| Merchant Marine | O23 | 14 | Wesley | 21 |
| Western Conn. St. ■ | O30 | 7 | Merchant Marine | 28 |
| Plymouth St. | N 6 | 16 | Western Conn. St. | 20 |
| Mass.-Lowell | N13 | 10 | Plymouth St. | 21 |
| St. John's (N.Y.) | N25 | 31 | Mass.-Lowell | 27 |

Colors: Scarlet & Gray. Nickname: Patriots.   III

### TRENTON STATE — Trenton, NJ 08650
*Eric Hamilton (16 yrs., 98-57-4)*

| 1993 Opponent | Date | Score | 1992 Opponent | Score |
|---|---|---|---|---|
| Wesley ■ | S 3* | 7 | Wesley | 21 |
| Salisbury St. ■ | S10* | 6 | Central Conn. St. | 14 |
| Wm. Paterson ■ | S17* | 13 | Wm. Paterson | 14 |
| Rowan | O 2* | 10 | Rowan | 26 |
| Frostburg St. | O 9 | 15 | FDU-Madison | 0 |
| LIU-C.W. Post ■ | O16 | 12 | Southern Conn. St. | 59 |
| Jersey City St. | O23 | 54 | Jersey City St. | 7 |
| Montclair St. ■ | O30 | 5 | Montclair St. | 17 |
| Springfield | N 6 | 6 | Kean | 12 |
| Kean | N13 | 30 | Ramapo | 7 |

Colors: Navy Blue & Gold. Nickname: Lions.   III

### SUSQUEHANNA — Selinsgrove, PA 17870
*Steve Briggs (3 yrs., 27-6-0)*

| 1993 Opponent | Date | Score | 1992 Opponent | Score |
|---|---|---|---|---|
| Lycoming ■ | S11 | 35 | Muhlenberg | 11 |
| Wash. & Jeff. | S18 | 20 | Moravian | 12 |
| King's (PA) ■ | S25 | 7 | Wilkes | 6 |
| Albright | O 2 | 27 | Lebanon Valley | 21 |
| Lebanon Valley ■ | O 9 | 25 | Delaware Valley | 21 |
| Moravian | O16 | 35 | Mass.-Lowell | 18 |
| Delaware Valley | O23 | 35 | Widener | 21 |
| Widener ■ | O30 | 35 | Juniata | 7 |
| Wilkes | N 6 | 19 | Lycoming | 23 |
| Juniata | N13 | 47 | Albright | 16 |

Colors: Orange & Maroon. Nickname: Crusaders.   III

### TRINITY (CONNECTICUT) — Hartford, CT 06106
*Don Miller (26 yrs., 140-63-5)*

| 1993 Opponent | Date | Score | 1992 Opponent | Score |
|---|---|---|---|---|
| Bates | S25 | 42 | Bates | 0 |
| Williams | O 2 | 33 | Williams | 40 |
| Hamilton ■ | O 9 | 21 | Hamilton | 17 |
| Tufts | O16 | 14 | Tufts | 0 |
| Bowdoin ■ | O23 | 3 | Bowdoin | 14 |
| Middlebury | O30 | 43 | Middlebury | 0 |
| Amherst | N 6 | 44 | Amherst | 21 |
| Wesleyan ■ | N13 | 37 | Wesleyan | 13 |

Colors: Blue & Gold. Nickname: Bantams.   III

■ Home games on each schedule.      *Night Games.

## TRINITY (TEXAS) ............. San Antonio, TX 78212
*Steven Mohr (3 yrs., 4-26-0)*

| Opponent | Date | | Opponent | |
|---|---|---|---|---|
| Claremont-M-S ■ | S11 | 30 | Tabor | 0 |
| Austin | S18 | 17 | Austin | 22 |
| Occidental ■ | S25* | 0 | Occidental | 39 |
| Washington (Mo.) ■ | O 2* | 27 | Washington (Mo.) | 21 |
| Carnegie Mellon | O 9 | 17 | Carnegie Mellon | 42 |
| Colorado Col. | O16 | 6 | Colorado Col. | 20 |
| Centre ■ | O23* | 7 | Centre | 27 |
| Rhodes | O30 | 19 | Rhodes | 31 |
| Sewanee | N 6 | 12 | Sewanee | 15 |
| Millsaps ■ | N13* | 17 | Millsaps | 40 |

Colors: Maroon & White.   Nickname: Tigers.   III

## TUFTS ............. Medford, MA 02155
*Duane Ford (8 yrs., 38-23-3)*

| Opponent | Date | | Opponent | |
|---|---|---|---|---|
| Wesleyan | S25 | 7 | Wesleyan | 14 |
| Bates | O 2 | 42 | Bates | 12 |
| Bowdoin ■ | O 9 | 0 | Trinity (Conn.) | 14 |
| Trinity (Conn.) ■ | O16 | 10 | Williams | 10 |
| Williams | O23 | 23 | Amherst | 0 |
| Amherst ■ | O30 | 23 | Colby | 13 |
| Colby | N 6 | 7 | Middlebury | 19 |
| Middlebury ■ | N13 | 6 | Bowdoin | 7 |

Colors: Brown & Blue.   Nickname: Jumbos.   III

## TUSKEGEE ............. Tuskegee Inst., AL 36088
*James Martin (9 yrs., 43-43-2)*

| Opponent | Date | | Opponent | |
|---|---|---|---|---|
| Jackson St. ■ | S 4 | 0 | Jackson St. | 30 |
| Savannah St. ■ | S11 | 24 | Savannah St. | 35 |
| Morris Brown ■ | S18 | 25 | Morris Brown | 20 |
| Miles | S25 | 40 | Miles | 6 |
| Albany St. (Ga.) ■ | O 2 | 14 | Albany St. (Ga.) | 14 |
| Clark Atlanta ■ | O 9 | 19 | Clark Atlanta | 30 |
| Morehouse† | O16* | 9 | Morehouse | 12 |
| Hampton | O23 | 41 | Hampton | 28 |
| Fort Valley St. ■ | O30 | 6 | Fort Valley St. | 38 |
| Alabama A&M | N13 | 14 | Alabama A&M | 26 |

Colors: Old Gold & Crimson.   Nickname: Golden Tigers.   II

## UC DAVIS ............. Davis, CA 95616
*Bob Biggs (1st yr. as head coach)*

| Opponent | Date | | Opponent | |
|---|---|---|---|---|
| Cal Poly SLO ■ | S11* | 14 | Cal St. Northridge | 16 |
| Cal St. Hayward ■ | S18* | 48 | Santa Clara | 44 |
| Southern Utah | S25* | 30 | St. Mary's (Cal.) | 26 |
| Humboldt St. ■ | O 2* | 21 | Cal St. Sacramento | 14 |
| Cal St. Chico | O 9* | 31 | Cal Poly SLO | 31 |
| Sonoma St. | O16 | 41 | Sonoma St. | 38 |
| Cal St. Northridge ■ | O23* | 58 | Humboldt St. | 31 |
| St. Mary's (Cal.) | O30 | 44 | Cal St. Chico | 37 |
| San Fran. St. | N 6* | 42 | San Fran. St. | 14 |
| Cal St. Sacramento | N13* | 38 | Cal St. Hayward | 27 |
| *II Championship* | | | | |
| | | 28 | Portland St. | 42 |

Colors: Blue & Gold.   Nickname: Aggies.   II

## UNION (NEW YORK) ......... Schenectady, NY 12308
*John Audino (3 yrs., 15-16-0)*

| Opponent | Date | | Opponent | |
|---|---|---|---|---|
| St. Lawrence | S11 | 41 | St. Lawrence | 14 |
| Worcester Tech ■ | S18 | 34 | Worcester Tech | 20 |
| Hobart | S25 | 24 | Hobart | 3 |
| Dickinson ■ | O 2 | 3 | Dickinson | 27 |
| Albany (N.Y.) ■ | O 9 | 17 | Albany (N.Y.) | 23 |
| Rensselaer | O16 | 8 | Rensselaer | 23 |
| Coast Guard | O23 | 21 | Coast Guard | 9 |
| Alfred ■ | O30 | 43 | Gettysburg | 7 |
| Rochester ■ | N 6 | 14 | Rochester | 20 |

Colors: Garnet.   Nickname: Dutchmen.   III

## UPPER IOWA ............. Fayette, IA 52142
*Paul Rudolph (2 yrs., 8-12-0)*

| Opponent | Date | | Opponent | |
|---|---|---|---|---|
| Wis.-Whitewater ■ | S11 | 26 | Wis.-Whitewater | 30 |
| Wartburg ■ | S18 | 14 | Wartburg | 17 |
| Luther | S25 | 20 | Luther | 28 |
| William Penn ■ | O 2 | 45 | William Penn | 7 |
| Dubuque ■ | O 9 | 54 | Dubuque | 12 |
| Buena Vista | O16 | 42 | Buena Vista | 24 |
| Mid-America Nazarene | O23 | 20 | Mid-America Nazarene | 10 |
| Central (Iowa) ■ | O30 | 20 | Central (Iowa) | 45 |
| Loras | N 6 | 57 | Loras | 38 |
| Simpson | N13 | 28 | Simpson | 20 |

Colors: Blue & White.   Nickname: Peacocks.   III

## UPSALA ............. East Orange, NJ 07019
*Mike Walsh (4 yrs., 14-25-1)*

| Opponent | Date | | Opponent | |
|---|---|---|---|---|
| Widener | S11 | 18 | Western Conn. St. | 13 |
| Kean ■ | S18 | 20 | Kean | 59 |
| Wilkes ■ | S25 | 8 | Rensselaer | 31 |
| Jersey City St. ■ | O 2 | 19 | Jersey City St. | 6 |
| King's (PA) ■ | O 9 | 13 | Wm. Paterson | 35 |
| Lycoming | O16 | 37 | Pace | 20 |
| Delaware Valley ■ | O30 | 20 | Wilkes | 31 |
| Lebanon Valley | N 6 | 16 | FDU-Madison | 22 |
| FDU-Madison | N12* | 13 | Bentley | 42 |
| | | 34 | Wesley | 28 |

Colors: Blue & Gray.   Nickname: Vikings.   III

## URSINUS ............. Collegeville, PA 19426
*Steve Gilbert (5 yrs., 21-28-0)*

| Opponent | Date | | Opponent | |
|---|---|---|---|---|
| Worcester Tech | S11 | 23 | Georgetown | 16 |
| Frank. & Marsh. ■ | S18 | 6 | Frank. & Marsh. | 13 |
| Western Md. | S25 | 21 | Western Md. | 35 |
| Swarthmore ■ | O 2 | 32 | Swarthmore | 34 |
| Johns Hopkins | O 9 | 34 | Johns Hopkins | 35 |
| Gettysburg ■ | O16 | 28 | Gettysburg | 6 |
| FDU-Madison ■ | O23 | 14 | FDU-Madison | 0 |
| Muhlenberg | N 6 | 10 | Worcester Tech | 24 |
| Dickinson | N13 | 6 | Muhlenberg | 3 |
| | | 0 | Dickinson | 21 |

Colors: Old Gold, Red & Black.   Nickname: Bears.   III

## VALDOSTA STATE ............. Valdosta, GA 31698
*Hal Mumme (4 yrs., 29-15-1)*

| Opponent | Date | | Opponent | |
|---|---|---|---|---|
| Mt. Senario ■ | S 2* | 13 | Ga. Southern | 24 |
| Central Fla. | S11 | 24 | Fort Valley St. | 17 |
| Fort Valley St. ■ | S18* | 6 | Jacksonville St. | 20 |
| Clark Atlanta ■ | S25* | 10 | Troy St. | 26 |
| Livingston ■ | O 2* | 42 | Livingston | 15 |
| Tarleton St. | O 9* | 28 | West Ga. | 42 |
| West Ga. | O16* | 31 | American Int'l | 21 |
| Mississippi Col. ■ | O23 | 28 | Mississippi Col. | 14 |
| Delta St. | O30* | 45 | Delta St. | 7 |
| North Ala. ■ | N 6* | 24 | North Ala. | 24 |
| Henderson St. | N13 | | | |

Colors: Red & Black.   Nickname: Blazers.   II

## VIRGINIA STATE ............. Ettrick, VA 23806
*Louis Anderson (2 yrs., 6-14-0)*

| Opponent | Date | | Opponent | |
|---|---|---|---|---|
| Norfolk St. ■ | S 4* | 28 | Norfolk St. | 21 |
| West Liberty St. | S11 | 7 | N.C. Central | 31 |
| N.C. Central ■ | S18 | 0 | Winston-Salem | 28 |
| Bowie St. ■ | S25 | 14 | Bowie St. | 28 |
| Livingstone | O 2 | 35 | Livingstone | 19 |
| Hampton | O 9 | 23 | Hampton | 55 |
| Fayetteville St. ■ | O16 | 15 | Fayetteville St. | 35 |
| Elizabeth City St. ■ | O23 | 28 | Elizabeth City St. | 27 |
| Virginia Union | O30 | 8 | Virginia Union | 23 |
| Lane ■ | N 6 | 0 | West Va. St. | 55 |
| Winston-Salem | N13 | | | |

Colors: Orange & Navy Blue.   Nickname: Trojans.   II

## VIRGINIA UNION ............. Richmond, VA 23220
*Henry Lattimore (14 yrs., 81-64-4)*

| Opponent | Date | | Opponent | |
|---|---|---|---|---|
| Howard | S 4 | 6 | Grambling | 54 |
| Livingstone | S11 | 20 | Hampton | 20 |
| Hampton ■ | S18* | 26 | New Haven | 80 |
| Bowie St. ■ | O 2 | 26 | Bowie St. | 6 |
| Elizabeth City St. ■ | O 9 | 6 | Elizabeth City St. | 38 |
| New Haven | O16 | 7 | Knoxville | 38 |
| Norfolk St. ■ | O23 | 41 | Norfolk St. | 38 |
| Virginia St. | O30 | 23 | Virginia St. | 8 |
| Winston-Salem ■ | N 6 | 6 | Central St. (Ohio) | 55 |
| N.C. Central | N13 | | | |

Colors: Steel Gray & Maroon.   Nickname: Panthers.   II

## WABASH ............. Crawfordsville, IN 47933
*Greg Carlson (10 yrs., 63-28-2)*

| Opponent | Date | | Opponent | |
|---|---|---|---|---|
| Wis.-Eau Claire | S11 | 24 | Albion | 25 |
| Albion | S18 | 10 | Hope | 8 |
| Hope ■ | S25 | 40 | Manchester | 8 |
| Manchester | O 2 | 16 | Franklin | 14 |
| Franklin | O 9 | 38 | Hanover | 33 |
| Hanover ■ | O16 | 42 | Anderson | 14 |
| Anderson ■ | O23 | 40 | Rose-Hulman | 13 |
| Rose-Hulman | O30 | 46 | Taylor | 14 |
| DePauw | N13 | 17 | DePauw | 8 |

Colors: Scarlet & White.   Nickname: Little Giants.   III

■ Home games on each schedule.          *Night Games.

## WARTBURG ...... Waverly, IA 50677
*Bob Nielson (4 yrs., 20-17-1)*

| 1993 Opponent | Date | 1992 Pts | 1992 Opponent | Opp |
|---|---|---|---|---|
| Coe | S11 | 16 | Coe | 20 |
| Upper Iowa | S18 | 17 | Upper Iowa | 14 |
| Central (Iowa) ■ | S25 | 21 | Central (Iowa) | 31 |
| Simpson | O 2 | 26 | Simpson | 48 |
| Luther | O 9 | 56 | Luther | 28 |
| William Penn ■ | O16 | 62 | William Penn | 3 |
| Buena Vista ■ | O23 | 28 | Buena Vista | 7 |
| Dubuque | O30 | 55 | Dubuque | 6 |
| Aurora ■ | N 6 | 14 | Aurora | 21 |
| Loras ■ | N13 | 22 | Loras | 33 |

Colors: Orange & Black.   Nickname: Knights.   III

## WASHBURN ...... Topeka, KS 66621
*Dennis Caryl (6 yrs., 23-39-0)*

| 1993 Opponent | Date | 1992 Pts | 1992 Opponent | Opp |
|---|---|---|---|---|
| Southern Ill. | S11 | 15 | Southwest Mo. St. | 66 |
| Missouri-Rolla ■ | S18* | 8 | Northeast Mo. St. | 42 |
| Central Mo. St. | S25 | 21 | Northwest Mo. St. | 22 |
| Pittsburg St. ■ | O 2* | 14 | Mo. Southern St. | 44 |
| Northwest Mo. St. | O 9 | 18 | Emporia St. | 25 |
| Northeast Mo. St. ■ | O16 | 13 | Central Mo. St. | 10 |
| Mo. Western St. | O23 | 21 | Missouri-Rolla | 26 |
| Mo. Southern St. ■ | O30 | 21 | Southwest Baptist | 17 |
| Emporia St. | N 6 | 29 | Pittsburg St. | 48 |
| Southwest Baptist | N13 | 17 | Mo. Western St. | 41 |

Colors: Yale Blue & White.   Nickname: Ichabods.   II

## WASHINGTON AND JEFFERSON  Washington, PA 15301
*John Luckhardt (11 yrs., 86-24-2)*

| 1993 Opponent | Date | 1992 Pts | 1992 Opponent | Opp |
|---|---|---|---|---|
| Frank. & Marsh. | S11 | 61 | Hiram | 6 |
| Susquehanna ■ | S18 | 35 | Widener | 0 |
| Bethany (W.Va.) ■ | S25 | 62 | Bethany (W.Va.) | 14 |
| Waynesburg | O 2 | 35 | Waynesburg | 0 |
| Thiel ■ | O 9 | 38 | Thiel | 0 |
| Gannon | O16 | 49 | Gannon | 16 |
| Grove City | O23 | 34 | Grove City | 13 |
| Cortland St. | O30 | 31 | Cortland St. | 6 |
| Ithaca ■ | N13 | 28 | Ithaca | 47 |
| | | | **III Championship** | |
| | | 33 | Lycoming | 0 |
| | | 51 | Emory & Henry | 15 |
| | | 18 | Rowan | 13 |
| | | 12 | Wis.-La Crosse | 16 |

Colors: Red & Black.   Nickname: Presidents.   III

## WASHINGTON AND LEE ...... Lexington, VA 24450
*Gary Fallon (15 yrs., 69-73-1)*

| 1993 Opponent | Date | 1992 Pts | 1992 Opponent | Opp |
|---|---|---|---|---|
| Emory & Henry | S11 | 13 | Emory & Henry | 41 |
| Centre ■ | S25 | 32 | Centre | 22 |
| Randolph-Macon | O 2 | 9 | Randolph-Macon | 31 |
| Davidson ■ | O 9 | 27 | Davidson | 12 |
| Hampden-Sydney | O16 | 24 | Hampden-Sydney | 21 |
| Sewanee ■ | O23 | 17 | Sewanee | 16 |
| Bridgewater (Va.) ■ | O30 | 12 | Bridgewater (Va.) | 20 |
| Guilford | N 6 | 21 | Guilford | 0 |
| Catholic ■ | N13 | 19 | Georgetown | 27 |
| Georgetown† | N20 | | | |

Colors: Royal Blue & White.   Nickname: Generals.   III

## WASHINGTON (MISSOURI) ...... St. Louis, MO 63130
*Larry Kindbom (10 yrs., 49-48-1)*

| 1993 Opponent | Date | 1992 Pts | 1992 Opponent | Opp |
|---|---|---|---|---|
| Rose-Hulman | S 4* | 15 | Rose-Hulman | 13 |
| Carnegie Mellon | S11 | 7 | Carnegie Mellon | 31 |
| Case Reserve | S18 | 21 | Case Reserve | 9 |
| Rochester ■ | S25 | 6 | Rochester | 42 |
| Trinity (Tex.) | O 2* | 27 | Trinity (Tex.) | 27 |
| Rhodes | O 9* | 19 | Rhodes | 26 |
| Central Meth. ■ | O16 | 3 | Central Meth. | 34 |
| Chicago | O23 | 23 | Chicago | 24 |
| Principia | O30 | 34 | Principia | 27 |
| Colorado Col. ■ | N 6 | 27 | Colorado Col. | 26 |

Colors: Red & Green.   Nickname: Bears.   III

## WAYNE STATE (MICHIGAN) ...... Detroit, MI 48202
*Brian VanGorder (1 yr., 4-7-0)*

| 1993 Opponent | Date | 1992 Pts | 1992 Opponent | Opp |
|---|---|---|---|---|
| Indianapolis | S 4 | 31 | Indianapolis | 26 |
| Saginaw Valley | S11 | 13 | Saginaw Valley | 32 |
| St. Francis (Ill.) ■ | S18 | 10 | Valparaiso | 23 |
| Ferris St. | S25 | 3 | Ferris St. | 21 |
| Ashland ■ | O 2 | 0 | Ashland | 14 |
| Northwood | O 9 | 21 | Butler | 31 |
| American Int'l | O16 | 21 | Northwood | 0 |
| Northern Mich. | O23 | 21 | Northern Mich. | 24 |
| St. Joseph's (Ind.) | O30 | 27 | St. Joseph's (Ind.) | 6 |
| Grand Valley St. ■ | N 6 | 14 | Grand Valley St. | 16 |
| Hillsdale ■ | N13 | 14 | Hillsdale | 41 |

Colors: Green & Gold.   Nickname: Tartars.   II

## WAYNE STATE (NEBRASKA) ...... Wayne, NE 68787
*Dennis Wagner (4 yrs., 19-22-1)*

| 1993 Opponent | Date | 1992 Pts | 1992 Opponent | Opp |
|---|---|---|---|---|
| Nebraska-Omaha | S 4 | 18 | Nebraska-Omaha | 20 |
| Morningside ■ | S11* | 7 | Morningside | 24 |
| Bemidji St. ■ | S18 | 44 | Bemidji St. | 7 |
| Mayville St. | S25* | 42 | Mayville St. | 7 |
| Iowa Wesleyan ■ | O 2 | 2 | Neb.-Kearney | 7 |
| Neb.-Kearney | O 9 | 35 | St. Francis (Ill.) | 21 |
| Southwest St. (Minn.) | O23 | 49 | Southwest St. (Minn.) | 29 |
| Michigan Tech | O30 | 38 | Michigan Tech | 48 |
| Peru St. ■ | N 6 | 17 | Peru St. | 17 |
| Minn.-Duluth† | N13 | 42 | Iowa Wesleyan | 11 |

Colors: Black & Gold.   Nickname: Wildcats.   II

## WAYNESBURG ...... Waynesburg, PA 15370
*Ty Clarke (5 yrs., 25-33-0)*

| 1993 Opponent | Date | 1992 Pts | 1992 Opponent | Opp |
|---|---|---|---|---|
| Gannon | S11 | 7 | Urbana | 17 |
| Grove City | | 3 | Gannon | 34 |
| Wash. & Jeff. ■ | O 2 | 3 | Grove City | 23 |
| Thomas More | O 9 | 0 | Wash. & Jeff. | 35 |
| Bethany (W.Va.) ■ | O16 | 0 | Thomas More | 10 |
| Thiel ■ | O23 | 16 | Bethany (W.Va.) | 27 |
| Kenyon | O30 | 19 | Thiel | 0 |
| Frostburg St. | N 6 | 26 | Kenyon | 21 |
| Wesley ■ | N13 | 0 | Frostburg St. | 14 |

Colors: Orange & Black.   Nickname: Yellow Jackets.   III

## WESLEY ...... Dover, DE 19901
*To be named*

| 1993 Opponent | Date | 1992 Pts | 1992 Opponent | Opp |
|---|---|---|---|---|
| Trenton St. | S 3* | 21 | Trenton St. | 7 |
| Bridgewater (Va.) ■ | S11 | 32 | Randolph-Macon | 20 |
| Geneva | S18 | 34 | Geneva | 15 |
| Randolph-Macon ■ | S25 | 26 | Bridgewater (Va.) | 13 |
| Thomas More | O 2 | 13 | Frostburg St. | 17 |
| Wm. Paterson ■ | O 9 | 47 | Gallaudet | 14 |
| Frostburg St. | O16 | 21 | Stony Brook | 14 |
| Salisbury St. ■ | O23 | 33 | Hampden-Sydney | 23 |
| Chowan ■ | O30 | 29 | Delaware Valley | 30 |
| Waynesburg | N13 | 38 | Upsala | 34 |

Colors: Blue & White.   Nickname: Wolverines.   III

## WESLEYAN ...... Middletown, CT 06457
*Frank Hauser (1 yr., 4-4-0)*

| 1993 Opponent | Date | 1992 Pts | 1992 Opponent | Opp |
|---|---|---|---|---|
| Tufts ■ | S25 | 14 | Tufts | 7 |
| Hamilton | O 2 | 14 | Hamilton | 24 |
| Colby ■ | O 9 | 21 | Colby | 28 |
| Bates ■ | O16 | 49 | Bates | 6 |
| Amherst | O23 | 46 | Amherst | 14 |
| Bowdoin | O30 | 40 | Bowdoin | 6 |
| Williams ■ | N 6 | 23 | Williams | 28 |
| Trinity (Conn.) | N13 | 13 | Trinity (Conn.) | 37 |

Colors: Red & Black.   Nickname: Cardinals.   III

## WEST CHESTER ...... West Chester, PA 19383
*Rick Daniels (4 yrs., 29-14-0)*

| 1993 Opponent | Date | 1992 Pts | 1992 Opponent | Opp |
|---|---|---|---|---|
| New Haven | S 4 | 6 | Villanova | 26 |
| Clarion | S11 | 38 | Wingate | 7 |
| Indiana (PA) ■ | S18 | 21 | Delaware | 20 |
| Delaware | S25 | 48 | Cheyney | 7 |
| Cheyney ■ | O 1* | 39 | Mansfield | 13 |
| Mansfield | O 9 | 38 | Millersville | 27 |
| Millersville ■ | O16 | 34 | Bloomsburg | 2 |
| Bloomsburg | O23 | 35 | Kutztown | 34 |
| Kutztown ■ | O30 | 35 | Shippensburg | 31 |
| Shippensburg | N 6 | 3 | East Stroudsburg | 0 |
| East Stroudsburg | N13 | | **II Championship** | |
| | | 26 | New Haven | 38 |

Colors: Purple & Gold.   Nickname: Golden Rams.   II

## WEST GEORGIA ...... Carrollton, GA 30118
*Ron Jurney (3 yrs., 12-21-0)*

| 1993 Opponent | Date | 1992 Pts | 1992 Opponent | Opp |
|---|---|---|---|---|
| Elon | S 4* | 16 | Samford | 44 |
| Tenn.-Martin | S11* | 18 | Livingstone | 12 |
| Albany St. (Ga.) ■ | S18 | 10 | Jacksonville St. | 17 |
| Central Ark. ■ | S25* | 26 | Clark Atlanta | 28 |
| Harding ■ | O 2 | 47 | Livingston | 13 |
| Livingston | O 9 | 38 | Mississippi Col. | 45 |
| Valdosta St. ■ | O16* | 42 | Valdosta St. | 28 |
| Mississippi Col. | O30* | 38 | Knoxville | 6 |
| Delta St. ■ | N 6 | 35 | Delta St. | 36 |
| North Ala. | N13 | 7 | North Ala. | 19 |
| | | 62 | Lane | 0 |

Colors: Red & Blue.   Nickname: Braves.   II

■ Home games on each schedule.          *Night Games.

## WEST LIBERTY STATE ........ West Liberty, WV 26074
*Bob Eaton (3 yrs., 11-18-1)*

| Opponent | Date | | Opponent | |
|---|---|---|---|---|
| Calif. (PA) ■ | S 4 | 9 | Calif. (PA) | 21 |
| Virginia St. ■ | S 18 | 28 | West Va. Tech | 14 |
| West Va. Tech ■ | S 25 | 29 | Shepherd | 35 |
| Shepherd | O 2 | 23 | Glenville St. | 28 |
| Glenville St. | O 9 | 14 | West Va. St. | 20 |
| West Va. St. ■ | O16 | 23 | Tiffin | 10 |
| Concord (W. Va.) ■ | O23 | 29 | Lenoir-Rhyne | 41 |
| West Va. Wesleyan | O30 | 13 | Concord (W. Va.) | 16 |
| Fairmont St. | N 6 | 21 | West Va. Wesleyan | 13 |
| Findlay | N13 | 10 | Fairmont St. | 12 |

Colors: Gold & Black.   Nickname: Hilltoppers.   **II**

## WEST TEXAS STATE ............. Canyon, TX 79016
*Ron Steele (1 yr., 1-9-0)*

| Opponent | Date | | Opponent | |
|---|---|---|---|---|
| Fort Lewis ■ | S11* | 0 | Southwestern Okla. | 37 |
| Panhandle St. ■ | S18* | 35 | Fort Lewis | 46 |
| Southwestern Okla. | S 25 | 10 | Cameron | 44 |
| Midwestern St. ■ | O 2* | 20 | Western N. Mex. | 30 |
| Prairie View | O 9 | 21 | Prairie View | 15 |
| Southeastern Okla. | O16 | 7 | Southeastern Okla. | 38 |
| Tarleton St. ■ | O30* | 14 | N.M. Highlands | 42 |
| Eastern N. Mex. | N 6 | 7 | Tarleton St. | 36 |
| Western N. Mex. | N13 | 0 | Eastern N. Mex. | 56 |
| | | 0 | Panhandle St. | 14 |

Colors: Maroon & White.   Nickname: Buffaloes.   **II**

## WEST VIRGINIA STATE .......... Institute, WV 25112
*Scott Tinsley (1 yr., 6-4-0)*

| Opponent | Date | | Opponent | |
|---|---|---|---|---|
| West Va. Tech† | S 4 | 42 | West Va. Tech | 8 |
| Elon | S11* | 22 | Morehead St. | 0 |
| Cheyney† | S18 | 34 | West Va. Wesleyan | 26 |
| Concord (W. Va.) | S 25 | 6 | Glenville St. | 35 |
| Glenville St. | O 2 | 0 | Shepherd | 19 |
| Fairmont St. ■ | O 9 | 20 | West Liberty St. | 14 |
| West Liberty St. | O16 | 40 | Fairmont St. | 14 |
| West Va. Wesleyan | O23 | 12 | Central St. (Ohio) | 42 |
| Catawba ■ | O30 | 55 | Virginia St. | 0 |
| Shepherd | N 6 | 6 | Concord (W. Va.) | 25 |

Colors: Gold & Black.   Nickname: Yellowjackets.   **II**

## WEST VIRGINIA TECH ....... Montgomery, WV 25136
*Bob Gobel (4 yrs., 17-23-1)*

| Opponent | Date | | Opponent | |
|---|---|---|---|---|
| West Va. St.† | S 4 | 8 | West Va. St. | 42 |
| Tiffin ■ | S11 | 24 | Tiffin | 28 |
| Morehead St. | S18* | 14 | West Liberty St. | 28 |
| West Liberty St. | S 25 | 8 | Va. Military | 48 |
| West Va. Wesleyan ■ | O 2 | 6 | Lees-McRae | 28 |
| Concord (W. Va.) | O 9 | 34 | West Va. Wesleyan | 41 |
| Fairmont St. ■ | O16 | 19 | Concord (W. Va.) | 37 |
| Shepherd | O23 | 26 | Fairmont St. | 40 |
| Glenville St. ■ | N 6 | 15 | Shepherd | 40 |
| Indiana St. | N13 | 7 | Glenville St. | 70 |

Colors: Gold & Blue.   Nickname: Golden Bears.   **II**

## WEST VIRGINIA WESLEYAN ... Buckannon, WV 26201
*Bill Struble (10 yrs., 40-59-0)*

| Opponent | Date | | Opponent | |
|---|---|---|---|---|
| Slippery Rock ■ | S 4 | 7 | Slippery Rock | 45 |
| Calif. (PA) ■ | S11 | 14 | Calif. (PA) | 12 |
| Fairmont St. ■ | S 25 | 26 | West Va. St. | 34 |
| West Va. Tech | O 2 | 14 | Concord (W. Va.) | 16 |
| Shepherd ■ | O 9 | 14 | Fairmont St. | 16 |
| Glenville St. | O16 | 41 | West Va. Tech | 34 |
| West Va. St. ■ | O23 | 13 | Shepherd | 19 |
| West Liberty St. ■ | O30 | 6 | Glenville St. | 30 |
| Concord (W. Va.) | N 6 | 24 | Geneva | 14 |
| Geneva ■ | N13 | 13 | West Liberty St. | 21 |

Colors: Orange & Black.   Nickname: Bobcats.   **II**

## WESTERN CONNECTICUT STATE .. Danbury, CT 06810
*John Cervino (1 yr., 2-8-0)*

| Opponent | Date | | Opponent | |
|---|---|---|---|---|
| Kean ■ | S 4* | 14 | Kean | 16 |
| Merchant Marine | S18 | 13 | Upsala | 18 |
| Wm. Paterson | S24* | 14 | Merchant Marine | 37 |
| Mass.-Dartmouth ■ | O 2* | 6 | Wm. Paterson | 17 |
| Plymouth St. | O 9 | 35 | Plymouth St. | 39 |
| Coast Guard ■ | O16 | 8 | Coast Guard | 6 |
| Mass.-Lowell ■ | O23 | 17 | Mass.-Lowell | 41 |
| Stony Brook | O30 | 20 | Stony Brook | 16 |
| Albany (N.Y.) ■ | N 6 | 0 | Albany (N.Y.) | 50 |
| Norwich | N13 | 21 | Norwich | 22 |

Colors: Blue & White.   Nickname: Colonials.   **III**

## WESTERN MARYLAND ....... Westminster, MD 21157
*Tim Keating (5 yrs., 25-23-0)*

| Opponent | Date | | Opponent | |
|---|---|---|---|---|
| Juniata ■ | S11 | 28 | Albright | 0 |
| Gettysburg | S18 | 38 | Gettysburg | 13 |
| Ursinus ■ | S 25 | 35 | Ursinus | 21 |
| Muhlenberg | O 2 | 39 | Muhlenberg | 0 |
| Randolph-Macon ■ | O 9 | 30 | Randolph-Macon | 48 |
| Dickinson | O16 | 17 | Dickinson | 14 |
| Frank. & Marsh. ■ | O23 | 27 | Frank. & Marsh. | 41 |
| Swarthmore | N 6 | 20 | Lebanon Valley | 22 |
| Johns Hopkins ■ | N13 | 20 | Swarthmore | 25 |
| | | 9 | Johns Hopkins | 21 |

Colors: Green & Gold.   Nickname: Green Terrors.   **III**

## WESTERN NEW ENGLAND...... Springfield, MA 01119
*Gerry Martin (2 yrs., 7-11-0)*

| Opponent | Date | | Opponent | |
|---|---|---|---|---|
| Fitchburg St. ■ | S11 | 28 | Fitchburg St. | 14 |
| Curry ■ | S18 | 25 | Curry | 22 |
| MIT ■ | S 25 | 9 | MIT | 27 |
| Salve Regina ■ | O 3 | 3 | St. Peter's | 19 |
| Stonehill ■ | O 9 | 21 | Stonehill | 54 |
| Bentley | O23 | 6 | Assumption | 13 |
| Nichols ■ | O30 | 6 | Bentley | 34 |
| Hartwick ■ | N 6 | 7 | Nichols | 35 |
| Assumption | N13 | 9 | Hartwick | 7 |
| | | 22 | Siena | 3 |

Colors: Blue & Gold.   Nickname: Golden Bears.   **III**

## WESTERN STATE ............... Gunnison, CO 81231
*Carl Iverson (9 yrs., 62-35-1)*

| Opponent | Date | | Opponent | |
|---|---|---|---|---|
| Northern Colo. ■ | S 4 | 27 | Northern Colo. | 30 |
| Eastern N. Mex. ■ | S11* | 57 | Eastern N. Mex. | 14 |
| Western Mont. ■ | S18 | 58 | Western Mont. | 24 |
| Neb.-Kearney ■ | S 25 | 64 | Adams St. | 31 |
| Colorado Mines ■ | O 2 | 39 | Colorado Mines | 32 |
| Fort Lewis | O 9 | 69 | Fort Lewis | 16 |
| Mesa St. ■ | O16 | 30 | Mesa St. | 3 |
| Chadron St. | O23 | 49 | Chadron St. | 21 |
| N.M. Highlands | O30 | 43 | N.M. Highlands | 15 |
| Fort Hays St. ■ | N 6 | 35 | Fort Hays St. | 10 |
| Adams St. | N13 | | **II Championship** | |
| | | 13 | Texas A&I. | 22 |

Colors: Crimson & Slate.   Nickname: Mountaineers.   **II**

## WESTFIELD STATE ............. Westfield, MA 01085
*Steve Marino (3 yrs., 13-16-0)*

| Opponent | Date | | Opponent | |
|---|---|---|---|---|
| Hartwick | S11* | 20 | Mass.-Boston | 34 |
| Mass.-Boston ■ | S17* | 41 | Fitchburg St. | 0 |
| Fitchburg St. | S 25 | 24 | Framingham St. | 6 |
| Framingham St. ■ | O 2 | 31 | MIT | 12 |
| MIT ■ | O 9 | 10 | Bri'water (Mass.) | 22 |
| Bri'water (Mass.) | O16 | 29 | Worcester St. | 0 |
| Worcester St. ■ | O22* | 13 | Mass. Maritime | 10 |
| Mass.-Dartmouth ■ | O30 | 14 | Mass.-Dartmouth | 21 |
| Mass.-Dartmouth ■ | N 5* | 22 | Maine Maritime | 13 |
| Maine Maritime | N13 | | | |

Colors: Navy & White.   Nickname: Owls.   **III**

## WHEATON (ILLINOIS) ............. Wheaton, IL 60187
*J. R. Bishop (11 yrs., 60-38-1)*

| Opponent | Date | | Opponent | |
|---|---|---|---|---|
| Lake Forest ■ | S11 | 29 | Lake Forest | 0 |
| Dayton | S18* | 3 | Dayton | 44 |
| Millikin ■ | O 2 | 21 | Millikin | 0 |
| Ill. Wesleyan | O 9 | 19 | Ill. Wesleyan | 33 |
| Carthage ■ | O16 | 28 | Carthage | 0 |
| North Park ■ | O23 | 24 | North Park | 0 |
| North Central | O30* | 33 | North Central | 6 |
| Elmhurst ■ | N 6 | 30 | Elmhurst | 0 |
| Augustana (Ill.) ■ | N13 | 15 | Augustana (Ill.) | 20 |

Colors: Orange & Blue.   Nickname: Crusaders.   **III**

## WHITTIER ...................... Whittier, CA 90608
*Ken Visser (2 yrs., 6-12-0)*

| Opponent | Date | | Opponent | |
|---|---|---|---|---|
| Cal St. Chico ■ | S11* | 18 | La Verne | 21 |
| Cal Lutheran | S18 | 24 | Menlo | 34 |
| Azusa Pacific ■ | S 25 | 6 | Occidental | 34 |
| Pomona-Pitzer ■ | O 2* | 21 | San Diego | 33 |
| Occidental ■ | O 9* | 21 | Pomona-Pitzer | 27 |
| Redlands | O16* | 39 | Azusa Pacific | 12 |
| Claremont-M-S ■ | O23 | 42 | Claremont-M-S | 19 |
| Menlo | O30 | 14 | Redlands | 45 |
| La Verne | N13 | 33 | Cal Lutheran | 30 |

Colors: Purple & Gold.   Nickname: Poets.   **III**

■ Home games on each schedule.          *Night Games.

## WIDENER ....................... Chester, PA 19013
*Bill Cubit (1 yr., 3-6-1)*

| Opponent | Date | | Opponent | Score |
|---|---|---|---|---|
| Upsala ■ | S 11 | 6 | Gettysburg | 40 |
| King's (PA) | S 18 | 0 | Wash. & Jeff. | 35 |
| Moravian | S 25 | 16 | Moravian | 7 |
| Juniata ■ | O 2 | 7 | Juniata | 13 |
| Delaware Valley ■ | O 9 | 16 | Lycoming | 28 |
| Albright | O 16 | 35 | Albright | 33 |
| Wilkes ■ | O 23 | 21 | Susquehanna | 35 |
| Susquehanna | O 30 | 14 | Wilkes | 14 |
| FDU-Madison | N 5* | 3 | Lebanon Valley | 30 |
| Lebanon Valley ■ | N 13 | 31 | Delaware Valley | 16 |

Colors: Widener Blue & Gold.  Nickname: Pioneers.  III

## WILKES ..................... Wilkes-Barre, PA 18766
*Joe DeMelfi (3 yrs., 7-22-1)*

| Opponent | Date | | Opponent | Score |
|---|---|---|---|---|
| Plymouth St. | S 11 | 35 | Plymouth St. | 24 |
| Lebanon Valley | S 18 | 19 | Albright | 10 |
| Upsala ■ | S 25 | 6 | Susquehanna | 7 |
| Delaware Valley ■ | O 2 | 14 | Moravian | 28 |
| Juniata | O 9 | 20 | Lebanon Valley | 26 |
| FDU-Madison ■ | O 16 | 17 | Delaware Valley | 13 |
| Widener | O 23 | 31 | Upsala | 20 |
| Lycoming ■ | O 30 | 14 | Widener | 14 |
| Susquehanna ■ | N 6 | 13 | Juniata | 6 |
| King's (PA) | N 13 | 0 | Lycoming | 33 |

Colors: Navy & Gold.  Nickname: Colonels.  III

## WILLIAM PATERSON ............... Wayne, NJ 07470
*Gerry Gallagher (7 yrs., 30-34-1)*

| Opponent | Date | | Opponent | Score |
|---|---|---|---|---|
| Geneva | S 4 | 20 | Geneva | 9 |
| Trenton St. ■ | S 17* | 14 | Trenton St. | 13 |
| Western Conn. St. ■ | S 24* | 17 | Western Conn. St. | 6 |
| Kean | O 2 | 26 | Kean | 21 |
| Wesley | O 9 | 35 | Upsala | 13 |
| Montclair St. ■ | O 16 | 19 | Montclair St. | 24 |
| Jersey City St. | O 30 | 23 | Ramapo | 0 |
| Rowan ■ | N 5* | 43 | Jersey City St. | 20 |
| Albany (N.Y.) | N 13* | 0 | Rowan | 30 |
| | | 27 | Central Conn. St. | 19 |

Colors: Orange & Black.  Nickname: Pioneers.  III

## WILLIAM PENN ................. Oskaloosa, IA 52577
*Ralph Young (7 yrs., 21-42-0)*

| Opponent | Date | | Opponent | Score |
|---|---|---|---|---|
| Concordia (St. Paul) | S 11 | 0 | Concordia (St. Paul) | 16 |
| Coe ■ | S 18 | 23 | Coe | 79 |
| Loras ■ | S 25 | 14 | Loras | 63 |
| Upper Iowa | O 2 | 7 | Upper Iowa | 45 |
| Central (Iowa) ■ | O 9 | 0 | Central (Iowa) | 55 |
| Wartburg ■ | O 16 | 3 | Wartburg | 62 |
| Luther ■ | O 23 | 7 | Luther | 42 |
| Buena Vista | O 30 | 0 | Buena Vista | 17 |
| Simpson ■ | N 6 | 21 | Simpson | 66 |
| Dubuque | N 13 | 28 | Dubuque | 26 |

Colors: Navy Blue & Gold.  Nickname: The Statesmen.  III

## WILLIAMS ................. Williamstown, MA 01267
*Dick Farley (6 yrs., 38-8-2)*

| Opponent | Date | | Opponent | Score |
|---|---|---|---|---|
| Colby | S 25 | 10 | Colby | 6 |
| Trinity (Conn.) | O 2 | 40 | Trinity (Conn.) | 33 |
| Bates | O 9 | 39 | Bates | 0 |
| Middlebury | O 16 | 0 | Middlebury | 3 |
| Tufts ■ | O 23 | 10 | Tufts | 10 |
| Hamilton ■ | O 30 | 33 | Hamilton | 34 |
| Wesleyan | N 6 | 28 | Wesleyan | 23 |
| Amherst ■ | N 13 | 41 | Amherst | 6 |

Colors: Purple.  Nickname: Ephs.  III

## WILMINGTON (OHIO) .......... Wilmington, OH 45177
*Mike Wallace (2 yrs., 3-17-0)*

| Opponent | Date | | Opponent | Score |
|---|---|---|---|---|
| Cumberland (Ky.) ■ | S 11 | 0 | Cumberland (Ky.) | 19 |
| Thomas More | S 18 | 21 | Thomas More | 52 |
| Tiffin | S 25 | 41 | Tiffin | 19 |
| Olivet ■ | O 2 | 27 | Olivet | 21 |
| Ohio Wesleyan | O 9 | 14 | Ohio Wesleyan | 50 |
| Defiance ■ | O 16 | 7 | Defiance | 45 |
| Geneva | O 23 | 28 | Geneva | 44 |
| Bluffton ■ | O 30 | 21 | Bluffton | 40 |
| Wooster | N 6 | 20 | Wooster | 30 |
| Mt. St. Joseph | N 13 | 21 | Mt. St. Joseph | 28 |

Colors: Green & White.  Nickname: Quakers.  III

## WINGATE ...................... Wingate, NC 28174
*Steve Wilt (7 yrs., 29-39-0)*

| Opponent | Date | | Opponent | Score |
|---|---|---|---|---|
| East Tenn. St. | S 4* | 33 | Kentucky St. | 35 |
| Wofford | S 11* | 7 | West Chester | 38 |
| Lees-McRae ■ | S 18 | 19 | Mars Hill | 16 |
| Mars Hill | S 25 | 33 | Gardner-Webb | 69 |
| Gardner-Webb ■ | O 2 | 28 | Carson-Newman | 36 |
| Carson-Newman ■ | O 9 | 7 | Lenoir-Rhyne | 49 |
| Lenoir-Rhyne | O 16* | 17 | Wofford | 24 |
| Chowan ■ | O 23 | 13 | Presbyterian | 34 |
| Presbyterian ■ | O 30 | 24 | Catawba | 27 |
| Catawba | N 6 | 21 | Elon | 55 |
| Elon | N 13 | | | |

Colors: Navy Blue & Old Gold.  Nickname: Bulldogs.  II

## WINONA STATE ................... Winona, MN 55987
*Tom Hosier (19 yrs., 68-114-3)*

| Opponent | Date | | Opponent | Score |
|---|---|---|---|---|
| Wis.-La Crosse | S 11* | 14 | Wis.-La Crosse | 31 |
| Wis.-Eau Claire ■ | S 18* | 19 | Wis.-Eau Claire | 21 |
| Moorhead St. ■ | S 25 | 13 | Moorhead St. | 38 |
| Michigan Tech | O 2 | 19 | Michigan Tech | 38 |
| Minn.-Morris | O 9 | 44 | Minn.-Morris | 7 |
| Northern St. (S.D.) ■ | O 16 | 16 | Northern St. (S.D.) | 21 |
| Bemidji St. | O 23 | 14 | Bemidji St. | 12 |
| Minn.-Duluth | O 30 | 0 | Minn.-Duluth | 21 |
| Southwest St. (Minn.) | N 6 | 17 | Southwest St. (Minn.) | 20 |
| Moorhead St.† | N 12 | 8 | Northern St. (S.D.) | 14 |

Colors: Purple & White.  Nickname: Warriors.  II

## WINSTON-SALEM STATE .. Winston-Salem, NC 27102
*Kermit Blount (1st yr. as head coach)*

| Opponent | Date | | Opponent | Score |
|---|---|---|---|---|
| Elizabeth City St. | S 4 | 27 | Elizabeth City St. | 18 |
| North Caro. A&T ■ | S 11* | 7 | North Caro. A&T | 21 |
| Howard | S 18 | 14 | Virginia St. | 0 |
| Livingstone | S 25 | 33 | Fayetteville St. | 8 |
| Fayetteville St. | O 2* | 40 | Johnson Smith | 13 |
| Norfolk St. ■ | O 9* | 14 | Southern-B.R. | 47 |
| N.C. Central ■ | O 16* | 48 | N.C. Central | 30 |
| Bowie St. | O 23 | 29 | Bowie St. | 0 |
| Johnson Smith ■ | O 30 | 35 | Wofford | 52 |
| Virginia Union | N 6 | 14 | Hampton | 27 |
| Virginia St. ■ | N 13 | 49 | Livingstone | 12 |

Colors: Scarlet & White.  Nickname: Rams.  II

## WISCONSIN-EAU CLAIRE ........ Eau Claire, WI 54702
*Greg Polnasek (1 yr., 4-5-0)*

| Opponent | Date | | Opponent | Score |
|---|---|---|---|---|
| Minn.-Duluth ■ | S 4* | 6 | Minn.-Duluth | 17 |
| Wabash | S 11 | 21 | Winona St. | 19 |
| Winona St. | S 18* | 3 | Wis.-River Falls | 38 |
| Wis.-Oshkosh | S 25* | 23 | Wis.-Stout | 14 |
| Wis.-Stevens Point | O 9 | 25 | Wis.-Oshkosh | 18 |
| Wis.-River Falls ■ | O 16 | 7 | Wis.-La Crosse | 35 |
| Wis.-Whitewater | O 23 | 35 | Wis.-Whitewater | 13 |
| Wis.-Platteville ■ | O 30 | 7 | Wis.-Stevens Point | 42 |
| Wis.-Stout | N 6 | 14 | Wis.-Platteville | 17 |
| Wis.-La Crosse ■ | N 13 | | | |

Colors: Navy Blue & Old Gold.  Nickname: Blugolds.  III

## WISCONSIN-LA CROSSE ........ La Crosse, WI 54601
*Roger Harring (24 yrs., 199-59-7)*

| Opponent | Date | | Opponent | Score |
|---|---|---|---|---|
| Winona St. | S 11* | 31 | Winona St. | 14 |
| Wis.-Oshkosh ■ | S 18 | 19 | Wis.-Stevens Point | 17 |
| Wis.-Platteville | S 25* | 35 | Wis.-Platteville | 7 |
| Wis.-Stevens Point ■ | O 2 | 32 | St. Ambrose | 7 |
| St. Ambrose | O 9 | 21 | Wis.-River Falls | 21 |
| Wis.-Stout | O 16* | 35 | Wis.-Eau Claire | 7 |
| Wis.-River Falls ■ | O 23 | 40 | Wis.-Oshkosh | 14 |
| Simpson | O 30 | 13 | Wis.-Whitewater | 3 |
| Wis.-Whitewater ■ | N 6 | 47 | Wis.-Stout | 23 |
| Wis.-Eau Claire | N 13 | | **III Championship** | |
| | | 47 | Redlands | 26 |
| | | 34 | Central (Iowa) | 9 |
| | | 29 | Mount Union | 24 |
| | | 16 | Wash. & Jeff. | 12 |

Colors: Maroon & Gray.  Nickname: Eagles.  III

## WISCONSIN-OSHKOSH ............ Oshkosh, WI 54901
*Ron Cardo (9 yrs., 34-52-4)*

| Opponent | Date | | Opponent | Score |
|---|---|---|---|---|
| St. Xavier (Ill.) ■ | S 4 | 20 | St. Norbert | 14 |
| St. Norbert | S 11* | 0 | Wis.-River Falls | 48 |
| Wis.-La Crosse | S 18 | 25 | Wis.-Stout | 31 |
| Wis.-Eau Claire ■ | S 25* | 14 | Wis.-Platteville | 19 |
| Wis.-Stout ■ | O 2 | 7 | Wis.-Stevens Point | 35 |
| Wis.-River Falls | O 9 | 18 | Wis.-Eau Claire | 25 |
| Wis.-Platteville ■ | O 16 | 14 | St. Ambrose | 36 |
| St. Ambrose ■ | O 23 | 14 | Wis.-La Crosse | 40 |
| Wis.-Stevens Point ■ | O 30 | 20 | Wis.-Whitewater | 34 |
| Wis.-Whitewater | N 13 | | | |

Colors: Gold, Black & White.  Nickname: Titans.  III

■ Home games on each schedule.  *Night Games.

## WISCONSIN-PLATTEVILLE......Platteville, WI 53818
*Jim Kinder (1st yr. as head coach)*

| Opponent | Date | Pts | Opponent | Pts |
|---|---|---|---|---|
| Dayton | S11* | 0 | Dayton | 48 |
| Wis.-River Falls | S18 | 0 | Wis.-Whitewater | 12 |
| Wis.-La Crosse ■ | S25* | 7 | Wis.-La Crosse | 35 |
| Wis.-Whitewater | O 2 | 19 | Wis.-Oshkosh | 14 |
| Wis.-Stout | O 9 | 10 | Wis.-River Falls | 0 |
| Wis.-Oshkosh ■ | O16 | 40 | Wis.-Stout | 17 |
| Iowa Wesleyan ■ | O23 | 7 | Wis.-Stevens Point | 31 |
| Wis.-Eau Claire | O30 | 24 | St. Ambrose | 0 |
| St. Ambrose | N 6 | 17 | Wis.-Eau Claire | 14 |
| Wis.-Stevens Point | N13 | | | |

Colors: Orange & Blue. Nickname: Pioneers.   III

## WISCONSIN-RIVER FALLS......River Falls, WI 54022
*John O'Grady (4 yrs., 22-14-3)*

| Opponent | Date | Pts | Opponent | Pts |
|---|---|---|---|---|
| Minn.-Morris | S 4 | 42 | Minn.-Morris | 20 |
| St. Thomas (Minn.) ■ | S11 | 36 | St. Thomas (Minn.) | 14 |
| Wis.-Platteville ■ | S18 | 48 | Wis.-Oshkosh | 0 |
| Alma ■ | S25 | 38 | Wis.-Eau Claire | 3 |
| Wis.-Oshkosh ■ | O 9 | 0 | Wis.-Platteville | 10 |
| Wis.-Eau Claire | O16 | 21 | Wis.-La Crosse | 21 |
| Wis.-La Crosse | O23 | 14 | Wis.-Whitewater | 21 |
| Wis.-Whitewater ■ | O30 | 62 | Wis.-Stout | 6 |
| Wis.-Stevens Point | N 6 | 44 | Wis.-Stevens Point | 24 |
| Wis.-Stout ■ | N13 | | | |

Colors: Red & White. Nickname: Falcons.   III

## WISCONSIN-STEVENS POINT Stevens Point, WI 54481
*John Miech (5 yrs., 32-17-2)*

| Opponent | Date | Pts | Opponent | Pts |
|---|---|---|---|---|
| Michigan Tech ■ | S 4 | 13 | Michigan Tech | 25 |
| Minn.-Morris | S11 | 42 | Minn.-Morris | 12 |
| Wis.-Platteville ■ | S18* | 17 | Wis.-La Crosse | 19 |
| Wis.-La Crosse | O 2 | 13 | Wis.-Whitewater | 14 |
| Wis.-Eau Claire ■ | O 9 | 35 | Wis.-Oshkosh | 7 |
| Thomas More ■ | O16 | 63 | Wis.-Stout | 6 |
| Wis.-Stout ■ | O23 | 31 | Wis.-Platteville | 7 |
| Wis.-Oshkosh | O30 | 42 | Wis.-Eau Claire | 7 |
| Wis.-River Falls ■ | N 6 | 24 | Wis.-River Falls | 44 |
| Wis.-Platteville | N13 | | | |

Colors: Purple & Gold. Nickname: Pointers.   III

## WISCONSIN-STOUT......Stout, WI 54751
*Ed Meierkort (1st yr. as head coach)*

| Opponent | Date | Pts | Opponent | Pts |
|---|---|---|---|---|
| Mayville St. ■ | S 4 | 21 | Mayville St. | 14 |
| Minn.-Duluth | S18 | 31 | Wis.-Oshkosh | 25 |
| Wis.-Whitewater | S25 | 14 | Wis.-Eau Claire | 23 |
| Wis.-Oshkosh | O 2 | 3 | Wis.-Whitewater | 42 |
| Wis.-Platteville ■ | O 9 | 6 | Wis.-Stevens Point | 63 |
| Wis.-La Crosse ■ | O16* | 17 | Wis.-Platteville | 40 |
| Wis.-Stevens Point | O23 | 9 | St. Ambrose | 10 |
| St. Ambrose ■ | O30 | 6 | Wis.-River Falls | 62 |
| Wis.-Eau Claire ■ | N 6 | 23 | Wis.-La Crosse | 47 |
| Wis.-River Falls | N13 | | | |

Colors: Navy Blue & White. Nickname: Blue Devils.   III

## WISCONSIN-SUPERIOR......Superior, WI 54880
*Dropped program after two games in 1992.*

| | | Pts | Opponent | Pts |
|---|---|---|---|---|
| | | 27 | Concordia (St. Paul) | 22 |
| | | 3 | Augsburg | 31 |

Colors: Orange & Black. Nickname: Yellowjackets.   III

## WISCONSIN-WHITEWATER.....Whitewater, WI 53190
*Bob Berezowitz (8 yrs., 53-29-4)*

| Opponent | Date | Pts | Opponent | Pts |
|---|---|---|---|---|
| Central Mo. St. ■ | S 4* | 30 | Upper Iowa | 26 |
| Upper Iowa | S11 | 12 | Wis.-Platteville | 0 |
| Wis.-Stevens Point ■ | S18* | 9 | Livingstone | 0 |
| Wis.-Stout ■ | S25 | 14 | Wis.-Stevens Point | 13 |
| Wis.-Platteville ■ | O 2 | 42 | Wis.-Stout | 3 |
| St. Ambrose ■ | O16 | 34 | St. Ambrose | 16 |
| Wis.-Eau Claire ■ | O23 | 21 | Wis.-River Falls | 14 |
| Wis.-River Falls | O30 | 13 | Wis.-Eau Claire | 35 |
| Wis.-La Crosse ■ | N 6 | 3 | Wis.-La Crosse | 13 |
| Wis.-Oshkosh ■ | N13 | 34 | Wis.-Oshkosh | 20 |

Colors: Purple & White. Nickname: Warhawks.   III

## WITTENBERG...............Springfield, OH 45501
*Doug Neibhur (4 yrs., 23-14-1)*

| Opponent | Date | Pts | Opponent | Pts |
|---|---|---|---|---|
| Muskingum | S11 | 0 | Baldwin-Wallace | 20 |
| Earlham ■ | S18* | 35 | Earlham | 3 |
| Wooster | S25 | 16 | Wooster | 3 |
| Case Reserve ■ | O 2 | 42 | Case Reserve | 10 |
| Allegheny | O 9 | 17 | Allegheny | 12 |
| Mercyhurst ■ | O16 | 20 | Mercyhurst | 20 |
| Kenyon ■ | O23 | 51 | Kenyon | 7 |
| Oberlin | O30 | 36 | Denison | 0 |
| Denison ■ | N 6 | 14 | Ohio Wesleyan | 7 |
| Ohio Wesleyan | N13 | | | |

Colors: Red & White. Nickname: Tigers.   III

## WOFFORD...............Spartanburg, SC 29303
*Mike Ayers (8 yrs., 42-41-1)*

| Opponent | Date | Pts | Opponent | Pts |
|---|---|---|---|---|
| Citadel ■ | S 4* | 27 | Elon | 41 |
| Wingate ■ | S11* | 13 | Citadel | 30 |
| Furman | S18 | 28 | Lenoir-Rhyne | 35 |
| Catawba ■ | S25* | 42 | Catawba | 17 |
| Presbyterian | O 2 | 27 | Presbyterian | 41 |
| Lees-McRae ■ | O 9 | 7 | Lees-McRae | 7 |
| Newberry ■ | O16* | 34 | Newberry | 16 |
| Lenoir-Rhyne | O23 | 2 | Wingate | 17 |
| Ala.-Birmingham ■ | O30* | 52 | Winston-Salem | 35 |
| Elon ■ | N 6 | 13 | Va. Military | 44 |
| Charleston So. | N13 | 24 | Bowie St. | 22 |

Colors: Old Gold & Black. Nickname: Terriers.   II

## WOOSTER........................Wooster, OH 44691
*Bob Tucker (8 yrs., 26-50-1)*

| Opponent | Date | Pts | Opponent | Pts |
|---|---|---|---|---|
| Kalamazoo | S11 | 17 | Kalamazoo | 27 |
| Allegheny | S18 | 7 | Allegheny | 56 |
| Wittenberg ■ | S25 | 3 | Wittenberg | 16 |
| Kenyon ■ | O 2 | 29 | Kenyon | 35 |
| Oberlin ■ | O 9 | 45 | Oberlin | 14 |
| Denison | O16 | 14 | Denison | 14 |
| Ohio Wesleyan ■ | O23 | 12 | Ohio Wesleyan | 41 |
| Earlham | O30 | 28 | Earlham | 21 |
| Wilmington (Ohio) ■ | N 6 | 30 | Wilmington (Ohio) | 20 |
| | | | Defiance | 62 |

Colors: Black & Old Gold. Nickname: Fighting Scots.   III

## WORCESTER POLYTECHNIC....Worcester, MA 01609
*Kevin Morris (1st yr. as head coach)*

| Opponent | Date | Pts | Opponent | Pts |
|---|---|---|---|---|
| Ursinus ■ | S11 | 56 | Worcester St. | 0 |
| Union (N.Y.) | S18 | 20 | Union (N.Y.) | 34 |
| Rensselaer ■ | O 2 | 13 | Mass.-Lowell | 9 |
| Norwich ■ | O 9 | 28 | Rensselaer | 14 |
| Merchant Marine ■ | O16 | 56 | Norwich | 6 |
| Mass.-Lowell ■ | O30 | 17 | Merchant Marine | 15 |
| Coast Guard | N 6 | 45 | Randolph-Macon | 0 |
| Plymouth St. ■ | N13 | 24 | Ursinus | 10 |
| | | 28 | Coast Guard | 10 |
| | | 43 | Plymouth St. | 20 |
| | | | **III Championship** | |
| | | 14 | Rowan | 41 |

Colors: Crimson & Gray. Nickname: Engineers.   III

## WORCESTER STATE...........Worcester, MA 01602
*Brien Cullen (8 yrs., 35-36-0)*

| Opponent | Date | Pts | Opponent | Pts |
|---|---|---|---|---|
| Mass.-Dartmouth ■ | S18 | 0 | Worcester Tech | 56 |
| Maine Maritime | S25 | 0 | Mass.-Dartmouth | 47 |
| Mass.-Boston ■ | O 2 | 14 | Maine Maritime | 20 |
| Fitchburg St. | O 9 | 27 | Mass.-Boston | 32 |
| Framingham St. ■ | O16 | 45 | Fitchburg St. | 0 |
| Westfield St. | O22* | 0 | Framingham St. | 14 |
| Bri'water (Mass.) ■ | O30 | 0 | Westfield St. | 29 |
| Nichols | N 6 | 12 | Bri'water (Mass.) | 24 |
| Mass. Maritime | N13 | 13 | Nichols | 19 |
| | | 6 | Mass. Maritime | 23 |

Colors: Royal Blue & Gold. Nickname: Lancers.   III

■ Home games on each schedule.   *Night Games.